Prisoners' Self-Help Litigation Manual

PRISONERS' SELF-HELP LITIGATION MANUAL

JOHN BOSTON AND DANIEL E. MANVILLE

FOURTH EDITION

Oceana®
NEW YORK

Oxford University Press, Inc., publishes works that further Oxford University's objective of excellence
in research, scholarship, and education.

Oxford   New York

Auckland   Cape Town   Dar es Salaam   Hong Kong   Karachi   Kuala Lumpur   Madrid   Melbourne
Mexico City   Nairobi   New Delhi   Shanghai   Taipei   Toronto

With offices in

Argentina   Austria   Brazil   Chile   Czech Republic   France   Greece   Guatemala   Hungary   Italy   Japan
Poland   Portugal   Singapore   South Korea   Switzerland   Thailand   Turkey   Ukraine   Vietnam

Published by Oxford University Press, Inc.
198 Madison Avenue, New York, New York 10016

Library of Congress Cataloging-in-Publication Data

Boston, John. 1948—
    Prisoners' self-help litigation manual./ John Boston, Daniel E. Manville. — 4th ed.
        p. cm.
    Includes bibliographical references and index.
    ISBN 978-0-19-537440-7 ((pbk.) : alk. paper)
    1. Prisoners—Legal status, laws, etc.—United States. 2. Actions and defenses—United States.
I. Manville, Daniel E. II. Title.
    KF9731.M36 2010
    344.7303'56—dc22   2010012899

Printed in Canada on acid-free paper

Note to Readers

This publication is designed to provide accurate and authoritative information in regard to the subject matter covered.
It is based upon sources believed to be accurate and reliable and is intended to be current as of the time it was written.
It is sold with the understanding that the publisher is not engaged in rendering legal, accounting, or other professional
services. If legal advice or other expert assistance is required, the services of a competent professional person should be
sought. Also, to confirm that the information has not been affected or changed by recent developments, traditional
legal research techniques should be used, including checking primary sources where appropriate.

*(Based on the Declaration of Principles jointly adopted by a Committee of the
American Bar Association and a Committee of Publishers and Associations.)*

Louis James Manville
December 19, 1921–November 23, 2009

To my Dad who, even though he was a prison guard, stood by me while I engaged in some very destructive behavior and while I was imprisoned. We had many disagreements but these did not impact on our love and respect for each other. He came to understand my drive to litigate on behalf of those imprisoned. I will miss him.

D.E.M.

For Dori and the guys.

J.B.

CONTENTS

CHAPTER 4

PROCEDURAL DUE PROCESS . 305

CHAPTER 5

EQUAL PROTECTION OF THE LAW . 413

CHAPTER 6

PRETRIAL DETAINEES' RIGHTS . 421

PART II: ENFORCING YOUR RIGHTS

CHAPTER 7

THE LEGAL SYSTEM . 427

PREFACE AND ACKNOWLEDGMENTS

We thank all of the advocates and prisoners who have encouraged us to produce a new edition of this book, including our colleagues at the Prisoners' Rights Project of the New York City Legal Aid Society, especially Dori A. Lewis, who read and criticized large parts of the manuscript, and also Legal Aid's patient and resourceful librarian, Alla Reznik. Others who provided valuable assistance include Amy Roemer and Richard McHugh, two lawyers and friends; Elizabeth Alexander, formerly of the ACLU National Prison Project and now in private practice representing prisoners; Randall C. Berg III and Peter Siegel of the Florida Justice Institute; Betsy R. Ginsberg of Cardozo Law School; and Deborah Golden of the D.C. Prisoners' Project of the Washington Lawyers' Committee for Civil Rights and Urban Affairs.

CHAPTER 1

Introduction
Using this Manual and Using the Courts

The last edition of this Manual appeared in 1995 and a lot has happened in the law of prisoners' rights and prison litigation since then. It has taken a long time to prepare this new edition, in part because the same developments that have made a new edition necessary were also keeping us busy in our practices.

Like the earlier editions of this Manual, this edition focuses on civil litigation. It does not deal with criminal law-related matters,[1] such as post-conviction remedies and detainers. It also does not deal with immigration law.[2] Other books that do address these subjects are listed in Appendix D.

A. THE STATE OF THE LAW

Since the last edition of this Manual, there have been tremendous changes in the procedural and substantive law affecting prisoners' rights. Many of the changes resulted from the enactment in 1996 of the Prison Litigation Reform Act (PLRA), which makes litigation by prisoners more difficult, more expensive, and less likely to succeed. Chapter 9 is devoted solely to the federal PLRA, and you should be sure you understand it *before* you file litigation, since it may have a major impact both on your present litigation and your ability to pursue litigation in the future. Most states have also enacted their own restrictions on state court prison litigation, some of them very similar to the federal PLRA.

One requirement of the PLRA is that you must *exhaust any available administrative remedies* at the prison or jail before you sue, even if you think you are in imminent danger.[3] Other major changes brought about by the PLRA and discussed in Chapter 9 include making indigent prisoners who are proceeding *in forma pauperis* pay the entire federal court filing fee (now $350) in installments; excluding prisoners who have had several lawsuits dismissed on certain grounds from proceeding *in forma pauperis* at all; and barring prisoners from recovering compensatory damages for "mental or emotional injury" unless they also suffered physical injury.

In the last edition, we told you that for prisoners, the Constitution wasn't what it used to be. The law continues to get worse. Over the last fifteen years, a more conservative Supreme Court has ruled against prisoners in case after case, cutting back or abolishing prisoners' rights with respect to due process protections,[4] access to the courts,[5] visiting,[6] participation in sex offender treatment,[7] clemency hearings,[8]

---

[1] This omission includes civil lawsuits arising from criminal arrests and prosecutions, such as suits alleging false arrest, malicious prosecution, or violation of civil rights during arrest or prosecution. These subjects are discussed in other manuals. *See, e.g.,* David Rudovsky, Karen Blum, Michael Avery, *Police Misconduct: Law and Litigation* (3d ed., Clark Boardman Callaghan), currently priced at $358.00. We do discuss suits alleging excessive force by police as well as jail and prison personnel, *see* Ch. 2, § G.2, and the differences among civil lawsuits, criminal appeals, and habeas corpus and other post-conviction proceedings. *See* Ch. 8, § H.

[2] There is a Supplement to the Seventh Edition of the Columbia Human Rights Law Review, *A Jailhouse Lawyer's Manual*, titled "Immigration and Consular Access." *See* Appendix D for more information on the *Jailhouse Lawyer's Manual*.

[3] *See* Ch. 9, § D. Exhaustion is also discussed briefly in § C of this chapter.

[4] *See* Sandin v. Conner, 515 U.S. 472, 484, 115 S. Ct. 2293 (1995) (due process protections are not required unless the prison "imposes atypical and significant hardship on the inmate in relation to the ordinary incidents of prison life").

[5] *See* Lewis v. Casey, 518 U.S. 343, 116 S. Ct. 2174 (1996) (restrictions on legal access do not violate right of access to the courts unless and until they hinder litigation of a non-frivolous legal claim).

[6] *See* Overton v. Bazzetta, 539 U.S. 126, 123 S. Ct. 2162 (2003) (upholding severe restrictions on visiting).

[7] *See* McKune v. Lile, 536 U.S. 24, 122 S. Ct. 2017 (2002) (Fifth Amendment right against self-incrimination is not applicable to disclosures required in sex offender programs).

[8] *See* Ohio Adult Parole Authority v. Woodard, 523 U.S. 272, 286–87, 118 S. Ct. 1244 (1998) (holding that there is no right to silence at a clemency interview).

parolees' rights,[9] remedies against private prison contractors,[10] and First Amendment rights.[11] The federal courts continue to emphasize the dangerousness of the prison environment and the importance of "deference" to the judgment of prison officials,[12] and have refused to hold prison officials to the same strict standards of conduct that apply in cases involving the constitutional rights of free citizens.[13]

Prisoners have retained or even gained some protection through federal statutes and state law. After the United Supreme Court held that the Religious Freedom Restoration Act was unconstitutional as applied to the States,[14] Congress enacted the Religious Land Use and Institutionalized Person Act (RLUIPA) so that state prisoners would have the same protections in practicing their religions as federal prisoners.[15] The Supreme Court acknowledged that prisoners are not excluded from the protections of the Americans with Disabilities Act.[16] Most states' law provides redress for prisoners against common law torts such as negligence, medical malpractice, assault and battery, invasion of privacy, and conversion of property.[17] In some cases, prisoners have rights under state constitutions that are more extensive than federal constitutional rights.[18]

To litigate effectively you must understand that not every wrong that prison officials subject you to violates legal rights enforceable by lawsuit. Verbal abuse, for example, almost never violates the law. You also must understand the difference between federal constitutional and statutory rights and rights that are based on state statutes, regulations, or constitutions. Violation of state law does not necessarily violate federal law and must generally be redressed in state court and not federal court.

In this single volume we cannot cover all the relevant tort law, statutes and regulations, and constitutions of the 50 states plus the federal government.[19] The Manual will focus on federal constitutional and statutory law, with limited discussion of state law where we think it is helpful. You must always keep in mind the possibility that state law may grant you more rights than the federal Constitution and statutes, and you must educate yourself carefully concerning *all* your rights before deciding whether to bring a lawsuit, what legal claims to assert, and in what court to file your case.

B. How to Use this Manual

There are no magical answers on how to become a successful jailhouse lawyer. You can achieve this only through hard work. This Manual is designed to provide you with basic information concerning your legal rights and how to enforce them. It is up to you to make use of this information. We do have one suggestion: work with others when you can. You can learn from those who are more knowledgeable than you; in addition, one of the best ways to understand something is to try to explain it to someone else.

There are several features of the Manual that are designed to make it easier to find what you need.

Table of Contents. We have broken the Manual up into chapters and divided the chapters into smaller sections and subsections, each with its own separate heading. All of the sections are listed in the Table of Contents. Scanning the Table of Contents is often the fastest way to locate the subject you want.

Index. At the end of the Manual, there is an alphabetical list of topics and the places in the book where they are discussed. Looking in the Index will help you find topics that do not have a special subsection (such as "John Doe defendants")

---

[9] *See* Samson v. California, 547 U.S. 843, 126 S. Ct. 2193 (2006) (Fourth Amendment rights of parolee not violated by suspicionless search).

[10] *See* Correctional Services Corp. v. Malesko, 534 U.S. 61, 122 S. Ct. 515 (2001) (civil rights suits not permitted against corporation contracting with federal government).

[11] *See, e.g.,* Beard v. Banks, 548 U.S. 521, 126 S. Ct. 2572 (2006) (First Amendment was not violated by restrictions on publications received by maximum security prisoners confined in segregation); Shaw v. Murphy, 532 U.S. 223, 121 S. Ct. 1475 (2001) (prisoner communications on legal matters could be restricted to the same extent as other prisoner speech).

[12] *See* Beard v. Banks, 548 U.S. 521, 530, 535, 126 S. Ct. 2572 (2006); Overton v. Bazzetta, 539 U.S. 126, 132, 123 S. Ct. 2162 (2003).

[13] *See* Beard v. Banks, 548 U.S. 521, 528, 126 S. Ct. 2572 (2006) ("the Constitution sometimes permits greater restriction of such rights in a prison than it would allow elsewhere" (citation omitted)).

[14] *See* City of Boerne v. Flores, 521 U.S. 507, 117 S. Ct. 2157 (1997).

[15] 42 U.S.C. § 2000cc, *et seq.; see* Cutter v. Wilkinson, 544 U.S. 709, 125 S. Ct. 2113 (2005) (upholding constitutionality of RLUIPA).

[16] Pennsylvania Dep't of Corrections v. Yeskey, 524 U.S. 206, 118 S. Ct. 1952 (1998).

[17] Torts in general, and these particular torts, are discussed in various sections of this Manual. *See* Ch. 2, §§ F.5, G.1.f, G.2.e, G.3; Ch. 3, § E.3.e; Ch. 4, §§ H.8.c, H.9; Ch. 8, § C. Consult the Index for references to specific torts.

[18] For example, under the New York State Constitution, pretrial detainees have a right to contact visits. Cooper v. Morin, 49 N.Y.2d 69 (1979), *cert. denied,* 446 U.S. 984 (1980). They do not have this right under the federal Constitution. Several state constitutions support a right to rehabilitation, *see* Ch. 2, § I, or more

---

extensive due process rights than the federal Constitution provides. *See* Ch. 4, § B.

[19] There are other manuals or publications that serve this purpose for a particular state. Two outstanding examples are: Heather MacKay and the Prison Law Office, *The California State Prisoners Handbook, A Comprehensive Practice Guide to California Prisons & Parole Law* (4th ed. 2008), available from Rayve Productions, POB 726, Windsor, CA 95492 for $40.00 for prisoners and $182.00 for non-prisoners; Columbia Human Rights Law Review, *A Jailhouse Lawyers' Manual* (7th ed. 2007) (covering New York State), availability information provided in Appendix D. State or local prisoners' rights or legal assistance offices may provide smaller guides, pamphlets, or information sheets about particular issues. These offices are listed in Appendix B.

in the Table of Contents, or that are mentioned in several places (such as "assaults").

Footnotes. At the bottom of each page are footnotes that contain case citations, statutory references, and other information backing up or explaining the statements on the page. These footnotes are a fast way of finding the law dealing with a particular subject. The references to cases and statutes are in standard legal citation form, which is explained in Chapter 11. The footnotes also contain cross-references to other sections of the Manual dealing with related topics.

In the footnotes we have mostly cited cases and statutes. We have tried to minimize citing materials such as law reviews and legal treatises and encyclopedias that are not likely to be available in most prison law libraries. When we have cited these materials, it is generally because they are particularly authoritative (such as *Moore's Federal Practice* on points of federal procedure), or because they deal with points that case law rarely addresses, such as many trial practice questions.

Forms. In Appendix C at the end of the Manual, there are actual examples of various kinds of legal papers that you may wish to use as models.

Sources of assistance. In Appendix B at the end of the Manual, there is a list of organizations that provide legal assistance to prisoners in each state.

Other books and publications. In the footnotes, we have cited a small number of other books that you may wish to buy or try to get the prison law library to obtain. Other useful books are recommended in the American Civil Liberties Union's Prisoners' Assistance Directory bibliography, which is included in Appendix D.

C. Before You Go to Court

There are certain basic ideas that you must grasp before undertaking any kind of *pro se* legal action.

1. *Exhaust the grievance system in your prison or jail.* The Prison Litigation Reform Act now requires prisoners to exhaust any available remedies prior to filing suit based on federal law.[20] Just writing a letter of complaint will not satisfy this requirement. You must follow the rules of the prison grievance procedure or any administrative appeal that will address the problem you are concerned about. If you do not, you may be found to have "procedurally defaulted," and your case may be dismissed as a result. Prison administrative remedies often have extremely short time deadlines, so you should find out about those remedies immediately if something happens that you may want to sue about—or, preferably, before anything happens.

2. *Keep records.* When facts are disputed, courts are not going to rule in your favor automatically. They will need to have enough information and will need to have some reason to believe you as opposed to prison officials. Courts and jurors are more likely to believe your testimony if you have a written record or a copy of letters or grievances that were created at the time of the incident to support your testimony.

For those reasons, if you think you may need to bring litigation about something that is happening to you in prison, you may want to keep notes, or even a diary, of the relevant events, such as your contacts with prison staff (including names and dates and what was said) in trying to get them to act on a risk of harm to you, or your efforts to obtain medical care and the symptoms or pain you experience each day, or whatever other problem you may have. Litigation can take a long time, and without a diary or other record to refresh your recollection, it will be hard for you to remember in sufficient detail all of what happened if your case goes to trial or you have to respond to a summary judgment motion months or years after the events.

Any time you write a kite or letter to prison staff about your problem, or file a grievance or an administrative appeal, you should keep a copy of it, and of the response. This will help you if prison staff deny ever receiving a complaint from you.[21] If you do not have access to a copying machine, you may have to make a carbon copy, or write out an identical copy of your complaint and keep it when you send the original to staff. Since your cell will probably be shaken down by prison staff from time to time, and since prisoners often complain that their legal papers are taken during searches, you should if possible send copies of your notes or diary and documents to someone on the outside who will keep them until they are needed. You should also not advertise to prison staff or anyone else that you are keeping records.

3. *Understand whom you are dealing with.* When you go to court, you will be dealing with judges. Even if you ultimately have a jury trial, there will be months—sometimes years—of pretrial proceedings supervised by the judge. Judges are mostly white, middle-class, middle-aged (and older), usually males, who have been successful lawyers or politicians. In short, they are members of the establishment. Even judges who are women, members of minority groups, or young are likely to have more in common with other judges than with prisoners. Very few of them will ever have been in a prison or jail except on a tour conducted by the warden.

This does not mean that judges cannot or will not be fair. It does mean that their experiences are very different from yours and you must understand where they are coming from in order to get through to them. They are likely to assume that authority figures, including prison officials, are honest people acting in good faith unless you prove otherwise. Thus, for example, they will not assume that prison guards falsify disciplinary reports to cover up their own misbehavior. If this is an element of your case, you must be prepared to prove to their satisfaction that it happened.

---

[20] *See* Ch. 9, § D., for a discussion of exhaustion of administrative remedies.

[21] *See* Ch. 9, § D.8, n. 513, for examples of cases where prison officials denied receiving grievances until prisoners produced copies of them.

Judges may have certain assumptions, biases, or prejudices about prisoners as well. They may assume that prisoners—people they think of as criminals—are likely to be irresponsible or dishonest people. You must conduct yourself in a restrained and dignified way or you will play directly into this stereotype. Do not use the courts as a place to blow off steam; do not make accusations you cannot prove; do your best to follow the rules of the court. Otherwise, you will not only guarantee losing your own case, but you may leave an impression that will hurt the next prisoner to bring a case in that court.

4. *Do not try to sound like a lawyer.* Prisoners often try to use the most formal and technical language they know in their legal papers because they think this is how lawyers do it and they can impress the court in that way. In fact, the tide has turned and the world in general is sick of lawyers and their jargon, and most good lawyers are doing their best to sound like ordinary sensible people. (Some states have even passed "plain English statutes" requiring that legal documents be written so ordinary people can understand them.) A judge reading your legal papers wants to know two things: What does this person want me to do? What facts does he have that will support what he wants me to do? The easier it is for the judge to find that out, the better off you are. But most importantly, the judge is going to be far more concerned with the facts of your case than with legal citations. The judge already knows something about the law, and can find out what he does not know by having his clerk go on the computer or into the library to find the law. However, the judge knows nothing about the facts except what the parties to the case say. Explain the facts, keep it simple, keep it short, and do not try to decorate it with fancy phrases.

5. *Follow through.* Do not bring a case unless you intend to pursue it. If you start a case and for some reason you cannot or do not wish to finish the litigation, do not just forget about it; try to dismiss it voluntarily.[22] There are a couple of reasons for this. First, if you bring a case and never follow it up, you will contribute to the stereotype many judges have of prisoners, which we referred to above. Second, the defendants' lawyer will make a motion to dismiss or a motion for summary judgment, and if you do not respond, the court will decide it based only on the defendants' submission. The result will be another bad precedent in the law books that may hurt later prisoner litigants. Third, if you don't defend against defendants' dismissal motion, it is more likely that the court will dismiss your lawsuit as frivolous or as not stating a claim for which relief can be granted, which will count as one of the "three strikes" that you are allowed before you are required under the Prison Litigation Reform Act to pay the entire filing fee before you can file a lawsuit.[23]

6. *Sue in the right court.* Many prisoners have their lawsuits dismissed because they go to federal court when they should go to state court, or because they go to the wrong state court. A dismissal for suing in the wrong court can

court as a strike against you under the Prison Litigation Reform Act.

The federal courts generally hear state prisoners' cases only if they raise issues of federal law, if the defendants are federal officials or employees, or if the plaintiff and defendants live in different states and the amount of money at issue is at least $75,000.[24] Many claims that state prisoners take to federal court—for example, accidents in the workplace or violation of state prison classification regulations—do not raise any federal law issues; these cases should be brought in state court. Some states require that claims against individuals be brought in one court and that claims against the state itself, or against state agencies, be brought in a different state court.[25] Find out before you sue what court the case belongs in.

7. *Sue the right defendants.* Many prisoners lose their cases because they sue the wrong people or agencies. In federal court, you generally cannot sue a state or its agencies; you can sue a city or county only under limited circumstances; and you can usually sue supervisory officials only for acts that they were personally involved in, not acts that their subordinates committed that they were not involved in. You can sue the United States itself only in certain circumstances; in other circumstances, you can only sue individual federal employees or officials. Sometimes you will have a choice of suing one defendant in one court and a different defendant in another court; for example, if an officer in a state prison assaults you with no justification, you may be able to sue the officer in federal court or the state government in a state court. Find out before you get started what lawsuit or suits you can legitimately bring, and who the proper defendants are for each.[26]

8. *Remember the statute of limitations.* Statutes of limitations are laws that state the time period in which you must file a lawsuit about an event, or you will lose the right to sue.[27] These statutes may provide for a long or short time period, and different kinds of suits are subject to different limitation periods even within the same state.

There is always a statute of limitations when you are suing for damages, and sometimes there are statutes of limitations for cases asking for an injunction or other court order. When you think your rights have been violated, find out right away how long you have to file a claim about it. If you miss this deadline, your lawsuit will be permanently barred.

In addition to having statutes of limitations, many counties and municipalities (and the federal government in tort cases) require you to give them notice within a certain

---

[22]Voluntary dismissals are discussed in Ch. 10, § I.

[23]The three strikes provision discussed in Ch. 9, § B.

[24]The kinds of cases that can be litigated in federal court are discussed in Ch. 8.

[25]In Michigan, for example, you must sue the State or its agencies for damages in the Court of Claims, but all lawsuits against prison officials in their individual capacities for damages must be filed in the court of general jurisdiction.

[26]These issues are discussed in Ch. 8.

[27]Statutes of limitations are discussed in Ch. 8, § N.

time period if you intend to sue them. If you do not file this "notice of claim" or "notice of intent," your case may be dismissed even if you file it before the statute of limitations has expired.

D. GETTING A LAWYER

You probably know the old saying that the person who represents himself has a fool for a client. That advice is obviously out of place in this Manual, if only because many prisoners do not have any option but representing themselves. However, nobody would dispute that having a good lawyer is better than representing yourself. Whether having a not so good lawyer is better depends on what kind of case you are bringing and what kinds of skills you have. There are certain kinds of cases—for example, medical damage suits—which require technical knowledge that no *pro se* litigant is likely to have. Also there are certain things that a *pro se* litigant cannot do, or cannot do as well as even a mediocre lawyer—for example, getting on the telephone to the other side's lawyers (and having them take the call), or persuading prison officials to turn over security-related documents that they do not want to have circulating in the prison.

Getting a lawyer for a prison case is frequently difficult, since most lawyers don't know much about prisons or prison law and many don't want to get involved with them. Also, private lawyers are out to make a living and they know that most prisoners do not have a lot of money to pay fees or to front the out-of-pocket costs even of meritorious cases.

There are a number of ways in which you can try to obtain a lawyer. You can ask the court to appoint a lawyer for you.[28] There is no right to a lawyer in civil cases, and it is generally left to the court's discretion whether to appoint counsel. Courts will be influenced in their decisions by a variety of factors: whether your case seems to have any merit; how complicated it is; whether you seem to be able to handle it yourself; and—probably the most important factor—how difficult it is to persuade a lawyer to represent you. Courts generally do not have any power to force private lawyers to take cases. However, the bar in some jurisdictions is more willing to get involved in representing prisoners and other poor people than in others. In New York City, for example, federal courts have counsel appointment programs that have arranged for many prisoners to be represented *pro bono* by prestigious law firms; but even these well-organized programs are overburdened and fail to provide lawyers for many cases in which the court wishes to appoint counsel. Courts in other areas may have no regular means at all for finding counsel, and the judge has only his personal knowledge of local lawyers to reply on.

A second avenue for finding counsel is civil rights, civil liberties, legal services, and legal aid offices.[29] Sometimes these organizations represent prisoners (though offices that receive federal Legal Services Corporation funds cannot);

even if you know they cannot, it is worth contacting them because they may be able to refer you to someone else. Bar associations (state, county, and city) often have referral services, although many are not very helpful to prisoners. Of course, you can also write directly to lawyers you know of or have had contact with.

Contacting an attorney involves some of the same practical considerations as writing legal papers. Lawyers are busy people, and they want to find out as quickly as possible what you want from them and why you think they should represent you. Private lawyers usually want to know what is in it for them. They also want to avoid involvement with situations that are complicated or non-productive, or with people who will be difficult and unreasonable as clients.

When you write to an attorney seeking representation, therefore, you should do your best to sound reasonable. Do not engage in name-calling or rhetoric. Tell the lawyer exactly what has happened that you think provided the basis for a lawsuit. You should do this as briefly as possible and still make yourself understood. (For example, "I was placed in punitive segregation after a hearing. I was found guilty of inciting a riot. The hearing board did not let me tell my side of the story. To my knowledge, none of the witnesses I asked for were called. They gave me a statement of reasons which says only 'We find you guilty based on all the evidence.'") Unless you know that the lawyer is knowledgeable about prison law, you should briefly mention what you believe is the legal basis of a suit—cases, statutes, regulations, etc.

If you have any kind of documentary evidence (*e.g.*, a disciplinary hearing disposition with a meaningless statement of reasons), it may help to send a copy with your letter. You should also tell the lawyer about any evidence you have to back up your story. However, it is not wise to send a big stack of papers, at least initially. If there are particular witnesses that you can identify, or if the prison keeps documents that would help prove your case, explain. You should explain in what way you were injured (physical injury, restrictive conditions in segregation, etc.), so the lawyer will be able to make a quick assessment about the likelihood of a money judgment.

Finally, if you are contacting a lawyer who may not be familiar with the kind of case you want to bring, you should mention any applicable attorneys' fee statutes, such as the Civil Rights Attorneys' Fees Award Act,[30] and the limitations on fees contained in the Prison Litigation Reform Act.[31] These statutes allow a court to award attorneys' fees to the plaintiff's lawyer if the plaintiff wins a civil rights suit against state or county officials. One thing you should never do is write to a lawyer and say "I need to see you. It's very important. Come visit me." Lawyers' time is their most valuable possession, and they are rarely willing to commit several hours of it without having some idea in advance of what they will be spending it on.

---

[28]Appointment of counsel is discussed in Ch. 10, § C.5.

[29]Many of these are listed in Appendix B.

[30]42 U.S.C. § 1988.

[31]42 U.S.C. § 1997e(d).

PART I

The Rights of Prisoners

CHAPTER 2

Conditions of Confinement

A. CRUEL AND UNUSUAL PUNISHMENT

The Eighth Amendment, which forbids "cruel and unusual punishments,"[1] governs the treatment of convicted prisoners. To win an Eighth Amendment case, you must establish both an "objective component," the seriousness of the challenged conditions, and a "subjective component," the state of mind of the officials who are responsible for them.[2]

1. The Objective Component: Cruel Conditions

Prison conditions that are "restrictive and even harsh are part of the penalty that criminal offenders pay for their offenses against society."[3] Conditions do not violate the Eighth Amendment unless they amount to "the unnecessary and wanton infliction of pain."[4]

That phrase can mean several different things in prison litigation. With respect to living conditions, prisoners must demonstrate "unquestioned and serious deprivations of basic human needs" or of the "minimal civilized measure of life's necessities" to establish an Eighth Amendment violation.[5] The Supreme Court has listed as basic human needs "food, clothing, shelter, medical care and reasonable safety"[6]

---

[1]U.S.Const., Amend. VIII.

[2]Farmer v. Brennan, 511 U.S. 825, 834, 114 S. Ct. 1970 (1994); Wilson v. Seiter, 501 U.S. 294, 298, 111 S. Ct. 2321 (1991).

[3]Rhodes v. Chapman, 452 U.S. 337, 347, 101 S. Ct. 2392 (1981).

[4]Rhodes v. Chapman, 452 U.S. at 347; Wilson v. Seiter, 501 U.S. at 297.

[5]Rhodes v. Chapman, 452 U.S. at 347; *accord,* Wilson v. Seiter, 501 U.S. at 308.

[6]Helling v. McKinney, 509 U.S. 25, 32, 113 S. Ct. 2475 (1993) (citing DeShaney v. Winnebago County Dep't of Social Services,

as well as "warmth [and] exercise."[7] The lower courts have also mentioned sanitation and personal hygiene[8] and sleep,[9] and may identify other basic needs in the future. The Supreme Court has held that the "temporary" (two years or more) deprivation of visiting rights does not deny basic necessities.[10] In our view, the prolonged idleness and deprivation of human contact in some segregation units denies basic human needs for companionship and meaningful activity, but the courts have not yet so held.[11] Even for issues that clearly raise Eighth Amendment concerns, the line between the "wanton infliction of pain" and conditions that are merely restrictive or harsh has not been clearly drawn.[12]

The malicious and sadistic use of force, even without significant injury, is an Eighth Amendment violation,[13] as is other treatment that unjustifiably inflicts pain or injury[14] or is humiliating or "antithetical to human dignity."[15] The Supreme Court has also held, in connection with cell searches, that "calculated harassment unrelated to prison needs" may constitute cruel and unusual punishment.[16]

The Court has not mentioned this holding in over 20 years, but has not overruled it, and presumably it is applicable to other forms of harassing conduct besides searches, though lower courts seem reluctant to apply it.[17]

Some recent Supreme Court decisions concerning prisoners' Eighth Amendment claims have emphasized physical harm, or the risk of it.[18] The Court has held that unsafe conditions that "pose an unreasonable risk of serious damage to [a prisoner's] future health" may violate the Eighth Amendment even if the damage has not yet occurred and may not affect every prisoner exposed to the conditions.[19] However, numerous decisions have held that conduct can violate the Eighth Amendment even if it does not inflict

---

489 U.S. 189, 199–200, 109 S. Ct. 998 (1989)). "Shelter" includes various aspects of physical conditions including lighting, ventilation, and structural deterioration. *See* § B of this chapter.

[7]Wilson v. Seiter, 501 U.S. at 304. "Shelter" includes various aspects of physical conditions including lighting, ventilation, and structural deterioration. *See* § B of this chapter.

[8]Palmer v. Johnson, 193 F.3d 346, 352 (5th Cir. 1999) (quoting Novak v. Beto, 453 F.2d 661, 665 (5th Cir. 1971)) (holding denial of toilet facilities for many inmates in a small area would be a "deprivation of basic elements of hygiene" violating the Eighth Amendment); Carver v. Bunch, 946 F.2d 451, 452 (6th Cir. 1991); Hoptowit v. Ray, 682 F.2d 1237, 1246 (9th Cir. 1982); Wolfish v. Levi, 573 F.2d 118, 125 (2d Cir. 1978), *rev'd on other grounds sub nom.* Bell v. Wolfish, 441 U.S. 520, 99 S. Ct. 1861 (1979); Newman v. Alabama, 559 F.2d 283, 291 (5th Cir. 1978).

[9]Harper v. Showers, 174 F.3d 716, 720 (5th Cir. 1999); Merritt v. Hawk, 153 F. Supp. 2d 1216, 1228 (D.Colo. 2001).

[10]Overton v. Bazzetta, 539 U.S. 126, 137, 123 S. Ct. 2162 (2003).

[11]*See* § J of this chapter.

[12]*Compare* Chandler v. Crosby, 379 F.3d 1278, 1296–97 (11th Cir. 2004) (holding that even "severe discomfort" from high inside temperatures during Florida summers did not violate the Eighth Amendment) *with* Dixon v. Godinez, 114 F.3d 640, 644 (7th Cir. 1997) (holding that the Eighth Amendment entitles prisoners "not to be confined in a cell at so low a temperature as to cause severe discomfort" (citation omitted)).

[13]Hudson v. McMillian, 502 U.S. 1, 7–9, 112 S. Ct. 995 (1992); *see* § G.2.a.1 of this chapter.

[14]Hope v. Pelzer, 536 U.S. 730, 738, 122 S. Ct. 2508 (2002) (citing unnecessary pain caused by handcuffs and the restricted position of confinement in holding the "hitching post" punishment unconstitutional).

[15]Hope v. Pelzer, 536 U.S. at 738, 745.

[16]Hudson v. Palmer, 468 U.S. 517, 530, 104 S. Ct. 3194 (1984); *see* Whitman v. Nesic, 368 F.3d 931, 934 (7th Cir. 2004) (equating "calculated harassment" to searches "maliciously motivated, unrelated to institutional security, and hence 'totally without penological justification'" (citation omitted)); Harper v. Showers, 174 F.3d 716, 720 (5th Cir. 1999) (holding allegation of frequent searches for

no purpose but to harass was not frivolous); Scher v. Engelke, 943 F.2d 921, 923–24 (8th Cir. 1991) (affirming verdict including punitive damages for repeated harassing cell searches done in retaliation for complaints about guard misconduct).

[17]*See* Dobbey v. Illinois Dep't of Corrections, 574 F.3d 443, 444–46 (7th Cir. 2009) (holding hanging a noose in housing area, though offensive, did not violate the Eighth Amendment under circumstances where it was not a threat); Johnson v. Dellatifa, 357 F.3d 539, 546 (6th Cir. 2004) (holding allegations that an officer continuously banged and kicked prisoner's cell door, threw food trays through the slot so hard the top came off, made aggravating remarks, insulted him about his hair length, growled and snarled through the cell window and smeared the window so he couldn't see out, behaved in a racially prejudiced manner towards him, and jerked and pulled him unnecessarily hard when escorting him from his cell would, if true, "demonstrate shameful and utterly unprofessional behavior by [the officer], but are insufficient to establish an Eighth Amendment violation"). *Cf.* Parrish v. Johnson, 800 F.2d 600, 604 (6th Cir. 1986) (holding that an officer's waving of a knife in a paraplegic prisoner's face, knife-point extortion of potato chips and cookies, incessant taunting, and failure to relay requests for medical care to the nurses violated the Eighth Amendment. The court emphasizes the plaintiff's paraplegic condition, his dependence on the officer who was abusing him, and the resulting "significant mental anguish.").

[18]Farmer v. Brennan, 511 U.S. 825, 836, 114 S. Ct. 1970 (1994) (addressing risk of inmate–inmate assault).

[19]Helling v. McKinney, 509 U.S. 25, 33, 113 S. Ct. 2475 (1993) ("a remedy for unsafe conditions need not await a tragic event"). *Helling* concerned exposure to tobacco smoke; other examples cited by the Court included exposure to the risk of infectious disease, unsafe drinking water, exposed wiring, deficient firefighting measures, and assault. *Id.*, 509 U.S. at 33–34; *see also* Hill v. Marshall, 962 F.2d 1209, 1213–14 (6th Cir. 1992) (risk of developing tuberculosis); Powell v. Lennon, 914 F.2d 1459, 1463 (11th Cir. 1990) (exposure to asbestos); Johnson-El v. Schoemehl, 878 F.2d 1043, 1045–55 (8th Cir. 1989) (pesticides); Clark v. Moran, 710 F.2d 4, 9–11 (1st Cir. 1983) (cancer-causing chemical). *See* §§ G.1 and G.3 of this chapter for further discussion of such issues.

physical injury[20] or cause lasting or permanent harm[21]—though the Prison Litigation Reform Act bars recovery of damages for mental or emotional injury in the absence of physical injury.[22]

Even conditions that are physically or mentally harmful, or that deprive prisoners of basic needs, may not violate the Eighth Amendment if they serve a legitimate correctional purpose.[23] Thus, one court has held that depriving "Close Management" prisoners of their two hours weekly outdoor recreation when they committed serious and dangerous misconduct did not violate the Eighth Amendment, even if it inflicted pain, in light of its penological justification.[24] Prison officials are entitled to deference in their decisions concerning order and security.[25] However, there are limits: one court has held that it is unconstitutional to inflict "serious psychological pain" on inmates to serve "minor [correctional] concerns," "routine and automatic

---

[20]*See, e.g.*, Hudson v. Palmer, 468 U.S. 517, 530, 104 S. Ct. 3194 (1984) (holding "calculated harassment unrelated to prison needs" through searches could violate the Eighth Amendment); Powers v. Snyder, 484 F.3d 929, 932–33 (7th Cir. 2007) (suggesting that plaintiffs need not prove a serious health risk in all second-hand smoke cases; "maybe there's a level of ambient tobacco smoke that, whether or not it creates a serious health hazard, inflicts acute discomfort amounting, especially if protracted, to punishment"); Benefield v. McDowall, 241 F.3d 1267, 1272 (10th Cir. 2001) (holding psychological harm actionable under Eighth Amendment); Hicks v. Frey, 992 F.2d 1450, 1457 (6th Cir. 1993) ("Extreme conduct by custodians that causes severe emotional distress is sufficient."); Scher v. Engelke, 943 F.2d 921, 924 (8th Cir. 1981) ("the scope of eighth amendment protection is broader than the mere infliction of physical pain"; evidence of "fear, mental anguish and misery" can establish the requisite injury for an Eighth Amendment claim); Kingsley v. Bureau of Prisons, 937 F.2d 26, 32 (2d Cir. 1991); White v. Napoleon, 897 F.2d 103, 111 (3d Cir. 1990); Parrish v. Johnson, 800 F.2d 600, 605 (6th Cir. 1986); Davenport v. DeRobertis, 653 F. Supp. 649, 656–58, 663–64 (N.D.Ill. 1987), *aff'd in pertinent part*, 844 F.2d 1310 (7th Cir. 1988); Mitchell v. Newryder, 245 F. Supp. 2d 200, 204 (D.Me. 2003) (holding prisoner denied access to toilet stated a valid claim that he was "purposefully subjected to dehumanizing prison conditions" regardless of any risk of harm); Colman v. Vasquez, 142 F. Supp. 2d 226, 236 (D.Conn. 2001) (cumulative emotional pain to a female sexual assault victim from pat frisking by male staff may be sufficient injury to support an Eighth Amendment claim); *see also* Hope v. Pelzer, 536 U.S. 730, 738, 745, 122 S. Ct. 2508 (2002) (citing "risk of particular discomfort and humiliation" from lack of bathroom breaks, in addition to pain and risk of injury, from "hitching post" restraints; stating prisoner was treated in a way "antithetical to human dignity"); Hudson v. McMillian, 503 U.S. 1, 7–8, 112 S. Ct. 995 (1992) (holding "significant injury" need not be shown to establish an Eighth Amendment violation for use of force). *But see In re* Long Term Administrative Segregation, 174 F.3d 464, 472 (4th Cir. 1999) ("A depressed mental state, without more, does not rise to the level of the 'serious or significant physical or emotional injury' that must be shown to withstand summary judgment on an Eighth Amendment charge.").

[21]Boretti v. Wiscomb, 930 F.2d 1150, 1154–55 (6th Cir. 1991); Jackson v. Cain, 864 F.2d 1235, 1247 (5th Cir. 1989); Foulds v. Corley, 833 F.2d 52, 55 (5th Cir. 1987); Corselli v. Coughlin, 842 F.2d 23, 26 (2d Cir. 1988); Gill v. Mooney, 824 F.2d 192, 196 (2d Cir. 1987); H.C. by Hewett v. Jarrard, 786 F.2d 1080, 1083, 1087 (11th Cir. 1986).

There is sometimes considerable confusion about the terms "pain" and "injury," and you may be faced with an argument that you may have suffered pain but the Eighth Amendment requires you to show injury. We think the best response is that if you have suffered the "wanton infliction of pain" sufficient to violate the Eighth Amendment, that pain causes injury, or *is* injury, as a legal matter. *See* McLaurin v. Prater, 30 F.3d 982, 984 (8th Cir. 1994) (pain is "sufficient injury to allow for recovery" under the Eighth Amendment); Strickler v. Waters, 989 F.2d 1375, 1381 (4th Cir. 1993) (holding that Eighth Amendment claims must be supported by "evidence of a serious or significant physical or emotional injury," but that pain sufficient to violate the Eighth Amendment would cause such injury); *see also* Hudson v. McMillian, 503 U.S. at 7–9 (holding that "significant injury" is not necessary for an Eighth

Amendment claim based on the malicious and sadistic use of force).

[22]*See* Ch. 9, § E.

[23]*See* Overton v. Bazzetta, 539 U.S. 126, 137, 123 S. Ct. 2162 (2003) (holding that temporary deprivation of visiting privileges as a means of effecting discipline did not violate the Eighth Amendment, though permanent or much longer deprivations might).

[24]Bass v. Perrin, 170 F.3d 1312, 1316–17 (11th Cir. 1999) (terming the deprivation "a rational, albeit debatable, response to the substantial threat posed by the plaintiffs"). Severe restrictions in high-security units, or on individual prisoners who persist in misconduct, are often found justified by the legitimate needs of security and discipline. *See, e.g.*, Trammell v. Keane, 338 F.3d 155, 163, 165–66 (2d Cir. 2003) (upholding deprivation of all property except one pair of shorts and denial of recreation, showers, hot water, and a cell bucket for about two weeks to a prisoner who persisted in misbehaving in a segregation unit); Rodriguez v. Briley, 403 F.3d 952, 952–53 (7th Cir. 2005) (holding that a rule requiring segregation prisoners to stow property in a box before leaving their cells could be enforced by refusing to let them leave their cells, even if the cost was missed meals and showers; the non-complying prisoner "punished himself"); Anderson v. Coughlin, 757 F.2d 33, 36 (2d Cir. 1985); Bono v. Saxbe, 620 F.2d 609, 614 (7th Cir. 1980). *But see* Williams v. Greifinger, 97 F.3d 699, 704–05 (2d Cir. 1996) (holding that treatment "otherwise . . . impermissible under the Eighth Amendment" is not acceptable for behavior control purposes); Williams v. Coughlin, 875 F. Supp. 1004, 1013 (W.D.N.Y. 1995) (holding two-day withholding of food for failure to return food tray could constitute disproportionate punishment where the prisoner had not engaged in conduct the rule was designed to curb).

If prison officials take steps to avoid harm caused by their restrictive measures, that fact will weigh against a finding of cruel and unusual punishment. Trammell v. Keane, 338 F.3d at 166 (noting that plaintiff was regularly observed by a nurse); Bass v. Perrin, 170 F.3d at 1317 (noting officials' daily cell-front medical and psychological examinations and instructions on in-cell exercise to prisoners denied all outside exercise).

[25]Norwood v. Vance, 572 F.3d 626, 630 (9th Cir. 2009) (holding jury should have received a deference instruction in case about lack of exercise during violence-related lockdowns).

security concerns," or "pragmatic interests of lesser significance."[26]

The Eighth Amendment standard "draw[s] its meaning from the evolving standards of decency that mark the progress of a maturing society."[27] In cases involving risks to health or safety, courts must "assess whether society considers the risk that the prisoner complains of to be so grave that it violates contemporary standards of decency to expose anyone unwillingly to such a risk. In other words, the prisoner must show that the risk of which he complains is not one that today's society chooses to tolerate."[28] However, judges are supposed to rely as much as possible on "objective factors" such as statutes and not on their personal opinions about standards of decency.[29] Some courts have held that state or federal prison regulations and health requirements, as well as statutes, are evidence of current standards of decency.[30]

However, statutes and regulations are only one factor in Eighth Amendment analysis, and violations of them do not always violate the Eighth Amendment.[31] The converse is also true: conditions may violate the Eighth Amendment even if they do not violate state laws.[32] Similarly, professional standards or expert opinions about how prisons should be run do not determine what is acceptable under the Eighth Amendment,[33] though they may assist the court in understanding the issues before it.[34] Several decisions have noted

---

[26]Jordan v. Gardner, 986 F.2d 1521, 1530 (9th Cir. 1993) (en banc).

[27]Rhodes v. Chapman, 452 U.S. 337, 346, 101 S. Ct. 2392, (quoting Trop v. Dulles, 356 U.S. 86, 101, 78 S. Ct. 590 (1958)); *accord*, Helling v. McKinney, 509 U.S. 25, 36, 113 S. Ct. 2475 (1993).

The courts have not said much about how these standards evolve. One court has stated that standards of decency in prison rise with society's standard of living. Davenport v. DeRobertis, 844 F.2d 1310, 1314–16 (7th Cir. 1988). The question has also been discussed in cases involving exposure to "second-hand" tobacco smoke. *See* § G.3.c of this chapter.

[28]Helling v. McKinney, 509 U.S. 25, 36, 113 S. Ct. 2475 (1993); *see* Baze v. Rees, 553 U.S. 35, 128 S. Ct. 1520, 1532 (2008) ("it is difficult to regard a practice as 'objectively intolerable' when it is in fact widely tolerated"; addressing lethal injection procedures).

[29]Rhodes v. Chapman, 452 U.S. at 346; Rodriguez v. McClenning, 399 F. Supp. 2d 228, 237–38 (S.D.N.Y. 2005) (relying on trend toward statutory prohibition of sexual contact between prison employees and prisoners in holding that "any sexual assault of a prisoner by a prison employee constitutes cruel and unusual punishment."); Schmidt v. Odell, 64 F. Supp. 2d 1014, 1031 (D.Kan. 1999) (holding Americans with Disabilities Act "reflects, to some degree, contemporary standards of decency concerning treatment of individuals with disabilities"); Gonyer v. McDonald, 874 F. Supp. 464, 466 (D.Mass. 1995) (citing health code violations for asbestos; "With respect to prison health hazards, state health codes reflect established public attitudes as to what those standards [of decency] are."); Morales Feliciano v. Romero Barcelo, 672 F. Supp. 591, 617–19 (D.P.R. 1986) (weighing statutes in Eighth Amendment analysis).

[30]Atkinson v. Taylor, 316 F.3d 257, 265 and n.7 (3d Cir. 2003) (holding that an executive order banning smoking in public buildings was some evidence of what society does not tolerate, and suggesting that a federal regulation prohibiting smoking in federal buildings and workplaces might be evidence of a national consensus); Lopez v. LeMaster, 172 F.3d 756, 761 (10th Cir. 1999) (holding that state Department of Health jail standard requiring 24-hour supervision and staffing sufficient to permit monitoring and response to calls for help "do not establish constitutional parameters for the reasonable measures necessary to insure inmate safety, [but] they do provide persuasive authority concerning what is required"); Pack v. Artuz, 348 F. Supp. 2d 63, 87–88 (S.D.N.Y. 2004)

(holding contemporary standards of decency are reflected in state Industrial Code and federal OSHA regulations governing asbestos exposure); Valdez v. Farmon, 766 F. Supp. 1529, 1537–38 (E.D.Cal. 1991) (state prison regulations); Dawson v. Kendrick, 527 F. Supp. 1252, 1294 (S.D.W.Va. 1981) (state fire code); Richardson v. Sheriff of Middlesex County, 407 Mass. 455, 553 N.E.2d 1286, 1289 (Mass. 1990) (state prison regulations); Inmates of Riverside County Jail v. Clark, 144 Cal.App.3d 850, 192 Cal.Rptr. 823, 828–29 (Cal.App. 1983) (state minimum standards for jails); Michaud v. Sheriff of Essex County, 390 Mass. 523, 458 N.E.2d 702, 706–07 (Mass. 1983) (same); Wilson v. State, 113 Idaho 563, 746 P.2d 1022, 1026–27 (Idaho 1987) (state haircutting sanitation regulations); *see* Capps v. Atiyeh, 559 F. Supp. 894, 914–15 (D.Or. 1982) (Constitution requires "substantial" compliance with fire code); *see also* Hall v. Bennett, 379 F.3d 462, 465 (7th Cir. 2004) (prison rule barring working with live wires and general safety codes that would be known to an electrical foreman was evidence of actual knowledge of a serious risk to safety).

[31]Carroll v. DeTella, 255 F.3d 470, 472–73 (7th Cir. 2001) (holding that contamination of water by radium and lead in almost twice the maximum amounts allowed by the federal Environmental Protection Agency did not violate the Eighth Amendment, since the *state* EPA was not planning any enforcement because the federal EPA was considering a more permissive standard; officials could defer to the environmental agencies); French v. Owens, 777 F.2d 1250, 1257 (7th Cir. 1985) (violations of state fire code and Occupational Safety and Health Administration regulations did not violate the Eighth Amendment); Masonoff v. DuBois, 899 F. Supp. 782, 799 (D.Mass. 1995) ("A court may look to state codes with respect to prison hazards in its effort to determine society's standard of decency, but these standards do not necessarily reflect the constitutional minimum.").

[32]McCord v. Maggio, 910 F.2d 1248, 1250 (5th Cir. 1990).

[33]Rhodes v. Chapman, 452 U.S. at 348 n.13; Inmates of Occoquan v. Barry, 844 F.2d 828, 836–37 (D.C. Cir.), *rehearing denied*, 850 F.2d 796 (D.C. Cir. 1988); Gary H. v. Hegstrom, 831 F.2d 1430, 1433 (9th Cir. 1987); Cody v. Hillard, 830 F.2d 912, 914 (8th Cir. 1987) (en banc); Green v. Ferrell, 801 F.2d 765, 771 (5th Cir. 1986); Alston v. Coughlin, 668 F. Supp. 822, 831, 836 (S.D.N.Y. 1987); *see also* Bell v. Wolfish, 441 U.S. 520, 543 n.27, 99 S. Ct. 1861 (1979) (same principle in case involving pretrial detainees).

[34]Rhodes v. Chapman, 452 U.S. at 363–64 and nn.11–12 (concurring opinion); Hall v. Bennett, 379 F.3d 462, 465 (7th Cir. 2004) (citing prison rules and National Electrical Safety Code as evidence that prison personnel knew of the risk of working with live electrical wires without gloves; Gates v. Cook, 376 F.3d 323, 339–42 (5th Cir. 2004) (affirming unconstitutionality of heat, sanitation, and lighting conditions based on expert testimony about their potential consequences); Inmates of Allegheny County Jail v. Wecht, 874 F.2d 147, 153–54 (3d Cir. 1989), *vacated and remanded on other grounds*, 493 U.S. 948 (1989); Davenport v. DeRobertis, 844 F.2d

that accreditation by organizations such as the American Correctional Association or the National Commission on Correctional Health Care does not establish that a prison or prison system is operating in a constitutional manner.[35]

Some courts have held that risks of a type that is commonplace outside prisons do not violate the Eighth Amendment.[36] We think this approach is wrong; after all, violent assault and exposure to environmental tobacco smoke, which the Supreme Court has said present Eighth Amendment concerns, also occur in civilian society.

In Eighth Amendment cases, courts inquire whether conditions, *"alone or in combination, . . . deprive inmates of the minimal civilized measure of life's necessities."*[37]

Under this "totality of the circumstances" approach,[38] merely unpleasant conditions do not automatically become unconstitutional when you add them together. Rather, conditions must have "a mutually enforcing effect that produces the deprivation of a single, identifiable human need" in order to become unconstitutional in combination.[39] Examples of this "mutually enforcing effect" include "a low cell temperature at night combined with a failure to issue blankets" or restrictions on outdoor exercise combined with long lock-in times.[40] Similarly, courts are more likely to find crowding unconstitutional if it occurs in combination with long lock-in times or contributes to other dangerous or deteriorated conditions.[41]

1310, 1315 (7th Cir. 1988); Inmates of Occoquan v. Barry, 850 F.2d at 801 (opinion concurring in denial of rehearing); Ramos v. Lamm, 639 F.2d 559, 567 n.10 (10th Cir. 1980); DeGidio v. Pung, 704 F. Supp. 922, 956 (D.Minn. 1989), *aff'd*, 920 F.2d 525 (8th Cir. 1990); Miles v. Bell, 621 F. Supp. 51, 60 (D.Conn. 1985).

In *Gates v. Cook*, 376 F.3d 323, 342–43 (5th Cir. 2004), the court affirmed an order to comply with the mental health care standards of the American Correctional Association and the National Commission on Correctional Health Care, based on the lower court's findings of an environment that was toxic to mental health and that caused mentally ill prisoners to deteriorate severely.

[35]*See* Gates v. Cook, 376 F.3d at 337 (stating "it is absurd to suggest that the federal courts should subvert their judgment as to alleged Eighth Amendment violations to the ACA whenever it has relevant standards. Additionally, the ACA's limited inspections are not be [sic] binding as factual findings on the magistrate or on this court. While compliance with ACA's standards may be a relevant consideration, it is not *per se* evidence of constitutionality."); Ruiz v. Estelle, 37 F. Supp. 2d 855, 901–02, 924–25 (S.D.Tex. 1999) (noting that NCCHC evaluation does not assess actual medical care but just written policies, bureaucracy, infrastructure, etc., and that ACA accreditation does not indicate whether the system is actually following its own procedures); LaMarca v. Turner, 662 F. Supp. 647, 655 (S.D.Fla. 1987) (finding ACA accreditation of "marginal relevance" in case about pattern of sexual assault), *appeal dismissed*, 861 F.2d 724 (11th Cir. 1988). *But see* Yellow Horse v. Pennington County, 225 F.3d 923, 928 (8th Cir. 2000) (weighing ACA accreditation in finding suicide prevention procedures constitutional); Grayson v. Peed, 195 F.3d 692, 697 (4th Cir. 1999) (weighing ACA and NCCHC accreditation in holding defendants not liable for death of restrained prisoner).

[36]*See* Christopher v. Buss, 384 F.3d 879, 882–83 (7th Cir. 2004) (rejecting the claim of a prisoner hit in the face with a softball because of a defect in the field; speculating that such defects "doubtless exist on subpar fields across the country" and noting that softball was a voluntary activity). In *Reynolds v. Powell*, 370 F.3d 1028, 1031–32 (10th Cir. 2004), the court held that a prisoner who alleged that he fell in the shower because the area did not drain properly did not state an Eighth Amendment claim because slippery floors are a common risk to members of the public at large; such claims, it said, are the province of tort law. *Contra*, Curry v. Kerik, 163 F. Supp. 2d 232, 236–37 (S.D.N.Y. 2001) (hazardous shower conditions can violate the Eighth Amendment).

[37]Rhodes v. Chapman, 452 U.S. at 347 (emphasis supplied); *accord*, Surprenant v. Rivas, 424 F.3d 5, 19–20 (1st Cir. 2005) (holding jury could find round-the-clock lock-in, denial of hygienic

products, limited access to water, and multiple daily strip searches unconstitutional taken together, even if case law was "in some disarray" about those conditions individually); Caldwell v. District of Columbia, 201 F. Supp. 2d 27, 34–35 (D.D.C. 2001) (holding jury could find that exposure to tobacco smoke combined with excessive heat, lack of ventilation, a plastic mattress, occasional lack of drinking water, flooding, and feces in the cells supported jury finding of an Eighth Amendment violation); Tillery v. Owens, 907 F.2d 418, 426–28 (3d Cir. 1990); Peterkin v. Jeffes, 855 F.2d 1021, 1024–25 (3d Cir. 1988).

[38]Rhodes v. Chapman, 452 U.S. at 363 (Brennan, J., concurring).

[39]Wilson v. Seiter, 501 U.S. 294, 304, 111 S. Ct. 2321 (1991); *see* Mitchell v. Maynard, 80 F.3d 1434, 1442 (10th Cir. 1996) (holding placement in a concrete cell with no heat, deprivation of clothing, mattress, blankets or any other bedding, prescription eyeglasses, out-of-cell exercise, utensils, adequate ventilation or hot water, and allowance only of minimal amounts of toilet paper, in combination, were "a significant departure from the 'healthy habilitative environment' the state is required to provide its inmates") (citation omitted); Ruiz v. Johnson, 37 F. Supp. 2d 855, 929 (S.D.Tex. 1999) ("the combination of inmates who are routinely subjected to violence, extortion, and rape, of officers who are aware of inmate-on-inmate victimization but fail to respond to the victims, of high barriers preventing inmates from seeking safekeeping or protective custody, and of a system that fails accurately to report, among other data, instances of requests for safekeeping and sexual assaults, and, as well, the obviousness of the risk to prison officials, when all are considered together, have the mutually enforcing effect of rendering prison conditions cruel and unusual by denying inmates safety from their fellow inmates"); Carty v. Farrelly, 957 F. Supp. 727, 735–36 (D.V.I. 1997) (finding shelter provided by jail constitutionally inadequate based on consideration of multiple factors).

[40]Wilson v. Seiter, 501 U.S. at 304; *see* Palmer v. Johnson, 193 F.3d 346, 353 (5th Cir. 1999) (holding totality of mutually enforcing circumstances—"overnight outdoor confinement with no shelter, jacket, blanket, or source of heat as the temperature dropped and the wind blew along with the total lack of bathroom facilities for forty-nine inmates sharing a small bounded area"—denied "the minimal civilized measure of life's necessities").

[41]*See* Tillery v. Owens, 907 F.2d at 428 (overcrowding may be "unbearable" in conjunction with deficiencies in physical plant and services even if it does not cause those deficiencies); Laube v. Haley, 234 F. Supp. 2d 1227, 1244–46 (M.D.Ala. 2002) (finding that "the combination of substantial overcrowding and significantly inadequate supervision," exacerbated by the crowding-related breakdown

Prison officials cannot "trade off" unconstitutional conditions under this theory. If one condition is cruel and unusual, the fact that other conditions are better will not save prison officials from Eighth Amendment liability.[42]

Often, the length of time prisoners are subjected to an unpleasant condition plays an important part in determining whether it is cruel and unusual.[43] But especially degrading or abusive conditions are unconstitutional even if imposed for short periods of time.[44]

The Supreme Court has held in criminal cases that punishments must not be "grossly disproportionate" to the crime.[45] This principle has played little part in Eighth Amendment analysis of prison conditions.[46]

2. The Subjective Component: Deliberate Indifference

In Eighth Amendment conditions cases, the plaintiff must prove that the defendants acted with "deliberate indifference."[47] The deliberate indifference standard does not apply to cases involving the use of force; in those

---

in classification, availability of weapons, and lack of segregation areas violated the Eighth Amendment right to protection from violence); *see also* § B.1 of this chapter.

[42]Spain v. Procunier, 600 F.2d 189, 195, 197, 199 (9th Cir. 1979) (constitutional violations found in use of tear gas and restraints and denial of recreation, even though physical structure and medical, nutritional, and sanitary practices were satisfactory); Fisher v. Koehler, 692 F. Supp. 1519, 1564 (S.D.N.Y. 1988) (unconstitutional levels of violence found although building seemed clean and in good condition), *aff'd*, 902 F.2d 2 (2d Cir. 1990); Frazier v. Ward, 426 F. Supp. 1354, 1357, 1372 (N.D.N.Y. 1977) (strip searches and denial of outdoor recreation found unconstitutional although other conditions were adequate); Michaud v. Sheriff of Essex County, 390 Mass. 523, 458 N.E.2d 702, 708 (Mass. 1983) (failure to provide toilet facilities was unconstitutional regardless of the "cumulative condition of the jail").

[43]Overton v. Bazzetta, 539 U.S. 126, 137, 123 S. Ct. 2162 (2003) (holding temporary deprivations of visiting did not violate the Eighth Amendment, stating that permanent or long-term deprivations might do so); Hutto v. Finney, 437 U.S. 678, 686–87, 98 S. Ct. 2565 (1978); Vinning-El v. Long, 482 F.3d 923, 924–25 (7th Cir. 2007) (holding six days' confinement in cell with floor covered in water, no working plumbing, walls smeared with blood and feces, no mattress, sheets, toilet paper, or other personal hygiene items violated the Eighth Amendment); Spencer v. Bouchard, 449 F.3d 721, 728–29 (6th Cir. 2006) (holding that the degree of exposure to cold that violates the Eighth Amendment would vary according to the length of the exposure); Alexander v. Tippah County, 351 F.3d 626, 630–31 (5th Cir. 2003) (questioning whether "deplorable" sanitary conditions imposed for 24 hours violated the Eighth Amendment; citing cases); Dixon v. Godinez, 114 F.3d 640, 643 (7th Cir. 1997) ("A condition which might not ordinarily violate the Eighth Amendment may nonetheless do so if it persists over an extended period of time."); Patchette v. Nix, 952 F.2d 158, 164 (8th Cir. 1991); Howard v. Adkison, 887 F.2d 134, 137 (8th Cir. 1989); Harris v. Fleming, 839 F.2d 1232, 1234–35 (7th Cir. 1988) (holding five-day deprivation of toilet paper and ten-day deprivation of toothbrush and toothpaste did not violate the Constitution); Martin v. Lane, 766 F. Supp. 641, 647–48 (N.D.Ill. 1991); Adams v. Kincheloe, 743 F. Supp. 1385, 1391–92 (E.D.Wash. 1990).

[44]*See, e.g.*, Hope v. Pelzer, 536 U.S. 730, 738, 122 S. Ct. 2508 (2002) (holding "hitching post" restraints for seven hours violated Eighth Amendment); Surprenant v. Rivas, 424 F.3d 5, 19–20 (1st Cir. 2005) (holding three weeks in segregation under unsanitary conditions would violate detainees' due process rights, which were held equal to Eighth Amendment protections); DeSpain v. Uphoff, 264 F.3d 965, 974 (10th Cir. 2001) (holding 36 hours' subjection to unsanitary flooding and exposure to human waste stated a claim; "exposure to human waste carries particular weight); Gaston v. Coughlin, 249 F.3d 156, 166 (2d Cir. 2001) (plaintiff's allegation that for several days the area in front of his cell was filled with feces,

urine, and sewage water stated an Eighth Amendment claim); McBride v. Deer, 240 F.3d 1287, 1291–92 (10th Cir. 2001) (three days in a feces-covered cell without cleaning materials stated a constitutional claim); Johnson v. Lewis, 217 F.3d 726, 734–35 (9th Cir. 2000) (holding that evidence that prisoners were held in the yard for 4 days in the summer and 17 hours in the winter, without toilet access, without drinking water for several hours, without warm clothing during subfreezing weather supported an Eighth Amendment claim); Palmer v. Johnson, 193 F.3d 346, 352–54 (5th Cir. 1999) (holding overnight stay outdoors without blankets or warm clothing or toilet facilities could violate the Eighth Amendment); Gordon v. Faber, 973 F.2d 686, 687–88 (8th Cir. 1992) (less than two hours' exposure to subfreezing outdoor weather without hats and gloves violated the Eighth Amendment; damages awarded); Henderson v. DeRobertis, 940 F.2d 1055 (7th Cir. 1991) (damages awarded for four days in subzero weather without heat or extra clothing or blankets); Johnson v. Pelker, 891 F.2d 136, 139 (7th Cir. 1989) (three days in a feces-smeared cell without running water and with no access to cleaning materials could violate the Eighth Amendment); Johnson v. Williams, 788 F.2d 1319, 1323 (8th Cir. 1986) (18-hour strip cell confinement could violate the Eighth Amendment depending on other conditions); LaReau v. Manson, 651 F.2d 96, 107–09 (2d Cir. 1981) (double-celling permitted for up to 30 days but use of floor mattresses forbidden for "any period of time"); McCray v. Burrell, 516 F.2d 357, 365–69 (4th Cir. 1975) (en banc) (two-day confinement in strip cell conditions with hole in the floor rather than a toilet violated the Eighth Amendment); *see also* cases cited in § D (Food), n.184, and § J (Segregation), nn.1327–1328, of this chapter.

[45]Ewing v. California, 538 U.S. 11, 30, 123 S. Ct. 1179 (2003).

[46]In a few cases courts have found prison disciplinary punishments disproportionate to the disciplinary offense. *See* Ch. 4, § H.1.p; *but see* Austin v. Johnson, 328 F.3d 204, 209 (5th Cir. 2003) (rejecting disproportionality argument where a minor stole a candy bar and was sent to a one-day boot camp, where after a day of exercise he suffered heat stroke and was hospitalized for two weeks with acute kidney failure; "[r]equiring youthful offenders to perform military-styled exercises for one day is neither cruel nor unusual; it is a deliberate policy choice to instill much-needed discipline.").

[47]Wilson v. Seiter, 501 U.S. 294, 303, 111 S. Ct. 2321 (1991). The Court reasoned that if deprivations are not specifically imposed as part of a prisoner's sentence, they are not really "punishment" unless the officials imposing them "possessed a sufficiently culpable state of mind." *Id.*, 501 U.S. at 297–98. The Court then decided that deliberate indifference was the appropriate state of mind requirement for conditions cases. *Accord*, Farmer v. Brennan, 511 U.S. 825, 834, 114 S. Ct. 1970 (1994) (inmate assault case). This

cases, the plaintiff must show that the defendants acted "maliciously and sadistically."[48]

Deliberate indifference in Eighth Amendment cases falls somewhere between mere negligence (carelessness) and actual malice (intent to cause harm).[49] That is, it amounts to recklessness.[50] Sometimes deliberate indifference is shown directly by evidence of prison personnel's bad motives or attitudes.[51] However, the Supreme Court has held that a prison official can be found reckless or deliberately

indifferent if "the official knows of and disregards an excessive risk to inmate health or safety. . . ."[52] This is the same standard of recklessness that is used in criminal law, and it is sometimes called the "subjective" approach to recklessness.[53] If prison officials know that conditions are "objectively cruel" and fail to act to remedy them, they are deliberately indifferent.[54] Prison officials are, however, allowed to impose severe hardships on prisoners for legitimate penological purposes, such as maintaining security and discipline, without being found deliberately indifferent.[55]

It is not enough in an Eighth Amendment case to show that the defendants *should* have known of a risk or of cruel conditions,[56] and older cases saying that are no longer good law. However, the fact that a condition or a risk was obvious is circumstantial evidence that will permit a judge or jury to conclude that a defendant did know about it, even if there is no direct evidence about what the defendant knew.[57]

---

reasoning has been justly criticized, *see Farmer*, 511 U.S. at 854–55 (Blackmun, J., concurring in result), but it is the law nonetheless.

A different deliberate indifference standard governs claims against city and county governments, regardless of whether the case involves the Eighth Amendment or an entirely different constitutional provision. *See* Ch. 8, § B.4.b.

[48]Hudson v. McMillian, 503 U.S. 1, 7, 112 S. Ct. 995 (1992); Whitley v. Albers, 475 U.S. 312, 320, 106 S. Ct. 1078 (1986), cited in Wilson v. Seiter, 501 U.S. at 302–03. These cases are discussed in §§ G.2.a.1 and G.2.b.3 of this chapter; *see also* § K of this chapter concerning emergencies and lockdowns.

The Supreme Court has stated that this standard applies only "in *one class* of prison cases: 'when officials stand accused of using excessive physical force.'" Farmer v. Brennan, 511 U.S. at 835 (citation omitted) (emphasis supplied). This suggests that certain pre-*Farmer* decisions were wrong in saying that the "malicious and sadistic" standard applies to other security-related issues, at least those where decisions must be made "in haste [and] under pressure." Jordan v. Gardner, 986 F.2d 1521, 1528 (9th Cir. 1993) (en banc) (stating the deliberate indifference standard applies to security policies that are "developed over time, with ample opportunity for reflection"); *accord*, Morgan v. District of Columbia, 824 F.2d 1049, 1062–63 (D.C. Cir. 1987); Fisher v. Koehler, 692 F. Supp. 1519, 1562 n.56 (S.D.N.Y. 1988), *aff'd*, 902 F.2d 2 (2d Cir. 1990). However, the Ninth Circuit has reiterated that view since *Farmer*. *See* Johnson v. Lewis, 217 F.3d 726, 734 (9th Cir. 2000) (when prison officials faced with a disturbance moved prisoners outside and made them lie down on the ground, they could not be held liable in those exigent circumstances unless they acted maliciously and sadistically; but once the prisoners were outside, handcuffed, prone, and under armed guard, deliberate indifference applied to failure to provide for sanitation, food, and drinking water).

The "malicious and sadistic" standard only applies to the conduct of persons actually using force. Claims against supervisors for failing to control subordinates' use of force, or against bystanding officers who do not intervene when other officers use excessive force, are subject to the deliberate indifference standard. *See* § G.2.d of this chapter.

[49]Farmer v. Brennan, 511 U.S. at 835–36; Wilson v. Seiter, 501 U.S. at 297–304.

Gross negligence" is a "nebulous" term that generally means something similar to the civil law recklessness standard. *Farmer*, 511 U.S. at 836 n.4; *see also* Canton v. Harris, 489 U.S. 378, 388 n.7, 109 S. Ct. 1197 (1989) (suggesting that gross negligence is not the same as deliberate indifference). In our opinion, using this term in a prisoners' rights case generally will not be helpful to the plaintiff.

[50]Farmer v. Brennan, 511 U.S. at 836.

[51]*See, e.g.*, Haley v. Gross, 86 F.3d 630, 642 (7th Cir. 1996) (stating that official who was told a prisoner had been threatening to set a fire and responded, "Well, go ahead, you nigger, burn your black asses. You've got to be in there," presented "a paradigm case

of deliberate indifference"); *see also* cases cited in § F.1.a, n.276, § G.1.b, nn.863–864, 882–883.

[52]*Farmer*, 511 U.S. at 837.

[53]*Farmer*, 511 U.S. at 840–41.

[54]Alberti v. Sheriff of Harris County, Texas, 937 F.2d 984, 998–99 (5th Cir. 1991); *accord*, Hope v. Pelzer, 536 U.S. 730, 738, 122 S. Ct. 2508 (2002) (finding Eighth Amendment violation where prison staff knowingly subjected the plaintiff to the obvious risks and pain of "hitching post" restraint); Williams v. Griffin, 952 F.2d 820, 826 (4th Cir. 1991).

In *Wilson v. Seiter*, 501 U.S. 294, 303–04, 111 S. Ct. 2321 (1991), the Supreme Court cited two deliberate indifference cases with approval. In one, the court held that a jury could have inferred deliberate indifference on the part of prison officials who transferred a known psychotic prisoner to a general population facility with no mental health care and who failed to segregate him, resulting in his murder by other inmates. Cortes-Quinones v. Jiminez-Nettleship, 842 F.2d 556, 559–60 (1st Cir. 1988). In another case involving a paraplegic prisoner, the court observed that there was no justification in the record for the failure to provide adequate toilet facilities and necessary physical therapy for months, and that the warden was the "responsible official in charge" of the prison and was "fully advised" of the problem. Therefore, the court concluded that her neglect constituted deliberate indifference. LaFaut v. Smith, 834 F.2d 389, 392–94 (4th Cir. 1987).

[55]Trammell v. Keane, 338 F.3d 155, 163 (2d Cir. 2003) (stating "the deliberate indifference standard must be applied in a way that accounts for the precise circumstances of the alleged misconduct and the competing institutional concerns"); *see* cases cited in nn.23–24, above.

[56]Farmer v. Brennan, 511 U.S. at 840–41.

This civil tort law or objective standard is applied in determining whether a municipality has a policy of deliberate indifference that caused a civil rights violation. *See* Ch. 8, § B.4.b.

[57]Farmer v. Brennan, 511 U.S. at 842–43; *id.* at 837 ("the official must both be aware of facts from which the inference could be drawn that a substantial risk of serious harm exists, and he must also draw the inference"); *see* Hope v. Pelzer, 536 U.S. 730, 738, 122 S. Ct. 2508 (2002); Vinning-El v. Long, 482 F.3d 923, 924–25 (7th Cir. 2007) (holding jury could infer that guards working in the area knew about grossly filthy cell conditions); Estate of Carter v. City of Detroit, 408 F.3d 305, 312–13 (6th Cir. 2005) (holding a jury could

Therefore, if you can show that officials disregarded a risk that was obvious, the court should not grant summary judgment against you, and you should have the right to a trial[58]—though you will not necessarily win in the end, since the court or jury may not find that the defendants "drew the inference" that you were at risk even if it was obvious.[59] Other kinds of facts may also be circumstantial evidence that the defendant had actual knowledge of a risk.[60]

Purposefully avoiding knowledge may also amount to deliberate indifference.[61]

A defendant need not know the precise nature of the risk to be found deliberately indifferent, as long as he or she knows that a serious risk exists.[62] A defendant also need not have knowledge of a specific risk to a specific individual from a specific source. For example, in an inmate–inmate assault case, "it does not matter whether the risk comes from a single source or multiple sources, any more than it matters whether a prisoner faces an excessive risk of attack for reasons personal to him or because all prisoners in his situation face such a risk."[63]

---

infer actual knowledge of a risk from a defendant's knowledge of a prisoner's condition, and could discount the defendant's claim he did not believe she was at risk); Lolli v. County of Orange, 351 F.3d 410, 420–21 (9th Cir. 2003) (holding officers' indifference to a diabetic prisoner's extreme behavior, sickly appearance, and explicit statements about his condition could support a finding of actual knowledge of a serious risk); Gates v. Cook, 376 F.3d 323, 343 (5th Cir. 2004) (holding deliberate indifference finding supported by "obvious and pervasive nature" of challenged conditions); Steele v. Shah, 87 F.3d 1266, 1270 (11th Cir. 1996) (denying summary judgment to prison doctor who had been told the plaintiff received psychiatric medication in part because of suicide risk, but discontinued it based on a cursory interview without reviewing medical records); Haley v. Gross, 86 F.3d 630, 641–42 (7th Cir. 1996); LaMarca v. Turner, 995 F.2d 1526, 1536–37 (11th Cir. 1993) (evidence that "painted . . . a picture that would be apparent to any knowledgeable observer" supported an inference of knowledge on the defendant's part); Goka v. Bobbitt, 862 F.2d 646, 651 (7th Cir. 1988) (the Eighth Amendment is violated in an inmate assault case "where defendants know of the danger or where the threat of violence is so substantial or pervasive that their knowledge could be inferred, and yet defendants fail to enforce a policy or take other reasonable steps which may have prevented the harm"); see also Wilson v. Seiter, 501 U.S. 294, 300, 111 S. Ct. 2321 (1991) ("The long duration of a cruel prison condition may make it easier to *establish* knowledge") (emphasis in original). *But see* Campbell v. Sikes, 169 F.3d 1353, 1372 (11th Cir. 1999) (dismissing medication discontinuation case because plaintiff's condition was not so obvious that knowledge could be inferred).

Direct and circumstantial evidence are discussed in Ch. 10, § S.1.a.

[58]Summary judgment is discussed in Ch. 10, § L.

[59]*See* Rich v. Bruce, 129 F.3d 336, 339–40 (4th Cir. 1997) (holding officer who was "too stupid" to understand the risk his actions created was not deliberately indifferent).

[60]Hope v. Pelzer, 536 U.S. 730, 738 n.8, 122 S. Ct. 2508 (2002) (holding particular defendants' awareness of a risk of harm "may be evaluated in part by considering the pattern of treatment that inmates generally received" as a result of the challenged practice); Hall v. Bennett, 379 F.3d 462, 465 (7th Cir. 2004) (holding knowledge of the risk of working with live electrical wires without gloves could be shown by a prison rule barring working with live wires and by general safety codes that would be known to an electrical foreman); LaMarca v. Turner, 995 F.2d 1526, 1536 n.21 (11th Cir. 1993) (holding warden's "supervisory role and the insular character of prison communities" supported inference of knowledge of "apparent" conditions).

Courts have disagreed over whether expert testimony concerning what a defendant could be expected to know supports an inference about what he or she did know. *Compare* Campbell v. Sikes, 169 F.3d 1353, 1368–73 (11th Cir. 1999) (rejecting proposition) *with* LeMarbe v. Wisneski, 266 F.3d 429, 436–38 & nn.4–6

(6th Cir. 2001) (holding testimony as to what any medical specialist would have known raised a jury issue as to defendant specialist's actual knowledge); Moore v. Duffy, 255 F.3d 543, 545 (8th Cir. 2001) (holding that expert evidence created a material factual dispute whether the prisoner's medical treatment deviated so far from professional standards as to constitute deliberate indifference).

[61]*Farmer*, 511 U.S. at 843 n.8; *see* Goebert v. Lee County, 510 F.3d 1312, 1327–28 (11th Cir. 2007) (jail captain had a duty to "look into" pregnant prisoner's complaint that she was leaking fluid, her condition was worsening, and she had not seen an obstetrician); Sanchez v. Taggart, 144 F.3d 1154, 1156 (8th Cir. 1998) (failure to try to verify claim of medical inability to perform work assignment supported deliberate indifference finding); Wallis v. Baldwin, 70 F.3d 1074, 1077 (9th Cir. 1995) (holding prison officials who had information about possible asbestos contamination had a duty to inspect before sending unprotected work crews to the location); Ginest v. Board of County Comm'rs of Carbon County, 333 F. Supp. 2d 1190, 1198 (D.Wyo. 2004) (officials have a duty to investigate information suggesting a risk of injury); *see also* Mayoral v. Sheahan, 245 F.3d 934, 940 (7th Cir. 2000) (holding jury could reject guard's testimony she knew nothing about gangs as "incredible and deliberately ignorant. The *Farmer* standard is not designed to give officials the motivation to 'take refuge' in the zone between ignorance and actual knowledge," and she could be seen "as trying to inhabit that zone.").

[62]Velez v. Johnson, 395 F.3d 732, 736 (7th Cir. 2005) (holding an officer who knew of a risk of assault could not escape liability by arguing that he didn't know the assault would be a rape).

[63]*Farmer*, 511 U.S. at 843; *see* Brown v. Budz, 398 F.3d 904, 914–15 (7th Cir. 2005) (holding deliberate indifference can be established by knowledge either of a victim's vulnerability or of an assailant's predatory nature; both are not required); Pierson v. Hartley, 391 F.3d 898, 903 (7th Cir. 2004) (holding that a prisoner could recover for assault by a violent prisoner assigned to a "meritorious housing" unit in violation of prison policy regardless of whether prison staff knew of the risk to the particular prisoner who was injured); Greene v. Bowles, 361 F.3d 290, 294–95 (6th Cir. 2004) (holding that a transgender prisoner could recover for assault by a known "predatory inmate" either because leaving her in a unit containing high-security inmates threatened her safety, or because placing that inmate in protective custody created a risk for its occupants generally); Marsh v. Butler County, Ala., 268 F.3d 1014, 1028–30 (11th Cir. 2001) (en banc) (holding prisoners assaulted in a county jail with no functioning cell locks or audio or visual surveillance, so dilapidated that inmates made weapons from pieces of the building, stated a claim against the county; similar allegations plus lack of segregation of violent from nonviolent inmates or

An official who has knowledge of a serious risk or a cruel condition must "take reasonable measures to abate it."[64] Prison officials who "respond[] reasonably to the risk" are not deliberately indifferent, "even if the harm ultimately was not averted."[65] However, they may be liable if their actions are "not adequate given the known risk,"[66] or if they

give "inconsequential logistical concerns that might be no more than matters of convenience" higher priority than prisoners' basic human needs.[67]

Some courts have said that prison officials cannot be found deliberately indifferent unless they possessed "actual knowledge of *impending* harm, *easily* preventable,"[68] or that they exposed the plaintiff to a risk "*because of,* rather than in *spite of,* the risk to him."[69] This is wrong. While actual knowledge must be shown under *Farmer,* the other items need not. You can sue under the Eighth Amendment for harm that is not "impending"; *Farmer* said that serious damage to prisoners' future health is actionable.[70] The harm does not have to be "easily preventable"; *Farmer* holds that prison officials must do what is reasonable,[71] not what is easy. In addition, *Farmer* specifically said that "it is enough that the official acted or failed to act *despite* his knowledge of a substantial risk of serious harm," and did not require proof that the official acted *because of* the risk.[72]

In deliberate indifference cases—especially individual damages cases—you must try to identify exactly *who* was deliberately indifferent.[73] In some cases, your claim may be against line staff who do not do their jobs.[74] In others, it may be against supervisors for

> knowing acquiescence in the unconstitutional behavior of
> . . . subordinates, . . . persistently violat[ing] a statutory

---

other classification, crowding, understaffing, lack of head counts, lack of staff surveillance in housing areas, lack of mental health screening, and lack of discipline for violent inmates stated a claim against the sheriff); Jensen v. Clarke, 94 F.3d 1191, 1198–1200 (8th Cir. 1996) (affirming injunction based on generalized increase in violence attributed to random assignment of cellmates); Hayes v. New York City Dep't of Correction, 84 F.3d 614, 621 (2d Cir. 1996) (prisoner's refusal to name his enemies to prison staff was not outcome determinative if staff knew of risk to him); LaMarca v. Turner, 995 F.2d at 1535 (liability can be based on "general danger arising from a prison environment that both stimulated and condoned violence"); Laube v. Haley, 234 F. Supp. 2d 1227, 1251 (M.D.Ala. 2002) (holding increase in programs and staff overtime, requests for more staff, etc., were inadequate responses to dangers posed by overcrowding); Coleman v. Wilson, 912 F. Supp. 1282, 1316 (E.D.Cal. 1995) (risk of harm to prisoners with mental illness from systemic medical care deficiencies is obvious), *appeal dismissed,* 101 F.3d 705 (9th Cir. 1996); Abrams v. Hunter, 910 F. Supp. 620, 625–26 (M.D.Fla. 1995) (acknowledging potential liability based on awareness of generalized, substantial risk of serious harm from inmate violence), *aff'd,* 100 F.3d 971 (11th Cir. 1996); Knowles v. New York City Dep't of Corrections, 904 F. Supp. 217, 221–22 (S.D.N.Y. 1995) (prison officials' knowledge of an ethnic "war" among inmates, that a Hispanic inmate who had been cut had been transferred to plaintiff's jail, and that plaintiff was part of a group at risk because of his accent and appearance was sufficient to withstand summary judgment).

[64]Farmer v. Brennan, 511 U.S. at 847; *see* Clem v. Lomeli, 566 F.3d 1177, 1181–82 (9th Cir. 2009) (jury instruction that defendant could be liable only if an "act of the defendant" harmed the plaintiff was erroneous; jury should have been told that failure to act may also support a deliberate indifference finding).

[65]*Farmer,* 511 U.S. at 844; *accord,* Erickson v. Holloway, 77 F.3d 1078, 1080–81 (8th Cir. 1996) (holding officer who learned of threat and notified officer on next shift before leaving was not deliberately indifferent); LaMarca v. Turner, 995 F.2d at 1535 (stating "if an official attempts to remedy a constitutionally deficient prison condition, but fails in that endeavor, he cannot be deliberately indifferent unless he knows of, but disregards, an appropriate and sufficient alternative").

[66]Riley v. Olk-Long, 282 F.3d 592, 597 (8th Cir. 2002); *accord,* Benjamin v. Fraser, 343 F.3d 35, 51–52 (2d Cir. 2003) (holding "largely ineffective" remedial efforts did not defeat liability for long-standing deficiencies; detainee case); Jensen v. Clarke, 94 F.3d 1191, 1200–01 (8th Cir. 1996) (holding injunction was appropriate despite defendants' post-complaint actions); Austin v. Hopper, 15 F. Supp. 2d 1210, 1262–63 (M.D.Ala. 1998) (order to follow a policy was not a sufficient response where officials knew it continued to be violated); Jones v. City and County of San Francisco, 976 F. Supp. 896, 908–09 (N.D.Cal. 1997) (holding correction of many fire safety deficiencies was a "less than reasonable" response where other serious inadequacies persisted); Coleman v. Wilson, 912 F. Supp. 1282, 1319 (E.D.Cal. 1995) (". . . [P]atently ineffective gestures purportedly directed towards remedying objectively unconstitutional

conditions do not prove a lack of deliberate indifference, they demonstrate it."), *appeal dismissed,* 101 F.3d 705 (9th Cir. 1996).

[67]Allen v. Sakai, 48 F.3d 1082, 1088 (9th Cir. 1995). In *Allen,* the court held that prison officials' own policy goal of five hours a week of recreation was evidence that they knew of the risks of depriving prisoners of exercise, and their failure to comply with it without good reason constituted deliberate indifference.

[68]*See* Feeney v. Correctional Medical Services, Inc., 464 F.3d 158, 162 (1st Cir. 2006) (citation and internal quotation marks omitted) (emphasis supplied); Palmer v. Marion County, 327 F.3d 588, 593 (7th Cir. 2003) (citations omitted). These two circuits appear to be the only ones to use this formula.

[69]McGill v. Duckworth, 944 F.2d 344, 348 (7th Cir. 1991) (emphasis in original) (citing Personnel Administrator v. Feeney, 442 U.S. 256, 279, 99 S. Ct. 2282 (1979)); *see McGill,* 944 F.2d at 350.

[70]Farmer v. Brennan, 511 U.S. at 845 (citing Helling v. McKinney, 509 U.S. 25, 33, 113 S. Ct. 2475 (1993)).

[71]*Farmer,* 511 U.S. at 847; *accord,* Hope v. Pelzer, 536 U.S. 730, 738, 122 S. Ct. 2508 (2002).

[72]*Farmer,* 511 U.S. at 842 (emphasis supplied). The Seventh Circuit has acknowledged that *Farmer* overruled some of its prior decisions in holding that the official need not be shown to have intended the harm that occurred. *See* Haley v. Gross, 86 F.3d 630, 641 (7th Cir. 1996).

[73]Naming the right defendants is one of the most important aspects of successful civil rights litigation. It is discussed generally in Ch. 8, § B.4, and specifically in connection with medical care (§ F.1.a), inmate assault (§ G.1.e), and use of force (§ G.2.d), in this chapter.

[74]*See* §§ F.1.a, G.1.b, and G.1.e on this point.

If line staff do not have adequate training, procedures, or resources with which to work, they may not be deliberately indifferent. Rivas v. Freeman, 940 F.2d 1491, 1495–96 (11th Cir. 1991)

duty to inquire about such behavior and to be responsible for preventing it, ... failure to train or supervise ... or an official acquiescence in the continued existence of prison conditions which, themselves, are so injurious to prisoners that they amount to a constitutional violation.[75]

In others, supervisors, or city, or county governments, may be found to have policies amounting to deliberate indifference.[76]

Where prisoners challenge institutional policies, practices, inadequate facilities, etc., rather than the individual misconduct of prison staff, courts have often held that deliberate indifference can be shown by "'repeated examples of negligent acts which disclose a pattern of conduct . . .' or by showing 'systematic or gross deficiencies in staffing, facilities, equipment or procedures,'"[77] regardless of prison officials' motives.[78]

In cases where prisoners seek injunctions, which are considered to be official capacity rather than individual capacity cases,[79] the court may find deliberate indifference even if particular officials are well motivated as individuals.[80] In such cases the focus is on "the institution's historical indifference" rather than the state of knowledge and the response of a particular individual.[81] In an injunctive case, the "actual knowledge" that is necessary to support a grant of relief may be provided by the judicial proceeding itself.[82]

In pleading an Eighth Amendment deliberate indifference claim, you should identify the right or risk to which the defendants were indifferent. With respect to medical care, the Supreme Court has held that prisoners must show "deliberate indifference to serious medical needs."[83] In other kinds of cases, you should use a similar phrase, identifying the particular "human need" you have been deprived of, using terms used by earlier Eighth Amendment cases. For example, if you were locked in a cell without a working toilet, you would refer to "deliberate indifference to the plaintiff's need for reasonably adequate sanitation"[84] or the need for "basic elements of hygiene."[85] If officials failed knowingly to protect you from assault, you would refer to "deliberate indifference to the plaintiff's need for safety."[86]

3. Other Legal Limits on Prison Conditions

The Eighth Amendment does not apply to pretrial detainees, who cannot be punished at all (at least in theory) under the Due Process Clause.[87] However, conditions or restrictions are not considered "punishment" if they are "reasonably

(Sheriff was responsible for a policy of deliberate indifference but his deputies were not liable because their actions "flowed from the lack of policies, procedures, and training"); Anderson v. City of Atlanta, 778 F.2d 678, 685–86 (11th Cir. 1985) (in medical care case, municipality held liable for inadequate staffing, but individual staff absolved).

[75]Villante v. Dep't of Corrections of City of New York, 786 F.2d 516, 519 (2d Cir. 1986); see Hill v. Marshall, 962 F.2d 1209, 1214 (6th Cir. 1992) (supervisor's failure to review and respond to inmates' medical complaints despite knowledge of a breakdown in services constituted deliberate indifference); see also cases cited in § G.1.e of this chapter, n.931.

[76]See §§ F.1.a and § G.1.e of this chapter.

If the local government has adequate policies and procedures, it cannot be held deliberately indifferent just because lower level employees violate them. Holmes v. Sheahan, 930 F.2d 1196, 1201–02 (7th Cir. 1991); see also Ch. 8, § B.4.b.

[77]French v. Owens, 777 F.2d 1250, 1254 (7th Cir. 1985) (medical care) (quoting Ramos v. Lamm, 639 F.2d 559, 575 (10th Cir. 1980)); accord, Harris v. Thigpen, 941 F.2d 1495, 1505 (11th Cir. 1991) (medical care); Todaro v. Ward, 565 F.2d 48, 52 (2d Cir. 1977) (medical care); Ginest v. Board of County Comm'rs of Carbon County, 333 F. Supp. 2d 1190, 1198–99 (D.Wyo. 2004); Gilland v. Owens, 718 F. Supp. 665, 687 (W.D.Tenn. 1989) (inmate violence); Fisher v. Koehler, 692 F. Supp. 1519, 1561-62 (S.D.N.Y. 1988), aff'd, 902 F.2d 2 (2d Cir. 1990) (inmate violence).

French v. Owens was cited with apparent approval by the Supreme Court in Wilson v. Seiter, 501 U.S. 294, 310 n.1, 111 S. Ct. 2321 (1991).

[78]See cases cited in § F.1, n.298, § F.3, nn.399–400 and G.1.c, n.895–896, in this chapter. But see Webb v. Goord, 340 F.3d 105, 110 (2d Cir. 2003) (holding that system-wide Eighth Amendment claim requires "evidence of a concerted intent among prison officials, one expressed through discernable regulations, policies, or practices"; "an accumulation of incidents," without a showing of systemic abuse, is not enough; plaintiffs' allegations of 40 unrelated incidents over 10 years at 13 prisons did not state a claim).

[79]An official capacity case is "in all respects other than name, to be treated as a suit against the entity." Kentucky v. Graham, 473

U.S. 159, 166, 105 S. Ct. 3099 (1985). See Ch. 8, § B.4.c, concerning capacity.

[80]Harris v. Angelina County, Texas, 31 F.3d 331, 335 (5th Cir. 1994) (deliberate indifference found "against the county"); LaMarca v. Turner, 995 F.2d 1526, 1542 (11th Cir. 1993) (in case involving an entrenched pattern of sexual assault, the district court properly entered injunctive relief against the new superintendent even though he seemed better motivated than the old superintendent); Fisher v. Koehler, 692 F. Supp. at 1562 (deliberate indifference found based on city government's "institutional failure" even though warden and commissioner were sincere and competent).

Capacity is discussed further in Ch. 8, §§ B.4.c and L.1.

[81]LaMarca v. Turner, 995 F.2d at 1542; accord, Alberti v. Sheriff of Harris County, Tex., 978 F.2d 893, 894–95 (5th Cir. 1992) (deliberate indifference supported by evidence "that the state knew" that refusal to accept felons caused serious local jail crowding); Terry v. Hill, 232 F. Supp. 2d 934, 944 (E.D.Ark. 2002) (finding "the State" deliberately indifferent).

[82]Farmer v. Brennan, 511 U.S. 825, 846 n.9, 114 S. Ct. 1970 (1994); see Hadix v. Johnson, 367 F.3d 513, 526 (6th Cir. 2004) (noting that same evidence showing unconstitutional conditions in court was available to prison officials).

[83]Estelle v. Gamble, 429 U.S. 97, 104, 97 S. Ct. 285 (1976).

[84]See Newman v. Alabama, 559 F.2d 283, 291 (5th Cir. 1978).

[85]Carver v. Bunch, 946 F.2d 451, 452 (6th Cir. 1991); Hoptowit v. Spellman, 753 F.2d 779, 783 (9th Cir. 1985).

[86]See Farmer, 511 U.S. at 832.

[87]City of Revere v. Mass. General Hospital, 463 U.S. 239, 244, 103 S. Ct. 2979 (1983).

related to a legitimate goal" and not "arbitrary or purposeless."[88] In practice, there is not much difference between the outcomes of convicts' and detainees' challenges to conditions of confinement, and we cite due process and Eighth Amendment cases more or less interchangeably in this chapter. The rights of detainees are discussed in more detail in Chapter 6.

Many state constitutions have clauses relevant to prison conditions. These clauses may provide greater protection than the federal Cruel and Unusual Punishments Clause[89] or

the federal Due Process Clause.[90] Even if a state constitutional provision is worded similarly to the federal provision, a state court could interpret the state constitution as providing more rights for prisoners.[91] So far, most courts have either rejected that view[92] or have avoided the question.[93]

State statutes and regulations may also provide more rights than the federal Constitution, and you may be able to enforce these in state court.[94] Federal statutes and regulations may also be enforceable in federal court through the Administrative Procedures Act[95] and otherwise.[96] Tort law may be enforced against state and local governments or prison personnel,[97] and against the federal government through the Federal Tort Claims Act (FTCA).[98]

---

[88]Bell v. Wolfish, 441 U.S. 520, 539, 99 S. Ct. 1861 (1979).

[89]For example, one state constitution provides that "[p]enal administration should be based on the principle of reformation and upon the need for protecting the public." Alaska Const. art. I, § 12. This provision creates a state constitutional right to rehabilitation, which does not exist under the federal Constitution. Ferguson v. Dep't of Corrections, 816 P.2d 134, 139–40 (Alaska 1991). State constitutional and statutory rights to rehabilitation are discussed further in §§ F.4.f and I.1 of this chapter.

The constitution of Utah forbids cruel and unusual punishments *and* provides: "Persons arrested or imprisoned shall not be treated with unnecessary rigor." Utah Const. art. I, § 9. The Utah Supreme Court, in a case where a prisoner was injured after staff failed to buckle his seat belt during transportation, has said:

> A prisoner suffers from unnecessary rigor when subject to unreasonably harsh, strict, or severe treatment. This may include being unnecessarily exposed to an increased risk of serious harm. . . . a violation of the prohibition on unnecessary rigor must arise from "treatment that is clearly excessive or deficient and unjustified, not merely the frustrations, inconveniences, and irritations that are common to prison life." When the claim of unnecessary rigor arises from an injury, a constitutional violation is made out only when the act complained of presented a substantial risk of serious injury for which there was no reasonable justification at the time.

The court went on to say that to recover damages, a plaintiff must show a "flagrant" violation, which means a violation of clearly established law, and added that such a violation requires that: "First, the nature of the act presents an obvious and known serious risk of harm to the arrested or imprisoned person; and second, knowing of that risk, the official acts without other reasonable justification." Dexter v. Bosko, 184 P.3d 592, 597–98 (Utah 2008) (citation and footnotes omitted). After reading this, we frankly are not sure whether the Utah Constitution provides more protection to prisoners than the Eighth Amendment deliberate indifference standard described in § A.2, nn.11–12 of this chapter. Other state courts have interpreted similar state constitutional provisions differently. For example, in *Sterling v. Cupp*, 290 Or. 611, 625 P.2d 123, 128–36 (1981), the court interpreted the state's "unnecessary rigor" clause to limit opposite-sex pat frisks to a greater degree than does federal law. However, it later held that claims of denial of adequate medical care should not be assessed under the unnecessary rigor clause, but instead under the state constitution's cruel and unusual punishments clause, which it interpreted to mean the same as the federal provision. Billings v. Gates, 323 Or. 167, 180–81, 916 P.2d 291 (1996).

[90]*See* Ch. 4, §§ A and A.1, and § H.1, n.287, for comments on state due process protections.

[91]For example, one court has held that the state constitution provides more protection for the rights of pretrial detainees than the federal Due Process Clause. Cooper v. Morin, 49 N.Y.2d 69, 399 N.E.2d 1188, 1194, 424 N.Y.S.2d 168 (N.Y. 1979). In addition, if a state constitution protects substantive interests that the federal Constitution does not, that state-protected interest may in turn be a liberty or property interest protected by the federal Due Process Clause. *See* Ch. 4, n.15.

[92]Grubbs v. Bradley, 552 F. Supp. 1052, 1124–25 (M.D.Tenn. 1982).

Some state courts simply assume without much discussion that their constitutional provisions mean the same thing as the Cruel and Unusual Punishments Clause or the Due Process Clause and then follow federal case law. *See, e.g.*, Crain v. Bordenkircher, 176 W.Va. 338, 342 S.E.2d 422, 437 (W.Va. 1986); Hickson v. Kellison, 170 W.Va. 732, 296 S.E.2d 855, 856 (W.Va. 1982); Wickham v. Fisher, 629 P.2d 896, 901 (Utah 1981). One state court has given state prison regulations great weight in making federal law decisions under the Eighth Amendment. Michaud v. Sheriff of Essex County, 390 Mass. 523, 458 N.E.2d 702, 706–07 (Mass. 1983); *see also* Inmates of Riverside County v. Clark, 144 Cal.App.3d 850, 192 Cal.Rptr. 823, 828–29 (Cal.App. 1983) (holding that federal due process standards apply under the state constitution, but giving weight to state correctional minimum standards in determining contemporary standards of decency).

[93]Michaud v. Sheriff of Essex County, 458 N.E.2d at 708.

[94]*See, e.g.*, § I.1 of this chapter, n.1220.

[95]*See* Ch. 8, § B.2.b, concerning the Administrative Procedures Act.

[96]For example, 18 U.S.C. § 4042, which sets out the duty of care of the Federal Bureau of Prisons to "provide for the safekeeping, care, and subsistence" and the "protection, instruction and discipline" of the prisoners, does not in itself create a private right of action. However, it does set out the standard of care in negligence cases under the Federal Tort Claims Act. Harper v. Williford, 96 F.3d 1526, 1528 (D.C. Cir. 1996); *see* Ch. 8, § C.2 (concerning FTCA).

[97]*See* in this chapter § F.5, concerning malpractice and medical negligence; § G.1, concerning tort claims for inmate assault; § G.2.e, concerning tort claims for excessive force; § G.3.d, concerning negligence claims for injuries caused by hazardous conditions; *see also* Ch. 8, § C, concerning tort claims generally.

[98]*See* Ch. 8, §§ C.2, H.2.b, concerning the FTCA.

There are also international laws and treaties that are intended to protect prisoners. These are beyond the scope of this Manual, chiefly because they do not in practice provide any additional protections for American prisoners. Though the United States has ratified the International Covenant on Civil and Political Rights and the Convention Against Torture and Other Cruel, Inhuman, or Degrading Treatment or Punishment, it has done so with "reservations" interpreting their language to go no further than American constitutional law. One commentator has said: "These reservations present perhaps the greatest obstacle to prisoners' rights in the United States."[99]

B. Shelter

A prisoner must be provided with "shelter which does not cause his degeneration or threaten his mental and physical well being."[100] Serious physical deterioration of the prison may violate the Eighth Amendment,[101] but ordinary wear and tear and delays in maintenance are not unconstitutional.[102] Dangerous conditions like fire hazards or exposure to asbestos may also violate the Eighth Amendment, as discussed in § G.3 of this chapter. A prison that fails to provide safe and adequate shelter may be ordered closed.[103] Confinement of prisoners outdoors without any shelter may be unconstitutional even for short periods.[104]

1. Crowding

One important aspect of shelter is whether it is adequate to the number of people confined in it. There are no fixed constitutional limits on prison crowding. In crowding cases courts examine the overall conditions of confinement as well as the amount of space per inmate to determine how crowding affects prisoners' existence. In *Rhodes v. Chapman*,[105] the Supreme Court held that double-celling in 63-square foot cells designed for one prisoner did not violate the Eighth Amendment in a prison which was a modern facility in good condition and in which "the prisoners [were] adequately sheltered, fed, and protected, and . . . opportunities for education, work and rehabilitation assistance [were] available."[106] Similarly, the Court held that crowding of pretrial detainees does not deny due process unless it imposes "genuine privations and hardship over an extended period of time. . . ."[107]

Thus, courts are more likely to find crowding unconstitutional if it is linked with violence and other safety hazards, breakdowns in classification, food services, or medical care, or deteriorated physical conditions.[108] Courts also look

[99]Elizabeth Vasiliades, *Solitary Confinement and International Human Rights: Why The U.S. Prison System Fails Global Standards*, 21 Am. U. Int'l L. Rev. 71, 84–85 (2005).

[100]Ramos v. Lamm, 639 F.2d 559, 568 (10th Cir. 1980).

[101]Carty v. Farrelly, 957 F. Supp. 727, 736 (D.V.I. 1997) ("the state of disrepair of the facilities (including plumbing, heating, ventilation, and showers) and the effect that substandard conditions have on the inmates' sanitation and health informs whether the prison provides an inhabitable shelter for Eighth Amendment purposes"); Morales Feliciano v. Hernandez Colon, 697 F. Supp. 37, 40–45 (D.P.R. 1988); Reece v. Gragg, 650 F. Supp. 1297, 1304 (D. Kan. 1986); Grubbs v. Bradley, 552 F. Supp. 1052, 1125–27 (M.D.Tenn. 1982); Battle v. Anderson, 447 F. Supp. 516, 525 (E.D.Okla.), aff'd, 564 F.2d 388 (10th Cir. 1977); Gates v. Collier, 390 F. Supp. 482, 486–489 (N.D.Miss. 1975), aff'd, 525 F.2d 965 (5th Cir. 1976).

[102]Shrader v. White, 761 F.2d 975, 983 (4th Cir. 1985); Peterkin v. Jeffes, 661 F. Supp. 895, 907–08 (E.D.Pa. 1987), aff'd in pertinent part, 855 F.2d 1021, 1026–28 (3d Cir. 1988); Alston v. Coughlin, 668 F. Supp. 822, 828–29 (S.D.N.Y. 1987).

[103]Inmates of Allegheny County Jail v. Wecht, 874 F.2d 147, 153–55 (3d Cir. 1989), *vacated and remanded on other grounds*, 493 U.S. 948 (1989); DiMarzo v. Cahill, 575 F.2d 15, 19–20 (1st Cir. 1978); Benjamin v. Fraser, 156 F. Supp. 2d 333, 189 (S.D.N.Y. 2001) (holding that "constitutionally substandard modular units" had to be phased out), *affirmed in part, vacated and remanded in part on other grounds*, 343 F.3d 35 (2d Cir. 2003); Jackson v. Gardner, 639 F. Supp. 1005, 1008, 1012 (E.D.Tenn. 1986); Grubbs v. Bradley, 552 F.2d at 1126–27; Battle v. Anderson, 447 F. Supp. at 525.

[104]Johnson v. Lewis, 217 F.3d 726, 732–33 (9th Cir. 2000) (confinement in yard for several days, once in hot weather and once in cold, along with other deprivations could support a finding

of Eighth Amendment violation); Palmer v. Johnson, 193 F.3d 346, 352–53 (5th Cir. 1999) (holding overnight outdoor confinement without protection from cold or access to bathroom facilities denied "life's necessities").

[105]452 U.S. 337, 101 S. Ct. 2392 (1981).

[106]*Rhodes*, 452 U.S. at 366 (Brennan, J., concurring). Or, as one court put it, "an allegation of overcrowding without more does not state a claim under the eighth amendment." Akao v. Shimoda, 832 F.2d 119, 120 (9th Cir. 1987) (emphasis supplied); *accord*, C.H. v. Sullivan, 920 F.2d 483, 485 (8th Cir. 1990); Lopez v. Robinson, 914 F.2d 486, 493 (4th Cir. 1990); Hoptowit v. Ray, 682 F.2d 1237, 1249 (9th Cir. 1982); Richards v. Cullen, 152 Wis.2d 710, 449 N.W.2d 318, 320 (Wis.App. 1989).

[107]Bell v. Wolfish, 441 U.S. 520, 542, 99 S. Ct. 1861 (1979). Conditions of pretrial detention are constitutionally acceptable if they are reasonably related to legitimate governmental objective. Bell v. Wolfish, 441 U.S. at 538–39. The economic motive of housing more prisoners without providing more space does not justify serious jail overcrowding. Morales Feliciano v. Parole Bd. of Puerto Rico, 887 F.2d 1, 5 (1st Cir. 1989); LaReau v. Manson, 651 F.2d 96, 104 (2d Cir. 1981); Campbell v. Cauthron, 623 F.2d 503, 508 (8th Cir. 1980); Reece v. Gragg, 650 F. Supp. 1297, 1303 (D.Kan. 1986); Richardson v. Sheriff of Middlesex County, 407 Mass. 455, 553 N.E.2d 1286, 1293 (Mass. 1990).

[108]Harris v. Angelina County, Texas, 31 F.3d 331, 335 (5th Cir. 1994); Williams v. Griffin, 952 F.2d 820, 824–25 (4th Cir. 1992) ("overcrowding accompanied by unsanitary and dangerous conditions can constitute an Eighth Amendment violation"); Tillery v. Owens, 907 F.2d 418, 427 (3d Cir. 1990) ("almost every element of the physical plant and provision of services . . . falls below constitutional norms"); French v. Owens, 777 F.2d 1250, 1252–53 (7th Cir. 1985) (poor physical conditions, lack of safety, breakdowns in medical and food services); Wellman v. Faulkner, 715 F.2d 269, 274 (7th Cir. 1983) (problems with physical plant, sanitation, food services, and recreation); Ruiz v. Estelle, 679 F.2d 1115, 1140–42 (5th Cir. 1982) (violence and understaffing); Coleman v. Schwarzenegger, 2009 WL 2430820 (E.D.Cal. 2009)

closely at the amount of lock-in time and are more likely to find a constitutional violation if prisoners are double-celled or otherwise crowded for long hours with little out-of-cell activity.[109] (In fact, single-celling in very small cells may

violate the Constitution if lock-in times are long.[110]) A particular degree of crowding may be unconstitutional for some groups of prisoners and not others, depending on their needs.[111] If prisoners are only subjected to crowding for a short time, courts are less likely to find it unconstitutional.[112] When overcrowding can be shown to have caused injury, for example from violence, damages may be awarded.[113]

The courts are divided on the constitutional acceptability of requiring prisoners to sleep on the floor, and it is hard to tell to what extent they disagree and to what extent their decisions reflect different circumstances. A number of decisions have held that overcrowding that results in prisoners' sleeping on the floor, even with mattresses,

---

(breakdown in medical and mental health services), *appeal dismissed*, 130 S.Ct. 1140 (2010); Jones v. City and County of San Francisco, 976 F. Supp. 896, 907 (N.D.Cal. 1997) (increased violence from inadequate supervision, deterioration of plumbing and sewage treatment, reduction in out-of-cell activities like recreation and religious services); Carty v. Farrelly, 957 F. Supp. 727, 735 (D.V.I. 1997) ("Overcrowding of inmates in correctional facilities can lead to violence among prisoners, breakdowns in classification systems, deterioration of the physical condition of the prison, and other safety hazards. When overcrowding causes such adverse effects, the overcrowding is unconstitutional."); Carver v. Knox County, Tenn., 753 F. Supp. 1370, 1386–87 (E.D.Tenn. 1989) (failure to provide "basic necessities," lack of recreation, breakdown of classification, failure to deliver medication), *remanded for reconsideration*, 887 F.2d 1287 (6th Cir. 1989), *adhered to on remand*, 753 F. Supp. 1398 (E.D.Tenn. 1990); Vazquez v. Carver, 729 F. Supp. 1063, 1069–70 (E.D.Pa. 1989) (violence, breakdowns in classification, use of program areas for housing); Fambro v. Fulton County, Ga., 713 F. Supp. 1426, 1430–31 (N.D.Ga. 1989) (surveillance and classification breakdowns, deficiencies in medical care, sanitation, and food service); Albro v. County of Onondaga, 681 F. Supp. 991, 994–95 (N.D.N.Y. 1988) (exacerbated threat of violence and fire hazards); Palmigiano v. Garrahy, 639 F. Supp. 244, 249–54 (D.R.I. 1986) (problems with safety, classification, idleness, food service, ventilation, plumbing, noise and medical care); Toussaint v. McCarthy, 597 F. Supp. 1388, 1408 (N.D.Cal. 1984) (old prisons with "deplorable" and "sordid" conditions and increased violence), *aff'd in part and rev'd in part on other grounds*, 801 F.2d 1080 (9th Cir. 1986); Grubbs v. Bradley, 552 F. Supp. 1052, 1125–27 (M.D.Tenn. 1982) (problems with noise, lighting, dilapidation, plumbing, safety, and idleness); Richardson v. Sheriff of Middlesex County, 553 N.E.2d at 1291–93 (sleeping on floor, inadequate bathroom facilities, crowding of inmates in non-housing areas). *But see* Benjamin v. Fraser, 343 F.3d 35, 53 (2d Cir. 2003) (reversing order that beds be spaced so that detainees' heads are six feet apart for protection from contagion because there was no showing of "actual or imminent substantial harm").

[109]Hall v. Dalton, 344 F.3d 648, 650 (8th Cir. 1994); Moore v. Morgan, 922 F.2d 1553, 1555 n.1 (11th Cir. 1991); Lyons v. Powell, 838 F.2d 28, 31 (1st Cir. 1988); French v. Owens, 777 F.2d at 1252–53 (double-celling with 24 square feet per inmate and 20–23 hour lock-in schedule); Hoptowit v. Ray, 682 F.2d at 1249 (court must consider lock-in time in assessing crowding); Campbell v. Cauthron, 623 F.2d at 506–07; Jones v. City and County of San Francisco, 976 F. Supp. at 907 (citing lock-in times of 16 to 23 or more hours a day in finding double-celling unconstitutional); Baker v. Holden, 787 F. Supp. 1008, 1017 (D.Utah 1992); Vazquez v. Carver, 729 F. Supp. at 1069–70 (long lock-in times weighed); Martino v. Carey, 563 F. Supp. 984, 1002 n.13 (D.Or. 1983) (in multiple-inmate cells, officials could provide either more space or more out-of-cell time); *see* Hubbard v. Taylor, 538 F.3d 229, 233–34 (3d Cir. 2008) (upholding extreme crowding in cells where prisoners had access to large dayrooms 14 hours a day). *But see* Smith v. Fairman, 690 F.2d 122, 125–26 (7th Cir. 1982); Chilcote v. Mitchell, 166 F. Supp. 2d 1313, 1315–18 (D.Ore. 2001) (holding confinement of three prisoners in 81 to 96 square feet with 20–21 hours lock-in

a day was not unconstitutional where there was no allegation of denial of basic needs).

[110]Hendrix v. Faulkner, 525 F. Supp. 435, 523, 525–27 (N.D.Ind. 1983) (37-square-foot cells, 17 square feet of floor space, 23-hour lock-in), *aff'd in pertinent part sub nom.* Wellman v. Faulkner, 715 F.2d 269, 274 (7th Cir. 1983); *see also* Inmates of Allegheny County v. Wecht, 874 F.2d 147, 154 (3d Cir. 1989) (cells "too small to provide humane living conditions"), *vacated and remanded on other grounds*, 493 U.S. 948 (1989). *But see* Bolton v. Goord, 992 F. Supp. 604, 609, 627–28 (S.D.N.Y. 1998) (holding confinement in cells of 53.3 and 58.6 square feet was not unconstitutional because inmates were only required to be in them for about two waking hours a day and had a variety of out-of-cell program activity).

[111]Balla v. Board of Corrections, 656 F. Supp. 1108, 1116–17 (D.Idaho 1987) (double-celling prohibited for maximum security and psychiatric housing); Delgado v. Cady, 576 F. Supp. 1446, 1457 (E.D.Wis. 1983) (limits placed on coerced double-celling of inmates with psychological problems or suicidal tendencies).

[112]Bell v. Wolfish, 441 U.S. at 543; Lyons v. Powell, 838 F.2d at 31; Union County Jail Inmates v. DiBuono, 713 F.2d 984, 1000 (3d Cir.), *rehearing denied*, 718 F.2d 1247 (3d Cir. 1983); Campbell v. Cauthron, 623 F.2d at 507; LaReau v. Manson, 651 F.2d at 105; Benjamin v. Malcolm, 646 F. Supp. 1550, 1554–55 (S.D.N.Y. 1986). *But see* Jones v. City and County of San Francisco, 976 F. Supp. at 907–08 (double-celling in 41-square foot cells with long lock-in times was unconstitutional where the average stay was 103 days).

[113]Morgan v. District of Columbia, 824 F.2d 1049, 1057–58 (D.C. Cir. 1987); Doe by and through Doe v. Washington County, 150 F.3d 920, 922–24 (8th Cir. 1998) (affirming jury award to juvenile plaintiff assaulted in his cell who was refused protection because the space was needed for other prisoners); Brown v. Mitchell, 327 F. Supp. 2d 615, 629–37 (E.D.Va. 2004) (allowing damages claim to go forward alleging that crowded and dilapidated conditions contributed to prisoner's death from disease); McKenna v. County of Nassau, 538 F. Supp. 737, 741 (E.D.N.Y. 1982), *aff'd*, 714 F.2d 115 (2d Cir. 1982); *see also* Redman v. County of San Diego, 942 F.2d 1435 (9th Cir. 1991) (en banc) (claim of prison rape caused in part by crowding should have gone to jury); Moore v. Morgan, 922 F.2d 1553, 1558 (11th Cir. 1991) (damages to be awarded for subjection to extreme crowding). *But see* Best v. Essex County, N.J., Hall of Records, 986 F.2d 54, 56–57 (3d Cir. 1993) (plaintiff failed to prove that his assault was caused by crowding); Brogsdale v. Barry, 926 F.2d 1184, 1188 (D.C. Cir. 1990) (crowding-related assault would not be actionable if the crowding was not unconstitutional).

is unconstitutional.[114] Most of them involve pretrial detainees, but some courts have reached the same conclusion as to the Eighth Amendment rights of convicts.[115] In most of these cases there were aggravating factors in addition to the fact of sleeping on the floor, such as prisoners' being held in areas not designed for housing[116] (though that is not unconstitutional in all circumstances[117]). Courts considering only the issue of sleeping on a floor mattress have often found it constitutional.[118] However, being required to sleep directly on the floor is unconstitutional.[119]

Some courts have held that if crowding results in unacceptable conditions, those conditions, and not the crowding itself, should be remedied.[120] That approach has been adopted in the Prison Litigation Reform Act, which provides that a "prisoner release order" (any order that limits or reduces prison population or directs release or nonadmission of prisoners) may be granted only after "less intrusive" relief has been tried and has failed to eliminate the constitutional violation.[121]

---

[114]Moore v. Morgan, 922 F.2d at 1555 n.1; Lyons v. Powell, 838 F.2d at 31 ("subjecting pretrial detainees to the use of a floor mattress for anything other than brief emergency circumstances may constitute an impermissible imposition of punishment"); Union County Jail Inmates v. Di Buono, 713 F.2d 984, 994 (3d Cir. 1983) (floor mattresses for more than a few days are unconstitutional); Lareau v. Manson, 651 F.2d 96, 105, 107–08 (2d Cir. 1981) (prison's use of floor mattresses for pretrial detainees unconstitutional "without regard to the number of days for which a prisoner is so confined"; for convicts, permissible only temporarily "in the event of a genuine emergency"); Maynor v. Morgan County, Ala., 147 F. Supp. 2d 1185, 1188, 1190 (N.D.Ala. 2001) (holding crowding that resulted in floor mattresses unconstitutional, requiring beds for all prisoners once crowding is relieved); Carty v. Farrelly, 957 F. Supp. 727, 735 (D.V.I. 1997) ("overcrowding which requires prisoners to sleep on mattresses on the floor on a consistent basis violates the Eighth and Fourteenth Amendments to the Constitution"); Zolnowski v. County of Erie, 944 F. Supp. 1096, 1113, 1115–16 (W.D.N.Y. 1996) (holding floor mattresses unconstitutional except in a less crowded area of the jail); Newkirk v. Sheers, 834 F. Supp. 772, 781–83 (E.D.Pa. 1993) (sleeping on floor mattresses for six nights or more violated detainees' rights); Balla v. Board of Corrections, 656 F. Supp. at 1118 (no floor mattresses any time for convicts); Monmouth County Correctional Institution Inmates v. Lanzaro, 595 F. Supp. 1417, 1440 (D.N.J. 1984) (floor mattresses limited to emergencies), *modified*, 695 F. Supp. 759 (D.N.J. 1988), *amended in part and clarified in part*, 717 F. Supp. 268 (D.N.J. 1989); Inmates of Allegheny County Jail v. Wecht, 565 F. Supp. 1278, 1296–97 (W.D.Pa. 1983), *aff'd in pertinent part*, 754 F.2d 120 (3d Cir. 1985); Martino v. Carey, 563 F. Supp. 984, 1002 (D.Or. 1983); Gross v. Tazewell County Jail, 533 F. Supp. 413, 416–17 (W.D.Va. 1982); Vazquez v. Gray, 523 F. Supp. 1359, 1365 (S.D.N.Y. 1981). *Contra*, Ferguson v. Cape Girardeau County, 88 F.3d 647, 650 (8th Cir. 1996) (13 nights on a floor mattress did not violate the Constitution under the circumstances); Antonelli v. Sheahan, 81 F.3d 1422, 1430 (7th Cir. 1996) (sleeping on the floor for one night did not violate the Constitution); Hamm v. DeKalb County, 774 F.2d 1567, 1575 (11th Cir. 1985); Castillo v. Bowles, 687 F. Supp. 277, 281 (N.D.Tex. 1988).

[115]Lareau v. Manson, 651 F.2d at 107–08; Maynor v. Morgan County, Ala., 147 F. Supp. 2d at 1190; Carty v. Farrelly, 957 F. Supp. at 735; Zolnowski v. County of Erie, 944 F. Supp. at 1113; Balla v. Board of Corrections, 656 F. Supp. at 1118.

[116]Mitchell v. Cuomo, 748 F.2d 804, 807 (2d Cir. 1984) ("temporary housing" consisting of infirmaries, program rooms, storage areas, etc.); LaReau v. Manson, 651 F.2d at 105–08 ("fishtank" dayroom, medical isolation cells); Zolnowski v. County of Erie, 944 F. Supp. at 1113–17 (court hold rooms, day rooms, atrium, chapel, and resource room unconstitutional; housing in gym, which was more spacious, was not); Young v. Keohane, 809 F. Supp. 1185, 1194–95 (M.D.Pa. 1992) (converted gym with no washing or toilet facilities, drinking water, tables or chairs, subject to flooding); Benjamin v. Sielaff, 752 F. Supp. 140, 141 n.3 (S.D.N.Y. 1990) (failure to provide "legitimate housing space"); Vazquez v. Carver, 729 F. Supp. at 1067, 1070 (holding cells, classroom, weight room); Balla v. Board of Corrections, 656 F. Supp. at 1118 (day rooms and other "non-designed cell areas"); Albro v. County of Onondaga, N.Y., 627 F. Supp. 1280, 1287 (N.D.N.Y. 1986) (corridor). Gross v. Tazewell County Jail, 533 F. Supp. at 416–17 (dayrooms); Vazquez v. Gray, 523 F. Supp. at 1365 (housing in dayrooms limited to five days); Richardson v. Sheriff of Middlesex County, 407 Mass. 455, 553 N.E.2d 1286, 1291-92 (Mass. 1990) (visiting rooms, common areas, temporary holding cells, and other areas not designed for housing).

[117]*See* Zolnowski v. County of Erie, 944 F. Supp. at 1116–17 (holding gym was sufficiently spacious that inmates could be held there); Alston v. Coughlin, 668 F. Supp. 822, 825-37 (S.D.N.Y. 1987) (finding conditions constitutionally acceptable despite the conversion of non-housing space to "temporary housing" with additional security staff, programs, food, clothing, housing, medical facilities, administrative staff, etc.).

[118]*Compare, e.g.*, Moore v. Morgan, 922 F.2d 1553, 1555 n.1, 1556–57 (11th Cir. 1991) (crowding with use of floor mattresses was unconstitutional) *with* Hubbard v. Taylor, 538 F.3d 229, 233–34 (3d Cir. 2008) (upholding triple-celling with extensive use of floor mattresses); Calhoun v. Thomas, 360 F. Supp. 2d 1264, 1287 (M.D.Ala. 2005); Robeson v. Squadrito, 57 F. Supp. 2d 642, 647 (N.D.Ind. 1999) ("Sleeping on a mattress on the floor, without aggravating circumstances (e.g., no mattress, low temperature without blankets, unreasonable vermin infestation), is not of constitutional magnitude.").

[119]Thompson v. City of Los Angeles, 885 F.2d 1439, 1448 (9th Cir. 1989); Anela v. Wildwood, 790 F.2d 1063, 1069 (3d Cir. 1986) (holding overnight detention without beds or mattresses appeared to deny due process); Oladipupo v. Austin, 104 F. Supp. 2d 626, 639 (W.D.La. 2000) ("A mattress is a basic human need, which must be provided to a detainee."). *But see* Stone-El v. Sheahan, 914 F. Supp. 202, 206 (N.D.Ill. 1995).

[120]Inmates of Occoquan v. Barry, 844 F.2d 828, 842-43 (D.C. Cir.), *rehearing denied*, 850 F.2d 796 (D.C. Cir. 1988); Cody v. Hillard, 830 F.2d 912, 914-15 (8th Cir. 1987) (en banc); *see* Laube v. Haley, 234 F. Supp. 2d 1227, 1251-52 (M.D.Ala. 2002) (directing measures to protect safety where the combination of jail crowding and lack of supervision in open dorms violated the Eighth Amendment).

[121]18 U.S.C. § 3626(a)(3). As we are finishing this book, a California court has granted the first such prisoner release order in a contested proceeding. Coleman v. Schwarzenegger, 2009 WL 2430820 (E.D.Cal. 2009), *appeal dismissed*, 130 S. Ct. 1140 (2010). The order resulting from this decision will likely be reviewed by the Supreme Court in the near future.

Several courts have held that state prison officials may be required to relieve local jail crowding that results from a backup of "state ready" convicted felons.[122]

2. Furnishings

The courts have not said much about the furnishings of cells and dormitories,[123] except to require that prisoners be provided with beds and reasonably sanitary bedding.[124]

Several courts have held that making prisoners sleep on mattresses on the floor violates the Eighth Amendment or due process.[125] Cells that prisoners are locked into must have toilets.[126] Courts have disagreed on whether prisoners have a right to have lockers in their cells.[127]

3. Ventilation and Heating

"Ventilation is a fundamental attribute of 'shelter' and 'sanitation', both of which are basic Eighth Amendment concerns."[128] Many courts have held that inadequate ventilation violates the Eighth Amendment or contributes to an unconstitutional combination of conditions.[129] Other courts

---

[122]Benjamin v. Malcolm, 803 F.2d 46, 50–54 (2d Cir. 1986); Tate v. Frey, 735 F.2d 986, 988–90 (6th Cir. 1984); Maynor v. Morgan County, Ala., 147 F. Supp. 2d 1185, 1187–90 (N.D.Ala. 2001) (requiring submission of a plan to remove state prisoners from county jail); *see also* Alberti v. Sheriff of Harris County, Texas, 937 F.2d 984, 999–1002 (5th Cir. 1991) (state required to pay costs of "ready-felon" backup). *Cf.* Hill v. Hutto, 537 F. Supp. 1185, 1189 (E.D.Va. 1982) (finding equal protection violation where state prisoners were backed up in local jail because of lack of state prison space).

Some states have statutes requiring state prison officials to accept convicted prisoners promptly. *See, e.g.,* Ayers v. Coughlin, 72 N.Y.2d 346, 533 N.Y.S.2d 849, 530 N.E.2d 373 (N.Y. 1988) (enforcing statute requiring transfer to state custody "forthwith"). If you have been convicted and want to get into state custody rather than stay in a local jail, you may be able to enforce such a statute in state court.

[123]*But see* Young v. Keohane, 809 F. Supp. 1185, 1194–95 (M.D.Pa. 1992) (lack of tables and chairs supported claim that conditions in converted gymnasium violated pretrial detainees' rights).

[124]Townsend v. Fuchs, 522 F.3d 765, 774 (7th Cir. 2008) (wet and moldy mattress was actionable under Eighth Amendment); Benjamin v. Fraser, 161 F. Supp. 2d 151, 180 (S.D.N.Y. 2001) (citing mattresses that were soiled, uncovered, or torn and uncleanable in finding a constitutional violation; detainee case), *aff'd in part, vacated in part and remanded on other grounds*, 343 F.3d 35 (2d Cir. 2003); Carver v. Knox County, Tenn., 753 F. Supp. 1370, 1389 (E.D.Tenn. 1989) ("The failure to regularly provide prisoners with clean bedding, towels, clothing and sanitary mattresses" is unconstitutional), *remanded for reconsideration*, 887 F.2d 1287 (6th Cir. 1989), *adhered to on remand*, 753 F. Supp. 1398 (E.D.Tenn. 1990); Toussaint v. McCarthy, 597 F. Supp. 1388, 1411 (N.D.Cal. 1984) ("Decency also requires that each cell be furnished with a clean, untorn pillow"), *aff'd in part and rev'd in part on other grounds*, 801 F.2d 1080 (9th Cir. 1986); Wabasha v. Solem, 580 F. Supp. 448, 451 (D.S.D. 1984) (cot, mattress, and bedding required); Dawson v. Kendrick, 527 F. Supp. 1252, 1288–89 (S.D.W.Va. 1981); O'Connor v. Keller, 510 F. Supp. 1359, 1372–73 (D.Md. 1981) (deprivation of mattress and bedding in isolation for 48 hours was unconstitutional); Hickson v. Kellison, 170 W.Va. 732, 296 S.E.2d 855, 858 (W.Va. 1982) (clean bedding and towels required); *see* LeMaire v. Maass, 12 F.2d 1444 (9th Cir. 1993) (when staff violated prison policy permitting deprivation of bedding only while misusing it, court should only have enjoined officials to follow their own policy. *But see* Green v. Baron, 879 F.2d 305, 309–10 (8th Cir. 1989) (deprivation of bedding as part of a behavior modification program might have been justified based on prisoner's mental condition); Ra Chaka v. Nash, 536 F. Supp. 613, 617 (N.D.Ill. 1982) (deprivation of bed in segregation was not unconstitutional); Sellers v. Roper, 554 F. Supp. 202, 209 (E.D.Va. 1982)

(rejecting claim of inadequate clean bedding); Williams v. Kelone, 560 So.2d 915 (La.App.) ("ideal bedding" not required; soiled blanket was not unconstitutional where clean sheets were provided and blankets were cleaned every few months), *writ denied*, 567 So.2d 107 (La. 1990). *Cf.* Peterkin v. Jeffes, 855 F.2d 1021, 1027 (3d Cir. 1988) (uncomfortable beds did not violate the Eighth Amendment unless they caused medical problems).

[125]*See* cases cited in § B.1 of this chapter, nn.114–116.

[126]*See* cases cited in § C of this chapter, n.180.

[127]*Compare* Peterkin v. Jeffes, 661 F. Supp. 895, 917 (E.D.Pa. 1987) (lockers not required), *aff'd in part and vacated in part on other grounds*, 855 F.2d 1021 (3d Cir. 1988) *with* Lightfoot v. Walker, 486 F. Supp. 504, 528 (S.D.Ill. 1980) ("personal storage units and refuse containers made of noncombustible materials" in cells). We think that prisoners in dormitories should have lockers or some other safe place to keep their property in order to avoid theft and resulting violence, but the only court to consider this issue was not convinced one way or the other. Fisher v. Koehler, 692 F. Supp. 1519, 1542 n.36 (S.D.N.Y. 1988), *aff'd*, 902 F.2d 2 (2d Cir. 1990).

[128]Minifield v. Butikofer, 298 F. Supp. 2d 900, 904 (N.D.Cal. 2004).

[129]Benjamin v. Fraser, 343 F.3d 35, 52 (2d Cir. 2003) (evidence of "large numbers of inoperable windows, clogged or dirty ventilation registers and exhaust vents in showers and cells, and poor air quality," plus findings concerning threatened and actual health hazards, supported finding of constitutionally inadequate ventilation; detainee case); Board v. Farnham, 394 F.3d 469, 486 (7th Cir. 2005) (holding evidence that ventilation system was contaminated with fiberglass dust and mold supported an Eighth Amendment claim); Keenan v. Hall, 83 F.3d 1083, 1090 (9th Cir. 1996) (holding allegations that the air was saturated with the fumes of feces, urine, and vomit supported an Eighth Amendment ventilation claim), *amended on other grounds*, 135 F.3d 1318 (9th Cir. 1998); Williams v. White, 897 F.2d 942, 944–45 (8th Cir. 1990); Gillespie v. Crawford, 833 F.2d 47, 50 (5th Cir. 1987), *on rehearing*, 858 F.2d 1101 (5th Cir. 1988); French v. Owens, 777 F.2d 1250, 1252–53 (7th Cir. 1985); Hoptowit v. Spellman, 753 F.2d 779, 784 (9th Cir. 1985); Madison County Jail Inmates v. Thompson, 773 F.2d 834, 839 (7th Cir. 1985); Ramos v. Lamm, 639 F.2d 559, 568–70 (10th Cir. 1980); Brown v. Mitchell, 327 F. Supp. 2d 615, 637 (E.D. Va. 2004) (holding expert testimony that poor ventilation was a contributing factor to prisoner's death from meningitis raised an issue for trial); Caldwell v. Hammonds, 53 F. Supp. 2d 1, 11 (D.D.C. 1999) (holding allegation that "smoke from tobacco and other contaminants fills the air, and . . . smoke from fires and mace is allowed to linger" states an Eighth Amendment claim); Jones v. City and County of

have rejected claims of lack of ventilation.[130] Inadequate ventilation may support a claim of unconstitutional exposure to environmental tobacco smoke.[131] Inadequate or excessive heat also violates the Eighth Amendment,[132] although mere variations in temperature or occasional breakdowns do not.[133] Several courts have ordered prison officials to repair broken windows and screens.[134]

The forced exposure of prisoners to extreme outdoor weather conditions can also violate the Eighth Amendment.[135]

4. Lighting

"Lighting is an indispensable aspect of adequate shelter and is required by the Eighth Amendment."[136] However, not

---

San Francisco, 976 F.Supp 896, 912–13 (N.D.Cal. 1997); Carver v. Knox County, Tenn., 753 F. Supp. 1370, 1393 (E.D.Tenn. 1989), *remanded for reconsideration*, 887 F.2d 1287 (6th Cir. 1989), *adhered to on remand*, 753 F. Supp. 1398 (E.D.Tenn. 1990); Tillery v. Owens, 719 F. Supp. 1256, 1271 (W.D.Pa. 1989), *aff'd*, 907 F.2d 418 (3d Cir. 1990); Inmates of Occoquan v. Barry, 717 F. Supp. 854, 866–67 (D.D.C. 1989); Reece v. Gragg, 650 F. Supp. 1297, 1304 (D.Kan. 1986); Toussaint v. McCarthy, 597 F. Supp. 1388, 1395–96, 1409 (N.D.Cal. 1984), *aff'd in part and rev'd in part on other grounds*, 801 F.2d 1080 (9th Cir. 1986); Monmouth County Correctional Institution Inmates v. Lanzaro, 595 F. Supp. 1417, 1436–38 (D.N.J. 1984), *modified*, 695 F. Supp. 759 (D.N.J. 1988), *amended in part and clarified in part*, 717 F. Supp. 268 (D.N.J. 1989); Ramos v. Lamm, 520 F. Supp. 1059, 1063 (D.Colo. 1981).

[130]Lopez v. Robinson, 914 F.2d 486, 490–91 (4th Cir. 1990) (evidence showed ventilation was adequate); Peterkin v. Jeffes, 855 F.2d 1021, 1026–27 (3d Cir. 1988) (no violation unless a health hazard is created); Shelby County Jail Inmates v. Westlake, 798 F.2d 1085, 1087–88 (7th Cir. 1986); Kitt v. Ferguson, 750 F. Supp. 1014, 1019–20 (D.Neb. 1990), *aff'd*, 950 F.2d 725 (8th Cir. 1991); Capps v. Atiyeh, 559 F. Supp. 894, 913 (D.Or. 1982) (similar to *Peterkin*); Biancone v. Kramer, 513 F. Supp. 908, 908–09 (E.D.Pa. 1981); Russell v. Enser, 496 F. Supp. 320, 325–26 (D.S.C. 1979), *aff'd*, 624 F.2d 1095 (4th Cir. 1980); Nadeau v. Helgemoe, 423 F. Supp. 1250, 1266–67 (D.N.H. 1976), *aff'd in part and vacated and remanded in part*, 561 F.2d 411 (1st Cir. 1977).

[131]Talal v. White, 403 F.3d 423, 427 (6th Cir. 2005). *See* § G.3.c of this chapter concerning environmental tobacco smoke.

[132]Wilson v. Seiter, 501 U.S. 304, 111 S. Ct. 2321 (1991) (warmth is a basic human need; low temperatures and no blankets would violate the Eighth Amendment); Gates v. Cook, 376 F.3d 323, 339–40 (5th Cir. 2004) (affirming finding of unconstitutional heat, requiring provision of fans, ice water, and daily showers when heat index is 90 or higher); Benjamin v. Fraser, 343 F.3d at 52 (affirming finding of unconstitutionality based on evidence of extreme temperatures, including no heat at times during winter; detainee case); Gaston v. Coughlin, 249 F.3d 156, 164–65 (2d Cir. 2001) (holding allegations of unrepaired broken windows throughout winter stated a constitutional claim); Dixon v. Godinez, 114 F.3d 640, 642–45 (7th Cir. 1997) ("... [P]risoners have a right to protection from extreme cold"; cold alone may violate the Eighth Amendment; "severe discomfort" can be unconstitutional without imminently threatening health); Henderson v. DeRobertis, 940 F.2d 1055, 1059 (7th Cir. 1991) ("constitutional rights don't come and go with the weather"); Foulds v. Corley, 833 F.2d 52, 54 (5th Cir. 1987); Corselli v. Coughlin, 842 F.2d 23, 27 (2d Cir. 1988); Beck v. Lynaugh, 842 F.2d 759, 761 (5th Cir. 1988); French v. Owens, 777 F.2d at 1252–53; Lewis v. Lane, 816 F.2d 1165, 1171 (7th Cir. 1987); Ramos v. Lamm, 639 F.2d at 568–70; Reece v. Gragg, 650 F. Supp. at 1304; Toussaint v. McCarthy, 597 F. Supp. at 1395–96, 1409; Monmouth County Correctional Institution Inmates v. Lanzaro, 595 F. Supp. at 1436–38; *see* Burchett v. Kiefer, 310 F.3d 937, 945 (6th Cir. 2002) (holding several hours' detention in an unventilated police car with windows rolled up in 90°F heat could violate the Fourth Amendment). *But see* Chandler v. Crosby, 379 F.3d 1278, 1295–98 (11th Cir. 2004) (holding that a showing of "severe discomfort" does not meet the constitutional standard, and subjection to temperatures that only exceeded 90°F 9% of the time during the summer and exceeded 95°F only seven times during the summer, with an effectively functioning ventilation system, was not unconstitutional.).

[133]Lopez v. Robinson, 914 F.2d at 492; Smith v. Sullivan, 553 F.2d 373, 381 (5th Cir. 1977); Booth v. King, 346 F. Supp. 2d 751, 729 (E.D.Pa. 2004) (15 days in a segregation cell with broken windows did not violate the Constitution); King v. Frank, 328 F. Supp. 2d 940, 947 (W.D.Wis. 2004) (allegation of "poor" temperature control did not state a claim); Wright v. Santoro, 714 F. Supp. 665, 668 (S.D.N.Y. 1989); Alston v. Coughlin, 668 F. Supp. 822, 829 (S.D.N.Y. 1987); Scot v. Merola, 555 F. Supp. 230, 233 (S.D.N.Y. 1983); Burks v. Walsh, 461 F. Supp. 454, 486 (W.D.Mo. 1978).

[134]Benjamin v. Fraser, 343 F.3d at 53–54; Palmigiano v. DiPrete, 737 F. Supp. 1257, 1260 (D.R.I. 1990); Inmates of Occoquan v. Barry, 717 F. Supp. 854, 866–67 (D.D.C. 1989); Mitchell v. Untreiner, 421 F. Supp. 886, 898 (N.D.Fla. 1976). "Operational windows are necessary for ventilation and temperature control." Benjamin v. Fraser, 156 F. Supp. 2d 333, 350 (S.D.N.Y. 2001), *aff'd in pertinent part*, 343 F.3d 35 (2d Cir. 2003).

[135]Johnson v. Lewis, 217 F.3d 726, 734–35 (9th Cir. 2000) (holding that evidence that prisoners were held in the yard for four days in the summer during hot humid weather, and 17 hours in the winter, without warm clothing during subfreezing weather, and other circumstances supported an Eighth Amendment claim); Palmer v. Johnson, 193 F.3d 346, 352–54 (5th Cir. 1999) (holding overnight stay outdoors with temperature falling below 59°F without blankets or warm clothing or toilet facilities could violate the Eighth Amendment); Gordon v. Faber, 973 F.2d 686, 687–88 (8th Cir. 1992) (forcing prisoners to go outside without adequate clothing in sub-freezing weather violated the Eighth Amendment). *But see* Woodbridge v. Dahlberg, 954 F.2d 1231, 1234 (6th Cir. 1992) (temporary placement in cold outdoor areas was justified by security needs).

[136]Toussaint v. McCarthy, 597 F. Supp. 1388, 1409 (N.D.Cal. 1984) ("[E]ach inmate must be afforded sufficient light to permit him to read comfortably while seated or lying on his bunk"), *aff'd in part and rev'd in part on other grounds*, 801 F.2d 1080 (9th Cir. 1986); *accord*, Keenan v. Hall, 83 F.3d 1083, 1090 (9th Cir. 1996) ("Adequate lighting is one of the fundamental attributes of 'adequate shelter' required by the Eighth Amendment."), *amended on other grounds*, 135 F.3d 1318 (9th Cir. 1998); Gates v. Cook, 376 F.3d 323, 341–42 (5th Cir. 2004) (affirming injunction requiring 20 foot candles of lighting in cells, based on evidence that lighting was grossly inadequate for sanitation, personal hygiene, and reading); Gillespie v. Crawford, 833 F.2d 47, 50 (5th Cir. 1987), *on rehearing*, 858 F.2d 1101 (5th Cir. 1988); French v. Owens, 777 F.2d 1250, 1252–53 (7th Cir. 1985); Hoptowit v. Spellman, 753 F.2d 779, 783 (9th Cir. 1985)

every defect in lighting is unconstitutional.[137] Some courts have held constant illumination unconstitutional,[138]

though decisions depend in part on how bright the light is and whether it is alleged or shown to interfere with sleep.[139]

5. Noise

Excessive noise "inflicts pain without penological justification" and violates the Eighth Amendment.[140] However, prisoners are not entitled to a "noise-free prison environment" or to freedom from noise that causes "mere discomfort or inconvenience."[141]

C. Sanitation and Personal Hygiene

"A sanitary environment is a basic human need that a penal institution must provide for all inmates."[142] The Eighth

---

(light inadequate for reading was unconstitutional); Bono v. Saxbe, 620 F.2d 609, 617 (7th Cir. 1980); Jones v. City and County of San Francisco, 976 F. Supp. 896, 915–16 (N.D.Cal. 1997) ("Where lighting appears so poor as to be inadequate for reading and to cause eyestrain and fatigue, the conditions appear unconstitutional even under the Eighth Amendment"; holding unconstitutional lighting conditions generally less than 5-foot candles); Tillery v. Owens, 719 F. Supp. 1256, 1271 (W.D.Pa. 1989), aff'd, 907 F.2d 418 (3d Cir. 1990); Calloway v. Fauver, 544 F. Supp. 584, 609 (D.N.J. 1982) (100-watt bulbs to be installed on request); Ramos v. Lamm, 520 F. Supp. 1059, 1063 (D.Colo. 1981) (lighting standards described); Dawson v. Kendrick, 527 F. Supp. 1252, 1288 (S.D.W.Va. 1981).

Courts have disagreed on the question whether transparent windows are required in jails. Compare Rutherford v. Pitchess, 710 F.2d 572, 579 (9th Cir. 1983), rev'd on other grounds sub nom. Block v. Rutherford, 468 U.S. 576, 108 S. Ct. 1975 (1984), with Rhem v. Malcolm, 371 F. Supp. 594, 610, 627 (S.D.N.Y. 1974), aff'd, 507 F.2d 333 (2d Cir. 1974).

[137]Peterkin v. Jeffes, 855 F.2d 1021, 1026–27 (3d Cir. 1988) (no constitutional violation found where there was no evidence of eye damage); Shelby County Jail Inmates v. Westlake, 798 F.2d 1085, 1088–89 (7th Cir. 1986); Shrader v. White, 761 F.2d 975, 984 (4th Cir. 1985); Vega v. Parsley, 700 F. Supp. 879, 883–84 (W.D.Tex. 1988) (burned out light bulb, promptly replaced, did not violate the Eighth Amendment); State v. Rouse, 229 Kan. 600, 629 P.2d 167, 172 (Kan. 1982) (two-week deprivation of light bulb in cell was not unconstitutional).

[138]Keenan v. Hall, 83 F.3d at 1090 ("Moreover, '[t]here is no legitimate penological justification for requiring [inmates] to suffer physical and psychological harm by living in constant illumination. This practice is unconstitutional."), amended on other grounds, 135 F.3d 1318 (9th Cir. 1998); King v. Frank, 328 F. Supp. 2d 940, 946–47 (W.D.Wis. 2004) ("Constant illumination may violate the Eighth Amendment if it causes sleep deprivation or leads to other serious physical or mental health problems"; noting previous holding that a 5-watt bulb doesn't violate the Eighth Amendment); Shepherd v. Ault, 982 F. Supp. 643, 647–48 (N.D.Iowa 1997) (holding allegation of cell illumination 24 hours a day by a 60-watt light bulb which prisoners were forbidden to cover stated a constitutional claim in view of allegations that the lighting made sleep very difficult, that the imposition for 283 and then 550 nights of "lighting so far removed from natural conditions" supported an inference of psychological harm); LeMaire v. Maass, 745 F. Supp. 623, 636 (D.Or. 1990), vacated and remanded on other grounds, 12 F.2d 1444 (9th Cir. 1993) (holding that keeping cell lights on 24 hours a day in segregation cells is unconstitutional).

In Shepherd v. Ault, the court noted that "the effectiveness of sleep deprivation as a tool of torture has long been recognized." 982 F. Supp. at 648 (citing Reck v. Pate, 367 U.S. 433, 81 S. Ct. 1541 (1961) (recognizing deprivation of food and sleep as unconstitutional punishment) and Ashcraft v. Tennessee, 322 U.S. 143, 150 n.6, 64 S. Ct. 921 (1944) (" 'It has been known since 1500 at least that deprivation of sleep is the most effective torture and certain to produce any confession desired,'" quoting Report of Committee on Lawless Enforcement of Law, Section of Criminal Law and Criminology of the American Bar Association, 1 American Journal Of Police Science 575, 579–80 (1930)).

[139]Ferguson v. Cape Girardeau County, 88 F.3d 647, 650 (8th Cir. 1996) (holding 14-day exposure to constant illumination did not violate Constitution); King v. Frank, 371 F. Supp. 2d 977, 985 (W.D.Wis. 2005) (holding constant illumination from 9 watt fluorescent bulb was not unconstitutional absent any evidence of adverse effects that outweighed the need to see in the cells).

[140]Toussaint v. McCarthy, 801 F.2d 1080, 1110 (9th Cir. 1986); accord, Antonelli v. Sheahan, 81 F.3d 1422, 1433 (7th Cir. 1996) (holding allegations that excessive noise "occurred every night, often all night, interrupting or preventing [plaintiff's] sleep," stated a constitutional claim); Benjamin v. Fraser, 161 F. Supp. 2d 151, 185 (S.D.N.Y. 2001) ("To the extent that excessive noise contributes to 'difficulty sleeping properly' it affects a 'basic daily living requirement' and thus may constitute a deprivation of the minimal requirements for federal constitutional purposes"; finding violation where Diesel generators near housing areas caused noise levels in excess of 45 decibels, and in some cases 70 decibels, 24 hours a day), affirmed in part, vacated and remanded in part on other grounds, 343 F.3d 35 (2d Cir. 2003); Jones v. City and County of San Francisco, 976 F. Supp. 896, 915 (N.D.Cal. 1997) (holding noise levels typically ranging from 73 to 96 decibels violated the Fourteenth Amendment); Reece v. Gragg, 650 F. Supp. 1297, 1304 (D.Kan. 1986); Ramos v. Lamm, 520 F. Supp. 1059, 1063 (D.Colo. 1981); Palmigiano v. Garrahy, 443 F. Supp. 956, 979 (D.R.I. 1977), remanded on other grounds, 599 F.2d 17 (1st Cir. 1979); Anderson v. Redman, 429 F. Supp. 1105, 1112 (D.Del. 1977), stay ordered, 480 F. Supp. 830 (D.Del. 1979); Rhem v. Malcolm, 371 F. Supp. 594, 627 (S.D.N.Y. 1974), aff'd, 507 F.2d 333 (2d Cir. 1974) (pretrial detention case).

[141]Johnson v. Lynaugh, 800 S.W.2d 936, 938 (Tex.App. 1990); accord, Givens v. Jones, 900 F.2d 1229, 1234 (8th Cir. 1990); Peterkin v. Jeffes, 855 F.2d 1021, 1027 (3d Cir. 1988); King v. Frank, 328 F. Supp. 2d 940, 946 (W.D.Wis. 2004) Griffin v. Coughlin, 743 F. Supp. 1006, 1018 (N.D.N.Y. 1990); Alston v. Coughlin, 668 F. Supp. 822, 837 (S.D.N.Y. 1987); Balla v. Board of Corrections, 656 F. Supp. 1108, 1119 (D.Idaho 1987).

[142]Toussaint v. McCarthy, 597 F. Supp. 1388, 1411 (N.D.Cal. 1984), aff'd in part and rev'd in part on other grounds, 801 F.2d 1080 (9th Cir. 1986); accord, Townsend v. Fuchs, 522 F.3d 765, 774 (7th Cir. 2008) (wet and moldy mattress was actionable under Eighth Amendment); Vinning-El v. Long, 482 F.3d 923, 924 (7th Cir. 2007) (holding confinement in filthy cell without bedding, toilet paper, or working plumbing denied "minimal civilized measure of life's necessities"); Gates v. Cook, 376 F.3d 323, 338 (5th Cir. 2004); Carty v. Farrelly, 957 F. Supp. 727, 736 (D.V.I. 1997)

Amendment requires adequate arrangements for cleaning and garbage disposal.[143] Prisons must also have functioning plumbing systems. "Inoperable plumbing systems contribute to both the risk of conveying waterborne disease and vermin infestation, and thus implicate constitutional violations."[144] Courts have found serious deficiencies in plumbing to violate the Eighth Amendment, both in individual housing locations[145] and in prisons or units as a whole.[146] Infestation by vermin may also violate the Eighth Amendment,[147] though the presence of some

---

("Generally, sanitation is one of the most basic human needs."); Sanford v. Brookshire, 879 F. Supp. 691, 693–94 (W.D.Tex. 1994) (holding six days in a filthy cell without working plumbing was unconstitutional); Fambro v. Fulton County, Ga., 713 F. Supp. 1426, 1431 (N.D.Ga. 1989); *see* Benjamin v. Fraser, 161 F. Supp. 2d 151, 180 (S.D.N.Y. 2001) (holding evidence of "soiled light shields, dirty or clogged ventilation registers, vermin activity, mildewed and decrepit bathroom and shower areas, clogged toilets, dirty janitor's closets, shortages of laundry detergent, and dirty prison cells in combination constitutes a clear deprivation of adequate sanitation"; also citing uncleanable and soiled mattresses and smoke-stained walls in cells; detainee case) (footnotes omitted), *aff'd in part, vacated in part and remanded on other grounds*, 343 F.3d 35 (2d Cir. 2003).

[143]Gates v. Cook, 376 F.3d at 338 (affirming injunction to clean cells between occupants and make cleaning supplies available weekly); Hoptowit v. Spellman, 753 F.2d 779, 784 (9th Cir. 1985) (failure to provide adequate cleaning supplies); Ramos v. Lamm, 639 F.2d 559, 569–70 (10th Cir. 1980) (citing "lack of routine maintenance and cleaning programs" and inadequate cleaning supplies for inmates to clean their own cells in finding constitutional violation); Marion County Jail Inmates v. Anderson, 270 F. Supp. 2d 1034, 1039, 1041 (S.D.Ind. 2003) (citing "unhealthy, unsanitary, dangerous, offensive conditions"; directing Sheriff to devise daily and weekly schedules for cleaning and maintenance of all housing areas; finding contempt of previous orders); Toussaint v. McCarthy, 597 F. Supp. at 1424 (directing measures to maintain sanitation including providing garbage cans, collecting garbage, and cleaning floors, pipe chases, and service areas); Palmigiano v. Garrahy, 443 F. Supp. 956, 963–64 (D.R.I. 1977) (citing breakdown of housekeeping), *remanded on other grounds*, 599 F.2d 17 (1st Cir. 1979); Dawson v. Kendrick, 527 F. Supp. 1252, 1264, 1289 (S.D.W.Va. 1981) ("The failure to provide for and require rudimentary housekeeping and cleaning at the jail has resulted in an unnecessarily filthy and denigrating environment which threatens the physical and mental well-being of the prisoners."). *But see* Wishon v. Gammon, 978 F.2d 446, 449 (8th Cir. 1992) (claim of unsanitary conditions rejected based on evidence that prison officials made adequate arrangements for inmates to clean their cells).

[144]Carty v. Farrelly, 957 F. Supp. at 736; *accord*, Benjamin v. Fraser, 161 F. Supp. 2d at 171 ("It is self-evident that access to adequate and functional plumbing is essential to a healthy jail environment because of the importance of water for drinking, personal hygiene, laundry, kitchen use, and housekeeping." No violation found."); Dennis v. Thurman, 959 F. Supp. 1253, 1261 (C.D.Cal. 1997) ("Water and functioning plumbing are basic necessities of civilized life.").

[145]Williams v. Griffin, 952 F.2d 820, 825 (4th Cir. 1991); McCord v. Maggio, 927 F.2d 844, 847 (5th Cir. 1991) (cell flooded with sewage and foul water was a "clear violation of the Eighth Amendment"); Thomas v. Jabe, 760 F. Supp. 120, 123 (E.D.Mich. 1991) (similar to *McCord*); Howard v. Wheaton, 668 F. Supp. 1140,

1142–43 (N.D.Ill. 1987) (holding allegation of 13 days in a cell without a working toilet and hot water stated a constitutional claim).

[146]Gates v. Cook, 376 F.3d at 341 (affirming order to correct "ping-pong" toilets in which raw sewage backs up in other cells when a toilet is flushed); Hoptowit v. Spellman, 753 F.2d at 783 (plumbing was "in such disrepair as to deprive inmates of basic elements of hygiene and seriously threaten their physical and mental well-being"); Ramos v. Lamm, 639 F.2d at 569; Jones v. City and County of San Francisco, 976 F. Supp. 896, 910 (N.D.Cal. 1997) (holding antiquated water supply system, sanitary fixtures in disrepair, deteriorated asbestos insulation, absence of vacuum breakers, sewage treatment deficiencies, among others, violated the Fourteenth Amendment, even without evidence that they caused disease); Morales Feliciano v. Hernandez Colon, 754 F. Supp. 942, 945 (D.P.R. 1991) (admissions to prison halted until running water was restored); Carver v. Knox County, Tenn., 753 F. Supp. 1370, 1389 (E.D.Tenn. 1989) ("functioning sinks, toilets and showers are basic necessities of modern life, particularly within the confines of a wholly self-contained environment such as a jail"), *remanded for reconsideration*, 887 F.2d 1287 (6th Cir. 1989), *adhered to on remand*, 753 F. Supp. 1398 (E.D.Tenn. 1990); Tillery v. Owens, 719 F. Supp. 1256, 1271 (W.D.Pa. 1989), *aff'd*, 907 F.2d 418 (3d Cir. 1990); Inmates of Occoquan v. Barry, 717 F. Supp. 854, 866–67 (D.D.C. 1989); Balla v. Board of Corrections, 656 F. Supp. 1108, 1118–19 (D.Idaho 1987); Dawson v. Kendrick, 527 F. Supp. at 1287. *But see* Shrader v. White, 761 F.2d 975, 984 (4th Cir. 1985) (holding substandard shower conditions did not violate the constitution where regular cleaning efforts were made and no health hazard was shown); Gilland v. Owens, 718 F. Supp. 665, 684 (W.D.Tenn. 1989) (frequent toilet and shower malfunctions were not unconstitutional where they were promptly repaired); Capps v. Atiyeh, 559 F. Supp. 894, 913 (D.Or. 1982).

[147]Gates v. Cook, 376 F.3d at 340 (affirming injunction to continue pest control efforts and repair and screen all windows, despite officials' claim of ongoing pest control efforts); Gaston v. Coughlin, 249 F.3d 156, 166 (2d Cir. 2001) (holding allegations of rodent infestation supported an Eighth Amendment claim); Antonelli v. Sheahan, 81 F.3d 1422, 1431 (7th Cir. 1996) (officials' claim that the prison was sprayed twice in 16 months does not negate deliberate indifference in light of allegations of continuing severe infestation); Williams v. Griffin, 952 F.2d at 825; Gillespie v. Crawford, 833 F.2d 47, 50 (5th Cir. 1987), *on rehearing*, 858 F.2d 1101 (5th Cir. 1988); Foulds v. Corley, 833 F.2d 52, 54 (5th Cir. 1987); Hoptowit v. Spellman, 753 F.2d at 783; Ramos v. Lamm, 639 F.2d at 569; Carty v. Farrelly, 957 F. Supp. 2d at 736 ("Conditions that generate infestation of vermin also do not comport with minimal civilized measures concerning a person's basic welfare."); Tillery v. Owens, 719 F. Supp. at 1271; Palmigiano v. Garrahy, 443 F. Supp. at 961. *But see* Wishon v. Gammon, 978 F.2d 446, 449 (8th Cir. 1992) (allegations of vermin infestation rejected in light of evidence that cells were sprayed regularly and more often on request); Dailey v. Byrnes, 605 F.2d 858, 859–60 (5th Cir. 1979) ("irremediable" infestation despite extermination efforts was not unconstitutional); Warren v. Stempson, 800 F. Supp. 991, 992–93 (D.D.C. 1992) (allegation of vermin infestation did not state an Eighth Amendment claim). *Cf.* Russell v. Richards, 384 F.3d 444, 447–50 (7th Cir. 2004) (upholding requirement that incoming inmates use a delousing shampoo).

vermin does not.[148] Proximity to human waste, even for relatively brief periods of time, has been of particular concern to courts in sanitation cases.[149]

Decisions applying these standards are often inconsistent. Some district courts brush off individual claims of seriously unsanitary conditions,[150] sometimes dismissing them as minor or temporary.[151] Be sure to cite any favorable decisions about sanitation by the federal appeals court for your circuit if you bring a case about sanitary conditions.[152] Courts also tend to hold that compensatory damages claims for unsanitary conditions are barred by the Prison Litigation Reform Act's provision concerning mental or emotional injury without physical injury.[153]

As with other prison conditions, under the deliberate indifference standard, officials must be shown to have known of unsanitary conditions to be held liable for them.[154] Prison officials cannot escape their responsibilities for maintaining sanitation by blaming the prisoners, either for causing unsanitary conditions or for failing to clean them up.[155] Prison officials can use inmate workers to keep the prison clean,[156] but it is still the officials' responsibility to provide adequate supplies, maintain fixtures and equipment, and organize cleaning activities.[157] However, courts have held

---

[148]Benjamin v. Fraser, 161 F. Supp. 2d 151, 174 (S.D.N.Y. 2001), *aff'd in pertinent part, vacated and remanded in part on other grounds,* 343 F.3d 35 (2d Cir. 2003). Vermin activity rises to the level of infestation if all growth stages of the organism are present. *Id.,* 161 F. Supp. 2d at 173.

[149]DeSpain v. Uphoff, 264 F.3d 965, 974 (10th Cir. 2001) (holding 36 hours' exposure stated an Eighth Amendment claim); Gaston v. Coughlin, 249 F.3d at 166 ("We are unwilling to adopt as a matter of law the principle that it is not cruel and unusual punishment for prison officials knowingly to allow an area to remain filled with sewage and excrement for days on end."); McBride v. Deer, 240 F.3d 1287, 1291–92 (10th Cir. 2001) and cases cited; Johnson v. Lewis, 217 F.3d 726, 732–33 (9th Cir. 2000).

[150]*See, e.g.,* Govan v. Campbell, 289 F. Supp. 2d 289, 296–97 (N.D.N.Y. 2003) (holding allegations that shower stalls were unclean and had rust bubbles, tier was infested with cockroaches, and "wild birds" flew around the jail did not state a constitutional claim); Roop v. Squadrito, 70 F. Supp. 2d 868, 875 (N.D.Ind. 1999) ("Plaintiff's complaint that his cell was filthy with dirt and fuzz on the floor' cannot be swept into a constitutional claim.").

[151]*See, e.g.,* Dellis v. Corrections Corporation of America, 257 F.3d 508, 511 (6th Cir. 2001) (prisoner subjected to flooded cell without working toilet alleged only temporary inconvenience); Oliver v. Powell, 250 F. Supp. 2d 593, 605 (E.D.Va. 2002) (holding allegations of roaches, leaky toilets, peeling paint, and writing on the wall did not violate the Eighth Amendment; "minor plumbing problems, and less than pristine cell conditions are ordinary incidents of prison life."); Wilson v. Cooper, 922 F. Supp. 1286, 1292 (N.D.Ill. 1996) (being held for days in a cell with virtually no running water and a leaking toilet that looked and smelled like it had been in a fire was "not sufficiently egregious" to violate the Constitution).

[152]One federal circuit held that six months' confinement allegedly under conditions of vermin infestation, cells smeared with human waste, and flooding from toilet leaks was not "grossly excessive punishment" under the Eighth Amendment. However, the court noted that the prisoners in that case challenged only the length of the punishment but did not allege that the conditions themselves violated the Eighth Amendment's Cruel and Unusual Punishments Clause, so the case does not hold that such conditions are constitutionally acceptable. Beverati v. Smith, 120 F.3d 500, 504–05 (4th Cir. 1997). The court did say that such a claim would probably fail because the prisoners didn't show that the conditions "resulted in serious physical or emotional injuries or the grave risk of such harm." *Id.,*120 F.3d at 504 n.5. That view is extreme, as shown by other cases cited in this section.

[153]*See* Ch. 9, § E; *see also* Sanford v. Brookshire, 879 F. Supp. 691, 694 (W.D.Tex. 1994) (awarding $1.00 in damages for six days in a filthy cell without working plumbing because the plaintiff showed no actual injury).

[154]*Compare* Gates v. Cook, 376 F.3d 323, 338 (5th Cir. 2004) (affirming deliberate indifference finding where conditions were "not atypical and easily observed"); DeSpain v. Uphoff, 264 F.3d 965, 975–77 (10th Cir. 2001) (holding Associate Warden's responsibility for supervising unit and fact that guards reported to him could support a finding of knowledge and deliberate indifference); Gaston v. Coughlin, 249 F.3d at166 (holding allegation that defendants "made daily rounds" of SHU supported claim of knowledge of conditions); Masonoff v. DuBois, 336 F. Supp. 2d 54, 59–60 (D.Mass. 2004) (holding officials could be found to have known about "obvious and substantial" risk from unsanitary conditions associated with chemical toilets) *with* Shannon v. Graves, 257 F.3d 1164, 1169 (10th Cir. 2001) (holding prison officials were not shown to have known of sewage backups and contamination of blankets and clothing); Arnold v. Moore, 980 F. Supp. 28, 34–35 (D.D.C. 1997) (holding warden and commissioner could not be held liable absent evidence of knowledge of filthy conditions).

[155]As one court observed, "We see no reason why well-behaved inmates should have to suffer cruel and unusual punishment because of the activities of some disruptive ones. . . . [T]he prison administration must bear the ultimate responsibility for cell block conditions." Blake v. Hall, 668 F.2d 52, 57–58 (1st Cir. 1981); *see also* McCord v. Maggio, 927 F.2d 844, 847 (5th Cir. 1991); Beck v. Lynaugh, 842 F.2d 759, 761 (5th Cir. 1988) (both cases holding that allegations of vandalism by inmates other than the plaintiff do not defeat an Eighth Amendment claim); Palmigiano v. Garrahy, 443 F. Supp. 956, 963–64 (D.R.I. 1977) (noting that even if some prisoners don't keep their cells clean, common areas "must be the basic responsibility of management"; citing "abdication" of any attempt to maintain cleanliness).

Confinement in an area where prisoners with mental illness cause unsanitary conditions may violate the Eighth Amendment. Thaddeus-X v. Blatter, 175 F.3d 378, 402–03 (6th Cir. 1999) (en banc); Bracewell v. Lobmiller, 938 F. Supp. 1571, 1578–79 (M.D.Ala. 1996), *aff'd,* 116 F.3d 1493 (11th Cir. 1997) (unpublished).

[156]*But see* Benjamin v. Fraser, 156 F. Supp. 2d 333, 355 (S.D.N.Y. 2001) (holding that patients cannot be relied upon to maintain sanitation in infirmary; "The fact that they can walk does not mean that they are capable of working with mops and scrub brushes."), *aff'd in part, vacated and remanded in part on other grounds,* 343 F.3d 35 (2d Cir. 2003).

[157]Hoptowit v. Spellman, 753 F.2d 779, 784 (9th Cir. 1985); Johnson v. Pelker, 891 F.2d 136, 139 (7th Cir. 1989) (citing lack of

that filthy conditions in an individual prisoner's cell do not violate the Constitution if she is given the means to clean it herself.[158]

Failure to conform to "free world" sanitation standards does not necessarily violate the Constitution.[159] However, you may be able to enforce state or local health, or sanitation codes in state court.[160]

Prisoners must also have reasonable opportunities for personal cleanliness.[161] However, there is little constitutional law concerning the availability of showers in general population under normal conditions. One court has held that a lack of shower facilities that resulted in inmates' being limited to three showers a week in general population in non-emergency conditions "deprives the inmates of basic hygiene and threatens their physical and mental well-being."[162] Most decisions about the frequency of showers deal with segregation units or with prolonged "lockdown" restrictions imposed after riots or other emergencies. One decision has held that one shower a week is required in segregation,[163]

but earlier decisions required more showers in segregation or lockdown situations.[164] Some recent decisions have upheld the deprivation of showers for reasons of behavior control; the limits of prison officials' power in this regard are not clear.[165] Inconvenience such as having to wait in line for a shower is not unconstitutional,[166] nor is failure to meet professional or public health standards for numbers of shower facilities.[167] State law may provide standards enforceable in state court.[168]

Courts have also required prison officials to provide water for washing as well as drinking,[169] and several courts

cleaning supplies); Howard v. Adkison, 887 F.2d 134, 137 (8th Cir. 1989) (same); Carty v. Farrelly, 957 F. Supp. 727, 736 (D.V.I. 1997) (noting threat to health caused by lack of plans for institutional housekeeping, kitchen maintenance, and sanitation); Carver v. Knox County, 753 F. Supp. 1370, 1388 (E.D.Tenn. 1989) ("The provision of basic cleaning supplies, such as mops, brooms, toilet brushes and cleaners are a basic necessity of civilized life"), *remanded for reconsideration*, 887 F.2d 1287 (6th Cir. 1989), *adhered to on remand*, 753 F. Supp. 1398 (E.D.Tenn. 1990); Tillery v. Owens, 719 F. Supp. 1256, 1271 (W.D.Pa. 1989) (citing lack of a formal housekeeping plan), *aff'd*, 907 F.2d 418 (3d Cir. 1990); Inmates of Occoquan v. Barry, 717 F. Supp. 854, 866–67 (D.D.C. 1989); Palmigiano v. Garrahy, 443 F. Supp. at 963–64.

[158]Davis v. Scott, 157 F.3d 1003, 1006 (5th Cir. 1998); Smith v. Copeland, 87 F.3d 265, 268 (8th Cir. 1996); *see* McBride v. Deer, 240 F.3d 1287, 1291–92 (10th Cir. 2001) (holding that three days' confinement in a feces-covered cell stated a claim, though it would not have if cleaning materials had been available to the plaintiff).

[159]Ruiz v. Estelle, 679 F.2d 1115, 1159 (5th Cir. 1982).

[160]*See* Wilson v. State, 113 Idaho 563, 746 P.2d 1022, 1026–27 (1987) (state haircutting sanitation regulations adopted as minimum constitutional standards); *see* § A.1 of this chapter, n.30, concerning regulations in Eighth Amendment analysis.

[161]*See* Bradley v. Puckett, 157 F.3d 1022, 1025 (5th Cir. 1998) (two-month denial of showers resulting from denial of shower chair to disabled prisoner stated an Eighth Amendment claim).

[162]Tillery v. Owens, 719 F. Supp. at 1272; *see* Richardson v. Sheriff of Middlesex County, 407 Mass. 455, 553 N.E.2d 1286, 1291 (Mass. 1990) (one shower for 60 prisoners violated pre-trial detainees' rights); *see also* Toussaint v. McCarthy, 801 F.2d 1080, 1180–81 (9th Cir. 1986) (showers required to have adjustable valves for hot and cold water); Carty v. Farrelly, 957 F. Supp.at 736 (noting lack of hot water in showers affects both personal hygiene and ability to clean eating utensils). *But see* Lopez v. Robinson, 914 F.2d 486, 492 (4th Cir. 1990) (right to hot showers was not "clearly established").

[163]Davenport v. DeRobertis, 844 F.2d 1310, 1316 (7th Cir. 1988) (one shower a week required for segregation prisoners). *But see* Beckford v. Portuondo, 151 F. Supp. 2d 204, 210–11 (N.D.N.Y. 2001) (deprivation of a single shower did not violate the Eighth

Amendment, but denial of all shower privileges for a week might, especially since the wheelchair-bound plaintiff had bladder problems and had to clean himself frequently to avoid bedsores).

[164]Walker v. Mintzes, 771 F.2d 920, 928–29 (6th Cir. 1985) (in lockdown case, three showers a week required for general population inmates, one for segregation inmates); Preston v. Thompson, 589 F.2d 300, 308 (7th Cir. 1978) (showers twice a week required for general population in lockdown case); Jefferson v. Southworth, 447 F. Supp. 179, 191 (D.R.I. 1978) (showers every other day required in lockdown case), *aff'd sub nom.* Palmigiano v. Garrahy, 616 F.2d 598 (1st Cir. 1980). *But see* Waring v. Meachum, 175 F. Supp. 2d 230, 241–42 (D.Conn. 2001) (holding failure to provide showers during a week's lockdown was not unconstitutional).

Several decisions have upheld the provision of three showers a week without deciding whether they were constitutionally required. Peterkin v. Jeffes, 661 F. Supp. 895, 914–15 (E.D.Pa. 1987) (three showers a week met constitutional requirements in death row unit), *aff'd in part and vacated in part on other grounds*, 855 F.2d 1021 (3d Cir. 1988); Dolphin v. Manson, 626 F. Supp. 229, 240 (D.Conn. 1986) (three showers a week met constitutional requirements in administrative segregation); Wojtczak v. Cuyler, 480 F. Supp. 1288, 1296, 1307 (E.D.Pa. 1979) (three showers a week enough in protective custody unit).

[165]In *Rodriguez v. Briley*, 403 F.3d 952 (7th Cir. 2005), a segregation prisoner missed 75 showers in 18 months because he repeatedly disobeyed a rule requiring him to store his property before leaving his cell; the court held that this did not violate the Constitution. In *Trammell v. Keane*, 338 F.3d 155, 163, 165–66 (2d Cir. 2003), the court held that prison officials were not deliberately indifferent for depriving a SHU prisoner of showers and other privileges for about two weeks in an effort to control his disruptive behavior. *See also* McCoy v. Goord, 255 F. Supp. 2d 233, 260 (S.D.N.Y. 2003) ("a two-week suspension of shower privileges does not suffice as a denial of 'basic hygiene needs'").

[166]Alston v. Coughlin, 668 F. Supp. 822, 831 (S.D.N.Y. 1987).

[167]Miles v. Bell, 621 F. Supp. 51, 59–60 (D.Conn. 1985).

[168]*See* Youngblood v. Gates, 200 Cal.App.3d 1302, 246 Cal. Rptr. 775, 790 (Cal.App. 1988) (state law required showers every other day in police lockups).

[169]Surprenant v. Rivas, 424 F.3d 5, 19–20 (1st Cir. 2005) (holding provision of water in cell only at officers' discretion contributed to a constitutional violation; prisoners were required to put their unwashed hands in their mouths during strip searches); Young v. Quinlan, 960 F.2d 351, 365 (3d Cir. 1992); Johnson v. Pelker, 891 F.2d 136, 139 (7th Cir. 1989) (three-day denial of water in filthy cell stated an Eighth Amendment claim); *see also* Cody v. Hillard, 599 F. Supp. 1025, 1050 (D.S.D. 1984) (excessively hot water in cell sinks did not violate the Constitution where inmates could mix it

have said that hot water must be provided.[170] Brief deprivations of water for valid security reasons are not unconstitutional,[171] and the lack of running water in cells is not unconstitutional if prisoners are provided with sufficient water in some other fashion.[172] Prisons are required to provide for clean clothing[173] and bedding,[174] and to make available toilet articles such as soap, toothbrush and toothpaste, sanitary napkins, and toilet paper.[175]

However, short-term deprivation of these items is not unconstitutional,[176] and deprivation of less basic items such

---

with cold water in the basin), *rev'd on other grounds*, 830 F.2d 912 (8th Cir. 1987) (en banc).

[170]French v. Owens, 777 F.2d 1250, 1252–53 (7th Cir. 1985) (lack of hot water in cells contributed to finding of an Eighth Amendment violation); Ramos v. Lamm, 639 F.2d 559, 568 (10th Cir. 1980) (holding state must provide hot and cold water in prison living space); Carty v. Farrelly, 957 F. Supp. 727, 736 (D.V.I. 1997) (noting lack of hot water in showers affects both personal hygiene and ability to clean eating utensils); Matthews v. Peters, 818 F. Supp. 224, 227 (N.D.Ill. 1993) (11-month denial of hot water stated an Eighth Amendment claim); Cody v. Hillard, 599 F. Supp. at 1030, 1050 (absence of hot running water in housing units was unconstitutional); Grubbs v. Bradley, 552 F. Supp. 1052, 1132 (M.D.Tenn. 1982) (hot water in cells required for prisoners with long lock-in schedules); Lightfoot v. Walker, 486 F. Supp. 504, 528 (S.D.Ill. 1980) (sink with hot water required in all cells). Some courts have emphasized lack of hot water in holding that segregation conditions raised Eighth Amendment concerns. *See* Mitchell v. Maynard, 80 F.3d 1433, 1443 (10th Cir. 1996) (holding placement in segregation without hot water, among other bad conditions, could be found to violate the Eighth Amendment); Williams v. White, 897 F.2d 942, 944–45 (8th Cir. 1990) (placement in solitary confinement without hot water, among other bad conditions, stated an Eighth Amendment claim). *But see* Mann v. Smith, 796 F.2d 79, 85 (5th Cir. 1986) (no constitutional right to hot water); Howard v. Wheaton, 668 F. Supp. 1140, 1143–44 (N.D.Ill. 1987) (confinement for 13 days without working toilet or hot water to clean himself stated a constitutional claim).

[171]Warren v. Irvin, 985 F. Supp. 350, 356–57 (W.D.N.Y. 1997) (deprivation of water for three days because the plaintiff was flooding his cell did not violate the Eighth Amendment); Dennis v. Thurman, 959 F. Supp. 1253, 1261 (C.D.Calif. 1997) (shutting off water to segregation unit for 36 hours did not violate the Eighth Amendment, since prisoners had used the water to flood the cell block); Smith v. Copeland, 892 F. Supp. 1218, 1229–30 (E.D.Mo. 1995) (turning off water in cell after prisoner had flooded his cell did not violate the Constitution where it was turned on three times a day for toilet flushing, and drinking water was provided with each meal).

[172]Atkins v. County of Orange, 372 F. Supp. 2d 377, 406 (S.D.N.Y. 2005) and cases cited; Carlyle v. Aubrey, 189 F. Supp. 2d 660, 665 (W.D.Ky. 2001); Reid v. Artus, 984 F. Supp. 191, 193–94 (S.D.N.Y. 1997) (eight-day water shut-off related to plumbing repairs did not state an Eighth Amendment claim, since the plaintiff got water when he needed it, several times a day, and was able to take showers).

[173]*See* cases cited in § E of this chapter, n.220.

[174]*See* cases cited in § B.2 of this chapter, n.124.

[175]Board v. Farnham, 394 F.3d 469, 481–82 (7th Cir. 2005) ("the right to toothpaste as an essential hygienic product is analogous to the established right to a nutritionally adequate diet"); Myers v. Hundley, 101 F.3d 542, 544 (8th Cir. 1996) ("a long-term,

repeated deprivation of adequate hygiene supplies violates inmates' Eighth Amendment rights. . . . Prisons may either regularly provide these supplies to inmates free of charge, or they may give inmates a suffient allowance with which to buy them."); Penrod v. Zavaras, 94 F.3d 1399, 1406 (10th Cir. 1996) (allegation of denial of free toothpaste and razors to indigent prisoner raised a factual issue under the Eighth Amendment where plaintiff alleged serious harm as a result); Keenan v. Hall, 83 F.3d 1083, 1091 (9th Cir. 1996) ("Indigent inmates have the right to personal hygiene supplies such as toothbrushes and soap"; allegation that plaintiff was denied such items except when he could pay for them, and that the indigency standard forced him to choose between hygiene items and legal supplies, stated a claim), *amended on other grounds*, 135 F.3d 1318 (9th Cir. 1998); Carver v. Bunch, 946 F.2d 451, 452 (6th Cir. 1991) (allegation of two-week denial of personal hygiene items stated an Eighth Amendment claim); Chandler v. Baird, 926 F.2d 1057, 1063–65 (11th Cir. 1991) (allegation of confinement without toilet paper, soap, and toothpaste supported an Eighth Amendment claim); Malone v. Colyer, 710 F.2d 258, 262 (6th Cir. 1983) (deprivation of toilet articles states a claim); Kimbrough v. O'Neil, 523 F.2d 1057, 1059 (7th Cir. 1975) (deprivation of soap and toilet paper in segregation was unconstitutional), *on rehearing*, 545 F.2d 1059 (7th Cir. 1976) (en banc); Atkins v. County of Orange, 372 F. Supp. 2d at 406 (allegation of denial of basic hygiene products such as toilet paper, toothbrush, and sanitary napkins raised a factual issue barring summary judgment); Carty v. Farrelly, 957 F. Supp. 727, 738 (D.V.I. 1997) (citing failure to supply items such as toothpaste and sanitary napkins in finding a constitutional violation); Williams v. ICC Committee, 812 F. Supp. 1029, 1032 (N.D.Cal. 1992) ("deliberate denial of toilet paper and soap for any extended period" would violate the Eighth Amendment); Carver v. Knox County, Tenn., 753 F. Supp. 1370, 1389 (E.D.Tenn. 1989) (failure to provide soap, razors, combs, toothpaste, toilet paper, access to mirror, sanitary napkins violated Constitution); Bird v. Figel, 725 F. Supp. 406 (N.D.Ind. 1986); Dawson v. Kendrick, 527 F. Supp. 1252, 1288 (S.D.W.Va. 1981); Heitman v. Gabriel, 524 F. Supp. 622, 628 (W.D.Mo. 1981); Feliciano v. Barcelo, 497 F. Supp. 14, 40 (D.P.R. 1979); Owens-El v. Robinson, 457 F. Supp. 984, 986 (W.D.Pa. 1978), *aff'd in part and vacated in part sub nom.* Inmates of Allegheny County Jail v. Pierce, 612 F.2d 754 (3d Cir. 1979); Youngblood v. Gates, 200 Cal.App.3d 1302, 246 Cal.Rptr. 775, 790 (Cal.App. 1988) (opportunity to shave and brush teeth required in police lockups); Hickson v. Kellison, 170 W.Va. 732, 296 S.E.2d 855, 858 (W.Va. 1982) (comb, toothbrush, toothpaste, shaving equipment required); *see also* Gluth v. Kangas, 951 F.2d 1504, 1508 (9th Cir. 1991) (policy that "forces inmates to choose between purchasing hygienic supplies and essential legal supplies, is 'unacceptable.'") *But see* Citro v. Zeek, 544 F. Supp. 829 (W.D.N.Y. 1982) (deprivation of toilet paper was not unconstitutional); Cassidy v. Superintendent, City Prison Farm, 392 F. Supp. 330, 333 (W.D.Va. 1975) (deprivation of toothpaste and toilet paper was not unconstitutional).

[176]Harris v. Fleming, 839 F.2d 1232, 1234–35 (7th Cir. 1988) (no toilet paper for five days, and no soap, toothbrush or toothpaste for ten days, was not unconstitutional because it was an "isolated incident"); Davidson v. Murray, 371 F. Supp. 2d 361, 372 (W.D.N.Y. 2005) ("occasional or temporary" deprivations of toothpaste, soap, toilet paper, etc., were not unconstitutional), *reconsideration denied on other grounds*, 2005 WL 1631056 (W.D.N.Y., July

as shampoo and deodorant may not be unconstitutional at all.[177]

Prisons must provide adequate functioning toilets for their populations,[178] and prisoners must be allowed access to them.[179] Many courts have held that prisoners may not be locked into cells without working toilets,[180] and the use of

---

1, 2005); Caudle-El v. Peters, 727 F. Supp. 1175, 1180–81 (N.D.Ill. 1989) (six-day delay not unconstitutional); Gilland v. Owens, 718 F. Supp. 665, 684 (W.D.Tenn. 1989) (short-term deprivation was not unconstitutional); Burnette v. Phelps, 621 F. Supp. 1157, 1160 (M.D.La. 1985) (same as *Gilland*).

[177]May v. Baldwin, 895 F. Supp. 1398, 1408 (D.Or. 1995), *aff'd*, 103 F.3d 557 (9th Cir. 1997); Scher v. Purkett, 758 F. Supp. 1316, 1317 (E.D.Mo. 1991).

[178]Fischer v. Winter, 564 F. Supp. 281, 302 (N.D.Cal. 1983) (failure to increase bathroom facilities while population was increasing was unconstitutional); Toussaint v. Rushen, 553 F. Supp. 1365, 1372, 1379–80 (N.D.Cal. 1983) (inadequate plumbing was unconstitutional; defendants were considering replacing leaking toilets with covered chamber pots), *aff'd in part and vacated in part on other grounds*, 722 F.2d 1490 (9th Cir. 1984); Richardson v. Sheriff of Middlesex County, 407 Mass. 455, 553 N.E.2d 1286, 1291 (Mass. 1990) (two toilets for 60 prisoners violated pretrial detainees' rights). *But see* Patchette v. Nix, 952 F.2d 158, 163 (8th Cir. 1991) (temporary violation of American Correctional Association standards for numbers of toilets did not violate the Eighth Amendment); Miles v. Bell, 621 F. Supp. 51, 60 (D.Conn. 1985) (failure to comply with correctional or public health standards regarding numbers of toilets did not violate the Constitution).

[179]Miller v. King, 384 F.3d 1248, 1262 (11th Cir. 2004) (holding that a paraplegic prisoner without access to wheelchair-accessible toilets, assistance in using toilets, and catheters could show he was denied "the basic levels of humane care and hygiene"), *vacated and superseded on other grounds*, 449 F.3d 1149 (11th Cir. 2006); Palmer v. Johnson, 193 F.3d 346, 353–54 (5th Cir. 1999) (citing lack of toilet access as supporting an Eighth Amendment claim for prisoners held outdoors overnight); Mitchell v. Newryder, 245 F. Supp. 2d 200, 204–05 (D.Me. 2003) (prisoner who was denied access to toilet, soiled himself, and then was not allowed to clean himself stated an Eighth Amendment claim); *see* Glaspy v. Malicoat, 134 F. Supp. 2d 890, 894–95 (W.D.Mich. 2001) (awarding compensatory and punitive damages to visitor who soiled himself after being denied the use of a toilet; "there are few activities that appear to be more at the heart of the liberty guaranteed by the Due Process Clause of the Fourteenth Amendment than the right to eliminate harmful wastes from one's body away from the observation of others"). *But see* Revels v. Vincenz, 382 F.3d 870, 875–76 (8th Cir. 2004) (holding the refusal to allow a mental patient to go to the bathroom immediately, causing him to urinate on himself, did not violate the Eighth Amendment, since the deprivation was momentary).

[180]Kimbrough v. O'Neil, 523 F.2d at 1058–59; Howard v. Wheaton, 668 F. Supp. 1140, 1142–44 (N.D.Ill. 1987); Heitman v. Gabriel, 524 F. Supp. at 626; Flakes v. Percy, 511 F. Supp. 1325, 1329 (W.D.Wis. 1981); Wolfish v. Levi, 439 F. Supp. 114, 157 (S.D.N.Y. 1977), *rev'd in part and remanded*, 573 F.2d 118 (2d Cir. 1978), *rev'd on other grounds sub nom.* Bell v. Wolfish, 441 U.S 520, 99 S. Ct. 1861 (1979); *see also* Attorney General v. Sheriff of Worcester County, 382 Mass. 57, 413 N.E.2d 722 (Mass. 1980) (state regulations required that all isolation cells contain toilets). *But see* Boland v. Coughlin, 622 F. Supp. 736, 737 (E.D.N.Y. 1985) (lack of toilet in

---

"Chinese toilets" (holes in the floor) or chamber pots has been condemned.[181] Even in extreme situations justifying denial of normal toilet facilities, the failure to allow the prisoner promptly to dispose of her wastes violates the Eighth Amendment.[182]

D. Food

"Food is one of the basic necessities of life protected by the Eighth Amendment."[183] Deprivation of food for any substantial period of time can violate the Constitution.[184]

---

segregation cell was not unconstitutional where the plaintiff never was denied access to a bathroom).

One court has recently held that it does not violate the Eighth Amendment to lock prisoners in cells with "nonflushable toilets" at night, since the drafters of the Eighth Amendment used them, as have many modern Americans. Knop v. Johnson, 977 F.2d 996, 1013 (6th Cir. 1992). The court fails to note that these non-prisoners were not locked into a small cell with their "nonflushable toilets." For this reason we think the *Knop* case was wrongly decided.

[181]Kirby v. Blackledge, 530 F.2d 583, 586 (4th Cir. 1976); LaReau v. MacDougall, 473 F.2d 974, 978 (2d Cir. 1972) and cases cited; Strachan v. Ashe, 548 F. Supp. 1193, 1202–03 (D.Mass. 1982); Bel v. Hall, 392 F. Supp. 274, 276–77 (D.Mass. 1975); Michaud v. Sheriff of Essex County, 390 Mass. 523, 458 N.E.2d 702, 708–09 (Mass. 1983) (citing state and federal constitutions). In *Masonoff v. DuBois*, 899 F. Supp. 782, 797 (D.Mass. 1995), the court held that the use of chemical toilets that prisoners must empty into slop sinks and that use toxic substances that cause health problems is unconstitutional.

[182]Young v. Quinlan, 960 F.2d 351, 364–65 (3d Cir. 1992) (even if placement in a "dry cell" was justified, the refusal to let the prisoner out to use a toilet and to empty his urinal would violate the Constitution); Wells v. Franzen, 777 F.2d 1258, 1263–64 (7th Cir. 1985) (the failure to release a restrained prisoner to go to the bathroom and the failure to remove his two-day-old bedpan full of urine raised a constitutional question).

[183]Knop v. Johnson, 667 F. Supp. 512, 525 (W.D.Mich. 1987), *aff'd in pertinent part*, 977 F.2d 996, 1000 (6th Cir. 1992); *accord*, Keenan v. Hall, 83 F.3d 1083, 1091 (9th Cir. 1996), *amended*, 135 F.3d 1318 (9th Cir. 1998).

[184]Reed v. McBride, 178 F.3d 849, 853 (7th Cir. 1999) (deprivation of food may violate the Eighth Amendment depending on the "amount and duration of the deprivation"; allegations of repeated three- to five-day deprivation of food stated a claim); Simmons v. Cook, 154 F.3d 805, 808–09 (8th Cir. 1998) (affirming damage award to paraplegic prisoners who missed four consecutive meals when placed where they could not get to their food trays in their wheelchairs); Green v. Johnson, 977 F.2d 1383, 1391 (10th Cir. 1992) (allegations of 72-hour reduction in rations stated a claim); Woods v. Thieret, 903 F.2d 1080, 1082 (7th Cir. 1990) (allegation of three-day denial of food stated a constitutional claim); Dearman v. Woodson, 429 F.2d 1288, 1290 (10th Cir. 1970) (two days' deprivation of food stated a constitutional claim); Hodge v. Ruperto, 739 F. Supp. 873, 876 (S.D.N.Y. 1990) (two and a half day denial of food prior to arraignment stated a constitutional claim); Willis v. Bell, 726 F. Supp. 1118, 1121–22 (N.D.Ill. 1989) (12-hour deprivation of food in police lockup, if intentional, was "obviously" unlawful).

The Supreme Court has identified deprivation of food to a suspect in custody as a type of "physical punishment" that can

Prison food must be nutritionally adequate.[185] If it is nutritionally adequate, courts will not get involved in the details of what is served.[186] (*E.g.*, there is no constitutional right to coffee.[187]) For short periods of time, particularly during lockdowns or other emergencies, prisons may serve food that would not be nutritionally adequate on a long-term basis.[188] Prison officials do have a constitutional

obligation to accommodate special diets required for medical reasons,[189] and to provide religious diets.[190]

Prison food must be "prepared and served under conditions which do not present an immediate danger to the health and well being of the inmates who consume it."[191] Numerous courts have found unsanitary food service to be unconstitutional.[192] Several have required food handlers to

---

render a confession involuntary. Schneckloth v. Bustamonte, 412 U.S. 218, 226, 93 S. Ct. 2041 (1973).

[185]Ramos v. Lamm, 639 F.2d 559, 570 (10th Cir. 1980); *accord*, Phelps v. Kapnolas, 308 F.3d 180, 186 (2d Cir. 2002); Thompson v. Gibson, 289 F.3d 1218, 1222 (10th Cir. 2002) (fact that a doctor prescribed double portions of food, which another doctor later discontinued, established only a medical disagreement and not inadequate food); Keenan v. Hall, 83 F.3d at 1091 (prison food must be "adequate to maintain health"); Antonelli v. Sheahan, 81 F.3d 1422, 1432 (7th Cir. 1996); Hazen v. Pasley, 768 F.2d 226, 228 n.2 (8th Cir. 1985) (diet causing "notable weight loss and mildly diminished health" was unconstitutional); Campbell v. Cauthron, 623 F.2d 503, 508–09 (8th Cir. 1980) (diet of sweet rolls and TV dinners was nutritionally inadequate; needs of inmates who work or exercise must be considered); Cunningham v. Jones, 567 F.2d 653, 657–60 (6th Cir. 1977) (prison officials must show that a restricted diet is nutritionally adequate); Caldwell v. Caesar, 150 F. Supp. 2d 50, 64–65 (D.D.C. 2001) (evidence that defendants did not provide a vegetarian diet, but just removed the meat and provided no alternative source of protein, supported a claim of nutritional inadequacy); Adams v. Mathis, 458 F. Supp. 302, 308 (M.D.Ala. 1978), *aff'd*, 614 F.2d 42 (5th Cir. 1980); *see also* Leeds v. Watson, 630 F.2d 674, 676 (9th Cir. 1980) (questioning adequacy of diet of TV dinners). *But see* Sivak v. Ada County, 115 Idaho 759, 769 P.2d 1131 (Idaho App. 1989) (weight loss of three pounds in a one-month stay did not establish that the diet was inadequate).

[186]Martin v. Scott, 156 F.3d 578, 580 (5th Cir. 1998) (use of "Vita-Pro" soy meat substitute did not violate Eighth Amendment, notwithstanding plaintiff's claim it made him sick); LaFevers v. Saffle, 936 F.2d 1117, 1120 (10th Cir. 1991) (failure to provide a vegetarian diet was not unconstitutional); Smith v. Sullivan, 553 F.2d 373, 379 (5th Cir. 1977) (court should not have prescribed contents of meals; "[a] well-balanced meal, containing sufficient nutritional value to preserve health, is all that is required"); Robeson v. Squadrito, 57 F. Supp. 2d 642, 647–48 (N.D.Ind. 1999) (rejecting plaintiff's complaint of small portions in light of a nutritionist's affidavit that the jail provided 3000 calories a day); Smith v. Harvey County Jail, 889 F. Supp. 426, 430 (D.Kan. 1995) ("plain but nutritious food" satisfies the Constitution).

[187]Lane v. Hutcheson, 794 F. Supp. 877, 882–83 (E.D.Mo. 1992); Miles v. Konvalenka, 791 F. Supp. 212, 214–15 (N.D.Ill. 1992).

[188]Rust v. Grammer, 858 F.2d 411, 414 (8th Cir. 1988) (upholding sandwich diet during a lockdown, but noting that "a diet, such as this one, without fruits and vegetables might violate the eighth amendment if it were the regular prison diet"); Craft v. Mann, 265 F. Supp. 2d 970, 972 (N.D.Ind. 2003) (two days of cheese sandwiches is not unconstitutional); Waring v. Meachum, 175 F. Supp. 2d 230, 239–40 (D.Conn. 2001) (holding a diet of cold cereal and sandwiches during a week-long lockdown was not unconstitutional, but agreeing with *Rust v. Grammer* on long-term diet); Islam v. Jackson, 782 F. Supp. 1111, 1114 (E.D.Va. 1992) ("Missing one meal as an isolated event does not deprive an inmate of basic

nutritional needs"); *see* Gwynn v. Transcor America, Inc., 26 F. Supp. 2d 1256, 1266–67 (D.Colo. 1998) (where 10 of 19 meals during interstate transportation were served at jails, plaintiff's allegation that the rest were from McDonald's or Arby's and she was coerced into giving them to the officers did not support a constitutional claim).

[189]*See* § F.4.e of this chapter concerning medical diets.

[190]*See* Ch. 3, § D.2.d, concerning religious diets.

[191]Ramos v. Lamm, 639 F.2d 559, 570–71 (10th Cir. 1980) and cases cited; *accord*, Johnson-El v. Schoemehl, 878 F.2d 1043, 1055 (8th Cir. 1989) (Constitution requires maintenance of kitchen sanitation and personal hygiene of kitchen workers); Jackson v. State of Arizona, 885 F.2d 639, 641 (9th Cir. 1989) (allegations of unsanitary food and polluted water stated an Eighth Amendment claim); Robles v. Coughlin, 725 F.2d 12, 16 (2d Cir. 1983) (allegation of contaminated food states a constititutional claim); Boyd v. Anderson, 265 F. Supp. 2d 952, 965 (N.D.Ind. 2003) (holding allegation that defendants "regularly served food that was inedible because it was spoiled or contaminated" stated an Eighth Amendment claim); Drake v. Velasco, 207 F. Supp. 2d 809, 812–13 (N.D.Ill. 2002) (allegation that Aramark food service company did not handle food properly and served food so unsanitary as to present a health risk stated an Eighth Amendment claim); Caldwell v. Caesar, 150 F. Supp. 2d 50, 62–63 (D.D.C. 2001) (holding expert evidence of unsanitary and unsafe food handling practices by Aramark supported an Eighth Amendment claim); Ingalls v. Florio, 968 F. Supp. 193, 198–99 (D.N.J. 1997) (allegation of food storage and preparation areas infested with vermin leading to contamination of food supported a constitutional claim); Malik v. Tanner, 697 F. Supp. 1294, 1304 (S.D.N.Y. 1988) (similar to *Robles*); Knop v. Johnson, 667 F. Supp. 512, 525 (W.D.Mich. 1987) (allegations of unsanitary and dangerous food preparation made out an Eighth Amendment claim), *aff'd in pertinent part*, 977 F.2d 996, 1000 (6th Cir. 1992); *see also* Rucker v. Ross Correctional Institution, 62 Ohio Misc.2d 372, 598 N.E.2d 918, 919 (Ohio Ct.Cl. 1992) (prison officials have a tort law duty "to use utmost care and caution in selling food for human consumption").

[192]French v. Owens, 777 F.2d 1250, 1255 (7th Cir. 1985); Ramos v. Lamm, 639 F.2d at 570–72; Alexander v. Boyd, 876 F. Supp. 773, 787 (D.S.C. 1995); Palmigiano v. DiPrete, 737 F. Supp. 1257, 1260, 1264 (D.R.I. 1990); Toussaint v. McCarthy, 597 F. Supp. 1388, 1401, 1412 (N.D.Cal. 1984), *aff'd in part and rev'd in part on other grounds*, 801 F.2d 1080 (9th Cir. 1986); Grubbs v. Bradley, 552 F. Supp. 1052, 1128 (M.D.Tenn. 1982); Dawson v. Kendrick, 527 F. Supp. 1252, 1297–98 (S.D.W.Va. 1981); Nicholson v. Choctaw County, Ala., 498 F. Supp. 295, 313 (S.D.Ala. 1980) ("No meat from an animal killed on the highway or road . . . shall be served in the jail."); Lightfoot v. Walker, 486 F. Supp. 504, 512–13, 524 (S.D.Ill. 1980); Palmigiano v. Garrahy, 443 F. Supp. 956, 962-63 (D.R.I. 1977) (filthy food service conditions were unconstitutional).

Most unsanitary food service cases involve a variety of unsanitary conditions. However, a single dangerous practice may be unconstitutional if it presents a serious risk. Capps v. Atiyeh, 559 F.

be medically certified.[193] If health hazards in food preparation and service are sufficiently gross, prisoners need not prove that serious food-borne illness has already occurred; the risk is enough.[194] Occasional contamination or unsanitary conditions do not violate the Constitution.[195] Nor must food handling and kitchen sanitation meet "free world" standards,[196] although these may be helpful to the court in deciding whether the Constitution has been violated.[197] Cold food,[198] unappetizing food,[199] or unpleasant schedules or dining conditions[200] do not violate the Constitution except in extreme circumstances.[201]

Supp. 894, 914 (D.Or. 1982) (unsafe milk pasteurization procedure found unconstitutional).

[193]Mitchell v. Untreiner, 421 F. Supp. 886, 900 (N.D.Fla. 1976); Campbell v. McGruder, 416 F. Supp. 100, 105–06 (D.D.C. 1975), aff'd in part and remanded, 580 F.2d 521 (D.C. Cir. 1978); Inmates of Suffolk County Jail v. Eisenstadt, 360 F. Supp. 676, 688 (D.Mass. 1973), aff'd, 494 F.2d 1196 (1st Cir. 1974).

[194]Benjamin v. Fraser, 343 F.3d 35, 56 (2d Cir. 2003); Drake v. Velasco, 207 F. Supp. 2d 809, 813 (N.D.Ill. 2002); Dawson v. Kendrick, 527 F. Supp. at 1298; see § A.1 of this chapter, n.19.

Most of the cases listed in the preceding footnotes do not cite specific evidence of illness. But see Kennibrew v. Russell, 578 F. Supp. 164, 168 (E.D.Tenn. 1983); Loren v. Jackson, 57 N.C.App. 216, 291 S.E.2d 310, 315 (N.C.App. 1982). If the health hazards are less overwhelming than in those cases, or the facts are in dispute, courts may cite a lack of evidence of food-borne illness as a reason to rule in prison officials' favor. Shrader v. White, 761 F.2d 975, 986–87 (4th Cir. 1985); Inmates of Occoquan v. Barry, 717 F. Supp. 854, 868 (D.D.C. 1989).

[195]Hamm v. DeKalb County, 774 F.2d 1567, 1575 (11th Cir. 1985); Shrader v. White, 761 F.2d at 986–87; Tucker v. Rose, 955 F. Supp. 810, 816 (S.D.Ohio 1997) ("The occasional presence of a rodent is insufficient to establish the objective component of an Eighth Amendment claim"); Islam v. Jackson, 782 F. Supp. 1111, 1114 (E.D.Va. 1992); Miles v. Bell, 621 F. Supp. 51, 62–63 (D.Conn. 1985); Danneman v. Schoemehl, 601 F. Supp. 1017, 1018 (E.D.Mo. 1985); Chase v. Quick, 596 F. Supp. 33, 34–35 (D.R.I. 1984); Freeman v. Trudell, 497 F. Supp. 481, 482 (E.D.Mich. 1980); Tuggle v. Egans, 457 F. Supp. 1015, 1017 (D.Colo. 1978); Boston v. Stanton, 450 F. Supp. 1049, 1055 (W.D.Mo. 1978); see also Johnson v. Bruce, 771 F. Supp. 327, 329 (D.Kan. 1991) (serving undercooked chicken on one occasion did not violate the Constitution absent evidence that the plaintiff consumed it and got sick), aff'd, 961 F.2d 220 (10th Cir. 1992).

[196]Ruiz v. Estelle, 679 F.2d 1115, 1159 (5th Cir. 1982); Miles v. Bell, 621 F. Supp. at 62–63. But see Caldwell v. Caesar, 150 F. Supp. 2d 50, 65–66 (D.D.C. 2001) (holding prisoner could pursue a negligence claim for violation of municipal regulations requiring regular handwashing and for serving unsanitary food).

[197]Ramos v. Lamm, 639 F.2d at 570–72; Palmigiano v. Garrahy, 443 F. Supp. at 980, 987.

[198]Brown-El v. Delo, 969 F.2d 644, 648 (8th Cir. 1992); Hamm v. DeKalb County, 774 F.2d at 1575; Hoitt v. Vitek, 497 F.2d 598, 601 (1st Cir. 1974); McCoy v. Goord, 255 F. Supp. 2d 233, 260 (S.D.N.Y. 2003); Harris v. Murray, 761 F. Supp. 409, 414–15 (E.D.Va. 1990); Boston v. Stanton, 450 F. Supp. at 1055.

In fact, the failure to keep food at the proper temperature can constitute a serious health hazard by permitting the growth of bacteria. Courts have recognized this fact in large-scale conditions cases involving the testimony of expert witnesses. See, e.g., Ramos v. Lamm, 639 F.2d at 571; Toussaint v. McCarthy, 597 F. Supp. 1388, 1401 (N.D.Cal. 1984), aff'd in part and rev'd in part on other grounds, 801 F.2d 1080 (9th Cir. 1986); Palmigiano v. Garrahy, 443 F. Supp. at 963; see also Caldwell v. Caesar, 150 F. Supp. 2d 50, 66 (D.D.C. 2001) (stating expert testimony is not needed to know that "hot food must be maintained at a minimum temperature to prevent the growth of harmful bacteria"). However, in a pro se case you probably will not get a court to take such a complaint seriously unless you have evidence that it is a widespread and consistent practice or that actual illness has resulted.

[199]U.S. v. State of Michigan, 680 F. Supp. 270, 275 (W.D.Mich. 1988); Zingmond v. Harger, 602 F. Supp. 256, 263 (N.D.Ind. 1985); Boston v. Stanton, 450 F. Supp. at 1055. But see cases cited in nn.204–214 of this section concerning the use of food as punishment.

[200]Green v. Ferrell, 801 F.2d 765, 770–71 (5th Cir. 1986) (two meals a day met constitutional standard if the diet was nutritionally adequate); Gardner v. Beale, 780 F. Supp. 1073, 1075–76 (E.D.Va. 1991) (serving two meals a day—brunch and dinner—on non-work days did not violate the Eighth Amendment); Armstrong v. Lane, 771 F. Supp. 943, 949 (C.D.Ill. 1991) (plastic utensils and styrofoam cups were not unconstitutional); Martin v. Lane, 766 F. Supp. 641, 648 (N.D.Ill. 1991) (lack of utensils during lockdown was not unconstitutional); Beardsley v. Moore, 765 F. Supp. 560, 563 (E.D.Mo. 1991) (serving food in a paper bag and not on a tray was not unconstitutional); Harris v. Murray, 761 F. Supp. 409, 415 (E.D.Va. 1990) (having to eat standing up occasionally is not unconstitutional); Tillery v. Owens, 719 F. Supp. 1256, 1272 (W.D.Pa. 1989) (food service that was "incredibly strained" by overcrowding was not unconstitutional), aff'd, 907 F.2d 418 (3d Cir. 1990); Robbins v. South, 595 F. Supp. 785, 790 (D.Mont. 1984) (15-minute meal periods upheld); Walker v. Johnson, 544 F. Supp. 345, 359 (E.D.Mich. 1982), aff'd in part and rev'd in part on other grounds sub nom. Walker v. Mintzes, 771 F.2d 920 (6th Cir. 1985) (dining hall security arrangements upheld); Merriweather v. Sherwood, 518 F. Supp. 355 (S.D.N.Y. 1981) (service of meals in housing tier, not dining room, upheld). But see Barnes v. Government of Virgin Islands, 415 F. Supp. 1218, 1234 (D.V.I. 1976) (requiring "three wholesome and nutritious meals per day").

[201]Rutherford v. Pitchess, 457 F. Supp. 104, 116 (C.D.Cal. 1978) (at least 15 minutes for meals required), aff'd in part and rev'd in part on other grounds, 710 F.2d 572 (9th Cir. 1979), rev'd on other grounds sub nom. Block v. Rutherford, 468 U.S. 589, 104 S. Ct. 3227 (1984).

One court has gone so far as to hold that one meal a day is constitutional as long as it provides enough nutrition. Cunningham v. Jones, 667 F.2d 565 (6th Cir. 1982). We disagree, and note that in Cunningham, no evidence was presented by the plaintiff's attorney. We think that evidence of the hunger pangs caused by 24 hours without food would demonstrate "the wanton and unnecessary infliction of pain" and the "unquestioned and serious deprivations of basic human needs" forbidden by the Eighth Amendment. Rhodes v. Chapman, 452 U.S. 337, 346, 101 S. Ct. 2392 (1981); see Willis v. Bell, 726 F. Supp. 1118, 1123-24 (N.D.Ill. 1989) (12 hours without food in police custody was "obviously" unlawful).

Prison officials are obligated to provide sufficient water,[202] and it must be fit to drink.[203]

The courts have placed some limits on prison officials' ability to use food as punishment or for behavior control. Clearly, they cannot impose a diet that is nutritionally inadequate.[204] Some older cases upheld bread and water punishment diets that were supplemented by regular meals every few days.[205] We think that evolving standards of decency have left these decisions behind.[206] Such punishments are rarely imposed nowadays; in fact, statutes or regulations in some jurisdictions forbid the use of food as punishment or require that segregated inmates receive the same meals as other prisoners.[207] However, prison officials may restrict prisoners' diets in order to control behavior such as throwing food.[208] The courts have generally upheld the use of "food loaf," an unappetizing substance made by mixing various foods and baking the mixture, as a "valid, temporary, safety measure" to control misuse of utensils, food, and human waste.[209] Some of them have warned that the use of such diets and other food deprivations must be restricted to controlling the kinds of behavior for which they were devised.[210] One court has held unconstitutional a similar diet ("grue"), even though it was nutritionally adequate in theory, because it was so revolting that many inmates would

---

[202]Clark-Murphy v. Foreback, 439 F.3d 280, 289–93 (6th Cir. 2006) (evidence that prisoner died of dehydration after his water was turned off for days supported an Eighth Amendment claim against staff members who knew but did not take action); Mabrey v. Farthing, 280 F.3d 400, 402–03 (4th Cir. 2002) (similar to *Clark-Murphy*); Johnson v. Lewis, 217 F.3d 726, 732 (9th Cir. 2000) (citing lack of drinking water for prisoners held outside after a disturbance in finding evidence supported an Eighth Amendment violation); Dellis v. Corrections Corporation of America, 257 F.3d 508, 512 (6th Cir. 2001) (holding that an allegation that the prison's water supply was out for three days and the plaintiff received only two half pints of milk and one 16.5 ounce bottle of water stated a constitutional claim); Atkins v. County of Orange, 372 F. Supp. 2d 377, 405–06 (S.D.N.Y. 2005) (prisoner's claim she was deprived of water to the point that her feet and legs swelled supported a constitutional claim). *But see* Johnson v. Commissioner of Correctional Services, 699 F. Supp. 1071, 1074 (S.D.N.Y. 1988) (eight days' confinement in a cell without running water did not violate the Eighth Amendment where the prisoner received a beverage with every meal); *see* § C of this chapter, n.171 concerning deprivations of water.

[203]Jackson v. Duckworth, 955 F.2d 21, 22 (7th Cir. 1992); Jackson v. State of Arizona, 885 F.2d 639, 641 (9th Cir. 1989); *see* Hearns v. Terhune, 413 F.3d 1036, 1043 (9th Cir. 2005) (holding failure to provide cold water in outside yard in 100°F weather stated an Eighth Amendment claim). *But see* Carroll v. DeTella, 255 F.3d 470, 472 (7th Cir. 2001) (lead from water pipes in the drinking water did not violate the Eighth Amendment where prisoners were told to let the water run in the morning before drinking it, which eliminated the hazard); Gholson v. Murry, 953 F. Supp. 709, 725 (E.D.Va. 1997) (similar to *Carroll*; defendants warned prisoners to let the water run for 15 to 30 seconds before drinking and not to drink hot water from the tap). In *Carroll v. DeTella*, the court also held that radium levels in the drinking water, which were twice the levels permitted by the federal Environmental Protection Agency, did not violate the Eighth Amendment, since the *state* EPA had declined to do anything about it on the ground that the federal agency might change its standard (as far as the court knew, it had not done so). 255 F.3d at 472-73. We frankly find this reasoning pretty shocking, and think that under the Eighth Amendment principles set out in Supreme Court cases, the court should have assessed the actual risk resulting from this contamination.

[204]Phelps v. Kapnolas, 308 F.3d 180, 186 (2d Cir. 2002); Cunningham v. Jones, 567 F.2d 653, 657–60 (6th Cir. 1977) (prison officials must show that a restricted diet is nutritionally adequate).

[205]Novak v. Beto, 453 F.2d 661, 668–71 (5th Cir. 1971); Ford v. Board of Managers of New Jersey State Prison, 407 F.2d 937 (3d Cir. 1969).

[206]*See* Jenkins v. Werger, 564 F. Supp. 806, 808–09 (D.Wyo. 1983) (five days' bread and water is unconstitutional); Landman v. Royster, 333 F. Supp. 621, 647 (E.D.Va. 1971) (bread and water diet

violated the Eighth Amendment), *supplemented*, 354 F. Supp. 1302 (E.D.Va. 1973); *see also* Finney v. Hutto, 410 F. Supp. 251, 275–76 (E.D.Ark. 1976) (diet of "grue" served to all punitive isolation inmates was unconstitutional even though they received regular meals every three days), *aff'd*, 548 F.2d 740 (8th Cir. 1977), *aff'd*, 437 U.S. 678, 98 S. Ct. 2565 (1978).

[207]*See, e.g.*, Rust v. Grammer, 858 F.2d 411, 413 (8th Cir. 1988) (citing Neb.Rev. Stat. § 83–4,114); Domegan v. Fair, 859 F.2d 1059, 1064 (1st Cir. 1988) (citing Mass.Gen.Laws Ch. 127, §§ 39–40).

[208]Burgin v. Nix, 899 F.2d 733, 734 (8th Cir. 1990); Rust v. Grammer, 858 F.2d at 414.

[209]LeMaire v. Maass, 745 F. Supp. 623, 633 (D.Or. 1990), *vacated and remanded on other grounds*, 12 F.3d 1444 (9th Cir. 1993); *accord*, Myers v. Milbert, 281 F. Supp. 2d 859, 865–66 (N.D.W.Va. 2003) (upholding use of food loaf with prisoner who threw his food tray out of his cell; the alleged adverse effects (vomiting, frequent bowel movements, burning in chest and throat) were not serious medical conditions, and defendants could rely on medical opinion as to when diet should be discontinued); Breazil v. Bartlett, 998 F. Supp. 236, 242 (W.D.N.Y. 1997) (". . . [T]he cruel and unusual punishment clause of the eighth amendment does not prohibit prison officials from restricting an inmate's diet as a punitive measure, as long as the inmate receives nutritionally adequate food that does not present an imminent health risk."); Adams v. Kincheloe, 743 F. Supp. 1385, 1390–92 (E.D.Wash. 1990); U.S. v. State of Michigan, 680 F. Supp. 270, 274-76 (W.D.Mich. 1988); Smith v. Oregon Dep't of Corrections, 101 Or.App. 539, 792 P.2d 109, 110 (Or.App. 1990), *review denied*, 310 Or. 475 (Or. 1990).

The *Adams* and *Michigan* cases both noted that the food loaf was nutritionally adequate and warned that if a food loaf diet presents an actual health threat, its use might well violate the Eighth Amendment.

[210]LeMaire v. Maass, 745 F. Supp. at 635–36; U.S. v. State of Michigan, 680 F. Supp. at 276; Moss v. Ward, 450 F. Supp. 591, 596 (W.D.N.Y. 1978) (complete deprivation of food); *see also* Green v. Johnson, 977 F.2d 1383, 1391 (10th Cir. 1992) (allegation that warden ordered reduced rations for 72 hours stated an Eighth Amendment claim).

In the *LeMaire* case, the appeals court held that the temporary use of "Nutraloaf" did not violate the Eighth Amendment, but held that prison officials could be enjoined to follow their own regulations limiting its use to food-related infractions and to a duration of no more than seven days. LeMaire v. Maass, 12 F.3d at 1456.

not eat it or would not eat enough of it.[211] Courts have disagreed over the conditioning of meal service on prisoners' compliance with prison rules related to meal service or to leaving one's cell.[212]

Some older decisions held that statutes or regulations limiting imposition of restricted diets to certain specified circumstances could create a liberty interest requiring due process protections. However, the Supreme Court appears to have overruled these decisions.[213] One court has held that deprivation of adequate food is "a form of corporal punishment" and that a hearing is required to impose it, without any reference to statutes or regulations.[214]

Prison officials are obliged to see that prisoners with mental illness are not harmed by malnutrition or thirst resulting from their illnesses, or from the official response to their illnesses.[215]

Most courts have held that a hunger-striking prisoner can be force-fed,[216] though there are some decisions to the contrary.[217] Since there is a liberty interest in avoiding unwanted medical treatment, including force-feeding, prisoners are entitled to due process before being subjected to it.[218]

---

[211]Finney v. Hutto, 410 F. Supp. at 276 n.12.

[212]In *Rodriguez v. Briley*, 403 F.3d 952 (7th Cir. 2005), a rule required prisoners to stow certain property in a box whenever they left their cell; the plaintiff repeatedly refused to do so, was not allowed out of his cell, and missed numerous meals as a result. The court upheld the enforcement of the rule, stating that the prisoner "punished himself," though it also said the prison might be obliged to act differently if the refusal to eat became suicidal or if the prisoner's actions resulted from mental illness. 403 F.3d at 952–53. *See* Berry v. Brady, 192 F.3d 504, 506–08 (5th Cir. 1999) (upholding denial of meals to prisoner who had refused to shave); Talib v. Gilley, 138 F.3d 211, 212, 214–215 (5th Cir. 1998) (upholding denial of meals because prisoner in lockdown refused to kneel with hands behind back before being served).

Other decisions have rejected this approach. *See* Cooper v. Sheriff, Lubbock County, Texas, 929 F.2d 1078, 1082–83 (5th Cir. 1991) (allegation that inmate was denied meals for 12 days because he would not "fully dress" stated Eighth Amendment and due process claims); Williams v. Coughlin, 875 F. Supp. 1004, 1013 (W.D.N.Y. 1995) (denying summary judgment where prisoner was denied five meals after refusing to return food tray); Moss v. Ward, 450 F. Supp. at 595–97 (several days' deprivation of food for refusing to return a cup violated the Eighth Amendment); Graves v. TDC Employees, 827 S.W.2d 47, 48 (Tex.App. 1992) (complaint alleging exclusion from dining hall for 98 of 120 meals in 40 days should not have been dismissed).

[213]*See* Ch. 4, § G.

[214]Cooper v. Sheriff, Lubbock County, Texas, 929 F.2d 1078, 1083–84 (5th Cir. 1991).

[215]Clark-Murphy v. Foreback, 439 F.3d 280, 289–90 (6th Cir. 2006) (holding that officials responsible for the death of a prisoner who died in an observation cell when his water was turned off during very hot weather could be found deliberately indifferent); Duffey v. Bryant, 950 F. Supp. 1168, 1177–78 (M.D.Ga. 1997) (holding that officials who allowed a prisoner with mental illness to die of malnutrition and dehydration could be found deliberately indifferent to his medical needs). *See* § F.4.a of this chapter concerning care of persons with mental illness.

[216]*In re* Grand Jury Subpoena John Doe, 150 F.3d 170, 172 (2d Cir. 1998) (upholding order that hunger-striking civil contemnor be force-fed; "the preservation of life, prevention of suicide, and enforcement of prison security, order, and discipline, outweigh the constitutional rights asserted by" the prisoner); Martinez v. Turner, 977 F.2d 421, 423 (8th Cir. 1992); *In re* Soliman, 134 F. Supp. 2d 1238, 1254 (N.D.Ala. 2001) (holding that officials may use a nasogastric tube or intravenous feeding, but that installing a feeding tube surgically would be an "exaggerated response"), *appeal dismissed as moot*, 296 F.3d 1237 (11th Cir. 2002) (per curiam); *In re* Sanchez, 577 F. Supp. 7 (S.D.N.Y. 1983); Lantz v. Coleman, 51 A.2d 99 (Conn.Super. 2009) (granting injunction allowing prison officials to force-feed); People ex rel. Illinois Dep't of Corrections v. Millard, 335 Ill.App.3d 1066, 782 N.E.2d 966 (2003), *appeal denied*, 204 Ill.2d 682, 792 N.E.2d 313 (2003); *In re* Caulk, 125 N.H. 226, 480 A.2d 93, 95–96 (N.H. 1984); Laurie v. Senecal, 666 A.2d 806, 809 (R.I. 1995) ("In respect to an incarcerated prisoner, we believe that there is no right under either the State or the Federal Constitution to override the compelling interest of the state in the preservation of his or her life and the prevention of suicide."); McNabb v. Dep't of Corrections, 163 Wash.2d 393, 406–11, 180 P.3d 1257 (Wash. 2008); State ex rel. White v. Narick, 170 W.Va. 195, 292 S.E.2d 54 (W.Va. 1982); *In re* Saenz, 299 Wis.2d 486, 500, 728 N.W.2d 765 (Wis.App. 2007); *see also* Garza v. Carlson, 877 F.2d 14, 17 (8th Cir. 1989) (threat of force-feeding was not unconstitutional).

In *Walker v. Horn*, 385 F.3d 321 (3d Cir. 2004), the plaintiff went nine days without food, allegedly as a religious fast, and prison officials obtained a state court order to force-feed him. His procedural due process claim was held barred by the state court proceeding, but his First and Eighth Amendment claims were tried to a jury, which ruled against him.

[217]Thor v. Superior Court, 5 Cal.4th 725, 732 855 P.2d 375 (1993) (in bank) ("under California law a competent, informed adult has a fundamental right of self-determination to refuse or demand the withdrawal of medical treatment of any form irrespective of the personal consequences," and this right is enjoyed by prisoners unless officials demonstrate a threat to institutional security or public safety); Singletary v. Costello, 665 So.2d 1099, 1109–10 (Fla.App. 1996) (affirming injunction against force-feeding under state constitution, noting absence of evidence of disruption in prison resulting from hunger strike); Zant v. Prevatte, 248 Ga. 832, 286 S.E.2d 715 (Ga. 1982); *see* In the Matter of Lilly, No. 07CV392, Memorandum Decision and Order Terminating Force Feeding and Injunction against Force Feeding (Wis. Circuit Ct., Dodge County, May 19, 2009) (holding there should be a "compelling circumstances" exception even if force-feeding is generally allowed). The argument that prisoner hunger strikes should be allowed is also detailed in a law review article. Mara Silver, *Testing Cruzan: Prisoners and the Constitutional Question of Self-Starvation*, 58 Stan. L. Rev. 631 (2005).

[218]*In re* Saenz, 299 Wis.2d 486, 728 N.W.2d 765 (Wis.App. 2007). That thoughtful decision held that due process calls for a hearing at which prison officials must show by a preponderance of the evidence that the prisoner has "refused to consume food and fluids sufficient to maintain his health for an extended period; . . . has been diagnosed by a physician as suffering from moderate to severe malnutrition, dehydration or other deleterious condition; . . . is in imminent danger of serious harm or death" without forced

E. Clothing

Prisoners are entitled to clothing that is "at least minimally adequate for the conditions under which they are confined."[219] They are entitled to clothing that is clean or to have an opportunity to clean it themselves,[220] and to enough clothing that they have something to wear while one change of clothing is being washed.[221] Clothing that fits badly or does not look good generally does not violate the Constitution.[222]

Prison officials may limit the amount of clothing an inmate possesses.[223]

Prisoners are not entitled to their choice of clothing,[224] and even pretrial detainees may be required to wear uniforms.[225] However, persons on trial in criminal courts are entitled to wear civilian clothes and not jail uniforms.[226]

---

hydration and/or forced feeding or other medical care. *Saenz*, 299 Wis.2d at 510–11. The prisoner must be allowed to attend, present evidence, compel witnesses to attend subject to court approval, and cross-examine. The prisoner may be represented by counsel, but appointment of counsel is not required; the court may require provision of a lay advisor or advocate. There is no due process right to an independent medical examination. Any order must be of limited duration or provide for periodic review. *Id.*, 299 Wis.2d at 512–516. These protections may be provided either in judicial proceedings, or prison officials may establish administrative procedures subject to judicial review. *Id.*, 299 Wis.2d at 516–17.

[219]Knop v. Johnson, 667 F. Supp. 467, 475–77 (W.D.Mich. 1987) (jackets found inadequate for Michigan winters; hats, gloves, or mittens, and boots or heavy socks also required), *aff'd in pertinent part*, 977 F.2d 996, 1012 (6th Cir. 1992); *accord*, Gordon v. Faber, 973 F.2d 686, 687–88 (8th Cir. 1992) (denial of hats and gloves in sub-freezing weather violated the Eighth Amendment); Davidson v. Coughlin, 920 F. Supp. 305 (N.D.N.Y. 1996); Williams v. Griffin, 952 F.2d 820, 825 (4th Cir. 1991) (allegation of deprivation of coats supported an Eighth Amendment claim); Balla v. Idaho State Bd. of Corrections, 595 F. Supp. 1558, 1575 (D.Idaho 1984) (inmates given lightweight uniforms must also get insulated underwear). *But see* Mays v. Springborn, 573 F.3d 643, 648–49 (7th Cir. 2009) (rejecting claim of inadequate winter clothing as no more than "the usual discomforts of winter"); Gerber v. Sweeney, 292 F. Supp. 2d 700, 709–10 (E.D.Pa. 2003) (upholding denial of hats and gloves in winter because they can be used to conceal contraband; allowing restriction of footwear to sandals because shoes would allow prisoners to gain "secure footing" from which to attack others). *See also* Hernandez v. Denton, 861 F.2d 1421, 1423–24 (9th Cir. 1988) (month-long deprivation of shoes could violate the Eighth Amendment), *vacated on other grounds*, 493 U.S. 81 (1989); Kendrick v. Bland, 659 F. Supp. 1188, 1196 (W.D.Ky. 1987) (raincoats and undershirts not constitutionally required), *aff'd sub nom.* Thompson v. Bland, 843 F.2d 1392, *and* Smith v. Bland, 856 F.2d 196 (6th Cir. 1988).

[220]Benjamin v. Fraser, 161 F. Supp. 2d 151, 178 (S.D.N.Y. 2001), *aff'd in in part, vacated and remanded in part on other grounds*, 343 F.3d 35, 52 (2d Cir. 2003); *accord*, Shannon v. Graves, 257 F.3d 1164, 1169 (10th Cir. 2001) (evidence of fecal contamination of blankets and clothing raised an Eighth Amendment issue, though officials were not shown to be deliberately indifferent); Divers v. Dep't of Corrections, 921 F.2d 191, 194 (8th Cir. 1990) ("adequate laundry facilities" required); Howard v. Adkison, 887 F.2d 134, 137 (8th Cir. 1989); Landfair v. Sheahan, 878 F. Supp. 1106, 1112 (N.D.Ill. 1995) (lack of clean clothing or means to launder clothing for an extended time could be unconstitutional); Wilson v. Cook County Bd. of Commissioners, 878 F. Supp. 1163, 1169 (N.D.Ill. 1995) (allegation that uniform had not been changed in a month, among other sanitary problems, stated a constitutional claim); Reece v. Gragg, 650 F. Supp. 1297, 1305 (D.Kan. 1986); Martino v. Carey, 563 F. Supp. 984, 1000 (D.Or. 1983); Toussaint v. Rushen, 553 F. Supp. 1365, 1371, 1379, 1385 (N.D.Cal. 1983) (lack of regular laundry service unconstitutional), *aff'd in part and vacated in*

part on other grounds, 722 F.2d 1490 (9th Cir. 1984); Dawson v. Kendrick, 527 F. Supp. 1252, 1288 (S.D.W.Va. 1981); Rutherford v. Pitchess, 457 F. Supp. 104, 116–17 (S.D.Cal. 1978), *aff'd in part and rev'd in part on other grounds*, 710 F.2d 572 (9th Cir. 1983), *rev'd on other grounds*, 468 U.S. 589 (1984); Hickson v. Kellison, 170 W.Va. 732, 296 S.E.2d 855, 858 (W.Va. 1982). *But see* McCorkle v. Walker, 871 F. Supp. 555, 557 (N.D.N.Y. 1995) (denial of change of underwear for 15 days was not unconstitutional); State v. Rouse, 229 Kan. 600, 629 P.2d 167, 172 (Kan. 1981) (two-week deprivation of clean clothing was not unconstitutional).

Prisoners may be required to do their own laundry. Green v. Ferrell, 801 F.2d 765, 771 (5th Cir. 1986); Shelby County Jail Inmates v. Westlake, 798 F.2d 1085, 1091 (7th Cir. 1986); Benjamin v. Fraser, 161 F. Supp. 2d at 178–79.

[221]Hazen v. Pasley, 768 F.2d 226, 228 n.2 (8th Cir. 1985); Evans v. Headley, 566 F. Supp. 1133, 1138 (S.D.N.Y. 1983); *see also* Hickson v. Kellison, 296 S.E.2d at 858 (failure to provide clothing other than what the prisoner was wearing when arrested is unconstitutional).

[222]Young v. Berks County Prison, 940 F. Supp. 121, 124 (E.D.Pa. 1996) (requiring the plaintiff to wear ill-fitting, dirty or torn clothes was "an indignity incidental to prison life that does not rise to the level of a constitutional violation"; he weighed 300 pounds and they didn't have much in his size); Knop v. Johnson, 667 F. Supp. 467, 475 (W.D.Mich. 1987).

[223]Rust v. Grammer, 858 F.2d 411, 414 (8th Cir. 1988); Lyons v. Farrier, 730 F.2d 525, 527 (8th Cir. 1984).

[224]Lopez v. City of New York, 2009 WL 229956, *13 (S.D.N.Y., Jan. 30, 2009) (rejecting argument that transgender prisoner had a right to wear clothing of opposite sex); Jones v. Warden of Stateville Correctional Center, 918 F. Supp. 1142, 1146 (N.D.Ill. 1995) ("Neither the Equal Protection Clause nor the First Amendment arguably accord [the male plaintiff] the right of access to women's clothing while confined to a state prison.").

[225]Wolfish v. Levi, 573 F.2d 118, 132–33 (2d Cir. 1978), *rev'd on other grounds sub nom.* Bell v. Wolfish, 441 U.S. 520, 99 S. Ct. 1861 (1979); Graham v. Perez, 121 F. Supp. 2d 317, 323 and n.10 (S.D.N.Y. 2000); *In re* Alcala, 222 Cal.App.3d 345, 271 Cal.Rptr. 674, 691–95 (Cal.App. 1990) (prohibition of most civilian clothing did not violate federal or state law).

[226]Estelle v. Williams, 425 U.S. 501, 96 S. Ct. 1691 (1976); Felts v. Estelle, 875 F.2d 785, 786 (9th Cir. 1989) (state must provide civilian clothing for indigent defendant); McFarland v. English, 111 F. Supp. 2d 591, 600–02 (E.D.Pa. 2000). *But see* U.S. v. Albritton, 75 F.3d 709, 711 (D.C. Cir. 1996) (being tried in prison garb did not deny due process where the prisoner did not object); Duckett v. Godinez, 67 F.3d 734, 747 (9th Cir. 1995) (being required to wear prison garb before a sentencing jury did not deny due process, since the defendant was no longer entitled to the presumption of innocence); Saenz v. Marshall, 791 F. Supp. 812, 814–15 (C.D.Cal. 1992) (appearance of a defense witness in prison garb did not

Some decisions have struck down the deprivation of clothing when it appears to have little or no justification.[227] However, most cases involving deprivation of clothing involve other deprivations as well, as when prisoners are thrown into "strip cells" without clothing, bedding, property, etc., after they have engaged or been accused of disruptive or violent behavior.[228] Decisions in those cases generally consider all the conditions to which the prisoner is subjected, as well as the prison officials' justification for their conduct. Some decisions hold that the prisoner's treatment is unlawful or that it raises constitutional issues,[229] and some

uphold it.[230] (A large number of these come from the federal appeals court for the Eighth Circuit.[231]) Either way, there is no clear constitutional rule about when officials may and

---

violate the defendants' rights); Wilson v. DeBruyn, 633 F. Supp. 1222 (W.D.N.Y. 1986) (federal court lacked jurisdiction to intervene in pending criminal cases on question of clothing at trial). The provision of poorly fitted civilian clothing does not deny due process. Adams v. Smith, 280 F. Supp. 2d 704, 717–18 (E.D.Mich. 2003).

[227]Rose v. Saginaw County, 353 F. Supp. 2d 900, 919–23 (E.D.Mich. 2005) (holding unconstitutional a policy of placing "uncooperative and disruptive" prisoners in administrative segregation naked); Beckford v. Portuondo, 151 F. Supp. 2d 204, 211–12 (N.D.N.Y. 2001) (deprivation of all clothing and bedding because prisoner would not cut a fingernail could be found "grossly disproportionate to the alleged infraction"); Wilson v. City of Kalamazoo, 127 F. Supp. 2d 855, 861 (W.D.Mich. 2000) (holding deprivation of all clothing including underwear to persons who would not answer questions about suicide risks stated Fourth and Fourteenth Amendment claims; the court notes that they could be left with their underwear); Inmates of Allegheny County Jail v. Wecht, 565 F. Supp. 1278, 1286 (W.D.Pa. 1983) (holding prisoners in restraints could not be deprived of clothing, since they were in no position to do anything dangerous with it); see also Walker v. Johnson, 544 F. Supp. 345, 361 (E.D.Mich. 1982) (prisoners in segregation could not be required to walk naked to the shower), aff'd in pertinent part sub nom. Walker v. Mintzes, 771 F.2d 920, 929 (6th Cir. 1985). Compare Johnson v. City of Kalamazoo, 124 F. Supp. 2d 1099, 1103–07 (W.D.Mich. 2000) (upholding removal of all clothing except underwear to prisoners who would not answer intake questions about suicide risk).

[228]See § J of this chapter, n.1327.

[229]Mitchell v. Maynard, 80 F.3d 1433, 1443 (10th Cir. 1996) (court cites deprivation of clothing among other conditions in holding that segregated confinement could violate the Eighth Amendment); Murphy v. Walker, 51 F.3d 714, 720–21 (7th Cir. 1995) (allegation that plaintiff was put in a cold cell in November with no bed, bedding, heat, or clothing stated a constitutional claim for inadequate heat and shelter); Wells v. Franzen, 777 F.2d 1258, 1264 (7th Cir. 1985) (where prisoner was held in underwear and restraints for nine days, the conditions "warrant further exploration"); Maxwell v. Mason, 668 F.2d 361, 363–65 (8th Cir. 1981) (holding unconstitutional 14 days in underwear, a cell with a mattress and nothing else); McCray v. Burrell, 622 F.2d 705, 706–07 (4th Cir. 1980) (holding that a prisoner's suicidal tendencies did not justify placing him naked in a barren cell without blankets, with nowhere to sleep or sit except bare concrete and only an encrusted hole in the floor for a toilet); DeMaio v. Mann, 877 F. Supp. 89, 93–94 (N.D.N.Y. 1995) (holding allegations of 12-day deprivations of food and clothing sufficient to withstand summary judgment), aff'd, 122 F.3d 1055 (2d Cir. 1995); and see cases cited in § J of this chapter, n.1327.

In LeMaire v. Maass, 745 F. Supp. 623, 639 (D.Or. 1990), vacated and remanded, 12 F.3d 1444 (9th Cir. 1993), the lower court held unconstitutional the practice of taking prisoners' clothing and returning it only after they "earned it back" through good behavior. This practice violated prison rules, and the appeals court held that prison officials should be enjoined only to follow their own rules. 12 F.3d at 1455.

[230]Trammell v. Keane, 338 F.3d 155, 163, 165–66 (2d Cir. 2002) (upholding deprivation of clothing other than shorts for two weeks to prisoner who defied ordinary disciplinary sanctions); Hawkins v. Hall, 644 F.2d 914, 917–18 (1st Cir. 1981) (deprivation of clothing for less than 24 hours pending medical and mental examinations upheld where ventilation, lighting, and heat were adequate); McMahon v. Beard, 583 F.2d 172, 174–75 (5th Cir. 1978) (three-month nude confinement without mattress, sheet, or blankets did not violate the Eighth Amendment where the prisoner continued to present a suicide risk).

[231]In Williams v. Delo, 49 F.3d 442, 445–46 (8th Cir. 1995), the plaintiff got into an altercation in the visiting room and was placed for three or four days in "temporary administrative segregation on limited property, that is, a strip cell," deprived of clothing, with no mattress and the water to his cell shut off; he was also denied a toothbrush and other hygiene items. The court said he was not deprived of "the minimal civilized measure of life's necessities." He got "three meals a day . . . and was sheltered from the elements. While he did not have any clothing or bedding, we have held there is no absolute Eighth Amendment right not to be put in a cell without clothes or bedding." 49 F.3d at 445–46; accord, Seltzer-Bey v. Delo, 66 F.3d 961, 964 (8th Cir. 1995) (holding two days in a strip cell without clothing did not deny a liberty interest or violate the Eighth Amendment). See Johnson v. Boreani, 946 F.2d 67, 70–72 (8th Cir. 1991) (officials were entitled to qualified immunity for repeated short deprivations of clothing); Porth v. Farrier, 934 F.2d 154, 156–57 (8th Cir. 1991) (unjustified 12-hour deprivation of clothing would have permitted, but did not require, a jury verdict for the plaintiff); Campbell v. Grammer, 889 F.2d 797, 802 (8th Cir. 1989) (inadvertent deprivation of clothing did not violate Eighth Amendment); Green v. Baron, 879 F.2d 305, 309–10 (8th Cir. 1989) (deprivation of clothing as part of a behavior modification program might have been justified by prisoner's mental condition); Rodgers v. Thomas, 879 F.2d 380, 385 (8th Cir. 1989) (unjustified deprivation of clothing was not unconstitutional where other conditions were adequate); Friends v. Moore, 776 F. Supp. 1382, 1390–91 (E.D.Mo. 1991) (leaving the plaintiff stripped naked and wet in a segregation yard area for two hours was not unconstitutional because the defendants intended to restore order rather than punish); see also O'Leary v. Iowa State Men's Reformatory, 79 F.3d 82, 83–84 (8th Cir. 1996) (upholding "progressive four-day behavior management program" which deprives prisoners of underwear but leaves them with jumpsuits). But see Wilkins v. Moore, 40 F.3d 954, 958 (8th Cir. 1994) (prisoner was kept naked for over 22 hours in a cell with unclean bedding and floors, poor lighting, and no blankets after he refused to write a statement favorable to prison guards concerning a use of force he had witnessed; court said the clothing deprivation had to be assessed as part of a "course of mistreatment" that included physical abuse, and previous Eighth Circuit cases did not bar it).

may not remove prisoners' clothing. Some courts have placed limits on the viewing of prisoners in the nude.[232]

F. MEDICAL CARE

Since prisoners cannot obtain their own medical services, the Constitution requires prison authorities to provide them with "reasonably adequate" medical care.[233] Courts have defined "adequate" medical services as "services at a level reasonably commensurate with modern medical science and of a quality acceptable within prudent professional standards,"[234] and as "a level of health services reasonably designed to meet routine and emergency medical, dental and psychological or psychiatric care."[235] It is not unlawful to incarcerate persons with serious medical problems as long as the necessary care will be provided in prison.[236]

In practice, providing care to prisoners generally means paying for the care, since most prisoners have little money and no medical insurance and are ineligible for public assistance.[237] The fact that the care may be expensive does not excuse prison officials from providing it.[238] State law will determine who is responsible for the costs.[239] If a prisoner does have money or insurance, it is not unconstitutional to bill the prisoner for the costs of medical care.[240] Some states have statutes to this effect, often covering prisoners in local jails who require treatment at outside hospitals.[241] But prison officials may not withhold medical care until the prisoner pays or agrees to pay; they must first provide the care and leave arguments about money until later.[242]

---

[232]*See* Ch. 3, § E.2, nn.923–925.

[233]Newman v. Alabama, 559 F.2d 283, 291 (5th Cir. 1978); *accord*, Hoptowit v. Ray, 682 F.2d 1237, 1246 (9th Cir. 1982); Wolfish v. Levi, 573 F.2d 118, 125 (2d Cir. 1978), *rev'd on other grounds sub nom.* Bell v. Wolfish, 441 U.S. 520, 99 S. Ct. 1861 (1979) (1979); *see also* Langley v. Coughlin, 888 F.2d 252, 254 (2d Cir. 1989) (officials must provide "reasonably necessary medical care . . . which would be available to [the prisoner] if not incarcerated").

[234]Fernandez v. U.S., 941 F.2d 1488, 1493 (11th Cir. 1991); *accord*, U.S. v. DeCologero, 821 F.2d 39, 43 (1st Cir. 1987); Tillery v. Owens, 719 F. Supp. 1256, 1305 (W.D.Pa. 1989), *aff'd*, 907 F.2d 418 (3d Cir. 1990); Howard v. City of Columbus, 239 Ga.App. 399, 405–06, 521 S.E.2d 51 (1999); *see* Barrett v. Coplan, 292 F. Supp. 2d 281, 285 (D.N.H. 2003) ("'Adequate medical care' requires treatment by qualified medical personnel who provide services that are of a quality acceptable when measured by prudent professional standards in the community, tailored to an inmate's particular needs, and that are based on medical considerations." (citing *DeCologero*)).

[235]Tillery v. Owens, 719 F. Supp. at 1301; *accord*, Riddle v. Mondragon, 83 F.3d 1197, 1203 (10th Cir. 1996); Ramos v. Lamm, 639 F.2d 559, 574 (10th Cir. 1980).

[236]U.S. v. Derbes, 369 F.3d 579, 581–83 (1st Cir. 2004) (appropriateness of downward departure from federal sentencing guidelines depends on whether prisoner would receive necessary mental health treatment in prison). Failure to provide adequate medical care may justify an injunction or damages, but not release from prison. Glaus v. Anderson, 408 F.3d 382, 387 (7th Cir. 2005); Caldwell v. U.S., 992 F. Supp. 363, 366 (S.D.N.Y. 1998).

[237]Monmouth County Correctional Institution Inmates v. Lanzaro, 834 F.2d 326, 350 (3d Cir. 1987) (citing City of Revere v. Mass. General Hospital, 463 U.S. 239, 245–46, 103 S. Ct. 2979 (1983)).

[238]Harris v. Thigpen, 941 F.2d 1495, 1509 (11th Cir. 1991); Langley v. Coughlin, 888 F.2d at 254; Ancata v. Prison Health Services, Inc., 769 F.2d 700, 705 (11th Cir. 1985); Rosado v. Alameida, 349 F. Supp. 2d 1340, 1348 (S.D.Cal. 2004); Kosilek v. Maloney, 221 F. Supp. 2d 156, 161 (D.Mass. 2002); Yarbaugh v. Roach, 736 F.

Supp. 318, 320 n.7 (D.D.C. 1990); *see* nn.299–300 of this chapter for further discussion of cost issues.

[239]Myrtle Beach Hosp., Inc. v. City of Myrtle Beach, 341 S.C. 1, 532 S.E.2d 868 (S.C. 2000) (holding city was not required to reimburse hospital for detainees' medical care under state statutes, public policy, or common law); Emergency Physicians Integrated Care v. Salt Lake County, 167 P.3d 1080, 1084–86 (Utah 2007) (county was obliged under common law *quantum meruit* rule to pay physicians the reasonable value of their services to county prisoners); Our Lady of Lourdes Hosp. v. Franklin County, 120 Wash.2d 439, 842 P.2d 956, 960–64 (Wash. 1993) (holding state statute required county to pay jail inmates' hospital bills, and required state agency to reimburse the county in full for patients eligible for public medical assistance).

[240]Smith v. Linn County, 342 N.W.2d 861, 863 (Iowa 1984); Metro. Dade County v. P.L. Dodge Foundations, 509 So.2d 1170, 1173 (Fla.App. 1987); Brown v. County Com'rs of Carroll County, 338 Md. 286, 658 A.2d 255, 265–66 (Md. 1995) (holding county should first seek reimbursement from Medicare for detainee's medical care but could recover costs from detainee for expenses Medicare did not cover); *see* City of Revere v. Mass. General Hospital, 463 U.S. 239, 245 n. 7, 103 S. Ct. 2979 (1983) (leaving question open). *But see* Matter of Commitment of F.H., 258 N.J. Super. 532, 610 A.2d 882, 884–85 (N.J.Super.A.D. 1992) (statute permitting state to recover costs of mental hospitalization from patient's assets did not apply to prisoners because of constitutional obligation to provide prison medical care).

[241]*See, e.g.*, Ancata v. Prison Health Services, Inc., 769 F.2d 700, 705 n.7 (11th Cir. 1985) (citing Florida statute); Smith v. Linn County, 342 N.W.2d at 863 (holding detainee treated at hospital was not entitled to reimbursement of hospital bills under Iowa statutes); Salem Hospital v. Marion County, 307 Or. 213, 766 P.2d 376, 378–81 (Or. 1988) (noting person who receives care has the first responsibility for paying the bills under Oregon statutes); Montana Deaconess Medical Center v. Johnson, 232 Mont. 474, 758 P.2d 756, 757–58 (Mont. 1988) (providing for county attorney to pursue payment from prisoners able to pay); Wisc. Stat. § 302.38(1) ("The sheriff, superintendent or other keeper may charge a prisoner for the costs of providing medical care to the prisoner while he or she is in the jail or house of correction. If the sheriff or other keeper maintains a personal money account for an inmate's use for payment for items from canteen, vending or similar services, the sheriff or other keeper may make deductions from the account to pay for the charges under this subsection."); *see also* Smith v. Dep't of Corrections, 105 Or.App. 61, 804 P.2d 482, 484 (Or.App. 1990) (upholding rules requiring inmates to pay for certain prosthetic devices; constitutional claims not raised).

[242]Monmouth County Correctional Institution Inmates v. Lanzaro, 834 F.2d at 351; *see also* Glover v. Johnson, 850 F. Supp. 592, 601–02 (E.D. Mich. 1994).

Some states have enacted statutes or administrative rules requiring prisoners to pay small amounts of money for medical visits or treatment.[243] These have mostly been upheld when challenged. One was found unconstitutional because it would have required days and even weeks at inmate pay rates to earn the money, and would have fallen particularly harshly on the chronically ill who require more medical care than other prisoners. The statute was then amended to charge only for physician visits made without a referral from a nurse or physician's assistant, and the revised version was upheld as constitutional.[244] Some other courts have emphasized the presence of similar protections in upholding medical fee statutes,[245] but certain others have upheld medical fees without reference to such restrictions, as long as care is provided to prisoners who cannot pay for it.[246] The removal of money from prisoners' accounts

to pay for medical care is a deprivation of property that requires due process, but courts have held that giving prisoners notice of the policy and an opportunity to dispute charges they think are erroneous satisfies due process.[247]

---

[243]*See, e.g.*, Mass. Gen. Law. 124 § 1(s); Ohio Adm.Cole 5120-5-13(A) (stating that "[n]o inmate shall be denied needed medical treatment because of a lack of ability to pay . . . [and] shall receive appropriate medical care based on their present need, without regard to financial status."); New Jersey A.C. 10A:16-1.5(b) and New Jersey A.C. 10A:2-2.2; North Dakota C.C. § 12-44.1-12.1(3)(e). The fees are not always small. *See* Wheeler v. Gardner, 708 N.W.2d 908, 911 (N.D. 2006) (statute authorized recovery of entire costs of medical and dental care from prison account).

[244]Collins v. Romer, 962 F.2d 1508, 1513–14 (10th Cir. 1992).

[245]Thus, in *Reynolds v. Wagner*, 128 F.3d 166, 174–75 (3d Cir. 1997), the court upheld charges of $3.00 per sick call visit in a system where doctor visits were free if referred by sick call staff but cost $5.00 if not; prescription medication and over-the-counter medication deemed necessary by medical staff were free, and over-the-counter medication was also available in the commissary; initial examinations were free; treatment for chronic conditions was free; some emergencies were free, others—like a twisted ankle from recreation—were not. Mental health services were free. No one was denied care because of lack of funds. Half of incoming monies were credited toward any negative balance. The court stated: "If a prisoner is able to pay for medical care, requiring such payment is not 'deliberate indifference to serious medical needs.'" 128 F.3d at 174. *See* Gardner v. Wilson, 959 F. Supp. 1224 (C.D.Calif. 1997) (upholding a $5.00 copayment requirement for medical visits, not applicable to inmates with no money, life-threatening or emergency situations, or follow-ups initiated by medical staff); Johnson v. Dep't of Public Safety and Correctional Services, 885 F. Supp. 817, 820 (D.Md. 1995) (finding no Eighth Amendment violation in "co-pay" system charging inmates $2.00 for certain non-emergency services, with exceptions for "emergency services, routine health assessments, continuing care visits necessary for follow-up treatments, infirmary care, chronic care or secondary care services (such as hospital care and diagnostic tests)," and no denial of treatment for lack of funds; equal protection challenge rejected as well).

[246]Roberson v. Bradshaw, 198 F.3d 645, 647 (8th Cir. 1999); Breakiron v. Neal, 166 F. Supp. 2d 1110, 1114–15 (N.D.Tex. 2001); Canell v. Multnomah County, 141 F. Supp. 2d 1046, 1057 (D.Or. 2001); Jones-Bey v. Cohen, 115 F. Supp. 2d 936, 940 (N.D.Ind. 2000); Hutchinson v. Belt, 957 F. Supp. 97, 100 (W.D.La. 1996) (upholding policy that did not deny medical care for lack of funds; "If an inmate is given access to medical services but chooses to

apply his resources elsewhere, it is the inmate, and not the prison official, who is indifferent to serious medical needs."); Robinson v. Fauver, 932 F. Supp. 639, 644 (D.N.J. 1996) (requiring prisoners to make medical co-payments if not indigent, and defining a prisoner as indigent who (1) has no funds in his or her account, (2) is unable to earn inmate wages because of prolonged illness or other uncontrollable circumstance, and (3) is "able to verify that he has no outside source from which to obtain funds," was not unlawful); Boblett v. Angelone, 942 F. Supp. 251, 254 (W.D.Va. 1996) (requiring "co-payment" for medical consultations is not unconstitutional as long as the prisoner receives the services; forcing the prisoner to choose between toiletries and medical care is not unlawful unless the lack of toiletries causes serious injury), *aff'd*, 121 F.3d 97 (4th Cir. 1997); Douglas v. DeBruyn, 936 F. Supp. 572, 578 (S.D.Ind. 1996); Bihms v. Klevenhagen, 928 F. Supp. 717, 718–19 (S.D.Tex. 1996) (upholding billing of $594 for medical care including kidney dialysis; indigents need not be exempted as long as the authorities provide the care first and attempt to collect later; court suggests jail should allow prisoner a "modest balance" for amenities but does not say this is required); Delverne v. Klevenhagen, 888 F. Supp. 64, 66–67 (S.D.Tex. 1995) (generally upholding fees of $10 to $16 per visit to a medical professional and $3 for each prescription, with exemptions for indigents, as not denying equal protection), *rev'd on other grounds sub nom.* Myers v. Klevenhagen, 97 F.3d 91 (5th Cir. 1996); *see also* Hudgins v. DeBruyn, 922 F. Supp. 144, 146 (S.D.Ind. 1996) (upholding requirement that many over-the-counter medications be purchased in the commissary, *except* when dispensed by medical staff "as part of a necessary treatment regimen for a serious medical condition" or "when an offender is an inpatient").

[247]Reynolds v. Wagner, 128 F.3d 166, 181–82 (3d Cir. 1997); *see also* Jensen v. Klecker, 648 F.2d 1179, 1183 (8th Cir. 1981) (no basis for due process claim where deductions from prisoner accounts were assessments for value received); Myers v. Klevenhagen, 97 F.3d 91, 95 (5th Cir. 1996) (existence of post-deprivation reimbursement procedure satisfied due process); Gardner v. Wilson, 959 F. Supp. 1224, 1229 (C.D.Calif. 1997) ("Due Process requires no more than notice and the post-deprivation grievance process."); Johnson v. Dep't of Public Safety and Correctional Services, 885 F. Supp. 817, 821–22 (D.Md. 1995) (holding policy providing for notice of charges, documentation of treatment, and signing of an authorization by the prisoner satisfied due process); Scott v. Angelone, 771 F. Supp. 1064, 1067–68 (D.Nev. 1991) (where state regulations authorized deductions for non-emergency medical visits, due process was satisfied by notifying inmates of the billing system, requiring the inmate's authorization before treatment was given, and providing "accounting inquiry" and grievance procedures to correct mistakes), *aff'd*, 980 F.2d 738 (9th Cir. 1982); Wheeler v. Gardner, 708 N.W.2d 908, 911 (N.D. 2006) (citing statute providing for notice and hearing before medical costs can be taken from inmate's account). One court has held that prisoners who alleged that a medical fees system claimed to exempt indigents, but in fact did not, failed to state a federal due process claim as long as state post-deprivation remedies were available to challenge the departure from state policy. Myers v. Klevenhagen, 97 F.3d 91, 95 (5th Cir. 1996). *But see* Delverne v. Klevenhagen, 888 F. Supp. 64, 67 (S.D.Tex. 1995) (stating that

When prisoners are released while receiving ongoing treatment, prisons are obliged to arrange for continuing treatment after release, for a period of time reasonably necessary to allow the prisoner to obtain treatment herself, to avoid the denial or interruption of treatment.[248]

Prisoners who are denied adequate medical care in state or local institutions may use 42 U.S.C. § 1983 to sue prison medical care providers, including private contractors.[249] However, suits against private corporations that provide medical care to state prisoners are treated like suits against municipalities. That is, to prevail against the corporation itself, the prisoner must show that the injury was caused by a policy of the corporation. If the injury was caused by the deliberate indifference of individual employees of the corporation, those employees must be sued individually, like employees of a state, county, or city.[250] State and local prisoners may also seek damages for medical malpractice under state law.[251]

Federal prisoners are in a different situation. Though they may bring "*Bivens* actions" for damages against prison employees,[252] the Supreme Court has held that corporations contracting with federal agencies, including the Bureau of Prisons, cannot be sued in federal court at all under the *Bivens* rule.[253] A federal prisoner's only constitutional remedy would be against individual employees of the corporation who violated her rights. However, several federal courts have now held that individual corporation employees cannot be sued if there is any other possible remedy, such as a state law suit.[254] Private contractors with the federal government are not subject to suit under the

Federal Tort Claims Act (FTCA).[255] However, a prisoner may be able to bring suit against a private corporation under state law for medical malpractice or other torts. If the prisoner also has a valid constitutional claim against another defendant in federal court arising from the same facts, the court may permit the state law claim to be joined with the federal claim under its supplemental jurisdiction.[256]

1. The Deliberate Indifference Standard

The Supreme Court has stated that "deliberate indifference to serious medical needs of prisoners constitutes the 'unnecessary and wanton infliction of pain' . . . proscribed by the Eighth Amendment."[257] Pretrial detainees' right to medical care is protected by the Due Process Clause rather than the Eighth Amendment, but most courts have simply applied the same Eighth Amendment deliberate indifference standard under the Due Process Clause.[258] A few courts have

---

"[t]he fact that an inmate may be declared non-indigent even though he has no funds in his prison account raises concerns about the method and criteria used for determining indigence—namely, whether that method comports with due process."). *Cf.* Collins v. Romer, 962 F.2d 1508, 1514 (10th Cir.1992) (noting district court ruling that inmate copayment statute which did not provide exceptions to copayment requirement would be unconstitutional).

[248]Wakefield v. Thompson, 177 F.3d 1160, 1164 (9th Cir. 1999) (where prisoner took psychotropic medication at the time of release, officials were required to provide him a supply sufficient to maintain him until he could arrange for a prescription after release); Lugo v. Senkowski, 114 F. Supp. 2d 111, 115 (N.D.N.Y. 2000) (where prisoner had kidney surgery and a stent was inserted, the allegation that prison officials released him without providing for removal of the stent and prevented him from returning to his treating physician stated a deliberate indifference claim).

[249]West v. Atkins, 487 U.S. 42, 108 S. Ct. 2250 (1988).

[250]Suits by state and local prisoners against private contractors and their employees are discussed further in Ch. 8, § B.1.c.

[251]*See* § F.5 of this chapter on negligence and malpractice.

[252]*See* Ch. 8, § B.2.c, concerning the *Bivens* rule, which permits suit against federal officials and employees who violate constitutional rights just as 42 U.S.C. § 1983 does for state officials and employees.

[253]Correctional Services Corporation v. Malesko, 534 U.S. 61, 69–71, 122 S. Ct. 515 (2002).

[254]These issues are discussed in Ch. 8, § B.2.d.

[255]28 U.S.C. § 2671; *see* Ch. 8, § C.2, n.300, on this point.

[256]Agyeman v. Corrections Corp. of America, 390 F.3d 1101, 1103–04 (9th Cir. 2004) (if prisoner has an FTCA claim against the United States, prisoner could also sue the corporation—presumably under state law—and ask that the claim be joined under the federal courts' supplemental jurisdiction). Supplemental jurisdiction is discussed in Ch. 8, § F.1.

[257]Estelle v. Gamble, 429 U.S. 97, 104, 97 S. Ct. 285 (1976); *see* Erickson v. Pardus, 551 U.S. 89, 94, 127 S. Ct. 2197 (2007) (per curiam) (allegation that a prison doctor stopped plaintiff's Hepatitis C medication even though he had commenced a one-year treatment program and needed treatment for the disease pled an Eighth Amendment claim).

[258]Martinez v. Beggs, 563 F.3d 1082, 1088 (10th Cir. 2009), *cert. denied*, 130 S.Ct. 259 (2009); Estate of Owensby v. City of Cincinnati, 414 F.3d 596, 602–03 (6th Cir. 2005); Miller v. Calhoun County, 408 F.3d 803, 812 (6th Cir. 2005); Garretson v. City of Madison Heights, 407 F.3d 789, 798 (6th Cir. 2005) (applying Eighth Amendment actual knowledge deliberate indifference requirement); Cuoco v. Moritsugu, 222 F.3d 99, 106–07 (2d Cir. 2000) (holding that pre-trial detainees' medical care claims invoke the Eighth Amendment deliberate indifference standard); Cottrell v. Caldwell, 85 F.3d 1480, 1490 (11th Cir. 1996) (Under Eighth Amendment and Due Process Clause, "the applicable standard is the same, so decisional law involving prison inmates applies equally to cases involving arrestees or pretrial detainees."); Salazar v. City of Chicago, 940 F.2d 233, 237–38 (7th Cir. 1991); Martin v. Board of County Comm'rs of Pueblo County, 909 F.2d 402, 406 (10th Cir. 1990); Molton v. City of Cleveland, 839 F.2d 240, 242–43 (6th Cir. 1988); Boring v. Kozakiewicz, 833 F.2d 468, 471–73 (3d Cir. 1987); Hamm v. DeKalb County, 774 F.2d 1567, 1574 (11th Cir. 1985) ("Distinguishing the eighth amendment and due process standards in this area would require courts to evaluate the details of slight differences in conditions. . . . That approach would result in the courts' becoming 'enmeshed in the minutiae of prison operations.' . . . Life and health are just as precious to convicted persons as to pretrial detainees.").

The Supreme Court has said only that detainees' due process rights are "at least as great" as Eighth Amendment protections, without saying what they actually are. City of Revere v. Mass. General Hospital, 463 U.S. 239, 244, 103 S. Ct. 2979 (1983).

tried to spell out some distinction between the medical care rights of convicts and those of pretrial detainees,[259] or of arrestees,[260] but some of these distinctions do not seem to make much difference.[261] Unless there is clear law to the contrary in your jurisdiction, you should probably assume that a detainee medical care claim will be treated like a convict's claim. State law—statutes, constitutions, or case law—may provide different standards.[262]

As with other Eighth Amendment claims, the deliberate indifference standard requires a plaintiff to show that the defendants had actual knowledge of an objectively cruel condition (in medical cases, a serious medical need) and did not respond reasonably to the risk.[263] Thus—bizarre as it sounds—a doctor who did not treat you properly because she didn't realize how sick you were, or what your problem was, may not be deliberately indifferent *because she failed to figure it out* and therefore didn't have actual knowledge of the risk.[264] Your only claim in a case like that may be for

---

Some lower courts also appear to have been no more specific than the Supreme Court. *See* Hartsfield v. Colburn, 371 F.3d 454, 457 (8th Cir. 2004). The rights of pre-trial detainees are discussed more generally in Ch. 6.

[259]The Ninth Circuit has suggested in dictum that in medical care cases, detainees might be entitled to the benefit of the standard it has held applicable to persons civilly committed, which requires committing physicians to "exercise judgment 'on the basis of substantive and procedural criteria that are not substantially below the standards generally accepted in the medical community.'" Lolli v. County of Orange, 351 F.3d 410, 415 (9th Cir. 2003) (quoting Jensen v. Lane County, 312 F.3d 1145, 1147 (9th Cir. 2002)); *see* Gibson v. County of Washoe, Nev., 290 F.3d 1175, 1188 n.10 (9th Cir. 2002) (noting the difference between Fourteenth Amendment "no punishment" rule and Eighth Amendment "no cruel and unusual punishment" rule; "It is quite possible, therefore, that the protections provided pretrial detainees by the Fourteenth Amendment in some instances exceed those provided convicted prisoners by the Eighth Amendment.").

[260]Some courts have held that denial of medical care to an arrestee who has not been arraigned is governed by a Fourth Amendment "objective reasonableness" standard. Williams v. Rodriguez, 509 F.3d 392, 403 (7th Cir. 2007); Freece v. Young, 756 F. Supp. 699, 705-04 (W.D.N.Y. 1991). *But see* Nerren v. Livingston Police Dep't, 86 F.3d 469, 472 (5th Cir. 1966) (rejecting *Freece*, holding arrestees and detainees are both subject to due process standard). In *Williams v. Rodriguez*, the Seventh Circuit explained that denial of medical care to an arrestee may be objectively unreasonable where the officer has notice of the arrestee's medical need, by word or observation, and where the medical need is serious, though not necessarily as serious as required by the deliberate indifference standard. The medical need is balanced against the scope of the treatment requested and the police interests in *not* providing medical care at that point (*e.g.*, where there is a need for investigation at the arrest site). Williams v. Rodriguez, 509 F.3d at 403 (citing Sides v. City of Champaign, 496 F.3d 820 (7th Cir.2007)).

[261]Two circuits have set out standards for detainees that they say are not much different from the Eighth Amendment deliberate indifference standard. The Seventh Circuit has held that the deliberate indifference standard applies to detainees' claims against correctional staff, but the due process "professional judgment" standard applies to claims against medical professionals. Chavez v. Cady, 207 F.3d 901, 905 (7th Cir. 2000). However, it has also said that this standard is "comparable" to the deliberate indifference standard and "requires 'essentially the same analysis.'" That is: "The trier of fact can conclude that the professional knew of the need from evidence that it was obvious and, further, it can be assumed that 'what might not be obvious to a lay person might be obvious to a professional acting within her area of expertise.'" *Id.* (citation omitted); *see* Estate of Cole by Pardue v. Fromm, 94 F.3d 254, 261-62 (7th Cir. 1996) (stating that deliberate indifference in a detainee case "may be inferred based upon a medical professional's erroneous treatment decision only when the medical professional's decision is such a substantial departure from accepted professional judgment, practice, or standards as to demonstrate that the person responsible did not base the decision on such a judgment"; stating

that this standard is borrowed from the due process/professional judgment standard of *Youngberg v. Romeo*, 457 U.S. 307, 323, 102 S. Ct. 2452 (1981)).

The Fifth Circuit has said that challenges to "general conditions, practices, rules, or restrictions of pretrial confinement" are governed by the "reasonable relationship" standard of *Bell v. Wolfish*, 441 U.S. 520, 99 S. Ct. 1861 (1979), discussed in Ch. 6, while jail officials' "episodic acts or omissions" are governed by the Eighth Amendment deliberate indifference standard. Hare v. City of Corinth, Miss., 74 F.3d 633, 643 (5th Cir. 1996) (en banc). To invoke the *Wolfish* analysis, a detainee must show that a challenged act or omission "implement[s] a rule or restriction or otherwise demonstrate[s] the existence of an identifiable intended condition or practice," or else show that acts or omissions "were sufficiently extended or pervasive, or otherwise typical of extended or pervasive misconduct by other officials, to prove an intended condition or practice to which the *Bell* test can be meaningfully applied." *Hare*, 74 F.3d at 645. Even if *Bell v. Wolfish* is shown to apply, it doesn't seem it will make much difference under this approach: the court said that "a proper application of *Bell*'s reasonable relationship test is functionally equivalent to a deliberate indifference inquiry." *Id.*, 74 F.3d at 643.

[262]*See, e.g.*, Jorgenson v. Schiedler, 87 Or.App. 100, 741 P.2d 528, 529 (Or.App. 1987) (state constitution requires "such medical care in the form of diagnosis and treatment as is reasonably available under the circumstances of [the prisoner's] confinement and medical condition").

State law claims of malpractice or negligence may be litigated as tort claims in state court; these are discussed in § F.5 of this chapter.

[263]Farmer v. Brennan, 511 U.S. 825, 837, 114 S. Ct. 1970 (1994); *see, e.g.*, Johnson v. Mullin, 422 F.3d 1184, 1187 (10th Cir. 2005) (warden, health services administrator, and dental assistant who were not informed that the plaintiff's dental problem was an emergency could not be found deliberately indifferent for failing to provide immediate treatment).

[264]Toguchi v. Chung, 391 F.3d 1051, 1059-60 (9th Cir. 2004) (dismissing an expert opinion that a prison doctor disregarded a serious risk of drug interactions because the expert "lacked any insight into [the prison doctor's] subjective knowledge"); Mata v. Saiz, 427 F.3d 745, 760 (10th Cir. 2005) (a nurse who subjectively believed the plaintiff was not having a heart attack and her chest pain had been relieved could not be found deliberately indifferent); Finnegan v. Maire, 405 F.3d 694, 696-97 (8th Cir. 2005) (per curiam) (holding that dentist who allegedly failed to recognize that

medical malpractice, since a misdiagnosis or nondiagnosis resulting from failure to exercise ordinary knowledge, skill, and care does constitute malpractice.[265]

However, the court does not have to accept medical staff's statements that they did not know you had a serious need if there is evidence (direct or indirect) to the contrary.[266] The same is true where non-medical personnel fail to act but there is evidence that they did know you were ill or at risk.[267] You don't have to show that the defendants knew

exactly what was wrong with you or what its consequences could be if it was clear you had a serious problem and the defendants disregarded it.[268] The fact that a risk was obvious

---

he had punctured an artery and merely sutured the area was not deliberately indifferent, given other allegations indicating that the dentist tried to exercise care); Johnson v. Quinones, 145 F.3d 164, 169 (4th Cir. 1998) (failure to diagnose pituitary tumor was not deliberate indifference since doctors did not "draw the inference" from the symptoms they observed).

[265]_See_ Coppage v. Mann, 906 F. Supp. 1025, 1040, 1049 (E.D.Va. 1995) (holding doctor could not be deliberately indifferent to a condition he mis-diagnosed, but could be liable for malpractice if he should have known what the problem was); _see_ § F.5 of this chapter for a discussion of malpractice.

[266]_See_ Vaughn v. Gray, 557 F.3d 904, 909 (8th Cir. 2009) (failure to respond to prisoner who vomited through the night could support finding of deliberate indifference despite defendants' claim that they thought the prisoner was vomiting because he had ingested shampoo; "Appellants' self-serving contention that they did not have the requisite knowledge does not provide an automatic bar to liability in light of the objective evidence to the contrary."); Scicluna v. Wells, 345 F.3d 441, 446 (6th Cir. 2003) (doctor's claim that there was no evidence he knew a patient was present in the prison could be overcome by inference that there was an emergency treatment request and he ignored it); Hudak v. Miller, 28 F. Supp. 2d 827, 832 (S.D.N.Y. 1998) (doctor's self-serving statement that he believed prisoner's headaches were caused by tension cannot defeat liability if the facts showed that the risk of a serious problem was so obvious that he must have known about it). In _LeMarbe v. Wisneski_, 266 F.3d 429, 440 (6th Cir. 2001), the plaintiff's medical expert said that any general surgeon would have known immediately upon finding bile in a patient's abdomen that there was a bile duct leak which needed to be stopped right away; the court said this evidence could show that the defendant surgeon "was aware of facts that supported an inference of a substantial risk of serious harm" and that he drew the inference and disregarded it when he failed to take action to stop the leak or refer the patient to a surgeon who could do so. _But see_ Campbell v. Sikes, 169 F.3d 1353, 1368–73 (11th Cir. 1999) (rejecting the idea that expert testimony about what a competent doctor would know can establish what a particular defendant did know).

[267]Estate of Carter v. City of Detroit, 408 F.3d 304, 310, 312–13 (6th Cir. 2005) (holding a defendant who knew the plaintiff was exhibiting "the classic symptoms of a heart attack" and did not arrange transportation to a hospital could be found deliberately indifferent); Clement v. Gomez, 298 F.3d 898, 905 (9th Cir. 2002) (correction staff could be found to have actual knowledge of prisoners' need for decontamination from pepper spray where officers themselves stepped out for fresh air, prisoners were heard coughing and gagging and made repeated requests for medical attention, and the officers opened the door and brought a fan in); Chavez v. Cady, 207 F.3d 901, 906 (7th Cir. 2000) (officers were on notice of seriousness of condition of prisoner with ruptured appendix because he "did his part to let the officers know he was suffering");

El-Uri v. City of Chicago, 186 F. Supp. 2d 844, 848–49 (N.D.Ill. 2002) (police officer who brutally beat a prisoner and observed the consequences could be found deliberately indifferent; "normally, screaming in pain will do to register a complaint").

[268]Dominguez v. Correctional Medical Services, 555 F.3d 543, 550 (6th Cir. 2009) (holding nurse need only be shown to have known that "serious risks accompany heat-related illnesses and dehydration," not that plaintiff could become quadriplegic as a result); Alsina-Ortiz v. LaBoy, 400 F.3d 77, 83 (1st Cir. 2005) (holding guard who knew of prisoner's "prolonged, manifest, and agonizing pain" and did nothing to get care for him could be found deliberately indifferent); Mata v. Saiz, 427 F.3d 745, 756 (10th Cir. 2005) (nurse who did not assess a prisoner suffering severe chest pains could be found deliberately indifferent); McElligott v. Foley, 182 F.3d 1248, 1256 (11th Cir. 1999) (doctor who failed to diagnose plaintiff's cancer could still be found to have actual knowledge of a substantial risk based on his "tremendous pain and illness" which the doctor observed); Hollenbaugh v. Maurer, 397 F. Supp. 2d 894, 904 (N.D.Ohio 2005) ("The plaintiff does not have to show that the defendants knew of the exact medical risk threatening Hollenbaugh"; the fact that he did not self-diagnose his heart attack or report his heart condition did not absolve defendants who observed ample evidence of his symptoms and complaints); Spencer v. Sheahan, 158 F. Supp. 2d 837, 849–50 (N.D.Ill. 2001) (doctor who knew that diabetics are at risk for foot problems and require prompt wound care to prevent long-term complications, but who waited two days before examining a patient with complaints of pain and discolored skin on foot and seven more days before referring patient to appropriate specialist, could be found deliberately indifferent where patient ultimately had partial foot amputation because of gangrene and infection); Hudak v. Miller, 28 F. Supp. 2d 827, 831 (S.D.N.Y. 1998) ("It should be noted that the knowledge which Hudak must show Dr. Miller had is not that Hudak had a brain aneurysm . . . but rather that Miller knew that Judak had some serious medical problem which bore further investigation"; plaintiff had complained for nine months of chronic headaches before receiving a CT scan).

Some decisions, in our view, take an unreasonably demanding view of who must be shown to have known what. For example, in _Zentmyer v. Kendall County, Ill._, 220 F.3d 805 (7th Cir. 2000), the plaintiff alleged that officers repeatedly failed to provide him with prescribed antibiotics, and as a result he suffered permanent hearing loss from an ear infection. The court held that he had failed to show that any of the defendants actually knew that he might suffer serious injury or pain from missing his medication, since he had no obvious outward symptoms and the doctors did not tell the officers that the medication had to be given regularly. _Zentmyer_, 220 F.3d at 811; _accord_, Mahan v. Plymouth County House of Corrections, 64 F.3d 14, 18 (1st Cir. 1995) (finding that failure to administer prescription medication did not constitute deliberate indifference absent evidence that prison officials knew the plaintiff would suffer serious medical consequences without medication). Under these decisions, if you are not receiving your prescribed medication from prison staff, you would have to make them aware of the harm that you could suffer from not receiving it as prescribed. We think that the only "actual knowledge" that correctional staff need to have in such a situation is that (a) medical staff

can support a finding that the defendants knew about it.[269] Further, prison staff can't automatically get off the hook just by claiming that they thought you were faking or malingering. The court or jury can reject that claim if there is other evidence that they knew you were ill or at risk.[270]

If defendants violate published professional standards of care or the prison's own procedures for medical care—though these do not by themselves show a constitutional violation—they may also be found to have had actual knowledge. The standards or procedures may "provide circumstantial evidence that a prison health care gatekeeper knew of a substantial risk of serious harm" in the situations for which they give instructions.[271]

You don't always have to show that the defendants had any knowledge of your medical condition. Deliberate indifference can be found if they had actual knowledge that there were deficiencies in the medical care system that created a risk of the kind of harm that happened to you. This approach is most likely to be useful for claims against higher level administrators or policymakers who have some ability to do something about the deficiencies.[272]

The courts' main concern in medical care cases seems to be distinguishing between deliberate indifference and "mere" (as they often put it) malpractice.[273] Under the deliberate indifference standard, courts will not take sides in disagreements with medical personnel's judgments or techniques.[274] In general, as long as there has been an exercise of professional judgment—even a mistaken or incompetent one—the courts will hold that the Constitution has been satisfied.[275]

---

have prescribed treatment, and (b) when people don't get prescribed medical treatment, their health may be damaged.

[269]Farmer v. Brennan, 511 U.S. 825, 842–43, 114 S. Ct. 1970 (1994).

[270]See, e.g., Conn v. City of Reno, 572 F.3d 1047, 1056 (9th Cir. 2009) (police officers' statements that they did not believe an arrestee's suicide threats and gestures were serious did not entitle them to summary judgment but presented a jury question); Estate of Carter v. City of Detroit, 408 F.3d 304, 310, 313 (6th Cir. 2005) (where defendant said he didn't really believe the plaintiff was ill despite her symptoms, jury "would be entitled to discount that explanation"); Foelker v. Outagamie County, 394 F.3d 510, 513–14 (7th Cir. 2005) (holding a jury could find that nurses who had observed the plaintiff's condition and the fact that he had defecated in his cell could be found to have known that he was going through drug withdrawal and to have done nothing about it, despite the claim of one defendant that he believed the plaintiff was "playing the system"); Hollenbaugh v. Maurer, 397 F. Supp. 2d 894, 904 (N.D.Ohio 2005) (defendants who said they believed the prisoner who died of a heart attack was drunk and faking illness could be held liable based on evidence that they heard his statements that he was not feeling well, had the flu or food poisoning, was having chest pains, and wanted to go to the hospital), aff'd, 221 Fed.Appx. 409 (6th Cir. 2007) (unpublished); Walker v. Benjamin, 293 F.3d 1030, 1039–40 (7th Cir. 2002) (claims that doctor and nurse withheld prescribed pain medication because they thought the prisoner was malingering and trying to get high presented a jury question of deliberate indifference); see also Greeno v. Daley, 414 F.3d 645, 655 (7th Cir. 2005) (absence of "objective" evidence of pain and suffering did not excuse refusal to treat it, since "self-reporting is often the only indicator a doctor has of a patient's condition").

[271]Mata v. Saiz, 427 F.3d 745, 757 (10th Cir. 2005). Even if there is no violation of policy, the policies may be evidence of the defendants' knowledge of the risks inherent in certain circumstances. Gibson v. County of Washoe, Nev., 290 F.3d 1175, 1190–91 (9th Cir. 2002) (policies concerning mentally ill prisoners showed that policymakers understood the risk presented by lack of prompt psychiatric attention for some new admissions). Courts may also be willing to presume knowledge of risks from medical professionals' training. See Dominguez v. Correctional Medical Services, 555 F.3d 543, 550 (6th Cir. 2009) ("As a trained medical professional, a registered nurse, Fletcher was aware or should have been aware of such dangers.").

[272]Alsina-Ortiz v. LaBoy, 400 F.3d 77, 81–82 (1st Cir. 2005) (holding high-level officials could be found deliberately indifferent if they "knew of a continuing pattern of culpable failures by guards or other prison staff to refer to health providers those prisoners with culpable complaints or manifest symptons"); Gibson v. County of Washoe, Nev., 290 F.3d 1175, 1190–91 (9th Cir. 2002) (holding that county policymakers could be held liable for policy that delayed psychiatric treatment for some new admissions when they knew that "inevitably some prisoners arrive at the jail with urgent health problems requiring hospitalization" and were "keenly aware" that mental illnesses could present urgent needs); Bass v. Wallenstein, 769 F.2d 1173, 1184–86 (7th Cir. 1985) (holding administrators could be held deliberately indifferent based on their knowledge of deficiencies in medical care system). See § F.3.a, below; see also § A.2 of this chapter concerning this point in other kinds of deliberate indifference cases, and Ch. 8, § B.4.a, for a discussion of when a supervisor can be liable.

[273]The two are not mutually exclusive. A particular set of facts may add up to deliberate indifference as well as malpractice, see Hathaway v. Coughlin, 99 F.3d 550 (2d Cir. 1996), and often does. See § F.5 of this chapter for a discussion of malpractice.

[274]Toguchi v. Chung, 391 F.3d 1051, 1059–60 (9th Cir. 2004); Ciarpaglini v. Saini, 352 F.3d 328, 331 (7th Cir. 2003); Hernandez v. Keane, 341 F.3d 137, 146–47 (2d Cir. 2003); Garvin v. Armstrong, 236 F.3d 896, 898 (7th Cir. 2001); Walker v. Peters, 233 F.3d 494, 499 (7th Cir. 2000); Varnado v. Collins, 920 F.2d 320, 321 (5th Cir. 1991); Long v. Nix, 86 F.3d 761, 766 (8th Cir. 1996); Smith v. Marcantonio, 910 F.2d 500, 502 (8th Cir. 1990). Cf. Bailey v. Gardebring, 940 F.2d 1150, 1155 (8th Cir. 1991) (failure to provide treatment is not deliberate indifference if there is no accepted form of treatment for the patient's condition).

There is an exception. Prison officials may not shop around until they get a medical opinion that suits their non-medical concerns, or intentionally rely on a medical opinion that is without adequate basis. Hamilton v. Endell, 981 F.2d 1063, 1066–67 (9th Cir. 1992). Courts have also held that when a prisoner's treating physicians recommend a course of action, and officials (even higher level medical administrators) ignore that recommendation, the result is not a mere disagreement over medical treatment but can be deliberate indifference. Johnson v. Wright, 412 F.3d 398, 406 (2d Cir. 2005).

[275]See Duckworth v. Ahmad, 532 F.3d 675, 681 (7th Cir. 2008) (failure to rule out cancer immediately in light of persistent bloody urine may have been malpractice but was not deliberate indifference); Jolly v. Knudsen, 205 F.3d 1094, 1097 (8th Cir. 2000)

There are several familiar fact patterns that courts have focused on in deciding whether a case presents a legitimate medical judgment or a question of deliberate indifference:

Direct evidence of deliberate indifference. Sometimes the acts or statements of prison personnel directly demonstrate an indifferent or hostile attitude toward prisoners' medical needs.[276]

Denial or delay of access to treatment.[277] Such conduct may include interference with access to medical personnel[278] or to a hospital,[279] or failure of medical personnel

---

(physician's increase in seizure medication to toxic levels was not deliberate indifference because he gave a reason for doing it); McElligott v. Foley, 182 F.3d 1248, 1256–57 (11th Cir. 1999) (holding failure to diagnose prisoner's cancer was not deliberate indifference, though failure to treat his worsening pain might be); Stewart v. Murphy, 174 F.3d 530, 535 (5th Cir. 1999); Perkins v. Kansas Dep't of Corrections, 165 F.3d 803, 811 (10th Cir. 1999) (denial of protease inhibitor to prisoner with HIV upheld, since other treatment was provided); Estate of Cole by Pardue v. Fromm, 94 F.3d 254, 261 (7th Cir. 1996); Starbeck v. Linn County Jail, 871 F. Supp. 1129, 1144–45 (N.D.Iowa 1994); Brown v. Borough of Chambersburg, 903 F.2d 274, 278 (3d Cir. 1990) (failure to diagnose broken ribs was not deliberate indifference); Givens v. Jones, 900 F.2d 1229, 1232–33 (8th Cir. 1990) (giving a prisoner medication to which he was allergic was negligence at worst); Benson v. Cady, 761 F.2d 335, 341 (7th Cir. 1985) (prescription of wrong drug was only malpractice); Owens-El v. U.S. Attorney General, 759 F.2d 349, 350 (4th Cir. 1985) (unnecessary continuation of dangerous drug was merely negligent); Supre v. Ricketts, 792 F.2d 958, 963 (10th Cir. 1986) (decision not to give female hormones to transgender prisoner was not deliberately indifferent); Martino v. Miller, 318 F. Supp. 2d 63, 66 (W.D.N.Y. 2004) (removing one kidney and part of bladder, even though tests showed plaintiff did *not* have cancer, was negligence at most); Gordon v. Higgs, 716 F. Supp. 1351, 1353 (D.Nev. 1989) (failure to take an x-ray was no more than negligent); Mastrota v. Robinson, 534 F. Supp. 434, 436, 438 (E.D. 1982) (claim of failure to diagnose vertebral fracture and failure to insert drainage tube after surgery did not state an Eighth Amendment violation); *see* Shakka v. Smith, 71 F.3d 162, 166 (4th Cir. 1995) (removal of plaintiff's wheelchair, done by psychologist to protect him and others, was not actionable). *But see* Boyce v. Alizaduh, 595 F.2d 948, 952–53 (4th Cir. 1979) (giving a prisoner medication to which he was allergic could be deliberate indifference); Thomas v. Pate, 493 F.2d 151, 158 (7th Cir. 1974) (same as *Boyce*).

[276]Greeno v. Daley, 414 F.3d 645, 654 (7th Cir. 2005) (nurse told prisoner that if he continued to "hassle" the medical staff he would be "locked up"); Hughes v. Joliet Correctional Center, 931 F.2d 425, 428 (7th Cir. 1991) (medical staff told prisoner with spinal injury he was "full of bullshit"); White v. Napoleon, 897 F.2d 103, 109 (3d Cir. 1990) (doctor allegedly burned the hand of an inmate who said he had lost feeling); Kersh v. Derozier, 851 F.2d 1509, 1510, 1513 (5th Cir. 1988) (the plaintiff lost sight in one eye because police and jail personnel would not let him wash something out of it); Meriwether v. Faulkner, 821 F.2d 408, 413 (7th Cir. 1987) (doctor ridiculed transgender prisoner and completely denied care); Mullen v. Smith, 738 F.2d 317, 318–19 (8th Cir. 1984) (prisoner was subjected to "ridicule and derision" in response to complaints of pain and inability to walk); Williams v. Vincent, 508 F.2d 541, 544 (2d Cir. 1974) (doctor refused to try to reattach the prisoner's severed ear and threw it away in front of him); Marcotte v. Monroe Corrections Complex, 394 F. Supp. 2d 1289, 1296 (W.D.Wash. 2005) (nurse threatened the plaintiff with "the hole" if

he kept complaining); Nelson v. Prison Health Services, 991 F. Supp. 1452, 1464 (N.D.Fla. 1997) (nurse insisted on finishing her breakfast before responding to urgent complaint of chest pain, then accused the prisoner of "theatrics"); Phillips v. Michigan Dep't of Corrections, 731 F. Supp. 792, 800 (W.D.Mich. 1990) (doctor directed ridicule and offensive remarks to a transgender prisoner), *aff'd*, 932 F.2d 969 (6th Cir. 1991); Langley v. Coughlin, 715 F. Supp. 522, 541 (S.D.N.Y. 1988) (deliberate indifference claim was supported by "displays of hostility by prison psychiatrists to their female patients . . . which sometimes led to outright refusals to treat"); Smallwood v. Renfro, 708 F. Supp. 182, 187–88 (N.D.Ill. 1989) (deliberate indifference claim was supported by evidence that a lieutenant overruled a decision to send the plaintiff to a hospital and later choked and hit the plaintiff). *But see* Means v. Cullen, 297 F. Supp. 2d 1148, 1154 (W.D.Wis. 2003) (mental health staff member's comment that no one would care if the plaintiff died did not show deliberate indifference where she also repeatedly recommended that he remain under clinical observation to ensure his safety).

[277]Estelle v. Gamble, 429 U.S. 97, 104, 97 S. Ct. 285 (1976).

[278]Goebert v. Lee County, 510 F.3d 1312, 1327–28, 1331 (11th Cir. 2007) (holding jail captain who decided to disbelieve inmate medical complaints could be found deliberately indifferent for not getting assistance for pregnant prisoner who complained she was leaking fluid); Alsina-Ortiz v. LaBoy, 400 F.3d 77, 83 (1st Cir. 2005) (holding guard who knew of prisoner's "prolonged, manifest, and agonizing pain" and did nothing to get care for him could be found deliberately indifferent); Scicluna v. Wells, 345 F.3d 441, 446 (6th Cir. 2003) ("Transferring a prisoner in need of urgent medical attention to a facility that the official knows is unable to provide the required treatment is conduct that would alert a reasonable person to the likelihood of personal liability."); Murphy v. Walker, 51 F.3d 714, 719 (7th Cir. 1995) (two-month failure to get prisoner with head injury to a doctor stated a claim); Fields v. City of South Houston, Texas, 922 F.2d 1183, 1192 n.10 (5th Cir. 1991) (evidence that police officers exercised wide discretion in summoning medical care for prisoners); H.C. by Hewett v. Jarrard, 786 F.2d 1080, 1083, 1087 (11th Cir. 1986) (isolation of injured inmate and deprivation of medical attention for three days); Robinson v. Moreland, 655 F.2d 887, 889–90 (8th Cir. 1981) (weekend's delay in treating a broken hand); Hurst v. Phelps, 579 F.2d 940, 941–42 (5th Cir. 1978) (refusal to take a prisoner to a doctor's appointment); McGill v. Mountainside Police Dep't 720 F. Supp. 418, 423 (D.N.J. 1989) (police officers' failure to get medical help for arrestee who was vomiting blood and had breathing difficulties); Tomarkin v. Ward, 534 F. Supp. 1224, 1235 (S.D.N.Y. 1982) (denial of medical care in solitary confinement); Isaac v. Jones, 529 F. Supp. 175, 180 (N.D.Ill. 1981) (delay by guards in providing care).

[279]Estate of Carter v. City of Detroit, 408 F.3d 304, 310, 312–13 (6th Cir. 2005) (holding a defendant who knew the plaintiff was exhibiting "the classic symptoms of a heart attack" and did not arrange transportation to a hospital could be found deliberately indifferent); Boswell v. Sherburne County, 849 F.2d 1117, 1122 (10th Cir. 1988) (delay in hospitalizing a miscarrying woman); Archer v. Dutcher, 733 F.2d 14, 16–17 (2d Cir. 1984) (similar to *Boswell*); *see* Gaines v. Choctaw County Commission, 242 F. Supp. 2d 1153, 1165 ((S.D.Ala. 2003) (Sheriff's removal of prisoner from

to deal with the prisoner's problem or to do so timely.[280] Refusal of treatment unless the prisoner complies with a seriously unreasonable condition constitutes deliberate indifference.[281] How much delay in treatment is tolerated depends on the seriousness and urgency of the medical need.[282] Some courts have held that delay is only actionable when it results in "substantial harm,"[283] but that standard is

---

[280]hospital against medical advice supported a deliberate indifference claim); Hodge v. Ruperto, 739 F. Supp. 873, 879 (S.D.N.Y. 1990) (police officers could be held liable for removing an arrestee from the hospital before his x-rays could be examined and his injuries treated).

[280]Scott v. Ambani, 575 F.3d 642 (6th Cir. 2009) (allegation that doctor refused to examine or provide pain medication to prisoner who had recently been treated for prostate cancer, had severe back and leg pain and a hard and painful testicular lump stated a deliberate indifference claim); Dominguez v. Correctional Medical Services, 555 F.3d 543, 551 (6th Cir. 2009) (holding nurse's failure to respond promptly to prisoner with symptoms of heat stroke could support a finding of deliberate indifference); Edwards v. Snyder, 478 F.3d 827, 832 (7th Cir. 2007) (holding an allegation of a doctor's gratuitous two-day delay in treating an injury stated a deliberate indifference claim regardless of the adequacy of later treatment); Spann v. Roper, 453 F.3d 1007, 1008–09 (8th Cir. 2006) (holding a nurse could be found deliberately indifferent for leaving a prisoner in his cell for three hours though she knew he had taken an overdose of mental health medications intended for another prisoner); Johnson v. Karnes, 398 F.3d 868, 875–76 (6th Cir. 2005) (holding jail doctor's failure to schedule surgery for severed tendons despite emergency room instruction to return prisoner in three to seven days could constitute deliberate indifference); McKenna v. Wright, 386 F.3d 432, 437 (2d Cir. 2004) (holding protracted delay in starting hepatitis C treatment stated a claim); Scicluna v. Wells, 345 F.3d 441, 446 (6th Cir. 2003) ("Knowingly waiting three weeks to examine a prisoner referred to one's care for urgent attention is conduct that a reasonable prison official . . . should have known would subject him to personal liability."); Farrow v. West, 320 F.3d 1235, 1247–48 (11th Cir. 2003) (holding delay of 15 months in providing dentures, with three- and eight-month hiatuses in treatment, by a dentist familiar with prisoner's painful condition, raised a jury question of deliberate indifference); LeMarbe v. Wisneski, 266 F.3d 429, 440 (6th Cir. 2001) (failure to make timely referral to specialist or tell the patient to seek one out was deliberate indifference); McElligott v. Foley, 182 F.3d 1248, 1256–57 (11th Cir. 1999) (holding repeated delays in doctor's seeing a patient with constant severe pain could constitute deliberate indifference); Miltier v. Beorn, 896 F.2d 848, 853–54 (4th Cir. 1990) (nurses' failure to attend infirmary patient who lost consciousness and fell); Lancaster v. Monroe County, Ala., 116 F.3d 1419, 1426 (11th Cir. 1997) ("[A] jail official who is aware of but ignores the dangers of acute alcohol withdrawal and waits for a manifest emergency before obtaining medical care is deliberately indifferent to the inmate's constitutional rights."); Sulton v. Wright, 265 F. Supp. 2d 292, 300 (S.D.N.Y. 2003) (four-year delay in treating torn knee ligaments supported a deliberate indifference claim); Lavender v. Lampert, 242 F. Supp. 2d 821, 848 (D.Or. 2002) (failure to provide continuous and effective pain-relieving medication for prisoner known to have severe chronic pain). *But see* Peterson v. Willie, 81 F.3d 1033, 1038 (11th Cir. 1996) (holding delay in providing the plaintiff with medication did not constitute deliberate indifference because the medication is toxic and the defendants were waiting to get his prior medical records, and because getting the medication would not have immediately changed the plaintiff's symptoms).

[281]Harrison v. Barkley, 219 F.3d 132, 138 (2d Cir. 2000) (prison dentist refused to fill a tooth unless the prisoner also contented to extraction of one of his few other teeth).

[282]*See, e.g.,* Bozeman v. Orum, 422 F.3d 1265, 1273 (11th Cir. 2005) (holding permissible delay for a prisoner unconscious from asphyxiation is measured in a few minutes, not hours); Austin v. Johnson, 328 F.3d 204, 210 (5th Cir. 2003) (given the serious medical consequences of dehydration, waiting nearly two hours to call an ambulance for a prisoner unconscious because of dehydration supported a deliberate indifference claim); Lancaster v. Monroe County, Ala., 116 F.3d 1419, 1425 (11th Cir. 1997) (holding that "a jail official who is aware of but ignores the dangers of acute alcohol withdrawal and waits for a manifest emergency before obtaining medical care is deliberately indifferent. . . ."); Weyant v. Okst, 101 F.3d 845, 856–57 (2d Cir. 1996) (delay of hours in getting medical attention for a diabetic in insulin shock raised a question of deliberate indifference); Bass by Lewis v. Wallenstein, 769 F.2d 1173, 1178, 1183 (7th Cir. 1985) (holding 10 to 15-minute delay in doctor's response to a patient in cardiac arrest supported liability); Patrick v. Lewis, 397 F. Supp. 2d 1134, 1142 (D.Minn. 2005) (a guard who observed a prisoner not breathing and then delayed medical response for 20 to 25 minutes while assisting another prisoner with a phone call could be found deliberately indifferent); Benjamin v. Schwartz, 299 F. Supp. 2d 196, 201 (S.D.N.Y. 2004) (where a plaintiff suffered from torn tendons, if a doctor "deliberately failed to schedule him for needed surgery for almost two years, well knowing that excessive delay could mean permanent disability, then he violated a clearly established constitutional right.").

One court has stated that "an unexplained delay of hours in treating a serious injury states a prima facie case of deliberate indifference." Brown v. Hughes, 894 F.2d 1533, 1538 (11th Cir. 1990) (four-hour delay in treating a broken foot); *accord,* Reed v. Dunham, 893 F.2d 285, 287 (10th Cir. 1990) (two-hour delay in treatment for stab wounds); Van Cleave v. U.S., 854 F.2d 82, 84 (5th Cir. 1988) (24-hour delay in treating injuries sustained during arrest); Loe v. Armistead, 582 F.2d 1291, 1296 (4th Cir. 1978) (22-hour delay in treating a broken arm); Calhoun v. Thomas, 360 F. Supp. 2d 1264, 1284 (M.D.Ala. 2005) (six-hour delay in treating gunshot wound); Johnson v. Summers, 411 Mass. 82, 577 N.E.2d 301, 305 (Mass. 1991) (delay of hours in taking prisoner with a broken leg to the hospital). *But see* Jenkins v. County of Hennepin, Minn., 557 F.3d 628, 632 (8th Cir. 1999) (day's delay in treatment of a broken jaw was not deliberate indifference); Mills v. Smith, 656 F.2d 337, 340 (8th Cir. 1981) (one and a half hour delay in hospitalizing a prisoner with a gunshot wound did not constitute deliberate indifference); Brown v. Commissioner of Cecil County Jail, 501 F. Supp. 1124, 1126–27 (D.Md. 1980) (delay of less than a week in treating gonorrhea was not deliberate indifference), *aff'd* 204 Fed. Appx. 979 (2d Cir. 2006) (unpublished).

[283]Sealock v. Colorado, 218 F.3d 1205, 1210 (10th Cir. 2000); Wynn v. Correctional Officer Mundo, 367 F. Supp. 2d 832, 835 (M.D.N.C. 2005), *aff'd,* 142 Fed.Appx. 193 (4th Cir. 2005) (unpublished); Clement v. California Dep't of Corrections, 220 F. Supp. 2d 1098, 1106 (N.D.Cal. 2002) (three months' delay in providing a colonoscopy did not cause substantial harm where plaintiff's

met if pain and suffering are unnecessarily prolonged.[284] Some courts have required "verifying medical evidence" to support a claim that delay has caused harm.[285]

Denial of access to medical personnel qualified to exercise judgment about a particular medical problem. There are several variations on this theme. In some cases, personnel may simply lack medical qualifications or training.[286] In others, prisoners are denied access to medical personnel with the necessary specialized expertise.[287] Sometimes

prisoners who need a physician's care are permitted to see only lower level, non-physician personnel.[288]

Failure to inquire into essential facts that are necessary to make a professional judgment. As one court put it, "We will defer to the informed judgment of prison officials as to an appropriate form of medical treatment. But if an informed judgment has not been made, the court may find that an eighth amendment claim has been stated."[289] Such cases may involve failure to conduct an adequate examination,[290] failure to ask necessary questions or take a

---

cancer surgery was successful; weight loss awaiting surgery was not substantial harm where his weight stabilized), *aff'd*, 364 F.3d 1148 (9th Cir. 2004); Smith v. Board of County Commissioners of County of Lyon, 216 F. Supp. 2d 1209, 1221–22 (D.Kan. 2002) (a month's delay in treating a spinal injury, resulting in incontinence, satisfied substantial harm requirement).

[284]Kikumura v. Osagie, 161 F.3d 1269 (10th Cir. 2006); Sealock v. Colorado, 218 F.3d at 1210 n.5.

[285]*See* Williams v. Liefer, 491 F.3d 710, 714–15 (7th Cir. 2007) and cases cited. Such evidence need not comprise expert testimony in all cases. *Id.*, 491 F.3d at 715–16.

[286]Williams v. Edwards, 547 F.2d 1206, 1216–18 (5th Cir. 1977) (Constitution was violated by medical staff consisting of mostly unlicensed doctors, untrained inmates and an untrained pharmacist.); Hartman v. Correctional Medical Services, Inc., 960 F. Supp. 1577, 1582–83 (M.D.Fla. 1996) (medical provider could be found deliberately indifferent for permitting a person with only a master's degree and no professional licenses to have authority over mental health referrals and suicide precautions); Casey v. Lewis, 834 F. Supp. 1477, 1545 (D.Ariz. 1993) (making of medical judgments by security staff could constitute deliberate indifference); *see* § 3.c, below, for a discussion of qualifications of medical staff, can be liable, and § 4.a, below, for a discussion of mental health care.

[287]Hayes v. Snyder, 546 F.3d 516, 526 (7th Cir. 2008) (refusal to refer to a specialist where doctor did not know cause of reported extreme pain made no sense and could support deliberate indifference finding); Mata v. Saiz, 427 F.3d 745, 756 (10th Cir. 2005) (holding nurse's failure to perform "gatekeeper" role by referring patient to a practitioner for symptoms of cardiac emergency could be deliberate indifference); Greeno v. Daley, 414 F.3d 645, 655 (7th Cir. 2005) (holding refusal to refer prisoner to a specialist or order an endoscopy for two years despite intense abdominal pain could be deliberate indifference); Hartsfield v. Colburn, 371 F.3d 454, 457 (8th Cir. 2004) (holding six weeks' delay in sending prisoner to a dentist, resulting in infection and loss of teeth, raised an Eighth Amendment claim); LeMarbe v. Wisneski, 266 F.3d 429, 440 (6th Cir. 2001) (failure to make timely referral to specialist or tell the patient to seek one out was deliberate indifference); Oxendine v. Kaplan, 241 F.3d 1272, 1278–79 (10th Cir. 2001) (prison doctor who reattached accidentally severed finger, which became gangrenous, could be found deliberately indifferent for failing to refer prisoner for specialist care at any point; denial of access to "medical personnel capable of evaluating the need for treatment" and performing surgery one is not qualified for can be deliberate indifference); Hemmings v. Gorczyk, 134 F.3d 104, 109 (2d Cir. 1998) (two-month refusal to send a prisoner with "classic" symptoms of a ruptured tendon to a specialist could constitute deliberate indifference); Parham v. Johnson, 126 F.3d 454, 458–57 n.7 (3d Cir. 1997) (denial of access to an ear specialist supported a deliberate indifference claim); Howell v. Evans, 922 F.2d 712, 723 (11th Cir. 1991) (failure to provide access to a respiratory therapist could

constitute deliberate indifference), *vacated as settled*, 931 F.2d 711 (11th Cir. 1991) (remand as to liability of supervisor); Smith v. Jenkins, 919 F.2d 90, 93 (8th Cir. 1990) (doctor's lack of evident qualifications to diagnose and treat mental illness supported a deliberate indifference claim); Mandel v. Doe, 888 F.2d 783, 789–90 (11th Cir. 1989) (damages awarded where physician's assistant failed to diagnose a broken hip, refused to order an x-ray, and prevented the prisoner from seeing a doctor); Waldrop v. Evans, 871 F.2d 1030, 1036 (11th Cir.) (non-psychiatrist was not competent to evaluate the significance of a prisoner's suicidal gesture; prison officials must "inform *competent* authorities" of medical or psychiatric needs (emphasis supplied)), *rehearing denied*, 880 F.2d 421 (11th Cir. 1989); Washington v. Dugger, 860 F.2d 1018, 1021 (11th Cir. 1988) (failure to return patient to VA hospital for treatment for Agent Orange exposure); Ancata v. Prison Health Services, Inc., 769 F.2d 700, 704–05 (11th Cir. 1985) (refusal to provide specialty consultations without a court order); Matzker v. Herr, 748 F.2d 1173, 1185 (7th Cir. 1984) (where inmate with broken teeth and an eye injury did not see a dentist or a "physician or surgeon much less an ophthalmologist," a constitutional claim was stated), *overruled on other grounds*, Salazar v. City of Chicago, 940 F.2d 233, 240 (7th Cir. 1991); Ancata v. Prison Health Services, Inc., 769 F.2d 700, 704–05 (11th Cir. 1985) (refusal to provide specialty consultations without a court order could constitute deliberate indifference); Inmates of Allegheny County Jail v. Pierce, 612 F.2d 754, 762–63 (3d Cir. 1979) (inmates with mental disorders are entitled to reasonable acces to medical personnel qualified to diagnose and treat those disorders); West v. Keve, 571 F.2d 158, 162 (3d Cir. 1978) (denial of access to a doctor capable of assessing the need for post-operative treatment stated a constitutional claim); Sulton v. Wright, 265 F. Supp. 2d 292, 300 (S.D.N.Y. 2003) (adoption of a utilization review system for specialist consultation and surgery approval that operated "to limit care as much as possible" and failure to correct tracking system so surgery had to be re-approved after transfers supported deliberate indifference claim); Spencer v. Sheahan, 158 F. Supp. 2d 837, 849–50 (N.D.Ill. 2001) (delay in referring diabetic with complications of a foot injury to the appropriate clinic could be found deliberately indifferent); Tillery v. Owens, 719 F. Supp. 1256, 1307 (W.D.Pa. 1989) (services of cardiologist and dermatologist should be provided), *aff'd*, 907 F.2d 418 (3d Cir. 1990). *Contra*, Duffield v. Jackson, 545 F.3d 1234, 1239 (8th Cir. 2008) (decision to refer to a specialist is a decision about course of treatment and not an Eighth Amendment violation).

[288]*See* § F.3.c of this chapter.

[289]Tillery v. Owens, 719 F. Supp. 1256, 1308 (W.D.Pa. 1989), *aff'd*, 907 F.2d 418 (3d Cir. 1990).

[290]Phillips v. Roane County, Tenn., 534 F.3d 531, 544 (6th Cir. 2008) (doctor's grossly perfunctory examination in the face of nausea, vomiting, and chest pain could evince deliberate indifference); Spruill v. Gillis, 372 F.3d 218, 237 (3d Cir. 2004) (allegations

history,[291] or failure to conduct tests that the prisoner's symptoms call for.[292]

Interference with medical judgment by factors unrelated to prisoners' medical needs.[293] These factors can include staffing so inadequate that medical staff lack the time to do their jobs,[294] facilities and procedures that do not allow for proper diagnosis and treatment,[295] and rules or policies restricting medical care on grounds unrelated to the prisoner's medical needs.[296] (There have been a few

---

that medical personnel refused to examine plaintiff on multiple occasions and accused him of "playing games" supported claims of deliberate indifference); Steele v. Shah, 87 F.3d 1266, 1270 (11th Cir. 1996) (denying summary judgment to prison doctor who had been told that the plaintiff received psychiatric medication in part because of suicide risk, but discontinued it based on a cursory interview without reviewing medical records); Jackson v. Fauver, 334 F. Supp. 2d 706, 722 (D.N.J. 2004) (HIV patient's complaints that medical staff did not examine him supported a deliberate indifference claim); Doe v. Gustavus, 294 F. Supp. 2d 1003, 1008–09 (E.D.Wis. 2003) (evidence that nurses never checked the pregnant plaintiff personally upon hearing that her water had broken, tested the plaintiff's pants to determine if her water had broken only after they had dried, and examined her only through the tray slot in the cell door supported a deliberate indifference claim); Seals v. Shah, 145 F. Supp. 2d 1378, 1385 (N.D.Ga. 2001) (citing failure to physically examine patient); Williams v. Patel, 104 F. Supp. 2d 984, 987 (C.D.Ill. 2000) (citing failure to physically examine patient with eye injury); Tillery v. Owens, 719 F. Supp. at 1306, 1308 (citing "cursory" sick call inquiries and intake physical examinations that were not "thorough" and in which the patient was never touched); see §§ F.3.a, F.3.b of this chapter. *But see* Brown v. Borough of Chambersburg, 903 F.2d 274, 278 (3d Cir. 1990) (failure to perform a physical examination, resulting in failure to diagnose broken ribs, was not deliberate indifference). In our opinion, *Brown* was incorrectly decided, and the failure to perform so obvious an examination should be considered deliberate indifference.

[291]Comstock v. McCrary, 273 F.3d 693, 709 (6th Cir. 2001) (psychologist's failure to follow up on indications of suicidality supported deliberate indifference claim); McElligott v. Foley, 182 F.3d 1248, 1256–57 (11th Cir. 1999) (holding failure to inquire into, and treat, plaintiff's severe pain, and repeated delays in doctor's seeing the patient, could be deliberate indifference); Boyce v. Alizaduh, 595 F.2d 948, 952–53 (4th Cir. 1979) (prison doctor ignored a complaint of allergy to medication).

[292]McKenna v. Wright, 386 F.3d 432, 437 (2d Cir. 2004) (allegation of repeated failures to test for Hepatitis C despite the presence of known "danger signs" supported a deliberate indifference claim); Miltier v. Beorn, 896 F.2d 848, 853 (4th Cir. 1990) (doctor failed to perform tests for cardiac disease in patient with symptoms that called for them); Hudak v. Miller, 28 F. Supp. 2d 827, 831 (S.D.N.Y. 1998) (failure to order CT scan for nine months for prisoner complaining of chronic headaches); Medcalf v. State of Kansas, 626 F. Supp. 1179, 1183 (D.Kan. 1986) (doctor failed to order tests that were suggested by "the elemental and classic symptoms of a brain tumor"); Weaver v. Jarvis, 611 F. Supp. 40, 44 (N.D.Ga. 1985) (prison doctor refused to conduct diagnostic tests on a prisoner with symptoms of optic disease leading to blindness).

[293]*See* West v. Atkins, 487 U.S. 42, 56 n.15, 108 S. Ct. 2250 (1988) (acknowledging that "the nonmedical functions of prison life inevitably influence the nature, timing and form of medical care provided to inmates"); McKenna v. Wright, 386 F.3d 432, 437 (2d Cir. 2004) (holding allegation that prisoner was "denied urgently needed treatment for a serious disease because he might be released within twelve months of starting the treatment" stated a deliberate indifference claim); Hartsfield v. Colburn, 371 F.3d 454, 457 (8th Cir. 2004) (holding that withholding of a dental referral for "nonmedical reasons—Hartsfield's behavioral problems"—raised a factual issue as to deliberate indifference); Durmer v. O'Carroll, 991 F.2d 64, 68–69 (3d Cir. 1993) (holding that delay of treatment for non-medical reasons could constitute deliberate indifference); Hamilton v. Endell, 981 F.2d 1063, 1066–67 (9th Cir. 1992) (holding that prison officials' disregarding a surgeon's recommendation on non-medical grounds could constitute deliberate indifference); Calhoun v. Thomas, 360 F. Supp. 2d 1264, 1284 (M.D.Ala. 2005) (delaying medical care to make an arrestee confess would support a deliberate indifference claim); Lavender v. Lampert, 242 F. Supp. 2d 821, 843 (D.Or. 2002) (reductions in medication for chronic pain while plaintiff was in disciplinary segregation supported deliberate indifference claim); Delker v. Maass, 843 F. Supp. 1390, 1398, 1401 (D.Or. 1994).

[294]*See* § F.3.c of this chapter.

[295]Natale v. Camden County Correctional Facility, 318 F.3d 575, 583 (3d Cir. 2003) (policy to see all new admissions within 72 hours, with no provision for prisoners with immediate medication needs, supported a deliberate indifference claim); Gibson v. County of Washoe, Nev., 290 F.3d 1175, 1189 (9th Cir. 2002) (policy to delay medical attention on intake for prisoners who were combative or uncooperative supported deliberate indifference claim on behalf of prisoner with mental illness who died for lack of medical care); Anderson v. County of Kern, 45 F.3d 1310 (9th Cir. 1995) (failure to provide a translator for medical encounters can constitute deliberate indifference); Matzker v. Herr, 748 F.2d 1142, 1147 (7th Cir. 1984) (lack of facilities), *overruled on other grounds*, Salazar v. City of Chicago, 940 F.2d 233, 240 (7th Cir. 1991); Green v. Carlson, 581 F.2d 669, 671, 675 (7th Cir. 1978) (failure to provide coverage for medical emergencies, failure to maintain working respirator, staff who did not know how to operate emergency equipment), *aff'd*, 446 U.S. 14, 100 S. Ct. 1468 (1980); Madrid v. Gomez, 889 F. Supp. 1146, 1221 (N.D.Cal. 1995) (lack of input by mental health staff concerning housing decisions even where they impact mental health supported deliberate indifference finding); Lightfoot v. Walker, 486 F. Supp. 504, 517, 527 (S.D.Ill. 1980) (inadequate system of medical records).

A number of cases have held that sick call procedures that did not permit adequate assessment of the prisoner's complaint are constitutionally inadequate. *See* § F.3.a of this chapter. Inadequate physical facilities and medical records systems have also been found to violate the Constitution. *See* §§ F.3.e and F.3.f of this chapter.

[296]This issue arises frequently in cases involving transgender prisoners. *See* § F.4.a of this chapter, n.492. *See also* Brock v. Wright, 315 F.3d 158, 163 (2d Cir. 2003) (holding policy forbidding treatment of keloid scars for purposes of alleviating moderate chronic pain could support deliberate indifference finding); Monmouth County Correctional Institution Inmates v. Lanzaro, 834 F.2d 326, 347 (3d Cir. 1987) (restrictions on abortion unrelated to individual treatment needs); Ancata v. Prison Health Services, Inc., 769 F.2d

situations in which courts have upheld security-based restrictions on medical treatment.[297]) As several courts have put it, "systemic deficiencies in staffing, facilities, or procedures [which] make unnecessary suffering inevitable" may support a finding of deliberate indifference.[298]

One non-medical ground for restricting treatment is cost, and many courts have said that care cannot be denied for that reason.[299] One federal appeals court has said that the

---

700, 704–05 (11th Cir. 1985) (refusal to provide specialty consultations without a court order); Johnson v. Pearson, 316 F. Supp. 2d 307, 316–19 (E.D.Va. 2004) (policy of double-celling non-smoking prisoners with smokers for administrative reasons regardless of their individual health issues violated Eighth Amendment); Sulton v. Wright, 265 F. Supp. 2d 292, 300 (S.D.N.Y. 2003) (allegations that the chief medical officer of the prison system "adopted a utilization review mechanism for specialist consultation and surgery approval that used a contractual vendor whose goal, in practice, was to limit care as much as possible" supported a deliberate indifference claim); Kenney v. Paderes, 217 F. Supp. 2d 1095, 1100 (D.Haw. 2002) (holding refusal to treat plaintiff with a particular medication that was a standard treatment for his condition could constitute deliberate indifference where there was compelling evidence of an unwritten policy against using that drug); Ramos v. O'Connell, 28 F. Supp. 2d 796, 803 (W.D.N.Y. 1998) (denial of medical and dental treatment to prisoners in medical quarantine for refusing tuberculosis test could be deliberate indifference); Casey v. Lewis, 834 F. Supp. 1477, 1545 (D.Ariz. 1993) (security staff's overruling of medical orders); U.S. v. State of Michigan, 680 F. Supp. 928, 1002, 1043–45 (W.D.Mich. 1987) (security or transportation constraints).

Prisons sometimes fail to provide prescribed medications because they don't routinely stock them—that is, they are not in the prison's "formulary." We are not aware of any decisions ruling on this practice. However, one federal court said it was "troubled" by such a claim, though it "reserve[d] for another day the issue of whether the government or a prison doctor may avoid liability for deliberate indifference by seeking shelter behind an inadequate formulary." Gil v. Reed, 381 F.3d 649, 663 n.3 (7th Cir. 2004).

[297]See Garvin v. Armstrong, 236 F.3d 896, 899 (7th Cir. 2001) (upholding policy of keeping asthma inhalers in a secure location was not deliberate indifference where it also called for producing them within four minutes). Prisons may limit the availability of narcotics and other addictive drugs because of their potential for abuse as long as they provide other treatment for prisoners' pain and other medical problems. Lawhorn v. Duckworth, 736 F. Supp. 1501, 1505 (N.D.Ind. 1987), aff'd, 902 F.2d 37 (7th Cir. 1990) (Valium); Wolfel v. Ferguson, 689 F. Supp. 756, 760 (S.D.Ohio 1987); see also Inmates of Allegheny County Jail v. Pierce, 612 F.2d 754, 760–61 (3d Cir. 1979) (jail officials could limit methadone treatment). One court has held that female hormone treatment may be denied to male transgender prisoner because of the security problems in placing them in either male or female prisons. White v. Farrier, 849 F.2d 322, 327 (8th Cir. 1988). See § F.4.a of this chapter for further discussion of treatment of transgender prisoners.

[298]Todaro v. Ward, 565 F.2d 48, 52 (2d Cir. 1977) (quoting Bishop v. Stoneman, 508 F.2d 1224, 1226 (2d Cir. 1974)); accord, Harris v. Thigpen, 941 F.2d 1495, 1505 (11th Cir. 1991); DeGidio v. Pung, 920 F.2d 525, 529 (8th Cir. 1990) (holding lack of "adequate organization and control in the administration of health services" supported a finding of Eighth Amendment violation); Free v. Granger, 887 F.2d 1552, 1556 (11th Cir. 1989) ("Proof of staffing or

procedural deficiencies may give rise to a finding of deliberate indifference); Eng v. Smith, 849 F.2d 80, 82 (2d Cir. 1988) (applying "systemic deficiencies" principle to mental health care); Morales Feliciano v. Rossello Gonzalez, 13 F. Supp. 2d 151, 206 (D.P.R. 1998); Coleman v. Wilson, 912 F. Supp. 1282, 1316–17 (E.D.Cal. 1995); Clarkson v. Coughlin, 898 F. Supp. 1019, 1042, 1049 (S.D.N.Y. 1995) (denial of interpreters to deaf prisoners during medical encounters constitutes "a systemic pattern of inadequacy of treatment . . . which is causing class members unwarranted suffering"); Madrid v. Gomez, 889 F. Supp. 1146, 1212–14 (N.D.Cal. 1995) (citing failure to "remedy the gross and obvious deficiencies of the system"); see Davis v. Carter, 452 F.3d 686, 691–94 (7th Cir. 2006) (holding plaintiff's deliberate indifference claim of a municipal policy of inordinate delay in providing methadone treatment was supported by evidence of an absence of policies and procedures to ensure timely treatment); Cabrales v. County of Los Angeles, 864 F.2d 1454, 1461 (9th Cir. 1988) (understaffing such that psychiatric staff could only spend "minutes per month" with disturbed inmates was unconstitutional), vacated, 494 U.S. 1091 (1989), reinstated, 886 F.2d 235 (9th Cir. 1989); Marcotte v. Monroe Corrections Complex, 394 F. Supp. 2d 1289, 1298 (W.D.Wash. 2005) (failure to remedy known deficient infirmary nursing procedures and other health department citations), reconsideration denied, 2005 WL 2978651 (W.D.Wash., Nov. 7, 2005); Jackson v. First Correctional Medical Services, 380 F. Supp. 2d 387, 392 (D.Del. 2005) (allegation of "the absence of basic policies to insure that the medical orders of treating physicians are reasonably followed and that the medical orders of physicians are reasonably transmitted" amounted to alleging that the treating physicians are unable to exercise informed professional judgment, resulting in deliberate indifference); Sulton v. Wright, 265 F. Supp. 2d 292, 300 (S.D.N.Y. 2003) (holding chief medical officer's failure to correct the failures of the medical tracking system which resulted in surgery having to be re-approved after transfers and to correct the failure of medical holds and coordination of patient work-up between prisons supported a deliberate indifference claim).

[299]Jones v. Johnson, 781 F.2d 769, 771 (9th Cir. 1986) (allegation of denial for budgetary reasons of surgery for painful and disabling condition stated a deliberate indifference claim); Kosilek v. Maloney, 221 F. Supp. 2d 156, 161 (D.Mass. 2002) ("It is not, however, permissible to deny an inmate adequate medical care because it is costly. In recognition of this, prison officials at times authorize CAT scans, dialysis, and other forms of expensive medical care required to diagnose or treat familiar forms of serious illness."); Wilson v. VanNatta, 291 F. Supp. 2d 811, 816 (N.D.Ind. 2003) (allegation that prescribed pain reliever and muscle relaxer and physical therapy were cancelled on grounds of cost states a deliberate indifference claim); Baker v. Blanchette, 186 F. Supp. 2d 100, 105 (D.Conn. 2001) (unexplained denial of colostomy closure until after the plaintiff's release, allegedly "not because of medical decisionmaking involving the use of professional judgment, but solely because of cost," supported a deliberate indifference claim); Kruger v. Jenne, 164 F. Supp. 2d 1330, 1334 (S.D.Fla. 2000) (allegation that medical provider refused and/or delayed treatment to save money stated a deliberate indifference claim); Taylor v. Barnett, 105 F. Supp. 2d 483, 489 & n.2 (E.D.Va. 2000) (allegation that HIV medication was changed solely for reason of cost, without medical

"civilized minimum" of medical care "is a function both of objective need and of cost. The lower the cost, the less need has to be shown, but the need must still be shown to be substantial."[300] However, neither that court nor any other that we are aware of has provided any clear guidance as to where the line is drawn or what role cost may play and under what circumstances.

Failure to carry out medical orders.[301] Such cases often involve the failure to provide prescribed medication[302] or the failure to act on medical recommendations for surgery or for other specialized care,[303] including

---

reason, stated a deliberate indifference claim); Taylor v. Plousis, 101 F. Supp. 2d 255, 268 (D.N.J. 2000) (delaying provision of a new leg prosthesis to avoid its cost would support a deliberate indifference claim); Starbeck v. Linn County Jail, 871 F. Supp. 1129, 1145–46 (N.D.Iowa 1994) (evidence that hernia surgery recommended by outside doctors was not performed because the county didn't want to pay for it could establish deliberate indifference).

In a recent case in which a prisoner sought a liver transplant, the defendants argued that it would be exorbitant to require prisons to pay for such care, but the plaintiff pointed out that state medical insurance ordinarily covered the cost of liver transplants. The court held that costs alone should not impede the provision of this necessary care, and added that "the Ninth Circuit expects lower courts to protect physical harm [sic] to an individual over monetary costs to government entities." Rosado v. Alameida, 349 F. Supp. 2d 1340, 1348 (S.D.Cal. 2004). Other decisions involving organ transplants suggest that the courts will apply standard deliberate indifference analysis to them. See Jackson v. McIntosh, 90 F.3d 330, 332 (9th Cir. 1996). Thus, a couple of decisions have suggested that the Federal Bureau of Prisons' policy of arranging for organ transplants only if the prisoner can pay for them is unconstitutional, though the question has not actually been decided yet. See Clark v. Hedrick, 233 F.3d 1093, 1094 (8th Cir. 2000); Barron v. Keohane, 216 F.3d 692, 693 (8th Cir. 2000).

[300]Ralston v. McGovern, 167 F.3d 1160, 1162 (7th Cir. 1999) (failure to provide already prescribed pain medication for the pain of cancer and cancer treatment "borders on the barbarous"). *But see* Maggert v. Hanks, 131 F.3d 670, 671–72 (7th Cir. 1997) (holding prisoner with gender identity disorder is not entitled to surgical and hormone treatment, "an esoteric medical treatment that only the wealthy can afford" and that is not presently provided at others' expense through Medicaid, insurance, etc.).

[301]Estelle v. Gamble, 429 U.S. 97, 105, 97 S. Ct. 285 (1976) ("intentionally interfering with the treatment once prescribed"); *see* Johnson v. Wright, 412 F.3d 398, 406 (2d Cir. 2005) (denial of Rebetron therapy for Hepatitis C contrary to the recommendations of all the plaintiff's treating physicians); Lawson v. Dallas County, 286 F.3d 257, 263 (5th Cir. 2002) (disregard for follow-up care instructions for paraplegic); Lopez v. Smith, 203 F.3d 1122, 1132 (9th Cir. 2000) (en banc) (failure to provide prescribed liquid diet for prisoner with a broken jaw, and substitution of a pureed diet that could not be drunk through a straw, stated a claim of interference with prescribed treatment); Koehl v. Dalsheim, 85 F.3d 86, 88 (2d Cir. 1996) (denial of prescription eyeglasses sufficiently alleged deliberate indifference); Erickson v. Holloway, 77 F.3d 1078, 1080–81 (8th Cir. 1996) (officer's refusal of emergency room doctor's request to admit the prisoner and take x-rays); Aswegan v. Bruhl, 965 F.2d 676, 677–68 (8th Cir. 1992) (failure to honor doctors' orders and refrain from cuffing the plaintiff's hands behind his back); Boretti v. Wiscomb, 930 F.2d 1150, 1156 (6th Cir. 1991) (nurse's failure to perform prescribed dressing change);

Martin v. Board of County Comm'rs of Pueblo County, 909 F.2d 402, 406 (10th Cir. 1990) (moving an arrestee with a broken neck against doctor's orders); Payne v. Lynaugh, 843 F.2d 177, 178 (5th Cir. 1988) (denial of access to recommended life-saving equipment); Gill v. Mooney, 824 F.2d 192, 195–96 (2d Cir. 1987) (denial of gymnasium time prescribed as rehabilitation therapy); McCorkle v. Walker, 871 F. Supp. 555, 558 (N.D.N.Y. 1995) (failure to obey a medical order to house asthmatic prisoner on a lower tier stated a claim); Arnold on behalf of H.B. v. Lewis, 803 F. Supp. 246, 257 (D.Ariz. 1992) (overriding of medical decisions by security staff); Jones v. Evans, 544 F. Supp. 769, 774–76 (N.D.Ga. 1982) (confiscation of prescribed back brace); Goodman v. Wagner, 553 F. Supp. 255, 257 (E.D.Pa. 1982) (failure to follow a doctor's orders for wound treatment); Johnson v. Harris, 479 F. Supp. 333, 335–37 (S.D.N.Y. 1979) (failure to provide special diet for diabetic). *But see* Williams v. O'Leary, 55 F.3d 320 (7th Cir. 1995) (two-year failure to provide correct osteomyelitis medication, resulting inter alia from failure to read medical records, was merely negligent).

One court has held that prison officials' failure to obey a medical order for showers and dressing changes did not constitute deliberate indifference. DesRosiers v. Moran, 949 F.2d 15, 19–20 (1st Cir. 1991). In our opinion this decision is contrary to *Estelle v. Gamble*'s reference, cited above, to "intentionally interfering with the treatment once prescribed" as a form of deliberate indifference.

[302]Board v. Farnham, 394 F.3d 469, 484 (7th Cir. 2005) (asthma inhaler); Gil v. Reed, 381 F.3d 649, 661 (7th Cir. 2004); Ralston v. McGovern, 167 F.3d 1160, 1161–62 (7th Cir. 1999); Aswegan v. Bruhl, 965 F.2d at 677–78; Hill v. Marshall, 962 F.2d 1209, 1213–14 (6th Cir. 1992); Johnson v. Hay, 931 F.2d 456, 461–62 (8th Cir. 1991); Boretti v. Wiscomb, 930 F.2d at 1156; Johnson v. Hardin County, Ky., 908 F.2d 1280, 1284 (6th Cir. 1990); Ellis v. Butler, 890 F.2d 1001, 1003–04 (8th Cir. 1989); Mitchell v. Aluisi, 872 F.2d 577, 581 (4th Cir. 1989) (confiscation of prescribed medication); Lowe v. Board of Comm'rs, County of Dauphin, 750 F. Supp. 697, 700 (M.D.Pa. 1990) (indiscriminate confiscation of medication from all incoming inmates); Goodman v. Wagner, 553 F. Supp. 255, 257 (E.D.Pa. 1982).

Some courts have held that denial or delay of prescribed medication does not violate the Eighth Amendment if the delay is short or the consequences are not serious. Mayweather v. Foti, 958 F.2d 91 (5th Cir. 1992); Martin v. New York City Dep't of Corrections, 522 F. Supp. 169, 170 (S.D.N.Y. 1981); Russell v. Enser, 496 F. Supp. 320, 326–28 (D.S.C. 1979), *aff'd*, 624 F.2d 1095 (4th Cir. 1980); Burrascano v. Levi, 452 F. Supp. 1066, 1069 (D.Md. 1978), *aff'd*, 612 F.2d 1306 (4th Cir. 1979); *see also* Harris v. Mapp, 719 F. Supp. 1317, 1324–25 (E.D.Va. 1989) (failure to provide prescribed Dilantin was merely negligent; the prisoner died), *aff'd*, 907 F.2d 1138 (4th Cir. 1990).

[303]Johnson v. Lockhart, 941 F.2d 705, 706–07 (8th Cir. 1991) (10-month delay in surgery that doctor recommended be done within days); Howell v. Evans, 922 F.2d 712, 723 (11th Cir. 1991) (failure to act on a medical judment that prisoners needed access to a respiratory therapist), *vacated as settled*, 931 F.2d 711 (11th Cir. 1991); Johnson v. Bowers, 884 F.2d 1053, 1056 (8th Cir. 1989) (failure to perform surgery recommended by prison doctor); Dace v. Solem, 858 F.2d 385, 387–88 (8th Cir. 1988) (failure of prison doctors to carry out surgery scheduled before plaintiff's

hospitalization or other care not available in the prison.[304] Courts in some cases have upheld security-based refusals to carry out medical orders where an alternative means of satisfying the prisoners' medical needs was provided.[305]

In addition to the situations described above, in which no genuine medical judgment was exercised, there are a number of decisions that say, in effect, that not every decision by a doctor reflects medical judgment.[306] Some such cases involve conduct by doctors that simply makes no sense and is not explained, such as failing to respond to apparently serious complaints or refusing to carry out prescribed or recommended treatments for no apparent reason.[307] Courts have said that the Constitution is

violated "if deliberate indifference cause[s] an easier and less efficacious treatment to be consciously chosen by the doctors."[308]

Courts have also acknowledged that extreme cases of bad judgment by medical personnel can constitute deliberate indifference. "Medical treatment that is 'so grossly incompetent, inadequate, or excessive as to shock the conscience or to be intolerable to fundamental fairness' constitutes deliberate indifference. . . . Additionally, when the need for medical treatment is obvious, medical care that is so cursory as to amount to no treatment at all may constitute deliberate indifference. . . ."[309] Gross departures from

---

incarceration); LaFaut v. Smith, 834 F.2d 389, 393–94 (4th Cir. 1987) (failure to provide rehabilitation therapy recommended by orthopedic specialist); Scott v. Garcia, 370 F. Supp. 2d 1056, 1068–69 (S.D.Cal. 2005) (failure of classification committee to act on medical direction to transfer prisoner with severe stomach and digestive problems to a prison with hospital facilities); Johnson-El v. District of Columbia, 579 A.2d 163, 169 (D.C. 1990) (failure to take prisoner to dermatologist).

[304]See § F.3.d of this chapter.

[305]Beck v. Skon, 253 F.3d 330, 334–35 (8th Cir. 2001) (refusal to house plaintiff nearer the cafeteria and infirmary because plaintiff did not meet the security criteria for that housing unit was not deliberately indifferent where officials offered to provide a wheelchair or deliver meals to him); Gerber v. Sweeney, 292 F. Supp. 2d 700, 648 (E.D.Pa. 2003) (prisoner who received a special hypertension diet calling for milk and juice could be provided cheese and fruit instead per a policy banning liquids and containers in segregation unit to curb throwing of urine and feces; diet substitution was done by a dietitian whose affidavit said it was nutritionally and medically adequate for the plaintiff).

[306]Johnson v. Doughty, 433 F.3d 1001, 1013 (7th Cir. 2006) ("a medical professional's erroneous treatment decision can lead to deliberate indifference liability if the decision was made in the absence of professional judgment").

[307]Scott v. Ambani, 575 F.3d 642, 648 (6th Cir. 2009) (holding doctor's refusal to examine or provide pain medication to prisoner who had recently been treated for prostate cancer, had severe back and leg pain and a hard and painful testicular lump, could constitute deliberate indifference); Hayes v. Snyder, 546 F.3d 516, 524–26 (7th Cir. 2008) (holding doctor's actions and testimony could support an inference that he was "hostile and dismissive" to plaintiff's needs and therefore deliberately indifferent); Greeno v. Daley, 414 F.3d 645, 654 (7th Cir. 2005) (holding medical staff's "obdurate refusal" to change prisoner's treatment despite his reports that his medication was not working and his condition was worsening could constitute deliberate indifference); Farrow v. West, 320 F.3d 1235, 1247–48 (11th Cir. 2003) (holding unexplained long delay in providing dentures by a dentist familiar with prisoner's painful condition could constitute deliberate indifference); Roberson v. Bradshaw, 198 F.3d 645, 648 (8th Cir. 1999) (holding doctor who ignored patient's complaint of adverse medication reaction and made no claim it was a medical judgment could be found deliberately indifferent); McElligott v. Foley, 182 F.3d 1248, 1256–57 (11th Cir. 1999) (holding failure to inquire further into, and treat, plaintiff's severe pain, and repeated delays in doctor's seeing the patient, could be deliberate indifference); Hunt v. Uphoff, 199 F.3d 1220,

1223–24 (10th Cir. 1999) (refusing to dismiss allegations that one doctor denied insulin prescribed by another doctor and that medically recommended procedures were not performed as mere differences of medical opinion); Hughes v. Joliet Correctional Center, 931 F.2d 425, 428 (7th Cir. 1991) (evidence that medical staff treated the plaintiff "not as a patient, but as a nuisance," and "were insufficiently interested in his health to take even minimal steps to guard against the possibility that the injury was severe" could support a finding of deliberate indifference).

[308]Williams v. Vincent, 508 F.2d 541, 544 (2d Cir. 1974); accord, McElligott v. Foley, 182 F.3d 1248, 1256–57 (11th Cir. 1999) (holding failure to inquire further into, and treat, plaintiff's severe pain, and repeated delays in doctor's seeing the patient, could support a finding of taking an "easier but less efficacious course of treatment"); Monmouth County Jail Inmates v. Lanzaro, 834 F.2d 326, 347 (3d Cir. 1987); Maynard v. New Jersey, 719 F. Supp. 292, 295 (D.N.J. 1989) (evidence that prisoner received only palliative treatment for severe complications of AIDS raised a factual question of deliberate indifference); see also Farrow v. West, 320 F.3d 1235, 1247–48 (11th Cir. 2003) (holding delay of 15 months in providing dentures, with three- and eight-month hiatuses in treatment, by a dentist familiar with prisoner's painful condition, raised a jury question of deliberate indifference).

[309]Adams v. Poag, 61 F.3d 1537, 1543–44 (11th Cir. 1995); see also Greeno v. Daley, 414 F.3d 645, 655 (7th Cir. 2005) (a doctor's persistence in a course of treatment known to be ineffective, and his ban on providing the prisoner with pain medication or gastroscopy, supported the argument that "the repeated refusal to uncover or effectively treat his condition was a 'gratuitous cruelty'"); Collignon v. Milwaukee County, 163 F.3d 982, 989 (7th Cir. 1998) ("A plaintiff can show that the professional disregarded the need only if the professional's subjective response was so inadequate that it demonstrated an absence of professional judgment, that is, that no minimally competent professional would have so responded under those circumstances."); Parham v. Johnson, 126 F.3d 454, 457–58 n.7 (3d Cir. 1997) (inappropriate treatment for no valid reason states a deliberate indifference claim; doctor continued medication for 114 days although the Physicians' Desk Reference says it should be used for no more than 10 days and plaintiff was experiencing adverse effects); Hughes v. Joliet Correctional Center, 931 F.2d 425, 428 (7th Cir. 1991) (evidence that medical staff treated the plaintiff "not as a patient, but as a nuisance," and "were insufficiently interested in his health to take even minimal steps to guards against the possibility that the injury was severe" could support a finding of deliberate indifference); White v. Napoleon, 897 F.2d 103, 109 (3d Cir. 1990) (deliberate indifference claim was stated by "allegations that the doctor intended to inflict pain on

accepted medical standards may be evidence of deliberate indifference.[310] The failure to follow professional standards, or even prison medical care protocols, may support a finding of deliberate indifference because the standards or protocols can be evidence of the practitioner's knowledge of the risk posed by particular symptoms or conditions.[311] In these cases, courts give substantial weight to expert testimony criticizing the prisoner's care, rather than dismissing it as a difference of opinion among doctors.[312]

The foregoing probably sounds inconsistent with the idea we started with—that courts don't get into disputes over medical judgment—and often it is. Courts sometimes seem willing to blur this line in extreme cases which involve not just bad care, but also very serious medical conditions, often leading to death, disability, or disfigurement.[313] Their reasoning may not be extended to less serious cases—or even all the serious cases.

A related issue is posed by cases in which prison medical personnel, having referred a prisoner to a specialist, fail to carry out the specialist's recommendations, or those of a specialist who directed treatment before the prisoner was incarcerated. Some decisions have held that such actions merely reflect differences of medical opinion and do not constitute deliberate indifference.[314] It seems to us that when prison officials or medical staff refer a prisoner to an outside consultant, they are in effect conceding that their own judgment is not sufficient to address the prisoner's medical condition, and if they disregard the consultant's directions, they should at a minimum be required to provide a convincing explanation for their choice, and not merely to label the matter as a difference of medical opinion. There are a number of decisions that are consistent with this view.[315]

---

prisoners without any medical justification and . . . the sheer number of specific instances in which the doctor allegedly insisted on continuing courses of treatment that the doctor knew were painful, ineffective, or entailed substantial risk of serious harm to the prisoners."); Rogers v. Evans, 792 F.2d 1052, 1058 (11th Cir. 1986) (treatment "so grossly incompetent, inadequate, or excessive as to shock the conscience" or "so inappropriate as to *evidence intentional maltreatment*" violates the Eighth Amendment (emphasis supplied)); Rosen v. Chang, 811 F. Supp. 754, 760–61 (D.R.I. 1993) ("Grossly incompetent and recklessly inadequate examination by a licensed physician" may constitute deliberate indifference).

[310]Howell v. Evans, 922 F.2d 712, 719 (11th Cir. 1991) ("the contemporary standards and opinions of the medical profession are highly relevant in determining what constitutes deliberate indifference"), *vacated as settled*, 931 F.2d 711 (11th Cir. 1991); Moore v. Duffy, 255 F.3d 543, 545 (8th Cir. 2001) (it is "clearly established" that medical treatment may so deviate from the applicable standard of care as to evidence deliberate indifference; conflicting expert opinions may create a factual question as to deliberate indifference); Smith v. Jenkins, 919 F.2d 90, 93 (8th Cir. 1990) (plaintiff should be permitted to prove that treatment "so deviated from professional standards that it amounted to deliberate indifference").

A recent decision granting a preliminary injunction to a prisoner who was declared ineligible for a liver transplant, without which he was at risk of early death, stated: "In order to prevail on a claim involving choices between alternative courses of treatment, a prisoner must show that the course of treatment the doctors chose was medically unacceptable in light of the circumstances and that they chose this course in conscious disregard of an excessive risk to plaintiff's health." Rosado v. Alameida, 349 F. Supp. 2d 1340, 1344–45 (S.D.Cal. 2004).

[311]Mata v. Saiz, 427 F.3d 745, 757–58 (10th Cir. 2005); *accord*, Phillips v. Roane County, Tenn., 534 F.3d 531, 541, 543–44 (6th Cir. 2008).

[312]"Whether an instance of medical misdiagnosis resulted from deliberate indifference or negligence is a factual question requiring exploration by expert witnesses." Rogers v. Evans, 792 F.2d at 1058; Smith v. Jenkins, 919 F.2d at 94 (suggesting that the district court "may" appoint an independent expert or obtain an opinion from the prisoner's pre-incarceration doctor); Miltier v. Beorn, 896 F.2d 848, 852 (4th Cir. 1990); Mandel v. Doe, 888 F.2d 783, 790 (11th Cir. 1989); Medcalf v. State of Kansas, 626 F. Supp. 1179, 1190 (D.Kan. 1986) (prisoner's expert's description of medical care as "gross negligence" raised a factual question for the jury); *see* § F.2.b of this chapter, nn.231–233, for a further comment on medical experts. *But see* Howell v. Evans, 922 F.2d at 722 (expert affidavit stating that a prison doctor "deviated from established standards" but not that his actions were "grossly inadequate" or

"plainly wrong" did not support a deliberate indifference claim), *vacated as settled*, 931 F.2d 711 (11th Cir. 1991).

[313]*See* Greeno v. Daley, 414 F.3d 645, 655 (7th Cir. 2005) (painful gastric condition that persisted for years as treatment was denied); Parham v. Johnson, 126 F.3d 454, 457–58 n.7 (3d Cir. 1997) (ear injury resulting in severe hearing loss after maltreatment); Waldrop v. Evans, 871 F.2d 1030, 1032–36 (11th Cir.) (severe self-mutilation following psychiatric neglect), *rehearing denied*, 880 F.2d 421 (11th Cir. 1989); Rogers v. Evans, 792 F.2d at 1060–62 (suicide following psychiatric neglect); Carswell v. Bay County, 854 F.2d 454, 455–57 (11th Cir. 1988) (treatment of diabetic suffering catastrophic weight loss with laxatives and pain-killers); Wood v. Sunn, 865 F.2d 982, 989–90 (9th Cir. 1988) (disregard of complaints because doctors assumed the prisoner's pain was psychological; he lost the ability to urinate), *vacated*, 880 F.2d 1011 (9th Cir. 1989); Rosen v. Chang, 811 F. Supp. 754, 760 (D.R.I. 1990) (death from untreated appendicitis); Joseph v. Brierton, 431 F. Supp. 50, 51–52 (N.D.Ill. 1976) (fatal administration of contra-indicated medication). Some of the cases cited in n.291 of this section concerning the failure to perform tests are similar.

One court has made this point explicit, stating that "life-threatening" or "fast-developing" conditions call for closer judicial scrutiny of prison medical care. Liscio v. Warren, 901 F.2d 274, 277 (2d Cir. 1990), *overruled on other grounds*, Caizzo v. Koreman, 581 F.3d 63 (2d Cir. 2009).

[314]*See, e.g.*, Dulany v. Carnahan, 132 F.3d 1234, 1240 (8th Cir. 1997); *see also* Lawhorn v. Duckworth, 736 F. Supp. 1501, 1504 (N.D.Ind. 1987) (prison doctors were considered "treating physicians" and outside hospital staff's judgments were only "recommendations"), *aff'd*, 902 F.2d 37 (7th Cir. 1990).

[315]*See* Gil v. Reed, 381 F.3d 649, 664 (7th Cir. 2004) ("On summary judgment, we find that prescribing on three occasions the very medication the specialist warned against . . . while simultaneously cancelling two of the three prescribed laxatives gives rise to a genuine issue of material fact about [the prison doctor's] state

It is medical judgment with respect to *the particular patient* to which courts defer under the deliberate indifference standard. Thus, the Second Circuit recently held that even though it might be generally appropriate to deny treatment for Hepatitis C to persons who present any evidence of substance abuse in the preceding two years, a jury could find that it was deliberately indifferent to apply that policy to a particular prisoner contrary to "the unanimous, express, and repeated recommendations of plaintiff's treating physicians, including prison physicians," to depart from the policy in the plaintiff's case.[316]

Prison personnel sometimes respond to allegations of deliberate indifference by saying that they did provide some medical care, or that your medical care was adequate in general. But prison officials must respond to all of your serious medical needs,[317] and the fact that you are properly treated on some occasions does not excuse deliberate indifference on others[318]—though isolated lapses in an overall pattern of adequate care will generally not constitute deliberate indifference.[319] A claim that officials "continuously assessed and monitored" a prisoner's condition does not excuse the failure to provide treatment when treatment is needed.[320]

---

of mind."); Jones v. Simek, 193 F.3d 485, 492 (7th Cir. 1999) (citing refusal to follow specialist's recommendations as supporting claim of deliberate indifference); Miller v. Schoenen, 75 F.3d 1305 (8th Cir. 1996) (expert evidence combined with recommendations from outside hospitals that were not followed supported deliberate indifference claim); Hamilton v. Endell, 981 F.2d 1063, 1066–67 (9th Cir. 1992) (disregard of treating ear surgeon's direction not to transfer prisoner by airplane could constitute deliberate indifference even though officials obtained a second opinion from their own physician; "By choosing to rely upon a medical opinion which a reasonable person would likely determine to be inferior, the prison officials took actions which may have amounted to the denial of medical treatment, and the 'unnecessary and wanton infliction of pain.'"); Verser v. Elyea, 113 F. Supp. 2d 1211, 1215 (N.D.Ill. 2000) (where a prison doctor "declined to follow the recommendations of an orthopedic specialist, which he is not, without even examining the patient, despite repeated complaints of pain and injury," claim could not be dismissed as a mere difference of medical opinion); Pugliese v. Cuomo, 911 F. Supp. 58, 63 (N.D.N.Y. 1996) (plaintiff entered prison with a recommendation for physical therapy; one prison doctor said he would never waste the state's money on such treatment); Starbeck v. Linn County Jail, 871 F. Supp. 1129, 1146–47 (N.D.Iowa 1994) (where outside doctors had recommended hernia surgery, prison officials who failed to provide the surgery could not claim a difference in medical judgment without providing an explanation of their decision).

In *Bender v. Regier*, 385 F.3d 1133, 1138 (8th Cir. 2004), a prison doctor was held not deliberately indifferent in failing to provide interferon treatment for Hepatitis C, in part because he was waiting for a specialist recommendation which did not arrive. The court didn't say whether the doctor would have been obliged to follow the recommendation had he received it.

[316]Johnson v. Wright, 412 F.3d 398, 406 (2d Cir. 2005). The prisoner had had a single urine scan that was positive for marijuana during the relevant two-year period. The court indicated that its holding is an extension of its previous holding "that a deliberate indifference claim can lie where prison officials deliberately ignore the medical recommendations of a prisoner's treating physicians." *Id.* at 404 (citing Gill v. Mooney, 824 F.2d 192, 196 (2d Cir. 1987)). Similarly, the court held that a policy forbidding treatment of chronically painful keloid scars could constitute deliberate indifference as applied to a prisoner who might have benefited from steroid injections. Brock v. Wright, 315 F.3d 158, 167 (2d Cir. 2003); *see* n.296, above.

[317]Matzker v. Herr, 748 F.2d 1142, 1147–48 (7th Cir. 1984), *overruled on other grounds*, Salazar v. City of Chicago, 940 F.2d 233, 240 (7th Cir. 1991) (prisoner who alleged that he suffered a broken nose, broken teeth, and an eye injury in a fight, but he only got treatment for the broken nose, stated a claim for deliberate indifference) *see also* Smith v. Jenkins, 919 F.2d 90, 93–94 (8th Cir. 1990) (mere proof of diagnosis by a doctor did not require dismissal of case; district court directed to review prisoner's medical records); Lavender v. Lampert, 242 F. Supp. 2d 821, 843 (D.Or. 2002) (the failure of medical staff to respond to ongoing complaints of chronic and debilitating pain could constitute deliberate indifference even though the prisoner regularly received medical services); Henderson v. Harris, 672 F. Supp. 1054, 1059 (N.D.Ill. 1987) (the fact that the prisoner received some care did not entitle the warden to have the case dismissed). *Cf.* Knop v. Johnson, 667 F. Supp. 512, 524–25 (W.D.Mich. 1987) (evidence that the prison system spends a lot of money and hires a lot of staff does not refute a deliberate indifference claim about the medical care system), *aff'd in part and rev'd in part on other grounds*, 977 F.2d 996 (6th Cir. 1992).

[318]Archer v. Dutcher, 733 F.2d 14, 16–17 (2d Cir. 1984) (pregnant woman who alleged a five-hour delay in taking her to the hospital when she began to miscarry raised a factual issue of deliberate indifference even though she received "extensive" medical attention on other occasions); Murrell v. Bennett, 615 F.2d 306, 310 n.4 (5th Cir. 1980) (the deliberate indifference standard "does not necessarily excuse one episode of gross misconduct merely because the overall pattern reflects general attentiveness"); *see* Comstock v. McCrary, 273 F.3d 693, 707 n.5 (6th Cir. 2001) ("Defendants' position is, apparently, that if a prison doctor offers some treatment, no matter how insignificant, he cannot be found deliberately indifferent. This is not the law. . . .").

[319]*See* Gutierrez v. Peters, 111 F.3d 1364, 1374–75 (7th Cir. 1997) (where prisoner received treatment for a cyst repeatedly over ten months with only isolated instances of delay, defendants were not deliberately indifferent; court must "examine the totality of an inmate's medical care"); McGuckin v. Smith, 974 F.2d 1050, 1060–61 (9th Cir. 1992) (a finding that maltreatment was an "isolated exception" to the prisoner's overall treatment militates against a finding of deliberate indifference, but a single "egregious" failure may support a deliberate indifference claim); Jones v. Evans, 544 F. Supp. 769, 775 (N.D.Ga. 1982) (a defendant may respond to a claim of denial of care or inadequate care by "establishing he was generally attentive to the prisoner's needs"; a claim of interference with prescribed care is less subject to that defense).

[320]McKenna v. Wright, 386 F.3d 432, 437 (2d Cir. 2004); *accord*, Shomo v. City of New York, 579 F.3d 175, 184 (2d Cir. 2009) (where plaintiff alleged a policy of disregarding medical recommendations for treatment, claim was not refuted by his having frequently seen doctors who administered tests); Sulton v. Wright, 265 F. Supp. 2d 292, 300 (S.D.N.Y. 2003) ("even if an inmate receives 'extensive' medical care, a claim is stated if . . . the gravamen of his problem is not addressed"); Lavender v. Lampert, 242 F. Supp. 2d 821, 843

Further, persisting in a course of treatment that is ineffective may itself constitute deliberate indifference.[321]

Some courts have said that "repeated examples of negligent acts which disclose a pattern of conduct by the prison medical staff" may add up to deliberate indifference.[322] But more recently, applying the "actual knowledge" courts have cautioned: "It may be, as quite a large number of cases state . . . that repeated acts of negligence are some evidence of deliberate indifference. . . . The only significance of multiple acts of negligence is that they may be evidence of the magnitude of the risk created by the defendants' conduct and the knowledge of the risk by the defendants. . . ."[323]

In some cases, prison officials have denied claims of deliberate indifference by arguing that their institutions have been accredited by the National Commission on Correctional Health Care or other professional organization. Accreditation focuses on written standards, policies, protocols, and facilities, and it may have some relevance to whether a prison's paper policies are constitutional.[324] However, it says nothing about whether the actual care provided is constitutional: "constitutional policies do not necessarily ensure constitutional practices."[325]

Showing deliberate indifference does not, as a matter of law, require expert testimony, as showing medical malpractice generally does.[326] However, as a practical matter, expert testimony will often be required to meet the plaintiff's burden of proof of deliberate indifference, and it is often required as a matter of law to prove that you had a serious medical need. This problem, and the courts' rarely-used power to appoint expert witnesses in prison medical care cases, are discussed elsewhere.[327]

a. Suing the Right Defendants In pursuing a deliberate indifference claim under § 1983 or *Bivens*, you must think closely about exactly who was deliberately indifferent—that is, who caused the constitutional violation and can be held liable for it.[328] In your complaint and other papers, you should be specific about the reasons you think a particular defendant is liable for a medical care deprivation.

Doctors and other medical personnel can be liable for the consequences of their own acts or omissions if they amount to deliberate indifference,[329] but in some cases the fault may be with correctional personnel who keep you from getting to see the medical staff or interfere with treatment that has been prescribed.[330] Wardens and other correctional supervisors are not deliberately indifferent when they act in reliance on the judgments of qualified medical personnel.[331]

(D.Or. 2002) (deliberate indifference claim was supported where plaintiff was examined regularly by medical staff but "there is an ongoing pattern of ignoring, and failing to timely respond to or effectively manage, plaintiff's chronic pain"); Hall v. Artuz, 954 F. Supp. 90, 94 (S.D.N.Y. 1997) ("The fact that Hall had many medical consultations concerning his knees . . . does not establish that he was not denied medically necessary physical therapy.").

[321]Greeno v. Daley, 414 F.3d 645, 655 (7th Cir. 2005); White v. Napoleon, 897 F.2d 103, 109 (3d Cir. 1990); Ruffin v. Deperio, 97 F. Supp. 2d 346, 353 (W.D.N.Y. 2000) (holding jury could find that treatment "consisted of little more than documenting [plaintiff's] worsening condition" and continuing ineffective treatment, notwithstanding frequent examinations and eventual referral to specialist).

[322]Ramos v. Lamm, 639 F.2d 559, 575 (10th Cir. 1980); *accord*, Harris v. Thigpen, 941 F.2d 1495, 1505 (11th Cir. 1991); DeGidio v. Pung, 920 F.2d 525, 533 (8th Cir. 1990) ("consistent pattern of reckless or negligent conduct" establishes deliberate indifference); Todaro v. Ward, 565 F.2d 48, 52 (2d Cir. 1977) (acts that appear negligent in isolation may constitute deliberate indifference if repeated); Diaz v. Broglin, 781 F. Supp. 566, 564 (N.D.Ind. 1991); Langley v. Coughlin, 715 F. Supp. 522, 541 (S.D.N.Y. 1988); Robert E. v. Lane, 530 F. Supp. 930, 940 (N.D.Ill. 1981) ("A pattern of similar instances presumptively indicates that prison administrators have, through their programs and procedures, created an environment in which negligence is unacceptably likely.").

[323]Sellers v. Henman, 41 F.3d 1100, 1102–03 (7th Cir. 1994); *accord*, Brooks v. Celeste, 39 F.3d 125, 128–29 (6th Cir. 1994).

[324]Grayson v. Peed, 195 F.3d 692, 697 (4th Cir. 1999) (rejecting challenge to training of staff because jails were accredited by American Correctional Association and the National Commission on Correctional Health Care, whose training requirements exceed constitutional standards), *rev'd on other grounds*, 243 F.3d 911 (5th Cir. 2001).

[325]Ruiz v. Estelle, 37 F. Supp. 2d 855 (S.D.Tex. 1999). For further discussion of accreditation, *see* § A.1 of this chapter, n.35.

[326]Hathaway v. Coughlin, 37 F.3d 63, 68 (2d Cir. 1994).

[327]*See* Ch. 10, § K.3, for a discussion of expert witnesses, including court-appointed experts.

[328]The "causation" or "personal involvement" requirement applied in civil rights actions is discussed in Ch. 8, § B.4.a.

[329]*See* § F.1 of this chapter.

The Supreme Court has held that physicians who are members of the federal Public Health Service are immune from individual liability, which makes the Federal Tort Claims Act (FTCA) the exclusive remedy against them for injuries resulting from the performance of medical or related functions within the scope of their employment. Hui v. Castaneda, ___ S. Ct. ___, 2010 WL 1740524 (2010).

[330]Estate of Carter v. City of Detroit, 408 F.3d 304, 310, 312–13 (6th Cir. 2005) (holding a jail supervisor who knew the plaintiff was exhibiting "the classic symptoms of a heart attack" and did not arrange transportation to a hospital could be found deliberately indifferent); Alsina-Ortiz v. LaBoy, 400 F.3d 77, 83 (1st Cir. 2005) (holding guard who knew of prisoner's "prolonged, manifest, and agonizing pain" and did nothing to get care for him could be found deliberately indifferent); Brown v. Hughes, 894 F.2d 1533, 1537–39 (11th Cir. 1990); Kelley v. McGinnis, 899 F.2d 612, 616 (7th Cir. 1990); Parrish v. Johnson, 800 F.2d 600, 605 (6th Cir. 1986); H.C. by Hewett v. Jarrard, 786 F.2d 1080, 1086–87 (11th Cir. 1986); Lewis v. Cooper, 771 F.2d 334, 336–37 (7th Cir. 1985); Scott v. Garcia, 370 F. Supp. 2d 1056, 1068–69 (S.D.Cal. 2005) (failure of classification committee to act on medical direction to transfer prisoner with severe stomach and digestive problems to a prison with hospital facilities); Harris v. O'Grady, 803 F. Supp. 1361, 1366 (N.D.Ill. 1992).

[331]As one court observed, a warden is "not responsible for second-guessing his medical staff." Tomarkin v. Ward, 534 F. Supp. 1224, 1232 (S.D.N.Y. 1982); *accord*, Spruill v. Gillis, 372 F.3d 218,

But they may be deliberately indifferent if they fail to provide adequate staff[332] or qualified staff,[333] if they maintain policies that interfere with adequate medical care,[334] if they fail to remedy unlawful conditions that they know about,[335]

or if they otherwise fail to carry out their responsibilities to make adequate medical care available.[336] City or county governments may be held liable on a similar basis if a plaintiff's injury was caused by a city or county policy.[337] Suits against

---

236 (3d Cir. 2004) (prison officials can't be held liable for medical mistreatment unless they have reason to believe, or actual knowledge, of mistreatment or non-treatment); Perkins v. Lawson, 312 F.3d 872, 875–76 (7th Cir. 2002); Miltier v. Beorn, 896 F.2d 848, 854–55 (4th Cir. 1990); White v. Farrier, 849 F.2d 322, 327 (8th Cir. 1988); Sires v. Berman, 834 F.2d 9, 13 (1st Cir. 1987); McCracken v. Jones, 562 F.2d 22, 24 (10th Cir. 1977); *see also* Estate of Cartwright v. City of Concord, Cal., 856 F.2d 1437, 1438 (9th Cir. 1988) (jail staff were not liable for waiting for an ambulance instead of personally administering CPR).

Prison officials may not, however, shop around until they get a medical opinion that suits their non-medical plans for a prisoner. *See* Hamilton v. Endell, 981 F.2d 1063, 1066–67 (9th Cir. 1992).

[332]Greason v. Kemp, 891 F.2d 829, 837–40 (11th Cir. 1990); Anderson v. City of Atlanta, 778 F.2d 678, 686–89 (11th Cir. 1985); Miranda v. Munoz, 770 F.2d 255, 260–62 (1st Cir. 1985).

[333]Howell v. Evans, 922 F.2d 712, 723 (11th Cir. 1991), *vacated as settled*, 931 F.2d 711 (11th Cir. 1991); Bass by Lewis v. Wallenstein, 769 F.2d 1173, 1184–86 (7th Cir. 1985); Langley v. Coughlin, 715 F. Supp. 522, 540 (S.D.N.Y. 1988); Medcalf v. State of Kansas, 626 F. Supp. 1179, 1186 (D.Kan. 1986); *see also* § F.3.c of this chapter.

[334]McKenna v. Wright, 386 F.3d 432, 437 (2d Cir. 2004) (medical supervisors could be held liable for applying a policy restricting Hepatitis C treatment); Brock v. Wright, 315 F.3d 158, 166 (2d Cir. 2003) (prisons' Chief Medical Officer could be held liable for promulgating a policy forbidding treatment of chronically painful keloid); Boswell v. Sherburne County, 849 F.2d 1117, 1123 (10th Cir. 1988) (chief jailer and sheriff could be held liable based on evidence that "inadequately trained jailers were directed to use their own judgment about the seriousness of prisoners' medical needs" and that medical care was restricted in order to save money); Meade v. Grubbs, 841 F.2d 1512, 1531 (10th Cir. 1988) (the failure of the state health commissioner to carry out statutory duties could be deliberate indifference); Jones v. Johnson, 781 F.2d 769, 771–72 (9th Cir. 1986) (supervisory officials could be liable for budgetary restrictions on medical care); Bass by Lewis v. Wallenstein, 769 F.2d at 1184–86 (damages awarded against assistant warden and medical administrator based on deficiencies in sick call procedure); Ancata v. Prison Health Services, Inc., 769 F.2d 700, 705–06 (11th Cir. 1985) (sheriff could be held liable for requiring court orders for outside medical care); Green v. Carlson, 581 F.2d 669, 671, 675 (7th Cir. 1978) (failure to provide emergency coverage when no doctor was on duty stated a claim against the chief medical officer), *aff'd*, 446 U.S. 14, 100 S. Ct. 1468 (1980); Sulton v. Wright, 265 F. Supp. 2d 292, 300 (S.D.N.Y. 2003) (prisons' chief medical officer could be held liable for adopting a utilization review system for specialist consultation and surgery approval whose goal in practice was "to limit care as much as possible").

[335]Alsina-Ortiz v. LaBoy, 400 F.3d 77, 81–82 (1st Cir. 2005) (high-level officials could be liable for line staff's failure to get medical care for an obviously sick prisoner if they "knew of a continuing pattern of culpable failures" to do so and made no reasonable attempt to remedy the problem); Aswegan v. Bruhl, 965 F.2d 676, 677–78 (8th Cir. 1992) (Deputy Warden and Security Director held liable for failure to correct known violations of doctors' orders); Hill v. Marshall, 962 F.2d 1209, 1213 (6th Cir. 1992)

(Deputy Superintendent of Treatment held liable for failure to respond to complaints despite his knowledge of a breakdown in the medical system); Greason v. Kemp, 891 F.2d 829, 839 (11th Cir. 1990) (prison system mental health director could be held liable for failure to remedy known deficiencies in mental health services); LaFaut v. Smith, 834 F.2d 389, 392–94 (4th Cir. 1987) (damages awarded against warden who was "fully advised" of failure to provide a paraplegic inmate with adequate toilet facilities and rehabilitation therapy); Thompkins v. Belt, 828 F.2d 298, 305 (5th Cir. 1987) (Sheriff could be held liable if he knew the plaintiff's requests for medical treatment were being ignored); Bass by Lewis v. Wallenstein, 769 F.2d at 1184–86 (assistant warden and medical administrator could be held liable for failure to act on previous warnings of inadequate medical care); Marcotte v. Monroe Corrections Complex, 394 F. Supp. 2d 1289, 1297 (W.D.Wash. 2005) (supervising doctor and and prison superintendent could be held liable if they "were aware of deficient infirmary nursing procedures and other health department citations and yet failed to take corrective action"); Sulton v. Wright, 265 F. Supp. 2d 292, 300 (S.D.N.Y. 2003) (holding chief medical officer's failure to correct the failures of the medical tracking system which resulted in surgery having to be re-approved after transfers and to correct the failure of medical holds and coordination of patient work-up between prisons supported a deliberate indifference claim); Lavender v. Lampert, 242 F. Supp. 2d 821, 840 (D.Or. 2002) (superintendent and health services manager who were notified repeatedly of failure to address the plaintiff's chronic pain could be found deliberately indifferent); Langley v. Coughlin, 715 F. Supp. at 544–49 (Commissioner, Superintendent, medical unit chief, and security captain could be held liable based on their knowledge of deficiencies in mental health care); Jones v. Evans, 544 F. Supp. 769, 777 (N.D.Ga. 1982) (warden and commissioner could be held liable for inadequate training, supervision, and direction of subordinate employees); Tomarkin v. Ward, 534 F. Supp. 1224, 1232 (S.D.N.Y. 1982) (warden could be responsible if he knew of denial of medical care in solitary confinement).

[336]Howell v. Burden, 12 F.3d 190, 192–94 (11th Cir. 1994) (Superintendent's "administrative authority" could support liability); Johnson v. Lockhart, 941 F.2d 705, 707 (8th Cir. 1991) ("Abdication of policy-making and oversight responsibilities can reach the level of deliberate indifference"; delays in prescribed surgery could support administrators' liability); Al-Jundi v. Mancusi, 926 F.2d 235, 239–40 (2d Cir. 1991) (Superintendent's failure to plan for medical care after violent suppression of prison disturbance would constitute deliberate indifference); Meade v. Grubbs, 841 F.2d at 1531 (the failure of the state health commissioner to carry out statutory duties could be deliberate indifference); Scott v. Garcia, 370 F. Supp. 2d 1056, 1068–69 (S.D.Cal. 2005) (classification committee could be held liable for failure to act on medical direction to transfer prisoner with severe stomach and digestive problems to a prison with hospital facilities); Brown v. Coughlin, 758 F. Supp. 876, 889 (S.D.N.Y. 1991) (Commissioner and Superintendent have personal duties to ensure adequate medical services).

[337]Davis v. Carter, 452 F.3d 686, 691–94 (7th Cir. 2006) (holding plaintiff's deliberate indifference claim of a municipal policy of

private corporations that provide medical care are treated like suits against municipalities: the prisoner must show that the injury was caused by a policy of the corporation.[338]

(The rule may be different in a state law malpractice or negligence suit.[339]) This option is available only against medical providers that contract with state or local governments; *Bivens* suits may not be brought against corporations that

---

inordinate delay in providing methadone treatment was supported by evidence of an absence of policies and procedures to ensure timely treatment); Gibson v. County of Washoe, Nev., 290 F.3d 1175, 1190–91 (9th Cir. 2002) (holding that county policymakers could be held liable for policy that delayed psychiatric treatment for new admissions with urgent needs); Lawson v. Dallas County, 286 F.3d 257, 263 (5th Cir. 2002) (neglect of paraplegic prisoner resulting from policies restricting nurses' ability to provide care, including failure to assess paraplegics on admission, restrictions on dressing changes, ban on foam mattresses, ban on nurses' entering prisoners' cells); Colle v. Brazos County, Tex., 981 F.2d 237, 245 (5th Cir. 1993) (inadequate monitoring, lack of arrangements for transfers to medical facilities); Cabrales v. County of Los Angeles, 864 F.2d 1454, 1460–61 (9th Cir. 1988) (inadequate staffing), *vacated*, 490 U.S. 1087 (1989), *reinstated*, 886 F.2d 235 (9th Cir. 1989); Anderson v. City of Atlanta, 778 F.2d at 685–89 (inadequate staffing); Ancata v. Prison Health Services, Inc., 769 F.2d 700, 705–06 (11th Cir. 1985) (policy of limited funding and requiring court orders for certain medical treatment); Garcia v. Salt Lake County, 768 F.2d 303, 307–08 (10th Cir. 1985) (inadequate staffing and policy of admitting unconscious persons to jail); Layman v. Alexander, 343 F. Supp. 2d 483, 489 (W.D.N.C. 2004) (Sheriff's Department could be held liable for lack of training for responding to prisoner injuries and medical problems, but not for staff's failure to follow policies that did exist for monitoring unconscious prisoners or those with head injuries); Nelson v. Prison Health Services, Inc., 991 F. Supp. 1452, 1465 (M.D.Fla. 1997) (court monitor's reports finding "pervasive and deep seated failures" including staff's "unwillingness to respond to inmates' requests for treatment" could support liability of county as well as medical provider).

If local governments establish adequate procedures for providing medical care to prisoners, they can't be held liable based on isolated failures of their employees to follow them. Holmes v. Sheahan, 930 F.2d 1196, 1201–02 (7th Cir. 1991); Bryant v. Maffucci, 923 F.2d 979, 986 (2d Cir. 1991).

Municipal liability in civil rights actions requires proof that the violation was caused by a municipal policy. This requirement is discussed in Ch. 8, § B.4.b.

[338]Johnson v. Karnes, 398 F.3d 868, 877 (6th Cir. 2005); Natale v. Camden County Correctional Facility, 318 F.3d 575, 583–85 (3d Cir. 2003) (policy to see all new admissions within 72 hours, with no provision for prisoners with immediate medication needs, supported a deliberate indifference claim against corporate provider); Jackson v. Illinois Medi-Car, Inc., 300 F.3d 760, 766 (7th Cir. 2002); Buckner v. Toro, 116 F.3d 450, 452 (11th Cir. 1997); Howell v. Evans, 922 F.2d 712, 723–25 (11th Cir.), *vacated as settled*, 931 F.2d 711 (11th Cir. 1991); Engelleiter v. Brevard County Sheriff's Dep't, 290 F. Supp. 2d 1300, 1313–14 (M.D.Fla. 2003) (prisoner who received inadequate diabetes care could not recover against corporation where corporation's policies for diabetic treatment were acceptable); Goodnow v. Palm, 264 F. Supp. 2d 125, 129–30 (D.Vt. 2003) (corporation's claim that seven-month delay in treating dental pain resulted from "administrative back-logs and patient prioritization" could support a finding of corporate liability); Wall v. Dion, 257 F. Supp. 2d 316, 319 (D.Me. 2003) (allegation that plaintiff was denied dental care despite

several requests sufficiently alleged a policy); Kruger v. Jenne, 164 F. Supp. 2d 1330, 1331 (S.D.Fla. 2000) (allegation that private provider denied care as a result of a policy to refuse and/or delay treatment to save money stated a deliberate indifference claim against corporation); Edwards v. Alabama Dep't of Corrections, 81 F. Supp. 2d 1242, 1254–55 (M.D. Ala. 2000) (CMS is to "be treated as a municipality for the purposes of the plaintiffs' § 1983 claims"; "In order to prove that CMS should be liable, the plaintiffs would have to demonstrate that CMS itself directly caused the violation of their constitutional rights through their adoption of some official policy or practice." (citations omitted)); Blumel v. Mylander, 954 F. Supp. 1547, 1556 (M.D.Fla. 1997) (Corrections Corporation of America could be held liable to a person held in a CCA jail without a probable cause hearing pursuant to a company policy not to release anyone without a judge's order to do so); Nelson v. Prison Health Services, Inc., 991 F. Supp. 1452, 1465 (M.D.Fla. 1997) (court monitor's reports finding "pervasive and deep seated failures" including staff's "unwillingness to respond to inmates' requests for treatment" could support liability of county as well as medical provider); Hartman v. Correctional Medical Services, Inc., 960 F. Supp. 1577, 1582–83 (M.D.Fla. 1996) (permitting a person with only a master's degree and no professional licenses to have authority over mental health referrals and suicide precautions supported claim of a policy of deliberate indifference by medical provider); McIlwain v. Prince William Hospital, 774 F. Supp. 986, 989–90 (E.D.Va. 1991); Moody v. Kearney, 380 F. Supp. 2d 393, 398 (D.Del. 2005); Miller v. Correctional Medical Systems, Inc., 802 F. Supp. 1126, 1132 (D.Del. 1992); *see* Green v. First Correctional Medical, 430 F. Supp. 2d 383, 386–87 (D.Del. 2006) (allegation that plaintiff's hand was fractured, corporation employees misplaced his files, denied diagnosing his fracture, left him without pain medication, and tried to bargain with him to drop his grievance sufficiently suggested a policy to defeat a motion to dismiss). *Contra*, Segler v. Clark County, 142 F. Supp. 2d 1264, 1269 (D.Nev. 2001) (holding private provider is not a municipality and should not be treated like one; plaintiff need not show a corporate policy and may recover punitive damages, which are not available against municipalities). *See* Ch. 8, § B.1.c, concerning corporate liability under § 1983.

One court has held that memos from the correction department expressing concern about a private contractor's failure to provide vital medication promptly, the difficulties of getting appointments with primary physicians and specialist referrals, and the failure adequately to maintain medical records could support a finding of deliberate indifference if the contractor failed to take affirmative steps to correct those problems. Jackson v. Fauver, 334 F. Supp. 2d 706, 739 (D.N.J. 2004).

[339]*See* Jackson v. Fauver, 334 F. Supp. 2d 697, 744 (D.N.J. 2004) (corporation providing medical care can be sued under state law despite its claim that medical personnel were independent contractors). Some courts have held that prisoners may sue as "third-party beneficiaries" of contracts between prisons or jails and private medical providers. *See* Ch. 8, § B.1.c, nn.42–44.

contract with federal agencies.[340] If the injury was caused by the deliberate indifference of individual employees of the corporation, those employees must be sued individually, like employees of a state, county, or city.[341]

b. Remedies for Deliberate Indifference Under the deliberate indifference standard, you may seek either an injunction requiring prison officials to give you proper medical care in the future,[342] or damages for their past failure to provide proper care,[343] or both. The two don't always go together. A court may find that you are not entitled to damages for what happened in the past, but you may still be entitled to an injunction to avoid harm in the future.[344]

Conversely, if you have received adequate care (or gotten well without it) by the time the court decides the case, you may not need an injunction, but you can still receive damages for any pain and suffering you experienced while waiting to receive proper treatment.[345]

2. Serious Medical Needs

Under the Constitution, prison officials need provide care only for "serious medical needs."[346] Many courts have held that a serious medical need is "one that has been diagnosed by a physician as mandating treatment or one that is so obvious that even a lay person would easily recognize the necessity of a doctor's attention."[347] However, the Eighth Amendment prohibits the "unnecessary and wanton infliction of pain,"[348] and many decisions—especially recent ones—have emphasized pain in determining what needs are serious.[349] Recent decisions have also emphasized whether a

---

[340]Correctional Services Corporation v. Malesko, 534 U.S. 61, 60–71, 122 S. Ct. 515 (2002); *see* Ch. 8, § B.2.d.

[341]*See* Natale v. Camden County Correctional Facility, 318 F.3d 575, 582–83 (3d Cir. 2003) (employees of private provider who did not act on diabetic's need for insulin could be found deliberately indifferent); Hicks v. Frey, 992 F.2d 1450, 1456–58 (6th Cir. 1993) (upholding judgment against employee and dismissal of claim against corporation). Some recent decisions have limited suits against employees of federal medical contractors. *See* Ch. 8, §§ B.1.c and B.2.d, for a discussion of acting under "color of law" and the liability of corporations and their employees for state or local and federal prisoners respectively.

[342]*See, e.g.,* Farnam v. Walker, 593 F. Supp. 2d 1000, 1011–19 (C.D.Ill. 2009) (requiring specialist care for cystic fibrosis); Rosado v. Alameida, 349 F. Supp. 2d 1340 (S.D.Cal. 2004) (enjoining prison officials to arrange plaintiff's evaluation for a liver transplant); Arnold on behalf of H.B. v. Lewis, 803 F. Supp. 246, 258–57 (D. Ariz. 1992); Yarbaugh v. Roach, 736 F. Supp. 318, 320 (D.D.C. 1990); Phillips v. Michigan Dep't of Corrections, 731 F. Supp. 792, 800–01 (W.D.Mich. 1990), *aff'd*, 932 F.2d 969 (6th Cir. 1991); *see also* Ch. 8, § O.2, concerning injunctions.

Courts have also granted injunctions in class actions requiring changes in the medical care system. *See, e.g.,* Gates v. Cook, 376 F.3d 323, 342–43 (5th Cir. 2004); Todaro v. Ward, 565 F.2d 48, 52 (2d Cir. 1977); Ginest v. Board of County Commissioners of Carbon County, 333 F. Supp. 2d 1190, 1209–10 (D.Wyo. 2004); Coleman v. Wilson, 912 F. Supp. 1282, 1304–04 (E.D.Cal. 1995); Madrid v. Gomez, 889 F. Supp. 1146, 129 (N.D.Cal. 1995). Prisoners may also seek injunctions against conditions that may cause illness in the future, such as exposure to infectious diseases or unsafe drinking water. Helling v. McKinney, 509 U.S. 25, 113 S. Ct. 2475 (1993). Such conditions are discussed further in § G.3.b of this chapter.

[343]*See, e.g.,* Coleman v. Rahija, 114 F.3d 778, 787 (8th Cir. 1997); Consolo v. George, 58 F.3d 791, 795 (1st Cir. 1995); Aswegan v. Bruhl, 965 F.2d 676, 677 (8th Cir. 1992); Hill v. Marshall, 962 F.2d 1209, 1215–17 (6th Cir. 1992); Leach v. Shelby County Sheriff, 891 F.2d 1241 (6th Cir. 1989); Mandel v. Doe, 888 F.2d 783 (11th Cir. 1989); Williams v. Patel, 104 F. Supp. 2d 984, 996 (C.D.Ill. 2000). Other cases involving damage awards are cited throughout the following sections on medical care.

[344]Koehl v. Dalsheim, 85 F.3d 86, 89 (2d Cir. 1996) (damage claim was properly dismissed against Superintendent, but injunctive claim should proceed because Superintendent had "overall responsibility to ensure that prisoners' basic needs were met"); Johnson v. Bowers, 884 F.2d 1053, 1056 (8th Cir. 1989); Crooks v.

Nix, 872 F.2d 800, 804–05 (8th Cir. 1989) (damage claim properly dismissed, but court should review current medical records before ruling on injunctive claim); *compare* Lee v. McManus, 543 F. Supp. 386, 391–93 (D.Kan. 1982) (granting injunction to paraplegic to avoid further medical neglect) *with* Lee v. McManus, 589 F. Supp. 633, 638–41 (D.Kan. 1984) (denying damages based on various defenses).

[345]Boretti v. Wiscomb, 930 F.2d 1150, 1154–55 (6th Cir. 1991) (prisoner could get damages for failure to treat his wound even though it had healed); Hathaway v. Coughlin, 841 F.2d 48 (2d Cir. 1988) (claim for delay in surgery should not have been dismissed after the surgery was performed); H.C. by Hewett v. Jarrard, 786 F.2d 1080, 1083, 1087 (11th Cir. 1986) (damages awarded for three-day denial of medical care with no permanent injury resulting); Robinson v. Moreland, 655 F.2d 887, 890 (8th Cir. 1981); West v. Keve, 571 F.2d 158 (3d Cir. 1978) (similar to *Hathaway*); Isaac v. Jones, 529 F. Supp. 175, 180 (N.D.Ill. 1981).

[346]Estelle v. Gamble, 429 U.S. 97, 104, 97 S. Ct. 285 (1976).

The seriousness of mental health needs is discussed in § F.4.a of this chapter, nn.456–462; *see also* cases cited in nn.489–492 concerning gender identity disorder, also called transsexualism.

[347]Brown v. Johnson, 387 F.3d 1344, 1351 (11th Cir. 2004); *accord,* Hayes v. Snyder, 546 F.3d 516, 522 (7th Cir. 2008); Johnson v. Busbee, 953 F.2d 349, 351 (8th Cir. 1991); Gaudreault v. Municipality of Salem, Mass., 923 F.2d 203, 208 (1st Cir. 1990); Monmouth County Correctional Institution Inmates v. Lanzaro, 834 F.2d 326, 347 (3d Cir. 1987); Ramos v. Lamm, 639 F.2d 559, 575 (10th Cir. 1980) and cases cited; Maynard v. New Jersey, 719 F. Supp. 292, 295 (D.N.J. 1989); Henderson v. Harris, 672 F. Supp. 1054, 1056, 1059 (N.D.Ill. 1987) (hemorrhoids); *see also* McGuckin v. Smith, 974 F.2d 1050, 1059–60 (9th Cir. 1992) ("the existence of an injury that a reasonable doctor or patient would find important and worthy of comment or treatment" supports a finding of seriousness); Davis v. Jones, 936 F.2d 971, 972 (7th Cir. 1991) (police are obligated to obtain medical care if an injury "reasonably appears to be serious"), *rehearing denied*, 946 F.2d 538 (7th Cir. 1991).

[348]Estelle v. Gamble, 429 U.S. at 104.

[349]Hayes v. Snyder, 546 F.3d 516, 523 (7th Cir. 2008) (holding that objective evidence of pain is not necessary; self-reporting may be the only evidence); Blackmore v. Kalamazoo County, 390 F.3d 890, 899–900 (6th Cir. 2004) (the plaintiff had an

medical condition disables the prisoner or interferes with daily activities in assessing seriousness.[350] A recent Second Circuit decision sums up all these factors, stating that the seriousness of a medical need is determined by factors including but not limited to "(1) whether a reasonable doctor or patient would perceive the medical need in question as 'important and worthy of comment or treatment,' (2) whether the medical condition significantly affects daily activities, and (3) 'the existence of chronic and substantial pain.'"[351]

"Eighth Amendment right to avoid the pain from the officers' deliberate indifference"; two-day delay in treating appendicitis was serious even though the appendix did not rupture); Spruill v. Gillis, 372 F.3d 218, 236 (3d Cir. 2004) (holding allegation of back condition causing pain so serious it has caused plaintiff to fall down sufficiently pled a serious need); Farrow v. West, 320 F.3d 1235, 1244–45 (11th Cir. 2003) (holding that pain, bleeding and swollen gums, and teeth slicing into gums of prisoner who needed dentures helped show serious medical need; "life long handicap or permanent loss" not required on these facts); Gutierrez v. Peters, 111 F.3d 1364, 1371 (7th Cir. 1997) ("delays in treating painful medical conditions that are not life-threatening can support Eighth Amendment claims"; infected pilonidal cyst); Cooper v. Casey, 97 F.3d 914, 916–17 (7th Cir. 1996) (subjective complaints of pain from beating verified by doctor's prescription of pain medication 48 hours later); McGuckin v. Smith, 974 F.2d 1050, 1060 (9th Cir. 1992) ("chronic and substantial pain"); Boretti v. Wiscomb, 930 F.2d 1150, 1154–55 (6th Cir. 1991) (needless pain even without permanent injury); Moreland v. Wharton, 899 F.2d 1168, 1170 (11th Cir. 1989) ("significant and uncomfortable health problem"); Johnson-El v. Schoemehl, 878 F.2d 1043, 1055 (8th Cir. 1989) (condition that is "medically serious or painful in nature"); Washington v. Dugger, 860 F.2d 1018, 1021 (11th Cir. 1988) (denial of treatments that "eliminated pain and suffering at least temporarily"); West v. Keve, 571 F.2d 158, 161–62 (3d Cir. 1978) (pain while awaiting a delayed operation); Lavender v. Lampert, 242 F. Supp. 2d 821, 845 (D.Or. 2002) ("'the existence of chronic and substantial pain' itself demonstrates a 'serious' medical need"); Kaminsky v. Rosenblum, 737 F. Supp. 1309, 1319 (S.D.N.Y. 1990) ("unnecessary pain and suffering"), appeal dismissed, 929 F.2d 922 (2d Cir. 1991); Bouchard v. Magnusson, 715 F. Supp. 1146, 1148 (D.Me. 1989); Young v. Harris, 509 F. Supp. 1111, 1113 (S.D.N.Y. 1981) (plaintiff could not walk without "substantial difficulty and discomfort"); see Case v. Bixler, 518 F. Supp. 1277, 1280 (S.D.Ohio 1981) (boil "in full flower" might be serious); see also McElligott v. Foley, 182 F.3d 1248, 1256–57 (11th Cir. 1999) (holding failure to treat severe pain could constitute deliberate indifference). But see Wilson v. Franchesci, 735 F. Supp. 395, 398 (M.D.Fla. 1990) (itching is not a serious medical need).

[350]Foelker v. Outagamie County, 394 F.3d 510, 513 (7th Cir. 2005) (prisoner suffering from acute delirium resulting from drug withdrawal, hallucinating, and defecating on the floor, had a serious medical need even though he was not in "distress"); Miller v. King, 384 F.3d 1248, 1261 (11th Cir. 2004) (holding paraplegia with incontinence is a serious medical need), vacated and superseded on other grounds, 449 F.3d 1149 (11th Cir. 2006); McBride v. Deer, 240 F.3d 1287, 1290–91 (10th Cir. 2001) (loss of full function in leg constituted "a lifelong handicap or a permanent loss"); Koehl v. Dalsheim, 85 F.3d 86, 88 (2d Cir. 1996) (loss of vision may not be "pain" but it is "suffering"); McGuckin v. Smith, 974 F.2d at 1050, 1060 (9th Cir. 1992) (condition that "significantly affects an individual's daily activities" is actionable); Johnson v. Bowers, 884 F.2d 1053, 1056 (8th Cir. 1989) (prison must treat a "substantial disability"); Monmouth County Correctional Institution Inmates v. Lanzaro, 834 F.2d 326, 347 (3d Cir. 1987) (medical need is serious if it imposes a "life-long handicap or permanent loss"); Lavender v. Lampert, 242 F. Supp. 2d 821, 849 (D.Or. 2002) ("To unnecessarily deny the use of a wheelchair to someone who obviously has an

injury, and who lacks mobility without it, would constitute deliberate indifference to a serious medical need."); Baker v. Blanchette, 186 F. Supp. 2d 100, 103 (D.Conn. 2001) (unrepaired colostomy was a serious need in part because it "prevented [plaintiff] from eliminating waste in a normal manner," required wearing a bag that emitted a foul odor, and required significant maintenance; even if they don't cause pain, these consequences cause suffering); Kenney v. Hawaii, 109 F. Supp. 2d 1271, 1279 (D.Haw. 2000) (a neurological disorder causing the plaintiff to shake violently "would support a claim that his daily activities would be affected and that his medical needs were serious"); Taylor v. Plousis, 101 F. Supp. 2d 255, 262 (D.N.J. 2000) ("a medical condition which threatens a plaintiff's ability to walk, even on a non-permanent basis, falls within the ambit of a 'serious medical need'"; plaintiff, a double amputee whose leg prosthesis was in disrepair, was denied a new one); Schmidt v. Odell, 64 F. Supp. 2d 1014, 1030 (D.Kan. 1999) (need of double amputee for a wheelchair was a serious medical need); Miller v. Michigan Dep't of Corrections, 986 F. Supp. 1073, 1080 (W.D.Mich. 1997) (bowel and bladder incontinence were serious); Hall v. Artuz, 954 F. Supp. 90, 94 (S.D.N.Y. 1997) (loss of function in leg); Kaufman v. Carter, 952 F. Supp. 520, 527 (W.D.Mich. 1996) (inability to walk, even temporarily); Pugliese v. Cuomo, 911 F. Supp. 58 (N.D.N.Y. 1996) (denial of physical therapy for pre-existing injury held serious); Tillery v. Owens, 719 F. Supp. 1256, 1286 (W.D.Pa. 1989) (citing definition of "serious" mental illness as one "that has caused significant disruption in an inmate's everyday life and which prevents his functioning in the general population without disturbing or endangering others or himself"), aff'd, 907 F.2d 418 (3d Cir. 1990); Young v. Harris, 509 F. Supp. 1111, 1113–14 (S.D.N.Y. 1981) (failure to provide leg brace was actionable). Other issues concerning prisoners with disabilities are addressed in § F.4.h of this chapter.

[351]Brock v. Wright, 315 F.3d 158, 162 (2d Cir. 2003) (citations omitted); accord, Suarez v. Keiser, 338 F. Supp. 2d 442, 444 (W.D.N.Y. 2004); see also Carnell v. Grimm, 872 F. Supp. 746, 755 (D.Haw. 1994), appeal dismissed in part, aff'd in part, 74 F.3d 977 (9th Cir. 1996).

The Second Circuit had earlier said that a serious medical need is "a condition of urgency, one that may produce death, degeneration, or extreme pain." Hathaway v. Coughlin, 37 F.3d 63, 66 (2d Cir. 1994) (quoting Nance v. Kelly, 912 F.2d 605, 607 (2d Cir.1990) (Pratt, J., dissenting)). In Brock, however, the court explicitly rejected the notion that "only 'extreme pain' or a degenerative condition would suffice to meet the legal standard," since "'the Eighth Amendment forbids not only deprivations of medical care that produce physical torture and lingering death, but also less serious denials which cause or perpetuate pain.'" Brock, 315 F.3d at 162. The court did repeat the "death, degeneration, or extreme pain" formula in a later case, see Johnson v. Wright, 412 F.3d 398, 403 (2d Cir. 2005), but did so in passing and did not purport to overrule Brock.

One federal appeals court has recently held that the seriousness of a medical need is not determined exclusively on the symptoms presented when the prisoner comes in contact with a prison employee, but on the "alleged harm to the prisoner"; the court makes reference to the prisoner's "selecting what harm to claim."[352] We are not too sure what this means, and suggest that in your complaint or other legal documents you always state (*briefly*) your whole medical complaint, from initial symptoms or history to your condition at the time you are preparing the document.

In cases where you are not completely denied treatment, but experience a temporary delay or interruption of treatment, the court may focus on the seriousness of the particular delay or interruption, "rather than the severity of the prisoner's underlying medical condition, considered in the abstract."[353] Thus, HIV is clearly a serious condition, but in a case where a prisoner had his HIV medication interrupted twice for several days at a time, which could theoretically have caused him harm, the court held that the prisoner did not demonstrate a serious medical need where in fact there were no adverse effects and no evidence of increased risk.[354] Some courts have said that a showing of "substantial harm" is necessary for delay in treatment to be considered serious, but pain and suffering resulting from the delay can satisfy that requirement.[355]

One court has stated, "Evidence of recent traumatic injury . . . has generally been sufficient to demonstrate a serious medical need."[356] However, courts have found some traumatic injuries too minor to be serious,[357] though in some such cases the plaintiff received some treatment, which the court seemed to consider adequate.[358]

Drug or alcohol withdrawal is a serious medical need.[359] Other complaints which courts have found serious include severe chest pain,[360] HIV,[361] hepatitis,[362] tuberculosis,[363] dental pain and loss of teeth,[364] asthma,[365] diabetes and its

---

[352]Mata v. Saiz, 427 F.3d 745, 753 (10th Cir. 2005); *accord*, Martinez v. Beggs, 563 F.3d 1082, 1088 (10th Cir. 2009), *cert. denied*, 130 S. Ct. 259 (2009).

[353]Kikumura v. Osagie, 461 F.3d 1269, 1291, 1296 (10th Cir. 2006) (holding delay must be shown to have caused "substantial harm," including pain suffered while awaiting treatment; two to three and a half hours delay in treating painful condition stated a claim); Spann v. Roper, 453 F.3d 1007, 1008–09 (8th Cir. 2006) (holding a jury could find a three-hour delay in addressing a medication overdose was objectively sufficiently serious, since immediate attention would have enabled medical staff to act to prevent the medication from becoming completely absorbed); Bozeman v. Orum, 422 F.3d 1265, 1273 (11th Cir. 2005) (noting that the tolerable delay for a prisoner known to be unconscious from asphyxiation is measured in minutes); Hill v. DeKalb Regional Youth Detention Center, 40 F.3d 1176, 1188 (11th Cir. 1994) (holding blood in prisoner's underwear was not a serious medical need inconsistent with four-hour delay in getting him to a hospital); Beyerbach v. Sears, 49 F.3d 1324, 1326 (8th Cir. 1995) (broken hand can be serious, but delay of two or three hours in treating it was not).

[354]Smith v. Carpenter, 316 F.3d 178, 186–89 (2d Cir. 2003). The court did warn that a showing of increased risk, even without presently detectable symptoms, might establish a serious medical need.

[355]Kikumura v. Osagie, 461 F.3d 1292, 1296 (10th Cir. 2006); Sealock v. Colorado, 218 F.3d 1205, 1210 & n.5 (10th Cir. 2000).

[356]Brown v. Hughes, 894 F.2d 1533, 1538 n.4 (11th Cir. 1990); *see* Murphy v. Walker, 51 F.3d 714, 719 (7th Cir. 1995) ("Any injury to the head unless obviously superficial should ordinarily be considered serious and merits attention until properly diagnosed as to severity."); Jones-Bey v. Conley, 144 F. Supp. 2d 1035, 1043 (N.D.Ind. 2000) (bruises and abrasions, bloody wrists, claim of permanent bone and nerve damage); Hill v. Algor, 85 F. Supp. 2d 391, 410 (D.N.J. 2000) (gash in head requiring sutures); Smallwood v. Renfro, 708 F. Supp. 182, 187 (N.D.Ill. 1989) (cut lip might be serious).

[357]Davis v. Reilly, 324 F. Supp. 2d 361, 368 (E.D.N.Y. 2004) (sprained back and neck, pain in testicle); Sonds v. St. Barnabas Hosp. Correctional Health Services, 151 F. Supp. 2d 303, 311 (S.D.N.Y. 2001) (bleeding finger); Shelton v. Angelone, 148 F. Supp. 2d 670, 679 (W.D.Va. 2001) (small cuts on the plaintiff's wrist and "signature marks" from a stun gun).

[358]Gaudreault v. Municipality of Salem, Mass., 923 F.2d 203, 208 (1st Cir. 1990); Williams-El v. Johnson, 872 F.2d 224, 230–31 (8th Cir. 1989); Wesson v. Oglesby, 910 F.2d 278, 284 (5th Cir. 1990); Martin v. Gentile, 849 F.2d 863, 871 (4th Cir. 1988) (cut over eye and piece of glass in hand were not so serious that a 14-hour delay in treating them was unconstitutional).

[359]*See* § F.4.g of this chapter concerning drug dependency treatment.

[360]Mata v. Saiz, 427 F.3d 745, 754 (10th Cir. 2005).

[361]Brown v. Johnson, 387 F.3d 1344, 1351 (11th Cir. 2004).

[362]Brown v. Johnson, 387 F.3d 1344, 1351 (11th Cir. 2004); Christy v. Robinson, 216 F. Supp. 2d 398, 413 (D.N.J. 2002).

[363]Maldonado v. Terhune, 28 F. Supp. 2d 284, 290 (D.N.J. 1998) ("As a general rule, it is not required that latent health problems blossom into full fledged disease before being considered serious.").

[364]*See* § F.4.c of this chapter concerning dental care.

[365]Board v. Farnham, 394 F.3d 469, 484 (7th Cir. 2005) (seriousness depends on the severity of the attacks). *But see* Oliver v. Dees, 77 F.3d 156, 160 (7th Cir. 1996) ("mild" asthma was not serious).

complications,[366] Crohn's disease,[367] severe arthritis,[368] osteomyelitis,[369] neurological disorders,[370] an unrepaired colostomy,[371] serious back pain,[372] a dislocated shoulder,[373] a painful calcium overgrowth in the wrist,[374] a painful growth on the ankle,[375] keloid scars causing chronic pain,[376] serious ear infection,[377] the need for post-surgical care,[378] the effects of pepper spray,[379] exposure of prisoners with respiratory problems to environmental tobacco smoke,[380] hemorrhoids

requiring surgery,[381] an infected pilonidal cyst,[382] ulcers,[383] seizure disorders,[384] complications of pregnancy,[385] rape,[386] and many mental illnesses including gender identity disorder.[387] This is of course a very incomplete list.[388]

Courts have dismissed many minor complaints—or complaints they deemed to be minor—as not serious.[389] However, courts have also recognized that "there can be a serious cumulative effect from the repeated denial of care with regard to even minor needs."[390] Thus, even a bad headache might not be serious by itself, but if you have them

[366]Lolli v. County of Orange, 351 F.3d 410, 420 (9th Cir. 2003) ("a constitutional violation may take place when the government does not respond to the legitimate medical needs of a detainee whom it has reason to believe is diabetic"); Natale v. Camden County Correctional Facility, 318 F.3d 575, 420 (3d Cir. 2003); Carrion v. Wilkinson, 309 F. Supp. 2d 1007, 1014 (N.D.Ohio 2004) ("a diabetic inmate's needs to control his diet are sufficient medical needs for purposes of the Eighth Amendment analysis"); Engelleiter v. Brevard County Sheriff's Dep't, 290 F. Supp. 2d 1300, 1307 (M.D.Fla. 2003); see Rouse v. Plantier,182 F.3d 192, 198–99 (3d Cir. 1999) (holding treatment of diabetics must be assessed in terms of the level of care that different individuals require). In *Ruffin v. Deperio*, 97 F. Supp. 2d 346, 351–52 (W.D.N.Y. 2000), the court held that pain and swelling to the plaintiff's foot was a serious medical need, in part because his diabetes could make his injury more severe than to a person without the disease (this plaintiff ultimately had to have part of his foot, and then part of his leg, amputated).

[367]Woulard v. Food Service, 294 F. Supp. 2d 596, 604 (D.Del. 2003).

[368]Christy v. Robinson, 216 F. Supp. 2d 398, 413 (D.N.J. 2002); Baumann v. Walsh, 36 F. Supp. 2d 508, 511 (N.D.N.Y. 1999); Finley v. Trent, 955 F. Supp. 642, 646 (N.D.W.Va. 1997).

[369]Gil v. Vogilano, 131 F. Supp. 2d 486, 492 (S.D.N.Y. 2001).

[370]Kenney v. Paderes, 217 F. Supp. 2d 1095, 1099 (D.Haw. 2002) (condition causing "present, detectable, and observable" tremors).

[371]Baker v. Blanchette, 186 F. Supp. 2d 100, 103 (D.Conn. 2001).

[372]Joyner v. Greiner, 195 F. Supp. 2d 500, 504 (S.D.N.Y. 2002); Palermo v. Correctional Medical Services, Inc., 133 F. Supp. 2d 1348, 1361 (S.D.Fla. 2001) (pain caused by a ruptured spinal disk which limited mobility); Dobbin v. Artuz, 143 F. Supp. 292, 302 (S.D.N.Y. 2001) ("severe and near constant pain").

[373]Higgins v. Correctional Medical Services of Ill., 178 F.3d 508, 511 (7th Cir. 1999); Petrichko v. Kurtz, 117 F. Supp. 2d 467, 470–71 (E.D.Pa. 2000).

[374]Adams v. DeTella, 994 F. Supp. 947, 949 (N.D.Ill. 1998).

[375]Dellairo v. Garland, 222 F. Supp. 2d 86, 91 (D.Me. 2002).

[376]Brock v. Wright, 315 F.d 158, 163 (2d Cir. 2003).

[377]Zentmyer v. Kendall County, Ill., 220 F.3d 805, 810 (7th Cir. 2000); Lewis v. Angelone, 926 F. Supp. 69, 73 (W.D.Va. 1996).

[378]Morales Feliciano v. Calderon Sierra, 300 F. Supp. 2d 321, 341 (D.P.R. 2004) ("the failure to provide appropriate post surgical care" implicates Eighth Amendment rights).

[379]Clement v. Gomez, 298 F.3d 898, 904 (9th Cir. 2002).

[380]Johnson v. Pearson, 316 F. Supp. 2d 307, 319 (E.D.Va. 2004) (prisoner with a respiratory condition, double-celled with a habitual smoker of cigars, sufficiently alleged a serious medical need based on mild headaches, difficulty breathing, eye irritation, runny nose, dizziness, and occasional stomach cramping).

[381]Jones v. Natesha, 151 F. Supp. 2d 938, 944 (N.D.Ill. 2001).

[382]Gutierrez v. Peters, 111 F.3d 1364, 1371 (7th Cir. 1997).

[383]Martin v. DeBruyn, 880 F. Supp. 610, 614 (N.D.Ind. 1995).

[384]Hudson v. McHugh, 148 F.3d 859, 864 (7th Cir. 1998).

[385]Pool v. Sebastian County, Ark., 418 F.3d 934, 945 (8th Cir. 2005) (bleeding, passing blood clots, extreme pain from cramping); Coleman v. Rahija, 114 F.3d 778, 785 (8th Cir. 1997) (preterm labor); see § F.4.f. of this chapter concerning pregnancy.

[386]Carnell v. Grimm, 872 F. Supp. 746, 756 (D.Haw. 1994), *appeal dismissed in part, aff'd in part*, 74 F.3d 977 (9th Cir. 1996).

[387]See § F.4.a. of this chapter.

[388]Compare Harris v. Murray, 761 F. Supp. 409, 414 (E.D.Va. 1990) (hair loss is not serious) with Johnson-El v. District of Columbia, 579 A.2d 163, 167–69 (D.C. 1990) (hair loss is serious; dermatological problem of scalp cited).

[389]Lomholt v. Holder, 287 F.3d 683, 684 (8th Cir. 2002) (sore feet from being kept barefoot in segregation was not serious); Qader v. New York, 396 F. Supp. 2d 466, 470 (S.D.N.Y. 2005) (dizziness and a "terrible headache" are not serious medical needs); Williams v. First Correctional Medical, 377 F. Supp. 2d 473, 476 (D.Del. 2005) (small hernia, which has resulted in no serious symptoms and has not affected plaintiff's daily activities, was not serious); Gerber v. Sweeney, 292 F. Supp. 2d 700, 708 (E.D.Pa. 2003) (failure to take blood pressure weekly, especially where hypertension was controlled by medication and plaintiff was on a special diet, did not implicate a serious need); Johnson v. Medford, 208 F. Supp. 2d 590, 592 (W.D.N.C. 2002) (fallen arches and flat feet); Shelton v. Angelone, 183 F. Supp. 2d 830, 840 (W.D.Va. 2002) (sensitivity to fluorescent cell lighting); Williams v. Elyea, 163 F. Supp. 2d 992, 998 (N.D.Ill. 2001) (mild mouth pain for which defendants did not provide medication); Palermo v. Correctional Medical Services, Inc., 133 F. Supp. 2d 1348, 1361 (S.D.Fla. 2001) (foot pain); Hall v. Conklin, 966 F. Supp. 546, 548 (W.D.Mich. 1996) (ingrown toenail); Ware v. Fairman, 884 F. Supp. 1201, 1206 (N.D.Ill. 1995) (delay in treating flu and refusal to provide medication for a rash and acne).

In some cases, courts have clearly applied the wrong standard in determining whether a need is serious. Thus, one court dismissed claims of tinnitus; allergies causing headaches, earaches, sinus congestion, soreness in throat and eyes, tearing, nasal infections, and breathing problems; and a need for contact lenses because the plaintiff's broken nose made wearing glasses painful, on the ground that none of these ailments caused "death, degeneration, or extreme pain." Davidson v. Scully, 155 F. Supp. 2d 77, 86 (S.D.N.Y. 2001). As noted above, in § F.2, that definition of serious medical need is not accurate.

[390]Jones v. Evans, 544 F. Supp. 769, 775 n.4 (N.D.Ga. 1982).

continually, we think you have a serious medical need.[391] A need may be serious even if prison officials have labelled care for it "elective"[392] or omitted it from their "serious needs list."[393]

Some courts have held that the seriousness of a medical need must be shown by "verifying medical evidence," at least where the seriousness of the injury is not apparent to a lay person.[394] One federal court has held that if the seriousness of a medical need is not apparent to a lay person, the plaintiff must submit *expert* medical evidence—an impossible task for most *pro se* litigants.[395] Other courts, however, have accepted other forms of evidence to meet this requirement.[396]

In drafting a complaint or other court papers, you should address the issue of "seriousness" by being very specific about the effects of the denial of medical care: how painful it is, whether its symptoms are visible, to what extent it interferes with your normal activities, how long you have had it, whether it is getting worse, etc.[397] Doing so will help make it clear to the court whether the seriousness of your condition is obvious to a lay person. If it is not obvious, and you are not in a position to provide "verifying medical evidence" through an expert or otherwise, you may also wish to ask the court to appoint a medical expert witness under Rule 706, Fed.R.Evid. Experts have been appointed in several prison medical cases, though most such requests are denied.[398]

3. The Medical Care System

In order to provide adequate medical care, prison officials must have an adequate system for identifying prisoners with medical needs and making sure that they are diagnosed and treated. "[S]ystemic deficiencies in staffing, facilities, or procedures [which] make unnecessary suffering inevitable" constitute deliberate indifference.[399] Sheer disorganization and dysfunction in a medical program can amount to deliberate indifference if it prevents prisoners from receiving necessary care.[400] In this connection, several courts have

---

[391]*See* Hudak v. Miller, 28 F. Supp. 2d 827, 830 (S.D.N.Y. 1998) (plaintiff complained of chronic headaches repeatedly for many months at one prison; he eventually proved to have a large aneurysm, which was surgically corrected).

[392]Johnson v. Bowers, 884 F.2d 1053, 1056 (8th Cir. 1989) (classifying surgery as elective "does not abrogate the prison's duty, or power, to promptly provide necessary medical treatment for prisoners. . . ."); Monmouth County Correctional Institution Inmates v. Lanzaro, 834 F.2d 326, 349 (3d Cir. 1987); Baker v. Blanchette, 186 F. Supp. 2d 100, 105 n.4 (D.Conn. 2001); Delker v. Maass, 843 F. Supp. 1390, 1399–1400 (D.Or. 1994). *But see* Boring v. Kozakiewicz, 833 F.2d 468, 473 (3d Cir. 1987) ("elective" surgery could be deferred for "presumably brief" period of pre-trial detention).

[393]Martin v. DeBruyn, 880 F. Supp. 610, 614 (N.D.Ind. 1995).

[394]Blackmore v. Kalamazoo County, 390 F.3d 890, 898 (6th Cir. 2004) (requirement held applicable only to "claims involving minor maladies or non-obvious complaints of a serious need for medical care"; signs of appendicitis were obvious); Estate of Carter v. City of Detroit, 408 F.3d 305, 310 (6th Cir. 2005) (no verifying medical evidence required since signs of a heart attack were obvious to a lay person); Johnson v. Karnes, 398 F.3d 868, 874 (6th Cir. 2005) (no verifying medical evidence needed since seriousness of severed hand tendons was obvious to a lay person); Pool v. Sebastian County, Ark., 418 F.3d 934, 945 (8th Cir. 2005) (verifying medical evidence was unnecessary where the plaintiff told prison officials she was pregnant, bleeding, and passing blood clots, and that she was in extreme pain from the cramping, presenting a need obvious to a layperson); Hartsfield v. Colburn, 371 F.3d 454, 457 (8th Cir. 2004) (dental pain, bleeding, swelling, etc., "constituted a need for medical attention that would have been obvious to a layperson, making submission of verifying medical evidence unnecessary"); Hill v. DeKalb Regional Youth Detention Center, 40 F.3d 1176, 1188 (11th Cir. 1994); McCabe v. Prison Health Services, 117 F. Supp. 2d 443, 452 (E.D.Pa. 1997) (expert testimony is sometimes needed to show seriousness, but "[n]o expert needs to tell a layperson that four years of suffering from chronic and severe leg pain is serious"). *Cf.* Napier v. Madison County, Kentucky, 238 F.3d 739, 743 (6th Cir. 2001) (holding prisoner who missed a number of scheduled dialysis appointments but had said missing them was "no big deal" was required to submit verifying medical evidence).

[395]Boring v. Kozakiewicz, 833 F.2d at 473–74. The dissenting judge in that case wrote, "The inhumanity of this paradoxical rule of law alone suggests a serious flaw." *Id.* at 474. We agree.

[396]*See* Garretson v. City of Madison Heights, 407 F.3d 789, 797 (6th Cir. 2005) (the plaintiff's "emergency hospital admission coupled with a stay of several days" satisfied the requirement); Richardson v. Nassau County, 277 F. Supp. 2d 196, 201 (E.D.N.Y. 2003) (evidence of a diagnosable eye condition is significant in determining seriousness; a plaintiff in a § 1983 suit is not required to produce expert medical testimony).

[397]The failure to provide such information can lead to the dismissal of your case. *See* Givens v. Jones, 900 F.2d 1229, 1233 (8th Cir. 1990) (claim of delay in treating leg pain dismissed where the prisoner did not allege "that his condition was acute or for any other reason required immediate attention nor that the [one-month] delay in treatment aggravated his condition"); Dixon v. Fox, 893 F.2d 1556, 1557 (8th Cir. 1990) (claim of suspension of medical diet dismissed where plaintiffs did not explain how their serious medical needs were compromised); Stinson v. Sheriff's Dep't of Sullivan County, 499 F. Supp. 259, 263 (S.D.N.Y. 1980) ("bruises and lacerations" were serious; vague claims of head pain and pain and suffering from unspecified "eye injury" were not).

[398]*See* Ch. 10, § K.3, nn.619–626 concerning appointment of experts.

The need for expert testimony is also a factor that weighs in favor of appointing counsel to represent you, and you should point this out in your motion for the appointment of counsel. *See* Ch. 10, § C.5, concerning appointment of counsel.

[399]Todaro v. Ward, 565 F.2d 48, 52 (2d Cir. 1977) (quoting Bishop v. Stoneman, 508 F.2d 1224, 1226 (2d Cir. 1974)).

[400]*See* DeGidio v. Pung, 920 F.2d 525, 529 (8th Cir. 1990) (lack of "adequate organization and control in the administration of health services" supported finding of Eighth Amendment violation); Greason v. Kemp, 891 F.2d 829, 839 (11th Cir. 1990) (state prison mental health director could be held liable for lack of mental health treatment plans, lack of policies and procedures for suicide prevention, and inadequate psychiatric staff leading to inmate suicide); French v. Owens, 777 F.2d 1250, 1254 (7th Cir. 1985); Bass by Lewis v. Wallenstein, 769 F.2d 1173, 1185 (7th Cir. 1985); Ramos v.

held that a quality assurance system is necessary to ensure adequate care in a large prison or prison system.[401]

In the next several sections, we will discuss what prison officials must do to meet their obligation to provide "a medical care system that meets minimal standards of adequacy."[402]

a. Communication of Medical Needs "Prison officials show deliberate indifference to serious medical needs if prisoners are unable to make their medical problems known to the medical staff."[403] Prisoners in isolated confinement must be able to communicate their medical needs to staff.[404] Sick call must be conducted in a fashion that permits prisoners' complaints to be evaluated in a professional manner.[405] Correctional personnel without medical training may be used to convey sick call requests[406] but they cannot be allowed to decide which prisoners will receive medical attention.[407] Prisons may use nurses, physicians' assistants, or medical technical assistants to determine priorities in seeing a doctor and to handle minor problems for which a doctor

---

Lamm, 639 F.2d 559, 575 (10th Cir. 1980); Newman v. Alabama, 503 F.2d 1320, 1331 (5th Cir. 1974) ("disorganized lines of therapeutic responsibility" contributed to an Eighth Amendment violation); Sulton v. Wright, 265 F. Supp. 2d 292, 300 (S.D.N.Y. 2003) (failure to correct tracking system, so surgery had to be re-approved after transfers, supported deliberate indifference claim); Alexander v. Boyd, 876 F. Supp. 773, 789 (D.S.C. 1995) ("Central to the issue of medical staffing is the necessity of a supervising physician to assure that the overall system is functioning properly to meet the health needs of the population."); Tillery v. Owens, 719 F. Supp. 1256, 1305–06 (W.D.Pa. 1989) (lack of proper administration of medical services and "general disorganization" of nursing services contributed to an Eighth Amendment violation), aff'd, 907 F.2d 418 (3d Cir. 1990); Inmates of Occoquan v. Barry, 717 F. Supp. 854, 867 (D.D.C. 1989) (lack of a follow-up system for treating chronic diseases cited as part of an Eighth Amendment violation); Lightfoot v. Walker, 486 F. Supp. 504, 522–24 (S.D.Ill. 1980) (organization and administration of health care generally found inadequate); see also cases cited in § F.1.a of this chapter, nn.295, 298.

[401]See § F.3.c of this chapter, n.430.

[402]Wellman v. Faulkner, 715 F.2d 269, 271 (7th Cir. 1983).

[403]Hoptowit v. Ray, 682 F.2d 1237, 1253 (9th Cir. 1982); accord, Johnson-El v. Schoemehl, 878 F.2d 1043, 1054–55 (8th Cir. 1989) (sick call only once a week stated a constitutional claim); Bass by Lewis v. Wallenstein, 769 F.2d 1173, 1184–85 (7th Cir. 1985) (known deficiencies in sick call system supported a finding of deliberate indifference); Morales Feliciano v. Calderon Sierra, 300 F. Supp. 2d 321, 341 (D.P.R. 2004) ("Failing to provide a sick call system that ensures access to care and that is capable of effectively handling emergencies" implicates Eighth Amendment rights); Alexander v. Boyd, 876 F. Supp. 773, 789 (D.S.C. 1995) (requiring nursing staff to be available daily to review sick call requests); Arnold on behalf of H.B. v. Lewis, 803 F. Supp. 246, 257 (D.Ariz. 1992) (lack of adequate system of psychiatric referrals supported a finding of deliberate indifference); Morales Feliciano v. Hernandez Colon, 697 F. Supp. 37, 41, 50 (D.P.R. 1988); Dawson v. Kendrick, 527 F. Supp. 1252, 1308 (D.W.Va. 1981); Lightfoot v. Walker, 486 F. Supp. 504, 516–17 (S.D.Ill. 1980); see Anderson v. County of Kern, 45 F.3d 1310, 1317 (9th Cir. 1995) (affirming requirement that non-inmate translator be provided on request for medical and psychiatric interviews of Spanish-speaking prisoners), amended, 75 F.3d 448 (9th Cir. 1995); Clarkson v. Coughlin, 898 F. Supp. 1019, 1049 (S.D.N.Y. 1995) (the lack of interpreters for deaf prisoners during medical encounters denies them adequate medical treatment); see also Wright v. Jones, 907 F.2d 848, 852 (8th Cir. 1990) (supervisory officials were not liable for denial of treatment where they had instituted policies and procedures for communication of medical requests).

[404]Todaro v. Ward, 565 F.2d 48, 51–52 (2d Cir. 1977) (infirmary patients in isolation rooms must be provided a way to summon nurses); Andrews v. Camden County, 95 F. Supp. 2d 217, 229–30 & n.6 (D.N.J. 2000) (holding absence of Medical Director and resulting failure to conduct daily rounds in segregation supported deliberate indifference claim); LeMaire v. Maass, 745 F. Supp. 623, 636 (D.Or. 1990) (segregation inmates could not be locked into cells from which they could not summon assistance), vacated and remanded, 12 F.2d 1444 (9th Cir. 1993). The appeals court in LeMaire did not disagree with the district court's finding of unconstitutionality, but merely held that its injunction was too broad.

[405]Hoptowit v. Ray, 682 F.2d at 1252–53 (evaluation of medical care complaints via written "kites" rather than examination of the patient was inadequate); Todaro v. Ward, 565 F.2d at 50–51) (nurse screening procedure that allowed 15–20 seconds per prisoner, did not permit physical examination, and assigned priorities based on "cryptic" written notes was inadequate); Tillery v. Owens, 719 F. Supp. 1256, 1306 (W.D.Pa. 1989) ("cursory" sick call and sick call conducted where the noise level prevented the doctor from hearing complaints were inadequate), aff'd, 907 F.2d 418 (3d Cir. 1990); U.S. v. State of Michigan, 680 F. Supp. 928, 1043–45, 1061 (W.D.Mich. 1987) (decisions about medical priorities cannot be made from the inmate's written complaint without an examination; court later accepts a written complaint system that requires all prisoners with non-routine complaints to be seen by a doctor within 24 hours).

[406]Miller v. Carson, 401 F. Supp. 835, 898 (M.D.Fla. 1975), aff'd in pertinent part, 563 F.2d 741 (5th Cir.), rehearing denied, 566 F.2d 106 (5th Cir. 1977). But see Andrews v. Camden County, 95 F. Supp. 2d 217, 229–30 (D.N.J. 2000) (noting inadequacy of system in which segregation prisoners told jail staff their medical problems and jail staff drafted memos notifying medical staff of them).

[407]Fields v. City of South Houston, Texas, 922 F.2d 1183, 1192 n.10 (5th Cir. 1991); Mitchell v. Aluisi, 872 F.2d 577, 581 (4th Cir. 1989) (allegation of medical screening by untrained lay personnel supported a claim of deliberate indifference); Kelley v. McGinnis, 899 F.2d 612, 616 (7th Cir. 1990) (allegation that non-medical personnel initially denied access to a doctor stated a deliberate indifference claim); Boswell v. Sherburne County, 849 F.2d 1117, 1123 (10th Cir. 1988) (deliberate indifference claim was supported by evidence that "inadequately trained jailers were directed to use their own judgment about the seriousness of prisoners' medical needs"); Hoptowit v. Ray, 682 F.2d at 1252; Carty v. Farrelly, 957 F. Supp. 727, 738 (D.V.I. 1997) (citing sick call administered by security staff instead of medical staff in finding a constitutional violation); Morales Feliciano v. Hernandez Colon, 697 F. Supp. 37, 41, 50 (D.P.R. 1988); Martino v. Carey, 563 F. Supp. 984, 989–90, 997–98 (D.Or. 1983).

is not necessary.[408] However, in such a system, the person doing the screening must have adequate training and physician supervision, and prisoners who need a physician's direct attention must receive it.[409]

A system that provides mental health care only to those who ask for it may be inadequate, since many prisoners with serious mental illness are incapable of making their needs known.[410]

b. Medical Examinations Many courts have held that medical examinations on intake, at least for the purpose of identifying persons with communicable diseases or immediate medical problems, are required.[411] Prisoners may be required to submit to these examinations.[412] However, prisons are generally not required to provide routine physical examinations.[413] Screening for infection with the AIDS virus is not constitutionally required, probably because AIDS is not easily communicated to people who do not engage in high-risk behavior.[414] Intake dental examinations are not required either.[415]

c. Medical Staff Prison officials must provide a medical staff that is "competent to examine prisoners and diagnose illnesses. It must be able to treat medical problems or to refer prisoners to others who can."[416] The rendering of medical

[408]Partee v. Lane, 528 F. Supp. 1254, 1259–61 (N.D.Ill. 1981); Burks v. Teasdale, 492 F. Supp. 650, 678–79 (W.D.Mo. 1980); see Toussaint v. McCarthy, 801 F.2d 1080, 1111–12 (9th Cir. 1986) (court should determine what services were performed by assistants, nurses, and inmates and whether they were qualified to perform them).

[409]See cases cited in § F.3.c of this chapter, n.420.

[410]Coleman v. Wilson, 912 F. Supp. 1282, 1305–06 (E.D.Cal. 1995).

[411]Gibson v. County of Washoe, Nev., 290 F.3d 1175, 1189 (9th Cir. 2002) (holding policy of delaying intake medical screening for prisoners who were uncooperative or combative could constitute deliberate indifference, since some such prisoners would need immediate psychiatric care or medication); LaReau v. Manson, 651 F.2d 96, 109–11 (2d Cir. 1981); Morales Feliciano v. Calderon Sierra, 300 F. Supp. 2d 321, 341 (D.P.R. 2004) ("Neglecting to fully screen incoming inmates or to detect mental health problems" implicates Eighth Amendment rights.); Maynor v. Morgan County, Ala., 147 F. Supp. 2d 1185, 1189 (N.D.Ala. 2001) (enjoining jail officials to screen each incoming prisoner for serious medical conditions, to provide prescribed medications within 24 hours of admission, and to provide immediate mental health care for those with indicia of serious mental illness); Morales Feliciano v. Rossello Gonzalez, 13 F. Supp. 2d 151, 210 (D.P.R. 1998) (failure to screen incoming inmates for infectious disease including tuberculosis is unconstitutional); Carty v. Farrelly, 957 F. Supp. 727, 737 (D.V.I. 1997) (lack of intake screening constitutes deliberate indifference; citing failure to screen for infectious diseases, mental illness, substance abuse and suicide risk, and failure to read tuberculosis tests within the required time frame); Madrid v. Gomez, 889 F. Supp. 1146, 1258 (N.D.Cal. 1995) (citing "woefully inadequate" intake health screening and "poorly implemented" communicable disease screening in finding that medical care system violated the Eighth Amendment); Hinton v. Patnaude, 162 F.R.D. 435, 438 (N.D.N.Y. 1995) (alleged failure to examine plaintiff for six days after his admission to jail stated a constitutional claim); Carver v. Knox County, Tenn., 753 F. Supp. 1370, 1391 (E.D.Tenn. 1989), remanded for reconsideration, 887 F.2d 1287 (6th Cir. 1989), adhered to on remand, 753 F. Supp. 1398 (E.D.Tenn. 1990); Tillery v. Owens, 719 F. Supp. 1256, 1306 (W.D.Pa. 1989) (cursory intake examinations were not adequate), aff'd, 907 F.2d 418 (3d Cir. 1990); Inmates of Occoquan v. Barry, 717 F. Supp. 854, 867 (D.D.C. 1989) (lack of reliable medical screening contributed to Eighth Amendment violation); Fambro v. Fulton County, Ga., 713 F. Supp. 1426, 1429 (N.D.Ga. 1989) (backlogs in intake examinations condemned); Morales Feliciano v. Hernandez Colon, 697 F. Supp. 37, 48

(D.P.R. 1988); Palmigiano v. Garrahy, 639 F. Supp. 244, 253 (D.R.I. 1986) (condemning lack of tuberculosis testing); Cody v. Hillard, 599 F. Supp. 1025, 1059 (D.S.D. 1984) (examination procedures found inadequate), aff'd in part and rev'd in part on other grounds, 830 F.2d 912 (8th Cir. 1987) (en banc); Monmouth County Correctional Institution Inmates v. Lanzaro, 595 F. Supp. 1417, 1440 (D.N.J. 1984), modified, 695 F. Supp. 759 (D.N.J. 1988), amended in part and clarified in part, 717 F. Supp. 268 (D.N.J. 1989); Dawson v. Kendrick, 527 F. Supp. 1252, 1307 (S.D.W.Va. 1981); Heitman v. Gabriel, 524 F. Supp. 622, 627–28 (W.D.Mo. 1981); Lightfoot v. Walker, 486 F. Supp. 504, 524 (S.D.Ill. 1980); Ahrens v. Thomas, 434 F. Supp. 873, 901 (W.D.Mo. 1977), aff'd in pertinent part, 570 F.2d 286, 289 (8th Cir. 1978). Contra, Smith v. Sullivan, 553 F.2d 373, 380 (5th Cir. 1977); Grim v. Moore, 745 F. Supp. 1280, 1284 (S.D.Ohio 1988), appeal dismissed, 869 F.2d 1490 (6th Cir. 1989); Lock v. Jenkins, 464 F. Supp. 541, 554 (N.D.Ind. 1978), aff'd in part and rev'd in part on other grounds, 641 F.2d 488 (7th Cir. 1981); Mawby v. Ambroyer, 568 F. Supp. 245, 250 (E.D.Mich. 1983). Cf. Suarez v. Camden County Bd. of Chosen Freeholders, 972 F. Supp. 269, 276–77 & n.11 (D.N.J. 1997) (failure to test on admission for adult onset diabetes is not deliberate indifference, since it usually presents with symptoms; tuberculosis is different).

A number of courts have held that prisoners must be screened on admission for mental disorders. See § F.4.a of this chapter, n.474.

[412]See § F.4.k of this chapter, n.779. This requirement is an exception to the right to refuse medical treatment discussed in that section. Screening and treatment for tuberculosis are discussed further in § F.4.d.1. Screening for HIV/AIDS is discussed in § F.4.d.2 of this chapter.

[413]Gibbs v. Grimmette, 254 F.3d 545, 550 (5th Cir. 2001) (restricting tuberculosis testing to persons who show symptoms of the disease or who have come in contact with an infected person is not deliberately indifferent); Featherman v. DiGiacinto, 617 F. Supp. 431, 435 (E.D.Pa. 1985); Tunnell v. Robinson, 486 F. Supp. 1265, 1271 (W.D.Pa. 1980).

[414]See § F.4.d of this chapter concerning infectious diseases including AIDS.

[415]See § F.4.c of this chapter concerning dental care.

[416]Hoptowit v. Ray, 682 F.2d 1237, 1253 (9th Cir. 1982); accord, Coleman v. Wilson, 912 F. Supp. 1282, 1307 (E.D.Cal. 1995) (proposal for "timely, responsible, and adequate care provided by qualified (and appropriately licensed) staff" was "not materially different from the constitutional requirement of ready access to competent medical staff"); Hartman v. Correctional Medical Services, Inc., 960 F. Supp. 1577, 1581–83 (M.D.Fla. 1996) (permitting a person

services by unqualified personnel is deliberate indifference,[417] as is the failure to provide access to specialist care that a particular prisoner's condition may require.[418] Medical personnel must be trained to respond to emergencies.[419] Non-physician staff like nurses and physicians' assistants cannot lawfully be assigned, or try to perform, tasks beyond their training, or be left without adequate supervision.[420] Prisoners whose medical needs call for a physician's attention must receive it,[421] and non-physicians may not refuse to carry out physicians' orders.[422] Prison or jail officials may be deliberately indifferent if they fail to provide guards with at least minimal training in recognizing and dealing with medical emergencies.[423]

Prison officials must provide enough medical staff coverage to meet the needs of the population.[424] However, as

---

with only a master's degree and no professional licenses to have authority over mental health referrals and suicide precautions supported claim of a policy of deliberate indifference by medical provider); Medcalf v. State of Kansas, 626 F. Supp. 1179, 1186 (D.Kan. 1986) (supervisor had a duty "to carefully hire, train and supervise adequate medical personnel capable of evaluating and meeting . . . reasonable medical needs").

[417]Oxendine v. Kaplan, 241 F.3d 1272, 1278–79 (10th Cir. 2001) (allegation that doctor peformed surgery he was not qualified for without seeking specialized assistance stated a deliberate indifference claim); Toussaint v. McCarthy, 801 F.2d 1080, 1112 (9th Cir. 1986); Williams v. Edwards, 547 F.2d 1206, 1216–18 (5th Cir. 1977); Petrichko v. Kurtz, 117 F. Supp. 2d 467, 471 (E.D.Pa. 2000) (officer who told another prisoner to set the plaintiff's dislocated shoulder could be found deliberately indifferent, since he "presided over the provision of medical care by an individual not qualified to provide such care"); Grubbs v. Bradley, 552 F. Supp. 1052, 1129 (M.D.Tenn. 1982); see § F.4.a of this chapter, n.481, concerning mental health staff. But see Breakiron v. Neal, 166 F. Supp. 2d 1110, 1116 (N.D.Tex. 2001) ("Prisoners have no constitutional right to have their medication dispensed by a licensed medical practitioner.").

[418]See § F.1 of this chapter, n.287.

[419]Bass by Lewis v. Wallenstein, 769 F.2d 1173, 1185 (7th Cir. 1985). But see Doe v. Gustavus, 294 F. Supp. 2d 1003, 1011 (E.D.Wis. 2003) (rejecting claim of failure to train nurses, given evidence that any licensed nurse would have known what to do about the plaintiff's pregnancy); Smith v. Lejeune, 203 F. Supp. 2d 1260, 1269 (D.Wyo. 2002) (rejecting claim of failure to train nurses about alcohol withdrawal; it is "not unreasonable for a doctor to rely on the training and experience of Licensed Practical Nurses").

[420]Toussaint v. McCarthy, 801 F.2d at 1111–12 (medical technical assistants, registered nurses, and inmates cannot lawfully render services they are not qualified for); Madrid v. Gomez, 889 F. Supp. 1146, 1258 (N.D.Cal. 1995) (noting inadequate training and supervision of medical technical assistants in deciding whether prisoners may see a doctor); Inmates of Occoquan v. Barry, 717 F. Supp. at 867 (medical technical assistants improperly diagnosed and dispensed medications without adequate supervision); Langley v. Coughlin, 715 F. Supp. 522, 540 (S.D.N.Y. 1988) ("apparently unqualified or untrained personnel were performing functions that should have been undertaken by a psychiatrist or under his close supervision"); Balla v. Idaho State Bd. of Corrections, 595 F. Supp. 1558, 1575–76 (D.Idaho 1984) (medical personnel were performing functions that should have been performed by a doctor and were providing treatment for which they were neither licensed nor trained); Capps v. Atiyeh, 559 F. Supp. 894, 912 (D.Or. 1982) (nurses and medical technicians were inadequately supervised); Lightfoot v. Walker, 486 F. Supp. 504, 516–17 (S.D.Ill. 1980) (nurses and medical technicians were inadequate supervised and trained); Palmigiano v. Garrahy, 443 F. Supp. 956, 974 (D.R.I. 1977) (nurses were inadequately trained and supervised), remanded on other grounds, 599 F.2d 17 (1st Cir. 1979). But see Harris v. Roberts, 719 F.

Supp. 879, 880 (N.D.Cal. 1989) (treatment by a physician's assistant rather than a doctor for two weeks was not deliberate indifference where there was no indication that the care given was substandard).

[421]Mandel v. Doe, 888 F.2d 783, 789–90 (11th Cir. 1989) (damages awarded where physician's assistant failed to diagnose a broken hip, refused to order an x-ray, and prevented the prisoner from seeing a doctor); Petrichko v. Kurtz, 117 F. Supp. 2d 467, 473 (E.D.Pa. 2000) (denial of access to a physician for two weeks could constitute deliberate indifference); Wolfel v. Ferguson, 689 F. Supp. 756, 759 (S.D.Ohio 1987) (damages awarded for denial by nurse of access to a doctor who could renew a prescription); see Natale v. Camden County Correctional Facility, 318 F.3d 575, 583 (3d Cir. 2003) (policy of seeing all prisoners within 72 hours of admission but making no provision for prisoners with more immediate needs supported a deliberate indifference claim).

[422]Johnson v. Hay, 931 F.2d 456, 461 (8th Cir. 1991) (pharmacist's refusal to fill prescriptions written by a doctor could constitute deliberate indifference); Boretti v. Wiscomb, 930 F.2d 1150, 1154–55 (6th Cir. 1981) (nurse's refusal to give pain medication and perform dressing changes as prescribed by doctor supported a deliberate indifference claim).

[423]Morrison v. Washington County, Ala., 700 F.2d 678, 685 (11th Cir. 1983); Layman v. Alexander, 343 F. Supp. 2d 483, 489 (W.D.N.C. 2004) (holding a jury could find lack of training to respond to injuries and medical conditions could support liability); King v. Frank, 328 F. Supp. 2d 940, 947–48 (W.D.Wis. 2004) (complaint that prisoner received no "mental health programming" and that there were not enough licensed mental health providers stated a claim; "Staff that are untrained or too few in numbers may contribute to an Eighth Amendment violation."); Brown v. Mitchell, 308 F. Supp. 2d 682, 706 (E.D.Va. 2004) (allegation that inadequate training led staff to allow obviously ill prisoner to die rather than to do anything for him stated a constitutional claim); Brock v. Warren County, Tenn., 713 F. Supp. 238, 243 (E.D.Tenn. 1989). But see Smith v. Board of County Commissioners of County of Lyon, 216 F. Supp. 2d 1209, 1224 (D.Kan. 2002) (rejecting claim of failure to provide medical training to jailers); Morris v. City of Alvin, Tex., 950 F. Supp. 804, 806 (S.D.Tex. 1997) ("There is no constitutional requirement that municipalities provide jailers and law enforcement personnel with sophisticated medical training so that they will detect hidden medical problems"; failure to provide training in recognizing "the ambiguous signs of drug overdose" was not a policy of deliberate indifference); Boston v. LaFayette County, Miss., 743 F. Supp. 462, 473 (N.D.Miss. 1990) (county was not required to train jailers to recognize "subtle" medical problems).

[424]Cabrales v. County of Los Angeles, 864 F.2d 1454, 1461 (9th Cir. 1988) (understaffing such that psychiatric staff could only spend "minutes per month" with disturbed inmates was unconstitutional), vacated, 494 U.S. 1091 (1989), reinstated, 886 F.2d 235 (9th Cir. 1989); Anderson v. City of Atlanta, 778 F.2d 678, 683–86 (11th Cir. 1985) (municipality could be held liable for death of

long as they succeed in meeting prisoners' medical needs, they have discretion whether to hire in-house medical staff or to contract for medical services outside the prison.[425]

Prisoners do not have a constitutional right to see the doctor of their choice.[426] In some states, statutes or regulations may provide such a right,[427] but these state rules must generally be enforced in state and not in federal court.[428]

Adequate supervision of medical staff is essential to the operation of a prison medical care system.[429] Some courts have held that large prison systems must provide some form of quality assurance in order to provide adequate medical care.[430]

d. Access to Outside Care   Prisons rarely provide the complete range of necessary medical services within their walls. If a prisoner requires care that is not available in the prison, the failure to obtain it elsewhere may constitute deliberate indifference.[431] Prison officials "may not allow security or transportation concerns to override a medical determination that a particular inmate is in need of prompt treatment and must be transported to an appropriate facility."[432]

---

neglected prisoner based on understaffing where jail had no medical personnel and too few officers on duty on night shift); Miranda v. Munoz, 770 F.2d 255, 261–62 (1st Cir. 1985); Garcia v. Salt Lake County, 768 F.2d 303, 308 (10th Cir. 1985); Wellman v. Faulkner, 715 F.2d at 272–74; Green v. Carlson, 581 F.2d 669, 671, 675 (7th Cir. 1978) (failure to provide coverage for medical emergencies when no doctor was present could constitute deliberate indifference), aff'd, 446 U.S. 14, 100 S. Ct. 1468 (1980); King v. Frank, 328 F. Supp. 2d 940, 947–48 (W.D.Wis. 2004) (complaint that prisoner received no "mental health programming" and that there were not enough licensed mental health providers stated a claim; "Staff that are untrained or too few in numbers may contribute to an Eighth Amendment violation."); Gaines v. Choctaw County Commission, 242 F. Supp. 2d 1153, 1163 (S.D.Ala. 2003) (claim of inadequate staffing to meet prisoners' medical needs); Morales Feliciano v. Rossello Gonzalez, 13 F. Supp. 2d 151, 209 (D.P.R. 1998) ("Defendants' manifest inability to adequately train, supervise or retain health care personnel which results in rampant under-staffing and the consequent impossibility to adequately meet the needs of the inmate population constitute deliberate indifference towards the health care needs of the plaintiff class."); Carty v. Farrelly, 957 F. Supp. 727, 737 (D.V.I. 1997) ("Providing *inadequate* medical staff effectively denied inmates access to diagnosis and treatment and constitutes deliberate indifference."); Coleman v. Wilson, 912 F. Supp. 1282, 1307 (E.D.Cal. 1995) (citing "constitutional requirement of ready access to competent medical staff," stating it is equivalent to "timely, responsible, and adequate care provided by qualified (and appropriately licensed) staff"); Madrid v. Gomez, 889 F. Supp. 1146, 1258 (N.D.Cal. 1995) (citing medical staffing levels that had progressed only from "abysmal" to "still insufficient" in finding Eighth Amendment violation); Tillery v. Owens, 719 F. Supp. 1256, 1305-06 (W.D.Pa. 1989); Inmates of Occoquan v. Barry, 717 F. Supp. at 868; Duran v. Anaya, 642 F. Supp. 510, 524–28 (D.N.M. 1986); Lightfoot v. Walker, 486 F. Supp. at 524–25; Battle v. Anderson, 457 F. Supp. 719, 728–29 (E.D.Okla. 1978). *But see* McDowell v. Brown, 392 F.3d 1283, 1290–91 (11th Cir. 2004) (plaintiff who alleged delay in emergency transportation because of policy of understaffing failed to prove a policy because he failed to show that emergency cases were consistently not transported to hospital timely; *Anderson v. Atlanta*, cited above, distinguished because in that case there were no medical personnel on the night shift when the plaintiff died).

[425]Hoptowit v. Ray, 682 F.2d at 1253–54; Smith v. Board of County Commissioners of County of Lyon, 216 F. Supp. 2d 1209, 1224 (D.Kan. 2002); Coleman v. Wilson, 912 F. Supp. 1282, 1308–09 (E.D.Cal. 1995) ("The Constitution requires either ready access to physicians at the prison or reasonably speedy access to outside physicians or facilities.").

[426]Roberts v. Spalding, 783 F.2d 867, 870 (9th Cir. 1986); U.S. v. Rovetuso, 768 F.2d 809, 825 (7th Cir. 1985); McCracken v. Jones, 562 F.2d 22, 24 (10th Cir. 1977); Hawley v. Evans, 716 F. Supp. 601, 603–04 (N.D.Ga. 1989); Apodaca v. Ommen, 807 P.2d 939, 943–44 (Wyo. 1991) (rejecting both state law and constitutional claims).

Whether there is a constitutional right to a second opinion depends on the circumstances. Clemens v. State, 112 Idaho 638, 733 P.2d 1263, 1265 (Idaho App. 1987) and cases cited.

[427]*See* West v. Atkins, 487 U.S. 42, 46 n.2, 108 S. Ct. 2250 (1988) (citing N.C. Gen. Stat. §§ 148–11, 148–19 (1987) (permitting minimum security prisoners to obtain medical care outside prison)); Roberts v. Spalding, 783 F. Supp. at 871 (citing Wash. Admin. Code R. 275-91-070); Smith v. Dep't of Corrections, 105 Or.App. 61, 804 P.2d 482, 484 (Or.App. 1991) (citing OAR 291-125-050[1], 291-124-085[2][d]).

[428]*See* Roberts v. Spalding, 783 F.2d at 871 (state regulation did not create a federally protected liberty interest).

[429]Alexander v. Boyd, 876 F. Supp. 773, 789 (D.S.C. 1995) ("Central to the issue of medical staffing is the necessity of a supervising physician to assure that the overall system is functioning properly to meet the health needs of the population.").

[430]Coleman v. Wilson, 912 F. Supp. 1282, 1308 (E.D.Cal. 1995); Madrid v. Gomez, 889 F. Supp. 1149, 1209, 1258–59 (N.D.Cal. 1995); Grubbs v. Bradley, 821 F. Supp. 496, 500 (M.D.Tenn. 1993).

[431]Kaminsky v. Rosenblum, 929 F.2d 922, 927 (2d Cir. 1991) (failure to act on recommendation of immediate hospitalization); Miltier v. Beorn, 896 F.2d 848, 853 (4th Cir. 1990) (failure to act on a recommendation for transfer to a cardiology unit); Ellis v. Butler, 890 F.2d 1001, 1004 (8th Cir. 1989) (cancellation of appointment with knee specialist); Washington v. Dugger, 860 F.2d 1018, 1021 (11th Cir. 1988) (failure to return patient to VA hospital for treatment for Agent Orange exposure); Payne v. Lynaugh, 843 F.2d 177, 178–79 (5th Cir. 1988) (failure to transfer prisoner to facility with oxygen equipment required for his emphysema); Morales Feliciano v. Calderon Sierra, 300 F. Supp. 2d 321, 341 (D.P.R. 2004) ("the failure to provide transportation to scheduled specialty appointments and other therapy" is an example of "interfering with the treatment once prescribed" forbidden by the Eighth Amendment); Carty v. Farrelly, 957 F. Supp. 727, 737 (D.V.I. 1997) ("failure to refer prisoners requiring medical care from an outside specialist to such providers also constitutes deliberate indifference"); Arnold on behalf of H.B. v. Lewis, 803 F. Supp. 246, 257 (D.Ariz. 1992) (delay or failure to act on referrals to a mental hospital).

[432]U.S. v. State of Michigan, 680 F. Supp. 928, 1002 (W.D.Mich. 1987); *accord*, Hurst v. Phelps, 579 F.2d 940, 941–42 (5th Cir. 1978); Morales Feliciano v. Rossello Gonzalez, 13 F. Supp. 2d 151, 211 (D.P.R. 1998); Inmates of Occoquan v. Barry, 717 F. Supp. 854, 867 (D.D.C. 1989) (Eighth Amendment violation found in part because

Nor may they deny necessary outside consultation or treatment on grounds of cost.[433] Necessary outside appointments must be provided without excessive delay,[434] as must hospitalization.[435] If prison officials send prisoners with special needs to outside specialists, one would think that they must follow the specialists' orders, but the courts are not unanimous on this point.[436] Prison officials are not necessarily required to

continue treatments started or recommended by prisoners' own physicians.[437]

e. Facilities, Equipment, and Supplies Prison officials must provide adequate facilities and equipment for necessary medical care.[438] The Constitution may be violated by dilapidated, dangerous or unsanitary physical conditions,[439] inadequate examination and treatment facilities,[440] defective or inadequate emergency equipment,[441] a malfunctioning x-ray machine[442] or other obsolete equipment,[443] or shortages or unavailability of medications, eyeglasses or prosthetic devices.[444]

f. Medical Records "The keeping of medical records is . . . a necessity."[445] Adequate and accurate records are of

"inmates wait months for appointments to specialty clinics"); Johnson-El v. District of Columbia, 579 A.2d 163, 169 (D.C. 1990) (allegation that dermatological treatment was delayed or denied by lack of transportation stated a deliberate indifference claim). *But see* Victoria W. v. Larpenter, 369 F.3d 475, 486 (5th Cir. 2004) (upholding policy requiring court order for "elective" care outside the jail, including abortion); Bush v. Ware, 589 F. Supp. 1454, 1464 (E.D.Wis. 1984) (medical appointment could be cancelled for security reasons when the prisoner was going to be transferred to a hospital in a few days).

[433]Monmouth County Correctional Institution Inmates v. Lanzaro, 834 F.2d 326, 336–37, 347 (3d Cir. 1987); Ancata v. Prison Health Services, Inc., 769 F.2d 700, 704 (11th Cir. 1985); *see* § F, n.238, and § F.1, nn.299–300, above.

[434]Morales Feliciano v. Rossello Gonzalez, 13 F. Supp. 2d 151, 211 (D.P.R. 1998); Casey v. Lewis, 834 F. Supp. 1477, 1546 (D.Ariz. 1993) (outside referrals must be "reasonably speedy"); Inmates of Occoquan v. Barry, 717 F. Supp. 854, 867 (D.D.C. 1989) (Eighth Amendment violation found in part because "inmates wait months for appointments to specialty clinics"). Outside facilities' scheduling priorities may not be used as an excuse not to provide necessary care promptly. Johnson v. Bowers, 884 F.2d 1053, 1056 (8th Cir. 1989).

[435]Brown v. District of Columbia, 514 F.3d 1279, 1284 (D.C. Cir. 2008) (failure to transfer prisoner with gallstones promptly to hospital); Sealock v. Colorado, 218 F.3d 1205, 1211 (10th Cir. 2000) (officer who refused to drive prisoner with apparent heart attack to hospital could be found deliberately indifferent); Chavez v. Cady, 207 F.3d 901, 906 (7th Cir. 2000) (holding correctional staff could be held liable for not acting timely on direction to hospitalize plaintiff); Coleman v. Rahia, 114 F.3d 778, 785 (8th Cir. 1997) (affirming damage award for two-hour delay in hospitalizing prisoner with pregnancy complications); Scott v. Garcia, 370 F. Supp. 2d 1056, 1068–69 (S.D.Cal. 2005) (failure of classification committee to act on medical direction to transfer prisoner with severe stomach and digestive problems to a prison with hospital facilities); *see* Gaines v. Choctaw County Commission, 242 F. Supp. 2d 1153, 1165 (S.D.Ala. 2003) (removal of acutely ill prisoner from hospital against medical advice supported a claim for deliberate indifference). *But see* McDowell v. Brown, 392 F.3d 1283, 1290–91 (11th Cir. 2004) (county could not be held liable for delay in hospitalization allegedly caused by understaffing in the absence of widespread delays); Schreter v. Bednosky, 963 F. Supp. 216, 217 (E.D.N.Y. 1997) (half hour delay in transportation to hospital did not constitute deliberate indifference).

[436]Some courts have accepted prison officials' claims that failure to follow specialist recommendations merely represents a difference of opinion that raises no constitutional issue. Others, however, have found failure to follow specialists' recommendations to support a claim of deliberate indifference. *See* § F.1, nn.314–315, above. When there is no claim of medical disagreement with specialists' recommendations, failure to follow them should certainly be viewed as deliberate indifference. *See* Washington v. Dugger,

860 F.2d 1018, 1020–21 (11th Cir. 1988) (failure to carry out undisputed recommendations of Veterans Administration hospital staff for prisoner exposed to Agent Orange could constitute deliberate indifference); Martinez v. Mancusi, 443 F.2d 921, 923–25 (2d Cir. 1970) (removal of surgical patient from hospital against doctor's orders could constitute deliberate indifference).

[437]Vaughan v. Lacey, 49 F.3d 1344, 1345–46 (8th Cir. 1995) (prison authorities could rely on their own physicians and not prisoner's civilian treating physician).

[438]Harris v. Thigpen, 941 F.2d 1495, 1509 (11th Cir. 1991); Langley v. Coughlin, 888 F.2d 252, 254 (2d Cir. 1989); Morales Feliciano v. Rossello Gonzalez, 13 F. Supp. 2d 151, 209, 211 (D.P.R. 1998) (citing failure to provide and maintain adequate facilities and equipment necessary for adequate health care in finding of constitutional violation).

[439]Newman v. Alabama, 503 F.2d 1320, 1331 (5th Cir. 1974); Williams v. Edwards, 547 F.2d 1206, 1217–18 (5th Cir. 1977); Benjamin v. Fraser, 161 F. Supp. 2d 151, 186–89 (S.D.N.Y. 2001) (finding lighting and sanitation constitutionally inadequate in jail medical areas), *aff'd in part, vacated and remanded in part on other grounds*, 343 F.3d 35, 52 (2d Cir. 2003); Lightfoot v. Walker, 486 F. Supp. 504, 512, 524 (S.D.Ill. 1980). *But see* Toussaint v. McCarthy, 801 F.2d 1080, 1112–13 (9th Cir. 1986) (sanitary standards of outside hospitals need not be met).

[440]Inmates of Allegheny County Jail v. Wecht, 874 F.2d 147, 153 (3d Cir. 1989) (inadequate space for mental health facilities supported an order closing the jail), *vacated and remanded on other grounds*, 110 S. Ct. 355 (1989); Tillery v. Owens, 719 F. Supp. 1256, 1307 (W.D.Pa. 1989) (condemning infirmary's lack of space, unsanitary conditions, and deficiencies in equipment and supplies), *aff'd*, 907 F.2d 418 (3d Cir. 1990); Jones v. Wittenberg, 330 F. Supp. 707, 718 (N.D.Ohio 1971), *aff'd*, 456 F.2d 854 (6th Cir. 1972).

[441]Green v. Carlson, 581 F.2d 669, 671, 675 (7th Cir. 1978), *aff'd*, 446 U.S. 14, 100 S. Ct. 1468 (1980); Carty v. Farrelly, 957 F. Supp. 727, 738 (D.V.I. 1997) (citing lack of emergency equipment, "critically important considering the high frequency of violent incidents," in finding a constitutional violation); Burks v. Teasdale, 492 F. Supp. 650, 678 (W.D.Mo. 1980).

[442]Todaro v. Ward, 431 F. Supp. 1129, 1139 (S.D.N.Y.), *aff'd*, 565 F.2d 48 (2d Cir. 1977).

[443]Newman v. Alabama, 503 F.2d 1320, 1331 (5th Cir. 1974).

[444]Newman v. Alabama, 503 F.2d at 1331.

[445]Johnson-El v. Schoemehl, 878 F.2d 1043, 1055 (8th Cir. 1989).

"critical importance . . . in any attempt to provide a continuity of medical care," and absent or deficient records create "the possibility for disaster."[446] Numerous courts have condemned the failure to maintain a reasonably complete and organized system of medical records[447] or the purposeful destruction of or tampering with medical records.[448]

---

[446]Burks v. Teasdale, 492 F. Supp. 650, 676 (W.D.Mo. 1980); *accord*, Morales Feliciano v. Calderon Sierra, 300 F. Supp. 2d 321, 341 (D.P.R. 2004) (record keeping and management are "critically important to the continuity of medical care, otherwise, the possibility for disaster is created"); Coleman v. Wilson, 912 F. Supp. 1282, 1314 (E.D.Cal. 1995) ("A necessary component of minimally adequate medical care is maintenance of complete and accurate medical records."); Madrid v. Gomez, 889 F. Supp. 1146, 1259 (N.D.Cal. 1995) (citing "utterly deficient" medical recordkeeping in finding constitutional violation).

[447]Ginest v. Board of County Commissioners of Carbon County, 333 F. Supp. 2d 1190, 1200, 1205 (D.Wyo. 2004); Morales Feliciano v. Rossello Gonzalez, 13 F. Supp. 2d 151, 210–11 (D.P.R. 1998); Fambro v. Fulton County, Ga., 713 F. Supp. 1426, 1429 (N.D.Ga. 1989); Cody v. Hillard, 599 F. Supp. 1025, 1040, 1057–58 (D.S.D. 1984), *aff'd in part and rev'd in part on other grounds*, 830 F.2d 912 (8th Cir. 1987) (en banc); Dawson v. Kendrick, 527 F. Supp. 1252, 1273, 1308 (S.D.W.Va. 1981); Ruiz v. Estelle, 503 F. Supp. 1265, 1323–24, 1331 (S.D.Tex. 1980), *aff'd in part, rev'd in part on other grounds*, 679 F.2d 1115 (5th Cir. 1982); Burks v. Teasdale, 492 F. Supp. at 676; Lightfoot v. Walker, 486 F. Supp. 504, 517, 527 (S.D.Ill. 1980); *see* Miranda v. Munoz, 770 F.2d 255, 261 (1st Cir. 1985) (prison officials' knowledge of continuing problem of prisoners arriving at hospital without their medical records cited as a basis for damage liability); Brown v. Coughlin, 758 F. Supp. 876, 882 (S.D.N.Y. 1991) ("failure to transfer necessary medical records in a timely fashion" supported a deliberate indifference claim); *see* U.S. v. Wallen, 177 F. Supp. 2d 455, 458–59 (D.Md. 2001) (citing unreliable prison medical record-keeping in ordering that criminal defendant with serious medical problems be held in a medical facility).

Courts have generally held that prison officials have no duty to obtain medical records from prior incarcerations or from before incarceration. Hott v. Hennepin County, Minn., 260 F.3d 901, 906 (8th Cir. 2001) (the failure to identify the plaintiff as a suicide risk by obtaining medical records from a county hospital did not violate the Constitution); Bozeman v. Orum, 199 F. Supp. 2d 1216, 1231–32 (M.D.Ala. 2002) (same), *aff'd*, 422 F.3d 1265 (11th Cir. 2005); McCabe v. Prison Health Services, 117 F. Supp. 2d 443, 455 (E.D.Pa. 1997) (state prison's failure to get county jail medical records was not deliberate indifference); *see* Campbell v. Sikes, 169 F.3d 1353 (11th Cir. 1999) (failure to review prior medical records was not deliberately indifferent where a summary was reviewed). *But see* Coleman v. Wilson, 912 F. Supp. 1282, 1314 (E.D.Cal. 1995) (affirming order to ensure that medical records are transferred with prisoners and that they are obtained for prisoners who are received from county jails).

[448]Montgomery v. Pintchak, 294 F.3d 492, 500–01 (3d Cir. 2002) (holding mere loss of medical records is not deliberate indifference, but ten-month refusal to recreate lost records followed by falsification of them stated a deliberate indifference claim); Wesley v. Davis, 333 F. Supp. 2d 888, 894 (C.D.Cal. 2004) (holding allegation of purposeful destruction of prisoner's medical records stated an Eighth Amendment claim).

Prison officials must maintain the privacy of prisoners' medical records.[449] Prisoners are generally entitled to have access to their own medical records.[450] Whether prisoners may be required to pay for them is determined by state law or regulations.[451]

4. Particular Medical Issues

a. Mental Health Care Mental health care is subject to the same constitutional standard as other forms of prison medical care: deliberate indifference to serious mental health needs violates the Eighth Amendment[452] or, for pretrial detainees, the Due Process Clause.[453] Some prisoners are not subject to these standards because they are neither convicts nor pretrial detainees in the usual sense. This category includes persons who are found incompetent to stand trial or not guilty by reason of insanity, or are civilly committed as sex offenders after their criminal sentence is finished. Their rights too are governed by the Due Process Clause, and their treatment is assessed by whether it is sufficiently related to the purpose of their confinement.[454] Persons found

---

[449]*See* § F.4.j of this chapter.

[450]*See* Benavides v. Bureau of Prisons, 995 F.2d 269 (D.C. Cir. 1993) (disclosure of medical records to physicians but not directly to the prisoner was permissible under the federal Privacy Act as long as the prisoner ultimately received them). *But see* Abdus-Samad v. Greiner, 158 F. Supp. 2d 307 (S.D.N.Y. 2001) (failure to assist the plaintiff in obtaining his medical records did not support an Eighth Amendment claim).

[451]*See* DeMarco v. Ginn, 137 F.R.D. 214 (D.N.J. 1990).

[452]Gates v. Cook, 376 F.3d 323, 343 (5th Cir. 2004); Dolihite v. Maughon by and through Videon, 74 F.3d 1027, 1042–43 (11th Cir. 1996); Smith v. Jenkins, 919 F.2d 90, 92–93 (8th Cir. 1990); Langley v. Coughlin, 888 F.2d 252, 254 (2d Cir. 1989); Waldrop v. Evans, 871 F.2d 1030, 1033 (11th Cir.), *rehearing denied*, 880 F.2d 421 (11th Cir. 1989); Eng v. Smith, 849 F.2d 80, 82 (2d Cir. 1988); Rogers v. Evans, 792 F.2d 1052, 1058 (11th Cir. 1986); Joseph v. Brierton, 739 F.2d 1244, 1246 (7th Cir. 1984); Wellman v. Faulkner, 715 F.2d 269, 272–73 (7th Cir. 1983); Ramos v. Lamm, 639 F.2d 559, 574 (10th Cir. 1980); Inmates of Allegheny County Jail v. Pierce, 612 F.2d 754, 761–63 (3d Cir. 1979); Bowring v. Godwin, 551 F.2d 44, 47 (4th Cir. 1977). *But see* Campbell v.Sikes, 169 F.3d 1353, 1367–68 (11th Cir. 1999) (holding there was no deliberate indifference in terminating patient's medication and restraining her absent evidence that the defendant psychiatrist knew the nature of her illness).

[453]Gibson v. County of Washoe, Nev., 290 F.3d 1175, 1187 (9th Cir. 2002); Lawson v. Trowbridge, 153 F.3d 368, 378 (7th Cir. 1998) (noting jury verdict for schizophrenic plaintiff who was jailed and denied mental health care for months and held in solitary confinement for 65 days). *See* nn.258–61, above, concerning detainees' medical care rights.

[454]Oregon Advocacy Center v. Mink, 322 F.3d 1101, 1121–22 (9th Cir. 2003) (persons found incompetent to stand trial but not timely admitted to a mental hospital, waiting one to five months in county jails without treatment, were not governed by the deliberate indifference standard; they may not be relegated to the level of treatment afforded to convicts, since they "have liberty interests in freedom from incarceration and in restorative treatment"; leaving them in county jails for months "violates their due process rights

"guilty but mentally ill" in states where the criminal law provides for such verdicts may be placed in a prison setting and provided mental health care by prison authorities.[455]

Not every mental health problem constitutes a serious need under the Constitution. One court has cited an expert's definition of a "serious" mental illness as one "that has caused significant disruption in an inmate's everyday life and which prevents his functioning in the general population without disturbing or endangering others or himself."[456] Complaints of depression are not necessarily serious,[457] but acute or serious depression may constitute a serious medical need,[458] and threats or risk of suicide certainly are.[459] Courts have held or assumed that manic-depressive or bipolar disorder and obsessive-compulsive disorder can be serious needs.[460] Immediate psychological trauma may also constitute a serious need.[461] Courts have held some other psychiatric disorders not to present serious needs.[462]

Prisoners with mental illness may bring suit concerning their treatment, or lack of it, like other prisoners, under 42 U.S.C. § 1983; in some cases, the federal disability statutes may also be relevant.[463] In addition, the Protection and Advocacy for Individuals with Mental Illness Act[464] (PAMII) provides for the creation of "protection and advocacy" (P&A) systems designed to "(A) protect and advocate the rights of individuals with mental illness; and (B) investigate incidents of abuse and neglect of individuals with mental illness if the incidents are reported to the system or if there is probable cause to believe that the incidents occurred."[465] These systems (which usually consist of private organizations funded by state governments) sometimes provide

---

because the nature and duration of their incarceration bear no reasonable relation to the evaluative and restorative purposes for which courts commit those individuals"; affirming seven-day limit on transferring them to a mental hospital); Barichello v. McDonald, 98 F.3d 948, 952–53 (7th Cir. 1996) (holding greater rights to movement off-ward for committed persons found not guilty by reason of insanity than those found unfit to stand trial was "matter[] of treatment" and no clearly established law forbade making the distinction between civilly and criminally committed persons); Phelps v. U.S. Bureau of Prisons, 62 F.3d 1020, 1023 (8th Cir. 1995) (insanity acquittee, required by statute to be placed in a "suitable facility," could be placed in Bureau of Prisons' Federal Medical Center despite its "prison-like conditions" given his dangerous criminal history, his mental diagnosis, and the reluctance of state officials to accept placement of someone who will need expensive long-term care); Huss v. Rogerson, 271 F. Supp. 2d 1118 (S.D.Iowa 2003) (holding person found not guilty by reason of insanity had a clearly established right to be held under non-punitive conditions, though delaying his admission to a mental hospital and keeping him in segregation during the interim was reasonable under the circumstances).

[455]Neely v. Newton, 149 F.3d 1074, 1083 (10th Cir. 1998).

[456]Tillery v. Owens, 719 F. Supp. 1256, 1286 (W.D.Pa. 1989), aff'd, 907 F.2d 418 (3d Cir. 1990).

[457]Partee v. Lane, 528 F. Supp. 1254, 1261 (N.D.Ill. 1981).

[458]Peterkin v. Jeffes, 661 F. Supp. 895, 917, 923 (E.D.Pa. 1987) (depression among "death row" inmates was serious), aff'd in pertinent part, 855 F.2d 1021 (3d Cir. 1988); Cody v. Hillard, 599 F. Supp. 1025, 1058–59 (D.S.D. 1984), aff'd in part and rev'd in part on other grounds, 830 F.2d 912 (8th Cir. 1987) (en banc); Robert E. v. Lane, 530 F. Supp. 930, 939 (N.D.Ill. 1981).

[459]Conn v. City of Reno, 572 F.3d 1047, 1055 (9th Cir. 2009).

[460]See Olsen v. Layton Hills Mall, 312 F.3d 1304, 1316 (10th Cir. 2002) (holding obsessive-compulsive disorder can be a serious need); Gibson v. County of Washoe, Nev., 290 F.3d 1175, 1191–92 (9th Cir. 2002) (treating person in manic phase of manic-depressive disorder as having a serious need); Page v. Norvell, 186 F. Supp. 2d 1134, 1136 (D.Ore. 2000) (noting lack of dispute that prisoner with diagnosis of bipolar disorder and with great anxiety had a serious need).

[461]Carnell v.Grimm, 872 F. Supp. 746, 756 (D.Haw. 1994) (holding that "an officer who has reason to believe someone has been raped and then fails to seek medical *and psychological* treatment after taking her into custody manifests deliberate indifference to a serious medical need"), *appeal dismissed in part, aff'd in part*, 74 F.3d 977 (9th Cir. 1996) (emphasis supplied). See Daniels v. State of Delaware, 120 F. Supp. 2d 411 (D.Del. 2000) (holding that officials who provided psychiatric care and medication to a prisoner raped by a correction officer were not deliberately indifferent); Carrigan v. State of Delaware, 957 F. Supp. 1376, 1384 (D.Del. 1997) (same; plaintiff was seen repeatedly by a doctor with training in psychology and was taken to a hospital for medical treatment and psychological evaluation, and then placed on a suicide watch, after she jumped off a tier).

[462]*But see* Stanley v. Litscher, 213 F.3d 340 (7th Cir. 2000) (stating "[i]t is difficult . . . to conceive of psychopathy as a 'serious medical need.' . . . Psychopaths are dangerous to others, not themselves"; noting that a psychiatrist had concluded that the plaintiff did not require "acute treatment"); Riddle v. Mondragon, 83 F.3d 1197, 1204 (10th Cir. 1996) (convicted sex offenders' complaints of inadequate treatment for their "addictive sexuality" do not raise serious medical needs absent "averments of diagnosis by a physician of a medical need mandating treatment, nor of a condition which a lay person would easily recognize as necessitating a doctor's attention. . . . Vague allegations of eroded self-esteem, apathy, fear and feelings of differentness, keeping a plaintiff in the 'addictive cycle,' do not amount to the basis for a constitutional claim."); Harris v. Lord, 957 F. Supp. 471, 476 (S.D.N.Y. 1997) (statements that plaintiff felt "unstable," fearful, and in need of help to "calm down" did not establish a serious medical need; the symptoms do not rise to the level or "pain, discomfort or risk to health" and her claim is not supported by "medical evidence, such as a physician's diagnosis.").

[463]The Rehabilitation Act and the Americans with Disabilities Act are discussed in § F.4.h.2 of this chapter. Mental impairments may constitute disabilities under those statutes.

[464]42 U.S.C. §§ 10801–10851.

[465]42 U.S.C. § 10803. Under the statute, "individual with a mental illness" is defined to include a person

(A) who has a significant mental illness or emotional impairment, as determined by a mental health professional qualified under the laws and regulations of the State; and

B)(i)(I) who is an inpatient or resident in a facility rendering care or treatment, even if the whereabouts of such inpatient or resident are unknown;

assistance or representation to prisoners.[466] There are similar systems for persons with developmental disabilities,[467] traumatic brain injury,[468] and other disabilities.[469] However, P&A organizations tend to be small, and they are responsible for assisting those in civilian institutions as well, so they cannot help everyone who requests their services, and some of them may not do prison-related work at all.

As with other kinds of medical care, prisoners are not entitled to their choice of treatment[470] or to the best possible treatment.[471] If professional judgment is exercised and some treatment is provided, courts will generally not find deliberate indifference.[472] A system of mental health care that has

some shortcomings but still provides care to those with "truly serious mental needs" is not unconstitutional.[473]

However, courts have found unconstitutional deficiencies in various aspects of psychiatric care and treatment of mentally ill prisoners, including the lack of mental health screening on intake,[474] the failure to follow up inmates with known or suspected mental disorders,[475] the failure to

___

(II) who is in the process of being admitted to a facility rendering care or treatment, including persons being transported to such a facility; or;

(III) who is involuntarily confined in a municipal detention facility for reasons other than serving a sentence resulting from conviction for a criminal offense. . . .

42 U.S.C. § 10802(4).

[466]*See* Oregon Advocacy Center v. Mink, 322 F.3d 1101, 1121–22 (9th Cir. 2003) (affirming injunction requiring prompt transfers of prisoners found incompetent to stand trial to mental hospitals). P&A organizations may represent prisoners directly, or they may sue in their own name on behalf of "representative constituents" with mental illness. Indiana Protection & Advocacy Servs. v. Indiana Family & Social Servs. Admin., ___ F.3d ___, 2010 WL 1610117, *8–12 (7th Cir. 2010) (en banc) (discussing P&A organizations' standing to bring suit); Oregon Advocacy Center v. Mink, 322 F.3d at 1109–13 (same); Aiken v. Nixon, 236 F. Supp. 2d 211, 224 (N.D.N.Y. 2002) (same).

[467]42 U.S.C. § 15043; *see* Tennessee Protection & Advocacy, Inc. v. Wells, 371 F.3d 342, 345 (6th Cir. 2004) (describing statutory scheme and operation of P&A system).

[468]42 U.S.C. § 300d-53.

[469]29 U.S.C. § 794e.

[470]Jackson v. Fair, 846 F.2d 811, 817–18 (1st Cir. 1988); Meriwether v. Faulkner, 821 F.2d 408, 413–14 (7th Cir. 1987).

[471]Some courts have stated that psychiatric treatment may be "limited to that which may be provided on a reasonable cost and time basis." Bowring v. Godwin, 551 F.2d 44, 48 (4th Cir. 1977); *accord*, Woodall v. Foti, 648 F.2d 268, 272 (5th Cir. 1981); *see also* U.S. v. Kidder, 869 F.2d 1328, 1331 (9th Cir. 1989) (the fact that the most appropriate care was not available in prison did not render a prison sentence unconstitutional). *But see* Langley v. Coughlin, 888 F.2d 252, 254 (2d Cir. 1989) (prison must provide "reasonably necessary" care that the prisoner could obtain if not incarcerated, even if it is expensive); *see also* § F.1 of this chapter, nn.299–300, concerning cost-based restrictions on medical care.

[472]Harris v. Thigpen, 941 F.2d 1495, 1510–11 (11th Cir. 1991); Murphy v. Lane, 833 F.2d 106, 108 (7th Cir. 1987) (receipt of some psychiatric care and prompt treatment by a prisoner who had tried to kill himself showed that there was no deliberate indifference); Supre v. Ricketts, 792 F.2d 958, 963 (10th Cir. 1986); Farmer v. Carlson, 685 F. Supp. 1335, 1341 (M.D.Pa. 1988) (two-month delay in responding to a transgender inmate's request for psychiatric care did not constitute deliberate indifference); Peterkin v. Jeffes, 661 F. Supp. 895, 917–19 (E.D.Pa. 1987) (where death row inmates had access to mental health staff, distrust of staff and lack of privacy in consultations did not render services unconstitutional), *aff'd in*

pertinent part, 855 F.2d 1021 (3d Cir. 1988); Capps v. Atiyeh, 559 F. Supp. 894, 921 (D.Or. 1982) (no constitutional violation found despite "infrequent" contact with treatment staff, lack of treatment plans, and useless records); Rodney v. Romano, 814 F. Supp. 311, 313 (E.D.N.Y. 1993). *But see* cases cited in nn.477, 485 of this section.

The failure to provide any treatment is not unconstitutional if there is no known cure or generally accepted treatment method for the prisoner's disorder. Bailey v. Gardebring, 940 F.2d 1150, 1155 (8th Cir. 1991).

[473]Grubbs v. Bradley, 552 F. Supp. 1052, 1129–30 (M.D.Tenn. 1982); *accord*, Capps v. Atiyeh, 559 F. Supp. 894, 920 (D.Or. 1982); *see* Atkins v. County of Orange, 372 F. Supp. 2d 377 (S.D.N.Y. 2005) (rejecting the plaintiffs' allegations of constitutionally deficient mental health care, stating disagreements about treatment do not raise a constitutional claim, temporary lapses and short delays do not constitute deliberate indifference, the plaintiffs do not show harm resulting from the delays, and overall they got a reasonable amount of care).

[474]Gibson v. County of Washoe, Nev., 290 F.3d 1175, 1189 (9th Cir. 2002) (jail's failure for several years to provide mental health screening on intake could be found deliberately indifferent, as could policy delaying medical attention and provision of psychiatric medication); Coleman v. Wilson, 912 F. Supp. 1282, 1298 & n.10, 1305–06 (E.D.Cal. 1995) (adequate prison mental health care requires "a systematic program for screening and evaluating inmates to identify those in need of mental health care"; a system that provided care only to those who self-report, who have medical records indicating prior psychiatric history, who exhibit bizarre behavior, or who ask to be seen by a psychiatrist, was constitutionally inadequate, since some seriously mentally ill inmates are incapable of making their needs for care known); Inmates of Occoquan v. Barry, 717 F. Supp. 854, 868 (D.D.C. 1989); Balla v. Idaho State Bd. of Correction, 595 F. Supp. 1558, 1577 (D.Idaho 1984); Ruiz v. Estelle, 503 F. Supp. 1265, 1339 (S.D.Tex. 1980), *aff'd in part, rev'd in part on other grounds*, 679 F.2d 1115 (5th Cir. 1982); Inmates of Allegheny County Jail v. Pierce, 487 F. Supp. 638, 642, 644 (W.D.Pa. 1980); Pugh v. Locke, 406 F. Supp. 318, 324 (M.D.Ala. 1976), *aff'd in part and modified sub nom.* Newman v. Alabama, 559 F.2d 283 (5th Cir. 1977).

In *Gates v. Cook*, 376 F.3d 323, 342–43 (5th Cir. 2004), involving conditions in a death row unit, the court affirmed an order requiring officials "to give each inmate private, comprehensive mental health examinations on a yearly basis."

[475]Clark-Murphy v. Foreback, 439 F.3d 280, 289–92 (6th Cir. 2006) (holding staff members were not entitled to qualified immunity for failing to get psychiatric assistance for an obviously deranged prisoner); Gibson v. County of Washoe, Nev., 290 F.3d 1175, 1190 (9th Cir. 2002) (policies that prevented a manic and disruptive prisoner from receiving medication and intake screening for 72 hours could be found deliberately indifferent); King v. Frank, 328 F. Supp. 2d 940, 947–48 (W.D.Wis. 2004) (complaint that plaintiff received no "mental health programming" and that

hospitalize inmates whose conditions cannot adequately be treated in prison,[476] gross departures from professional standards in treatment,[477] and the failure to separate severely mentally ill inmates from the mentally healthy.[478]

(Mixing mentally ill inmates with those who are not mentally ill may violate the rights of both groups. [479]) Courts have also held that housing mentally ill prisoners under conditions of extreme isolation is unconstitutional.[480]

---

there were not enough licensed mental health providers stated a claim); Duffey v. Bryant, 950 F. Supp. 1168, 1177–78 (M.D.Ga. 1997) (jail staff could be held liable for failing to get care for a manic-depressive prisoner who died in jail of malnutrition and dehydration); Arnold on behalf of H.B. v. Lewis, 803 F. Supp. 246, 257 (D.Ariz. 1992).

[476]Oregon Advocacy Center v. Mink, 322 F.3d 1101, 1121–22 (9th Cir. 2003) (holding months-long delays in moving persons found incompetent to stand trial to mental hospital denied due process); Terry v. Hill, 232 F. Supp. 2d 934, 943–44 (E.D.Ark. 2002) (holding lengthy delays in transferring mentally ill detainees to mental hospital were unconstitutional); Casey v. Lewis, 834 F. Supp. 1477, 1548–49 (D.Ariz. 1993); Arnold on behalf of H.B. v. Lewis, 803 F. Supp. at 257.

[477]Smith v. Jenkins, 919 F.2d 90, 93 (8th Cir. 1990) (care that "so deviated from professional standards that it amounted to deliberate indifference" would violate the Constitution); Waldrop v. Evans, 871 F.2d 1030, 1033 (11th Cir.), rehearing denied, 880 F.2d 421 (11th Cir. 1989) ("grossly incompetent or inadequate care" can constitute deliberate indifference; the prisoner's medication was discontinued abruptly and without justification); Greason v. Kemp, 891 F.2d 829, 835 (11th Cir. 1990) (similar to Waldrop; "grossly inadequate psychiatric care" can be deliberate indifference); Page v. Norvell, 186 F. Supp. 2d 1134, 1138 (D.Ore. 2000) (holding allegation that a mental health professional downgraded the plaintiff's mental health diagnosis after meeting with him for only two minutes, there was no evidence to support his "clinical findings," and may have purposefully misdiagnosed him, supported a deliberate indifference claim); Langley v. Coughlin, 715 F. Supp. 522, 537–41 (S.D.N.Y. 1988) ("consistent and repeated failures . . . over an extended period of time" could establish deliberate indifference).

[478]Gates v. Cook, 376 F.3d 323, 342–43 (5th Cir. 2004) (affirming order "to house the inmates with psychosis and severe mental illnesses separately from the other inmates" in death row unit); Cortes-Quinones v. Jiminez-Nettleship, 842 F.2d 556, 560–61 (1st Cir. 1988) (transferring a mentally ill inmate to general population in a crowded jail with no psychiatric facilities constituted deliberate indifference); Morales Feliciano v. Rossello Gonzalez, 13 F. Supp. 2d 151, 209, 211 (D.P.R. 1998) (leaving severely mentally ill patients in general population and failing to hospitalize prisoners whose mental health condition requires it constitute deliberate indifference); Casey v. Lewis, 834 F. Supp. at 1548–49 (condemning delays that resulted in psychotic inmates remaining in lockdown); Tillery v. Owens, 719 F. Supp. 1256, 1303–04 (W.D.Pa. 1989) (Constitution requires separate unit for severely mentally ill, i.e., those who will not take their medication regularly, maintain normal hygienic practices, accept dietary restrictions, or report symptoms of illness.), aff'd, 907 F.2d 418 (3d Cir. 1990); Inmates of Occoquan v. Barry, 717 F. Supp. 854, 868 (D.D.C. 1989) (inmates with mental health problems must be placed in a separate area or a hospital and not in administrative/punitive segregation area); Langley v. Coughlin, 709 F. Supp. 482, 484–85 (S.D.N.Y.) (placement of mentally ill in punitive segregation resulted in conditions that might violate the Eighth Amendment), appeal dismissed, 888 F.2d 252 (2d Cir. 1989); Langley v. Coughlin, 715 F. Supp. at 543–44

(same); Finney v. Mabry, 534 F. Supp. 1026, 1036–37 (E.D.Ark. 1982) (separate facility for "most severely mentally disturbed" required); Inmates of Allegheny County Jail v. Pierce, 487 F. Supp. at 644; see also Morales Feliciano v. Hernandez Colon, 697 F. Supp. 37, 48 (D.P.R. 1988) (mentally ill inmates barred from a jail). Contra, Delgado v. Cady, 576 F. Supp. 1446, 1456 (E.D.Wis. 1983) (housing of psychotics in segregation unit upheld).

Some courts have suggested that a prisoner's mental condition must be considered in connection with disciplinary proceedings. See Ch. 4, § D.1.o.

[479]Gates v. Cook, 376 F.3d 323, 342–43 (5th Cir. 2004) (citing findings from death row unit of severe psychiatric deterioration of mentally ill prisoners whose behavior aggravates the problems of sanitation and sleep deprivation for other prisoners); Thaddeus-X v. Blatter, 175 F.3d 378, 403 (6th Cir. 1999) (en banc) (allegation of placement where mentally ill patients are kept, where prisoners throw human waste and urine at each other and at staff, there is a constant foul odor, the prisoners repeatedly flood the gallery and bang their footlockers, some refuse to bathe or flush their toilets, and the area is cleaned only rarely, states an Eighth Amendment claim); DeMallory v. Cullen, 855 F.2d 442, 444–45 (7th Cir. 1988) (allegation that mentally ill inmates were knowingly housed with non-mentally ill in a high-security unit and that they caused filthy and dangerous conditions stated an Eighth Amendment claim against prison officials); Goff v. Harper, 59 F. Supp. 2d 910, 913 (S.D.Iowa 1999) (noting prior finding of Eighth Amendment violation resulting from "the pandemonium and bedlam the mentally-stable inmates must suffer" from confinement with mentally ill inmates who can't or don't control their behavior); Carty v. Farrelly, 957 F. Supp. 727, 738–39 (D.V.I. 1997) ("Failure to house mentally ill inmates apart from the general prison population also violates the constitutional rights of both groups."); Nolley v. County of Erie, 776 F. Supp. 715, 738–40 (W.D.N.Y. 1991); Tillery v. Owens, 719 F. Supp. at 1303 (citing increased tension for psychologically normal inmates and danger of retaliation against mentally ill); Langley v. Coughlin, 709 F. Supp. at 484–85; Langley v. Coughlin, 715 F. Supp. at 543–44; see Hassine v. Jeffes, 846 F.2d 169, 178 n.5 (3d Cir. 1988) (prisoners could seek relief from the consequences of other inmates' failure to receive adequate mental health services); see Bracewell v. Lobmiller, 938 F. Supp. 1571, 1579 (M.D.Ala. 1996) (holding that exposure to deranged and unsanitary actions of prisoners with mental illness were serious enough to violate Eighth Amendment, but defendants were not shown to have sufficient knowledge to be deliberately indifferent), aff'd, 116 F.3d 1493 (11th Cir. 1997) (table).

[480]Jones'El v. Berge, 164 F. Supp. 2d 1096, 1116–25 (W.D.Wis. 2001) (granting preliminary injunction requiring removal of seriously mentally ill from "supermax" prison); Ruiz v. Estelle, 37 F. Supp. 2d 855, 915 (S.D.Tex. 1999) (holding "administrative segregation is being utilized unconstitutionally to house mentally ill inmates—inmates whose illness can only be exacerbated by the depravity of their confinement"), rev'd and remanded on other grounds, 243 F.3d 941 (5th Cir. 2001), adhered to on remand, 154 F. Supp. 2d 975, 984–86 (S.D.Tex. 2001); Coleman v. Wilson, 912 F. Supp. 1282, 1320–21 (E.D.Cal. 1995) (inappropriate disciplinary treatment and placement in segregation units of prisoners with mental illness was unconstitutional); Madrid v. Gomez, 889 F.

Many prison mental health care cases focus on the lack of adequate and qualified staff.[481] Several courts have concluded that the lack of an on-site psychiatrist in a large prison is unconstitutional.[482] The failure to train correctional staff to deal with mentally ill prisoners can also constitute deliberate indifference.[483] A recent decision holds that the use of chemical agents against prisoners with mental illness who engage in disruptive behavior as a result of their illness violates the Eighth Amendment.[484]

Psychiatric medication is an essential element of mental health care. The unjustified discontinuation of medications, which can have disastrous results, may be found unconstitutional[485]—though, as with other kinds of medical care, mere differences of opinion over appropriate medication do not

---

Supp. 1146, 1265 (N.D.Cal. 1995) (holding retention of mentally ill prisoners in Pelican Bay isolation unit unconstitutional); Casey v. Lewis, 834 F. Supp. 1477, 1548–49 (D.Ariz. 1993) (condemning placement and retention of mentally ill prisoners in lockdown status); Langley v. Coughlin, 715 F. Supp. 522, 540 (S.D.N.Y. 1988) (holding that psychiatric evidence that prison officials fail to screen out from SHU "those individuals who, by virtue of their mental condition, are likely to be severely and adversely affected by placement there" raises a triable Eighth Amendment issue); Inmates of Occoquan v. Barry, 717 F. Supp. 854, 868 (D.D.C. 1989) (holding that inmates with mental health problems must be placed in a separate area or a hospital and not in administrative/punitive segregation area). *But see* Scarver v. Litscher, 434 F.3d 972, 976–77 (7th Cir. 2006) (holding that prison officials who were not shown to have known that keeping a psychotic prisoner under conditions of extreme isolation and heat would aggravate his mental illness could not be found deliberately indifferent); Horne v. Coughlin, 155 F.3d 26, 31 (2d Cir. 1998) (six months' SHU confinement of prisoner with mental retardation did not violate the Eighth Amendment).

[481]Greason v. Kemp, 891 F.2d at 837–40 (prison clinic director, prison system mental health director, and prison warden could be found deliberately indifferent based on their knowing toleration of a "clearly inadequate" mental health staff); Waldrop v. Evans, 871 F.2d at 1036 (physician's failure to refer a suicidal prisoner to a psychiatrist could constitute deliberate indifference); Cabrales v. County of Los Angeles, 864 F.2d 1454, 1461 (9th Cir. 1988) (deliberate indifference was established where mental health staff could only spend "minutes per month" with disturbed inmates), *vacated*, 490 U.S. 1087 (1989), *reinstated*, 886 F.2d 235 (9th Cir. 1989); Casey v. Lewis, 834 F. Supp. at 1548–49; King v. Frank, 328 F. Supp. 2d 940, 947–48 (W.D.Wis. 2004) ("Staff that are untrained or too few in numbers may contribute to an Eighth Amendment violation."); Goff v. Harper, 59 F. Supp. 2d 910, 924 (S.D.Iowa 1999) (directing officials to fill vacant psychologist positions); Morales Feliciano v. Rossello Gonzalez, 13 F. Supp. 2d 151, 210 (D.P.R. 1998) (failure to provide mental health staff sufficient to meet the needs of the prison population is unconstitutional); Carty v. Farrelly, 957 F. Supp. 727, 739 (D.V.I. 1997) (citing lack of on-site mental health staff and identification of prisoners requiring mental health care by unqualified persons); Hartman v. Correctional Medical Services, Inc., 960 F. Supp. 1577, 1582–83 (M.D.Fla. 1996) (holding medical provider could be found deliberately indifferent based on evidence that it permitted a person with only a master's degree and no professional licenses to have authority over mental health referrals and suicide precautions); Coleman v. Wilson, 912 F. Supp. 1282, 1298 & n.10, 1306–07 (E.D.Cal. 1995) (stating adequate prison mental health care requires "employment of a sufficient number of trained mental health professionals"; holding recommendation of "timely, responsible, and adequate care provided by qualified (and appropriately licensed) staff," was "not materially different from the constitutional requirement of ready access to competent medical staff"); Tillery v. Owens, 719 F. Supp. at 1302–03 ("gross staffing deficiencies" and lack of mental health training of nurses supported finding of deliberate indifference); Inmates of Occoquan v. Barry, 717 F. Supp. at 868 ("woefully short" mental health staff supported a finding of unconstitutionality); Langley v. Coughlin, 715 F. Supp. at 540 (use of untrained or unqualified personnel with inadequate supervision by psychiatrist supported constitutional

claims); Inmates of Allegheny County Jail v. Pierce, 487 F. Supp. at 640–45; Ruiz v. Estelle, 503 F. Supp. 1265, 1339 (S.D.Tex. 1980), *aff'd in part and rev'd in part on other grounds*, 679 F.2d 1115 (5th Cir. 1982).

[482]Wellman v. Faulkner, 715 F.2d 269, 272–73 (7th Cir. 1983); Ramos v. Lamm, 639 F.2d 559, 578 (10th Cir. 1980); Cody v. Hillard, 599 F. Supp. 1025, 1044 (D.S.D. 1984), *aff'd in part and rev'd in part on other grounds*, 830 F.2d 912 (8th Cir. 1987) (en banc); Balla v. Idaho State Bd. of Correction, 595 F. Supp. 1558, 1577–78 (D.Idaho 1984). *Contra*, Capps v. Atiyeh, 559 F. Supp. 894, 917–21 (D.Or. 1982); *see also* Young v. City of Augusta, Ga. through DeVaney, 59 F.3d 1160, 1171 (11th Cir. 1995) (rejecting argument that local jails must be able to provide on-site expert psychiatric care).

[483]Young v. City of Augusta, Ga. through DeVaney, 59 F.3d 1160, 1171 (11th Cir. 1995) (claim that "jail employees are inadequately selected or trained to recognize the need to remove a mentally ill inmate to a hospital or to dispense medication as prescribed" could support municipal liability if deliberate indifference were shown); Langley v. Coughlin, 709 F. Supp. at 483–85; Kendrick v. Bland, 541 F. Supp. 21, 25–26 (W.D.Ky. 1981); *see also* Allen v. Muskogee, Okla., 119 F.3d 837, 841–42 (10th Cir. 1997) (evidence of failure to train police to deal with mentally disturbed, armed individuals supported claim against municipality); Sharpe v. City of Lewisburg, Tenn., 677 F. Supp. 1362, 1367–68 (M.D.Tenn. 1988) (failure to train police to deal with mentally disturbed individual supported damage award).

[484]Thomas v. McNeil, 2009 WL 64616, *25–27 (M.D.Fla., Jan. 9, 2009), *judgment entered*, 2009 WL 605306 (M.D.Fla., Mar. 9, 2009).

[485]*See* Steele v. Shah, 87 F.3d 1266, 1269–70 (11th Cir. 1996) (holding abrupt discontinuation of medications, with no explanation, examination, or review of records, could constitute deliberate indifference); Greason v. Kemp, 891 F.2d 829 (11th Cir. 1990) (prisoner killed himself); Waldrop v. Evans, 871 F.2d 1030 (11th Cir. 1989) (prisoner blinded and castrated himself); McDuffie v. Hopper, 982 F. Supp. 817, 829 (M.D.Ala. 1997) (prisoner killed himself). *But see* Campbell v. Sikes, 169 F.3d 1353, 1367–68 (11th Cir. 1999) (holding discontinuation of medication by doctor who did not know the prisoner's diagnosis, having not obtained her medical records but having read a summary, was not deliberately indifferent); Vaughan v. Lacey, 49 F.3d 1344, 1346 (8th Cir. 1995) (substantial reduction in medications after transfer was only a difference of medical opinion). *Cf.* Wakefield v. Thompson, 177 F.3d 1160, 1164 (9th Cir. 1999) (holding Eighth Amendment requires prison officials to provide mentally ill prisoners with a supply of medication upon release).

raise a constitutional issue.[486] The use of these medications requires continuing monitoring and assessment of their effects.[487] Prisoners who are taking psychotropic medications at the time of their release must be provided with a sufficient supply to ensure availability until the prisoner has an opportunity to arrange for their continuance after release.[488]

The courts are agreed that transsexualism, referred to medically as gender identity disorder (GID), is a serious medical need.[489] The denial of any treatment at all for it constitutes deliberate indifference.[490] Most cases hold that the prisoner has no right to any specific form of treatment such as female hormone therapy.[491] However, more recent decisions have emphasized the need for an individualized determination of each person's treatment needs and the unacceptability of blanket rules governing particular types of treatment.[492]

---

[486]Toguchi v. Chung, 391 F.3d 1051, 1059–60 (9th Cir. 2004) (finding no deliberate indifference where drug interaction killed the prisoner); Ciarpaglini v. Saini, 352 F.3d 328, 331 (7th Cir. 2003).

[487]Gates v. Cook, 376 F.3d 323, 342–43 (5th Cir. 2004) (affirming injunction requiring monitoring and assessment of medication levels of inmates receiving psychotropic medications); Wellman v. Faulkner, 715 F.2d at 272–73 (noting need for a psychiatrist to supervise medications); Ginest v. Board of County Commissioners of Carbon County, 333 F. Supp. 2d 1190, 1201 (D.Wyo. 2004) ("all patients on psychotropic medical [sic] must be monitored in a periodic basis to determine (1) if the drug is causing any harmful side-effects, and (2) if the drug is working the way the doctor intends for it to work"; "Prison officials have a constitutional duty to adequately monitor inmates [sic] prescribed psychotropic medication, whether they request such monitoring or not."); Page v. Norvell, 186 F. Supp. 2d 1134, 1139 (D.Ore. 2000) (holding that a mental health professional could be found deliberately indifferent for denying a prisoner a review of medication); Coleman v. Wilson, 912 F. Supp. 1282, 1298 & n.10, 1309–12 (E.D.Cal. 1995) (holding adequate prison mental health care requires "administration of psychotropic medication only with appropriate supervision and periodic evaluation"; finding supervision inadequate); Lelsz v. Kavanagh, 673 F. Supp. 828, 843 (N.D.Tex. 1987) (non-prisoner case); Ruiz v. Estelle, 503 F. Supp. at 1339; see also U.S. v. State of Michigan, 680 F. Supp. 928, 979–83, 1005–07 (W.D.Mich. 1987) (describing safeguards for use of psychotropic medications).

[488]Wakefield v. Thompson, 177 F.3d 1160, 1164 (9th Cir. 1999).

[489]Cuoco v. Moritsugu, 222 F.3d 99, 106 (2d Cir. 2000) and cases cited; White v. Farrier, 849 F.2d 322, 325 (8th Cir. 1988); Meriwether v. Faulkner, 821 F.2d 408, 411–13 (7th Cir. 1987); Phillips v. Michigan Dep't of Corrections, 731 F. Supp. 792, 799–800 (W.D.Mich. 1990), aff'd, 932 F.2d 969 (6th Cir. 1991).

[490]Meriwether v. Faulkner, 821 F.2d at 414.

[491]See Praylor v. Texas Dep't of Criminal Justice, 430 F.3d 1208, 1209 (5th Cir. 2005) (per curiam) (upholding denial of hormone therapy under the circumstances, noting that system provided hormone therapy in some cases); De'Lonta v. Angelone, 330 F.3d 630, 635 (4th Cir. 2003) (holding prisoner with GID was entitled to treatment for compulsion to self-mutilate); Maggert v. Hanks, 131 F.3d 670, 671–72 (7th Cir. 1997) (stating in dictum that prison officials need not provide hormonal and surgical procedures to "cure" GID); White v. Farrier, 849 F.2d at 327–28; Meriwether v. Faulkner, 821 F.2d at 413; Supre v. Ricketts, 792 F.2d 958, 963 (10th Cir. 1986); Farmer v. Carlson, 685 F. Supp. 1335, 1340–41 (M.D.Pa. 1988); Lamb v. Maschner, 633 F. Supp. 351, 353–54

(D.Kan. 1986). But see Phillips v. Michigan Dep't of Corrections, 731 F. Supp. at 800–01 (granting preliminary injunction requiring continued estrogen treatment based on a record of ridicule and mistreatment by prison medical staff).

[492]See De'Lonta v. Angelone, 330 F.3d at 635 (holding termination of estrogen therapy for gender identity disorder "based solely on the Policy rather than on a medical judgment concerning [the plaintiff's] specific circumstances" could support a deliberate indifference finding); Allard v. Gomez, 9 Fed.Appx. 793, 794 (9th Cir. 2001) (unpublished) (holding the record raised an Eighth Amendment question whether a transgender prisoner was denied hormone therapy based on "an individualized medical evaluation or as a result of a blanket rule, the application of which constituted deliberate indifference"); South v. Gomez, 211 F.3d 1275, 2000 WL 222611, *2 (9th Cir. 2000) (unpublished) (holding that abrupt termination of hormone therapy, rather than tapering it off as recommended by all doctors involved, could be deliberate indifference); Fields v. Smith, 2010 WL 1325165 (E.D. Wis., March 31, 2010) (holding state Inmate Sex Change Prevention Act is unconstitutional because it bars funding for hormone treatment without regard to individuals' medical condition); Sundstrom v. Frank, 2007 WL 3046240, *18, *21 (E.D.Wis., Oct. 15, 2007) (holding state Inmate Sex Change Prevention Act might be unconstitutional on its face because it bars both hormonal and surgical treatment without regard to individual determinations of medical need; rejecting argument that such treatment presents security risks in light of evidence that many transgender prisoners will continue to present as female through appearance, mannerism, etc.); Barrett v. Coplan, 292 F. Supp. 2d 281, 286 (D.N.H. 2003) (allegation that transgender prisoner was denied even an evaluation for psychological, medical, or surgical treatment contrary to recognized professional standards stated an Eighth Amendment claim; "the Eighth Amendment does not permit necessary medical care to be denied to a prisoner because the care is expensive or because it might be controversial or unpopular. . . . A blanket policy that prohibits a prison's medical staff from making a medical determination of an individual inmate's medical needs and prescribing and providing adequate care to treat those needs violates the Eighth Amendment."); Brooks v. Berg, 270 F. Supp. 2d 302, 310 (N.D.N.Y.) (holding persons with GID entitled to some form of treatment determined by medical professionals and not by prison administrators; holding a policy to treat transgender only for those diagnosed before incarceration "contrary to a decided body of law"), vacated in part on other grounds, 289 F. Supp. 2d 286 (N.D.N.Y. 2003); Kosilek v. Maloney, 221 F. Supp. 2d 156 (D.Mass. 2002) (holding an individualized determination by medical professionals is required; a blanket policy denying initiation of hormone therapy in prison is impermissible); Wolfe v. Horn, 130 F. Supp. 2d 648, 652–53 (E.D.Pa. 2001) (holding that refusal to continue hormone treatment commenced before incarceration may constitute deliberate indifference). Even courts that deny gender-affecting relief to transgender prisoners seem to acknowledge that under some circumstances it might be appropriate. Compare Praylor v. Texas Dep't of Criminal Justice, 430 F.3d at 1209 ("based upon the instant record and circumstances of Praylor's complaint, the denial of his specific request for hormone therapy does not constitute deliberate indifference") with Maggert v. Hanks, 131 F.3d 670,

Sometimes you may wish to avoid psychiatric treatment you don't want and don't think you need. You are entitled to notice and a hearing before being committed to a mental hospital, since the stigma attached to psychiatric commitment and the possibility of involuntary subjection to psychiatric treatment constitute a deprivation of liberty requiring due process.[493] This is true even if the mental hospital is part of the correction department.[494] The process due before commitment to a mental hospital includes written notice, an adversary hearing including the right to present witnesses and confront and cross-examine adverse witnesses, an independent decision-maker, a written decision, and assistance from a qualified and independent adviser.[495] Based on the same reasoning, it has been held that subjection of all prisoners to a behavior modification program without a showing of individual need denies due process.[496] If you have been involuntarily committed to a hospital for the criminally insane because you were incompetent to stand trial, you can only be kept there long enough to determine if you will become competent in the foreseeable future.[497] Officials have a duty to inform the court when you

no longer require treatment.[498] Return to prison from a mental hospital requires only the most minimal procedural protections,[499] or none at all.[500]

Transfer to a mental hospital for evaluation only and not for treatment does not require due process.[501] Neither does placement in mental health-related programs that do not amount to psychiatric commitment.[502] Whether transfer to a particular mental health unit is subject to due process requirements under *Vitek* depends on the nature of the unit, and the plaintiff must submit evidence on that subject.[503] Prisoners may be required to participate in mental health-related programs for reasons of rehabilitation.[504]

Psychiatric treatment may not be used for disciplinary purposes,[505] nor may psychiatric confinement or isolation be imposed under degrading or excessively restrictive conditions.[506] The courts have required that the use of seclusion

---

671–72 (7th Cir. 1997) (stating in dictum that prison officials need not provide hormonal and surgical procedures to "cure" GID).

[493]Vitek v. Jones, 445 U.S. 480, 494–96, 100 S. Ct. 1254 (1980); *accord*, Young v. Breeding, 929 F. Supp. 1103, 1108 (N.D.Ill. 1996) (allegation of transfer to a mental hospital without a hearing states a constitutional claim).

One federal court has held that temporary transfers to a mental hospital do not require due process. Gay v. Turner, 994 F.2d 425, 427 (8th Cir. 1993). We think this decision is inconsistent with *Vitek.* Another has held that commitment to a mental institution at the end of a prison sentence requires the protections of *Vitek.* Alston v. Parker, 363 F.3d 229, 231 (3d Cir. 2004).

At least one court has held that transfer to a psychiatric facility can be a sufficiently adverse action that it is unconstitutional to threaten such transfer in retaliation for engaging in First Amendment-protected activity such as filing grievances. Morales v. Mackalm, 278 F.3d 126, 132 (2d Cir. 2002); *see also* Thaddeus-X v. Blatter, 175 F.3d 378, 398 (6th Cir. 1999) (en banc) ("transfer to the area of the prison used to house mentally disturbed inmates, especially combined with the conditions allegedly present there," could deter protected activity).

[494]Baugh v. Woodard, 808 F.2d 333, 335 n.2 (4th Cir. 1987); Witzke v. Johnson, 656 F. Supp. 294, 297–98 (W.D.Mich. 1987); *see also* State v. Harris, 236 Neb. 783, 463 N.W. 2d 829, 833–36 (Neb. 1990) (same rule applied to criminal defendant committed by court as a "mentally disturbed sex offender").

[495]Miller v. Vitek, 437 F. Supp. 569, 575 (D.Neb. 1977), *aff'd as modified sub nom.* Vitek v. Jones, 480, 496–500, 100 S. Ct. 1254 (1980). Such hearings may be conducted by videoconferencing. U.S. v. Baker, 45 F.3d 837 (4th Cir. 1994).

[496]Canterino v. Wilson, 546 F. Supp. 174, 208–09 (W.D.Ky. 1982), *vacated and remanded on other grounds*, 869 F.2d 948 (6th Cir. 1989). *Cf.* Davie v. Wingard, 958 F. Supp. 1244, 1257–58 (S.D.Ohio 1997) (placement in "Progressive Readjustment Inmate Development Environment" ("PRIDE") behavior modification program after a disciplinary conviction did not violate the Eighth Amendment).

[497]Jackson v. Indiana, 406 U.S. 715, 738, 92 S. Ct. 1845 (1972); *see* O'Connor v. Donaldson, 422 U.S. 563, 95 S. Ct. 2486 (1975)

(unjustified confinement in a civil mental hospital is unconstitutional).

[498]Stuebig v. Hammel, 446 F. Supp. 31, 32–34 (M.D.Pa. 1977). *But see* Stuebig v. Hammel, 714 F.2d 292 (3d Cir. 1983) (damage claims dismissed because right was not "clearly established").

[499]Cruz v. Ward, 558 F.2d 658, 662–63 (2d Cir. 1977).

[500]Jackson v. Fair, 846 F.2d 811, 815–17 (1st Cir. 1988).

[501]U.S. v. Jones, 811 F.2d 444, 447–48 (8th Cir. 1987).

[502]Hall v. Unknown Agents of New York State Dep't of Correctional Services, 825 F.2d 642, 644–47 (2d Cir. 1977). In *Nwaokocha v. Sadowski*, 369 F. Supp. 362, 365, 373–74 (E.D.N.Y. 2005), the court upheld transfer to a federal medical center for "special care and treatment" without referring to any procedural protections or to *Vitek.*

[503]Okumoto v. Lattin, 649 F. Supp. 55, 57–58 (D.Nev. 1986).

[504]*See* cases cited in § F.4.b of this chapter, nn.522–526.

[505]Nelson v. Heyne, 491 F.2d 352, 356–57 (7th Cir. 1974) (tranquilizers could not be used to keep order); Knecht v. Gillman, 488 F.2d 1136, 1139–40 (8th Cir. 1973) (punitive use of drugs is unlawful); Wheeler v. Glass, 473 F.2d 983, 987 (7th Cir. 1973) (use of restraints for discipline of mentally retarded youths violated the Eighth Amendment); Wright v. McMann, 460 F.2d 126, 129 (2d Cir. 1972) (psychiatric isolation cells could not be used for disciplinary purposes); Breads v. Moehrle, 781 F. Supp. 953, 957 (W.D.N.Y. 1991) (claim that prisoner was a "disciplinary nightmare" did not justify involuntary medication); Negron v. Ward, 458 F. Supp. 748, 760–61 (S.D.N.Y. 1978) (damages awarded for disciplinary placement on seclusion ward).

[506]Young v. City of Augusta, Ga. through DeVaney, 59 F.3d 1160, 1173 (11th Cir. 1995) (allegation that plaintiff was held in isolation naked and chained to a bed among filth and excrement stated an Eighth Amendment claim); Scott v. Plante, 641 F.2d 117, 128 (3d Cir. 1981) (confinement in psychiatric hospital under inhuman conditions constituted "punishment" of a former detainee whose charges had been dismissed), *vacated*, 458 U.S. 1101 (1982), *on remand*, 691 F.2d 634, 637 (3d Cir. 1982); McCray v. Burrell, 516 F.2d 357, 369 (4th Cir. 1975) (en banc) (conditions of mental observation cell condemned); Martyr v. Bachik, 770 F. Supp. 1406 (D.Or. 1991) (restrictions on official correspondence enjoined); Tillery v. Owens, 719 F. Supp. 1256, 1303–04 (W.D.Pa. 1989) (psychiatric cells that were filthy, infested, and without furniture violated the Eighth Amendment), *aff'd*, 907 F.2d 418 (3d Cir. 1990); Flakes v. Percy, 511 F. Supp. 1325, 1330–41 (W.D.Wis. 1981)

and restraint be restricted to legitimate mental health purposes, subjected to close medical supervision, and conducted in a humane manner.[507]

(prisoners could not be locked in mental hospital cells without toilets for more than one hour); Feliciano v. Barcelo, 497 F. Supp. 14, 35 (D.P.R. 1979) (isolation without clothes or bedding with inadequate space, light, and ventilation condemned); Johnson v. Levine, 450 F. Supp. 648, 657–58 (D.Md. 1978) (psychiatric isolation cells similar to punitive segregation found unconstitutional), *aff'd in pertinent part*, 588 F.2d 1378, 1381 (4th Cir. 1978); *see also* Rascon v. Hardiman, 803 F.2d 269, 274–75 (7th Cir. 1986) (toleration of physical abuse to keep order in a prison psychiatric unit could violate the Constitution). *But see* Anderson v. County of Kern, 45 F.3d 1310, 1315 (9th Cir. 1995) (upholding the use of "safety cells" (padded cells with "pit toilets") for suicidal and violent inmates for brief periods of time, notwithstanding sanitation problems); Green v. Baron, 879 F.2d 305, 309–10 (8th Cir. 1989) (deprivation of bedding and hot meals and of clothing except underwear when the plaintiff was in his cell might be justified by the circumstances); Hawkins v. Hall, 644 F.2d 914, 916–18 (1st Cir. 1981) (brief confinement in a strip cell with a hole in the floor for a toilet did not violate the Eighth Amendment); McMahon v. Beard, 583 F.2d 172, 174–75 (5th Cir. 1978) (90 days' confinement in strip cell after suicide attempt was not unconstitutional).

[507]Buckley v. Rogerson, 133 F.3d 1125, 1127–30 (8th Cir. 1998) (evidence that the plaintiff was repeatedly placed in restraints and segregation without medical approval during his confinement in a prison mental hospital, that correction officers were allowed to develop "treatment plans" and that "treatment" also included depriving the plaintiff of clothing, blankets, bed and mattress in segregation, and that the plaintiff's treating doctor checked on him every 90 days supported a constitutional claim; there is a constitutional right to medical approval of restraints and segregation; "the freedom from bodily restraint is at the core of the liberty interest protected by the due process clause."); Wells v. Franzen, 777 F.2d 1258, 1261–62 (7th Cir. 1985) (restraint must be based on professional judgment; nature and duration must be reasonably related to its purpose); Campbell v. McGruder, 580 F.2d 521, 551 (D.C. Cir. 1978) (doctor's authorization, written records required); Ziemba v. Armstrong, 343 F. Supp. 2d 173, 184–85 (D.Conn. 2004) (allegation that plaintiff was restrained for 22 hours with only cursory examinations, despite his history of mental illness and obvious anxiety and agitation supported an Eighth Amendment claim), *aff'd in pertinent part*, 430 F.3d 623, 626 (2d Cir. 2005); Zigmund v. Foster, 106 F. Supp. 2d 352, 361 (D.Conn. 2000) (placement in four-point restraints and seclusion did not deny due process, but failure to have a physician assess plaintiff during 17 hours in restraints might be a "substantial departure from accepted professional judgment, practice, or standards"); Swans v. City of Lansing, 65 F. Supp. 2d 625, 638 (W.D.Mich. 1999) (affirming damage award where prisoner with mental illness died of asphyxia from being "hog-tied" pursuant to "unstated city policy of using maximum restraints on non-compliant prisoners" and where officer booked him rather than getting medical care); Jones v. Thompson, 818 F. Supp. 1263, 1268 (S.D.Ind. 1993) (five-day "hog-tying" of detainee was unconstitutional); U.S. v. State of Michigan, 680 F. Supp. 928, 977, 982–83 (W.D.Mich. 1987) (similar to *Campbell*); Inmates of Allegheny County Jail v. Wecht, 565 F. Supp. 1278, 1285 (W.D.Pa. 1983) (inmates not to be restrained without clothes or mattress); Wheeler v. Glass, 473 F.2d 983, 987 (7th Cir. 1973) (use of restraints

Prisoners have a right under the Due Process Clause to avoid the involuntary use of antipsychotic medication (Haldol, Prolixin, Mellaril, and similar drugs), but prison officials may force the prisoner to submit to them if she has a "serious mental illness . . ., if the inmate is dangerous to himself or others and the treatment is in the inmate's medical interest."[508] This holding is an exception to the general

---

for discipline was unconstitutional); Ferola v. Moran, 622 F. Supp. 814, 821–25 (D.R.I. 1985) (conditions of shackling, lack of medical supervision, and absence of policy held unconstitutional); Burks v. Teasdale, 492 F. Supp. 650, 679 (W.D.Mo. 1980) (lack of written policy governing restraint and seclusion was unconstitutional); Gawreys v. D.C. General Hospital, 480 F. Supp. 853, 855–56 (D.D.C. 1979) (metal restraints banned except for transportation); Owens-El v. Robinson, 457 F. Supp. 984, 990–91 (W.D.Pa. 1978) (inmates in restraints to have mattresses and clean bedding; medical authorization and record-keeping required), *aff'd in part and rev'd in part on other grounds sub nom.* Inmates of Allegheny County Jail v. Pierce, 612 F.2d 754 (3d Cir. 1979); Negron v. Preiser, 382 F. Supp. 535, 542–43 (S.D.N.Y. 1974) (records to be kept of reasons for seclusion). *But see* Campbell v. Sikes, 169 F.3d 1353 (11th Cir. 1999) (repeated placement in "L-shaped restraints" (hog-tying), for up to 27 hours, was not unconstitutional, since the plaintiff was undisputedly a danger to herself and others and had shown great ingenuity in escaping from less severe restraints; she was monitored every 15 minutes; she got meals, bathroom breaks, and sometimes a mattress to lie on; defendants complied with all their own procedures, including documentation, and in some cases refused requests to restrain her); O'Donnell v. Thomas, 826 F.2d 788, 790 (8th Cir. 1987) (use of restraints for five days was not unconstitutional where a doctor had ordered them after a suicide attempt).

[508]Washington v. Harper, 494 U.S. 210, 227, 110 S. Ct. 1028 (1990); *see* Maul v. Constan, 928 F.2d 784, 785 (7th Cir. 1991) (lower court found that forcible administration of psychotropics denied due process); Bee v. Greaves, 910 F.2d 686, 687–88 (10th Cir. 1990) (upholding damages for the unjustified administration of thorazine); Roberson v. Goodman, 296 F. Supp. 2d 1051, 1054–55 (D.N.D. 2003) (upholding involuntary medication, after a hearing, based on prisoner's uncontrolled assaultive behavior and his evident paranoia and its consequences); Blissett v. Eisensmidt, 940 F. Supp. 449, 456 (N.D.N.Y. 1996) (forcible injection could constitute excessive force and battery; jury verdict upheld); Breads v. Moehrle, 781 F. Supp. at 957. *But see* Sullivan v. Flannigan, 8 F.3d 591, 599 (7th Cir. 1993) (prisoner was not entitled to a drug-free period so he could prove he could function without medication); Williams v. Anderson, 959 F.2d 1411, 1414–17 (7th Cir. 1992) (defendants were protected by qualified immunity for involuntary medication before the *Washington* decision).

The liberty interest in avoiding unwanted psychotropic medications is applicable to persons on parole or supervised release as well. *See* U.S. v. Williams, 356 F.3d 1045, 1057 (9th Cir. 2004) (holding that supervised release condition to take whatever medications the defendant's doctor prescribed must be made only on a "medically-informed record" and must meet the statutory requirement that supervised release restrictions impose "no greater deprivation of liberty than is reasonably necessary"); Felcer v. Fiedler, 974 F.2d 1484, 1496–1500 (7th Cir. 1992) (involuntary medication of parolee denied due process).

rule that competent adults are entitled to refuse medical treatment.[509]

When prisoners are involuntarily medicated because of dangerousness, due process requires procedural protections, but not a judicial hearing.[510] It is enough if there is a decision by medical professionals who are not currently involved in the prisoner's diagnosis or treatment, along with notice, an adversary hearing, the right to present and cross-examine witnesses, and the assistance of an "independent lay advisor who understands the psychiatric issues involved" (not a lawyer).[511] These protections are the minimum required by the federal Constitution; state law may provide greater safeguards.[512] Under both state and federal law, authorities are permitted to use antipsychotic medications over the patients' objections for safety reasons in emergencies.[513]

Government may medicate criminal defendants to render them competent to stand trial, but only for serious charges and on a showing that the treatment will be medically appropriate, is unlikely to have side effects undermining a fair trial, and is necessary "significantly to further important governmental trial-related interests."[514] In such cases, authorization must be obtained from the trial court, and lower court decisions have required the prosecution to make a strong and specific showing of need.[515]

_____

[509]See § F.4.k of this chapter concerning the right to refuse medical treatment.

[510]See U.S. v. Keeves, 115 F. Supp. 2d 1152, 1140 (E.D.Mo. 2000) (since medication was primarily to manage dangerousness, not to restore competency, no judicial hearing was necessary).

[511]Washington v. Harper, 494 U.S. at 233–36; see Morgan v. Rabun, 128 F.3d 694, 696 (8th Cir. 1997) (applying Washington holding to person acquitted by reason of insanity and civilly committed); Doby v. Hickerson, 120 F.3d 111, 114 (8th Cir. 1997) (affirming damage award for medication without procedural protections); Roberson v. Goodman, 296 F. Supp. at 1056 (upholding state's medication procedures). But see Washington v. Silber, 805 F. Supp. 379, 383–85 (W.D.Va. 1992) (court construes findings made to justify commitment as sufficient also to justify medication at a later date), aff'd, 993 F.2d 1541 (4th Cir. 1993).

[512]Most states will have statutes and administrative regulations governing these medications. There are also relevant judicial decisions in some states. See, e.g., Large v. Superior Court, 148 Ariz. 229, 714 P.2d 399, 408–09 (Ariz. 1986) (en banc) (for prisoners, valid medical, not security or administrative, reasons are required, along with a treatment plan that complies with state statutes governing civilly committed patients; citing state constitution); Riese v. St. Mary's Hospital and Medical Center, 209 Cal.App. 3d 1303, 271 Cal.Rptr. 199, 210–13 (Cal.App. 1987), review dismissed, 259 Cal.Rptr. 669, 774 P.2d 698 (Cal. 1989) (competent patients can refuse; incompetence must be determined judicially, and medication of incompetent person for more than 14 days requires consent of relative, guardian, or conservator; state statutes cited); People v. Medina, 705 P.2d 961 (Colo. 1985) (en banc) (competent patients can refuse; incompetence must be determined judicially by clear and convincing evidence; patients have the right to counsel; state statutes and common law cited); Rogers v. Commissioner of Dep't of Mental Health, 390 Mass. 489, 458 N.E.2d 308 (Mass. 1983) (competent patients may refuse; incompetence must be determined judicially, and the court shall make the treatment decision; state statutes cited); Rivers v. Katz, 67 N.Y.2d 485, 495 N.E.2d 337, 343–44, 504 N.Y.S.2d 74, 81–82 (N.Y. 1986) (judicial determination of incompetence required; state constitution cited); In re K.K.B., 609 P.2d 747, 751–52 (Okla. 1980) (a competent patient may refuse; incompetency must be decided by a court and a guardian appointed to make informed decision whether to consent).

[513]See, e.g., Hogan v. Carter, 85 F.3d 1113, 1177 (4th Cir. 1996) (en banc) (emergency telephone order by psychiatrist of single

dose of Thorazine in emergency did not require Washington procedural protections; due process required only an exercise of professional judgment by a licensed psychiatrist personally familiar with the patient, his condition, and his history, that it was in his medical interest to receive the medication in order to avoid harming himself); Dancy v. Simms, 116 F. Supp. 2d 652, 655 (D.Md. 2000) (involuntary medication pursuant to a professional medical decision in an emergency requires no procedural protections); Wilson v. Chang, 955 F. Supp. 18, 21 (D.R.I. 1997) ("a prison doctor, if he has reasonable grounds to believe that an inmate is a danger to himself or others, utilizing his medical judgment in a medically appropriate manner, may inject the inmate with a sedative to deal with an emergency situation"; Washington v. Harper procedural requirements do not apply); Large v. Superior Court, 714 P.2d at 408; People v. Medina, 705 P.2d at 974–75 (emergency treatment permitted but judicial authorization must be obtained "as soon as practicable after the emergency" to continue it).

[514]Sell v. U.S., 539 U.S. 166, 179, 123 S. Ct. 2174 (2003); see Riggins v. Nevada, 504 U.S. 127, 138, 112 S. Ct. 1810 (1992) (pretrial detainees may not be medicated for trial without a finding that it is "necessary to accomplish an essential state policy" such as safety or ensuring that the detainee remains competent for trial).

[515]U.S. v. Rivera-Guerrero, 426 F.3d 1130, 1138, 1140 (9th Cir. 2005) (holding involuntary medication orders should be issued "only after both sides have had a fair opportunity to present their case and develop a complete and reliable record"; "Specificity as to the medications to be administered is critical."); U.S. v. Evans, 404 F.3d 227, 242 (4th Cir. 2005) (holding that even where the crime charged was serious and there were no special circumstances weighing against medication, government was obliged to propose a specific course of treatment and explain how that treatment would "specifically further" its goals and be "medically appropriate" for the specific defendant under the specific circumstances); U.S. v. Miller, 292 F. Supp. 2d 163, 164–65 (D.Me. 2003) (government failed to justify involuntary medication of defendant; it did not address whether such medication is medically appropriate, did not adequately consider the potential side-effects to the particular defendant's ability to cooperate with counsel before and at trial, and "most importantly" failed to show why it was so important to bring the defendant to trial quickly); U.S. v. Kourey, 276 F. Supp. 2d 580, 585 (S.D.W.Va. 2003) (involuntary medication refused because the charges, violation of supervised release on a misdemeanor conviction, are not serious enough); Rickman v. Dutton, 864 F. Supp. 686, 713–14 (M.D.Tenn. 1994) (state murder conviction reversed because of failure to show that medication during trial was in the defendant's medical interest and supported compelling interests of the state; making the defendant competent was not enough by itself); see U.S. v. Rivera-Guerrero, 377 F.3d 1064, 1070 (9th Cir. 2004) (federal magistrate judges may not exercise final review over medication decisions; district court must engage in de novo review).

Some states have special sentencing statutes for defendants found to be mentally ill or in need of treatment which provide for potentially longer terms of incarceration and permit the prisoner to be released only after she has been "cured."[516] One court has held that persons sentenced under such a statute have a right to "a treatment program that will address their particular needs with the reasonable objective of rehabilitation."[517] This rule is an exception to the general rule that there is no constitutional right to rehabilitation in prison,[518] and its scope is narrow. It does not apply to prisoners who have been given an ordinary criminal sentence, even if they are required to receive a psychological examination before being paroled,[519] or to prisoners who merely claim that their crime was caused by mental illness.[520] Other courts have declined to adopt even this limited "right to treatment" rule.[521] Similar issues have been explored in more detail in connection with sex offender programs, discussed in the next section.

b. Sex Offender Programs In recent years there has been an explosion of programs, rules, regulations, and statutes affecting sex offenders. These fall into three broad categories: (a) treatment programs and special provisions for sex offenders in prison; (b) schemes for civil commitment of sex offenders, usually after completion of their criminal sentences; and (3) requirements of notification to victims and communities of the release of sex offenders, and post-release restrictions on them.

In prison, sex offenders may be required to participate in programs of treatment for their disorders.[522] That is so even if the program requires them to admit guilt of offenses for which they have not been prosecuted or convicted, or for which their convictions are not final, and does not grant them immunity, as long as the consequences of non-participation are not so serious as to "compel" self-incrimination.[523] Denial of prison privileges has so far been held not serious enough to compel self-incrimination.[524] Most decisions to

---

One federal appeals court has held that the trial court must remain involved even after allowing involuntary medication: the court "must closely monitor the process to ensure that the dosage is properly individualized to the defendant, that it continues to be medically appropriate, and that it does not deprive him of a fair trial or the effective assistance of counsel." U.S. v. Gomes, 289 F.3d 71, 82 (2d Cir. 2002).

[516]*See* State v. Harris, 236 Neb. 783, 463 N.W.2d 829, 833–35 (Neb. 1990), for a discussion of such statutes. These sentencing schemes are beyond the scope of this Manual except insofar as they affect prisoners' rights to mental health treatment.

[517]Ohlinger v. Watson, 652 F.2d 775, 777–79 (9th Cir. 1980); *accord*, Leamer v. Fauver, 288 F.3d 532, 544 (3d Cir. 2002) (prisoner sentenced under a statute that imposed an indeterminate prison term, provided for therapeutic treatment, and permitted release only when the prisoner "is capable of making an acceptable social adjustment in the community" created a liberty interest in receiving the therapy); *see* State v. Cruz, 125 N.J. 550, 593 A.2d 1169, 1171–72 (N.J. 1991) (interpreting state statutes); *see also* Young v. Armontrout, 795 F.2d 55, 56 (8th Cir. 1986) (failure to provide rehabilitative services required by sentencing court should have been treated as a § 1983 claim).

The Supreme Court has suggested that indefinite incarceration may be permissible without treatment if a person has an untreatable disorder. Kansas v. Hendricks, 521 U.S. 346, 365–66, 117 S. Ct. 2072 (1997). This case involved a sex offender program and is discussed in the next section.

[518]*See* § I, n.1233, of this chapter concerning rehabilitation generally, and § F.4.b of this chapter concerning rehabilitative programs for sex offenders.

[519]Balla v. Idaho State Bd. of Corrections, 869 F.2d 461, 468–70 (9th Cir. 1989).

[520]U.S. v. Kidder, 869 F.2d 1328, 1332 (9th Cir. 1989).

[521]Cameron v. Tomes, 990 F.2d 14, 19 (1st Cir. 1993) (disapproving lower court's "right to treatment" analysis because the facts of the case did not show a lack of treatment); Bailey v. Gardebring, 940 F.2d 1150, 1155 (8th Cir. 1991) (prisoner under civil commitment as a "psychopathic personality" in addition to his criminal sentence was not entitled to psychiatric treatment to overcome his "sexual offender condition"); Knight v. Mills, 836 F.2d 659, 666–69 (1st Cir. 1987) (the right to treatment, if any, for persons incarcerated for psychiatric reasons was not "clearly established" as of 1981).

The lower court in *Cameron v. Tomes* had held that confinement under a statute that makes release depend on improvement in the prisoner's mental condition is a type of civil confinement and that mental health issues in such cases are governed by a "professional judgment" standard, which is generally considered to be more favorable to the prisoner than the deliberate indifference standard. 783 F. Supp. 1511, 1515 (D.Mass. 1992) (citing Youngberg v. Romeo, 457 U.S. 307, 102 S. Ct. 2452 (1981)). *But see* Houghton v. South, 965 F.2d 1532, 1536 (9th Cir. 1992) (suggesting that there is not much difference between the two standards). The appeals court in *Cameron*, which observed that the plaintiff's claims did not really involve treatment issues, held that his living conditions must not fall below "the minimum standards of civilized decency." The court added that it was unclear whether any civil commitment right to treatment would apply to persons who were also under criminal commitment. *Cameron*, 990 F.2d at 19.

[522]Sundby v. Fiedler, 827 F. Supp. 580, 583 (W.D.Wis. 1993) (upholding mandatory sex offender program because the state's interest in rehabilitating sex offenders outweighed their liberty interest in avoiding treatment). *See also* Patterson v. Webster, 760 F. Supp. 150, 153–54 (E.D.Mo. 1991) (requirement that certain prisoners complete sexual offenders program before being paroled was not unconstitutional).

[523]McKune v. Lile, 536 U.S. 24, 35–36, 122 S. Ct. 2017 (2002). *See* Callender v. Sioux City Residential Treatment Facility, 88 F.3d 666, 668 (8th Cir. 1996) (holding sex offender could be removed from work release for refusing to take responsibility for offense of which he claimed innocence); Molesky v. Walter, 931 F. Supp. 1506, 1514 (E.D.Wash. 1996) (holding a sex offender whose appeal was pending could be required under threat of discipline to submit to a psychological evaluation, required to determine his eligibility for camp, work release, or pre-release placement; his claim of possible self-incrimination was too speculative, and due process and other legal arguments were also rejected).

[524]*McKune*, 536 U.S. at 36 ("The consequences in question here—a transfer to another prison where television sets are not placed in each inmate's cell, where exercise facilities are not readily available, and where work and wage opportunities are more

date have held that the loss of good time, or even denial of parole, does not constitute compulsion.[525] Courts have held that the use of the penile plethysmograph, which measures sexual response, in the course of sex offender treatment does not violate the Fourth Amendment or other privacy right.[526]

Classification as a sex offender may be based on past offenses as well as the current one.[527] Persons not actually convicted of sex offenses may nonetheless be found to be sex offenders, and compelled to participate in treatment, based on other evidence that they have committed sex offenses.[528] Courts have differed over whether classification as a sex offender in prison requires due process protections; the differences may be related to the different consequences of such classification in different prisons.[529] New restrictions

---

limited—are not ones that compel a prisoner to speak about his past crimes despite a desire to remain silent."). The *McKune* plurality equated the threshold with the *Sandin v. Conner* "atypical and significant" test, *id.* at 37, but Justice O'Connor rejected that test while agreeing that the particular deprivations were not sufficiently serious to constitute compulsion. *Id.* at 52. As a result, the precise legal standard governing such questions is not settled. *See* Wirsching v. Colorado, 360 F.3d 1191, 1203–04 (10th Cir. 2004) (holding total denial of visiting with children and denial of opportunity to earn good time at the usual rate was not coercion); Johnson v. Baker, 108 F.3d 10, 11 (2d Cir. 1997) (per curiam) (exclusion from sex offender program and therefore from Family Reunion Program for failure to admit his crime did not violate plaintiff's privilege against self-incrimination; pre-*McKune* case); Nicolaison v. Erickson, 425 N.W.2d 597, 599 (Minn.App. 1988) (denial of "incentive" job assignments to an inmate who refused to participate in a sex offender treatment program was not unconstitutional).

[525]Entzi v. Redmann, 485 F.3d 998, 1004 (8th Cir. 2007) (holding loss of opportunity to earn good time is not compulsion), *cert. denied*, 128 S. Ct. 1714 (2008); Gwinn v. Awmiller, 354 F.3d 1211, 1225–26 (10th Cir. 2004) (withholding of good time is not sufficient to constitute compulsion); Ainsworth v. Stanley, 317 F.3d 1, 6 (1st Cir. 2002) (finding no self-incrimination violation where parole was denied to almost all prisoners who refused treatment); Searcy v. Simmons, 299 F.3d 1220, 1224 (10th Cir. 2002) (loss of opportunity to earn good time is not compulsion); Wolfe v. Pennsylvania Dep't of Corrections, 334 F. Supp. 2d 762, 772 (E.D.Pa. 2004) (denial of parole for refusing to disclose sexual history did not violate the privilege against self-incrimination; Russell v. Eaves, 722 F. Supp. 558, 560 (E.D.Mo. 1989) (requirement that prisoner complete Missouri Sex Offender Program before becoming parole eligible did not deny equal protection and did not violate the Fifth Amendment by requiring participants to "accept responsibility" for their crimes). In *Donhauser v. Goord*, 314 F. Supp. 2d 119 (N.D.N.Y.), *preliminary injunction granted*, 314 F. Supp. 2d 139 (N.D.N.Y.), *amended*, 317 F. Supp. 2d 160 (N.D.N.Y. 2004), *vacated and remanded*, 181 Fed.Appx. 11 (2d Cir. 2006) (unpublished), the lower court held that a practice of depriving prisoners of good time for refusing to participate in such a program by disclosing sexual history violated the privilege against self-incrimination. On appeal, however, the Second Circuit returned the case to the lower court for clearer findings on whether loss of good time was an "automatic and direct" result of refusal to participate. 181 Fed.Appx. at 12.

In *Hydrick v. Hunter*, 500 F.3d 978, 991–92 (9th Cir. 2007), *cert. granted, judgment vacated on other grounds*, 129 S. Ct. 2431 (2009), the court stated in dictum that a requirement that civilly committed sex offenders acknowledge their illnesses on pain of never being released might violate the *First* Amendment by compelling speech.

[526]*See* Ch. 3, § E.2, n.920.

[527]Montalvo v. Snyder, 207 F. Supp. 2d 581, 587 (E.D.Ky. 2002) (classification is supported by prison policy and does not violate the Ex Post Facto Clause because it is not punitive; classification issues do not raise constitutional questions), *aff'd*, 84 Fed.App. 521 (6th Cir. 2003).

[528]Gwinn v. Awmiller, 354 F.3d at 1219–20 (upholding classification based on a statement in the plaintiff's pre-sentence report by the victim); *Cf.* Fox v. Lappin, 409 F. Supp. 2d 79, 87 n.12, 90 (D.Mass. 2006) (while federal prisoners must have been convicted of federal sex offenses for purposes of community notice, federal prisons may rely on state sex offenses for internal classification purposes).

[529]Gwinn v. Awmiller, 354 F.3d at 1218–20 (reduction in ability to earn good time for sex offenders required due process protections, but the mere stigma of labelling did not); Chambers v. Colorado Dep't of Corrections, 205 F.3d 1237, 1242–43 (10th Cir. 2000) (following *Neal*); Kirby v. Siegelman, 195 F.3d 1285, 1288, 1291–92 (11th Cir. 1999) (finding a liberty interest where sex offenders were required to participate in group therapy and admit past sexual offenses and were barred from minimum custody and therefore excluded from work release and community custody programs); Neal v. Shimoda, 131 F.3d 818, 827 (9th Cir. 1997) (stigmatization and mandatory treatment, which was required for parole eligibility, created a liberty interest in avoiding sex offender classification); Kritenbrink v. Crawford, 313 F. Supp. 2d 1043, 1049–50 (D.Nev. 2004) (classification as a sex offender did not implicate a liberty interest where it caused the plaintiff to be confined in a higher security prison and to lose the opportunity to go to a work camp and obtain early release credit; court gives plaintiff the opportunity to show that conditions for sex offenders are atypical and significant compared to ordinary confinement); Jones v. Puckett, 160 F. Supp. 2d 1016, 1023 (W.D.Wis. 2001) (holding classification as a sex offender did not require due process since evaluation of criminal behavior and treatment needs is common in prisons); Cooper v. Garcia, 55 F. Supp. 2d 1090, 1098 (S.D.Cal. 1999) (sex offender classification did not require due process because it only excluded the plaintiff from the family visiting program; *Neal v. Shimoda* distinguished because no liberty interest is at issue here).

The "process due" for sex offender classification, if any, is the same as for prison disciplinary proceedings. Gwinn v. Awmiller, 354 F.3d at 1218–19; Neal v. Shimoda, 131 F.3d at 830–31. *But see* Jones v. Puckett, 160 F. Supp. 2d 1016, 1024 (W.D.Wis. 2001) (holding appearance before classification committee with notice and statement of reasons satisfied due process). A prisoner who has actually been convicted of a sex offense has already received all the process required. Neal v. Shimoda, 131 F.3d at 831.

Other decisions address whether there is a liberty interest in avoiding identification as a sex offender for purposes of post-release community notification, residence restrictions, etc. *See* § F.4.b of this chapter, nn.554–555.

and requirements based on previously committed sex offenses are generally held not to violate the Ex Post Facto Clause because they are deemed not to be punitive.[530]

Complaints about the adequacy of prison sex offender treatment are assessed under the usual standard of deliberate indifference to serious medical needs.[531] Exclusion from sex offender programs generally does not deny due process,[532] but may raise other constitutional issues, especially if prisoners must complete the programs to obtain release on parole or otherwise.[533] Complaints that sex offenders are treated more harshly or restrictively than other prisoners are generally evaluated under the "rational basis" equal protection standard, under which governmental actions are almost always upheld,[534] or the *Turner v. Safley* reasonable

relationship standard.[535] Special requirements for release of sex offenders on parole or other forms of release are generally upheld.[536] Requirements that sex offenders provide DNA samples have generally been upheld, though at this point such requirements have also been upheld for many other categories of offenders.[537]

Many states and the federal government[538] now have laws providing for civil commitment of sex offenders after completion of their sentences. In *Kansas v. Hendricks*,[539] the Supreme Court broadly approved such statutes, upholding a Sexually Violent Predator Act which provided for the civil commitment of persons who because of a "mental abnormality" or a "personality disorder" are likely to engage in "predatory acts of sexual violence."[540] "Mental abnormality" was defined in the statute as a "congenital or acquired condition affecting the emotional or volitional capacity which predisposes the person to commit sexually violent offenses in a degree constituting such person a menace to the health and safety of others." The Court held that it did not deny due process to incarcerate persons indefinitely based on that standard, even without a finding of

[530]Neal v. Shimoda, 131 F.3d 818, 825–26 (9th Cir. 1977); Dominique v. Weld, 73 F.3d 1156, 1163 (1st Cir. 1996) (exclusion from work release until completion of sex offender treatment program); Shaffer v. Meyers, 338 F. Supp. 2d 562, 565–66 (M.D.Pa. 2004) (denial of parole), *aff'd*, 163 Fed.Appx. 111 (3d Cir. 2006) (unpublished); Johnstone v. Simmons, 45 F. Supp. 2d 1220, 1224 (D.Kan. 1999) (denial of parole).

[531]Riddle v. Mondragon, 83 F.3d 1197, 1204 (10th Cir. 1996) (complaints of inadequate treatment for "addictive sexuality" do not rise to the level of "serious medical needs" without diagnosis by a physician of a medical need mandating treatment, nor of a condition which a lay person would easily recognize as necessitating a doctor's attention. . . . Vague allegations of eroded self-esteem, apathy, fear and feelings of differentness, keeping a plaintiff in the 'addictive cycle,' do not amount to the basis for a constitutional claim." Nor do the plaintiffs show deliberate indifference; they get a weekly group session staffed by a psychologist, and the lack of further response does not amount to the unnecessary and wanton infliction of pain.).

[532]*See* Ch. 4, § H.5.b concerning due process issues in sex offender programs.

[533]Beebe v. Heil, 333 F. Supp. 2d 1011, 1015–18 (D.Colo. 2004) (state law that requires the state to provide convicted sex offenders with a treatment program and makes parole eligibility contingent on completing it, creates a liberty interest, and failure to provide the program could "shock the conscience" for purposes of substantive due process analysis). *But see* Stanley v. Litscher, 213 F.3d 340, 342 (7th Cir. 2000) (prisoner diagnosed as a psychopath could be excluded from sex offender treatment program, since his medical need was not shown to be serious; his disability discrimination claim is rejected because officials could rationally decide that psychopaths do not benefit from such programs and they spoil them for others; his due process claim is rejected because there is no liberty or property interest in participating in the program); Richmond v. Cagle, 920 F. Supp. 955 (E.D.Wis. 1996) (exclusion from program for refusing to accept responsibility for a charge not leading to conviction did not raise a constitutional claim).

[534]Riddle v. Mondragon, 83 F.3d 1197, 1208 (10th Cir. 1996) (holding sex offenders are not a suspect class; classification of all sex offenders as "violent" offenders, their exclusion from rehabilitation and treatment programs, and the imposition of longer sentences on them do not deny equal protection because they have a rational basis).

[535]Wirsching v. Colorado, 360 F.3d 1191 (10th Cir. 2004) (upholding denial to plaintiff of all visits with his children); Waterman v. Farmer, 183 F.3d 208, 214 (3d Cir. 1999) (upholding broad denial of "sexually oriented" materials in institution for sex offenders); Odenwalt v. Gillis, 327 F. Supp. 2d 502, 508–09 (M.D.Pa. 2004) (upholding rule barring all prisoners ever convicted of sex offenses against minors from contact visits with any children, including their own).

[536]Doe v. Simon, 221 F.3d 137, 139–40 (2d Cir. 2000) (upholding requirement that residence be approved even though it resulted in three months' delay in plaintiff's conditional release); Glauner v. Miller, 184 F.3d 1053, 1054 (9th Cir. 1999) (upholding requirement that sex offenders be certified by a special panel not to be a "menace to health, safety, or morals" to be parole-eligible; "heightened recidivism concerns" provided rational basis for treating sex offenders differently from others); *see also* Prevard v. Fauver, 47 F. Supp. 2d 539, 543 (D.N.J. 1999) (upholding denial of "custodial reduction credits" for sex offenders sentenced to indeterminate terms, since indeterminate-sentenced prisoners could be released any time, and the state had a legitimate interest in making sure they were rehabilitated before release).

[537]*See* Ch. 3, § E.2, n.917.

[538]The federal civil commitment program, authorized by the Adam Walsh Child Protection and Safety Act, was recently upheld by the Supreme Court, which rejected the argument that it exceeds the federal government's powers and therefore violates the Tenth Amendment. U.S. v. Comstock, ___ S.Ct. ___, 2010 WL 1946729 (2010).

[539]521 U.S. 346, 117 S. Ct. 2072 (1997).

[540]The statute applies not only to prisoners convicted of sexually violent offenses scheduled for release, but also to persons charged with such offenses but incompetent to stand trial, and persons found not guilty by reason of insanity *or not guilty at all* of such an offense. Kansas v. Hendricks, 521 U.S. 346, 352, 117 S. Ct. 2072 (1997) (citing statute).

mental illness.[541] It also held that the statute does not impose criminal liability or punishment, and therefore does not violate the Ex Post Facto Clause or the Double Jeopardy Clause. It said that the alleged lack of meaningful treatment does not make the statute punitive, since incapacitation—keeping people out of circulation—is a legitimate purpose if their dangerous disorders are untreatable.[542] In *Seling v. Young*,[543] it added that an individual prisoner's complaint that she is being treated punitively does not make civil commitment criminal in nature.[544]

The Supreme Court did state that where a civil commitment statute is designed to incapacitate and to treat, "due process requires that the conditions and duration of confinement under the Act bear some reasonable relation to the purpose for which persons are committed."[545] Consistently with this statement, a lower court has stated that civilly committed persons must be provided with treatment programs that give them "a reasonable opportunity to be cured or improve the mental condition for which they were confined" and "more considerate treatment and conditions of confinement" than convicts.[546]

Despite these fine words, in practice, civilly committed sex offenders seem generally to be treated like prisoners, often very high security prisoners,[547] and decisions concerning their permissible conditions of confinement have varied widely. One federal appellate court held it did not deny due process to require all civilly committed sex offenders to be restrained with a waist belt and leg chains as well as handcuffs during transportation, with no individualized determination of the danger or escape risk posed by each.[548] However, a second decision by the same appellate court held that the use of "therapeutic seclusion" (strip cell confinement) for periods up to 82 days by mental health professionals against civilly committed sex offenders could deny due process if it exceeded the bounds of professional judgment: "all the Constitution requires is that punishment be avoided and medical judgment be exercised. But this is a far cry from saying that anything goes."[549] Another lower court decision held that sex offenders who have finished their criminal

---

[541]Kansas v. Hendricks, 521 U.S. at 356–60.

Later, in *Kansas v. Crane*, 534 U.S. 407, 122 S. Ct. 867 (2002), which involved the same statute, the Court further held that a prisoner need not be shown to be *completely* unable to control her behavior to justify civil commitment: "It is enough to say that there must be proof of serious difficulty in controlling behavior. And this, when viewed in light of such features of the case as the nature of the psychiatric diagnosis, and the severity of the mental abnormality itself, must be sufficient to distinguish the dangerous sexual offender whose serious mental illness, abnormality, or disorder subjects him to civil commitment from the dangerous but typical recidivist convicted in an ordinary criminal case." 534 U.S. at 413.

[542]Kansas v. Hendricks, 521 U.S. at 365–66. This last point is probably dictum, since the Court also says that Mr. Hendricks did receive some treatment, but it does suggest the Supreme Court's thinking on this subject.

[543]531 U.S. 250, 121 S. Ct. 727 (2000).

[544]Seling v. Young, 531 U.S. at 262–65. The plaintiff alleged that the sex offenders unit was on the grounds of a prison and relied on prison facilities for essential services including library services, medical care, food, and security, and the plaintiffs alleged that they were punitively abused, confined to their rooms, subjected to random searches of rooms and units, and placed under excessive security.

[545]*Seling*, 531 U.S. at 255.

[546]Sharp v. Weston, 233 F.3d 1166, 1171–72 (9th Cir. 2000) ("Although the state enjoys wide latitude in developing treatment regimens, the courts may take action when there is a substantial departure from accepted professional judgment or when there has been no exercise of professional judgment at all."); *accord*, Turay v. Seling, 108 F. Supp. 2d 1148, 1151 (W.D.Wash. 2000) ("This rule applies to sex offenders, and '[l]ack of funds, staff or facilities cannot justify the State's failure to provide [those confined] with that treatment necessary for rehabilitation.' . . . Accordingly, these plaintiffs, and others involuntarily confined through civil proceedings, cannot simply be warehoused and put out of sight; they must be afforded adequate treatment. Although confined, they are not prisoners," and are entitled to "more considerate

treatment and conditions of confinement" than convicted criminals.); *see* Williams v. Nelson, 398 F. Supp. 2d 977, 987 (W.D.Wis. 2005) (civilly committed sex offenders must be provided treatment, but treatment decisions need only be the product of professional judgment).

[547]*See* King v. Greenblatt, 149 F.3d 9, 19 (1st Cir. 1998) (noting "a significant change in the philosophical approach to treatment of civilly committed sex offenders in programs operated by correctional departments" from a "more permissive mental health approach to the more restrictive behavior control approach."). In that case, the court modified an earlier consent decree to permit "a new approach to behavior management, featuring definite sanctions for defined unacceptable behavior," a much restricted community access program, easier transfers back to correctional institutions, reduction in privileges, etc. *Id.*, 149 F.3d at 16–17.

[548]Thielman v. Leean, 282 F.3d 478, 481 (7th Cir. 2002). In this case, the court said that the due process standard of *Sandin v. Conner*, 515 U.S. 472, 115 S. Ct. 2293 (1995), *see* Ch. 4, § A, applied to this civil commitment case because facilities dealing with sexual offenders are "volatile" environments similar to prisons, and the additional restraints did not constitute an "atypical and significant deprivation." *Thielman*, 282 F.3d at 483. The application of *Sandin* appears inconsistent with the general statement in *Seling v. Young* that conditions must be reasonably related to the purpose of the confinement. The *Thielman* court also said that the more restrictive treatment of committed sexual offenders than of other mental patients does not deny equal protection, since defendants could rationally consider sex offenders more dangerous than other mental patients. 282 F.3d at 485.

[549]West v. Schwebke, 333 F.3d 745, 748–49 (7th Cir. 2003). The court added: "What sets this case apart from others . . . is that respected experts have opined, on plaintiffs' behalf, that the defendants' choices exceed the scope of honest professional disagreement." 333 F.3d at 749. This decision applied only to the mental health professionals who were defendants. The lower court in that case said that claims against administrative defendants would be governed by the "no punishment" standard of *Bell v. Wolfish*, which governs the rights of pre-trial detainees. West v. Macht, 235 F. Supp. 2d 966, 974 (E.D.Wis. 2002). *Accord*, Serna v. Goodno, 567 F.3d 944, 948–49 (8th Cir. 2009) (holding that strip searches of civilly committed sex offenders were governed by law applying to

sentences, but remain in state prison (though they are in effect pretrial detainees) awaiting proceedings for civil commitment, were subjected to punishment denying due process when they were held in conditions significantly *more* restrictive than in the preceding months when they were serving criminal sentences, without any mental health treatment or counseling, with extremely limited access to program and other activities, and with no legitimate interest cited for the greater restrictions.[550] Another decision held that sex offenders are not similarly situated to other civilly committed persons, and it was not unconstitutional to require them to be held in county jails, rather than mental health facilities, after expiration of their sentences pending their civil commitment proceedings, as long as conditions in those jails did not expose a prisoner to an "excessive risk to his health and safety."[551]

Many states now have laws requiring community and/ or victim notification of the release of sex offenders on parole or otherwise, and restricting sex offenders in various ways once they are released. These laws are generally beyond the scope of this Manual. However, the Supreme Court has made several relevant decisions. In *Smith v. Doe I*,[552] the Court upheld a Sex Offender Registration Act which required registration, photography, fingerprinting, notification of changes of address, etc., with information on the offenders and their whereabouts made public. The Court said the statute did not violate the Ex Post Facto Clause because it was not intended to impose punishment, but to protect the public from new crimes by sex offenders, and because its provisions did not have a punitive effect even though they were adverse for sex offenders.[553] The Court also upheld the placement of convicted sex offenders on a registry posted on the Internet, stating that even if there is a liberty interest in avoiding stigmatization as a sex offender, no hearing is required where the statute applied solely to persons who already had criminal convictions for

sex offenses.[554] However, several cases, both before and after *Smith v. Doe I*, have held that a person who has not actually been convicted of a sex offense has a liberty interest protected by due process in avoiding being labelled as a sex offender upon release.[555]

---

detainees; upholding searches of entire facility population based on fear that an unidentified resident had a cellphone).

[550]Atwood v. Vilsack, 338 F. Supp. 2d 985, 1003–05 (S.D.Iowa 2004). The court also held that the denial of bail between the expiration of the criminal sentence and the civil commitment was not unconstitutional because it was based on a finding of probable cause to believe that the person is a sexually violent predator who is likely to reoffend if not incarcerated. 338 F. Supp. 2d at 998–99.

[551]Munoz v. Kolender, 208 F. Supp. 2d 1125, 1141–44, 1147 (S.D.Cal. 2002); *see* Thiel v. Wisconsin, 399 F. Supp. 2d 929, 933 (W.D.Wis. 2005) (" . . . [N]othing in the United States Constitution prevents state officials from temporarily detaining a civil committee in conditions normally reserved for inmates so that he may attend court proceedings concerning his commitment.") In *Thiel*, the court held that strip searching a civilly detained sex offender, dressing him in prison clothing, and restraining him before sending him to court did not deny due process.

[552]538 U.S. 84, 123 S. Ct. 1140 (2003).

[553]Smith v. Doe I, 538 U.S. at 90–103.

---

[554]Connecticut Dep't of Public Safety v. Doe, 538 U.S. 1, 7–8, 123 S. Ct. 1160 (2003).

[555]In *Gwinn v. Awmiller*, 354 F.3d 1211 (10th Cir. 2004), the court held that mere stigmatization was not enough to implicate a liberty interest *in prison* (though the reduction in ability to earn good time was). However, it said that upon release, sex offender registration might constitute a deprivation of liberty under the "stigma-plus" test, which requires a plaintiff to show that "(1) the government made a statement about him or her that is sufficiently derogatory to injure his or her reputation, that is capable of being proved false, and that he or she asserts is false, and (2) the plaintiff experienced some governmentally imposed burden that 'significantly altered [his or] her status as a matter of state law.'" *Gwinn*, 354 F.3d at 1216. Similarly, in *Coleman v. Dretke*, 395 F.3d 216, 221–23 (5th Cir. 2004), the court held that a statute that required registered sex offenders to submit to intrusive behavior-modifying treatment after release created a liberty interest requiring due process protections as applied to persons who had not actually been convicted of sex offenses. The decision required only procedural protections; it held that requiring sex offender registration of people not convicted of sex offenses did not "shock the conscience" because it has a legitimate purpose and is not designed to injury, and therefore does not deny substantive due process. *Coleman*, 395 F.3d at 222–23. An earlier, pre-*Smith* decision held that a prisoner has a liberty interest in avoiding labelling as a sex offender on release, by analogy with the rule that commitment to a mental hospital, with its stigmatization and subjection to behavior modification programs, creates a liberty interest. Kirby v. Siegelman, 195 F.3d 1285, 1291 (11th Cir. 1999). (The *Kirby* court applied the *Sandin v. Conner* due process analysis, which is usually restricted to prison conditions, *see* Ch. 4, § A.3, and which seems inappropriate applied to post-release restrictions.) *Accord*, Doe v. Pryor, 61 F. Supp. 2d 1224, 1231 (M.D.Ala. 1999) (holding sex offenders' community notification statute is a deprivation of liberty, since it will damage the plaintiff's reputation and standing in the community and deprive him of state law rights to move without notifying state officials, to live with a minor or in certain locations, and to change his name; will also foreclose employment and housing opportunities beyond those explicitly forbidden; and will deprive the plaintiff of his legitimate privacy interest in his home address, satisfying the "stigma-plus" test; Roe v. Farwell, 999 F. Supp. 174, 195–96 (D. Mass. 1998) (finding liberty interest protected by due process in avoiding public labelling as a sex offender based on state court decisions).

However, in *Smith v. Siegelman*, 322 F.3d 1290 (11th Cir. 2003), which involved a non-prisoner designated as a sex offender on a statewide Central Registry on Child Abuse and Neglect, the court held that there was no liberty interest because the plaintiff had not been denied anything; the only consequence of designation was appearing on a list. 322 F.3d at 1297. This decision appears inconsistent with the same court's decision in *Kirby v. Siegelman*, cited above; it does not cite *Kirby*.

c. Dental Care   Deliberate indifference to serious dental needs is unconstitutional.[556] The presence of a serious dental need may be "based on various factors, such as the pain suffered by the plaintiff, . . . the deterioration of the teeth due to a lack of treatment, . . . or the inability to engage in normal activities."[557] Thus, the restoration or extraction of painful decayed teeth, and the making of dentures for patients who need them to eat properly, are serious needs.[558] The failure to provide reasonable, and reasonably prompt, attention for these conditions, and the failure to provide follow-up care that is ordered by dental or medical personnel, violate the Constitution.[559] Limiting care to pulling teeth that could be

saved has been held unconstitutional.[560] Intake dental examinations are not required so long as the prison provides a means for inmates to communicate their dental needs and

---

[556]Board v. Farnham, 394 F.3d 469, 481–82 (7th Cir. 2005) (holding that breaking off teeth rather than extracting them, and denial of toothpaste for protracted periods, supported an Eighth Amendment claim); Hartsfield v. Colburn, 371 F.3d 454, 457 (8th Cir. 2004); Farrow v. West, 320 F.3d 1235, 1244–47 (11th Cir. 2003); Wynn v. Southward, 251 F.3d 588, 593 (7th Cir. 2001) (dental care is "one of the most important medical needs of inmates"); Harrison v. Barkley, 219 F.3d 132, 137–39 (2d Cir. 2000) (holding refusal to fill a cavity violated the Eighth Amendment); Hunt v. Dental Dep't, 865 F.2d 198, 200 (9th Cir. 1989); Ramos v. Lamm, 639 F.2d 559, 574 (10th Cir. 1980); Matzker v. Herr, 748 F.2d 1142, 1147–48 (7th Cir. 1984), *overruled on other grounds*, Salazar v. City of Chicago, 940 F.2d 233, 240 (7th Cir. 1991); Dean v. Coughlin, 623 F. Supp. 392, 400–01 (S.D.N.Y. 1985). *But see* Johnson v. Mullin, 422 F.3d 1184, 1187 (10th Cir. 2005) (defendants were not deliberately indifferent to dental emergency because they did not have actual knowledge that it was an emergency).

[557]Chance v. Armstrong, 143 F.3d 698, 703 (2d Cir. 1998); Dean v. Coughlin, 623 F. Supp. at 404 (dental conditions are serious if they "cause pain, discomfort or threat to good health").

[558]*Dean*, 623 F. Supp. at 404; *see* Hartsfield v. Colburn, 371 F.3d 454, 457 (8th Cir. 2004) (dental pain, bleeding, and swelling were a serious need because the need would have been obvious to a layperson); Farrow v. West, 320 F.3d 1235, 1244–45 (11th Cir. 2003) (prisoner with only two remaining teeth, bleeding, swollen gums, weight loss, etc., had serious need for dentures; he need not show a "life-long handicap or permanent loss"); Wynn v. Southward, 251 F.3d 588, 593 (7th Cir. 2001) (allegation of inability to chew, bleeding, headaches, disfigurement from lack of dentures states a serious medical need); Harrison v. Barkley, 219 F.3d 132, 137 (2d Cir. 2000) (a cavity presents a serious medical need if it is not treated); Goodnow v. Palm, 264 F. Supp.2d125, 132–33 (D.Vt. 2003) (painful broken tooth was a serious need); Williamson v. Brewington-Carr, 173 F. Supp. 2d 235, 239 (D.Del. 2001) (infected tooth was a serious need). *Cf.* Jackson v. Wharton, 687 F. Supp. 595, 597 (M.D.Ga. 1988) (complaint about dentures that served mainly cosmetic purposes was not a serious need).

[559]Hartsfield v. Colburn, 371 F.3d 454, 457 (8th Cir. 2004) (withholding of care for a painful dental condition because prisoner had been threatening and argumentative supported a deliberate indifference claim); Farrow v. West, 320 F.3d 1235, 1247 (11th Cir. 2003) (15-month delay in providing dentures for prisoner with bleeding, swelling, etc., could support deliberate indifference claim); Wynn v. Southward, 251 F.3d 588, 593 (7th Cir. 2001) (allegation of knowing failure to provide dentures stated a deliberate indifference claim); Harrison v. Barkley, 219 F.3d 132, 138 (2d Cir. 2000) (refusal to fill a cavity unless the plaintiff consented to extraction of other teeth

stated a claim); Brownlee v. Conine, 957 F.2d 353, 354 (7th Cir. 1992) (claim of denial of dental care for a painful condition was not frivolous); Matzker v. Herr, 748 F.2d at 1147–48 (inmate with broken teeth should receive a "thorough dental examination"); Goodnow v. Palm, 264 F.3d 125, 130, 134 (D.Vt. 2003) (seven-month delay in addressing broken tooth supported deliberate indifference claim against private medical provider); Wall v. Dion, 257 F. Supp. 2d 316, 319 (D.Me. 2003) (allegation of refusal to treat infected tooth despite several complaints sufficiently pled a policy of deliberate indifference by private medical provider); Moore v. Jackson, 123 F.3d 1082, 1087 n.3 (8th Cir. 1997) (holding three-month delay in treating a toothache in the face of the prisoner's repeated complaints supported deliberate indifference claim; complaints supported an inference of actual knowledge by the dentist); Williamson v. Brewington-Carr, 173 F. Supp. 2d 235, 239 (D.Del. 2001) (three-year denial of extraction of tooth which then became infected supported a deliberate indifference claim); Manney v. Monroe, 151 F. Supp. 2d 976, 989 (N.D.Ill. 2001) (allegation that dentist only gave pain medication for toothache and dental hygienist who scheduled examinations ignored plaintiff's complaints stated a deliberate indifference claim); Ramos v. O'Connell, 28 F. Supp. 2d 796, 803–04 (W.D.N.Y. 1998) (refusal to treat abscessed tooth because he had refused a tuberculosis test and was not allowed out of his cell stated a deliberate indifference claim); Fields v. Gander, 734 F.2d 1313, 1315 (8th Cir. 1984) (three-week delay in treatment of a painful condition stated a claim); Carver v. Knox County, Tenn., 753 F. Supp. 1370, 1391 (E.D.Tenn. 1989) ("substantial delay" in "necessary dental treatment" violates the Constitution), *remanded for reconsideration*, 887 F.2d 1287 (6th Cir. 1989), *adhered to on remand*, 753 F. Supp. 1398 (E.D.Tenn. 1990); Tillery v. Owens, 719 F. Supp. 1256, 1309 (W.D.Pa. 1989) (dental care delays of up to a year condemned), *aff'd*, 907 F.2d 418 (3d Cir. 1990); Inmates of Occoquan v. Barry, 717 F. Supp. 854, 868 (D.D.C. 1989) ("significant delays" in dental appointments cited); Fambro v. Fulton County, Ga., 713 F. Supp. 1426, 1429–31 (N.D.Ga. 1989) (three-week delays in dental care cited in finding an Eighth Amendment violation); Dean v. Coughlin, 623 F. Supp. at 403–04 (denial of and delays in filling cavities, performing root canals, providing crowns, extracting teeth, and providing bridges and dentures violates the Eighth Amendment); Morgan v. Sproat, 432 F. Supp. 1130, 1156–57 (S.D.Miss. 1977) (in juvenile institution, dental care could not be limited to emergencies). *But see* Vester v. Murray, 683 F. Supp. 140, 141 (E.D.Va. 1988) (complaints of delay that amounted only to inconvenience did not constitute a serious need), *aff'd in part, vacated in part*, 878 F.2d 380 (1989); Grubbs v. Bradley, 552 F. Supp. 1052, 1129 (M.D.Tenn. 1982) (delays in access to non-emergency care were not unconstitutional); Clifton v. Robinson, 500 F. Supp. 30, 35 (E.D.Pa. 1980) (five-day delay in treating a toothache was acceptable during an emergency); Stokes v. Hurdle, 393 F. Supp. 757, 761–62 (D.Md. 1975) (three-week delay in treatment for a non-emergency condition was not deliberate indifference; policy of providing only emergency services to segregation inmates upheld), *aff'd sub nom.* Stokes v. Brown, 535 F.2d 1250 (4th Cir. 1976).

[560]Dean v. Coughlin, 623 F. Supp. 392, 405 (S.D.N.Y. 1985); *see* Chance v. Armstrong, 143 F.3d at 703–04 (holding allegation that dentists proposed extraction, rather than saving teeth, for financial

delivers treatment for those who need it.[561] Courts have disagreed over whether preventive services are constitutionally mandated.[562] As with other forms of medical care, mere malpractice or negligence or difference of opinion over proper care do not violate the Constitution, though it may be actionable under state law.[563]

County jails that hold inmates for relatively short periods may not be required to provide the full range of dental services that a prison must supply.[564] However, even jails cannot restrict dental services to extractions,[565] and at least one court has required a jail to provide more than emergency dental services.[566]

d. Infectious Diseases Prison officials have an obligation to protect prisoners from the risk of infectious diseases.[567] A number of courts have held that prisons and jails are obliged to conduct intake examinations for this purpose.[568] It violates the Eighth Amendment to expose prisoners to sources of infection such as raw sewage or human waste.[569]

1) Tuberculosis Tuberculosis (TB) is a disease that can damage a person's lungs or other parts of the body and can cause serious illness. TB germs are spread when people with the active disease cough or sneeze and others breathe the germs into their lungs, though it usually takes close,

day-to-day contact with someone who has active TB to spread it. TB infection is often "latent," which means that the TB germs are present but are controlled by the body's defenses. Persons with latent TB infection are not sick and cannot spread the disease. If the body's defenses weaken (which can result from HIV infection and other causes), TB germs can begin multiplying and can cause illness and infect others.

Tuberculosis infection is detected with the Mantoux skin test. If the skin test shows infection, a chest x-ray will reveal damage to the lungs if any, and a sputum test will show if there are TB germs in the lungs. There is also a Quantiferon TB test that gives results very rapidly.

Tuberculosis can be cured if patients take their medication as prescribed (often for several months). If they don't take it, they can become seriously ill, and may even die. Some TB germs are "resistant" to one or more TB medicines, so doctors have to use combinations of other TB medicines, and it may take longer to cure than regular TB. Drug-resistant TB can develop if people with active TB take their medicine incorrectly, or if they have not been given the right TB medicines. A person with untreated drug-resistant TB of the lungs or throat can spread drug-resistant germs to other people.[570]

Both active and latent TB are serious medical needs.[571] Prison officials have been found deliberately indifferent in failing to respond to tuberculosis exposure and outbreaks of the disease in order to protect prisoners from infection.[572] They are allowed to require prisoners to submit to TB testing for this purpose.[573] Persons who have or are suspected of active TB may be isolated to avoid spreading the disease. Prison officials also isolate persons who have refused TB testing.

---

reasons stated an Eighth Amendment claim). *But see* Hogan v. Russ, 890 F. Supp. 146, 148 (N.D.N.Y. 1995) (holding defendants' offer to pull teeth or allow the prisoner to pay for periodontal treatment was not deliberately indifferent; they said it was not prison policy to pay such specialized care).

[561]Dean v. Coughlin, 623 F. Supp. at 398, 404.

[562]*Compare* Board v. Farnham, 394 F.3d 469, 482 (7th Cir. 2005) (recognizing right to toothpaste as an "essential hygienic product . . . analogous to the established right to a nutritionally adequate diet"); Barnes v. Government of Virgin Islands, 415 F. Supp. 1218, 1235 (D.V.I. 1976) (curative and preventive services required) *with* Rial v. McGinnis, 756 F. Supp. 1070, 1073 (N.D.Ill. 1991); Dean v. Coughlin, 623 F. Supp. at 404; Jackson v. Lane, 688 F. Supp. 1291 (N.D.Ill. 1988).

[563]*See, e.g.,* Green v. Khrisnaswamy, 328 F. Supp. 2d 417, 419 (W.D.N.Y. 2004), *aff'd*, 134 Fed.Appx. 465 (2d Cir. 2005) (unpublished); Majors v. Ridley-Turner, 277 F. Supp. 2d 916, 918 (N.D.Ind. 2003); Rivera v. Goord, 253 F. Supp. 2d 735, 748 (S.D.N.Y. 2003); Sirois v. Prison Health Services, 233 F. Supp. 2d 52, 57–58 (D.Me. 2002) (examples of dental care claims dismissed as malpractice or differences of opinion at most).

[564]*See* Nicholson v. Choctaw County, Ala., 498 F. Supp. 295, 308 (S.D.Ala. 1980) (dentures need not be provided).

[565]Heitman v. Gabriel, 524 F. Supp. 622, 627 (W.D.Mo. 1981) (emergency fillings and pain relief measures required).

[566]Miller v. Carson, 401 F. Supp. 835, 878 (M.D.Fla. 1975), *aff'd in pertinent part*, 563 F.2d 741 (5th Cir. 1977).

[567]Jolly v. Coughlin, 76 F.3d 468, 477 (2d Cir. 1996); *see* Helling v. McKinney, 509 U.S. 25, 33, 113 S. Ct. 2475 (1993) (citing cases condemning the failure to separate prisoners with contagious diseases from others).

[568]*See* § F.3.b of this chapter.

[569]*See* § G.3.b of this chapter, n.1168.

[570]This information is summarized from the New York City Department of Health fact sheet on tuberculosis, available on its Web site at www.nyc.gov/html/doh/html/tb/tb-facts.shtml(last visited February 6, 2010).

[571]Maldonado v. Terhune, 28 F. Supp. 2d 284, 290 (D.N.J. 1998).

[572]DeGidio v. Pung, 704 F. Supp. 922, 937–51, 956–59 (D. Minn. 1989) (deliberate indifference was shown by persistent failure to respond to the obvious complaints and symptoms of the first case, the failure to advise inmates of their exposure, the failure to develop a policy and protocol and the failure of administrators, Health Department, or physicians to take responsibility, the failure to test all inmates when they tested all staff, and leaving patient education to a laboratory technician). *Cf.* McCroy v. Sheahan, 383 F. Supp. 2d 1010, 1014 (N.D.Ill. 2005) (delay in preventive treatment was not deliberately indifferent where jail TB policies are based on CDC and American Thoracic Society guidelines, incoming inmates are screened for active TB, and prisoners found to have it are immediately isolated); Wright v. Baker, 849 F. Supp. 569, 573–74 (N.D.Ohio 1994) (prison officials could not be held liable for TB exposure where they had appropriate screening, prevention, and isolation procedures in place).

[573]Jones-Bey v. Wright, 944 F. Supp. 723, 733 (N.D.Ind. 1996) (use of force to administer a TB test was not unlawful where officers acted with "professionalism and restraint").

This practice is generally upheld, but some isolation practices have been found excessive for their purpose and therefore unconstitutional.[574] They have also been found liable for failing to provide adequate care to those who contract the disease.[575]

2) HIV and AIDS

AIDS (acquired immuno-deficiency syndrome) is a serious illness that is caused by the human immunodeficiency virus (HIV). It attacks the immune system, the body's natural defense against disease, leaving the body vulnerable to other illnesses that can be fatal.

HIV is mainly spread through unprotected sex or sharing needles to inject drugs with an HIV-infected person, or from HIV-infected mothers to their infants before, during, and after birth (breast feeding). It is not spread by casual contact such as touching, hugging, and shaking hands, breathing and coughing, using toilets, telephones, drinking fountains, etc.

You can be infected with HIV for many years before there are any signs of illness. As HIV weakens the immune system, signs and symptoms may appear, such as swollen lymph glands in the neck, underarm, and groin area; recurrent fever, including "night sweats"; rapid weight loss for no apparent reason; constant fatigue; diarrhea and decreased appetite; white spots or unusual blemishes in the mouth.[576]

It is wise to be tested for HIV, even if you don't feel sick, if you have any reason to believe you might have been infected—or even if you don't. Though there is no known cure for the disease, there are now treatments available that control the disease and allow most people to remain healthy for many years if they take their medication regularly as prescribed.

Courts have given wide latitude to prison officials in matters related to AIDS and infection with HIV. Prison officials have broad discretion to segregate HIV-infected prisoners and to require screening for HIV infection.[577] However, they are not required to take either of these steps for the benefit of non-infected prisoners.[578] Extreme and unjustified security measures or other restrictions affecting people with HIV may violate the Constitution.[579] However, some courts have upheld as constitutional the exclusion of those

---

[574]In *Jolly v. Coughlin*, 76 F.3d 468 (2d Cir. 1996), a Rastafarian prisoner who refused a screening test for latent (inactive and non-contagious) tuberculosis was placed in "medical keeplock" and allowed out of his cell only ten minutes a week. After three and a half years of this treatment, the court held that he was entitled to a preliminary injunction on First and Eighth Amendment grounds, stating that the policy made no sense because the prisoner was treated more harshly than he would have been if he had been known to *have* latent tuberculosis and to refuse medication for it; requiring him to submit to chest x-rays and sputum samples would provide adequate protection. *Jolly*, 76 F.3d at 478; *accord*, Williams v. Greifinger, 97 F.3d 699 (2d Cir. 1996); Selah v. Goord, 255 F. Supp. 2d 42, 55–56 (N.D.N.Y. 2003) (granting preliminary injunction to prisoner placed in isolation for a year after refusing PPD skin test on religious grounds, but who was willing to take a sputum test and who had previously had a negative PPD); Reynolds v. Goord, 103 F. Supp. 2d 316, 337–38 (S.D.N.Y. 2000) (if the plaintiff cooperates with other diagnostic tools, like chest x-rays, sputum testing, and examination for physical symptoms of TB, his presence in general population presents no realistic threat of contagion); *see also* Pacheco v. Comisse, 897 F. Supp. 671 (N.D.N.Y. 1995) (holding officials were not entitled to summary judgment for refusing to send a prisoner to a court appearance, allegedly because he had refused to take a tuberculosis test and was in "quarantine"; he said it was pretextual and in retaliation for his complaints and lawsuits). *But see* Karolis v. New Jersey Dep't of Corrections, 935 F. Supp. 523, 530 (D.N.J. 1996) (refusing to follow *Jolly* because here the segregation imposed for refusing the TB test did provide medical protection).

[575]Hill v. Marshall, 962 F.2d 1209, 1213–15 (6th Cir. 1992) (affirming damages for increased risk of TB resulting from failure to ensure that prisoner with positive TB test received medication). *But see* Maldonado v. Terhune, 28 F. Supp. 2d 284, 290 (D.N.J. 1998) ("Prescribing medication that may have side effects does not amount to 'deliberate indifference' to serious medical needs as is necessary to support a claim under *Estelle*. . . . What is required is that prison officials be mindful of side effects and take reasonable steps to avoid serious harm.").

[576]The foregoing information is summarized from the New York City Department of Health's Web site (http://www.nyc.gov/html/doh/html/ah/ahbasic.shtml, last visited May 5, 2010).

[577]Harris v. Thigpen, 941 F.2d 1495, 1513–21 (11th Cir. 1991); Dunn v. White, 880 F.2d 1188 (10th Cir. 1989) (HIV testing of all inmates upheld); Muhammad v. Carlson, 845 F.2d 175 (8th Cir. 1988) (isolation of HIV positive prisoner did not deny due process); Judd v. Packard, 669 F. Supp. 741, 743 (D.Md. 1987) (isolation upheld); McDuffie v. Rikers Island Medical Dep't, 668 F. Supp. 328, 330 (S.D.N.Y. 1987) (same); Cordero v. Coughlin, 607 F. Supp. 9, 10–11 (S.D.N.Y. 1984); People v. Adams, 149 Ill.2d 331, 173 Ill. Dec. 600, 597 N.E.2d 574, 579–86 (Ill. 1992) (upholding mandatory HIV testing of persons convicted of prostitution). *But see* Barlow v. Ground, 943 F.2d 1132, 1136–39 (9th Cir. 1991) (warrantless taking of blood sample for HIV test from arrestee not admitted to jail violated the Fourth Amendment); Nolley v. County of Erie, 776 F. Supp. 715, 735–36 (W.D.N.Y. 1991) (placement of HIV positive prisoner in segregation was unreasonable and denied due process).

[578]Glick v. Henderson, 855 F.2d 536, 539–40 (8th Cir. 1988); Oladipupo v. Austin, 104 F. Supp. 2d 626, 635 (W.D.La. 2000); Myers v. Maryland Div. of Correction, 782 F. Supp. 1095, 1096–97 (D.Md. 1992); Feigley v. Fulcomer, 720 F. Supp. 475, 477–82 (M.D.Pa. 1989); Cameron v. Metcuz, 705 F. Supp. 454, 458–60 (N.D.Ind. 1989); Jarrett v. Faulkner, 662 F. Supp. 928, 929 (S.D.Ind. 1987); *see* Bolton v. Goord, 992 F. Supp. 604, 628–29 (S.D.N.Y. 1998) (double-celling prisoners with HIV presents no unconstitutional risk of spreading the disease). *But see* Billman v. Indiana Dep't of Corrections, 56 F.3d 785, 788 (7th Cir. 1995) (allegation of rape by an HIV-positive prisoner whose propensity for rape was known stated a claim; though plaintiff did not contract AIDS, fear of it could be an element of damages).

[579]May v. Sheahan, 226 F.3d 876, 882 (7th Cir. 2000) (shackling prisoner with AIDS to hospital bed despite presence of an armed guard, failure to produce him in court, and restrictions on access to counsel stated a constitutional claim); Perkins v. Kansas Dep't of Corrections, 165 F.3d 803, 809 (10th Cir. 1999) (prolonged denial of outdoor exercise and requirement to wear a spit mask stated an Eighth Amendment claim); Anderson v. Romero, 72 F.3d

with AIDS or HIV infection from programs such as family reunion (trailer visits)[580] and temporary release.[581] HIV-infected prisoners are "handicapped" within the meaning of the federal Rehabilitation Act and the Americans with Disabilities Act (ADA), and under those statutes they may not be excluded from programs for which they are "otherwise qualified."[582] However, one federal appeals court has upheld a broad exclusion of prisoners with HIV from recreational, religious, and educational programs on the ground that any factually supported possibility of transmitting an inevitably fatal disease justified the policy of segregation,[583] and another upheld their exclusion from food service jobs on the ground that other inmates' incorrect perceptions of risk and the "particular sensitivity of prisoners to food service" justified their policy.[584]

AIDS and HIV present serious medical needs,[585] though some courts prefer to ask whether a plaintiff's need for particular treatment at a particular time is serious. One federal appeals court has held that interruptions in HIV medication, though potentially dangerous, can be found non-serious if they do not have any adverse effects including increased drug resistance.[586] Claims of inadequate medical

care for AIDS and HIV infection are evaluated under the same deliberate indifference standard as other medical care claims.[587] Such claims must be evaluated in light of current developments in HIV treatment.[588] Denial of HIV treatment to a prisoner who refuses to be tested for HIV is not unconstitutional.[589]

518, 526 (7th Cir. 1995) (denial of haircuts and outdoor recreation may deny equal protection).

[580]Doe v. Coughlin, 71 N.Y.2d 48, 518 N.E.2d 536, 523 N.Y.S.2d 782 (N.Y. 1987). *Contra*, Bullock v. Gomez, 929 F. Supp. 1299, 1306–07 (C.D.Cal. 1996) (holding exclusion from overnight visiting must be done case by case and not by blanket policy; policy could be irrational as applied to prisoner and wife who were both HIV-positive).

The policy upheld in *Doe* was subsequently discontinued by prison officials while additional federal court litigation was pending.

[581]Harris v. Thigpen, 727 F. Supp. 1564, 1580–82 (M.D.Ala. 1990), *aff'd in part, vacated and remanded in part on other grounds*, 941 F.2d 1495 (11th Cir. 1991). *But see* Lopez v. Coughlin, 139 Misc.2d 851, 529 N.Y.S.2d 247 (N.Y.Sup. 1988) (denial of temporary release to AIDS patient struck down as not rationally related to its purported medical justification).

[582]Gates v. Rowland, 39 F.3d 1439, 1446 (9th Cir. 1994); Harris v. Thigpen, 941 F.2d at 1522–24; Dean v. Knowles, 912 F. Supp. 519, 521 (S.D.Fla. 1996) (denial of trustee status to asymptomatic prisoner with HIV for unexplained "medical" reasons raised a material factual issue under the ADA). *But see* Murdock v. Washington, 193 F.3d 510 (7th Cir. 1999) (per curiam) (prisoner who was excluded from a "culinary arts" program because he refused an HIV test, but said he did not have HIV, was not a "qualified individual with a disability").

These statutes are discussed further in § F.4.h of this chapter.

[583]Onishea v. Hopper, 171 F.3d 1289, 1299 (11th Cir. 1999).

[584]Gates v. Rowland, 39 F.3d 1439, 1447 (9th Cir. 1994).

[585]Brown v. Johnson, 387 F.3d 1344, 1351 (11th Cir. 2004); Perkins v. Kansas Dep't of Corrections, 165 F.3d 803, 811 (10th Cir. 1999); Rivera v. Alvarado, 240 F. Supp. 2d 136, 142–43 (D.P.R. 2003).

[586]Smith v. Carpenter, 316 F.3d 178, 186–89 (2d Cir. 2003); *accord*, Evans v. Bonner, 196 F. Supp. 2d 252, 256 (E.D.N.Y. 2002); *see* Taylor v. Barnett, 105 F. Supp. 2d 483, 487 (E.D.Va. 2000) (HIV

is a serious medical need, but mere failure to provide prescribed medication timely does not establish deliberate indifference, even though "withholding life-sustaining AIDS medication clearly is sufficiently objectively serious"). *But see* Murphy v. Bray, 51 F. Supp. 2d 877, 882 (S.D.Ohio 1999) (holding nine-day failure to provide prescribed HIV medications supported a deliberate indifference claim); McNally v. Prison Health Services, 28 F. Supp. 2d 671, 674 (D.Me. 1998) (holding failure to provide prescribed medication to prisoner who was suffering from fever, night chills, and night sweats stated a constitutional claim; citing "psychological stress over being forced to endure a potentially fatal deprivation of prescribed medication" in addition); *see also* McNally v. Prison Health Services, 52 F. Supp. 2d 147, 148–49 (D.Me. 1999) (holding evidence of fever, chills, and flu-like symptoms and increased risk of drug resistance in the future were sufficient to withstand summary judgment). Even if interruption of medication does have adverse effects, it does not violate the Constitution if it was merely negligent. Callaway v. Smith County, 991 F. Supp. 801, 809 (E.D.Tex. 1998).

Unless it has an adverse effect on the prisoner's health, the failure to provide medication also does not constitute the "physical injury" required to recover compensatory damages for mental or emotional injury under the Prison Litigation Reform Act. Leon v. Johnson, 96 F. Supp. 2d 244, 248 (W.D.N.Y. 2000).

[587]Brown v. Johnson, 387 F.3d 1344, 1351 (11th Cir. 2004) (withdrawal of HIV treatment stated a constitutional claim); Moore v. Mabus, 976 F.2d 268, 271 (5th Cir. 1992); Harris v. Thigpen, 941 F.2d at 1504–09 (treatment of HIV-infected prisoners was not systemically inadequate); Taylor v. Barnett, 105 F. Supp. 2d 483, 489 (E.D.Va. 2000) (allegation that HIV treatment was limited by cost considerations and did not reflect medical judgment stated a claim); Maynard v. New Jersey, 719 F. Supp. 292, 295–96 (D.N.J. 1989) (allegation that AIDS patient received only palliative treatment stated a constitutional claim); Tillery v. Owens, 719 F. Supp. 1256, 1309 (W.D.Pa. 1989) (prison officials ordered to promulgate AIDS treatment procedures), *aff'd*, 907 F.2d 418 (3d Cir. 1990); Hawley v. Evans, 716 F. Supp. 601, 602–04 (N.D.Ga. 1989) (denial of AZT until patients showed symptoms was not deliberate indifference given state of medical knowledge; patients did not have a right to treatment by their private physicians or a right to experimental drugs).

[588]Edwards v. Alabama Dep't of Corrections, 81 F. Supp. 2d 1242, 1250 (M.D.Ala. 2000) (stating that "new information about the kinds, costs, and availability of new treatments for HIV patients, bears directly on what levels of care are currently reasonable, and thus on what constitutes cruel and unusual punishment"). Thus, the decision in *Perkins v. Kansas Dep't of Corrections*, 165 F.3d 803, 811 (10th Cir. 1999), in which the court dismissed the plaintiff's complaint of failure to provide protease inhibitors in addition to AZT and 3TC, as a mere disagreement about the proper treatment, might come out differently today.

[589]Walker v. Peters, 233 F.3d 494, 499 (7th Cir. 2000) (refusing to dispense potentially dangerous medication without verifying

Prisoners have a right to privacy in medical information generally,[590] and especially in their diagnoses of AIDS or HIV infection, which is violated by disclosure either directly, or indirectly by the way HIV-prisoners are housed or receive medical treatment.[591] Some states have statutes protecting the confidentiality of HIV-related information, and these may support claims for damages.[592]

3) *Hepatitis C* Hepatitis C[593] is a viral infection that causes liver disease, which in some cases may progress to cirrhosis (serious scarring of the liver), which can be fatal. It may be many years after infection before the disease is advanced enough to make the person feel sick, though some people experience symptoms such as appetite loss, fatigue, nausea and vomiting, vague stomach pain, and jaundice (a yellowing of the skin and whites of the eyes) within two weeks to six months after infection. Hepatitis C may progress faster in people who are HIV positive.

The disease is spread by direct exposure to blood from an infected person, such as through sharing injection drug equipment, or by blood transfusions before 1992. The risk of sexual transmission or transmission from mother to child appears to be small. There is no evidence that it can be transmitted by casual contact, through foods, or by coughing or sneezing.

Hepatitis C is diagnosed by a positive blood test for Hepatitis C antibody. Testing is recommended for anyone at risk for infection. Everyone who has Hepatitis C should seek medical advice even if they don't have symptoms. Treatment with a combination of two drugs, interferon and ribavirin, is available for people infected with Hepatitis C who have active inflammation of their liver.[594]

Hepatitis C does, of course, present a serious medical need,[595] though some courts prefer to look at the specific need presented by a particular prisoner in determining seriousness.[596] Many prisoners have complained that it is very difficult to obtain treatment for Hepatitis C, possibly because some of the treatments are expensive. Complaints about Hepatitis C treatment are decided under the same deliberate indifference standard applied to other medical care claims.[597] Several decisions have held that restrictive rules and practices that prevent prisoners from receiving treatment for this disease raise substantial Eighth Amendment issues.[598]

---

the need for it is reasonable, and failure to force a competent prisoner to take a test he refused was not deliberate indifference).

[590]*See* § F.4.j of this chapter for a discussion of medical privacy.

[591]Doe v. Delie, 257 F.3d 309, 316–17 (3d Cir. 2001) (prison officials failed to justify jail staff's informing medical escort officers of his condition, leaving the door open during his medical appointments allowing others to eavesdrop, and announcing his medication loudly enough for others to hear); Doe v. City of Cleveland, 788 F. Supp. 979, 985 (N.D.Ohio 1991); Nolley v. County of Erie, 776 F. Supp. 715, 729 (W.D.N.Y. 1991); Doe v. Meachum, 126 F.R.D. 437, 439 (D.Conn. 1988); Doe v. Coughlin, 697 F. Supp. 1234, 1236–38 (N.D.N.Y. 1988); Woods v. White, 689 F. Supp. 874, 875–77 (W.D.Wis. 1988), *aff'd*, 899 F.2d 17 (7th Cir. 1990); Hillman v. Columbia County, 164 Wis.2d 376, 474 N.W.2d 913, 922–23 (Wis.App. 1991), *review granted*, 482 N.W.2d 105 (Wis. 1992); *see also* Doe v. Borough of Barrington, 729 F. Supp. 376, 382–85 (D.N.J. 1990) (non-prisoner case). *But see* Anderson v. Romero, 72 F.3d 518, 525–26 (7th Cir. 1995) (warning other prisoners and staff that a prisoner is an "HIV carrier" does not violate privacy rights); Harris v. Thigpen, 941 F.2d at 1513–21 (prison authorities' decision to segregate HIV positive inmates overcame the inmates' privacy rights); *see also* Leon v. Johnson, 96 F. Supp. 2d 244, 250 (W.D.N.Y. 2000) (having to disclose status to get a Spanish interpreter did not violate privacy rights since he only had to disclose it to staff); Doe v. Marsh, 918 F. Supp. 580, 586 (N.D.N.Y. 1996) (disclosure did not violate rights where plaintiffs were involved in HIV advocacy and their status was widely known); Baez v. Rapping, 680 F. Supp. 112, 115 (S.D.N.Y. 1988) (privacy rights not violated by ordinary reporting of medical findings).

[592]*See, e.g.,* Nolley v. County of Erie, 776 F. Supp. at 733–34. *But see* Hillman v. Columbia County, 474 N.W.2d at 917–18 (state HIV privacy statute did not apply to jail personnel).

[593]There are a number of different types of Hepatitis. Hepatitis C is the variety that is most widespread in the prison population.

[594]This information is summarized from the New York City Department of Health's Web site, http://www.nyc.gov/html/doh/html/cd/cdhepc-fact.shtml (last visited March 2, 2008). That file has been replaced by http://www.nyc.gov/html/doh/downloads/pdf/cd/cd-hepc-bro.pdf (last visited February 6, 2010), a simpler document that says substantially the same things.

[595]Brown v. Johnson, 387 F.3d 1344, 1351 (11th Cir. 2004).

[596]Bender v. Regier, 385 F.3d 1133, 1137 (8th Cir. 2004) (while Hepatitis C infection is clearly a serious medical problem, the Eighth Amendment question is whether the plaintiff had a serious medical need for prompt interferon treatment).

[597]Brown v. Johnson, 387 F.3d 1344, (11th Cir. 2004). Bender v. Regier, 385 F.3d 1133, 1138 (8th Cir. 2004) ("inadvertent failure" to provide adequate Hepatitis C treatment is not deliberate indifference); Christy v. Robinson, 216 F. Supp. 2d 398, 404–05, 411, 414–16 (D.N.J. 2002) (noting that the court had ordered an examination to see if the plaintiff should receive interferon treatment; stating that it did not appear to be indicated for the plaintiff); *see* Erickson v. Pardus, 551 U.S. 89, 94, 127 S. Ct. 2197, 2200 (2007) (per curiam) (holding that allegation that a prison doctor stopped plaintiff's Hepatitis C medication even though he had commenced a one-year treatment program and needed treatment for the disease pled an Eighth Amendment claim).

[598]Johnson v. Wright, 412 F.3d 398, 406 (2d Cir. 2005) (applying a rule that no one with a recent history of substance abuse could receive Rebetron therapy for Hepatitis C to a prisoner whose abuse history was very minor and whose treating doctors all recommended treatment could constitute deliberate indifference); McKenna v. Wright, 386 F.3d 432, 437 (2d Cir. 2004) (allegation of refusal to provide Hepatitis C treatment because plaintiff might be released within a year stated a deliberate indifference claim).

In *Glaus v. Anderson*, 408 F.3d 382 (7th Cir. 2005), the plaintiff challenged a Federal Bureau of Prisons policy that provided for the continuation of interferon treatment only if the patient's viral load dropped below one million; the plaintiff's dropped from 21 million to a little over one million, and his viral load increased drastically when treatment was stopped. The court dismissed his claim because it was improperly filed as a habeas corpus petition. *Glaus*, 408 F.3d at 387–88.

In at least one case, a court has ordered a prison system to take steps to assess a prisoner for a liver transplant.[599] A requirement that prisoners seeking Hepatitis C treatment submit to a psychological evaluation has been upheld, since it is related to potential side effects of certain medications and is "part and parcel of the treatment."[600] Liver function may now be a "major life activity" for purposes of the federal disability statutes.[601]

4) Methicillin-Resistant Staphylococcus Aureus (MRSA)

MRSA is a variation (actually, several variations) of the common *Staphylococcus aureus* bacterium that causes infections. It can be spread through direct contact with infected individuals or through contact with materials that have been exposed to the bacteria. The risk of transmission is increased by conditions such as overcrowding, shared facilities, close contact between inmates, and unsanitary conditions.[602] Exposure to MRSA is a serious medical need.[603]

There have been a number of MRSA outbreaks in prisons and jails in recent years, but there is little reported case law about them. In one unreported case, the court declined to disturb a jury verdict for prisoners who contracted MRSA against jail officials, stating that there was "ample evidence" that the defendants knew of the spreading MRSA infection and "failed to take necessary steps to minimize the number of inmates affected"; the record showed "grossly inadequate medical treatment, a failure to keep the showers and food handling areas in a sanitary condition, and a failure to instruct inmates on prevention of infectious diseases."[604] Another unreported decision held that an allegation that a prisoner with MRSA who was released from the infirmary to general population with open sores stated a claim of deliberate indifference to the risk of transmitting the disease to other prisoners including the plaintiff.[605] However, many prisoner claims of MRSA infection have been dismissed because of the lack of evidence as to how the prisoner was infected.[606]

e. Medical Diets Prison officials must provide special diets that are medically necessary.[607] However, brief or harmless delays and interruptions in providing prescribed diets are not unconstitutional.[608] As with any other form of medical care, disagreements with medical personnel about your dietary needs do not raise a constitutional issue.[609] In most

---

[599]Rosado v. Alameida, 349 F. Supp. 2d 1340, 1348 (S.D.Cal. 2004).

[600]Iseley v. Dragovich, 236 F. Supp. 472, 477 (E.D.Pa. 2002).

[601]*See* § F.4.h(2) of this chapter, n.687.

[602]Kaucher v. County of Bucks, 455 F.3d 418, 421 (3d Cir. 2006); *see* Bowers v. City of Philadelphia, 2007 WL 219651, *15 (E.D.Pa., Jan. 25, 2007) (citing risk of transmission of MRSA among other diseases in enjoining crowded conditions in police lockup and intake units).

[603]Lopez v. McGrath, 2007 WL 1577893, *5 (N.D.Cal., May 31, 2007).

[604]Keller v. County of Bucks, 2005 WL 675831, *1 (E.D.Pa., Mar. 22, 2005), *aff'd*, 209 Fed.Appx. 201 (3d Cir. 2006) (unpublished). Correction officers sued over the same outbreak, but their claims were rejected. Kaucher v. County of Bucks, 455 F.3d at 429–30 (the cited conditions "did not affect corrections officers, who were free to seek outside medical treatment, who did not live in the jail, and who received detailed instructions on infectious disease prevention in the jail's standard operating procedures").

[605]Kimble v. Tennis, 2006 WL 1548950, *4 (M.D.Pa., June 5, 2006).

[606]*See, e.g.*, Lopez v. McGrath, 2007 WL 1577893, *6–8 (citing lack of evidence that plaintiff was infected with MRSA by his cellmate); Kalina v. King County Jail, 2006 WL 4093686, *7 (W.D.Wash., Dec. 26, 2006) (citing lack of evidence that the plaintiff was infected with MRSA in the jail).

[607]Sellers v. Henman, 41 F.3d 1100, 1102 (7th Cir. 1994); Morales Feliciano v. Calderon Sierra, 300 F. Supp. 2d 321, 341 (D.P.R. 2004) (failing to provide prescribed diets implicates Eighth Amendment rights); Woulard v. Food Service, 294 F. Supp. 2d 596, 604 (D.Del. 2003) (holding failure to provide six small meals a day prescribed for Crohn's disease could be deliberate indifference; the need was serious because a doctor prescribed for it); Mandala v. Coughlin, 920 F. Supp. 342, 355 (E.D.N.Y. 1996) (year's delay in providing high-fiber diet prescribed after abdominal surgery supported a deliberate indifference claim); Coades v. Jeffes, 822 F.Sup. 1189, 1191–92 (E.D.Pa. 1993) (denial of special diet for ulcers implicated a serious need and could be found deliberately indifferent); McCargo v. Vaughn, 778 F. Supp. 1341, 1342 (E.D.Pa. 1991); Kyle v. Allen, 732 F. Supp. 1157, 1159 (S.D.Fla. 1990); Balla v. Idaho State Bd. of Corrections, 595 F. Supp. 1558, 1574–75 (D.Idaho 1984); Riddick v. Bass, 586 F. Supp. 881, 883 (E.D.Va. 1984); Johnson v. Harris, 479 F. Supp. 333, 336–37 (S.D.N.Y. 1979). *But see* Abdush-Shahid v. Coughlin, 933 F. Supp. 168, 180 (N.D.N.Y. 1996) (it was not deliberately indifferent to remove the plaintiff from his special diet, since he was not eating the special meals and the doctor authorized the removal).

[608]Dixon v. Fox, 893 F.2d 1556, 1557 (8th Cir. 1990) (interruption of medical diets was not unconstitutional where plaintiffs did not explain how their serious medical needs were compromised); Hunt v. Dental Dep't, 865 F.2d 198, 201 n.2 (9th Cir. 1989) (failure to put the plaintiff on a soft diet was not unconstitutional where after a short delay he was transferred to a prison where he could get it); Toussaint v. McCarthy, 801 F.2d 1080, 1112 (9th Cir. 1986) (delays in providing special diets were not unconstitutional); Twyman v. Crisp, 584 F.2d 352, 354–55 (10th Cir. 1978) (temporary suspension of diet was not unconstitutional); Clement v. California Dep't of Corrections, 220 F. Supp. 2d 1098, 1107 (N.D.Cal. 2002) (two-month delay in providing prescribed high-fiber, low-fat diet was not deliberate indifference absent proof of harm); Waring v. Meachum, 175 F. Supp. 2d 230 (D.Conn. 2001) (six-day failure to provide prescribed diet during lockdown was not deliberate indifference); Robeson v. Squadrito, 57 F. Supp. 2d 642, 649–50 (N.D.Ind. 1999) (five-day delay in providing hypoglycemic diet did not violate the Constitution; a later, longer delay in which his blood sugar was tested each day and was normal did not support a deliberate indifference claim).

[609]Martinez v. Griffin, 840 F.2d 314, 315 (5th Cir. 1988); Gerber v. Sweeney, 292 F. Supp. 700, 704–05 (E.D.Pa. 2003) (substitution of cheese and fruit for prescribed diet calling for milk and juice was not unconstitutional where a dietician approved it); Williams v. Coughlin, 650 F. Supp. 955, 956–57 (S.D.N.Y. 1987).

cases you will only be entitled to a medical diet if medical staff have prescribed one. However, deliberate indifference may exist if medical or correctional personnel simply ignore your dietary needs and no medical judgment about them is made.[610]

f. Pregnancy, Childbirth, Abortion, and Reproduction

The courts have not fully explored the medical care rights of pregnant women.[611] It is clear that actual complications of pregnancy are serious medical needs, and cases involving them are treated similarly to other prison medical care cases.[612] Courts have held the shackling of women in labor in or the late stages of pregnancy unconstitutional.[613] We believe that women are also constitutionally entitled to reasonably adequate preventive pre-natal care, on the ground that the need to bear a healthy child and avoid complications of pregnancy is a serious medical need.[614]

As part of the constitutional protection of personal privacy, women have a limited constitutional right to end their pregnancies through abortion. Restrictions are

---

See also Cody v. Hillard, 599 F. Supp. 1025, 1039, 1057 (D.S.D. 1984) (absence of a special diet line for diabetics was not unconstitutional where medical staff gave proper dietary counseling), *aff'd in part and rev'd in part on other grounds*, 830 F.2d 912 (8th Cir. 1987) (en banc).

[610]Lolli v. County of Orange, 351 F.3d 410, 420–21 (9th Cir. 2003) (a prisoner who was arrested, informed security staff and a nurse that he was diabetic and needed to eat quickly, and was instead put in a holding cell and beaten when he complained, sufficiently supported a deliberate indifference claim). The *Lolli* court stated: "Diabetes is a common yet serious illness that can produce harmful consequences if left untreated for even a relatively short period of time. . . . We therefore join our sister circuits in acknowledging that a constitutional violation may take place when the government does not respond to the legitimate medical needs of a detainee whom it has reason to believe is diabetic." 351 F.3d at 419–20; *accord*, Sellers v. Henman, 41 F.3d 1100, 1102 (7th Cir. 1994); Taylor v. Anderson, 868 F. Supp. 1024, 1025–26 (N.D.Ill. 1994). *But see* Carrion v. Wilkinson, 309 F. Supp. 2d 1007, 1014 (N.D.Ohio 2004) (stating "Courts have recognized that a diabetic inmate's needs to control his diet are sufficient medical needs for purposes of the Eighth Amendment analysis," but holding that defendants were not deliberately indifferent where they explained to him that his diet was "self-monitored" and how to make the necessary choices, prescribed insulin and other medications, and counseled him on his diet).

[611]There have been several class actions challenging the treatment of pregnant prisoners, but these have been settled without formal decisions by the courts involved. E.M. Barry, Pregnant Prisoners, in Robbins, *Prisoners and the Law* § 17C (Clark Boardman ed. 1990), *reprinted from* 12 HARV. WOMEN'S L.J. 189 (1989). One federal court entered extensive requirements for gynecological examination and testing, STD testing, follow-up care, health education, pre-natal care, protocols, and education based on local law rather than the Constitution, *see* Women Prisoners of the District of Columbia Dep't of Corrections v. District of Columbia, 877 F. Supp. 634, 681–84 (D.D.C. 1994), but an appellate court held that the use of local law for that purpose was an abuse of discretion. Women Prisoners of the District of Columbia Dep't of Corrections v. District of Columbia, 93 F.3d 910, 920–23 (D.C. Cir. 1996).

The number of pregnant prisoners is substantial. In one federal prison housing 1300 women, the government estimated that about 50 are pregnant at any one time. Berrios-Berrios v. Thornburgh, 716 F. Supp. 987, 988 (E.D.Ky. 1989).

[612]*See, e.g.*, Pool v. Sebastian County, Ark., 418 F.3d 934, 945 (8th Cir. 2005) (pregnant prisoner who told prison staff she was pregnant, bleeding, and passing blood clots, and that she was in extreme pain from the cramping, showed "a need for medical attention that would have been obvious to a layperson, making submission of verifying medical evidence unnecessary"); Coleman v. Rahija, 114 F.3d 778, 785 (8th Cir. 1997) (pre-term labor is a serious medical need; "[a] layperson would have recognized the necessity for a doctor's attention" when the plaintiff appeared in the clinic bleeding and in pain; upholding damage award for delay in hospitalization); Boswell v. Sherburne County, 849 F.2d 1117, 1121–22 (10th Cir. 1988) (pregnant woman's vaginal bleeding treated as serious); Archer v. Dutcher, 733 F.2d 14, 16–17 (2d Cir. 1984) (similar to *Boswell*); Doe v. Gustavus, 294 F. Supp. 2d 1003, 1008 (E.D.Wis. 2003) ("Having medical assistance immediately preceding and during a birth is, in today's society, taken for granted." Jail staff's disregard of plaintiff's symptoms of impending birth could be deliberate indifference.); Williams v. Delcambre, 413 So.2d 324, 326 (La. App. 1982) ("Having elected to carry the child through term she was entitled to medical assistance in furtherance of her maternal goal."), *writ denied*, 416 So.2d 115 (La. 1982).

[613]*See* Nelson v. Correctional Medical Services, 583 F.3d 522, 534 (8th Cir. 2009) (en banc) (holding it clearly established that a woman "in the final stages of labor cannot be shackled absent clear evidence that she is a security or flight risk"). At least one court has struck down a practice of shackling women in their third trimester with leg shackles, handcuffs, belly chain and "black box" as violating the Eighth Amendment; it held that leg shackles provide sufficient security, and these must be removed during labor and shortly thereafter. Women Prisoners of the District of Columbia Dep't of Corrections v. District of Columbia, 877 F. Supp. 634, 668–69 (D.D.C. 1994), *vacated in part and remanded*, 93 F.3d 910, 920–23 (D.C. Cir. 1996). These provisions were explicitly preserved by the appellate court. 93 F.3d at 969, 973. *See also* Women Prisoners of the District of Columbia Dep't of Corrections v. District of Columbia, 968 F. Supp. 744 (D.D.C. 1997) (describing settlement after appellate proceedings).

[614]In *Monmouth County Correctional Institutional Inmates v. Lanzaro*, 834 F.2d 326, 348–49 (3d Cir. 1987), the court held that pregnancy was a serious medical need in the context of the right to abortion, citing both the physical and the psychological consequences of pregnancy. We think that the same conclusion follows when a pregnant woman chooses to bear her child.

One court has stated, "The knowledge of [a prisoner's] advanced stage of pregnancy is insufficient by itself to put a reasonable jail commander on notice that [she] has a serious medical condition." Hartbarger v. Blackford County Dep't of Public Welfare, 733 F. Supp. 300, 303 (N.D.Ind. 1990). We don't think that case is inconsistent with our view. In *Hartbarger*, the plaintiff was only in jail for eight days, and her complaints related to pain and discomfort, inability to sleep, and emotional upset; she did not allege either acute complications of pregnancy or a long-term denial of pre-natal care. We think that pregnancy of a longer term prisoner, or one close to delivery or with symptoms of complications, should be regarded as a serious need.

unconstitutional if they impose an "undue burden" on the right to abortion. "An undue burden exists, and therefore a provision of law is invalid, if its purpose or effect is to place a substantial obstacle in the path of a woman seeking an abortion before the fetus attains viability."[615] After the fetus is viable, abortion may be regulated or even banned except to preserve the life or health of the mother.[616]

In prison or jail, the right to abortion has been held protected both as a matter of privacy and as an aspect of the Eighth Amendment right to medical care. The leading decision on abortions for prisoners held that unwanted pregnancy constitutes a serious medical need and that the denial of an abortion constitutes deliberate indifference.[617] It also concluded that restrictions on abortions that were not applied to other medical procedures were irrational and therefore unconstitutional under the *Turner v. Safley* "reasonableness" test,[618] and that jail or prison officials must provide for abortions regardless of the prisoner's ability or willingness to pay.[619] However, a recent decision upheld a policy requiring a court order for "elective" medical procedures, and held that the denial of an abortion for failure to follow that procedure was not unconstitutional.[620]

You may have trouble obtaining an abortion in jail or prison because many people are opposed to abortion on religious or moral grounds, and many jail and prison systems have rules designed to prevent prisoners from getting them and to get around earlier decisions affirming prisoners' right to abortions.[621] You may also have problems in getting an abortion scheduled because in most cases it will require a trip to an outside clinic or hospital and because it may be an unfamiliar request in many prisons and jails. There may also be special rules or procedures you must follow. Since abortions can be banned, and are also more dangerous, later in pregnancy,[622] delay may result in your being denied an abortion.[623]

For these reasons, if you think you may be pregnant, request a pregnancy test *immediately*. If you learn that you are pregnant and want an abortion, request it *immediately* and ask specifically what procedures must be followed. If you do not get prompt responses to these requests, complain to higher authority or use the grievance process *quickly*.[624] If jail or prison officials deny your request or fail to act on it promptly, you may have to seek a temporary restraining order or preliminary injunction[625] if you are to obtain an abortion safely and legally.

[615]Planned Parenthood of Southeastern Pennsylvania v. Casey, 505 U.S. 833, 877–78, 112 S. Ct. 2791 (1992).

[616]Planned Parenthood v. Casey, 505 U.S. at 877.

Viability" refers to the point at which a fetus can live outside its mother's body and can occur as early as the 23d or 24th week of pregnancy. *Id.* at 860.

[617]Monmouth County Correctional Institution Inmates v. Lanzaro, 834 F.2d at 346–49; *see also* Gibson v. Matthews, 926 F.2d 532, 536–37 (6th Cir. 1991) (prison officials were not shown to be deliberately indifferent with respect to the denial of a prisoner's abortion); Bryant v. Maffucci, 923 F.2d 979, 983–84 (2d Cir. 1991) (negligent denial of an abortion did not violate detainee's rights). However, one federal circuit has recently held that elective, non-therapeutic abortions do not represent a serious medical need and their denial is not deliberate indifference. Roe v. Crawford, 514 F.3d 789, 798–801 (8th Cir. 2008), *cert. denied*, 129 S. Ct. 109 (2008).

[618]Monmouth County Correctional Institution Inmates v. Lanzaro, 834 F.2d at 336–44; *accord*, Roe v. Crawford, 514 F.3d at 798–801 (holding the *Turner* test and not the undue burden test governs in prison abortion cases).

[619]*Monmouth County*, 834 F.2d at 351. *Contra*, Roe v. Crawford, 514 F.3d at 800–01.

The Supreme Court has upheld a statute forbidding public employees to "perform or assist" abortions except to save the mother's life. Webster v. Reproductive Health Services, 492 U.S. 490, 109 S. Ct. 3040 (1989). The Supreme Court reasoned that women were free to go elsewhere for abortions besides public hospitals. 492 U.S. at 509. Since prisoners are not free, the *Webster* case should have no application to prison abortion cases. The lower court in *Webster* specifically noted that prisoners' right to public funding of abortions was not an issue in that case. Reproductive Health Services v. Webster, 851 F.2d 1071, 1084 and n.17 (8th Cir. 1988), *rev'd on other grounds*, 492 U.S. 490, 109 S. Ct. 3040 (1989). The conclusion that prison officials must provide for prisoners' abortions is also supported by the fact that the Supreme Court in *Webster* cited the case of *DeShaney v. Winnebago County Dep't of Social Services*, 489 U.S. 189, 198, 109 S. Ct. 998 (1989), which emphasizes that government has obligations to provide services like medical care to incarcerated persons but not free individuals.

[620]Victoria W. v. Larpenter, 369 F.3d 475, 486 (5th Cir. 2004). This court unconvincingly distinguished the *Monmouth County* case on the grounds that the policy at issue dealt with all "elective" procedures and did not single out abortions, and the justifications raised included security and avoidance of liability as well as cost. The court also said that "while an abortion is time-sensitive and unique in its constitutional protection, a non-therapeutic abortion is not a medical emergency. . . . The constitutional right to choose to abort one's pregnancy does not necessarily categorize it as an emergency." *Victoria W.*, 369 F.3d at 487 n.52.

[621]The *Victoria W.* decision cited above provides an example of such a rule.

[622]Planned Parenthood v. Casey, 505 U.S. 833, 877–78, 112 S. Ct. 2791 (1992); Roe v. Wade, 410 U.S. 113, 163–65, 93 S.Ct. 705 (1973).

[623]This is what happened to the plaintiffs in the *Bryant* and *Gibson* cases cited in n.617, above.

[624]You are best advised at least to start the grievance process, even if it won't be completed in time. You will certainly have a good argument if you go into court and say the grievance process is not an "available remedy" for a problem that requires urgent action. However, the law is not clear on this point, *see* Ch. 9, § D, nn.232–237, and officials may argue that your failure even to start the process should disqualify you from judicial relief.

[625]*See* Roe v. Crawford, 396 F. Supp. 2d 1041 (W.D.Mo. 2005) (granting preliminary injunction), *stay denied*, 546 U.S. 959 (2005); Doe v. Barron, 92 F. Supp. 2d 694, 696–97 (S.D.Ohio 1999) (granting TRO where jail officials said they would not arrange for an abortion without a court order; stating it is in the public interest to uphold the right declared in *Roe v. Wade* when it is "arbitrarily denied by prison officials absent medical or other

The same advice applies to preventive pre-natal care. In some prisons and jails, the administration and medical staff may not be accustomed to providing such care, and it may take them a while to arrange it. The sooner you ask, the sooner you are likely to get it.

Once your child is born, there is no constitutional right to keep it in prison, even if you wish to breast-feed the child.[626] A few states do have statutes that allow women to keep newborn children with them for limited periods of time.[627] One federal court has required prison officials to permit a prisoner to breast-feed her newborn child during regular visiting hours, but declined to require them to make arrangements to deliver her milk to the child's custodian for use at other times.[628] Another court has held that denial of child visiting and lack of child placement counselling to mothers who deliver in jail do not violate the Eighth Amendment.[629]

One federal appeals court has held that a male prisoner serving a life sentence, and therefore ineligible for family visits, was not constitutionally entitled to impregnate his wife by providing a sperm sample for artificial insemination. The court ruled very broadly, stating: "Our conclusion that the right to procreate is inconsistent with incarceration is not dependent on the science of artificial insemination, or on how easy or difficult it is to accomplish. Rather, it is a conclusion that stems from consideration of the nature and goals of the correctional system, including isolating prisoners, deterring crime, punishing offenders, and providing rehabilitation."[630]

g. Drug Dependency Treatment[631] Drug or alcohol withdrawal is a serious medical need,[632] and prisons and jails are constitutionally required to provide some form of treatment for it.[633] However, there is no constitutional right to treatment for the addiction itself.[634] Thus, most decisions have held that prisons and jails need not provide methadone

---

legitimate concerns."). Temporary restraining orders and preliminary injunctions are discussed in Ch. 8, § O.2.a.

[626]Southerland v. Thigpen, 784 F.2d 713, 717 (5th Cir. 1986) (finding the right to breast-feed "fundamentally inconsistent with imprisonment itself").

Prisoners' parental rights are discussed in more detail in Ch. 3, § G.3.

[627]See Ch. 3, § G.3, n.1019.

[628]Berrios-Berrios v. Thornburgh, 716 F. Supp. 987, 990–91 (E.D.Ky. 1989).

[629]Women Prisoners of District of Columbia Dep't of Corrections v. District of Columbia, 899 F. Supp. 659, 674–75 (D.D.C. 1995).

[630]Gerber v. Hickman, 291 F.3d 617, 622 (9th Cir. 2002) (en banc). The claim that some rights are inherently inconsistent with incarceration is arguably contrary to the "reasonable relationship" analysis the Supreme Court has said applies to all restrictions on prisoners' fundamental rights. See Ch. 3, § A. It is also contrary to reality, since conjugal or "family" visiting is widespread in American corrections, but that did not seem to bother the *Gerber* court: "The fact that California prison officials may choose to permit some inmates the privilege of conjugal visits is simply irrelevant to whether there is a constitutional right to conjugal visits or a right to procreate while in prison." 291 F.3d at 621–22.

[631]In some states, courts may direct drug or alcohol treatment as part of or instead of a criminal sentence. These issues of criminal law and procedure are beyond the scope of this Manual.

[632]Lancaster v. Monroe County, Ala., 116 F.3d 1419, 1426 (11th Cir. 1997) (" . . . [A] jail official who is aware of but ignores the dangers of acute alcohol withdrawal and waits for a manifest emergency before obtaining medical care is deliberately indifferent to the inmate's constitutional rights."); Ledford v. Sullivan, 105 F.3d 354, 359 (7th Cir. 1997) (nausea, dizziness, vomiting, a crawling sensation on his skin, unspecified emotional and mental regression, and depression resulting from deprivation of anti-depressant medication); Kelley v. County of Wayne, 325 F. Supp. 2d 788, 792 (E.D.Mich. 2004) ("Heroin withdrawal is a serious medical condition."); Gonzalez v. Cecil County, Md., 221 F. Supp. 2d 611, 616 (D.Md. 2002) (heroin addiction); see Foelker v. Outagamie County, 394 F.3d 510, 513 (7th Cir. 2005) (prisoner suffering acute delirium from drug withdrawal had serious medical need).

[633]Foelker v. Outagamie County, 394 F.3d 510, 513 (7th Cir. 2005) (evidence of knowing failure to treat drug withdrawal supported a deliberate indifference claim); Pedraza v. Meyer, 919 F.2d 317, 318–19 (5th Cir. 1990) (allegation of four-day refusal to provide treatment for drug withdrawal was not frivolous under the deliberate indifference standard); Gonzalez v. Cecil County, Md., 221 F. Supp. 2d 611, 617 (D.Md. 2002) (treating heroin withdrawal only with Kaopectate and a blood pressure medication stated a deliberate indifference claim; providing some treatment is no defense if the treatment is completely inappropriate); U.S. ex rel. Walker v. Fayette County, Pa., 599 F.2d 573, 575–76 (3d Cir. 1979) (10-day denial of medical care during withdrawal would constitute deliberate indifference); Palmigiano v. Garrahy, 443 F. Supp. 956, 989 (D.R.I. 1977) (Constitution requires treatment other than "abrupt denial or 'cold turkey'"), *remanded on other grounds*, 599 F.2d 17 (1st Cir. 1979); Laaman v. Helgemoe, 437 F. Supp. 269, 314–15 (D.N.H. 1977) ("symptoms such as withdrawal pains" are serious medical needs). *But see* Thompson v. Upshur County, Texas, 245 F.3d 447, 458–59 (5th Cir. 2001) (finding no deliberate indifference for most defendants where prisoner who died of alcohol withdrawal had refused hospitalization and was returned to a jail better equipped to deal with his problems; one defendant who knew he was injuring himself and did not act to protect him could be deliberately indifferent); Kelley v. County of Wayne, 325 F. Supp. 2d 788, 792 (E.D.Mich. 2004) (although heroin addiction is a serious medical need, defendants who did not know of the plaintiff's condition could not be found deliberately indifferent); Smith v. Lejeune, 203 F. Supp. 2d 1260, 1268 (D.Wyo. 2002) (finding no deliberate indifference where prisoner died of alcohol withdrawal but did not display usual symptoms or admit history of alcohol use).

[634]Smith v. Schneckloth, 414 F.2d 680, 682 (9th Cir. 1969); Counts v. Newhart, 951 F. Supp. 579, 587 (E.D.Va. 1996); Laaman v. Helgemoe, 437 F. Supp. at 314–15; Ladetto v. Commissioner of Correction, 7 Mass.App. 1, 385 N.E.2d 273, 275 (App. 1979); Bresolin v. Morris, 88 Wash.2d 167, 558 P.2d 1350, 1353 (1977). The courts generally construe drug addiction treatment as a matter of rehabilitation rather than medical care. There is no right to

maintenance even for persons who were in methadone programs outside prison.[635] The courts have taken a similar approach to alcoholism treatment.[636]

Drug addiction that significantly limits a major life activity is a recognized disability under the Americans with Disabilities Act (ADA); persons currently engaging in the illegal use of drugs are not protected against discrimination by the ADA, but it protects persons who have successfully completed or are participating in a supervised drug rehabilitation program and are no longer using illegal drugs.[637]

Prisons may, of course, provide treatment for drug or alcohol addiction voluntarily. If they do, they have substantial discretion in their content and operation,[638] with the exception that some such programs have been found to violate the Establishment Clause of the First Amendment because of their religious component.[639] There has been considerable litigation about the Federal Bureau of Prisons' implementation of a statute providing for early release for some prisoners who complete a drug treatment program.[640]

State statutes or constitutional provisions may provide for a right to drug or alcohol treatment.[641] However, state laws on those subjects do not always provide enforceable rights for prisoners.[642]

---

rehabilitation under the federal Constitution, although some states' laws provide for such a right. *See* § I of this chapter.

One court has held that the lack of drug addiction treatment was unconstitutional under the circumstances because of its consequences for increased violence, suicidal gestures, and inmates' becoming addicted while in prison. Palmigiano v. Garrahy, 443 F. Supp. at 971–73. Similarly, another court held that the failure to provide drug and alcohol treatment "contributes to the totality of conditions which make degeneration probable and self-improvement unlikely." Ramos v. Lamm, 485 F. Supp. 122, 146 (D.Colo. 1980), *aff'd in part, vacated in part on other grounds*, 639 F.2d 559 (10th Cir. 1980).

[635]Fredericks v. Huggins, 711 F.2d 31, 33–34 (4th Cir. 1983); Inmates of Allegheny County Jail v. Pierce, 612 F.2d 754, 760–61 (3d Cir. 1979); U.S. ex rel. Walker v. Fayette County, Pa., 599 F.2d 573, 575–76 (3d Cir. 1979); Holly v. Rapone, 476 F. Supp. 226, 231 (E.D.Pa. 1979). *But see* Cudnik v. Krieger, 392 F. Supp. 305, 312–13 (N.D. Ohio 1974) (methadone required for prisoner who had previously received it). *Cf.* Messina v. Mazzeo, 854 F. Supp. 116, 139–41 (E.D.N.Y. 1994) (allegation that plaintiff was denied methadone for withdrawal symptoms on admission to jail stated a deliberate indifference claim; court distinguishes cases rejecting demands for methadone maintenance).

[636]Pace v. Fauver, 479 F. Supp. 456, 457–58 (D.N.J. 1979) (desire for treatment for alcoholism was a matter of rehabilitation and not a serious medical need), *aff'd*, 649 F.2d 860 (3d Cir. 1981); State v. Puga, 111 Idaho App. 874, 728 P.2d 398, 400–01 (Idaho App. 1986).

[637]Thompson v. Davis, 295 F.3d 890, 896 (9th Cir. 2002) (refusing to dismiss challenge to policy of denying parole to persons with substance abuse histories); *see* § F.4.h of this chapter concerning the disability statutes.

[638]*See* Kerr v. Puckett, 138 F.3d 321, 323–24 (7th Cir. 1998) (rejecting claim that prison drug programs constituted "brainwashing"; programs designed to change people's values are not unconstitutional); Munir v. Kearney, 377 F. Supp. 2d 468, 472 (D.Del. 2005) (upholding removal of Muslim prisoner who said that a writing assignment violated his religious beliefs; it would be unduly burdensome to provide alternative essay questions); Garvin v. Terhune, 157 F. Supp. 2d 416, 418 (D.N.J. 2001) (holding officials could require drug program participation and reduce plaintiff's custody status for refusing; "Prison officials must and should make decisions concerning the types of programs in which prisoners should participate."); Ross v. Keelings, 2 F. Supp. 2d 810, 815–20 (E.D.Va. 1998) (coerced participation in rehabilitative Therapeutic Community program was not unlawful, though court ruled against

religious component of program); Pryor-El v. Kelly, 892 F. Supp. 261, 273 (D.D.C. 1995) (finding no liberty interest implicated by exclusion from drug program); Rodriguez v. Goord, 50 A.D.3d 1328, 855 N.Y.S.2d 309 (2008) (holding requirement that prisoner who had been off drugs for 10 years or more participate in alcohol and substance abuse training program was not arbitrary and capricious).

[639]*See* Ch. 3, § D.4, nn.862–865.

[640]18 U.S.C.A. § 3621(e)(2)(B) provides that persons convicted of non-violent crimes may obtain release a year early by completing a drug treatment program. In *Lopez v. Davis*, 531 U.S. 230, 121 S. Ct. 714 (2001), the Supreme Court upheld a Bureau of Prisons regulation excluding persons convicted of drug trafficking offenses enhanced under the sentencing guidelines for possession of a dangerous weapon during the crime. The Court held that since the statute says the Bureau "may" grant early release, not "must," the Bureau retains discretion to exclude prisoners either by category or individually as long as they act reasonably, and this exclusion is reasonable in light of concerns for public safety from persons whose criminal conduct suggests readiness to resort to life-endangering violence. *Lopez*, 531 U.S. at 239–41. However, courts have subsequently held that the regulation was enacted in violation of procedural requirements. *See* Paulsen v. Daniels, 413 F.3d 999, 1005 (9th Cir. 2005); Bohner v. Daniels, 243 F. Supp. 2d 1171 (D.Or. 2003). The application of the regulation continues to be a source of controversy. *See* Richardson v. Joslin, 397 F. Supp. 2d 830, 833–34 (N.D.Tex. 2005) (presence of guns does not permit disqualifying a prisoner who was convicted of money laundering and not a drug offense and there was no finding that he used or possessed the guns during the crime); Galle v. Clark, 346 F. Supp. 2d 1052, 1058 (N.D.Cal. 2004) (prisoner found eligible for early release program can't be made ineligible retroactively by a change in the rules); Kuna v. Daniels, 234 F. Supp. 2d 1168 (D.Or. 2002) (prisoner who completed drug program was eligible for early release despite Bureau's claim he really did not show "abuse or dependence"; all that is required is use of drugs).

[641]*See, e.g.*, Abraham v. State, 585 P.2d 526, 533 (Alaska 1978); People v. Ryan, 12 Cal.Rptr.2d 395, 396–97 (Cal.App. 1992); State v. Armstrong, 175 W.Va. 381, 332 S.E.2d 837, 844 (W.Va. 1985).

[642]Aripa v. Dep't of Social and Health Services, 91 Wash.2d 135, 588 P.2d 185, 187–89 (Wash. 1978) (state statutes requiring alcohol treatment programs did not create a right to an individualized treatment program); Bresolin v. Morris, 88 Wash.2d 167, 558 P.2d 1350, 1352–53 (Wash. 1977) (state laws concerning rehabilitation created a governmental interest but no enforceable right to drug treatment).

h. Prisoners with Disabilities Prisoners with disabilities or handicaps are protected both by the Constitution and by federal statutes. State and local statutes and prison regulations may also provide some protections for disabled prisoners.

1) Constitutional Protections Under the Eighth Amendment, prison officials must meet the medical needs of prisoners with disabilities and furnish the assistance that they require in order to live a minimally decent life in prison. As one court put it, "the prison authorities must take the prisoner as they find him and provide facilities compatible with his physical condition that meet civilized standards of decency."[643] In determining whether a prisoner has a serious medical need, courts consider whether her medical condition causes disability or interferes with daily activities.[644] Paralyzed or bedridden prisoners are entitled to receive appropriate medical treatment as well as adequate toilet facilities and means to keep themselves clean.[645] A number of decisions have disapproved the denial of physical therapy to those who require it.[646] Prisoners who cannot walk are entitled to necessary prostheses, resulting in denial of a wheelchair and inability to keep himself clean, violated the Eighth Amendment); Leach v. Shelby County Sheriff, 891 F.2d 1241, 1243–44 (6th Cir. 1989) (failure to bathe paraplegic inmate, provide catheter supplies and a hospital mattress, and aid with his bowel training violated the Eighth Amendment); LaFaut v. Smith, 834 F.2d 389, 392–94 (4th Cir. 1987) (deprivation of prescribed rehabilitation therapy and failure to provide adequate toilet facilities violated the Eighth Amendment); Parrish v. Johnson, 800 F.2d 600, 605 (6th Cir. 1986) (leaving paraplegic lying in his own feces violated the Eighth Amendment); Cummings v. Roberts, 628 F.2d 1065, 1068 (8th Cir. 1980) (denial of means of personal hygiene to bedridden prisoner stated a constitutional claim); Beckford v. Irvin, 49 F. Supp. 2d 170, 178–79 (W.D.N.Y. 1999) (upholding jury verdict for prisoner for deprivation of wheelchair and failure to provide access to showers and recreation); Kaufman v. Carter, 952 F. Supp. 520, 526 (W.D.Mich. 1996) (failure to provide bilateral amputee with rubbing alcohol to clean his prosthetic limbs and "ace wraps" to maintain the size of his stumps, resulting in inability to use his prostheses and confinement to a wheelchair, supported an Eighth Amendment claim); Casey v. Lewis, 834 F. Supp. 1569, 1581 (D.Ariz. 1993); Candelaria v. Coughlin, 787 F. Supp. 368, 378 (S.D.N.Y. 1992) (denial of orthopedic treatment and dietary supplement to paralyzed prisoner stated a claim), aff'd, 979 F.2d 845 (2d Cir. 1992); Yarbaugh v. Roach, 736 F. Supp. 318, 319–20 (D.D.C. 1990) (preliminary injunction granted to prisoner with multiple sclerosis who had not received physical therapy, had not been bathed, etc.); Ruiz v. Estelle, 503 F. Supp. at 1346 (proper hygiene, nursing care and physical therapy required); *see also* Brown v. State, 392 So.2d 113, 114–15 (La.App. 1980) (locking a paraplegic in a room without an adequate toilet or shower for nine days was not "reasonable" under state law). *But see* Evans v. Dugger, 908 F.2d 801, 803–04 (11th Cir. 1990) (deliberate indifference standard applied; jury verdict for prison officials); Shockley v. Jones, 823 F.2d 1068, 1072 (7th Cir. 1987) (delay in dressing changes and other treatment did not constitute deliberate indifference); Green v. McKaskle, 788 F.2d 1116, 1126–27 (5th Cir. 1986) (failure to provide specialist care and a specially designed bed did not constitute deliberate indifference); Palermo v. Correctional Medical Services, Inc., 133 F. Supp. 2d 1348, (S.D.Fla. 2001) (refusal to authorize a wheelchair for a prisoner with constant, severe back pain which limited mobility, and for whom using crutches was painful, was a matter for medical judgment).

One state has promulgated regulations requiring prisoners to pay for prostheses unless they are "medically necessary interventions that correct pathological or functional defects." Smith v. Dep't of Corrections, 105 Or.App. 61, 804 P.2d 482, 484 (Or.App. 1991) (upholding rules on state law grounds).

[646]Miller v. King, 384 F.3d at 1261–62; Hicks v. Frey, 992 F.2d 1450, 1456–57 (6th Cir. 1993); LaFaut v. Smith, 834 F.2d 389, 392–94 (4th Cir. 1987); McCarthy v. Weinberg, 753 F.2d 836, 839 (10th Cir. 1985) (denial of physical therapy for multiple sclerosis stated a constitutional claim); Candelaria v. Coughlin, 787 F. Supp. 368, 378 (S.D.N.Y. 1992), aff'd, 979 F.2d 845 (2d Cir. 1992); Yarbaugh v. Roach, 736 F. Supp. 318, 319–20 (D.D.C. 1990) (granting injunction); Lee v. McManus, 543 F. Supp. 386, 391–93 (D.Kan. 1982) (granting injunction); Ruiz v. Estelle, 503 F. Supp. at 1346.

---

[643]*In re* Coca, 85 Cal.App.3d 493, 149 Cal.Rptr. 465, 470–71 (Cal.App. 1978) (prisoner with a colostomy was entitled to adequate private facilities to defecate and clean himself); *accord,* Cameron v. Tomes, 990 F.2d 14, 21 (1st Cir. 1993) (affirming order requiring a handicapped accessible room for an amputee); Blankenship v. Kerr County, Texas, 878 F.2d 893, 895–96 (5th Cir. 1989) (placement of known epileptic arrestee in an unpadded cell, where he was injured during a seizure, stated a deliberate indifference claim); Ruiz v. Estelle, 503 F. Supp. 1265, 1345 (S.D.Tex. 1980) ("The fact that unusual accommodations may be necessary, in light of their special needs, to accomplish the provision of minimal conditions of incarceration does not absolve prison officials of their duty toward handicapped inmates."), *aff'd in part and vacated in part on other grounds,* 679 F.2d 1115 (5th Cir. 1982).

[644]*See* § F.2 of this chapter, nn.350–351.

[645]Miller v. King, 384 F.3d 1248, 1261–62 (11th Cir. 2004) (allegations by wheelchair-bound paraplegic of denial of medical consultations, leg braces and orthopedic shoes, wheelchair-accessible showers and toilets, opportunity to bathe, urinary catheters, and assistance in using the toilet raised a material factual issue under the Eighth Amendment), *vacated and superseded on other grounds,* 449 F.3d 1149 (11th Cir. 2006); Lawson v. Dallas County, 286 F.3d 257 (5th Cir. 2002) (affirming damages for medical neglect and inhumane treatment of paraplegic prisoner); Bradley v. Puckett, 157 F.3d 1022, 1025–26 (5th Cir. 1998) (two-month denial of shower chair to prisoner with leg brace stated an Eighth Amendment claim); Simmons v. Cook, 154 F.3d 805, 808 (8th Cir. 1998) (affirming damage award for placement of paraplegics in solitary for 32 hours without their egg crate mattresses contrary to medical orders; they missed four consecutive meals because their wheelchairs could not maneuver to where their food trays were placed, and they were unable to eliminate their bodily wastes); Frost v. Agnos, 152 F.3d 1124, 1129 (9th Cir. 1998) (failure to provide safe and accessible shower facilities to prisoner with leg in a long cast stated an Eighth Amendment claim); Hicks v. Frey, 992 F.2d 1450, 1456–57 (6th Cir. 1993) (failure to turn paraplegic prisoner or keep him clean, denial of showers and exercise, and placement in cell that could not accommodate wheelchair violated Eighth Amendment); Weeks v. Chaboudy, 984 F.2d 185, 187–88 (6th Cir. 1993) (exclusion of paralyzed inmate from the prison infirmary,

wheelchairs, or other mobility aids,[647] and to be protected from conditions that are unsafe in light of their physical condition.[648] Prisons are subjected to a limited Eighth Amendment obligation to make prison facilities accessible to inmates with impaired mobility.[649] Prisoners with impaired vision or hearing are entitled to some assistance with their disabilities, although not necessarily to the care of their choice.[650] Courts have held that the failure to accommodate other disabilities raises Eighth Amendment or other constitutional

[647]Miller v. King, 384 F.3d at 1261–62 (allegations of denial of wheelchair repairs, leg braces, and orthopedic shoes raised a material factual issue under the Eighth Amendment); Hemmings v. Gorczyk, 134 F.3d 104, 108 (2d Cir. 1998) (deprivation of crutches to prisoner with serious leg injury stated an Eighth Amendment claim); Johnson v. Hardin County, Ky., 908 F.2d 1280, 1284 (6th Cir. 1990) (denial of crutches and proper bedding supported a finding of deliberate indifference); Cummings v. Roberts, 628 F.2d 1065, 1068 (8th Cir. 1980) (denial of wheelchair to bedridden patient stated a constitutional claim); Lavender v. Lampert, 242 F. Supp. 2d 821, 843, 849 (D.Or. 2002) (holding failure to provide orthopedic footwear for prisoner with spastic paralysis of one foot supported a deliberate indifference claim; further, "To unnecessarily deny the use of a wheelchair to someone who obviously has an injury, and who lacks mobility without it, would constitute deliberate indifference to a serious medical need."); Navedo v. Maloney, 172 F. Supp. 2d 276, 284 (D.Mass. 2001) (denial of wheelchair, accessible shower, physical therapy, and transfer to an accessible facility to wheelchair-dependent prisoner stated an Eighth Amendment claim); Beckford v. Irvin, 49 F. Supp. 2d 170, 182–83 (W.D.N.Y. 1999) (upholding jury verdict for prisoner deprived of wheelchair); Schmidt v. Odell, 64 F. Supp. 2d 1014, 1031 (D.Kan. 1999) (refusing to provide a wheelchair to an amputee was not unconstitutional in itself, but "the ability of the plaintiff to move himself about the jail in an appropriate manner—to use the toilet, to use the shower, to obtain his meals, and to obtain suitable recreation and exercise—was a basic need—part of the 'minimal civilized measure of life's necessities'—that the defendants were obligated to help provide under the Eighth Amendment," and it wasn't satisfied by making him get around on knee pads); Hallett v. New York State Dep't of Correctional Services, 109 F. Supp. 2d 190 (S.D.N.Y. 2000) (five-month deprivation of personal wheelchair and provision of standard wheelchair unsuitable for his medical condition that caused pain and injury stated Eighth Amendment claim); Taylor v. Plousis, 101 F. Supp. 2d 255, 261 (D.N.J. 2000) (intentional delay in providing leg prosthesis would constitute deliberate indifference); Rosales v. Coughlin, 10 F. Supp. 2d 261, 269 (W.D.N.Y. 1998) (deprivation of medically prescribed cane stated a constitutional claim); Casey v. Lewis, 834 F. Supp. at 1581; Candelaria v. Coughlin, 787 F. Supp. at 378 (alleged denial of adequate wheelchair for paraplegic stated a claim); Young v. Harris, 509 F. Supp. 1111, 1113–14 (S.D.N.Y. 1981) (failure to provide prescribed leg brace stated an Eighth Amendment claim); Ruiz v. Estelle, 503 F. Supp. at 1340 (denial of canes, braces, and wheelchairs condemned); see also Serrano v. Francis, 345 F.3d 1071, 1079 (9th Cir. 2003) (placement of wheelchair-reliant prisoner in segregation unit for two months without a wheelchair and without means of showering was an atypical and significant deprivation requiring due process protections); Mullen v. Smith, 738 F.2d 317, 318 (8th Cir. 1984) (allegation that injured prisoner was ordered to walk and verbally abused when he fell down stated an Eighth Amendment claim). But see Shakka v. Smith, 71 F.3d 162 (4th Cir. 1995) (brief deprivation of a wheelchair ordered by a psychiatrist for safety reasons was not unconstitutional); Donald v. Wilson, 847 F.2d 1191, 1194 (6th Cir. 1988) (confiscation of leg prosthesis was not unconstitutional in a jail with limited movement where the plaintiff had used the prosthesis as a weapon and to carry contraband); Lowrence v. Scully, 575 F. Supp. 39, 40 (S.D.N.Y. 1983)

(denial of wheelchair upheld where medical evidence showed the plaintiff could walk).

[648]Allah v. Goord, 405 F. Supp. 2d 265, 275–76 (S.D.N.Y. 2005) (holding an allegation by a wheelchair-using prisoner that he was strapped in too loosely in a vehicle and was injured in sudden stops stated an Eighth Amendment claim).

[649]Ruiz v. Estelle, 503 F. Supp. at 1346 (officials have "no obligation to make prison life the same for physically handicapped inmates as it is for others," but the failure to make minor adjustments resulting in deprivation of virtually all opportunity for activity was unconstitutional).

[650]Robertson v. Las Animas County Sheriff's Dep't, 500 F.3d 1185, 1193–99 (10th Cir. 2007) (holding law enforcement officials were obliged to provide deaf arrestee with assistive devices if they knew of his disability and his need for accommodation); Tanney v. Boles, 400 F. Supp. 2d 1027, 1041–42 (E.D.Mich. 2005) (holding deaf inmate's complaint of inadequate access to a TDD/TTY telephone device raised a First Amendment issue); Clarkson v. Coughlin, 898 F. Supp. 1019 (S.D.N.Y. 1995) (holding failure to provide deaf and hearing-impaired interpretive services during disciplinary, grievance and parole proceedings, exclusion from education programs, absence of interpreters during medical encounters denied due process; absence of a Sensorially Disabled Unit for women as well as men denied due process; Casey v. Lewis, 834 F. Supp. at 1583; Williams v. ICC Committee, 812 F. Supp. 1029, 1032 (N.D.Cal. 1992) (allegation that legally blind inmate was deprived of eyeglasses stated a deliberate indifference claim); Harris v. O'Grady, 803 F. Supp. 1361, 1366 (N.D.Ill. 1992) (legally blind inmate's allegations of denial of glasses, medical attention, and handicapped housing stated a deliberate indifference claim); Bonner v. Arizona Dep't of Corrections, 714 F. Supp. 420, 425–26 (D.Ariz. 1989) (refusal to provide a sign language interpreter at a deaf-mute prisoner's disciplinary hearing denied due process); Ruiz v. Estelle, 503 F. Supp. at 1340 (deprivation of sight and hearing aids condemned); Perry v. State, 511 So.2d 268, 269 (Ala. Cr.App. 1987) (deprivation of legally blind prisoner's visual aids and failure to provide assistance in disciplinary proceeding violated Constitution). But see Stevens v. Harper, 213 F.R.D. 358, 375 (E.D.Cal. 2002) (hearing-impaired prisoner's allegation that staff members "make fun of him, swear at him, and treat him disrespectfully" does not state a claim because verbal harassment generally does not violate the Eighth Amendment).

issues as well.[651] Mistreatment of disabled prisoners may also constitute negligence, actionable under state tort law.[652]

It is not unlawful to send a seriously disabled person to prison as long as proper care is provided.[653] Some courts have suggested that if a particular prison is unable to provide the necessary care, the prisoner must be moved to a facility that can provide it.[654]

Discrimination against prisoners with disabilities may deny equal protection of the laws, but prison officials need only show that their actions have a rational basis in order to defeat an equal protection claim.[655] The disability statutes, discussed in the next section, provide a more favorable legal standard for disability discrimination claims.

2) The Federal Disability Statutes The federal ADA[656] and Section 504 of the Rehabilitation Act[657] apply to prisoners.[658]

---

[651]Bane v. Virginia Dep't of Corrections, 267 F. Supp. 2d 514, 520–21 (W.D.Va. 2003) (holding failure to honor an order to front-cuff rather than rear-cuff a prisoner with a shoulder injury that limited his range of motion raised an Eighth Amendment claim).

In *Hargis v. Foster*, 312 F.3d 404 (9th Cir. 2002), a prisoner with a neurological disorder that caused jerking and shaking refused to shave with a bladed razor because it was dangerous; officials refused to provide an electric razor and charged the prisoner with "coercion" when he said the issue might come up in litigation. The court held that the prisoner raised a material issue of fact under the First Amendment as to whether the defendants' action was an unconstitutional "exaggerated response." *Hargis*, 312 F.3d at 406.

[652]*See* Muhammad v. U.S., 6 F. Supp. 2d 582, 594–95 (N.D.Tex. 1998) (awarding damages for negligent failure to place a prisoner with mobility and neurological problems in a suitable facility).

[653]People v. Superior Court (Beasley), 159 Cal.App.3d 131, 205 Cal.Rptr. 413, 416 (Cal.App. 1984); Commissioner v. Coburn, 336 Pa.Super. 203, 485 A.2d 502, 505 (Pa.Super. 1984).

[654]Payne v. Lynaugh, 843 F.2d 177, 178–79 (5th Cir. 1988); Yarbaugh v. Roach, 736 F. Supp. 318, 320 n.7 (D.D.C. 1990); Villa v. Franzen, 511 F. Supp. 231, 233–34 (N.D.Ill. 1981).

[655]More v. Farrier, 984 F.2d 269, 271–72 (8th Cir. 1993); Bonner v. Lewis, 857 F.2d 559, 565 (9th Cir. 1988); Green v. McKaskle, 788 F.2d 1116, 1125–26 (5th Cir. 1986); Judd v. Packard, 669 F. Supp. 741, 743 (D.Md. 1987) (medically directed segregation of HIV positive prisoner did not deny equal protection); Rowe v. Fauver, 533 F. Supp. 1239, 1247–48 (D.N.J. 1982) (regulation barring medically disabled prisoners from earning work credit against their sentences was not unconstitutional as applied to paralyzed prisoners); *see also* Joihner v. McEvers, 898 F.2d 569, 571–73 (7th Cir. 1989) (exclusion of prisoner from a work camp because of his medical condition did not deny due process).

[656]42 U.S.C. § 12101 *et seq.*

[657]29 U.S.C. § 794.

[658]Pennsylvania Dep't of Corrections v. Yeskey, 524 U.S. 206, 118 S. Ct. 1952 (1998) (ADA); Crawford v. Indiana Dep't of Corrections, 115 F.3d 481, 486 (7th Cir. 1997) ("Rights against discrimination are among the few rights that prisoners do not park at the prison gates"; prisoners "have the same interest in access to the programs, services, and activities available to the other inmates of their prison as disabled people on the outside have to the counterpart programs, services, and activities available to free people."); Harris v. Thigpen, 941 F.3d 1495, 1522 n.41 (11th Cir. 1991) (Rehabilitation Act); Bonner v. Lewis, 857 F.2d 559 (9th Cir. 1988)

Courts have heard claims under these statutes, and in some cases granted significant relief, in cases involving prisoners with hearing impairments,[659] visual impairments,[660]

(Rehabilitation Act). This is true for short-term facilities and prisoners jailed for short periods. Chisolm v. McManimon, 275 F.3d 315, 327 (3d Cir. 2001).

The statutes apply to parolees as well. Armstrong v. Davis, 275 F.3d 849, 871 (9th Cir. 2001) (affirming injunction requiring accommodation of disabilities in the parole process); Thompson v. Davis, 295 F.3d 890, 897 (9th Cir. 2002) (holding prisoners could challenge exclusion from parole of persons with drug abuse histories; stating ADA applies to "substantive decision making process in the criminal law context.").

[659]Chisolm v. McManimon, 275 F.3d 315, 329 (3d Cir. 2001) (holding defendants were not entitled to summary judgment for denying a deaf prisoner a sign language interpreter at jail intake and for failing to provide access to a TDD); Armstrong v. Davis, 275 F.3d 849, 859, 879 (9th Cir. 2001) (affirming injunction against failures to accommodate hearing impairments during parole or parole revocation proceedings); Randolph v. Rodgers, 170 F.3d 850, 858 (8th Cir. 1999) (holding failure to provide hearing-impaired prisoner with sign language interpreter during disciplinary and classification proceedings violated ADA); Duffy v. Riveland, 98 F.3d 447 (9th Cir. 1996) (holding deaf prisoner might be entitled to certified interpreter in disciplinary hearings); Clarkson v. Coughlin, 898 F. Supp. 1019 (S.D.N.Y. 1995) (ADA and Rehabilitation Act rights of deaf and hearing-impaired prisoners were violated by practice including failure to provide interpretive services during reception and classification, failure to provide telephone devices for the deaf and closed caption decoders wherever other inmates have the right to use telephones and televisions, failure to provide safety alarms adequate for deaf inmates, failure to provide proper accommodations for vocational and academic education and alcohol and drug rehabilitation counseling, failure to provide interpretive services during disciplinary, grievance, and parole proceedings); Rewolinski v. Morgan, 896 F. Supp. 879, 881 (E.D.Wis. 1995) (deaf plaintiff who alleged denial of closed captioned videos, a sign language interpreter for disciplinary hearings and medical appointments, enough visiting time to communicate in sign language, a telephone device for the deaf after 9:00 p.m., a visual alarm clock, and visual fire alarms stated a non-frivolous ADA claim).

[660]Armstrong v. Davis, 275 F.3d at 859 (affirming injunction against failures to accommodate visual impairments during parole or parole revocation proceedings); Arlt v. Missouri Dep't of Correction, 229 F. Supp. 2d 938, 943–44 (E.D.Mo. 2002); Kruger v. Jenne, 164 F. Supp. 2d 1330 (S.D.Fla. 2000) (prisoner's allegations that he is blind, has a serious need for a personal aide and/or a cane to get around, and that he fell and was injured as a result of not having them; that his electric shaver and talking book were confiscated; and that as a result of his disability he was unable to participate in activities and programs such as outdoor and indoor exercise and recreation and the law library, stated a claim under the ADA); Williams v. Illinois Dep't of Corrections, 1999 WL 1068669 (N.D. Ill. 1999) (granting injunction to accommodate blind prisoner). *But see* Mason v. Correctional Medical Services, Inc., 559 F.3d 880, 887–88 (8th Cir. 2009) (declining to order Braille materials, computer software, and other accommodations where prison provided blind prisoner with an inmate assistant to accompany him everywhere and assist with all reading and writing tasks); Canell v. Multnomah County, 141 F. Supp. 2d 1046, 1057 (D.Or. 2001) (need for reading glasses is not a disability).

mobility impairments,[661] mental illness,[662] alcoholism,[663] drug addiction that does not involve current use of drugs,[664] arm and shoulder impairments,[665] diabetes,[666] and other disabilities.[667] The Individuals with Disabilities in Education Act (IDEA) protects the rights of young prisoners with learning disabilities to have access to educational programs.[668]

Title II of the ADA, the "public entity" section, provides that "no qualified individual with a disability shall, by reason of such disability, be excluded from participation in or be denied the benefits of the services, programs, or activities of a public entity, or be subjected to discrimination by any such entity."[669] Section 504 of the Rehabilitation Act

---

[661]Pierce v. County of Orange, 526 F.3d 1190, 1217–23, 1226 (9th Cir. 2008) (holding mobility- and dexterity-impaired inmates were entitled to injunctive relief to accommodate their disabilities), *cert. denied* 129 S. Ct. 597 (2008); Kiman v. New Hampshire Dep't of Corrections, 451 F.3d 274, 285–87 (1st Cir. 2006) (holding evidence of denial of access to prescribed medications and a shower chair, handcuffing in front rather than behind the back, and denial of a bottom bunk to a prisoner with amyotrophic lateral sclerosis raised a material factual issue of ADA violation; upholding denial of cane for security reasons, finding that plaintiff was not actually denied access to programs as a result); Armstrong v. Davis, 275 F.3d at 879 (9th Cir. 2001) (affirming injunction against failures to accommodate mobility impairments during parole or parole revocation proceedings); Love v. Westville Correctional Center, 103 F.3d 558 (7th Cir. 1996); Navedo v. Maloney, 172 F. Supp. 2d 276, 283 (D.Mass. 2001) (denial of wheelchair, accessible shower, physical therapy, and transfer to an accessible facility to wheelchair-dependent prisoner stated an ADA claim); Becker v. Oregon, 170 F. Supp. 2d 1061, 1068–69 (D.Ore. 2001) (allegation of placement in a disciplinary unit lacking handicap-accessible showers stated an ADA claim); Schmidt v. Odell, 64 F. Supp. 2d 1014, 1033 (D.Kan. 1999) (evidence that amputee was denied wheelchair or any means of mobility other than knee pads, was denied a shower chair and had to crawl in the shower, etc., supported an ADA claim); Beckford v. Irvin, 49 F. Supp. 2d 170, 181 (W.D.N.Y. 1999) (upholding jury verdict for prisoner for deprivation of wheelchair and failure to provide access to showers and recreation); Saunders v. Horn, 959 F. Supp. 689, 698 (E.D.Pa. 1996), *recommendation adopted*, Saunders v. Horn, 960 F. Supp. 893 (E.D.Pa. 1997) (complaint by prisoner with degenerative disk disorder that limited his walking, showering, etc., of failure to provide an accessible bathroom stated an ADA claim). *But see* Beckford v. Portuondo, 151 F. Supp. 2d 204, 220–22 (N.D.N.Y. 2001) (placing wheelchair-using prisoner into a segregation cell that was not wheelchair accessible did not violate the disability statutes because it was brief, no cell was available that was wheelchair accessible and equipped with a plexiglass shield, and there is no evidence of intent to discriminate).

[662]Thompson v. Davis, 295 F.3d 890, 898 n.4 (9th Cir. 2002) (court held that "categorically" denying parole to a prisoner based upon his mental illness would violate the ADA, but denying parole for that prisoner after considering his disability of mental illness through an individual assessment of his potential to recidivate if paroled would not violate the ADA or RA); Sites v. McKenzie, 423 F. Supp. 1190, 1197 (N.D.W.Va. 1976) (excluding prisoner with mental illness from vocational rehabilitation programs violated Rehabilitation Act); *see* Atkins v. County of Orange, 251 F. Supp. 2d 1225, 1231–1232 (S.D.N.Y. 2003) (finding that placement of mentally ill inmates within "keeplock isolation" did not equate to a denial of services under the ADA in the absence of an allegation of such denial; mentally ill inmates were not disparately treated from other inmates who were also a "danger to [themselves] or others").

[663]Regional Economic Community Action Program, Inc. v. City of Middletown, 294 F.3d 35, 47 (2d Cir. 2002) (noting alcohol addiction substantially limited plaintiffs' ability to live independently and to live with their families, which is a substantial limitation on the major life activity of caring for themselves); Parker v. Michigan Department of Corrections, 2001 WL 1736637, *1–2 (W.D. Mich. 2001) (injunctive relief claim pursuant to ADA stated for denial of access to treatment for alcoholism).

[664]Thompson v. Davis, 295 F.3d 890, 896 (9th Cir. 2002) (noting the ADA protects persons who have successfully completed or are participating in a supervised drug rehabilitation program and are no longer using illegal drugs). *But see* Brashear v. Simms, 138 F. Supp. 2d 693, 695 (D.Md. 2001) (smoking is not a disability under the ADA because it is readily remediable by an effort of will or by using items like nicotine patches or chewing gum).

[665]Bane v. Virginia Dep't of Corrections, 267 F. Supp. 2d 514, 520 n.2 (W.D.Va. 2003).

[666]Rouse v. Plantier, 997 F. Supp. 575, 582 (D.N.J. 1998) (evidence that by failing to treat their diabetes, the defendants excluded prisoners from participation in some programs supported a claim under the ADA), *vacated on other grounds*, 182 F.3d 192 (3d Cir. 1999). *See* Erjavac v. Holy Family Health Plus, 13 F. Supp. 2d 737, 746 (N.D. Ill. 1998) (insulin-dependent diabetes in its untreated form "meets all three prongs of the ADA's disability definition"). *But see* Burger v. Bloomberg, 418 F.3d 882, 883 (8th Cir. 2005) (complaint about medical care provided for diabetes was not actionable under ADA or Rehabilitation Act).

[667]Raines v. State of Florida, 983 F. Supp. 1362 (N.D.Fla. 1997) (various disabilities; court held their exclusion from the highest class of "incentive gain time" violated the ADA); Armstrong v. Wilson, 942 F. Supp. 1252 (N.D.Cal. 1996), *aff'd*, 124 F.3d 1019 (9th Cir. 1997) (mobility, hearing, vision, kidney, and learning disabilities); *see* Scott v. Garcia, 370 F. Supp. 2d 1056, 1074–75 (S.D.Cal. 2005) (holding that eating is a major life activity, and a plaintiff with stomach and digestive problems raised a material factual issue under the ADA where he submitted evidence that he was denied access to the prison meal service by not being given enough time to eat or the option to eat small frequent meals).

[668]*See* § I.1 of this chapter for further discussion of education in prison.

[669]42 U.S.C. § 12132. Public entities include "any department, agency, special purpose district, or other instrumentality of a State or States or local government." 42 U.S.C. § 12132(1)(B). *See* Thompson v. Davis, 295 F.3d 890, 897–98 (9th Cir. 2002) (state parole boards fall squarely within the statutory definition of public entity).

The ADA also has provisions addressing employment discrimination, referred to as Title I. 42 U.S.C. § 12112. An "employer" is defined as "a person engaged in an industry affecting commerce" who has more than 15 employees each working day, and an "employee" is defined as "an individual employed by an employer." Courts have often interpreted statutes referring to "employees" to exclude prisoners. *See* § I.2 of this chapter, nn.1279–1283; Ch. 5, § A; Ch. 8, § E.1, n.408. Therefore, if you have a complaint concerning prison job discrimination or exclusion based on disability, you should cite the "public entity" provisions of the ADA in addition to the employment discrimination provisions, since prison

provides that "[n]o otherwise qualified individual with a disability in the United States, . . . shall, solely by reason of her or his disability, be excluded from the participation in, be denied the benefits of, or be subjected to discrimination under any program or activity receiving Federal financial assistance or under any program or activity conducted by any Executive agency. . . ."[670] This means that any agency—including a department of correction, Sheriff's office, etc.—that receives any federal funding is covered by the Rehabilitation Act for all of its services, programs, and activities.[671] Federal agencies and prisons are not subject to the ADA, but they are subject to the Rehabilitation Act.[672] Department of Justice regulations promulgated under the statutes are applicable to prisons and jails.[673]

To take advantage of the ADA, you must generally be a "qualified individual with a disability."[674] "Disability" under the ADA means:

(A) a physical or mental impairment that substantially limits one or more of the major life activities of [an] individual;

(B) a record of such impairment; or

(C) being regarded as having such an impairment (as described in paragraph (3)).[675]

This definition is comparable to the definition of "handicap" under the Rehabilitation Act,[676] so Rehabilitation Act case law on this point will be very relevant in ADA cases. Expert medical testimony is not necessary to establish the existence of a disability.[677]

To qualify as a disability an impairment must be one that "substantially limits one or more major life activities."[678] Congress broadened the meaning of these terms in the ADA Amendments Act of 2008, effective January 1, 2009,[679] to overrule restrictive interpretations of these terms by the Supreme Court.[680]

The ADA Amendments Act stated generally: "The definition of disability in this chapter shall be construed in favor of broad coverage of individuals under this chapter, to the maximum extent permitted by the terms of this chapter."[681]

---

employment is a program subject to the Title II public entity provisions. Northrop v. Carucci, 2007 WL 685173, *4 (D.Conn., March 5, 2007); Montez v. Romer, 32 F. Supp. 2d 1235, 1239–40 (D. Colo.1999). One federal circuit has held that prison employment is not subject to the disability statutes, see White v. Colorado, 82 F.3d 364, 367 (10th Cir. 1996), but that decision has been overruled by the Supreme Court's Yeskey decision cited above. Montez v. Romer, 32 F. Supp. 2d at 1240.

[670]29 U.S.C. § 794(a). "Executive agency" in this statute refers to federal agencies.

[671]See Schroeder v. City of Chicago, 927 F.2d 957, 962 (7th Cir. 1991). But see Nolley v. County of Erie, 776 F. Supp. 715, 742–43 (W.D.N.Y. 1991) (local jail was not subject to the Rehabilitation Act because the federal funds it received were no more than payment for housing federal prisoners).

[672]Yeskey v. Penn. Dep't of Corr., 118 F.3d 168, 171 (3d Cir. 1997), aff'd, 524 U.S. 206, 118 S. Ct. 1952 (1998).

[673]Amos v. Maryland Dep't of Public Safety and Correctional Services, 178 F.3d 212, 221 (4th Cir. 1999), dismissed as settled, 205 F.3d 687 (4th Cir. 2000); Yeskey v. Penn. Dep't of Corr., 118 F.3d at 170–71; Onishea v. Hopper, 171 F.3d 1289, 1301–04 (11th Cir. 1999); see Chisolm v. McManimon, 275 F.3d 315, 328 (3d Cir. 2001) (giving a deaf prisoner pencil and paper rather than an American Sign Language interpreter at jail intake may not comply with the ADA, in part because of failure to follow Department of Justice regulation); Bullock v. Gomez, 929 F. Supp. 1299, 1302–03 (C.D. Cal. 1996) (citing DOJ regulations).

[674]42 U.S.C. § 12132.

There can be exceptions where a non-disabled prisoner is affected by the failure to accommodate someone else's disability. It works the other way too: a disabled non-prisoner who is in some way excluded from a program, service, or activity of a prison can bring suit about it. Thus, in Niece v. Fitzner, 922 F. Supp. 1208 (E.D.Mich. 1996), a prisoner challenged the prison's failure to provide a Telecommunications Device for the Deaf so he could communicate with his deaf fiancé; the court held that both the prisoner and his fiancé had standing to sue under the ADA.

[675]42 U.S.C. § 12102(1). "Paragraph (3)" means 42 U.S.C. § 12102(3), which says:

(A) An individual meets the requirement of "being regarded as having such an impairment" if the individual establishes that he or she has been subjected to an action prohibited under this chapter because of an actual or perceived physical or mental impairment whether or not the impairment limits or is perceived to limit a major life activity.

(B) Paragraph (1)(C) shall not apply to impairments that are transitory and minor. A transitory impairment is an impairment with an actual or expected duration of 6 months or less.

See Mitchell v. Massachusetts Dep't of Correction, 190 F. Supp. 2d 204, 212 (D.Mass. 2002) (where prison officials excluded plaintiff from programs because of his diabetes and heart condition, they couldn't defend by arguing that he wasn't in such bad shape and therefore wasn't disabled, since they "regarded" him as disabled and treated him as such).

[676]See 29 U.S.C. § 706(7)(B).

[677]Colwell v. Suffolk County Police Dep't, 967 F. Supp. 1419, 1425 (E.D.N.Y. 1997), rev'd on other grounds, 158 F.3d 635 (2d Cir. 1998).

[678]42 U.S.C. § 12102(1)(A).

[679]The amendments are not retroactive, i.e., they do not apply to conduct that occurred before their effective date. Lytes v. DC Water and Sewer Authority, 572 F.3d 936, 939–42 (D.C. Cir. 2009); Milholland v. Sumner County Bd. of Educ., 569 F.3d 562, 565 (6th Cir. 2009). However, they do apply to plaintiffs who seek only prospective relief for ongoing problems even if the problems started before the amendments were enacted. Jenkins v. National Bd. of Medical Examiners, 2009 WL 331638, *1–2 (6th Cir. 2009) (unpublished).

[680]When the Supreme Court interprets the Constitution, Congress has no power to overrule it. But when it interprets a statute Congress has passed, Congress is free to change the statute so the Court's interpretation of the prior version no longer has any effect.

[681]42 U.S.C. § 12102(4)(A).

Specifically, it redefined "substantially limits" as follows:

> (B) The term "substantially limits" shall be interpreted consistently with the findings and purposes of the ADA Amendments Act of 2008.[682]
>
> (C) An impairment that substantially limits one major life activity need not limit other major life activities in order to be considered a disability.
>
> (D) An impairment that is episodic or in remission is a disability if it would substantially limit a major life activity when active.
>
> (E)(i) The determination of whether an impairment substantially limits a major life activity shall be made without regard to the ameliorative effects of mitigating measures such as—
>
>> (I) medication, medical supplies, equipment, or appliances, low-vision devices (which do not include ordinary eyeglasses or contact lenses), prosthetics including limbs and devices, hearing aids and cochlear implants or other implantable hearing devices, mobility devices, or oxygen therapy equipment and supplies;
>>
>> (II) use of assistive technology;
>>
>> (III) reasonable accommodations or auxiliary aids or services; or
>>
>> (IV) learned behavioral or adaptive neurological modifications.[683]

However, not every impairment that affects a major life activity will "substantially limit" it as required for an ADA claim, either under the amendments or under prior law.[684]

The ADA Amendments Act also redefined major life activities as follows:

> (A) In general
>
> For purposes of paragraph (1), major life activities include, but are not limited to, caring for oneself, performing manual tasks, seeing, hearing, eating, sleeping, walking, standing, lifting, bending, speaking, breathing, learning, reading, concentrating, thinking, communicating, and working.
>
> (B) Major bodily functions
>
> For purposes of paragraph (1), a major life activity also includes the operation of a major bodily function, including but not limited to, functions of the immune system, normal cell growth, digestive, bowel, bladder, neurological, brain, respiratory, circulatory, endocrine, and reproductive functions.[685]

Before the ADA Amendments Act, courts had to determine case by case what are major life activities under the statute; now, the statute includes most of the activities previously recognized in case law,[686] but still allows for the case-by-case identification of other major life activities by saying "including but not limited to" the items listed. The amendments overrule some earlier decisions finding an impairment did not affect a major life activity. For example, one appeals court held that liver function is not a major life activity.[687] However, the amendments specifically include "major bodily functions" as major life activities, and liver

---

[682]The findings and purposes are in Pub. L. No. 110-325, § 2, Sept. 25, 2008, 122 Stat. 3553. This part of the ADA Amendments Act has not been "codified" into sections of the U.S. Code. However, it is printed in the U.S. Code's Historical and Statutory Notes after 42 U.S.C. § 12101. The findings say that certain Supreme Court decisions (discussed below) have limited the scope of the ADA in ways not consistent with congressional intent, Pub. L. No. 110-325, § 2(a), and the purposes are to reject those interpretations and "to carry out the ADA's objectives of providing 'a clear and comprehensive national mandate for the elimination of discrimination' by reinstating a broad scope of protection to be available under the ADA." Id., § 2(b).

[683]42 U.S.C. § 12102(4). There is one exception: "The ameliorative effects of the mitigating measures of ordinary eyeglasses or contact lenses shall be considered in determining whether an impairment substantially limits a major life activity." 42 U.S.C. § 12102(4)(E)(ii). That is, if they give you glasses or contacts and you can see reasonably well with them, you're probably not an individual with a disability.

[684]See, e.g., Pritchett v. Ellers, 2009 WL 1132343, *1 (3d Cir. 2009) (unpublished) (papilloma of larynx, which made the plaintiff's voice raspy and was aggravated by second-hand smoke, did not substantially limit the major life activity of speech, since there was no evidence it kept him from being understood); Rohr v. Salt River Project Agricultural Imp. and Power Dist., 555 F.3d 850, 860 (9th Cir. 2009) (whether diabetes substantially limited the major life activity of eating depended on whether the plaintiff's case was controlled with insulin alone or whether it required adjustment of diet and meal schedule too).

[685]42 U.S.C. § 12102(2). When the Supreme Court interprets the Constitution, Congress has no power to overrule it. But when it interprets a statute Congress has passed, Congress is free to change the statute so the Court's interpretation of the prior version no longer has any effect.

[686]These include, e.g.:

- walking, seeing, and hearing, Toyota Motor Manufacturing, Kentucky v. Williams, 534 U.S. 184, 197-98, 122 S. Ct. 681 (2002); Degrafinreid v. Ricks, 417 F. Supp. 2d 403, 412 (S.D.N.Y. 2006).
- eating, Scott v. Garcia, 370 F. Supp. 2d 1056, 1074 (S.D.Cal. 2005) (serious digestive disorders and resulting dietary restrictions were a substantial limitation; failure to allow plaintiff time to eat or small frequent meals raised an ADA issue).
- reproduction and childbearing, Bragdon v. Abbott, 524 U.S. 624, 632, 118 S. Ct. 2196 (1998) (holding HIV is an "impairment" under the ADA from the moment of infection because of its interference with reproduction and childbearing).
- thinking and concentrating, Battle v. United Parcel Service, Inc., 438 F.3d 856, 861 (8th Cir. 2006).
- sleeping, interacting with others, and reading. Head v. Glacier Northwest Inc., 413 F.3d 1053, 1060–61 (9th Cir. 2005).
- kidney function. Fiscus v. Wal-Mart Stores, Inc., 385 F.3d 378, 385 (3d Cir. 2004).

[687]Furnish v. SVI Systems, Inc., 270 F.3d 445, 449–50 (7th Cir. 2001).

function is "major" enough that you can't survive without it. The amended statute also mentions digestive and circulatory functions, to which the liver contributes. So it looks to us like liver function is now a major life activity under the amendment. Other pre-amendment decisions finding no effect on a major life activity will probably remain good law under the amendments.[688]

These amendments were intended to overturn two Supreme Court decisions. The *Toyota Motor* case said there must be "a demanding standard for qualifying as disabled," and that the term "major life activity" is limited to impairments that "prevent[] or severely restrict[] the individual from doing activities that are of central importance to most people's daily lives" and have an impact that is "permanent or long term."[689] *Sutton v. United Airlines* held that a person may not be "substantially limited" by an impairment if she has the benefit of corrective devices.[690] *Sutton* also narrowly defined being "regarded" as having an impairment.[691] Congress made it clear that it disapproved of these interpretations and was amending the statute to reflect its intentions accurately.[692] Be sure to point that out if defendants make arguments based on those cases, or on cases that in turn rely on *Sutton* or *Toyota Motor*.

Persons with infectious diseases are considered "handicapped" under the Rehabilitation Act[693] and to have an impairment under the ADA as well.[694] However, courts will weigh the risk of transmission of the disease, and its seriousness, heavily in determining whether a person is "otherwise qualified" and whether an accommodation is reasonable.[695]

To pursue an ADA claim, you must be a *"qualified person with a disability,"* which means a person who

> with or without reasonable modifications to rules, policies, or practices, the removal of architectural, communication, or transportation barriers, or the provision of auxiliary aids and services, meets the essential eligibility requirements for the receipt of services or the participation in programs or activities. . . .[696]

The Rehabilitation Act uses the phrase "otherwise qualified"[697] (*i.e.,* qualified except for their disabilities), which means the same thing, and courts often use this phrase in ADA cases as well.[698]

---

[688]*See, e.g.,* Yeskey v. Pennsylvania, 76 F. Supp. 2d 572, 577 (M.D.Pa. 1999) (the strenuous physical exercise required by a prison boot camp program is not a "major life activity" compared to such activities as walking, seeing, hearing, speaking, breathing, learning, and working; major life activities are those that the average person in the general population can perform with little or no difficulty).

[689]Toyota Motor Manufacturing, Kentucky v. Williams, 534 U.S. 184, 202, 122 S. Ct. 681 (2002). The Court said that "performing manual tasks" was not a major life activity unless the particular tasks in which a person is limited were "central to daily life," either individually or taken together. *Id.* It held that even though the plaintiff could not perform repetitive work with hands and arms extended at or above shoulder levels for extended periods of time, evidence that she could still brush her teeth, wash her face, bathe, garden, fix breakfast, do laundry, and pick up around the house meant she probably was not disabled.

[690]Sutton v. United Airlines, Inc., 527 U.S. 471, 483, 119 S. Ct. 2139 (1999); *accord,* Murphy v. United Parcel Service, Inc., 527 U.S. 516, 521–22, 119 S. Ct. 2133 (1999) (person whose high blood pressure was controlled by medication was not disabled). *But see* Gorman v. Easley, 257 F.3d 738, 742 (8th Cir. 2001) (rejecting claim that a wheelchair-using arrestee was not disabled; his wheelchair did not substitute for his legs, and anyway he was not allowed to use it in the police van where he was injured), *rev'd on other grounds sub nom.* Barnes v. Gorman, 536 U.S. 181, 122 S. Ct. 2097 (2002).

[691]Sutton v. United Airlines, Inc., 527 U.S. at 490.

[692]Pub. L. No. 110-325, § 2, Sept. 25, 2008, 122 Stat. 3553. This part of the ADA Amendments Act has not been "codified" into sections of the U.S. Code. However, it is printed in the U.S. Code's Historical and Statutory Notes after 42 U.S.C. § 12101.

[693]School Bd. of Nassau County v. Arline, 480 U.S. 273, 282–86, 107 S. Ct. 1123 (1987). This category includes persons with HIV.

Harris v. Thigpen, 941 F.3d 1495, 1522-24 (11th Cir. 1991).

[694]Bragdon v. Abbott, 524 U.S. 624, 118 S. Ct. 2196 (1998). Though the ADA Amendments Act does not specifically mention infectious diseases, it includes "major bodily functions" in the definition of major life activities, 42 U.S.C. § 12102(2)(b), so a disease that interferes with any of those functions would be covered by the amendments.

[695]The Supreme Court held that "[a] person who poses a significant risk of communicating an infectious disease to others in the workplace will not be otherwise qualified for his or her job if reasonable accommodation will not eliminate that risk." School Bd. of Nassau County v. Arline, 480 U.S. at 287 n.16. For the application of this holding to persons with HIV in prison, *see* § F.4.d.2 of this chapter.

[696]42 U.S.C. § 12131(2); *see* Miller v. King, 384 F.3d 1248, 1266 (11th Cir. 2004) (discussing "qualified" requirement in prison context); Casey v. Lewis, 834 F. Supp. 1569, 1584-85 (D.Ariz. 1993) (plaintiffs failed to establish that hearing-impaired inmates were qualified for certain programs).

[697]29 U.S.C. 794(a).

[698]*See* Thompson v. Davis, 295 F.3d 890, 896 (9th Cir. 2002) (holding that persons who were statutorily eligible for parole sufficiently pled they were "otherwise qualified" for the public benefit of parole consideration); Onishea v. Hopper, 171 F.3d 1289, 1297 (11th Cir. 1999) (en banc) (holding prisoners with infectious diseases are "otherwise qualified" for prison jobs only if reasonable accommodation will eliminate the risk); Veloz v. New York, 339 F. Supp. 2d 505, 528–29 (S.D.N.Y. 2004) (plaintiff was not "otherwise qualified" for a Unit for the Physically Disabled because his condition did not interfere with activities of daily living as required by the UPD admission criteria).

In *Raines v. State of Florida*, 983 F. Supp. 1362 (N.D.Fla. 1997), a state statute provided for gain time for a prisoner who "works diligently, participates in training, uses time constructively, or otherwise engages in positive activities." Prison officials separated the four listed activities and limited the gain time available to prisoners unable to engage in any work, recreational or training activities because of physical or mental impairment, because they were receiving mental health treatment, or because they were housed at a reception and medical center for treatment. The court held that these groups were "otherwise qualified" under the authorizing statute, since even if they couldn't work, they could "use time

The disability statutes require that the prisoner show she has been excluded from or denied the benefits of a service, program, or activity.[699] Services, programs, and activities include, essentially, "anything a public entity does"; though incarceration itself is not a service, program, or activity, almost any official activity in which prisoners participate or are required to participate, in prisons, jails, and other custodial or correctional institutions is within the scope of the ADA.[700]

Claims of mistreatment by prisoners with disabilities do not state disability statute claims if they do not involve an element of discrimination based on disability or exclusion from services, programs, or activities.[701] Claims of deprivation of adequate medical care often are dismissed on this ground.[702] However, if you can show how the denial of medical care amounts to an exclusion from medical services, which is a program, service, or activity,[703] or that a medical

---

constructively" and engage in "positive activities," and the state's practice of separating the statutory requirement into four separate activities and denying the maximum gain time to disabled prisoners who cannot engage in all four activities violated the ADA. The court noted that the plaintiffs sought no accommodation and there were no financial and administrative burdens on the defendant from allowing them to earn the maximum gain time. *Raines*, 983 F. Supp. at 1374.

[699]Kiman v. New Hampshire Dep't of Corrections, 451 F.3d 274, 284–85 (1st Cir. 2006) (prisoner deprived of cane was not denied access to programs, services, or activities where defendants said they would have helped him to the shower if he had asked and doctor wrote a pass to allow him to have recreation in the day room since he couldn't go outside); Atkins v. County of Orange, 251 F. Supp. 2d 1225, 1232 (S.D.N.Y. 2003) (plaintiffs who alleged inadequate mental health care did not state a claim under the disability statutes because they did not allege that they were denied the benefit of a program, service, or activity; allegation that violent and self-destructive mentally ill prisoners were placed in keeplock isolation did not state a claim absent any allegation that they were treated any differently from non-mentally ill violent and self-destructive prisoners).

[700]Lee v. City of Los Angeles, 250 F.3d 668, 691 (9th Cir. 2001); *accord*, Pennsylvania Dep't of Corrections v. Yeskey, 524 U.S. 206, 211, 118 S. Ct. 1952 (1998) (citing prison law library and boot camp program as programs under the ADA); Crawford v. Indiana Dep't of Corrections, 115 F.3d 481, 483–84 (7th Cir. 1997) (educational programs and use of library and dining hall are programs of a public entity); Duffy v. Riveland, 98 F.3d 447, 454–55 (9th Cir. 1996) (treating disciplinary hearing as a program for Rehabilitation Act and ADA purposes); Bane v. Virginia Dep't of Corrections, 267 F. Supp. 2d 514, 522–23 (W.D.Va. 2003) (holding general rehabilitative and correctional activities of prisons are "programs" under the statute, and prison officials are obliged to accommodate disabilities in day-to-day prison operations). *But see* Aswegan v. Bruhl, 113 F.3d 109, 110 (8th Cir. 1997) (cable TV is not a service, program, or activity); *see also* McCray v. City of Dothan, 169 F. Supp. 2d 1260, 1275 (M.D.Ala. 2001) (police investigative activities are "government programs" under the ADA, as long as the circumstances are secure and there is no threat to safety; police were obliged to accommodate a deaf individual in the course of arresting him); Calloway v. Boro of Glassboro Dep't of Police, 89 F. Supp. 2d 543, 554 (D.N.J. 2000) (investigative questioning at a police station is a program, service, or activity of the Police Department under the ADA); Hanson v. Sangamon County Sheriff's Dep't, 991 F. Supp. 1059, 1061 (C.D.Ill. 1998) (deaf plaintiff's allegation that he was arrested, the officers did not try to communicate with him, he was not told his bail amount, and a telephone device for the deaf was not provided, resulting in his spending unnecessary hours in jail stated an ADA claim; the county jail is a public entity and the plaintiff alleged denial of services and activities in the form of an

opportunity to post bond and to make a telephone call). *But see* Hainze v. Richards, 207 F.3d 795, 801–02 (5th Cir. 2000) (police shooting and arrest of a violent mentally ill person, in which the police did not use their training in nonviolent techniques, did not violate the ADA; the plaintiff was not denied the benefits and protections of police mental health training by the officers, but by his own actions in assaulting an officer; "Title II [of the ADA] does not apply to an officer's on-the-street responses to reported disturbances or other similar incidents; once the area was secure and safety was not threatened, defendants would have been obliged to reasonably accommodate the plaintiff's disability in handling and transporting him to a mental health facility."); *accord*, Thompson v. Williamson County, Tennessee, 219 F.3d 555, 558 (6th Cir. 2000); Patrice v. Murphy, 43 F. Supp. 2d 1156, 1159–60 (W.D.Wash. 1999) (an arrest is not a "program or service" under the ADA, though arresting a person because of behavior caused by a disability could give rise to an ADA claim for discrimination).

[701]*See, e.g.*, Dukes v. State of Georgia, 428 F. Supp. 2d 1298, 1324 (N.D.Ga. 2006) (complaints of failure to provide food, water, and hygiene, to provide clean clothes, and to act when he was lying in his own urine did not state ADA claims; "Failure to meet needs, however, is more appropriately addressed through the Eighth Amendment."); McIntyre v. Robinson, 126 F. Supp. 2d 394, 408–09 (D.Md. 2000) (complaints about environmental tobacco smoke by prisoners with asthma, hypertension, and heart disease did not support disability statute claims absent evidence that they had been excluded from prison programs as a result of their disabilities).

[702]Burger v. Bloomberg, 418 F.3d 882, 883 (8th Cir. 2005) (per curiam); Fitzgerald v. Corrections Corp. of America, 403 F.3d 1134, 1144 (10th Cir. 2005); Smith v. Franklin County, 227 F. Supp. 2d 667, 675 (E.D.Ky. 2002) (plaintiff denied seizure medications in jail did not state an ADA claim because she failed to specify the programs, facilities, services, activities, or benefits she was denied); Moore v. Prison Health Services, 24 F. Supp. 2d 1164, 1167 (D.Kan. 1998) (plaintiff who was given a wheelchair that collapsed under him did not raise a disability statute claim without evidence he was excluded from services or benefits provided to others), *aff'd*, 201 F.3d 448 (10th Cir. 1999).

[703]In *Kiman v. New Hampshire Dep't of Corrections*, 451 F.3d 274, 284, 286–87 (1st Cir. 2006), the court noted the distinction between ADA claims based on negligent medical care and those based on discriminatory medical care, and held that a claim of denial of prescription medications was not just a matter of medical judgment, which is not litigable under the ADA. Rather, it presented a discrimination claim, *i.e.*, of denial of access to part of the prison's program of medical services, that could be pursued under the ADA. Similarly, in *Allah v. Goord*, 405 F. Supp. 2d 265 (S.D.N.Y. 2005), the court held that a wheelchair-using prisoner's complaint that he was not provided safe transportation to outside medical appointments stated an ADA claim for exclusion from medical appointments: "Although plaintiff is not wholly precluded from participating in this service, if he is at risk of incurring serious

deprivation causes you to be excluded from other services, programs, or activities,[704] or constitutes discrimination based on your disability,[705] you may be able to pursue your medical claim under the disability statutes as well as the Eighth Amendment.

To show exclusion from or denial of the benefits of a service, program, or activity, you must show one of several things.

1. *Disparate treatment.* This means intentional discrimination, and requires a showing that hostility towards disabled persons was a significant factor in the defendants' actions (under the ADA) or the only factor (under the Rehabilitation Act).[706]

2. *Disparate impact.* This means "application of facially neutral standards that have an unlawful discriminatory effect upon a protected class."[707]

3. *Failure to make reasonable accommodation for the plaintiff's disabilities.* This is the most common basis for prisoner disability claims. The ADA protects qualified individuals with disabilities, which means persons with disabilities "who, *with or without reasonable modifications to rules, policies, or practices, the removal of architectural, communication, or transportation barriers, or the provision of auxiliary aids and services,* meet[] the essential eligibility requirements for the receipt of services or the participation in programs or activities provided by a public entity."[708] The Rehabilitation Act similarly requires "reasonable accommodations" for disabled persons.[709] Accommodations are deemed unreasonable only if they impose "undue financial

and administrative burdens"[710] or require "a fundamental alteration in the nature of [the] program."[711] Thus, under both statutes, defendants can be required, at least to some degree, to change the way they operate, change physical structures, provide affirmative assistance so that disabled persons can have access to their programs, services, and activities.[712] An accommodation may be unreasonable because it fails without justification to comply with Department of Justice regulations under the ADA or Rehabilitation Act.[713]

You do not have to show disparate treatment or disparate impact to establish a lack of reasonable accommodation.

---

injuries each time he attempts to take advantage of outside medical attention, surely he is being denied the *benefits* of this service." *Allah,* 405 F. Supp. 2d at 280–81.

[704]Kiman v. New Hampshire Dep't of Corrections, 451 F.3d 274, 288–89 (1st Cir. 2006) (pain from rear-cuffing of prisoner who had a medical order for front-cuffing supported an ADA claim because it "affected his access" to a variety of services, programs, and activities).

[705]McNally v. Prison Health Services, 46 F. Supp. 2d 49, 58–59 (D.Me. 1999) (prisoner with HIV who said he did not receive his medication while other prisoners received theirs stated an ADA claim).

[706]Regional Economic Community Action Program, Inc. v. City of Middletown, 294 F.3d 35, 49 (2d Cir. 2002). *See* Love v. Westville Correctional Center, 103 F.3d 558, 560 (7th Cir. 1996) (affirming damage award where quadriplegic prisoner was held in infirmary and was unable to use recreational, dining, and visitation facilities and unable to participate in prison programs; since defendants did not argue no accommodation was possible or that he was unqualified for the programs, they were shown to have engaged in intentional discrimination).

[707]Regional Economic Community Action Program, Inc., 294 F.3d at 52–53; Alexander v. Choate, 469 U.S. 287, 299,105 S. Ct. 712 (1985) (noting that some but not all disparate impact claims are actionable under the Rehabilitation Act).

[708]42 U.S.C. § 12131 (emphasis supplied).

[709]School Bd. of Nassau County v. Arline, 480 U.S. 273, 288 n.17, 107 S. Ct. 1123 (1987).

[710]Southeastern Community College v. Davis, 442 U.S. 397, 412, 99 S. Ct. 2361 (1979) (quoted in Harris v. Thigpen, 941 F.3d 1495, 1527 (11th Cir. 1991); *see* Love v. Westville Correctional Center, 103 F.3d 558, 561 (7th Cir. 1996) ("If Westville means that reasonable accommodations existed, but it did not want to spend the money to implement them, this argument is inconsistent with the premise of the ADA."). *But see* Spurlock v. Simmons, 88 F. Supp. 2d 1189, 1196 (D. Kan. 2000) (allowing deaf prisoner to use a Telephone Device for the Deaf whenever he wanted to would have placed an undue burden on prison officials, even though hearing prisoners could use the phone whenever they wanted).

[711]School Bd. of Nassau County v. Arline, 480 U.S. 273, 275, 107 S. Ct. 1123 (1987) (quoted in Harris v. Thigpen, 941 F.2d at 1527). *See* Henrietta D. v. Bloomberg, 331 F.3d 261, 273 (2d Cir. 2003) (being required to follow agency's own regulations was a reasonable accommodation); Arlt v. Missouri Dep't of Correction, 229 F. Supp. 2d 938, 944 (E.D.Mo. 2002) (holding that initial denial of accommodation of visually impaired and learning-disabled prisoner taking a GED exam was unreasonable because defendants later did what he asked, showing it was reasonable).

[712]*See* Gorman v. Easley, 257 F.3d 738, 751 (8th Cir. 2001), *rev'd on other grounds sub nom. Barnes v. Gorman,* 536 U.S. 181, 122 S. Ct. 2097 (2002) (reasonable accommodation for transporting a wheelchair-bound arrestee required modifying defendants' practices to transport him in a manner that was "safe and appropriate consistent with his disability"; affirming jury verdict for plaintiff where police did not use van with wheelchair locks, but strapped him onto a bench in a van where he was injured); Partelow v. Massachusetts, 442 F. Supp. 2d 41, 49 (D.Mass. 2006) (wheelchair-bound prisoner was not denied a reasonable accommodation where the handicap-accessible shower in his unit was closed for renovations, where defendants provided a shower chair, moved him to another unit which had an accessible shower, moved him back on his request, and then let him shower in the medical unit); Estate of Alcalde v. Deaton Specialty Hosp. Home, Inc., 133 F. Supp. 2d 702, 707 (D.Md. 2001) (while there is no *per se* rule requiring sign language interpreters in hospital settings, "[t]he test is whether an interpreter was necessary to provide the hearing-impaired individual with an equal opportunity to benefit from the services provided by defendants to patients who do not suffer from a hearing impairment.").

[713]Chisolm v. McManimon, 275 F.3d 315, 332 (3d Cir. 2001) (giving a deaf prisoner pencil and paper rather than an American Sign Language interpreter at jail intake may not comply with the ADA; defendants failed to follow Department of Justice regulation requiring a choice of auxiliary aids and did not show that their alternative was effective).

It is not a defense for defendants to say—as they actually have in some cases—that they don't discriminate against the disabled, but treat everybody badly. The statutes require public entities to reasonably accommodate disabilities regardless of whether they are treating people the same or differently.[714]

The reasonable accommodation rule requires defendants to provide "meaningful access" to programs that persons with disabilities are otherwise entitled to.[715] You don't have to be completely excluded from a service, program, or activity to have a claim. It is enough if your access is made unusually difficult, painful, or dangerous by the failure to accommodate your disabilities.[716] However, accommodations do not have to be the best possible in order to satisfy the statutes.[717]

The disability statutes arguably provide a more favorable standard for prisoners than does the Constitution.[718]

The reasonable accommodation requirement described above contrasts sharply with the reasonableness standard applied to other prisoner claims by *Turner v. Safley*,[719] which requires that prisoners come up with "*de minimis* cost" solutions in order to prevail. While cost is a consideration under the disability statutes, there is no general rule that only "*de minimis* cost" can be required.[720]

However, some courts have held that in prison cases, the ADA/Rehabilitation Act standard must be interpreted consistently with the *Turner* reasonable relationship standard,[721] or that the factors discussed in *Turner* may appropriately be considered in disability cases.[722] Even courts that do not so hold will certainly consider security concerns and other factors peculiar to the prison

---

[714]Henrietta D. v. Bloomberg, 331 F.3d 261, 276–77 (2d Cir. 2003) ("[W]e hold that a claim of discrimination based on a failure reasonably to accommodate is distinct from a claim of discrimination based on disparate impact. Quite simply, the demonstration that a disability makes it difficult for a plaintiff to access benefits that are available to both those with and without disabilities is sufficient to sustain a claim for a reasonable accommodation.")

[715]Alexander v. Choate, 469 U.S. 287, 301, 105 S. Ct. 712 (1985) (under the Rehabilitation Act, "an otherwise qualified handicapped individual must be provided with meaningful access to the benefit that the grantee offers. . . . [T]o assure meaningful access, reasonable accommodations in the grantee's program or benefit may have to be made."); *accord*, Henrietta D. v. Bloomberg, 331 F.3d at 273–78 (applying *Choate* under ADA).

[716]Thus, in a case where the amputee prisoner was denied a wheelchair and had no way of getting around except knee pads, the court held: "The fact that plaintiff was actually able to use most of the jail services does not preclude his claim in light of the fact that he was able to do so only by virtue of exceptional and painful exertion which was contrary to a physician's instructions concerning his disability." Schmidt v. Odell, 64 F. Supp. 2d 1014, 1033 (D.Kan. 1999); *accord*, Kiman v. New Hampshire Dep't of Corrections, 451 F.3d 274, 288–89 (1st Cir. 2006) (pain from rear-cuffing of prisoner who had a medical order for front-cuffing supported an ADA claim because it "affected his access" to a variety of services, programs, and activities); Allah v. Goord, 405 F. Supp. 2d 265, 280–81 (S.D.N.Y. 2005) (failure to provide safe transportation to wheelchair-using prisoner stated an ADA claim for exclusion from medical appointments: "Although plaintiff is not wholly precluded from participating in this service, if he is at risk of incurring serious injuries each time he attempts to take advantage of outside medical attention, surely he is being denied the *benefits* of this service.").

[717]*See, e.g.,* Mason v. Correctional Medical Services, Inc., 559 F.3d 880, 887–88 (8th Cir. 2009) (where prison provided blind prisoner with an inmate assistant to accompany him everywhere, read and write for him as needed, and read written material into a tape recorder for him, access to programs was meaningful; prison need not also supply Braille materials, computer software, etc.).

[718]They certainly do in certain kinds of due process cases. Prisoners generally must show that they were subjected to "atypical and significant hardship" in order to pursue a claim for deprivation

of liberty without due process. *See* Ch. 4, § A. That means that most exclusion from programs and much prison discipline does not present a due process issue. *See* Ch. 4, §§ F, H.5. However, [under the disability statutes, prisoners need only show that their disabilities were not reasonably accommodated. Thus, in *Randolph v. Rogers*, 980 F. Supp. 1051, 1058 (E.D.Mo. 1997), *reversed in part, vacated in part on other grounds*, 170 F.3d 850 (8th Cir.1999), the court held that failure to provide a sign language interpreter did not deny due process because the prisoner's 30-day segregation terms were not atypical and significant, but his ADA claim was allowed to go forward.

[719]*See* Ch. 3, § A, for a discussion of the *Turner* standard.

[720]The cost issue under the statutes is assessed under the "undue hardship" requirement. The Supreme Court has said that this inquiry

> requires not simply an assessment of the cost of the accommodation in relation to the recipient's overall budget, but a case-by-case analysis weighing factors that include: (1) [t]he overall size of the recipient's program with respect to number of employees, number and type of facilities, and size of budget; (2) [t]he type of the recipient's operation, including the composition and structure of the recipient's workforce; and (3) [t]he nature and cost of the accommodation needed.

Olmstead v. L.C., 527 U.S. 581, 606 n.16, 119 S. Ct. 2176 (1998) (internal citation and quotation marks omitted); *see* Pennsylvania Protection and Advocacy, Inc. v. Pennsylvania Dep't of Public Welfare, 402 F.2d 374, 380–81 (3d Cir. 2005) (holding that budget constraints do not establish a fundamental alteration defense; non-prison case). Onishea v. Harper, 171 F.3d 1289, 1304 (11th Cir. 1999) (holding that "undue hardship" standard of Rehabilitation Act allowed consideration of cost; $1.7 million staffing increase relative to a $163 million prison budget would be an undue hardship).

[721]Gates v. Rowland, 39 F.3d 1439, 1446–47 (9th Cir. 1994) (holding ADA standard "equivalent to" *Turner* standard). *Contra*, Amos v. Maryland Dep't of Public Safety and Correctional Services, 178 F.3d 212, 220 (4th Cir. 1999) (rejecting application of *Turner* as inconsistent with *Yeskey*), *dismissed as settled*, 205 F.3d 687 (4th Cir. 2000).

[722]Onishea v. Hopper, 171 F.3d 1289, 1300–01 (11th Cir. 1999) (en banc) (holding consideration of the *Turner* factors helpful in applying ADA).

environment in deciding whether an accommodation is reasonable.[723]

Compensatory damages are available under the disability statutes, but not punitive damages.[724] There are some complications in seeking compensatory damages. The first concerns whom the statutes allow you to sue. Unlike the rules under 42 U.S.C. § 1983,[725] most courts have held that officials cannot be sued in their individual capacities, but only in their official capacities, under the statutes[726]

(though there is disagreement, discussed below, over the circumstances in which official capacity damage suits are allowed). Some have held that you can sue governments or government agencies directly,[727] which is also unlike the § 1983 rule.[728] Some have said that you cannot sue individuals at all, since you can sue government agencies.[729] Confusing as this is, it is also to prisoners' benefit, since under any of these differing rules, you won't have to satisfy the "personal involvement" requirement of 42 U.S.C. § 1983.[730] If there is a clear statement by your federal circuit of who the proper defendants are under these statutes, follow it. If there isn't, you should name the prison personnel you think are directly responsible for your problem, and their superiors in the chain of command, in their official capacities, and also name the agency (sheriff's office, department of correction, private contractor, etc.) that operates the institution. This should leave you with some viable defendants no matter what position your court adopts on the "sue whom?" question.

Unfortunately, suing states, state agencies, and state employees in their official capacities raises questions of sovereign immunity under the Eleventh Amendment.[731] Courts have sharply disagreed about how far Congress can go, and how far it has gone, in overriding state sovereign immunity

---

[723]*See* Mason v. Correctional Medical Services, Inc., 559 F.3d 880, 887–88 (8th Cir. 2009) (where prison provided blind prisoner with an inmate assistant, failure to provide trained civilian assistant from outside prison was justified because security would require an officer escort for an outside civilian); Kiman v. New Hampshire Dep't of Corrections, 451 F.3d 274, 285 (1st Cir. 2006) (holding depriving prisoner of a cane in a segregation unit did not violate the ADA). *But see* Chisolm v. McManimon, 275 F.3d 315, 329 (3d Cir. 2001) (court refuses to credit defendants' mere repetition of security without support for their claims of security problems; claim that TDD device would present a security problem on a housing unit did not explain why it couldn't be provided at another location).

[724]Barnes v. Gorman, 536 U.S. 181, 188–89, 122 S. Ct. 2097 (2002).

[725]Under § 1983, claims can be brought against state officials or employees in their official capacities only for declaratory and injunctive relief; damages claims must be brought against them in their individual capacities. City or county officials or employees can be sued in their official capacities for injunctive relief, and for damages where your injury resulted from an official policy and not just from misconduct by individuals. *See* Ch. 8, § B.4.b. The "policy" requirement does not apply to official capacity claims under the disability statutes, unlike § 1983. Delano-Pyle v. Victoria County, Texas, 302 F.3d 567, 575 (5th Cir. 2002). The law is unsettled as to whether damages can be recovered against official capacity defendants, and under what circumstances, under the federal statutes protecting religious rights. *See* Ch. 3, § D.1.b.4.

[726]Everson v. Leis, 556 F.3d 484, 501 n.7 (6th Cir. 2009); Radaszewski v. Maram, 383 F.3d 599, 606 (7th Cir. 2004); Garcia v. S.U.N.Y. Health Sciences Center of Brooklyn, 280 F.3d 98, 107 (2d Cir. 2001); Alsbrook v. City of Maumelle, 184 F.3d 999, 1004 n.8 (8th Cir. 1999) (en banc); Walker v. Snyder, 213 F.3d 344, 346 (7th Cir. 2000); Jordan v. Delaware by and through the Delaware Dep't of Corrections, 433 F. Supp. 2d 433, 440 (D.Del. 2006); Degrafinreid v. Ricks, 417 F. Supp. 2d 403, 411 (S.D.N.Y. 2006); Tanney v. Boles, 400 F. Supp. 2d 1027, 1044 (E.D.Mich. 2005); Roque v. Armstrong, 392 F. Supp. 2d 382, 388 (D.Conn. 2005); Atkins v. County of Orange, 251 F. Supp. 2d 1225 (S.D.N.Y. 2003); Candelaria v. Cunningham, 2000 WL 798636, *2 (S.D.N.Y., June 20, 2000); Mitchell v. Mass. Dep't of Correction, 190 F. Supp. 2d, 204, 211 & n.6 (D. Mass. 2002); Becker v. Oregon, 170 F. Supp. 2d 1061, 1067 (D.Ore. 2001); Romand v. Zimmerman, 881 F. Supp. 806 (N.D.N.Y. 1995); Niece v. Fitzner, 922 F. Supp. 594 (E.D. Mich. 1996).

There is one exception to this rule. Several courts have held that you may sue individuals under the anti-retaliation provisions of the ADA. *See* Shotz v. City of Plantation, Fla., 344 F.3d 1161, 1179–80 (11th Cir. 2003); Alston v. District of Columbia, 561 F. Supp. 2d 29, 42 (D.D.C. 2008); Key v. Grayson, 163 F. Supp. 2d 697, 716–717 (E.D.Mich. 2001). Others have disagreed. *See* Baird ex rel. Baird v. Rose, 192 F.3d 462, 471 (4th Cir. 1999). However, most

cases rejecting individual liability are in the employment context, not the Title II public entity context, *Shotz*, 344 F.3d at 1173–74, and *Baird* relied on cases from the employment context. Prisoner disability cases are generally brought under Title II.

[727]Everson v. Leis, 556 F.3d at 501 n.7 (proper defendants under ADA Title II can include the "public entity *or* an official acting in his official capacity" (emphasis supplied)); Hallett v. New York State Dep't of Correctional Services, 109 F. Supp. 2d 190, 199–200 (S.D.N.Y. 2000) (noting that the statute refers to public *entities* and not individuals). The Supreme Court confirmed this view, at least as to ADA claims that are based on conduct that would also violate the Constitution. U.S. v. Georgia, 546 U.S. 151, 159, 126 S. Ct. 877 (2006) (". . . [I]nsofar as Title II creates a private cause of action for damages against the States for conduct that *actually* violates the Fourteenth Amendment, Title II validly abrogates state sovereign immunity.").

[728]Under § 1983, you cannot sue states or state agencies by name, and you can sue city or county governments only if your complaint is based on an official policy rather than mere misconduct by employees. *See* Ch. 8, § B.4.b., concerning municipal liability, and L.1.a, concerning suits against state and their agencies.

[729]Fox v. State University of New York, 497 F. Supp. 2d 446, 451 (E.D.N.Y. 2007); Carrasquillo v. City of New York, 324 F. Supp. 2d 428, 441–42 (S.D.N.Y. 2004); Key v. Grayson, 163 F. Supp. 2d 697, 716 (E.D.Mich. 2001); Hallett v. New York State Dep't of Correctional Services, 109 F. Supp. 2d 190, 199–200 (S.D.N.Y. 2000).

[730]For a discussion of personal involvement, *see* Ch. 8, § B.4.a.

[731]*See* Ch. 8, § L.1.a, for further discussion of the Eleventh Amendment. City and county governments are not protected by the Eleventh Amendment, so there's no problem suing them for damages under the disability statutes. *See* Board of Trustees of University of Alabama v. Garrett, 531 U.S. 356, 364, 121 S. Ct. 955 (2001).

in the ADA. The Supreme Court has issued two decisions which overrule many earlier lower court decisions, and there will probably be more because matters are still not completely resolved. Be sure you read the most recent decisions from the Supreme Court and courts in your federal circuit if you wish to bring disability statute litigation. Following is the state of the law as we are finishing this Manual in 2009.

It is clear that Congress has abrogated the states' Eleventh Amendment protection for declaratory and injunctive relief under Title II of the ADA.[732] Congress has also abrogated it at least for prisoners' ADA damage claims that also involve actual violations of the Constitution.[733] That means that if your complaint asserts conduct that violates the ADA *and* the Constitution, you can bring ADA damage claims against defendants in their official capacities, or against the governments they work for, in addition to constitutional damages claims under § 1983.

It is not yet clear whether states or official capacity defendants can be held liable for damages for prison ADA violations that do not also violate the Constitution.[734] The Supreme Court has said that if conduct violates the ADA but not the Constitution, lower courts must decide "whether Congress's purported abrogation of sovereign immunity as to that class of conduct is nevertheless valid."[735]

So far, the lower courts have not settled that question for prison ADA cases, though a couple of decisions have held that Eleventh Amendment immunity is not abrogated for claims that do not involve constitutional violations.[736] However, in an earlier case, the Supreme Court held that the ADA requirement of program accessibility (which is broader than constitutional requirements) applies to cases involving the right of access to courts, because the long record of constitutional violations with respect to access to courts entitled Congress to take "added prophylactic measures in response."[737] In reaching that conclusion, the Court noted "a pattern of unequal treatment in the administration of a wide range of public services, programs, and activities, *including the penal system*," and cited examples from lower court prison decisions.[738] This reference supports the argument that Eleventh Amendment immunity from damages should

---

[732]U.S. v. Georgia, 546 U.S. 151, 160, 126 S. Ct. 877 (2006) (concurring opinion); Miller v. King, 384 F.3d 1248, 1263–67 (11th Cir. 2004), *vacated and superseded on other grounds*, 449 F.3d 1149 (11th Cir. 2006); McCarthy v. Hawkins, 381 F.3d 407, 413 (5th Cir. 2004).

[733]U.S. v. Georgia, 546 U.S. at 155–60.

The Court in that case specifically referred to Fourteenth Amendment rights. In fact, virtually all constitutional claims by state prisoners are Fourteenth Amendment claims in part, because the Fourteenth Amendment "incorporates" the Eighth Amendment's protection against cruel and unusual punishments and makes it applicable to the states, *Georgia*, 546 U.S. at 157 (citation omitted), and also incorporates the First, Fourth, and Sixth Amendments. *See* Ch. 4, n.2. The Fourteenth Amendment's Equal Protection Clause applies directly to states, so almost any constitutional claim a state prisoner might raise is also a Fourteenth Amendment claim. *See also Georgia*, 563 U.S. at 162 (Stevens, J., concurring) (suggesting that Court's holding should be extended generally to claims about the mistreatment of disabled prisoners, stating that "courts have also reviewed myriad other types of claims by disabled prisoners, such as allegations of the abridgment of religious liberties, undue censorship, interference with access to the judicial process, and procedural due process violations").

[734]The reason this is an issue is that the Supreme Court has held that Congressional abrogation of states' Eleventh Amendment protection against damage awards, based on its authority under section 5 of the Fourteenth Amendment, must display "congruence and proportionality" to the problem Congress was trying to remedy, and not be an attempt to change substantive constitutional law. Tennessee v. Lane, 541 U.S. 509, 520–21, 124 S. Ct. 1978 (2004). So the courts have to decide how far the statute can go in imposing damage liability on the states and still be "congruent and proportional." *See* Goonewardena v. New York, 475 F. Supp. 2d 310, 322–27 (S.D.N.Y. 2007), for a useful discussion of the "congruent and proportional" test.

[735]U.S. v. Georgia, 546 U.S. at 159.

Some courts seem to think, wrongly, that *U.S. v. Georgia* restricted prison ADA damages claims to those that also allege constitutional violations. *See, e.g.*, Nails v. Laplante, 596 F. Supp. 2d 475, 481 (D.Conn. 2009); Rhodan v. Schofield, 2007 WL 1810147, *16 (N.D.Ga., June 19, 2007). If your case raises this question, be sure to point out the language quoted above from *U.S. v. Georgia* indicating that this question remains for the lower courts to decide.

[736]*See* Hale v. Mississippi, 2007 WL 3357562, *8 (S.D.Miss. 2007) (holding ADA Title II is "not a 'congruent and proportional' response in the context of state prisons"; prisoner's claim concerned exclusion from work, education, and transfers because of medical and mental health classification); Chase v. Baskerville, 508 F. Supp. 2d 492, 503–04 (E.D.Va. 2007) (holding ADA Title II is not a congruent and proportional means of enforcing Eighth Amendment or Equal Protection Clause), *aff'd*, 305 Fed.Appx. 135 (4th Cir. 2008) (unpublished). Our research during the summer of 2009 discovered no cases to the contrary, and a number saying they needed more information to decide the question. One court has said that the question is sufficiently difficult to warrant assignment of counsel to a *pro se* litigant. Muhammad v. Department of Corrections, 2007 WL 1695702, *2 (D.N.J., June 12, 2007).

There are some post-*U.S. v. Georgia* decisions finding the ADA damages remedy "congruent and proportional" with respect to public education. Toledo v. Sanchez, 454 F.3d 24, 33–40 (1st Cir. 2006), *cert. denied*, 549 U.S. 1301 (2007); Goonewardena v. New York, 475 F. Supp. 2d 310, 326 (S.D.N.Y. 2007).

[737]Tennessee v. Lane, 541 U.S. 509, 528–31, 124 S. Ct. 1978 (2004). In that decision, the Court held that courts should determine what damages claims against states can be heard under the ADA based on the particular right asserted in the case before them, rather than for the ADA as a whole. It is arguable, based on *Lane*, that damages may be awarded for prison ADA violations affecting access to courts even if they do not meet the stiff requirements for constitutional court access claims. *See* Ch. 3, § C, concerning access to courts. Examples of such possible claims are law libraries that are not accessible to those with mobility impairments, or lack of assistance for persons with visual or cognitive disabilities. We are not aware of any case law on this point.

[738]Tennessee v. Lane, 541 U.S. at 525 (emphasis supplied).

be held to be abrogated for the full range of prison ADA claims; be sure to cite it if your case involves that issue.

The Eleventh Amendment defense is not available for claims under the Rehabilitation Act. Ongoing acceptance of federal funds waives the Eleventh Amendment defense to Rehabilitation Act claims.[739] As far as we know, virtually every state and local correction department or Sheriff's office receives some federal funding, so you can probably sue any of them under the Rehabilitation Act. Reading this, you might ask, "Why bother with the ADA, if I can sue under the Rehabilitation Act and avoid all these Eleventh Amendment complications?" That's a good question; while there are differences between the statutes, they are unlikely to be important in most prisoner cases.[740] One difference is that the Rehabilitation Act prohibits discrimination "solely by reason of" disability,[741] while the ADA prohibits discrimination "by reason of . . . disability," leaving out "solely."[742] However, this should not make a difference if your complaint is about failure to provide a reasonable accommodation for your disability.[743] Expert witness fees can be recovered under the ADA but not the RA,[744] but this will not matter to you unless you are in a position to retain an expert. It is theoretically possible that the ADA might in some

instances provide a more favorable legal standard.[745] We have not seen an actual case in which this has happened. The practical application of the ADA is guided by regulations enacted by the Department of Justice (see 28 C.F.R. § 35.101 et seq.), which may be helpful to prisoners.[746]

Some courts have held that a showing of deliberate indifference or intentional discrimination is required to recover damages under either the ADA or the Rehabilitation Act.[747]

i. Prison Assignments and Regulations The Eighth Amendment forbids exposure of prisoners to conditions that pose "an unreasonable risk of serious damage to [their] future health."[748] A prisoner may not be required to perform a work assignment inconsistent with her medical condition. However, if prison medical personnel authorize the assignment the courts will not second-guess their judgment.[749] Similarly, prison housing assignments that are inconsistent with or aggravate a prisoner's medical condition may

---

[739]Phiffer v. Columbia River Correctional Institute, 384 F.3d 791 (9th Cir. 2004) (per curiam); Garrett v. University of Ala. at Birmingham Bd. of Trustees, 344 F.3d 1288, 1293 (11th Cir. 2003); Armstrong v. Davis, 275 F.3d 849, 878 (9th Cir. 2001); Arlt v. Missouri Dep't of Correction, 229 F. Supp. 2d 938, 942 (E.D.Mo. 2002). The reason this rule is different from the ADA rule is that the Rehabilitation Act was based on Congress's Spending Clause authority to set conditions on receipt of federal funding, and not just on its authority under section 5 of the Fourteenth Amendment. Lovell v. Chandler, 303 F.3d 1039, 1051 (9th Cir. 2002); Koslow v. Commonwealth of Pa., 302 F.3d 161, 167 (3d Cir. 2002).

[740]See Chase v. Baskerville, 508 F. Supp. 2d 492, 507 (E.D.Va. 2007) (rejecting ADA damage liability under the Eleventh Amendment but upholding RA liability), aff'd, 305 Fed.Appx. 135 (4th Cir. 2008) (unpublished); see also Bennett-Nelson v. Louisiana Bd. of Regents, 431 F.3d 448, 455 (5th Cir.2005) (declining to decide ADA Eleventh Amendment question since RA claim was nearly identical and would go forward regardless).

This discussion has been informed by Betsy Ginsberg, *Out with the New, in with the Old: The Importance of Section 504 of the Rehabilitation Act to Prisoners with Disabilities*, 36 FORDHAM URB. L.J. 713 (2009).

[741]29 U.S.C. § 794.

[742]42 U.S.C. § 12132; see New Directions Treatment Svcs. v. City of Reading, 490 F.3d 293, 301 n.4 (3d Cir. 2007); Regional Econ. Cmty. Action Program (RECAP) v. City of Middleton, 294 F.3d 35, 49 (2d Cir. 2002) (both citing the difference in standards).

[743]Ginsberg, *Out with the New, in with the Old*, 36 FORDHAM URB. L.J. 713, 737–38 (noting that causation is not an issue in reasonable accommodation cases) (citing Bennett-Nelson v. Louisiana Bd. of Regents, 431 F.3d 448, 454 (5th Cir. 2005)).

[744]Compare Lovell v. Chandler, 303 F.3d 1039, 1058 (9th Cir. 2002) (holding expert fees recoverable under the ADA) with M.P., ex rel. K.P. v. Independent School Dist. No. 721, 2007 WL 844688, *4 (D.Minn. 2007) (expert fees not recoverable under RA).

[745]Part of the ADA says: "Except as otherwise provided in this chapter, nothing in this chapter shall be construed to apply a lesser standard than the standards applied under title V of the Rehabilitation Act of 1973 (29 U.S.C. 790 et seq.) or the regulations issued by Federal agencies pursuant to such title." 42 U.S.C. 12201(a). So the ADA can't provide a worse outcome than the Rehabilitation Act, but it might in theory provide a better one.

[746]See Yeskey v. Penn. Dep't of Corr., 118 F.3d 168, 170–71 (3d Cir. 1997), aff'd, 524 U.S. 206, 118 S. Ct. 1952 (1998); Onishea v. Hopper, 171 F.3d 1289, 1301–04 (11th Cir. 1999). There are regulations under the Rehabilitation Act as well, and the ADA regulations (like the ADA itself) "shall not be construed to apply a lesser standard" than is applied under the Rehabilitation Act and its regulations. 28 C.F.R. § 35.103. So, for the issue you are concerned with, you would have to compare the ADA regulations (which are as noted in 28 C.F.R. part 35) with the Rehabilitation Act regulations, which are scattered around in different places in the Code of Federal Regulations. The Department of Health and Human Services regulations are in 45 C.F.R. Part 84; the Department of Justice regulations are in 28 C.F.R. Part 42.501 et seq.; the Department of Education Regulations are in 34 C.F.R. Part 104. We're sorry this is so complicated; if we made the law, we'd try to make it simpler.

[747]Garcia v. S.U.N.Y. Health Sciences Center of Brooklyn, 280 F.3d 98, 112 (2d Cir. 2001); Ferguson v. City of Phoenix, 157 F.3d 668, 674–75 (9th Cir. 1998) (requiring proof of intent to discriminate). Some courts have suggested (and we agree) that the basis for the Garcia holding was undermined by the Supreme Court's decision in Tennessee v. Lane, 541 U.S. 509, 124 S. Ct. 1978 (2004). See Degrafinreid v. Ricks, 417 F. Supp. 2d 403, 409–11 (S.D.N.Y. 2006). The court that decided Garcia has so far declined to consider that question, but has very recently held that Garcia requirement that the plaintiff show discriminatory animus applies only to cases involving claims of denial of equal protection, not of substantive rights. Bolmer v. Oliveira, 594 F.3d 134, 147 (2d Cir. 2010).

[748]Helling v. McKinney, 509 U.S.25, 33–35, 113 S. Ct. 2475 (1993). The Court made this statement in a case about exposure to environmental tobacco smoke. This issue, and exposure to other environmental hazards, are discussed in § G.3.b of this chapter.

[749]See § I.2 of this chapter, nn.1264–1266.

constitute deliberate indifference.[750] Prison regulations or security measures may be unconstitutional if they have adverse medical consequences.[751] Prisoners may not be transferred if their medical condition makes it dangerous to their health,[752] and conversely, if their health requires transfer to a different facility, failure to do so may be deliberate indifference.[753]

j. Medical Privacy Most courts have held that there is a constitutional right to privacy, extending to prisoners, in medical diagnoses and other medical information.[754] That right is not violated by the reporting of medical findings in the ordinary course of prison medical care operations.[755] Some courts have also upheld fairly wide disclosure to prison administrations as well,[756] or held that privacy rights depend on how sensitive the particular information is.[757] However, the "[c]asual, unjustified dissemination of confidential medical information to non-medical staff and other prisoners" is unconstitutional.[758]

Several courts have condemned the lack of confidentiality resulting from the use of inmates as medical records clerks.[759] Courts have reached different conclusions about other prison practices or actions that indirectly disclose

---

[750]Payne v. Lynaugh, 843 F.2d 177, 178–79 (5th Cir. 1988) (failure to transfer prisoner to facility with oxygen equipment required for his emphysema stated a deliberate indifference claim); Johnson v. Pearson, 316 F. Supp. 2d 307, 316–19 (E.D.Va. 2004) (persistently double-celling prisoner with respiratory problems with smokers could constitute deliberate indifference); Lavender v. Lampert, 242 F. Supp. 2d 821, 849 (D.Or. 2002) (allegation that prisoner with severe orthopedic problems was housed in hilly terrain that exacerbated them raised a factual issue of deliberate indifference); *see* § G.3.c of this chapter for further discussion of environmental tobacco smoke.

[751]Vaughan v. Ricketts, 859 F.2d 736, 741–42 (9th Cir. 1988) (mass digital rectal searches without regard to individuals' medical condition would violate the Eighth Amendment); Monroe v. Bombard, 422 F. Supp. 211, 214–15 (S.D.N.Y. 1976) ("no beard" rule could not be applied to a prisoner whose skin condition did not permit shaving).

[752]Hamilton v. Endell, 981 F.2d 1063, 1066–67 (9th Cir. 1992); Roba v. U.S., 604 F.2d 215, 218–19 (2d Cir. 1979); *see* Scicluna v. Wells, 345 F.3d 441, 446 (6th Cir. 2003) ("Transferring a prisoner in need of urgent medical attention to a facility that the official knows is unable to provide the required treatment is conduct that would alert a reasonable person to the likelihood of personal liability.").

[753]Payne v. Lynaugh, 843 F.2d 177, 178–79 (5th Cir. 1988) (failure to transfer prisoner to facility with oxygen equipment required for his emphysema); Scott v. Garcia, 370 F. Supp. 2d 1056, 1068–69 (S.D.Cal. 2005) (failure of classification committee to act on medical direction to transfer prisoner with severe stomach and digestive problems to a prison with hospital facilities); *see* §§ F.1.a, nn.279; F.3.d., n.435; F.4.a., n.476, concerning failure to hospitalize or to do so timely.

[754]Most courts have held that this right is based on the Due Process Clause of the Fourteenth or Fifth Amendment. *See* Doe v. Delie, 257 F.3d 309, 316 (3d Cir. 2001) (Fourteenth Amendment right of privacy extends to prescription records and is "especially strong" with respect to HIV status; right survives incarceration and is subject to *Turner v. Safley* reasonableness standard); Powell v. Schriver, 175 F.3d 107, 111–12 (2d Cir. 1999) (right of privacy extends to transsexualism; *Turner* applies); A.L.A. v. West Valley City, 26 F.3d 989, 990 (10th Cir. 1994); Nolley v. County of Erie, 776 F. Supp. 715, 729 (W.D.N.Y. 1991); Woods v. White, 689 F. Supp. 874, 875–76 (W.D.Wis. 1988), *aff'd*, 899 F.2d 17 (7th Cir. 1990); Doe v. Coughlin, 697 F. Supp. 1234, 1237–38 (N.D.N.Y. 1988); Doe v. Meachum, 126 F.R.D. 437, 439 (D.Conn. 1988); *see also* Doe v. Borough of Barrington, 729 F. Supp. 376, 382–85 (D.N.J. 1990) (non-prisoner case); Matter of Rules Adoption Regarding Inmate-Therapist Confidentiality, 224 N.J.Super. 252, 540 A.2d 212, 216–18 (N.J.Super.App.Div. 1988) (policies requiring disclosures by prison psychotherapists struck down). *Contra*, Jarvis v. Wellman, 52 F.3d 125, 126 (6th Cir. 1995) (holding there is no general right to privacy in medical records).

The Supreme Court also held in a non-prisoner case that turning hospital drug test results over to the police violated the *Fourth* Amendment, stating that "[t]he reasonable expectation of privacy enjoyed by the typical patient undergoing diagnostic tests in a hospital is that the results of those tests will not be shared with nonmedical personnel without her consent." Ferguson v. City of Charleston, 532 U.S. 67, 78, 121 S. Ct. 1281 (2001).

[755]Baez v. Rapping, 680 F. Supp. 112, 115 (S.D.N.Y. 1988); *see also* Dean v. Roane General Hospital, 578 F. Supp. 408, 410 (S.D.W.Va. 1984) (hospital's disclosure of medical records to Sheriff who had sent prisoner to the hospital did not violate the Constitution).

[756]One federal appeals court has said that "the Bureau of Prisons is entitled to up-to-date medical information about persons in its custody," and it was therefore permissible for the plaintiff's prison doctor to talk to the U.S. Attorney who was defending the plaintiff's civil suit about injuries from a traffic accident. Ueland v. U.S., 291 F.3d 993, 999 (7th Cir. 2002). Another court has upheld a required medical release that permitted disclosure "if it is believed that the plaintiff poses a threat to his own health and safety, the health and safety of others or the orderly operation of the prison facility," and to prepare reports and recommendations or to make decisions about housing, work or program status, pre-release, or parole. Iseley v. Dragovich, 236 F. Supp. 2d 472, 479 (E.D.Pa. 2002).

[757]Cortes v. Johnson, 114 F. Supp. 1182, 1185 (W.D.N.Y. 2000) (distinguishing between disclosure of HIV status or transsexuality, which carry a risk of harm, and disclosure of the plaintiff's back and leg problems); Webb v. Goldstein, 117 F. Supp. 2d 289, 294 (E.D.N.Y. 2000) (holding disclosure of records that did not contain sensitive information such as HIV-positive status or psychiatric diagnosis did not violate the right of privacy).

[758]Woods v. White, 689 F. Supp. at 877; *see* Ueland v. U.S., 291 F.3d at 999 (stating government could not "gratuitously reveal a prisoner's medical information to third parties").

[759]Williams v. Edwards, 547 F.2d 1206, 1217 (5th Cir. 1977); Cody v. Hillard, 599 F. Supp. 1025, 1036, 1056 (D.S.D. 1984), *aff'd in part and rev'd in part on other grounds*, 830 F.2d 912 (8th Cir. 1987) (en banc); Tillery v. Owens, 719 F. Supp. 1256, 1305 (W.D.Pa. 1989), *aff'd*, 907 F.2d 418 (3d Cir. 1990). *But see* Toussaint v. McCarthy, 801 F.2d 1080, 1112 (9th Cir. 1986) (court rejects claim that lack of confidentiality of medical records makes medical care inadequate; right to privacy not discussed).

medical information without justification.[760] Courts have also differed about whether the use of correctional staff or other prisoners as interpreters during medical encounters violates the right of privacy.[761]

The federal Health Insurance Portability and Accountability Act (HIPAA) contains provisions protecting the privacy of medical records.[762] In a nutshell, the statute requires "covered entities" to keep people's health information private except as specified by federal regulations[763] or as authorized by the person who is the subject of the information. A covered entity is anyone who provides health care and transmits records electronically, so prisons and prison systems can be covered entities subject to the HIPAA restrictions. So far most courts have held that HIPAA does not create a private cause of action, so you cannot bring suit for violation of it.[764] The Office for Civil Rights of the U.S. Department of Health and Human Services has authority to receive and investigate complaints of HIPAA privacy violations.

Disclosure of medical information about a prisoner may also violate state law. The medical profession recognizes an ethical obligation to preserve patients' confidentiality, and many states have statutes or regulations protecting the privacy of medical records[765] and making doctor–patient communications privileged. Some statutes or regulations forbid disclosure of certain kinds of medical information.[766] Disclosure of medical information may also constitute the "public disclosure of private facts," which is one variety of the tort of invasion of privacy in some states.[767] In a number of states the breach of doctor–patient confidentiality is a tort for which damages may be awarded.[768]

There is a psychotherapist–patient privilege, recognized by the federal courts as well as many states, that exempts from forced disclosure or use in court proceedings confidential communications made to licensed psychiatrists, psychologists, and clinical social workers in the course of psychotherapy.[769] Many (but not all) states recognize a similar physician–patient privilege for communications with physicians about one's medical condition or treatment.[770]

k. The Right to Refuse Treatment A mentally competent adult has a right under both the common law and the Fourteenth Amendment to refuse medical

---

[760]Casey v. Lewis, 834 F. Supp. 1477, 1546 (D.Ariz. 1993) (condemning sick call system that required inmates to discuss medical problems); Nolley v. County of Erie, 776 F. Supp. 715, 734-36 (W.D.N.Y. 1991); Doe v. Coughlin, 697 F. Supp. 1234, 1239-42 (N.D.N.Y. 1988). *But see* Harris v. Thigpen, 941 F.2d 1495, 1521 (11th Cir. 1991) (prison policy of segregating HIV positive inmates upheld in spite of plaintiffs' privacy rights); Rodriguez v. Ames, 287 F. Supp. 2d 213, 219-21 (W.D.N.Y. 2003) (holding that performing a rectal examination in a prisoner's cell in the presence of his cellmate did not violate the Constitution; although prisoners retain a limited right to bodily privacy, "there are many unfortunate and embarrassing circumstances prisoners must endure as part of their daily lives"; the interest in keeping a particular medical condition private varies with the condition, and there was no indication that word of his condition spread throughout the prison or he experienced discriminatory or violent action from other inmates).

[761]*Compare* Clarkson v. Coughlin, 898 F. Supp. 1019, 1041 (S.D.N.Y. 1995) (holding use of persons as sign language interpreters who are not under a duty to maintain medical confidentiality violated deaf prisoners' privacy rights) *with* Franklin v. District of Columbia, 163 F.3d 625, 637-39 (D.C. Cir. 1998) (holding Spanish-speaking prisoners are not entitled to medical providers who speak Spanish); Cortes v. Johnson, 114 F. Supp. 2d 182, 184 (W.D.N.Y. 2000) (rejecting *Clarkson* holding).

[762]42 U.S.C. §§ 1320d *et seq.*

[763]These regulations appear at 45 C.F.R. § 164.512.

[764]Acara v. Banks, 470 F.3d 569, 571-72 (5th Cir. 2006) and cases cited.

[765]*See, e.g.*, Nolley v. County of Erie, 776 F. Supp. at 733-34 (citing N.Y.Pub.Health Law § 2780 *et seq.* (McKinney 1991 Supp.)); Davidson v. State, 3 A.D.3d 623, 771 N.Y.S.2d 197 (3d Dep't 2004) (affirming damage award for release of medical records in violation of prison system's regulations). After the *Davidson* decision, which involved unauthorized disclosure to the state Attorney General's

office, the New York State prison system changed its regulations to allow disclosure of health information for purposes of defending itself against prisoner lawsuits. 7 N.Y.C.R.R. § 5.24(b).

[766]In New York, state law provides special protection to HIV-related information. McKinney's Public Health Law, Article 27-F; *see* Melendez v. Strong Memorial Hosp., 9 Misc.3d 938, 804 N.Y.S.2d 626, 627 (N.Y.Sup. 2005).

[767]*See, e.g.*, Hillman v. Columbia County, 164 Wis.2d 376, 474 N.W.2d 913, 919-20 (Wis.App. 1991), *review granted*, 382 N.W.2d 105 (Wis. 1992). *But see* Wilson v. Ohio Dep't of Rehabilitation and Correction, 73 Ohio App.3d 496, 597 N.E.2d 1148, 1150 (Ohio App. 1991) (disclosure to court of medical records of prisoner who had put his medical condition in issue in a lawsuit did not violate his privacy rights). Invasion of privacy is discussed further in Ch. 3, § E.3.

[768]Vassiliades v. Garfinckel's, Brooks Bros., 492 A.2d 580, 592 (D.C. 1985); Alberts v. Devine, 395 Mass. 59, 479 N.E.2d 113, 120 (Mass. 1985); MacDonald v. Clinger, 84 A.D.2d 482, 446 N.Y.S.2d 801, 803-04 (N.Y.App.Div. 1982); Humphers v. First Interstate Bank, 298 Or. 706, 696 P.2d 527, 534-35 (Or. 1985); Horne v. Patton, 291 Ala. 701, 287 So.2d 824, 830 (Ala. 1974); Hammonds v. Aetna Casualty & Surety Co., 243 F. Supp. 793, 801-02 (N.D.Ohio 1965); Watts v. Cumberland County Hospital System, Inc., 75 N.C.App. 1, 330 S.E.2d 242, 248-50 (N.C.App. 1985), *rev'd on other grounds*, 317 N.C. 321, 345 S.E.2d 201 (N.C. 1986).

[769]Jaffee v. Redmond, 518 U.S. 1, 15, 116 S. Ct. 1923 (1996). This privilege is applicable to prison psychotherapy. *See, e.g., In re* Sims, 534 F.3d 117, 134-41 (2d Cir. 2008) (holding prisoner plaintiff had not forfeited the privilege). However, it is limited to communications made to a licensed psychotherapist, in confidence, and in the course of diagnosis and treatment. *See* U.S. v. Romo, 413 F.3d 1044, 1049 (9th Cir. 2005) (confession to prison counselor that was not in the course of counseling, treatment, or a therapy session was not privileged even though the counselor had treated the prisoner in the past).

[770]Whalen v. Roe, 429 U.S. 589, 602 n.28, 97 S. Ct. 869 (1977). Federal courts are not governed by that privilege in cases based on federal law. Northwestern Memorial Hosp. v. Ashcroft, 362 F.3d 923, 926 (7th Cir. 2004); Gilbreath v. Guadalupe Hosp. Foundation Inc., 5 F.3d 785, 791 (5th Cir. 1993).

treatment.[771] Medical treatment to which the patient has not consented may constitute an assault and/or battery.[772] The right is not absolute and may be overridden under some circumstances, *e.g.*, where there is a strong public health reason to administer the treatment.[773] Whether persons can be made to submit to medical procedures for law enforcement purposes depends on the intrusiveness of the procedure and the strength of the law enforcement need.[774]

The right to refuse treatment extends to prisoners.[775] However, it may be restricted for valid reasons. Claims of compelled treatment are usually assessed under the *Turner v. Safley*[776] reasonable relationship standard.[777] The Supreme Court, applying *Turner*, has held that prisoners with "serious mental illness" may be involuntarily medicated with antipsychotic drugs if "the inmate is dangerous to himself or others and the treatment is in the inmate's medical interest."[778] Prisoners may not refuse examinations or treatment for communicable diseases even if they have religious objections to them.[779] The majority of courts have held that prisoners may not refuse treatment that is necessary to save

---

[771]Cruzan by Cruzan v. Director, Mo. Dep't of Health, 497 U.S. 261, 277–78, 110 S. Ct. 2841 (1990).

[772]*See* § F.5, n.792, below.

[773]Jacobson v. Massachusetts, 197 U.S. 11, 25–39, 25 S. Ct. 358 (1905) (smallpox vaccination could be required despite religious objections).

[774]Winston v. Lee, 470 U.S. 753, 759–66, 105 S. Ct. 1611 (1985). In *Winston*, the Court held that under the Fourth Amendment's protection against unreasonable searches, a criminal defendant could not be forced to submit to the surgical removal under general anesthesia of a bullet that might be evidence of a crime. It contrasted this serious intrusion to the minor intrusion involved in taking a blood sample, which is permissible for law enforcement purposes under *Schmerber v. California*, 384 U.S. 757, 86 S. Ct. 1826 (1966). *See also* U.S. v. Husband, 226 F.3d 626, 636 (7th Cir. 2000) (permissibility of anesthetizing an arrestee to recover drugs held in mouth depends on the magnitude of the risk presented, the imminence of the potential loss of evidence to the prosecution, and the extent of the supposed medical risk faced by the arrestee without the medical intrusion).

[775]The Supreme Court, in finding that there is a right to refuse treatment in the *Cruzan* case, 497 U.S. at 277, relied on two prison cases: *Washington v. Harper*, 494 U.S. 210, 221, 110 S. Ct. 1028 (1989) (holding that prisoners have "a significant liberty interest in avoiding the unwanted administration of antipsychotic drugs") and *Vitek v. Jones*, 445 U.S. 480, 494 100 S. Ct. 1254 (1980) (holding that transfer to a mental hospital coupled with mandatory behavior modification treatment implicated a constitutional liberty interest). *See* White v. Napoleon, 897 F.2d 103, 113 (3d Cir. 1990); Runnels v. Rosendale, 499 F.2d 733, 735 (9th Cir. 1974) (allegation of surgery without consent stated a constitutional claim); Clarkson v. Coughlin, 898 F. Supp. 1019, 1049 (S.D.N.Y. 1995) (lack of sign language interpreters denied deaf prisoners the right to refuse treatment).

[776]482 U.S. 78, 107 S. Ct. 2254 (1987). This standard is discussed in Ch. 3, § A.

[777]Russell v. Richards, 384 F.3d 444, 447–48 (7th Cir. 2004); Iseley v. Dragovich, 236 F. Supp. 2d 472, 479 (E.D.Pa. 2002); *In re* Soliman, 134 F. Supp. 2d 1238, 1253 (N.D.Ala. 2001). In *Russell v. Richards*, the court upheld a requirement that prisoners newly admitted to jail use a delousing shampoo, and explained that officials need not meet the higher standards required for involuntary psychotropic medication because delousing "poses a much less serious intrusion on an inmate's autonomy," since it is applied externally and is not "mind-altering." Russell v. Richards, 384 F.3d at 450.

In *White v. Napoleon*, the court held that the right to refuse may be overcome "when prison officials, in the exercise of professional judgment, deem it necessary to carry out valid medical or penological objectives. . . . [T]he judgment of prison authorities will be presumed valid unless it is shown to be such a substantial departure from accepted professional judgment, practice or standards as to demonstrate that the person responsible actually did not base the decision on such judgment." 897 F.2d at 113. The court did not explain what kinds of objectives might justify forcible treatment. Similarly, in *Roper v. Grayson*, 81 F.3d 124 (10th Cir. 1996), the diabetic plaintiff was forced to take insulin, and the court said: "The defendants' interest in protecting Plaintiff and their constitutional duty to provide him with adequate medical care outweighed his interest to reject the medical treatment." 81 F.3d at 125. The court did not indicate what limits there might be on prison officials' power to impose "adequate medical treatment," and its broad statement appears to be inconsistent with *Cruzan* and other decisions that recognize a right to refuse treatment.

[778]Washington v. Harper, 494 U.S. 210, 227, 110 S. Ct. 1028 (1990). The Court based this holding on application of the *Turner v. Safley* standard. 494 U.S. at 224–28; *see* § F.4.a of this chapter for further discussion of forced medication. Compelled participation in sex offender treatment is discussed in § F.4.b of this chapter.

In *Johnson v. Meltzer*, 134 F.3d 1393, 1397 (9th Cir. 1998), the court applied *Washington*'s "medically appropriate" requirement to a case where an arrestee who was unconscious and could not consent was administered a drug not yet approved by the Food and Drug Administration. The court said that if the drug was given for the plaintiff's benefit, it was lawful, but if it was done for research purposes, it was not.

[779]McCormick v. Stalder, 105 F.3d 1059, 1061 (10th Cir. 1997) (prisoner who tested positive for tuberculosis could be required to submit to INH medication therapy or be isolated); Thompson v. City of Los Angeles, 885 F.2d 1439, 1447 (9th Cir. 1989) (x-ray and blood sample can be required); Zaire v. Dalsheim, 698 F. Supp. 57, 59–60 (S.D.N.Y. 1988) (no right to refuse diphtheria-tetanus injection), *aff'd*, 904 F.2d 33 (2d Cir. 1990); Ballard v. Woodard, 641 F. Supp. 432, 436–37 (W.D.N.C. 1986) (no right to refuse tuberculosis test); Smallwood-El v. Coughlin, 589 F. Supp. 692, 699–700 (S.D.N.Y. 1984) (no right to refuse intake examination for communicable diseases; prisoner could be segregated for refusing); Ormond v. State, 599 So.2d 951, 957–58 (Miss. 1992); *see also* cases cited in § F.4.d of this chapter, n.577, holding that prison officials may screen inmates for HIV infection.

That does not mean that prison officials can conduct medical tests at will on unwilling prisoners. In *Walker v. Sumner*, 917 F.2d 382, 386–88 (9th Cir. 1990), the court held that compulsory blood tests for AIDS, allegedly intended only to help train state medical workers, might be unconstitutional unless prison officials explained their relevance to a legitimate penological objective. *See also* Irwin v. Arrendale, 117 Ga.App. 1, 159 S.E.2d 719, 726 (Ga.App. Nov 16, 1967) (compulsory x-ray done without good cause would state a claim for "technical assault and battery").

their lives, citing the danger to prison order if an inmate is allowed to die as well as the danger that prisoners may use the threat of death to manipulate prison officials or the criminal justice system.[780] Courts have reached varying results in cases where prison officials or medical staff demanded that prisoners accept an unwanted form of treatment in order to receive other treatment that they needed and wanted.[781] Security or law enforcement personnel who assist in forcing medical care on prisoners in reliance on instructions from medical personnel are generally not held liable.[782]

A prisoner's refusal of treatment will often absolve officials of any responsibility for the consequences.[783]

_____

[780]Polk County Sheriff v. Iowa Dist. Court for Polk County, 594 N.W.2d 421 (Iowa 1999); Commissioner of Correction v. Myers, 379 Mass. 255, 399 N.E.2d 452, 457 (Mass. 1979); Von Holden v. Chapman, 87 A.D.2d 66, 450 N.Y.S.2d 623, 625–27 (N.Y. App.Div. 1982); State ex rel. Schuetzle v. Vogel, 537 N.W.2d 358 (N.D. 1995); Pennsylvania Dep't of Public Welfare v. Kallinger, 134 Pa.Cmwlth. 415, 580 A.2d 887, 889–92 (Pa.Commw. 1990), *appeal dismissed*, 615 A.2d 730 (Pa. 1992). *Contra*, Zant v. Prevatte, 248 Ga. 832, 286 S.E.2d 715 (Ga. 1982); Stouffer v. Reid, ___ A.2d ___, 2010 WL 1526472 (Md. 2010). Similarly, the majority of courts have held that a hunger-striking prisoner can be force-fed. *See* cases cited in § D of this chapter, n.216.

[781]The different outcomes probably reflect the great difference in facts. In *Iseley v. Dragovich*, 236 F. Supp. 2d 472, 479 (E.D.Pa. 2002), the court upheld a requirement that prisoners seeking Hepatitis C treatment undergo a psychological evaluation. The purpose of the examination was to assess the risk of psychological side effects from the medication; the court said it was "part and parcel of the treatment." In *Harrison v. Barkley*, 219 F.3d 132, 138 (2d Cir. 2000), however, the court held that refusing to fill a dental cavity unless the prisoner agreed to the extraction of some of his few other remaining teeth constituted deliberate indifference, describing it as "imposition of a seriously unreasonable condition" on treatment of a painful degenerative medical problem.

[782]*See* Sullivan v. Bornemann, 384 F.3d 372, 377–78 (7th Cir. 2004) (where officers assisted in forcible catherization, court refuses to place them "in the impossible position of having to second-guess the medical judgments of emergency room physicians"; stating *Cruzan* holding has little application in view of the state's interest in "assuring the medical stability of its pretrial detainees"); Tinius v. Carroll County Sheriff Dep't, 321 F. Supp. 2d 1064, 1074–75 (N.D.Iowa 2004) (deputies who forcibly assisted in catheterization were engaged in "community caretaking" in which "reasonableness has a fluid quality"); Saulsberry v. Maricopa County, 151 F. Supp. 2d 1109, 1116, 1118 (D.Ariz. 2001) (rejecting Fourth Amendment claim on the grounds that a medical intrusion is not a search; holding defendants were entitled to qualified immunity on right to refuse claim, for restraining a prisoner for involuntary catheterization).

[783]Walker v. Peters, 233 F.3d 494, 502 (7th Cir. 2000) (prison officials could not be held liable for refusing AIDS treatment to a prisoner who refused to be tested for the disease); Groman v. Township of Manalapan, 47 F.3d 628, 633 (3d Cir. 1985); Higgins v. Correctional Medical Services of Ill., 8 F. Supp. 2d 821, 826 (N.D.Ill. 1998) (prisoner's refusal to let medical personnel palpate his arm,

The circumstances, if any, under which prison officials might be *required* to impose treatment over objection are not well defined.[784]

The common law right to refuse treatment is part of the doctrine of "informed consent."[785] Courts have held that the Constitution protects prisoners' right of informed consent, *i.e.*, "a right to such information as is reasonably necessary to make an informed decision to accept or reject proposed treatment, as well as a reasonable explanation of the viable alternative treatments that can be made available in a prison setting."[786]

5. Negligence and Malpractice

Negligence by medical personnel does not violate the Constitution, but it is generally a tort under state law. The negligence of doctors is called medical malpractice. A doctor commits malpractice if she causes injury by failing "to have and use the knowledge, skill and care ordinarily possessed and employed by members of the profession in good standing."[787] To avoid malpractice, the doctor must utilize ordinary knowledge, skill, and care both in diagnosis and in treatment.[788] The mere fact that treatment is unsuccessful or has a bad result does not make it malpractice,[789] and malpractice is not proven just because you or a different doctor disagree with a course of

_____

the preferred method for assessing an alleged dislocation, is an effective bar to liability); Dias v. Vose, 865 F. Supp. 53, 58 (D.Mass. 1994).

[784]*See* Sanville v. McCaughtry, 266 F.3d 724, 734 (7th Cir. 2001) (allowing a prisoner with mental illness to refuse treatment despite his bizarre behavior was a medical judgment and not deliberate indifference); Thompson v. Upshur County, Texas, 245 F.3d 447, 459 (5th Cir. 2001) (holding defendants entitled to qualified immunity for failing to treat delirium tremens of prisoner who refused treatment and died); Walker v. Peters, 233 F.3d 494, 500 (7th Cir. 2000) (holding that refusal to make a competent adult prisoner take an HIV test—which was necessary in order for him to receive HIV treatment—over his objection was not deliberate indifference).

[785]Cruzan by Cruzan v. Director, Mo. Dep't of Health, 497 U.S. 261, 267-70, 110 S. Ct. 2841 (1990).

[786]White v. Napoleon, 897 F.2d 103, 113 (3d Cir. 1990); Clarkson v. Coughlin, 898 F. Supp. 1019, 1049 (S.D.N.Y. 1995) (lack of sign language interpreters denied deaf inmates the right to informed consent). *But see* McAleese v. Owens, 770 F. Supp. 255, 263 (M.D.Pa. 1991) (deliberate indifference standard applied to failure to inform prisoner of adverse consequences of medication). *See also* n. 791 in the next section concerning informed consent.

[787]W. Page Keeton et al., *Prosser and Keeton on the Law of Torts* § 32, at 187 (5th ed. 1984). The same idea is phrased in various ways in different states. *See, e.g.*, Chambers v. Ingram, 858 F.2d 351, 355 (7th Cir. 1988) (Illinois law); Hutchinson v. U.S., 838 F.2d 390, 392 (9th Cir. 1988) (California law); Berman v. U.S., 205 F. Supp. 2d 362, 364 (M.D.Pa. 2002).

[788]Yosuf v. U.S., 642 F. Supp. 415, 428 (M.D.Pa. 1986).

[789]Todd v. U.S., 570 F. Supp. 670, 677 (D.S.C. 1983); Lemke v. U.S., 557 F. Supp. 1205, 1212 (D.N.D. 1983); *see* Marricone v. U.S., 703 F. Supp. 384, 388 (E.D.Pa. 1989) (the patient died but there was no evidence of negligence).

treatment.[790] Under the "informed consent" doctrine, doctors must also provide their patients with enough information about the risks of medical treatment that they can decide sensibly whether to submit to the treatment.[791] Performing a medical procedure against a patient's will may be an assault and/or battery.[792]

The plaintiff in a malpractice case must submit evidence of what the standard of care is—*i.e.*, what the doctor should have done consistent with ordinary skill, care, and knowledge. Some states' law measures the standard of care by local medical practice, some use a "similar locality" standard, and some use national standards of practice.[793] The duty of care owed to prisoners is the same as that owed to private patients.[794] Medical personnel who undertake to treat specialized problems are held to the standard of care applicable to those specialties, even if they do not claim specialized expertise.[795] Expert evidence is required to establish the standard of care unless the issue is one that is within the common knowledge of lay people[796]—*e.g.*, failure to dispense an antibiotic prescribed for an infected surgical site.[797] Expert evidence is also generally needed to show that there was a deviation from the standard,[798] again unless common knowledge suffices to decide the question.[799] You will probably not be excused from this expert evidence requirement just because you are a *pro se* prisoner.[800] Under some circumstances, however, you can satisfy the expert requirement with something less than your own retained expert witness.[801]

---

[790]Fitzgerald v. Manning, 679 F.2d 341, 347 (4th Cir. 1982); *Prosser and Keeton on the Law of Torts* § 32, at 187.

[791]Cruzan by Cruzan v. Director, Mo. Dep't of Health, 497 U.S. 261, 269–77, 110 S. Ct. 2841 (1990); Marino v. Ballestas, 749 F.2d 162, 167 (3d Cir. 1984); Harbeson v. Parke Davis, Inc., 746 F.2d 517, 521–22 (9th Cir. 1984); Matter of Conroy, 98 N.J. 321, 486 A.2d 1209, 1222 (N.J. 1985); *Prosser and Keeton on the Law of Torts* § 32 at 189–90. *See also* n. 786 in the previous section concerning informed consent.

[792]*Cruzan*, 497 U.S. at 269–70 (citing W. Page Keeton et al., *Prosser and Keeton on the Law of Torts* § 9, at 39–42 (5th ed. 1984)); Gindraw v. Dendler, 967 F. Supp. 833, 840 (E.D.Pa. 1997) (extracting the wrong tooth might be a battery by the dentist; "Performing a medical procedure without informed consent is a technical assault and battery."); Irwin v. Arrendale, 159 S.E.2d at 726 (compulsory x-ray done without good cause would state a claim for "technical assault and battery"); *see* Blissett v. Eisensmidt, 940 F. Supp. 449, 451(N.D.N.Y. 1996) (noting jury verdict finding battery based on forcible injection by nurse).

[793]*Prosser and Keeton on the Law of Torts* § 32, at 187–88; *see* Chambers v. Ingram, 858 F.2d at 356 (citing Illinois "similar locality" rule); Morrison v. Washington County, Ala., 700 F. Supp. 678, 684–85 (11th Cir. 1983) (citing Alabama's "national medical community" standard).

[794]District of Columbia v. Mitchell, 533 A.2d 629, 648 (D.C.1987); Moss v. Miller, 254 Ill.App.3d 174, 625 N.E.2d 1044, 1052 (1993); Calloway v. City of New Orleans, 524 So.2d 182, 186–87 (La.App. 4 Cir. 1988) (medical "corpsman" was obliged to exercise the same standard of care while working in a prison as while working in a hospital); Matter of Rules Adoption Regarding Inmate-Therapist Confidentiality N.J.A.C. 10A:16-4.4, 224 N.J.Super. 252, 261–62, 540 A.2d 212, 217 (1988); Harrell v. City of Belen, 93 N.M. 612, 620, 603 P.2d 722, 729 (N.M.App., 1979): Douglas v. County of Oswego, 151 Misc.2d 239, 573 N.Y.S.2d 236, 238 (N.Y.Sup. 1991); Bowers v. County of Essex, 118 Misc.2d 943, 461 N.Y.S.2d 959, 961 (N.Y.Sup. 1983) (doctor must prescribe appropriate care even if the Sheriff refuses to approve it); Sloan v. Ohio Dep't of Rehab. & Corr., 119 Ohio App.3d 331, 334, 695 N.E.2d 298 (Ohio App. 1997); Shea v. City of Spokane, 17 Wash. App. 236, 562 P.2d 264, 270 (Wash.App. 1977), *aff'd*, 90 Wash.2d 43, 578 P.2d 42 (1978). *But see* Cole v. Acadia Parish Sheriff's Dep't, 998 So.2d 212, 216–17 (La.App. 2008) (duty under state statutes was to provide "reasonable care"), *writ denied*, 999 So.2d 784 (La. 2009).

[795]Williams v. U.S., 747 F. Supp. 967, 1009 (S.D.N.Y. 1990).

[796]Chambers v. Ingram, 858 F.2d at 356–57; Hutchinson v. U.S., 838 F.2d 390, 392–93 (9th Cir. 1988); *Prosser and Keeton on the Law of Torts* § 32, at 188–89. *But see* Fitzgerald v. Corrections Corp. of America, 403 F.3d 1134, 1144–45 (10th Cir. 2005) (plaintiff was not required to produce expert evidence to defend a summary judgment motion where defendants' evidence was completely inadequate to support the motion).

[797]Gil v. Reed, 381 F.3d 649, 660–61 (7th Cir. 2004) (comparing that failure to leaving a sponge inside the patient during surgery); *see* Bryan v. Shah, 351 F. Supp. 2d 295, 301–02 (D.N.J. 2005) (lay people would know that disregarding orders from a treating doctor deviates from the standard of care).

[798]Wolfe v. Horn, 130 F. Supp. 2d 648, 659 (E.D.Pa. 2001) (requiring expert testimony that the disputed treatment fell below the applicable standard of care, to a reasonable degree of medical certainty); Gindraw v. Dendler, 967 F. Supp. 833, 838–39 (E.D.Pa. 1997) (expert evidence needed to show that breaking a tooth and leaving the roots in the jaw, and using more force than necessary to extract a tooth, constitute malpractice).

[799]Gindraw v. Bendler, 967 F. Supp. at 837–38 (noting that leaving sponges or surgical instruments in the body or operating on the wrong body part may be sufficiently obvious to the lay person that expert testimony may be unnecessary).

[800]*See* Gunter v. State, 153 Ariz. 386, 736 P.2d 1193, 1200 (Ariz. App. 1987); Buerger v. Ohio Dep't of Rehabilitation and Correction, 64 Ohio App.3d 394, 581 N.E.2d 1114, 1116–18 (Ohio App. 1989).

Some courts have relaxed the requirement a bit. *See* Jackson v. Fauver, 334 F. Supp. 2d 697, 740 (D.N.J. 2004) (accepting testimony of one physician for multiple problems even though he was not a specialist in all of them; "requiring indigent inmates with complaints about substandard medical treatment to obtain specialists in every applicable medical field is unreasonably burdensome."), *reconsideration granted on other grounds*, 2005 WL 1677513 (D.N.J., June 29, 2005).

[801]In one case, where the issue was the failure of prison personnel to follow a surgeon's directions, the court held that the surgeon's "angry reaction and reassertion of his earlier instructions [when he learned prison personnel were not following them]" were enough to raise a genuine factual issue barring summary judgment. Gil v. Reed, 381 F.3d 649, 660 (7th Cir. 2004) ("We hold that Gil may rely on his treating physicians to establish the standard of care, even if those physicians are agents of defendants.").

The plaintiff must show that the injuries for which she seeks damages were the cause of the injury she claims.[802]

The main difference between the malpractice standard and deliberate indifference is that malpractice includes ordinary mistakes and inadvertence, while deliberate indifference does not.[803] For example, in one case a prison doctor was held not to be deliberately indifferent for failing to diagnose spinal cancer, since by missing the diagnosis he lacked the "actual knowledge" required for deliberate indifference. However, he could be found negligent, and to have committed malpractice, if he *should* have known that the plaintiff's spinal cord was being compressed.[804] Other typical examples of malpractice include leaving sponges inside the patient after an operation,[805] failing to give necessary medication,[806] prescribing inappropriate medication,[807] failing to perform appropriate diagnostic tests,[808] delaying examination and treatment,[809] etc.[810] These actions may or may not constitute deliberate indifference as well, depending on their seriousness and other circumstances.

In most cases, if you are complaining about a doctor's inadequate treatment or diagnosis, your claim on the merits will be stronger in a malpractice suit than a civil rights suit. If you are complaining about the system's failure to get you to medical staff for diagnosis and treatment, or failure to see that you receive care that has been ordered, your chances may be better in a federal civil rights action, or in a state law action for negligence by administrative personnel. However, in order to decide which claims to bring, you must also take into account the immunity rules and the rules concerning who can be sued that govern negligence and malpractice cases in your state.[811] In some cases these rules will mean that you cannot bring suit even if negligence or malpractice occurred.[812]

Non-physicians performing medical services—nurses, physicians' assistants, technicians, etc.—may be found liable for malpractice or negligence if they fail to have and to use the knowledge, skill, and care expected of their professions[813] or if they disobey physicians' directions.[814] They may not be held to the same standard as a physician[815] and generally

---

[802]Miller v. Corrections Corp. of America, 375 F. Supp. 2d 889, 901–02 (D.Alaska 2005) (rejecting claim of negligence in providing speech therapy where plaintiff's expert couldn't say with certainty that the lack of therapy made his condition worse).

[803]The facts that establish deliberate indifference are likely also to establish malpractice or negligence. Wolfe v. Horn, 130 F. Supp. 2d 648, 659 (E.D.Pa. 2001); Nelson v. Prison Health Services, 991 F. Supp. 1452, 1466 (N.D.Fla. 1997). The opposite is not necessarily true; there are many sets of facts that establish malpractice or negligence but not deliberate indifference. However, a finding of malpractice does not preclude a finding of deliberate indifference. Hathaway v. Coughlin, 99 F.3d 550, 553–54 (2d Cir. 1996).

[804]Coppage v. Mann, 906 F. Supp. 1025, 1040, 1049 (E.D.Va. 1995); *see* Toombs v. Bell, 915 F.2d 345, 347 (8th Cir. 1991) (medical technician's failure to examine or treat a prisoner with abdominal pain was malpractice; constitutional claim had been dismissed); Chambers v. Ingram, 858 F.2d 351, 357-59 (7th Cir. 1988) (psychiatrist's failure to conduct a thorough examination and to make adequate reports of her observations and treatment was found to constitute malpractice but not deliberate indifference); Lynsky v. City of Boston, 761 F. Supp. 858, 864–66 (D.Mass. 1990) (failure to order additional diagnostic tests for heart disease based on EKG abnormalities was not deliberate indifference but may have been grossly negligent); Gunter v. State, 153 Ariz. 386, 736 P.2d 1198, 1199 (Ariz.App. 1987) (denial of medication stated a negligence claim even if not "significant" enough to constitute deliberate indifference).

[805]*Prosser and Keeton on the Law of Torts* § 32, at 189.

[806]Jacques v. State, 127 Misc.2d 769, 487 N.Y.S.2d 463, 466 (N.Y.Ct.Cl. 1984); District of Columbia v. Anderson, 597 A.2d 1295, 1298 (D.C.App. 1991).

[807]Haught v. Maceluch, 681 F.2d 291, 303–04 (5th Cir.), *rehearing denied*, 685 F.2d 1385 (5th Cir. 1982).

[808]Sewell v. U.S., 629 F. Supp. 448, 457–58 (W.D.La. 1986).

[809]Tomcik v. Ohio Dep't of Rehabilitation and Correction, 62 Ohio Misc.2d 324, 598 N.E.2d 900, 903–04 (Ohio Ct.Cl. 1991).

[810]*See, e.g.*, Ashker v. California Dep't of Corrections, 112 F.3d 392, 393 (9th Cir. 1997) (noting malpractice verdict for prisoner who was shot in the arm and was treated with a cast rather than being sent to the hospital as the treating surgeon recommended); Haley v. U.S., 739 F.2d 1502, 1505 (10th Cir. 1984) (failure to obtain and review medical records); Powers v. U.S., 589 F. Supp. 1084,

1101 (D.Conn. 1984) (failure to recognize and respond to post-operative complications); Jackson v. U.S., 577 F. Supp. 1377, 1379 (E.D.Mo. 1983) (failure to render proper emergency care).

[811]These subjects are discussed in Ch. 8, §§ C and L.5, concerning tort claims and tort immunities.

[812]*See, e.g.*, Phillips v. Monroe County, Miss., 311 F.3d 369, 375 (5th Cir. 2002) (noting that the waiver of sovereign immunity allowing negligence suits against the state excludes prisoners); Cooper v. Office of the Sheriff of Will County, 333 F. Supp. 2d 728, 732–33 (N.D.Ill. 2004) (state law negligence claim for untreated asthma attack was barred by the state Tort Immunity Act which bars liability for failure to furnish or obtain medical care, except where the employee knows from observation that the prisoner is in need of immediate attention and through willful and wanton conduct doesn't take reasonable action to get it; claim of willful and wanton conduct could go forward, since the statute didn't bar it); Lanford v. Prince George's County, Md., 199 F. Supp. 2d 297, 302 (D.Md. 2002) (negligence claims against a county based on the acts of officers and the jail doctor are barred by state law rules providing immunity for discretionary acts (a category which includes provision of medical care) unless they are done with malice).

[813]Toombs v. Bell, 915 F.2d 345, 348-49 (8th Cir. 1991) (medical technician found negligent); Nelson v. Prison Health Services, 991 F. Supp. 1452, 1466 (N.D.Fla. 1997) (nurses who did not respond to complaint of chest pain could be found liable for malpractice); Drew v. Knowles, 511 So.2d 393, 396 (Fla.App. 1987) (nurse); France v. State, 132 Misc.2d 1031, 506 N.Y.S.2d 254 (N.Y.Ct.Cl. 1986) (prison druggist held negligent for a month's failure to refill anti-itch prescription; ordinary care for a druggist is "the highest practicable degree of prudence, thoughtfulness and vigilance"); Hight v. State, 35 Misc.2d 926, 231 N.Y.S.2d 361, 362–63 (N.Y.Ct.Cl. 1962) (nurse was negligent for leaving prisoner unattended after an enema; the prisoner fainted and was injured).

[814]Abille v. U.S., 482 F. Supp. 703, 706–07 (N.D.Cal. 1980) (nurses were negligent in not following physician's directions regarding safety of mental patient).

[815]Fein v. Permanente Medical Group, 38 Cal.3d 137, 211 Cal. Rptr. 368, 695 P.2d 665, 673–74 (Cal. 1985), *appeal dismissed*, 474

may not be held liable for acts performed at a physician's direction.[816] Their failure to follow state statutes limiting their practice may constitute negligence *per se*.[817]

Prison and jail administrators and other non-medical personnel may be found negligent for acts or omissions that do not involve medical training or judgment but that interfere with medical treatment.[818] The standard applied in such cases is one of ordinary care.[819]

Claims for malpractice and medical negligence that occur while you are in state or local custody can be brought in state court as provided by the statutes and court rules of the particular state.[820] You may be able to join such a claim with a constitutional claim for deliberate indifference if state court rules permit. If you file a constitutional "deliberate indifference" claim in federal court, you may also be able to add a state law tort claim under the supplemental (formerly called "pendent") jurisdiction of the federal court.[821] If the negligence or malpractice occurred when you were in federal custody, you may bring suit in federal court under the Federal Tort Claims Act (FTCA).[822] State law will be applied in such a case.[823] You may join claims under the FTCA and civil rights claims alleging deliberate indifference in the same federal court action.[824]

Many states have instituted requirements that plaintiffs in malpractice or medical negligence cases meet certain requirements, such as submitting their complaints to a screening panel before filing them, or submitting an affidavit from a physician that the case has merit. You will have to comply with such requirements even if you bring your malpractice or negligence case in federal court under the court's supplemental or diversity jurisdiction.[825] Such requirements

U.S. 892 (1985); Calloway v. City of New Orleans, 524 So.2d 182, 186 (La.App.) (jail corpsman is held to a standard of care lower than a physician's but higher than a lay person's), *writ denied*, 530 So.2d 84 (La. 1988); Paris v. Michael Kreitz, Jr., P.A., 75 N.C.App. 365, 331 S.E.2d 234, 245, 247 (N.C.App.), *review denied*, 315 N.C. 185, 337 S.E.2d 858 (N.C. 1985); Morena v. South Hills Health System, 501 Pa. 634, 462 A.2d 680, 685 (Pa. 1983) (ambulance paramedics were not capable of making medical diagnoses).

[816]Lewis v. Sauvey, 708 F. Supp. 167, 168 (E.D.Mich. 1989); Paris v. Michael Kreitz, Jr., P.A., 75 N.C.App. 365, 331 S.E.2d 234, 245, 247 (N.C.App.) (nurses are not liable for obeying doctors' instructions unless they are obviously wrong and harmful), *review denied*, 315 N.C. 185, 337 S.E.2d 858 (N.C. 1985).

[817]Central Anesthesia Assoc., P.C. v. Worthy, 254 Ga. 728, 333 S.E.2d 829, 831–33 (Ga. 1985) (anesthesia performed by a student nurse without a doctor's supervision contrary to a state statute was negligence *per se*).

[818]Kikumura v. Osagie, 461 F.3d 1269, 1301 (10th Cir. 2006) (officers' failure to contact infirmary about visibly ill prisoner supported a negligence claim); Miller v. Corrections Corp. of America, 375 F. Supp. 2d 889 (D.Alaska 2005) (year's delay in providing speech therapy supported negligence claim for failure to meet state law duty to provide prisoners with reasonable medical care); Banks v. Yokemick, 177 F. Supp. 2d 239, 245–46, 253–54 (S.D.N.Y. 2001) (police officer could be found negligent for failing to disclose that he had struck arrestee in the head with a radio, resulting in misdiagnosis and delay in treatment); Muhammed v. U.S., 6 F. Supp. 2d 582, 594 (N.D.Tex. 1998) (finding government negligent in failing to place disabled prisoner in a facility consistent with his medical condition); Finkelstein v. District of Columbia, 593 A.2d 591, 595 (D.C.App. 1991) (officers were negligent in failing to assist inmate having an asthma attack); Ferguson v. Perry, 593 So.2d 273, 277 (Fla.App. 1992) (evidence that police failed to obtain medical care for arrestee who needed it presented a jury question of negligence); Calloway v. City of New Orleans, 524 So.2d at 185–86 (Sheriff was negligent in not transporting miscarrying woman to a hospital); Harris County, Texas v. Jenkins, 678 S.W.2d 639, 644 (Tex.App. 1984) (Sheriff was negligent in failing to provide prescribed medication); Countryman v. County of Winnebago, 90 Ill.Dec. 344, 135 Ill.App. 384, 481 N.E.2d 1255, 1261 (Ill.App. 1985) (jail employees were negligent in taking no action to get injured prisoner to a doctor and failing to see that intake medical questionnaire was completed); Muhammed v. U.S., 6 F. Supp. 2d 582, 594–95 (N.D.Tex. 1998) (awarding damages for failure to place disabled prisoner in a facility consistent with his medical condition). *But see* Perotti v. Ohio Dep't of Rehabilitation and Correction, 61 Ohio App.3d 86, 572 N.E.2d 172, 176–77 (Ohio App. 1989) (providing non-narcotic pain medications in place of prescribed narcotic medications for security reasons was not negligence).

[819]Countryman v. County of Winnebago, 481 N.E.2d at 1261 ("ordinary and reasonable care for the preservation of [prisoners'] health and life"); Gordon v. City of New York, 120 A.D.2d 562, 502

N.Y.S.2d 215, 216 (N.Y.App.Div. 1986) ("ordinary care . . . to provide for the health and care" of prisoners); Heumphreus v. State, 334 N.W.2d 757, 759 (Iowa 1983) ("reasonable diligence with reference to the care of injured, ill, or diseased inmates").

[820]*See, e.g.*, Herbert v. District of Columbia, 716 A.2d 196, 198–201 (D.C. 1988) (holding the District's duty to exercise reasonable care in providing medical treatment to prisoners could be delegated to a private provider, and the District could not be held liable for the provider's negligence); *see* Ch. 8, § C.1, concerning state tort claims. You may also file such a claim in federal court based on federal diversity jurisdiction if you are a resident of a different state from the one where the negligence or malpractice occurred. *See* Ch. 8, § F.2, concerning diversity jurisdiction.

[821]You cannot do this if the defendant under state law is the state itself, though you may be able to do so if the defendants are state employees or city or county government or employees *See* Ch. 8, § F.1, on supplemental jurisdiction.

[822]*See* Ch. 8, § C.2, H.2.b, on the FTCA; *see, e.g.*, Berman v. U.S., 205 F. Supp. 2d 362 (M.D.Pa. 2002) (awarding substantial damages for failure to provide adequate follow-up treatment for ileostomy).

[823]There is one exception. A federal statute requires the Bureau of Prisons to "provide suitable quarters and provide for the safekeeping, care, and subsistence" of federal prisoners. 18 U.S.C. § 4042. Where the prisoner's complaint involves that duty, as opposed to pure medical malpractice, the federal statute governs regardless of state law, and state law serves only to "flesh out" the elements of liability. Muhammed v. U.S., 6 F. Supp. 2d 582, 594 (N.D.Tex. 1998) (awarding substantial damages for failure to place disabled prisoner in a facility consistent with his medical condition).

[824]*See* Ch. 8, § H.2.b, for a discussion of the consequences of this strategy.

[825]Little v. Tall, 195 F. Supp. 2d 199, 201 (D.Me. 2002) (dismissing negligence claim for failure to comply with statute requiring submission to a pre-litigation panel); Turner v. Sullivan, 937 F.

are also applied to claims under the FTCA, which are governed by state law.[826] State malpractice procedural requirements do not apply to constitutional civil rights claims in federal court[827] (or in state court § 1983 actions either, it would appear[828]).

G. PERSONAL SAFETY

The Constitution requires prison and jail officials to provide "reasonable safety" for prisoners.[829] They must protect them from assault by other inmates and from unreasonably hazardous living and working conditions, and must refrain from subjecting them to the unnecessary and excessive use of force. In the next three sections we discuss each of these issues in detail.

Supp. 79, 80 (D.Mass. 1996) (referring malpractice claim to state panel as state statute required); Jolly v. Klein, 923 F. Supp. 931, 948 (S.D.Tex. 1996) (staying, rather than dismissing, to give plaintiff the opportunity to comply with the state malpractice notice statute).

Requirements of an affidavit or certificate of merit may not apply where the plaintiff's claim is one that is supported by common sense or common knowledge. *See* Natale v. Camden County Correctional Facility, 318 F.3d 575, 580 (3d Cir. 2003) (common sense would tell laypeople that medical personnel charged with caring for an insulin-dependent diabetic should determine how often the diabetic needs insulin"); Bryan v. Shah, 351 F. Supp. 2d 295, 301–02 (D.N.J. 2005) (lay people would know that disregarding orders from a treating doctor deviates from the standard of care).

You must read these statutes closely to see whether they are actually applicable to your claim. *See, e.g.,* Freeman v. Fairman, 916 F. Supp. 786, 792 (N.D.Ill. 1996) (claim against non-physicians for breaching statutory duty to "exercise ordinary and reasonable care for the preservation of [prisoners'] health and life" was not a malpractice claim and not subject to the procedural requirements for such claims).

[826]Callahan v. Cho, 437 F. Supp. 2d 557, 561–62 (E.D.Va. 2006); LaFramboise v. Thompson, 329 F. Supp. 2d 1054, 1057–58 (D.N.D. 2004), *aff'd,* 439 F.3d 792 (8th Cir. 2006); Stanley v. U.S., 321 F. Supp. 2d 805, 808–09 (N.D.W.Va. 2004).

[827]Faulkingham v. Penobscot County Jail, 350 F. Supp. 2d 285, 287–88 (D.Me. 2004); Cordray v. County of Lincoln, 320 F. Supp. 2d 1171, 1173–74 (D.N.M. 2004).

[828]In *Felder v. Casey,* 487 U.S. 131, 108 S. Ct. 2302 (1988), the Supreme Court held that a state "notice of claim" requirement for suits against state agencies or officials did not apply to § 1983 suits filed in state court because it was in conflict with the purposes of § 1983. That holding appears to bar application of state malpractice requirements to § 1983 suits. Congress has provided for exhaustion of administrative remedies in prison cases, but completing the prison grievance process should satisfy that requirement. *See* Ch. 10, § D.

[829]Farmer v. Brennan, 511 U.S. 825, 844, 114 S. Ct. 1970 (1994); Helling v. McKinney, 509 U.S. 25, 33, 113 S. Ct. 2475 (1993) (quoting DeShaney v. Winnebago County Dep't of Social Services, 489 U.S. 189, 200, 109 S. Ct. 998 (1989)).

1. Protection from Inmate Assault

Prison officials must take reasonable measures to protect prisoners from assault by other inmates, including sexual assault.[830] If they fail to do so, courts may award damages to injured prisoners[831] or injunctions to prisoners who are in danger.[832]

a. The Deliberate Indifference Standard Prison officials are not automatically liable for all inmate assaults.

---

[830]Farmer v. Brennan, 511 U.S. 825, 833, 114 S. Ct. 1970 (1994). The plaintiff in *Farmer* complained of rape as well as of being beaten,.511 U.S. at 831.

[831]*See, e.g.,* Cantu v. Jones, 293 F.3d 839, 843–44 (5th Cir. 2002) (affirming award of $22,500 for razor blade assault resulting in 52 stitches); Newman v. Holmes, 122 F.3d 650, 651 (8th Cir. 1997) (affirming $500 each for two prisoners who were assaulted and cut); Wright v. Jones, 907 F.2d 848, 850, 852 (8th Cir. 1990) ($1000 compensatory damages, and $225 punitive damages against each defendant, for severe beating); Mayberry v. Walters, 862 F.2d 1040, 1041–42 (3d Cir. 1990); Walsh v. Mellas, 837 F.2d 789, 791, 801–02 (7th Cir. 1988); Stokes v. Delcambre, 710 F.2d 1120, 1124–28 (5th Cir. 1983); Hutchinson v. McCabee, 168 F. Supp. 2d 101, 102–04 (S.D.N.Y. 2001) (noting award of $392,000 for permanent injury that limited plaintiff's future ability to work); Miller v. Shelby County, 93 F. Supp. 2d 892, 902 (W.D.Tenn. 2000) (awarding $40,000 for impairment of the right shoulder, a scalp puncture wound, and a frozen right shoulder, headaches, and blurred vision).

Some decisions hold that a prisoner who is subjected to a risk of assault, but is not actually assaulted, cannot recover damages. *See, e.g.,* Babcock v. White, 102 F.3d 267, 273–74 (7th Cir. 1996). Other decisions are to the contrary. *See, e.g.,* Benefield v. McDowall, 241 F.3d 1267, 1271 (10th Cir. 2001); Hobbs v. Lockhart, 46 F.3d 864, 866, 869 (8th Cir. 1995) (plaintiff was chased by assailant but escaped). Under the Prison Litigation Reform Act, however, claims of exposure to a risk of assault that does not lead to injury are generally held subject to 42 U.S.C. § 1997e(e), which prohibits recovery of compensatory damages for mental or emotional injury without physical injury. *See* Ch. 9, § E.

[832]Farmer v. Brennan, 511 U.S. at 845–46; *see, e.g.,* Jensen v. Clarke, 94 F.3d 1191, 1200–01 (8th Cir. 1996) (enjoining officials to use classification process in assigning cellmates); Ruiz v. Estelle, 679 F.2d 1115, 1140–42 (5th Cir. 1982) (overcrowding to be reduced); Skinner v. Uphoff, 234 F. Supp. 2d 1208, 1217–18 (D. Wyo. 2002) (injunction to be formulated to control violence in jail); Fisher v. Koehler, 692 F. Supp. 1519, 1565–66 (S.D.N.Y. 1988), *aff'd,* 902 F.2d 2 (2d Cir. 1990); Withers v. Levine, 449 F. Supp. 473, 479 (D.Md. 1978) (procedures for safe placement to be promulgated), *aff'd,* 615 F.2d 158 (4th Cir. 1980); Doe v. Lally, 467 F. Supp. 1339, 1354–57 (D.Md. 1979) (classification required).

A prisoner need not wait until an assault has occurred before obtaining injunctive relief. Farmer v. Brennan, 511 U.S. at 845; Riley v. Jeffes, 777 F.2d 143, 147 (3d Cir. 1985). However, courts will consider whether a prisoner has used the appropriate internal prison procedures in deciding whether to grant an injunction. *Farmer,* 511 U.S. at 847. Since *Farmer,* the Prison Litigation Reform Act has added a requirement of exhausting administrative remedies before filing any prison conditions suit under federal law. *See* Ch. 9, § D, concerning the exhaustion requirement.

Mere negligence or carelessness do not violate the Constitution.[833] Instead, you must show that prison officials displayed "deliberate indifference" or "reckless disregard" for safety by failing to "act reasonably" in response to danger.[834] In Eighth Amendment cases, this means you must show that prison personnel "[knew] of and disregard[ed] an excessive risk to inmate health or safety; the official must both be aware of facts from which the inference could be drawn that a substantial risk of serious harm exists, and he must also draw the inference."[835] This standard is also generally applied to inmate assault cases involving pretrial detainees, which are brought under the Due Process Clause and not under the Eighth Amendment.[836]

Under this standard, the facts of how an assault happened and what the defendants knew are all-important. Defendants must be shown to have had actual knowledge of the risk; it is not enough that they *should* have known of the risk.[837] Thus, in one case where an officer in a high-security unit violated four separate security rules resulting in a prisoner's being attacked by another prisoner with a known grudge against him, the court held he could not be found deliberately indifferent because he was too stupid to understand the added risk his conduct was creating (he did not "draw the inference").[838] On the other hand, if there is evidence that a risk was obvious, a judge or jury *can* (but are not required to) conclude that defendants had actual knowledge of it.[839] Purposefully avoiding knowledge can also

---

[833]Davidson v. Cannon, 474 U.S. 344, 347–48. 106 S. Ct. 668 (1986); Boyce v. Moore, 314 F.3d 884, 889 (7th Cir. 2002) (failing to review a logbook that would have informed prison staff of a risk to the plaintiff was negligence at most); Tucker v. Evans, 276 F.3d 999, 1001–02 (8th Cir. 2002) (evidence that officer did not pay attention to activities in dormitory showed only negligence); Lewis v. Richards, 107 F.3d 549, 554 (7th Cir. 1997) ("Exercising poor judgment . . . falls short of meeting the standard of consciously disregarding a known risk to [prisoners'] safety."); Gibson v. Foltz, 963 F.2d 851, 854 (6th Cir. 1992); Glenn v. Berndt, 289 F. Supp. 2d 1120, 1125 (N.D.Cal. 2003) (officer who let black and white segregation prisoners out at the same time during a period of racial conflict but said it was an accident was merely negligent and not deliberately indifferent).

Negligence in permitting an assault may constitute a tort under state law. Tort claims based on inmate assault are discussed in § G.1.f of this chapter.

[834]Farmer v. Brennan, 511 U.S. at 828, 834–47, 114 S. Ct. 1970 (1994); *accord*, Goka v. Bobbitt, 862 F.2d 646, 651 (7th Cir. 1988) (the Constitution is violated "where defendants know of the danger or where the threat of violence is so substantial or pervasive that their knowledge could be inferred, and yet defendants fail to embrace a policy or take other reasonable steps which may have prevented the harm"); *see* Clem v. Lomeli, 566 F.3d 1177, 1181–82 (9th Cir. 2009) (jury in assault case should have been instructed that defendants' failure to act, as well as acting, could support finding of deliberate indifference).

Sometimes prison officials argue that in dangerous situations involving inmate–inmate violence, the more demanding "malicious and sadistic" standard applicable to use of force cases, *see* § G.2.a.1 of this chapter, should be applied. However, the Supreme Court has said that deliberate indifference governs Eighth Amendment prison cases except for "*one class* of prison cases: when 'officials stand accused of using excessive physical force.'" Farmer v. Brennan, 511 U.S. at 835 (emphasis supplied); *accord*, MacKay v. Farnsworth, 48 F.3d 491, 492–93 (10th Cir. 1995).

[835]Farmer v. Brennan, 511 U.S. at 837; *see, e.g.*, Taylor v. Michigan Dep't of Corrections, 69 F.3d 76, 84 (6th Cir. 1995) (obvious risk of placing a small, vulnerable prisoner in an open, unstructured camp setting in a system with a pervasive problem of sexual assault could support an inference of knowledge); Reece v. Groose, 60 F.3d 487, 491 (8th Cir. 1995) (prisoner who had been labelled a snitch and placed in protective custody as a result was subjected to a risk sufficiently obvious to support a finding of knowledge).

[836]*See, e.g.*, Crow v. Montgomery, 403 F.3d 598, 601–02 (8th Cir. 2005); Hart v. Sheahan, 396 F.3d 887, 892–93 (7th Cir. 2005);

see also Ch. 6 concerning the rights of pre-trial detainees.

[837]*See, e.g.*, Verdecia v. Adams, 327 F.3d 1171, 1175–76 (10th Cir. 2003) (plaintiff was assaulted by gang members because he was Cuban; the recent occurrence of two incidents of violence between the Latin Kings and Cuban prisoners did not support a deliberate indifference finding because they did not show that prison officials were aware of a risk of further such violence); Mendez v. Walker, 110 F. Supp. 2d 209, 214–16 (W.D.N.Y. 2000) (officer who opened plaintiff's cell, allowing a prisoner who had previously assaulted him to do so again, could not be held liable if he didn't know about the prior fight; the court rejects the argument that it was written in the logbook and the officer should have read it).

Of course, even if they didn't know about the risk at the time of a particular assault, they will presumably know about it after being sued over it and will know about it in the future. Madrid v. Gomez, 889 F. Supp. 1146, 1269–70 (N.D.Cal. 1995) (so holding about the risk of assigning prisoners to double cells without assessing prior assaultive record).

[838]Rich v. Bruce, 129 F.3d 336, 339–40 (4th Cir. 1997); *see* Smith v. Gray, 259 F.3d 933, 934 (8th Cir. 2001) (segregation prisoners flooded their cells in protest, plaintiff was ordered to clean up the water, and the segregation prisoners threatened him; officers who let out one of the prisoners, who then attacked the plaintiff, could not be found liable because they weren't shown to have known there was a risk of assault).

There are cases that take this idea to an even more absurd extreme. Thus, in *Nichols v. Maryland Correctional Institution—Jessup*, 186 F. Supp. 2d 575 (D.Md. 2002), where a prisoner informed an officer about his cellmate's threat of assault, the court said that the officer's failure to do anything about it must have meant that he did not "draw the inference" that his lack of action would increase the danger to the plaintiff. 186 F. Supp. at 581–82. Fortunately, most courts do not reason that way, or prisoners could never win a case of this type.

[839]Farmer v. Brennan, 511 U.S. at 842–43; Horton v. Cockrell, 70 F.3d 397, 401 (5th Cir. 1995) (prisoner who had assaulted multiple other prisoners and tried to start a race riot presented an obvious risk); Taylor v. Michigan Dep't of Corrections, 69 F.3d 76, 84 (6th Cir. 1995) (obvious risk of placing a small, vulnerable prisoner in an open, unstructured camp setting in a system with a pervasive problem of sexual assault could support an inference of knowledge); Reece v. Groose, 60 F.3d 487, 491 (8th Cir. 1995) (prisoner who had been labelled a snitch and placed in protective custody as a result was subjected to a risk sufficiently obvious to support a finding of knowledge). *But see* Washington v. LaPorte County

amount to deliberate indifference.[840] The defendants do not have to know the precise nature of the risk, as long as they know that there is a serious risk to your safety.[841] They do not have to harbor a purpose of harming prisoners, or believe that harm will actually occur, as long as they have actual knowledge of the risk.[842]

To be held liable, prison officials must disregard a risk that is "excessive" or poses a "substantial risk of serious harm";[843] the ordinary risk of running a prison does not violate the Eighth Amendment. Courts assume that prisons are full of dangerous people and they will not hold prison officials responsible for every risk that results in an assault.[844]

They often dismiss isolated failures to protect as "mere negligence" and not as deliberate indifference, even in cases where prison officials failed to act on or pay attention to information in their possession.[845]

In addition, prison officials will not be held liable if they "responded reasonably to the risk, even if the harm ultimately was not averted."[846] However, measures that are not

---

Sheriff's Dep't, 306 F.3d 515, 519 (7th Cir. 2002) (risk resulting from allowing prisoners to choose their own cellmates was not obvious); *see* § I.A of this chapter concerning the deliberate indifference standard.

[840]Farmer v. Brennan, 511 U.S. at 843 n.8; *see* Velez v. Johnson, 395 F.3d 732, 736 (7th Cir. 2005) (officer notified of risk could be held liable even if he didn't know the details of the risk; to hold otherwise "would essentially reward guards who put their heads in the sand by making them immune from suit—the less a guard knows the better. That view is inconsistent with *Farmer*."); Mayoral v. Sheahan, 245 F.3d 934, 940 (7th Cir. 2000) (jury could find officer's testimony that she knew nothing about gangs "incredible and deliberately ignorant"; the *Farmer* standard "is not designed to give officials the motivation to 'take refuge' in the zone between ignorance and actual knowledge"); *see* § I.A of this chapter concerning the deliberate indifference standard.

[841]Velez v. Johnson, 395 F.3d 732, 736 (7th Cir. 2005) (where prisoner pushed an emergency call button and told staff he was having a conflict with his cellmate, officer's claim that he did not know the cellmate was holding a razor blade to the plaintiff's neck, or that the plaintiff would be raped, did not show he lacked knowledge of the risk).

[842]Farmer v. Brennan, 511 U.S. at 836, 842. The Seventh Circuit has said that a prisoner would have to show that staff members have "the motive of allowing or helping prisoners to injure one another." Weiss v. Cooley, 230 F.3d 1027, 1033 (7th Cir. 2000). This holding is contrary to *Farmer*, as the Seventh Circuit itself has conceded in an earlier case. Haley v. Gross, 86 F.3d 630, 641 (7th Cir. 1996).

[843]Farmer v. Brennan, 511 U.S. at 834, 837; *see* Berry v. City of Muskogee, 900 F.2d 1489, 1496 (10th Cir. 1990) (risk that is "very likely to result in a violation of a prisoner's constitutional rights"); Brown v. Hughes, 894 F.2d 1533, 1537 (11th Cir. 1990) ("'a strong likelihood, rather than a mere possibility' of injury"); Frett v. Government of Virgin Islands, 839 F.2d 968, 978 (3d Cir. 1988) (risk "of such a nature and degree that to disregard it was a gross deviation from the standard of care a corrections officer should have exercised in the situation"); Morgan v. District of Columbia, 824 F.2d 1049, 1058 (D.C. Cir. 1987) ("obvious unreasonable risk of violent harm"); Pressly v. Hutto, 816 F.2d 977, 979 (4th Cir. 1987) ("real and imminent risk of harm").

[844]*See, e.g.*, Herndon v. Armontrout, 986 F.2d 1237, 1241–42 (8th Cir. 1993) (officers who left the plaintiffs in a dangerous situation while they controlled another dangerous situation were not liable); Gardner v. Cato, 841 F.2d 105, 107 (5th Cir. 1988) (double-celling the plaintiff with a mentally unstable inmate who had access to cleaning chemicals was not deliberate indifference); Berg v.

Kincheloe, 794 F.2d 457, 461–62 (9th Cir. 1986) (discussing prison officials' difficulties in protecting inmates); Robinson v. U.S. Bureau of Prisons, 244 F. Supp. 2d 57, 64 (S.D.N.Y. 2003) ("The mere allegation that having one corrections officer supervise 219 inmates with violent proclivities, without more, is an insufficient basis upon which a fair minded trier of fact could reasonably conclude that defendants were aware of an excessive risk to Miller's safety or the FCI Ray Brook prison population in general."); Heine v. Receiving Area Personnel, 711 F. Supp. 178, 183–85 (D.Del. 1989) (leaving newly admitted prisoner alone with an inmate worker, who sexually assaulted him, was not deliberate indifference).

[845]For example, in *Davidson v. Cannon*, 474 U.S. 344, 106 S. Ct. 668 (1986), the prisoner sent prison officials a note saying he had been threatened; the assistant superintendent did not view the matter as urgent, and the sergeant to whom he forwarded it forgot about it and went home without telling anyone about it. The lower court found that this conduct was negligent but did not constitute deliberate indifference. 474 U.S. at 346; *see* Fisher v. Lovejoy, 414 F.3d 659, 663–64 (7th Cir. 2005) (holding officer was not deliberately indifferent in leaving a prisoner who had been attacked in proximity to the 18 others who had attacked him, since he didn't anticipate that a second prisoner would have a knife or that they would attack again after being ordered against the wall); Johnston v. Lucas, 786 F.2d 1254, 1258–59 (5th Cir. 1986) (failure to keep plaintiff separate from a prisoner known to have previously threatened him was not deliberate indifference); Cline v. U.S. Dep't of Justice, 525 F. Supp. 825, 827 (D.S.D. 1981) (marshals' failure to act on a judge's instructions to separate the plaintiff from Native American prisoners was merely negligent).

[846]Farmer v. Brennan, 511 U.S. at 844; *accord*, Borello v. Allison, 446 F.3d 742, 748–49 (7th Cir. 2006) (where prisoner had complained that his cellmate was showing signs of mental illness, and officials had him examined by a psychiatrist who found no risk, and then interviewed the two prisoners and concluded the conflict had subsided, they had acted reasonably and were not liable for a later assault); Erickson v. Holloway, 77 F.3d 1078, 1080–81 (8th Cir. 1996) (holding officer who learned of threat and notified officer on next shift before leaving was not deliberately indifferent); Lee v. Carlson, 564 F. Supp. 1048, 1052–53 (M.D.Pa. 1983).

Some courts have said that the lack of a reasonable response does not show an Eighth Amendment violation because reasonableness is a negligence standard. Pagels v. Morrison, 335 F.3d 736, 742 (8th Cir. 2003); Gibbs v. Franklin, 49 F.3d 1206, 1208 (7th Cir. 1995). Such decisions directly contradict *Farmer v. Brennan*.

Similarly, one federal appellate court persists in stating that prison officials can only be held liable if they could "easily" have prevented the assault. Case v. Ahitow, 301 F.3d 605, 607 (7th Cir. 2002). *Farmer* says prison officials must act reasonably, and doesn't limit that holding to situations where it is easy for them to act—a rule that would be very odd in situations where prisoners' lives and safety are at stake. This point is discussed further in § A.2 of this chapter, nn.68–72.

reasonably calculated to ensure safety from violence do not satisfy that obligation.[847] If protective measures prove inadequate in practice, of course, officials are obliged to take further action.[848] Refusing to place a prisoner in protective custody, or removing her from it, may constitute deliberate indifference,[849] though not in all circumstances.[850] Offering to place a prisoner in protective custody may satisfy officials'

legal obligation in some cases[851] (but again, not in all circumstances[852]), and some courts have even held that failing to request protective custody may weigh against holding prison officials liable.[853] However, deliberate indifference may be shown or supported by evidence of obstacles to admission to protective custody[854] or of failure of protective custody actually to provide safety.[855]

Officials' failure to follow their own rules, regulations, or policies concerning protection of prisoners may support a deliberate indifference claim,[856] although violation of

---

[847]Riley v. Olk-Long, 282 F.3d 592, 597 (8th Cir. 2002) (actions that are "not adequate given the known risk" do not defeat liability); Hayes v. New York City Dep't of Correction, 84 F.3d 614, 621 (2d Cir. 1996) (holding official response that did not include transferring the plaintiff or issuing a timely separation order did not defeat liability as a matter of law); Winton v. Board of Commissioners of Tulsa County, Okla., 88 F. Supp. 2d 1247, 1266 (N.D.Okla. 2000); Fisher v. Koehler, 692 F. Supp. 1519, 1565–66 (S.D.N.Y. 1988) (officials' actions to curb jail violence were not sufficient to obviate the need for an injunction), aff'd, 902 F.2d 2 (2d Cir. 1990); see also § A.2 of this chapter, n.66.

[848]See Jensen v. Clarke, 94 F.3d 1191, 1200–01 (8th Cir. 1996) (holding injunction was appropriate despite defendants' post-complaint actions). Cf. Benjamin v. Fraser, 343 F.3d 35, 51–52 (2d Cir. 2003) (holding "largely ineffective" remedial efforts did not defeat liability for long-standing deficiencies in detainee case involving physical conditions).

[849]Hamilton v. Leavy, 117 F.3d 742, 748 (3d Cir. 1997) (holding failure of officials to place plaintiff in protective custody promptly after an officer told other prisoners he was a snitch could be deliberate indifference); Hutchinson v. McCabee, 168 F. Supp. 2d 101, 103 (S.D.N.Y. 2001) (evidence would support finding that official should at least have offered protection while investigating prisoner's account of threat; Boyce v. Fairman, 24 F. Supp. 2d 880, 884, 886 (N.D.Ill. 1998); Hill v. Godinez, 955 F. Supp. 945, 949 (N.D.Ill. 1997) (evidence that plaintiff was attacked after being denied protective custody by members of a gang that defendants knew he must be protected from supported a deliberate indifference claim); see Mayoral v. Sheahan, 245 F.3d 934, 940 (7th Cir. 2000) (evidence that a tier officer brushed off a request for protective custody supported plaintiff's deliberate indifference claim).

[850]Boyce v. Moore, 314 F.3d 884, 890 (7th Cir. 2002) (officials did not know who the attackers were, their motive, or their possible gang affiliation); Lewis v. Richards, 107 F.3d 549, 553–54 (7th Cir. 1997) (denial of protective custody does not establish deliberate indifference; plaintiff must show that the defendants either took no precautions to avoid a known hazard, or that the precautions they took ignored the risk he faced); Jelinek v. Greer, 90 F.3d 242, 244–45 (7th Cir. 1996) (removing plaintiff from protective custody was not deliberate indifference where his own disciplinary offenses provided justification for it, and where defendants sent him to an intermediate "kick-out unit" and not to general population); Davis v. Scott, 94 F.3d 444, 446–47 (8th Cir. 1996) (removal from PC because the prisoners plaintiff feared were not in the prison any more was not deliberate indifference; plaintiff's statements that their friends remained was "vague and unsubstantiated" and did not put defendants on notice of a risk to him); Jones v. Russell, 950 F. Supp. 855, 857 (N.D.Ill. 1996) ("Prison officials have a duty to protect inmates, but prisoners are not entitled to be housed in protective custody on demand"; plaintiff failed to show that defendants knew of a risk to him).

[851]Berry v. Sherman, 365 F.3d 631, 634 (8th Cir. 2004) (plaintiff's refusal to go to protective custody showed there was no substantial risk); Allgood v. Morris, 724 F.2d 1098, 1100 (4th Cir. 1984); Leach v. Dufrain, 103 F. Supp. 2d 542, 550 (N.D.N.Y. 2000); Harris v. Roberts, 719 F. Supp. 879, 881 (N.D.Cal. 1989) (leaving prisoner in a prison in which she had to ask for protective custody was not unconstitutional).

[852]Dellis v. Corrections Corporation of America, 257 F.3d 508, 512 (6th Cir. 2001) (the fact that the prisoner had refused protective custody a year previously did not necessarily excuse a subsequent failure to protect).

[853]Burrell v. Hampshire County, 307 F.3d 1, 9 (1st Cir. 2002) (failure to request protective custody supported reasonableness of defendants' inaction); Blankenship v. Meachum, 840 F.2d 741, 743 (10th Cir. 1988); Freeman v. Godinez, 996 F. Supp. 822, 825 (N.D.Ill. 1998) (whether the plaintiff sought PC is relevant to defendants' knowledge of the risk to him); Artis v. Petrovsky, 638 F. Supp. 51, 54 (W.D.Mo. 1986).

[854]Butler v. Dowd, 979 F.2d 661, 675 (8th Cir. 1992) (en banc); Ruiz v. Estelle, 37 F. Supp. 2d 855, 929 (S.D.Tex. 1999) (citing "high barriers preventing inmates from seeking safekeeping or protective custody" in finding constitutional violation), rev'd on other grounds and remanded, Ruiz v. U.S., 243 F.3d 941 (5th Cir. 2001).

[855]Greene v. Bowles, 361 F.3d 290, 294–95 (6th Cir. 2004) (defendants could be found deliberately indifferent for assault on transgender prisoner by "predatory inmate" housed in protective custody unit); Doe v. Bowles, 254 F.3d 617, 622 (6th Cir. 2001) (staff could be deliberately indifferent for failing to protect prisoner from assault in protective custody); Fischl v. Armitage, 128 F.3d 50, 56–59 (2d Cir. 1997) (evidence that officers in protective custody allowed plaintiff to be assaulted supported a deliberate indifference claim); Reece v. Groose, 60 F.3d 487, 491 (8th Cir. 1995) (placing a prisoner who had been labelled a snitch in protective custody was reasonable, but allowing another prisoner with a history of violence to work there might not have been reasonable); Miller v. Shelby County, 93 F. Supp. 2d 892, 900–01 (W.D.Tenn. 2000) (awarding damages for assault on protective custody prisoner who was assaulted by gang members permitted out of their cells at the same time); see Fisher v. Koehler, 692 F. Supp. 1519, 1528-29 (S.D.N.Y. 1988) (noting high assault rates in protective custody dormitories), aff'd, 902 F.2d 2 (2d Cir. 1990).

[856]Pierson v. Hartley, 391 F.3d 898, 903–04 (7th Cir. 2004) (defendants knew the plaintiff's assailant was in a "meritorious assignment" dorm with him in violation of prison rules); Scicluna v. Wells, 345 F.3d 441, 445 (6th Cir. 2003) (violation of rules requiring separation of co-defendants); Lopez v. LeMaster, 172 F.3d 756, 761 (10th Cir. 1999) ("While [the Oklahoma Department of Health jail standards] do not establish constitutional parameters for the reasonable measures necessary to insure inmate safety, they do provide persuasive authority concerning what is required.");

prison policies does not by itself establish a constitutional violation.[857] The lack of a prison policy addressing a particular problem may be evidence of deliberate indifference[858]— or, if the problem is a particularly unusual one, it may be evidence that defendants do not have knowledge of the risk.[859]

The Supreme Court has said that "it does not matter whether the risk comes from a single source or multiple sources, any more than it matters whether a prisoner faces an excessive risk of attack for reasons personal to him or because all prisoners in his situation face such a risk."[860] Thus there are two kinds of fact situations that can establish deliberate indifference in a prisoner assault case. You can show that prison officials failed to respond to a particular threat or danger to you. Or you can show that you were assaulted as a result of prison conditions or practices that are dangerous to all prisoners or to an identifiable group of them.[861] It is possible for both kinds of facts to be present in the same case.

If prison officials are liable for an assault under the foregoing standards, that liability may extend not only to the intended victim of the assault but to prisoners who are injured trying to stop the assault.[862]

b. Risks to a Particular Prisoner Prison officials or employees may obviously be held liable for an inmate assault if they actively permit or encourage it.[863] They may also be

found deliberately indifferent if they stand by and do nothing about an assault that they witness.[864] However, officers are not required to rush in and physically stop every prison assault regardless of the risk of injury to themselves or the risk that their actions might make the situation more dangerous.[865]

Skinner v. Uphoff, 234 F. Supp. 2d 1208, 1214–15 (D.Wyo. 2002) (failure to follow policy requiring investigation of violent incidents supported deliberate indifference finding); Gulett v. Haines, 229 F. Supp. 2d 806, 821–24 (S.D.Ohio 2002) (failure to follow rule to keep segregation prisoners apart supported deliberate indifference claim); *see* Benner v. McAdory, 165 F. Supp. 2d 773, 778 (N.D.Ill. 2001) ("a systemic lapse in enforcement of a policy critical to ensuring prisoner safety could be sufficient to show deliberate indifference"), *aff'd*, 34 Fed.Appx. 483 (7th Cir. 2002) (unpublished).

[857]Langston v. Peters, 100 F.3d 1235, 1239 (7th Cir. 1996) (double-celling segregation prisoners contrary to prison rules did not show deliberate indifference where prisoners were screened first).

[858]A.M. v. Luzerne County Juvenile Detention Center, 372 F.3d 572, 583 (3d Cir. 2004) (evidence of the lack of a policy or procedure for reviewing and following up on incident reports supported plaintiff's deliberate indifference claim).

[859]Grimsley v. MacKay, 93 F.3d 676, 682 (10th Cir. 1996) (prisoner locked into a maximum security cell was injured by a prisoner who broke his cell window with a scrub brush handle, which had not happened previously).

[860]Farmer v. Brennan, 511 U.S. 825, 843, 114 S.Ct. 1970 (1994).

[861]*Farmer*, 511 U.S. at 843.

[862]Pool v. Missouri Dep't of Corrections and Human Resources, 883 F.2d 640, 645 (8th Cir. 1989).

[863]Leary v. Livingston County Jail, 528 F.3d 438, 442 (7th Cir. 2008) (telling other prisoners that the plaintiff was charged with raping a child supported a deliberate indifference claim); Cantu v. Jones, 293 F.3d 839, 844–45 (5th Cir. 2002) (defendants were liable and were not entitled to immunity where they "essentially

orchestrated the attack"); Snider v. Dylag, 188 F.3d 51, 55 (2d Cir. 1999) (assault invited by staff member's statements to other inmates is actionable); Fischl v. Armitage, 128 F.3d 50, 56–59 (2d Cir. 1997) (assault made possible by officer's actions is actionable); Pavlick v. Mifflin, 90 F.3d 205, 208–10 (7th Cir. 1996) (affirming damages based on evidence that officer actively aided the assault or at least permitted it by opening the plaintiff's cell while he was asleep); Northington v. Jackson, 973 F.2d 1518, 1525 (10th Cir. 1992); Durre v. Dempsey, 869 F.2d 543, 548 (10th Cir. 1989); Smith-Bey v. Hospital Administrator, 841 F.2d 751, 758 (7th Cir. 1988); Vaughn v. Willis, 853 F.2d 1372, 1377 (7th Cir. 1988); Glover v. Alabama Department of Corrections, 734 F.2d 691, 693–94 (11th Cir. 1984) (affirming liability of official who publicly offered a reward for assaulting the plaintiff), *cert. granted, vacated and remanded on other grounds*, 474 U.S. 806 (1985); Montero v. Crusie, 153 F. Supp. 2d 368, 376–77 (S.D.N.Y. 2001) (allegation that officers released another prisoner into a recreation area with the plaintiff in hopes he would attack him supported an Eighth Amendment claim); *see* Newsome v. Lee County, Ala., 431 F. Supp. 2d 1189, 1199 (M.D.Ala. 2006) (deputy who allowed male prisoners to rape a female prisoner could be held liable for "physical coercion").

[864]Odom v. South Carolina Dep't of Corrections, 349 F.3d 765, 772 (4th Cir. 2003) (officers who failed to take action when they saw other prisoners trying to get through a fence to attack him could be liable under the Eighth Amendment); Peate v. McCann, 294 F.3d 879, 882–84 (7th Cir. 2002) (officer who returned assailant's weapon to him and did nothing when he assaulted the plaintiff again could be held liable); Walker v. Norris, 917 F.2d 1449, 1453 (6th Cir. 1990); Ayala Serrano v. Lebron Gonzales, 909 F.2d 8, 14 (1st Cir. 1990); Stubbs v. Dudley, 849 F.2d 83, 87 (2d Cir. 1988) (the Constitution requires "human decency, not superhuman courage"); Morales v. New York State Dep't of Corrections, 842 F.2d 27, 30 (2d Cir. 1988); Richardson v. Penfold, 839 F.2d 392, 396 (7th Cir. 1988); Davis v. Zahradnick, 600 F.2d 458, 459–60 (4th Cir. 1979); Payne v. Collins, 986 F. Supp. 1036, 1061 (E.D.Tex. 1997) (officer is not required to intervene physically but must take *some* action on witnessing an assault); Mendez-Suarez v. Veles, 698 F. Supp. 905, 908 (N.D.Ga. 1988); *see also* Stokes v. Delcambre, 710 F.2d 1120, 1125 (5th Cir. 1983) (jailer refused to investigate screams of victims).

[865]MacKay v. Farnsworth, 48 F.3d 491, 493 (10th Cir. 1995) (officers who intervened verbally and called for assistance and medical personnel were not deliberately indifferent); Arnold v. Jones, 891 F.2d 1370, 1373–74 (8th Cir. 1989); Williams v. Willits, 853 F.2d 586, 591 (8th Cir. 1988); Sinnett v. Simmons, 45 F. Supp. 2d 1210, 1219 (D.Kan. 1999) (officer who called for help rather than physically intervening was not deliberately indifferent).

The same rule applies in tort cases, which are discussed in § G.1.e of this chapter. *See* Hernandez v. Ohio Dep't of Rehabilitation and Correction, 62 Ohio Misc.2d 249, 598 N.E.2d 211, 212–14 (Ohio Ct.Cl. 1990) (officers' failure to intervene in knife fight was not negligence).

Prison officials may be found deliberately indifferent if they fail to protect prisoners who are obvious victims[866] or have been identified as at risk,[867] or if they place a prisoner in a situation of danger from others who are known to be aggressive and violent.[868] Of course, many prisoners have engaged in aggressive or violent behavior, and the assailant must have an unusually violent history for prison officials to be required to treat her specially.[869] It may be deliberate indifference if prison officials fail to take measures to control a prisoner whom they themselves have already identified as unusually dangerous.[870]

---

[866]Farmer v. Brennan, 511 U.S. 825, 114 S. Ct. 1970 (1994) (placing a young, non-violent, feminine-appearing transgender prisoner in general population in a high-security prison with a history of violence); Greene v. Bowles, 361 F.3d 290, 294–95 (6th Cir. 2004) (placing a transgender prisoner in a "protective custody" unit containing high-security prisoners); Weiss v. Cooley, 230 F.3d 1027, 1032 (7th Cir. 2000) (placing a prisoner accused of a highly publicized rape in general population even though other prisoners shouted threats and insults at him when he entered the jail; knowledge of risk can be based on "knowledge of the victim's characteristics, not the assailants"); Taylor v. Michigan Dep't of Corrections, 69 F.3d 76, 78, 81–82 (6th Cir. 1995) (transfer of young, small, mentally retarded prisoner to a camp with dormitory-style housing); Swofford v. Mandrell, 969 F.2d 547, 549 (7th Cir. 1992) (placing a sex offender in an unsupervised holding cell); Cortes-Quinones v. Jiminez-Nettleship, 842 F.2d 556, 559–60 (1st Cir. 1988) (transferring a mentally disturbed inmate to an overcrowded general population with no psychiatric care); Stokes v. Delcambre, 710 F.2d 1120, 1125 (5th Cir. 1983) (failure to separate young white males); Gullatte v. Potts, 654 F.2d 1007, 1013 (5th Cir. 1981) (releasing a known informant to a high-security general population); Heisler v. Kralik, 981 F. Supp. 830, 834, 838 (S.D.N.Y. 1997) (failure to protect prisoner charged with sexual assault on a minor), aff'd, 164 F.3d 618 (2d Cir. 1998) (unpublished); Reece v. Groose, 60 F.3d 487, 491–92 (8th Cir. 1995) (prisoner who had been labelled a snitch and had been placed in protective custody was subjected to a risk sufficiently obvious to support a finding of knowledge; allowing a prisoner with a history of violence to work in that unit could be deliberate indifference); Harris v. O'Grady, 803 F. Supp. 1361, 1366 (N.D.Ill. 1992) (placement of legally blind inmate in general population); Bellamy v. McMickens, 692 F. Supp. 205, 211 (S.D.N.Y. 1988) (permitting another inmate access to the cell of a prisoner known to be at risk of being murdered); Blizzard v. Quillen, 579 F. Supp. 1446, 1449–50 (D.Del. 1984) (similar to *Gullatte*).

The Eighth Amendment does not bar sentencing particularly victim-prone individuals to prison. The prisoner's remedy is a suit directed to correcting any dangerous conditions that may exist. State v. Krieger, 163 Wis.2d 241, 471 N.W.2d 599, 606 (Wis.App.), *review denied*, 474 N.W.2d 107 (Wis. 1991).

[867]Johnson v. Johnson, 385 F.3d 503, 526–27 (5th Cir. 2004) (holding allegation that classification officials, informed of repeated rapes of plaintiff, took no action and told him to "learn to f*** or fight" stated an Eighth Amendment claim); Giroux v. Somerset County, 178 F.3d 28, 30, 33 (1st Cir. 1999) (supervisor who knew "cell feed" status was often protective in nature, but left a "cell feed" prisoner in a waiting area with the brother of a prisoner who had threatened him, could be found deliberately indifferent); Spruce v. Sargent, 149 F.3d 783, 785–86 (8th Cir. 1998) (warden could be found deliberately indifferent where he reviewed plaintiff's complaints of sexual assault and denied his request to be moved; warden acknowledged that prisoners had to fight against sexual aggression).

[868]Hearns v. Terhune, 413 F.3d 1036, 1041 (9th Cir. 2005) (allegation that prison officials knew, but did nothing, about a "ruling group" of Muslim prisoners who assaulted those who questioned their authority, stated a deliberate indifference claim); Nei v. Dooley, 372 F.3d 1003, 1006–07 (8th Cir. 2004) (per curiam) (failure to curb a prisoner who was assaulting others and threatening to infect them with HIV supported a deliberate indifference claim); Cottone v. Jenne, 326 F.3d 1352, 1358–59 (11th Cir. 2003) (staff's failure to monitor prisoner with a record of "violent, schizophrenic outbursts" stated a deliberate indifference claim); Parker v. Carpenter, 978 F.2d 190, 192 (5th Cir. 1992) (placement of low-security inmate in high-security area); Redman v. City of San Diego, 942 F.2d 1435, 1444 (9th Cir. 1991) (en banc) (double-celling an "aggressive homosexual" with another inmate); Frett v. Government of Virgin Islands, 839 F.2d 968, 978 (3d Cir. 1988); Saunders v. Chatham County Bd. of Comm'rs, 728 F.2d 1367, 1368 (11th Cir. 1984) (failure to segregate an inmate who displayed a "violent pattern of behavior"); Wade v. Haynes, 663 F.2d 778, 780–82 (8th Cir. 1981) (putting a violent inmate in a segregation cell with a young and small inmate), aff'd on other grounds sub nom. Smith v. Wade, 461 U.S. 30, 103 S. Ct. 1625 (1983); Harris v. Roberts, 719 F. Supp. 879, 880 (N.D.Cal. 1989); Ryan v. Burlington County, 708 F. Supp. 623, 633–35 (D.N.J. 1989), aff'd on other grounds, 889 F.2d 1286 (3d Cir. 1989); McCaw v. Frame, 499 F. Supp. 424, 425 (E.D.Pa. 1980) (plaintiff placed in a cell with a known rapist); *see* Robinson v. Prunty, 249 F.3d 862, 866–67 (9th Cir. 2001) (placing prisoners of different races in the yard together could constitute deliberate indifference where gang-based racial rivalries were so intense as to create a "gladiator-like scenario").

[869]Estate of Ford v. Ramirez-Palmer, 301 F.3d 1043, 1052–53 (9th Cir. 2002) (officials could not be held liable for double-celling the plaintiff with a person who had a substantial record of violence and was on a list for transfer to a special unit for "extremely dangerous inmates," since he had been double-celled before, with the plaintiff among others, without problems, and though he was classified as a "predator," the plaintiff was not classified as a "victim"); Street v. Corrections Corporation of America, 102 F.3d 810, 817 (6th Cir. 1996) (noting that although assailant had a history of violence, so did the plaintiff); Cowart v. U.S., 617 F.2d 112, 116–17 (5th Cir. 1980) (negligence case); Hanna v. Lane, 610 F. Supp. 32, 35 (C.D.Ill. 1985); Wheeler v. Sullivan, 599 F. Supp. 630, 641–42 (D.Del. 1984).]

Even a prisoner who does have an unusually violent history need not be segregated indefinitely. *See* Curry v. Crist, 226 F.3d 974, 978–79 (8th Cir. 2000) (officials were not deliberately indifferent for leaving in general population a prisoner convicted of murdering his two sons, his girlfriend, and a prostitute, since he had remained nonviolent for several years in prison).

[870]Thus, in *Gulett v. Haines*, 229 F. Supp. 2d 806, 821–24 (S.D.Ohio 2002), the plaintiff was held in a unit for assaultive and combative inmates in which only one prisoner was ever supposed to be out at a time and the officer on duty controlled the cell doors; the fact that he was nonetheless attacked by another prisoner

Prison officials may be held liable if they fail to act on a specific warning of danger to a particular prisoner.[871] However, such a specific warning is not necessary. The Supreme Court has held that "the failure to give advance notice is not dispositive" if there is other evidence that prison officials know of the risk.[872] Of course, if the prisoner's failure to complain or warn means that prison officials do not know of the risk, the prisoner will lose.[873] Similarly, a warning that is not specific enough to put officials on notice of the risk of assault will not support a finding of liability.[874] Prison officials may also not be liable if they simply disbelieve a warning of a risk to safety,[875] though the jury (or the court in a bench trial) is not required to believe officials' testimony to that effect.[876]

Several courts have held that failing to separate prisoners who have fought in the past can constitute deliberate indifference.[877] However, the fact that a prisoner has been attacked in the past by someone does not make prison officials liable for future attacks by others, unless there is some identifiable reason for them to have known of the risk of the second attack.[878] Failure to protect prisoners targeted by gangs can be deliberate indifference,[879] though officials are not required to treat any past history of conflict with gangs

---

supported a deliberate indifference claim. *Accord*, Hobbs v. Lockhart, 46 F.3d 864, 868–69 (8th Cir. 1995). *But see* Rich v. Bruce, 129 F.3d 336, 339–40 (4th Cir. 1997) (finding no deliberate indifference on facts similar to *Gulett's* because the officer failed to appreciate the risk he was creating).

[871]Case v. Ahitow, 301 F.3d 605, 606–07 (7th Cir. 2002) (defendants could be held liable where they knew another prisoner had it in for the plaintiff and didn't act to keep them separate); Flint v. Kentucky Department of Corrections, 270 F.3d 340, 353–54 (6th Cir. 2001) (officials who knew of threats against a prisoner but did nothing to protect him could be found deliberately indifferent when he was murdered); Weiss v. Cooley, 230 F.3d 1027, 1029–30, 1032–33 (7th Cir. 2000) (officer who heard other prisoners shouting threats and insults at prisoner accused of highly publicized rape but put him in general population could be found deliberately indifferent); Young v. Quinlan, 960 F.2d 351, 363 (3d Cir. 1992) ("prison officials should, at a minimum, investigate each allegation of violence or threat of violence"); Hendricks v. Coughlin, 942 F.2d 109, 111–12 (2d Cir. 1991); Roland v. Johnson, 856 F.2d 764, 770 (6th Cir. 1988); Harris by and through Harris v. Maynard, 843 F.2d 414, 417 (10th Cir. 1988); Anderson v. Gutschenritter, 836 F.2d 346, 349 (7th Cir. 1988); Berg v. Kincheloe, 794 F.2d 457, 460–61 (9th Cir. 1986); Watts v. Laurent, 774 F.2d 168, 171–73 (7th Cir. 1985); Miller v. Shelby County, 93 F. Supp. 2d 892, 899–900 (W.D.Tenn. 2000) (failure to keep plaintiff separated from gang members in protective custody after he had expressed fear of gang attack was deliberate indifference); Mastrota v. Robinson, 534 F. Supp. 434, 436–38 (E.D.Pa. 1982); West v. Rowe, 448 F. Supp. 58, 60–61 (N.D.Ill. 1978).

[872]Farmer v. Brennan, 511 U.S. 825, 848 114 S. Ct. 1970 (1994); *see* Woods v. Lecureux, 110 F.3d 1215, 1223–24 (6th Cir. 1997) (official's receipt of an incident report documenting the risk to the plaintiff could support a deliberate indifference finding without complaint from the plaintiff); Hayes v. New York City Dep't of Correction, 84 F.3d 614, 621 (2d Cir. 1996) (prisoner's refusal to name his enemies to prison staff was not outcome determinative if staff knew of risk to him); Richardson v. Penfold, 839 F.2d 392, 395–96 (7th Cir. 1988); Gullatte v. Potts, 654 F.2d 1007, 1013 (5th Cir. 1981); Baker v. Lehman, 932 F. Supp. 666, 670–71 (E.D.Pa. 1996) (the question is not whether the plaintiff perceived a threat and told the defendants, but whether the defendants were aware of facts from which they could draw the inference that a substantial risk of serious harm existed, and whether they drew that inference).

Earlier decisions holding that prison officials must know of a specific danger from a specific assailant are now overruled. Krein v. Norris, 309 F.3d 487, 491–92 (8th Cir. 2002).

[873]*See, e.g.*, Brown v. Hughes, 894 F.2d 1533, 1537 (11th Cir. 1990) (where the plaintiff complained about a "racial problem" but did not say he was personally in danger, prison officials were not liable for a subsequent assault on him); Mullen v. Unit Manager Weber, 730 F. Supp. 640, 644–45 (M.D.Pa. 1990) (plaintiff did not

say he had been threatened and did not identify the inmates he was afraid of); *see also* Moore v. Dowd, 731 F. Supp. 921, 924 (E.D.Mo. 1990) (prison officials were not liable where the inmates who assaulted the plaintiff were not the ones he had complained to them about).

[874]Klebanowski v. Sheahan, 540 F.3d 633, 639–40 (7th Cir. 2008) (prison staff were not liable to prisoner who told them he feared for his life, but didn't say he had actually been threatened by gang members because he wasn't in a gang); Carter v. Galloway, 352 F.3d 1346, 1349–50 (11th Cir. 2003) (per curiam) (officials were not liable for assault where plaintiff had warned that his cellmate was "acting crazy" and planning to fake a hanging and said the plaintiff would help him "one way or another," but didn't tell prison staff he viewed this as a threat); Butera v. Cottey, 285 F.3d 601, 605–07 (7th Cir. 2002) (a complaint of "having problems" and wanting off the block was not sufficient to convey knowledge of a risk of serious harm); Delgado–Brunet v. Clark, 93 F.3d 339, 345 (7th Cir. 1996) (the plaintiff's vague complaints and the fact that his assailant was a "known gang member" did not put officials on notice of the risk to him); Nunez v. Goord, 172 F. Supp. 2d 417, 430–31 (S.D.N.Y. 2001) (plaintiff's statement that he was "experiencing problems and feared that he was going to have trouble" was insufficient to warn defendants of a risk of assault); *see* Lindell v. Houser, 442 F.3d 1033, 1036 (7th Cir. 2006) (court declines to construe complaint about "racial/cultural conflict" with cellmate as a warning of risk of assault).

[875]Lindell v. Houser, 442 F.3d at 1035.

[876]*See* § F.1 of this chapter, n.270, for examples of this point in medical deliberate indifference cases.

[877]Morales v. New York State Dep't of Corrections, 842 F.2d 27, 30 (2d Cir. 1988); Frett v. Government of Virgin Islands, 839 F.2d 968, 978 (3d Cir. 1988); Pressly v. Hutto, 816 F.2d 977, 978–79 (4th Cir. 1987); Holmes v. Goldin, 615 F.2d 83, 84–85 (2d Cir. 1980); *see* Ashford v. District of Columbia, 306 F. Supp. 2d 8, 14 (D.D.C. 2004) (allegation that D.C. failed to notify prisons to which D.C. prisoners were transferred of separation orders arising from prior fights could state a deliberate indifference claim).

[878]Boyce v. Moore, 314 F.3d 884, 888–87, 889–91 (7th Cir. 2002).

[879]Walsh v. Mellas, 837 F.2d 789, 797–98 (7th Cir. 1988).

as a current risk,[880] and they are not required to separate all gang members in the absence of a specific risk.[881]

A number of courts have held that prison staff's calling a prisoner a "snitch" or otherwise informing other prisoners that she has cooperated with law enforcement, or has complained to prison staff about the conduct of another prisoner, can constitute deliberate indifference.[882] Courts have also held that prison staff's disclosing information or making accusations about a prisoner that might lead other prisoners to attack her can be deliberate indifference.[883]

c. Group Risks[884] Even if prison officials don't know about the risk to a particular prisoner, they can be held liable for policies or conditions that are dangerous to all prisoners or to an identifiable group of prisoners.[885] Groups may be "identifiable" because of prisoners' personal characteristics, their records or backgrounds, or the way they are treated or housed by the prison system. Identifiable groups acknowledged by the courts so far include accused or convicted sexual offenders;[886] prisoners who are young, small, naive, or passive and therefore vulnerable to intimidation;[887] new admissions;[888] transgender (transsexual) prisoners;[889] prisoners targeted by gangs;[890] members of ethnic groups;[891]

---

[880]Lindell v. Houser, 442 F.3d 1033, 1035 (7th Cir. 2006) (defendants were not liable for double-celling plaintiff with a member of the Gangster Disciples, one of whom he had assaulted 18 months earlier).

[881]See § G.1.c of this chapter, n.898.

[882]Flint v. Kentucky Department of Corrections, 270 F.3d 340, 344, 353 (6th Cir. 2001) (accusing prisoner of "ratting" on inmate-staff misconduct constituted deliberate indifference); Benefield v. McDowall, 241 F.3d 1267, 1271 (10th Cir. 2001) (it is clearly established in this circuit that labelling a prisoner as a snitch constitutes deliberate indifference; citing cases from several jurisdictions); Northington v. Marin, 102 F.3d 1564, 1567(10th Cir. 1996) (noting defendant's admission that if he spread such a rumor, the prisoner would probably be attacked); Thomas v. Hill, 963 F. Supp. 753, 755–56 (N.D.Ind. 1997) (officer arrested for dealing drugs in prison who told other officer and prisoners that the plaintiff had set him up could be found deliberately indifferent); see also Hamilton v. Leavy, 117 F.3d 742, 748 (3d Cir. 1997) (holding failure of officials to place plaintiff in protective custody promptly after an officer told other prisoners he was a snitch could be deliberate indifference). But see Williams v. McGinnis, 192 F. Supp. 2d 757, 760 (E.D.Mich. 2002) (hearing officer who named plaintiff as an informant in a disciplinary report could not be held liable absent evidence that he was aware of a significant risk), aff'd, 57 Fed.Appx. 662 (6th Cir. 2003) (unpublished). At least one court has said that pressuring a prisoner to become an informant can violate the Constitution. David v. Hill, 401 F. Supp. 2d 749, 756–57 (S.D.Tex. 2005).

One federal circuit, in a non-Eighth Amendment case, has refused to assume without evidence that calling a prisoner a "rat" in public would invite attacks by other prisoners. Dawes v. Walker, 239 F.3d 489, 492–93 (2d Cir. 2001) (holding prisoner was not subjected to "adverse" action for First Amendment retaliation purposes). Within the Second Circuit, if you bring such a case under the Eighth Amendment and are faced with a summary judgment motion or trial, you should try to present such evidence—for example, if you were attacked and your attackers made comments indicating a belief you were an informant, you should explain that in your affidavit or testimony.

[883]Hearns v. Terhune, 413 F.3d 1036, 1041–42 (9th Cir. 2005) (chaplain allegedly told other prisoners that the plaintiff held heretical beliefs and must be killed); Montero v. Crusie, 153 F. Supp. 368, 377 (S.D.N.Y. 2001) (plaintiff alleged that officers spread rumors that the plaintiff was gay, a child molester, and a rapist, resulting in threats of harm to him).

[884]In the previous edition of this book, we referred to risks to all prisoners or an identifiable group of them as "generalized risks."

However, one federal appeals court has now used that term in a different way and said that "general risks" are not actionable under the Eighth Amendment. See Pierson v. Hartley, 391 F.3d 898, 903 (7th Cir. 2004). To avoid confusion, we have changed our term to "group risk."

[885]Farmer v. Brennan, 511 U.S. 825, 843, 114 S. Ct. 1970 (1994) ("it does not matter whether a prisoner faces an excessive risk of attack for reasons personal to him or because all prisoners in his situation face such a risk"); Janes v. Hernandez, 215 F.3d 541, 542–43 (5th Cir. 2000) (per curiam) (where Sheriff maintained a policy of mixing nonviolent prisoners with dangerous ones, plaintiffs need not show that the Sheriff knew the specific prisoners who injured the plaintiff were a danger to him); Doe by and through Doe v. Washington County, 150 F.3d 920, 923 (8th Cir. 1998) (plaintiff need not establish knowledge of a risk to the plaintiff; a risk to "all juveniles in Doe's situation" was sufficient); Taylor v. Michigan Dep't of Corrections, 69 F.3d 76, 81 (6th Cir. 1995) (under Farmer v. Brennan, the question is whether warden "had knowledge about the substantial risk of serious harm to a particular class of persons, not whether he knew who the particular victim turned out to be"); LaMarca v. Turner, 995 F.2d 1526, 1535 (11th Cir. 1993) (deliberate indifference could be found based on failure to protect from the "general danger arising from a prison environment that both stimulated and condoned violence"); Winton v. Board of Commissioners of Tulsa County, Okla., 88 F. Supp. 2d 1247, 1265 (N.D.Okla. 2000) (knowledge of a "particularized risk" need not be shown to establish deliberate indifference if there is knowledge of a long-standing, pervasive,and well-documented risk).

The Seventh Circuit has held that policymakers can be held liable only for risks posed by, or to, a specific detainee, and not "general" risks. Brown v. Budz, 398 F.3d 904, 909–10 (7th Cir. 2005). This holding appears to be contrary to Farmer v. Brennan.

[886]Weiss v. Cooley, 230 F.3d 1027, 1029–30, 1032 (7th Cir. 2000).

[887]Taylor v. Michigan Dep't of Corrections 69 F.3d 76, 82 (6th Cir. 1995); Redman v. County of San Diego, 942 F.2d 1435, 1448 (9th Cir. 1991) (en banc); Butler v. Dowd, 979 F.2d 661, 667 (8th Cir.1992); Vosburg v. Solem 845 F.2d 763, 766 (8th Cir. 1988); Withers v. Levine, 615 F.2d 158 (4th Cir. 1980).

[888]Martin v. White, 742 F.2d 469, 475 n.6 (8th Cir. 1984).

[889]Greene v. Bowles, 361 F.3d 290, 294 (6th Cir. 2004); Randolph v. State, 74 F. Supp. 2d 537, 542 (D.Md.1999) (citing Farmer, 511 U.S. at 843).

[890]Walsh v. Mellas, 837 F.2d 789, 797–98 (7th Cir. 1988).

[891]Knowles v. New York City Dep't of Corrections, 904 F. Supp. 217, 222 (S.D.N.Y. 1995) (plaintiff was recognizably Jamaican because of his physical characteristics and accent).

former co-defendants;[892] informants;[893] and prisoners in mental observation units.[894]

In some such cases, lower court have held that deliberate indifference may be shown by "a series of incidents closely related in time" or by "systematic deficiencies in staffing, facilities or procedures [that] make suffering inevitable. . . ."[895] Officials must be shown to have known about the resulting risks (which courts and juries can conclude from a showing that the risks were obvious).[896]

A variety of risk factors have been found to support findings of deliberate indifference in group risk cases. Examples are:

- Failure to classify inmates and separate the particularly violent or vulnerable[897] (though prison

---

[892]Scicluna v. Wells, 345 F.3d 441, 445 (6th Cir. 2003).

[893]Cimino v. Gomez, 1995 WL 55319, *2–3 (N.D.Cal., Feb. 7,1995); *see* § G.1.b of this chapter, n.882, concerning the risks to prisoners who become known as informants.

[894]Byrd v. Abate, 945 F. Supp. 581, 585–86 (S.D.N.Y. 1996).

[895]Fisher v. Koehler, 692 F. Supp. at 1561 (citations omitted); *accord*, Villante v. Dep't of Corrections of City of New York, 786 F.2d 516, 519 (2d Cir. 1986) (deliberate indifference may be shown by "knowing acquiescence in the unconstitutional behavior of . . . subordinates, . . . persistently violat[ing] a statutory duty to inquire about such behavior and to be responsible for preventing it, . . . failure to train or supervise . . . or an official acquiescence in the continued existence of prison conditions which, themselves, are so injurious to prisoners that they amount to a constitutional violation"); Gilland v. Owens, 718 F. Supp. 665, 687 (W.D.Tenn. 1989) ("intentional and deliberate decisions and procedures [that do] not protect inmates' rights to personal safety" or "[s]ystematic deficiencies in facilities, procedures or staffing" can constitute deliberate indifference).

[896]Thus, in *Jensen v. Clarke*, 94 F.3d 1191 (8th Cir. 1996), the court found actual knowledge of a risk of violence resulting from random double-celling of new admissions based on evidence that officials knew of the increase in violence, knew that reported assaults understate actual levels of violence, were aware of obstacles to surveillance in the cells, knew that prison rules acted as a disincentive to reporting assaults, and acknowledged that double-celling erodes manageability and increases the potential for violence. In addition, it found that the paper classification process was not really used and that later classification meetings rarely resulted in cell assignment changes, and that the defendants knew all of this because they had worked their way up through the system. 94 F.3d at 1199; *see* Taylor v. Michigan Dep't of Corrections, 69 F.3d 76, 80–84 (6th Cir. 1995) (where vulnerable prisoner was subjected to sexual assault in a camp with open barracks housing, evidence that the warden knew that authority to review transfers was being delegated without adequate review, and that the unstructured conditions in camps created a greater risk, supported deliberate indifference finding); Hale v. Tallapoosa County, 50 F.3d 1579, 1583–84 (11th Cir. 1995) (where crowding led to jail violence, evidence that the Sheriff knew of the violence and its consequences, including expert testimony that given the conditions "it was plainly foreseeable to a reasonable law enforcement official that a violent act was likely to occur," sufficiently established the Sheriff's subjective knowledge of the risk).

[897]Brown v. Budz, 398 F.3d 904, 914–16 (7th Cir. 2005) (allowing a prisoner with a history of assaulting white inmates to be placed unsupervised into a unit containing white inmates could constitute deliberate indifference; "a deliberate indifference claim may be predicated on custodial officers' knowledge that a specific individual poses a heightened risk of assault to even a large class of detainees"); Pierson v. Hartley, 391 F.3d 898, 903 (7th Cir. 2004) (prisoner could recover for assault by a violent prisoner assigned to a "meritorious housing" unit in violation of prison policy, regardless of whether prison staff knew of the risk to the particular prisoner who was injured); Greene v. Bowles, 361 F.3d 290, 294–95 (6th Cir. 2004) (transgender prisoner could recover for assault by a known "predatory inmate" either because leaving her in a unit containing high-security inmates threatened her safety, or because placing that inmate in protective custody created a risk for its occupants generally); Scicluna v. Wells, 345 F.3d 441, 445 (6th Cir. 2003) (prisoner who was assaulted by his former co-defendant, from whom prison policy required his separation, was "a member of an identifiable group of prisoners for whom risk of assault was a serious problem"); Marsh v. Butler County, Ala., 268 F.3d 1014, 1029–30 (11th Cir. 2001) (en banc) (lack of classification and separation of violent prisoners supported a deliberate indifference claim); Janes v. Hernandez, 215 F.3d 541, 542–43 (5th Cir. 2000) (per curiam) (policy of mixing nonviolent prisoners with dangerous ones could support county liability for assault); Newman v. Holmes, 122 F.3d 650, 652 (8th Cir. 1997) (affirming damage award to plaintiffs assaulted by a prisoner who was supposed to be in disciplinary lockup); Jensen v. Clarke, 94 F.3d 1191, 1198–1201 (8th Cir. 1996) (affirming injunction based on overall increase in violence attributed to random assignment of cellmates); Butler v. Dowd, 979 F.2d 661, 675 (8th Cir. 1992) (en banc) (random housing assignments of vulnerable prisoners and obstacles to admission to protective custody); Redman v. County of San Diego, 942 F.2d 1435, 1445, 1448 (9th Cir. 1991) (en banc) (failure to segregate "aggressive homosexuals"); Berry v. City of Muskogee, 900 F.2d 1489, 1497–98 (10th Cir. 1990) (failure to separate crime partners); Ryan v. Burlington County, N.J., 889 F.2d 1286, 1293 (3d Cir. 1989) (failure to implement classification system); Walsh v. Mellas, 837 F.2d 789, 797–98 (7th Cir. 1988) (failure to screen for gang involvement); Redman v. County of San Diego, 942 F.2d 1435, 1445, 1448 (9th Cir. 1991) (en banc) (failure to segregate "aggressive homosexuals"); Stokes v. Delcambre, 710 F.2d 1120, 1124–25 (5th Cir. 1983); Laube v. Haley, 234 F. Supp. 2d 1227, 1246–47 (M.D.Ala. 2002) (compromise of classification system by overcrowding contributed to excessive violence); Winton v. Board of Commissioners of Tulsa County, Okla., 88 F. Supp. 2d 1247, 1268 (N.D.Okla. 2000) ("lack of inmate segregation and classification" could constitute a "*de facto* polic[y] of inaction" supporting liability); Taylor v. Foltz, 803 F. Supp. 1261, 1266 (E.D.Mich. 1992), *aff'd*, 990 F.2d 1260 (6th Cir. 1993); Tillery v. Owens, 719 F. Supp. at 1276 (permitting different classifications, including protective custody and punitive segregation, to mingle during showers and exercise); Gilland v. Owens, 718 F. Supp. 665, 686–89 (W.D.Tenn. 1989); Fisher v. Koehler, 692 F. Supp. at 1547, 1562; Withers v. Levine, 449 F. Supp. 473, 477–78 (D.Md. 1978), *aff'd*, 615 F.2d 158 (4th Cir. 1980); Doe v. Lally, 467 F. Supp. 1339, 1349–50 (D.Md. 1979). *But see* James v. Milwaukee County, 956 F.2d 696, 702–03 (7th Cir. 1992) (policy of mixing parole and probation

officials are not required always to separate inmates by gangs[898]).

- Failure to provide adequate supervision of inmates.[899]

- Overreliance on open dormitory housing.[900]
- Overcrowding.[901]

---

violators did not constitute deliberate indifference); Falls v. Nesbit, 966 F.2d 375, 379–80 (8th Cir. 1992) (housing protective custody and non-PC inmates together was not unconstitutional).

[898]Mayoral v. Sheahan, 245 F.3d 934, 939 (7th Cir. 2000); Mooring v. San Francisco Sheriff's Dep't, 289 F. Supp. 2d 1110, 1117–18 (N.D.Cal. 2003).

Gang affiliation may be relevant to protecting prisoners from assault, but there must be some showing of a more specific risk than the mere fact of gang membership to establish a sufficiently serious risk in a particular case. Mooring v. San Francisco Sheriff's Dep't, 289 F. Supp. 2d at 1117–18; see, e.g., Walsh v. Mellas, 837 F.2d 789, 797–98 (7th Cir. 1988) (plaintiff had been targeted by gang); Rodriguez v. Connecticut, 169 F. Supp. 2d 39, 45 (D.Conn. 2001) (officials could be held liable based on a policy of housing rival gangs together in a "Close Custody" unit); Miller v. Shelby County, 93 F. Supp. 2d 892, 899 (W.D.Tenn. 2000) (failing to separate gang members from others during lock-out time in segregation unit constituted deliberate indifference).

[899]Hart v. Sheahan, 396 F.3d 887, 894 (7th Cir. 2005) (plaintiffs' allegations of regular lockdowns in double cells, with no staff present because they are searching other housing units, stated a constitutional claim for "subjecting them to a risk of serious harm by an unreasonably protracted detention of them out of sight and hearing of guards"); Cottone v. Jenne, 326 F.3d 1352, 1358–59 (11th Cir. 2003) (staff's failure to monitor prisoner with a record of "violent, schizophrenic outbursts" stated a deliberate indifference claim); Krein v. Norris, 309 F.3d 487, 489–91 (8th Cir. 2002) (evidence that officials provided only one guard for three barracks housing 150 inmates, and did not change staffing even though one barracks was known to be extremely violent, supported an Eighth Amendment claim; Lawrence v. Norris, 307 F.3d 745, 747 (8th Cir. 2002) (prisoner who was attacked at a time when the only guard on duty was controlling traffic in the hallway stated an Eighth Amendment claim); Marsh v. Butler County, Ala., 268 F.3d 1014, 1029 (11th Cir. 2001) (en banc) ("Conditions like those in this case, where violent prisoners are allowed free reign of a jail with easy access to weapons without proper supervision by guards could be found to have caused the assaults on Plaintiffs."); Lopez v. LeMaster, 172 F.3d 756, 762 (10th Cir. 1999) (acknowledged deficiencies in staffing and supervision); Smith v. Arkansas Dep't of Correction, 103 F.3d 637, 645 (8th Cir. 1996) (failure to provide supervision in open barracks); Berry v. City of Muskogee, 900 F.2d 1489, 1497–98 (10th Cir. 1990) (inadequate staffing, failure to lock inmates in at night); Ryan v. Burlington County, N.J., 889 F.2d 1286, 1294 (3d Cir. 1989) (inadequate staffing); Pool v. Mo. Dep't of Corrections and Human Resources, 883 F.2d 640, 645 (8th Cir. 1989) (inadequate supervision); Vosburg v. Solem, 845 F.2d 763, 766–67 (8th Cir. 1988) (limited guard coverage at night, guards stationed where they could not see into cells); Alberti v. Klevenhagen, 790 F.2d 1220, 1224 (5th Cir. 1986) (inadequate staffing and observation), rehearing denied, 799 F.2d 992 (5th Cir. 1986); Riley v. Jeffes, 777 F.2d 143, 148 (3d Cir. 1985) (giving inmates keys and permitting them to keep cell block doors open); Martin v. White, 742 F.2d 469, 471 (8th Cir. 1984) (inadequate observation by staff); Stokes v. Delcambre, 710 F.2d 1120, 1124–25 (5th Cir. 1983) (lack of observation of cell block, acceptance of fighting); Laube v. Haley, 234 F. Supp. 2d 1227, 1244–46 (M.D.Ala.

2002) (inadequate supervision related to overcrowding of dormitories); Rodriguez v. Connecticut, 169 F. Supp. 2d 39, 48 (D.Conn. 2001) (proof that officers were off their posts and watching television rather than supervising a "Close Custody" unit would support a deliberate indifference claim); Winton v. Board of Commissioners of Tulsa County, Okla., 88 F. Supp. 2d 1247, 1268 (N.D.Okla. 2000) (understaffing could be a "de facto polic[y] of inaction" supporting liability); Byrd v. Abate, 945 F. Supp. 581, 585–86 (S.D.N.Y. 1996) (prisoner in a mental observation unit "belonged to an identifiable group of prisoners who were at risk of substantial harm," and absence of officer from post could be deliberate indiffeence); Tillery v. Owens, 719 F. Supp. at 1276 (inadequate staffing, failure to monitor shower area); Gilland v. Owens, 718 F. Supp. at 688 (deficiencies in staffing); Fisher v. Koehler, 692 F. Supp. at 1549, 1562 (inadequate staffing, poor sight lines aggravated by double bunks); Benjamin v. Malcolm, 564 F. Supp. 668, 672 (S.D.N.Y. 1983) (lack of observation caused by structure of tiers); LaMarca v. Turner, 662 F. Supp. 647, 657–58 (S.D.Fla. 1987) (similar to Fisher), vacated and remanded on other grounds, 995 F.2d 1526 (11th Cir. 1993); Ramos v. Lamm, 485 F. Supp. 122, 156 (D.Colo. 1979) (architectural "blind spots"), aff'd in pertinent part, 639 F.2d 559 (10th Cir. 1980); Fischer v. Winter, 564 F. Supp. 281, 292–93 (N.D.Cal. 1983) (double bunks in dormitories). But see Santiago v. Lane, 894 F.2d 218, 221–22 (7th Cir. 1990) (prison officials were not liable for an assault in a "dangerously concealed" area because there was no evidence of prior attacks there).

[900]Fisher v. Koehler, 692 F. Supp. at 1546–47, 1562; see Smith v. Arkansas Dep't of Correction, 103 F.3d 637, 644–45 (8th Cir. 1996) (noting dangers of open barracks); Winton v. Board of Commissioners of Tulsa County, Okla., 88 F. Supp. 2d 1247, 1266 n.13, 1268 (N.D.Okla. 2000) (noting evidence that violent offenders should be kept in cells rather than open dormitories); Ruiz v. Estelle, 503 F. Supp. 1265, 1282 (S.D.Tex. 1980) (noting particular dangers of dormitories), aff'd in pertinent part, 679 F.2d 1115 (5th Cir. 1982); Taylor v. Foltz, 803 F. Supp. 1261, 1264 (E.D.Mich. 1992) (officials' failure to review files to determine if plaintiff could be held safely in an unsupervised dormitory stated a claim), aff'd, 990 F.2d 1260 (6th Cir. 1993).

Several cases acknowledge the need for constant guard supervision in dormitories, or the consequences of its absence. Smith v. Arkansas Dep't of Correction, 103 F.3d at 644–45; Williams v. Edwards, 547 F.2d 1206, 1213–14 (5th Cir. 1977); Gates v. Collier, 501 F.2d 1291, 1309 (5th Cir. 1974); Laube v. Haley, 234 F. Supp. 2d 1227, 1244–46 (M.D.Ala. 2002) ("the combination of substantial overcrowding and significantly inadequate supervision in open dorms" violates the Eighth Amendment right to protection from violence); Finney v. Mabry, 534 F. Supp. 1026, 1040–41 (E.D.Ark. 1982).

A classification system should place more aggressive, higher security inmates in cell housing rather than open dormitories. Fisher v. Koehler, 692 F. Supp. at 1546–47; U.S. ex rel. Wolfish v. Levi, 439 F. Supp. 114, 126 (S.D.N.Y. 1977), aff'd in pertinent part, 573 F.2d 118, 133 n.31 (2d Cir. 1978), rev'd on other grounds, 441 U.S. 520, 99 S. Ct. 1861 (1979).

[901]Doe by and through Doe v. Washington County, 150 F.3d 920, 923–24 (8th Cir. 1998) (crowding that resulted in five juvenile prisoners in one cell and in the plaintiff's being returned to that cell

- Failure to control tools or other items that can be used as weapons[902] (including pieces of a dilapidated building).[903]
- Failure to maintain locks in working order.[904]
- Placement of inmates in positions of supervisory or disciplinary authority over other inmates.[905]
- Failure to take corrective action in response to high rates of assault or to particular patterns of assault.[906]

Not every case where one of these conditions exists will result in a deliberate indifference finding, since a court or jury may conclude that the defendants did not have sufficient actual knowledge to be held liable, or that they responded reasonably to the problem, or that the risk was not large enough to violate the Eighth Amendment. In damage cases, courts may be unwilling to hold officials liable for conditions over which they do not entirely have control,[907] or which they are working to correct or mitigate.[908]

To win based on a group risk, you must show that the risk is "substantial or pervasive,"[909] a "constant threat of violence,"[910] or a "pervasive risk of harm."[911] A pervasive or constant risk may be shown either for the whole prison or for a particular, identifiable group of prisoners.[912] "A pervasive risk of harm may not ordinarily be shown by pointing to a single incident or to isolated incidents, but it may be

---

an hour after asking for protection supported deliberate indifference finding); Redman v. County of San Diego, 942 F.2d 1435, 1445, 1447 (9th Cir. 1991) (en banc; Ryan v. Burlington County, N.J., 860 F.2d 1204, 1209 (3d Cir. 1988); Morgan v. District of Columbia, 824 F.2d 1049, 1060–61 (D.C. Cir. 1987); Toussaint v. Yockey, 722 F.2d 1490, 1492 (9th Cir. 1986); Mitchell v. Cuomo, 748 F.2d 804, 805–07 (2d Cir. 1984); Laube v. Haley, 234 F. Supp. 2d 1227, 1244–46 (M.D.Ala. 2002) (crowding combined with inadequate supervision in overcrowded dorms violated the Eighth Amendment); Winton v. Board of Commissioners of Tulsa County, Okla., 88 F. Supp. 2d 1247, 1268 (N.D.Okla. 2000) (persistent crowding could be a *de facto* polic[y] of inaction" supporting deliberate indifference claim); Fisher v. Koehler, 692 F. Supp. at 1541–46, 1562; McKenna v. County of Nassau, 538 F. Supp. 737, 741 (E.D.N.Y. 1982), *aff'd*, 714 F.2d 115 (2d Cir. 1982).

[902]Marsh v. Butler County, Ala., 268 F.3d 1014, 1029 (11th Cir. 2001) (en banc) (conditions "where violent prisoners are allowed free reign of a jail with easy access to weapons without proper supervision by guards could be found to have caused the assaults on Plaintiffs"); Berry v. City of Muskogee, 900 F.2d at 1498 (failure to maintain control of wire brooms); Goka v. Bobbitt, 862 F.2d 646, 652 (7th Cir. 1988) (failure to enforce a tool control policy); Shrader v. White, 761 F.2d 975, 982 (4th Cir. 1985) (failure to curb manufacture of weapons from scrap metal); Tillery v. Owens, 719 F. Supp. at 1276 (failure to search inmates leaving industry area).

[903]Marsh v. Butler County, Ala., 268 F.3d 1014, 1027–28 (11th Cir. 2001) (en banc).

[904]Marsh v. Butler County, Ala., 268 F.3d at 1027–28 (lack of working cell locks contributed to pattern of violence); Earrey v. Chickasaw County, Miss., 965 F. Supp. 870, 872–73, 877 (N.D.Miss. 1997) (officials were not entitled to summary judgment where prisoner was assaulted in a jail without functioning cell locks).

[905]McDuffie v. Estelle, 935 F.2d 682, 686 n.6 (5th Cir. 1991) and cases cited.

Several courts have held that staff tolerance of inmates' "running" housing areas may support a deliberate indifference claim. Bass v. Jackson, 790 F.2d 260, 263 (2d Cir. 1986); Stokes v. Delcambre, 710 F.2d 1120, 1124–25 (5th Cir. 1983); Gilland v. Owens, 718 F. Supp. at 688. In *Mayoral v. Sheahan*, 245 F.3d 934 (7th Cir. 2000), the court held that evidence that a tier officer told an inmate in a rowdy cell block to "control 'his guys,'" thus seeming "to have deliberately abdicated his responsibility and put the fate of the inmates in the hands of another inmate," could support a claim of deliberate indifference. 254 F.3d at 940.

[906]Krein v. Norris, 309 F.3d 487, 489–91 (8th Cir. 2002) (failure to keep track of number and location of assaults, failure to enhance staffing for housing area with elevated violence level); Butler v. Dowd, 979 F.2d at 675 (failure to investigate or prosecute rapes, failure to train staff or warn inmates of danger); Roland v. Johnson, 856 F.2d 764, 770 (6th Cir. 1988) (failure to reclassify exploitative inmates); Vosburg v. Solem, 845 F.2d 763, 767 (8th Cir.

1988) (failure to develop policies to protect inmates in high-risk areas; failure to discipline or prosecute assailants); Matzker v. Herr, 748 F.2d 1142, 1149 (7th Cir. 1984) (failure to "exercise proper supervisory authority or direction" to remedy known violence problem), *overruled on other grounds*, Salazar v. City of Chicago, 940 F.2d 233, 240 (7th Cir. 1991); Skinner v. Uphoff, 234 F. Supp. 2d 1208, 1215–16 (D.Wyo. 2002) (failure to investigate assaults and a "code of silence" about staff misconduct that contributes to assault constituted deliberate indifference); Abrams v. Hunter, 910 F. Supp. 620, 625–26 (M.D.Fla. 1995) (acknowledging potential liability based on awareness of overall substantial risk of serious harm from inmate violence), *aff'd*, 100 F.3d 971 (11th Cir. 1996); Knowles v. New York City Dept. of Corrections, 904 F. Supp. 217, 222 (S.D.N.Y. 1995) (prison officials' knowledge of an ethnic "war" among inmates, that a Hispanic inmate who had been cut had been transferred to plaintiff's jail, and that plaintiff was part of a group at risk because of his accent and appearance was sufficient to withstand summary judgment); LaMarca v. Turner, 662 F. Supp. 647, 663–64 (S.D.Fla. 1987) (little action against contraband, no system for investigating rapes), *vacated and remanded on other grounds*, 995 F.2d 1526 (11th Cir. 1993); Randall v. Thompson, 635 F. Supp. 145, 148 (N.D.Ill. 1986) (sealing of exits in area where many inmates had been attacked); Redmond v. Baxley, 475 F. Supp. 1111, 1120–21 (E.D.Mich. 1979) (inadequate response to known pattern of rape); Stevens v. County of Dutchess, 445 F. Supp. 89, 93 (S.D.N.Y. 1977) (lack of "therapeutic action" in response to pattern of violence).

[907]*See, e.g.*, Crow v. Montgomery, 403 F.3d 598, 602–03 (8th Cir. 2005) (holding defendants were entitled to summary judgment despite allegations that the jail was overcrowded, poorly supervised and understaffed, and the detainees were inadequately classified).

[908]*See, e.g.*, Hedrick v. Roberts, 183 F. Supp. 2d 814, 821–22 (E.D.Va. 2001) (new Sheriff who inherited an aged, overcrowded jail but was striving to improve it could not be held deliberately indifferent).

[909]Goka v. Bobbitt, 862 F.2d 646, 651–52 (7th Cir. 1988).

[910]Ruiz v. Estelle, 679 F.2d 1115, 1142 (5th Cir. 1982); Woodhous v. Commonwealth of Virginia, 487 F.2d 889, 890 (4th Cir. 1973).

[911]Withers v. Levine, 615 F.2d 158, 161 (4th Cir. 1980).

[912]Farmer v. Brennan, 511 U.S. 825, 843,114 S. Ct. 1970 (1994); *see* n.886–894 earlier in this section.

established by much less than proof of a reign of violence and terror in the particular institution."[913] A pervasive risk may be shown "by proving that violence and sexual assaults occur with sufficient frequency, that prisoners are put in reasonable fear for their safety, and to reasonably apprise prison officials of the existence of the problem and the need for protective measures."[914] It may be shown by sheer numbers of incidents as documented by prison records,[915] although these records do not always reflect the full extent of prison violence.[916] A pervasive risk may also be shown by testimony and other evidence showing "that serious violence has become almost a feature of institutional life. . . ."[917]

---

[913]Withers v. Levine, 615 F.2d 158, 161 (4th Cir. 1980); *accord,* Hearns v. Terhune, 413 F.3d 1036, 1041 (9th Cir. 2005) (citing a series of planned attacks and religious-related violence by a Muslim "ruling group" against other Muslims as "longstanding, pervasive, [and] well-documented"); Falls v. Nesbit, 966 F.2d 375, 378 (8th Cir. 1992); Fisher v. Koehler, 692 F. Supp. 1519, 1560 (S.D.N.Y. 1988), *aff'd,* 902 F.2d 2 (2d Cir. 1990) and cases cited.

[914]Matzker v. Herr, 748 F.2d 1142, 1149 (7th Cir. 1984), *overruled on other grounds,* Salazar v. City of Chicago, 940 F.2d 233, 240 (7th Cir. 1991); *accord,* Withers v. Levine, 615 F.2d at 161.

One court has held that "fear amounting to mental pain" must be shown to establish a pervasive risk. Shrader v. White, 761 F.2d 975, 979 (4th Cir. 1985). Other federal courts have not adopted this view. Fisher v. Koehler, 692 F. Supp. 1519, 1560 n.52 (S.D.N.Y. 1988), *aff'd,* 902 F.2d 2 (2d Cir. 1990).

[915]*See, e.g.,* Butler v. Dowd, 979 F.2d at 675 (at least 100 sexual assaults in three years supported jury finding of pervasive risk); Doe v. Sullivan County, Tenn., 956 F.2d 545, 554 (6th Cir. 1992) (four incidents a month per 100 inmates supported an Eighth Amendment claim); Gilland v. Owens, 718 F. Supp. 665, 686–87 (W.D.Tenn. 1989) (685 altercations in six months in a population around 2300 showed a pervasive risk); Fisher v. Koehler, 692 F. Supp. at 1529–32, 1560–61 (1300 reported violent incidents annually in a population of 2500–2600 showed pervasive risk); Alberti v. Klevenhagen, 790 F.2d 1220, 1225–26 (5th Cir. 1986) (over 1200 acts of violence annually in a population over 4000 showed pervasive risk), *rehearing denied,* 799 F.2d 992 (5th Cir. 1986); Ruiz v. Estelle, 37 F. Supp. 2d 855, 916 (S.D.Tex. 1999) (noting increase in reported assault rate from 6.4 per thousand inmates to 10.5), *rev'd on other grounds and remanded,* Ruiz v. U.S., 243 F.3d 941 (5th Cir. 2001); Jensen v. Gunter, 807 F. Supp. at 1472–73, 1483 (179 disciplinary convictions in six months for assault and threats in a population around 523), *remanded on other grounds sub nom.,* Jensen v. Clarke, 73 F.3d 808 (8th Cir. 1996); *see also* Vosburg v. Solem, 845 F.2d 763, 766–67 (8th Cir. 1988) (citing disciplinary convictions for fighting and assault); Laube v. Haley, 234 F. Supp. 2d 1227, 1246 (M.D.Ala. 2002) (citing "extremely high" assault rate, without giving data); Grubbs v. Bradley, 552 F. Supp. 1052, 1078–79 (M.D.Tenn. 1982) (citing disciplinary convictions); Ramos v. Lamm, 485 F. Supp. 122, 141 (D.Colo. 1979) (citing numbers of requests for protective custody), *aff'd in pertinent part,* 639 F.2d 559, 567 n.10 (10th Cir. 1980). *But see* Butera v. Cottey, 285 F.3d 601, 607–08 (7th Cir. 2002) (evidence of about 50 fights and 10–15 allegations of sexual assault in a five-year period, none of them in the cellblock at issue, did not show a pervasive risk); McGhee v. Foltz, 852 F.2d 876, 880 (6th Cir. 1988) (reported violence failed to establish a pervasive risk); Westmoreland v. Brown, 883 F. Supp. 67, 75–76 (E.D.Va. 1995) (in a jail population of up to 1355, the occurrence of 42–78 assaults a month (1.4 to 2.5 a day) was not sufficient to create a "substantial" risk of inmate–inmate assault under *Farmer);* Wheeler v. Sullivan, 599 F. Supp. 630, 646, 652 (D.Del. 1984) (fewer than ten assaults a month in a population reaching 900 did not establish pervasive risk).

[916]It is well known that many incidents of prison violence are not reported because prisoners are afraid to "snitch" or because prison officials discourage their reporting or fail to observe them or to report them accurately. *See, e.g.,* Roland v. Johnson, 856 F.2d 764, 770 (6th Cir. 1988); Ruiz v. Estelle, 37 F. Supp. 2d 855, 928 (S.D.Tex. 1999) (noting underreporting of sexual assaults because of official inaction and discouragement), *rev'd on other grounds and remanded,* Ruiz v. U.S., 243 F.3d 941 (5th Cir. 2001); Alberti v. Klevenhagen, 790 F.2d at 1226; Tillery v. Owens, 719 F. Supp. 1256, 1274 (W.D.Pa. 1989), *aff'd,* 907 F.2d 418 (3d Cir. 1990); Gilland v. Owens, 718 F. Supp. at 687; Fisher v. Koehler, 692 F. Supp. at 1529–30; Benjamin v. Malcolm, 564 F. Supp. 668, 672 (S.D.N.Y. 1983). Also, different prison and jail systems use different kinds of reporting systems, so that an "assault" might mean one thing in one system and something else in another, and incidents that get reported in one system do not get reported elsewhere. If prison records or statistics are used in an inmate assault case—either by you or by prison officials—be sure you find out how they are compiled, what they mean, and especially what is left out. *Compare* Fisher v. Koehler, 692 F. Supp. 1530–32 (court heard extensive evidence concerning the basis of violence data) *with* McGriff v. Coughlin, 640 F. Supp. 877, 880 (S.D.N.Y. 1986) (court compares "assault ratios" for state and federal prisons without asking any questions about their basis).

[917]Fisher v. Koehler, 692 F. Supp. 1519, 1561 (S.D.N.Y. 1988), *aff'd,* 902 F.2d 2 (2d Cir. 1990); *see, e.g.,* Hale v. Tallapoosa County, 50 F.3d 1579, 1583 (11th Cir. 1995) (evidence that inmate–inmate violence "occurred regularly when the jail was overcrowded," as had been the case for two years, and that the violence was severe enough to require medical attention and even hospitalization on occasion, was sufficient to establish a "substantial risk of serious harm"); Jensen v. Clarke, 94 F.3d 1191, 1198 (8th Cir. 1996) (pervasive risk properly found based on prisoners' anecdotal testimony about violence and evidence that tensions are increased by the cell size, lack of privacy, the ineffective surveillance system, deterrents to reporting, a contraband rule, and the excessive amount of time spent on lockdown status); Doe v. Sullivan County, Tenn., 956 F.2d at 554 (testimony that inmates complained of danger every day supported a finding of deliberate indifference); Morgan v. District of Columbia, 824 F.2d 1049, 1060–61 (D.C. Cir. 1987); Ruiz v. Estelle, 37 F. Supp. 2d 855, 929 (S.D.Tex. 1999) (citing "the combination of inmates who are routinely subjected to violence, extortion, and rape, of officers who are aware of inmate-on-inmate victimization but fail to respond to the victims, of high barriers preventing inmates from seeking safekeeping or protective custody, and of a system that fails accurately to report, among other data, instances of requests for safekeeping and sexual assaults, and, as well, the obviousness of the risk to prison officials"), *rev'd on other grounds and remanded,* Ruiz v. U.S., 243 F.3d 941 (5th Cir. 2001); LaMarca v. Turner, 662 F. Supp. 647, 656–62, 679–704, 706 (S.D.Fla. 1987), *vacated and remanded on other grounds,* 995 F.2d 1526 (11th Cir. 1993); Withers v. Levine, 449 F. Supp. 473, 478 (D.Md. 1978), *aff'd,* 615 F.2d 158 (4th Cir. 1980); Pugh v. Locke, 406 F. Supp. 318, 325 (M.D.Ala. 1976), *aff'd and remanded sub nom.* Newman v. Alabama, 559 F.2d 283 (5th Cir. 1977).

If a risk is obvious or evident, you need not show that it has caused such a large amount of prior violence. Thus, one court held that a jail's failure to lock down prisoners at night, to maintain control of wire brooms, to separate crime partners, and to have more than one officer on duty in the jail at night created a risk sufficiently obvious to establish deliberate indifference, even though there was little evidence of prior violence in the jail.[918] Similarly, another court held that prison officials' failure to enforce their "tool control" policy created a risk that was "evident" both on its face and from a record of 13 prior attacks with broom handles in two years in a large prison.[919]

d. Sexual Assault Claims of sexual assault by other prisoners are governed by the same rules as other kinds of assault: the plaintiff must show deliberate indifference to an excessive risk of serious harm, meaning that the defendants must have failed to act reasonably in response to a risk of which they had actual knowledge.[920] The cases applying these rules to any assault will be relevant to sexual assault claims as well.

Courts assume without much discussion that rape and sexual coercion constitute serious harm.

Prison officials who do not take action with respect to sexual assaults they are informed of, or patterns of sexual assault that they know about, can be found deliberately indifferent.[921] Courts have acknowledged in numerous cases that transgender (transsexual) prisoners and prisoners who are small, young, and/or naive about prison life are at particular risk for sexual assault, and that prison officials may be held liable based on their knowledge of those risks.[922]

Officials may also be held liable for failure to provide protection against prisoners who are known to be sexually aggressive.[923]

Congress has recently enacted the Prison Rape Elimination Act of 2003 (PREA),[924] which does not provide direct benefits for persons who have been raped and wish to bring litigation about it (*i.e.*, if you get raped, PREA does not provide the basis for a lawsuit, even if it is prison officials' fault that it happened). PREA provides for information-gathering, studies, reports, and grants to state and local governments. However, it also calls for the U.S. Attorney General to promulgate national standards for the detection, prevention, reduction, and punishment of prison rape.[925] It may be that once these standards are completed (which is supposed to occur by mid-2010), officials' compliance or failure to comply with them may be given some weight by courts in deciding prison sexual assault lawsuits.[926]

e. Causation and Suing the Right Defendants To obtain damages from prison officials[927] for an inmate assault, you must show that the actions or practices you complain about actually caused the assault.[928] For example, if you claim that

---

[918]Berry v. City of Muskogee, 900 F.2d 1489, 1498–99 (10th Cir. 1990).

[919]Goka v. Bobbitt, 862 F.2d 646, 652 (7th Cir. 1988); *see also* Shrader v. White, 761 F.2d 975, 982 (4th Cir. 1985) (failure to safeguard scrap metal and restrict the making of weapons could indicate a "pervasive risk" even if there was little evidence of injury from weapons); Stokes v. Delcambre, 710 F.2d 1120, 1124–25 (5th Cir. 1983) (inadequate surveillance, lack of classification, acceptance of fighting in jail by administrators created an unconstitutional risk of assault).

[920]Farmer v. Brennan, 511 U.S. 825, 833, 114 S. Ct. 1970 (1994). This case, the Supreme Court's decision concerning assaults by other prisoners, involved allegations of rape as well as beating. 511 U.S. at 831. *But see* Newsome v. Lee County, Ala., 431 F. Supp. 2d 1189, 1199 (M.D.Ala. 2006) (assessing claim against deputy who allowed male prisoners to rape a female prisoner under standards normally applicable to use of force claims).

[921]Johnson v. Johnson, 385 F.3d 503, 526–27 (5th Cir. 2004); Spruce v. Sargent, 149 F.3d 783, 785–86 (8th Cir. 1998); LaMarca v. Turner, 995 F.2d 1526, 1535 (11th Cir. 1993); Butler v. Dowd, 979 F.2d 661, 675 (8th Cir. 1992) (en banc); Vosburg v. Solem, 845 F.2d 763, 767 (8th Cir. 1988); Withers v. Levine, 615 F.2d 158, 161 (4th Cir. 1980).

[922]Farmer v. Brennan, 511 U.S. at 848–49; Green v. Bowles, 361 F.3d 290, 294 (6th Cir. 2004); Taylor v. Michigan Dept. of Corrections, 69 F.3d 76, 84 (6th Cir. 1995); Butler v. Dowd, 979 F.2d 661, 667 (8th Cir.1992); Redman v. County of San Diego, 942

F.2d 1435, 1448 (9th Cir. 1991) (en banc); Vosburg v. Solem 845 F.2d 763, 766 (8th Cir. 1988); Withers v. Levine, 615 F.2d at 161.

Courts have held that transgender prisoners may be housed with their anatomical gender and not the gender they identify as. Lopez v. City of New York, 2009 WL 229956, *13 (S.D.N.Y., Jan. 30, 2009) (pre-operative transwoman prisoner could be housed with males).

[923]Redman v. City of San Diego, 942 F.2d 1435, 1444 (9th Cir. 1991) (en banc); Roland v. Johnson, 856 F.2d 764, 770 (6th Cir. 1988) (failure to reclassify exploitative inmates); Vosburg v. Solem, 845 F.2d 763, 767 (8th Cir. 1988).

[924]42 U.S.C.A. § 15601 *et seq.*

[925]42 U.S.C.A. § 15607.

[926]*See* § A.1 of this chapter, nn.30–34, concerning the use of regulations and standards in determining contemporary standards of decency under the Eighth Amendment.

[927]You can also sue the prisoner who attacked you, though such a suit would have to be a tort suit for assault and battery. Other prisoners generally can't be sued under 42 U.S.C. § 1983 or the *Bivens* doctrine, see Ch. 8, §§ B.1.c, B.2, because they do not act under color of state or federal law. See Figalora v. Smith, 238 F. Supp. 2d 658, 661 (D.Del. 2002).

[928]Tucker v. Evans, 276 F.3d 999, 1002 (8th Cir. 2002) (prison policy forbidding officers to enter barracks until assistance arrived could not support liability, since the assault was over by the time the officer on duty knew anything was wrong); Best v. Essex County, N.J., Hall of Records, 986 F.2d 54, 56–57 (3d Cir. 1993); Doe v. Sullivan County, Tenn., 956 F.2d 545, 550 (6th Cir. 1992) (plaintiff failed to prove that "offensive" prison conditions caused him to be assaulted); Leer v. Murphy, 844 F.2d 628, 633–34 (9th Cir. 1988); Williams v. Willits, 853 F.2d 586, 589–90 (8th Cir. 1988); Moore v. Sheahan, 38 F. Supp. 2d 695, 697–98 (N.D.Ill. 1999) (plaintiff could not base claim on placement in a cell with a defective lock because he was assaulted during a period when the cells were unlocked anyway). This "causation" requirement applies to all actions under 42 U.S.C. § 1983. *See* Ch. 8, § B.4.

lack of classification created a pervasive risk of harm, but you and your assailant have similar records and would have been housed together even if properly classified, prison officials will probably not be held liable for your assault based on lack of classification.[929] You must be prepared to make the connection between what the defendants did or failed to do and what happened to you.

You must also be sure to name the right defendants—those who are actually responsible for your injuries. These may include line correctional officers who observe an assault or know of a risk to you and do nothing.[920] They may also include middle or higher level supervisors who make policies, or fail to make or to enforce policies, or fail to act on risks they know about, resulting in your being assaulted[931]—

though "referring the matter for further investigation or taking similar administrative steps" rather than immediately intervening personally may be "a reasonable discharge of their duty to protect the inmates in their care."[932] City or county government itself may be liable if your assault results from a governmental policy.[933] Private corporations

_____

[929]See Armon v. Jones, 580 F. Supp. 917, 924 (N.D.Tex. 1983) (it was not deliberate indifference to place a felony detainee with a long criminal record in a cell with other accused felons); see also Collins v. County of Kern, 390 F. Supp. 2d 964, 973–74 (E.D.Cal. 2005) (prisoner who had said he was a Crip and shouldn't be placed in a housing unit with Bloods could not recover damages where the people who assaulted him were not Bloods).

[930]Velez v. Johnson, 395 F.3d 732, 736 (7th Cir. 2005) (officer who knew of risk of assault could be liable for not acting to prevent it); Cottone v. Jenne, 326 F.3d 1352, 1358–59 (11th Cir. 2003) (officers who failed to monitor a unit for prisoners with severe mental illness could be held liable for resulting assault); Odom v. South Carolina Dep't of Corrections, 349 F.3d 765, 772 (4th Cir. 2003) (officers who saw prisoners trying to assault the plaintiff and did not act could be held liable); Peate v. McCann, 294 F.3d 879, 882–84 (7th Cir. 2002) (officer who returned assailant's weapon to him and did nothing when he assaulted the plaintiff again could be held liable); Northington v. Marin, 102 F.3d 1564, 1567–68 (10th Cir. 1996) (affirming damages against a deputy who told other prisoners the plaintiff was an informant); Wright v. Jones, 907 F.3d 848, 850–52 (8th Cir. 1990); Ayala Serrano v. Lebron Gonzales, 909 F.2d 8, 14 (1st Cir. 1990); Walker v. Norris, 917 F.2d 1449, 1453 (6th Cir. 1990); Frett v. Government of Virgin Islands, 839 F.2d 968, 978 (3d Cir. 1988); Gulett v. Haines, 229 F. Supp. 2d 806, 821–24 (S.D.Ohio 2002) (officer who allowed two prisoners to come into physical contact on a high-security unit where such contact was forbidden could be held liable).

[931]Pierson v. Hartley, 391 F.3d 898, 903–04 (7th Cir. 2004) (reinstating jury verdict against unit team manager and casework manager who placed prisoner with violent history in a "meritorious assignment" unit); Brown v. Budz, 398 F.3d 904, 909, 916 (7th Cir. 2005) (allegation that prison supervisors knew of the risk posed by a prisoner with a history of racial assaults stated a claim); Greene v. Bowles, 361 F.3d 290, 294–95 (6th Cir. 2004) (warden who knew record of "predatory inmate" could be liable for placing him in the same unit as a transgender prisoner); Taylor v. Michigan Dep't of Corrections, 69 F.3d 76, 80–82 (6th Cir. 1995) (warden who knew transfer review procedures had broken down and did not act to correct the problem could be liable for rape of a vulnerable prisoner transferred into a high-risk situation); Redman v. County of San Diego, 942 F.2d 1435, 1447–48 (9th Cir. 1991) (en banc) (Sheriff could be held liable for acquiescing in dangerous classification policies; captains could be liable for originating them); Santiago v. Lane, 894 F.2d 218, 223 (7th Cir. 1990) (corrections director, warden, and chief of security could be held liable for

transferring the plaintiff for safety reasons without notifying the receiving prison of the danger); Ryan v. Burlington County, N.J., 889 F.2d 1286, 1293 (3d Cir. 1989) (members of county Board of Freeholders could be held liable for failure to provide adequate security personnel); Pool v. Mo. Dep't of Corrections and Human Resources, 883 F.2d 640, 645 (8th Cir. 1989) (allegation that prison supervisor knew of assaults resulting from inadequate staffing but did nothing stated a claim against him); Roland v. Johnson, 856 F.2d 764, 770 (6th Cir. 1988) (warden and corrections director could be held liable for a policy discouraging the reporting and prosecution of assault, failing to act on their knowledge of a high rate of assault, and permitting aggressive inmates to hold "honor" positions in medium security); Cortes-Quinones v. Jiminez-Nettleship, 842 F.2d 556, 559–61 (1st Cir. 1988) (damages awarded against corrections director and administrator and jail superintendent for transferring mentally ill inmate to an overcrowded jail with no psychiatric facilities); Walsh v. Mellas, 837 F.2d 789, 797–98 (7th Cir. 1988) (damages awarded against security officials for failure to institute screening procedures to protect prisoners from gang-related violence); Boone v. Elrod, 706 F. Supp. 636, 638 (N.D.Ill. 1989) (captain, corrections director, and sheriff "cannot hide behind their underlings" when they actually had notice of threats to the plaintiff); see Wilks v. Young, 897 F.2d 896, 898 (7th Cir. 1990) (it was error to refuse to instruct the jury concerning supervisory liability).

The Seventh Circuit has held that policymakers can be held liable only for risks posed by, or to, a specific detainee, and not "general" risks. Brown v. Budz, 398 F.3d 904, 909–10 (7th Cir. 2005). This holding appears to be contrary to Farmer v. Brennan.

[932]Johnson v. Johnson, 385 F.3d 503, 526–27 (5th Cir. 2004) (Executive Director, Senior Warden, and Director of Classification, who knew of plaintiff's sexual assault complaints but referred them, were entitled to qualified immunity).

[933]Janes v. Hernandez, 215 F.3d 541, 542–43 (5th Cir. 2000) (per curiam) (policy of mixing nonviolent prisoners with dangerous ones could support county liability for assault); Lopez v. LeMaster, 172 F.3d 756, 763 (10th Cir. 1999) (county could be held liable for policy of understaffing and failure to monitor); Doe by and through Doe v. Washington County, 150 F.3d 920, 924 (8th Cir. 1998) (county could be held liable for policy of crowding); Redman v. County of San Diego, 942 F.2d 1435, 1444–45 (9th Cir. 1991) (en banc) (municipality could be held liable for policies of crowding and placement of aggressive inmates in general population); Berry v. City of Muskogee, 900 F.2d 1489, 1497–99 (10th Cir. 1990) (municipality could be held liable for policies of failing to lock down prisoners at night, failing to control wire brooms, allowing crime partners to commingle, and failing to provide enough staff); Anderson v. Gutschenritter, 836 F.2d 346, 349 (7th Cir. 1988) (where Sheriff was county policymaker for jail, county could be held liable for his actions); Morgan v. District of Columbia, 824 F.2d 1049, 1058–61 (D.C. Cir. 1987); Villante v. Dep't of Corrections of City of New York, 786 F.2d 516, 519 (2d Cir. 1986); Winton v. Board of Commissioners of Tulsa County, Okla., 88 F. Supp. 2d 1247, 1268 (N.D.Okla. 2000) ("overcrowding, understaffing, lack of

operating prisons can be held liable on the same basis as municipalities—if an assault was caused by a corporate policy.[934] If not, their employees are generally subject to suit individually on the same basis as correctional staff employed by a government.[935] Supervisors or municipal governments are not liable in a civil rights suit solely for the acts or omissions of their subordinates or for matters not within their control.[936]

Claims against municipalities are subject to a deliberate indifference standard, but it may be slightly different from the standard discussed in § G.a.1 of this chapter.[937]

In our experience, naming the wrong defendants, or failing to explain why they are the right defendants, is the most common mistake of *pro se* plaintiffs in assault cases. In your complaint and other court papers, you should be specific about the reasons you believe each named defendant is liable.[938]

f. Tort Claims for Inmate Assault Assaults caused by negligence do not violate the Constitution, but they may be torts under state law. It is generally recognized that there is a tort duty on the part of prison authorities to protect prisoners from assault by other prisoners,[939] though some states have enacted statutes abolishing or limiting tort liability for some or all prisoner assaults.[940] Each state has its own rules about tort suits—which court to sue in, who are the proper defendants, etc.[941] Federal prisoners may sue for negligence under the OK.[942] Under some circumstances, prisoners can join both tort claims and civil rights claims in the same suit in state or federal court.[943]

Prison officials are negligent if they fail to exercise "reasonable" or "ordinary" care to protect prisoners from assault.[944] In some jurisdictions, the standard of care may be

---

adequate inmate supervision, lack of inmate segregation and classification, lack of inmate exercise time, dormitory-style housing, all of which existed over a long period of time" could be "*de facto* policies of inaction by the County which created and or contributed to the conditions which created a serious risk of harm in the jail"); Saunders v. Chatham County Bd. of Comm'rs, 728 F.2d 1367, 1368 (11th Cir. 1984) (damages awarded against municipality based on assault resulting from understaffing); McKenna v. County of Nassau, 538 F. Supp. 737, 741 (E.D.N.Y. 1982) (assault caused by policy of overcrowding and failure to respond to its consequences), *aff'd*, 714 F.2d 115 (2d Cir. 1982).

When an assault is caused or made possible by a *violation* of policy, a city or county normally cannot be held liable. In some instances, however, a practice that violates policy on paper may in fact represent the actual *de facto* policy, and the city or county may be liable for it. *Compare* Redman v. County of San Diego, 942 F.3d 1435, 1445 (9th Cir. 1991) (en banc) (routine practice of leaving sexually aggressive prisoners in general population and double-celling them with other prisoners because of crowding could be the municipal custom and policy even if it contradicted policy on paper) *with* Gregory v. Shelby County, Tenn., 220 F.3d 433, 442 (6th Cir. 2000) (where policy prohibited opening more than one cell door in protective custody unit, plaintiff failed to show that violating it was "so widespread as to have the force of law" and make it the real policy). *See* Ch. 8, §§ B.4.a., B.4.b.

[934]Street v. Corrections Corporation of America, 102 F.3d 810, 818 (6th Cir. 1996); *see* Ch. 8, §§ B.1.c, B.4.b.

[935]Flint v. Kentucky Dep't of Corrections, 270 F.3d 340, 351–52 (6th Cir. 2001) (holding prison print shop supervisor, who worked for a private entity, acted under color of law because he "performed functions typically attributed to the State: housing and providing security for individuals who had been convicted of a crime and sentenced to a term of imprisonment").

[936]Walker v. Norris, 917 F.2d 1449, 1455–56 (6th Cir. 1990) (superintendent and commissioner were not responsible for guards' misconduct where they provided proper training); Bailey v. Wood, 909 F.2d 1197, 1200 (8th Cir. 1990) (warden was not liable for an assault resulting from a guard's leaving his post); Alvarez Kerkado v. Otero de Ramos, 693 F. Supp. 1366, 1369–71 (D.P.R. 1988) (supervisory officials were not liable for assault caused by overcrowding and understaffing that they could not control).

[937]*See* Ch. 8, § B.4.b.

[938]*See* Leer v. Murphy, 844 F.2d 628, 633–34 (9th Cir. 1988); *see also* Roland v. Johnson, 856 F.2d 764, 770 (6th Cir. 1988) (explaining bases of liability of several defendants in the same incident); Morales v. New York State Dep't of Corrections, 842 F.2d 27, 29 (2d Cir. 1988) (same).

[939]*See* Giraldo v. California Dep't of Corrections and Rehabilitation, 168 Cal.App.4th 231, 246–53, 85 Cal.Rptr.3d 371 (2008) and cases and treatises cited; Sanchez v. State, 36 A.D.3d 1065, 827 N.Y.S.2d 338, 339 (N.Y. App.Div. 2007).

[940]*See* Davidson v. Cannon, 474 U.S. 344, 346, 106 S. Ct. 668 (1986) (citing N.J.S.A. 59:5-2(b)(4)) (forbidding tort suits against public employers or governmental bodies based on "any injury caused by . . . a prisoner to any other prisoner"); Taylor v. Buff, 172 Cal.App.3d 384, 388, 218 Cal.Rptr. 249, 251 (Cal.App. 1985) (citing Cal. Government Code at § 840.2) (government employees could be held liable for dangerous conditions only if they had immediately available the authority, funds and other means to correct them); Webb v. Lawrence County, 144 F.3d 1131, 1139 (8th Cir. 1998) (citing S.D.Codified Laws § 3-21-9) (providing that no person or political subdivision is liable for any injury to a prisoner by another prisoner).

[941]State tort suits are discussed further in Ch. 8, § C.1 and § H.2.a.

[942]*See* Ch. 8, § C.2 for a discussion of the FTCA.

[943]*See* Ch. 8, § F for discussions of litigating state law claims in federal court.

[944]Frett v. Government of Virgin Islands, 839 F.2d 968, 975–76 (3d Cir. 1988); McGill v. Duckworth, 726 F. Supp. 1144, 1157 (N.D.Ind. 1989) (prison officials had a state law duty to "take reasonable precautions under the circumstances to preserve [prisoner's] life, health and safety"), *rev'd on other grounds*, 944 F.2d 344 (7th Cir. 1991); Sanchez v. State, 99 N.Y.2d 247, 252–53, 784 N.E.2d 675 (N.Y. 2002); Upchurch v. State, 51 Haw. 150, 454 P.2d 112, 114 (Haw. 1969); City of Lexington v. Greenhow, 451 S.W.2d 424, 425 (Ky. 1970); Spann v. State, Dep't of Corrections, 421 So.2d 1090, 1092 (Fla.App. 1982), *review denied*, 430 So.2d 452 (Fla. 1983); Shields v. State through Dep't of Corrections, 380 So.2d 123, 125 (La.App. 1979), *writ denied*, 382 So.2d 164 (La. 1980) (quoting Parker v. State, 282 So.2d 483, 486 (La. 1973)); Saunders v. State, 446 A.2d 748, 750 (R.I. 1982); Sebastiano v. State, 112 A.D.2d 562, 491 N.Y.S.2d 499, 501 (App. Div. 1985); Methola v. County of Eddy,

made more specific by state or local law.[945] The duty of care of the federal Bureau of Prisons, for purposes of suits under the Federal Tort Claims Act (FTCA), is fixed by a federal statute requiring it to "provide suitable quarters and provide for the safekeeping, care and subsistence" of federal prisoners, and to "provide for [their] protection,"[946] regardless of state law to the contrary (even though state law usually governs FTCA suits).[947]

Negligence is generally considered easier to prove than deliberate indifference, since simple carelessness by prison personnel may establish negligence.[948] (Acts or omissions that do constitute deliberate indifference will usually be negligent as well.[949]) But prison officials are not negligent every time they make a mistake, even if a serious assault results.[950] Nor are they required to eliminate every foreseeable risk regardless of the effect on prison operations.[951] In addition, if prison officials establish proper security procedures, they are not negligent every time the procedures fail.[952]

Sometimes it is obvious what "ordinary care" means; for example, guards must pay attention to what is going on in front of them.[953] In other cases it is not so obvious.

---

96 N.M. 274, 629 P.2d 350, 353 (N.M.App. 1981) (quoting City of Belen v. Harrell, 93 N.M. 601, 603 P.2d 711, 713 (N.M.App. 1979)); Merritt for Merritt v. State, 108 Idaho 20, 696 P.2d 871, 875 (Idaho 1985).

One court has held that a prisoner who was intoxicated on admission was owed "a high degree of care" by jail officials, not just ordinary care. Daniels v. Andersen, 195 Neb. 95, 237 N.W.2d 397, 401 (Neb. 1975). *Contra*, City of Louisville v. Humphrey, 461 S.W.2d 352, 354 (Ky. 1970).

[945]For example, one court applied a New York statute (subsequently repealed) requiring the Sheriff "'to take reasonable steps' to ensure that the assignment of housing unit personnel will afford 'appropriate precautions for the personal safety and welfare of persons in custody,' and [] that 'particular attention' be paid 'to those who are known to be vulnerable to assault or any physical or mental abuse.'" Arnold v. County of Nassau, 89 F. Supp. 2d 285, 298–99 (E.D.N.Y. 2000), *rev'd on other grounds*, 252 F.3d 599 (2d Cir. 2001). That court also cited violation of state regulations as constituting evidence that the jury could consider in determining negligence, 89 F. Supp. at 299 (though the appellate court said it failed to explain them sufficiently to the jury, 252 F.3d at 603–04).

[946]18 U.S.C. § 4042.

[947]U.S. v. Muniz, 374 U.S. 150, 164–65, 83 S. Ct. 1850 (1963) (holding statute applicable under the FTCA); *see* Ch. 8, §§ C.2, H.2.b, concerning the FTCA.

This standard is the same as the usual "ordinary care" standard. Williams v. U.S., 384 F. Supp. 579, 583 (D.D.C. 1974); Cohen v. U.S., 252 F. Supp. 679, 687 (N.D.Ga. 1966), *rev'd on other grounds*, 389 F.2d 689 (5th Cir. 1967). It will make a difference for federal prisoners in states where the law provides that there is no duty of care or a more limited duty of care to prisoners.

[948]*See, e.g.,* Davidson v. Cannon, 474 U.S. 344, 346–47, 106 S. Ct. 668 (1986) (where prison officials were warned of danger but one forgot and another decided it wasn't urgent, the lower court found negligence but not deliberate indifference); Rangolan v. County of Nassau, 217 F.3d 77, 79–80 (2d Cir. 2000) (where the county put a notice in the plaintiff's file to keep him separated from another prisoner, but an officer failed to carry it out, there was no deliberate indifference; negligence verdict was not challenged); Estate of Davis v. Johnson, 745 F.2d 1066, 1072 (7th Cir. 1984) (officer's failure to follow rule requiring two cell inspections an hour constituted negligence but not deliberate indifference); Davis v. Pringle, 642 F. Supp. 171, 177–78 (N.D.Ga. 1986) (failure to take greater precautions in light of "possibility" of attack might evidence lack of due care but was not deliberate indifference); Earle v. Gunnell, 78 Md.App. 648, 554 A.2d 1256, 1262–64 (Md.App. 1989) (officer who improperly opened the plaintiff's protective custody cell to "locked-tier" inmates was negligent but not deliberately indifferent); City of Waco v. Hester, 805 S.W.2d 807, 816 (Tex.App. 1990) (failure to act on an unclear warning was negligence but not cruel and unusual punishment).

[949]*See, e.g.,* Ashford v. District of Columbia, 306 F. Supp. 2d 8, 14–15 (D.D.C. 2004) (failure to notify receiving prison of separation orders for transferred prisoner could be negligence as well as deliberate indifference).

[950]Marshall v. U.S., 242 F. Supp. 2d 395, 397–98 (S.D.N.Y. 2003) (where officer saw an earlier part of a dispute but no staff saw the assailant carrying a weapon or knew of any prior incident or existing relationship that would have made the assault foreseeable, or saw any part of the incident that would have provided an opportunity to prevent the injury, there was no negligence); Williams v. U.S., 384 F. Supp. at 582–84 (decision to leave two inmates who had fought in the same housing unit was not negligent where they falsely assured prison officials the dispute was over).

[951]For example, knowledge of prisoners' ingenuity in "turning innocent products into dangerous weapons . . . does not mean that prison authorities must deprive inmates of essential commodities . . . simply because of the ever-present danger that some devious prisoner may pervert or misuse this normally safe product to harm someone." Moore v. Foti, 440 So.2d 530, 532 (La.App. 1983) (permitting liquid deodorant was not negligent), *writ denied*, 444 So.2d 1224 (La. 1984). Similarly, prison officials were held not to be negligent in giving prisoners with bad disciplinary records a "fresh start" after transfer, since doing so might assist in rehabilitation, or in leaving fire extinguishers accessible to inmates, since inmates might be required to fight fires. Fleishour v. U.S., 365 F.2d 126, 128 (7th Cir. 1966); *see also* Robinson v. U.S. Bureau of Prisons, 244 F. Supp. 2d 57, 65 (S.D.N.Y. 2003) (having one officer supervise 219 violent prisoners did not depart from ordinary care); Hernandez v. Ohio Dep't of Rehabilitation and Correction, 62 Ohio Misc.2d 249, 598 N.E.2d 211, 212–14 (Ohio Ct.Cl. 1990).

[952]Cowart v. U.S., 617 F.2d 112, 117 (5th Cir. 1980) (failure to give especially close supervision to an inmate who was "no worse than the general run of prison inmates" was not negligent); Williams v. U.S., 384 F. Supp. at 584 (where the prison had reasonable policies to control flammables and contraband, the fact that one prisoner obtained gasoline did not show negligence). *Contra*, Bourgeois v. U.S., 375 F. Supp. 133, 135–36 (N.D.Tex. 1974) (permitting unsupervised access to flammable liquids was negligent).

[953]*See, e.g.,* Bourgeois v. U.S., 375 F. Supp. at 135–36 (officer was negligent in failing to take precautionary action when he saw a prisoner tampering with the locking mechanism); Huertas v. State, 84 A.D.2d 650, 444 N.Y.S.2d 307, 309 (N.Y.App.Div. 1981) (finding

One court has held that prison safety and security is not "within the realm of the everyday experiences of a lay person" and that the plaintiff must therefore "show by competent expert testimony, or other supporting proof," the meaning of ordinary care in prison and how the defendants' conduct departed from it.[954] Statutes and regulations, or even internal rules, governing jail or prison operations may help establish exactly what ordinary care requires in a particular case; violation of them may be evidence of negligence[955] or in some circumstances may be negligence *per se*.[956]

Prison officials may only be held liable for assaults that are "reasonably foreseeable"[957] or that they "know or have reason to anticipate will occur."[958] If an assault is foreseeable, the precise form of injury you suffer need not have been foreseeable.[959] Courts in some states focus on whether there was any reason for prison officials to know about the risk of assault by a particular attacker on a particular victim.[960]

---

staff negligent where the assailant had walked past five officers and a civilian with a two and a half foot iron bar under his work apron; "with adequate and proper supervision by correctional officers reasonably attentive to their duties," the assault could have been prevented); Finkelstein v. District of Columbia, 593 A.2d 591, 594 (D.C.App. 1991) (holding failure to intervene in group sexual activity negligent); Wackenhut Corrections Corporation v. de la Rosa, 305 S.W.2d 594, 623 (Tex.App. 2009) (failure to pat search prisoners leaving housing area as policy required was negligent); *see also* Cohen v. U.S., 252 F. Supp. 679, 687 (N.D.Ga. 1966) (ordinary care requires closer supervision of psychotic and assaultive prisoner than of other prisoners), *rev'd on other grounds*, 389 F.2d 689 (5th Cir. 1967).

[954]Hughes v. District of Columbia, 425 A.2d 1299, 1303 (D.C. 1981) (failure to return plaintiff to protective custody was not shown to be negligent); *see also* Garza v. U.S., 413 F. Supp. 23, 25–26 (W.D.Okla. 1975) (expert testimony was needed to establish that security staffing was inadequate); District of Columbia v. Carmichael, 577 A.2d 312, 314 (D.C. 1990) (expert's opinion that did not clearly state a standard of care for prison contraband control was insufficient to establish negligence). *Contra*, Wackenhut Corrections Corporation v. de la Rosa, 305 S.W.2d at 623 (no expert testimony needed to establish negligence and causation in failure to search prisoners leaving housing area). *See* City of Lexington v. Greenhow, 451 S.W.2d 424, 426 (Ky. 1970) (lack of television surveillance in drunk tank did not show negligence without evidence that such systems are "commonly used"); Baker v. State Dep't of Rehabilitation, 28 Ohio App.3d 99, 502 N.E.2d 261, 263 (Ohio App. 1986) (guards' failure to remain on a tier when the cells were open was not negligence where there was no "formal written rule" requiring it and an expert witness testified that the procedures used were adequate).

[955]Estate of Davis v. Johnson, 745 F.2d 1066, 1072 (7th Cir. 1984) (police regulation requiring two cell inspections per hour was "evidence" of required standard of care); Murphy v. U.S., 653 F.2d 637, 646–50 (D.C. Cir. 1981) (evidence of violation of prison's count and tool control procedures, supported by expert testimony, could establish negligence); District of Columbia v. Bethel, 567 A.2d 1331, 1335 (D.C. 1990) (American Correctional Association standards and jail's own policies and procedures do not automatically set a duty of care, but an expert opinion that is partly based on them can do so); Sanchez v. State, 99 N.Y.2d 247, 254–55, 784 N.E.2d 675 (N.Y. 2002) (state regulations and security post description describing officer's surveillance duties were relevant to negligence determination); Lyons v. State by Humphrey by Pung, 366 N.W.2d 621, 624 (Minn. App. 1985) (alleged failure to supervise a gym "according to plans" raised a material factual issue of negligence; Daniels v. Andersen, 195 Neb. 95, 237 N.W.2d 397, 401 (Neb. 1975) (duty of care was established by jail rule requiring "constant" surveillance of "drunk tank"). *But see* Mobley v. State, 1 A.D.2d 731, 147 N.Y.S.2d 414 (N.Y.App.Div. 1955) (violation of state prison rules did not establish

negligence where the rules were designed to regulate employees from the prison administration's viewpoint and not to set the standard of care owed to prisoners), *reargument and appeal denied*, 1 A.D.2d 928, 150 N.Y.S.2d 561 (N.Y.App.Div. 1956).

[956]Thus, in *Baker v. State Dep't of Rehabilitation*, 28 Ohio App.3d 99, 502 N.E.2d 261 (Ohio App. 1986), the court stated that under Ohio law "when a statute mandates a particular procedure and creates a duty, the failure to conform to the statute is negligence *per se*." 502 N.E.2d at 263 (finding no written rule that was violated, and therefore no negligence). Under New York law, if a statute is designed to protect a class of persons of which the plaintiff is a member, violation of it "generally constitutes conclusive evidence of negligence," or "negligence *per se*." Where the statute is not designed to protect a class including the plaintiff, its violation is "evidence of negligence which the jury may consider in conjunction with all other relevant proven facts." Daggett v. Keshner, 284 A.D. 733, 735–36, 324 N.Y.S.2d 524 (N.Y.A.D. 1954) (quoted in Arnold v. County of Nassau, 89 F. Supp. 2d 285, 298–99 (E.D.N.Y. 2000), *rev'd on other grounds*, 252 F.3d 599 (2d Cir. 2001)). *But see* Walden v. State, 430 So.2d 1224, 1227 (La.App.) (internal prison policy was not a "duty imposed by law" and its violation was not negligence *per se*), *writ denied*, 435 So.2d 430 (La. 1983); McGee v. State through Dep't of Corrections, 417 So.2d 416, 419 (La.App.) (violation of federal court staffing order was not negligence *per se*), *writ denied*, 420 So.2d 981 (1982).

[957]Sanchez v. State, 99 N.Y.2d 247, 253, 784 N.E.2d 675 (N.Y. 2002).

[958]Shields v. State through Dep't of Correction, 380 So.2d 123, 125 (La.App. 1979), *writ. denied*, 382 So.2d 164 (La. 1980) (quoting Parker v. State, 282 So.2d 483, 486 (La. 1973)); *accord*, McGill v. Duckworth, 726 F. Supp. 1144, 1157 (N.D.Ind. 1989), *rev'd on other grounds*, 944 F.2d 344 (7th Cir. 1991); Barnard v. State, 265 N.W.2d 620, 621 (Iowa 1978) (plaintiff must show that "some danger was, or should have been, apparent"); Saunders v. State, 446 A.2d 748, 751 (R.I. 1982) (the danger must be one that is "known or, in the exercise of ordinary care, should have been known by the prison official"); City of Lexington v. Greenhow, 451 S.W.2d at 425 (jailer was not negligent for "failing to prevent what he could not reasonably anticipate").

[959]Palay v. U.S., 349 F.3d 418, 433–34 (7th Cir. 2003) (prisoner was injured when he raised his head abruptly when a fire extinguisher was discharged into his face).

[960]Walden v. State, 430 So.2d 1224, 1227 (La.App.) (referring to foreseeability requirement as the "bad blood" rule), *writ denied*, 435 So.2d 430 (La. 1983); McGee v. State through Dep't of Corrections, 417 So.2d 416, 418 (La.App. 1982) (emphasizing lack of knowledge of "prior threats or previous confrontations between these two inmates"), *writ denied*, 420 So.2d 981 (La. 1982); Saunders v. State, 446 A.2d 748, 751 (R.I. 1982) (even if prison officials know about the attacker's dangerous propensities, the victim must show that they "would be likely to give rise to an attack upon [the victim]

These courts may not be receptive to suits based on a group risk to all prisoners such as inadequate staffing or supervision. In those states, depending on the facts of your case, you may have a better chance in a federal civil rights action, where liability may be based on a risk to all or an identifiable group of prisoners, though you will have to meet the higher deliberate indifference standard. Courts in other states have permitted tort suits based on group risks.[961] One recent decision states that the defendant need not have known that the victim was vulnerable or the assailant was dangerous, or known that the assault was about to occur and had a chance to intervene. Liability can be based on what the state "reasonably *should have known*" based on its "knowledge of risks to a class of inmates based on the institution's expertise or prior experience, or from its own policies and practices designed to address such risks."[962]

A court may rule against you if it thinks you somehow brought an assault on yourself, by attacking or provoking other inmates,[963] by failing to inform prison officials of a danger to you,[964] or in some other way.[965] Sometimes the courts call such behavior contributory negligence.[966] In some states a plaintiff who is contributorily negligent cannot recover any damages. Other states utilize a "comparative negligence" rule under which a plaintiff who is negligent

---

as a specific identifiable victim or as a member of a group of identifiable victims").

[961]One court observed, "'Foreseeability' does not require the anticipation of a particular injury to a particular person, . . . but only the anticipation of a general type or category of harm which in ordinary experience might be expected to flow from a particular type of negligence." Garrett v. U.S., 501 F. Supp. 337, 339 (N.D.Ga. 1980) (finding government negligent in housing an inmate with an exceptionally assaultive prison record in general population); *accord*, Kemp v. Waldron, 115 A.D.2d 869, 497 N.Y.S.2d 158 (N.Y.App.Div. 1985) (court rejects claim that sheriff and deputy owed a duty only if there was a "special responsibility to safeguard the specific victim"; plaintiff had alleged inadequate guard supervision in jail), *aff'g* 125 Misc.2d 197, 479 N.Y.S.2d 440, 441 (N.Y.Sup. 1984); *see also* Frett v. Government of Virgin Islands, 839 F.2d 968, 979 (3d Cir. 1988); Estate of Davis v. Johnson, 745 F.2d 1066, 1072 (7th Cir. 1984) (violation of police regulations requiring constant supervision of mentally disturbed detainees supported negligence verdict); Brown v. U.S., 486 F.2d 284, 288–89 (8th Cir. 1973) (overcrowding and understaffing could support negligence finding if plaintiff could prove they caused his assault); Bourgeois v. U.S., 375 F. Supp. 133, 136 (N.D.Tex. 1974) (permitting unsupervised access to flammable liquids, failing to provide adequate supervision, and failing to take precautions when a prisoner was caught tampering with the locking system were negligent); Spann v. State Dep't of Corrections, 421 So.2d 1090, 1092-93 (Fla.App. 1982) (negligence could be found if prison officials made flammable liquids available to prisoners), *review denied*, 430 So.2d 452 (Fla. 1983); Hampton v. State through Dep't of Corrections, 361 So.2d 257, 259 (La.App. 1978) (distribution of acid without close supervision would be negligence); Lyons v. State by Humphrey by Pung, 366 N.W.2d 621 (Minn.App. 1985) (failure to provide guard supervision in a gymnasium could constitute negligence); Daniels v. Andersen, 195 Neb. 95, 237 N.W.2d 397, 401 (Neb. 1975) (inadequate surveillance of "drunk tank" was negligent where fights admittedly "were to be expected"); Methola v. County of Eddy, 96 N.M. 274, 629 P.2d 350, 353 (N.M.App. 1981) (failure to provide adequate monitoring and inspection of cells); City of Waco v. Hester, 805 S.W.2d 807, 816 (Tex.App. 1990) (city was negligent in failing to segregate a "violent homosexual").

[962]Sanchez v. State, 99 N.Y.2d 247, 254–55, 784 N.E.2d 675 (N.Y. 2002) (holding plaintiff was entitled to a trial where State habitually placed maximum security prisoners out of sight of any

officer during periods of movement). Note that in *Sanchez*, violation of the State's own post description for officers and of state regulations was held to be relevant to foreseeability; as noted above, such violations may also be relevant to deciding what ordinary care requires.

[963]Johnson v. U.S. Government, 258 F. Supp. 372, 377 (E.D.Va. 1966) (prisoner who had "approached and bothered" other inmates could not recover damages for resulting assault); State ex rel. Miser v. Hay, 328 S.W.2d 672, 674–75 (Mo. 1959) (where a drunken inmate's aggressive actions provoked other inmates to attack him, the jury was properly instructed to consider contributory negligence). *But see* District of Columbia v. Bethel, 567 A.2d 1331, 1335 (D.C. 1990) (jury could find that prisoner who slapped another prisoner and did not then seek protective custody was not contributorily negligent); Lamb v. Clark, 282 Ky. 167, 138 S.W.2d 350, 352–53 (Ky. 1940) (loud, disturbing, and unsanitary conduct by drunken arrestee, not including assault, was not contributory negligence); Methola v. County of Eddy, 629 P.2d at 354 (prisoner who did not tell jail officials about prior disputes with his cellmates or ask for transfer was not contributorily negligent where it was defendants' duty to assign cells and the plaintiff was too badly injured to be held accountable for his actions).

[964]Hackett v. U.S., 462 F. Supp. 131, 133 (N.D.Tex. 1978) (plaintiff who failed to notify defendants of danger to him was negligent and assumed the risk), *aff'd*, 606 F.2d 319 (5th Cir. 1979); Walker v. U.S., 437 F. Supp. 1081, 1083 (D.Or. 1977) (plaintiff who failed to notify prison officials of danger could not recover); Bell v. State, 143 Ariz. 305, 693 P.2d 960, 964–65 (Ariz.App. 1984) (evidence of plaintiff's knowledge of prison life and his failure to disclose danger to officials was relevant to contributory negligence; evidence of his alleged violent propensities was not relevant).

[965]McGill v. Duckworth, 944 F.2d 344, 351–52 (7th Cir. 1991) (plaintiff "incurred the risk" of assault by accompanying his assailant to the shower after the assailant pushed him and threatened him); Jackson v. U.S., 413 F. Supp. 516, 520 (N.D.Ohio 1976) (prisoner who smuggled liquor into honor camp and was assaulted by an inmate who had been drinking it was contributorily negligent); Burdick v. State, 206 Misc.2d 839, 135 N.Y.S.2d 548, 549 (N.Y.Ct. Cl. 1954) (prisoner who stopped in line to speak to a locked-in inmate could not recover for injuries inflicted by him), *aff'd*, 286 A.D.2d 988, 144 N.Y.S.2d 740 (N.Y.App.Div. 1955). *But see* City of Waco v. Hester, 805 S.W.2d at 815 (prisoner was not contributorily negligent in entering a shower area after being intimidated by his assailant).

[966]"Contributory negligence is conduct on the part of the plaintiff, contributing as a legal cause to the harm he has suffered, which falls below the standard to which he is required to conform for his own protection." W. Page Keeton et al., *Prosser and Keeton on the Law of Torts* § 65 at 451 (5th ed. 1984).

may recover partial damages if the defendant is also negligent.[967]

Depending on the facts of your case and whom you are suing, tort law immunity rules may prevent you from recovering damages.[968] In inmate assault cases, plaintiffs frequently have problems with the immunity rule covering acts that are "discretionary" (involve judgment) and not "ministerial."[969] Thus, in a case where a prisoner was assaulted with a large pin used to close laundry bags, a court said the prisoner couldn't pursue damages for officials' negligence in providing the pins, since that decision involved discretion. However, he could seek damages on the ground that prison officials had failed to follow their own staffing plan and had left the gymnasium where the assault occurred unsupervised.[970]

Some courts have held that a discretionary act "is one which requires a balancing of complex and competing

---

[967]*Prosser and Keeton on the Law of Torts* § 67 at 468–79; *see, e.g.,* White v. State, 167 A.D.2d 646, 563 N.Y.S.2d 239, 241 (N.Y.App. Div. 1990) (plaintiff's conduct was not "superseding negligence" barring recovery but was contributory negligence reducing damages by 40%); Saunders v. State of Rhode Island, 731 F.2d 81, 82 (1st Cir. 1984) (jury found plaintiff and State each 50% negligent).

Contributory negligence is not a defense to an allegation of intentional or reckless conduct by prison staff. Santiago v. Lane, 894 F.2d 218, 224 (7th Cir. 1990).

[968]Tort immunities are discussed further in Ch. 8, § L.5.

[969]As one court put it, "an official duty is ministerial when it is absolute, certain and imperative, involving merely execution of a specific duty arising from fixed and designated facts. Discretionary or judicial duties are such as necessarily require the exercise of reason in the adaptation of the means to an end, and discretion in determining how or whether the act shall be done or the course pursued." Travis v. Pinto, 87 N.J.Super. 263, 208 A.2d 828, 831 (N.J.Super. 1965).

This immunity generally does not apply to grossly negligent acts, Jackson v. Dep't of Corrections, 301 S.C. 125, 390 S.E.2d 467, 469 (S.C.App. 1989), *aff'd,* 302 S.C. 519, 397 S.E.2d 377 (S.C. 1990), or those based on "corrupt or malicious motives." Thiele v. Kennedy, 18 Ill.App.3d 465, 309 N.E.2d 394, 395–96 (Ill.App. 1974).

[970]Lyons v. State by Humphrey by Pung, 366 N.W.2d 621, 623-24 (Minn.App. 1985); *see* Newton v. Black, 133 F.3d 301, 306–07 (5th Cir. 1998) (officer who failed to report a threat was immune because reporting threats was discretionary and not ministerial); Wilks v. Young, 897 F.2d 896, 899–900 (7th Cir. 1990) (policy to follow separation orders only in general population and not in special housing was not ministerial; Wisconsin law); Davis v. Pringle, 642 F. Supp. 171, 178-79 (N.D.Ga. 1986) (warden's and supervisors' failure to take greater security precautions was discretionary; officers' lapses in guarding plaintiff were non-discretionary; warden's failure to obey statute requiring "comprehensive plans" for such incidents was non-discretionary); Upchurch v. State, 51 Haw. 150, 454 P.2d 112, 115 (Haw. 1989) (rules for protective custody placement were discretionary; failure to carry them out, or negligence in applying them, was not discretionary); *see also* City of Waco v. Hester, 805 S.W.2d at 812–13 ("police-protection exemption" for negligent formulation of policy did not bar a suit based on the failure to implement a segregation policy). *But see* Keeland v. Yamhill County, 24 Or.App. 85, 545 P.2d 137, 139 (Or. App. 1976) (decision to permit inmates in dormitory to possess razor blades was ministerial and not discretionary).

---

factors at the planning, rather than the operational, stage of development."[971] In practice, however, many courts apply discretionary immunity to ordinary day-to-day decisions of prison officials.[972] That immunity is a particular problem under the Federal Tort Claims Act (FTCA), where it is called the "discretionary function exception" to the FTCA's waiver of the government's sovereign immunity against suit.[973] One appellate decision says it bars liability for conduct that "involves an element of judgment or choice" that in turn "involves considerations of social, economic, and political policy."[974] In that case, the court held that the failure of prison staff to perform a Central Inmate Monitoring (CIM) evaluation of a prisoner's cellmate, who threatened and then strangled him, was actionable under the FTCA, since the cellmate was a state prisoner who was subject to CIM requirements by mandatory (*i.e.,* non-discretionary) regulation. However, the failure to search the "SENTRY" database was subject to the discretionary exception because there is no mandatory duty to perform such a search. The failure to take action other than a cell search when the prisoner reported his cellmate's threat was protected by the discretionary function exception, since prison regulations gave staff discretion in

---

[971]Lyons v. State by Humphrey by Pung, 366 N.W.2d at 623; *accord,* Taylor v. Buff, 172 Cal.App.3d 384, 389, 218 Cal.Rptr. 249, 252 (Cal.App. 1985).

Discretionary immunity is also discussed in Ch. 8, § L.5.

[972]*See, e.g.,* Thiele v. Kennedy, 309 N.E.2d at 395–96; Travis v. Pinto, 208 A.2d at 831 (holding release from protective custody discretionary); Hann v. State, 137 Misc.2d 605, 521 N.Y.S.2d 973, 977 (Sup.Ct. 1987) (early return of segregation inmate to general population based on psychiatric discharge was discretionary).

[973]*See* 28 U.S.C. § 2680(a) (the United States has not consented to suit where the claim is "based upon the exercise or performance or the failure to exercise or perform a discretionary function or duty on the part of a federal agency or an employee of the Government, whether or not the discretion involved be abused"). This immunity is discussed further in Ch. 8, § C.2.a.

[974]Alfrey v. U.S., 276 F.3d 557, 561 (9th Cir. 2002). Thus, in *Montez v. U.S.,* 359 F.3d 392 (6th Cir. 2004), the court held that placing a former protective custody prisoner in a prison where he could not be kept safe involved a discretionary function. The court reasoned that the statute requiring the Bureau of Prisons to "provide for the safekeeping" and "provide for the protection" of federal prisoners, 18 U.S.C. § 4042(a), doesn't tell the Bureau how to fulfill that duty. The court said it presumed that when policy confers discretion, the exercise of that discretion is grounded in policy and therefore is immunized. Montez v. U.S., 359 F.3d at 395, 397–98; *see* Palay v. U.S., 349 F.3d 418, 427–31 (7th Cir. 2003) (exception applies only where the alleged negligent act involves an element of judgment or choice that is "based on considerations of public policy"; a decisionmaker must be charged with making such policy-related judgments for choices to qualify for the exception; the exception does not apply to persons making decisions they are not authorized to make); Cohen v. U.S., 151 F.3d 1338, 1343–44 (11th Cir. 1998) (classification is a discretionary activity and plaintiff could not recover for placement of his assailant, who had a serious criminal history, in a minimum security institution; court notes that actions performed at the "operational level" may still be entitled to the discretionary function exception).

deciding how to respond, and that discretion involved policy considerations such as how intrusive a search should be conducted and how to set priorities among different risks.[975]

Discretionary immunity does not apply in federal civil rights actions alleging deliberate indifference. You should research your state's law on this immunity before deciding whether to proceed by tort suit or by civil rights action. Some cases that are barred by discretionary immunity may be successfully pursued as deliberate indifference claims.[976]

State statutes may provide other immunities for prison officials,[977] or establish other rules of law that have the same effect as immunity.[978]

---

[975]Alfrey v. U.S., 276 F.3d at 562–66.

[976]For example, in *White v. County of Palm Beach*, 404 So.2d 123, 125 (Fla.App. 1981), the plaintiff complained that the jail was "old, inadequately funded and overcrowded"; the court held that the county was immune for the planning decision not to provide better facilities. By contrast, damages have been awarded in civil rights suits in which assaults were shown to have been caused by municipal policies of overcrowding. *See* Morgan v. District of Columbia, 824 F.2d 1049, 1060–61 (D.C. Cir. 1987); McKenna v. County of Nassau, 538 F. Supp. 737, 741 (E.D.N.Y. 1982), *aff'd*, 714 F.2d 115 (2d Cir. 1982).

In *Taylor v. Buff*, 172 Cal.App.3d 384, 218 Cal.Rptr. 249 (Cal. App. 1985), other prisoners were able to assault the plaintiff because the jail's locking system did not work. The court held that the county supervisors were immune for their failure to provide an improved monitoring system in the jail, despite a state regulation requiring it, because "[a] decision involving the allocation of limited funds is a purely discretionary one." 218 Cal.Rptr. at 253. The sheriff was immune for his failure to fix the locks because of a state statute and also enjoyed discretionary immunity for deciding to leave the doors open at night rather than chaining them shut. The county itself was protected by a state statute immunizing counties from liability for prisoner-inflicted injuries. In our opinion, since the problem of broken locks was well known to the county government, a federal court could have awarded damages against the county government or other responsible parties for the failure either to repair the locks or to take alternative safety precautions.

[977]Many states hold public employees or agencies immune from tort liability for acts performed within the scope of their authority unless they were done maliciously, in bad faith, wantonly or recklessly. *See, e.g.*, Gulett v. Haines, 229 F. Supp. 2d 806, 819–20 (S.D.Ohio 2002). There are other varieties of immunity that vary from state to state. *See, e.g.*, Newton v. Black, 133 F.3d 301, 306 (5th Cir. 1998) (under state qualified immunity law, in a negligence case, the defendant must be shown to have breached a ministerial duty or to have substantially exceeded his authority; failing to report a threat was not ministerial, since policy allowed staff discretion to determine the seriousness of the threat, and there is no evidence that the defendant exceeded his authority); Taylor v. Buff, 218 Cal.Rptr. at 252 (citing Cal.Govt. Code § 821) (government employees are immune for failure to comply with state jail minimum standards); Bollinger v. Schneider, 64 Ill.App.3d 758, 21 Ill. Dec. 522, 381 N.E.2d 849, 851–54 (1978) (citing Ill.Rev.Stat. 1975, ch. 85, §§ 4-103, 9-103) (public entities and employees are immune from liability for "failure to provide sufficient equipment, personnel or facilities" in jails and prisons, but this immunity is waived if the public entity purchases insurance).

[978]*See* Ch. 8, § L.5, nn.877–879.

2. Use of Force by Staff

Excessive or unnecessary force by police or prison staff violates the Constitution, and may be remedied by damages[979] or injunctive relief.[980] In serious cases the officers or supervisors may be criminally prosecuted.[981] Prisoners, too, are sometimes criminally prosecuted and convicted in

---

[979]Many cases cited in this section involve awards of compensatory or punitive damages or both. *See* Wright v. Sheppard, 919 F.2d 665, 669–73 (11th Cir. 1990), for a discussion of damage issues in a use of force case; *see* Ch. 8, § O.1, for a more general discussion of damages for civil rights violations, and Ch. 9, § E, for discussion of the effect of the Prison Litigation Reform Act on damages in prisoners' actions.

[980]Injunctive relief is generally granted only when prisoners prove a widespread pattern or practice of unconstitutional use of force. *See* Hoptowit v. Ray, 682 F.2d 1237, 1249–51 (9th Cir. 1982); Finney v. Arkansas Bd. of Correction, 505 F.2d 194, 205 (8th Cir. 1974); Inmates of Attica v. Rockefeller, 453 F.2d 12, 22–23 (2d Cir. 1971); Von Colln v. County of Ventura, 189 F.R.D. 583, 597–99 (C.D.Cal.1999) (granting preliminary injunction against use of restraint chairs); Madrid v. Gomez, 889 F. Supp. 1146, 1280–82 (N.D.Cal. 1995); Fisher v. Koehler, 692 F. Supp. 1519, 1562–65 (S.D.N.Y. 1988), *injunction entered*, 718 F. Supp. 1111 (S.D.N.Y. 1989), *aff'd*, 902 F.2d 2 (2d Cir. 1990); Ruiz v. Estelle, 503 F. Supp. 1265, 1299–1307 (S.D.Tex. 1980), *aff'd in pertinent part*, 679 F.2d 1115 (5th Cir. 1982); *see also* Hawkins v. Comparet-Cassani, 251 F.3d 1230, 1239–44 (9th Cir. 2001) (upholding injunction against use of stun belts in court in part, directing modification in part); Ruiz v. Johnson, 154 F. Supp. 2d 975, 991–94, 999–1000 (S.D.Tex. 2001) (continuing injunction governing use of force, indicating further relief needed). There are some cases in which injunctions have been issued without such a showing. Commonwealth of Pennsylvania v. Porter, 659 F.2d 306, 312–13, 321–22 (3d Cir. 1981) (individual police officer limited to desk duty based on history of unconstitutional misuse of force); Cohen v. Coahoma County, Miss., 805 F. Supp. 398, 405–06 (N.D.Miss. 1992) (granting injunction based on a single incident because the Sheriff said he would do the same thing under similar circumstances). *See* Ch. I, § O.2, concerning injunctions.

[981]*See, e.g.*, U.S. v. LaVallee, 439 F.3d 670 (10th Cir. 2006) (affirming convictions of officers who beat prisoners and fabricated reports and self-inflicted injuries to cover up); U.S. v. Serrata, 425 F.3d 886 (10th Cir. 2005) (affirming convictions of officers and a lieutenant for beating a prisoner and falsifying reports and an assault charge; noting an officer's work boots were properly classified as a dangerous weapon for sentencing); U.S. v. Donnelly, 370 F.3d 87 (1st Cir. 2004) (affirming sentence of officer for conspiracy and violation of civil rights for unwritten agreement to use excessive force on prisoners who "disrespected" staff "to teach the inmates a lesson"); U.S. v. Walsh, 194 F.3d 37, 41–42, 48–51 (2d Cir. 1999) (affirming conviction of officer for demanding that mentally ill prisoner allow him to step on the prisoner's penis in return for giving him a cigarette); U.S. v. Strange, 370 F. Supp. 2d 644, 651 (N.D.Ohio 2005) (sentencing former sheriff's deputy for retaliatory jail beating, noting that such beatings "were apparently condoned and even ordered by superior officers"); U.S. v. Clayton, 172 F.3d 347, 351 n.4 (5th Cir. 1999) (affirming conviction for kicking an arrestee in the head as she lay unresisting in handcuffs).

connection with use of force incidents, which may limit their ability to seek relief in subsequent lawsuits.[982]

a. The Constitutional Standards The precise constitutional standard applicable to a use of force claim depends on whether the plaintiff is a convict, a pretrial detainee, or an arrestee at the time force is used, though it is open to question how different the standards really are in practice.

1) Convicts Convicted prisoners are protected from misuse of force by the Cruel and Unusual Punishments Clause of the Eighth Amendment. The Supreme Court has held that "whenever prison officials stand accused of using excessive physical force in violation of the Cruel and Unusual Punishments Clause, the core judicial inquiry is . . . whether force was applied in a good-faith effort to maintain or restore discipline, or maliciously and sadistically to cause harm."[983]

In deciding whether force was used "maliciously or sadistically," the extent of injury inflicted is "one factor," and "[t]he absence of serious injury is therefore relevant to the Eighth Amendment inquiry, but does not end it."[984] Other factors that the Court said may be relevant are "the need for application of force, the relationship between that need and the amount of force used, the threat 'reasonably perceived by the responsible officials,' and 'any efforts made to temper the severity of a forceful response.'"[985]

The "malicious and sadistic" standard applies to the actions of staff who are directly using force.[986] The deliberate

indifference standard applies to staff members who stand by and do not intervene in an illegal beating, and to claims of inadequate policy, supervision, training, or control by supervisors or local governments.[987]

2) Pretrial Detainees Detainees are protected against excessive force by the Due Process Clause of the Fourteenth Amendment or (for federal detainees) the Fifth Amendment. The standard governing detainees' use of force claims is not settled. For many years, most courts followed the Second Circuit's decision in *Johnson v. Glick*, which held:

> Not every push or shove . . . violates a prisoner's constitutional rights. . . . [A] court must look to such factors as the need for the application of force, the relationship between the need and the amount of force that was used, the extent of injury inflicted, and whether force was applied in a good faith effort to maintain or restore discipline or maliciously and sadistically for the very purpose of causing harm.[988]

These factors were also cited in the Supreme Court's *Hudson v. McMillian* decision, discussed in the previous section, concerning convicts' Eighth Amendment claims. The difference is that in *Hudson*, all the other factors are weighed only to decide whether force was used "maliciously and sadistically," but under *Johnson v. Glick*, all of them including malicious and sadistic intent are given equal status.

Some courts have continued to use the *Johnson v. Glick* standard.[989] However, since *Hudson v. McMillian* was decided, several federal circuits have applied its "malicious and sadistic" standard to detainees under the Due Process Clause as well as to convicts under the Eighth Amendment.[990]

---

[982]Rules of *res judicata* may limit prisoners' ability to dispute the facts underlying a criminal conviction. Further, claims inconsistent with a criminal conviction cannot be pursued in a civil action unless the criminal conviction is first overturned in a state forum or a federal habeas corpus proceeding. The latter rule also applies to disciplinary convictions that resulted in a loss of good time. These issues are discussed in Ch. 8, §§ H.1, M.

[983]Hudson v. McMillian, 503 U.S. 1, 6–7, 112 S. Ct. 995 (1992); *accord*, Wilkins v. Gaddy, ___ U.S. ___, 130 S. Ct. 1175, 1178 (2010) (per curiam); *see* Baskerville v. Mulvaney, 411 F.3d 45, 47–48 (2d Cir. 2005) (quoting and discussing jury instructions); Johnson v. Breeden, 280 F.3d 1308, 1313–16 (11th Cir. 2002) (same).

The Court had previously applied this rule to riots and disturbances in prison, *see* Whitley v. Albers, 475 U.S. 312, 320–21, 106 S. Ct. 1078 (1986), but in *Hudson* it extended it to all use of force cases involving convicts. Cases holding otherwise are now overruled, at least on that point. Blyden v. Mancusi, 186 F.3d 252, 263 n.4 (2d Cir. 1999).

Some older cases had held that "spontaneous, isolated" or "unprovoked" attacks are not "punishment," but these are no longer good law. U.S. v. Walsh, 194 F.3d at 48–49 (dictum); Pelfrey v. Chambers, 43 F.3d 1034, 1036–37 (6th Cir. 1995). *But see* Cain v. Rock, 67 F. Supp. 2d 544, 552 (D.Md. 1999) (holding random sexual assault was not "punishment").

[984]Hudson v. McMillian, 503 U.S. at 7; *accord*, Wilkins v. Gaddy, 130 S. Ct. at 1178–79; Wright v. Goord, 554 F.3d 255, 269 (2d Cir. 2009).

[985]*Hudson*, 503 U.S. at 7 (quoting *Whitley v. Albers, supra*).

[986]*Hudson*, 503 U.S. at 7–8 (standard applies "whenever prison officials stand accused of *using* excessive physical force in violation

of the Cruel and Unusual Punishments Clause") (emphasis supplied).

[987]*See* § G.2.d of this chapter, nn.1125–1133.

[988]Johnson v. Glick, 481 F.2d 1028, 1033 (2d Cir. 1973); *see* the following cases which all apply some variations of the *Johnson v. Glick* standard: White v. Roper, 901 F.2d 1501, 1507 (9th Cir. 1990); U.S. v. Cobb, 905 F.2d 784, 787 (4th Cir. 1990); Meade v. Grubbs, 841 F.2d 1512, 1527 (10th Cir. 1988); Brooks v. Pembroke City Jail, 722 F. Supp. 1294, 1299–1300 (E.D.N.C. 1989).

The Supreme Court stated that "the Due Process Clause protects a pretrial detainee from the use of excessive force that amounts to punishment." Graham v. Connor, 490 U.S. 386, 395 n.10, 109 S. Ct. 1865 (1989). It did not explain what "amounts to punishment" means. In *U.S. v. Cobb*, the court defined "punitive" by reference to the *Johnson v. Glick* standard. 905 F.2d at 789. The question of what constitutes "punishment" of a pre-trial detainee is discussed generally in Ch. 6.

[989]*See* Beltran v. O'Mara, 405 F. Supp. 2d 140, 160 (D.N.H. 2005), *reconsideration denied on other grounds*, 2006 WL 240558 (D.N.H., Jan 31, 2006); Garcia v. City of Boston, 115 F. Supp. 2d 74, 81 (D.Mass. 2000), *aff'd on other grounds*, 253 F.3d 147 (1st Cir. 2001).

[990]*See* Fennell v. Gilstrap, 559 F.3d 1212, 1217 (11th Cir. 2009) (per curiam); Fuentes v. Wagner, 206 F.3d 335, 347 (3d Cir. 2000)

Others have tried to apply the *Bell v. Wolfish*[991] detainee conditions of confinement standard to use of force cases,[992] or have devised other standards.[993] One circuit has said

generally that detainees' use of force claims are governed by the Fourth Amendment standard of objective reasonableness that is applied to uses of force during arrest, but this holding probably refers only to persons who have not yet been arraigned.[994]

3) Arrestees and Others "Seized" by the Police

Police use of force is almost always analyzed under the Fourth Amendment "reasonableness" standard, which governs "all claims that law enforcement officers have used excessive force—deadly or not—in the course of an arrest, investigatory stop, or other 'seizure' of a free citizen. . . ."[995] Under the Fourth Amendment, you need not show malicious intent because the officer's state of mind is not important. The question is "whether the officers' actions are 'objectively reasonable' in light of the facts and circumstances confronting them, without regard to their underlying intent or motivation."[996] Concerning deadly force, the Supreme Court has held that it may only be used against a fleeing suspect "[w]here the officer has probable cause to believe that the suspect poses a threat of serious physical harm, either to the officer or to others. . . ."[997]

(*Hudson* standard applies, at least in cases involving prison disturbances); U.S. v. Walsh, 194 F.3d 37, 47–48 (2d Cir. 1999); Valencia v. Wiggins, 981 F.2d 1440, 1446 (5th Cir. 1993); *see also* Bozeman v. Orum, 422 F.3d 1265, 1271 (11th Cir. 2005) (stating that the *Johnson* standard turns on good faith versus malicious and sadistic intent, like the Eighth Amendment standard).

[991]441 U.S. 520, 99 S. Ct. 1861 (1979).

[992]*See* Birdine v. Gray, 375 F. Supp. 2d 874, 879 (D.Neb. 2005) (whether the action was done for a punitive purpose, was rationally related to a legitimate purpose, and was excessive relative to that purpose); Sulkowska v. City of New York, 129 F. Supp. 2d 274, 291–92 (S.D.N.Y. 2001) (court applies *Bell v. Wolfish*, does not cite *Hudson v. McMillian*, and says that plaintiff must show that defendants had reason to know of facts creating a high degree of risk of physical harm and acted in conscious disregard or indifference to that risk); Simms v. Hardesty, 303 F. Supp. 2d 656, 667–68 (D.Md. 2003) (plaintiff must show that officers' use of force was intended as punishment, was not merely an incident of some other legitimate purpose, and the resulting injury was more than *de minimis*), *aff'd*, 104 Fed.Appx. 853 (4th Cir. 2004) (unpublished); Miller v. Fairman, 872 F. Supp. 498, 505–06 (N.D.Ill. 1994) ("Pretrial detainees have a Fourteenth Amendment due process right against being subjected by jail guards to excessive force that amounts to punishment."); *see also* Lewis v. Downey, 581 F.3d 467, 474 (7th Cir. 2009) (assuming due process standard provides greater protections than Eighth Amendment, but not saying what they are because plaintiff waived the argument).

[993]*See* Andrews v. Neer, 253 F.3d 1052, 1060–61 (10th Cir. 2001) (detainees are entitled to an "objective reasonableness" standard under the Due Process Clause similar to arrestees under the Fourth Amendment); Wilson v. Williams, 83 F.3d 870, 875–76 (7th Cir. 1996) (detainees are arguably entitled to a higher standard of conduct in the use of force than are convicts; actual intent or reckless disregard must be shown, but may be inferred from objective factors, including the extent of injury, the need for force, relationship between need and amount of force, the threat reasonably perceived by staff, and any attempt to temper the severity of the response); Hill v. Algor, 85 F. Supp. 2d 391, 401 (D.N.J. 2000) ("The standard for § 1983 excessive force claims governed by the Fourteenth Amendment—that the officer's conduct 'shock the conscience'—is much higher than the 'objective reasonableness' standard imposed by the Fourth Amendment."); Moore v. Hosier, 43 F. Supp. 2d 978, 985 (N.D.Ind. 1998) (detainees arguably are entitled to a higher degree of legal protection than the Eighth Amendment; plaintiff must prove that the defendants "acted with deliberate or callous indifference, evidenced by an actual intent to violate [the plaintiff's] rights or reckless disregard for his rights").

One court has suggested the following standard for detainee use of force claims:

> First, search for evidence that the use of force was intended to punish the detainee. . . . This intent inquiry is not substantially different than the current Eighth Amendment requirement, although intentionally easier for a plaintiff to meet. Second, if there is no direct evidence of intent, determine (1) whether a legitimate interest in the use of force is evident from the circumstances, and (2) if so, whether the force used was necessary to further that interest. . . . As in *Hudson v. McMillian*, the detainee

would not be required to show severe injuries. . . . If the jail official fails either prong, his conduct violated the pretrial detainee's due process rights under the Fourteenth Amendment.

Telfair v. Gilberg, 868 F. Supp. 1396, 1412 (N.D.Ga. 1994), *aff'd*, 87 F.3d 1330 (11th Cir. 1996) (unpublished). Whatever its merit, this decision appears to be overruled by the Eleventh Circuit cases cited in n.990, above.

[994]Lolli v. County of Orange, 351 F.3d 410, 415 (9th Cir. 2003). In *Lolli*, the court relied on *Gibson v. County of Washoe, Nev.*, 290 F.3d 1175, 1197 (9th Cir. 2002), and *Pierce v. Multnomah County*, 76 F.3d 1032 (9th Cir. 1996). *Pierce* actually says that the Fourth Amendment applies to arrestees before they are arraigned or released, after it acknowledged the due process "no punishment" standard. 76 F.3d at 1042–43. *Gibson*, like *Lolli*, actually involved a pre-arraignment arrestee. It is likely that the Ninth Circuit will make a different ruling in a case involving use of force against a post-arraignment detainee.

[995]Graham v. Connor, 490 U.S. 386, 395, 109 S. Ct. 1865 (1989); Parker v. Gerrish, 547 F.3d 1, 11 (1st Cir. 2008) (Fourth Amendment analysis of tasering incident); U.S. v. Schatzle, 901 F.2d 252, 254 (2d Cir. 1990). In *Graham*, the Supreme Court overruled a large number of earlier cases that had applied the Due Process Clause to claims of police brutality.

[996]Graham v. Connor, 490 U.S. at 397. Evidence that officers acted out of malice may, however, help prove that their actions were not reasonable. Williams v. Bramer, 180 F.3d 699, 704 (5th Cir.), *clarified*, 186 F.3d 633 (5th Cir. 1999).

At least one federal court has tried more than once to make this requirement more demanding for plaintiffs. In *Williams v. Bramer*, the court held that a plaintiff must show "(1) an injury (2) which resulted directly and only from the use of force that was clearly excessive to the need and (3) the force used was objectively unreasonable." 180 F.3d at 703.

[997]Tennessee v. Garner, 471 U.S. 1, 11, 105 S. Ct. 1694 (1985); *see* Mercado v. City of Orlando, 407 F.3d 1152, 1157–58 (11th Cir. 2005) (shooting a person in the head at close range with a "Sage Launcher,"

The courts do not agree about when a person ceases to be an "arrestee" protected by the Fourth Amendment.[998] Some courts say the Fourth Amendment applies until the arrestee receives a probable cause determination in court,[999] or as long as she remains in the custody of the arresting officers,[1000] or some combination of these or other factors.[1001] Other courts have limited Fourth Amendment scrutiny of use of force to the time and place of arrest.[1002]

In cases where force by police does not involve any sort of seizure, the Due Process Clause protects persons against excessive force.[1003]

b. Applying the Standards   It is open to question how different these standards really are in practice.[1004] Whether you are arguing that force was objectively unreasonable in a Fourth Amendment case or used maliciously and sadistically in an Eighth Amendment case, you must usually show that it was not justified by any legitimate law enforcement or prison management need, or was completely out of proportion to that need.

There are several issues that frequently arise in use of force cases of all types.

1) Amount of Force   There is no fixed line for how much force violates the Constitution; it depends on all the circumstances. "When prison officials maliciously and sadistically use force to cause harm, contemporary standards of decency always are violated," unless the force is "*de minimis*" (minimal).[1005] But even *de miminis* force may

---

which shoots a projectile that delivers about the energy of a thrown baseball, was deadly force and could violate the Fourth Amendment where the arrestee, though he had a knife, did not make any threatening move towards the police and was not committing a crime or resisting arrest, and there were alternatives such as using a crisis negotiation team); Deorle v. Rutherford, 272 F.3d 1272, 1286–87 (9th Cir. 2001) (holding use of a "less lethal" "beanbag" round consisting of lead shot in a cloth bag could constitute excessive force where the suspect was walking towards police but was unarmed and had been given no warning).

[998]*See* Graham v. Connor, 490 U.S. at 395 n.10 (declining to decide the issue).

[999]Pierce v. Multnomah County, Oregon, 76 F.3d 1032, 1042–43 (9th Cir.1996); Frohmader v. Wayne, 958 F.2d 1024, 1026–27 (10th Cir. 1992); Hill v. Algor, 85 F. Supp. 2d 391, 402–03 (D.N.J. 2000); Fournier v. Joyce, 753 F. Supp. 989, 991–93 (D.Me. 1990) (Fourth Amendment standard applied to arrest made in jail waiting area); Henson v. Thezan, 717 F. Supp. 1330 (N.D.Ill. 1989) (post-arrest abuse is governed by the Fourth Amendment until first appearance in court).

Under this reasoning, a person arrested pursuant to a warrant, who had already had a determination of probable cause, might be subject to the due process standard for detainees immediately after arrest. *See* Riley v. Dorton, 115 F.3d 1159, 1161–62 (4th Cir. 1997) (en banc).

[1000]McDowell v. Rogers, 863 F.2d 1302, 1306 (6th Cir.1988); Robins v. Harum, 773 F.2d 1004, 1010 (9th Cir.1985).

[1001]Gutierrez v. City of San Antonio, 139 F.3d 441, 452 (5th Cir. 1998) (Fourth Amendment applies until "*after* the incidents of arrest are completed, *after* the plaintiff has been released from the arresting officer's custody, and *after* the plaintiff has been in detention awaiting trial for a significant period of time") (quoting Valencia v. Wiggins, 981 F.2d 1440, 1443–44 (5th Cir.1993)); Titran v. Ackman, 893 F.2d 145, 147 (7th Cir. 1990) (arrestee's presence in jail and completion of booking invoked due process standard); Powell v. Gardner, 891 F.2d 1039, 1044 (2d Cir. 1989) (dictum) (Fourth Amendment "probably should be applied at least to the period prior to the time when the person arrested is arraigned or formally charged, and remains in the custody (sole or joint) of the arresting officer"); Calhoun v. Thomas, 360 F. Supp. 2d 1264, 1271–74 (M.D.Ala. 2005) (person not formally arrested, not arraigned, in arresting officer's custody and being interrogated in handcuffs was governed by the Fourth Amendment). In *Wilson v. Spain*, 209 F.3d 713, 715–16 (8th Cir. 2000), the court did not define the dividing line between arrest and detention, but applied the Fourth Amendment to a case in which the prisoner had been booked and placed in a cell and the arresting officer then opened the cell and hit him with the cell door.

[1002]*See* Orem v. Rephann, 523 F.3d 442, 446 (4th Cir. 2008) (due process governed force used while transporting arrestee in patrol car); Riley v. Dorton, 115 F.3d 1159, 1161–62 (4th Cir. 1997) (en banc) (Fourth Amendment scrutiny limited to the time and

place of arrest); Brothers v. Klevenhagen, 28 F.3d 452, 457 (5th Cir. 1994) (persons in police custody are protected by due process standards); Wilkins v. May, 872 F.2d 190, 195 (7th Cir. 1989) (excessive force during interrogation of an arrestee is governed by due process).

As stated in the previous section, *see* n.994, one court has said that the Fourth Amendment protects pre-trial detainees, but it probably didn't really mean it.

[1003]Cummings v. McIntyre, 271 F.3d 341, 345 (1st Cir. 2001) (noting court "substantially agree[s]" with *Johnson v. Glick* standard in this context).

[1004]Davis v. Little, 851 F.2d 605, 610 (2d Cir. 1988) (stating that the similarities between due process and Fourth Amendment standards "far outweigh the differences"); *accord,* Titran v. Ackman, 893 F.2d 145, 147 (7th Cir. 1990).

[1005]Hudson v. McMillian, 503 U.S. 1, 9–10, 112 S. Ct. 995 (1992); *see* Samuels v. Hawkins, 157 F.3d 557, 558 (8th Cir. 1998) (throwing a cup of water on a prisoner, even accompanied by threats, was *de minimis*); Riley v. Dorton, 115 F.3d 1159, 1161, 1167–68 (4th Cir. 1997) (en banc) (force was *de minimis* where police officer stuck a pen a quarter of an inch into arrestee's nose, threatening to rip it open, and slapped him across the face with "medium force"); McClanahan v. City of Moberly, 35 F. Supp. 2d 744, 745–46 (E.D.Mo. 1998) (slaps to the face were *de minimis*), *aff'd,* 168 F.3d 494 (8th Cir. 1998) (unpublished); Aziz Zarif Shabazz v. Pico, 994 F. Supp. 460, 471 (S.D.N.Y. 1998) (kicking a prisoner's feet is *de minimis* even if it should not be done). *But see* Griffin v. Crippen, 193 F.3d 89, 91–92 (2d Cir. 1999) (dismissal of Fourth Amendment case on ground that bruised shin and swelling over knee were *de minimis* was wrong); Atkins v. County of Orange, 372 F. Supp. 2d 377, 400–01 (S.D.N.Y. 2005) (claim that prisoner was slammed into doors and walls, resulting in severe pain in his shoulder which lasted three to five days, could not be dismissed as *de minimis*); Watts v. County of Sacramento, 65 F. Supp. 2d 1111, 1119–20 (E.D.Cal. 1999) (lifting a suspect by the handcuffs was not *de minimis*), *reversed and remanded on other grounds,* 256 F.3d 886 (9th Cir. 2001).

be unconstitutional if it is "repugnant to the conscience of mankind."[1006] If there is no need for force, the Constitution may be violated by relatively small amounts of force,[1007]

even a push or a shove.[1008] However, serious and even deadly force does not violate the Constitution if the necessity for force is serious enough and the officers did not intend to cause needless harm.[1009] Even when there is a need to use some force,

---

In some cases, courts have held rather substantial force to be *de minimis*. *See, e.g.*, Nolin v. Isbell, 207 F.3d 1253, 1258 & n.4 (11th Cir. 2000) (allegation that a police officer grabbed the plaintiff from behind by shoulder and wrist, threw him against a van several feet away, kneed him in the back and pushed his head into the side of the van, resulting in bruises to forehead, chest, and wrists, alleged only minimal force); Nowell v. Arcadian Ambulance Service, 147 F. Supp. 2d 495, 509–10 (W.D.La. 2001) (police officer who put knee in the face of an arrestee who kept spitting at him used *de minimis* force); Ostrander v. Horn, 145 F. Supp. 2d 614, 617–19 (M.D.Pa. 2001) (finding *de minimis* force where prisoner who had done nothing wrong, as part of a *training exercise*, was forcefully dragged from his cell, placed in a cage with his hands cuffed behind his back, then dragged back, strip-searched, and returned to his cell; officers shoved his face into a corner while screaming at him not to turn around, twisting his arms while cuffing and uncuffing him), *aff'd*, 49 Fed.Appx. 391 (3d Cir. 2002) (unpublished).

[1006]Hudson v. McMillian, 503 U.S. at 9–10; *see* U.S. v. Walsh, 194 F.3d 37, 50 (2d Cir. 1997) (conduct of officer who required mentally ill prisoner to let him step on the prisoner's penis before giving him a cigarette was "repugnant to the conscience of mankind"); Laury v. Greenfield, 87 F. Supp. 2d 1210, 1217 (D.Kan. 2000) (assault with no penological justification is repugnant; plaintiff alleged he was assaulted after reporting staff misconduct).

[1007]Wilkins v. Gaddy, ___ U.S. ___, 130 S.Ct. 1175, 1178–79 (2010) (per curiam) ("An inmate who is gratuitously beaten by guards does not lose his ability to pursue an excessive force claim merely because he has the good fortune to escape without serious injury."); Pelfrey v. Chambers, 43 F.3d 1034, 1037 (6th Cir. 1995) (allegation that officers forcibly cut off the plaintiff's hair with a knife stated an Eighth Amendment claim; actions seemed "designed to frighten and degrade"); Felix v. McCarthy, 939 F.2d 699, 701–02 (9th Cir. 1991) (throwing a prisoner across a hallway into a wall without reason violated the Eighth Amendment); Campbell v. Grammer, 889 F.2d 797, 802 (8th Cir. 1989) (completely unjustified spraying with fire hose violated Eighth Amendment); Romaine v. Rawson, 140 F. Supp. 2d 204, 211–12 (N.D.N.Y. 2001) (slaps to the face violated the Eighth Amendment where there was no justification for any force); Tesoro v. Zavaras, 46 F. Supp. 2d 1118, 1123–24 (D.Colo. 1999) (allegation that officers grabbed and twisted plaintiff's genitals during a strip search while he was handcuffed and offering no resistance supported an Eighth Amendment claim); Mitchell v. Keane, 974 F. Supp. 332, 340–41 (S.D.N.Y. 1997) (twisting a baton in a restrained inmate's shackles, inflicting pain, supported an Eighth Amendment claim; the fact that the plaintiff had assaulted an officer earlier did not justify it), *aff'd*, 175 F.3d 1008 (2d Cir. 1999); Jones v. Huff, 789 F. Supp. 526, 536 (N.D.N.Y. 1992) ("unwarranted and cavalier" kicks in the buttocks violated the Eighth Amendment); Bee v. DeKalb County, 679 F. Supp. 1107, 1109, 1113 (N.D.Ga. 1988) (allegation of unprovoked blow to the face created a factual issue as to excessive force); Burris v. Kirkpatrick, 649 F. Supp. 740, 744–46 (N.D.Ind. 1986) (officer who threw hot water at another inmate and burned the plaintiff, leaving no permanent injury, violated the Eighth Amendment). *But see* Jackson v. Culbertson, 984 F.2d 699, 700 (5th Cir. 1993) (per curiam) (spraying with fire extinguisher that caused no injury was *de minimis*);

DeMallory v. Cullen, 855 F.2d 442, 444 (7th Cir. 1988) (spitting on an inmate did not violate the Constitution).

[1008]Abreu v. Nicholls, 2010 WL 726520, *3 (2d Cir. 2010) (unpublished) (pushing a prisoner's head halfway back with a rubber hammer, where circumstances indicated force was intended to humiliate, was not *de minimis* and supported an Eighth Amendment claim); H.C. by Hewett v. Jarrard, 786 F.2d 1080, 1085–86 (11th Cir. 1986) (a guard who pushed a juvenile inmate who was giggling and protesting the treatment of another inmate violated the Eighth Amendment); Harris v. Adams, 410 F. Supp. 2d 707, 713–14 (S.D.Ohio 2005) (arrestee who was pushed into a cell and injured his knee badly stated a Fourth Amendment and due process claim); Glisson v. Sangamon County Sheriff's Dep't, 408 F. Supp. 2d 609, 625–26 (C.D.Ill. 2006) (arrestee who was pushed into a wall and suffered a laceration on his back stated a Fourth Amendment claim); Hicks v. Weed, 90 F. Supp. 2d 260, 263 (W.D.N.Y. 260) (pushing a shackled prisoner against cells repeatedly was not *de minimis* force); Arroyo Lopez v. Nuttall, 25 F. Supp. 2d 407, 409–10 (S.D.N.Y. 1998) (awarding damages against an officer who shoved a prisoner without justification while he was praying); Winder v. Leak, 790 F. Supp. 1403, 1407 (N.D.Ill. 1992) (pushing a disabled inmate and causing him to fall violated the Eighth Amendment); Lindsey v. City of St. Paul, 732 F. Supp. 1000, 1002–03 (D.Minn. 1990) (constitutional claim was stated by an allegation that an elderly woman was pushed to the ground by police).

[1009]Whitley v. Albers, 475 U.S. 312, 322–26, 106 S. Ct. 1078 (1986) (use of shotgun in a riot/hostage situation did not violate the Eighth Amendment); Fennell v. Gilstrap, 559 F.3d 1212, 1218–19 (11th Cir. 2009) (per curiam) (kick to the face that caused three fractures, and for which deputy was fired, was not unconstitutional where the prisoner was resisting other officers and the defendant intended to kick him in the arm); Marquez v. Gutierrez, 322 F.3d 689, 692–93 (9th Cir. 2003) (prisoner's claim that he was shot, although uninvolved in the inmate fight that prompted the shooting, stated a claim under *Whitley*, but officers who could have perceived him as involved and threatening an assault victim were entitled to qualified immunity); Jeffers v. Gomez, 267 F.3d 895, 911–12 (9th Cir. 2001) (shooting of prisoner, apparently accidentally, while staff were trying to suppress a disturbance did not violate the Constitution absent malicious and sadistic intent); Grayson v. Peed, 195 F.3d 692, 696–97 (4th Cir. 1999) (officers were justified in restraining, punching, pepper-spraying, and placing in four-point restraints a disruptive prisoner, even though he died); Kinney v. Indiana Youth Center, 950 F.2d 462, 465–66 (7th Cir. 1991) (shooting of a prisoner trying to escape was not unlawful); Henry v. Perry, 866 F.2d 657, 659 (3d Cir. 1989) (officers could shoot to prevent the escape of a dangerous prisoner); Brown v. Smith, 813 F.2d 1187, 1188–89 (11th Cir.) (officer was justified in pinning a handcuffed inmate's neck against a wall with a baton where he refused to go back into his cell), *rehearing denied*, 818 F.2d 871 (11th Cir. 1987); Williams v. Kelley, 624 F.2d 695, 698 (5th Cir. 1980) (officers were not liable for accidentally strangling a prisoner while trying to subdue him); Hayes v. Wimberly, 625 F. Supp. 967, 969–70 (E.D.Ark. 1986) (officers were not liable in using a riot stick and gas to subdue a prisoner who had armed himself with a

the use of force completely excessive to the circumstances violates the Constitution.[1010] Conversely, "any efforts made to temper the severity of a forceful response" will weigh against a finding of liability.[1011]

2) Injury Prisoners need not prove a serious or significant injury to establish excessive force. In Eighth Amendment cases, the degree of injury is "relevant to the . . . inquiry but does not end it,"[1012] and nothing in the Fourth Amendment concept of an "unreasonable" seizure requires physical injury; it simply requires unreasonableness.[1013] As for pretrial detainees, officials are forbidden to inflict any punishment, not just injurious punishment, on them.[1014]

The extent of injury is therefore "but one of the factors to be considered. Even if the injuries suffered 'were not permanent or severe,' a plaintiff may still recover if 'the force used was unreasonable and excessive.'"[1015] Many courts have upheld constitutional use of force claims in which no physical injury was alleged, although most such cases involve a serious threat of injury or death[1016] or other

---

broken light bulb), *aff'd*, 815 F.2d 710 (8th Cir. 1987); Peebles v. Frey, 617 F. Supp. 1072, 1074 (E.D.Mo. 1985) (it was not excessive to punch an inmate in the head when he grabbed and shoved a captain who was trying to calm him down).

[1010]A good example is *Musgrove v. Broglin*, 651 F. Supp. 769, 773–76 (N.D.Ind. 1986), in which a prisoner failed to get out of bed and the officer dumped him out onto the floor, injuring him substantially; the court found an Eighth Amendment violation. *See also* Harris v. Chapman, 97 F.3d 499, 505–06 (11th Cir. 1996) (where officer snapped the plaintiff's head back in a towel, kicked him, and subjected him to racial abuse, jury finding for plaintiff upheld); Hickey v. Reeder, 12 F.3d 754, 758–59 (8th Cir. 1993) (shooting a prisoner with a taser gun because he refused to clean his cell violated the Eighth Amendment); Wilson v. Lambert, 789 F.2d 656, 657–58 (8th Cir. 1986) (beating of inmate who refused to return to a housing unit where he had been threatened with sexual assault violated the Eighth Amendment; damages awarded); Patzner v. Burkett, 779 F.2d 1363, 1371 (8th Cir. 1985) (jury question presented where legless man had been dragged out of his house without asking whether he had artificial legs or a wheelchair); Lewis v. Downs, 774 F.2d 711, 714–15 (6th Cir. 1985) (some force was justified but striking and kicking handcuffed persons was not); Martinez v. Rosado, 614 F.2d 829, 830–32 (2d Cir. 1980) (prisoners' refusal of orders did not justify an assault by officers); Brown v. Triche, 660 F. Supp. 281, 286 (N.D.Ill. 1987) (damages awarded to handcuffed inmate who was pushed against a wall, hit several times in the face and hit or kicked in the neck when he failed to sit down when ordered); Smith v. Dooley, 591 F. Supp. 1157, 1168–69 (W.D.La. 1984) (it was reasonable to use force to get an armed inmate out of his cell, but not to continue after he was disarmed and handcuffed); Bush v. Ware, 589 F. Supp. 1454, 1461–62 (E.D.Wis. 1984) (guards were justified in trying to take a metal object from a prisoner locked in his cell, but not in striking him with a flashlight and restraints).

[1011]Hudson v. McMillian, 503 U.S. at 7 (quoting *Whitley v. Albers*). *But see* Treats v. Morgan, 308 F.3d 868, 874 (8th Cir. 2002) (providing medical care after an unjustified pepper-spraying was not "tempering" the response; following the prison's rule to warn prisoners before spraying them would have tempered it).

[1012]Hudson v. McMillian, 503 U.S. at 7; *accord*, McHenry v. Chadwick, 896 F.2d 184, 187 (6th Cir. 1990).

[1013]Lester v. City of Chicago, 830 F.2d 706, 712–13 (7th Cir. 1987); Bibum v. Prince George's County, 85 F. Supp. 2d 557, 563 (D.Md. 2000) ("actual injury . . . physical or otherwise" will support a Fourth Amendment claim). Despite these holdings, some courts continue to assume that some degree of injury must be shown under the Fourth Amendment. *See, e.g.*, Williams v. Bramer, 180 F.3d 699, 704 (5th Cir.) (use of force plaintiff must show

"(1) an injury (2) which resulted directly and only from the use of force that was clearly excessive to the need and (3) the force used was objectively unreasonable"), *clarified*, 186 F.3d 633 (5th Cir. 1999).

[1014]Williams v. Boles, 841 F.2d 181, 183 (7th Cir. 1988).

[1015]Brooks v. Kyler, 204 F.3d 102, 108–09 (3d Cir. 2000) (jury could find Eighth Amendment violation based on superficial lacerations and abrasions; objective evidence of any particular degree of injury is not required); Felix v. McCarthy, 939 F.2d 699, 702 (9th Cir. 1991) (minor injuries are actionable when force is completely unjustified); Gray v. Spillman, 925 F.2d 90, 93 (4th Cir. 1991) (extent of injury is relevant to damages but is not a prerequisite to suit); Campbell v. Grammer, 889 F.2d 797, 802 (8th Cir. 1989) (injuries from completely unjustified spraying with a fire hose were actionable even though not severe); Corselli v. Coughlin, 842 F.2d 23, 26 (2d Cir. 1988) (citation omitted) (jury question was presented where inmate was allegedly knocked unconscious and sustained cuts, swelling, dizziness, and blurred vision); U.S. v. Bigham, 812 F.2d 943, 949 (5th Cir.) and cases cited in n.4 (severity of injury "tends to prove degree of force and the existence or absence of its justification"), *rehearing denied*, 816 F.2d 677 (5th Cir. 1987); Byrd v. Clark, 783 F.2d 1002, 1006 (11th Cir. 1986) (severity of injury is not determinative of constitutional violation but is probative of the amount of force used); Winder v. Leak, 790 F. Supp. 1403, 1407 (N.D.Ill. 1992) (pushing a handicapped inmate to the floor, causing pain, could violate the Eighth Amendment); Johnson v. Doherty, 713 F. Supp. 69, 71 (S.D.N.Y. 1989) (where injury is minor, court must "consider the context in which the incident occurred"); Bowman v. Casler, 622 F. Supp. 836, 838 (N.D.N.Y. 1985).

[1016]*See, e.g.*, Chandler v. District of Columbia Dep't of Corrections, 145 F.3d 1355, 1360 (D.C. Cir. 1998) ("the repeated threat of physical harm, . . . sexual harassment, . . . or a threat accompanied by conduct supporting the credibility of the threat" may violate the Eighth Amendment); Northington v. Jackson, 973 F.2d 1518, 1524 (10th Cir. 1992) (putting a gun to a prisoner's head and threatening to kill him may violate the Eighth Amendment); Martin v. Board of County Comm'rs of Pueblo County, 909 F.2d 402, 406–07 (10th Cir. 1990) (the threat of physical coercion stated a Fourth Amendment claim where the police disregarded medical orders by arresting and moving a woman hospitalized with a neck fracture); Jackson v. Crews, 873 F.2d 1105, 1108 (8th Cir. 1989) (threat to break the plaintiff's neck could violate the Fourth Amendment); Wilkins v. May, 872 F.2d 190, 195 (7th Cir. 1989) (interrogation at gunpoint may deny due process); Parrish v. Johnson, 800 F.2d 600, 605 (6th Cir. 1986) (verbal threats and waving of knife violated the Eighth Amendment; damages awarded); Burton v. Livingston, 791 F.2d 97, 100 (8th Cir. 1986) (death threat made at gunpoint by a prison guard was "a wanton act of cruelty which . . . was brutal despite the fact that it resulted in no measurable physical injury"); Black v. Stephens, 662 F.2d 181, 189 (3d Cir. 1981) (damages awarded against officer who

extreme circumstances.[1017] Courts have also held that force used during interrogation when the suspect poses no threat is excessive regardless of injury.[1018] Courts recognize that mental pain can be as real and serious as physical pain,[1019] though under the Prison Litigation Reform Act you cannot recover compensatory damages for such injury unless you have also suffered physical injury.[1020]

Despite these principles, defendants frequently argue that use of force cases should be dismissed because the injury (as opposed to the force) was *de minimis*, and sometimes the courts accept the argument.[1021] However, the Supreme Court has strongly rejected the idea that *de minimis* injury means *de minimis* force, stating:

> Injury and force . . . are only imperfectly correlated, and it is the latter that ultimately counts. An inmate who is gratuitously beaten by guards does not lose his ability to pursue an excessive force claim merely because he has the good fortune to escape without serious injury.[1022]

As a practical matter, even when courts analyze the issues correctly, infliction of minor injuries such as bruises and abrasions will be found unconstitutional only if there was no need to use force at all or if there is other evidence of malicious or sadistic behavior by the defendants.[1023] If you

---

brandished a loaded gun at point-blank range); Oses v. Fair, 739 F. Supp. 707, 709 (D.Mass. 1990) (Eighth Amendment was violated when an officer struck inmate with a gun, stuck gun barrel into his mouth, and made him kiss the officer's wife's shoes); Parker v. Asher, 701 F. Supp. 192, 194–95 (D.Nev. 1988) (threatening a prisoner with a taser gun solely to inflict fear stated an Eighth Amendment claim); Douglas v. Marino, 684 F. Supp. 395, 398 (D.N.J. 1988) (similar to *Parrish*); *see* Hopson v. Fredericksen, 961 F.2d 1374, 1378–79 (8th Cir. 1992) (threats unaccompanied by a weapon or physical gesture do not violate the Constitution). *Contra*, Knight v. Caldwell, 970 F.2d 1430, 1432 (5th Cir. 1992) (assault without injury accompanied by death threats did not violate the Constitution).

[1017]Hickey v. Reeder, 12 F.3d 754, 758–59 (8th Cir. 1993) (shooting a prisoner with a stun gun to make him clean his cell violated the Eighth Amendent); Davis v. Locke, 936 F.2d 1208, 1212 (11th Cir. 1991) (dropping a shackled inmate so he hit his head violated the Fourteenth Amendment); Jones v. Huff, 789 F. Supp. 526, 536 (N.D.N.Y. 1992) (ripping a prisoner's clothes off was unconstitutional because "done maliciously with the intent to humiliate him"); Henson v. Thezan, 698 F. Supp. 150, 152 (N.D.Ill. 1988) (allegation that a prisoner was abused for hours could not be dismissed based on absence of injury), *reconsideration denied on other grounds*, 717 F. Supp. 1330 (N.D.Ill. 1989).

[1018]Calhoun v. Thomas, 360 F. Supp. 2d 1264, 1276 (M.D.Ala. 2005).

[1019]Northington v. Jackson, 973 F.2d at 1524; Parrish v. Johnson, 800 F.2d 600, 605 (6th Cir. 1986) ("significant mental anguish"); Burton v. Livingston, 791 F.2d at 100–01 ("terror of instant and unexpected death"); Parker v. Asher, 701 F. Supp. 192, 194 (D.Nev. 1988) ("gratuitous fear").

As one court observed: "Many things—beating with a rubber truncheon, water torture, electric shock, incessant noise, reruns of 'Space 1999'–may cause agony as they occur yet leave no enduring injury." Williams v. Boles, 841 F.2d at 183.

[1020]42 U.S.C. § 1997e(e); *see* Ch. 9, § E, for a discussion of the limitations placed by the Prison Litigation Reform Act on recovery of compensatory damages.

[1021]Taylor v. McDuffie, 155 F.3d 479, 483–85 (4th Cir. 1998) (slight swelling in the jaw and some irritation inside mouth, abrasions to wrists and ankles, and tenderness over ribs, were *de minimis*); Siglar v. Hightower, 112 F.3d 191, 192–94 (5th Cir. 1997) (complaint that officer twisted arm and ear and ear was sore for three days was *de minimis*); Nowell v. Arcadian Ambulance Service, 147 F. Supp. 2d 495, 509–10 (W.D.La. 2001) (abrasions inside the mouth and a bruise near the eye, allegedly from a police officer's knee in the face, were *de minimis*).

[1022]Wilkins v. Gaddy, ___ U.S. ___, 130 S.Ct. 1175, 1179 (2010) (per curiam) (holding prisoner who alleged he suffered a bruised heel, lower back pain, increased blood pressure, migraine headaches, dizziness and psychological trauma when he was "punched, kicked, kneed, choked, and body slammed 'maliciously and sadistically' and '[w]ithout any provocation," stated an Eighth Amendment claim); *accord*, U.S. v. LaVallee, 439 F.3d 670, 687–88 (10th Cir. 2006) (rejecting *Siglar v. Hightower* analysis); Oliver v. Keller, 289 F.3d 623, 628–29 (9th Cir. 2002); Watford v. Bruce, 126 F. Supp. 2d 425, 427 (E.D.Va. 2001) (noting that *Hudson v. McMillian* analysis asks whether force, not injury, was *de minimis*); Merritt v. Hawk, 153 F. Supp. 2d 1216, 1223 (D.Colo. 2001) (same). The *Oliver* case points out the difference between the physical injury requirement of the Prison Litigation Reform Act, 42 U.S.C. § 1997e(e), which requires more than a *de minimis* injury to recover compensatory damages, and the *Hudson v. McMillian* requirement that *force* must generally be more than *de minimis* to support an Eighth Amendment excessive force claim.

[1023]Hudson v. McMillian, 503 U.S. 1, 10, 112 S. Ct. 995 (1992) (bruises, swelling, loosened teeth); Valencia v. Wiggins, 981 F.2d 1440, 1443, 1447 (5th Cir. 1993) (affirming liability for infliction of scratches, cuts and bruises not requiring medical attention on unresisting prisoner); Oliver v. Collins, 914 F.2d 56, 59 (5th Cir. 1990) (contusions, edema, lumps, bruises, etc., stated a claim where the plaintiff alleged that the force was completely unprovoked); Molton v. City of Cleveland, 839 F.2d 240, 249–50 (6th Cir. 1988) (bruises, abrasions, and a nosebleed stated a claim where an arrestee was knocked down and kicked while handcuffed); Franklin v. Aycock, 795 F.2d 1253, 1256–57 (6th Cir. 1986) (damages awarded for "trauma and abrasions" of back, shoulder, and ankle; no force was actually needed); Harrison v. Byrd, 765 F.2d 501, 504 (5th Cir. 1985) (bruises and knots were actionable where the plaintiff alleged he was repeatedly stomped while in handcuffs); Simpson v. Saroff, 741 F. Supp. 1073, 1078 (S.D.N.Y. 1990) (allegations of a punched stomach, swollen and bleeding wrists from tight handcuffs, and a faintly detectable scar on the wrist stated a Fourth Amendment claim); Smallwood v. Renfro, 708 F. Supp. 182, 188 (N.D.Ill. 1989) (no requirement of "serious injury" where force was used gratuitously; choking the plaintiff and hitting him in the arm with a radio for no reason stated an Eighth Amendment claim); Zumbroegel v. City of Dearborn Heights, 705 F. Supp. 358, 363 (E.D.Mich. 1989) (slamming the plaintiff against a police car, handcuffing him too tightly, and striking him in the face after he had been handcuffed could violate the Constitution); Bellamy v. McMickens, 692 F. Supp. 205, 213 (S.D.N.Y. 1988) (where the plaintiff had broken some light fixtures but claimed he did not resist the officers and was beaten after he was handcuffed and

were physically resisting authority in some way, or if there was some other justification for using force, the court will probably not rule in your favor if your injuries were minor.[1024] And if the defendants were responding to a major threat to safety or security, the infliction of crippling or life-threatening injuries may not be unconstitutional.[1025]

Courts may not grant summary judgment based on prison medical records that minimize injury to prisoners where there are sworn allegations or other evidence of more serious injury.[1026]

---

sustained bruises and embedded glass fragments, officers were not entitled to summary judgment); Burris v. Kirkpatrick, 649 F. Supp. 740, 745 (N.D.Ind. 1986) (damages awarded for a non-permanent burn where a guard threw hot water at another inmate and hit the plaintiff); Williams v. Omodt, 640 F. Supp. 120, 121–23 (D.Minn. 1986) (damages awarded for "bruises, contusions, swelling and considerable pain" where there was no justification for any force); Velleff v. Cantwell, 630 F. Supp. 346, 347 (N.D.Ill. 1986) (infliction of lacerated lip and bruised eye and jaw by sheriff who hit the plaintiff in the face while two deputies held him raised a jury question); Brown v. Triche, 660 F. Supp. 281, 284–87 (N.D.Ill. 1987) (swelling, abrasions, small laceration, loss of consciousness inflicted against a handcuffed inmate who did not sit down when ordered violated the Constitution).

[1024]Stanley v. Hejirika, 134 F.3d 629, 634–37 (4th Cir. 1998) (force causing bruises to arm, jaw, wrists, and back, and a loosened tooth, was justified by the need to move a prisoner who was inciting other inmates to set fires after an earlier disturbance); Culver v. Town of Torrington, Wyo., 930 F.2d 1456, 1459–61 (10th Cir. 1991) (force was justified by the need to search an arrestee for drugs); White v. Roper, 901 F.2d 1501, 1507 (9th Cir. 1990); Gassner v. City of Garland, Texas, 864 F.2d 394, 400 (5th Cir. 1989); Pressly v. Gregory, 831 F.2d 514, 517–18 (4th Cir. 1987); Roberson v. Goodman, 296 F. Supp. 2d 1051, 1060 (D.N.D. 2003) (kicking the plaintiff's food slot closed on his fingers did not violate the Constitution where the plaintiff was threatening to kill the officer, refused to put his hands out to be cuffed, tried to punch the officer's groin through the food slot, and engaged in other violent or recalcitrant conduct), aff'd, 114 Fed.Appx. 772 (8th Cir. 2004) (unpublished); Friends v. Moore, 776 F. Supp. 1382, 1389 (E.D.Mo. 1991); Bony v. Brandenburg, 735 F. Supp. 913, 915 (S.D.Ind. 1990); Brooks v. Pembroke City Jail, 722 F. Supp. 1294, 1300 (E.D.N.C. 1989); Francis v. Pike County, Ohio, 708 F. Supp. 170, 171–72 (S.D.Ohio 1988), aff'd, 875 F.2d 863 (6th Cir. 1989).

[1025]See § G.2.b(1) of this chapter, n.1009.

[1026]Scott v. Coughlin, 344 F.3d 282, 289–90 (2d Cir. 2003); see Calhoun v. Thomas, 360 F. Supp. 2d 1264, 1280 (M.D.Ala. 2005) (failure of an emergency room physician to notice visible injuries did not show force used was de minimis, since the doctor's main concern was an earlier gunshot wound, and other evidence showed severe swelling and discoloration); Sanders-El v. Spielman, 38 F. Supp. 2d 438, 439 n.1 (D.Md. 1999) ("it would seem that the law must entertain the possibility that health care providers in a prison setting might bring certain biases to their occupation"); see also Green v. Branson, 108 F.3d 1296, 1304 (10th Cir. 1997) (noting claim of falsification of medical records after a use of force).

3) Malice In Fourth Amendment cases, you need not show that the officer acted with malicious intent.[1027] By contrast, in Eighth Amendment cases, "whether force was applied in a good-faith effort to maintain or restore discipline, or maliciously and sadistically to cause harm," is the primary question.[1028] In pretrial detainee cases, some courts require a showing of malice and some do not.[1029]

To establish malice, you need not be able to prove directly what was in the officers' mind. Malice is generally inferred from the officers' actions and the circumstances in which they take place.[1030]

[1027]Graham v. Connor, 490 U.S. 386, 397, 109 S. Ct. 1865 (1989) ("underlying intent or motivation" are not relevant under Fourth Amendment).

[1028]Hudson v. McMillian, 503 U.S. 7, 112 S. Ct. 995 (1992); accord, Wilkins v. Gaddy, ___ U.S. ___, 130 S.Ct. 1175, 1178 (2010) (per curiam); Whitley v. Albers, 475 U.S. 312, 320–21, 106 S. Ct. 1078 (1986); Cummings v. Malone, 995 F.2d 817, 822 (8th Cir. 1993); Romano v. Howarth, 998 F.2d 101, 106–07 (2d Cir. 1993). You must show malice only on the part of those who are using force; you should not have to prove malice in a case against supervisors of those who use force, or against local governments whose policies result in excessive force. See § G.2.d of this chapter, nn.1125, 1130; Ch. 8, § B.4.a.

There is a lot of territory between "good faith" and "malice and sadism." One court found an Eighth Amendment violation where "the officers acted, if not 'maliciously and sadistically,' with at least a viciousness going beyond 'a good faith effort to maintain or restore discipline.'" Fisher v. Koehler, 692 F. Supp. 1519, 1563 (S.D.N.Y. 1988), aff'd, 902 F.2d 2 (2d Cir. 1990). However, you should assume that you will need to prove malice on the officers' part in any Eighth Amendment use of force case. See Thomas v. Ferguson, 361 F. Supp. 2d 435, 441 (D.N.J. 2004) (force that might be "uncivil and immoral" but not malicious and sadistic did not violate the Eighth Amendment).

One court has held that "sadistic" means "extreme or excessive cruelty or delighting in cruelty" as opposed to "regular cruelty," Parkus v. Delo, 135 F.3d 1232, 1234 (8th Cir. 1995), and that "'maliciously' and 'sadistically,' have different meanings, and the two together establish a higher level of intent than would either alone." Howard v. Barnett, 21 F.3d 868, 872 (8th Cir. 1994). Courts have not said much about this idea in later cases.

[1029]See § G.2.a.2 of this chapter concerning use of force claims by detainees.

[1030]Skrtich v. Thornton, 280 F.3d 1295, 1300–02 (11th Cir. 2002); Sims v. Artuz, 230 F.3d 14, 22 (2d Cir. 2000) (holding Eighth Amendment claim requires facts "from which it could be inferred that prison officials subjected [plaintiff] to excessive force"); U.S. v. Walsh, 194 F.3d 37, 50 (2d Cir. 1997) (force was "wanton" since there was absolutely no perceived need for it); Thomas v. Stalter, 20 F.3d 298, 302 (7th Cir. 1994); Hill v. Shelander, 992 F.2d 714, 717 (7th Cir. 1993); Valencia v. Wiggins, 981 F.2d 1440, 1446 (5th Cir. 1993); Miller v. Leathers, 913 F.2d 1085, 1088 (4th Cir. 1990) (en banc) (the fact that the plaintiff had previously filed a grievance against the officer and that the officer removed him from his cell without a supervisor present in violation of prison regulations could support an inference that the officer intended to retaliate against the plaintiff); Oliver v. Collins, 914 F.2d 56, 59 (5th Cir. 1990) (testimony that a beating was completely gratuitous and that

If staff act maliciously and sadistically, they can be held liable if the person they injured was not the person against whom their malice was directed.[1031]

4) Justifications for Use of Force Force may be used to restore or maintain order in a jail or prison—not to punish prisoners or to retaliate against them.[1032] Keeping order does not mean that once a prisoner has misbehaved, anything goes; force that is unnecessary, or excessive to the need, may still be unconstitutional.[1033] As a practical matter, it will

be harder for you to win such a case, since prison officials will argue that your misbehavior justified their actions.[1034] Many courts show very little patience with misbehaving prisoners.[1035] However, if officers used substantial force after you had stopped, or been stopped from, whatever you were doing, or when you were restrained or locked in a cell, their actions may be unconstitutional.[1036] If that is what happened

---

no force at all was necessary would support a finding of malice); Lewis v. Downs, 774 F.2d 711, 714 (6th Cir. 1985) (evidence that an officer kicked a handcuffed person who was lying on the ground showed malicious motivation); Orwat v. Maloney, 360 F. Supp. 2d 146, 154 (D.Mass. 2005) (holding malicious intent may be inferred from the extent of injury inflicted, here a broken jaw requiring three and a half weeks in the infirmary); Bozeman v. Estate of Haggard, 302 F. Supp. 2d 1310, 1312–14 (M.D.Ala. 2004) (officers' continuing to press a prisoner into his mattress, suffocating him, after he had stopped resisting, supported claim of malicious intent), *aff'd sub nom.* Bozeman v. Orum, 422 F.3d 1265 (11th Cir. 2005). *But see* Fennell v. Gilstrap, 559 F.3d 1212, 1218–19 (11th Cir. 2009) (per curiam) (injurious kick to the face did not show malice where other deputies had failed to subdue resisting prisoner and deputy intended to kick him in the arm).

[1031]Robins v. Meecham, 60 F.3d 1436, 1441–42 (9th Cir. 1995) (if officer acted maliciously and sadistically in shooting at one prisoner, he could be liable to another prisoner who was injured by a ricochet even if the officer did not intend to shoot him).

[1032]Jackson v. Bishop, 404 F.2d 571, 579–81 (8th Cir. 1968) (holding corporal punishment unconstitutional); Skrtich v. Thornton, 280 F.3d 1295, 1302 (11th Cir. 2002) ("It is not constitutionally permissible for officers to administer a beating as punishment for a prisoner's past misconduct."); Romaine v. Rawson, 140 F. Supp. 2d 204, 211–12 (N.D.N.Y. 2001) (repeatedly slapping a prisoner because he had been disrespectful violated the Eighth Amendment); Evans v. Hennessy, 934 F. Supp. 127, 133 (D.Del. 1996) (striking a prisoner with fists because he had previously been verbally abusive violated the Eighth Amendment).

[1033]Orem v. Rephann, 523 F.3d 442, 446 (4th Cir. 2008) (tasering a verbally abusive arrestee who was handcuffed and hobbled in a patrol car supported claim of due process denial); Johnson v. Blaukat, 453 F.3d 1108, 1112–13 (8th Cir. 2006) (where officers used injurious force and pepper spray in a multi-prisoner cell, after one prisoner had behaved disruptively, against another prisoner who said she had ceased resisting, whether malicious and sadistic force was a jury question); Sikes v. Gaytan, 218 F.3d 491, 492 (5th Cir. 2000) (affirming verdict against guard who repeatedly punched prisoner and jumped on his arm until it broke after prisoner spit on him); Hickey v. Reeder, 12 F.3d 754, 758–59 (8th Cir. 1993) (refusing to sweep his cell does not justify shooting a prisoner with a stun gun); Miller v. Leathers, 913 F.2d 1085, 1089 (4th Cir. 1990) (en banc) (verbal provocations would not justify breaking a prisoner's arm with a baton); U.S. v. Cobb, 905 F.2d 784 (4th Cir. 1990) (verbal provocation does not excuse a physical assault by a law enforcement officer); Corselli v. Coughlin, 842 F.2d 23, 26–27 (2d Cir. 1988) (jury could find for prisoner even if he had refused an order); King v. Blankenship, 636 F.2d 70, 73 (4th Cir. 1980); Martinez v. Rosado, 614 F.2d 829, 831 (2d Cir. 1980); Orwat v. Maloney, 360 F. Supp. 2d 146, 154 (D.Mass. 2005) (even if prisoner thrust his finger

into officer's face, breaking the prisoner's jaw might not have been justified).

One court has suggested that force may not be used against a prisoner who has refused an unlawful order. Valdez v. Farmon, 766 F. Supp. 1529, 1535 (E.D.Cal. 1991). We don't recommend that you test this holding.

[1034]*See* § G.2.b.2 of this chapter, n.1024, for cases in which the prisoner's misconduct was held to justify the use of force.

[1035]*See, e.g.,* Caldwell v. Moore, 968 F.2d 595, 600 (6th Cir. 1992) (upholding use of taser and restraints against a prisoner who created a disturbance in his cell); Stenzel v. Ellis, 916 F.2d 423, 426–28 (8th Cir. 1990) (injurious force was justified against a prisoner locked in his cell who insisted on sleeping completely covered with a blanket); Bennett v. Parker, 898 F.2d 1530, 1533–34 (11th Cir. 1990) (force was properly used against a prisoner who the court believes was "creating a disturbance" by refusing to enter his cell); Pittman v. Kurtz, 165 F. Supp. 2d 1243, 1246 (D.Kan. 2001) (allegations that defendants hit plaintiff in the head and beat his head against the floor "must be considered in light of the fact" that the plaintiff apparently refused to go to his cell after multiple orders and that he repeatedly struck a defendant with a pencil).

[1036]*See* Giles v. Kearney, 571 F.3d 318, 327 (3d Cir. 2009) (prisoner's resistance and strikiing an officer "do not provide a blank check justification" for excessive force later; blow that caused a broken rib and collapsed lung would violate Eighth Amendment if done after prisoner was subdued); Parker v. Gerrish, 547 F.3d 1, 11 (1st Cir. 2008) (affirming jury verdict against police who tasered a motorist who did not significantly resist); Thompson v. Zimmerman, 350 F.3d 734, 735 (8th Cir. 2003) (the fact that a prisoner had previously been yelling and kicking the walls did not justify staff's entering his cell and using force after he had stopped); Skrtich v. Thornton, 280 F.3d 1295, 1302 (11th Cir. 2002) ("It is not constitutionally permissible for officers to administer a beating as punishment for a prisoner's past misconduct."); Bogan v. Stroud, 958 F.2d 180, 185 (7th Cir. 1992) (beating a prisoner after he had been subdued was unconstitutional even though he had stabbed an officer); Miller v. Glanz, 948 F.2d 1562, 1564, 1567 (10th Cir. 1991) (allegation that officers knocked down an inmate who resisted handcuffing did not state an Eighth Amendment claim; allegation that they came back later and beat him up in his cell did state a claim); Slakan v. Porter, 737 F.2d 368, 372 (4th Cir. 1984) (prisoner's abusive language justified discipline, but not use of high-powered water hoses and beating with clubs, when inmate was locked in cell); Bafford v. Nelson, 241 F. Supp. 2d 1192, 1205 (D.Kan. 2002) (initial use of force was justified, but later beating while restrained raised an Eighth Amendment claim); Concepcion v. Morton, 125 F. Supp. 2d 111, 126 (D.N.J. 2000) (allegations of being struck and kicked while handcuffed after an earlier assault incident supported an excessive force claim), *rev'd on other grounds,* 306 F.3d 1347 (3d Cir. 2002); Ruble v. King, 911 F. Supp. 1544, 1557 (N.D.Ga. 1995); Jones v. Huff, 789 F. Supp. 526, 536 (N.D.N.Y. 1992) (slapping and punching a handcuffed inmate violated the Eighth Amendment); Caudle-El v. Peters, 727 F. Supp. 1175, 1180 (N.D.Ill. 1989)

to you, you should make that fact clear in your complaint and other litigation papers.

The same principles apply if force was used to control a "prison disturbance." The legal standard is the same in "disturbance" cases as in other force cases under the Eighth Amendment,[1037] but in practice courts will give prison officials more leeway when they are faced with a riot, a takeover of a housing area, or any other serious loss of control. This will be true in cases involving arrestees and detainees as well as convicts. However, even in a "disturbance," prison officials are not entitled to do anything they want to prisoners. They still have to present some justification for their actions.[1038] They may not rely on a "disturbance" that was already over when the force was used.[1039] Nor can they get your case dismissed simply by invoking the word "disturbance." If there is a factual dispute whether force was used against you in quelling a disturbance, prison officials are not entitled to summary judgment,[1040] and a court or jury may rule in your favor after a trial.[1041]

Physical abuse may not be used to extract information from prisoners,[1042] even when the information is related to institutional security.[1043]

c. Types of Force

1) *Weapons* The use of weapons by prison and jail staff and police is generally assessed by the same standards as other uses of force.[1044] The use of firearms in cases of prison disturbances has been upheld, though it will not necessarily be valid in all circumstances.[1045] The use of stun devices has been upheld where they are used to restore order[1046] but held

---

(allegation that the plaintiff was choked, thrown to the ground, and kneed in the back after he was handcuffed and secured stated an Eighth Amendment claim); *see* § G.2.b(1) of this chapter, n.540, for additional cases of this nature; *see also* Williams v. Burton, 943 F.2d 1572, 1576 (11th Cir. 1991) (Constitution may be violated "if prison officials continue to use force after the necessity for the coercive action has ceased"). *But see* Olson v. Coleman, 804 F. Supp. 148, 150 (D.Kan. 1992) (single blow to a handcuffed inmate did not violate the Constitution).

[1037]Hudson v. McMillian, 503 U.S. 1, 6, 112 S. Ct. 995 (1992).

[1038]Campbell v. Grammer, 889 F.2d 797, 802 (8th Cir. 1989) (spraying inmates with a high-pressure fire hose without justification violated the Eighth Amendment even though a disturbance was going on); Smith v. Marcellus, 917 F. Supp. 168, 173–74 (W.D.N.Y. 1995) (existence of an emergency "does not . . . automatically justify whatever steps might have been taken"; allegation that plaintiff was struck with batons and a radio and forcibly pinned with a shield even though he was sitting on his bed presented a factual issue as to the necessity of the force used); McCullough v. Cady, 640 F. Supp. 1012, 1017–18 (E.D.Mich. 1986) (an arbitrary shooting during a multiple-inmate fight in the yard violated the Constitution).

[1039]Al-Jundi v. Mancusi, 926 F.2d 235, 240 (2d Cir. 1991); Bolin v. Black, 875 F.2d 1343, 1350 (8th Cir. 1989); Unwin v. Campbell, 863 F.2d 124, 130 (1st Cir. 1988). *But see* Stanley v. Hejirika, 134 F.3d 629, 634–37 (4th Cir. 1998) (considering earlier disturbance in assessing force used in extracting prisoner who was inciting other inmates to set fires).

The *Al-Jundi* and *Unwin* cases held that the "malicious and sadistic" standard did not apply unless there was a disturbance going on at the time force was used. They have been overruled in this respect by *Hudson v. McMillian*. But their basic reasoning, that a disturbance does not justify force after it is over, is still valid.

[1040]Unwin v. Campbell, 863 F.2d at 130.

[1041]Meriwether v. Coughlin, 879 F.2d 1037, 1047–48 (2d Cir. 1989).

[1042]Gray v. Spillman, 925 F.2d 90, 93 (4th Cir. 1991); Ware v. Reed, 709 F.2d 345, 351 (5th Cir. 1983); Calhoun v. Thomas, 360 F. Supp. 2d 1264, 1276 (M.D.Ala. 2005) ("any amount of force used during an interrogation when the suspect poses no threat may violate a person's constitutional rights"); Coleman v. Rieck, 253 F. Supp. 2d 1101, 1107–08 (D.Neb. 2003) ("the Constitution does not sanction kicking a suspect until he turns over evidence"), *aff'd*, 154 Fed.Appx. 546 (8th Cir. 2005) (unpublished); *see* Brown v. Mississippi, 297 U.S. 278, 286, 56 S. Ct. 461 (1936) (the use of violence to extract confessions from suspects in custody denies due process).

Coercive questioning does not violate the privilege against self-incrimination unless statements are compelled and used in a criminal prosecution. Chavez v. Martinez, 538 U.S. 760, 766–67, 123 S. Ct. 1994 (2003).

[1043]Cohen v. Coahoma County, Miss., 805 F. Supp. 398, 403–04 (N.D.Miss. 1992).

[1044]The Supreme Court has held that the police may use deadly force (which usually, but not always, involves weapons) against a fleeing suspect only "[w]here the officer has probable cause to believe that the suspect poses a threat of serious physical harm, either to the officer or to others. . . ." Tennessee v. Garner, 471 U.S. 1, 11, 105 S. Ct. 1694 (1985) (holding deadly force permissible); *see* § G.2.a.3 of this chapter, n.997, on this subject.

[1045]Whitley v. Albers, 475 U.S. 312, 322–26, 106 S. Ct. 1078 (1986) (applying "malicious and sadistic" standard to prisoner shooting); Marquez v. Gutierrez, 322 F.3d 689, 692–93 (9th Cir. 2003) (prisoner's claim that he was shot, although uninvolved in the inmate fight that prompted the shooting, stated a claim under *Whitley*, but officers who could have thought he was involved and threatening an assault victim were entitled to qualified immunity); Jeffers v. Gomez, 267 F.3d 895, 911–12 (9th Cir. 2001) (shooting of prisoner, apparently accidentally, while staff were trying to suppress a disturbance did not violate the Constitution absent malicious and sadistic intent; Avratin v. Bermudez, 420 F. Supp. 2d 1121, 1124–27 (S.D.Cal. 2006) (similar to *Marquez*; officer shot a prisoner directly with a wooden projectile, rather than bouncing it off the ground as prison rules required and with no effort to use lesser means first).

[1046]Caldwell v. Moore, 968 F.2d 595, 596–97, 600 (6th Cir. 1992) (upholding use of stun gun against prisoner who shouted and kicked his cell door); Michenfelder v. Sumner, 860 F.2d 328, 335–36 (9th Cir. 1988); Manier v. Cook, 394 F. Supp. 2d 1282, 1288 (E.D.Wash. 2005) (upholding use of taser against prisoner who refused to return to his cell until he spoke to a supervisor, after becoming verbally abusive when a staff member would not notarize his legal documents); Birdine v. Gray, 375 F. Supp. 874, 880–81 (D.Neb. 2005) (upholding use of stun gun against prisoner

unconstitutional where their use has been clearly excessive to the need.[1047] Courts have acknowledged that requiring prisoners in court to wear "stun belts," which administer a severe shock when activated, can deter criminal defendants from participating in their own defense and conferring with their attorneys, and have held that their use must be limited, similarly to the limits on the use of restraints in court.[1048]

The unjustified use of water hoses and fire extinguishers against prisoners has been condemned by several courts.[1049]

2) Chemical Agents The use of chemical agents, too, is governed by the same standards as other uses of force.[1050] It is usually upheld when prison staff are attempting to restore order or subdue recalcitrant prisoners or arrestees,[1051] including in some cases persons in restraints[1052] or locked in their cells.[1053] However, the unnecessary use of tear gas or

---

who was physically resisting, and subsequent use of electronic restraint shield when he kicked and banged his door and tried to damage a light fixture); Collins v. Scott, 961 F. Supp. 1009, 1016–17 (E.D.Tex. 1997) (upholding use of stun shield against Muslim prisoner who objected to a strip search by a female officer on religious grounds); Alford v. Osei-Kwesi, 203 Ga.App. 716, 418 S.E.2d 79, 84–85 (Ga.App. 1992).

[1047]Hickey v. Reeder, 12 F.3d 754, 758–59 (8th Cir. 1999) (shooting a prisoner with a stun gun to make him clean his room was unconstitutional); Shelton v. Angelone, 183 F. Supp. 2d 830, 835–36 (W.D.Va. 2002) (evidence of use of a stun gun without justification on a prisoner who was in handcuffs was sufficient to withstand summary judgment); see Brown v. City of Golden Valley, 574 F.3d 491, 496–98 (8th Cir. 2009) (tasering a car passenger who was not resisting and was suspected of a minor offense could violate the Fourth Amendment); Parker v. Gerrish, 547 F.3d 1, 11 (1st Cir. 2008) (tasering of unresisting motorist violated the Fourth Amendment); McKenzie v. City of Milpitas, 738 F. Supp. 1293, 1299–01 (N.D.Cal. 1990) (jury question was presented by evidence of inadequate training and supervision of police officers in use of tasers).

[1048]In *U.S. v. Durham*, 287 F.3d 1297 (11th Cir. 2002), an appeals court held that a trial court contemplating use of a stun belt

> will likely need to make factual findings about the operation of the stun belt, addressing issues such as the criteria for triggering the belt and the possibility of accidental discharge. A court will also need to assess whether an essential state interest is served by compelling a particular defendant to wear such a device, and must consider less restrictive methods of restraint. Furthermore, the court's rationale must be placed on the record to enable us to determine if the use of the stun belt was an abuse of the court's discretion.

287 F.3d at 1306–07; see Hawkins v. Comparet-Cassani, 251 F.3d 1230, 1242 (9th Cir. 2001) (stun belts may be used to maintain security, but not to prevent courtroom disruption).The use of restraints in court is discussed in Ch. 10, § Q.

[1049]Campbell v. Grammer, 889 F.2d 797, 802–03 (8th Cir. 1989) (affirming damage award for unjustified spraying with high-pressure water hose); Slakan v. Porter, 737 F.2d 368, 372 (4th Cir. 1984) (affirming damage award for use of high-pressure water hoses against an inmate locked in cell who used abusive language); Beckford v. Portuondo, 151 F. Supp. 2d 204, 215–16 (N.D.N.Y. 2001) (spraying with a fire extinguisher as punishment, causing minor injury, supported an Eighth Amendment claim). *But see* Jackson v. Culbertson, 984 F.2d 699, 700 (5th Cir. 1993) (per curiam) (holding spraying with fire extinguisher was *de minimis* force).

[1050]*See, e.g.,* Champion v. Outlook Nashville, Inc., 380 F.3d 893, 901 (6th Cir. 2004) (Fourth Amendment standards applied to use of pepper spray during arrest); Clement v. Gomez, 298 F.3d 898, 903–04 (9th Cir. 2002) (applying "malicious and sadistic" Eighth Amendment standard to gassing in prison); Thomas v. McNeil, 2009 WL 64616, *25–27 (M.D.Fla., Jan. 9, 2009) (applying deliberate indifference standard to policy of using chemical agents against prisoners with mental illness behaving disruptively because of their illness), *judgment entered*, 2009 WL 605306 (M.D.Fla., Mar. 9, 2009); see Colon v. Schneider, 899 F.2d 660, 666–69 (7th Cir. 1990) (prison use of force regulations limiting use of mace did not create a liberty interest).

[1051]*See* Monday v. Oullette, 118 F.3d 1099, 1104–05 (6th Cir. 1997) (use of pepper spray upheld against person who was large and drunk and refused to go to a hospital, and who police had probable cause to believe was trying to kill himself); Soto v. Dickey, 744 F.2d 1260, 1270 (7th Cir. 1984) (use of chemical agents is permissible when "reasonably necessary . . . to subdue recalcitrant prisoners"); Dayton v. Sapp, 668 F. Supp. 385, 388 (D.Del. 1987) (jury properly upheld use of mace against a drunken arrestee struggling with police).

The use of chemical agents has been upheld to make prisoners enter their cells, *see* Fairweather v. Giles Dalby Correctional Facility, 154 F. Supp. 2d 921, 926 (N.D.Tex. 2001); Norris v. Detrick, 918 F. Supp. 977, 982 (N.D.W.Va. 1996), *aff'd*, 108 F.3d 1373 (4th Cir. 1997) (unpublished); Norris v. District of Columbia, 614 F. Supp. 294, 296, 301 (D.D.C. 1985), or to leave their cells or housing units as directed. Morgan v. Ward, 699 F. Supp. 1025, 1054–55 (N.D.N.Y. 1988) (tear gas may be used "to move a rebellious inmate"); Peterson v. Davis, 551 F. Supp. 137, 134–35 (D.Md. 1982) (use of tear gas upheld where inmates refused to leave a housing area), *aff'd*, 729 F.2d 1453 (4th Cir. 1984).

[1052]Justice v. Dennis, 834 F.2d 380, 383 (4th Cir. 1987) (en banc) (use of mace on a handcuffed prisoner who was drunk and capable of "strenuous" resistance), *vacated on other grounds*, 490 U.S. 1087 (1989).

[1053]Clement v. Gomez, 298 F.3d 898, 903–04 (9th Cir. 2002) (use of pepper spray against prisoners fighting in their cell was not shown to be malicious and sadistic); Combs v. Wilkinson, 315 F.3d 548, 557 (6th Cir. 2002) (officer's use of mace after a disturbance against a prisoner who placed his face near an open window was made in haste and under pressure, and is therefore entitled to deference); Williams v. Benjamin, 77 F.3d 756, 762–63 (4th Cir. 1996) (use of mace upheld against prisoner who along with others had thrown water out of his cell and refused to remove his arm from the food service window); Soto v. Dickey, 744 F.2d 1260, 1265–67 (7th Cir. 1984) (upholding use of mace to get segregation prisoners to submit to being handcuffed); Lock v. Jenkins, 641 F.2d 488, 495–96 (7th Cir. 1981) (tear gas upheld against locked-in prisoners who were "inciting a riot at a time of tremendous tension," but not to retrieve a metal tray or to make prisoners stop shouting and uttering threats); Bailey v. Turner, 736 F.2d 963, 966–72 (4th Cir. 1984) (tear gassing of locked-in prisoners is not *per se* unconstitutional); Price v. Dixon, 961 F. Supp. 894, 900 (E.D.N.C. 1997)

other chemical agents has been held unlawful by a number of courts.[1054] Officers may not use chemical agents against a person who poses no risk,[1055] or continue to use chemical agents on a person who has been secured or has stopped resisting.[1056] Once chemical agents have been used, prisoners (including bystanders who have been exposed) must be allowed a reasonable opportunity for decontamination.[1057]

(upholding use of mace against prisoner who threw urine on officer; "it is accepted that prisoners may be subdued with mace when acting disorderly as long as the use is neither excessive nor applied solely for the purpose of inflicting pain or punishment"); Blair-El v. Tinsman, 666 F. Supp. 1218, 1221–22 (S.D.Ill. 1987) (tear gas was properly used against a plaintiff who refused to stop yelling and chanting gang slogans in his cell). *But see* McCargo v. Mister, 462 F. Supp. 813, 818–20 (D.Md. 1978) (damages awarded for use of tear gas on prisoners locked in cell).

[1054]*See* Spain v. Procunier, 600 F.2d 189, 196 (9th Cir. 1979) (tear gas may be used in "dangerous quantities" only when there is a threat of injury to persons or to "substantial amounts of valuable property"); Ruiz v. Estelle, 503 F. Supp. 1265, 1305 (S.D.Tex. 1980), *aff'd in part and rev'd in part on other grounds*, 679 F.2d 1115 (5th Cir. 1982); Battle v. Anderson, 376 F. Supp. 402, 433 (E.D.Okla. 1974) (limiting chemical agents to situations involving the imminent threat of bodily harm, or a riot or escape). In a case involving juvenile facilities, the court held that CS gas "should be used only when a genuine risk of serious bodily harm to another exists and other less intrusive methods of restraint are not reasonably available." Alexander v. Boyd, 876 F. Supp. 773, 786 (D.S.C. 1995).

One appellate decision said that a burst of Capstun was *de minimis* force, since the effects were dissipated in 45 minutes and the plaintiff received infirmary treatment. Jones v. Shields, 207 F.3d 491, 495 (8th Cir. 2000). In subsequent decisions, that court has emphasized that it did *not* hold that all uses of pepper spray are *de minimis. See* Lawrence v. Bowersox, 297 F.3d 727, 731–32 (8th Cir. 2002) (noting that in *Jones*, the prisoner had refused direct orders, become threatening, and was large and out of his cell); Treats v. Morgan, 308 F.3d 868, 872–73 (8th Cir. 2002) (*Jones* did not immunize all uses of Capstun against "disobedient or querulous" prisoners). Other courts have rejected the notion that use of chemical agents is *de minimis. See* Headwaters Forest Defense v. County of Humboldt, 240 F.3d 1185, 1199–1200 (9th Cir. 2000) (lack of significant or permanent injury was only one factor to be considered, and pain was excruciating), *judgment vacated on other grounds*, 534 U.S. 801 (2001).

[1055]One court has held that "use of pepper spray will not be justified every time an inmate questions orders or seeks redress for an officer's actions. . . . A basis for an Eighth Amendment claim exists when, as alleged here, an officer uses pepper spray without warning on an inmate who may have questioned his actions but who otherwise poses no threat." Treats v. Morgan, 308 F.3d 868, 873 (8th Cir. 2002) (using Capstun against a prisoner who merely refused to accept a property receipt but posed no threat could violate the Eighth Amendment); *accord*, Walker v. Bowersox, 526 F.3d 1186, 1189 (8th Cir. 2008) (use of pepper spray against prisoner locked in his cell who was refusing to return a food tray presented an Eighth Amendment jury question); Johnson v. Blaukat, 453 F.3d 1108, 1113 (8th Cir. 2006) (use of pepper spray against a prisoner who alleged she was not resisting presented a jury question of excessive force); Lawrence v. Bowersox, 297 F.3d 727, 732–33 (8th Cir. 2002) (affirming punitive damages for prisoners who were pepper-sprayed after questioning an officer's racist remark but who were confined to their cells and did not disobey orders); DeSpain v. Uphoff, 264 F.3d 965, 978 (10th Cir. 2001) (officer could be held liable for spraying pepper spray indiscriminately along a tier;

"We will not require inmates to be subjected to the malicious whims of prison guards"); Foulk v. Charrier, 262 F.3d 687, 701–02 (8th Cir. 2001) (evidence that officer enticed plaintiff to put his face to cell door window and sprayed pepper spray into his face supported a finding of malicious and sadistic force); Lock v. Jenkins, 641 F.2d 488, 495–96 (7th Cir. 1981) (tear gas upheld against locked-in prisoners who were "inciting a riot at a time of tremendous tension," but not to retrieve a metal tray or to make prisoners stop shouting and uttering threats); *see* Headwaters Forest Defense v. County of Humboldt, 276 F.3d 1125, 1130–31 (9th Cir. 2002) (use of pepper spray against peaceful protesters who posed no risk and were under control could support a Fourth Amendment claim); Thomas v. McNeil, 2009 WL 64616, *25–27 (M.D.Fla., Jan. 9, 2009) (holding policy of using chemical agents against prisoners with mental illness behaving disruptively because of their illness was unconstitutional), *judgment entered*, 2009 WL 605306 (M.D.Fla., Mar. 9, 2009).

[1056]Norton v. City of Marietta, 432 F.3d 1145, 1153–54 (10th Cir. 2005) (per curiam) (plaintiff who said he had kicked his cell door earlier but was not combative when officers entered his cell and pepper sprayed him presented a jury question under the Eighth Amendment); Henderson v. Munn, 439 F.3d 497, 502–03 (8th Cir. 2006) (pepper-spraying an arrestee who was on the ground with both hands cuffed behind him and in pain from a dislocated ankle supports a Fourth Amendment claim even if he had previously been resisting arrest); Champion v. Outlook Nashville, Inc., 380 F.3d 893, 901 (6th Cir. 2004) (use of pepper spray on restrained and unresisting arrestee could violate Fourth Amendment); Vinyard v. Wilson, 311 F.3d 1340, 1348–49 (11th Cir. 2002) (same, as to person arrested for minor offense secured in the back of a patrol car); Blackledge v. Carlone, 126 F. Supp. 2d 224, 229–31 (D.Conn. 2001) (similar to *Vinyard*, punitive damages upheld).

[1057]Walker v. Bowersox, 526 F.3d 1186, 1189 (8th Cir. 2008) (plaintiff was denied shower or clean clothing for three days after use of pepper spray); Clement v. Gomez, 298 F.3d 898, 904–05 (9th Cir. 2002) (failure to provide for decontamination could be deliberate indifference); Headwaters Forest Defense v. County of Humboldt, 276 F.3d 1125, 1131–32 (9th Cir. 2002) (denial of decontamination could violate Fourth Amendment reasonableness standard); LaLonde v. County of Riverside, 204 F.3d 947, 961 (9th Cir. 2000) (plaintiff was left with pepper spray on face and in eyes for 20–30 minutes with no offer of medical assistance; when "an arrestee surrenders and is rendered helpless, . . . a refusal without cause to alleviate [a weapon's] harmful effects constitutes excessive force."); Williams v. Benjamin, 77 F.3d 756, 764–66 (4th Cir. 1996) (keeping prisoner restrained and unable to wash off mace for eight hours may have violated the Eighth Amendment since he had done nothing threatening during that period). *But see* Baldwin v. Stalder, 137 F.3d 836, 840–41 (5th Cir. 1998) (failure to allow prisoners to wash off mace for three hours was reasonable because the prisoners had previously been involved in a disturbance and no one was asking for medical attention); *see also* Norris v. Detrick, 918 F. Supp. 977, 984 (N.D.W.Va. 1996) (nurse who tried but failed to mitigate effects of close-range CN gas was not deliberately indifferent), *aff'd*, 108 F.3d 1373 (4th Cir. 1997) (unpublished).

3) Restraints Prison officials may use restraints for security purposes,[1058] but the courts have curbed some extreme or abusive restraint practices. For example, in *Hope v. Pelzer*[1059] the Supreme Court held that the Alabama "hitching post" practice, in which prisoners who were accused of refusing to work were handcuffed for long periods to a horizontal bar, exposed to the sun and without access to drinking water or toilets, violated the Eighth Amendment. The Court emphasized that the practice was painful, humiliating, and dangerous, and that it was clearly intended as punishment for past conduct and not to ensure safety.[1060]

In *Hope v. Pelzer* the Court held that prison officials had been deliberately indifferent to the risk of harm to prisoners,[1061] but it did not say whether all restraint cases are supposed to be decided under the deliberate indifference standard. In fact, courts have taken several different approaches. Some have treated restraints as a form of use of force and have applied the *Hudson v. McMillian* "malicious and sadistic" standard that governs other prisoner use of force claims.[1062] Some years ago the Supreme Court held that "[l]iberty from bodily restraint always has been recognized as the core of the liberty protected by the Due Process Clause from arbitrary government action," and that this interest survives criminal conviction and incarceration as well as civil commitment.[1063] Some courts have applied the *Youngberg* due process standard to prisoners.[1064] Some have asked whether incidents or practices of restraint meet the *Sandin v. Conner* "atypical and significant hardship" test (and they have come up with different answers).[1065]

Others have applied different due process theories, mostly in cases involving pretrial detainees.[1066] Restraint issues in arrest or search cases are governed by the Fourth Amendment's requirement of reasonable searches and seizures.[1067]

Since the courts have not agreed on the right legal theory in restraint cases, the best course for a convict or detainee may be just to plead them all—deliberate indifference, malicious and sadistic intent, deprivation of the right of bodily liberty, and atypical and significant hardship—and be sure you make the facts clear in your complaint, since there are some clear fact-based patterns in the way courts decide restraint cases. The most important factor appears to

---

[1058]This section addresses restraints used to maintain security and order in prison. The use of psychiatric restraints is discussed in § F.4.a of this chapter; the use of restraints in connection with court appearances is discussed in Ch. 10, § Q, nn.780–781.

[1059]536 U.S. 730, 122 S. Ct. 2508 (2002).

[1060]Hope v. Pelzer, 536 U.S. at 736–38, 745.

[1061]*Hope*, 536 U.S. at 737–38.

[1062]Walker v. Bowersox, 526 F.3d 1186, 1188 (8th Cir. 2008); Williams v. Benjamin, 77 F.3d 756, 761–65 (4th Cir. 1996); Sadler v. Young, 325 F. Supp. 2d 689, 700–01 (W.D.Va. 2004), *rev'd and remanded on other grounds*, 118 Fed.Appx. 762 (4th Cir. 2005) (unpublished); Casaburro v. Giuliani, 986 F. Supp. 176, 180–81 (S.D.N.Y. 1997). The Supreme Court itself described restraint as a form of use of force in *Muehler v. Mena*, 544 U.S. 93, 99, 125 S. Ct. 1465 (2005).

[1063]Youngberg v. Romeo, 457 U.S. 307, 316, 102 S. Ct. 2452 (1982) (citation omitted).

[1064]Benjamin v. Fraser, 264 F.3d 175, 188 (2d Cir. 2001) (holding use of restraints against detainees believed to have used or possessed weapons required due process protection); Buckley v. Rogerson, 133 F.3d 1125, 1129 (8th Cir. 1998) (holding placement in restraints without medical approval in a prison mental hospital denied due process); Murphy v. Walker, 51 F.3d 714, 718 (7th Cir. 1995) (detainees have a liberty interest in freedom from restraint and government must have a legitimate penological or medical reason for using it).

[1065]*See* Thielman v. Leean, 282 F.3d 478, 484 (7th Cir. 2002) (requirement to wear waist belt and leg chains in addition to handcuffs during transportation is not atypical and significant

but "the stuff of nickels and dimes"); Key v. McKinney, 176 F.3d 1083, 1086–87 (8th Cir. 1999) (24 hours in handcuffs and leg shackles was not atypical and significant, since prisoners can expect to spend time in restraints during their sentences); Williams v. Benjamin, 77 F.3d 756, 768–70 (4th Cir. 1996) (placement in four-point restraints is atypical and significant; process is not required for initial placement but may be required for retention); Sadler v. Young, 325 F. Supp. 2d 689, 705–06 (W.D.Va. 2004) (placement in four-point restraints is atypical and significant and also deprived prisoner of an interest protected directly by the Due Process Clause), *rev'd and remanded on other grounds*, 118 Fed.Appx. 762 (4th Cir. 2005) (unpublished); Davis v. Lester, 156 F. Supp. 2d 588, 595–96 (W.D.Va. 2001) (48 hours in five-point restraints is atypical and significant); *see* Harrison v. Dretke, 865 F. Supp. 385, 386–87 (W.D.Tex. 1994) (Constitution does not create a liberty interest protected by due process in avoiding restraints), *aff'd*, 68 F.3d 469 (5th Cir. 1995) (unpublished); *see also* Laws v. Cleaver, 140 F. Supp. 2d 145, 155 (D.Conn. 2001) (court could not find four hours in four-point restraints atypical and significant absent evidence of the frequency with which prisoners are so restrained, how tight the restraints were, what effect they had on the plaintiff, etc.).

The standard of *Sandin v. Conner*, 515 U.S. 472, 115 S. Ct. 2293 (1995), is discussed in Ch. 4, § A.

[1066]*See* Lumley v. City of Dade City, Florida, 327 F.3d 1186, 1196 (11th Cir. 2003) (where plaintiff had been arrested after a shootout with police and restrained to a bed for days, the court said the due process question was whether his restraint "shocked the conscience"); Robles v. Prince George's County, Md., 302 F.3d 262, 269 (4th Cir. 2002) (applying *Bell v. Wolfish* reasonable relationship standard to handcuffing of detainee to a fence); Benjamin v. Fraser, 264 F.3d 175, 188 (2d Cir. 2001) (finding liberty interest in avoiding excessive restraints based on *Youngberg v. Romeo* holding); May v. Sheahan, 226 F.3d 876, 884 (7th Cir. 2000) (applying *Bell v. Wolfish* rational relationship test to practice of shackling all hospitalized detainees to their beds); Jones v. Mabry, 723 F.2d 590, 593 (8th Cir. 1983) (under the pre-*Sandin* law of due process, high-security prisoners were not deprived of liberty by being required to wear leg irons whenever they left their cells); Beltran v. O'Mara, 405 F. Supp. 2d 140, 160–61 (D.N.H. 2005) (applying *Johnson v. Glick* due process standard to detainee's placement in restraint chair), *reconsideration denied on other grounds*, 2006 WL 240558 (D.N.H., Jan 31, 2006).

Courts have not fully resolved what the "process due" should be in connection with restraints. *See* Ch. 4, § H.3, concerning due process in the use of restraints.

[1067]*See* Muehler v. Mena, 544 U.S. 93, 98–101,125 S. Ct. 1465 (2005).

be whether there is a plausible safety reason for the restraints.[1068] Courts have generally upheld the use of restraints on segregation or other high-security inmates when they are out of their cells,[1069] or in some cases in their cells where they have committed serious misconduct.[1070] Prisoners may generally be restrained when they are out of the prison and there is a danger of escape.[1071] However, even in that context, excessive and indiscriminate restraint practices may be struck down.[1072]

Prisoners who are actively disruptive may be restrained, including by placement in a restraint chair or four- or five-point restraints.[1073] Prolonged restraint may be lawful if the prisoner is seriously disruptive and if the prisoner receives food, water, bathroom breaks, and medical attention.[1074] However, the use

---

[1068]*See* Muehler v. Mena, 544 U.S. 93, 99–100, 125 S. Ct. 1465 (2005) (citing safety reasons for handcuffing occupants during a residential search); Hope v. Pelzer, 536 U.S. 730, 738, 122 S. Ct. 2508 (2002) (emphasizing lack of safety concerns in holding "hitching post" restraints unconstitutional).

[1069]Keenan v. Hall, 83 F.3d 1083, 1092 (9th Cir. 1996), *amended*, 135 F.3d 1318 (9th Cir. 1998); Bruscino v. Carlson, 854 F.2d 162, 164, 166 (7th Cir. 1988) (handcuffing with box over cuffs and leg shackles when outside cell); Benson v. Cady, 761 F.2d 335, 341 n.1 (7th Cir. 1985) (handcuffing during medical examinations); Tubwell v. Griffith, 742 F.2d 250, 252–53 (5th Cir. 1984) (leg shackles and waist chains required to use law library; hands released when necessary); Jones v. Mabry, 723 F.2d 590, 592 (8th Cir. 1983) (use of leg irons whenever out of cell, including exercise, for several months after a disturbance); Bono v. Saxbe, 620 F.2d 609, 613–15 (7th Cir. 1980) (handcuffing when out of cells except for showers and recreation); Pendergrass v. Hodge, 53 F. Supp. 2d 838, 842 (E.D.Va. 1999) (requiring a segregation prisoner to be taken to recreation in restraints was reasonable even though he fell down the stairs); Dawes v. Coughlin, 964 F. Supp. 652, 658–59 (N.D.N.Y. 1997) (restraining a persistently violent prisoner during recreation periods did not violate the Eighth Amendment), *aff'd*, 159 F.3d 1346 (2d Cir. 1998) (unpublished); Young v. Larkin, 871 F. Supp. 772, 781 (M.D.Pa. 1994) (being in segregation was sufficient justification to require handcuffing during visits), *aff'd*, 47 F.3d 1163 (3d Cir. 1995) (unpublished); Armstrong v. Lane, 771 F. Supp. 943, 949 (C.D.Ill. 1991) (use of restraints during visits and when out of the cell); Hanna v. Lane, 610 F. Supp. 32, 35–36 (C.D.Ill. 1985) (security belt and handcuffs during visits); Freeman v. Trudell, 497 F. Supp. 481 (E.D.Mich. 1980) (handcuffing during a shower and a visit). *But see* Washington v. Israel, 513 F. Supp. 1061, 1062 (E.D.Wis. 1981) (complaint that inmate was handcuffed to cell while restraint belt was attached before being moved in the prison states Eighth Amendment claim).

[1070]LeMaire v. Maass, 12 F.3d 1444, 1459–60 (9th Cir. 1993); Caldwell v. Moore, 968 F.2d 595, 601–02, (6th Cir. 1992); Miller v. Glanz, 948 F.2d 1562, 1569–70 (10th Cir. 1991); Stenzel v. Ellis, 916 F.2d 423, 428–29 (8th Cir. 1990) (inmate restrained after blocking surveillance camera in cell); Bruscino v. Carlson, 854 F.2d at 164 (upholding restraint of inmates who had engaged in food-throwing and other in-cell misbehavior). However, several courts have condemned this practice when it is employed for prolonged periods or without appropriate supervision. *See* n.1078, below.

[1071]Moody v. Proctor, 986 F.2d 239, 241 (8th Cir. 1993) (upholding use of "black box" restraints over handcuffs during transportation); Fulford v. King, 692 F.2d 11, 14–15 (5th Cir. 1982) (same); Occhino v. U.S., 686 F.2d 1302, 1305–06 (8th Cir. 1982) (shackling during transfer was not disproportionate to legitimate objectives); Spain v. Procunier, 600 F.2d 189, 198 (9th Cir. 1979) (leg manacles and waist chains could be used during movement outside the prison); Datz v. Hudson, 806 F. Supp. 982, 989–90 (N.D.Ga. 1992) (upholding use of waist chains in court holding cells); Young v. City of Atlanta, 631 F. Supp. 1498, 1503–05

(N.D.Ga. 1986) (use of handcuffs and ankle chains on arrestee during hospital visit was not unconstitutional); Guerrero v. Cain, 574 F. Supp. 1012, 1015 (D.Or. 1983) (chaining of escape risk inmate to hospital bed for several days was not unconstitutional; chain was long enough that he could eat, sleep, move around, and get to the toilet); *see* Thielman v. Leean, 282 F.3d 478 (7th Cir. 2002) (upholding requirement that prisoner civilly committed as a sexual offender wear full restraints and not just handcuffs during transportation).

In *Freeman v. Arpaio*, 125 F.3d 732 (9th Cir. 1997), the court held that requiring Muslim prisoners to be handcuffed or shackled on their way to religious services satisfied the *Turner v. Safley* "reasonable relationship" test, *see* Ch. 3, § A, but might deny equal protection because the reason for singling out Muslims was not sufficiently explained. *Freeman*, 125 F.3d at 737–38.

[1072]In *May v. Sheahan*, 226 F.3d 876, 884 (7th Cir. 2000), the court held that a practice of shackling all hospitalized detainees to their beds 24 hours a day despite the presence of an armed guard was "plainly excessive in the absence of any indication that the detainee poses some sort of security risk." 226 F.3d at 884. *But see* Haslar v. Megerman, 104 F.3d 178, 180 (8th Cir. 1997) (policy of shackling prisoners to bed when hospitalized did not constitute deliberate indifference where it provided for safeguards such as wrapping legs in gauze, checking complaints of tightness, etc., even though officers failed to follow the safeguards).

In *Benjamin v. Fraser*, 264 F.3d 175 (2d Cir. 2001), the court limited a jail system's "Red ID" and "enhanced restraint" policies, under which pre-trial detainees believed to have used or possessed weapons or engaged in violent conduct were required to be shackled, rear-handcuffed, and placed in "black box" restraints and "security mitts" which made it impossible to use their hands, during the entire time they were out of the jail for court appearances (up to 14 hours in some cases). The court held that this painful and sometimes injurious practice had "a severe and deleterious effect . . . tantamount to punishment" and significantly restricted the due process liberty interest in freedom from bodily restraint, and therefore required procedural protections to ensure it was only imposed on persons who had actually committed the conduct charged. *Benjamin*, 264 F.3d at 188.

[1073]Williams v. Benjamin, 77 F.3d 756, 763–64 (4th Cir. 1996) (placing a prisoner in four-point restraints minutes after subduing him with mace did not violate the Eighth Amendment); Sadler v. Young, 325 F. Supp. 2d 689, 701–02 (W.D.Va. 2004) (prisoner who had slapped food tray could be strapped to a bed immediately thereafter), *rev'd and remanded on other grounds*, 118 Fed.Appx. 762 (4th Cir. 2005) (unpublished). *But see* Davis v. Lester, 156 F. Supp. 2d 588, 594 (W.D.Va. 2001) (use of four-point restraints is upheld only after in-depth examination of facts and justifications).

[1074]Fuentes v. Wagner, 206 F.3d 335, 344–46 (3d Cir. 2000) (eight hours in a restraint chair did not violate the Eighth Amendment where defendants observed the prisoner, released him periodically, etc., and there was no evidence of malicious and sadistic intent); Birdine v. Gray, 375 F. Supp. 2d 874, 881(D.Neb. 2005) (several hours' placement in restraint chair did not violate

of restraints may be unlawful if they are applied in a manner that is dangerous, painful or injurious,[1075] degrading,[1076]

done for a punitive or retaliatory purpose,[1077] or continued for longer than safety requires.[1078]

---

plaintiff's rights where he had physically resisted staff, refused to agree to be compliant, and was constantly monitored and observed and extended restraint authorized by the superintendent); Myers v. Milbert, 281 F. Supp. 2d 859, 862–63 (N.D.W.Va. 2003) (20-hour restraint in "stokes basket" (a metal stretcher) did not violate the Eighth Amendment for prisoner who had assaulted an officer, kicked a door, and was "out of control," and who received bathroom breaks, medications, food, and liquids); see Zigmund v. Foster, 106 F. Supp. 2d 352, 362 (D.Conn. 2000) (17 hours in restraints for person institutionalized after insanity acquittal might deny due process as a "substantial departure from accepted professional judgment, practice, or standards").

[1075]Hope v. Pelzer, 536 U.S. 730, 738, 122 S. Ct. 2508 (2002) (citing risk of physical harm, unnecessary pain from handcuffs and restricted position, unnecessary exposure to heat of the sun, and prolonged thirst); Walker v. Bowersox, 526 F.3d 1186, 1188 (8th Cir. 2008) (20-hour confinement upright in restraint chair without toilet access, pain or heartburn medication, aggravating chronic back pain and PTSD);Williams v. Benjamin, 77 F.3d 756, 765–68 (4th Cir. 1996) (leaving a prisoner in four-point restraints for eight hours without toilet access, medical attention, or ability to wash off mace, and "hollering with pain," could violate the Eighth Amendment); Aswegan v. Bruhl, 965 F.2d 676, 678 (8th Cir. 1992) (per curiam) (violation of medical orders not to cuff the plaintiff's hands behind his back supported a finding of Eighth Amendment violation); Spain v. Procunier, 600 F.2d at 197 (use of neck chains in addition to other restraints, over a period of years, with no showing of necessity violated the Eighth Amendment); Williams v. Goord, 142 F. Supp. 2d 416, 425–29 (S.D.N.Y. 2001) (restraint during exercise periods might result in an unconstitutional denial of exercise); Swans v. City of Lansing, 65 F. Supp. 2d 625, 638 (W.D.Mich. 1999) (upholding damage verdict for fatal use of "kick-stop" restraints to hog-tie prisoner pursuant to "unstated city policy of using maximum restraints on non-compliance [sic] prisoners"); Picariello v. Fenton, 491 F. Supp. 1020, 1023 (M.D.Pa. 1980) (jury could find that leaving a prisoner face down in restraints for an hour or two was unconstitutional; defendants held immune); Gawreys v. D.C. General Hospital, 480 F. Supp. 853, 854–56 (D.D.C. 1979) (use of metal restraints was unconstitutional); Gates v. Collier, 349 F. Supp. 881, 890, 900 (N.D.Miss. 1972) (prisoners not to be handcuffed to fences, bars, or other fixtures), aff'd, 501 F.2d 1291 (5th Cir. 1974). But see LeMaire v. Maass, 12 F.3d 1444, 1457 (9th Cir. 1993) (requiring violent prisoner to shower in restraints was not unconstitutional); Williams v. Burton, 943 F.2d 1572, 1575–77 (11th Cir. 1991) (28 hours in four-point restraints with mouth taped shut was not unconstitutional); Holloway v. Dobbs, 715 F.2d 390, 392–93 (8th Cir. 1983) (failure to wrap ankles in bandages before long-distance travel in fetters was not unconstitutional); Reimann v. Frank, 397 F. Supp. 2d 1059, 1077–78 (W.D.Wis. 2005) (nurse practitioner's decision to continue using metal restraints on plaintiff could prevail over two physicians' recommendations for soft restraints if based on nurse practitioner's medical judgment); Pendergrass v. Hodge, 53 F. Supp. 2d 838, 842 (E.D.Va. 1999) (requiring a segregation prisoner to be taken to recreation in restraints was reasonable even though he fell down the stairs).

[1076]Hope v. Pelzer, 536 U.S. at 738 (noting denial of toilet access to prisoners on hitching post); Glisson v. Sangamon County Sheriff's

Dep't, 408 F. Supp. 2d 609, 621-23 (C.D.Ill. 2006) (prisoner strapped into wheelchair for hours and left in his own urine stated an Eighth Amendment claim); Ziemba v. Armstrong, 343 F. Supp. 2d 173, 185 (D.Conn. 2004) (citing lack of bathroom access to prisoner in restraints), rev'd in part on other grounds, 430 F.3d 623 (2d Cir. 2005); Fieldcamp v. City of New York, 242 F. Supp. 2d 388, 390–91 (S.D.N.Y. 2003) (handcuffing arrestee so she couldn't pull clothing over exposed breast stated a Fourth Amendment claim); Von Colln v. County of Ventura, 189 F.R.D. 583, 597 (C.D.Cal. 1999) (citing denial to detainees of bathroom breaks and an opportunity to clean up after soiling themselves in enjoining restraint chair policy).

[1077]Hope v. Pelzer, 536 U.S. at 744-45 (noting punitive purpose of hitching post practice); Williams v. Dep't of Corrections, 208 F.3d 681, 680 (8th Cir. 2000) (allegation that officers put leg irons on too tightly to retaliate for plaintiff's court testimony stated a claim); Perkins v. Kansas Dep't of Corrections, 165 F.3d 803, 811 (10th Cir. 1999) (allegedly punitive requirement that HIV-positive prisoner wear a face mask that covered his entire head stated an Eighth Amendment claim); Murphy v. Walker, 51 F.3d 714, 718 (7th Cir. 1995) ("bodily restraints may not be used as punishment; they may only be used on violent inmates who pose a threat to others or suicidal inmates who pose a threat to themselves"); Putman v. Gerloff, 639 F.2d 415, 419-20 (8th Cir. 1981) (jury could award damages if overnight shackling was done with punitive intent); Davis v. Milwaukee County, 225 F. Supp. 2d 967, 976–77 (E.D.Wis. 2002) (claim that plaintiff was painfully restrained in retaliation for a complaint was not frivolous); Davis v. Lester, 156 F. Supp. 2d 588, 594 (W.D.Va. 2001) (inferring that 48 hours in five-point restraints for kicking a door was punitive); Von Colln v. County of Ventura, 189 F.R.D. 583, 595–97 (C.D.Cal. 1999) (placing detainees in a restraint chair for "kicking cell walls," "bad attitude," "resistance," etc., as opposed to violent behavior, was punitive and denied due process); Madrid v. Gomez, 889 F. Supp. 1146, 1168–71, 1254–55 (N.D.Cal. 1995) (leaving prisoners in "fetal restraints" as punishment violated the Eighth Amendment); Stewart v. Rhodes, 473 F. Supp. 1185, 1193-94 (S.D.Ohio 1979) (punitive use of restraints enjoined); see Littlewind v. Rayl, 839 F. Supp. 1369, 1373–75 (D.N.D. 1993) (restraints under harsh conditions were punitive), appeal dismissed, 33 F.3d 985 (8th Cir. 1994).

Exactly what "punitive" means is not entirely clear. In Key v. McKinney, 176 F.3d 1083 (8th Cir. 1999), the prison rule prescribed that anyone caught spitting, throwing objects, or starting fires would be held in handcuffs and leg shackles for 24 hours. One would think that restraint for a specified time period after specified misconduct is punitive, but the lower court found that the policy was intended to "manage behavior" rather than punish, and the appeals court said the policy was not unduly severe and there was no deliberate indifference. Key, 176 F.3d at 1086; cf. Walker v. Bowersox, 526 F.3d 1186, 1188 (8th Cir. 2008) (20-hour confinement in restraint chair after disruptive incident could violate the Eighth Amendment where prisoner was denied food, water, prescribed medication, and toilet access); Fuentes v. Wagner, 206 F.3d 335, 342-43 (3d Cir. 2000) (statements that there was nothing the prisoner could do to affect the time he remained in a restraint chair once placed there would support a conclusion it was used as punishment, though other evidence supported a jury verdict to the contrary).

[1078]Hope v. Pelzer, 536 U.S. at 737-38 (noting lack of ongoing safety concern behind placement on hitching post); Guerra v.

Handcuffing may be unconstitutional if it inflicts injury because the cuffs are excessively tight[1079] or for

_____

Drake, 371 F.3d 404, 405–06 (8th Cir. 2004) (per curiam) (noting damage award to prisoner left in a restraint chair for long periods, even though he had disobeyed orders and resisted deputies); Williams v. Benjamin, 77 F.3d 756, 765–68 (4th Cir. 1996) (leaving a prisoner in four-point restraints for eight hours, absent evidence that he had done anything threatening since being placed in them, could violate the Eighth Amendment); Ziemba v. Armstrong, 343 F. Supp. 2d 173, 185 (D.Conn. 2004) (holding 22-hour restraint without food, water, or bathroom access could violate Eighth Amendment), _rev'd in part on other grounds_, 430 F.3d 623 (2d Cir. 2005); Davis v. Lester, 156 F. Supp. 2d 588, 593–94 (W.D.Va. 2001) (48-hour five-point restraint for kicking a door stated an Eighth Amendment claim); Von Colln v. County of Ventura, 189 F.R.D. 583, 597 (C.D.Cal. 1999) (keeping detainees in restraint chair long after any justification had abated cited in enjoining practice); French v. Owens, 777 F.2d 1250, 1253–54 (7th Cir. 1985) (chaining prisoners to beds for 12 hours and longer with hard shackles violated the Eighth Amendment); Galluccio v. Holmes, 724 F.2d 301, 304 (2d Cir. 1983) (chaining prisoner to a bed for two days after he refused an anal cavity search presented a jury issue under the Fourth Amendment); Putman v. Gerloff, 639 F.2d 415, 419–20 (8th Cir. 1981) (jury could find overnight chaining and handcuffing of prisoners locked in cells unconstitutional); Sadler v. Young, 325 F. Supp. 2d 689, 702–04 (W.D.Va. 2004), _rev'd and remanded on other grounds_, 118 Fed.Appx. 762 (4th Cir. 2005) (unpublished) (holding restraint for over 47 hours could be found unconstitutional where prisoner was calm after three hours; court finds a policy of punitive 48-hour restraints); Picariello v. Fenton, 491 F. Supp. 1020, 1024 (M.D.Pa. 1980) (jury could find that three to five days in restraints in cell was unconstitutional; defendants held immune); Picariello v. Fenton, 491 F. Supp. 1026, 1039–40 (M.D.Pa. 1980) (three to five days in restraints in cell constituted tort of battery); Stewart v. Rhodes, 473 F. Supp. 1185 (S.D.Ohio 1979) (restraint for more than three hours requires doctor's authorization), appeal dismissed, 661 F.2d 934 (6th Cir. 1981); Tate v. Kassulke, 409 F. Supp. 651, 654 (W.D.Ky. 1976) (dictum) ("protracted" chaining to bed would violate the Eighth Amendment); Landman v. Royster, 333 F. Supp. 621, 647–48 (E.D.Va. 1971) (shackling of inmates in cells, interfering with eating, sleeping, and using the toilet, was unconstitutional), _supplemented_, 354 F. Supp. 1302 (E.D.Va. 1973).

[1079]Lyons v. City of Xenia, 417 F.3d 565, 575–76 (6th Cir. 2005) ("The Fourth Amendment . . . prohibits unduly tight handcuffing in the course of an arrest. . . . In order to reach a jury on this claim, the plaintiff must allege some physical injury from the handcuffing, . . . and must show that officers ignored plaintiff's complaints that the handcuffs were too tight. . . ."); Hanig v. Lee, 415 F.3d 822, 824 (8th Cir. 2005) ("For the application of handcuffs to amount to excessive force, there must be something beyond minor injuries."); Wall v. County of Orange, 364 F.3d 1107, 1112 (9th Cir. 2004) ("It is well-established that overly tight handcuffing can constitute excessive force."); Kopec v. Tate, 361 F.3d 772, 777 (3d Cir. 2004) (placing excessively tight handcuffs on an arrestee and needlessly failing to loosen them for 10 minutes, resulting in permanent nerve damage, would violate the Fourth Amendment where the officer was not in a dangerous situation); Bastien v. Goddard, 279 F.3d 10, 16 (1st Cir. 2002) (claim of "lengthy, painful handcuffing, which had lingering physical effects" was actionable under the Fourth Amendment; plaintiff need not show "serious" injury); Davidson v.

other reasons.[1080] Handcuffing prisoners to stationary objects has been found unconstitutional.[1081] The use of "black box" restraints over handcuffs during transportation has generally been upheld.[1082] "Hog-tying" (securing a handcuffed

_____

Flynn, 32 F.3d 27, 30 (2d Cir. 1994) (allegation of injurious tight handcuffing done for an improper motive stated an Eighth Amendment claim); _see_ Johnson v. City of Ecorse, 137 F. Supp. 2d 886, 893 (E.D.Mich. 2001) ("it is long-established that where the arrestee suffers from a physical ailment that makes handcuffing especially painful, and advises the officers of this condition before tight handcuffs cause the arrestee injury, there is a clearly established right to be free of excessively-tight handcuffs").

[1080]Kiman v. New Hampshire Dep't of Corrections, 451 F.3d 274, 288–89 (1st Cir. 2006) (evidence that prison staff refused to honor plaintiff's "front-cuff pass," issued because rear-cuffing was painful in light of his physical condition, supported a claim under the Americans with Disabilities Act); Benjamin v. Fraser, 264 F.3d 175, 188 (2d Cir. 2001) (holding painful and injurious rear-cuffing and other enhanced restraints during transportation for prisoners who have possessed or used weapons is a deprivation of liberty requiring due process protections); Carroll v. City of Quincy, 441 F. Supp. 2d 215, 221–23 (D.Mass. 2006) (rear-handcuffing an arrestee who was so drunk he had trouble standing, and leaving him by himself, was deliberate indifference to an excessive risk to safety); Bane v. Virginia Dep't of Corrections, 267 F. Supp. 2d 514, 520–23, 530–32 (W.D.Va. 2003) (allegation that prison staff ignored a medical order not to rear-handcuff a prisoner, dislocating his shoulder, raised factual issues under the Eighth Amendment and the Rehabilitation Act); Aceto v. Kachajian, 240 F. Supp. 2d 121, 124–25 (D.Mass. 2003) (handcuffing a non-threatening arrestee behind her back and aggravating a known injury stated an excessive force claim); Jackson v. Sheriff of Ellis County, Texas, 154 F. Supp. 2d 917, 920 (N.D.Tex. 2001) (handcuffing an arrestee who needed a cane to walk, causing him to fall down stairs, stated a deliberate indifference claim); Ferguson v. Hall, 33 F. Supp. 2d 608, 612 (E.D.Mich. 1999) (rear-cuffing a non-disruptive arrestee who asked to be front-cuffed because of a previous visible injury and whose arm was broken when he was rear-cuffed anyway supported a Fourth Amendment claim); Casaburro v. Giuliani, 986 F. Supp. 176, 180 (S.D.N.Y. 1997) (keeping prisoner handcuffed in holding cell for seven hours after arrest may deny due process). _But see_ Rodriguez v. Farrell, 294 F.3d 1276, 1278 (11th Cir. 2002) (rejecting complaint that plaintiff was handcuffed behind his back for a long time despite telling the arresting officer that he had an arm injury; the officer was not obliged to believe what a suspect told him).

[1081]Gates v. Collier, 349 F. Supp. 881, 890, 900 (N.D.Miss. 1972) (prisoners not to be handcuffed to fences, bars, or other fixtures), _aff'd_, 501 F.2d 1291 (5th Cir. 1974); Madrid v. Gomez, 889 F. Supp. 1146, 1168–71, 1254–55 (N.D.Cal. 1995) (leaving prisoners in "fetal restraints," sometimes chained to toilets or other objects, violated the Eighth Amendment); _see_ Hope v. Pelzer, 536 U.S. 730, 742–43, 122 S. Ct. 2508 (2002) (finding _Gates_ holding to be clearly established law). _But see_ Stewart v. McManus, 924 F.2d 138, 143 (8th Cir. 1991) ("flex-cuffing" a prisoner to his cell bars during a post-disturbance shakedown was not unconstitutional where prison officials had run out of handcuffs).

[1082]Moody v. Proctor, 986 F.2d 239, 241 (8th Cir. 1993); Fulford v. King, 692 F.2d 11, 14–15 (5th Cir. 1982); Burnette v. Phelps, 621 F. Supp. 1157, 1161 (M.D.La. 1985); _see_ Gomm v. DeLand, 729 F. Supp. 767, 781 (D.Utah 1990) (subjecting a prisoner to "black box"

person's ankles to the handcuffs) has been found unconstitutional in some circumstances.[1083] Failure to supervise and protect persons in handcuffs may be unlawful if injury results.[1084] The Supreme Court has held that non-prisoners may be detained for safety reasons in handcuffs during the course of a search, even if the search takes hours.[1085]

State statutes or regulations may restrict the use of physical restraints; these restrictions may be enforceable in state court.[1086] The use of restraints in federal prisons is governed by regulation.[1087]

4) Sexual Abuse by Staff Sexual abuse of prisoners by staff can violate the Constitution.[1088] This rule is not limited to correctional staff, but also applies to other staff who have authority over prisoners or access to them because of their positions.[1089] It applies regardless of the gender of the abuser and the victim.[1090]

To establish an Eighth Amendment violation, prisoners must show that prison staff have a sufficiently "wanton" state of mind. Since there is no legitimate purpose for sexual abuse, the behavior itself is generally enough to show wantonness.[1091] It is not completely settled how serious the sexual misconduct must be to be unconstitutional. One federal appeals court held that sexual abuse can violate the Eighth Amendment if it is "severe or repetitive,"[1092] but others have

---

restraints contrary to medical orders was merely negligent and not unconstitutional), *aff'd*, 931 F.2d 62 (10th Cir. 1991).

[1083]Cruz v. City of Laramie, Wyo., 239 F.3d 1183, 1188–89 (10th Cir. 2001) (hog-tying an obviously mentally deranged suspect constituted excessive force); Gutierrez v. City of San Antonio, 139 F.3d 441, 446–52 (5th Cir. 1998) (citing evidence that hog-tying is sufficiently dangerous to constitute deadly force in some circumstances); *see* Madrid v. Gomez, 889 F. Supp. 1146, 1168–71, 1254–55 (N.D.Cal. 1995) (leaving prisoners in "fetal restraints," similar to hog-tying, as punishment violated the Eighth Amendment). *But see* Garrett v. Unified Government of Athens-Clarke County, 378 F.3d 1274, 1279 (11th Cir. 2004) (per curiam) (hog-tying (which the court calls "fettering") a compliant arrestee was not unreasonable where the arrestee had previously led police on a high-speed chase).

[1084]Warren v. Swanson, 69 F. Supp. 2d 1047, 1050 (N.D.Ill. 1999) (arrestee who was handcuffed to a wall and suffered injury when no one responded to calls for help stated a Fourth Amendment claim).

[1085]Muehler v. Mena, 544 U.S. 93, 100, 125 S. Ct. 1465 (2005).

[1086]*See* Roudette v. Jones, 101 Misc.2d 136, 420 N.Y.S.2d 616 (N.Y.Sup. 1979) (prison officials must obey regulation limiting restraints to transportation within and outside the prison and to cases involving a physician's order). The regulation was subsequently amended to permit the prison superintendent to authorize restraints. 7 N.Y.C.R.R. § 250.3(h).

State tort law may provide a remedy for abuse of restraint procedures under some circumstances. *See* Phillips v. State, Dep't of Public Safety and Corrections, 978 So.2d 1223, 1230 (La.App. 2008) (awarding damages to arrestee negligently kept in shackles for 36 hours without medical attention for resulting injuries).

[1087]28 C.F.R. § 552.21(a) (cited in Bruscino v. Carlson, 654 F. Supp. 609, 614 (S.D.Ill. 1987), *aff'd*, 854 F.2d 162 (7th Cir. 1988)). The enforcement of federal law against federal prison officials is discussed in Ch. 8, § B.2.

[1088]Smith v. Cochran, 339 F.3d 1205, 1212–13 (10th Cir. 2003) (holding that sexual abuse or rape by staff is "malicious and sadistic" by definition because there is no legitimate purpose for it); Riley v. Olk-Long, 282 F.3d 592 (8th Cir. 2002) (affirming damage award against supervisors found deliberately indifferent to risk of sexual assault by guard); Fontana v. Haskin, 262 F.3d 871, 878–81 (9th Cir. 2001) (sexual harassment during arrest states a Fourth Amendment claim); Mathie v. Fries, 121 F.3d 808, 811–12 (2d Cir. 1997) (affirming trial court's finding of Eighth Amendment violation); K.M. v. Alabama Dep't of Youth Services, 360 F. Supp. 2d 1253, 1257–58 (M.D.Ala. 2005) (sexual assault violates Eighth and

Fourteenth Amendments); Thomas v. City of Clanton, 285 F. Supp. 2d 1275, 1280–81 (M.D.Ala. 2003) (the Fourteenth Amendment protects unconvicted persons from sexually motivated assaults); Women Prisoners of the District of Columbia Dep't of Corrections v. District of Columbia, 877 F. Supp. 634, 664–65 (D.D.C. 1994) (court finds pattern of sexual harassment violating the Eighth Amendment based on evidence of rape, physical touching, vulgar sexual comments, and lack of privacy from opposite-sex staff), *remanded on other grounds*, 93 F.3d 910 (D.C. Cir. 1996).

Sometimes prisoners refer to intrusive body searches as sexual assaults, or allege that sexual misconduct occurs during searches. Searches are discussed in Ch. 3, § E.2.

[1089]In *Smith v. Cochran*, the court held that a state drivers' license examiner for whom the plaintiff was working while on work release could be held liable for sexual abuse because the prison system had delegated custodial or supervisory authority over her to him. 339 F.3d at 1213–16 & n.5; *see* Walker v. Taylorville Correctional Center, 129 F.3d 410, 413–14 (7th Cir. 1997) (counselor could be held liable for sexual abuse; he acted under color of law even though he was pursuing his own purposes); Paz v. Weir, 137 F. Supp. 2d 782, 803–05 (S.D.Tex. 2001) (jail chaplain who abused prisoner acted under color of state law); *see also* Giron v. Correction Corp. of America, 14 F. Supp. 2d 1245, 1248–51 (D.N.M. 1998) (officer employed by private corporation acted under color of state law and could be held liable for sexual abuse).

[1090]Schwenk v. Hartford, 204 F.3d 1187, 1197 (9th Cir. 2000).

[1091]Giron v. Corrections Corp. of America, 191 F.3d 1281, 1290 (10th Cir. 1999) ("Where no legitimate penological purpose can be inferred from a prison employee's alleged conduct, including but not limited to sexual abuse or rape, the conduct itself constitutes sufficient evidence that force was used 'maliciously and sadistically for the very purpose of causing harm.'" (citation omitted)); Boddie v. Schneider, 105 F.3d 857, 861 (2d Cir. 1997).

[1092]Boddie v. Schneider, 105 F.3d 857, 861 (2d Cir. 1997) (allegations that prisoner was "verbally harassed, touched, and pressed against without his consent" several times did not state an Eighth Amendment violation). Under *Boddie*, a number of claims of physical sexual abuse have been dismissed as not serious enough to violate the Eighth Amendment. *See* Morrison v. Cortright, 397 F. Supp. 2d 424, 425 (W.D.N.Y. 2005) (running finger between buttocks and pressing against plaintiff during strip frisk); Davis v. Castleberry, 364 F. Supp. 2d 319, 321 (W.D.N.Y. 2005) (grabbing a prisoner's penis during a pat frisk); Montero v. Crusie, 153 F. Supp. 2d 368, 373, 375 (S.D.N.Y. 2001) (allegations that an officer squeezed the plaintiff's genitalia and made sexual propositions during pat frisks).

omitted the "severe or repetitive" limit,[1093] and it may be obsolete. A more recent district court decision held that contemporary standards of decency have now evolved to the point that "any sexual assault of a prisoner by a prison employee constitutes cruel and unusual punishment."[1094] Under any version of the standard, any form of actual sexual penetration is likely to be unconstitutional.[1095] Sexual harassment that does not involve physical contact generally is not unconstitutional.[1096] Courts have disagreed over the status

of less intrusive actions.[1097] The Fourth Amendment probably provides a more favorable standard for arrestees than the Eighth Amendment standard does for convicts; one court has held in a Fourth Amendment case that "unreasonable, non-consensual, inappropriate touching and propositioning" is unlawful and that "[t]here is no situation that would justify any amount of purposeful sexual verbal and physical predation against a handcuffed arrestee."[1098]

A prisoner need not show physical injury to pursue a claim for sexual abuse by staff.[1099] It is not clear whether sexual abuse by itself satisfies the Prison Litigation Reform Act's requirement that prisoners show physical injury in

---

[1093]*See* Schwenk v. Hartford, 204 F.3d 1187, 1197 (9th Cir. 2000) (stating generally that "[r]ape, coerced sodomy, unsolicited touching of women prisoners' vaginas, breasts and buttocks by prison employees are 'simply not part of the penalty that criminal offenders pay for their offenses against society.'"); Walker v. Taylorville Correctional Center, 129 F.3d 410, 411, 414 (7th Cir. 1997) (allegations of rubbing arm, stroking penis, and making suggestive comments "appear to satisfy the threshold standard for sexual harassment claims in a § 1983 case").

[1094]Rodriguez v. McClenning, 399 F. Supp. 2d 228, 237–38 (S.D.N.Y. 2005) (relying on trend toward statutory prohibition of sexual contact between prison employees and prisoners). The court held that the plaintiff's allegations, that an officer pat searched him in a sexually suggestive manner, caressing his chest and repeatedly groping his genitals and buttocks, stated an Eighth Amendment claim even though they were similar to the allegations held not to state a claim in *Boddie*. *Rodriguez*, 399 F. Supp. 2d at 237.

[1095]Smith v. Cochran, 339 F.3d 1205, 1212–13 (10th Cir. 2003) (forcible rape); White v. Ottinger, 442 F. Supp. 2d 236, 245, 248 (E.D.Pa. 2006) (forcible oral sex); K.M. v. Alabama Dep't of Youth Services, 360 F. Supp. 2d 1253, 1258–59 (M.D.Ala. 2005) (evidence that a staff member put a finger in a juvenile detainee's vagina); Hammond v. Gordon County, 316 F. Supp. 2d 1262, 1285, 1287 (N.D.Ga. 2002) (allegation that officer instructed prisoner to engage in oral sex with another prisoner for cigarettes, in addition to instructing her to strip and exposing his penis, and allegation that officer inserted fingers into prisoner's vagina in addition to telling her to strip or flash); Goode v. Correctional Medical Services, Inc., 168 F. Supp. 2d 289, 291 n.1, 293 (D.Del. 2001) (allegation that nurses conducted an internal examination without gloves); Carrigan v. Davis, 70 F. Supp. 2d 448, 452–53 (D.Del. 1999) ("an act of vaginal intercourse and/or fellatio between a prison inmate and a prison guard, whether consensual or not, is a *per se* violation of the Eighth Amendment").

[1096]Boxer X v. Harris, 437 F.3d 1107, 1111 (11th Cir. 2006) (ordering a male prisoner to masturbate under threat of reprisal was *de minimis* harm); Austin v. Terhune, 367 F.3d 1167, 1171 (9th Cir. 2004) (officer's "verbal sexual harassment" of exposing himself and making offensive comments was not actionable under the Eighth Amendment); Morales v. Mackalm, 278 F.3d 126, 132 (2d Cir. 2002) (allegation that a female staff member asked the male plaintiff to have sex with her and to masturbate in front of her and other female staff did not state a constitutional claim); Blueford v. Prunty, 108 F.3d 251, 254 (9th Cir. 1997) ("same-sex trash talk" is not unconstitutional); Ornelas v. Giurbino, 358 F. Supp. 2d 955, 963 (S.D.Cal. 2005) (guard's attempt to solicit sexual favors in exchange for privileges did not state a claim); Minifield v. Butikofer, 298 F. Supp. 2d 900, 903–04 (N.D.Cal. 2004) (officer's unzipping clothing and telling a prisoner to grab his penis was merely verbal abuse); Hammond v. Gordon County, 316 F. Supp. 2d 1262, 1282

(N.D.Ga. 2002) (officer's asking a prisoner to "flash" in exchange for cigarettes amounts only to verbal harassment).

One court has held that non-physical sexual harassment can be constitutionally significant where there is also widespread physical sexual abuse:

> There is a substantial risk of injury when officers make sexual remarks in an environment where sexual assaults of women prisoners by officers are well known and inadequately addressed. In free society, a woman who experiences harassment may seek the protection of police officers, friends, coworkers or relevant social service agencies. She may also have the option of moving to locations where the harassment would no longer occur. In sharp contrast, the safety of women prisoners is entrusted to prison officials, some of whom harass women prisoners and many of whom tolerate the harassment. Furthermore, the women are tightly confined, making their escape from harassment as unlikely as escape from the jail itself.
>
> Routine invasions of bodily privacy, such as men peering into women's cells at CTF or the unannounced presence of male guards in female living areas provide a reminder to women prisoners that their exposure to abuse is almost endless. . . .

Women Prisoners of the District of Columbia Dep't of Corrections v. District of Columbia, 877 F. Supp. 634, 665 (D.D.C. 1994), *remanded on other grounds*, 93 F.3d 910 (D.C. Cir. 1996).

[1097]*Compare* Turner v. Huibregtse, 421 F. Supp. 2d 1149, 1151–52 (W.D.Wis. 2006) (grabbing buttocks and fondling penis could violate the Eighth Amendment); Rodriguez v. McClenning, 399 F. Supp. 2d 228, 237–38 (S.D.N.Y. 2005) (caressing chest and groping genitals and buttocks stated an Eighth Amendment claim); Gilson v. Cox, 711 F. Supp. 354, 356 (E.D.Mich. 1989) (allegation that an officer reached for the prisoner's groin area and grabbed his buttocks might violate his interest in "personal bodily integrity," including "the right to be free from sexual abuse" (citation omitted)) *with* Carrigan v. Davis, 70 F. Supp. 2d 448, 454 & n.5 (D.Del. 1999) citing cases, *and with* cases cited in n.1092, above.

[1098]Fontana v. Haskin, 262 F.3d 871, 880–81 (9th Cir. 2001). *But see* Hicks v. Moore, 422 F.3d 1246, 1253–54 (11th Cir. 2005) (slight touching of female arrestee's body during fingerprinting unaccompanied by any other sexual comment or action did not violate the Fourth Amendment).

[1099]Daskalea v. District of Columbia, 227 F.3d 433, 443–44 (D.C. Cir. 2000); Schwenk v. Hartford, 204 F.3d 1187, 1196 & n.6 (9th Cir. 2000).

order to recover compensatory damages for mental or emotional injury.[1100]

Courts have disagreed whether a prisoner's consent or submission to staff sexual misconduct is a defense for the staff member in a civil rights suit. One federal appeals court has held that a prisoner who voluntarily engages in sexual activity is not subjected to the infliction of pain that is a necessary element of an Eighth Amendment claim.[1101] Other courts have emphasized that in most states, where sex between prisoners and prison staff is unlawful, it is impossible for a prisoner validly to consent to sex,[1102] or have said that the circumstances of imprisonment mean that prisoners' consent is not voluntary.[1103]

Sexual abuse claims may be asserted against supervisors or against municipalities on the same basis as other supervisory or municipal liability claims.[1104] One court has

held that when an officer presents a known risk of sexual assault, a collective bargaining agreement with a prison staff union cannot serve as an excuse for doing nothing about that person.[1105]

The Prison Rape Elimination Act of 2003 (PREA) directs the U.S. Attorney General to promulgate national standards for the detection, prevention, reduction, and punishment of prison rape, by staff as well as by other prisoners.[1106]

Prisoners who have been sexually abused may need medical attention or psychological counselling. Claims that such care was denied are governed by the same deliberate indifference standard applied to other medical and mental health care claims.[1107]

Sexual abuse may constitute the torts of assault and battery[1108] or intentional infliction of emotional distress

---

[1100]42 U.S.C. § 1997e(e) has been interpreted as meaning that prisoners cannot recover compensatory damages for mental or emotional injury unless they also show physical injury. Courts have disagreed whether sexual abuse constitutes physical injury for this purpose. *See* Ch. 9, § E.3, n.592.

[1101]Freitas v. Ault, 109 F.3d 1335, 1338–39 (8th Cir.1997); *accord,* Fisher v. Goord, 981 F. Supp. 140, 174–75 (W.D.N.Y.1997); *see* Giron v. Corrections Corp. of America, 191 F.3d 1281, 1287–88 (10th Cir. 1999) (apparently accepting that consent is relevant, not resolving whether plaintiff or defendant has the burden of proof).

[1102]Hammond v. Gordon County, 316 F. Supp. 2d 1262, 1285 n.6 (N.D.Ga. 2002); Carrigan v. Davis, 70 F. Supp. 2d 448, 459–60 (D.Del. 1999); *see* Paz v. Weir, 137 F. Supp. 2d 782, 807–09 (S.D.Tex. 2001) (court finds a factual dispute whether sexual activity was consensual, and notes Texas law making it non-consensual if done by a public servant who coerces the other person or by a clergyman who exploits the other person); Fisher v. Goord, 981 F. Supp.140, 175 (W.D.N.Y. 1997) (noting that a subsequently passed New York statute making sex between prison staff and inmates illegal might eliminate the consent defense).

[1103]White v. Ottinger, 442 F. Supp. 2d 236, 247–48 (E.D.Pa. 2006) (citing evidence that officer's power made sexual relationship nonconsensual); Carrigan v. Davis, 70 F. Supp. 2d 448, 460 (D.Del. 1999) ("Examining the totality of the Plaintiff's circumstances as a prisoner, the control the institution necessarily maintained over her, and the lack of control which she maintained over her own life, the Court concludes, as a matter of law, that the Plaintiff was incapable of giving a voluntary waiver.")

[1104]*See* Tafoya v. Salazar, 516 F.3d 912 (10th Cir. 2008) (holding sheriff could be found deliberately indifferent to risk of sexual assault by staff because of deficiencies in supervision and training and failure to enforce protective policies); Gonzales v. Martinez, 403 F.3d 1179, 1186–88 (10th Cir. 2005) (evidence that the jail was generally out of control and that sheriff and jail administrator ignored or dismissed complaints, supported a deliberate indifference claim against the municipality); Riley v. Olk-Long, 282 F.3d 592, 596–97 (8th Cir. 2002) (affirming damage award against supervisors found deliberately indifferent to known risk of sexual assault by guard); Daskalea v. District of Columbia, 227 F.3d 433, 441–43 (D.C. Cir. 2000) (affirming finding of municipal liability); White v. Ottinger, 442 F. Supp. 2d 236, 248–50 (E.D.Pa. 2006) (finding basis for liability of various supervisors); Faas v. Washington County, 260 F. Supp. 2d 198, 204–08 (D.Me. 2003)

(evidence of a history of prior sexual misconduct by jail officers supported claim against the county; training claim dismissed); Hammond v. Gordon County, 316 F. Supp. 2d 1262, 1288–90 (N.D.Ga. 2002) (plaintiffs raised a claim against sheriff and jail administrator with evidence that jailers received no formal training concerning sexual harassment or proper contact with inmates, there was no formal policy on the subject, jailers were unsupervised and "essentially did as they pleased," and there was a history of complaints about sexual misconduct); Ortiz v. Voinovich, 211 F. Supp. 2d 917, 924–26 (S.D.Ohio 2002) (supervisor who told prisoner at risk of sexual assault to stay around her friends and "do anything you have to do to protect yourself" could be found liable for not doing more); Colman v. Vasquez, 142 F. Supp. 2d 226, 237–38 (D.Conn. 2001) (failure to investigate complaints meaningfully while plaintiff remained subject to officer's sexual harassment stated a claim of supervisory deliberate indifference); Paz v. Weir, 137 F. Supp. 2d 782, 814–16 (S.D.Tex. 2001) (jail administrator could be held liable based on evidence of a custom allowing the chaplain access to female prisoners in violation of formal procedure and evidence of a cover-up of his prior misconduct). *But see* Beers-Capitol v. Whetzel, 256 F.3d 120, 135–44 (3d Cir. 2001) (holding supervisors could not be found liable for sexual assaults in juvenile facility; one counselor with some knowledge of risk could be held liable); Morris v. Eversley, 282 F. Supp. 2d 196, 204–08 (S.D.N.Y. 2003) (finding no basis for liability of superintendent and assistant deputy superintendent); Thomas v. City of Clanton, 285 F. Supp. 2d 1275, 1283 (M.D.Ala. 2003) (rejecting municipal liability claim absent evidence of "widespread prior abuse"). Supervisory and municipal liability are discussed in Ch. 8, §§ B.4.a, B.4.b.

[1105]Riley v. Olk-Long, 282 F.3d 592, 597 (8th Cir. 2002).

[1106]42 U.S.C.A. § 15607; *see* § G.1.d of this chapter, nn.924–925, concerning PREA.

[1107]Giron v. Corrections Corp. of America, 191 F.3d 1281, 1286 (10th Cir. 1999); Carrigan v. State of Delaware, 957 F. Supp. 1376, 1383–85 (D.Del. 1997).

[1108]K.M. v. Alabama Dep't of Youth Services, 360 F. Supp. 2d 1253, 1263 (M.D.Ala. 2005) (state battery law requires a "rude or angry" touching, and indecency is a kind of rudeness); Bolton v. U.S., 347 F. Supp. 2d 1218, 1222–213 (N.D.Fla. 2004) (allowing sexual battery claim to go forward); Hammond v. Gordon County, 316 F. Supp. 2d 1262, 1293–94 (N.D.Ga. 2002) (putting fingers into a prisoner's vagina would constitute assault and battery). *But see* Austin v. Terhune, 367 F.3d 1167, 1172 (9th Cir. 2004) (also known as outrage),[1109] or it may support a claim of negligence by supervisors,[1110] any of which may be actionable under the Federal Tort Claims Act (FTCA)[1111] as well as directly under state law. It may be hard to recover for staff sexual abuse against the abuser's employer based on *respondeat superior*, the tort rule which means that the employer often pays for the employee's misconduct. That rule usually applies only when the employee's conduct was within the scope of employment, and sexually abusing prisoners is not generally within prison employees' scope of employment.[1112]

However, if the employer itself was negligent in some fashion, it can be liable without the need for a *respondeat superior* argument.

5) *Verbal Abuse* Most courts hold that verbal abuse by itself does not violate the Constitution.[1113] That holding includes racial epithets and other racial abuse.[1114] However, verbal threats of force may be unconstitutional in extreme cases usually involving plausible threats of death or injury,[1115] or where they are in retaliation for constitutionally protected conduct.[1116] Verbal abuse may be an aggravating factor where physical abuse is also established,[1117] and it

---

(officer's exposing himself to a prisoner was not assault where the officer was inside a control booth and there was no evidence the prisoner was placed in fear). Assault and battery claims are discussed further in § G.2.e of this chapter.

Consent is likely to be relevant to an assault and battery claim, since you must generally show an *unpermitted* contact to prove that tort. *See* Giron v. Corrections Corp. of America, 191 F.3d 1281, 1288 (10th Cir. 1999).

[1109]White v. Ottinger, 442 F. Supp. 2d 236, 251 (E.D.Pa. 2006) (coerced oral sex supported claim for intentional infliction of emotional distress); K.M. v. Alabama Dep't of Youth Services, 360 F. Supp. 2d 1253, 1260 (M.D.Ala. 2005) (Alabama law makes sexual harassment actionable in "particularly egregious cases"; the fact that the plaintiff was a minor and in state custody and the assailant was entrusted with her care made this case egregious); Faas v. Washington County, 260 F. Supp. 2d 198, 208 (D.Me. 2003) (finding evidence to support negligent infliction of emotional distress but not intentional infliction); Hammond v. Gordon County, 316 F. Supp. 2d 1262, 1292–93 (N.D.Ga. 2002) (putting fingers into a prisoner's vagina would constitute intentional infliction of emotional distress); Brown v. Youth Services Intern. of South Dakota, Inc., 89 F. Supp. 2d 1095, 1105 (D.S.D. 2000) (corporation's keeping counselor in his job after prior incidents of sexual abuse by him was sufficiently outrageous to support a finding of intentional infliction of emotional distress). *But see* Austin v. Terhune, 367 F.3d 1167, 1172 (9th Cir. 2004) (claims for intentional and negligent infliction of emotional distress fail absent any evidence of severe distress or damage). The elements of intentional infliction of emotional distress are discussed in Ch. 8, § C, n.273.

[1110]Bolton v. U.S., 347 F. Supp. 2d 1218, 1221–22 (N.D.Fla. 2004); Brown v. Youth Services Intern. of South Dakota, Inc., 89 F. Supp. 2d 1095, 1103–04 (D.S.D. 2000) (claims for negligent hiring, retention, and supervision of employee who abused juvenile prisoners could go forward).

[1111]Bolton v. U.S., 347 F. Supp. 2d 1218, 1222 (N.D.Fla. 2004) (battery and negligence); *see* Ch. 8, §§ C.2, H.2.b, concerning the FTCA.

[1112]Adorno v. Correctional Services Corporation, 312 F. Supp. 2d 505, 516–18 (S.D.N.Y. 2004); *see* Grager v. Schudar, 770 N.W.2d 692, 699 (N.D. 2009) (upholding standard scope of employment jury instruction despite plaintiff's argument that it allowed defendants to argue that their officer was not employed to sexually assault prisoners).

This is not a problem under the FTCA, since that statute allows battery claims against the United States for actions taken by federal law enforcement officers "within the scope of their authority *or* under color of Federal law," 28 U.S.C. § 2680(h), and prison and jail staff will almost always be operating under color of law. *See* Bolton v. U.S., 347 F. Supp. 2d 1218, 1222–23 (N.D.Fla. 2004). *But see* Vallo v. U.S., 298 F. Supp. 2d 1231, 1237 (D.N.M. 2003)

(prisoner's battery claims were not actionable under the FTCA because the tribal detention officer was not a federal "investigative or law enforcement officer"). Scope of employment is discussed further in § G.2.e of this chapter, n.1148.

There may be other rules of state law that benefit sexually abused prisoners. In some states, employers may be held liable for the actions of employees who acted with "apparent authority" even if they were not genuinely acting within the scope of their employment. *See* Brown v. Youth Services Intern. of South Dakota, Inc., 89 F. Supp. 2d 1095, 1105–06 (D.S.D. 2000) (finding counselor in juvenile institution who molested residents acted with apparent authority).

[1113]Skinner v. Cunningham, 430 F.3d 483, 489 (1st Cir. 2005) (allegations including threats and false charges suggested "a sorry story of mis-administration by the prison" but did not violate the Eighth Amendment); Johnson v. Dellatifa, 357 F.3d 539, 546 (6th Cir. 2004) (similar to *Skinner*); Austin v. Terhune, 367 F.3d 1167, 1171 (9th Cir. 2004) (verbal sexual harassment did not violate the Eighth Amendment); Cumbey v. Meachum, 684 F.2d 712, 714 (10th Cir. 1982); Morrison v. Martin, 755 F. Supp. 683, 687 (E.D.N.C.), *aff'd*, 917 F.2d 1302 (4th Cir. 1990); Williams v. Pecchio, 543 F. Supp. 878, 879 (W.D.N.Y. 1982); Freeman v. Trudell, 497 F. Supp. 481, 482 (E.D.Mich. 1980). *Contra*, Parker v. Asher, 701 F. Supp. 192, 194 (D.Nev. 1988) ("[S]ince the purpose of the eighth amendment is to prevent prison authorities from inflicting grossly undue punishment it applies to wanton and unnecessary verbal abuse as well as physical abuse.").

[1114]Blades v. Schuetzle, 302 F.3d 801, 805 (8th Cir. 2002) (racially derogatory language does not violate the Fourteenth Amendment unless it is so pervasive or severe to amount to racial harassment); DeWalt v. Carter, 224 F.3d 607, 612 (7th Cir. 2000).

One court has held that the use of racial slurs with such frequency that they create an "atmosphere of racial harassment" violates the Constitution, but the appeals court held that supervisory officials could not be held responsible unless they actually encouraged this conduct. Knop v. Johnson, 667 F. Supp. 467, 505–08 (W.D.Mich. 1987), *rev'd in pertinent part*, 977 F.2d 996, 1014 (6th Cir. 1992); *see also* Finney v. Mabry, 534 F. Supp. 1026, 1043 (E.D.Ark. 1982) (racial slurs to be eliminated as part of a comprehensive injunction).

[1115]*See* § G.2.b.2 of this chapter, n.1016.

[1116]Proctor v. Harmon, 257 F.3d 867, 869 (8th Cir. 2001); Burton v. Livingston, 791 F.2d 97, 100–01 (8th Cir. 1986); Hudspeth v. Figgins, 584 F.2d 1345, 1348 (4th Cir. 1978). *Contra*, Gaut v. Sunn, 810 F.2d 923, 925 (9th Cir. 1987).

[1117]Harris v. Chapman, 97 F.3d 499, 505–06 (11th Cir. 1996) (where officer snapped the plaintiff's head back in a towel, kicked

may help prove malicious intent or unreasonableness of the force used.[1118] Verbal abuse that subjects a prisoner to attack by other prisoners may violate the Constitution.[1119] Under some circumstances, certain kinds of verbal abuse can constitute the tort of defamation, which is addressed in another chapter.[1120]

d. Liability for Force: Bystanders, Supervisors, and Municipalities Law enforcement officers may be held liable not only for using excessive force but for failing to intervene when others are doing so.[1121] This principle, first asserted in police cases, applies equally in prisons and jails,[1122] and to line staff as well as supervisors.[1123] Under this rule, you may be able to recover from all the guards involved in a beating even if you don't know which ones actually struck you or who struck which blows.[1124]

Claims against bystanders are decided under the deliberate indifference standard rather than the malicious and sadistic standard that applies to persons actually using force.[1125] However, the bystanders must have had a "realistic opportunity" to prevent or stop the beating in order to be held liable.[1126]

Supervisory officials who were not even present at the beating may sometimes be held liable if you can show

him, and subjected him to racial abuse, jury finding for plaintiff upheld); Herrera v. Valentine, 653 F.2d 1220, 1225–26 (8th Cir. 1981); R.G. v. Koller, 415 F. Supp. 2d 1129, 1156–57 (D.Haw. 2006) (holding "relentless campaign of harassment based on their sexual orientation that included threats of violence, physical and sexual assault, imposed social isolation, and near constant use of homophobic slurs" against gay youth in a juvenile facility denied due process); Women Prisoners of the District of Columbia Dep't of Corrections v. District of Columbia, 877 F. Supp. 634, 665 (D.D.C. 1994) (holding verbal sexual harassment contributed to an Eighth Amendment violation where there was also a pattern of physical sexual abuse), *remanded on other grounds*, 93 F.3d 910 (D.C. Cir. 1996).

[1118]*See, e.g.*, Bozeman v. Orum, 422 F.3d 1265, 1271 n.11 (11th Cir. 2005) ("threatening language as part of a totality of circumstances can be relevant to what is constitutionally reasonable or, as in this case, to the determination of reasonable inferences about the Officers' subjective state of mind"); Kerman v. City of New York, 261 F.3d 229, 239–40 (2d Cir. 2001) (verbal abuse and other factors might support a claim of objectively unreasonable force); Williams v. Bramer, 180 F.3d 699, 706 (5th Cir. 1999) (use of racial epithets is "strong evidence that a comment or action is racially motivated"), *clarified*, 186 F.3d 633 (5th Cir. 1999); Estate of Davis by Ostenfeld v. Delo, 115 F.3d 1388, 1394 (8th Cir. 1997) (officer's taunting and threatening the plaintiff the day after a use of force incident could help prove malicious intent in using force); Albritten v. Dougherty County, Ga., 973 F. Supp. 1455, 1465 (M.D.Ga. 1997) (racial epithets could help show that use of force was based on racial animus and was therefore unreasonable).

[1119]*See* § G.1.b of this chapter, nn.882–883.

[1120]*See* Ch. 3, § E.3, nn.955–960 and accompanying text.

[1121]Randall v. Prince George's County, Md., 302 F.3d 188, 203–04 (4th Cir. 2002); Mick v. Brewer, 76 F.3d 1127, 1136 (10th Cir. 1996); Anderson v. Branen, 17 F.3d 552, 557 (2d Cir. 1994); Bruner v. Dunaway, 684 F.2d 422, 425–26 (6th Cir. 1982); Harris v. Chanclor, 537 F.2d 203, 206 (5th Cir. 1976); Byrd v. Brishke, 466 F.2d 6, 11 (7th Cir. 1972); Thomas v. Frederick, 766 F. Supp. 540, 555 (W.D.La. 1991); *see* U.S. v. Serrata, 425 F.3d 886, 895–96 (10th Cir. 2005) (affirming officer's criminal conviction of civil rights violation for failing to intervene).

[1122]Smith v. Mensinger, 293 F.3d 641, 650 (3d Cir. 2002); Skrtich v. Thornton, 280 F.3d 1295, 1302 (11th Cir. 2002); Estate of Davis by Ostenfeld v. Delo, 115 F.3d 1388, 1395 (8th Cir. 1997); Robins v. Meecham, 60 F.3d 1436, 1442 (9th Cir. 1995); Buckner v. Hollins, 983 F.2d 119, 121–22 (8th Cir. 1993); Bolin v. Black, 875 F.2d 1343, 1347–48 (8th Cir. 1989); Putman v. Gerloff, 639 F.2d 415, 423–24 (8th Cir. 1981); Pizzuto v. County of Nassau, 239 F.

Supp. 2d 301, 312 (E.D.N.Y. 2003) (supervisor who directed a prisoner be subdued by force if necessary, opened the cell door, heard what happened from 40 feet away, but did not act could be held liable for officers' beating him to death); Moore v. Hosier, 43 F. Supp. 2d 978, 985–87 (N.D.Ind. 1998); Kesler v. King, 29 F. Supp. 2d 356, 371–72 (S.D.Tex. 1998) ("Plaintiffs contend, and this Court agrees, that the duty to intercede is heightened in a prison setting, where the state has restrained an individual's liberty to such a degree that he can no longer care for or protect himself."); Jackson v. Austin, 241 F. Supp. 2d 1313, 1322–23 (D.Kan. 2003); *see also* Davis v. Rennie, 264 F.3d 86, 98, 102 (1st Cir. 2002) (applying rule to mental patients).

[1123]Smith v. Mensinger, 293 F.3d at 651 ("The duty to uphold the law does not turn upon an officer's rank."); Byrd v. Brishke, 466 F.2d at 10–11.

[1124]Skrtich v. Thornton, 280 F.3d 1295, 1302 (11th Cir. 2002) ("we reject the argument that the force administered by each defendant in this collective beating must be analyzed separately to determine which of the defendants' blows, if any, used excessive force"); Miller v. Smith, 220 F.3d 491, 495 (7th Cir. 2000); Simpson v. Hines, 903 F.2d 400, 403 (5th Cir. 1990) (10 officers could be held liable where they acted as a unit); Rutherford v. City of Berkeley, 780 F.2d 1444, 1448 (9th Cir. 1986) (jury could infer that three officers who were present during a beating participated in it); Grandstaff v. City of Borger, Texas, 767 F.2d 161, 168 (5th Cir. 1985) (where numerous officers fired shots, plaintiff's estate need not identify whose bullet killed him); Davis v. Hill, 173 F. Supp. 2d 1136, 1144 (D.Kan. 2001); Merritt v. Hawk, 153 F. Supp. 2d 1216, 1223–24 (D.Colo. 2001) (describing the beating and identifying those present was sufficient to allege their direct participation); Skorupski v. Suffolk County, 652 F. Supp. 690, 694 (E.D.N.Y. 1987). *But see* Lolli v. County of Orange, 351 F.3d 410, 417 (9th Cir. 2003) (noting that plaintiff did not "assert a group liability theory" but relied on evidence that each deputy exerted some physical force).

[1125]Estate of Davis by Ostenfeld v. Delo, 115 F.3d 1388, 1395 (8th Cir. 1997) (noting that failure to report can be evidence of deliberate indifference); Buckner v. Hollins, 983 F.2d 119, 121–23 (8th Cir. 1993); Jackson v. Austin, 241 F. Supp. 2d 1313, 1322–23 (D.Kan. 2003).

[1126]Smith v. Mensinger, 293 F.3d at 652; *accord*, Robins v. Meecham, 60 F.3d 1436, 1442 (9th Cir. 1995); Anderson v. Branen, 17 F.3d 552, 557–58 (2d Cir. 1994); Gaudreault v. Municipality of Salem, Mass., 923 F.2d 203, 207 n.3 (1st Cir. 1990); O'Neill v. Krzeminski, 839 F.2d 9, 11 (2d Cir. 1988); Taylor v. Kveton, 684 F. Supp. 179, 183–84 (N.D.Ill. 1988); *see also* Rascon v. Hardiman, 803 F.2d 269, 276–77 (7th Cir. 1986) (bystanding officer must actually see and permit unlawful conduct to be held liable).

that their actions or inactions (such as failure to act against officers with records of misusing force) led to excessive force against you.[1127] Several courts have found police supervisors liable for misuse of force by officers based on histories of inadequate training or inadequate investigation of citizen complaints.[1128] City or county governments can be held liable if you can show that the beating was caused by a municipal policy, *e.g.*, of failing adequately to train and supervise staff and investigate use of force complaints.[1129] Maintaining or tolerating a "code of silence" about staff misconduct can support supervisory or municipal liability.[1130]

Claims of supervisory or municipal liability are generally governed by the deliberate indifference standard, rather

---

[1127]Danley v. Allen, 540 F.3d 1298, 1315 (11th Cir. 2008) (allegations that defendants, through "force reports and similar documents, inmate complaints, jailer complaints, attorney complaints, judicial officer complaints, and personal observation" knew that jailers "regularly used pepper spray excessively as a means of punishment and not for legitimate reasons" adequately stated supervisory liability claim); Valdes v. Crosby, 450 F.3d 1231, 1237–44 (11th Cir. 2006) (warden could be held liable for prisoner's beating death based on evidence he was on notice of a pattern of excessive force and did not act to curb it), *cert. dismissed*, 549 U.S. 1249 (2007); Curry v. Scott, 249 F.3d 493, 507–08 (6th Cir. 2001) (supervisors could be liable for assault by racist officer based on their knowledge of his employment record and its implications and statements by other staff about his conduct and attitude); Estate of Davis by Ostenfeld v. Delo, 115 F.3d 1388, 1396 (8th Cir. 1997) (superintendent was properly held liable based on evidence that he knew of the main officer defendant's propensity to use excessive force); Meriwether v. Coughlin, 879 F.2d 1037, 1048 (2d Cir. 1989) (damages awarded against Commissioner who was aware of the risk of beatings but did nothing); Bolin v. Black, 875 F.2d at 1347–48 (associate warden liable on facts similar to *Meriwether*); Parker v. Williams, 862 F.2d 1471, 1477 (11th Cir. 1989) (sheriff could be held liable for a beating by a deputy who had a known history of criminal behavior, mental problems, and drug abuse); Kesler v. King, 29 F. Supp. 2d 356, 368–69 (S.D.Tex. 1998) (Sheriff could be held liable for abusive emergency search of jail unit based on inadequate training and supervision of staff); Murray v. Koehler, 734 F. Supp. 605, 607 (S.D.N.Y. 1990) (warden could be held liable based on officers' history of retaliatory beatings); Haynes v. Marshall, 704 F. Supp. 788, 793–94 (S.D.Ohio 1988) (warden could be held liable for giving guards unsupervised authority to use force to enforce rules and punish inmates), *aff'd in part, rev'd in part on other grounds*, 887 F.2d 700 (6th Cir. 1989); Musgrove v. Broglin, 651 F. Supp. 769, 774–76 (N.D.Ind. 1986) (superintendent could be liable where the officer had not been disciplined for his prior misconduct). *But see* Serna v. Colorado Dep't of Corrections, 455 F.3d 1146 (10th Cir. 2006) (prison director who authorized "special operations response team" (SORT) search could not be held liable for officers' conduct that violated SORT procedures where he did not plan or direct the search or directly supervise it, and had no duty to supervise because others had that duty).

[1128]*See* Gutierrez-Rodriguez v. Cartagena, 882 F.2d 553, 562–61 (1st Cir. 1989); Kerr v. City of West Palm Beach, 875 F.2d 1546, 1556–57 (11th Cir. 1989); Bordanaro v. McLeod, 871 F.2d 1151, 1159–63 (1st Cir. 1989); Fiacco v. Rensselaer, N.Y., 783 F.2d 319, 329 (2d Cir. 1986); Commonwealth of Pennsylvania v. Porter, 659 F.2d 306, 321–22 (3d Cir. 1981); Madrid v. Gomez, 889 F. Supp. 1146, 1249 (N.D.Cal. 1995) (prison officials liable for "abdicating their duty to supervise and monitor the use of force and deliberately permitting a pattern of excessive force to develop and persist."); Thomas v. Frederick, 766 F. Supp. 540, 555–56 (W.D.La. 1991).

Supervisory officials cannot be held liable for a use of force based solely on their failure adequately to investigate that same incident. Williams v. Omodt, 640 F. Supp. 120, 123–24 (D.Minn. 1986). However, their failure to investigate the current incident has some probative value in establishing past investigative policies and practices. Bordanaro v. McLeod, 871 F.2d at 1167. The failure to investigate may also be relevant to other issues such as malicious intent and the appropriateness of punitive damages. McHenry v. Chadwick, 896 F.2d 184, 189 (6th Cir. 1990). Punitive damages are discussed further in Ch. 8, § O.1.c.

[1129]Beck v. City of Pittsburgh, 89 F.3d 966, 974 (3d Cir. 1996) (police department process "structured to curtail disciplinary action and stifle investigations" could support municipal liability); Vann v. City of New York, 72 F.3d 1040, 1050–51 (2d Cir. 1995) (inadequate monitoring of identified "problem" officers could support liability); Kopf v. Wing, 942 F.2d 765, 269 (4th Cir. 1991) ("circle the tents" approach to police brutality complaints could help show a county policy of excessive force); Davis v. Mason County, 927 F.2d 1473, 1480–83 (9th Cir. 1991) (policy of inadequate police training); Kerr v. City of West Palm Beach, 875 F.2d at 1556–57 (policy of inadequate police training); Bordanaro v. McLeod, 871 F.2d at 1159–63 (inadequate police training and inadequate investigation of citizen complaints); Depew v. City of St. Marys, Ga., 787 F.2d 1496, 1499 (11th Cir. 1986) (inadequate investigation of complaints against police); Fiacco v. Rensselaer, N.Y., 783 F.2d at 329 (inadequate investigation of complaints against police); Rymer v. Davis, 754 F.2d 198, 200–01 (6th Cir. 1985) (inadequate police training), *vacated sub nom.* City of Shepherdsville, Ky. v. Rymer, 473 U.S. 901 (1985); Phebus v. City of Memphis, 340 F. Supp. 2d 874, 879 (W.D.Tenn. 2004) (allegation of failure to train, discipline, monitor and evaluate police officers in the use of force, refusal to adequately investigate civilian complaints, and instructing officers to make false statements about such claims supported a claim against the city); Galindez v. Miller, 285 F. Supp. 2d 190, 199 (D.Conn. 2003) (evidence of failure to investigate excessive force complaints reasonably and the failure to discipline officers supported a claim against the city); Kesler v. King, 29 F. Supp. 2d 356, 374 (S.D.Tex. 1998) (county could be held liable for inadequate training and supervision of emergency team); Berry v. City of Phillipsburg, Kan., 796 F. Supp. 1400, 1408 (D.Kan. 1992) (knowing employment of Sheriff who misused force); McLin by and through Harvey v. City of Chicago, 742 F. Supp. 994, 998–1002 (N.D.Ill. 1990) (failure to discipline police officers that resulted in further abusive behavior by them); Mosier v. Robinson, 722 F. Supp. 555, 557–58 (W.D.Ark. 1989) (municipality liable for a beating by a drunken sheriff where municipal officials knew of his habits and did nothing); *see also* Hammer v. Gross, 932 F.2d 842, 850 (9th Cir. 1991) (where the option to conduct forcible blood extractions was left to police officers' discretion, there was evidence of a city policy permitting excessive force). Municipal liability is discussed further in Ch. 8, § B.4.b.

[1130]Sledd v. Lindsay, 102 F.3d 282, 289 (7th Cir. 1996); Madrid v. Gomez, 889 F. Supp. 1146, 1156–57, 1199–1200, 1251 (N.D.Cal. 1995).

than the "malicious and sadistic" standard.[1131] That is because the reason the "malicious and sadistic" standard was adopted is that decisions concerning use of force are often made "in haste, under pressure, and frequently without the luxury of a second chance."[1132] The failure to train or to discipline officers, to investigate complaints, or to have an appropriate written use of force policy generally involve long-term practices and not split-second decisions. Claims based on such policies or practices are similar to prison "conditions of confinement" cases, in which the prisoner need only prove deliberate indifference.[1133]

e. Tort Claims for Excessive Force Excessive force by prison staff may constitute assault and battery under state tort law. It may also constitute other torts, such as negligence[1134] or the intentional infliction of emotional distress,[1135] but assault and battery is the most common state law claim for physical abuse by prison staff.[1136]

Generally, battery is any harmful or offensive contact with a person that is done intentionally; an assault is an act that is intended to cause, and does cause, a reasonable fear that a battery is about to occur.[1137] A leading torts treatise observes that "it is an assault when the defendant swings a fist to strike the plaintiff, and the plaintiff sees the movement; a battery when the fist comes in contact with the plaintiff's nose."[1138] An act need not be a blow, kick, or use of a weapon, and it need not cause physical harm, to constitute a battery.[1139]

There are limits on these tort principles in prisons and jails; not every push or shove by an officer constitutes an assault and battery. As one court put it, "The incidental and necessary touchings by correctional officers of inmates in the performance of their duties are not batteries, but are privileged contacts. . . . [O]fficials charged with the custody of prisoners are privileged to use force which is reasonable

---

[1131]Valdes v. Crosby, 450 F.3d 1231, 1243–44 (11th Cir. 2006), *cert. dismissed*, 549 U.S. 1249 (2007); Curry v. Scott, 249 F.3d 493, 506 n.5 (6th Cir. 2001); Blyden v. Mancusi, 186 F.3d 252, 264 (2d Cir. 1999); White v. Holmes, 21 F.3d 277, 280 (8th Cir. 1994) (claim against supervisor in use of force case decided under deliberate indifference standard); Gutierrez-Rodriguez v. Cartagena, 882 F.2d at 562 (supervisory liability for police shooting); Meriwether v. Coughlin, 879 F.2d at 1048 (supervisory liability for prison beatings); Madrid v. Gomez, 889 F. Supp. 1146, 1249–51 (N.D.Cal. 1995); *see* Canton v. Harris, 489 U.S. 378, 389–90, 109 S. Ct. 1197 (1989) (applying deliberate indifference to claim against municipality in pre-trial detainee suicide case).

[1132]Whitley v. Albers, 475 U.S. 312, 320–21, 106 S. Ct. 1078 (1986) (cited in Hudson v. McMillian, 503 U.S. 1, 6, 112 S. Ct. 995 (1992)).

[1133]*See* cases cited in § A.2 of this chapter, nn.75–81.

[1134]In some cases it may also support a state law negligence claim. *See* Ansley v. Heinrich, 925 F.2d 1339, 1342–44 (11th Cir. 1991) (jury found police officers liable for negligence but not assault and battery or civil rights violation); Roberts v. State, 159 Ind.App. 456, 307 N.E.2d 501, 505 (Ind.App. 1974) (allegation that guards fired into a crowd during a prisoner protest and injured an innocent bystander stated a claim for negligence as well as for assault).

[1135]Alexander v. Newman, 345 F. Supp. 2d 876, 888 (W.D.Tenn. 2004). *But see* Ruble v. King, 911 F. Supp. 1544, 1558–59 (N.D.Ga. 1995) (rejecting claim in the absence of evidence of extreme emotional distress). This tort is more frequently invoked in connection with sexual abuse. *See* § G.2.c.4 of this chapter, n.1109. The elements of intentional infliction of emotional distress are discussed in Ch. 8, § C, n.273.

[1136]State statutes or constitutions may also contain restrictions on the use of force that state courts may enforce. *See, e.g.,* Fernelius v. Pierce, 22 Cal.2d 226, 138 P.2d 12, 16 (1943) (state statute forbade "any cruel, corporal or unusual punishment" or any treatment "which would injure or impair the health of the prisoner"); Farmer v. Rutherford, 136 Kan. 298, 15 P.2d 474, 478 (1932) (state statute provided that "prisoners shall be treated with humanity"); Harrah v. Leverette, 165 W.Va. 665, 271 S.E.2d 322, 330–31 (1980) (state constitution prohibits prison personnel from using physical force

"absent imminent and present danger of harm to others, themselves, or state property").

[1137]W. Page Keeton et al., *Prosser and Keeton on the Law of Torts* § 9, at 39 (5th ed. 1984). The definitions of these torts may vary slightly from state to state, but the general idea is usually similar. *See, e.g.,* Jackson v. Austin, 241 F. Supp. 2d 1313, 1323 (D.Kan. 2003); Evicci v. Baker, 190 F. Supp. 2d 233, 239 (D.Mass. 2002) ("An assault is a threatening gesture coupled with the apparent ability to injure a person with force or violence; a battery is an accomplished assault."); Picariello v. Fenton, 491 F. Supp. 1026, 1037 (1980). *But see* Thomas v. Holder, 836 S.W.2d 351, 353 (Tex.App. 1992) ("A civil assault is committed if a person knowingly, intentionally, or recklessly causes bodily injury to another.").

Assault and battery claims for sexual abuse are discussed in § G.2.c.4 of this chapter, n.1108.

[1138]*Prosser and Keeton on the Law of Torts* § 10 at 46.

[1139]One court stated that the common law action for battery "makes actionable *any* intentional and unpermitted contact with the plaintiff's person or anything attached to it." Johnson v. Glick, 481 F.2d 1028, 1033 (2d Cir. 1973) (emphasis supplied). *But see* Beckwith v. Hart, 263 F. Supp. 2d 1018, 1023 (D.Md. 2003) (closing a door on the plaintiff's foot was not a battery where it was intended only to exclude him from the room). In *Picariello v. Fenton*, the court found that unnecessarily leaving a prisoner confined in restraints in his cell for over 36 hours was a battery. 491 F. Supp. at 1038–39. *But see* Coppage v. Mann, 906 F. Supp. 1025, 1050 (E.D.Va. 1995) (handcuffing plaintiff to his hospital bed was not a battery because it was not done with wantonness, malice, or anger, but to assist in treating his bedsore). Medical treatment administered over the patient's objection may be a battery. *See* § F.5 of this chapter, n.792.

Unlike the rule in civil rights actions, courts have held that a bystanding officer who does not intervene in excessive force cannot be liable for battery because commission of a violent act is a necessary element of the tort. Ruble v. King, 911 F. Supp. 1544, 1558–59 (N.D.Ga. 1995). However, a bystanding officer may be found negligent for failing to intervene. Jean-Laurent v. Wilkerson, 438 F. Supp. 2d 318, 327–28 (S.D.N.Y. 2006) (holding officers were not negligent because they lacked time to intervene).

under the circumstances to maintain control of their charges."[1140]

The assault and battery standard, which focuses on what is "reasonable" and "necessary" rather than on what the officer intended, appears similar to the Fourth Amendment "objective reasonableness" standard applied to uses of force against arrestees.[1141] Thus it is more favorable to prisoners than the *Hudson v. McMillian* Eighth Amendment standard, which requires the plaintiff to prove malicious intent.[1142] Whether it is more favorable than the standard applied in pretrial detainees' cases will depend on the facts and on which standard the court uses.[1143] Courts have also

suggested that the law of assault and battery may make it easier to recover for relatively minor injuries.[1144]

Depending on which state you are in, there may be other legal rules that make assault and battery claims easier or harder to win than civil rights claims for use of force. For example, in some states, defendants have the burden of proving that a battery was justified, but in civil rights cases the plaintiff always has the burden of proving that a use of force was not justified.[1145] In some states, you may be able to sue the state, city, or county directly for the officers' acts under the doctrine of *respondeat superior*,[1146] which is not available in a federal civil rights action.[1147] *Respondeat superior* allows recovery against the employer when an employee violates someone's legal rights while acting within the scope of her employment.[1148] State law immunity rules, however,

---

[1140]Picariello v. Fenton, 491 F. Supp. at 1038; *accord*, State v. Bojorquez, 138 Ariz. 495, 675 P.2d 1314, 1317 (Ariz. 1984) (citation omitted) (prison officials have "statutory right to use that amount of physical force necessary to maintain order within the prison"); Roberts v. State, 159 Ind.App. 456, 307 N.E.2d 501, 506 (Ind.App. 1974) (citation omitted) (police officers "may exercise reasonable means for the safe-keeping of prisoners, to preserve discipline and to secure obedience to reasonable orders"); Polizzi v. Trist, 154 So.2d 84, 85 (La.App. 1963) (deputy sheriff would be liable for striking a prisoner "when there was no need for it"); Mason v. Ohio Dep't of Rehabilitation and Correction, 62 Misc.2d 96, 593 N.E.2d 482, 486 (Ct.Cl. Ohio 1990) ("force must be used in the performance of official duties and cannot exceed the amount of force which is reasonably necessary under the circumstances"); Johnson v. Peterson, 799 S.W.2d 345, 347 (Tex.App. 1990) (under state statute, "guard is privileged in using reasonable force to maintain the security of the penal institution"; claim that guard placed his finger on prisoner's nose in an offensive manner was frivolous); *see* Roskop v. Trent, 250 Or. 397, 443 P.2d 174, 175 (Or. 1963) (deputy was entitled to raise a claim of self-defense where he inflicted injury on a prisoner after the prisoner attacked him).

[1141]*See* Dean v. City of Worcester, 924 F.2d 364, 369 (1st Cir. 1991) (state law assault standard is essentially the same as the Fourth Amendment standard).

This may not be true in every state or in every case. *See, e.g.,* Carter v. Chicago Police Officers, 165 F.3d 1071, 1080–81 (7th Cir. 1998) (actions by police officers that were not "objectively reasonable" would not constitute a battery under Illinois law unless done with "willful and wanton" intent); Jarvis v. Government of Virgin Islands, 919 F. Supp. 717, 183 (D.V.I. 1996) (twisting the plaintiff's arm may not have been an assault because the officer did not intend to cause harm, but could have been objectively unreasonable).

[1142]*See* Neal v. Miller, 778 F. Supp. 378, 381–85 (W.D.Mich. 1991) (officer who struck inmate with "playful or mischievous" intent committed battery but did not violate the Eighth Amendment).

This advantage may not exist in every state. For example, in some states law enforcement officers are immune from suit unless they commit "willful or malicious wrong." *See* Yang v. Murphy, 796 F. Supp. 1245, 1252 (D.Minn. 1992); Johnson v. Peterson, 799 S.W.2d at 347. Such an immunity rule makes proving an assault and battery as difficult as proving an Eighth Amendment violation.

[1143]*See, e.g.,* Trujillo v. Goodman, 825 F.2d 1453, 1459–60 (10th Cir. 1987) (a police officer who "spontaneousl[ly]" threw a flashlight at the plaintiff was properly found to have committed a

battery but not a due process violation); Whitlock v. Jackson, 754 F. Supp. 1394, 1400 (S.D.Ind. 1991) (upholding jury verdict that plaintiff had been subjected to battery but not a due process violation). The use of force standards applicable to detainees are discussed in § G.2.a.2 of this chapter.

[1144]Davis v. Lane, 814 F.2d 397, 400 (7th Cir. 1987); *see* Myrick v. Cooley, 91 N.C.App. 209, 371 S.E.2d 492, 497 (N.C.App. 1988) (forcible arrest resulting in a minor cut and scratches was not unconstitutional but presented a jury question as to assault and battery by police officer), *review denied*, 323 N.C. 477, 373 S.E.2d 865 (N.C. 1988).

If a battery does not cause physical injury at all, the plaintiff may still recover nominal damages for the battery itself, compensatory damages for "the resulting mental disturbance, such as fright, revulsion, or humiliation," and in some cases, punitive damages. *Prosser and Keeton on the Law of Torts* § 9, at 40–41.

[1145]Davis v. Lane, 814 F.2d at 401 (Illinois law). *But see* Wing v. Britton, 748 F.2d 494, 497 (8th Cir. 1984) (under Arkansas law, plaintiff has the burden of showing that force used in an arrest was excessive).

[1146]*See, e.g.,* Roberts v. State, 307 N.E.2d at 504–06 (state could be held liable for guards' shooting of a prisoner during a disturbance); Gullette v. State through Dep't of Corrections, 383 So.2d 1287, 1289 (La.App. 1980) (damages awarded against state for assault by guard); Jones v. State, 33 N.Y.2d 275, 352 N.Y.S.2d 169, 307 N.E.2d 236, 237–38 (N.Y. 1973) (state could be liable in Court of Claims for injuries inflicted by state police in suppressing a prison disturbance). *But see* Bayer v. Almstadt, 29 Mich.App. 171, 185 N.W.2d 40, 41 (Mich.App. 1970) (sheriff was not liable for acts of deputies). *Cf.* Alexander v. Newman, 345 F. Supp. 2d 876, 885–86 (W.D.Tenn. 2004) (state law provided individual police officers and supervisors were immune under state law if the municipality was not immune).

[1147]*See* Ch. 8, § B.4.a. n.141.

[1148]Sometimes defendants argue that employees were not acting within the scope of their employment because they are not hired to break the law. That is not the standard. Scope of employment usually includes actions that take place while employees are on the job and generally performing their duties, even if they break the law while doing them. *See, e.g.,* Wilson v. City of Chicago, 120 F.3d 681, 685 (7th Cir. 1997) (police officer who tortured a suspect was acting within the scope of his employment); Pizzuto v. County of Nassau, 239 F. Supp. 2d 301, 313–16 (E.D.N.Y. 2003) (officers who beat a prisoner to death acted within the scope of their

may make it difficult or even impossible to bring some excessive force suits in state court.[1149]

Assault and battery claims against federal law enforcement officers may be brought under the Federal Tort Claims Act (FTCA), which allows *respondeat superior* recovery against the federal government for some of the torts of its employees.[1150]

You may be able to join civil rights and assault and battery claims in the same lawsuit, either in federal court[1151]

or in state court. If you do join the two claims in one suit, the court must instruct the jury separately on each claim.[1152]

There are surprisingly few reported decisions involving prison assault and battery claims. However, state law, unlike constitutional law, generally seems to treat uses of force in prison similarly to police use of force on the streets.[1153] You may therefore find useful guidance in assault and battery cases involving police officers.

3. Hazardous Conditions

Prison officials must provide a reasonably safe living and working environment for prisoners.[1154] In extreme cases courts may order unsafe facilities closed.[1155] However, prisoners alleging that unsafe conditions violate the Eighth Amendment must show that the defendants have been deliberately indifferent to their safety.[1156]

a. Fire Safety "Prisoners have the right not to be subjected to the unreasonable threat of injury or death by fire and need not wait until actual casualties occur in order to obtain relief from such conditions."[1157] But prisoners are not entitled to a

---

employment because they were on duty in their assigned work area and carrying out their duties in furthering the employer's business by keeping order on the housing unit; the officers had historically been granted considerable discretion in keeping order, including use of force, and the use of force was foreseeable); Moore v. Hosier, 43 F. Supp. 2d 978, 992 (N.D.Ind. 1998) (officer who helped subdue the plaintiff and then beat him after he was restrained may have acted within the scope of his employment, since the later attack was not "divorced in time, place, and purpose" from the earlier use of force, which was clearly within the scope of employment); *see also* Jones v. Patrick & Assoc. Detective Agency, 442 F.3d 533, 535–36 (7th Cir. 2006) (private security guard who had a run-in with the plaintiff, went to the police station where he was held, got admitted to the holding cells, and assaulted the plaintiff presented a jury question as to scope of employment, since the dispute had its origin in a work-related incident, the guard was still on duty, wearing his uniform, and carrying his employer-issued weapons, and he probably would never have gotten into the holding cells if he hadn't been a security guard in uniform). Scope of employment in sexual abuse cases is discussed at § G.2.c.4, n.1112, and under the FTCA in Ch. 8, § C.2.a, nn.313–319.

[1149]*See, e.g.,* Yang v. Murphy, 796 F. Supp. 1245, 1252 (D.Minn. 1992) (municipality was immune for training and supervision of police officers); Alford v. Osei-Kwesi, 203 Ga.App. 716, 418 S.E.2d 79, 85 (Ga.App. 1992) (jail lieutenant was immune because he exercised discretion and his actions were not "wilful, malicious, or corrupt"). Tort law immunities are discussed in Ch. 8, § L.5.

[1150]*See, e.g.,* Harris v. U.S., 677 F. Supp. 403, 405–06 (W.D.N.C. 1988); Picariello v. Fenton, 491 F. Supp. 1026, 1037 (1980).

The FTCA mostly does not cover intentional torts such as assault and battery, but a provision of the statute allows such claims against federal investigative or law enforcement officers, which most courts have interpreted to allow suit against federal correctional staff. *See* Ortiz v. Pearson, 88 F. Supp. 2d 151, 154–55 (S.D.N.Y. 2000) (citing 28 U.S.C. § 2680(h)). It does not allow assault and battery claims against prison staff who are not investigative or law enforcement officers. *See* Barber v. Grow, 929 F. Supp. 820, 824 (E.D.Pa. 1996) (dismissing claim of assault and battery by work supervisor, who was not alleged to be an investigative or law enforcement officer). The FTCA is discussed in more detail in Ch. 8, §§ C.2 and H.2.b.

[1151]State law claims against state or local officials and employees and county governments may be brought along with § 1983 claims under the doctrine of supplemental (formerly "pendent") jurisdiction. Miller v. Lovett, 879 F.2d 1066, 1073 (2d Cir. 1989) (district court should have heard a pendent assault and battery claim in a § 1983 use of force case); Lohr v. State of Florida Dep't of Corrections, 835 F.2d 1404, 1405 (11th Cir. 1988) (jury found assault and battery on two plaintiffs, civil rights violation on one); Ware v. Reed, 709 F.2d 345, 354 (5th Cir. 1983) (judge should have submitted assault and battery claim as well as § 1983 claim to the

jury); Stewart v. Roe, 776 F. Supp. 1304, 1307–08 (N.D.Ill. 1991) (court exercises supplemental jurisdiction over battery claim); *see* Ch. 8, § F.1, for further discussion of supplemental and pendent jurisdiction.

Prisoners suing for uses of force by federal prison personnel may bring constitutional claims and claims under the FTCA in the same action. Sanchez v. Rowe, 651 F. Supp. 571, 573–74 (N.D.Tex. 1986); Picariello v. Fenton, 491 F. Supp. 1026, 1027–28 (1980).

[1152]Davis v. Lane, 814 F.2d 397, 400 (7th Cir. 1987).

[1153]*See, e.g.,* Roberts v. State, 159 Ind.App. 456, 307 N.E.2d 501, 506 (Ind.App. 1974); Jones v. State, 307 N.E.2d 236, 237–38 (N.Y. 1973).

[1154]Helling v. McKinney, 509 U.S. 25, 33, 113 S. Ct. 2475 (1993); Hoptowit v. Spellman, 753 F.2d 779, 784 (9th Cir. 1985); Ramos v. Lamm, 639 F.2d 559, 568 (10th Cir. 1980) (prisoners are entitled to "shelter which does not . . . threaten [their] mental and physical well being"). *But see* Toussaint v. McCarthy, 597 F. Supp. 1388, 1410 (N.D.Cal. 1984) (lack of "seismic" [earthquake] safety did not violate the Eighth Amendment), *aff'd*, 801 F.2d 1080 (9th Cir. 1986).

[1155]*See* § B of this chapter.

[1156]Helling v. McKinney, 509 U.S. at 32–33; Wilson v. Seiter, 501 U.S. 294, 303,111 S. Ct. 2321 (1991).

The meaning of deliberate indifference is discussed in § A.2 of this chapter. The deliberate indifference standard has long been used in medical care and inmate assault cases, and is also discussed in the sections on those subjects. *See* §§ F.1, G.1.a of this chapter.

[1157]Hoptowit v. Spellman, 753 F.2d at 784; *accord*, Hadix v. Johnson, 367 F.3d 513, 525 (6th Cir. 2004); Dimarzo v. Cahill, 575 F.2d 15, 18 (1st Cir. 1978); Jones v. City and County of San Francisco, 976 F. Supp. 896, 908–09 (N.D.Cal. 1997) (even if officials made substantial efforts to improve safety, court must consider whether inmates are actually reasonably safe in assessing deliberate indifference); Tillery v. Owens, 719 F. Supp. 1256, 1279 (W.D.Pa. 1989), *aff'd*, 907 F.2d 418 (3d Cir. 1990); Knop v. Johnson, 667 F. Supp. 512, 526 (W.D.Mich. 1987), *aff'd in part and rev'd in part on other grounds*, 977 F.2d 996, 1013 (6th Cir. 1992); Fischer v. Winter, 564 F. Supp. 281, 300 (N.D.Cal. 1983). *But see* Ruiz v.

risk-free environment, and prison officials are not liable for fire hazards that are not reasonably predictable.[1158] Courts have found a variety of fire safety deficiencies to violate the Constitution.[1159]

Prisons are not required by the Constitution to comply in every respect with civilian fire codes,[1160] though their provisions may be helpful in determining Eighth Amendment standards.[1161] However, if you think that fire regulations are being violated, complaining to state or local fire officials may help get such violations corrected,[1162] and you may be able to get the regulations enforced in state court.

b. Environmental Hazards   Exposing prisoners to dangerous conditions or toxic substances may also violate the Constitution.[1163] Courts have cited exposure to friable asbestos[1164] as raising constitutional questions,[1165] though the

---

Estelle, 679 F.2d 1115, 1152–53 (5th Cir. 1982) (reversing a lower court's injunction because no one had yet been killed or seriously injured by fire and the risk of fire seemed small); *accord,* Standish v. Bommel, 82 F.3d 190, 191–92 (8th Cir. 1996).

[1158]Duckworth v. Franzen, 780 F.2d 645, 653–56 (7th Cir. 1985); Knop v. Johnson, 667 F. Supp. at 526.

[1159]*See, e.g.,* Inmates of the Allegheny County Jail v. Wecht, 874 F.2d 147, 154 (3d Cir. 1989) (antiquated heating system that would channel smoke and fumes to cells, lack of a sprinkler system, faulty wiring, unreliable locking system contributed to a finding that the jail as a whole was unconstitutional and must be closed), *vacated and remanded on other grounds,* 493 U.S. 948 (1989); Leeds v. Watson, 630 F.2d 674, 675–76 (9th Cir. 1980) (cell area must be provided with a fire exit even if rarely used); Maynor v. Morgan County, Ala., 147 F. Supp. 2d 1185, 1186–87, 1189 (N.D.Ala. 2001) (officials ordered to repair and maintain fire safety equipment); White v. Cooper, 55 F. Supp. 2d 848, 858 (N.D.Ill. 1999) ("The absence of fire safety and prevention devices, which are necessary in a correctional facility to notify staff that a fire has started and to aid in the evacuation of smoke, is an obvious risk of serious harm."); Carty v. Farrelly, 957 F. Supp. 727, 737 (D.V.I. 1997) ("Failure to provide functional fire safety systems subjects prisoners to life-threatening conditions." Court cites inoperable cell locking devices, manual alarm systems, smoke dampers, and heat detectors); Jones v. City and County of San Francisco, 976 F. Supp. 896, 908–09 (N.D.Cal. 1997) (lack of fire-rated doors, lack of sprinklers in critical areas, use of flammable mattresses, combustible storage, lack of staff for evacuation, deteriorating electrical system); Alexander v. Boyd, 876 F. Supp. 773, 786 (D.S.C. 1995) (individual padlocks on cells cited as unsafe); Tillery v. Owens, 719 F. Supp. 1271, 1277–80 (W.D.Pa. 1989) (absence of fire barriers, fire alarms, standpipes, smoke alarms, sprinklers or smoke exhaust systems, combined with presence of combustible materials, a high inmate population and a small staff, presented an unconstitutional risk of fire), *aff'd,* 907 F.2d 418 (3d Cir. 1990); Inmates of Occoquan v. Barry, 717 F. Supp. 854, 867 (D.D.C. 1989) (jail officials directed to repair inoperative fire alarms and smoke detectors, post proper evacuation plans, change exit doors to open outward rather than inward, develop emergency plan for releasing segregation inmates during fires); Rogers v. Etowah County, 717 F. Supp. 778, 779, 781 (N.D.Ala. 1989) (replacement of defective locks with chains and padlocks presented serious risk in case of fire and was unconstitutional); Coniglio v. Thomas, 657 F. Supp. 409, 414 (S.D.N.Y. 1987) (smoke barriers required, sprinklers not required in segregation unit); Jackson v. Gardner, 639 F. Supp. 1005, 1012 (E.D.Tenn. 1986) (posting of fire escape plans required in jail); Toussaint v. McCarthy, 597 F. Supp. 1388, 1410 (N.D.Cal. 1984) (defective electrical wiring and lack of evacuation procedures presented unconstitutional fire hazards), *aff'd in part and rev'd in part on other grounds,* 801 F.2d 1080 (9th Cir. 1986); *see also* Facility Review Panel v. Holden, 177 W.Va. 703, 356 S.E.2d 457, 459–60 (W.Va. 1987) (lack of evacuation plans, fire drills, sprinkler system, and padlocked outside exits violated jail officials' state statutory duties). *But see* Kitt v. Ferguson, 750 F. Supp. 1014, 1020 (D.Neb. 1990) (fire exits that required staff with keys to open were not unconstitutional), *aff'd,* 950 F.2d 725 (8th Cir. 1991); Miles v. Bell, 621 F. Supp. 51, 64–65 (D.Conn. 1985)

(lack of fire door and sprinklers in laundry not unconstitutional); Grubbs v. Bradley, 552 F. Supp. 1052, 1075–76, 1090, 1113, 1127 (M.D.Tenn. 1982) (no constitutional violation presented by "serious" fire hazards including extensive use of polyurethane foam pillows and mattresses, lack of a central cell unlocking mechanism, etc.); Mawby v. Ambroyer, 568 F. Supp. 245, 251 (E.D.Mich. 1983) (lack of smoke detectors in maximum security was not unconstitutional).

[1160]Hadix v. Johnson, 367 F.3d 513, 527–28 (6th Cir. 2004) (Constitution does not require compliance with private Life Safety Code.); French v. Owens, 777 F.2d 1250, 1257 (7th Cir. 1985); Shrader v. White, 761 F.2d 975, 985–86 (4th Cir. 1985); Miles v. Bell, 621 F. Supp. at 65.

[1161]Masonoff v. DuBois, 899 F. Supp. 782, 799 (D.Mass. 1995) ("A court may look to state codes with respect to prison hazards in its effort to determine society's standard of decency, but these standards do not necessarily reflect the constitutional minimum." Plaintiffs were not entitled to summary judgment based on lack of automatic locks and a functioning sprinkler system.); Capps v. Atiyeh, 559 F. Supp. 894, 914–15 (D.Or. 1982) ("substantial" rather than "literal" compliance with fire code required by Constitution); Dawson v. Kendrick, 527 F. Supp. 1252, 1294 (S.D.W.Va. 1981) (fire regulations may be an "indicator" of Eighth Amendment standards). If prison officials do comply with state and local fire regulations, courts are unlikely to find a constitutional violation. Mawby v. Ambroyer, 568 F. Supp. at 251.

[1162]Or they may not. *See* Capps v. Atiyeh, 559 F. Supp. 894, 914–15 (D.Or. 1982) (Fire Marshal declined to prosecute violations and extended the prison's time to comply for budgetary reasons).

Even if state or local officials do not enforce the law, it is worthwhile asking them to inspect and make a record of violations.

[1163]Helling v. McKinney, 509 U.S. 25, 35, 113 S. Ct. 2475 (1993) (Eighth Amendment bars exposure, with deliberate indifference, to conditions "that pose an unreasonable risk of serious damage to [the plaintiff's] future health"); Jackson v. State of Arizona, 885 F.2d 639, 641 (9th Cir. 1989) (allegations of polluted water stated an Eighth Amendment claim); Davis v. Stanley, 740 F. Supp. 815, 817–18 (N.D.Ala. 1987) (allegations that deputies engaged in a high-speed chase while transporting the plaintiff between jails did not state a constitutional claim).

[1164]"Friable" asbestos means asbestos fibers floating in the air where people can inhale them. Asbestos that is not friable is not dangerous.

[1165]Smith v. U.S., 561 F.3d 1090, 1094, 1105 (10th Cir. 2009) (allegation of knowing exposure to asbestos dust stated an Eighth

level of exposure must be shown to present a genuine health hazard,[1166] and defendants must be shown to have been deliberately indifferent to the risk.[1167] Deliberately

indifferent exposure of prisoners to sewage or other forms of human waste may violate the Eighth Amendment.[1168] Contaminated drinking water can violate the Eighth Amendment.[1169] Exposure to other types of toxic fumes and

---

Amendment claim); Herman v. Holiday, 238 F.3d 660, 663–65 (5th Cir. 2001) (allegation of routine exposure to asbestos presented factual issues under the Eighth Amendment); LaBounty v. Coughlin, 137 F.3d 68, 73 (2d Cir. 1998) (same as *Herman*); Wallis v. Baldwin, 70 F.3d 1074, 1076 (9th Cir. 1995) (evidence that plaintiff was required to clean an asbestos-laden area for 45 hours without adequate protective gear supported an Eighth Amendment claim); Powell v. Lennon, 914 F.2d 1459, 1463 (11th Cir. 1990) (exposure to asbestos during building renovations constituted deliberate indifference to medical needs); Gonyer v. McDonald, 874 F. Supp. 464, 466–67 (D.Mass. 1995) (allegation of free-floating asbestos fibers in the prison environment raised an Eighth Amendment claim); Inmates of Occoquan v. Barry, 717 F. Supp. 854, 866 (D.D.C. 1989) (court requires documentation of asbestos removal before housing unit renovations are undertaken); *see also* Webster v. Sowders, 846 F.2d 1032, 1034 (6th Cir. 1988) (noting that district court had enjoined unsafe asbestos removal practices).

[1166]Pack v. Artuz, 348 F. Supp. 2d 63, 79–80 (S.D.N.Y. 2004) ("The health risk posed by friable asbestos has been acknowledged by various courts, which have held that inmates' unwilling exposure to an unreasonably high concentration of air-borne asbestos particles constitutes a cognizable claim under the Eighth Amendment.... For exposure to airborne asbestos fibers to create a substantial risk of serious harm, however, the intensity and duration of the exposure must both be significant." Where the level of exposure was within the limits of the state Industrial Code and OSHA regulations, there was no constitutional violation absent evidence that the plaintiff suffers from an asbestos-related disease or is likely to do so in the future.); *see* McNeil v. Lane, 16 F.3d 123, 125 (7th Cir. 1994) (exposure to "moderate levels of asbestos" was not cruel and unusual); Crawford v. Artuz, 143 F. Supp. 2d 249, 259–60 (S.D.N.Y. 2001) (citing lack of evidence of risk of asbestos-related injury).

There is a question whether 42 U.S.C. § 1997e(e), which bars compensatory damages for mental or emotional injury without physical injury, means that prisoners cannot recover compensatory damages for the future risk of asbestos-related illness. *See* Ch. 9, § E; *see also* Fontroy v. Owens, 150 F.3d 239, 244–45 (3d Cir. 1998) (prisoner could not recover emotional injury damages under Eighth Amendment, § 1997e(e) not cited).

[1167]Wallis v. Baldwin, 70 F.3d 1074, 1076–77 (9th Cir. 1995) (evidence that defendants had been informed of asbestos risk from an inspection report, an order to abate it from the state fire marshal, etc., established deliberate indifference); Gonyer v. McDonald, 874 F. Supp. 464, 466–67 (D.Mass. 1995) (allegation that the warden had known of the asbestos problem for several years satisfied the deliberate indifference requirement). *See* Smith v. Montefiore Med. Center-Health Services, 22 F. Supp. 2d 275, 282 (S.D.N.Y. 1998) (finding no deliberate indifference where circumstances of exposure were not foreseeable), *reconsideration denied*, 1998 WL 851529 (S.D.N.Y., Dec. 7, 1998); Napoleoni v. Scully, 932 F. Supp. 559, 562–63 (S.D.N.Y. 1996) (officials could not be held liable without evidence they knew of the presence of asbestos). *Cf.* Castor v. U.S., 883 F. Supp. 344, 353–54 (S.D. Ind. 1995) (under FTCA, decision whether to abate or encapsulate asbestos in a prison was subject to discretionary function immunity).

[1168]Gates v. Cook, 376 F.3d 323, 340–41 (5th Cir. 2004) (affirming injunction to correct malfunctioning toilets that backed up raw sewage into cells); Burton v. Armontrout, 975 F.2d 543, 545 n.2 (8th Cir. 1992) (prison officials enjoined to supply protective clothing and masks to prisoners cleaning up medically contaminated sewage); Fruit v. Norris, 905 F.2d 1147, 1150–51 (8th Cir. 1990) (Eighth Amendment violated when prisoners were ordered to clean out a raw sewage facility at temperatures of up to 125 degrees without the protective clothing and equipment called for by the operations manual; prison officials held to a standard of "common sense"); Masonoff v. DuBois, 899 F. Supp. 782, 797 (D.Mass. 1995) (holding use of chemical toilets which prisoners must empty into slop sinks violated the Eighth Amendment). One court stated:

> Inmate exposure to sewage can constitute a serious risk to inmate health and safety and satisfy the objective component [of the Eighth Amendment]. . . . Evidence in the record confirms what is obvious: exposure to the human waste of others carries a significant risk of contracting infectious diseases such as Hepatitis A, shigella, and others. . . . There is no requirement that an inmate suffer serious medical problems before the condition is actionable. . . .

Shannon v. Graves, 257 F.3d 1164, 1168 (10th Cir. 2001) (footnote omitted). However, the defendants were found not to be deliberately indifferent under the circumstances. *See* Rish v. Johnson, 131 F.3d 1092, 1095–1100 (4th Cir. 1996) (holding officials who failed to provide prisoner hospital orderlies adequate protective clothing to protect them from exposure to bodily fluids were not shown to have had knowledge of the risk); Smith v. Copeland, 87 F.3d 265, 269 (8th Cir. 1996) (four days with an overflowing toilet did not establish an Eighth Amendment violation under the circumstances); Good v. Olk-Long, 71 F.3d 314, 315–16 (8th Cir. 1995) (holding officials who required prisoners to clean up raw sewage without adequate protective clothing were entitled to qualified immunity).

[1169]Jackson v. Duckworth, 955 F.2d 21, 22 (7th Cir. 1992); Jackson v. Arizona, 885 F.2d 639, 641 (9th Cir. 1989); *see* Robinson v. Page, 170 F.3d 747, 748–49 (7th Cir. 1999) (holding prisoner alleging physical injury from contaminated water could seek damages notwithstanding Prison Litigation Reform Act). *But see* Carroll v. DeTella, 255 F.3d 470, 472–73 (7th Cir. 2001) (lead contamination in water did not violate the Eighth Amendment because it results from corrosion in the pipes, and prison officials warned prisoners to run the water for a few minutes before drinking it; also holding radium contamination twice the maximum level set by the Environmental Protection Agency did not violate the Eighth Amendment because the EPA wasn't doing anything about it); Gholson v. Murry, 953 F. Supp. 709, 725 (E.D.Va. 1997) (defendants were not deliberately indifferent to lead in the water supply because they had reviewed the situation "intensely" and had warned prisoners to let the water run for 30 seconds before drinking and not to drink hot water from the tap).

In *Carroll v. DeTella*, the court stated: "If the prison authorities are violating federal antipollution laws, the plaintiff may have a remedy under those laws." 255 F.3d at 473. It cited 42 U.S.C. § 9659; Schalk v. Reilly, 900 F.2d 1091, 1094–95 (7th Cir.1990); Clinton

substances has also been found to present Eighth Amendment concerns.[1170]

One court has suggested that dangerous conditions are constitutionally acceptable if workers in the surrounding community also have to put up with them.[1171] We think these decisions are wrong. If that was the law, the Supreme Court could not have held exposure to environmental tobacco smoke violates the Eighth Amendment under some circumstances,[1172] since people are often exposed to environmental tobacco smoke outside prison.

Prisons are not required by the Constitution to comply with all civilian environmental regulations.[1173] However, you may be able to argue that these regulations are evidence of

contemporary standards of decency.[1174] As with fire safety, it may also be helpful to complain to state or local health departments, Occupational Safety and Health Administrations, or other relevant agencies.[1175] State or local regulations may be enforceable in state courts.

c. Environmental Tobacco Smoke The Supreme Court held in *Helling v. McKinney* that exposure to environmental tobacco smoke ("ETS" or "second-hand smoke") may violate the Eighth Amendment if it is done with deliberate indifference, if it poses an "unreasonable risk of serious damage to [prisoners'] health" (including harm that may occur in the future), and if the risk is sufficient to violate contemporary standards of decency.[1176] Those standards of decency are continuing to evolve, as states and localities continue to impose new restrictions on smoking, even within the prison setting.[1177]

County Comm'rs v. EPA, 116 F.3d 1018, 1024–25 (3d Cir. 1997) (en banc); Conservation Law Foundation v. Reilly, 950 F.2d 38, 40 (1st Cir. 1991)."

[1170]Board v. Farnham, 394 F.3d 469, 485–87 (7th Cir. 2005) (allegations that ventilation system was contaminated with black mold and fiberglass liner, which were hazardous to health and aggravated prisoners' asthma, and defendants did nothing when notified but vacuum the grates, supported a deliberate indifference claim); Kelley v. Borg, 60 F.3d 664, 667 (9th Cir. 1995) (refusing to let prisoner out of cell who was overcome by fumes from nearly construction could constitute deliberate indifference); Johnson-El v. Schoemehl, 878 F.2d 1043, 1054–55 (8th Cir. 1989) (an allegation that pesticides were sprayed in housing units so that inmates had to breathe the fumes stated a claim under the deliberate indifference standard); Clark v. Moran, 710 F.2d 4, 9–11 (1st Cir. 1983) (conduct by state police of a skin test using a potent carcinogen was unconstitutional); Crawford v. Coughlin, 43 F. Supp. 2d 319, 325–26 (W.D.N.Y. 1999) (exposure to dangerous chemicals in a prison industrial shop because dust masks ran out, goggles were supplied only intermittently, plaintiff was never supplied with work gloves or work clothing and received no safety instructions raised an Eighth Amendment factual issue); Cody v. Hillard, 599 F. Supp. 1025, 1032, 1051 (D.S.D. 1984) (inadequate ventilation of toxic fumes in inmate workplaces was unconstitutional), *aff'd in part and rev'd in part on other grounds*, 830 F.2d 912 (8th Cir. 1987) (en banc); *But see* Givens v. Jones, 900 F.2d 1229, 1234 (8th Cir. 1990) (subjection for three weeks to noise and fumes from housing unit renovations did not violate the Eighth Amendment even if they gave the plaintiff migraine headaches).

[1171]Jackson v. Cain, 864 F.2d 1235, 1245 (5th Cir. 1989) (allegation that the plaintiff was forced to work without a mask in heavy corn dust, causing nosebleeds, hair loss, and sores on his face, did not state an Eighth Amendment claim unless "the practice differed from that of the surrounding agricultural community or violated a clearly established law"); Sampson v. King, 693 F.2d 566, 569 (5th Cir. 1982) (exposure to pesticide Parathion did not violate the Eighth Amendment where it violated only non-mandatory regulations and was not shown to be any different from practices in the surrounding agricultural community).

[1172]*See* Helling v. McKinney, 509 U.S. 25, 35, 113 S. Ct. 2475 (1993).

[1173]French v. Owens, 777 F.2d 1250, 1257 (7th Cir. 1985) (Occupational Safety and Health Administration [OSHA] regulations); Ruiz v. Estelle, 679 F.2d 1115, 1159 (5th Cir. 1982); *see* Carroll v. DeTella, 255 F.3d 470, 473 (7th Cir. 2001) ("If the prison authorities are violating federal antipollution laws, the plaintiff

may have a remedy under those laws. . . . His remedy is not under the Eighth Amendment.").

[1174]*See* § A.1 of this chapter, nn.30–34.

[1175]*But see* Coupar v. U.S. Dep't of Labor, 105 F.3d 1263, 1265–67 (9th Cir. 1997) (dismissing prisoner complaint under the whistleblower protection provisions of the Clean Air Act and the Toxic Substances Control Act, since prisoners are not employees). If an agency's job is to protect the health and safety of workers, not prisoners, you should point out that correctional employees are subjected to the same hazardous conditions as the prisoners. In fact, you may be able to persuade prison employees to make the complaint themselves, either individually or through their union or employee association.

[1176]Helling v. McKinney, 509 U.S. 25, 33–35, 113 S. Ct. 2475 (1993).

Helling overruled prior decisions holding that "[t]he Eighth Amendment does not sweep so broadly as to include possible latent harms to health." Clemmons v. Bohannon, 956 F.2d 1523, 1527 (10th Cir. 1992) (en banc). It also overruled a prior decision holding that exposure to ETS is not "punishment" unless the prisoner has an allergy or other medical condition caused by smoke. Steading v. Thompson, 941 F.2d 498, 500 (7th Cir. 1991).

[1177]Thus, one recent decision goes further than *Helling* by suggesting that plaintiffs need not prove a serious health risk in all ETS cases; "maybe there's a level of ambient tobacco smoke that, whether or not it creates a serious health hazard, inflicts acute discomfort amounting, especially if protracted, to punishment." Powers v. Snyder, 484 F.3d 929, 932–33 (7th Cir. 2007) (dictum). *Compare* Wilson v. Lynaugh, 878 F.2d 846, 852 (5th Cir. 1989) (holding that at that time, standards had not evolved to provide any protection against ETS); *see* Atkinson v. Taylor, 316 F.3d 257, 265 n.7 (3d Cir. 2003) (noting prohibitions on smoking in public buildings and workplaces as evidence that society has become less tolerant of unwanted ETS); McIntyre v. Robinson, 126 F. Supp. 2d 394, 406 (D.Md. 2000) (stating "the relevant question is not whether current standards of decency allow society to expose prisoners, specifically, to ETS against their will, but rather whether those standards allow 'anyone' to be so exposed"); McPherson v. Coombe, 29 F. Supp. 2d 141, 145 (W.D.N.Y. 1998) (noting "growing recognition" of health risks of second-hand smoke; "A fact-finder could determine that the risk of future harm faced by plaintiff, given the

There is no right to a smoke-free environment for all prisoners. Cases finding ETS to raise a constitutional claim generally involve either an extreme degree of exposure to ETS or a plaintiff whose medical condition makes her especially vulnerable to it medically, or both.[1178] Though *Helling*

involved a prisoner who was double-celled with a heavy smoker, courts have also held that other forms of ETS exposure can raise constitutional questions.[1179] However, limited exposure of healthy persons to ETS does not violate the Constitution.[1180] Most courts so far have focused on the immediate consequences of ETS exposure and not the potential long-term consequences, even though the latter were emphasized in *Helling v. McKinney*.[1181] Courts have disagreed about how serious the consequences of ETS

---

conditions under which he is confined, is not a risk that society chooses to tolerate.").

[1178]Talal v. White, 403 F.3d 423, 427 (6th Cir. 2005) (allegation that plaintiff is allergic to tobacco smoke, medical staff recommended no-smoking housing, defendants fail to enforce a no-smoking rule, and they retaliated by exposing him to more smoke when he complained); Kelley v. Hicks, 400 F.3d 1282, 1284 (11th Cir. 2005) (per curiam) ("a prisoner can state a cause of action under the Eighth Amendment for exposure to ETS by 'alleging that [prison officials] have, with deliberate indifference, exposed him to levels of ETS that pose an unreasonable risk of serious damage to his future health.'"); Lehn v. Holmes, 364 F.3d 862, 871 (7th Cir. 2004) (plaintiff complained of being double-celled with smokers); Atkinson v. Taylor, 316 F.3d 257, 260–61, 264 (3d Cir. 2003) (diabetic plaintiff complained of being double-celled with heavy smokers); Davis v. New York, 316 F.3d 93, 100–01 (2d Cir. 2002) (plaintiff alleged that he had been housed for years where most prisoners smoked, that in the honor block he was surrounded by chain or frequent smokers, resulting in dizziness, breathing difficulties, blackouts, and respiratory problems); Reilly v. Grayson, 310 F.3d 519, 521 (6th Cir. 2002) (damages awarded where officials disregarded medical recommendations to place the asthmatic plaintiff in a smoke-free environment); Alvarado v. Litscher, 267 F.3d 648, 649–53 (7th Cir. 2001) (asthmatic plaintiff held in units where no-smoking rules were not enforced, and unable to participate in programs needed for parole because of smoke in common areas, stated an Eighth Amendment claim); Warren v. Keane, 196 F.3d 330, 333 (2d Cir. 1999) (claim of atmosphere "permeated with smoke" from failure to enforce inadequate smoking rules stated a claim); Whitley v. Hunt, 158 F.3d 882, 884, 887–88 (5th Cir. 1998) (claim that prisoner was subjected to ETS for 13 weeks and became seriously ill was not frivolous); Johnson v. Pearson, 316 F. Supp. 2d 307, 316–17 (E.D.Va. 2004) (plaintiff complained of being double-celled with a pack-a-day cigar smoker, and suffered respiratory problems which worsened with smoke exposure); Gill v. Smith, 283 F. Supp. 2d 763, 768–69 (N.D.N.Y. 2003) (evidence that officer persistently smoked at his law library post, resulting in exposure of the asthmatic plaintiff for hours at a time, and that the plaintiff had an asthma attack after one law library visit, was sufficient to present a jury question whether society was willing to tolerate the exposure); Walker v. Godinez, 912 F. Supp. 307, 310–12 (N.D.Ill. 1993) (allegation that officers blew cigarette smoke in face of prisoner with asthma, emphysema, and diabetes, causing violent asthma attacks, stated a claim). Some pre-*Helling* cases are similar. *See* Hunt v. Reynolds, 974 F.2d 734, 735 (6th Cir. 1992) ("forcing a prisoner with a serious medical need for a smoke-free environment to share his cell with an inmate who smokes" could violate the Eighth Amendment); Franklin v. State of Oregon, State Welfare Division, 662 F.2d 1337, 1346–47 (9th Cir. 1981) (allegation that cigarette smoke endangered the health of a prisoner with a throat tumor stated a constitutional claim); Beeson v. Johnson, 668 F. Supp. 498, 501–04 (E.D.N.C. 1987) (prisoner suffering from a medical condition requiring a smoke-free environment presented a factual question whether his Eighth Amendment rights were violated), *rev'd in part on other grounds*, 894 F.2d 401 (4th Cir. 1990).

[1179]Davis v. New York, 316 F.3d 93, 100–01 (2d Cir. 2002) (smoking in housing area generally); Reilly v. Grayson, 310 F.3d 519, 521 (6th Cir. 2002) (right is broader than not being celled with a smoker, includes being removed "from places where smoke hovers"); Alvarado v. Litscher, 267 F.3d 648, 649–53 (7th Cir. 2001) (smoking in housing area generally and in common and program areas); Warren v. Keane, 196 F.3d 330, 332–33 (2d Cir. 1999) (cells and common areas "permeated with smoke"); Gill v. Smith, 283 F. Supp. 2d 763, 768–69 (N.D.N.Y. 2003) (smoking by law library officer); McPherson v. Coombe, 29 F. Supp. 2d 141, 145 (W.D.N.Y. 1998) (dormitories).

[1180]Powers v. Snyder, 484 F.3d 929, 932 (7th Cir. 2007) ("A prison is not required to provide a completely smoke-free environment, except for prisoners who have asthma or some other serious respiratory condition that even a low level of ambient smoke would aggravate."); Gill v. Pidlypchak, 389 F.3d 379, 380 (2d Cir.2004) (affirming a district court's finding that three brief encounters with second-hand smoke were insufficient to state a constitutional claim); Richardson v. Spurlock, 260 F.3d 495, 499–500 (5th Cir. 2001) (holding intermittent exposure on bus rides was frivolous; plaintiff "does not share living quarters with a smoker, nor does he work in a smoke-filled environment"); Bacon v. Taylor, 414 F. Supp. 2d 475, 480–81 (D.Del. 2006) (a few instances of one officer smoking in a housing area did not state a constitutional claim); Boblett v. Angelone, 957 F. Supp. 808, 815 (W.D.Va. 1997) (four days' placement in a smoking area did not violate the Eighth Amendment); Davidson v. Coughlin, 920 F. Supp. 305, 308–09 (N.D.N.Y. 1996) (ETS exposure of prisoner in single cell with no evidence of medical problems did not violate the Eighth Amendment).

[1181]*But see* Atkinson v. Taylor, 316 F.3d 257, 265–66 (3d Cir. 2003) (citing plaintiff's evidence supporting a claim for future injury); Warren v. Keane, 196 F.3d 330, 332–33 (2d Cir. 1999) (allegation that ETS exposure "creates serious long-term health risks" sufficiently supported a claim for future injury); Hunt v. Reynolds, 974 F.2d 734, 735 (6th Cir.1992) (cognizable claim for future injury requires showing of a serious medical need for a smoke free environment); Johnson v. Pearson, 316 F. Supp. 2d 307, 316–18 (E.D.Va. 2004) (plaintiff raised material issue of fact with respect to deliberate indifference to future injury from ETS).

In *Henderson v. Sheahan*, 196 F.3d 389, 851–52 (7th Cir. 1999), the court said that a claim of future injury is not actionable without evidence that the plaintiff with "reasonable medical certainty" faced some defined level of increased risk of developing a serious medical condition from ETS exposure. Such evidence must show that the individual plaintiff bears such a risk, and not just that there is an increased risk to people in general. *Henderson*, 196 F.3d at 848–49 n.3 (relying on state tort law); *accord*, Atkinson v. Taylor, 316 F.3d at 277 (dissenting opinion) (arguing general statement about risks of ETS, with nothing specific concerning the plaintiff, did not sufficiently support a future injury claim).

exposure must be to violate the Constitution.[1182] Anecdotal accounts of how much smoke there is and how harmful it is may be adequate at the pleading stage, but the plaintiff will have to provide more substantial evidence of harmful exposure by the time of summary judgment or trial.[1183] Part of your case will have to be "a scientific and statistical inquiry into the seriousness of the potential harm and the likelihood that such injury to health will actually be caused by exposure. . . ."[1184]

Plaintiffs in ETS cases must provide evidence of deliberate indifference, which means evidence that prison officials knew of the risk and did not act to stop it.[1185] Courts have disagreed over whether banning smoking, and then failing consistently to enforce the ban, supports a finding of deliberate indifference or not.[1186] Courts have also differed

---

[1182]*Compare* Powers v. Snyder, 484 F.3d 929, 932–33 (7th Cir. 2007) (suggesting that plaintiffs need not prove a serious health risk in all ETS cases; "maybe there's a level of ambient tobacco smoke that, whether or not it creates a serious health hazard, inflicts acute discomfort amounting, especially if protracted, to punishment") *with* Bartlett v. Pearson, 406 F. Supp. 2d 626, 633 (E.D.Va. 2005) ("An inmate states a valid ETS claim only when the inmate experiences severe physical symptoms, but is denied access to medical care."). *See also* Atkinson v. Taylor, 316 F.3d at 268 ("When a susceptible prisoner is confined to a cell, a small and confined space, with a 'constant' smoker for an extended period of time, such symptoms may transform what would otherwise be a passing annoyance into a serious ongoing medical need." Plaintiff who alleged nausea, inability to eat, headaches, chest pains, difficulty breathing, numbness in limbs, teary eyes, itching and burning skin, dizziness, sore throat, coughing, and production of sputum stated an Eighth Amendment claim, even if some other people voluntarily tolerate such exposure.); Davis v. New York, 316 F.3d 93, 100–01 (2d Cir. 2002) (allegation of dizziness, breathing difficulties, blackouts, and respiratory problems); Warren v. Keane, 196 F.3d 330, 332 (2d Cir. 1999) (allegations of sinus problems, headaches, dizziness, asthma, shortness of breath, chest pains); Johnson v. Pearson, 316 F. Supp. 2d 307, 319–20 (E.D.Va. 2004) (allegation of mild headaches, difficulty breathing, eye irritation, runny nose, dizziness, and occasional stomach cramping supported an Eighth Amendment claim based on serious medical needs). *But see* Henderson v. Sheahan, 196 F.3d 839, 846 (7th Cir. 1999) (holding "breathing problems, chest pains, dizziness, sinus problems, headaches and a loss of energy" do not meet the standard definition of "serious medical need" since no physician diagnosed the plaintiff as having a medical condition that required a smoke-free environment, or treated him for consequences of exposure to smoke, and no layperson would consider the injuries so serious as to require medical care and attention).

Note that the Seventh Circuit's statement in *Powers v. Snyder*, quoted above, seems to take a very different approach to the degree of injury required than does its earlier decision in *Henderson v. Sheahan*, discussed in n.1181, above.

[1183]Larson v. Kempker, 414 F.3d 936, 940 (8th Cir. 2005) (denying preliminary injunction in the absence of evidence concerning the level of ETS exposure or its future health consequences); Scott v. District of Columbia, 139 F.3d 940, 942–43 (D.C. Cir. 1998) (ruling against plaintiff who provided no objective evidence of ETS levels, where defendants showed that they were within OSHA and American Society of Heating, Refrigerating, and Air Conditioning Engineers standards); Jones v. Goord, 435 F. Supp. 2d 221, 249–51 (S.D.N.Y. 2006); Abdullah v. Washington, 437 F. Supp. 2d 137, 140–41 (D.D.C. 2006).

[1184]*Helling*, 509 U.S. 25, 36, 113 S. Ct. 2475 (1993); Atkinson v. Taylor, 316 F.3d 257, 276–77 (3d Cir. 2003) (discussion of use of scientific and statistical evidence). This kind of case is very difficult

for a *pro se* prisoner to present. You should therefore request the court to appoint counsel, *see* Ch. 10, § C.5, and to appoint an expert witness, as the lower court in *Helling* had recommended at an earlier stage of the case. McKinney v. Anderson, 924 F.2d 1500, 1510–11 (9th Cir.), *vacated and remanded*, 502 U.S. 903 (1991), *reinstated*, 959 F.2d 853 (9th Cir. 1992), *aff'd sub nom.* Helling v. McKinney, 509 U.S. 25, 113 S. Ct. 2475 (1993). Court-appointed experts are discussed briefly in Ch. 10, § K.3.

[1185]*See, e.g.*, Talal v. White, 403 F.3d 423, 428 (6th Cir. 2005) (holding allegations that officers smoke and allowed prisoners to smoke and that plaintiff had filed grievances and a request for a cell change supported a deliberate indifference claim); Lehn v. Holmes, 364 F.3d 862, 872 (7th Cir. 2004) (holding allegation that prisoner had written to the warden about his ETS exposure without remedy supported a deliberate indifference claim); Atkinson v. Taylor, 316 F.3d 257, 269 (3d Cir. 2003) (holding failure to move prisoner from cell with a smoker after plaintiff's complaints showed deliberate indifference); Reilly v. Grayson, 310 F.3d 519, 521 (6th Cir. 2002) (lack of response to medical recommendations for a smoke-free environment showed reckless disregard). *But see* Weaver v. Clarke, 120 F.3d 852, 854 (8th Cir. 1997) (finding no deliberate indifference where defendants took steps to put the plaintiff in a non-smoking cell and to enforce smoking rules).

[1186]*Compare* Talal v. White, 403 F.3d 423, 428 (6th Cir. 2005) (allegation of failure to enforce policy supported a deliberate indifference claim); Gill v. Smith, 283 F. Supp. 2d 763, 769 (N.D.N.Y. 2003) (existence of policy is evidence that the defendant knew of the risk posed by his smoking on the job); Caldwell v. Hammonds, 53 F. Supp. 2d 1, 9 (D.D.C. 1999) ("Governments can not adopt a 'policy' that is plainly ignored and then claim that violations are not officially sanctioned and therefore not sanctionable"; noting that despite the policy tobacco products were sold in the commissary) *with* Scott v. District of Columbia, 139 F.3d 940, 944 (D.C. Cir. 1998) (" . . . [I]t is hard to see how imperfect enforcement of a nonsmoking policy can, alone, satisfy *Helling*'s subjective element. That the District even has such a policy militates against a finding of deliberate indifference."); *accord,* Franklin v. District of Columbia, 163 F.3d 625, 636 (D.C. Cir. 1998); *see* Jones v. Goord, 435 F. Supp. 2d 221, 250 (S.D.N.Y. 2006) ("the mere existence of a policy proscribing smoking in prisons does not deprive this Court of jurisdiction to hear plaintiffs' claims if plaintiffs allege . . . that the policy is routinely ignored"; the policy does weigh against a deliberate indifference finding if there is only a small degree of noncompliance).

At least one court has held in a Federal Tort Claims Act (FTCA) case the government is immune from tort liability for non-enforcement of smoking policies because "the extent to which the BOP chooses to apply its resources to enforce the regulation against smoking . . . and the extent to which the BOP chooses to apply its resources elsewhere . . . are discretionary choices made among many alternatives." Santos v. U.S., 2006 WL 1050512, *2 (5th Cir., Apr. 21, 2006) (unpublished). For a discussion of the FTCA, *see* Ch. 8, §§ C.2, H.2.b.

over whether prisoners may be denied non-smoking housing because of prison security or operational problems.[1187]

Prison officials should only rarely be entitled to the defense of qualified immunity in ETS cases, since the right to be free from excessive ETS exposure was clearly established by the Supreme Court in *Helling* well over a decade ago.[1188]

Smoking may be banned entirely in prisons and jails,[1189] and many of them have done so.

d. Risks of Injury Deliberate indifference or callous disregard for prisoners' safety violates the Eighth Amendment if it creates an unreasonable risk of injury in living,[1190]

working,[1191] or transportation conditions.[1192] Negligence—ordinary carelessness—by prison officials does not violate the constitution even if it results in serious accidental injury to a prisoner.[1193] Violation of prison rules or civilian safety codes may help establish deliberate indifference.[1194] A few courts have held that risks that are common to the general public do not violate the Eighth Amendment and are the province of tort law.[1195] This appears to be wrong, at least

---

[1187]*Compare* Johnson v. Pearson, 316 F. Supp. 2d 307, 317–18 (E.D.Va. 2004) (holding policy making accommodating non-smokers the last priority in housing "is in direct conflict with *Helling*"; defendants were "only concerned with administrative convenience"); McPherson v. Coombe, 29 F. Supp. 2d 141, 146 (W.D.N.Y. 1998) (holding denial of non-smoking housing based on "logistical concerns" of running a crowded prison could support deliberate indifference) *with* Bartlett v. Pearson, 406 F. Supp. 2d 626, 630–31 (E.D.Va. 2005) (finding no deliberate indifference where prisoner waited months for non-smoking housing because of crowding; officials offered to let him return to segregation, and they did have a policy to protect non-smokers even if they couldn't carry it out).

[1188]*See* Warren v. Keane, 196 F.3d 330, 333 (2d Cir. 1999) (denying qualified immunity because it is "clearly established that prison officials [can] violate the Eighth Amendment through deliberate indifference to an inmate's exposure to levels of ETS that pose[] an unreasonable risk of future harm to the inmate's health").

[1189]Brashear v. Simms, 138 F. Supp. 2d 693, 694–95 (D.Md. 2001) (upholding ban on tobacco as a rational means of protecting non-smokers from ETS; holding smoking is not a disability under Americans with Disabilities Act); Austin v. Lehman, 893 F. Supp. 448, 451–53 (E.D.Pa. 1995) (Eighth Amendment does not shield "an activity as marginally related to prisoners' basic well-being as cigarette smoking," and there is no due process liberty interest in smoking); Washington v. Tinsley, 809 F. Supp. 504, 506–08 (S.D.Tex. 1992); Doughty v. Board of County Comm'rs for County of Weld, Colo., 731 F. Supp. 423 (D.Colo. 1989); Elliott v. Board of Weld County Comm'rs, 796 P.2d 71, 72 (Colo.App. 1990); *see* Grass v. Sargent, 903 F.2d 1206 (8th Cir. 1990) (no-smoking rule during prison visits was not unconstitutional); Addison v. Pash, 961 F.2d 731, 732 (8th Cir. 1992) (denial of cigarettes did not violate the Eighth Amendment); Casteel v. McCaughtry, 168 Wis.2d 758, 484 N.W.2d 579, 582 (Wis.App. 1992), *aff'd in part and rev'd in part on other grounds*, 500 N.W.2d 277 (Wis. 1993).

[1190]Phillips v. Jasper County Jail, 437 F.3d 791, 796 (8th Cir. 2006) (allegation that a prisoner with a known seizure disorder was housed in a top bunk and was injured falling out of bed supported an Eighth Amendment claim); Brown v. Bargery, 207 F.3d 863, 865–67 (6th Cir. 2000) (allegation that mis-installed beds presented a danger of injury could raise Eighth Amendment concerns); Curry v. Kerik, 163 F. Supp. 2d 232, 236–37 (S.D.N.Y. 2001) (hazardous shower conditions).

[1191]Ambrose v. Young, 474 F.3d 1070, 1078 (8th Cir. 2007) (ordering prisoner work crew to stomp out a grass fire adjacent to a downed power line constituted deliberate indifference); Morgan v. Morgensen, 465 F.3d 1041, 1045–47 (9th Cir. 2006) (forcing prisoner to work with defective equipment supported an Eighth Amendment claim; the fact that the prisoner had sought the work assignment was not a defense); Bibbs v. Armontrout, 943 F.2d 26, 27 (8th Cir. 1991); Gill v. Mooney, 824 F.2d 192, 195 (2d Cir. 1987) (knowingly requiring a prisoner to climb an unsafe ladder would violate the Eighth Amendment); Jones v. Morris, 777 F.2d 1277, 1280 (7th Cir. 1985) (prison officials could be held liable for a fall if they knew of dangerous working conditions and acted with deliberate indifference in failing to cure them); Onnette v. Reed, 832 S.W.2d 450, 453 (Tex.App. 1992) (allegation that the plaintiff was made to work on an unsafe scaffold as a result of deliberate indifference stated a constitutional claim).

[1192]Brown v. Missouri Dep't of Corrections, 353 F.3d 1038, 1040 (8th Cir. 2004) (per curiam) (allegation that transportation officers refused to fasten the seat belt of a restrained prisoner and then drove recklessly stated a deliberate indifference claim).

[1193]Daniels v. Williams, 474 U.S. 327, 331–33, 106 S. Ct. 662 (1986) (negligence that caused a prisoner to fall on stairs did not violate the Constitution); Bowie v. Procunier, 808 F.2d 1142, 1143 (5th Cir. 1987) (allegation that plaintiff lost an eye because of negligent failure to provide safe wood-chopping equipment did not state an Eighth Amendment claim); Wright v. Collins, 766 F.2d 841, 849 (4th Cir. 1985); Major v. Benton, 647 F.2d 110, 112–13 (10th Cir. 1981) (negligent failure to formulate safety measures for working in ditches did not violate the Constitution); Rocheleau v. Cumberland County Sheriff's Dept, 733 F. Supp. 140 (D.Me. 1990) (fall over an open floor drain resulted only from negligence and did not state a claim); Thaxton v. Rose, 563 F. Supp. 1361, 1362 (M.D.Tenn. 1983) (hand injury caused by defective laundry press did not violate the Eighth Amendment); Hickman v. Hudson, 557 F. Supp. 1341, 1345 (W.D.Va. 1983) (negligent closing of cell door on plaintiff's hand did not violate the Eighth Amendment); Mitchell v. State of West Virginia, 554 F. Supp. 1215, 1217 (N.D.W.Va. 1983) (slip and fall caused by butter on the floor did not violate the Constitution).

In *Curry v. Kerik*, 163 F. Supp. 2d 232, 237 (S.D.N.Y. 2001), the defendants said a complaint about hazardous shower conditions should be dismissed because the plaintiff alleged they were negligent, but the court held that even though he used that word, the facts he alleged—that the defendants failed to make repairs over nine months despite being informed of the conditions—supported a claim of deliberate indifference.

[1194]Hall v. Bennett, 379 F.3d 462, 465 (7th Cir. 2004) (citing prison rule barring working with live wires and general safety codes that would be known to an electrical foreman; *see* § A.1 of this chapter, n.30.

[1195]Christopher v. Buss, 384 F.3d 879, 882–83 (7th Cir. 2004) (rejecting the claim of a prisoner hit in the face with a softball

in cases of deliberate indifference to safety, since exposure to environmental tobacco smoke is a common experience outside prison, yet the Supreme Court has said it can violate the Eighth Amendment.[1196]

Prisoners may be able to recover damages for prison personnel's negligence through tort actions. Prison officials and personnel have a tort law duty to provide safe living and working conditions for prisoners.[1197] State and local prisoners may bring tort actions in state court if state law permits,[1198]

and federal prisoners may use the Federal Tort Claims Act (FTCA).[1199] To show negligence, you must establish that prison personnel[1200] failed to use "reasonable care"[1201] to avoid a foreseeable risk.

Even under a negligence standard, prison officials are not liable for everything that goes wrong and hurts somebody.[1202] Negligence actions are subject to the defenses that state law provides, such as immunity[1203] or contributory or

---

because of a defect in the field; speculating that such defects "doubtless exist on subpar fields across the country"); Reynolds v. Powell, 370 F.3d 1028, 1031 (10th Cir. 2004) (holding that a fall in the shower caused by inadequate drainage did not state an Eighth Amendment claim because slippery floors are a common risk to members of the public at large). *Contra*, Curry v. Kerik, 163 F. Supp. 2d 232, 236–37 (S.D.N.Y. 2001) (hazardous shower conditions can violate the Eighth Amendment).

[1196]Helling v. McKinney, 509 U.S. 25, 33–35, 113 S. Ct. 2475 (1993); *see* the previous section concerning ETS risks.

[1197]*See, e.g.*, Bridgewater v. State through Dep't of Corrections, 434 So.2d 383, 384 (La. 1983) (department "owes prison inmates the duty of providing equipment and machinery which is safe for the tasks the inmates are required to perform"); Monroe v. Ohio Dep't of Rehabilitation and Correction, 66 Ohio App.3d 236, 583 N.E.2d 1102, 1105 (Ohio App. 1990) (prison has "common-law duty . . . to provide a safe and secure place to plaintiff while he was in defendant's custody"); Watkins v. Dep't of Rehabilitation and Correction, 61 Ohio Misc.2d 295, 578 N.E.2d 896, 899 (Ohio Ct. Cl. 1988) (officials "had the duty to provide plaintiff with a safe place to work and with safe equipment with which to work" and "to adequately train plaintiff" to use the equipment); McAfee v. Overberg, 51 Ohio Misc.86, 367 N.E.2d 942, 944 (Ohio Ct.Cl. 1977) (state was negligent in failing to furnish the plaintiff with a "safe and adequate means of transportation" to his prison job).

[1198]*See, e.g.*, Bradley v. County of Albany, 161 A.D.2d 1050, 559 N.Y.S.2d 590, 591–92 (N.Y.App.Div. 1990) (allegation that the plaintiff's hand was caught in a mechanical gate stated a claim against the county); Giles v. State, 106 Misc.2d 329, 431 N.Y.S.2d 781, 784–85 (N.Y.Ct.Cl. 1980) (damages awarded to inmate kicked by a cow based on state's failure to train him adequately in handling dairy animals); Callahan v. State, 19 A.D.2d 437, 243 N.Y.S.2d 881, 882–83 (N.Y.App.Div. 1963) (damages awarded for injuries resulting from a defective machine safety device; state labor law used to establish a standard of care), *aff'd*, 14 N.Y.2d 665, 249 N.Y.S.2d 871, 198 N.E.2d 903 (N.Y. 1964); Monroe v. Ohio Dep't of Rehabilitation and Correction, 66 Ohio App.3d 236, 583 N.E.2d 1102, 1105 (Ohio App. 1990) (placing a seizure-prone inmate in a cell with a sharp protruding edge of metal would constitute negligence); Keil v. Dep't of Rehabilitation and Correction, 57 Ohio Misc.2d 40, 567 N.E.2d 324 (Ohio Ct.Cl. 1989) (damages awarded to a prisoner who fell from a scaffolding that had no guard rail); Fondern v. Dep't of Rehabilitation and Correction, 51 Ohio App.2d 180, 367 N.E.2d 901, 903–05 (Ohio App. 1977) (damages awarded for injuries caused by a malfunctioning machine); Onnette v. Reed, 832 S.W.2d 450, 451–52 (Tex.App. 1992) (allegation that the plaintiff was forced to work on an unsafe scaffold stated a claim under the Texas Tort Claims Act); *see also* Bishop v. John Doe 1, 902 F.2d 809, 810 (10th Cir. 1990) (prisoner injured by improperly installed and maintained "speed bag" must pursue his tort claims in state court under New Mexico Tort Claims Act); Solomon v. Dixon, 724 F.

Supp. 1193, 1195–96 (E.D.N.C. 1989) (describing state tort claims procedure), *aff'd*, 904 F.2d 701 (4th Cir. 1990).

[1199]*See* Ch. 8, §§ C.2, H.2.b, concerning the FTCA.

[1200]"Prison personnel" can include other prisoners who are negligent in performing their work assignments. Duhon v. Calcasieu Parish Police Jury, 517 So.2d 1016, 1017 (La.App. 1987); Baker v. North Carolina Dep't of Correction, 85 N.C. App. 345, 354 S.E.2d 733 (N.C.App. 1987); Zawitz v. Ohio Dep't of Rehabilitation and Correction, 61 Ohio Misc.2d 798, 585 N.E.2d 573, 577 (Ohio Ct.Cl. 1990).

[1201]District of Columbia v. Mitchell, 533 A.2d 629, 639 (D.C. 1987); Hille v. Wright County, 400 N.W.2d 744, 747 (Minn.App. 1987); Haworth v. State, 592 P.2d 820, 825 (Haw. 1979); *see* Becnel v. Charlet, 569 So.2d 9, 11 (La.App. 1990) (work supervisor had a duty to use reasonable care in handling dangerous tools), *writ denied*, 572 So.2d 65 (La. 1991); McCoy v. Ohio Dep't of Rehabilitation and Corrections, 31 Ohio App.3d 228, 511 N.E.2d 398, 401–03 (Ohio App. 1986) (state "safe employment" statute did not define the standard of care for prison work assignments).

[1202]Fournier v. City of New Orleans, 533 So.2d 1044, 1046 (La. App. 1988) (injury caused by security door blown shut by a freak gust of wind was not foreseeable), *writ denied*, 536 So.2d 1215 (La. 1989); Epps v. State, 151 A.D.2d 545, 542 N.Y.S.2d 319, 320 (N.Y.App.Div. 1989) (state was not liable for malfunctioning power saw blade where prison personnel had no notice and no reason to know of the defective condition); Troche v. State, 130 A.D.2d 573, 515 N.Y.S.2d 293, 294 (N.Y.App.Div. 1987) (state was not negligent where inmate tripped over a rope marking off a flower bed); Manross v. Ohio Dep't of Rehabilitation and Correction, 62 Ohio Misc.2d 273, 598 N.E.2d 226, 228 (Ohio Ct.Cl. 1991) (prison was not liable for inmate's fall on ice without proof that the defendant knew or should have known the ice was there).

In rare cases, where prison officials create or maintain an "unreasonable risk" of injury, they may be held to a standard of "strict liability" and be held liable without proof of negligence. Perro v. State, 517 So.2d 258, 263 (La.App. 1987) (Department of Correction was strictly liable for maintaining a homemade table saw without a guard), *writ denied*, 518 So.2d 510 (La. 1988).

[1203]Immunity rules for state and local governments and their officials vary widely from state to state. Sometimes they are established by statute and sometimes by case law. In Michigan, for example, statutes provide that government agencies are immune from tort liability for all "governmental functions" except in cases involving structural conditions of government buildings, highway maintenance, operation of motor vehicles, and the performance of "proprietary functions." Wade v. Dep't of Corrections, 439 Mich. 158, 483 N.W.2d 26 (Mich. 1992) (barring damage claim by prisoner who slipped on floor because of negligent janitorial care). For further discussion of tort immunities, *see* Ch. 8, § L.5; *see also* § G.1.f of this chapter, nn.968–978, for examples of the application of state law immunity rules in prisoner assault cases.

comparative negligence.[1204] Several courts have declined to find prisoners contributorily negligent in accident cases because prison life restricted their freedom of action.[1205]

In some states and in the federal prison system, prisoners are barred from suing for work accidents and are instead eligible for a form of workers' compensation.[1206]

H. Classification

Classification decisions about individual prisoners are generally left to prison officials' discretion.[1207] There is no constitutional right to a particular classification status.[1208] This is true even if the prisoner loses privileges as a result of a change in classification.[1209] Classification decisions do not deny equal protection of the laws as long as there is a rational basis for them.[1210] It is not unconstitutional to classify prisoners by factors such as membership in a gang or "security threat group,"[1211] conviction of a sex offense,[1212] alien status or presence of a detainer,[1213] or other security risk.[1214]

Classification decisions are unconstitutional if they are done for unconstitutional reasons, such as retaliation for exercise of First Amendment rights, or racial, religious, or political discrimination.[1215] Prisoners may be required to

---

[1204]See, e.g., State Dep't of Corrections v. Romero, 524 So.2d 1032, 1033–34 (Fla.App. 1988) (prisoner who fell off a tractor that did not have a seat belt was partly negligent because he had stopped to tie his shoe; damages to be reduced), review denied, 534 So.2d 401 (Fla. 1988); Perro v. State, 517 So.2d at 261–62 (prisoner injured by a saw without a safety guard was not entitled to any damages because of contributory negligence; he used the machine for the wrong purpose and there was other equipment available); Hille v. Wright County, 400 N.W.2d at 747–48 (drunken arrestee who injured himself on exposed duct was contributorily negligent); Hicks v. State, 124 A.D.2d 949, 509 N.Y.S.2d 152, 153 (N.Y.App.Div. 1986) (prisoner injured by a machine with the safety guard off that was sitting on an unstable base was 50% negligent where he did not use the machine properly); Telfair v. State, 87 A.D.2d 610, 448 N.Y.S.2d 41, 42 (N.Y.App.Div. 1982) (prisoner who slipped on water on the floor was 50% negligent). But see District of Columbia v. Mitchell, 533 A.2d 629, 642–47 (D.C. 1987) (prisoner injured by a falling ventilator cover was not contributorily negligent because prison officials should have discovered the dangerous condition through their own regular maintenance procedures).

[1205]District of Columbia v. Mitchell, 533 A.2d at 644 (prisoner was not contributorily negligent in sitting under a loose ventilator cover because he had no choice in where he lived or how the dormitory was arranged); Dawson v. State through Dep't of Corrections, 452 So.2d 357, 359 (La.App. 1984) (prisoner injured by a machine he knew was defective was not contributorily negligent; he was told to work and "acted in the manner expected of him as an inmate"); Stilley v. State, 376 So.2d 1007, 1008 (La.App. 1979) (prisoner injured by exploding tire was not contributorily negligent for using a defective lock rim when ordered to do so; "the plaintiff, as an inmate, was not in a position to refuse to perform a job known to be dangerous"), writ denied, 378 So.2d 1389 (La. 1980); Mariano v. State, 31 Misc.2d 241, 222 N.Y.S.2d 968, 971 (N.Y.Ct.Cl. 1961) (prisoner injured by a defective machine was not contributorily negligent because he had been ordered to keep working).

A related defense, assumption of risk, is generally held inapplicable to prisoners' work accidents because it assumes a freedom of choice that prisoners do not have. District of Columbia v. Mitchell, 533 A.2d at 640; Haworth v. State, 592 P.2d at 823–24.

[1206]See Ch. 8, § E, for a discussion of workers' compensation.

[1207]Wilkerson v. Stalder, 329 F.3d 431, 436 (5th Cir. 2003); Frost v. Agnos, 152 F.3d 1124, 1130 (9th Cir. 1998); see Cohen v. U.S., 151 F.3d 1338, 1344 (11th Cir. 1998) (holding prisoner classification is subject to the discretionary function exception in FTCA cases, so federal prisoners cannot recover damages for it under the FTCA); see Ch. 8, §§ C.2.a, nn.335–343, concerning the FTCA discretionary function exception, and § G.1.f of this chapter, nn.973–975.

[1208]Moody v. Daggett, 429 U.S. 78, 88 n.9, 97 S. Ct. 274 (1976); Harbin-Bey v. Rutter, 420 F.3d 571, 576 (6th Cir. 2005); Hernandez v. Johnston, 833 F.2d 1316, 1318 (9th Cir. 1987); Tubwell v. Griffith, 742 F.2d 250, 253 (5th Cir. 1984); see also Ra Chaka v. Franzen, 727 F. Supp. 454, 457–59 (N.D.Ill. 1989) (upholding a system that separated population into classification levels and limited their mixing at religious services).

[1209]Limas v. McNary, 799 F. Supp. 1259, 1263–64 (D.Mass. 1992) (upholding exclusion from minimum security of prisoner with immigration detainer); Isaraphanich v. Coughlin, 716 F. Supp. 119, 121 (S.D.N.Y. 1989) (upholding exclusion of high-security inmate from "family visiting" program upheld); Wheway v. Warden, State Prison, 215 Conn. 418, 576 A.2d 494, 501 (Conn. 1990) (prisoner could be classified maximum security and denied temporary release based on out-of-state parole detainer); see also Sher v. Coughlin, 739 F.2d 77, 80 (2d Cir. 1984) (denial of wages during reclassification process did not violate the Constitution).

[1210]Riddle v. Mondragon, 83 F.3d 1197, 1207 (10th Cir. 1996); Paoli v. Lally, 812 F.2d 1489, 1493 (4th Cir. 1987); Hendking v. Smith, 781 F.2d 850, 851–52 (11th Cir. 1986). But see Hluchan v. Fauver, 480 F. Supp. 103, 109–11 (D.N.J. 1979) (classification restrictions on sex offenders denied equal protection by failing to define "sex offenses" clearly).

[1211]Westefer v. Snyder, 422 F.3d 570, 575 (7th Cir. 2005) (noting gang membership is not protected by the Constitution); Harbin-Bey v. Rutter, 420 F.3d 571, 575–77 (6th Cir. 2005); In re Long Term Administrative Segregation, 174 F.3d 464, 469–71 (4th Cir. 1999) (upholding classification of Five Percenters as "security threat group" members); Torres v. Stewart, 263 F. Supp. 2d 463, 469 (D. Conn. 2003) (upholding classification in Close Custody program based on designation as a "Security Risk Group Safety Threat Member").

[1212]See § F.4.b of this chapter.

[1213]Thye v. U.S., 109 F.3d 127, 130 (2d Cir. 1997) (alien status); Posey v. DeWalt, 86 F. Supp. 2d 565, 571–72 (E.D.Va. 1999), appeal dismissed, 215 F.3d 1320 (4th Cir. 2000).

[1214]Harper v. Showers, 174 F.3d 716, 718–19 (5th Cir. 1999) (prisoner could be classified as an extreme security risk based on successful escape and unsuccessful attempts to escape); Batts v. Richards, 4 F. Supp. 2d 96, 98–99 (D.Conn. 1998) (enhancing the level of assaults for classification purposes because of the prisoner's large size was within officials' discretion).

[1215]Lucien v. DeTella, 141 F.3d 773, 774 (7th Cir. 1998); Dace v. Solem, 858 F.2d 385, 388 (8th Cir. 1988); Whittington v. Lynaugh, 842 F.2d 818, 820 (5th Cir. 1988); Koch v. Lewis, 96 F. Supp. 2d 949, 955–57 (D.Ariz. 2000), vacated as moot, 399 F.3d 1099 (9th Cir. 2005)

cooperate with classification procedures and disciplined for refusing to do so.[1216]

Classification decisions and changes in classification rarely require due process protections.[1217] Reliance on erroneous information in classification does not deny due process except in very limited circumstances.[1218] Retroactive application of changes in a classification system does not violate the Constitution's Ex Post Facto Clause.[1219] State classification statutes or regulations may provide greater rights than the federal constitution; these must generally be enforced in state court.[1220]

The lack of classification may be unconstitutional in some circumstances. Jails and prisons must classify inmates sufficiently to control the risk of violence.[1221] Courts have

not required the segregation of gang members or the separation of prisoners from different gangs unless there is some more specific warning of a risk of violence.[1222] Courts have cited the breakdown of classification systems caused by crowding as one basis for finding crowded conditions unconstitutional.[1223] Courts have also required the separation of seriously mentally ill inmates from the general population.[1224] Courts have disagreed over whether the Constitution requires pretrial detainees to be segregated from convicts.[1225]

(classification as a gang member based on flimsy and outdated evidence after plaintiff won lawsuits against prison officials established a *prima facie* case of retaliation); Pratt v. Rowland, 769 F. Supp. 1128, 1135 (N.D.Cal. 1991).

Prisoners may, however, be classified based on their past associations with groups that have assisted in prison escapes, Baraldini v. Thornburgh, 884 F.2d 615, 620 (D.C. Cir. 1989); Bukhari v. Hutto, 487 F. Supp. 1162, 1166–67 (E.D.Va. 1980), or on statements that suggest the prisoner may foment unrest or violence in prison. Rosenberg v. Meese, 622 F. Supp. 1451, 1473 (S.D.N.Y. 1985).

[1216]Taylor v. Best, 746 F.2d 220, 223–25 (4th Cir. 1984) (classification interview procedure did not violate prisoner's privacy or Fifth Amendment right against self-incrimination).

[1217]Moody v. Daggett, 429 U.S. 78, 88 n.9, 97 S. Ct. 274 (1976). Under current law, classification decisions generally do not deprive prisoners of liberty interests unless they affect release dates. *See* Ch. 4, § H.5, concerning due process issues in classification.

[1218]Whitley v. Hunt, 158 F.3d 882, 889–90 (5th Cir. 1998) (claim that officials relied on inaccurate records to raise plaintiff's security classification was frivolous; "Inmates have no protectable property or liberty interest in custodial classification."); *see* Ch. 4, § H.7, concerning officials' reliance on inaccurate information.

[1219]*See* Dyke v. Meachum, 785 F.2d 267, 268 (10th Cir. 1986); Julien v. Meachum, 618 F. Supp. 49, 52 (W.D.Okla. 1985); Morris v. Meachum, 718 P.2d 1354, 1355 (Okla. 1986). The Ex Post Facto Clause says: "No State shall . . . pass any . . . *ex post facto* Law. . . ." U.S. Const. art. I, § 10, cl. 1.

[1220]*See In re* Wilson, 202 Cal.App.3d 661, 249 Cal.Rptr. 36, 40–42 (Cal.App. 1988) (reviewing but upholding classification decision); *see also* Jones v. Connell, 833 F.2d 503, 505 (3d Cir. 1987) (federal court could not enforce state law classification rules); Noren v. Straw, 578 F. Supp. 1, 6–7 (D.Mont. 1982) (declining pendent jurisdiction over claim that failure to segregate detainees and convicts in county jail violated state statutes). State law will determine whether classification decisions can be judicially reviewed in state court. *See* Ch. 8, § D.2, concerning state judicial review.

Some courts have held that prison officials must comply with state Administrative Procedure Acts in promulgating classification systems. Stoneham v. Rushen, 156 Cal.App.3d 302, 203 Cal.Rptr. 20, 22–25 (Cal.App. 1984); Malumphy v. MacDougall, 125 Ariz. 483, 610 P.2d 1044 (Ariz. 1980).

[1221]*See* § G.1.c of this chapter for discussion of classification and its relationship to violence among prisoners; *see also* Hackl v. Dale, 171 W.Va. 415, 299 S.E.2d 26, 29–30 (W.Va. 1982) (citing state classification statute).

Cases requiring local jails to establish classification systems have stressed the need to protect prisoners from violence. *See, e.g.,* Jones v. Diamond, 636 F.2d 1364, 1374 (5th Cir. 1981) (en banc); Carver v. Knox County, Tenn., 753 F. Supp. 1370, 1388 (E.D.Tenn.1989), *remanded for reconsideration,* 887 F.2d 1287 (6th Cir. 1989), *adhered to on remand,* 753 F. Supp. 1398 (E.D.Tenn. 1990); Dawson v. Kendrick, 527 F. Supp. 1252, 1294 (S.D.W.Va. 1981); Nicholson v. Choctaw County, Ala., 498 F. Supp. 295, 309–10, 314 (S.D.Ala. 1980).

[1222]*See* §.G.1.c of this chapter, n.898.

[1223]Harris v. Angelina County, Tex., 31 F.3d 331, 335 (5th Cir. 1994); Laube v. Haley, 234 F. Supp. 2d 1227, 1245–46 (M.D.Ala. 2002); Carty v. Farrelly, 957 F. Supp. 727, 735 (D.V.I. 1997); Gilland v. Owens, 718 F. Supp. 665, 688 (W.D.Tenn. 1989).

[1224]*See* § F.4.a of this chapter, nn.478–479.

[1225]*Holding separation required:* Pembroke v. Wood County, Tex., 981 F. Supp. 225, 229 (5th Cir. 1993); Ryan v. Burlington County, N.J., 860 F.2d 1199, 1204 (3d Cir. 1988) (detainees have a clearly established right to be separated from convicted felons); Pulliam v. Shelby County, Tenn., 902 F. Supp. 797, 801 (W.D.Tenn. 1995); Barnes v. Government of the Virgin Islands, 415 F. Supp. 1218, 1235 (D.V.I. 1976) (separation required); Alberti v. Sheriff of Harris County, 406 F. Supp. 649, 678 (S.D.Tex. 1975) (separate cellblocks required). *Holding separation not required:* Martin v. Tyson, 845 F.2d 1451, 1456 (7th Cir. 1988); Shelby County Jail Inmates v. Westlake, 798 F.2d 1085, 1089–90 (7th Cir. 1986) (jury could find that failure to separate detainees and convicts did not violate Constitution); Burciaga v. County of Lenawee, 123 F. Supp. 2d 1076, 1078 (E.D.Mich. 2000) (no right to separation unless the state has an intent to punish or is indifferent to possible harm); Faulcon v. City of Philadelphia, 18 F. Supp. 2d 537, 540 (E.D.Pa. 1998) (citing lack of evidence that commingling convicted and sentenced prisoners with detainees is especially dangerous to detainees), *aff'd,* 185 F.3d 861 (3d Cir. 1999); Chapman v. Guessford, 924 F. Supp. 30, 33 (D.Del. 1996); Heath v. DeCourcy, 704 F. Supp. 799, 801 (S.D.Ohio 1988) ("classification should be based on propensity for violence and may disregard whether an inmate is being held pretrial or has been sentenced"), *aff'd,* 888 F.2d 1105 (6th Cir. 1989); Monmouth County Correctional Institution Inmates v. Lanzaro, 695 F. Supp. 759, 774 (D.N.J. 1988) (no right to separation if all are given the rights of detainees), *amended in part and clarified in part,* 717 F. Supp. 268 (D.N.J. 1989); Armon v. Jones, 580 F. Supp. 917, 924 (N.D.Tex. 1983) (placement of high-security detainee in cell with convicted persons was not unconstitutional); Bradford v. Gardner, 578 F. Supp. 382, 383 (E.D.Tenn. 1984) (placement of detainee in housing block with convicted felons did not amount to a "serious" constitutional issue), *appeal dismissed,* 786 F.2d 1163 (6th Cir. 1986); Campbell v. Bergeron, 486 F. Supp. 1246, 1249–50 (M.D.La. 1980), *aff'd,* 654 F.2d 719 (5th Cir. 1981); Johnston v. Ciccone, 260 F. Supp. 553, 556 (W.D.Mo. 1966) (mixing of detainees and convicts in prison medical center upheld);

Several courts have required the segregation of juveniles from adults.[1226] Women must generally be separated from men.[1227] Transgender prisoners may be housed with their anatomical gender and not with the gender they identify as.[1228] Racial segregation, of course, is unconstitutional.[1229] So far, the courts have upheld the segregation of inmates with AIDS or HIV infection.[1230]

---

see Jones v. Diamond, 636 F.2d 1364, 1376 (5th Cir. 1981) (en banc) (separation required, but separate cells are sufficient); *see also* Albro v. Onondaga County, 681 F. Supp. 991, 994 (N.D.N.Y. 1988) (where detainees and convicts were mixed, the legal standards applicable to detainees would be applied to the entire population).

State law commonly requires separation of convicts from detainees. *See, e.g.,* Wickham v. Fisher, 629 P.2d 896, 902 (Utah 1981); Hickson v. Kellison, 170 W.Va. 732, 296 S.E.2d 855, 857 (W.Va. 1982).

[1226]Reece v. Gragg, 650 F. Supp. 1297, 1304–05 (D.Kan. 1986) (failure to separate juveniles contributed to a finding of constitutional violation); Ahrens v. Thomas, 434 F. Supp. 873, 901 (W.D.Mo. 1977) (juveniles barred from jail except for short periods awaiting transfer), *aff'd in pertinent part*, 570 F.2d 286, 289–96 (8th Cir. 1978); Patterson v. Hopkins, 350 F. Supp. 676, 684 (N.D.Miss. 1972) (juveniles must be kept in separate quarters in county jail), *aff'd*, 481 F.2d 640 (5th Cir. 1973); Baker v. Hamilton, 345 F. Supp. 345, 352 (W.D.Ky. 1972) (juveniles barred from adult jail); *see* Osorio v. Rios, 429 F. Supp. 570, 574–77 (D.P.R. 1976) (disruptive juveniles may be put in adult institutions only after notice and hearing).

The federal Juvenile Justice and Delinquency Prevention Act, 42 U.S.C. 5633(a)(12–14), requires states obtaining certain federal funding to separate juveniles from adults in jails and prisons and to remove juveniles from adult institutions. This statute creates a private right of action (right to sue) under 42 U.S.C. § 1983, but only against state and local agencies eligible for funding and not against low-level police or corrections personnel. Doe v. Borough of Clifton Heights, 719 F. Supp. 382, 384 (E.D.Pa.), *aff'd*, 902 F.2d 1558 and 1559 (3d Cir. 1989); *accord*, Horn v. Parks v. Madison County Fiscal Court, 22 F.3d 653, 657–59 (6th Cir. 1994) and cases cited; Hendrickson v. Griggs, 672 F. Supp. 1126, 1139–45 (N.D.Iowa 1987) (directing submission of a plan to comply with statute's prohibition of placing juveniles in adult jails), *appeal dismissed*, 856 F.2d 1041 (8th Cir. 1988).

[1227]Ahrens v. Thomas, 434 F. Supp. 873, 901 (W.D.Mo. 1977) (women barred from jail except for short periods while their transfer was arranged), *aff'd in pertinent part*, 570 F.2d 286, 289–96 (8th Cir. 1978); Mitchell v. Untreiner, 421 F. Supp. 886, 899 (N.D.Fla. 1976). *But see* Moore v. Marketplace Restaurant, Inc., 754 F.2d 1336, 1349 (7th Cir. 1985) (failure to segregate by sex in jail holding cell was not unconstitutional); Crosby v. Reynolds, 763 F. Supp. 666, 669–70 (D.Neb. 1991) (housing a pre-operative male transgender prisoner receiving hormone treatment in a women's housing unit did not violate clearly established rights).

[1228]Lopez v. City of New York, 2009 WL 229956, *13 (S.D.N.Y., Jan. 30, 2009) (pre-operative transwoman prisoner could be housed with males).

[1229]*See* Ch. 5, nn.32–37.

[1230]*See* § F.4.d.2 of this chapter.

I. ACTIVITIES

Idleness, by itself, does not violate the Constitution.[1231] Courts will only find idleness unconstitutional if it has serious consequences like mental deterioration or increased violence.[1232] Moreover, adult prisoners have no federal constitutional right to rehabilitation in prison except under very limited circumstances.[1233]

1. Program Activities

Prisons are not generally required by the Constitution to provide educational, vocational, or counselling programs.[1234]

[1231]Women Prisoners of the District of Columbia Dep't of Corrections v. District of Columbia, 93 F.3d 910, 927 (D.C. Cir. 1996); Peterkin v. Jeffes, 855 F.2d 1021, 1029–30 (3d Cir. 1988); Toussaint v. McCarthy, 801 F.2d 1080, 1106–07 (9th Cir. 1986) and cases cited; Griffin v. Coughlin, 743 F. Supp. 1006, 1017 (N.D.N.Y. 1990); Inmates of Occoquan v. Barry, 717 F. Supp. 854, 868 (D.D.C. 1989).

[1232]Madrid v. Gomez, 889 F. Supp. 1146, 1262–65 (N.D.Cal. 1995); Morales Feliciano v. Romero Barcelo, 672 F. Supp. 591, 619–20 (D.P.R. 1986); Knop v. Johnson, 667 F. Supp. 512, 522–23 (E.D.Mich. 1987), *aff'd in part and rev'd in part on other grounds*, 977 F.2d 996 (6th Cir. 1992); Capps v. Atiyeh, 559 F. Supp. 894, 908–09 (D.Or. 1982); Palmigiano v. Garrahy, 443 F. Supp. 956, 981 (D.R.I 1977), *remanded on other grounds*, 599 F.2d 17 (1st Cir. 1979).

In segregation units, courts have generally upheld long periods of unrelieved cell confinement, requiring only that regular out-of-cell exercise be provided. *See* § I.3 of this chapter, nn.1293–1298, on exercise, and § J, concerning segregation.

[1233]Hoptowit v. Ray, 682 F.2d 1237, 1254 (9th Cir. 1982); French v. Heyne, 547 F.2d 994, 1002 (7th Cir. 1976); Morales Feliciano v. Romero Barcelo, 672 F. Supp. at 619–20; Termunde v. Cook, 684 F. Supp. 255, 259 (D.Utah 1988); McBride v. Illinois Dep't of Corrections, 677 F. Supp. 537, 539 (N.D.Ill. 1987). State law relevant to rehabilitation is discussed in the next section.

Adult prisoners sentenced to longer terms under statutes specifically intended for purposes of rehabilitation have a right to rehabilitative treatment. *See* § F.4.a of this chapter, nn.516–521. Persons sentenced to long or indefinite terms as sex offenders for treatment purposes, or whose parole depends on receiving sex offender treatment, may have a right to such treatment. *See* § F.4.b of this chapter, nn.533, 546. In some cases in which the totality of conditions violated the Eighth Amendment, courts have required the establishment of rehabilitative programs as part of a remedy. Finney v. Arkansas Bd. of Corrections, 505 F.2d 194, 209 (8th Cir. 1974).

Statutes governing juvenile justice sometimes provide that rehabilitation is one of the purposes of juvenile incarceration. In such instances, the conditions of juveniles' confinement must be reasonably related to rehabilitation, and rehabilitative programs may be required. *See* Alexander v. Boyd, 876 F. Supp. 773, 796 (D.S.C. 1995) and cases cited.

[1234]Zimmerman v. Tribble, 226 F.3d 568, 571 (7th Cir. 2000); Newman v. Alabama, 559 F.2d 283, 292 (5th Cir. 1977); Hoptowit v. Ray, 682 F.2d 1237, 1254–55 (9th Cir. 1982); Williams v. McGinnis, 755 F. Supp. 230, 231 (N.D.Ill. 1991); Inmates of Occoquan v. Barry, 717 F. Supp. 854, 868 (D.D.C. 1989); Gabel v.

Courts will generally not interfere with prison officials' decisions about who may participate in those programs that they do provide.[1235] There may be exceptions to those rules where denial of or exclusion from a particular kind of program results in a violation of a separate constitutional right.[1236]

Federal statutes may create rights to programs for some prisoners.[1237] Under the Rehabilitation Act and the

Americans with Disabilities Act, prisons must make their programs accessible to prisoners with disabilities by providing reasonable accommodations of those disabilities.[1238] The Individuals with Disabilities Education Act[1239] requires prisons and jails to provide special education services for those prisoners who are eligible and in need of them.[1240]

State law may provide a right to rehabilitation or program activities,[1241] though the relevant laws may or may not be enforceable by prisoners through lawsuits.[1242] If they are enforceable, they will generally have to be enforced in state court.[1243] Some courts have held that these state law rights create liberty interests protected by the Due Process Clause of the federal Constitution,[1244] but most decisions have been to the contrary after the Supreme Court's decision in *Sandin v. Conner.*[1245] However, a state constitutional right to

---

Estelle, 677 F. Supp. 514, 515 (S.D.Tex. 1987); Spencer v. Snell, 626 F. Supp. 1096 (E.D.Mo.), *aff'd*, 786 F.2d 1171 (8th Cir. 1986); Burnette v. Phelps, 621 F. Supp. 1157, 1159 (M.D.La. 1985); *see* Palomino v. Federal Bureau of Prisons, 408 F. Supp. 2d 282, 290–91 (S.D.Tex. 2005) (Federal Bureau of Prisons had discretion under regulations to terminate its boot camp program). *But see* Lewis v. Washington, 197 F.R.D. 611, 615 (N.D.Ill. 2000) (denial of access to vocational, rehabilitative, and educational opportunities may contribute to a finding that the totality of conditions constitutes cruel and unusual punishment, even if the lack of programs is not unconstitutional by itself).

The rights of young prisoners to basic educational services are discussed later in this section.

[1235]*See, e.g.*, Tanner v. Federal Bureau of Prisons, 433 F. Supp. 2d 117, 123–26 (D.D.C. 2006) (prison officials could transfer a prisoner and interrupt his vocational programming even though he showed that the loss of his program would cause irreparable harm to him); Stewart v. Davies, 954 F.2d 515, 516 (8th Cir. 1992); Billups v. New York State, 885 F. Supp. 38, 42 (N.D.N.Y. 1995) (officials could remove a prisoner from a vocational program that had a waiting list based on his excessive absences for law library visits); *see also* § J of this chapter. Several decisions have held that courts will not interfere with the Federal Bureau of Prisons' decisions about which prisoners are placed in shock incarceration programs. Gissendanner v. Menifee, 975 F. Supp. 249, 250–51 (W.D.N.Y. 1997); U.S. v. Sutton, 973 F. Supp. 488, 491 (D.N.J. 1997), *aff'd*, 156 F.3d 1226 (3d Cir. 1998) (unpublished); U.S. v. Zigon, 772 F. Supp. 820, 821 (S.D.N.Y. 1991).

[1236]Thus, exclusion from a law library or other legal access program could result in a denial of the right of access to courts if it impeded litigation of a non-frivolous claim, *see* Ch. 3, §§ C.1.a.1, C.2.a., nn.504–505. In some instances, absence of or exclusion from counseling might constitute deliberate indifference to a serious medical or mental health need. *See* Hetzel v. Swartz, 909 F. Supp. 261, 266 (M.D.Pa. 1995) (holding deprivation of counseling to prisoner with terminal illness and declining mental capacity might deny treatment for a serious medical need); Carnell v. Grimm, 872 F. Supp. 746, 756 (D.Haw. 1994) ("an officer who has reason to believe someone has been raped and then fails to seek medical *and psychological* treatment after taking her into custody manifests deliberate indifference to a serious medical need" (emphasis supplied)), *appeal dismissed in part, aff'd in part*, 74 F.3d 977 (9th Cir. 1996); *see also* § F.4.a of this chapter concerning mental health care.

[1237]Federal law formerly provided for financial assistance to prisoners seeking education through "Pell grants," but the statute was amended to exclude prisoners some years ago. The exclusion does not deny equal protection or due process of law and does not violate the Eighth Amendment or the Ex Post Facto Clause. Tremblay v. Riley, 917 F. Supp. 195, 196–201 (W.D.N.Y. 1996); Nicholas v. Riley, 874 F. Supp. 10, 12–14 (D.D.C. 1995), *aff'd*, 1995 WL 686227 (D.C. Cir., Oct .10, 1995) (unpublished).

[1238]The federal disability statutes are discussed in § F.4.h.2 of this chapter.

[1239]20 U.S.C. § 1400 *et seq.*

[1240]*See* Handberry v. Thompson, 446 F.3d 335, 347–51 (2d Cir. 2006) (affirming injunctive provisions enforcing IDEA in jail system); Paul Y. by and through Kathy Y. v. Singletary, 979 F. Supp. 1422, 1426–27 (S.D.Fla. 1997) (granting injunction requiring prison officials to comply with IDEA in changing prisoner plaintiff's Individual Education Plan); Alexander S. v. Boyd, 876 F. Supp. 773, 788, 800 (D.S.C. 1995); Donnell v. Illinois State Bd. Of Educ., 829 F. Supp. 1016, 1020 (N.D.Ill. 1993).

[1241]*See, e.g.*, Abraham v. State, 585 P.2d 526, 530–33 (Alaska 1978); Cooper v. Gwinn, 171 W.Va. 245, 298 S.E.2d 781, 795 (W.Va. 1981) (state statutes required classification, education, and treatment programs and created an interest enforceable through the state constitution).

Issues concerning alcohol and drug rehabilitation are discussed in § F.4.g of this chapter.

[1242]Concerning state rehabilitation laws, *see* Hoptowit v. Ray, 682 F.2d 1237, 1255 (9th Cir. 1982); Capps v. Atiyeh, 559 F. Supp. 894, 908 (D.Or. 1982); Grubbs v. Bradley, 552 F. Supp. 1052, 1125 (M.D.Tenn. 1982). State laws regarding programs may not give prisoners a right to any particular program as long as some programs are available. State v. Evans, 127 N.H. 501, 506 A.2d 695, 698–99 (N.H. 1985); Sullivan v. South Carolina Dep't of Corrections, 355 S.C. 437, 444, 586 S.E.2d 124 (2003) ("Even if this provision is read to require some rehabilitation for inmates, it does not mandate any specific programs that must be provided by the General Assembly or the SCDC and, more importantly, it does not mandate any particular timetable for the furnishing of any rehabilitative services."); Nash v. Coxon, 155 Vt. 336, 583 A.2d 96, 98 (Vt. 1990).

[1243]Under the Prison Litigation Reform Act, federal courts may not enter orders requiring prison officials to comply with state law requirements. 18 U.S.C. § 3626(a)(1) (limiting prospective relief to violations of federal rights); *see* Handberry v. Thompson, 446 F.3d 335, 344–46 (2d Cir. 2006).

[1244]*See, e.g.*, Williams v. Lane, 851 F.2d 867, 880–81 (7th Cir. 1988); Association for the Reduction of Violence v. Hall, 558 F. Supp. 661, 663–64 (D.Mass. 1983), *vacated on other grounds*, 734 F.2d 63 (1st Cir. 1984); Ferguson v. Dep't of Corrections, 816 P.2d 134, 139–40 (Alaska 1991). *Contra*, Lane v. Reid, 575 F. Supp. 37, 39 (S.D.N.Y. 1983).

[1245]515 U.S. 472, 115 S. Ct. 2293 (1995). *Sandin* held that most deprivations in prison do not require due process protections to

education has been treated by the Supreme Court as a *property* interest and not a liberty interest,[1246] and courts have held that prisoners (usually young prisoners who have not completed high school) may challenge the deprivation of that property interest at least to a limited degree in federal court.[1247]

State law may require that prisoners participate in rehabilitation programs.[1248] Required participation in programs that have a religious component may violate the First Amendment's prohibition on "establishment of religion."[1249]

Racial or sex discrimination in prison programs violates the Equal Protection Clause of the Constitution,[1250] as do completely irrational distinctions in access to programs.[1251] Exclusion from programs in retaliation for exercising constitutional rights may also be unconstitutional.[1252] Denial of programs to prisoners in segregation has usually been upheld.[1253]

2. Work

The Thirteenth Amendment to the federal Constitution forbids "slavery [or] involuntary servitude, *except* as a punishment for crime whereof the party shall have been duly convicted. . . ."[1254] Thus, convicted prisoners may be required to work[1255] and may be disciplined if they refuse.[1256] Persons who are not convicts are protected by the Thirteenth

---

unless they impose "atypical and significant hardship on the inmate in relation to the ordinary incidents of prison life." 515 U.S. at 483–84. The application of this holding to program issues is discussed in Ch. 4, § H.5.

[1246]Goss v. Lopez, 419 U.S. 565, 574, 95 S. Ct. 729 (1975).

[1247]Handberry v. Thompson, 446 F.3d 335, 354–55 (2d Cir. 2006) (holding state statutes created a property interest only in receiving educational services not "wholly unsuited" to legislative purpose, and requiring provision of 15 hours of school weekly to young jail prisoners without high school diplomas or GEDs); Clarkson v. Coughlin, 898 F. Supp. 1019, 1040–41 (S.D.N.Y. 1995) (exclusion of deaf prisoners from educational programs denied due process); Donnell C. v. Illinois State Bd. of Educ., 829 F. Supp. 1016, 1019–20 (N.D.Ill. 1993).

The Supreme Court has also said that it is possible that there is an independent constitutional right to minimal educational services as a prerequisite for meaningful exercise of First Amendment rights. San Antonio Independent School District v. Rodriguez, 411 U.S. 1, 35–37, 93 S. Ct. 1278 (1973). At least one court has held that under this theory, the complete denial of education to school age detainees stated a constitutional claim. Donnell C. v. Illinois State Bd. of Educ., 829 F. Supp. 1016, 1018–19 (N.D.Ill. 1993).

[1248]*See* Davie v. Wingard, 958 F. Supp. 1244, 1257–58 (S.D.Ohio 1997) (placement in "Progressive Readjustment Inmate Development Environment" ("PRIDE") behavior modification program after a disciplinary conviction did not violate the Eighth Amendment). Many states now have mandatory treatment programs for sex offenders. These are discussed in § F.4.b of this chapter.

[1249]This issue and the Establishment Clause generally are discussed in Ch. 3, § D.4.

[1250]*See* Ch. 5 for a discussion of the Equal Protection Clause and its application to prison programs.

[1251]French v. Heyne, 547 F.2d 994, 998–99 (7th Cir. 1976) (restriction of vocational programs to prisoners with short indeterminate sentences stated an equal protection claim in the absence of a rational justification in the record); Damron v. North Dakota Commissioner of Corrections, 299 F. Supp. 2d 970, 981 (D.N.D. 2004) (". . . [W]hile a state has no obligation to provide inmates with access to educational opportunities while imprisoned, if a state chooses to provide or allow inmates access to educational opportunities, it cannot deny an inmate equal access to such opportunities without a rational basis for such discriminatory treatment."), *aff'd*, 127 Fed.Appx. 909 (8th Cir. 2005) (unpublished); Little v. Terhune, 200 F. Supp. 2d 445, 450 (D.N.J. 2002)

("Although inmates do not have a constitutional right to educational and work programs, once the state grants such rights to prisoners it may not invidiously discriminate against a class of inmates in connection with those programs unless the difference in treatment is rationally related to the legitimate governmental interest used to justify the disparate treatment.").

If prison officials do come forward with a rational basis for distinctions in program access, they will prevail. *See, e.g.*, Brian B. ex rel. Lois B. v. Commonwealth of Pennsylvania Dep't of Educ., 230 F.3d 582, 586–88 (3d Cir. 2000) (upholding limits on educational services to adult offenders in county jails compared to adults in state prisons and juveniles in either prisons or jails); Riddle v. Mondragon, 83 F.3d 1197, 1207 (10th Cir. 1996) (upholding exclusion of sex offenders from various programs and benefits).

[1252]Harris v. Fleming, 839 F.2d 1232, 1236–38 (7th Cir. 1988); Rizzo v. Dawson, 778 F.2d 527, 531 (9th Cir. 1985).

[1253]Toussaint v. McCarthy, 801 F.2d 1080, 1106–08 (9th Cir. 1986); Beck v. Lynaugh, 842 F.2d 759, 762 (5th Cir. 1988); McGruder v. Phelps, 608 F.2d 1023, 1026 (5th Cir. 1979); Little v. Terhune, 200 F. Supp. 2d 445, 450–57 (D.N.J. 2002) (upholding deprivation of educational opportunities in segregation, as applied to prisoner held in segregation for 15 years).

[1254]U.S.Const., Amend. XIII (emphasis supplied).

[1255]Ali v. Johnson, 259 F.3d 317, 318 (5th Cir. 2001) (prisoners could be made to work even though state law did not explicitly require them to do so; earlier decision stating that a prisoner not sentenced to hard labor retains Thirteenth Amendment protections is no longer good law); Wendt v. Lynaugh, 841 F.2d 619, 620–21 (5th Cir. 1988); Canell v. Multnomah County, 141 F. Supp. 2d 1046, 1058 (D.Or. 2001) ("Compelling an inmate to clean his surroundings is permissible." Plaintiff was required to wash chairs in his living unit.); Alexander v. Schenk, 118 F. Supp. 2d 298, 302 (N.D.N.Y. 2000); Patrick v. Staples, 780 F. Supp. 1528, 1546 (N.D.Ind. 1990).

A convicted prisoner whose appeal is still pending may be required to work. Plaisance v. Phelps, 845 F.2d 107, 108 (5th Cir. 1988).

[1256]Glick v. Lockhart, 759 F.2d 675, 676 (8th Cir. 1985); Mosby v. Mabry, 697 F.2d 213, 215 (8th Cir. 1982); Laaman v. Hancock, 351 F. Supp. 1265, 1270 (D.N.H. 1972); *see also* Mikeska v. Collins, 900 F.2d 833, 837 (5th Cir. 1990) (prisoners who refused to work could be placed in administrative segregation), *withdrawn and superseded on rehearing on other grounds*, 928 F.2d 126 (5th Cir. 1991).

Such discipline must, of course, be permissible under the Eighth Amendment. *See* Hope v. Pelzer, 536 U.S. 730, 122 S. Ct. 2508 (2002) (restraining prisoners to a "hitching post" if they refused to work was unconstitutional).

Amendment from mandatory work,[1257] except that they may be required to perform "general housekeeping responsibilities" that "for health and safety must be routinely observed in any multiple living unit."[1258] Some courts have expanded this last idea beyond helping keep up one's own living area to include institutional tasks such as working in jail food service.[1259]

It is unconstitutional to give inmates jobs involving supervisory or disciplinary authority over other inmates because of the risk of violence or exploitation.[1260] Prisoners may not be required to do work that is unsafe,[1261] beyond their physical capabilities,[1262] or contrary to their religious beliefs.[1263] They may not be given work assignments that are medically inappropriate.[1264] To prevail on a claim of medically inappropriate work, you must spell out the nature of your medical problem and explain why it makes your work assignment inappropriate,[1265] and courts will generally not second-guess prison medical personnel's judgments in these cases.[1266] Prisoners may not be subjected to intentional racial discrimination in prison jobs; decisions are divided on whether the anti-employment discrimination provisions of Title VII of the federal Civil Rights Act apply to prisoners.[1267] Prisoners may not be denied work assignments, removed

---

[1257]Martinez v. Turner, 977 F.2d 421, 423 (8th Cir. 1992); Johnston v. Ciccone, 260 F. Supp. 553, 556 (W.D.Mo. 1966); *see also* Cokely v. Endell, 27 F.3d 331, 332 (8th Cir. 1994) (claim that convict who had won his habeas corpus proceeding and was held pending further proceedings could not be forced to work was not frivolous).

A prisoner who cannot be required to work, but who works voluntarily, is not subjected to involuntary servitude. Brooks v. George County, Miss., 84 F.3d 157, 162–63 (5th Cir. 1996).

[1258]Bijeol v. Nelson, 579 F.2d 423, 424–25 (7th Cir. 1978) (noting that chores took from 45 minutes to two hours daily and were rotated); *accord*, Martinez v. Turner, 977 F.2d 421, 423 (8th Cir. 1992).

[1259]Channer v. Hall, 112 F.3d 214, 218–19 (5th Cir. 1997) (prisoner who finished sentence but remained in prison as an immigration detainee could be forced to continue working in prison food service because of the "civic duty" exception to the Thirteenth Amendment which applies to compulsory jury and military services; working in food service is analogous to "housekeeping tasks"); Ford v. Nassau County Executive, 41 F. Supp. 2d 392, 401 (E.D.N.Y. 1999) (forcing detainee to work as "food cart worker" did not violate Thirteenth Amendment because it was not "compulsory labor akin to African slavery"); *see* Tourscher v. McCullough, 184 F.3d 236, 242 (3d Cir. 1999) (prisoner whose conviction was reversed, but who remained in prison pending a new trial and was compelled to continue working in the cafeteria, might have a Thirteenth Amendment claim if the work was more than "general housekeeping responsiblities").

[1260]McDuffie v. Estelle, 935 F.2d 682, 686 n.6 (5th Cir. 1991) and cases cited.

[1261]The right to safe working conditions is discussed in § G.3 of this chapter.

[1262]Franklin v. Lockhart, 890 F.2d 96, 97 (8th Cir. 1989); Martin v. Sargent, 780 F.2d 1334, 1337 (8th Cir. 1985); Johnson v. Clinton, 763 F.2d 326, 328 (8th Cir. 1985); East v. Lemons, 768 F.2d 1000 (8th Cir. 1985); Howard v. King, 707 F.2d 215, 219–20 (5th Cir. 1983), *rehearing denied*, 719 F.2d 787 (5th Cir. 1983); Ray v. Mabry, 556 F.2d 881, 882 (8th Cir. 1977).

[1263]Franklin v. Lockhart, 890 F.2d at 97 (allegation that the plaintiff was required to handle manure and dead animals in violation of his Muslim beliefs stated a constitutional claim); Chapman v. Pickett, 491 F. Supp. 967, 972 (C.D.Ill. 1980), *rev'd and remanded on other grounds*, 645 F.2d 73 (7th Cir. 1980), *rev'd*, 676 F.2d 1097 (7th Cir. 1982); Williams v. Bitner, 359 F. Supp. 2d 370, 375–79 (M.D.Pa. 2005) (holding that punishing a Muslim prisoner for refusing to touch or assist in preparing pork could violate both

Religious Land Use and Institutionalized Persons Act and the First Amendment), *aff'd*, 455 F.3d 186 (3d Cir. 2006); *see* Chapman v. Pickett, 801 F.2d 912, 913–15 (7th Cir. 1986) (clarifying history of the case), *vacated*, 484 U.S. 807 (1987), *remanded*, 840 F.2d 20 (7th Cir. 1988). *But see* Ray v. Mabry, 556 F.2d at 882 (allegation of Sunday work did not state a claim where the plaintiff did not allege that his religion forbade Sunday work).

[1264]Williams v. Norris, Arkansas Dep't of Corrections, 148 F.3d 983, 986–88 (8th Cir. 1998) (damages awarded to prisoner classified for light work who was assigned to construction without checking his medical records); Sanchez v. Taggart, 144 F.3d 1154, 1156 (8th Cir. 1998) (an officer who was informed that the plaintiff was barred from hard labor, failed to check the records, and ordered the plaintiff to do the work anyway, causing injury, supported an Eighth Amendment claim); Madewell v. Roberts, 909 F.2d 1203, 1207 (8th Cir. 1990) (making an inmate with arthritis work under cold conditions could support a finding of Eighth Amendment violation); East v. Lemons, 768 F.2d 1000 (8th Cir. 1985); Toombs v. Hicks, 773 F.2d 995, 996–97 (8th Cir. 1985); Howard v. Headly, 72 F. Supp. 2d 118, 123 (E.D.N.Y. 1999) (prisoner assigned to sanitation work against doctor's orders stated a deliberate indifference claim); Jackson v. O'Leary, 689 F. Supp. 846, 850 (N.D.Ill. 1988); *see* Finney v. Mabry, 534 F. Supp. 1026, 1033 (E.D.Ark. 1982) (medical personnel must be consulted before a prisoner is disciplined for a medically based refusal of assignment); *see also* Roy v. Phelps, 488 So.2d 468, 470 (La.App. 1986) (assigning an inmate to heavy labor while he was recovering from a back injury was negligent; damages awarded). *But see* Mikeska v. Collins, 900 F.2d 833, 837 (5th Cir. 1990) (Eighth Amendment was not violated by requiring an inmate with a stomach ulcer to work where there was no indication that defendants knowingly gave him work that would aggravate his condition and where he received adequate medical care), *withdrawn and superseded on rehearing on other grounds*, 928 F.2d 126 (5th Cir. 1991).

[1265]Farinaro v. Coughlin, 642 F. Supp. 276, 279 (S.D.N.Y. 1986) (vague and unexplained complaints rejected).

[1266]Lewis v. Lynn, 236 F.3d 766, 767–68 (5th Cir. 2001) (rejecting claim that prisoner with asthma was inappropriately assigned to hoeing, digging, and spreading dirt, since officials first consulted with medical personnel); Morin v. Dep't of Corrections, 727 F. Supp. 699, 701 (D.Me. 1990) (job assignment that was consistent with medical restrictions did not violate the Constitution); Shepard v. Stidham, 502 F. Supp. 1275, 1281 (M.D.Ala. 1980) (if medical personnel have authorized the assignment, prison officials may rely on their judgments).

[1267]*See* Ch. 5, concerning equal protection of the laws and related issues of discrimination.

from them, or given particularly undesirable ones, in retaliation for constitutionally protected activities.[1268]

Apart from these limitations, courts generally do not intervene in prison work issues. The Constitution is not violated by hard work,[1269] long hours,[1270] removal from a job with or without a hearing,[1271] or denial of opportunities to work,[1272] although state law may create a right to work.[1273]

There is no constitutional right to be paid for prison work,[1274] although prisoners may have a right to be paid under state law or prison regulations, and this right may be enforceable in state court or may create an entitlement protected by the federal Due Process Clause.[1275] Disparities in hours or rates of pay are not unconstitutional.[1276] Prisoners who work inside the prison are not covered by the Fair Labor Standards Act (FLSA),[1277] the federal minimum wage law,[1278] because they are not considered "employees" of the state or of the prison system.[1279] This rule applies to privately operated prisons as well as government-operated ones,[1280] and to pretrial detainees as well as convicts.[1281] When prisoners work for private companies or other agencies external to the prison, the courts apply an "economic realities" test to determine whether the outside party is really an "employer."[1282]

[1268]DeWalt v. Carter, 224 F.3d 607, 618–19 (7th Cir. 2000); Williams v. Meese, 926 F.2d 994, 998 (10th Cir. 1991); Pate v. Peel, 256 F. Supp. 2d 1326, 1336–40 (N.D.Fla. 2003) (noting that adverse action—here, assignment to a medically unsuitable job—in retaliation for filing grievances would be unconstitutional, though this plaintiff's claim is found unsupported); Hunter v. Heath, 95 F. Supp. 2d 1140, 1149–51 (D.Or. 2000).

[1269]Franklin v. Lockhart, 890 F.2d 96, 97 (8th Cir. 1989) (claim that assignment to "hoe squad" was *per se* cruel and unusual was frivolous); Jackson v. O'Leary, 689 F. Supp. 846, 849–50 (N.D.Ill. 1988).

[1270]Howard v. King, 719 F.2d 787, 788 (5th Cir. 1983); Woodall v. Partilla, 581 F. Supp. 1066, 1077 (N.D.Ill. 1984); Coxson v. Godwin, 405 F. Supp. 1099, 1101 (W.D.Va. 1976).

[1271]*See* Ch. 4, § H.5, for a discussion of due process issues related to removal from jobs and other programs.

[1272]Penrod v. Zavaras, 94 F.3d 1399, 1407 (10th Cir. 1996); Frazier v. Coughlin, 81 F.3d 313, 318 (2d Cir. 1996) (exclusion from certain jobs in "Close Supervision Unit" did not deprive plaintiff of a liberty interest); Kalka v. Vasquez, 867 F.2d 546, 547 (9th Cir. 1989) (denying work opportunities to a prisoner whose transfer was delayed by crowding, and denying "work credit" even though the prisoner was willing to work, did not deny equal protection); Garza v. Miller, 688 F.2d 480, 486 (7th Cir. 1982); Byrd v. Vitek, 689 F.2d 770, 771 (8th Cir. 1982); Jackson v. O'Leary, 689 F. Supp. at 848.

Denial of work opportunities in administrative segregation or protective custody does not violate the Constitution. Toussaint v. McCarthy, 801 F.2d 1080, 1106–08 (9th Cir. 1986); Taylor v. Rogers, 781 F.2d 1047, 1049–50 (4th Cir. 1986); Manley v. Bronson, 657 F. Supp. 832, 840 (D.Conn. 1987); *see also* § J of this chapter.

[1273]*See, e.g.,* Laaman v. Helgemoe, 437 F. Supp. 269, 318 (D.N.H. 1977) (state statutes provided a right to work); Hays v. State, 830 P.2d 783, 785 (Alaska 1992) (state constitution and statute confers a right to work, but prison officials have discretion to determine particular inmates' assignments); Cooper v. Gwinn, 171 W.Va. 245, 298 S.E.2d 781, 787–89 (W.Va. 1981) (lack of work opportunities violated state statutes and constitution).

[1274]Loving v. Johnson, 455 F.3d 562, 563 (5th Cir. 2006) (per curiam); Mikeska v. Collins, 900 F.2d at 837; Wendt v. Lynaugh, 841 F.2d 619, 620 (5th Cir. 1988); Piatt v. MacDougall, 773 F.2d 1032, 1035 (9th Cir. 1985); Omasta v. Wainwright, 696 F.2d 1304, 1305 (11th Cir. 1983) (prisoner whose conviction was reversed was not entitled to be paid for prison work he had done); Manning v. Lockhart, 623 F.2d 536, 538 (8th Cir. 1980); Kennibrew v. Russell, 578 F. Supp. 164, 169 (E.D.Tenn. 1983); *see also* Murray v. Mississippi Dep't of Corrections, 911 F.2d 1167 (5th Cir. 1990) (making a prisoner work without pay on private property does not violate the Constitution even if it violates state statutes); Craine v. Alexander, 756 F.2d 1070, 1074–75 (5th Cir. 1985) (work outside jail did not violate federal Anti-Peonage Act because it was not compelled by a

state policy). *Cf.* Jennings v. Lombardi, 70 F.3d 994, 995–97 (8th Cir. 1995) (prisoner transferred under the Interstate Corrections Compact from a state where prisoners are paid to a state where they are not did not have a federal law right to be paid).

[1275]*See* Ch. 4, §§ D.7.d, H.8.b; Brooks v. George County, Miss., 84 F.3d 157, 164 (5th Cir. 1996) (prisoner who had not been convicted and who did work voluntarily on public property had a legitimate expectation under state law of wages for it).

[1276]Salahuddin v. Coughlin, 674 F. Supp. 1049, 1056–58 (S.D.N.Y. 1987); Finney v. Mabry, 534 F. Supp. 1026, 1034 (E.D.Ark. 1982); Newell v. Davis, 437 F. Supp. 1059, 1061 (E.D.Va. 1977), *aff'd*, 563 F.2d 123 (4th Cir. 1977).

[1277]29 U.S.C. § 201 *et seq.*

[1278]Some states have their own minimum wage laws, but they tend to be interpreted in the same way as the federal law. *See* McGinnis v. Stevens, 543 P.2d 1221, 1238–39 (Alaska 1976); Prieur v. D.C.I. Plasma Center of Nevada, Inc., 726 P.2d 1372, 1373, 102 Nev. 472 (1986).

[1279]Loving v. Johnson, 455 F.3d 562, 563 (5th Cir. 2006) (per curiam); Morgan v. McDonald, 41 F.3d 1291, 1293 (9th Cir. 1994) (prisoner's high level of skill and training and allegedly educational and rehabilitative purpose of his work did not bring him under the FLSA); Hale v. State of Arizona, 993 F.2d 1387, 1393–95 (9th Cir. 1993) (en banc); Harker v. State Use Industries, 990 F.2d 131, 133–36 (4th Cir. 1993); Vanskike v. Peters, 974 F.2d 806, 808–12 (7th Cir. 1992); Miller v. Dukakis, 961 F.2d 7, 8–9 (1st Cir. 1992); McGinnis v. Stevens, 543 P.2d at 1238–39. The *Vanskike* case notes that if prisoners were treated as employees entitled to the minimum wage, the cost of their board and lodging might be deductible from their wages. 974 F.2d at 812 n.6.

[1280]Bennett v. Frank, 395 F.3d 409, 410 (7th Cir. 2005).

[1281]Tourscher v. McCullough, 184 F.3d 236, 242–43 (3d Cir. 1999) (noting that detainees' work in jail is unlike traditional free-market employment); Villareal v. Woodham, 113 F.3d 202, 207 (11th Cir. 1997).

[1282]This test generally focuses on whether the employer has the power to hire and fire, supervises and controls employee work schedules and conditions of employment, determines the rate and method of payment, and maintains employment records. Carter v. Dutchess Community College, 735 F.2d 8, 12–14 (2d Cir. 1984); Woodall v. Partilla, 581 F. Supp. 1066, 1077–78 (N.D.Ill. 1984). This test is limited to the relationship between the prisoner and an external employer and is not applicable to the relationship between the prisoner and jail or prison officials. *See* Reimonenq v. Foti, 72 F.3d 472, 475 (5th Cir. 1996) (rejecting economic reality test as "unserviceable" in addressing the relationship between work

In most cases, the courts have found that the FLSA did not apply.[1283]

Prisoners have no constitutional right to unionize[1284] or to operate their own businesses while imprisoned.[1285]

3. Recreation and Exercise

Exercise is one of the basic human needs that prison officials must provide for under the Eighth Amendment.[1286] "Given current norms, exercise is no longer considered an optional form of recreation, but is instead a necessary requirement for physical and mental well-being."[1287] Courts have not required an actual showing of physical injury when exercise is denied for a significant period of time.[1288] Claims of

deprivation of exercise require the same showing of deliberate indifference that is generally required for Eighth Amendment conditions of confinement claims.[1289]

Courts' rulings on exercise and recreation issues vary widely, partly because courts don't always agree and partly because they are dealing with different fact situations.

In recreation cases, courts will look closely at how long prisoners are deprived of exercise. Some courts have held that the Constitution is not violated for short periods of time by the complete lack of exercise[1290] or severe restrictions on the ability to exercise.[1291] Deprivation or severe

---

release prisoners and the Sheriff); Manville v. Wayne State University, 85 Mich.App. 628, 632–33, 272 N.W.2d 162 (1978) (prisoner employed at a non-prison state agency stated claim under economic reality test).

[1283]These courts have generally found that the outside agency is not an "employer" because prison officials retained control over the selection of employees and the operation of the program, or simply because state law dictated that result. Gilbreath v. Cutter Biological, 931 F.2d 1320, 1326 (9th Cir. 1991); Alexander v. Sara, Inc., 559 F. Supp. 42, 44 (M.D.La.), aff'd, 721 F.2d 149 (5th Cir. 1983); Sims v. Parke Davis & Co., 334 F. Supp. 774, 786–88 (E.D.Mich. 1971), aff'd, 453 F.2d 1259 (6th Cir. 1971) (per curiam); Prieur v. D.C.I. Plasma Center of Nevada, Inc., 102 Nev. 472, 726 P.2d 1372, 1373 (Nev. 1986); Manville v. Wayne State University, 85 Mich. App. at 634. In one case, the court held the FLSA inapplicable because the corporation for whom the prisoner worked, though supposedly independent, was a state entity, the state appointed the board of directors, the corporation's assets would revert to state ownership when the corporation dissolved, etc. Gambetta v. Pride, 112 F.3d 1119, 1123–24 (11th Cir. 1997).

The court did find that prisoners were employees entitled to the minimum wage in Watson v. Graves, 909 F.2d 1549, 1553–56 (5th Cir. 1990), where the prisoners were supervised by a private employer that could hire and fire and were in competition with non-prisoner workers.

[1284]Jones v. North Carolina Prisoners' Labor Union, 433 U.S. 119, 129–34, 97 S. Ct. 2532 (1977).

[1285]French v. Butterworth, 614 F.2d 23, 24 (1st Cir. 1980); Robbins v. South, 555 F. Supp. 785, 791 (D.Mont. 1984).

[1286]Wilson v. Seiter, 501 U.S. 294, 304, 111 S. Ct. 2321 (1991).

[1287]Delaney v. DeTella, 256 F.3d 679, 683 (7th Cir. 2001); accord, Perkins v. Kansas Dep't of Corrections, 165 F.3d 803, 810 (10th Cir. 1999) ("some form of regular outdoor exercise is extremely important to the psychological and physical well being of inmates"); Dawson v. Kendrick, 527 F. Supp. 1252, 1298 (S.D.W.Va. 1981) ("Undue restrictions on prisoners' opportunities for physical exercise may constitute cruel and unusual punishment in violation of the Eighth Amendment when they pose an unreasonable threat to the prisoners' physical and mental health."); Gilland v. Owens, 718 F. Supp. 665, 685 (W.D.Tenn. 1989) (crowding and lack of staff do not provide penological justification for lack of exercise).

[1288]See Delaney v. DeTella, 256 F.3d 679, 685 (7th Cir. 2001) ("we have acknowledged the strong likelihood of psychological injury when segregated prisoners are denied all access to exercise for more than 90 days"); Lopez v. Smith, 203 F.3d 1122, 1133 n.15

(9th Cir.2000) (no showing of adverse medical effects required where prisoner alleged denial of exercise for more than six weeks). But see Wishon v. Gammon, 978 F.2d 446, 449 (8th Cir. 1992) (rejecting challenge to 45 minutes a week of recreation where plaintiff showed no injury; length of confinement not stated).

The Prison Litigation Reform Act, 42 U.S.C. § 1997e(e), limits the recovery of damages for mental or emotional injury sustained while in custody. See Ch. 9, § E.

[1289]Fogle v. Pierson, 435 F.3d 1252, 1260 (10th Cir. 2006); Delaney v. DeTella, 256 F.3d 679, 685–86 (7th Cir. 2001); Allen v. Sakai, 48 F.3d 1082, 1088 (9th Cir. 1995); Jones v. Garcia, 430 F. Supp. 2d 1095, 1103 (S.D.Cal. 2006) (finding no deliberate indifference where prolonged deprivation of exercise resulted from efforts to keep prisoners safe). In Allen v. Sakai, the court held that prison officials' own goal of five hours a week of recreation was evidence that they knew of the risks of depriving prisoners of exercise, and giving "inconsequential logistical concerns that might be no more than matters of convenience" higher priority than prisoners' exercise needs could constitute deliberate indifference. Allen, 48 F.3d at 1088.

[1290]Phillips v. Norris, 320 F.3d 844 (8th Cir. 2003) (holding that 37 days in segregation without exercise "is perhaps pushing the outer limits of acceptable restrictions" but is not atypical and significant for purposes of due process analysis); Vinson v. Texas Bd. of Corrections, 901 F.2d 474, 475 (5th Cir. 1990) (claims of occasional denial of recreation were "frivolous"); Knight v. Armontrout, 878 F.2d 1093, 1095–96 (1989) (13-day deprivation of recreation did not violate the Constitution); Harris v. Fleming, 839 F.2d 1232, 1236 (7th Cir. 1988) (28-day deprivation upheld); Leonard v. Norris, 797 F.2d 683, 685 (8th Cir. 1988) (denial of recreation for the first 15 days of punitive segregation upheld); Toussaint v. McCarthy, 597 F. Supp. 1388, 1412 (N.D.Cal. 1984) (recreation could be suspended for up to ten days), aff'd in part and rev'd in part on other grounds, 801 F.2d 1080 (9th Cir. 1986); Brown v. Copeland, 780 S.W.2d 68 (Mo.App. 1989) (three-day deprivation of exercise was not unconstitutional). But see Patterson v. Mintzes, 717 F.2d 284, 289 (6th Cir. 1983) (46-day denial stated an Eighth Amendment claim); Adams v. Wolff, 624 F. Supp. 1036, 1038–39 (D.Nev. 1985) (damages awarded for six-week denial of recreation); Grubbs v. Bradley, 552 F. Supp. 1052, 1131 (M.D.Tenn. 1982) (suspension of recreation limited to three days).

[1291]Shelby County Jail Inmates v. Westlake, 798 F.2d 1085, 1089 (7th Cir. 1986); Green v. Ferrell, 801 F.2d 765, 771–72 (5th Cir. 1986); Maillett v. Phinney, 741 F. Supp. 288, 292 (D.Me. 1990) (two and a half weeks with exercise limited to walking inside the jail did not violate the Constitution); But see Gilland v. Owens, 718 F. Supp. 665, 685 (W.D.Tenn. 1989) (lack of exercise was not justified where

restrictions for longer periods (usually of months) have been held to violate the Constitution or at least to state a constitutional claim.[1292]

Most cases striking down restricted exercise opportunities involve inmates who are locked in their cells most of the time, either in segregation units or in local jails that do not provide jobs, programs, or other activities. In such cases, many courts have held that prison officials must permit at least five hours a week of out-of-cell exercise.[1293] If lock-in

times are long, it is irrelevant that prisoners can do exercises in their cells; they are entitled to some relief from uninterrupted cell confinement.[1294] However, if prisoners are allowed other out-of-cell activities, very limited yard or gymnasium opportunities (or none) may be upheld,[1295] especially in local jails.[1296] Courts have held that prisoners who present extreme behavior problems may be denied even the small amount of out-of-cell exercise time usually required in segregation units,[1297] though some have cautioned that such deprivations must be reserved for "unusual circumstances" and situations where it is "impossible" to

---

some inmates stayed short times but others stayed for "months or longer").

[1292]Hearns v. Terhune, 413 F.3d 1036, 1042–43 (9th Cir. 2005) (nine months); Delaney v. DeTella, 256 F.3d 679, 683–85 (7th Cir. 2001) (six months; court acknowledges the strong likelihood of psychological injury after 90 days); Lopez v. Smith, 203 F.3d 1122, 1133 (9th Cir. 2000) (six and a half months); Perkins v. Kansas Dep't of Corrections, 165 F.3d 803, 805, 810 (10th Cir. 1999) (nine months); Jolly v. Coughlin, 76 F.3d 468, 481 (2d Cir. 1996) (three years limited to ten minutes out of cell a week); Antonelli v. Sheahan, 81 F.3d 1422, 1432 (7th Cir. 1996) (allegations of no recreation for seven weeks and being called for an hour once every two weeks stated a constitutional claim); Allen v. Sakai, 48 F.3d 1082, 1087–88 (9th Cir. 1994) (45 minutes of exercise a week for six weeks); Housley v. Dodson, 41 F.3d 597, 599 (10th Cir. 1994) (three months with only 30 minutes of exercise); Williams v. Goord, 142 F. Supp. 2d 416, 425–26 (S.D.N.Y. 2001) (claim that prisoner was placed in mechanical restraints during recreation for 28 days "presents a close constitutional case" under standard that plaintiff must show he was "denied all meaningful exercise for a substantial period of time"). In Pearson v. Ramos, 237 F.3d 881, 884–85 (7th Cir. 2001), the court held that in general 90 days is the dividing line between permissible and impermissible deprivations of exercise, but that consecutive 90-day deprivations could be imposed based on separate instances of serious misconduct.

[1293]Davenport v. DeRobertis, 844 F.2d 1310, 1315 (7th Cir. 1988) and cases cited; Pierce v. County of Orange, 526 F.3d 1190, 1212 (9th Cir. 2008) (declining to terminate requirement of two hours' exercise weekly, noting most courts have required five to seven hours), cert. denied, 129 S. Ct. 597 (2008); Morales Feliciano v. Hernandez Colon, 697 F. Supp. 37, 50 (D.P.R. 1988) (three hours twice a week of "active physical recreation" required); Albro v. Onondaga County, 681 F. Supp. 991, 995 (N.D.N.Y. 1988) (one hour a day required for pre-trial detainees); Toussaint v. McCarthy, 597 F. Supp. 1388, 1402, 1412 (N.D.Cal. 1984) (requiring eight hours a week), affirmed in part, reversed in part on other grounds, 801 F.2d 1080 (9th Cir. 1986); see Divers v. Dep't of Corrections, 921 F.2d 191, 194 (8th Cir. 1990) (recreation of only 45 minutes a week in protective custody stated a constitutional claim); Gumpl v. Seiter, 689 F. Supp. 754, 755–56 (S.D.Ohio 1987) (two hours a week out of cell would violate the Eighth Amendment if there was any feasible alternative); see also French v. Owens, 777 F.2d 1250, 1255–56 (7th Cir. 1982) (two and a half hours twice a week upheld); Termunde v. Cook, 684 F. Supp. 255, 259–60 (D.Utah 1988) (five hours a week for recreation, showers, and phone calls upheld); Farmer v. Carlson, 685 F. Supp. 1335, 1343 (M.D.Pa. 1988) (five hours a week upheld); Manley v. Bronson, 657 F. Supp. 832, 839–40 (D.Conn. 1987) (one hour daily upheld). But see Rahman X v. Morgan, 300 F.3d 970, 973–74 (8th Cir. 2002) (three hours a week in a dayroom with exercise equipment did not impose atypical and significant hardship for due process purposes); Hosna v. Groose,

80 F.3d 298, 306 (8th Cir. 1996) (three hours a week of out-of-cell exercise does not necessarily violate the Constitution, nor does requiring a prisoner to exercise in an enclosed area (in this case, 3×7×20 feet)); Henderson v. Lane, 979 F.2d 466, 469 (7th Cir. 1992) (right to more than an hour a week of recreation was not clearly established); Torres Garcia v. Puerto Rico, 402 F. Supp. 2d 373, 383 (D.P.R. 2005) (upholding one hour a week out of cell); Wishon v. Gammon, 978 F.2d 446, 449 (8th Cir. 1992) (upholding 45 minutes a week for protective custody prisoners).

[1294]Delaney v. DeTella, 256 F.3d at 684; Davenport v. DeRobertis, 844 F.2d at 1314. But see Roop v. Squadrito, 70 F. Supp. 2d 868, 875 (N.D.Ind. 1999) (holding lack of recreation was not unconstitutional because plaintiff could do push-ups and sit-ups in his cell; he was held only 30 days); McClung v. Camp County, Texas, 627 F. Supp. 528, 532 (E.D.Tex. 1986) (denial of out-of-cell exercise upheld in jail with cells large enough to exercise in).

[1295]See Johnson v. Williams, 768 F. Supp. 1161, 1167 (E.D.Va. 1991) (two hours a week outdoors upheld during a 10-week lockdown during which prisoners were out of their cells two hours a day); see Walker v. Mintzes, 771 F.2d 920, 927–28 (6th Cir. 1985) (suggesting that inmates living under greater restrictions have a greater need for yard time).

[1296]Wilson v. Blankenship, 163 F.3d 1284, 1292–93 (11th Cir. 1998) (lack of indoor or outdoor exercise program at crowded jail was not unconstitutional since prisoners had access to a (crowded) dayroom during the day); Green v. Ferrell, 801 F.2d 765, 771–72 (5th Cir. 1986) (lack of indoor or outdoor exercise facilities upheld in a jail where stays were short and inmates had five hours a day in a day room); Shelby County Jail Inmates v. Westlake, 798 F.2d 1085, 1089 (7th Cir. 1986) (lack of recreation program upheld in jail where inmates had access to a "bullpen" with an exercise bicycle all day); Lane v. Hutcheson, 794 F. Supp. 877, 885 (E.D.Mo. 1992) (similar to Green).

[1297]Pearson v. Ramos, 237 F.3d 881, 884–86 (7th Cir. 2001) (prisoner could be subjected to four consecutive 90-day deprivations of yard privileges for separate incidents of serious misconduct); Bass v. Perrin, 170 F.3d 1312, 1316–17 (11th Cir. 1999) (suspension of yard privileges for serious misconduct in "Close Management" unit upheld); LeMaire v. Maass, 12 F.3d 1444, 1457–58 (9th Cir. 1993) (upholding denial of out-of-cell exercise to violent prisoner); McGuiness v. DuBois, 893 F. Supp. 2, 4 (D.Mass. 1995) (upholding loss of yard time as a disciplinary sanction for prisoners already in segregation), aff'd, 86 F.3d 1146 (1st Cir. 1996) (table); Armstrong v. Lane, 771 F. Supp. 943, 949–50 (C.D.Ill. 1991) (upholding one hour a week out of cell for prisoner presenting extraordinary security problems).

allow exercise.[1298] Deprivations of exercise during facility lockdowns have also been upheld.[1299]

A number of courts have held that prisoners—at least, those who are confined for long periods—are constitutionally entitled to regular exercise outdoors.[1300] Some have held

that conditions that make it difficult or impossible to use an outdoor yard violate that right,[1301] but courts generally do not intervene concerning the size, equipment, etc., of outdoor facilities.[1302] Others, however, have held that indoor exercise satisfies the Constitution.[1303]

[1298]Williams v. Greifinger, 97 F.3d 699, 704–05 (2d Cir. 1996); *see* Mitchell v. Rice, 954 F.2d 187, 191–92 (4th Cir. 1992) (18-month denial of exercise to an extremely assaultive prisoner must be justified by a showing that there were no feasible alternatives); Spain v. Procunier, 600 F.2d 189, 199 (9th Cir. 1979); Williams v. Goord, 142 F. Supp. 2d 416, 429 (S.D.N.Y. 2001) (even an unusual security risk cannot be subjected to a blanket policy of denial of exercise); *see also* Pressley v. Brown, 754 F. Supp. 112, 117 (W.D.Mich. 1990) (prison officials must present penological justification for deprivation of recreation to segregated inmate). Similarly, in *Lopez v. Smith*, 203 F.3d 1122 (9th Cir. 2000) (en banc), the court held that it was not enough for officials to say that they kept a prisoner from the yard for his own protection; they must justify why they did not provide some other opportunity for outdoor recreation. 203 F.3d at 1133.

[1299]*See* § K, n.1366, below.

[1300]Fogle v. Pierson, 435 F.3d 1252, 1260 (10th Cir. 2006) (three years with no outdoor exercise at all presented an arguable Eighth Amendment claim; this court has previously noted "substantial agreement" that regular outdoor exercise is important to psychological and physical well-being and that some courts hold denial of "fresh air and exercise" to be cruel and unusual under some circumstances); Hearns v. Terhune, 413 F.3d 1036, 1042–43 (9th Cir. 2005) (long-term deprivation of outdoor exercise is unconstitutional); Lopez v. Smith, 203 F.3d 1122, 1133 (9th Cir. 2000) (en banc) (six and a half month deprivation of outdoor exercise could violate the Eighth Amendment); Perkins v. Kansas Dep't of Corrections, 165 F.3d 803, 810 (10th Cir. 1999) (denial of all outdoor exercise for months could violate Eighth Amendment); Toussaint v. Yockey, 722 F.2d 1490, 1492–93 (9th Cir. 1984); Spain v. Procunier, 600 F.2d 189, 199 (9th Cir. 1979) (five hours a week required); Carver v. Knox County, Tenn., 753 F. Supp. 1370, 1389–90 (E.D.Tenn. 1989) (outdoor exercise required for inmates held in jail for more than a year), *aff'd in part and rev'd in part*, 887 F.2d 1287 (6th Cir. 1989); Adams v. Wolff, 624 F. Supp. 1036, 1039–41 (D.Nev. 1985) damages awarded for six weeks' deprivation of outdoor recreation in local jail); Martino v. Carey, 563 F. Supp. 984, 1000–01 (D.Or. 1983); Frazier v. Ward, 426 F. Supp. 1354, 1369 (N.D.N.Y. 1977) (five hours a week required); *see* Toussaint v. McCarthy, 597 F. Supp. 1388, 1402, 1412 (N.D.Cal. 1984) (eight hours a week required; outdoor exercise might not be required if more indoor exercise was provided), *affirmed in part, reversed in part on other grounds*, 801 F.2d 1080 (9th Cir. 1986); Gumpl v. Seiter, 689 F. Supp. 754, 755–56 (S.D.Ohio 1987) (complete denial of outdoor exercise would violate the Eighth Amendment if there was any feasible alternative). *But see* May v. Baldwin, 109 F.3d 537, 565 (9th Cir. 1997) ("a temporary denial of outdoor exercise with no medical effects is not a substantial deprivation").

Areas that are merely open to the outside do not provide outdoor recreation. *See* Keenan v. Hall, 83 F.3d 1083, 1090 (9th Cir. 1996) (exercise comprising a room with a roof and one wall of "perforated steel admitting sunlight only through the top third" did not meet requirement of outdoor recreation); Frazier v. Ward, 426 F. Supp. 1354, 1369 (N.D.N.Y. 1977) (covered "back door cell"

area with "no grass, no dirt, no rain" was inadequate); Mathis v. Henderson, 108 Misc.2d 63, 437 N.Y.S.2d 34 (N.Y.Sup. 1980) (covered structure on the prison roof was not "out of doors" for purpose of complying with state regulation).

[1301]Hearns v. Terhune, 413 F.3d 1036, 1042–43 (9th Cir. 2005) (lack of drinking water where yard temperatures regularly exceeded 100 degrees could violate the Eighth Amendment for prisoner in segregation); Davidson v. Scully, 914 F. Supp. 1011, 1017 (S.D.N.Y. 1996) (refusal to provide reasonably warm clothing for outdoor exercise during upstate New York winters is unconstitutional). *But see* Gates v. Cook, 376 F.3d 323, 343–44 (5th Cir. 2004) (lack of shade or water for an hour is not of constitutional stature); Gerber v. Sweeney, 292 F. Supp. 2d 700, 709–10 (E.D.Pa. 2003) (denial of winter coats, hats, gloves, and shoes in the recreation yard during winter did not violate the Eighth Amendment. Defendants provided prisoners with sandals, not shoes, "in order to prevent prisoners from getting a secure footing off which they can physically attack guards or inmates."); Jones v. City and County of San Francisco, 976 F. Supp. 896, 916 (N.D.Cal. 1997) (inadequate clothing for cold weather exercise did not violate the Constitution where it did not prevent use of the yard).

[1302]Anderson v. Coughlin, 757 F.2d 33, 35–36 (2d Cir. 1985) (where inmates got outside regularly, lack of equipment and lack of indoor facilities did not violate the Constitution); Gholson v. Murry, 953 F. Supp. 709, 722–24 (E.D.Va. 1997) (recreation in 8×20 foot cages without restrooms for six weeks does not violate the Eighth Amendment). *But see* Parnell v. Waldrep, 511 F. Supp. 764, 771 (W.D.N.C. 1981) (requiring equipment for "full-fledged physical exercise"); Crain v. Bordenkircher, 178 W.Va. 264, 342 S.E.2d 422, 439–40 (W.Va. 1986) ("planned and organized recreation with adequate space, equipment and time" required where overall conditions were unconstitutional).

[1303]*See* Anderson v. Romero, 72 F.3d 518, 528 (7th Cir. 1996); Wilson v. Blankenship, 163 F.3d 1284, 1292–93 (11th Cir. 1998) (upholding lack of outdoor and indoor exercise areas in overcrowded jail, noting plaintiff could exercise in crowded day room); Martin v. Tyson, 845 F.2d 1451, 1456 (5th Cir. 1988) (lack of outdoor exercise upheld where a local jail had no facilities, the cell was large enough to exercise in, and the prisoner was an escape risk); Green v. Ferrell, 801 F.2d 765, 771–72 (5th Cir. 1986) (lack of outdoor exercise upheld where cells were large, inmates had access to a day room, and stays were short); Shelby County Jail Inmates v. Westlake, 798 F.2d 1085, 1089 (7th Cir. 1986) (lack of outdoor recreation upheld where inmates had access to exercise bicycles and stays were short); Wilkerson v. Maggio, 703 F.2d 909, 911–12 (5th Cir. 1983); Clay v. Miller, 626 F.2d 345, 347 (4th Cir. 1986) (outdoor recreation not required where prisoners had access to a dayroom 18 hours a day); Torres Garcia v. Puerto Rico, 402 F. Supp. 2d 373, 383 (D.P.R. 2005) ("Deprivation of outdoor exercise does not raise a constitutional issue."); Grace v. Wainwright, 761 F. Supp. 1520, 1525 (M.D.Fla. 1991) (outdoor recreation was not required because the plaintiff could exercise in his cell); *see* Bass v. Perrin, 170 F.3d 1312, 1316–17 (11th Cir. 1999) (denying "Close Management" prisoners who misbehave in segregation unit the two hours of outdoor exercise a week they were otherwise entitled

If a constitutional minimum of exercise is provided, courts will generally not intervene in the details of prison recreation programs, at least on federal constitutional grounds.[1304] Courts have differed over whether scheduling recreation periods in conflict with other constitutionally mandated activities is unlawful.[1305] Disparities in exercise opportunities in different prisons are generally not held to deny equal protection of the laws.[1306] State statutes or regulations sometimes provide more rights to exercise and recreation than the federal Constitution. These rights may be enforced in state court.[1307]

---

to did not violate the Eighth Amendment; defendants were not deliberately indifferent where they took steps to prevent potential harm).

[1304]Gates v. Cook, 376 F.3d 323, 343–44 (5th Cir. 2004) (provision of flip-flops, in which it is hard to exercise, was not of constitutional stature); Peterkin v. Jeffes, 855 F.2d 1021, 1031–32 (3d Cir. 1988) (where death row inmates got two hours outside daily, limited area and lack of indoor recreation was not unconstitutional); French v. Owens, 777 F.2d 1250, 1255–56 (7th Cir. 1982) (where inmates usually got five hours a week outdoors, use of "cramped and noisy gym" in inclement weather was not unconstitutional); Gerber v. Sweeney, 292 F. Supp. 2d 700, 709–10 (E.D.Pa. 2003) (providing sandals for recreation to make it harder to attack others was not unconstitutional); Allah v. al-Hafeez, 208 F. Supp. 2d 520, 532–33 (E.D.Pa. 2002) (policy forbidding more than ten inmates in a group in the yard upheld); Miles v. Bell, 621 F. Supp. 51, 63–64 (D.Conn. 1985) (where inmates spent little time in their living units, inadequate or overcrowded recreation facilities did not violate the Constitution); Shoats v. Owen, 128 Pa.Cmwlth. 427, 563 A.2d 963, 965 (Pa.Commw. 1989) (segregation inmates could be denied indoor recreation on days where outdoor recreation was not possible).

[1305]See Allen v. City & County of Honolulu, 39 F.3d 936, 939–40 (9th Cir. 1994) (holding that prisoner was entitled both to exercise and to law library access and should not have to forego one for the other). Contra, Thomas v. Ramos, 130 F.3d 754, 764 (7th Cir. 1997) (holding that schedule conflicts between exercise and medical visits reflected the prisoner's choice); Douglas v. DeBruyn, 936 F. Supp. 572, 578–79 (S.D.Ind. 1996) (conflict between recreation and law library periods does not violate the Eighth Amendment). But see Thomas v. Ramos, 130 F.3d at 765 (objecting to notion that prisoners may be required to trade off one right for another).

[1306]Williams v. Price, 25 F. Supp. 2d 605, 620 (W.D.Pa. 1997) (applying rational basis standard to prisoners' equal protection claims); see Ch. 5 concerning equal protection of the laws.

[1307]New York State Com'n of Correction v. Ruffo, 157 A.D.2d 987, 550 N.Y.S.2d 746 (App. Div. 3d Dep't 1990) (enforcing state regulation requiring local jails to provide outdoor recreation); Inmates of B-Block v. Jeffes, 79 Pa.Commw. 275, 470 A.2d 176, 178–80 (Pa.Commw. 1983) (enforcing state statute requiring two hours of outdoor recreation daily; rejecting constitutional claim), aff'd, 504 Pa. 509, 475 A.2d 743 (1984); Bowe v. Smith, 119 Misc.2d 453, 465 N.Y.S.2d 391, 394–95 (N.Y.Sup. 1983) (enforcing state regulation requiring daily exercise; "exercise" means more than movement to the dining hall and participation in programs); Mathis v. Henderson, 108 Misc.2d 63, 437 N.Y.S.2d 34 (N.Y.Sup. 1980) (enforcing state regulation calling for outdoor recreation).

J. Segregation: Punitive, Administrative, Protective, and "Supermax"

There are different kinds of prison segregation,[1308] but they look a lot alike, with long lock-in times, severe restrictions on activities and on contact with other inmates, and extreme security measures such as frequent cell and body searches. Even though administrative and protective segregation are not supposed to punish, they are often operated in similar ways to punitive segregation. There has been a trend for some years to create larger segregation units, and sometimes entire prisons, specially designed to provide more complete isolation and to operate with more restrictions and security procedures, and given names like "control unit," "close management unit," or (the current fashion) "supermax."[1309]

In this section we discuss the length and conditions of segregated confinement. The procedural requirements for placement in segregation are discussed elsewhere in this Manual.[1310]

Long ago, courts recognized that prolonged isolation and sensory deprivation can be psychologically damaging.[1311] Modern courts have also acknowledged "what anyway seems pretty obvious, that isolating a human being from other human beings year after year or even month

---

[1308]Prison officials use a variety of terms to describe segregation units. In this section we refer to segregation meant to discipline inmates for breaking the rules as "punitive segregation." We refer to segregation that is intended to prevent prisoners from committing future misconduct or threatening security as "administrative segregation." We refer to segregation intended to protect prisoners from assault as "protective custody."

[1309]The U.S. Department of Justice has defined a supermax facility as "a highly restrictive, high-custody housing unit within a secure facility, or an entire secure facility, that isolates inmates from the general population and from each other." U.S. Dep't of Justice, National Institute of Corrections, Supermax Prisons: Overview and General Considerations (1999) (quoted in Michael B. Mushlin, 1 Rights of Prisoners § 2.3 at 87 (2002)).

[1310]See Ch. 4, §§ F.2, H.2. A number of courts have held that evidence of the harmful effects of prolonged isolation shows that it is sufficiently "atypical and significant" that subjection to it is a deprivation of liberty requiring due process under the rule of Sandin v. Conner, 515 U.S. 472, 484, 115 S. Ct. 2293 (1995); See Ch. 4, §§ F.2, H.2.

[1311]The Supreme Court said of Nineteenth Century solitary confinement that "[a] considerable number of prisoners fell, after even a short confinement, into a semi-fatuous condition, from which it was next to impossible to arouse them, and others became violently insane; others still, committed suicide; while those who stood the ordeal better were not generally reformed, and in most cases did not recover sufficient mental activity to be of any subsequent service to the community." In re Medley, 134 U.S. 160, 168, 10 S. Ct. 384 (1890) (striking down a statute retroactively imposing solitary confinement as an ex post facto law).

after month can cause substantial psychological damage, even if the isolation is not total."[1312]

Despite this recognition, courts have not been willing to prohibit isolated confinement, either in conventional segregation units[1313] or in "supermax"-type facilities.[1314]

Some courts have said that persons who are already psychiatrically vulnerable to the effects of isolation must be excluded from it.[1315] Some have held that prolonged isolated confinement is unconstitutional for juvenile prisoners.[1316]

Courts have generally declined to place any fixed time limit on segregation time based on constitutional concerns,[1317] though statutes or administrative regulations may provide a limit.[1318] Some cases have placed limits on punitive segregation time when segregation conditions were unacceptably bad,[1319] and courts occasionally find a segregation sentence to be disproportionate to the offense.[1320] Administrative segregation, however, is said to be preventive in nature, and may generally continue as long as the

---

[1312]Davenport v. DeRobertis, 844 F.2d 1310, 1313, 1316 (7th Cir. 1988); *accord*, Madrid v. Gomez, 889 F. Supp. 1146, 1235 (N.D.Cal. 1995) ("many, if not most, inmates in the SHU experience some degree of psychological trauma in reaction to their extreme social isolation and the severely restricted environmental stimulation in SHU"); Langley v. Coughlin, 715 F. Supp. 522, 540 (S.D.N.Y. 1989); Baraldini v. Meese, 691 F. Supp. 432, 446–47 (D.D.C. 1988) (citing testimony re sensory disturbance, perceptual distortions, and other psychological effects of segregation), *rev'd on other grounds*, 884 F.2d 615 (D.C. Cir. 1989); Bono v. Saxbe, 450 F. Supp. 934, 946–47 (E.D.Ill. 1978), *aff'd in part and remanded in part on other grounds*, 620 F.2d 609 (7th Cir. 1980). *But see* Freeman v. Berge, 283 F. Supp. 2d 1009, 1016–17 (W.D.Wis. 2003) (officials were entitled to qualified immunity from the plaintiff's claim of social and sensory isolation; though the court agrees that "harm caused by lack of human contact and sensory stimulation may violate 'contemporary standards of decency' in some instances" and that "evidence has accumulated regarding the harm that depriving inmates of social interaction and sensory stimulation can cause.... However, agreement among mental health professionals regarding the deleterious effects of solitary confinement does not translate into legal notice that defendants may have been violating the Eighth Amendment."), *reconsideration denied*, 2003 WL 23208945 (W.D.Wis., June 19, 2003). Several of the cited cases rely on the research and testimony of psychiatrist Stuart Grassian. *See* Stuart Grassian, M.D., *Psychopathological Effects of Solitary Confinement*, 140 AM. J. PSYCHIATRY 11 (1983); Stuart Grassian and Nancy Friedman, *Effects of Sensory Deprivation in Psychiatric Seclusion and Solitary Confinement*, 8 INT'L J. OF LAW AND PSYCHIATRY 49 (1986).

[1313]*See In re* Long Term Administrative Segregation, 174 F.3d 464, 471–72 (4th Cir. 1999) (administrative segregation with 23-hour lockup, no radio or TV, five hours of exercise a week, and exclusion from all programs did not violate the Eighth Amendment because it did not deny a "basic human need"; "A depressed mental state, without more, does not rise to the level of the 'serious or significant physical or emotional injury' that must be shown" under the Eighth Amendment.); Bruscino v. Carlson, 854 F.2d 162, 166–67 (7th Cir. 1988) (holding that conditions in Marion federal penitentiary "control unit" and "permanent lockdown" at Marion federal penitentiary, including long lock-in times, use of restraints when out of cell, restricted access to law libraries, digital rectal searches were "sordid and horrible" but not unconstitutional).

[1314]In *Madrid v. Gomez*, 889 F. Supp. 1146 (N.D.Cal. 1995), concerning California's Pelican Bay supermax facility, the court found an unconstitutional pattern of excessive force and also found that medical and mental health care were constitutionally inadequate, but did not find the general isolation and idleness of supermax life unconstitutional, except for persons with mental illness or certain other kinds of psychiatric problems, as discussed below. The court said that "the conditions of extreme social isolation and reduced environmental stimulation found in the Pelican Bay SHU will likely inflict some degree of psychological trauma upon most inmates confined there for more than brief periods.... [But] we are not persuaded ... that the risk of developing an injury to mental

health of *sufficiently serious magnitude* ... is high enough for the SHU population as a whole, to find that current conditions in the SHU are *per se* violative of the Eighth Amendment with respect to all potential inmates." *Madrid*, 889 F. Supp. at 1265 (emphasis in original).

Other recent challenges to supermax conditions have resulted in few rulings, since they have tended to be settled in whole or in part. In *Jones'El v. Berge*, 164 F. Supp. 2d 1096, 1116–25 (W.D.Wis. 2001), the court similarly ruled that prisoners with mental illness could not be held in the Wisconsin supermax facility, but the prisoners' other challenges to supermax conditions were later settled, so there is no broader ruling on those conditions. *See* Jones-El v. Berge, 374 F.3d 541, 543 (7th Cir. 2004) (describing history of case). In litigation about the Ohio supermax prison, the question of prisoners' due process rights went to the Supreme Court, but the challenges to conditions of confinement were settled without a court ruling on them. Wilkinson v. Austin, 545 U.S. 209, 218, 125 S. Ct. 2384 (2005). A major challenge to supermax conditions in Indiana was also settled without any ruling on the legal challenge to supermax conditions or procedures. *See* Isby v. Bayh, 75 F.3d 1191, 1195 (7th Cir. 1996) (settlement "provides for a commissary, expands access to radio and television, increases visitation and telephone rights, makes more reading materials available and expands recreational opportunities, allows prisoners to have more personal property and greater access to items of personal hygiene, improves the bedding material assigned to prisoners, decreases the intensity of twenty-four hour lights in the cells, limits the use of force by DOC personnel, expands medical care, provides a comprehensive law library with improved prisoner access, provides educational opportunities and substance abuse programs when necessary, and improves the prisoner grievance procedures").

[1315]*See* § F.4.a of this chapter, n.480.

[1316]R.G. v. Koller, 415 F. Supp. 2d 1129, 1154–55 (D.Haw. 2006) and cases cited.

[1317]Torres v. Commissioner of Correction, 427 Mass. 611, 614–15, 695 N.E.2d 200 (1998).

[1318]*See, e.g.*, Tate v. Carlson, 609 F. Supp. 7, 10 (S.D.N.Y. 1984) (13-month segregation confinement violated federal prison regulations requiring that prisoners be released to general population or transferred within 90 days); Libby v. Commissioner of Correction, 385 Mass. 421, 432 N.E.2d 486, 490 (Mass. 1982) (noting 15-day limit on "isolation time" for inmates committing further offenses in segregation).

[1319]*See* Ch. 4, § H.1.p, n.555.

[1320]*See* Ch. 4, § H.1.p, n.553–554.

reason for it continues to exist.[1321] Serious past misconduct can justify continued administrative segregation for substantial periods,[1322] but not indefinitely[1323]—though we don't know of a case in which a court actually found that segregation was unconstitutional because its length outran the justification for it.[1324]

Due process requires that prison officials periodically review prisoners' status to determine if there is still a reason to keep them in administrative segregation.[1325] In some cases, prisoners are segregated for long periods of time without having done anything wrong. The courts have acknowledged that this situation presents "a very difficult question" but have not done anything about it.[1326]

Courts have often condemned segregation conditions that are unsanitary, unhealthful, or degrading, such as "strip cell" confinement involving deprivation of clothing, washing and toilet facilities, and proper bedding.[1327] They have

---

[1321]Hewitt v. Helms, 459 U.S. 460, 477 n.9, 103 S. Ct. 864 (1983); *In re* Long Term Administrative Segregation, 174 F.3d 464, 469–71 (4th Cir. 1999) (Five Percenters, considered a "Security Threat Group" by officials, could be kept in segregation indefinitely or until they renounced their affiliation); Smith v. Shettle, 946 F.2d 1250, 1254 (7th Cir. 1991); Bono v. Saxbe, 620 F.2d 609, 614 (7th Cir. 1980); Sostre v. McGinnis, 442 F.2d 178, 192–93 (2d Cir. 1971); Todd v. Commissioner of Correction, 27 Mass.App. 1199, 543 N.E.2d 1152, 1153–54 (Mass.App. 1989). *See also* Ch. 4, §§ F, H.2.

[1322]Mims v. Shapp, 744 F.2d 946, 951–52 (3d Cir. 1984) (five-year confinement of a prisoner who had killed an officer did not deny due process).

[1323]Sheley v. Dugger, 833 F.2d 1420, 1427 (11th Cir. 1987) (allegation of 10-year segregation after escape and weapons violations, with no further justification, stated a due process claim); Morris v. Travisono, 549 F. Supp. 291, 295–96 (D.R.I. 1982) (refusing to stand up in court and sleeping at the wrong end of the bed did not justify continuing segregation after eight and a half years), *aff'd*, 707 F.2d 28 (1st Cir. 1983).

[1324]This issue is raised in the "Angola Three" litigation, in which the plaintiffs, who had been affiliated with the Black Panther Party, and two of whom had been convicted of murdering a prison guard, were held for 28–35 years in administrative segregation despite their lack of any continuing disciplinary record. The court denied summary judgment for prison officials, holding that a reasonable fact finder could "determine that the cumulative effect of over 28 years of confinement in lockdown at LSP constitutes a sufficiently serious deprivation of at least one basic human need, including but not limited to sleep, exercise, social contact and environmental stimulation. It is obvious that being housed in isolation in a tiny cell for 23 hours a day for over three decades results in serious deprivations of basic human needs." Wilkerson v. Stalder, 639 F. Supp. 2d 654, 680, 681-82 (M.D.La. 2007).

[1325]*See* Ch. 4, § H.2.

[1326]Meriwether v. Faulkner, 821 F.2d 408, 416 (7th Cir. 1987).

[1327]Surprenant v. Rivas, 424 F.3d 5, 19–20 (1st Cir. 2005) (upholding jury verdict for the plaintiff based on evidence that he was allowed only a five-minute shower every day, was denied all hygienic products, had access to water, including to flush his toilet, only at the guards' discretion, and was subjected daily to multiple strip searches that required him to place his unwashed fingers into his mouth); Dixon v. Godinez, 114 F.3d 640, 644–45 (7th Cir. 1997)

(allegations that cell got so cold in winter that ice formed on the walls supported an Eighth Amendment claim); Mitchell v. Maynard, 80 F.3d 1434, 1442 (10th Cir. 1996) (allegations that plaintiff was stripped of his clothing, placed in a concrete cell with no heat, provided with no mattress, blankets, or bedding of any kind, deprived of his prescription eyeglasses, not allowed out-of-cell exercise, not provided with writing utensils, not provided adequate ventilation or hot water, and allowed minimal amounts of toilet paper supported a claim of Eighth Amendment violation); Blissett v. Coughlin, 66 F.3d 531, 537 (2d Cir. 1995) (jury verdict upheld for prisoner placed naked in a feces-smeared mental observation cell for eight days); Chandler v. Baird, 926 F.2d 1057, 1063 (11th Cir. 1991) (allegation of confinement in undershorts without bedding, toilet paper, running water, soap, and toothpaste in a cold and filthy cell stated an Eighth Amendment claim); Maxwell v. Mason, 668 F.2d 361, 363–65 (8th Cir. 1981) (14-day confinement with only undershorts and mattress violated the Eighth Amendment; damages awarded); McCray v. Burrell, 622 F.2d 705, 706 (4th Cir. 1980) (confinement without clothing or personal hygiene items for two days violated the Eighth Amendment); Kirby v. Blackledge, 530 F.2d 583, 586–87 (4th Cir. 1976) (cell with no bedding, no light, and a hole in the floor for a toilet violated the Eighth Amendment); Kimbrough v. O'Neil, 523 F.2d 1057, 1059 (7th Cir. 1975) (alleged three-day confinement in a cell without toilet, water, bedding or mattress, soap or toilet paper stated an Eighth Amendment claim), *aff'd on other grounds*, 545 F.2d 1059 (7th Cir. 1976) (en banc); LaReau v. MacDougall, 473 F.2d 974, 978 n.2 (2d Cir. 1972) (five-day confinement with "Chinese toilet" [hole in the floor] flushed from outside and with no means of personal cleanliness violated the Eighth Amendment) and cases cited; Wright v. McMann, 460 F.2d 126, 129 (2d Cir. 1972) (11- and 21-day periods in unsanitary cell with no clothing, bedding, soap, toilet paper, or heat violated the Eighth Amendment); Young v. Breeding, 929 F. Supp. 1103, 1108 (N.D.Ill. 1996) (placement in a strip cell for 20 days with no clothing for the first night and no bedding for some time thereafter stated an Eighth Amendment claim); Howard v. Wheaton, 668 F. Supp. 1140, 1142–44 (N.D.Ill. 1987) (allegation of 13-day confinement in protective custody cell without working toilet or hot water stated an Eighth Amendment claim); Lovell v. Brennan, 566 F. Supp. 672, 695–96 (D.Me. 1983) ("restraint cells" with Chinese toilets and without furniture or water violated the Eighth Amendment), *aff'd*, 728 F.2d 560 (1st Cir. 1984); Griffin v. DeRobertis, 557 F. Supp. 302, 304–06 (N.D.Ill. 1983) (allegation of 12-day confinement without bedding or working toilet stated an Eighth Amendment claim); O'Connor v. Keller, 510 F. Supp. 1359, 1371–74 (D.Md. 1981) two-day confinement without mattress, blanket, or toilet paper violated the Eighth Amendment); Flakes v. Percy, 511 F. Supp. 1325, 1329 (W.D.Wis. 1981) (locked cells without toilets or sinks violate the Eighth Amendment); Strachan v. Ashe, 548 F. Supp. 1193, 1202 (D.Mass. 1982) (use of "soil pots" is unconstitutional); Berch v. Stahl, 373 F. Supp. 412, 421 (E.D.N.C. 1974). *But see* Williams v. Delo, 49 F.3d 442, 445–46 (8th Cir. 1995) (three- to four-day deprivation of clothing, mattress, water, toothbrush, and other hygiene items did not violate the Eighth Amendment); Johnson v. Boreani, 946 F.2d 67, 71 (8th Cir. 1991) (placement in "quiet" room without clothing or bedding did not violate clearly established rights); Porth v. Farrier, 934 F.2d 154, 156–57 (8th Cir. 1991) (confinement for 12 hours without clothing, bedding, or mattress would have permitted, but did not require, a jury verdict for the plaintiff); Owen v.

also condemned absence of light, heat, and ventilation and poor sanitation in segregation.[1328] Segregated prisoners must

receive adequate food, although cold food or a monotonous diet do not violate the Constitution.[1329] Courts have upheld some deprivations that might otherwise cross the constitutional line when prisoners who are already in segregation commit further disciplinary violations.[1330]

Several courts have found the confinement of mentally ill prisoners in segregation to be unconstitutional, not just in its effect on those prisoners, but also insofar as it exposes other inmates to dangerous or deranged behavior.[1331] Extremes of isolation, in the form of solitary confinement behind solid or "boxcar" doors, have also been held unconstitutional.[1332] But increasing the isolation of those who

---

Heyne, 473 F. Supp. 345, 348 (N.D.Ind. 1978) (unintentional deprivation of mattress and bedding, commode controlled from outside the cell were not unconstitutional), *aff'd*, 605 F.2d 559 (7th Cir. 1979).

Additional relevant cases will be found in § B.2 of this chapter, n.124 (bedding), § C, nn.163–165, 169–170, 178–183 (showers, water for washing, access to toilets), § E, nn.229–231 (clothing).

[1328]Hutto v. Finney, 437 U.S. 678, 686–87, 98 S. Ct. 2565 (1978); Gates v. Cook, 376 F.3d 323, 338–44 (5th Cir. 2004) (affirming injunction requiring improved cell cleaning procedures, provision of fans, ice water, and daily showers during hot weather, added pest control measures including repairing window screens, correction of unsanitary "ping-pong toilets," improvement of lighting, and enhanced mental health services); Keenan v. Hall, 83 F.3d 1083, 1090 (9th Cir. 1996) (inadequate ventilation can violate the Eighth Amendment; "If the air was in fact saturated with the fumes of feces, urine, and vomit, it could undermine health and sanitation."), *amended on other grounds*, 135 F.3d 1318 (9th Cir. 1998); Williams v. Adams, 935 F.2d 960, 962 (8th Cir. 1991) (13-day confinement in a cell with a broken toilet leaking waste stated a constitutional claim); McCord v. Maggio, 927 F.2d 844, 848 (5th Cir. 1991) (confinement in a segregation cell flooded with sewage and foul water was a "clear violation of the Eighth Amendment"); Williams v. White, 897 F.2d 942, 944–45 (8th Cir. 1990) (allegation of lack of ventilation and mattress infested with bugs and insects stated an Eighth Amendment claim); Foulds v. Corley, 833 F.2d 52, 52–54 (5th Cir. 1987) (allegation that segregation was extremely cold and that the plaintiff had to sleep on the floor where rats crawled over him stated an Eighth Amendment claim); Bono v. Saxbe, 620 F.2d 609, 615 (7th Cir. 1980) (inadequate lighting might violate the Constitution); Kirby v. Blackledge, 530 F.2d 583, 587 (4th Cir. 1976) (lack of sanitation and ventilation violated the Eighth Amendment); LaReau v. MacDougall, 473 F.2d 974, 978 (2d Cir. 1972) (almost continuous darkness violated the Eighth Amendment); Thomas v. Jabe, 760 F. Supp. 120, 123 (E.D.Mich. 1991) (placement in segregation cell flooded with water and human waste was unconstitutional); Lovell v. Brennan, 566 F. Supp. 672, 695–96 (D.Me. 1983) ("restraint cells" without windows, inside lights, heat, or ventilation violated the Eighth Amendment), *aff'd*, 728 F.2d 560 (1st Cir. 1984); Imprisoned Citizens Union v. Shapp, 451 F. Supp. 893, 898 (E.D.Pa. 1978) (absence of light and ventilation); Hancock v. Avery, 301 F. Supp. 786, 791–92 (M.D.Tenn. 1969) (absence of light and ventilation). *But see* Davis v. Scott, 157 F.3d 1003, 1006 (5th Cir. 1998) (three-day placement in a "crisis management cell" that was filthy, with blood on the walls, excrement on the floors and bread loaf on the floor, was not unconstitutional where the plaintiff was given cleaning supplies); Beverati v. Smith, 120 F.3d 500, 504 (4th Cir. 1997) (holding allegations that cells were infested with vermin and smeared with human feces and urine, flooded with water from a toilet leak upstairs, and unbearably hot; that the food was cold; that prisoners did not receive clean clothing, linen or bedding, as often as regulations prescribed; that they were out of their cells only three or four times a week and never allowed outside; that there were no educational or religious services available; and that prisoners received less food than in general population did not state a claim of atypical and significant conditions requiring due process protections; court says the prisoners did not argue the conditions violated the Eighth Amendment).

Some segregation units have constant illumination in cells, even during sleeping hours; some courts have held that practice unconstitutional. *See* § B.4 of this chapter, nn.138–139.

Additional relevant cases are cited in §§ B.3, B.4, and C of this chapter.

[1329]*See* § D of this chapter.

[1330]Thus, one court upheld the deprivation of all property except one pair of shorts and denial of recreation, showers, hot water, and a cell bucket for about two weeks to a prisoner who persisted in misbehaving in a segregation unit. The court noted that the plaintiff's condition was regularly monitored by a nurse and that the purpose of the measures was to control ongoing misconduct by the prisoner. Trammell v. Keane, 338 F.3d 155, 163, 165–66 (2d Cir. 2003). Another allowed the deprivation of all remaining outdoor recreation to prisoners who committed serious misconduct in a "Close Management" unit where they were already restricted to two hours a week outside. Bass v. Perrin, 170 F.3d 1312, 1316–17 (11th Cir. 1999); *see* LeMaire v. Maass, 12 F.3d 1444, 1454–55 (9th Cir. 1993) (upholding rule providing: "A disciplinary-segregated inmate may be required to forfeit or be temporarily deprived of any service or activity when the inmate is using them to destroy or damage property, obstruct security, or threatens physical violence to himself/herself or others. . . ."); *see also* O'Leary v. Iowa State Men's Reformatory, 79 F.3d 82, 83–84 (8th Cir. 1996) (upholding "progressive four-day behavior management program" for prisoners who commit disciplinary offenses in the segregation unit; they are deprived of underwear, blankets, and mattress, exercise and visits and allowed to read, but not retain, their mail; the items are gradually restored assuming the prisoner behaves correctly). *But see* Beckford v. Portuondo, 151 F. Supp. 2d 204, 212 (N.D.N.Y. 2001) (an allegation that the plaintiff was deprived of all clothing and bedding and forced to sleep on cold steel because he would not cut a fingernail stated an Eighth Amendment claim; a jury could find that these actions were "grossly out of proportion to the alleged infraction, [and defendants] were acting with the intent to at least deprive him of his most basic necessities.").

[1331]*See* § F.4.a of this chapter, nn.478–479.

[1332]Hoptowit v. Ray, 682 F.2d 1237, 1257–58 (9th Cir. 1982) (solid doors that excluded nearly all fresh air and light, limited access to medical care, and caused sanitary problems violated the Eighth Amendment); LeMaire v. Maass, 745 F. Supp. 623, 636 (D. Or. 1990) ("quiet cells" with steel doors were unconstitutional because they made it impossible to call for medical attention), *vacated and remanded on other grounds*, 12 F.2d 1444 (9th Cir. 1993); Toussaint v. McCarthy, 597 F. Supp. 1388, 1408 (N.D.Cal. 1984) ("quiet cells" with closed solid doors were unconstitutional), *aff'd in part and rev'd in part on other grounds*, 801 F.2d 1080,

commit misconduct in the segregation unit has been upheld.[1333]

Segregation conditions that are merely boring or restrictive are not unconstitutional.[1334] In fact, a plurality of the Supreme Court has recently endorsed the idea that administrative segregation conditions, which in theory are not supposed to be punitive, can be purposefully made unpleasant in order to create incentives for prisoners to behave better so they can stay out of such units.[1335] It is not clear how far this reasoning will go. The *Beard* plurality said the prison officials' arguments prevailed in part because the plaintiffs submitted no evidence to contradict them, and in future cases courts might reach different conclusions on different records. The plurality also stressed that the restrictions at issue were imposed "only upon those with serious prison-behavior problems (here the 40 most intractable inmates in the [state])," and "prison officials, relying on their professional judgment, reached an experience-based conclusion that the policies help to further legitimate prison objectives."[1336]

Thus, *Beard* can be read as saying that severe constitutional deprivations intended to induce compliance with prison rules may pass muster only if they are imposed as a matter of considered policy, and restricted to persons with the most serious records of misbehavior. Certainly that is the argument you should make if prison officials impose extremely severe deprivations on a wide range of prisoners, for example on a state's entire administrative segregation population, or on all prisoners in a segregation unit much bigger than the one in *Beard*. Also, the *Beard* plurality reached its conclusions applying the "reasonable relationship" test that governs restrictions on constitutional rights by the decision in *Turner v. Safley.*[1337] *Beard* did not address Eighth Amendment claims, and there is no indication that its reasoning would apply to deprivations or restrictions serious enough to violate the Eighth Amendment.

The restrictions upheld in *Beard* consisted of a ban on newspapers, magazines, and photographs for prisoners in the state's "Long Term Segregation Unit."[1338] In earlier decisions, restrictions on reading matter and correspondence met with varying responses from the courts.[1339] Restrictions on visiting that do not amount to a complete denial of visits are usually upheld.[1340] Segregated prisoners generally need not be permitted to go to the law library as long as adequate provisions are made for their access to courts.[1341] Most recent decisions hold that segregation inmates can be denied the right to attend group religious services, but others have required individualized determinations, or have required alternate arrangements for religious exercise.[1342] Limits on possession of personal property are generally upheld.[1343] Strip searches of segregation inmates are permissible as long as there is a correctional justification for them.[1344]

1106–07 (9th Cir. 1986); Bono v. Saxbe, 527 F. Supp. 1187 (S.D.Ill. 1981); Bono v. Saxbe, 450 F. Supp. 934, 946–48 (E.D.Ill. 1978), *aff'd in part and remanded in part on other grounds*, 620 F.2d 609 (7th Cir. 1980); Berch v. Stahl, 373 F. Supp. 412, 421 (E.D.N.C. 1974) (solid-door confinement limited to 15 days); *see also* U.S. v. Koch, 552 F.2d 1216, 1218–19 (7th Cir. 1977) (six-hour confinement in boxcar cell to obtain confession was unconstitutionally coercive; confession suppressed). *But see* Tyler v. Black, 865 F.2d 181 (8th Cir. 1989) (en banc) (boxcar doors were not unconstitutional); Libby v. Commissioner of Correction, 385 Mass. 421, 432 N.E.2d 486, 492–95 (Mass. 1982) (confinement for 15-day periods behind solid doors was not unconstitutional where medical surveillance and other conditions were adequate).

[1333]Beckford v. Portuondo, 151 F. Supp. 2d 204, 211–12 (N.D.N.Y. 2001) (placement in a plexiglass-front strip cell after the plaintiff had smeared feces on his cell walls did not violate the Eighth Amendment, especially since the plaintiff had previously thrown urine and feces at officers); DeMaio v. Mann, 877 F. Supp. 89, 93 (N.D.N.Y. 1995) (use of plexiglass cell shields that do not stop ventilation does not violate the Eighth Amendment), *aff'd*, 122 F.3d 1055 (2d Cir. 1995) (unpublished); Killen v. McBride, 907 F. Supp. 302, 304–05 (N.D.Ind. 1994) (upholding eight-day placement in a cell with a shield or bubble in front of it after plaintiff stabbed another prisoner through his cell bars; the bubble was designed to permit ventilation), *aff'd*, 70 F.3d 1274 (7th Cir. 1995) (unpublished).

[1334]Martin v. Scott, 156 F.3d 578, 579–80 (5th Cir. 1998) (limited recreation and visit time, limited possession of property and commissary purchases, requirement to wear a jumpsuit, denial of desserts with meals, handcuffing whenever out of cell, and substitution of a soy product called Vita-Pro for meat were not unconstitutional); Peterkin v. Jeffes, 855 F.2d 1021, 1030 n.15 (3d Cir. 1988); Toussaint v. McCarthy, 801 F.2d 1080, 1106–07 (9th Cir. 1986); Jackson v. Meachum, 699 F.2d 578, 582–84 (1st Cir. 1983), and cases cited. The possibility that psychological harm or deterioration might result from such conditions does not make them unconstitutional. The courts have left open the possibility that such conditions might be found unconstitutional based on proof that they actually do cause harm. Peterkin v. Jeffes, 855 F.2d at 1030 n.15.

[1335]Beard v. Banks, 548 U.S. 521, 530–35, 126 S. Ct. 2572 (2006).

When the Supreme Court decides a case by a plurality, that means there is no opinion joined by a majority (five or more) of the Justices. When "no single rationale explaining the result enjoys the assent of five Justices, 'the holding of the Court may be viewed as that position taken by those Members who concurred in the judgments on the narrowest grounds.'" Marks v. U.S., 430 U.S. 188, 193, 97 S. Ct. 990 (1977) (citations omitted). In *Beard*, a four-Justice plurality endorsed the reasoning stated above, while two other Justices concurred in the judgment (*i.e.*, agreed that the prison officials should win), but did so on grounds so different from those relied on by the plurality that it seems to us the "narrowest ground" goes no further than saying that the specific rule at issue in *Beard* is not unconstitutional.

[1336]*Beard*, 548 U.S. at 532–33.

[1337]Turner v. Safley, 482 U.S. 78, 107 S. Ct. 2254 (1987). *See* Ch. III, § A, for further discussion of the *Turner* standard.

[1338]*Beard*, 548 U.S. at 523–26.

[1339]*See* Ch. 3, §§ B.1.d nn.144–149, B.2.c. nn.207–209.

[1340]*See* Ch. 3, § B.7.

[1341]*See* Ch. 3, § C.2.a, nn.534–535.

[1342]*See* Ch. 3, § D.2.b, nn.776–780.

[1343]*See* Ch. 3, § F, nn.974–975.

[1344]*See* Ch. 3, § E.2, n.896.

Under the Eighth Amendment, courts have required at least minimal opportunities for exercise in segregation units.[1345] But the lack of program opportunities in segregation does not violate the Constitution.[1346] Physical restraints may be used when segregated prisoners are out of their cells, though some courts have placed limits on their use.[1347]

In protective custody (PC) cases, the courts have rejected claims that conditions more restrictive than general population deny equal protection.[1348] Security restrictions and exclusion of PC inmates from group and program activities are generally upheld,[1349] but restrictions without a rational basis[1350] and extremely oppressive PC conditions have been found unconstitutional.[1351] Several courts have held that double-celling protective custody inmates under crowded and oppressive conditions is unconstitutional.[1352]

[1345]*See* § I.3 of this chapter, nn.1293–1298. Separate exercise facilities for segregation prisoners must be kept in safe and usable condition. Hearns v. Terhune, 413 F.3d 1036, 1042–43 (9th Cir. 2005) (holding that segregation yard where temperatures regularly exceeded 100 degrees and no water was available could violate the Eighth Amendment).

[1346]Toussaint v. McCarthy, 801 F.2d 1080, 1106–08 (9th Cir. 1986); Beck v. Lynaugh, 842 F.2d 759, 762 (5th Cir. 1988); McGruder v. Phelps, 608 F.2d 1023, 1026 (5th Cir. 1979); Little v. Terhune, 200 F. Supp. 2d 445, 450–57 (D.N.J. 2002) (upholding deprivation of educational opportunities to prisoner held in segregation for 15 years).

[1347]*See* § G.2.c.3 of this chapter.

[1348]Wishon v. Gammon, 978 F.2d 446, 449–50 (8th Cir. 1992); Taylor v. Rogers, 781 F.2d 1047, 1050 (4th Cir. 1986); French v. Owens, 777 F.2d 1250, 1256 (7th Cir. 1985); Lyons v. Farrier, 730 F.2d 525, 527 (8th Cir. 1984); Griffin v. Coughlin, 743 F. Supp. 1006, 1009–16 (N.D.N.Y. 1990); Crozier v. Shillinger, 710 F. Supp. 760, 764 (D.Wyo. 1989). *But see* Williams v. Lane, 851 F.2d 867, 880–82 (7th Cir. 1988) (restrictions that had no rational basis denied equal protection; a regulation entitling protective custody inmates to equal housing and program activities created a liberty interest protected by due process); Madden v. Kemna, 739 F. Supp. 1358, 1361–63 (W.D.Mo. 1990) (noncompliance with state regulations requiring "substantial equality" of privileges for protective custody inmates denied due process); *see also* Divers v. Dep't of Corrections, 921 F.2d 191, 193 (8th Cir. 1990) (allegation that "lockdown" PC inmates received worse treatment than "general population" PC inmates was not frivolous).

One court held that excessive restrictions in protective custody are unconstitutional because they make the prisoner choose between regular prison privileges and the constitutional right to safe conditions. Wojtczak v. Cuyler, 480 F. Supp. 1288, 1302–05 (E.D.Pa. 1979). Other courts have not followed *Wojtczak's* reasoning. *See* Taylor v. Rogers, 781 F.2d at 1050; Griffin v. Coughlin, 743 F. Supp. at 1019.

[1349]Wishon v. Gammon, 978 F.2d at 449–50 (upholding restrictions on recreation and program activities); Franklin v. Lockhart, 883 F.2d 654 (8th Cir. 1989) (upholding strip search practices in punitive, administrative, and protective units); Taylor v. Rogers, 781 F.2d 1047 (4th Cir. 1986) (upholding restrictions on religious services, recreation, programs, work assignments, visiting, telephone access, canteen visits, and access to library and law library); French v. Owens, 777 F.2d at 1256 (upholding denial of access to vocational, academic, and rehabilitation programs); Shrader v. White, 761 F.2d 975, 981 (4th Cir. 1985) (cell confinement was not unconstitutional); Allgood v. Morris, 724 F.2d 1098, 1099–1100 (4th Cir. 1984); Sweet v. South Carolina Dep't of Corrections, 529 F.2d 854,

863–66 (4th Cir. 1975) (en banc); Graham v. Perez, 121 F. Supp. 2d 317, 323 & n.10 (S.D.N.Y. 2000) (dismissing claims of only two and a half hours a day out-of-cell time, lack of job opportunities and prison wages, limited location and content of meals, lack of hot water and electrical outlets in cells, inadequate lighting, inadequate recreation opportunities, limits on stamps, newspapers, and phone calls, requiring prison-issued clothing, and limited personal grooming opportunities); Gawloski v. Dallman, 803 F. Supp. 103 (S.D.Ohio 1992); Griffin v. Coughlin, 743 F. Supp. at 1009–19; Crozier v. Shillinger, 710 F. Supp. at 763–64; Termunde v. Cook, 684 F. Supp. 255, 259–62 (D.Utah 1988); Cody v. Hillard, 599 F. Supp. 1025, 1034–35, 1054–55 (D.S.D. 1984), *aff'd in part and rev'd in part on other grounds*, 830 F.2d 912 (8th Cir. 1987) (en banc); M.C.I. Concord Advisory Bd. v. Hall, 447 F. Supp. 398, 404 (D.Mass. 1978). *But see* Lewis v. Washington, 197 F.R.D. 611, 615 (N.D.Ill. 2000) (exclusion from vocational, rehabilitative, and educational opportunities and denial of access to a gymnasium may constitute cruel and unusual punishment as part of the totality of the circumstances).

Segregation prisoners, including those in protective custody, may be denied physical access to law libraries, but courts have required that other measures be taken to protect their right of access to courts. *See* Ch. 3, § C.2.a, nn.534–536.

[1350]Williams v. Lane, 851 F.2d at 877–82 (denial of opportunities for communal worship, religious instruction and religious counseling, and restrictions on law library access lacked a rational basis and were unconstitutional); Nadeau v. Helgemoe, 561 F.2d 411, 417–18 (1st Cir. 1977) (law library privileges ordered expanded); Griffin v. Coughlin, 743 F. Supp. at 1025–28 (lack of private consultation with religious advisors was unconstitutional); Wojtczak v. Cuyler, 480 F. Supp. at 1307; *see* Sweet v. South Carolina Dep't of Corrections, 529 F.2d 854, 863–66 (4th Cir. 1975) (en banc) (restrictions on showers and exercise might be unconstitutional if they threatened health or if greater opportunities were practical).

[1351]Morales Feliciano v. Romero Barcelo, 672 F. Supp. 591, 603–04 (D.P.R. 1986) (conditions including 24-hour lock-in and complete absence of program activity and lack of medical supervision "wantonly inflicts . . . considerable pain"); Battle v. Anderson, 457 F. Supp. 719, 738 (E.D.Okla. 1978) (excessive heat, "primitive" physical conditions were unconstitutional), *remanded*, 594 F.2d 486 (10th Cir. 1979); *see* Dixon v. Godinez, 114 F.3d 640, 643–44 (7th Cir. 1997) (allegations of extreme cold in winter supported an Eighth Amendment claim); Lewis v. Washington, 197 F.R.D. 611, 616 (N.D.Ill. 2000) (exclusion from vocational, rehabilitative, and educational opportunities, denial of access to a gymnasium, deprivation of access to toilets or water during recreation, and cold food may constitute cruel and unusual punishment as part of the totality of the circumstances).

[1352]*See* Nami v. Fauver, 82 F.3d 63, 65–68 (3d Cir. 1996) (protective custody prisoners at a "Youth Correctional Facility" stated a claim in alleging that they were double-celled in 80-square foot cells with only one bed, so one inmate had to sleep on the floor by the toilet; that the cells had solid doors and it was difficult to summon help; that inmates were double-celled with others who had psychiatric problems, were violent, or who smoked; that the

Protective custody conditions that do not provide adequate protection, such as mixing protective custody and punitive segregation inmates, are unconstitutional.[1353]

Courts have generally upheld strict isolation and security practices in capital offender or "death row" units,[1354]

though they will strike down unsanitary and unhealthful conditions in them just as they do in other unit.[1355]

State statutes and regulations may provide more favorable legal standards than the Constitution for protective custody and other segregated prisoners.[1356] These may be enforced in state court.[1357] Under current law, state statutes

---

ventilation system was inadequate; that double-celling had resulted in rapes and other assaults; that they were confined to their cells except for recreation and half-hour to hour-long job assignments, and recreation was limited to one to two and a half hour period twice a week; that they were not allowed access to bathrooms during recreation; that they were provided less access to jobs and educational programs, as well as drug and alcohol programs required by the parole board, than general population inmates; that general population inmates worked in protective custody despite a statute to the contrary; and that they must wear the "black box" when transported to other locations such as medical appointments); Balla v. Idaho State Bd. of Corrections, 595 F. Supp. 1558, 1575 (D.Idaho 1984) (double-celling combined with limited movement and recreation were unconstitutional); French v. Owens, 538 F. Supp. 910, 916, 925–26 (S.D.Ind. 1982), *aff'd in pertinent part*, 777 F.2d 1250, 1257 (7th Cir. 1985); Burks v. Walsh, 461 F. Supp. 454, 486–89 (W.D.Mo. 1978); Battle v. Anderson, 457 F. Supp. at 738; M.C.I. Concord Advisory Bd. v. Hall, 447 F. Supp. 398, 401, 404 (D.Mass. 1978). *Contra*, C.H. v. Sullivan, 920 F.2d 483, 485 (8th Cir. 1990); Cody v. Hillard, 830 F.2d 912, 915–16 (8th Cir. 1987) (en banc).

[1353]Little v. Walker, 552 F.2d 193, 195–97 (7th Cir. 1977) (placement of inmates needing protection in same unit with violence-prone inmates supported an Eighth Amendment claim); Miller v. Shelby County, 93 F. Supp. 2d 892, 899–900 (W.D.Tenn. 2000) (custom of mixing PC prisoners with violent gang members during out-of-cell time was a policy of deliberate indifference); Steffenhagen v. Armontrout, 749 F. Supp. 997, 999–1000 (W.D.Mo. 1990) (allegations of a history of unauthorized access to PC unit by other inmates supported an Eighth Amendment claim); Inmates of Occoquan v. Barry, 717 F. Supp. 854, 867 (D.D.C. 1989) (prohibiting placement of protective custody and punitive segregation inmates in same unit); Tillery v. Owens, 719 F. Supp. 1271, 1276 (W.D.Pa. 1989) (permitting different classifications, including protective custody and punitive segregation, to mingle during showers and exercise, violated the Eighth Amendment), *aff'd*, 907 F.2d 418 (3d Cir. 1990); Balla v. Idaho State Bd. of Corrections, 595 F. Supp. at 1580 (permitting other inmates access to protective custody unit violated the Eighth Amendment); *see also* Lovell v. Brennan, 728 F.2d 560, 565 (1st Cir. 1984) (requirement of some corroboration of the basis of a request for protective custody was not unconstitutional); Fisher v. Koehler, 718 F. Supp. 1111, 1113–14, 1120–22 (S.D.N.Y. 1989) (setting out requirements for safe housing of protective custody inmates), *aff'd*, 902 F.2d 2 (2d Cir. 1990). *Contra*, McGill v. Duckworth, 944 F.2d 344, 350 (7th Cir. 1991); *see* Falls v. Nesbitt, 966 F.2d 375, 379 (8th Cir. 1992) (double-celling a protective custody inmate with a general population inmate did not deny the Eighth Amendment).

[1354]Solomon v. Zant, 888 F.2d 1579, 1582 (11th Cir. 1989) (death row inmate could be denied attorney visits because he did not comply with a "no beard" rule); Peterkin v. Jeffes, 855 F.2d 1021, 1028–33 (3d Cir. 1988) (long lock-in times and restricted activity and recreation were not unconstitutional); Smith v. Coughlin, 748 F.2d 783, 784–89 (2d Cir. 1984) (restricted visiting list, denial of contact visits, and denial of congregate religious

services upheld; refusal to permit visits by paralegals held unconstitutional); Wrinkles v. Davis, 311 F. Supp. 2d 735, 740–42 (N.D.Ind. 2004) (79-day lockdown with exclusion of religious volunteers who conducted services, suspension of visiting, frequent shakedown searches, and deprivations of telephones, hygiene services, hot meals, and exercise equipment did not violate the Constitution; deprivation of out-of-cell exercise might violate the Eighth Amendment if there were no opportunities to exercise in the cells); Williams v. Price, 25 F. Supp. 2d 605, 615 (W.D.Pa. 1997) (strip searches before and after counsel visits did not violate capital prisoners' Fourth Amendment rights); Rawls v. Sundquist, 929 F. Supp. 284, 287–91 (M.D.Tenn. 1996) (removal by Governor of TV satellite dish donated for death row unit did not violate the Constitution), *aff'd*, 113 F.3d 1235 (6th Cir. 1997); Card v. Dugger, 709 F. Supp. 1098, 1102–11 (M.D.Fla. 1988) (denial of contact visits with priest, limited visiting schedule, and failure to provide Catholic priest for death sentenced inmates upheld), *aff'd*, 871 F.2d 1023 (11th Cir. 1989); Jeffries v. Reed, 631 F. Supp. 1212, 1215–19 (E.D.Wash. 1986) (restrictions on court access, confiscation of certain personal property, strip search practices, denial of contact visits, telephone restrictions upheld); *see also* McDonald v. Armontrout, 908 F.2d 388, 391–93 (8th Cir. 1990) (modifications in consent decree governing death row conditions were properly granted on prison officials' request); Thompson v. Enomoto, 915 F.2d 1383, 1391 (9th Cir. 1990) (affirming district court's grant of modifications to death row consent judgment). *But see* Burgess v. Lowry, 201 F.3d 942, 947–48 (7th Cir. 2000) (striking down practice of requiring visitors to death row prisoners to submit to strip searches without reasonable suspicion); Mann v. Reynolds, 46 F.3d 1055, 1060–61 (10th Cir. 1995) (striking down a ban on contact visits with counsel); Lewis v. Lane, 816 F.2d 1165, 1171 (7th Cir. 1987) (practice of banging on bars to test them might implicate the Eighth Amendment if it were done "in a manner designed to harass prisoners"); Williams v. Price, 25 F. Supp. 2d 605, 619 (W.D.Pa. 1997) (holding lack of confidentiality in attorney–client consultations supported a claim for violation of due process right of privacy); Buehl v. Lehman, 802 F. Supp. 1266, 1271 (E.D.Pa. 1992) (prison officials must justify the refusal to permit a death row inmate to marry).

[1355]Gates v. Cook, 376 F.3d 323, 338–44 (5th Cir. 2004) (affirming injunction requiring improved cell cleaning procedures, provision of fans, ice water, and daily showers during hot weather, added pest control measures including repairing window screens, correction of unsanitary "ping-pong toilets," improvement of lighting, and enhanced mental health services). *But see* Chandler v. Crosby, 379 F.3d 1278, 1294–98 (11th Cir. 2004) (rejecting challenge to excessive heat in death row unit).

[1356]Williams v. Lane, 548 F. Supp. 927, 932 (N.D.Ill. 1982); Wojtczak v. Cuyler, 480 F. Supp. 1288, 1301-02 (E.D.Pa. 1979).

[1357]Blaney v. Commissioner of Correction, 374 Mass. 337, 372 N.E.2d 770, 773–74 (Mass. 1978) (state statute entitled protective custody inmates to the same treatment as general population except as necessary to maintain security; improved exercise, visiting, and lock-out privileges ordered).

and regulations will only rarely create "liberty interests" enforceable under the Constitution.[1358]

K. EMERGENCIES AND LOCKDOWNS

Prison officials have wide discretion in responding to emergencies. The Supreme Court has emphasized that courts must exercise "hesitancy to critique in hindsight decisions necessarily made in haste, under pressure, and frequently without the luxury of a second chance."[1359] Courts generally defer to prison officials' decisions concerning the use of force and riot control measures[1360] as well as "lockdowns"[1361] and other suspensions of normal activities. As one court put it, "[W]hen a genuine emergency exists, prison officials may be more restrictive than they otherwise may be, and certain services may be suspended temporarily. The more basic the particular need, the shorter time it can be withheld."[1362] Thus, in emergencies courts have upheld major restrictions on religious activity,[1363] property,[1364]

due process rights,[1365] exercise,[1366] routine medical services,[1367] food service,[1368] and other rights and activities.[1369]

[1358]*See* cases cited in Ch. 4, §§ A, B.

[1359]Whitley v. Albers, 475 U.S. 312, 320, 106 S. Ct. 1078 (1986) (holding that emergency measures must be "wanton and obdurate" to violate the Constitution).

[1360]Rust v. Grammer, 858 F.2d 411, 414 (8th Cir. 1988) (quoting Whitley v. Albers, 475 U.S. at 322 (emergency measures are lawful unless they are enacted "in bad faith and for no legitimate purpose")). Even actions that in retrospect were clearly mistaken may be excused in an emergency. *See* Campbell v. Grammar, 889 F.2d 797, 802 (8th Cir. 1989) (Constitution was not violated where prisoners were left without jumpsuits for a week after a lockdown and search through "misunderstanding, inexperience, oversight, inadvertence, and fecklessness".); *see also* §§ G.2.b(4), nn.1039–1041, and G.2.c, nn.1045, 1053, of this chapter, concerning use of force during disturbances.

[1361]Lopez v. Robinson, 914 F.2d 486, 491–92 (4th Cir. 1990) (lockdown after mess hall disturbance upheld); Anderson v. Coughlin, 700 F.2d 37, 44 (2d Cir. 1982) (keeplocking prisoners during an officers' job action was reasonable); Vallina v. Meese, 704 F. Supp. 769, 772–74 (E.D.Mich. 1989) (it was "reasonable" to place Cuban inmates in administrative detention during riots by Cubans at other federal prisons); Jordan v. Robinson, 464 F. Supp. 223, 226 (W.D.Pa. 1979) (lockup of all Muslim prisoners upheld after conflicts among Muslims).

[1362]Hoptowit v. Ray, 682 F.2d 1237, 1258 (9th Cir. 1982).

[1363]Walker v. Mintzes, 771 F.2d 920, 929–30 (6th Cir. 1985) (ban on group services upheld during lockdown); Wrinkles v. Davis, 311 F. Supp. 2d 735, 740 (N.D.Ind. 2004) (temporary exclusion of religious volunteers during lockdown after murder of prisoner on death row unit upheld); Ra Chaka v. Franzen, 727 F. Supp. 454, 457–59 (N.D.Ill. 1989) (restrictions on religious services during lockdown and transition to "unit management" system upheld); Collins v. Ward, 544 F. Supp. 408, 413–14 (S.D.N.Y. 1982) (denial of group services for 15 days to inmates transferred after a disturbance was not unconstitutional).

[1364]Rust v. Grammer, 858 F.2d at 414 (removal of inmates' property was not unlawful where they had used it to start fires); Ashford v. Barry, 737 F. Supp. 1, 2 (D.D.C. 1990) (seizure of sheets, blankets, and toiletries and failure to give receipts immediately for

seized property was not unconstitutional in connection with a disturbance in which property had been thrown and set on fire).

[1365]Graham v. Baughman, 772 F.2d 441, 445–46 (8th Cir. 1985) (prison officials need not call witnesses in disciplinary hearings immediately after an emergency, but should have contacted them later); Gabel v. Estelle, 677 F. Supp. 514, 515 (S.D.Tex. 1987) (locking down striking inmates without notice and hearing was justified by emergency conditions); Ponds v. Cuyler, 541 F. Supp. 291, 292 (E.D.Pa. 1982) (upholding suspension of time limits for disciplinary hearings).

[1366]Norwood v. Vance, 572 F.3d 626, 633 (9th Cir. 2009) (officials were not liable for repeated lockdowns without exercise of three to four and a half months done in response to violent incidents); Rust v. Grammer, 858 F.2d at 414 (two-week cancellation of yard privileges during lockdown upheld); Hayward v. Procunier, 629 F.2d 599, 600, 633 (9th Cir. 1980) (suspension and gradual restoration of yard exercise upheld); Jones v. Garcia, 430 F. Supp. 2d 1095, 1103 (S.D.Cal. 2006) (10-month deprivation of outdoor recreation did not violate the Eighth Amendment where prison officials were trying to bring racial violence under control and opening the yard would have endangered the plaintiff); Wrinkles v. Davis, 311 F. Supp. 2d 735, 741 (N.D.Ind. 2004) (removal of exercise equipment from housing units upheld); Johnson v. Williams, 768 F. Supp. 1161, 1167 (E.D.Va. 1991). *But see* Delaney v. DeTella, 256 F.3d 679, 684 (7th Cir. 2001) (six-month deprivation of exercise during lockdown was not shown to have a legitimate penological justification); Wrinkles v. Davis, 311 F. Supp. 2d at 741–42 (suspension of out-of-cell exercise during 79-day lockdown could violate Eighth Amendment if cells provided no opportunity for in-cell exercise).

[1367]Lucien v. Gomez, 841 F. Supp. 754, 756 (N.D.Ill. 1993) (two-week postponement of non-emergency medical appointments did not violate Constitution); Gray v. Levine, 455 F. Supp. 267, 270 (D.Md. 1978) (Constitution was not violated by temporary limits on medical services where medications were distributed and emergency hospital services available.), *aff'd*, 605 F.2d 1201 and 1202 (4th Cir. 1979). *But see* Al-Jundi v. Mancusi, 926 F.2d 235, 239 (2d Cir. 1991) (even after a major disturbance, prison officials were obligated to make provision for medical needs); Hoptowit v. Ray, 682 F.2d at 1258 ("It is doubtful . . . that any circumstance would permit a denial of access to emergency medical care."); Labatt v. Twomey, 513 F.3d 641, 649–51 (7th Cir. 1975) (allegation of denial of treatment of serious medical needs during "deadlock" should not have been dismissed).

[1368]Rust v. Grammer, 858 F.2d at 414 (diet of water and cold sandwiches "might violate the eighth amendment if it were the regular prison diet," but not as a short-term response to food-throwing and similar misconduct); Hayward v. Procunier, 629 F.2d at 600, 603 (two weeks of sack lunches, with regular meal service gradually restored over six months, upheld during lockdown after prison murders); Waring v. Meachum, 175 F. Supp. 2d 230, 239–40 (D.Conn. 2001) (similar to *Rust*; six-day suspension of special diet also upheld).

[1369]Hayward v. Procunier, 629 F.2d at 600, 603 (restricted showers, visits); Labatt v. Twomey, 513 F.2d at 648 (reduction in food, lack of showers, laundry, toilet articles, programs, sanitation); Wrinkles v. Davis, 311 F. Supp. 2d 735, 740–41 (N.D.Ind.

The courts generally will not second-guess prison officials' decision that an emergency exists unless the officials are shown to have acted in bad faith or on a pretext.[1370] "The unreviewable discretion of prison authorities in what they deem to be an emergency is not open-ended or time unlimited."[1371] Prisoners have had some success in challenging the prolonged continuation of emergency measures.[1372] Thus, when prison officials faced with a disturbance moved prisoners outside and made them lie down on the ground, the court held that they could not be held liable in those exigent circumstances unless they acted maliciously and sadistically. But once the prisoners were outside, handcuffed, prone, and under armed guard, officials could be held liable under the deliberate indifference standard for failure to provide for sanitation, food, and drinking water.[1373]

Another court concluded that three months after a riot, the emergency was over, and required prison officials to resume providing showers and yard recreation.[1374] However, after an emergency, prison officials are not necessarily required to restore all privileges that were restricted; they may change their policies to prevent further security threats as long as the new policies are not unconstitutional.[1375]

One court has suggested that prisoners have due process rights to procedural protections if emergency restrictions continue for a long time.[1376] Others have rejected this view,[1377] especially since the Supreme Court's decision in *Sandin v. Conner.*[1378]

2004) (suspension of visiting, deprivation of telephones, and hygiene services); Liles v. Camden County Dep't of Corrections, 225 F. Supp. 2d 450, 461 (D.N.J. 2002) (three-week restriction to 20 minutes a day out of cell upheld during lockdown to make repairs after an escape attempt); Waring v. Meachum, 175 F. Supp. 2d 230, 241–42 (D.Conn. 2001) (one-week suspension of showers and clean clothing); Miller v. Campbell, 804 F. Supp. 159, 162–63 (D.Kan. 1992) (shutting off water to stop flooding and shutting off electricity after a light fixture was broken); Collins v. Ward, 544 F. Supp. 408, 414 (S.D.N.Y. 1982) (short-term denial of law library access).

[1370]Collins v. Ward, 544 F. Supp. at 412, and cases cited. *But see* DeSpain v. Uphoff, 264 F.3d 965, 974–76 (10th Cir. 2001) (36-hour refusal to allow cleaning up of flooding and human waste supported an Eighth Amendment claim where it was not clear there was an ongoing safety threat, since prisoners were locked in and staff came and went).

In *Sanchez v. Taggart*, 144 F.3d 1154 (8th Cir. 1998), an officer directed a prisoner to perform sandbagging duty during a flood, refusing to verify his statement that he was barred from hard labor for medical reasons. The court held that the officer would be held liable for the resulting injury despite his claim of an emergency, since an hour and a half passed between the initial order and the commencement of work, and there were other prisoners available to help with the work. 144 F.3d 1156–67.

[1371]Hoitt v. Vitek, 497 F.2d 598, 600 (1st Cir. 1974); *see* Caldwell v. Miller, 790 F.2d 589, 598 (7th Cir. 1986) (restrictions necessary immediately after an emergency may not be necessary permanently); Liles v. Camden County Dep't of Corrections, 225 F. Supp. 2d 450, 461 (D.N.J. 2002) ("Courts have recognized that extended periods of lock-down can violate the Eighth Amendment. . . . Lockdown periods of less than thirty days ... generally do not violate the Eighth Amendment."); Termunde v. Cook, 684 F. Supp. 255, 262 (D.Utah 1988) (post-lockdown denial of religious services upheld, but court notes that future conditions might justify relief).

[1372]*See* Graham v. Baughmann, 772 F.2d 441, 445–46 (8th Cir. 1985) (claim that prison officials could not call witnesses for disciplinary hearings after a riot might have had merit in the short run, but they should have contacted the witnesses later).

[1373]Johnson v. Lewis, 217 F.3d 726, 734 (9th Cir. 2000); *see* Jones v. Brown, 461 F.3d 333, 362–33 (3d Cir. 2006) (practice of opening legal mail outside prisoners' presence, introduced after

the September 11, 2001 terrorist attacks and the later incidents of anthrax-containing mail, might have been reasonable at the time, but its continuation was unreasonable and unconstitutional three years later in the absence of any anthrax attacks), *cert. denied*, 549 U.S. 1286 (2007).

[1374]Preston v. Thompson, 589 F.2d 300, 302–03 (7th Cir. 1978); *accord*, Delaney v. DeTella, 256 F.3d 679, 684 (7th Cir. 2001) (holding six-month denial of all out-of-cell exercise during lockdown required legitimate penological justification, not just conclusory statement that allowing yard time would pose a "potential security threat"); Jefferson v. Southworth, 447 F. Supp. 179, 188–90 (D.R.I. 1978), *aff'd sub nom.* Palmigiano v. Garrahy, 616 F.2d 598 (1st Cir. 1980). *But see* Hayward v. Procunier, 629 F.2d at 603 (continuation of lockdown for five months was not unconstitutional).

[1375]Walker v. Mintzes, 771 F.2d 920, 926–28, 931 (6th Cir. 1985); Ra Chaka v. Franzen, 727 F. Supp. 454, 457–59 (N.D.Ill. 1989); Termunde v. Cook, 684 F. Supp. at 259–61.

[1376]Labatt v. Twomey, 513 F.3d 641, 646 (7th Cir. 1975).

[1377]Abdul-Wadood v. Duckworth, 860 F.2d 280, 285 (7th Cir. 1988) (restrictions "imposed upon the unit as a whole, [in] response to an emergency, . . . continued to ensure the security of the unit" do not require due process protections); Caldwell v. Miller, 790 F.2d 589, 601–05 (7th Cir. 1986); Hayward v. Procunier, 629 F.2d at 601–02; Saunders v. Packel, 436 F. Supp. 618, 624–25 (E.D.Pa. 1977); *see also* Rust v. Grammer, 858 F.2d 411, 413 (8th Cir. 1988) (state regulations forbidding restricted diet, clothing, visits, etc., for punishment were not applicable to lockdown conducted for security and not disciplinary purposes).

[1378]515 U.S. 472, 116 S. Ct. 2293 (1995); *see* Wrinkles v. Davis, 311 F. Supp. 2d 735, 739–40 (N.D.Ind. 2004) ("Institutional lockdowns, like disciplinary segregation, fall within the expected parameters of an inmate's sentence, and do not present the type of 'atypical' deprivation in which a state might conceivably create a liberty interest."); Alley v. Angelone, 962 F. Supp. 827, 833 (E.D.Va. 1997).

CHAPTER 3

Civil Liberties in Prison

The Supreme Court has said that "[t]here is no iron curtain drawn between the Constitution and the prisons of this country,"[1] and that prisoners do not lose all of the fundamental rights of Americans like free speech, religious freedom, and freedom from unreasonable searches and seizures. But these civil liberties are severely restricted in prison.

A. THE REASONABLE RELATIONSHIP STANDARD

In *Turner v. Safley*, the Supreme Court held that "when a prison regulation impinges on inmates' constitutional rights, the regulation is valid if it is reasonably related to legitimate penological interests. . . ."[2] There are several factors that determine whether a regulation is reasonable:

1) [Whether there is] a "valid, rational connection" between the prison regulation and the legitimate governmental interest put forward to justify it. . . . [A] regulation cannot be sustained where the logical connection between the regulation and the asserted goal is so remote as to render the policy arbitrary or irrational.

Moreover, the governmental objective must be a legitimate and neutral one. . . .

2) . . . [W]hether there are alternative means of exercising the right that remain open to prison inmates. . . .

3) . . . [T]he impact accommodation of the asserted constitutional right will have on guards and other inmates, and on the allocation of prison resources generally. . . . When accommodation of an asserted right will have a significant "ripple effect" on fellow inmates or on prison staff, courts should be particularly deferential to the informed discretion of prison officials. . . .

4) . . . [T]he absence of ready alternatives is evidence of the reasonableness of a prison regulation. . . . But if an inmate claimant can point to an alternative that fully accommodates the prisoner's rights at *de minimis* [minimal] cost to valid penological interests, a court may consider that as evidence that the regulation does not satisfy the reasonable relationship standard.[3]

The *Turner* standard has been applied to prison restrictions on marriage,[4] religious exercise,[5] access to publications and inmate–inmate correspondence,[6] refusal of psychotropic medications,[7] visiting,[8] and many other matters.[9]

---

[1]Wolff v. McDonnell, 418 U.S. 539, 555–56, 94 S. Ct. 2963 (1974).

[2]Turner v. Safley, 482 U.S. 78, 89, 107 S. Ct. 2254 (1987); *accord*, O'Lone v. Estate of Shabazz, 482 U.S. 342, 349, 107 S. Ct. 2400 (1987).

State constitutions may provide greater protections to prisoners than the federal Constitution. Thus, in *Sterling v. Cupp*, 290 Or. 611, 625 P.2d 123, 128–36 (Or. 1981), the court held that its state constitution's prohibition of "unnecessary rigor" in the treatment of prisoners provided a better basis for analyzing prisoners' privacy rights than federal law, and concluded that pat frisks by opposite-sex staff must be "justified by necessity," and the justification must exist for the particular search. This holding appears more favorable to prisoners than the reasonable relationship standard. *See* § E.2 of this chapter, nn.911–912, concerning the federal law governing such searches.

---

[3]Turner v. Safley, 482 U.S. at 89–91.

[4]Turner v. Safley, 482 U.S. at 91–99.

[5]O'Lone v. Estate of Shabazz, 482 U.S. at 349.

[6]Beard v. Banks, 548 U.S. 521, 126 S. Ct. 2572 (2006); Shaw v. Murphy, 532 U.S. 223, 121 S. Ct. 1475 (2001); Thornburgh v. Abbott, 490 U.S. 401, 109 S. Ct. 1874 (1989).

[7]Washington v. Harper, 494 U.S. 210, 110 S. Ct. 1028 (1990).

[8]Overton v. Bazzetta, 539 U.S. 126, 131–32, 123 S. Ct. 2162 (2003).

[9]*See, e.g.*, Schreiber v. Ault, 280 F.3d 891, 892–93 (8th Cir. 2002) (disposition of blood samples over religious objection); Wolf v. Ashcroft, 297 F.3d 305, 306–10 (3d Cir. 2002) (prohibition on showing R and NC-17 rated movies); Oliver v. Scott, 276 F.3d 736, 745–46 (5th Cir. 2002) (cross-gender housing area surveillance); Walker v. Sumner, 917 F.2d 382, 385–88 (9th Cir. 1990) (compulsory and duplicative HIV testing); Goodwin v. Turner, 908 F.2d 1395, 1398–99 (8th Cir. 1990) (restrictions on artificial insemination); Benzel v.

In fact, the Supreme Court has said that it applies to all claims that a prison regulation infringes on constitutional rights,[10] but that is not quite true. It does not apply to "conditions of confinement" cases governed by the Eighth Amendment's Cruel and Unusual Punishments Clause,[11] to issues of procedural due process,[12] or to claims of racial discrimination.[13] Nor does it apply to claims brought by pre-trial detainees.[14]

The *Turner* standard also does not apply to claims based on statutes that prescribe a different standard, such as the Religious Freedom Restoration Act and the Religious Land Use and Institutionalized Persons Act,[15] and may not apply to claims under the Americans with Disabilities Act and the Rehabilitation Act.[16]

Though *Turner* said its standard applied to challenges to "prison regulations," it has also been applied to cases challenging state and federal statutes[17] as well as to informal

---

Grammer, 869 F.2d 1105, 1108 (8th Cir. 1989) (restrictions on telephone use); Robinson v. Palmer, 841 F.2d 1151, 1156 (D.C. Cir. 1988) (suspension of visits); Woods v. O'Leary, 890 F.2d 883, 885 (7th Cir. 1989) (restrictions on inmate businesses); Dunn v. White, 880 F.2d 1188, 1194 (10th Cir. 1989) (mandatory HIV virus testing).

[10]Washington v. Harper, 494 U.S. 210, 223–24, 110 S. Ct. 1028 (1990).

One federal court recently questioned whether the *Turner* standard applies to "a claim of constitutional protection from state action such as a strip search," noting that *Turner* and other Supreme Court cases applying it concerned prisoners' assertion of affirmative rights to correspond, marry, organize a union, and order books. N.G. v. State, 382 F.3d 225, 235–36 (2d Cir. 2004). We do not think this is right. In *Washington v. Harper*, the *Turner* standard was applied to the right to refuse the involuntary administration of psychotropic medications, which is "a claim of constitutional protection from state action" that is as intrusive as a strip search.

At least one recent decision holds that certain rights are "fundamentally inconsistent" with incarceration, and the *Turner* analysis is not applicable in cases involving them. Gerber v. Hickman, 291 F.3d 617, 620 (9th Cir. 2002) (en banc) (addressing prisoner's claimed right to reproduce through artificial insemination). This argument, which appears inconsistent with the Supreme Court's post-*Turner* decisions, was recently presented to the Supreme Court and was not accepted, though it was not conclusively ruled out either. Overton v. Bazzetta, 539 U.S. 126, 131–32, 123 S. Ct. 2162 (2003). *But see* Stewart v. Alameida, 418 F. Supp. 2d 1154, 1162 (N.D.Cal. 2006) (in light of *Overton*, court considers reasonableness of restriction rather than whether right survives incarceration as *Gerber* directs). However, more recently the Court has said that it has applied *Turner* "*only* to rights that are 'inconsistent with proper incarceration.' . . . This is because certain privileges and rights must necessarily be limited in the prison context," a rationale the Court said was not true of freedom from racial discrimination. Johnson v. California, 543 U.S. 499, 510, 125 S. Ct. 1141 (2005). Another recent decision initially held that *Turner* was inapplicable to a statutory prohibition on prisoners' use or possession of electric musical instruments because these instruments impose costs, *e.g.*, the electricity to operate them, and government need not subsidize First Amendment exercise. In the face of a vigorous dissent on this point, the panel agreed to rest its decision on its alternate *Turner* analysis instead. Kimberlin v. U.S. Dep't of Justice, 318 F.3d 228, 232–33 (D.C. Cir.), *rehearing denied*, 351 F.3d 1166 (D.C. Cir. 2003); *see id.*, 318 F.3d at 237–38 (concurring and dissenting opinion).

[11]Wilson v. Seiter, 501 U.S. 294, 302–03, 111 S. Ct. 2321 (1991) (adopting "deliberate indifference" standard for conditions cases); *see* Hope v. Pelzer, 536 U.S. 730, 122 S. Ct. 2508 (2002) (applying deliberate indifference standard to Eighth Amendment challenge to prison restraint practice). Conditions of confinement are discussed in Ch. 2.

[12]The extent of required procedural protections is governed by *Mathews v. Eldridge*, 424 U.S. 319, 335, 96 S. Ct. 893 (1976). *See* Wilkinson v. Austin, 545 U.S. 209, 224–25, 125 S. Ct. 2384 (2005); Washington v. Harper, 494 U.S. 210, 110 S. Ct. 1028 (1990) (applying *Turner* to substantive claims and *Mathews* to procedural claims). *But see* Powell v. Coughlin, 953 F.2d 744, 749 (2d Cir. 1991) (applying *Turner* to a due process claim—incorrectly, we believe).

Procedural due process is discussed more generally in Ch. 4.

[13]Johnson v. California, 543 U.S. 499, 510–14, 125 S. Ct. 1141 (2005). The Court did not say whether its ruling would apply to other kinds of discrimination or denial of equal protection of the laws. Some lower courts have held that *Turner* does not apply to claims of gender discrimination either. McCoy v. Nevada Dep't of Prisons, 776 F. Supp. 521, 523 n.2 (D.Nev. 1991). Gender discrimination is discussed in Ch. 5.

[14]In *Bell v. Wolfish*, 441 U.S. 520, 535, 99 S. Ct. 1861 (1979), the Supreme Court held that persons held in jail who have not been convicted of anything cannot be punished. Whether conditions or practices amount to punishment may depend on whether they bear a reasonable relationship to legitimate governmental interests. *Wolfish*, 441 U.S. at 539. The Supreme Court has never clarified the differences, if any, between the *Wolfish* reasonable relationship standard and the *Turner* reasonable relationship standard. One federal court has pointed out that the "penological interests" with which *Turner* was concerned include "interests that related to the treatment (including punishment, deterrence, rehabilitation, etc.) of persons convicted of crimes." Benjamin v. Fraser, 264 F.3d 175, 187 n.10 (2d Cir. 2001). Another federal court has contradicted itself on the point. *Compare* Mauro v. Arpaio, 188 F.3d 1054, 1059 n.1 (9th Cir. 1999) (en banc) (applying *Turner* to censorship of publications in a jail housing both sentenced prisoners and detainees, though the rehabilitative rationale it relied on has no application to detainees) *with* Demery v. Arpaio, 378 F.3d 1020, 1028–29 (9th Cir. 2004) (applying *Wolfish*, ignoring *Mauro*, in detainee case); *see* Mauro, 188 F.3d at 1067 (dissenting opinion) (pointing out inappropriateness of *Turner* standard in detainee case).

The same federal court that decided the *Benjamin* case has also held in a strip search case that *Turner* applies to prisons and not jails, regardless of whether the particular plaintiffs are convicts or detainees. Shain v. Ellison, 273 F.3d 56, 65–66 (2d Cir. 2001).

[15]These statutes were intended by Congress to provide greater protection to religious rights than does the *Turner* standard. *See* § D.1.b of this chapter.

[16]Some courts have said that the *Turner* standard should apply under these standards, and some have not. *See* Ch. 2, § F.4.h.2, concerning these statutes.

[17]*See* Waterman v. Farmer, 183 F.3d 208, 212–20 (3d Cir. 1999); Amatel v. Reno, 156 F.3d 192, 195–203 (D.C. Cir. 1998); Langone v. Coughlin, 712 F. Supp. 1061, 1064–66 (N.D.N.Y. 1989).

policies and practices[18] and to individual actions by prison personnel[19]—including those that are contrary to prison regulations.[20]

The *Turner* standard is less favorable to prisoners than some earlier case law. Previously, courts applied a "less restrictive alternative" rule in many First Amendment cases, holding that restrictions must be "no greater than is necessary or essential" to protect an "important or substantial" interest.[21] That rule is now limited to restrictions on outgoing correspondence to non-prisoners.[22] Cases applying the less restrictive alternative rule to issues such as incoming correspondence, publication censorship, and constitutional claims concerning religious rights have been overruled.[23]

Weighing the *Turner* factors is not a scientific process,[24] and courts have not always agreed on how to do it. The lower

courts have differed with each other, and sometimes with themselves, over whether prison officials must provide evidence or merely assertion in support of their positions.[25] Most have held that defendants must produce evidence,[26]

One recent decision asserts that the *Turner* standard does not apply to statutes. Padgett v. Donald, 401 F.3d 1273, 1281 n.7 (11th Cir. 2005). This is contrary to other courts' decisions and we do not think it is correct.

[18] *See* Jones v. Salt Lake County, 503 F.3d 1147, 1159 n.3 (10th Cir. 2007) (unwritten "publisher only" rule); Cornwell v. Dahlberg, 963 F.2d 912, 917 (6th Cir. 1992) ("unwritten prison policies," in that case the conduct of strip searches); Tanney v. Boles, 400 F. Supp. 2d 1027, 1043 (E.D.Mich. 2005) (practice that was "regularly enforced and at least implicitly endorsed by [defendant's] superiors"); Griffin v. Coughlin, 743 F. Supp. 1006, 1010–16, 1028 (N.D.N.Y. 1990) (protective custody recreation schedule and failure to provide for private consultation with religious advisors).

[19] *See* Boles v. Neet, 486 F.3d 1177, 1181 n.4 (10th Cir. 2007) (denial of religious garb during medical visit); Ford v. McGinnis, 352 F.3d 582, 595 n.15 (2d Cir. 2003) (denial of religious meal); Frazier v. DuBois, 922 F.2d 560, 562 (10th Cir. 1990) (allegedly retaliatory transfer).

[20] In *Shakur v. Selsky*, 391 F.3d 106 (2d Cir. 2004), a publication was seized pursuant to a disciplinary rule, even though questions of what publications were allowed were the province of the facility Media Review Committee. The court applied *Turner* and stated that "a failure to abide by established procedures or standards can evince an improper objective." *Shakur*, 391 F.3d at 116; *see* Nolley v. County of Erie, 776 F. Supp. 715, 736 (N.D.N.Y. 1991) (segregation of HIV-positive inmate contrary to jail's own policies struck down under *Turner*).

[21] Procunier v. Martinez, 416 U.S. 396, 413–14, 94 S. Ct. 1800 (1974).

[22] Thornburgh v. Abbott, 490 U.S. 401, 413-14, 109 S. Ct. 1874 (1989).

In *Abbott*, the Court rejected its earlier view that the involvement of non-prisoners required the application of a more lenient standard to incoming letters as well. *Id.* at 410 n.9. Correspondence is discussed in more detail in § B.1 of this chapter.

[23] These issues are discussed in §§ B.1, B.2, and D of this chapter.

[24] "*Turner* does not call for placing each factor in one of two columns and tallying a numerical result. . . . *Turner* does contemplate a judgment by the court regarding the reasonableness of the defendants' conduct under all of the circumstances reflected in the record." DeHart v. Horn, 227 F.3d 47, 59 (3d Cir. 2000) (en

banc); *accord*, Beard v. Banks, 548 U.S. 521, 126 S. Ct. 2572 (2006) (plurality opinion) ("The real task . . . is not balancing these factors" but assessing whether the record shows a reasonable, not just logical, relationship).

[25] *Compare* Morrison v. Garraghty, 239 F.3d 648, 661 (4th Cir. 2001) (affirming district court's entry of relief in part because defendants failed to substantiate their argument that their policy promoted security) *with* Veney v. Wyche, 293 F.3d 726, 730–35 & n.1 (4th Cir. 2002) (affirming under *Turner* the district court's dismissal on initial screening, with no response from defendants, of a challenge to a policy that on appeal prison officials *denied existed*). *Cf.* Lindell v. Frank, 377 F.3d 655, 657–58 (7th Cir. 2004) (holding a *Turner* claim cannot be assessed without knowing that the prison's policy actually was).

[26] *See* Ramirez v. Pugh, 379 F.3d 122, 130 (3d Cir. 2004) (holding that the second, third, and fourth *Turner* factors are "fact-intensive" requiring a "contextual, record-sensitive analysis," though "[w]here the link between the regulation at issue and the legitimate government interest is sufficiently obvious, no evidence may be necessary to evaluate the other *Turner* prongs"); Beerheide v. Suthers, 286 F.3d 1179, 1189 (10th Cir. 2002) ("In order to warrant deference, prison officials *must present credible evidence* to support their stated penological goals."); Ford v. McGinnis, 352 F.3d 582, 596–97 (2d Cir. 2003) (declining to consider *Turner* factors for the first time on appeal, remanding for development of an appropriate record); Armstrong v. Davis, 275 F.3d 849, 874 (9th Cir. 2001) (rejecting argument that defendants who failed to justify policies in the district court could do so with arguments developed later); Davis v. Norris, 249 F.3d 800, 801 (8th Cir. 2001) (holding court cannot apply *Turner* standard where defendants did not submit evidence supporting their argument); Flagner v. Wilkinson, 241 F.3d 475, 486 (6th Cir. 2001) (holding that defendants were not entitled to summary judgment on an as-applied challenge to a religious restriction without evidence supporting their arguments that related to the individual plaintiff); Nicholas v. Miller, 189 F.3d 191, 194–95 (2d Cir. 1999) (per curiam) (finding material factual disputes concerning prison's denial of a request to form a Prisoners' Legal Defense Center, despite conclusory claims that permitting it would undermine safety and security); Shimer v. Washington, 100 F.3d 506, 509–10 (7th Cir. 1996) (requiring evidence and not mere assertion); Salahuddin v. Coughlin, 993 F.2d 306, 309–10 (2d Cir. 1993) (rejecting conclusory justifications for denying congregate religious services in newly opened prison where construction had not been completed); Walker v. Sumner, 917 F.2d 382, 386–87 (9th Cir. 1990) (prison officials may not obtain summary judgment based on conclusory assertions without explanation or factual support); Salaam v. Lockhart, 905 F.2d 1168, 1174 (8th Cir. 1990) (officials may not "pil[e] conjecture upon conjecture" to justify their policies) (quoting Reed v. Faulkner, 842 F.2d 960, 963–64 (7th Cir. 1988)); Canadian Coalition against the Death Penalty v. Ryan, 269 F. Supp. 2d 1199, 1203 (D.Ariz. 2003) ("Although prison authorities are permitted to establish regulations in anticipation of potential problems, 'they must as a minimum supply some evidence that such potential problems are real, not imagined.'"). *But see* Fraise v. Terhune, 283 F.3d 506,

though a recent Supreme Court decision makes it clear that the opinions of prison officials *are* evidence, at least if they are "experience-based conclusions"–even if they are not supported by facts showing that the officials' opinions were correct, or that the policies they followed based on their opinions actually succeeded in serving their intended purposes.[27] Some courts have held that prison officials initially need only assert a "common sense connection" between policy and challenged practice. If plaintiffs fail to refute that connection, it is sufficient if prison officials reasonably could have thought the policy would advance legitimate penological interests; if plaintiffs do refute the common-sense connection, prison officials must then "demonstrate that the relationship is not so 'remote as to render the policy arbitrary or irrational.'"[28] Courts have also differed over how much to question the logic and consistency of prison officials' positions,[29] and whether prison rules must be assessed

only on their face or also as applied to particular prisoners.[30] At least one court has held that when prison officials change a pre-existing rule, the *Turner* analysis is applied to the change, and not to the rule as a whole—that is, if officials make an unreasonable change, the fact that the rule is generally reasonable will not insulate the change from constitutional challenge.[31]

It is hard for prisoners to prevail under the *Turner* standard. One reason is that the Supreme Court has emphasized the need to defer to the judgment of prison officials.[32] However, the Court has also said the standard is not

---

[27]Beard v. Banks, 548 U.S. 521, 533, 126 S. Ct. 2572 (2006).

[28]Prison Legal News v. Cook, 238 F.3d 1145, 1150 (9th Cir. 2001); *accord*, Wolf v. Ashcroft, 297 F.3d 305, 308–09 (3d Cir. 2002); *see* Jones v. Brown, 461 F.3d 353, 360–61 (3d Cir. 2006) (applying *Wolf v. Ashcroft* holding after *Beard v. Banks*), *cert. denied*, 549 U.S. 1286 (2007).

[29]*See* Shakur v. Selsky, 391 F.3d 106, 115–16 (2d Cir. 2004) (questioning whether a ban on all materials from "unauthorized organizations" was rationally related to maintaining security, since officials had the obvious alternative of sending the materials to the already-existing Media Review Committee for individual examination pursuant to established procedures); California First Amendment Coalition v. Woodford, 299 F.3d 868, 879 (9th Cir. 2002) (emphasizing the "exaggerated response" component of the *Turner* standard, noting that some governmental interests require "a closer fit between the regulation and the purpose it serves"); Beerheide v. Suthers, 286 F.3d 1179, 1186–92 (10th Cir. 2002) (closely examining prison officials' justifications for failure to provide a kosher diet); Pope v. Hightower, 101 F.3d 1382, 1384–85 (11th Cir. 1996) (holding once district judge had determined that restriction of prisoner's telephone list to 10 persons was rationally related to curtailing criminal activity and the harassment of judges and jurors, inquiry was over); Hakim v. Hicks, 223 F.3d 1244, 1248–49 (11th Cir. 2000) (affirming rejection of officials' claim that adding religious names to ID cards would undermine order and security); Allen v. Coughlin, 64 F.3d 77, 80–81 (2d Cir. 1995) (rejecting justification for a ban on clippings enclosed in correspondence, since prisoners were allowed to receive entire newspapers); Bradley v. Hall, 64 F.3d 1276, 1280 (9th Cir. 1995) ("[D]eference does not mean abdication." (citation omitted)). *Compare* Morrison v. Garraghty, 239 F.3d 648, 660–61 (4th Cir.

2001) (rejecting defendants' argument that certain religious items sought by plaintiff could be dangerous, since other inmates were allowed them) *with* Hammons v. Saffle, 348 F.3d 1250, 1255 (10th Cir. 2003) (upholding ban on personal possession of Muslim oils, but not other oils, because government "can, in some circumstances, implement policies that are logical but yet experiment with solutions and address problems one step at a time"). *Cf.* Fromer v. Scully, 874 F.2d 69, 74 (2d Cir. 1989) (upholding requirement that beards be shaved for intake photograph and thereafter limited to one inch; rejecting argument that since only a complete ban would fully serve officials' concerns, the partial ban was irrational; "We reject that approach as leading to perverse incentives for prison officials not to compromise with inmate desires. . . .").

[30]*Compare* Pope v. Hightower, 101 F.3d at 1384–85 (disapproving district court's inquiry into whether a telephone rule generally valid under *Turner* was constitutional as applied to a prisoner whose family was in a distant state and who therefore relied more on the telephone for family contact than other prisoners) *with* Lindell v. Frank, 377 F.3d 655, 659 (7th Cir. 2004) (assessing validity of rule prohibiting clippings in prisoners' mail in light of the plaintiff's confinement in a high-security unit with no access to the prison library); Flagner v. Wilkinson, 241 F.3d 475, 486 (6th Cir. 2001) (prison officials failed to support restrictions on religious practice with evidence supporting their application to the individual plaintiff).

[31]Levitan v. Ashcroft, 281 F.3d 1313, 1322 (D.C. Cir. 2002) (where prison officials banned prisoners from consuming wine during Catholic Communion services, which had formerly been permitted, lower court should assess that change in light of the fact that alcohol would still be consumed on the prison grounds and in prisoners' presence by the chaplain).

[32]Turner v. Safley, 482 U.S. 78, 90, 107 S. Ct. 2254 (1987) ("When accommodation of an asserted right will have a significant "ripple effect" on fellow inmates or on prison staff, courts should be particularly deferential to the informed discretion of prison officials. . . ."); *see* Shaw v. Murphy, 532 U.S. 223, 229, 121 S. Ct. 1475 (2001) (describing standard as "a unitary, deferential standard"). In declining to apply the *Turner* standard to a claim of racial discrimination, the Court characterized it as extremely undemanding, stating that it "would allow prison officials to use race-based policies even when there are race-neutral means to accomplish the same goal, and even when the race-based policy does not in practice advance the goal," and that the blanket racial segregation policy struck down years earlier "might stand a chance of survival if prison officials simply asserted that it was necessary to prison management." Johnson v. California, 543 U.S. 499, 514, 125 S. Ct. 1141 (2005).

"toothless,"[33] and *Turner* itself struck down one of the policies before it, a prohibition on marriage without official permission.[34] In its most recent decision applying *Turner*, the Supreme Court ruled against the prisoners but pointed out that they "did not offer any fact-based or expert-based refutation [of the prison officials' motion] in the manner the rules provide.[35] It continued:

> . . . [W]e do not suggest that the deference owed prison authorities makes it impossible for prisoners or others attacking a prison policy like the present one ever to succeed or to survive summary judgment. After all, the constitutional interest here is an important one. *Turner* requires prison authorities to show more than a formalistic logical connection between a regulation and a penological objective. A prisoner may be able to marshal substantial evidence that, given the importance of the interest, the Policy is not a reasonable one. . . . And with or without the assistance that public interest law firms or clinics may provide, it is not inconceivable that a plaintiff's counsel, through rigorous questioning of officials by means of depositions, could demonstrate genuine issues of fact for trial.[36]

When prisoners have won cases under the *Turner* standard, they have done so by showing that some or all of the factors cited in *Turner* and described at the beginning of this section weigh in their favor.

(a) Prisoners can try to show that here is no "valid, rational connection" between the policy or action under challenge and the purpose it is intended to serve.[37] In some cases, the relationship between the policy and its purpose is too remote to establish a "valid, rational connection."[38]

In others, the policy simply makes no logical sense at all.[39] Sometimes policies make no sense because they, or the arguments in favor of them, are inconsistent with other prison policies or practices,[40] or because other policies and

---

[33]Thornburgh v. Abbott, 490 U.S. 401, 414, 109 S. Ct. 1874 (1989).

[34]Turner v. Safley, 482 U.S. 78, 94–99, 107 S. Ct. 2254 (1987).

[35]Beard v. Banks, 548 U.S. 521, 534, 126 S. Ct. 2572 (2006).

[36]*Beard*, 548 U.S. at 535–36.
Note that the Court emphasizes the role of counsel and of experts in these comments. You should cite them to the court if your case involves application of the *Turner* standard and you are asking the court to appoint counsel or to appoint an expert witness. *See* Ch. 10, § C.5, concerning appointment of counsel, and § K.3, which discusses court-appointed experts.

[37]*Turner*, 482 U.S. at 89; Ramirez v. Pugh, 379 F.3d 122, 128 (3d Cir. 2004) (holding the district court must "identify with particularity" the claimed interest in rehabilitation underlying the ban on delivery to prisoners of material that is "sexually explicit or contains nudity" so the parties can adduce sufficient evidence whether there is a rational connection between ends and means); Shimer v. Washington, 100 F.3d 506, 510 (7th Cir. 1996) (questioning connection of defendants' policy with its objectives).

[38]*See* Jones v. Brown, 461 F.3d 353, 363–64 (3d Cir. 2006) (holding a policy of opening legal mail outside prisoners' presence was not shown to be reasonably connected to protecting against anthrax attacks, absent some significant risk of an anthrax attack; noting a policy that might have appeared reasonable immediately after 9/11/01 and subsequent anthrax attacks ceased to be reasonable with the passage of time), *cert. denied*, 549 U.S. 1286 (2007);

Hunafa v. Murphy, 907 F.2d 46, 47 (7th Cir. 1990) (prison officials could not obtain summary judgment on failure to provide pork-free meals based on arguments that "seem[ed] trivial" or were "implausible, though not impossible" or "speculative"); Canadian Coalition against the Death Penalty v. Ryan, 269 F. Supp. 2d 1199, 1203 (D.Ariz. 2003) (rejecting "reflexive, rote assertions" such as society and crime victims may perceive prison as not punitive enough and deterrence may be impaired if prisoners are not forbidden to communicate with communications service providers); Nolley v. County of Erie, 776 F. Supp. 715, 736 (N.D.N.Y. 1991) (segregation of HIV-positive inmate contrary to jail's own policies was an "exaggerated response" and was only remotely connected to correctional goals); Casey v. Lewis, 773 F. Supp. 1365, 1367–70 (D.Ariz. 1991) (suspension of contact attorney visits struck down because there was no evidence of security problems when such visits were permitted).

[39]Turner v. Safley, 482 U.S. at 98 (restrictions on marriage had no logical connection with prevention of "love triangles" and were an "exaggerated response" to security concerns); Clement v. California Dept of Corrections, 364 F.3d 1148, 1152 (9th Cir. 2003) (holding that a ban on receipt of material printed from the Internet was an arbitrary way of reducing the volume of mail and had no rational relation to security risks); Prison Legal News v. Lehman, 397 F.3d 692, 700 (9th Cir. 2005) (ban on non-subscription bulk mail and catalogs as determined by postage rates lacked a rational relationship to reducing contraband, since contraband is more likely to appear in first class mail, and lacked a rational relationship to controlling risk of fire because the total amount of property was already restricted); Jacklovich v. Simmons, 392 F.3d 420, 429 (10th Cir. 2004) (questioning whether a four-month ban on receiving publications furthers behavior management or rehabilitation when imposed without regard to behavior); *see* Thompson v. Vilsack, 328 F. Supp. 2d 974, 978–79 (S.D.Iowa 2004) (rejecting the argument for requiring a co-payment by Jewish prisoners for kosher food to teach financial responsibility since other prisoners were not asked to pay for their food).

[40]Conyers v. Abitz, 416 F.3d 580, 585 (7th Cir. 2005) (denying summary judgment to officials based on their "rigid and unsupported" assumption that a sign-up deadline for Ramadan participation was *per se* reasonable, where other categories of prisoners were excused from the deadline); Jacklovich v. Simmons, 392 F.3d 420, 429 (10th Cir. 2004) (questioning whether a prohibition on gift publications is rationally connected with prevention of "strong-arming" when prison policy placed no limit on funds that could be deposited to a prisoner's account and allowed canteen expenditures of $180 a month); Allen v. Coughlin, 64 F.3d 77, 80 (2d Cir. 1995) (alleged danger of inflammatory material did not justify ban on newspaper clippings in letters when entire newspapers were allowed in); Griffin v. Lombardi, 946 F.2d 604, 607–08 (8th Cir. 1991) (evidence that a rule officials claimed was necessary was not followed in dealing with other prisoners or at other prisons raised a factual issue whether the rule met the *Turner* standard); Whitney v. Brown, 882 F.2d 1068, 1074, 1076 (6th Cir. 1989) ("glaring" inconsistencies between security arguments for restricting religious services and other practices of defendants rendered restrictions irrational; "flurry of disconnected and self-conflicting points"

practices already serve the interests at stake.[41] In a few cases, there is no valid, rational connection with the purpose of a policy or action because prison officials' statements of its purpose are not true.[42]

If the "valid, rational connection" requirement is not met, the regulation or practice is unconstitutional regardless of the other factors.[43] Conversely, meeting that requirement does not, by itself, validate a challenged policy.[44]

(b) Prisoners can try to show that the asserted goal of a regulation, practice or action is not legitimate[45]

and neutral.[46] Some courts have said that prison officials' interests are not legitimate if their actions are contrary to state law[47] or to their own policies.[48]

(c) Prisoners can try to show that they have no alternative means of exercising the constitutional right that the challenged policy or practice restricts.[49] Courts have disagreed over what is an acceptable alternative. For example, in religious exercise cases, some courts have said that if one religious practice is restricted, the ability to engage in other religious practices is an alternative means of exercising the First Amendment right of religious exercise.[50] Others have

---

cannot justify serious restrictions); Monmouth County Correctional Institution Inmates v. Lanzaro, 834 F.2d 326, 338 (3d Cir. 1987) (restrictions on abortion were not rationally related to security where jail officials did not apply them to other outside medical procedures); Berrios-Berrios v. Thornburgh, 716 F. Supp. 987, 990 (E.D.Ky. 1989) (ban on breast-feeding in a visiting room where bottle-feeding was allowed was not rational); Langone v. Coughlin, 712 F. Supp. 1061, 1067 (N.D.N.Y. 1989) (statute that prevented prisoners with life sentences from marrying, but did not invalidate already existing marriages, did not rationally serve interests in punishment, regulation of marriage and support, or clarification of marital status).

[41] Canadian Coalition against the Death Penalty v. Ryan, 269 F. Supp. 2d 1199, 1202 (D.Ariz. 2003) (forbidding prisoners to communicate with communication service providers lacked a rational connection with goals of preventing defrauding the public and inappropriate contact with minors, victims, or other prisoners because these were already served by multiple other means).

[42] Quinn v. Nix, 983 F.2d 115, 118 (8th Cir. 1993) (restrictions on inmates' haircuts were not justified by their interest in curtailing gang activity because that was not the actual motivation for the restrictions); Williams v. Lane, 851 F.2d 867, 872–73 (7th Cir. 1988) (court need not defer to prison officials' views if they are unworthy of belief); Wares v. vanBebber, 319 F. Supp. 2d 1237, 1248–50 (D.Kan. 2004) (holding "defendants are not entitled to the deference afforded to them under the Turner framework if their conduct was not actually motivated by legitimate penological interests at the time they acted"; citing other cases rejecting pretextual justifications); see Swift v. Lewis, 901 F.2d 730, 731–32 (9th Cir. 1990) (prison officials must submit evidence that the interests they cite are the actual reasons for the policy).

[43] Shaw v. Murphy, 532 U.S. 223, 229–30, 121 S. Ct. 1475 (2001); Canadian Coalition against the Death Penalty v. Ryan, 269 F. Supp. 2d 1199, 1203 (D.Ariz. 2003).

[44] Beard v. Banks, 548 U.S. 521, 533, 126 S. Ct. 2572 (2006) (plurality opinion) ("The real task . . . is . . . determining whether the Secretary [of Corrections] shows more than simply a logical relation, that is, whether he shows a reasonable relation." (emphasis in original)).

[45] See Walker v. Sumner, 917 F.2d 382, 387 (9th Cir. 1990) (stating that training of state health care workers would be a "highly dubious" justification for mandatory AIDS testing); Goodwin v. Turner, 908 F.2d 1395, 1399 n.7 (8th Cir. 1990) (stating that concerns such as decreasing welfare rolls were not legitimate penological interests); Monmouth County Correctional Institution Inmates v. Lanzaro, 834 F.2d 326, 342–43 (3d Cir. 1987) (holding abortion restrictions were not justified by state's interest in childbirth because that interest does not further rehabilitation, security, or deterrence); Langone v. Coughlin, 712 F. Supp. 1061, 1066 n.6 (N.D.N.Y. 1989) (questioning whether regulation of marriage and

support and the clarification of marital status are legitimate penological interests); see also Turner v. Safley, 482 U.S. 78, 98–99, 107 S. Ct. 2254 (1987) (striking down ban on marriage, noting officials' rehabilitation concern was "suspect" where applied with paternalism towards women).

[46] See Freeman v. Texas Dep't of Criminal Justice, 369 F.3d 854, 860–62 (5th Cir. 2004) (holding rule classifying Church of Christ as part of the Christian non-Catholic "major faith sub-group," rather than recognizing it as a separate entity, was neutral because it did not target that church or favor one group over another). Bahrampour v. Lampert, 356 F.3d 969, 976 (9th Cir. 2004) ("These categorical restrictions [on publications] are neutral because they target the effects of the particular types of materials, rather than simply prohibiting broad selections of innocuous materials."). Policies must be neutral as applied, as well as facially, to pass muster under the Turner standard. Mayfield v. Texas Dep't of Criminal Justice, 529 F.3d 599, 608–09 (5th Cir. 2008).

[47] Salaam v. Lockhart, 905 F.2d 1168, 1174–75 (8th Cir. 1990) (rejecting officials' refusal to acknowledge name changes that were allowed by state law); Salahuddin v. Harris, 657 F. Supp. 369, 376–77 (S.D.N.Y. 1987) (where state statutes and regulations protected an inmate's right to write to state officials about officers' misconduct, the inmate's action "was compatible with New York's penological objectives at the time of the communication"), adhered to, 684 F. Supp. 1224 (S.D.N.Y. 1988).

[48] The Second Circuit has noted that when the challenge is to a discrete action by prison staff, as opposed to a regulation or policy, "a failure to abide by established procedures or standards can evince an improper objective." Shakur v. Selsky, 391 F.3d 106, 116 (2d Cir. 2004).

[49] Turner, 482 U.S. at 90; see Lindell v. Frank, 377 F.3d 655, 659–60 (7th Cir. 2004) (holding that prisoner did not have an alternative to receiving clippings in the mail because he was in a restrictive unit and denied access to the prison library, and subscriptions were not a meaningful alternative because he would not know in advance what to subscribe to); Allen v. Coughlin, 64 F.3d 77, 80 (2d Cir. 1995) (striking down ban on clippings enclosed in correspondence, noting that subscriptions and inter-library loan were not shown to be adequate alternatives); Monmouth County Correctional Institution Inmates v. Lanzaro, 834 F.2d at 338–39 (no alternative to timely abortions); Langone v. Coughlin, 712 F. Supp. at 1068 (no way to exercise the right to marry other than by marrying).

[50] See O'Lone v. Estate of Shabazz, 482 U.S. 342, 351–52, 107 S. Ct. 2400 (1987) (upholding exclusion of Muslim prisoners from Jumu'ah services during working hours, in part because they could engage in congregate prayer or religious discussion at other times, they received pork-free meals, Ramadan observance was

refused to require prisoners to sacrifice important elements of their religious practice just because there were other religious observances still available to them.[51] The same issue arises with reading material: if prisoners are denied the right to read what they want, is it a sufficient alternative to let them read something else?[52] The absence of any alternative

for the prisoner does not, however, necessarily invalidate the challenged practice.[53]

(d) Prisoners can try to show that accommodating their rights will not have much effect on prison operations.[54] Conversely, if doing so will have a "significant 'ripple effect' on fellow inmates or on prison staff," prisoners are less likely to prevail.[55]

---

accommodated, etc.); Baranowski v. Hart, 486 F.3d 112, 121 (5th Cir. 2007) (ability to worship in one's cell using religious materials, and to access the chapel and lockers containing religious materials on certain days and times, constituted an alternative for prisoners excluded from congregate services), *cert. denied*, 128 S. Ct. 707 (2007); Fraise v. Terhune, 283 F.3d 506, 519 (3d Cir. 2002) (holding that Five Percenters seeking to study religious material that was banned had alternatives because the Bible and Koran are also acknowledged as "lessons" by the Five Percenters and they were allowed to "discuss [] and seek[] to achieve self-knowledge, self-respect, responsible conduct, [and] righteous living."); DeHart v. Horn, 227 F.3d 47, 54 (3d Cir. 1999) (holding that a Buddhist denied a religious diet had alternatives because he was permitted to pray, to recite the Sutras, to meditate, to correspond with the City of 10,000 Buddhas, a center of Buddhist teaching, and to purchase non-leather sneakers); Goff v. Graves, 362 F.3d 543, 549–50 (8th Cir. 2004) (upholding refusal to allow food trays prepared for religious banquet to be delivered to members in segregation unit; noting that members could practice other aspects of their religion).

[51] *See* Beerheide v. Suthers, 286 F.3d 1179, 1188–89 (10th Cir. 2002) (holding plaintiffs denied a kosher diet lacked alternative ways of maintaining a kosher diet; paying for it themselves was not an alternative because even those with some money would have to sacrifice communication with family and legal representatives to pay for the food); Flagner v. Wilkinson, 241 F.3d 475, 486 (6th Cir. 2001) (holding that a Jewish prisoner required to cut his beard and sidelocks had no alternatives because no other aspects of his religion could compensate for having to violate an essential tenet); Washington v. Garcia, 977 F. Supp. 1067, 1073 (S.D.Cal. 1997) (refusing to accept fasting and praying as an alternative to receiving Muslim diet during Ramadan; under that approach, the alternatives factor "would have no meaning because an inmate would always be able to pray privately"). In *Sutton v. Rasheed*, 323 F.3d 236, 255–56 (3d Cir. 2003), the court held that members of the Nation of Islam did not have alternatives when deprived of religious texts "which provide critical religious instruction and without which they could not practice their religion generally." The court distinguished its own decision in *Fraise v. Terhune* (cited in previous note), stating that the materials that the Five Percenters in *Fraise* were denied lacked the "sacrosanct and fundamental quality which the writings of the prophet, Elijah Muhammad, or the writings of Minister Farrakhan, have for members of one or another sect of the Nation of Islam." 323 F.3d at 255.

[52] *See* Ramirez v. Pugh, 379 F.3d 122, 130 n.4 (3d Cir. 2004) (prisoners denied "sexually explicit" material have the alternative of reading something else); Bahrampour v. Lampert, 356 F.3d 969, 976 (9th Cir. 2004) (a plaintiff denied role-playing materials can play or read about chess, and can receive bodybuilding publications without the simulated sexual activity in magazines he was denied); Chriceol v. Phillips, 169 F.3d 313, 316 (5th Cir. 1999) (the right to read other materials was an alternative for a prisoner who wanted Aryan Nations material); Giano v. Senkowski, 54 F.3d 1050, 1056 (2d Cir. 1995) ("If Giano's right is framed as the right to

graphic sexual imagery to satisfy carnal desires and expressions, commercially produced erotica and sexually graphic written notes from wives or girlfriends are adequate substitutes for semi-nude personal photographs. If, on the other hand, the right is seen as reinforcing the emotional bond between loved ones and similar affective links, conventional photographs and romantic letters would adequately satisfy this need."); *see also* Morrison v. Hall, 261 F.3d 896, 904 and n.6 (9th Cir. 2001) (prisoners challenging a ban on magazines sent by third and fourth class mail had no alternative because they could not make publishers use different mailing rates, radio and TV are not alternatives to reading, and many prisoners can't afford higher rates anyway); Allen v. Coughlin, 64 F.3d 77, 80 (2d Cir. 1995) (subscriptions and interlibrary loan were not necessarily adequate alternatives to receiving newspaper clippings in correspondence).

[53] Beard v. Banks, 548 U.S. 521, 532, 126 S. Ct. 2572 (2006) (plurality opinion).

Some courts have rather extreme ideas of what constitutes an alternative. In *Fontroy v. Beard*, 559 F.3d 173 (3d Cir. 2009), the court upheld a policy requiring courts and lawyers to obtain a "control number" in order to have their mail to prisoners treated as privileged. The court said that getting a control number was an alternative even though many lawyers and all courts refused to get one. It stated: "We acknowledge that these problems make the DOC's new mail policy a less-than-ideal means of accommodating the Inmates' important First Amendment rights. . . . Alternatives . . . need not be ideal, . . .; they need only be available." *Fontroy*, 559 F.3d at 180–81 (citation and internal quotation marks omitted). The court did not explain how an alternative can be "available" when the prisoner has no way of taking advantage of it.

[54] Turner v. Safley, 482 U.S. 78, 90, 107 S. Ct. 2254 (1987); *see* Jacklovich v. Simmons, 392 F.3d 420, 431–32 (10th Cir. 2004) (delivering gift publications would not be unduly burdensome since prison officials already delivered other publications and expended significant time and effort tracking receipt of other publications); Lindell v. Frank, 377 F.3d 655, 659–60 (7th Cir. 2004) (allowing prisoners to receive clippings in the mail would not unduly burden prison staff because they already inspected the mail); Mayweathers v. Newland, 258 F.3d 930, 938 (9th Cir. 2001) (allowing absence of Muslims from work assignments for Jumu'ah services had no "ripple effect"; they were just marked absent but not penalized); Canadian Coalition against the Death Penalty v. Ryan, 269 F. Supp. 2d 1199, 1202 (D.Ariz. 2003) (forbidding prisoners to communicate with communication service providers was not necessary because goals of preventing defrauding the public and inappropriate contact with minors, victims, or other prisoners were served by other statutes and regulations and means to enforce them).

[55] *Turner*, 482 U.S. at 90; *see, e.g.*, Oliver v. Scott, 276 F.3d 736, 746 (5th Cir. 2002) (holding that ending cross-sex surveillance in bathrooms and showers would have "ripple effect" of reassignment of staff, with cost to security and gender equity of staff).

(e) Prisoners can try to show that there are "obvious, easy alternative" for prison officials to the challenged policy or practice—that is, they "can point to an alternative that fully accommodates the prisoner's rights at *de minimis* cost to valid penological interests."[56] Courts do not agree on exactly what *de minimis* cost means.[57]

[56]*Turner*, 482 U.S. at 90–91; *see Turner, id.* at 98 (permitting women inmates to marry would be easy for prison officials); Shakur v. Selsky, 391 F.3d 106, 115–16 (2d Cir. 2004) (questioning whether a ban on all materials from "unauthorized organizations" was rationally related to maintaining security, since officials had the obvious alternative of sending the materials to the already-existing Media Review Committee for individual examination pursuant to established procedures); Morrison v. Hall, 261 F.3d 896, 905 (9th Cir. 2001) (the easy, obvious alternative to banning third and fourth class mail because of a concern for "junk mail" is to distinguish between junk mail and magazine subscriptions); Hakim v. Hicks, 223 F.3d 1244, 1249 (11th Cir. 2000) (adding religious names to ID cards was a *de minimis* cost alternative); Benjamin v. Coughlin, 905 F.2d 571, 576–77 (2d Cir. 1990) (a requirement of intake haircuts for Rastafarians for purposes of ID photos was unconstitutional because taking the photo with the hair held back was a nearly costless alternative); Salaam v. Lockhart, 905 F.2d 1168, 1173-74 (8th Cir. 1990) (permitting use of Muslim names with "a/k/a" designations was an "obvious, easy alternative" to banning them entirely); Monmouth County Correctional Institution Inmates v. Lanzaro, 834 F.2d 326, 341-42 (3d Cir. 1987) (providing abortions to pregnant prisoners was no more burdensome than providing medical care for childbirth); Williams v. Bitner, 359 F. Supp. 2d 370, 378–79 (M.D.Pa. 2005) (disciplining a Muslim prisoner who refused to help prepare pork could violate the First Amendment where officials had the alternative of simply removing him from his job), *aff'd*, 455 F.3d 186 (3d Cir. 2006). *Compare* Hammons v. Saffle, 348 F.3d 1250, 1257 (10th Cir. 2003) (there was no *de minimis* cost alternative to prohibiting possession of Muslim oils in cells; the lack of incident under the former permissive policy did not establish that nothing bad would happen in the future); Nasir v. Morgan, 350 F.3d 366, 373 (3d Cir. 2003) (there was no easy, obvious alternative to banning correspondence with former prisoners; prison staff would have to read the mail); Onishea v. Hopper, 171 F.3d 1289, 1301 (11th Cir. 1999) (en banc) (holding that excluding potentially violent prisoners rather than HIV-positive prisoners from programs, in order to avoid exposure to HIV-infected blood, was not an "easy alternative"); Giano v. Senkowski, 54 F.3d 1050, 1056 (2d Cir. 1995) (prohibiting display and sharing of nude or semi-nude photos of loved ones was not an obvious, easy alternative to banning the photos entirely because imposing it would disregard prison officials' judgment and it would require "difficult line-drawing"); Covino v. Patrissi, 967 F.2d 73 (2d Cir. 1992) (strip searches on reasonable suspicion were not an easy, obvious alternative because foregoing random searches would affect security); Nolley v. County of Erie, 776 F. Supp. 715, 736, 741 (W.D.N.Y. 1991) (when jail officials violated their own regulations, or later changed their regulations to accommodate prisoners, following the regulations constituted an alternative to restricting the plaintiff's rights).

[57]Thus, one court held that there was no *de minimis* cost alternative for providing 225 Muslims with Halal food where it would cost $280 a year apiece, even though officials spent $3650 a year per person for kosher food for observant Jews, since the number of

The *Turner* analysis has been made more complicated by the recent Supreme Court decision in *Beard v. Banks*, which upheld the denial of magazines, newspapers, and photographs to prisoners in a high-security unit.[58] *Beard* holds that prison officials' desire to provide incentives (i.e., make things worse) for difficult prisoners, so maybe they will behave better in the future, is a legitimate interest that may justify restrictions on constitutional rights.[59] Some Justices expressed the concern that this interest cannot sensibly be analyzed using the *Turner* factors: "This justification has no limiting principle; if sufficient, it would provide a 'rational basis' for any regulation that deprives a prisoner of a constitutional right so long as there is at least a theoretical possibility that the prisoner can regain the right at some future time by modifying his behavior." Further, "there could never be a 'ready alternative' for furthering the government interest, because the government interest is tied directly to depriving the prisoner of the constitutional right at issue."[60] The plurality in *Beard* acknowledged this point, stating: "In fact, the second, third, and fourth factors [of the *Turner* analysis], being in a sense logically related to the [restriction on rights] itself, here add little, one way or another, to the first factor's basic logical rationale. . . . The real task in this case is not balancing these factors, but rather determining whether the [defendant] shows more than simply a logical relation, that is, whether he shows a reasonable relation."[61] The Court did not explain how courts are to make that determination if the *Turner* factors do not work.

It is not clear how far the reasoning of *Beard* will be taken. In theory, prison officials could use it to try to make prison life as unpleasant as possible for everyone, and claim doing so was reasonably related to the legitimate interests in rehabilitation and deterrence, since released prisoners

Jews was much smaller. Williams v. Morton, 343 F.3d 212, 217–18 (3d Cir. 2002). In another case brought by observant Jews, however, a different court compared the amount of money involved in providing them with kosher food to the total food service budget of the Department of Corrections, holding that $13,000 a year would have *de minimis* impact because it amounted to 0.158% of an $8.25 million total budget. Beerheide v. Suthers, 286 F.3d 1179, 1191–92 (10th Cir. 2002).

A particularly extreme weighing of costs and alternatives appears in *Kimberlin v. U.S. Dep't of Justice*, 318 F.3d 228 (D.C. Cir.), *rehearing denied*, 351 F.3d 1166 (D.C. Cir. 2003), in which a statute barring prisoners' use or possession of electrical musical instruments was held justified under the first three *Turner* factors—and by implication the fourth factor as well—by the costs of electricity, storage, upkeep, and supervision.

[58]Beard v. Banks, 548 U.S. 521, 126 S. Ct. 2572 (2006).

[59]*Beard*, 548 U.S. at 530–32 (plurality opinion).

[60]*Beard*, 548 U.S. at 547 (Stevens, J., dissenting); *accord*, Kimberlin v. U.S. Dep't of Justice, 318 F.3d 228, 239–40 (D.C. Cir.) (concurring and dissenting opinion), *rehearing denied*, 351 F.3d 1166 (D.C. Cir. 2003) (noting incompatibility of punitive rationale and *Turner* standard); Jewell v. Gonzales, 420 F. Supp. 2d 406, 424–27 (W.D.Pa. 2006) (same).

[61]*Beard*, 548 U.S. at 532–33.

might try harder to stay out of prison. The *Beard* Court did emphasize that the measures it upheld were imposed only upon "those with serious prison-behavior problems (here the 40 most intractable inmates in [Pennsylvania]),"[62] and it may be possible to restrict its reasoning to cases involving punitive and administrative segregation units.

B. FREEDOM OF EXPRESSION

The First Amendment forbids laws "abridging the freedom of speech, or of the press; or the right of the people peaceably to assemble, and to petition the Government for a redress of grievances."[63] Prisoners retain these rights, but they are significantly restricted in prison.

1. Correspondence

Prisoners have a First Amendment right to communicate by mail,[64] and non-prisoners also have a First Amendment right to correspond with prisoners.[65] However, these rights may be restricted by prison officials.[66]

Prison officials have greater power to restrict, inspect, and censor "general" correspondence (like letters to and from family members, friends, and businesses) than "privileged" correspondence (like attorney–client mail and some other legal and governmental mail).

a. General Correspondence Prison officials can restrict *incoming* correspondence from prisoners' family and friends if the restrictions are "reasonably related" to legitimate interests, but restrictions on *outgoing* correspondence cannot be greater than "necessary or essential" to protect "important or substantial" interests.[67] This difference in legal standards between incoming and outgoing mail is sometimes overlooked,[68] so be sure to call it to the court's attention if your case involves outgoing mail.

Courts have struck down a variety of restrictions on prisoners' general correspondence. Several courts have held that requiring prior approval of everyone you correspond with is unconstitutional;[69] using a "negative mail list" to forbid you from corresponding with particular individuals is not.[70] Others have struck down prohibitions on writing to religious leaders,[71] minors,[72] former correctional

---

[62]*Beard*, 548 U.S. at 533.

[63]U.S.Const., Amend. I.

Technically, the First Amendment only restricts Congress, but it has long been interpreted to forbid restrictions of free speech by all agencies of government. *See* Fiske v. Kansas, 274 U.S. 380, 386–87 (1927).

[64]Davis v. Goord, 320 F.3d 346, 351 (2d Cir. 2003); Morrison v. Hall, 261 F.3d 896, 906 (9th Cir. 2001); Zimmerman v. Tribble, 226 F.3d 568, 572 (7th Cir. 2000).

[65]Procunier v. Martinez, 416 U.S. 396, 408–09, 94 S. Ct. 1800 (1974); Nasir v. Morgan, 350 F.3d 366, 369 n.3 (3d Cir. 2003); Rowe v. Shake, 196 F.3d 778, 783 (7th Cir. 1999).

The Supreme Court in *Procunier* ruled based on the rights of the outside correspondents and not the prisoner, stating that their rights were "inextricably intertwined" and there was no issue of the prisoner's standing to assert the correspondent's rights. Procunier v. Martinez, 416 U.S. at 409. Some later decisions have limited the extent of prisoners' and their correspondents' ability to assert their rights, but have not disturbed the basic idea that both prisoner and correspondent have First Amendment rights to communicate with each other. *See* Nasir v. Morgan, 350 F.3d at 369 n.3, 376 (holding prisoner could assert outside correspondent's First Amendment rights but not due process rights); Massey v. Helman, 221 F.3d 1030, 1034–37 (7th Cir. 2000) (holding outside correspondent could not assert prisoner's correspondence rights, but ruling on the merits of correspondent's own claim); Rowe v. Shake, 196 F.3d at 783 (outside correspondent had standing to assert his own First Amendment rights in complaining about delays in delivery of his letters to prisoners).

[66]A federal statute that prohibits obstructing correspondence does not apply to prison mail restrictions. Crofton v. Roe, 170 F.3d 957, 961 (9th Cir. 1999) (citing 18 U.S.C. § 1702); *see* U.S. v. Felipe, 148 F.3d 101, 108–09 (2d Cir. 1998) (noting that federal postal regulations contain an exemption for prisons that makes mail delivery subject to prison rules).

[67]Thornburgh v. Abbott, 490 U.S. 401, 413–14, 109 S. Ct. 1874 (1989); Procunier v. Martinez, 416 U.S. 396, 413–14, 94 S. Ct. 1800 (1974); Barrett v. Belleque, 544 F.3d 1060, 1062 (9th Cir. 2008); Nasir v. Morgan, 350 F.3d 366, 373 (3d Cir. 2003) (applying the two standards); Martucci v. Johnson, 944 F.2d 291, 295–96 (6th Cir. 1991).

[68]*See* Woods v. O'Leary, 890 F.2d 883, 885–87 (7th Cir. 1989) (erroneously applying the *Turner* reasonableness standard in an outgoing mail case); Canadian Coalition against the Death Penalty v. Ryan, 269 F. Supp. 2d 1199, 1201–02 (D.Ariz. 2003) (assessing rule against communicating with Internet service providers under *Turner*).

Several federal circuits have affirmatively held that *Turner* is applicable to outgoing correspondence. *See* Samford v. Dretke, 562 F.3d 674, 679 (5th Cir. 2009) (stating that *Procunier/Thornburgh* standard is limited to assessing security risk of outgoing correspondence); Ortiz v. Fort Dodge Correctional Facility, 368 F.3d 1024, 1026 n.2 (8th Cir. 2004) (stating that *Thornburgh* merely "left open the possibility" of applying a stricter standard); Altizer v. Deeds, 191 F.3d 540, 548 (4th Cir. 1999); Blaise v. Fenn, 48 F.3d 337, 339 n.4 (8th Cir. 1995). We believe these holdings are contrary to *Thornburgh v. Abbott*.

[69]Guajardo v. Estelle, 580 F.2d 748, 754–55 (5th Cir. 1978); Finney v. Arkansas Board of Correction, 505 F.2d 194, 211–212 (8th Cir. 1974); Intersimone v. Carlson, 512 F. Supp. 526, 531 (M.D.Pa. 1980); Powlowski v. Wullich, 81 Misc.2d 895, 366 N.Y.S.2d 584, 591 (N.Y.Sup.Ct. 1975). *Contra*, Savage v. Snow, 575 F. Supp. 828, 835–36 (S.D.N.Y. 1983); *see also* Woods v. O'Leary, 890 F.2d at 885–88 (prison officials could bar correspondence about establishing a Universal Life Church congregation until the plaintiff complied with regulations requiring approval of inmate business ventures and submission of information about the business).

[70]Samford v. Dretke, 562 F.3d 674, 680 (5th Cir. 2009) (citing Jones v. Diamond, 594 F.2d 997, 1014 (5th Cir. 1979)).

[71]Walker v. Blackwell, 411 F.2d 23, 29 (5th Cir. 1969) (Elijah Muhammad); Peek v. Ciccone, 288 F. Supp. 329, 333–34 (W.D.Mo. 1968) (the Pope).

[72]Hearn v. Morris, 526 F. Supp. 267, 269–72 (E.D.Cal. 1981). The court held that requiring the parents' prior consent was unconstitutional, but that if the parents objected the correspondence

officers,[73] and persons the prisoner did not know before he was incarcerated.[74] Prisoners are also entitled to correspond with the media[75] and with communication service providers.[76] Correspondence with family members may be prohibited where there is a good enough correctional reason.[77]

Other restrictions have been upheld. Correspondence between prisoners may generally be prohibited,[78] and if permitted is subject to reasonable restriction.[79] Inmate–inmate correspondence providing legal assistance enjoys no more constitutional protection than other inmate–inmate correspondence.[80] Prisons may forbid corresponding with persons who have been released from prison.[81]

Prisoners may be forbidden to communicate with victims, witnesses, or jurors in their criminal cases, or subjected to other restrictions that are rationally related to their criminal convictions or pending charges.[82] They may be limited to corresponding only with identified individuals, barring them from responding to "personal" advertisements or using "pen pal" correspondence services.[83] They may be forbidden to write to people who have requested not to get mail from them.[84]

The Constitution permits incoming non-privileged mail to be opened outside the inmate's presence.[85] Prison officials can also read non-privileged mail for security or other correctional purposes without probable cause and without obtaining a warrant,[86] although some courts have

---

could be stopped. *But see* Lucas v. Scully, 71 N.Y.2d 401, 408, 526 N.Y.S.2d 927, 932 (N.Y. 1988) (state regulations required prior approval of correspondence with unrelated minors).

[73]Stevens v. Ralston, 674 F.2d 759, 760–61 (8th Cir. 1982). The court cited the "special facts of the case," including the facts that the prisoner involved was paraplegic and unlikely to escape.

[74]Owen v. Lash, 682 F.2d 648, 650–53 (7th Cir. 1982).

[75]*See* § B.4 of this chapter.

[76]Canadian Coalition against the Death Penalty v. Ryan, 269 F. Supp. 2d 1199, 1202–03 (D.Ariz. 2003).

[77]Samford v. Dretke, 562 F.3d 674, 680–82 (5th Cir. 2009) (upholding bar on prisoner's communicating with his children where he had assaulted their mother in their presence).

[78]Turner v. Safley, 482 U.S. 78, 91–93, 107 S. Ct. 2254 (1987); Purnell v. Lord, 952 F.2d 679, 682–83 (2d Cir. 1992) (upholding suspension of inmate–inmate correspondence based on one inmate's threatening letter); Farrell v. Peters, 951 F.2d 862, 863 (7th Cir. 1991) (correspondence between plaintiff and his imprisoned "common law wife" could be banned).

[79]*See* Lindell v. Casperson, 360 F. Supp. 2d 932, 955 (W.D.Wis. 2005) (upholding refusal to deliver inmate–inmate letters about Wotanism because they contained contraband and concerned an activity which would violate the law), *aff'd*, 169 Fed.Appx. 999 (7th Cir. 2006) (unpublished); Maberry v. McKune, 24 F. Supp. 2d 1222, 1228 (D.Kan. 1998) (upholding censorship of inmate–inmate correspondence concerning blood sacrifices).

[80]Shaw v. Murphy, 532 U.S. 223, 230, 121 S. Ct. 1475 (2001). *But see* Goff v. Nix, 113 F.3d 887, 892 (8th Cir. 1997) (upholding policy prohibiting legal correspondence between prisoners at different facilities, but requiring officials to provide for returning documents to their owners when the prisoner in possession of them is transferred).

Earlier, one federal appeals court had held that a complete prohibition on corresponding with a prison "writ writer" violated the First Amendment. Storseth v. Spellman, 654 F.2d 1349, 1355–56 (9th Cir. 1981). That holding is doubtful after *Shaw*. Storseth also held that such correspondence is not privileged and can be read by prison officials. 654 F.2d at 1356. *See* Gometz v. Henman, 807 F.2d 113, 115–16 (7th Cir. 1986) (a jailhouse lawyer and his "client" who had been involved in joint criminal activity could be kept from corresponding); Weaver v. Toombs, 756 F. Supp. 335, 338–40 (W.D.Mich. 1989) (inmate–inmate legal correspondence could be confiscated where the prisoners failed to follow prison policies governing legal assistance), *aff'd*, 915 F.2d 1574 (6th Cir. 1990).

[81]Nasir v. Morgan, 350 F.3d 366, 370–76 (3d Cir. 2003).

[82]Samford v. Dretke, 562 F.3d 674, 680 (5th Cir. 2009) (upholding bar on correspondence with children where prisoner had assaulted their mother in their presence; "Prisons have a legitimate interest in protecting crime victims and their families from the unwanted communications of prisoners when a victim requests that the prison prevent such communications."); U.S. v. Felipe, 148 F.3d 101, 109–11 (2d Cir. 1998) (affirming criminal sentence containing drastic restrictions on correspondence rights of gang leader who had used the mail for illegal purposes while incarcerated); Wheeler v. U.S., 640 F.2d 1116, 1123–26 (9th Cir. 1981); U.S. v. Flores, 214 F. Supp. 2d 1193, 1197 (D.Utah 2002) (court requires correspondence of defendant in gang–related prosecution to be read for threats, conspiracy, criminal plots or obstruction efforts); Intersimone v. Carlson, 512 F. Supp. 526, 530–33 (M.D.Pa. 1980). *But see* U.S. v. Holloway, 740 F.2d 1373, 1383 (6th Cir. 1984) (a defendant convicted of a fraudulent scheme involving communication with prisoners could be barred from communicating with prisoners as a condition of probation; during her six months' incarceration, a ban on communicating with *anyone* except relatives, legal counselors, and "other recognized counselors" was overbroad).

In all of the foregoing cases, the restriction was imposed by, or at the request of, a court rather than prison officials.

[83]Rodriguez v. Ames, 224 F. Supp. 2d 555, 565 (W.D.N.Y. 2002); Lucas v. Scully, 71 N.Y.2d 401, 408, 526 N.Y.S.2d 927, 932 (N.Y. 1988).

[84]Berdella v. Delo, 972 F.2d 204, 209 (8th Cir. 1992); Guajardo v. Estelle, 580 F.2d 748, 755 & n.4 (5th Cir. 1978); Malsh v. Garcia, 971 F. Supp. 133, 137–38 (S.D.N.Y. 1997) (upholding discipline of prisoner who communicated with a person on his "negative correspondence list"); Hardwick v. Ault, 447 F. Supp. 116, 129 (M.D.Ga. 1978).

[85]Martin v. Tyson, 845 F.2d 1451, 1456–57 (5th Cir. 1988); Bumgarner v. Bloodworth, 768 F.2d 297, 301 (8th Cir. 1985); Mosby v. Mabry, 697 F.2d 213, 215 (8th Cir. 1982); Word v. Croce, 230 F. Supp. 2d 504, 514 (S.D.N.Y. 2002) (non-legal mail could be opened outside prisoner's presence), *reconsideration denied*, 2004 WL 434038 (S.D.N.Y., Mar. 9, 2004).

[86]Duamutef v. Hollins, 297 F.3d 108, 113 (2d Cir. 2002) (upholding 30-day "mail watch" involving stopping, opening, and reading all plaintiff's non-privileged correspondence); Beville v. Ednie, 74 F.3d 210, 213–14 (10th Cir. 1996) (reading outgoing non-legal mail without cause was not unconstitutional); Smith v. Boyd, 945 F.2d 1041, 1043 (8th Cir. 1991); U.S. v. Brown, 878 F.2d 222, 225–26 (8th Cir. 1989) (mail could be read with "reasonable justification," which was provided by evidence that the prisoner was a suicide risk); Rodriguez v. James, 823 F.2d 8, 11–13 (2d Cir. 1987) (upholding a requirement that outgoing "business mail" must be left unsealed); U.S. v. Kelton, 791 F.2d 101, 103 (8th Cir. 1986); Gaines v. Lane, 790 F.2d 1299, 1304

restricted the reading of outgoing mail.[87] Thus, if you or your correspondents are so foolish as to discuss criminal activities in letters, the letters can and probably will be used in a criminal prosecution.[88] In some states, statutes

or regulations limit the reading of prisoners' general correspondence.[89] These may be enforceable in state court.[90]

Outgoing non-privileged letters cannot be censored except to serve important correctional interests, and the censorship cannot be any more restrictive than necessary.[91] Prison officials may not censor letters or punish or retaliate against prisoners just because they criticize prison conditions or personnel or offend them in some way,[92] though if your correspondence contains serious abuse, courts will not be sympathetic and may find a different way to look at the case and rule against you.[93]

(7th Cir. 1986) (all non-privileged mail may be "spot checked and read"); Meadows v. Hopkins, 713 F.2d 206, 209–11 (6th Cir. 1983); Guajardo v. Estelle, 580 F.2d at 756–57; Feeley v. Sampson, 570 F.2d 364, 374 (1st Cir. 1978); Smith v. Shimp, 562 F.2d 423, 426 (7th Cir. 1977); Oliver v. Powell, 250 F. Supp. 2d 593, 606–08 (E.D.Va. 2002) (prison could require prisoners to consent to inspection and reading of general correspondence before it would be delivered); DiRose v. McClennan, 26 F. Supp. 2d 550, 554 (W.D.N.Y. 1998) ("mail watch" was justified based on finding the plaintiff with letters discussing escape plans); Sumlin v. State, 260 Ark. 709, 587 S.W.2d 571 (Ark. 1979); Gross v. State, 460 N.W.2d 882, 884 (Iowa App. 1990); State v. Dunn, 478 So.2d 659, 663 (La.App. 1985); State v. Cuypers, 481 N.W.2d 553, 555–56 (Minn. 1992) (upholding regulation permitting reading of outgoing non-legal mail); see also Nakao v. Rushen, 635 F. Supp. 1362, 1365 (N.D.Cal. 1986) (personal letters seized and read in cell search could not be sent to a third party, but official letters could be sent to the agency from which they were sent). But see Heimerle v. Attorney General, 753 F.2d 10, 13–14 (2d Cir. 1985) (questioning security justification for reading mail).

[87]Wolfish v. Levi, 573 F.2d 118, 130 (2d Cir. 1978), rev'd in part on other grounds sub nom. Bell v. Wolfish, 441 U.S. 520, 99 S. Ct. 1861 (1979); Martino v. Carey, 563 F. Supp. 984, 1004–05 (D.Or. 1983) (outgoing mail cannot be read); State v. Sheriff, 619 P.2d 181, 183 (Mont. 1980); see Oliver v. Powell, 250 F. Supp. 2d 593, 608–09 (E.D.Va. 2002) (upholding policy of reading outgoing mail upon reasonable suspicion of illegal activity, since policy was narrowly drawn and did not confer unchecked, subjective discretion); see also Jolivet v. Deland, 966 F.2d 573, 577–78 (10th Cir. 1992) (damages awarded against officials who copied prisoner's outgoing mail and showed it to another prisoner). But see Altizer v. Deeds, 191 F.3d 540, 548 (4th Cir. 1999) (Procunier's holding that some outgoing correspondence can be censored means that generally it can be read); Beville v. Ednie, 74 F.3d 210, 213–14 (10th Cir. 1996) (reading of outgoing non-legal mail without cause is not unconstitutional).

[88]See, e.g., U.S. v. Gordon, 168 F.3d 1222, 1228 (10th Cir. 1999) (holding non-prisoner had no expectation of privacy in a letter depicting him with large amounts of cash since it was sent to a prisoner); U.S. v. Felipe, 148 F.3d 101, 107–09 (2d Cir. 1998) (upholding use of prison correspondence in criminal trial); U.S. v. Whalen, 940 F.2d 1027, 1034–35 (7th Cir. 1991); U.S. v. Kelton, 791 F.2d at 102–03; U.S. v. Brown, 878 F.2d 222, 225–26 (8th Cir. 1989); U.S. v. Carrozza, 2 F. Supp. 2d 126, 127–28 (D.Mass. 1998) (prison could forward letter discussing criminal activity to law enforcement officials, who could use it in a criminal prosecution, even though prison's internal rules had been violated); Jeffers v. Ricketts, 627 F. Supp. 1334, 1345–46 (D.Ariz. 1986), aff'd in part, rev'd in part on other grounds, 832 F.2d 476 (9th Cir. 1987), rev'd on other grounds sub nom Lewis v. Jeffers, 479 U.S. 764 (1990); People v. Oaks, 216 Ill.App.3d 1072, 159 Ill.Dec. 630, 576 N.E.2d 299, 301 (Ill.App. 1991); see also Gross v. State, 460 N.W.2d 882, 884 (Iowa App. 1990) (prisoner disciplined for threats in an outgoing letter). But see U.S. v. Heatley, 41 F. Supp. 2d 284, 289 (S.D.N.Y. 1999) (stating prison authorities' right to read incoming non-legal mail "is not boundless," but refusing to suppress materials copied under a broad warrant authorizing copying of all prisoner's incoming and outgoing mail).

[89]See, e.g., In re Gonzales, 212 Cal.App.3d 459, 260 Cal.Rptr. 506, 507 (Cal.App. 1989) (citing Cal.Code Regs., Title 15, § 3138(a)); Matter of Rules Adoption Regarding Inmate Mail to Attorneys, etc., 120 N.J. 137, 576 A.2d 274, 275 (N.J. 1990) (citing N.J.A.C. § 10A:18–2.6(g)); Lucas v. Scully, 71 N.Y.2d 401, 408, 526 N.Y.S.2d 927, 930–31 (N.Y. 1988).

[90]Such regulations may create liberty interests enforceable in federal court. Martyr v. Mazur-Hart, 789 F. Supp. 1081, 1087 (D. Or. 1991) (state regulation providing that mental patients may freely send and receive sealed mail); Balabin v. Scully, 606 F. Supp. 176, 183 (S.D.N.Y. 1985) (regulation requiring "reasonable suspicion" to open outgoing mail).

[91]Procunier v. Martinez, 416 U.S. 396, 413, 94 S. Ct. 1800 (1974); see Thornburgh v. Abbott, 490 U.S. 401, 411–12, 109 S. Ct. 1874 (1989) (limiting Procunier to outgoing correspondence). As noted above, some courts have rejected this distinction between incoming and outgoing. See n.68 of this section.

[92]Procunier v. Martinez, 416 U.S. at 413–16 (striking down regulations that barred letters that "unduly complain," "magnify grievances," or express "inflammatory political, racial, religious or other views" or "defamatory matter"); Todaro v. Bowman, 872 F.2d 43, 49 (3d Cir. 1989); Brooks v. Andolina, 826 F.2d 1266, 1268 (3d Cir. 1987); Milonas v. Williams, 691 F.2d 931, 941–43 (10th Cir. 1982) (juvenile institution could not censor "negative thinking" and statements considered "untrue"); McNamara v. Moody, 606 F.2d 621, 623–24 (5th Cir. 1979) (nominal damages awarded for censorship of a letter accusing the mail censor of engaging in masturbation and having sex with a cat); Gee v. Ruettgers, 872 F. Supp. 915, 918 (D.Wyo. 1994) (holding prison officials failed to justify censorship of outgoing letter; they failed to explain how allegedly false information about prison conditions sent to a prisoner's family member threatened security and order); Hardwick v. Ault, 447 F. Supp. 116, 129 (M.D.Ga. 1978) (forbidding censorship of criticism of prison conditions, profanity, or obscenity); Cavey v. Levine, 435 F. Supp. 475, 481–83 (D.Md. 1977), aff'd sub nom. Cavey v. Williams, 580 F.2d 1047 (4th Cir. 1978).

[93]In Morgan v. Quarterman, 570 F.3d 663 (5th Cir. 2009), the prisoner sent a vulgar note on toilet paper to the Assistant Attorney General opposing his habeas petition, and another AAG returned it to the prison, which disciplined him. The court said that its earlier decision in McNamara v. Moody, cited in the previous footnote, did not apply, because in this case, unlike McNamara, prison officials had said punishing the prisoner served the interest in rehabilitation, and because the letter in McNamara was a private message to the prisoner's girlfriend and not to opposing counsel. Morgan, 570 F.3d at 666–67; see also Leonard v. Nix, 55 F.3d 370, 375 (8th Cir. 1995) (upholding discipline of prisoner for writing vulgar, obscene, and racist epithets against the prison warden in a

Officials may censor letters that contain gang symbols or references.[94]

Courts have upheld rules forbidding prisoners to solicit money or goods except from family members[95] and forbidding outgoing mail pertaining to inmate business ventures that had not been officially approved.[96]

Incoming letters may be censored if there is a reasonable relationship between the censorship and some legitimate correctional purpose.[97] In *Thornburgh v. Abbott*, the Supreme Court upheld the censorship of publications that are "detrimental to the security, good order, or discipline of the institution or . . . might facilitate criminal activity."[98] The courts have taken a similar approach to letters,[99] upholding censorship of mail containing threats, blackmail, extortion, escape plans, or code.[100] Courts have limited prison officials'

power to withhold mail that they think might disturb inmates.[101] The majority of courts that have considered the question have held that nude photographs may be barred from correspondence.[102] Prison officials may also bar chain letters.[103] Courts have struck down bans on receiving newspaper clippings[104] and any information downloaded from the Internet.[105]

The Constitution does not require free postage for non-legal mail.[106] Reasonable restrictions on the purchase of postage and supplies by non-indigent prisoners will be upheld.[107]

---

letter to an outside correspondent; they were not genuine communication with the correspondent but were really directed towards to prison staff); Wilder v. Tanouye, 71 Haw. 30, 779 P.2d 390, 393–94 (Haw. 1989) (threat to return prisoner to segregation based on letter to Congressman may have violated First Amendment, but damages could not be awarded after threat was rescinded).

[94]Koutnik v. Brown, 396 F. Supp. 2d 978, 984–86 (W.D.Wis. 2005) (upholding rule against mail that "teaches or advocates illegal activity, disruption, or behavior consistent with a gang or a violent ritualistic group"; ". . . [P]rison officials have every right to censor mail to the extent needed to prevent inmates from helping run, direct or support outside illegal activities, including outside gang activity."), *aff'd*, 189 Fed.Appx. 546 (7th Cir. 2006) (unpublished).

[95]Gaines v. Lane, 790 F.2d 1299, 1305 n.4 (7th Cir. 1986).

[96]Woods v. O'Leary, 890 F.2d 883, 885–87 (7th Cir. 1989). This decision erroneously applies the *Turner* reasonable relationship standard to outgoing mail.

[97]An example of an illegitimate purpose is "capricious interference . . . based upon a guard's personal prejudices." Parrish v. Johnson, 800 F.2d 600, 604 (6th Cir. 1986). A possible example of a lack of a reasonable relationship is prison officials' refusal to let a prisoner receive his original grade transcript and diploma from a school program in order to prevent forgery of documents, after many other inmates had been permitted to receive these items. Griffin v. Lombardi, 946 F.2d 604, 607–08 (8th Cir. 1991).

[98]Thornburgh v. Abbott, 490 U.S. 404, 419, 109 S. Ct. 1874 (1989).

[99]*See* Valiant-Bey v. Morris, 829 F.2d 1441, 1443–44 (8th Cir. 1987) (policy permitting censorship based on institutional security and employee and inmate safety is not overbroad); Martin v. Kelley, 803 F.2d 236, 242 (6th Cir. 1986) (upholding regulation prohibiting mail that is a "clear and present danger to institutional security"); Gaines v. Lane, 790 F.2d at 1304–05 (upholding regulation barring mail that threatens security or safety).

[100]Gaines v. Lane, *id.*; *accord*, Heimerle v. Attorney General, 558 F. Supp. 1292, 1296 (S.D.N.Y. 1983) (plans for escapes or other prohibited activities, conducting a business, threats, obscenity, code, contraband), *rev'd on other grounds*, 753 F.2d 10 (2d Cir. 1985); *see* Hallal v. Hopkins, 947 F. Supp. 978, 998 (S.D.Miss. 1995) (presence of a "foreign substance" in letters justified inspecting and confiscating them, but did not automatically justify refusal to deliver them unless the contraband was infused in the paper); *see also* Allen v. Wood, 970 F. Supp. 824, 831 (E.D.Wash. 1997)

(upholding ban on oversize greeting cards because of storage concerns and because they provided a place to hide contraband).

[101]Ramos v. Lamm, 639 F.2d 559, 581 (10th Cir. 1980) (mail cannot be censored on the ground that it will cause psychiatric or emotional disturbance except by qualified mental health personnel); Guajardo v. Estelle, 580 F.2d 748, 757 (5th Cir. 1978) (striking down practice of delaying "disturbing" mail until a chaplain or psychologist could be notified).

[102]The reason for this rule is to prevent violence that might occur when photos of one prisoner's nude spouse or lover are viewed by other prisoners. Giano v. Senkowski, 54 F.3d 1050, 1055–56 (2d Cir. 1995); Trapnell v. Riggsby, 622 F.2d 290, 293 (7th Cir. 1980); Hunter v. Koehler, 618 F. Supp. 13, 16–18 (W.D.Mich. 1984). *Contra*, Pepperling v. Crist, 678 F.2d 787, 790–91 (9th Cir. 1982); *see also* Thomas v. Scully, 943 F.2d 259, 260 (2d Cir. 1991) (a complaint that a ban on noncommercial nude photos violated the First Amendment was not frivolous).

[103]Smith v. Maschner, 899 F.2d 940, 944 (10th Cir. 1990).

[104]Lindell v. Frank, 377 F.3d 655, 658–60 (7th Cir. 2004); Allen v. Coughlin, 64 F.3d 77, 80–81 (2d Cir. 1995).

[105]Clement v. California Dep't of Corrections, 364 F.3d 1148 (9th Cir. 2004) (per curiam); *accord*, West v. Frank, 2005 WL 701703, *5–7 (W.D.Wis., Mar. 25, 2005). In *Clement*, the court rejected the claim that Internet materials presented special security risks, observing that prison officials didn't show that coded messages were more likely in Internet-generated materials than in other documents, and that it is usually easier to trace the origins of a printed e-mail than to track handwritten or typed mail. 364 F.3d at 1151–52. A couple of lower courts have upheld the rejection of Internet-generated materials based on prisons' rules allowing receipt of publications only from the publisher, a commercial vendor, or attorney of record. Williams v. Donald, 2007 WL 4287718, *4–7 (M.D.Ga., Dec. 4, 2007), *vacated as moot*, 322 Fed.Appx. 876 (11th Cir. 2009) (unpublished) (noting the case was moot because the regulation was amended); Waterman v. Commandant, U.S. Disciplinary Barracks, 337 F. Supp. 2d 1237, 1241–42 (D.Kan. 2004) (citing Rogers v. Morris, 34 Fed. Appx. 481 (7th Cir. 2002) (unpublished)).

[106]Johnson v. Goord, 445 F.3d 532, 535 (2d Cir. 2006) (per curiam) (holding that a rule prohibiting prisoners from receiving stamps through the mail and providing them only one free stamp a month for personal use did not violate rights of indigent prisoners); Van Poyck v. Singletary, 106 F.3d 1558, 1559 (11th Cir. 1997); Kaestel v. Lockhart, 746 F.2d 1323, 1325 (8th Cir. 1984); Everhart v. Shuler, 652 F. Supp. 1504, 1511 (N.D.Ind.), *aff'd*, 834 F.2d 173 (7th Cir. 1987).

[107]Davidson v. Mann, 129 F.3d 700, 702 (2d Cir. 1997) (upholding limit of 50 stamps every 2 weeks for non-legal mail).

b. Privileged Correspondence "Privileged" mail is entitled to greater confidentiality and freedom from censorship than general correspondence.[108] Mail to and from attorneys, courts, paralegals, and legal organizations must be treated as privileged,[109] at least when it is actually legal in nature.[110] Some federal courts have said that mail from courts, which consists of public documents, should not be considered privileged.[111] Other courts have rejected this view, correctly

in our view.[112] Mail addressed to other recipients does not become privileged just because it discusses legal subjects.[113] Some courts have also accorded privileged status to mail to and from various public officials and agencies of state, local, and federal government.[114] However, not all such mail is privileged; one court has recently held that the privilege "does not encompass 'general communications' with public officials that do not implicate the right to petition for [redress of] grievances and the right of access to the courts."[115] There is

---

[108]Evans v. Vare, 402 F. Supp. 2d 1188, 1194–96 (D.Nev. 2005) (holding restrictions on prisoners' legal mail are subject to heightened scrutiny and must be no greater than necessary to serve a substantial governmental interest; relying on Second and Sixth Circuit decisions), *affirmed in part, reversed in part, and remanded on other grounds*, 203 Fed.Appx. 95 (9th Cir. 2006) (unpublished).

[109]Kaufman v. McCaughtry, 419 F.3d 678, 685–86 (7th Cir. 2005) (properly marked mail from an identified attorney must be opened only in the prisoner's presence); Sallier v. Brooks, 343 F.3d 868, 877 (6th Cir. 2003) ("mail from a court constitutes 'legal mail'"; so does attorney correspondence); Taylor v. Sterrett, 532 F.2d 462, 474 (5th Cir. 1976) (mail from "any identifiable attorney either representing or being asked to represent a prisoner in relation to any criminal or civil problem") (cited in Guajardo v. Estelle, 580 F.2d 748, 757-58 (5th Cir. 1978)); Faulkner v. McLocklin, 727 F. Supp. 486, 489–90 (N.D.Ind. 1989) (mail from American Civil Liberties Union and Legal Services program offices); Knop v. Johnson, 685 F. Supp. 636, 644 (W.D.Mich. 1988), *aff'd in part and rev'd in part on other grounds*, 977 F.2d 996 (6th Cir. 1992); Giarratano v. Bass, 596 F. Supp. 818, 819–20 (E.D.Va. 1984); Carty v. Fenton, 440 F. Supp. 1161, 1163–64 (M.D.Pa. 1977) (mail from state courts is privileged and confidential); *see also* Davidson v. Scully, 694 F.2d 50 (2d Cir. 1982) (when sued, prison officials revised their rule to treat mail to ACLU and other legal organizations as privileged); Ramos v. Lamm, 639 F.2d 559, 582 (10th Cir. 1980) (privileged correspondence could not be confined to matters relating to criminal convictions or complaints about prison administration); *In re Gonzales*, 212 Cal.App.3d 459, 260 Cal.Rptr. 506, 508 (Cal.App. 1989) (correspondence with Canadian attorney treated as privileged; privileged status extended to correspondence about child custody matter).

[110]*See* Kaufman v. McCaughtry, 419 F.3d 678, 685–86 (7th Cir. 2005) (holding that prisoner failed to describe mail from the Department of Justice, the ACLU, a legal services office, a law firm, and a county sheriff's office, and to a court enclosing papers and to an assistant attorney general, so as to establish that it merited treatment as legal mail; he conceded that he was neither represented nor seeking to be represented by an attorney from any of the organizations involved); Sallier v. Brooks, 343 F.3d 868, 874–75 (6th Cir. 2003) (holding mail from an organization like the American Bar Association can be opened outside the prisoner's presence unless there is a specific indication to the contrary).

Mail to a non-attorney does not become privileged if a prisoner declares that person to be a legal representative or sends that person materials intended for use in a legal proceeding. Zimmerman v. Tribble, 226 F.3d 568, 573 n.2 (7th Cir. 2000).

[111]Keenan v. Hall, 83 F.3d 1083, 1094 (9th Cir. 1996) (holding it is not legal mail); Martin v. Brewer, 830 F.2d 76, 78 (7th Cir. 1987) (dictum); McCain v. Reno, 98 F. Supp. 2d 5, 7–8 (D.D.C. 2000) (holding court mail need not be opened in prisoner's presence); *see* Sanders v. Dep't of Correction, 815 F. Supp. 1148, 1149

(N.D.Ill. 1991) (under *Martin*, letters from court clerks are not constitutionally privileged).

[112]*See* Sallier v. Brooks, 343 F.3d 868, 876–77 (6th Cir. 2003) ("In order to guard against the possibility of a chilling effect on a prisoner's exercise of his or her First Amendment rights and to protect the right of access to the courts, we hold that mail from a court constitutes 'legal mail' and cannot be opened outside the presence of a prisoner who has specifically requested otherwise."); Castillo v. Cook County Mail Room Dep't, 990 F.2d 304, 306–07 (7th Cir. 1993). We think the view expressed in *Sallier* is more realistic. There is a large practical difference between a prisoner's legal matters being available in courthouse files somewhere and their being scrutinized by prison staff in the prison where he is confined.

[113]Malsh v. Garcia, 971 F. Supp. 133, 138 (S.D.N.Y. 1997).

[114]Davidson v. Scully, 694 F.2d at 53–54 n.5 (military authorities); Guajardo v. Estelle, 580 F.2d at 759 (government agencies); Taylor v. Sterrett, 532 F.2d 462, 473–74 (5th Cir. 1976) (parole and probation departments); Burt v. Carlson, 752 F. Supp. 346, 348 (C.D.Cal. 1990) ("various government agencies"); Faulkner v. McLocklin, 727 F. Supp. at 490 (elected officials, government agencies); Knop v. Johnson, 685 F. Supp. at 644 (Legislative Corrections Ombudsman); Mawby v. Ambroyer, 568 F. Supp. 245, 249–50 (E.D.Mich. 1983) (Attorney Grievance Commission); Stover v. Carlson, 413 F. Supp. 718, 723 (D.Conn. 1976) (Justice Department and other prosecutorial authorities, governor, and foreign embassies).

[115]Jones v. Caruso, 569 F.3d 258, 268 (6th Cir. 2009) (mail to state Secretary of State asking for information about copyrighting and trademark registration was not privileged); *accord*, Sallier v. Brooks, 343 F.3d 868, 876 (6th Cir. 2003) (mail from county clerks is not privileged because they do not provide legal advice or direct legal services and do not have authority to act on a prisoner's behalf; the matters they deal with such as birth, marriage, or death certificates, tax and real estate services, automobile title, etc., "are not the types of legal matters that raise heightened concern or constitutional protection"); *see* O'Keefe v. Van Boening, 82 F.3d 322, 326 (9th Cir. 1996) (holding grievance mail to state officials need not be treated as privileged); Smith v. Maschner, 899 F.2d 940, 944 (10th Cir. 1990) (alleged opening of mail from the Post Office and Internal Revenue Service did not interfere with legal communication); Moore v. Schuetzle, 354 F. Supp. 2d 1065, 1079–80 & n.6 (D.N.D. 2005) (mail from police department and correction department were not privileged; mail from Innocence Project presented a "closer question" without a description of its contents, and probably would not be legal mail without an attorney's name on the return address), *aff'd*, 172 Fed.Appx. 133 (8th Cir. 2006) (unpublished); Stone-El v. Fairman, 785 F. Supp. 711, 716 (N.D.Ill. 1991) (mail to state or federal officials is not privileged); Jackson v. Norris, 748 F. Supp. 570, 573 (M.D.Tenn. 1990) (letters from Jesse Jackson presidential campaign were not privileged); Jackson v. Mowery, 743 F. Supp. 600, 606 (N.D.Ind. 1990) ("legal mail"

disagreement as to whether mail to and from the media is privileged.[116] Business or commercial mail need not be treated as privileged.[117]

Interference with or invasion of privacy of legal mail cannot be successfully challenged as a denial of access to courts unless the plaintiff can show that the infringement caused actual injury to the assertion of a legal claim.[118] Such claims should be pled as First Amendment or Fourth Amendment claims instead.[119]

Privileged mail may not be read in the ordinary course of prison routine.[120] Except in emergencies,[121] officials must

obtain a warrant based on probable cause to read privileged mail.[122] It may be opened and inspected for contraband, but only in the prisoner's presence[123] (though one federal appeals court has held that prisoners can be required to request such treatment of their legal mail[124]). Outgoing privileged mail may generally be sent unopened.[125]

In order for mail to be treated as privileged, it must be clearly marked.[126] Privileged mail may be held briefly to

---

includes only communications between inmates and attorneys); Campbell v. Sumner, 587 F. Supp. 376, 379 (D.Nev. 1984) (unclear if FBI mail is privileged).

[116]See § B.4 of this chapter, n.230.

[117]Lucas v. Scully, 71 N.Y.2d 401, 406, 526 N.Y.S.2d 927 (N.Y. 1988).

[118]Davis v. Goord, 320 F.3d 346, 351 (2d Cir. 2003); Gardner v. Howard, 109 F.3d 427, 430–31 (8th Cir. 1997) ("The act of opening incoming mail does not injure an inmate's right to access the courts. The policy that incoming confidential legal mail should be opened in inmates' presence instead serves the prophylactic purpose of assuring them that confidential attorney–client mail has not been improperly read in the guise of searching for contraband."). Compare Simkins v. Bruce, 406 F.3d 1239, 1242–44 (10th Cir. 2005) (holding that failure to forward legal mail, as prison procedure required, to a prisoner temporarily held in a county jail, resulting in his failing to receive notice and to respond to a summary judgment motion, denied the right of access to court); Gramegna v. Johnson, 846 F.2d 675, 677 (11th Cir. 1988) (holding practice of allowing inmate mail to accumulate until "a sizable bundle has amassed," then forwarding it, violated the right of access to courts where a six-week delay caused the plaintiff to miss his appeal deadline) with Pearson v. Simms, 345 F. Supp. 2d 515, 519–20 (D.Md. 2003) (rejecting claim of legal mail delay in the absence of specific allegations of actual injury to litigation), aff'd, 88 Fed.Appx. 639 (4th Cir. 2004) (unpublished).

The "actual injury" requirement for court access claims is discussed in § C.1.a(1) of this chapter.

[119]See § C.3 of this chapter concerning legal communications.

[120]Reneer v. Sewell, 975 F.2d 258, 260 (6th Cir. 1992); Lemon v. Dugger, 931 F.2d 1465, 1467–68 (11th Cir. 1991); Proudfoot v. Williams, 803 F. Supp. 1048, 1052 (E.D.Pa. 1992) and cases cited; Chinchello v. Fenton, 763 F. Supp. 793, 795 (M.D.Pa. 1991); see also U.S. v. DeFonte, 441 F.3d 92, 95–96 (2d Cir. 2006) (per curiam) (holding attorney–client privilege is applicable to materials retained in a prisoner's cell that comprise or recount conversations with counsel or outline matters that the client intends to discuss with counsel); Sturm v. Clark, 835 F.2d 1009, 1015 n.13 (3d Cir. 1987) (reading of confidential correspondence in an attorney's briefcase raised First Amendment and attorney–client privilege issues).

One court has held that in order to determine if mail is eligible for free postage as legal mail, "[w]hen a question arises," officials may take "a cursory look at the contents." Kendrick v. Bland, 586 F. Supp. 1536, 1554 (W.D.Ky. 1984). We think this decision is dead wrong, since it gives greater weight to the price of a postage stamp than it does to the attorney–client privilege.

[121]See Burton v. Nault, 902 F.2d 4, 5 (6th Cir. 1990) (where an inmate tried to kill himself and left a letter to his lawyer, prison

officials properly opened it and read it to see if it contained information about drugs he might have taken).

[122]Guajardo v. Estelle, 580 F.2d 748, 759 (5th Cir. 1978); Burton v. Foltz, 599 F. Supp. 114, 117 (E.D.Mich. 1984). Cf. Com. v. Moore, 928 A.2d 1092 (Pa.Super. 2007) (upholding warrantless search, emphasizing repeatedly that correspondence searched was non-privileged).

[123]In Wolff v. McDonnell, 418 U.S. 539, 577, 94 S. Ct. 2963 (1974), the Supreme Court approved inspection in the prisoner's presence without stating that it was required. The lower courts, however, have held that it is a constitutional requirement. Merriweather v. Zamora, 569 F.3d 307, 316–17 (6th Cir. 2009) (holding requirement to be clearly established law); Al-Amin v. Smith, 511 F.3d 1317, 1333–34 (11th Cir. 2008), cert. denied, 129 S. Ct. 104 (2008); Jones v. Brown, 461 F.3d 353, 358–64 (3d Cir. 2006) (holding unconstitutional post-9/11/01 rules allowing opening of legal mail outside prisoners' presence), cert. denied, 549 U.S. 1286 (2007); Sallier v. Brooks, 343 F.3d 868, 874 (6th Cir. 2003); Davis v. Goord, 320 F.3d at 351; see Gaines v. Lane, 790 F.2d 1299, 1305-06 (7th Cir. 1986); Royse v. Superior Court of State of Washington, 779 F.2d 573, 574–75 (9th Cir. 1985); Jensen v. Klecker, 648 F.2d 1179, 1182 (8th Cir. 1981); Guajardo v. Estelle, 580 F.2d at 757–59; Hinderliter v. Hungerford, 814 F. Supp. 66, 68 (D.Kan. 1993); Young v. Keohane, 809 F. Supp. 1185, 1197 (M.D.Pa. 1992); Burt v. Carlson, 752 F. Supp. 346, 348 (C.D.Cal. 1990); Faulkner v. McLocklin, 727 F. Supp. 486, 489–92 (N.D.Ind. 1989); McChriston v. Duckworth, 610 F. Supp. 791, 795–96 (N.D.Ind. 1985); see also Guyer v. Beard, 907 F.2d 1424, 1428–29 (3d Cir. 1990) (prisoner could be required to sign a power of attorney consenting to opening of legal mail in his presence). But see Stone-El v. Fairman, 785 F. Supp. 711, 715 (N.D.Ill. 1991) (incoming mail from courts may be opened outside inmate's presence but not read).

[124]Sallier v. Brooks, 343 F.3d 868, 874 (6th Cir. 2003) ("opt-in" systems are constitutionally sound as long as prisoners receive notice of the policy, do not have to renew their request upon transfer, and need not designate particular attorneys as their counsel); Knop v. Johnson, 685 F. Supp. 636, 644 (W.D.Mich. 1988), aff'd in pertinent part, 977 F.2d 996, 1012 (6th Cir. 1992). Contra, Guajardo v. Estelle, 580 F.2d at 757–58.

[125]Davidson v. Scully, 694 F.2d 50, 53 (2d Cir. 1982); Guajardo v. Estelle, 580 F.2d at 759; Smith v. Shimp, 562 F.2d 423, 424 (7th Cir. 1977); Mawby v. Ambroyer, 568 F. Supp. 245, 249–50 (E.D.Mich. 1983). But see Witherow v. Paff, 52 F.3d 264, 265–66 (7th Cir. 1995) (providing for "cursory visual inspection" without reading of outgoing mail to public officials); Royse v. Superior Court of State of Washington, 779 F.2d at 574–75 (outgoing mail to court could be inspected for contraband in the inmate's presence); Ramos v. Lamm, 639 F.2d 559, 582 (10th Cir. 1980) (outgoing privileged mail could be opened in the inmate's presence in "exceptional circumstances").

[126]Kaufman v. McCaughtry, 419 F.3d 678, 686 (7th Cir. 2005) ("... [W]hen a prison receives a letter for an inmate that is marked

verify the identity of the addressee.[127] Isolated or negligent instances of opening privileged mail may not violate the Constitution.[128]

with an attorney's name and a warning that the letter is legal mail, officials potentially violate the inmate's rights if they open the letter outside of the inmate's presence."); Boswell v. Mayer, 169 F.3d 384, 388 (6th Cir. 1999) (holding mail from Attorney General's office not containing the return address of an attorney and marked as privileged need not be treated as privileged); O'Donnell v. Thomas, 826 F.2d 788, 790 (8th Cir. 1987); Harrod v. Halford, 773 F.2d 234, 235–36 (8th Cir. 1985); Faulkner v. McLocklin, 727 F. Supp. at 491.

This rule is subject to abuse, and in our view a recent decision upholds an abuse of it. The Pennsylvania prison system requires lawyers and courts to obtain a "control number" in order for their correspondence to be opened in the prisoner's presence. A federal court has upheld that policy, despite the fact that many lawyers and all courts have refused to obtain control numbers, holding that getting a control number was an adequate alternative for protecting prisoners' privacy *even though the prisoners had no way of getting courts and lawyers to do so.* Fontroy v. Beard, 559 F.3d 173, 180–81 (3d Cir. 2009) ("We acknowledge that these problems make the DOC's new mail policy a less-than-ideal means of accommodating the Inmates' important First Amendment rights. . . . Alternatives . . . need not be ideal, . . .; they need only be available." (citation and internal quotation marks omitted)).

Federal prison regulations require that envelopes be marked with the words "Special Mail—Open Only in the Presence of the Inmate" to be treated as privileged mail. *See* Merriweather v. Zamora, 569 F.3d 307, 313–14 (6th Cir. 2009) (discussing application of rule). The courts have disagreed over the lawfulness of that requirement. *Compare* Henthorn v. Swinson, 955 F.2d 351, 353–54 (5th Cir. 1992) (upholding regulation); Martin v. Brewer, 830 F.2d 76, 78 (7th Cir. 1987) (requirement upheld as to attorneys; case remanded for further proceedings as to public officials); Bruscino v. Carlson, 654 F. Supp. 609, 617–18 (S.D.Ill. 1987), *aff'd,* 854 F.2d 162 (7th Cir. 1988); Bagguley v. Barr, 893 F. Supp. 967, 972 (D.Kan. 1995) (applying requirement), not questioning constitutionally *with* Burt v. Carlson, 752 F. Supp. 346, 347–49 (C.D.Cal. 1990) (enjoining requirement); Thornley v. Edwards, 671 F. Supp. 339, 341–43 (M.D.Pa. 1987) (holding requirement unconstitutional under the Sixth Amendment); *see also* U.S. v. Stotts, 925 F.2d 83, 87–90 (4th Cir. 1991) (upholding a relaxed version of the requirement that did not insist on the exact "Special Mail" wording).

[127]Guajardo v. Estelle, 580 F.2d at 758–59 (quoting Taylor v. Sterrett, 532 F.2d 462, 473–74 (5th Cir. 1976)); Burton v. Foltz, 599 F. Supp. 114, 117 (E.D.Mich. 1984); *see also* Wolff v. McDonnell, 418 U.S. 539, 576–77, 94 S. Ct. 2963 (1974) (lawyer wishing to correspond confidentially could be required to identify himself in advance).

[128]Davis v. Goord, 320 F.3d 346, 351–52 (2d Cir. 2003); Gardner v. Howard, 109 F.3d 427, 430–31 (8th Cir. 1997); Smith v. Maschner, 899 F.2d 940, 944 (10th Cir. 1990); Stevenson v. Koskey, 877 F.2d 1435, 1440–41 (9th Cir. 1989); Haston v. Galetka, 799 F. Supp. 1129, 1131–32 (D.Utah 1992); Bryant v. Winston, 750 F. Supp. 733, 734 (E.D.Va. 1990); Jackson v. Norris, 748 F. Supp. 570, 573–74 (M.D. Tenn. 1990); Williams v. McClain, 708 F. Supp. 1086, 1089 (W.D.Mo. 1989); Averhart v. Shuler, 652 F. Supp. 1504, 1507–10 (N.D.Ind.), *aff'd,* 834 F.2d 173 (7th Cir. 1987). *But see* Faulkner v. McLocklin, 727 F. Supp. at 491–92 (negligence was not a defense where letters were opened intentionally).

Prison officials must provide indigent inmates with basic correspondence supplies and postage for legal mail.[129]

c. Procedural Protections in Restricting Correspondence

The right to correspond is a liberty interest protected by due process, and prisoners are entitled to notice when an incoming or outgoing letter is rejected, a "reasonable opportunity to protest" for the author of the letter, and referral of complaints to someone other than the censor.[130] Courts have disagreed whether providing access to a prison grievance process meets due process requirements.[131]

d. Other Rules Governing Prisoner Correspondence

Prison officials may impose reasonable restrictions on how correspondence is carried out, though they must come forward with some penological justification for restrictive policies.[132] They may require that outgoing

[129]*See* § C.2.b of this chapter.

[130]The Supreme Court held that these protections were sufficient in *Procunier v. Martinez,* 416 U.S. 396, 417–19, 94 S. Ct. 1800 (1974). The lower courts have held that they are required. Murphy v. Missouri Dep't of Corrections, 814 F.2d 1252, 1258 (8th Cir. 1987); Martin v. Kelley, 803 F.2d 236, 243–44 (6th Cir. 1986); Gregory v. Auger, 768 F.2d 287, 291 (8th Cir. 1985); Davis v. Milwaukee County, 225 F. Supp. 2d 967, 979 (E.D.Wis. 2002) (claim of rejection of mail without notification was not frivolous); Hardwick v. Ault, 447 F. Supp. 116, 129 (M.D.Ga. 1978); Laaman v. Helgemoe, 437 F. Supp. 269, 322 (D.N.H. 1977); *see* Bonner v. Outlaw, 552 F.3d 673, 676–79 (8th Cir. 2009) (holding notice requirement applicable to all mail, including packages). *But see* Wilson v. Holman, 793 F. Supp. 920, 922–23 (E.D.Mo. 1992) (letters that violated ban on inmate–inmate correspondence could be seized without notice); Yancey v. Jenkins, 638 F. Supp. 340, 341–42 (N.D.Ill. 1986) (notice not required when the mail contains plans for criminal conduct. Procedural protections are required when the censorship is directed by a court as well as when prison officials do it. Wheeler v. U.S., 640 F.2d 1116, 1121 (9th Cir. 1981); Intersimone v. Carlson, 512 F. Supp. 526, 531 (M.D.Pa. 1980).

One federal appeals court has held that returning mail to the sender without providing procedural protections is constitutional under *Thornburgh v. Abbott.* Holloway v. Pigman, 884 F.2d 365, 367 (8th Cir. 1989); *accord,* Harris v. Bolin, 950 F.2d 547, 550 (8th Cir. 1991). We think that this decision is wrong. The portion of *Procunier v. Martinez* that requires procedural protections was not overruled by *Thornburgh,* and the issue of due process was not even mentioned in that case. The Eighth Circuit has subsequently acknowledged that notice may be required when correspondence is seized. Knight v. Lombardi, 952 F.2d 177, 179 (8th Cir. 1992) (due process was "arguably" violated by lack of notice).

[131]Martin v. Kelley, 803 F.2d at 237–38 (no); Gaines v. Lane, 790 F.2d 1299, 1305 (7th Cir. 1986) (yes); Gregory v. Auger, 768 F.2d 287, 291 (8th Cir. 1985) (no).

[132]*See, e.g.,* Smith v. Erickson, 884 F.2d 1108, 1111 (8th Cir. 1989) (prison officials must explain why they refused to mail legal mail that was not in envelopes from the prison canteen); *see also* Smith v. Erickson, 961 F.2d 1387, 1388 (8th Cir. 1992) (accepting prison officials' explanation for requiring use of envelopes from the prison canteen); Hall v. Johnson, 224 F. Supp. 2d 1058, 1060–61 (E.D.Va. 2002) (upholding policy limiting items of general

correspondence carry the prison's name or otherwise be identified as coming from a prisoner.[133] They may require that incoming mail bear a return address.[134] They may ban enclosures intended for someone other than the addressee ("kiting" mail).[135] They may ban possession of stamps as long as they provide another means of paying postage.[136] They are not required to provide receipts for certified mail.[137] However, prison officials may not refuse to deliver incoming mail addressed to prisoners by their religious names as long as the address is sufficient for officials to deliver it.[138] Decisions are mixed as to whether prison officials may refuse to deliver mail because it is written in a language other than English.[139]

Some courts have held that there is a constitutional right to have mail promptly delivered or forwarded.[140] But mail delays that are brief, occasional, or accidental are seldom held unconstitutional, especially if there are no harmful consequences.[141] Realistically, the courts know that mail is often mishandled outside prison, too. To win a mail delay case, you will probably have to show that the delay was intentional or resulted from an unreasonable policy and that it actually caused serious harm such as missing a court deadline.[142]

---

correspondence, not including legal, educational, vendor, governmental, or "special purpose" mail, to one ounce each), *aff'd*, 53 Fed. Appx. 292 (4th Cir. 2002) (unpublished); Avery v. Powell, 806 F. Supp. 7, 10–11 (D.N.H. 1992) (upholding prohibition on receipt of blank greeting cards except from vendors based on concerns about contraband).

[133]Rogers v. Isom, 709 F. Supp. 115, 116–17 (E.D.Va. 1989); Theriault v. Magnusson, 698 F. Supp. 369, 370–73 (D.Me. 1988); Nachtigall v. Board of Charities and Corrections, 590 F. Supp. 1223, 1224 (D.S.D. 1984); *see* Turner v. Ralls, 770 F. Supp. 605, 606 (D.Kan. 1991) (where a convicted sex offender abused his mail privileges to get in contact with high school girls, prison officials could place a notice in his outgoing correspondence concerning his identity and his criminal record).

[134]Morrison v. Hall, 261 F.3d 896, 906–07 (9th Cir. 2001) (noting requirement helps return to sender if necessary, allows the prison to notify the sender of prison mail rules, and helps in investigations).

[135]Lucas v. Scully, 71 N.Y.2d 401, 408, 526 N.Y.S.2d 927, 932 (N.Y. 1988).

[136]Little v. Norris, 787 F.2d 1241, 1243 (8th Cir. 1986); Kaestel v. Lockhart, 746 F.2d 1323, 1325 (8th Cir. 1984); *see also* Rentschler v. Campbell, 739 F. Supp. 561, 563–64 (D.Kan. 1990) (upholding rule requiring inmates to pay for postage over 25 cents by releasing funds from their accounts rather than attaching more than one stamp to it).

[137]Smith v. Maschner, 899 F.2d 940, 944 (10th Cir. 1990).

[138]Salaam v. Lockhart, 905 F.2d 1168, 1172–74 (8th Cir. 1990); Masjid Muhammad-D.C.C. v. Keve, 479 F. Supp. 1311, 1326 (D.Del. 1979); *see also* Diamontiney v. Borg, 918 F.2d 793, 795–96 (9th Cir. 1990) (preliminary injunction affirmed requiring prison officials to deliver court correspondence under non-religious changed name so prisoner could litigate whether he was entitled to use the name). *But see* Fawaad v. Jones, 81 F.3d 1084, 1086–87 (11th Cir. 1996) (prisoners may be required to use prior name as well as religious name in correspondence); Thacker v. Dixon, 784 F. Supp. 286, 305–06 (E.D.N.C. 1991) (prison officials may use former name as well as new name in correspondence), *aff'd*, 953 F.2d 639 (4th Cir. 1992). Religious name changes are discussed in § D.2.f of this chapter.

[139]In *Ramos v. Lamm*, 639 F.2d 559, 581 (10th Cir. 1980), the court held that an English-only correspondence policy was unconstitutional where prison officials presented no justification for it. In *Thongvanh v. Thalacker*, 17 F.3d 256, 259–60 (8th Cir.1994), the court held similarly where the record showed that the prison could get the Laotian plaintiff's letters translated at a local refugee center

so they could be read for security purposes, and where German and Spanish-speaking prisoners were exempted from the rule. However, in *Ortiz v. Fort Dodge Correctional Facility*, 368 F.3d 1024, 1027 (8th Cir. 2004), the same court upheld an English-only rule that exempted persons who could only communicate in another language; it noted that this plaintiff, unlike Thongvanh, did not identify a cost-free way for the prison to read his Spanish-language correspondence—even though by the time the court ruled, the prison system had abandoned its policy. *Accord*, Sisneros v. Nix, 884 F. Supp. 1313, 1331–33 (S.D.Iowa 1995), *aff'd in part, remanded in part on other grounds*, 95 F.3d 749 (8th Cir. 1996).

[140]Zimmerman v. Tribble, 226 F.3d 568, 572–73 (7th Cir. 2000) (a "continuing pattern or repeated occurrences" of delayed mail would state a First Amendment claim, but sporadic and short-term delays do not); Nicholson v. Choctaw County, Ala., 498 F. Supp. 295, 311 (S.D.Ala. 1980); Taylor v. Leidig, 484 F. Supp. 1330, 1332 (D.Colo. 1980); *see* Sherman v. McDougall, 656 F.2d 527, 528 (9th Cir. 1981) (approving a rule requiring delivery within 24 hours); *see also* Simkins v. Bruce, 406 F.3d 1239, 1242–44 (10th Cir. 2005) (holding that failure to forward legal mail, as prison procedure required, to a prisoner temporarily held in a county jail, resulting in his failing to receive notice and to respond to a summary judgment motion, denied the right of access to court). *But see* Clark v. Schumacher, 109 Or.App. 354, 820 P.2d 3, 5 (1991) (no right to have mail forwarded by prison officials).

[141]Rowe v. Shake, 196 F.3d 778, 782 (7th Cir. 1999); Martucci v. Johnson, 944 F.2d 291, 295–96 (6th Cir. 1991) (upholding brief withholding of incoming and outgoing mail during investigation of alleged escape plan); Richardson v. McDonnell, 841 F.2d 120, 122 (5th Cir. 1988) (delays are not unconstitutional unless they prejudice the prisoner's legal proceedings); Hines v. Boothe, 841 F.2d 623, 624 (5th Cir. 1988) (negligent loss of legal mail was not unconstitutional); Grady v. Wilken, 735 F.2d 303, 306 (8th Cir. 1984) (20-day delay resulting from transfer was not unconstitutional where there was no delay in court access); Oliver v. Powell, 250 F. Supp. 2d 593, 602 (E.D.Va. 2002) (mail delivery late at night did not violate any federal right); Armstrong v. Lane, 771 F. Supp. 943, 948 (C.D.Ill. 1991); Gorman v. Moody, 710 F. Supp. 1256, 1266 (N.D.Ind. 1989); Alston v. Coughlin, 668 F. Supp. 822, 847 (S.D.N.Y. 1987); Odom v. Tripp, 575 F. Supp. 1491, 1493 (E.D.Mo. 1983); Guffey v. Trago, 572 F. Supp. 782, 784–86 (N.D.Ind. 1983); Owen v. Schuler, 466 F. Supp. 5, 7 (N.D.Ind. 1977), *aff'd*, 594 F.2d 867 (7th Cir. 1979); Pickett v. Schaefer, 503 F. Supp. 27, 28 (S.D.N.Y. 1980); Stinson v. Sheriff's Dep't of Sullivan County, 499 F. Supp. 259, 264 (S.D.N.Y. 1980).

[142]*See* Gramegna v. Johnson, 846 F.2d 675, 677 (11th Cir. 1988), in which the court held that allowing inmate mail to accumulate at a central location until "a sizable bundle has amassed," then forwarding it, violated the right of access to courts. The plaintiff in that

Courts have upheld some restrictions on correspondence in segregation that are designed to make segregation more unpleasant. The Supreme Court upheld the denial of photographs, as well as magazines and newspapers, in incoming mail in a high-security unit.[143] Earlier decisions affirmed other restrictions.[144] The courts have not spelled out how far prison officials can go. Most of the cases cited involved limited periods of time,[145] and several of them stressed that the mail was not destroyed or returned but was given to the prisoner on release from segregation. The Supreme Court case involved a long-term segregation unit, but emphasized that this unit contained "the 40 most intractable inmates" in the state.[146] It can be argued that significant restrictions on the ability to communicate by letter must be limited to short durations or to extreme prisoner misbehavior.

Also, in most of these cases the restriction was only on incoming mail and not outgoing mail.[147] In our view, broad restrictions on outgoing mail from segregation should be held unconstitutional. Outgoing mail is generally entitled to more constitutional protection than incoming mail.[148] Restrictions on outgoing mail can prevent prisoners from exposing or protesting abusive treatment or conditions—the danger of which is particularly great for prisoners in segregation. In administrative segregation, punitive reasons for limiting correspondence have no application, and prisoners should be entitled to the same mail privileges as in general population unless prison officials have a non-punitive justification for restricting them.[149]

2. Publications

Prisoners have a First Amendment right to read, and publishers and others have a right to send them reading material.[150] However, prison officials have a long history of censoring publications, sometimes for good reason, but sometimes because they express unorthodox political, sexual, racial, or religious views, and especially views that are critical of prison officials.[151]

a. What Can Be Censored   The censorship of books, magazines, and newspapers sent to prisoners is governed by the same *Turner v. Safley* "reasonableness" standard that governs censorship of incoming letters and most other prison restrictions on constitutional rights.[152] Applying that standard, the Supreme Court in *Thornburgh v. Abbott* upheld a regulation permitting censorship of any publication "determined detrimental to the security, good order, or discipline of the institution or if it might facilitate criminal activity," but barring censorship "solely because [the publication's] content is religious, philosophical, political, social, or sexual, or because its content is unpopular or repugnant."[153] The Court held

---

case had missed his appeal deadline because his mail was held up for six weeks by this policy.

[143]Beard v. Banks, 548 U.S. 521, 126 S. Ct. 2572 (2006).

[144]One court stated, "Left free to write to anyone in the world and to receive literature of any kind, a prisoner might find punitive isolation desirable, offering solitude and leisure as an alternative to the ordinary conditions of prison work and life." Daigre v. Maggio, 719 F.2d 1310, 1312–13 (5th Cir. 1983) (ban on outgoing personal mail and incoming bulk mailings, newspapers and magazines); *accord*, Leonard v. Norris, 797 F.2d 683, 685 (8th Cir. 1986) ("personal" mail denied, legal mail and "media" permitted); Little v. Norris, 787 F.2d 1241, 1243–44 (8th Cir. 1986) (same as *Leonard*); Gregory v. Auger, 768 F.2d 287, 290–91 (8th Cir. 1985) ("personal, legal or religious" first-class mail permitted, all other mail denied); Jackson v. Brookhart, 640 F. Supp. 241 (S.D.Iowa 1986) (policy permitting only religious, legal or educational materials and personal correspondence is upheld). *But see* Jones v. Sargent, 737 F.2d 766, 767–68 (8th Cir. 1984) (denial of personal correspondence in punitive segregation raised "potentially important first amendment concerns").

[145]In *Leonard v. Norris* and *Little v. Norris*, there was a 30-day limit on segregation terms; in *Gregory v. Auger*, the limit was 60 days. In *Jackson v. Brookhart*, although the restriction was imposed for 286 days, the prisoner was convicted of 38 separate offenses, none of which carried a sentence of more than 30 days. In *Daigre v. Maggio*, no time limit was mentioned but the prisoner was serving only 10 days.

[146]Beard v. Banks, 548 U.S. at 533.

[147]The exception is *Daigre v. Maggio*.

[148]*See* § B.1.a of this chapter, n.67.

[149]*See* Hardwick v. Ault, 447 F. Supp. 116, 128–30 (M.D.Ga. 1978) (striking down mail restrictions). *But see* Beard v. Banks, 548 U.S. at 530–32 (upholding restrictions of mail in administrative segregation as a means of altering prisoners' behavior).

[150]Thornburgh v. Abbott, 490 U.S. 401, 407–08, 109 S. Ct. 1874 (1989); King v. Federal Bureau of Prisons, 415 F.3d 634, 638 (7th Cir. 2005) ("Freedom of speech is not merely freedom to speak; it is often freedom to read. . . . Forbid a person to read and you shut him out of the marketplace of ideas and opinions that it is the purpose of the free-speech clause to protect."); Prison Legal News v. Lehman, 397 F.3d 692, 699 (9th Cir. 2005).

[151]Lyon v. Grossheim, 803 F. Supp. 1538, 1550–51 (S.D.Iowa 1992) and cases cited.

[152]Thornburgh v. Abbott, 490 U.S. 401, 409–19, 109 S. Ct. 1874 (1989).

[153]*Thornburgh*, 490 U.S. at 404–05, 414–19. The regulation also mentioned several categories of material that could be excluded if sufficiently "detrimental": material concerning making or using weapons, alcohol, or drugs; methods of escape or maps or drawings of prisons; material written in code; material that "encourages or instructs" in criminal activity; material that "may lead to the use of physical violence or group disruption"; and sexually explicit material that threatens security, order, or discipline. 490 U.S. at 405, 415–17.

Before *Thornburgh*, courts had applied the more favorable "less restrictive alternative" standard of *Procunier v. Martinez*, which held that censorship must be "no greater than is necessary or essential" to protect an "important or substantial" interest, in publications as well as correspondence cases. Procunier v. Martinez, 416 U.S. 396, 413–14, 94 S. Ct. 1800 (1974). Under that standard, courts struck down much prison censorship. *See, e.g.,* McCabe v. Arave, 827 F.2d 634, 638 (9th Cir. 1987) (white supremacist literature); Abdul Wali v. Coughlin, 754 F.2d 1015, 1020–21 (2d Cir. 1985) (report of prisoners' rights group on conditions at Attica);

that the "broad discretion" granted wardens by that regulation was "appropriate."[154] In pursuing a censorship claim, you must give the court enough information about what was censored that the court can evaluate your claim and prison officials' defenses under the foregoing standards.[155]

Courts have upheld a variety of censorship rules under *Thornburgh*,[156] though they have also found some unconstitutionally overbroad even in the prison context.[157]

_____

Pepperling v. Crist, 678 F.2d 787, 790 (9th Cir. 1982) (*Hustler* and *High Times*); Hopkins v. Collins, 548 F.2d 503, 504 (4th Cir. 1977) (Black Panther newspaper); Jackson v. Ward, 458 F. Supp. 546, 559 (W.D.N.Y. 1978) (literature that criticizes police or corrections officials).

[154]*Thornburgh*, 490 U.S. at 416.

[155]George v. Smith, 507 F.3d 605, 608 (7th Cir. 2007). This may present some problems if you have not been allowed to see the publication. The *George* court complained that the plaintiff had not "described the book in the complaint, produced it in discovery, or provided a title or ISBN that would allow the court to evaluate the prison's cliams about its potential effect on security." *Id.* Presumably, if you provide a brief explanation of what you understand the publication to be and why you don't think it presents any reason for censorship, you will satisfy the court's concerns.

[156]*See, e.g.,* Jones v. Salt Lake County, 503 F.3d 1147, 1155–56 (10th Cir. 2007) (bans on "sexually explicit material" (referring to photographs of breasts and genitals) and "technical publications" (those containing information on weapons, escapes, making alcohol, hiding and moving contraband)); Harbin-Bey v. Rutter, 420 F.3d 571, 578–79 (6th Cir. 2005) (ban on material portraying gang symbols or signs); Prison Legal News v. Lehman, 397 F.3d 692, 702–03 (9th Cir. 2005) (rule prohibiting "third-party legal material" containing information that "could create a risk of violence and/or physical harm to any person); Bahrampour v. Lampert, 356 F.3d 969, 974–76 (9th Cir. 2004) (upholding regulations barring "sexually explicit" material, meaning "'[p]ortrayal of actual or simulated, penetration or stimulation, sexual violence, sexual contact between two people, or sexual contact between a person and an animal," and "role-playing or similar fantasy games or materials"; latter rule "intended to prevent inmates from placing themselves in fantasy roles that reduce accountability and substitute raw power for legitimate authority"); Mauro v. Arpaio, 188 F.3d 1054, 1060–63 (9th Cir. 1999) (en banc) (upholding restriction on sexually explicit but non-obscene materials, including all depictions of frontal nudity; stating it did not matter if prohibition took in artistic and scientific journals); Chriceol v. Phillips, 169 F.3d 313, 314–17 (5th Cir. 1999) (upholding a ban on material that presents "an immediate and tangible threat to the security and order of the facility or to inmate rehabilitation," and specifically material that "advocates racial, religious, or national hatred in such a way so as to create a serious danger of violence in the facility"); Willson v. Buss, 370 F. Supp. 2d 782, 787–91 (N.D.Ind. 2005) (upholding a rule against "blatant homosexual materials," explained as meaning "if it's obvious, it's clear, by reading it or looking at it, that it's homosexual material"); Lyon v. Grossheim, 803 F. Supp. 1538, 1548–50 (S.D.Iowa 1992) (upholding a regulation excluding material that is "likely to be disruptive or produce violence").

[157]*See, e.g.,* Shakur v. Selsky, 391 F.3d 106, 115–16 (2d Cir. 2004) (ban on all materials from "unauthorized organizations" did not appear to be rationally related to security; individualized review through the existing Media Review Committee appeared to

(Courts have disagreed over whether a censorship rule can be unconstitutionally vague.[158]) However, courts must not only assess whether censorship rules are valid on their face, but whether they are valid as applied—that is, whether a particular item was properly censored under them.[159]

_____

be an obvious alternative); Cline v. Fox, 319 F. Supp. 2d 685, 692–95 (N.D.W.Va. 2004) (striking down policy barring all depictions of sexual conduct, including work of literary value such as *Sophie's Choice, Myra Breckinridge,* and books by John Updike, while allowing commercial pornography such as *Playboy* or *Maxim*); Aiello v. Litscher, 104 F. Supp. 2d 1068, 1073, 1075–82 (W.D.Wis. 2000) (striking down ban on anything that was "in whole or in part, pornography," defined as "any material, whether written, visual, or audio representation or reproduction that depicts any of the following: (a) Human sexual behavior. (b) Sadomasochistic abuse. . . . (d) Nudity which appeals to the prurient interest in sex," etc.; rule was used to bar letters and books with a single sexual reference, an issue of *Cosmopolitan,* a picture of the Sistine Chapel, the *Sports Illustrated* swimsuit issue, and issues of *Vanity Fair, Rolling Stone, Maxim,* and various fitness and motorcycle magazines that contained ads of photo showing a portion of a buttock or a breast).

[158]A regulation may be unconstitutionally vague if it fails to provide "fair warning" regarding what conduct violates it or if it fails to provide those charged with enforcing it with an "explicit and ascertainable standard" to prevent its enforcement in arbitrary manner. Aiello v. Litscher, 104 F. Supp. 2d 1068, 1082 (W.D.Wis. 2000) (quoting Karlin v. Foust, 188 F.3d 446, 458–59 (7th Cir. 1999)). While one federal court has said that the "substantial overlap" between the *Turner* test and the vagueness and overbreadth doctrines "suggests that the Supreme Court did not intend for those doctrines to apply with independent force in the prison-litigation context," Waterman v. Farmer, 183 F.3d 208, 213 (3d Cir. 1999), others have applied vagueness analysis to prison censorship rules. Aiello v. Litscher, 104 F. Supp. 2d 1068, 1083 (W.D.Wis. 2000) (holding rule against material that is "in whole or part, pornography" was vague where even the defendants said it did not mean what it said); *see* Amatel v. Reno, 156 F.3d 192, 203 (D.C. Cir. 1998) (noting that vagueness challenge may have "independent force" and remanding for consideration of it); Willson v. Buss, 370 F. Supp. 2d 782, 791 (N.D.Ind. 2005) (holding a rule against "blatant homosexual materials," which defendants said applies "if it's obvious, it's clear, by reading it or looking at it, that it's homosexual material," was not vague; vagueness scrutiny is relaxed in prisons); *see* Ch. 4, § H.1.q, concerning vagueness in disciplinary rules.

[159]Thornburgh v. Abbott, 490 U.S. 401, 404, 419, 109 S. Ct. 1874 (1989); *accord,* Prison Legal News v. Lehman, 397 F.3d 692, 702–03 (9th Cir. 2005) (rule prohibiting "third-party legal material" containing information that could create a risk of violence or physical harm was constitutional, but its application to suppress materials that would embarrass the agency and educate prisoners on how to assert their rights would violate the First Amendment); Shakur v. Selsky, 391 F.3d 106, 117–18 (2d Cir. 2004) (allegation that censorship of particular materials was not supported by prisons' own censorship rules stated a First Amendment claim; earlier decision upholding censorship of certain New Afrikan Liberation Movement materials did not validate the censorship of other New Afrikan materials that had not been specifically ruled on); Murphy v. Missouri Dep't of Correction, 372 F.3d 979, 986 (8th Cir. 2004) (court must review the contents of each item to determine whether its censorship is an "exaggerated response"); Bahrampour v.

Under the *Turner* standard, officials' "failure to abide by established procedures and standards can evince an improper objective" in acts of censorship that are contrary to their own rules.[160] Also, the rules prison officials make presumably reflect what they think is reasonably necessary to serve security or other legitimate penological interests, which suggests that departure from those rules is arguably unreasonable under *Turner*. There is also an argument that failure to follow censorship rules is in itself a violation of the First Amendment.[161] When state or local prison censors violate their own rules, you may also have the option of asking a state court to strike down the censorship on that ground, instead of or in addition to claiming that the censorship violates the First Amendment.[162]

Prison censorship controversies tend repetitively to involve certain kinds of publications, and the results are mixed, with some courts allowing censorship of strongly expressed views or allegations that the censors find distasteful or threatening, while others hold that there must actually be some advocacy or concrete risk of violent or other unlawful action to justify censorship. With respect to racist

---

Lampert, 356 F.3d 969, 974, 976 (9th Cir. 2004) (determining that publications actually violated challenged rule, in addition to examining constitutionality of rule); Lyon v. Grossheim, 803 F. Supp. 1538, 1550–55 (S.D.Iowa 1992) (upholding rule against materials "likely to produce disruption or violence" but finding that censored publications did not violate it).

Prison officials cannot escape the need to justify censorship of a particular publication by declaring it "contraband." Shaheed-Muhammad v. DiPaolo, 393 F. Supp. 2d 80, 104 (D.Mass. 2005).

[160]Shakur v. Selsky, 391 F.3d 106, 116 (2d Cir. 2004); *accord,* Farid v. Goord, 200 F. Supp. 2d 220, 241 (W.D.N.Y. 2002) (fact that articles prisoner had written were not sent to the "media review" committee, as prison rules required, supported claim that he was improperly disciplined for them).

[161]Generally, state officials' violation of state law and regulations does not violate the Constitution and cannot be remedied in federal court. *See* Ch. 8, § F.1, on supplemental jurisdiction. But censorship may be an exception to this rule. Even before *Turner,* some courts held that the Constitution requires prison officials to follow their own censorship standards. *See* Thibodeaux v. State of South Dakota, 553 F.2d 558, 560 (8th Cir. 1977); Hardwick v. Ault, 447 F. Supp. 116, 131 (M.D.Ga. 1978). This is consistent with general First Amendment law, where the Supreme Court has stated, "[p]recision of regulation must be the touchstone," NAACP v. Button, 371 U.S. 415, 438, 83 S. Ct. 328 (1963); *accord,* Interstate Circuit v. Dallas, 390 U.S. 676, 672, 88 S. Ct. 1298 (1968), and official discretion in censorship must be guided by "narrowly drawn, reasonable and definite standards. . . ." Niemotko v. Maryland, 340 U.S. 268, 271, 71 S. Ct. 325 (1951). *Thornburgh v. Abbott* upheld regulations permitting greater discretion than would be allowed under non-prison censorship rules, 490 U.S. at 416, but even so, if the Constitution requires officials to have standards at all, it would seem to follow that they must obey the standards rather than ignore them.

[162]*Cf.* Bailey v. Loggins, 32 Cal.3d 907, 920–22, 654 P.2d 758 (1982) (censorship regulations "must be framed and applied uniformly with due regard for constitutionally protected rights of free expression").

---

publications (many of which also purport to be religious), most courts have held that there must be some advocacy or risk of violence to justify censorship, in addition to the expression of racist views.[163] Officials often censor material

---

[163]*See* Borzych v. Frank, 439 F.3d 388, 390–91 (7th Cir. 2006) (upholding censorship of Odinist books *Creed of Iron, Temple of Wotan,* and *The NPKA Book of Blotar* because they "promote violence to exalt the status of whites and demean other races; it is the means rather than the underlying racist views that the defendants contend (and we hold) may be forbidden in prisoners' reading matter"); Murphy v. Missouri Dep't of Correction, 372 F.3d 979, 986 (8th Cir. 2004) ("We have previously held that a total ban on publications that espouse white supremacy is overly broad and does not closely conform to the purpose of upholding the security of the prison." Claim that *The Way,* published by the Christian Separatist Church Society, was "so racially inflammatory as to be reasonably likely to cause violence" did not justify censorship where court's review of the publication showed it "did not appear to counsel violence."); Chriceol v. Phillips, 169 F.3d 313, 314–16 (5th Cir. 1999) (upholding censorship of materials from Aryan Nations/Church of Jesus Christ Christian under rule forbidding material that presents "an immediate and tangible threat to the security and order of the facility or to inmate rehabilitation," and specifically material that "advocates racial, religious, or national hatred in such a way so as to create a serious danger of violence in the facility"; this material was found "incendiary to the point of being almost certain to cause interracial violence, and nearly all of them openly advocate violence or other illegal activities"); Williams v. Brimeyer, 116 F.3d 351, 354 (8th Cir. 1997) (striking down ban on all materials from Church of Jesus Christ Christian, awarding punitive damages; publications that "did not counsel violence" or cause disruption could not be banned solely because of racist and separatist views); Stefanow v. McFadden, 103 F.3d 1466, 1472–73 (9th Cir. 1996) (censorship of anti-Semitic *Christianies [sic] Ancient Enemy* upheld; merely "advocating racial purity" does not justify censorship, but this book "issues a call to arms for white Christians to fight back in a 'war for survival'" and was reasonably concluded to be "so inflammatory it is reasonably likely to incite violence in the prison."); Haff v. Cooke, 923 F. Supp. 1104, 1112 (E.D.Wis. 1996) (upholding seizure of Aryan Nations material; "implicitly and explicitly, the documents advocate violence"); Reimann v. Murphy, 897 F. Supp. 398, 402–03 (E.D.Wis. 1995) (upholding censorship of materials from Church of the Creator that "are so replete with racial hatred and language inciting violence that there is no way they could be redacted and leave anything more than sentence fragments"); Thomas v. U.S. Secretary of Defense, 730 F. Supp. 362, 365 (D.Kan. 1990) (publications of White Aryan Resistance could be censored under a regulation barring material that "communicates information designed to encourage prisoners to disrupt the institution by strikes, riots, racial or religious hatred"; censorship followed "an individualized determination that the rejected publication might encourage inmates to disrupt the security and order of the institution.")

There are cases seeming to suggest that racist views, without more, may justify censorship. *See, e.g.,* Van Dyke v. Washington, 896 F. Supp. 183, 189 (C.D.Ill. 1995) (upholding censorship of publications containing "overt negative racial commentary, constant use of pejorative racial terms, constant reinforcement of a 'them against us' philosophy, and a 'call to action' regarding protection of the Aryan race," without evidence of actual racial confrontation);

containing what prison officials consider to be gang signs or symbols, or to be produced by gangs, or by other "unauthorized organizations," especially African-American nationalist groups.[164] Material offering sharp criticism of prisons or prison personnel recurrently encounters censorship.[165] Satanist literature has been censored,[166] as has material

expressing hostility to particular religious groups.[167] Prisons may censor materials that encourage, or contain instructions or helpful information for, actions that present security or other risks or are contrary to prison rules.[168]

George v. Sullivan, 896 F. Supp. 895, 896–99 (W.D.Wis. 1995) (upholding censorship of material from Church of Jesus Christ Christian which "fosters animosity among people of different races and cultures"). We think these cases are overruled by the Seventh Circuit's *Borzych* decision, cited above.

[164]Mays v. Springborn, 575 F.3d 643, 649 (7th Cir. 2009) (upholding censorship of pages of *Vibe* magazine displaying gang signs); Harbin-Bey v. Rutter, 420 F.3d 571, 578–79 (6th Cir. 2005) (upholding censorship of *FHM* magazine because of article containing gang signs); Shakur v. Selsky, 391 F.3d 106 (2d Cir. 2004) (holding censorship of what plaintiff called "New Afrikan political literature" and staff called "Nubian gang materials" stated a First Amendment claim where prison relied on overbroad rule prohibiting possessing "unauthorized organizational insignia or materials"; "unauthorized organization" is "any gang or any organization which has not been approved by the deputy commissioner for program services"); Fraise v. Terhune, 283 F.3d 506, 516–21 (3d Cir. 2002) (upholding ban on Five Percenter literature, in part because they also recognize the Bible and Koran and could study those instead); Shaheed-Muhammad v. DiPaolo, 393 F. Supp. 2d 80, 104 (D.Mass. 2005) (holding prison officials failed to justify censorship of *The Five Percenter* where they failed to explain "why these particular editions of *The Five Percenter* posed a security risk;" court rejects claim that their mere presence, regardless of contents, presented a threat); Marria v. Broaddus, 2003 WL 21782633, *6 & n.12, 18–20 (S.D.N.Y., July 31, 2003) (striking down ban on Five Percenter literature in the absence of a showing it advocated violence), *relief entered*, 2004 WL 1724984 (S.D.N.Y., July 30, 2004).

[165]Olson v. Loy, 951 F. Supp. 225, 229–30 (S.D.Ga. 1996) (upholding censorship of *Prison Life* issue that contained allegations of illegal activities by Federal Prison Industries and information about the plaintiff's own lawsuit and his activities with respect to these allegations, plus the names of prison staff members, and an allegation that FPI employed illegal aliens, whose warden feared that these illegal aliens might be mistreated by other inmates); Malik v. Coughlin, 154 A.D.2d 135, 552 N.Y.S.2d 182, 183–84 (N.Y.App.Div. 1990) (upholding censorship of "inflammatory accusations" against prison personnel, citing allegations that medical staff use inmates as "guinea pigs" for experimental drugs and that prison officials perpetrated "mass genocide" against black and Hispanic prisoners). *Thornburgh v. Abbott* itself involved, among other publications, one that was sharply critical of Bureau of Prisons medical care. Thornburgh v. Abbott, 490 U.S. 401, 420–22, 109 S. Ct. 1874 (1989) (concurring/dissenting opinion).

[166]McCorkle v. Johnson, 881 F.2d 993, 995–96 (11th Cir. 1989); *see* Doty v. Lewis, 995 F. Supp. 1081, 1085–87 (D.Ariz. 1998) (upholding denial of *The Satanic Bible* because of the "selfish and brutal" philosophy it advocates and its endorsement of human sacrifice, and because the plaintiff might use it to cast spells that other inmates would believe in); Carpenter v. Wilkinson, 946 F. Supp. 522, 529–30 (N.D.Ohio 1996) (upholding censorship of *The Satanic Bible* because it has "great potential for fomenting trouble of all kinds in a prison setting, leading to difficulty in maintaining security and order and in delivering rehabilitative services in the

prisons"; court cites alleged advocacy of preying on the weak among other passages). *Cf.* Borzych v. Frank, 340 F. Supp. 2d 955, 961, 967 (W.D.Wis. 2004) (upholding denial of a catalog that included products for Satanists to use in ritualistic killings where plaintiff did not allege it was essential to his religious practice), *reconsideration denied*, 2004 WL 2491597 (W.D.Wis., Oct. 28, 2004). *See* § D.1.a of this chapter, n.638, concerning Satanism.

[167]Weir v. Nix, 890 F. Supp. 769, 781–82 (S.D. Iowa 1995) (holding censorship of religious comic books from Chick Publications that were anti-Catholic but did not espouse violence violated the First Amendment), *aff'd on other grounds, appeal dismissed in part*, 114 F.3d 817 (8th Cir. 1997); Lyon v. Grossheim, 803 F. Supp. 1538, 1552–55 (S.D. Iowa) (striking down censorship of anti-Catholic comic books).

[168]*See, e.g.*, Mays v. Springborn, 575 F.3d 643, 649 (7th Cir. 2009) (upholding censorship of *Vibe* magazine article on prison riot); George v. Smith, 507 F.3d 605, 608–09 (7th Cir. 2007) (a newsletter containing a fund-raising proposal could be censored because prisoners are not allowed to raise funds from each other); King v. Federal Bureau of Prisons, 415 F.3d 634, 638 (7th Cir. 2005) ("A prison need not allow prisoners to buy books detailing famous prison escapes, . . . or even, we suppose, books on how to make yourself as strong as Mike Tyson through exercise. . . .") (dictum); Bahrampour v. Lampert, 356 F.3d 969, 973, 976 (9th Cir. 2004) (upholding censorship of role-playing magazine *White Dwarf* in part because such material promotes gambling and leads to a risk of violent debt collection); Lawson v. Singletary, 85 F.3d 502, 511–13 (11th Cir. 1996) (upholding ban on material that "depicts, describes or encourages activities which may lead to the use of physical violence or group disruption" or "otherwise presents a threat to the security, order, or rehabilitative objectives of the correctional system or the safety of any person"); Guajardo v. Estelle, 580 F.2d 748, 761 (5th Cir. 1978) ("They may censor portions of publications that contain information regarding the manufacture of explosives, weapons or drugs. They may also censor portions of publications that a reasonable person would construe as written solely for the purpose of communicating information designed to achieve the break down of prisons through inmate disruption such as strikes or riots. They may not censor inmate publications that advocate the legitimate use of prison grievance procedures or that urge prisoners to contact public representatives about prison conditions."); Sherman v. McDougall, 656 F.2d 527, 528 (9th Cir. 1981) (*American Rifleman* magazine); Maberry v. McKune, 24 F. Supp. 2d 1222, 1228 (D.Kan. 1998) (upholding censorship of chapter 12 of Aleister Crowley's *Magick in Theory and Practice* because it discusses blood sacrifices, "a topic that could clearly pose a threat to prison safety and security"); Packett v. Clarke, 910 F. Supp. 469, 474–76 (D.Neb. 1996) (catalog offering lock-picking gear, umbrellas with hidden blades, restraining devices and keys, etc., could be banned under rule prohibiting "a threat to the safety, security, or good order of the facility" to prevent prisoners from getting ideas about making weapons or means of escape); Knecht v. Collins, 903 F. Supp. 1193, 1200 (S.D.Ohio 1995) (issues of *Prison News Service* stating that "[t]he affirmative defense of self defense/justification should be a viable option for the Brothers to illustrate that the conditions were so oppressive that the takeover was necessary to save

Officials may ban materials concerning the Uniform Commercial Code that prisoners have used to file fraudulent liens and financing statements against prison personnel and other government officials, though there is some question about how broad the prohibition can be.[169] Material that is considered damaging to rehabilitation may also be censored.[170] The *Prison Legal News* has been repeatedly

excluded from prisons, generally for reasons supposedly unrelated to its contents, and courts have generally overturned those exclusions.[171]

Before *Thornburgh*, courts disagreed on whether sexual literature could be censored if it was not actually obscene.[172] After *Thornburgh*, it seems clear that prison officials have some ability to censor non-obscene publications; the regulation upheld in *Thornburgh* permitted censorship of "sexually explicit" material that might threaten security, order, or discipline or facilitate criminal activity.[173] Recent decisions have generally upheld the exclusion of material explicitly depicting sexual activity or nudity,[174] as well as some

---

their lives," advocating that prisoners "break the walls down," and encouraging people to "act" and "resist" and overthrow the white supremacist regime, including prison authorities, were properly censored; issues that merely encouraged peaceful protests, such as letters to the Governor or prison officials, or were described as "anti-government" and anti-establishment" and allegedly "could provoke violence," but did not actually incite violence, could not be censored), *aff'd in part and rev'd in part*, 187 F.3d 636 (6th Cir. 1999) (unpublished); Brown v. Hilton, 492 F. Supp. 771, 776 (D.N.J. 1980) (diagrams and instructions concerning infantry weapons); Mayberry v. Robinson, 427 F. Supp. 297, 309 (M.D.Pa. 1977) (Air Force Survival Manual). *But see* Smith v. Miller, 423 F. Supp. 2d 859, 860–61 (N.D.Ind. 2006) (holding officials were not entitled to summary judgment on plaintiff's right to possess anarchist publications that do not advocate violence and are devoid of "fighting words"; court says it is a "close case" and it will seek to appoint counsel).

[169]*See* Jones v. Caruso, 569 F.3d 258, 273–75 (6th Cir. 2009) (granting preliminary injunction against broad prohibition on UCC materials which "could be used to harass or threaten" others where narrower disciplinary rules would accomplish officials' purpose); Monroe v. Beard, 536 F.3d 198 (3d Cir. 2008) (upholding rule barring various UCC-related materials), *cert. denied*, 129 S. Ct. 1647 (2009). For information on prior litigation imposing sanctions on prisoners for these fraudulent activities, *see* Jones v. Caruso, 569 F.3d at 261 (citing cases involving prisoners' fraudulent UCC filings); Monroe v. Beard, 536 F.3d at 208 n.11 (citing criminal convictions of prisoners and others for filing fraudulent UCC filings).

[170]*See, e.g.*, King v. Federal Bureau of Prisons, 415 F.3d 634, 639 (7th Cir. 2005) ("Were King in prison for computer hacking or other computer-related crimes, the prison could, in the interest of rehabilitation (i.e., preventing recidivism), . . . forbid him to buy a book that would enable him to increase his ability as a hacker when he's released. . . ."). In *Bahrampour v. Lampert*, 356 F.3d 969 (9th Cir. 2004), the court upheld the censorship of the magazine *White Dwarf* under a regulation restricting "role playing or similar fantasy games or materials" which was "intended to prevent inmates from placing themselves in fantasy roles that reduce accountability and substitute raw power for legitimate authority." 356 F.3d at 973, 976. Though the court doesn't specifically mention rehabilitation, that would seem to be part of this rule's concern.

In *Ramirez v. Pugh*, 379 F.3d 122 (3d Cir. 2004), the court observed that the interest in rehabilitation has never been defined by the Supreme Court. Policies targeting the specific behavioral patterns that led to a prisoner's incarceration, or that emerge during incarceration and present a threat of lawbreaking, are certainly legitimate, it said. But it warned: "To say, however, that rehabilitation legitimately includes the promotion of 'values,' broadly defined, with no particularized identification of an existing harm towards which the rehabilitative efforts are addressed, would essentially be to acknowledge that prisoners' First Amendment rights are subject to the pleasure of their custodians." *Ramirez*, 379 F.3d at 128.

Ramirez concerned the censorship of sexual material, which is discussed further in the next paragraph.

[171]*See* Prison Legal News v. Lehman, 397 F.3d 692 (9th Cir. 2005); Jacklovich v. Simmons, 392 F.3d 420 (10th Cir. 2004); Prison Legal News v. Cook, 238 F.3d 1145 (9th Cir. 2001); Waterman v. Commandant, U.S. Disciplinary Barracks, 337 F. Supp. 2d 1237, 1242–43 (D.Kan. 2004); Miniken v. Walter, 978 F. Supp. 1356 (E.D.Wash. 1997). Some of these cases are discussed elsewhere in this section. *PLN* has prevailed by settlement in several other cases.

[172]*Compare* Pepperling v. Crist, 678 F.2d 787, 790 (9th Cir. 1982) (non-obscene material cannot be banned) *with* Carpenter v. State of South Dakota, 536 F.2d 759, 761–63 (8th Cir. 1976) (upholding rejection of non-obscene materials that "would have a detrimental effect upon rehabilitation"); Aikens v. Jenkins, 534 F.2d 751, 756 n.4 (7th Cir. 1976); Guajardo v. Estelle, 580 F.2d at 762 (non-obscene materials that "encourage deviate, criminal sexual behavior" may be rejected); *see* Miller v. California, 413 U.S. 15, 24, 93 S. Ct. 2607 (1973) (defining obscenity).

[173]*See* Lawson v. Singletary, 85 F.3d 502, 507 n.7 (11th Cir. 1996) (holding *Miller v. California* obscenity standard does not apply to prison censorship).

In *Thornburgh v. Abbott*, the brief reference to "sexually explicit" material had been supplemented by a complicated formula giving the warden discretion over homosexual, sadomasochistic, and bestial material; providing that ordinarily, explicit heterosexual material would be admitted; reiterating that homosexual material must be sexually explicit to be banned and permitting gay rights material; and barring all sexually explicit material involving children. Thornburgh v. Abbott, 490 U.S. 401, 405 n.6, 109 S. Ct. 1874 (1989).

[174]*See* Bahrampour v. Lampert, 356 F.3d 969, 972, 974, 976 (9th Cir. 2004) (upholding ban on "any '[p]ortrayal of actual or simulated' penetration or stimulation, sexual violence, sexual contact between two people, or sexual contact between a person and an animal," unless it has "scholarly value, or general social or literary value"; upholding censorship of *Muscle Elegance* magazine featuring ads for videos promising "Painful, Erotic Domination"); Frost v. Symington, 197 F.3d 348, 357–58 (9th Cir. 1999) (upholding rule barring depictions of sexual penetration, citing concerns for safety of staff and prisoners, protection of female staff from sexual harassment, and disputes over possession of materials); Mauro v. Arpaio, 188 F.3d 1054, 1059–63 (9th Cir. 1999) (en banc) (upholding ban on "sexually explicit" materials, defined as "personal photographs, drawings, and magazines and pictorials that show frontal nudity," under which *Playboy* was censored; noting it would not matter if policy excluded artistic and scientific journals); Waterman v.

gay-oriented publications.[175] However, some extreme instances of censorship on sexual grounds have been struck down.[176] When material is objectionable on sexual grounds, officials may censor it for everyone; they are not required to make individual determinations of whether it is safe for particular prisoners, especially since prisoners may circulate it from person to person.[177]

Censorship of religious publications is not just a "right to read" issue. It can also be challenged as a violation of the right of free exercise of religion.[178] Doing so has the benefit that prisoners can take advantage of the more favorable legal standards of the Religious Freedom Restoration Act (for federal prisoners) or the Religious Land Use and Institutionalized Persons Act (for state and local prisoners), both of which protect prisoners against "substantial burdens" on their religious exercise.[179] However, courts do not always agree that all reading of religious material qualifies as

---

Farmer, 183 F.3d 208, 214–20 (3d Cir. 1999) (upholding ban on "sexually oriented and obscene materials," defined in regulations to mean "a picture or other representation, publication, sound recording, live performance or film that contains a description or depiction of sexual activity or associated anatomical area" (exposed genitalia or female breasts), and is "predominantly oriented to such depictions or descriptions," as applied to sex offenders at a diagnostic and treatment facility); Amatel v. Reno, 156 F.3d 192, 199–203 (D.C. Cir. 1998) (upholding Ensign Amendment, a statute barring the Federal Bureau of Prisons from using federal funds to "distribute or make available" material that is "sexually explicit or featuring nudity," such as *Playboy* and *Penthouse*); Owen v. Wille, 117 F.3d 1235, 1237–38 (11th Cir. 1997) (upholding censorship of publications containing nude photos, though officials admitted that a blanket ban would be unconstitutional); Dawson v. Scurr, 986 F.2d 257, 260–62 (8th Cir. 1993) (upholding rule-barring portrayals of child sex acts, sadomasochism, or bestiality, and permitting other sexually explicit material to be read only by "psychologically fit" inmates under supervision); Thompson v. Patteson, 985 F.2d 202, 205–07 (5th Cir. 1993) (upholding rule-barring "graphic descriptions of homosexuality, sodo-masochism [sic], bestiality, incest or sex with children" and allowing publications "primarily covering the activities of any sexual or political rights groups or organizations"); Moses v. Dennehy, 523 F. Supp. 2d 57, 60–65 (D.Mass. 2007) (upholding ban on the receipt, possession, and display of nearly all materials containing nude or semi-nude images or sexually explicit content except for those illustrative of "medical, educational, or anthropological content"; upholding application to publications including *VIBE*, The "Master Piece" postcards, *GQ*, *Teen Vogue*, *Teen People*, *Elle*, *Interview*, *American Photo*, *Details*, *I and Eye*, *National Geographic: Faces of Africa*, *Diana and Nikon: Essays on Photography*, *National Enquirer (Thirty Years of Unforgettable Images)*, and *Passages*), aff'd sub. nom Josselyn v. Dennehy, 2009 WL 1587695 (1st Cir., June 9, 2009) (unpublished); Ramirez v. Pugh, 486 F. Supp. 2d 421, 426–37 (M.D.Pa. 2007) (upholding Ensign Amendment), *appeal dismissed as moot*, 273 Fed.Appx. 159, 2008 WL 934054 (3d Cir. 2008); Snelling v. Riveland, 983 F. Supp. 930, 933–37 (E.D.Wash. 1997) (upholding detailed ban on "sexually explicit" materials under which *Genesis* magazine was censored; court cites evidence that 24% of the prison population is incarcerated for sex crimes, there is an ongoing problem of sexual assaults, consensual sexual behavior, and sexual harassment of female staff, and a "significant number" of inmates are infected with HIV or hepatitis, and that "inmates exposed to pornography become desensitized and require more and more graphic material which may ultimately result in acting out sexual fantasies"), aff'd, 165 F.3d 917 (9th Cir. 1998) (unpublished); Powell v. Riveland, 991 F. Supp. 1249, 1253–56 (W.D.Wash. 1997) (upholding same policy as *Snelling* on same grounds, upholding censorship of magazines *Swank* and *Fox*).

[175]*See* Espinoza v. Wilson, 814 F.2d 1093, 1098 (6th Cir. 1987) (censorship of publications that "condone" homosexuality, like *Gay Community News*, upheld); Willson v. Buss, 370 F. Supp. 2d 782, 787–91 (N.D.Ind. 2005) (upholding censorship of *Out* and *The Advocate* under rule forbidding "blatant homosexual materials"; court holds it is reasonably related to the legitimate purpose of keeping prisoners safe, since anyone believed to be homosexual based on reading choices could be targeted for sexual and physical abuse and extortion).

In *Harper v. Wallingford*, 877 F.2d 728, 733 (9th Cir. 1989), the court upheld censorship of publications of the North American Man/Boy Love Association, citing evidence that such material could lead to violence involving its recipients and could impair some prisoners' rehabilitation, though it added, "Merely advocating homosexual activity is not a sufficient basis for a ban."

[176]Cline v. Fox, 319 F. Supp. 2d 685, 692–95 (N.D.W.Va. 2004) (holding policy banning anything that depicts "explicit sexual activity" including works of recognized literary value by authors such as John Updike, William Styron, and Gore Vidal, but permitted "magazines such as *Playboy* or *Maxim*, which objectify women in order to sexually arouse or gratify men," had no reasonable relationship to security, safety, or rehabilitation); Aiello v. Litscher, 104 F. Supp. 2d 1068, 1075–81 (W.D.Wis. 2000) (striking down ban on anything that was "in whole or in part, pornography," defined as "any material, whether written, visual, or audio representation or reproduction that depicts any of the following: (a) Human sexual behavior. (b) Sadomasochistic abuse. . . . (d) Nudity which appeals to the prurient interest in sex," etc.; rule was used to ban letters and books with a single sexual reference, an issue of *Cosmopolitan*, a picture of the Sistine Chapel, the *Sports Illustrated* swimsuit issue, and issues of *Vanity Fair*, *Rolling Stone*, *Maxim*, and various fitness and motorcycle magazines that contained ads of photo showing a portion of a buttock or a breast).

[177]Amatel v. Reno, 156 F.3d 192, 201 (D.C. Cir. 1998).

[178]*See, e.g.*, Iqbal v. Hasty, 490 F.3d 143, 173–74 (2d Cir. 2007) (holding repeated confiscation of Koran stated a First Amendment claim), *aff'd in part, rev'd in part, and remanded on other grounds sub nom.* Ashcroft v. Iqbal, ___ U.S. ___, 129 S. Ct. 1937 (2009); Sutton v. Rasheed, 323 F.3d 236, 252–54 (3d Cir. 2003) (per curiam) (denial of Nation of Islam materials which "provide religious instruction and without which they could not practice their religion generally" violated free exercise rights under the *Turner/O'Lone* standard); Taylor v. Cox, 912 F. Supp. 140, 145–46 (E.D.Pa. 1995) (allegation that confiscation of Koran kept plaintiff from carrying out Ramadan observances stated RFRA and free exercise claims). *But see* Neal v. Lewis, 414 F.3d 1244, 1246–48 (10th Cir. 2005) (holding that allowance of 12 books plus a dictionary, a thesaurus, and a "primary religious text" sufficiently accommodated the Muslim plaintiff's right to exercise his religion).

[179]*See* Washington v. Klem, 497 F.3d 272, 282–86 (3d Cir. 2007); Rowe v. Davis, 373 F. Supp. 2d 822, 825–26 (N.D.Ind. 2005), both holding that reading religious literature was part of plaintiff's

a protected exercise of religion.[180] Further, some cases involving religious literature have considered its censorship very generally in the context of prisoners' overall opportunities for religious exercise, rather than reviewing each challenged item to see if there is really a basis to censor it.[181] At least one federal court has taken the view that only the specific act of censorship may be addressed under RLUIPA, and that courts may not strike down censorship rules under it.[182] If you challenge the denial to you of religious material, you should generally allege a violation of the First Amendment free speech clause that is applicable to all reading material, of the Religious Land Use and Institutionalized Persons Act or the Religious Freedom Restoration Act, and of the Free Exercise Clause of the First Amendment.

Courts have disagreed whether prisoners have a right to receive catalogs.[183] Some decisions have upheld rules

---

[180]*See* Borzych v. Frank, 439 F.3d 388, 390 (7th Cir. 2006) (questioning whether denial of certain books substantially burdens Odinist religious exercise); Tarpley v. Allen County, Indiana, 312 F.3d 895, 898–99 (7th Cir. 2002) (upholding confiscation of plaintiff's Bible where jail provided him with an institutional copy of the same version, but without the interpretive commentary in his copy); Wares v. Simmons, 524 F. Supp. 2d 1313, 1320–21 (D.Kan. 2007) (holding denial of the *Tehillim* (daily reading of Psalms according to days of Jewish month) and *Tanya* (Chabad teachings of a Rabbi Zalman) did not substantially burden plaintiff's religious exercise in light of other religious items and activities available to him).

Earlier, some courts dismissed religious literature claims under RFRA on the ground that RFRA's "substantial burden" requirement meant that prisoners had to show that a practice that they were prevented from engaging in was mandated by their religion or was a "central" tenet or belief. *See, e.g.,* Stefanow v. McFadden, 103 F.3d 1466, 1471 (9th Cir. 1996) (plaintiff failed to show that anti-Semitic book was essential to his Christian Identity religious exercise). Those decisions are no longer good law, since "substantial burden" is now defined in both RFRA and RLUIPA as "any exercise of religion, whether or not compelled by, or central to, a system of religious belief." Navajo Nation v. U.S. Forest Service, 479 F.3d 1024, 1033 (9th Cir. 2007) (noting cases based on narrower view of religious exercise are not good law), *on rehearing on other grounds,* 535 F.3d 1058 (9th Cir. 2008), *cert. denied,* 129 S. Ct. 2763 (2009); *see* § D.1.b(2) of this chapter. The argument for why religious reading should be protected by RLUIPA and RFRA is well stated by *Rowe v. Davis,* 373 F. Supp. 2d 822, 825–26 (N.D.Ind. 2005):

> Reading religious literature may not be compelled by or central to Mr. Rowe's system of religious belief, but he alleges that it is a part of his exercise of religion. That is to say that reading religious literature is a part of the way Mr. Rowe practices and expresses his religious beliefs. Therefore, reading religious literature is a religious exercise. Taking his religious literature was directly, primarily, and fundamentally responsible for rendering that religious exercise effectively impracticable. Therefore taking his religious literature was a substantial burden on his religious exercise of reading religious literature.

[181]*See* Fraise v. Terhune, 283 F.3d 506, 519–21 (3d Cir. 2002) (affirming ban on Five Percenter literature in connection with treatment of Five Percenters as a "security risk group"). We think this approach is wrong.

[182]*See* Borzych v. Frank, 439 F.3d 388, 391 (7th Cir. 2006).

[183]*Compare* Prison Legal News v. Lehman, 397 F.3d 692, 699–700 (9th Cir. 2005) (striking down rule prohibiting receipt of non-subscription bulk mail and catalogs); Allen v. Higgins, 902 F.2d 682, 684 (10th Cir. 1990) (finding the denial of a catalogue unconstitutional where prison officials made the decision without examining the catalogue, which did not present a security threat) *with* Smith v. Maschner, 899 F.2d 940, 944 (10th Cir. 1990) (return of catalogues sent to the prisoner, along with denial of incoming stickers, labels, and chain letters, upheld); Pepper v. Carroll, 423 F. Supp. 2d 442, 448 (D.Del. 2006) (upholding exclusion of catalog of books and magazines); Dixon v. Kirby, 210 F. Supp. 2d 792, 799–801 (S.D.W.Va. 2002) (upholding ban on catalogs, imposed to avoid overwhelming volume of mail, where prison made selected catalogs available in the commissary), *aff'd,* 48 Fed.Appx. 93 (4th Cir. 2002) (unpublished); Sutton v. Stewart, 22 F. Supp. 2d 1097, 1109–10 (D.Ariz. 1998) (upholding denial of brochure from merchant that was not an "approved vendor" from whom prisoners could order), *aff'd,* 185 F.3d 869 (9th Cir. 1999) (unpublished); Allen v. Wood, 970 F. Supp. 824, 829–30 (E.D.Wash. 1997) (upholding ban on catalogs); *see* Jones v. Salt Lake County, 503 F.3d 1147, 1159–60 (10th Cir. 2007) (remanding for *Turner* analysis, but strongly suggesting a catalog ban would be upheld); Sheets v. Moore, 97 F.3d 164, 168–69 (6th Cir. 1996) (upholding policy prohibiting receipt of "free advertising material, fliers and other bulk rate mail" except from a recognized religious organization sent via the prison chaplain; prisoners could pay the postage to receive them by second class mail). In some of these cases, courts have noted that officials made catalogs available to prisoners in the commissary or elsewhere in support of upholding a ban on individuals' receipt of catalogs. *See Sheets v. Moore,* 97 F.3d at 168–69; *Dixon v. Kirby,* 210 F. Supp. 2d at 800–01; *Allen v. Wood,* 970 F. Supp. at 829–30.

We think the *Lehman* and *Allen v. Higgins* decisions are correct. "Commercial speech" enjoys some degree of First Amendment protection, and that right may be asserted by those who wish to receive commercial information as well as those who communicate it. *See* Virginia State Board of Pharmacy v. Virginia Consumer Council, 475 U.S. 748, 756, 762–65 (1976). Prison officials should therefore be required to give some penological justification for denying you a particular catalog. The concerns for contraband, volume of incoming mail, amount of property, etc., that some decisions rely on in upholding such bans can be addressed in other ways, as the *Lehman* decision shows. As a practical matter, we see no reason why catalogs should be assessed any differently than, for example, a magazine full of advertisements. *But see* Sutton v. Stewart, 22 F. Supp. 2d at 1110 (distinguishing catalogs containing nothing but offers of sale of unauthorized items from magazines containing other content in addition to advertisements). Prison officials can forbid you to order merchandise from catalogues, but that is no reason to keep you from reading about it. *Cf.* Eckford-el v. Toombs, 760 F. Supp. 1267, 1271–72 (W.D.Mich. 1991) (rule against entering into contracts did not justify censorship of a brochure from a correspondence school). Of course, some catalogs

prohibiting possession of certain publications but permitting prisoners to read them under supervision,[184] though courts have declined to require prison officials to offer such a procedure as an alternative to denying publications altogether.[185]

Prison officials have wide latitude in censoring publications that are produced in prison by prisoners.[186]

b. Censorship Procedures Prison censors must observe procedural safeguards.[187] First, there must be an "individualized" determination that a particular publication violates the rules at the time it is censored. The prison cannot simply establish an "excluded list" of publications or ban broad categories of materials without regard to their actual contents.[188] Most courts have required additional safeguards

---

may contain material that is objectionable for other reasons. Packett v. Clarke, 910 F. Supp. 469, 474–77 (D.Neb. 1996) (upholding ban on catalog that might suggest ways of concealing weapons).

[184]Dawson v. Scurr, 986 F.2d 257, 260–62 (8th Cir. 1993) (sexually explicit publications); Grooms v. Caldwell, 806 F. Supp. 807, 810 (N.D.Ind. 1991) (Ku Klux Klan materials).

[185]Mauro v. Arpaio, 188 F.3d 1054, 1062–63 (9th Cir. 1999) (en banc).

[186]Pittman v. Hutto, 594 F.2d 407, 411–12 (4th Cir. 1979). *But see* Bailey v. Loggins, 32 Cal.3d 907, 920, 187 Cal.Rptr. 575, 654 P.2d 758 (Cal. 1982) (prison administration cannot censor newspaper "merely because it disagrees with the views presented, objects to inmate criticism of administration policy, or seeks to avoid discussion of controversial issues"; court relies on state statute as well as First Amendment).

[187]Krug v. Lutz, 329 F.3d 692, 696–97 & n.4 (9th Cir. 2003) (prisoner has a "liberty interest in the receipt of his subscription mailings sufficient to trigger procedural due process guarantees"; defendants' claim that there is no liberty interest in obscene material misses the point, since the plaintiff "has a right to receive his nonobscene subscription materials and a corresponding right to fair procedures governing the withholding of allegedly obscene materials").

[188]The Supreme Court in *Thornburgh* relied heavily on the existence of this protection, stating that it was "comforted" in upholding the federal prisons' censorship regulations by the "individualized" determinations and the lack of "shortcuts that would lead to needless exclusions." Thornburgh v. Abbott, 490 U.S. 401, 416-17, 109 S. Ct. 1874 (1989). Later decisions have treated individualized decisions as a constitutional requirement and not just as "comfort." *See* Shakur v. Selsky, 391 F.3d 106, 115–16 (2d Cir. 2004) (citing the above quoted *Thornburgh* language, holding that a ban on all publications from "unauthorized organizations" was a "shortcut" that "greatly circumscribes the universe of reading materials accessible to inmates" and appears "not sufficiently related to any legitimate and neutral penological objective"); Murphy v. Missouri Dep't of Corrections, 372 F.3d 979, 986 (8th Cir. 2004) ("Before the prison authorities censor materials, they must review the content of each particular item received."); Williams v. Brimeyer, 116 F.3d 351, 354 (8th Cir. 1997) (striking down blanket ban on materials from the Church of Jesus Christ Christian); Shaheed-Muhammad v. DiPaolo, 393 F. Supp. 2d 80,

as well, including notice of the censorship, an opportunity to be heard, a meaningful statement of reasons for the censorship, a prompt decision, and the right to appeal to an official other than the censor.[189] Where a prison has such procedures in place, and then disregards them, officials'

---

104 (D.Mass. 2005) (blanket ban rejected on *The Five Percenter* magazine; defendants argued that "it is not the content of the publication that poses a threat to penological interests, but rather the mere presence of it within the facility," but court said they failed to explain "why these particular editions of *The Five Percenter* posed a security risk"); *see also* Owen v. Wille, 117 F.3d 1235, 1237–38 (11th Cir. 1997) (noting defendants did not dispute that a blanket ban on publications with nude photos would be unconstitutional, upholding exclusion of publications after individualized review); Thomas v. U.S. Secretary of Defense, 730 F. Supp. 362, 365 (D.Kan. 1990) (upholding censorship where officials made a "conscientious review" of the material and pointed to "particular portions . . . which could legitimately raise concerns regarding the potential for racial or religious confrontation"). Even before *Thornburgh*, courts had held that prison officials cannot impose a blanket ban on all issues of particular newspapers and magazines; they must review each issue individually. Guajardo v. Estelle, 580 F.2d 748, 762 (5th Cir. 1978); Hardwick v. Ault, 447 F. Supp. 116, 131 (M.D.Ga. 1978); Cofone v. Manson, 409 F. Supp. 1033, 1041–42 (D.Conn. 1976); McCleary v. Kelly, 376 F. Supp. 1186, 1190–91 (M.D.Pa. 1974); Laaman v. Hancock, 351 F. Supp. 1265, 1269 (D.N.H. 1972).

One recent decision does hold that officials need not review individual issues of certain magazines that the court takes judicial notice "invariably contain nude or semi-nude depictions, or sexually explicit content," listing *Purely 18, Fox, Hustler, Adult Cinema Review, House Roses, Black Tail, Black Gold, De Unique, Black Video Illustrated, Celebrity Skin, Plumpers, Over 40, Over 50, High Society, Chic, Oui, Lollypops, Asian Beauties, Shaved Orientals, Barely Legal, Asian Fever, Asian Lace, Penthouse, Salsa, Celebrity Sleuth, Hawk, Gallery, Easy Rider, Biker, Outlaw Biker, In The Wind, American Curves, Spanish Maxim, Paper Wings, Stuff, Maxim,* and *FHM.* Moses v. Dennehy, 523 F. Supp. 2d 57, 63–64 (D.Mass. 2007), *aff'd sub. nom* Josselyn v. Dennehy, 2009 WL 1587695 (1st Cir., June 9, 2009) (unpublished). Even if this decision is accepted, we don't think its reasoning could be extended to other types of periodicals with a greater variety of contents.

[189]Prison Legal News v. Lehman, 397 F.3d 692, 700–01 (9th Cir. 2005) (notice and review of rejections required for materials sent by first class, periodical, or subscription bulk mail); Krug v. Lutz, 329 F.3d 692, 697 (9th Cir. 2003) (holding due process for rejection of correspondence extends to receipt of publications; appeal to someone other than the censor is a due process requirement); Frost v. Symington, 197 F.3d 348, 353–54 (9th Cir. 1999) (holding notice of withholding of publication required); Murphy v. Missouri Dep't of Corrections, 814 F.2d 1252, 1258 (8th Cir. 1987); Hopkins v. Collins, 548 F.2d 503, 504 (4th Cir. 1977); Dooley v. Quick, 598 F. Supp. 607, 622 (D.R.I. 1984), *aff'd,* 787 F.2d 579 (1st Cir. 1986); Jackson v. Ward, 458 F. Supp. 546, 565 (W.D.N.Y. 1978); Hardwick v. Ault, 447 F. Supp. at 131; Cofone v. Manson, 409 F. Supp. at 1041; Aikens v. Lash, 390 F. Supp. 663, 672 (N.D.Ind. 1975), *aff'd* as modified, 547 F.2d 372 (7th Cir. 1976); Battle v. Anderson, 376 F. Supp. 402, 426 (E.D.Okla. 1974); Laaman v. Hancock, 351 F. Supp. at 1268; Sostre v. Otis, 330 F. Supp. 941, 946 (S.D.N.Y. 1971).

"failure to abide by established procedures and standards can evince an improper objective" in any resulting censorship decision.[190]

Some courts have held that the sender of literature should also receive notice and an opportunity to be heard[191]—a conclusion that is hard to argue with, since publishers have First Amendment rights to communicate with the prisoner audience.[192] A requirement of notice to the sender is consistent with the Supreme Court's holding that the author of a censored letter should get a chance to protest.[193] Notice to the sender is also consistent with common sense. The prisoner is hardly in a position to dispute the censorship of a publication he has not been allowed to see. The sender, who knows what is in the publication or can find out, is better able to explain why the publication should not have been censored.

Prison officials are not constitutionally required to engage in "item censorship"; if one part of a publication is objectionable, they can ban the entire publication.[194]

c. Non-Content-Based Restrictions on Publications

Some restrictions on reading matter are not based on the content of the publications. The Supreme Court has upheld a prohibition on receiving hardcover books from anyone but the publisher, a book club, or a bookstore.[195] The lower courts have upheld broader "publisher only" rules,[196] although the Supreme Court's holding suggests that such a rule could be struck down if you showed that it did not allow sufficient alternative means for obtaining reading material.[197] Prohibitions on hardcover books are not unconstitutional if paperback books are permitted.[198] Restrictions on the number of books a prisoner can possess have been upheld.[199] Courts

---

In *Shakur v. Selsky,* in which the prisoner had been disciplined for possessing a publication, the court held that failure to send the publication to the Media Review Committee did not deny due process because the prisoner had received a disciplinary hearing consistent with the requirements of *Wolff v. McDonnell. Shakur,* 391 F.3d at 118–19. The court does not appear to have considered what process would be due where publications were censored absent a disciplinary proceeding.

[190]Shakur v. Selsky, 391 F.3d at 116; *see* Williams v. Brimeyer, 116 F.3d 351, 354 (8th Cir. 1997) (holding rejection of publications appeared to be an exaggerated response where officials bypassed their own publication review procedure, which had approved similar materials).

[191]Jacklovich v. Simmons, 392 F.3d 420, 433–34 (10th Cir. 2004) (holding sender of publication is entitled to notice of nondelivery); Montcalm Publishing Co. v. Beck, 80 F.3d 105, 109 (4th Cir. 1996); Lawson v. Dugger, 840 F.2d 781, 786 (11th Cir. 1987), *rehearing denied,* 840 F.2d 779 (11th Cir. 1988), *vacated and remanded on other grounds,* 490 U.S. 1078 (1989); Hopkins v. Collins, 548 F.2d at 504; Cofone v. Manson, 409 F. Supp. at 1041; *see also* Vodicka v. Phelps, 624 F.2d 569, 575 (5th Cir. 1980) (notice to sender could replace notice to prisoner under the circumstances).

[192]Thornburgh v. Abbott, 490 U.S. 401, 408, 109 S. Ct. 1874 (1989); Montcalm Publishing Co. v. Beck, 80 F.3d 105, 109 (4th Cir. 1996). Further, as a practical matter, "[a]n inmate who cannot even see the publication can hardly mount an effective challenge to the decision to withhold that publication, and while the inmate is free to notify the publisher and ask for help in challenging the prison authorities' decision, the publisher's First Amendment right must not depend on that." *Montcalm,* 80 F.3d at 109.

[193]Procunier v. Martinez, 416 U.S. 396, 417–19, 94 S. Ct. 1800 (1974). (The procedural part of *Procunier* was not overruled by *Thornburgh v. Abbott*).

[194]Thornburgh v. Abbott, 490 U.S. at 418–19; Harbin-Bey v. Rutter, 420 F.3d 571, 579 (6th Cir. 2005); Shabazz v. Parsons, 127 F.3d 1246, 1249 (10th Cir. 1997).

We think it may be worthwhile to argue to state courts that item censorship should be required by the state constitution. It was instituted in the New York State prisons in response to litigation and has apparently worked well.

[195]Bell v. Wolfish, 441 U.S. 520, 550–52, 99 S. Ct. 1861 (1979).

[196]Jones v. Salt Lake County, 503 F.3d 1147, 1156–59 (10th Cir. 2007) (upholding policy limiting donations of paperback books to the jail library and allowing them to be ordered only from the publisher with permission; upholding prohibition on catalogs); Ward v. Washtenaw County Sheriff's Dep't, 881 F.2d 325, 328–30 (6th Cir. 1989) (publisher only rule applied to magazines); Hurd v. Williams, 755 F.2d 306, 308–09 (3d Cir. 1985) (rule applied to newspapers, periodicals, and softbound books); Zaczek v. Hutto, 642 F.2d 74, 75 (4th Cir. 1981) (all publications must come from publisher or a "legitimate bookstore"); Cotton v. Lockhart, 620 F.2d 670, 672 (8th Cir. 1980); Avery v. Powell, 806 F. Supp. 7, 11 (D.N.H. 1992) (all publications must come from publishers or bookstores); Rich v. Luther, 514 F. Supp. 481, 482–83 (W.D.N.C. 1981) (rule applied to all publications for higher security inmates); Ramos v. Lamm, 485 F. Supp. 122, 163 (D.Colo. 1979) (all publications must be obtained from a publisher or an "established vendor or distributor"), *modified on other grounds,* 639 F.2d 559 (10th Cir. 1980).

[197]*See* Keenan v. Hall, 83 F.3d 1083, 1093 (9th Cir. 1996) (publisher only rule may be unconstitutional where it combines with other circumstances to impose severe limits on availability of reading material; rule at issue applied to paperbacks as well as hardcovers, plaintiffs complained of limited library and access to it, prisoners were forbidden to pass books to one another); Pratt v. Sumner, 807 F.2d 817, 819–20 (9th Cir. 1987) (a complaint that a "publisher or bookstore only" policy was applied to softcover books was held not to be frivolous where there was no information on alternative means of obtaining the books and the plaintiff's confinement was longer than that in *Wolfish*); Kines v. Day, 754 F.2d 28, 30–31 (1st Cir. 1985) (similar rule upheld as constitutional on its face, but court declined to hear a challenge to its application (i.e., its effect) because the plaintiff did not show that he was actually denied access to identifiable publications).

In our opinion, to win a challenge to a rule of this type, you must identify a particular publication or a type of reading material that you can't get under the rule.

[198]Skelton v. Pri-Cor, Inc., 963 F.2d 100, 103 (6th Cir. 1991); Brownlee v. Conine, 957 F.2d 353, 354 (7th Cir. 1992); Cosby v. Purkett, 782 F. Supp. 1324, 1330 (E.D.Mo. 1992).

[199]Neal v. Lewis, 414 F.3d 1244, 1248 (10th Cir. 2005) (restriction to 12 books plus the primary text of prisoner's religion upheld); Weir v. Nix, 114 F.3d 817, 821 (8th Cir. 1997) (limit of 25 books does not violate Religious Freedom Restoration Act; plaintiff's request to maintain a "well-rounded research library" is "outlandish"); *see* Tarpley v. Allen County, Indiana, 312 F.3d 895, 898–99 (7th Cir. 2002) (upholding jail policy of barring retention of personal reading materials to avoid fights over ownership and

have struck down other restrictions that make no sense, or that make it impossible or excessively difficult to obtain reading material, or a particular kind of reading material.[200] One court has suggested that the issue in assessing a non-content-related limit on publications is "whether the regulations and policies here still 'permit a broad range of publications to be sent, received, and read.'"[201] Courts have struck down prohibitions on newspapers,[202] as well as bans on newspaper clippings received in correspondence.[203] Courts have struck down prohibitions on material downloaded and printed from the Internet.[204] Several decisions have struck down prohibitions on material sent in particular postage classes.[205] Courts have held unconstitutional the failure to provide enough light to read by.[206]

Prison officials may restrict reading material in punitive segregation, although most cases upholding this practice have involved short periods of time.[207] However, the Supreme Court has upheld a prohibition on magazines, newspapers, and personal photographs in a high-security administrative segregation unit housing "the 40 most intractable inmates" in a state prison system for

---

claims for compensation for lost or stolen books; upholding confiscation of plaintiff's Bible where jail provided him with an institutional copy of the same version, but without the interpretive commentary in his copy).

[200]Prison Legal News v. Lehman, 397 F.3d 692, 699–700 (9th Cir. 2005) (ban on non-subscription bulk mail and catalogs struck down as having no rational relationship to controlling contraband, since contraband is more likely to be contained in first class mail, and no rational relationship to limiting property and fire hazards, since there was already a rule limiting the amount of property); Jacklovich v. Simmons, 392 F.3d 420, 429–32 (10th Cir. 2004) (questioning reasonableness of prohibition on receiving any publications for the first 120 days after intake and banning the receipt of gift publications and subscriptions); Ashker v. California Dep't of Corrections, 350 F.3d 917, 923–24 (9th Cir. 2003) (striking down requirement of "approved vendor" labels which added nothing to security and obstructed receipt of reading material); Crofton v. Roe, 170 F.3d 957, 960–61 (9th Cir. 1999) (striking down prohibition on receipt of publications as gifts); Pembroke v. Wood County, Tex., 981 F.2d 225, 229 (5th Cir. 1993) (restriction of reading material to one Bible was unconstitutional); Jackson v. Elrod, 881 F.2d 441, 444–46 (7th Cir. 1989) (denial of right to receive hardcover books even from the publisher and with the covers removed was unconstitutional); Kincaid v. Rusk, 670 F.2d 737, 743–45 (7th Cir. 1982) (ban on pictorial magazines, newspapers, and hardcover books, designed to prevent fires and protect plumbing, violated the First Amendment); Parnell v. Waldrep, 511 F. Supp. 764, 767–68 (W.D.N.C. 1981) (similar to *Kincaid*).

[201]Jacklovich v. Simmons, 392 F.3d 420, 431 (10th Cir. 2004); *accord*, Ashker v. California Dep't of Corrections, 224 F. Supp. 2d 1253, 1259 (N.D.Cal. 2002) (under *Turner*, "[r]egulations to be viewed with caution include those which categorically prohibit access to a broad range of materials"), *aff'd*, 350 F.3d 917, 923–24 (9th Cir. 2003).

[202]Green v. Ferrell, 801 F.2d 765, 772 (5th Cir. 1986); Mann v. Smith, 796 F.2d 79, 82–83 (5th Cir. 1986) (ban on all newspapers and magazines violated First Amendment); Hutchings v. Corum, 501 F. Supp. 1276, 1299 (W.D.Mo. 1980); Mitchell v. Untreiner, 421 F. Supp. 886, 895 (N.D.Fla. 1976); Manicone v. Corso, 365 F. Supp. 576, 577 (E.D.N.Y. 1973); Powlowski v. Wullich, 81 Misc.2d 895, 366 N.Y.S.2d 584, 590 (N.Y.Sup. 1975); *see* Van Cleave v. U.S., 854 F.2d 82, 84 (5th Cir. 1988) (ban on newspapers stated a constitutional claim); Martin v. Tyson, 845 F.2d 1451, 1454 (5th Cir. 1988) (ban on newspapers raised a triable issue).

[203]Lindell v. Frank, 377 F.3d 655, 658–60 (7th Cir. 2004) (striking down application of publisher only rule to clippings received in correspondence); Allen v. Coughlin, 64 F.3d 77, 80–81 (2d Cir. 1995) (denying summary judgment to prison officials who maintained a publisher only rule for newspapers and prohibited enclosure of newspaper clippings in correspondence).

[204]*See* § B.1.a of this chapter, n.105.

[205]Prison Legal News v. Lehman, 397 F.3d 692, 700–01 (9th Cir. 2005) (striking down a prohibition on receipt of non-subscription bulk mail and catalogs; noting that it didn't matter whether the prisoner had paid for the material as long as he had requested it); Morrison v. Hall, 261 F.3d 896, 903–05 (9th Cir. 2001) (striking down prohibition on publications sent third or fourth class); Prison Legal News v. Cook, 238 F.3d 1145, 1149–50 (9th Cir. 2001) (striking down prohibition on "standard rate" (bulk) mail as applied to subscription non-profit newsletters). *But see* Sheets v. Moore, 97 F.3d 164, 168–69 (6th Cir. 1996) (upholding policy prohibiting receipt of "free advertising material, fliers and other bulk rate mail" except from a recognized religious organization sent via the prison chaplain, based on concerns that large influx of mail would make it difficult to search and result in fire hazards; officials made catalogs available in the prison store, and prisoners could pay the postage to receive them by second class mail); Clark v. Schumacher, 109 Or.App. 354, 820 P.2d 3, 5 (Or.App. 1991) (prohibition on third and fourth class and bulk mail upheld).

[206]Antonelli v. Sheahan, 81 F.3d 1422, 1433 (7th Cir. 1996) ("Any right to access to printed materials protected by the First Amendment and (in the case of a pre-trial detainee) the Due Process Clause is necessarily implicated where there is objectively insufficient lighting to enable reading.")

[207]Gregory v. Auger, 768 F.2d 287, 289–91 (8th Cir. 1985) (inmates in disciplinary detention could be deprived of all but first class mail of a "personal, legal or religious" nature where detention was limited to 60 days); Daigre v. Maggio, 719 F.2d 1310, 1312–13 (5th Cir. 1983) (ban on newspapers and magazines in segregation upheld as applied to an inmate who served 10 days); Pendleton v. Housewright, 651 F. Supp. 631, 635 (D.Nev. 1986) (denial of reading materials upheld when limited to a few days at a time); Jackson v. Brookhart, 640 F. Supp. 241 (S.D.Iowa 1986) (upholding the deprivation of all reading material except for religious, legal, or educational materials, correspondence, and a newspaper for an hour a day, to an inmate serving 286 days for 38 infractions); Guajardo v. Estelle, 568 F. Supp. 1354, 1366–68 (S.D.Tex. 1983) (deprivation of publications except for legal and religious materials in solitary confinement upheld where limited to 15 days); Johnson v. Anderson, 370 F. Supp. 1373, 1391–94 (D.Del. 1974) (deprivation of reading matter permissible). *But see* Hardwick v. Ault, 447 F. Supp. 116, 128–31 (M.D.Ga. 1978) (mail and reading matter restrictions in administrative segregation held unconstitutional).

indefinite periods.[208] It is not clear whether this holding would apply to all prisoners in segregation units.[209]

Prison officials are not generally required to provide reading materials for prisoners.[210] But if they do provide libraries, the "selective removal of library books restricts an inmate's right to receive information" and must pass muster under the *Turner* standard.[211] If the prison provides religious

literature, the failure to do so on a reasonably equal basis for different religions may be unconstitutional.[212]

3. Access to Non-Print Media

Courts have held that prisons cannot justify excessive restrictions on reading material by allowing prisoners to watch television or listen to the radio.[213] They have also held that there is no constitutional right to watch TV or movies or listen to the radio in prison.[214] It is not clear why that should be the case, since at this point radio and television are at least as important as books and magazines as sources of information and entertainment. Insofar as prisons do

---

[208]Beard v. Banks, 548 U.S. 521, 533, 126 S. Ct. 2572 (2006) (plurality opinion). *Beard* is discussed extensively in § A of this chapter, nn.58–62.

[209]In *Jacklovich v. Simmons*, 392 F.3d 420 (10th Cir. 2004), newly admitted prisoners in "Level I" were forbidden any publications except a "primary religious text" for the first 120 days of their confinement. Though the policy was initially upheld, on appeal the court reversed and remanded, stating: "We fail to see how a four-month complete denial of access to constitutionally protected materials (regardless of behavior) furthers behavior management or rehabilitation." *Jacklovich*, 392 F.3d at 429. In *Spellman v. Hopper*, 95 F. Supp. 2d 1267 (M.D.Ala. 1999), the court struck down a ban on magazine and newspaper subscriptions in administrative segregation, rejecting an argument that this was needed for "discipline" by observing that administrative segregation is not a disciplinary classification. *Spellman*, 95 F. Supp. 2d at 1279–80. In *Wares v. Simmons*, 524 F. Supp. 2d 1313 (D.Kan. 2007), a sex offender who refused to participate in a "Sex Abuse Treatment Program" was subjected to the Kansas Level I restrictions addressed in *Jacklovich v. Simmons*, which denied him religious publications other than a "primary religious text." The defendants initially claimed that this policy was justified by the need to enforce the demand for program participation, and then added the argument that property needed to be kept to a minimum for high-security classifications (which the plaintiff was in because he had refused the program) for security reasons. The court held that the policy did not violate either the First Amendment or RLUIPA. *Wares*, 524 F. Supp. 2d at 1320–25.

[210]Hunnicutt v. Armstrong, 305 F. Supp. 2d 175, 188 (D.Conn. 2004) (complaint about procedure for distributing books in segregation unit rejected; "Research has revealed no constitutional right to unlimited pleasure reading."), *affirmed in part, vacated in part, remanded on other grounds*, 152 Fed.Appx. 34 (2d Cir. 2005) (unpublished); Counts v. Newhart, 951 F. Supp. 579, 587 (E.D.Va. 1996) (there is no right to a "general-literary library" in jail), *aff'd*, 116 F.3d 1473 (4th Cir. 1997) (unpublished); Stewart v. McGinnis, 800 F. Supp. 604, 618 (N.D.Ill. 1992); Inmates of Occoquan v. Barry, 717 F. Supp. 854, 868 (D.D.C. 1989) (library deficiencies do not come within the purview of the eighth amendment); Griffin v. Smith, 493 F. Supp. 129, 131 (W.D.N.Y. 1980) (complaints of limit on books in segregation cells and inadequate library did not state constitutional claims). In some older cases, courts have directed that reading material be provided in local jails or in segregation units. Dawson v. Kendrick, 527 F. Supp. 1252, 1316 (S.D.W.Va. 1981); Mitchell v. Untreiner, 421 F. Supp. 886, 901 (N.D.Fla. 1976); Giampetruzzi v. Malcolm, 406 F. Supp. 836, 846 (S.D.N.Y. 1975) (greater library access required for prisoners in administrative segregation); Brenneman v. Madigan, 343 F. Supp. 128, 140 (N.D.Cal. 1972).

[211]Cline v. Fox, 319 F. Supp. 2d 685, 690–91 (N.D.W.Va. 2004) (holding that removal from library of all materials that depict "explicit sexual activity," including works by authors such as Gore

Vidal and John Updike, while allowing "commercial pornography" such as *Playboy* and *Maxim*, was unconstitutional).

[212]McElyea v. Babbitt, 833 F.2d 196, 199 (9th Cir. 1987); Pitts v. Knowles, 339 F. Supp. 1183, 1185–86 (W.D.Wis. 1972), *aff'd*, 478 F.2d 1405 (7th Cir. 1973). *But see* Neal v. Lewis, 325 F. Supp. 2d 1231, 1238 (D.Kan. 2004) (absence of Shi'ite texts from prison library did not deny equal protection because plaintiff could not prove intentional discrimination), *aff'd*, 414 F.3d 1244 (10th Cir. 2005); *see* § D.3 of this chapter on the equal treatment of religions.

[213]Jacklovich v. Simmons, 392 F.3d 420, 431 (10th Cir. 2004); Morrison v. Hall, 261 F.3d 896, 904 (9th Cir. 2001); Mann v. Smith, 796 F.2d 79, 83 (5th Cir. 1986); *see* Spellman v. Hopper, 95 F. Supp. 2d 1267, 1283 n.28 (M.D.Ala. 1999) (noting literature distinguishing experience of reading from that of TV or radio).

[214]Montana v. Commissioners' Court, 659 F.2d 19, 23 (5th Cir. 1981); Pepper v. Carroll, 423 F. Supp. 2d 442, 447 (D.Del. 2006) (plaintiff's religious rights were not violated by failure to provide a TV so he could watch religious services); Riley v. Snyder, 72 F. Supp. 2d 456, 460 (D.Del. 1999); Manley v. Fordice, 945 F. Supp. 132, 136–37 (S.D.Miss. 1996) (upholding rule restricting TVs to prisoners in work programs or ineligible for them), *aff'd*, 132 F.3d 1455 (5th Cir. 1997) (unpublished); Gawloski v. Dallman, 803 F. Supp. 103, 111 (S.D.Ohio 1992); Terrell v. State, 573 So.2d 730, 732 (Miss. 1990); *see also* Aswegan v. Bruhl, 113 F.3d 109, 110 (8th Cir. 1997) (holding cable TV is not a service, program, or activity under the Americans with Disabilities Act); More v. Farrier, 984 F.2d 269, 271–72 (8th Cir. 1993) (prison officials need not provide the same level of TV service to wheelchair-bound inmates as to the rest of the population); Rial v. McGinnis, 756 F. Supp. 1070, 1073–74 (N.D.Ill. 1991) (ban on televisions with built-in video players did not violate the Constitution). If officials do permit such viewing by prisoners, restrictions on it are governed by the *Turner v. Safley* reasonable relationship standard. *See* Jewell v. Gonzales, 420 F. Supp. 2d 406, 427–37 (W.D.Pa. 2006) (upholding regulations enacted under the Zimmerman Amendment barring showing of "R"-rated films in federal prisons). Permitting prisoners in some programs but not others to have TV access does not deny equal protection, since it is rational to provide incentives for prisoners to enter particular programs and to behave well in order to stay in them. Manley v. Fordice, 945 F. Supp. at 137–38.

One court has held that the provision of a religious channel in a prison's closed-circuit television channel did not violate the First Amendment's ban on establishment of religion. Henderson v. Berge, 362 F. Supp. 2d 1030, 1032–34 (W.D.Wis. 2005), *reconsideration denied*, 2005 WL 1261970 (W.D.Wis., May 26, 2005), *aff'd*, 190 Fed.Appx. 507, 509–10, 2006 WL 2267092 (7th Cir. 2006) (unpublished).

permit access to radio, TV, or movies, restrictions on that access are subject to the *Turner v. Safley* reasonable relationship analysis.[215]

We do not know of any court decision holding that prisoners have a right of access to recorded music,[216] but if prisons allow it, restrictions on access are subject to the *Turner v. Safley* reasonable relationship analysis.[217] One court has held that there is no right to possess CD and tape equipment in order to learn languages for religious purposes, unless it is shown that they cannot be learned from books.[218]

We also do not know of any court decision holding that prisoners have a right to Internet access.[219] However, one court has held that it is irrational for prisons to ban material that has been printed out from the Internet.[220]

4. Communication with Media and Writing for Publication

Prisoners have a First Amendment right to "be free from governmental interference with [their] contacts with the press if that interference is based on the content of [their] speech or proposed speech."[221] However, prison officials have substantial discretion over how press contacts are made as long as they leave open adequate alternatives. Thus, they may ban interviews of prisoners by media representatives as long as prisoners are free to write letters to the press or communicate via their other visitors.[222] In general, the press has no more right to enter jails or prisons than does the general public.[223] But if officials choose to permit some press conferences and interviews, they must have non-discriminatory guidelines and fair procedures for granting or denying permission for them.[224]

---

[215]*See* Wolf v. Ashcroft, 297 F.3d 305, 308–10 (3d Cir. 2002) (directing lower court to apply *Turner* to the "Zimmer Amendment," which prohibits expenditure of funds for viewing movies rated R or NC-17); Jewell v. Gonzales, 420 F. Supp. 2d 406, 424–41 (W.D.Pa. 2006) (upholding Amendment under *Turner*).

[216]*See* Saahir v. Estelle, 47 F.3d 758, 761 (5th Cir. 1995) (no federal law creates a right to listen to musical tapes in prison).

[217]Herlein v. Higgins, 172 F.3d 1089, 1090–91 (8th Cir. 1999) (ban on music cassettes labelled "parental advisory—explicit lyrics" is not unconstitutional, since the court found that exposing gang members and sex offenders to music with explicit lyrics can cause a security threat); Golden v. McCaughtrey, 937 F. Supp. 818, 821–22 (E.D.Wis. 1996) (upholding forwarding of cassette tapes with parental advisory warnings for review and prohibition of those with lyrics which encourage or advocate violence or disrespect for an ethnic or racial group; "Rap music constitutes speech protected by the First Amendment," but censorship policy satisfied the *Turner* standard.).

[218]Lindell v. Casperson, 360 F. Supp. 2d 932, 953 (W.D.Wis. 2005), *aff'd*, 169 Fed.Appx. 999 (7th Cir. 2006) (unpublished).

[219]*Cf.* Damron v. North Dakota Commissioner of Corrections, 299 F. Supp. 2d 970, 986 (D.N.D. 2004) (upholding deprivation of access to educational computers, which did not have Internet access, because prisoner had downloaded pictures of women in bikinis from a CD given to him by staff), *aff'd*, 127 Fed.Appx. 909 (8th Cir. 2005). One court has held that prisoners may not be forbidden to communicate with persons who may place material on the Internet on their behalf. *See* Canadian Coalition against the Death Penalty v. Ryan, 269 F. Supp. 2d 1199, 1202–03 (D.Ariz. 2003); *see also* Cassels v. Stalder, 342 F. Supp. 2d 555, 564–67 (M.D.La. 2004) (punishing a prisoner for a complaint about medical care that his mother put on the Internet violated the First Amendment).

[220]*See* § B.1.a of this chapter, n.105.

[221]Kimberlin v. Quinlan, 199 F.3d 496, 502 (D.C. Cir. 1999).

[222]Pell v. Procunier, 417 U.S. 817, 822–28, 94 S. Ct. 2800 (1974); Hammer v. Ashcroft, 570 F.3d 798, 801–05 (7th Cir. 2009) (en banc) (upholding denial of face-to-face media interviews by prisoners in special confinement units); Johnson v. Stephan, 816 F. Supp. 677, 679 (D.Kan. 1993) (upholding denial of interview with TV journalists); U.S. v. Hinckley, 725 F. Supp. 616, 629–30 (D.D.C. 1989) (person acquitted of presidential assassination attempt by reason of insanity could be denied press interviews); *see* Mujahid v. Sumner, 807 F. Supp. 1505, 1509–11 (D.Haw. 1992) (rule barring both visits and correspondence with members of the press was unconstitutional), *aff'd*, 996 F.2d 1226 (9th Cir. 1993) (unpublished); *see also* Houchins v. KQED, Inc., 438 U.S. 1, 98 S. Ct. 2588 (1978) (reversing an injunction granting television station access to jail; no majority opinion); State v. Olson, 586 So.2d 1239, 1244 (Fla.App. 1991) (statute forbidding the receipt of unauthorized written communication from prisoner could be applied to a reporter who received notes from a prisoner during a visit).

[223]Pell v. Procunier, 417 U.S. at 834; Saxbe v. Washington Post Co., 417 U.S. 843, 849–50, 94 S. Ct. 1811 (1974); Sidebottom v. Schriro, 927 F. Supp. 1221, 1223–25 (E.D.Mo. 1996) (upholding officials' temporary suspension of media interviews until they could meet with media and determine what the demand for interviews was going to be; upholding exclusion of the mother of an executed prisoner as a reporter). *But see* The Chicago Reader v. Sheahan, 141 F. Supp. 2d 1142, 1145–47 (N.D.Ill. 2001) (holding exclusion of reporter from jail access based on the content of her prior stories violated the First Amendment; she must be admitted on the same basis as other reporters). Courts have issued conflicting decisions concerning media access to executions. *Compare* California First Amendment Coalition v. Woodford, 299 F.3d 868, 873–85 (9th Cir. 2002) (holding the public and press are entitled to view executions by lethal injection in their entirety in light of the First Amendment "qualified right of access to governmental proceedings"; officials' desire to "conceal the harsh reality of executions from the public" did not justify exclusion) *with* Rice v. Kempker, 374 F.3d 675, 678–81 (8th Cir. 2004) (upholding ban on videotaping of executions against challenge by religious organization); Entertainment Network, Inc. v. Lappin, 134 F. Supp. 2d 1002, 1010–18 (S.D.Ind. 2001) (upholding refusal to allow recording and broadcast of execution based on purposes of preventing sensationalizing of executions, preserving their solemnity, maintaining security and order in prison, and protecting privacy of condemned persons, their families, victims, and participants in the execution).

[224]Main Road v. Aytch, 522 F.2d 1080, 1088–90 (3d Cir. 1975), *remedy approved*, 565 F.2d 54 (3d Cir. 1977).

One court has upheld a rule permitting interviews only to journalists who have jobs with radio or television stations, excluding a producer of public access cable programs. Jersawitz v. Hanberry, 783 F.2d 1532, 1534–35 (11th Cir. 1986).

Prisoners are entitled to write letters to the press[225] and to write for publication.[226] Some courts have held that such communications are properly assessed under the "less restrictive alternative" standard applied to outgoing mail,[227] but others have applied the "reasonable relationship" standard that is applied to other prison restrictions on expression in situations where it is expected that a published communication would be read within the prison.[228] If you

bring a case alleging that your communications with the media have been censored, you should provide the communication to the court, or if that is not possible, describe it sufficiently that the court will be able to determine whether interfering with it was unconstitutional.[229]

Courts have disagreed over whether mail to the media is entitled to the same confidentiality as "privileged" legal mail.[230] If you are litigating this issue, be sure to remind the court that prison officials have a long history of retaliating against prisoners who criticize them to people or agencies on the outside,[231] even though such retaliation is unlawful.[232] It is therefore essential to permit media mail to be sent confidentially in order to protect prisoners' right to complain to the press about prison conditions.[233]

---

[225]Owen v. Lash, 682 F.2d 648, 650–53 (7th Cir. 1982) (ban on correspondence with newspaper reporter was unconstitutional); Spruytte v. Hoffner, 181 F. Supp. 2d 736, 742–45 (W.D.Mich. 2001) (transfer in retaliation for letter to newspaper was unconstitutional; damages awarded); Castle v. Clymer, 15 F. Supp. 2d 640, 662–63 (E.D.Pa. 1998) (holding prisoner's transfer for interview and letters to a newspaper reporter violated the First Amendment even though the prisoner's comments were "confrontational and inflammatory"); Mujahid v. Sumner, 807 F. Supp. 1505, 1509–11 (D.Haw. 1992) (ban on correspondence with members of the press unless they had been friends before the prisoner was incarcerated was unconstitutional), aff'd, 996 F.2d 1226 (9th Cir. 1993) (unpublished); Martyr v. Mazur-Hart, 789 F. Supp. 1081, 1089 (D.Or. 1992) (enjoining interference with a mental patient's letters to the media).

[226]Abu-Jamal v. Price, 154 F.3d 128, 134–36 (3d Cir. 1998) (granting preliminary injunction against use of a rule against engaging in a business or profession to interfere with prisoner's writing for publication); Tyler v. Ciccone, 299 F. Supp. 684, 688 (W.D.Mo. 1969) (restrictions on detainee's preparation of manuscripts struck down).

A recent decision struck down a prohibition on federal prisoners' writing for the news media under a byline. Jordan v. Pugh, 504 F. Supp. 2d 1109, 1119–20 (D.Colo. 2007), motion to amend denied, motion for findings granted, 2007 WL 2908931 (D.Colo., Oct. 4, 2007). An earlier decision upheld an older version of that regulation, which forbade prisoners to write for payment, act as reporters, or publish under a byline in the news media, but permitting them to write letters to the media. Martin v. Rison, 741 F. Supp. 1406, 1410–18 (N.D.Cal. 1990), vacated as moot sub nom. Chronicle Publishing Co. v. Rison, 962 F.2d 959 (9th Cir. 1992).

Prisoners generally do not have direct access to the Internet, but they may get others to place material on the Internet for them, or others may write about them on the Internet. One court has struck down a statute that forbade prisoners from contact by mail with communication service providers or from having access to the Internet through a provider. Canadian Coalition against the Death Penalty v. Ryan, 269 F. Supp. 2d 1199, 1202–03 (D. Ariz. 2003); see also Cassels v. Stalder, 342 F. Supp. 2d 555, 564–67 (M.D.La. 2004) (holding rule prohibiting "spreading rumors" vague and overbroad on its face and as applied to a prisoner who told his mother he had been denied medical care, resulting in her putting the information on the Internet).

[227]Jordan v. Pugh, 504 F. Supp. 2d 1109, 1119–20 (D.Colo. 2007), motion to amend denied, motion for findings granted, 2007 WL 2908931 (D.Colo., Oct. 4, 2007); Spruytte v. Hoffner, 181 F. Supp. 2d 736, 742 (W.D.Mich. 2001).

[228]Martin v. Rison, 741 F. Supp. 1406, 1412–13 (N.D.Cal. 1990), vacated as moot sub nom. Chronicle Publishing Co. v. Rison, 962 F.2d 959 (9th Cir. 1992); Lomax v. Fiedler, 554 N.W.2d 841, 848–49, 204 Wis.2d 196, 216–19 (Wis.App. 1996) (upholding discipline against prisoner for articles which could be read as

"condoning or advocating violence and were rife with name-calling and false accusations against prison officials"), review denied, 208 Wis.2d 212, 562 N.W.2d 601 (1997). The court in Abu-Jamal v. Price, 154 F.3d 128, 132–35 (3d Cir. 1998), also applied Turner to a prisoner's writing for publication, but did not explain why.

[229]George v. Smith, 507 F.3d 605, 609 (7th Cir. 2007) (acknowledging that advertisements can be protected speech, but rejecting the plaintiff's claim he was barred from placing ads because he didn't say what the content of the ads would have been).

[230]Compare Guajardo v. Estelle, 580 F.2d 748, 759 (5th Cir. 1978); Taylor v. Sterrett, 532 F.2d 462, 481–82 (5th Cir. 1976); Travis v. Lockhart, 607 F. Supp. 1083, 1085–86 (E.D.Ark. 1985); Burton v. Foltz, 599 F. Supp. 114, 116–17 (E.D.Mich. 1984) (all holding media mail privileged) with Gaines v. Lane, 790 F.2d 1299, 1307 (7th Cir. 1986); Moore v. Branson, 755 F. Supp. 268, 269 (E.D.Mo. 1991) (holding media mail non-privileged), aff'd, 950 F.2d 728 (8th Cir. 1991). At least two courts have held that incoming media mail need not be treated as privileged, but outgoing mail must be. Mann v. Adams, 846 F.2d 589, 591 (9th Cir. 1988); Matter of Rules Adoption Regarding Inmate Mail, 120 N.J. 137, 576 A.2d 274, 279–82 (N.J. 1990) (citing Thornburgh v. Abbott).

Some letters addressed to publications need not be treated as media mail. Lucas v. Scully, 71 N.Y.2d 401, 403 n.3, 526 N.Y.S.2d 927, 932 (N.Y. 1988) (citing regulation excluding mail addressed to a box number in care of a "media entity" from the media mail category).

[231]See, e.g., Meriwether v. Coughlin, 879 F.2d 1037, 1046 (2d Cir. 1989) (affirming jury verdict for prisoners who were transferred for complaining to state agencies and public interest organizations); Cruz v. Beto, 603 F.2d 1178, 1180–81, 1186 (5th Cir. 1979) (affirming damage award for retaliation against attorney who criticized prisons and inmates who were her clients); Cavey v. Levine, 435 F. Supp. 475, 483 (D.Md. 1977) (prisoner punished for threatening to write to the press), aff'd sub nom. Cavey v. Williams, 580 F.2d 1047 (4th Cir. 1978).

[232]Kimberlin v. Quinlan, 774 F. Supp. 1, 4 n.6 (D.D.C. 1991) and cases cited; Cavey v. Levine, 435 F. Supp. at 483; see also Pratt v. Rowland, 770 F. Supp. 1399, 1406 (N.D.Cal. 1991) (defendants enjoined from threatening, harassing or punishing the plaintiff because of his media attention).

[233]See Procunier v. Martinez, 416 U.S. 396, 424, 94 S. Ct. 1800 (1974) (Marshall, J., concurring) ("Allowing inspection of media mail will chill open communication by these residents with the media since it allows critics to be identified, creating fear of reprisals").

Involuntary media exposure may violate your state law rights,[234] and in some cases may violate the Constitution.[235]

5. Organizations, Protests, Grievances, and Complaints

The First Amendment protects "the right of the people peaceably to assemble, and to petition the Government for a redress of grievances."[236] These rights are severely restricted in prison.

Prison officials may ban prisoner organizations that oppose or criticize prison policies,[237] and court decisions have generally upheld restrictions on those prisoner organizations that are permitted.[238] There is no constitutional right to belong

to a gang, or "Security Threat Group" as prison officials often call them,[239] and officials may impose restrictions or take disciplinary action based on gang membership[240] or the use of gang signs or symbols.[241] In some instances courts have declared religious organizations to be security threat groups.[242]

---

[234]Huskey v. National Broadcasting Co., Inc., 632 F. Supp. 1282, 1286–94 (N.D.Ill. 1986) (inmate filmed without his consent while working out in his gym shorts had claims for the state law tort of invasion of privacy and for violation of NBC's contract with the prison to protect inmates' privacy). Rights of privacy are discussed in § E of this chapter.

[235]Demery v. Arpaio, 378 F.3d 1020, 1029–33 (9th Cir. 2004) (broadcasting live video images over the Internet from inside jail constituted unlawful punishment of pre-trial detainees); Lauro v. Charles, 219 F.3d 202, 203 (2d Cir. 2000) (the "perp walk," i.e., parading an arrestee before the media for no law enforcement purpose, "exacerbates the seizure of the arrestee unreasonably and therefore violates the Fourth Amendment").

[236]U.S.Const., Amend. I.

[237]Jones v. North Carolina Prisoners' Labor Union, Inc., 433 U.S. 119, 97 S. Ct. 2532 (1977). In Jones, the Supreme Court upheld prison officials' ban on solicitation for union meetings, union membership, and bulk mailings of union literature into the prison, even though no strike or work stoppage was actually imminent. The Court stressed that prisoners' status and the realities of prison life required restrictions on the right to associate, that prison officials' decisions should be granted deference, and that the prison environment is not a "public forum" open to all groups including those that wish to pursue an "adversary relationship" with the prison administration. Jones, 433 U.S. at 129–35. But see Shakur v. Selsky, 391 F.3d 106, 115–16 (2d Cir. 2004) (questioning constitutionality of law barring materials concerning any organization not authorized by the Commissioner). Contra, Leitzsey v. Coombe, 998 F. Supp. 282, 285–88 (W.D.N.Y. 1998) (upholding discipline of prisoner for his own writings concerning the "Black-A-Moor Kings and Queens Knights Nation" under rule referred to in Shakur).

[238]Preast v. Cox, 628 F.2d 292, 294 (4th Cir. 1980) (prisoner groups could be required to receive official recognition before engaging in joint activities; denial of recognition would be virtually unreviewable by court); Akbar v. Borgen, 803 F. Supp. 1479, 1485–86 (E.D.Wis. 1992) (upholding a rule forbidding "unsanctioned group activity" on its face and as applied to a prisoner seeking to form a Muslim organization); Hudson v. Thornburgh, 770 F. Supp. 1030, 1036 (W.D. Pa. 1991) (disbanding of Association of Lifers upheld because prison officials believed it was a security threat), aff'd, 980 F.2d 723 (3d Cir. 1992); Thomas v. U.S. Secretary of Defense, 730 F. Supp. 362, 366 (D.Kan. 1990) (white inmates could be denied the right to form a "European Heritage Club"); McCabe v. Arave, 626 F. Supp. 1199, 1206 (D.Idaho 1986) (prison could ban formal study classes of white racist religious group in

"close custody"), aff'd in pertinent part, 827 F.2d 634 (9th Cir. 1987); see also Salahuddin v. Coughlin, 591 F. Supp. 353, 361 (S.D.N.Y. 1984) (prison officials could restrict association rights of Inmate Liaison Committee); Cabassa v. Kuhlmann, 173 A.D.2d 973, 569 N.Y.S.2d 825, 825 (N.Y.App.Div. 1991) (president of inmate student group could be disciplined for threatening a boycott of a college program), appeal denied, 78 N.Y.2d 858 (1991). But see Dawson v. Delaware, 503 U.S. 159, 165–69, 112 S. Ct. 1093 (1992) (use in a criminal trial of prisoner's membership in the Aryan Brotherhood violated the First Amendment); Nicholas v. Miller, 189 F.3d 191, 194–95 (2d Cir. 1999) (per curiam) (holding prison officials were not entitled to summary judgment after prohibiting formation of Prisoners' Legal Defense Center); Castle v. Clymer, 15 F. Supp. 2d 640, 665–66 (E.D.Pa. 1998) (prisoner could not be transferred for activities as head of Lifers organization that had been authorized).

[239]Westefer v. Snyder, 422 F.3d 570, 574–75 (7th Cir. 2005).

[240]Westefer v. Snyder, 422 F.3d 575 (segregation of gang members and their transfer to supermax prison did not violate the First Amendment); Harbin-Bey v. Rutter, 420 F.3d 571, 576–79 (6th Cir. 2005) (upholding censorship of mail and publications with gang references and designation of prisoner who received and sent them as a "Security Threat Group" leader with restrictions on visiting, community placement, and other privileges); Stewart v. Almeida, 418 F. Supp. 2d 1154, 1162–63 (N.D.Cal. 2006) (upholding "gang validation" procedure by which gang members were usually placed in SHU); Koch v. Lewis, 96 F. Supp. 2d 949, 960–66 (D.Ariz. 2000) (holding prisoners could be segregated as gang members and denied parole eligibility and earned early release credit based on past conduct as long as it supported current gang membership; upholding requirement that they renounce gang membership and inform on other members to get out of segregation), vacated as moot, 399 F.3d 1099 (9th Cir. 2005).

Due process considerations in classifying prisoners as security threat group members and segregating them are addressed in Ch. 4, § H.5.a.

[241]Koutnik v. Brown, 396 F. Supp. 2d 978, 986 (W.D.Wis. 2005) (upholding censorship of letters referring to gang allegiance), aff'd, 189 Fed.Appx. 546 (7th Cir. 2006) (unpublished); State ex rel. Whiting v. Kolb, 158 Wis.2d 226, 461 N.W.2d 816, 820–21 (Wis. App. 1990) (ban on "ritualistic greetings" including embracing and kissing upheld as a means of prohibiting "gang symbolism").

[242]Some courts have upheld classification of the Five Percenters as a "Security Threat Group" and the segregation of prisoners who refuse to renounce all ties with it. Fraise v. Terhune, 283 F.3d 506, 518–23 (3d Cir. 2002); In re Long Term Admin. Segregation of Inmates Designated as Five Percenters, 174 F.3d 464, 466–69 (4th Cir.1999). These cases relied only on the First Amendment's Free Exercise Clause. Courts considering the Religious Land Use and Institutionalized Persons Act have placed limits on prison officials' ability to restrict religious groups under STG policies. See Marria v. Broaddus, 2003 WL 21782633, *13–21 (S.D.N.Y., July 31, 2003) (holding Five Percenters' classification as a Security Threat Group and absolute ban on Five Percenter literature violated the Religious Land Use and Institutionalized Persons Act); see also Hardaway v.

Courts have also upheld restrictions on informal or social association by prisoners.[243]

Courts have disagreed on the constitutional status of petitions in prison. Some courts have held that they are protected by the First Amendment,[244] while others have approved restrictions or bans on them.[245] Whether prisoners can be punished for circulating or signing petitions will depend on whether prison rules give notice that such activity is forbidden.[246]

Grievances filed through an official grievance procedure are constitutionally protected,[247] even though there is no constitutional requirement that prisons have a grievance system,[248] or that they follow its procedures if they do have

---

Haggerty, 2007 WL 2868100 (E.D.Mich., Sept. 27, 2007) (following *Marria*, denying summary judgment to prison officials on classification of Five Percenters as STG); Johnson v. Martin, 2005 WL 3312566, *6–8 (W.D.Mich., Dec. 7, 2005) (denial of all literature produced by Melanic Islamic Palace of the Rising Sun, which prison classified as a Security Threat Group, violated the Religious Land Use and Institutionalized Persons Act), *reconsideration denied*, 2006 WL 223108 (W.D.Mich., Jan. 30, 2006). Freedom of religion is discussed in § D of this chapter.

[243]Burnette v. Phelps, 621 F. Supp. 1157, 1159–60 (M.D.La. 1985) (rule against speaking in dining hall did not violate First Amendment); Dooley v. Quick, 598 F. Supp. 607, 612 (D.R.I. 1984) (as long as there is some opportunity for human contact, "decisions about how and when inmates may see and/or contact other inmates" are up to prison officials), *aff'd*, 787 F.2d 579 (1st Cir. 1986); *see also* Brew v. School Board of Orange County, Florida, 626 F. Supp. 709, 716–18 (M.D.Fla. 1985) (fraternization on school premises between teacher and work release prisoners was not a form of association protected by the First Amendment), *aff'd*, 802 F.2d 1397 (11th Cir. 1986). *But see* Franklin v. Murphy, 745 F.2d 1221, 1230 (9th Cir. 1984) (claim that prison hospital ordered other inmates not to associate with plaintiff and threatened to punish plaintiff for such association "arguably" stated a claim for denial of freedom of association).

[244]*See, e.g.*, Bridges v. Russell, 757 F.2d 1155, 1156–57 (11th Cir. 1985) (allegation of transfer in retaliation for a petition stated a claim); Haymes v. Montanye, 547 F.2d 188, 191 (2d Cir. 1976); Stoval v. Bennett, 471 F. Supp. 1286, 1290 (M.D.Ala. 1979).

[245]Duamutef v. O'Keefe, 98 F.3d 22, 24 (2d Cir. 1996) (holding petitions may be prohibited as long as there is a grievance process); Wolfel v. Morris, 972 F.2d 712, 716–17 (6th Cir. 1992); Nickens v. White, 622 F.2d 967, 971–72 (8th Cir. 1980) (upholding regulation forbidding "mass protest petitions," noting that prisoners have alternative methods of expressing their views, i.e., correspondence and an internal grievance procedure); Edwards v. White, 501 F. Supp. 8, 12 (M.D.Pa. 1979) (dictum) (stating that a ban is permissible because the process of gathering signatures might lead to violence); Williams v. Stacy, 468 F. Supp. 1206, 1209–11 (E.D.Va. 1979) (petition describing guards as "Nazis" and "maniacs" and warning of "another Attica" could be suppressed, even if true).

[246]Gayle v. Gonyea, 313 F.3d 677, 680 n.3 (2d Cir. 2002) (questioning whether prison rule gave notice that petitions were forbidden); Farid v. Goord, 200 F. Supp. 2d 220, 236 (W.D.N.Y. 2002) (petition was constitutionally protected where no rule forbade it); Richardson v. Coughlin, 763 F. Supp. 1228, 1234–37 (S.D.N.Y. 1991) (prisoner could not be punished merely for gathering signatures on a petition where prison rules did not specifically prohibit such action).

[247]Hoskins v. Lenear, 395 F.3d 372, 375 (7th Cir. 2005) (per curiam); Gayle v. Gonyea, 313 F.3d 677, 682 (2d Cir. 2002); Williams v. Meese, 926 F.2d 994, 998 (10th Cir. 1991); Johnson-El v. Schoemehl, 878 F.2d 1043, 1053–54 (8th Cir. 1989); Sprouse v. Babcock, 870 F.2d 450, 452 (8th Cir. 1989); Jackson v. Cain, 864 F.2d 1235, 1248–49 (5th Cir. 1989); Wildberger v. Bracknell, 869 F.2d 1467, 1468 (11th Cir. 1989); Bridges v. Russell, 757 F.2d 1155, 1157 (11th Cir. 1985). *But see* Hadden v. Howard, 713 F.2d 1003, 1007 (3d Cir. 1983) (upholding punishment for "maliciously untrue" statements in grievance despite regulation forbidding such punishment); Ward v. Dyke, 58 F.3d 271, 274–75 (6th Cir. 1995) (transferring a prisoner who had filed 115 grievances in less than five months did not violate the First Amendment); Williams v. Smith, 717 F. Supp. 523, 524–25 (W.D.Mich. 1989) (retaliatory disciplinary charge of which the prisoner was cleared did not violate substantive due process). *Cf.* Hamilton v. County of San Bernardino, 325 F. Supp. 2d 1087, 1090–94 (C.D.Cal. 2004) (striking down statute making it a misdemeanor knowingly to file a false misconduct allegation against a police officer). *Compare* Rouse v. Benson, 193 F.3d 936, 941 (8th Cir. 1999) (prisoners do not have the right to "incite other inmates to file grievances") *with* Graham v. Henderson, 89 F.3d 75, 80 (2d Cir. 1996) (filing a grievance and attempting to find inmates to represent the grievants is constitutionally protected).

[248]Antonelli v. Sheahan, 81 F.3d 1422, 1430 (7th Cir. 1996); Spencer v. Moore, 638 F. Supp. 315, 316 (E.D.Mo. 1986); Hutchings v. Corum, 501 F. Supp. 1276, 1298 (W.D.Mo. 1980), and cases cited; *see also* Lopez v. Robinson, 914 F.2d 486, 494–95 (4th Cir. 1990) (the failure to make grievance forms readily available and officers' practice of requiring inmates to tell them why they wanted the form did not violate "clearly established" rights). *But see* Canterino v. Wilson, 546 F. Supp. 174, 215–16 (W.D.Ky. 1982) (disparities in grievance procedures between men's and women's prisons denied equal protection), *vacated and remanded on other grounds*, 869 F.2d 948 (6th Cir. 1989).

Some courts have approved or encouraged the creation of grievance procedures or required them in order to protect other rights. Hoptowit v. Ray, 682 F.2d 1237, 1251 (9th Cir. 1982) (court could require establishment of a grievance procedure for brutality complaints, but went too far in spelling out its details); Finney v. Mabry, 458 F. Supp. 720, 721 (E.D.Ark. 1978) (consent judgment containing grievance procedure approved); Miller v. Carson, 563 F.2d 741, 752–54 (5th Cir.) (jail "ombudsman" could be ordered by federal court on a temporary basis only), *rehearing denied*, 566 F.2d 106 (5th Cir. 1977); Laaman v. Helgemoe, 437 F. Supp. 269, 320 (D.N.H. 977) (grievance procedure required to prevent abuse and mistreatment). State law may create a right to a grievance procedure; under some circumstances, officials' failure to comply with such a state law mandate may state a constitutional claim. Lucas v. Wasser, 425 F. Supp. 955, 961–62 (S.D.N.Y. 1976); *see also* Johnson v. Ward, 64 A.D.2d 186, 409 N.Y.S.2d 670, 672–73 (N.Y.App.Div. 1978) (state statute creating grievance procedure created liberty interest restricting transfers of grievance representatives). *Contra*, Mann v. Adams, 855 F.2d 639, 640 (9th Cir. 1988) (unpublished administrative policy statements do not create a

one,[249] or that they issue decisions that fairly resolve prisoners' problems.[250]

Other forms of individual protest and criticism may be constitutionally protected, though advocacy of violating prison rules is not.[251] How complaints are made is as important as what they say. Criticisms made in outgoing letters generally are protected by the First Amendment.[252] The First Amendment also protects communication with official agencies,[253] orderly participation in forums designed for prisoners to express their views,[254] complaints addressed directly to prison officials,[255] and other activities that do not

threaten security.[256] However, protests and complaints that involve a direct confrontation with prison personnel enjoy less constitutional protection, even if the staff members are doing something wrong.[257] Such confrontations may present the danger of a disturbance, especially if there are other inmates present. Prisoners do not have a right to express themselves by engaging in group action that is disruptive of prison activities.[258]

Most courts hold or assume that prisoners have a right to speak up for other prisoners or to help them speak up for themselves[259]—especially if that is part of their job

liberty interest in a grievance procedure); *accord*, Flick v. Alba, 932 F.2d 728, 729 (8th Cir. 1991).

[249]Wildberger v. Bracknell, 869 F.2d 1467 (11th Cir. 1989); Spencer v. Moore, 638 F. Supp. at 316; Azeez v. DeRobertis, 568 F. Supp. 8, 10 (N.D.Ill. 1982); Watts v. Morgan, 572 F. Supp. 1385, 1391 (N.D.Ill. 1983).

[250]Geiger v. Jowers, 404 F.3d 371, 374 (5th Cir. 2005) (per curiam) ("[A prisoner] does not have a federally protected liberty interest in having those grievances resolved to his satisfaction.").

[251]Pilgrim v. Luther, 571 F.3d 201, 204–05 (2d Cir. 2009) (upholding discipline for pamphlet advocating work stoppage).

[252]*See* cases cited in § B.1.a of this chapter, nn.67, 91.

[253]Brown v. Crowley, 312 F.3d 782, 789–91 (6th Cir. 2002) (complaint to state police); Cornell v. Woods, 69 F.3d 1383, 1388 (8th Cir. 1995) (cooperation with internal affairs investigation); Meriwether v. Coughlin, 879 F.2d 1037, 1046 (2d Cir. 1989) (correspondence with state officials and public interest organizations); Franco v. Kelly, 854 F.2d 584, 589–90 (2d Cir. 1988) (cooperation with Inspector General investigating staff misconduct); *see also* Frazier v. King, 873 F.2d 820, 825–27 (5th Cir. 1989) (nurse's disclosure to State Nursing Board of violations of state nursing standards in a prison infirmary was constitutionally protected).

[254]*See* Meriwether v. Coughlin, 879 F.2d at 1046 (meetings with Superintendent to discuss problems in prison). Prisoners who participate in approved forums can be required to follow prison rules governing these activities and can be disciplined if they do not do so. Brookins v. Kolb, 990 F.2d 308, 315 (7th Cir. 1993) (upholding transfer of member of Paralegal Base Committee for violating rules requiring committee correspondence to be reviewed by Group Advisor).

[255]Pearson v. Welborn, 471 F.3d 732, 741 (7th Cir.2006) (oral complaint protected); Mitchell v. Farcass, 112 F.3d 1483, 1485, 1490 (11th Cir. 1997) (declining to dismiss where prisoner met with officials and presented inmates' complaints); Newsom v. Morris, 888 F.2d 371, 375–77 (6th Cir. 1989) (inmate disciplinary assistants who lost their jobs for complaining to the warden about the disciplinary board chairman were entitled to reinstatement); Ustrak v. Fairman, 781 F.2d 573, 577–78 (7th Cir. 1986) (denial of transfer because of letters to warden was unconstitutional); King v. Ditter, 432 F. Supp. 813, 818–19 (W.D.Wis. 2006) (letters to prison officials, like grievances, are protected); Salahuddin v. Harris, 684 F. Supp. 1224, 1226–27 (S.D.N.Y. 1988) (letter to Superintendent and other officials protesting the discipline of another inmate was constitutionally protected); *see* Salahuddin v. Harris, 657 F. Supp. 369, 376–77 (S.D.N.Y. 1987) (citing state statutes and regulations to show that the inmate's conduct was not incompatible with state penological objectives); Collins v. Schoonfield, 344 F. Supp. 257, 270–71 (D.Md. 1972); *see also* Cale v. Johnson, 861 F.2d 943, 951

(6th Cir. 1988) (allegation of false disciplinary charge in retaliation for complaints about food stated a constitutional claim); Wolfel v. Bates, 707 F.2d 932, 934 (6th Cir. 1983) (punishment for "making unfounded complaints or charges against staff members . . . with malicious intent" violates the First Amendment in the absence of findings that the statements were actually false or malicious). *But see* Ross v. Reed, 719 F.2d 689, 695 (4th Cir. 1983) (court expresses "grave doubt" that false accusations designed to pressure an employee into changing prisoner's parole eligibility date were protected).

[256]Cain v. Lane, 857 F.2d 1139, 1143 (7th Cir. 1988) (discipline for trying to document inmate complaints about conditions stated a First Amendment claim); Cassels v. Stalder, 342 F. Supp. 2d 555, 564–67 (M.D.La. 2004) (holding rule prohibiting "spreading rumors" vague and overbroad on its face and as applied to a prisoner who told his mother he had been denied medical care, resulting in her putting the information on the Internet).

[257]Several cases have found such face-to-face protests unprotected by the Constitution. *See* Freeman v. Texas Dep't of Criminal Justice, 369 F.3d 854, 864 (5th Cir. 2004) (holding plaintiff's public rebuke of chaplain, which caused other prisoners to walk out of service, was not "consistent with his status as a prisoner" and was not protected; "Prison officials may legitimately punish inmates who verbally confront institutional authority without running afoul of the First Amendment."); Garrido v. Coughlin, 716 F. Supp. 98, 101 (S.D.N.Y. 1989) ("verbal confrontation" of officers over their treatment of another inmate); Pollard v. Baskerville, 481 F. Supp. 1157, 1160 (E.D.Va. 1979) (accusation that a guard brought in contraband), *aff'd*, 620 F.2d 294 (4th Cir. 1980); Riggs v. Miller, 480 F. Supp. 799, 804 (E.D.Va. 1979) ("bickering, argumentative conversation"); Craig v. Franke, 478 F. Supp. 19, 21 (E.D.Wis. 1979) (accusation that an officer was drunk); Durkin v. Taylor, 444 F. Supp. 879, 881–83 (E.D.Va. 1979) (statement that "I am tired of chickenshit rules").

[258]Graham v. Henderson, 89 F.3d 75, 80 (2d Cir. 1996) (there is no constitutional right to organize a prison work slowdown).

[259]Bridges v. Gilbert, 557 F.3d 541, 551 (7th Cir. 2009) (allegation of retaliation for submitting an affidavit in a lawsuit about a prisoner's death stated a First Amendment claim); Scott v. Coughlin, 344 F.3d 282, 288 (2d Cir. 2003) (plaintiff alleged that he suffered retaliation for submitting a statement in support of another prisoner's excessive force claim; "involvement in filing claims against prison officials and helping others do so was protected activity, as it was an exercise of his right to petition the government for redress of grievances under the First Amendment"); Lodato v. Ortiz, 314 F. Supp. 2d 379, 382, 386–87 (D.N.J. 2004) (holding filing grievances is constitutionally protected; plaintiff's grievance was about excessive force against another prisoner).

assignment.[260] One court has said that prisoners "do not have a constitutional right to incite other inmates to file grievances."[261] We don't think that makes any sense; if filing grievances or making other complaints is a constitutional right, then advocating that other prisoners do so, or helping them to do so, should also be constitutionally protected. A couple of decisions have held that prisoners have a constitutional right to assist others with grievances only if the other prisoner could not pursue his claim without that assistance.[262] This rule is borrowed from the law of the right of access to courts,[263] and we think it is inappropriate. The right to file a grievance is part of the general right to speak freely and petition for redress of grievances; it does not depend on whether the prisoner wishes to file a lawsuit or is complaining about something that would support a lawsuit. We do not see any basis for forbidding prisoners to speak up on each other's behalf, or help each other speak, as long as they do not disrupt the orderly operation of the prison.

One federal appeals court held, for a while, that the First Amendment does not protect prisoners' speech about matters "personal to" them that are not matters of "public interest or concern."[264] This is an idea that had previously been applied only to public employees' free speech rights at work.[265] That court has now abandoned the idea for prisoners,[266] and other courts have rejected it as well, correctly in our view.[267] If you are faced with this argument, point out that the rule about public employees applies only

when one of them "speaks . . . as an employee upon matters only of personal interest. . . ."[268] Thus it only limits speech in a part of an employee's life. Since a prisoner is a prisoner around the clock and in all aspects of life, to apply that rule to prisoners is a much broader and more sweeping limitation, and one that is not justified by the special concerns related to speech in the workplace.[269]

Prison officials may require you to be civil and respectful in making complaints within the prison, even if you make them in letters or other non-disruptive forms. (They do not have that power with respect to letters to outside correspondents.[270]) Courts have held that prisons may forbid "derogatory or degrading remarks" about employees, "abusive conversation, correspondence, or phone calls," etc., in communications made within the prison[271]—though one

---

[260]Auleta v. LaFrance, 233 F. Supp. 2d 396, 399–400 (N.D.N.Y. 2002) (holding an inmate legal assistant who said he was placed in keeplock for helping another prisoner file a grievance appeal as part of his assigned job stated a First Amendment claim). In *Auleta*, the defendants argued that the Supreme Court decision in *Shaw v. Murphy*, 532 U.S. 223, 231, 121 S. Ct. 1475 (2001), held that prisoners have no right to provide legal assistance to each other. The *Auleta* court rejected the argument, stating that *Shaw* only said that there is no *special* constitutional right to provide such assistance, and that restrictions on it must be evaluated under the *Turner v. Safley* reasonableness standard like any other prison free speech claim. *Auleta, id.*

[261]Rouse v. Benson, 193 F.3d 936, 941 (8th Cir. 1999).

[262]Herron v. Harrison, 203 F.3d 410, 416–17 (6th Cir. 2000); Purkey v. CCA Detention Center, 339 F. Supp. 2d 1145, 1152–53 (D.Kan. 2004).

[263]*See* § C.2.c of this chapter.

[264]Brookins v. Kolb, 990 F.2d 308, 313 (7th Cir. 1993); *see* Pearson v. Welborn, 471 F.3d 732, 740 (7th Cir. 2006) (plaintiff's "complaints about the use of shackles in group therapy and the denial of yard time related to matters of concern to all J pod prisoners" and were not just "personal gripes").

[265]*See, e.g.,* Connick v. Myers, 461 U.S. 138, 145, 103 S. Ct. 1684 (1983).

[266]Watkins v. Kasper, 599 F.3d 791, 795–96 (7th Cir. 2010).

[267]*See* Friedl v. City of New York, 210 F.3d 79, 87 (2d Cir. 2000) ("The 'public concern' requirement, developed in the context of public employee speech, has no place in the context of prisoner petitions for redress of grievances, which typically address matters

of personal concern."); Thaddeus X v. Blatter, 175 F.3d 378, 392 (6th Cir. 1999) (same, in access to courts retaliation case).

[268]Connick v. Myers, 461 U.S. at 147 (emphasis supplied).

[269]As the Seventh Circuit acknowledged, to draw an analogy to public employee speech "would be to remove protection from nearly everything a prisoner says." Bridges v. Gilbert, 557 F.3d 541, 550 (7th Cir. 2009). That decision did leave open whether the "public concern" standard might still have some application to prisoners' work-related claims, but the court has now decisively rejected the public concern test from prisoner cases. Watkins v. Kasper, 599 F.3d at 795–96.

[270]Brooks v. Andolina, 826 F.2d 1266, 1268 (3d Cir. 1987) (disciplinary action against a prisoner who accused staff of misconduct in an outgoing letter was unconstitutional); McNamara v. Moody, 606 F.2d 621, 624 (5th Cir. 1979) (refusal to mail a letter containing derogatory remarks about the mail censor was unconstitutional). *See* § B.1.a of this chapter, nn.92–93, concerning this subject.

[271]Lockett v. Suardini, 526 F.3d 866, 874 (6th Cir. 2008) (calling disciplinary hearing officer "a foul and corrupted bitch" violated rule against insolent speech and was not protected); Gibbs v. King, 779 F.2d 1040, 1045–46 (5th Cir. 1986); *accord,* Hale v. Scott, 371 F.3d 917, 918–19 (7th Cir. 2004) (holding complaint letter embellished with a statement that an officer was rumored to be "screwing a lot of the officers on the midnight shift" was not protected); Smith v. Campbell, 250 F.3d 1032, 1037 (6th Cir. 2001) (prisoner could be transferred for "aggressive attitudes" and "attempts to intimidate staff members" in connection with grievances); Cowans v. Warren, 150 F.3d 910, 911 (8th Cir. 1998) (upholding disciplinary conviction for calling officers "racists," "supremacists," and "dogs" in a grievance); Ustrak v. Fairman, 781 F.2d 573, 580 (7th Cir. 1986) (regulation forbidding "being disrespectful" or verbally abusing employees); Goff v. Dailey, 789 F. Supp. 978, 980–81 (S.D.Iowa 1992) (inmate's comment that an officer "did not get any pussy before work" was not protected by the First Amendment), *aff'd in part and rev'd in part on other grounds,* 991 F.2d 1437 (8th Cir. 1993); Scarpa v. Ponte, 638 F. Supp. 1019, 1028 (D.Mass. 1986) (prisoner could be disciplined for "disrespectful" letter); Savage v. Snow, 575 F. Supp. 828, 836 (S.D.N.Y. 1983) (prisoner could be disciplined for addressing an officer in an "abusive" manner); Franklin v. State of Oregon, 563 F. Supp. 1310, 1326 (D.Or. 1983) (use of "expletives" toward a guard was not

federal appeals court has held that such rules cannot be enforced in connection with formal grievances.[272]

Some courts have held that prisoners may be punished for lying if they make false statements about prison staff.[273] This rule creates a danger that prisons will suppress criticism simply by saying that any prisoner who complains is lying. One district court has held that in order to avoid "an unconstitutional chill on complaints that matter," prisoners cannot be punished for making false statements (or statements prison officials claim are false) in formal grievances, or in direct complaints to the warden.[274] In any event, if the prisoner submits evidence that his statements were true, the court may not assume otherwise; the factual dispute is an issue for trial,[275] notwithstanding any findings that prison officials may have made.[276]

Threats of unlawful or improper action are not constitutionally protected.[277] A "threat" to take a constitutionally protected action is itself constitutionally protected.[278] However, including a threat to sue or take other protected action will not protect you if your communication is otherwise abusive or disruptive.[279]

---

protected by the First Amendment), *aff'd in part and rev'd in part*, 745 F.2d 1221 (9th Cir. 1984); Harry v. Smith, 148 Misc.2d 629, 561 N.Y.S.2d 374, 376–77 (N.Y.Sup. 1990) (prisoner could be found guilty of verbal harassment for saying "shit" while complaining of commissary delays); *see also* Respress v. Coughlin, 585 F. Supp. 854, 860–62 (S.D.N.Y. 1984) (transfer of prisoner for spreading "rumors" about misconduct by prison officials was not unconstitutional, since such rumors could interfere with order and rehabilitation).

[272]Bradley v. Hall, 64 F.3d 1276, 1279–81 (9th Cir. 1995). The *Bradley* court said that applying a rule against "hostile, sexual, abusive or threatening" language to written grievances was an exaggerated response, and that a "threat of punishment for an impolitic choice of words" was an unacceptable burden on court access (since filing a grievance is now required before filing a lawsuit). "If there is any time a prisoner should be permitted to speak freely, it is at the bar of justice." *Bradley*, 64 F.3d at 1281. However, at least one court has said that *Bradley* is undermined by a later Supreme Court decision which disapproves the Ninth Circuit's approach to such questions and holds that courts may not give special value to a particular kind of communication. *In re* Parmelee, 115 Wash. App. 273, 284, 63 P.3d 800 (2003), *review denied*, 151 Wash.2d 1017 (2004) (citing Shaw v. Murphy, 532 U.S. 223, 121 S. Ct. 1475 (2001)). In *Parmelee*, the court held that a prisoner whose grievance had referred to officers with terms including "asshole," "pissant," "prick," "shitheads," etc., could be punished under a rule prohibiting insolent language; the prisoner's statement that an officer should be "fired before his attitude gets him fucked up" could be punished as a threat. *In re* Parmelee, 115 Wash.App. at 286–88.

[273]Hasan v. U.S. Dep't of Labor, 400 F.3d 1001, 1005 (7th Cir. 2005).

[274]Hancock v. Thalacker, 933 F. Supp. 1449, 1487–93 (N.D.Iowa 1996). The court reasoned that the grievance process contains sufficient safeguards for prison officials to deal with false complaints. Denying the grievance is sufficient.

[275]Hart v. Hairston, 343 F.3d 762, 765 (5th Cir. 2003) (per curiam). The plaintiff's sworn statement (in that case, a verified complaint) that his complaint or grievance was true is sufficient evidence to defeat summary judgment on that point. By contrast, in *Hasan v. U.S. Dep't of Labor*, where the disciplinary conviction for lying was upheld, it was apparently undisputed that the prisoner had lied. *Hasan*, 400 F.3d at 1005.

[276]Courts have generally held that prison disciplinary findings are not preclusive in later judicial proceedings (*i.e.*, they are not binding on courts). *See* Ch. 8, § M, nn.932–935. Courts have also noted the dangers that would arise from giving internal prison findings preclusive effect. *See* Simpson v. Nickel, 450 F.3d 303, 308 (7th Cir. 2006) (courts must address factual disputes notwithstanding prison administrative findings, "otherwise prison disciplinary boards could immunize guards who violate prisoners' rights, and the act of penalizing speech would be self-vindicating"); Johnson v. Freeburn, 144 F.Supp.2d 817, 823 (E.D.Mich. 2001) (noting that allowing disciplinary hearings to preclude litigation of retaliation claims would put pressure on hearing officers to avoid dismissing marginal disciplinary charges to protect officers from litigation).

[277]Chavis v. Struebel, 317 F. Supp. 2d 232, 238 (W.D.N.Y. 2004) (holding prisoner could be disciplined for complaint letter threatening to "get even with" officers who searched his cell and to "deal with" a lieutenant for being racist); Jones v. State, 447 N.W.2d 556, 557–58 (Iowa App. 1989) (obscenities about prison staff and threat to "get even" could be punished); Nieves v. Coughlin, 157 A.D.2d 945, 550 N.Y.S.2d 205, 206 (N.Y.App.Div. 1990) (statement "I'll do a year in the box and then come out strong on you" could be punished under rule against threats). Courts may interpret "threat" very broadly in the prison context, or may allow prison officials to do so. *See, e.g., In re* Parmelee, 115 Wash.App. 273, 288, 63 P.3d 800 (2003) (upholding disciplinary conviction for saying an officer should be fired "before his attitude gets him fucked up," even though prisoner said he just meant he might file a lawsuit), *review denied*, 151 Wash.2d 1017 (2004).

[278]*See* Cavey v. Levine, 435 F. Supp. 475, 481–83 (D.Md. 1977) (prisoner could not be punished for threats to write to the press about an inmate suicide), *aff'd sub nom.* Cavey v. Williams, 580 F.2d 1047 (4th Cir. 1978); *see also* Hargis v. Foster, 312 F.3d 404, 411 (9th Cir. 2002) (holding that a disciplinary conviction for "coercion" for mentioning pending litigation to an officer presented a jury question as to reasonableness). One court held that a rule forbidding prisoners to threaten employees with litigation during "confrontation situations" was unconstitutional, but on rehearing the court held that it could not decide the case because loss of good time was involved and the prisoner had not gotten the disciplinary conviction overturned in a state proceeding or via federal habeas corpus. Clarke v. Stalder, 121 F.3d 222, 228–31 (5th Cir. 1997), *on rehearing*, 154 F.3d 186 (5th Cir. 1998) (en banc).

[279]Howard v. Cherish, 575 F. Supp. 34, 35–36 (S.D.N.Y. 1983) (loud and disruptive complaints about work conditions could be

Prisoners cannot be punished for possession of their own writings as long as these do not threaten prison security or other legitimate penological interests.[280]

6. Retaliation for Speech

"The First Amendment forbids prison officials from retaliating against prisoners for exercising the right of free speech."[281] In some cases, prison officials openly discipline, transfer, or take other action against prisoners for something they have said or written, claiming that it violated a prison rule. In these cases, the main issues are often the legal questions whether the prisoner's speech was constitutionally protected, whether the disciplinary rule is constitutional on its face or as applied to the prisoner's conduct, whether there is "some evidence" that the conduct violated the rule, or whether the rule gave the prisoner sufficient notice that his expressive conduct would violate it. Cases of this type are discussed in the preceding section and in the chapter on procedural due process.[282] In this section we deal with cases in which prisoners allege that officials have covertly retaliated against them with false disciplinary charges or other

improper measures. In these cases, the major factual issue is usually what the real reason for those actions was.

It is also unconstitutional to retaliate against prisoners for exercising the right of access to courts. Although we discuss that subject in another section,[283] many of the same legal principles govern both types of retaliation cases, so we have cited many court access retaliation cases here.

Unconstitutional retaliation may be remedied by an injunction, even if the practices are not formally part of official policy,[284] or by an award of damages.[285]

To state a retaliation claim, you must allege "(1) that the speech or conduct at issue was protected, (2) that the defendant took adverse action against the plaintiff, and (3) that there was a causal connection between the protected speech and the adverse action."[286] To prevail, of course, you will

_____

the subject of discipline even though the prisoner had also threatened to sue about them).

[280]Farid v. Goord, 200 F. Supp. 2d 220, 241–43 (W.D.N.Y. 2002) (prisoner could not be punished for possessing his own writings, which were satirical political and social commentaries that did not threaten security). _But see_ Pilgrim v. Luther, 571 F.3d 201, 204–05 (2d Cir. 2009) (upholding discipline for writing and possessing a pamphlet advocating a work stoppage); Turner v. Johnson, 46 F. Supp. 2d 655, 660–63 (S.D.Tex. 1999) (similar to _Pilgrim_; matter addressed as due process rather than free speech claim).

[281]Farrow v. West, 320 F.3d 1235, 1248 (11th Cir. 2003); _accord_, Crawford-El v. Britton, 523 U.S. 574, 588 n.10, 118 S. Ct. 1584 (1998) ("The reason why such retaliation offends the Constitution is that it threatens to inhibit exercise of the protected right."); Hoskins v. Lenear, 395 F.3d 372, 375 (7th Cir. 2005) (per curiam) ("Prisoners are entitled to utilize available grievance procedures without threat of recrimination. . . ."); Scott v. Coughlin, 344 F.3d 282, 287–88 (2d Cir. 2003) (". . . [Plaintiff's] involvement in filing claims against prison officials and helping others do so was protected activity, as it was an exercise of his right to petition the government for redress of grievances under the First Amendment."); Mitchell v. Farcass, 112 F.3d 1483, 1485, 1490 (11th Cir. 1997) (holding allegation that plaintiff was placed in segregation after complaining to the NAACP stated a claim); Frazier v. Dubois, 922 F.2d 560, 561–62 (10th Cir. 1990) and cases cited; Thomas v. Evans, 880 F.2d 1235, 1241–42 (11th Cir. 1989); Pratt v. Rowland, 770 F. Supp. 1399, 1406 (N.D.Cal. 1991) (granting injunction).

There may be circumstances where the exercise of other rights may also support a retaliation claim. _See_ Vance v. Barrett, 345 F.3d 1083, 1093–94 (9th Cir. 2003) (firing prisoners from their jobs for refusing to sign an agreement to waive interest on their savings accounts, to which they were constitutionally entitled under the due process clause, was unconstitutional); Rouse v. Benson, 193 F.3d 936, 941 (8th Cir. 1999) (allegation of transfer in retaliation for Native American religious exercise stated a constitutional claim).

[282]_See_ Ch. 4, § H.1.q.

[283]_See_ § C.1.c of this chapter.

[284]Gomez v. Vernon, 255 F.3d 1118, 1127, 1129–30 (9th Cir. 2001); Ruiz v. Estelle, 679 F.2d 1115, 1154 (5th Cir. 1982); Pratt v. Rowland, 770 F. Supp. 1399, 1406 (N.D.Cal. 1991).

[285]Dannenberg v. Valadez, 338 F.3d 1070, 1072 (9th Cir. 2003) (noting jury verdict of $6500 compensatory and $2500 punitive damages for retaliation for assisting another prisoner with litigation; noting injunction requiring expungement of material related to disciplinary action); Walker v. Bain, 257 F.3d 660, 663–64 (6th Cir. 2001) (noting jury verdict for plaintiff whose legal papers were confiscated in retaliation for filing grievances); Trobaugh v. Hall, 176 F.3d 1087 (8th Cir. 1999) (directing award of compensatory damages to prisoner placed in isolation for filing grievances); Hines v. Gomez, 108 F.3d 265 (9th Cir. 1997) (affirming jury verdict for plaintiff subjected to retaliation for filing grievances); Coleman v. Turner, 838 F.2d 1004, 1005 (8th Cir. 1988) (nominal damages only); Lamar v. Steele, 693 F.2d 559, 562 (5th Cir. 1982) (nominal damages), _on rehearing_, 698 F.2d 1286 (5th Cir. 1983); Cruz v. Beto, 603 F.2d 1178, 1181, 1186 (5th Cir. 1979); Maurer v. Patterson, 197 F.R.D. 244 (S.D.N.Y. 2000) (upholding jury verdict for plaintiff who was subjected to retaliatory disciplinary charge for complaining about operation of grievance program); Gaston v. Coughlin, 81 F. Supp. 2d 381 (N.D.N.Y. 1999) (awarding damages for trumped-up disciplinary charge made in retaliation for prisoner's complaining about state law violations in mess hall work hours), _on reconsideration_, 102 F. Supp. 2d 81 (N.D.N.Y. 2000).

[286]Espinal v. Goord, 558 F.3d 119, 128 (2d Cir. 2009); _accord_, Thaddeus-X v. Blatter, 175 F.3d 378, 394 (6th Cir. 1999) (en banc). Other courts have stated the standard in different ways, but they generally amount to the same thing or close to it. _See, e.g._, Rhodes v. Robinson, 408 F.3d 559, 567–68 (9th Cir. 2005) (retaliation claims require "five basic elements: (1) an assertion that a state actor took some adverse action against an inmate (2) because of (3) that prisoner's protected conduct, and that such action (4) chilled the inmate's exercise of his First Amendment rights, and (5) the action did not reasonably advance a legitimate correctional goal"); Revels v. Vincenz, 382 F.3d 870, 876 (8th Cir. 2004) (plaintiff must show "(1) he engaged in a protected activity, (2) the government official took adverse action against him that would chill a person of ordinary firmness from continuing in this activity, and (3) the adverse action was motivated at least in part by the exercise of the protected activity"); Hart v. Hairston, 343 F.3d 762, 764 (5th Cir. 2003) (per curiam) (retaliation claims require a prisoner to allege "(1) a specific constitutional right, (2) the defendant's intent to

have to prove all these elements. Some courts have said that in pleading such a claim, you must at a minimum allege "a chronology of events from which retaliation may plausibly be inferred,"[287] but others have disagreed that this is a pleading requirement at all[288] or have indicated that it is only one way of pleading the necessary causal relationship between protected speech and adverse action.[289] As a practical matter, when you plead a retaliation claim, you should briefly state whatever factual basis you have for believing that the adverse action taken against you was done for retaliatory reasons and not for a legitimate correctional purpose. The time sequence of your protected activity and the adverse action is one possible factual basis.

One federal appeals court formerly held that a retaliation claim must "shock the conscience" to state a constitutional violation, but that rule has been abandoned.[290] Some courts have also said that retaliation claims should be approached with skepticism, since prisoners can characterize any adverse action as retaliation.[291] However, retaliation claims are allowed to go forward as long as the prisoner properly pleads the required elements and provides some factual support for them on summary judgment.

To support a retaliation claim, adverse action must be sufficient to deter or "chill" a person of "ordinary firmness" in the exercise of constitutional rights.[292] However, prisoners do not have to show that they were actually deterred from exercising their rights; if that were the law, the fact that a prisoner kept complaining or filed suit about the retaliation would defeat the claim.[293] The question whether a particular action would deter a person of ordinary firmness is an objective one and does not depend on how a particular plaintiff reacts; the question is whether the defendants' actions are capable of deterring a person of ordinary firmness.[294] Adverse action need not independently violate the Constitution to support a retaliation claim.[295] Nor need it impose "atypical and significant hardship on the inmate in relation to the ordinary incidents of prison life"[296] as is required to support a claim of deprivation of liberty denying due process.[297]

Among the actions that courts have found sufficiently adverse to support a retaliation claim are assaults and

retaliate against the prisoner for his or her exercise of that right, (3) a retaliatory adverse act, and (4) causation"); Rauser v. Horn, 241 F.3d 330, 333 (3d Cir. 2001) (prisoner must allege constitutionally protected conduct, adverse action, and a causal link between the two).

If you are pleading a First Amendment retaliation claim, obviously you should mention the First Amendment. However, courts have held that this is not legally necessary as long as you plead facts showing that you were subjected to adverse action as a result of engaging in protected speech. Austin v. Terhune, 367 F.3d 1167, 1171 (9th Cir. 2004).

[287]Cain v. Lane, 857 F.2d 1139, 1143 n.6 (7th Cir. 1988).

[288]McElroy v. Lopac, 403 F.3d 855, 858 (7th Cir. 2005) (per curiam) (for pleading purposes, it was sufficient to state the retaliatory conduct and the allegedly constitutionally protected activity that motivated it).

[289]Allen v. Thomas, 388 F.3d 147, 149 (5th Cir. 2004) ("To state a valid claim for retaliation, an inmate must either produce direct evidence of motivation or allege a chronology of events from which retaliation may plausibly be inferred." (citation and internal quotation marks omitted)).

A recent Supreme Court decision appears to increase the factual detail required in complaints alleging improper intent, such as retaliation claims. See Ashcroft v. Iqbal, ___ U.S. ___, 129 S. Ct. 1937 (2009). This decision, and pleading requirements in general, are discussed in Ch. 10, § B.1.

[290]Walker v. Bain, 257 F.3d 660, 672 (6th Cir. 2001) (citing Thaddeus-X v. Blatter, 175 F.3d 378, 388 (6th Cir.1999)).

[291]Davis v. Goord, 320 F.3d 346, 352 (2d Cir. 2003); Dawes v. Walker, 239 F.3d 489, 491 (2d Cir. 2001).

[292]Morris v. Powell, 449 F.3d 682, 685–86 (5th Cir. 2006) (describing "ordinary firmness" rule as a "*de minimis* standard"); Rhodes v. Robinson, 408 F.3d 559, 568–69 (9th Cir. 2005); Revels v.

Vincenz, 382 F.3d 870, 876 (8th Cir. 2004); Davis v. Goord, 320 F.3d 346, 353 (2d Cir. 2003); Toolasprashad v. Bureau of Prisons, 286 F.3d 576, 585 (D.C. Cir. 2002); Rauser v. Horn, 241 F.3d 330, 333 (3d Cir. 2001); Thaddeus-X v. Blatter, 175 F.3d 378, 398 (6th Cir. 1999) (en banc) (noting the standard is intended to weed out "inconsequential" actions and may require prisoners to tolerate more than public employees or "average citizens"); Osterback v. Kemp, 300 F. Supp. 2d 1238, 1256 (N.D.Fla. 2003), *on reconsideration*, 300 F. Supp. 2d 1263 (N.D.Fla. 2003).

[293]Rhodes v. Robinson, 408 F.3d 559, 569 (9th Cir. 2005); *see* Espinal v. Goord, 558 F.3d 119, 128 n.7 (2d Cir. 2009); Lashley v. Wakefield, 367 F. Supp. 2d 461, 467 (W.D.N.Y. 2005).

[294]Bell v. Johnson, 308 F.3d 594, 605–06 (6th Cir. 2002). In a case tried to a jury, that question is to be decided by the jury, *id.*, 308 F.3d at 603, and the claim need not be supported by expert testimony. *Id.* at 605–07.

[295]Hoskins v. Lenear, 395 F.3d 372, 375 (7th Cir. 2005) (per curiam); Cody v. Weber, 256 F.3d 764, 771 (8th Cir. 2001); DeWalt v. Carter, 224 F.3d 607, 618 (7th Cir. 2000) (citing Babcock v. White, 102 F.3d 267, 275 (7th Cir. 1996)); Mitchell v. Farcass, 112 F.3d 1483, 1490 (11th Cir. 1997); Wilson v. Silcox, 151 F. Supp. 2d 1345, 1351 (N.D.Fla. 2001)(citing Thomas v. Evans, 880 F.2d 1235, 1242 (11th Cir. 1989)); *see* Zimmerman v. Tribble, 226 F.3d 568, 573 (7th Cir. 2000) (allegation that plaintiff was excluded from the law library in retaliation for his complaints did not state a claim of denial of access to courts, but did state a retaliation claim); Price v. Wall, 428 F. Supp. 2d 52, 56 (D.R.I. 2006) (allegation of retaliatory refusal to upgrade classification stated a claim; officials' broad discretion to classify prisoners "does not swallow the right of access to courts"). *Contra*, Jones v. Greninger, 188 F.3d 322, 326 (5th Cir. 1999) (holding restriction on law library access that did not deny access to courts could not support a retaliation claim).

[296]Sandin v. Conner, 515 U.S. 472, 484, 115 S. Ct. 2293 (1995).

[297]Austin v. Terhune, 367 F.3d 1167, 1170–71 (9th Cir. 2004); Hines v. Gomez, 108 F.3d 265, 269 (9th Cir. 1997); Allah v. Sieverling, 229 F.3d 220, 224 (3d Cir. 2000); Williams v. Manternach, 192 F. Supp. 2d 980, 985, 987 (N.D.Iowa 2002) (dismissing due process claim under *Sandin*, holding retaliation claim could go forward); *see* Gill v. Pidlypchak, 389 F.3d 379, 384 (2d Cir. 2004) (holding retaliation claim could go forward based on false misbehavior reports resulting in three weeks of keeplock); Scott v. Churchill, 377 F.3d 565, 567, 569 (6th Cir. 2004) (holding retaliation claim could go forward based on disciplinary charges that were dismissed).

threats,[298] placement in segregated confinement,[299] the filing of false disciplinary charges,[300] confiscation or destruction of property,[301] denial of or interference with medical care,[302] transfer or denial of transfer,[303] placement in a psychiatric facility,[304] termination from or denial of jobs or programs,[305] unfavorable classification,[306] actions affecting parole prospects,[307] and others.[308] Courts have found other actions insufficiently serious.[309] To our surprise, courts have disagreed

---

[298]Burgess v. Moore, 39 F.3d 216, 218 (8th Cir. 1994); Hudspeth v. Figgins, 584 F.2d 1345, 1348 (4th Cir. 1978) (death threat); Wilson v. Silcox, 151 F. Supp. 2d 1345, 1350–51 (N.D. Fla. 2001) (verbal harassment and threats of bodily harm); Rivera v. Goord, 119 F. Supp. 2d 327, 340 (S.D.N.Y. 2000); Carter v. Newburgh Police Dep't, 523 F. Supp. 16, 20 (S.D.N.Y. 1980) (threats and beatings). *But see* Gaut v. Sunn, 810 F.2d 923, 925 (9th Cir. 1987) (threats of bodily harm alone, even in retaliation for litigation activities, do not state a constitutional claim).

[299]Trobaugh v. Hall, 176 F.3d 1087, 1088 (8th Cir. 1999) (three days of isolation for persisting in pursuing grievances conceded to violate First Amendment); Cruz v. Beto, 603 F.2d 1178, 1185–86 (5th Cir. 1979) (placement of attorney's clients in segregated unit); Auletta v. France, 233 F. Supp. 2d 396, 402 (N.D.N.Y. 2002) (seven and a half days' keeplock).

[300]Austin v. Terhune, 367 F.3d 1167, 1170–71 (9th Cir. 2004); Hart v. Hairston, 343 F.3d 762, 764 (5th Cir. 2003) (per curiam) (discipline resulting in 27 days loss of privileges was adverse); Brown v. Crowley, 312 F.3d 782, 789 (6th Cir. 2002) (holding disciplinary charges that were dismissed were sufficiently adverse because they "subjected [plaintiff] to the risk of significant sanctions"); Milhouse v. Carlson, 652 F.2d 371, 373 (3d Cir. 1981) (conspiratorially planned disciplinary actions); Lashley v. Wakefield, 367 F. Supp. 2d 461, 466–67 (W.D.N.Y. 2005) (repeated disciplinary charges that were dismissed but resulted in 20 days of pre-hearing confinement).

[301]Allen v. Thomas, 388 F.3d 147, 150 (5th Cir. 2004); Bell v. Johnson, 308 F.3d 594, 604–05 (6th Cir. 2002); Thomas v. Evans, 880 F.2d 1235, 1241–42 (11th Cir. 1989) (confiscation of legal materials); Wright v. Newsome, 795 F.2d 964, 968 (11th Cir. 1986); Hall v. Sutton, 755 F.2d 786, 787 (11th Cir. 1985); Collins v. Goord, 438 F. Supp. 2d 399, 419 (S.D.N.Y. 2006) and cases cited.

[302]Davis v. Goord, 320 F.3d 346, 353 (2d Cir. 2003) (denial of high fiber diet, delay of medical appointment); Bell v. Johnson, 308 F.3d 594, 604–05 (6th Cir. 2002) (confiscation of dietary supplements prescribed for AIDS); Thomas v. Evans, 880 F.2d 1235, 1241–42 (11th Cir. 1989) (assignment to a job inconsistent with medical condition); Ferranti v. Moran, 618 F.2d 888, 892 (1st Cir. 1980).

[303]Morris v. Powell, 449 F.3d 682, 687 (5th Cir. 2006) (transfer to a more dangerous prison); Siggers-El v. Barlow, 412 F.3d 693, 701–02 (6th Cir. 2005) (transfer to a similar prison that caused the prisoner to lose the high-paying job he needed to pay his attorney and made it more difficult for the attorney to visit him); Toolasprashad v. Bureau of Prisons, 286 F.3d 576, 585 (D.C. Cir. 2002) (transfer to a prison more distant from his ill parents and from staff members who could have testified at his parole hearing, and where he lost access to jobs); Rauser v. Horn, 241 F.3d 330, 333 (3d Cir. 2001) (transfer to a more distant prison); Murphy v. Lane, 833 F.2d 106, 108–09 (7th Cir. 1987); Rizzo v. Dawson, 778 F.2d 527, 531–32 (9th Cir. 1985); Ferranti v. Moran, 618 F.2d 888, 892 (1st Cir. 1980) (denial of transfer); Price v. Wall, 428 F. Supp. 2d 52, 55 (D.R.I. 2006) (transfer to another state where plaintiff could not get required rehabilitative treatment; refusal to reclassify despite official's own board's recommendation); *see* Gomez v. Vernon, 255 F.3d 1118, 1127, 1130 (9th Cir. 2001) (threats of

transfer causing prisoner to quit law library job); Spruytte v. Hoffner, 181 F. Supp. 2d 736, 742–45 (W.D.Mich. 2001) (transfer alone was not sufficiently adverse, but combined with loss of higher paying jobs, being labelled as security threats, and loss of personal property, satisfied the "ordinary firmness" standard; damages awarded).

[304]Morales v. Mackalm, 278 F.3d 126, 132 (2d Cir. 2002); Tyler v. Carnahan, 230 F.3d 1066, 1067 (8th Cir. 2000) (plaintiff also alleged he was "locked down" and "terrorized" when he continued to complain).

[305]Siggers-El v. Barlow, 412 F.3d 693, 701–02 (6th Cir. 2005) (loss of high-paying job resulting from retaliatory transfer); Williams v. Meese, 926 F.2d 994, 998 (10th Cir. 1991) (job denials and transfers); Thomas v. Evans, 880 F.2d 1235, 1241–42 (11th Cir. 1989) (assignment to a job inconsistent with medical condition); Harris v. Fleming, 839 F.2d 1232, 1236–37 (7th Cir. 1988) (discrimination in job and cell assignments); Rizzo v. Dawson, 778 F.2d 527, 531–32 (9th Cir. 1985) (exclusion from programs); Price v. Wall, 428 F. Supp. 2d 52, 55 (D.R.I. 2006) (transfer resulting in denial of required rehabilitative treatment).

[306]Madewell v. Roberts, 909 F.2d 1203, 1206 (8th Cir. 1990) (blocking reclassification opportunities, worsening living and working conditions); Dace v. Solem, 858 F.2d 385, 388 (8th Cir. 1988) (reclassification); Whittington v. Lynaugh, 842 F.2d 818, 819–20 (5th Cir. 1988) (dictum); Purcell v. Coughlin, 790 F.2d 263, 265 (2d Cir. 1986) (central monitoring classification); Price v. Wall, 428 F. Supp. 2d 52, 55 (D.R.I. 2006) (refusal to reclassify despite official's own board's recommendation).

[307]Toolasprashad v. Bureau of Prisons, 286 F.3d 576, 585 (D.C. Cir. 2002) (transfer away from prison where staff members would have supported parole application); Rauser v. Horn, 241 F.3d 330, 333 (3d Cir. 2001) (denial of parole); Wolfe v. Pennsylvania Dep't of Corrections, 334 F. Supp. 2d 762, 774 (E.D.Pa. 2004) (imposition of new prerequisites for parole); McDaniel v. Rhodes, 512 F. Supp. 117, 120 (S.D.Ohio 1981) (threats of adverse parole action); Inmates of Nebraska Penal and Correctional Complex v. Greenholtz, 436 F. Supp. 432, 437 (D.Neb. 1976) (refusal of parole consideration), *aff'd*, 567 F.2d 1381 (8th Cir. 1977).

[308]Davis v. Goord, 320 F.3d 346, 353 (2d Cir. 2003) (obstruction of grievances); Walker v. Thompson, 288 F.3d 1005, 1008–09 (7th Cir. 2002) (denial of out-of-cell exercise); Cooper v. Schriro, 189 F.3d 781, 784 (8th Cir. 1999) (shutting off plaintiff's water, threatening his safety); Purkey v. CCA Detention Center, 339 F. Supp. 2d 1145, 1154–55 (D.Kan. 2004) (harassment, threats, placement in segregation, scattering and disassembling of papers, denial of visits with wife, confiscation of legal materials); Martin v. Ezeagu, 816 F. Supp. 20, 24 (D.D.C. 1993) ("ongoing pattern of harassment and arbitrary exclusion" from law library).

[309]Morris v. Powell, 449 F.3d 682, 687 (5th Cir. 2006) (requiring prisoner to work a week in the kitchen and a day in a particularly unpleasant assignment was *de minimis*); Davis v. Goord, 320 F.3d 346, 353 (2d Cir. 2003) (insulting or disrespectful comments).

whether labelling a prisoner as an informer is sufficiently serious to support a retaliation claim.[310]

Some courts have held that a retaliation plaintiff must prove that "but for" the retaliation, the adverse action would not have occurred.[311] Most, however, have held that the plaintiff need only show that protected speech was a "motivating factor" for retaliation, at which point the burden of proof shifts and the defendant must show that the adverse action would have been taken anyway.[312]

Under either of these standards, the plaintiff must produce evidence that the adverse action was in fact done for retaliatory reasons.[313] Such evidence may be direct, such as statements by prison officials or staff indicating their motive for taking the adverse action,[314]

or your own sworn statements based on personal knowledge, or those of other prisoners, recounting facts (not suspicions or guesses) that support the claim of retaliatory motive.[315] Often there is no direct evidence, so prisoners must rely on circumstantial evidence.[316] Types of evidence that have been found to support retaliation claims include the suspicious timing of adverse action shortly after the prisoner has made complaints or filed grievances,[317]

---

[310]The Second Circuit has held it is not. Morales v. Mackalm, 278 F.3d 126, 132 (2d Cir. 2002) (calling the plaintiff a "stoolie" in front of other prisoners); Dawes v. Walker, 239 F.3d 489, 492–93 (2d Cir. 2001) (calling the plaintiff a "rat" in front of others, in the absence of evidence that other prisoners would be incited to attack him). Several district courts have held to the contrary. *See* Thomas v. Hill, 963 F. Supp. 753, 755 (N.D. Ind. 1997) (plaintiff accused of informing on drug trafficking in the prison); Knecht v. Collins, 903 F. Supp. 1193, 1203 (S.D.Ohio 1998) (plaintiffs called "snitches"), *aff'd in pertinent part*, 187 F.3d 636 (6th Cir. 1999); Thomas v. D.C., 887 F. Supp. 1, 4–5 (D.D.C. 1995) (plaintiff called a homosexual and a "snitch"). We think the risk to a prisoner's safety from being labelled as an informer is potentially very serious and should be considered "adverse."

[311]Peterson v. Shanks, 149 F.3d 1140, 1144 (10th Cir.1998); Woods v. Smith, 60 F.3d 1161, 1166 (5th Cir.1995); Goff v. Burton, 7 F.3d 734, 737–38 (8th Cir.1993); Layne v. Vinzant, 657 F.2d 468, 475 (1st Cir.1981) (citing McDonald v. Hall, 610 F.2d 16, 18–19 (1st Cir. 1979)).

[312]Hasan v. U.S. Dep't of Labor, 400 F.3d 1001, 1006 (7th Cir. 2005); *accord*, Scott v. Coughlin, 344 F.3d 282, 287–88 (2d Cir. 2003) (plaintiff must show "improper motivation" played a "substantial part" in defendant's decision); Rauser v. Horn, 241 F.3d 330, 333–34 (3d Cir. 2001); Reynolds v. Green, 184 F.3d 589, 594 (6th Cir. 1999) (plaintiff need show protected conduct was "a substantial or motivating factor" in adverse action); Adams v. Wainwright, 875 F.2d 1536, 1537 (11th Cir. 1989) (per curiam) (rejecting "but for" burden on plaintiff).

This "burden-shifting" rule is the rule in retaliation cases involving employment. Mt. Healthy City School District Board of Education v. Doyle, 429 U.S. 274, 287, 97 S. Ct. 568 (1977). The court in *Hasan v. U.S. Dep't of Labor, supra*, said: "We cannot think of a reason why a stricter standard for proof of causation should apply when the plaintiff is a prisoner rather than an employee. A prisoner has less freedom of speech than a free person, but less is not zero, and if he is a victim of retaliation for the exercise of what free speech he does have, he should have the same right to a remedy as his free counterpart." 400 F.3d at 1006.

[313]Richardson v. McDonnell, 841 F.2d 120, 122–23 (5th Cir. 1988); Jones v. Coughlin, 696 F. Supp. 916, 920–22 (S.D.N.Y. 1988).

[314]*See, e.g.,* Bruce v. Ylst, 351 F.3d 1283, 1288–89 (9th Cir. 2003) (citing statement by person who validated plaintiff as a gang member that plaintiff had "pissed off higher-ups"); Hart v. Hairston, 343 F.3d 762, 764 (5th Cir. 2003) (per curiam) (disciplinary charge

for allegedly lying in a grievance showed a direct link between complaint and punishment); Rauser v. Horn, 241 F.3d 330 (3d Cir. 2001) (prison staff warned plaintiff not to disrupt their programs with constitutional challenges, threatened that he would be denied parole, and admitted that his adverse parole recommendation came from refusal to complete the program that he was protesting); Baskerville v. Blot, 224 F. Supp. 2d 723, 733 (W.D.N.Y. 2002) (holding evidence that the officers made statements suggesting retaliatory motive supported a claim of retaliation despite passage of three years before retaliatory acts).

[315]*See, e.g.,* Mays v. Springborn, 575 F.3d 643, 650 (7th Cir. 2009) (at trial, plaintiff's plausible testimony created a jury question as to retaliatory motive); Muhammad v. Close, 379 F.3d 413, 416–17 (6th Cir. 2004) (an affidavit from a prisoner who reported overhearing a conversation between the defendant and another officer about the need to "get [the plaintiff's] ass" supported the plaintiff's retaliation claim). *Compare* Vega v. DeRobertis, 598 F. Supp. 501, 506 (N.D.Ill. 1984) (prisoner's belief unsupported by specific facts did not establish retaliatory motive), *aff'd*, 774 F.2d 1167 (7th Cir. 1985).

[316]Bennett v. Goord, 343 F.3d 133, 138–39 (2d Cir. 2003) (direct evidence of retaliatory motive is not required where circumstantial evidence is sufficiently compelling); Hines v. Gomez, 108 F.3d 265, 268 (9th Cir. 1997) (jury could infer retaliatory motive from evidence from prison staff that the plaintiff had a reputation for "complaining" or "whining," from his having filed many grievances, and from his having told the defendant he would be filing a grievance against him); Smith v. Maschner, 899 F.2d 940, 947–49 (10th Cir. 1990); Shabazz v. Cole, 69 F. Supp. 2d 177, 197–98 (D.Mass. 1999).

[317]Mays v. Springborn, 575 F.3d at 650 (commencement of more onerous searches immediately after plaintiff complained of searches); Espinal v. Goord, 558 F.3d 119, 129 (2d Cir. 2009) (passage of six months between lawsuit and beating by officers including one of the defendants supported an inference of causation); Allen v. Thomas, 388 F.3d 147, 149–50 (5th Cir. 2004) (confiscation of property shortly after the prisoner sent letters critical of the prison to the mail room); Muhammad v. Close, 379 F.3d 413, 417–18 (6th Cir. 2004) (stating that temporal proximity alone may be significant enough to constitute direct evidence of retaliatory motive); Bruce v. Ylst, 351 F.3d 1283, 1288 (9th Cir. 2003) (citing "suspect timing" of gang validation that closely followed plaintiff's success in grievances); Bennett v. Goord, 343 F.3d 133, 138–39 (2d Cir. 2003) (filing of disciplinary actions after plaintiff successfully settled claims of retaliation on prior occasions, and filing of additional charges when he filed a grievance about noncompliance with the settlement); Gayle v. Gonyea, 313 F.3d 677, 683 (2d Cir. 2002) (disciplinary charge filed six days after plaintiff filed a grievance); Harris v. Fleming, 839 F.2d 1232, 1236–38 (7th Cir. 1988); Rodriguez v. McClenning, 399 F. Supp. 2d 228, 239–40 (S.D.N.Y. 2005) (disciplinary charge following a grievance); Farid v. Goord, 200 F. Supp. 2d 220, 237 (W.D.N.Y. 2002) (retaliation claim was

adverse action that is based on flimsy or suspect evidence,[318] departures from the usual prison

procedures in acting against the prisoner,[319] and others.[320]

The fact that there is "some evidence" to support adverse action does not automatically mean it was not retaliatory.[321] However, if officials show that you in fact committed an offense for which you were disciplined, that will generally meet defendants' burden to show that their actions were not retaliatory.[322] Claims of retaliatory discipline appear to be subject to the rule that loss of good time can only be challenged in a civil action in federal court if the disciplinary proceeding has already been set aside in a state administrative or court proceeding, or by federal habeas corpus.[323]

---

supported by evidence that officer who initiated disciplinary action disliked Muslims and acted a few days after the plaintiff was found with a petition); *see* Withrow v. Donnelly, 356 F. Supp. 2d 273, 275–76 (W.D.N.Y. 2005) (passage of six months between complaint and retaliation did not defeat the claim; there is no bright line rule, and anyway the plaintiff had continued to make oral complaints in the interim).

Suspicious timing, however, will not support your retaliation claim if the defendants show legitimate reasons for their actions. Jackson v. Fair, 846 F.2d 811, 820 (1st Cir. 1988); Howland v. Kilquist, 833 F.2d 639, 644–45 (7th Cir. 1987); Hilliard v. Scully, 648 F. Supp. 1479, 1487–88 (S.D.N.Y. 1986).

[318]Bruce v. Ylst, 351 F.3d 1283, 1288 (9th Cir. 2003) (noting that the plaintiff had been validated as a gang member after winning grievances based on the same evidence that had been found insufficient before the grievance); Bennett v. Goord, 343 F.3d 133, 138–39 (2d Cir. 2003) (claim that discipline was retaliatory was supported by fact that all relevant disciplinary actions were later found unjustified); Gayle v. Gonyea, 313 F.3d 677, 683 (2d Cir. 2002) (same as *Bennett*; also, court notes that the accusing officer's testimony did not support all charges); Flaherty v. Coughlin, 713 F.2d 10, 13–14 (2d Cir. 1983) (denial of temporary release despite plaintiff's improved overall record, the minor nature of his most recent disciplinary violations, his constructive activities, etc.); Rodriguez v. McClenning, 399 F. Supp. 2d 228, 239–40 (S.D.N.Y. 2005) (plaintiff had a record of good behavior, all but one charge was dismissed at a hearing, and that one was expunged later); Kounelis v. Sherrer, 396 F. Supp. 2d 525, 531 (D.N.J. 2005) (claim that searches were retaliatory was supported by the fact that resulting disciplinary charges were dismissed); Lashley v. Wakefield, 367 F. Supp. 2d 461, 467–68 (W.D.N.Y. 2005) (findings that there was insufficient evidence to support discipline); Baskerville v. Blot, 224 F. Supp. 2d 723, 733 (W.D.N.Y. 2002) (holding that the fact the alleged retaliatory disciplinary charges were dismissed supported a claim of retaliation despite passage of three years before retaliatory acts); Farid v. Goord, 200 F. Supp. 2d 220, 237–38 (W.D.N.Y. 2002) (retaliation claim was supported by evidence that gravity of disciplinary charges was grossly disparate to evidence supporting them); Maurer v. Patterson, 197 F.R.D. 244, 247 (S.D.N.Y. 2000) (retaliation claim was supported by the fact that of 30 prisoners charged with an offense, only the two who were part of the grievance program were convicted, and the only evidence was supposed confidential hearsay informant information as to which there were credibility questions); Koch v. Lewis, 96 F. Supp. 2d 949, 956 (D. Ariz. 2000) (classification as a gang member based on "flimsy and outdated" evidence supported a claim of retaliation for legal activities), *vacated as moot*, 399 F.3d 1099 (9th Cir. 2005); Jones v. Coughlin, 696 F. Supp. 916, 923 (S.D.N.Y. 1988) (denial of temporary release, supposedly based on criminal record, where the facts showed that others denied for that reason had much worse records than the plaintiff).

If some staff members fabricate evidence to punish a prisoner for retaliatory reasons, the fact that other staff members reasonably rely on that evidence in making decisions about the prisoner does not defeat a retaliation claim. Toolasprashad v. Bureau of Prisons, 286 F.3d 576, 584–87 (D.C. Cir. 2002).

[319]Cornell v. Woods, 69 F.3d 1383, 1388–89 (8th Cir. 1995) (disciplinary charges were delayed a month and filed even though the plaintiff had been promised immunity; the plaintiff was transferred immediately even though the usual procedure was to keep the prisoner in the same location pending resolution of a disciplinary report; it was claimed this was for investigative purposes but no investigation was conducted); Segretti v. Gillen, 259 F. Supp. 2d 733, 736 (N.D.Ill. 2003) (prisoner alleged that officer against whom he had filed a grievance filed a false disciplinary report and was then allowed to participate in his disciplinary hearing and dictate the result); Gaston v. Coughlin, 81 F. Supp. 2d 381, 389–90 (N.D.N.Y. 1999) (prisoner was fired from his job after making a complaint, allegedly because he was planning a work stoppage, but there were no log entries or required security reports about the stoppage and the prisoner was not issued a misbehavior report), *reconsideration denied*, 102 F. Supp. 2d 81 (N.D.N.Y. 2000).

[320]Collins v. Goord, 438 F. Supp. 2d 399, 419 (S.D.N.Y. 2006) (extensive damage to plaintiff's typewriter supported an inference of malicious destruction); Hunter v. Heath, 95 F. Supp. 2d 1140, 1150–51 (D.Or. 2000) (removal from law library job supported retaliation claim), *rev'd on other grounds*, 26 Fed.Appx. 754 (9th Cir. 2002).

[321]"The 'some evidence' standard applies only to due process claims attacking the result of a disciplinary board's proceeding, not the correctional officer's retaliatory accusation." Bruce v. Ylst, 351 F.3d at 1289; *accord*, Hines v. Gomez, 108 F.3d 265, 268–69 (9th Cir. 1997). One federal circuit has taken the opposite position. *See* Moots v. Lombardi, 453 F.3d 1020, 1023 (8th Cir. 2006) ("Conduct violations cannot be deemed retaliatory when they were issued for actual violations of prison rules"; if a defendant shows there was some evidence of the infraction, claim of retaliation is barred. "The fact that the conduct violation was later expunged does not mean that there was not some evidence for its imposition."); Moore v. Plaster, 313 F.3d 442, 444 (8th Cir. 2002) (unpublished).

[322]Gayle v. Gonyea, 313 F.3d 677, 682 (2d Cir. 2002) (holding that officials can defeat a retaliation claim by showing it is undisputed that the plaintiff "committed the most serious, if not all, of the prohibited conduct charged in the misbehavior report"); Hynes v. Squillace, 143 F.3d 653, 657 (2d Cir. 1998).

[323]*See, e.g.*, Skinner v. Bolden, 89 Fed.Appx. 579, 580, 2004 WL 504343 (6th Cir. 2004) (unpublished); Norris v. Eicher, 2007 WL 3174020, *3 (W.D.Mich., Oct. 29, 2007), *reconsideration denied*, 2007 WL 4465266 (W.D.Mich., Dec. 18, 2007); Newsome v. Wexford Health Services, 2007 WL 581812, *7 (C.D.Ill., Feb. 20, 2007); Johnson v. Freeburn, 29 F. Supp. 2d 764, 773 (E.D.Mich. 1998). These decisions rely on the Supreme Court decision in *Edwards v. Balisok*, 520 U.S. 641, 117 S. Ct. 1584 (1997), which

In some cases, courts have held that retaliation for expressive activity will be upheld if it satisfies the *Turner v. Safley* standard by being reasonably related to legitimate penological interests.[324] We are not sure how retaliation for First Amendment-protected activity could ever meet that standard, so what the courts must mean is that in those cases, the expressive activity was not really protected in light of the limits on the First Amendment rights of prisoners.

7. Visiting

The federal Constitution provides very little protection for visiting in prison. Although prison visiting is an aspect of the constitutional right of free association, the Supreme Court in *Overton v. Bazzetta* said that "freedom of association is among the rights least compatible with incarceration."[325] It added: "We do not hold, and we do not imply, that any right to intimate association is altogether terminated by incarceration or is always irrelevant to claims made by prisoners."[326] However, applying the *Turner v. Safley* "reasonable relationship" standard, *Overton* upheld several very restrictive visiting practices on security and other grounds. It upheld rules barring visits by minors except for children, stepchildren, grandchildren, or brothers and sisters of the prisoner, and barring the prisoner's own children if his parental rights had been terminated; all minors had to be accompanied by a parent or legal guardian in order to visit.[327] It upheld a prohibition on visiting by former prisoners, except for those who were members of a prisoner's immediate family *and* had been approved by the warden. The Court said that this rule "bears a self evident connection

to the State's interest in maintaining prison security and preventing future crimes."[328]

Overton also upheld a rule providing that prisoners with two disciplinary violations for substance abuse could be barred from visiting entirely, with no fixed time limit, since "[d]rug smuggling and drug use in prison are intractable problems."[329] It justified these conclusions in part by stating that prisoners have alternative means of exercising their claimed right of association: letters, telephone calls, and messages sent through those persons who are allowed to visit.[330] It also stated that the prisoners failed to point to ready alternatives that accommodated their free association rights without more than a *de minimis* cost to the security and other goals of the regulations.[331]

In addition to these holdings about the right of free association, *Overton* held that the ban on visits for prisoners with substance abuse convictions did not constitute cruel and unusual punishment under the Eighth Amendment.[332] It did say that "[I]f the withdrawal of all visitation privileges were permanent or for a much longer period, or if it were applied in an arbitrary manner to a particular inmate, the case would present different considerations."[333]

Under *Overton*—and for that matter, before *Overton*—relatively few federal constitutional challenges to visiting restrictions have been successful. Several courts have struck

---

involved a due process claim and not a retaliation claim. One circuit had reached the contrary conclusion before *Edwards* was decided. Woods v. Smith, 60 F.3d 1161, 1164–66 (5th Cir. 1995).

[324]Rhodes v. Robinson, 408 F.3d 559, 567–68 (9th Cir. 2005) (holding that prisoners must prove both that adverse action was taken because of a "prisoner's protected conduct," and that it "did not reasonably advance a legitimate correctional goal"); Osterback v. Kemp, 300 F. Supp. 2d 1238, 1257–58 (N.D.Fla. 2003) (prisoner could be transferred because of filing multiple grievances and complaints even though found "right every time," since staff morale might have been affected), *on reconsideration*, 300 F. Supp. 2d 1263 (N.D.Fla. 2003).

[325]Overton v. Bazzetta, 539 U.S. 126, 131, 123 S. Ct. 2162 (2003).

[326]Overton v. Bazzetta, *id.* Before *Overton*, some courts did say that there is no constitutional right to visiting. *See, e.g.*, Berry v. Brady, 192 F.3d 504, 508 (5th Cir. 1999) ("Berry has no constitutional right to visitation privileges.") The status of these holdings after *Overton* is not clear.

[327]Overton, 539 U.S. at 133 (stating "we conclude that the regulations bear a rational relation to MDOC's valid interests in maintaining internal security and protecting child visitors from exposure to sexual or other misconduct or from accidental injury"; holding that reducing the number of children is a legitimate goal because it makes supervision easier and lessens disruption).

[328]Overton, 539 U.S. at 133; *see* Safley v. Turner, 586 F. Supp. 589, 596 (W.D.Mo. 1984) (prohibition on former inmates for six months after their release upheld), *aff'd on other grounds*, 777 F.2d 1307 (8th Cir. 1985), *aff'd in part and rev'd in part on other grounds*, 482 U.S. 78, 107 S. Ct. 2254 (1987).

[329]Overton, 539 U.S. at 134. Though the Court said the ban "may be removed after two years," it noted that reinstatement was not automatic. *Id.* It did say that "if faced with evidence that MDOC's regulation is treated as a *de facto* permanent ban on all visitation for certain inmates, we might reach a different conclusion in a challenge to a particular application of the regulation," but that situation was not before it. *Id.*; *see* Alkebulanyahh v. Bush, 2008 WL 2690123, *2 (D.S.C., July 1, 2008) (allowing claim of *de facto* permanent ban on visiting to go forward).

[330]Overton, 539 U.S. at 135. The Court added: "Respondents protest that letter writing is inadequate for illiterate inmates and for communications with young children. They say, too, that phone calls are brief and expensive, so that these alternatives are not sufficient. Alternatives to visitation need not be ideal, however; they need only be available." *Id.*

[331]Overton, 539 U.S. at 136.

[332]Overton, 539 U.S. at 136–37. Specifically, it said:

Michigan, like many other States, uses withdrawal of visitation privileges for a limited period as a regular means of effecting prison discipline. This is not a dramatic departure from accepted standards for conditions of confinement.... Nor does the regulation create inhumane prison conditions, deprive inmates of basic necessities or fail to protect their health or safety. Nor does it involve the infliction of pain or injury, or deliberate indifference to the risk that it might occur.

Id., 539 U.S. at 137.

[333]Overton, 539 U.S. at 137.

down broad prohibitions on visiting by children,[334] and we do not think these decisions are overruled by *Overton's* allowance of narrower restrictions on children's visiting. It seems clear that any constitutional protection of prison visiting is strongest when it involves members of the prisoner's immediate family.[335] But even close family members may be

barred from visiting based on good cause.[336] Several courts have upheld restrictions on sex offenders' visiting with children, including their own.[337] In extreme cases prisoners may be denied all or nearly all visits based on severe threats to prison security[338] or to public safety.[339] One court has upheld

---

[334]Morrow v. Harwell, 768 F.2d 619, 626–27 (5th Cir. 1985); McMurry v. Phelps, 533 F. Supp. 742, 764 (W.D.La. 1982); Nicholson v. Choctaw County, Ala., 498 F. Supp. 295, 310 (S.D.Ala. 1980); Valentine v. Englehardt, 474 F. Supp. 294, 301–02 (D.N.J. 1979); Stewart v. Gates, 450 F. Supp. 583, 586 (C.D.Cal. 1978), *remanded*, 618 F.2d 117 (9th Cir. 1980); *In re* Smith, 112 Cal.App.3d 956, 169 Cal.Rptr. 564, 570 (Cal.App. 2 Dist. 1980) (holding "ban on child visitation is an excessive response to the limited risk presented by child visitation in these particular facilities, and therefore not reasonably related to a legitimate governmental objective, influenced as we are by the fundamental nature of the rights between parent and child and the interest of the state in maintaining that delicate relationship"); Powlowski v. Wullich, 81 Misc.2d 895, 366 N.Y.S.2d 584, 591 (N.Y.Sup. 1975); *see* Buie v. Jones, 717 F.2d 925, 929 (4th Cir. 1983) (". . . [T]hose who operate detention facilities, whether in the form of local jails or prisons, should be aware that the absolute prohibition on visitation by a detainee's minor children . . . is almost certainly unconstitutional." (concurring opinion)); Hallal v. Hopkins, 947 F. Supp. 978, 996–97 (S.D.Miss. 1995) (questioning basis for ban on visits by children under 12, ordering evidentiary hearing); Smith v. McDonald, 869 F. Supp. 918, 919 (D.Kan. 1994) ("While under existing case law the court would carefully scrutinize a policy which created a blanket prohibition on visitation by minors," this policy has been changed so the court denies relief.); *see also* Ross v. Owens, 720 F. Supp. 490, 491 (E.D.Pa. 1989) (prison officials could not keep the plaintiff's 16-year-old son from visiting without the consent of his legal guardian). *But see* N.E.W. v. Kennard, 952 F. Supp. 714, 719–20 (D.Utah 1997) (upholding complete ban on visits by children under eight years old); Ford v. Beister, 657 F. Supp. 607, 611 (M.D.Pa. 1986) (prohibition on visits by minors upheld based on unique security problems).

[335]Keenan v. Hall, 83 F.3d 1083, 1092 (9th Cir. 1996) (denial of visits from anyone other than immediate family did not violate the Constitution), *amended*, 135 F.3d 1318 (9th Cir. 1998); Ramos v. Lamm, 639 F.2d 559, 580 (10th Cir. 1981) (greater restrictions on non-family visitors than family upheld); Hamilton v. Saxbe, 428 F. Supp. 1101, 1111–12 (N.D.Ga. 1976), *aff'd sub nom.* Hamilton v. Bell, 551 F.2d 1056 (5th Cir. 1977). One court has held that a husband and wife who were both pre-trial detainees and co-defendants must be permitted to visit each other. Perkins v. Wagner, 513 F. Supp. 904, 906–07 (E.D.Pa. 1981). *Contra,* Hallal v. Hopkins, 947 F. Supp. 978, 996 (S.D.Miss. 1995). Husband–wife visits have been denied where both were convicts. Wallace v. Hutto, 80 F.R.D. 739, 740–41 (W.D.Va. 1978), *aff'd*, 601 F.2d 583 (4th Cir. 1979); McFadden v. State, 580 So.2d 1210, 1216 (Miss. 1991).

Officials may limit visiting privileges to those who actually have a lawful family relationship. *See* Africa v. Vaughan, 998 F. Supp. 552, 555–56 (E.D.Pa. 1998) (upholding refusal to allow visit by woman to whom plaintiff was not married and who did not meet the state law requirements for common law marriage, notwithstanding the plaintiff's argument that he has his own system of marriage).

[336]Samford v. Dretke, 562 F.3d 674, 682 (5th Cir. 2009) (upholding exclusion of children of prisoner from visiting list where prisoner had assaulted their mother in their presence); Ware v. Morrison, 276 F.3d 385, 387–88 (8th Cir. 2002) (upholding 18-month suspension of visits with wife and others after plaintiff was found, following visits, with contraband including five freshly cut steaks, one four-pound box of frozen shrimp, four one-pound packages of linguine, and bottles of tequila and cognac); Robinson v. Palmer, 841 F.2d 1151, 1155–56 (D.C. Cir. 1988) (permanent suspension of wife's visits for trying to smuggle marijuana to her husband upheld); U.S. v. Ali, 396 F. Supp. 2d 703, 708–10 (E.D.Va. 2005) (upholding limitation of terrorist suspect's visits to family and counsel); Smith v. Matthews, 793 F. Supp. 998, 1000 (D.Kan. 1992) (upholding permanent suspension of wife's visits after she refused a search); Patterson v. Walters, 363 F. Supp. 486, 488–89 (W.D.Pa. 1973) (wife was barred after smuggling drugs); Rowland v. Wolff, 336 F. Supp. 257, 260 (D.Neb. 1971) (prisoner's half-sister was barred after bringing a gun into the prison); Victory v. Coughlin, 165 A.D.2d 402, 568 N.Y.S.2d 186, 187–88 (N.Y.App. Div. 1991) (wife who had helped prisoner escape was barred).

[337]Wirsching v. Colorado, 360 F.3d 1191, 1199–1201 (10th Cir. 2004) (upholding under *Overton* the denial of all visits with his own children to a sex offender who refused to participate in a treatment program, based on evidence that visiting might harm the child and undermine the plaintiff's rehabilitation); Odenwalt v. Gillis, 327 F. Supp. 2d 502, 508–09 (M.D.Pa. 2004) (upholding denial of contact visits with his own children to a sex offender convicted of a crime against his stepdaughter, under a rule denying contact visits to all sex offenders ever convicted of sex offenses against minors).

[338]Hernandez v. McGinnis, 272 F. Supp. 2d 223, 228 (W.D.N.Y. 2003) (upholding, under *Turner* and Eighth Amendment, permanent revocation of visiting privileges, with leave to seek reconsideration, which was granted after three years, to a prisoner who was found bringing a shank to the visiting room).

[339]U.S. v. Felipe, 148 F.3d 101, 109–12 (2d Cir. 1998) (prisoner convicted of gang-related crimes who had used the mail from prison to help commit them was properly barred from visits with anyone but his attorney and close family members approved by the court with notice to the U.S. Attorney's office, with all visits monitored); U.S. v. DeSoto, 885 F.2d 354, 363–64 (7th Cir. 1989) (pre-trial detainee indicted for trying to kill a prosecution witness, her children, and the prosecutor was properly denied all visits except from counsel); U.S. v. Flores, 214 F. Supp. 2d 1195, 1197–98 (D.Utah 2002) (detainee indicted for crimes including gang murder was first denied all but counsel visits, then permitted to visit with only one person, to protect witnesses where one had already been assaulted). *But see* Kentucky Dep't of Corrections v. Thompson, 490 U.S. 454, 465, 109 S. Ct. 1904 (1989) (Kennedy, J., concurring) (agreeing to uphold "precise and individualized" visiting restrictions without foreclosing a claim that permanently forbidding visits to some or all prisoners is unconstitutional).

the denial of all visiting in a 90-day "shock" program in which prisoners worked on a chain gang.[340]

Courts have upheld other reasonable rules governing who may visit,[341] including requirements that visitors be approved in advance[342] and that they provide identification.[343] Visits by religious advisors may be governed by the more favorable "compelling interest" test of the Religious Freedom Restoration Act and the Religious Land Use and Institutionalized Persons Act and not just the weaker reasonable relationship test of *Turner v. Safley*.[344] Some courts have struck down or questioned restrictions on visiting by same-sex partners.[345]

Restrictions on time, place, and manner of visiting have generally been upheld,[346] as have distinctions in visiting conditions between general population prisoners and those in segregation or protective custody.[347] Courts have been more willing to intervene in cases involving county jails with extremely limited visiting opportunities or oppressive conditions.[348] However, it is not unconstitutional to place convicts in a prison so distant that it is difficult or impossible for them to receive visits.[349] Nor does the suspension of visits during emergencies and lockdowns violate the Constitution.[350]

The Supreme Court long ago held that contact visits are not constitutionally required, even for pre-trial detainees,[351]

---

[340]Austin v. Hopper, 15 F. Supp. 2d 1210, 1233–39 (M.D.Ala. 1998) (holding purposes of making the program as austere as possible to deter inmates from future crimes or parole violations, and to remove distractions from the program's objectives, were legitimate and justified the denial of visiting).

[341]Smith v. Coughlin, 748 F.2d 783, 788–89 (2d Cir. 1984) (death row inmate could be limited to visits with family, lawyers, doctors, and clergy); Beasley v. Wharton, 682 F. Supp. 1234, 1236–37 (M.D.Ga. 1988) (visiting could be limited to persons who knew the inmate before his incarceration); Alim v. Byrne, 521 F. Supp. 1039, 1045 (D.N.J. 1980); Carey v. Beans, 500 F. Supp. 580, 585 (E.D.Pa. 1980) (prohibition on unlicensed bondspersons upheld), *aff'd*, 659 F.2d 1065 (3d Cir. 1981); Stewart v. Gates, 450 F. Supp. 583, 586 (C.D.Cal. 1978), *remanded*, 618 F.2d 117 (9th Cir. 1980). *But see* O'Malley v. Brierley, 477 F.2d 785, 795–96 (3d Cir. 1973) (racial or religious discrimination prohibited); Hardaway v. Kerr, 573 F. Supp. 419, 423–24 (W.D.Wis. 1983) (blanket ban on former jail volunteer workers enjoined on First Amendment grounds).

[342]Ramos v. Lamm, 639 F.2d 559, 580 (10th Cir. 1981).

[343]Ross v. Owens, 720 F. Supp. 490, 491 (E.D.Pa. 1989).

[344]Kikumura v. Hurley, 242 F.3d 950, 960–62 (10th Cir. 2001). These statutes are discussed in § C.1.b of this chapter.

[345]Whitmire v. State of Arizona, 298 F.3d 1134, 1136 (9th Cir. 2002) (reversing dismissal of complaint concerning a rule forbidding same-sex "kissing, embracing (with the exception of relatives or immediate family) or petting"; it was not supported by common sense); Doe v. Sparks, 733 F. Supp. 227, 234 (W.D.Pa. 1990) (in a state where homosexual conduct was legal, banning same-sex "boy/girlfriends" while permitting those of the opposite sex was irrational and denied equal protection).

[346]*See, e.g.*, Martin v. Tyson, 845 F.2d 1451, 1455–56 (5th Cir. 1988) (upholding scheduling and length of visits); Butler-Bey v. Frey, 811 F.2d 449, 451 (8th Cir. 1987) (upholding prohibition on religious headgear in visiting room); Ramos v. Lamm, 639 F.2d 559, 580 (10th Cir. 1981) (upholding five days or ten half-days a month); Henry v. Coughlin, 940 F. Supp. 639, 643–44 (S.D.N.Y. 1996) (upholding rule that prisoner who had had family visit could not have another visit on the day the family visit ended); Benson v. County of Orange, 788 F. Supp. 1123, 1125–26 (C.D.Cal. 1992) (reduction of visiting schedule to two days a week was not unconstitutional); Hallal v. Hopkins, 947 F. Supp. 978, 996 (S.D.Miss. 1995) (limit of visiting periods to 20 minutes upheld); Walker v. Johnson, 544 F. Supp. 345, 361 (E.D.Mich. 1982) (upholding three hours of visiting a week), *aff'd in part, rev'd in part on other grounds*,

771 F.2d 920 (6th Cir. 1985); Tunnell v. Robinson, 486 F. Supp. 1265, 1270–71 (W.D.Pa. 1980) (upholding a limit of five visitors at a time); Louis v. Ward, 444 F. Supp. 1107, 1108–09 (S.D.N.Y. 1978) (upholding limits on numbers of visits and visitors); Adams v. Aaron, 421 F. Supp. 430, 431 (E.D.Ill. 1976) (upholding limit on visits by particular individual).

[347]Beck v. Lynaugh, 842 F.2d 759, 762 (5th Cir. 1988) (administrative segregation); Taylor v. Rogers, 781 F.2d 1047, 1049–50 (4th Cir. 1986) (protective custody); Smith v. Coughlin, 748 F.2d 783, 788 (2d Cir. 1984) (death row); Ramos v. Lamm, 639 F.2d 559, 580 (10th Cir. 1981) (denial of contact visits in segregation); Bono v. Saxbe, 620 F.2d 609, 613–15 (7th Cir. 1980) (same); Smith v. Copeland, 892 F. Supp. 1218, 1234 (E.D.Mo. 1995) (policy denying visits to prisoners in isolation upheld as reasonable), *aff'd on other grounds*, 87 F.3d 265 (8th Cir. 1996); Robinson v. Illinois State Correctional Center (Stateville), 890 F. Supp. 715, 718–19 (N.D.Ill. 1995) (reducing visiting for segregation prisoners from two hours to one hour a week); Morrison v. Martin, 755 F. Supp. 683, 687 (E.D.N.C. 1990) (same), *aff'd*, 917 F.2d 1302 (4th Cir. 1990); Brooks v. Kleiman, 743 F. Supp. 350, 351 (E.D.Pa. 1989) (same); Crozier v. Shillinger, 710 F. Supp. 760, 764 (D.Wyo. 1989) (protective custody); Card v. Dugger, 709 F. Supp. 1098, 1103–09 (M.D.Fla. 1988) (death row), *aff'd*, 871 F.2d 1023 (11th Cir. 1989); Wilson v. Nevada Dep't of Prisons, 511 F. Supp. 750, 753 (D.Nev. 1981) (limits on non-family visitors for death row inmates); Freeman v. Trudell, 497 F. Supp. 481, 482 (E.D.Mich. 1980) (handcuffing of punitive segregation inmate for visits); Griffin v. Smith, 493 F. Supp. 129, 131 (W.D.N.Y. 1980) (exclusion from general population visiting room); Wojtczak v. Cuyler, 480 F. Supp. 1288, 1307 (E.D.Pa. 1979) (protective custody); Malik v. Coughlin, 157 A.D.2d 961, 550 N.Y.S.2d 219, 220 (N.Y.App.Div. 1990) (one non-legal visit a week for punitive segregation inmates).

[348]Morrow v. Harwell, 768 F.2d 619, 626–27 (5th Cir. 1985) (weekend visiting required); Jackson v. Gardner, 639 F. Supp. 1005, 1012 (E.D.Tenn. 1986) (increased visiting ordered); McMurry v. Phelps, 533 F. Supp. 742, 764 (W.D.La. 1982) (30 minutes a week was inadequate; hours accessible to working people required; lack of privacy and inability to see and hear condemned); Dawson v. Kendrick, 527 F. Supp. 1252, 1309 (S.D.W.Va. 1981) (obstructions to sight and hearing to be corrected); Nicholson v. Choctaw County, Ala., 498 F. Supp. 295, 310 (S.D.Ala. 1980) (two sessions of two hours weekly were inadequate; weekend, evening, and holiday visits required).

[349]*See* Ch. 4, § H.4, n.759.

[350]Wrinkles v. Davis, 311 F. Supp. 2d 735, 740 (N.D.Ind. 2004).

[351]Block v. Rutherford, 468 U.S. 576, 585–89, 104 S. Ct. 3227 (1984); *see* Toussaint v. McCarthy, 801 F.2d 1080, 1113–14 (9th Cir.

Conjugal or "family" visits are not constitutionally required,[352] and in prisons that have such visits, prison officials may lawfully exclude higher security inmates[353] and impose other restrictions.[354] There is no liberty interest requiring due process protections in avoiding removal from a family visiting program.[355]

_____

1986) (contact visits not required for convicts); Smith v. Coughlin, 748 F.2d 783, 788 (2d Cir. 1984) (contact visits not required for death row prisoners).

[352]Hernandez v. Coughlin, 18 F.3d 133, 137 (2d Cir. 1994) ("[t]he Constitution . . . does not create any protected guarantee to conjugal visitation privileges while incarcerated."); Davis v. Carlson, 837 F.2d 1318, 1319 (5th Cir. 1988); McCray v. Sullivan, 509 F.2d 1332, 1334 (5th Cir. 1975); Ramos v. Lamm, 485 F. Supp. 122, 162 (D.Colo. 1979), aff'd in part and set aside in part on other grounds, 639 F.2d 559 (10th Cir. 1980); Payne v. District of Columbia, 253 F.2d 867, 868 (D.C. Cir. 1958) (per curiam) (no right to conjugal visits in jail); Wilkinson v. McManus, 298 Minn. 541, 541, 214 N.W.2d 671, 672 (1974) (Minnesota prisoners do not have the right to conjugal visits during incarceration); see Gerber v. Hickman, 291 F.3d 617, 620–22 (9th Cir. 2002) (en banc) (holding a prisoner denied conjugal visits also had no right to impregnate his wife by artificial insemination); see also § G.1 of this chapter.

[353]Peterson v. Shanks, 149 F.3d 1140, 1145 (10th Cir. 1998) (ineligibility for family visiting resulting from safety-related transfer did not violate plaintiff's rights); Cooper v. Garcia, 55 F. Supp. 2d 1090, 1098–99 (S.D.Cal. 1999) (upholding exclusion of plaintiff from family visits on the ground he was a sex offender, even though not prosecuted as one, since there is no liberty interest in family visits); Isaraphanich v. Coughlin, 716 F. Supp. 119, 121 (S.D.N.Y. 1989) (upholding the denial of participation in the "Family Reunion Program" based on an Immigration and Naturalization Service detainer that caused the plaintiff to be placed in a high security classification); Toussaint v. McCarthy, 597 F. Supp. 1388, 1402, 1413 (N.D.Cal. 1984) (upholding the exclusion of segregated inmates from "family visits"), aff'd in part and rev'd in part on other grounds, 801 F.2d 1080 (9th Cir. 1986); see also Doe v. Coughlin, 71 N.Y.2d 48, 523 N.Y.S.2d 782, 518 N.E.2d 536 (N.Y. 1987) (upholding exclusion of inmates with AIDS from Family Reunion Program). The policy upheld in Doe v. Coughlin has since been abandoned by the prison system.

[354]Champion v. Artuz, 76 F.3d 483, 486 (2d Cir. 1996) (exclusion of wife who was an ex-offender upheld); Daniel v. Rolfs, 29 F. Supp. 2d 1184, 1188–89 (E.D.Wash. 1998) (upholding limitation of "extended family visits" to persons legally married before incarceration); In re Cummings, 30 Cal.3d 870, 640 P.2d 1101, 1102–03, 180 Cal.Rptr. 826 (Cal. 1982) (upholding exclusion of common law spouses from conjugal visiting program); Mary of Oakknoll v. Coughlin, 101 A.D.2d 931, 932, 475 N.Y.S.2d 644, 646 (N.Y. A.D. 3 Dep't 1984) (upholding requirement of valid marriage license to qualify for family visits). But see Bullock v. Gomez, 929 F. Supp. 1299, 1304–08 (C.D.Cal. 1996) (exclusion of HIV-positive prisoner from overnight visits with his HIV-positive wife raised a material issue under the disability statutes).

[355]Champion v. Artuz, 76 F.3d 483, 486 (2d Cir. 1996); Giano v. Goord, 9 F. Supp. 2d 235, 241 (W.D.N.Y. 1998), affirmed in part, vacated in part on other grounds, 250 F.3d 146 (2d Cir. 2001); Torricellas v. Poole, 954 F. Supp. 1405, 1414–15 (C.D.Cal. 1997), aff'd, 141 F.3d 1179 (9th Cir. 1998) (unpublished).

One court has held that surveillance and monitoring of detainees' visits to gather evidence for criminal prosecution violated state law, but monitoring could be permitted as necessary "to insure the security of the prison and the protection of the public."[356] Strip searches of prisoners may be required in connection with contact visiting. Strip searches of visitors generally require reasonable suspicion that the visitor is bringing in contraband.[357]

Prisoners have a right to visit in privacy with attorneys, law students, and legal paraprofessionals, and legal visits are generally required to be contact visits unless there is a particular security reason to the contrary.[358]

Given the limits of federal constitutional protections of visiting rights, you may have more chance of success if you proceed in state court relying on state constitutions, statutes, case law, and prison regulations.[359] Federal prisoners may

_____

[356]DeLancie v. Superior Court, 31 Cal.3d 865, 183 Cal.Rptr. 866, 647 P.2d 142, 147 (Cal. 1982). But see Shell v. U.S., 448 F.3d 951, 955–56 (7th Cir. 2006) (surveillance of visits pursuant to warrant by bugging visitor's badge was a reasonable search and not a search of the person); People v. Gallego, 52 C.3d 115, 276 Cal.Rptr. 679, 802 P.2d 169, 194–95 (Cal. 1990) (monitoring and recording visit conversations of a detainee who was a "major security risk" did not violate state or federal law).

[357]See § E.2 of this chapter for a discussion of strip searches.

[358]See § C.3 of this chapter, nn.587–592, for a discussion of legal visits.

[359]See, e.g., Adkins v. Stansel, 204 P.3d 1031, 1033–36 (Alaska 2009) (noting right to visiting is "an important component of the fundamental right to rehabilitation" under the state constitution; though state courts have upheld restrictions on visiting, allegation that private prison denied plaintiff a visit as part of a pattern of discouraging visiting stated a claim); In re French, 106 Cal. App.3d 74, 164 Cal.Rptr. 800, 807 (Cal.App. 1980) (citing 15 Cal. Admin.Code, § 3170(d)) (state regulations required contact visits except in particular cases involving security or punishment); Cooper v. Morin, 49 N.Y.2d 69, 424 N.Y.S.2d 168, 399 N.E.2d 1188, 1193–96 (N.Y. 1979) (state constitution required contact visits for detainees); Scott v. New Jersey Dep't of Corrections, 2009 WL 88133, *1–2 (N.J.Super.App.Div., Jan. 15, 2009) (holding permanent deprivation of contact visits based on disciplinary offenses was forbidden by state regulations); Rivera v. New York City Dep't of Correction, 24 Misc.3d 536, 876 N.Y.S.2d 631 (Sup. Ct. 2009) ("When . . . inmates are granted [visiting] rights by regulation, any restriction of them must then be subject to administrative and judicial review. . . . Thus, while the Department maintains authority to revoke or limit an inmate's visitation rights, it must first demonstrate reasonable cause to believe that such action is necessary to maintain safety, security, and good order of a correctional facility. . . ." Court holds denial of contact visits starting six months after a positive drug test lacked any reasonable basis); Dawes v. State, 194 Misc.2d 617, 618–19, 755 N.Y.S.2d 221 (N.Y.Co.Ct. 2003) (under state regulations, prisoner could not be deprived of contact visits because of misbehavior unrelated to visits); Chambers v. Coughlin, 76 A.D.2d 980, 429 N.Y.S.2d 74 (N.Y.App.Div. 1980) (state regulations forbade visiting deprivations as punishments); Gordon v. Oregon State Dep't of Corrections, 104 Or.App. 436, 801 P.2d 892 (Or.App. 1990) (state

also be able to rely on federal prison regulations concerning visits.[360]

With respect to procedural protections for visit denial or suspension, the Supreme Court has held that there is no constitutionally based liberty interest in visiting that requires due process protections if prison officials try to take it away.[361] That decision acknowledged that state law might create a liberty interest that due process would protect,[362] but later the Supreme Court drastically restricted liberty interest analysis. Under current law a deprivation must impose "atypical and significant hardship on the inmate in relation to the ordinary incidents of prison life" to call for due process protections.[363] The Court made it clear in *Overton* that suspension of visits does not meet that standard.[364]

Pre-trial detainees may be entitled to due process in connection with visiting deprivations, since the "atypical and significant" standard does not apply to them,[365] though we are not aware of any case where this point has been decided. In older cases where a liberty interest in visiting was found, courts disagreed over what procedural protections were required.[366] Where the atypical and significant standard does not apply, if a deprivation of visits is imposed as punishment for a disciplinary offense, the prisoner is presumably entitled to the usual safeguards of prison disciplinary hearings.[367] But once a prisoner has received a disciplinary hearing and has been convicted of a contraband or visit-related offense, due process does not require further hearings before visits can be suspended or limited.[368]

8. Telephones

Courts have said that prisoners have a First Amendment right to telephone access subject to reasonable limitations.[369]

---

regulations limited length of visiting suspensions). *But see* Victory v. Coughlin, 165 A.D.2d 402, 568 N.Y.S.2d 186, 187–88 (N.Y.App. Div. 1991) (state constitution does not protect visiting rights of convicts).

[360]*See* Boudin v. Thomas, 533 F. Supp. 786, 792–93 (S.D.N.Y.) (federal prison regulation required contact visits in most circumstances), *appeal dismissed, remanded*, 697 F.2d 288 (2d Cir. 1982).

[361]Kentucky Dep't of Corrections v. Thompson, 490 U.S. 454, 460–61, 109 S. Ct. 1904 (1989); *see also* Smith v. Matthews, 793 F. Supp. 998, 1000 (D.Kan. 1992) (federal regulations do not create a liberty interest in visiting); Milan v. Duckworth, 756 F. Supp. 381, 383 (N.D.Ind. 1989) (state visiting regulations did not create a liberty interest), *aff'd*, 920 F.2d 935 (7th Cir. 1990); White v. O'Leary, 742 F. Supp. 990, 994 (N.D.Ill. 1990) (barring the civilian plaintiffs from visiting prisons did not deny due process); Brisbon v. Lane, 554 F. Supp. 426, 428–29 (N.D.Ill. 1983) (prisoner's girlfriend could be barred based on unproven allegations that she had assisted another prisoner's escape attempt).

[362]Kentucky Dep't of Corrections v. Thompson, 490 U.S. 454, 460–61, 109 S. Ct. 1904 (1989). A number of courts found such a liberty interest in state law after *Thompson*. *See* Mendoza v. Blodgett, 960 F.2d 1425, 1431–33 (9th Cir. 1992) (state regulations); Patchette v. Nix, 952 F.2d 158, 161–62 (8th Cir. 1991) (state regulations); Taylor v. Armontrout, 894 F.2d 961, 963–64 (8th Cir. 1989) (Department of Corrections rule); Van Poyck v. Dugger, 779 F. Supp. 571, 576 (M.D.Fla. 1991) (state regulations); U.S. ex rel. Adams v. O'Leary, 659 F. Supp. 736, 738–39 (N.D.Ill. 1987) (state statute); Jackson v. Illinois Dep't of Corrections, 567 F. Supp. 1021, 1024–26 (N.D.Ill. 1983) (state regulation); Kozlowski v. Coughlin, 539 F. Supp. 852, 856–57 (S.D.N.Y. 1982) (state judicial decision and administrative regulations).

[363]Sandin v. Conner, 515 U.S. 472, 484, 115 S. Ct. 2293 (1995).

[364]Overton v. Bazzetta, 539 U.S. 126, 137, 123 S. Ct. 2162 (2003) (stating "withdrawal of visiting privileges for a limited period as a regular means of effecting prison discipline . . . is not a dramatic departure from accepted standards for conditions of confinement. *Cf. Sandin* . . ."); *accord*, Phillips v. Norris, 320 F.3d 844, 847 (8th Cir. 2003) (denial of contact visits did not deprive prisoner of a liberty interest); Torres Garcia v. Puerto Rico, 402 F. Supp. 2d 373, 381 (D.P.R. 2005) (a three-month deprivation of visiting with family members "fall[s] well below" the atypical and

significant hardship line); Ware v. Morrison, 276 F.3d 385, 387 (8th Cir. 2002) (loss of visiting did not deny liberty interest even if punitive); Henry v. Coughlin, 940 F. Supp. 639, 643 (S.D.N.Y. 1996).

[365]*See* Ch. 4, § C, n.78.

Prisoners, either convicted or pre-trial, may have procedural protections against deprivation of visiting rights under state law. *See* Rivera v. New York City Dep't of Correction, 24 Misc.3d 536, 540, 876 N.Y.S.2d 631 (Sup. Ct. 2009) (notice and hearing were required under jail regulations for deprivation of contact visits).

[366]In one case, the court preliminarily required that procedural safeguards comparable to those in a prison disciplinary hearing were required. Kozlowski v. Coughlin, 539 F. Supp. 852, 858 (S.D.N.Y. 1982). The case was settled before there was a final ruling. *See* Kozlowski v. Coughlin, 871 F.2d 241 (2d Cir. 1989) (adhering to settlement).

Other courts held that the "process due" is limited to "meaningful written responses to the prisoner's request and an opportunity to seek review of a denial from an officer other than the one who initially denied the prisoner's request." Hamilton v. Saxbe, 428 F. Supp. 1101, 1110 (N.D.Ga. 1976) (emphasis in original), *aff'd sub nom.* Hamilton v. Bell, 551 F.2d 1056 (5th Cir. 1977); *accord*, Laaman v. Helgemoe, 437 F. Supp. 269, 321 (D.N.H. 1977). *See* Ch. 4, § 4.D for a general discussion of determining what procedures are required by due process.

[367]*See* Czajka v. Moore, 708 F. Supp. 253, 254 (E.D.Mo. 1989) (where deprivation of visits was based on an unconstitutional disciplinary hearing, the court granted a preliminary injunction restoring visiting rights).

[368]Harmon v. Auger, 768 F.2d 270, 273 (8th Cir. 1985) (contact visits automatically suspended); Inman v. Coughlin, 156 A.D.2d 786, 549 N.Y.S.2d 207, 208 (N.Y.App.Div. 1989) (contact visits could be suspended after a disciplinary conviction for visiting room offense; the wife received a separate hearing).

[369]Johnson v. State of California, 207 F.3d 650, 656 (9th Cir. 2000); Washington v. Reno, 35 F.3d 1093, 1100 (6th Cir. 1994); King v. Frank, 328 F. Supp. 2d 940, 945 (W.D.Wis. 2004) ("Inmates have a First Amendment right both to communicate with

However, those cases where courts have actually found that restrictions on telephone access violated the Constitution generally involve pre-trial detainees and emphasize the effect of the restrictions on attorney–client telephone contact.[370] In cases involving convicts (and in some pre-trial

detainee cases[371]), courts have been unwilling to intervene as long as some level of telephone access was provided.[372] We are not aware of cases in which courts have actually found telephone access limits for convicted persons unconstitutional.[373] Courts have generally upheld the restriction of

---

[370]Lynch v. Leis, 382 F.3d 642 (6th Cir. 2004) (noting that lower court had granted an injunction against a collect-only telephone system where the Public Defender did not accept collect calls); Johnson-El v. Schoemehl, 878 F.2d 1043, 1052–53 (8th Cir. 1989) (one chance every two weeks to try to call an attorney under excessively noisy conditions was "patently inadequate"); Johnson by Johnson v. Brelje, 701 F.2d 1201, 1207–08 (7th Cir. 1983) (a weekly limit of two outgoing calls and no incoming calls was unreasonable where most of the detainees were from a city 370 miles away from the jail); McClendon v. City of Albuquerque, 272 F. Supp. 2d 1250, 1258 (D.N.M. 2003) (newly imposed five-minute limit on calls to attorneys, combined with ban on visits by class counsel, would "unjustifiably obstruct the availability of professional representation" and deny access to courts); Tuggle v. Barksdale, 641 F. Supp. 34, 37 (W.D.Tenn. 1985) (requiring that all telephone calls be made collect at a cost of 75 cents is "arbitrary, unduly harsh and primitive to many inmates or their families"); Johnson v. Galli, 596 F. Supp. 135, 138 (D.Nev. 1984) (telephone access only once a week, sometimes less often, presented a triable constitutional claim); Inmates of Allegheny County Jail v. Wecht, 565 F. Supp. 1278, 1284 (W.D.Pa. 1983) (detainees must be permitted to make non-collect calls to government agencies and lawyers); Dawson v. Kendrick, 527 F. Supp. 1252, 1314 (S.D.W.Va. 1981) (failure to provide "sufficient and regular telephone service" denied detainees adequate access to counsel); Stewart v. Gates, 450 F. Supp. 583, 586 (C.D.Cal. 1978) (requiring addition of telephones at accessible locations and available "at reasonable times on request"), *remanded*, 618 F.2d 117 (9th Cir. 1980); Moore v. Janing, 427 F. Supp. 567, 576 (D.Neb. 1976) (requiring privacy for attorney–client calls; declining to disturb limit of three phone calls every five days); Mitchell v. Untreiner, 421 F. Supp. 886, 902 (N.D.Fla. 1976) (daily phone access required); Inmates of the Suffolk County Jail v. Eisenstadt, 360 F. Supp. 676, 690 (D.Mass. 1973) (daily access to pay telephones required), *aff'd*, 494 F.2d 1196 (1st Cir. 1974); Brenneman v. Madigan, 343 F. Supp. 128, 141 (N.D.Cal. 1972) ("eavesdropping, accomplished either by means of electronic equipment or the presence of a custodial officer, would raise serious constitutional questions"); In re Grimes, 208 Cal.App.3d 1175, 256 Cal.Rptr. 690, 694–95 (Cal.App. 1989) ("collect only" telephone system denied court access; jail directed to install free line to public defender's office); *see* Feeley v. Sampson, 570 F.2d 364, 374 (1st Cir. 1978) (noting that a complete ban on calls to non-attorneys would "limit the ability of a detainee to investigate and prepare his defense"); Johnson v. Galli, 596 F. Supp. 135, 138 (D.Nev. 1984) ("Ofttimes use of a telephone is essential for a pretrial detainee to contact a lawyer, bail bondsman or other person in order to prepare his case or otherwise exercise his rights."). *But see* Lane v. Hutcheson, 794 F. Supp. 877, 881 (E.D.Mo. 1992) (upholding telephone system providing only collect calls).

Pre-trial detainees' right to communicate with the outside world is discussed further in Ch. 6.

---

[371]Martin v. Tyson, 845 F.2d 1451, 1458 (5th Cir. 1988) (one monitored telephone call every other day, with a non-monitored line for legal calls, met constitutional requirements); Simpson v. Gallant, 223 F. Supp. 2d 286, 295 (D.Me. 2002) (refusal to allow disciplinary segregation prisoners to make telephone calls except for a "bona fide" reason, not including "[r]outine lawyer calls," upheld), *aff'd*, 62 Fed.Appx. 368 (1st Cir. 2003) (unpublished); Bellamy v. McMickens, 692 F. Supp. 205, 214 (S.D.N.Y. 1988) (delays of no more than a day in telephone access did not violate the Constitution); Moore v. Janing, 427 F. Supp. 567, 576–77 (D. Neb. 1976) (three five-minute phone calls every five days, with unlimited calls for the purpose of obtaining counsel, was reasonable).

[372]Washington v. Reno, 35 F.3d 1093, 1100 (6th Cir. 1994) ("The exact nature of telephone service to be provided to inmates is generally to be determined by prison administrators, subject to court scrutiny for unreasonable restrictions." (citations omitted)); Aswegan v. Henry, 981 F.2d 313, 314 (8th Cir. 1992) (upholding ban on phone calls to attorneys' "800" numbers); Wooden v. Norris, 637 F. Supp. 543, 545, 557–58 (M.D.Tenn. 1986) (upholding replacement of coin-operated telephones with more expensive operator-assisted collect system); Jeffries v. Reed, 631 F. Supp. 1212, 1219 (E.D.Wash. 1986) (three opportunities a week for death row inmate to make collect calls to attorneys were sufficient); Peterkin v. Jeffes, 661 F. Supp. 895, 915 (E.D.Pa. 1987) (phone calls once a week or once a month did not violate rights of death row inmates), *aff'd in pertinent part*, 855 F.2d 1021, 1028, 1032 (3d Cir. 1988); Robbins v. South, 595 F. Supp. 785, 789 (D.Mont. 1984) (upholding requirement of prior authorization of phone calls and limitation to one call a week on weekdays only); Pino v. Dalsheim, 558 F. Supp. 673, 675 (S.D.N.Y. 1983) (prisoner who could make two telephone calls a month and was able to correspond and be visited was not entitled to an order providing additional telephone time for long-distance consultation with counsel); Mastrota v. Robinson, 534 F. Supp. 434, 437 (E.D.Pa. 1982) (upholding denial of phone calls before a transfer); *see* Wrinkles v. Davis, 311 F. Supp. 2d 735, 741 (N.D.Ind. 2004) (upholding denial of telephone access during most of 79-day lockdown).

[373]In *Washington v. Reno*, 35 F.3d 1093 (6th Cir. 1994), the court cited constitutional concerns with a proposed telephone system that required prisoners to list 20 persons they wished to call and required those persons who were not family members or approved visitors to fill out an intrusive questionnaire before the prisoner could call them. However, it held that expanding the list to 30 people and eliminating the questionnair requirement, along with evidence that "prison authorities may not now, without justification, routinely eliminate courts, elected officials, and members of the news media from inmate call lists," led the court to hold it was unlikely that plaintiffs would prevail on their constitutional challenge. Washington v. Reno, 35 F.3d at 1100. Thus the court did not actually rule on these "concerns." *See also* Divers v. Dep't of Corrections, 921 F.2d 191, 193–94 (8th Cir. 1990) (complaint alleging that protective custody inmates could only call their attorneys if they proved they had a court appearance within 30 days was not frivolous).

telephone calls to a specified list of persons,[374] and the denial or restriction of telephone privileges to persons in segregation units.[375] Courts have upheld severe telephone restrictions where prisoners have used the telephone to intimidate witnesses or engage in or promote other illegal activity, or there is concern that they may do so.[376] Short-term or inadvertent denials of telephone access do not violate the Constitution.[377] The failure to make adequate telephone equipment available for hearing-impaired prisoners may violate the First Amendment or the disability statutes.[378]

There is some disagreement about the right of a newly arrested person to have access to a telephone. Courts have held that arrested persons in custody have the right to telephone an attorney under the Fourteenth Amendment,[379] but some have also held that delaying that right does not violate the Sixth Amendment right to counsel as long as no accusatorial questioning or adversarial proceedings take place in the interim.[380] Others have held that the right to call an attorney does not "attach" until the commencement of adversary judicial proceedings.[381] Still others have said that there is a general due process right not to be held incommunicado, and have not limited the right to post-arrest telephone access to calling a lawyer.[382] Arrestees may be required to complete the booking process before using the telephone.[383] Courts have disagreed whether state statutes

---

[374]Pope v. Hightower, 101 F.3d 1382, 1384–86 (11th Cir. 1996) (upholding limit of 10 people on telephone calling list, with the option of changing the list every six months); Arney v. Simmons, 26 F. Supp. 2d 1288, 1293–96 (D.Kan. 1998) (upholding telephone system limited to collect calls to an approved list of 10 persons that can be changed every 120 days, with recording and monitoring of non-legal calls); Carter v. O'Sullivan, 924 F. Supp. 903, 909–11 (C.D.Ill. 1996) (upholding system with a call list limited to 30 people, changed weekly, with non-attorney calls monitored and recorded, and calls cut off if transferred to a third party).

[375]Benzel v. Grammer, 869 F.2d 1105, 1108 (8th Cir. 1989) (upholding restricted telephone list for segregation inmates); Armstrong v. Lane, 771 F. Supp. 943, 949 (C.D.Ill. 1991) (upholding deprivation of telephone privileges to segregation inmates); Toussaint v. McCarthy, 597 F. Supp. 1388, 1413 (N.D.Cal. 1984) (denial of telephone access to segregation inmates did not violate the Eighth Amendment), *aff'd in part and rev'd in part on other grounds*, 801 F.2d 1080 (9th Cir. 1986).

[376]*See* U.S. v. Felipe, 148 F.3d 101, 110–11 (2d Cir. 1998) (detainee convicted of gang activities could be limited to telephone calls to his attorney); U.S. v. DeSoto, 885 F.2d 354, 363–64 (7th Cir. 1989) (detainee who had been indicted for trying to kill a prosecution witness, her children, and the prosecutor was properly denied all telephone calls except to counsel); U.S. v. Ali, 396 F. Supp. 2d 703, 708–10 (E.D.Va. 2005) (upholding restriction of terrorism suspect's calls to a small number of family and counsel only); U.S. v. Flores, 214 F. Supp. 2d 1193, 1198 (D.Utah 2002) (same restriction, where one witness had been attacked). In *Valdez v. Rosenbaum*, 302 F.3d 1039, 1043–49 (9th Cir. 2002), the court upheld a four and a half month ban on any telephone access, except to the detainee's attorney upon written request, based on the fact that the plaintiff's superseding indictment named five new defendants who were not yet in custody and he might warn them.

[377]Williams v. McClain, 708 F. Supp. 1086, 1087–88 (W.D.Mo. 1989) (16-day denial of phone access contrary to jail policy did not state a constitutional claim).

[378]Tanney v. Boles, 400 F. Supp. 2d 1027, 1041–44, 1047 (E.D.Mich. 2005) (holding deaf inmate's complaint of inadequate access to a TDD/TTY telephone device raised a factual issue under the First Amendment and supported a Rehabilitation Act claim); Hanson v. Sangamon County Sheriff's Dep't, 991 F. Supp. 1059, 1064 (C.D.Ill. 1998) (failure to provide a telephone device for the deaf for an arrestee stated an ADA claim); Clarkson v. Coughlin, 898 F. Supp. 1019, 1046–47 (S.D.N.Y. 1995) (lack of TDD/TTY devices violated the disability statutes); Rewolinski v. Morgan, 896 F. Supp. 879, 881 (E.D.Wis. 1995) (restricted availability of telephone devices for the deaf stated an ADA claim); *see* Ch. 4, § F.4.h(2), concerning the disability statutes. *But see* Spurlock v. Simmons, 88 F. Supp. 2d 1189, 1196 (D. Kan. 2000) (allowing deaf prisoner to use a telephone device for the deaf whenever he

wanted to would have placed an undue burden on prison officials, even though hearing prisoners could use the phone whenever they wanted).

[379]Tucker v. Randall, 948 F.2d 388, 390–91 (7th Cir. 1991) ("Denying a pre-trial detainee access to a telephone for four days would violate the Constitution in certain circumstances. The Sixth Amendment right to counsel would be implicated if plaintiff was not allowed to talk to his lawyer for the entire four-day period. . . . In addition, unreasonable restrictions on prisoner's telephone access may also violate the First and Fourteenth Amendments."); Moore v. Marketplace Restaurant, Inc., 754 F.2d 1336, 1349 & n.19 (7th Cir. 1985). *But see* Collins v. Ainsworth, 382 F.3d 529, 545 (5th Cir. 2004) (arrestees who were deprived of telephone access for less than 24 hours in a mass arrest situation "were not subjected to impermissible punishment").

[380]Moore v. Marketplace Restaurant, Inc., 754 F.2d 1336, 1349 & n.19 (7th Cir. 1985) (citing State Bank of St. Charles v. Camic, 712 F.2d 1140, 1144 (7th Cir.1983)).

[381]Fridley v. Horrigs, 162 F. Supp. 2d 772, 778 n.4 (S.D.Ohio 2000) (arrestee had no right to call his attorney from jail, since the right to counsel had not yet attached), *aff'd on other grounds*, 291 F.3d 867 (6th Cir. 2002); Johnson v. Carroll, 694 F. Supp. 500, 505 (N.D.Ill. 1988) (so holding, even though the arrestee was interrogated for 30 hours).

[382]Carlo v. City of Chino, 105 F.3d 493, 495–500 (9th Cir. 1997) ("the right of an arrestee not to be held incommunicado involves a substantial liberty interest"; court upholds right without limiting it to communication with counsel); *see* Kis v. County of Schuylkill, 866 F. Supp. 1462, 1478 (E.D.Pa. 1994) (policy of permitting detainees to make a telephone call upon admission, then denying them telephone access during a 48-hours "isolation period," then permitting them access "within reason" after their release to general population was not unconstitutional). *But see* Harrill v. Blount County, Tenn., 55 F.3d 1123, 1125 (6th Cir. 1995) (holding police did not violate the plaintiff's rights when they prevented her from immediately telephoning her father after her arrest, since he was being investigated for the same criminal activity; they told her she could telephone an attorney. "The right to make a phone call immediately upon arrest is not a recognized property right, nor is it a traditional liberty interest recognized by federal law.").

[383]Strandberg v. City of Helena, 791 F.2d 744, 747 (9th Cir. 1986); State Bank of St. Charles v. Camic, 712 F.2d 1140, 1144 (7th Cir. 1983) (refusal to permit an arrestee a phone call until he

governing post-arrest telephone access create liberty interests enforceable in federal court.[384]

Prisoners have a right of privacy in telephone calls to their attorneys, but not in telephone calls to other persons.[385] Federal statutes prohibit the recording of telephone conversations without a warrant and forbid the use of such recordings as evidence under most circumstances.[386] However, if prison officials provide notice that your calls will be monitored, you will be deemed to have consented to the monitoring, and anything you say over the telephone can be used against you in criminal proceedings.[387]

---

cooperated with booking procedures did not violate the Sixth Amendment or due process).

[384]Compare Carlo v. City of Chino, 105 F.3d 493, 495–97 (9th Cir. 1997) (holding yes) with Harrill v. Blount County, Tenn., 55 F.3d 1123, 1125 (6th Cir. 1995) (holding no).

[385]Prison officials satisfy their obligation to respect attorney–client privacy if they surveill telephone calls generally but make available another means of private telephone access for attorney calls. Martin v. Tyson, 845 F.2d 1451, 1458 (5th Cir. 1988) (monitored line for social calls and non-monitored line for attorney calls met constitutional requirements); Arney v. Simmons, 26 F. Supp. 2d 1288, 1296–97 (D.Kan. 1998) (similar to Martin); U.S. v. Noriega, 764 F. Supp. 1480, 1485–90 (S.D.Fla. 1991) (monitoring of attorney–client telephone calls did not violate the Sixth Amendment because the prisoner had been informed of the monitoring and had had the opportunity to make special arrangements for unmonitored calls); Lee v. Carlson, 645 F. Supp. 1430, 1438–39 (S.D.N.Y. 1986), aff'd, 812 F.2d 712 (2d Cir. 1987); Tuggle v. Barksdale, 641 F. Supp. 34, 37–38 (W.D.Tenn. 1985); State v. Trevino, 833 P.2d 1170, 1176 (N.M.App.), aff'd in part sub nom. State v. Orosco, 833 P.2d 1146 (N.M. 1992) (upholding videotaping of telephone calls). Cf. Tucker v. Randall, 948 F.2d 388, 391 (7th Cir. 1991) ("Prison officials may tape a prisoner's telephone conversations with an attorney only if such taping does not substantially affect the prisoner's right to confer with counsel"); U.S. v. Noriega, 917 F.2d 1543, 1551 n.10 (11th Cir. 1990) (prisoner may have waived attorney–client privilege by signing a telephone usage release form).

At least one court has held (correctly, in our view) that prisoners also have a right to private telephone calls with persons such as medical practitioners or clergy. See Breest v. Dubois, 7 Mass.L.Rptr. 246, 1997 WL 449898, *5–6 (Mass. Super. 1997) (order to show cause why calls to pre-approved medicals personnel and clergy are not privileged).

[386]18 U.S.C. §§ 2510–2521 (Title VII, Omnibus Crime Control and Safe Streets Act of 1968). These protections also apply to other forms of communication. Lonegan v. Hasty, 436 F. Supp. 2d 419, 432 (E.D.N.Y. 2006) (applying statute to oral conversations that were tape-recorded by prison staff; stating "the Wiretap Act prohibits prison officers from intercepting communications involving prisoners without court authorization. . . . [I]n the prison setting, attorney–client communications generally are distinguished from other kinds of communications and exempted from routine monitoring.").

[387]U.S. v. Novak, 531 F.3d 99, 101–03 (1st Cir. 2008) (O'Connor, J.) (mistaken surveillance of attorney–client calls did not violate Fourth Amendment in light of client's consent to monitoring generally; Sixth Amendment claims waived); U.S. v. Moore, 452 F.3d 382, 386–87 (5th Cir. 2006); U.S. v. Workman, 80 F.3d 688, 693–94

In recent years, many prisons and jails have contracted with private telephone service providers, which often charge excessive rates to prisoners or those who receive prisoners' calls, and kick back part of the money to the prison authorities. Prisoners' challenges to these arrangements have led to mixed results under the Constitution[388] and under federal

---

(2d Cir. 1996) (prisoner received notice from an orientation handbook and a sign over the telephone); U.S. v. van Poyck, 77 F.3d 285, 290–92 (9th Cir. 1996) (prisoner with notice of surveillance did not have a reasonable expectation of privacy in his telephone calls, in addition to impliedly consenting to surveillance); U.S. v. Horr, 963 F.2d 1124, 1126 (8th Cir. 1992); U.S. v. Rivera, 292 F. Supp. 2d 838, 844 (E.D.Va. 2003); U.S. v. Noriega, 764 F. Supp.1480, 1491 (S.D.Fla. 1991); see Huguenin v. Ponte, 29 F. Supp. 2d 57, 66–67 (D.R.I. 1998) (where officials did not put warning signs over the telephones, but said they gave other kinds of warnings, there was an issue of fact whether they had given sufficient notice).

Courts have also held that the statutory restrictions do not apply to prison telephone monitoring at all because it falls within an exception in the statute for law enforcement officers acting in the ordinary course of their duties. U.S. v. Lewis, 406 F.3d 11, 17–19 (1st Cir. 2005); U.S. v. Friedman, 300 F.3d 111, 122–23 (2d Cir. 2002); U.S. v. van Poyck, 77 F.3d 285, 291–92 (9th Cir. 1996); U.S. v. Noriega, 764 F. Supp.1480, 1490–91 (S.D.Fla. 1991); U.S. v. Vasta, 649 F. Supp. 974, 989 (S.D.N.Y. 1986); U.S. v. Clark, 651 F. Supp. 76, 78–80 (M.D.Pa. 1986), aff'd, 857 F.2d 1464 (3d Cir. 1988). Contra, Kimberlin v. Quinlan, 774 F. Supp. 1, 10 (D.D.C. 1991); Crooker v. U.S. Dep't of Justice, 497 F. Supp. 500, 502–03 (D.Conn. 1980) and cases cited. Compare Huguenin v. Ponte, 29 F. Supp. 2d 57, 64–66 (D.R.I. 1998) (personnel of a private prison are not "investigative or law enforcement officers" who are exempt from the statutory prohibition) with U.S. v. Rivera, 292 F. Supp. 2d 838, 842–43 (E.D.Va. 2003) (applying "ordinary course" exception to surveillance by private telephone provider acting under the supervision of law enforcement).

Some courts have held that there must be "some notice" to prisoners of the surveillance in order for the ordinary course exception to apply, but it need not be notice sufficient to support a finding that the prisoner consented. Adams v. City of Battle Creek, 250 F.3d 980, 984 (6th Cir. 2001); see U.S. v. Friedman, 300 F.3d 111, 122–23 (2d Cir. 2002) (holding that if notice is required, it need not be sufficient to show consent).

[388]Gilmore v. County of Douglas, State of Nebraska, 406 F.3d 935, 940 (8th Cir. 2005) (a 45% commission paid to the county by the jail telephone provider and surcharged to prisoners' relatives did not deny them equal protection relative to other telephone users who receive collect calls from non-prisoners, since the charge was reasonably related to defraying the costs of providing the service—even though there was no evidence supporting that claim); Arsberry v. Illinois, 244 F.3d 558, 564–66 (7th Cir. 2001) (rejecting First Amendment, due process, and equal protection attacks on sole-source contracts for prison telephone service); Johnson v. State of California, 207 F.3d 650, 656 (9th Cir. 2000) (allegation that prison officials conspired with telephone companies to overcharge prisoners in exchange for kickbacks did not state a claim absent allegations that the charges were so exorbitant as to deprive prisoners of telephone access altogether); McGuire v. Ameritech Services, Inc., 253 F. Supp. 988–1006 (S.D.Ohio 2003) (rejecting due process and part of equal protection challenge to exclusive contracts for prison telephone services which made collect calls more expensive than those from non-prisoners; rejecting claim

statutes and regulations.[389] In at least one case, a state Public Service Commission has struck down prison telephone rates as exorbitant.[390]

9. Voting

The Constitution permits states to disenfranchise (exclude from voting) persons convicted of "participation in rebellion, or other crimes."[391] The Supreme Court has held that this means states may disenfranchise convicted felons.[392] Challenges to felon disenfranchisement statutes have generally been unsuccessful under both the Equal Protection Clause and other constitutional provisions[393] and the federal Voting Rights Act.[394] Felons should therefore look to state election laws to determine their right to vote, and disputes about those laws' application should generally be taken to state court rather than federal court.[395]

At present, all states except for Maine and Vermont bar convicted felons serving prison sentences from voting; 35 disenfranchise felons on parole and 30 disenfranchise felons on probation; 2 states disenfranchise all felons even after they have completed their sentences and any period of parole.[396] Some states provide for disenfranchisement based on any felony conviction, while others permit some convicted felons to vote.[397]

under Contracts Clause; but holding that First Amendment claim that high rates made communication impossible, and equal protection claim based on denial of a fundamental right, could go forward); Daleure v. Kentucky, 119 F. Supp. 2d 683, 691 (W.D.Ky. 2000) (rejecting equal protection challenge to high rates), *appeal dismissed*, 269 F.3d 540 (6th Cir. 2001).

[389]Arsberry v. Illinois, 244 F.3d 558, 564–68 (7th Cir. 2001) ("filed rate" doctrine did not bar challenge to telephone contracts, rather than rates; rejecting antitrust claim because statutes do not restrict acts of government or of contractors with governmen); McGuire v. Ameritech Services, Inc., 253 F. Supp. 2d 988, 1006–10, 1012–15 (S.D.Ohio 2003) (rejecting Sherman Act antitrust claim because that statute was not intended to restrain state governments and policies; rejecting claim under federal Telecommunications Act based on "filed rate" doctrine, which means companies can charge whatever the relevant regulatory agency has approved); Daleure v. Kentucky, 119 F. Supp. 2d 683, 687–90, 692–94 (W.D.Ky. 2000) (dismissing antitrust claims for damages under "filed rate" doctrine, but allowing injunctive antitrust claims to go forward), *appeal dismissed*, 269 F.3d 540 (6th Cir. 2001).

[390]Daleure v. Kentucky, 119 F. Supp. 2d 683, 686 n.5 (W.D.Ky. 2000), *appeal dismissed*, 269 F.3d 540 (6th Cir. 2001). *Cf.* Dep't of Corrections v. Public Utilities Com'n, 968 A.2d 1047 (Me. 2009) (state Public Utilities Commission did not have jurisdiction over telephone rates where the prison department and not contractors operated the telephone system).

[391]U.S. Const., Amend. XIV.

[392]Richardson v. Ramirez, 418 U.S. 24, 55–56, 94 S. Ct. 2655 (1974); *accord*, Wesley v. Collins, 791 F.2d 1255, 1261–62 (6th Cir. 1986); Franklin v. Murphy, 745 F.2d 1221, 1231 (9th Cir. 1984); Texas Supporters of Workers World Party Presidential Candidates v. Strake, 511 F. Supp. 149, 153 (S.D.Tex. 1981); *see* Danielson v. Dennis, 139 P.3d 688, 691–95 (Colo. 2006) (holding that statute disenfranchising felony parolees did not conflict with state constitution). A recent decision holds that disenfranchisement is not limited to "common-law felonies." Coronado v. Napolitano, 2008 WL 191987, *8–9 (D.Ariz., Jan. 22, 2008).

Most states provide for the restoration of voting rights by pardon or other procedure. *See, e.g.*, Richardson v. Ramirez, 418 U.S. at 30 (California law); Wesley v. Collins, 791 F.2d at 1258 n.3 (Tennessee law).

[393]Simmons v. Galvin, 573 F.3d 24, 42–45 (1st Cir. 2009) (Massachusetts constitutional amendment disqualifying prisoners from voting did not violate the Ex Post Facto Clause), *pet. for cert. filed*, No. 09-920, 78 U.S.L.W. 3461 (Feb. 1, 2010); Johnson v. Governor of State of Florida, 405 F.3d 1214, 1223–27 (11th Cir. 2005) (holding any discriminatory effect of Florida's

nineteenth-century felon disenfranchisement law had been cured by later amendments); Cotton v. Fordice, 157 F.3d 388, 391–92 (5th Cir. 1988) (similar to *Johnson*); King v. City of Boston, 2004 WL 1070573, *1 (D. Mass. 2004) (disenfranchisement statute did not violate Ex Post Facto Clause as applied to persons convicted before its enactment); Jones v. Edgar, 3 F. Supp. 2d 979, 981 (C.D.Ill. 1998) (Illinois disenfranchisement law did not violate the Fifteenth Amendment); Perry v. Beamer, 933 F. Supp. 556, 559–60 (E.D. Va. 1996) (Virginia statute did not deny equal protection), *aff'd*, 99 F.3d 1130 (4th Cir. 1996); Madison v. State, 161 Wash.2d 85, 103–09, 163 P.3d 757 (2007) (upholding Washington State disenfranchisement law).

The Supreme Court struck down a state statute that disenfranchised certain *misdemeanants* as racially discriminatory. Hunter v. Underwood, 471 U.S. 222, 105 S. Ct. 1916 (1985).

[394]*See* Simmons v. Galvin, 573 F.3d at 35–42; Hayden v. Pataki, 449 F.3d 305, 314–28 (2d Cir. 2006) (en banc) (Voting Rights Act does not encompass prisoner disenfranchisement statutes); Johnson v. Governor of State of Florida, 405 F.3d 1214, 1228 (11th Cir. 2005) (Voting Rights Act "does not prohibit all voting restrictions that may have a racially disproportionate effect," and felon disenfranchisement statutes are "deeply rooted in this Nation's history").

A federal appeals court recently held that the Washington felon disenfranchisement statute violated the Voting Rights Act; however, the court will rehear the case *en banc*. Farrakhan v. Gregoire, 590 F.3d 989 (9th Cir. 2010), *rehearing en banc granted*, ___ F.3d ___, 2010 WL 1766232 (9th Cir. 2010).

[395]*See, e.g.*, Cepulonis v. Secretary of Commonwealth, 389 Mass. 930, 452 N.E.2d 1137 (Mass. 1983) (incarcerated state residents must be permitted to register and vote by absentee ballot); Dane v. Board of Registrars of Voters of Concord, 374 Mass. 152, 371 N.E.2d 1358 (Mass. 1978) (prisoners are presumed to retain the domicil they had before their incarceration but can change their domicil to the location of the prison based on sufficient proof of intent); Hitchner v. Cumberland County Board of Elections, 163 N.J.Super. 560, 395 A.2d 270 (N.J.County Ct. 1978) (convicted criminal released pending a future surrender date was entitled to vote under state law).

[396]The Sentencing Project, Felony Disenfranchisement Laws in the United States, *available at* http://www.sentencingproject.org/pdfs/1046.pdf.

[397]*See, e.g.*, U.S. v. Dahms, 938 F.2d 131, 133–34 (9th Cir. 1991) (incarcerated felons disenfranchised, but rights restored upon release); Wesley v. Collins, 791 F.2d 1255, 1258 (6th Cir. 1986) (all felons disenfranchised in Tennessee); Franklin v. Murphy, 745 F.2d 1221, 1231 (9th Cir. 1984) (felons barred from voting while imprisoned in Oregon); Maryland Election Code Ann., art. 33, § 3–4 (1984) (disenfranchisement on second offense only); New

Pre-trial detainees and misdemeanants are generally eligible to vote.[398]

Those prisoners who are eligible to vote must be provided with some practical means of voting, usually absentee ballots.[399]

C. Access to the Courts

The right of access to courts is a very important right, since it theoretically protects all your other rights.[400] This right extends to all categories of prisoners,[401] and it is supposed to be "adequate, effective, and meaningful."[402]

That sounds good, but recent Supreme Court decisions have made it very difficult for prisoners to pursue claims based on the right of court access. These days, most prisoner court access claims are thrown out immediately, costing the prisoner a filing fee and a "strike" for nothing.[403] This section tells you what cases you can bring and how to plead them to avoid that outcome.

There are three basic kinds of court access claims that prisoners can assert:

1. **Right to assistance claims.** These are claims that prison officials failed to assist prisoners in bringing legal actions, by providing law libraries or legal assistance, as required by the decision in *Bounds v. Smith*.[404]

2. **Interference claims.** These are claims that prison officials or other officials interfered with prisoners' attempts to bring or pursue legal actions.

3. **Retaliation claims.** These are claims that officials retaliated against prisoners who brought or tried to bring legal actions.

Hampshire Const., Pt. I, art. II (disenfranchisement only for treason, bribery, and election offenses).

Recent decisions hold that it is not unconstitutional to require that felons pay all fines and restitution included in their sentences before their right to vote is restored. Coronado v. Napolitano, 2008 WL 191987, *3–4 (D.Ariz., Jan. 22, 2008); Madison v. State, 161 Wash.2d 85, 103–09, 163 P.3d 757 (2007).

[398]In *O'Brien v. Skinner*, 414 U.S. 524, 533 n.2, 94 S. Ct. 740 (1974), the Supreme Court observed that the state law under consideration did not disenfranchise detainees and misdemeanants and that it "therefore need not confront . . . the very substantial constitutional problems presented if a State did seek to exclude these classes from the franchise." The *O'Brien* Court went on to strike down laws that permitted detainees and misdemeanants to vote by absentee ballot only if they were confined outside their home counties. Later, the Court struck down a statute disenfranchising certain misdemeanants, holding that the statute had been intended as a means of racial discrimination. Hunter v. Underwood, 471 U.S. 222, 105 S. Ct. 1916 (1985). It is not clear whether a state could lawfully choose to disenfranchise certain misdemeanants for non-discriminatory reasons. *But see In re* Interrogatories of the U.S. District Court Pursuant to Rule 21.1, 642 P.2d 496, 497–98 (Colo. 1982) (state constitution and statute disenfranchised all convicted persons held in prisons or jails, but not pre-trial detainees).

[399]O'Brien v. Skinner, 414 U.S. at 530–31; Murphree v. Winter, 589 F. Supp. 374, 380–82 (S.D.Miss. 1984); Dawson v. Kendrick, 527 F. Supp. 1252, 1316 (S.D.W.Va. 1981); Tate v. Collins, 496 F. Supp. 205, 208–10 (W.D.Tenn. 1980).

In at least one state, imprisoned felons have been disenfranchised in practice by a statute making them ineligible for absentee ballots. Both state and federal courts have upheld the statute. Owens v. Barnes, 711 F.2d 25, 27–28 (3d Cir. 1983); Martin v. Haggerty, 120 Pa.Cmwlth. 134, 548 A.2d 371 (Pa.Commw. 1988), *appeal denied*, 520 Pa. 621, 554 A.2d 512 (1989).

[400]"Because a prisoner ordinarily is divested of the privilege to vote, the right to file a court action might be said to be his remaining most 'fundamental political right, because preservative of all rights.'" McCarthy v. Madigan, 503 U.S. 140, 153, 112 S. Ct. 1081 (1992) (quoting Yick Wo v. Hopkins, 118 U.S. 356, 370 (1886)).

Despite its importance, the courts are not too clear about where this right comes from; they have cited the Privileges and Immunities Clause of Article IV of the Constitution, the First Amendment Petition Clause, the Fifth Amendment Due Process Clause, and the Fourteenth Amendment Equal Protection and Due Process Clauses. Christopher v. Harbury, 536 U.S. 403, 415 n.12, 122 S. Ct. 2179 (2002).

[401]*See* John L. v. Adams, 969 F.2d 228, 232–33 (6th Cir. 1992) and cases cited (juvenile prisoners); Johnson v. Brelje, 701 F.2d 1201, 1207 (7th Cir.1983) (persons detained as unfit to stand trial); Orantes-Hernandez v. Smith, 541 F. Supp. 351, 384 (C.D.Cal. 1982) (immigration detainees). The same is true of persons acquitted by reason of insanity but then committed to a mental institution, King v. Atiyeh, 814 F.2d 565, 568 (9th Cir.1987); Ward v. Kort, 762 F.2d 856, 858 (10th Cir.1985); Hatch v. Yamauchi, 809 F. Supp. 59, 61 (E.D.Ark. 1992) (prisoners held in a mental hospital), and for that matter of psychiatric patients in general. Murray v. Didario, 762 F. Supp. 109, 109–10 (E.D.Pa. 1991); Robbins v. Budke, 739 F. Supp. 1479, 1485 (D.N.M.1990).

[402]Bounds v. Smith, 430 U.S. 817, 822, 97 S. Ct. 1491 (1977).

[403]*See* Ch. 9, §§ A, B, concerning the filing fees and "three strikes" provisions of the Prison Litigation Reform Act.

Many state constitutions have "open courts" clauses, which in some states may confer greater rights than the federal law of court access. In Indiana, the Open Courts Clause states: "'All courts shall be open; and every person, for injury done to him in his person, property, or reputation, shall have remedy by due course of law. Justice shall be administered freely, and without purchase; completely, and without denial; speedily, and without delay." The state Supreme Court held that a state "three strikes" provision, which was even more restrictive than the federal statute, violated that Clause. Smith v. Indiana Dep't of Correction, 883 N.E.2d 802 (Ind. 2008); *see* Ch. 9, § B, concerning the federal provision. In *Smith v. Fisher*, 965 So.2d 205 (Fla.App. 2007), *review denied*, 980 So.2d 490 (Fla. 2008), the court held that the state constitution's open courts clause was not violated by a law providing that prisoners declared "vexatious litigants" could be required to post security at the outset of a case unless their lawsuits appeared to have merit; however, the court held that the state must satisfy the very demanding compelling interest/least restrictive alternative test in assessing that kind of statute.

[404]Bounds v. Smith, 430 U.S. at 828.

We will discuss each type of claim separately in the next few sections.

In addition, there are other issues connected with going to court and getting legal information and advice that are probably best presented as claims under other constitutional provisions (the First Amendment right of free speech, the Fourth Amendment protection against unreasonable searches and seizures, etc.), and not as court access claims. We will discuss those issues as well.

The right of court access in civil cases is distinct from the right of indigent persons to have lawyers appointed for their defense under the Sixth Amendment or the Due Process Clause. This constitutional right to appointed counsel is mostly limited to criminal trial and appellate proceedings,[405] and to civil proceedings that may deprive a non-prisoner of liberty or other interests of compelling importance.[406] (State statutes or case law may provide for a broader right to appointed counsel for indigents.[407]) There is no constitutional right to appointed counsel in civil lawsuits brought by prisoners about prison conditions or restrictions.[408] At most, the court may have discretion to request an attorney to represent you in such a case.[409] In some states, statutes provide for the appointment of a trustee or a guardian *ad litem* to defend or prosecute certain civil lawsuits involving prisoners.[410]

Sometimes court access issues arise in connection with the timeliness of federal post-conviction proceedings, which under the Anti-Terrorism and Effective Death Penalty Act (AEDPA) are now governed by a one-year statute of limitations.[411] In some cases, courts have held that the time limit was "equitably tolled" for prisoners who missed the deadline because of interference or inadequate facilities or assistance from prison officials.[412] (The same equitable tolling rules apply to statutes of limitations for ordinary civil rights claims.[413]) However, such claims require a showing of "extraordinary circumstances that are both beyond [the litigant's] control and unavoidable even with diligence."[414]

---

[405] *See* Murray v. Giarratano, 492 U.S. 1, 7, 109 S. Ct. 2765 (1989).

[406] *See* Lassiter v. Dep't of Social Services, 452 U.S. 18, 32–33, 101 S. Ct. 2153 (1981) (holding counsel is not required in all proceedings to terminate parental rights).

[407] *See* Lassiter v. Dep't of Social Services, 452 U.S. at 30 (citing state court decisions requiring appointed counsel for parental rights termination).

[408] Montgomery v. Pinchak, 294 F.3d 492, 498 (3d Cir. 2002); Lewis v. Lynn, 236 F.3d 766, 768 (5th Cir. 2001); Jackson v. County of McLean, 953 F.2d 1070, 1071 (7th Cir. 1992); Glick v. Henderson, 855 F.2d 536, 541 (8th Cir. 1988).

[409] *See* Ch. 10, § C.5 concerning the appointment of counsel.

[410] *See, e.g.,* Garcia v. Wibholm, 461 N.W.2d 166, 169–70 (Iowa 1990) (barring entry of a judgment against a prisoner unless a guardian ad litem is appointed and provides a defense); England v. Laird, 2008 WL 399758, *1–2 (Ky. App., Feb. 15, 2008) (state law requires appointment of guardian ad litem to defend civil action against prisoner unless he waives that appointment) (unpublished); Berdella v. Pender, 821 S.W.2d 846, 850–51 (Mo. 1992) (describing provisions for appointment of a trustee to defend or prosecute civil suits involving a convict's estate; noting purpose to protect creditors, and other "interested persons," from the potential squandering of an inmate's estate while the inmate was incarcerated); Schrader v. Summerville, 763 S.W.2d 717 (Mo.App. 1989) (holding trustee should have been appointed for prisoner sued civilly), *superseded by statute as stated in* Phillips v. Edmundson, 240 S.W.3d 691, 693 (Mo. 2007) (noting current law did not make appointment mandatory); Bulter v. Madison County Jail, 109 S.W.3d 360, 369 (Tenn.Ct.App. 2002) (noting state law requires appointment of guardian for an infant or incompetent person who does not already have a representative).

[411] 28 U.S.C. § 2244(d)(1); 28 U.S.C. § 2255(f).

[412] *See, e.g.,* Ramirez v. Yates, 471 F.3d 993, 998 (9th Cir. 2009) (prisoner's four-month deprivation of his legal file in segregation might warrant equitable tolling if it made filing impossible and he pursued his rights diligently); Roy v. Lampert, 465 F.3d 964, 970–72 (9th Cir. 2006) (absence of AEDPA and Oregon law in library of Arizona prison petitioners were transferred to supported their "extraordinary circumstances" claim), *cert. denied sub nom.* Belleque v. Kephart, 549 U.S. 1317 (2007); Egerton v. Cockrell, 334 F.3d 433, 438 (5th Cir. 2003) (absence of a copy of AEDPA in the prison law library resulted in tolling the time limit); *see* Mendoza v. Carey, 449 F.3d 1065, 1069–71 & n.6 (9th Cir. 2006) (allegation that prisoner was denied access to Spanish-language legal materials or Spanish-speaking persons who could assist him, preventing him from learning about AEDPA's one-year limitations period and thereby preventing his timely filing of a habeas petition, could constitute the extraordinary circumstances required to invoke equitable tolling of that time limit). *But see* Jones v. Hulick, 449 F.3d 784, 789 (7th Cir. 2006) (denying equitable tolling where prisoner alleged he missed the AEDPA deadline because he was placed in segregation for 60 days without access to a law library as a result of a false allegation, Illinois limits law library access for all prisoners anyway, the state interferes with prisoners' mail, and he was defrauded by an organization which promised to file his habeas petition), *cert. denied,* 449 F.3d 784 (2007); Gant v. Goord, 430 F. Supp. 2d 135, 139 (W.D.N.Y. 2006) ("In general, the difficulties attendant on prison life, such as transfers between facilities, solitary confinement, lockdowns, restricted access to the law library, and an inability to secure court documents, do not by themselves qualify as extraordinary circumstances" that would support equitable tolling of the one-year AEDPA limitations period.), *reconsideration denied,* 2007 WL 2712344 (W.D.N.Y., Sept. 13, 2007); Jones v. Gundy, 100 F. Supp. 2d 485, 488–89 (W.D.Mich. 2000) (refusing to toll the time limit for prisoner who had been in segregation with little access to legal materials, and who got out of segregation only to find that the relevant books had been stolen; ignorance of the law does not excuse prompt filing).

[413] Fogle v. Pierson, 435 F.3d 1252, 1258–59 (10th Cir. 2006) (plaintiff's allegation that he was kept in 23-hour lock-in 5 days a week and 24-hour lock-in for the other 2, with no access to law library clerks or prison lawyers, might meet the "extraordinary circumstances" test for equitable tolling of claim based on segregation conditions), *cert. denied,* 549 U.S. 1059 (2007).

[414] Akins v. U.S., 204 F.3d 1086, 1089–90 (11th Cir. 2000) (refusing equitable tolling where the prisoner had had time to get his action filed before he was placed in lockdown with limited law library access).

Courts will rule against prisoners if they cannot show that the interference made it impossible for them to file on time.[415] For example, if the prisoner waited until the last minute, or failed to take all available steps to file a timely petition, the court will probably not find extraordinary circumstances.[416]

Sometimes court rules and procedures restrict access to court. These issues are discussed in other sections of this book.[417]

1. Types of Court Access Claims

a. The Right to Assistance in Bringing Legal Claims The Supreme Court held in *Bounds v. Smith* that prison authorities have an affirmative obligation to "*assist* inmates in the preparation and filing of meaningful legal papers by providing prisoners with adequate law libraries or adequate assistance from persons trained in the law."[418] It has also held that "indigent inmates must be provided at state expense with paper and pen to draft legal documents, with notarial services to authenticate them, and with stamps to mail them."[419]

However, in *Lewis v. Casey*, the Supreme Court imposed several restrictions on prisoners' ability to enforce the *Bounds v. Smith* obligation. *Lewis* held that a prisoner complaining of a *Bounds* violation must show that:

(1) he was, or is, suffering "actual injury" by being "frustrated" or "impeded"[420]

(2) in bringing a non-frivolous claim[421]

(3) about his criminal conviction or sentence or the conditions of his confinement.[422]

We will discuss each of these requirements in turn, as well as other aspects of *Lewis*. We will also discuss, in the later sections, whether these requirements also apply to interference and retaliation cases.

1) The "Actual Injury" Requirement *Lewis v. Casey* says it is not enough for prisoners to show that prison officials do not provide adequate law libraries, legal assistance, or legal supplies, or that they impose unreasonable restrictions on prisoners who try to use them. Prisoners must show that the inadequacies or restrictions caused them "actual injury," *i.e.*, "that a nonfrivolous legal claim had been frustrated or was being impeded."[423] Huge numbers of prisoners' access to court claims are dismissed for failure to meet this requirement.

Exactly what "frustrated or impeded" means is not completely clear. *Lewis* gave two examples:

> [The inmate] might show, for example, that a complaint he prepared was dismissed for failure to satisfy some technical requirement which, because of deficiencies in the prison's legal assistance facilities, he could not have known. Or that he had suffered arguably actionable harm that he wished to bring before the courts, but was so stymied by inadequacies of the law library that he was unable even to file a complaint.[424]

If you experience interference with your efforts to get a post-conviction proceeding filed, a court may simply treat the limitations period as starting to run when an unconstitutional government-created impediment to filing is removed. However, mere inability to get to the law library will not automatically have this result; the prisoner must explain how that inability actually caused harm. *Akins*, 204 F.3d at 1090.

[415]Ramirez v. Yates, 471 F.3d 993, 998 (9th Cir. 2009) (limited access to law library and copy machine in segregation did not justify tolling, since such occurrences were common and did not make filing impossible); U.S. v. Rodriguez, 438 F. Supp. 2d 449, 452–55 (S.D.N.Y. 2006) (intentional confiscation of legal papers could constitute the required "extraordinary circumstances," but this prisoner failed to show that the absence of legal papers prevented filing a timely motion, since his claim of medical incompetence to stand trial would depend on his personal account of his disabilities and medical evidence rather than legal files), *certificate of appealability denied*, 2007 WL 998197 (S.D.N.Y., Apr. 2, 2007); Jones v. Gundy, 100 F. Supp. 2d 485, 488 (W.D.Mich. 2000) (denying relief where plaintiff failed to explain how the lack of particular materials prevented him from going forward).

[416]Mendoza v. Carey, 449 F.3d 1065, 1071 n.6 (9th Cir. 2006) (to qualify for tolling, Spanish-speaking prisoner denied access to Spanish legal materials or Spanish-speaking assistance would have to show that he tried diligently to get a translator); U.S. ex rel. Santiago v. Hinsley, 297 F. Supp. 2d 1065, 1067–68 (N.D.Ill. 2003) (denying relief to prisoner who waited until the last minute to get started); Howze v. Zon, 319 F. Supp. 2d 344, 346–47 (W.D.N.Y. 2004) (equitable tolling requires a showing of extraordinary circumstances and reasonable diligence, and the prisoner did not show the latter, since there were steps he could have taken to get his papers in timely); Jones v. Gundy, 100 F. Supp. 2d 485, 488 (W.D.Mich. 2000) (noting plaintiff had four years before AEDPA to get his case in).

[417]*See* Ch. 10, § Q, concerning court appearances, and Ch. 10, § X, concerning restrictions on *pro se* litigants; *see also* Ch. 9, concerning the various restrictions found in the Prison Litigation Reform Act.

[418]Bounds v. Smith, 430 U.S. 817, 828, 97 U.S. 1491 (1977) (emphasis supplied).

[419]*Bounds*, 430 U.S. at 824–25.

[420]Lewis v. Casey, 518 U.S. 343, 351–53, 116 S. Ct. 2174 (1996).

[421]*Lewis*, 518 U.S. at 353.

[422]*Lewis*, 518 U.S. at 355.

[423]*Lewis*, 518 U.S. at 351–53; *see* Akins v. U.S., 204 F.3d 1086, 1090 (11th Cir. 2000) ("The mere inability of a prisoner to access the law library is not, in itself, an unconstitutional impediment. The inmate must show that this inability caused an actual harm. . . .").

[424]*Lewis*, 518 U.S. at 351; *see* Simkins v. Bruce, 406 F.3d 1239, 1243–44 (10th Cir. 2005) (plaintiff was actually injured where failure to forward his legal mail prevented his receiving notice of a summary judgment motion, resulting in the dismissal of his case and loss of the right to appeal); Lehn v. Holmes, 364 F.3d 862, 870 (7th Cir. 2004) (holding that failure to make out-of-state legal materials available to prisoner, so he could not file a challenge to his indictment in that state, satisfied the actual injury requirement);

Some courts seem to assume that the prisoner's case must be dismissed, or prevented from being filed, in order to be "frustrated or impeded."[425] Others assume that obstacles that impair the ability to present one's case effectively are also actionable.[426] The latter view appears to be the correct one. The Supreme Court said in a later decision that cases that were inadequately tried or settled, or where a particular kind of relief could not be sought, as a result of officials' actions, could support a claim of denial of court access, in addition to those that were dismissed or never filed.[427]

Allegations of actual injury must be specific, explaining how your litigation was harmed, or will be harmed,[428] in order to support a court access claim.[429] Courts have held generally that delay by itself is not sufficient injury to constitute a denial of court access,[430] though we think that holding would be wrong in a case where the delay resulted in a prisoner's spending unnecessary time in prison, in segregated confinement, or in unlawful conditions that timely court access would have remedied.[431]

If your claim is that you were injured because denial of access to courts caused you to be convicted or kept you from getting your conviction or sentence overturned, you cannot attack the conviction or sentence through a § 1983 action. Under the rule of Heck v. Humphrey,[432] you have to exhaust state judicial remedies (or show that those remedies were not available), and if unsuccessful, then proceed via federal habeas corpus to get your conviction or

---

Davis v. Milwaukee County, 225 F. Supp. 2d 967, 976–77 (E.D.Wis. 2002) (holding that a prisoner whose case was dismissed for failure to exhaust administrative remedies was denied access to courts because the jail lacked legal materials from which he could have learned about the exhaustion requirement, or materials about the jail grievance procedure).

[425]See Ingalls v. Florio, 968 F. Supp. 193, 203 (D.N.J. 1997); Smith v. Armstrong, 968 F. Supp. 40, 48–49 (D.Conn. 1996) (holding in class action that individuals who had managed to file complaints despite lack of assistance had not been injured); Stewart v. Sheahan, 1997 WL 392073, *3 (N.D.Ill. 1997) ("If the judge ruled against him because Stewart did not have the resources to disabuse him of his misunderstanding of the law, this is a matter of effective argument, not inability to present a claim at all." The plaintiff alleged that he was denied access to authority that would have demonstrated that a state court had jurisdiction over his claim.)

[426]See Cody v. Weber, 256 F.3d 764, 768 (8th Cir. 2001) (holding the advantage defendants obtained by reading the plaintiff's private legal papers constituted actual injury); Goff v. Nix, 113 F.3d 887, 890–92 (8th Cir. 1997) (holding that inability of co-plaintiffs to coordinate recruitment of witnesses for trial "impeded" a non-frivolous claim, though upholding rule barring their correspondence under the Turner standard; holding that plaintiff who "lost legal papers critical to his post-conviction proceeding" was actually injured); Purkey v. CCA Detention Center, 339 F. Supp. 2d 1145, 1152 (D.Kan. 2004) (holding that defendants' alleged discarding of notes of interrogations essential for the plaintiff's challenge to his conviction sufficiently pled actual injury); King v. Barone, 1997 WL 337032, *4 (E.D.Pa. 1997) (declining to dismiss claim based on confiscation of alleged exculpatory documentation since it is "conceivable" this may have impeded the plaintiff's petition for post-conviction relief).

Other courts have explicitly rejected the notion that inability to present a case well constitutes injury. See Curtis v. Fairman, 1997 WL 159319, *5 (N.D.Ill. 1997) (holding that denial of law library access to respond to a motion to dismiss is not actual injury because case citations and legal arguments are not absolutely necessary at this stage); Kain v. Bradley, 959 F. Supp. 463, 468 (M.D.Tenn. 1997) (holding that plaintiff's inability to discover a legal argument more successful than the one he made was not injury where he was able to submit some response to a motion).

[427]Christopher v. Harbury, 536 U.S. 403, 414, 416 n.13, 122 S. Ct. 2179 (2002). Christopher was not a prison case, and it referred to a case which was "tried to an inadequate result due to missing or fabricated evidence in an official cover-up," rather than dismissed or not filed because of inadequate law library access or other prison shortcomings. But it cites Lewis v. Casey repeatedly, and its holdings would seem to be applicable to prison cases governed by Lewis. See also Marshall v. Knight, 445 F.3d 965, 968–69 (7th Cir. 2006) (holding that "because of my inability to prepare I was

Denied credit Time that I was entitled to" sufficiently pled actual injury).

[428]In theory, there is no reason you should not be able to get an injunction to prevent denial of access in future cases. However, you will need to demonstrate with specificity what case or cases you expect to be bringing, and why the existing facilities will be inadequate for those cases. See Bausch v. Cox, 32 F. Supp. 2d 1057, 1059 (E.D.Wis. 1998) (holding that claim of inadequate law library facilities was too speculative to support relief without a description of claims presently being hindered by them).

[429]Ali v. District of Columbia, 278 F.3d 1, 8 (D.C. Cir. 2002) (holding prisoner's allegation that his litigation was "set back" was insufficient to establish actual injury); Graham v. Perez, 121 F. Supp. 2d 317, 324 (S.D.N.Y. 2000) (holding allegation of restrictions on legal materials should be supported with specific facts supporting the claim, including each of the defendants' actions, the case to which the actions were related, how they affected the case, and the outcome of the case).

[430]Johnson v. Barczak, 338 F.3d 771, 773 (7th Cir. 2003) ("But a delay becomes an injury only if it results in 'actual substantial prejudice to specific litigation.'" (citation omitted)); Lebron v. Armstrong, 289 F. Supp. 2d 56, 61 (D.Conn. 2003); Konigsberg v. LeFevre, 267 F. Supp. 2d 255, 261 (N.D.N.Y. 2003) ("Interferences that merely delay an inmate's ability to work on a pending action or to communicate with the courts [do] not rise to the level of a constitutional violation."); Griffin v. DeTella, 21 F. Supp. 2d 843, 847 (N.D.Ill. 1998) ("Standing alone, delay and inconvenience to not rise to the level of a constitutional deficiency.")

[431]See May v. Sheahan, 226 F.3d 876, 883 (7th Cir. 2000) (holding that a hospitalized pre-trial detainee's allegations that refusal to take him to court would result in delay in disposition resulting in longer incarceration, inability to seek lower bail, delay in other motions, and restricted attorney access met the actual injury requirement); Simpson v. Gallant, 231 F. Supp. 2d 341, 348–49 (D.Me. 2002) (holding that restrictions that prevented plaintiff from making bail and proceeding with a scheduled trial stated a court access claim); Taylor v. Cox, 912 F. Supp. 140, 142, 144 (E.D.Pa. 1995) (holding allegation that seizure of legal materials resulted in an extra month's incarceration stated a court access claim).

[432]512 U.S. 477, 114 S. Ct. 2364 (1994); see Ch. 8, § H.1.a, concerning the Heck rule.

sentence overturned.[433] Until that time, you cannot bring a § 1983 suit about the conviction or sentence. However, if you were being prevented in some way from getting into state court or filing a habeas petition, you would be able to seek an injunction under § 1983 to remove the obstacle.[434]

2) The Non-Frivolous Claim Requirement

To violate the right of court access, deficiencies in prison facilities or services must "frustrate or impede" a claim that is not frivolous.[435] That merely means your claim must be "arguable."[436] You do not have to prove that you would have won the case[437]—though you may have to prove that to obtain compensatory damages.[438] You do have to be very specific about what your claim was so the court can tell if the claim is frivolous or not[439]—in fact, you have to plead

that claim, as well as the court access claim, in your complaint.[440]

3) The Criminal Sentence/Conditions of Confinement Requirement

Lewis v. Casey says that the affirmative obligation to help prisoners bring lawsuits extends only to what prisoners need "in order to attack their sentences, directly or collaterally, and in order to challenge the conditions of their confinement. Impairment of any *other* litigating capacity is simply one of the incidental (and perfectly constitutional) consequences of conviction and incarceration."[441] Thus, prison officials need not provide assistance to prisoners with respect to child custody, divorce, suits against them by crime victims, civil suits for false arrest, or other police misconduct, etc.[442] —though that does not mean prison officials can obstruct such claims or retaliate against prisoners who file them.[443] One court has said that prisoners have no right to law libraries or other assistance to pursue anything other than "direct appeal, collateral attack, and § 1983 civil rights actions."[444] We think that holding is too narrow. For example, conditions of confinement cases may be based on state law[445] or on statutory rights enforced in other ways than §1983 actions.[446]

---

[433]Hoard v. Reddy, 175 F.3d 531, 533 (7th Cir. 1999) (denying injunction to make state court reopen a post-conviction proceeding).

[434]Hoard v. Reddy, 175 F.3d at 133.

[435]Lewis v. Casey, 518 U.S. 343, 353, 116 S. Ct. 2174 (1996). The *Bounds* right to assistance does not extend to frivolous cases. *Id.* at n.3. Courts have upheld statutes in some jurisdictions that deprive prisoners of good time when courts find their cases frivolous. *See* People v. Shaw, 386 Ill.App.3d 704, 714–20, 898 N.E.2d 755 (2008) (rejecting constitutional challenge), *appeal denied*, 232 Ill.2d 593, 910 N.E.2d 1131 (2009); Holt v. State, 757 So.2d 1088, 1090 (Miss.App. 2000) (upholding application of statute). There is a similar provision for federal prisoners in the Prison Litigation Reform Act; to our knowledge its constitutionality has not been tested. *See* Ch. 9, § I.

[436]Lewis v. Casey, 518 U.S. at 353 n.3. A frivolous claim is defined as one that "lacks an arguable basis either in law or fact." Neitzke v. Williams, 490 U.S. 319, 325, 109 S. Ct. 1827 (1989).

[437]Simkins v. Bruce, 406 F.3d 1239, 1244 (10th Cir. 2005) ("*Lewis* does not suggest that the plaintiff must prove a case within a case to show that the claim hindered or impeded by the defendant necessarily would have prevailed."); Gomez v. Vernon, 962 F. Supp. 1296, 1302 (D.Idaho 1997); *see* Bell v. Johnson, 308 F.3d 594, 607 (6th Cir. 2002) (holding that losing a case on summary judgment does not make it frivolous, and that it could be the basis of a court access claim).

[438]*See* Simkins v. Bruce, 406 F.3d at 1244 n.5; Davis v. Milwaukee County, 225 F. Supp. 2d 967, 980–81 (E.D.Wis. 2002). If your case would have come out the same way even without the denial of access to court, you haven't really lost anything, so there is nothing to award compensatory damages about, though you might have an argument for punitive damages. In order to win compensatory damages for the denial of court access, you will have to show that it made a difference to the outcome. A similar issue is presented in disciplinary due process cases, where you can't get compensatory damages if your disciplinary hearing would have come out the same way if due process had been observed. *See* Ch. 4, § H.1.r.4 for a discussion of this point.

[439]Tarpley v. Allen County, Ind., 312 F.3d 895, 899 (7th Cir. 2002) (holding a prisoner who provided no detail about the cases he was unable to bring did not state a court access claim); Moore v. Plaster, 266 F.3d 928, 933 (8th Cir. 2001) (rejecting court access claim because the plaintiff did not show his case was not frivolous).

[440]*See* § C.1.a(4) of this chapter.

[441]Lewis v. Casey, 518 U.S. 343, 355, 116 S. Ct. 2174 (1996). One court has held that the right to assistance extends to challenging a pending indictment that may lead to a sentence, as well as to the current sentence. Lehn v. Holmes, 364 F.3d 862, 868–69 (7th Cir. 2004).

[442]*See* Wilson v. Blankenship, 163 F.3d 1284, 1291 (11th Cir. 1998) (holding that there is no right to law library access for a civil forfeiture proceeding); Canell v. Multnomah County, 141 F. Supp. 2d 1046, 1056 (D.Or. 2001) (finding no right to assistance for civil cases not involving conditions of confinement).

There are other laws besides the *Bounds v. Smith* right to legal assistance that provide a right to some legal assistance in certain proceedings. For example, if you are charged with a new criminal offense while in prison, you will have a right to counsel for your defense under the Sixth Amendment. *See* § C.1.a(7) of this chapter. There is a constitutional right to counsel in many probation and parole revocation proceedings. Gagnon v. Scarpelli, 411 U.S. 778, 92 S. Ct. 1756 (1973). You may also have the right to counsel under state law in a proceeding to terminate your parental rights, *see* Lassiter v. Dep't of Social Services, 452 U.S. 18, 30, 101 S. Ct. 2153 (1981) (citing state decisions), or other proceedings.

[443]*See* §§ C.1.b, C.1.c of this chapter.

[444]*See* Thaddeus-X v. Blatter, 175 F.3d 378, 392 (6th Cir. 1999) (en banc) (stating the right is so limited).

[445]*See* Arce v. Walker, 58 F. Supp. 2d 39, 44 (W.D.N.Y. 1999) (noting open question whether the *Bounds* right to assistance applies to claims based on state law).

[446]*See* Friedl v. City of New York, 210 F.3d 79, 86 (2d Cir. 2000) (noting that "not every 'challenge to the conditions of confinement' takes the form of a civil rights action"; holding a work release prisoner's administrative application for public assistance, which is provided for by federal statute, was constitutionally protected). Similarly, suits under the federal disability statutes, the Religious Freedom Restoration Act, and the Religious Land Use and

4) The Requirement to Plead the "Frustrated or Impeded" Claim In *Christopher v. Harbury*, the Supreme Court added another requirement: you must *plead* the claim that you say was "frustrated or impeded," *i.e.*, your complaint about denial of court access must also set out the claim that you say was "frustrated or impeded."[447] For example, if you were beaten by staff members and then were kept away from all legal facilities and materials until the statute of limitations had run on your claim about the assault, your complaint would have to describe the beating and say who did it, just as you would have done in a complaint about the beating itself, in addition to describing the interference with your legal work.[448] You must also describe any remedy that you were prevented from getting, and that you can only get now as part of your court access claim.[449] (In the beating example, you would say that in your court access suit you are seeking the damages that you would have sought in the assault suit, which you can't get now because the statute of limitations has run on the assault claim.)

5) Does the Right to Court Access Stop When You File a Complaint? *Lewis* also contains statements that, some courts say, limit the requirement of law libraries or legal assistance to the initial preparation of complaints and petitions. What *Lewis* actually says is that the right of court access is the right to "bring to court a grievance that the inmate wishe[s] to present"; the government need not "enable the prisoner to *discover* grievances" or "to *litigate effectively* once in court."[450] Some courts have held that this means the right of court access is only a "right of initial access to commence

a lawsuit."[451] That would mean that once you get the complaint filed, you're on your own and have no further right to a law library or legal assistance.

We don't think *Lewis v. Casey* really means that. We think it means that the government is not obligated to make prisoners, many of whom are poorly educated and legally unsophisticated, into "effective[]" litigators.[452] The notion that the obligation to assist prisoners extends beyond the filing of the complaint is supported by *Lewis*'s statement that: "It is the role of courts to *provide relief* to claimants, in individual or class actions, who have suffered, or will imminently suffer, actual harm. . . ."[453] A court does not "provide relief" based only on a complaint; obtaining relief from a court requires both defending the claim (*e.g.*, by responding to motions to dismiss and for summary judgment) and moving it toward judgment (*e.g.*, by discovery, motion practice, and ultimately trial).[454] We think the correct rule was stated in a recent appellate decision interpreting *Lewis*: "A prisoner states an access-to-courts claim when he alleges that even though he successfully got into court by filing a complaint or petition challenging his conviction, sentence,

Institutionalized Persons Act may address prison conditions even though they are not brought under § 1983. *See* Ch. 2, § 4.h.2 concerning the disability statutes, and § D.1.b of this chapter concerning the religion statutes.

[447]Christopher v. Harbury, 536 U.S. 403, 415–16, 122 S. Ct. 2179 (2002). The claim must "be described well enough to apply the 'nonfrivolous' test and to show that the 'arguable' nature of the underlying claim is more than hope." 536 U.S. at 416.

Some courts seem not to have noticed the *Christopher* pleading requirement. In *Thomson v. Washington*, 362 F.3d 969, 970–71 (7th Cir. 2004), the court held that failure to identify the allegedly thwarted lawsuits did not support dismissal, since "[f]ederal judges are forbidden to supplement the federal rules for requiring 'heightened' pleading of claims not listed in Rule 9." Since the *Christopher* pleading rule was announced by the Supreme Court, it is the law and you should follow it.

[448]The claim on which you were denied access to court must "be described well enough to apply the 'nonfrivolous' test and to show that the 'arguable' nature of the underlying claim is more than hope." Christopher v. Harbury, 536 U.S. at 416.

[449]Christopher v. Harbury, 536 U.S. at 415; *see* Small v. City of New York, 274 F. Supp. 2d 271, 278–79 (E.D.N.Y. 2003) (plaintiffs argued that intimidating witnesses and destroying evidence would impair their ability to recover damages for conscious pain and suffering and punitive damages), *clarified, reconsideration denied*, 304 F. Supp. 2d 401 (E.D.N.Y. 2004).

[450]Lewis v. Casey, 518 U.S. 343, 354, 116 S. Ct. 2174 (1996).

[451]Benjamin v. Jacobson, 935 F. Supp. 332, 352 (S.D.N.Y. 1996), *aff'd in part, rev'd in part and remanded on other grounds*, 172 F.3d 144 (2d Cir. 1999) (en banc); *accord*, Zigmund v. Foster, 106 F. Supp. 2d 352, 359 (D.Conn. 2000); Stewart v. Sheahan, 1997 WL 392073, *3–4 (N.D.Ill. 1997) (" . . . Stewart did succeed in putting his petition before the court. If the judge ruled against him because Stewart did not have the resources to disabuse him of his misunderstanding of the law, this is a matter of effective argument. . . . Institutions are not required to provide inmates with the ability to argue the legal basis of their claims in court."). Some courts had reached this conclusion or something similar before *Lewis v. Casey*. *See* Knop v. Johnson, 977 F.2d 996, 1000, 1007 (6th Cir. 1992) (holding the right limited to the "pleading stage," which apparently includes "not only the drafting of complaints and petitions for relief but also the drafting of responses to motions to dismiss and the drafting of objections to magistrates' reports and recommendations"); Cornett v. Donovan, 51 F.3d 894, 899 (9th Cir. 1995) (holding the right limited to "pleading stage" including reply to a counterclaim or answer to a cross-claim if one is asserted); Nordgren v. Milliken, 762 F.2d 851, 855 (10th Cir. 1985) (right limited to filing of complaint or petition).

[452]What *Lewis* says is: "To demand the conferral of such sophisticated legal capabilities upon a mostly uneducated and indeed largely illiterate prison population is effectively to demand permanent provision of counsel, which we do not believe the Constitution requires." Lewis v. Casey, 518 U.S. at 354.

[453]*Lewis*, 518 U.S. at 349 (emphasis supplied).

[454]*See* Bonner v. City of Pritchard, Ala., 661 F.2d 1206, 1212–13 (11th Cir. 1981) (en banc) (holding that the right of court access was not satisfied by permitting prisoner to file a complaint and then dismissing his case until the end of his 10-year sentence); NAACP v. Meese, 615 F. Supp. 200, 206 n.18 (D.D.C. 1985) (holding the right of court access extends past pleading stage); Gilmore v. Lynch, 319 F. Supp. 105, 111 (N.D.Cal. 1970) holding the (right entails "all the means a defendant or petitioner might require to get a fair hearing from the judiciary"), *aff'd sub nom.* Younger v. Gilmore, 404 U.S. 15, 92 S.Ct. 250 (1971) (per curiam).

or conditions of confinement, his denial of access to legal materials caused a potentially meritorious claim to fail."[455] *Bounds v. Smith* itself supports this view,[456] and so does the more recent decision in *Christopher v. Harbury.* [457]

6) *The Reasonable Relationship Standard* The operation of prison law library or legal assistance programs is governed by the "reasonable relationship" standard, which lets prison officials adopt whatever practices or restrictions they choose as long as they are reasonably related to legitimate penological interests.[458] That means that even if restrictions do cause actual harm to prisoners' litigation, they do not violate the right of court access if they are reasonably related to legitimate ends.[459] As a practical matter, that means you should never wait until the last minute to prepare and file legal papers; if prison officials do something that causes you to miss the deadline, and they can defend their actions, you may be left with no remedy at all.[460]

7) *Prisoners with Pending Criminal Cases* Some courts have held that a prisoner who is represented by criminal defense counsel has no right to a law library or any other means of court access.[461] We think that conclusion is wrong, because an attorney handling a criminal case is not always prepared to deal with all of the client's other legal problems and proceedings.[462] Of course having a criminal defense lawyer does satisfy the right of court access for purposes of the criminal case itself.[463] (There is a difference between the Sixth Amendment right to counsel, which requires appointment of counsel for indigents and requires the *effective* assistance of counsel; the right of court access does not include either requirement.[464])

The right to court access with respect to the criminal case is satisfied when a criminal defendant is offered appointed counsel, whether he takes it or not.[465] However, there is also a separate Sixth Amendment right to defend

---

[455]Marshall v. Knight, 445 F.3d 965, 969 (7th Cir. 2006). In *Marshall*, the plaintiff alleged that his law library time was so restricted that he was unable to research and prepare for a court hearing, causing him to lose time credits that would have shortened his incarceration. If the right to assistance through law libraries only applied to filing complaints, the court would presumably have dismissed his case.

[456]*Bounds* said: "Moreover, if the State files a response to a *pro se* pleading, it will undoubtedly contain seemingly authoritative citations. Without a library, an inmate will be unable to rebut the State's argument." Bounds v. Smith, 430 U.S. 817, 825–26, 97 S. Ct. 1491 (1977). If the right of court access ended with the filing of a complaint, rebutting the State's response would not be part of the right. As one court pointed out: "The inmates' ability to file is not dispositive of the access question, because the Court in *Bounds* explained that for access to be meaningful, post-filing needs, such as the research tools necessary to effectively rebut authorities cited by an adversary in responsive pleadings, should be met." Morrow v. Harwell, 768 F.2d 619, 623 (5th Cir. 1985); *see* Michael B. Mushlin, 2 *Rights of Prisoners* at § 11:4 (Thomson West, 3d ed. 2002).

[457]536 U.S. 403, 414, 416 n.13, 122 S. Ct. 2179 (2002). *Christopher* referred to cases which "ended poorly, or could not have commenced, or could have produced a remedy subsequently unobtainable," 536 U.S. at 414, or were "tried to an inadequate result due to missing or fabricated evidence in an official cover-up," 536 U.S. at 416 n.13, as examples of potentially meritorious denial of court access claims. That is inconsistent with the view that the right of court access only protects the right to file a complaint. *Christopher* was not a prison case, but it cites *Lewis v. Casey* repeatedly, and its principles would seem to be applicable to prison cases governed by *Lewis*.

[458]*Lewis*, 518 U.S. at 361–62 (citing Turner v. Safley, 482 U.S. 78, 107 S. Ct. 2254 (1987)); *see* § A of this chapter.

[459]*Lewis, id.*; *see, e.g.*, Goff v. Nix, 113 F.3d 887, 890–92 (8th Cir. 1997) (upholding policy prohibiting legal correspondence between prisoners at different facilities); Green v. Johnson, 977 F.2d 1383, 1390 (10th Cir. 1992) (upholding rule limiting possession of legal materials in cells to two cubic feet).

[460]Akins v. U.S., 204 F.3d 1086, 1090 (11th Cir. 2000) (holding that a prisoner who missed a deadline because a long lockdown kept him from getting to the law library could not establish a court

access violation without showing that the lockdown itself was unreasonable).

[461]Johnson by Johnson v. Brelje, 701 F.2d 1201, 1208 (7th Cir. 1983); Jones v. Lexington County Detention Center, 586 F. Supp. 2d 444, 452 (D.S.C. 2008); Canell v. Multnomah County, 141 F. Supp. 2d 1046, 1056 (D.Or. 2001); Maillett v. Phinney, 755 F. Supp. 463, 465–66 (D.Me. 1991); Bell v. Hopper, 511 F. Supp. 452, 453 (S.D.Ga. 1981).

[462]Ortiz v. Downey, 561 F.3d 664, 671 (7th Cir. 2009) ("the assistance of counsel in [a] criminal case did not diminish [plaintiff's] right to adequate legal resources for the purpose of pursuing his civil suit"); Peterkin v. Jeffes, 855 F.2d 1021, 1042–47 (3d Cir. 1988) (noting that availability of counsel to death row inmates did not necessarily extend to federal habeas or civil rights matters); Green v. Ferrell, 801 F.2d 765, 772 (5th Cir. 1986) (noting that availability of defense trial counsel was irrelevant to need for court access for post-conviction relief); Mann v. Smith, 796 F.2d 79, 83–84 (5th Cir.1986) (holding that access to a court-appointed defense lawyer who refused to pursue a civil rights claim did not satisfy the court access requirement); Gilland v. Owens, 718 F. Supp. 665, 688–89 (W.D.Tenn. 1989) (holding that availability of criminal defense lawyers did not address the right of access with respect to non-criminal matters). *Cf.* Martucci v. Johnson, 944 F.2d 291, 295 (6th Cir. 1991) (holding that availability of appointed counsel plus provision of legal materials "on request" satisfied court access requirement in the absence of evidence that the plaintiff was barred from discussing his other problems with the criminal attorney).

[463]Bourdon v. Loughren, 386 F.3d 88, 96, 99 (2d Cir. 2004); Perez v. Metropolitan Correctional Center Warden, 5 F. Supp. 2d 208, 211–12 (S.D.N.Y. 1998), aff'd, 181 F.3d 83 (2d Cir. 1999) (unpublished); Ingalls v. Florio, 968 F. Supp. 193, 203 (D.N.J. 1997) (holding that denial of law library access does not establish actual injury in the form of inability to assist one's criminal defense lawyer, since defendants assist their attorneys with factual issues and not legal issues).

[464]Bourdon v. Loughren, 386 F.3d at 98. The *Bourdon* decision discusses the difference between the two rights in detail.

[465]U.S. v. Wilson, 690 F.2d 1267, 1271–72 (9th Cir. 1982); *see also* Sahagian v. Dickey, 827 F.2d 90, 90–98 (7th Cir. 1987) (prison officials had no obligation to provide law library or legal materials for discretionary direct review of a criminal conviction, since the

oneself *pro se*.[466] One federal appeals court has stated: "An incarcerated criminal defendant who chooses to represent himself has a constitutional right to access to 'law books . . . or other tools' to assist him in preparing a defense."[467] Most other circuits have held to the contrary.[468] Before you decide to represent yourself in a criminal prosecution, it is wise to know what access to law libraries you will have at the jail where you will be held, since most likely that's what you will be stuck with because the court may not direct anything different for you. Also, if the court offers to appoint standby counsel to assist you in defending yourself, you should carefully consider that offer, since you may discover that you need information or assistance that are not realistically available to you otherwise.[469]

b. The Right to Be Free from Interference with Court Access Government is prohibited from interfering with people's (including prisoners') efforts to use the courts.[470]

As with other constitutional violations, such interference must be intentional to violate the Constitution.[471]

Sometimes such interference results from prison policy. The Supreme Court has said: "Regulations and practices that unjustifiably obstruct the availability of professional representation or other aspects of the right of access to the courts are invalid."[472] Thus, the Supreme Court has struck down a prison rule that allowed prisoners to file only those legal papers that prison and parole officials determined were "properly drawn,"[473] and another rule forbidding prisoners to obtain help from other prisoners if there is no other way of getting legal assistance.[474] However, restrictions will be upheld if they satisfy the *Turner v. Safley* standard of a "reasonable relationship" to legitimate penological goals.[475] Courts have upheld a variety of rules and actions that make litigation more difficult for prisoners,[476] including limits on the amount of legal materials a prisoner may possess.[477]

---

prisoner already had the benefit of a transcript, initial appellate brief, and appellate opinion).

[466]Bribiesca v. Galaza, 215 F.3d 1015, 1020 (9th Cir. 2000) (dictum); *accord*, Taylor v. List, 880 F.2d 1040, 1047 (9th Cir. 1989) ("An incarcerated defendant may not meaningfully exercise his right to represent himself without access to law books, witnesses, or other tools to prepare a defense."); Milton v. Morris, 767 F.2d 1443, 1447 (9th Cir. 1985)) (holding that the right to a *pro se* criminal defense requires officials to provide "some access to materials and witnesses"); Kaiser v. City of Sacramento, 780 F. Supp. 1309, 1314–15 (E.D.Cal. 1992) (provision of information packets plus cell delivery systems satisfied the Sixth Amendment).

[467]Bribiesca v. Galaza, 215 F.3d 1015, 1020 (9th Cir. 2000) (dictum); *accord*, Taylor v. List, 880 F.2d 1040, 1047 (9th Cir. 1989) ("An incarcerated defendant may not meaningfully exercise his right to represent himself without access to law books, witnesses, or other tools to prepare a defense") (citing Milton v. Morris, 767 F.2d 1443, 1447 (9th Cir. 1985)) (holding that the right to a *pro se* criminal defense requires officials to provide "some access to materials and witnesses"); Kaiser v. City of Sacramento, 780 F. Supp. 1309, 1314–15 (E.D.Cal. 1992) (provision of information packets plus cell delivery systems satisfied the Sixth Amendment).

[468]*See* U.S. v. Cooper, 375 F.3d 1041, 1052 (10th Cir. 2004) ("When a prisoner voluntarily, knowingly and intelligently waives his right to counsel in a criminal proceeding, he is not entitled to access to a law library or other legal materials.") (citing U.S. v. Taylor, 183 F.3d 1199, 1205 (10th Cir. 1999) (citing cases)); Degrate v. Godwin, 84 F.3d 768, 768–69 (5th Cir. 1996) (per curiam) (citing cases); Davis v. Milwaukee County, 225 F. Supp. 2d 967, 973 (E.D.Wis. 2002) (holding that exercising the right to a *pro se* defense does not give rise to alternative rights such as access to a law library).

[469]U.S. v. Cooper, 375 F.3d at 1052 (noting that standby counsel provided the assistance the criminal defendant sought from a law library).

[470]As one court put it:

> First, . . . in order to assure that incarcerated persons have meaningful access to courts, states are required to provide affirmative assistance in the preparation of legal papers in cases involving constitutional rights and other civil rights actions related to their incarceration. . . .

> Second, in all other types of civil actions, states may not erect barriers that impede the right of access of incarcerated persons.

John L. v. Adams, 969 F.2d 228, 235 (6th Cir. 1992).

[471]Simkins v. Bruce, 406 F.3d 1239, 1242–43 (10th Cir. 2005) (mail room supervisor's statement that she acted consistently with her training showed intentional action; negligence would not be sufficient, and malice is not required).

[472]Procunier v. Martinez, 416 U.S. 396, 419, 94 S. Ct.1800 (1974) (striking down a rule barring attorneys from using students and paraprofessionals to conduct prisoner interviews); *see* U.S. v. Mikhel, 552 F.3d 961, 963–64 (9th Cir. 2009) (striking down "Special Administrative Measures" barring use of translator at interviews and barring public defender's investigator from meeting with criminal defendant without an attorney or paralegal present).

[473]*Ex parte* Hull, 312 U.S. 546, 549, 61 S. Ct. 640 (1941) (striking down regulation permitting officials to screen prisoners' submissions to court).

[474]Johnson v. Avery, 393 U.S. 483, 490, 89 S. Ct. 747 (1969); *see* § C.2.c of this chapter.

[475]Lewis v. Casey, 518 U.S. 343, 361–62, 116 S. Ct. 2174 (1996) (citing Turner v. Safley, 482 U.S. 87, 107 S. Ct. 2254 (1987)) (upholding restrictions on "lockdown" prisoners' access to legal materials and assistance); *see* § A of this chapter concerning the *Turner* standard).

[476]*See, e.g.*, Smith v. Erickson, 961 F.2d 1387, 1388 (8th Cir. 1992) (holding refusal to send plaintiff's legal mail was justified by his failure to comply with valid correspondence rules); *see also* Prison Legal News v. Lehman, 397 F.3d 692, 703 (9th Cir. 2005) (holding constitutional under the First Amendment a "third party legal material" policy that prohibited delivery of mail, including judicial decisions and litigation documents, which could create a risk of violence or harm, but holding that its discriminatory application to suppress materials that would embarrass prison officials or educate prisoners about their rights would violate the First Amendment); *see also* § C.1.a. of this chapter.

[477]Green v. Johnson, 977 F.2d 1383, 1390 (10th Cir. 1992) (upholding rule limiting possession of legal materials in cells to two cubic feet); Howard v. Snyder, 389 F. Supp. 589, 593–94 (D.Del. 2005) (upholding rule limiting legal papers to two boxes except with permission for a third); Hewes v. Magnusson, 350 F.

Individual acts of interference that do not represent regulations or practices can also violate the right of court access. For example, the confiscation or destruction of prisoners' legal papers and books, not pursuant to a valid rule, may violate the right.[478] So may the destruction or fabrication

of evidence or cover-ups of misconduct that deprive its victims of the means to challenge unlawful conduct in court.[479]

The *Lewis v. Casey* rule that plaintiffs must show "actual injury," *i.e.*, that they were "frustrated . . . or impeded" in pursuing a non-frivolous claim,[480] applies to interference cases.[481]

Supp. 2d 222, 237–38 (D.Me. 2004) (holding confiscation of legal papers was not unlawful where plaintiff admitted he had had more than the two accordion folders of papers permitted); Savko v. Rollins, 749 F. Supp. 1403, 1407–09 (D.Md. 1990) (regulation limiting possession of written material, including legal papers, to 1.5 cubic feet upheld), *aff'd sub nom.* Simmons v. Rollins, 924 F.2d 1053 (4th Cir. 1991); Murphy v. Dowd, 757 F. Supp. 1019, 1021–22 (E.D.Mo. 1990) (similar to *Savko*); McClaflin v. Pearce, 739 F. Supp. 537, 539–40 (D.Or.1990) (similar rule applied in segregation unit); Hadix v. Johnson, 712 F. Supp. 550, 552 (E.D.Mich. 1989) (upholding restriction of legal papers to one footlocker holding over 100 pounds of paper); Cooper v. Corderman, 809 S.W.2d 11, 13–14 (Mo.App. 1990) (upholding restriction to two "legal boxes").

We regard these restrictions (except for those in *Hadix*) as being excessive and unrealistic for a prisoner who is engaged in any substantial litigation project, or in several cases. If you litigate about such a rule, be sure to explain to the court what the consequences of the rule are—i.e., what materials you need and do not have access to. If prison officials claim that they will store your materials and make them available when you need them, you should try it and see if it works before going to court. *See* Sowell v. Vose, 941 F.2d 32, 35 (1st Cir. 1991) (prisoner's complaint about limited access to legal papers dismissed because he did not show how he was injured by it).

[478]Thomson v. Washington, 362 F.3d 969, 970 (7th Cir. 2004); Brownlee v. Conine, 957 F.2d 353, 354 (7th Cir. 1992); Roman v. Jeffes, 904 F.2d 192, 198 (3d Cir. 1990); Morello v. James, 810 F.2d 344, 347 (2d Cir. 1987); Simmons v. Dickhaut, 804 F.2d 182, 183–85 (1st Cir. 1986); Wright v. Newsome, 795 F.2d 964, 968 (11th Cir. 1986); Carter v. Hutto, 781 F.2d 1028, 1032 (4th Cir. 1986); Patterson v. Mintzes, 717 F.2d 284, 288 (6th Cir. 1983); Tyler v. Woodson, 597 F.2d 643, 644 (8th Cir. 1979); Purkey v. CCA Detention Center, 339 F. Supp. 2d 1145, 1151–52 (D.Kan. 2004); Williams v. ICC Committee, 812 F. Supp. 1029, 1032–33 (N.D.Cal. 1992); Gallipeau v. Berard, 734 F. Supp. 48, 53 (D.R.I. 1990); Balabin v. Scully, 606 F. Supp. 176, 183–84 (S.D.N.Y. 1985); Stringer v. Thompson, 537 F. Supp. 133, 137 (N.D.Ill. 1982); Slie v. Bordenkircher, 526 F. Supp. 1264, 1265 (N.D.W.Va. 1981). *But see* Chavers v. Abrahamson, 803 F. Supp. 1512, 1514 (E.D.Wis. 1992) (deprivation of legal materials denies court access only if they are "crucial or essential to a pending or contemplated appeal"); Weaver v. Toombs, 756 F. Supp. 335, 340 (W.D.Mich. 1989) (legal papers sent between inmates could be confiscated because the inmates had not followed the rules for inmate–inmate legal assistance), *aff'd,* 915 F.2d 1574 (6th Cir. 1990).

Generally, prisoners complaining that property has been seized must pursue their claims in state court (*see* Ch. 4, § H.8, concerning property deprivations), but materials essential to court access are not just property; their intentional confiscation states a federal law claim that may be litigated in federal court. Zilich v. Lucht, 981 F.2d 694, 696 (3d Cir. 1992); Morello v. James, 810 F.2d 344, 347–48 (2d Cir. 1987). However, merely negligent deprivations of legal papers do not deny access to courts. Crawford-El v. Britton, 951 F.2d 1314, 1318–19 (D.C. Cir. 1991); Morello v. James, 797 F. Supp. 223, 227 (W.D.N.Y. 1992); Duff v. Coughlin, 794 F. Supp. 521, 524 (S.D.N.Y. 1992). Negligence cases must be brought in state court.

[479]Christopher v. Harbury, 536 U.S. 403, 414, 416 n.13, 122 S. Ct. 2179 (2002); Chappell v. Rich, 340 F.3d 1279, 1283 (11th Cir. 2003) (per curiam) (" . . . [I]nterference with the right of court access by state agents who intentionally conceal the true facts about a crime may be actionable as a deprivation of constitutional rights."); Swekel v. City of River Rouge, 119 F.3d 1259, 1261–64 (6th Cir. 1997); Small v. City of New York, 274 F. Supp. 2d 271, 278–79 (E.D.N.Y. 2003) (allegations that after a drunken police officer ran over the decedent, other police officers conspired to select a sobriety test the officer might beat, delayed administration of the test, intimidated witnesses, and destroyed material evidence at the crime scene, stated a claim for denial of access to courts), *clarified, reconsideration denied,* 304 F. Supp. 2d 401 (E.D.N.Y. 2004); Heinrich ex rel. Heinrich v. Sweet, 62 F. Supp. 2d 282, 315 (D.Mass. 1999) and cases cited (stating that the right of court access is violated when government officials wrongfully and intentionally conceal information crucial to judicial redress, do so in order to frustrate the right, and substantially reduce the likelihood of obtaining redress).

Cover-up attempts that do not succeed do not deny court access. Orwat v. Maloney, 360 F. Supp. 2d 146, 159–60 (D.Mass. 2005); Pizzuto v. County of Nassau, 240 F. Supp. 2d 203, 213 (E.D.N.Y. 2002).

In some states, prisoners may have a claim for spoliation of evidence if officials intentionally or negligently destroy evidence that might have permitted the successful litigation of an otherwise valid legal claim. *See* Perez-Garcia v. Village of Mundelein, 396 F. Supp. 2d 907, 912–13 (N.D.Ill. 2005). Under federal law applicable in federal court, spoliation of evidence may result in sanctions. *See* Adkins v. Wolever, 554 F.3d 650 (6th Cir. 2009) (en banc); *see also* Ch. 10, § S.1.c, n.910.

[480]*See* Lewis v. Casey, 518 U.S. at 351–53; *see also* § C.1.a(1) of this chapter.

[481]Christopher v. Harbury, 536 U.S. 403, 415, 122 S. Ct. 2179 (2002); *see* Johnson v. Hamilton, 452 F.3d 967, 973–74 (8th Cir. 2006) (claim of denial of access to legal papers fails absent evidence of injury or prejudice); Ortloff v. U.S., 335 F.3d 652, 656 (7th Cir. 2003) (affirming dismissal of claim that prison officials destroyed materials related to pending lawsuits; a plaintiff "must usually plead specific prejudice to state a claim, such as by alleging that he missed court deadlines, failed to make timely filings, or that legitimate claims were dismissed because of the denial of reasonable access to legal resources."); Ali v. District of Columbia, 278 F.3d 1, 8 (D.C. Cir. 2003) (applying actual injury rule to a claim that plaintiff had to send legal documents out of the prison); Cody v. Weber, 256 F.3d 764, 769–70 (8th Cir. 2001) (holding deprivation of access to legal documents did not meet the actual injury standard without explanation of what the documents were and how they affected litigation); McBride v. Deer, 240 F.3d 1287, 1290 (10th Cir. 2001) (holding allegation that prison official's refusal to disburse a prisoner's money so he could buy legal materials did not state a court access claim without an explanation of what materials he needed, how the prison law library failed to provide what he needed, or how his legal claim was non-frivolous); Chriceol v. Phillips, 169

Lewis v. Casey also said that the *Bounds* right to law libraries or legal assistance is limited to cases about your criminal conviction and sentence and about convictions of confinement. In our view, that rule should not apply to interference cases. *Lewis's* discussion of that restriction focused on the *Bounds v. Smith* assistance requirement and not the rule against interference with court access.[482] It was not intended to allow officials to interfere with other kinds of cases besides criminal and prison conditions matters.[483] Some courts have said that the *Bounds* right to law libraries or legal assistance stops when you get your complaint filed. As explained above,[484] we think that is wrong. But even if it is right, we do not think it applies to interference cases, and at least one court has agreed. It held that even if *Lewis* does limit the state's *Bounds* obligation to assisting with the filing of complaints, it "cannot, however, be read to give officials license to thwart that litigation once it is filed."[485]

F.3d 313, 314, 317 (5th Cir. 1999) (refusing to disburse court fees from prisoner's account could deny court access, but where the plaintiff's parents paid his fees and his suit was filed, there was no actual injury); Livingston v. Goord, 225 F. Supp. 2d 321, 331 (W.D.N.Y. 2003) (dismissing claim of deprivation of legal papers in the absence of any showing of harm; the plaintiff won the relevant case), *aff'd*, 153 Fed.Appx. 769 (2d Cir. 2005) (unpublished); Leach v. Dufrain, 103 F. Supp. 2d 542, 548 (N.D.N.Y. 2000) (holding confiscation of legal papers does not state a court access claim without sufficient information about the quantity and contents of the papers to determine whether the confiscation "impermissibly compromised" a legal action). *Compare* Lueck v. Wathen, 262 F. Supp. 2d 690, 695 (N.D.Tex. 2003) (holding that confiscation of the affidavit of a key witness that plaintiff's defense lawyer never interviewed, which was necessary in his post-conviction proceeding to show that the witness had evidence material to his claim of ineffectiveness of counsel, constituted actual injury).

[482]*Lewis* said: "The tools [*Bounds v. Smith*] requires to be provided are those that inmates need in order to attack their sentences, directly or collaterally, and in order to challenge the conditions of their confinement." 518 U.S. at 355.

[483]In *Snyder v. Nolen*, 380 F.3d 279 (7th Cir. 2004) (per curiam), the court said:

In one line of cases, the Supreme Court has held that the fundamental right of access to the courts requires prison authorities to provide prisoners with the tools necessary "to attack their sentences, directly or collaterally, and in order to challenge the conditions of their confinement." *Lewis v. Casey*. . . .

However, the Supreme Court also has held that the First Amendment right to petition the government includes the right to file other civil actions in court that have a reasonable basis in law or fact. . . .

380 F.3d at 290. *Snyder* relied in part on an earlier, pre-*Lewis* case which acknowledged that the *Bounds* right was limited to challenges to convictions, sentences, and prison conditions, but cautioned that "in all other types of civil actions, states may not erect barriers that impede the right of access of incarcerated persons." John L. v. Adams, 969 F.2d 228, 235 (6th Cir. 1992), cited in *Snyder*, 380 F.3d at 290–91.

[484]*See* § C.1.a.5 of this chapter.

[485]Rhoden v. Godinez, 1996 WL 559954, *3 (N.D.Ill. 1996).

c. The Right to Be Free from Retaliation for Using the Court System Prison officials may not retaliate against prisoners for using the courts or trying to do so,[486] whatever the form of the retaliation.[487] The Supreme Court has explained: "The reason why such retaliation offends the Constitution is that it threatens to inhibit exercise of the protected right. . . . Retaliation is thus akin to an 'unconstitutional condition' demanded for the receipt of a government-provided benefit."[488] Unconstitutional retaliation may be remedied by an injunction or by an award of damages.[489] Claims of retaliation for exercising the right of court access are generally governed by the same rules as claims of retaliation for other forms of speech (letters, grievances, etc.), and we discuss retaliation claims in more detail in the free speech section of this book.[490]

Courts have stated the requirements of a retaliation claim in various ways. Here is a typical one:

A retaliation claim essentially entails three elements: (1) the plaintiff engaged in protected conduct; (2) an adverse action was taken against the plaintiff that would deter a person of ordinary firmness from continuing to engage in that conduct; and (3) there is a causal connection between elements one and two–that is, the adverse action was motivated at least in part by the plaintiff's protected conduct.[491]

Retaliatory action must be serious enough to deter a "person of ordinary firmness" from exercising First Amendment rights.[492] However, the "adverse action" need not be unconstitutional all by itself in order to violate the

---

[486]The protected act of trying to gain court access should include whatever actions a prisoner needs to take in order to get his claim into court. In *Siggers-El v. Barlow*, 412 F.3d 693 (6th Cir. 2005), a prison employee refused to process a disbursement the plaintiff needed in order to retain a lawyer to file a court action; the prisoner went over the employee's head to his supervisor, and suffered retaliation as a result. The court rejected defendants' claim that going to a higher official was not constitutionally protected, holding that it was "part of his attempt to access the courts." 412 F.3d at 699.

[487]DeTomaso v. McGinnis, 970 F.2d 211, 214 (7th Cir. 1992) ("whether the retaliation takes the form of property or privileges does not matter") (dictum); *see* § B.6 of this chapter for discussion of different types of actions that may constitute retaliation.

[488]Crawford-El v. Britton, 523 U.S. 574, 588 n.10, 118 S. Ct. 1584 (1998). An unconstitutional condition is a demand that you give up a constitutional right in return for some benefit—for example, if prison officials told you they would only let you have family visits if you stopped filing lawsuits. Retaliation reverses the time sequence—for example, you do file lawsuits, and as a result they deny you family visits.

[489]*See* § B.6 of this chapter.

[490]*See* § B.6 of this chapter.

[491]Thaddeus-X v. Blatter, 175 F.3d 378, 394 (6th Cir. 1999) (en banc). Courts have stated the retaliation standard in different ways, but they generally amount to the same thing or close to it. *See* § B.6 of this chapter for further discussion.

[492]*See* § B.6 of this chapter.

rule against retaliation.[493] For example, disciplinary charges for which the punishment was not sufficiently "atypical and significant" to require due process protections[494] may still be unconstitutional if they were made for retaliatory reasons.[495] Courts have held a variety of actions sufficiently "adverse" to support a suit for retaliation.[496]

The biggest problem in retaliation cases is proving that the adverse action was, in fact, retaliatory. Courts are inclined to be suspicious of retaliation claims.[497] Without some concrete evidence to support your claim, the court will rule against you—probably on summary judgment, without a trial. That evidence can include either direct evidence, or sufficiently convincing circumstantial evidence, such as the time sequence of your legal action and the alleged retaliation.[498]

Courts are divided over the burden of proof in retaliation claims. Some say that the plaintiff must prove both that the defendants retaliated against him *and* that they would not have taken the same action without the retaliatiory motive. Others say that once the plaintiff proves retaliation, the defendants have to show that they would have done the same thing anyway in order to avoid being found liable.[499]

Retaliation claims, logically, should not be subject to the *Lewis v. Casey* requirements that the plaintiff show "actual injury" in the form of impairment of litigation of a non-frivolous claim. "In a retaliation claim . . ., the harm suffered is the adverse consequences which flow from the inmate's constitutionally protected action. Instead of being *denied* access to the courts, the prisoner is penalized for actually exercising that right."[500]

Retaliation claims should also not be limited to retaliation for suits challenging criminal convictions or conditions of confinement, since that requirement in *Lewis v. Casey* was intended to apply only to prison officials' affirmative obligation to assist prisoners with law libraries or legal assistance.[501] At least that's what we think, and you can make the argument if the issue comes up in your case. Unfortunately, court decisions to date are to the contrary.[502]

---

[493]*See* § B.6 of this chapter.

[494]*See* Ch. 4, § A.3.

[495]*See* § B.6 of this chapter.

[496]*See* § B.6 of this chapter.

[497]*See, e.g.,* Dawes v. Walker, 239 F.3d 489, 491 (2d Cir. 2001) (". . . [C]ourts must approach prisoner claims of retaliation with skepticism and particular care.").

[498]Types of evidence that have been found to support retaliation claims are discussed in § B.6 of this chapter.

[499]*See* § B.6 of this chapter

[500]Thaddeus-X v. Blatter, 175 F.3d 378, 394 (6th Cir. 1999) (en banc); *accord,* Nei v. Dooley, 372 F.3d 1003, 1007 (8th Cir. 2004) (per curiam); Poole v. County of Otero, 271 F.3d 955, 960 (10th Cir. 2001). *But see* Oliver v. Powell, 250 F. Supp. 2d 593, 600 (E.D.Va. 2002) (holding that a prisoner who continued to file suits after retaliatory acts had no claim for unconstitutional retaliation).

[501]*See* § C.1.b of this chapter.

[502]*See* Johnson v. Rodriguez, 110 F.3d 299, 311 (5th Cir. 1997) (applying *Lewis v. Casey* rule to hold that retaliation for bringing

2. Specific Issues in Court Access Cases

a. Law Libraries and Legal Assistance Before *Lewis v. Casey*, the Supreme Court held in *Bounds v. Smith* that prison officials must "assist inmates in the preparation and filing of meaningful legal papers by providing prisoners with adequate law libraries or adequate assistance from persons trained in the law."[503] That statement is still good law, but in order to enforce it you must satisfy the *Lewis v. Casey* "actual injury" requirement. Unless you can show that the lack of an adequate library or legal assistance has frustrated or impeded your bringing a non-frivolous claim about your criminal conviction or sentence or about your conditions of confinement, as previously described,[504] you will lose no matter how bad the law library or the legal assistance program is.[505]

The following discussion of the law of law libraries and legal assistance is mostly from before *Lewis v. Casey*. Because it is so hard to show actual injury, there has been very little case law since *Lewis* concerning what prison officials must do to meet their *Bounds* obligations. You can expect that defendants will argue that pre-*Lewis* case law is no longer valid. Even if you persuade the court that that law is valid in general, you will also have to persuade it that your claim satisfies the above-described requirements of *Lewis v. Casey*.

Bounds, as noted, said prison officials must provide law libraries or legal assistance. Some courts have strictly

---

lawsuits other than those challenging convictions and conditions of confinement does not violate the Constitution); *see also* Herron v. Harrison, 203 F.3d 410, 415 (6th Cir. 2000) (holding retaliation for a frivolous complaint is not actionable).

[503]430 U.S. 817, 828, 97 S. Ct. 1491 (1977).

[504]*See* §§ C.1.a(1–3) of this chapter.

[505]*See* Johnson v. Barczak, 338 F.3d 771, 772–73 (7th Cir. 2003) (holding a prisoner's claim of an inadequate jail law library did not meet the actual injury requirement, because the court granted him an extension of time to file and his post-conviction proceeding eventually went forward); Hains v. Washington, 131 F.3d 1248, 1249 (7th Cir. 1997) (holding complaint about restrictive law library practices, unaccompanied by allegations of actual injury to plaintiff's own court access, did not state a court access claim); Klinger v. Dept. of Corrections, 107 F.3d 609, 616–17 (8th Cir. 1997) (holding that even a law library so inadequate and disorganized as to amount to a "complete and systemic denial of access" did not violate the Constitution without proof of injury); Rienholtz v. Campbell, 64 F. Supp. 2d 721, 730–31 (W.D.Tenn.) (holding that allowing the law library collection to deteriorate did not state a court access claim where the plaintiff did not show injury to himself), *aff'd*, 198 F.3d 247 (6th Cir. 1999) (unpublished); Bausch v. Cox, 32 F. Supp. 2d 1057, 1058–59 (E.D.Wis. 1998) (holding complaints of missing books and lack of Shepard's, digests, and other materials do not state a court access claim absent a showing of actual injury to identified litigation); Harksen v. Garratt, 29 F. Supp. 2d 265, 269, 272 (E.D.Va. 1998) (holding that a claim of pathetically inadequate law library services fails without allegations showing how the plaintiff was impeded in the pursuit of a nonfrivolous claim).

followed the "either/or" approach of *Bounds*, holding that if the state provides adequate legal assistance, it need not also provide you with a law library.[506] After *Lewis v. Casey*, some prison systems have abolished or stopped updating their prison law libraries and have provided limited legal assistance programs instead, so this issue will probably come up more frequently.[507] If there is a legal assistance program that serves your prison, a court may find that you have no right to a law library unless you show that your case has been rejected by the program,[508] that the program does not assist with the kind of case you wish to bring,[509] or that its resources or services are inadequate to serve the prison population.[510]

One court has held that a program that excluded "lawsuits against public agencies or public officials to change social or public policy" was adequate to meet prison officials' court access obligations and that no law library was required.[511] We think that decision is inconsistent with *Lewis v. Casey*'s holding that the right to court access encompasses challenges to the conditions of confinement,[512] which are almost always against public agencies or officials and often seek to change policy. (One thing that does seem clear is that if the court appoints counsel for you in a civil case, you have adequate access to court for that case, and no right to law library access in addition.[513])

Some courts have also held that if prison officials provide a law library, they need not provide any further assistance.[514] Other courts, however, have looked more closely at this version of the "either/or" question, and have concluded that establishment of a law library, by itself, does not provide adequate court access to prisoners who lack the ability to use it, such as those who are illiterate, poorly educated, or non-English-speaking. These courts have concluded that prisons must provide some legal assistance in addition to a law library.[515] That idea finds support in *Lewis v. Casey* itself, which says that *Bounds v. Smith* "guarantees no particular

[506]Blake v. Berman, 877 F.2d 145, 147 (1st Cir. 1989) (failure to provide legal materials was not unconstitutional where the plaintiff had not fully pursued assistance from local Defender Project); Houtz v. Deland, 718 F. Supp. 1497, 1499 (D.Utah 1989) (system of "contract attorneys" met constitutional standards and no law library was required); Falzerano v. Collier, 535 F. Supp. 800, 802–03 (D.N.J. 1982) (claim of lack of law library was frivolous in a jurisdiction with public defenders and a Public Advocate).

[507]*See, e.g.*, White v. Kautzky, 269 F. Supp. 2d 1054, 1056 (N.D.Iowa 2003) (noting Iowa stopped updating its libraries and hired "contract attorneys"), *rev'd and vacated on other grounds*, 494 F.3d 677 (8th Cir. 2007).

Lewis v. Casey itself suggested that prison systems "might replace libraries with some minimal access to legal advice and a system of court-provided forms [for complaints] . . . that asked the inmates to provide only the facts and not to attempt any legal analysis." Such a system, *Lewis* said, could remain in place until and unless a prisoner showed that a non-frivolous claim was being frustrated or impeded. Lewis v. Casey, 518 U.S. 343, 352–53, 116 S. Ct. 2174 (1996). We are not aware of any prison that has adopted such a system. The above-cited decision in *White v. Kautzky* says, in the context of a "contract attorney" system, that "handing an inmate an application for post-conviction relief, standing alone, does not appear to be nearly enough" to provide meaningful access to courts. 269 F. Supp. 2d at 1062.

[508]Spates v. Manson, 644 F.2d 80, 84 (2d Cir. 1981) (denial of access was not proven without showing that "prisoners with nonfrivolous claims" had been rejected by legal assistance programs).

[509]Peterkin v. Jeffes, 855 F.2d 1021, 1046 (3d Cir. 1988) (*Bounds* obligation is not satisfied by provision of counsel unless they are available "for all relevant proceedings"); Carter v. Mandel, 573 F.2d 172, 173 (4th Cir. 1978) (assistance program must address civil rights claims to be adequate); Griffin v. Coughlin, 743 F. Supp. 1006, 1024 (N.D.N.Y. 1990) (existence of Prisoners' Legal Services program did not substitute for law library access because it was not shown to be "available for all relevant proceedings").

[510]*See* Bear v. Kautzky, 305 F.3d 802, 804–05 (8th Cir. 2002) (holding that testimony that a contract attorney had a conflict of interest with one prisoner, that a second prisoner tried to meet with the attorney for a year without success, and that the attorney couldn't help a third prisoner because he knew nothing about criminal law, showed that the program was inadequate); Leeds v. Watson, 630 F.2d 674, 676–77 (9th Cir. 1980) (if legal aid program does not provide adequate services for the prison population, a law library must be provided); Hooks v. Wainwright, 578 F.2d 1102, 1103 (5th Cir. 1978) (assistance program that served only 25% of the prison population was not adequate); White v. Kautzky, 269 F.

Supp. 2d 1054, 1062 (N.D.Iowa 2003) (holding that an allegation that a contract attorney who was supposed to provide assistance and advice with post-conviction proceedings merely handed the prisoner a form stated a claim of denial of court access; " . . . [H]anding an inmate an application for post-conviction relief, standing alone, does not appear to be nearly enough."), *rev'd and vacated on other grounds*, 494 F.3d 677 (8th Cir. 2007); John L. v. Adams, 750 F. Supp. 288, 293–95 (M.D.Tenn. 1990) (referring prisoners to local legal and legal services offices and public defenders did not meet court access requirements where these agencies did not actually assist most prisoners), *aff'd in pertinent part*, 969 F.2d 228 (6th Cir. 1992); Ruiz v. Estelle, 503 F. Supp. 1265, 1371 (S.D.Tex. 1980), *aff'd in pertinent part, rev'd on other grounds*, 679 F.2d 1115, 1153–55 (5th Cir. 1982).

[511]Kelsey v. State of Minnesota, 622 F.2d 956, 958–59 (8th Cir. 1980).

[512]*Lewis*, 518 U.S. at 354–55.

[513]Arce v. Walker, 58 F. Supp. 2d 39, 45 (W.D.N.Y. 1999).

[514]Tineo v. U.S., 977 F. Supp. 245, 254 (S.D.N.Y. 1996).

[515]Knop v. Johnson, 977 F.2d 996, 1005 (6th Cir. 1992); Valentine v. Beyer, 850 F.2d 951, 956–57 (3d Cir. 1988) (affirming injunction against dismantling of inmate paralegal system partly because of the needs of illiterate and non-English-speaking inmates); Lindquist v. Idaho State Board of Correction, 776 F.2d 851, 855–56 (9th Cir. 1985); Cruz v. Hauck, 627 F.2d 710, 721 (5th Cir. 1980); U.S. ex rel. Para-Professional Law Clinic v. Kane, 656 F. Supp. 1099, 1104 (E.D.Pa.), *aff'd*, 835 F.2d 285 (3d Cir. 1987); Cody v. Hillard, 599 F. Supp. 1025, 1060–61 (D.S.D. 1984), *rev'd on other grounds*, 830 F.2d 912, 914 (10th Cir. 1987) (en banc); Canterino v. Wilson, 562 F. Supp. 106, 111 (W.D.Ky. 1983); Glover v. Johnson, 478 F. Supp. 1075, 1097 (E.D.Mich. 1979). *But see* Cepulonis v. Fair, 732 F.2d 1, 6–7 (1st Cir. 1984) (legal assistance may be required only based on evidence that a law library program is inadequate); White v. Lewis, 167 Ariz. 76, 804 P.2d 805, 810 (Ariz.App. 1990) (prisoner who was "articulate and able to make appropriate use of

methodology but rather the conferral of a capability—the capability of bringing contemplated challenges to sentences or conditions of confinement before the courts."[516] So if, in fact, a prisoner is unable to to file such claims without legal assistance in addition to access to law books, logically, that assistance must be provided.

The legal assistance that courts have mandated generally consists of trained inmate paralegals, and they have not been very specific about the training required.[517] There is no right to the legal assistant of one's choice.[518] Assistance from attorneys has only been required in unusual circumstances,[519] and even then actual representation by counsel is not required.[520]

In several cases, courts have enjoined attempts to terminate or reduce legal assistance programs until prison officials provided adequate alternative means of court access.[521] If inmates are dependent on a legal assistance program, there must be a workable system to ensure that they have access to it.[522] However, after *Lewis v. Casey*, prisoners would have to show that they have suffered or will suffer actual injury, as defined in *Lewis*, in order to obtain such relief.[523]

A law library must be "adequate."[524] Courts have reached various conclusions about what an adequate law library must contain.[525] After *Lewis v. Casey*, it must contain what

---

legal authority" was not entitled to a legal assistant in addition to a law library).

[516]*Lewis*, 518 U.S. at 356–57 (adding that "it is that capability, rather than the capability of turning pages in a law library, that is the touchstone").

[517]*See* Knop v. Johnson, 977 F.2d at 1005 (requiring "intelligent laypeople who can write coherent English and who have had some modicum of exposure to legal research and to the rudiments of prisoner-rights law"); Lindquist v. Idaho State Board of Correction, 776 F.2d at 855–56 (holding inmate law clerks to be sufficient to assist illiterate and non-English-speaking inmates; attorney assistance was not required).

[518]Gometz v. Henman, 807 F.2d 113, 116 (7th Cir. 1986); Storseth v. Spellman, 654 F.2d 1349, 1353 (9th Cir. 1981); White v. Lewis, 167 Ariz. 76, 804 P.2d 805, 810 (Ariz.App. 1990).

[519]John L. v. Adams, 969 F.2d 228, 234 (6th Cir. 1992) (juvenile prisoners required access to attorneys); Smith v. Bounds, 813 F.2d 1299, 1301–02 (4th Cir. 1987) (state could be required to provide attorney assistance where it had failed for years to implement adequate law library access), *aff'd on other grounds on rehearing*, 841 F.2d 77 (4th Cir. 1988) (en banc); Canterino v. Wilson, 644 F. Supp. 738, 740–41 (W.D.Ky. 1986) (requiring some attorney assistance for women inmates). *But see* Hooks v. Wainwright, 775 F.2d 1433, 1436–37 (11th Cir. 1985) (attorney assistance need not be provided as part of court access program), *rehearing denied*, 781 F.2d 1550 (11th Cir. 1985).

[520]Murray v. Giarratano, 492 U.S. 1, 10–13, 109 S. Ct. 2765 (1989); Knop v. Johnson, 977 F.2d at 1005–07; *see* Nordgren v. Mitchell, 716 F.2d 1335, 1338 (10th Cir. 1983) (despite inadequacies of the prison library, prisoners were not entitled to the assistance of counsel in defending paternity suits).

In *Murray v. Giarratano*, the lower court held that in capital cases, even prisoners with law library access must have individual counsel appointed to prepare state post-conviction proceedings. The Supreme Court reversed, holding that the right to counsel does not extend to post-conviction proceedings, and that problems in law library access can be remedied "without any need to enlarge the holding of *Bounds*." 492 U.S. at 13. However, the prison system involved in *Murray* already had trained legal assistance in the form of "unit attorneys" who served as legal advisors. *Id.*, 492 U.S. at 5–6. Thus, *Murray* is not inconsistent with the cases that hold that some trained legal assistance is required. Courts have continued to hold that even in capital cases, appointed counsel is not required to investigate and prepare post-conviction challenges to convictions and sentences. *See* Barbour v. Haley, 471 F.3d 1222, 1230 (11th Cir. 2006) ("*Giarratano*, however, established a categorical rule that

there is no federal constitutional right to postconviction counsel."), *cert. denied*, 551 U.S. 1134 (2007).

[521]Valentine v. Beyer, 850 F.2d at 956–58; Hooks v. Wainwright, 578 F.2d 1102, 1103 (5th Cir. 1978); U.S. ex rel. Para-Professional Law Clinic v. Kane, 656 F. Supp. at 1107–08; Wade v. Kane, 448 F. Supp. 678, 685 (E.D.Pa. 1978), *aff'd*, 591 F.2d 1338 (3d Cir. 1979).

[522]Watson v. Norris, 729 F. Supp. 581, 586 (M.D.Tenn. 1989); Tuggle v. Barksdale, 641 F. Supp. 34, 37 (W.D.Tenn. 1985).

[523]*See In re* Para-Professional Law Clinic at SCI-Graterford, 334 F.3d 301, 305–06 (3d Cir. 2003) (allowing termination of legal assistance program under Prison Litigation Reform Act because there was no denial of access to court ongoing at the time); Hadix v. Johnson, 182 F.3d 400, 405–06 (6th Cir. 1999) (holding that an injunction continuing a legal services program requires a showing of actual injury).

[524]Bounds v. Smith, 430 U.S. 817, 828, 97 S. Ct. 1491 (1977).

[525]*See, e.g.*, Egerton v. Cockrell, 334 F.3d 433, 438 (5th Cir. 2003) ("The absence of all federal materials from a prison library (without making some alternative arrangements to apprise prisoners of their rights) violates the First Amendment right, through the Fourteenth Amendment, to access to the courts." The absence of a copy of the Anti-Terrorism and Effective Death Penalty Act from the prison law library was a state-created impediment that tolled the AEDPA limitations period.); Johnson v. Moore, 948 F.2d 517, 521 (9th Cir. 1991) (absence of certain titles of the U.S. Code did not deny the plaintiff's court access rights); Battle v. Anderson, 788 F.2d 1421, 1424 (10th Cir. 1986) ("substantial volume of basic materials" was sufficient); Caldwell v. Miller, 790 F.2d 589, 607, 610 (7th Cir. 1986) (listing contents of "basic" library for segregation unit); Lindquist v. Idaho State Board of Corrections, 776 F.2d 851, 856 n.1 (9th Cir. 1985); Wattson v. Olsen, 660 F.2d 358, 359 n.2 (8th Cir. 1981) (state and federal case law and statutes and other materials were sufficient); Ramos v. Lamm, 639 F.2d 559, 584 (10th Cir. 1980) (libraries without federal cases or with many missing volumes were inadequate); Cruz v. Hauck, 627 F.2d 710, 720 (5th Cir. 1980) ("Federal Supplement from 1960 or so on should probably be available"); Johnson v. State of Nebraska Dep't of Correctional Services, 806 F. Supp. 1412, 1420–21 (D.Neb. 1992) (missing volumes of state case reports did not deny court access unless the material was unavailable from other sources); Abdul-Akbar v. Watson, 775 F. Supp. 735, 749–50 (D.Del. 1991) (in "satellite" library, current digests and treatises are required; federal materials are needed for civil rights and habeas cases); Griffin v. Coughlin, 743 F. Supp. 1006, 1020 n.14 (N.D.N.Y. 1990) (law library contents were adequate; absence of Shepard's is not unconstitutional if digests are available); Maillett v. Phinney, 741 F. Supp. 288, 291–92 (D.Me. 1990) (allegation that the law library contained nothing but court rules and "nutshell" books raised a factual issue as to its

the prisoner who wishes to file suit about his conviction, sentence, or conditions of confinement needs in order to do so.

County jails may have smaller law libraries than state prisons, but they must provide some access to legal materials.[526] Prisoners who are transferred from one state to another, or from state to federal custody, have a right of access to legal materials from their home states.[527] Most courts have held that it is the responsibility of the sending state to make these materials available.[528]

Reasonable limits on prisoners' law library access may be imposed,[529] but restrictions that deny meaningful law

library access will be struck down,[530] subject to the requirement that prisoners must show they suffered actual injury from those restrictions.[531] As a practical matter, few prisoners can show that law library restrictions caused them actual harm to their cases.[532]

---

adequacy); Tuggle v. Barksdale, 641 F. Supp. at 38–39 (various statutes, court rules, federal procedure materials, and other books required; missing or damaged books must be repaired or replaced); Hooks v. Wainwright, 536 F. Supp. 1330, 1342 (M.D.Fla. 1982) (libraries without federal case reporters or federal statutes would be inadequate), rev'd on other grounds, 775 F.2d 1433 (11th Cir. 1985); Hardwick v. Ault, 447 F. Supp. 116, 133–34 (M.D.Ga. 1978) (listing required library contents); Miller v. Evans, 832 P.2d 786, 788–89 (Nev. 1991) (holding library contents adequate and listing them).

[526]Penland v. Warren County Jail, 797 F.2d 332, 335–36 (6th Cir. 1986) (concurring opinion); Morrow v. Harwell, 768 F.2d 619, 622–24 (5th Cir. 1985), on remand, 640 F. Supp. 225 (W.D.Tex. 1986); Leeds v. Watson, 630 F.2d 674, 677 (9th Cir. 1980); Tuggle v. Barksdale, 641 F. Supp. at 38; Brown v. Manning, 630 F. Supp. 391, 397 (E.D.Wash. 1985); Noren v. Straw, 578 F. Supp. 1, 5 (D.Mont. 1982); Parnell v. Waldrep, 511 F. Supp. 764, 769 (W.D.N.C. 1981); Fluhr v. Roberts, 460 F. Supp. 536, 537 (W.D.Ky. 1978). But see Strickler v. Waters, 989 F.2d 1375, 1384–88 and n.17 (4th Cir. 1993) (upholding adequacy of a county jail law library containing only statutes and a legal encyclopedia; case reporters could be obtained from outside the jail; these facilities might be inadequate for an inmate held longer than six months); Williams v. Leeke, 584 F.2d 1336, 1340 (4th Cir. 1978) ("We should not be understood to say that every small jail must have a law library, but misdemeanants serving sentences of up to 12 months in local jails should not be left wholly without resources. . . .").

[527]Sahagian v. Dickey, 827 F.2d 90, 93–94 (7th Cir. 1987) (citing district court holding); Sills v. Bureau of Prisons, 761 F.2d 792, 796 (D.C. Cir. 1985); Caldwell v. Miller, 790 F.2d 589, 606–07 (7th Cir. 1986); Rich v. Zitnay, 644 F.2d 41, 43 (1st Cir. 1981); Luce v. Magnuson, 675 F. Supp. 681, 683 (D.Me. 1987); Cooper v. Sumner, 672 F. Supp. 1361, 1365 (D.Nev. 1987); Benjamin v. Potter, 635 F. Supp. 243, 244–45 (D.V.I. 1986), aff'd, 838 F.2d 1205 (1st Cir. 1988); Shoats v. Commissioner, Pa. Dep't of Correction, 139 Pa.Cmwlth. 607, 591 A.2d 326, 329 (Pa.Commw. 1991).

[528]Story v. Morgan, 786 F. Supp. 523, 527–28 n.3 (W.D.Pa. 1992) and cases cited; Messere v. Fair, 752 F. Supp. 48, 52 (D.Mass. 1990). But see Lehn v. Holmes, 364 F.3d 862, 867–69 (7th Cir. 2004) (where Illinois used a Maryland indictment to justify increasing the plaintiff's security level, Illinois was required to provide him with the means to challenge the Maryland indictment).

[529]Geder v. Roth, 765 F.Supp.1357, 1358 (N.D. Ill. 1991) (10 hours of library time in 3 months was not unconstitutional without a showing of prejudice); Housley v. Killinger, 747 F. Supp. 1405, 1408 (D.Or. 1990) (six or more hours a day, seven days a week provided adequate access); Bellamy v. McMickens, 692 F. Supp. 205,

214 (S.D.N.Y. 1988) (temporary deprivation of access was not unconstitutional); Robbins v. South, 595 F. Supp. 785, 789 (D.Mont. 1984) (17 hours access a month upheld); Collins v. Ward, 544 F. Supp. 408, 414 (S.D.N.Y. 1982) (two-week deprivation of law library access did not violate the Constitution); Rucker v. Grider, 526 F. Supp. 617, 620 (W.D.Okla. 1980) (restrictions on access in Assessment and Reception Center were reasonable because confinement there was short and provisions were made for filing deadlines and other exceptional circumstances). But see Berry v. Dep't of Corrections, 144 Ariz. 318, 697 P.2d 711, 714 (Ariz.App. 1985) (law library or legal assistance must be provided at Reception and Treatment Center where inmates remained for 60 to 90 days).

[530]"[P]risoners must receive sufficient access to prison libraries which will enable them to research law and to determine what facts may be necessary to state a cause of action." Zamora v. Pierson, 158 F. Supp. 2d 830, 836 (N.D.Ill. 2001). Most such cases involve restricted time in the law library. See, e.g., Gluth v. Kangas, 951 F.2d 1504, 1508, 1511 (9th Cir. 1991) (arbitrary denials of access and failure to allow a "reasonable amount" of time in the library denied access); Johnson-El v. Schoemehl, 878 F.2d 1043, 1053 (8th Cir. 1989) (one hour twice a week in the law library was "obviously inadequate to research most legal claims"); Williams v. Leeke, 584 F.2d at 1340 ("meaningful legal research" cannot be done in 45–minute intervals); Cruz v. Hauck, 627 F.2d at 720 (two or three hours a week might be inadequate; "the paramount consideration is whether the . . . hours of availability are sufficient to provide for meaningful legal research); Tillery v. Owens, 719 F. Supp. 1256, 1284 (W.D.Pa. 1989) (four hours a month were inadequate for segregated clinic inmates; four hours a week required), aff'd, 907 F.2d 418 (3d Cir. 1990); Ramos v. Lamm, 485 F. Supp. 122, 166 (D.Colo. 1979) (three hours every four to six weeks was inadequate), aff'd in part and rev'd in part, 639 F.2d 559 (10th Cir. 1980); see Pembroke v. Wood County, Tex., 981 F.2d 225, 229 (5th Cir. 1993) (seven-month deprivation of law library access was unconstitutional).

[531]Marshall v. Knight, 445 F.3d 965, 969 (7th Cir. 2006) (plaintiff who alleged that defendants reduced his law library access to a "non-existent" level, making him unable to research and prepare for a court hearing and therefore to lose time credits that would have shortened his incarceration, stated a court access claim); Walker v. Mintzes, 771 F.2d 920, 931–32 (6th Cir. 1985) (court should determine whether restricted hours actually denied anyone court access).

[532]Michau v. Charleston County, South Carolina, 434 F.3d 725, 728 (4th Cir. 2006) (lack of access to law library did not deny court access without a showing of prejudice); Twyman v. Crisp, 584 F.2d 352, 358 (10th Cir. 1978) (restricted hours did not result in harm to the plaintiff); Auguste v. Dep't of Corrections, 424 F. Supp. 2d 363, 369–70 (D.Conn. 2006) (prisoner who got an hour every other day during the relevant 13-month period, and was granted additional time on 63 occasions, was not denied access to court); Pepper v. Carroll, 423 F. Supp. 2d 442, 446 (D.Del. 2006) (rejecting claim of prisoner who in two and a half months in SHU received law library services on 23 occasions and went to the library 77 times); Oliver v. Powell, 250 F. Supp. 2d 593, 601 (E.D.Va. 2002) (holding that

In general, physical access to the law library is required.[533] Segregation inmates may be excluded from physical access on security grounds, but their court access rights remain "undiminished."[534] A number of decisions hold that if segregation inmates are denied physical access to the library, they must receive additional assistance—either a basic law library on the housing unit or assistance from legally trained persons.[535] Courts understand that a

"cell delivery" or "paging" system, by itself, does not provide adequate court access because prisoners who cannot visit the library generally will not know what materials to ask for.[536] If prison officials do permit segregation inmates to have physical access to the law library, that access must be adequate.[537]

Several courts have upheld severe security measures in connection with high-security inmates' visiting the law library.[538] However, harassment in the guise of security is unlawful.[539] Special restrictions on particular individuals will be upheld if they are imposed for legitimate reasons, but not if they are arbitrary or retaliatory.[540]

---

depriving plaintiff of some of his allotted law library time did not deny access to courts absent proof of actual injury).

[533]Toussaint v. McCarthy, 801 F.2d 1080, 1108–10 (9th Cir. 1986); Green v. Ferrell, 801 F.2d 765, 772 (5th Cir. 1986); Williams v. Leeke, 584 F.2d at 1339; Wolfish v. Levi, 573 F.2d 118, 133 (2d Cir. 1978), *rev'd on other grounds sub nom.* Bell v. Wolfish, 441 U.S. 520, 99 S. Ct. 1861 (1979); Hooks v. Wainwright, 536 F. Supp. 1330, 1342-43 (M.D.Fla. 1982), *rev'd on other grounds,* 775 F.2d 1433 (11th Cir. 1985). *But see* Stewart v. Gates, 450 F. Supp. 583, 589 (C.D.Cal. 1978) ("runner" system upheld for inmates who also had access to the public defender), *remanded,* 618 F.2d 117 (9th Cir. 1980).

[534]Peterkin v. Jeffes, 855 F.2d 1021, 1038 (3d Cir. 1988); *see* Harris v. Thigpen, 941 F.2d 1495, 1527 (11th Cir. 1991) (segregated HIV positive prisoners retained court access rights); Abdul-Akbar v. Watson, 775 F. Supp. 735, 748 (D.Del. 1991) (alternative to direct access "must be of at least equal caliber" to direct access).

[535]Knop v. Johnson, 977 F.2d 996, 1005–08 (6th Cir. 1992) (paralegal assistance required); Toussaint v. McCarthy, 926 F.2d 800, 803–04 (9th Cir. 1990) (provision of a separate library for administrative segregation inmates met constitutional standards); Wood v. Housewright, 900 F.2d 1332, 1335 (9th Cir. 1990) (system of "satellite" libraries and inmate law clerks satisfied constitutional requirements); DeMallory v. Cullen, 855 F.2d 442, 447 (7th Cir. 1988) (cell delivery system is adequate only when prisoners have "starter" or "basic" libraries or "assistance by trained, skilled and independent legal personnel"); Toussaint v. McCarthy, 801 F.2d at 1108–10 (documented security risks could be excluded from the library but must receive "research assistance" as well as cell delivery); Campbell v. Miller, 787 F.2d 217, 227 (7th Cir. 1986); Cepulonis v. Fair, 732 F.2d 1, 5–7 (1st Cir. 1984) (satellite law library required in segregation unit); Abdul-Akbar v. Watson, 775 F. Supp. at 752 ("an expanded paging system, if properly supplemented by real legal research assistance from paralegals and a library containing a full and updated set of digests or treatises from which citations may be located" could meet constitutional standards); Gluth v. Kangas, 773 F. Supp. 1309, 1311 (D.Ariz. 1988) (untrained inmate legal assistants did not provide adequate access), *aff'd,* 951 F.2d 1504 (9th Cir. 1991); Griffin v. Coughlin, 743 F. Supp. 1006, 1019-25 (N.D.N.Y. 1990) (cell delivery system limited to two books a day, supplemented only by written communication with clerks, some of whom were untrained, was inadequate in protective custody unit); Watson v. Norris, 729 F. Supp. 581, 585–86 (M.D.Tenn. 1989) (protective custody inmates who had to depend on jailhouse lawyers who had sole discretion whether to help a particular inmate were denied adequate court access); Tillery v. Owens, 719 F. Supp. 1256, 1282-84 (W.D.Pa. 1989), *aff'd on other grounds,* 907 F.2d 418 (3d Cir. 1990) (restrictive housing inmates who lacked physical access and had no assistance by legally trained persons were not provided adequate court access); Reutcke v. Dahm, 707 F. Supp. 1121, 1130 (D.Neb. 1988) (where inmates are barred from physical access, "the state must provide research

assistance in the form of persons trained in the law"); Long v. Beyer, 676 F. Supp. 75, 76–77 (D.N.J. 1988) (cell delivery system must be supplemented by access to inmate paralegals, a logging system and a deadline for delivery, or else a small library on the unit); Kendrick v. Bland, 586 F. Supp. 1536, 1550-52 (W.D.Ky. 1984) (access to attorneys and paralegals required); Johnson v. Galli, 596 F. Supp. 135, 138 (D.Nev. 1984) (physical access or expert assistance required); Knight v. Superior Court, 161 Ariz. 551, 779 P.2d 1290, 1293 (Ariz.App. 1989) ("paging" system is adequate for a criminal defendant only if "adequate advisory counsel assistance" is provided; a paralegal was adequate); *see also* Green v. McKaskle, 788 F.2d 1116, 1126 (5th Cir. 1986) (limit of checking out 2–3 books a day stated a constitutional claim). *But see* Jones v. Smith, 784 F.2d 149, 151–52 (2d Cir. 1986) (refusal to provide advance sheets in segregation upheld where the plaintiff was only there for 30 days).

[536]Knop v. Johnson, 977 F.2d at 1006–07; DeMallory v. Cullen, 855 F.2d at 446–47; Kaiser v. City of Sacramento, 780 F. Supp. 1309, 1316 (E.D.Cal. 1992); Nolley v. County of Erie, 776 F. Supp. 715, 716 (W.D.N.Y. 1991); Messere v. Fair, 752 F. Supp. 48, 50 (D.Mass. 1990); Maillett v. Phinney, 741 F. Supp. 288, 292 (D.Me. 1990); Johnson v. Galli, 596 F. Supp. at 138; Martino v. Carey, 563 F. Supp. 984, 1003–04 (D.Or. 1983); *see* LaPlante v. Pepe, 307 F. Supp. 2d 219, 220–21 (D.Mass. 2004) (noting court's previous finding that excluding plaintiff from the law library and requiring him to designate needed materials by citation violated the right of court access). *But see* Williams v. Lehigh Dep't of Correction, 79 F. Supp. 2d 514, 518 (E.D.Pa. 1998) (holding reliance on a request slip system did not violate the right to court access without a showing of prejudice).

[537]Williams v. Lane, 851 F.2d 867, 874-75, 878-79 (7th Cir. 1988) (restrictions on protective custody inmates' law library access lacked a rational basis and were unconstitutional); Nadeau v. Helgemoe, 561 F.2d 411, 417–18 (1st Cir. 1977) (protective custody inmates must be given more than one hour a week in the law library).

[538]Rickman v. Avanti, 854 F.2d 327, 328–29 (9th Cir. 1988) (segregated prisoners could be strip searched before going to the library); Tubwell v. Griffith, 742 F.2d 250, 252 (5th Cir. 1984) (upholding the use of restraints on high-security inmates using the law library); Arruda v. Fair, 710 F.2d 886 (1st Cir. 1983).

[539]Ruiz v. Estelle, 679 F.2d 1115, 1154 (5th Cir. 1982) (harassing strip searches at law library enjoined).

[540]*Compare* Martin v. Ezeagu, 816 F. Supp. 20, 24 (D.D.C. 1993) (allegation of "ongoing pattern of harassment and arbitrary exclusion" from the law library stated a constitutional claim) *with* Caddell v. Allenbrand, 804 F. Supp. 200, 201 (D.Kan. 1992)

The case law discussed above deals with access to physical law libraries. Outside prisons and jails, legal research is increasingly done in electronic databases such as Westlaw and Lexis, which we doubt that most prisoners have access to. In some cases, opposing litigants and courts rely on material that is available *only* in electronic databases,[541] which puts *pro se* prisoners at an even greater disadvantage.[542] Some courts have rules requiring litigants who cite such materials to provide *pro se* litigants with printed copies of them. If your adversary cites such materials and does *not* provide them to you, whether or not there is such a rule in your jurisdiction, you should ask for copies of the cited materials, and ask the court to direct that you be provided them and that if necessary your time to respond be extended so you will have time to receive and review them. You should do the same if the court cites material you have no access to (but if you need to file a notice of appeal, motion to reconsider, etc., don't miss the deadline waiting to receive the materials).

Prisoners are of course permitted to possess their own legal books and other legal information, subject to rules bearing a reasonable relationship to legitimate correctional purposes.[543] If you wish to challenge confiscation or prohibition of legal books or information, you should probably

assert a First Amendment claim based on the right to read as well as or instead of a claim of denial of access to the courts, for the reasons explained elsewhere.[544]

b. Postage, Materials, and Services The Supreme Court has stated, "It is indisputable that indigent inmates must be provided at state expense with paper and pen to draft legal documents, with notarial services to authenticate them, and with stamps to mail them."[545] Courts have made various rulings on free postage and materials,[546] and some have

---

(upholding restrictions on access by a prisoner who had torn pages out of a book).

[541]Many lower court cases are unpublished. In the federal appellate courts, many cases are unpublished in the sense that the court declares them to be non-precedential, but in fact some of these are published in the Federal Appendix, a set of books which may or may not be in law libraries that have the Federal Reporter and Federal Supplement. *See* Ch. 11 for further discussion of case reporters and of electronic research.

[542]To our knowledge, no court has held that prisoners' inability to get such materials is a denial of access to court. One recent decision does express concern about "the impact on the appearance of justice when *pro se* litigants may not have financial access to case authorities that form the basis of a court's decision, thereby hampering the litigants' opportunities to understand and assert their legal rights." Lebron v. Sanders, 557 F.3d 76, 78 (2d Cir. 2009). The court said the circuit's Judicial Conference was best suited to consider the issue, and meanwhile "hope[d] that district courts will be sensitive both to ensuring that their local rules are strictly enforced and and to considerations of whether *pro se* indigent litigants will have access, without cost, to review the case law relied upon by a district court in ruling upon the litigants' claims." *Id.* at 79.

[543]Certain legal materials can be prohibited. Materials concerning the Uniform Commercial Code which prisoners have used to harass prison personnel and other officials with fraudulent liens and other filings can be banned. Jones v. Caruso, 569 F.3d 258, 273–75 (6th Cir. 2009) (accepting legitimacy of such prohibitions, granting preliminary injunction against particular overly broad rule); Monroe v. Beard, 536 F.3d 198 (3d Cir. 2008, *cert. denied*, 129 S. Ct. 1647 (2009). A rule prohibiting "third-party legal material" containing information that "could create a risk of violence and/or physical harm to any person" has been upheld. Prison Legal News v. Lehman, 397 F.3d 692, 702–03 (9th Cir. 2005).

[544]A court access claim requires you to show actual injury to non-frivolous litigation, which you may not be able to do. Other applicable legal claims do not. *See* § C.3 of this chapter for a discussion of this point in connection with legal communication and privacy issues. The right to read is discussed in § B.2 of this chapter.

[545]Bounds v. Smith, 430 U.S. 817, 824–25, 97 S. Ct. 1491 (1977); *accord*, Smith v. Erickson, 884 F.2d 1108, 1111 (8th Cir. 1989); Chandler v. Coughlin, 763 F.2d 110, 114 (2d Cir. 1985) ("reasonably adequate" amount of free postage must be provided); Phillips v. Hust, 338 F. Supp. 2d 1148, 1162–63 (D.Or. 2004) (holding that denial of access to a binder necessary to comply with court filing rules denied access to courts), *aff'd in pertinent part*, 477 F.3d 1070 (9th Cir. 2007), *cert. granted, judgment vacated on other grounds*, 129 S. Ct. 1036 (2009); Ruiz v. Estelle, 503 F. Supp. 1265, 1371 n.206 (S.D.Tex. 1980) (notarial services required), *aff'd in pertinent part, rev'd on other grounds*, 679 F.2d 1115, 1153–55 (5th Cir. 1982); Morgan v. Nevada Board of State Prison Commissioners, 593 F. Supp. 621, 624 (D.Nev. 1984) (unavailability of paper and envelopes for days or weeks at a time denied court access); Dawson v. Kendrick, 527 F. Supp. 1252, 1313–14 (S.D.W.Va. 1981) (denial of postage, writing materials, notarial services denied court access).

One federal court has said that prisoners have "'no constitutional entitlement to subsidy' . . . to prosecute a civil suit," Lindell v. McCallum, 352 F.3d 1107, 1111 (7th Cir. 2003), which appears directly contrary to the holding of *Bounds v. Smith* quoted in the text above.

[546]*See, e.g.*, Bell-Bey v. Williams, 87 F.3d 832, 839 (6th Cir. 1996) (upholding policy providing 10 first-class stamps per month, with additional postage provided on proof that it was for existing pending litigation); Blaise v. Fenn, 48 F.3d 337, 339–41 (8th Cir. 1995) (upholding provision of $7.70 a month to all inmates to use as they wished, with advances of up to $3.50 for legal expenses, or more for "exceptional need"); Gluth v. Kangas, 951 F.2d 1504, 1509–10 (9th Cir. 1991) (upholding lower court's order that free materials be provided to prisoners with less than $12 in their accounts); Smith v. Erickson, 961 F.2d 1387, 1388 (8th Cir. 1992) (the Constitution was satisfied by one free mailing a week, plus allowing inmates to maintain a negative account balance for legal postage and providing "reasonable amounts of free paper and pens"); Gittens v. Sullivan, 848 F.2d 389, 390 (2d Cir. 1988) ($1.10 a week postage plus a $36.00 advance against future earnings upheld for a segregation inmate); King v. Atiyeh, 814 F.2d 565, 568 (9th Cir. 1987) (limit of three free stamps a week stated a claim for denial of court access); Gaines v. Lane, 790 F.2d 1299, 1308 (7th Cir. 1986) (provision for "reasonable" amounts of free legal mail upheld); Chandler v. Coughlin, 763 F.2d at 115 (dicta) (rules providing five one-ounce letters a week but not permitting accumulation of postage to mail larger items appeared arbitrary); Kershner v. Mazurkiewicz, 670 F.2d 440, 444 (3d Cir. 1982) (10 first-class

approved restrictions that we think are quite unreasonable for prisoners who are actually engaged in litigation.[547] Under *Lewis v. Casey*, such restrictions can only be effectively challenged if prisoners can show that they frustrate or impede efforts to bring non-frivolous cases.[548] Inmates who are not indigent are not constitutionally entitled to free postage and materials for legal mail.[549] Courts have not settled what "indigent" means for this purpose. One court has held that an indigency policy that "forces inmates to choose between purchasing hygienic supplies and essential legal supplies is 'unacceptable.'"[550]

Courts have held that the Constitution does not require access to typewriters.[551] However, we think that if court rules require papers to be typed, meaningful court access requires giving the prisoner a means to comply.[552] Typewriters, of course, are mostly obsolete outside prison; almost everyone uses computers with word processing programs. The courts have not to our knowledge required computer access for preparing papers.[553]

Prison officials must provide a means for prisoners to make sufficient copies of papers to comply with court rules.[554] However, prisoners are not entitled to unlimited free copying, and charges and restrictions will be upheld as long as prisoners are actually able to get their papers filed.[555]

---

[547]letters a month upheld); Chandler v. Coughlin, 733 F. Supp. 641, 644, 647 (S.D.N.Y. 1990) (equivalent of five first-class letters a week, with advances available for legal mail only, upheld), *on remand from* 763 F.2d 110 (2d Cir. 1985); Accoolla v. Angelone, 186 F. Supp. 2d 670, 671–72 (W.D.Va. 2002) ("The mere fact that [the plaintiff] has consent to pursue four lawsuits at one time does not require prison officials to alter the amount of free materials to be provided to him."); Wrenn v. Freeman, 894 F. Supp. 244, 251 (E.D.N.C. 1995) (questioning whether free postage only for those who have nothing in their accounts and have not removed more than $10.00 in the preceding 30 days is adequate); Peterkin v. Jeffes, 661 F. Supp. 895, 916 (E.D.Pa. 1987) (10 free letters a month upheld), *affirmed in pertinent part*, 855 F.2d 1021, 1028, 1032 (3d Cir. 1988).

[547]Hoppins v. Wallace, 751 F.2d 1161, 1162 (11th Cir. 1985) (two free stamps a week upheld); Robbins v. South, 595 F. Supp. 785, 789 (D.Mont. 1984) (four envelopes and eight sheets of paper a month upheld).

[548]518 U.S. 343, 351–53, 116 S. Ct. 2174 (1996); *see* Collins v. Goord, 438 F. Supp. 399, 418 (S.D.N.Y. 2006) (deprivation of stiff-barreled pens in SHU did not deny court access since they did not cause actual prejudice to plaintiff); § C.1.a(1) of this chapter. In fact, cases about inadequate supplies were dismissed in the absence of actual harm long before *Lewis*. *See* Purcell v. Coughlin, 790 F.2d 263, 265 (2d Cir. 1986); Hudson v. Robinson, 678 F.2d 462, 466 (3d Cir. 1982); Kershner v. Mazurkiewicz, 670 F.2d 440, 444 (3d Cir. 1982).

[549]Glick v. Lockhart, 769 F.2d 471, 472 (8th Cir. 1985); Lyons v. Clark, 694 F. Supp. 184, 189 (E.D.Va. 1988), *aff'd*, 887 F.2d 1080 (4th Cir. 1990); *see also* Chilton v. Atwood, 769 F. Supp. 267, 269 (M.D.Tenn. 1991) (a non-indigent inmate who ran out of stamps, which he had a chance to buy every week, thereby missing his appeal deadline, was not denied access to courts by the refusal to mail his notice of appeal).

[550]Gluth v. Kangas, 951 F.2d at 1508 (holding inmates entitled to indigent status if they had less than $12 in their accounts and had received $12 or less in the preceding 30 days). Other courts have upheld more stringent rules in the absence of evidence that anyone had been harmed by them. White v. White, 886 F.2d 721, 722–23 (4th Cir. 1989) (free postage denied to plaintiff who had had $5.00 in his account 10 days previously); Kendrick v. Bland, 586 F. Supp. 1536, 1553–54 (W.D.Ky. 1984) (free copying denied to anyone with $5.00 in prison account). Other courts have also rejected the argument that prisoners should not have to balance expenditures for legal supplies against other commissary expenditures. Lebron v. Armstrong, 289 F. Supp. 2d 56, 61 (D.Conn. 2003).

[551]American Inmate Paralegal Ass'n v. Cline, 859 F.2d 59, 61 (8th Cir. 1988); Lindquist v. Idaho State Bd. of Correction, 776 F.2d 851, 858 (9th Cir. 1985); Twyman v. Crisp, 584 F.2d 352, 358 (10th Cir. 1978); Wolfish v. Levi, 573 F.2d 118, 132 (2d Cir. 1978), *rev'd on other grounds sub nom.* Bell v. Wolfish, 441 U.S. 520, 99 S. Ct. 1861 (1979); Roberts v. Cohn, 63 F. Supp. 2d 921, 924–25 (N.D.Ind. 1999) (holding prisoners do not have a right to possess typewriters and word processors; the right of court access is satisfied by basic materials such as pens and paper), *aff'd*, 215 F.3d 1330 (7th Cir. 2000); Kendrick v. Bland, 586 F. Supp. at 1554; *see* Collins v. Goord, 438 F. Supp. 2d 399, 418 (S.D.N.Y. 2006) (destruction of typewriter did not deny court access where prisoner was filing typed documents anyway).

[552]Johnston v. Lehman, 609 A.2d 880, 883 (Pa.Cmwlth. 1992) (if court rules required documents to be typewritten, the denial of a typewriter would deny court access).

[553]The Federal Rules of Appellate Procedure now require that briefs be "reproduced with a clarity that equals or exceeds the output of a laser printer," Fed.R.App.P. 32(a)(1)(B), but they also provide that courts may by "local rule or order in a particular case . . . accept documents that do not meet all of the form requirements of this rule." Fed.R.App.P. 32(e).

[554]Collins v. Goord, 438 F. Supp. 399, 417 (S.D.N.Y. 2006) (allegation that plaintiff was denied necessary copies and his action was dismissed as a result stated a court access claim); Canell v. Multnomah County, 141 F. Supp. 2d 1046, 1056 (D.Or. 2001) ("Officials must also provide photocopying when the plaintiff is obliged to provide copies in connection with the rights of action recognized under *Bounds*."); Giles v. Tate, 907 F. Supp. 1135, 1138 (S.D.Ohio 1995) (holding "some reasonable means of access to a photocopy machine" is required; prison's charge of 35 cents a page, without provision to advance funds against plaintiff's pay of $9.00 a month, denied the plaintiff court access because he could not pay for the medical records and other documents necessary to his civil rights suit; those facts sufficiently showed actual injury); Gluth v. Kangas, 951 F.2d at 1510 (upholding order requiring free photocopying for indigents); Harrington v. Holshouser, 741 F.2d 66, 69 (4th Cir. 1984) (free copying required for indigents); Johnson v. Parke, 642 F.2d 377, 379–80 (10th Cir. 1981) (refusal to make copies at prisoner's expense sufficient to comply with court rules may deny court access); *see also* Ramos v. Lamm, 485 F. Supp. 122, 166 (D.Colo. 1979) (access to photocopier might be required given the limited law library hours and other restrictions), *aff'd in pertinent part*, 639 F.2d 559 (10th Cir. 1980).

[555]Keenan v. Hall, 83 F.3d 1083, 1094 (9th Cir. 1996) (complaints of slow and expensive photocopying do not raise a constitutional

Access to notarial services must be reasonable but need not be continuous,[556] so don't wait until the last minute if you need to get documents notarized in time for a court deadline.

c. "Jailhouse Lawyers"   Some inmates—often referred to as "jailhouse lawyers" or "writ-writers"—try to help others with their legal problems even if they are not part of an official legal assistance program. The Supreme Court has held that prison authorities cannot prohibit prisoners from helping each other with legal matters unless they provide reasonable alternative forms of assistance.[557] But the opposite is also true:

if prison authorities *do* provide reasonable alternative assistance, they can obstruct or prohibit jailhouse lawyering,[558] or limit it to prisoners who have job assignments as inmate legal assistants or law clerks.[559] Since this limited right to jailhouse lawyering is generally part of the right to affirmative assistance described in *Bounds v. Smith* and limited in *Lewis v. Casey*, the *Lewis* "actual injury" requirement is applicable to claims of interference with jailhouse lawyering.[560]

Some courts have recognized an exception to these principles, holding: "Litigation undertaken in good faith by a prisoner motivated to bring about social change and protect constitutional rights in the prison is a 'form of political expression' and 'political association' much as the Supreme Court has held litigation to be for certain organizations outside the prison setting."[561] In that kind of case, a prisoner

---

issue absent specific instances of actual injury), *amended*, 135 F.3d 1318 (9th Cir. 1998); Scott v. Kelly, 107 F. Supp. 2d 706, 709 (E.D.Va. 2000) (holding prisoners do not have "unlimited rights to photocopies or photocopying machines"; there is no denial of court access claim unless the prisoner shows litigation was impeded), *aff'd*, 6 Fed. Appx. 187 (4th Cir. 2001) (unpublished); Beck v. Lynaugh, 842 F.2d 759, 762 (5th Cir. 1988); Jones v. Franzen, 697 F.2d 801, 803–04 (7th Cir. 1983); Gibson v. McEvers, 631 F.2d 95, 97–98 (7th Cir. 1980); Harrell v. Keohane, 621 F.2d 1059, 1061 (10th Cir. 1980); Rhodes v. Robinson, 612 F.2d 766, 771 (3d Cir. 1979) (including a profit margin in the price of copies did not deny court access); Hewes v. Magnusson, 350 F. Supp. 2d 222, 237 (D.Me. 2004) (a policy providing 100 free copies is not unconstitutional); Lyons v. Clark, 694 F. Supp. 184, 188 (E.D.Va. 1988), *aff'd*, 887 F.2d 1080 (4th Cir. 1990); Dugar v. Coughlin, 613 F. Supp. 849, 854 (S.D.N.Y. 1985).

Courts have held that if prisoners have access to carbon paper, restrictions on photocopying do not deny court access. Johnson v. Moore, 926 F.2d 921, 925 (9th Cir.), *dismissed as moot*, 948 F.2d 517 (9th Cir. 1991); Gittens v. Sullivan, 670 F. Supp. 119, 122 (S.D.N.Y. 1987), *aff'd*, 848 F.2d 389 (2d Cir. 1988); Salahuddin v. Coughlin, 591 F. Supp. 353, 361 (S.D.N.Y. 1984). Whether these cases are good law now, when carbon paper is almost extinct, we do not know.

[556]Dugar v. Coughlin, 613 F. Supp. 849, 854 (S.D.N.Y. 1985) (five days a week was not required); Robbins v. South, 595 F. Supp. 785, 789 (D.Mont. 1984) (two days a week was sufficient); Kendrick v. Bland, 586 F. Supp. at 1554 (delays in notarization were not unconstitutional); *see also* Rodriguez v. Barreiro, 165 A.D.2d 969, 561 N.Y.S.2d 857 (N.Y.App.Div. 1990) (notary services two days a week did not violate state regulations).

Keep in mind that in federal court and in some other federal proceedings, notarization is not required; you may submit a declaration under penalty of perjury under 28 U.S.C. § 1746. Duncan v. Foti, 828 F.2d 297 (5th Cir. 1987). One court has held that in a state whose statutes, like federal statutes, permitted the filing of non-notarized documents, refusal to notarize does not deny court access. Martin v. Davies, 917 F.2d 336, 341 (7th Cir. 1990).

[557]Johnson v. Avery, 393 U.S. 483, 490, 89 S. Ct. 747 (1969); *accord*, Bear v. Kautzky, 305 F.3d 802, 805 (8th Cir. 2002) (holding that evidence of inadequacy of contract lawyer program supported an injunction allowing assistance by jailhouse lawyers); Thaddeus-X v. Blatter, 175 F.3d 378, 395–96 (6th Cir. 1999) (en banc) (holding that allegations that a prisoner could not get help from the prison law librarians (who "are such in name only") or the state Prison Legal Services, and could not help himself with law books because he was ignorant of the law and in segregation where he could not go to the law library, supported a claim that he had a right to

assistance from a jailhouse lawyer); Munz v. Nix, 908 F.2d 267, 268 n.3 (8th Cir. 1990); Corpus v. Estelle, 551 F.2d 68 (5th Cir. 1977); Wetmore v. Fields, 458 F. Supp. 1131, 1144 (W.D.Wis. 1978); Wade v. Kane, 448 F. Supp. 678, 684 (E.D.Pa. 1978), *aff'd*, 591 F.2d 1338 (3d Cir. 1979).

Jailhouse lawyers are viewed by many courts as having standing to assert the rights of the inmates who need their help. Rhodes v. Robinson, 612 F.2d 766, 769 (3d Cir. 1979); Buise v. Hudkins, 584 F.2d 223, 227–28 (7th Cir. 1978); Munz v. Nix, 908 F.2d 267, 268 n.3 (8th Cir. 1990). *But see* Goff v. Nix, 113 F.3d 887, 890 (8th Cir. 1997) (holding that jailhouse lawyers transferred away from their "clients" did not have standing to assert the clients' claims without a finding that the clients could not find other assistants or means of court access); Gometz v. Henman, 807 F.2d 113, 115 (7th Cir. 1986) (questioning earlier standing decisions); Adams v. James, 784 F.2d 1077, 1080 (11th Cir. 1986) ("In a non-class-action context a prisoner has no standing to litigate another prisoner's claim of denial of access to the courts."). *See* Ch. 8, § I.1, concerning standing.

[558]Shaw v. Murphy, 532 U.S. 223, 231 n.3, 121 S. Ct. 1475 (2001); Herron v. Harrison, 203 F.3d 410, 415 (6th Cir. 2000) (stating that "an inmate does not generally have an independent right to help other prisoners with their legal claims. . . . Such assistance is protected, however, when the inmate receiving the assistance would otherwise be unable to pursue legal redress."); Smith v. Maschner, 899 F.2d 940, 950 (10th Cir. 1990); Gassler v. Rayl, 862 F.2d 706, 708 & n.3 (8th Cir. 1988); Flittie v. Solem, 827 F.2d 276, 280 (8th Cir. 1987); Gallipeau v. Berard, 734 F. Supp. 48, 53 (D.R.I. 1990); Farmer v. Carlson, 685 F. Supp. 1335, 1344–45 (M.D.Pa. 1988); Jeffries v. Reed, 631 F. Supp. 1212, 1217 (E.D.Wash. 1986); Graham v. Hutto, 437 F. Supp. 118, 119 (E.D.Va. 1977), *appeal dismissed*, 571 F.2d 575 (4th Cir. 1978).

[559]Sizemore v. Lee, 20 F. Supp. 2d 956, 958–59 (W.D.Va. 1998) (holding that a prisoner who had paralegal training could be disciplined for refusing to stop giving legal help to other prisoners, since the prison has a law library with inmate law clerks), *appeal dismissed*, 173 F.3d 425 (4th Cir. 1999).

[560]Bass v. Singletary, 143 F.3d 1442, 1445–46 (11th Cir. 1998) (holding policy that inhibited mutual legal assistance by barring prisoners from possessing legal papers with other prisoners' names on them did not deny access to courts without evidence of harm to particular litigation).

[561]Adams v. James, 784 F.2d 1077, 1081 (11th Cir. 1986); *accord*, Smith v. Maschner, 899 F.2d 940, 950 (10th Cir. 1990); Osterback v. Kemp, 300 F. Supp. 2d 1238, 1240, 1254 (N.D.Fla. 2003)

helping someone else would be exercising his own First Amendment rights as well as the other prisoner's.

Even where jailhouse lawyering is not against the rules, jailhouse lawyers may be disciplined for their activities if they violate other prison rules, if doing so meets the *Turner v. Safley* standard of reasonable relationship to a legitimate penological interest.[562] However, prison officials may not retaliate against prisoners who give legal assistance if they do not break prison rules in doing so.[563] Nor may they apply disciplinary rules to punish prisoners who give legal assistance for conduct that they had no prior notice was prohibited.[564]

Jailhouse lawyers may be required to obey reasonable rules governing their activities.[565] They are not really lawyers and do not have the right to practice law as a lawyer would. They need not be allowed to assist other inmates in court or to file papers on their behalf.[566] In general, communications between "jailhouse lawyers" and their inmate "clients" are not privileged,[567] although some courts have suggested that the activities of prison-sponsored legal assistance programs are entitled to more confidentiality.[568] Correspondence between jailhouse lawyers and their "clients" is entitled to no more constitutional protection than any other inmate–inmate correspondence.[569] Prison authorities may prohibit

---

(applying *Adams v. James* holding to prisoner transferred for filing a bar grievance against the prison law librarian), *on reconsideration,* Osterback v. Kemp, 300 F. Supp. 2d 1263 (N.D.Fla. 2003).

[562]Shaw v. Murphy, 532 U.S. at 229–31. In *Shaw,* an inmate law clerk—knowing his services had been requested—wrote to an inmate in segregation and advised him that the officer on whose word he was being prosecuted had a record of misconduct, and the other prisoner's defense lawyer should contact the clerk about it. The clerk was charged with "insolence" and "interference with due process hearings." The Supreme Court did not decide the question whether the clerk could be disciplined. It held generally that there is no special protection for legal assistance that is greater than the protection of any other kind of speech by prisoners under *Turner v. Safley,* 482 U.S. 78, 107 S. Ct. 2254 (1987), and left the final determination to the lower courts.

[563]Auleta v. LaFrance, 233 F. Supp. 2d 396, 400 (N.D.N.Y. 2002) (holding that there is no legitimate interest under *Turner* in punishing prisoners for providing authorized assistance to other prisoners; plaintiff was assigned as an inmate legal assistant); Adams v. James, 784 F.2d at 1880–82; Buise v. Hudkins, Buise v. Hudkins, 584 F.2d 223, 227–31 (7th Cir. 1978); Vaughn v. Trotter, 516 F. Supp. 886, 893–99 (M.D.Tenn. 1980); Wetmore v. Fields, 458 F. Supp. 1131, 1145 (W.D.Wis. 1978).

[564]Newell v. Sauser, 79 F.3d 115, 117–18 (9th Cir. 1995) (holding an inmate law librarian, who was authorized to help other prisoners with their legal work, could not be disciplined for possessing other prisoners' legal papers under a rule forbidding possession of anything not authorized or issued by the prison); *see* Shaw v. Murphy, 532 U.S. at 232–33 (Ginsburg, J., concurring) (noting the plaintiff's allegations that rules forbidding insolence and interference with due process hearings were vague and overbroad as applied to his providing legal advice to another prisoner). The requirement that disciplinary rules give adequate notice of what is prohibited is discussed in Ch. 8, § H.1.q.

[565]Johnson v. Avery, 393 U.S. 483, 490, 89 S. Ct. 747 (1969) (time and location of legal activities can be regulated); Weaver v. Toombs, 756 F. Supp. 335, 340 (W.D.Mich. 1989) (legal materials could be confiscated from inmates who had not complied with the rules for inmate–inmate legal assistance), *aff'd,* 915 F.2d 1574 (6th Cir. 1990); Smith v. Halford, 570 F. Supp. 1187, 1194 (D.Kan. 1983) (prisoner could be transferred for refusing to abide by time limits on legal assistance to others). *But see* People ex rel. Hicks v. James, 150 Misc.2d 950, 571 N.Y.S.2d 367, 369 (N.Y.Sup. 1991) (once an inmate has received permission to act as a law clerk, permission cannot be withdrawn arbitrarily).

[566]Bonacci v. Kindt, 868 F.2d 1442, 1443 (5th Cir. 1989); Storseth v. Spellman, 654 F.2d 1349, 1355 (9th Cir. 1981) (jailhouse lawyers may assist in preparing and filing pleadings but may not file them on behalf of others); *see also* Thomas v. Estelle, 603 F.2d 488, 489 (5th Cir.) (appeals court lacked jurisdiction over appeal by jailhouse lawyer on behalf of another inmate), *rehearing denied,* 606 F.2d 321 (5th Cir. 1979); Williams v. Frame, 145 F.R.D. 65 (E.D.Pa. 1992) (complaint submitted by two prisoners must be signed by both because one non-attorney cannot act in behalf of another); Cummings v. Chiles, 600 So.2d 1135, 1137 (Fla.App. 1992) (jailhouse lawyer helping another inmate need not be served with litigation papers in that inmate's case). *But see* Santiago v. C.O. Campisi Shield 4592, 91 F. Supp. 2d 665, 671 (S.D.N.Y. 2000) (refusing defendants' request to disregard papers prepared for the plaintiff by another prisoner, and submitted by that prisoner without the plaintiff's signature after the plaintiff had been transferred and could not sign them).

On rare occasions, courts have permitted in-court representation of one prisoner by another. Williamson v. State of Indiana, Dep't of Correction, 577 F. Supp. 983 (N.D.Ind. 1984); Thurman v. Rose, 575 F. Supp. 1488, 1489 n.1 (N.D.Ind. 1983). However, courts have also expressed disapproval of this practice, *see* Hahn v. McLey, 737 F.2d 771, 772 (8th Cir. 1984); Miller v. Duffin, 637 F. Supp. 496, 498 (N.D.Ind. 1986), *aff'd,* 812 F.2d 1410 (7th Cir. 1989), and it is unlikely to be allowed.

[567]Storseth v. Spellman, 654 F.2d 1349, 1356 (9th Cir. 1981); Moorhead v. Lane, 125 F.R.D. 680, 686 (C.D.Ill. 1989); People v. Velasquez, 192 Cal.App.3d 319, 237 Cal.Rptr. 366, 371 (1987); People v. Barber, 116 Ill.App.3d 767, 72 Ill.Dec. 472, 452 N.E.2d 725, 731–32 (Ill.App. 1983); State v. Spell, 399 So.2d 551, 556 (La. 1981); Richardson v. Texas, 744 S.W.2d 65, 74–75 (Tex.Cr.App. 1987), *vacated on other grounds,* 492 U.S. 914 (1989).

[568]*See* Knop v. Johnson, 685 F. Supp. 636, 641–42 (W.D.Mich. 1988) (searches of legal access program offices must be limited to protect privacy of legal papers), *aff'd in part and rev'd in part on other grounds,* 977 F.2d 996 (6th Cir. 1992); Walker v. Johnson, 544 F. Supp. 345, 365 (E.D.Mich. 1982) (officials directed to stop screening legal material circulated between inmates and jailhouse lawyers), *aff'd in part and rev'd in part on other grounds sub nom.* Walker v. Mintzes, 771 F.2d 920 (6th Cir. 1985). *But see* State v. Spell, 399 So.2d at 556 (communications with inmate assigned to assist other inmates in the law library were not privileged); People v. Brisbon, 89 Ill.App.3d 513, 44 Ill.Dec. 590, 411 N.E.2d 956, 964 (Ill.App. 1980) (if a privilege existed, it did not apply to statements unrelated to the case the prison law clerk was helping with).

[569]Shaw v. Murphy, 532 U.S. 223, 230–31, 121 S. Ct. 1475 (2001); *see* Turner v. Safley, 482 U.S. 78, 91–93, 107 S. Ct. 2254 (1987) (holding inmate–inmate correspondence may be prohibited entirely). *But see* Goff v. Nix, 113 F.3d 887, 890–92 (8th Cir. 1997) (upholding policy prohibiting legal correspondence between

jailhouse lawyers from charging fees.[570] Courts may enjoin the activities of particular jailhouse lawyers if they abuse the judicial process.[571]

One court has held that co-plaintiffs in litigation have a limited constitutional right to meet to discuss their joint litigation.[572]

Whether prisoners have a right to organize to discuss legal issues, unrelated to providing assistance in specific cases, is unsettled.[573]

3. Legal Communication and Privacy

Prisoners have long been held entitled to unobstructed and confidential communication with courts and with attorneys and their assistants.[574] Interference with such communications may violate the right of court access.[575] However, court

access claims require that the plaintiff show actual injury to a non-frivolous legal claim.[576] You will not be able to show this if your claim is about communicating with a lawyer for advice or assistance about a non-litigation matter, or just to find out if you have a non-frivolous claim, or if you are able to litigate your claim despite interference or intrusion in your communications with counsel.[577]

It makes much more sense to plead a claim about communication with attorneys as a simple First Amendment claim.

> The right to hire and consult an attorney is protected by the First Amendment's guarantee of freedom of speech, association and petition.... [T]he state cannot impede an individual's ability to consult with counsel on legal matters.... Furthermore, the right to obtain legal advice does not depend on the purpose for which the advice was sought.... In sum, the First Amendment protects the right of an individual or group to consult with an attorney on any legal matter.[578]

---

prisoners at different facilities, but striking down prohibition on jailhouse lawyers' returning documents to their owners after transfer); *see also* § B.1.b concerning inmate–inmate legal correspondence.

[570]Johnson v. Avery, 393 U.S. 483, 490, 89 S. Ct. 747 (1969); Henderson v. Ricketts, 499 F. Supp. 1066, 1068–69 (D.Colo. 1980).

[571]Storseth v. Spellman, 654 F.2d 1349, 1354 (9th Cir. 1981) (court properly enjoined "writ writer" from interfering in a case in which the court had appointed an attorney); Matter of Green, 586 F.2d 1247, 1251–53 (8th Cir. 1978); *In re* Tyler, 677 F. Supp. 1410, 1414 (D.Neb. 1987) (prisoner who had abused court system barred from drafting complaints for other inmates), *aff'd*, 839 F.2d 1290 (8th Cir. 1988).

The power of courts to limit prisoners' ability to use the courts is discussed at greater length in Ch. 10, § X.

[572]Dooley v. Quick, 598 F. Supp. 607, 617–18 (D.R.I. 1984) (prison officials must formulate rules defining when such meetings will be permitted), *aff'd*, 787 F.2d 579 (1st Cir. 1986). *But see* Beck v. Lynaugh, 842 F.2d 759, 762 (5th Cir. 1988) (upholding denial of such meetings in segregation unit).

[573]Nicholas v. Miller, 189 F.3d 191, 195 (2d Cir. 1999) (per curiam) ("We express no view as to the extent, if any, that a First Amendment associational right could protect the right to associate for the purpose of discussing law-related issues short of practicing law....").

[574]Procunier v. Martinez, 416 U.S. 396, 419-22, 94 S. Ct.1800 (1974) (interviewing privileges must be extended to law students and paralegals employed by attorneys); *Ex parte* Hull, 312 U.S. 546, 549, 61 S. Ct. 640 (1941) (striking down regulation permitting prison officials to screen prisoners' submissions to court); Simkins v. Bruce, 406 F.3d 1239, 1243 (10th Cir. 2005) (". . . [T]he principle that unimpeded transmission of inmate legal mail is the 'most obvious and formal manifestation' of the right of access to the courts, . . . has been clearly established for some time now."); Smith v. Coughlin, 748 F.2d 783, 789 (2d Cir. 1984) (refusal to permit visiting by paralegal was unconstitutional); Orantes-Hernandez v. Smith, 541 F. Supp. 351, 385 (C.D.Cal. 1982) (interviews by paralegals must be permitted); *see also* § B.1.b of this chapter for a discussion of "privileged" legal mail.

[575]*See, e.g.*, U.S. v. Mikhel, 552 F.3d 961, 963–64 (9th Cir. 2009) (striking down "Special Administrative Measures" barring use of translator at interviews and barring public defender's investigator from meeting with criminal defendant without an attorney or paralegal present); Simkins v. Bruce, 406 F.3d 1239, 1242–44

(10th Cir. 2005) (holding that failure to forward legal mail, as prison procedure required, to a prisoner temporarily held in a county jail, resulting in his failing to receive notice and to respond to a summary judgment motion, denied the right of access to court); Gramegna v. Johnson, 846 F.2d 675, 677 (11th Cir. 1988) (allowing inmate mail to accumulate at a central location until "a sizable bundle has amassed," then forwarding it, violated the right of access to courts of a prisoner who missed his appeal deadline as a result of a six-week delay caused by this policy).

[576]Lewis v. Casey, 518 U.S. 343, 351–53, 116 S. Ct. 2174 (1996); *see* Gardner v. Howard, 109 F.3d 427, 431 (8th Cir. 1997) ("The act of opening incoming mail does not injure an inmate's right to access the courts. The policy that incoming confidential legal mail should be opened in inmates' presence instead serves the prophylactic purpose of assuring them that confidential attorney–client mail has not been improperly read in the guise of searching for contraband."). The actual injury requirement is discussed at § C.1.a.1 of this chapter.

[577]Oliver v. Fauver, 118 F.3d 175, 177–78 (3d Cir. 1997) (opening of legal mail does not deny court access without a showing of actual injury to legal claims; this plaintiff's papers arrived in court and his claim was adjudicated); Thomsen v. Ross, 368 F. Supp. 2d 961, 973–75 (D.Minn. 2005) (improper opening of legal correspondence did not deny access to court without a showing of actual injury to legal claims); Arney v. Simmons, 26 F. Supp. 2d 1288, 1296–97 (D.Kan. 1998) (holding that monitoring attorney–client telephone calls would not deny access to courts in the absence of actual injury as required by *Lewis v. Casey*); Williams v. Price, 25 F. Supp. 2d 605, 619 (W.D.Pa. 1997) (holding confidentiality of attorney–client communications does not present a court access claim after *Lewis v. Casey*; it must be asserted under the First Amendment, Sixth Amendment, or the due process right of privacy).

Invasion of legal privacy can inflict "actual injury" under some circumstances. *See* Cody v. Weber, 256 F.3d 764, 768–69 (8th Cir. 2001) (holding allegation that defendants obtained an unfair advantage in defending themselves against his claims by reading his legal papers stated a court access claim).

[578]Denius v. Dunlap, 209 F.3d 944, 954 (7th Cir. 2000); *accord*, Poole v. County of Otero, 271 F.3d 955, 961 (10th Cir. 2001)

The First Amendment right to consult with an attorney has been recognized in prison cases as well,[579] and it is not subject to the *Lewis v. Casey* requirements that the challenged action have caused actual injury by impeding the litigation of a non-frivolous legal claim concerning prison conditions or a criminal conviction or sentence.[580]

If you have pending criminal charges, you are additionally protected by the Sixth Amendment right to the effective assistance of counsel, and jail procedures that cause "unreasonable interference with the accused person's ability to consult counsel" violate that right.[581] Sixth Amendment claims, unlike court access claims, do not require a showing of actual injury to a non-frivolous claim.[582] However, such a claim will be subject to all the limitations of the Sixth Amendment right to counsel.[583]

At least one court has held that restrictions on attorney telephone calls that prevent a detainee from making bail can violate the Fourteenth Amendment's Due Process Clause.[584]

Whether viewed as court access, free speech, or Sixth Amendment issues, "[r]egulations and practices that unjustifiably obstruct the availability of professional representation . . . are invalid."[585] The right to communicate with lawyers "is not limited to those already represented by an attorney, but extends equally to prisoners seeking any form of legal advice or assistance."[586] Prisons and jails must provide reasonable schedules and facilities for legal visits[587] and must provide for them to be conducted confidentially.[588]

("First Amendment rights of association and free speech extend to the right to retain and consult with an attorney."); Cipriani v. Lycoming Housing Auth., 177 F. Supp. 2d 303, 324 (M.D.Pa. 2001).

[579]*See* Massey v. Wheeler, 221 F.3d 1030, 1035–36 (7th Cir. 2000) (acknowledging attorney's First Amendment claim, though rejecting it on the merits); Sturm v. Clark, 835 F.2d 1009, 1015 and n.3 (3d Cir. 1987) (holding special restrictions on one attorney's prisoner consultation stated a violation of her First Amendment rights); Williams v. Price, 25 F. Supp. 2d 623, 629–30 (W.D.Pa. 1998) (holding that lack of confidentiality in attorney–client consultation violated the First Amendment). In *Cassels v. Stalder*, 342 F. Supp. 2d 555 (M.D.La. 2004), the plaintiff complained to his mother about his medical care; when she put the information on the Internet in an effort to find him a lawyer, prison officials disciplined him for "spreading rumors." The court held that this action was an unconstitutional restriction on the right to seek legal assistance. 342 F. Supp. 2d at 564–67.

[580]Al-Amin v. Smith, 511 F.3d 1317, 1334 (11th Cir. 2008), *cert. denied*, 129 S. Ct. 104 (2008); Jones v. Brown, 461 F.3d 353, 359–60 (3d Cir. 2006), *cert. denied*, 549 U.S. 1286 (2007).

[581]Benjamin v. Fraser, 264 F.3d 175, 185–86 (2d Cir. 2001) (requiring improvements in attorney visiting procedures that imposed unnecessary delays); *see* Simpson v. Gallant, 231 F. Supp. 2d 341, 348–49 (D.Me. 2002) (holding a claim of inability to use the jail telephone to seek the assistance of counsel states a Sixth Amendment claim).

[582]U.S. v. Mikhel, 552 F.3d 961, 963–64 (9th Cir. 2009) (striking down "Special Administrative Measures" barring use of translator at interviews as violating criminal defendant's Sixth Amendment and due process rights); Benjamin v. Fraser, 264 F.3d at 186 ("It is not clear to us what 'actual injury' would even mean as applied to a pretrial detainee's right to counsel."); Jones v. City and County of San Francisco, 976 F. Supp. 896, 913–14 & n.17 (N.D.Cal. 1997) (pre-trial detainees could pursue Sixth Amendment claim even if they did not show injury required for court access claim); *see* Iqbal v. Hasty, 490 F.3d 143, 170 (2d Cir. 2007) (detainee's allegations of interference with attorney–client communication pled a Sixth Amendment claim), *aff'd in part, rev'd in part, and remanded on other grounds sub nom.* Ashcroft v. Iqbal, __ U.S. __, 129 S. Ct. 1937 (2009).

[583]*See* Lumley v. City of Dade City, Florida, 327 F.3d 1186, 1195 (11th Cir. 2003) (holding the refusal to let an arrestee see a lawyer while he was held in a hospital under guard after arrest did

not violate the Sixth Amendment because the prosecution did not formally start until after he was out of the hospital).

[584]Simpson v. Gallant, 231 F. Supp. 2d 341, 348 (D.Me. 2002).

[585]Procunier v. Martinez, 416 U.S. 396, 419, 94 S. Ct. 1800 (1974); *accord*, Benjamin v. Fraser, 264 F.3d at 184; *see* Foster v. Basham, 932 F.2d 732, 734–35 (8th Cir. 1991) (removal of telephone directory pages listing attorneys was unconstitutional); Sims v. Brierton, 500 F. Supp. 813, 815–17 (N.D.Ill. 1980) (prisoner must be allowed to meet with law student assistant to prepare for his deposition without being subjected to a strip search).

[586]Ruiz v. Estelle, 503 F. Supp. 1265, 1372 (S.D.Tex. 1980), *aff'd in pertinent part, rev'd on other grounds*, 679 F.2d 1115, 1153–55 (5th Cir. 1982).

[587]Benjamin v. Fraser, 264 F.3d 175, 187–88 (2d Cir. 2001) (affirming relief against delays in counsel visiting for which defendants provided no security or other justification); Orantes-Hernandez v. Smith, 541 F. Supp. 351, 384 (C.D.Cal. 1982) (immigration detainees held at an isolated location are entitled to receive legal visits at night); Nunez v. Boldin, 537 F. Supp. 578, 582 (S.D.Tex.) (same), *appeal dismissed*, 692 F.2d 755 (5th Cir. 1982); Jones v. Wittenberg, 440 F. Supp. 60, 64 (N.D.Ohio 1977) (attorney consultation facilities ordered renovated for contact visits, soundproofed, and provided with adequate ventilation and furnishings); Mitchell v. Untreiner, 421 F. Supp. 886, 902 (N.D.Fla. 1976) (attorneys must be permitted to visit within 12 hours of arrest and from 6:00 a.m. to 10:00 p.m. daily); Inmates of the Suffolk County Jail v. Eisenstadt, 360 F. Supp. 676, 689–90 (D.Mass. 1973) (jail must provide evening and weekend counsel visits), *aff'd*, 494 F.2d 1196 (1st Cir. 1974); Collins v. Schoonfield, 344 F. Supp. 257, 280–81 (D.Md. 1972) ("lack of facilitation on an unreasonable basis" of attorney visits violates the Constitution).

[588]Johnson-El v. Schoemehl, 878 F.2d 1043, 1051–52 (8th Cir. 1989); Ruiz v. Estelle, 679 F.2d 1115, 1154–55 (5th Cir. 1982); Dawson v. Kendrick, 527 F. Supp. 1252, 1314 (S.D.W.Va. 1981); Nicholson v. Choctaw County, Ala., 498 F. Supp. 295, 310 (S.D.Ala. 1980); Jones v. Wittenberg, 440 F. Supp. 60, 64 (N.D.Ohio 1977) (attorney consultation facilities ordered soundproofed); Moore v. Janing, 427 F. Supp. 567, 575–76 (D.Neb. 1976); Mitchell v. Untreiner, 421 F. Supp. 886, 902 (N.D.Fla. 1976); People v. Torres, 218 Cal. App.3d 700, 219 Cal.App.3d 234C, 267 Cal.Rptr. 213, 217–18 (Cal. App. 1990) (privacy was required even when prison officials had confidential information that the attorney might be involved in an escape attempt; restrictions such as searches and non-contact visits could be imposed); *see also* Sturm v. Clark, 835 F.2d 1009, 1015 n.13 (3d Cir. 1987) (officers' reading of confidential correspondence in visiting attorney's briefcase raised issues of attorney–client privilege and the attorney's First Amendment rights). *But see* Lopez v.

Legal visits must be permitted to all inmates,[589] and they must generally be contact visits,[590] though courts have upheld non-contact visits in particularly secure prisons or units[591] or for persons whom officials believed presented particular risks.[592] Reasonable telephone access to counsel is required for pre-trial detainees and possibly for convicts as well.[593] Transfers of pre-trial detainees to remote locations may violate their rights if access to counsel is obstructed,[594] though the remedy may be to improve access rather than to rescind the transfer.[595] Other inconvenient restrictions that do not actually obstruct court access are generally upheld.[596]

Prisoners may communicate with attorneys of their choice; prison officials may not impose special restrictions on attorneys they do not like.[597] Prisoners may not be restricted to communicating with the counsel of record in their criminal cases.[598] In particular, prisoners may consult with legal staff of prisoners' rights groups and other advocacy organizations[599] and with attorneys handling class action litigation about prison conditions.[600] However, legal

---

Robinson, 914 F.2d 486, 494 (4th Cir. 1990) (privacy was sufficient where attorney visits could be visually observed by officers but not overheard, listened to, or recorded).

[589]Inmates of the Suffolk County Jail v. Eisenstadt, 360 F. Supp. at 693 (inmates in isolation cannot be denied legal visits); Collins v. Schoonfield, 344 F. Supp. at 269 (non-suicidal inmates and inmates not presenting an immediate threat to life, safety, or property may not be denied attorney visits as a means of discipline); see also Giampetruzzi v. Malcolm, 406 F. Supp. 836, 845 (S.D.N.Y. 1975) (administrative segregation inmates may confer with their attorneys in such numbers as may be shown necessary to prepare their defenses).

[590]Ching v. Lewis, 895 F.2d 608, 610 (9th Cir. 1990); Jones v. Wittenberg, 440 F. Supp. 60, 64 (N.D.Ohio 1977) (ordering attorney consultation facilities renovated for contact visits).

[591]Casey v. Lewis, 4 F.3d 1516, 1520–24 (9th Cir. 1993) (upholding denial of contact attorney visits to prisoners in lockdown units); Mitchell v. Dixon, 862 F. Supp. 95, 96–97 (E.D.N.C., Aug. 18, 1994) (upholding denial of contact attorney visits in state's most secure prison); Jeffries v. Reed, 631 F. Supp. 1212, 1218 (E.D.Wash. 1986) (upholding denial of contact attorney visits to prisoners in capital unit).

[592]McMaster v. Pung, 984 F.2d 948, 953 (8th Cir. 1993) (upholding ban on contact visits with female attorney who had been observed engaging in sexual activity with prisoner); Williams v. Wyrick, 747 F.2d 1231, 1232 (8th Cir. 1984) (investigator who worked for the prisoner, not an attorney, could be required to visit in the non-contact general visiting area); People v. Torres, 218 Cal. App.3d 700, 219 Cal.App.3d 234C, 267 Cal.Rptr. 213, 217–18 (Cal. App. 1990) (non-contact attorney visit could be required when jail officials had information that attorney presented a security risk).

[593]See § B.8 of this chapter for a discussion of telephone access.

[594]Covino v. Vermont Dep't of Corrections, 933 F.2d 128, 130 (2d Cir. 1991) (court should examine whether transfer impaired the right to counsel); Cobb v. Aytch, 643 F.2d 946, 957–62 (3d Cir. 1981) (transfer of pre-trial detainees to state prison impinged on Sixth Amendment rights; notice and a hearing required). But see U.S. v. Johnson, 225 F. Supp. 2d 982, 1006 (N.D.Iowa 2002) (holding that detainee's placement was not an "unjustifiable obstruction" of representation); Mingo v. Patterson, 455 F. Supp. 1358, 1361–62 (D.Colo. 1978) (transfer of detainee between jails upheld as long as attorney was not barred from the new jail).

Transfers are discussed further in Ch. 4, § H.4.

[595]Johnson by Johnson v. Brelje, 701 F.2d 1201, 1207–08 (7th Cir. 1983) (increased telephone access required); U.S. v. Parker-Taramona, 778 F. Supp. 21, 22–23 (D.Haw. 1991) (permitting Hawaiian detainees to be transferred to the mainland, but requiring the government to return them 21 days before trial and to pay for their lawyers to travel to visit them).

[596]Bruscino v. Carlson, 854 F.2d 162, 167 (7th Cir. 1988) (delays in arranging for legal visits to a maximum security prison did not deny court access); Campbell v. Miller, 787 F.2d 217, 225–27 (7th Cir. 1986) (restriction of attorney visits in maximum security Control Unit to Thursday through Sunday and requirement of 24 hours' notice upheld). But see Benjamin v. Fraser, 264 F.3d 175, 187–88 (2d Cir. 2001) (affirming relief against delays in counsel visiting for which defendants provided no security or other justification).

Strip searches in connection with attorney visits have drawn mixed results from the courts. Compare Williams v. Price, 25 F. Supp. 2d 605, 615 (W.D.Pa. 1997) and cases cited (requiring visual strip searches before and after non-contact counsel visits does not violate the Fourth Amendment in capital unit) with Wood v. Hancock County, 245 F. Supp. 2d 231, 239 (D.Me. 2003) (jails are not automatically entitled to strip search prisoners after contact visits with attorneys; they must present evidence about the jail population, the facility's experience with contraband (especially in connection with contact visits, in particular with attorneys), how contact visits work, whether the plaintiff had access to other prisoners, etc.).

[597]Sturm v. Clark, 835 F.2d 1009, 1015 (3d Cir. 1987) (allegation that attorney was restricted because she had publicized staff misconduct stated a First Amendment claim); Cruz v. Beto, 603 F.2d 1178, 1180–81, 1186 (5th Cir. 1979) (damages awarded against officials who cut off access to a particular attorney and punished inmates who remained her clients).

[598]Ruiz v. Estelle, 503 F. Supp. 1265, 1372 (S.D.Tex. 1980), aff'd in pertinent part, rev'd on other grounds, 679 F.2d 1115, 1153–55 (5th Cir. 1982) (citing Nolan v. Scafati, 430 F.2d 548 (1st Cir. 1970)); Manicone v. Cleary, No. 74-575 (E.D.N.Y., June 30, 1975), Memorandum and Opinion (unreported) at 13, 38.

[599]Abel v. Miller, 824 F.2d 1522, 1534 (7th Cir. 1987) (staff of a prisoners' rights organization could not be barred from visiting and correspondence in response to their criticisms and litigation); Jean v. Nelson, 711 F.2d 1455, 1508–09 (11th Cir. 1982) (attorneys for Haitian Refugee Center had a right to inform Haitians detained by Immigration and Naturalization Service of their legal rights), on rehearing, 727 F.2d 957 (11th Cir. 1984) (en banc), rev'd on other grounds, 472 U.S. 846 (1985); Dreher v. Sielaff, 636 F.2d 1141, 1145 (7th Cir. 1980) (prison officials should be directed to prepare a plan for reasonable access by staff of Prison Legal Aid program).

[600]McClendon v. City of Albuquerque, 272 F. Supp. 2d 1250, 1258 (D.N.M. 2003) (newly imposed five-minute limit on calls to attorneys, combined with ban on visits by class counsel, would "unjustifiably obstruct the availability of professional representation" and deny access to courts); Valvano v. McGrath, 325 F. Supp. 408, 412 (E.D.N.Y. 1971).

A number of courts have entered unreported orders enjoining prison officials from interfering with class counsel's interviews of

visitors may be barred if they have engaged in serious misconduct.[601] At least one court has held that prisoners are not entitled to meet as a group with an attorney.[602]

Prisoners have a right of privacy in their legal communications, though courts have said different things about the basis of the right. Invasion of attorney–client privacy[603] will not usually present a court access claim, since usually it will not cause the kind of "actual injury" required under *Lewis v. Casey*.[604] This right of privacy, like the right to communicate with lawyers, is probably best viewed as a First Amendment right.[605] Invasion of attorney–client privacy may also be viewed as an unreasonable search under the Fourth Amendment.[606] It may violate a Fourteenth Amendment right of privacy.[607] It may also invade the attorney–client

privilege.[608] The right of privacy in attorney–client communications applies whether the communication is by visit,[609] telephone,[610] or mail. Privileged legal correspondence may not be read by prison officials or opened outside the prisoner's presence.[611] Nor may prison staff read prisoners' legal papers under other circumstances such as cell searches,[612] though they may search them for contraband.[613] The Supreme Court's holding that prisoners have no general expectation of privacy in their living quarters, and that there is no Fourth Amendment claim based on unreasonable cell

---

clients and witnesses. *See, e.g.,* Brenneman v. Madigan, No. C-70 1911AJ2 (N.D.Cal., November 16, 1970), Findings of Fact and Conclusions of Law in Support of Preliminary Injunction at 3; Smith v. Carberry, No. C-70 1244LHB (N.D.Cal., August 5, 1970), Preliminary Injunction at 2; Wayne County Jail Inmates v. Wayne County Board of Commissioners, Civil Action No. 71-173217-C (Mich.Circuit Ct., Dec. 1, 1975), Order Granting Plaintiffs' Motion for Limited Access to the County Jail.

[601]Crusoe v. DeRobertis, 714 F.2d 752, 756–57 (7th Cir. 1983) (paralegal who had engaged in misconduct could be barred from prison); Phillips v. Bureau of Prisons, 591 F.2d 966, 970–76 (D.C. Cir. 1979) (ex-inmate paralegal could be barred based on his prison disciplinary record); Reed v. Evans, 455 F. Supp. 1139, 1143 (S.D.Ga. 1978) (a paralegal who had falsely claimed to be an attorney could be excluded), *aff'd,* 592 F.2d 1189 (5th Cir. 1979); *see* McMaster v. Pung, 984 F.2d 948, 953 (8th Cir. 1993) (attorney who had engaged in sexual activity with a prisoner could be denied contact visits); Benson v. County of Orange, 788 F. Supp. 1123, 1126 (C.D.Cal. 1992) (annual "background checks" of counsel before their admission to visiting are not unconstitutional).

[602]Boyd v. Anderson, 265 F. Supp. 2d 952, 969 (N.D.Ind. 2003).

[603]Communications with inmate legal assistants or "jailhouse lawyers" are not privileged, though some courts have granted them some protections under certain circumstances. *See* § C.2.c. of this chapter, nn.567–569.

[604]*See* nn.576–577 in this section.

[605]Denius v. Dunlap, 209 F.3d 944, 954 (7th Cir. 2000) ("Because the maintenance of confidentiality in attorney-client communications is vital to the ability of an attorney to effectively counsel her client, interference with this confidentiality impedes the client's First Amendment, [sic] right to obtain legal advice."); Sturm v. Clark, 835 F.2d 1009, 1015 n.13 (3d Cir. 1987) (reading of prisoner's legal correspondence in attorney's briefcase raised a First Amendment issue); Williams v. Price, 25 F. Supp. 2d 623, 629–30 (W.D.Pa. 1998) (holding that lack of confidentiality in attorney-client consultation violated the First Amendment).

[606]*See* Lonegan v. Hasty, 436 F. Supp. 2d 419, 433–36 (E.D.N.Y. 2006) and cases cited (attorneys had an expectation of privacy in attorney-client consultation based on attorney-client privilege, and did not lose it because the communications took place in a prison).

[607]*See* Williams v. Price, 25 F. Supp. 2d 623, 628 (W.D.Pa. 1998).

[608]This point is a little confusing. The above-cited cases holding that attorney–client privacy is protected by the First or Fourth Amendment base their decisions in part on the attorney–client privilege and its importance. *See* Denius v. Dunlap, 209 F.3d at 953–54; Lonegan v. Hasty, 436 F. Supp. at 434. However, courts may enforce the attorney–client privilege independently of any constitutional interest. U.S. v. DeFonte, 441 F.3d 92, 94 (2d Cir. 2006) (per curiam) (prisoners retain the attorney–client privilege regardless of whether there is a Fourth Amendment expectation of privacy); Gomez v. Vernon, 255 F.3d 1118, 1131–34 (9th Cir. 2001) (attorney–client privilege is a matter of federal common law; court imposes sanctions on prison officials' counsel for reading prisoners' legal privileged correspondence).

The attorney–client privilege does have limits. There is a "crime-fraud exception" to the attorney–client privilege under which communications that are made for an unlawful purpose or to further an illegal scheme are not privileged. *See* U.S. v. Lentz, 419 Supp.2d 820, 829–32 (E.D.Va. 2005) and cases cited.

The attorney–client privilege can be waived if you do not keep the communications private. *See, e.g.,* Commonwealth v. Boyd, 397 Pa.Super. 468, 580 A.2d 393, 394 (Pa.Super. 1990) (attorney–client privilege did not apply to a letter the prisoner hung on his cell wall). However, you do not waive the privilege just because the limitations of prison life make it impossible to for you to maintain absolute privacy. Gomez v. Vernon, 255 F.3d 1118, 1133 (9th Cir. 2001) (where prisoners did what they could to keep documents private, they did not waive the privilege). *Cf.* U.S. v. Johnson, 378 F. Supp. 2d 1041, 1047–49 (N.D.Iowa 2005) (capital defendant did not waive work product privilege by disclosing information to a third party in a way that did not increase the likelihood of prosecutors' obtaining it). The work product privilege is explained in Ch. 10, § K.1.b.

[609]*See* n.588, above.

[610]*See* § B.8 of this chapter, n.385.

[611]*See* § B.1.b of this chapter for a discussion of privileged correspondence.

[612]U.S. v. DeFonte, 441 F.3d 92, 94–95 (2d Cir. 2006) (per curiam); Cody v. Weber, 256 F.3d 764, 768–69 (8th Cir. 2001) (holding allegation that prison staff read plaintiff's legal papers during searches stated a constitutional claim); Bayron v. Trudeau, 702 F.2d 43, 45 (2d Cir. 1983) (same). *But see* Giba v. Cook, 232 F. Supp. 2d 1171, 1187 (D.Or. 2002) (reading during cell search of letters to and from prisoner's sister, an attorney, was not improper where the sister was not providing legal representation to him).

[613]Kalka v. Megathlin, 10 F. Supp. 2d 1117, 1121 (D.Ariz. 1998), *aff'd,* 188 F.3d 513 (9th Cir. 1999); *see* Mitchell v. Dupnik, 75 F.3d 517, 522 (9th Cir.1996) (prisoner had no Fourth Amendment right to be present when his legal materials were searched).

searches,[614] was based on the need for prison officials to have "[u]nfettered access" to search for contraband.[615] This holding does not in our view defeat the strong expectation of privacy in one's legal communications, since prison personnel can search for contraband as thoroughly as they want without reading prisoners' legal correspondence.[616]

D. RELIGIOUS FREEDOM

1. Free Exercise of Religion

The First Amendment to the Constitution protects the "free exercise" of religion.[617] Under that Amendment, you have an absolute right to believe what you want.[618] But what you can do about it is more limited. The Supreme Court has held that "reasonable opportunities must be afforded to all prisoners to exercise the religious freedom guaranteed by the First and Fourteenth Amendments without fear of penalty."[619] However, later Supreme Court decisions have permitted severe restrictions on prisoners' religious practice.

Two federal statutes, the Religious Freedom Restoration Act (RFRA), which governs federal institutions, and the Religious Land Use and Institutionalized Persons Act (RLUIPA), which governs state and local institutions, provide greater protection to prisoners' religious rights. We address both First Amendment and RFRA/RLUIPA claims in the following sections, and directly compare their requirements and benefits in § D.1.b of this chapter.

a. What Beliefs Are Protected? To be protected by the Free Exercise Clause of the First Amendment, or by RFRA and RLUIPA,[620] beliefs must meet two requirements: they must be religious, and they must be sincerely held.

Courts have not always agreed on what constitutes a religion. One court has held that a belief system is religious if it addresses "fundamental and ultimate questions," is "comprehensive in nature," and presents "certain formal and external signs."[621] Others have "jettisoned the objective, content-based approach . . . in favor of a more subjective definition of religion, which examines an individual's inward attitudes towards a particular belief system."[622]

Beliefs may be religious even if they are non-traditional or unfamiliar to mainstream America,[623] and even if they do not include belief in a God.[624] Courts may not pass

---

[614]Hudson v. Palmer, 468 U.S. 517, 530, 104 S. Ct. 3194 (1984).

[615]Hudson v. Palmer, 468 U.S. at 527.

[616]*But see* Nash v. McGinnis, 315 F. Supp. 2d 318, 320 (W.D.N.Y. 2004) (dismissing claims of confiscation of "legal letters" from prison officials insofar as they were raised under the Fourth Amendment); Barstow v. Kennebec County Jail, 115 F. Supp. 2d 3, 7 n.8 (D.Me. 2000) ("Courts are unclear about whether legal mail or materials maintained in a prisoner's cell loses its Sixth Amendment protection under the rationale of *Hudson*."); Schenck v. Edwards, 921 F. Supp. 679, 689–90 (E.D.Wash. 1996) (under *Hudson*, inspection of legal papers seized in cell searches need not be done in inmate's presence), *aff'd*, 133 F.3d 929 (9th Cir. 1998) (unpublished).

[617]U.S.Const., Amend. I. The First Amendment also protects against the "establishment of religion," which means government support or sponsorship of religion. That subject is discussed in § D.4 of this chapter.

[618]Employment Division v. Smith, 494 U.S. 872, 877, 110 S. Ct. 1595 (1990); Braunfeld v. Brown, 366 U.S. 599, 603, 81 S. Ct. 1144 (1961).

[619]Cruz v. Beto, 405 U.S. 319, 322 n.2, 92 S. Ct. 1079 (1972).

[620]While neither statute defines religion, RLUIPA says that religious exercise "includes any exercise of religion, whether or not compelled by, or central to, a system of religious belief," 42 U.S.C.

§ 2000cc-5(7)(A), and that definition now applies under RFRA too. 42 U.S.C. § 2000bb-2(4). RLUIPA also says: "This Act shall be construed in favor of a broad protection of religious exercise, to the maximum extent permitted by the terms of this Act and the Constitution." 42 U.S.C. § 2000bb-2(4). It therefore seems reasonable to conclude that anything the courts have found to be protected by the Free Exercise Clause is also protected by RLUIPA and RFRA.

[621]Africa v. Commonwealth of Pennsylvania, 662 F.2d 1025, 1032 (3d Cir. 1981); *accord*, Dettmer v. Landon, 799 F.2d 929, 931–32 (4th Cir. 1986) (applying similar analysis).

[622]Patrick v. LeFevre, 745 F.2d 153, 157 (2d Cir. 1984). The court went on to quote the definition of religion by the philosopher William James: "the feelings, acts, and experiences of individual men in their solitude, so far as they apprehend themselves to stand in relation to whatever they may consider the divine." *Id.* at 158 (quoting W. James, *The Varieties of Religious Experience* 31 (1910)); *see* Ford v. McGinnis, 352 F.3d 582, 589–90 (2d Cir. 2003) (reaffirming subjective approach); *see also* U.S. v. Myers, 906 F. Supp. 1494, 1502–04 (D.Wyo. 1995) (defining religion for two pages), *aff'd*, 95 F.3d 1475 (10th Cir. 1996); Alabama and Coushatta Tribes v. Big Sandy Sch. Dist., 817 F. Supp. 1319, 1329 (E.D.Tex. 1993) ("Whenever a belief system encompasses fundamental questions of the nature of reality and relationship of human beings to reality, it deals with essentially religious questions."), *remanded on other grounds*, 20 F.3d 469 (5th Cir. 1994) (unpublished).

This subjective view seems consistent with the Supreme Court's definition of religion as an individual's sincere belief, even though not theistic in nature, "based upon a power or being, or upon a faith, to which all else is ultimately dependent." U.S. v. Seeger, 380 U.S. 163, 176, 85 S. Ct. 850 (1965); *accord*, Welsh v. U.S., 398 U.S. 333, 339–40, 90 S. Ct. 1792 (1970). *Seeger* was not defining religion for constitutional purposes but was interpreting the Universal Military Training and Service Act.

[623]As one court observed, "the mere fact that a belief may be unusual does not strip it of constitutional protection." Dettmer v. Landon, 617 F. Supp. 592, 596 (E.D.Va. 1985), *aff'd in pertinent part*, 799 F.2d 929 (4th Cir. 1986).

[624]Torcaso v. Watkins, 367 U.S. 488, 495 n.11, 81 S. Ct. 1680 (1961); Kaufman v. McCaughtry, 419 F.3d 678, 681–82 (7th Cir. 2005) (non-theistic and even atheistic views may merit Free Exercise Clause protection as long as they deal with issues of "ultimate concern" and occupy a "place parallel to that filled by . . . God in traditionally religious persons."); Marria v. Broaddus, 200 F. Supp. 2d 280, 292–93 (S.D.N.Y. 2002) (where plaintiff said that the Five Percenters are not a religion but a way of life, there was a triable issue whether the plaintiff sincerely believes what he says and whether his beliefs are religious. "Plaintiff explains that although he would not use the word 'religion' to describe the Nation, the

judgment on the truth, falsity, or rationality of beliefs in determining whether they are religious.[625] A belief system can be religious even if it includes some secular (non-religious) elements.[626]

For First Amendment and RFRA/RLUIPA purposes, courts have treated a variety of belief systems as religions, including Rastafari,[627] Sikhism,[628] Taoism,[629] Native American religions,[630] Santeria,[631] the Hebrew Israelite

religion,[632] Wotanism (also known as Odinism or Asatru),[633] Wicca,[634] the Moorish Science Temple,[635] and many others besides the more familiar Muslim, Jewish, Buddhist, and Christian beliefs.[636] Courts' rulings have been inconclusive in connection with the Church of the New Song,[637] Satanism,[638] the Aryan Nations/Church of Jesus Christ

---

Nation holds the same significance in his life as Christianity to an observant Christian."). *But see* Kalka v. Hawk, 215 F.3d 90, 99 (D.C. Cir. 2000) (Supreme Court's statement in *Torcaso* that Secular Humanism is a religion "does not stand for the proposition that humanism, no matter in what form and no matter how practiced, amounts to a religion under the First Amendment.").

[625]Thomas v. Review Board, Indiana Employment Security Division, 450 U.S. 707, 714, 101 S. Ct. 1425 (1981); Searles v. DeChant, 393 F.3d 1126, 1131 n.6 (10th Cir. 2004) ("It is not within the judicial ken to question the centrality of particular beliefs or practices to a faith, or the validity of particular litigants' interpretations of those creeds." (citation omitted)); Ford v. McGinnis, 352 F.3d 582, 590–91 (2d Cir. 2004); Martinelli v. Dugger, 817 F.2d 1499, 1504 (11th Cir. 1987) ("[T]he Supreme Court has admonished federal courts not to sit as arbiters of religious orthodoxy."); Dettmer v. Landon, 799 F.2d at 932; Malnak v. Yogi, 592 F.2d 197, 208 (3d Cir. 1979).

[626]Wiggins v. Sargent, 753 F.2d 663, 666 (8th Cir. 1985) (belief in white supremacy did not make beliefs of Church of Jesus Christ Christian non-religious); *see also* Welsh v. U.S., 398 U.S. 333, 342, 90 S. Ct. 1792 (1970) (beliefs can be religious even if they have a "political dimension" or reflect "considerations of public policy").

[627]Reed v. Faulkner, 842 F.2d 960, 961–62 (7th Cir. 1988); Overton v. Coughlin, 131 Misc.2d 295, 499 N.Y.S.2d 860, 863–64 (N.Y.Sup. 1986), *aff'd*, 133 A.D.2d 744, 520 N.Y.S.2d 32 (N.Y.App. Div. 1987), *appeal dismissed*, 72 N.Y.2d 838 (1988); *see also* Benjamin v. Coughlin, 905 F.2d 571, 573 n.1 (2d Cir. 1990) (holding question settled by *Overton*). *But see* Wilson v. Schillinger, 761 F.2d 921, 930 (3d Cir. 1985) (it was not "clearly established" that Rastafarianism is a religion).

[628]Singh v. Goord, 520 F. Supp. 2d 487, 499–509 (S.D.N.Y. 2007).

[629]Adams v. Stanley, 237 F. Supp. 2d 136, 139–47 (D.N.H. 2003).

[630]Warsoldier v. Woodford, 418 F.3d 989, 991–92, 994–1001 (9th Cir. 2005; Iron Eyes v. Henry, 907 F.2d 810, 814–16 (8th Cir. 1990); Holloway v. Pigman, 884 F.2d 365, 366 (8th Cir. 1989); Pollock v. Marshall, 845 F.2d 656, 657 (6th Cir. 1988); SapaNajin v. Gunter, 857 F.2d 463, 464 (8th Cir. 1988); Standing Deer v. Carlson, 831 F.2d 1525, 1527 (9th Cir. 1987); Allen v. Toombs, 827 F.2d 563, 565 (9th Cir. 1987); Cole v. Flick, 758 F.2d 124, 125 (3d Cir. 1985); Brown v. Schuetzle, 368 F. Supp. 2d 1009, 1020–24 (D.N.D. 2005); Sample v. Borg, 675 F. Supp. 574, 575 (E.D.Cal. 1987), *vacated as moot*, 870 F.2d 563 (9th Cir. 1989); Cole v. Fulcomer, 588 F. Supp. 772, 773 (M.D.Pa. 1984), *rev'd on other grounds sub nom.* Cole v. Flick, 758 F.2d 124 (3d Cir. 1985); Reinert v. Haas, 585 F. Supp. 477, 480–81 (S.D.Iowa 1984); Battle v. Anderson, 457 F. Supp. 719, 738 (E.D.Okla. 1978), *aff'd*, 564 F.2d 388 (10th Cir. 1979).

There is a federal American Indian Religious Freedom Act, 42 U.S.C. § 1996, but it does not create a cause of action for individuals or any judicially enforceable individual rights. Lyng v. Northwest Indian Cemetery Protective Ass'n, 485 U.S. 439, 455, 108 S. Ct. 1319 (1988); Combs v. Corrections Corp. of America, 977 F. Supp. 799, 801 (W.D.La. 1997).

[631]Campos v. Coughlin, 854 F. Supp. 194 (S.D.N.Y. 1994).

[632]Lawson v. Wainwright, 641 F. Supp. 312, 315 (S.D.Fla. 1986) (parties stipulated that it is a bonafide religion), *aff'd in part and remanded*, 840 F.2d 781 (11th Cir. 1987), *rehearing denied*, 840 F.2d 779 (11th Cir. 1988), *vacated and remanded on other grounds*, 490 U.S. 1078 (1989).

[633]Lindell v. McCallum, 352 F.3d 1107, 1108 (7th Cir. 2003) ("It is an obscure religion, but he didn't make it up.").

[634]O'Bryan v. Bureau of Prisons, 349 F.3d 399, 400 (7th Cir. 2003); Dettmer v. Landon, 799 F.2d 929, 932 (4th Cir. 1986).

[635]Mack v. O'Leary, 80 F.3d 1175, 1177–78 (7th Cir. 1996), *cert. granted, judgment vacated on other grounds*, 522 U.S. 801 (1997); Gilmore-Bey v. Coughlin, 929 F. Supp. 146, 152–52 (S.D.N.Y. 1996) (noting the religion was recognized and accommodated after suit was filed), *aff'd in part*, 122 F.3d 1056 (2d Cir. 1997).

[636]Torcaso v. Watkins, 367 U.S. 488, 495 n.11, 81 S. Ct. 1680 (1961) ("Buddhism, Taoism, Ethical Culture, Secular Humanism and others"); Washington v. Klem, 497 F.3d 272, 275 (3d Cir. 2007) (Children of the Sun Church); Adkins v. Kaspar, 393 F.3d 559, 562–65 (5th Cir. 2004) (Yahweh Evangelical Assembly); Richards v. White, 957 F.2d 471, 475 n.4 (7th Cir. 1992) ("Thelemic" faith conceded to be a bonafide religion); Malnak v. Yogi, 592 F.2d 197, 198-200 (3d Cir. 1979) (Transcendental Meditation); Founding Church of Scientology v. U.S., 409 F.2d 1146, 1160 (D.C. Cir. 1969) (Scientology); Coronel v. Paul, 316 F. Supp. 2d 868, 870–81 (D. Ariz. 2004) (Dianic paganism); Johnson v. Martin, 223 F. Supp. 2d 820, 823 (W.D.Mich. 2002) (Melanic Islamic Palace of the Rising Sun); Luckette v. Lewis, 883 F. Supp. 471, 477–83 (D.Ariz.1995) (Freedom Church of Revelation); Osgood v. District of Columbia, 567 F. Supp. 1026, 1034–36 (D.D.C. 1983) (Christian Science); Alim v. Byrne, 521 F. Supp. 1039, 1044 (D.N.J. 1980) (United Against Racism, Discrimination and Social Injustice); Williams v. Warden, Federal Correctional Inst., 470 F. Supp. 1123, 1127 (D. Conn. 1979) (Christian Adamic faith).

[637]One court has held the Church to be a religion. Loney v. Scurr, 474 F.Supp. 1186, 1192–95 (S.D.Iowa 1979); Remmers v. Brewer, 361 F.Supp. 537, 540–42 (S.D.Iowa 1973), *aff'd*, 494 F.2d 1277 (8th Cir. 1974) (per curiam). Others have disagreed. Theriault v. Carlson, 495 F.2d 390, 395 (5th Cir. 1974); Theriault v. Silber, 453 F. Supp. 254, 260 (W.D.Tex. 1978) (Church of the New Song was "a masquerade designed to obtain First Amendment protection"), *appeal dismissed*, 579 F.2d 302 (5th Cir. 1978). The appeals court in the circuit where it has been found to be a religion has said that prison officials could file a motion to modify the earlier Iowa decisions, since "prison officials now appear to have gathered substantial evidence that CONS functions not as a religious organization but as a racist prison gang. . . ." Goff v. Graves, 362 F.3d 543, 551 (8th Cir. 2004).

[638]*Compare* Ramirez v. Coughlin, 919 F. Supp. 617, 623 (N.D.N.Y. 1996) (claim of restriction and non-recognition of Satanism raised "important First Amendment issues"); Howard v. U.S., 864 F. Supp. 1019, 1025–29 (D.Colo. 1994) (granting preliminary injunction requiring prison officials to accommodate plaintiff's Satanic rituals and allow him access to candles, candle holders, incense, a gong or bell, a black robe, a chalice, and an object

Christian,[639] the Five Percenters,[640] the Universal Life Church,[641] and others.[642] A few cases have held groups or belief systems not to be genuinely religious,[643] including some deemed to be bogus religions, or devised to gain concessions from prison officials or disrupt prison life.[644]

The Constitution and RFRA/RLUIPA protect each individual's religious beliefs. You need not belong to an established church or sect,[645] and if you do, your beliefs need not be shared by all of its members, or be part of any orthodox or official interpretation of church doctrine.[646]

suitable for pointing, to the same extent as other religious groups) *with* Kennedy v. Meachum, 540 F.2d 1057, 1061 (10th Cir. 1976) (case remanded to determine whether Satanism is a religion); Childs v. Duckworth, 509 F. Supp. 1254, 1528–60 (N.D.Ind. 1981), *aff'd*, 705 F.2d 915, 919–20 (7th Cir. 1983) (district court found it "doubtful" whether Satanism is a religion; the appellate court did not reach the question).

Some courts have said they do not need to determine whether Satanism is a religion because restrictions on it are lawful even if it is. McCorkle v. Johnson, 881 F.2d 993, 995 (11th Cir. 1989) (court did not determine whether Satanism is a religion because prison restrictions on Satanic practice were lawful); Doty v. Lewis, 995 F. Supp. 1081, 1086 (D.Ariz. 1998) (officials' testimony "demonstrates that the Satanic Bible in the hands of Plaintiff presents a serious threat to the safety and security of the prison" because of the "selfish and brutal" philosophy it advocates and its endorsement of human sacrifice, and because the plaintiff might use it to cast spells that other inmates would believe in); Carpenter v. Wilkinson, 946 F. Supp. 522, 529 (N.D.Ohio 1996) ("large portions of *The Satanic Bible* have great potential for fomenting trouble of all kinds in a prison setting, leading to difficulty in maintaining security and order and in delivering rehabilitative services in the prisons."). *But see* Howard v. U.S., 864 F. Supp. 1019, 1026 (D.Colo. 1994) (rejecting claim that Satanism is counter-rehabilitative, since plaintiff's version of it omits drinking blood and eating flesh).

[639] McCabe v. Arave, 827 F.2d 634, 637 n.2 (9th Cir. 1987) (assuming church to be a religion); Murphy v. Missouri Dep't of Corrections, 814 F.2d 1252, 1255–56 (8th Cir. 1987) (district court assumed Aryan Nations to be a religion); Wiggins v. Sargent, 753 F.2d 663, 666-67 (8th Cir. 1985) (district court directed to reexamine whether group's beliefs are religious).

[640] In *Marria v. Broaddus*, 200 F. Supp. 2d 280 (S.D.N.Y. 2002), the court rejected the defendants' claim that the Five Percenters are not entitled to RLUIPA protections because the plaintiff said that they are not a religion but a way of life. The court said that is semantics; there is a triable issue whether the plaintiff sincerely believes what he says and whether his beliefs are religious. "Plaintiff explains that although he would not use the word 'religion' to describe the Nation, the Nation holds the same significance in his life as Christianity to an observant Christian." 200 F. Supp. 2d at 292–93. In a later decision, the court held that the Five Percenters' beliefs are religious in nature. Marria v. Broaddus, 2003 WL 21782633, *11–12 (S.D.N.Y., July 31, 2003); *see* Patrick v. LeFevre, 745 F.2d 153, 159-60 (2d Cir. 1984) (reversing and remanding for reconsideration a lower court decision that this group is not a religion).

In at least two states, prison officials have declared Five Percenters to be a "Security Threat Group" based on their alleged violent acts and other misconduct, and placed them in administrative segregation until and unless they renounce their affiliation. The courts have upheld this practice without disputing that the group is a religion. *See* Fraise v. Terhune, 283 F.3d 506 (3d Cir. 2002); *In re* Long Term Administrative Segregation, 174 F.3d 464 (4th Cir. 1999). *But see* Hetsberger v. Dept. of Corrections, 395 N.J.Super. 548, 929 A.2d 1139 (N.J.Super.A.D. 2007) (requiring policy upheld in *Fraise* to be assessed under RLUIPA). In *Marria v. Broaddus*, 200 F. Supp. 2d at 294–95, the court held that the fact that some Five Percenters had acted violently did not justify banning the whole group.

[641] Woods v. O'Leary, 890 F.2d 883, 885 (7th Cir. 1989) (court need not decide whether Universal Life Church is a religion); Jones v. Bradley, 590 F.2d 294, 295–96 (9th Cir. 1979) (district court had decided Church is not a religion; appellate court did not reach the issue); Jacques v. Hilton, 569 F. Supp. 730 (D.N.J. 1983) (United Church of St. Dennis, affiliated with Universal Life Church, is not a religion), *aff'd*, 738 F.2d 422 (3d Cir. 1984).

[642] Swift v. Lewis, 901 F.2d 730 (9th Cir. 1990) (reserving the question whether the Vow of the Nazarite is religious); Theriault v. A Religious Office, 895 F.2d 104, 107 (2d Cir. 1990) (district court should have determined whether the Holy Mizanic faith is a religion); Brightly v. Wainwright, 814 F.2d 612 (11th Cir. 1987); Dreibelbeis v. Marks, 675 F.2d 579, 581–82 (3d Cir. 1982) (court did not decide if Church of Prophetic Meditation is a religion).

[643] Abdool-Rashaad v. Seiter, 690 F. Supp. 598, 601–02 (S.D.Ohio 1987) (Universalism); Johnson v. Pa. Bureau of Corrections, 661 F. Supp. 425, 436–37 (M.D.Pa. 1987) (Spiritual Order of Universal Beings).

[644] *See* Green v. White, 525 F. Supp. 81, 83 (E.D.Mo. 1981) (Human Awareness Life Church was not a religion; prisoner had demanded conjugal visits, banquets, and payment as a chaplain), *aff'd*, 693 F.2d 45 (8th Cir. 1982); *see also* n.637, above, concerning Church of the New Song.

[645] Frazee v. Illinois Dep't of Employment Security, 489 U.S. 829, 833, 109 S. Ct. 1514 (1989); U.S. v. Zimmerman, 514 F.3d 851, 853–54 (9th Cir. 2007) (holding beliefs based on prisoner's "Catholic upbringing, his time spent studying other religions such as Buddhism and a passage from the Bible" were protected by the Religious Freedom Restoration Act); Mosier v. Maynard, 937 F.2d 1521, 1523 (10th Cir. 1991).

[646] Thomas v. Review Board, Indiana Employment Security Division, 450 U.S. 707, 715–16, 101 S. Ct. 1425 (1981) (religious freedom "is not limited to beliefs which are shared by all of the members of a religious sect"; "it is not within the judicial function and judicial competence to inquire whether the petitioner or his fellow worker more correctly perceived the commands of their common faith. Courts are not arbiters of scriptural interpretation."); Nelson v. Miller, 570 F.3d 868, 878–79 (7th Cir. 2009) (requirement that prisoner show dietary practice was compelled by religion was contrary to RLUIPA and substantially burdened his religious exercise); Ortiz v. Downey, 561 F.3d 664, 669 (7th Cir. 2009) (jail official's statement to prisoner that he too was Roman Catholic and therefore knew that a rosary and prayer book were not "vital to worship" did not by itself justify refusing them to the plaintiff); Fifth Ave. Presbyterian Church v. City of New York, 293 F.3d 570, 574 (2d Cir. 2002) (courts are not permitted to inquire into the centrality of a professed belief to the adherent's religion or to question its validity in determining whether a religious practice exists. The only requirement is that the plaintiff "demonstrate that the beliefs professed are 'sincerely held' and in the individual's 'own scheme of things, religious.'"); LaFevers v. Saffle, 936 F.2d 1117,

(Some courts have been very resistant to this proposition.[647]) If your beliefs are unique or unusual, that fact may weigh heavily in determining how far prison officials have to go to

accommodate them.[648] Conversely, if you adhere to the beliefs of a particular group, it does not matter that you are not, or some religious authority says you are not, really a member of the group.[649] Beliefs are protected even if the individual is "struggling" with his position or his beliefs "are not articulated with the clarity and precision that a more sophisticated person might employ."[650] That does not mean you can simply claim that some prison practice violates your religious beliefs, without explanation. You must be specific as to what your religious belief is and why you think it is being violated.[651]

1119 (10th Cir. 1991); Martinelli v. Dugger, 817 F.2d 1499, 1504–05 (11th Cir. 1987); Dettmer v. Landon, 799 F.2d 929, 932 (4th Cir. 1986); Hudson v. Maloney, 326 F. Supp. 2d 206, 211 n.3 (D.Mass. 2004) (rejecting testimony of Muslim scholar that plaintiffs misunderstood their religion: "The issue in free exercise cases, however, is not whether an adherent has correctly divined the religious commands of his faith, but whether his understanding of what his religion requires, however unorthodox, is based on a sincerely held religious belief."); Coronel v. Paul, 316 F. Supp. 2d 868, 881 (D.Ariz. 2004) ("[I]ndividuals have the right to exercise their faith in unique and nontraditional ways. . . . Resort to tests to determine the scope of a believer's faith is impermissible—courts are not competent to resolve matters of religious doctrine." The plaintiff, a Dianic pagan, sought to attend Pasqui Yaqui and Hawaiian pagan services, and the court rejects defendants' claim that *Modern Day Dianic Practices* shows that this is not part of his religious exercise.); Williams v. Bitner, 359 F. Supp. 2d 370, 376 (M.D.Pa. 2005) ("And, for purposes of the RLUIPA, it matters not whether the inmate's religious belief is shared by ten or tens of millions. All that matters is whether the inmate is sincere in his or her own views."), *aff'd*, 455 F.3d 186 (3d Cir. 2006); Thacker v. Dixon, 784 F. Supp. 286, 295 (E.D.N.C. 1991) ("Except in the most extreme cases, a court must confine itself to a determination of whether the practice in question has a basis in religious belief as the individual sees it."), *aff'd*, 953 F.2d 639 (4th Cir. 1992); Moskowitz v. Wilkinson, 432 F. Supp. 947, 949 (D.Conn. 1977); Monroe v. Bombard, 422 F. Supp. 211, 215 n.4 (S.D.N.Y. 1976); *see* Koger v. Bryan, 523 F.3d 789, 800–02 (7th Cir. 2008) (requirement that religious diets be religiously required and verified by clergy substantially burdened plaintiff's religious exercise and was not shown to be least restrictive as required by RLUIPA). *But see* Levitan v. Ashcroft, 281 F.3d 1313, 1321 (D.C. Cir. 2002) ("A court may also consider whether the litigants' beliefs find any support in the religion to which they subscribe, or whether the litigants are merely relying on a self-serving view of religious practice. This inquiry is not a matter of deciding whether appellants' beliefs accord in every particular with the religious orthodoxy of their church. . . . Instead, a court may determine whether the litigants' views have any basis whatsoever in the creed or community on which they purport to rest their claim.")

[647]In *Goff v. Graves*, 362 F.3d 543, 548 (8th Cir. 2004), the court held that plaintiffs in a free exercise case must show that the practice allegedly infringed is based on a teaching of the religion, and reversed the district court because the practice was not "grounded" in the religion's "theology or its prescribed rituals." *Accord*, U.S. v. Brown, 330 F.3d 1073, 1077 n.3 (8th Cir. 2003) (holding plaintiff "failed to show that forbidding blood samples is a 'central tenet' of the Jehovah's Witness religion"). However, that court has finally acknowledged that this view is wrong. Gladson v. Iowa Dep't of Corrections, 551 F.3d 825, 832–33 (2009). Unfortunately it may be popping up again elsewhere. *See* Smith v. Allen, 502 F.3d 1255, 1278–80 (11th Cir. 2007) (finding no substantial burden for RLUIPA purposes where no evidence, including the third-party religious writings plaintiff submitted, supported the centrality of the disputed practices to his religious exercise).

---

[648]*See* Kahey v. Jones, 836 F.2d 948, 950–51 (5th Cir. 1988) (prison officials were not obliged to provide individualized religious diets). One court has upheld a "rule of five" requiring five documented members to qualify a religion for official recognition, congregate services, etc. Spies v. Voinovich, 173 F.3d 398, 404–05 (6th Cir. 1999).

If you openly disagree with the beliefs expressed in the services of a religious group, you can be excluded from the services of that group. *See* § D.2.b of this chapter, n.762.

[649]Love v. Reed, 216 F.3d 682, 688 (8th Cir. 2000) (prisoner who was not Jewish, but believed he should follow original Hebrew Sabbath rules, was entitled to do so where officials failed to justify their failure to accommodate his beliefs); Jackson v. Mann, 196 F.3d 316, 320 (2d Cir. 1999) (plaintiff's entitlement to a kosher diet depended on whether he sincerely believed he should keep kosher, not on whether a prison rabbi agreed that he was Jewish).

Several courts have held that prisoners who adhere to Native American beliefs cannot be excluded from Native American religious observance because they do not have Native American ancestry. Morrison v. Garraghty, 239 F.3d 648, 657–59 (4th Cir. 2001) (holding exclusion denied equal protection); Brown v. Schuetzle, 368 F. Supp. 2d 1009, 1023–24 (D.N.D. 2005) (holding policy would violate First Amendment); Mitchell v. Angelone, 82 F. Supp. 2d 485, 492 (E.D.Va. 1999) (finding equal protection violation); Combs v. Corrections Corp. of America, 977 F. Supp. 799, 802–03 (W.D.La. 1997) (finding First Amendment religious freedom violation). *But see* Bear v. Nix, 977 F.2d 1291, 1293 (8th Cir. 1992) (upholding exclusions of non-Native Americans from religious observances where done by an independent religious consultant hired pursuant to a consent judgment).

[650]Thomas v. Review Board, 450 U.S. at 715; *accord*, Love v. Reed, 216 F.3d 682, 688 (8th Cir. 2000) ("It is not the place of the courts to deny a man the right to his religion simply because he is still struggling to assimilate the full scope of its doctrine."); Faheem-El v. Lane, 657 F. Supp. 638, 644 (C.D.Ill. 1986) (fact that beliefs were changing did not mean they were not religious).

[651]Johnson v. Moore, 948 F.2d 517, 520 (9th Cir. 1991); Holloway v. Pigman, 884 F.2d 365, 367 (8th Cir. 1989); Dunn v. White, 880 F.2d 1188, 1197 (10th Cir. 1989) ("The mere assertion of generic religious objections is not sufficient to invoke first amendment protection").

Beliefs must be sincerely held to be protected by the Free Exercise Clause[652] or RFRA and RLUIPA.[653] In determining the sincerity of beliefs, courts sometimes consider evidence of how long and how consistently the prisoner has adhered to them.[654] But beliefs cannot be found insincere just because you acquired them recently or while in prison.[655] Displaying interest in other religions does not show that one's own beliefs are insincere.[656] Nor does the fact that you have violated your religious beliefs mean you are not sincere; it just means that you are a sinner.[657] Courts are generally reluctant to find beliefs insincere on summary judgment.[658]

b. Standards for Religious Freedom Claims

1) *RFRA, RLUIPA, the First Amendment, and State Law*

Under the First Amendment's Free Exercise Clause, as long as a prison restriction is reasonably related to a legitimate correctional purpose, it must be upheld.[659] We discuss this "reasonable relationship" standard (the *Turner/O'Lone* standard) earlier in this chapter.[660]

---

[652]Murphy v. Missouri Dep't of Correction, 372 F.3d 979, 983 (8th Cir. 2004); Ford v. McGinnis, 352 F.3d 582, 588 (2d Cir. 2003); Sutton v. Rasheed, 323 F.3d 236, 250–51 (3d Cir. 2003) (per curiam).

Sincerity is not an issue in claims under the Establishment Clause of the First Amendment. Alexander v. Schenk, 118 F. Supp. 2d 298, 301 (N.D.N.Y. 2000) (the Establishment Clause was drafted to prevent government from coercing *anyone* to support or participate in religious exercise). The Establishment Clause is discussed in § D.4 of this chapter.

[653]Gonzales v. O Centro Espirita Beneficente Uniao do Vegetal, 546 U.S. 418, 430–31, 126 S. Ct. 1211 (2006); Cutter v. Wilkinson, 544 U.S. 709, 725 n.13, 125 S. Ct. 2113 (2005).

[654]Jackson v. Mann, 196 F.3d 316, 320 (2d Cir. 1999) (plaintiff supported claim of sincerity by showing his past self-identification as Jewish, previous participation in the kosher program, and going without food for several days when first denied kosher meals, as well as submitting his mother's affidavit concerning his religious upbringing); Sourbeer v. Robinson, 791 F.2d 1094, 1102 (3d Cir. 1986) (district court could find plaintiff insincere based on his failure to attend services and to designate a religious advisor); Singh v. Goord, 520 F. Supp. 2d 487, 499–500 (S.D.N.Y. 2007) (noting that plaintiff was born and raised as a Sikh, regularly attended Sikh services growing up, consistently asserted his beliefs in prison, engaged in hunger strikes in support of his beliefs, and adhered to Sikh teachings despite being punished); Vaughn v. Garrison, 534 F. Supp. 90, 92 (E.D.N.C. 1981) (prison officials could limit Muslim prayer rugs to persons who had submitted request for the pork-free diet required by Muslim tenets), *aff'd*, 673 F.2d 1319 (4th Cir. 1982); Gallahan v. Hollyfield, 516 F.Supp. 1004, 1006 (E.D.Va. 1981) (prisoner who had adhered to beliefs since childhood was sincere), *aff'd*, 670 F.2d 1345 (4th Cir. 1982); Moskowitz v. Wilkinson, 432 F. Supp. 947, 950 (D.Conn. 1977) (prisoner's sincerity was demonstrated by his receipt of four disciplinary tickets and loss of good time for refusing to cut his hair in violation of his beliefs).

[655]Sample v. Lappin, 424 F. Supp. 187, 193 & n.6 (D.D.C. 2006) (the fact that plaintiff didn't indicate his religious preference on admission did not make him insincere; "The accuracy or inaccuracy of BOP records does not necessarily reflect the sincerity of plaintiff's religious beliefs."), *reconsideration denied*, 479 F. Supp. 2d 120 (D.D.C. 2007); Shaheed-Muhammad v. DiPaolo, 393 F. Supp. 2d 80, 91–92 (D.Mass. 2005) (plaintiff's identification as Christian upon admission in 1992 did not make his later Muslim beliefs insincere); Cole v. Fulcomer, 588 F. Supp. 772, 774–75 (M.D.Pa. 1984) (plaintiff could be sincere adherent of Native American religion even though he had not practiced it all his life and did not engage in formal observances), *rev'd on other grounds sub nom.* Cole v. Flick, 758 F.2d 124 (3d Cir. 1985); Maguire v. Wilkinson, 405 F. Supp. 637, 640 (D.Conn. 1975); *see also* Masjid Muhammad-D.C.C. v. Keve, 479 F. Supp. 1311, 1321–22 (D.Del. 1979) (relief granted to Muslims who changed their names after conversion in prison). *Cf.* Searles v. van Bebber, 251 F.3d 869, 880 (10th Cir. 2001) (evidence supported punitive damages against a chaplain who excluded the plaintiff from Jewish services without examining or weighing evidence of his sincerity).

[656]Shaheed-Muhammad v. DiPaolo, 393 F. Supp. 2d 80, 92 (D.Mass. 2005) (plaintiff had read books about other religions); Howard v. U.S., 864 F. Supp. 1019, 1024 (D.Colo. 1994) (plaintiff had attended services of other religions).

[657]Reed v. Faulkner, 842 F.2d 960, 963 (7th Cir. 1988) ("the fact that a person does not adhere steadfastly to every tenet of his faith does not mark him as insincere"); McElyea v. Babbitt, 833 F.2d 196, 198 (9th Cir. 1987) (prisoner cannot be found insincere based on "second-hand knowledge of past behavior"); Weir v. Nix, 890 F. Supp. 769, 776 (S.D. Iowa 1995) (alleged receipt of pornography did not prove Christian fundamentalist insincere; "the gap between the ideal and reality is a universal feature of human experience"), *aff'd, appeal dismissed in part*, 114 F.3d 817 (8th Cir. 1997); Young v. Lane, 733 F. Supp. 1205, 1209 (N.D.Ill. 1990) (allegation that some Jewish plaintiffs had been seen eating non-kosher food did not mean they were insincere), *rev'd on other grounds*, 922 F.2d 370 (7th Cir. 1991); *see* Luke 7:36–50 ("Let him without sin cast the first stone"); *see also* Matthew 7:1–14.

Courts have barred prison officials from depriving sincerely religious prisoners of religious exercise as a result of their violating their sincere beliefs. *See* Lovelace v. Lee, 472 F.3d 174, 190–92, 200 (4th Cir. 2006) (holding exclusion of sincere Muslim prisoner from all religious observance after he broke Ramadan fast raised material issues under RLUIPA and First Amendment); Kuperman v. New Hampshire Dept. of Corrections, 2007 WL 1200092, *3–5 (D.N.H. 2007) (holding Orthodox Jewish prisoner who sincerely believed in keeping kosher could not be barred from the kosher diet for six months because he purchased some non-kosher food).

[658]Murphy v. Missouri Dep't of Correction, 372 F.3d 979, 983 (8th Cir. 2004); Shaheed-Muhammad v. DiPaolo, 393 F. Supp. 2d 80, 90 (D.Mass. 2005); Coronel v. Paul, 316 F. Supp. 2d 868, 881 (D.Ariz. 2004); *see* Storm v. Town of Woodstock, 32 F. Supp. 2d 520, 527 (N.D.N.Y. 1998) ("As with any credibility assessment, the sincerity of plaintiffs' religious claims is evaluated by considering all the evidence presented at trial and appraising plaintiffs' demeanor during direct and cross-examination."), *aff'd*, 165 F.3d 15 (2d Cir. 1998). *But see* Singh v. Goord, 520 F. Supp. 2d 487, 499–500 (S.D.N.Y. 2007) (finding plaintiff sincere on summary judgment where defendants put forth no evidence to the contrary).

[659]O'Lone v. Estate of Shabazz, 482 U.S. 342, 349, 107 S. Ct. 2400 (1987) (quoting Turner v. Safley, 482 U.S. 78, 89, 107 S. Ct. 2254 (1987). This is the same reasonableness standard that governs other prison civil liberties claims.

[660]*See* § A of this chapter.

To provide greater protection for everyone's religious rights, Congress in 1993 passed the Religious Freedom Restoration Act (RFRA),[661] which says that a government may not "substantially burden" a person's exercise of religion unless it "demonstrates" that doing so "(1) is in furtherance of a compelling governmental interest; and (2) is the least restrictive means of furthering that compelling governmental interest."[662] But the Supreme Court held that RFRA was unconstitutional as applied to states and their agencies, because it exceeded Congress's power under Section 5 of the Fourteenth Amendment to enforce that Amendment's protections.[663] RFRA remains in effect as applied to federal prisons.[664]

In 2000, Congress tried again. It passed the Religious Land Use and Institutionalized Persons Act (RLUIPA), which reinstated the "compelling interest/least restrictive means" standard of RFRA for states and their agencies. Congress avoided the constitutional problem that RFRA had by basing RLUIPA on Congress's power under the Spending Clause of the Constitution rather than the Fourteenth Amendment.[665] That is, if state or local governments accept federal funds for their correctional programs, they must satisfy the compelling interest/least restrictive means standard to justify placing substantial burdens on prisoners' religious exercise.[666] Virtually all agencies that run prisons or jails accept some federal funds,[667] so RLUIPA applies to virtually all prisons and jails. Privately operated prisons are subject to RLUIPA if they contract with government agencies that receive federal funds.[668] So far, RLUIPA has survived constitutional challenges.[669]

RFRA and RLUIPA provide a more favorable legal standard for prisoners than do the First Amendment and the reasonable relationship standard, but there are some open questions under the statutes (discussed later in this section) about what remedies prisoners can obtain, and against what defendants.[670] It may therefore be wise to plead both a

---

[661]42 U.S.C. § 2000bb.

[662]42 U.S.C. § 2000bb-1.

[663]City of Boerne v. Flores, 521 U.S. 507, 532–36, 117 S. Ct. 2157 (1997).

[664]O'Bryan v. Bureau of Prisons, 349 F.3d 399, 401 (7th Cir. 2003) (noting RFRA's application to internal federal government operations rests on art. I, § 8, clause 18 of the Constitution); Kikumura v. Hurley, 242 F.3d 950, 959–60 (10th Cir. 2001); Jama v. U.S.I.N.S., 343 F. Supp. 2d 338, 369–70 (D.N.J. 2004) (immigration detainees).

[665]U.S. Const. art. I, § 8, cl. 1.

RLUIPA is also based on Congress's power over interstate commerce, U.S. Const. art. I, § 8, cl. 3. *See* DeHart v. Horn, 390 F.3d 262, 275 (3d Cir. 2004) (describing RLUIPA's purpose and intent). That means if you were in a prison or jail run by an agency that did not take federal money, you could establish RLUIPA jurisdiction by showing that the restriction you wished to challenge had a substantial effect on interstate commerce. For example, if you were denied a religious diet, you would argue that this denial to you and all the other similarly situated prisoners in the prison system had a substantial effect on, say, the market for Kosher or Halal food. You could also argue that prison system's use of out-of-state transfers of prisoners meant that prison practices generally affected interstate commerce. *See* Derek L. Gaubatz, *RLUIPA at Four: Evaluating the Success and Constitutionality of RLUIPA's Prisoner Provisions*, 28 Harvard Journal of Law and Public Policy 501, 537–38 (2005). However, some courts have said that RLUIPA's provisions concerning prisoners' religious exercise rest only on the Spending Clause. Nelson v. Miller, 570 F.3d 868, 886 (7th Cir. 2009) (noting lack of evidence prisoner's diet claim affected interstate commerce); Smith v. Allen, 502 F.3d 1255, 1274 n.9 (11th Cir. 2007); Sisney v. Reisch, 533 F. Supp. 2d 952, 968 n.1 (D.S.D. 2008), *aff'd in part, rev'd in part sub nom.* Van Wyhe v. Reisch, 581 F.3d 639 (8th Cir. 2009). *But see* Charles v. Verhagen, 348 F.3d 601, 609 n.3 (7th Cir. 2003) (suggesting that a prison system that transfers prisoners out of state engages in interstate commerce in meeting their religious needs); Corey v. South Carolina Dep't of Corrections, 2007 WL 29024, *7 (D.S.C. 2007) (suggesting that prison's returning books to a publisher might involve interstate commerce); Johnson v. Martin, 223 F. Supp. 2d 820, 829 (W.D.Mich. 2002) (". . . [T]he free exercise of religion affects interstate commerce in a multitude of ways including: use of the airwaves to advertise various religions and to seek charitable donations for domestic and international concerns; use of the interstate highway system for traveling choirs and missionary groups; and, use of the mail system to buy and sell ceremonial items and religious literature. . . . [But] it must still be shown at trial that in the particular case at issue, there is a connection to interstate commerce."). There remains a question whether RLUIPA is valid as an exercise of the interstate commerce power. Daker v. Ferrero, 475 F. Supp. 2d 1325, 1342–47 (N.D.Ga. Feb 26, 2007), *vacated in part on other grounds on reconsideration*, 506 F. Supp. 2d 1295 (N.D.Ga. 2007).

[666]42 U.S.C. § 2000cc-1.

[667]*See* Cutter v. Wilkinson, 544 U.S. 709, 725 n.4, 125 S. Ct. 2113 (2005) ("Every State, including Ohio, accepts federal funding for its prisons."). There may be some county sheriff's offices and other local correctional agencies that do not take any federal money.

[668]Dean v. Corrections Corp. of America, 540 F. Supp. 2d 691, 693–94 (N.D.Miss. 2008). Companies that operate private prisons are also likely to engage in interstate commerce and to be subject to RLUIPA for that reason.

[669]The Supreme Court has upheld RLUIPA against an argument that it violates the Establishment Clause of the Constitution. Cutter v. Wilkinson, 544 U.S. 709, 125 S. Ct. 2113 (2005). The Court in *Cutter* did not reach arguments that RLUIPA exceeds Congress's authority under the Spending and Commerce Clauses and violates the Tenth Amendment, and the argument that "in the space between the Free Exercise and Establishment Clauses, the States' choices are not subject to congressional oversight." 544 U.S. at 718 n.7. These arguments have been unsuccessful in the lower courts. *See, e.g.*, Cutter v. Wilkinson, 423 F.3d 579 (6th Cir. 2005) (on remand from Supreme Court, rejecting Spending Clause and Tenth Amendment arguments); Benning v. Georgia, 391 F.3d 1299 (11th Cir. 2004) (same).

[670]There is one question about what defendants can be sued for religious freedom violation that affects both RFRA/RLUIPA and First Amendment claims. Some courts have held that a prison chaplain was not a "state actor" who could be sued for civil rights violations when performing "inherently ecclesiastical functions" as opposed to "administrative and managerial tasks." Montano v. Hedgepeth, 120 F.3d 844, 850–51 (8th Cir. 1997). We think that is wrong, and that another federal court was correct in holding that a

First Amendment violation and a RFRA/RLUIPA violation when you are challenging a restriction on religious exercise.[671]

Some states also have their own statutes, regulations, or state constitutional rules that protect the religious rights of prisoners or of all citizens. This state law will generally have to be enforced in state court.[672]

2) "Substantial Burdens" on Religious Rights

In any religious rights case, one of the basic questions is whether some government action has "substantially burdened" a person's religious exercise. RLUIPA does not define substantial burden, since Congress intended that it mean the same thing under RLUIPA as in First Amendment religious rights cases.[673] This has resulted in some confusion, since courts in First Amendment cases were not always consistent in using this term.[674] Some recent decisions have said that a substantial burden exists where a prisoner will lose benefits available to other prisoners by following his religious precepts, or where government puts substantial pressure on a prisoner to substantially modify his behavior and violate his beliefs.[675] Others have omitted the "loss of benefits" aspect and have referred only to pressure or coercion.[676] It is not clear whether this really makes much difference, since obviously loss of benefits can be a kind of pressure. Government action that is merely offensive to someone's religious beliefs, but does not penalize them or coerce them to change their behavior or beliefs, does not substantially burden religious exercise.[677]

Some courts had previously said under the First Amendment and RFRA that a substantial burden on religious exercise must involve a "central tenet" [678] or a mandatory

---

volunteer prison chaplain was a state actor when he prevented a prisoner from giving testimony during a religious service because his right to conduct religious services at the prison was a privilege created by the state. Phelps v. Dunn, 965 F.2d 93, 102 (6th Cir.1992). Since RLUIPA and RFRA provide for liability for government agencies or persons acting under "color of law" (who are usually state actors), 42 U.S.C. § 2000cc-5(4)(A), 42 U.S.C. § 2000bb-2(1), this question affects cases brought under those statutes as well as under 42 U.S.C. § 1983. It is discussed in more detail in Ch. 8, § B.1.c, nn.27–28.

[671]Some decisions have said that courts should consider RFRA or RLUIPA, even if they are not pled, as long as the prisoner alleges facts showing a substantial burden on their religious exercise. Ortiz v. Downey, 561 F.3d 664, 670 (7th Cir. 1999); McEachin v. McGuinnis, 357 F.3d 197, 199 n.2 (2d Cir. 2003); Small v. Lehman, 98 F.3d 762, 766 (3d Cir. 1996); see Alvarez v. Hill, 518 F.3d 1152, 1157–58 (9th Cir. 2008) (considering RLUIPA claim not pled in the complaint where prisoners' further filings gave notice of it). Other courts may not entertain a RFRA or RLUIPA claim if it has not been pled. See Pierce v. County of Orange, 526 F.3d 1190, 1209 n.19 (9th Cir. 2008), cert. denied, 129 S. Ct. 597 (2008). One argument in favor of considering the statutory claim is that if the plaintiff wins, the court does not have do address the constitutional claim. Koger v. Bryan, 523 F.3d 789, 801 (7th Cir. 2008).

[672]See Johnson v. Horn, 150 F.3d 276, 283, 288 (3d Cir. 1998) (citing state regulation providing for "reasonable accommodations for dietary restrictions," and wondering why prisoners didn't go to state court to enforce it); Benjamin v. Coughlin, 905 F.2d 571, 577 (2d Cir. 1990) (requirement of free-world sponsor for religious services might be inconsistent with state statutes, but issue must be resolved in state court); Wilson v. Moore, 270 F. Supp. 2d 1328, 1355–57 (N.D.Fla. 2003) (declining to hear claims under Florida Religious Freedom Restoration Act); Cancel v. Goord, 278 A.D.2d 321, 717 N.Y.S.2d 610, 611–12 (2d Dep't 2000) (holding that Muslim services conducted so as to denigrate Shi'a faith violated religious freedom protections of state Correction Law), leave to appeal denied, 96 N.Y.2d 778, 725 N.Y.S.2d 633, 749 N.E.2d 203 (2001). But see Shaheed-Muhammad v. DiPaolo, 393 F. Supp. 2d 80, 93–94, 101–02, 105 (D.Mass. 2005) (declining to dismiss claims under state Civil Rights Act, state Constitution, or state statute concerning prison religious exercise).

Favorable state law on prison religious exercise cannot be enforced in federal court because (a) federal courts are not permitted to enforce state law against state governments, see Pennhurst State Sch. & Hosp. v. Halderman, 465 U.S. 89, 122–123, 104 S. Ct. 900 (1984), and (b) the Prison Litigation Reform Act prevents federal courts from granting injunctions against prison or jail officials except for violations of "Federal rights." Handberry v. Thompson, 446 F.3d 335, 344–46 (2d Cir. 2006).

[673]Washington v. Klem, 497 F.3d 272, 278 (3d Cir. 2007).

[674]Washington v. Klem, 497 F.3d at 278–80; see McEachin v. McGuinnis, 357 F.3d 197, 202–03 (2d Cir. 2004) (noting divergent views on substantial burden question); Ford v. McGinnis, 352 F.3d 582, 592–93 (2d Cir. 2004).

[675]Washington v. Klem, 497 F.3d at 280; accord, Lovelace v. Lee, 472 F.3d 174, 187 (4th Cir. 2006); Adkins v. Kaspar, 393 F.3d 559, 570 (5th Cir. 2004) (burden is substantial if it "truly pressures the adherent to significantly modify his religious behavior and significantly violate his religious beliefs," which occurs "when it either (1) influences the adherent to act in a way that violates his religious beliefs, or (2) forces the adherent to choose between, on the one hand, enjoying some generally available, non-trivial benefit, and, on the other hand, following his religious beliefs"); Gartrell v. Ashcroft, 191 F. Supp. 2d 23, 37 (D.D.C. 2002), appeal dismissed, 2003 WL 1873847 (D.C. Cir., Apr. 11, 2003).

[676]Jolly v. Coughlin, 76 F.3d 468, 477 (2d Cir.1996) (substantial burden means situations where "the state 'puts substantial pressure on an adherent to modify his behavior and to violate his beliefs.'") (quoting Thomas v. Review Bd. of the Indiana Employment Sec. Div., 450 U.S. 707, 718, 101 S. Ct. 1425 (1981)) (a First Amendment case); accord, Vision Church v. Village of Long Grove, 468 F.3d 975, 997 (7th Cir. 2006), cert. denied, 128 S. Ct. 77 (2007); Midrash Sephardi, Inc. v. Town of Surfside, 366 F.3d 1214, 1227 (11th Cir. 2004) (describing substantial burden as "akin to significant pressure which directly coerces the religious adherent to conform his or her behavior accordingly. Thus, a substantial burden can result from pressure that tends to force adherents to forego religious precepts or from pressure that mandates religious conduct.").

[677]Navajo Nation v. U.S. Forest Service, 535 F.3d 1058, 1070 (9th Cir. 2008) (the use of recycled waste water to make artificial snow in a small part of a large area considered sacred by Native Americans was not a substantial burden even if it "diminish[ed] . . . spiritual fulfillment"), cert. denied, 129 S. Ct. 2763 (2009).

[678]Mack v. O'Leary, 80 F.3d 1175, 1179 (7th Cir. 1996), cert. granted, judgment vacated on other grounds, 522 U.S. 801 (1997); accord, Freeman v. Arpaio, 125 F.3d 732, 737 (9th Cir. 1997).

requirement[679] of the person's religion. The Supreme Court long ago rejected that view under the First Amendment,[680] and RLUIPA did the same by defining "religious exercise" to include "any exercise of religion, whether or not compelled by, or central to, a system of religious belief,"[681] and applying that definition to RFRA as well.[682] Therefore, officials should not get very far by arguing that a burden is not substantial because the particular religious practice it affects is not important or not required by orthodox doctrine.[683] However, you do need to show that the practice is important to your own religious practice.[684]

Courts have found a substantial burden in a wide variety of situations, for example: firing and disciplining a Muslim prisoner who refused to handle pork in his food service job;[685] requiring prisoners to keep their hair cut short, and forcibly cutting it where prisoners did not comply;[686] refusing to allow a prisoner to preach;[687] excluding a Native American prisoner from group services for a period of three months;[688] denying wine during Jewish services that normally called for it;[689] confiscating religious literature;[690] refusal to grant a nutritionally adequate non-meat diet during the 40 days of Lent;[691] requiring clergy verification of religious diets, as applied to prisoner whose religion had no clergy and where dietary rules were not prescribed but left to individual conscience;[692] and refusing to allow a Dianic pagan prisoner to attend services of other religious groups that he said were necessary for him to "achieve meaningful satisfactory religious exercise."[693] Examples of restrictions that courts found *not* to be substantial burdens include: failure to conduct services every Sabbath for the Yahweh Evangelical Assembly, where prison officials had not located enough outside volunteers to provide weekly services; [694] requiring an Orthodox Jewish prisoner to submit an application to receive kosher food; [695] denying Muslims a full-size prayer rug, allowing instead a prayer towel that is the same size but thinner.[696]

---

[679]Bryant v. Gomez, 46 F.3d 948, 949 (9th Cir. 1995).

[680]Employment Div. v. Smith, 494 U.S. 872, 886–87, 110 S. Ct. 1595 (1990); *accord*, Shakur v. Schriro, 514 F.3d 878, 884–85 (9th Cir. 2008).

[681]42 U.S.C. § 2000cc-5(7)(A); *see* Nelson v. Miller, 570 F.3d 868, 878–79 (7th Cir. 2009) (requirement that prisoner show dietary practice was compelled by religion was contrary to RLUIPA); Grace United Methodist Church v. City of Cheyenne, 451 F.3d 643, 662–63 (10th Cir. 2006) (holding court's pre-RLUIPA requirement that plaintiff show interference with a practice "fundamental" to his religion is not applicable under RLUIPA); Coronel v. Paul, 316 F. Supp. 2d 868, 876–77 (D.Ariz. 2004) (noting that RLUIPA was intended in part to get rid of RFRA interpretations limited to "central tenets" and practices that were "mandated or compelled" by the religion).

[682]42 U.S.C. § 2000bb-2(4); *see* Kikumura v. Hurley, 242 F.3d 950, 960 (10th Cir. 2001).

[683]*See* § D.1.a of this chapter, nn.646–647, for further discussion of this issue.

[684]Smith v. Allen, 502 F.3d 1255, 1278–80 (11th Cir. 2007) (finding no substantial burden where plaintiff did not show the importance of the disputed practices to his religious exercise); Adkins v. Kaspar, 393 F.3d 559, 570 (5th Cir. 2004) (plaintiff must demonstrate "honesty and accuracy of his contention that the religious practice at issue is important to the free exercise of his religion"); *see* Borzych v. Frank, 439 F.3d 388, 390 (7th Cir. 2006) (questioning whether denial to Odinist plaintiff of books *Creed of Iron*, *Temple of Wotan*, and *The NPKA Book of Blotar* substantially burdened his religious exercise where the only evidence was his and other prisoners' "unreasoned say-so," with no "objective evidence . . . that the books are important to Odinism," and where defendants' expert on folklore and Old Norse language and literature said they were not Odinic or even religious but were secular works promoting racism).

The fact that a prisoner has complied with prison rules contrary to his religious beliefs does not mean that there is no substantial burden from the rules; there is no "use it or lose it" principle governing prisoners' religious rights. May v. Baldwin, 109 F.3d 557, 563 (9th Cir. 1997).

[685]Williams v. Bitner, 359 F. Supp. 2d 370, 376 (M.D.Pa. 2005) ("Williams was placed in the unenviable position of choosing between punishment by prison officials or observance of religious teachings. This is the type of choice that the RLUIPA was enacted to prevent."), *aff'd on other grounds*, 455 F.3d 186 (3d Cir. 2006).

Similarly, punitive measures including loss of privileges and expulsion from programs against a Native American prisoner who refused to cut his hair were substantial burdens, even if officials did not physically force him to cut his hair. Warsoldier v. Woodford, 418 F.3d 989, 995–96 (9th Cir. 2005); *see* McEachin v. McGuinnis, 357 F.3d 197, 205 (2d Cir. 2004) ("Precedent suggests that inmates have a right not to be disciplined for refusing to perform tasks that violate their religious beliefs.").

[686]Smith v. Ozmint, 578 F.3d 246, 251-52 (4th Cir. 2009).

[687]Spratt v. Rhode Island Dep't of Corrections, 482 F.3d 33, 38 (1st Cir. 2007).

[688]Meyer v. Teslik, 411 F. Supp. 2d 983, 989–90 (W.D.Wis. 2006).

[689]Sample v. Lappin, 424 F. Supp. 2d 187, 194–95 (D.D.C. 2006), *reconsideration denied*, 479 F. Supp. 2d 120 (D.D.C. 2007).

[690]Rowe v. Davis, 373 F. Supp. 2d 822, 826 (N.D.Ind. 2005) (" . . . [R]eading religious literature is a part of the way Mr. Rowe practices and expresses his religious beliefs. Therefore, reading religious literature is a religious exercise. . . . Therefore taking his religious literature was a substantial burden on his religious exercise of reading religious literature.").

[691]Nelson v. Miller, 570 F.3d 868, 880 (7th Cir. 2009).

[692]Koger v. Bryan, 523 F.3d 789, 800–02 (7th Cir. 2008); *accord*, Nelson v. Miller, 570 F.3d 868, 878 (7th Cir. 2009).

[693]Coronel v. Paul, 316 F. Supp. 2d 868, 880–81 (D.Ariz. 2004).

[694]Adkins v. Kaspar, 393 F.3d 559, 571 (5th Cir. 2004).

[695]Resnick v. Adams, 348 F.3d 763, 767–68 & n.6 (9th Cir. 2003); *see* Jackson-Bey v. Hanslmaier, 115 F.3d 1091, 1097 (2d Cir. 1997) (requiring prisoners to register religious preference in order to receive religious accommodations places only a "slight burden" on religious exercise).

[696]Hudson v. Dennehy, 538 F. Supp. 2d 400, 411–12 (D.Mass. 2008), *aff'd sub nom* Crawford v. Clarke, 578 F.3d 59 (1st Cir. 2009).

3) RFRA/RLUIPA and the First Amendment Standard Compared

The RFRA/RLUIPA standard—often referred to as "strict scrutiny"—is more favorable to prisoners than the *Turner/O'Lone* reasonableness standard,[697] and a number of cases have ruled against prisoners under *Turner/O'Lone* but in favor of them under RFRA/RLUIPA.[698] Advantages of the statutory standard include:

1. Under RLUIPA and RFRA, prison officials have the burden of proof; they must "demonstrate" that their rules are valid under the statutes.[699] Under the reasonableness standard, in contrast, the burden is on prisoners to "point to an alternative that fully accommodates the prisoner's rights at *de minimis* cost to valid penological interests" in order to prevail.[700]

2. RFRA and RLUIPA require prison officials to justify their policies by showing they are necessary to serve a "compelling" interest, while the *Turner/O'Lone* standard only requires a valid or legitimate interest. Prison security is considered a compelling interest,[701] though enforcing authority in every aspect of prison operations may not be.[702] Beyond that, it's a bit murky what is and isn't compelling.[703]

As to cost, the statutes themselves say they "may require a government to incur expenses in its own operation to avoid imposing a substantial burden on religious exercise,"[704] which should limit officials' ability to use cost as a reason not to accommodate your religions exercise. Some decisions—mostly from outside the prison context—have said that administrative convenience and cost-cutting are not compelling interests.[705] However, the Supreme Court has said that Congress "anticipated that courts would apply [RLUIPA's] standard with 'due deference to the experience and expertise of prison and jail administrators in establishing

---

[697]Jova v. Smith, 582 F.3d 410, 415 (2d Cir. 2009) ("As a general matter, the RLUIPA imposes duties on prison officials that exceed those imposed by the First Amendment."); Borzych v. Frank, 439 F.3d 388, 390 (7th Cir. 2006) ("RLUIPA . . . prohibits prisons that receive federal funding from substantially burdening an inmate's religious exercise unless the step in question is the least restrictive way to advance a compelling state interest. . . . The first amendment, by contrast, does not require the accommodation of religious practice: states may enforce neutral rules."); Freeman v. Texas Dep't of Criminal Justice, 369 F.3d 854, 858 n.1 (5th Cir. 2004) ("The RLUIPA standard poses a far greater challenge than does *Turner* to prison regulations that impinge on inmates' free exercise of religion.").

[698]*See* Murphy v. Missouri Dep't of Correction, 372 F.3d 979, 983–85, 989 (8th Cir. 2004) (prohibition on group worship by Christian Separatist Church Society did not violate the First Amendment since defendants claimed "racial segregation will spark violence" and CSC members had the alternative of studying scriptures and CSC writings, praying, etc.; however, under RLUIPA, officials would have to justify their restrictions at trial and "provide some basis for their concern that racial violence will result from any accommodation of CSC's request"); Kikumura v. Hurley, 242 F.3d 950, 957–58, 960–62 (10th Cir. 2001) (upholding the exclusion of a religious adviser under *Turner/O'Lone*, but stating prisoner might prevail under the RFRA standard; advisor had been excluded because he rather than the plaintiff had initiated the contact); Charles v. Verhagen, 220 F. Supp. 2d 937, 951–52 (W.D.Wis. 2002) (striking down prohibition on Islamic prayer oil under the "exacting" least restrictive means test of RLUIPA, upholding it under the First Amendment), *aff'd*, 348 F.3d 601 (7th Cir. 2003).

[699]42 U.S.C.A. § 2000cc-1(a) (RLUIPA); 42 U.S.C.A. § 2000bb-1(a) (RFRA); *see* Spratt v. Rhode Island Dep't of Corrections, 482 F.3d 33, 38–40 (1st Cir. 2007); O'Bryan v. Bureau of Prisons, 349 F.3d 399, 401 (7th Cir. 2003) (officials "must demonstrate, and not just assert, that the rule at issue is the least restrictive means of achieving a compelling interest"; refusing to assume without proof that rule against "casting of spells/curses" was necessary to avoid fights); *see also* Smith v. Ozmint, 578 F.3d 246, 252-54 (4th Cir. 2009) (requirement of short haircuts was not adequately supported by an affidavit prepared in another case for another prison of a different security level); Shakur v. Schriro, 514 F.3d 878, 889–90 (9th Cir. 2008) (holding affidavit from religious official, rather than food service or procurement official, which was partly based on hearsay from other prison personnel, was insufficient to establish expense of providing Halal or kosher meat to Muslims).

[700]Turner v. Safley, 482 U.S. 78, 91, 107 S. Ct. 2254 (1987); *see* O'Lone v. Estate of Shabazz, 482 U.S. 342, 350, 107 S. Ct. 2400 (1987) (rejecting placement of burden on officials).

[701]Cutter v. Wilkinson, 544 U.S. 709, 725 n.13, 125 S. Ct. 2113 (2005); Jova v. Smith, 582 F.3d 410, 415–16 (2d Cir. 2009); Warsoldier v. Woodford, 418 F.3d 989, 998 (9th Cir. 2005); *see* Lawson v. Singletary, 85 F.3d 502, 506, 512–13 (11th Cir. 1996) (upholding under RFRA, as applied to religious publications, a rule censoring material that "depicts, describes, or encourages activities which may lead to the use of physical violence or group disruption" or "otherwise presents a threat to the security, order or rehabilitative objectives of the correctional system or the safety of any person").

[702]*See* Jova v. Smith, 582 F.3d at 146 (upholding refusal to comply with dietary requests that specified particular foods and portions for particular days and required that they be prepared by adherents of the religion on grounds of "administrative burden"); Koger v. Bryan, 523 F.3d 789, 800 (7th Cir. 2008) (noting that orderly administration of prison dietary system has been held to be a legitimate penological interest, but not a compelling interest); Lovelace v. Lee, 472 F.3d 174, 190 (4th Cir. 2006) (interest in "removing inmates from religious dietary programs where the inmate flouts prison rules" is not on its face a compelling interest). *Jova* and *Koger* seem to contradict each other on whether administrative concerns can be a compelling interest. However, the administrative burden in *Jova* was much greater than in *Koger*. We think that administrative burden will be compelling, or not, depending on how large it is on the facts of a particular case.

[703]The Supreme Court has "never set forth a general test to determine what constitutes a compelling state interest." Waters v. Churchill, 511 U.S. 661, 671, 114 S. Ct. 1878 (1994).

[704]42 U.S.C. § 2000cc-3(c) (RLUIPA). This provision was also made applicable to federal agencies, officials, etc., so it is applicable in RFRA cases. 42 U.S.C. § 2000cc-5(4)(B).

[705]Memorial Hospital v. Maricopa County, 415 U.S. 250, 263-69 94 S. Ct. 1076 (1974) ("conservation of the taxpayers' purse" held not sufficient under a compelling interest standard); Frontiero v. Richardson, 411 U.S. 677, 690–91, 93 S. Ct. 1764 (1973) (administrative convenience does not meet strict scrutiny standard).

necessary regulations and procedures to maintain good order, security and discipline, consistent with consideration of costs and limited resources.'"[706] Courts will probably hold administrative and cost issues to be compelling in RLUIPA or RFRA cases, or not, depending on how serious they are.[707] You may have more success in persuading a court that a particular policy is not necessary to serve a compelling interest, or that there is a less restrictive alternative, than that there is no compelling interest at stake. However, the statutes' acknowledgment that defendants may be required to "incur expenses" to comply does appear more favorable than the *Turner/O'Lone* standard, which requires prisoners to show that there is an alternative that "fully accommodates the prisoner's rights at *de minimis* cost to valid penological interests"[708]—which some courts have interpreted as meaning a "cost-free" alternative.[709]

3. Officials must show under RFRA and RLUIPA that their policy is the "least restrictive means" of serving the compelling interest that they claim—that is, that there is no way to accomplish some necessary purpose that is more respectful of prisoners' religious rights than the practice that is being challenged.[710] Under this standard, courts have held

that prison officials must show that they have "actually considered and rejected the efficacy of less restrictive measures."[711] That is quite different from the reasonable relationship standard, which the Supreme Court has said "is not a 'least restrictive alternative' test: prison officials do not have to set up and then shoot down every conceivable alternative method of accommodating the claimant's constitutional complaint."[712] The existence of less restrictive practices at other institutions[713] (or with respect to other prisoners in

---

[706]Cutter v. Wilkinson, 544 U.S. at 723 (citing legislative history).

[707]*See, e.g.,* Shakur v. Schriro, 514 F.3d 878, 890–91 (9th Cir. 2008) (questioning how large the expense of making Halal or kosher meat available to Muslims would actually be); Baranowski v. Hart, 486 F.3d 112, 125–26 (5th Cir. 2007) ("controlling costs" is a compelling interest; providing kosher food would be a threat to "maintaining good order" because it would trigger resentment among other prisoners and cause increased demand by other groups for religious diets), *cert. denied,* 128 S.Ct. 707 (2007); Spavone v. City of New York, 420 F. Supp. 2d 236, 240 (S.D.N.Y. 2005) (jail system has a compelling interest in trying to restrict movement of inmates to maintain proper order; court upholds requirement that prisoners register their religious affiliation and restricts them to a single religious choice); Ingalls v. Florio, 968 F. Supp. 193, 204–05 (D.N.J. 1997) ("the fair apportionment of access to prison resources for the benefit of inmates of all faiths constitutes a compelling governmental interest"); Rust v. Clarke, 883 F. Supp. 1293, 1307 (D.Neb. 1995) (upholding under RFRA various restrictions on Asatru practice as "protecting the rights of *all . . .* inmates to freely exercise their religion by equitably allocating finite resources among the numerous denominations. . . ."), *aff'd,* 89 F.3d 841 (8th Cir. 1996) (unpublished). *But see* Luckette v. Lewis, 883 F. Supp. 471, 480–81 (D.Ariz. 1995) (though budgetary concerns are compelling, the alleged greater cost of kosher food for a few prisoners is not large enough to justify denial).

[708]Turner v. Safley, 482 U.S. 78, 90–91, 107 S. Ct. 2254 (1987).

[709]Ortiz v. Fort Dodge Correctional Facility, 368 F.3d 1024, 1027 (8th Cir. 2004).

[710]For example, in *Williams v. Bitner,* 359 F. Supp. 2d 370 (M.D.Pa. 2005), *aff'd on other grounds,* 455 F.3d 186 (3d Cir. 2006), where a Muslim prisoner was disciplined for refusing to handle pork in his food service job, the court agreed with prison officials that maintaining order and security was a compelling interest, but said that disciplining the prisoner was not necessarily the least restrictive alternative, since he was not being disruptive and other

prisoners were available to prepare the pork. 359 F. Supp. 2d at 376–77. Similarly, in *Sample v. Lappin,* 424 F. Supp. 2d 187 (D.D.C. 2006), *reconsideration denied,* 479 F. Supp. 2d 120 (D.D.C. 2007), the Jewish plaintiff alleged that the refusal to provide wine at Jewish services substantially burdened his religious exercise. The court agreed that controlling alcohol consumption in prison is a compelling governmental interest, but held that a complete prohibition was not shown to be the least restrictive means, since Bureau of Prisons policy allows inmates to receive small amounts of wine as part of religious rituals under certain controlled circumstances, and the warden's reasons for not following that policy were not adequately explained. 424 F. Supp. 2d at 195–96. *See* Warsoldier v. Woodford, 418 F.3d 989, 998–99 (9th Cir. 2005) (holding officials' security justifications for restricting hair length were not shown to be necessary at the plaintiff's minimum security prison); Hudson v. Dennehy, 538 F. Supp. 2d 400, 412 (D.Mass. 2008) (upholding exclusion of segregation prisoners from Jumu'ah services based on compelling interests of rehabilitation and good order, but holding that denying them video participation is not the least restrictive means), *aff'd sub nom* Crawford v. Clarke, 578 F.3d 39 (1st Cir. 2009); Mayweathers v. Terhune, 328 F. Supp. 2d 1086, 1094–96 (E.D.Cal. 2004) (ban on beards was not the least restrictive means to identify prisoners reliably; instead, officials could visually inspect facial hair daily, as their regulations already required, and require photos both clean shaven and with a beard); Gartrell v. Ashcroft, 191 F. Supp. 2d 23, 38–40 (D.D.C. 2002) (placing prisoners with religious objections in a prison system that forbids beards and long hair is not the least restrictive means of managing D.C. prison population; they should not send prisoners whose religious beliefs would be burdened to that system), *appeal dismissed,* 2003 WL 1873847 (D.C. Cir. 2003).

[711]Warsoldier v. Woodford, 418 F.3d 989, 999 (9th Cir. 2005); *accord,* Jova v. Smith, 582 F.3d 410, 416 (2d Cir. 2009); Washington v. Klem, 497 F.3d 272, 284 (3d Cir. 2007); Spratt v. Rhode Island Dep't of Corrections, 482 F.3d 33, 40–41 (1st Cir. 2007) (blanket assertion that alternatives are unfeasible does not meet officials' burden); Gartrell v. Ashcroft, 191 F. Supp. 2d at 39–40.

[712]Turner v. Safley, 482 U.S. 78, 90–91, 107 S. Ct. 2254 (1987).

[713]Warsoldier v. Woodford, 418 F.3d 989, 1000 (9th Cir. 2005) ("Indeed, the failure of a defendant to explain why another institution with the same compelling interests was able to accommodate the same religious practices may constitute a failure to establish that the defendant was using the least restrictive means."). In *Warsoldier,* the court noted that prison officials failed to explain why it did not restrict hair length at women's prisons as well as men's prisons, since its claimed interests in health and security were just as compelling for women, and the rate of assault among women was not greatly different from that among men. 418 F.3d at 1000; *accord,* Smith v. Ozmint, 578 F.3d 246, 253 (4th Cir. 2009) (noting failure to explain why long hair was acceptable at women's

the same institution[714]) may also be an important consideration.[715] By contrast, the Supreme Court has said that in a reasonable relationship analysis there is no "'lowest common denominator' security standard, whereby a practice permitted at one penal institution must be permitted at all institutions."[716] Under RFRA/RLUIPA, the alternatives that must be considered include granting religious exemptions from otherwise valid rules and policies.[717] Under *Turner/O'Lone*,

prison officials are generally not required to create religious exemptions to otherwise valid policies.[718]

4. RLUIPA and RFRA apply the compelling interest/least restrictive means test to any "substantial burden" on religious exercise,[719] and they define "religious exercise" as "any exercise of religion, whether or not compelled by, or central to, a system of religious belief."[720] These provisions rule out the approach that some courts had taken under the First Amendment and *Turner/O'Lone* standard of ruling against prisoners if they thought that a particular religious practice was not sufficiently "central" or supported by religious authorities.[721] Under *Turner/O'Lone*, courts sometimes held that restricting some religious practices is all right as long as other practices—"alternative means" of religious exercise—were permitted.[722] That argument should not be valid under RLUIPA or RFRA.[723]

Despite these differences between the constitutional and statutory standards, some courts have been reluctant to interpret the statutes as they are written, and have applied them in ways that are more consistent with the *Turner/O'Lone* standard than with the actual language of RLUIPA and RFRA. For example, one court upheld the denial to Jewish prisoners of a kosher diet, stating that "controlling costs" is a compelling governmental interest,[724] without reference to

---

prison); *see* Shakur v. Schriro, 514 F.3d 878, 890–91 (9th Cir. 2008) (holding that evidence of an out-of-state prison that served Halal meat to Muslims at only minimal extra cost over regular meals, and cheaper than kosher meals, was relevant to whether denial of Halal meat to plaintiff was the least restrictive means).

[714]Rowe v. Davis, 373 F. Supp. 2d 822, 827 (N.D.Ind. 2005) (denial of Celtic Cross would not be the least restrictive alternative if prisoners of other religions were permitted to have them); Mayweathers v. Terhune, 328 F. Supp. 2d 1086, 1096–97 (E.D.Cal. 2004) (denial of work exemptions for Jumu'ah services was not the least restrictive means of administering the prison work program where prisoners were allowed up to 16 hours a month off work for visits, special services, and other events); Luckette v. Lewis, 883 F. Supp. 471, 481 (D.Ariz. 1995) (granting injunction to allow plaintiff to wear a quarter-inch beard, as was allowed to other prisoners for medical reasons).

[715]Warsoldier v. Woodford, 418 F.3d at 1000; *accord*, Jova v. Smith, 582 F.3d 410, 416 (2d Cir. 2009); Spratt v. Rhode Island Dep't of Corrections, 482 F.3d at 42 ("evidence of policies at one prison is not conclusive proof that the same policies would work at another institution," but it does require explanation from officials as to why they won't work at the prison under suit).

[716]Turner v. Safley, 482 U.S. 78, 93 n.*, 107 S. Ct. 2254 (1987) (quoting Bell v. Wolfish, 441 U.S. 520, 554, 99 S. Ct. 1861 (1979)); *see* Fromer v. Scully, 874 F.2d 69, 74–75 (2d Cir. 1989) (holding that more lenient practices in other prison systems did not determine whether ban on beards was unconstitutional under *Turner*); Wilson v. Moore, 270 F. Supp. 2d 1328, 1353 (N.D.Fla. 2003) (under *Turner/O'Lone*, dismissing argument that other prisons in other states allow sweat lodges for Native American worship).

[717]Gonzales v. O Centro Espirita Beneficente Uniao do Vegetal, 546 U.S. 418, 430–32, 436, 126 S. Ct. 1211 (2006) (requiring exemption from controlled substance statute for religious group that used a Schedule I drug sacramentally; under RFRA, government cannot merely "echo[] the classic rejoinder of bureaucrats throughout history: If I make an exception for you, I'll have to make one for everybody, so no exceptions."); Smith v. Ozmint, 578 F.3d 246, 253 (4th Cir. 2009) (prison officials failed to show why short hair requirement must be uniform); Shakur v. Schriro, 514 F.3d 878, 890 (9th Cir. 2008) (prison officials failed to show that denial of Halal or kosher meat to Muslims was the least restrictive alternative where they failed to consider an exemption for the plaintiff, who had gastrointestinal problems on the Muslim vegetarian diet); Gartrell v. Ashcroft, 191 F. Supp. 2d 23, 38–40 (D.D.C. 2002) (requiring officials to exempt prisoners with religious objections to cutting hair and shaving beards from transfer to a prison system which forbade long hair and beards), *appeal dismissed*, 2003 WL 1873847 (D.C. Cir., Apr. 11, 2003).

[718]Green v. Polunsky, 229 F.3d 486, 491 (5th Cir. 2000) (holding religious exemption from no-beard rule is not required even though there was a medical exemption); Friedman v. State of Arizona, 912 F.2d 328, 332 (9th Cir. 1990). *But see* Flagner v. Wilkinson, 241 F.3d 475, 487 (6th Cir. 2001) (suggesting need for a religious exemption under *Turner/O'Lone*).

[719]42 U.S.C.A. § 2000cc(a)(1).

[720]42 U.S.C.A. § 2000cc-5(7)(A) (emphasis supplied); *see, e.g.*, Rowe v. Davis, 373 F. Supp. 2d 822, 825–26 (N.D.Ind. 2005) (holding that reading religious literature "is a part of the way Mr. Rowe practices and expresses his religious beliefs. Therefore, reading religious literature is a religious exercise," and preventing him from doing it is a substantial burden).

[721]*See* § D.1.b(2) of this chapter, nn.646–649.

[722]O'Lone v. Estate of Shabazz, 482 U.S. 342, 351–52, 107 S. Ct. 2400 (1987) (upholding exclusion of Muslim prisoners from Jumu'ah services during working hours, in part because they could engage in congregate prayer or religious discussion at other times, they received pork-free meals, Ramadan observance was accommodated, etc.); *see* § A of this chapter, nn.49–53.

[723]Greene v. Solano County Jail, 513 F.3d 982, 987 (9th Cir. 2008) (rejecting argument that RLUIPA allows banning some aspects of religious exercise as long as "in the aggregate" the restrictions do not substantially burden religious exercise); Meyer v. Teslik, 411 F. Supp. 2d 983, 989–90 (W.D.Wis. 2006) ("Unlike the First Amendment, RLUIPA protects more than the right to practice one's faith; it protects the right to engage in specific, meaningful acts of religious expression in the absence of a compelling reason to limit the expression"; where prisoner was excluded from several religious services, the fact that he remained free to meditate silently, fast, or correspond with other believers was irrelevant to the question of substantial burden).

[724]Baranowski v. Hart, 486 F.3d 112, 125–26 (5th Cir. 2007), *cert. denied*, 128 S. Ct. 707 (2007). *Baranowski* also accepted

RLUIPA's provision stating that it "may require a government to incur expenses in its own operations to avoid imposing a substantial burden on religious exercise."[725] Another court upheld restrictions on prisoners' hair length, stating the lower court "improperly substituted its judgment for that of prison officials" in applying the least restrictive means test,[726] though that is essentially what the least restrictive means test requires.

4) Remedies and Defendants under RFRA/RLUIPA

There are some unsettled issues that may limit the usefulness of RFRA and RLUIPA. The statutes provide for "appropriate relief" but they don't say what that means. It seems clear that injunctive relief is "appropriate" to end practices that are found illegal under the statutes,[727] though there may be some special rules about injunctions under RLUIPA. The statute says:

> A government may avoid the preemptive force of any provision of this chapter by changing the policy or practice that results in a substantial burden on religious exercise, by retaining the policy or practice and exempting the substantially burdened religious exercise, by providing exemptions from the policy or practice for applications that substantially burden religious exercise, or by any other means that eliminates the substantial burden.[728]

Some courts have interpreted that provision to mean that officials may avoid a court order by changing their practices after they are sued to accommodate religious exercise.[729] That is different from the usual rule, under which

reforms made under pressure of litigation do not make a case moot or preclude the grant of injunctive relief.[730]

Decisions are divided on the availability of damages. Some courts have held that damages are included in the phrase "appropriate relief,"[731] which makes sense, because the Supreme Court has previously held exactly that, and because generally courts can award damages when a federal statute creates a private cause of action unless Congress forbids damages.[732] Further, RLUIPA itself says: "This Act shall be construed in favor of a broad protection of religious exercise, to the maximum extent permitted by the terms of this Act and the Constitution,"[733] which suggests that all the remedies usually available in litigation should be available. A few courts have held that "appropriate relief" does not include damages.[734]

However, a number of courts have recently held that the sovereign immunity of state governments[735] prevents damages awards against governments or against official capacity defendants under RLUIPA and RFRA. The basic idea of RLUIPA is that states waive their sovereign immunity by accepting federal funds. These recent decisions say that the phrase "appropriate relief" does not give sufficient notice that by accepting the funds the states are waiving their sovereign immunity from RLUIPA damages claims.[736]

---

officials' argument that providing kosher food would be a threat to "maintaining good order" because it would trigger resentment among other prisoners and cause increased demand by other groups for religious diets. *Id.*

[725]42 U.S.C. § 2000cc-3(c).

[726]Hoevenaar v. Lazaroff, 422 F.3d 366, 370 (6th Cir. 2006); *see* Fegans v. Norris, 537 F.3d 897, 902–06 (8th Cir. 2008) (upholding hair length restriction and prohibition on beards, rejecting usual RLUIPA requirement of religious exemptions).

[727]Smith v. Allen, 502 F.3d 1255, 1269 (11th Cir. 2007).

[728]42 U.S.C. § 2000cc-3(e).

[729]Boles v. Neet, 402 F. Supp. 2d 1237, 1241 (D.Colo. 2005), *aff'd*, 486 F.3d 1177 (10th Cir. 2007) (citing Civil Liberties for Urban Believers v. City of Chicago, 342 F.3d 752, 762 (7th Cir. 2003)). *But see* Family Life Church v. City of Elgin, 2007 WL 2790763, *5 (N.D.Ill., Sept. 24, 2007) (holding policy change by defendants did not eliminate damage claim for injuries sustained under old policy).

Also, one court has suggested that analysis under the statutes is "specific," meaning that it requires courts to examine the situation of the individual plaintiff; courts cannot "nullify whole regulations just because they have a potential for improper application to a particular faith or belief." Borzych v. Frank, 439 F.3d 388, 392 (7th Cir. 2006) (citing Gonzales v. O Centro Espirita Beneficente Uniao do Vegetal, 546 U.S. 418, 126 S. Ct. 1211 (2006)). The *Gonzales* case does indeed call for a focus on the individual plaintiff. However, the Supreme Court's point seems to be to place a greater burden of justification on the *defendants*, not to limit the courts'

injunctive powers. That is, defendants must not only show that their policy is well founded in general, but that they have compelling reasons for insisting on applying it to individuals who have religious objections, rather than exempting them from the policy. *Gonzales*, 546 U.S. at 430–31.

[730]*See* Ch. 8, § I.2, concerning mootness.

[731]Smith v. Allen, 502 F.3d at 1270–71 and cases cited; Jama v. U.S. Immigration and Naturalization Service, 343 F. Supp. 2d 338, 371–76 (D.N.J. 2004) (RFRA case); *see* Lighthouse Institute for Evangelism, Inc. v. City of Long Branch, 510 F.3d 253, 272–73 (3d Cir. 2007), *cert. denied*, 128 S.Ct. 2503 (2008); Shidler v. Moore, 409 F. Supp. 2d 1060, 1069 (N.D.Ind.2006) (both assuming damages are available under RLUIPA).

[732]Franklin v. Gwinnett County Public Schools, 503 U.S. 60, 66, 70–71, 76, 112 S. Ct. 1028, 1034–35 (1992); *accord*, Smith v. Allen, 502 F.3d at 1270.

[733]42 U.S.C. § 2000cc-3(g).

[734]Bock v. Gold, 2008 WL 345890, *1, *5–7 (D.Vt. 2008); Boles v. Neet, 402 F. Supp. 2d 1237, 1241 (D.Colo.2005), *aff'd on other grounds*, 486 F.3d 1177 (10th Cir. 2007).

[735]*See* Ch. 8, § L.1, for a discussion of the Eleventh Amendment and sovereign immunity from damages.

[736]The Supreme Court has accepted a case that may resolve this question. *See* Sossamon v. Lone Star State of Texas, 560 F.3d 316, 330–31 (5th Cir. 2009), *cert. granted in part*, 2010 WL 2025142 (May 24, 2010); *see also* Van Wyhe v. Reisch, 581 F.3d 639, 653–54 (8th Cir. 2009); Nelson v. Miller, 570 F.3d 868, 884–85 (7th Cir. 2009); Cardinal v. Metrish, 564 F.3d 794, 801 (6th Cir. 2009), pet. for cert. filed, No. 09-109 (July 22, 2009); Scott v. Beard, 252 Fed.Appx. 491, 492–93 (3rd Cir. 2007) (unpublished); Madison v. Virginia, 474 F.3d 118, 129–33 (4th Cir. 2006); Pugh v. Goord, 571 F. Supp. 2d 477, 507–09 (S.D.N.Y. 2008); Williams v. Beltran, 569 F. Supp. 2d 1057, 1063–65 (C.D. Cal. 2008); Bock v. Gold, 2008 WL 345890, *1, *5–7 (D.Vt., Feb. 7, 2008); Toler v. Leopold, 2007 WL 2907889, *1–2 (E.D.Mo., Oct.1, 2007); Dean v. Blum, 2007 WL

Some courts have held similarly concerning federal government sovereign immunity and RFRA.[737] Others have held that states do waive their sovereign immunity from RLUIPA damages claims by accepting federal money.[738]

There is also a question against whom, if anybody, RLUIPA is intended to authorize damage awards. The statute allows relief against a "government," and defines that term to include State, county, city, and other governments and branches and agencies of governments as well as individuals.[739] Some courts have held that the statute does not permit damages against defendants in their individual capacity.[740] If that is the case, then you cannot recover damages at all in a jurisdiction where the courts have held states do not waive their sovereign immunity under RLUIPA, since official capacity awards would also be barred. Other courts have held that damages can be awarded against officials in their individual capacity,[741] as is the case under 42 U.S.C. § 1983.

It makes a difference whether RFRA and RLUIPA claims are prosecuted against governmental bodies or officials in their official capacity, or against officials in their individual capacity. If you sue officials in their individual capacity, they will be entitled to the defense of qualified immunity unless the rights you assert are "clearly established."[742] Official capacity defendants, like municipalities, are generally not entitled to the defense of qualified immunity,[743] so you should be able to recover damages against them even if the rights you assert are not "clearly established." However, you probably cannot recover punitive damages against governmental units or against official capacity defendants even if official capacity damages suits are permitted.[744] If you sue officials in their individual capacities, you will probably have to satisfy the same "personal involvement" requirement as applies under 42 U.S.C. § 1983.[745] If you sue them in their official capacities, you may not face that requirement. For all these reasons, you should be sure you know whether RLUIPA damage liability is individual capacity or official capacity in the court where you are filing suit, if it exists at all.

Even if a court is persuaded that damages are permitted by RLUIPA or RFRA, they will probably be limited because many courts have interpreted the Prison Litigation Reform Act's prohibition on compensatory damages for mental or emotional injury without physical injury[746] as prohibiting compensatory damages (though not nominal and punitive damages) for violations of religious rights.[747]

Attorneys' fees are available to the prevailing party in a RLUIPA suit on the same terms as under other civil

---

2264615, *7 (D.Neb., Aug. 6, 2007), *reconsideration denied*, 2007 WL 3225382 (D.Neb., Oct. 29, 2007).

[737]Webman v. Fed. Bureau of Prisons, 441 F.3d 1022, 1026 (D.C. Cir. 2006) (holding language in Religious Freedom Restoration Act, similar to that in RLUIPA, permitting suit for "appropriate relief," did not waive federal government's immunity to suits for damages; citing cases); Jama v. U.S. Immigration and Naturalization Service, 343 F. Supp. 2d 338, 373–76 (D.N.J. 2004).

[738]Smith v. Allen, 502 F.3d 1255, 1275–76 (11th Cir. 2007); Price v. Caruso, 451 F. Supp. 2d 889, 902 (E.D.Mich.2006).

One decision, later reversed, held that RLUIPA is governed by the Civil Rights Remedies Equalization Act of 1986, 42 U.S.C. § 2000d-7, which says that the Eleventh Amendment is no defense for states from claims under federal discrimination statutes. Sisney v. Reisch, 533 F. Supp. 2d 952, 969–72 (D.S.D. 2008), *aff'd in part, rev'd in pertinent part sub nom.* Van Wyhe v. Reisch, 581 F.3d 639 (8th Cir. 2009). Other courts have rejected that line of reasoning. Madison v. Virginia, 474 F.3d 118, 133 (4th Cir. 2006) (holding that RLUIPA is not really a discrimination statute).

[739]42 U.S.C. § 2000cc-5(4)(A); *see* 42 U.S.C. § 2000bb-2(1) (defining government for RFRA cases as "a branch, department, agency, instrumentality, and official (or other person acting under color of law) of the United States" or of the District of Columbia, the Commonwealth of Puerto Rico, and United States territories and possessions).

[740]Nelson v. Miller, 570 F.3d 868, 886–89 (7th Cir. 2009) (rejecting individual capacity damages to avoid serious constitutional question whether Spending Clause authority extended to creating damages remedies against individuals); Rendelman v. Rouse, 569 F.3d 182, 187–89 (4th Cir. 2009) (holding RLUIPA did not give sufficient notice to state officials that they could be liable individually if they accepted federal funds); Sossamon v. Lone Star State of Texas, 560 F.3d 316, 328–29 (5th Cir. 2009) (similar to *Nelson*), *cert. granted in part*, 2010 WL 2025142 (May 24, 2010); Smith v. Allen, 502 F.3d at 1276 & n.12 (similar to *Nelson*); Pugh v. Goord, 571 F. Supp. 2d 477, 506–07 (S.D.N.Y. 2008); Gooden v. Crain, 405 F. Supp. 2d 714, 723 (E.D.Tex.2005) ("RLUIPA does not contemplate recovering damages from individuals. . . ."), *aff'd in part, vacated in part on other grounds*, 2007 WL 4166145 (5th Cir. 2007) (unpublished); Jama v. U.S. Immigration and Naturalization Service, 343 F. Supp. 2d 338, 373–76 (D.N.J. 2004) (RFRA case).

[741]Shidler v. Moore, 409 F. Supp. 2d 1060, 1071 (N.D.Ind. 2006); Charles v. Verhagen, 220 F. Supp. 2d 937, 953 (W.D.Wis. 2002), *aff'd*, 348 F.3d 601 (7th Cir. 2003); Daker v. Ferrero, 2006 WL 346440, *8–10 (N.D.Ga., Feb.13, 2006); Orafan v. Goord, 2003 WL 21972735, *9 (N.D.N.Y., Aug. 11, 2003).

[742]Lovelace v. Lee, 472 F.3d 174, 196–99 (4th Cir 2006); Ahmad v. Furlong, 435 F.3d 1196, 1198 (10th Cir. 2006); *see* Ch. 8, § L.4, concerning qualified immunity.

[743]Brandon v. Holt, 469 U.S. 464, 472, 105 S. Ct. 873 (1985).

[744]*See* City of Newport v. Fact Concerts, Inc., 453 U.S. 247, 101 S. Ct. 2748 (1981) (denying punitive damages against a municipality under § 1983); Powell v. Alexander, 391 F.3d 1, 23 (1st Cir. 2004) (official capacity defendants were not subject to punitive damages).

[745]*See* Ch. 8, § B.4.a, concerning the personal involvement requirement.

[746]42 U.S.C. § 1997e(e).

[747]*See, e.g.*, Mayfield v. Texas Dep't of Criminal Justice, 529 F.3d 599, 605–06 (5th Cir. 2008); Fegans v. Norris, 537 F.3d 897, 908 (8th Cir. 2008); Smith v. Allen, 502 F.3d 1255, 1270 (11th Cir. 2007). *Smith* says that both compensatory and punitive damages are limited by the PLRA. Other courts have held that only compensatory damages are so limited. *See* Ch. 9, § E.

rights statutes.[748] However, attorneys' fees in prisoners' RLUIPA cases are limited by the Prison Litigation Reform Act.[749]

2. Particular Religious Practices and Issues

a. Contact with Clergy and Religious Advisors Prisoners are entitled to receive visits from clergy and religious advisors and to confer privately with prison religious personnel.[750] Court decisions under the First Amendment *Turner/O'Lone* standard have left prison officials with substantial control over how and when these rights are exercised.[751] Prisoners may be more successful under RFRA and RLUIPA in challenges to restrictive practices.[752]

Prisoners have a right to correspond with religious leaders and advisors.[753]

Prison officials have not been required to employ staff chaplains of every religious group regardless of size.[754] In some cases, courts have ruled in favor of prison officials at least in part because they tried but were not able to obtain outside clergy to conduct religious observances.[755]

b. Religious Services and Groups Group worship services are "essential parts of the right to the free exercise of religion."[756] However, under the First Amendment *Turner/O'Lone* standard, the courts have left prison officials with

---

[748]42 U.S.C. § 1988, as amended by RFRA.

[749]*See* Ch. 9, § F.

[750]Griffin v. Coughlin, 743 F. Supp. 1006, 1025–29 (N.D.N.Y. 1990) (protective custody inmates were entitled to religious consultations in a private setting rather than at the bars of their cells); Wojtczak v. Cuyler, 480 F. Supp. 1288, 1300 (E.D.Pa. 1979) (protective custody prisoner was entitled to see a chaplain and receive communion or mass in his cell); Finney v. Hutto, 410 F. Supp. 251, 281 (E.D.Ark. 1976) (Muslims were entitled to visits from outside clergy on the same terms as other inmates), *aff'd in part on other grounds*, 548 F.2d 740 (8th Cir. 1977), *aff'd on other grounds*, 437 U.S. 678 (1978); *see also* Saleem v. Evans, 866 F.2d 1313, 1314 (11th Cir. 1989) (allegation by a member of the Nation of Islam that the only Muslim minister authorized to enter the prison was from the American Muslim Mission stated a constitutional claim); Burks-Bey v. Stevenson, 328 F. Supp. 2d 928, 937–38 (N.D.Ind. 2004) (denial of all spiritual and pastoral care states a First Amendment claim).

[751]Reimers v. State of Oregon, 863 F.2d 630, 631–32 (9th Cir. 1988) (Pentecostal minister could be barred because of his proselytizing activities; prisoners do not have the right to the clergy of their choice); McClaflin v. Pearce, 739 F. Supp. 537, 541 (D.Or. 1990) (segregation inmate could be denied extended visits with priest); Card v. Dugger, 709 F. Supp. 1098, 1102–09 (M.D.Fla. 1988) (death row inmate could be denied contact visits with his priest and required to take Communion through bars), *aff'd*, 871 F.2d 1023 (11th Cir. 1989); Wrinkles v. Davis, 311 F. Supp. 2d 735, 740 (N.D.Ind. 2004) (upholding exclusion of religious volunteers during lockdown after murder of a prisoner; "A permanent ban on religious services and visits by religious counselors might violate the First Amendment, but the complaint establishes that religious services and visits by religious counselors resumed long before the lockdown was lifted."); Alim v. Byrne, 521 F. Supp. 1039, 1045 (D.N.J. 1980) (visits could be denied with an ex-prisoner who had been a religious leader while confined).

[752]*See* Kikumura v. Hurley, 242 F.3d 950, 957–58, 960–62 (10th Cir. 2001) (upholding the exclusion of a religious adviser under *Turner/O'Lone*, but stating prisoner might prevail under the RFRA standard; advisor had been excluded because he rather than the plaintiff had initiated the contact); Rowe v. Davis, 373 F. Supp. 2d 822, 826–27 (N.D.Ind. 2005) (exclusion of spiritual advisor with a criminal record substantially burdened plaintiff's religious exercise and might not be the least restrictive alternative where others with criminal histories are allowed to visit).

[753]Neal v. Georgia, 469 F.2d 446, 449–50 (5th Cir. 1972) (claim of suspension of correspondence with "spiritual advisor" was not frivolous); Walker v. Blackwell, 411 F.2d 23, 29 (5th Cir. 1969); Peek v. Ciccone, 288 F. Supp. 329, 333–34 (W.D.Mo. 1968).

[754]*See* cases cited in § D.3 of this chapter, n.841.

[755]Wilson v. Moore, 270 F. Supp. 2d 1328, 1351-52 (N.D.Fla. 2003) (officials couldn't be held liable under First Amendment for their inability to get a Native American religious figure to work in prison); *see* Brown v. Schuetzle, 368 F. Supp. 2d 1009, 1020–23 (D.N.D. 2005) (failure to provide a pipe keeper who could communicate with the Sacred Grandfathers in their native language and who had completed the Vision Quest and the four days and four years of the Sundance did not violate the First Amendment or RLUIPA).

[756]Freeman v. Arpaio, 125 F.3d 732, 736–37 (9th Cir. 1997) (allegation of refusal to permit Muslim service attendance raised a First Amendment claim); *accord*, Williams v. Lane, 646 F. Supp. 1379, 1407 (N.D.Ill. 1986) (denial of group worship in protective custody was unconstitutional), *aff'd*, 851 F.2d 867, 877–78 (7th Cir. 1988); *see* Salahuddin v. Coughlin, 993 F.2d 306, 308 (2d Cir. 1993); Phelps v. Dunn, 965 F.2d 93, 100 (6th Cir. 1992) (trial would be required to determine whether gay inmate was justifiably excluded from services); Whitney v. Brown, 882 F.2d 1068, 1073–78 (6th Cir. 1989) (officials' desire to limit movement between prison units did not justify limits on Sabbath services and ban on congregate Passover Seders for Jewish inmates); Young v. Coughlin, 866 F.2d 567, 570 (2d Cir. 1989) (prisoners "should be afforded every reasonable opportunity to attend religious services, whenever possible"); Salahuddin v. Cuomo, 861 F.2d 40, 43 (2d Cir. 1988) (allegation of denial of religious services was not frivolous); McElyea v. Babbitt, 833 F.2d 196, 198 (9th Cir. 1987) (allegation of denial of Jewish services raised a factual question); Harris v. Lord, 957 F. Supp. 471, 474–75 (S.D.N.Y. 1997) (denial of religious services on a single occasion, without justification, violated both First Amendment and RFRA); Nolley v. County of Erie, 776 F. Supp. 715, 741–42 (W.D.N.Y. 1991) (exclusion from services violated First Amendment); Vanscoy v. Hicks, 691 F. Supp. 1336, 1337–38 (M.D.Ala. 1988) (damages awarded for exclusion from religious services). *But see* Kaufman v. McCaughtry, 419 F.3d 678, 683 (7th Cir. 2005) (refusal to allow atheist study group did not violate the Free Exercise Clause, even though atheism is a religion for First Amendment purposes, where plaintiff "failed utterly" to show that he would be unable to practice atheism effectively without group meetings; but the court struck the prohibition down on Establishment Clause grounds).

substantial discretion in how they are provided.[757] The majority of cases cited in this section are First Amendment cases; prisoners may be more successful under RFRA and RLUIPA.[758]

Officials have been allowed to ban inmate-led services and to require religious groups to obtain "free world"

sponsors or leaders, even if that proves impossible to accomplish.[759] (As already noted, prisons themselves are not required to employ or provide chaplains for every religious group regardless of size.[760]) They have been able to prohibit services and group activities of some groups entirely where there was a reasonable fear that violence would result from them,[761] and may exclude individuals from services where

---

[757]See, e.g., O'Lone v. Estate of Shabazz, 482 U.S. 342, 349–53, 107 S. Ct. 2400 (1987) (upholding refusal to allow Muslims to return from outside assignments for Jumu'ah services); Mumin v. Phelps, 857 F.2d 1055, 1057–58 (5th Cir. 1988) (similar to O'Lone); Hadi v. Horn, 830 F.2d 779, 787–88 (7th Cir. 1987) (occasional cancellation of services because of scheduling conflicts with other activities did not violate First Amendment); Roberts v. Champion, 255 F. Supp. 2d 1272, 1289 (N.D.Okla. 2003) (restriction of Muslim services to 10 participants, with Jumu'ah services only every other week on Monday, upheld), aff'd, 91 Fed.Appx. 108 (10th Cir. 2004) (unpublished); Johnson v. Bruce, 771 F. Supp. 327, 329 (D.Kan. 1991) (upholding conduct of Muslim services in the evening after completion of program activities), aff'd, 961 F.2d 220 (10th Cir. 1992); Indian Inmates of Nebraska Penitentiary v. Grammer, 649 F. Supp. 1374, 1378–79 (D.Neb. 1986) (prison officials were not required to permit peyote ceremonies in prison), aff'd, 831 F.2d 301 (8th Cir. 1987). But see Mayweathers v. Newland, 258 F.3d 930, 937–38 (9th Cir. 2001) (affirming injunction under First Amendment requiring officials to excuse Muslims from work assignments for Jumu'ah services; distinguishing O'Lone, which involved prisoners working outside the prison).

[758]See, e.g., Sossamon v. Lone State State of Texas, 560 F.3d 316, 331–37 (5th Cir. 2009) (exclusion of prisoner from worshiping in chapel with cross and altar was not shown to be the least restrictive alternative under RLUIPA where the chapel was used for many other purposes involving similar demands on officials; noting RLUIPA standard is more favorable than First Amendment standard), cert. granted in part, 2010 WL 2025142 (May 24, 2010); Spratt v. Rhode Island Dep't of Corrections, 482 F.3d 33, 41–43 & n.12 (1st Cir. 2007) (holding under RLUIPA that officials failed to justify total ban on prisoners' preaching, noting contrary case law under Turner/O'Lone); Murphy v. Missouri Dep't of Correction, 372 F.3d 979, 983–85, 988–89 (8th Cir. 2004) (upholding summary judgment for defendants under Turner standard but finding a triable issue under RLUIPA as to right of Christian Separatist Church to group worship); Mayweathers v. Terhune, 328 F. Supp. 2d 1086, 1096–97 (E.D.Cal. 2004) (requiring officials under RLUIPA to excuse Muslim prisoners from work assignments to attend Jumu'ah services, despite the supposed need to keep up work incentives; noting policy would probably be upheld under Turner/O'Lone); see also Greene v. Solano County Jail, 513 F.3d 982, 987–90 (9th Cir. 2008) (under RLUIPA, officials failed to show the need for a total ban on group worship by maximum security prisoners; First Amendment claim not sufficiently addressed by defendant); Hyde v. Fisher, 146 Idaho 782, 799, 203 P.3d 712 (App. 2009) (under RLUIPA, holding that officials could not bar Native American services for lack of an outside volunteer to supervise them; prison must provide a chaplain or other staff member for supervision). But see Gladson v. Iowa Dep't of Corrections, 551 F.3d 825, 834 (8th Cir. 2009) (upholding three-hour limit on Wiccan Samhita celebration in the absence of evidence why three hours was too short and eight hours was needed); Fowler v. Crawford, 534 F.3d 931 (8th Cir. 2008) (upholding denial of sweat lodge to Native American prisoners under RLUIPA), cert. denied, 129 S. Ct. 1585 (2008).

[759]Adkins v. Kaspar, 393 F.3d 559, 571 (5th Cir. 2004) (requirement of outside volunteers to conduct congregate services, applied to all religious groups, did not violate RLUIPA); Spies v. Voinovich, 173 F.3d 398, 405–06 (6th Cir. 1999); Anderson v. Angelone, 123 F.3d 1197, 1198–99 (9th Cir. 1997); Benjamin v. Coughlin, 905 F.2d 571, 577–78 (2d Cir. 1990); Hadi v. Horn, 830 F.2d at 784–87; Tisdale v. Dobbs, 807 F.2d 734, 737–39 (8th Cir. 1986); McRoy v. Cook County Dep't of Corrections, 366 F. Supp. 2d 662, 678–79 (N.D.Ill. 2005), aff'd, 205 Fed.Appx. 462 (7th Cir. 2006) (unpublished), cert. denied, 128 S. Ct. 624 (2007); Burks-Bey v. Stevenson, 328 F. Supp. 2d 928, 933–34 (N.D.Ind. 2004); Hobbs v. Pennell, 754 F. Supp. 1040, 1047–50 (D.Del. 1991) (Nation of Islam could be required to utilize outside Imam even if other Muslim sects were not); see Allen v. Toombs, 827 F.2d 563, 567–68 (9th Cir. 1987) (court did not decide whether outside sponsor rule was unconstitutional because there was no evidence it had actually interfered with services). But see Spratt v. Rhode Island Dep't Of Corrections, 482 F.3d 33, 41–43 & n.12 (1st Cir. 2007) (holding ban in prisoners' preaching was not sufficiently justified under RLUIPA where prisoners were allowed to exercise leadership in other contexts); Johnson-Bey v. Lane, 863 F.2d 1308, 1312 (7th Cir. 1988) (arbitrary enforcement of ban on inmate-led services might be unlawful); Hyde v. Texas Dep't of Criminal Justice, 948 F. Supp. 625, 626 (S.D.Tex. 1996) (Jehovah's Witnesses must be allowed to meet without an outside sponsor as are other groups); Abdul Jabbar-al Samad v. Horn, 913 F. Supp. 373, 374–76 (E.D.Pa. 1995) (requirement of outside leaders for religious services raises a First Amendment claim); Hyde v. Fisher, 146 Idaho 782, 798–99, 203 P.3d 712 (App. 2009) (Native American group must be allowed to have services with a prison staff member supervising where an outside volunteer proved impossible to find).

In one recent decision under RLUIPA, the court upheld a requirement that congregate services be directed by a prison-affiliated chaplain or an outside sponsor, allowing inmates to serve as "facilitators" only if the religion is "known outside the institution." The court said that this policy "strikes a delicate balance between respecting inmates' demands to participate in congregational activities, while ensuring that those meetings do not serve as proxies for gang recruitment or organization." Jova v. Smith, 582 F.3d 410, 417 (2d Cir. 2009).

[760]See § D.3 of this chapter, n.841.

[761]Murphy v. Missouri Dep't of Correction, 372 F.3d 979, 983, 989 (8th Cir. 2004) (prohibition on group worship by Christian Separatist Church Society did not violate the First Amendment since "racial segregation will spark violence" and CSC members had the alternative of studying scriptures and CSC writings, praying, etc.; however, under RLUIPA, officials would have to justify their restrictions at trial and "provide some basis for their concern that racial violence will result from any accommodation of CSC's request"); Brown v. Johnson, 743 F.2d 408, 412–13 (6th Cir. 1984) (complete ban on worship services by homosexual-oriented church was justified by the danger of violence to prisoners identified as homosexuals). But see Kaufman v. McCaughtry, 419 F.3d 678, 684

they reasonably fear conflict.[762] They may require close supervision of services by prison staff.[763] They may require prisoners of different security levels to attend services separately.[764] They have not been required to provide services, or a full program of services, for religious groups with only a few members.[765] They have been allowed to require different

denominations or sects of the same religion to share services,[766] though services conducted so as to denigrate or discriminate against members of a particular sect may

---

(7th Cir. 2005) (rejecting claim that atheist group meetings would raise security concerns, since they were the same security concerns that applied to other religious groups that were allowed to meet).

[762]Allah v. al-Hafeez, 208 F. Supp. 2d 520, 529–31 (E.D.Pa. 2002); *see* Freeman v. Texas Dep't of Criminal Justice, 369 F.3d 854 (5th Cir. 2004) (upholding transfer of prisoner who verbally confronted chaplain during service and incited a walkout); Abdur-Rahman v. Michigan Dep't of Corrections, 65 F.3d 489, 491–92 (6th Cir. 1995) (upholding security-related exclusion from services); Best v. Kelly, 879 F. Supp. 305, 309 (W.D.N.Y. 1995) (upholding exclusion of prisoner who persisted in disputing rabbi's interpretation of Judaism); *see also* Crocker v. Durkin, 159 F. Supp. 2d 1258, 1274–75 (D.Kan. 2001) (holding interruption of services to remove prisoners thought to be planning a work stoppage and to confiscate fezes with the initials of Fruit of Islam, thought to be a paramilitary organization, did not violate the Constitution), *reconsideration denied*, 204 F.R.D. 696 (D.Kan. 2002).

[763]Cooper v. Tard, 855 F.2d 125, 128–30 (3d Cir. 1988) (upholding ban on group prayer in "management unit" without prison officials' supervision); Butler-Bey v. Frey, 811 F.2d 449, 452 (8th Cir. 1987) (upholding requirement that guards be present at religious meetings and that minutes and membership lists be provided to the prison administration); McRoy v. Cook County Dep't of Corrections, 366 F. Supp. 2d 662, 680–81 (N.D.Ill. 2005) (frequent cancellation of religious services because of lockdowns and staff shortages did not violate the First Amendment; prisoners had alternative means of religious observance such as praying in their cells or dayrooms), *aff'd*, 205 Fed.Appx. 462 (7th Cir. 2006) (unpublished), *cert. denied*, 128 S. Ct. 624 (2007); *see also* Woods v. O'Leary, 890 F.2d 883, 885–87 (7th Cir. 1989) (prisoners who wanted to establish a congregation of the Universal Life Church could be required to comply with regulations requiring submission of information to prison officials); Childs v. Duckworth, 705 F.2d 915, 921 (7th Cir. 1983) (prisoners could be denied the right to conduct Satanic services until they provided requisite information about what would happen at them).

[764]McRoy v. Cook County Dep't of Corrections, 366 F. Supp. 2d 662, 680 (N.D.Ill. 2005) (upholding restriction of group activities including religious services to prisoners from a single pod to keep classifications separated), *aff'd*, 205 Fed.Appx. 462 (7th Cir. 2006) (unpublished), *cert. denied*, 128 S. Ct. 624 (2007); Garcia v. Board of County Comm'rs of Lehigh County, 276 F. Supp. 2d 404, 408–10 (E.D.Pa. 2003) (First Amendment case); Ra Chaka v. Franzen, 727 F. Supp. 454, 457–59 (N.D.Ill. 1989) (prison authorities could require that Muslim services be held separately for each classification level).

[765]Adkins v. Kaspar, 393 F.3d 559, 563–71 (5th Cir. 2004) (failure to provide Saturday Sabbath services every week and organize observance of various holy days for 25-member Yahweh Evangelical Assembly upheld under First Amendment and RLUIPA); Spies v. Voinovich, 173 F.3d 398, 404–05 (6th Cir. 1999) (upholding rule that a religious group must have at least five members to be recognized, hold services, etc.); Tart v. Young, 168 F. Supp. 2d 590, 594 (W.D.Va. 2001) (upholding rule allowing group religious meetings

only when there is more than one member in each pod); Jaben v. Moore, 788 F. Supp. 500, 502 (D.Kan. 1992). *But see* Hyde v. Texas Dep't of Criminal Justice, 948 F. Supp. 625, 626 (S.D.Tex. 1996) (Jehovah's Witnesses must be allowed to meet in groups of less than 15 as are other groups); *see* § D.3 of this chapter concerning differences in the treatment of religious groups).

[766]Freeman v. Texas Dep't of Criminal Justice, 369 F.3d 854, 858–61 (5th Cir. 2004) (policy of providing combined services for five "major faith sub-groups" did not violate First Amendment, despite objection of Church of Christ adherents to being part of a "Christian non-Catholic" group because it was "too ecumenical," used music in services, etc.); Weir v. Nix, 114 F.3d 817, 820–21 (8th Cir. 1997) (under RFRA, Christian fundamentalist separatist prisoner was not entitled to services separate from other fundamentalists; "Only when a prisoner's sole opportunity for group worship arises under the guidance of someone whose beliefs are significantly different from his own is there a possibility that the plaintiff's free exercise rights are substantially burdened in this manner."); Small v. Lehman, 98 F.3d 762, 766–68 (3d Cir. 1996) (failure to provide Sunni Muslims services separate from other Muslim sects stated a claim under RFRA); Clifton v. Craig, 924 F.2d 182, 183–84 (10th Cir. 1991) (Church of Christ members, who do not believe in musical instruments in church, could be denied separate services from other Christian sects who used musical instruments); Allah v. al-Hafeez, 208 F. Supp. 2d 520, 531–32 (E.D.Pa. 2002) (refusal to provide separate Muslim services for Nation of Islam prisoners upheld under *Turner/O'Lone*); Pugh v. Goord, 184 F. Supp. 2d 326, 336 (S.D.N.Y. 2002) (upholding combined Sunni and Shi'a services under *Turner/O'Lone*; ". . . [P]rison officials have documented that multiplying the number of sects or groupings entitled to separate services would have an adverse impact upon security . . . by increasing opportunities for inmates to exchange contraband and carry on gang-related activity under the cloak of religion."), *vacated*, 345 F.3d 121 (2d Cir. 2003) (vacating dismissal on the ground that plaintiffs received insufficient notice that dismissal was under consideration); Muhammad v. City of New York Dep't of Corrections, 904 F. Supp. 161, 191 (S.D.N.Y. 1995) (upholding "generic" Muslim services; Nation of Islam plaintiffs failed to show that the service "offends or ignores particular practices or beliefs that are *mandated* by NOI teachings"), *aff'd on other grounds*, 126 F.3d 119 (2d Cir. 1997); Matiyn v. Commissioner, Dep't of Corrections, 726 F. Supp. 42, 44 (W.D.N.Y. 1989) (prison authorities could require Sunni and Shia Muslims to attend same services); Faheem-El v. Lane, 657 F. Supp. 638, 645–46 (C.D.Ill. 1986) (members of particular mosque could be denied separate Muslim services where prison authorities had identified this mosque as a street gang and there were other Muslim services they could attend); *see* Orafan v. Goord, 411 F. Supp. 2d 153 (N.D.N.Y. 2006), *vacated and remanded*, 249 Fed.Appx. 217 (2d Cir. 2007) (unpublished) (vacating decision upholding joint Shi'a and Sunni services). *But see* SapaNajin v. Gunter, 857 F.2d 463, 465 (8th Cir. 1988) (Sioux prisoner's rights were violated where the only available medicine man was a member of a "deviant" sect; officials required to provide some services by other medicine men).

violate the law.[767] They have been permitted to ban group religious activities in prison yards and other common locations[768] and to suspend services entirely in emergencies[769] or as a result of misuse of the services for non-religious purposes.[770]

Decisions are divided as to whether prisons must provide sweat lodges for Native American religious exercise.[771]

Courts have held that prison officials' refusal to allow wine at religious services that call for it raises material First Amendment or RLUIPA issues.[772] They have been permitted to delegate decisions about individuals' eligibility to participate in a religious group's services to a religious authority.[773] Prisoners leaving living areas for religious services can be required to submit to a strip search.[774]

One court has held that under RLUIPA, forbidding a prisoner to attend the services of other religions was a substantial burden, since he said doing so was necessary for him to "achieve meaningful satisfactory religious exercise."[775]

---

[767]Cancel v. Mazzuca, 205 F. Supp. 2d 128, 140–41 (S.D.N.Y. 2002) (allegation that Sunni Imam engaged in an active campaign of hostility towards Shi'ites states a First Amendment claim); Cancel v. Goord, 278 A.D.2d 321, 717 N.Y.S.2d 610, 611–12 (2d Dep't 2000) (where Sunni Imam routinely proselytized Shi'ite inmates and denigrated Shi'a beliefs, religious freedom protections of state Correction Law were violated), *leave to appeal denied*, 96 N.Y.2d 778, 725 N.Y.S.2d 633, 749 N.E.2d 203 (2001); *see* Pugh v. Goord, 184 F. Supp. 2d at 334 ("While the First and Fourteenth Amendments do not require that prison inmates have access to religious advisors whose own views are completely congruent to their own, their protections are certainly not satisfied where the religious leader purportedly responsible for inmates' spiritual guidance overtly despises the deeply held beliefs of inmates under his charge.").

[768]Cooper v. Tard, 855 F.2d 125, 128–30 (3d Cir. 1988); Ahmad v. Erhmann, 339 F. Supp. 2d 1134, 1137–38 (D.Colo. 2004) (ban on group prayer and "individual demonstrative prayer" in open areas of housing units upheld under First Amendment; court notes that prisoners have alternatives such as Jumu'ah services, reading the Qu'ran, and observing Ramadan; RLUIPA claim not decided), *rev'd and remanded on other grounds*, 435 F.3d 1196 (10th Cir. 2006) (holding defendants could raise qualified immunity as to RLUIPA claim); *see also* Shabazz v. Coughlin, 852 F.2d 697, 700–02 (2d Cir. 1988) (ban on prayer in yard did not violate "clearly established" rights).

[769]Walker v. Mintzes, 771 F.2d 920, 929–30 (6th Cir. 1985); Wrinkles v. Davis, 311 F. Supp. 2d 735, 740 (N.D.Ind. 2004) (suspension of services during lockdown of a death row unit did not violate the First Amendment, though "[a] permanent ban on religious services and visits by religious counselors might violate the First Amendment"); Alim v. Byrne, 521 F. Supp. 1039, 1045 (D.N.J. 1980); *see* McRoy v. Cook County Dep't of Corrections, 366 F. Supp. 2d 662, 677–78 (N.D.Ill. 2005) (frequent cancellation of religious services during lockdowns did not violate First Amendment), *aff'd*, 205 Fed.Appx. 462 (7th Cir. 2006) (unpublished), *cert. denied*, 128 S. Ct. 624 (2007).

[770]Leonard v. Norris, 797 F.2d 683, 684–85 (8th Cir. 1986); Thomas v. Norris, 596 F. Supp. 422 (E.D.Ark. 1984).

[771]Werner v. McCotter, 49 F.3d 1476, 1480 (10th Cir. 1995) (denial of access of high-security prisoner to sweat lodge raised a material issue under RFRA); Youngbear v. Thalacker, 174 F. Supp. 2d 902, 914–15 (N.D.Iowa 2001) (a year's delay in providing a sweat lodge violated the First Amendment; noting that the availability of alternative religious activities such as meeting in the chapel and possession of medicine bags, eagle feathers, etc., did not substitute for the lack of a facility to perform "a central tenet of the Native American religion, the purification ceremony"; defendants never disputed that they were willing to provide the lodge). *Contra*, Fowler v. Crawford, 534 F.3d 931, 939–43 (8th Cir. 2008) (upholding denial of sweat lodge under RLUIPA), *cert. denied*, 129 S. Ct. 1585 (2008); Hamilton v. Schriro, 74 F.3d 1545, 1555–56 (8th Cir. 1996) (sweat lodge ceremony could be prohibited under RFRA

because it would provide an opportunity for assault, escape, drug use, and homosexual conduct outside the view of prison guards, and other prisoners might consider it favoritism for the Native Americans to get their own religious facility); Wilson v. Moore, 270 F. Supp. 2d 1328, 1353 (N.D.Fla. 2003) (refusing under *Turner/O'Lone* to require construction and use of a sweat lodge; "the court can see how non-Native Americans might view this as a sauna and demand their own"; the sacred nature of such a structure would restrict access by prison officials; and there are concerns about allowing fires on prison grounds. The fact that other prisons in other states allow sweat lodges does not require a different conclusion.); Tart v. Young, 168 F. Supp. 2d 590, 594 (W.D.Va. 2001); Combs v. Corrections Corp. of America, 977 F. Supp. 799, 803 (W.D.La. 1997) (upholding restrictions on sweat lodge under First Amendment); Hyde v. Fisher, 146 Idaho 782, 798–99, 203 P.3d 712 (App. 2009) (upholding denial of sweat lodge under RLUIPA).

One recent decision holds that a complete ban on "smudging" (producing smoke for prayers) did not satisfy RLUIPA. Hyde v. Fisher, 146 Idaho at 799–800.

[772]Levitan v. Ashcroft, 281 F.3d 1313, 1321–23 (D.C. Cir. 2002) (denial of wine at Catholic services raised a material First Amendment issue); Sample v. Lappin, 424 F. Supp. 2d 187, 195–96 (D.D.C. 2006) (complete denial of wine to Orthodox Jew for services raised a RFRA claim because it may not be the least restrictive means of controlling alcohol in prison; regulations allowed small amounts of wine for religious rituals, but warden did not permit it), *reconsideration denied*, 479 F. Supp. 2d 120 (D.D.C. 2007).

[773]Bear v. Nix, 977 F.2d 1291, 1294 (8th Cir. 1992).

[774]McRoy v. Cook County Dep't of Corrections, 366 F. Supp. 2d 662, 681–82 (N.D.Ill. 2005) (First Amendment case), *aff'd*, 205 Fed.Appx. 462 (7th Cir. 2006) (unpublished), *cert. denied*, 128 S. Ct. 624 (2007).

[775]Coronel v. Paul, 316 F. Supp. 2d 868, 881 (D.Ariz. 2004) (holding defendants would have the option of showing that a compelling interest required excluding him from those services). *But see* Spavone v. City of New York, 420 F. Supp. 2d 236, 240 (S.D.N.Y. 2005) (holding under RLUIPA that prisoner who designated himself Catholic could be excluded from Protestant Bible study where officials allowed him to meet with the Catholic chaplain, giving him an opportunity for Bible study; requirement of religious registration served the compelling interest of minimizing inmate movement on Rikers Island); Burks-Bey v. Stevenson, 328 F. Supp. 2d 928, 933 (N.D.Ind. 2004) (refusing to allow Moorish Science Temple adherent to attend services of other religions to "honor all of the divine prophets and teachings" did not violate the Constitution); Woods v. Evatt, 876 F. Supp. 756, 764 (D.S.C. 1995)

Several courts have held that inmates from segregation or other high-security units may be excluded from group worship services.[776] Some of these decisions have noted that the inmates were provided with other opportunities for religious exercise.[777] We think it can be argued that such alternative opportunities are constitutionally required, and indeed some courts have required them.[778] Some courts have also suggested that blanket exclusions of all segregated

inmates may not be permissible, and prison officials may have to consider inmates case by case.[779] These arguments should carry considerable weight in cases brought under RFRA or RLUIPA, which require that prison officials pursue their goals by the "least restrictive means."[780]

Prison officials may be required to accommodate other kinds of religious observances besides services.[781] They have not been required to permit other religious gatherings such as banquets.[782]

(upholding restriction of Muslim services to prisoners registered as Muslims, since services were on a work day for non-Muslims), *aff'd*, 68 F.3d 463 (4th Cir. 1995) (unpublished).

[776]Pedraza v. Meyer, 919 F.2d 317, 320 (5th Cir. 1990); Garza v. Carlson, 877 F.2d 14, 11 (8th Cir. 1989); Matiyn v. Henderson, 841 F.2d 31, 37 (2d Cir. 1988); McCabe v. Arave, 827 F.2d 634, 637 (9th Cir. 1987); Little v. Norris, 787 F.2d 1241, 1244 (8th Cir. 1986); Taylor v. Rogers, 781 F.2d 1047, 1049–50 (4th Cir. 1986); Otey v. Best, 680 F.2d 1231, 1234 (8th Cir. 1982); Sweet v. South Carolina Dep't of Corrections, 529 F.2d 854, 863 (4th Cir. 1975) and cases cited; Gonzalez v. Litscher, 230 F. Supp. 2d 950, 960 (W.D.Wis. 2002) ("no reasonable person" could find that denial of access to sweat lodge violated the First Amendment as applied to a prisoner in the most restrictive status at the state's Supermax prison), *aff'd*, 79 Fed.Appx. 215 (7th Cir. 2003) (unpublished); Woods v. Evatt, 876 F. Supp. 756, 768 (D.S.C. 1995), *aff'd*, 68 F.3d 463 (4th Cir.1995) (unpublished); Stroud v. Roth, 741 F. Supp. 559, 560–63 (E.D.Pa. 1990); Aliym v. Miles, 679 F. Supp. 1, 2 (W.D.N.Y. 1988); Bellamy v. McMickens, 692 F. Supp. 205, 214–15 (S.D.N.Y. 1988); Peterkin v. Jeffes, 661 F. Supp. 895, 912–13, 926–27 (E.D.Pa. 1987), *aff'd*, 855 F.2d 1021 (3d Cir. 1988); Bruscino v. Carlson, 654 F. Supp. 609, 618 (S.D.Ill. 1987), *aff'd*, 854 F.2d 162, 166 (7th Cir. 1988); Powell v. Dep't of Corrections, State of Okla., 647 F. Supp. 968, 971 (N.D.Okla. 1986); Dominguez v. Figel, 626 F. Supp. 368, 371 (N.D.Ind. 1986); *see* Pepper v. Carroll, 423 F. Supp. 2d 442, 447 (D.Del. 2006) (rejecting claim that prisoner in segregation had a right to a TV to watch religious services). *But see* Fogle v. Pierson, 435 F.3d 1252, 1264 (10th Cir. 2006) (allegation that prisoner was denied all opportunity for "Christian fellowship" during three years in administrative segregation was not frivolous); Ford v. McGinnis, 352 F.3d 582, 597 (2d Cir. 2003) ("a prisoner's free exercise right to participate in religious services is not extinguished by his or her confinement in special housing or keeplock"); Salahuddin v. Coughlin, 993 F.2d 306, 308–10 (2d Cir. 1993) (inmates in "keeplock" may not automatically be excluded from services); Divers v. Dep't of Corrections, 921 F.2d 191, 194 (8th Cir. 1990) (denial of all religious services in protective custody stated a constitutional claim); Williams v. Lane, 851 F.2d 867, 877–78 (7th Cir. 1988) (prison officials did not sufficiently justify denial of communal worship opportunities).

[777]*See, e.g.,* McCabe v. Arave; Little v. Norris; Peterkin v. Jeffes; Bruscino v. Carlson; Powell v. Dep't of Corrections, all cited in the preceding footnote; *see also* Gawloski v. Dallman, 803 F. Supp. 103, 113 (S.D.Ohio 1992).

[778]*See* Pierce v. County of Orange, 526 F.3d 1190, 1211 (9th Cir. 2008) (administrative segregation prisoners must be allowed religious worship unless they are disruptive or violent; they may be provided individual chapel visits or meetings with religious advisers rather than group services), *cert. denied*, 129 S. Ct. 597 (2008); Sample v. Borg, 675 F. Supp. 574, 580 (E.D.Cal. 1987) (Native American in "security housing" should have been permitted to participate in pipe ceremony at his cell door), *vacated as moot*, 870 F.2d 563 (9th Cir. 1989); Wojtczak v. Cuyler, 480 F. Supp. 1288,

1300 (E.D.Pa. 1979) (protective custody prisoner was entitled to see a chaplain and receive communion or mass in his cell).

[779]Young v. Coughlin, 866 F.2d 567, 570 (2d Cir. 1989); Beck v. Lynaugh, 842 F.2d 759, 761 (5th Cir. 1988); *see* Salahuddin v. Coughlin, 992 F.2d 447, 449 (2d Cir. 1993) (inmate in segregation for fighting could be excluded under *Young* holding); Termunde v. Cook, 684 F. Supp. 255, 262 (D.Utah 1988) (court refuses to order services for protective and administrative segregation prisoners, but suggests that a policy of individual screening or small group services should be tried).

[780]*See* Greene v. Solano County Jail, 513 F.3d 982, 987–90 (9th Cir. 2008) (questioning whether a total ban on group worship by maximum security prisoners is the least restrictive means of maintaining security, since a law library down the hall was already used by those prisoners and could be used for religious services); Hudson v. Dennehy, 538 F. Supp. 2d 400, 412 (D.Mass. 2008) (exclusion of segregation prisoners from attending Jumu'ah services substantially burdens religious exercise but serves the compelling interest of rehabilitation and good order, but barring them from video participation as well is not the least restrictive alternative), *aff'd sub nom* Crawford v. Clarke, 578 F.3d 39 (1st Cir. 2009); Rowe v. Davis, 373 F. Supp. 2d 822, 827–28 (N.D.Ind. 2005) (allegation that all administrative segregation prisoners are excluded from religious services, without individualized determination of risk, states a claim under RLUIPA).

[781]Ford v. McGinnis, 352 F.3d 582, 594–96 (2d Cir. 2003) (holding that denial of Eid ul Fitr meal to keeplocked Muslim prisoner raised a material factual issue under the First Amendment); Wares v. vanBebber, 319 F. Supp. 2d 1237, 1245–50 (D.Kan. 2004) (holding that denial of Sukkot observance—which requires Jews to dine in a booth, or Sukkah—raised a factual issue under *Turner/O'Lone*); Howard v. U.S., 864 F. Supp. 1019, 1027–30 (D.Colo. 1994) (officials required to make provision for Satanist to perform rituals; their staffing concerns, while legitimate, appeared selective, since other small groups had been accommodated, and plaintiff asked only for an hour a month in a space the size of a broom closet).

[782]Mack v. O'Leary, 80 F.3d 1175, 1180–81 (7th Cir. 1996) (under RFRA, officials need not accommodate Moorish Science Temple banquet request; there were 300 religious denominations, making it impossible for everyone to have a banquet), *cert. granted, judgment vacated on other grounds*, 522 U.S. 801 (1997); Charles v. Verhagen, 220 F. Supp. 2d 937, 946–47 (W.D.Wis. 2002) (upholding under RLUIPA limit of one religious feast a year given the security, management, and resources problems connected with them), *aff'd*, 348 F.3d 601 (7th Cir. 2003); Glasshofer v. Thornburgh, 514 F. Supp. 1242, 1248 (E.D.Pa. 1981), *aff'd*, 688 F.2d 821 (3d Cir. 1982). If prison officials do permit religious banquets, reasonable restrictions about their operation will be upheld. *See, e.g.,* Pierce v. Smith, 347 F. Supp. 2d 1143, 1154–56 (M.D.Ala. 2004) (upholding policy that food for religious feasts must be commercially prepared and sealed and not home-prepared).

Religious groups may be required to seek official recognition and to follow rules limiting their independence.[783]

c. Religious Dress, Hair, and Beards Courts' decisions have been mixed in cases involving hair and beard restrictions, in large part because of changes in legal standards. Some early decisions had struck down hair and beard restrictions to which prisoners had religious objections,[784] though others had upheld them.[785] After *Turner* and *O'Lone* were decided, courts in First Amendment cases almost always upheld such restrictions despite prisoners' religious objections,[786] with a few exceptions,[787]

and earlier favorable decisions were overruled.[788] Decisions have been mixed under RFRA and RLUIPA. Prisoners have prevailed in some cases,[789] but in others, courts have assessed

[783]Akbar v. Borgen, 803 F. Supp. 1479, 1484–86 (E.D.Wis. 1992); *see* Woods v. O'Leary, 890 F.2d 883, 885–88 (7th Cir. 1989) (prison officials could bar correspondence about establishing a Universal Life Church congregation until the plaintiff complied with regulations requiring prior approval of inmate business ventures).

[784]Fromer v. Scully, 817 F.2d 227 (2d Cir. 1987); Teterud v. Burns, 522 F.2d 357 (8th Cir. 1975).

[785]Martinelli v. Dugger, 817 F.2d 1499, 1506 (11th Cir. 1987); Brightly v. Wainwright, 814 F.2d 612, 613 (11th Cir. 1987); Shabazz v. Barnauskas, 790 F.2d 1536, 1538–40 (11th Cir. 1986) (Muslim); Wilson v. Schillinger, 761 F.2d 921, 928 (3d Cir. 1985) (Rastafarian); Cole v. Flick, 758 F.2d 124, 130–31 (3d Cir. 1985) (Native American); Dreibelbeis v. Marks, 742 F.2d 792, 794–96 (3d Cir. 1984).

[786]Henderson v. Terhune, 379 F.3d 709, 713–15 (9th Cir. 2004) (ban on long hair upheld as applied to Native American prisoner); Hines v. South Carolina Dep't of Corrections, 148 F.3d 353, 358–59 (4th Cir. 1998) (upholding ban on beards, long hair, and "extreme" hair styles); Taylor v. Johnson, 257 F.3d 470, 472–74 (5th Cir. 2001) (rejecting free exercise challenge to prohibition on beards; but holding lower court should have considered his equal protection claim relative to persons who can't shave for medical reasons); Green v. Polunsky, 229 F.3d 486, 489–91 (5th Cir. 2000) (upholding policy barring all beards except for medical reasons); Sours v. Long, 978 F.2d 1086, 1087 (8th Cir. 1992) (haircut requirement could be applied to adherents of the "Vow of the Nazarite"); Powell v. Estelle, 959 F.2d 22, 25–26 (8th Cir. 1992); Campbell v. Purkett, 957 F.2d 535, 536–37 (8th Cir. 1992) (same as *Sours*); Friedman v. State of Arizona, 912 F.2d 328, 331–33 (9th Cir. 1990) (ban on beards except where medically required could be applied to Jewish inmate); Dunavant v. Moore, 907 F.2d 77, 79 (8th Cir. 1990) (rule limiting beard to two inches in length could be applied to member of the Church of Jesus Christ Christian/Aryan Nation); Iron Eyes v. Henry, 907 F.2d 810, 814–16 (8th Cir. 1990) (rule requiring inmates to wear their hair above their collars could be applied to a Native American prisoner even though the rule provided for religious exemptions); Fromer v. Scully, 874 F.2d 69, 73–76 (2d Cir. 1989) (requirement of clean-shaven intake photo and one-inch limit on beards could be applied to a Jewish prisoner); Pollock v. Marshall, 845 F.2d 656, 658–60 (6th Cir. 1988) (Lakota Indian could be required to cut his hair even though the rules provided for a religious exception); Perry v. Davies, 757 F. Supp. 1223, 1224 (D.Kan. 1991) (requirement of clean-shaven ID photo upheld); Trussel v. Maynard, 813 P.2d 532, 533–34 (Okla.App. 1991) (beard restrictions upheld as applied to a non-denominational Christian).

[787]Flagner v. Wilkinson, 241 F.3d 475, 486–87 (6th Cir. 2001) (allowing "as applied" challenge to grooming regulation to go

forward where a Hasidic Jewish plaintiff had been allowed to keep his beard and sidelocks for years and none of the alleged bad effects of allowing beards—concealing contraband, supressing gang identifiers, avoiding clogged drains—had ever been attributed to him); Benjamin v. Coughlin, 905 F.2d 571, 576–77 (2d Cir. 1990) (Rastafarian inmates could not be made to cut their hair on intake because an adequate ID photograph could be taken with the hair pulled back); Goodman v. Money, 180 F. Supp. 2d 946, 947 (N.D.Ohio 2001) (granting temporary restraining order to Orthodox Jewish prisoners who had been permitted to maintain beards and sidelocks until recently, despite prison system's grooming policy; relying on *Flagner*).

[788]Fromer v. Scully, 874 F.2d at 73–74, *overruling* Fromer v. Scully, 817 F.2d 227 (2d Cir. 1987); Iron Eyes v. Henry, 907 F.2d at 813, *overruling* Teterud v. Burns, 522 F.2d 357 (8th Cir. 1975).

[789]Smith v. Ozmint, 578 F.3d 246, 252–54 (4th Cir. 2009) (holding state officials had not sufficiently justified their short-hair rule, reversing summary judgment; noting that affidavit from another case about another prison was not helpful); Warsoldier v. Woodford, 418 F.3d 989, 998–1001 (9th Cir. 2005) (holding a three-inch limit on hair length was not shown to be the least restrictive alternative, since the plaintiff was at a minimum security prison, there was no indication that officials had even considered alternatives such as the creation of religious exemptions, and other prison systems, including the Federal Bureau of Prisons, either do not have such hair length policies or do provide religious exemptions); Mayweathers v. Terhune, 328 F. Supp. 2d 1086, 1094–96 (E.D.Cal. 2004) (rejecting argument that beards must be banned so prisoners can be identified reliably, holding that the less restrictive alternative is to require mandatory visual inspections of prisoners' facial hair, as regulations already require, and require photos both clean shaven and with a beard); Gartrell v. Ashcroft, 191 F. Supp. 2d 23, 38–40 (D.D.C. 2002) (holding that placement of D.C. prisoners whose religion forbade cutting hair and shaving beards in Virginia prison system, which forbade long hair and beards, was not the least restrictive alternative; plaintiffs with such beliefs could be housed in Bureau of Prisons institutions or in systems that did not burden their religious beliefs), *appeal dismissed*, 2003 WL 1873847 (D.C. Cir., Apr. 11, 2003); Estep v. Dent, 914 F. Supp. 1462, 1466–67 (W.D.Ky. 1996) (granting preliminary injunction against cutting earlocks of Orthodox Jewish plaintiff; the fact that defendants waited three months weakened their claim of a compelling interest); Luckette v. Lewis, 883 F. Supp. 471, 481 (D.Ariz. 1995) (granting injunction to allow plaintiff to wear a quarter-inch beard, as was also allowed for medical reasons); *see* Fluellen v. Goord, 2007 WL 4560597, *4–8 (W.D.N.Y., Mar.12, 2007), *report and recommendation adopted*, Amaker v. Goord, 2007 WL 4560595, *2 (W.D.N.Y., Dec. 18, 2007) (granting injunction against preventing prisoner with dreadlocks from attending Nation of Islam services); *see also* State v. Whitaker, 2007 WL 625931, *3–7 (Ohio App. 6 Dist., Mar. 2, 2007) (vacating conviction of violation of "community control" (probation) of person residing in treatment center who refused to cut his hair based on Native American religion; applying strict scrutiny standard similar to RLUIPA), *appeal not allowed*, 114 Ohio St.3d 1508, 872 N.E.2d 950 (Ohio, Aug. 29, 2007). In *Helbrans v. Coombe*, 890 F. Supp. 227, 230 (S.D.N.Y. 1995), prison officials dropped their demand that the Orthodox

the issues in much the same way that they did under *Turner/O'Lone*, and have upheld restrictive rules.[790]

Restrictions on religious headgear and other attire were also generally upheld before RFRA and RLUIPA.[791]

It may be easier for prisoners to win such cases under the statutes.[792]

Even under the reasonableness standard, prison officials must present factual justifications for their rules.[793] If the rules are not enforced against all religious groups, or if some inmates are exempted from them, courts may require stronger justifications from prison officials.[794]

d. Diet Courts have held that "a prisoner has a right to a diet consistent with his or her religious scruples."[795]

Jewish prisoner shave his beard after viewing computer-generated photographs of him without facial hair.

[790]Hoevenaar v. Lazaroff, 422 F.3d 366, 370–71 (6th Cir. 2006) (holding that even low-security prisoners could be forbidden to grow kouplocks under a rule against long hair); Diaz v. Collins, 114 F.3d 69, 72–73 (5th Cir. 1997) (upholding hair length restrictions under RFRA); Harris v. Chapman, 97 F.3d 499, 503–04 (11th Cir. 1996) (haircut requirement did not violate RFRA); Hamilton v. Schriro, 74 F.3d 1545, 1554–55 (8th Cir. 1996) (upholding hair length regulations under RFRA); Ragland v. Angelone, 420 F. Supp. 2d 507, 513–19 (W.D.Va. 2006), *aff'd*, 193 Fed.Appx. 218 (4th Cir. 2006) (unpublished); Davie v. Wingard, 958 F. Supp. 1244, 1248–52 (S.D.Ohio 1997) (upholding ban on long hair under RFRA).

[791]Muhammad v. Lynaugh, 966 F.2d 901, 902–03 (5th Cir. 1992) (upholding ban on kufis except in cells and chapel, and ban on religious patches or insignia); Young v. Lane, 922 F.2d 370, 375–77 (7th Cir. 1991) (upholding ban on wearing yarmulkes except in cells and at religious services since they can be used to hide contraband and as gang identification, even though baseball caps were permitted); Benjamin v. Coughlin, 905 F.2d at 578–79 (Rastafarian "crowns" could be banned, even though yarmulkes and kufis were permitted, because they were larger and looser fitting and presented a greater danger of hiding contraband); Butler-Bey v. Frey, 811 F.2d 449, 451 (8th Cir. 1987) (prison could ban fezes in visiting room and other common areas); Standing Deer v. Carlson, 831 F.2d 1525, 1528–29 (9th Cir. 1987) (prison could ban Native American headbands in the dining hall); Dettmer v. Landon, 799 F.2d 929, 933–34 (4th Cir. 1986) (adherent of Church of Wicca could be denied possession of white hooded robe); Abdullah v. Kinnison, 769 F.2d 345, 349–51 (6th Cir. 1985) (rule that required Hanafi Muslims to keep their white prayer robes in the chapel rather than their cells upheld); Sutton v. Stewart, 22 F. Supp. 2d 1097, 1102–03 (D.Ariz. 1998) (upholding rule that kufis may be worn only in cells, in designated living areas, and during religious ceremonies), *aff'd*, 185 F.3d 869 (9th Cir. 1999) (unpublished); Aqueel v. Seiter, 781 F. Supp. 517, 520–23 (S.D.Ohio 1991) (upholding requirement that Muslim remove his tarboosh in dining hall and before the Rules Infraction Board), *aff'd*, 966 F.2d 1451 (6th Cir. 1992); Faheem-El v. Lane, 657 F. Supp. 638, 646 (C.D.Ill. 1986) (members of particular mosque that prison officials concluded was really a street gang could be denied the right to wear that mosque's religious symbols). *But see* Burgin v. Henderson, 536 F.2d 501, 504 (2d Cir. 1976) (factual record was necessary to determine whether a rule barring all hats was necessary to prevent hiding weapons); Ali v. Szabo, 81 F. Supp. 2d 447, 470 (S.D.N.Y. 2000) (denying summary judgment to Sheriff on prohibition of kufi where he put forward no legitimate purpose for the policy); Sample v. Borg, 675 F. Supp. 574, 582 (E.D.Cal. 1987) (Native American segregation inmate could be prohibited from wearing hairwraps but not headband), *vacated as moot*, 870 F.2d 563 (9th Cir. 1989); Reinert v. Haas, 585 F. Supp. 477, 481–82 (S.D.Iowa 1984) (Native American prisoners granted preliminary injunction permitting them to wear headbands).

[792]*See* Muslim v. Frame, 891 F. Supp. 226, 232–33 (E.D.Pa. 1995) (in RFRA challenge to rule against wearing kufis in common areas, prison officials failed to produce evidence of the costs that would result from performing additional searches, or evidence that kufis were gang symbols or obstructions to identifying prisoners); Luckette v. Lewis, 883 F. Supp. 471, 481–82 (D.Ariz. 1995) (where prison officials in RFRA case did not identify any safety concerns with head coverings other than gang colors, defendants and plaintiff directed to agree on an acceptable head covering).

[793]Boles v. Neet, 486 F.3d 1177, 1182–83 (10th Cir. 2007) (officials failed to identify legitimate penological interests served by forbidding the Jewish plaintiff to wear a yarmulke and *tallit katan* (religious undergarments) on a medical visit).

[794]McKinney v. Maynard, 952 F.2d 350, 352–53 (10th Cir. 1991) (allegation of unequal treatment of religions should not have been dismissed as frivolous); Swift v. Lewis, 901 F.2d 730, 731–32 (9th Cir. 1990) (where prison permitted long hair and beards to Sikhs and American Indians, but not to Nazarite Christians, they must present evidence supporting this unequal treatment); Reed v. Faulkner, 842 F.2d 960, 964 (7th Cir. 1988) (where Native Americans were allowed long hair, prison officials were required to show why Rastafarians were denied it); Wilson v. Moore, 270 F. Supp. 2d 1328, 1347 (N.D.Fla. 2003) (allegation that Native Americans were more restricted in their religious garb than other prisoners should proceed to trial); *see also* Mosier v. Maynard, 937 F.2d 1521, 1527 (10th Cir. 1991) (prison officials must justify demanding outside references before granting a religious exemption from a hair length rule). *But see* Davie v. Wingard, 958 F. Supp. 1244, 1252–53 (S.D.Ohio 1997) (allowing long hair to women prisoners but not men upheld because men present more serious security issues than women); Abordo v. State of Hawaii, 938 F. Supp. 656, 659 (D.Haw. 1996) (same).

Unequal treatment of religious groups is discussed further in § D.3 of this chapter.

[795]Ford v. McGinnis, 352 F.3d 582, 597 (2d Cir. 2003); *accord*, Beerheide v. Suthers, 286 F.3d 1179, 1185 (10th Cir. 2002); Jackson v. Mann, 196 F.3d 316, 321 (2d Cir. 1999) (holding right clearly established); McElyea v. Babbitt, 833 F.2d 196, 198 (9th Cir. 1987) ("Inmates . . . have the right to be provided with food sufficient to sustain them in good health that satisfies the dietary laws of their religion."); *see also* LaFevers v. Saffle, 936 F.2d 1117, 1119 (10th Cir. 1991) (claim of denial of vegetarian diet was not frivolous); Hunafa v. Murphy, 907 F.2d 46, 47 (7th Cir. 1990) (prison officials must present evidence supporting the reasons they refused to stop serving pork to Muslims in segregation); Omar v. Casterline, 288 F. Supp. 2d 775, 781–82 (W.D.La. 2003) (allegation that Muslim plaintiff was repeatedly served pork and pork products raised a material issue under the First Amendment). *But see* Benjamin v. Coughlin, 905 F.2d 571, 579–80 (2d Cir. 1990) (holding denial of

However, the actual outcomes of prison religious diet cases have been inconsistent under the *Turner* standard. Many courts have held that prison officials must provide diets required by prisoners' religions,[796] or accommodate other religious concerns about food service.[797] Others have held that prisoners' complaints about religious diets at least raised valid First Amendment claims.[798] But other courts

have ruled against prisoners in diet cases, usually holding that denying religious diets was reasonably related to budgetary and administrative concerns given the cost[799] and/or complication[800] of providing the desired diet. Prisons have not been required under *Turner/O'Lone* to provide diets that would require individualized preparation.[801] Where prisons provide a nutritionally adequate religious diet, courts will generally not get involved in disputes about the details.[802]

Rastafarian Ital diet was not unconstitutional where the required diet was never clearly defined).

[796]Beerheide v. Suthers, 286 F.3d 1179, 1188–89 (10th Cir. 2002) (holding plaintiffs denied a kosher diet lacked alternative ways of maintaining a kosher diet; paying for it themselves was not an alternative because even those with some money would have to sacrifice communication with family and legal representatives to pay for the food); Ashelman v. Wawrzaszek, 111 F.3d 674, 677–78 (9th Cir. 1997) (provision of only one kosher meal, with a choice of vegetarian or pork-free meals for the other two, violated the First Amendment where a full kosher diet could be provided by using whole fruits, vegetables, nuts, and cereals, with disposable utensils, at modest cost, and where other religions' dietary requirements were accommodated); Moorish Science Temple of America, Inc. v. Smith, 693 F.2d 987, 990 (2d Cir. 1982) (failure to provide diet conforming to Muslim religious beliefs stated a claim); Kahane v. Carlson, 527 F.2d 492, 495 (2d Cir. 1980) (Orthodox Jews must receive kosher diets); Ross v. Blackledge, 477 F.2d 616, 618–19 (4th Cir. 1972) (Muslims are entitled to a nutritionally adequate pork-free diet); Thompson v. Vilsack, 328 F. Supp. 2d 974, 978–80 (S.D.Iowa 2004) (striking down requirement of co-payment from Jewish prisoners for kosher meals under *Turner* standard); Prushinowski v. Hambrick, 570 F. Supp. 863, 866–69 (E.D.N.C. 1983) (failure to provide diet required by Ultra Orthodox Satmar Hasidic sect violated First Amendment and federal prison regulations); Masjid Muhammad-D.C.C. v. Keve, 479 F. Supp. 1311, 1319 (D.Del. 1979) (if prison menu, without pork items, will provide a nutritionally adequate diet, prison officials must inform Muslims of which items contain pork); Battle v. Anderson, 376 F. Supp. 402, 427, 436 (E.D.Okla. 1974) (similar to *Masjid*).

[797]Love v. Reed, 216 F.3d 682, 690–91 (8th Cir. 2000) (holding unconstitutional the refusal to provide food on Saturday for consumption on Sunday per the plaintiff's idiosyncratic "Hebrew" belief system); Makin v. Colorado Dept. of Correction, 183 F.3d 1205, 1211–14 (10th Cir. 1999) (holding failure to adjust meal schedule for Ramadan violated the First Amendment); Schlesinger v. Carlson, 489 F. Supp. 612, 616–19 (M.D.Pa. 1980) (Hasidic Jew entitled to special cooking facilities).

[798]Shakur v. Schriro, 514 F.3d 878, 885–88 (9th Cir. 2008) (holding prisoner's request for Halal or kosher meat, based on gastrointestinal distress caused by vegetarian Muslim diets, required more complete analysis under *Turner* standard); Conyers v. Abitz, 416 F.3d 580, 585–86 (7th Cir. 2005) (defendants were not entitled to summary judgment where they did not explain why they could not have accommodated a segregation prisoner who had missed the deadline for receiving Ramadan meals); McEachin v. McGuinnis, 357 F.3d 197, 203–05 (2003) (allegation that plaintiff was subjected to a "food loaf" diet during Ramadan, when Muslims are required to break their fast with Halal food, should not have been dismissed); Lewis v. Mitchell, 416 F. Supp. 2d 935, 944 (S.D.Cal. 2005) (allegation that Muslim prisoner was intentionally misled into consuming pork-containing food stated a First Amendment claim); Shaheed-Muhammad v. DiPaolo, 393 F. Supp.

2d 80, 99 (D.Mass. 2005) (holding defendants' desire for efficiency and cost-effectiveness in their food program, used to justify denial of vegetarian meals, were undermined for *Turner/O'Lone* purposes by the fact that they had later started to provide vegetarian diets); Caldwell v. Caesar, 150 F. Supp. 2d 50, 56–57 (D.D.C. 2001) (holding requirement that prisoners renew their religious diets every 90 days raised an issue for trial under *Turner/O'Lone*, especially as applied to a prisoner in segregation); Muhammad v. McMickens, 708 F. Supp. 607, 608, 610 (S.D.N.Y. 1989) (evidence that Halal food was not actually prepared in a manner consistent with the dictates of the plaintiff's religion established issues of fact precluding summary judgment); Ross v. Coughlin, 669 F. Supp. 1235, 1241–42 (S.D.N.Y. 1987) (failure to provide kosher food prepared according to the laws of Kashrut stated a constitutional claim); Javeri v. McMickens, 660 F. Supp. 325, 326 (S.D.N.Y. 1987) (allegation that Muslim Halal meals were prepared in pots used to cook pork presented "an issue of substance").

[799]Williams v. Morton, 343 F.3d 212, 217–18 (3d Cir. 2002) (holding that there was no *de minimis* cost alternative where providing 225 Muslims with Halal food would cost $280 a year apiece, compared with $3650 a year per person for kosher food for a smaller number of observant Jews); Martinelli v. Dugger, 817 F.2d 1499, 1507 n.29 (11th Cir. 1987) (failure to provide a full kosher diet was justified by expense). *But see* Beerheide v. Suthers, 286 F.3d 1179, 1189–92 (10th Cir. 2002) (holding that $13,000 a year— 0.158% of an $8.25 million budget—for kosher food for Jewish prisoners had *de minimis* impact on the overall prison food budget).

[800]Goff v. Graves, 362 F.3d 543, 549–50 (8th Cir. 2004) (upholding refusal to allow food trays prepared for religious banquet to be delivered to members in segregation unit, noting that members had sent contraband to unit before); Williams v. Morton, 343 F.3d 212, 218 (3d Cir. 2002) (serving Halal food would be a "considerable disruption" and cause "additional security concerns").

[801]DeHart v. Horn, 390 F.3d 262, 269–70 (3d Cir. 2004) (citing need for "individualized preparation" of Mahayana Buddhist diet, which requires avoidance of "pungent vegetables" such as garlic, onions, etc.); Benjamin v. Coughlin, 905 F.2d at 579–80 (failure to provide an Ital diet for Rastafarians was not unconstitutional where the nature of the diet varied among individuals and sects and the plaintiffs "failed to clearly define the claim"); Kahey v. Jones, 836 F.2d 948, 949–50 (5th Cir. 1988) (officials were not required to provide an individualized diet cooked and served in utensils that had never come into contact with pork byproducts); Udey v. Kastner, 805 F.2d 1218, 1219–20 (5th Cir. 1986) (prisoner had no right to an individualized diet of organically grown products washed in distilled water; pre-*O'Lone* case).

[802]*See* Al-Alamin v. Gramley, 926 F.2d 680, 687 (7th Cir. 1991) (ban on non-commercial Halal food upheld since commercial Halal food was available); Tisdale v. Dobbs, 807 F.2d 734, 740 (8th Cir. 1986) (Muslim inmates observing Ramadan could be fed

Some courts have held that the existence of alternative means of religious expression supported the denial of religious diets.[803] Courts will not intervene against food service rules or procedures that do not actually interfere with access to religious diets.[804]

Prisoners may be more successful in religious diet cases under RLUIPA and RFRA.[805] In enacting RLUIPA, Congress expressed specific concern about dietary issues, such as the denial of Halal food even when Kosher food was

provided, and the failure to accommodate religious fasting schedules.[806]

Prisoners are entitled to refrain from food service work that is contrary to their religious beliefs.[807]

e. Religious Objects Under the *Turner/O'Lone* First Amendment standard, prison officials have generally been allowed to bar religious objects and artifacts if they present security problems,[808] or may allow them to be used only during

---

bologna sandwiches at night like other inmates who missed meals during the day); Singh v. Goord, 520 F. Supp. 2d 487, 506 (S.D.N.Y. 2007) (where Sikh prisoner received a vegetarian diet and was able to identify occasional items that contained eggs, his religious exercise was not substantially burdened); Cooper v. Rogers, 788 F. Supp. 255, 258–60 (D.Md.), *aff'd*, 959 F.2d 231 (4th Cir. 1991) (where prison provided kosher lunches and dinners, and there were kosher items available for breakfast, failure to provide a complete kosher breakfast did not violate the First Amendment).

[803]DeHart v. Horn, 390 F.3d 262, 266–67, 269 n.7 (3d Cir. 2004) (noting district court holding that a Buddhist denied a religious diet had alternatives because he was permitted to pray, to recite the Sutras, to meditate, to correspond with the City of 10,000 Buddhas, a center of Buddhist teaching, and to purchase non-leather sneakers); Goff v. Graves, 362 F.3d 543, 549–50 (8th Cir. 2004) (upholding refusal to allow food trays prepared for religious banquet to be delivered to members in segregation unit; noting that members could practice other aspects of their religion). *Contra*, Williams v. Bitner, 359 F. Supp. 2d 370, 379 (M.D.Pa. 2005) (holding that other religious practices did not substitute for Muslim's "faith-based interest in avoiding contact with pork"), *aff'd*, 455 F.3d 186 (3d Cir. 2006); Washington v. Garcia, 977 F. Supp. 1067, 1073 (S.D.Cal. 1997) (refusing to accept fasting and praying as an alternative to receiving Muslim diet during Ramadan; under that approach, the alternatives factor "would have no meaning because an inmate would always be able to pray privately").

[804]Resnick v. Adams, 348 F.3d 763, 767–72 & n.6 (9th Cir. 2003) (requirement that Jewish prisoners submit an application in order to receive kosher food did not violate First Amendment or RLUIPA).

[805]*See* Jova v. Smith, 582 F.3d 410, 416 (2009) (upholding refusal to satisfy "highly detailed" dietary requests calling for specific foods and portions on individual days of the week, prepared by adherents of the religion, on grounds of administrative burden; holding defendants failed to justify refusal to provide vegan diet); Koger v. Bryan, 523 F.3d 789, 800–02 (7th Cir. 2008) (noting that orderly administration of prison dietary system has been held to be a legitimate penological interest, but not a compelling one; requirement that religious diets be religiously required and verified by clergy substantially burdened plaintiff's religious exercise and was not shown to be least restrictive); Shakur v. Schriro, 514 F.3d 878, 888–90 (9th Cir. 2008) (holding prisoner's request for Halal or kosher meat, based on gastrointestinal distress caused by vegetarian Muslim diets, required more complete analysis under RLUIPA); Hudson v. Dennehy, 538 F. Supp. 2d 400, 411 (D.Mass. 2008) (failure to provide Halal food to Muslim prisoners violated RLUIPA), *aff'd sub nom* Crawford v. Clarke, 578 F.3d 39 (1st Cir. 2009). *But see* Baranowski v. Hart, 486 F.3d 112, 124–25 (5th Cir. 2007) (upholding refusal under RLUIPA to provide kosher diet to Jewish prisoners on ground of "controlling costs" among others), *cert. denied*, 128 S. Ct. 707 (2007).

[806]Cutter v. Wilkinson, 544 U.S. 709, 716 n.5, 125 S. Ct. 2113 (2005). In *Nelson v. Miller*, 570 F.3d 868 (7th Cir. 2009), the court held that denial of a non-meat diet to a prisoner who objected to eating four-footed animals was not generally a substantial burden under RLUIPA because the regular diet would still be adequate if he skipped the four-footed animals and ate the other meat. However, during the 40 days of Lent, when he ate *no* meat, the regular diet was not adequate and he was entitled to receive an adequate non-meat diet. 570 F.3d at 879–80.

[807]*See* Kenner v. Phelps, 605 F.2d 850, 851 (5th Cir. 1979) (per curiam) (allegation that Muslim prisoner was punished for refusing to handle pork stated a constitutional claim); Hayes v. Long, 72 F.3d 70, 73–74 (8th Cir. 1995); Williams v. Bitner, 359 F. Supp. 2d 370, 375–79 (M.D.Pa. 2005) (holding that punishing a Muslim prisoner for refusing to touch or assist in preparing pork could violate both RLUIPA and the First Amendment), *aff'd*, 455 F.3d 186 (3d Cir. 2006); Chapman v. Pickett, 491 F. Supp. 967, 971–72 (C.D.Ill. 1980) (punishing a Muslim for refusing to handle pork was unconstitutional), *rev'd and remanded on other grounds*, 645 F.2d 73 (7th Cir. 1980), *rev'd*, 676 F.2d 1097 (7th Cir. 1982), *damage award affirmed*, 801 F.2d 912 (7th Cir. 1986), *vacated on other grounds*, 484 U.S. 807 (1987), *remanded*, 840 F.2d 20 (7th Cir. 1988); *see also* Beyah v. Coughlin, 789 F.2d 986, 989–90 (2d Cir. 1986) (allegation that Muslim prisoner was denied the right to use soap products that contained no pork products raised a factual issue barring summary judgment).

[808]Mark v. Nix, 983 F.2d 138, 139 (8th Cir. 1993) (upholding confiscation of a rosary with a plastic crucifix that could be used to open handcuffs); Hall v. Bellmon, 935 F.2d 1106, 1113 (10th Cir. 1991) (upholding ban on sharp objects or items worn around the neck as applied to Native American religious objects); Friend v. Kolodzieczak, 923 F.2d 126, 127–28 (9th Cir. 1991) (upholding ban on rosaries and scapulars from jail pursuant to a rule that prohibited all property not supplied or approved by the jail administration); McCorkle v. Johnson, 881 F.2d 993, 995–96 (11th Cir. 1989) (upholding denial of Satanic medallions and books); Dettmer v. Landon, 799 F.2d 929, 933 (4th Cir. 1986) (upholding denial to adherent of Church of Wicca possession of candles, hollow statues, sulphur, incense, and kitchen timer); Childs v. Duckworth, 705 F.2d 915, 921 (7th Cir. 1983) (upholding denial to Satanists of candles, incense, and a crystal ball); Hudson v. Maloney, 326 F. Supp. 2d 206, 209 n.2 (D.Mass. 2004) (upholding denial of full-size prayer rug based on fire hazards, sanitation problems, and their use to conceal contraband; prayer towels were permitted); Doty v. Lewis, 995 F. Supp. 1081, 1085–87 (D.Ariz. 1998) (upholding denial to Satanist in Special Management Unit possession of candles, incense, religious books, and a Baphomet tapestry); Sutton v. Stewart, 22 F. Supp. 2d 1097, 1101–02 (D.Ariz. 1998) (upholding ban on Muslim oils, since they are flammable and their possession only by Muslims led to bartering and threats), *aff'd*, 185 F.3d 869 (9th Cir. 1999) (unpublished); McClaflin v. Pearce, 739 F.

ceremonies and meetings[809] or under other restrictions.[810] Courts are most likely to question officials' judgments where it appears that restrictions are being applied inconsistently.[811] RFRA and RLUIPA may provide more favorable results for prisoners.[812]

Prison authorities are not generally obligated to provide inmates with religious objects as long as they are free to obtain them on their own.[813] Unjustified deprivation of a prisoner's own religious items violates the First Amendment and/or RFRA/RLUIPA and is directly actionable in federal court; the due process rule requiring the use of state tort remedies for ordinary property deprivations is not applicable.[814]

f. Names Prison officials must acknowledge genuine religious name changes for purposes such as delivering mail and other services.[815] They have not been required to eliminate the old name from their records; neither the continued use of the old name by prison staff[816] or the requirement that

---

Supp. 537, 541 (D.Or. 1990) (upholding denial of rosary in segregation; religious calendar could be barred if it did not conform to segregation rules); Sample v. Borg, 675 F. Supp. 574, 581 (E.D.Cal. 1987) (upholding denial to Native American segregation inmate of medicine bags but not tobacco ties), *vacated as moot*, 870 F.2d 563 (9th Cir. 1989); Mathes v. Carlson, 534 F. Supp. 226, 228 (W.D.Mo. 1982) (upholding ban on medicine bundles unless inspected by prison personnel); *see also* Holloway v. Pigman, 884 F.2d 365, 367 (8th Cir. 1989) (granting summary judgment against Native American prisoner who was denied sage and sweet grass where he failed to detail what his religious practice required).

[809]Wilson v. Moore, 270 F. Supp. 2d 1328, 1351–54 (N.D.Fla. 2003) (refusal to allow prisoner to have a prayer pipe in his cell upheld, but refusal to let him keep it in the chapel for supervised or group use raised an issue for trial under *Turner/O'Lone* standard; officials could prohibit personal possession of drums and rattles); Combs v. Corrections Corp. of America, 977 F. Supp. 799, 803 (W.D.La. 1997) (upholding policy requiring Native American religious objects to be secured in the chaplain's office, but requiring that prisoners have access to them as often as before the rule was introduced).

[810]Hammons v. Saffle, 348 F.3d 1250, 1255–58 (10th Cir. 2003) (upholding policy under First Amendment barring personal possession of prayer oils, allowing prisoners to obtain them from chaplains or keep them in designated worship areas); *see* Higgins v. Burroughs, 834 F.2d 76, 77–78 (3d Cir. 1987) (prison policy barring prisoner from carrying rosary beads into the visiting room presented a factual issue under the *O'Lone* standard).

[811]Sasnett v. Litscher, 197 F.3d 290, 292–93 (7th Cir. 1999) (ban on possession of crosses except when attached to rosaries, a specifically Catholic device, violated the First Amendment; government can't pick and choose among religions); Singh v. Goord, 520 F. Supp. 2d 487, 500, 502–03, 508–09 (S.D.N.Y. 2007) (admission that Sikh *Kara* (thin steel bracelet) posed no more security risk than metal crucifix, which was allowed; fact that prisoners possessed bed sheets, scarves, and religious items larger than plaintiff's nine-foot turban; fact that other prisoners were allowed to wear religious headgear on outside transports; all supported RLUIPA and First Amendment challenges to denial of those items); Kilaab al Ghashiya (Khan) v. Dept. of Corrections of the State of Wisconsin, 250 F. Supp. 2d 1016, 1035 (E.D.Wis. 2003) (refusing to dismiss challenge to ban on deprivation of oil, incense, and candles; officials' claims of fire hazards and the bad effects of smoke in the prison were undermined by the fact that "ceremonial smoking, smudging, and the use of incense" were allowed to others, consistently with policy concerning smoking materials), *dismissed on other grounds* (Jan. 15, 2004); Campos v. Coughlin, 854 F. Supp. 194, 208–12 (S.D.N.Y. 1994) (striking down prohibition on Santeria beads when worn under clothing under RFRA and First Amendment, since the security issue was no different from that presented by crucifixes or medals, which were permitted).

[812]Craddick v. Duckworth, 113 F.3d 83, 85 (7th Cir. 1997) (prohibition of Native American medicine bags violated RFRA); Sasnett v. Sullivan, 91 F.3d 1018, 1019, 1022–23 (7th Cir. 1996) (rule barring "items which because of shape or configuration are apt to cause a laceration if applied to the skin with force" violated RFRA as applied to crucifixes that were too small or light to be a weapon, too inexpensive to barter for a weapon, invisible because worn under clothing, and not gang symbols; rule was not the least restrictive means as applied), *cert. granted, vacated on other grounds*, 521 U.S. 1114 (1997); Perez v. Frank, 433 F. Supp. 2d 955, 964 (W.D.Wis. 2006) (allegation that plaintiff was denied uninterrupted access to prayer oils stated a RLUIPA claim); Rowe v. Davis, 373 F. Supp. 2d 822, 827 (N.D.Ind. 2005) (denial of Celtic Cross to plaintiff would not be the least restrictive alternative if prisoners of other religions were permitted to have them); Charles v. Verhagen, 220 F. Supp. 2d 937, 951–52 (W.D.Wis. 2002) (striking down prohibition on Islamic prayer oil under the "exacting" least restrictive means test of RLUIPA), *aff'd*, 348 F.3d 601 (7th Cir. 2003); Ramirez v. Coughlin, 919 F. Supp. 617, 622 (N.D.N.Y. 1996) (denying summary judgment to defendants under RFRA as to their denial to Satanist plaintiff of a three-inch metal bell for ceremonies); Alameen v. Coughlin, 892 F. Supp. 440, 449–50 (E.D.N.Y. 1995) (granting injunction under RFRA against prohibition of display of Sufi Muslim dhikr beads; concern about their being used as gang symbols was addressed by permitting black beads only). *But see* Hyde v. Fisher, 146 Idaho 782, 800–01, 203 P.3d 712 (App. 2009) (upholding uniform property limits under RLUIPA even though these restricted Native American religious practice). *Cf.* Shaheed-Muhammad v. DiPaolo, 393 F. Supp. 2d 80, 93–94 (D.Mass. 2005) (deprivation of a religious medal accompanied by threats stated a claim under the Massachusetts Civil Rights Act).

[813]Frank v. Terrell, 858 F.2d 1090, 1091 (5th Cir. 1988).

[814]Smith v. Smith, 578 F. Supp. 1373, 1375 (E.D.Pa. 1984); *see* § IV. H.8.b. *But see* Booth v. King, 346 F. Supp. 2d 751, 759–60 (E.D.Pa. 2004) (applying post-conviction remedy rule to religious property).

[815]Hakim v. Hicks, 223 F.3d 1244, 1250–51 (11th Cir. 2000) (requiring religious names to be added to ID cards under *Turner/O'Lone*); Malik v. Brown, 71 F.3d 724, 728–30 (9th Cir. 1995) (allowing prisoner to use both names on outgoing mail held required under *Turner*); Ali v. Dixon, 912 F.2d 86, 89–90 (4th Cir. 1990); Salaam v. Lockhart, 905 F.2d 1168, 1172–76 (8th Cir. 1990); Barrett v. Commonwealth of Virginia, 689 F.2d 498, 501–03 (4th Cir. 1982); Masjid Muhammad-D.C.C. v. Keve, 479 F. Supp. 1311, 1324 (D.Del. 1979).

[816]Fawaad v. Jones, 81 F.3d 1084, 1086–87 (11th Cir. 1996) (requiring prisoner to use both names on correspondence upheld under RFRA); Ali v. Dixon, 912 F.2d 86, 90–91 (4th Cir. 1990); Imam Ali Abdullah Adba v. Cannery, 634 F.2d 339, 340 (6th Cir.

the prisoner continue in some instances to respond to the old name[817] violate the Constitution. (Prisoners may fare better on these questions under RFRA or RLUIPA.) Prisoners may be required to go through the state's official name change procedure, if there is one, before their new names are acknowledged.[818]

g. Religious Literature The right to read religious publications is protected by the First Amendment, like the right to read anything else. Reading religious publications can also be treated as part of the free exercise of religion, so restrictions can be challenged under the more favorable standard of RFRA and RLUIPA. These issues are discussed in more detail in another section.[819]

h. Other Religious Issues Prison officials may require prisoners to submit to medical examination or treatment over their religious objections,[820] though punitive measures against prisoners who refuse may be struck down if they do not actually serve a medical purpose.[821] Courts have held that prisoners who are executed may not be subjected to autopsies over their previously stated religious objections.[822] So far, prisoners have had little success in religious challenges to the taking of blood or other bodily tissue or fluids for DNA samples.[823] Prisoners may be required to submit to legitimate security procedures such as searches despite religious objections.[824] However, work assignments that require prisoners to violate their religious beliefs may violate the First Amendment or RFRA/RLUIPA.[825]

Prison officials may not retaliate against prisoners for their religious beliefs or their attempts to practice them.[826] An officer who shoved a prisoner without justification while he was praying violated the First Amendment.[827] One court has held that alleged refusal to tell a Muslim prisoner the

---

1980); Masjid Muhammad-D.C.C. v. Keve, 479 F. Supp. at 1322–24; *see* U.S. v. Baker, 415 F.3d 1273, 1274 (11th Cir. 2005) (per curiam) (criminal defendant was not entitled to a new commitment order under his religious name; he was entitled to have his name change recognized prospectively by the prison system through a dual-name policy). *But see* Spies v. Voinovich, 173 F.3d 398, 405–06 (6th Cir. 1999) (refusal to use Buddhist name upheld because prisoners have no rights with respect to the way prisons keep their records).

[817]Muhammad v. Wainwright, 839 F.2d 1422, 1424–25 (11th Cir. 1987) (disciplining an inmate who had obtained a legal name change for refusing to respond to his old name did not violate a "clearly established" right). Felix v. Rolan, 833 F.2d 517, 519 (5th Cir. 1987) (prisoner could be required to sign in to law library using both Muslim and birth names); Ephraim v. Angelone, 313 F. Supp. 2d 569, 576–77 (E.D.Va. 2003), *aff'd*, 313 F. Supp. 2d 569 (4th Cir. 2004); Thacker v. Dixon, 784 F. Supp. 286, 303 (E.D.N.C. 1991) (prisoner could be required to provide his old name as well as the new name to obtain services), *aff'd*, 953 F.2d 639 (4th Cir. 1992). *But see* Bilal v. Davis, 918 F.2d 723 (8th Cir. 1990) (allegation that prisoner was expelled from a disciplinary hearing for refusing to respond to his committed name stated a First Amendment claim).

[818]Azeez v. Fairman, 795 F.2d 1296, 1299 (7th Cir. 1986); Rahman v. Stephenson, 626 F. Supp. 886, 887–88 (W.D.Tenn. 1986); Salahuddin v. Coughlin, 591 F. Supp. 353, 359 (S.D.N.Y. 1984).

[819]*See* §§ B.2.a, nn.178–181, and B.2.c, n.212, above.

[820]Karolis v. New Jersey Dep't of Corrections, 935 F. Supp. 523, 527–28 (D.N.J.1996) (involuntary administration of tuberculosis test to prisoner upheld under RFRA because there is a compelling state interest in stopping the spread of tuberculosis); Ballard v. Woodard, 641 F. Supp. 432, 436–37 (W.D.N.C. 1986) (no right to refuse tuberculosis test under First Amendment); Smallwood-El v. Coughlin, 589 F. Supp. 692, 699–700 (S.D.N.Y. 1984) (no right to refuse intake examination for communicable diseases; prisoner could be segregated for refusing); *see* Jacobson v. Massachusetts, 197 U.S. 11, 25–39, 25 S. Ct. 358 (1905) (smallpox vaccination could be required of non-prisoners despite religious objections).

One court has held that prison officials did not violate the First Amendment when they failed to dispose of the medical blood samples of a Jehovah's Witness consistently with his religious beliefs (*i.e.*, by pouring it on the ground and covering it with dust), given

the health risks of infection from blood. Schreiber v. Ault, 280 F.3d 891, 892–93 (8th Cir. 2002).

[821]*See* Ch. 2, § F.4.k., concerning placement in isolation for refusing PPD test for tuberculosis.

[822]Workman v. Levy, 136 F. Supp. 2d 899, 900–01 (M.D.Tenn. 2001); U.S. v. Hammer, 121 F. Supp. 2d 794, 801–02 (M.D.Pa. 2000).

[823]In *U.S. v. Holmes*, 2007 WL 529830 (E.D.Cal., Feb. 20, 2007), the court ruled that a requirement of extracting blood for a DNA sample, rather than taking a less intrusive buccal (cheek) swab, substantially burdened a defendant's religious exercise and was not justified by a compelling interest, and ordered that the buccal swab be taken. Courts have rejected challenges to any taking of a DNA sample. *See* U.S. v. Hilsenrath, 2008 WL 2620909, *4 (N.D.Cal., July 1, 2008) (upholding probation condition requiring provision of blood sample); Loparo v. Unnamed Defendants, 2006 WL 3359586, *2 (W.D.Va., Nov. 20, 2006) (finding compelling interest in taking blood sample and no substantial burden on religious exercise); *see also* Kaemmerling v. Lappin, 553 F.3d 669, 679 (D.C. Cir. 2008) (prisoner who objected to DNA analysis, but not to taking of fluid or tissue samples, failed to identify a burden on religious observance); U.S. v. Zimmerman, 514 F.3d 851, 854 (9th Cir. 2007) (criminal defendant's claim of religious objection must be assessed under RLUIPA).

[824]*See* § E.2 of this chapter, nn.931–933.

[825]Franklin v. Lockhart, 890 F.2d 96, 97 (8th Cir. 1989) (if the plaintiff was required to handle manure and dead animals in his "hoe squad" job, contrary to his Muslim beliefs, First Amendment would be violated); *see* cases cited in § D.2.d of this chapter, n.807, concerning prisoners required to handle pork in food service jobs.

In *Murphy v. Carroll*, 202 F. Supp. 2d 421 (D.Md. 2002), the court held that designating Saturday as "cell clean-up day" violated the First Amendment as applied to an Orthodox Jewish prisoner who observed the Sabbath on Saturday. The court said prison officials had "obvious, readily available alternatives" such as providing cleaning materials to the plaintiff on Sunday. 202 F. Supp. 2d at 424. *But see* Rowold v. McBride, 973 F. Supp. 829, 836–37 (N.D.Ind. 1997) (upholding requirement that Seventh Day Adventist/ Messianic Jew work on his Sabbath).

[826]Rouse v. Benson, 193 F.3d 936, 941 (8th Cir. 1999).

[827]Arroyo Lopez v. Nuttall, 25 F. Supp. 2d 407, 409–10 (S.D.N.Y. 1998) (awarding damages).

time of day so he could follow his prayer schedule raised a factual issue under the First Amendment.[828]

The refusal to designate "Holy Ground" for Native American religious practice did not violate the First Amendent, since prisons "cannot be expected to set aside and police patches of land for every religious sect."[829] A rule against casting spells, applied to Wiccan prisoners, raised a claim under RFRA.[830] Tape-recording a detainee's confession to a priest in jail violated the *priest's* rights under RFRA.[831] Prison officials' ability to restrict religious donations from prisoners' accounts is in dispute.[832] Religious objections to racial integration need not be respected.[833] A prohibition on sparring and receiving martial arts training, claimed to be a religious requirement, is permissible under RLUIPA in order to further safety and institutional security.[834]

Parole or probation conditions that infringe on religious freedom may be upheld if the factual justification is strong enough.[835]

3. Equal Treatment of Religions

Prison officials are obligated to treat religions in an even-handed manner,[836] but absolute equality of treatment is not always required, and most claims of unequal treatment have been unsuccessful. The Supreme Court stated, "We do not suggest . . . that every religious sect or group within a prison—however few in number—must have identical facilities or personnel. A special chapel or place of worship need not be provided for every faith regardless of size, nor must a chaplain, priest, or minister be provided without regard to the extent of the demand."[837]

Under the Equal Protection Clauses,[838] distinctions between religious groups are usually assessed under a "reasonableness" standard.[839] Special treatment for a particular religious sect may also violate the Establishment Clause.[840]

Under these rules, courts have usually sustained differences in the availability of religious personnel[841] and in

---

[828]Omar v. Casterline, 288 F. Supp. 2d 775, 781–82 (W.D.La. 2003).

[829]Wilson v. Moore, 270 F. Supp. 2d 1328, 1350 (N.D.Fla. 2003).

[830]O'Bryan v. Bureau of Prisons, 349 F.3d 399, 401 (7th Cir. 2003).

[831]Mockaitis v. Harcleroad, 104 F.3d 1522, 1530 (9th Cir. 1997).

[832]In *Blankenship v. Gunter*, 898 F.2d 625, 627–28 (8th Cir. 1990), a rule forbidding such donations was upheld. However, the plaintiff in *Blankenship* failed to dispute evidence that alternative means of making donations were available. In *Abdullah v. Gunter*, 949 F.2d 1032, 1036 (8th Cir. 1991), the court held that a challenge to the same rule presented factual issues that could not be resolved on summary judgment and that counsel should be appointed for the plaintiff.

[833]Ochs v. Thalacker, 90 F.3d 293, 296–97 (8th Cir. 1996); Taylor v. Thornton, 107 F. Supp. 2d 1061, 1063–64 (W.D.Mo. 2000); White v. Morris, 811 F. Supp. 341, 344 (S.D.Ohio 1992).

[834]Jova v. Smith, 582 F.3d 410, 416 (2d Cir. 2009).

[835]Yahweh v. U.S. Parole Comm'n, 158 F. Supp. 2d 1332, 1345–51 (S.D.Fla. 2001) (upholding a parole condition requiring religious leader to have no contact with his followers, since his prior involvement with them led to criminal acts including murder).

[836]Cruz v. Beto, 405 U.S. 319, 322, 92 S. Ct. 1079 (1972) (Buddhist prisoner is entitled to "a reasonable opportunity of pursuing his faith comparable to the opportunity afforded fellow prisoners who adhere to conventional religious precepts. . . ."); Al-Alamin v. Gramley, 926 F.2d 680, 686 (7th Cir. 1991) ("qualitatively comparable" treatment required); Lindell v. Casperson, 360 F. Supp. 2d 932, 958 (W.D.Wis. 2005) ("The denial of a privilege to adherents of one religion while granting it to others is discrimination on the basis of religion in violation of the equal protection clause of the Constitution."), *aff'd*, 169 Fed.Appx. 999 (7th Cir. 2006) (unpublished); Lucero v. Hensley, 920 F. Supp. 1067, 1075 (C.D.Calif. 1996) (allegation that there are as many Native American as Jewish inmates and that there is a full-time rabbi, but not a full-time Native American chaplain, states an equal protection claim; defendants must show they have "made a good faith attempt to treat different religious groups equally").

[837]Cruz v. Beto, 405 U.S. at 322 n.2.

[838]U.S. Const., amend. V, XIV; *see* Ch. 5 concerning the law of equal protection.

[839]Shakur v. Schriro, 514 F.3d 878, 891 (9th Cir. 2008) (applying *Turner* reasonableness standard and not "rational basis" equal protection standard); DeHart v. Horn, 227 F.3d 47, 61 (3d Cir. 2000) (en banc); Benjamin v. Coughlin, 905 F.2d 571, 575 (2d Cir. 1990).

Some courts in equal protection cases have held that religious groups were not "similarly situated" and therefore the Equal Protection Clause afforded them *no* protection against unequal treatment. *See, e.g.*, DeHart v. Horn, 390 F.3d 262, 272 (3d Cir. 2004) (holding plaintiff's unusual religious diet demands were so burdensome that he was not "similarly situated" to anyone else); Murphy v. Missouri Dep't of Correction, 372 F.3d 979, 984–85 (8th Cir. 2004) (refusal to permit services of Christian Separatist Church did not deny equal protection because it was not similarly situated to other churches to which racial separatism was not central). Other courts have said that differences in treatment do not deny equal protection if prison officials do not act with discriminatory purpose. *See, e.g.*, Freeman v. Texas Dep't of Criminal Justice, 369 F.3d 854, 863 (5th Cir. 2004); Shaheed v. Winston, 885 F. Supp. 861, 869 (E.D.Va. 1995), *aff'd*, 161 F.3d 3 (4th Cir.1998).

The exclusion of particular individuals from religious exercise may violate the Equal Protection Clause. Morrison v. Garraghty, 239 F.3d 648, 657–59 (4th Cir. 2001); Mitchell v. Angelone, 82 F. Supp. 2d 485, 492 (E.D.Va. 1999) (both striking down the exclusion from Native American religious practice of persons without Native American ancestry).

[840]Cutter v. Wilkinson, 544 U.S. 709, 724–25, 125 S. Ct. 2113 (2005). The Establishment Clause is discussed in the next section.

[841]Werner v. McCotter, 49 F.3d 1476, 1481 (10th Cir. 1995) (lack of Cherokee religious advisor did not violate plaintiff's rights under RFRA where the prison had six nondenominational part-time chaplains and two Native American spiritual advisors, who were Lakota Sioux); Lucero v. Hensley, 920 F. Supp. 1067, 1074 (C.D.Cal. 1996) (lack of a full-time Native American chaplain did not violate RFRA because services could be conducted by inmates, who were ordained by the part-time chaplain, and there was no showing they could not perform the mandates of the religion); Wilson v. Moore, 270 F. Supp. 2d 1328, 1351 (N.D.Fla. 2003) ("Defendants do not have the obligation to hire a minister of every faith to conduct religious services for prisoners, nor do they have

facilities or budgets provided to different religious groups.[842] Differences in the accommodation of religious dietary

needs have met with mixed responses.[843] Differences between groups in the application of restrictive rules have been met with greater suspicion from the courts.[844] However, officials

---

the obligation to drum up volunteers"; First Amendment case); *see also* Duffy v. California State Personnel Board, 232 Cal.App.3d 1, 283 Cal.Rptr. 622, 625–34 (Cal.App. 1991) (prison could limit Catholic chaplain position to priests in good standing with the Roman Catholic Church). *But see* SapaNajin v. Gunter, 857 F.2d 463, 465 (8th Cir. 1988) (First Amendment rights of Sioux prisoner were violated where only medicine man provided by prison authorities was a member of a "deviant" sect).

[842]Baranowski v. Hart, 486 F.3d 112, 122–23 (5th Cir. 2007) (less frequent services and less access to the chapel for Jewish prisoners than others was justified by small number of Jews in population), *cert. denied*, 128 S. Ct. 707 (2007); Blair-Bey v. Nix, 963 F.2d 162, 163–64 (8th Cir. 1992) (Moorish Science Temple was not entitled to a separate religious advisor from other Muslim groups); Johnson v. Moore, 948 F.2d 517, 520 (9th Cir. 1991) (upholding failure to provide a Unitarian Universalist chaplain); Al-Alamin v. Gramley, 926 F.2d 680, 687–88 (7th Cir. 1991) (prison need not employ full-time Imam even though it had a chaplain); Butler-Bey v. Frey, 811 F.2d 449, 453–54 (8th Cir. 1987); Thompson v. Commonwealth of Ky., 712 F.2d 1078, 1081–82 (6th Cir. 1983); Jaben v. Moore, 788 F. Supp. 500, 502 (D.Kan. 1992) (Jewish services need not be provided given the small number of Jewish inmates and the availability of a rabbi; Ra Chaka v. Franzen, 727 F. Supp. 454, 460 (N.D.Ill. 1989); Card v. Dugger, 709 F. Supp. 1098, 1109 (M.D.Fla. 1988) (Catholic chaplain need not be provided since outside clergy were allowed to visit; every inmate was not entitled to a clergyperson of his own faith; predominance of Protestant chaplains in Florida prisons was not unlawful where they were not selected based on religious affiliation and Catholic priests rarely applied), *aff'd*, 871 F.2d 1023 (11th Cir. 1989); Glasshofer v. Thornburgh, 514 F. Supp. 1242, 1245–47 (E.D.Pa. 1981) (differences in physical facilities and lack of a Jewish chaplain on staff did not violate the Constitution since adequate accommodations were provided and Jewish chaplains were allowed to visit), *aff'd*, 688 F.2d 821 (3d Cir. 1982); *see also* Young v. Lane, 922 F.2d 370, 377–78 (7th Cir. 1991) (failure to reimburse Jewish rabbis for travel expenses, while other religious leaders were reimbursed, did not violate any "clearly established" rights). *But see* McElyea v. Babbitt, 833 F.2d 196, 199 (9th Cir. 1987) (allegation of prison library's failure to provide Jewish literature raised First Amendment and equal protection issues); Lucero v. Hensley, 920 F. Supp. 1067, 1075 (C.D.Calif. 1996) (allegation that there are as many Native American as Jewish inmates and that there is a full-time rabbi, but not a full-time Native American chaplain, states an equal protection claim; defendants must show they have "made a good faith attempt to treat different religious groups equally"); Rasul v. District of Columbia, 680 F. Supp. 436, 439–42 (D.D.C. 1988) (rejection of a Muslim Imam for chaplain's post because he was not a Protestant constituted religious discrimination where the job involved directing a program of religious activity for all inmates, not just Protestants); Cochran v. Rowe, 438 F. Supp. 566, 571 (N.D.Ill. 1977) (Muslim clergy should be compensated in the same manner as other clergy, and prison funds allocated for religious purposes should be distributed proportionately to all groups); Pitts v. Knowles, 339 F. Supp. 1183, 1185–86 (W.D.Wis. 1972) (prison's provision of 700 Bibles and only two Qu'rans was unconstitutional), *aff'd without opinion*, 478 F.2d 1405 (7th Cir. 1973); Northern v. Nelson, 315 F. Supp. 687, 688 (N.D.Cal. 1970) (Muslim

clergy must be compensated in a similar manner to other clergy), *aff'd on other grounds*, 448 F.2d 1266 (9th Cir. 1971).

[843]Shakur v. Schriro, 514 F.3d 878, 891–92 (9th Cir. 2008) (questioning cost justification for denying Halal or kosher meat to Muslims, given large expense of providing kosher diet with meat to Jewish prisoners); Williams v. Morton, 343 F.3d 212, 221–22 (3d Cir. 2003) (providing kosher food but not Halal food did not deny equal protection because the kosher diet did not include meat); Johnson v. Horn, 150 F.3d 276, 284–85 (3d Cir. 1998) (providing a hot pork alternative to Muslims but only a cold kosher diet to Jews did not deny equal protection because a hot kosher diet would have required more effort from officials, making Jews and Muslims not similarly situated); LaFevers v. Saffle, 936 F.2d 1117, 1120 (10th Cir. 1991) (allegation that prison provided Muslim diet but not vegetarian diet was not frivolous under the First Amendment); Moorish Science Temple of America, Inc., v. Smith, 693 F.2d 987, 990 (2d Cir. 1982) (allegation that Muslims were not provided with their dietary requirements, while other religious groups were, stated a constitutional claim); *see* Baranowski v. Hart, 486 F.3d 112, 123 n.6 (5th Cir. 2007) (dismissing Jewish prisoners' equal protection claim concerning kosher diet on the ground that no one else received a kosher diet), *cert. denied*, 128 S. Ct. 707 (2007).

[844]McKinney v. Maynard, 952 F.2d 350, 352–53 (10th Cir. 1991) (allegation of denial of Native American religious rights was not frivolous, since the plaintiff alleged that other religions were treated differently); Swift v. Lewis, 901 F.2d 730, 732–33 (9th Cir. 1990) (prison officials must show why Christian Nazarites were not entitled to the same exemption from hair and beard rules granted to Sikhs and American Indians); Johnson-Bey v. Lane, 863 F.2d 1308, 1311–12 (7th Cir. 1988) (evidence that ban on inmate-conducted services was enforced unequally and that defendants delayed unreasonably in arranging for outside ministers stated a constitutional claim); Reed v. Faulkner, 842 F.2d 960, 964 (7th Cir. 1988) (prison officials were required to produce evidence justifying making Rastafarians but not Native Americans cut their hair); Valiant-Bey v. Morris, 829 F.2d 1441, 1444 (8th Cir. 1987) (allegation that mail from Moorish Science Temple was singled out for special handling stated a claim of religious discrimination); Walker v. Blackwell, 411 F.2d 23, 29 (5th Cir. 1969) (Muslims must be permitted to receive religious publications "in the same manner that other newspapers are allowed to other inmates"); Wilson v. Moore, 270 F. Supp. 2d 1328, 1353 (N.D.Fla. 2003) (evidence that Native American prisoners were allowed to wear headbands only during services while Jews and Muslims were allowed to wear religious headgear at all times supported an equal protection claim); Hyde v. Texas Dep't of Criminal Justice, 948 F. Supp. 625, 626 (S.D.Tex. 1996) (Jehovah's Witnesses must be allowed to meet in groups of less than 15 and without an outside sponsor as are other groups); Abordo v. State of Hawai'I, 902 F. Supp. 1220, 1226 (D.Haw. 1995) (allegation that Native American was required to cut hair while Hawaiians and women were allowed to wear long hair stated an equal protection claim); *see also* Freeman v. Abdullah, 925 F.2d 266, 267 (8th Cir. 1991) (allegation that prison officials had dissolved a particular Muslim sect was not frivolous). *But see* Benjamin v. Coughlin, 905 F.2d 571, 578–79 (2d Cir. 1990) (Rastafarian "crowns" could be banned, though kufis and yarmulkes were permitted, because crowns were larger and looser fitting and presented

have been upheld in denying recognition and imposing severe restrictions on religious groups that they viewed as posing serious risks to prison order or security.[845]

If religious groups are treated unequally, it may be possible to argue that the better treatment given one group shows that the worse treatment given to the other does not meet the reasonable relationship standard of *Turner/O'Lone*. Such arguments should be even stronger under the "least restrictive means" standards of RFRA and RLUIPA, since if prison officials allow one religious group a particular benefit, denying it to another group does not seem to be "least restrictive."[846] The Supreme Court said in upholding RLUIPA that courts "must be satisfied that the Act's proscriptions are and will be administered neutrally among different faiths,"[847] and cited the provision of Kosher food for Jews but not Halal food for Muslims as an example of the kind of restriction RLUIPA was intended to correct.[848]

4. Establishment of Religion

The First Amendment prohibits the "establishment of religion."[849] The exact meaning of this phrase is hotly debated, but the basic idea is that government may not give official sanction or sponsorship to particular religious beliefs or to religion in general[850]—though the heightened protection afforded religious exercise by the Religious Land Use and Institutionalized Persons Act does not violate the Establishment Clause.[851] Nor can government coerce anyone to participate in religious activities.[852]

Establishment Clause standards differ from Free Exercise Clause standards in important respects. A plaintiff need not demonstrate sincerity of beliefs in an Establishment Clause case.[853] In addition, several courts have held that the *Turner/O'Lone* reasonable relationship standard does not govern Establishment Clause cases.[854] We think this is correct. As one court explained: "The 'exercise' of Establishment Clause rights differs from the exercise of most other constitutional rights, in that it is in essence a public matter: The inmate is not claiming a right to do something, but rather insisting the institution cannot expend public money to support religion." Therefore the *Turner/O'Lone* limitations on prisoners' constitutional rights are not relevant.[855]

Hiring clergy and funding religious activities in prison do not violate the Establishment Clause, since these actions are necessary in order for prisoners to engage in religious exercise.[856] However, the Establishment Clause may be

---

a greater danger of hiding contraband); Hobbs v. Pennell, 754 F. Supp. 1040, 1047–50 (D.Del. 1991) (Nation of Islam could be required to have outside Imam for services, even if other Muslims were not, because of its militant and confrontational beliefs); Faheem-El v. Lane, 657 F. Supp. 638, 644–46 (C.D.Ill. 1986) (prison officials could deny recognition to a religious sect that also functioned as a street gang).

[845]Murphy v. Missouri Dep't of Correction, 372 F.3d 979, 983–85, 989 (8th Cir. 2004) (upholding denial under First Amendment of group services to Christian Separatist Church because its emphasis on racial separatism posed a risk of violence; noting the result might be different under RLUIPA); Brown v. Johnson, 743 F.2d 408, 413 (6th Cir. 1984) (prison could bar services by homosexual-oriented church group because of danger of violence); Faheem-El v. Lane, 657 F. Supp. 638, 644–46 (C.D.Ill. 1986) (prison officials could deny recognition to a religious sect that also functioned as a street gang); *see* § B.5 of this chapter, n.242, concerning the classification of some religious groups as "security threat groups." *But see* Bryant v. McGinnis, 463 F. Supp. 373, 386–88 (W.D.N.Y. 1978) (damages awarded for failure to recognize Black Muslim religious rights).

[846]Hudson v. Dennehy, 538 F. Supp. 2d 400, 411 (D.Mass. 2008) (citing dietary accommodations to Jewish, Buddhist, and Seventh Day Adventist inmates in finding denial of Halal food violated RLUIPA), *aff'd sub nom* Crawford v. Clarke, 578 F.3d 39 (1st Cir. 2009).

[847]Cutter v. Wilkinson, 544 U.S. 709, 723, 125 S. Ct. 2113 (2005). "Finally, RLUIPA does not differentiate among bona fide faiths." *Id.* at 723.

[848]*Cutter*, 544 U.S. at 716 n.5 (citing legislative history).

[849]U.S. Const., Amend. I.

[850]The Supreme Court has held that in Establishment Clause cases, courts should inquire whether the challenged law or conduct has a "secular purpose," whether "its principal or primary effect . . . advances or inhibits religion," and whether it creates an "excessive entanglement of government with religion." Lemon v. Kurtzman, 403 U.S. 602, 612–13, 91 S. Ct. 2105 (1971). Though this standard has been criticized, *see* Cutter v. Wilkinson, 544 U.S. 709, 727 n.1, 125 S. Ct. 2113 (2005) (Thomas, J., dissenting) (referring to "discredited test" of *Lemon*), it has not been overruled. *See* McCreary County, Ky. v. American Civil Liberties Union of Ky., 545 U.S. 844, 859, 125 S. Ct. 2722 (2005) (applying *Lemon*); Kaufman v. McCaughtry, 419 F.3d 678, 683–84 (7th Cir. 2005) (same).

[851]Cutter v. Wilkinson, 544 U.S. 709, 719–24, 125 S. Ct. 2113 (2005).

[852]Lee v. Weisman, 505 U.S. 577, 587, 112 S. Ct. 2649 (1992); *see* Kerr v. Farrey, 95 F.3d 472, 479 (7th Cir. 1996) (when a plaintiff alleges religious coercion, "three points are crucial: first, has the state acted; second, does the action amount to coercion; and third, is the object of the coercion religious or secular?"); Turner v. Hickman, 342 F. Supp. 2d 887, 893–95 (E.D.Cal. 2004) (discussing coercion test at length).

[853]Alexander v. Schenk, 118 F. Supp. 2d 298, 301 (N.D.N.Y. 2000) (Establishment Clause prevents government from coercing *anyone* to support or participate in religious exercise).

[854]Americans United for Separation of Church and State v. Prison Fellowship Ministries, Inc., 509 F.3d 406, 426 (8th Cir. 2007); Ross v. Keelings, 2 F. Supp. 2d 810, 818 (E.D.Va. 1998); Scarpino v. Grosshiem, 852 F. Supp. 798, 804 (S.D. Iowa 1994).

[855]Scarpino v. Grosshiem, 852 F. Supp. at 804. Nonetheless, some courts have applied *Turner/O'Lone* in Establishment Clause cases without much discussion. *See, e.g.*, Alexander v. Schenk, 118 F. Supp. 2d 298, 301 (N.D.N.Y. 2000).

[856]Carter v. Broadlawns Medical Center, 857 F.2d 448, 457 (8th Cir. 1988) (restrictions on prisoners and involuntarily committed mental patients "constitute a state-imposed burden on the patients' religious practices that the state may appropriately adjust for" by providing chaplains); Johnson-Bey v. Lane, 863 F.2d 1308, 1312 (7th Cir. 1988); Henderson v. Berge, 362 F. Supp. 2d 1030, 1032–33 (W.D.Wis. 2005) (providing religious as well as secular channels in a prison TV system did not violate the Establishment Clause; alleviating governmental interference with religious

violated if religious functionaries exercise non-religious authority over prisoners.[857] It may also be violated if particular religious viewpoints are favored by prison authorities,[858] though precise equality in treatment is not required.[859]

Prisoners may not be coerced to hear or submit to religious views,[860] though exposure to celebration of traditional religious holidays does not violate the Establishment Clause in the absence of actual religious observance.[861] Coercing participation or penalizing non-participation in prison programs of a religious nature does violate the Establishment Clause.[862] The limits on prisons' sponsorship

---

exercise can be a secular purpose), *reconsideration denied*, 2005 WL 1261970 (W.D.Wis., May 26, 2005), *aff'd*, 190 Fed.Appx. 507 (7th Cir. 2006) (unpublished); Duffy v. California State Personnel Board, 232 Cal.App.3d 1, 283 Cal.Rptr. 622, 628–31 (Cal.App. 1991); *see* Cutter v. Wilkinson, 544 U.S. 709, 724–25, 125 S. Ct. 2113 (2005) (noting that if states could not give greater accommodation to religious concerns than others, prisons could not provide chaplains).

[857]Theriault v. A Religious Office, 895 F.2d 104, 106–07 (2d Cir. 1990) (allegation that chaplains exercised non-religious authority raised "significant" questions under the Establishment Clause); Theriault v. Carlson, 339 F. Supp. 375, 381–82 (N.D.Ga. 1972) (prison chaplains' filing of reports on inmates' religious activities was unconstitutional), *vacated on other grounds*, 495 F.2d 390 (5th Cir. 1974). *But see* Remmers v. Brewer, 494 F.2d 1277, 1278 (8th Cir. 1974) (chaplains' reports could be used in parole decisions because they did not deal "solely or primarily" with religious activities or the lack of them).

[858]Cutter v. Wilkinson, 544 U.S. at 724–25 ("singl[ing] out a particular religious sect for special treatment" violates the Establishment Clause (citation omitted)); Kaufman v. McCaughtry, 419 F.3d 678, 683–84 (7th Cir. 2005) (banning an atheist study group while permitting other religious groups violated the Establishment Clause); Perez v. Frank, 433 F. Supp. 2d 955, 966 (W.D.Wis. 2006) ("To the extent petitioner contends that the religious traditions of other inmates are being accommodated while Islamic traditions are not, his allegations state a claim under the establishment clause."); Parnell v. Waldrep, 511 F. Supp. 764, 768 (W.D.N.C. 1981) (permitting Bibles and "little Christian tracts" while banning other books violated the Establishment Clause); *see also* McElyea v. Babbitt, 833 F.2d 196, 199 (9th Cir. 1987) (allegation of failure to provide Jewish literature in prison libraries might be subject to Establishment Clause defense).

[859]Murphy v. Missouri Dep't of Correction, 372 F.3d 979, 985 (8th Cir. 2004) (providing an internal religious TV channel with a "broad spectrum" of religious ideas, but excluding the Christian Separatist Church, did not violate the Establishment Clause); Henderson v. Berge, 362 F. Supp. 2d 1030, 1032–33 (W.D.Wis. 2005) (providing the Sky-Angel Trinity religious TV channel, among other cable channels, did not violate the Establishment Clause; the prison provided additional closed-circuit channels with religious programming, including non-Christian religions), *reconsideration denied*, 2005 WL 1261970 (W.D.Wis., May 26, 2005), *aff'd*, 190 Fed.Appx. 507 (7th Cir. 2006) (unpublished); *see* § D.3 of this chapter for further discussion of unequal treatment of religions.

[860]Campbell v. Cauthron, 623 F.2d 503, 509 (8th Cir. 1980) ("lay witnessing" in jail could violate Establishment Clause if conducted so inmates could not avoid it); Byar v. Lee, 336 F. Supp. 2d 896, 905–06 (W.D.Ark. 2004) (disciplinary rules modeled after the Ten Commandments violated the Establishment Clause); Campbell v. Thornton, 644 F. Supp. 103, 106 (W.D.Mo. 1986) (evidence that proprietors of "halfway house" forced their religion on the plaintiff established a constitutional violation); *see also* Spratt v. County of

Kent, 621 F. Supp. 594, 600–01 (W.D.Mich. 1985) (jail social worker could be fired for persisting in using religious methods, including casting out demons; the Sheriff "chose to walk the narrow line between the free exercise and establishment clauses by forbidding county paid social workers from using religious counseling techniques while, at the same time, allowing inmates access to voluntary chaplains of all faiths who services the jail"), *aff'd*, 810 F.2d 203 (6th Cir. 1986). *But see* Canell v. Lightner, 143 F.3d 1210, 1214 (9th Cir. 1998) (proselytizing by officer was not an establishment of religion where he did not act pursuant to policy and he was transferred when the plaintiff complained); R.G. v. Koller, 415 F. Supp. 2d 1129, 1159–60 (D.Haw. 2006) (prisoners who complained that staff engaged in "Bible discussions" did not show "*government endorsement* of religion").

[861]Blagman v. White, 112 F. Supp. 2d 534, 540–41 (E.D.Va. 2000), *aff'd*, 3 Fed.Appx. 23 (4th Cir. 2001) (unpublished); Torricellas v. Poole, 954 F. Supp. 1405, 1411–12 (C.D.Cal. 1997) (Christmas party in prison visiting room did not violate the Establishment Clause; it had a secular purpose (to let prisoners and their families celebrate the holidays in a festive atmosphere), its primary purpose was neither to advance nor inhibit religion (citing elf costumes), and state entanglement was minimal because the party was proposed by an inmate representative group), *aff'd*, 141 F.3d 1179 (9th Cir. 1998) (unpublished).

[862]Kerr v. Farrey, 95 F.3d 472, 478–80 (7th Cir. 1996) (holding that a prisoner could not be required to participate in Narcotics Anonymous or have his security classification raised); Owens v. Kelley, 681 F.2d 1362, 1365 (11th Cir. 1982) ("a condition of probation which requires the probationer to submit himself to a course advocating the adoption of religion or a particular religion . . . transgresses the First Amendment"); Turner v. Hickman, 342 F. Supp. 2d 887, 895–98 (E.D.Cal. 2004) (holding requirement to participate in Narcotics Anonymous to be eligible for parole violated Establishment Clause, even where the religious views expressed were similar to the plaintiff's); Clanton v. Glover, 280 F. Supp. 2d 1360, 1366 (M.D.Fla. 2003) (holding allegation that prison drug program required prayer ceremony supported an Establishment Clause claim); Nusbaum v. Terrangi, 210 F. Supp. 2d 784, 788–89 (E.D.Va. 2002) (substance abuse program required in order to obtain good time credits and containing religious emphasis on "higher power" violated Establishment Clause); Bausch v. Sumiec, 139 F. Supp. 2d 1029, 1033–35 (E.D.Wis. 2001) (requiring participation in religion-based substance abuse program as a condition of staying out of prison on parole violation violated Establishment Clause); Alexander v. Schenk, 118 F. Supp. 2d 298, 301 (N.D.N.Y. 2000) (coercion to participate in religious Alcohol and Substance Abuse Treatment program violated the Establishment Clause regardless of the plaintiff's religious sincerity); Ross v. Keelings, 2 F. Supp. 2d 810, 816–18 (E.D.Va. 1998) (similar to *Nusbaum*); Warburton v. Underwood, 2 F. Supp. 2d 306, 315–18 (W.D.N.Y. 1998) (allegation that good time was withheld unless plaintiff participated in Narcotics Anonymous stated an Establishment Clause claim); Griffin v. Coughlin, 88 N.Y.2d 674, 673 N.E.2d 98, 649 N.Y.S.2d 903 (1996) (holding that participation in family visiting program could not be conditioned on participation in Alcoholics

of non-coercive religious programs have not been fully explored. However, a recent decision holds that a program (the "InnerChange" program) dominated by Bible study, Christian classes, religious revivals, and church services, which was housed by the prison in superior living quarters (the former "honor unit" of the prison, which afforded greater privacy than other living units), and whose participants received greater visiting and other privileges than other prisoners, violated the Establishment Clause.[863] Even though the program had a secular purpose (providing programming and reducing recidivism), the court found that it had the effect of advancing or endorsing religion, since it clearly involved religious indoctrination, and it defined recipients with reference to religion, admitting only those willing to participate in Christian programs.[864] The court also found that prisoners could not choose to direct the funding for their participation away from the religious organization and to another program.[865]

Anonymous); *see also* Warner v. Orange County Dep't of Probation, 115 F.3d 1068, 1074–77 (2d Cir. 1997) (holding compelled attendance at Alcoholics Anonymous as a probation condition violated the Establishment Clause; county was required to make available a secular alternative). *But see* Gray v. Johnson, 436 F. Supp. 2d 795, 801–02 (W.D.Va. 2006) (rejecting claim where court found religious discussion came from prisoners and not staff); State v. Emery, 593 A.2d 77, 79–80 (Vt. 1991) (probation requirement of participation in a sex offenders' program upheld over the probationer's religious objection); *see also* Stafford v. Harrison, 766 F. Supp. 1014, 1017 (D.Kan. 1991) (a Chemical Dependency Recovery Program featuring "God as we understood him" was not a religion, and requiring the plaintiff to complete it did not violate the Establishment Clause). We think *Stafford* is erroneous because it uses too narrow a definition of religion. *See* § D.1.a of this chapter, nn.621–626.

[863]Americans United for Separation of Church and State v. Prison Fellowship Ministries, 509 F.3d 406, 423–26 (8th Cir. 2007) ("*Americans United*").

[864]*Americans United*, 509 F.3d at 423–25. These findings showed that the program violated the Establishment Clause standard for "direct aid" to religious organizations set out in *Agostini v. Felton*, 521 U.S. 203, 234–35, 117 S. Ct. 1997 (1997). *Cf.* DeStefano v. Emergency Housing Group, Inc., 247 F.3d 397, 408–19 (2d Cir. 2001) (holding that inclusion of Alcoholics Anonymous among services offered by a state-funded facility did not violate the Establishment Clause, but the participation of staff members in religious indoctrination would).

[865]It made this finding because during the litigation, the financial arrangement was changed so that InnerChange was paid based on the number of prisoners who chose the program, which they claimed made it an "indirect aid" program subject to a more lenient legal standard under the Establishment Clause. However, the lack of ability to direct the aid to a secular or other alternative meant that the program failed the "indirect aid" test as well. *Americans United*, 509 F.3d at 425–26. *Compare* Freedom from Religion Foundation, Inc. v. McCallum, 324 F.3d 880, 883–84 (7th Cir. 2003) (holding sponsorship of halfway house program operated by a religious institution did not violate the Establishment Clause since prisoners could freely choose secular alternatives, even if they weren't as good as the religious one).

E. SEARCHES, SEIZURES, AND PRIVACY

The Fourth Amendment provides that "[t]he right of the people to be secure in their persons, houses, papers, and effects, against unreasonable searches and seizures, shall not be violated, and no Warrants shall issue, but upon probable cause. . . ."[866] The Due Process Clause's protection of liberty also includes certain privacy-related interests, including "the individual interest in avoiding disclosure of personal matters" and "the interest in making certain kinds of important decisions"[867] State law generally protects broader rights of privacy than the federal Constitution.[868] However, privacy rights are very drastically restricted in jails and prisons.

1. Searches of Living Quarters

The Supreme Court held in *Hudson v. Palmer* that a prisoner has no "reasonable expectation of privacy" in his living quarters; thus, the protection against unreasonable searches and seizures does not apply to housing searches at all, even if they are abusive and unjustified.[869] The Court reasoned that prison security requires that prison officials have "[u]nfettered access" to prisoners' cells to search for contraband.[870] It had previously ruled that prisoners need not be permitted to observe cell searches in order to minimize the risk of improper seizures.[871] However, it did say in *Hudson* that cell searches amounting to "calculated harassment unrelated to prison needs" may constitute cruel and unusual punishment in violation of the Eighth Amendment.[872]

---

[866]U.S.Const., Amend. V.

[867]Whalen v. Roe, 429 U.S. 589, 599, 97 S. Ct. 869 (1977) (footnotes omitted).

[868]*See* § E.3 of this chapter.

[869]Hudson v. Palmer, 468 U.S. 517, 530, 104 S. Ct. 3194 (1984); *accord*, Booth v. King, 346 F. Supp. 2d 751, 759–60 (E.D.Pa. 2004); Wrinkles v. Davis, 311 F. Supp. 2d 735, 741 (N.D.Ind. 2004); Martin v. Lane, 766 F. Supp. 641, 646 (N.D.Ill. 1991). In *Hudson*, the Court held that no constitutional claim was stated even though the complaint alleged that an officer "maliciously took and destroyed a quantity of Palmer's property, including legal materials and letters, for no reason other than harassment." 568 U.S. at 541 (dissenting opinion). *But see* Rodriguez v. McClenning, 399 F. Supp. 2d 228, 239–40 (S.D.N.Y. 2005) (holding that a cell search was not actionable but that the retaliatory planting of contraband and disciplinary charges related to it were).

One court has held that electronic surveillance (conducted pursuant to warrant with probable cause) of a criminal defendant talking to himself in his cell was not a custodial interrogation. U.S. v. Moody, 977 F.2d 1425, 1434–35 (11th Cir. 1992).

[870]Hudson v. Palmer, 468 U.S. at 517.

[871]Bell v. Wolfish, 441 U.S. 520, 555–61, 99 S. Ct. 1861 (1979). That ruling was reaffirmed in a decision issued simultaneously with *Hudson*. Block v. Rutherford, 468 U.S. 576, 589–91, 104 S. Ct. 3227 (1984).

[872]Hudson v. Palmer, 468 U.S. at 530; *see* Harper v. Showers, 174 F.3d 716, 720 (5th Cir. 1999) (allegation of searches for no purpose but harassment raised a non-frivolous Eighth Amendment claim); Scher v. Engelke, 943 F.2d 921, 923–24 (8th Cir. 1991)

Some courts have held that if a search is initiated by prosecutors for law enforcement purposes and not by prison officials for security purposes, prisoners do retain Fourth Amendment rights (though they are "much diminished in scope"), and a warrant is required.[873] Some courts have restricted this rule to pre-trial detainees.[874] At least one state court has held that prisoners retain a degree of protection against cell searches under the *state* constitution.[875] However, most state courts have simply applied *Hudson v. Palmer* to law enforcement-related living quarters searches.[876]

_____

(repeated harassing cell searches done in retaliation for a prisoner's complaints about guard misconduct violated the Eighth Amendment; punitive damages awarded); Wright v. Newsome, 795 F.2d 964, 968 (11th Cir. 1986) (allegation that cell searches and seizures were done in retaliation for lawsuits and grievances stated a constitutional claim); Blanks v. Smith, 790 F. Supp. 192, 194 (E.D.Wis. 1992) (allegation of daily strip and cell searches for two weeks stated an Eighth Amendment claim). *But see* Proudfoot v. Williams, 803 F. Supp. 1048, 1051 (E.D.Pa. 1992) (three cell searches in eight days did not violate the Eighth Amendment, since each search was properly motivated).

A few decisions have held that searches done for retaliatory reasons are not included in the "harassment" searches that are actionable under *Hudson*. *See* Lashley v. Wakefield, 367 F. Supp. 2d 461, 470 (W.D.N.Y. 2005). In our view this makes no sense—a retaliatory search is surely a kind of harassment unrelated to prison needs—and the *Scher* and *Wright* decisions cited above support such claims. *See also* Harding v. Vilmer, 72 F.3d 91, 92 (8th Cir. 1995) (per curiam) (it was clearly established that retaliatory searches could violate the Eighth Amendment).

[873]U.S. v. Cohen, 796 F.2d 20, 24 (2d Cir. 1986); Rogers v. State, 783 So.2d 980, 992 (Fla. 2001) (stating *Hudson* did not authorize law enforcement searches of jail cell, in context of motion to disqualify State Attorney from prosecution), *denial of post-conviction relief aff'd*, 957 So.2d 538 (Fla. 2007); Lowe v. State, 203 Ga.App. 277, 416 S.E.2d 750, 752 (Ga.App. 1992); *see also* State v. Neely, 236 Neb. 527, 462 N.W.2d 105, 112 (Neb. 1990) (warrantless search of suitcase seized on arrest and held in jail's locked inventory violated detainee's Fourth Amendment rights). *Contra*, State v. Spirko, 59 Ohio St.3d 1, 570 N.E.2d 229, 256 (Ohio 1991); *see also* State v. Matthews, 296 S.C. 379, 373 S.E.2d 587, 593–94 (S.C. 1988) (where prosecutor had received threats from the prisoner, a resulting cell search was security-related and raised no Fourth Amendment issue).

[874]Willis v. Artuz, 301 F.3d 65, 69 (2d Cir. 2002); U.S. v. Reece, 797 F. Supp. 843, 846 (D.Colo. 1992); State v. Jackson, 321 N.J.Super. 365, 379–80, 729 A.2d 55 (1999).

[875]State v. Berard, 576 A.2d 118, 120–21 (Vt. 1990).

[876]*See* State v. Apelt, 176 Ariz. 349, 861 P.2d 634, 649 (1993); State v. Melendez, 168 Ariz. 275, 812 P.2d 1093, 1094–95 (Ariz. App.) (search of cell after violent incident upheld), *review denied in pertinent part*, 812 P.2d 996 (1991), *vacated on other grounds*, 834 P.2d 154 (Ariz. 1992); People v. Davis, 36 Cal.4th 510, 31 Cal. Rptr.3d 96, 115 P.3d 417, 429–30 (2005) (holding tape-recording a conversation in a defendant's cell did not infringe any Fourth Amendment expectation of privacy); Cleveland v. State, 557 So.2d 959, 960 (Fla.App. 1990) (no expectation of privacy in a toilet stall in a Probation and Restitution Center); State v. O'Rourke, 792 A.2d 262, 267 (Me.2001); People v. Phillips, 219 Mich.App. 159, 555 N.W.2d 742, 743–44 (1996); People v. Frye, 144 A.D.2d 714, 534

If legal materials in your cell are inspected or confiscated, that fact does not bring the search within the scope of the Fourth Amendment.[877] If the removal or inspection of such materials actually results in interference with your ability to file or prosecute a legal action, you may have a claim for denial of access to courts.[878] If privileged materials are read, and not just inspected for contraband, you may have a claim for violation of the First Amendment or the attorney–client privilege.[879]

The Due Process Clause provides some limited protection against seizures of property.[880] Other constitutional provisions may protect prisoners against the confiscation of certain types of property, such as religious objects[881] or books.[882]

2. Body Searches and Bodily Privacy

Prisoners retain a limited expectation of privacy in their persons.[883] Body searches must therefore be reasonable.

_____

N.Y.S.2d 735, 736 (N.Y.App.Div. 1988) (routine search of cell and person upheld), *appeal denied*, 73 N.Y. 891 (1989); State v. Martin, 322 N.C. 229, 367 S.E.2d 618, 621–22 (1988); Commonwealth v. Boyd, 397 Pa.Super. 468, 580 A.2d 393, 395 (Pa. Super. 1990); State v. Andujar, 899 A.2d 1209, 1224–25 (R.I. 2006); State v. Williams, 690 S.W.2d 517, 524 (Tenn. 1985) (police tape-recording of conversations in jail cell did not violate any reasonable expectation of privacy); *see also* Loden v. State, 199 Ga.App. 683, 406 S.E.2d 103, 107 (Ga.App. 1991) (property an arrestee chooses to take to jail may be subjected to an inventory search).

[877]Kalka v. Megathlin, 10 F. Supp. 2d 1117, 1121 (D.Ariz. 1998), *aff'd*, 188 F.3d 513 (9th Cir. 1999); Zimmerman v. Hoard, 5 F. Supp. 2d 633, 637 (N.D.Ind. 1998); *see* Hudson v. Palmer, 468 U.S. 517, 530, 541, 104 S. Ct. 3194 (1984) (dissenting opinion) (noting that legal materials were allegedly taken in search that Supreme Court said raised no Fourth Amendment issue); *see also* Mitchell v. Dupnik, 75 F.3d 517, 522 (9th Cir.1996) (prisoner had no Fourth Amendment right to be present when his legal materials were searched); Barstow v. Kennebec County Jail, 115 F. Supp. 2d 3, 7 n.8 (D.Me. 2000) (stating law is unclear whether legal materials in a detainee's jail cell lose their *Sixth* Amendment protection).

[878]*See* § C.1.b of this chapter, nn.477–481.

[879]*See* § C.3 of this chapter, nn.605–608.

[880]*See* Ch. 4, § H.8 concerning these due process protections.

[881]*See* § D.2.e of this chapter; Ch. 4, § H.8.b.

[882]*See* § B.2 of this chapter.

[883]Levine v. Roebuck, 550 F.3d 684, 687 (8th Cir. 2008); Nicholas v. Goord, 430 F.3d 652, 658 (2d Cir. 2005); Peckham v. Wisconsin Dep't of Correction, 141 F.3d 694, 696–97 (7th Cir. 1998); Fortner v. Thomas, 983 F.2d 1024, 1030 (11th Cir. 1993) ("We are persuaded to join other circuits in recognizing a prisoner's constitutional right to bodily privacy because most people have 'a special sense of privacy in their genitals, and involuntary exposure of them in the presence of people of the other sex may be especially demeaning and humiliating.'"); Forbes v. Trigg, 976 F.2d 308, 312 (7th Cir. 1992); Covino v. Patrissi, 967 F.2d 73, 78 (2d Cir. 1992); Cornwell v. Dahlberg, 963 F.2d 912, 916 (6th Cir. 1992); Dunn v. White, 880 F.2d 1188, 1191 (10th Cir. 1989); Smith v. Chrans, 629 F. Supp. 606, 610–11 (C.D.Ill. 1986); Tucker v. Dickey, 613 F. Supp. 1124, 1128 (W.D.Wis. 1985); Storms v. Coughlin, 600

Deciding what is reasonable "requires a balancing of the need for the particular search against the invasion of rights that the search entails."[884]

There has been much litigation over prison strip searches. Sometimes officials argue that they are not really engaging in strip searches by giving their practices a different name or claiming they have a different purpose. Courts have responded differently to these claims.[885]

Persons newly arrested on minor charges cannot be strip searched pursuant to a blanket policy; there must be reasonable suspicion that the person is concealing contraband,[886] which can be based on the person's behavior

___

F. Supp. 1214, 1223–24 (S.D.N.Y. 1984). One federal circuit decision seemed to hold that prisoners never have any expectation of privacy, Johnson v. Phelan, 69 F.3d 144, 150 (7th Cir.1995), but a later decision corrected that impression. Peckham v. Wisconsin Dep't of Correction, cited above. See Oliver v. Scott, 276 F.3d 736, 744 (5th Cir. 2002) ("Prisoners retain, at best, a very minimal Fourth Amendment interest in privacy after incarceration.").

Courts have disagreed over whether the Fourteenth Amendment's due process clause provides any separate protection of bodily privacy. Compare Oliver v. Scott, 276 F.3d at 744–45 (no) with Poe v. Leonard, 282 F.3d 123, 136–39 (2d Cir. 2002) (yes; non-prison case involving police surveillance of civilian dressing).

[884]Bell v. Wolfish, 441 U.S. 520, 559, 99 S. Ct. 1861 (1979).

[885]Compare Wood v. Hancock County Sheriff's Dep't, 354 F.3d 57, 59–61, 63, 65 (1st Cir. 2003) (fact that officials called procedure a "clothing search" did not mean it wasn't a strip search; "The critical question is whether viewing the naked body was an objective of the search, rather than an unavoidable and incidental by-product."); Marriott v. County of Montgomery, 227 F.R.D. 159, 168–70 (N.D.N.Y. 2005) ("change-out" procedure was a strip search; "the admittees are required to strip naked in front of a CO and submit to the observation of their body by the CO"), aff'd, 2005 WL 3117194 (2d Cir., Nov. 22, 2005) (unpublished); Doan v. Watson, 168 F. Supp. 2d 932, 935–36 (S.D.Ind. 2001) (search was called "delousing procedure") with Kelsey v. County of Schoharie, 567 F.3d 54, 64 (2d Cir. 2009) (upholding "change-out" procedure involving only "incidental observation" of the body).

Sometimes strip searches are referred to as "visual body cavity searches," and these may involve a closer inspection of anal and genital areas, or prisoners may be required to spread their buttocks, lift their genitals, etc. See, e.g., Covino v. Patrissi, 967 F.2d 73, 75 (2d Cir. 1992). As far as we can tell, any difference between a strip search and a visual body cavity search has little or no bearing on the legality of searches of prisoners under current law. See Chapman v. Nichols, 989 F.2d 393, 397–98 (10th Cir. 1993); Weber v. Dell, 804 F.2d 796, 802 (2d Cir.1986) (referring to "strip/body cavity searches" without distinction). But see Frazier v. Ward, 426 F. Supp. 1354, 1366 (N.D.N.Y. 1977) (routine anal and testicular searches, carried out in an abusive manner, violated the Eighth Amendment); see also Security and Law Enforcement Employees, Dist. Council 82 v. Carey, 737 F.2d 187, 207–09 (2d Cir. 1984) (holding staff may be strip searched on reasonable suspicion but visual body cavity searches require a warrant based on probable cause).

[886]"[T]he Fourth Amendment precludes prison officials from performing strip/body cavity searches of arrestees charged with misdemeanors or other minor offenses unless the officials have a

___

or on the nature of the charges at arrest.[887] Some courts have

___

reasonable suspicion that the arrestee is concealing weapons or other contraband based on the crime charged, the particular characteristics of the arrestee, and/or the circumstances of the arrest." Weber v. Dell, 804 F.2d 796, 802 (2d Cir. 1986); accord, Hartline v. Gallo, 546 F.3d 95, 100–02 (2d Cir. 2008); N.G. v. Connecticut, 382 F.3d 225, 232 (2d Cir. 2004) (citing cases); Shain v. Ellison, 273 F.3d 56, 62–66 (2d Cir. 2001); Wilson v. Jones, 251 F.3d 1340, 1343 (11th Cir. 2001); Roberts v. Rhode Island, 239 F.3d 107, 113 (1st Cir. 2001) (applying same holding where detainees were placed in same institution as convicts); Chapman v. Nichols, 989 F.2d 393, 395 (10th Cir. 1993) and cases cited; Kennedy v. Los Angeles Police Dep't, 901 F.2d 702, 713–16 (9th Cir. 1989); Masters v. Crouch, 872 F.2d 1248, 1255 (6th Cir. 1989); Doe v. Calumet City, Ill., 754 F. Supp. 1211, 1219–20 (N.D.Ill. 1990); see Bynum v. District of Columbia, 257 F. Supp. 2d 1, 2 (D.D.C. 2002) (holding that inmates strip searched upon return to the jail from court after receiving release orders, who were to be held only for brief processing before release, stated a Fourth Amendment claim).

[887]See, e.g., Hicks v. Moore, 422 F.3d 1246, 1252 (11th Cir. 2005) (charge for a crime of violence supports reasonable suspicion); Skurstenis v. Jones, 236 F.3d 678, 682 (11th Cir. 2000) (upholding strip search of a person who was carrying a pistol on arrest); Kelly v. Foti, 77 F.3d 819, 821 (5th Cir. 1996) (lack of a photo ID and failure to post $200 bond within five hours did not justify a strip search); Franklin v. County of Dutchess, 225 F.R.D. 487, 498 (S.D.N.Y. 2005) (felony arrest or prior felony conviction do not, without more, support a strip search); Tardiff v. Knox County, 397 F. Supp. 2d 115, 131 (D.Me. 2005) (felony charge not involving violence, weapons, or drugs did not, without more, support a strip search), reconsideration denied, 425 F. Supp. 2d 159 (D.Me. 2006), certificate of appealability denied, 451 F. Supp. 2d 253 (D.Me. 2006); George v. City of Wichita, 348 F. Supp. 2d 1232, 1240–41 (D.Kan. 2004) (charge of violent felony supported a strip search); Dodge v. County of Orange, 282 F. Supp. 2d 41, 83–86 (S.D.N.Y. 2003) (alcohol intoxication, parole violation charge, or felony charge did not support strip search by themselves; individualized determinations required), appeal dismissed, remanded on other grounds, 103 Fed.Appx. 688 (2d Cir. 2004) (unpublished); Murcia v. County of Orange, 226 F. Supp. 2d 489, 494 (S.D.N.Y.2002) (individualized suspicion required to strip search felony arrestees); Dodge v. County of Orange, 209 F.R.D. 65, 75–77 (S.D.N.Y. 2002) (strip search was not justified by detainees' activating a metal detector before they had emptied their pockets, since it can be activated by innocuous items: by appearing to be under the influence of alcohol or drugs; or by admission for violation of probation or parole); Ford v. City of Boston, 154 F. Supp. 2d 131, 143–44 (D. Mass. 2001) (strip searching all arrestees with felony charges or who had defaulted on a court appearance violated the Fourth Amendment).

While some drug charges may support a strip search, Warner v. Grand County, 57 F.3d 962, 964 (10th Cir. 1995) (arrest for drug possession); Bradley v. Village of Greenwood Lake, 376 F. Supp. 2d 528, 536 (S.D.N.Y. 2005) (drug possession charge plus evasion of the police before arrest supported a strip search), the mere fact or suspicion of being under the influence or alcohol or drugs does not support a reasonable suspicion that the arrestee is hiding contraband and must be strip searched. Foote v. Spiegel, 118 F.3d 1416, 1425–26 (10th Cir. 1997); accord, Way v. County of Ventura, 445 F.3d 1157, 1161–62 (9th Cir. 2006) (striking down blanket policy of

extended this rule only to persons not placed in the general jail population,[888] but others have rejected that distinction.[889] Less intrusive routine searches of arrestees may be upheld.[890]

Courts generally defer to prison officials when they come up with a reasonable security justification for strip search practices,[891] and sometimes when it seems they don't.[892] Challenges to search practices are usually decided under the reasonable relationship standards applying to detainees and convicts.[893] Detainees and convicts alike can ordinarily be made to submit to strip searches in connection

with transfers[894] or contact visits[895] and when entering or leaving high-security areas of the prison,[896] as well as when there is specific reason for the search either of a person[897] or a group.[898] One federal appeals court court has upheld a policy of random visual body cavity searches in a state prison,[899] though the same court has also held that in jails,

---

[888]strip searching all persons arrested for all drug offenses, including being under the influence of a drug); Thomsen v. Ross, 368 F. Supp. 2d 961, 970–71 (D.Minn. 2005) (aggravated DUI charge did not support strip search).

[888]Powell v. Barrett, 541 F.3d 1298, 1314–15 (11th Cir. 2008) (en banc) (upholding blanket strip search policy for persons admitted to jail's general population); Foote v. Spiegel, 118 F.3d 1416, 1425 (10th Cir. 1997); Warner v. Grand County, 57 F.3d 962, 964 (10th Cir. 1995); Dobrowolskyj v. Jefferson County, Ky., 823 F.2d 955, 959 (6th Cir. 1987); Logan v. Shealy, 660 F.2d 1007, 1013 (4th Cir. 1981).

[889]Shain v. Ellison, 273 F.3d 56, 620–66 (2d Cir. 2001) (refusing to distinguish between pre- and post-arraignment cases); Roberts v. Rhode Island, 239 F.3d 107, 112 (1st Cir. 2001) and cases cited.

[890]Stanley v. Henson, 337 F.3d 961, 963–64 (7th Cir. 2003) (upholding requirement that arrestees change clothes, stripping only to their underwear, in the presence of a same-sex officer); accord, Smook v. Minnehaha County, 457 F.3d 806, 811–12 (8th Cir. 2006) (same holding as to juvenile arrestee), cert. denied, 549 U.S. 1317 (2007).

[891]Conyers v. Abitz, 416 F.3d 580, 584 (7th Cir. 2005) ("We generally defer to the judgment of prison officials when they are evaluating what is necessary to preserve institutional order and discipline. . . ."). But see N.G. v. Connecticut, 382 F.3d 225, 234 (2d Cir. 2004) (holding search for a missing pencil did not justify strip searches because the possibility it could be concealed in a body cavity and then used as a weapon was too unlikely). Warrantless searches of pre-trial detainees for general law enforcement, as opposed to prison security, purposes violates the Fourth Amendment. Friedman v. Boucher, 580 F.3d 847, 857 (9th Cir. 2009).

[892]Peckham v. Wisconsin Dep't of Correction, 141 F.3d 694, 695–97 (7th Cir. 1998) (upholding strip searches when prisoners' time in segregation was extended even if they did not leave the unit; no explanation given).

[893]Serna v. Goodno, 567 F.3d 944, 949–51 (8th Cir. 2009) (applying Bell v. Wolfish standard to civilly committed sex offenders); Stanley v. Henson, 337 F.3d 961, 964 (7th Cir. 2003) (applying Bell v. Wolfish standard to detainee claim); Skundor v. McBride, 280 F. Supp. 2d 524, 526–28 (S.D.W.Va. 2003) (applying Turner v. Safley standard to convict claim), aff'd, 98 Fed.Appx. 257 (4th Cir. 2004) (unpublished).

[894]Omar v. Casterline, 288 F. Supp. 2d 775, 780 (W.D.La. 2003). But see N.G. v. Connecticut, 382 F.3d 225, 233–34 (2d Cir. 2004) (holding strip searches of juveniles transferred from another detention center where they had already been strip searched were not justified).

[895]Bell v. Wolfish, 441 U.S. 520, 559, 99 S. Ct. 1861 (1979); see also Wood v. Hancock County Sheriff's Dep't, 354 F.3d 57, 67–69 (1st Cir. 2003) (strip search after contact visit with attorney upheld); Williams v. Price, 25 F. Supp. 2d 605, 615 (W.D.Pa. 1997) (upholding strip searches before and after counsel visits for high security prisoners); Bono v. Saxbe, 527 F. Supp. 1182, 1184–86 (S.D.Ill. 1980) (upholding strip searches before and after non-contact visits for segregated prisoners). But see Wabasha v. Solem, 580 F. Supp. 448, 452 (D.S.D. 1984) (routine strip searches after non-contact visits violated the Eighth Amendment).

[896]See, e.g., Bruscino v. Carlson, 854 F.2d 162, 164–66 (7th Cir. 1988) (Marion Control Unit); Rickman v. Avanti, 854 F.2d 327, 328 (9th Cir. 1988) (administrative segregation); Goff v. Nix, 803 F.2d 358, 366–71 (8th Cir. 1986) (segregation); Skundor v. McBride, 280 F. Supp. 2d 524, 527–28 (S.D.W.Va. 2003) (upholding routine searches of high-security prisoners upon leaving recreation yard), aff'd, 98 Fed.Appx. 257 (4th Cir. 2004) (unpublished); Terrovona v. Brown, 783 F. Supp. 1281, 1284–86 (W.D.Wash. 1991) (digital rectal searches in "Intensive Management Unit"); Sanders v. Heitzkey, 757 F. Supp. 981, 983, 987 (E.D.Wis. 1991) (segregation), aff'd, 962 F.2d 10 (7th Cir. 1992); Merritt-Bey v. Salts, 747 F. Supp. 536, 538 (E.D.Mo. 1990) (segregation); Gomez v. Coughlin, 685 F. Supp. 1291, 1300 (S.D.N.Y. 1988) (administrative segregation); Langton v. Commissioner of Correction, 404 Mass. 165, 533 N.E.2d 1375, 1376–77 (Mass. 1989) (disciplinary and administrative segregation unit); see also Franklin v. Lockhart, 883 F.2d 654, 655–57 (8th Cir. 1989) (upholding various searches of punitive, administrative and protective segregation inmates). The court in McRoy v. Cook County Dep't of Corrections, 366 F. Supp. 2d 662, 681–82 (N.D.Ill. 2005), aff'd, 205 Fed.Appx. 462 (7th Cir. 2006) (unpublished), cert. denied, 128 S. Ct. 624 (2007), went further, upholding strip searches of all prisoners leaving the inmate housing areas for any reason. See Conyers v. Abitz, 416 F.3d 580, 584 (7th Cir. 2005) (upholding frisking of prisoners as they leave the prison chapel because the chapel is "a hotbed of contraband exchange").

[897]Thompson v. Souza, 111 F.3d 694, 700–01 (9th Cir. 1997) (upholding strip searches in connection with search for drugs); Vaughan v. Ricketts, 950 F.2d 1464, 1468–69 (9th Cir. 1991) ("reasonable cause" required to justify digital rectal searches); Gonzalez v. State, 541 So.2d 1354, 1356 (Fla.App. 1989) (disappearance of keys justified strip search of inmate working in the area); see Reynolds v. City of Anchorage, 379 F.3d 358, 365–66 (6th Cir. 2004) (upholding strip search of juvenile offender based on circumstances suggesting drug use).

[898]Serna v. Goodno, 567 F.3d 944, 949–51 (8th Cir. 2009) (upholding strip search of sex offender facility population based on evidence that someone had a cellphone).

[899]Covino v. Patrissi, 967 F.2d 73, 77-80 (2d Cir. 1992). In Covino, the court noted that these searches were conducted privately in the inmates' rooms.

strip searches must be justified by individualized reasonable suspicion.[900] Strip searches that are not related to legitimate security needs or are designed to harass may be found unconstitutional under the Fourth Amendment or the Eighth Amendment.[901] Searches that are more intrusive than

visual inspection must generally be justified by individualized suspicion of contraband.[902]

Visitors may be strip searched only if there is reason to believe that the particular visitor is carrying contraband. Several courts have held that "reasonable cause" or "reasonable suspicion" is required to justify strip-searching visitors.[903] Less intrusive searches of visitors may be

---

[900]Shain v. Ellison, 273 F.3d 56, 65–66 (2d Cir. 2001). Most recently, this court has extended suspicionless strip searches based on a reasonable relationship to legitimate goals to the claim of a detainee held "in a prison-like environment" and *charged* with felonies. Iqbal v. Hasty, 490 F.3d 143, 172 (2d Cir. 2007), *aff'd in part, rev'd in part, and remanded on other grounds sub nom.* Ashcroft v. Iqbal, ___ U.S. ___, 129 S. Ct. 1937 (2009). By contrast, another court has held that the rule against suspicionless strip searches of minor arrestees is applicable to an institution that houses both convicts and pre-trial detainees. Roberts v. Rhode Island, 239 F.3d 107, 113 (1st Cir. 2001).

[901]Harris v. Ostrout, 65 F.3d 912, 916 (11th Cir. 1995) (stating that if strip searches "are devoid of penological merit and imposed simply to inflict pain, the federal courts should intervene," and that they may not be used to retaliate against First Amendment-protected activity); *accord*, Peckham v. Wisconsin Dep't of Correction, 141 F.3d 694, 697 (7th Cir. 1998) (holding that prisoners retain some Fourth Amendment rights but Eighth Amendment is "more properly posed" to protect against unconstitutional strip searches); Tribble v. Gardner, 860 F.2d 321, 325–27 (9th Cir. 1988) (evidence of digital rectal searches unrelated to security needs supported Fourth and Eighth Amendment claims); Hay v. Waldron, 834 F.2d 481, 487 (5th Cir. 1987) (retaliatory use of strip searches stated a claim); Meriwether v. Faulkner, 821 F.2d 408, 418 (7th Cir. 1987) (allegation of harassment by strip searches stated Eighth Amendment claim); Franklin v. Lockhart, 769 F.2d 509, 510–11 (8th Cir. 1985) (allegation of twice-daily strip searches of inmate who did not leave segregation unit stated a claim); U.S. v. Smith, 774 F.2d 1005, 1006–07 (10th Cir. 1985) (digital or instrument search of rectal cavity was not justified by tip from informant as to whom there was no evidence of reliability); Hodges v. Stanley, 712 F.2d 34, 35 (2d Cir. 1983) (allegation of a strip search that was unnecessary because it immediately followed another strip search stated a Fourth Amendment claim); Burton v. Kuchel, 865 F. Supp. 456, 466 (N.D.Ill. 1994) (evidence of daily strip searches justified "an inference of calculated harassment" for summary judgment purposes; "such forced chronic strip and body cavity searches are fairly construed as unacceptable torment"); Ruiz v. Estelle, 679 F.2d 1115, 1154–55 (5th Cir. 1982) (strip searches in connection with law library visits were "unwarranted harassment"); Lipton v. County of Orange, N.Y., 315 F. Supp. 2d 434, 446 (S.D.N.Y. 2004) (stating that allegations of a strip search on *release* from jail "present an appalling abuse of the power afforded to corrections officers") (dictum); Duffy v. County of Bucks, 7 F. Supp. 2d 569, 579–81 (E.D.Pa. 1998) (repeated strip searches for no apparent purpose, including one after release had been ordered, stated a constitutional claim); Morgan v. Ward, 699 F. Supp. 1025, 1051–54 (N.D.N.Y. 1988) (strip searches of segregation inmates before contact visits violated the Fourth Amendment); Wabasha v. Solem, 580 F. Supp. 448, 451 (D.S.D. 1984) (routine strip searches after non-contact visits violated the Eighth Amendment). *But see* Skurstenis v. Jones, 236 F.3d 678, 683–84 (11th Cir. 2000) (upholding medical search for pubic lice conducted only minutes before the plaintiff was released).

[902]Prisoners may lawfully be subjected to digital and x-ray searches and placed in "dry cells" based on individualized suspicion of contraband possession. U.S. v. Holloway, 128 F.3d 1254, 1256 (8th Cir. 1997) (placement in dry cell based on reliable information of intent to smuggle drugs upheld as a "proportionate response"); Vaughan v. Ricketts, 950 F.2d 1464, 1468–69 (9th Cir. 1991) (requiring "reasonable cause" to justify digital rectal searches); U.S. v. Caldwell, 750 F.2d 341, 345–46 (5th Cir. 1984); Cameron v. Hendricks, 942 F. Supp. 499, 502–03 (D.Kan. 1996) (prisoner suspected of concealing contraband could be x-rayed, and when a contraband handcuff key was observed, he could be subjected to attempts to remove it with surgical tools and an enema); U.S. v. Oakley, 731 F. Supp. 1363, 1369–72 (S.D.Ind. 1990). *But see* Pena v. Gardner, 976 F.2d 469, 471 (9th Cir. 1992) (generalized vague allegations of digital search without probable cause did not state a claim).

One federal appeals court held based on a prison rule that prisoners had a liberty interest protected by due process in avoiding "Feces Watch" in a dry cell except upon reasonable suspicion of contraband. Mendoza v. Blodgett, 960 F.2d 1425, 1429 (9th Cir. 1992). Later, the Supreme Court changed the law of prison due process to hold that only deprivations that raised constitutional issues or imposed "atypical and significant hardship in relation to the ordinary incidents of prison life" constituted deprivations of liberty without due process. Sandin v. Conner, 515 U.S. 472, 484, 115 S. Ct. 2293 (1995). We think being placed in a cell without water and having one's feces scrutinized should qualify as a deprivation of a liberty interest on both grounds, but the issue remains open. *See* Ch. 4, § A.3, for discussion of the *Sandin* "atypical and significant" standard.

[903]Burgess v. Lowry, 201 F.3d 942, 945 (7th Cir. 2000) (citing cases); Varrone v. Bilotti, 123 F.3d 75, 78–79 (2d Cir. 1997); Wood v. Clemons, 89 F.3d 922, 929 (1st Cir. 1996) (reasonable suspicion is "something stronger than a mere 'hunch,' . . . but something weaker than probable cause"; at a minimum, it requires "articulable factual information bearing at least some indicia of reliability"); Spear v. Sowders, 71 F.3d 626, 630–31 (6th Cir. 1995) (en banc) (reasonable suspicion "requires only specific objective facts upon which a prudent official, in light of his experience, would conclude that illicit activity might be in progress"); Daugherty v. Campbell, 935 F.2d 780, 784 (6th Cir. 1991); Thorne v. Jones, 765 F.2d 1270, 1276–77 (5th Cir. 1985); Hunter v. Auger, 672 F.2d 668, 674 (8th Cir. 1982); Commonwealth v. Gumby, 398 Pa.Super. 155, 580 A.2d 1110, 1111–12 (Pa.Super. 1990); *see* Boren v. Deland, 958 F.2d 987, 988 (10th Cir. 1992) (partial strip search was justified by reasonable suspicion that visitor was wearing "inappropriate" clothing); Smothers v. Gibson, 778 F.2d 470, 473 (8th Cir.1985) (inmate's mother was strip searched based on an uncorroborated tip; jury question of reasonableness of search was presented). The same standard is generally applied to strip searches of prison staff. *See, e.g.,* Security and Law Enforcement Employees, etc. v. Carey, 737 F.2d 187, 203–05 (2d Cir. 1984). *Cf.* State v. Custodio, 607 P.2d

conducted routinely, without cause.[904] Visitors who refuse searches can have their visits suspended; courts have reached different conclusions about how long such a suspension can be.[905]

Even searches that are justified must be conducted in a reasonable manner.[906] Strip and other searches may be unconstitutional if they are needlessly intrusive,[907]

1048, 1050–52 (Haw. 1980) (visitor was deemed to have voluntarily consented to a strip search that was required in order to visit).

A manual body cavity search of a visitor, because it is more intrusive, must be supported by probable cause and a legitimate security purpose. Laughter v. Kay, 986 F. Supp. 1362, 1373–74 (D. Utah 1997) (holding search was not justified by security, since plaintiff was not allowed to visit even after undergoing the search with no contraband found).

A visitor cannot be searched without a warrant after leaving the prison and no longer being in a position to smuggle in contraband. Marriott by and through Marriott v. Smith, 931 F.2d 517, 520 (8th Cir. 1991).

[904]Ybarra v. Nevada Board of State Prison Commissioners, 520 F. Supp. 1000, 1003 (D.Nev. 1981) (pat-down searches of visitors and removal of shoes, jackets, etc. upheld without probable cause or "real suspicion"). Searches of visitors' automobiles do not require individualized suspicion. Neumeyer v. Beard, 421 F.3d 210, 214–15 (3d Cir. 2005) (random searches of visitors' vehicles in the prison parking lot upheld under "special needs" doctrine); Spear v. Sowders, 71 F.3d 626, 631–32 (6th Cir. 1995) (en banc); see Romo v. Champion, 46 F.3d 1013, 1018–20 (10th Cir. 1995) (roadblock and requirement to open trunk and car doors and submit to a dog sniff search did not require individualized suspicion; once the dog had barked at a visitor, there was reasonable suspicion justifying a strip search). Cf. Jordan v. Taylor, 310 F.3d 1068, 1069 (8th Cir. 2002) (upholding requirement that eight-year-old child, who set off the metal detector probably because of her overall buttons, remove the overalls and go through the metal detector in her grandmother's jacket; the search was consensual since the visitors could have left).

[905]Challenging visit suspension probably has a better chance of success under state law or regulations than the federal Constitution. Compare Smith v. Matthews, 793 F. Supp. 998, 1000 (D.Kan. 1992) (upholding permanent suspension of wife's visits after she refused a search) with In re French, 106 Cal.App.3d 74, 164 Cal.Rptr. 800, 804–06 (Cal.App. 1980) (holding that barring visitor indefinitely for refusing a strip search on one occasion was unreasonable); Gordon v. Oregon State Dep't of Corrections, 104 Or.App. 436, 801 P.2d 892 (Or.App. 1990) (state regulations permitted visitor who refused a strip search to be barred from visiting for only six months). For further discussion of visiting, see § B.7 of this chapter.

[906]Bell v. Wolfish, 441 U.S. 520, 559–60, 99 S. Ct. 1861 (1979); Mays v. Springborn, 575 F.3d 643, 649 (7th Cir. 2009); Thompson v. City of Los Angeles, 885 F.2d 1439, 1447 n.7 (9th Cir. 1989). But see Muehler v. Mena, 544 U.S. 93, 100–01, 125 S. Ct. 1465 (2005) (upholding handcuffing a resident for two to three hours during a search of her house for weapons and evidence of gang membership).

[907]Amaechi v. West, 237 F.3d 356, 360–62 (4th Cir. 2001) (holding officer was not entitled to qualified immunity for a pat search under the clothing of a female misdemeanor arrestee during which his fingertip penetrated her genitals); Hill v. Koon, 732 F.

abusively performed,[908] or conducted in an unnecessarily public manner or with the unnecessary involvement or presence of opposite-sex staff.[909] Abusive strip searches may

---

Supp. 1076, 1082–83 (D.Nev. 1990) (digital rectal search was not justified when less intrusive searches had not been tried first); Knop v. Johnson, 685 F. Supp. 636, 640–43 (W.D.Mich. 1988) (searches of inmate paralegals made subject to supervision to protect privacy of legal papers), aff'd in part and rev'd in part on other grounds, 977 F.2d 996 (6th Cir. 1992).

[908]See Mays v. Springborn, 575 F.3d at 649–50 (evidence of searches conducted with demeaning comments, dirty gloves, and in a cold room supported a constitutional claim); Hutchins v. McDaniels, 512 F.3d 193, 195–96 (5th Cir. 2007) (holding strip search conducted in front of numerous inmates and a female guard and requiring the prisoner to engage in humiliating acts could violate the Fourth Amendment); Evans v. Stephens, 407 F.3d 1272, 1281–82 (11th Cir. 2005) (en banc) (holding search in police lockup conducted in broom closet and accompanied by ridicule, threatening language, and anal penetration with an object, violated Fourth Amendment); Calhoun v. DeTella, 319 F.3d 936, 940 (7th Cir. 2003) (holding strip searches accompanied by sexual harassment, with opposite-sex staff as invited spectators, would be "designed to demean and humiliate" and would state an Eighth Amendment claim); Vaughan v. Ricketts, 859 F.2d 736, 741–42 (9th Cir. 1988) (mass digital rectal searches under public and unsanitary conditions; Fourth and Eighth Amendment claims stated); Goff v. Nix, 803 F.2d 358, 365 n.9 (8th Cir. 1986) (verbal harassment during otherwise proper strip searches enjoined); Bonitz v. Fair, 804 F.2d 164, 170–73 (1st Cir. 1986) (similar to Vaughan, above); Galluccio v. Holmes, 724 F.2d 301, 304 (2d Cir. 1983) (evidence that inmate who resisted digital and proctoscopic searches because they hurt was then chained to a bed for two days presented a jury question as to reasonableness).

[909]Mays v. Springborn, 575 F.3d at 649–50 (evidence of searches conducted publicly without reason and against prison rules supported a constitutional claim); Hutchins v. McDaniels, 512 F.3d 193, 195–96 (5th Cir. 2007) (citing presence of numerous inmates and an opposite-sex guard at strip search); Calhoun v. DeTella, 319 F.3d 936, 940 (7th Cir. 2003) (citing presence of opposite-sex staff as invited spectators at strip search as supporting an Eighth Amendment claim); Farmer v. Perrill, 288 F.3d 1254, 1260–61 (10th Cir. 2002) (affirming denial of summary judgment as to a challenge to visual strip searches en route to the recreation yard conducted in view of other inmates; government may not simply justify the searches, but must justify doing them in the open); Moore v. Carwell, 168 F.3d 234, 237 (5th Cir. 1999) (holding allegation of strip and body cavity searches performed by an opposite-sex officer absent an emergency, at a time when same sex officers were available to conduct the search, was not frivolous; "We must balance the need for the particular search against the invasion of the prisoner's personal rights caused by the search."); Hayes v. Marriott, 70 F.3d 1144, 1147–48 (10th Cir. 1995) (holding summary judgment was inappropriate given allegation that plaintiff was subjected to a body cavity search in the presence of numerous witnesses, including female correctional officers and case managers and secretaries); Vaughan v. Ricketts, 859 F.2d at 741–42; Bonitz v. Fair, 804 F.2d at 170–73; Estes-El v. State of New York, 552 F. Supp. 885, 889 (S.D.N.Y. 1982) (strip search without privacy presented a factual issue of reasonableness); see Skundor v. McBride, 280 F. Supp. 2d 524, 527 (S.D.W.Va. 2003) (citing absence

violate the Eighth Amendment as well as the Fourth Amendment.[910]

Several courts have held that clothed pat frisks by guards of the opposite sex do not violate the Fourth Amendment or the religious rights of inmates whose beliefs forbid them.[911] However, an important decision held that intrusive pat frisks of female inmates by male staff violated the Eighth Amendment, based on evidence that many women inmates had long histories of verbal, physical, and sexual abuse by men.[912]

Taking samples of bodily fluids is a search for Fourth Amendment purposes.[913] Prison officials may require prisoners to provide urine samples for drug testing either with reasonable, individualized cause, or pursuant to a program that is designed to prevent selective enforcement or harassment.[914] Unnecessary lack of privacy in taking urine samples is unreasonable.[915] Prisoners may be required to give blood samples or submit to other medical tests for legitimate

---

of opposite-sex staff and avoidance of unnecessary viewers in upholding strip search practice), *aff'd*, 98 Fed.Appx. 257 (4th Cir. 2004) (unpublished); Fernandez v. Rapone, 926 F. Supp. 255, 261–62 (D.Mass. 1996) (upholding post-visit strip searches conducted in the presence of other prisoners where exposure was brief and same-sex staff conducted the searches). *But see* Somers v. Thurman, 109 F.3d 614, 620 (9th Cir. 1997) (defendants were entitled to qualified immunity from Fourth Amendment claim that female staff members subjected plaintiff to visual body cavity searches on a regular basis, watched him shower, pointed at him and made jokes about him; dismissing Eighth Amendment claim); Jackson v. Wiley, 352 F. Supp. 2d 666, 681–82 (E.D.Va. 2004) (presence of female nurses at strip and rectal search was not unconstitutional, since medical professionals commonly examine persons of the opposite sex), *aff'd*, 103 Fed.Appx. 505 (4th Cir. 2004) (unpublished); Show v. Patterson, 955 F. Supp. 182, 187–92 (S.D.N.Y. 1997) (allegation that after a disturbance, Muslim prisoners were kept with others naked in a holding cell, in view of about 15 staff members, for half an hour, did not support an Eighth Amendment claim, but did support a religious freedom claim).

[910]Calhoun v. DeTella, 319 F.3d 936, 940 (7th Cir. 2003); Tribble v. Gardner, 860 F.2d 321, 325 n.6 (9th Cir. 1988); Vaughan v. Ricketts, 859 F.2d at 741–42; Meriwether v. Faulkner, 821 F.2d 408, 418 (7th Cir. 1987); *see* Hudson v. Palmer, 468 U.S. 517, 530, 104 S. Ct. 3194 (1984). At least one court has said the Eighth Amendment is a preferable basis for addressing prison strip searches. Peckham v. Wisconsin Dep't of Correction, 141 F.3d 694, 697 (7th Cir. 1998) (holding that prisoners retain some Fourth Amendment rights but Eighth Amendment is "more properly posed" to protect against unconstitutional strip searches). *But see* Somers v. Thurman, 109 F.3d 614, 624 (9th Cir. 1997) ("To hold that gawking, pointing, and joking violates the prohibition against cruel and unusual punishment would trivialize" the Eighth Amendment standard.)

[911]Timm v. Gunter, 917 F.2d 1093, 1099-1101 (8th Cir. 1990); Madyun v. Franzen, 704 F.2d 954, 957 (7th Cir. 1983); Sam'i v. Mintzes, 554 F. Supp. 416, 417 (E.D.Mich. 1983) (similar to *Madyun*). *But see* Sterling v. Cupp, 290 Or. 611, 625 P.2d 123, 128–36 (Or. 1981) (barring such searches under the state constitution). *Cf.* Bagley v. Watson, 579 F. Supp. 1099, 1103–05 (D.Or. 1983) (state law ban on such searches could not prevail against women's federal statutory right to equal employment opportunity). Religious objections to search procedures are discussed further at nn.931–933, below.

[912]Jordan v. Gardner, 986 F.2d 1521, 1526–27 (9th Cir. 1993) (en banc). This decision depended on extensive expert testimony of the sort that a *pro se* litigant will probably not be able to present. If you bring a claim of this kind, be sure to request the appointment of counsel, and point out to the court that the need for expert testimony supports your request. *See* Ch. 10, § C.5. *See also*

Colman v. Vasquez, 142 F. Supp. 2d 226, 234–36 (D.Conn. 2001) (challenge by female prisoner in "sexual trauma unit" to pat frisks by male staff stated Fourth and Eighth Amendment claims).

[913]Skinner v. Railway Labor Executives' Assn., 489 U.S. 602, 616, 109 S. Ct. 1402 (1989); Forbes v. Trigg, 976 F.2d 308, 312–13 (7th Cir. 1992); Ramey v. Hawk, 730 F. Supp. 1366, 1369 (E.D.N.C. 1989).

[914]Thompson v. Souza, 111 F.3d 694, 702–03 (9th Cir. 1997) ("where prison officials select a large number of inmates for testing based on legitimate criteria," the danger of harassment of individuals does not exist; upholding urine testing of group of 124 inmates); Lucero v. Gunter, 52 F.3d 874, 877 (10th Cir. 1995) (" . . . [A]lthough random urine testing of inmates does not violate the Fourth Amendment, . . . the procedures for selecting inmates for testing must be truly random." A procedure leaving selection to the discretion of line staff would violate the Fourth Amendment.); Forbes v. Trigg, 976 F.2d at 314–15 (upholding a program of testing all inmates in a particular job); Spence v. Farrier, 807 F.2d 753, 755 (8th Cir. 1986) (random urinalysis upheld, but court cautions that procedures must be "truly random"); Wade v. Farley, 869 F. Supp. 1365, 1369 (N.D.Ind. 1994) (smell of marijuana from plaintiff's cell justified taking urine sample); Harris v. Keane, 962 F. Supp. 397, 407 (S.D.N.Y. 1997) (similar to *Wade*); Abdul-Akbar v. Dep't of Corrections, 910 F. Supp. 986, 1007 (D.Del. 1995) (tip that plaintiff was smoking marijuana combined with his long history of drug abuse justified non-random drug screening), *aff'd*, 111 F.3d 125 (3d Cir. 1997); Ramey v. Hawk, 730 F. Supp. 1366, 1369–73 (E.D.N.C. 1989) (upholding random searches); Lomax v. McCaughtry, 731 F. Supp. 1388, 1393 (E.D.Wis. 1990) (information from confidential informant established reasonable suspicion); Storms v. Coughlin, 600 F. Supp. 1214, 1222–26 (S.D.N.Y. 1984) (searches without individual cause must be based on a genuinely "blind" choice); Grochulski v. Kuhlmann, 176 A.D.2d 1111, 575 N.Y.S.2d 722, 723 (N.Y.App.Div. 1991) (upholding regulation permitting urinalysis based on information from unconfirmed sources), *leave denied*, 79 N.Y.2d 755 (1992). *See* Ch. 4, § H.1.j for a discussion of the use of urinalysis results in prison disciplinary proceedings. *Cf.* Sparks v. Stutler, 71 F.3d 259, 261–62 (7th Cir. 1995) (officials were entitled to qualified immunity where they had cause to take a urine sample, the plaintiff said he couldn't supply one, and they catheterized him, finding his bladder empty).

[915]Sepulveda v. Ramirez, 967 F.2d 1413, 1416 (9th Cir. 1992); Storms v. Coughlin, 600 F. Supp. at 1222 (dictum). This view is supported by the cases cited in nn.923–925 of this section holding that unnecessary viewing of prisoners undressed or performing bodily functions is unconstitutional. *But see* Whitman v. Nesic, 368 F.3d 931, 934–35 (7th Cir. 2004) (upholding requirement that prisoners stand naked in a bathroom stall until they produce a sample). *Cf.* Nelson v. McBride, 912 F. Supp. 403, 408 (N.D.Ind. 1996) (having officers rather than medical staff take urine samples does not violate the Fourth Amendment).

correctional purposes.[916] In recent years, that rule has been extended to the provision of DNA samples pursuant to state or federal statute.[917] However, more intrusive medical procedures require greater justification from government and must be balanced against the seriousness of the intrusion.[918] Urinalysis, blood samples, etc., do not raise any issue of self-incrimination under the Fifth Amendment because they are not considered testimonial.[919] Courts have held that the use of the penile plethysmograph, which measures sexual response, in the course of sex offender treatment does not violate the Fourth Amendment or other privacy right.[920]

---

[916]Thompson v. City of Los Angeles, 885 F.2d 1439, 1447 (9th Cir. 1989) (upholding requirement of blood sample and x-ray); Dunn v. White, 880 F.2d 1188, 1195 (10th Cir. 1989) (upholding requirement of HIV tests); People v. Pifer, 216 Cal.App.3d 956, 265 Cal.Rptr. 237 (Cal.App. 1989) (upholding routine x-ray search of transferred inmates); People v. Adams, 149 Ill.2d 331, 173 Ill.Dec. 600, 597 N.E.2d 574, 579–86 (Ill. 1992) (upholding required HIV testing of persons convicted of prostitution); see Woods v. Lemonds, 804 F. Supp. 1106, 1109–10 (E.D.Mo. 1992) (upholding forcible taking of blood sample pursuant to a warrant); see Saulsberry v. Maricopa County, 151 F. Supp. 2d 1109, 1116–18 (D.Ariz. 2001) (defendants were entitled to qualified immunity for involuntary catheterization to remove urine for medical purposes), aff'd, 41 Fed.Appx. 953 (9th Cir. 2002) (unpublished); see also Ch. 2, § F.4.k. But see Barlow v. Ground, 943 F.2d 1132, 1136–39 (9th Cir. 1991) (warrantless taking of blood sample from arrestee violated the Fourth Amendment); Walker v. Sumner, 917 F.2d 382, 387 (9th Cir. 1990) (purpose of training state health workers may not be sufficient justification for involuntary seizure of blood specimens); Henry v. Ryan, 775 F. Supp. 247, 253 (N.D.Ill. 1991) (coerced blood and saliva samples taken from a person who was not a suspect raised a Fourth Amendment issue).

[917]Wilson v. Collins, 517 F.3d 421, 424–28 (6th Cir. 2008) (upholding state statute requiring DNA samples from convicted felons); U.S. v. Kriesel, 508 F.3d 941, 946–49 (9th Cir. 2007) (upholding federal statute requiring DNA sampling of everyone convicted of a federal felony, including those on supervised release); Banks v. U.S., 490 F.3d 1178, 1188–93 (10th Cir. 2007) (upholding application of sampling requirement of federal DNA Backlog Elimination Act to nonviolent felons on parole, probation, or supervised release); U.S. v. Hook, 471 F.3d 766, 771–73 (7th Cir. 2006) (similar to Kriesel), cert. denied, 549 U.S. 1343 (2007); Padgett v. Donald, 401 F.3d 1273, 1278–79 (11th Cir. 2005) (upholding state statute requiring DNA sampling of all convicted incarcerated felons); Nicholas v. Goord, 430 F.3d 652 (2d Cir. 2005) (upholding statute applying to assault, homicide, rape, incest, escape, attempted murder, kidnaping, arson, and burglary, suggesting its rationale applies to all convicted felons); Jones v. Murray, 962 F.2d 302, 306–08 (4th Cir. 1992) (upholding statute requiring prisoners to give blood samples for DNA analysis for future law enforcement purposes); see Groceman v. U.S. Dep't of Justice, 354 F.3d 411, 413 n.2 (5th Cir. 2004) (per curiam) (noting variety of approaches taken by courts to DNA statutes); see also Sanders v. Coman, 864 F. Supp. 496, 500–01 (E.D.N.C. 1994) (use of force to obtain blood samples does not violate the Eighth Amendment).

Some older decisions involved statutes that were limited to certain offenses, see, e.g., Shaffer v. Saffle, 148 F.3d 1180 (10th Cir. 1998); Gilbert v. Peters, 55 F.3d 237 (7th Cir. 1995). Some decisions suggested that mandatory DNA sampling would not be lawful for all offenses. See, e.g., Roe v. Marcotte, 193 F.3d 72, 81–82 (2d Cir. 1999) (upholding statute applying to sex offenders; rejecting rationale that would extend to all offenses). However, the cases cited earlier in this footnote upheld DNA sampling of all convicted felons, including those not sentenced to prison. It is not clear where the line will ultimately be drawn, or whether there will be one. But see Friedman v. Boucher, 568 F.3d 1119, 1124–30 (9th Cir. 2009) (holding warrantless, suspicionless, forcible extraction of a DNA sample from a person who had served a sentence for a sex offense in another state and was held as a pre-trial detainee on unrelated charges violated clearly established Fourth Amendment rights). Challenges to DNA collection based on religious objections have mostly been unsuccessful. See § D.2.g of this chapter, n.823.

[918]Winston v. Lee, 470 U.S. 753, 760, 105 S. Ct. 1611 (1985) (holding criminal defendant could refuse surgery to remove a bullet that would require general anesthesia; "The reasonableness of surgical intrusions beneath the skin depends on a case-by-case approach, in which the individual's interests in privacy and security are weighed against society's interests in conducting the procedure."); U.S. v. Husband, 226 F.3d 626, 636 (7th Cir. 2000) (permissibility of anesthetizing an arrestee to recover drugs from his mouth depends on the magnitude of the risk presented, the imminence of the potential loss of evidence to the prosecution, and the extent of the supposed medical risk faced by the arrestee without the medical intrusion); see U.S. v. Husband, 312 F.3d 247 (7th Cir. 2002) (on remand, finding search reasonable in light of safety of sedative used and danger to arrestee from drugs held in mouth).

[919]Schmerber v. California, 384 U.S. 757, 760–65, 86 S. Ct. 1826 (1966) (blood sample for alcohol test); (DNA); Wilson v. Collins, 517 F.3d at 431; U.S. v. Zimmerman, 514 F.3d 851, 855 (9th Cir. 2007) (DNA); U.S. v. Hook, 471 F.3d 766, 773–74 (7th Cir. 2006) (DNA); Boling v. Romer, 101 F.3d 1336, 1340–41 (10th Cir. 1996) (DNA sample); Lucero v. Gunter, 17 F.3d 1347, 1350 (10th Cir. 1994) (urinalysis); Hampson v. Satran, 319 N.W.2d 796, 800 (N.D. 1982) (drug test). But see U.S. v. Zimmerman, 514 F.3d 851, 853–54 (9th Cir. 2007) (religious objection to giving blood sample should be considered under Religious Freedom Restoration Act).

[920]Searcy v. Simmons, 97 F. Supp. 2d 1055, 1063–64 (D.Kan. 2000), aff'd on other grounds, 299 F.3d 1220 (10th Cir. 2002); Lile v. McKune, 24 F. Supp. 2d 1152, 1161–64 (D.Kan. 1998), vacated as moot in pertinent part, 224 F.3d 1175, 1193 (10th Cir. 2000), rev'd on other grounds, 536 U.S. 24 (2002); Pool v. McKune, 267 Kan. 797, 987 P.2d 1073, 1078–80 (Kan. 1999); see Walrath v. U.S., 830 F. Supp. 444, 447 (N.D.Ill. 1993) (upholding plethysmography as a probation condition). But see U.S. v. Cope, 527 F.3d 944, 954 (9th Cir. 2008) (court must make individual determination of need, and explain why less intrusive means are not adequate, in order to to impose penile plethysmograph testing as a condition of supervised release in light of "known flaws and intrusiveness of plethysmograph testing" (citing U.S. v. Weber, 451 F.3d 552 (9th Cir. 2006)); cf. U.S. v. Rhodes, 552 F.3d 624 (7th Cir. 2009) (declining to adopt Weber rule where plethysmograph testing had not actually been ordered).

One court has stated that there is a constitutional right to refuse unlawful prison searches.[921] Others disagree,[922] and we don't recommend this practice, since you will risk injury and are likely to be charged and convicted of disciplinary offenses or new crimes. Even if you ultimately prevail in court you will suffer a lot in the interim. It is more prudent to obey orders and then seek administrative or judicial relief.

Outside the context of searches, courts have said that prisoners have the right not to be viewed unnecessarily in the nude or while performing private bodily functions, especially by persons of the opposite sex.[923] However, "infrequent and casual observation, or observation at a distance . . . reasonably related to prison needs" are not unconstitutional,[924] and particular security or other administrative needs may justify viewing of unclothed prisoners by opposite-sex staff.[925] (The question of when prisoners may be deprived of clothing is addressed elsewhere in this book.[926]) Courts have generally upheld prohibitions on prisoners' covering their cell windows for privacy when undressed, on the toilet, etc.[927] The loss of privacy that is inherent in prison life—especially under crowded conditions—does not violate the Constitution.[928]

Some cases taking restrictive views of inmates' privacy rights are employment discrimination cases in which inmates were not represented and their interests were not seriously considered by the courts.[929] But some courts in

[921]Valdez v. Farmon, 766 F. Supp. 1529, 1534 (E.D.Cal. 1991).

[922]Koss v. Dep't of Corrections, 184 Mich.App. 614, 459 N.W.2d 34, 35–36 (Mich.App. 1990) (prisoner could be disciplined for refusing a search that was not authorized by prison regulation).

[923]Mills v. City of Barbourville, 389 F.3d 568, 579 (6th Cir. 2004) (stating "we have recognized that a prison policy forcing prisoners to be searched by members of the opposite sex or to be exposed to regular surveillance by officers of the opposite sex while naked . . . would provide the basis of a claim on which relief could be granted"); Sepulveda v. Ramirez, 967 F.2d 1413, 1416 (9th Cir. 1992); Walker v. Mintzes, 771 F.2d 920, 929 (6th Cir. 1985) (prisoners must be permitted to wear appropriate clothing while walking to showers); Cumbey v. Meachum, 684 F.2d 712, 714 (10th Cir. 1982); Galvan v. Carothers, 855 F. Supp. 285, 291–92 (D.Alaska 1994), aff'd, 122 F.3d 1071 (9th Cir. 1997) (unpublished); Klein v. Pyle, 767 F. Supp. 215, 218 (D.Colo. 1991); Valdez v. Farmon, 766 F. Supp. at 1535; Thomas v. Jabe, 760 F. Supp. 120, 123 (E.D.Mich. 1991); DiLoreto v. Borough of Oaklyn, 744 F. Supp. 610, 621–22 (D.N.J. 1990); Clark v. Tinnin, 731 F. Supp. 998, 1007 (D.Colo. 1990); Lumpkin v. Burns, 702 F. Supp. 242, 243 (D.Nev. 1988); D.B. v. Tewksbury, 545 F. Supp. 896, 905 (D.Or. 1982); Rushing v. Wayne County, 436 Mich. 247, 462 N.W.2d 23, 32 (Mich. 1990); see Fortner v. Thomas, 983 F.2d 1024, 1030 (11th Cir. 1993) (noting that exposure of genitals to persons of opposite sex may be especially demeaning and humiliating); Forts v. Ward, 621 F.2d 1210, 1216–17 (2d Cir. 1980) (male guards could work night shift in female housing units where women could wear "satisfactory sleepwear" and cover their cell windows for 15-minute periods); see Ch. 2, § E, concerning clothing.

[924]Michenfelder v. Sumner, 860 F.2d 328, 333–34 (9th Cir. 1988) (occasional viewing of strip searches by female officers did not violate the Constitution where they did not actually conduct the searches and staffing policy reasonably accommodated privacy rights); accord, Strickler v. Waters, 989 F.2d 1375, 1387–88 (4th Cir. 1993); Letcher v. Turner, 968 F.2d 508, 510 (5th Cir. 1992); Cookish v. Powell, 945 F.2d 441, 447 (1st Cir. 1991); Timm v. Gunter, 917 F.2d 1093, 1101 (8th Cir. 1990) (assignment of opposite-sex guards to most housing units did not violate privacy rights); Grummett v. Rushen, 779 F.2d 491, 493–95 (9th Cir. 1985); Zunker v. Bertrand, 798 F. Supp. 1365, 1369–70 (E.D.Wis. 1992) (upholding post-visit strip searches in view of other inmates in light of security reasons for not providing more privacy); Rodriguez v. Kincheloe, 763 F. Supp. 463, 471 (E.D.Wash. 1991), aff'd, 967 F.2d 590 (9th Cir. 1992);

Merritt-Bey v. Salts, 747 F. Supp. 536, 539 (E.D.Mo. 1990); Csizmadia v. Fauver, 746 F. Supp. 483, 489–90 (D.N.J. 1990) (reviewing case law); Johnson v. Pa. Dep't of Corrections, 661 F. Supp. 425, 430–35 (W.D.Pa. 1987); Smith v. Chrans, 629 F. Supp. 606, 611 (C.D.Ill. 1986); Miles v. Bell, 621 F. Supp. 51, 66 (D.Conn. 1985); see also Crosby v. Reynolds, 763 F. Supp. 666, 669–70 (D. Neb. 1991) (defendants were immune from damages for placing a pre-operative male transsexual in women's housing). But see Canedy v. Boardman, 801 F. Supp. 254, 256–57 (W.D.Wis. 1992) (rejecting cases limiting opposite-sex searches to inadvertent, infrequent, or random observation).

One federal circuit has said that disparate treatment of men and women with respect to opposite-sex surveillance (women supervising men, but not vice versa) did not deny equal protection of the law. Oliver v. Scott, 276 F.3d 736, 746–47 (5th Cir. 2002).

[925]Hill v. McKinley, 311 F.3d 899, 903–05 (8th Cir. 2002) (holding both male and female staff could participate in transfer of unruly naked female prisoner, since not enough female guards were available; holding that leaving the prisoner exposed on a restraint board in male officers' presence violated the Fourth Amendment); Oliver v. Scott, 276 F.3d 736, 744–46 (5th Cir. 2002) (upholding under the Turner reasonable relationship standard a policy "permitting all guards to monitor all inmates at all times" because it "increases the overall level of surveillance," and bathrooms and showers can be the site of violence); Birdine v. Gray, 375 F. Supp. 2d 874, 879 (D.Neb. 2005) (holding transporting an unruly prisoner naked to an area where he could be observed continuously did not violate his rights, since he refused to put on his clothes).

[926]See Ch. 2, § E.

[927]Birdine v. Gray, 375 F. Supp. 2d 874, 879 n.14 (D.Neb. 2005); see MacDonald v. Angelone, 69 F. Supp. 2d 787, 793–94 (E.D.Va. 1999) (holding there was no clearly established right).

[928]Bolton v. Goord, 992 F. Supp. 604, 627 (S.D.N.Y. 1998) (the embarrassment and discomfort of having to use the toilet in front of a cellmate "does not approach the standard of inhumane conditions that violate the Eighth Amendment").

[929]See, e.g., Griffin v. Michigan Dep't of Corrections, 654 F. Supp. 690, 702–03 (E.D.Mich. 1982); compare Forts v. Ward, 621 F.2d 1210, 1212 (2d Cir. 1980) (inmates sued prison officials and officers' union).

If prison officials try to rely on cases in which prisoners were not parties, you should point this out to the court and suggest that such cases should not be given precedential weight because prisoners' privacy interests did not receive a fair hearing.

such employment cases have held that prison officials may legitimately restrict supervision by opposite-sex staff.[930]

One issue that has not been explored much is the effect, if any, of religious objections to prison searches or other bodily privacy invasions. Under the Constitution, such claims have rarely prevailed.[931] The Religious Freedom Restoration Act and the Religious Land Use and Institutionalized Persons Act provide greater protection for prisoners' religious claims than does the reasonable relationship standard applied under the Constitution.[932] However, to date most decisions applying these statutes to prison searches have been unfavorable to prisoners.[933]

3. Other Privacy Issues

Prisoners are constitutionally entitled to privacy in their correspondence, visits, and telephone calls with attorneys and their assistants.[934] They have a constitutional right of privacy in their medical diagnoses and treatment, especially information concerning HIV infection, and in communications with mental health professionals.[935] Otherwise, the disclosure of information about a prisoner generally does not violate the Constitution.[936] There may be exceptions in extreme cases[937] or when a state or federal statute creates a reasonable expectation of privacy.[938] Such disclosures by federal agencies may also directly violate the federal

---

[930]See Dothard v. Rawlinson, 433 U.S. 321, 97 S. Ct. 2720 (1977) (upholding exclusion of female staff from male prisons because of their "jungle atmosphere" and likelihood of assaults on women staff); Everson v. Michigan Dep't of Corrections, 391 F.3d 737, 748–52 (6th Cir. 2004) (holding female gender could be a "bona fide occupational qualification" (BFOQ) for working in women's housing units where the prison system had a "grave problem of sexual abuse of female inmates"); Robino v. Iranon, 145 F.3d 1109, 1111 (9th Cir. 1998) (per curiam) (similar to Everson, but applying to only six posts in a women's prison); Torres v. Wisc. Dep't of Health & Social Serv., 859 F.2d 1523, 1530 (7th Cir.1988) (en banc). In Everson, the court said: "The privacy rights of Michigan's female inmates also weigh in favor of a BFOQ." 391 F.3d at 757. In Robino, it said: "Whether or not the inmates could successfully assert their own right to privacy is immaterial to this case. We are concerned here with a considered prison policy that takes into account security, rehabilitation, and morale." 145 F.3d at 1111.

[931]Madyun v. Franzen, 704 F.2d 954, 957 (7th Cir. 1983); Show v. Patterson, 955 F. Supp. 182, 187–91 (S.D.N.Y. 1997) (allegation that after a disturbance, Muslim prisoners were kept with others naked in a holding cell, in view of about 15 staff members, for half an hour, stated a claim under the First Amendment); Hill v. Blum, 916 F. Supp. 470, 472–73 (E.D.Pa. 1996) (pat search including genitalia did not violate the First Amendment rights of a Muslim prisoner); Johnson v. Pa. Bureau of Corrections, 661 F. Supp. 425, 438 (W.D.Pa. 1987) (occasional nude viewing of Muslim inmates by opposite-sex guards was not unconstitutional); Sam'i v. Mintzes, 554 F. Supp. 416, 417 (E.D.Mich. 1983) (similar to Madyun). But see Sterling v. Cupp, 290 Or. 611, 625 P.2d 123, 128–36 (Or. 1981) (barring such searches under the state constitution).

[932]See § D.1.b of this chapter concerning these statutes.

[933]See Jova v. Smith, 582 F.3d 410, 416 (2d Cir. 2009) (under RLUIPA, upholding refusal to respect demand of Tulukeesh adherents that they not appear nude before persons who were not followers of their religion, given the institutional necessity for strip frisks); May v. Baldwin, 109 F.3d 557, 562–64 (9th Cir. 1997) (under RFRA, requiring a Rastafarian to loosen his dreadlocks was a substantial burden on his religious exercise, but it was also the least restrictive means of searching for contraband); Levinson-Roth v. Parries, 872 F. Supp. 1439, 1542 (D.Md. 1995) (requiring the Orthodox plaintiff to remove her wig for purposes of an intake photograph did not violate the Religious Freedom Restoration Act; since she was given a towel to cover her head except for momentary exposure, the interference with religious rights was not substantial); Collins v. Scott, 961 F. Supp. 1009, 1014–15 (E.D.Tex. 1997) (rejecting RFRA claim by Muslim prisoner of strip search

over religious objection; court says the Muslim modesty rule applies to either sex, and plaintiff was willing to be strip searched by males). But see Show v. Patterson, 955 F. Supp. 182, 187–91 (S.D.N.Y. 1997) (allegation that after a disturbance, Muslim prisoners were kept with others naked in a holding cell, in view of about 15 staff members, for half an hour, stated a claim under the Religious Freedom Restoration Act). In our view the Collins case is a gross misinterpretation of RFRA.

[934]See § C.3 of this chapter.

[935]See Ch. 2, § F.4.j.

[936]Kimberlin v. U.S. Dep't of Justice, 788 F.2d 434, 438 (7th Cir. 1986) (disclosure of prisoner's financial affairs did not violate the Constitution); Ferguson v. Dier-Zimmel, 809 F. Supp. 668, 670 (E.D.Wis. 1992) (there is no constitutional right of privacy in records related to criminal proceedings or incarceration); Barry v. Whalen, 796 F. Supp. 885, 894 (E.D.Va. 1992) (responding to press inquiries about a prisoner did not violate clearly established rights); Jones/Seymour v. LeFebvre, 781 F. Supp. 355, 357–58 (E.D.Pa. 1991) (filming a prisoner walking in a corridor did not violate his Fourth Amendment or privacy rights; the fact that he was imprisoned was a matter of public record), aff'd, 961 F.2d 1567 (3d Cir. 1992); Smith v. Coughlin, 727 F. Supp. 834, 843 (S.D.N.Y. 1989) (notification to prison by child welfare officials that a prisoner was being investigated for assaulting his daughter did not violate his privacy rights); see also Davis v. Bucher, 853 F.2d 718, 720 (9th Cir. 1988) (officer did not violate the Constitution by showing nude photos of the plaintiff's wife to other inmates).

[937]See Lattany v. Four Unknown U.S.Marshals, 845 F. Supp. 262, 266 (E.D.Pa. 1994) (allegation that a defendant was photographed with no law enforcement justification stated a constitutional claim for privacy violation); Best v. District of Columbia, 743 F. Supp. 44, 48 (D.D.C. 1990) (videotaping of inmates being transported in shackles stated a constitutional claim and required prison officials to show some institutional justification for it); Smith v. Fairman, 98 F.R.D. 445, 450–51 (C.D.Ill. 1982) (allowing a prisoner to be filmed involuntarily in his cell violated constitutional rights of privacy). But see Harding v. Jones, 768 F. Supp. 275, 277–78 (E.D.Mo. 1991) (a caseworker who gave the plaintiff's mother's telephone number to another inmate, who harassed her, was entitled to qualified immunity).

[938]See Soucie v. County of Monroe, 736 F. Supp. 33, 35–37 (W.D.N.Y. 1990) (unauthorized disclosure of Youthful Offender conviction stated a constitutional claim because state statutes created an expectation of privacy). But see Jones/Seymour v. LeFebvre, 781 F. Supp. at 359 (prison directive governing media relations did not create a liberty interest).

Privacy Act.[939] Notification to the public or to local law enforcement official of the release of prisoners with particular criminal histories has generally been upheld.[940] Prisoners may be required to disclose information to prison personnel in connection with legitimate prison procedures, although the Fifth Amendment may bar the state from using it in a subsequent criminal prosecution.[941] Prisoners may not be put on display for the entertainment of the media or the public.[942]

Prisoners have rights of private choice in refusing medical treatment,[943] terminating pregnancy by abortion,[944] marriage and the maintenance of family relationships,[945] and personal appearance.[946] Rights of private choice to

engage in sexual activity have not been extended to the prison setting.[947] There is no privacy right in name changes made for personal and not religious reasons.[948] One court has held that the covert surveillance of a detainee's confession to a priest violated the *priest's* religious and privacy rights, even if there was some doubt that the prisoner had an expectation of privacy.[949]

A broader right of privacy is protected by most states' law, either by common law (i.e., court decisions) or by statute.[950] State law rights of privacy may encompass freedom from "intentional interference with another's interest in solitude or seclusion,"[951] from "public disclosure of private facts,"[952] and from publicity that places the plaintiff in a

---

[939]5 U.S.C. § 552a; *see* Reyes v. Supervisor of Drug Enforcement Agency, 834 F.2d 1093, 1095 (1st Cir. 1987) (disclosure of information by DEA to prison officials in violation of federal Privacy Act could support a damage claim). *But see* Maydak v. U.S., 363 F.3d 512, 516 (D.C. Cir. 2004) (holding that prison officials' retention of copies of photographs made during inmate visits could violate Privacy Act unless related to law enforcement activity); Kimberlin v. U.S. Dep't of Justice, 788 F.2d at 436–38 (disclosures did not violate Privacy Act because Bureau of Prisons regulations authorized them as a "routine use").

The Privacy Act provides for damages for violations in a minimum amount of $1,000. However, the plaintiff must show evidence of actual damages to recover anything. Doe v. Chao, 540 U.S. 614, 620–23, 124 S. Ct. 1204, 1207 (2004). For persons who are prisoners at the time they file suit, the Prison Litigation Reform Act's provision concerning mental or emotional injury may bar recovery for emotional distress unaccompanied by physical injury. *See* Ch. 9, § E.

The Privacy Act also provides some protections against the maintenance of inaccurate records by prison officials, and permits individuals to obtain records concerning themselves. *See* Ch. 4, § H.7, nn.940–952, and Ch. 10, § K.1, n.405.

[940]*See* Ch. 2, § F.4.b, nn.552–555, concerning sex offender notification requirements; *see also* Rem v. U.S. Bureau of Prisons, 320 F.3d 791, 794 (8th Cir. 2003) (plaintiff did not have a liberty interest in avoiding notification pursuant to statute to local law enforcement officials of early release of prisoners convicted of drug trafficking or violent offenses).

[941]Taylor v. Best, 746 F.2d 220, 223–25 (4th Cir. 1984) (classification interview procedure did not violate prisoner's privacy or Fifth Amendment right against self-incrimination). Self-incrimination issues related to sex offender treatment are discussed in Ch. 2, § F.4.b, nn. 523–525.

[942]Demery v. Arpaio, 378 F.3d 1020, 1029–32 (9th Cir. 2004) (striking down policy of broadcasting live images via the Internet of pre-trial detainees in non-public areas of a jail); Lauro v. Charles, 219 F.3d 202, 203 (2d Cir. 2000) (holding the "perp walk"— displaying an arrested person to the media with no other legitimate law enforcement purpose—"exacerbates the seizure of the arrestee unreasonably and therefore violates the Fourth Amendment.").

[943]*See* Ch. 2, § F.4.k.

[944]*See* Ch. 2, § F.4.f.

[945]*See* § G of this chapter.

[946]Quinn v. Nix, 983 F.2d 115, 118 (8th Cir. 1992) (requiring prisoners to cut their "shag" hairstyles with no correctional justification was unconstitutional). *But see* Star v. Gramley, 815 F. Supp. 276, 278–79 (C.D.Ill. 1993) (prison officials had a rational basis for

preventing a male prisoner from wearing female clothing and makeup).

[947]People v. Santibanez, 91 Cal.App.3d 287, 154 Cal.Rptr. 74, 75–76 (Cal.App. 1979); People v. Coulter, 94 Mich.App. 531, 288 N.W.2d 448, 451 (Mich.App. 1980); Rodgers v. Ohio Dep't of Rehab. & Corr., 91 Ohio App.3d 565, 632 N.E.2d 1355, 1356–57 (1993).

[948]Kirwan v. Larned Mental Health, 816 F. Supp. 672, 674 (D.Kan. 1993). *But see* Diamontiney v. Borg, 918 F.2d 793, 795–96 (9th Cir. 1990) (affirming preliminary injunction requiring delivery of mail addressed to plaintiff in his changed name pending decision of the case).

[949]Mockaitis v. Harcleroad, 104 F.3d 1522, 1530, 1532–33 (9th Cir. 1997). On the peculiar facts of that case, the prisoner might not have had an expectation of privacy. *Mockaitis*, 104 F.3d at 1533. We would expect that in the usual case the prisoner would be found to have an expectation of privacy, given the court's statement that "the history of the nation has shown a uniform respect for the character of sacramental confession as inviolable by government agents interested in securing evidence of crime from the lips of criminal." 104 F.3d at 1532.

[950]W. Page Keeton et al., *Prosser and Keeton on the Law of Torts* § 117, at 854–63 (5th ed. 1984).

[951]Hill v. McKinley, 311 F.3d 899, 905–06 (8th Cir. 2002) (damages awarded for "intrusion upon seclusion" by leaving female prisoner naked on a restraint board); Helton v. U.S., 191 F. Supp. 2d 179, 182–83 (D.D.C. 2002) (unlawful strip search stated a claim for invasion of privacy); Huskey v. National Broadcasting Co., Inc., 632 F. Supp. 1282, 1286–89 (N.D.Ill. 1986) (allegation that TV crew filmed an inmate without his consent while he was wearing only gym shorts in a secluded exercise area stated a claim for violation of state law right of privacy). In *Helton*, the court said the elements of this tort are "(1) an invasion or interference by physical intrusion, by use of a defendant's sense of sight or hearing, or by use of some other form of investigation or examination; (2) into a place where the plaintiff has secluded himself, or into his private or secret concerns; (3) that would be highly offensive to an ordinary, reasonable person." *Helton*, 191 F. Supp. 2d at 181 (citation omitted); *accord*, Hill v. McKinley, 311 F.3d at 906.

[952]One court stated that the elements of this tort are: "(1) a public disclosure of facts regarding the plaintiff; (2) the facts disclosed must be private facts; (3) the private matter made public must be one which would be highly offensive to a reasonable person of ordinary sensibilities; and (4) the defendant must act either unreasonably or recklessly as to whether there was a legitimate public interest in the matter, or with actual knowledge that none

"false light in the public eye."[953] The facts that someone has been convicted of a crime and imprisoned are matters of public record, and publicizing them is not an invasion of privacy.[954]

The law of "false light" privacy invasions is designed to protect people's reputations. So is the tort of defamation,[955] which includes libel (written defamation) and slander (oral defamation). A leading tort treatise says that "a communication is defamatory if it tends so to harm the reputation of another so as to lower him in the estimation of the

community or to deter third persons from associating or dealing with him."[956]

Defamation cases are hard for prisoners to win for several reasons. Statements that a prisoner engaged in prison misconduct made in connection with disciplinary proceedings are privileged, whether uttered by staff or by other inmates.[957] Prisoners with substantial criminal records may be "libel proof," meaning that the court thinks they have no reputation left to lose.[958] A prisoner may make himself a "limited public figure" by engaging in newsworthy conduct, meaning that he will have to show that the allegedly defamatory statement was made with actual malice.[959] A statement that discredits a prisoner among the prison population but not among the public is not defamatory.[960]

F. PERSONAL PROPERTY

Under the Constitution, prison officials have broad discretion to restrict the property prisoners may get and keep,[961] though state law and prison regulations may create greater

---

existed." Hillman v. Columbia County, 164 Wis.2d 376, 474 N.W.2d 913, 919–20 (Wis.App. 1991) (holding that disclosure of HIV infection to jail employees and inmates stated a claim), *review granted*, 482 N.W.2d 105 (1992); *see also* Board of Pardons v. Freedom of Information Commission, 19 Conn.App. 539, 563 A.2d 314, 317–18 (1989). (Records of prisoners seeking pardons and Board's deliberations about them need not be disclosed under state Freedom of Information Law), *cert. denied*, 212 Conn. 819 (Conn. 1989); Wilson v. Ohio Dep't of Rehabilitation and Correction, 73 Ohio App.3d 496, 597 N.E.2d 1148, 1150 (Ohio App. 1991) (unauthorized disclosure of prisoner's medical records can invade privacy, but not when the plaintiff brought a lawsuit about his medical condition).

[953]The elements of the false light tort include: "(1) communication to the public at large in such a manner as to make the untrue statement public knowledge; (2) the individual is placed in a false light which would be highly offensive to a reasonable person; and (3) the actor had knowledge, or acted in reckless disregard, of the falsity of the publicized matter and the false light in which the plaintiff would be placed." Clarke v. Denton Publishing Co., 793 S.W.2d 329, 331 (Tex.App. 1990) (citing Restatement (Second) of Torts, § 652 E (1976)).

[954]Romer v. Morgenthau, 119 F. Supp. 2d 346, 352, 361 (S.D.N.Y. 2000); Griffin-El v. MCI Telecommunications Corp., 835 F. Supp. 1114, 1122 (E.D.Mo. 1993), *aff'd*, 43 F.3d 1476 (8th Cir. 1994) (unpublished); Huskey v. National Broadcasting Co., Inc., 632 F. Supp. at 1287; *see* De Lesline v. State, 91 A.D.2d 785, 458 N.Y.S.2d 79, 80 (N.Y.App.Div. 1982) (a photograph of a college class for prisoners that included the plaintiff "permissibly illustrated an article of general interest" and did not violate state privacy statutes). *But see* Brady-Lunny v. Massey, 185 F. Supp. 2d 928, 932 (C.D.Ill. 2002) (refusing to require disclosure of prisoners' names under state Freedom of Information Act; "Like disclosing a 'rap sheet,' providing a list of inmates' names here would be an unreasonable invasion of privacy." For witnesses and persons not charged or convicted, disclosure "would stigmatize these individuals and cause what could be irreparable damage to their reputations.").

[955]The Constitution does not protect reputation, so defamation is not unconstitutional even when committed by prison personnel or other public employees or officials. Ellingburg v. Lucas, 518 F.2d 1196, 1197 (8th Cir. 1975); Sorenson v. Zapien, 455 F. Supp. 1207, 1209 (D.Colo. 1978); *see* Paul v. Davis, 424 U.S. 693, 701–13, 96 S. Ct. 1155 (1976).

There appears to be no remedy for prisoners for defamation by federal prison or other personnel. Federal employees are immune from tort liability individually, and the Federal Tort Claims Act provides no remedy for defamation. 28 U.S.C. § 2680(h); *see* Ch. 8, § C.2.a, concerning FTCA liability.

[956]W. Page Keeton et al., *Prosser and Keeton on the Law of Torts* § 111 at 774 (5th ed. 1984). This is a general definition; the details of defamation law vary considerably from state to state. *Id.* at 773.

[957]Couch v. Schultz, 193 Mich.App. 292, 483 N.W.2d 684, 686–87 (Mich.App.), *appeal denied*, 489 N.W.2d 764 (Mich. 1992); Hatcher v. Sumpter, 825 P.2d 638, 639–40 (Okla.App. 1992); *see also* Carlson v. Pima County, 141 Ariz. 487, 687 P.2d 1242 (Ariz. 1984) (disciplinary report was a public record and disclosure of it was privileged unless done with malice).

[958]Ray v. Time, Inc., 452 F. Supp. 618, 622 (W.D.Tenn. 1976), *aff'd*, 528 F.2d 1280 (6th Cir. 1978); Cofield v. Advertiser Co., 486 So.2d 434, 435 (Ala. 1986); Jackson v. Longcope, 394 Mass. 577, 476 N.E.2d 617, 619–20 (Mass. 1985).

[959]Ali v. Daily News Pub.Co., Inc., 540 F. Supp. 142, 144–46 (D.V.I. 1982) (prisoner who acted as spokesman for inmate population and who sought contact with the press was a limited public figure); Van Straten v. Milwaukee Journal, 151 Wis.2d 905, 447 N.W.2d 105, 109–10 (Wis.App. 1989) (inmate who slit his wrists, causing jail staff to fear AIDS, was a limited public figure), *review denied*, 451 N.W.2d 597 (1989).

The actual malice requirement means that the statement must have been made "with knowledge that it was false or with reckless disregard of whether it was false or not." New York Times Co. v. Sullivan, 376 U.S. 254, 280, 84 S. Ct. 710 (1964). This standard is very difficult for a plaintiff to meet. *See* McFarland v. Hearst Corp., 332 F. Supp. 746, 749–50 (D.Md. 1971) (description of plaintiff as a "vicious" criminal based on an FBI report describing him as "dangerous" was not made with actual malice).

[960]Saunders v. Board of Directors, WHYY-TV, 382 A.2d 257, 259 (Del.Super. 1978) ("A statement that a person is an informant of a law enforcement agency does not label one with unlawful or improper conduct.").

[961]"Prison officials are free to dictate what personal effects inmates may have . . . unless these effects, such as mail, enjoy some constitutional protection." Franklin v. State of Oregon, 563 F. Supp. 1310, 1330 (D.Or. 1983) (citations omitted), *aff'd*, 745 F.2d 1221 (9th Cir. 1984); *accord*, Bannan v. Angelone, 962 F. Supp. 71, 74 (W.D.Va. 1996) ("Unless other rights such as religion or speech are

property rights for prisoners.[962] (Taking away property is discussed in another chapter.[963])

There are certain kinds of property that prisoners are constitutionally entitled to obtain, or have provided, such as reading material,[964] materials and supplies necessary for access to courts,[965] religious objects,[966] clothing,[967] and personal hygiene articles.[968] Deprivation or limitation of property in retaliation for the exercise of constitutional rights is unconstitutional.[969] Outside of those circumstances, courts generally uphold limits on the kinds of items prisoners may obtain or possess[970] as well as the total amount of property

they can have[971] and the way that property is stored.[972] Prison officials may withdraw permission to possess particular kinds of property as long as they allow prisoners an opportunity to send it to someone outside prison or otherwise dispose of it.[973] Courts have generally upheld rules imposing greater property restrictions in segregation units than in general population.[974] Deprivation of all property, especially

involved, jails may thus constitutionally disallow the possession of personal property.").

[962]See, e.g., Blaisdell v. Dep't of Public Safety, 119 Hawai'i 275, 285, 196 P.3d 277 (2008) (state statute did not authorize prison officials to divide trust account and restrict withdrawals from one part); Spruytte v. Dep't of Corrections, 184 Mich.App. 423, 459 N.W.2d 52, 54–55 (Mich.App. 1990) (state law created a constitutionally protected property interest in possessing personal computers); see also Faunce v. Denton, 167 Cal.App.3d 191, 213 Cal. Rptr. 122 (Cal.App. 1985) (property limits struck down because of noncompliance with state Administrative Procedures Act).

[963]See Ch. 4, § D.8, concerning due process requirements and other protections against the confiscation and destruction of property.

[964]See § B.2 of this chapter.

[965]See §§ C.3, C.6 of this chapter.

[966]See § D.2.e of this chapter.

[967]See Ch. 2, § E.

[968]See Ch. 2, § C.

[969]Crawford-El v. Britton, 93 F.3d 813, 826 (D.C. Cir. 1996) (en banc); see Davis v. Norris, 249 F.3d 800, 801 (8th Cir. 2001) (officials must justify limit of personal photographs to five where plaintiff alleged that the policy was in retaliation for inmates' filing claims about lost photographs); see § B.6 of this chapter for further discussion of retaliation cases.

[970]Bell v. Wolfish, 441 U.S. 520, 553–55, 99 S. Ct. 1861 (1979) (ban on all packages from family members upheld); Mason v. Clark, 920 F.2d 493, 495 (8th Cir. 1990) (AM/FM radios could be barred on security grounds); Gaston v. Taylor, 918 F.2d 25, 29 (4th Cir. 1990) (upholding rule barring all items not "approved"), superseded on other grounds, 946 F.2d 340 (4th Cir. 1991) (en banc); Roberts v. Cohn, 63 F. Supp. 2d 921, 924–25 (N.D.Ind. 1999) (officials may prohibit possession of typewriters and word processors; the right of court access is satisfied by basic materials such as pens and paper), aff'd, 215 F.3d 1330 (7th Cir. 2000); Maberry v. McKune, 24 F. Supp. 2d 1222, 1228–29 (D.Kan. 1998) (limit on number and value of books plaintiff can possess did not deny due process or equal protection); Jensen v. Klecker, 648 F.2d 1179, 1183 (8th Cir. 1981) (upholding ban on food parcels); Washington v. Tinsley, 809 F. Supp. 504, 508 (S.D.Tex. 1992) (upholding ban on tobacco products); Lane v. Hutcheson, 794 F. Supp. 877, 883 (E.D.Mo. 1992) (upholding ban on mirrors); Savko v. Rollins, 749 F. Supp. 1403, 1415 (D.Md. 1990) (upholding ban on electric hot pots), aff'd sub nom. Simmons v. Rollins, 924 F.2d 1053 (4th Cir. 1991); Gabel v. Estelle, 677 F. Supp. 514, 515 (S.D.Tex. 1987) (upholding ban on typewriters); Burnette v. Phelps, 621 F. Supp. 1157, 1160 (M.D.La. 1985) (property rules need not be the same at every prison); Sanchez v. Warden, State Prison, 214 Conn. 23, 570 A.2d 673, 677

(Conn. 1990) (upholding ban on radios with speakers); Armstead v. Phelps, 449 So.2d 1049, 1051–52 (La.App. 1984) (styrofoam cups, typewriter covers, butter, and flammable substances could be banned); Jordan v. Dep't of Corrections, 185 Mich.App. 59, 460 N.W.2d 227, 229 (Mich.App. 1990) (upholding rule barring all unauthorized property as applied to a paper punch); Blades v. Twomey, 159 A.D.2d 868, 553 N.Y.S.2d 215 (N.Y.App.Div. 1990) (rule barring items valued over $200 upheld); Flowers v. Sullivan, 149 A.D.2d 287, 545 N.Y.S.2d 289, 293 (N.Y.App.Div. 1989) (restrictions on radio, stereo, and electrical equipment upheld), appeal dismissed, 75 N.Y.2d 850 (1990) and 75 N.Y.2d 1004 (N.Y. 1990). But see Feeley v. Sampson, 570 F.2d 364, 375 (1st Cir. 1978) (complete ban on all personal property in jail was unconstitutional).

The courts have disagreed whether prisoners can be barred from buying state lottery tickets. Compare Aiello v. Kingston, 947 F.2d 834, 836 (7th Cir. 1991); Hatch v. Sharp, 919 F.2d 1266 (7th Cir. 1990) (upholding ban) with Williams v. Manson, 499 F. Supp. 773 (D.Conn. 1980) (striking ban down). We doubt courts would follow Williams v. Manson today.

[971]Howard v. Snyder, 389 F. Supp. 2d 589, 593–95 (D.Del. 2005) (upholding rule limiting prisoners to two boxes of property and confiscating additional property unless they obtained permission for it); Bannan v. Angelone, 962 F. Supp. 71, 74 (W.D.Va. 1996) (upholding ban on word processors and typewriters); Garrett v. Gilmore, 926 F. Supp. 554 (W.D.Va. 1996) (upholding limit of one standing locker and one foot locker of property, with excess property maintained for limited periods at a central location); Nitcher v. Armontrout, 778 S.W.2d 231, 232 (Mo.App. 1989) (upholding a rule requiring prisoners to dispose of "excess" property within 90 days); see also Long v. Collins, 917 F.2d 3, 4 (5th Cir. 1990) (challenge to limit of four cubic feet of property storage "highly dubious"); Salahuddin v. Coughlin, 591 F. Supp. 353, 358 (S.D.N.Y. 1984) (limit on property that prison officials would pay to have transferred upheld).

[972]Rodriguez v. Briley, 403 F.3d 952, 953 (7th Cir. 2005) (rule requiring prisoners to stow certain property in a box whenever they leave their cells could be enforced by not letting the prisoner leave his cell, even for meals and showers).

[973]See Ch. 4, § H.8.a, n.975.

[974]Beard v. Banks, 548 U.S. 521, 531–36, 126 S. Ct. 2572 (2006); Hosna v. Groose, 80 F.3d 298, 304–05 (8th Cir. 1996); Beck v. Lynaugh, 842 F.2d 759, 762 (5th Cir. 1988); Taylor v. Rogers, 781 F.2d 1047, 1049–50 (4th Cir. 1986); Lyon v. Farrier, 730 F.2d 525, 527 (8th Cir. 1984); Bono v. Saxbe, 620 F.2d 609, 613 (7th Cir. 1980); Armstrong v. Lane, 771 F. Supp. 943, 949 (C.D.Ill. 1991); Crozier v. Shillinger, 710 F. Supp. 760, 763–65 (D.Wyo. 1989); Griffin v. Smith, 493 F. Supp. 129, 131 (W.D.N.Y. 1980); Malik v. Coughlin, 157 A.D.2d 961, 550 N.Y.S.2d 219, 220 (N.Y.App.Div. 1990). But see Ruiz v. McCotter, 661 F. Supp. 112, 151 (S.D.Tex. 1986) (refusing to impose harsher restrictions on segregation to improve staff morale).

clothing, may be unlawful even in segregation.[975] However, prison officials may remove property in emergencies or to prevent injury or property damage.[976] They may restrict the ways in which property is obtained,[977] including banning the transfer of property among prisoners.[978] Prisoners may be required to register their personal property.[979]

Money is property, and prison officials have substantial discretion in handling and regulating prisoners' money,[980] though they must observe due process requirements in taking money.[981] Prison officials and governments have devised a number of ways to take away prisoners' money; these are discussed elsewhere.[982] Cash is contraband and subject to confiscation in most prisons.[983]

The extent of prison officials' ability to control what prisoners do with or about property they own outside prison is not clear.[984]

G. Family Life

The right to maintain family relationships is fundamental under our Constitution.[985] In practice, however, most family issues are governed by state law and decided in state courts.[986] Federal courts generally do not get involved in disputes about marriage, divorce, child custody, etc., unless a state rule or procedure violates the Constitution.[987] Your first

---

[975]See Ch. 2, § J, concerning segregation units.

[976]LeMaire v. Maass, 12 F.3d 1444, 1454–55 (9th Cir. 1993) (upholding rule providing: "A disciplinary-segregated inmate may be required to forfeit or be temporarily deprived of any service or activity when the inmate is using them to destroy or damage property, obstruct security, or threatens physical violence to himself/herself or others. . . ."); Rust v. Grammer, 858 F.2d 411, 414 8th Cir. 1988) (upholding removal of inmate property except for bedding and clothing because some inmates had started fires in segregation unit); Ashford v. Barry, 737 F. Supp. 1, 2 (D.D.C. 1990) (seizure of bedding and toiletries in response to a disturbance in which property was thrown and set on fire was not unconstitutional); see also cases cited in Ch. 2, § K, concerning emergencies and lockdowns.

[977]Weiler v. Purkett, 137 F.3d 1047, 1050–51 (8th Cir. 1998) (en banc) (upholding rule limiting packages to those from "approved vendors," upholding application to package labelled legal materials sent by a family member); Stewart v. McGinnis, 800 F. Supp. 604, 618–19 (N.D.Ill. 1992) (suspension of commissary privileges does not deny any constitutional right); Tunnell v. Robinson, 486 F. Supp. 1265, 1272 (W.D.Pa. 1980) (restriction of mail orders to certain companies upheld); Vaughn v. Garrison, 534 F. Supp. 90, 93 (E.D.N.C. 1981) (same), aff'd, 673 F.2d 1319 (4th Cir. 1982); Hertz v. Carothers, 784 P.2d 659, 660 (Alaska 1990) (filling of commissary orders through a store that added a 5% handling fee did not raise a constitutional issue).

[978]Lyon v. Farrier, 730 F.2d 525, 527 (8th Cir. 1984); Ford v. Schmidt, 577 F.2d 408, 410 (7th Cir. 1978); McWhorter v. Jones, 573 F. Supp. 33, 35 (E.D.Tenn. 1983); Velarde v. Ricketts, 480 F. Supp. 261, 262 (D.Colo. 1979).

[979]Bryant v. Barbara, 11 Kan.App.2d 165, 717 P.2d 522, 526 (Kan.App. 1986).

[980]Foster v. Hughes, 979 F.2d 130, 132–33 (8th Cir. 1992) (upholding a rule barring individual interest-bearing accounts; inmates were allowed to buy savings bonds); Blankenship v. Gunter, 898 F.2d 625, 627–28 (8th Cir. 1990) (upholding a rule barring disbursements from inmate accounts to anyone besides family members and the commissary); Maberry v. McKune, 24 F. Supp. 2d 1222, 1228 (D.Kan. 1998) (different limits on expenditures, depending on how far the prisoner had advanced in programs, did not deny equal protection); Sahagian v. Dickey, 646 F. Supp. 1502, 1508–10 (W.D.Wis. 1986) (upholding restrictions on sending money to persons outside prison and requirement that 15% of incoming funds be placed in a "release account"); Tunnell v. Robinson, 486 F. Supp. at 1271–72 (various restrictions on bank accounts upheld); Henderson v. Ricketts, 499 F. Supp. 1066, 1068–69 (D.Colo. 1980) (ban on fund transfers between prisoners upheld); Nix v. Paderick, 407 F. Supp. 844, 846 (E.D.Va. 1976) (prisoners could be denied possession of checks and other documents related to bank accounts); Meis v. Grammer, 226 Neb. 360, 411 N.W.2d 355, 360 (Neb. 1987) (same as Blankenship); Richards v. Cullen, 150 Wis.2d 935, 442 N.W.2d 574 (Wis.App. 1989) (upholding requirement that 15% of incoming funds be saved for

release), review denied, 449 N.W.2d 277 (Wis. 1989). But see Chriceol v. Phillips, 169 F.3d 313, 317 (5th Cir. 1999) (withholding access to a prison account to pay legal fees could deny access to courts); Abdullah v. Gunter, 949 F.2d 1032, 1036 (8th Cir. 1991) (denying summary judgment and directing appointment of counsel in challenge to denial of right to make religious donations); Doty v. Doyle, 182 F. Supp. 2d 750, 752–55 (E.D.Wis. 2002) (requiring payment of an appellate fee out of prison "release account" for prisoner transferred out of state, and barring replenishment of the release account from his out-of-state income; noting that prisoners' money is held in trust and the terms of the trust are set when it is created).

[981]See Ch. 4, § D.7.d for a discussion of due process issues related to prisoners' money.

[982]See Ch. 4, § D.7.d for a discussion of fees assessed against prisoners.

[983]See Ch. 4, § D.7.d for a discussion of confiscation of money.

[984]See King v. Federal Bureau of Prisons, 415 F.3d 634, 637–38 (7th Cir. 2005) (preventing or delaying a prisoner's communication with his stockbroker, resulting in his assets losing value, could constitute an unlawful deprivation of property).

[985]Roberts v. U.S. Jaycees, 468 U.S. 609, 618, 104 S. Ct. 3244 (1984) (recognizing constitutional protection of "highly personal relationships" "that attend the creation and sustenance of a family—marriage, . . . childbirth, . . . the raising and education of children, . . . and cohabitation with one's relatives. . . .").

[986]Sosna v. Iowa, 419 U.S. 393, 404, 95 S. Ct. 553 (1975) (domestic relations have "long been regarded as a virtually exclusive province of the States").

[987]Ankenbrandt v. Richards, 504 U.S. 689, 703, 112 S. Ct. 2206 (1992) ("[t]he whole subject of the domestic relations of husband and wife, parent and child, belongs to the laws of the States and not to the laws of the United States. . . ." (citation omitted)). In Ankenbrandt, the Supreme Court held that federal diversity jurisdiction (the power to hear cases involving residents of different states) did not apply to domestic relations cases so as to bring them into federal court. So even if you and your spouse or other family member live in different states, you will have to proceed in state court on litigation about family matters. See Ch. 8, § F.2, concerning diversity jurisdiction.

resort in such cases must usually be to your state's family law and other relevant statutes and to the state courts.

1. Marriage

There is a constitutional right to marry,[988] and prisoners retain it despite their incarceration. The Supreme Court has held that prison regulations limiting inmate marriages must satisfy the *Turner v. Safley* standard requiring a reasonable relationship to legitimate penological interests.[989] Applying this standard, federal courts have struck down some direct and serious restrictions on the right to marry.[990] Where officials refuse to provide assistance that is necessary as a practical matter for prisoners to get married, their refusal will also be assessed under the *Turner* standard.[991]

Incidental restrictions on the right to marry appear to be constitutional.[992]

Prisoners who are married are not constitutionally entitled to conjugal visits to have sexual relations with their spouses.[993] Many states have such programs, but prison rules as to who may participate in them and under what restrictions are generally upheld.[994]

A few states recognize "common law marriage," in which people live together and agree to be married without going through an official marriage ceremony. Other states require that all marriages be "solemnized" with the official ceremony.[995] If you have a valid common law marriage in your home state, other states may be obliged to recognize it.[996]

It is not unconstitutional for states to maintain "anti-fraternization" policies and terminate staff members who marry or cohabit with prisoners or former prisoners.[997]

---

[988]Zablocki v. Redhail, 434 U.S. 374, 383–86, 98 S. Ct. 673 (1976).

[989]Turner v. Safley, 482 U.S. 78, 97, 107 S. Ct. 2254 (1987). In *Turner*, the Supreme Court struck down a regulation forbidding prisoners to marry unless the prison superintendent found "compelling reasons" to approve the marriage. *See also* Buehl v. Lehman, 802 F. Supp. 1266, 1270–71 (E.D.Pa. 1992) (prison officials must demonstrate a reasonable basis for forbidding a death row inmate to marry a woman who had been barred from visiting).

[990]Langone v. Coughlin, 712 F. Supp. 1061, 1066–69 (N.D.N.Y. 1989) (statute that forbade prisoners with life sentences to marry, but did not invalidate marriages entered into before sentencing, was so irrational as to be unconstitutional); Vazquez v. New Jersey Dep't of Corrections, 348 N.J.Super. 70, 76–77, 791 A.2d 281 (2002) (lack of pre-incarceration relationship between the parties seeking to marry and officials' view that they had an unrealistic view of when the prisoner would be released did not justify denial of marriage); *see* Carter v. Dutton, 16 F.3d 1218, 1994 WL 18006, *1 (6th Cir. 1994) (unpublished) (noting lower court holding that regulation imposing a one-year waiting period on inmates who wished to marry was unconstitutional); U.S. v. Norris, 2007 WL 4335459, *3 (N.D.Ind., Dec. 7, 2007) (holding government's concern that allowing a jailed defendant to marry might allow a witness to claim the marital privilege did not justify preventing the marriage).

A predecessor statute to the one struck down in *Langone*, which forbade inmates serving life sentences to marry, was upheld because the marriage restriction was intended as part of the punishment for the crime. Turner v. Safley, 482 U.S. at 97, *interpreting* Butler v. Wilson, 415 U.S. 953, 94 S. Ct. 1479 (1974).

[991]Toms v. Taft, 338 F.3d 519, 527 (6th Cir. 2003) (". . . [W]e now hold that the distinction between actively prohibiting an inmate's exercise of his right to marry and failing to assist is untenable in a case in which the inmate's right will be completely frustrated without officials' involvement. . . . The inmate's right to marry may be curtailed only where the officials' refusal to assist the inmate is reasonably related to legitimate penological interests."). In *Toms*, the plaintiffs could not get married because state law required both prospective spouses to appear for an interview; prison officials would not agree to have a prison employee appointed as a deputy clerk to interview them, and the county clerk refused to send a staff member to the prison. The court did not actually decide the constitutionality of these refusals, because the claim for an injunction was moot and the damages claims were barred by qualified immunity. *But see In re* Coats, 849 A.2d 254

(Pa. Super. 2004) (holding court clerk owes no duty to inmate to implement video conferencing or to travel to prison to conduct required oral examination so that inmate could obtain marriage license, resulting in inability to marry).

[992]Martin v. Snyder, 329 F.3d 919, 920 (7th Cir. 2003) (12-month delay of marriage resulting from suspension of visits); *see* Williams v. Wisconsin, 336 F.3d 576, 582 (7th Cir. 2003) (rule which affected the timing or the place of marriage plans of parolee is type of incidental interference with the right to marry [that] does not give rise to a constitutional claim if there is "some justification" for the interference"; plaintiff was forbidden to travel out of the country to get married).

[993]*See* § B.7, n.352; *see* Turner v. Safley, 482 U.S. at 95–96 (noting most prisoner marriages are "formed in the expectation that they ultimately will be fully consummated," *i.e.*, after release).

[994]*See* cases cited in § B.7 of this chapter, nn.353–354.

[995]*See, e.g.*, N.Y.Dom.Rel.Law § 11 (McKinney 1988).

[996]Farrell v. Peters, 951 F.2d 862, 863 (7th Cir. 1991) (per curiam) (prison officials need not recognize claimed common law marriage not valid under state law); Africa v. Vaughan, 998 F. Supp. 552, 556 (E.D.Pa. 1998) (same); *see In re* Cummings, 30 Cal.3d 870, 640 P.2d 1101, 1102–03, 180 Cal.Rptr. 826 (Cal. 1982) (common law spouses can be excluded from conjugal visiting program).

Most states require cohabitation as one of the factors in determining whether a common-law marriage exists; the intent of two prisoners to cohabit after their release from prison has been held insufficient. Canady v. Russell, 138 S.W.3d 412, 414 (Tex. App.-Tyler 2004) ("Without legally and/or factually sufficient evidence of cohabitation between a man and woman, an alleged informal marriage does not exist in a form recognized by the State of Texas.").

[997]Poirier v. Massachusetts Dep't of Correction, 558 F.3d 92, 95–96 (1st Cir. 2009); Keeney v. Heath, 57 F.3d 579, 581–82 (7th Cir. 1995); Wolford v. Angelone, 38 F. Supp. 2d 452, 459–63 (W.D. Va. 1999). *Cf.* Akers v. McGinnis, 352 F.3d 1030 (6th Cir. 2003) (court upheld prison rule that prohibits prison staff from having any nonwork-related contact with prisoners, parolees, probationers (offenders), their relatives, and visitors).

2. Divorce

The constitutional right of court access protects prisoners' right to bring an action seeking a divorce.[998] States have substantial discretion to regulate divorce and set conditions on it.[999] However, since divorce can only be obtained through the state courts, states may not impose rules that make it impossible to obtain.[1000]

Prisoners must be provided a fair opportunity both to pursue divorce proceedings and to oppose or to respond to them.[1001] Courts have disagreed whether this means an actual appearance in court.[1002] If the prisoner is not allowed to appear personally, other means must be considered for the prisoner to present his case.[1003] Prisoners must receive notice of divorce proceedings early enough to prepare for them.[1004] Some courts have held that service upon a prison officer does not meet the criteria for effective service of process on a prisoner.[1005]

Prisoners are not constitutionally entitled to have counsel appointed to defend a divorce proceeding,[1006] though state courts may be authorized to do so under state law in some circumstances.[1007]

The grounds and procedures for divorce vary widely from state to state, as do the rules governing the division of property and child custody and visitation. On these subjects you must consult the statutes and case law of your state. Imprisonment or conviction of a felony constitutes grounds for divorce in many states.[1008] Some courts have held that a

---

[998]Snyder v. Nolen, 380 F.3d 279, 290 (7th Cir. 2004) (per curiam); Hall v. Hall, 128 Mich. App. 757, 760, 341 N.W.2d 206 (1983) (prisoner right of access to court included right to bring action for divorce and court abused discretion by denying prisoners request to testify by deposition).

In *Lewis v. Casey*, 518 U.S. 343, 361–62, 116 S. Ct. 2174 (1996), the Supreme Court held that the right to be provided assistance in filing court actions, through law libraries or otherwise, applies only to cases challenging convictions, sentences, or conditions of confinement. However, the right not to have prison officials interfere with your pursuing a court action extends to civil actions generally, including divorce and other family law-related matters. Snyder v. Nolen, 380 F.3d at 290. See § C.1.b of this chapter for further discussion of this issue.

[999]*See* Sosna v. Iowa, 419 U.S. 393, 95 S.Ct. 553 (1975) (upholding a one-year residency requirement for divorce in state).

[1000]Boddie v. Connecticut, 401 U.S. 371, 380–82, 91 S. Ct. 780 (1971) (state cannot require filing fees for divorce from indigents who cannot pay them); Lynk v. LaPorte Superior Court No. 2, 789 F.2d 554, 567 (7th Cir. 1986) (state cannot require prisoner to appear personally in court to have a non-contested divorce granted but refuse to provide means for that appearance) (dictum); State ex rel. Kittrell v. Carr, 878 S.W.2d 859, 861–64 (Mo. Ct. App. 1994) (similar to *Lynk*).

Property division related to a divorce is not part of a fundamental right, and states may require filing fees in connection with that subject. *See* Sirbaugh v. Young, 25 Fed.Appx. 266, 267 (6th Cir. 2001) (unpublished). Many states have adopted statutes similar to the federal Prison Litigation Reform Act, which requires the payment of filing fees by indigent prisoners. You will have to check your local statutes to determine whether your state has adopted such a plan.

[1001]Wilson v. Wilson, 238 Neb. 219, 469 N.W.2d 750, 752–53 (Neb. 1991) ("a prison inmate must be given a meaningful opportunity to be heard in responding to a marriage dissolution action"; court should not have granted divorce petition without "some form of evidence"); Nichols v. Martin, 776 S.W.2d 621, 623 (Tex.App. 1989) (court cannot refuse to permit a prisoner who cannot obtain counsel to go forward with a divorce proceeding).

[1002]Some courts have held that prisoners have no right to be released from prison to attend such proceedings, but that they can present their cases through depositions or written testimony. *See, e.g.,* Belser v. Belser, 575 So.2d 1139 (Ala.Civ.App. 1991); Wilson v. Wilson, 469 N.W.2d at 752–53; State ex rel. Gladden v. Sloper, 209 Or. 346, 306 P.2d 418, 419 (1957). Others have held that the court must specifically consider whether the interest of the prisoner in appearing outweighs the interest of the state in not producing the prisoner. *See, e.g.,* Strube v. Strube, 158 Ariz. 602, 764 P.2d 731, 735

(1988) (a prisoner who asked to appear in a divorce case to assert his property and child visiting rights is presumed "entitled to be personally present at critical proceedings, such as the trial itself"); *In re* Marriage of Allison, 126 Ill.App.3d 453, 81 Ill.Dec. 610, 467 N.E.2d 310, 317 (1984); Hall v. Hall, 128 Mich.App. 757, 341 N.W.2d 206, 209 (1983); Zuniga v. Zuniga, 13 S.W. 3d 798, 803 (Tex. App. 1999) (default judgment against prisoner was improper where it was entered because prisoner failed to appear after the trial court ignored his request to be brought to court).

Court appearances are discussed further in Ch. 10, § Q.

[1003]Kocaya v. Kocaya, 347 S.C. 26, 29 (S.C. Ct. App. 2001) (refusal to produce prisoner or consider alternatives for providing him court access denied right of access to courts); Knight v. Knight, 11 S.W.3d 898, 903–06 (Tenn. Ct. App. 1999) (vacating divorce decree obtained by prisoner's spouse where court failed to rule on prisoner's request to be transported to the hearing or to have the hearing postponed until his release; lower court should consider options such as testimony by video or telephone, holding the trial at the prison, or delaying it until release); Dodd v. Dodd, 17 S.W.3d 714, 717 (Tex. App.-Houston [1st Dist.] 2000, no pet.) ("Should the court find that the *pro se* . . . inmate in a civil action is not entitled to leave prison to appear personally in court, then the prisoner *should be allowed to proceed by affidavit, deposition, telephone, or other effective means.*" (emphasis in original; citations omitted)); *In re* B.R.G., 48 S.W. 3d 812, 820 (Tex. App.-El Paso 2001).

[1004]Tolbert v. Tolbert, 1994 WL 705230, *2 (Tenn. Ct. App. 1994) (four days notice of a divorce trial given to a prisoner was insufficient, and continuance should have been granted).

[1005]Garcia v. Garcia, 712 P.2d 288, 289–90 (Utah 1986).

[1006]*See, e.g.,* Lyon v. Lyon, 765 S.W.2d 759, 763 (Tenn. Ct. App. 1988); *see* Lassiter v. Dept. of Social Services, 452 U.S. 18, 48 n.17, 101 S. Ct. 2153 (1981) (dissenting opinion) (noting lack of constitutional right to appointed counsel to address child custody issues in a divorce proceeding).

[1007]*See, e.g.,* Murfitt v. Murfitt, 809 N.E. 2d 332, 334–35 (Ind. Ct. App. 2004) (state law authorized appointment based on type and complexity of legal issues and facts, applicant's ability to present the claim without an attorney, and likelihood of applicant prevailing on the merits of the defense in deciding whether to appoint counsel).

[1008]In New York, for example, imprisonment for three or more years is a ground for divorce. N.Y. Dom. Rel. Law § 170(3); *see* Miss. Code Annotated Section 93-5-1 (ground for divorce that

spouse's criminal activities and incarceration can be taken into account in resolving money issues in a divorce.[1009] Whether trial by jury is available in a divorce action varies among states.[1010]

Many states require that a person seeking a divorce be a resident of a county for a certain number of days before filing for divorce. The problem for prisoners is that the county where they are confined is generally not considered their residency for the purpose of seeking divorce.[1011] For prisoners, courts have held that the proper venue in a divorce is the county in which the prisoner lived at the time of his incarceration.[1012] However, some courts have held that this presumption is rebuttable if the prisoner proves an intent to live in the county where the prison is located upon release.[1013] Establishing that where you are confined is your place of residency for a divorce may be very hard since prison officials can transfer you at any time out of that county.[1014]

3. Children

There is no constitutional right to conceive a child in prison.[1015]

A pregnant prisoner is entitled to have an abortion rather than bear the child; this subject is addressed elsewhere in this book.[1016]

There is no constitutional right to keep physical custody of a child in prison, although a few states have statutes permitting women to keep newborn children for a limited period of time.[1017] Children are generally permitted to visit

---

spouse was sentenced to a penitentiary and not pardoned before incarceration); Tenn. Code Ann. Section 36-4-101 (6) ("a criminal activity resulting in conviction and incarceration is clearly inappropriate marital conduct."); *see also* Budnick v. Budnick, 42 Va. App. 823, 836–38, 595 S.E.2d 50 (2004) ("husband's criminal activities and convictions irreparably harmed the marriage"). *But see* Scheu v. Vargas, 778 N.Y.S.2d 663 (N.Y. Sup. 2004) (husband's continued incarceration for a period of three or more years after marriage did not constitute fault necessary to be a ground for divorce because he was already incarcerated at the time of the marriage).

[1009]*See, e.g.*, Budnick v. Budnick, 42 Va.App. 823, 836–38, 595 S.E.2d 50 (2004) ("husband's criminal activities and convictions" constituted "negative nonmonetary contributions" which were properly considered in awarding bulk of marital assets to wife).

[1010]*Compare* Peters-Riemers v. Riemers, 644 N.W.2d 197, 202 (N.D. 2002); Arbino v. Johnson & Johnson, 116 Ohio St.3d 468, 880 N.E.2d 420, 445 (Ohio 2007) (both noting absence of jury right in divorce actions) *with* Walker v. Walker, 280 Ga. 696, 631 S.E.2d 697, 698 (Ga. 2006) (applying jury right in divorce action); Taylor v. Taylor, 63 S.W.3d 93, 99–101 (Tex. App. 2001) (state constitution and statutes protect right to jury trial in divorce proceedings). In *Taylor*, the court held that a prisoner does not waive the right to jury trial by involuntarily failing to appear in court. 63 S.W.3d at 102.

[1011]*See, e.g.*, Gonzales v. Gonzales, 2003 WL 23015065 (Tex. App.-Tyler 2003) (application of statutory residency requirements to preclude divorce filing by husband did not violate his constitutional rights to reasonable access to the courts (citing LeFebvre v. LeFebvre, 510 S.W.2d 29, 30–31 (Tex.Civ.App.-Beaumont 1974, no writ)); Fowler v. Fowler, 191 Mich.App. 318, 319, 477 N.W.2d 112 (1991) ("The issue of legal residency is principally one of intent, and it is presumed that a prisoner cannot establish a new domicile in the county or state of his imprisonment because the relocation was involuntary.").

[1012]*See, e.g.*, Fowler v. Fowler, 191 Mich.App. at 319 (inmate who resided in Florida prior to incarceration failed to establish county of place of confinement in Michigan as his new domicile for purpose of obtaining a divorce); State ex rel. Henderson v. Blaeuer, 723 S.W.2d 589, 590 (Mo. App. 1987).

[1013]Stifel v. Hopkins, 477 F.2d 1116, 1124 (6th Cir. 1973) (recognized that prisoner could adopt an intent to remain in a particular state even though the prisoner had moved there only as a result of incarceration); Fowler v. Fowler, 191 Mich.App. at 319.

[1014]You may be able to waive venue, which some courts consider a personal privilege that parties can waive. *See* State ex rel. Kittrell v. Carr, 878 S.W.2d 859, 861 (Mo. Ct. App. 1994).

[1015]Gerber v. Hickman, 291 F.3d 617, 620–22 (9th Cir. 2002) (en banc); Goodwin v. Turner, 908 F.2d 1395, 1399–1400 (8th Cir. 1990); Anderson v. Vasquez, 827 F. Supp. 617, 619–22 (N.D. Cal. 1992) (holding that inmates condemned to death had no right to conjugal visits and that the prison had no obligation to provide artificial insemination services), *aff'd in pertinent part, rev'd in part*, 28 F.3d 104 (9th Cir. 1994) (unpublished); Percy v. N.J. Dep't of Corrections, 278 N.J. Super. 543, 549, 651 A.2d 1044 (1995).

Both *Gerber* and *Goodwin* involved male prisoners who were not permitted to artificially inseminate their wives. In *Gerber*, the court did not analyse the restriction under the *Turner v. Safley* reasonableness test; it declared that a right to procreation is inconsistent with incarceration and therefore it did not even engage in the *Turner* analysis. We think this approach is questionable. *See* § A of this chapter, n.9 In *Goodwin*, the court ruled against the prisoner based on the *Turner* standard, in large part because it said if prison officials allowed male prisoners to procreate, it would have to let women do so also, and that would create serious medical and other problems. *Accord*, Percy v. N.J. Dep't of Corrections, *id.*

Some courts have upheld probation conditions providing that a probationer refrain from having more children based on certain extreme circumstances. State v. Oakley, 245 Wis.2d 447, 478, 629 N.W.2d 200 (2001) (defendant ordered not to procreate until he showed that he could support his existing children as well as a new one; he had a history of willfully evading child support), *modified*, 248 Wis.2d 654, 655, 635 N.W.2d 760 (Wis. 2001); Trammell v. State, 751 N.E.2d 283 (Ind. App. 2001) (same); *But see* State v. Talty, 103 Ohio St. 3d 177, 182–83, 814 N.E.2d 1201 (2004) (antiprocreation order imposed on probationer was overbroad where it did not provide for its termination if prisoner paid his child support); People v. Pointer, 151 Cal.App.3d 1128, 199 Cal.Rptr. 357, 365 (1984) (order not to conceive during five-year probationary period was overbroad as applied to defendant convicted of child endangerment for imposing a strict macrobiotic diet on her children).

[1016]Pregnancy, childbirth, and abortion are discussed in Ch. 2, § F.4.f.

[1017]*See* Cal. Penal Code §§ 3416–22; Wainwright v. Moore, 374 So.2d 586, 587–88 (Fla.App. 1979) (citing Fla. Stat. § 944.24 (1977)) (statute permitting children born to incarcerated mothers to remain with their mothers for the first 18 months was subject to a court determination of the child's best interests); Bailey v. Lombard, 101 Misc.2d 56, 420 N.Y.S.2d 650, 654–56 (N.Y.Sup. 1979) (despite statute, it was in the child's best interests not to stay in jail with its mother)

their parents in prison, and some courts have held that prison officials are constitutionally required to permit such visits.[1018] Courts have held that prison officials must permit a new mother to breast-feed her child in the visiting room during regular visiting hours,[1019] but are not required to allow her to keep the child in prison or to be released for that purpose.[1020] A divorced parent in prison should retain reasonable visitation rights with his or her children unless a court finds visiting would not be in the children's best interest.[1021]

Parents who go to prison, or women who give birth while in prison, are usually permitted to make arrangements for physical custody of their children, most often with their spouses, relatives, or friends.[1022]

If you want to keep your children, you should do your best to make your own arrangements for their care, and do so before you go to prison (or before giving birth, if you are pregnant in prison).[1023] It is probably wise to establish a formal guardianship.[1024] Don't wait until the state has your children or has started court proceedings. If you do, child welfare or social services agencies will usually place the children in foster care,[1025] and the court will be guided by its own view of the child's best interests.[1026] If your child is in

---

(citing McKinney's N.Y. Corr.L. § 611); Apgar v. Beauter, 75 Misc.2d 439, 347 N.Y.S.2d 872, 875–77 (N.Y.Sup. 1973) (under state statute, sheriff did not have complete discretion to refuse to admit child to jail).

[1018]See § B.7 of this chapter.

[1019]Berrios-Berrios v. Thornburgh, 716 F. Supp. 987, 990–91 (E.D.Ky. 1989). The court held that the mother was not entitled to have prison officials arrange to deliver her breast milk to the child's caretaker.

[1020]Southerland v. Thigpen, 784 F.2d 713, 716–18 (5th Cir. 1986); Pendergrass v. Toombs, 24 Or.App. 719, 546 P.2d 1103 (1976).

[1021]Hoversten v. Superior Court, 74 Cal.App. 4th 636, 640, 88 Cal. Rptr. 2d 197 (1998); In re Sims, 308 Ill. App. 3d 311, 313–314; 719 N. E. 2d 1166 (4th Dist. 1999) (incarcerated parent who provided no evidence about his relationship to his daughter, facilities available for visitation, how it would occur or who would transport his daughter, or how far the child would be required to travel failed to show it was in his child's best interests to have visits with him in prison); Skillett v. Sierra, 30 Kan.App.2d 1041, 1048–49, 53 P.3d 1234 (2002), rev. denied, 275 Kan. 965 (2002) (visitation denied where father was found to have sexually abused child's half-sisters); Thomas v. Thomas, 715 N.Y.S. 2d 818, 819, 277 A.D. 2d 935 (4th Dep't 2000) ("Unless there is a compelling reason or substantial evidence that visitation with an incarcerated parent is detrimental to a child's welfare, such visitation should not be denied."); McCrone v. Parker, 265 A.D.2d 757, 758, 697 N.Y.S.2d 379 (3d Dep't 1999) (increasing visitation from once to three times a year); Ellett v. Ellett, 265 A.D. 2d 747, 748, 698 N.Y.S. 2d 740, 741–42 (1999) (visitation denied as not in the child's best interest where it required a 10-hour round trip by automobile, the prisoner's sentence was severe, the child was very young, and the prior relationship between prisoner and child was almost nonexistent); Wise v. Del Toro, 505 N.Y. S. 2d 880, 881, 122 A.D. 2d 714, 714–715 (1986) (fact of a parent's incarceration, standing alone, does not make visitation of that parent's child inappropriate); Pacheco v. Bedford, 787 A. 2d 1210, 1213–14 (R.I. 2002) ("Visitation rights are to be strongly favored and will be denied only in an extreme situation in which the children's physical, mental, or moral health would be endangered by contact with the parent in question." Mere incarceration, standing alone, does not justify the denial of visitation rights; visits were terminated in this case because of lack of significant bond between prisoner and daughter and fact that prisoner had been convicted of victimizing a child.); see Wolfe v. Wolfe, 899 P.2d 46, 47–48 (Wyo. 1995) (it is abuse of discretion for trial court to modify visitation provisions of divorce decree without affording incarcerated father an opportunity to be heard or otherwise providing for development of an evidentiary record).

[1022]See, e.g., In re State in the Interest of Valdez, 29 Utah 2d 63, 504 P.2d 1372, 1375–76 (Utah 1973) (children were not "dependent" and juvenile court lacked jurisdiction over children of incarcerated parent who had arranged for his sister and brother-in-law to care for them); accord, Welfare Commissioner v. Anonymous, 33 Conn.Sup. 100, 364 A.2d 250 (1976).

[1023]The rest of this section relies heavily on Philip M. Genty, Procedural Due Process Rights of Incarcerated Parents in Termination of Parental Rights Proceedings: A Fifty State Analysis, 30 J. Family Law 757 (1991–92).

[1024]A guardianship is a legal arrangement intended to safeguard the rights and interests of minors or other legally incompetent persons. Parents are generally referred to as the "natural guardians" of their children. Naming someone else as a child's guardian does not terminate parental rights; it is a temporary arrangement. See, e.g., In re Guardianship of Zyla, 251 Neb. 163, 555 N.W.2d 768 (1996). If a court proposed to terminate parental rights in connection with a guardianship proceeding, the prisoner would be entitled to the legal protections available in a termination proceeding. Cf. Shappy v. Knight, 251 Ark. 943, 945–46, 475 S.W.2d 704 (1972). As with other family law matters, guardianship law will vary from state to state. Guardianship must be authorized by a court. See, e.g., In re Guardianship of Workman, 171 Neb. 554, 106 N.W.2d 722 (1960). The petitioner must generally show that the guardianship is reasonable and necessary. See, e.g., In re Guardianship of Harp, 6 Wash. App. 701, 495 P.2d 1059 (1972). The court does not have to appoint the person you propose as guardian. See, e.g., In re Estate and Guardianship of Brown, 199 Cal.App.2d 262, 266, 18 Cal.Rptr. 613 (Cal.App. 1962) (citing In re Iler, 16 Ariz. 323, 145 P. 143 (1914)).

[1025]See Matter of Taurus F., 415 Mich. 512, 330 N.W.2d 23, 52 (1982) (mother and aunt failed to agree on custody before the child was born; the child was still in foster care after five years of litigation), appeal dismissed sub nom. Finney v. Mich. Dep't of Social Services, 464 U.S. 923 (1983).

[1026]Courts making a "best interests" determination are not necessarily required to give preference to placing a child with relatives. See Stanley B. v. State, DFYS, 93 P.3d 403, 406 (Alaska 2004); In Interest of Price, 7 Kan.App. 2d 477, 644 P.2d 467, 473 (1982) (refusing to place children with the parents of a prisoner the court found to be an unfit father); V.S. v. Com., Cabinet for Human Resources, 706 S.W.2d 420, 426 (Ky. App. 1986) (placement with relatives is only one option for consideration in the best interests of the child once the conditions of terminating parental rights are met; non-prisoner case); In re McIntyre, 192 Mich.App. 47, 52, 480

foster care or another form of state custody, the state may go to court to terminate your parental rights if you will be unable to resume caring for your child within a reasonably short period of time. In fact, federal law—the Adoption and Safe Families Act (ASFA), passed in 1997—now *requires* states to seek termination of parental rights for children who have been in foster care for 15 of the preceding 22 months, unless the child is already being cared for by a relative, the state agency has documented a compelling reason why parental rights should not be terminated, or the state agency has not provided the family with the services necessary to achieve safe reunification.[1027] That doesn't mean your parental rights will automatically be terminated. The state will still have to prove by clear and convincing evidence that the state's criteria for termination are met. But you will have to defend your parental rights.

One purpose of ASFA is to keep children from spending long periods in foster care by freeing them for permanent adoption.[1028] If your parental rights are terminated, the child can be adopted without your consent. Adoption decisions are based primarily on what the court thinks is the best interest of the child.[1029] Some states permit "open" adoption in which the original parent has some continuing contact with the child.[1030] Others do not.[1031] Even if your state permits such post-adoption visitation arrangements, don't count on getting them. If you have an open adoption agreement or order, you will have standing to ask a court to enforce its terms. However, it is ultimately up to the court to decide whether enforcement of these provisions is in the best interests of your child at the time the court is considering the matter.[1032] This may be difficult to show if you are serving a long prison sentence. For these reasons, if you want to maintain any relationship with your child, you should contest any proceeding that is brought to terminate your parental rights at the time it is brought. In a later adoption proceeding, or after you are released from prison, it may be too late.

There is some risk that you will lose your parental rights even if the child is not in state custody. Another person may seek to adopt the child, ending your parental rights. For example, when the other parent marries someone else, the new spouse may seek to adopt the child. If you have had only minimal prior contact with your child, have failed to support the child financially, or, in the case of a father, have not established paternity, the new spouse may be able to adopt your child without your consent. However, this is presumably less likely to happen if your children are with someone you know and trust than if they are in state custody.

The rules and procedures for termination of parental rights vary from state to state, and are generally governed by statute.[1033] There are some basic constitutional requirements. The state must show by clear and convincing evidence that you are in some way unfit as a parent.[1034] The meaning of "unfit" is generally a matter of state law,[1035] and states have taken various approaches in cases involving prisoners. State statutes and court decisions often focus on whether the parent has "neglected" or "abandoned" the child.[1036]

N.W.2d 293 (1991) (non-prison case); *In re* D.H., 173 P.3d 365, 369 (Wyo. 2007) (non-prisoner case).

This varies from state to state. In some states, child welfare authorities are obligated to try and place the child with relatives of the parents. *See, e.g., In re* Terry E., 180 Cal.App.3d 932, 225 Cal. Rptr. 803, 812 (Cal.App. 1986); Matter of Christina T., 590 P.2d 189, 192 (Okla. 1979).

[1027]42 U.S.C. § 675(5)(E).

[1028]Adoption generally means that the parent is completely and permanently replaced by another person. If your child is adopted, you may never see or hear from the child again.

[1029]*See, e.g.,* Hooper v. Rockwell, 334 S.C. 281, 295–96, 513 S.E.2d 358 (1999).

[1030]*See, e.g.,* N.Y. Social Services Law § 383-c; Matter of Jacob, 86 N.Y.2d 651, 636 N.Y.S.2d 716, 660 N.E.2d 397, 404 (1995) (discussing New York Statute statute); *see also* Petition of Dep't of Social Services to Dispense with Consent to Adoption, 392 Mass. 696, 467 N.E.2d 861, 866 (Mass. 1984) (state statutes do not eliminate court's discretion to direct post-adoption visitation by pre-adoption family members). The New York statute was intended to overrule a court decision that rejected the possibility of open adoption. *See* Matter of Gregory B., 74 N.Y.2d 77, 89–91, 542 N.E.2d 1052, 1058–59 (N.Y. 1989) ("to judicially require such contacts arguably may be seen as threatening the integrity of the adoptive family unit"). *Compare In re* C.R.H., 620 N.W.2d 175, 180 (N.D. 2000) (noting that state legislature had not provided for open adoption).

[1031]*See, e.g., In re* C.R.H., 620 N.W.2d 175, 179–80 (N.D. 2000) (noting lack of legislative provision for open adoption).

[1032]*See, e.g.,* Re Adoption of Children by F., 170 N.J.Super. 419, 406 A.2d 986, 989 (1979); *In re* Rebecca O., 46 A.D.3d 687, 688, 847 N.Y.S.2d 610, 612 (N.Y.App.Div. 2007).

[1033]Despite this fact, we don't cite many statutes in the rest of this discussion because it's not practical to discuss the statutes of all 50 states. We have mostly cited examples of case law that show how courts in different states have applied their states' statutes, and which may be helpful in understanding how courts will apply similar statutes in other states.

[1034]Santosky v. Kramer, 455 U.S. 745, 760, 769–70, 102 S. Ct. 1388 (1982). *But see* Quilloin v. Walcott, 434 U.S. 246, 255, 98 S. Ct. 549 (1978) (state need not prove unfitness of unmarried father who had never before taken any significant responsibility for the child).

[1035]*See, e.g., In re* Christina P., 175 Cal.App.3d 115, 220 Cal. Rptr. 525, 535 (Cal.App. 1985) ("Unfitness means a probability that the parent will fail in a substantial degree to discharge parental duties toward the child."); Conn v. Conn, 15 Neb.App. 77, 722 N.W.2d 507, 512 (2006) ("Parental unfitness means a personal deficiency or incapacity which has prevented, or will probably prevent, performance of a reasonable parental obligation in child rearing and which has caused, or probably will result in, detriment to a child's well-being." (citation omitted)); State in Interest of C.Y. v. Yates, 765 P.2d 251, 255 (Utah App. 1988) ("An unfit or incompetent parent is one who 'substantially and repeatedly refuse[s] or fail[s] to render proper parental care and protection.'" (citations omitted)).

[1036]*See, e.g., In re* Juvenile Appeal, 187 Conn. 431, 446 A.2d 808, 814 (Conn. 1982) (abandonment defined as "such conscious disregard and indifference [by a parent] to his parental obligations

In most states, conviction of a felony or imprisonment by itself does not justify termination of parental rights,[1037] and some courts emphasize the importance of determining whether the parent is presently unfit at the time of the termination proceeding.[1038] Courts have weighed factors such as the nature of the parent's crimes or bad acts (especially those involving harm to children),[1039] the length of time the

parent has been or will be imprisoned[1040] (which is addressed explicitly in many states' statutes[1041]), and the conduct of the parent toward the child, both in and out of prison. In some cases, courts have held that a parent's imprisonment, or the

_____

as to evince a settled purpose to forego his obligation and duties to his child" (citations omitted)); Matter of Welfare of Udstuen, 349 N.W.2d 300, 303–04 (Minn.App. 1984) (child found "neglected and in foster care"); In Interest of F.H., 283 N.W.2d 202, 214 (N.D. 1979) (child found to be "abandoned").

[1037]Adoption of Coffee, 59 Cal.App.3d 593, 130 Cal.Rptr. 887, 891 (Cal.App. 1976); Harden v. Thomas, 329 So.2d 389, 391 (Fla. App. 1976); In Interest of Sanders, 77 Ill.App.3d 78, 32 Ill.Dec. 847, 395 N.E.2d 1228, 1233 (1979); Murphy v. Vanderver, 169 Ind.App. 528, 349 N.E.2d 202, 203 (Ind.App. 1976); Adoption of Rapp, 348 So.2d 107, 109–10 (La.App. 1977); Petition of Boston Children's Service Assn., 20 Mass.App. 566, 481 N.E.2d 516, 520–21 (Mass. App.), _review denied_, 396 Mass. 1102, 484 N.E.2d 102 (Mass. 1985); _In re_ DeWayne G., Jr., 263 Neb. 43, 638 N.W.2d 510, 521 (Neb. 2002); _In re_ Parental Rights to Q.L.R., 118 Nev. 602, 54 P.3d 56, 58–59 (Nev. 2002); _In re_ Yocum, 158 N.C.App. 198, 207–08, 580 S.E.2d 399, 405 (2003) ("[i]ncarceration, standing alone, is neither a sword nor a shield in a termination of parental rights decision."), _aff'd_, 357 N.C. 568, 597 S.E.2d 674 (N.C. 2003); Re Adoption of Schoeppner, 46 Ohio St.2d 21, 75 Ohio Ops. 2d 12, 345 N.E.2d 608, 610 (Ohio 1976); Matter of Qq., 78 A.D.2d 741, 432 N.Y.S.2d 649, 651 (N.Y.App.Div. 1980); Matter of Adoption of Maynor, 38 N.C.App.724, 248 S.E.2d 875, 877 (N.C.App. 1978); _In re_ Adoption of C.D.M., 39 P.3d 802, 808 (Okla. 2001); Re Adoption of McCray, 460 Pa.210, 331 A.2d 652, 655 (Pa. 1975); Elliott v. Maddox, 510 S.W.2d 105, 107–08 (Tex.Civ.App. 1974) (incarcerated father had not abandoned his child); Re Adoption of Jameson, 20 Utah 2d 53, 432 P.2d 881, 882 (Utah 1967) (imprisonment did not amount to desertion).

[1038]_See, e.g._, Interest of S.M., 169 Ga.App. 364, 312 S.E.2d 829, 831 (Ga.App. 1983) (mother's rights should not have been terminated despite her history of drug abuse); Interest of H.L.T., 164 Ga.App. 517, 298 S.E.2d 33, 35 (Ga.App. 1982); Matter of Welfare of Udstuen, 349 N.W.2d 300, 303–04 (Minn.App. 1984); In re L.H., 336 Mont. 405, 154 P.3d 622, 625–27 (Mont. 2007) (finding factors making parent unfit, including incarceration among others, "not likely to change within a reasonable time"); State v. Grady, 231 Or.App. 65, 371 P.2d 68, 69–70 (Or.App. 1962); _In re_ Sego, 82 Wash.2d 736, 513 P.2d 831, 833–34 (Wash. 1973); _In re_ FM, 163 P.3d 844, 849 & n.4 (Wyo. 2007). _But see_ In the Interest of S.F., 32 S.W.3d 318, 322 (Tex. App. 2000) (state "need only show incarceration was part of a course of conduct endangering the child"; course of conduct can include events before the child's birth).

[1039]_See, e.g._, People v. Ray, 88 Ill.App.3d 1010, 44 Ill.Dec. 182, 411 N.E.2d 88, 91–92 (1980) (parental rights terminated of parent who had fatally physically abused another child), _appeal dismissed_, 452 U.S. 956 (1981); J. v. M., 157 N.J.Super. 478, 385 A.2d 240, 247–48 (App.Div. 1978) (rights terminated of parents convicted of manslaughter and child abuse of other children). All states permit termination based on child abuse or other crimes committed against children. _See, e.g._, N.Y. Soc.Serv. Law § 384-b(8). In fact, the federal Adoption and Safe Families Act (ASFA) now requires states to provide for termination based on crimes involving

children. 42 U.S.C. § 671(a)(15)(D). _But see In re_ Christina P., 175 Cal.App.3d 115, 220 Cal.Rptr. 525, 535 (Cal.App. 1985) (conviction for escape and for lewd and lascivious acts with a minor did not show unfitness without "[a]mplification of the facts").

[1040]_See, e.g., In re_ Brannon, 340 So.2d 654, 655–56 (La.App. 1976); Matter of Gregory B., 74 N.Y.2d 77, 89–91, 542 N.E.2d 1052, 1058–59 (N.Y. 1989); _In re_ Hederson, 30 Ohio App.3d 187, 507 N.E.2d 418, 420–21 (Ohio App. 1986) (life sentence with parole eligibility in 14 years supported termination of parent's rights); Stursa v. Kyle, 99 Or.App. 236, 782 P.2d 158, 159–60 (Or.App. 1989) (upholding statute permitting adoption without consent of a parent incarcerated for more than three years); Hamby v. Hamby, 264 S.C. 614, 216 S.E.2d 536, 538 (S.C. 1975) (repeated crimes resulting in years of imprisonment supported a finding of abandonment); Matter of Adoption of J.L.P., 774 P.2d 624, 630 (Wyo. 1989) ("unfitness might be deduced from an extended prison term"). _But see_ Harden v. Thomas, 329 So.2d 389, 391 (Fla.App. 1976) (life imprisonment "does not, as a matter of law, constitute abandonment"); Petition of Boston Children's Service Assn., 20 Mass.App. 566, 481 N.E.2d 516, 521 (Mass.App. 1985), _review denied_, 396 Mass. 1102, 484 N.E.2d 102 (Mass. 1985) (mother serving life sentence and ineligible for parole for 15 years was not shown to be unfit).

[1041]These statutes vary and you will need to learn the provisions of your own state. At present, 25 states' statutes address the length of incarceration as a factor in parental termination decisions. Some of them are stated in general terms. _See, e.g._, Alaska Statutes § 47.10.080, 47.10.086 (it is a ground for termination that the parent is scheduled to serve a period of incarceration during the child's minority that is "significant, considering the child's age and need for adult care and supervision"); _see also_ Ariz. Rev. Stat. § 8-533 (such length that the child will be deprived of a normal home for a period of years); Ark. Code. Annot. § 9-27-341; 13 Del. Code Annot. § 1103; 5 Fla. Annot. Stat. § 39.806; Idaho Code § 16-2005 (incarceration without chance of parole); Annot. L. Mass. § 26; Miss. Code § 93-15-103; 12 Miss. Annot. Stat. § 211.447; XII N.H. Rev.Stat. Annot. § 169-C.3; N.M. Annot. Stat. § 32A-4-28 (incarceration, which is unlikely to change in the future); R.I.Gen.L. § 419B.504; S.D.Codified L. Annot. § 26-8A-21.1.

Other statutes are stated in terms of particular time periods. _See, e.g._, Colo. Rev. Stat. § 19-3-604 (incarceration such that the parent would not be eligible for release for six years or more after the court makes a finding of dependency (three years if the child is less than six years old); Ill. Comp. Stat. § 750.1.D (incarceration will prevent discharging parental responsibilities for more than two years after the parental termination proceeding); VI Iowa Annot. Stat. § 232.116 (unlikely to be released within five years); LI K.R.S. § 600.020; 10 La. Children's Code Art. 1015, 1036; Mich. Comp.L. § 712 A.19b (child deprived of normal home for more than two years); Mont. Code. Annot. § 41-3-609; 21 Ohio Rev. Code Annot. § 2151.414 (unable to care for child for at least 18 months after filing of motion or dispositional hearing); Tenn.Code Annot. §§ 36-1-102, 36-1-113; 5 Tex.Stat.Ann. § 161.001; Utah Code Annot. § 78-3a-408 (child deprived of normal home for more than one year). This information was compiled by Prof. Philip M. Genty in unpublished materials.

failure to support the child, amounts to, or helps establish, abandonment or desertion of the child.[1042]

In practice, the rules concerning prisoners' parental rights are seldom crystal clear, and courts exercise a great deal of discretion. They often look at the overall conduct of an imprisoned parent toward the child in determining whether to terminate parental rights. Therefore, if you want to retain your rights, you should make every practical effort to maintain a relationship with your child by letters, telephone calls, and visits, to participate in decisions about the child's life, to help plan for the child's future, and to provide some financial support, however small, if you can.[1043] If you believe you are the father of a child, but have not been married to the mother, and are not listed on the birth certificate, you should immediately seek to establish that you are the father if you wish to retain paternal rights.[1044] If you don't do this, and later someone seeks to adopt that child, it may be very difficult, if not impossible, to establish that you are the father and prevent the adoption from taking place.

State child care agencies are generally required to provide reasonable efforts to assist in maintaining and strengthening parent–child relationships or parenting skills,[1045]

[1042]*In re* Adoption of Baby Boy, 106 Ariz. 195, 472 P.2d 64, 70 (Ariz. 1970) (child was "dependent" and could be adopted by relatives where the natural mother was in prison and the father was dead); Matter of Adoption of Titsworth, 11 Ark.App. 197, 669 S.W.2d 8, 10–11 (Ark.App. 1984); *In re* Welfare of Children of R.W., 678 N.W.2d 49, 56 (Minn. 2004) (abandonment found where prisoner failed to maintain any direct contact with the children, failed to inquire about their welfare after learning they had been placed in foster care, relied on the children's mother to assume sole responsibility for having the children returned to her, failed to respond legal action); Interest of H.M., 770 S.W.2d 442, 444–45 (Mo.App. 1989); Interest of F.H., 283 N.W.2d 202, 212–14 (N.D. 1979) (abandonment found based on parent's "confinement coupled with other factors"); Adoption of T.M., 389 Pa.Super. 303, 566 A.2d 1256, 1257–58 (Pa.Super. 1989); Dep't of Social Services v. Henry, 296 S.C. 507, 374 S.E.2d 298, 299–300 (S.C. 1988); *In re* Adoption of Dobbs, 12 Wash.App. 676, 531 P.2d 303, 305–06 (Wash.App. 1975); *see also* Keeney v. Prince George's County Dep't of Social Services, 43 Md.App. 688, 406 A.2d 955 (Md.Spec.App. 1979) (statute presuming that a parent's rights should be terminated if a child has been in foster care for two years upheld as applied to an imprisoned parent).

[1043]For cases in which such factors influenced the court to rule in the prisoner-parent's favor, *see In re* T.M.R., 116 Cal.Rptr. 292, 41 Cal.App.3d 694, 698–99 (1974) (finding no abandonment where incarcerated mother wrote to her children twice a month, even though her children were too young to read); Petition of Boston Children's Service Assn., 20 Mass.App. 566, 481 N.E.2d 516, 520 (Mass.App. 1985) (incarcerated mother "made every effort to maintain contact with the children"), *review denied*, 396 Mass. 1102, 484 N.E.2d 102 (Mass. 1985); *In re* Parental Rights to Q.L.R., 118 Nev. 602, 54 P.3d 56, 58–59 (Nev. 2002) (noting parent's efforts to provide some financial support and to keep in contact with child); *In re* Yocum, 158 N.C.App. 198, 207–08, 580 S.E.2d 399, 405 (2003) (citing father's efforts to maintain relationship in light of his limited income), *aff'd*, 357 N.C. 568, 597 S.E.2d 674 (N.C. 2003); *In re* K.L.J., 607 S.E.2d 55, 2005 WL 89109, *7 (N.C. App. 2005) (lower court termination decision reversed; father had numerous prison visits with child, attended parenting classes, and sought potential guardians for the child while he was in prison); *In re* Adoption of M.J.H., 348 Pa.Super. 65, 501 A.2d 648, 653–54 (Pa.Super. 1985) (emphasizing parent's "consistent efforts . . . 'to take and maintain a place of importance in the child's life'" and to take some responsibility for parenthood), *appeal denied*, 522 A.2d 1105 (Pa.), *appeal dismissed*, 484 U.S. 804 (1987); *see also* In Interest of Sanders, 77 Ill. App.3d 78, 32 Ill.Dec. 847, 395 N.E.2d 1228, 1233 (Ill.App. 1979)

(imprisoned father held not to have abandoned children because he had cared for them while out of prison).

For cases in which the prisoner's failure to maintain a relationship with the child supported termination of parental rights, *see* Matter of Adoption of Titsworth, 11 Ark.App. 197, 669 S.W.2d 8, 10–11 (Ark.App. 1984) (adoption should be permitted over mother's objection in part because the mother had not communicated with the child or tried to support him); Petition of R.H.N., 710 P.2d 482, 486–87 (Colo. 1985) (failure to provide any financial support supported termination of rights); Turner v. Adoption of Turner, 352 So.2d 957, 959–60 (Fla.App. 1977) (father deemed to have abandoned his child by failing to try to communicate with her); *In re* Daniel C., 480 A.2d 766, 767–69 (Me. 1984) (father's rights were properly terminated at request of Department of Human Services where during 10 years all he had done for the child was give him a toy truck at age three); *In re* Caldwell, 228 Mich. App. 116, 121, 576 N.W.2d 724, 727–28 (1998) (failure to communicate with child except infrequently supported termination), *appeal denied*, 457 Mich. 866, 581 N.W.2d 732 (Mich. 1998) (unpublished); *In re* T.D.P., 164 N.C. App. 287, 595 S.E.2d 735 (2004) (holding that, although earning meager wages in the prison kitchen, the respondent nevertheless "had an ability to pay some portion of the costs of [his child's] foster care[,]" and failure to do so constituted "sufficient grounds . . . for termination of [his] parental rights under N.C. Gen.Stat. § 7B-1111(a)(3)"); *In re* D.J.S., 737 A.2d 283, 286 (Pa. Super. 1999) (citing father's failure to maintain "proactive" relationship with child supported termination); In the Interest of A.P., 692 A.2d 240, 245 (Pa. Super. 1997) (parental rights terminated where father made limited efforts to keep in touch with child); *In re* Adoption of McCray, 460 Pa.210, 331 A.2d 652, 655 (1975) (approving adoption over the objection of an imprisoned parent who did not show any interest in the child until an adoption petition was filed); *see also* Matter of Gregory B., 74 N.Y.2d 77, 89–91, 542 N.E.2d 1052, 1058–59 (N.Y. 1989) (holding termination appropriate for prisoners who could offer no plan for the children other than indefinite foster care until their release from prison).

[1044]For example, Michigan allows a parent to file a complaint under the Paternity Act, Mich. Compiled Law § 722.711, to establish his paternity of the minor child. *See* Afshar v. Zamarron, 209 Mich.App. 86, 89–90, 530 N.W.2d 490 (1995).

[1045]*See, e.g.*, Matter of Juvenile Action No. S-624, 126 Ariz. 488, 616 P.2d 948, 950 (Ariz.App. 1980) (state "should do everything in their power to keep the family together and not destroy it"); People in Interest of M.C.C., 641 P.2d 306, 308–09 (Colo.App. 1982); *In re* Daniel C., 480 A.2d 766, 769–71 (Me. 1984) (Dep't of Human Services must make "reunification efforts," but these need not be proven in a termination proceeding); *In re* M.A.E., 297 Mont. 434, 991 P.2d 972, 980 (Mont. 1999) (terminating rights after agency "made reasonable efforts in formulating treatment plans" that might have led to mother's rehabilitation and improved

and you should try to take advantage of such services. However, such requirements for reunification services and plans do not always apply fully in cases involving prisoners.[1046] Where such plans are utilized, the parent's non-cooperation, or a lack of success in fulfilling the plan, may be weighed in a subsequent proceeding to terminate parental rights.[1047]

Prison counselling or social services personnel may also be able to assist you in trying to maintain a relationship with your child (and even if they don't help you, they may at least make a record of your efforts and requests).

It is important to make these efforts even if they are unsuccessful, since a court may some day look back on your behavior in determining whether you are fit to keep your parental rights. What you must not do is engage in threats or misconduct against persons who you believe are obstructing your efforts or failing to cooperate. Such behavior will only hurt your chances of keeping your parental rights.

Proceedings to terminate parental rights must be conducted in accordance with due process.[1048] You are entitled to a hearing, but state law varies as to whether an incarcerated person has the right to be physically present at the hearing,[1049] whether other means of participation are acceptable,[1050] and whether the "hearing" can be limited to a

---

parenting but were thwarted by her own misconduct); Matter of Gregory B., 74 N.Y.2d 77, 542 N.E.2d 1052, 1056 (N.Y. 1989) (citing N.Y. Soc. Serv. Law § 348-b[7]) (agency was required to make "diligent efforts" including counseling and arranging visitation); Matter of Harris, 87 N.C.App. 179, 360 S.E.2d 485, 488–89 (N.C.App. 1987) (Department of Social Services was required to make "diligent efforts to encourage respondents to strengthen their parental relationships or undertake planning for their children's future"); In re N.H., 632 N.W.2d 451, 457 (N.D. 2001) (statute required reasonable efforts to prevent removal of a child or to reunify the child with the child's family, and reasonable efforts to preserve and reunify families); State in Interest of C.Y. v. Yates, 765 P.2d 251, 255 (Utah App. 1988) ("treatment plan" required); Cain v. Commonwealth of Va., 12 Va.App. 42, 402 S.E.2d 682, 684 (Va. App. 1991) (statute requires "reasonable and appropriate efforts of social, medical, mental health or other rehabilitative agencies to remedy the conditions leading to foster care placement"); Welfare of Ferguson, 98 Wash.2d 589, 656 P.2d 503 (Wash. 1983) (citing RCW § 13.34 (statute requires that parent be offered "all necessary services, reasonably available, capable of correcting the parental deficiencies within the foreseeable future")); In re HC, 983 P.2d 1205, 1210-11 (Wyo. 1999) (reversing termination of parental rights where Department of Family Services provided inadequate evidence of its rehabilitative efforts).

[1046]See, e.g., Matter of Welfare of Udstuen, 349 N.W.2d 300, 303–04 (Minn.App. 1984) (lack of a "case plan" was excusable because the father had been convicted and imprisoned for battering his child); In re Guardianship of B. Children, 168 A.D.2d 312, 562 N.Y.S.2d 643, 644 (N.Y.App.Div. 1990) (Department of Social Services need not attempt to strengthen the parent–child relationship after the parent murdered one of the children); In re Hederson, 30 Ohio App.3d 187, 189, 507 N.E.2d 418, 420 (Ohio App. 1986) ("unification plan" that made no provision for contact with the imprisoned father was adequate; child had been placed with relatives); Interest of Wagner, 209 Neb. 33, 305 N.W.2d 900, 902 (Neb. 1981) (after a previous court finding of neglect, a rehabilitation plan is no longer required); People in Interest of T.H., 396 N.W.2d 145, 151 (S.D. 1986) (program to rehabilitate parent not required in every case of incarcerated parent).

[1047]Interest of R.H.S., 737 S.W.2d 227, 234–36 (Mo.App. 1987) (parental rights could be terminated even though the father had made "some progress" in complying with a social service plan); In re Parental Rights as to N.D.O., 121 Nev. 379, 115 P.3d 223, 224, 227 (Nev. 2005) (weighing lack of progress under agency case plan); In re B.J.K., 701 N.W.2d 924, 927–28 (N.D. 2005); State in Interest of C.Y. v. Yates, 765 P.2d 251, 255 (Utah Ct.App. 1988) (parental rights terminated where there was no significant improvement in parental skills).

[1048]This right extends to fathers who have not married the children's mother if they have come forward to participate in the rearing of their children. Stanley v. Illinois, 405 U.S. 645, 657–59, 92 S. Ct. 1208 (1972) (unmarried father could not be presumed unfit and was entitled to notice and a hearing in child custody proceedings). But see Lehr v. Robertson, 463 U.S. 248, 261, 103 S. Ct. 2985 (1983) (unmarried father who had never had substantial relationship with child and left the mother with sole responsibility did not have a right to notice of adoption proceedings); see also Quilloin v. Walcott, 434 U.S. 246, 254–55, 98 S. Ct. 549 (1978) (adoption could not be blocked by an unmarried father who had not legitimated the child, had not supported it regularly, and had never lived with it). If the child's mother was married to someone else when the child was born and the husband wishes to raise the child as his own, a state law that makes the husband the presumptive father of the child as a matter of law does not violate the biological father's constitutional rights. Michael H. v. Gerald D., 491 U.S. 110, 127–30, 109 S. Ct. 2333 (1989).

[1049]Compare In re S.R.B. 270 Ga.App. 466, 467, 606 S.E.2d 655 (Ga. App. 2004) ("We know of no constitutional entitlement mandating the father's right to appear personally at the termination hearing." (citation omitted)); In Interest of S.K.S., 648 S.W.2d 402, 405 (Tex.App. 1983) (a prisoner had no right to be produced for a termination proceeding where he had been permitted to appear through counsel and by deposition) with Cal. Penal Code § 2525 (no termination hearing can be conducted without the prisoner present). Court appearances are discussed generally in Ch. 10, § Q.

Courts have generally held that a prisoner confined in a different state from the termination proceeding has no right to be produced for the hearing. See In re Gary U., 136 Cal.App.3d 494, 186 Cal.Rptr. 316 (1982); In re Juvenile Appeal, 187 Conn. 431, 446 A.2d 808, 812–13 (1982); In re J.L.D., 14 Kan.App.2d 487, 794 P.2d 319, 321–22 (1980); In re Randy Scott B., 511 A.2d 450, 452–54 (Me. 1986); In Interest of F.H., 283 N.W.2d 202, 208–10 (N.D. 1979); State ex rel. Juvenile Dep't of Lane County v. Stevens, 100 Or.App. 481, 786 P.2d 1296, 1299–1300 (1999), rev. denied, 310 Or. 71, 792 P.2d 104 (1990); In Interest of Darrow, 32 Wash.App. 803, 649 P.2d 858, 860–61 (1982). In most of these cases, the court stresses that the imprisoned parent was represented by counsel and had an opportunity to testify in writing or by telephone.

[1050]See In re Adoption/Guardianship No. 6Z980001 in Dist. Court for Montgomery County, 131 Md.App. 187, 748 A.2d 1020, 1023 (Md.App. 2000) (telephone appearance was not required where prisoner was represented by counsel); In Interest of F. H.,

summary judgment proceeding conducted on paper.[1051] The federal Constitution does not guarantee a right to counsel at all termination proceedings; the question must be decided case by case.[1052] However, most states now provide for the appointment of counsel for indigents in all termination proceedings.[1053] If the state provides an appeal from termination decisions, indigents must be allowed to proceed without payment of fees they cannot afford.[1054]

Parents are responsible for supporting their children financially, and imprisonment does not automatically end that obligation.[1055] If you do have income or assets outside

prison, child support orders can be enforced against them while you are incarcerated,[1056] and in some states these orders may be enforceable against prison wages.[1057] If you have an order for child support that you can't pay because you are in prison, the debt will just keep piling up unless you do something about it, and the authorities may try to enforce it after you are out of prison and earning money. If you don't pay, you can be prosecuted and possibly imprisoned.[1058] To prevent this from happening, in some states you can get the court to suspend or reduce child support obligations based on your incarceration and loss of income. However, state courts are sharply divided on this question.[1059] Some have a "no justification" rule (holding incarceration does not justify eliminating or reducing child support obligations),[1060] some have a "complete justification" rule (holding incarceration

---

283 N.W.2d 202, 209–10 (N.D.1979) (prisoner's right to appear satisfied by appearance through counsel or by deposition).

[1051]Some courts have held that the Constitution forbids resolving parental termination issues purely on paper submissions. *See* Matter of Christina T., 590 P.2d 189, 192 (Okla. 1979) (holding due process requires a hearing; "Juvenile actions are not, and were never intended to be, the sort of proceeding capable of resolution upon a flurry of pleadings."); *accord, In re* Mark K., 159 Cal.App.3d 94, 205 Cal.Rptr. 393, 396–98 (Cal.App. 1984). Other courts have simply asked whether the state's summary judgment rules are intended to apply to termination proceedings. *See* People in Interest of A.E., 914 P.2d 534, 537–39 (Colo.App. 1996) (reviewing cases). In *People in Interest of A.E.*, the court held that the state summary judgment rules were applicable to termination cases, but said they will rarely be appropriate because the "clear and convincing evidence" standard is required in termination cases and will seldom be met when the facts are contested. 914 P.2d at 538–39; *see* Matter of Adoption of J.L.P., 774 P.2d 624, 628–32 (Wyo. 1989) (summary judgment is "generally" not compatible with due process, but this parent was so clearly unfit that an evidentiary hearing was not required); *see also* People v. Ray, 88 Ill.App. 1010, 411 N.E.2d 88, 92 (1980) (summary judgment granted), *appeal dismissed*, 452 U.S. 956 (1981). Summary judgment (at least as it operates in federal courts) is discussed in Ch. 10, § L.

[1052]Lassiter v. Dep't of Social Services, 452 U.S. 18, 31–32, 101 S. Ct. 2153 (1981); *accord, In re* Christina P., 175 Cal.App.3d 115, 220 Cal.Rptr. 525, 531–32 (Cal.App. 1985) (under *Lassiter*, counsel was required in this case); Matter of Carolyn S.S., 498 A.2d 1095, 1097–98 (Del. 1984).

[1053]Lassiter v. Dep't of Social Services, 452 U.S. at 34 (noting that 33 states had such statutes); Matter of Carolyn S.S., 498 A.2d at 1098 (noting that more states passed statutes after *Lassiter*). Some courts have held that their state constitutions require counsel in all termination cases. *See* Matter of K.L.J., 813 P.2d 276 (Alaska 1991); M.E.K. v. R.L.K., 921 So.2d 787, 789–91 (Fla.App. 2006) (holding state constitution requires counsel); Matter of Adoption of K.A.S., 499 N.W.2d 558, 563–67 (N.D. 1993) (interpreting state statute and constitution as requiring appointment of counsel). *But see* Matter of A.B., 234 Mont. 344, 780 P.2d 622, 625 (Mont. 1989) (due process requires counsel only prior to permanent custody hearings, not during initial stages); Casper v. Huber, 456 P.2d 436 (Nev. 1969) (no right to counsel on appeal in termination proceeding where the court found the appeal frivolous).

[1054]M.L.B. v. S.L.J. 519 U.S. 102, 119–20, 117 S. Ct. 555 (U.S. 1996) (holding indigent parent who could not afford $2353 transcript fee required to appeal must be allowed to appeal anyway).

[1055]*In re* Adoption of ADA, 132 P.3d 196, 202 (Wyo. 2006) ("even when a parent is incarcerated, he must pay child support if he has the means to do so").

[1056]Avery v. Avery, 864 So.2d 1054, 1057 (Miss.App. 2004) (upholding child support of $225 a month against prisoner who had assets that could be used to pay); Division of Child Support Enforcement ex rel. Harper v. Barrows, 570 A.2d 1180, 1183–84 (Del.Super. 1990) and cases cited; Proctor v. Proctor, 773 P.2d 1389, 1391 (Utah App. 1989).

[1057]Smith v. State, Dep't of Revenue, Child Support Enforcement Div., 790 P.2d 1352 (Alaska 1990).

[1058]*See* Little v. Streater, 452 U.S. 1, 10, 101 S. Ct. 2202 (1981); Kennedy v. Wood, 439 N.E.2d 1367, 1370 (Ind. 1982).

[1059]For discussion of the different approaches, *see* Yerkes v. Yerkes, 573 Pa. 294, 299–305, 824 A.2d 1169 (Pa. 2003).

[1060]*Yerkes v. Yerkes* adopts this approach for Pennsylvania 573 Pa. at 306–08. *Yerkes* also (573 Pa. at 299 n.3) lists additional states following this approach including Arizona, *see* State ex rel. Dep't of Econ. Sec. v. Ayala, 185 Ariz. 314, 916 P.2d 504, 508 (Ct.App.1996); Arkansas, *see* Reid v. Reid, 57 Ark.App. 289, 944 S.W.2d 559, 562 (1997); Connecticut, *see* Shipman v. Roberts, No. FA000630559, 2001 WL 761030, *6 (Conn.Super.Ct. June 7, 2001); Delaware, *see* Division of Child Support Enf. ex rel. Harper v. Barrows, 570 A.2d 1180, 1183 (Del.1990); Indiana, *see* Davis v. Vance, 574 N.E.2d 330, 331 (Ind.Ct.App.1991); Kansas, *see In re* Marriage of Thurmond, 265 Kan. 715, 962 P.2d 1064, 1073 (1998); Kentucky, *see* Commonwealth ex rel. Marshall v. Marshall, 15 S.W.3d 396, 401 (Ky.Ct.App.2000); Louisiana, *see* State v. Nelson, 587 So.2d 176, 178 (La.Ct.App.1991); Montana, *see* Mooney v. Brennan, 257 Mont. 197, 848 P.2d 1020, 1023–24 (1993); New Hampshire, *see* Noddin v. Noddin, 123 N.H. 73, 455 A.2d 1051, 1053–54 (1983); New York, *see* Matter of Knights, 71 N.Y.2d 865, 527 N.Y.S.2d 748, 522 N.E.2d 1045, 1046 (1988); North Dakota, *see* Koch v. Williams, 456 N.W.2d 299, 302 (N.D.1990); Ohio, *see* Richardson v. Ballard, 113 Ohio App.3d 552, 681 N.E.2d 507, 508 (1996); Oklahoma, *see* State ex rel. Jones v. Baggett, 990 P.2d 235, 245–46 (Okla.1999); and Utah, *see* Proctor v. Proctor, 773 P.2d 1389, 1391 (Utah App.1989); *see also* State ex rel. Longnecker v. Longnecker, 11 Neb.App. 773, 777, 660 N.W.2d 544 (2003). In Pennsylvania, at least one court has held that a later-enacted rule allows courts, despite the *Yerkes* decision, to consider prisoners' income while in prison as a basis for modification of child support obligations. Nash v. Herbster, 932 A.2d 183, 187–88 (Pa.Super. 2007).

does justify relief from child support),[1061] others have a "one factor" rule which requires incarceration to be considered along with other circumstances,[1062] and there are other variations.[1063] This is a subject of ongoing debate and you should always be sure you have your state's current law.

We cannot state too strongly that you must deal with this issue as quickly as possible. Depending on your state's law, doing so may save you from having an overwhelming debt when you are released (even in states that allow reductions for incarcerated persons, the courts may not be able to give relief retroactively against payments already due.[1064])

[1061]Yerkes v. Yerkes, 573 Pa. at 300 n.4, lists states following this approach including California, *see In re* Marriage of Smith, 90 Cal.App.4th 74, 108 Cal.Rptr.2d 537, 543–45 (2001); Idaho, *see* Nab v. Nab, 114 Idaho 512, 757 P.2d 1231, 1238 (1988); Maryland, *see* Wills v. Jones, 340 Md. 480, 667 A.2d 331, 339 (1995); Michigan, *see* Pierce v. Pierce, 162 Mich.App. 367, 412 N.W.2d 291, 292–93 (1987); Minnesota, *see* Franzen v. Borders, 521 N.W.2d 626, 629–30 (Minn.Ct.App.1994); Oregon, *see In re* Marriage of Willis & Willis, 314 Or. 566, 840 P.2d 697, 699 (1992); and Washington, *see In re* the Marriage of Blickenstaff & Blickenstaff, 71 Wash.App. 489, 859 P.2d 646, 650–51 (1993).

[1062]Yerkes v. Yerkes, 573 Pa. at 300 n.5, lists states following this approach including Alabama, *see* Alred v. Alred, 678 So.2d 1144, 1146 (Ala.Civ. App.1996); Alaska, *see* Bendixen v. Bendixen, 962 P.2d 170, 173 (Alaska 1998); Colorado, *see In re* Marriage of Hamilton, 857 P.2d 542, 544 (Colo.Ct.App. 1993); Illinois, *see In re* Burbridge, 317 Ill.App.3d 190, 250 Ill.Dec. 510, 738 N.E.2d 979, 982 (2000); Iowa, *see In re* Marriage of Walters, 575 N.W.2d 739, 743 (Iowa 1998); Missouri, *see* Oberg v. Oberg, 869 S.W.2d 235, 238 (Mo.Ct.App. 1993); New Mexico, *see* Thomasson v. Johnson, 120 N.M. 512, 903 P.2d 254, 256–57 (Ct.App. 1995); Texas, *see* Hollifield v. Hollifield, 925 S.W.2d 153, 156 (Tex.App. 1996); and Wisconsin, *see* Parker v. Parker, 152 Wis.2d 1, 447 N.W.2d 64, 65–66 (App. 1989).

The factors taken into account include the reason the obligated parent entered prison, the length of incarceration, the financial circumstances, the potential for work release, the amount of the existing child support award, and the total amount of child support that will have accumulated upon the incarcerated parent's discharge." Yerkes v. Yerkes, *id.*; *see* Naranjo v. Naranjo, 63 Mass. App.Ct. 256, 258–59, 825 N.E.2d 551 (2005) (noting that state law would have automatically adjusted child support payments during incarceration).

[1063]Some courts have modified the "no justification" rule to reflect state law that child support obligations are to be adjusted to current income for all persons including prisoners. Adkins v. Adkins, 221 W.Va. 602, 656 S.E.2d 47, 52–54 (W.D.Va. 2007); Lambert v. Lambert, 861 N.E.2d 1176, 1181–82 (Ind. 2007); *see also* Gisi v. Gisi, 731 N.W.2d 223, 229–30 (S.D. 2007) (holding payments could be reduced to a level based on the minimum wage, but not further). Some courts have held that requests to modify child support during incarceration should be deferred until release from prison, and a realistic payment plan should be determined based on the facts at that time. Dep't of Revenue v. Jackson, 846 So.2d 486, 490–93 (Fla. 2003); Halliwell v. Halliwell, 326 N.J.Super. 442, 741 A.2d 638, 646 (App.Div. 1999),

[1064]*See* Mich. Compiled Law § 552.603(2); *see also* McLaughlin v. McLaughlin, 255 Mich.App. 475, 477, 660 N.W.2d 784 (2003)

If you let unpaid child support pile up, your non-payment may also be cited as a reason to terminate your parental rights.

The obligation to support children extends to unmarried fathers and their illegitimate children. Most states have a procedure by which you can acknowledge paternity of your illegitimate child and voluntarily accept your obligations. If you do not do this, you may be sued in a paternity action, which can result in an order requiring you to pay child support.[1065] Don't assume that the mother of the children will not bring suit. She may have no choice. Typically, mothers receiving public assistance (welfare) are required by law to cooperate in proceedings to establish paternity; the state then prosecutes the case and receives the child support payments. Federal law requires states to establish programs of this type.[1066]

If you are sued in a paternity action, and you claim that you are not really the child's father, you must contest the case when it is brought, or you may be subjected to a child support order. You cannot decide after you are out of prison to claim that you are not really the child's father. Once it has been decided that you are the father of the child, the matter is *res judicata*, and you will probably not be permitted to dispute paternity at a later point if the state tries to enforce a support order against you.[1067]

If you dispute that you are the father of the child, you are entitled to due process rights. The Supreme Court long ago noted that the blood tests then available could often determine with certainty that a paternity defendant is not the father of a particular child, and held that due process requires providing those tests to indigent paternity defendants.[1068] (Since that decision, determination of paternity

---

("defendant's child-support order is not subject to retroactive modification for the time that he was incarcerated."); County of Santa Clara v. Wilson, 111 Cal.App.4th 1324, 1327 (2003) (court has no power to retroactively modify past child support obligations or eliminate accrued interest on unpaid arrearages); Dep't of Revenue v. Jackson, 846 So.2d 486, 490 (Fla. 2003).

[1065]This can have serious consequences. In one case, the prisoner was subject to a support order of $100 a month, and owed $6300 by the time his case got to the state supreme court. Allen v. Division of Child Support Enforcement, 575 A.2d 1176, 1177–78 (Del. Super. 1990).

[1066]*See* Little v. Streater, 452 U.S. 1, 9 n.6, 101 S. Ct. 2202 (1981) (citing 42 U.S.C. § 654(4)).

[1067]*Ex parte* W.J., 622 So.2d 358, 362–63 (Ala. 1993); Gardner v. Gardner, 371 Pa.Super. 256, 538 A.2d 4, 8 (Pa.Super. 1988), *appeal denied*, 555 A.2d 115 (Pa. 1989).

[1068]Little v. Streater, 452 U.S. at 16. In *Little*, the Court emphasized that in the case before it, the state put the burden of proof on the paternity defendant. However, many states have held that due process requires provision of blood tests in state-prosecuted paternity proceedings regardless of the burden of proof. *See, e.g.*, Peterson v. Moffitt ex rel. Dep't of Human Resources, 253 Ga. 253, 319 S.E.2d 449, 451 (Ga. 1984); People v. Askew, 74 Ill.App.3d 743, 30 Ill.Dec. 777, 393 N.E.2d 1124, 1127 (Ill.App. 1979) (criminal case); Kennedy v. Wood, 439 N.E.2d 1367, 1369–73 (Ind.App. 1982); Shaw v. Seward, 689 S.W.2d 37, 39–41 (Ky.App. 1985);

has become even more reliable through DNA analysis.) Some states provide for the right to a jury trial in paternity cases.[1069] Numerous courts have held that indigents must be provided appointed counsel to defend state-prosecuted paternity proceedings,[1070] but others have held that the right to counsel in paternity cases is to be decided on a case by case basis.[1071] Paternity can be proven by a preponderance of the evidence, unlike termination of parental rights, which as noted above requires clear and convincing evidence.[1072]

Paternity and support proceedings raise the same issues of appearance in court versus other means of presenting a defense that divorce and parental rights proceedings do.[1073]

Anderson v. Jacobs, 68 Ohio St.2d 67, 22 Ohio Ops.3d 268, 428 N.E.2d 419, 425 (Ohio 1981); State ex rel. Fox v. Hicks, 69 Or.App. 348, 686 P.2d 431, 436 (Or.App. 1984); Johnson v. Brinker, 326 Pa.Super. 464, 474 A.2d 333, 336–37 (Pa.Super. 1984); *see also* Boone v. State, Dep't of Human Resources, 250 Ga. 379, 297 S.E.2d 727, 728–29 (Ga. 1982) (non-indigent defendant could be compelled to submit to blood tests but not to pay for them unless paternity was proved). *But see Ex parte* Calloway, 456 So.2d 306, 308 (Ala.Civ.App. 1983) (since one inconclusive blood test had been performed, the refusal to pay for the series of seven blood tests referred to in *Little v. Streater* did not deny due process), *aff'd*, 456 So.2d 308 (Ala. 1984).

[1069]*Compare* Amendments to Florida Family Law Rules of Procedure, 723 So.2d 208, 211 (Fla. 1998) (acknowledging jury right in paternity proceedings); People ex rel. Raines v. Biggs, 135 Ill.App.3d 200, 90 Ill.Dec. 99, 481 N.E.2d 899, 902–03 (Ill.App. 1985); Re Paternity of J.S.C., 135 Wis.2d 280, 400 N.W.2d 48, 54 (Wis.App. 1986) (defendant had right to a jury trial), *review denied*, 407 N.W.2d 559 (Wis. 1987) *with* Banks v. Hopson, 275 Ga. 758, 760, 571 S.E.2d 730 (Ga. 2002) (noting statutory abolition of jury trial in paternity cases); Evans v. Wilson, 382 Md. 614, 648 n.5, 856 A.2d 679 (Md. 2004) (same); Smeido v. Jansons, 23 A.D.2d 796, 259 N.Y.S.2d 169, 170 (N.Y.App.Div. 1965); State ex rel. Goodner v. Speed, 96 Wash.2d 838, 640 P.2d 13 (Wash. 1982).

[1070]County of Mendocino v. Ted S., 217 Cal.App.3d 1202, 266 Cal.Rptr. 452, 454 (Cal.App. 1990); Lavertue v. Niman, 196 Conn. 403, 493 A.2d 213, 216–17 (Conn. 1985); Allen v. Division of Child Support Enforcement, 575 A.2d 1176, 1185 (Del. Super. 1990); Kennedy v. Wood, 439 N.E.2d 1367, 1369–73 (Ind.App. 1982); Kenner v. Watha, 115 Mich.App. 521, 323 N.W.2d 8, 10–11 (Mich. App. 1982); State ex rel. Cody v. Toner, 8 Ohio St.3d 22, 456 N.E.2d 813, 815 (Ohio 1983); Corra v. Coll, 305 Pa.Super. 179, 451 A.2d 480, 483 (Pa.Super. 1982); *see also* Gardner v. Gardner, 371 Pa. Super. 256, 538 A.2d 4, 9 (Pa.Super. 1988) (counsel required only where the father denies paternity), *appeal denied*, 555 A.2d 115 (Pa. 1989).

[1071]Nordgren v. Mitchell, 716 F.2d 1335, 1339 (10th Cir. 1983); Wake County ex rel. Carrington v. Townes, 306 N.C. 333, 293 S.E.2d 95, 99–100 (1982); State v. James, 38 Wash.App. 264, 686 P.2d 1097, 1100–02 (1984). A few have held that there is no right to counsel in paternity cases at all. State Dep't of Health and Welfare ex rel. State of Or. v. Conley, 132 Idaho 266, 971 P.2d 332, 270 (1999); State ex rel. Hamilton v. Snodgrass, 325 N.W.2d 740, 743 (Iowa 1982) (no right to counsel unless provided by statute); Franks v. Mercer, 401 So.2d 470, 472 (La.App. 1981); *see also* State ex rel. Adult & Family Services Civ. v. Stoutt, 57 Or.App. 303, 644 P.2d 1132, 1136–38 (1982) (counsel not required in this case; court does not reach question whether counsel is ever required), *petition denied*, 653 P.2d 999 (Or. 1982).

[1072]Rivera v. Minnich, 483 U.S. 574, 577–82, 107 S. Ct. 3001 (1987).

[1073]*See, e.g.,* Barnes v. Fucci, 563 So.2d 175, 176 (Fla. App. 4 Dist. 1990) (imprisoned mother entitled to appear for hearing on child support and custody); In the Interest of Z.L.T., 124 S.W.3d 163, 165 (Tex Sup. Ct. 2003) (requiring balancing of prisoner's interest in appearing against state's interest in not producing only if prisoner requests to appear and gives reasons).

CHAPTER 4

Procedural Due Process

The Due Process Clauses prohibit governments, including prison officials, from depriving you of "life, liberty, or property without due process of law."[1] There are two kinds of due process issues: procedural and substantive. Procedural due process means the procedures that the Constitution requires before government can deprive you of life, liberty, or property. Substantive due process "bars certain arbitrary, wrongful government actions 'regardless of the fairness of the procedures used to implement them.'"[2]

Substantive due process protections are limited. If an issue is governed by a more specifically relevant provision of the Constitution, such as the Cruel and Unusual Punishments Clause of the Eighth Amendment, substantive due process does not provide any greater protection.[3] Substantive due

process has been held to forbid conditions that constitute "punishment" of pretrial detainees,[4] to protect against forced psychotropic medication without justification[5] and more generally to protect the right to refuse unwanted medical treatment,[6] and to protect limited rights of privacy.[7] The Supreme Court has stated that action by executive branch officials may deny substantive due process if it "shocks the conscience."[8] What shocks the conscience depends on the situation.[9] Substantive due process challenges to legislation

---

[1] U.S. Const, Amends. V, XIV. The Fifth Amendment's Due Process Clause applies to federal officials; the Fourteenth Amendment applies to state and local officials.

[2] See Zinermon v. Burch, 494 U.S. 113, 125, 110 S. Ct. 975 (1990) (citation omitted); accord, County of Sacramento v. Lewis, 523 U.S. 833, 840, 118 S. Ct. 1708 (1998).

"Substantive due process" also sometimes refers to the protections of the First, Fourth, Sixth, and Eighth Amendments. That is because these Amendments initially applied only to the federal government. They now apply to the states because they are considered to be "incorporated" in the Fourteenth Amendment's Due Process Clause, which does apply to the states. See Duncan v. Louisiana, 391 U.S. 145, 147–48, 88 S. Ct. 1444 (1968); Duncan v. Poythress, 657 F.2d 691, 704 (5th Cir. 1981).

You don't need to worry about this theoretical point in writing your legal papers. We explain it so you won't be confused by discussions in some of the cases.

[3] County of Sacramento v. Lewis, 523 U.S. 833, 842–43, 118 S. Ct. 1708 (1998); Whitley v. Albers, 475 U.S. 312, 326–27, 106 S. Ct. 1078 (1986); see also Graham v. Connor, 490 U.S. 386, 395, 109 S. Ct. 1865 (1989) (holding Fourth Amendment rather than Due Process Clause governs claims of excessive force during arrest).

[4] See Bell v. Wolfish, 441 U.S. 520, 99 S. Ct. 1861 (1979); see also Ch. 6 for a discussion of pretrial detainees' rights.

[5] See Washington v. Harper, 494 U.S. 210, 221–22, 110 S. Ct. 1028 (1990). Psychotropic medications are discussed in Ch. 2, § 4.a.

[6] See White v. Napoleon, 897 F.2d 103, 111 (3d Cir. 1990) (holding that due process protects both a right to refuse treatment and a right to receive sufficient information to exercise the former right intelligently). The right to refuse treatment is discussed in Ch. 2, § 4.k.

[7] See Lawrence v. Texas, 539 U.S. 558, 564–579, 123 S. Ct. 2472 (2003) (finding substantive due process right of private choice in sexual matters); Poe v. Leonard, 282 F.3d 123, 136–39 (2d Cir. 2002) (finding substantive due process right to be protected from photography of one's naked body); Doe v. Delie, 257 F.3d 309, 316–17 (3d Cir. 2001) (finding due process right of privacy in medical information, especially about HIV status). Privacy issues are discussed in Ch. 3, § E; medical privacy is discussed in Ch. 2, § 4.j.

[8] County of Sacramento v. Lewis, 523 U.S. 833, 848–49, 118 S. Ct. 1708 (1998).

[9] The Court said that conduct amounting to deliberate indifference may shock the conscience where the officials realistically have time to deliberate; but "when unforeseen circumstances demand . . . instant judgment," intent to cause harm must be shown in order to shock the conscience. Sacramento v. Lewis, 523 U.S. at 852–53. That case involved a high-speed

do not require a showing of conduct that shocks the conscience.[10] Further, some courts take the approach that conduct that "shocks the conscience" need not be shown in cases about the substantive due process protections of privacy, refusal of medical treatment, etc.[11]

This chapter focuses primarily on procedural due process.[12] Questions of procedural due process involve "two steps: the first asks whether there exists a liberty or property interest which has been interfered with by the State . . .; the second examines whether the procedures attendant upon that deprivation were constitutionally sufficient. . . ."[13] That is, are prison officials taking liberty or property from you, and if so, are they using fair procedures to make that decision?

The following sections elaborate on these points. Keep in mind that they apply to the interpretation of the federal Constitution by federal courts. State courts may take a different approach in interpreting state constitutions' due process protections.[14] State constitutions may also protect a broader range of rights than the federal Constitution, and these may in turn be protected by state due process clauses.[15]

The Due Process Clauses protect persons from being "deprived" of life, liberty, or property without due process. The word "deprived" in due process cases generally has its commonsense meaning, with one major exception. Negligence—i.e., lack of ordinary care—does not constitute a "deprivation" of liberty or property.[16] However, if the deprivation of liberty or property is intentional, it is a deprivation for due process purposes, and it is no defense that officials were only negligent in denying you due process for that deprivation. Thus, if prison officials intentionally take away your good time (deprive you of liberty), but claim that they negligently failed to afford you the proper procedures, they can still be held liable for denying you due process.[17] Not every interference with a liberty interest is serious enough to constitute a deprivation.[18]

Actions that affect a large group of people equally are often not considered to deny due process even if they infringe upon liberty or property interests.[19] Thus, when a legislature changes temporary release standards and makes

---

police chase. (Police misconduct during arrest is governed by the Fourth Amendment. *Id.*, 523 U.S. at 842–45.)

[10]Dias v. City and County of Denver, 567 F.3d 1169, 1182 (10th Cir. 2009); County Concrete Corp. v. Town of Roxbury, 442 F.3d 159, 169 (3d Cir. 2006); Hawkins v. Freeman, 195 F.3d 732, 739 (4th Cir. 1999); *see* Sacramento v. Lewis, 523 U.S. at 846 (emphasizing that "shock the conscience" standard applies to executive action). Thus, in *Lawrence v. Texas*, which struck down a state statute on substantive due process grounds, the Supreme Court did not find that the statute shocked the conscience. 539 U.S. at 564–79.

[11]Cruz-Erazo v. Rivera-Montanez, 212 F.3d 617, 622 (1st Cir. 2000) (holding that conduct that "shocks the conscience" is necessary to a due process claim only if the plaintiffs cannot show that they have been deprived of a specific liberty or property interest). *But see* Leamer v. Fauver, 288 F.3d 532, 546–47 (3d Cir. 2002) (holding that the "shock the conscience" standard "typically" applies to challenges to executive action).

[12]Rights protected by substantive due process are mostly discussed in Chapters 2 and 3, as indicated in nn. 5–7, above. On a few subjects, we address substantive law as well as procedural requirements in this chapter, generally because we didn't find another good place to put the substantive material. That is the case with transfers, discussed in § H.4 of this chapter.

[13]Kentucky Dep't of Corrections v. Thompson, 490 U.S. 454, 460, 109 S. Ct. 1904 (1989).

[14]For example, under the California Constitution, "freedom from arbitrary adjudication is a substantive element of one's liberty," People v. Ramirez, 25 Cal.3d 260, 158 Cal.Rptr. 316, 599 P.2d 622, 627 (Cal. 1979), at least where there is a statutory benefit or interest at stake. Ryan v. California Interscholastic Federation-San Diego Section, 114 Cal.Rptr.2d 798, 94 Cal.App.4th 1048, 1071 (2001). In that state, therefore, due process is required whenever government takes "deprivatory action" against an individual, regardless of whether there is a liberty or property interest that federal law would recognize. *See* Toussaint v. McCarthy, 801 F.2d 1080, 1096 (9th Cir. 1986) (explaining California law).

[15]For example, the Alaska Constitution creates a right to rehabilitation, and due process therefore requires officials to provide procedural protections when they remove prisoners from rehabilitative programs. Ferguson v. Dep't of Corrections, 816 P.2d 134, 139–40 (Alaska 1991).

[16]Daniels v. Williams, 474 U.S. 327, 328, 106 S. Ct. 662 (1986); Davidson v. Cannon, 474 U.S. 344, 349, 106 S. Ct. 668 (1986).

[17]Daniels v. Williams, 474 U.S. at 333–34; Franklin v. Aycock, 795 F.2d 1253, 1261–62 (6th Cir. 1986); Sourbeer v. Robinson, 791 F.2d 1094, 1105 (3d Cir. 1986); *see* Maldonado Santiago v. Velasquez Garcia, 821 F.2d 822, 828 (1st Cir. 1987) (same rule applied to transfer); *see also* Sample v. Diecks, 885 F.2d 1099, 1114 (3d Cir. 1989) (if officials authorize a system to deprive persons of life, liberty, or property, it is irrelevant whether they intend that it violate due process); Williams v. Wilkinson, 122 F. Supp. 2d 894, 904 & n.10 (S.D.Ohio 2000) (intentionally disallowing plaintiff's witnesses supported a due process claim). *Contra*, Camardo v. Walker, 794 F. Supp. 65, 66–67 (D.R.I. 1992).

[18]*See, e.g.*, Sturm v. Clark, 835 F.2d 1009, 1013 (3d Cir. 1987) (though an attorney had a liberty interest in practicing law, prison visiting restrictions that made visiting her clients difficult did not deprive her of a liberty interest because they did not "significantly alter or extinguish" that right).

[19]Warren v. City of Athens, Ohio, 411 F.3d 697, 710 (6th Cir. 2005) ("Governmental determinations of a general nature that affect all equally do not give rise to a due process right to be heard. But, when a relatively small number of persons are affected on individual grounds, the right to a hearing is triggered. . . ." (citation omitted)); Foster v. Hughes, 979 F.2d 130, 132 (8th Cir. 1992) ("Persons are entitled to procedural due process, in the form of an individual opportunity to be heard, only when the government makes an individualized determination, not when the government commits a legislative act affecting all those similarly situated."); Stewart v. McGinnis, 800 F. Supp. 604, 614 (N.D.Ill. 1992); Sahagian v. Dickey, 646 F. Supp. 1502, 1510 (W.D.Wis. 1986); *see* O'Bannon v. Town Court Nursing Center, 447 U.S. 773, 799–801, 100 S. Ct. 2467 (1980) (Blackmun, J., concurring).

some of the prisoners already in the program ineligible, due process protections are not required, even though they would be required if a prisoner's "individualized record" was considered.[20] Restrictions that might require due process if imposed on an individual prisoner do not require due process when imposed on an entire prison or housing unit in a "lockdown" or other emergency security measure.[21]

A. What Liberty Means for Prisoners

In the 1995 decision in *Sandin v. Conner*,[22] the Supreme Court restricted the legal definition of "liberty" for prisoners. Before *Sandin*, courts had said that if statutes or regulations sufficiently restricted the discretion of prison officials, they created a "liberty interest" and prison officials had to provide fair procedures in order to take that interest away.[23] These were often referred to as "state-created liberty interests," though federal statutes and regulations could also create liberty interests.

Sandin disapproved of that kind of analysis, saying it discouraged states from codifying their rules and led to greater federal court intervention in day-to-day prison management.[24] The Court had previously held that "given a valid conviction, the criminal defendant has been constitutionally deprived of his liberty to the extent that the State may confine him and subject him to the rules of its prison system so long as the conditions of confinement do not otherwise violate the Constitution. . . . Confinement in any of the State's

institutions is within the normal limits or range of custody which the conviction has authorized the State to impose."[25]

For these reasons, *Sandin* said that prisoners should only be found to have liberty interests in three circumstances: (1) when the right at issue is independently protected by the Constitution, (2) when the challenged action causes the prisoner to spend more time in prison, or (3) when the action imposes "atypical and significant hardship on the inmate in relation to the ordinary incidents of prison life."[26]

1. Rights Independently Protected by the Constitution

Sandin says that some prison conditions "exceed[] the sentence in such an unexpected manner as to give rise to protection by the Due Process Clause of its own force."[27] That is, they are "so severe in kind or degree (or so removed from the original terms of confinement) that they amount to deprivations of liberty," regardless of the terms of state law.[28] For example, the Supreme Court has said that "involuntary commitment to a mental hospital is not within the range of conditions of confinement to which a prison sentence subjects an individual." Therefore, prisoners have a liberty interest arising from the Constitution in not being classified and treated as mentally ill, and the state has to provide due process protections before committing a prisoner to a mental hospital.[29] Similarly, prisoners have liberty interests based on the Constitution in avoiding the unwanted administration of antipsychotic drugs[30] and the unjustified censorship of letters,[31] and prisoners are entitled to due process protections in both instances.

2. Actions that Make the Prisoner Spend More Time in Prison

In *Sandin*, the Supreme Court reaffirmed its earlier holding that good time, which was conferred by state statute and could only be revoked on a finding that the prisoner had committed serious misconduct, was an interest of "real substance" protected by due process.[32] Courts since *Sandin* have continued to hold that deprivation of good time requires due process protections where the relevant statutes or regulations sufficiently limit prison officials' discretion in

---

[20]Jenkins v. Fauver, 108 N.J. 239, 528 A.2d 563, 569 (N.J. 1987). *But see* Tracy v. Salamack, 572 F.2d 393, 396–97 (2d Cir. 1978) (statutory change requiring Commissioner's written approval for temporary release but not changing eligibility standards was permissible, but each prisoner was entitled to an individual reevaluation before temporary release was revoked).

[21]Abdul-Wadood v. Duckworth, 860 F.2d 280, 285 (7th Cir. 1988); Rust v. Grammer, 858 F.2d 411, 413 (8th Cir. 1988); Hayward v. Procunier, 629 F.2d 599, 602 (9th Cir. 1980); Wrinkles v. Davis, 311 F. Supp. 2d 735, 739–40 (N.D.Ind. 2004) ("Institutional lockdowns, like disciplinary segregation, fall within the expected parameters of an inmate's sentence, and do not present the type of 'atypical' deprivation in which a state might conceivably create a liberty interest."); Alley v. Angelone, 962 F. Supp. 827, 833 (E.D.Va. 1997). *But see* Labatt v. Twomey, 513 F.2d 641, 646 (7th Cir. 1975) (prolonged continuation of lockdown may require due process protections); *see also* Ch. 2, § K, concerning lockdowns.

This does not mean that officials can do whatever they want without due process as long as it involves a group of inmates. In one case where prison officials put all Cuban "Marielito" prisoners into administrative segregation because they thought these prisoners presented special security risks, the court held that due process was required and that each inmate was entitled to an individualized decision. Perez v. Neubert, 611 F. Supp. 830, 839–40 (D.N.J. 1985).

[22]515 U.S. 472, 115 S. Ct. 2293 (1995).

[23]*See, e.g.,* Kentucky Dep't of Corrections v. Thompson, 490 U.S. 454, 462, 109 S. Ct. 1904 (1989).

[24]Sandin v. Conner, 515 U.S. at 482.

[25]Meachum v. Fano, 427 U.S. 215, 224–25, 96 S. Ct. 2532 (1976); *see Sandin*, 515 U.S. 478–79 (citing *Meachum* reasoning).

[26]*Sandin*, 515 U.S. at 484.

[27]*Sandin*, 515 U.S. at 484.

[28]*Sandin*, 515 U.S. at 497 (Breyer, J., dissenting).

[29]Vitek v. Jones, 445 U.S. 480, 491–94, 100 S. Ct. 1254 (1980).

[30]Washington v. Harper, 494 U.S. 210, 221–22, 110 S. Ct. 1028 (1990).

[31]Procunier v. Martinez, 416 U.S. 396, 417–19, 94 S. Ct. 1800 (1974).

[32]Sandin v. Conner, 515 U.S. 472, 477–78, 115 S. Ct. 2293 (1995) (citing Wolff v. McDonnell, 418 U.S. 539, 557–58 (1974)).

taking good time.[33] (Some have held that after *Sandin*, the deprivation of earned good time credit is a deprivation of liberty even if statutes and regulations do not limit discretion to take it away.[34]) Some courts have said that a change in classification that restricts prisoners' ability to earn good time in the future is a deprivation of liberty;[35] some have said that is the case only if state law and regulations create a liberty interest in obtaining good time,[36] while others have simply said that the ability to earn good time is too speculative to call for due process protections.[37]

Actions that make prisoners ineligible for parole have been held to deprive them of a liberty interest.[38] Actions that *may*, or may not, have some effect on discretionary parole release have "too attenuated" a relationship with the length of incarceration to constitute a deprivation of liberty invoking due process protections.[39] Parole release itself is not governed by *Sandin*, but by the liberty interest analysis that existed before *Sandin*.[40] Revocation of parole requires due process protections, and so may revocation of other forms of release from prison, depending on how similar they are to parole conditions.[41]

In order to bring a damage suit for action that subjects you to more time in prison, you will generally have to get that action overturned, administratively or judicially, in state court, or in a habeas corpus proceeding, before you can bring a § 1983 action to seek damages for it.[42]

3. Actions that Impose "Atypical and Significant Hardship on the Inmate in Relation to the Ordinary Incidents of Prison Life"[43]

The big change *Sandin v. Conner* made was eliminating due process protections for interests that are not independently protected by the Constitution and don't affect the length of time in prison, but that courts had previously found to be state-created liberty interests. *Sandin* drastically restricted these, holding: "States may under certain circumstances create liberty interests which are protected by the Due Process Clauses. . . . [b]ut these interests will be generally limited to freedom from restraint which . . . nonetheless imposes atypical and significant hardship on the inmate in relation to the ordinary incidents of prison life."[44]

---

[33]*See* Teague v. Quarterman, 482 F.3d 769, 777–80 (5th Cir. 2007) (holding that deprivation of any amount of good time is a liberty deprivation, rejecting argument that good time loss can be *de minimis*); *see* Brooks v. Shanks, 118 N.M. 716, 885 P.2d 637, 641 (1994) (pre-*Sandin* case holding that New Mexico's good time statute sufficiently limits discretion to create a liberty interest). *But see* Moorman v. Thalacker, 83 F.3d 970, 973 (8th Cir. 1996) (expressing doubt whether the Iowa good time statute creates a liberty interest, since it says only that inmates are "eligible" for good time and allows it to be revoked for any rule violation, not restricted to serious misbehavior).

[34]*See, e.g.*, Sanford v. Manternach, 601 N.W.2d 360, 366–68 (Iowa 1999) (holding that Iowa's good time statute creates a liberty interest because it would inevitably affect the length of time the prisoner served; after *Sandin*, the statute need not be mandatory to create a liberty interest).

[35]Gwinn v. Awmiller, 354 F.3d 1211, 1219 (10th Cir. 2004); Chambers v. Colorado Dep't of Corrections, 205 F.3d 1237, 1242–43 (10th Cir. 2000) (holding that a decision to reduce the rate at which a prisoner could earn good time based on his sex offender classification deprived him of liberty, though the court does not find that state statutes and regulations create a liberty interest in earning good time).

[36]*See* Cardoso v. Calbone, 490 F.3d 1194, 1197–98 (10th Cir. 2007 (citing Wilson v. Jones, 430 F.3d 1113, 1120–21, 1123 (10th Cir. 2005) (holding that a discretionary decision to reclassify a prisoner and reduce rate of earning good time after a disciplinary conviction did not deny a liberty interest, distinguishing earlier authority holding that a mandatory reclassification and reduction of good time did deny a liberty interest)); Fogle v. Pierson, 435 F.3d 1252, 1262 (10th Cir. 2006) (segregation and loss of ability to earn good time did not raise a due process claim where the credits were discretionary and there was no liberty interest in them); Montgomery v. Anderson, 262 F.3d 641, 645 (7th Cir. 2001) (stating that loss of opportunity to earn good time does not deny liberty unless state system creates a liberty interest in good time); Abed v. Armstrong, 209 F.3d 63, 66–67 (2d Cir. 2000) (holding prisoners have no liberty interest in the opportunity to earn good time where prison officials had discretion to determine eligibility for good time).

[37]*See* Malchi v. Thaler, 211 F.3d 953, 958–59 (5th Cir. 2000) (citing Luken v. Scott, 71 F.3d 192, 193 (5th Cir. 1995)) (holding the opportunity to earn good time credits does not create a liberty interest because its effect on release date is speculative); Alley v. Angelone, 962 F. Supp. 827, 834 (E.D.Va. 1997) (holding that the potential effect on good time of restrictions on employment and program participation is not a liberty interest protected by due process).

[38]Wilkinson v. Austin, 545 U.S. 209, 223, 125 S. Ct. 2384 (2005) (parole ineligibility was one factor making placement in "supermax" prison the deprivation of a liberty interest); Neal v. Shimoda, 131 F.3d 818, 829 (9th Cir. 1997) (sex offender classification that removed parole eligibility); Beebe v. Heil, 333 F. Supp. 2d 1011, 1015–18 (D.Colo. 2004) (state law that requires the state to provide convicted sex offenders with a treatment program and makes parole eligibility contingent on completing it, creates a liberty interest, and failure to provide the program could "shock the conscience" for purposes of substantive due process analysis); *see* Green v. Black, 755 F.2d 687, 688–89 (8th Cir. 1985) (holding that exclusion from sex offenders program that resulted in parole ineligibility might violate a state-created liberty interest).

[39]Sandin v. Conner, 515 U.S. 472, 487, 115 S. Ct. 2293 (1995); *accord*, Quartararo v. Catterson, 917 F. Supp. 919, 938–39 (E.D.N.Y. 1996).

[40]*See* § H.6.a of this chapter concerning due process in parole release.

[41]Due process issues connected with release on or revocation of parole and temporary release are addressed in § H.6 of this chapter.

[42]*See* Ch. 8, § H.1.a.

[43]Sandin v. Conner, 515 U.S. at 484.

[44]*Sandin*, 515 U.S. at 483–84. The category of "atypical and significant hardship" has been described as "a broad middle category of imposed restraints or deprivations that, considered by

Sandin cited several examples of the kind of liberty interest it was trying to get rid of: cases where courts had found, or prisoners claimed, liberty interests in participating in boot camp programs, being excused from prison furlough rules, receiving tray lunches rather than sack lunches, receiving a dictionary, avoiding transfer to cells without electrical outlets for TVs, having a prison job, and avoiding placement on a "food loaf" diet.[45] Consistently with *Sandin*, courts have generally held that deprivation of prison jobs, exclusion from programs, and detrimental changes in classification do not constitute atypical and significant hardship and do not merit due process protections.[46]

Since *Sandin*, the most significant area of prison due process litigation has involved segregated confinement; courts have sharply disagreed whether and under what circumstances due process is required under *Sandin* in order to place or retain a prisoner in segregation.[47] Aside from segregation, examples of the small number of prison conditions issues that have been held by at least one court to be atypical and significant include placement in five-point restraints;[48] deprivation of two hours a week of yard time for prisoners who were already held in Close Management, a form of solitary confinement;[49] and placement in a prison sex offender program that makes the prisoner ineligible for parole unless she participates in a treatment program.[50]

The *Sandin* analysis focuses on "atypical and significant hardship on the inmate in relation to the ordinary incidents of *prison life*,"[51] and the decision as a whole focuses on the supposed bad effects of the prior liberty interest law on

prison administration.[52] That would seem to mean that *Sandin* does not affect due process law concerning matters that are not part of "prison life," and you should emphasize that point if you are bringing litigation about something that will have its effect outside prison. Courts have not always observed this distinction.[53]

B. STATE-CREATED LIBERTY INTERESTS

Sandin did not abolish state-created liberty interests; it just changed the requirements for finding one in cases about conditions of confinement for convicted prisoners. So it would seem that the pre-*Sandin* liberty interest analysis is still valid in cases involving people who are not convicts or deprivations that do not involve prison conditions.[54] First we will describe how the pre-*Sandin* liberty interest analysis worked, and presumably still works in those other types of cases, and then we will discuss the effects of *Sandin* on liberty interest analysis in cases involving convicted prisoners' conditions.

1. The Pre-*Sandin* Liberty Interest Analysis

The basic idea of state-created liberty interests is that when state law—regulations, statutes, or state constitution—limits the discretion of officials to do as they please by telling them that they can only take certain actions, or that they must take certain actions, under certain defined circumstances, the people affected by that state law have a liberty interest in having that state law followed. Due process then requires fair procedures to determine whether the defined circumstances exist.

For example, in a 1983 case involving administrative segregation,[55] a state statute said that an inmate "may" be placed in segregation based on "the need for control," the "threat of a serious disturbance, or a serious threat to the individual or others."[56] The Supreme Court said that was the same as saying officials would *not* put a prisoner in administrative segregation unless one of those reasons

---

themselves, are neither obviously so serious as to fall within, nor obviously so insignificant as to fall without, the Clause's protection." *Sandin*, 515 U.S. at 497 (Breyer, J., dissenting).

[45]*Sandin*, 515 U.S. at 483; *see, e.g.*, Phillips v. Norris, 320 F.3d 844, 847 (8th Cir. 2003) (limits on religious services, at least short-term, were not atypical and significant); King v. Frank, 328 F. Supp. 2d 940, 944 (W.D.Wis. 2004) (placement on "paper gown restriction" was not atypical and significant).

[46]*See* § H.5 of this chapter.

[47]*See* § F of this chapter.

[48]Williams v. Benjamin, 77 F.3d 756, 769 (4th Cir. 1996) (holding prisoner's arguments "persuasive and forceful" but not deciding the issue); Davis v. Lester, 156 F. Supp. 2d 588, 596 (W.D.Va. 2001). *Contra*, Key v. McKinney, 176 F.3d 1083, 1086–87 (8th Cir. 1999). The use of restraints is discussed in more detail in § H.3 of this chapter and in Ch. 2, § G.2.c.3.

[49]Bass v. Perrin, 170 F.3d 1312, 1318 (11th Cir. 1999). This case stands for the important principle that the "marginal value" of small deprivations may be atypical and significant for people who are already in situations of great deprivation. However, other courts have come to different conclusions about enhanced punishments for prisoners already in segregation. *See* § G of this chapter.

[50]Neal v. Shimoda, 131 F.3d 818, 829 (9th Cir. 1997). Due process issues affecting sex offenders are discussed in § H.5.b of this chapter; other issues concerning sex offenders are discussed in Ch. 2, § F.4.b.

[51]Sandin v. Conner, 515 U.S. at 483–84 (emphasis supplied).

[52]*Sandin*, 515 U.S. at 482.

[53]*See, e.g.*, Kirby v. Siegelman, 195 F.3d 1285, 1291 (11th Cir. 1999). In *Kirby*, the court applied the "atypical and significant" analysis to labelling prisoners as sex offenders in a program that had no effect on prison life but required notification of victims and neighbors 30 days after release. This appears to be wrong under *Sandin*, which as noted focuses on prison life.

[54]As to pretrial detainees and persons who are civilly committed, *see* § C of this chapter. The pre-*Sandin* analysis still applies to cases about parole release, *see* McQuillion v. Duncan, 306 F.3d 895, 903 (9th Cir. 2002); Ellis v. District of Columbia, 84 F.3d 1413, 1417–18 (D.C. Cir. 1996); *id.*, 84 F.3d at 1425–26 (concurring and dissenting opinion); Orellana v. Kyle, 65 F.3d 29, 32 (5th Cir. 1995), and may apply to some temporary release cases. *See* § H.6.d of this chapter.

[55]Hewitt v. Helms, 459 U.S. 460,103 S. Ct. 864 (1983).

[56]37 Pa. Code § 95.104(b)(1) (quoted in Hewitt v. Helms, 459 U.S. at 470 n.6).

was present. This created a liberty interest in staying out of administrative segregation. Therefore the prisoner was entitled to procedural protections to make sure that the reason for segregation—the "need for control," the "threat of a serious disturbance," etc. —actually existed.[57] Similarly, a statute that says a prisoner "shall" be released on parole "unless" parole officials find that certain specified circumstances exist creates a liberty interest in parole release, and due process therefore requires a proceeding to determine if those reasons for denying release do exist.[58]

To determine whether there was a liberty interest in cases decided before *Sandin*, courts looked in statutes and regulations for "mandatory language" (the words that limit officials' discretion, often words like "shall," "will," or "must") and "substantive predicates" (the conditions or circumstances that must exist in order for prison officials to take a certain action, like deny parole or place a prisoner in administrative segregation).[59] Using this method, courts sometimes found that prisoners had a liberty interest and were entitled to a hearing in connection with transfers,[60] classification decisions,[61] program assignments,[62] prison jobs,[63] etc.

Here are some pointers about how that method works:

(1) Words like "shall" and "unless" are not absolutely necessary to create a liberty interest. Mandatory language can take various forms. Courts will examine the statute or regulation as a whole to determine whether "the inmate could reasonably

expect to enforce the regulations against the official."[64]

(2) Language is not mandatory if it contains loopholes or "escape clauses," such as requiring officials to do something under specified circumstances "insofar as possible"[65] or under circumstances "including but not limited to" those specified in the regulations.[66] Language that leaves prison officials significant discretion does not create a liberty interest.[67]

(3) Criteria in statutes and regulations can be "substantive predicates" even if they require the decision-maker to exercise subjective judgment. For example, the Supreme Court held that "a substantial risk that [the inmate] will not conform to the conditions of parole," or a "substantially adverse effect on institutional discipline," were sufficient to create a liberty interest in being paroled.[68] As long as the decision-maker is required to take some action, or forbidden to take some action, if she decides that the criteria are met, a liberty interest is created.[69]

---

[57]*Hewitt*, 459 U.S. at 471–72.

[58]Greenholtz v. Inmates of the Nebraska Penal and Correctional Complex, 442 U.S. 1, 12–13, 99 S. Ct. 2100 (1979) (citing Neb.Rev. Stat. §§ 83-1, 114(1) (1976)).

[59]*See* Hewitt v. Helms, 459 U.S. at 471–72; *accord*, Kentucky Dep't of Corrections v. Thompson, 490 U.S. 454, 462, 109 S. Ct. 1904 (1989); Board of Pardons v. Allen, 482 U.S. 369, 374–80, 107 S. Ct. 2415 (1987).

[60]*See, e.g.*, Maldonado Santiago v. Velazquez Garcia, 821 F.2d 822, 827–28 (1st Cir. 1987) (holding a regulation limiting emergency transfers created a liberty interest); Reese v. Sparks, 760 F.2d 64, 67 (3d Cir. 1985) (finding state law liberty interest in avoiding punitive transfers).

[61]*See, e.g.*, Howard v. Grinage, 6 F.3d 410, 413 (6th Cir. 1993) (holding regulations created a liberty interest in classification); Doe v. Sullivan County, Tenn., 956 F.2d 545, 557–58 (6th Cir. 1992) (holding classification procedures created a liberty interest in being classified with regard to safety and mental disability).

[62]*See, e.g.*, Williams v. Lane, 851 F.2d 867, 880–81 (7th Cir. 1988) (finding liberty interest created by regulations requiring equal programs and housing opportunities for protective custody inmates); Green v. Black, 755 F.2d 687, 688–89 (8th Cir. 1985) (holding statutes and regulations could create a liberty interest in participating in a sex offender program).

[63]*See, e.g.*, Baptist v. O'Leary, 742 F. Supp. 975, 978–79 (N.D.Ill. 1990).

[64]Layton v. Beyer, 953 F.3d 839, 849 (3d Cir. 1992); *accord*, Banks v. Fauver, 801 F. Supp. 1422, 1428–30 (D.N.J. 1992) (holding rules stating the purpose of protective custody and requiring officials to determine if there was evidence supporting the need for it created a liberty interest). One court said: "No magic form of words is required to make a regulation mandatory" as long as it sets out criteria that are "binding," "exhaustive," and "definite." It added: "[A]ll that is required is that it be clear that if X (the substantive predicate), then Y (the specified outcome, from which the enforcement officials are not free to depart.)" Smith v. Shettle, 946 F.2d 1250, 1250–52 (7th Cir. 1991).

Not all courts accept this point. At least one has maintained that the "'shall/unless' formula" is "dispositive" in deciding whether there is a liberty interest. Toussaint v. McCarthy, 801 F.2d 1080, 1095 (9th Cir. 1986).

[65]Joihner v. McEvers, 898 F.2d 569, 572 (7th Cir. 1990); *accord*, Lyle v. Sivley, 805 F. Supp. 755, 761 (D.Ariz. 1992) (holding the phrase "to the extent practicable" did not create a liberty interest).

[66]Jackson v. O'Leary, 689 F. Supp. 846, 849 (N.D.Ill. 1988), *reconsideration denied*, 1988 WL 84704 (N.D.Ill., Aug. 10, 1988); *accord*, Kentucky Dep't of Corrections v. Thompson, 490 U.S. 454, 464–65,109 S. Ct. 1904 (1989) (finding no liberty interest, noting that visitors could be excluded even if they did not fit one of the categories in the prison's visiting regulation); Baptist v. Lane, 708 F. Supp. 920, 921–22 (N.D.Ill. 1989) (holding no liberty interest is created if there is a nonexclusive list of criteria), *reconsideration denied*, 1989 WL 31065 (N.D.Ill., Mar 31, 1989).

[67]*See* Valdez v. Rosenbaum, 302 F.3d 1039, 1045 (9th Cir. 2002) (holding that a statute requiring "reasonable access" for detainees to a telephone left officials with discretion to determine what "reasonable" meant and did not create a liberty interest).

[68]Greenholtz v. Inmates of the Nebraska Penal and Correctional Complex, 442 U.S. 1, 11, 99 S. Ct. 2100 (1979).

[69]*See* Board of Pardons v. Allen, 482 U.S. 369, 375–77, 107 S. Ct. 2415 (1987) (holding liberty interest in parole release was

(4) Procedural rules by themselves do not create liberty interests; only an actual restriction on prison officials' decisions (a substantive predicate) will do so.[70] When officials violate their own procedural rules, a state court suit to enforce those rules is generally the only remedy.

(5) Liberty interests can be created at any level of law, or at more than one. For example, a statute might seem to grant too much discretion to create a liberty interest, but regulations promulgated under the statute may contain the necessary mandatory language and substantive predicates.[71] State constitutions or common law, as interpreted by state courts, may create liberty or property interests.[72]

2. State-Created Liberty Interests Where *Sandin* Applies

The foregoing discussion does not apply to cases about convicts' conditions of confinement, since as we have stated, *Sandin* changed the law for those cases. *Sandin* did say that "[s]tates may under certain circumstances create liberty interests," but the "atypical and significant" standard restricts those circumstances.

So what if there *is* atypical and significant hardship? How does the court decide if the state *has* created a liberty interest?

Many courts have said or assumed that *Sandin* meant that they were to find a liberty interest if there was atypical and significant hardship *and* state statutes or regulations limited discretion sufficiently to create a liberty interest under the pre-*Sandin* law,[73] despite the fact that *Sandin* had harshly criticized that method.[74] But in the later *Wilkinson v. Austin* decision, the Supreme Court repeated its criticism, stating that "[a]fter *Sandin*, it is clear that the touchstone of the inquiry into the existence of a protected, state-created liberty interest in avoiding restrictive conditions of confinement is not the language of regulations regarding those conditions but the nature of those conditions themselves 'in relation to the ordinary incidents of prison life.'"[75] Exactly what this means is not clear. It may be as simple as saying that any time the state creates prison conditions that are so extreme as to be atypical and significant by comparison to ordinary conditions, there is a state-created liberty interest.[76] Or it may be that if statutes and prison regulations place *any* limits on official discretion in placing prisoners in those condition, there is a state-created liberty interest, even if those statutes and regulations would not have created a liberty interest under the pre-*Sandin* analysis.[77]

---

created by statutes stating that the Board *shall* grant parole "when in its opinion there is reasonable probability that the prisoner can be released without detriment to the prisoner or to the community. . . . [and] when the board believes that he is able and willing to fulfill the obligations of a law-abiding citizen."); Hewitt v. Helms, 459 U.S. 460, 470 n.6, 103 S. Ct. 864 (1983) (holding vague phrases like "the need for control" and "the threat of a serious disturbance" were sufficient to create a liberty interest).

[70]*See* Olim v. Wakinekona, 461 U.S. 238, 249–50, 103 S. Ct. 1741 (1983) (holding that regulations requiring a pre-transfer hearing, but not restricting the grounds for transfer, did not create a liberty interest, so the failure to provide the pre-transfer hearing did not deny due process); Bonner v. Lewis, 857 F.2d 559, 564 (9th Cir. 1988) (holding a statute requiring sign language interpreters in administrative proceedings did not create a liberty interest); *see* Cleveland Bd. of Educ. v. Loudermill, 470 U.S. 532, 541, 105 S. Ct. 1487 (1985) (stating that "[t]he categories of substance and procedure" are distinct for purposes of due process analysis).

[71]*See* Lewis v. Thigpen, 767 F.2d 252, 262 (5th Cir. 1985); Mayes v. Trammell, 751 F.2d 175, 178–79 (6th Cir. 1986); *see also* Board of Pardons v. Allen, 482 U.S. at 378 n.9 (recognizing relevance of regulations promulgated under a statute); Hewitt v. Helms, 459 U.S. at 470–71 (considering statute and regulations together); Goss v. Lopez, 419 U.S. 565, 573–74, 95 S. Ct. 729 (1975) (considering education statute together with school rules).

[72]Memphis Light, Gas and Water Division v. Craft, 436 U.S. 1, 9–12, 98 S. Ct. 1554 (1978); Kozlowski v. Coughlin, 539 F. Supp. 852, 855–56 (S.D.N.Y. 1982) (state constitutional right to contact visits); Ferguson v. Dep't of Corrections, 816 P.2d 134, 139–40 (Alaska 1991) (state constitutional right to rehabilitation).

[73]*See* Magluta v. Samples, 375 F.3d 1269, 1277–82 (11th Cir. 2004); Sealey v. Giltner, 197 F.3d 578, 584 (2d Cir. 1999) (holding that *Sandin* did not abolish liberty interest analysis, just limited it to atypical and significant deprivations); Frazier v. Coughlin, 81 F.3d 313, 317 (2d Cir. 1996) (holding a plaintiff must show "both that the confinement or restraint creates an 'atypical and significant hardship' under *Sandin*, and that the state has granted its inmates, by regulation or by statute, a protected liberty interest in remaining free from that confinement or restraint."); Williams v. Benjamin, 77 F.3d 756, 769 (4th Cir. 1996) (citing state regulations in *Sandin* analysis); Jones v. Moran, 900 F. Supp. 1267, 1273–74 (N.D.Cal. 1995).

[74]There was some basis for believing that was what *Sandin* meant, since the Court at one point cited *Board of Pardons v. Allen*, 482 U.S. 369, 107 S. Ct. 2415 (1987), as an example of a surviving state-created liberty interest. That case is a classic example of liberty interest analysis based on analysis of the language of state laws. The dissenting opinion in *Sandin* interprets the majority opinion the same way. Sandin v. Conner, 515 U.S. 472, 497–99, 115 S. Ct. 2293 (1995).

[75]Wilkinson v. Austin, 545 U.S. 209, 223, 125 S. Ct. 2384 (2005) (quoting *Sandin*).

[76]This view might be consistent with the statement in *Wilkinson* that "a liberty interest in avoiding particular conditions of confinement may arise from state *policies or* regulations, subject to the important limitations set forth in *Sandin v. Conner.* . . ." *Wilkinson*, 545 U.S. at 222 (emphasis supplied). The reference to "policies" would amount to saying that a liberty interest can arise from what the state *does*, in addition to what it writes down in regulations.

[77]*See* Tellier v. Fields, 280 F.3d 69, 83 (2d Cir. 2000) (stating that the liberty interest analysis is a little different after *Sandin*, because *Sandin* "shifted the emphasis of the inquiry from the strict language of the statute to an analysis of the right safeguarded by the statute."); Carter v. Munoz 2008 WL 4057846, *4 (E.D.Cal., Aug. 28, 2008) ("harsh conditions of management cell status" may

C. Due Process for Pretrial Detainees and the Civilly Committed

As we said above, *Sandin v. Conner's* restrictive ruling about prison due process is based on the idea that a criminal conviction and prison sentence mostly extinguishes a prisoner's liberty. What if you haven't been convicted of anything, but are in jail awaiting trial? Courts have generally held that the rule of *Sandin v. Conner* does not apply to pretrial detainees.[78] Some courts have said that the pre-*Sandin* liberty interest analysis still applies to detainees, so that a statute or regulation that contains "mandatory language" and "substantive predicates" calls for due process protections.[79] The trouble with that approach is that *Sandin* severely criticized liberty interest analysis on grounds that seem applicable to detainees as well as convicts. Other courts have held that detainees are entitled to a due process hearing if they are threatened with punishment.[80]

If, as *Sandin* says, its standard is based on the loss of liberty resulting from a criminal conviction, one would think that persons in civil confinement of any sort would not be subject to it. However, at least one federal appeals court has applied *Sandin* to civil confinement.[81]

---

support claim of liberty interest; no discussion of extent to which regulations limit discretion), *report and recommendation adopted*, 2008 WL 4601106 (E.D.Cal., Oct. 15, 2008); Koch v. Lewis, 216 F. Supp. 2d 994, 999 (D.Ariz. 2001) ("While some form of state regulation may yet be necessary to trigger a liberty interest, the sort of mandatory language necessary under *Hewitt* is no longer a prerequisite."), *vacated as moot*, 399 F.3d 1099 (9th Cir. 2005). In *Koch*, the court observed that the prison rules contained specific procedures for "security threat group validation" and added: "Although [the state's policies] were not mandatory enough to support a liberty interest under *Hewitt*, they are sufficient to form the bases [sic] of a liberty interest under *Sandin*. That is not to say that regulatory language retains much significance in the modern due process analysis." *Koch*, 216 F. Supp. 2d at 1000.

In *Iqbal v. Hasty*, 490 F.3d 143, 161–62 (2d Cir. 2007), *aff'd in part, rev'd in part, and remanded on other grounds sub nom.* Ashcroft v. Iqbal, ___ U.S. ___, 129 S. Ct. 1937 (2009), the court held that *Tellier v. Fields, supra*, is not abrogated by *Wilkinson v. Austin*, and cited *Wilkinson's* statement that liberty interests "arise from state policies or regulations," but it didn't explain how or whether *Wilkinson* changed the analysis. The Supreme Court did not address that issue in its decision.

[78]Iqbal v. Hasty, 490 F.3d at 162–63; Surprenant v. Rivas, 424 F.3d 5, 17 (1st Cir. 2005); Peoples v. CCA Detention Centers, 422 F.3d 1090, 1106 n.2 (10th Cir. 2005) (*Sandin* leaves Bell v. Wolfish, which governs detainees' rights, "untouched"), *vacated in part on other grounds*, 449 F.3d 1097 (10th Cir. 2006); Valdez v. Rosenbaum, 302 F.3d 1039, 1044 n.3 (9th Cir. 2002); Benjamin v. Fraser, 264 F.3d 175, 188–89 (2d Cir. 2001); Fuentes v. Wagner, 206 F.3d 335, 342 n.9 (3d Cir. 2000); Rapier v. Harris, 172 F.3d 999, 1004–05 (7th Cir. 1999); Mitchell v. Dupnik, 75 F.3d 517, 523–24 (9th Cir. 1995) (holding that since *Sandin* is based on "the expected parameters of the sentence imposed by a court of law," detainees are entitled to a due process hearing before being restrained for reasons other than to assure their appearance at trial). *Contra*, Cephas v. Truitt, 940 F. Supp. 674, 680 (D.Del. 1996).

In some cases, courts have applied the *Sandin* analysis to pretrial detainees without realizing that there is a question whether it is applicable. *See, e.g.*, Magluta v. Samples, 375 F.3d 1269, 1278–82 (11th Cir. 2004). If you are in a jurisdiction where the courts have done that, point out to the court in your case that they really didn't decide whether *Sandin* applies to detainees, that that the issue is still open.

Courts have differed over whether convicted but unsentenced prisoners should be treated like sentenced prisoners or detainees for purposes of disciplinary due process claims. *Compare* Tilmon v. Prator, 368 F.3d 521, 523–24 (5th Cir. 2004) (per curiam); Resnick v. Hayes, 213 F.3d 443, 448 (9th Cir. 2000) and cases cited (holding they should be treated like convicts) *with* Fuentes v. Wagner, 206

F.3d 335, 340 (3d Cir. 2000) (citing Cobb v. Aytch, 643 F.2d 946, 962 (3d Cir. 1980) (holding they should be treated like detainees)).

[79]Valdez v. Rosenbaum, 302 F.3d at 1044–45 (applying liberty interest analysis to state telephone access statute and regulations); Carlo v. City of Chino, 105 F.3d 493, 499–500 (9th Cir. 1997) (applying liberty interest analysis to restriction on arrestees' telephone calls); Benjamin v. Kerik, 102 F. Supp. 2d 157, 173 (S.D.N.Y. 2000) (applying liberty interest analysis, holding classification directive left too much discretion to create a liberty interest), *aff'd on other grounds*, 264 F.3d 175 (2d Cir. 2001).

[80]Iqbal v. Hasty, 490 F.3d 143, 165 (2d Cir. 2007) (holding that detainee was entitled to procedural protections based directly upon the Due Process Clause where he was subjected to conditions so harsh as to comprise punishment, as well as under federal regulations that created a liberty interest, regardless of defendants' punitive intent), *aff'd in part, rev'd in part, and remanded on other grounds sub nom.* Ashcroft v. Iqbal, ___ U.S. ___, 129 S. Ct. 1937 (2009); Surprenant v. Rivas, 424 F.3d 5, 17 (1st Cir. 2005) (holding detainees have a liberty interest in avoiding punishment); Holly v. Woolfolk, 415 F.3d 678, 679–80 (7th Cir. 2005) (noting holdings that "any nontrivial punishment of a person not yet convicted [is] a sufficient deprivation of liberty to entitle him to due process of law"); Rapier v. Harris, 172 F.3d at 1005 (applying *Bell v. Wolfish* punishment analysis to due process claim); Mitchell v. Dupnik, 75 F.3d 517, 523–24 (9th Cir. 1995); Zarnes v. Rhodes, 64 F.3d 285, 292 (7th Cir. 1995). The First Circuit has held that detainees are denied due process when they are punished as a result of false charges made by staff members with the intent to cause them to be punished. Surprenant v. Rivas, 424 F.3d at 13–14.

One federal circuit has said: "Although pretrial detainees do not have a liberty interest in being confined in the general prison population, they do have a liberty interest in not being detained indefinitely in the SHU without explanation or review of their confinement" because "the protections due to sentenced inmates provide a floor for what pretrial detainees may expect." Stevenson v. Carroll, 495 F.3d 62, 69 (3d Cir. 2007), *cert. denied*, 128 S. Ct. 1223 (2008). It added that detainees are entitled to the usual procedural safeguards for administrative or disciplinary confinement, and possibly "a higher level of procedure" for persons accused of participating in a riot. 495 F.3d at 70–71. It did not state any minimum period of confinement required to trigger those due process rights.

[81]*See* Thielman v. Leean, 282 F.3d 478, 483–84 (7th Cir. 2002) (applying *Sandin* to person committed as a "sexually violent person" after completion of criminal sentence).

D. What Due Process of Law Means

The basic requirement of due process is the right to notice and an opportunity to be heard "at a meaningful time and in a meaningful manner."[82] The "process that is due" can take different forms in different kinds of cases. For example, some cases require a face-to-face hearing, but in others, it is enough for the prisoner to be "heard" in writing.[83]

The requirements of due process in a given type of case are determined by balancing three factors: (1) how serious the deprivation is, (2) how much good additional procedures are likely to do, and (3) how expensive or difficult additional procedures would be for the officials who must carry them out.[84] This "balancing test" determines what due process requires, even if state law or prison regulations call for something different.[85] The requirements of due process in particular kinds of cases are discussed later in this chapter.

In the past, some courts have held that when official discretion is limited by substantive criteria or "predicates,"[86] due process requires that decisions actually be made based on those criteria.[87] Nowadays, for convicted prisoners, that principle would appear to be limited to cases where there is a liberty interest under the principles of *Sandin v. Conner*.[88]

E. Post-Deprivation Remedies

An important aspect of due process is *when* you have a right to be heard. In some cases, you must receive a hearing before you are deprived of liberty or property.[89] In other cases, a hearing must be provided within a short time after the deprivation.[90] In still other cases, however, due process is satisfied if you have available a "post-deprivation remedy" such as a state court damage lawsuit, a Federal Tort Claims Act (FTCA) suit, or an administrative grievance procedure. In these cases, you must use the post-deprivation remedy; you cannot bring a civil rights suit.[91] This rule most often applies to property claims,[92] but it applies to some liberty deprivations as well.[93]

The law of post-deprivation remedies is confusing, but it can be summarized in a few rules:

(1) If the courts have already held that a pre-deprivation, or reasonably prompt, hearing is required, a post-deprivation remedy does not satisfy due process.[94]

(2) If the deprivation was "random and unauthorized" or "unpredictable," a post-deprivation remedy is sufficient. The courts have reasoned that in such cases, it is impossible to provide a hearing in advance, so due process is satisfied by a hearing afterwards.[95] If pre-deprivation

---

[82]Hamdi v. Rumsfeld, 542 U.S. 507, 533, 124 S. Ct. 2633 (2004); Logan v. Zimmerman Brush Co., 455 U.S. 422, 437, 102 S. Ct. 1148 (1982) (citation omitted); *see* Goss v. Lopez, 419 U.S. 565, 579, 95 S. Ct. 729 (1975) and cases cited.

[83]*See, e.g.*, Mendoza v. Blodgett, 960 F.2d 1425, 1431 (9th Cir. 1992) (referring to placement on "feces watch").

[84]Mathews v. Eldridge, 424 U.S. 319, 335, 96 S. Ct. 843 (1976); *accord*, Hamdi v. Rumsfeld, 542 U.S. at 529.

The *Mathews v. Eldridge* standard, and not the "reasonable relationship" standard of *Turner v. Safley*, governs prison due process issues. Washington v. Harper, 494 U.S. 210, 229, 110 S. Ct. 1028 (1990); *see* Ch. 3, § A for a discussion of the "reasonable relationship" standard. Some courts have applied the "reasonable relationship" standard to due process cases, *see, e.g.*, Powell v. Coughlin, 953 F.2d 744, 749 (2d Cir. 1991), but these decisions appear to be erroneous in light of *Washington v. Harper*.

[85]Cleveland Bd. of Educ. v. Loudermill, 470 U.S. 532, 541, 105 S. Ct. 1487 (1985); Vitek v. Jones, 445 U.S. 480, 491, 100 S. Ct. 1254 (1980); *see* Shakur v. Selsky, 391 F.3d 106, 118 (2d Cir. 2004) (where a prisoner received a disciplinary hearing, additional state law procedural safeguards were not relevant to his due process claim).

[86]*See* § B of this chapter for a discussion of substantive predicates.

[87]*See, e.g.*, Brennan v. Cunningham, 813 F.2d 1, 11–12 (1st Cir. 1987) (temporary release decision based on public pressure and not statutory criteria would be improper); Winsett v. McGinnes, 617 F.2d 996, 1007–08 (3d Cir. 1980) (en banc); *see* Mickens-Thomas v. Vaughn, 321 F.3d 374, 386–87 (3d Cir. 2003) (citing *Winsett* with approval); *see also* nn.832, 881, below. *Contra*, Francis v. Fox, 838 F.2d 1147, 1149 n.8 (11th Cir. 1988); Baumann v. Arizona Dep't of Corrections, 754 F.2d 841, 844–45 (9th Cir.1985).

[88]*See* §§ A, B, of this chapter.

[89]*See, e.g.*, Gilbert v. Frazier, 931 F.2d 1581, 1582 (7th Cir. 1991) (holding a hearing is required before prisoner is convicted of a disciplinary offense); Sample v. Diecks, 885 F.2d 1099, 1116 (3d Cir. 1989) (holding pre-deprivation process is required when prisoners complain that their release dates have been miscalculated).

[90]*See* Morrissey v. Brewer, 408 U.S. 471, 485, 92 S. Ct. 2593 (1972) (holding that preliminary parole revocation hearing must be held "as promptly as convenient after arrest"); Hewitt v. Helms, 459 U.S. 460, 472, 103 S. Ct. 864 (1983) (holding prisoner placed in administrative segregation must be heard within a "reasonable time" after confinement); Mendoza v. Blodgett, 960 F.2d 1425, 1431 (9th Cir. 1992) (holding prisoner subjected to extremely unpleasant "feces watch" procedures was entitled to a hearing within a "reasonable time" after it started; five days afterward was not sufficient).

[91]*See, e.g.*, Friedman v. Young, 702 F. Supp. 433, 437 (S.D.N.Y. 1988) (holding the availability of the Federal Tort Claims Act barred the plaintiff's civil rights suit for property loss).

[92]Hudson v. Palmer, 468 U.S. 517, 533–35, 104 S. Ct. 3194 (1984). Property claims are discussed in much more detail in § H.8 of this chapter.

[93]Zinermon v. Burch, 494 U.S. 113, 131–32, 110 S. Ct. 975 (1990).

[94]Patterson v. Coughlin, 761 F.2d 886, 892–93 (2d Cir. 1985); McClendon v. Turner, 765 F. Supp. 251, 254–55 (W.D.Pa. 1991); Jones v. Smith, 607 F. Supp. 251, 256–57 (E.D.Pa. 1984) (claim for deprivation of property through misuse of disciplinary procedure was not barred by the existence of state remedies).

[95]Zinermon v. Burch, 494 U.S. 113, 129–32, 110 S. Ct. 975 (1990); Warren v. City of Athens, Ohio, 411 F.3d 697, 709–10 (6th Cir. 2005) ("In this context, 'unauthorized' means that the official

process is possible, post-deprivation process does not meet due process requirements.[96]

(3) A post-deprivation hearing does not satisfy due process requirements if the deprivation resulted from "established state procedure"[97] or "policy,"[98] or if it was "predictable"[99] or "authorized."[100] A practice can constitute a policy or established procedure even if it is contrary to state or local law,[101] or if it amounts to a "policy" of failing to enforce the law.[102]

(4) If the people who denied you a proper hearing were the same people who had the ability and authority to give you a hearing, a post-deprivation remedy does not satisfy due process.[103]

This last point has not been accepted by all the lower courts. Some cases have interpreted *Zinermon* and *Parratt* to mean that if the state has rules providing for hearings that satisfy the Constitution, it does not deny due process for officials to ignore or violate those rules, as long as you are able to bring a post-deprivation suit for damages in state court.[104] We think this view is wrong. The Supreme Court in *Zinermon* emphasized that it is the unauthorized deprivation of liberty or property, not the unauthorized denial of due process, that brings the post-deprivation remedies rule into play.[105]

Here is how this distinction would work in a disciplinary case. The hearing officer is authorized to deprive you of your liberty; that is part of her job. She is also required to follow certain rules of due process. Even if she violates those rules and denies you due process, the resulting deprivation of liberty is authorized. It is the due process denial, not the deprivation of liberty, that is unauthorized. You should therefore be entitled to bring a civil rights suit and are not restricted to the state's post-deprivation remedies.

The post-deprivation remedy rule applies only to deprivations of procedural due process. It does not apply to issues of substantive due process or to other substantive

---

in question did not have the power or authority to effect the deprivation, not that the act was contrary to law. . . .").

[96]Zinermon v. Burch, 494 U.S. at 136–40; Burtnieks v. City of New York, 716 F.2d 982, 988–89 (2d Cir. 1983) (pre-deprivation process is required where there is no "necessity for quick action" or "impracticality of providing any pre-deprivation process"). *But see* Ellis v. Sheahan, 412 F.3d 754, 757–58 (7th Cir. 2005) (holding that a post-deprivation hearing was adequate where the *status quo* had been restored and the remaining dispute was over money owed).

[97]Logan v. Zimmerman Brush Co., 455 U.S. 422, 436, 102 S. Ct. 1148 (1982); Honey v. Distelrath, 195 F.3d 531, 534 (9th Cir. 1999); Wright v. Newsome, 795 F.2d 964, 967 (11th Cir. 1986) (allegation that property was taken pursuant to the "sanctioned standard operating procedure" of the prison stated a constitutional claim); Burtnieks v. City of New York, 716 F.2d at 988; *see* Lavicky v. Burnett, 758 F.2d 468, 472 (10th Cir. 1985) (act requiring some degree of planning and coordination was not random and unauthorized). *But see* Carcamo v. Miami-Dade County, 375 F.3d 1104, 1105 n.4 (11th Cir. 2004) (holding under some circumstances "post-deprivation remedies may be acceptable even in contexts involving a state policy or procedure" if pre-deprivation process is not feasible); Love v. Coughlin, 714 F.2d 207, 208–09 (2d Cir. 1983) (prisoner's allegation of "recurring" property losses did not state a due process claim if post-deprivation remedies were available).

[98]Piatt v. MacDougall, 773 F.2d 1032, 1036–37 (9th Cir. 1985) (en banc); Spruytte v. Walters, 753 F.2d 498, 509–10 (6th Cir. 1985); Loukas v. Hofbauer, 784 F. Supp. 377, 383 (E.D.Mich. 1991).

[99]Zinermon v. Burch, 494 U.S. at 138.

[100]New Windsor Volunteer Ambulance Corps., Inc. v. Meyer, 442 F.3d 101, 115–16 (2d Cir. 2006) (actions were not random and unauthorized when performed by officials with final decision-making authority); McClendon v. Turner, 765 F. Supp. 251, 254 (W.D.Pa. 1991).

[101]Honey v. Distelrath, 195 F.3d 531, 534 (9th Cir. 1999); Hicks v. Feeney, 770 F.2d 375, 378–79 (3d Cir. 1985); Spruytte v. Walters, 753 F.2d at 509–10; Burtnieks v. City of New York, 716 F.2d at 988.

[102]Anderson v. City of New York, 611 F. Supp. 481, 492 (S.D.N.Y. 1985) (failure to promulgate and enforce policy to execute state law may be an established procedure). *But see* Lewis v. Young, 162 Wis.2d 574, 470 N.W.2d 328, 331 (Wis.App. 1991) (misinterpretation or disregard for prison rules must be pursued in state court).

[103]Zinermon v. Burch, 494 U.S. 113, 138, 110 S. Ct. 975 (1990); Honey v. Distelrath, 195 F.3d 531 at 534; Plumer v. State of

Maryland, 915 F.2d 927, 931 (4th Cir. 1990) ("In short, when a state government can and does provide a predeprivation hearing and charges its employees with effecting the deprivation complained of, the availability of an adequate state postdeprivation remedy does not, standing alone, satisfy the Due Process Clause." (citing Zinermon v. Burch, *supra*)); Smith v. McCaughtry, 801 F. Supp. 239, 243 (E.D.Wis. 1992); Loukas v. Hofbauer, 784 F. Supp. at 382.

[104]*See* Bogart v. Chapell, 396 F.3d 548, 563 (4th Cir. 2005) (where the people who took the plaintiff's property were empowered to enforce the law, but their unlawful actions were not predictable, and they did not have the duty to provide procedural safeguards, post-deprivation safeguards were sufficient); Caine v. Hardy, 943 F.2d 1406, 1414–15 (5th Cir. 1991) (en banc); Easter House v. Felder, 910 F.2d 1387, 1404 (7th Cir. 1990) (en banc). Some courts have applied this reasoning to prison disciplinary cases. *See* Hamlin v. Vaudenberg, 95 F.3d 580, 585 (7th Cir. 1996); Irby v. Macht, 184 Wis.2d 831, 847–51, 522 N.W.2d 9, 15–17 (1994) (involving same prison and court system).

[105]The Court's own words were:

. . . [P]etitioners cannot characterize their conduct as "unauthorized" in the sense the term is used in *Parratt* and *Hudson*. The State delegated to them the power and authority to effect the very deprivation complained of here . . . and also delegated to them the concomitant duty to initiate the procedural safeguards set up by state law to guard against unlawful confinement. In *Parratt* and *Hudson*, the state employees had no similar broad authority to deprive prisoners of their personal property, and no similar duty to initiate . . . the procedural safeguards required before deprivations occur. The deprivation here is "unauthorized" only in the sense that it was not an act sanctioned by state law, but, instead, was a "depriv[ation] of constitutional rights . . . by an official's abuse of his position."

494 U.S. at 138 (citation and footnote omitted).

constitutional violations.[106] If you have been unlawfully beaten up, deprived of religious rights, denied medical care or access to courts, subjected to an unlawful search, etc., it doesn't matter what remedies the state provides. You are entitled to bring a civil rights suit in federal court.[107]

A post-deprivation remedy must be "adequate" to satisfy due process requirements. A remedy is adequate if it is capable of providing full compensation for your loss.[108] It may be adequate even if it lacks some of the features of a federal civil rights lawsuit, such as punitive damages or trial by jury.[109] It is not clear whether a remedy that provides only for damages is inadequate if you have reason to seek an injunction.[110]

A remedy may be adequate even if it is administrative rather than judicial in nature,[111] and regardless of whether it provides for a judgment against a governmental body or against individual employees.[112]

The courts have not yet developed firm rules for deciding when a post-deprivation remedy is inadequate, but it is clear that you must show[113] either that the procedure is unfair, that it was not really available to you, or that you used it and it failed to address the merits of your claim.[114] Circumstances that may make a remedy inadequate include the failure to give notice of its existence,[115] refusal to waive filing fees for indigents,[116] immunity rules,[117] lack of

---

[106]Zinermon v. Burch, 494 U.S. at 125–27.

[107]McCullah v. Gadert, 344 F.3d 655, 660 (7th Cir. 2003) (Fourth Amendment violation); Williams-El v. Johnson, 872 F.2d 224, 229 (8th Cir. 1989) (use of force); Love v. Sheffield, 777 F.2d 1453, 1454 (11th Cir. 1985) (inmate assault and denial of medical care); Augustine v. Doe, 740 F.2d 322, 325–27 (5th Cir. 1984) (unlawful search); Smith v. Smith, 578 F. Supp. 1373, 1375 (E.D.Pa. 1984) (denial of access to courts and freedom of religion). This is true even if part of your damages include a loss of property. Zilich v. Lucht, 981 F.2d 694, 695 (3d Cir. 1992) (deprivation of legal materials); Morello v. James, 810 F.2d 344, 347–48 (2d Cir. 1987) (same); Simmons v. Dickhaut, 804 F.2d 182, 184–85 (1st Cir. 1986) (same); Mann v. City of Tucson, Dep't of Police, 782 F.2d 790, 793 (9th Cir. 1986) (unlawful search resulting in property loss).

[108]Parratt v. Taylor, 451 U.S. 527, 544, 101 S. Ct. 1908 (1981); see Orebaugh v. Caspari, 910 F.2d 526, 527–28 (8th Cir. 1990) (holding procedure for replacing property, rather than paying for it, did not deny due process); McClary v. O'Hare, 786 F.2d 83, 87–88 (2d Cir. 1986) (holding workers' compensation procedure with limited damages was adequate). But see Hamlin v. Vaudenberg, 95 F.3d 580, 585 (7th Cir. 1996) (holding inmate complaint procedure and judicial review proceeding provided adequate due process for disciplinary proceeding, despite the unavailability of damages, because they were "neither meaningless nor nonexistent"); accord, Irby v. Macht, 184 Wis.2d 831, 847–51, 522 N.W.2d 9 (1994) (involving same prison and court system). These decisions do not appear to have been followed in other jurisdictions. In addition, the *Hamlin* decision appears to have involved only the violation of state regulations and not federal due process standards. More importantly, most courts hold that where disciplinary charges carry a serious enough penalty to require due process, the prisoner must receive pre-deprivation process, so it doesn't matter how adequate post-deprivation remedies may be. See nn.89, 94, in this section.

[109]Parratt v. Taylor, 451 U.S. 527, 544, 101 S. Ct. 1908 (1981).

[110]Compare Bumgarner v. Bloodworth, 738 F.2d 966, 968 (8th Cir. 1984) (state remedy that did not provide for return of property was inadequate) with Shango v. Jurich, 681 F.2d 1091, 1105 (7th Cir. 1982) (loss of unique property did not constitute irreparable harm justifying an injunction).

[111]Hamlin v. Vaudenberg, 95 F.3d 580, 585 (7th Cir. 1996) (prison complaint procedure with right of judicial review); Al-Ra'id v. Ingle, 69 F.3d 28, 31–32 (5th Cir. 1995) (prison grievance procedure); McClary v. O'Hare, 786 F.2d 83, 86–87 (2d Cir. 1986)

(workers' compensation procedure); Ausley v. Mitchell, 748 F.2d 224, n.2 (4th Cir. 1984) (en banc); Phelps v. Anderson and Langford, 700 F.2d 147, 149 (4th Cir. 1983); Steffen v. Housewright, 665 F.2d 245, 247–48 (8th Cir. 1981).

[112]Parratt v. Taylor, 451 U.S. at 543–44 (government body); Graham v. Mitchell, 529 F. Supp. 622, 625 (E.D.Va. 1982) (individual officer).

[113] See Myers v. Klevenhagen, 97 F.3d 91, 94–95 (5th Cir. 1996) (holding plaintiff has the burden of showing remedies are inadequate).

[114]One court has stated that if relief is denied for any reason other than the lack of merit of the claim, due process is denied and the matter can be heard by a federal court. Loftin v. Thomas, 681 F.2d 364, 365 (5th Cir. 1982). Another court stated that "specific facts suggesting that the state post-deprivation remedies were effectively denied" to the plaintiff sufficiently supported a claim of an inadequate remedy. Freeman v. Dep't of Corrections, 949 F.2d 360, 362 (10th Cir. 1991). Other courts have asserted more demanding standards. See Easter House v. Felder, 910 F.2d 1387, 1406 (7th Cir. 1990) (en banc) (remedy must be shown "inadequate to the point that it is meaningless or nonexistent"); Campbell v. Shearer, 732 F.2d 531, 534 (6th Cir. 1984) (plaintiff must show "a procedural deficiency in state law or a systemic problem with the state's corrective process").

[115]Butler v. Castro, 896 F.2d 698, 700–03 (2d Cir. 1990) (state remedy for obtaining return of seized property from Police Department was inadequate where it was not in the municipal code, affected persons did not receive notice of it, and part of the municipal code gave misinformation about the required procedures).

[116]Williams v. St. Louis County, 812 F.2d 1079, 1082–83 (8th Cir. 1987); Walker v. Scurr, 617 F. Supp. 679, 681 (S.D.Iowa 1985). But see Piatt v. MacDougall, 773 F.2d 1032, 1034 (9th Cir. 1985) (en banc) (refusal to waive an appellate filing fee did not make the remedy inadequate where the prisoner received an adequate hearing in the trial court); accord, Nickens v. Melton, 38 F.3d 183, 184-85 (5th Cir. 1994).

[117]Belcher v. Norton, 497 F.3d 742, 753 (7th Cir. 2007); Larramendy v. Newton, 994 F. Supp. 1211, 1216 (E.D.Cal. 1998); Soto v. Lord, 693 F. Supp. 8, 15–16 (S.D.N.Y. 1988); Madden v. City of Meriden, 602 F. Supp. 1160, 1169 (D.Conn. 1985); Harper v. Scott, 577 F. Supp. 15, 17 (E.D.Mich. 1984). However, several courts have held that a remedy can be adequate even if the defendants are immune. Powell v. Georgia Dep't of Human Resources, 114 F.3d 1074, 1082, n.11 (11th Cir.1997) (holding that state's invocation of sovereign immunity did not make remedies inadequate; Hamlin v. Vaudenberg, 95 F.3d 580, 585 n.3 (7th Cir. 1996) (stating otherwise adequate remedies are not made inadequate by immunity defenses); Al-Mustafa Irshad v. Spann, 543 F. Supp. 922, 927–28

timeliness,[118] severe limits on recovery,[119] the failure to provide a hearing,[120] and other practical obstacles to imprisoned litigants.[121] The fact that you tried the remedy and were not satisfied with the result does not by itself make the remedy inadequate.[122] Nor is a remedy inadequate if you have lost your chance to use it by failing to comply with procedural requirements such as filing a notice of claim.[123] Most courts have held that you should plead in your complaint the circumstances that make the post-deprivation remedy inadequate.[124]

F. WHEN IS SEGREGATED CONFINEMENT A LIBERTY DEPRIVATION?

Before *Sandin v. Conner*, federal courts generally held that any significant punitive or disciplinary action required due

process protections.[125] There was no issue whether such action deprived the prisoner of a liberty interest, since courts found that the disciplinary rules themselves create a liberty interest; a prison rulebook says, in effect, "if you don't break these rules, we won't punish you."[126] Administrative segregation also called for due process if the relevant statutes and regulations contained sufficiently definite limits on discretion to give rise to a state-created liberty interest.[127]

Now, under *Sandin*, the placement of convicts[128] in segregation is a deprivation of liberty requiring due process protections only if they are subjected to "atypical and significant hardship . . . in relation to the ordinary incidents of prison life,"[129] and if there is also a state-created liberty interest.[130] In *Sandin* itself, a prisoner sentenced to 30 days' punitive segregation was found not to have been deprived of liberty for due process purposes, and many lower courts

---

(E.D.Va. 1982) (a remedy could be adequate even if defendants were immune).

[118]Holman v. Hilton, 712 F.2d 854, 858–59 (3d Cir. 1983) (a remedy that could not be pursued until after release was inadequate); Fink v. Supreme Court of Pa., 654 F. Supp. 437 (M.D.Pa. 1987) (remedy must be offered in a timely fashion), *aff'd*, 838 F.2d 1205 (3d Cir. 1988).

[119]Parrett v. City of Connersville, Ind., 737 F.2d 690, 697 (7th Cir. 1984); Williams v. Morris, 697 F.2d 1349, 1351 (10th Cir. 1982) (procedure that automatically denied compensation for items not listed in a "property book" was probably inadequate). *But see* Price v. Harris, 722 F.2d 427, 428 (8th Cir. 1983) (where state claims procedure awarded only part of the amount claimed by the prisoner, the claim could not be relitigated in federal court).

[120]Holman v. Hilton, 712 F.2d 854, 862 (3d Cir. 1983) (administrative procedure permitting only written presentations was inadequate).

[121]Pena v. Mattox, 84 F.3d 894, 898 (7th Cir. 1996) (holding defendants cannot rely on the existence of post-deprivation remedies if their conduct prevented the plaintiff from using them; this plaintiff did not receive notice); Coleman v. Faulkner, 697 F.2d 1347, 1349 (10th Cir. 1982) (holding remedy was inadequate where plaintiff could not afford counsel and prison officials would not let him appear *pro se*).

[122]Robinson v. Ridge, 996 F. Supp. 447, 450 (E.D.Pa. 1997) (holding prisoner offered $50 for his destroyed religious items had an adequate remedy, even though he said they were worth more), *aff'd*, 175 F.3d 1011 (3d Cir. 1999); Willoughby v. Luster, 717 F. Supp. 1439, 1443 (D.Nev. 1989).

[123]Howland v. State, 169 Ariz. 293, 818 P.2d 1169, 1173 (Ariz. App. 1991).

[124]Gudema v. Nassau County, 163 F.3d 717, 724 (2d Cir. 1998) (" . . . [T]he unavailability of an appropriate remedy is part of a due process plaintiff's claim. . . ."); Pilgrim v. Littlefield, 92 F.3d 413, 417 (6th Cir. 1996) (affirming dismissal because plaintiff did not plead inadequacy of post-deprivation remedies); Antonelli v. Sheahan, 81 F.3d 1422, 1430 (7th Cir. 1996) (plaintiff's failure to allege either that property confiscation took place according to established procedure, or that post-deprivation remedies were inadequate, did not state a due process claim); Durre v. Dempsey, 869 F.2d 543, 548 (10th Cir. 1989) (holding plaintiff must allege that defendants "have in fact denied him an adequate state remedy"); Barstow v. Kennebec County Jail, 115 F. Supp. 2d 3, 8 (D.Me. 2000).

[125]*See, e.g.*, Pletka v. Nix, 957 F.2d 1480, 1484 (8th Cir. 1992) ("It has always been true that a person may not be punished by government without due process of law."); McCann v. Coughlin, 698 F.2d 112, 121 (2d Cir. 1982) (holding that any time in SHU or 14 days or more of any other disciplinary confinement required due process).

[126]Gilbert v. Frazier, 931 F.2d 1581, 1582 (7th Cir. 1991); Green v. Ferrell, 801 F.2d 765, 768–69 (5th Cir. 1986) (holding that punishment always implicates a liberty interest because the requirement of guilt is a substantive limit on official discretion); Sher v. Coughlin, 739 F.2d 77, 81 (2d Cir. 1984) (holding "state statutes and regulations authorizing restrictive confinement *as punishment upon a finding of disciplinary infraction* will *invariably* provide sufficient limitation on the discretion of prison officials to create a liberty interest" (emphasis supplied)). Sometimes this is made explicit in the rules. *See* Wright v. Coughlin, 31 F. Supp. 2d 301, 311 (W.D.N.Y. 1998) (quoting state regulations provision that disciplinary sentences may be imposed only "upon an adverse disposition at a hearing conducted in accordance with the regulations"), *vacated and remanded on other grounds*, 225 F.3d 647 (2d Cir. 2000).

[127]*See* Hewitt v. Helms, 459 U.S. 460, 468, 470–72, 103 S. Ct. 864 (1983).

[128]Pretrial detainees are in a different legal situation, as described in § C of this chapter.

[129]Segregation would also require due process if it deprived prisoners of something independently protected by the Constitution. *See* § A.1 of this chapter. However, it does not. It is possible that very long periods of segregation will be found to be protected by due process under the Constitution itself because of the psychological harm that can result from prolonged isolated confinement, *see* § F.2 of this chapter, just as the Supreme Court has held that the use of mind-altering medications requires due process. *See* Washington v. Harper, 494 U.S. 210, 221–22, 110 S. Ct. 1028 (1990). So far courts have not found that to be the case for prisoners who do not already suffer from mental illness. *See* Williams v. Armontrout, 852 F.2d 377, 378–79 (8th Cir. 1988) (finding no liberty interest in administrative confinement after 13 years); *see also* §§ F.2, nn.152-155, F.3, n.159, and H.1.o of this chapter, nn.548–550.

[130]Sandin v. Conner, 515 U.S. 472, 484, 115 S. Ct. 2293 (1995). *See* §§ A, B of this chapter concerning the meaning of these terms.

have held that much longer segregation terms are not liberty deprivations either.

As to administrative segregation, before *Sandin* many courts had held that placement in it was not a liberty deprivation, because statutes and prison regulations left prison officials too much discretion to give rise to a liberty interest.[131] Now, under *Sandin*, administrative segregation too must be shown to impose atypical and significant hardship relative to ordinary prison conditions in order to create a liberty interest protected by due process.[132] However, if conditions are sufficiently harsh compared to ordinary prison conditions, courts applying *Sandin* may now find a liberty interest regardless of whether the regulation strictly limits officials' discretion.[133]

The law on what constitutes an atypical and significant hardship in segregation cases varies so much from one federal court to another that we are going to have to deal with each circuit separately. But first we want to identify the basic questions that *Sandin* presents for challenges to isolated confinement—some of which the courts have not clearly answered.

In *Sandin*, the prisoner served 30 days in punitive segregation, locked in his cell except for daily 50-minute exercise and shower periods, and isolated and restrained with leg irons and waist chains during those periods.[134] The Court said, in effect, that this was not a big deal—*i.e.*, that these conditions did not present

> a dramatic departure from the basic conditions of Conner's indeterminate sentence. . . . We hold that Conner's discipline in segregated confinement did not present the type of atypical, significant deprivation in which a State might conceivably create a liberty interest. The record shows that, at the time of Conner's punishment, disciplinary segregation, with insignificant exceptions, mirrored those conditions imposed upon inmates in administrative segregation and protective custody. We note also that the State expunged Conner's disciplinary record with

respect to the "high misconduct" charge nine months after Conner served time in segregation. Thus, Conner's confinement did not exceed similar, but totally discretionary, confinement in either duration or degree of restriction. Indeed, the conditions at Halawa involve significant amounts of "lockdown time" even for inmates in the general population. Based on a comparison between inmates inside and outside disciplinary segregation, the State's actions in placing him there for 30 days did not work a major disruption in his environment.[135]

The Court added that general population inmates "are confined to cells for anywhere between 12 and 16 hours a day, depending on their classification."[136] Of course, as the dissenting opinion pointed out, in general population the prisoner could have worked, taken classes, or mingled with others for eight hours a day.[137] Yet the Supreme Court said that placement in segregation was not a "dramatic departure" from the basic conditions of his sentence, and concluded: "The regime to which he was subjected as a result of the misconduct hearing was within the range of confinement to be normally expected for one serving an indeterminate term of 30 years to life."[138]

Sandin left the lower courts with very little guidance in determining what constitutes "atypical and significant hardship . . . in relation to the ordinary incidents of prison life,"[139] except that 30 days in 23-hour lock-up doesn't meet that standard. The Supreme Court later decided another case under the "atypical and significant" standard, holding that confinement in a "Supermax" prison is atypical and significant where

> almost all human contact is prohibited, even to the point that conversation is not permitted from cell to cell; the light, though it may be dimmed, is on for 24 hours; exercise is for 1 hour per day, but only in a small indoor room. Save perhaps for the especially severe limitations on all human contact, these conditions likely would apply to most solitary confinement facilities, but here there are two added components. First is the duration. Unlike the 30 day placement in *Sandin*, placement at OSP is indefinite and, after an initial 30 day review, is reviewed just annually. Second is that placement disqualifies an otherwise eligible inmate for parole consideration. . . . While any of these conditions standing alone might not be sufficient to create a liberty interest, taken together they impose an atypical and significant hardship within the correctional context. It follows that respondents have a liberty interest in avoiding assignment to OSP.[140]

---

[131]*See, e.g.*, Templeman v. Gunter, 16 F.3d 367, 369 (10th Cir. 1994); O'Bar v. Pinion, 953 F.2d 74, 84–85 (4th Cir. 1991); Williams v. Sweeney, 882 F. Supp. 1520, 1522–23 (E.D.Pa. 1995) (holding that jail regulations permitting placement in administrative segregation for certain reasons or "for other reasons as determined by the Warden" allowed so much discretion that no liberty interest was created).

[132]*See* Sealey v. Giltner, 197 F.3d 578, 585 (2d Cir. 1999); Hatch v. District of Columbia, 184 F.3d 846, 853 (D.C. Cir. 1999) (holding that regulations permitting administrative segregation in four circumstances created a liberty interest); Lee v Coughlin, 26 F. Supp. 2d 615, 633–35 (S.D.N.Y. 1998). In at least one case, a court has found that there is no liberty interest in avoiding initial placement in administrative segregation, but the regulations create one in avoiding prolonged retention there. *See* Tellier v. Fields, 280 F.3d 69, 82–83 (2d Cir. 2000) (analyzing federal prison regulations).

[133]*See* § F of this chapter, n.77.

[134]*Sandin v. Conner*, 515 U.S. 472, 494, 115 S. Ct. 2293 (1995) (dissenting opinion).

[135]*Sandin*, 515 U.S. at 485–86 (footnotes omitted).

[136]*Id.*, 515 U.S. at 486 n.8.

[137]*Id.*, 515 U.S. at 494.

[138]*Id.*, 515 U.S. at 487.

[139]*Id.*, 515 U.S. at 484.

[140]Wilkinson v. Austin, 545 U.S. 209, 223–24, 125 S. Ct. 2384 (2005); *see* Iqbal v. Hasty, 400 F.3d 143, 163 (2d Cir. 2007) (holding that under *Wilkinson*, alleged conditions including

The *Wilkinson* decision still did not do much to clarify where the line is between atypical and significant conditions and the "ordinary incidents of prison life." The unanswered questions are addressed in the following subsections.

1. What Does "Atypical" Mean?

The usual meaning of "atypical" is "unusual." In *Sandin*, as mentioned above, the Supreme Court emphasized that the conditions of disciplinary segregation the plaintiff was subjected to "mirrored" those in administrative segregation and protective custody, and were not all that different from general population.[141] You would think that courts would want to know what proportion of prisoners are subjected to a particular condition in determining whether it is atypical and significant. Only a few courts have taken that approach,[142] though hardly any have explicitly said it

is wrong.[143] One court has held that a punishment or restriction is not atypical if it is "routinely" imposed by prison officials—not that it is more likely than not to happen, but that there must be a "substantial chance" of its occurrence.[144] Some courts seem to assume that as long as whatever happens to the prisoner is authorized by prison rules, it is not atypical, without even asking how often it really happens.[145] At least one court has explicitly rejected that view.[146]

2. What Does "Significant" Mean?

In *Sandin*, the Court dismissed the 30-day placement of a general population prisoner in 23-hour isolated lock-up, with restraints during the hour out of cell, as not atypical and significant. Some courts have dismissed much worse conditions as not being atypical and significant even though they were imposed for much longer.[147] Other courts, however, consider "normal SHU conditions" atypical and significant if they last long enough.[148] One court in particular has held that courts must give suitable weight to the difference between being confined 23 hours a day and half the day,[149] even though the Supreme Court in *Sandin* seemed not to be impressed by that difference.[150] Several courts have

---

"solitary confinement, repeated strip and body-cavity searches, beatings, exposure to excessive heat and cold, very limited exercise, and almost constant lighting—as well as the initially indefinite duration of confinement" sufficiently pled atypical and significant hardship), *aff'd in part, rev'd in part, and remanded on other grounds sub nom.* Ashcroft v. Iqbal, ___ U.S. ___, 129 S. Ct. 1937 (2009); Westefer v. Snyder, 422 F.3d 570, 590 (7th Cir. 2005) (stating that claiming *Wilkinson*'s liberty interest turned exclusively on the absence of parole is "far too crabbed a reading of the decision"; plaintiffs' claim should not have been dismissed even though Illinois supermax cells have windows, the doors are mesh rather than solid steel, the exercise yard is partly outdoors, and visiting is not as limited as in *Wilkinson*).

[141]*Sandin*, 515 U.S. at 485–86.

[142]*See* Colon v. Howard, 215 F.3d 227, 232 (2d Cir. 2000) (stating courts might consider "the precise frequency of SHU confinements of varying durations" in the atypical and significant determination); Scott v. Coughlin, 78 F. Supp. 2d 299, 311 n.12 (S.D.N.Y. 2000) (stating that data showing only 1.58% of the prison population were placed in administrative segregation or involuntary protective custody and only 0.55% stayed as long as 60 days would support plaintiff's claim that 60 days' confinement was atypical and significant); Lee v. Coughlin, 26 F. Supp. 2d 615, 635 (S.D.N.Y. 1998) (weighing fact that plaintiff's segregation sentence was longer than 99% of disciplinary confinement sentences); McClary v. Kelly, 4 F. Supp. 2d 195 (W.D.N.Y. 1998) (using similar analysis for prisoner held in administrative segregation for four years). *Contra*, Edmonson v. Coughlin, 21 F. Supp. 2d 242, 249–50 (W.D.N.Y. 1998) (holding eight months' administrative segregation not atypical and significant since about 2% of the population serves as much as six months).

One recent appeal decision said: "Whatever the 'ordinary incidents of prison life' may encompass, they must be decided with reference to the particular prison system at issue, and can only be truly 'ordinary' when experienced by a significant proportion of the prison population." Austin v. Wilkinson, 372 F.3d 346, 355 (6th Cir. 2004), *aff'd in part and rev'd in part on other grounds*, 545 U.S. 209, 125 S. Ct. 2384 (2005). However, that court did not actually look at what proportion of the prison population experienced the conditions, and the Supreme Court, in reviewing the decision, did not address whether the proportion of prison population subject to

the challenged conditions plays a part in the "atypical and significant" analysis.

[143]One court has cautioned that a disciplinary punishment can be atypical and significant even if it is not unusual compared to other disciplinary punishments. It said that the point of *Sandin* is that deprivations are not serious enough to require due process if they "are typically endured by other prisoners, not as a penalty for misbehavior, but simply as the result of ordinary prison administration." Welch v. Bartlett, 196 F.3d 389, 394 (2d Cir. 1999); *accord*, Kalwasinski v. Morse, 201 F.3d 103, 107 (2d Cir. 1999).

[144]Hatch v. District of Columbia, 184 F.3d 846, 857–58 (D.C. Cir. 1999).

[145]*See* Griffin v. Vaughn, 112 F.3d 703, 707–09 (3d Cir. 1997).

[146]Hatch v. District of Columbia, 184 F.3d at 857.

[147]*See* Fraise v. Terhune, 283 F.3d 506, 523 & n.1 (3d Cir. 2002) (holding that placement in "maximum custody" in "Security Threat Group Management Unit" did not deprive prisoners of liberty although prisoners received only five hours out of cell a week, shower or shave every third day, strip searches every time they left their cells, one non-contact visit a month, one monitored phone call a month, all meals in cells, denial of all regular programs); Beverati v. Smith, 120 F.3d 500, 504 (4th Cir. 1997) (holding that filthy, vermin-infested, and flooded conditions, with unbearably hot cells, cold food, and smaller portions, no clean clothing or bedding, no outdoor recreation, etc., for six months were not atypical and significant).

[148]*See, e.g.*, Palmer v. Richards, 364 F.3d 60, 65 (2d Cir. 2004). The issue of duration is discussed below in § F.5 of this chapter.

[149]*See* Kawalsinski v. Morse, 201 F.3d 103, 106 (2d Cir. 1999).

[150]One court has pointed out major differences between the Hawaii's prison system at issue in *Sandin* and the New York prison system which justify different results in applying the atypical and significant standard. Among other things, the difference between general population and segregation appears to be larger in New York, and there is less discretion to place prisoners in segregation;

held that "supermax" confinement conditions, characterized by even greater isolation, lock-in time, idleness, property restrictions, etc., than in the usual segregation units, are atypical and significant.[151]

One issue that has not been explored very much is whether the recognized psychological impact of isolated confinement makes it "significant" for due process purposes. Though they were not mentioned in *Sandin* or in *Wilkinson*, the Supreme Court recognized these effects long ago,[152] and modern courts have done so as well, mostly in cases addressing whether certain conditions of confinement are so extreme as to violate the Eighth Amendment.[153] These consequences of isolation are arguably comparable to other psychological impacts that the Supreme Court has held cognizable under the Due Process Clause based on the Constitution itself.[154] A few decisions have cited these effects

as reasons for considering long terms in segregation as "significant" and therefore as calling for due process.[155]

One court has suggested that if a punishment appears disproportionately harsh for the offense, that fact "weighs in favor of an atypical and significant hardship."[156]

3. Significant Hardship for Everybody? Or Just the Plaintiff?

The same conditions may affect different people in different ways; can conditions be significant for due process purposes because of their particular effect on one individual? One court has held that placing a wheelchair-bound prisoner in a non-wheelchair-accessible SHU for a couple of months created an atypical and significant hardship for that person.[157] Another court said that placing a prisoner in SHU who was so tall that the cramped quarters and short bed aggravated a medical problem in his back could also be atypical and significant.[158] A similar argument might be made about people with mental illness. Courts have held that placing such persons in segregation can violate the Eighth Amendment because they are particularly susceptible to the psychological effects of isolation,[159] so placement

---

though there is a catchall provision allowing segregation in circumstances not spelled out by the rules, that provision is limited to "emergency or unusual situations." Punitive segregation is significantly different from administrative security. For those reasons, punitive confinement in New York does impose a "major disruption" on the prisoner's environment. Lee v. Coughlin, 26 F. Supp. 2d 615, 633–35 (S.D.N.Y. 1998).

[151]Wilkinson v. Austin, 545 U.S. 209, 223–24, 125 S. Ct. 2384 (2005); Gillis v. Litscher, 468 F.3d 495 (7th Cir. 2006); Westefer v. Snyder, 422 F.3d 570, 589–90 (7th Cir. 2005); Farmer v. Kavanagh, 494 F. Supp. 2d 345, 357 (D.Md. 2007); Koch v. Lewis, 216 F. Supp. 2d 994, 1000–01 (D.Ariz. 2001), *vacated as moot*, 399 F.3d 1099 (9th Cir. 2005).

[152]In solitary confinement, the Court said, "[a] considerable number of prisoners fell, after even a short confinement, into a semifatuous condition, from which it was next to impossible to arouse them, and others became violently insane; others still, committed suicide; while those who stood the ordeal better were not generally reformed, and in most cases did not recover sufficient mental activity to be of any subsequent service to the community." *In re* Medley, 134 U.S. 160, 168, 10 S. Ct. 384 (1890) (striking down a statute retroactively imposing solitary confinement as an *ex post facto* law).

[153]*See* Davenport v. DeRobertis, 844 F.2d 1310, 1313, 1316 (7th Cir. 1988) ("the record shows, what anyway seems pretty obvious, that isolating a human being from other human beings year after year or even month after month can cause substantial psychological damage, even if the isolation is not total"); Madrid v. Gomez, 889 F. Supp. 1146, 1235 (N.D.Cal. 1995); Langley v. Coughlin, 715 F. Supp. 522, 540 (S.D.N.Y. 1989); Bono v. Saxbe, 450 F. Supp. 934, 946–47 (E.D.Ill. 1978), *aff'd in part and remanded in part on other grounds*, 620 F.2d 609 (7th Cir. 1980). Several of these cases rely on the research and testimony of psychiatrist Stuart Grassian. *See* Stuart Grassian, M.D., *Psychopathological Effects of Solitary Confinement*, 140 AM.J.PSYCHIATRY 11 (1983); Stuart Grassian and Nancy Friedman, *Effects of Sensory Deprivation in Psychiatric Seclusion and Solitary Confinement*, 8 INT'L J. OF LAW AND PSYCHIATRY 49 (1986).

[154]*See* Washington v. Harper, 494 U.S. 210, 221–22, 110 S. Ct. 1028 (1990) (holding that prisoners possess "a significant liberty interest in avoiding the unwanted administration of antipsychotic drugs. . . ."); Vitek v. Jones, 445 U.S. 480, 492, 100 S. Ct. 1254 (1980) (citing exposure to "[c]ompelled treatment in the form of mandatory behavior modification programs" in holding that a prisoner's commitment to a mental hospital is a deprivation of liberty).

[155]*See* Colon v. Howard, 215 F.3d 227, 232 (2d Cir. 2000) (stating courts might consider "evidence of the psychological effects of prolonged confinement in isolation"); Shoats v. Horn, 213 F.3d 140, 144 (3d Cir. 2000) (citing evidence that prison officials would be concerned about psychological harm after 90 days of extreme isolation); Koch v. Lewis, 216 F. Supp. 2d 994, 1001 (D. Ariz. 2001) (citing "detrimental pathological effect" in finding extreme isolated confinement atypical and significant), *vacated as moot*, 399 F.3d 1099 (9th Cir. 2005); Lee v. Coughlin, 26 F. Supp. 2d 615, 637 (S.D.N.Y. 1998) ("The effect of prolonged isolation on inmates has been repeatedly confirmed in medical and scientific studies."); McClary v. Kelly, 4 F. Supp. 2d 195, 205–09 (W.D.N.Y. 1998) (holding the mental health risks of prolonged incarceration created atypical and significant hardship); Garcia v. Gomez, 1996 WL 390320, *3 (N.D.Cal., July 3, 1996) ("The SHU is stark to the point of being akin to a sensory deprivation tank. Almost exclusively, prisoners see nothing, do nothing and interact with no one, experiencing abject tedium"; finding a liberty interest in avoiding confinement in a particular SHU.), *vacated on other grounds*, 164 F.3d 630 (9th Cir. 1998).

[156]Cox v. Malone, 199 F. Supp. 2d 135, 143 (S.D.N.Y. 2002) (dictum), *aff'd*, 56 Fed.Appx. 43 (2d Cir. 2003) (unpublished).

[157]Serrano v. Francis, 345 F.3d 1071, 1079 (9th Cir. 2003) (stating "the conditions imposed on Serrano in the SHU, *by virtue of his disability*, constituted an atypical and significant hardship on him." (emphasis supplied)).

[158]Delany v. Selsky, 899 F. Supp. 923, 927–28 (N.D.N.Y. 1995).

[159]*See* Madrid v. Gomez, 889 F. Supp. 1146, 1265–66 (N.D.Cal. 1995) (holding unconstitutional placement of the mentally ill in Pelican Bay isolation unit); Casey v. Lewis, 834 F. Supp. 1477, 1548–49 (D.Ariz. 1993) (condemning placement and retention of mentally ill prisoners in lockdown status); Langley v. Coughlin, 715 F. Supp. 522, 540 (S.D.N.Y. 1988) (holding that psychiatric evidence that prison officials fail to screen out from SHU "those individuals who, by virtue of their mental condition, are likely to be severely and adversely affected by placement there" raises a

in segregation might be atypical and significant for them where it would not be for a person without mental illness.

4. Atypical and Significant Compared to What?

Sandin said that to require due process, conditions must "impose[] atypical and significant hardship . . . in relation to the ordinary incidents of prison life."[160] What are those "ordinary incidents" that conditions are to be compared to? The Supreme Court has acknowledged this question without answering it.[161] *Sandin* said that the prisoner's disciplinary segregation, "with insignificant exceptions, mirrored those conditions imposed upon inmates in administrative segregation and protective custody. . . . Thus, [his] confinement did not exceed similar, but totally discretionary, confinement in either duration or degree of restriction."[162] Some courts have held that this means administrative segregation and conditions similar to administrative segregation are never atypical and significant.[163] That in turn would mean that conditions must be atypical and significant compared to administrative segregation in order to require due process. Others have rejected this view, holding that if administrative segregation is *not* totally discretionary, it can be atypical and significant,[164] or simply that segregation conditions should be compared with general population conditions to decide if they are atypical and significant.[165]

Courts have also held that the ordinary conditions of administrative segregation can be atypical and significant if they last for an atypical length of time.[166]

5. Does Duration Matter?

Sandin said that the prisoner's 30-day confinement "did not exceed similar, but totally discretionary, confinement in either duration or degree of restriction."[167] That seems to imply that even ordinary segregation conditions can become atypical and significant if they go on long enough. Some courts have ruled to that effect.[168] Other courts appear not to think that length of confinement matters.[169] Courts that do consider the length of confinement have come out very differently in deciding how much segregation time it takes to be atypical and significant.[170] Obviously, after *Sandin*, time periods less than or only slightly more than 30 days will not be considered atypical and significant unless the conditions are extreme.[171] In administrative segregation cases, the Supreme Court has said that the potentially indefinite nature of the confinement weighs in favor of finding atypical and

triable Eighth Amendment issue); *see also* Inmates of Occoquan v. Barry, 717 F. Supp. 854, 868 (D.D.C. 1989) (holding that inmates with mental health problems must be placed in a separate area or a hospital and not in administrative/punitive segregation area). Discipline and mental health are discussed further in § H.1.o of this chapter.

[160]Sandin v. Conner, 515 U.S. 472, 484, 115 S. Ct. 2293 (1995).

[161]Wilkinson v. Austin, 545 U.S. 209, 223,125 S. Ct. 2384 (2005) (stating that the "supermax" conditions before it were atypical and significant "under any plausible baseline").

[162]Sandin, 515 U.S. at 486 (footnote omitted). The difference between administrative and punitive segregation conditions amounted to one extra phone call and one extra visit. *Id.* at 476 n.2.

[163]See Hatch v. District of Columbia, 184 F.3d 846, 857–58 (D.C. Cir. 1999); Wagner v. Hanks, 128 F.3d 1173, 1174–75 (7th Cir. 1997) (holding that segregated confinement is atypical and significant only if it is substantially more restrictive than any non-punitive confinement in the state's prison system).

In *Hatch*, the court acknowledged that many District of Columbia prisoners are transferred out of D.C. institutions, but rejected the jail officials' argument that "atypical and significant" should be assessed in relation to the most restrictive conditions routinely imposed at any prison in the country. 184 F.3d at 856–57. Instead, it said that conditions at other prisons should be considered only if it is "likely both that inmates serving sentenced similar to [the plaintiff's] and that once transferred they will actually face such conditions." *Id.* at 858.

[164]See Sealey v. Giltner, 197 F.3d 578, 585 (2d Cir. 1999).

[165]Palmer v. Richards, 364 F.3d 60, 65, 66 (2d Cir. 2004) (quoting Welch v. Bartlett, 196 F.3d 389, 393 (2d Cir. 1999)); Phillips v. Norris, 320 F.3d 844, 847 (8th Cir. 2003). *Contra*, Wagner

v. Hanks, 128 F.3d at 1175; Griffin v. Vaughn, 112 F.3d 703, 706 n.2 (3d Cir. 1997) (rejecting the use of general population as a basis for comparison). In *Jackson v. Carey*, 353 F.3d 750, 755 (9th Cir. 2003), the court referred to comparisons with general population or administrative segregation, "whichever is applicable."

[166]See, e.g., Hatch v. District of Columbia, 184 F.3d at 858. This point is discussed further in the next section.

[167]Sandin v. Conner, 515 U.S. 472, 486, 115 S. Ct. 2293 (1995).

[168]See Marion v. Columbia Correctional Institution, 559 F.3d 693, 697 (7th Cir. 2009); Palmer v. Richards, 364 F.3d 60, 64 (2d Cir. 2004); Mitchell v. Horn, 318 F.3d 523, 532 (3d Cir. 2003); Gaines v. Stenseng, 292 F.3d 1222, 1226 (10th Cir. 2002); Hatch v. District of Columbia, 184 F.3d 846, 858 (D.C. Cir. 1999).

[169]One circuit has said that "extended lockdown" for *30 years* would not be atypical and significant if it was imposed as part of initial classification into the prison, though it might if it was imposed for some other reason. Wilkerson v. Stalder, 329 F.3d 431, 435–36 (5th Cir. 2003).

[170]Compare Palmer v. Richards, 364 F.3d at 64 (holding 77 days under aggravated conditions could be atypical and significant); Colon v. Howard, 215 F.3d 227, 231–32 (2d Cir. 2000) (holding that confinement for less than 101 days under normal SHU conditions is probably not atypical and significant, 305 days is, and anything in between requires close examination of the first) *with* Smith v. Mensinger, 293 F.3d 641, 654 (3d Cir. 2002) (holding seven months not atypical and significant); Griffin v. Vaughn, 112 F.3d 703, 708 (3d Cir. 1997) (holding 15 months in segregation not atypical and significant).

[171]See Gillis v. Litscher, 468 F.3d 495, 490–91 (7th Cir. 2006) (holding 12 days in a "supermax" "Behavior Modification Program," with no property, no mail, phone, visitors, canteen items, writing materials, clothing, or bedding, limited toilet paper, and "nutri-loaf" for food, raised a jury question under the atypical and significant standard); Mitchell v. Horn, 318 F.3d 523, 527–28, 532 n.6 (3d Cir. 2003) (directing district court to consider whether four days confinement in a cell smeared with feces and infested with flies, in an area populated by mentally ill prisoners, was atypical and significant).

significant hardship.[172] One court has held that where a prisoner does not serve an entire disciplinary term, the relevant time period is the time actually served,[173] and where separate disciplinary sentences "constitute a sustained period of confinement," they should be aggregated (considered together) to decide if they are atypical and significant.[174] Similarly, where a prisoner has been held in pre-hearing segregation and then is kept in segregation after a hearing that denies due process, the entire period should be considered to determine whether it was atypical and significant.[175]

6. Does the Prisoner's Criminal Sentence Matter?

Sandin said that a punishment of 30 days in 23-hour lock-up was "well within the range of confinement to be normally expected for one serving an indeterminate term of 30 years to life."[176] It is hard to know what the Supreme Court meant by that statement. Why would 30 days in punitive segregation be any more or less "expected" for someone doing 30 to life than for someone doing one year? Some courts have applied this statement in *Sandin* and have given the prisoner's criminal sentence weight in determining whether a segregation term was atypical and significant.[177] Most courts simply have not mentioned the issue.

---

[172]Wilkinson v. Austin, 545 U.S. 209, 224, 125 S. Ct. 2384 (2005); *accord*, Koch v. Lewis, 216 F. Supp. 2d 994, 1001–02 (D. Ariz. 2001), *vacated as moot*, 399 F.3d 1099 (9th Cir. 2005). *But see* Johnston v. Vaughn, 2000 WL 1694029, *2 (E.D.Pa., Nov. 3, 2000) (noting that any administrative segregation prisoner can claim potentially indefinite confinement, and actual time served must be the "threshold consideration" in deciding whether there is a liberty interest).

[173]Hanrahan v. Doling, 331 F.3d 93, 97 (2d Cir. 2003); Colon v. Howard, 215 F.3d 227, 231 n.4 (2d Cir. 2000).

[174]*See* Giano v. Selsky, 238 F.3d 223, 226 (2d Cir. 2001) (holding that 92 days in administrative segregation was atypical and significant since it followed 670 days segregation at another prison); Sims v. Artuz, 230 F.3d 14, 23–24 (2d Cir. 2000) (noting that some or all of plaintiff's multiple disciplinary proceedings might properly be aggregated for determining atypical and significant question).

[175]Sealey v. Giltner, 197 F.3d 578, 587 (2d Cir. 1999) ("Whatever the point is beyond which confinement in harsh conditions constitutes atypicality, a prison official must not be permitted to extend such confinement beyond that point without according procedural due process.").

[176]Sandin v. Conner, 515 U.S. 472, 487, 115 S. Ct. 2293 (1995).

[177]*See, e.g.*, Hatch v. District of Columbia, 184 F.3d 846, 856 (D.C. Cir. 1999); Thomas v. Ramos, 130 F.3d 754, 761 (7th Cir. 1997) (noting, in holding segregation time not atypical and significant, that 70 days segregation is relatively short compared to the plaintiff's 12-year prison sentence); Rimmer-Bey v. Brown, 62 F.3d 789, 791 (6th Cir. 1995) (holding several years in administrative segregation was not atypical and significant "within the context of his life sentence," without explanation); Edmonson v. Coughlin, 21 F. Supp. 2d 242, 250 (W.D.N.Y. 1998) (noting that a prisoner with a longer sentence is more likely to have the chance to serve a longer segregation sentence, and therefore such a sentence is more typical and less significant than for someone with a shorter sentence);

7. Segregated Confinement and the Atypical and Significant Standard, Circuit by Circuit

As we have mentioned, the post-*Sandin* due process law varies considerably among jurisdictions. The most favorable and well-developed law is in the Second Circuit (New York, Vermont, and Connecticut). While Second Circuit decisions are the law only in the Second Circuit, they may be persuasive to courts in other circuits where significant questions are not yet settled. Below, we discuss the state of the law in each circuit.

First Circuit: This court has not yet made any substantial rulings applying the "atypical and significant" standard to segregated confinement.[178] Its main statement about the meaning of "atypical and significant" came in a case in which the prisoner was not put in segregation, but was removed from work release and placed in a medium security prison. The court said:

> As in *Sandin*, the state's action here did not in any way affect the duration of Dominique's state sentence. . . . Additionally, his transfer to a more secure facility subjected him to conditions no different from those ordinarily experienced by large numbers of other inmates serving their sentences in customary fashion. In *Sandin*, the Supreme Court observed that conditions in the segregated confinement at issue "mirrored those conditions imposed upon inmates in administrative segregation and protective custody." . . . The Court found support in this similarity for the proposition that "[b]ased on a comparison between inmates inside and outside disciplinary segregation, the State's actions in placing him there for 30 days did not work a major disruption in his environment." . . . Similarly here, any hardship was not "atypical" in relation to the ordinary incidents of prison life.[179]

This statement suggests that the First Circuit would not find disciplinary segregation conditions atypical and significant unless they were much more oppressive than conditions in other types of segregation. However, since disciplinary segregation was not actually at issue in *Dominique*, the question whether there is a liberty interest in avoiding segregated confinement is still an open one. Also, *Dominique* was decided the year after *Sandin*, so it is possible to argue that the law has developed significantly

---

Quartararo v. Catterson, 917 F. Supp. 919, 936–37 (E.D.N.Y. 1996) (weighing sentence length).

[178]In *Skinner v. Cunningham*, 430 F.3d 483 (1st Cir. 2005), the plaintiff was involved in a fight, and the other prisoner died as a result. He was placed in segregation for 40 days, then was acquitted of the criminal charges resulting from the death, and was returned to general population without ever receiving a hearing. The court noted the various interpretations of *Sandin* and said: "We think it is enough here that Skinner's segregation was rational, that its duration was not excessive, and that the central condition—isolation from other prisoners—was essential to its purpose." 430 F.3d at 487.

[179]Dominique v. Weld, 73 F.3d 1156, 1160 (1st Cir. 1996).

since then, and the First Circuit should adopt rules like the Second Circuit rules discussed below.[180] *Dominique* also did not address at all the question whether the long duration of segregated confinement may make it atypical and significant. Most district court cases in the First Circuit addressing due process requirements for segregated confinement have involved relatively short periods of segregation and have made no attempt to explore the broader question whether segregation can ever be atypical and significant.[181]

Second Circuit: The Second Circuit has said that courts must consider both the duration and the conditions of segregated confinement to decide what is atypical and significant.[182] It has also said that in making that judgment, the court must consider segregation conditions as compared to general population, not just to other segregation conditions.[183] It must give suitable weight to the difference between being confined 23 hours a day in segregation and half the day in general population, and must examine the extent of interruptions of prison programming.[184] In general, confinement in a "special housing unit" (SHU) for 305 days or more is atypical and significant; confinement for less than 101 days under "normal SHU conditions" is probably not atypical and significant; and confinement for any period of time in between requires a close examination of the conditions of confinement and detailed findings by the district court, preferably after appointment of counsel to develop the necessary record.[185] Confinement for shorter periods than 101 days can be atypical and significant if the conditions are worse than normal SHU conditions,[186] as they are at certain SHU-only prisons.[187] If the plaintiff alleges that the actual conditions diverge from those provided by

---

[180]In a slightly later case, the court stated: "In *Sandin*, the Court concluded that solitary confinement did not present the type of atypical, significant deprivation in which a state might conceivably create a liberty interest." McGuinness v. Dubois, 75 F.3d 794, 797 n.3 (1st Cir. 1996). That statement, which is more disadvantageous to prisoners than *Dominique*'s, and which also goes further than what the Supreme Court actually said in *Sandin*, is dictum—not precedent—because the prisoner in that case had lost good time, and was entitled to due process for that reason, so the court did not need to rule on anything related to segregated confinement. By now, a number of courts have held that there can be a liberty interest in avoiding segregated confinement under some circumstances, so you can argue that this statement in *McGuinness*—which was made only a year after *Sandin*—is simply wrong as a statement of current law.

[181]*See, e.g.*, Hewes v. Magnusson, 350 F. Supp. 2d 222, 235 (D.Me. 2004) (holding segregation for periods of one month and two weeks not atypical and significant); DeWitt v. Wall, 2004 WL 235445, *5 (D.R.I. 2004) (30 days), *aff'd as modified*, 121 Fed.Appx. 398 (1st Cir. 2004) (unpublished); Childers v. Maloney, 247 F. Supp. 2d 32, 36 (D.Mass. 2003) (10 days).

Some decisions in the District of Massachusetts have held longer segregation terms not to be atypical and significant, adopting the Seventh Circuit's view that since *Sandin*, "the right to litigate disciplinary confinements has become vanishingly small." Balsavich v. Mahoney, 2004 WL 1497687, *3 (D.Mass., July 6, 2004) (12 months) (quoting Wagner v. Hanks, 128 F.3d 1173, 1175 (7th Cir. 1997)); *accord*, Orwat v. Maloney, 360 F. Supp. 2d 146, 160–61 (D.Mass. 2005) (eight months).

[182]Palmer v. Richards, 364 F.3d 60, 64 (2d Cir. 2004).

The plaintiff's testimony can be sufficient to establish what the conditions are. Sealey v. Giltner, 197 F.3d 578, 586 (2d Cir. 1999).

[183]Palmer v. Richards, 364 F.3d at 65, 66 (quoting Welch v. Bartlett, 196 F.3d 389, 393 (2d Cir. 1999)); *accord*, Davis v. Barrett, 576 F.3d 129, 135 (2d Cir. 2009); *see* Lee v. Coughlin, 26 F. Supp. 2d 615, 633–35 (S.D.N.Y. 1998) (noting that New York's prison system differs from the Hawaii system addressed in *Sandin* in that the difference between general population and segregation is larger in New York, punitive segregation is significantly different from administrative segregation, and there is less discretion to place prisoners in segregation; therefore punitive confinement in

New York, unlike Hawaii does impose a "major disruption" on the prisoner's environment).

[184]Kalwasinski v. Morse, 201 F.3d 103, 106–07 (2d Cir. 1999); *see* Ramirez v. McGinnis, 75 F. Supp. 2d 147, 152 (S.D.N.Y. 1999) (weighing loss of programs interrupted by SHU placement).

[185]Colon v. Howard, 215 F.3d 227, 231–32 (2d Cir. 2000); *accord*, Palmer v. Richards, 364 F.3d at 64–65.

A detailed factual inquiry is not necessary "in cases involving shorter periods of segregated confinement where the plaintiff has not alleged any unusual conditions." Hynes v. Squillace, 143 F.3d 653, 658 (2d Cir. 1998) (six weeks in SHU following 21 days in pre-hearing "keeplock").

[186]*See* Davis v. Barrett, 576 F.3d at 134–35 (court must examine actual conditions of 55-day stay where plaintiff alleged abnormal conditions including no out-of-cell exercise, denial of cell study and commissary privileges afforded other prisoners, no furnishings, and grossly unsanitary conditions); Palmer v. Richards, 364 F.3d at 65–66 (holding that 77 days in SHU could be atypical and significant where the prisoner alleged deprivation of personal clothing, grooming equipment, hygiene products, reading and writing materials, and other items; mechanical restraints when out of his cell; lack of communication with family); Ortiz v. McBride, 380 F.3d 649, 651–52, 654–55 (2d Cir. 2004) (holding 90-day SHU confinement where the prisoner alleged, among other aggravating conditions, that he spent 3 weeks of 24-hour lock-in, denial of personal hygiene items, and meals served without utensils and with no ability to wash his hands, sufficiently alleged atypical and significant hardship); Welch v. Bartlett, 196 F.3d 389, 393 (2d Cir. 1999) (holding that allegations of 90 days' SHU confinement with inadequate amounts of toilet paper, soap, and cleaning materials, a filthy mattress, and infrequent changes of clothing stated a claim of atypical and significant hardship); Smart v. Goord, 441 F. Supp. 2d 631, 640 (S.D.N.Y. 2006) (70-day stay in involuntary protective custody stated a claim), *reconsideration granted in part and denied in part on other grounds*, 2008 WL 591230 (S.D.N.Y. 2008); Ramirez v. McGinnis, 75 F. Supp. 2d 147, 151–52 (S.D.N.Y. 1999) (holding allegation of 60 days SHU sufficiently alleged atypical and significant hardship; weighing allegations of conditions inconsistent with SHU regulations, and loss of programs interrupted by SHU placement). *But see* Beckford v. Portuondo, 151 F. Supp. 2d 204, 218–19 (N.D.N.Y. 2001) (holding that restricted diet, limited water, and placement behind a plexiglass shield for periods not exceeding a week were not atypical and significant).

[187]*Colon*, 215 F.3d at 234 n.7 (citing Lee v. Coughlin, 26 F. Supp. 2d 615, 632–33 (S.D.N.Y. 1998)) (noting greater use of

regulation, the court must examine the actual conditions.[188] The record might also include "evidence of the psychological effects of prolonged confinement in isolation and the precise frequency of SHU confinements of varying durations."[189] The relevant time period is the time actually served in cases where the prisoner does not serve the entire sentence.[190] "Normal SHU conditions" means those authorized by the prison regulations: 23-hour lock-up with one hour of exercise, two showers a week, denial of work and education, reduced frequency of visits, limited property, etc.[191] Where the prisoner serves more than one SHU term consecutively, the terms should be aggregated (considered together) for purposes of deciding whether the confinement was atypical and significant.[192]

New York also employs the sanction of "keeplock," which used to mean locking the prisoner in his or her own cell rather than in SHU.[193] Nowadays, some prisoners nominally sentenced to keeplock actually serve part or all of their time in SHU,[194] and others are placed in separate "keeplock blocks."[195] To date, the lower courts have mostly treated keeplock the same as SHU in their *Sandin* analyses.[196]

Third Circuit: This court, like the Second Circuit, has stated: "In deciding whether a protected liberty interest exists under *Sandin*, we consider the duration of the disciplinary confinement and the conditions of that confinement in relation to other prison conditions," and that the *Sandin* test is a "fact-specific" one.[197] However, the results in the Third Circuit so far have been much less favorable to prisoners than in the Second Circuit. In *Griffin v. Vaughn*,[198] the plaintiff was held in administrative segregation for 15 months on suspicion of raping a correctional officer. The court said this treatment was not atypical and significant, because state regulations provided for administrative segregation and prescribe the conditions under which the plaintiff was kept, and these are applicable to prisoners in a variety of circumstances. It said: "It is also apparent that it is not atypical for inmates to be exposed to those conditions"[199]— even though the regulations say that segregation for investigative purposes shall not exceed 10 days, renewable by the Superintendent for another 10 days. The court did not examine how many prisoners were actually subjected to the conditions at issue for as long as 15 months. The court rejected the proposition that general population is the proper basis of comparison for determining what is atypical and significant.[200] It said: "If an inmate is committed for an atypical period of time to undesirable conditions in violation of state law, that is clearly a factor to be considered in determining whether he has been subjected to atypical and significant hardship and, accordingly, whether due process protection has been triggered."[201] Later decisions are consistent with *Griffin*, holding periods of months in segregation not atypical and significant.[202] The only prisoner to win on the atypical and significant issue in a Third Circuit case had been held in segregation under uniquely harsh conditions for *eight years*.[203]

---

restraints, solitary exercise in restraints, limited visiting at high-security segregation facility).

[188]Davis v. Barrett, 576 F.3d at 135.

[189]*Colon*, 215 F.3d at 232.

[190]*Colon*, 215 F.3d at 231 n.4; *accord,* Hanrahan v. Doling, 331 F.3d 93, 97 (2d Cir. 2003). (But for purposes of analyzing the qualified immunity of the hearing officer, the focus should be on the sentence imposed by the hearing officer, regardless of whether it was later modified. *Hanrahan,* 331 F.3d at 98.).

[191]Palmer v. Richards, 364 F.3d at 65 (quoting prison regulations).

[192]Giano v. Selsky, 238 F.3d 223, 226 (2d Cir. 2001) (holding that 92 days in administrative segregation was atypical and significant since it followed 670 days segregation at another prison); Sims v. Artuz, 230 F.3d 14, 23–24 (2d Cir. 2000) (multiple disciplinary proceedings might properly be aggregated for atypical and significant determination); Sealey v. Giltner, 197 F.3d 578, 587 (2d Cir. 1999) (pre- and post-hearing confinement should both be considered).

[193]*See* McKinnon v. Patterson, 568 F.2d 930 (2d Cir. 1977).

[194]*See* Samuels v. Selsky, 2002 WL 31040370, *9 (S.D.N.Y. 2002); Rivera v. Wohlrab, 232 F. Supp. 2d 117, 122 (S.D.N.Y. 2002) (noting similar allegation).

[195]*See* Muhammad v. Pico, 2003 WL 21792158, *4 (S.D.N.Y. 2003) (alleging confinement in "long-term keeplock block").

[196]*See, e.g.,* Muhammad v. Pico, *id.,* at *14–15; Bunting v. Nagy, 2003 WL 21305339, *3 (S.D.N.Y., June 6, 2003); Jackson v. Johnson, 15 F. Supp. 2d 341, 346 (S.D.N.Y. 1998) (holding 99 days in keeplock followed by denial of parole was sufficient to withstand summary judgment under the atypical and significant standard). *But see* Beckford v. Portuondo, 151 F. Supp. 2d 204, 219 (N.D.N.Y. 2001) (holding that six months of keeplock did not implicate a liberty interest).

[197]Mitchell v. Horn, 318 F.3d 523, 532 (3d Cir. 2003).

[198]112 F.3d 703 (3d Cir. 1997).

[199]Griffin v. Vaughn, 112 F.3d at 708.

[200]*Griffin,*112 F.3d at 706 n.2.

[201]*Griffin*, 112 F.3d at 708–09; *see* Mitchell v. Horn, 318 F.3d 523, 527, 533 n.6 (3d Cir. 2003) (directing district court to consider whether four days confinement in a cell smeared with feces and infested with flies, in an area populated by mentally ill prisoners, was atypical and significant).

[202]Smith v. Mensinger, 293 F.3d 641, 654 (3d Cir. 2002) (seven months); Torres v. Fauver, 292 F.3d 141, 151–52 (3d Cir. 2002) (15 days disciplinary detention followed by 120 days of administrative segregation); *see* Mitchell v. Horn, 318 F.3d at 531–33 (noting similarity of case to *Griffin*, but remanding for more factual development).

In *Fraise v. Terhune*, 283 F.3d 506, 522–23 (3d Cir. 2002), the court held it was not atypical and significant to place members of the Five Percenters in a "Security Threat Group Management Unit," since such custody is within the terms of their sentences. The conditions in this unit were comparable to many segregation units: five hours out of cell a week, shower or shave every third day, strip searches every time prisoners leave their cells, one non-contact visit a month, one monitored phone call a week, all meals in cells, no access to regular prison programs. *Fraise*, 283 F.3d at 523 n.1 (dissenting opinion). The court does not say how long prisoners spent in that unit; they were required to complete a "three-phase behavior modification and education program" and must renounce in writing all affiliations with Security Threat Groups in order to be eligible to return population. *Fraise*, 283 F.3d at 511.

[203]Shoats v. Horn, 213 F.3d 140, 144 (3d Cir. 2000). The plaintiff was subject to 23-hour lock-in and denied radio and TV, phone

Fourth Circuit: In this circuit, which has been notoriously unfavorable to prisoners' civil rights claims, the leading case applying *Sandin* to segregated confinement held that prisoners sentenced to a month in segregation, then kept there for five or six months more after their terms expired, were not subjected to atypical and significant hardship. First, the court said that the regulations say that conditions are mostly similar to those in general population and that "even those conditions that are more restrictive are not particularly onerous. Indeed, the differences in conditions specified in the prison regulations appear to be fairly common ones, leading the other courts of appeals to conclude that confinement to administrative segregation does not implicate a liberty interest."[204] The prisoners alleged that the actual conditions did not conform to the regulations and that

> ... [T]heir cells were infested with vermin; were smeared with human feces and urine; and were flooded with water from a leak in the toilet on the floor above.... In addition, inmates maintain that their cells were unbearably hot and that the food they received was cold.... [They] did not receive clean clothing, linen or bedding, as often as required by the regulations governing administrative segregation; that they were permitted to leave their cells three to four times per week, rather than seven, and that no outside recreation was permitted; that there were no educational or religious services available; and that food was served in considerably smaller portions....

The court said that while these alleged conditions "were more burdensome than those imposed on the general prison population, they were not so atypical that exposure to them for six months imposed a significant hardship in relation to the ordinary incidents of prison life."[205] If the Fourth Circuit does not consider those conditions atypical and significant, it is hard to imagine what conditions would meet that standard in that court. However, a more recent unpublished decision states that claims of segregation conditions involving deprivation of out-of-cell exercise for seven months "have an arguable basis in law and fact" and the lower court must consider whether they implicated a liberty interest.[206] A later district court decision decided after *Wilkinson v. Austin* focused entirely on segregation conditions, holding

that a prisoner transferred to Maryland's "supermax" prison was deprived of a liberty interest without discussing the nine-month length of confinement.[207]

Fifth Circuit: This circuit initially held that *Sandin* "establishes that [the prisoner's] administrative segregation, without more, does not constitute a deprivation of a constitutionally cognizable liberty interest," without paying any attention either to the duration of confinement or to the conditions.[208] Some years later, it reviewed the case of prisoners held in "extended lockdown" (23-hour lock-up in small cells, 3 hours solitary outdoor exercise a week, restricted property, reading materials, legal access, etc.) for about *thirty years* and held that if their placement resulted from their initial classification upon entering the prison, there was no due process claim because prisoners have no protectable liberty interest in classification.[209] However, if their placement was not based on initial classification, the lower court would have to apply the *Sandin* test and would have to decide what to compare the extended lockdown conditions to in order to determine if they were "atypical."[210] In a later case, the court held that "confinement to a shared cell for twelve months with permission to leave only for showers, medical appointments, and family visits," with no out-of-cell exercise at all, was not atypical and significant.[211]

---

calls except in emergencies, books other than legal and religious, contact with his family, all program activities, and access to the library. *See also* Young v. Beard, 227 Fed.Appx. 138 (3d Cir.2007) (unpublished) (930 days in segregation is not atypical and significant); Pressley v. Blaine, 544 F. Supp. 2d 446, 455 (W.D.Pa. 2008) (1080 days; "If 930 days does not continue an atypical hardship, a mere five months more does not either."); Blackwell v. Vaughn, 2001 WL 872777, *4 (E.D.Pa. 2001) (stating that a prisoner who had been in administrative segregation for five years following a disciplinary segregation sentence "could conceivably have a protected liberty interest").

[204]Beverati v. Smith, 120 F.3d 500, 503–04 (4th Cir. 1997).

[205]*Beverati*, 120 F.3d at 504.

[206]McNeill v. Currie, 84 Fed.Appx. 276, 278 (4th Cir. 2003) (unpublished).

[207]Farmer v. Kavanagh, 494 F. Supp. 2d 345, 357 (D.Md. 2007) ("In light of the prohibition of 'almost all human contact,' coupled with severe restrictions on movement or any type of activity, both of which may last for the duration of some inmates' underlying sentences, and may be less likely to be relieved by parole than the less arduous conditions at other facilities, the conditions at MCAC create such a hardship when judged against 'any plausible baseline.'"). In Ajaj v. U.S., 479 F. Supp. 2d 501, 515 (D.S.C. 2007), the court held that confinement in SHU did not deprive the plaintiff of liberty, since the conditions there were "not nearly so restrictive and atypical as those at issue in *Wilkinson*." The court did not refer to the length of his confinement, which was only five days. *Ajaj*, 479 F. Supp. 2d at 505. *See* Gambrell v. Turner, 2009 WL 789777 (D.S.C., March 23, 2009) (holding 173-day confinement in "Special Management Unit" with no allegation of harsh conditions was not atypical and significant).

[208]Luken v. Scott, 71 F.3d 192, 193 (5th Cir. 1995) (per curiam); *accord*, Madison v. Parker, 104 F.3d 765, 768 (5th Cir. 1997) (holding that 30-day cell restriction and commissary restriction are "merely changes in the conditions of his confinement and do not implicate due process concerns"); Pichardo v. Kinker, 73 F.3d 612, 613 (5th Cir. 1996) (holding placement in administrative segregation was not a liberty deprivation, without mentioning conditions or duration). In a case about parole rights, the court said that "it is difficult to see that any other deprivations in the prison context, short of those that clearly impinge on the duration of confinement, will henceforth qualify for constitutional 'liberty' status." Orellana v. Kyle, 65 F.3d 29, 31–32 (5th Cir. 1995).

[209]Wilkerson v. Stalder, 329 F.3d 431, 435–36 (5th Cir. 2003).

[210]*Wilkerson*, 329 F.3d at 436.

[211]Hernandez v. Velasquez, 522 F.3d 556, 562–63 (5th Cir. 2008).

Sixth Circuit: This court has recently tried to clear up some of the confusion caused by its earlier cases. In its most recent decision, *Harden-Bey v. Rutter*,[212] it held that a prisoner's allegation that he had been held in administrative segregation without a hearing for three years and that his confinement was "indefinite" stated a due process claim, and that both conditions and duration play a part in determining what is atypical and significant.[213] It repudiated the statement in an earlier case that administrative segregation does not involve atypical and significant hardship "without regard to duration."[214] That earlier decision, the court said, addressed a situation where prison authorities segregated a prison murder suspect for two and a half years during investigation and pending a hearing; the present case was different because the prisoner had been confined longer, confinement was indefinite rather than awaiting a hearing, and no reason had yet been presented with the reason for the prison authorities' actions.[215] It dismissed other earlier cases[216] as addressing only the question whether initial placement in administrative segregation, or a relatively brief stay (117 days[217]), is atypical and significant, and not the question "whether the placement may last into perpetuity without becoming 'atypical and significant.'"[218] *Harden-Bey* left standing the idea that the existence of a liberty interest requiring due process protections is determined in part by whether the defendants had "good reason" for the confinement.[219] This idea that due process is not required because officials have a good reason for their actions seems backwards to us, and to miss the point of due process, which is to provide fair procedures to determine whether "good reason" actually exists.

Harden-Bey told the lower court to examine the "nature" as well as the duration of the plaintiff's

confinement,[220] but didn't say how to do that. Earlier, however, the court found segregated confinement atypical and significant in a case involving the state's "supermax" segregation facility. The court didn't say exactly what conditions the "supermax" should be compared to in determining whether they were atypical and significant, but it rejected state officials' arguments that the proper basis of comparison was "supermax" prisons in other states. "Whatever the 'ordinary incidents of prison life' may encompass, they must be decided with reference to the particular prison system at issue, and can only be truly 'ordinary' when experienced by a significant proportion of the prison population."[221] In finding the conditions atypical and significant, the Sixth Circuit noted that the lower court had compared them to those in the segregation units of maximum security prisons.[222] However, since *Harden-Bey* told the lower court to consider the conditions in ordinary administrative segregation and not maximum security punitive segregation, it may be that extreme "supermax" conditions are not necessary to establish a liberty interest in avoiding long terms in segregation.

Seventh Circuit: This court has gone back and forth in its statements about segregation and liberty interests. Early in 2009, it stated in a case involving 240 days of segregation: "The Supreme Court's decisions in *Sandin* and *Wilkinson* establish that disciplinary segregation *can* trigger due process protections depending on the duration and conditions of segregation."[223] In prior cases, it had said that segregation could almost never be a deprivation of a liberty interest,[224]

---

[212]524 F.3d 789 (6th Cir. 2008).

[213]Harden-Bey v. Rutter, 524 F.3d at 793.

[214]*Harden-Bey*, 524 F.3d at 794 (citing Jones v. Baker, 155 F.3d 810, 812 (6th Cir.1998)).

[215]*Harden-Bey*, 524 F.3d at 794 (citing Jones v. Baker).

[216]*Harden-Bey*, 524 F.3d at 794–95 (citing Harbin-Bey v. Rutter, 420 F.3d 571, 577 (6th Cir. 2005)); Mackey v. Dyke, 111 F.3d 460, 461 (6th Cir.1997); Rimmer-Bey v. Brown, 62 F.3d 789, 789 (6th Cir.1995).

[217]Mackey v. Dyke, 111 F.3d at 161.

[218]*Harden-Bey*, 524 F.3d at 795; *See* Gibbs v. Ball, 2009 WL 331604, *8 (E.D.Mich., Feb. 11, 2009) (6–18 months was not atypical and significant).

[219]*Harden-Bey*, 524 F.3d at 794 (citing Jones v. Baker, 155 F.3d at 812, which noted the serious charge—murder of a prison staff member—against the plaintiff); *see* Bey v. Luoma, 2008 WL 4534427, *6 (W.D.Mich., Sept. 30, 2008) (three years' segregation based on serious accusations of misconduct was not atypical and significant). One lower court has turned this idea in the plaintiff's favor and held that placement in administrative segregation as retaliation for complaining about sexual assault was atypical and significant because it was not justified. Ortiz v. Voinovich, 211 F. Supp. 2d 917, 928–29 (S.D.Ohio 2002).

[220]*Harden-Bey*, 524 F.3d at 795.

[221]Austin v. Wilkinson, 372 F.3d 346, 355 (6th Cir. 2004), *aff'd in part and rev'd in part on other grounds*, 545 U.S. 209, 125 S. Ct. 2384 (2005).

[222]*Austin*, 372 F.3d at 353 (noting lower court's finding that "the extreme isolation visited upon the inmates at OSP, the lack of any outdoor recreation, the limitations upon personal property rights and access to telephones and counsel and, finally, the ineligibility of OSP inmates for parole, all combined to create a significant and atypical hardship"). The Supreme Court affirmed that conditions were atypical and significant, but did not address the reasoning that conditions must be experienced by a "significant proportion of the prison population" to constitute the "ordinary incidents of prison life" which form the basis of comparison and determination of what is atypical and significant. Rather, the Court said that "we are satisfied that assignment to OSP imposes an atypical and significant hardship under any plausible baseline." Wilkinson v. Austin, 545 U.S. 209, 223, 125 S. Ct. 2384 (2005).

[223]Marion v. Columbia Correctional Institution, 559 F.3d 693, 697 (7th Cir. 2009).

[224]The court said in 2008:

> . . . [I]nmates have no liberty interest in avoiding transfer to discretionary segregation—that is, segregation imposed for administrative, protective, or investigative purposes. . . . [T]here is nothing "atypical" about discretionary segregation; [it] is instead an "ordinary incident of prison life" that inmates should expect to experience during their time in prison.

Townsend v. Fuchs, 522 F.3d 765, 771 (7th Cir. 2008) (citations omitted).

and that the liberty interest found by the Supreme Court in *Wilkinson* was based "largely on the fact that placement was indefinite and disqualified otherwise eligible inmates from consideration for parole."[225] On the other hand, a plaintiff placed for 12 days in the extremely harsh conditions of a "Behavior Modification Program" within a "Supermax" prison was held entitled to a trial under the atypical and significant standard.[226] The 2009 *Marion* decision, however, said that earlier decisions taking a very restrictive approach involved much shorter periods of time than 240 days, and cited even earlier cases, and decisions from other courts, that took a more liberal view of when segregation might be a liberty deprivation.[227] It concluded that a term of segregation as long as 240 days "requires scrutiny of the actual conditions of segregation" to determine if it is atypical and significant.[228]

The Seventh Circuit has said that segregated confinement is atypical and significant only if it is substantially more restrictive than *any* non-punitive confinement anywhere in the state's prison system; the proper comparison is not with general population.[229] The *Marion* decision acknowledged that point, but said it was premature, since under the Supreme Court's *Wilkinson* decision, "whether an inmate has a protected liberty interest must be determined from the *actual* conditions of confinement and not simply from a review of state regulations."[230]

The law in the Seventh Circuit must be viewed as unsettled, given the sharp differences between *Marion* and some earlier decisions. Be sure you have seen the court's most recent decisions if you are considering a segregation due process challenge in that circuit.[231]

Eighth Circuit: This court has generally rejected prisoners' claims that their segregated confinement was atypical and significant, without providing much explanation of how it reaches its conclusions or how lower courts should approach the question.[232] Most recently, however, it said: "We have consistently held that a demotion to segregation, even without cause, is not itself atypical and significant hardship. . . . Thus, in order for [a prisoner] to assert a liberty interest, he must show some difference between his new conditions in segregation and the conditions in the general population which amounts to an atypical and significant hardship."[233] Thus, it appears that this court now thinks the proper standard of comparison (the "ordinary incidents of prison life") is conditions in the general population—at least for prisoners who are sent to segregation from general population.[234] However, it held that the conditions cited by the plaintiff—denial of contact visits, exercise, and religious

---

[225]Townsend v. Fuchs, 522 F.3d at 772; *accord*, Gillis v. Litscher, 468 F.3d 488, 492 (7th Cir. 2006) (adding that "*Wilkinson* does not answer the question as to when the denial of life's necessities alone could give rise to a liberty interest but still fall short of violating the Eighth Amendment"; there is "a 'small space' between the two." (quoting Wagner v. Hanks, 128 F.3d 1173, 1174 (7th Cir. 1997)); *see* Westefer v. Snyder, 422 F.3d 570, 589–90 (7th Cir. 2005) (holding confinement in a "Supermax" unit where the prisoners were eligible for parole but restricted in their ability to earn good time, and where confinement was potentially indefinite, stated a due process claim under the atypical and significant standard).

[226]Gillis v. Litscher, 468 F.3d 495 (7th Cir. 2006). In stage one of the program, the plaintiff had no property, no privileges (no mail, phone, visitors, canteen items, writing materials), and no clothing, slept on a concrete slab with no bedding, was provided very limited quantities of toilet paper, and was fed "nutri-loaf." Stage two was somewhat less harsh. *Gillis*, 468 F.3d at 490–91.

[227]Marion v. Columbia Correctional Institution, 559 F.3d at 697–99.

The *Marion* decision noted that other circuits "have held that periods of confinement that approach or exceed one year may trigger a cognizable liberty interest without any reference to conditions," and cited cases from the Second Circuit. 559 F.3d at 698–99 & nn.3–4. Previously, the court had said that the Second Circuit's decisions "leave the door open a bit wider than *Sandin* . . . appears to allow." Wagner v. Hanks, 128 F.3d 1173, 1175 (7th Cir. 1997).

[228]*Marion*, 559 F.3d at 698.

[229]Wagner v. Hanks, 128 F.3d 1173, 1175 (7th Cir. 1997); *accord*, Lekas v. Briley, 405 F.3d 602, 608–09 (7th Cir. 2005) (holding that a comparison with general population is the same as with discretionary segregation, since anyone in general population may be placed in discretionary segregation).

[230]*Marion*, 559 F.3d at 699 (emphasis supplied) (citing Wilkinson v. Austin, 545 U.S. 209, 223, 125 S. Ct. 2384 (2005)).

[231]As we write this, there are only a few district court decisions assessing such claims after *Marion*. Mustache v. Johnson, 2009 WL 1683207, *3 (E.D.Wis., June 16, 2009) (35 days not atypical and significant); Williams v. Humphrey, 2009 WL 1444160, *2, 5 (W.D.Wis., May 20, 2009) (180 days is long enough to require inquiry into conditions).

[232]"We have consistently held that administrative and disciplinary segregation are not atypical and significant hardships under *Sandin*." Portley-El v. Brill, 288 F.3d 1063, 1065 (8th Cir. 2002) (citations omitted). In *Portley*, the plaintiff was placed in punitive segregation for 30 days and then returned to the state he had come from, where he was placed in administrative segregation. The court held that his failure to spell out what he thought was atypical and significant about his treatment meant that his claim was "defectively pleaded" and had to be dismissed. *Id.*

[233]Phillips v. Norris, 320 F.3d 844, 847 (8th Cir. 2003); *accord*, Johnson v. Hamilton, 452 F.3d 967, 973 (8th Cir. 2006); *see* Wycoff v. Nichols, 94 F.3d 1187, 1190 (8th Cir. 1996) (holding 45 days in segregation was not actionable without evidence in the record that the conditions "were atypical of the ordinary conditions of confinement or that they rose to the level of a significant deprivation").

[234]In earlier cases where prisoners were sent to punitive segregation from another form of segregation, the court used the previous form of segregation as the basis of comparison. *See* Rahman X. v. Morgan, 300 F.3d 970, 973–74 (8th Cir. 2002) (holding that 15 months in a segregation cell was not atypical and significant for a death row prisoner since the actual conditions of his confinement were not much different from death row); Kennedy v. Blankenship, 100 F.3d 640, 642–43 (8th Cir. 1996) (holding that "demotion" from administrative segregation to punitive isolation for 30 days (as happened to the plaintiff in *Sandin*) was not atypical

services—were not atypical and significant; it is impossible to tell how much weight the court gave the conditions, and how much it gave their relatively short duration.[235] In an earlier case, the court held that segregation for 15 days in the most restrictive level of disciplinary detention and 107 days in less restrictive detention conditions was not atypical and significant, without much explanation.[236] The only segregation cases in which the Eighth Circuit has actually ruled for prisoners on the atypical and significant issue are unpublished decisions involving confinement of a decade or more.[237]

Ninth Circuit: This court appears to take a more flexible approach to the atypical and significant question than most other circuits. It has said:

> Rather than invoking a single standard for determining whether a prison hardship is atypical and significant, we rely on a "condition or combination of conditions or factors [that] requires case by case, fact by fact consideration." . . . Specifically, we look to three guideposts by which to frame the inquiry: (1) whether the challenged condition "mirrored those conditions imposed upon inmates in administrative segregation and protective custody," and thus comported with the prison's discretionary authority; (2) the duration of the condition, and the degree of restraint imposed; and (3) whether the state's action will invariably affect the duration of the prisoner's sentence.[238]

Applying that approach, it has also said: "Typically, administrative segregation in and of itself does not implicate a protected liberty interest. . . ."[239] However, it has also said:

> *Sandin* requires a factual comparison between conditions in general population or administrative segregation (whichever is applicable) and disciplinary segregation, examining the hardship caused by the challenged action in relation to the basic conditions of life as a prisoner. . . . "What less egregious condition or combination of conditions or factors would meet the test requires case by case, fact by fact consideration."[240]

So it appears that there are no hard and fast rules in this circuit, and segregation may under some circumstances be atypical and significant. In one recent case, the court held that a prisoner who was sentenced to 10 days of disciplinary detention and then placed for 24 months in an administrative segregation unit had stated a claim of atypical and significant hardship: "Most significantly, [the prisoner] was segregated for a period of two years, and 'the length of confinement cannot be ignored in deciding whether the confinement meets constitutional standards.'"[241] In another recent case, it said that a prisoner who spent five months in punitive confinement. and alleged that his conditions were materially different both from general population and from administrative segregation, had stated a claim under the atypical and significant standard regardless of whether the appropriate comparison was general population or administrative segregation.[242] In a third case, the court held that a two-month stay in SHU was atypical and significant because

---

and significant; focusing on the difference between the two sorts of segregation).

[235]Phillips v. Norris, 320 F.3d at 847. The court first said prisoners do not have a liberty interest in contact visitation, which seems beside the point. Presumably the question whether conditions are atypical and significant relates to conditions as a whole, not to each condition considered separately. With respect to exercise, the court said 37 days' deprivation was not atypical and significant, though it "is perhaps pushing the outer limits of acceptable restriction." *Id.* The court also mentioned the relatively brief duration in connection with finding that the denial of religious services was not atypical and significant.

[236]Moorman v. Thalacker, 83 F.3d 970, 971–73 (8th Cir. 1996).

[237]Williams v. Norris, 277 Fed.Appx. 647, 648-49 (8th Cir. 2008) (unpublished) (12 years in administrative segregation held atypical and significant); Herron v. Wright, 116 F.3d 480 (8th Cir. 1997) (unpublished) (stating length of confinement is a "significant factor" in determining what is atypical and significant, and 10 years in administrative segregation appeared to be "beyond typical and insignificant," even though the initial placement in segregation was not). On remand, the district court agreed that the length of confinement—by then more than thirteen years—was atypical and significant, and the appeals court affirmed. Herron v. Schriro, 11 Fed. Appx. 659 (8th Cir. 2001) (unpublished). *See* Bunch v. Long, 2008 WL 5082861, *3 (W.D.Mo., Nov. 24, 2008) (22 months is not atypical and significant); Taylor v. Crawford, 2008 WL 3890379, *3 (E.D.Mo., Aug. 18, 2008) (holding eight years in administrative segregation is atypical and significant).

[238]Serrano v. Francis, 345 F.3d 1071, 1078 (9th Cir. 2003); *accord*, Jackson v. Carey, 353 F.3d 750, 755 (9th Cir. 2003); Ramirez v. Galaza, 334 F.3d 850, 861 (9th Cir. 2002).

[239]*Serrano*, 345 F.3d at 1078.

[240]*Jackson*, 353 F.3d at 755 (citation omitted).

[241]Ramirez v. Galaza, 334 F.3d at 861 (citations omitted); *see* Koch v. Lewis, 216 F. Supp. 2d 994, 1000–01 (D.Ariz. 2001) (holding "draconian" and extremely isolating conditions of "supermax" Special Management Unit II, which were indefinite in time and had gone on for five and a half years, were atypical and significant; stating *Sandin* "requires a case-by-case examination of both the conditions . . . and the duration of the deprivation at issue"), *vacated as moot*, 399 F.3d 1099 (9th Cir. 2005). *But see* Jones v. McDaniel, 552 F. Supp. 2d 1141, 1144, 1146 (D.Nev. 2008) (segregated confinement is not atypical and significant; plaintiff served 180 days in administrative segregation); Bryant v. Cortez, 536 F. Supp. 2d 1160, 1167 (C.D.Cal. 2008) (18 months in administrative segregation did not deprive plaintiff of a liberty interest).

[242]Jackson v. Carey, 353 F.3d at 756 (emphasis in original). The court appeared to be leaving open either the question of which comparison was appropriate, or the possibility that a prisoner could prevail by making a strong showing on either one. Earlier, the court said that a "major difference" between segregation and general population could meet the atypical and significant standard,

of the particular circumstances of the plaintiff: he needed a wheelchair and was placed for two months in a segregation unit where he couldn't use his wheelchair.[243] Another prisoner who spent 70 days in disciplinary segregation was held not to have stated a claim of atypical and significant hardship because, though he alleged limited recreational opportunities, limited access to showers, a flat and dirty mattress with no pillow, lack of access to the library, and cold food, he did not allege that administrative segregation was any different and did not explain how his conditions differed from those of general population.[244]

The Ninth Circuit has also held that when the prisoner's allegation is that a disciplinary charge is completely unsupported by evidence, due process is violated regardless of whether there is a liberty interest under the atypical and significant test.[245] This rule appears to us to be contrary to *Sandin v. Conner*, but it's the law in the Ninth Circuit and may be persuasive to some courts elsewhere.

Tenth Circuit: This court recently held that courts determining whether conditions are atypical or significant should not rely on comparisons with general population or other kinds of housing units.[246] Instead, they should "look at a few key factors, none dispositive," as in *Wilkinson v. Austin*.

> Relevant factors might include whether (1) the segregation relates to and furthers a legitimate penological interest, such as safety or rehabilitation; (2) the conditions of placement are extreme; (3) the placement increases the duration of confinement, as it did in *Wilkinson*; and (4) the placement is indeterminate (in *Wilkinson* the placement was reviewed only annually).[247]

In that case, the plaintiff was a transgender prisoner who was held for 14 months in administrative segregation. The court held that she was not deprived of a liberty interest because the defendants had good reasons to segregate her,[248] the conditions were "spartan, but not atypical of protective

custody" (*e.g.*, she had five and a half hours out of cell each day), and the overall length of her incarceration was not extended. As to "indeterminate" placement, the court noted that she got a status review including an interview every 90 days, even though it was clear she was not going to be released to general population.[249] The length of the confinement did not play a part in the analysis; the court noted that it had previously held that up to five years in administrative segregation did not deprive the plaintiff of liberty.[250] However, only the previous year—and, like *DiMarco*, after *Wilkinson v. Austin*—the court had held that for long periods of confinement (750 days in that case) "the duration of that confinement may itself be atypical and significant."[251] This was consistent with its previous decision stating that the district court must determine whether 75 days' confinement in punitive segregation is itself 'atypical and significant,'" citing an earlier case which said that court must address *both* the duration and degree of plaintiff's restrictions compared to other inmates.[252] These decisions seemed to suggest that confinement under ordinary punitive or administrative segregation conditions can be atypical or significant if they go on long enough, and to overrule an earlier decision stating that "*Sandin* makes clear that placement in administrative segregation such as occurred here does not give rise to a liberty interest."[253]

---

as could the duration of confinement. Keenan v. Hall, 83 F.3d 1083, 1089 (9th Cir. 1996), *amended*, 135 F.3d 1318 (9th Cir. 1998).

[243]Serrano v. Francis, 345 F.3d 1071, 1079 (9th Cir. 2003) ("The removal of his wheelchair dropped him from the relative baseline status that he maintained outside administrative segregation and forced him to endure a situation far worse than a non-disabled prisoner sent to the SHU would have to face.").

[244]Resnick v. Hayes, 213 F.3d 443, 448 and n.3 (9th Cir. 2000).

[245]Nonnette v. Small, 316 F.3d 872, 878–79 (9th Cir. 2002); Burnsworth v. Gunderson, 179 F.3d 771, 775 (9th Cir. 1999).

[246]Estate of DiMarco v. Wyoming Dep't of Corrections, Div. of Prisons, 473 F.3d 1334, 1340 (10th Cir. 2007) (noting that prior decisions had been inconsistent in making comparisons with other segregation units or with general population).

[247]Estate of DiMarco v. Wyoming Dep't of Corrections, Div. of Prisons, 473 F.3d at 1342.

[248]As we said above, *see* n.219 in this chapter, the idea that having a good reason to lock someone up means that due process is less necessary seems backwards to us. The point of due process protections is to test whether there *is* an adequate reason for the deprivation of liberty.

[249]*Estate of DiMarco*, 473 F.3d at 1342–44.

[250]*Estate of DiMarco*, 473 F.3d at 1340–41; Hunt v. Sapien, 480 F. Supp. 2d 1271 (D.Kan. 2007) (holding 850-day administrative segregation not atypical and significant under *DiMarco*; stating confinement was not indefinite because it was reviewed more frequently than annually), *reconsideration denied*, 2007 WL 1520906 (D.Kan., May 23, 2007).

[251]Trujillo v. Williams, 465 F.3d 1210, 1225 (10th Cir. 2006).

[252]Gaines v. Stenseng, 292 F.3d 1222, 1226 (10th Cir. 2002) (citing Perkins v. Kansas Dep't of Corrections, 165 F.3d 803, 809 (10th Cir. 1999)); *see also* Fogle v. Pierson, 435 F.3d 1252, 1259 (10th Cir. 2006) (district court erred in holding that three years' administrative segregation with only five hours a week out of cell could not state a claim; allegations of daily cell searches, 24-hour electric lighting, and no privacy should be considered in determining if confinement was atypical and significant).

Confinement of shorter duration would not be atypical and significant and such claims could be disposed of on motions to dismiss. Gaines v. Stenseng, 292 F.3d at 1226; *see* Grossman v. Bruce, 447 F.3d 801, 805–06 (10th Cir. 2006) (7 days in segregation and 30 days of "restriction time" were not atypical and significant).

In the *Perkins* case, the plaintiff alleged that he had been confined for over a year in an 8 by 14-foot concrete cell for 23 1/2 hours a day, released only for showers, denied out-of-cell exercise, and required to wear a face mask when out of his cell. The court said the lower court should not have dismissed that claim, and that defendants' claim that lots of prisoners were locked up and isolated did not address "both the duration and degree of plaintiff's restrictions as compared with other inmates." *Perkins*, 165 F.3d at 809. The court also cited Colon v. Howard, 215 F.3d 227, 231–32 (2d Cir. 2000), one of the Second Circuit cases emphasizing duration of confinement.

[253]Talley v. Hesse, 91 F.3d 1411, 1413 (10th Cir. 1996).

Eleventh Circuit: The Eleventh Circuit has said very little about segregation and *Sandin*. Most recently, it held that an allegation that a prisoner in administrative segregation who "was confined under extremely harsh conditions—in solitary confinement (under conditions unlike other pretrial detainees or even convicted prisoners), locked in an extremely small, closet-sized space, and with minimal contact with other human beings for a prolonged time exceeding 500 days" sufficiently pled atypical and significant hardship.[254] In earlier decisions, the court had "assume[d]" that a full year of solitary confinement would be atypical and significant,[255] and held that two months in segregation was not atypical and significant.[256] In another very important decision, this court found that prisoners in "Close Management" who were deprived of the two hours' yard time a week that such prisoners usually received had been subjected to atypical and significant hardship.[257] The court said that to people already under the restrictions of Close Management, the "marginal value of those two hours . . . is substantial."[258] The court did not rule on the question whether placement in Close Management (apparently a form of administrative segregation) was itself atypical and significant.

District of Columbia Circuit: This court has said "atypical and significant hardship" is assessed in comparison to "the most restrictive conditions that prison officials, exercising their administrative authority to ensure institutional safety and good order, routinely impose on inmates serving similar sentences."[259] To be atypical and significant, conditions must be worse than "the usual conditions of administrative segregation" at the prison where the plaintiff is held, or "more restrictive conditions at other prisons if it is likely both that inmates serving sentences similar to appellant's will actually be transferred to such prisons and that once transferred they will actually face such conditions."[260]

The court said that being locked in 23 and a half hours a day and all 48 hours of the weekend, restrained whenever leaving the cell block, denied all outside recreation, isolated when out of the cell, and denied legal telephone calls might be atypical and significant, contrasting these conditions to an earlier decision which said that a prisoner who had lost only his work and other privileges and half of his out-of-cell time by being moved to segregation was not subjected to atypical and significant hardship.[261]

Even if the conditions were not atypical and significant, their duration may be; this court directed the lower court to consider whether a 29-week term in segregation was atypical compared to terms "routinely" imposed.[262] "Routinely," to this court, does not mean that something is more likely to happen than not, but that there must be a "substantial chance" of its occurrence.[263] The mere fact that prison regulations permit a prisoner to be treated in a certain way does not mean it isn't atypical and significant in fact.[264] The court also said that the length of the prisoner's sentence must be considered—though it did not explain how.[265]

G. Additional Punishments for Segregated Prisoners

Before *Sandin v. Conner*, some courts held that when prisoners already in segregation are subjected to enhanced punishments, due process requires additional procedural protections.[266] However, *Sandin* cited a decision holding

---

[254]Magluta v. Samples, 375 F.3d 1269, 1282 (11th Cir. 2004).

[255]Williams v. Fountain, 77 F.3d 372, 374 n.3 (11th Cir. 1996). *But see* Al-Amin v. Donald, 165 Fed.Appx. 733, 736, 738–39 (11th Cir. 2006) (unpublished) (holding three years in administrative segregation did not deprive plaintiff of a liberty interest since the conditions were similar to those in general population).

[256]Rodgers v. Singletary, 142 F.3d 1252, 1253 (11th Cir. 1998) (per curiam).

[257]Bass v. Perrin, 170 F.3d 1312, 1318 (11th Cir. 1999).

[258]Bass v. Perrin, *id.*

[259]Hatch v. District of Columbia, 184 F.3d 846, 856 (D.C. Cir. 1999).

[260]Specifically, the court said:

In evaluating whether Hatch had a liberty interest in avoiding adjustment segregation, the district court should begin by determining the usual conditions of administrative segregation at Lorton. It should treat those conditions as the baseline for evaluating whether Hatch's two-week adjustment segregation was an "atypical and significant hardship." If using that comparison the court finds that his adjustment segregation was "atypical and significant," it should then take into account the possibility that Hatch will be transferred to other prisons.

The district court should redefine the comparative baseline by reference to more restrictive conditions at other prisons if it finds that it is likely both that inmates serving sentences similar to Hatch's will actually be transferred to such prisons and that once transferred they will actually face such conditions. The term "likely," as we use it here, means not that the combination of events must be more probable than not, but that there must be a substantial chance of its occurrence.

Hatch, 184 F.3d at 858.

[261]*Hatch*, 184 F.3d at 854 (citing Neal v. District of Columbia, 131 F.3d 172, 175 (D.C. Cir.1997)).

[262]*Hatch*, 184 F.3d at 858; *see* Brown v. District of Columbia, 66 F. Supp. 2d 41, 46 (D.D.C. 1999) (holding that administrative segregation conditions cannot be atypical and significant, but its duration can be).

[263]*Hatch*, 184 F.3d at 857.

[264]*Hatch*, 184 F.3d at 857 ("Properly constructed, *Sandin's* baseline requires not mere inquiry into the most restrictive conditions prison officials have legal authority to impose for administrative reasons, but a factual determination of the most restrictive conditions prison officials 'ordinarily' or 'routinely' impose.").

[265]*Hatch*, 184 F.3d at 856; *accord*, Franklin v. District of Columbia, 163 F.3d 625, 634 (D.C. Cir.1998) (stating that courts must consider not only "the discipline involved" but also the "nature of the prisoner's term of incarceration" in determining "whether a prisoner's 'liberty' is threatened.").

[266]Cooper v. Sheriff, Lubbock County, Texas, 929 F.2d 1078, 1083–84 (5th Cir. 1991) (deprivation of adequate food is "a form of

that prisoners could not be placed on a "food loaf" diet without due process as an example of the kind of due process decisions it was trying to put a stop to.[267] Not surprisingly, courts since *Sandin* have not held the use of food loaf or other restricted diet punishments to constitute atypical and significant hardship requiring due process,[268] though it is possible for such restrictions to violate other constitutional rights.[269] Similarly, courts have generally found that placing a prisoner in a cell with a plexiglass shield over the door (which severely restricts ventilation) is not atypical and significant.[270] On the other hand, one of the most important post-*Sandin* due process decisions holds that prisoners who are already in "Close Management" status have a liberty interest in not being deprived of their two hours a week of yard time; because it is almost the only relief from cell confinement that these prisoners receive, its "marginal value" is substantial, and deprivation of it is therefore atypical and significant.[271] It seems to us that avoiding a food loaf diet or having the ventilation in one's cell obstructed should also have great "marginal value." It also seems to us that these punishments are very literally atypical and significant, since they represent an extreme form of punishment that is generally supposed to be used in cases of extreme misconduct. The food loaf and cell shield cases generally involve short periods of time, and it may be that a court would consider such punishments atypical and significant if they continued for more than a week or two.

H. Particular Due Process Issues

In the next several sections, we will discuss the application of due process principles in particular kinds of cases. Some due process issues, such as those connected with suspension of visits and censorship of correspondence and publications, are not discussed here; they are dealt with in the sections on those subjects.[272]

1. Disciplinary Proceedings

Whether you are entitled to due process protections when you are faced with disciplinary action depends on what that disciplinary action is. The Supreme Court held in *Wolff v. McDonnell* that prisoners who lose statutory good time in disciplinary proceedings are entitled to notice, a written statement of the evidence behind a decision and the reasons for the punishment imposed, a limited right to call witnesses and present documentary evidence at a hearing, and in certain cases the assistance of a counsel substitute.[273] Until the mid-1990s, most courts held that any significant amount of segregated confinement also called for due process protections,[274] though some held that punishments that did not include loss of good time did not call for all the protections of *Wolff*, but only for the more informal procedures

---

corporal punishment" and a hearing is required to impose it); Domegan v. Fair, 859 F.2d 1059, 1063–64 (1st Cir. 1988) (deprivation of water and electricity implicated state-created liberty interest); Eng v. Coughlin, 684 F. Supp. 56, 63–64 (S.D.N.Y. 1988) (prisoner had a liberty interest based on regulations in avoiding placement in plexiglass front cell).

[267] Sandin v. Conner, 515 U.S. 472, 483, 115 S. Ct. 2293 (1995) (citing U.S. v. Michigan, 680 F. Supp. 270, 277 (W.D. Mich. 1988)).

[268] *See* McEachin v. McGuinnis, 357 F.3d 197, 201 (2d Cir. 2004) (affirming holding that restricted diet for a week did not require due process safeguards); Turnboe v. Gundy, 25 Fed.Appx. 292, 293 (6th Cir.2001) (unpublished); Beckford v. Portuondo, 151 F. Supp. 2d 204, 218–19 (N.D.N.Y. 2001) (holding restricted diet and limited water for periods not exceeding a week were not atypical and significant under *Sandin*); Amaral v. Greis, 2001 WL 1705112, *2 (W.D.N.Y. 2001) ("As applied to a due process claim involving a prisoner's diet, in order to allege an atypical and significant hardship, it is not sufficient merely to allege a dietary restriction, but rather, a plaintiff must allege that the restricted diet is nutritionally inadequate or otherwise poses a threat to his physical well-being."); Doucett v. Warden, Maryland Correctional Adjustment Center, 2001 WL 604187, *1 (D.Md., May 31, 2001) (food loaf diet was not atypical and significant absent evidence of physical harm).

State law may entitle prisoners to procedural protections when these added punishments are imposed. *See* Borden v. Hofmann, 974 A.2d 1249, 1253–56 (Vt. 2009) (holding use of Nutraloaf was at least partly punitive and therefore required due process under state statutes).

[269] *See, e.g.*, McEachin v. McGuinnis, 357 F.3d at 201–04 (holding imposition of a food loaf diet during Ramadan might violate right to free exercise of religion); Phelps v. Kapnolas, 308 F.3d 180, 186 (2d Cir. 2002) (imposition of a nutritionally inadequate diet could violate the Eighth Amendment). Food is discussed more generally in Ch. 2, § D.

[270] *See* Beckford v. Portuondo, 151 F. Supp. 2d at 218–19 (holding placement behind a plexiglass shield for periods not exceeding a week were not atypical and significant under *Sandin*); DeMaio v. Mann, 877 F. Supp. 89, 93 (N.D.N.Y.) (finding no liberty interest in New York's prison regulation in staying out of a plexiglass-shielded cell; regulations permit the use of cell shields for "good cause"), *aff'd*, 122 F.3d 1055 (2d Cir. 1995).

[271] Bass v. Perrin, 170 F.3d 1312, 1318 (11th Cir. 1999); *accord*, Perkins v. Kansas Dep't of Corrections, 2004 WL 825299, *7–8 (D.Kan., March 29, 2004) (finding a factual question whether denial of all outdoor exercise for 13 months in segregation was atypical and significant).

[272] *See* Ch. 3, §§ B.1 (correspondence), B.2 (publications), B.7 (visiting).

[273] Wolff v. McDonnell, 418 U.S. 539, 556–59, 563–71, 94 S. Ct. 2963 (1974). One court has recently suggested that loss of the opportunity to earn good time credits "likely" requires "less elaborate" process than required by *Wolff* for actual deprivation of good time, though it did not actually rule on the point. *See* Montgomery v. Anderson, 262 F.3d 641, 646 (7th Cir. 2002). For further discussion of due process issues affecting good time, *see* §§ A.2, H.1.r(3) of this chapter.

Some additional due process requirements have been identified by the lower courts. These are discussed in later sections of this chapter.

[274] *See, e.g.*, McKinnon v. Patterson, 568 F.2d 930, 939 (2d Cir. 1977) (holding that the threat of disciplinary confinement of 14 days or longer, in segregation or the prisoner's own cell, called for *Wolff* process).

usually associated with placement in administrative segregation.[275]

In 1995, however, the Supreme Court held in *Sandin v. Conner* that punishments other than loss of good time constitute deprivations of liberty requiring due process safeguards only if they impose "atypical and significant hardship . . . in relation to the ordinary incidents of prison life."[276] What constitutes atypical and significant hardship is discussed earlier in this chapter.[277]

It seems to us that any punishment severe enough to be described as "atypical and significant hardship"—which means, at a minimum, months of segregated confinement or extremely bad conditions for shorter periods[278]—should call for all the protections of *Wolff*, which after all are not much. *Wolff* itself assumed that "solitary confinement" requires the same protections as loss of good time.[279] *Wolff* also acknowledged that disciplinary proceedings "are certainly likely to be considered by the state parole authorities in making parole decisions" and that they may have other serious "collateral consequences" in addition to the disciplinary sentence itself.[280] Given those high stakes for the prisoner, the already limited due process protections of *Wolff* should not be further watered down. In any case, the less formal procedures used for administrative segregation placement are not appropriate for disciplinary proceedings in any case. The Supreme Court has noted that "the stigma of wrongdoing or misconduct does not attach to administrative segregation" and that "there is no indication that [it] will have any significant effect on parole opportunities."[281] This is obviously not true of disciplinary action. Equally important, the safeguards of *Hewitt v. Helms* were designed for the "subjective" and "intuitive" judgments involved in

placement in administrative segregation, for which "trial-type procedural safeguards" are not helpful.[282] By contrast, the Supreme Court has said that in proceedings about "specific, serious misbehavior, . . . more formal, adversary-type procedures might be useful."[283]

In some disciplinary cases, the sanction may not be severe enough to amount to a deprivation of liberty, but due process may be required because the prisoner has been deprived of property.[284] Most courts to consider the question have said that deprivations of property are not subject to the "atypical and significant hardship" rule of *Sandin v. Conner*, which was entirely about liberty.[285] Courts have assumed that a disciplinary deprivation of property requires the procedural protections of *Wolff v. McDonnell*.[286]

You may have more rights under prison regulations, state statutes or even the state Constitution than you do under the federal Due Process Clause.[287] You must be careful to distinguish between federal due process violations, which can be remedied in either federal or in state court, and acts that only violate state law or administrative regulations, which generally can only be challenged in state court.[288]

---

[275]Hensley v. Wilson, 850 F.2d 269, 283 (6th Cir. 1988) (holding only loss of good time requires *Wolff* rights); Bryant v. Miller, 637 F. Supp. 226, 228 (M.D.Pa. 1984) (similar to *Hensley*); Mujahid v. Apao, 795 F. Supp. 1020, 1026 (D.Haw. 1992) (similar to *Hensley*). *Contra*, Ramirez v. Turner, 991 F.2d 351, 354 (7th Cir. 1993) (rejecting the argument that *Wolff* applies only to deprivations of good time). *See* Walker v. Navarro County Jail, 4 F.3d 410, 412 (5th Cir. 1998) (holding that *Wolff* applies to placement in solitary confinement and loss of good time in prison, and "arguably" to solitary confinement in a county jail, while "a mere few days administrative segregation" is governed by *Hewitt*); Dzana v. Foti, 829 F.2d 558, 562 (5th Cir. 1987) (holding an immigration detainee who was segregated for a month and whose disciplinary record was sent to the Immigration and Naturalization Service was entitled to *Wolff* process because of the potential dire consequences of INS action).

The requirements of due process for administrative segregation are discussed in more detail in § H.2 of this chapter.

[276]Sandin v. Conner, 515 U.S. 472, 484, 115 S. Ct. 2293 (1995).

[277]*See* § A.3 of this chapter.

[278]*See* § A.3 of this chapter.

[279]Wolff v. McDonnell, 418 U.S. 539, 571 n.19, 94 S. Ct. 2963 (1974).

[280]Wolff v. McDonnell, 418 U.S. at 565.

[281]Hewitt v. Helms, 459 U.S. 460 473, 103 S. Ct. 864 (1983).

[282]Hewitt v. Helms, 459 U.S. at 474.

[283]Wilkinson v. Austin, 545 U.S. 209, 229, 125 S. Ct. 2384 (2005) (citing Wolff v. McDonnell, 418 U.S. 539, 94 S. Ct. 2963 (1974)).

[284]Jeffries v. Tennessee Dep't of Correction, 108 S.W.3d 862, 872–73 (Tenn.Ct.App. 2002) ($810 restitution order).

[285]The majority of courts to address the question have held that *Sandin* is not applicable to deprivations of property. *See* § H.8 of this chapter, n.955. *But see* Barone v. Hatcher, 984 F. Supp. 1304, 1311–12 (D.Nev. 1997) (holding that $33.48 restitution order deprived prisoner of a property interest under *Sandin* because it was atypical and significant, so the failure to give a proper statement of reasons denied due process).

[286]*Barone, id.; Jeffries*, 108 S.W.3d at 872–76; *see* § H.1.p of this chapter, nn.556–558, concerning monetary sanctions in disciplinary cases.

[287]For example, in New Jersey the state law principle of "fairness and rightness" has been interpreted to require more procedural protections for prisoners than *Wolff v. McDonnell* called for. Avant v. Clifford, 67 N.J. 496, 341 A.2d 629, 642–43 (N.J. 1975). The Alaska Constitution also provides greater rights than the federal Due Process Clauses. McGinnis v. Stevens, 543 P.2d 1221 (Alaska 1975). In this section we have cited numerous cases enforcing state statutes and regulations governing disciplinary proceedings. State court remedies in disciplinary cases are discussed at § H.1.r of this chapter.

[288]Violation of administrative regulations generally does not by itself deny due process. *See, e.g.*, Gaines v. Stenseng, 292 F.3d 1222, 1225 (10th Cir. 2002); Crosby-Bey v. District of Columbia, 786 F.2d 1182, 1186 (D.C. Cir. 1986); Dixon v. Goord, 224 F. Supp. 2d 739, 744–45 (S.D.N.Y. 2002); LaBoy v. Coughlin, 822 F.2d 3 (2d Cir. 1987); *see* U.S. v. Caceres, 440 U.S. 741, 752–53, 99 S. Ct. 1465 (1979) (describing limited circumstances under which violation of regulations denies due process); Moore v. Stotts, 804 F. Supp. 202, 203 (D.Kan. 1992) (applying *Caceres* to disciplinary case).

Often, the prison disciplinary procedures will comply with the requirements of due process on paper, but your argument will be that prison officials did not follow those procedures. In such a case, the officials' statement of general policy or usual practice will not entitle them to get your case dismissed if you have made specific allegations in the complaint, or sworn statements in response to a summary judgment motion, that the policy or practice was not followed in your case.[289]

If you want to challenge a disciplinary proceeding in court, do not refuse to attend or to participate in your hearing, even if you think it will be conducted unfairly. If you do refuse, the court may hold that you waived your right to object to the result.[290] You should also make whatever requests you have (*e.g.*, for witnesses or documents) *before* the hearing, and make any objections to the hearing procedures *at* the hearing. If you wait until later, a court may rule that you waived them.[291]

In the rest of this section, we will discuss each of the *Wolff* due process requirements, along with some other issues raised in Supreme Court decisions and by the lower courts in disciplinary cases. Since prisons have many different names for their disciplinary bodies, we will use the terms "committee" or "hearing officer" throughout.[292]

a. Notice Inmates must receive written notice of the charges against them at least 24 hours before the hearing.[293] The notice may be given after the prisoner is placed in pre-hearing segregation.[294]

The purpose of the notice is "to inform [the inmate] of the charges and to enable him to marshal the facts and prepare a defense."[295] Accordingly, the prisoner must be allowed to retain possession of the notice pending the hearing.[296] The notice should also be in a language the prisoner can understand.[297] It must be reasonably specific about what the prisoner is accused of doing.[298] If the notice describes the

---

A federal court may not order state officials to comply with state law. Pennhurst State School and Hospital v. Halderman, 465 U.S. 89, 104 S. Ct. 900 (1984). The *Pennhurst* rule does not affect damage suits brought against state officials in their individual capacities. *See* Ch. 8, § F.1, n.464.

[289]Mayers v. Anderson, 93 F. Supp. 2d 962, 968 (N.D.Ind. 2000); Brown v. District of Columbia, 66 F. Supp. 2d 41, 44 (D.D.C. 1999).

[290]Jones v. Smith, 116 A.D.2d 993, 498 N.Y.S.2d 713 (N.Y.App. Div. 1986); Saenz v. Murphy, 162 Wis.2d 54, 469 N.W.2d 611, 615–16 (Wis. 1991) (holding inmate who walked out of his hearing waived the right to object to the absence of witnesses); *see also* Scott v. Kelly, 962 F.2d 145, 147 (2d Cir. 1992) (prisoner's refusal to testify justified refusing to call witnesses and finding the plaintiff guilty); Perry v. Davies, 757 F. Supp. 1223, 1224 (D.Kan. 1991) (holding prisoner who pleaded guilty could not challenge his disciplinary conviction in court). *But see* Howard v. Wilkerson, 768 F. Supp. 1002, 1006 (S.D.N.Y. 1991) (refusal to attend might not waive due process objections if it was prompted by prison personnel's threatening behavior).

[291]*See, e.g.*, Sweeney v. Parke, 113 F.3d 716, 720 (7th Cir. 1997) (holding prisoner who waited until the hearing to ask for witnesses waived them); Bedoya v. Coughlin, 91 F.3d 349, 352–53 (2d Cir. 1996) (prisoner who agreed it was "time for a disposition" even though one of his witnesses had not been called waived that witness); Cox v. Malone, 199 F. Supp. 2d 135, 143–44 (S.D.N.Y. 2002) (prisoner who failed to ask that a witness be interviewed, even when asked at the end of the hearing if he had any procedural objections, waived the issue), *aff'd*, 56 Fed.Appx. 43 (2d Cir. 2003) (unpublished); Shakoor v. Coughlin, 165 A.D.2d 917, 560 N.Y.S.2d 528, 529 (N.Y.App.Div. 1990) (prisoner who failed to argue at the hearing that there was inadequate evidence supporting an infraction waived the argument).

[292]Disciplinary proceedings may be conducted by a single hearing officer and not a committee without denying due process. Cosby v. Purkett, 782 F. Supp. 1324, 1330–31 (E.D.Mo. 1992); Proffitt v. U.S., 758 F. Supp. 342, 347 (E.D.Va. 1990)

[293]Wolff v. McDonnell, 418 U.S. 539, 564, 94 S. Ct. 2963 (1974); *see* Payne v. Axelrod, 871 F. Supp. 1551, 1557 (N.D.N.Y. 1995) (holding failure to give notice before the hearing was cured by adjourning the hearing when the lack of notice was discovered).

[294]Smith v. Maschner, 899 F.2d 940, 946 (10th Cir. 1990).

[295]Wolff v. McDonnell, 418 U.S. at 564; *see* Brown v. District of Columbia, 66 F. Supp. 2d 41, 45 (D.D.C. 1999) (stating "plaintiff was simply not afforded the most basic process—an opportunity to know the basis on which a decision will be made and to present his views on that issue or issues.").

[296]Benitez v. Wolff, 985 F.2d 662, 665 (2d Cir. 1993).

[297]Powell v. Ward, 562 F. Supp. 274, 277 (S.D.N.Y. 1983); Reyes v. Henderson, 121 Misc.2d 970, 971–72, 469 N.Y.S.2d 520 (N.Y.Sup. 1983). *But see* Wong v. Coughlin, 138 A.D.2d 899, 526 N.Y.S.2d 640, 642 (N.Y.App.Div. 1988) (inmate who could understand the charge in English but was "more comfortable" in Chinese had no right to notice in Chinese).

[298]Sira v. Morton, 380 F.3d 57, 72 (2d Cir. 2004) (holding "there must be sufficient factual specificity to permit a reasonable person to understand what conduct is at issue so that he may identify relevant evidence and present a defense"); Spaulding v. Collins, 867 F. Supp. 499, 507 (S.D.Tex. 1993) ("The adequacy of notice hinges upon whether it is sufficiently detailed to allow the inmate to understand the charges and to marshal the facts in his defense."); U.S. ex rel. Speller v. Lane, 509 F. Supp. 796, 798–99 (S.D.Ill. 1981) (holding notice must describe the "specific conduct on which the charges are based"); Rinehart v. Brewer, 483 F. Supp. 165, 169 (S.D.Iowa 1980) (holding notice must contain date, general time and location of incident, a general description of the incident, citation to rules violated, and identification of other persons involved); Needs v. State, 118 Idaho 207, 795 P.2d 912, 913 (Idaho App. 1990) (holding notice lacking any description of the alleged violation denied due process); Harrah v. Leverette, 165 W.Va. 665, 271 S.E.2d 322, 327 (W.Va. 1980) (holding notice that failed to state the specific acts charged and the correct times of occurrence was not adequate); *see* Clayton-El v. Lane, 203 Ill. App.3d 895, 148 Ill.Dec. 877, 561 N.E.2d 183, 187 (Ill. App. 1990) (holding "notice of the specific crime, the date and place of the crime and the alleged infractions stemming from that crime" were sufficient), *appeal denied*, 135 Ill.2d 554, 151 Ill.Dec. 381, 564

conduct the prisoner is accused of and states the rule she is charged with breaking, technical errors that do not affect the inmate's ability to understand the charges do not deny due process.[299] Merely listing the number or name of the rule that the prisoner allegedly violated is not enough.[300] The actual evidence against the prisoner need not be disclosed in the notice.[301]

Some courts have held that a prisoner can be convicted of an offense she was not charged with as long as the notice described what she allegedly did.[302] We think those cases

are wrong. A prisoner must know the rule she is alleged to have broken in order to know how to "marshal the facts and present a defense" at a hearing.[303] Changing the charge and giving the prisoner no opportunity to respond and prepare is fundamentally unfair.[304]

Inadequate notice denies due process even if the prisoner goes forward at the hearing and tries to present a defense.[305]

b. Hearings: The Right to Hear and to Be Heard

The most basic due process right is the right to be heard. If the committee refuses even to listen to you, they violate due process.[306] You also have the right to hear—*i.e.*, to be informed of the evidence against you so you can

---

N.E.2d 836 (Ill. 1990); Vogelsang v. Coombe, 105 A.D.2d 913, 482 N.Y.S.2d 348 (N.Y.App.Div. 1984) (holding notice that described the prisoner's acts during a riot was sufficient), *aff'd*, 66 N.Y.2d 835, 489 N.E.2d 251, 498 N.Y.S.2d 364 (1985). *But see* Harmon v. Auger, 768 F.2d 270, 276 (8th Cir. 1985) (holding inmates charged with drug offenses based on an EMIT test are not entitled to notice of a specific date that they used drugs); Pino v. Dalsheim, 605 F. Supp. 1305, 1316 (S.D.N.Y. 1985) (holding notice need not explain the technical elements of the charges, the difference in degrees of misbehavior, and the range of possible punishments); Lahey v. Kelly, 71 N.Y.2d 135, 524 N.Y.S.2d 30, 518 N.E.2d 924, 929 (N.Y. 1987) (similar to *Harmon*).

The major exception to the specificity requirement is cases involving confidential informants, which are discussed in greater detail in § H.1.m of this chapter.

[299]Holt v. Caspari, 961 F.2d 1370, 1373 (8th Cir. 1992) (notice that charged "possession of contraband" rather than "possession of dangerous contraband" was adequate since the factual basis of the charges was the same); Wright v. Dixon, 409 F. Supp. 2d 210, 214 (W.D.N.Y. 2006) (90-minute error in time of incident did not deprive plaintiff of adequate notice where notice was "otherwise sufficiently detailed to put plaintiff on notice of the misconduct alleged"); Espinal v. Goord, 180 F. Supp. 2d 532, 538 (S.D.N.Y. 2002) (notice charging both fighting and assault was sufficient); Nicholas v. Tucker, 89 F. Supp. 2d 475, 478 (S.D.N.Y. 2000) (notice that clearly explained the prisoner's alleged misconduct and identified the rule under which he was charged was sufficient), *aff'd*, 40 Fed.Appx. 642 (2d Cir. 2002) (unpublished); Armstrong v. Lane, 771 F. Supp. 943, 946–47 (C.D.Ill. 1991) (holding notice giving the wrong rule number but the right name of the offense and describing what the prisoner had done was sufficient); Warren v. Irvin, 184 A.D.2d 1059, 584 N.Y.S.2d 365, 366 (N.Y.App.Div. 1992) (holding wrong date on misbehavior report did not deny due process because it did not prejudice the inmate's defense).

[300]Pino v. Dalsheim, 605 F. Supp. at 1315; Powell v. Ward, 487 F. Supp. 917, 926–27 (S.D.N.Y. 1980), *aff'd as modified*, 643 F.2d 924 (2d Cir. 1981).

[301]Alnutt v. Cleary, 913 F. Supp. 160, 166–67 (W.D.N.Y. 1996).

[302]*See* Kalwasinski v. Morse, 201 F.3d 103, 108 (2d Cir. 1999) (holding notice was sufficient that said the plaintiff had threatened to kill an officer, even if the death threat was not confirmed at the hearing; he had had sufficient notice he was accused of making verbal threats); Bostic v. Carlson, 884 F.2d 1267, 1270–71 (9th Cir. 1989) (holding charge of stealing followed by conviction for possession of contraband did not deny due process because the notice described the facts alleged); Northern v. Hanks, 326 F.3d 909, 911 (7th Cir. 2003) (holding change in charges did not deny due process, since an investigative report the prisoner was provided supplied all the facts needed to defend against the new charge); Jones v. Brown, 300 F. Supp. 2d 674, 679 (N.D.Ind. 2003)

("If an inmate is found guilty of a charge that is factually related to the notice he received, then the notice requirement of *Wolff v. McDonnell* . . . is satisfied."); Nicholas v. Tucker, 89 F. Supp. 2d 475, 478 (S.D.N.Y. 2000) (holding the fact that the prisoner was charged with misuse of property, convicted of causing property damage or loss, then on appeal found to have misused property, did not invalidate the conviction), *aff'd*, 40 Fed.Appx. 642 (2d Cir. 2002) (unpublished); Townes v. Hewitt, 84 Pa.Commw. 151, 478 A.2d 548, 550 (Pa.Commw. 1984) (holding inmates charged with assaulting officers and conspiring to disrupt routine by taking over part of the prison, but found guilty of disobeying orders, were not denied due process because the notice described the facts of the offense).

[303]Wolff v. McDonnell, 418 U.S. 539, 564, 94 S.Ct. 2963 (1974); *see* Evans v. Deuth, 8 F. Supp. 2d 1135, 1137 (N.D.Ind. 1998) (holding change in charge from "giving anything of value" in the notice to "extortion" in the hearing denied due process); Massop v. LeFevre, 127 Misc.2d 910, 911, 487 N.Y.S.2d 925 (N.Y.Sup. 1985) (holding that giving notice of a violation of one rule and convicting the inmate under a different rule violated state regulations). *See also* Sira v. Morton, 380 F.3d 57, 71 (2d Cir. 2004) (" . . . [U]nlike *Kalwasinski*, this is not a case where one discrepancy in a misbehavior report can be excused because other details provided adequate notice of the conduct at issue."); Northern v. Hanks, 326 F.3d at 1109 (distinguishing *Evans v. Deuth* because Evans did not get sufficient notice of what his charge would be changed to).

[304]*But see* Scruggs v. Jordon, 435 F. Supp. 2d 869, 873 (N.D.Ind. 2006) (where charge was changed between notice and hearing, but prisoner got 24 hours' notice of the change, due process was not violated).

[305]Needs v. State, 118 Idaho 207, 795 P.2d 912, 914 (Idaho App. 1990).

[306]Jackson v. Cain, 864 F.2d 1235, 1252 (5th Cir. 1989); McCann v. Coughlin, 698 F.2d 112, 123 (2d Cir. 1983) (prisoner tried to present a defense to one charge, was interrupted and told that the committee was moving on to the next charge); Mack v. Johnson, 430 F. Supp. 1139, 1145 (E.D.Pa. 1977) (committee refused to let the prisoner explain why he denied the charges), *aff'd*, 582 F.2d 1275 (3d Cir. 1978); *see* Pino v. Dalsheim, 605 F. Supp. at 1318 (fact-finder is required to "consider in good faith the substance of the inmate's defense"). This issue is closely related to the right to an impartial fact-finder, discussed in more detail in § H.1.h of this chapter.

respond to it.[307] (It is not necessary to disclose the evidence before the hearing.[308]) Prison officials are obligated to take the necessary steps so you can hear and be heard,[309] including provisions for prisoners who do not speak English or who are hearing-impaired.[310] If witnesses are "called" by

telephone, the accused prisoner must be able to hear their testimony, *e.g.*, by speakerphone.[311]

In order to hear and be heard, you have a right to be present at the hearing.[312] However, there are exceptions. Because there is no right to confrontation and cross-examination, the testimony of some witnesses may be taken outside your presence.[313] Under exceptional circumstances, an accused prisoner may be excluded entirely from the disciplinary hearing if the hearing officer "reasonably concludes that his presence would unduly threaten institutional safety or undermine correctional goals."[314] Even then, however, the hearing officer must attempt to hear the inmate's version of the facts in some manner.[315]

The Constitution does not require that the decision be based only on the evidence presented at the hearing. "Due to the peculiar environment of the prison setting, it may be that certain facts relevant to the disciplinary determination do not come to light until after the formal hearing. It would be unduly restrictive to require that such facts be excluded from consideration. . . ."[316] Such evidence should, however,

[307]Sira v. Morton, 380 F.3d 57, 74 (2d Cir. 2004) ("An inmate's due process right to know the evidence upon which a discipline ruling is based is well established. . . . Such disclosure affords the inmate a reasonable opportunity to explain his actions and to alert officials to possible defects in the evidence."); Francis v. Coughlin, 891 F.2d 43, 47 (2d Cir. 1989) (holding evidence must be disclosed at the hearing and not after it); Young v. Kann, 926 F.2d 1396, 1401–03 (3d Cir. 1991); Daigle v. Hall, 387 F. Supp. 652, 660 (D. Mass. 1975); Rosario v. Selsky, 169 A.D.2d 955, 564 N.Y.S.2d 851, 852 (N.Y.App.Div. 1991) (prisoner should have been informed of photo array from which he was identified; failure to do so deprived him of the opportunity to defend himself and denied due process).

In cases involving confidential informants, prison officials have not always been required to disclose all the evidence against the prisoner. *See* § H.1.m of this chapter. Disclosure of evidence may be denied for reasons of safety. *See, e.g.*, Thomas v. McBride, 306 F. Supp. 2d 855, 862 (N.D.Ind. 2004) (upholding refusal to disclose documentary evidence supporting charge of attempt to traffic in contraband), *aff'd*, 118 Fed.Appx. 977 (7th Cir. 2004) (unpublished).

[308]Leacock v. DuBois, 937 F. Supp. 81, 84 (D.Mass. 1996); Alnutt v. Cleary, 913 F. Supp. 160, 166–67 (W.D.N.Y. 1996); Wade v. Farley, 869 F. Supp. 1365, 1371 (N.D.Ind. 1994).

[309]*See* Dean v. Thomas, 933 F. Supp. 600, 604–07 (S.D.Miss. 1996) (holding the fact that the jail was new and officials had not "formally established" a disciplinary process or had the staff present to conduct hearings did not justify failing to give hearings for the first six months the jail was open).

[310]Clarkson v. Coughlin, 898 F. Supp. 1019, 1049–50 (S.D.N.Y. 1995) (holding failure to provide interpretive services for deaf and hearing-impaired prisoners at hearings denied due process); Bonner v. Arizona Dep't of Corrections, 714 F. Supp. 420, 425–26 (D.Ariz. 1989) (holding refusal to provide a sign language interpreter at a deaf-mute prisoner's disciplinary hearing denied due process); Powell v. Ward, 487 F. Supp. 917, 932 (S.D.N.Y. 1980) (holding inmates who speak only Spanish must be provided translators at the hearing), *aff'd as modified*, 643 F.2d 924 (2d Cir.1981); Santana v. Coughlin, 90 A.D.2d 947, 457 N.Y.S.2d 944 (N.Y.App.Div. 1982) (holding lack of accurate Spanish translation denied due process); *see also* Pyles v. Kamka, 491 F. Supp. 204 (D.Md. 1980) (consent judgment required sign language interpreter for hearing impaired). *But see* Gonzales-Perez v. Harper, 241 F.3d 633, 637–38 (8th Cir. 2001) (holding a Spanish-speaking prisoner was not denied due process by lack of an interpreter where he received one whenever he asked and understood enough English to understand the proceedings anyway); Maldonado v. Racette, 175 A.D.2d 963, 573 N.Y.S.2d 544, 545 (N.Y.App.Div. 1991) (holding due process did not require an interpreter for an inmate who understood the proceedings without one).

Deaf and hearing-impaired prisoners may have greater rights to accommodation in disciplinary proceedings under the Americans with Disabilities Act and the Rehabilitation Act than under the Due Process Clause. The disability statutes are discussed in Ch. 2, § F.4.h.2. *See* Randolph v. Rogers, 980 F. Supp. 1051, 1058

(E.D.Mo. 1997) (failure to provide a sign language interpreter did not deny due process because the prisoner's 30-day segregation terms were not atypical and significant), *reversed in part, vacated in part on other grounds*, 170 F.3d 850 (8th Cir.1999).

[311]*See* § H.1.c of this chapter, n.329.

[312]Battle v. Barton, 970 F.2d 779, 782 (11th Cir. 1992) (stating inmate's presence "is one of the essential due process protections afforded by the Fourteenth Amendment").

[313]Geder v. Godinez, 875 F. Supp. 1334, 1336–37, 1339 (N.D.Ill. 1995) (holding prisoner could be excluded from second day of his hearing where only staff witnesses testified); Wade v. Farley, 869 F. Supp. 1365, 1375 (N.D.Ind. 1994) (holding exclusion of prisoner while a staff witness was testifying did not deny due process). *See* § H.1.d of this chapter concerning confrontation and cross-examination and § H.1.m concerning evidence from confidential informants.

[314]Malik v. Tanner, 697 F. Supp. 1294, 1302–03 (S.D.N.Y. 1988); *accord*, Battle v. Barton, 970 F.2d at 782–83 (upholding refusal to allow prisoner to testify who refused to state his name and prison number); Payne v. Axelrod, 871 F. Supp. 1551, 1557 (N.D.N.Y. 1995) (holding threats of violence justified exclusion from hearing); Dawes v. Carpenter, 899 F.Sup. 892, 897 (N.D.N.Y. 1995) (same); *see* Beyah v. Leonardo, 182 A.D.2d 868, 581 N.Y.S.2d 896, 897 (N.Y.App.Div. 1992); Sanders v. Coughlin, 168 A.D.2d 719, 564 N.Y.S.2d 496, 498 (N.Y.App.Div.) (holding prisoner's refusal to comply with required frisk and restraint procedures justified proceeding without him), *appeal denied*, 77 N.Y.2d 806 (1991); Samuels v. LeFevre, 120 A.D.2d 894, 503 N.Y.S.2d 163 (N.Y.App. Div. 1986) (inmate who misbehaved at a hearing could be made to leave).

The courts have disagreed whether prison officials can be required to adjourn a hearing to permit a hospitalized inmate to attend. *Compare* Davis v. Lane, 814 F.2d 397, 402 (7th Cir. 1987) *with* Moody v. Miller, 864 F.2d 1178, 1181 (5th Cir. 1989).

[315]Malik v. Tanner, 697 F.2d at 1302–03.

[316]Baxter v. Palmigiano, 425 U.S. 308, 322 n.5, 96 S. Ct. 1551 (1976).

be in the administrative record[317] and reflected in the written disposition.[318] The case law also suggests that such evidence must be disclosed to the prisoner, with a chance to respond to it, before a decision is made.[319] State law may require that the committee rely only on the evidence presented at the hearing.[320]

If due process entitles you to a hearing before you can be punished, one would think that if you receive a favorable decision at the hearing, it's over and you can't be punished based on the same accusations. However, the courts have not barred prison officials from subjecting prisoners to repeat hearings if the prisoner wins the first time.[321]

c. Witnesses　Prisoners have the right to call witnesses when doing so is not "unduly hazardous to institutional safety or correctional goals."[322] Courts have disagreed whether witnesses called by the accused prisoner must appear

---

[317]Riggins v. Walter, 279 F.3d 422, 428–29 (7th Cir. 1995) (holding determination whether there was some evidence to support a disciplinary conviction must be limited to evidence in the administrative record).

[318]Baxter v. Palmigiano, 425 U.S. at 322 n.5.

[319]See nn.307, 309 of this section and 329–330 of the next section.

[320]See Lonski on behalf of Colby v. Coughlin, 126 A.D.2d 981, 511 N.Y.S.2d 957 (N.Y.App.Div. 1987); Matter of Hunter, 43 Wash. App. 174, 715 P.2d 1146, 1147 (Wash.App. 1986).

[321]In *Meeks v. McBride*, 81 F.3d 717, 722 (7th Cir. 1996), the court said that the Double Jeopardy Clause does not apply to prison disciplinary proceedings at all:

> . . . [T]o apply double jeopardy protection to prohibit a subsequent disciplinary hearing after acquittal would impose an extreme burden on prison administrators. If an acquittal in an earlier hearing were to preclude a subsequent hearing on the same charge, the overriding interest of prison administrators to act swiftly to maintain institutional order could be compromised in the interest of developing the evidence needed to obtain a conviction.

Accord, Turner v. Johnson, 46 F. Supp. 2d 655, 666–67 (S.D.Tex. 1999) (stating that successive prison disciplinary hearings for repetition of the same offense would not constitute double jeopardy (dictum)); *see* Howard v. Pierce, 981 F. Supp. 190, 193–95 (W.D.N.Y. 1997) (holding that a second disciplinary proceeding against a prisoner whose first proceeding had been expunged, after he had been convicted of murder in court for the same act, was not "arbitrary, conscience-shocking, or oppressive in a constitutional sense," though it might have been "incorrect or ill-advised"), *aff'd*, 175 F.3d 1008 (2d Cir. 1999). *Compare* Russo v. New Jersey Dep't of Corrections, 324 N.J.Super. 576, 737 A.2d 183, 187–88 (1999) (holding that repeat disciplinary prosecutions do not impose double jeopardy and are not *per se* forbidden by state law fairness principles) *with* Balagun v. New Jersey Dep't of Corrections, 361 N.J.Super. 199, 824 A.2d 1109, 1112–13 (2003) (holding that if prisoner was punished for possessing certain materials, they were nonetheless returned to him, and then he was punished for them again, action would be "fundamentally unfair"). *See* § H.1.s of this chapter, nn.653–658, for more on double jeopardy issues.

[322]Wolff v. McDonnell, 418 U.S. 539, 566, 94 S. Ct. 2963 (1974); *see* Edwards v. Balisok, 520 U.S. 641, 646–47, 117 S. Ct.

---

and testify at the hearing or can be interviewed by prison personnel outside your presence.[323]

We think that witnesses should testify at the hearing, not have their statements taken outside the hearing, unless there is a good correctional reason for failing to do so in a particular case. This is the commonsense meaning of "calling" a witness.[324] Having your own witnesses testify at the hearing is also consistent with the Supreme Court's holding in *Wolff v. McDonnell* that there is no right to confront witnesses testifying "against" the inmate. If the Court had meant to extend this rule to other witnesses, presumably it would have said so,[325] and the reasons not to require confrontation and cross-examination of adverse witnesses do

---

1584 (1997) (refusal to call any witnesses was "an obvious procedural defect").

State law may provide a more favorable standard. *See* McGinnis v. Stevens, 543 P.2d 1221, 1230–31 (Alaska 1975) (holding witnesses to be allowed unless repetitious or irrelevant, except for "exceptional cases" and "compelling reasons"); *accord*, Abruska v. Dep't of Corrections, State of Alaska, 902 P.2d 319, 322 (Alaska 1995) (holding hearing committee erred in refusing to call inmate witnesses who would have impeached an officer's credibility).

[323]*Compare* Kalwasinski v. Morse, 201 F.3d 103, 109 (2d Cir. 1999); Francis v. Coughlin, 891 F.2d 43, 48 (2d Cir. 1989) (holding witnesses may be interviewed outside the hearing by the hearing officer) *with* Serrano v. Francis, 345 F.3d 1071, 1079–80 (9th Cir. 2003) (holding a blanket denial of live witnesses at a disciplinary hearing is impermissible; exclusions must be justified individually); Whitlock v. Johnson, 153 F.3d 380, 387–88 (7th Cir. 1998) (holding policies excluding appearance at hearing of categories of witnesses "presumptively disfavored"); Mitchell v. Dupnik, 75 F.3d 517, 525–26 (9th Cir. 1996) (holding prison officials may not use interviews of witnesses as a substitute for calling them at the hearing); Bartholomew v. Watson, 665 F.2d 915, 917–18 (9th Cir. 1982) (holding witnesses must appear at the hearing); Hrbek v. State, 478 N.W.2d 617, 619 (Iowa 1991) ("An unjustified refusal to permit live testimony of a defense witness . . . will warrant reversal"); Mahers v. State, 437 N.W.2d 565, 569 (Iowa 1989).

The *Francis* case relied on a prior decision from the same court which in turn relied on a Supreme Court case dealing only with witnesses against the inmate. *See* Bolden v. Alston, 810 F.2d 353, 358 (2d Cir. 1987) (citing Baxter v. Palmigiano, 425 U.S. 308, 322, 96 S. Ct. 1551 (1976)). As we state in the text below, the Supreme Court in *Wolff v. McDonnell* treated witnesses against the inmate and witnesses called by the inmate differently, and we think *Francis v. Coughlin* is in error in failing to make that distinction.

[324]*See* Mitchell v. Dupnik, 75 F.3d 517, 525–26 (9th Cir. 1996).

[325]*See* Wolff v. McDonnell, 418 U.S. at 567–69. As one court stated:

> We are not persuaded that *Wolff* supports a blanket policy against allowing witnesses to be present at the hearing. The Court appears to have contemplated individualized determinations of the potential threat to security created by the presence of the inmate at the interview. . . . Requiring prison officials to determine on an individual basis whether witnesses can be present encourages them to exercise their discretion to strike the appropriate balance between the prisoner's right to call witnesses and the prison's need to maintain order.

not apply to the prisoner's calling her own witnesses.[326] Allowing witnesses to appear live is also important for purposes of fairness. "Particularly since witnesses are often the only means for an inmate to attempt to prove his version of events, the opportunity for the [committee] to evaluate the credibility and demeanor of the inmate's defense witnesses should not be discounted."[327] Besides, as a practical matter, it is important for the accused prisoner to have the option of questioning a witness she calls—or at least of hearing the witness and suggesting questions to the hearing committee—to be sure that all the relevant information is brought out.[328] The committee, which was not present at the incident, is not likely to be able to do this effectively. The prisoner must also hear the testimony in order to have an opportunity to respond to it.[329] Even if there is a good reason not to "call" the witness in your presence, the committee should hear the witness outside your presence and inform you of the substance of the testimony.[330]

Powell v. Ward, 487 F. Supp. 917, 928–29 (S.D.N.Y. 1980), *aff'd as modified*, 643 F.2d 924 (2d Cir. 1981). This decision has been overruled by *Francis v. Coughlin*, but we think its reasoning remains persuasive. *See* Mahers v. State, 437 N.W.2d 565, 568–69 (Iowa 1989).

[326]One court stated:

The witnesses at issue in *Baxter*, and in the portion of *Wolff* that *Baxter* analyzed, were prosecution witnesses, and not the inmate's witnesses. An entirely different balancing of concerns applied to confrontation and cross-examination of those witnesses: greater likelihood of hostility and resentment between the accused and the witness, which would erode discipline and threaten corrective aims; lengthening of the proceedings; and a lesser due process interest for the inmate in confronting these witnesses than in calling his own to provide exculpatory evidence.... The *Baxter* Court, as well as the *Wolff* Court, determined that on this issue the balance tipped in favor of the prison authorities' concerns for pursuing their safety and correctional goals.... Those concerns, and that balance, do not apply to the present case, in which [the prisoner] sought to call his own witnesses.

Mitchell v. Dupnik, 75 F.3d at 526.

[327]Whitlock v. Johnson, 153 F.3d at 388.

[328]*See* Mahers v. State, 437 N.W.2d at 568–69.

[329]The courts have acknowledged these necessities in connection with witnesses who testify by telephone. Balla v. Murphy, 116 Idaho 257, 775 P.2d 149, 152 (Idaho App. 1987) (holding witnesses may be interviewed by telephone only if the accused prisoner can speak directly to the witness and hear his answers); Matter of Plunkett, 57 Wash.App. 230, 788 P.2d 1090, 1093 (Wash.App. 1990) ("If a telephonic hearing is used, the inmate ordinarily should have the same opportunity to hear testimony as does the hearing officer. Only then can the prisoner be assured of having an opportunity to give responsive testimony in his or her defense.").

[330]Espinoza v. Peterson, 283 F.3d 949, 953 (8th Cir. 2002) (upholding refusal to return a transferred inmate to the prison to testify where his presence would have been a security risk and prison officials obtained a written statement from him); Francis v. Coughlin, 891 F.2d 43, 47-8 (2d Cir. 1989); Rosales v. Bennett, 297 F.

Prison officials can decline to call witnesses if their reasons are "logically related to preventing undue hazards to 'institutional safety or correctional goals.'"[331] Witnesses may be denied for reasons such as "irrelevance, lack of necessity, or the hazards presented in individual cases."[332] Mere convenience does not justify refusing to call witnesses.[333]

Supp. 2d 637, 642 (W.D.N.Y. 2004) (upholding refusal to call witnesses in protective custody where they were asked questions prepared by the plaintiff and their answers tape-recorded for the hearing); Abrazinski v. DuBois, 940 F. Supp. 361, 364 (D.Mass. 1996) (holding refusal to permit calling witnesses held at other prisons did not deny due process; the prisoner was able to get affidavits from them); Vasquez v. Coughlin, 726 F. Supp. 466, 469–70 (S.D.N.Y. 1989); Powell v. Ward, 487 F. Supp. at 928–29; Daigle v. Hall, 387 F. Supp. 652, 660 (D.Mass. 1975) (stating if testimony is not presented directly by witnesses, "it nevertheless must be revealed to the inmate with sufficient detail to permit the inmate to rebut it intelligently"); Torres v. Coughlin, 166 A.D.2d 793, 563 N.Y.S.2d 152, 153 (N.Y.App.Div. 1990) (holding officer who was off duty because of injury should have testified by telephone); Alvarado v. LeFevre, 111 A.D.2d 475, 488 N.Y.S.2d 856, 857 (N.Y.App.Div. 1985); *see also* Wilkerson v. Oregon State Correctional Institution, 24 Or.App. 61, 544 P.2d 198, 200 (Or.App. 1976) (under state regulations, prisoner's request that witnesses be interviewed should have been granted). This had been done in several of the cases in which courts upheld the failure to produce witnesses at the hearing. *See, e.g.*, Green v. Coughlin, 633 F. Supp. 1166, 1168–70 (S.D.N.Y. 1986); Lewis v. Faulkner, 559 F. Supp. 1316, 1320 (N.D.Ind. 1983); Devaney v. Hall, 509 F. Supp. 497, 500 (D.Mass. 1981); Homer v. Morris, 684 P.2d 64, 68 (Utah 1984).

[331]Ponte v. Real, 471 U.S. 491, 497, 105 S. Ct. 2192 (1985).

[332]Wolff v. McDonnell, 418 U.S. 539, 566, 94 S. Ct. 2963 (1974); *see* Brown v. Braxton, 373 F.3d 501, 507–08 (4th Cir. 2004) (upholding exclusion of assault victim housed in protective custody where written testimony was submitted); Kalwasinski v. Morse, 201 F.3d 103, 109 (2d Cir. 1999) (upholding the exclusion of officer witnesses who were not present at the incident); McMaster v. Pung, 984 F.2d 948, 952 (8th Cir. 1993) (upholding refusal to call the plaintiff's wife on the ground that her presence in the prison was a security risk); Miller v. Duckworth, 963 F.2d 1002, 1005 (7th Cir. 1992) (holding witnesses need not be called if doing so would require returning the accused prisoner to a prison from which he had escaped); Green v. Coughlin, 633 F. Supp. 1166, 1168–70 (S.D.N.Y. 1986) (upholding denial of witnesses who had been involved in the same riot plaintiff was accused of; their written statements had been obtained).

[333]Vasquez v. Coughlin, 726 F. Supp. at 469–70 (holding the fact that the victim of a stabbing was thought to be out of the prison did not justify refusing to call him; given the witness's importance, prison officials must show why the hearing could not have been adjourned or the witness interviewed separately); *Ex parte* Bland, 441 So.2d 122, 125 (Ala. 1983) (holding refusal to call a witness because he was off duty or could not be reached by phone denied due process); Torres v. Coughlin, 166 A.D.2d 793, 563 N.Y.S.2d 152, 153 (N.Y.App.Div. 1990) (holding fact that officer was off duty indefinitely because of injury did not justify failure to call him, by phone if necessary); DeMauro v. LeFevre, 91 A.D.2d 1156, 458 N.Y.S.2d 749 (N.Y.App.Div. 1983); *see also* Silva v. Scully, 138 A.D.2d 717, 526 N.Y.S.2d 532, 533–34 (N.Y.App.Div. 1988) (holding the fact that an inmate witness checked a box on a form

Witnesses may be denied if they would be cumulative (repetitive) of other witnesses.[334] But prison officials may not automatically refuse to call multiple witnesses,[335] especially when a prisoner "faces a credibility problem trying to disprove the charges of a prison guard."[336] Certainly, the refusal to hear any witnesses corroborating the accused inmate will deny due process if the facts are in dispute.[337] The refusal to call a particularly important witness is also likely to deny due process.[338] However, witnesses may be denied where they would only testify concerning irrelevant matters or side issues.[339] You should be prepared to say why the witness is important and what you think he or she will establish, both to prison officials when you request the witness[340] and to the court if you challenge the disciplinary proceeding.[341] However, the fact that a person was an eyewitness to all or part of the incident or conduct for which you are charged should be sufficient to require that the witness be called, or at least interviewed by prison staff to determine whether she would give relevant testimony, even if you can't say for sure what the witness would say.[342]

---

[334]Hudson v. Hedgepeth, 92 F.3d 748, 752 (8th Cir. 1996) (denying witnesses whose testimony prison officials determined would be cumulative as to the relevant issue did not deny due process); Bostic v. Carlson, 884 F.2d 1267, 1273–74 (9th Cir. 1989) (denying some witnesses did not deny due process where other witnesses were called); Rodgers v. Thomas, 879 F.2d 380, 383 (8th Cir. 1989) (where three witnesses had been called, holding the refusal to call a fourth did not deny due process); Langton v. Berman, 667 F.2d 231, 234 (1st Cir. 1981) (holding where several witnesses testified, 11 other witnesses need not be called in the absence of any suggestion that they would have provided additional information); Malek v. Camp, 822 F.2d 812, 815 (8th Cir. 1987) (holding denial of 13 witnesses upheld where the plaintiff testified and submitted another inmate's written statement); Wright v. Coughlin, 31 F. Supp. 2d 301, 328–29 (W.D.N.Y. 1998) (holding denial of two of three witnesses, based on the prisoner's concession that their testimony would be similar to that of the witness who was called, did not deny due process), *vacated and remanded on other grounds*, 225 F.3d 647 (2d Cir. 2000).

[335]Fox v. Coughlin, 893 F.2d 475, 478 (2d Cir. 1990) (holding denial of two witnesses out of seven was not justified; they could not be assumed to be cumulative just because they signed the disciplinary report); Fox v. Dalsheim, 112 A.D.2d 368, 491 N.Y.S.2d 820, 821 (N.Y.App.Div. 1985) (holding where two officers had testified, two others should have been called, because their testimony might not have agreed with the others').

[336]Ramer v. Kerby, 936 F.2d 1102, 1104 (10th Cir. 1991).

[337]Edwards v. Balisok, 520 U.S. 641, 646–47, 117 S. Ct. 1584 (1997) (refusal to call any witnesses was "an obvious procedural defect"); Graham v. Baughman, 772 F.2d 441, 445 (8th Cir. 1985); Green v. Nelson, 442 F. Supp. 1047, 1057 (D.Conn. 1977).

[338]Pannell v. McBride, 306 F.3d 499, 503 (7th Cir. 2002) (per curiam) (refusal to call officers present at a search where contraband was found might deny due process); Bryan v. Duckworth, 88 F.3d 431, 434 (7th Cir. 1996) (noting question whether refusal to call a nurse, the only potential non-prisoner witness except the complaining officer, denied due process); Smith v. Maschner, 899 F.2d 940, 946–47 (10th Cir. 1990) (holding where an inmate was charged with disrespect, the refusal to call the person he was disrespectful to raised a material due process question), *on remand*, 915 F. Supp. 2d 263 (D.Kan. 1996) (denying qualified immunity); Gilbert v. Selsky, 867 F. Supp. 159, 165–66 (S.D.N.Y. 1994) (in theft case, holding refusal to call the officer who allegedly let the prisoner into the area where it occurred, other officers who could vouch for his whereabouts at the time, and other inmates who had access to the stolen materials, denied due process); Vasquez v. Coughlin, 726 F. Supp. at 469–70 (holding where the prisoner was charged with a

stabbing, the failure to call the alleged victim raised a due process issue); Young v. State, 584 So.2d 553 (Ala.Cr.App. 1991) (holding refusal to call eyewitness to incident denied due process); Torres v. Coughlin, 166 A.D.2d 793, 563 N.Y.S.2d 152, 153 (N.Y.App.Div. 1990) (holding officer allegedly assaulted by prisoner should have been called); Cruz v. Oregon State Penitentiary Corrections Division, 48 Or.App. 473, 617 P.2d 650, 652 (Or.App. 1980) (committee should have heard a witness whose testimony was crucial as to whether a rule was actually broken).

[339]Morgan v. Quarterman, 570 F.3d 663, 668 (5th Cir. 2009) (upholding exclusion of witnesses to matters irrelevant to the facts underlying the charges); Miller v. Duckworth, 963 F.2d 1002, 1004-05 (7th Cir. 1992) (witnesses who would only testify to the plaintiff's motive in escaping need not be called); Felton v. Lincoln, 429 F. Supp. 2d 226, 241 (D.Mass. 2006) (witnesses need not be called to testify to matters not in dispute); Pino v. Dalsheim, 605 F. Supp. 1305, 1315–16 (S.D.N.Y. 1985) (where the prisoner admitted the charges, the committee could refuse to hear witnesses concerning mitigating circumstances); Ra Chaka v. Nash, 536 F. Supp. 613, 616 (N.D.Ill. 1982) (witnesses need not be heard on prisoner's motivations where the issue was whether he had broken a rule). *But see* Coleman v. Coombe, 65 N.Y.2d 777, 492 N.Y.S.2d 944, 482 N.E.2d 562 (N.Y. 1985) (mitigating testimony should have been permitted); Crippen v. Coughlin, 109 A.D.2d 951, 486 N.Y.S.2d 442 (N.Y.App.Div. 1985) (witnesses who would have confirmed the prisoner's story should have been called even if they could not swear he was innocent).

One court has held that the right to call witnesses applies only to witnesses who will "produce affirmatively supportive evidence." Owens v. Libhart, 729 F. Supp. 1510, 1513 (M.D.Pa. 1990), *aff'd*, 925 F.2d 419 (3d Cir. 1991). We do not think this rule is supported by *Wolff v. McDonnell*, and we don't think anyone can be sure what a witness will say until the witness is called.

[340]Walker v. McClellan, 126 F.3d 127, 129–30 (2d Cir. 1997) (holding denial of witnesses did not violate clearly established right where the prisoner wouldn't tell the hearing officer why they were relevant); Sanchez v. Roth, 891 F. Supp. 452, 457 (N.D.Ill. 1995) (holding prisoner's failure to explain relevance of witnesses justified failure to call them).

[341]Piggie v. Cotton, 344 F.3d 674, 678 (7th Cir. 2003); Liner v. Goord, 115 F. Supp. 2d 432, 436 (S.D.N.Y. 2000) (holding failure to call some witnesses did not deny due process in part because of failure to explain what testimony was lost); Breazil v. Bartlett, 998 F. Supp. 236, 243 (W.D.N.Y. 1997) (holding failure to call a witness did not deny due process absent evidence that the witness would have made a difference in the hearing officer's findings).

[342]*See* Ayers v. Ryan, 152 F.3d 77, 81 (2d Cir. 1998) (holding prisoner who admitted he knew of no witnesses who could support

---

indicating that he did not want to get involved, without further inquiry, was insufficient reason not to call the witness); *accord*, Codrington v. Mann, 174 A.D.2d 868, 571 N.Y.S.2d 160, 161 (N.Y. App.Div. 1991).

Blanket policies of denying witnesses, or types of witnesses, have generally been held unconstitutional. Some courts have said that any exclusion of witnesses must be related to the specific facts of a disciplinary case.[343] Others have said that blanket rules may be permissible, but only in very limited circumstances.[344] Rules forbidding the calling of staff witnesses have been held unconstitutional by some federal courts,[345] as have rules permitting witnesses to refuse to appear without explanation.[346] The courts have disagreed whether character witnesses may be excluded across the board.[347] Courts have upheld restrictions on witnesses when they were held on segregation units or the hearing was to be held there.[348] One court has upheld a blanket policy permitting mental health staff to be consulted by the hearing officer but not called as witnesses.[349]

If prison officials refuse to call witnesses you request, the burden is on them to explain their decision at least "in a limited manner."[350] However, they need not explain it to you

---

his defense did not waive his claim, since he had identified persons who might have witnessed the incident and they had not been interviewed).

[343]As one court put it, "If there is preclusion of an entire class of witnesses . . . the right is dissipated in a cloud of verbiage." Dalton v. Hutto, 713 F.2d 75, 76 (4th Cir. 1983); *accord*, Grossman v. Bruce, 447 F.3d 801, 805 (10th Cir. 2006) (due process requires an individualized determination whether calling a witness is unduly hazardous to correctional goals); Forbes v. Trigg, 976 F.2d 308, 316–17 (7th Cir. 1992); McFarland v. Cassady, 779 F.2d 1426, 1428 (9th Cir. 1986); King v. Wells, 760 F.2d 89, 93 (6th Cir. 1985); McCann v. Coughlin, 698 F.2d 112, 122–23 (2d Cir. 1983); Bartholomew v. Watson, 665 F.2d 915 (9th Cir. 1982); Winnie v. Clarke, 893 F. Supp. 875, 879, 882 (D.Neb. 1995) (stating blanket rule that only eyewitnesses could be called at disciplinary hearings appeared to deny due process (the plaintiff had been charged with refusing to give a urine sample and the witnesses were a psychologist's assistant and a physician's assistant); then stating that the right was not clearly established); Williams v. Wilkinson, 132 F. Supp. 2d 601, 603–04 (S.D.Ohio 2001) (striking down unwritten policy to exclude witnesses based on a pre-judgment of credibility); Hendrix v. Faulkner, 525 F. Supp. 435, 446 (N.D.Ind. 1981), *aff'd in part and vacated in part on other grounds sub nom.* Wellman v. Faulkner, 715 F.2d 269 (7th Cir. 1983). In *Pizarro Calderon v. Chavez*, 327 F. Supp. 2d 131, 137 (D.P.R. 2004), the court observed that Bureau of Prisons policy calls for individualized assessment of witness requests, but the disciplinary form says no witnesses are permitted other than prison staff; the court questioned whether the latter policy would withstand constitutional scrutiny.

[344]These courts acknowledge that the Supreme Court has rejected the idea that "'across-the-board' policies denying witness requests are invariably proper," *Ponte v. Real*, 471 U.S. 491, 496, 105 S. Ct. 2192 (1985), but point out that it has not ruled that such policies are invariably improper. *See* Whitlock v. Johnson, 153 F.3d 380, 386 (7th Cir. 1998). However, *Whitlock* concluded that "a rule excluding a class or category of witnesses is presumptively disfavored and is only justified if the prison officials demonstrate that the reasons for excluding the class apply with equal force to all potential witnesses falling within that category." 153 F.3d at 388. *Whitlock* then struck down as unconstitutional a policy of excluding all live defense witness testimony unless the witness was already present for other reasons and was available when called. *Id.* at 389. In *Brown v. Braxton*, 373 F.3d 501 (4th Cir. 2004), the court upheld a regulation authorizing the use of written statements, rather than live testimony, from inmate witnesses at higher security prisons and segregation units because it called for case-by-case discretion in cases involving this class of prisoners. *Id.* at 504-07.

[345]Ramer v. Kerby, 936 F.2d 1102, 1104 (10th Cir. 1991); Dalton v. Hutto, 713 F.2d at 76. *But see* White v. Wyrick, 727 F.2d 757 (8th Cir. 1984) (officers' refusal to appear did not deny due process where the possible penalty was limited).

One court has held that prison officials could refuse to call staff witnesses "because to do so would undermine prison authority by having one guard testify against another guard." Brown v. Frey, 889 F.2d 159, 167–68 (8th Cir. 1989). We think this decision is pretty shocking, since in effect it promotes cover-ups even if some staff members are prepared to tell the truth. Further, staff testimony will always be more credible to a prison hearing officer than prisoner testimony, and cases in which staff testimony supports the prisoner are the cases in which the prisoner is most likely to be innocent of the offense. To deprive prisoners of the benefit of such testimony amounts to abandoning any pretense that the hearing is intended to uncover the truth.

[346]Piggie v. Cotton, 342 F.3d 660, 666 (7th Cir. 2003) (per curiam); Forbes v. Trigg, 976 F.2d at 316–18.

[347]*Compare* Graham v. Baughman, 772 F.2d 441, 445 (8th Cir. 1985); Oswalt v. Godinez, 894 F. Supp. 1181, 1187 (N.D.Ill. 1995); Wright v. Caspari, 779 F. Supp. 1025, 1028 (E.D.Mo. 1992) (all upholding exclusion of character witnesses) *with* Spellmon-Bey v. Lynaugh, 778 F. Supp. 338, 343–44 (E.D.Tex. 1991) (holding character evidence is subject to the same standards as other testimony; where charges based on confidential information are vague, character evidence may be particularly relevant).

[348]Lewis v. Faulkner, 559 F. Supp. 1316, 1320 (N.D.Ind. 1983) (refusal to call witnesses held in disciplinary segregation upheld where their written statements were permitted); Devaney v. Hall, 509 F. Supp. 497, 500–01 (D.Mass. 1981) (prohibition of witnesses upheld for hearings held in disciplinary segregation unit); Cortez v. Coughlin, 67 N.Y.2d 907, 501 N.Y.S.2d 809, 492 N.E.2d 1225 (N.Y. 1986); People ex rel. Bradley v. Smith, 115 A.D.2d 225, 496 N.Y.S.2d 126 (N.Y.App.Div. 1985), *leave denied*, 67 N.Y.2d 604 (N.Y. 1986); *see* McGuinness v. DuBois, 75 F.3d 794, 799–800 (1st Cir. 1996) (upholding exclusion of live inmate witnesses in hearings held in the disciplinary unit based on the facts of the case, though holding that the blanket policy might deny due process under other circumstances).

[349]Powell v. Coughlin, 953 F.2d 744, 749 (2d Cir. 1991).

[350]Ponte v. Real, 471 U.S. 491, 497, 105 S. Ct. 2192 (1985); *see* Ayers v. Ryan, 152 F.3d 77, 81 (2d Cir. 1998) (holding prison officials who refuse to interview a witness have the burden of showing that their conduct was rational; "oversight" is not an adequate justification); Smith v. Mass. Dep't of Correction, 936 F.2d 1390, 1399-1400 (1st Cir. 1991) (holding argument, unsupported by evidence, concerning the reason a witness was not called did not meet officials' burden); Ferreira v. DuBois, 963 F. Supp. 1244, 1253 (D.Mass. 1996) (holding prison officials who offered no explanation for failing to call a witness were not entitled to summary judgment); Smith v. Maschner, 915 F. Supp. 263, 270 (D.Kan. 1996) (holding prison officials had the burden of going forward and burden of proof of the legitimacy of refusal to call a witness); Barnes v. LeFevre, 69 N.Y.2d 649, 511 N.Y.S.2d 591, 503

or write it down at the time of the hearing; if you sue them, they may present their explanation then.[351] State law may require that the reasons be documented at the time of the hearing.[352]

It is your responsibility to ask that witnesses be called and to comply with prison procedures for doing so,[353] as long as those procedures are reasonable.[354] However, manipulation of the procedures by prison officials to exclude witnesses may deny due process.[355] Prison officials may be required to make reasonable efforts to identify and locate witnesses that you cannot completely identify.[356]

As a matter of common sense, as well as to avoid waiving your rights, you should tell prison officials what witnesses you want called and what you expect them to say—and, if you ask for a lot of witnesses, which ones are the most important to you. If the officials are acting in good faith, you are more likely to get a fair hearing this way. If they are not acting in good faith and you sue them, they will have no excuse for having failed to call at least some of your witnesses.

When witnesses are called, the hearing officer has substantial discretion to control the questioning so "the examination of witnesses is conducted in a professional manner and relates only to germane subjects."[357]

d. Confrontation and Cross-Examination There is no constitutional right to "confrontation and cross-examination of those furnishing evidence against the inmate."[358] Prison officials are therefore not required to present the testimony of their witnesses—staff members or inmates—at the hearing in your presence.[359] In the case of staff members, some courts have held that they need not personally testify or be interviewed at all, and that a written report can be sufficient evidence to convict.[360] You may be able in some

---

N.E.2d 1022, 1023 (N.Y. 1986) (officer's hearsay report that an inmate was unwilling to testify, without further explanation, was insufficient to justify the witness's non-appearance).

[351]Ponte v. Real, 471 U.S. at 497.

[352]People ex rel. Vega v. Smith, 66 N.Y.2d 130, 139, 495 N.Y.S.2d 332, 485 N.E.2d 997 (N.Y. 1985); McGinnis v. Stevens, 543 P.2d 1221, 1230 (Alaska 1975); see Afrika v. Selsky, 750 F. Supp. 595, 601 (S.D.N.Y. 1990) (holding failure to note reasons for not calling witnesses violated state regulations but not due process).

[353]Sweeney v. Parke, 113 F.3d 716, 719–20 (7th Cir. 1997) (holding prisoner waived witnesses by not requesting them before the hearing); Scott v. Kelly, 962 F.2d 145, 146–47 (2d Cir. 1992) (holding hearing officer could refuse to call witnesses when the prisoner refused to say what their testimony would be); Ramer v. Kerby, 936 F.2d 1102, 1105 (10th Cir. 1991) (holding inmate can be required to submit questions in advance); Bostic v. Carlson, 884 F.2d 1267, 1273–74 (9th Cir. 1989) (holding inmate can be required to tell disciplinary committee what he expects witnesses to say so the committee can know whom to call); Carter v. Fairman, 675 F. Supp. 449, 451–52 (N.D.Ill. 1987); Garfield v. Davis, 566 F. Supp. 1069, 1073 (E.D.Pa. 1983); Williams v. Schulte, 605 F. Supp. 498, 500–01 (E.D.Mo. 1984); see Lebron v. Coughlin, 169 A.D.2d 859, 564 N.Y.S.2d 587, 588 (N.Y.App.Div.) (holding inmate waived witness's appearance by agreeing to proceed without him), appeal dismissed, 78 N.Y.2d 852 (N.Y. 1991).

Courts have said this rule does not apply if prison officials have a policy of denying all witness requests and you do not ask for witnesses because it would be futile. McCann v. Coughlin, 698 F.2d 112, 122–23 (2d Cir. 1983); Pino v. Dalsheim, 605 F. Supp. 1305, 1317 (S.D.N.Y. 1984). However, that may not be reliable under the Prison Litigation Reform Act requirement of exhaustion of administrative remedies, so you should ask for your witnesses even if you know they will be denied, and raise the matter on administrative appeal. See Ch. 9, § D, concerning the administrative exhaustion requirement.

[354]See Miller v. Duckworth, 963 F.2d 1002, 1004–05 n.2 (7th Cir. 1992) (prisoners cannot be required to identify witnesses immediately upon receiving notice of charges).

[355]Brooks v. Andolino, 826 F.2d 1266, 1269 (3d Cir. 1987); Grandison v. Cuyler, 774 F.2d 598, 604 (3d Cir. 1985); Feagin v. Broglin, 693 F. Supp. 736, 740–41 (N.D.Ind. 1988).

[356]Kingsley v. Bureau of Prisons, 937 F.2d 26, 31 (2d Cir. 1991) (prisoner did not know witnesses' names, but officials had a list of them); Grandison v. Cuyler, 774 F.2d at 604 (inmate gave witness's name but got his number wrong); Pino v. Dalsheim, 605 F. Supp. at 1317–18 (officials first refused to identify, then refused to interview, previous occupants of cell where contraband was found); People ex rel. Cooper v. Smith, 115 Misc.2d 689, 690, 454 N.Y.S.2d 635

(N.Y.Sup. 1983) (cell location and nickname should be enough to locate a witness). But see Dixon v. Goord, 224 F. Supp. 2d 739, 746–47 (S.D.N.Y. 2002) (holding the hearing officer was not obliged to identify the "Latino [officer] . . . who does transportation," even though there were only 10 or 12 Latino officers in the prison); Strickland v. Delo, 758 F. Supp. 1319, 1321 (E.D.Mo. 1991) (failure to call witnesses upheld because the prisoner did not identify them with specificity); Brown v. Scully, 110 A.D.2d 835, 488 N.Y.S.2d 84 (N.Y.App.Div. 1985) (officials were not required to call "members of the Mosque" without more specific identification).

[357]Sand v. Steele, 218 F. Supp. 2d 788, 792 (E.D.Va. 2002) (hearing officer is "under a duty to maintain an environment during a hearing where the examination of witnesses is conducted in a professional manner and relates only to germane subjects"), aff'd, 71 Fed.Appx. 234 (4th Cir. 2003) (unpublished); Odom v. Goord, 238 A.D.2d 816, 817–18, 656 N.Y.S.2d 524, 526 (N.Y.A.D. 3d Dep't 1997) (hearing officer who admonished prisoner who interrupted witnesses was not biased).

[358]Wolff v. McDonnell, 418 U.S. 539, 567–69, 94 S. Ct. 2963 (1974) (emphasis supplied); accord, Baxter v. Palmigiano, 425 U.S. 308, 320–23, 96 S. Ct. 1551 (1976); see also Murphy v. Superintendent, Massachusetts Correctional Institution, 396 Mass. 830, 489 N.E.2d 661, 662 (1986) (holding confrontation not required by state constitution).

[359]Brown-Bey v. U.S., 720 F.2d 467, 469 (7th Cir. 1983) (holding prisoner accused of assault could be required to leave the hearing during the victim's testimony); Spaulding v. Collins, 867 F. Supp. 499, 508–09 (S.D.Tex. 1993) (holding prisoner could be excluded from officer's testimony about an informant); U.S. ex rel. Speller v. Lane, 509 F. Supp. 796, 800 (S.D.Ill. 1981) (holding adverse witnesses could be interviewed over the telephone rather than called at the hearing).

[360]People ex rel. Vega v. Smith, 66 N.Y.2d 130, 495 N.Y.S.2d 332, 485 N.E.2d 997, 1002–04 (N.Y. 1985); Carter v. Kane, 938 F. Supp. 282, 287 (E.D.Pa. 1996) (holding a misbehavior report by an

cases to obtain the equivalent of confrontation and cross-examination by calling adverse witnesses yourself.[361]

If witnesses are presented outside the prisoner's presence, due process requires that the prisoner be informed of what they said.[362]

Some states' law calls for confrontation and cross-examination on a limited basis.[363] You will generally be able to challenge denial of those rights only in a state court proceeding.

e. Documentary and Physical Evidence Documentary evidence, like witness testimony, may be presented where doing so would not be "unduly hazardous to institutional safety or correctional goals."[364] State law may also require disclosure of relevant documentation; if so, that law may be enforceable in state court.[365] If you already have documentary evidence, it should pose no risks for you to offer it at the hearing. However, prison officials have the discretion "to limit access to other inmates to collect statements or to compile other documentary evidence" that you don't

already have.[366] You should ask for documents in advance of the hearing or you may be held to have waived them.[367]

Numerous courts have held that there is a limited due process right to examine, or to have produced at the hearing, documents in prison officials' possession that may help determine whether you are guilty.[368] Some courts have held that the "*Brady* rule," which requires the disclosure of material exculpatory evidence in criminal prosecutions, also applies to prison disciplinary proceedings.[369] Videotapes are

---

officer who witnessed the misconduct can support a disciplinary conviction); Harrison v. Pyle, 612 F. Supp. 850, 855 (D.Nev. 1985); *see* nn.451–452, below, for more on this subject.

In *Vega*, the court limited its ruling to written reports based on personal knowledge and properly dated and signed, and noted that the inmate would generally have the right to call the officer who wrote the report as a witness if she so chose. To support a conviction, written reports must state with specificity what the particular inmate did that violated the rules. Bryant v. Coughlin, 77 N.Y.2d 642, 569 N.Y.S.2d 582, 572 N.E.2d 23, 26 (N.Y. 1991) (reports stating that "all inmates in the Messhall were actively participating in this riot" did not constitute substantial evidence of particular prisoners' guilt).

[361]Perez v. Wilmot, 67 N.Y.2d 615, 499 N.Y.S.2d 659, 490 N.E.2d 526, 527 (N.Y. 1986). However, prison officials may not allow you to call your accusers as your own witnesses, and such a decision will probably be held not to deny due process. *See* Piggie v. Hanks, 98 F. Supp. 2d 1003, 1006 (N.D.Ind. 2000) (upholding hearing officer's refusal to call reporting officer and reliance on the officer's report), *vacated on other grounds*, 2001 WL 34124549 (N.D.Ind., Feb 23, 2001).

[362]*See* cases cited in § H.1.b of this chapter, nn.307, 309, and § H.1.c, nn.329–330.

[363]Avant v. Clifford, 67 N.J. 496, 341 A.2d 629, 647 (N.J. 1975) (requiring an explanation when confrontation and cross-examination are denied); McGinnis v. Stevens, 543 P.2d 1221, 1231 (Alaska 1975) (cross-examination permitted unless there are "compelling reasons" to forbid it); Flowers v. Phelps, 595 So.2d 668, 669 (La.App. 1991) (prison rules required cross-examination); Harrah v. Leverette, 165 W.Va. 665, 271 S.E.2d 322, 327 (W.Va. 1980) (confrontation and cross-examination allowed unless "good cause" is found to deny it).

[364]Wolff v. McDonnell, 418 U.S. 539, 566, 94 S. Ct. 2963 (1974).

[365]*See, e.g.,* Tocco v. Marquette Prison Warden, 123 Mich.App. 395, 333 N.W.2d 295, 297–98 (Mich.App. 1983) (reversing hearing because of non-disclosure of report); Hodges v. Scully, 141 A.D.2d 729, 529 N.Y.S.2d 832, 833–34 (N.Y.App.Div. 1988) (holding refusal to introduce use of force report violated state regulations).

[366]*Id.; see also* Frankenberry v. Williams, 677 F. Supp. 793, 797–98 (M.D.Pa. 1988) (hearing need not be delayed so plaintiff could obtain documents from drug testing company and utilize Freedom of Information Act), *aff'd*, 860 F.2d 1074 (3d Cir. 1988).

[367]Piggie v. McBride, 277 F.3d 922, 925 (7th Cir. 2002).

[368]Piggie v. Cotton, 344 F.3d 674, 678 (7th Cir. 2003) (holding "an inmate is entitled to disclosure of material, exculpatory evidence in prison disciplinary hearings unless such disclosure would unduly threaten institutional concerns"); Smith v. Mass. Dep't of Correction, 936 F.2d 1390, 1401 (1st Cir. 1991) (holding prison officials must explain denial of "relevant and important documents central to the construction of a defense"); Campbell v. Henman, 931 F.2d 1212, 1214 (7th Cir. 1991) (holding exculpatory evidence must be disclosed to the prisoner); Chavis v. Rowe, 643 F.2d 1281, 1285–86 (7th Cir. 1981) (holding report that tended to show the prisoner was not guilty should have been disclosed); Pace v. Oliver, 634 F.2d 302, 304–05 (5th Cir. 1981) (holding absolute bar on presentation of documentary evidence and production of prison records denied due process); Spellmon-Bey v. Lynaugh, 778 F. Supp. 338, 344 (E.D.Tex. 1991) (holding absent threat to safety or correctional goals, officials must produce documents that might show that the prisoner could not have committed the offense); Giano v. Sullivan, 709 F. Supp. 1209, 1215 (S.D.N.Y. 1989) (holding unjustified refusal to produce officers' eyewitness reports of the incident denied due process); Pino v. Dalsheim, 605 F. Supp. 1305, 1317–18 (S.D.N.Y. 1985) (holding due process was violated by failure to check prison logs for relevant information); Brooks v. Coughlin, 182 A.D.2d 1115, 583 N.Y.S.2d 91 (N.Y.App.Div. 1991) (holding hearing officer's refusal to look at a videotape of the incident denied due process); *see also* Harper v. Lee, 938 F.2d 104, 105–06 (8th Cir. 1991) (holding after a prisoner was denied access to documents and convicted, a rehearing at which the documents were produced satisfied due process). *But see* Rasheed-Bey v. Duckworth, 969 F.2d 357, 362 (7th Cir. 1992) (holding failure to disclose investigator's confidential file, which was reviewed by the hearing committee, did not deny due process since the plaintiff was notified of the underlying facts, the material was not exculpatory, and it had sufficient guarantees of reliability); Withrow v. Goord, 374 F. Supp. 2d 326, 328 (W.D.N.Y. 2005) (refusal to turn over photographs and records of officer's injuries to prisoner was reasonable); Thomas v. McBride, 306 F. Supp. 2d 855, 862 (N.D.Ind. 2004) (upholding refusal to disclose documents supporting attempted contraband trafficking charge based on "safety and confidentiality concerns"), *aff'd*, 118 Fed.Appx. 977 (7th Cir. 2004) (unpublished); Moore v. Selsky, 900 F. Supp. 670, 675 (S.D.N.Y. 1995) (failure to examine medical records of a prisoner charged with drug use, in violation of prison rules, did not deny due process), *aff'd*, 101 F.3d 683 (2d Cir. 1996).

[369]Piggie v. Cotton, 344 F.3d at 678 (citing Brady v. Maryland, 373 U.S. 83, 83 S. Ct. 1194 (1963)); Thompson v. Hawk, 978 F. Supp. 1421, 1424 (D.Kan. 1997).

a type of document, and courts have held that disciplinary bodies must review relevant videotapes, and prisoners must be shown videotapes that are used as evidence against them,[370] unless there is a specific security reason not to do so.[371] (Such reasons need not be explained at the hearing, but in a later lawsuit the officials will have the burden of showing that their action was not arbitrary.[372]) Several decisions have held that if a prisoner is disciplined for a document that she allegedly wrote herself, the document must be produced at the hearing.[373] However, several courts

have held that due process does not require production of documentation of drug tests.[374]

Courts are unlikely to require document production if the documents you want do not bear directly on the question of whether you did what you are accused of. For example, prison officials will probably not be required to produce an officer's disciplinary record so you can argue that the officer is not credible.

Courts have said that there may also be a limited due process right to have physical evidence produced at the hearing when it is particularly important to determining guilt or innocence.[375]

---

[370]Howard v. U.S. Bureau of Prisons, 487 F.3d 808, 813–15 (7th Cir. 2007) (where plaintiff alleged that a videotape existed and would exculpate him, failure to review it denied due process); Piggie v. Cotton, 344 F.3d 674, 678–79 (7th Cir. 2003) ("We have never approved of a blanket policy of keeping confidential security camera videotapes for safety reasons. . . ."; where it is not apparent whether the tape is exculpatory or not, "minimal due process" requires that the district court review the tape *in camera*.); Phelps v. Tucker, 370 F. Supp. 2d 792, 797 (N.D.Ind. 2005) (refusal to review videotape denied due process notwithstanding officials' claim that it wasn't very clear); Mayers v. Anderson, 93 F. Supp. 2d 962, 965–68 (N.D.Ill. 2000) (failure to review a requested videotape without a stated reason denied due process).

[371]Ordinarily the prisoner should have an opportunity to see the videotape to point out to the hearing officer the points the prisoner considers important. *Piggie*, 344 F.3d at 679. If there is a security justification, the prisoner may be denied the right to see a videotape that is viewed by the hearing officer. *Id.;* Wright v. Coughlin, 31 F. Supp. 301, 327 (W.D.N.Y. 1998) (holding refusal to show the prisoner a videotape of a prison disturbance which the hearing officer viewed did not deny due process, since the defendants claimed a security justification and the tape did not include the plaintiff), *vacated on other grounds,* 225 F.3d 647 (2d Cir. 2000). In *White v. Indiana Parole Bd.,* 266 F.3d 759, 768 (7th Cir. 2001), the court held that non-disclosure of a videotaped witness interview did not deny due process where it was before the hearing officer, since it "likely" involved discussion of security-related matters. The court's speculation about what the tape was "likely" to contain seems a flimsy basis for denying the prisoner knowledge of the evidence against him, and this decision seems inconsistent with the same court's later decision in *Piggie v. Cotton,* which required the district court to review a disputed tape *in camera. See also* Scruggs v. Jordan, 485 F.3d 934, 940 (7th Cir. 2007) (denial to prisoner of access to videotape did not deny due process where the prisoner had admitted the conduct he was charged with).

[372]Piggie v. McBride, 277 F.3d 922, 925 (7th Cir. 2002).

[373]Young v. Kann, 926 F.2d 1396, 1400–02 (3d Cir. 1991) (holding inmate charged with writing a threatening letter should have been permitted to see the letter, and the hearing officer should have read the letter himself rather than relying on a second-hand description of it); Scarpa v. Ponte, 638 F. Supp. 1019, 1023 (D.Mass. 1986) (holding inmate charged with writing a "mocking, taunting and disrespectful" letter should have been permitted to inspect the letter); McIntosh v. Carter, 578 F. Supp. 96, 98–99 (W.D.Ky. 1983) (holding disciplinary committee should have made its own judgment about whether a handwritten note was actually written by the prisoner, and should have let the prisoner see it). *But see* Griffin-Bey v. Bowersox, 978 F.2d 455, 456–57 (8th Cir. 1992) (holding letter need not be produced when the prisoner more or

less admitted the offense and failed to show that the outcome of the hearing would have been different if he had seen the letter).

[374]Holt v. Caspari, 961 F.2d 1370, 1372 (8th Cir. 1992) (holding lab analysis need not be produced for pills that were plainly marked); Harrison v. Dahm, 911 F.2d 37, 41 (8th Cir. 1990) (holding failure to provide documentation of EMIT test results and evidence log did not deny due process); Rucker v. Johnson, 724 F. Supp. 568, 571 (N.D.Ill. 1989) (holding failure to provide drug test report did not deny due process because the prisoner was told what it said and turning it over would not have affected the outcome of the hearing); Holm v. Haines, 734 F. Supp. 366, 372 (W.D.Wis. 1990) (holding failure to produce drug test results did not deny due process because *Wolff* does not require production of physical evidence); Works v. State, 575 So.2d 622, 624 (Ala.Crim.App. 1991) (holding EMIT test documentation need not be placed in evidence); King v. Gorczyk, 175 Vt. 220, 225, 825 A.2d 16, 21 (Vt. 2003).

Drug testing is discussed further in § H.1.j of this chapter and Ch. 2, § E.2.

[375]Young v. Lynch, 846 F.2d 960, 963 (4th Cir. 1988) (due process may require production of evidence "when it is the dispositive item of proof, it is critical to the inmate's defense, it is in the custody of prison officials, and it could be produced without impairing institutional concerns"); Ross v. Franzen, 777 F.2d 1216, 1218 (7th Cir. 1985) (claim that committee refused to place contraband screwdriver in evidence raised a due process question). *But see* Hoskins v. McBride, 202 F. Supp. 2d 839, 845 (N.D.Ind. 2002) (it was sufficient for the disciplinary board to see the contraband items and for them to be described to the prisoner), *aff'd,* 66 Fed.Appx. 47 (7th Cir. 2003) (unpublished).

In *Young v. Lynch,* the inmate was accused of smoking a marijuana cigarette, which he said was only tobacco, and the disciplinary committee refused to produce the butt. There was apparently no evidence except an officer's opinion that the substance was marijuana. If there is other evidence identifying drugs or other contraband, courts are unlikely to require that the physical evidence be produced. *See, e.g.,* Berrios v. Kuhlmann, 143 A.D.2d 475, 532 N.Y.S.2d 593 (N.Y.App.Div. 1988) (holding a positive urinalysis result meant there was no need to produce the specimen at the hearing); *see also* Locher v. Plagemann, 765 F. Supp. 1260, 1262 (W.D.Va. 1991) (holding containers of contraband sugar need not be produced at the hearing since no laboratory test was required to identify the sugar). Drug and alcohol testing is discussed further in § H.1.j of this chapter.

One court has held that even if there is a right to have existing evidence produced at the hearing, the destruction of such evidence before the hearing does not deny due process unless prison officials

f. Assistance with a Defense There is no constitutional right to an attorney, retained or appointed, in the disciplinary process,[376] though state law may provide a right to counsel under some circumstances.[377] However, if an inmate is illiterate or the issues are so complex that it is unlikely she can present her case adequately, assistance from a staff member or another inmate may be required by due process.[378] Prisoners with significant mental problems should also be entitled to such assistance,[379] since they too are unlikely to

be able to present a defense. Common sense suggests that prisoners who do not speak English should also be entitled to assistance.[380] Federal courts have disagreed over whether prisoners who are placed in segregation before their hearings have a right to assistance from a staff member; we think they should, since an inmate who is locked up is prevented from effectively preparing her case, just like an inmate who is illiterate or one faced with extremely complex issues.[381] State law or regulations may provide for assistance in other situations.[382]

The Court in *Wolff v. McDonnell* did not spell out exactly what the role of an assistant should be. One federal court has held that staff assistance must be provided "in good faith and in the best interests of the inmate" and "should include gathering evidence, obtaining documents and relevant tapes, and interviewing witnesses. At a minimum, an assistant should perform the investigatory tasks which the inmate, were he able, could perform for himself."[383] In New York, the courts have held that the assistant's job is to investigate and gather evidence, not to act like a lawyer at

---

act in bad faith. Griffin v. Spratt, 969 F.2d 16, 20–21 (3d Cir. 1992).

[376]Baxter v. Palmigiano, 425 U.S. 308, 315, 96 S. Ct. 1551 (1976); Wolff v. McDonnell, 418 U.S. 539, 569–70, 94 S. Ct. 2963 (1974). This is true even if there is a likelihood of criminal prosecution for the same acts that the disciplinary proceeding is based on. *See* § H.1.s of this chapter. *But see In re* Pierpoint, 271 Kan. 620, 634, 24 P.3d 128, 138 (2001) (stating that "in the exceptional case, where . . . the inmate faces possible felony charges as a result of the disciplinary violation, . . . due process requires an attorney to represent the interest of such inmates," but in the ordinary case, holding that neither the Constitution nor state regulations requires counsel in disciplinary proceedings).

[377]*See* Harrah v. Leverette, 165 W.Va. 665, 271 S.E.2d 322, 327–28 (W.Va. 1980) (holding the presence of a state prosecutor at the hearings entitled the prisoners to counsel); McGinnis v. Stevens, 543 P.2d 1221, 1232 (Alaska 1975) (holding prisoners under investigation for felony prosecution were entitled to counsel under the Alaska Constitution); *see also* Moore v. Gaither, 767 A.2d 278, 283–88 (D.C. 2001) (holding that D.C. regulations allowing prisoners to obtain counsel for disciplinary hearings did not apply to a private prison holding D.C. prisoners). The Mississippi Supreme Court held as a matter of state administrative law that "common sense and the interest of justice dictate that, where one takes the initiative and goes to the expense of hiring an attorney to speak for him, the attorney should be allowed to represent his client," and the refusal to do so at a "classification" (disciplinary) hearing was arbitrary and capricious. Edwards v. Booker, 796 So.2d 991, 995 (2001). *But see* Maghee v. State, 639 N.W.2d 28, 30 (Iowa 2002) (holding neither federal nor state constitution required provision of counsel either at a disciplinary hearing or in a subsequent judicial review proceeding). *Cf.* Felton v. Lincoln, 429 F. Supp. 2d 226, 242 (D.Mass. 2006) (regulation allowing counsel at state prison disciplinary hearings did not apply to county jails).

[378]Wolff v. McDonnell, 418 U.S. at 570–71; *see* Brown v. O'Keefe, 141 A.D.2d 915, 529 N.Y.S.2d 48 (N.Y.App.Div. 1988) (holding accusation of drug use based on urinalysis was a "complex case" requiring assistance).

So far, courts have rejected the argument that prisoners are entitled to an assistant in cases involving confidential informants where a lot of the relevant information is withheld from the prisoner. Hudson v. Hedgepeth, 92 F.3d 748, 751 (8th Cir. 1996); Sauls v. State, 467 N.W.2d 1, 3 (Iowa App. 1990).

[379]The Supreme Court has not addressed this issue directly in the context of prison disciplinary proceedings, but it held that counsel is required when a prisoner is committed to a mental institution, observing that someone "thought to be suffering from a mental disease or defect" presumably needs help even more than an illiterate or uneducated one. Vitek v. Jones, 445 U.S. 480, 496–97, 100 S. Ct. 1254 (1980). We think this reasoning is equally applicable to disciplinary hearings. *See* People ex rel. Reed v. Scully, 140

Misc.2d 379, 531 N.Y.S.2d 196 (N.Y.Sup. 1988) (holding an inmate acquitted by reason of mental disease in a criminal trial should have had an assistant appointed to help present an insanity defense at his disciplinary hearing); *see also* U.S. ex rel. Ross v. Warden, 428 F. Supp. 443, 445–46 (E.D.Ill. 1977) (holding that a staff assistant, who would only follow the prisoner's direction, was not sufficient to satisfy due process for a paranoid schizophrenic prisoner who was incompetent to provide direction). *But see* Horne v. Coughlin, 191 F.3d 244, 249–50 (2d Cir. 1999) (declining to decide whether a mentally retarded prisoner was entitled to assistance); Whittington v. Vaughn, 289 F. Supp. 2d 621, 626–27 (E.D.Pa. 2003) (upholding punishment of schizophrenic prisoner for acts committed after refusing medication; rejecting claims he should have had counsel or other assistance because he didn't claim he was illiterate or couldn't understand the questions presented; ignoring the question whether mental illness should also call for assistance).

[380]State law or prison regulations sometimes require this. *See, e.g.,* Rivera v. Smith, 110 A.D.2d 1043, 489 N.Y.S.2d 131 (N.Y.App. Div. 1985).

Prisoners may be entitled to the assistance of an interpreter if one is necessary for them to understand the proceedings. *See* § H.1.b of this chapter, n.309. One court has held that a legally blind inmate is entitled to assistance. Perry v. State, 511 So.2d 268, 269 (Ala.Crim.App. 1987).

[381]*Compare* Eng v. Coughlin, 858 F.2d 889, 898 (2d Cir. 1988) (requiring assistance for prisoners in pre-hearing segregation) *with* Miller v. Duckworth, 963 F.2d 1002, 1004 (7th Cir. 1992) (not requiring assistance for segregated prisoners).

[382]*See* State v. Melendez, 172 Ariz. 68, 834 P.2d 154, 155 n.1 (Ariz. 1992) (noting that state regulations permitted representation by retained counsel, willing staff member, or by another prisoner); McGinnis v. Stevens, 543 P.2d 1221, 1232 (Alaska 1975) (holding prisoners under investigation for felony prosecution were entitled to counsel under the Alaska Constitution); Harrah v. Leverette, 165 W.Va. 665, 271 S.E.2d 322, 327–28 (W.Va. 1980) (holding the presence of a state prosecutor at disciplinary hearings entitled the prisoners to counsel).

[383]Eng v. Coughlin, 858 F.2d at 898.

the hearing.[384] The hearing officer cannot properly serve as the prisoner's assistant.[385] One court has held that statements made to a counsel substitute provided by the prison may not be used at a subsequent criminal prosecution.[386]

There is no due process right to *effective* assistance at a disciplinary hearing.[387] However, if a staff member is appointed as your assistant and then does not actually assist you, that failure to assist denies due process,[388] though it will not invalidate a disciplinary conviction unless there is reason to believe it affected the outcome.[389] Some decisions have

held that if the case is not one in which *Wolff* requires an assistant, an assistant's failure to do her job does not deny due process.[390] We think that the latter cases are wrong. It is true that a violation of prison regulations by itself usually does not deny due process.[391] But the Supreme Court has held that due process is violated when "an individual has reasonably relied on agency regulations promulgated for his guidance or benefit, and has suffered substantially because of their violation by the agency."[392] That is exactly what happens if you rely on an assistant to prepare your defense, she does nothing, and you are convicted as a result.

If you are entitled to assistance but not provided with it, you should object at the hearing or you will likely be held to have waived the issue.[393]

g. Prompt Hearing and Pre-Hearing Segregation The law has never been well settled concerning how quickly a disciplinary hearing must be held. Some older cases held or suggested that hearings must occur within a relatively short time,[394] especially if the prisoner was in pre-hearing segregation.[395] Some decisions held that time limits in state law

---

[384]Gunn v. Ward, 52 N.Y.2d 1017, 1018, 438 N.Y.S.2d 302, 420 N.E.2d 100 (N.Y. 1981); *see* Lee v. Coughlin, 902 F. Supp. 424, 433 (S.D.N.Y. 1995) (holding that an assistant is supposed to *prepare* a defense, not just assist after the hearing begins).

In a case where the prisoner was sufficiently mentally ill he could not direct an assistant, the court held that due process required an assistant who was an "effective spokesman, specifically someone who will take the initiative in representing petitioner"; officials could, but were not required to, allow his attorney to represent him at the hearing. U.S. ex rel. Ross v. Warden, 428 F. Supp. at 446–47.

[385]Lee v. Coughlin, 902 F. Supp. at 433 ("Were I to adopt defendants' position that a hearing officer and an inmate assistant could be the same person, the confined inmate's right to an assistant and an impartial hearing officer would be rendered meaningless."); *see* Ayers v. Ryan, 152 F.3d 77, 81 (2d Cir. 1998) (holding prisoner did not waive the right to an assistant by agreeing to the hearing officer's "irregular" proposal to act as an assistant).

[386]State v. Melendez, 172 Ariz. 68, 834 P.2d 154, 157–59 (1992).

The *Melendez* case held that it denied due process for the state to offer assistance to the prisoner and then turn it into a "trap." 834 P.2d at 158. It did not hold that the attorney–client privilege protects statements made to prisoners who provide legal assistance to other prisoners. Most courts have held that such statements are not privileged. *Id.* at 158–59; *see* cases cited in Ch. 3, § C.2.c, n.567.

[387]McKinney v. Hanks, 911 F. Supp. 359, 363 (N.D.Ind. 1995).

[388]Grandison v. Cuyler, 774 F.2d 598, 604 (3d Cir. 1985) (holding allowance of only five minutes consultation with an inmate assistant was inadequately justified); McConnell v. Selsky, 877 F. Supp. 117, 123 (S.D.N.Y. 1994) (holding refusal of employee assistant to interview two officers because they worked on a different shift, combined with hearing officer's refusal to appoint another assistant or interview the officers, denied due process); Giano v. Sullivan, 709 F. Supp. 1209, 1215 (S.D.N.Y. 1989) (holding failure of assistant to help the prisoner denied due process); Pino v. Dalsheim, 605 F. Supp. 1305, 1318 (S.D.N.Y. 1985) (holding due process was violated by assistant's failure to carry out "basic, reasonable and non-disruptive requests"); Balla v. Idaho State Bd. of Correction, 595 F. Supp. 1558, 1582 (D.Idaho 1984) (similar to *Grandison*); *see also* Ayers v. Ryan, 152 F.3d 77, 81 (2d Cir. 1998) (holding hearing officer's statement that he would assist the plaintiff by calling witnesses, and then failure to do so, denied due process); Hendricks v. State of New York Dep't of Correctional Services, 165 A.D.2d 923, 560 N.Y.S.2d 534, 535 (N.Y.App.Div. 1990) (holding assistant's failure to assist violated state regulations).

[389]Pilgrim v. Luther, 571 F.3d 201, 206 (2d Cir. 2009) (holding assistant's alleged non-performance was harmless error where plaintiff failed to identify any evidence not presented as a result and where there was plenty of evidence of guilt).

[390]Bostic v. Carlson, 884 F.2d 1267, 1274 (9th Cir. 1989); *see also* Abdul-Wadood v. Duckworth, 860 F.2d 280, 283–84 (7th Cir. 1988) (same holding in an administrative segregation case).

[391]*See* n.288 of this chapter, above.

[392]U.S. v. Caceres, 440 U.S. 741, 752–53, 99 S. Ct. 1465 (1979).

[393]Jackson v. Johnson, 30 F. Supp. 2d 613, 619–20 (S.D.N.Y. 1998). *But see* Ayers v. Ryan, 152 F.3d 77, 81 (2d Cir. 1998) (holding prisoner did not waive his right to assistance by agreeing to the irregular proposal that the hearing officer provide assistance); Lee v. Coughlin, 902 F. Supp. 424, 432–33 (S.D.N.Y. 1995) (holding where prisoner designated several choices of assistant but was assigned someone else, said he'd prefer an assistant of his own choice, and the designated assistant did nothing, the prisoner did not waive assistance; he asked for it repeatedly).

[394]*See* Bostic v. Carlson, 884 F.2d 1267, 1270, 1274 (9th Cir. 1989) (holding delays of eight and ten days did not deny due process); Pitts v. Kee, 511 F. Supp. 497, 501–02 (D.Del. 1981) (holding 13-day delay was not justified); Dowdy v. Johnson, 510 F. Supp. 836, 838–39 (E.D.Va. 1981) (upholding month's delay); Battle v. Anderson, 376 F. Supp. 402, 422 (E.D.Okla. 1974) (imposing 72-hour limit); *In re* Davis, 25 Cal.3d 384, 158 Cal.Rptr. 384, 599 P.2d 690, 699 (Cal. 1979) (holding 33–83 days was excessive); *see also* Willoughby v. Luster, 717 F. Supp. 1439, 1441 (D.Nev. 1989) (holding 48-day delay raised question whether confinement was administrative or disciplinary); State v. Luke, 382 So.2d 1265 (Fla. App. 1980) (holding administrative confinement pending criminal indictment did not deny due process).

A number of these older cases held that emergency conditions will justify longer delays than usual in providing hearings. *See* U.S. ex rel. Houston v. Warden, Stateville Correctional Center, 635 F.2d 656, 658–59 (7th Cir. 1980) (two months during institutional lockdown); Ponds v. Cuyler, 541 F. Supp. 291, 292 (E.D.Pa. 1982) (nine days during "state of emergency"); Keenan v. Bordenkircher, 294 S.E.2d 175, 176 (W.Va. 1982) (55 days under emergency conditions).

[395]Owens v. Maschner, 811 F.2d 1365 (10th Cir. 1987) (holding 20-day delay for confined inmate may have denied due process);

or prison regulations gave rise to liberty interests protected by due process,[396] but others disagreed.[397] In any case, the Supreme Court's decision that only "atypical and significant hardship" in connection with a state-created liberty interest denies due process[398] would seem to have buried the idea that violation of state time limits does so.[399]

Similarly, decisions imposing due process limits on hearing delay because the prisoner is in segregation pending the hearing[400] are overruled as a practical matter under *Sandin*, since the periods of segregation involved generally would not be considered atypical and significant hardship.[401] For the same reason, pre-*Sandin* decisions holding that when there is a state-created liberty interest, pre-hearing segregation requires separate due process protections within a "reasonable time"[402] and that the prisoner cannot be required to wait until a later disciplinary hearing for these protections,[403] are probably no longer good law except in cases where the delay is so long as to be "atypical and significant" under *Sandin*. However, pre-hearing segregation will be considered along with post-hearing segregation for purposes of determining if the prisoner has suffered atypical and significant hardship overall as a result of a disciplinary proceeding.[404]

As a practical matter, it will probably be hard to convince a court that pre-hearing delay has denied due process unless the delay was extreme (*i.e.*, at least several months) or you can show that it somehow harmed your defense.[405] For these reasons you are probably more likely to succeed on a claim based on a delayed hearing if there is a state law or regulation providing for a time limit and if you challenge its violation in state court.[406]

Russell v. Coughlin, 774 F. Supp. 189, 197 (S.D.N.Y. 1991) ("Due process requires that a disciplinary hearing be commenced within a reasonable time after an inmate is placed in administrative segregation."; 11 days was reasonable under the circumstances), *reargument granted on other grounds*, 782 F. Supp. 876 (S.D.N.Y. 1991); Majid v. Henderson, 533 F. Supp. 1257, 1271–73 (N.D.N.Y.) (holding that due process requires that the hearing begin "as soon as is reasonably practicable" and generally within seven days), *aff'd*, 714 F.2d 115 (2d Cir. 1982); Powell v. Ward, 392 F. Supp. 628, 632 (S.D.N.Y.), *aff'd as modified*, 542 F.2d 101, 103–04 (2d Cir. 1976) (imposing seven-day time limit where prisoner is confined pending hearing); Tasker v. Griffith, 238 S.E.2d 229, 234–35 (W.Va. 1977) (holding three-day limit "ordinarily" applicable where the prisoner is segregated).

[396]Brown v. Frey, 889 F.2d 159, 166 (8th Cir. 1989) (state statute requiring a hearing within three days created a liberty interest in getting a hearing within a "reasonable time"); Maldonado Santiago v. Velazquez Garcia, 821 F.2d 822, 827–28 (1st Cir. 1987); King v. Hilton, 525 F. Supp. 1192, 1199 (D.N.J. 1981); *see also* Meeker v. Manning, 540 F. Supp. 131, 139 (D.Conn. 1982) (time limit in welfare regulation created a right to a timely eligibility determination).

[397]*See* Bostic v. Carlson, 884 F.2d at 1270; Gutierrez v. Coughlin, 841 F.2d 484, 486 (2d Cir. 1988) (per curiam); Caruth v. Pinkney, 683 F.2d 1044, 1052 (7th Cir. 1982).

[398]Sandin v. Conner, 515 U.S. 472, 484, 115 S. Ct. 2293 (1995); *see* § A.3 of this chapter for further discussion.

[399]*See* Shell v. Brzezniak, 365 F. Supp. 2d 362, 376 (W.D.N.Y. 2005); Orwat v. Maloney, 360 F. Supp. 2d 146, 161–62 (D.Mass. 2005) (three months' delay in serving disciplinary report and three more months' delay in scheduling a hearing, resulting in eight months' pre-hearing segregaton, was not atypical and significant and did not deprive plaintiff of a liberty interest).

[400]*See, e.g.*, Owens v. Maschner, 811 F.2d 1365 (10th Cir. 1987) (20-day delay for confined inmate may have denied due process); Russell v. Coughlin, 774 F. Supp. 189, 197 (S.D.N.Y. 1991) ("Due process requires that a disciplinary hearing be commenced within a reasonable time after an inmate is placed in administrative segregation."; 11 days was reasonable under the circumstances), *reargument granted on other grounds*, 782 F. Supp. 876 (S.D.N.Y. 1991).

[401]Baskerville v. Blot, 224 F. Supp. 2d 723, 736 (S.D.N.Y. 2002); Jenner v. Curtin, 979 F. Supp. 153, 154 (N.D.N.Y. 1997); Clark v. Neal, 890 F. Supp. 345, 350–51 (D.Del. 1995); *see* § F.1 of this chapter for discussion of the significance of length of stay in segregation due process cases.

[402]Russell v. Coughlin, 910 F.2d 75, 77–78 (2d Cir. 1990) (citing Hewitt v. Helms, 459 U.S. 460, 476, 103 S. Ct. 864 (1983)); *see* § H.2 of this chapter concerning administrative segregation. *Cf.* Pardo v. Hosier, 946 F.2d 1278, 1281–83 (7th Cir. 1991) (finding no liberty interest under state law regulations governing pre-hearing segregation).

[403]Gittens v. LeFevre, 891 F.2d 38, 41 (2d Cir. 1989). *Contra*, Riggins v. Walter, 279 F.3d 422, 426 (7th Cir. 1995) (holding that a prisoner placed in pre-hearing segregation was provided due process by the "postdeprivation" disciplinary hearing he received).

[404]Sealey v. Giltner, 197 F.3d 578, 587 (2d Cir. 1999).

[405]*See* Jordan v. Federal Bureau of Prisons, 191 Fed.Appx. 639 (10th Cir. 2006) (unpublished) (holding that five years in segregation pending criminal investigation was not "atypical and significant"); Jones v. Baker, 155 F.3d 810, 812–13 (6th Cir. 1998) (holding that two and a half years in segregation before a disciplinary hearing was not "atypical and significant" for due process purposes where the prisoner was being investigated for violent misconduct); Oswalt v. Godinez, 894 F. Supp. 1181, 1185-86 (N.D.Ill. 1995) (holding that a three-month delay in concluding an investigation while the plaintiff was segregated did not deny due process under *Sandin*); Dowdy v. Johnson, 510 F. Supp. 836, 839 (E.D.Va. 1981); People ex rel. Friedrich v. Smith, 106 A.D.2d 911, 483 N.Y.S.2d 134 (N.Y.App.Div. 1984) (holding seven-year delay did not deny due process where the prisoner had admitted the charges and had been in federal custody during the seven years); *see* White v. Booker, 598 F. Supp. 984, 986–87 (E.D.Va. 1984) (holding pre-hearing confinement did not deny due process where the time was credited against the punitive segregation sentence).

[406]For example, the New York prisons' requirement that hearings commence within seven days has been enforced against prison officials in the New York state courts because it is embodied in a state regulation. *See, e.g.*, Brito v. Sullivan, 141 A.D.2d 819, 530 N.Y.S.2d 28 (N.Y.App.Div. 1988); Coley v. Sullivan, 126 A.D.2d 641, 511 N.Y.S.2d 78 (N.Y.App.Div. 1987); *see also* Smith v. Coughlin, 182 A.D.2d 990, 582 N.Y.S.2d 567, 568 (N.Y.App.Div. 1992) (noting state regulation permits extension of time limit with proper authorization); Johnson v. Vitek, 205 Neb. 745, 290 N.W.2d 190 (Neb. 1980) (noting state law required hearings to be commenced within eight days but not completed within that time); Hopkins v. Maryland Inmate Grievance Comm'n, 40 Md.App. 329,

In cases involving pretrial detainees, where *Sandin* does not apply, delay in disciplinary hearings for prisoners held in pre-hearing segregation may be more constitutionally significant.[407]

h. Impartial Decision-Maker You are entitled to a hearing before an impartial fact-finder[408]—that is, one whose mind is not already made up and who can give you a fair hearing.[409] However, the courts have held that "[t]he degree of impartiality required of prison officials does not rise to the level of that required of judges generally,"[410] and that prison officials in general can be impartial.[411] A hearing officer can

be impartial even if she has previously presided over hearings involving the same prisoner.[412] However, someone who was involved in the current incident or the filing of charges, witnessed the incident, or investigated it is generally not considered impartial.[413] Other facts about a specific committee member may disqualify that person from conducting your hearing. One court held that the father of the officer who wrote the misconduct report was not impartial.[414] Others have held that a staff member who has been the subject of suits or complaints by a prisoner cannot be impartial in

---

391 A.D.2d 1213 (Md.App. 1978). *But see* Clayton-El v. Lane, 203 Ill.App. 895, 148 Ill.Dec. 877, 561 N.E.2d 183, 186 (Ill.App. 1990) (violation of state regulations did not require dismissal of proceeding), *appeal denied*, 135 Ill.2d 554, 151 Ill.Dec. 381, 564 N.E.2d 836 (Ill. 1990); Billups v. Dep't of Correctional Services Appeals Bd., 238 Neb. 39, 469 N.W.2d 120, 123-24 (Neb. 1991) (same).

[407]*See* Wilson v. Philadelphia Detention Center, 986 F. Supp. 282, 288-90 (E.D.Pa. 1997) (upholding a damage award to a prisoner who was put in segregation and had his hearing delayed for 10 days under circumstances a jury could find punitive); *see also* Surprenant v. Rivas, 424 F.3d 5, 14-15 (1st Cir. 2005) (affirming jury verdict for plaintiff against officer who fabricated charges knowing the plaintiff would be placed immediately into segregation). *But see* Holly v. Woolfolk, 415 F.3d 678, 681 (7th Cir. 2005) (holding pre-hearing segregation does not deny due process, just as arrest before a hearing does not deny due process; a post-deprivation hearing satisfies due process; court notes pre-hearing detention for much longer periods than the plaintiff's 48 hours, doesn't say what might be acceptable); *see* § C of this chapter concerning due process rights of detainees.

[408]Edwards v. Balisok, 520 U.S. 641, 647, 117 S. Ct. 1584 (1997) (stating due process requirements "are not so lax as to let stand the decision of a biased hearing officer who dishonestly suppresses evidence of innocence").

[409]An impartial decisionmaker "does not prejudge the evidence and . . . cannot say . . . how he would assess evidence he has not yet seen." Patterson v. Coughlin, 905 F.2d 564, 570 (2d Cir. 1990); *see* Surprenant v. Rivas, 424 F.3d 5, 17-18 (1st Cir. 2005) (a hearing officer who refused to interview an alibi witness based on a preconceived and subjective belief the witness would lie was not impartial); Hodges v. Scully, 141 A.D.2d 729, 529 N.Y.S.2d 832, 834 (N.Y.App.Div. 1988) (holding a hearing officer who already had a written and signed disposition in front of him while he conducted the hearing committed a "patent violation" of the right to impartiality). *But see* Moore v. Selsky, 900 F. Supp. 670, 676 (S.D.N.Y. 1995) (holding hearing officer did not lack impartiality because he wrote out his disposition between the first day of the hearing and the second; the plaintiff had presented all his evidence by then), *aff'd*, 101 F.3d 683 (2d Cir.1996).

[410]Allen v. Cuomo, 100 F.3d 253, 259 (2d Cir. 1996).

[411]Wolff v. McDonnell, 418 U.S. 539, 570-71, 94 S. Ct. 2963 (1974). Officials may not be disqualified simply because they have security responsibilities. Powell v. Ward, 542 F.2d 101, 103 (2d Cir. 1976). *But see* Avant v. Clifford, 67 N.J. 496, 341 A.2d 629, 646 (N.J. 1975) (holding under state Constitution that no more than one-third of the committee can be correctional officers, and in the

future staff from outside the particular prison must sit on committees).

[412]Pannell v. McBride, 306 F.3d 499, 502 (7th Cir. 2002) (per curiam); Black v. Selsky, 15 F. Supp. 2d 311, 317 (W.D.N.Y. 1998) (holding hearing officer was not biased based on having denied the plaintiff a time cut on an unrelated charge).

[413]Diercks v. Durham, 959 F.2d 710, 713 (8th Cir. 1992); Merritt v. De Los Santos, 721 F.2d 598, 600-01 (7th Cir. 1983); Rhodes v. Robinson, 612 F.2d 766, 773 (3d Cir. 1979); Willoughby v. Luster, 717 F. Supp. 1439, 1441-42 (D.Nev. 1989); Czajka v. Moore, 708 F. Supp. 253, 255 (E.D.Mo. 1989); Staples v. Traut, 675 F. Supp. 460, 464 (W.D.Wis. 1986); Powell v. Ward, 487 F. Supp. 917, 931 (S.D.N.Y. 1980), *aff'd as modified*, 643 F.2d 924 (2d Cir. 1981); Bradham v. State, 476 N.W.2d 369, 372-73 (Iowa App. 1991) (holding committee member who received warden's statement and passed it on to the committee was not impartial). *But see* Gaither v. Anderson, 236 F.3d 817, 820 (7th Cir. 2000) (holding the fact that committee members who heard a charge that the prisoner had stolen a mattress had seen him with a mattress earlier that day were only "tangentially involved" and remained impartial), *disapproved on other grounds by* White v. Indiana Parole Bd., 266 F.3d 759 (7th Cir. 2001); Whitford v. Boglino, 63 F.3d 527, 534 (7th Cir. 1995) (holding supervisor who signed a disciplinary report as shift supervisor had only "tangential involvement" and was not disqualified from presiding at the hearing); Madera v. Goord, 103 F. Supp. 2d 536, 540-41 (N.D.N.Y. 2000) (holding hearing officer who had authorized the search which found the contraband for which the prisoner was charged was sufficiently impartial because he was not "*directly* involved in the search or its execution"); Russell v. Coughlin, 774 F. Supp. 189, 197 (S.D.N.Y.) (holding hearing officer who had previously reviewed the disciplinary charges was not necessarily biased), *reargument granted on other grounds*, 782 F. Supp. 876 (S.D.N.Y. 1991). *Contra*, People v. Superior Court (Hamilton), 230 Cal.App.3d 1592, 281 Cal.Rptr. 900, 903-04 (1991) (holding hearing officer who had previously reviewed and classified the charge had acted in a prosecutorial role and due process required her disqualification).

[414]Vines v. Howard, 676 F. Supp. 608, 614-15 (E.D.Pa. 1987); *see* Eads v. Hanks, 280 F.3d 728, 729 (7th Cir. 2002) (stating in dictum that the spouse or "significant other" of a witness might not be impartial). *But see* Brown v. Frey, 889 F.2d 159, 170 (8th Cir. 1989) (holding the fact that a member of the hearing panel and a member of the administrative review committee were married to each other did not deny due process); Scott v. Coughlin, 78 F. Supp. 2d 299, 315-16 (S.D.N.Y. 2000) (holding the fact that the hearing officer was friendly with the judge whose courtroom the prisoner was charged with refusing to enter did not impair his impartiality).

that prisoner's disciplinary hearing.[415] External pressures on hearing officers can also prevent them from being impartial.[416]

Committees or hearing officers may display lack of impartiality by their statements and actions at the hearings or in connection with them.[417]

Sometimes state law or prison regulations prescribe who may sit on a disciplinary committee. Violations of these rules do not necessarily deny due process,[418] but you may be able to challenge them in state court.

i. Standards of Proof The question of how much evidence is required in a disciplinary hearing is not settled. To understand the issues, you must distinguish between the "burden of proof" and the "standard of review."

The burden of proof is applied at the initial, fact-finding stage of a proceeding. It is the amount of evidence that the fact-finding body (in this case, the disciplinary committee or hearing officer) must believe is present in order to convict. The standard of review is applied when a court is asked to review the proceeding after a lower court or an administrative body has already done the fact-finding and made a decision.

The burden of proof and the standard of review are not necessarily the same.[419] For example, in a civil trial, the plaintiff must usually prove her case to the trial court by a "preponderance of the evidence." That is the burden of proof.

---

[415]Malek v. Camp, 822 F.2d 812, 815–16 (8th Cir. 1987) (holding allegation that a hearing officer knew the plaintiff had helped another inmate sue him stated a due process claim); Edwards v. White, 501 F. Supp. 8, 11 (M.D.Pa. 1979) (holding that where an inmate was charged with possessing a petition calling for a particular official to be fired, that official could not be impartial), aff'd, 633 F.2d 212 (3d Cir. 1980). But see Adams v. Gunnell, 729 F.2d 362, 370 (5th Cir. 1984) (holding disciplinary board member could still be impartial even though the inmate had filed a grievance against him); Redding v. Fairman, 717 F.2d 1105, 1112–13 (7th Cir. 1983) (holding a prison official who had been sued by the plaintiff could be impartial in some circumstances). Cf. Goff v. Harper, 60 F.3d 518, 521 (8th Cir. 1995) (disapproving preliminary injunction barring persons against whom civil rights suits had been filed from sitting on those inmates' disciplinary proceedings, since it was speculative whether there would be any disciplinary proceedings against them).

[416]In Perry v. McGinnis, 209 F.3d 597 (6th Cir. 2000), the court found that "overwhelming evidence suggests that there was, at the very least, a strong expectation that the not-guilty/dismissal rate should not rise above 10%" and stated that "[i]f hearing officers focus on finding 90% of the defendants before them guilty, as the evidence adduced thus far suggests, they cannot possibly be impartial, as is required by Wolff." 209 F.3d at 606; see Heit v. van Ochten, 126 F. Supp. 2d 487 (W.D.Mich. 2001) (approving settlement forbidding the 10% quota). But see Allen v. Cuomo, 100 F.3d 253, 259 (2d Cir. 1996) (holding that any incentive for hearing officers to find prisoners guilty or upgrade their violations based on the perception that a $5.00 surcharge on all disciplinary convictions might raise revenue to prevent prison staff layoffs was "too remote and attenuated to deprive the inmates of due process").

[417]Edwards v. Balisok, 520 U.S. 641, 647, 117 S. Ct. 1584 (1997) (holding decision of a "biased hearing officer who dishonestly suppresses evidence of innocence" cannot stand); Francis v. Coughlin, 891 F.2d 43, 46–47 (2d Cir. 1989) (allegations that hearing officer suppressed evidence, distorted testimony, and never informed the plaintiff of evidence against him raised a material issue of lack of impartiality); Farid v. Goord, 200 F. Supp. 2d 220, 243–44 (W.D.N.Y. 2002) (citing allegation of bias against Muslims as supporting a due process claim); Giano v. Sullivan, 709 F. Supp. 1209, 1217 (S.D.N.Y. 1989) (holding continued presence of staff witnesses, including the lieutenant who drafted the misbehavior report, who interrupted the prisoner while he testified and stayed with the hearing officer while he drafted his findings, created an "unacceptable risk of unfairness"); Lonski on behalf of Colby v. Coughlin, 126 A.D.2d 981, 511 N.Y.S.2d 757, 758 (N.Y.App.Div. 1987) (holding hearing officer's "prosecutorial" questioning suggested lack of impartiality); Tumminia v. Kuhlmann, 139 Misc.2d 394, 527 N.Y.S.2d 673 (N.Y.Sup. 1988) (holding hearing officer's statement, "Okay now. You have to convince me that you're not guilty," raised a "strong suspicion that he did not have an open mind."); People ex rel. Cooper v. Smith, 115 Misc.2d 689, 454 N.Y.S.2d 635 (N.Y.Sup. 1982) (holding hearing officer's comments

raised "serious question" about his impartiality); see Pino v. Dalsheim, 605 F. Supp. 1305, 1318 (S.D.N.Y. 1984) (holding fact-finder is required to "consider in good faith the substance of the inmate's defense"); see also Surprenant v. Rivas, 424 F.3d 5, 17–18 (1st Cir. 2005) (holding that a hearing officer who rushed to impose punishment despite a request from officials to await the results of an investigation could be found to lack impartiality); Serrano v. Francis, 345 F.3d 1071, 1083 (9th Cir. 2003) (holding that hearing officer's statement that he didn't "know how black people think" and references to the ongoing O.J. Simpson trial presented sufficient factual basis for trial on whether the disallowance of live testimony was racially motivated); Colon v. Coughlin, 58 F.3d 865, 871 (2d Cir. 1995) (holding that hearing officer's statement, when asked if he thought an officer could fabricate charges, that "I believe the staff here is professional and I don't think anyone would deal along those lines," showed he was "far from unbiased"). But see White v. Indiana Parole Bd., 266 F.3d 759, 766–67 (7th Cir. 2001) (committee did not lose impartiality where the officer who wrote the misconduct charge remained in the hearing room; "Because prison disciplinary boards are entitled to receive, and act on, information that is withheld from the prisoner and the public, they must be entitled to discuss that evidence off the record with persons who know its significance."); Orwat v. Maloney, 360 F. Supp. 146, 163 n.13 (D.Mass. 2005) (the fact that the hearing officer addressed the officers by their first names and apologized for taking their time did not show bias); Espinal v. Goord, 180 F. Supp. 2d 532, 539 (S.D.N.Y. 2002) (holding hearing officer was not biased because he was the supervisor of the involved security staff); Moore v. Selsky, 900 F. Supp. 670, 676–77 (S.D.N.Y. 1995) (holding hearing officer was not impartial because he said he believed the system's drug tests were reliable; he would have lacked impartiality only if unwilling to consider impartially the possibility of error), aff'd, 101 F.3d 683 (2d Cir. 1996).

[418]Glick v. Walker, 834 F.2d 709, 711 (8th Cir. 1987).

[419]Plunk v. Givens, 234 F.3d 1128, 1130 (10th Cir. 2003); accord, Hamdi v. Rumsfeld, 542 U.S. 507, 537, 124 S. Ct. 2633 (2004).

However, on appeal, the appellate court must uphold the trial court's decision on the factual issues unless it is "clearly erroneous." That is the standard of review.[420]

"Some evidence" is the standard of review that the Due Process Clause requires courts to apply when they review prison disciplinary proceedings.[421] That means the court will uphold the conviction as long as there was some evidence to support it, regardless of how much other evidence there was supporting a different conclusion. States may provide in their statutes and regulations for a higher standard of review by state courts, but the Constitution does not require them to do so.

The courts are divided concerning the burden of proof that must be applied by the hearing officer or committee. In *Goff v. Dailey*, a federal appeals court held that "some evidence" is the burden of proof, as well as the standard of review, in disciplinary proceedings.[422] In other words, this court held that if there is *any* evidence that you are guilty, the committee can convict you, even if there is overwhelming evidence that you are innocent.

Later, the Vermont Supreme Court found the *Goff* decision "unpersuasive" and held that due process requires the burden of proof to be the "preponderance of the evidence."[423] The preponderance standard simply requires that for a fact-finder to convict someone, it must be convinced that she is more likely guilty than innocent.[424] Very few other courts have addressed the issue since *Goff* and *LaFaso*.[425]

We think the preponderance standard is the proper burden of proof for a variety of reasons, which you should cite to the court if the issue arises in your case. First, the "some evidence" test, while useful in reviewing a decision that has already been made, is simply not designed for the initial fact-finding. As the Vermont court observed, the Supreme Court in *Superintendent v. Hill*

> stated that its "some evidence" standard "does not require examination of the entire record, independent assessment of the credibility of witnesses, or weighing of the evidence." . . . We find incredible the suggestion that a *de novo* proceeding intended to determine the guilt or innocence of any individual could dispense with these procedures and retain a semblance of "fundamental fairness."[426]

As the lower court in *Goff* pointed out, and the Vermont court agreed, the accepted due process "balancing test" supports the use of a higher standard than "some evidence." ". . . [T]he inmate's interest in not being erroneously disciplined is an important one; the risk of error with use of a 'some evidence' standard is high; and the state's interest in swift and certain punishment is not impeded by the use of the preponderance standard of proof." In addition, the state has no interest in treating innocent people as if they were guilty.[427]

---

[420]These burdens are discussed in Ch. 10, §§ S.1.f and U.1.a.

[421]Superintendent v. Hill, 472 U.S. 445, 457, 105 S. Ct. 2768 (1985); *see* LaFaso v. Patrissi, 161 Vt. 46, 633 A.2d 695, 697 (1993) (noting that *Superintendent v. Hill* addressed the standard of review and not the standard of proof).

[422]Goff v. Dailey, 991 F.2d 1437, 1440–43 (8th Cir. 1993).

[423]LaFaso v. Patrissi, 633 A.2d at 699–700; *accord,* Carrillo v. Fabian, 701 N.W.2d 763, 776–77 (Minn. 2005); *see* Brown v. Fauver, 819 F.2d 395, 399 n.4 (3d Cir. 1987) (expressing doubt whether a "some evidence" burden of proof meets due process standards (dictum)).

[424]*In re* Winship, 397 U.S. 358, 371, 90 S. Ct. 1068 (1970) (Harlan, J., concurring) (stating the preponderance standard "simply requires the trier of fact 'to believe that the existence of a fact is more probable than its nonexistence'" (citation omitted)).

[425]The Supreme Court of Iowa, the state where *Goff* originated, has agreed with *Goff*. Backstrom v. Iowa District Ct. for Jones County, 508 N.W.2d 705, 710–11 (Iowa 1993). More recently, several judges of that court realized that *Goff* and *Backstrom* were wrongly decided, but they did not persuade the court majority. Marshall v. State, 524 N.W.2d 150, 152–53 (Iowa 1994). The Supreme Court of Nebraska has endorsed the *Goff* analysis, but it is not clear whether that court actually focused on the difference between the standard of review and the standard of proof. *See* Lynch v. Nebraska Dep't of Correctional Services, 245 Neb. 603, 610, 514 N.W.2d 310 (1994).

One federal appeals court, while not deciding the standard of proof question, has stated: "The Supreme Court has never held that the Due Process Clause requires . . . some narrowly-worded standard of evidence such as . . . '[t]he greater weight of the

evidence' standard." Henderson v. U.S. Parole Comm'n, 13 F.3d 1073, 1079 (7th Cir. 1994). That is true, but misleading. The Supreme Court has never said what the standard of proof in prison discipline is, so the question is open.

[426]LaFaso v. Patrissi, 161 Vt. 46, 50, 633 A.2d 695, 698 (1993); *see* Valmonte v. Bane, 18 F.3d 992, 1004 (2d Cir. 1994) (noting that a "some credible evidence" standard "does not require the factfinder to weigh conflicting evidence"). In *Carrillo v. Fabian*, 701 N.W.2d at 776, the court pointed out that procedural protections such as notice and the opportunity to respond are of little value if the prisoner can be convicted when the balance of evidence fails to prove she committed the offense.

[427]Goff v. Dailey, 991 F.2d at 1444 (dissenting opinion) (citations omitted); *accord,* Brown v. Fauver, 819 F.2d at 399 n.4 (expressing "grave doubts" whether it is constitutional to punish a prisoner for acts "which he in all probability did not commit"); LaFaso v. Patrissi, 633 A.2d at 698–700 ("We conclude there is a very significant risk of erroneous discipline of an innocent inmate under a 'some evidence' standard of proof."); Carrillo v. Fabian, 701 N.W.2d at 776 (stating "the government derives no benefit from disciplining inmates who have committed no offense"). The due process balancing test is discussed in § D of this chapter.

If prison officials have reason to believe that a prisoner is involved in activities that threaten security, but they can't immediately convict her of a disciplinary offense by the preponderance of the evidence, the law allows them to place her in administrative segregation, which does not require proof of "specific, serious misbehavior." Wilkinson v. Austin, 545 U.S. 209, 228, 125 S. Ct. 2384 (2005); *accord,* Hewitt v. Helms, 459 U.S. 460, 473–74, 103 S. Ct. 864 (1983) (noting subjective and predictive nature of administrative segregation decisions); *see* § H.2 of this chapter concerning administrative segregation.

The dissenting opinion in *Goff* pointed out that no cases applying the due process balancing test have previously upheld a standard of proof less than a preponderance of the evidence.[428] The Supreme Court has recently confirmed that it has only "utilized the 'some evidence' standard in the past as a standard of review, not as a standard of proof."[429] Cases cited in *Goff* as supporting the use of a standard lower than the preponderance of the evidence did not actually deal with the standard of proof. Rather, they dealt only with the procedural nature of the hearing that was required,[430] or were off the point for some other reason.[431]

In addition to the foregoing arguments, the use of a low standard of proof in prison disciplinary hearings is unfair because these proceedings are already so one-sided. For example, a prisoner may be convicted on nothing more than an officer's written report.[432] Thus, there will be some evidence in almost every disciplinary case.

The standard of proof issue arises in cases where a disciplinary violation (usually involving contraband) could have been committed by a number of prisoners. In *Hamilton v. O'Leary*, all four prisoners in a cell were found guilty of possessing contraband found in a vent when their cell was searched; the disciplinary decision said that prisoners are "responsible for whatever is found in the cell." The court said that this "constructive possession" could provide some evidence of guilt "when contraband is found where only a few inmates have access," and that a 25% likelihood of guilt satisfied the "some evidence" standard.[433] It acknowledged that if it had to consider the prisoner's claim that 32 prisoners actually had access to the vent, the resulting 3.1% likelihood of guilt would not be "some evidence." It did not explain where the line is drawn between a small number that is "some evidence" and a small number that is "no evidence."[434] If you have a case where you have been found guilty based purely on a probability less than 51%, you should argue that the proper standard of proof is the preponderance of the

[428]Goff v. Dailey, 991 F.2d 1437, 1443 (8th Cir. 1993) and cases cited.

[429]Hamdi v. Rumsfeld, 542 U.S. 507, 537, 124 S. Ct. 2633 (2004). The Court acknowledged that the "some evidence" standard is "ill suited" to a situation in which a habeas corpus petitioner has received no prior proceedings and no opportunity to "rebut the executive's factual assertions before a neutral decisionmaker." *Id.* We think the same argument is applicable to prison disciplinary hearings.

[430]In *Goss v. Lopez*, 419 U.S. 565, 95 S. Ct. 729 (1975), the Supreme Court held that a school principal could suspend a student after telling the student what she was accused of doing and informally discussing the charges with her. It did not say whether the principal did or did not have to be convinced that the student was more likely guilty than innocent. Similarly, in *Cleveland Bd. of Educ. v. Loudermill*, 470 U.S. 532, 105 S. Ct. 1487 (1985), the Court held that public employees may be terminated after giving them notice of the charges, an explanation of the evidence, and a chance to respond to it. It did not address the burden of proof that had to be met in this proceeding. In addition, these cases dealt with temporary deprivations: suspension for no more than ten days in *Goss* and a preliminary "pre-termination" hearing, followed by a final administrative hearing providing greater due process rights, in *Loudermill*.

Hewitt v. Helms, which concerns administrative segregation, also dealt with procedural requirements rather than the standard of proof. In addition, it specifically stated that administrative segregation involved "subjective" and "intuitive" judgments for which "trial-type procedural safeguards" are not helpful. 459 U.S. at 474. Thus, *Hewitt* has no application to disciplinary proceedings, which are intended to make the factual determination whether a prisoner has broken a rule or not. *See* § H.2 of this chapter concerning administrative segregation.

[431]Cases involving civil forfeiture of property do not support the holding in *Goff* because they are based on the concept of an "in rem" proceeding against the property itself, *see* Calero-Toledo v. Pearson Yacht Leasing Co., 416 U.S. 663, 684–87, 94 S. Ct. 2080 (1974) (citing The Palmyra, 12 Wheat 1 (1827)), which does not apply to deprivations of a person's liberty. For this reason, civil forfeiture law only requires the government to show that the property was involved in illegal activity and does not require evidence that the property owner committed any unlawful act. *See* Calero-Toledo v. Pearson Yacht Leasing Co., 416 U.S. at 686–87; *see* U.S. v. 92 Buena Vista Ave., Rumson, N.J., 507 U.S. 111, 119–21,113 S. Ct. 1126 (1993). Such a proceeding is clearly different from one to determine whether a prisoner is personally guilty of a disciplinary offense. In addition, *Goff's* statement that forfeitures may be based only on a showing of probable cause, 991 F.2d at 1441, is not the

whole story. An initial seizure may be justified by a showing of probable cause, but a permanent forfeiture requires a subsequent hearing at which either party may have the burden of proof by a preponderance of the evidence. *See* U.S. v. One Assortment of 89 Firearms, 465 U.S. 354, 362, 104 S. Ct. 1099 (1984); U.S. v. $12,390, 956 F.2d 801, 806 (8th Cir. 1992). Under *Goff*, a prisoner whose claim of innocence was supported by a preponderance of the evidence could still be convicted.

[432]*See* n.451 of this section, below.

[433]Hamilton v. O'Leary, 976 F.2d 341, 345–46 (7th Cir. 1992); *accord*, Thompson v. Hawk, 978 F. Supp. 1421, 1424 (D.Kan. 1997); *see* Jensen v. Gunter, 807 F. Supp. 1463, 1479–80 (D.Neb. 1992) (upholding rule presuming all inmates in a multiple occupancy housing unit guilty of possessing contraband found there, though holding prisoners might still challenge adequacy of evidence in individual cases), *appeal dismissed on other grounds*, 992 F.2d 183 (8th Cir. 1993); *see also* Howard v. U.S. Bureau of Prisons, 487 F.3d 808, 812 (7th Cir. 2007) (finding of contraband in prisoner's property met "some evidence" standard notwithstanding the argument that other prisoners had access to his property, which had been stored while he was in segregation).

[434]The dissenting judge in *Hamilton* said that it was clear that eight inmates had access to the immediate area of the vent, and that the resulting 12.5% probability of guilt "is not my idea of some evidence. . . ." 976 F.2d at 347. *See* Cardenas v. Wigen, 921 F. Supp. 286, 288–89 n.4 (E.D.Pa. 1996) (stating in dictum that the 8.3% likelihood of guilt arising where contraband was found in an area shared by 12 inmates was not "some evidence"). Similarly, in *Broussard v. Johnson*, 253 F.3d 874, 877 (5th Cir. 2001), the only valid evidence that the prisoner possessed escape-related contraband was the presence of a pair of bolt cutters in his work area, but they were not "some evidence" of the offense since 100 inmates had access to that area.

evidence, and that under that standard you cannot lawfully be found guilty if the evidence shows that you are less likely to be guilty than innocent. Obviously that argument will not succeed in a jurisdiction where courts have already held that the standard of proof is only "some evidence." Courts may also respond that it does not deny due process for prison officials to make rules based on collective guilt.[435]

Turning to standards of judicial review, the "some evidence" standard is the lowest possible standard of review.[436] Under it, courts have said they will not make an "independent assessment of the credibility of witnesses"[437] or otherwise get involved in weighing the evidence or second-guessing the disciplinary committee's decision that you are guilty.[438] As a result, many disciplinary convictions are upheld by courts on very flimsy or questionable proof.[439] The courts

will intervene only if there is no evidence at all to support the charge,[440] or an element of the charge.[441] (Usually, there

---

[435]The dissenting judge in *Hamilton v. O'Leary* said that such a rule might be acceptable in prison, even though the prison officials did not rely on it in that case. 976 F.2d 347. The idea of collective guilt seems to us fundamentally inconsistent with due process, and we are not aware of any court that has actually upheld its application.

[436]One court has refused to credit prison disciplinary hearings in determining whether to terminate a prisoner's parental rights because of the low evidentiary requirements and the use of evidence which would not be admissible in other kinds of proceedings. *In re M.S.*, 239 Ill.App.3d 938, 945–49, 606 N.E.2d 768 (Ill.App. 1992).

[437]Superintendent v. Hill, 472 U.S. 445, 455, 105 S. Ct. 2768 (1985).

[438]Hudson v. Johnson, 242 F.3d 534, 537 (5th Cir. 2001); Cummings v. Dunn, 630 F.2d 649, 650 (8th Cir. 1980); Walsh v. Finn, 865 F. Supp. 126, 129 (S.D.N.Y. 1994) (stating that under the "some evidence" standard, "[o]nce the court determines that the evidence is reliable, its inquiry ends—it should not look further to see whether other evidence in the record may have suggested a contrary conclusion."); Rogers v. Oestreich, 736 F. Supp. 964, 967 (E.D.Wis. 1990); *see* McPherson v. McBride, 188 F.3d 784, 787 (7th Cir. 1999) (rejecting proposition that the "some evidence" standard is not applicable when an officer submits a false report). *But see* Propst v. Leapley, 886 F.2d 1068, 1070–71 (8th Cir. 1989) (holding disciplinary decision based on racial bias was unlawful).

[439]*See, e.g.*, Sweeney v. Parke, 113 F.3d 716, 720–21 (7th Cir. 1997) (there was some evidence of tampering with a cell lock where an officer reported seeing that a blanket blocked his view of the cell, then plaintiff walked into his cell and tried to close the door unnoticed, and cell door was later found unlocked); Mason v. Sargent, 898 F.2d 679, 680 (8th Cir. 1990) (holding there was "some evidence" that the plaintiff possessed contraband where it was found in a locker he shared with another inmate, even though the other inmate admitted it was his); Turner v. Scroggy, 831 F.2d 135, 140 (6th Cir. 1987) (holding evidence that prisoner touched a female staff member on the shoulder and side with his hands and knee was "some evidence" of sexual assault); Hoskins v. McBride, 202 F. Supp. 2d 839, 845–46 (N.D.Ind. 2002) (holding videotape of a child throwing something into the trash can where drugs were found, and the fact that the prisoner was the only one who had a child visitor at the time, were sufficient, though "[t]his is not much evidence"), *aff'd*, 66 Fed.Appx. 47 (7th Cir. 2003) (unpublished); Zimmerman v. Tippecanoe Sheriff's Dep't, 25 F. Supp. 2d 915, 921 (N.D.Ind. 1998) (holding staff members' statement that the plaintiff

confessed was some evidence); Ramey v. Hawk, 730 F. Supp. 1366, 1372–73 (E.D.N.C. 1989) (holding failure to urinate within two hours was "some evidence" of refusal to supply a urine sample even though the plaintiff testified he had trouble urinating while being watched); Quinlan v. Fairman, 663 F. Supp. 24, 27 (N.D.Ill. 1987) (holding officer's testimony that the plaintiff committed an assault was "some evidence" even though the victim of the assault denied it); LuGrain v. State, 479 N.W.2d 312, 316–18 (Iowa 1991) (similar to *Ramey*).

[440]*See, e.g.*, Teague v. Quarterman, 482 F.3d 769, 780 (5th Cir. 2007) (invalidating disciplinary conviction for a "trafficking and trading" offense where there was no evidence the prisoner knew that another prisoner had deposited money into his account; refusing to interpret disciplinary rule as one of strict liability); Wilson v. Jones, 430 F.3d 1113, 1123–24 (10th Cir. 2005) (finding no evidence to support a conviction of obtaining money under false pretenses where state law allowed the disbursement that the prisoner requested); Burnsworth v. Gunderson, 179 F.3d 771, 772–73 (9th Cir. 1999) (holding there was no evidence that a prisoner who said that if he did not get protective custody, his only option would be to "hit the fence," actually escaped or attempted to escape); Lenea v. Lane, 882 F.2d 1171, 1175–76 (7th Cir. 1989) (holding there was no evidence that the prisoner had aided an escape based on the facts that he knew the escapees, had spoken to one on the day of the escape, was legitimately in the general area when they escaped, and was found to be "deceptive" during a polygraph test); Cerda v. O'Leary, 746 F. Supp. 820, 825 (N.D.Ill. 1990) (holding evidence discrediting the prisoner's alibi but not affirmatively supporting his guilt was not any evidence of the infraction); Adams v. Wolff, 624 F. Supp. 1036, 1040 (D.Nev. 1985) (holding stab wounds alone did not constitute evidence of fighting); Edwards v. White, 501 F. Supp. 8, 11 (M.D.Pa. 1979) (holding possession of a petition with no signatures was no evidence of a "conspiracy to disrupt prison routine"), *aff'd*, 633 F.2d 209 (3d Cir. 1980); U.S. ex rel. Smith v. Robinson, 495 F. Supp. 696, 701 (E.D.Pa. 1980) (holding contraband charge was not supported by any evidence that seized items were really contraband); Harper v. State, 463 N.W.2d 418, 420–21 (Iowa 1990) (holding the fact that an inmate broke a minor rule was no evidence that he disobeyed a lawful order); Matter of Reismiller, 101 Wash.2d 291, 678 P.2d 323, 326 (Wash. 1984) (holding no evidence was produced linking the prisoner with the contraband).

In *Baxter v. Palmigiano*, 425 U.S. 308, 317–18, 96 S. Ct. 1551 (1976), the Supreme Court held that a prisoner's silence at a hearing could be used as evidence of guilt. This point is discussed in § H.1.s of this chapter.

[441]In *Gamble v. Calbone*, 375 F.3d 1021, 1032 (10th Cir. 2004), the court held that a disciplinary conviction for violating a criminal offense required some evidence of the intent required to commit that criminal offense. It rejected the argument that as long as there was some evidence of *some* of the elements of the offense, due process was satisfied. Prison officials may argue that *Gamble's* holding is limited to cases involving disciplinary charges for criminal offenses. *But see* Morgan v. Dretke, 433 F.3d 455, 458 (5th Cir. 2005) (holding that a disciplinary conviction of assault inflicting non-serious injury could not stand absent any evidence of injury). At least one court has rejected the argument that there must be some evidence of every element of a prison disciplinary offense.

Particular Due Process Issues 351

is some evidence in these "no evidence" cases, but the evidence doesn't really show that the prisoner committed the offense.) Some cases have held that disciplinary decisions requiring restitution for damage to property must have at least some evidence of the value or cost of the property.[442]

Despite courts' strong statements about not weighing evidence in disciplinary cases, many courts have interpreted the "some evidence" standard to require some *reliable* evidence[443]—i.e., they hold that some evidence is so completely insubstantial as to amount to no evidence. One court has said that if "'some evidence' is to be distinguished from 'no evidence,' it must possess at least some minimal probative value . . . to satisfy the requirement of the Due Process Clause that the decisions of prison administrators must have some basis in fact." Evidence may be "rendered so suspect by the manner and circumstances in which given as to fall short of constituting a basis in fact" for imposing discipline. The "some evidence" standard does not "require that credence be given to that evidence which common sense and experience suggest is incredible"[444] or "blatantly implausible."[445]

Under the "some evidence" standard of review, the presence of evidence supporting the prisoner does not invalidate the conviction as long as there is evidence against the prisoner as well.[446] However, some courts have held that the existence of exculpatory evidence may be more significant when that evidence "directly undercuts the reliability of the evidence on which the disciplinary authority relied or there are other extra-ordinary circumstances."[447] In such cases there must be sufficient evidence of the reliability of the evidence against the prisoner, and an explanation of why the exculpatory evidence is rejected.[448]

"Evidence" is defined broadly, and prison hearings need not follow the rules of evidence applied in courts. For example, testimony need not be under oath,[449] and hearsay is admissible.[450] In particular, written reports by prison staff—a type of hearsay—can be sufficient evidence to prove a disciplinary violation,[451] at least as long as they are based on personal knowledge and properly signed and dated.[452]

Hamilton v. Scott, 762 F. Supp. 794, 800 (N.D.Ill.), *aff'd sub nom.* Hamilton v. O'Leary, 976 F.2d 341 (7th Cir. 1991).

[442]Keeling v. Schaefer, 181 F. Supp. 2d 1206, 1224–25 (D.Kan. 2001); Artway v. Scheidemantel, 671 F. Supp. 330 (D.N.J. 1987).

[443]Sira v. Morton, 380 F.3d 57, 76–77 (2d Cir. 2004).

[444]Goff v. Burton, 91 F.3d 1188, 1192 (8th Cir. 1996) (holding the some evidence standard was not met where a confidential informant gave hearsay testimony and no staff member spoke with the source of the hearsay, and the victim of the alleged assault made inconsistent statements, never testified under oath, did not appear at the disciplinary hearing, and gave statements in response to leading questions and the promise of a transfer to a more desirable prison); *see* Moore v. Plaster, 266 F.3d 928, 932 (8th Cir. 2001) (holding staff member's report that contained accusations, but was not based on personal knowledge and did not even name persons who witnessed the alleged violation, was "only an accusation" that "does not qualify as 'evidence'"); Broussard v. Johnson, 253 F.3d 874, 876–77 (5th Cir. 2001) (holding that after unreliable informant evidence was eliminated, the presence of bolt cutters in an area where 100 inmates had access was not "some evidence" of possession of escape contraband); Hayes v. McBride, 965 F. Supp. 1186, 1189–90 (N.D.Ind. 1997) (officer said the prisoner admitted a substance was an intoxicant, the prisoner denied it; without any other evidence that the substance was an intoxicant, the "some evidence" standard was not met); Gilbert v. Selsky, 867 F. Supp. 159, 164–65 (S.D.N.Y. 1994) (similar to *Broussard*); *see also* § H.1.j of this chapter concerning reliability of evidence from scientific tests.

[445]Zavaro v. Coughlin, 970 F.2d 1148, 1153–54 (2d Cir. 1992) (holding statements that "every inmate" out of 100 in the mess hall participated in a disturbance were so "blatantly implausible" that they did not constitute some evidence of a particular inmate's guilt); *see* Bryant v. Coughlin, 77 N.Y.2d 642, 569 N.Y.S.2d 582, 572 N.E.2d 23, 26 (N.Y. 1991) (holding similar evidence did not support individual findings of guilt under a "substantial evidence" standard).

[446]Rice v. McBride, 967 F. Supp. 1097, 1103 (N.D.Ind. 1997).

[447]Viens v. Daniels, 871 F.2d 1328, 1335 (7th Cir. 1989).

[448]Meeks v. McBride, 81 F.3d 717, 720–21 (7th Cir. 1996) (holding toxicology report of drug use did not meet the "some evidence" standard because there were two instances of unreliable identifying information in the report and the plaintiff showed there was another inmate with the same name who had been confused with him in prior disciplinary proceedings, and the defendants submitted no evidence bolstering the reliability of the report).

[449]Ruley v. Nevada Bd. of Prison Comm'rs, 628 F. Supp. 108, 111–12 (D.Nev. 1986).

[450]Rodgers v. Thomas, 879 F.2d 380, 383 (8th Cir. 1989) (hearsay verified by the disciplinary committee did not deny due process); Rudd v. Sargent, 866 F.2d 260, 262 (8th Cir. 1989); Moore v. Selsky, 900 F. Supp. 670, 674–75 (S.D.N.Y. 1995) (holding letter from a drug test manufacturer, which stated that no drugs or diseases had been identified which produce a false positive reaction for cocaine or cannabinoids, was hearsay but was "some evidence"); Wolfe v. Carlson, 583 F. Supp. 977, 980–81 (S.D.N.Y. 1984); Flythe v. Davis, 407 F. Supp. 137, 138 (E.D.Va. 1976); Murphy v. Superintendent, Massachusetts Correctional Institution, 396 Mass. 830, 489 N.E.2d 661, 663 (Mass. 1986).

[451]McPherson v. McBride, 188 F.3d 784, 786–87 (7th Cir. 1999) (holding report was sufficient to support disciplinary conviction, despite its brevity, where it described the infraction in sufficient detail and the conduct clearly violated prison rules); Carter v. Kane, 938 F. Supp. 282, 287 (E.D.Pa. 1996) (holding a misbehavior report by an officer who witnessed the misconduct can support a disciplinary conviction); Harrison v. Pyle, 612 F. Supp. 850, 855 (D.Nev. 1985); People ex rel. Vega v. Smith, 66 N.Y.2d 130, 495 N.Y.S.2d 332, 485 N.E.2d 997, 1002–04 (N.Y. 1985).

[452]People ex rel. Vega v. Smith, 485 N.E.2d at 1002–04; *see* Walsh v. Finn, 865 F. Supp. 126, 129–30 (S.D.N.Y. 1994) (holding a misbehavior report written by an officer who did not actually see the alleged misconduct is not some evidence); Rodriguez v. Coughlin, 176 A.D.2d 1234, 577 N.Y.S.2d 190, 191 (N.Y.App.Div. 1991) (holding misbehavior reports not based on personal knowledge were not substantial evidence). *But see* Stone-Bey v. Swihart, 898 F. Supp. 1287, 1297 (N.D.Ind. 1995) (holding officer's failure to sign reports and properly document them did not make the reports inadmissible); Palacio v. Dep't of Correctional Services,

However, courts have cautioned that hearsay that is completely uncorroborated and has no other indications of reliability does not constitute some evidence.[453] The determination whether there was some evidence to support a disciplinary conviction must be limited to evidence in the administrative record.[454]

In some states, the standard of review under state law is "substantial evidence," which means "evidence on which reasonable persons are accustomed to rely in the conduct of serious affairs."[455] This standard is more favorable to prisoners than "some evidence," but it is hard to pin down exactly what the practical difference is between the "substantial evidence" test and the "some evidence" test, since courts rarely apply both standards in the same case.[456]

If your state has a "substantial evidence" standard, a federal court will probably not enforce it, so you are best advised to bring your case in state court if the main problem with your disciplinary hearing is the adequacy of the evidence. Federal prison regulations, which used to prescribe a "substantial evidence" standard of review, now state that a disciplinary conviction must be based on "at least some facts, and if there is conflicting evidence, it must be based on the greater weight of the evidence."[457]

j. Urinalysis, Polygraphy, and Other Scientific Tests The use of urinalysis evidence to support disciplinary charges of drug use is now well established. Courts have held that use of a fluorescence polarization immunoassay (FPIA), said to be 95% accurate, satisfies due process without a second confirmatory test.[458] Most courts have held that the "Enzyme Multiple Immunoassay Test" (EMIT) or other reliable test, confirmed by a second test, is sufficient to support a disciplinary conviction.[459] These decisions imply, though they do not explicitly say, that a single test is inadequate, and some courts have so held.[460] Other courts have upheld convictions based on a single unconfirmed test.[461] Failure to provide a urine sample within a reasonable time has also been held to be sufficient evidence to support a charge of drug use.[462]

The EMIT test gives "false positive" results in reaction with some over-the-counter medications and other substances.

---

182 A.D.2d 900, 901, 582 N.Y.S. 2d 42 (N.Y.App.Div. 1992) (holding report of officer who did not witness an assault, but who witnessed the victim's identification of the assailant and recorded the victim's story, was substantial evidence).

[453]Sira v. Morton, 380 F.3d 57, 78–80 (2d Cir. 2004); *accord*, Luna v. Pico, 356 F.3d 481, 489 (2d Cir. 2004) (holding due process violated when a prisoner "is punished solely on the basis of a victim's hearsay accusation without any indication in the record as to why the victim should be credited"; accuser had refused to confirm his allegation and there was no other evidence or assessment of credibility); Young v. Kann, 926 F.2d 1396, 1402 (3d Cir. 1991) (holding reliance on a prison employee's oral summary of an allegedly threatening letter, without reading the letter, may deny due process); Howard v. Wilkerson, 768 F. Supp. 1002, 1008 (S.D.N.Y. 1991) (holding hearsay information with no evidence supporting its credibility was not "some evidence"); Parker v. State, 597 So.2d 753, 754 (Ala.Cr.App. 1992) (holding staff member's report based on what other inmates told him was not "some evidence"); Johnson v. State, 576 So.2d 1289, 1290 (Ala.Crim.App. 1991) (similar to *Howard*); Ex parte Floyd, 457 So.2d 961, 962 (Ala. 1984) (holding "supposition based upon supposition, stemming from hearsay" was inadequate to support a conviction); Farrell v. Oregon State Penitentiary, Corrections Div., 51 Or.App. 465, 625 P.2d 1380, 1382 (Or.App. 1981) (holding anonymous note did not meet state regulations' requirement that evidence "be of such credibility as would be considered by reasonable persons in the conduct of their affairs"); *see also* cases cited in nn.443–445, above.

Many such cases involve the use of confidential informants without evidence of their reliability. Confidential informants are discussed in more detail in § H.1.m of this chapter.

[454]Riggins v. Walter, 279 F.3d 422, 428–29 (7th Cir. 1995).

[455]Murphy v. Superintendent, Massachusetts Correctional Institution, 396 Mass. 830, 489 N.E.2d 661, 663 (1986); *accord*, People ex rel. Vega v. Smith, 485 N.E.2d at 1002.

[456]In one New York case, the court held that evidence that the prisoner was "standing around" when two other inmates committed an extortive assault was not "substantial evidence" to support his conviction for extortion. Lopez v. Smith, 105 A.D.2d 1124, 482 N.Y.S.2d 583 (N.Y.App.Div. 1984). In our opinion, that evidence would not have met the "some evidence" test either, but the court did not comment on that question. *See also* Solar v. Oregon State Penitentiary, 87 Or.App. 222, 742 P.2d 611 (Or.App. 1987) (finding lack of substantial evidence in several cases), *review denied*, 744 P.2d 1004 (Or. 1987).

---

[457]28 C.F.R. § 541.17; *see* Henderson v. Carlson, 812 F.2d 874, 879 (3d Cir. 1987) (citing predecessor 28 C.F.R. § 541.17(f) (1986)).

[458]Louis v. Dep't of Correctional Services of Nebraska, 437 F.3d 697, 700–01 (8th Cir. 2006).

[459]Higgs v. Bland, 888 F.2d 443, 445, 448–49 (6th Cir. 1989); Peranzo v. Coughlin, 850 F.2d 125 (2d Cir. 1988) (per curiam); Spence v. Farrier, 807 F.2d 753, 756 (8th Cir. 1986); Pella v. Adams, 702 F. Supp. 244, 247 (D.Nev. 1988) and cases cited; Works v. State, 575 So.2d 622, 624 (Ala.Crim.App. 1991); Lahey v. Kelly, 71 N.Y.2d 135, 524 N.Y.S.2d 30, 32–34, 518 N.E.2d 924 (N.Y. 1987).

[460]Wykoff v. Resig, 613 F. Supp. 1504, 1512 (N.D.Ind. 1985) (holding "all positive EMIT results in the future should be confirmed by a second EMIT test or its equivalent"), *aff'd*, 819 F.2d 1143 (7th Cir. 1987); *see* Holm v. Haines, 734 F. Supp. 366, 371 (W.D.Wis. 1990) (stating EMIT test without corroboration may not meet the "some evidence" standard); Bourgeois v. Murphy, 119 Idaho 611, 809 P.2d 472, 480 (Idaho 1991) (finding "considerable merit" in argument that a single uncorroborated test is not "some evidence").

[461]Henson v. U.S. Bureau of Prisons, 213 F.3d 897, 898–99 (5th Cir. 2000) (per curiam) (holding there was no need for a confirming test and in any case the initial test met the "some evidence" standard); Thompson v. Owens, 889 F.2d 500, 501–02 (3d Cir. 1989); Harrison v. Dahm, 911 F.2d 37, 41–42 (8th Cir. 1990); Petition of Johnston, 109 Wash.2d 493, 745 P.2d 864, 868 (Wash. 1987); Hoeppner v. Iowa, 379 N.W.2d 23, 25–26 (Iowa Ct.App. 1985) (holding urine sample need not be preserved for independent testing); *see also* Ballard v. Carlson, 882 F.2d 93, 96 (4th Cir. 1989) (holding reliance on unconfirmed EMIT test did not violate "clearly established constitutional rights").

[462]LuGrain v. State, 479 N.W.2d 312, 317–18 (Iowa 1991).

A second EMIT test does not eliminate this risk; to verify the EMIT test completely, it is necessary to perform a test that is based on a different methodology.[463] So far most courts have not required this type of confirmation.[464] Nor are prison officials required to let a prisoner have a different test done at her own expense.[465]

Most courts have held that a "reasonably reliable chain of custody" for urine samples must be maintained,[466] though the chain of custody need not be perfect.[467] At least one court has rejected the view that a chain of custody is required on the ground that a drug test is "some evidence" even if the chain of custody was not properly maintained.[468] In our opinion, this holding misses the point. As we pointed out in the previous section, many courts have held that due process requires some *reliable* evidence to support a disciplinary conviction. Drug test evidence may be very reliable if it is properly handled, but if prison staff mix up or mishandle the samples, it ceases to be reliable but there is no practical way for the prisoner to refute it. Due process thus requires special precautions to address this special risk of unreliability, just as the use of confidential informants requires special precautions to ensure the informants' reliability.[469]

The courts have generally not required actual laboratory test results to be produced at the disciplinary hearing[470] and have not required laboratory technicians or other technical personnel to be called as witnesses.[471] Officials are not required to set threshold levels for drug testing to distinguish between drug use and second-hand smoke exposure.[472]

The failure to perform scientific tests to establish facts in a disciplinary proceeding does not deny due process if there is enough other evidence to support the conviction. Drug and alcohol tests are not required if other evidence indicates that a substance is a drug or alcohol.[473] When a

---

[463]Adkins v. Martin, 699 F. Supp. 1510, 1513–14 (W.D.Okla. 1988); Frankenberry v. Williams, 677 F. Supp. 793, 799–801 (M.D.Pa.) (noting different test eliminated issue of cross-reactivity with the prisoner's prescription medication), *aff'd*, 860 F.2d 1074 (3d Cir. 1988).

[464]We know of one exception. Ferguson v. Dep't of Corrections, 816 P.2d 134, 140 (Alaska 1991).

[465]Henson v. U.S. Bureau of Prisons, 213 F.3d 897, 898–99 (5th Cir. 2000) (per curiam) and cases cited; Koenig v. Vannelli, 971 F.2d 422, 423 (9th Cir. 1992); Pella v. Adams, 723 F.Supp. 1394, 1396 (D.Nev. 1989); Hoeppner v. Iowa, 379 N.W.2d 23, 26 (Iowa Ct.App. 1985).

[466]Soto v. Lord, 693 F. Supp. 8, 17–20 (S.D.N.Y. 1988); *accord*, Thomas v. McBride, 3 F. Supp. 2d 989, 992 (N.D.Ind. 1998) and cases cited; Wykoff v. Resig, 613 F. Supp. 1504, 1513 (N.D.Ind. 1985); Ex parte Shabazz, 989 So.2d 524, 525–26 (Ala. 2008); Bourgeois v. Murphy, 119 Idaho 611, 809 P.2d 472, 481 (1991) (". . . [W]hen there is no documentation of the chain of custody to show that that which was analyzed by the laboratory came from the inmate in question, there is no test from a legal standpoint."); Byerly v. Ashley, 825 S.W.2d 286, 288 (Ky.App. 1991) (holding it must be "established with reasonable certainty that the specimen tested was the same as that taken from the [prisoner]"); *see* Elkin v. Fauver, 969 F.2d 48 (3d Cir. 1992) (applying a consent decree requiring maintenance of a chain of custody); Satchell v. Coughlin, 178 A.D.2d 795, 577 N.Y.S.2d 696, 697 (N.Y.App.Div. 1991) (holding record is sufficient if it shows the steps taken in the chain of custody).

[467]Webb v. Anderson, 224 F.3d 649, 652–53 (7th Cir. 2000) (holding omissions from chain of custody documentation did not preclude relying on the test results where there was no basis for thinking the sample was mishandled or a mistake made); Higgs v. Bland, 888 F.2d 443, 445, 449 (6th Cir. 1989) (upholding conviction despite "some lapses" in chain of custody); Alicea v. Howell, 387 F. Supp. 2d 227, 233 (W.D.N.Y. 2005) (violation of prison rules for handling urine samples did not deny due process); *see* Louis v. Dep't of Correctional Services of Nebraska, 437 F.3d 697, 700 (8th Cir. 2006) (refusing to require that the prisoner be allowed to sign and seal the specimen, in the absence of evidence that the current procedures have led to serious errors).

[468]Thompson v. Owens, 889 F.2d 500, 502 (3d Cir. 1989).

[469]*See* Meeks v. McBride, 81 F.3d 717, 720–21 (7th Cir. 1996) (holding that toxicology report did not meet "some evidence" standard since chain of custody documentation suggested it might have been for the wrong prisoner's sample); *see* § H.1.m of this chapter concerning confidential informants.

[470]*See* § D.1.e of this chapter, n.374.

[471]Louis v. Dep't of Correctional Services of Nebraska, 437 F.3d 697, 701 (8th Cir. 2006) (upholding refusal to require lab technicians to be called as witnesses); Alicea v. Howell, 387 F. Supp. 2d 227, 233–34 (W.D.N.Y. 2005) (similar to *Mathews*); Mathews v. Selsky, 870 F. Supp. 66 (S.D.N.Y. 1994) (holding that the refusal to call a representative of the Syva Company did not violate clearly established rights).

The Supreme Court has recently held that laboratory analysts must be called as witnesses in order for the results of their tests to be admitted into evidence in criminal trials. Melendez-Diaz v. Massachusetts, ___ U.S. ___, 129 S.Ct. 2527 (2009). This decision is unlikely to be applicable to prison disciplinary hearings because it is based on the Confrontation Clause of the Sixth Amendment to the Constitution, and as we have already noted, the right to confrontation of adverse witnesses is not applicable to prison disciplinary proceedings as a matter of due process. *See* § H.1.d of this chapter, above.

[472]King v. Gorczyk, 175 Vt. 220, 226, 825 A.2d 16 (2003).

[473]Griffin v. Spratt, 969 F.2d 16, 22 (3d Cir. 1992) (holding officer's testimony that he believed material was fermented could support a conviction); Clark v. State, 462 So.2d 1065 (Ala.Crim. App. 1985) (holding officer's testimony about the smell of alcohol on the prisoner's breath could establish alcohol use without a blood test); Barker v. State, 437 So.2d 1375, 1377 (Ala.Crim.App. 1983) (holding officer "qualified from study, experience, or observation" could identify marijuana without scientific proof); Olds v. Oregon State Penitentiary, Corrections Division, 48 Or.App. 481, 617 P.2d 643 (1988) (holding a "person of common experience" could identify alcoholic beverage, no testing required); Matter of Reismiller, 101 Wash.2d 291, 678 P.2d 323, 325 1984) (same as *Barker*). *But see* Hayes v. McBride, 965 F. Supp. 1186, 1189–90 (N.D.Ind. 1997) (holding the "some evidence" standard was not met where an officer said the prisoner admitted a substance was an intoxicant, the prisoner denied making the admission, and there was no other evidence that it was an intoxicant); Williams v. State, 461 So.2d 1335, 1338 (Ala.Crim.App.) (holding unqualified officer's statement that material "appeared to be marijuana" was not

weapon is found in a prisoner's cell, the failure to examine it for fingerprints does not deny due process.[474] The failure to use handwriting analysis of disputed documents does not deny due process.[475]

The use of polygraph testing for investigative purposes is within the discretion of prison officials; you are not entitled to such a test,[476] even if prison officials give one to your accuser,[477] and you are not entitled to have witnesses against you polygraphed.[478] Most courts hold that polygraph evidence is admissible in disciplinary hearings.[479] However, a polygraph test that shows only that you are not telling the truth is not evidence that you are guilty of the disciplinary charge; it is only evidence that your story is not credible.[480]

Similarly, refusal to take a polygraph test cannot, by itself, show that you are guilty of the offense.[481] Polygraphs are most often used to corroborate other evidence[482] or in cases where no one objects.[483] So far the courts have not determined whether polygraph evidence by itself can meet the "some evidence" standard.[484]

A polygraph is not really a "lie detector"; it measures various physiological signs that are only indirectly related to truthfulness, and its results require a great deal of interpretation by the polygraph operator.[485] Consequently, in criminal cases, some courts have held that polygraph evidence is too unreliable to be admitted into evidence at all,[486] while others admit it only under limited circumstances with a foundation establishing its reliability.[487] Some courts have required safeguards in using polygraphs in disciplinary proceedings—e.g., holding evidence admissible only when

---

substantial evidence); Wightman v. Superintendent, Massachusetts Correctional Institution, Walpole, 19 Mass.App. 442, 475 N.E.2d 85, 88–89 (1985) (holding statement by unqualified person that he "believed" an unknown substance to be "angel dust" was insufficient to support a drug conviction).

[474]Flanagan v. Warden, U.S. Penitentiary, 784 F. Supp. 178, 180–81 (M.D.Pa. 1992); White v. Booker, 598 F. Supp. 984, 986 (E.D.Va. 1984); see Okocci v. Klein, C.O., 270 F. Supp. 2d 603, 610–11 (E.D.Pa. 2003) (holding failure to perform fingerprint analysis did not deny clearly established rights), aff'd, 100 Fed. Appx. 127 (3d Cir. 2004) (unpublished).

[475]Spaulding v. Collins, 867 F. Supp. 499, 509 (S.D.Tex. 1993).

[476]Wright v. Caspari, 779 F. Supp. 1025, 1028–29 (E.D.Mo. 1992); Johnson v. New Jersey Dep't of Correction, 298 N.J. Super. 79, 83, 688 A.2d 1123 (N.J.Super.App.Div. 1997). Cf. U.S. ex rel. Wilson v. DeRobertis, 508 F. Supp. 360, 362 (N.D.Ill. 1981) (holding polygraph might sometimes be necessary to ensure fairness, but not under the circumstances of this case). But see Caron v. Oregon State Penitentiary, 143 Or.App. 238, 923 P.2d 672 (1996) (holding that where a hearing officer offered the prisoner a polygraph test but then proceeded without it, the proceeding was rendered unfair; reversal ordered).

[477]Losee v. State, 374 N.W.2d 402, 404–05 (Iowa 1985); Pruitt v. State, 274 S.C. 565, 266 S.E.2d 779, 782 (S.C. 1980).

[478]Hester v. McBride, 966 F. Supp. 765, 773 (N.D.Ind. 1997).

[479]Toussaint v. McCarthy, 926 F.2d 800, 802–03 (9th Cir. 1991); Lenea v. Lane, 882 F.2d 1171, 1174 (7th Cir. 1989) and cases cited. In Oregon, the Court of Appeals has repeatedly held polygraph evidence admissible for various purposes, but the state Supreme Court has held only that such evidence is admissible when the prisoner requests the examination and does not object to the evidence, leaving open the question whether it is admissible under other circumstances. Snow v. Oregon State Penitentiary, Corrections Div., 308 Or. 259, 262 n.2, 267–68, 780 P.2d 215, 216 n.2, 219 (1989). In Iowa, the appeals court has held that polygraph evidence should not be used as evidence in disciplinary cases unless the parties agree to its use, and that refusal to take a polygraph test should not be used as evidence. Bradley v. State, 473 N.W.2d 224, 226 (Iowa App. 1991).

One court has said that voice stress analysis is admissible, by analogy with polygraph evidence. Stone-Bey v. Swihart, 898 F. Supp. 1287, 1299–1300 (N.D.Ind. 1995). We expect that voice stress analysis will generally be treated as similar to polygraph evidence by the courts.

[480]Lenea v. Lane, 882 F.2d at 1176; Parker v. Oregon State Correctional Institution, 87 Or.App. 354, 742 P.2d 617 (1987);

see Brown v. Smith, 828 F.2d 1493, 1495 (10th Cir. 1987) (holding one "inconclusive" polygraph test, plus a second one interpreted as showing that the prisoner was withholding information, did not support a conviction for assault); see also Johnson v. State, 576 So.2d 1289, 1290 (Ala.Crim.App. 1991) (holding polygraph evidence supporting the hearsay statement of a witness who was not produced was not "some evidence" of guilt). But see Terrell v. Godinez, 966 F. Supp. 679, 684 (N.D.Ill. 1997) (holding that failing a polygraph was evidence of guilt).

[481]Backstrom v. Iowa District Court for Jones County, 508 N.W.2d 705, 709–10 (Iowa 1993) (upholding convictions, noting that refusal of polygraph was only a "small part" of the evidence).

[482]See Viens v. Daniels, 871 F.2d 1328, 1335 (7th Cir. 1989) (noting polygraph used to corroborate confidential informant); Wiggett v. Oregon State Penitentiary, 85 Or.App. 635, 738 P.2d 580, 582–83 (Or.App. 1987), review denied, 304 Or. 186, 743 P.2d 736 (Or. 1987).

[483]See Graham v. Oregon State Penitentiary, 83 Or.App. 567, 733 P.2d 39, 40 (1987), review denied, 303 Or. 590, 739 P.2d 570 (1987).

[484]See Lenea v. Lane, 882 F.2d at 1175–76 (declining to decide the question). In Toussaint v. McCarthy, 926 F.2d 800, 802 (9th Cir. 1990), the court held that "[a]s used at San Quentin," polygraph results meet the some evidence standard for purposes of testing whether prisoners had given up gang associations.

[485]"A polygraph test, which records certain physiological phenomena, such as changes in pulse rate, blood pressure, respiration, and electrodermal response, operates on the theory that a person giving a deceitful answer will undergo a significant physiological reaction, while a person telling the truth will have a normal reaction. . . . Among other things, the accuracy of the polygraph depends upon the type of the test given and the expertise of the examiner." Snow v. Oregon State Penitentiary, Corrections Division, 308 Or. 259, 263 n.4, 780 P.2d 215 (Or. 1989).

[486]See, e.g., U.S. v. Prince-Oyibo, 320 F.3d 494, 501 (4th Cir. 2003).

[487]See, e.g., U.S. v. Piccinonna, 885 F.2d 1529, 1536–37 (11th Cir. 1989) (holding that polygraph evidence could be admitted pursuant to a stipulation spelling out how the examination would be conducted and who would perform it); U.S. v. Falsia, 724 F.2d 1339, 1341–42 (9th Cir. 1983).

obtained by a state certified and licensed examiner.[488] However, in the restricted setting of a prison disciplinary hearing, which is not designed to explore complicated technical issues and where there is generally no right to cross-examination, we think the use of polygraph evidence creates great risks of mistaken convictions.[489] For these reasons, you should consider objecting to the use of polygraph evidence against you in a disciplinary hearing. It is doubtful that you have the right to refuse polygraph testing entirely, although you have a right under the Fifth Amendment to refuse to answer questions that are potentially incriminating.[490]

k. Written Disposition If you are found guilty, you are entitled to a "'written statement by the factfinders as to the evidence relied on and the reasons' for the disciplinary action."[491] The Supreme Court added:

> It may be that there will be occasions when personal or institutional safety are so implicated, that the statement may properly exclude certain items of evidence, but in that event the statement should indicate the fact of the omission.[492]

Several courts have said that the written statement must be reasonably specific and may not simply adopt the officer's report by stating, for example, "Inmate is guilty of misconduct as written."[493] One court held that "each item of evidence relied on by the hearing officer should be included in the report unless safety concerns dictate otherwise."[494]

Another held that a statement of reasons should point out facts, mention evidence, and explain credibility judgments.[495] The committee must also give reasons for the disciplinary action taken.[496]

Other courts have set lower standards. One federal court has held that as long as the officers' reports are not so long or so contradictory or ambiguous that you can't tell what the committee relied on, the disposition can merely incorporate them by reference.[497] Others have held that credibility judgments need not be explained.[498] A third court has stated that "the kind of statements that will satisfy the constitutional minimum will vary from case to case depending on the severity of the charges and the complexity of the factual circumstances and proof offered by both sides. . . ."[499] This court held that in a case where there was substantial evidence that the prisoner was innocent, and in a complex case involving severe punishment, dispositions that merely adopted the officer's and investigator's reports did not meet due process standards.[500] However, it held that in a simple case where the only issue is the relative credibility of an inmate and an officer, the disciplinary committee may merely refer to the officer's report.[501]

---

[488]Wiggett v. Oregon State Penitentiary, 85 Or.App. 635, 738 P.2d 580, 583 (Or.App. 1987), *review denied*, 304 Or. 186, 743 P.2d 736 (Or. 1987).

[489]The possibility for unfairness in the use of polygraph evidence is illustrated in *Bucklin v. State*, 342 N.W.2d 896, 897–98 (Iowa App. 1983), in which a prisoner was convicted of lying based only on polygraph results. (His request to cross-examine the polygrapher was denied.)

[490]Riggins v. Walter, 279 F.3d 422, 431 (7th Cir. 1995).

[491]Wolff v. McDonnell, 418 U.S. 539, 565, 94 S. Ct. 2963 (1974) (quoting Morrissey v. Brewer, 408 U.S. 471, 489, 92 S. Ct. 2593 (1972)).

[492]Wolff v. McDonnell, 418 U.S. at 565. Such omissions will most often occur in cases involving confidential informants, discussed in § H.1.m of this chapter.

[493]Scruggs v. Jordan, 485 F.3d 934, 941 (7th Cir. 2007) ("We have repeatedly upheld the sufficiency of written statements that indicate only what evidence was relied on to make the decision, *and why*." (emphasis supplied)); Dyson v. Kocik, 689 F.2d 466, 467–68 (3d Cir. 1982); *accord*, King v. Wells, 760 F.2d 89, 93 (6th Cir. 1985); Chavis v. Rowe, 643 F.2d 1281, 1286–87 (7th Cir. 1981); Hayes v. Walker, 555 F.2d 625, 633 (7th Cir.1977); Owens v. State, 507 So.2d 576, 578 (Ala.Cr.App. 1987); State ex rel. Meeks v. Gagnon, 95 Wis.2d 115, 289 N.W.2d 357, 362–63 (Wis.App. 1986). *But see* Hudson v. Edmonson, 848 F.2d 682, 685–88 (6th Cir. 1988) (holding right to a more specific disposition was not clearly established in 1983).

[494]King v. Wells, 760 F.2d at 93 (emphasis in original); *see* Freitas v. Auger, 837 F.2d 806, 809–10 (8th Cir. 1988) (holding statement that cited the inmate's admissions and statements and

---

confidential statements of informants and stated that a polygraph test was not relied on was sufficient).

There is a limit to this principle. A disposition "need not discuss and analyze every argument raised by the inmate." Pino v. Dalsheim, 605 F. Supp. 1305, 1316 (S.D.N.Y. 1984).

[495]Robinson v. Young, 674 F. Supp. 1356, 1368 (W.D.Wis. 1987); *accord*, Whitford v. Boglino, 63 F.3d 527, 536–37 (7th Cir. 1995) (holding failure to explain why committee did not credit exculpatory evidence supports a due process claim); Stone-Bey v. Swihart, 898 F. Supp. 1287, 1299–1300 (N.D.Ind. 1995) (holding hearing officer must explain why he chose to reject a witness's recantation of an earlier statement); Washington v. Chrans, 769 F. Supp. 1045, 1052 (C.D.Ill. 1991); Staples v. Traut, 675 F. Supp. 460, 465–68 (W.D.Wis. 1986); *see also* Scarpa v. Ponte, 638 F. Supp. 1019, 1025 (D.Mass. 1986) (holding inmate disciplined for a letter to the Superintendent should have been informed which parts of the letter violated the rules).

[496]Wolff v. McDonnell, 418 U.S. at 565; Dedrick v. Wallman, 617 F. Supp. 178, 183 (S.D.Iowa 1985); Ivey v. Wilson, 577 F. Supp. 169, 173 (W.D.Ky. 1983).

Some courts have rejected this view. Pardo v. Hosier, 946 F.2d 1278, 1284–85 (7th Cir. 1991); Bucklin v. State, 342 N.W.2d 896, 898 (Iowa App. 1983). We think that their holdings are contrary to the plain language of *Wolff v. McDonnell*.

[497]Brown v. Frey, 807 F.2d 1407, 1409–13 (8th Cir. 1986); *accord*, Mujahid v. Apao, 795 F. Supp. 1020, 1027 (D.Haw. 1992).

[498]Hensley v. Wilson, 850 F.2d 269, 278 (6th Cir. 1988); Ferreira v. DuBois, 963 F. Supp. 1244, 1254 (D.Mass. 1996).

[499]Culbert v. Young, 834 F.2d 624, 631 (7th Cir. 1987).

[500]Culbert v. Young, 834 F.2d at 630 (citing Chavis v. Rowe, 643 F.2d at 1286–87, and Hayes v. Walker, 555 F.2d at 633).

[501]Culbert v. Young, 834 F.2d at 631; *accord*, Moffatt v. Broyles, 288 F.3d 978, 981 (7th Cir. 2002) (holding that "Based on the preponderance of the evidence, the CAB finds the offender guilty" sufficed where it was clear that credibility was the only issue). In another case, the same court said that the committee's failure to

In our opinion, specificity—including explanation of credibility judgments—should be required in all statements of reasons because it will encourage fairer decisions. In prison and elsewhere, "[a] reasons requirement promotes thought by the decision-maker, focuses attention on the relevant points and further protects against arbitrary and capricious decisions grounded upon impermissible or erroneous considerations."[502] In prison, it is all too easy for a factfinder simply to assume that officers are always telling the truth and inmates are always lying, and to issue rubber-stamp decisions on that basis without giving each case serious and individualized attention.[503] The very lenient "some evidence" standard of judicial review makes it easy for prison officials to get away with such a practice.[504]

We believe that especially where the only issue, or the main issue, is who is telling the truth, prison disciplinary committees should be required to explain themselves clearly and fully.

Due process does not require that disciplinary proceedings be tape-recorded or transcribed or that these records be provided to the prisoner if made,[505] although prison regulations or state law may require that a record be made and provided.[506]

l. Appeal Several courts have held that due process does not require prison authorities to provide an administrative appeal of disciplinary convictions.[507] However, many prison systems do provide for such appeals, and you may be able to challenge violations of appeal rules in a state court lawsuit.[508] You *must* use the administrative appeal process to exhaust your administrative remedies if you wish to bring a lawsuit at some later point,[509] and you

---

provide a reasoned explanation why it believed the evidence against the plaintiff rather than the exculpatory affidavits that he submitted supported a due process claim. Whitford v. Boglino, 63 F.3d 527, 536–37 (7th Cir. 1995).

[502]Jackson v. Ward, 458 F. Supp. 546, 565 (W.D.N.Y. 1978) and cases cited; *accord*, State ex rel. Meeks v. Gagnon, 289 N.W.2d at 363; *see* Dunlop v. Bachowski, 421 U.S. 560, 572, 95 S. Ct. 1851 (1975) (same conclusion in a non-constitutional case). An example of this point is *Chavis v. Rowe*, 643 F.2d at 1287, in which a prisoner was convicted of assault and put in segregation for five months before a review board cleared him. The court observed that if the committee had made detailed findings in the first place, the prisoner might never have been wrongfully punished.

From this perspective, we think the court was in error in *Smith v. Maschner*, 899 F.2d 940, 946 (10th Cir. 1990), in holding that "providing a written transcript of the hearing more than suffices to insure adequate review of the proceedings, to protect the inmate against collateral consequences, and to guarantee that officials, faced with outside scrutiny, will act fairly." A transcript certainly provides adequate information about what happened at the hearing, but it does not explain how the committee reached its decision, and providing a transcript does not force them to think more carefully in making it.

[503]The Supreme Court has acknowledged that credibility judgments in prison disciplinary hearings are often between inmates and the committee's co-workers and that they "thus are under obvious pressure to resolve a disciplinary dispute in favor of the institution and their fellow employee. . . . It is the old situational problem of the relationship between the keeper and the kept, a relationship that hardly is conducive to a truly adjudicatory performance." Cleavinger v. Saxner, 474 U.S. 193, 204, 106 S. Ct. 496 (1985); *see* Greene v. Secretary of Public Safety and Correctional Services, 68 Md.App. 147, 510 A.2d 613, 619 (Md.App. 1986) (court is disturbed by a committee member's "negative response" to the question "Is an inmate ever right?").

[504]In *Culbert*, the court cited this low standard of review as a factor supporting a low standard for statements of reasons. 834 F.2d at 630. A similar observation was made in *Hudson v. Edmonson*, 848 F.2d 682, 688 (6th Cir. 1988) ("it is difficult to show how the written finding under *Wolff* can be more demanding than the minimal evidentiary finding upheld in *Hill*"). As indicated, we think this is backwards. The leniency of the "some evidence" standard actually supports a requirement of greater specificity in dispositions. *See* § H.1.i of this chapter concerning standards of judicial review.

[505]Felton v. Lincoln, 429 F. Supp. 2d 226, 242 (D.Mass. 2006); Dixon v. Goord, 224 F. Supp. 2d 739, 744 (S.D.N.Y. 2002); Brown v. State, 592 So.2d 621, 623–24 (Ala. 1991); Balla v. Murphy, 116 Idaho 257, 775 P.2d 149, 153 (Idaho App. 1989); Greene v. Secretary of Public Safety, 68 Md.App. 147, 510 A.2d 613, 618 (Md.App. 1986); Negron v. Dep't of Corrections, 220 N.J.Super. 425, 532 A.2d 735, 738 (N.J.Super.App.Div. 1987); Rivera v. Smith, 137 A.D.2d 281, 528 N.Y.S.2d 930, 931 (N.Y.App.Div. 1988). *Cf.* Ruiz v. Estelle, 679 F.2d 1115, 1155 (5th Cir. 1982) (holding that tape recording or transcripts could be required in prison system where statements of reasons were shown to be inadequate), *amended in part, vacated in part on other grounds*, 688 F.2d 266 (5th Cir. 1983).

[506]Flowers v. Phelps, 595 So.2d 668, 669–70 (La.App. 1991) (reversing disciplinary conviction because officials failed to preserve the tape as regulations required).

[507]Brown v. Angelone, 938 F. Supp. 340, 345 (W.D.Va. 1996); Chance v. Compton, 873 F. Supp. 82, 86 (W.D.Tenn. 1994); Bell v. Lane, 657 F. Supp. 815, 817 (N.D.Ill. 1987); Grandison v. Cuyler, 600 F. Supp. 967, 975 (E.D.Pa. 1984), *rev'd on other grounds*, 774 F.2d 598 (3d Cir. 1985); Garfield v. Davis, 566 F. Supp. 1069, 1074 (E.D.Pa. 1983); *see* Giovanni v. Lynn, 48 F.3d 908, 911–12 (5th Cir. 1995) (holding the same in an administrative segregation case). *But see* Forbes v. Trigg, 976 F.2d 308, 319–20 (7th Cir. 1992) (holding that administrative review must be "meaningful"); Carter v. Thompson, 808 F. Supp. 1548, 1555 (M.D.Fla. 1992) (allegation that plaintiff was denied a form for an administrative appeal raised a factual question precluding summary judgment).

Review is required of administrative segregation, but this requirement is designed to serve entirely different purposes and has no application to disciplinary cases. Grandison v. Cuyler, 600 F. Supp. at 975.

[508]Compare Burke v. Coughlin, 97 A.D.2d 862, 469 N.Y.S.2d 240 (N.Y.App.Div. 1983) (enforcing time limit) *with* Sheppard v. LeFevre, 116 A.D.2d 867, 498 N.Y.S.2d 190 (N.Y.App.Div. 1986) (not enforcing time limit).

[509]The Prison Litigation Reform Act requires that you exhaust "available" administrative remedies before bringing a federal court civil action. You may also need to file a grievance in addition to appealing the disciplinary conviction in order to exhaust with respect to all the issues arising from a disciplinary proceeding. *See* Ch. 9, § D. In many states you will have to exhaust administrative

must raise all issues in the appeal that you wish to raise later in court.[510]

If there is an appeal process, the official who handles the appeals may be liable for failure to correct due process violations, at least if they are obvious in the administrative record.[511]

Some courts have held that if due process violations are remedied by an administrative reversal of the conviction, the prisoner has no due process claim.[512] We think that holding goes too far. Due process requires a hearing *before* punishment is imposed,[513] and that hearing must meet due process standards. A post-deprivation hearing—in the form of an administrative review or otherwise—therefore does not cancel out due process violations in the original hearing.[514] If your punishment takes effect before the administrative reversal, you should be able to recover for the harm

you sustained.[515] (Of course your actual punishment, *e.g.*, segregation time served, must be serious enough to constitute "atypical and significant hardship,"[516] or must affect your release date, in order to call for due process at all.[517]) If your punishment does not take effect before the reversal, then you will not actually have been deprived of liberty and will not have a due process claim.[518]

---

remedies before you can bring a state court challenge to your discipline. If you lose good time and have to challenge your disciplinary conviction via federal habeas corpus, you must exhaust whatever administrative or judicial remedies are available in your state. *See* Ch. 8, § H.1.a.

[510]Eads v. Hanks, 280 F.3d 728, 729 (7th Cir. 2002); Moffatt v. Broyles, 288 F.3d 978, 982 (7th Cir. 2002) (holding it would have been enough if he had "expressed disgruntlement about the generic reason").

[511]Lewis v. Smith, 855 F.2d 736, 738 (11th Cir. 1988); King v. Higgins, 702 F.2d 18, 21 (1st Cir. 1983); Williams v. Bitner, 359 F. Supp. 2d 370, 377 (M.D.Pa. 2005), *aff'd*, 455 F.3d 186 (3d Cir. 2006); Johnson v. Coombe, 156 F. Supp. 2d 273, 278 (S.D.N.Y. 2000); Gabai v. Jacoby, 800 F. Supp. 1149, 1156 (S.D.N.Y. 1992); Feagin v. Broglin, 693 F. Supp. 736, 740 (N.D.Ind. 1988); Pino v. Dalsheim, 605 F. Supp. 1305, 1319 (S.D.N.Y. 1984); Dyson v. Kocik, 564 F. Supp. 109, 120 (M.D.Pa. 1983), *aff'd*, 740 F.2d 956 (3d Cir. 1984). *But see* Wright v. Collins, 766 F.2d 841, 850 (4th Cir. 1985) (holding warden not liable based on inmate's letter complaining of due process violations); King v. Cuyler, 541 F. Supp. 1230, 1233–34 (E.D.Pa. 1982) (holding reviewing official was not liable where the due process violation was not evident in the record). In *James v. Aidala*, 389 F. Supp. 2d 451, 453 (W.D.N.Y. 2005), the court held that an alleged practice of affirming constitutionally infirm disciplinary convictions on administrative appeal, and then reversing them if the plaintiff went to court, stated a due process claim.

[512]Wycoff v. Nichols, 94 F.3d 1187, 1198 (8th Cir. 1996) (holding administrative appeal process was "part of the due process" the plaintiff received, and it cured the alleged violation); Terrell v. Bassett, 353 F. Supp. 2d 658, 661 (E.D.Va. 2005) and cases cited; Vega v. DeRobertis, 598 F. Supp. 501, 505 (N.D.Ill. 1984), *aff'd*, 774 F.2d 1167 (7th Cir. 1985).

[513]Gilbert v. Frazier, 931 F.2d 1581, 1582 (7th Cir. 1991); *see* Phelps v. Tucker, 370 F. Supp. 2d 792, 797 (N.D.Ind. 2005) (holding defendants' argument was "legally backwards" since the plaintiff lost good time and did not have a cause of action until the administrative reversal; noting that an appeal is not one of the rights required by *Wolff v. McDonnell*).

[514]*See* § E of this chapter for a discussion of post-deprivation remedies.

[515]Walker v. Bates, 23 F.3d 652, 658–59 (2d Cir.1994) ("The rule is that once prison officials deprive an inmate of his constitutional procedural rights at a disciplinary hearing and the prisoner commences to serve a punitive sentence imposed at the conclusion of the hearing, the prison official responsible for the due process deprivation must respond in damages, absent the successful interposition of a qualified immunity defense."); *see* Chavis v. Rowe, 643 F.2d 1281, 1287–88 (7th Cir. 1981) (administrative reversal of disciplinary conviction did not moot claim for damages); Gayle v. Lucas, 133 F. Supp. 2d 266, 271 (S.D.N.Y. 2001) ("Reversal of a charge on administrative appeal will not cure a § 1983 violation in connection with that charge if the prisoner began serving his punishment before the appeal."); Justice v. Coughlin, 941 F. Supp. 1312, 1324 (N.D.N.Y. 1996) (similar to *Gayle*); Sanford v. Manternach, 601 N.W.2d 360, 368–69 (Iowa 1999) (holding reversal of loss of good time did not eliminate the due process violation where the prisoner had already served additional prison time).

[516]*See* Hanrahan v. Doling, 331 F.3d 93, 97 (2d Cir. 2003).

[517]*See* § A of this chapter; *see also* § H.1.r.(4) of this chapter on damages in disciplinary cases.

[518]Laws v. Cleaver, 140 F. Supp. 2d 145, 153 (D.Conn. 2001) (holding prisoner whose loss of good time was reversed administratively was not deprived of liberty); Wright v. Coughlin, 31 F. Supp. 2d 301, 312 (W.D.N.Y. 1998) (holding loss of good time that was corrected before it affected the length of incarceration was not a deprivation of liberty); Cespedes v. Coughlin, 956 F. Supp. 454, 472–73 (S.D.N.Y.) (" … [A] prisoner's successful administrative appeal cures the deprivation of due process where that appeal corrects the constitutional error before the prisoner begins to serve his improperly imposed sentence."), *on reconsideration*, 969 F. Supp. 254 (S.D.N.Y. 1997).

In *Young v. Hoffman*, 970 F.2d 1154, 1156 (2d Cir. 1992) (per curiam), the court said generally that an administrative appeal "cured any procedural defect" in the hearing. However, the court later clarified that in *Young* the crucial point was that the plaintiff never served any additional time and was not deprived of liberty as a result of the defective hearing. Walker v. Bates, 23 F.3d at 657–58.

In *Morissette v. Peters*, 45 F.3d 1119 (7th Cir. 1995), the court stated broadly that "[t]here is no denial of due process if the error the inmate complains of is corrected in the administrative appeal process," but it also noted that the prisoner did not serve any extra segregation time because his time was all credited to another sentence. 45 F.3d at 1122. Since the court cited both *Young v. Hoffman* and *Walker v. Bates* without expressing disagreement with *Walker*, Morrison, 45 F.3d at 1122 n.4, it appears that this court takes the same approach as *Walker*. That would be consistent with its earlier decision holding that administrative reversal does not moot a damage claim growing out of the hearing. Chavis v. Rowe, 643 F.2d at 1287–88.

m. Confidential Informants Prison officials sometimes rely on information from informants whom they do not produce or identify. Often they do not even disclose the nature of the confidential information. In our view this practice undermines the due process protections of *Wolff v. McDonnell* (especially the requirements of notice and a statement of reasons), makes it impossible to defend against many disciplinary charges,[519] and "invites disciplinary sanctions on the basis of trumped up charges."[520] Nonetheless, the courts have permitted it because they believe prison life is dangerous and violent, and informants may be assaulted or even killed if their identities are disclosed.[521]

Some courts have set minimal standards for notice of charges in informant cases, holding that even in a confidential informant case, the prisoner must receive notice with "sufficient factual specificity to permit a reasonable person to understand what conduct is at issue so that he may identify relevant evidence and present a defense"; even if some details are unknown, "an inmate can at least be given any general information regarding the relevant time and place that is known to the authorities."[522] Other courts have not been willing to go even that far.[523] At the hearing itself, the

"due process right to know the evidence upon which a discipline ruling is based"[524] may have to be compromised, but prison officials who do so "must offer a reasonable justification for their actions, if not contemporaneously, then when challenged in a court action."[525]

The courts do recognize that if the usual due process safeguards are bypassed, other safeguards become more necessary.[526] Due process therefore requires that prison officials independently establish the reliability of confidential informants.[527] "A bald assertion by an unidentified person, without more, cannot constitute some evidence of guilt."[528]

---

[519]*See* Franklin v. Israel, 537 F. Supp. 1112, 1118–21 (W.D.Wis. 1982) for a discussion of this problem.

[520]Helms v. Hewitt, 655 F.2d 487, 502 (3d Cir. 1981), *rev'd on other grounds sub nom.* Hewitt v. Helms, 459 U.S. 460, 103 S. Ct. 864 (1983); *see also* McCollum v. Miller, 695 F.2d 1044, 1049 (7th Cir. 1982) (noting danger of use of disciplinary hearings for "schemes of revenge").

[521]Sira v. Morton, 380 F.3d 57, 78 (2d Cir. 2004); McCollum v. Miller, 695 F.2d at 1048; Smith v. Rabalais, 659 F.2d 539, 544 (5th Cir. 1981); *see* Wolff v. McDonnell, 418 U.S. 539, 568–69, 94 S. Ct. 2963 (1974) (acknowledging dangers of disclosure of some witness identities).

[522]Sira v. Morton, 380 F.3d at 72; *see* Dible v. Scholl, 506 F.3d 1106, 1108–1111 (8th Cir. 2007) (holding notice stating only that confidential information indicated that plaintiff "threatened and choked a citizen of the State of Iowa" was insufficient where no justification was given for withholding time, place, or identity of victim); Rinehart v. Brewer, 483 F. Supp. 165, 169 (S.D.Iowa 1980) (holding that prison officials should usually give notice of the date, "general time" and place of the incident, a general description of the incident, and the identity of other persons involved, deleting from the notice only those specific facts that would cause security problems if disclosed, and giving the inmate notice that certain types of facts were deleted). *But see* Freitas v. Auger, 837 F.2d 806, 809 (8th Cir. 1988) (holding notice sufficient where it generally described the accused prisoner's conduct without giving dates, places, or the identities of others involved); Zimmerlee v. Keeney, 831 F.2d 183, 188 (9th Cir. 1987) (holding notice was sufficient that charged the prisoner with smuggling marijuana and amphetamines with members of a prison club at some time during a five-month period; Pratt v. Rowland, 770 F. Supp. 1399, 1402–03 (N.D.Calif. 1991) (holding notice supplemented with a more specific "Confidential Information Disclosure Form" was sufficient).

[523]For example, in *Smith v. Rabalais*, 659 F.2d at 541–44, the court upheld a disciplinary conviction in which the prisoner was accused of selling an unspecified amount of drugs, which were not

described, to unidentified persons at an undisclosed number of undisclosed times and places. *Accord*, McCollum v. Miller, 695 F.2d at 1048. *But see* Spellmon-Bey v. Lynaugh, 778 F. Supp. 338, 342–43 (E.D.Tex. 1991) (holding defendants must articulate "specific security concerns" for refusing to give notice of time and place of offenses).

[524]Sira v. Morton, 380 F.3d at 74.

[525]Sira v. Morton, 380 F.3d at 75 (citing Ponte v. Real, 471 U.S. 491, 498, 105 S. Ct. 2192 (1985)). In *Sira*, the court noted that it appeared from the record that much of the evidence withheld from the plaintiff could have been disclosed without identifying the informants.

[526]Sira v. Morton, 380 F.3d at 78; McCollum v. Miller, 695 F.2d at 1048–49.

[527]Sira v. Morton, 380 F.3d at 77–78 (stating "when sound discretion forecloses confrontation and cross-examination, the need for the hearing officer to conduct an independent assessment of informant credibility to ensure fairness to the accused inmate is heightened"); Whitford v. Boglino, 63 F.3d 527, 534–36 (7th Cir. 1995) (holding that the use of confidential informant testimony without some evidence of reliability would deny due process, and defendants' failure to come forward with such evidence amounted to an admission they did not meet legal requirements); Williams v. Fountain, 77 F.3d 372, 375 (11th Cir. 1996) (noting that this requirement's purpose is both to foster reliable prison investigations and to enable meaningful appellate review); Zavaro v. Coughlin, 970 F.2d 1148, 1153–54 and n.1 (2d Cir. 1992); Taylor v. Wallace, 931 F.2d 698, 702 (10th Cir. 1991); Wells v. Israel, 854 F.2d 995, 998–99 (7th Cir. 1988); Hensley v. Wilson, 850 F.2d 269, 276 (6th Cir. 1988); Zimmerlee v. Keeney, 831 F.2d at 186; Gomez v. Kaplan, 964 F. Supp. 830, 835 (S.D.N.Y. 1997) (requiring hearing officers to make an "independent assessment of the reliability of confidential informants, and to create and preserve a record of that assessment"); Spellmon-Bey v. Lynaugh, 778 F. Supp. at 345–47; Vasquez v. Coughlin, 726 F. Supp. 466, 470–71 (S.D.N.Y. 1989); Gittens v. Sullivan, 720 F. Supp. 40, 43 (S.D.N.Y. 1989); *In re* Jackson, 43 Cal.3d 501, 233 Cal.Rptr. 911, 731 P.2d 36, 46 (Cal. 1987) (ruling on state constitutional grounds).

One federal court has rejected any requirement that informant reliability be assessed. *See* Baker v. Lyles, 904 F.2d 925, 931–33 (4th Cir. 1990).

[528]Freitas v. Auger, 837 F.2d at 810; *accord*, Broussard v. Johnson, 253 F.3d 874, 876–77 (5th Cir. 2001) (per curiam) (holding reliability was not established where the investigating officer testified only to what the warden had told him about the informant and the hearing officer did not receive any other evidence of reliability); Brown v. Smith, 828 F.2d 1493, 1495 (10th Cir. 1987); Cato v. Rushen, 824 F.2d 703, 705 (9th Cir. 1987)

However, the authorities are given wide latitude in establishing reliability. One court has suggested several ways that reliability may be established:

> (1) the oath of the investigating officer as to the truth of his report containing confidential information and his appearance before the disciplinary committee . . .; (2) corroborating testimony . . .; (3) a statement on the record by the chairman of the disciplinary committee that, "he had firsthand knowledge of the sources of information and considered them reliable on the basis of 'their past record of reliability,'" . . .; or (4) in camera[529] review of material documenting the investigator's assessment of the credibility of the confidential informant.[530]

Some courts have held that the evidence on reliability must provide some corroboration for the current information and not just establish that the informant has provided reliable information in the past.[531]

The evidence establishing the reliability of informants need not be disclosed to the accused prisoner at the hearing or in the statement of reasons because it would risk disclosing the informant's identity.[532] Courts have disagreed over whether "the detailed evidence and the basis and reasons for the committee's determinations of informant reliability" must be documented at the time of the hearing,[533] or whether prison officials can reconstruct it after the fact if you bring a lawsuit.[534] State law may require greater safeguards.[535]

(holding hearsay provided via a confidential informant who was later polygraphed inconclusively did not meet the "some evidence" test); Cerda v. O'Leary, 746 F. Supp. 820, 825 (N.D.Ill. 1990).

[529]*In camera* means "in chambers"; the court means that a court may review material submitted by prison officials privately without disclosing it to the prisoner or the public.

[530]Mendoza v. Miller, 779 F.2d 1287, 1293 (7th Cir. 1985); *accord*, Richards v. Dretke, 394 F.3d 291, 295 (5th Cir. 2004) (holding reliability established in a proceeding about a racial fight by evidence of the race of each witness, the fact that each was present and had first-hand knowledge, and the reports tended to corroborate one another); Hensley v. Wilson, 850 F.2d 269, 277 (6th Cir. 1988) (holding committee may rely on an investigator's report if it states that the informant "has proved reliable in specific past instances or that the informant's story has been independently corroborated on specific material points."); Freitas v. Auger, 837 F.2d at 811 (reluctantly upholding magistrate's finding of reliability where informant statements contained some factual background, were consistent, and one was "against the informant's penal interest"); Zimmerlee v. Keeney, 831 F.2d at 186–87; Pratt v. Rowland, 770 F. Supp. 1399, 1403-04 (N.D.Calif. 1991) (holding informant's testimony could be corroborated by information he gave concerning other inmates); Carter v. Duckworth, 739 F. Supp. 1259, 1262 (N.D.Ind. 1989) (upholding disciplinary conviction based on informant testimony where the hearing board examined material documenting the investigator's credibility assessment). Polygraph evidence has been used to corroborate informants' reliability in some cases. *See* § H.1.j of this chapter, n.482.

[531]Sira v. Morton, 380 F.3d at 78 (holding hearing officers must consider the totality of the circumstances and not just past record for credibility); Williams v. Fountain, 77 F.3d 372, 375 (11th Cir. 1996) (stating there must be support for "the credibility of confidential informants *and* the reliability of the information provided by them" (emphasis supplied)). Other courts appear to accept past reliability alone as one alternative means of establishing credibility. *See* Hensley v. Wilson, 850 F.2d at 277 (holding committee may rely on an investigator's report if it states that the informant "has proved reliable in specific past instances *or* that the informant's story has been independently corroborated on specific material points." (emphasis supplied)).

[532]Hensley v. Wilson, 850 F.2d at 279. When the identities of witnesses are known to the investigating officer and the hearing officer, they are not really confidential informants whose testimony requires evidence to establish reliability. Richards v. Dretke, 394 F.3d 291, 294–95 (5th Cir. 2004).

[533]Hensley v. Wilson, 850 F.2d at 280–83; *accord*, Williams v. Fountain, 77 F.3d at 375 (holding use of confidential informants requires documentation in the record of some good faith investigation and findings as to their credibility and the reliability of their information); Freitas v. Auger, 837 F.2d at 811 n.11 (quoting Rinehart v. Brewer, 483 F. Supp. 165, 170 (S.D. Iowa 1980) (directing prison officials to comply with rather detailed directions for preparing a summary of confidential information that they rely on)). We think such a requirement is appropriate, since it "eliminates the possibility that officials might later search around for evidence which would have warranted a committee in deeming an informant reliable," *Hensley*, 850 F.2d at 283—not to mention the possibility that they might make something up.

[534]Riggins v. Walter, 279 F.3d 422, 429 n.11 (7th Cir. 1995); Taylor v. Wallace, 931 F.2d 698, 702 (10th Cir. 1991).

In *Broussard v. Johnson*, 253 F.3d 874, 876–77 (5th Cir. 2001), the court refused to follow *Taylor v. Wallace*, holding that it is necessary for there to be some evidence before the disciplinary body to support reliability, though that information may be supplemented later in a court proceeding. Some courts, *e.g., Taylor v. Wallace*, 931 F.2d at 702, have said that a requirement of contemporaneous documentation is contrary to the Supreme Court decision in *Ponte v. Real*, 471 U.S. 491, 105 S. Ct. 2192 (1985), which holds that if the hearing body refuses to call witnesses you request, they need not explain their refusal at the time of the hearing. The court in *Hensley v. Wilson* explained at length why that argument is wrong. 850 F.2d at 279–80.

[535]Shea v. Edwards, 221 Ill.App. 219, 163 Ill.Dec. 668, 581 N.E.2d 822, 823 (Ill.App. 1991) (holding reasons for not disclosing confidential source must be stated on the face of the disciplinary ticket); Alvarado v. LeFevre, 111 A.D.2d 475, 488 N.Y.S.2d 2d 856 (N.Y.App.Div. 1985) (holding hearing officer should have interviewed informants; officer's assessment of their credibility was not "substantial evidence"); Solar v. Oregon State Penitentiary, 87 Or.App. 222, 742 P.2d 611, 614–16 (Or.App. 1987) (requiring some evidence both of the reliability of the informant and the truthfulness of the evidence), *review denied*, 744 P.2d 1004 (Or. 1987); State ex rel. Staples v. Dep't of Health and Social Services, Division of Corrections, 115 Wis.2d 363, 340 N.W.2d 194, 198 (Wis. 1983) (statements of informants must be taken under oath and corroborated, and cannot be used unless the committee finds that the informants would be subject to a significant risk of bodily harm if they appeared). *But see In re* Jackson, 43 Cal.3d 501, 233 Cal.Rptr. 911, 731 P.2d 36, 46 (Cal. 1987) (hearing officer need not personally interview informants).

Some courts have said that if there is other evidence to support a disciplinary conviction, the reliability of the informant need not be established.[536] We think those decisions are mistaken. The question should be not whether the factfinder *could* have convicted without unreliable informant information, but whether it *would* have done so. If you are convicted of a disciplinary offense after a hearing in which unreliable information played a significant part, the court should not automatically assume you would have been convicted anyway at a hearing where unreliable evidence was excluded.[537]

We think that a case relying on confidential informants is a complex case in which the prisoner should have the right to a staff assistant who can examine the informant evidence and the alleged basis for its reliability. So far, the courts have not adopted this position.[538]

n. False Charges   Under the Due Process Clause the courts will not independently assess the merits of disciplinary convictions, as long as there is some evidence to support them and minimal procedural rules are followed.[539] Most courts have gone a step further and held that false or unfounded charges do not deny due process as long as prison officials go through the required procedural motions.[540]

We think that this rule makes a sham of due process, and we agree with the court that said:

> However minimal may be the process due to prisoners before segregation, that process is insufficient when it has been contaminated by the introduction through state action of false inculpatory evidence. The introduction of false evidence in itself violates the due process clause. . . . The fact that prisoners are not entitled to the full panoply of procedural protections afforded at trial when they are subject to internal prison discipline does not deprive them of the fundamental right not to have state officials make purposely false statements about them.[541]

But even if you are stuck with the majority view that prison staff are generally privileged to make up disciplinary charges with impunity, if you are substantially punished based on false charges and do not receive a hearing, you should have a due process claim.[542]

Even if false charges do not deny due process, they may violate other rights. The courts are in agreement that disciplinary charges brought in retaliation for filing grievances, making complaints, pursuing lawsuits, or engaging in other activities protected by the Constitution violate the substantive constitutional right in question.[543] At least one court has held that an officer's false testimony, made with knowledge that it would lead to disciplinary confinement, could constitute the tort of intentional infliction of emotional distress.[544]

You should understand that the real issue in a "false charge" case is that the courts know how easy it is for an angry prisoner to call her accuser a liar. Courts are extremely suspicious of such claims and reluctant to get into these disputes. For that reason, you had better have solid evidence in addition to your own say-so if you bring a case alleging false charges, and you had better be prepared to support your claim in response to a motion for summary judgment very quickly after you file.

---

[536]Espinoza v. Peterson, 283 F.3d 949, 952 (8th Cir. 2002); Williams v. Fountain, 77 F.3d at 375 (citing Young v. Jones, 37 F.3d 1457 (11th Cir. 1994)).

[537]The question what *would* have happened if you had been given a lawful hearing is crucial to your ability to recover damages for due process violations. *See* § H.1.r.4 of this chapter.

[538]*See* Hudson v. Hedgepeth, 92 F.3d 748, 751 (8th Cir. 1996); Sauls v. State, 467 N.W.2d 1, 3 (Iowa App. 1990). Assistance with a defense is discussed in § H.1.f of this chapter.

[539]*See* § H.1.i of this chapter.

[540]Sprouse v. Babcock, 870 F.2d 450, 452 (8th Cir. 1989); Freeman v. Rideout, 808 F.2d 949, 951–53 (2d Cir. 1986); Hanrahan v. Lane, 747 F.2d 1137, 1140–41 (7th Cir. 1984); Orwat v. Maloney, 360 F. Supp. 2d 146, 157 (D.Mass. 2005) ("The constitutional corrective for such things is the subsequent hearing that the inmate receives on those charges."); Banks v. Klapish, 717 F. Supp. 520, 522 (W.D.Mich. 1989); Garrido v. Coughlin, 716 F. Supp. 98, 101 (S.D.N.Y. 1989); Wilson v. Maben, 676 F. Supp. 581, 584 (M.D.Pa. 1987).

One court stated that a disciplinary hearing "terminates an officer's possible liability for the filing of a false disciplinary report." Hawkins v. O'Leary, 729 F. Supp. 600, 602 (N.D.Ill. 1990). We think that is wrong. When prison staff "ma[ke] false reports and recommendations with the purpose or expectation that they [will] lead to segregated confinement," they should be subject to liability under the usual principles that individuals can be held liable for the foreseeable consequences of their actions. Furtado v. Bishop, 604 F.2d 80, 89 (1st Cir. 1979). The standards of due process and of evidence are so low in prison disciplinary proceedings, where a prisoner can be found guilty on nothing more than an officer's written report, *see* § H.1.i of this chapter, that it is always foreseeable that filing a disciplinary report will result in discipline after a hearing even if the report is fabricated.

[541]Morrison v. LeFevre, 592 F. Supp. 1052, 1073 (S.D.N.Y. 1984). This opinion has been limited by the decision in *Freeman v. Rideout*, 808 F.2d at 952. In that case, the court observed that in *Morrison* the plaintiff never received any hearing at all.

A few other courts have made statements similar to *Morrison*'s, but they are in a minority. *See* Cale v. Johnson, 861 F.2d 943, 949–50 (6th Cir. 1988); Furtado v. Bishop, 604 F.2d 80, 89 (1st Cir. 1979); U.S. v. Wallace, 673 F. Supp. 205, 207–08 (S.D.Tex. 1987); Douglas v. Marino, 684 F. Supp. 395, 398–99 (D.N.J. 1988); King v. Cuyler, 541 F. Supp. 1230, 1235 (E.D.Pa. 1982); *see also* Foulds v. Courley, 833 F.2d 52, 54 (5th Cir. 1987) (holding allegation that false charges were brought to compel a prisoner to disclose information about other inmates stated a due process claim).

[542]Surprenant v. Rivas, 424 F.3d 5, 13–14 (1st Cir. 2005); Freeman v. Rideout, 808 F.2d at 952.

[543]*See* Ch. 3, §§ B.6, C.1.c, concerning retaliation claims; *see also* Winston v. Coughlin, 789 F. Supp. 118, 120–21 (W.D.N.Y. 1992) (holding allegation that officers filed fabricated reports to conceal their Eighth Amendment violations stated a claim).

[544]Orwat v. Maloney, 360 F. Supp. 2d 146, 165 (D.Mass. 2005).

o. Discipline and Mental Health The courts have not fully explored the constitutional issues involved in disciplining prisoners who have mental disorders. Courts in one state have held that in a "disciplinary proceeding in which a prisoner's mental state is at issue, a hearing officer is required to consider evidence regarding the prisoner's mental condition,"[545] but did not say whether that requirement is based on due process considerations or on state law. Nor did the court explain exactly how the court is supposed to weigh mental health evidence, though subsequent decisions have focused on whether the prisoner was properly found "responsible for his actions."[546] We think the right to assistance at a disciplinary hearing, now applicable to persons who are illiterate or faced with issues too complex for them to understand, should also extend to persons with serious mental illness, but court decisions on that point are mixed.[547]

Some courts have held that the Constitution forbids punishment for behavior caused or influenced by mental illness.[548] Courts have also condemned the housing of mentally disturbed inmates in punitive segregation units.[549] There is ample support for the idea that placing mentally ill inmates in punitive segregation can constitute cruel and unusual punishment,[550] and at a minimum such inmates must be screened by qualified mental health staff before they are placed in segregation. If they are segregated, they are entitled to adequate access to mental health care.[551]

The arguments we have suggested will probably require the support of expert witnesses, and it is unlikely that you can make them successfully unless you obtain counsel to present expert testimony.

---

[545]Matter of Huggins v. Coughlin, 76 N.Y.2d 904, 561 N.Y.S.2d 910, 563 N.E.2d 281, 282 (N.Y. 1990); *see* Rosado v. Kuhlmann, 164 A.D.2d 199, 563 N.Y.S.2d 295, 297 (N.Y.App.Div. 1990) (holding that "the mental competence and mental illness of a prisoner must be considered during the prison disciplinary process where a [mental disease or defect] adjudication has been made or a well-documented history of serious psychiatric problems calls the prisoner's mental health into question"; applying holding to a case in which the prisoner assaulted staff in the course of an emergency referral to the psychiatric unit), *appeal denied*, 77 N.Y.2d 806 (1991). *But see* Zamakshari v. Dvoskin, 899 F. Supp. 1097, 1107 (S.D.N.Y. 1994) (holding the failure to consider mental health status did not violate clearly established law as of 1988). *Cf.* Powell v. Coughlin, 953 F.2d 744, 749 (2d Cir. 1991) (upholding a policy permitting mental health staff to be consulted by the hearing officer but not called as witnesses); Ryan v. Pico, 227 A.D.2d 806, 642 N.Y.S.2d 436 (App.Div. 1996) (affirming disciplinary conviction in which prisoner's mental health therapist testified out of the prisoner's presence; "the reasons for this proceeding . . . were adequately explained . . ., and no more is required").

[546]*See, e.g.*, Mawhinney v. Goord, 281 A.D.2d 670, 720 N.Y.S.2d 855 (N.Y.App.Div. 2001); *see also* People ex rel. Reed v. Scully, 140 Misc.2d 379, 531 N.Y.S.2d 196 (N.Y.Sup. 1988) (holding a prisoner found insane in a criminal trial should be able to present an insanity defense when charged with a disciplinary offense for the same actions).

[547]*See* § H.1.f of this chapter, n.379.

[548]*See* Coleman v. Wilson, 912 F. Supp. 1282, 1320–22 (E.D.Cal. 1995) (Eighth Amendment was violated by practices including punitive treatment of prisoners acting out because of their mental illness); Arnold on behalf of H.B. v. Lewis, 803 F. Supp. 246, 256 (D.Ariz. 1992) (holding placement in lockdown "as punishment for the symptoms of [the plaintiff's] mental illness and as an alternative to providing mental health care" violated the Eighth Amendment); Cameron v. Tomes, 783 F. Supp. 1511, 1524–25 (D.Mass. 1992) (holding application of standard disciplinary procedures to a sex offender in a "Treatment Center for the Sexually Dangerous" amounted to punishing him for his psychological problems and, when done without consultation with mental health staff, violated the "professional judgment" standard applied to civilly committed persons), *aff'd as modified*, 990 F.2d 14, 21 (1st Cir. 1993). *Cf.* Pryor v. New Jersey Dep't of Corrections, 672 A.2d 717, 718 (N.J.Sup.App.Div. 1996) (holding that rule against "abusive or obscene language to a staff member" could not be applied to statements made by a prisoner at a psychotherapy session), *cert. denied*, 145 N.J. 375, 678 A.2d 716 (N.J. 1996). *But see* Whittington v. Vaughn, 289 F. Supp. 2d 621, 625–26 (E.D.Pa. 2003) (upholding disciplinary confinement of schizophrenic prisoner for conduct he engaged in after refusing his medication); Trammell v. Coombe, 649 N.Y.S.2d 964 (Sup.Ct. 1996) (holding prisoner subject to discipline failed to show his violent acts were "attributable to mental disease" where a psychiatric evaluation suggested that he "experiences paranoid ideations, [but] he is not psychotic. He is fully aware of his actions and his conduct is volitional"); Parrilla v. Senkowski, 300 A.D.2d 870, 754 N.Y.S.2d 684 (App.Div. 2002) (rejecting argument that prisoner who resisted being double-celled could not be disciplined because he believed his mental health condition made him a bad candidate for double-celling), *leave denied*, 99 N.Y.2d 510 (2003); Colantonio v. Coughlin, 194 A.D.2d 1015, 599 N.Y.S.2d 667 (App.Div. 1993) (upholding disciplinary punishment for self-mutilation prompted by depression where the prisoner was "responsible for his actions").

[549]*See* Inmates of Occoquan v. Barry, 717 F. Supp. 854, 868 (D.D.C. 1989); Langley v. Coughlin, 715 F. Supp. 522, 543–44 (S.D.N.Y. 1989); Langley v. Coughlin, 709 F. Supp. 482, 484–85 (S.D.N.Y. 1989), *appeal dismissed*, 888 F.2d 252 (2d Cir. 1989); Walker v. Montana, 316 Mont. 103, 107–10, 116–22, 68 P.2d 872, 875–77, 881–84 (2003) (condemning, under state constitutional provisions, punitive "Behavior Modification Plans" imposed on mentally ill prisoner in disciplinary unit).

[550]*See* Coleman v. Wilson, 912 F. Supp. 1282, 1320–22 (E.D.Cal. 1995); Arnold on behalf of H.B. v. Lewis, 803 F. Supp. at 256. One court held the Eighth Amendment was violated by placement in the extremely isolating conditions at the Pelican Bay administrative segregation unit in California of "the already mentally ill, as well as persons with borderline personality disordered, brain damage or mental retardation, impulse-ridden personalities, or a history of prior psychiatric problems or chronic depression. For these inmates, placing them in the SHU is the mental equivalent of putting an asthmatic in a place with little air to breathe." Madrid v. Gomez, 889 F. Supp. 1146, 1265 (N.D.Cal. 1995). *But see* Scarver v. Litscher, 434 F.3d 972, 976–77 (7th Cir. 2006) (holding that prison officials who were not shown to have known that keeping a psychotic prisoner under conditions of extreme isolation and heat would aggravate his mental illness could not be found deliberately indifferent).

[551]Mental health care is discussed in Ch. 2, § F.4.a.

p. Punishment In general, the Due Process Clause does not limit the punishments that may be imposed after a disciplinary hearing. Only if a punishment is "cruel and unusual" under the Eighth Amendment will prison officials be forbidden to utilize it. Thus, physical abuse and foul and degrading conditions of punitive confinement are unconstitutional.[552]

Punishments may also be held to be cruel and unusual if they are grossly disproportionate to the offense,[553] but courts are "extremely reluctant" to find prison punishments to be disproportionate.[554] The Supreme Court upheld a 30-day limit on punitive segregation in one case, but that decision was based mostly on the extremely bad conditions of confinement.[555]

Monetary restitution for property damage or other offenses that cost the prison money is a legitimate form of punishment if authorized by statute or regulation,[556] and one court has held that monetary fines for prison rule violations do not deny due process on their face.[557] Restitution orders

---

[552]*See* Hope v. Pelzer, 536 U.S. 730, 738, 122 S. Ct. 2508 (2002) (holding unconstitutional the practice of restraining prisoners to "hitching post"); Hutto v. Finney, 437 U.S. 678, 686–88, 98 S. Ct. 2565 (1978) (affirming injunction limiting confinement in foul segregation conditions); Jackson v. Bishop, 404 F.2d 571, 579 (8th Cir. 1968) (holding use of the "strap" unconstitutional). The Eighth Amendment is discussed generally in Ch. 2, § A; conditions of punitive segregation are discussed in more detail in Ch. 2, § J. Limits on the use of food as punishment are discussed in Ch. 2, §§ D, G of this Manual.

Sometimes particular kinds of punishment, like deprivation of mail, visits, or religious rights, raise other kinds of constitutional questions. These are discussed in the appropriate sections. *See, e.g.,* Ch. 2, §§ B.1 (correspondence), B.7 (visits), D.2.b (religious services).

[553]Pearson v. Ramos, 237 F.3d 881, 885 (7th Cir. 2001) (stating that court "continue[s] to recognize" norm of proportionality); Adams v. Carlson, 368 F. Supp. 1050, 1053 (E.D.Ill.) (holding 16 months' segregation excessive for involvement in a work stoppage), *on remand from* 488 F.2d 619 (7th Cir. 1973); Black v. Brown, 524 F. Supp. 856, 858 (N.D.Ill. 1981) (holding 18 months' segregation excessive for running in the yard), *aff'd in part and rev'd in part,* 688 F.2d 841 (7th Cir. 1982); Hardwick v. Ault, 447 F. Supp. 116, 125–26 (M.D.Ga. 1978) (holding indefinite segregation *per se* disproportionate); Fulwood v. Clemmer, 206 F. Supp. 370, 379 (D.D.C. 1962) (holding two years' segregation excessive for disruptive preaching); Keenan v. Bordenkircher, 294 S.E.2d 175, 177 (W.Va. 1982) (holding 10 years' segregation was excessive for escape; sentence limited to 2 years already served); *see* Leslie v. Doyle, 125 F.3d 1132, 1135 (7th Cir. 1997) (holding 15-day segregation sentence, though literally disproportionate if there was *no* offense, did not raise an Eighth Amendment issue); *see also* Haynes v. Lambor, 785 F. Supp. 754, 757 (N.D.Ill. 1992) (holding Eighth Amendment disproportionality claim requires proof of culpable mental state on the part of defendants). In *Surprenant v. Rivas,* 424 F.3d 5, 13 (1st Cir. 2005), the court said that pretrial detainees may be punished for jail infractions, but "the discipline imposed must be roughly proportionate to the gravity of the infraction. . . . An arbitrary, or disproportionate sanction, or one that furthers no legitimate penological objective, constitutes punishment (and, thus, is proscribed by the Fourteenth Amendment)."

[554]Savage v. Snow, 575 F. Supp. 828, 836 (S.D.N.Y. 1983) (upholding 90 days' loss of good time and confinement in segregation for abuse of correspondence privileges); *see* Pearson v. Ramos, 237 F.3d 881, 885 (7th Cir. 2001) (upholding 4 consecutive 90-day sentences to loss of yard time for a segregation prisoner based on assaulting an officer, setting a fire, spitting in an officer's face, and throwing a broom and "bodily fluids" on a staff member); Grady v. Wilken, 735 F.2d 303, 305 (8th Cir. 1984)

(upholding six months' segregation for extortion); Madyun v. Franzen, 704 F.2d 954, 960–61 (7th Cir. 1983) (upholding 15 days in segregation for refusing a strip search); Rhodes v. Robinson, 612 F.2d 766, 774 (3d Cir. 1979) (upholding one month's segregation for threatening to kill another prisoner); Glouser v. Parratt, 605 F.2d 419, 420–21 (8th Cir. 1979) (upholding 30 days' segregation and 60 days' loss of good time for marijuana possession); Dixon v. Goord, 224 F. Supp. 2d 739, 748 (S.D.N.Y. 2002) (upholding seven months for assaulting an officer); Bates v. Wright, 738 F. Supp. 386, 389 (D.Or. 1990) (upholding four weeks' segregation for possessing medication the plaintiff should have taken and claiming the nurse had authorized him to keep it); Tyra v. Harger, 587 F. Supp. 1336, 1341 (N.D.Ind. 1984) (upholding 15 days' confinement to cell for blocking a locking device); Woodall v. Partilla, 581 F. Supp. 1066, 1075 (N.D.Ill. 1984) (upholding 360 days' segregation and loss of good time for conviction of assault and sexual misconduct); Mtambuzi v. Coughlin, 176 A.D.2d 1110, 575 N.Y.S.2d 412, 413 (N.Y.App.Div. 1991) (upholding a year's segregation and loss of good time for striking an officer), *appeal denied,* 580 N.Y.S.2d 199 (N.Y.App.Div. 1992).

[555]Hutto v. Finney, 437 U.S. 678, 686–87, 98 S. Ct. 2565 (1978); *accord,* Pugh v. Locke, 406 F. Supp. 318, 327–28, 332–33 (M.D.Ala. 1976) (imposing 21-day limit), *aff'd as modified sub nom.* Newman v. Alabama, 559 F.2d 283 (5th Cir. 1977); Berch v. Stahl, 373 F. Supp. 412, 420–21 (W.D.N.C. 1974) (limiting segregation to 15 or 30 days depending on conditions). *See also* Sostre v. McGinnis, 442 F.2d 178, 192–93 (2d Cir. 1971) (refusing to impose a limit on segregation time); Capps v. Atiyeh, 559 F. Supp. 894, 906 (D.Ore. 1982) (refusing to limit segregation time unless conditions were unconstitutional).

[556]Longmire v. Guste, 921 F.2d 620, 623–24 (5th Cir. 1991) (upholding state statute providing for restitution); Campbell v. Miller, 787 F.2d 217, 224–25 (7th Cir. 1986) (upholding impoundment of prisoner's account pending compliance with $1445 restitution order imposed after a *Wolff* hearing); Ruley v. Nevada Bd. of Prison Comm'rs, 628 F. Supp. 108 (D.Nev. 1986); Sauls v. State, 467 N.W.2d 1, 2–3 (Iowa App. 1990); Ciampi v. Commissioner of Correction, 452 Mass. 162, 892 N.E.2d 270 (2008); VanCleave v. Oregon State Penitentiary, 93 Or.App.326, 761 P.2d 1366 (Or.App. 1988), *review denied,* 307 Or. 405, 769 P.2d 779 (Or. 1989); Burlett v. Holden, 835 P.2d 989, 991 (Utah App. 1992); *see* Wilson v. TDCJ-ID, 268 S.W.3d 756, 759 (Tex.App. 2008) (where prisoner had received an assessment of damages in a disciplinary hearing, prison need not have used state garnishment procedures to remove money from his account). *But see* Conklin v. Zant, 202 Ga.App. 214, 413 S.E.2d 536, 537–38 (Ga.App. 1991) (holding restitution orders must be authorized by state law).

In some prison systems, money found in prisoners' possession is confiscated, usually without a hearing. The relevant due process issues are discussed in § H.8.d of this chapter.

[557]Clark v. Schumacher, 103 Or.App. 1, 795 P.2d 1093, 1096 (Or.App. 1990); *see also* Allen v. Cuomo, 100 F.3d 253, 259–60

must be supported by evidence that the prisoner actually destroyed or damaged the property and of the value of the items.[558]

Disparities in punishment do not deny due process unless they are so extreme as to be completely irrational[559] or are based on unlawful considerations.[560]

In a few cases, courts have found that state law or prison regulations that limit disciplinary punishments create "entitlements" or "liberty interests" protected by the federal Due Process Clause.[561] These decisions are questionable after

Sandin v. Conner's holding that only "atypical and significant hardship" suffices to create a liberty interest in prison.[562] The same is true of decisions finding a liberty interest in not having a disciplinary charge "upgraded" to a more severe level,[563] unless the consequences of that "upgrade" are extremely severe.

Whether enhanced punishments imposed on prisoners already in segregation require additional procedural protections in light of *Sandin v. Conner* is discussed in an earlier section.[564]

State law or prison regulations may limit punishments in ways that can be enforced in state courts.[565]

q. Disciplinary Rules Many things can be forbidden in prison that could not be forbidden in the "free world."[566] Courts rarely strike down a prison disciplinary rule as unconstitutional on its face unless it severely restricts basic constitutional rights.[567] They are somewhat more willing to

---

(2d Cir. 1996) (upholding $5.00 surcharge on disciplinary convictions). The court did not address arguments concerning the possible impact of the rules. *But see* State v. Murray, 621 P.2d 334, 339–40 (Haw. 1980) (holding state law prohibited the taking of prisoners' earned money as punishment).

[558]Burns v. Pa. Dep't of Correction, 544 F.3d 279, 291 (3d Cir. 2008) (assessment of prisoner account for restitution after disciplinary conviction was a deprivation of property requiring due process even though officials never actually took the money); Quick v. Jones, 754 F.2d 1521 (9th Cir. 1985) (holding inmate could not be sentenced to restitution for destroying property without findings that he destroyed it); Keeling v. Schaefer, 181 F. Supp. 2d 1206, 1224–25 (D.Kan. 2001) (holding restitution order must be supported by evidence of the amount required for restitution); Artway v. Scheidemantel, 671 F. Supp. 330 (D.N.J. 1987) (holding inmate could not be sentenced to restitution without a hearing that addressed the value of the property); *see* Vickers v. Oregon State Correctional Institution, 90 Or.App. 226, 751 P.2d 1125 (Or.App. 1988) (holding order of restitution that did not specify the amount was "clear error").

[559]*See* Ferreira v. Duval, 887 F. Supp. 374, 379 (D.Mass. 1995) (holding prisoner who received more severe sentence than others involved in the same incident was not denied equal protection; he was identified as a leader, had a worse disciplinary record than the others, and did not accept responsibility for the incident); Mazzanti v. Bogan, 866 F. Supp. 1029, 1033 (E.D.Mich. 1994) (holding allegations that other inmates with positive drug tests were treated less harshly than the plaintiff did not state a constitutional claim without details of their infractions and punishments); Phillips v. Gathright, 468 F. Supp. 1211, 1212 (W.D.Va.), *aff'd*, 603 F.2d 219 (4th Cir. 1979); McCray v. Bennett, 467 F. Supp. 187, 193 (M.D.Ala. 1978). *But see* Hinebaugh v. Wiley, 137 F. Supp. 2d 69, 79 (N.D.N.Y. 2001) (refusing to dismiss without an explanation where the plaintiff received 15 days SHU and 14 days lost good time for receiving a copy of a case, while the person who gave it to him received only a reprimand); Ivey v. Wilson, 577 F. Supp. 169, 173 (W.D.Ky. 1983) (holding the statement of reasons must explain the more severe sentence where two prisoners received extremely different sentences for the same misconduct).

[560]Henard v. Parke, 5 F. Supp. 2d 641, 642–44 (N.D.Ind. 1998) (finding disparity in punishment reflected racial discrimination), *vacated as moot*, 191 F.3d 456 (7th Cir. 1999); Santiago v. Miles, 774 F. Supp. 775, 786–87, 800–01 (W.D.N.Y. 1991) (finding class-wide racial discrimination in disciplinary sanctions).

[561]Jackson v. Cain, 864 F.2d 1235, 1250–51 (5th Cir. 1989); Sanders v. Borgert, 711 F. Supp. 889, 893 (E.D.Mich.), *aff'd*, 891 F.2d 292 (6th Cir. 1989); Morgan v. District of Columbia, 647 F. Supp. 694, 697 (D.D.C. 1986); *see* Haynes v. Lambor, 785 F. Supp. 754, 759 (N.D.Ill. 1992) (assuming there is a liberty interest in timely release from segregation, due process requires "a relatively prompt resolution").

[562]Sandin v. Conner, 515 U.S. 472, 484, 115 S. Ct. 2293 (1995); *see* § B of this chapter concerning state-created liberty interests.

[563]*See* Staples v. Young, 679 F. Supp. 884, 885–88 (W.D.Wis. 1988) (holding upgrading of offense from "minor" to "major" requires due process in the form of a statement of reasons); *compare* Culbert v. Young, 834 F.2d 624, 627–28 (7th Cir. 1987) (finding no liberty interest in regulation that did not clearly limit officials' discretion to upgrade charge). *See* Holt v. Caspari, 961 F.2d 1370, 1373 (8th Cir. 1992) (holding there is no right to notice of whether a disciplinary offense is "serious" or "minor"); *accord*, Jensen v. Satran, 651 F.2d 605, 607 (8th Cir. 1981) (per curiam).

[564]*See* § G of this chapter.

[565]*See* Alvarez v. State Dep't of Corrections, 638 P.2d 804, 806–07 (Colo.App. 1981) (holding prison officials' completely unlimited discretion to determine punishment violated the state constitution); Trammell v. Coombe, 170 Misc.2d 471, 476, 649 N.Y.S.2d 964, 967–68 (Sup.Ct. 1996) (holding that "deprivation orders" removing toilet paper, soap, clothing, etc., could not be used for punitive purposes under prison regulations); Chambers v. Coughlin, 76 A.D.2d 980, 429 N.Y.S.2d 74, 76 (N.Y.App.Div. 1980) (holding denial of contact visitation for non-segregated inmates unlawful under state regulations); *see also* Massop v. LeFevre, 127 Misc.2d 910, 487 N.Y.S. 2d 925 (N.Y.Sup. 1985) (holding 60-day punishment excessive where prison regulations only authorized 30 days for the infraction listed on the notice).

[566]*See, e.g.*, Scruggs v. Jordan, 485 F.3d 934, 938–39 (7th Cir. 2007) (officials can prohibit inmates from using violence to defend themselves or others, and can discipline them for doing so); Pedraza v. Meyer, 919 F.2d 318, 320 (5th Cir. 1990) (holding prisoner could be disciplined for violating a rule against writing to other prisoners even though the other prisoner was his wife); Withrow v. Bartlett, 15 F. Supp. 2d 292, 296–99 (W.D.N.Y. 1998) (holding prisoner could be disciplined for praying in the yard contrary to prison rules); Leitzsey v. Coombe, 998 F. Supp. 282, 287 (W.D.N.Y. 1998) (upholding a rule prohibiting materials concerning any organization not approved by the Commissioner as applied to the prisoner's own organization).

[567]A rare exception is *Hancock v. Thalacker*, 933 F. Supp. 1449, 1487–90 (N.D.Iowa 1996), which holds that prisoners cannot be punished for false statements in grievances and other complaints

strike down particular applications of rules,[568] including—in very rare circumstances—instances where conduct by prison staff unjustifiably caused the violation.[569]

"Due process requires that inmates receive fair notice of a rule before they can be sanctioned for its violation."[570]

This requirement of notice does not apply if the conduct in question also violates criminal statutes.[571] One court has held that lack of notice of the penalties for violating prison rules before the prisoner breaks them does not deny due process, but notice of the penalties must be given before the hearing.[572] As long as prisoners do have notice of the rules, prison authorities' failure to follow state law procedures for rule-making will not deny due process,[573] although it may make the rules unenforceable under state law.[574]

Due process forbids rules that are so vague that people of ordinary intelligence must guess at their meaning,[575] or that fail to provide explicit standards for those who enforce the rules.[576] A rule may be vague "on its face," meaning that under no circumstances can it be applied constitutionally.[577] It may also be vague "as applied," meaning that it does not

---

to prison officials unless the statements are shown by a preponderance of the evidence to have been made with knowledge they were false. cases cited in n.577, below, striking down prison rules as vague

[568]*See, e.g.,* Hargis v. Foster, 312 F.3d 404, 406 (9th Cir. 2002) (holding rule prohibiting "involvement in any disorderly conduct by coercing or attempting to coerce any official action" is not unconstitutional on its face, but as applied to a statement that an officer's actions could come up in pending litigation, it raised a material question whether it had a rational connection with security concerns or was an "exaggerated response"); Bradley v. Hall, 64 F.3d 1276, 1279–81 (9th Cir. 1995) (holding rule against "disrespect" could not be applied to statements in written grievances). *But see* Hale v. Scott, 371 F.3d 917, 918–19 (7th Cir. 2004) (upholding discipline under rule forbidding "insolence" for falsely accusing an officer of sexual misconduct); Edwards v. Johnson, 209 F.3d 772, 779 (9th Cir. 2000) (upholding discipline of plaintiff for "unauthorized contact with members of the general public" for handing visitors a flyer, making disparaging remarks about the institution, and suggesting visitors should not believe what officials told them).

The extent to which prisoners' free expression by speech and writing can be restricted by prison rules is discussed further in Ch. 3, § B; disciplinary retaliation for constitutionally protected activity is discussed in Ch. 3, §§ B.6, C.1.c.

[569]For example, if prison staff order prisoners to do something that violates their religious rights and then discipline them for refusing to do it, their First Amendment religious rights may be violated. *See* Warsoldier v. Woodford, 418 F.3d 989, 995–96, 1001–02 (9th Cir. 2005) (holding punishment for Native American prisoner for refusing to cut his hair on religious grounds unlawfully burdened his religious rights, holding rule should be enjoined); McEachin v. McGuinnis, 357 F.3d 197, 204–05 (2d Cir. 2003) (allegation that officer ordered plaintiff to return his food tray and cup while he was performing *salat* in his cell, and then issued a misbehavior report when he continued his prayers, stated a First Amendment claim); Williams v. Bitner, 359 F. Supp. 2d 370, 376 (M.D.Pa. 2005) (disciplining a Muslim prisoner for refusing to handle pork in his food service job violated his religious rights), *aff'd on other grounds,* 455 F.3d 186 (3d Cir. 2006); *see* additional cases cited in Ch. 3, § D.2.d, n.807. In *O'Connor v. Huard,* 117 F.3d 12, 16 (1st Cir. 1997), the court held that it denied due process for an officer to taunt a detainee with an anxiety disorder in order to provoke "rage attacks" that would result in disciplinary segregation.

As noted, these are very rare situations, involving extreme facts. Do not get the idea that if an officer provokes you or behaves in a way you think is improper, you are entitled to disobey the rules in response. If you do, you may subject yourself to harsh discipline in which courts will not intervene.

[570]Forbes v. Trigg, 976 F.2d 308, 314 (7th Cir. 1992); *accord,* Coffman v. Trickey, 884 F.2d 1057, 1060 (8th Cir. 1989) (conviction for "knowingly failing to abide by any published institutional rule" denied due process where no institutional rule actually forbade the prisoner's conduct); Meis v. Gunter, 906 F.2d 364, 367 (8th Cir. 1990) (dictum); Frazier v. Coughlin, 850 F.2d 129, 130 (2d Cir.

1988); Oswalt v. Godinez, 894 F. Supp. 1181, 1189 (N.D.Ill. 1995) (holding allegation that prisoner was convicted of "conspiracy to attempt escape" but there was no such offense in the rule book stated a due process claim); Robles v. Coughlin, 725 F.2d 12, 16 (2d Cir. 1983) and cases cited; Hodges v. Jones, 873 F. Supp. 737, 745–46 (N.D.N.Y. 1995) (holding allegation that prisoner was disciplined under a rule that was not posted and that was announced on a day he was not present supported a due process claim); Richardson v. Coughlin, 763 F. Supp. 1228, 1235 (S.D.N.Y. 1991); Noren v. Straw, 578 F. Supp. 1, 6 (D.Mont. 1982); *see also* Gibbs v. King, 779 F.2d 1040, 1045 (5th Cir. 1986) (where rule required that prisoners obey posted policies, evidence of posting must be offered at the disciplinary hearing).

[571]Frazier v. Coughlin, 850 F.2d at 130. State law, however, may require notice of prison rules even when the conduct does violate criminal statutes. Collins v. Hammock, 52 N.Y.2d 798, 800, 436 N.Y.S.2d 704, 417 N.E.2d 1245 (N.Y. 1980).

[572]McMillan v. Healy, 739 F. Supp. 153, 156–57 (S.D.N.Y. 1990); *see* Bryan v. Dep't of Corrections, 258 N.J.Super. 546, 610 A.2d 889, 892 (1992) (state law required that notice of sanctions be given before an offense is committed). *But see* Heide v. Oregon State Correctional Institution, 107 Or.App. 445, 812 P.2d 35 (1991) (erroneous notice of maximum penalty did not deny due process but might violate state law).

[573]LaBoy v. Coughlin, 822 F.2d 3, 4 (2d Cir. 1987) (per curiam).

[574]*See* Jones v. Smith, 64 N.Y.2d 1003, 1005–06, 478 N.E.2d 1191, 466 N.Y.S.2d 175 (N.Y. 1985) (disciplinary rules not filed with Secretary of State could not be enforced); Dep't of Correction v. McNeil, 209 N.J.Super. 120, 506 A.2d 1291 (1986) (requiring compliance with state Administrative Procedure Act, but refusing to overturn past convictions).

[575]Chatin v. Coombe, 186 F.3d 82, 89 (2d Cir. 1999); Rios v. Lane, 812 F.2d 1032, 1038 (7th Cir. 1987); Soto v. City of Sacramento, 567 F. Supp. 662, 684–85 (E.D.Calif. 1983) and cases cited.

[576]Chatin v. Coombe, 186 F.3d at 87; Aiello v. Litscher, 104 F. Supp. 2d 1068, 1083 (W.D.Wis. 2000).

[577]Cassels v. Stalder, 342 F. Supp. 2d 555, 564–67 (M.D.La. 2004) (striking down rule forbidding "spreading rumors" as vague and overbroad on its face); Noren v. Straw, 578 F. Supp. 1, 6 (D.Mont. 1982) (rule requiring inmates to act in an "orderly, decent manner with respect for the rights of the other inmates" was vague; new rules required); Jenkins v. Werger, 564 F. Supp. 806, 807–08 (D.Wyo. 1983) (statute barring "unruly or disorderly" conduct was void for vagueness).

give adequate notice that it prohibits the conduct with which a particular prisoner is charged.[578] The courts scrutinize rules for vagueness most closely when they impinge on First Amendment freedoms.[579]

Courts may tolerate a greater degree of vagueness in prison rules than they do in criminal statutes.[580] For example, one court upheld a rule banning "derogatory or degrading remarks" against employees, "insults, unwarranted and uncalled for remarks, or other clearly intrusive verbal behavior" against employees on duty, and "unsolicited, non-threatening, abusive conversation, correspondence or phone calls" to employees.[581]

r. Remedies for Unlawful Disciplinary Proceedings

Courts may grant several different kinds of remedies if you show that a disciplinary conviction was unlawfully obtained.[582] However, you cannot always get all the relief you want in the same proceeding; be sure you understand what restrictions apply in both the federal courts and the state courts in your jurisdiction.

The scope of state court judicial review and remedial powers varies from state to state.[583] In some states, it appears that there are no state court remedies for unlawful disciplinary proceedings.[584] Other states permit judicial review of

---

[578]Farid v. Ellen, 593 F.3d 233, 241–44 (2d Cir. 2010) (holding a rule against contraband was vague as applied where charges required prisoner to interpret the rule to include violation of internal rules of a prisoner organization); Gayle v. Gonyea, 313 F.3d 677, 680 n.3 (2d Cir. 2002) (questioning whether a rule forbidding work stoppages, sit-ins, lock-ins, or "other actions which may be detrimental to the order of the facility" gave adequate notice that circulating petitions or encouraging others to file grievances is barred); Chatin v. Coombe, 186 F.3d at 87–88 (holding that a rule prohibiting unauthorized religious services and speeches was vague as applied to silent, individual demonstrative prayer (*i.e.*, Muslim *salat*)); Newell v. Sauser, 79 F.3d 115, 117–18 (9th Cir. 1995) (holding rule against possessing anything not authorized or issued by the facility could not be applied to law librarian in possession of legal work prepared for other inmates, since as law librarian he was authorized to possess it); Wolfel v. Morris, 972 F.2d 712, 717–18 (6th Cir. 1992) (rule barring unauthorized group organizing was vague as applied to circulating a petition); Rios v. Lane, 812 F.2d at 1038–39 ("gang activity" rule was vague as applied to plaintiff's conduct); Smith v. Rowe, 761 F.2d 360, 364 (7th Cir. 1985) (contraband rule vague as applied); Adams v. Gunnell, 729 F.2d 362, 369 (5th Cir. 1984) (rule prohibiting "disruptive conduct" did not give adequate notice as applied); Cassels v. Stalder, 342 F. Supp. 2d 555, 566–67 (M.D.La. 2004) (holding rule forbidding "spreading rumors" vague as applied to reading a grievance document to prisoner's mother); Gee v. Ruettgers, 872 F. Supp. 915, 920 (D.Wyo. 1994) (holding prohibition on providing "false information to any official, court, news media, penitentiary employee, or the general public" is not unconstitutionally vague on its face, but was vague as applied to letters to a prisoner's immediate family). *But see* Nicholas v. Tucker, 89 F. Supp. 2d 475, 477 (S.D.N.Y. 2000) (rule that inmates shall not "lose, destroy, steal, misuse, damage, or waste any type of state property" for personal use was not vague as applied to a prisoner who used a prison computer to do personal legal work), *aff'd in part and remanded in part on other grounds*, 40 Fed.Appx. 642 (2d Cir. 2002) (unpublished); Schenck v. Edwards, 921 F. Supp. 679, 688 (E.D.Wash. 1996) (rule against unauthorized use of the mail was properly applied against prisoner who mailed pleadings he had drafted to another prisoner, even though the rule did not specifically prohibit drafting pleadings or label them as contraband), *aff'd*, 133 F.3d 929 (9th Cir. 1998); *see also* Moorman v. Thalacker, 83 F.3d 970, 974–75 (8th Cir. 1996) (holding that disciplining a prisoner for attempt to possess a firearm as a convicted felon, based on his statement that he would try to get a gun after his release, was a reasonable enough interpretation of the rule to confer qualified immunity on the defendants; not mentioning vagueness).

[579]Chatin v. Coombe, 186 F.3d at 86 (citing Grayned v. City of Rockford, 408 U.S. 104, 109, 92 S. Ct. 2294 (1972)).

[580]Fichtner v. Iowa State Penitentiary, 285 N.W.2d 751, 759 (Iowa 1979). *But see* Chatin v. Coombe, 186 F.3d at 86–87 (holding that prison punishments are more like criminal penalties than civil ones and therefore call for close scrutiny of rules for vagueness); Rios v. Lane, 812 F.2d at 1038 (stating "where prohibited conduct does not carry with it its own indicia of wrongdoing the need for clearly drawn prison regulations is particularly acute").

At least one court has suggested that a prison rule is not vague if it satisfies the *Turner v. Safley* reasonable relationship test. *See* Waterman v. Farmer, 183 F.3d 208, 213 (3d Cir. 1999). We think this is wrong. The question whether a rule is reasonably related to legitimate penological interests under *Turner* is different from whether it is drafted to give adequate notice of what conduct it forbids. Aiello v. Litscher, 104 F. Supp. 2d 1068, 1083 (W.D.Wis. 2000).

[581]Gibbs v. King, 779 F.2d 1040, 1045–46 (5th Cir. 1986); *see* Murphy v. Shaw, 195 F.3d 1121, 1128 (9th Cir 2000) (upholding rules against "insolence," defined as "words . . . intended to harass or cause alarm in an employee," and "interference with due process hearings," supplemented with examples, though "clearer language could be imagined"), *rev'd on other grounds*, 532 U.S. 223, 121 S. Ct. 1475 (2001); Gaston v. Taylor, 946 F.2d 340, 342 (4th Cir. 1991) (en banc) (rule barring possession of "anything not specifically approved for the specific inmate who has possession of the item" was not unconstitutional); Landman v. Royster, 333 F. Supp. 621, 655–56 (E.D.Va. 1971) (striking down rules against "misbehavior," "misconduct," and "agitation," but upholding rules against insolence, harassment, and insubordination); Gittens v. Coughlin, 184 A.D.2d 812, 584 N.Y.S.2d 670, 671 (N.Y.App.Div. 1991) (similar to *Gaston*); Rabi v. LeFevre, 120 A.D.2d 875, 502 N.Y.S.2d 546, 547 (N.Y.App.Div. 1986) (upholding a rule forbidding "possession of any article or paraphernalia which by its unusual nature gives reasonable grounds to believe escape is planned"). *Compare* Tate v. Kassulke, 409 F. Supp. 651, 659 (W.D.Ky. 1976) (holding rule against "disturbances" vague) *with* Witherspoon v. LeFevre, 82 A.D.2d 959, 440 N.Y.S. 2d 375 (N.Y.App.Div. 1981) (upholding a similar rule that contained a definition of "disturbance").

[582]Courts will be extremely reluctant to grant an injunction preventing a disciplinary hearing even if you can show that there is some likelihood of a constitutional violation. They will prefer to wait and see what happens. If you are not convicted, the case will go away, and if you are convicted, the facts that emerge at the hearing will help clarify the issues. *See* Gomes v. Fair, 738 F.2d 517, 528–29 (1st Cir. 1984).

[583]*See* Ch. 8, § D, for further discussion of state court remedies.

[584]Moffatt v. Director, TDCJ-CID, 390 F. Supp. 2d 560, 561 (E.D.Tex. 2005); Zimmerman v. State, 750 N.E.2d 337, 338 (Ind. 2001) (citing Hasty v. Broglin, 531 N.E.2d 200 (Ind. 1988)). *But see*

disciplinary hearings in the same manner as other administrative decisions are reviewed.[585] Some states' courts have
held that prison disciplinary proceedings are not subject to
judicial review under the state's administrative procedures
act.[586] Other forms of judicial review may be available in
these states.[587] In most states you will be required to exhaust
any available administrative remedies before challenging a
disciplinary proceeding in court,[588] and the same rule now
applies in federal court too under the Prison Litigation
Reform Act.[589]

The most important thing to keep in mind is that you
may have broader rights under state law than under the federal Constitution, and there are limits on federal courts'
power to enforce state law.[590] State courts, on the other hand,
can generally enforce federal constitutional rights.

1) New Hearing   If your hearing was procedurally defective,
the court can order prison officials to give you a new one that
complies with the law. This is commonly done by state courts
enforcing state rules of procedure.[591] One court has held that
expungement, rather than a new hearing, is required when
there has been a "substantial" violation, meaning a violation

---

Magar v. Parker, 490 F.3d 816, 818–19 (10th Cir. 2007) (noting that
legislature has newly created a remedy for Oklahoma prisoners);
Waters v. State, 691 N.E.2d 1228 (Ind.App. 1997) (holding that
court could enforce a statute providing that disciplinary charges of
which the prisoner was found not guilty must be expunged).

[585]*See* Shea v. Edwards, 221 Ill.App. 219, 163 Ill.Dec. 668, 581
N.E.2d 822, 823 (Ill.App. 1991) (mandamus was an appropriate
remedy to compel Department of Corrections to follow its own
regulations); Tocco v. Marquette Prison Warden, 123 Mich.App.
395, 333 N.W.2d 295, 296–97 (Mich.App. 1983); *see also* New York
State cases cited throughout this section.

[586]*See* Rose v. Arizona Dep't of Corrections, 167 Ariz. 116, 804
P.2d 845, 849 (Ariz.App. 1991) and cases cited; Singleton v. D.C.
Dep't of Corrections, 596 A.2d 56 (D.C.App. 1991); Hill v.
Superintendent, 392 Mass. 198, 466 N.E.2d 818, 821–22 (Mass.
1984), *rev'd on other grounds*, 472 U.S. 445, 105 S. Ct. 2768 (1985);
Zeltner v. N.J. Dep't of Corrections, 201 N.J.Super. 195, 492 A.2d
1084 (App.Div. 1985) (APA review limited to disciplinary
proceedings resulting in loss of a year's good time or more),
certification denied, 102 N.J. 299 (1985).

[587]*See, e.g.*, Davis v. State, 345 N.W.2d 97, 99–100 (Iowa 1984)
(permitting claims based on state or federal law or prison
regulations to be pursued via action for postconviction relief);
Holsey v. Inmate Grievance Comm'n, 296 Md. 601, 464 A.2d 1017
(Md.App. 1983) (grievance procedure held subject to judicial
review limited to the grievance record); Prock v. District Court of
Pittsburg County, 630 P.2d 772, 775–76 (Okla. 1981) (judicial
review limited to federal constitutional claims); Moore v. Black,
368 N.W.2d 488, 220 Neb. 122 (Neb. 1985) (proceeding in error,
not declaratory judgment action, was proper remedy).

[588]*See, e.g.*, James v. State, 479 N.W.2d 287, 292 (Iowa 1991).

[589]*See* Ch. 9, § D.

[590]*See* Ch. 8, § F.1.

[591]*See, e.g.*, Shea v. Edwards, 221 Ill.App. 219, 163 Ill.Dec. 668,
581 N.E.2d 822, 823 (Ill.App. 1991); Coleman v. Coombe, 65
N.Y.2d 777, 492 N.Y.S.2d 944, 482 N.E.2d 562 (N.Y. 1985).

---

of a procedural rule that "(1) directly protects the integrity
of the adjudication of guilt or innocence, or (2) prevents
the inmate from gaining access to evidence."[592] Other states
have developed different criteria for deciding when to order
a new hearing and when to throw out a disciplinary charge
altogether.[593]

Some prison systems administratively reverse defective
disciplinary convictions and hold new hearings.[594] This
practice does not deny due process.[595] Federal courts in civil
actions rarely order new hearings, probably because most
prisoners will have served most or all of their penalties by
the time a federal case is decided.[596] It is more common in
federal habeas corpus proceedings, where good time has
been taken, for the court to give prison officials a choice of
giving back the good time or providing a new hearing conducted consistently with due process requirements.[597]

In a case where the prisoner is seeking damages, we
think a new hearing is an inappropriate remedy because
there is a built-in bias. Under the damages rules discussed
below,[598] if you are cleared or get a lighter sentence in the

---

[592]Hrbek v. State, 478 N.W.2d 617, 619 (Iowa 1991).

[593]*See, e.g.*, Hartje v. Coughlin, 70 N.Y.2d 866, 868, 523
N.Y.S.2d 463, 517 N.E.2d 1348 (N.Y. 1987) (new hearing was
improper where prison officials had not produced enough evidence,
even though they said they could produce more); Allah v. LeFevre,
132 A.D.2d 293, 522 N.Y.S.2d 321 (N.Y.App.Div. 1987) (passage of
time precluded a meaningful new hearing); Lonski on behalf of
Colby v. Coughlin, 126 A.D.2d 981, 511 N.Y.S.2d 757 (N.Y.App.
Div. 1987) (new hearing appropriate for recent misconduct;
different hearing officer required); Cunningham v. LeFevre, 130
A.D.2d 809, 514 N.Y.S.2d 833 (N.Y.App.Div. 1987) (new hearing
was inappropriate where two years had passed, a key witness had
been paroled, and the prisoner had served two-thirds of his
sentence); Campbell v. Marquette Prison Warden, 119 Mich.App.
377, 326 N.W.2d 516, 518 (Mich.App. 1982) (rehearing was proper
where there was enough evidence to convict but the hearing
officer's findings were inadequate).

[594]*See, e.g.*, Benny v. O'Brien, 736 F. Supp. 242, 245 (D.Kan.
1990) (federal regulations permitted new hearing after conviction
was reversed on administrative appeal); Benadum v. Scurr, 320
N.W.2d 578, 580 (Iowa 1982) (same holding under state
regulations).

[595]Harper v. Lee, 938 F.2d 104, 105–06 (8th Cir. 1991); Russell
v. Coughlin, 774 F. Supp. 189, 198 (S.D.N.Y.), *reargument granted
on other grounds*, 782 F. Supp. 876 (S.D.N.Y. 1991); *see* Hoskins v.
McBride, 202 F. Supp. 2d 839, 846 (N.D.Ind. 2002) (holding it does
not deny due process to be given a harsher sentence after a new
hearing than after the first one), *aff'd*, 66 Fed.Appx. 47 (7th Cir.
2003) (unpublished).

[596]There are exceptions. *See, e.g.*, Giano v. Sullivan, 709 F.
Supp. 1209, 1218 (S.D.N.Y. 1989) (expungement and release from
segregation ordered "unless and until respondents promptly afford
him a new disciplinary hearing"); Ivey v. Wilson, 577 F. Supp. 169
(W.D.Ky. 1983).

[597]*See, e.g.*, Mayers v. Anderson, 93 F. Supp. 2d 962, 968
(N.D.Ind. 2000); Evans v. Deuth, 8 F. Supp. 2d 1135, 1137 (N.D.Ind.
1998).

[598]*See* nn.616–620 below, and Ch. 8, § O.1, concerning
damages. Keep in mind that many courts have held that

new hearing, prison officials are in effect admitting that you were injured by the old hearing, which would support your argument for damages.[599] This may create an incentive to find you guilty and to impose a severe penalty.

2) Release from Disciplinary Confinement

If you are sent to punitive segregation based on an unlawful disciplinary conviction, a court can direct that you be released.

Some decisions say that a petition for a writ of federal habeas corpus may be used to seek release from segregation.[600] Others hold habeas may not be used,[601] and the Supreme Court has recently strongly suggested that habeas is not available for that purpose.[602] You should be able to seek release from segregation in an ordinary civil rights action.[603] In any case, even if you could proceed via federal

habeas corpus to challenge placement in segregation or other conditions of confinement issues, there would be no advantage in doing so, since it would subject you to the requirement of exhausting state court remedies in addition to state administrative procedures, and to other restrictive habeas corpus rules.[604]

State courts will have their own rules as to what remedy is proper. In New York, for example, a state court habeas proceeding cannot be used to obtain release from segregation; instead, an "Article 78" proceeding for judicial review of administrative action must be employed.[605]

3) Restoration of Good Time

If you have lost good time in a disciplinary proceeding, you cannot bring a § 1983 action about it without first getting the decision set aside (getting a "favorable termination"), either in a state court or state administrative process or by federal habeas corpus.[606] That is because anything that affects the fact or duration of your imprisonment is within the "core of habeas corpus" and subject to the habeas corpus requirement that you exhaust state court remedies, as well as state administrative remedies, before you can proceed in federal court.[607] This rule is not limited to cases where you are asking for your good time back; it applies if a favorable decision would "necessarily imply the invalidity" of a disciplinary proceeding where you lost good time.[608] It does not apply to challenges to

---

compensatory damages may not be awarded for segregated confinement under the Prison Litigation Reform Act. *See* Ch. 9, § E.2.

[599]*See* Staples v. Traut, 675 F. Supp. 460, 465–66 (W.D.Wis. 1986) (refusing to order a new hearing since the plaintiff sought only damages). *But see* King v. Higgins, 702 F.2d 18, 22 (1st Cir. 1983) (holding that where a new hearing led to a better result for the prisoner, damages were proper for the result of the prior hearing that denied due process).

[600]*See, e.g.,* Medberry v. Crosby, 351 F.3d 1049, 1053 (11th Cir. 2003); Bostic v. Carlson, 884 F.2d 1267, 1269 (9th Cir. 1989); Boudin v. Thomas, 732 F.2d 1107, 1111 (2d Cir.), *reh'g denied,* 737 F.2d 261, 262 (2d Cir. 1984); Krist v. Ricketts, 504 F.2d 887, 887–88 (5th Cir. 1974) (per curiam); *see* Abdul-Hakeem v. Koehler, 910 F.2d 66, 69–70 (2d Cir. 1990) (clarifying *Boudin,* holding that habeas or § 1983 may be used to challenge the place of confinement).

[601]*See* Montgomery v. Anderson, 262 F.3d 641, 643–44 (7th Cir. 2001) ("Disciplinary segregation affects the severity rather than duration of custody. More-restrictive custody must be challenged under § 1983, in the uncommon circumstances when it can be challenged at all."); Brown v. Plaut, 131 F.3d 163, 167–68 (D.C. Cir. 1997); Toussaint v. McCarthy, 801 F.2d 1080, 1102–03 (9th Cir. 1986).

[602]"Challenges to the validity of any confinement or to particulars affecting its duration are the province of habeas corpus, . . . ; requests for relief turning on circumstances of confinement may be presented in a § 1983 action." Muhammad v. Close, 540 U.S. 749, 750, 124 S. Ct. 1303 (2004) (per curiam). It added: "This Court has never followed the speculation in *Preiser v. Rodriguez,* 411 U.S. 475, 499, 93 S. Ct. 1827 (1973), that such a prisoner subject to 'additional and unconstitutional restraint' might have a habeas claim independent of § 1983. . . ." *Muhammad,* 540 U.S. at 751 n.1. *But see* Levine v. Apker, 455 F.3d 71, 78 (2d Cir. 2006) (stating, after *Muhammad,* that federal prisoners may use a habeas petition under 28 U.S.C. § 2241 to challenge the execution of sentence, a category it says "includes matters such as 'the administration of parole, computation of a prisoner's sentence by prison officials, prison disciplinary actions, prison transfers, type of detention and prison conditions'" (quoting Jiminian v. Nash, 245 F.3d 144, 146 (2d Cir. 2001)).

[603]*See* Stringer-El v. Nix, 945 F.2d 1015, 1016 (8th Cir. 1991) (affirming preliminary injunction releasing the plaintiff from segregation); Espinal v. Goord, 180 F. Supp. 2d 532, 536, 541

(S.D.N.Y. 2002) (denying preliminary injunction releasing plaintiff from punitive segregation only because he failed to show it was likely he would prevail on his due process claim). Federal prisoners generally must exhaust their administrative remedies before seeking any kind of court order concerning their treatment in prison. *See* Ch. 8, § K, and Ch. 9, § D, concerning exhaustion of administrative remedies.

[604]For example, most courts hold that state prisoners challenging administrative decisions must satisfy the one-year limitations period of 28 U.S.C. § 2244(d)(1). Some have held that state prisoners using § 2254 are also governed by the AEDPA limitation that relief can be granted only if the adverse state court decision was "contrary to, or involved an unreasonable application of, clearly established Federal law, as determined by the Supreme Court of the United States." 28 U.S.C. § 2254(d)(1). *See* Ch. 8, § H.1.a, n.548.

[605]People ex rel. Dawson v. Smith, 69 N.Y.2d 689, 512 N.Y.S.2d 19, 504 N.E.2d 386 (N.Y. 1986); *see* Palaia v. Oregon State Penitentiary, 66 Or.App. 225, 673 P.2d 578 (Or.App. 1983) (identifying authority for state judicial review of disciplinary confinement).

[606]Muhammad v. Close, 540 U.S. 749, 751, 124 S. Ct. 1303 (2004). The same rule applies to federal prisoners, who must use federal administrative and habeas procedures to obtain a favorable termination. This rule is discussed further in Ch. 8, § H.1.

[607]Preiser v. Rodriguez, 411 U.S. 475, 494, 93 S. Ct. 1827 (1973).

[608]Edwards v. Balisok, 520 U.S. 641, 648, 117 S. Ct. 1584 (1997); *see, e.g.,* Clarke v. Stalder, 154 F.3d 186, 189–90 (5th Cir. 1998) (en banc) (holding prisoner could not challenge the constitutionality of a disciplinary rule because the issue was so intertwined with his

disciplinary proceedings where no good time was taken.[609] Nor does it apply to challenges to procedures in which the prisoner seeks only an order requiring that future hearings be conducted under different rules, and does not seek to invalidate particular proceedings in which good time has been taken.[610] In addition, one federal court has held that if a prisoner abandons forever any challenge to loss of good time or other sanction affecting the length of confinement, the favorable termination rule does not apply, and a challenge to other sanctions such as segregated confinement may go forward without first getting the decision overturned.[611]

Federal prisoners seeking the return of good time must proceed via habeas corpus under 28 U.S.C. § 2241,[612] after exhaustion of administrative remedies.[613]

4) Damages If a disciplinary hearing denies due process, you can seek damages in a federal civil rights action against prison officials who were personally involved in the violation.[614] In general, prison disciplinary officials are entitled only to "qualified immunity" from damages in federal court, and not to the absolute immunity afforded to quasi-judicial officials.[615] If they knew or should have known that they were violating the Constitution, you can recover damages from them.

If the court finds that, given a proper hearing, you would have been cleared or would have received a less severe sentence, you may be entitled to damages for the punishment that you were erroneously subjected to.[616] Damages have been awarded for the loss of freedom and privileges in punitive segregation, lost wages, or any other consequences of the wrongful conviction.[617] Some courts have interpreted the Prison Litigation Reform Act's provision prohibiting compensatory damages for mental or emotional injury without a showing of physical injury as barring compensatory damages for wrongful placement in segregation; we explain in another chapter why we believe that holding is wrong.[618]

---

challenge to a disciplinary conviction where he had lost good time).

[609]Muhammad v. Close, 540 U.S. 749, 754–55, 124 S. Ct. 1303 (2004) (holding that where no good time was taken, a § 1983 suit "could not therefore be construed as seeking a judgment at odds with his conviction or with the State's calculation of time to be served in accordance with the underlying sentence.").

[610]See Wilkinson v. Dotson, 544 U.S. 74, 82, 125 S. Ct. 1242, 1248–49 (2005). *Wilkinson* was a challenge to parole hearing procedures, but its holding should be equally applicable to disciplinary proceedings that result in the loss of good time. This point is illustrated by *Whitlock v. Johnson*, 153 F.3d 380 (7th Cir. 1998), which preceded *Wilkinson* but makes a similar distinction. In *Whitlock*, the appeals court said that the lower federal courts have power to order that witness testimony be permitted in future disciplinary hearings, but it could not order either that good time be restored, or that new hearings be held, in cases where prisoners had previously lost good time at hearings where they were not permitted witnesses. 153 F.3d at 389–90.

[611]Peralta v. Vasquez, 467 F.3d 98, 104–06 (2d Cir. 2006) *cert. denied*, 551 U.S. 1145 (2007).

[612]See, e.g., Carmona v. U.S. Bureau of Prisons, 243 F.3d 629, 632 (2d Cir. 2001) (holding that § 2241 is available for challenges to the execution of sentence after conviction); Walker v. O'Brien, 216 F.3d 626, 629 (7th Cir. 2000); Brown v. Smith, 828 F.2d 1493, 1495 (10th Cir. 1987).

The differences among habeas corpus under 28 U.S.C. §§ 2241 and 2254, and federal post-conviction relief under § 2255, are discussed in Ch. 8, §§ H.1, .2.

[613]Carmona v. U.S. Bureau of Prisons, 243 F.3d at 634; Seehausen v. van Buren, 243 F. Supp. 2d 1165, 1167 (D.Or. 2002).

[614]See Ch. 8, § B.4.a, concerning the personal involvement requirement, and Ch. 8, § 0.1, concerning damages.

[615]Cleavinger v. Saxner, 474 U.S. 193, 106 S. Ct. 496 (1985); Tulloch v. Coughlin, 50 F.3d 114, 116–17 (2d Cir. 1995) (applying same rule to a private attorney who served as a hearing officer);Young v. Selsky, 41 F.3d 47, 52–54 (2d Cir. 1994)

(applying same rule to official who reviews disciplinary appeals); Zavaro v. Coughlin, 970 F.2d 1148, 1153 n.2 (1992); Barry v. Whalen, 796 F. Supp. 885, 893–94 (E.D.Va. 1992) (holding reforms since *Cleavinger* did not entitle federal prison hearing officers to absolute immunity).

One federal appeals court has held that in Michigan, because the state provides so many quasi-judicial safeguards, disciplinary hearing personnel, who are licensed attorneys, are entitled to the same absolute immunity as judges. Shelly v. Johnson, 849 F.2d 228 (6th Cir. 1988); *accord*, Branham v. Spurgis, 720 F. Supp. 605, 607 (W.D.Mich. 1989); Banks v. Klapish, 717 F. Supp. 520, 521 (W.D.Mich. 1989). In reality, it appears that prison officials exerted considerable pressure on Michigan hearing officers not to find too many prisoners not guilty, keeping statistical records on them and using disciplinary threats to keep their not guilty rulings to no more than 10%. This allegation was never proven, since the Michigan prison system settled the litigation when they were sued over this practice. *See* Heit v. van Ochten, 126 F. Supp. 2d 487 (W.D.Mich. 2001) (approving settlement forbidding the challenged practices); *see also* Perry v. McGinnis, 209 F.3d 597, 606 (6th Cir. 2000) (noting "overwhelming evidence suggests that there was, at the very least, a strong expectation that the not-guilty/dismissal rate should not rise above 10%"; holding that hearing officer who alleged he was subject to retaliation for deciding too many hearings in prisoners' favor stated a First Amendment claim).

See generally Ch. 8, § L, on immunity questions.

[616]King v. Higgins, 702 F.2d 18, 22 (1st Cir. 1983) (holding that where a new hearing led to a better result for the prisoner, damages were proper for the result of the prior hearing that denied due process).

[617]See, e.g., Trobaugh v. Hall, 176 F.3d 1087, 1089 (8th Cir. 1999) ($100 a day and consideration of punitive damages); Maurer v. Patterson, 197 F.R.D. 244, 249–50 (S.D.N.Y. 2000) ($25,000 lump sum for 30 days in segregation and removal from grievance committee; punitives reduced to $20,000); Soto v. Lord, 693 F. Supp. 8, 22 (S.D.N.Y. 1988) ($50 a day for 60 days punitive segregation, plus lost wages); *see also* Patterson v. Coughlin, 905 F.2d 564, 570 (2d Cir. 1990) (amount of damages was a factual issue and prison officials were entitled to a jury trial even after summary judgment was granted against them on liability). Damages in segregation cases are discussed further in Ch. 8, § 0.1, nn.1011, 1029–1032.

[618]See Ch. 9, § E.2.

Courts have disagreed over who bears the burden of proof on how a properly conducted hearing would have turned out. Some courts have held that once a due process violation has occurred, "the burden of proof shift[s] to the officials to demonstrate that the procedural violation did not cause [the prisoner's] injury."[619] Other courts have held that the plaintiff has the burden of proof that a proper hearing would have come out differently.[620]

One court has held that as long as there is "some evidence" to support the disciplinary charge, damages for the punishment cannot be awarded.[621] We think that this holding is wrong. The presence of "some evidence" means only that if the prisoner had been convicted, the conviction would have stood up under judicial review.[622] The proper question, however, is whether the prisoner *would* have been convicted in a proper hearing conducted by an impartial fact-finder. Presumably this does not happen in every case where there is "some evidence."[623]

Whether a court will find that your punishment was caused by the due process violations may depend on the nature of the violations and the way they affected the hearing. If you are improperly denied witnesses or an impartial fact-finder, or if the fairness of the hearing itself is compromised in some other way, a court is more likely to find that the due process violation caused your conviction than if the violation is merely technical or has no obvious effect on the way the hearing was conducted.[624] An inadequate statement of reasons, even though it comes at the end of the proceeding, can also cause improper convictions;[625] after all, one purpose of statements of reasons is to make the decision-maker think the case through correctly.[626] In any disciplinary case, you must explain to the court in practical terms how the due process violations you complain about affected the outcome of the hearing. This can sometimes get complicated if you have had multiple disciplinary proceedings, since you can only recover damages for things that resulted from the hearing that the court has found unlawful.[627]

In the past, courts have held that even if you would have received the same result at a proper hearing, you could recover damages for any emotional injury you could show was caused by the denial of your due process rights.[628] If you couldn't show that the due process violation caused either a worse result or emotional injury, you would be entitled to nominal damages of one dollar.[629] You might also recover punitive damages, with or without compensatory damages, if you could show that prison officials exhibited malice, ill will, a desire to injure, or reckless indifference to your rights.[630] Now, under the Prison Litigation Reform Act, prisoners may not recover compensatory damages for mental or emotional injury unless they have also suffered physical injury.[631] Courts have generally held that prisoners can receive nominal damages for mental or emotional injury without physical injury, and most have held that they can recover punitive damages.[632]

You may be entitled to recover damages in state court under state law for unlawful discipline, but the law on this point will vary from state to state and you must research the matter carefully. You will have to determine:

- Whether state law recognizes a damage claim for violation of prison regulations;

---

[619]King v. Wells, 760 F.2d 89, 94 n.4 (6th Cir. 1985); *accord,* Franklin v. Aycock, 795 F.2d 1253, 1263–64 (6th Cir. 1986); Staples v. Traut, 675 F. Supp. 460, 466 (W.D.Wis. 1986).

In the Supreme Court case that addressed this question in the context of school suspensions, the lower court had taken this position, holding that the defendant school officials would be expected to prove that the students would have been suspended even if a proper hearing had been held. The Supreme Court did not express disagreement. Carey v. Piphus, 435 U.S. 247, 260, 98 S. Ct. 1042 (1978) (citing Piphus v. Carey, 545 F.2d 30, 32 (7th Cir. 1976)).

[620]Graham v. Baughman, 772 F.2d 441, 446 (8th Cir. 1985); McCann v. Coughlin, 698 F.2d 112, 126–27 (2d Cir. 1982). *But see* Morgan v. Ward, 699 F. Supp. 1025, 1045 (N.D.N.Y. 1988) (awarding damages in a case where the trial testimony "did not adequately establish that plaintiff committed these violations," suggesting that the defendants have the burden of showing that the prisoner was guilty); Pino v. Dalsheim, 605 F. Supp. 1305, 1319 (S.D.N.Y. 1984) ("there is reason to believe that if [the prisoner] had been afforded those rights which he was wrongly denied, he might well have been acquitted of the entire charge," without reference to a burden of proof).

In one case, the court held that the plaintiff usually has the burden of proof, but when the defendants' failure to identify and call witnesses had made it impossible to find them years later, the burden shifted to them. Patterson v. Coughlin, 905 F.2d at 570.

[621]Adams v. Wolff, 624 F. Supp. 1036, 1038 (D.Nev. 1985).

[622]*See* § H.1.i of this chapter.

[623]*See* Patterson v. Coughlin, 905 F.2d at 569 (court refuses to assume that a hearing officer would not believe inmate witnesses).

[624]McCann v. Coughlin, 698 F.2d at 126–27; Pino v. Dalsheim, 605 F. Supp. at 1319.

[625]*See* Franklin v. Aycock, 795 F.2d at 1263–64 (defendants had to show that the plaintiff could not have had his conviction reversed on administrative appeal with a better statement of reasons); Chavis v. Rowe, 643 F.2d 1281, 1287 (7th Cir. 1981) (prisoner might never have been convicted had the committee made detailed findings). *Contra,* Akbar v. Fairman, 788 F.2d 1273, 1278 (7th Cir. 1986).

[626]*See* § H.1.k of this chapter.

[627]*See, e.g.,* Gaston v. Coughlin, 249 F.3d 156, 164 (2d Cir. 2001) (holding where first hearing was reversed, and second hearing complied with the law, and the prisoner got credit for time served on the sentence after the second hearing, all his SHU time was caused by the second hearing, since he would have served that time without the violations at the first hearing).

[628]Lewis v. Smith, 855 F.2d 736, 738 (11th Cir. 1988) ($500 awarded); King v. Wells, 760 F.2d 89, 94 (6th Cir. 1985) ($1000 awarded).

[629]Shango v. Jurich, 965 F.2d 289, 294–95 (7th Cir. 1992); Franklin v. Aycock, 795 F.2d at 1263–64.

[630]Smith v. Wade, 461 U.S. 30, 51, 103 S. Ct. 1625 (1983); *see* Ch. 8, § O.1.d, concerning punitive damages.

[631]42 U.S.C. § 1997e(e).

[632]*See* Ch. 9, § E.1.

- Whether state law recognizes common law tort claims based on improper prison disciplinary proceedings;
- Whether state courts can award damages for federal constitutional violations;
- Whether state rules of immunity, including sovereign immunity, protect either the state or prison officials from damage liability.

This can get pretty complicated. In New York state courts, for example, prison officials cannot be sued personally for damages; suits must be brought against the State itself in the Court of Claims,[633] which only hears state law tort claims and state constitutional claims, not federal constitutional claims.[634] As a matter of tort law, New York courts have held that placing a prisoner in punitive segregation for no legitimate reason and without any process stated a claim for "intentional and malicious action,"[635] but that if the prisoner received any procedural protections, there was no claim for the tort of false imprisonment.[636] They also ruled that improper disciplinary proceedings cannot constitute the tort of malicious prosecution.[637] The state Court of Appeals then held that the State is immune from liability for disciplinary proceedings conducted "under the authority of and in full compliance with the governing statutes and regulations,"[638] and that immunity has been applied even where the disciplinary proceeding was administratively reversed.[639] That immunity ruling would seem to apply to state constitutional torts as well as other state law torts. It seems that New York prisoners can only recover damages for disciplinary confinement if they are not released from segregation at the end of their sentences.[640] So most New York prisoners bring their damage claims based on disciplinary proceedings in federal court under § 1983. These issues do not seem to have been explored very much in other states.[641]

5) *Expungement of Conviction* Since disciplinary convictions may affect parole eligibility or have other "collateral consequences"[642] besides the actual punishment, courts can order the expungement (or "expunction") of the record of your conviction.[643] They will not do this in all cases. Federal courts have held that expungement, like damages, is not appropriate if the prisoner would have been convicted in a properly conducted hearing.[644] However, the conviction should be expunged when there was no evidence to support it,[645] or the due process violations "significantly affected

---

[633]N.Y. Correction Law § 24; *see* Cepeda v. Coughlin, 128 A.D.2d 995, 513 N.Y.S.2d 528, 530 (N.Y.App.Div. 1987), *appeal denied*, 70 N.Y.2d 602 (N.Y. 1987). This statute was recently held unconstitutional as applied to federal § 1983 claims in state court, *see* Haywood v. Drown, ___ U.S. ___, 129 S. Ct. 2108 (2009), but it will probably remain applicable to state law claims in state court.

[634]Brown v. State, 89 N.Y.2d 172, 179–84, 674 N.E.2d 1129, 1133–36 (N.Y. 1996); Gittens v. State, 132 Misc.2d 399, 504 N.Y.S.2d 969, 972 (N.Y.Ct.Cl. 1986).

[635]Wilkinson v. Skinner, 34 N.Y.2d 53, 57–61, 356 N.Y.S.2d 15, 312 N.E.2d 158 (N.Y. 1974).

[636]Gittens v. State, 132 Misc.2d 399, 504 N.Y.S.2d 969 (N.Y.Ct. Cl. 1986); Treacy v. State, 131 Misc.2d 849, 501 N.Y.S.2d 1005 (N.Y.Ct.Cl. 1986), *aff'd on other grounds sub nom.* Arteaga v. State, 72 N.Y.2d 212, 532 N.Y.S.2d 57, 527 N.E.2d 1194 (N.Y. 1988).

The elements of the tort of false imprisonment are (1) detention or imprisonment that is (2) unlawful or not legally justifiable. Hart v. Walker, 720 F.2d 1436, 1439 (5th Cir. 1983); Weisman v. LeLandais, 532 F.2d 308, 311 (2d Cir. 1976).

[637]Gittens v. State, 504 N.Y.S.2d at 974; Treacy v. State, 501 N.Y.S.2d at 1006; *accord*, Greer v. DeRobertis, 568 F. Supp. 1370, 1376 (N.D.Ill. 1983).

The elements of the tort of malicious prosecution are (1) a criminal proceeding (2) instituted by the defendant without probable cause (3) with malice or other improper purpose that (4) terminates in favor of the accused. W. Page Keeton et al., *Prosser and Keeton on the Law of Torts* § 119 (5th ed. 1984). The proper defendant in a malicious prosecution case is the complainant, not the court that hears the case. *Id.* Even if a state recognized a malicious prosecution claim for prison disciplinary proceedings, you would have to get the conviction overturned (have it "terminate in favor of the accused") before you could sue for malicious prosecution.

[638]Arteaga v. State, 527 N.E.2d 1194; *see also* Shivers v. Barnes, 813 S.W.2d 121, 123 (Mo.App. 1991) (official who recommended disciplinary sanction was entitled to immunity for performing a discretionary function).

[639]Minieri v. State, 204 A.D.2d 982, 613 N.Y.S.2d 510 (N.Y.App. Div. .1994).

[640]Minieri v. State, 613 N.Y.S.2d at 511; Gittens v. State, 504 N.Y.S.2d at 974 (failure to release an inmate at the end of his term of punitive confinement was actionable as "wrongful excessive confinement," a "species" of false imprisonment).

[641]*But see* Collier v. Evans, 199 Ga.App. 763, 406 S.E.2d 90 (Ga. App. 1991) (involving false imprisonment claim based on excessive detention resulting from improper disciplinary hearings); Saxton v. Ohio Dep't of Rehab. & Corr., 80 Ohio App.3d 389, 609 N.E.2d 245, 246 (Ohio App. 1992) (erroneous placement in segregation does not constitute the tort of false imprisonment; plaintiff did not challenge his imprisonment); Irby v. Macht, 184 Wis.2d 831, 851, 522 N.W.2d 9, 17 (Wis. 1994) (noting absence of a damage remedy in Wisconsin).

[642]Wolff v. McDonnell, 418 U.S. 539, 565, 94 S. Ct. 2963 (1974).

[643]Del Raine v. Carlson, 826 F.2d 698, 707 (7th Cir. 1987); Powell v. Ward, 643 F.2d 924, 934 (2d Cir. 1981); Fromer v. Scully, 693 F. Supp. 1536, n.4 (S.D.N.Y. 1988); Walker v. U.S., 116 F.R.D. 149, 150–51 (S.D.N.Y. 1987); *see also* Beard v. Livesay, 798 F.2d 874, 880 (6th Cir. 1986) (unlawful reclassification ordered expunged).

[644]Elkin v. Fauver, 969 F.2d 48, 53 (3d Cir. 1993) (employing "harmless error" standard); Powell v. Coughlin, 953 F.2d 744, 750–52 (2d Cir. 1991) (same as *Elkin*); Wells v. Israel, 629 F. Supp. 498 (E.D.Wis. 1986), *aff'd*, 854 F.2d 995 (7th Cir. 1988); Shango v. Jurich, 608 F. Supp. 931, 940 (N.D.Ill. 1985); Coles v. Levine, 561 F. Supp. 146, 153–54 (D.Md. 1983), *aff'd*, 725 F.2d 674 (4th Cir. 1984).

[645]Wilson v. Jones, 430 F.3d 1113, 1124 (10th Cir. 2005); Burnsworth v. Gunderson, 179 F.3d 771, 775 (9th Cir. 1999) (affirming expungement order); Lenea v. Lane, 882 F.2d 1171, 1176

[the prisoner's] ability to demonstrate his innocence."[646] The courts have disagreed whether expungement is appropriate if the officials did not realize they were violating due process.[647] State courts may develop their own standards for when expungement will be required.[648]

6) Injunction If you show that prison officials are employing an unconstitutional procedure as a matter of policy or practice, you may be able to get an injunction telling them to stop it,[649] if you can show that you are at risk of being subjected to the unlawful procedure in the future.[650] Injunctions against disciplinary procedures that deny due process are most often granted in class actions,[651] but they can also be granted in an

individual case if you can establish that what happened to you actually represents prison policy or practice and not just a particular prison employee violating the rules.[652]

s. Disciplinary Proceedings and Criminal Prosecution
Courts have held that the Double Jeopardy Clause of the Constitution[653] does not apply to prison disciplinary proceedings.[654] That means that criminal acts may subject a prisoner both to prison discipline and to criminal prosecution.[655] In fact, you can be subject to prison discipline even if you were acquitted of criminal charges,[656] and vice versa.[657] If you were convicted of criminal charges, you can be disciplined for the criminal acts based solely on the fact that you were convicted.[658]

The fact that a disciplinary charge is also a criminal offense does not mean that your disciplinary hearing must

---

(7th Cir. 1989) (noting record ordered expunged by the lower court).

[646]Hayes v. Thompson, 637 F.2d 483, 493 (7th Cir. 1980); *see* Morgan v. Ellerthorpe, 785 F. Supp. 295, 303 (D.R.I. 1992) (expungement may be appropriate when the prisoner was improperly denied witnesses); Dedrick v. Wallman, 617 F. Supp. 178, 184–86 (S.D.Iowa 1985) (expungement ordered where reasons for finding of guilt were inadequate but not where reasons for the punishment imposed were inadequate); Pino v. Dalsheim, 605 F. Supp. 1305, 1319–20 (S.D.N.Y. 1985) (conviction expunged where inmate was denied witnesses, ability to prepare defense, and impartial fact-finder; conviction not expunged for lack of adequate notice where the prisoner had actual knowledge of the charges and the ability to present a defense); Martin v. Foti, 561 F. Supp. 252, 261–62 (E.D.La. 1983) (conviction expunged based on lack of notice of charges).

[647]*Compare* Hayes v. Thompson, 637 F.2d at 493 (expungement ordered) *with* McKinnon v. Patterson, 568 F.2d 930, 935 (2d Cir. 1977) (expungement denied).

[648]Kenney v. Commissioner of Corrections, 393 Mass. 28, 468 N.E.2d 616, 621 (Mass. 1984) (expungement was proper where inmate had already served part of sentence); Miller v. Iowa District Court for Jones County, 603 N.W.2d 86, 89 (Iowa 1999) (violation of internal policy to delay disciplinary proceedings until related criminal charges were disposed of deprived prisoner of a substantial right, but not a constitutional one, and therefore called for a new hearing but not expungement); Torres v. Coughlin, 166 A.D.2d 793, 563 N.Y.S.2d 152, 153 (N.Y.App.Div. 1990) (denial of right to call witnesses required expungement); Cunningham v. LeFevre, 130 A.D.2d 809, 514 N.Y.S.2d 833 (N.Y.App.Div. 1987) (expungement proper where a new hearing would not be appropriate because of the passage of time); Grant v. LeFevre, 135 Misc.2d 476, 515 N.Y.S.2d 960 (N.Y.Sup. 1987) ("gross abuse" of rights supports expungement); Loveland v. Gorczyk, 173 Vt. 501, 502, 786 A.2d 418, 419 (Vt. 2001) (expungement denied where prisoner's complaint was late response to an administrative appeal).

[649]Wolff v. McDonnell, 418 U.S. 539, 554–55, 94 S. Ct. 2963 (1974). As noted above at n.582, courts are unlikely to grant an injunction to prevent a disciplinary hearing.

[650]*See* Ch. 8, § I, for discussions of standing, mootness, and ripeness.

[651]*See, e.g.*, Austin v. Wilkinson, 372 F.3d 346 (6th Cir. 2004), *aff'd in part and rev'd in part on other grounds*, 545 U.S. 209, 125 S. Ct. 2384 (2005); Whitlock v. Johnson, 153 F.3d 380, 389–90 (7th Cir. 1998) (partly affirming an injunction against a policy of refusing to call witnesses in disciplinary proceedings); Powell v. Ward, 487 F. Supp. 917 (S.D.N.Y. 1980) (entering comprehensive

injunction concerning disciplinary proceedings), *aff'd and modified*, 643 F.2d 924 (2d Cir. 1981).

[652]*See, e.g.*, Williams v. Wilkinson, 132 F. Supp. 2d 601, 611–12 (S.D.Ohio 2001) (enjoining an informal policy of refusing to call witnesses in disciplinary hearings); Muhammad v. Butler, 655 F. Supp. 1466, 1469 (D.N.J. 1985) (officials ordered to provide a disciplinary hearing or restore custody status), *appeal dismissed*, 802 F.2d 447 (3d Cir. 1986) (unpublished); Vines v. Howard, 676 F. Supp. 608, 615–16 (E.D.Pa. 1987) (enjoining hearing officer from sitting in cases in which his son, a prison employee, initiated the charge or was called as a witness).

[653]The Double Jeopardy Clause provides that no person shall "be subject for the same offence to be twice put in jeopardy of life or limb." U.S. Const., Amend. V. *See* § H.1.b of this chapter, n.321, for further discussion of double jeopardy.

[654]Porter v. Coughlin, 421 F.3d 141, 146–48 (2d Cir. 2005); Fogle v. Pierson, 435 F.3d 1252, 1261–62 (10th Cir. 2006); Wirsching v. Colorado, 360 F.3d 1191, 1205 (10th Cir. 2004); Meeks v. McBride, 81 F.3d 717, 722 (7th Cir. 1996); Turner v. Johnson, 46 F. Supp. 2d 655, 666–67 (S.D.Tex. 1999).

[655]Porter v. Coughlin, 421 F.3d at 146–46 (prisoner can be disciplined for the same acts after successful criminal prosecution); U.S. v. Brown, 59 F.3d 102, 104–06 (9th Cir. 1995) (prisoner can be prosecuted for the same acts after disciplinary prosecution); Caudle-El v. Peters, 727 F. Supp. 1175, 1178 (N.D.Ill. 1989); Sierra v. Lehigh County, Pa., 617 F. Supp. 427, 431 (E.D.Pa. 1985); State v. Killebrew, 109 Wis.2d 611, 327 N.W.2d 155 (Wis.App. 1982), *aff'd*, 115 Wis.2d 243, 340 N.W.2d 470 (1983); *see also* U.S. ex rel. Conklin v. Beyer, 678 F. Supp. 1109, 1111 (D.N.J. 1988) (statute permitting parole board to postpone parole eligibility based on disciplinary convictions did not subject prisoners to double jeopardy, violate due process, or constitute a bill of attainder).

[656]Rusher v. Arnold, 550 F.2d 896, 897–98 (3d Cir. 1977); Wilson v. Farrier, 372 N.W.2d 499, 502 (Iowa 1985); People v. Sylvester, 165 A.D.2d 920, 560 N.Y.S.2d 530, 532 (N.Y.App.Div. 1990).

[657]People v. Jones, 301 Ill.App.3d 608, 703 N.E.2d 994 (App. 1998) (holding a prisoner cleared of an offense at a disciplinary hearing could still be prosecuted criminally for it).

[658]Porter v. Coughlin, 964 F. Supp. 97, 103–04 (W.D.N.Y. 1997) (holding that the criminal trial provided due process, so it didn't matter if witnesses were denied at the disciplinary hearing), *aff'd*, 421 F.3d 141 (2d Cir. 2005).

provide the safeguards of a criminal trial.[659] Under the fed-eral Constitution, you are not entitled to a retained or appointed attorney in a disciplinary proceeding even if you could be prosecuted for the same conduct,[660] though state law may allow for counsel in such cases.[661] Disciplinary action by prison officials also does not make you an "accused" and trigger your rights to counsel and to a speedy trial even if you are later criminally prosecuted.[662]

---

[659]Ramer v. Kerby, 936 F.2d 1102, 1105 (10th Cir. 1991); *see* Cerda v. O'Leary, 746 F. Supp. 820, 826 (N.D.Ill. 1990) (rule prohibiting acts that would violate state or federal law did not require that the prisoner first be convicted of the criminal offense beyond a reasonable doubt).

[660]Baxter v. Palmigiano, 425 U.S. 308, 315, 96 S. Ct. 1551 (1976) (rejecting the view that prisoners are entitled to representation at disciplinary hearings where the charges involve conduct punishable as a crime under state law); *see* Wolff v. McDonnell, 418 U.S. 539, 569–70, 94 S. Ct. 2963 (1974). Some state courts have said in dicta that there may be a right to counsel in this situation. *See In re* Pierpoint, 271 Kan. 620, 634, 24 P.3d 128, 138 (2001) (stating that "in the exceptional case, where . . . the inmate faces possible felony charges as a result of the disciplinary violation, . . . due process requires an attorney to represent the interest of such inmates"); Witter v. State, 112 Nev. 908, 920–21, 921 P.2d 886, 895 (1996) (stating that there may be a Sixth Amendment right to counsel when the disciplinary charge involves conduct punishable under state law). However, such statements appear contrary to *Baxter v. Palmigiano.*

In *Witter v. State,* the court held that a prison disciplinary conviction for possessing a knife could be put in evidence in the penalty phase of a capital prosecution notwithstanding that the prisoner had not had a lawyer in the disciplinary proceeding, since his action was not a punishable offense under state law.

[661]*See* Harrah v. Leverette, 165 W.Va. 665, 271 S.E.2d 322, 327–28 (W.Va. 1980) (holding the presence of a state prosecutor at the hearings entitled the prisoners to counsel); McGinnis v. Stevens, 543 P.2d 1221, 1232 (Alaska 1975) (holding prisoners under investigation for felony prosecution were entitled to counsel under the Alaska Constitution).

Under some circumstances, prisoners are entitled to assis-tance in disciplinary proceedings from a staff member or another inmate. *See* § H.1.f of this chapter. In some prison systems, such assistance is provided in all or most serious disciplinary cases. One court has held that if the prison system offers you an assistant, statements you make to the assistant cannot then be used against you in a criminal prosecution. State v. Melendez, 172 Ariz. 68, 834 P.2d 154, 157–59 (Ariz. 1992). *But see* State v. Foster, 199 Ariz. 39, 42–43, 13 P.3d 781, 784–85 (Ariz.App. 2000) (refusing to apply *Melendez* where the State did not offer the assistant). However, statements you make to "jailhouse lawyers" or assistants who are not appointed by prison authorities are not privileged and can be used against you. *See* Ch. 3, § C.2.c, n.567.

[662]U.S. v. Gouveia, 467 U.S. 180, 104 S. Ct. 2292 (1984) (holding prisoners were not entitled to the appointment of counsel until they were indicted and arraigned even though they had been in administrative detention for 19 months).

The Court in *Gouveia* did not decide the question of when the right to speedy trial attaches, but noted that lower courts have held that it was not triggered by segregation of a prisoner. 467 U.S. at 190, n.6; *see* U.S. v. Harris, 12 F.3d 735, 736 (7th Cir. 1994) (holding

The Fifth Amendment to the Constitution says: "No person . . . shall be compelled in any criminal case to be a witness against himself. . . ."[663] In disciplinary proceedings you are only partially protected by this "privilege against self-incrimination" because prison disciplinary hearings are not criminal proceedings.[664] The state cannot force you to testify at the disciplinary hearing without granting you some degree of immunity.[665] However, if you don't testify, your silence can be used as evidence against you at the

---

retention in disciplinary segregation pending commencement of criminal proceedings was not an arrest under Speedy Trial Act or Sixth Amendment); U.S. v. Duke, 527 F.2d 386, 389–90 (5th Cir.1976); U.S. v. Moore, 299 F. Supp. 2d 623, 628 (S.D.W.Va. 2004) (administrative segregation did not trigger speedy trial right), *aff'd,* 116 Fed.Appx. 421 (4th Cir. 2004) (unpublished); State v. Luke, 382 So.2d 1265, 1267 (Fla.App. 1980) (holding pre-indictment delay while prisoners remained in administrative segregation did not deny due process without a showing of prejudice in the criminal proceeding).

You should also be aware of the Supreme Court's decision in *Kuhlmann v. Wilson,* 477 U.S. 436, 106 S. Ct. 2616 (1986), that the prosecution may use statements a prisoner makes even after arraignment to an informant placed in the prisoner's cell as long as the informant does not actually question the accused prisoner. *But see* Arizona v. Fulminante, 499 U.S. 279, 111 S. Ct. 1247 (1991) (holding that a confession obtained by a prison informant who offered to protect the defendant from other inmates if he would talk about his crime was inadmissible).

[663]U.S.Const., Amend. V.

Strictly speaking, the Fifth Amendment by itself only applies to the federal government, but the Fourteenth Amendment's Due Process Clause makes the privilege against self-incrimination binding on state officials. Malloy v. Hogan, 378 U.S. 1, 84 S. Ct. 1489 (1964).

[664]Baxter v. Palmigiano, 425 U.S. 308, 317, 96 S. Ct. 1551 (1976).

[665]Baxter v. Palmigiano, 425 U.S. at 316–17; Tinch v. Henderson, 430 F. Supp. 964, 968–69 (M.D. Tenn. 1977).

A grant of immunity, for purposes of the privilege against self-incrimination, is a promise that testimony or information you give will not be used against you in a criminal proceeding. There are two kinds of immunity. "Use and derivative use" immunity means that the information you give, or any information that is obtained based on it, cannot be used against you. "Transactional immunity," by contrast, would protect you from any criminal pros-ecution for any acts you disclose, regardless of what other evidence the prosecutor may obtain from other sources. *See* Kastigar v. U.S., 406 U.S. 441, 92 S. Ct. 1653 (1972) (distinguishing two types of immunity). It is unlikely that you will be granted transactional immunity to testify in a disciplinary hearing. An example of a grant of use and derivative use immunity is the statement included in misbehavior reports issued in the New York State prisons: "You are hereby advised that no statement made by you in response to the charge, or information derived therefrom may be used against you in a criminal proceeding." 7 N.Y.C.R.R. § 251–3.1(c)(d)(1) (1992); *see* Cliff v. Kingsley, 293 A.D.2d 954, 742 N.Y.S.2d 408 (App.Div. 2002) (holding that use and derivative use immunity satisfies Fifth Amendment; transactional immunity need not be granted).

disciplinary hearing.[666] If you do testify without a grant of immunity, it is possible that anything you say could be used against you in a subsequent criminal prosecution, depending on the law of your state.[667] Some state courts have held that disciplinary hearing testimony may not be used at all in criminal cases.[668] Others have held that disciplinary hearing testimony may be used in criminal cases only if the inmate receives *Miranda* warnings.[669] In other states, prisoners are informed before their hearings that their testimony cannot be used in subsequent criminal proceedings, and the courts will enforce these promises.[670]

The privilege against self-incrimination applies only to statements. Physical evidence such as blood, urine, or DNA samples is not "testimonial" in nature and therefore raises no issue of self-incrimination.[671]

Self-incrimination issues in prison are not limited to disciplinary proceedings.[672] Prison sexual offender programs often raise significant self-incrimination issues, which are discussed in another chapter.[673]

Whether *Miranda* warnings are required during investigations of prison misconduct that may result either in disciplinary charges or in criminal charges depends on all the circumstances of the prisoner's interrogation.[674] Courts have held that if prison personnel question you "on the scene" or spontaneously and non-coercively, the interrogation is not "custodial" and you are not entitled to *Miranda* warnings.[675] *Miranda* warnings are required when you are being investigated for criminal conduct unrelated to prison discipline; interrogation of a prisoner under those circumstances is considered "custodial" under *Miranda*.[676] The failure to give you *Miranda* warnings is important only in connection with a subsequent criminal prosecution; it does not affect the validity of prison disciplinary proceedings.[677]

---

[666]Baxter v. Palmigiano, 425 U.S. at 317–19.

In *Baxter*, the court emphasized that there was other evidence of guilt in addition to the prisoner's silence. We think it is fair to conclude that your silence alone is not enough to support a conviction; prison officials must come up with some evidence other than your silence. However, one court has held that a prisoner's refusal to testify "created such a strong adverse presumption as to render further testimony irrelevant." Scott v. Kelly, 962 F.2d 145, 147 (2d Cir. 1992). We think this decision is extreme and that other courts are not likely to go that far.

[667]*See* People v. Wyngaard, 462 Mich. 659, 672–74, 614 N.W.2d 143, 149–50 (2000) (holding that a prisoner's choice between testifying in a disciplinary hearing, and possibly incriminating themselves, and giving up the chance to testify on her own behalf, does not compel prisoners to incriminate themselves).

[668]Avant v. Clifford, 67 N.J. 496, 341 A.2d 629, 653–54 (N.J. 1975). *But see* People v. Wyngaard, 462 Mich. 659, 672–74, 614 N.W.2d 143, 149–50 (2000) (overruling its prior decision barring the use of prison hearing testimony in criminal prosecutions).

[669]Grant v. State, 154 Ga.App. 758, 270 S.E.2d 42 (Ga.App. 1980); State v. Harris, 176 Mont. 70, 576 P.2d 257 (Mont. 1978).

Miranda v. Arizona, 384 U.S. 436, 467–74, 86 S. Ct. 1601 (1966), requires that arrested suspects be warned that they have the right to remain silent, that anything they say can be used against them in court, that they have the right to talk to a lawyer and have her present during the questioning, and that counsel will be appointed if they cannot afford a lawyer. If you are not given *Miranda* warnings when they are required, any statements you make at that time may have to be suppressed in a later criminal prosecution. However, the *Miranda* protections do not prevent prosecutors from using statements that you made without the proper warnings for the purpose of impeaching your testimony if you testify at your criminal trial. Harris v. New York, 401 U.S. 222, 91 S. Ct. 643 (1971).

[670]*See, e.g.,* People v. Nunez-Ramos, 160 A.D.2d 1029, 554 N.Y.S.2d 947, 949 (N.Y.App.Div.), *appeal denied*, 76 N.Y.2d 793 (N.Y. 1990). In *People v. Wyngaard*, 462 Mich. 659, 664–69, 614 N.W.2d 143, 145–48 (2000), the court overruled its earlier decision holding that testimony from disciplinary proceedings can't be used in criminal prosecutions. However, it held that in the case before it, since the prisoner had been told his testimony could not be used criminally, that promise had to be kept.

[671]*See* Ch. 3, § E.2, n.919.

[672]*See, e.g.,* State v. Canas, 597 N.W.2d 488, 496–97 (Iowa 1999) (holding an arrestee who had drugs on his person and failed to disclose them on entry to the jail could be prosecuted for introducing a controlled substance into a detention facility, despite his claim that to disclose them would have incriminated himself).

[673]*See* Ch. 2, § F.4.b, nn.523–525.

[674]People v. Patterson, 146 Ill.2d 445, 167 Ill.Dec. 1045, 588 N.E.2d 1175, 1180–81 (Ill.1992) (*Miranda* warnings were not required for prisoner who was questioned in restraints in investigator's office about security-related matters); *see* Arthur v. State, 575 So.2d 1165, 1187–91 (Ala.Cr.App. 1991) (prisoner who had been removed from work release to county jail was entitled to *Miranda* warnings when interrogated by work release supervisor); State v. DePue, 237 Mont. 428, 774 P.2d 386, 388 (Mont. 1989) (reclassification hearing was not an interrogation for *Miranda* purposes); Walker v. State, 102 Nev. 290, 720 P.2d 700, 701 (Nev. 1986) (statements elicited by counselor investigating offense could not be used in prosecution because *Miranda* warnings had not been given).

[675]*See, e.g.,* U.S. v. Conley, 779 F.2d 970, 974 (4th Cir. 1985); U.S. v. Scalf, 725 F.2d 1272, 1275–76 (10th Cir. 1984); Cervantes v. Walker, 589 F.2d 424, 427–28 (9th Cir. 1978).

[676]Mathis v. U.S., 391 U.S. 1, 4–5, 88 S. Ct. 1503 (1968).

[677]Montgomery v. Anderson, 262 F.3d 641, 646 (7th Cir. 2002) (holding failure to give *Miranda* warnings is "irrelevant to prison discipline"); Tinch v. Henderson, 430 F. Supp. 964, 967 (M.D. Tenn. 1977); *see* Bradley v. State, 473 N.W.2d 224, 226–29 (Iowa App. 1991) (holding lack of *Miranda* warnings during pre-hearing investigation did not invalidate disciplinary proceeding because the prisoner was not considered "in custody").

2. Administrative Segregation[678]

As explained earlier,[679] placement in administrative segregation requires due process protections only if (a) the confinement "imposes atypical and significant hardship . . . in relation to the ordinary incidents of prison life,"[680] *and* there is a state-created liberty interest in staying out of segregation,[681] or in not being kept there for long periods.[682] The law varies from state to state as to when and whether placement or retention in segregation is "atypical and significant" enough to require due process.[683] There were many decisions on this point before *Sandin v. Conner*, but they are not reliable after *Sandin*. In the absence of a liberty interest, the only protection against arbitrary imposition of administrative segregation will be enforcement of state law in state courts.

Even where there is a liberty interest, the Supreme Court has held that less procedural protection is required for administrative segregation than for disciplinary hearings, stating that being put in segregation was not "of great consequence" because the prisoner was "merely transferred from one extremely restricted environment to an even more confined situation. Unlike disciplinary confinement the stigma of wrongdoing or misconduct does not attach to administrative segregation . . . [and] there is no indication that administrative segregation will have any significant effect on parole opportunities."[684] It also said that putting someone in administrative segregation "turns largely on 'purely subjective evaluations and on predictions of future behavior'" and on "intuitive judgments" that "would not be appreciably fostered by the trial-type procedural safeguards" of disciplinary hearings.[685] In other words, the Supreme Court thought that since administrative segregation is not really based on facts, fact-finding procedures are not helpful.

For these reasons, the Court said, due process requires only "an informal nonadversary review of the information supporting [the prisoner's] administrative confinement."[686] Officials must provide:

(1) "[S]ome notice of the charges."[687] Courts have generally held that this notice may be less formal and detailed than the notice required for disciplinary charges.[688] However, one recent decision held that due process requires "a notice that is something more than a mere formality. . . . The effect of the notice should be to

---

[678]Administrative segregation is segregation that is supposedly not punitive but is imposed pending investigation of misconduct charges, to prevent future misconduct or other violations of security and order, or to protect the person who is segregated, or while a prisoner is awaiting transfer or classification. Sometimes different names are used: "maximum security," "involuntary protective admission," "close custody," etc.

This section discusses only the due process aspects of confinement in administrative segregation. Limits on the conditions and restrictions of segregation units are discussed in Ch. 2, § J.

[679]*See* §§ A, F of this chapter.

[680]Sandin v. Conner, 515 U.S. 472, 484, 115 S. Ct. 2293 (1995).

[681]Decisions to date have found no constitutionally based liberty interest even if the confinement is of extremely long duration. Williams v. Armontrout, 852 F.2d 377, 378–79 (8th Cir. 1988) (13 years).

[682]*See* Tellier v. Fields, 280 F.3d 69, 82–83 (2d Cir. 2000) (analyzing federal prison regulations); *accord*, Iqbal v. Hasty, 490 F.3d 143, 161–62 (2d Cir. 2007) (holding *Tellier* is not abrogated by *Wilkinson v. Austin*), *aff'd in part, rev'd in part, and remanded on other grounds sub nom.* Ashcroft v. Iqbal, ___ U.S. ___, 129 S. Ct. 1937 (2009).

[683]*See* § F.7 of this chapter.

[684]Hewitt v. Helms, 459 U.S. 460, 473, 103 S. Ct. 864 (1983). In the Court's later "supermax" decision, conditions were much more restrictive than in *Hewitt*, and the Court did not say that supermax confinement is "not . . . of great importance" in that case. But it did say that "[t]he private interest at stake here, while more than minimal, must be evaluated, nonetheless, within the context of the prison system and its attendant curtailment of liberties." Wilkinson v. Austin, 545 U.S. 209, 225, 125 S. Ct. 2384 (2005). Conversely, it

---

held that the State's interest was "a dominant consideration. . . . The State's first obligation must be to ensure the safety of guards and prison personnel, the public, and the prisoners themselves." *Id.* at 227. It also gave weight to scarce resources and the high cost of incarceration, stating that "courts must give substantial deference to prison management decisions before mandating additional expenditures for elaborate procedural safeguards when correctional officials conclude that a prisoner has engaged in disruptive behavior." *Id.* at 228.

[685]Hewitt v. Helms, 459 U.S. at 474; *accord, Wilkinson*, 545 U.S. at 228; Toussaint v. McCarthy, 801 F.2d 1080, 1100 (9th Cir. 1986).

[686]*Hewitt*, 459 U.S. at 472; *accord, Wilkinson*, 545 U.S. at 229; Banks v. Fauver, 801 F. Supp. at 1430–31.

[687]*Hewitt*, 459 U.S. at 476; *see* Brown v. Plaut, 131 F.3d 163, 171 n.9 (D.D.C. 1997) (holding that notice need not be in advance of the hearing); Matiyn v. Henderson, 841 F.2d at 36 (if inmate was placed in segregation for four days without receiving notice, due process was violated); Brown v. District of Columbia, 66 F. Supp. 2d 41, 45 (D.D.C. 1999) (holding that prisoner who did not get notice before or during his hearing of the alleged misconduct for which he was to be segregated "was not afforded the most basic process—an opportunity to know the basis on which a decision will be made and to present his views on that issue or issues"); Loukas v. Hofbauer, 784 F. Supp. 377, 380 (E.D.Mich. 1991) (explaining the charge at the hearing and offering an adjournment provided sufficient notice). *But see* Rahman X v. Morgan, 300 F.3d 970, 974 (8th Cir. 2002) (rejecting the plaintiff's claim that he did not receive notice on the ground that he knew enough to request a hearing).

[688]Stringfellow v. Perry, 869 F.2d 1140, 1142–43 (8th Cir. 1989) (statements that "more extensive investigation" was needed were sufficient); Toussaint v. McCarthy, 801 F.2d 1080, 1100–01 (9th Cir. 1986) ("detailed written notice of charges" is not required); Dell'Orfano v. Scully, 692 F. Supp. 226 (S.D.N.Y. 1988) (notice that plaintiff was suspected of using drugs because he had needle marks was adequate). *But see* Pardo v. Hosier, 611 F. Supp. 693, 698 (C.D.Ill. 1985) (notice that a prisoner was being investigated, but not what for, was insufficient), *rev'd on other grounds*, 946 F.2d 1278 (7th Cir. 1991).

compel 'the charging officer to be [sufficiently] specific as to the misconduct with which the inmate is charged" to inform the inmate of what is is accused of doing so that he can prepare a defense to those charges and not be made to explain away vague charges set out in a misbehavior report."[689] More recently, the Supreme Court said that "[r]equiring officials to provide a brief summary of the factual basis for the classification review and allowing the inmate a rebuttal opportunity safeguards against the inmate's being mistaken for another or singled out for insufficient reason."[690]

(2) "[A]n opportunity [for the prisoner] to present his views" to the decision-maker, orally or in writing.[691] Prisoners must be able to present their views directly to the person who actually makes the decision.[692] This must occur "within a reasonable time" after the confinement.[693] What is "reasonable" depends on the reason for delay.[694]

(3) "[S]ome sort of periodic review" to determine if there is a need for continued segregation. This need not involve new evidence or statements.[695] The courts have not pinpointed

---

[689]Taylor v. Rodriguez, 238 F.3d 188, 192–93 (2d Cir. 2001) (holding that a notice referring only to "past admission to outside law enforcement," "recent tension . . . involving gang activity," and "statements by independent confidential informants" were too vague; officials must provide specific allegations of conduct involving current gang involvement); *accord*, Brown v. Plaut, 131 F.3d 163, 172 (D.D.C. 1997) ("If Brown was not provided an accurate picture of what was at stake in the hearing, then he was not given his due process."); Brown v. District of Columbia, 66 F. Supp. 2d 41, 45 (D.D.C. 1999) (holding that prisoner who was not informed of the alleged misconduct for which he was to be segregated "was not afforded the most basic process—an opportunity to know the basis on which a decision will be made and to present his views on that issue or issues"); Nettles v. Griffith, 883 F.Supp. 136, 143, 145 (E.D.Tex. 1995) (holding that conversation with jail official in which he was not told of any charges against him or that he would be segregated did not meet due process standards; damages awarded).

[690]Wilkinson v. Austin, 545 U.S. 209, 226, 125 S. Ct. 2384 (2005).

[691]Hewitt v. Helms, 459 U.S. 460, 476, 103 S. Ct. 864 (1983); Jackson v. Cain, 864 F.2d 1235, 1252 (5th Cir. 1989); *see* Wilkinson v. Austin, 545 U.S. 209, 226, 125 S. Ct. 2384 (2005) (noting the importance of "a fair opportunity for rebuttal" and approving a system that provided "the opportunity to be heard at the Classification Committee [initial] stage" and "to submit objections prior to the final level of review"). *Wilkinson* also noted that if one reviewer recommended against placement, a later reviewer could not overturn that recommendation, though the Court did not say this safeguard is constitutionally required. 545 U.S. at 226.

We believe that a prisoner who is not literate, or not literate in a language the prison officials can read, is entitled as a matter of due process to present her views orally, since a written presentation is not meaningful for an inmate in that position. We are not aware of any case law on that issue.

[692]Hatch v. District of Columbia, 184 F.3d 846, 852 (D.C. Cir. 1999) (holding that prisoner who was not allowed to attend his hearing and had an exchange of letters with other prison officials had not had an opportunity to present his views to the decision-maker); Toussaint v. McCarthy, 926 F.2d 800, 803 (9th Cir. 1990); Gittens v. LeFevre, 891 F.2d 38, 41–42 (2d Cir. 1989); *see* Stewart v. Almeida, 418 F. Supp. 2d 1154, 1167 (N.D.Cal. 2006) (where the person who interviewed the plaintiff was the same person who had submitted the gang validation request, plaintiff "had a meaningful opportunity to present his views to the critical decisionmaker" even though someone else formally validated him).

[693]Hewitt v. Helms, 459 U.S. at 472. Since a hearing within a "reasonable time" is required, a post-deprivation remedy like a damage claim does not satisfy due process. Loukas v. Hofbauer, 784 F. Supp. at 382.

Time limits on segregation before disciplinary hearings are discussed further at § D.1.g of this chapter.

[694]Hatch v. District of Columbia, 184 F.3d 846, 852 (D.C. Cir. 1999) (holding an exchange of letters between prison officials, seven weeks after initial placement, was not "a reasonable time following his transfer"); Layton v. Beyer, 953 F.2d at 850–51 (20 days might be unreasonable depending on the justification); Russell v. Coughlin, 910 F.2d 75, 78 (2d Cir. 1990) (10 days' delay with no explanation except inadvertence was not reasonable); Matiyn v. Henderson, 841 F.2d 31, 36 (2d Cir. 1988) (confinement for four days with no hearing denied due process; state regulation providing for no hearing for those held less than 14 days would be unconstitutional); Sourbeer v. Robinson, 791 F.2d 1094, 1100 (3d Cir. 1986) (35 days presents a "close question" but is approved); Hayes v. Lockhart, 754 F.2d 281 (8th Cir. 1985) (15-day delay approved); Green v. Bauvi, 792 F. Supp. 928, 938–39 (S.D.N.Y. 1992) (disobeying prison's own time limit was not reasonable); Russell v. Coughlin, 774 F. Supp. 189, 197 (S.D.N.Y.) (11 days delay did not deny due process because prison officials explained it satisfactorily), *reargument granted on other grounds*, 782 F. Supp. 876 (S.D.N.Y. 1991); Scott v. Coughlin, 727 F. Supp. 806, 809 (W.D.N.Y. 1990) (six and eight days without justification denied due process); Nelson v. Bryan, 607 F. Supp. 959 (D.Nev. 1985) (5–8 days approved); Perez v. Neubert, 611 F. Supp. 830 (D.N.J. 1985) (three weeks upheld where 170 inmates were involved); *see also* Gittens v. LeFevre, 891 F.2d at 41–42 (due process requirements for pre-hearing keeplock were not satisfied by a disciplinary hearing after several days).

[695]Hewitt v. Helms, 459 U.S. at 477 n.9; Magluta v. Samples, 375 F.3d 1269, 1278–79 & n.7, 1283 (11th Cir. 2004); Ramsey v. Squires, 879 F. Supp. 270, 283 (W.D.N.Y. 1995) (holding regulations that did not provide for periodic review unconstitutional), *aff'd*, 71 F.3d 405 (2d Cir. 1995) (unpublished); *see* Knight v. Armontrout, 878 F.2d 1093, 1095 (8th Cir. 1989) (lack of personal appearance at periodic review did not deny due process); Hameed v. Coughlin, 37 F. Supp. 2d 133, 138–39 (N.D.N.Y. 1999) (holding periodic review did not require input from the prisoner, and could be based on facts determined at initial placement and the review officer's general knowledge of prison conditions and tensions; "disrespectful attitude" justified continuing segregation); Edmonson v. Coughlin, 21 F. Supp. 2d 242, 253–54 (W.D.N.Y. 1998) (upholding review process that did not permit the prisoner to submit information); Eggleton v. Gluch, 717 F. Supp. 1230, 1234–35 (E.D.Mich. 1989) (administrative review could be denied because there was a pending investigation that justified continued segregation, and nothing the plaintiff could say would have affected the FBI's pending investigation), *aff'd*,

how often this review must be conducted. One court has held that every 120 days is sufficient.[696] Others have held that intervals of around a month are adequate[697] but intervals approaching a year deny due process.[698] Review must be meaningful; due process is not satisfied by perfunctory review and rote reiteration of stale justifications.[699] Prison officials should give notice if new evidence is to be presented at review hearings or if the

hearings are not conducted on a regular and frequent schedule.[700]

The Court in *Hewitt* did not say anything about written dispositions or about impartial decision-makers. A few courts have held that statements of reasons are not required by due process.[701] However, the Supreme Court said in *Wilkinson v. Austin* that Ohio "requires that the decision-maker provide a short statement of reasons. This requirement guards against arbitrary decisionmaking while also providing the inmate a basis for objection before the next decisionmaker or in a subsequent classification review."[702] This explanation suggests that the statement of reasons is a due process requirement, even though the Court did not say so explicitly. This reasoning makes sense for review hearings as well as initial hearings; without a statement of reasons, it is impossible to determine whether a prisoner's continuing confinement is based on a continuing justification or whether it is just the "rote reiteration of stale justifications" that courts have condemned.[703] The courts have not resolved whether an impartial decisionmaker is required for administrative segregation decisions.[704]

Common reasons for placing or retaining prisoners in administrative segregation include pending investigations or disciplinary charges,[705] risk of escape or other security threats,[706] involvement in gangs or other "security threat

---

916 F.2d 712 (6th Cir. 1990). Periodic review was not addressed by the Supreme Court in the *Wilkinson v. Austin* decision.

If you are being kept in segregation for reasons different than the ones for which you were first placed there, we think that you should have the right to submit new evidence or statements and, in some cases, appear personally. For example, if you were first put in segregation for investigation of some offense, and then kept in on the basis that your attitude is still dangerous, it is hard to see how prison officials can assess your attitude without talking with you.

[696]Toussaint v. McCarthy, 926 F.2d at 803; *see* Smith v. Shettle, 946 F.2d 1250, 1255 (7th Cir. 1991) (30-day intervals are not constitutionally required). *But see* Hatori v. Haga, 751 F. Supp. 1401, 1407–08 (D.Haw. 1989) (30-day review required in conformity with defendants' own regulations).

[697]Rahman X v. Morgan, 300 F.3d 970, 974 (8th Cir. 2002) (holding 60-day review satisfied due process); Luken v. Scott, 71 F.3d 192, 194 (5th Cir. 1995) (holding 90-day review adequate); Garza v. Carlson, 877 F.2d 14, 17 (8th Cir. 1989) (monthly reviews upheld); Clark v. Brewer, 776 F.2d 226, 234 (8th Cir. 1985) (weekly hearings for two months and monthly hearings thereafter upheld); Mims v. Shapp, 744 F.2d 946, 952–54 (3d Cir. 1984) (30–day review adequate).

[698]McQueen v. Tabah, 839 F.2d 1525, 1529 (11th Cir. 1988) (11 months without review stated a due process claim); Toussaint v. McCarthy, 801 F.2d 1080, 1101 (9th Cir. 1986) (12 months without review denied due process).

[699]Sourbeer v. Robinson, 791 F.2d 1094, 1101 (3d Cir. 1986); McClary v. Kelly, 87 F. Supp. 2d 205, 214 (W.D.N.Y. 2000) (stating that review must be "'meaningful'" and not a "sham or fraud," upholding damage verdict for sham review), *aff'd*, 237 F.3d 185 (2d Cir. 2001); Smart v. Goord, 441 F. Supp. 2d 631, 642 (S.D.N.Y. 2006) (allegation that review hearings were a "hollow formality" and officials did not actually consider releasing plaintiff stated a due process claim); Giano v. Kelly, 869 F. Supp. 143, 150 (W.D.N.Y. 1994) (stating that "prison officials must be prepared to offer evidence that the periodic reviews held are substantive and legitimate, not merely a 'sham'"); *see* Thompson-El v. Jones, 876 F.2d 66, 69 n.6 (8th Cir. 1989) (dictum) (a claim that there was an "ongoing investigation" might not justify six months' segregation when there was little or no actual investigation going on). *But see* Edmonson v. Coughlin, 21 F. Supp. 2d 242, 253–54 (W.D.N.Y. 1998) ("The fact that the ASRC repeated the same rationale each week, and did not enable Edmonson to submit information is not a basis for finding that the ASRC violated due process." Though the process should have been "better documented," it need not be "formalized."); Golub v. Coughlin, 885 F. Supp. 42, 45–46 (N.D.N.Y. 1995) (holding that review that cited nothing but the crime the prisoner had committed and the resulting publicity was adequate).

[700]Clark v. Brewer, 776 F.2d at 234.

[701]Toussaint v. McCarthy, 801 F.2d 1080, 1101 (9th Cir. 1986); *accord*, Jones v. Moran, 900 F. Supp. 1267, 1275 (N.D.Cal. 1995).

[702]Wilkinson v. Austin, 545 U.S. 209, 226, 125 S. Ct. 2384 (2005) (citing Greenholtz v. Inmates of Nebraska Penal and Correctional Complex, 442 U.S. 1, 16, 99 S. Ct. 2100 (1979)).

[703]*See* Sourbeer v. Robinson, 791 F.2d 1101, 1104 (3d Cir. 1986); *see* Sheley v. Duger, 833 F.2d 1420, 1427 (11th Cir. 1987) (hearing ordered to determine if there was continuing justification for 12-year confinement); *cf.* Wolff v. McDonnell, 418 U.S. 539, 565, 94 S. Ct. 2963 (1974) (explaining the need for written records).

[704]*See* Shoats v. Horn, 213 F.3d 140, 146 (3d Cir. 2000) (rejecting claim of bias because there were many decision-makers who all reached the same conclusion; not deciding whether an impartial fact-finder is required); Woods v. Edwards, 51 F.3d 577, 582–82 (5th Cir. 1995) (noting lack of evidence to support claim of biased periodic review; "tribunal having at least 'an apparent impartiality towards the charges'" required); Parenti v. Ponte, 727 F.2d 21, 25 (1st Cir. 1984) (Classification Board members whose recommendations were nonbinding did not have to be impartial.); Gomez v. Coughlin, 685 F. Supp. 1291, 1297 (S.D.N.Y. 1988) (due process may require a decisionmaker with an "open mind").

[705]Skinner v. Cunningham, 430 F.3d 483, 486–87 (1st Cir. 2005) (40 days' segregation pending murder investigation of prisoner was appropriate); Pardo v. Hosier, 946 F.2d 1278, 1281–83 (7th Cir. 1991); Russell v. Coughlin, 910 F.2d 75, 77–78 (2d Cir. 1990); *see* Bowe v. Smith, 119 Misc.2d 453, 465 N.Y.S.2d 391, 393 (N.Y.Sup. 1983) (regulations permit pre-hearing confinement "whenever an officer reasonably believes a rule has been violated").

[706]*See, e.g.*, Martin v. Tyson, 845 F.2d 1451, 1457 (5th Cir. 1988).

groups,"[707] protection of the segregated inmate,[708] and recent transfer.[709] Prison officials' reasons deny due process only if they are clearly arbitrary or the segregation is clearly excessive.[710] Some courts have suggested that as the length of segregation increases, prison officials' burden of justification for continued segregation also increases.[711]

The Supreme Court said in *Hewitt* that in making segregation decisions, prison officials may consider "the character of the inmates confined in the institution, recent and longstanding relations between prisoners and guards, prisoners *inter se* [among themselves], and the like . . .; rumor, reputation, and even more imponderable factors . . . 'purely subjective evaluations' . . . intuitive judgments."[712] Officials therefore need not promulgate objective criteria for release

from administrative segregation.[713] However, despite the endorsement of "rumor, reputation, . . . [and] intuitive judgments" as a basis for segregation, several courts have applied the same requirement of "reliable" evidence to administrative segregation decisions that courts have applied to disciplinary proceedings.[714]

State law may provide additional safeguards not required by the *Hewitt* decision. Violation of state law rules generally does not deny due process,[715] and you will have to enforce such rules in state court.[716] It may also be possible to convince a state court that the state constitution requires more procedural protections than *Hewitt v. Helms* provides.[717]

---

[707]Taylor v. Rodriguez, 238 F.3d 188, 193 (2d Cir. 2001); Toussaint v. McCarthy, 926 F.2d 800, 802 (9th Cir. 1990); *see* Koch v. Lewis, 216 F. Supp. 2d 994, 1004–07 (D.Ariz. 2001) (holding that actions and not mere membership in a gang must be shown to justify placement in indefinite administrative confinement), *vacated as moot*, 399 F.3d 1099 (9th Cir. 2005).

[708]*See, e.g.*, Meriwether v. Faulkner, 821 F.2d 408, 416 (7th Cir. 1987) (transsexual prisoner segregated for own protection); Golub v. Coughlin, 885 F. Supp. 42, 45–46 (N.D.N.Y. 1995) (holding that a charge for a heinous murder was sufficient reason to keep a prisoner in involuntary protective custody).

[709]*See* § H.4 of this chapter.

[710]*See* Clark v. Brewer, 776 F.2d 226, 234–35 (8th Cir. 1985) (fear of adverse staff or inmate reaction may be considered, but the mere possibility of such reaction cannot by itself justify segregation); Perez v. Neubert, 611 F. Supp. 830, 839–40 (D.N.J. 1985) (defendants could not continue the segregation of all "Marielito" prisoners based only on their group membership). Some courts have held that placing a detainee in administrative segregation solely because the prosecution has decided to seek the death penalty is improper. U.S. v. Catalan-Roman, 329 F. Supp. 2d 240, 253 (D.P.R. 2004); U.S. v. Lopez, 327 F. Supp. 2d 138, 143 (D.P.R. 2004); *see* Lopez, *id.* at 144 ("Placement in SHU limits the amount and kind of mitigating evidence that a capital defendant might bring to the penalty phase.").

[711]Sheley v. Dugger, 833 F.2d 1420, 1427 (11th Cir. 1987) (allegation of 10-year segregation with no new information stated a due process claim); Meriwether v. Faulkner, 821 F.2d 408, 416 (7th Cir. 1987) (protracted segregation unrelated to misconduct presents "a very difficult question"); Mims v. Shapp, 744 F.2d 946, 951-52 (3d Cir. 1984).

[712]Hewitt v. Helms, 459 U.S. 460, 474, 103 S. Ct. 864 (1983) (citations omitted); *accord*, Shoats v. Horn, 213 F.3d 140, 146 (3d Cir. 2000) (holding prison officials' conclusion that plaintiff was a current threat to security and good order justified retention in segregation); Mims v. Shapp, 744 F.2d 946, 952–53 (3d Cir. 1984); Crosby-Bey v. District of Columbia, 598 F. Supp. 270 (D.D.C. 1984) (prisoner could be segregated because of injuries suggesting he had been in a fight). *But see* Ryan v. Sargent, 969 F.2d 638, 640–41 (8th Cir. 1992) (use of confidential informant information requires the same safeguards of reliability as in disciplinary cases); Jackson v. Bostick, 760 F. Supp. 524, 530–31 (D.Md. 1991) (substantive due process requires an independent determination based on reliable information before a prisoner can be segregated as an escape risk); U.S. v. Gotti, 755 F. Supp. 1159, 1164 (E.D.N.Y. 1991) ("subjective

belief' of what was in a detainee's mind, without more" did not justify administrative detention).

[713]Clark v. Brewer, 776 F.2d at 236; Mims v. Shapp, 744 F.2d at 952–53.

[714]Taylor v. Rodriguez, 238 F.3d 188, 194 (2d Cir. 2001) (holding requirement not met by confidential informant information not supported by any indicia of reliability); *accord*, Bruce v. Ylst, 351 F.3d 1283, 1288 (9th Cir. 2003) (holding evidence of plaintiff's gang involvement had "sufficient indicia of reliability" to justify segregation); Ryan v. Sargent, 969 F.2d 638, 640–41 (8th Cir. 1992) (use of confidential informant information requires the same safeguards of reliability as in disciplinary cases); Koch v. Lewis, 216 F. Supp. 2d 994, 1003 (D.Ariz. 2001) (holding that confinement in supermax unit required evidence with sufficient "indicia of reliability" to justify indefinite confinement), *vacated as moot*, 399 F.3d 1099 (9th Cir. 2005); Jackson v. Bostick, 760 F. Supp. 524, 530–31 (D.Md. 1991); *see* U.S. v. Gotti, 755 F. Supp. 1159, 1164 (E.D.N.Y. 1991) (subjective belief of what was in a detainee's mind, without more' did not justify administrative detention). *But see* Edmonson v. Coughlin, 21 F. Supp. 2d 242, 252 (W.D.N.Y. 1998) (what "evidence" means must be understood in light of the predictive function of administrative segregation; "a judgment call based on evidence that might not be admissible in a civil trial can constitute 'some evidence' in support of AS confinement;" upholding segregation based on newspaper reports and the actions of state and federal authorities in response to escape plans; holding that hearing officer must have decided that confidential information was reliable, since he said he relied on it). *Edmonson* was overruled by *Taylor v. Rodriguez*, cited above, but may still be persuasive to some courts.

[715]Drayton v. Robinson, 719 F.2d 1214, 1218–19 (3d Cir. 1983); Nelson v. Bryan, 607 F. Supp. 959, 961 (D.Nev. 1985); Smallwood-El v. Coughlin, 589 F. Supp. 692, 698–99 (S.D.N.Y. 1984); Monahan v. Wolff, 585 F. Supp. 1198, 1201 (D.Nev. 1984).

[716]*See, e.g.*, Kenney v. Commissioner of Correction, 393 Mass. 28, 468 N.E.2d 616, 619–20 (Mass. 1984) (prisoner's placement in disciplinary unit pending a hearing and the failure to obtain the Commissioner's authorization for pre-hearing confinement violated state regulations).

[717]The California courts have held that their state constitution requires procedural protections for administrative segregation placement similar to those required in disciplinary hearings. *In re* Davis, 25 Cal.3d 384, 158 Cal.Rptr. 384, 599 P.2d 690, 695 (Cal. 1979); *In re* Carr, 116 Cal.App.3d 962, 967–71, 172 Cal.Rptr. 417, 420–23 (1981); Inmates of Sybil Brand Institute for Women v. County of Los Angeles, 130 Cal.App.3d 89, 108, 181 Cal.Rptr. 599,

In theory, administrative segregation cannot be used as a pretext for punitive confinement.[718] Thus, keeping a prisoner in administrative segregation based on a misconduct charge of which she has been cleared denies due process.[719] But making the distinction between punitive and non-punitive confinement can be difficult, partly because a rules violation and a security threat may arise from the same conduct,[720] and partly because prison officials have a history of trying to "avoid their due process responsibilities simply by relabelling the punishments imposed on prisoners."[721]

Courts have taken different approaches to this problem. One court has held that confinement that is partly punitive in intent is governed by *Hewitt* and not by *Wolff v. McDonnell* if the inmate would have been segregated anyway without the punitive motive.[722] This rule invites abuse, since prison officials can always claim they would have confined the prisoner anyway. Another federal court has held that segregation for violating a rule requires *Wolff v. McDonnell* rights even if it is labelled "administrative."[723] A third decision holds that if a prisoner is already in administrative segregation and prison officials wish to keep her there based on a new act of misconduct for which no disciplinary hearing has been held, they must permit witness testimony on the same basis as in an ordinary disciplinary hearing.[724] We think that the last two decisions are correct, since any case involving the factual question whether or not an inmate broke a rule is one for which the fact-finding procedures of *Wolff v. McDonnell* are appropriate.[725]

3. Restraints

Most litigation about the use of restraints is about whether restraint practices violate the substantive law.[726] Practices that apply to all prisoners, or all prisoners in a particular group (*e.g.*, restraining all prisoners during transportation outside the prison, or all segregation prisoners whenever they are out of their cells) will not present procedural due process issues. However, policies that apply selectively to individual prisoners based on their actions, their histories, etc., may present procedural due process questions, and the courts are divided over how to approach them.

We think the best approach is that prolonged or extreme physical restraint deprives prisoners of liberty that is directly protected by the Constitution. The Supreme Court has stated: "[L]iberty from bodily restraint always has been recognized as the core of the liberty protected by the Due Process Clause from arbitrary governmental action," and it survives criminal conviction and incarceration, pretrial detention, or involuntary civil commitment.[727] That principle applies to prison restraint practices, though it is "highly qualified" in prison and must be balanced against the justifications for the practices.[728] That means every

---

609 (1982); *see also* Tasker v. Griffith, 238 S.E.2d 229, 234 (W.Va. 1978) (limiting reasons for administrative segregation).

In arguing for a better due process standard in state court, you should rely on the arguments made by earlier federal court cases that were overruled by *Hewitt. See, e.g.*, Wright v. Enomoto, 462 F. Supp. 397, 402–04 (N.D.Calif. 1976), *summarily affirmed*, 434 U.S. 1052, 98 S. Ct. 1223 (1978); Helms v. Hewitt, 655 F.2d 487, 497–500 (3d Cir. 1981), *rev'd*, 459 U.S. 460, 103 S. Ct. 864 (1983); Bono v. Saxbe, 450 F. Supp. 934, 942–43 (E.D.Ill. 1978), *aff'd in pertinent part*, 620 F.2d 609, 618 (7th Cir. 1982).

[718]Brown-El v. Delo, 969 F.2d 644, 648–49 (8th Cir. 1992); Sheley v. Duger, 833 F.2d 1420, 1427 (11th Cir. 1987); Toussaint v. McCarthy, 801 F.2d 1080, 1102 (9th Cir. 1986); Van Poyck v. Dugger, 582 So.2d 108, 109 (Fla.App. 1991); *see also* Willoughby v. Luster, 717 F. Supp. 1439, 1441 (D.Nev. 1989) (whether detention was administrative or disciplinary in nature was a factual question for the court).

[719]Childs v. Pellegrin, 822 F.2d 1382, 1388 (6th Cir. 1988). *But see* Dell'Orfano v. Scully, 692 F. Supp. 226, 230 (S.D.N.Y. 1988) (prison officials conceded that inmates were sometimes placed in administrative segregation when there wasn't enough proof to support "formal charges"); Adams v. Wolff, 624 F. Supp. 1036, 1038–39 (D.Nev. 1985) (upholding retention of prisoner in protective custody after his disciplinary term was over).

[720]If you are found guilty of a disciplinary offense after a proper hearing, prison officials may place you in administrative segregation based on the conviction without giving you a separate hearing. Walker v. Mintzes, 771 F.2d 920, 933 (6th Cir. 1985).

[721]Taylor v. Clement, 433 F. Supp. 585, 586–87 (S.D.N.Y. 1977); *accord*, Sanders v. Woodruff, 908 F.2d 310, 316 (8th Cir. 1990) (dissenting opinion) ("One of the unanticipated and unfortunate consequences of *Wolff v. McDonnell* has been the tendency of prison administrators to label disciplinary actions administrative rather than punitive to avoid having to comply with the due process requirements of *Wolff*."); *see* Hendrix v. Faulkner, 525 F. Supp. 435, 462 (N.D.Ind. 1981) (repeated short lockups for "investigation" without charges or hearing denied due process), *aff'd in part and vacated and remanded in part on other grounds sub nom.* Wellman v. Faulkner, 715 F.2d 269 (7th Cir. 1983).

[722]Matiyn v. Henderson, 841 F.2d 31, 37 (2d Cir. 1988).

[723]Woodson v. Lack, 865 F.2d 107, 109–10 (6th Cir. 1989); *see* Sheley v. Duger, 833 F.2d at 1427 (allegation of 10-year confinement with no new evidence "raises the possibility that Sheley is being disciplined for prior conduct"). *Contra*, Nelson v. Bryan, 607 F. Supp. 959, 961 (D.Nev. 1985) (segregation for a fixed period based on a rule violation is not necessarily punitive).

[724]Clark v. Brewer, 776 F.2d 226, 235 (8th Cir. 1985).

[725]*See* § H.1 of this chapter, n.283, and § H.2 of this chapter, n.685, concerning this distinction.

[726]Restraint practices may violate the Eighth Amendment for convicts or substantive due process for pretrial detainees. *See* Ch. 2, § G.2.c.(3).

[727]Youngberg v. Romeo, 457 U.S. 307, 316, 102 S. Ct. 2452 (1982) (internal quotation marks and citation omitted).

[728]Benjamin v. Fraser, 264 F.3d 175, 188 (2d Cir. 2001). This decision involved pretrial detainees, and the court said that the *Sandin* "atypical and significant" analysis does not apply to detainees because that analysis starts with the idea that a criminal *conviction* broadly extinguishes prisoners' liberty. However, the decision explicitly states that the particular right to freedom from bodily restraint survives a criminal conviction, so its reasoning should apply to cases involving convicts. *See also* Murphy v. Walker, 51 F.3d 714, 718 (7th Cir. 1995) (detainees have a liberty interest in freedom from restraint and government must have a legitimate

routine instance of restraint, such as being restrained after a disturbance or use of force, will not require due process. However, restraint practices that are unusual or prolonged should do so. For example, one jail system's "Red ID" policy provided that prisoners who used or possessed weapons in jail, or had a prior record of doing so, were kept shackled, rear-handcuffed and in "tube mitts" for periods of many hours when taken to court; the court directed jail officials to provide due process protections to determine whether the accused prisoner had actually used or possessed weapons.[729]

If the use or continuation of restraints requires due process, what process is due? The courts have not fully explored this question. In the above-mentioned "Red ID" decision, officials were subjecting prisoners to restraints whenever they left the prison because of misconduct they had supposedly engaged in. In that situation, prison officials were required to provide the safeguards required by *Wolff v. McDonnell* to determine whether prisoners have committed acts of misconduct for disciplinary purposes.[730] Other restraint situations are intended to address what prison staff considers an immediate risk of violent or disruptive conduct. One federal appeals court held that in such a situation, pre-hearing process was impractical and post-deprivation process was sufficient, meaning that at some point (it didn't say when) the continuation of restraints would require due process.[731] However, a lower court has suggested that pre-deprivation process may be possible, and

post-deprivation process inadequate, in some situations where staff seek to restrain prisoners immediately.[732]

When restraints are used for medical or psychiatric purposes, they must be authorized and supervised by medical or psychiatric personnel.[733] When prisoners are restrained during court proceedings for security reasons, the decision is supposed to be made by the court.[734]

4. Transfers

Transfers between prisons[735] can usually be done without due process protections.[736] This principle is not limited to transfers within states. Due process is generally not constitutionally required in connection with transfers between state and federal custody;[737] from one state to another;[738] from county or city jail to state prison;[739] to a private

---

penological or medical reason for using it); Branham v. Meachum, 77 F.3d 626, 629–30 (2d Cir. 1996) (allegation of placement in restraints without a hearing or administrative review stated a due process claim under pre-*Sandin* law; prisoner should have a chance to address *Sandin*).

[729]Benjamin v. Fraser, 264 F.3d at 181–82, 189–90.

[730]*See Benjamin*, 264 F.3d at 189–90. The lower court had also required a mandatory medical examination to determine whether there were medical reasons prisoners could not be kept in the restraints for long periods; the appeals court expressed its doubt that this measure was necessary, but did not reverse it. *Benjamin*, 264 F.3d at 191 n.13. In *Dawes v. Coughlin*, 964 F. Supp. 652, 658 (N.D.N.Y. 1997), *aff'd*, 159 F.3d 1346 (2d Cir. 1998) (unpublished), defendants issued "restraint orders" to a segregation prisoner based on his violent and threatening behavior. The court held that the weekly review of restraint orders, the availability of the grievance program, and the availability of a judicial remedy in state court provide the process due.

[731]Williams v. Benjamin, 77 F.3d 756, 769–70 & n.10 (4th Cir. 1996). The plaintiff in *Williams* was restrained for eight hours. *See also* Sadler v. Young, 325 F. Supp. 2d 689, 705–06 (W.D.Va. 2004) (a prisoner placed in four-point restraints had a right to procedural protection during his confinement to ensure that its continuation was not arbitrary and capricious; court does not say what protections; a chance to tell his story before restraint, and a disciplinary hearing for the underlying incident, are irrelevant), *rev'd and remanded on other grounds*, 118 Fed.Appx. 762 (4th Cir. 2005) (unpublished); Davis v. Lester, 156 F. Supp. 2d 588, 595–96 (W.D.Va. 2001) (finding a due process claim in connection with five-point restraints, not stating the process due).

[732]Fitts v. Witkowski, 920 F. Supp. 679, 684–85 (D.S.C. 1996) (noting relative lack of urgency where staff wanted to place prisoner in four-point restraints because he had spit on an officer, and staff spent 20 minutes getting approval and signatures, showing that some process was not impossible).

[733]*See* Ch. 2, § F.4.a, n.507.

[734]*See* Ch. 10, § Q.

[735]This chapter deals with transfers that are done for purposes of prison administration. If you have pending criminal charges or an outstanding sentence or warrant in another jurisdiction, that jurisdiction may attempt to extradite you or may lodge a detainer. Detainer and extradition proceedings are beyond the scope of this Manual.

[736]Meachum v. Fano, 427 U.S. 215, 224–25, 96 S. Ct. 2532 (1976) (a criminal conviction "has sufficiently extinguished the defendant's liberty interest to empower the state to confine him in *any* of its prisons" (emphasis supplied)); *see* Sandin v. Conner, 515 U.S. 472, 484, 115 S. Ct. 2293 (1995) (statutes and prison regulations do not create a liberty interest unless they impose "atypical and significant hardship" on prisoners); Cochran v. Morris, 73 F.3d 1310, 1318 (4th Cir. 1996) (en banc) (applying *Sandin* to reaffirm that transfers do not require due process).

Meachum and *Sandin* mean that even if prison officials choose to provide hearings in connection with transfers, unfairness or failure to follow rules in those hearings will not deny constitutional rights, *see Cochran, id.*, though they may violate state law.

[737]Johnson v. Moore, 948 F.2d 517, 519 (9th Cir. 1991); Sisbarro v. Warden, Massachusetts State Penitentiary, 592 F.2d 1, 4 (1st Cir. 1979); Fletcher v. Warden, 467 F. Supp. 777 (D.Kan. 1979) and cases cited.

The statutory basis for state-federal transfers is discussed later in this section.

[738]Olim v. Wakinekona, 461 U.S. 238, 245–48, 103 S. Ct. 1741 (1983); White v. Lambert, 370 F.3d 1002, 1013 (9th Cir. 2004); Sisbarro v. Warden, Massachusetts State Penitentiary, 592 F.2d at 3; Tucker v. Angelone, 954 F. Supp. 134, 136 (E.D.Va. 1997), *aff'd*, 116 F.3d 473 (4th Cir. 1997) (unpublished); Tyson v. Tilghman, 764 F. Supp. 251, 253 (D.Conn. 1991). The Interstate Corrections Compact, under which many such transfers are arranged, is discussed later in this section.

[739]Cobb v. Aytch, 643 F.2d 946, 953–56 (3d Cir. 1981); Dolphin v. Manson, 626 F. Supp. 229, 236 (D.Conn. 1986); Epps v. Levine, 457 F. Supp. 561, 564 (D.Md. 1978). Pretrial detainees may,

prison;[740] or to a distant location and an alien cultural climate.[741] This rule applies even if the transfer is to a higher security institution,[742] is done in response to alleged misconduct,[743] or causes you to lose program opportunities.[744] Nor is due process generally required in connection with transfers between housing units in the same prison,[745]

_____

however, have constitutional liberty interests related to their criminal defense that are infringed by such transfers. *See* n.753 in this section.

The failure to transfer a prisoner promptly from a local jail to a prison after conviction does not violate his due process or other constitutional rights. Waters v. Bass, 304 F. Supp. 2d 803, 805–06 (E.D.Va. 2004). It may be illegal for other reasons. *See* Ch. 2, § B.1, n.122.

[740]Overturf v. Massie, 385 F.3d 1276, 1279 (10th Cir. 2004); White v. Lambert, 370 F.3d 1002, 1013 (9th Cir. 2004); Pischke v. Litscher, 178 F.3d 497, 500 (7th Cir. 1999).

[741]Olim v. Wakinekona, 461 U.S. at 247–48; Ali v. Gibson, 631 F.2d 1126, 1134–35 (3d Cir. 1980); *see also* Lyons v. Clark, 694 F. Supp. 184, 187 (E.D.Va. 1988) (holding sentencing judge's recommendation that a federal prisoner be kept "in this area" was not binding on prison officials).

[742]Meachum v. Fano, 427 U.S. 236, 216–25, 96 S. Ct. 2532 (1976); Freitas v. Ault, 109 F.3d 1335, 1337 (8th Cir. 1997); Bruscino v. Carlson, 854 F.2d 162, 167 (7th Cir. 1988); Harris v. McDonald, 737 F.2d 662, 663–65 (7th Cir. 1984); Williams v. Wells, 744 F.2d 1345, 1346 (8th Cir. 1984); Gilmore v. Goord, 415 F. Supp. 2d 220, 223 (W.D.N.Y. 2006); Gomez v. Carlson, 685 F. Supp. 1291, 1297–98 (S.D.N.Y. 1988); Paoli v. Lally, 636 F. Supp. 1252, 1256–66 (D.Md. 1986), *aff'd*, 812 F.3d 1489 (4th Cir. 1987); *see* Armstrong v. Lane, 771 F. Supp. 943, 948 (C.D.Ill. 1991) (holding placement on "circuit rider" program of repeated transfers among segregation units did not deny due process).

[743]Montanye v. Haymes, 427 U.S. 235, 242, 96 S. Ct. 2543 (1976); Meachum v. Fano, 427 U.S. at 228; Castaneda v. Henman, 914 F.2d 981, 983 (7th Cir. 1990); Gatson v. Coughlin, 679 F. Supp. 270, 272 (W.D.N.Y. 1988).

[744]Zimmerman v. Tribble, 226 F.3d 568, 571–72 (7th Cir. 2000) (holding transfer to prison where the plaintiff could not participate in programs and earn good time did not require due process protections); Tanner v. Federal Bureau of Prisons, 433 F. Supp. 2d 117, 123–24 (D.D.C. 2006); Fort v. Reed, 623 F. Supp. 1106, 1108 (E.D.Wash. 1985) (holding reduced chances for a furlough did not require due process before transfer); Smith v. Halford, 570 F. Supp. 1187, 1191 (D.Kan. 1983) (same, for loss of work release program); Burnside v. Frey, 563 F. Supp. 1344, 1345 (E.D.Mo. 1983) (same, for loss of sex offender treatment program); Clark v. Commissioner of Corrections, 512 A.2d 327, 329 (Me. 1986) (same, for loss of opportunity to earn discretionary good time).

[745]Williams v. Faulkner, 837 F.2d 304, 308–09 (7th Cir. 1988), *aff'd on other grounds sub nom.* Nietzke v. Williams, 490 U.S. 319, 109 S. Ct. 1827 (1989); Mathews v. Fairman, 779 F.2d 409, 411–15 (7th Cir. 1985); Sorenson v. Murphy, 874 F. Supp. 461, 463 (D.Mass. 1995); Chandler v. Lord, 601 F. Supp. 681, 683 (S.D.N.Y. 1985), *aff'd*, 767 F.2d 907 (2d Cir. 1985).

If the "transfer" is to disciplinary or administrative segregation, of course, a different question may be presented depending on the severity of conditions and length of confinement. *See* § F of this chapter.

or with the denial of a transfer.[746] Contrary to what some prisoners believe, interstate transfers or transfers to private prisons do not cause the sentencing state to "lose jurisdiction" over the prisoner.[747]

The Due Process Clauses will only require procedural protections in connection with a transfer of a convicted prisoner if the transfer deprives the prisoner of a right that is independently protected by the Constitution, or if it imposes "atypical and significant hardship" relative to ordinary prison conditions.[748] An example of the first category (the only example we know of at this point) is transfer to a mental hospital, which requires due process protections in the form of a commitment hearing.[749] An example of the second (again, the only one we know of) is transfer to a high-security "supermax" unit for a potentially indefinite period of time under extremely harsh and restrictive conditions.[750] If you argue that your transfer imposes atypical and significant hardship, you will probably also have to show that there is a state-created liberty interest. Exactly how this is done after *Sandin v. Conner* is not entirely clear.[751]

_____

[746]Paoli v. Lally, 812 F.2d 1489, 1493 (4th Cir. 1987); Nash v. Black, 781 F.2d 665, 668 (8th Cir. 1986); Marshall v. Reno, 915 F. Supp. 426, 430–31 (D.D.C. 1996) (holding a Canadian prisoner had no liberty interest in being transferred to Canada to serve his sentence).

[747]Overturf v. Massie, 385 F.2d 1276, 1279 (10th Cir. 2004) (criminal jurisdiction remains with the sentencing jurisdiction regardless of transfers; transfers do not result in "constructive pardon"); White v. Lambert, 370 F.3d 1002, 1013 n.10 (9th Cir. 2004); Koos v. Holm, 204 F. Supp. 2d 1099, 1103 (W.D.Tenn. 2002); Slater v. McKinna, 997 P.2d 1196, 1200 (Colo. 2000); Hunt v. State Dep't of Corrections, 985 P.2d 651, 652–53 (Colo. 1999).

[748]Sandin v. Conner, 515 U.S. 472, 484, 115 S. Ct. 2293 (1995); *see* § A of this chapter.

[749]Vitek v. Jones, 445 U.S. 480, 494–96, 100 S. Ct. 1254 (1980); *see* § A.1, n.29 of this chapter; *see also* Ch. 2, § F.4.a, nn.493–498. The process due before a prisoner is committed to a mental hospital includes written notice, an adversary hearing including the right to present witnesses and confront and cross-examine adverse witnesses, an independent decision-maker, a written decision, and assistance from a qualified and independent adviser. Miller v. Vitek, 437 F. Supp. 569, 575 (D.Neb. 1977), *aff'd as modified sub nom.* Vitek v. Jones, 445 U.S. 480, 496–500, 100 S. Ct. 1254 (1980).

[750]Wilkinson v. Austin, 545 U.S. 209, 223–24, 125 S. Ct. 2384 (2005). This case, though it involved transfer to a different institution, is really more like an administrative segregation due process case than the usual transfer case. *See* § H.2 of this chapter.

[751]*See* § B of this chapter. Even before *Sandin*, most transfer statutes and regulations were held not to create a liberty interest. *See, e.g.*, Schroeder v. McDonald, 55 F.3d 454, 462 (9th Cir. 1995) (holding a policy that prisoners must be held in the least restrictive environment consistent with their classification did not create a liberty interest because the policies permit exceptions and deviations); Smith v. Massachusetts Dep't of Correction, 936 F.2d 1390, 1397 (1st Cir. 1991); Matiyn v. Henderson, 841 F.2d 31, 34 (2d Cir. 1988); Beard v. Livesay, 798 F.2d 874, 879 (6th Cir. 1986) (finding liberty interest in classification but not in transfer); Leonard v. Norris, 797 F.2d 683, 684 (8th Cir. 1986); Rizzo v. Dawson, 778 F.2d 527, 530–31 (9th Cir. 1985). There were a few

State law may provide greater protections against transfers than the federal Constitution; generally you will have to enforce such state law in state court.[752]

Pretrial detainees may be in a slightly different situation from convicts with respect to transfers. Some courts have held that detainees are entitled to due process protections if they are transferred to state prisons and the result is interference with their Sixth Amendment rights to effective assistance of counsel and to a speedy trial.[753]

Prisoners are often held in segregation before or after being transferred. Such segregation is a form of administrative segregation and will only require due process protection under limited circumstances.[754]

Transfers may violate substantive constitutional rights even if they do not present a due process issue. Transfers in retaliation for bringing litigation or for exercising other constitutional rights are unlawful,[755] as are transfers that

seriously threaten a prisoner's life or safety.[756] In some circumstances, transfers may be constitutionally required to protect life and safety.[757] One court has held that transferring prisoners to a state where their religious rights would be less well accommodated than in their home state could violate the Religious Land Use and Institutionalized Persons Act.[758] However, transfers to distant locations that interfere with visiting do not violate the Constitution.[759]

Transfers between different prison systems are usually authorized by statute or contract. Many transfers between states are arranged through the Interstate Corrections Compact (ICC),[760] under which groups of states adopt uniform statutes governing interstate transfers and then make contracts among themselves.[761] Courts have generally held

---

[752]*See, e.g.*, Blake v. Commissioner of Correction, 390 Mass. 537, 457 N.E.2d 281, 282 (Mass. 1983) (enforcing regulation requiring notice and hearing before transfer); Watson v. Whyte, 162 W.Va. 26, 245 S.E.2d 916 (W.Va. 1978) (holding state constitution required the same procedural protections as for a parole revocation proceeding in order to transfer a prisoner from a "forestry center" to a penitentiary); *see also* People v. Ramirez, 25 Cal.3d 260, 268–69, 599 P.2d 622 (1979) (finding state constitutional liberty interest in avoiding transfer from California Rehabilitation Commission facility to prison).

[753]Cobb v. Aytch, 643 F.2d 995, 955–56 (4th Cir. 1981); Muslim v. Frame, 854 F. Supp. 1215, 1228–29 (E.D.Pa. 1994); *see* Epps v. Levine, 457 F. Supp. 561, 564–67 (D.Md. 1978) (holding state law created a due process right to a court determination before a detainee was transferred to state prison). *But see* Falcon v. Knowles, 807 F. Supp. 1531, 1533 (S.D.Fla. 1992) (holding transfer of federal detainees to a federal prison in another state did not violate the Constitution); Black v. Delbello, 575 F. Supp. 28, 29–30 (S.D.N.Y. 1983) (holding transfer of detainee to another county jail to relieve overcrowding was within officials' discretion); *accord*, Lyons v. Papontomiou, 558 F. Supp. 4 (E.D.Tenn.), *aff'd*, 705 F.2d 455 (6th Cir. 1982).

[754]*See* § H.1.g of this chapter.

[755]*See* Ch. 3, §§ B.6, C.1.c, concerning retaliation claims.

exceptions, often in very specialized transfer situations. *See* Barfield v. Brierton, 883 F.2d 923, 936–37 (11th Cir. 1989) (holding state statutes and regulations appeared to create a liberty interest in a youthful offender's remaining in a youth institution); Maldonado Santiago v. Velazquez Garcia, 821 F.2d 822, 827–28 (1st Cir. 1987) (holding regulation limiting emergency transfers created a liberty interest); Reese v. Sparks, 760 F.2d 64, 67 (3d Cir. 1985) (finding state law liberty interest in avoiding punitive transfer); Angell v. Henneberry, 92 Md.App. 279, 607 A.2d 590, 597–98 (Md.App. 1992) (holding that statute created a liberty interest in remaining in a treatment facility); Johnson v. Ward, 64 A.D.2d 186, 409 N.Y.S.2d 670 (N.Y.App.Div. 1978) (state statute gave inmate grievance representative a liberty interest in avoiding transfer); Kelly v. Powers, 477 N.W.2d 586, 588–89 (N.D. 1991) (holding statute required a hearing before out-of-state transfer if the inmate did not consent).

[756]Fitzharris v. Wolff, 702 F.2d 836, 839 (9th Cir. 1983); Gullatte v. Potts, 654 F.2d 1007, 1012–13 (5th Cir. 1981); Roba v. U.S., 604 F.2d 215, 218–19 (2d Cir. 1979). These cases will generally be evaluated under the "deliberate indifference" test. *See* Ch. 2, §§ G.1, G.3 concerning personal safety. *See also* Ross v. U.S., 641 F. Supp. 368, 372 (D.D.C. 1986) (in a proper case, claim of negligent transfer resulting in assault could be litigated under Federal Tort Claims Act).

[757]Walker v. Lockhart, 713 F.2d 1378, 1383 (8th Cir. 1983); Streeter v. Hopper, 618 F.2d 1178, 1182 (5th Cir. 1980). *But see* Moore v. Schuetzle, 486 F. Supp. 2d 969, 481–82 (D.N.D. 2007) (federal courts' power to order transfers does not extend to making federal prisons take custody of state prisoners), *aff'd as modified*, 289 Fed. Appx. 962 (8th Cir. 2008) (unpublished); People v. Brack, 821 P.2d 928, 930 (Colo.App. 1991) (prisoner could be retained in protective custody rather than given an interstate transfer).

[758]Gartrell v. Ashcroft, 191 F. Supp. 2d 23, 39 (D.D.C. 2002), *appeal dismissed*, 2003 WL 1873847 (D.C. Cir., Apr. 11, 2003) (unpublished) (requiring D.C. prisoners whose Rastafarian or other religious practice was burdened by Virginia hair and beard rules to be returned to D.C.).

[759]Olim v. Wakinekona, 461 U.S. 238, 248 n.9, 103 S. Ct. 1741 (1983); Davis v. Carlson, 837 F.2d 1318, 1319 (5th Cir. 1988); Brown-Bey v. U.S., 720 F.2d 467, 470 (7th Cir. 1983); Lyons v. Clark, 694 F. Supp. 184, 186–88 (E.D.Va. 1988) (no liberty interest in staying near one's family and community); Pitts v. Meese, 684 F. Supp. 303, 315 (D.D.C. 1987), *aff'd*, 866 F.2d 1450 (D.C. Cir. 1989); Dozier v. Hilton, 507 F. Supp. 1299, 1307 (D.N.J. 1981); Johnson v. Brelje, 482 F. Supp. 125, 132 (N.D.Ill. 1979); *see* Ali v. Gibson, 631 F.2d 1126 (3d Cir. 1980) (upholding transfer from Virgin Islands to mainland).

[760]Prisoners may also be transferred between states pursuant to executive agreements or other contracts not made under the ICC. Merchant v. State Dep't of Corrections, 168 P.3d 856, 865 (Wyo. 2007); Daye v. State, 171 Vt. 475, 478–79, 769 A.2d 630 (Vt. 2000) (prison commissioner's power to contract for out-of-state transfer was not limited to contracts conforming to the ICC); Transfers may be arranged under the Interstate Agreement on Detainers (IAD) for the limited purpose of resolving out-of-state criminal proceedings. Prisoners transferred under the IAD may be held in county jails and not admitted to the state's prison system. *See* Merchant v. State Dep't of Corrections, *supra*.

[761]Trujillo v. Williams, 465 F.3d 1210, 1218 n.8 (10th Cir. 2006). If a state adopts the ICC, it will enact it as part of its own statutes. *Id.* (citing statutes).

that the ICC does not constitute federal law enforceable under § 1983.[762]

The terms of the ICC generally relate to arrangements among state governments and do not confer any rights on prisoners.[763] The Compact does provide that a transferred inmate may not be deprived "of any legal rights which said inmate would have had if confined in an appropriate institution of the sending state," that hearings to which the prisoner is entitled are to be conducted according to the law of the sending state, and that a transferred inmate shall have any benefits she would have been accorded in prison in the sending state.[764] Despite this language, courts have generally held that states receiving prisoners under the ICC may treat them according to their own policies and do not have to give them the benefit of the policies of their home states,[765] unless the prisoner has a liberty or property interest in those benefits (which is usually not the case).[766] That result may seem inconsistent with the above-cited provisions of the ICC, but it is consistent with the statute's provision that transferred prisoners "shall be treated equally with such similar inmates of the receiving state as may be confined in the same institution."[767] That means that ordinarily, challenges to treatment in prison after an interstate transfer must be brought in the receiving state.[768] However, if in fact the receiving state follows directions or decisions from the sending state in its treatment of a particular prisoner, the prisoner may be able to challenge that treatment in an action against the sending state's officials in the sending state's courts.[769]

State-to-federal transfers have generally been accomplished pursuant to a statute which authorizes the Attorney General to contract with states "for the custody, care,

---

[762]Smith v. Cummings, 445 F.3d 1254, 1259 (10th Cir. 2006); Garcia v. LeMaster, 439 F.3d 1215, 1219 (10th Cir. 2006); Ghana v. Pearce, 159 F.3d 1206, 1208 (9th Cir. 1998); Stewart v. McManus, 924 F.2d 138, 142 (8th Cir. 1991). An interstate agreement constitutes federal law enforceable under § 1983 only if "the subject matter of that agreement is an appropriate subject for congressional legislation," Cuyler v. Adams, 449 U.S. 433, 440, 101 S. Ct. 703 (1981) (holding Interstate Agreement on Detainers to constitute federal law), and courts have held that interstate transfer of prisoners is not appropriate for congressional legislation. Ghana v. Pearce, 159 F.3d at 1208 ("[T]he Compact's procedures are a purely local concern and there is no federal interest absent some constitutional violation in the treatment of these prisoners." (citations omitted)); accord, Stewart v. McManus, 924 F.2d 138, 142 (8th Cir. 1991).

[763]Cooper v. Sumner, 672 F. Supp. 1361, 1365 (D.Nev. 1987).

[764]Ghana v. Pearce, 159 F.3d at 1207–08 (citing Oregon ICC); see Hayes v. Lockhart, 754 F.2d 281, 283 (8th Cir. 1985) (citing Arkansas ICC; Arkansas inmate transferred to Florida was entitled to good time and other benefits earned in Florida on the same basis as if he had earned them in Arkansas, but had to exhaust his state remedies before seeking a writ of habeas corpus in federal court); Sayles v. Thompson, 99 Ill.2d 122, 457 N.E.2d 440, 441 (Ill. 1983) ("Under the compact a transferred inmate retains all the rights and privileges he possessed while confined within the Illinois prison system."). Cf. Pletka v. Nix, 957 F.2d 1480, 1483–85 (8th Cir. 1992) (en banc) (release of prisoner from punitive segregation in the receiving state did not bar the sending state from continuing his segregation after he was returned).

[765]Garcia v. LeMaster, 439 F.3d 1215, 1220 (10th Cir. 2006) (Compact "does not command California to administer the classification and recreation rules of the various states from which its prisoners have been transferred."); Ghana v. Pearce, 159 F.3d 1206, 1209 (9th Cir. 1998) (prisoner not entitled to be disciplined according to sending state's law); Jennings v. Lombardi, 70 F.3d 994, 996 (8th Cir. 1995) (prisoner not entitled to be paid wages he would have received in sending state); Stewart v. McManus, 924 F.2d 138, 141–42 (8th Cir. 1991) (prisoner not entitled to be disciplined according to sending state's law); Abrazinski v. Dubois, 876 F. Supp. 313, 317–19 (D.Mass. 1996) (prisoner not entitled to be disciplined according to sending state's law, since it was the receiving state's rules that he was breaking; court notes that if the sending state provided more frequent parole consideration, transferred prisoner might be entitled to that aspect of sending

state law); Cranford v. State, 471 N.W.2d 904, 905–06 (Iowa App. 1991) (same as Stewart v. McManus); Daye v. State, 171 Vt. 475, 481–82, 769 A.2d 630 (Vt. 2000) (Vermont prisoners transferred to Virginia were properly subject to Virginia visiting policies.).

[766]Garcia v. LeMaster, 439 F.3d at 1219–1220 (New Mexico prisoner had no liberty interest in that state's classification procedures); Ghana v. Pearce, 159 F.3d at 1209 (New Jersey prisoner had no liberty interest in New Jersey disciplinary rules as long as the Oregon disciplinary rules did not deny due process); Jennings v. Lombardi, 70 F.3d at 996 (Missouri prisoner had no property interest in receiving the wages he would have received in Missouri); see § A of this chapter concerning liberty interests.

[767]Ghana v. Pearce, 159 F.3d at 1207; Garcia v. LeMaster, 439 F.3d at 1219 (citing New Mexico and California ICCs); see Jennings v.Lombardi, 70 F.3d at 996–97 (citing ICC provision stating that transferred inmates shall receive wages on the same basis as prisoners of the state to which they are transferred).

The Garcia court also noted that New Mexico in its own policies had "authorized" California to apply its policies related to classification, case management, discipline, etc. Garcia, 439 F.3d at 1218. It agreed with the plaintiff that New Mexico "retain[ed] jurisdiction" over him, but said that jurisdiction related to transfer decisions and his New Mexico conviction and sentence. Id., 439 F.3d at 1220. Consistently with this last point, another federal court held that a Maryland prisoner transferred to Florida could not use the Florida courts to challenge Maryland's use of his Florida convictions to enhance his Maryland sentence. Unger v. Moore, 258 F.3d 1260, 1263–64 (11th Cir. 2001). That is, the state in which he was sentenced retained authority over his sentence.

[768]There are occasional exceptions. In Joslyn v. Armstrong, 2001 WL 1464780 (D.Conn., May 16, 2001), Connecticut prisoners alleged that they were transferred to a Virginia supermax prison and subjected to excessive force with the knowledge and acquiescence of Connecticut authorities; the court allowed the case to proceed in Connecticut, rather than transferring it to Virginia as the Connecticut Commissioner requested.

Another exception is that courts generally have held that the sending state is responsible for making state legal materials available for purposes of the prisoner's access to courts. See Ch. 3, § C.2.a, nn.527–528.

[769]Barrett v. Belleque, 344 Or. 91, 101–03, 176 P.3d 1272 (2008).

subsistence, education, treatment and training" of persons convicted in state courts, after certifying that "proper and adequate treatment facilities and personnel are available."[770] The Supreme Court has held that this statute does not limit state-to-federal transfers to prisoners who have a specific need for specialized treatment, but gives the Attorney General broad discretion to accept state prisoners as long as there is space available.[771] Persons convicted of crimes in the District of Columbia are committed to the custody of the Attorney General, who has discretion to place and transfer them within the District of Columbia and federal prison systems.[772] Transfer agreements between the federal government and state governments or the District of Columbia are not subject to the Compact Clause of the Constitution.[773]

State law may prohibit or restrict out-of-state transfers of prisoners.[774] For example, several states have "anti-transportation" clauses in their constitutions.[775] These provisions may be interpreted differently in different states.[776] They will be enforceable, if anywhere, in state courts.

5. Programs, Work, and Classification

As a general rule, there is no constitutional right to be in a particular status or activity in prison,[777] and being assigned to or excluded from a particular program (including visiting), job, or classification is generally not "atypical and significant hardship" that might require procedural protections.[778] There are a few exceptions. If prison officials'

action or inaction with respect to program, job, or classification matters affects your parole eligibility or good time credits, you may be deprived of a liberty interest requiring due process protections.[779] In such situations where classification does require due process protections, the process due is likely to be similar to that required for administrative segregation.[780]

a. Gangs and "Security Threat Groups" Prison officials often take action against prisoners for being involved with prison gangs or "security threat groups" (STGs). Since there is no constitutional right to belong to a gang or other prohibited group in prison,[781] such action does not necessarily deprive the prisoner of liberty. Unless the prisoner is subjected to "atypical and significant hardship . . . in relation to the ordinary incidents of prison life,"[782] prison officials need not provide procedural safeguards when they place members of gangs or other prohibited groups under special restrictions.[783] In some cases, the wholesale placement of gang or STG members in administrative segregation has been held

---

[770]18 U.S.C. § 5003(a).

[771]Howe v. Smith, 452 U.S. 473, 101 S. Ct. 2468 (1981).

[772]Blango v. Thornburgh, 942 F.2d 1487, 1488 (10th Cir. 1991) (citing D.C. Code, § 24–425).

[773]Stevenson v. Thornburgh, 943 F.2d 1214, 1216 (10th Cir. 1991); Blango v. Thornburgh, 942 F.2d at 1490.

[774]Brandon v. Alaska Dep't of Corrections, 938 P.2d 1029, 1033 (Alaska 1997) (out-of-state transfer was subject to judicial review for consistency with state constitutional right to rehabilitation).

[775]Ala.Const., Art. I, § 30; Ark.Const., Art. II, § 21; Ga.Const., Art. I, § 7; Ill.Const., Art.II, § 11; Kan.Const. BR 12; Neb.Const., Art.I, § 15; Ohio Const., Art. I, § 12; Tex. Const., Art. I, § 20; W. Va.Const., Art. III, § 5; Okla. Const., Art. II, § 29.

[776]Compare Ray v. McCoy, 321 S.E.2d 90, (W.Va. 1984) (state constitution prohibited out-of-state transfers) with Sayles v. Thompson, 99 Ill. 2d 122, 457 N.E.2d 440, 443–44 (Ill. 1983) (similar state constitutional prohibition applied only when an out-of-state transfer would constitute cruel and unusual punishment); Daye v. State, 171 Vt. 475, 483–85, 769 A.2d 630 (Vt. 2000) (neither transportation clause nor "visible punishments" clause of state constitution barred out-of-state transfers).

[777]Moody v. Daggett, 429 U.S. 78, 88 n.9, 97 S. Ct. 274 (1976) (due process is not required in connection with prisoner classification and eligibility for rehabilitative programs); Whitley v. Hunt, 158 F.3d 882, 889 (5th Cir. 1998) ("Inmates have no protectable property or liberty interests in custodial classification.").

[778]See, e.g., Johnson v. Rowley, 569 F.3d 40, 44 (2d Cir. 2009) (UNICOR job assignment); Harbin-Bey v. Rutter, 420 F.3d 571,

577 (6th Cir. 2005) (security classification); Ware v. Morrison, 276 F.3d 385, 387–88 (8th Cir. 2002) (visiting); DeWalt v. Carter, 224 F.3d 607, 613 (7th Cir. 2000) (jobs); Tanner v. Federal Bureau of Prisons, 433 F. Supp. 2d 117, 123 (D.D.C. 2006) (educational and vocational programs); Palomino v. Federal Bureau of Prisons, 408 F. Supp. 2d 282, 292–93 (S.D.Tex. 2005) (cancellation of "shock incarceration" program did not deny due process to prisoner even though the sentencing judge had expected him to be placed in it); Williams v. Manternach, 192 F. Supp. 2d 980, 985 (N.D.Iowa 2002) (loss of "level" status and job); Cooper v. Garcia, 55 F. Supp. 2d 1090, 1097 (S.D.Cal. 1999) (eligibility for family visiting program); James v. Reno, 39 F. Supp. 2d 37, 40 (D.D.C. 1999) (classification), aff'd, 1999 WL 615084 (D.C. Cir., July 2, 1999) (unpublished); Ross v. Keelilngs, 2 F. Supp. 2d 810, 815 (E.D.Va. 1998) (placement in "Therapeutic Community" drug program); Hines v. Fabian, 764 N.W.2d 849, 855 (Minn.App. 2009) (termination from rehabilitative program).

[779]Neal v. Shimoda, 131 F.3d 818, 828–30 (9th Cir. 1997) (holding that classification as a sex offender deprived prisoner of a liberty interest where refusing sex offender treatment made one ineligible for parole); Hernandez v. Johnson, 833 F.2d 1316, 1318 (9th Cir. 1987) (dicta; not deciding question); Green v. Black, 755 F.2d 687, 688–89 (8th Cir. 1985); Morales Feliciano v. Romelo Barcelo, 672 F. Supp. 591, 619–20 (D.P.R. 1986). The circumstances under which effects on parole and good time are discussed in more detail in § A.2 of this chapter.

[780]Barnett v. Centoni, 31 F.3d 813, 815 (9th Cir. 1994); Kulow v. Nix, 28 F.3d 855, 858 (8th Cir. 1994); see § H.2 of this chapter concerning due process requirements for administrative segregation. But see Neal v. Shimoda, 131 F.3d at 830–31 (holding that prisoners labelled as sex offenders who had not been criminally convicted of a sex offense are entitled to the same procedural protections as for a prison disciplinary proceeding).

[781]Westefer v. Snyder, 422 F.3d 570, 575 (7th Cir. 2005) (citing Jones v. North Carolina Prisoners' Labor Union, Inc., 433 U.S. 119, 132, 97 S. Ct. 2532 (1977)).

[782]Sandin v. Conner, 515 U.S. 472, 484, 115 S. Ct. 2293 (1995).

[783]Harbin-Bey v. Rutter, 420 F.3d 571, 576–77 (6th Cir. 2005).

not to be atypical and significant.[784] In such cases officials may, without procedural protections, hold persons they believe to be gang or STG members in segregation until they renounce their affiliation[785] and "debrief" (provide information about gang or STG activities and other members).[786] They may take such actions even against groups that claim to be religious in nature if the groups are shown to promote violence.[787]

If prison officials' actions against gang members are found to impose "atypical and significant hardship," due process protections apply. Usually, the action taken is placement in administrative segregation or other high-security confinement, and the due process requirements will be the same as for any placement in such units.[788] Officials need only produce "some evidence" of gang membership to justify segregation,[789] though even under that standard, evidence must bear some indications of reliability.[790]

At least one court has held that reliable evidence of *current* gang activity or affiliation is required.[791]

b. Sex Offender Programs The proliferation of restrictive laws and practices directed at sex offenders is addressed elsewhere in this Manual.[792] In this section, we address only due process questions related to the treatment of sex offenders in prison.

If you have actually been convicted of a sex offense, classification as a sex offender in prison will generally not raise a due process issue, since your criminal proceeding—which provides more procedural protections than prison proceedings—will have provided the "process due."[793] However, prison officials sometimes rely on charges of which the prisoner was not convicted, or on other information, in classifying prisoners as sex offenders. For prisoners in that situation, the question is whether the classification deprives them of a liberty interest protected by due process.

In-prison classification as a sex offender does not, by itself, deprive prisoners of a liberty interest protected by due process.[794] However, the consequences of that classification

---

[784]Fraise v. Terhune, 283 F.3d 506, 516–21 (3d Cir. 2002); *In re* Long Term Administrative Segregation, 174 F.3d 464, 469–70 (4th Cir. 1999) (holding that officials need not make individualized determinations of members' dangerousness); Madrid v. Gomez, 889 F. Supp. 1146, 1275 (N.D.Cal. 1995).

[785]Fraise v. Terhune, 283 F.3d at 520; *In re* Long Term Administrative Segregation, 174 F.3d at 471; Koch v. Lewis, 96 F. Supp. 2d 949, 966 (D.Ariz. 2000), *vacated as moot*, 399 F.3d 1099 (9th Cir. 2005).

[786]Madrid v. Gomez, 889 F. Supp. 1146, 1278 (N.D.Cal. 1995).

[787]Fraise v. Terhune, 283 F.3d at 520; *In re* Long Term Administrative Segregation, 174 F.3d at 469–70. Those decisions uphold the segregation of all members of the Five Percenters, based on what seems to us to be a pretty thin factual basis. *See Fraise*, 283 F.3d at 526–27 (dissenting opinion).

[788]*See* § H.2 of this chapter concerning administrative segregation due process.

[789]Bruce v. Ylst, 351 F.3d 1283, 1288–89 (9th Cir. 2003); Taylor v. Rodriguez, 238 F.3d 188, 193 (2d Cir. 2001); Toussaint v. Rowland, 926 F.2d 800, 802–03 (9th Cir. 1991) (allowing use of polygraph evidence under "some evidence" standard).

[790]Taylor v. Rodriguez, 238 F.3d at 194; Koch v. Lewis, 96 F. Supp. 2d 949, 965–66 (D.Ariz. 2000), *vacated as moot*, 399 F.3d 1099 (9th Cir. 2005); *see* Stewart v. Alameida, 418 F. Supp. 2d 1154, 1168 (N.D.Cal. 2006) (stating that reliability of evidence had been shown *in camera* (confidentially)). In *Madrid v. Gomez*, the court further required prison officials to make a record when they reject a piece of evidence as failing to support gang membership, so it will not be relied on in the future. 889 F. Supp. at 1273–74.

One court has held that there must be evidence of actual gang activity, not just membership, to support indefinite "supermax" placement. Koch v. Lewis, 216 F. Supp. 2d at 1004–07. *Contra*, Stewart v. Alameida, 418 F. Supp. 2d at 1167–68 (upholding finding of gang affiliation based on photographs of him with gang members and interview with confidential informant, despite lack of any evidence of actual gang-related actions); *see In re* Long Term Administrative Segregation, 174 F.3d at 470 (holding prison officials need not make "an individual assessment of [each] inmate's dangerousness" in classifying Five Percenters as security threat group).

[791]Taylor v. Rodriguez, 238 F.3d at 193.

Another court rejected a requirement that retention in a supermax prison be supported by evidence of recent gang involvement. It stated that the question of current vs. past gang involvement is about the substantive criteria for placement and that *procedural* due process does not have anything to do with such questions. It left open the possibility that protracted confinement based on old evidence of gang involvement might violate *substantive* due process or the Eighth Amendment. Austin v. Wilkinson, 372 F.3d 346, 356 (6th Cir. 2004), *aff'd in part, rev'd in part on other grounds*, 545 U.S. 209, 125 S. Ct. 2384 (2005).

[792]*See* Ch. 2, § F.4.b.

[793]Neal v. Shimoda, 131 F.3d 818, 831 (9th Cir. 1997); *see* Connecticut Dep't of Public Safety v. Doe, 538 U.S. 1, 7, 123 S. Ct. 1160 (2003) (holding that convicted sex offenders are not entitled to a hearing under a statute that required all convicted sex offenders to register).

[794]Gwinn v. Awmiller, 354 F.3d 1211, 1216 (10th Cir. 2004). The court viewed the plaintiff's claim as an assertion that his good name, reputation, honor, or integrity had been impugned, which only raises a due process issue if the plaintiff shows that "(1) the government made a statement about him or her that is sufficiently derogatory to injure his or her reputation, that is capable of being proved false, and that he or she asserts is false, and (2) the plaintiff experienced some governmentally imposed burden that 'significantly altered [his or] her status as a matter of state law.'" *Id.* (quoting Paul v. Davis, 424 U.S. 693, 710–11, 96 S. Ct. 1155 (1996)). This is sometimes described as the "stigma plus" standard.

The requirement that sex offenders register after their release from prison has been held to constitute a liberty deprivation, since the registration requirement itself alters the status of a non-prisoner. *See* Gwinn v. Awmiller, 354 F.3d at 1222–24 and cases cited; Doe v. Dep't of Public Safety, 271 F.3d 38, 47–59 (2d Cir.2001) (holding that the stigma of being listed on a sex offender registry that contained false information, combined with the "extensive and onerous" registration duties imposed by Connecticut's

may be serious enough to constitute a deprivation of liberty if it affects the prisoner's ability to earn good time or parole release[795] or if it subjects the prisoner to a mandatory, intrusive therapy program.[796] Without such consequences, the sex offender classification by itself is not a deprivation of liberty.[797] Nor is it a liberty deprivation to exclude persons

classified as sex offenders from prison programs and benefits unless there is a liberty interest in participating in them[798]—which, as noted earlier, is usually not the case.

In instances where in-prison sex offender classification does require due process protections, most courts have said that the "process due" is the same as required for a prison disciplinary hearing.[799]

One court has held that retaining a sex offender past his conditional release date because his residence had not been approved did not deny due process; due process required only that the prisoner be informed that he would not be released without an approved residence and that he receive an explanation of why the condition was imposed by parole authorities and an opportunity to dispute those reasons.[800]

6. Parole and Temporary Release

This section focuses on programs of release from prison that are under the authority of prison officials or other administrative personnel. It does not deal with probation, since probation is an aspect of criminal sentencing that is beyond the scope of this Manual. For the same reason, it does not deal with temporary release programs that are under the authority of the sentencing court.[801]

In the past, most prisoners received "indeterminate" sentences, under which an administrative body, usually called a parole board, decided when to release the prisoner, subject to conditions. If the prisoner was accused of violating parole conditions, the parole board would decide whether to revoke her parole. In recent years, a number of states and the federal government have abolished parole; the

---

sex offender statute, were sufficient to implicate a liberty interest), *rev'd on other grounds*, 538 U.S. 1, 123 S. Ct. 1160 (2003).

[795]Gwinn v. Awmiller, 354 F.3d at 1217 (good time); Chambers v. Colorado Dep't of Corrections, 205 F.3d 1237, 1242–43 (10th Cir. 2000) (good time); Neal v. Shimoda, 131 F.3d 818, 828–29 (9th Cir. 1997) (parole eligibility); Green v. Black, 755 F.2d 687, 688–89 (8th Cir. 1985) (parole eligibility); Beebe v. Heil, 333 F. Supp. 2d 1011, 1015–18 (D.Colo. 2004) (state law that requires the state to provide convicted sex offenders with a treatment program and makes parole eligibility contingent on completing it, creates a liberty interest, and that failure to provide the program could "shock the conscience" for purposes of substantive due process analysis); *see* § I.A.2 of this chapter concerning due process issues related to earning parole and good time.

[796]Kirby v. Siegelman, 195 F.3d 1285, 1288, 1291–92 (11th Cir. 1999) (finding a liberty interest where sex offenders were required to participate in group therapy and admit past sexual offenses and were barred from minimum custody and therefore excluded from work release and community custody programs); Neal v. Shimoda, 131 F.3d 818, 828–29 (9th Cir. 1997) (finding a liberty interest in avoiding sex offender classification where sex offenders were required to admit the sex offense and go through a treatment program); Cooper v. Garcia, 55 F. Supp. 2d 1090, 1101–02 (S.D.Cal. 1999) (holding *Neal* applies only where the classification is coupled with mandatory, coercive treatment that affects a liberty interest); Schuyler v. Roberts, 285 Kan. 677, 685–87, 175 P.3d 259 (Kan. 2008) (applying *Gwinn* "stigma plus" test, holding that labelling plaintiff a sex offender and requiring him to undergo sex offender treatment required due process). These decisions say that the stigma and the treatment requirement of sex offender classification are similar to commitment to a mental hospital, which the Supreme Court held in *Vitek v. Jones*, 445 U.S. 480, 100 S. Ct. 1254 (1980), called for due process protections. *See* Kirby v. Siegelman, 195 F.3d at 1291–92; Neal v. Shimoda, 131 F.3d at 828–29.

In *Chambers v. Colorado Dep't of Corrections*, 205 F.3d 1237, 1243 (10th Cir. 2000), a very confusing opinion, the court seemed to endorse the reasoning of *Neal v. Shimoda*. The later Tenth Circuit decision in *Gwinn v. Awmiller*, discussed above, interprets *Chambers* as based on the loss of opportunity to earn good time at a higher rate. *Gwinn*, 354 F.3d at 1217.

[797]Thiel v. Wisconsin, 399 F. Supp. 2d 929, 932–34 (W.D.Wis. 2005) (classifying all civilly detained sex offenders as maximum security and treating them as such does not deny due process); Kritenbrink v. Crawford, 313 F. Supp. 2d 1043, 1049–50 (D.Nev. 2004) (classification as a sex offender did not implicate a liberty interest where it caused the plaintiff to be confined in a higher security prison and to lose the opportunity to go to a work camp and obtain early release credit; court gives plaintiff the opportunity to show that conditions for sex offenders are atypical and significant compared to ordinary confinement); Jones v. Puckett, 160 F. Supp. 2d 1016, 1023–24 (W.D.Wis. 2001) (identifying a prisoner as in need of sex offender treatment, without mandating the treatment or denying parole eligibility for not accepting it, was not a liberty deprivation).

[798]*See* Callender v. Sioux City Residential Treatment Facility, 88 F.3d 666, 668–69 (8th Cir. 1996) (exclusion from a work release program after refusing to acknowledge guilt of sex offense); Riddle v. Mondragon, 83 F.3d 1197, 1206–07 (10th Cir. 1996) (exclusion from various programs and benefits); Jones v. Moore, 996 F.2d 943, 945–46 (8th Cir. 1993) (refusing to transfer prisoner to a prison with a sex offenders program because of his escape history did not deny due process); Mahfouz v. Lockhart, 826 F.2d 791, 793–94 (8th Cir. 1987) (exclusion from work/study release program); Cooper v. Garcia, 55 F. Supp. 2d 1090, 1098 (S.D.Cal. 1999) (exclusion from family visiting program); Richmond v. Cagle, 920 F. Supp. 955, 958 (E.D.Wis. 1996); Martinkoski v. Wisconsin Dep't of Corrections, 896 F. Supp. 882, 884 (E.D.Wis. 1995).

[799]Gwinn v. Awmiller, 354 F.3d 1211, 1219 (10th Cir. 2004) (holding *Wolff v. McDonnell* rights plus the "some evidence" standard are required); Neal v. Shimoda, 131 F.3d 818, 830 (9th Cir. 1997). *But see* Jones v. Puckett, 160 F. Supp. 2d 1016, 1024 (W.D.Wis. 2001) (holding due process was satisfied by notice, an opportunity to be heard, and a statement of reasons by the prison program committee).

[800]Doe v. Simon, 221 F.3d 137, 140 (2d Cir. 2000). "Conditional release" in New York means release based on good time credits; the releasee is subject to parole supervision.

[801]*See, e.g.*, State v. Shield, 368 N.W.2d 721 (Iowa 1985); People v. Malmquist, 155 Mich.App. 521, 400 N.W.2d 317 (1986); State v. Larson, 393 N.W.2d 238, 243 (Minn.App. 1986); State v. Hunt, 80 N.C.App. 190, 341 S.E.2d 350, 354 (N.C.App. 1986).

time the prisoner must serve is dictated by statute or decided by the court.[802] However, in many of these no-parole jurisdictions, prisoners must still serve a term of "supervised release" or "post-release supervision" which is similar to parole, since it may be revoked if they violate the conditions of release.[803] The federal government has adopted this system.[804] Supervised release for federal offenders is now under the authority of the sentencing court.[805]

As explained in greater detail in the following subsections, prisoners' federal constitutional rights with respect to parole and temporary release are limited. Often, state statutes and regulations will provide greater rights. These must generally be enforced in state court.[806] Even when a prisoner has a federal constitutional claim related to parole, if success would result in immediate or earlier release, she will be required to exhaust her state court remedies (for federal prisoners, administrative remedies) and file a habeas corpus petition before a federal court will hear the claim. There are some serious limitations to the habeas remedy.[807] Parole personnel are often held immune from suit for damages even if their actions violate the Constitution.[808]

a. Parole Release　The federal Constitution does not require states to maintain a parole system and does not create a right to parole release.[809] There is no right to due process in release proceedings unless state statutes or regulations create a liberty interest in parole release.[810] In *Greenholtz v. Inmates of Nebraska Penal Correctional Complex*, the Supreme Court examined Nebraska's statute and found that a prisoner being considered for parole is "entitled to some measure of constitutional protection" since the statute created an expectation of release on parole "unless" the statutory reasons for parole denials are found. The Court emphasized that "this statute has unique structure and language and thus whether any other state provides a protectible entitlement must be decided on a case-by-case basis."[811] You must therefore examine your state statutes closely in determining whether they create a liberty interest in being paroled. Parole practices and procedures that are not set out in statutes or regulations do not create liberty interests.[812]

Parole statutes in some states have been held to create a liberty interest.[813] In other states, there is no liberty interest in obtaining parole.[814] If there is no such liberty interest,

---

[802]Many of these states enacted "truth-in-sentencing" laws, which requires an inmate to serve every day of the imposed minimum sentence. *See, e.g.*, State v. Plank, 282 Wis.2d 522, 699 N.W.2d 235, 239–40 (Wis. App. 2005); Evans v. State, 872 A.2d 539, 554–55 (Del. Supr. 2005).

[803]*See, e.g.*, People v. Sitkowski, 382 Ill.App.3d 1072, 1075–76, 891 N.E.2d 879 (2008).

[804]A 1984 statute essentially abolished parole for federal prisoners as of November 1, 1992. Sentencing Reform Act of 1984, Pub. L. No. 98-473, §§ 212, 218(a)(5), 235. The history of this statute and the functions of its various sections are discussed in Romano v. Luther, 816 F.2d 832, 834–39 (2d Cir. 1987); *see also* Lightsey v. Kastner, 846 F.2d 329, 331–33 (5th Cir. 1988).

The United States Parole Commission remains in existence primarily to supervise persons released on parole pursuant to the old parole statutes, and has also been given responsibility for administering the parole system for District of Columbia Code offenders for offenses committed before August 5, 2000, and the supervised release of D.C. Code offenders sentenced for offenses committed after August 4, 2000. *See* http://www.usdoj.gov/uspc/ (U.S. Parole Commission web site, visited June 16, 2008). The Commission also has responsibility for military offenders, prisoners sentenced in foreign countries, and transferred to the United States to serve their sentences, and state prisoners in the federal Witness Protection Program. *Id.*

[805]18 U.S.C. § 3583; 21 U.S.C. § 841 (drug offenses); *see* Johnson v. U.S., 529 U.S. 694, 696–99, 120 S. Ct. 1795 (2000).

[806]*See, e.g.*, Siao-Pao v. Mazzucca, 442 F. Supp. 2d 148, 156 (S.D.N.Y. 2006) (violation of state law requirement that prisoners denied parole be told the reasons "in detail and not in conclusory terms" is not for federal courts to address); Quinteros v. Hernandez, 419 F. Supp. 2d 1209, 1214 (C.D.Cal. 2006) (petitioner "may not transform a state-law issue into a federal one merely by asserting a violation of [a constitutional right]" (citation omitted)).

[807]*See* Ch. 8, § H.1.a. Temporary release cases are generally not subject to this requirement. *See id.*, n.561.

[808]*See* Ch. 8, § L.2.

[809]Greenholtz v. Inmates of Nebraska Penal Correctional Complex, 442 U.S. 1, 7, 99 S. Ct. 2100 (1979).

State constitutions may differ. *See, e.g.*, In re Trantino, 177 N.J. Super. 499, 427 A.2d 91 (1981) (legislature is obligated by state constitution to provide for parole).

[810]*See* § B of this chapter for a discussion of how a liberty interest is created.

[811]Greenholtz v. Inmates of Nebraska Penal Correctional Complex, 442 U.S. at 12.

[812]Jago v. Van Curen, 454 U.S. 14, 19–21, 102 S. Ct. 31 (1981); Barna v. Travis, 239 F.3d 169, 170–71 (2d Cir. 2001) (per curiam); Slocum v. Georgia State Bd. of Pardons and Paroles, 678 F.2d 940, 941 n.3 (11th Cir. 1982); *see* Connecticut Bd. of Pardons v. Dumschat, 452 U.S. 458, 465, 101 S. Ct. 2460 (1981) (same holding as to commutation of sentences).

[813]Board of Pardons v. Allen, 482 U.S. 369, 376–80 & n.10, 107 S. Ct. 2414 (1987) and cases cited; Sass v. California Bd. of Prison Terms, 461 F.3d 1123, 1127–28 (9th Cir. 2006); Bermudez v. Duenas, 936 F.2d 1064, 1067 (9th Cir. 1991) (per curiam); Felce v. Fiedler, 974 F.2d 1484, 1490–92 (9th Cir. 1992); Sonntag v. Paparozzi, 256 F. Supp. 2d 320, 325 (D.N.J. 2003), *aff'd as modified*, 94 Fed.Appx. 970 (3d Cir. 2004) (unpublished); Stogsdill v. Board of Parole, 342 Or. 332, 336–37, 154 P.3d 91 (2007); *see* Cooper v. South Carolina Dep't of Probation, Parole and Pardon Services, 661 S.E.2d 106, 111–12 (S.C. 2008) (prisoner had liberty interest in having parole board decide based on the factors dictated by the state parole statute).

[814]*See, e.g.*, cases cited in Board of Pardons v. Allen, 482 U.S. at 378–79 n.10; Thompson v. Veach, 501 F.3d 832, 835–37 (7th Cir. 2007) (Illinois); Barna v. Travis, 239 F.3d 169, 171 (2d Cir. 2001) (per curiam) (New York); Ellis v. District of Columbia, 84 F.3d 1413, 1418–20 (D.C. Cir. 1996); Inmates v. Ohio State Adult Parole Auth., 929 F.2d 233, 235–36 (6th Cir. 1991); Brandon v. District of Columbia Bd. of Parole, 823 F.2d 644, 648 (D.C. Cir. 1987); Huggins v. Isenbarger, 798 F.2d 203, 206 (7th Cir. 1986) (per curiam) (Indiana); Staton v. Wainwright, 665 F.2d 686 (5th Cir. 1982) (Florida); Shirley v. Chestnut, 603 F.2d 805 (10th Cir. 1979)

your only procedural protections in the parole release process are those provided by state law.[815]

The Supreme Court's decision in *Sandin v. Conner*,[816] which substantially limited prisoners' due process rights, affects cases pertaining to treatment in prison. *Sandin* has, or should have, no application to due process requirements in determining whether someone should be released from prison entirely.[817] In those cases, the pre-*Sandin* law of liberty interests should still be valid.[818]

In states where there is a liberty interest in parole, due process requires certain procedural protections, but these are limited. Since parole decisions are generally "subjective in part and predictive in part," "[p]rocedures designed to elicit specific facts" are not necessarily required.[819] Due process does not require a formal hearing, but is satisfied if the prisoner is provided an informal interview with the board, has the opportunity to ensure that the board is considering her record, and is able to present any special factors meriting consideration.[820] The board need not provide a summary of evidence on which the decision is based as long as it "informs the inmate in what respects he falls short of qualifying for parole."[821] Some courts have held there must be

"some evidence" to support the decision,[822] but others have rejected that argument on the ground that parole release decisions are not really about evidence, as *Greenholtz* suggests.[823] The requirements of due process may vary to some degree depending on the terms of a particular parole statute.[824] However, the particular requirements of each state's parole procedures will generally have to be enforced in state court.

The Constitution does not place many limits on the decisions of parole boards or the factors they may consider. Parole authorities may rely on allegations of conduct of which the prisoner was not convicted, or was even acquitted.[825] However, some courts have held that it denies due process for them to rely on erroneous or

---

(Oklahoma); Lynch v. Hubbard, 47 F. Supp. 2d 125, 127–28 (D. Mass. 1999), *aff'd*, 248 F.3d 1127 (1st Cir. 2000) (unpublished).

[815]*See, e.g.*, N.Y. Executive Law § 259-i(2)(a) (requiring statement of reasons for parole denial).

[816]515 U.S. 472, 115 S. Ct. 2293 (1995).

[817]*See* Michael v. Ghee, 498 F.3d 372, 378 (6th Cir. 2007), *cert. denied*, 128 S. Ct. 2067 (2008); McQuillion v. Duncan, 306 F.3d 895, 903 (9th Cir. 2002) (holding *Sandin* deals with "internal prison disciplinary regulations" and not whether due process is required in parole release proceedings); Ellis v. District of Columbia, 84 F.3d 1413, 1417–18 (D.C. Cir. 1996) (stating *Sandin* test is "ill-fitted to parole eligibility determinations," adhering to Supreme Court parole precedents until Supreme Court rules otherwise).

[818]*See* McQuillion v. Duncan, 306 F.3d at 903; Ellis v. District of Columbia, 84 F.3d at 1418; *id.* at 1425–26 (concurring and dissenting opinion); Watson v. Disabato, 933 F. Supp. 390, 393 (D.N.J. 1996).

[819]Greenholtz v. Inmates of Nebraska Penal Correctional Complex, 442 U.S. 1, 13-14, 99 S. Ct. 2100 (1979).

[820]*Greenholtz*, 442 U.S. at 14–15; *see* Watson v. Disabato, 933 F. Supp. 390, 393–94 (D.N.J. 1996) (due process requires "notice of the pendency of the parole determination, a statement by the government showing that the prisoner is substantially likely to recidivate, and an opportunity for the prisoner to submit a written response to the state's reasons," and an explanation of the reasons for parole denial). *See* Ch. 4, § D, for a discussion of how the extent of due process procedures is determined.

One federal circuit has held that "[a]t most, . . . parole authorities must 'furnish to the prisoner a statement of its reasons for denial of parole.'" Vann v. Angelone, 73 F.3d 519, 522 (4th Cir. 1996). This decision is inconsistent with *Greenholtz* and in fact relied on an earlier circuit decision that preceded *Greenholtz*. *Vann, id.* (citing Franklin v. Shields, 569 F.2d 784 (4th Cir. 1977)).

[821]*Greenholtz*, 442 U.S. at 15. If a particular parole statute made parole release contingent on a particular *factual* finding, as opposed to a subjective and predictive judgment by the Board, the

requirements of due process might be different for that parole system.

[822]*See* Hayward v. Marshall, ___ F.3d ___, 2010 WL 1664977, *10–11 (9th Cir. 2010) (en banc) (noting California courts' adoption of requirement of "some evidence" of dangerousness for denial of parole, holding there is no such federal constitutional requirement).

[823]*See, e.g.*, Schwartz v. Dennison, 518 F. Supp. 2d 560, 573 (S.D.N.Y. 2007), *aff'd*, 339 Fed.Appx. 28 (2d Cir. 2009) (unpublished). *See* Hayward v. Marshall, 2010 WL 1664977 at *8–10.

[824]*See, e.g.*, Watson v. Disabato, 933 F. Supp. 390, 394–95 (D.N.J. 1996) (parole statute created a liberty interest in having a future parole eligibility date set when parole is denied, and due process requires that a date be set unless a statutory exception applies). *Compare* Quinteros v. Hernandez, 419 F. Supp. 2d 1209, 1217 (C.D.Cal. 2006) (failure to set a parole date did not deny due process where statute did not require a date until after the board found the prisoner suitable for parole).

[825]Fiumara v. O'Brien, 889 F.2d 254, 257–58 (10th Cir. 1989) (prosecutor's letters); Castillo-Sicairos v. U.S. Parole Comm'n, 866 F.2d 262, 264 (8th Cir. 1989) (counts dismissed in a plea bargain and information not relied on by the sentencing court); Maddox v. U.S. Parole Comm'n, 821 F.2d 997, 999–1000 (5th Cir. 1987) (noting Parole Commission's broad authority in materials it considers for parole decisions, including dismissed counts of an indictment, hearsay evidence, and allegations of criminal activity for which prisoner was not even charged); Billiteri v. U.S. Bd. of Parole, 541 F.2d 938, 944–45 (2d Cir. 1976); *see* Jackson v. Walters, 733 F. Supp. 33, 34–35 (W.D. Pa. 1989) (acquittals could be considered in furlough decisions), *aff'd*, 899 F.2d 1217 (3d Cir. 1990).

Use of such information may be limited in particular parole systems. *See, e.g.*, Dunn v. U.S. Parole Com'n, 818 F.2d 742, 745 (10th Cir. 1987) (holding insanity acquittal could be considered for purposes of assessing whether release would jeopardize public welfare, but not for whether it would encourage disrespect for law or depreciate the seriousness of the offense, since an insanity acquittal meant that the prisoner was incapable at the time of understanding that his conduct violated the law); Layne v. Ohio Adult Parole Auth., 97 Ohio St.3d 456, 464, 780 N.E.2d 548, 555 (2002) (requiring parole board to use only offense of conviction in calculating an "offense category score" for parole purposes, but holding that the board, "when considering an inmate for parole, still retains its discretion to consider any circumstances relating to the offense or offenses of conviction, including crimes that did not result in conviction, as well as any other factors the APA deems relevant").

inaccurate information.[826] Prison conditions that arbitrarily interfere with parole opportunities may be unconstitutional.[827]

One issue that concerns many prisoners is the tendency of some parole boards to deny parole repeatedly based on the person's original offense, with little or no consideration given to what the person may have done while in prison to merit release. In general, courts have held that due process scrutiny of the substance of parole board decisions is extremely limited,[828] and parole boards do not deny due process if they base denial of parole solely on the seriousness of the prisoner's criminal offense and record.[829] They need not give good institutional behavior more weight than the seriousness of the offense.[830]

Some recent decisions have questioned whether there is a constitutional limit to reliance on the seriousness of the criminal record. One federal circuit suggested there was such a limit, but now appears to have backed away from that conclusion.[831] In another state, prisoners filed a class action alleging that for a certain class of violent felons, state officials had adopted a policy of denying parole based exclusively on the offense, despite state law requiring the parole board to consider other factors including the prisoner's institutional record. The court held that even in the absence of a state-created liberty interest in parole release, "there is an entitlement to a process of decision-making, which comports with the statutory guidelines of consideration to *all* relevant statutory factors."[832]

At least one court has held that due process requires that a person not convicted of a sex offense be provided at least the due process required for a prison disciplinary hearing before being labelled a sex offender and required to complete a sex offender program before becoming parole eligible. Neal v. Shimoda, 131 F.3d 818, 830–32 (9th Cir. 1997).

[826]One federal circuit has so held, even where there is no liberty interest in parole, if the prisoner makes specific allegations of reliance on false information. Jones v. Ray, 279 F.3d 944, 946 (11th Cir.2001); *see* Monroe v. Thigpen, 932 F.2d 1437, 1441–42 (11th Cir. 1991) (defendants admitted falsity of information). Other courts have limited any right to challenge false information to systems where there is a liberty interest in parole release. Johnson v. Rodriguez, 110 F.3d 299, 308–309 n.13 (5th Cir.1997); Reffitt v. Nixon, 917 F. Supp. 409, 413–14 (E.D.Va. 1996) (right not to have parole release decisions based on false information exists only if there is a liberty interest in getting parole), *aff'd*, 121 F.3d 699 (4th Cir. 1997) (unpublished); *see* Drennon v. Craven, 141 Idaho 34, 38, 105 P.3d 694, 698 (Idaho App. 2004) (rejecting claim because prisoner did not show that erroneous information was relied upon). *Cf. Greenholtz*, 442 U.S. at 13 (noting that inaccurate information in parole files increases the risk of erroneous parole decisions).

Before you bring suit, you must use any available statutory or administrative procedure to try to get your file corrected. *See* § D.7 of this chapter. You may be able to get access to part or all of your parole file through state freedom of information laws, as is the case with the federal Freedom of Information Act. *See* U.S. Dep't of Justice v. Julian, 486 U.S. 1, 103 S. Ct. 1606 (1988) (concerning access to pre-sentence reports used by parole authorities); Rule 32(d), Fed.R.Crim.P. (requiring disclosure of pre-sentence report to defendant).

[827]Morales Feliciano v. Romero Barcelo, 672 F. Supp. 591, 606–07, 619–20 (D.P.R. 1986) (loss of right to be heard by parole board because of overburdened staff); Williams v. Lane, 646 F. Supp. 1379, 1408–09 (N.D.Ill. 1986) (deprivation of parole opportunities to protective custody inmates), *aff'd*, 851 F.2d 867, 873–74, 885 (7th Cir. 1988).

[828]Some courts have held that denial of release may deny due process if it is done for "arbitrary or impermissible reasons." Boddie v. New York State Div. of Parole, 288 F. Supp. 2d 431, 440 (S.D.N.Y.2003) and cases cited; *see also* Cartagena v. Connelly, 2006 WL 2627567, *7 (S.D.N.Y., Sept. 14, 2006) (citing cases), *report and recommendation adopted*, 2008 WL 2169659 (S.D.N.Y., May 23, 2008). Other courts have questioned whether due process provides for any substantive review of parole decisions. *See* Tatta v. Miller, 2005 WL 2806236, *3 n.2 (E.D.N.Y., Oct. 27, 2005) and cases cited.

[829]Resnick v. U.S. Parole Comm'n., 835 F.2d 1297, 1300 (10th Cir. 1989) (parole commission could deny parole based on "enormity or magnitude of the offense"); Manley v. Thomas, 255 F. Supp. 2d 263, 267 (S.D.N.Y. 2003). Denial of parole based on the seriousness of the offense does not constitute double jeopardy. Averhart v. Tutsie, 618 F.2d 479, 483 (7th Cir. 1980) (inmate denied parole five times based upon seriousness of crime).

[830]Schiselman v. U.S. Parole Comm'n, 858 F.2d 1232, 1240 (7th Cir. 1988); Siao-Pao v. Mazzucca, 442 F. Supp. 2d 148, 155 (S.D.N.Y. 2006) (where state law allowed parole board to give each factor "whatever weight it deems appropriate," it could give more weight to seriousness of the underlying crime than record in prison).

[831]The Ninth Circuit refused to disturb a parole board's finding that a prisoner's exemplary prison record was outweighed by the gravity of the his crime and prior conduct, but said that "[o]ver time," if that exemplary behavior continued, the continued denial of parole based only on prior conduct would raise serious questions. Biggs v. Terhune, 334 F.3d 910, 916 (9th Cir. 2003); *accord*, Irons v. Carey, 505 F.3d 846, 854 (9th Cir. 2007) ("We hope that the Board will come to recognize that in some cases, indefinite detention based solely on an inmate's commitment offense, regardless of the extent of his rehabilitation, will at some point violate due process, given the liberty interest in parole that flows from the relevant California statutes."). In a later case, however, the same court said that any right to release in the absence of evidence of future dangerousness would have to arise from substantive state law, and it overruled *Biggs* and *Irons* to the extent they suggested that there was an independent federal constitutional right to release. Hayward v. Marshall, ___ F.3d ___, 2010 WL 1664977, *5 (9th Cir. 2010) (en banc). The court declined to decide whether the federal Constitution requires "some evidence" of dangerousness to deny parole release, since the state Supreme Court had already held that the state constitution had such a requirement, and there was some evidence of dangerousness in the case before it. *Id.*, *10–11.

[832]Graziano v. Pataki, 2006 WL 2023082, *7 (S.D.N.Y., July 17, 2006) (emphasis supplied); *see id.*, *9 ("while there is no due process right to being granted parole, there is a due process right to have the decision made only in accordance with the statutory criteria"); *see also* Graziano v. Pataki, 2007 WL 4302483, *2–4 (S.D.N.Y., Dec. 5, 2007) (certifying case as a class action); Villaronga

Other courts have rejected this view, and the question remains open.[833]

In some instances, parole practices may violate other constitutional rights besides the Due Process Clauses. Discrimination without rational basis in parole practices may violate the Equal Protection Clause;[834] individual parole decisions may also deny equal protection if they involve intentional discrimination or an improper purpose,[835] including racial discrimination.[836] (Simple disparities between inmates with similar records are not unlawful.[837]) Parole practices or decisions may violate the right of court access.[838]

The federal disability statutes[839] apply to parole and require that prisoners' disabilities be accommodated in parole proceedings.[840]

The state has broad authority to place conditions on granting parole.[841] Parole conditions do not violate the Constitution unless they significantly infringe on substantial constitutional rights.[842] States may permit parole for some offenses and not others,[843] or impose special requirements on particular offenders or types of offenders, as long as the requirements have a rational basis.[844] The federal

---

v. New York State Div. of Parole, 13 Misc.3d 1228(A), 1228(A), 831 N.Y.S.2d 357, 357 (N.Y.Sup. 2006) (unpublished) (describing *Graziano* arguments as "compelling"). *Accord,* Cooper v. South Carolina Dep't of Probation, Parole and Pardon Services, 661 S.E.2d 106, 111–12 (S.C. 2008) (prisoner had liberty interest in having parole board decide based on the factors dictated by the state parole statute).

[833]Farid v. Bouey, 554 F. Supp. 2d 301, 307 (N.D.N.Y. 2008); Wilmas v. Blunt, 2007 WL 4372817, *2 (E.D.Mo. 2007), *aff'd as modified,* 2009 WL 1175525 (8th Cir., May 4, 2009) (unpublished); Standley v. Dennison, 2007 WL 2406909, *10–12 (N.D.N.Y., Aug. 21, 2007); Mathie v. Dennison, 2007 WL 2351072, *6–8 & n.4 (S.D.N.Y., Aug. 16, 2007) (stating that violation of the state's parole statutes violates only state law and not the Due Process Clause).

[834]*See* Bishop v. Moran, 676 F. Supp. 416, 421–23 (D.R.I. 1987) (denial of personal appearance at parole hearing to prisoners incarcerated out of state denied equal protection). *But see* Jaben v. Moore, 788 F. Supp. 500, 504 (D.Kan. 1992) (disagreeing with *Bishop*). The Equal Protection Clause is discussed in Ch. 5

[835]Clark v. State of Ga. Pardons and Paroles Bd., 915 F.2d 636, 639 (11th Cir. 1990); Brandon v. District of Columbia Bd. of Parole, 823 F.2d 644, 650-51 (D.C. Cir. 1987; Hilliard v. Bd. of Pardons and Paroles, 759 F.2d 1190, 1193 (5th Cir. 1985).

[836]Block v. Potter, 631 F.2d 233, 240–41 (3d Cir. 1980).

[837]Patten v. North Dakota Parole Bd., 783 F.2d 140, 143–44 (8th Cir. 1986); Augustine v. Brewer, 821 F.2d 365, 372 (7th Cir. 1987).

[838]Rauser v. Horn, 241 F.3d 330, 333 (3d Cir. 2001) (alleged retaliatory denial of parole stated a court access claim); Wolfe v. Pennsylvania Dep't of Corrections, 334 F. Supp. 2d 762, 774 (E.D.Pa. 2004) (allegation that new prerequisites for parole were imposed based on plaintiff's grievances and litigation stated a First Amendment claim); Buhrman v. Wilkinson, 257 F. Supp. 2d 1110, 1120 (S.D.Ohio 2003) ("It should go without saying that if a parole board acts against a prisoner because he exercised his right to file a civil complaint, such conduct is actionable as a violation of the First Amendment."); McDaniel v. Rhodes, 512 F. Supp. 117, 120 (S.D.Ohio 1981) (threats of adverse parole action in retaliation for litigation stated a court access claim); Inmates of Nebraska Penal and Correctional Complex v. Greenholtz, 436 F. Supp. 432, 437 (D.Neb. 1976) (parole consideration cannot be denied because inmates have pending litigation), *aff'd,* 567 F.2d 1381 (8th Cir. 1977); *see* Johnson v. Rodriguez, 110 F.3d 299, 311–14 (5th Cir. 1997) (holding that to support a retaliation claim plaintiffs must show that they were retaliated against by denial of parole for actual litigation that was not frivolous). *Cf.* Toolasprashad v. Bureau of Prisons, 286 F.3d 576, 585 (D.C. Cir. 2002) (allegation of retaliatory

transfer away from prison where staff members would have supported parole application stated a court access claim).

[839]*See* Ch. 2, § F.4.h(2) concerning the disability statutes.

[840]Armstrong v. Davis, 275 F.3d 849, 858–59, 871 (9th Cir. 2001) (affirming injunction requiring accommodation of disabilities in the parole process); Clarkson v. Coughlin, 898 F. Supp. 1019, 1040, 1050 (S.D.N.Y. 1995) (due process and the federal disability statutes require provision of sign language interpreters for deaf or hearing-impaired prisoners during parole proceedings).

[841]Board of Pardons v. Allen, 482 U.S. 369, 377 n.8, 107 S. Ct. 2415 (1987); *see, e.g.,* U.S. ex rel. Conklin v. Beyer, 678 F. Supp. 1109, 1111 (D.N.J. 1988) (upholding statute permitting parole board to postpone eligibility based on disciplinary record); Alessi v. Thomas, 620 F. Supp. 589, 593–94 (S.D.N.Y. 1985) (ban on associating with persons with criminal records was not vague as applied).

[842]Farrell v. Burke, 449 F.3d 470, 486–87 (2d Cir. 20006) (holding parole condition barring possession of "pornographic material" was unconstitutionally vague, though not vague as applied, since material possessed by plaintiff was pornographic under any definition of the term); Coleman v. Dretke, 395 F.3d 216, 222–23 (5th Cir. 2004) (requiring person not convicted of sex offense to register as a sex offender and attend sex offender therapy, without notice or hearing, denied due process because there is a liberty interest in freedom from such conditions); Felce v. Fiedler, 974 F.2d 1484, 1493-96 (9th Cir. 1992) (restricting involuntary psychotropic medication of parolees); Hyland v. Procunier, 311 F. Supp. 749, 750 (N.D.Cal. 1970) (enjoining limits on public speeches by parolee). *But see* Grennier v. Frank, 453 F.3d 442, 446 (7th Cir. 2006) (in a parole system where there is no liberty interest in release, requiring prisoner to complete sex offender program before release did not require further process).

[843]U.S. v. Zavala-Serra, 853 F.2d 1512, 1518 (9th Cir. 1988) (parole ineligibility for large-scale drug trafficking operation did not constitute cruel and unusual punishment).

[844]*See, e.g.,* U.S. v. Bender, 566 F.3d 748, 751–54 (8th Cir. 2009) (offender who met an under-aged woman on-line and had sex with her, and who used a library computer to view pornography, could be forbidden to use computers and the internet without probation officer's permission; ban on all "sexually stimulating materials" was not sufficiently tailored to facts of case; absolute ban on entering libraries was overly broad); U.S. v. Voelker, 489 F.3d 139, 150–153 (3d Cir. 2007) (striking down prohibition on possession of any sexually explicit material, since the ban affected some constitutionally protected material and the offender's history did not support prohibition of material other than child pornography); U.S. v. Simmons, 343 F.3d 72, 82–83 (2d Cir. 2003) (offender whose crime involved minors could be forbidden to possess or view any pornography, not just child pornography, since his history indicated

disability statutes prevent states from excluding prisoners from parole based on their disabilities.[845] Parolees may be required to agree to be searched at any time without cause, and such searches do not violate the Fourth Amendment.[846] Charging parolees fees for their own supervision has been upheld by the courts,[847] as have other fees and charges,[848] though it would appear that you can't be reincarcerated just for being unable to pay them.[849]

A recurrent issue in parole cases is whether changes in parole statutes, regulations, or practices violate the constitutional prohibition against *ex post facto* laws,[850] which forbids imposing punishment[851] for an act that was not punishable when it was committed, or imposing more severe punishment than the law prescribed at the time of the offense.[852] Parole statutes, rules, etc.,[853] that change the standards for granting parole or dictate longer periods of incarceration violate the Ex Post Facto Clause if applied retroactively to offenses committed before the change in law.[854]

---

that there was a connection between his criminal behavior and possession of any sexually explicit material); Boling v. Romer, 101 F.3d 1336, 1340–41 (10th Cir. 1996) (sex offenders could be required to provide DNA samples before parole release); Folk v. Attorney General of the Commonwealth of Pa., 425 F. Supp. 2d 663, 672 (W.D.Pa. 2006) (sex offender could be denied parole unless he acknowledged guilt of his crimes; "Progress by the parole applicant in the process of rehabilitation is a legitimate consideration for the Board."); McColpin v. Davies, 778 F. Supp. 516, 518 (D.Kan. 1991) (requirement to attend sex offender program for a third time upheld), *aff'd*, 961 F.2d 220 (10th Cir. 1992). Sex offender programs are discussed further in § H.5.b of this chapter and in Ch. 2, § F.4.b.

[845]*See* Thompson v. Davis, 295 F.3d 890, 897 (9th Cir. 2002) (holding prisoners could challenge exclusion from parole of persons with drug abuse histories; stating Americans with Disabilities Act applies to "substantive decision making process in the criminal law context"). The federal disability statutes are discussed in Ch. 2, § F.4.h(2).

[846]Samson v. California, 547 U.S. 843, 852–56, 126 S. Ct. 2193 (2006).

[847]Owens v. Sebelius, 357 F. Supp. 2d 1281, 1285–90 (D.Kan. 2005); Taylor v. Sebelius, 350 F. Supp. 2d 888, 894–900 (D.Kan. 2004), *aff'd*, 189 Fed.Appx. 752, 756–59 (10th Cir. 2006) (unpublished).

[848]Alexander v. Johnson, 742 F.2d 117, 123–25 (4th Cir. 1984) (upholding requirement that prisoners who can afford it repay the costs of their criminal defense).

[849]The Supreme Court has so held concerning monetary conditions of probation, *see* Bearden v. Georgia, 461 U.S. 660, 668–72, 103 S. Ct. 2064 (1983), and that rule applies to parole conditions as well. Com. v. Dorsey, 328 Pa.Super. 241, 248–49, 476 A.2d 1308, 1312 (Pa.Super. 1984); State v. Haught, 179 W.Va. 557, 562, 371 S.E.2d 54, 59 (W.Va. 1988).

[850]U.S. Const., Art. I, § 9, cl. 3, and § 10, cl. 1.

[851]Measures that are not considered punishment are not subject to the Ex Post Facto Clause. *See* Smith v. Doe, 538 U.S. 84, 123 S. Ct. 1140 (2003) (holding sex offender registration requirement is not punitive either in intent or in operation); *see* Neal v. Shimoda, 131 F.3d 818, 826–27 (9th Cir. 1997) (requirement that sex offenders complete a treatment program before becoming parole eligible does not violate the Ex Post Facto Clause because it is rehabilitative and not punitive); Jones v. Murray, 962 F.2d 302, 310 (4th Cir. 1992) (requirement of providing blood sample before parole release is not punitive).

[852]Weaver v. Graham, 450 U.S. 24, 28, 101 S. Ct. 960 (1981). *Cf.* Stogner v. California, 539 U.S. 607, 610–21, 123 S. Ct. 2446 (2003) (applying a law extending a statute of limitations to permit prosecution of a crime that had become time-barred before the statute was enacted violated the Ex Post Facto Clause); Carmell v. Texas, 529 U.S. 513, 120 S. Ct. 1620 (2000) (change in law requiring less evidence to convict violated the Ex Post Facto Clause as applied to previously committed offense).

[853]The Supreme Court has held that Ex Post Facto Clause analysis requires courts to consider not only the relevant statutes, but also relevant administrative rules, regulations, guidelines, and practices. Garner v. Jones, 529 U.S. 244, 255, 120 S. Ct. 1362 (2000). Before *Garner*, some courts had said that administrative guidelines and the like were not "laws" for this purpose, or that rules that merely affected the way parole authorities exercised their discretion were not "laws." Some courts have now said that *Garner* erases this distinction entirely. *See* Fletcher v. Reilly, 433 F.3d 867, 876–77 (D.C. Cir. 2006); *accord*, Michael v. Ghee, 498 F.3d 372, 382–84 (6th Cir. 2007), *cert. denied*, 128 S. Ct. 2067 (2008). Others have disagreed. *See* U.S. v. Demaree, 459 F.3d 791, 795 (7th Cir.2006) ("We conclude that the ex post facto clause should apply only to laws and regulations that bind rather than advise, a principle well established with reference to parole guidelines whose retroactive application is challenged under the ex post facto clause."), *cert. denied*, 551 U.S. 1167 (2007).

[854]Lynce v. Mathis, 519 U.S. 433, 117 S. Ct. 891 (1997) (state statute which retroactively cancelled provisional early release credits awarded to a state prisoner violated the Ex Post Facto Clause, even though the purpose of the credits was to reduce overcrowding); Fletcher v. Reilly, 433 F.3d 867, 876–77, 879 (D.C. Cir. 2006) ("The controlling inquiry under *Garner* is how the Board or the Commissioner exercises discretion in practice, and whether differences between the exercise of discretion in two systems actually 'create[] a significant risk of prolonging [an inmate's] incarceration." Where a regulation gave less weight to post-incarceration behavior than its predecessor, there was a *prima facie* case of *ex post facto* violation.); McKissick v. U.S. Parole Com'n, 295 F. Supp. 2d 643, 648–49 (S.D.W.Va. 2003) (use of new "salient factor score" in denying parole was not an *ex post facto* violation where it represented a way of structuring discretion that had previously existed, and petitioner did not show it actually made him serve more time), *aff'd*, 67 Fed.Appx. 824 (4th Cir. 2003) (unpublished); Jones v. Murray, 962 F.2d at 310. Wolfe v. Pennsylvania Dep't of Corrections, 334 F. Supp. 2d 762, 774–75 (E.D.Pa. 2004) (allegation that changed standards for parole release placed greater weight on public safety stated an Ex Post Facto Clause claim); Miller v. Ignacio, 112 Nev. 930, 934–35, 921 P.2d 882, 884–85 (1996) (withdrawal of Pardons Board's power to commute life without parole to life with the possibility of parole violated the Ex Post Facto Clause); Shelton v. Armenakis, 146 Or. App. 521, 525, 934 P.2d 512, 514 (1997) (applying a new statute providing for postponement of parole would violate the Ex Post Facto Clause applied to someone whose offense predated the statute); Christenson v. Thompson, 143 Or. App. 483, 923 P.2d 1316 (1996) (applying a new statute to determine release date for prisoner whose offense predated the statute). *But see* Inmates of the

This rule applies to changes in good time statutes that result in postponing parole or other release eligibility[855] and to measures that extend the period that must be served on parole.[856] It does not apply to new requirements that are justified in terms of rehabilitation, law enforcement, or other non-punitive purposes.[857] A change in law reducing the frequency of parole consideration does not violate the Ex Post Facto Clause unless it creates a "significant risk of increasing [the prisoner's] punishment" in actual operation.[858] Changes that are merely procedural do not constitute

ex post facto laws.[859] Changes in officials' attitudes resulting in a harsher application of the same laws do not violate the Ex Post Facto Clause.[860]

State statutes and regulations governing parole release may provide greater rights to prisoners than the federal Constitution. These will generally have to be enforced in state court.[861]

b. Parole Rescission Parole rescission means having your parole release date taken from you before you are actually released on parole. Like parole release, and unlike parole revocation, parole rescission does not entitle you to due process protections unless the state has created a liberty interest in parole release.[862] The *Sandin v. Conner* limitations on due process rights do not apply to parole rescission.[863]

Pennsylvania Dep't of Corrections v. Corbett, 484 F. Supp. 2d 359 (E.D.Pa. 2007) (granting summary judgment in case previously captioned *Wolfe v. Pennsylvania Dep't of Corrections, supra,* on the ground that applying the new parole standard did not actually disadvantage the plaintiff).

Changes in statutes and regulations can violate the Ex Post Facto Clause even if the state's parole statutes and regulations do not create a liberty interest or entitlement protected by due process. *See* Raske v. Martinez, 876 F.2d 1496, 1499 (11th Cir. 1989); Alston v. Robinson, 791 F. Supp. 569, 588 (D.Md. 1992), *aff'd,* 19 F.3d 10 (4th Cir.1994) (unpublished) (citing Weaver v. Graham, 450 U.S. at 29–30).

[855]Weaver v. Graham, 450 U.S. 24, 35–36, 101 S. Ct. 960 (1981); Hunter v. Ayers, 336 F.3d 1007, 1011 (9th Cir. 2003); Smith v. Scott, 223 F.3d 1191, 1194–96 (10th Cir. 2000) (unforeseeable new amendment to good time regulations violated Ex Post Facto Clause); Arnold v. Cody, 951 F.2d 280, 282–83 (10th Cir. 1991); Raske v. Martinez, 876 F.2d 1496,1498–1502 (11th Cir. 1989). *But see* Shabazz v. Gabry, 123 F.3d 909, 912 (6th Cir.1997) (finding no *ex post facto* violation in Michigan amendments reducing frequency of parole hearings); Hallmark v. Johnson, 118 F.3d 1073, 1077–79 (5th Cir. 1997) (regulation restricting return of good time taken in disciplinary proceeding did not violate Ex Post Facto Clause where return had been discretionary, unlike *Hunter v. Ayers* where there were objective criteria for return); Abed v. Armstrong, 209 F.3d 63, 65–66 (2d Cir. 2000) (directive making prisoners viewed as safety threats ineligible for good time was not an *ex post facto* violation since good time had been discretionary).

[856]Combs v. Board of Parole and Post-Prison Supervision, 141 Or. App. 219, 917 P.2d 74 (1996).

[857]*See, e.g.,* Neal v. Shimoda, 131 F.3d 818, 826–27 (9th Cir. 1977) (requirement that sex offenders go through a treatment program to become parole eligible did not violate Ex Post Facto Clause); Gilbert v. Peters, 55 F.3d 237, 238–39 (7th Cir. 1995) (requirement to provide blood sample for DNA testing before release did not violate Ex Post Facto Clause); *see* Smith v. Doe I, 538 U.S. 84, 92–106, 123 S. Ct. 1140 (2003) (sex offender registration provisions were not punitive and therefore did not violate the Ex Post Facto Clause).

[858]Garner v. Jones, 529 U.S. 244, 255, 120 S. Ct. 1362 (2000) (change in parole board's rules was subject to Ex Post Facto Clause scrutiny, but should have been considered in combination with board's internal policy statement and its actual practices); *accord,* California Dep't of Corrections v. Morales, 514 U.S. 499, 510–12, 115 S. Ct. 1597 (1995); Jernigan v. State, 340 S.C. 256, 264 & n.5, 531 S.E.2d 507 (S.C. 2000) (holding statute that extended time between parole hearings, without a provision for expedited review based on changed circumstances or new information, violated the Ex Post Facto Clause).

[859]Weaver v. Graham, 450 U.S. 24, 29, 101 S. Ct. 960 (1981); Barna v. Travis, 239 F.3d 169, 171 (2d Cir. 2001) (per curiam); *see* Alston v. Robinson, 791 F. Supp. at 590–92 (increase in required parole board vote for release and provisions for victim notice and response were procedural); *see also* Johnson v. Gomez, 92 F.3d 964, 967–68 (9th Cir. 1996) (statute allowing governor to overrule parole board decisions, but not changing the standards for release, did not violate the Ex Post Facto Clause where there was no showing it resulted in a less favorable decision).

[860]Grennier v. Frank, 453 F.3d 442, 445 (7th Cir. 2006).

[861]Boling v. Romer, 101 F.3d 1336, 1338 n.2 (10th Cir. 1996).

[862]Jago v. Van Curen, 454 U.S. 14, 17–21, 102 S. Ct. 31 (1981) (rescission of parole did not constitute a deprivation of liberty); *accord,* Hess v. Board of Parole and Post-Prison Supervision, 514 F.3d 909, 915 (9th Cir. 2008) (parole board could rescind parole date based upon "present severe emotional disturbance such as to constitute a danger to the health and safety of the community."), *cert. denied,* 128 S. Ct. 2972 (2008); Bill v. U.S. Parole Com'n, 53 Fed.Appx. 29 (10th Cir. 2002) (unpublished) (presumptive parole date can be changed based upon institutional misconduct behavior); Gilbertson v. Texas Bd. of Pardons and Parole, 993 F.2d 74, 75 (5th Cir. 1993); Inmates v. Ohio State Adult Parole Auth., 929 F.2d 233, 235–37 (6th Cir. 1991) (prisoners granted parole release "on or after" certain future dates were not entitled to due process protections when those dates were rescinded). *Compare* McQuillion v. Duncan, 306 F.3d 895, 901–02 (9th Cir. 2002) (holding parole rescission deprived prisoner of a liberty interest where state law permitted rescission only for "good cause" including "(1) any disciplinary conduct subsequent to the grant of parole, (2) psychiatric deterioration of the prisoner, and (3) new information indicating parole should not occur, such as an inability to meet a special condition of parole, information significant to the original grant of parole being fraudulently withheld from the Board, or fundamental errors which resulted in the improvident grant of parole" (citation omitted)). In *Hess v. Board of Parole and Post-Prison Supervision,* 514 F.3d at 913, the court held that a parole rescission statute denies due process if it is excessively vague about the criteria for rescission, though it upheld the statute before it.

[863]McQuillion v. Duncan, 306 F.3d 895, 902–03 (9th Cir. 2002) (*Sandin* applies only to "internal prison disciplinary regulations").

Parole rescission requires only "some evidence" supporting rescission.[864] State law or regulations may provide procedural protections enforceable in state court.[865]

c. Parole Revocation The Supreme Court held that a parolee enjoys a "conditional liberty" protected by due process in *Morrissey v. Brewer*.[866] Revocation of parole requires two types of hearing: (1) a preliminary hearing to determine whether there is probable cause or reasonable ground to believe that the parolee has violated the terms of parole, and (2) a final revocation hearing to determine any contested relevant facts and to consider whether those facts support revocation.[867] Even when there is no dispute that the parolee committed a violation, if the parole board has any discretion not to revoke parole, she is generally entitled to an opportunity to present mitigating evidence at the final hearing to argue that parole should not be revoked for it.[868] Court-imposed supervised release that involves parole-type supervision is generally governed by the same rules as parole and probation revocation.[869]

At the preliminary hearing, you are minimally entitled to: (1) a hearing conducted by someone not involved in initiating the revocation charges; (2) notice of the facts upon which the revocation charges are based; (3) the right to be present and to be heard on your behalf; (4) a written summary of the evidence and arguments presented; (5) a written decision containing the facts and reasoning for finding probable cause; and (6) the right to confront those providing adverse information unless the hearing officer determines that the informant would be subjected to risk of harm if her identity was disclosed.[870]

At the final hearing, you are entitled to:[871] (1) a hearing before a neutral and detached body, usually the parole board or a hearing officer working for it;[872] (2) written notice listing your alleged parole violations; (3) disclosure of all the evidence to be used against you; (4) an opportunity to speak to the parole board to state why your parole should not be revoked, including an opportunity to present witnesses and documentary evidence; (5) an opportunity to confront and cross-examine adverse witnesses unless the parole board specifically finds good cause why you should not be allowed to;[873] (6) a written decision stating the facts and the reasoning upon which your parole was revoked; and (7) a reasonably prompt hearing.[874] Parole revocation charges need only

---

[864]Caswell v. Calderon, 363 F.3d 832, 838–39 (9th Cir. 2004); McQuillion v. Duncan, 306 F.3d 895, 904–05 (9th Cir. 2002); McCarns v. Dexter, 534 F. Supp. 2d 1138, 1149–56 (C.D.Cal. 2008) (finding Governor's rescission of parole date denied due process). In *McQuillion*, the court also held that refusing to let the petitioner call members of the panel that had paroled him at the rescission hearing did not deny due process. 306 F.3d at 900.

[865]For example, a New York regulation provides for notice, a hearing with counsel and cross-examination, and an administrative appeal in parole rescission cases. 9 N.Y.C.R.R. § 8002.5 *et seq.*

[866]408 U.S. 471, 480–82, 92 S. Ct. 2593 (1971). The same is true of prisoners released to a program that is virtually identical to parole except in name. Young v. Harper, 520 U.S. 143, 147–52, 117 S. Ct. 1148 (1997) (holding persons in "pre-parole" program were entitled to same due process rights as parolees).

[867]Morrissey v. Brewer, 408 U.S. at 485–89.

[868]*See* Black v. Romano, 471 U.S. 606, 612–13, 105 S. Ct. 2254 (1985); U.S. v. Cornog, 945 F.2d 1504, 1512 (11th Cir. 1991); Preston v. Piggman, 496 F.2d 270, 274–75 (6th Cir. 1974); Witzke v. Withrow, 702 F. Supp. 1338, 1351–53 (W.D.Mich. 1988) and cases cited; Ex parte Martinez, 742 S.W.2d 289, 290–92 (Tex.Cr.App. 1987) (citing state and federal constitutions); *see also* Pope v. Chew, 521 F.2d 400, 405 (4th Cir. 1975) (same holding as to conditional pardon). This rule applies where the parolee has been convicted of a new crime and can no longer dispute committing that crime. Witzke v. Withrow, 702 F. Supp. at 1352–53 (citing Moss v. Patterson, 555 F.2d 137 (6th Cir. 1977) (per curiam)); Ex parte Martinez, *supra*. If state law makes revocation mandatory under certain circumstances, there is no right to such a hearing if the circumstances are not disputed. *See, e.g.*, Pickens v. Butler, 814 F.2d 237, 239–41 (5th Cir. 1987) (state law and regulations made revocation mandatory upon conviction of a felony); Ringor v. State, 88 Hawaii 229, 238, 965 P.2d 162, 171 (Haw. App. 1998); Alevras v. Neubert, 727 F. Supp. 852, 853–54 (S.D.N.Y. 1990).

[869]U.S. v. Kelley, 446 F.3d 688, 690–91 (7th Cir. 2006); U.S. v. Hall, 419 F.3d 980, 985 n.4 (9th Cir. 2005).

[870]Morrissey v. Brewer, 408 U.S. at 485–88.

A parole officer not involved in bringing the charges against you can be the hearing officer. *Morrissey*, 408 U.S. at 486. The parolee may present "letters, documents, or individuals who can give relevant information to the hearing officer." *Id.* at 487.

[871]*See* Morrissey v. Brewer, 408 U.S. at 487–89.

[872]*See* Sonntag v. Papparozzi, 256 F. Supp. 2d 320, 325–26 (D.N.J. 2003) (holding decisions of temporary parole members, appointed by Governor without legislative confirmation allegedly in violation of state law, did not deny due process), *aff'd as modified*, 94 Fed.Appx. 970 (3d Cir. 2004) (unpublished).

[873]*See, e.g.*, Ash v. Reilly, 431 F.3d 826, 830 (D.C. Cir. 2005); White v. White, 925 F.2d 287, 290–91 (9th Cir. 1991); Downie v. Klincar, 759 F. Supp. 425, 426–27 (N.D. Ill. 1991) (good cause for not allowing confrontation and cross-examination of adverse witnesses is determined by balancing test which weighs reliability of hearsay evidence and difficulty or costs of procuring and producing witnesses); *see also* Gholston v. Jones, 848 F.2d 1156 (11th Cir. 1988) (waiver of right to confrontation and cross-examination cannot be presumed if not on the hearing record). Some courts have held that even without good cause to exclude a witness, a parolee must show "prejudice from his inability to cross-examine" the missing witness to invalidate the hearing result. Ash v. Reilly, 431 F.3d at 830.

The courts have disagreed whether the parole authority must make an explicit finding of good cause for not allowing a parolee to confront an adverse witness. *See* Singletary v. Reilly, 452 F.3d 868, 872 (D.C. Cir. 2006) (citing cases; not requiring such a finding, but placing the burden on parole authorities to ensure sufficient indicia of reliability to protect due process).

[874]Morrissey v. Brewer, 408 U.S. at 485–88 ("A lapse of two months . . . would not appear to be unreasonable."). Courts generally hold that delay in parole revocation hearings does not deny due process unless some prejudice, other than incarceration in the interim, is shown—*e.g.*, inability to present a case because evidence is unavailable. Villarreal v. U.S. Parole Comm'n, 985 F.2d

be proved by a preponderance of the evidence, not beyond a reasonable doubt.[875] Parole revocation hearings are not bound strictly by the rules of evidence; "the process should be flexible enough to consider evidence including letters, affidavits, and other material that would not be admissible in an adversary criminal trial."[876] One court has held that the standard concerning hearsay in parole revocation proceedings is not whether it would be admissible at a criminal trial but "whether the evidence considered as a whole, including the hearsay evidence, was both sufficient in quantity and reliability to ensure fundamental due process rights."[877] However, "the use of unsubstantiated or unreliable hearsay" would be inconsistent with due process.[878] The federal Constitution does not require that evidence obtained in violation of the Fourth Amendment be excluded from parole hearings,[879] though some state courts do apply the exclusionary rule to parole revocation.[880] The decision-making body may also be required by due process to follow its own rules and standards in deciding to revoke parole.[881]

A parolee is constitutionally entitled to counsel for a revocation proceeding if a substantial issue is raised as to whether parole or probation was actually violated, or if the issues to be raised in mitigation of any violations are so complex that the parolee is not capable of handling them effectively.[882] The parolee should be informed by the parole revocation hearing officer of the limited right to appointment of counsel. It is then the parolee's responsibility to make a timely request for appointed counsel and to state why counsel is needed. If the parolee does not appear to be capable of "speaking effectively for himself" (*e.g.*, because of limited mental capacity or a mental disorder), counsel should be appointed.[883] Some states have dispensed with these distinctions and have enacted statutes providing for counsel in all parole revocation proceedings.[884]

The preliminary hearing must be conducted at, or reasonably near, the place of the alleged parole violation or arrest.[885] Since some states do not provide the parole board, or their hearing officers, with the power to compel witnesses to attend revocation hearings,[886] this requirement makes it easier for parolees to get necessary witnesses and other evidence to the hearing.

If a parolee is convicted of a new criminal offense, a preliminary hearing is not required, since probable cause that you have violated your parole will exist at the moment of conviction.[887] Even if you are acquitted of the criminal charge, your parole may be revoked based on the same incident.[888] The authorities are barred from revoking parole on

---

835, 837 (5th Cir. 1993) (154-day delay between arrest and final hearing did not violate due process absent showing of prejudice); Meador v. Knowles, 990 F.2d 503, 506 (9th Cir. 1993); Covington v. State, 938 P.2d 1085, 1088 n.2 (Alaska App. 1997); *see* Ellis v. District of Columbia, 84 F.3d 1413, 1424 (D.C. Cir. 1996) (policy of revocation hearings within 60 days of the preliminary interview and within 30 days after notice of a warrant's execution satisfied due process). If prejudicial delay is established, due process requires quashing of the parole violation warrant. U.S. ex rel. Sims v. Sielaff, 563 F.2d 821, 828 (7th Cir. 1977); Flenoy v. Ohio Adult Parole Authority, 56 Ohio St.3d 131, 134, 564 N.E.2d 1060, 1063 (Ohio 1990). The Supreme Court has tolerated long periods of delay in cases involving prisoners incarcerated on other charges. *See* nn.891–892 in this section, below.

[875]Faheem-El v. Klincar, 841 F.2d 712, 731 (7th Cir. 1988); Johnson v. Kelsh, 664 F. Supp. 162, 164 n.5 (S.D.N.Y. 1987) (preponderance of evidence required to establish parole revocation; burden on state to prove parole violation); *see* U.S. v. Armstrong, 187 F.3d 392, 394 (4th Cir. 1999) (same, for federal supervised release). Though the parole board must use a preponderance standard of proof in deciding whether to revoke parole, if it applies that standard, for purposes of judicial review, due process requires only that there be *some* evidence in the record supporting its conclusion. Moore v. Olson, 368 F.3d 757, 760 (7th Cir. 2004); *see* § H.1.i of this chapter concerning the relationship between the standard of proof and the standard of judicial review.

[876]Morrissey v. Brewer, 408 U.S. at 489; *see* Vargas v. U.S. Parole Comm'n, 865 F.2d 191, 195 (9th Cir. 1988) (arrest report relied on in parole revocation). However, the right of confrontation may be violated by the use of documentary evidence in place of live testimony. Gholston v. Jones, 848 F.2d at 1159–60 and cases cited; Downie v. Klincar, 759 F. Supp. at 426–27.

[877]Singletary v. Reilly, 452 F.3d 868, 872 (D.C. Cir. 2006) (quoting Crawford v. Jackson, 323 F.3d 123, 128 (D.C. Cir. 2003)). Courts have disagreed whether there must be "good cause" to admit hearsay in parole revocation hearings or whether courts should balance the government's need for the evidence against the interest of the parolee in confronting witnesses against her. *See* U.S. v. Kelley, 446 F.3d 688, 691 n.4 (7th Cir. 2006) (collecting cases).

[878]Singletary v. Reilly, 452 F.3d at 872.

[879]Pennsylvania Bd. of Probation and Parole v. Scott, 524 U.S. 357, 364–69, 118 S. Ct. 2014 (1998).

[880]*See, e.g.*, People ex rel. Picarillo v. New York State Bd. of Parole, 48 N.Y.2d 76, 421 N.Y.S.2d 842, 394 N.E.2d 354 (N.Y. 1979).

[881]*See* Collins v. Hendrickson, 371 F. Supp. 2d 1326, 1328–29 (M.D.Fla. 2005) (where state law required parole commission to base decisions on the parole examiner's factual findings, there was a liberty interest in having that law followed, and revocation for reasons contradicting parole examiner's findings denied due process).

[882]Gagnon v. Scarpelli, 411 U.S. 778, 92 S. Ct. 1756 (1973). *Gagnon* actually dealt with probation revocation, but it treated probation and parole as equivalent for this purpose.

[883]Gagnon v. Scarpelli, 411 U.S. at 790–91; *see also* Smith v. U.S. Parole Comm'n, 875 F.2d 1361, 1368 (9th Cir. 1988) (no absolute right to counsel during parole revocation hearing).

[884]*See, e.g.*, In re Wayne County Prosecutor, 232 Mich. App. 482, 485, 591 N.W.2d 359 (1998) (citing Michigan statute).

[885]Morrissey v. Brewer, 408 U.S. 471, 485, 92 S. Ct. 2593 (1972).

[886]Other states do provide this power. *See, e.g.*, N.Y. Executive Law § 259(i)(3)(c)(iii) (providing for subpoena power).

[887]Moody v. Daggett, 429 U.S. 78, 86 n.7, 92 S. Ct. 274 (1976).

[888]Whitehead v. U.S. Parole Com'n, 755 F.2d 1536, 1537 (11th Cir. 1985) (noting parole revocation requires lower standard of proof than criminal conviction); Standlee v. Rhay, 557 F.2d 1303, 1305–07 (9th Cir. 1977) (parole revocation after acquittal does not

such grounds only if, as a matter of law, the dismissal of criminal charges removes all factual basis from the claim that you committed a parole violation.[889]

Parole authorities are not required to hold revocation hearings immediately when a parolee is convicted of another crime. In *Moody v. Daggett*,[890] the federal parole board had issued a parole violation warrant which was lodged as a detainer against a prisoner convicted of another crime, but the board refused to execute it until he was released from the sentence he was presently serving. This meant that he lost the opportunity to serve the two sentences concurrently. The Supreme Court upheld the parole board's refusal to execute the warrant.[891] It added that if a prisoner is concerned that evidence mitigating the parole violation charge would be lost if the hearing was delayed, the prisoner can identify the evidence that may be lost, giving parole authorities the opportunity to schedule an earlier hearing.[892]

States must accommodate prisoners' disabilities in parole revocation proceedings under the federal disability statutes.[893]

d. Temporary Release The current law of temporary release[894] is generally similar to the law of parole. Most courts say that prisoners who are in work release or other temporary release programs have a liberty interest in staying in them, requiring due process protections when officials try to remove them, if they live in the community and not in an institutional setting; but if they continue to live in a prison, halfway house, or other institution, they do not have a liberty interest in staying in the program.[895] The Supreme Court has held in *Young v. Harper* that persons released to a "pre-parole" program in which they lived at home under conditions similar to parole were entitled to the same due process protections as regular parolees when officials sought to revoke their status.[896] A number of courts have said that the *Young* decision confirms that there is a liberty interest in staying in temporary release programs where participants live in the community, but not in programs where the prisoner continues to live in the prison or other institution.[897]

Some older cases say that there is no liberty interest in staying on temporary release, but many of these cases involved programs where the prisoner remained in an institution.[898] Other older decisions concerning temporary release focus on whether state statutes and regulations

---

constitute double jeopardy); State v. Johnson, 92 Wash.2d 598, 600 n.2, 599 P.2d 529 (Wash. 1979).

[889]Flenoy v. Ohio Adult Parole Auth., 56 Ohio St.3d 131, 564 N.E.2d 1060, 1062 (Ohio 1990).

[890]429 U.S. 78, 97 S. Ct. 274 (1976).

[891]Moody v. Daggett, 429 U.S. at 87.

Federal courts have similarly held that a state prisoner is not entitled to an immediate violation hearing when a federal detainer is lodged with the state prison officials alleging violation of federal parole because of a state felony conviction. *See, e.g.,* Heath v. U.S. Parole Com'n, 788 F.2d 85, 90–91 (2d Cir. 1986); U.S. ex rel Hahn v. Revis, 560 F.2d 264 (7th Cir. 1977); Hicks v. Board of Parole, 550 F.2d 401 (8th Cir. 1977). The same result has been reached when a state parole violation warrant was lodged as a detainer with prison officials of another state. *See* Larson v. McKenzie, 554 F.2d 131 (4th Cir. 1977) (per curiam).

[892]Moody v. Daggett, 429 U.S. at 88 n.9. In one case, the court held that a parolee could force the Parole Commission to place the mitigating evidence on the record preserving it for subsequent revocation hearing. *See* U.S. ex rel Caruso v. U.S. Bd. of Parole, 570 F.2d 1150, 1154 n.9 (3d Cir. 1978).

[893]*See* § H.6.a, n.840 of this chapter.

[894]In this section, we use the term "temporary release" to include work or education release, furloughs, halfway houses, and all other programs that permit prisoners to get out of ordinary confinement.

[895]Anderson v. Recore, 446 F.3d 324, 328–29 (2d Cir. 2006); Paige v. Hudson, 341 F.3d 642, 643–44 (7th Cir. 2003) (holding that removal from "home detention" to jail was a liberty deprivation requiring due process); Anderson v. Recore, 317 F.3d 194, 200 (2d Cir. 2003); Friedl v. City of New York, 210 F.3d 79, 84 (2d Cir. 2000); Asquith v. Dep't of Corrections, 186 F.3d 407, 410–11 (3d Cir. 1999) (holding that prisoner in work release in a halfway house was still in institutional confinement and had no liberty interest); Kim v. Hurston, 182 F.3d 113, 117 (2d Cir. 1999); Callender v. Sioux City Residential Treatment Facility, 88 F.3d 666, 668 (8th Cir. 1996) (holding a prisoner in a work release program more analogous to institutional life than parole or probation did not have a liberty interest protected by due process); Edwards v. Lockhart, 908 F.2d 299, 301–03 (8th Cir. 1990) (holding temporary release program in which the plaintiff lived at home and not in an institution was similar to parole and there was a constitutionally based liberty interest in avoiding termination); Whitehorn v. Harrelson, 758 F.2d 1416, 1421 (11th Cir. 1985) (holding prisoner held in work release center had no liberty interest because he remained institutionalized); Weller v. Grant County Sheriff, 75 F. Supp. 2d 927, 932–33 (N.D.Ind. 1999) (holding that work release participant who remained in jail while not working had no liberty interest in staying in the program); Quartararo v. Catterson, 73 F. Supp. 2d 270, 273–74 (E.D.N.Y. 1999); Wright v. Coughlin, 31 F. Supp. 2d 301, 312 (W.D.N.Y. 1998) (finding a liberty interest in remaining in an extra-institutional work release program), *vacated on other grounds*, 225 F.3d 647 (2d Cir. 2000) (unpublished). Some courts have held that where work release is part of the criminal sentence and placement and removal are under the control of the sentencing court, there is no liberty interest. *See* McGoue v. Janecka, 211 F. Supp. 2d 627, 631 (E.D.Pa. 2002).

[896]Young v. Harper, 520 U.S. 143, 117 S. Ct. 1148 (1997).

[897]Asquith v. Dep't of Corrections, 186 F.3d at 410–11; Friedl v. City of New York, 210 F.3d at 84; Kim v. Hurston, 182 F.3d 113, 118 (2d Cir. 1999); Paige v. Hudson, 234 F. Supp. 2d 893, 901–03 (N.D.Ind. 2002), *aff'd*, 341 F.3d 642 (7th Cir. 2003); Carter v. McCaleb, 29 F. Supp. 2d 423, 427 (W.D.Mich. 1998).

[898]*See* Dominique v. Weld, 73 F.3d 1156, 1160 (1st Cir. 1996), *aff'g* 880 F. Supp. 928, 933 (D.Mass. 1995) (involving prisoner living in a minimum security prison); Bowser v. Vose, 968 F.2d 105, 106–09 (1st Cir. 1992) (involving prisoner in furlough program who was released for brief periods but remained in prison most of the time); Brennan v. Cunningham, 813 F.2d 1, 5–7 (1st Cir. 1987) (involving prisoner in halfway house); Whitehorn v. Harrelson, 758 F.2d 1416, 1421 (11th Cir. 1985) (involving prisoner held in work release center).

created a liberty interest protected by due process.[899] However, the Supreme Court has now held that a prisoner can only establish a state-created liberty interest if she is subjected to "atypical and significant hardship" compared to ordinary prison conditions.[900] Since removal from temporary release merely puts a prisoner back in ordinary prison conditions, most (though not all) courts have held that it does not constitute atypical and significant hardship.[901] You are much better off relying on the *Young v. Harper* holding, if it applies to your situation, than on the liberty interest argument.

There is no constitutionally based liberty interest in obtaining temporary release.[902] Can statutes and regulations create a liberty interest in obtaining temporary release, as is the case with parole?[903] Before *Sandin v. Conner*, some courts had found liberty interests in admission to temporary release in statutes and regulations,[904] though most had not,

because in most cases the statutes and regulations left prison officials with too much discretion in granting temporary release to create a liberty interest.[905] If *Sandin v. Conner's* requirement that prisoners show "atypical and significant hardship" compared to ordinary prison conditions[906] applies to admission to temporary release, prisoners do not have a liberty interest, because denial of temporary release just means the prisoner stays in ordinary prison conditions.[907] On the other hand, if temporary release programs in which the prisoner lives in the community are constitutionally similar to parole, as courts have said since the Supreme Court decided *Young v. Harper*,[908] it would seem that statutes and regulations could create a liberty interest in being admitted to them,[909] just as some parole statutes and regulations do.

Temporary release is very unpopular with politicians and much of the public, and it is often subject to cutbacks and new restrictions in the face of bad publicity, like when a prisoner on temporary release is accused of a highly publicized crime. The courts have placed some limits on this process. If the legislature chooses to change the eligibility criteria so you no longer meet them, you may be removed from temporary release.[910] However, some courts have held that if officials try to bar or remove you based on criteria

---

[899]A number of courts found liberty interests using this approach. *See, e.g.,* Lanier v. Fair, 876 F.2d 243, 247–48 (1st Cir. 1989) (liberty interest created by "Manual of Operations" and "Program Statement" that governed contract with private halfway house operator); Brennan v. Cunningham, 813 F.2d at 6–7; Tracy v. Salamack, 572 F.2d 393, 395–96 (2d Cir. 1978) (citing practices as well as regulations); U.S. ex rel. Flores v. Cuyler, 511 F. Supp. 386, 389–90 (E.D.Pa. 1981); Smith v. Stoner, 594 F. Supp. 1091, 1105–06 (N.D.Ind. 1984) (liberty interest in staying on work release created by state court's sentence); Gray v. Wisconsin Dep't of Health and Social Services, 495 F. Supp. 321, 322–23 (E.D.Wis. 1980); Perrote v. Percy, 465 F. Supp. 112, 114 (W.D.Wis. 1979), *modified,* 489 F. Supp. 212, 214 (E.D.Wis. 1980). Others did not. *See* Bowser v. Vose, 968 F.2d at 106–09; Coakley v. Murphy, 884 F.2d 1218, 1221 (9th Cir. 1989); Vinson v. Barkley, 646 F. Supp. 39, 42 (W.D.N.Y. 1986); Williams v. Sumner, 648 F. Supp. 510, 512 (D.Nev. 1986); Holmes v. Robinson, 84 Md.App. 144, 578 A.2d 294, 298 (Md.Spec.App. 1990), *cert. denied,* 321 Md. 501, 583 A.2d 275 (1991).

[900]Sandin v. Conner, 515 U.S. 472, 484, 115 S. Ct. 2293 (1995); *see* § A.3 of this chapter.

[901]*See* Asquith v. Dep't of Corrections, 186 F.3d at 409–11; Callender v. Sioux City Residential Treatment Facility, 88 F.3d 666, 669 (8th Cir. 1996); Dominique v. Weld, 73 F.3d 1156, 1160 (1st Cir. 1996); McGoue v. Janecka, 211 F. Supp. 2d 627, 631 (E.D.Pa. 2002), all holding that returning a work release participant to prison is not atypical and significant. *Contra,* Segretti v. Gillen, 259 F. Supp. 2d 733, 737–38 (N.D.Ill. 2003); Quartararo v. Catterson, 917 F. Supp. 919, 940–41 (E.D.N.Y. 1996); Roucchio v. Coughlin, 923 F. Supp. 360, 374–75 & n.6 (S.D.N.Y. 1996).

[902]Kitchen v. Upshaw, 286 F.3d 179, 186–87 (4th Cir. 2002); Lee v. Governor of State of New York, 87 F.3d 55, 58 (2d Cir. 1996); Mahfouz v. Lockhart, 826 F.2d 791, 792 (8th Cir. 1987); Baumann v. Arizona Dep't of Corrections, 754 F.2d 841, 843–45 (9th Cir. 1985); Romer v. Morgenthau, 119 F. Supp. 2d 346, 357–58 (S.D.N.Y. 2000).

[903]As discussed above, statutes and regulations governing parole release can create a liberty interest if they place sufficient limits on official discretion (though most do not). *See* § H.6.a of this chapter.

[904]*See* Winsett v. McGinnes, 617 F.2d 996, 1007–08 (3d Cir. 1980) (en banc) (holding that where discretion to release is governed by certain criteria, an eligible inmate has a liberty interest

that is violated by consideration of factors outside those criteria); Olynick v. Taylor County, 643 F. Supp. 1100, 1103–04 (W.D.Wis. 1986) (denial of work release that was mandated by sentencing judge denied due process); In re Head, 147 Cal.App.3d 1125, 195 Cal.Rptr. 593, 596–98 (1983).

[905]*See, e.g.,* DeTomaso v. McGinnis, 970 F.2d 211, 212–13 (7th Cir. 1992); Gaston v. Taylor, 946 F.2d 340, 344 (4th Cir.1991) (en banc); Canterino v. Wilson, 869 F.2d 948, 953 (6th Cir. 1989); Francis v. Fox, 838 F.2d 1147, 1149–50 (11th Cir. 1988); Mahfouz v. Lockhart, 826 F.2d at 793; Nash v. Black, 781 F.2d 665, 668 (8th Cir. 1986); Baumann v. Arizona Dep't of Corrections, 754 F.2d at 844–45; Johnson v. Stark, 717 F.2d 1550, 1551 (8th Cir. 1983); Cruz v. Sielaff, 767 F. Supp. 547, 550 (S.D.N.Y. 1991); Rial v. McGinnis, 756 F. Supp. 1070, 1073 (N.D.Ill. 1991); Fuller v. Lane, 686 F. Supp. 686, 688–89 (C.D.Ill. 1988); Dugar v. Coughlin, 613 F. Supp. 849, 855–56 (S.D.N.Y. 1985); Martino v. Gard, 526 F. Supp. 958, 966 (E.D.N.Y. 1981); *see also* Hickson v. Burkhart, 651 F. Supp. 355, 356 (S.D.W.Va. 1987), *aff'd in part, vacated in part,* 838 F.2d 1209 (4th Cir. 1988); Jones v. Lane, 568 F. Supp. 1113, 1115 (N.D.Ill. 1983); Young v. Hunt, 507 F. Supp. 785, 787–89 (N.D.Ind. 1981) (finding no liberty interest on various grounds).

[906]*See* § A.3 of this chapter.

[907]*See* Kitchen v. Upshaw, 286 F.3d 179, 186–87 (4th Cir. 2002).

[908]*See* nn.896–897, above.

[909]*But see* Gambino v. Gerlinski, 96 F. Supp. 2d 456, 459–60 (M.D.Pa. 2000) (holding federal work release statute did not create a liberty interest because it was not explicitly mandatory and did not contain specified substantive predicates), *aff'd,* 216 F.3d 1075 (3d Cir. 2000) (unpublished).

[910]Tracy v. Salamack, 572 F.3d 393, 396 (2d Cir. 1978).

that are not permitted under their own statutes and regulations, due process is violated.[911]

Some courts hold that where there is a liberty interest in staying on temporary release, revocation proceedings need only meet the due process standards of prison disciplinary hearings.[912] Others have held that the higher standards of parole or probation revocation are required.[913] The *Young v. Harper* decision discussed above, with its holding that release that looks like parole should be treated like parole,

___

[911]Brennan v. Cunningham, 813 F.2d 1, 11–12 (1st Cir. 1987); Winsett v. McGinnes, 617 F.2d 996, 1007–08 (3d Cir. 1980) (en banc).

[912]*See* Lanier v. Fair, 876 F.2d 243, 248-49 (1st Cir. 1989); Brennan v. Cunningham, 813 F.2d at 8–9; Tracy v. Salamack, 572 F.2d at 397; Perrote v. Percy, 465 F. Supp. 112, 114 (W.D.Wis. 1979), *modified*, 489 F. Supp. 212, 214 (E.D.Wis. 1980); People ex rel. Cunningham v. Metz, 61 A.D.2d 590, 403 N.Y.S.2d 330, 332 (N.Y.App.Div. 1978).

[913]Edwards v. Lockhart, 908 F.2d 299, 303 (8th Cir. 1990) (parole revocation procedures were required to revoke temporary release in which the plaintiff lived at home); Quartararo v. Hoy, 113 F. Supp. 2d 405, 412–13 (E.D.N.Y. 2000) (parole revocation procedures); Smith v. Stoner, 594 F. Supp. 1091, 1107 (N.D.Ind. 1984) (parole revocation procedures required); U.S. ex rel. Flores v. Cuyler, 511 F. Supp. 386, 391 (E.D.Pa. 1981) (witnesses and confrontation required); *see also* Perrote v. Percy, 489 F. Supp. at 214–16 (requiring hearings within 14 days; pre-hearing confinement only upon a finding of need; immediate reinstatement upon a finding of not guilty of the disciplinary offense).

The parole/probation revocation due process standards require

> (1) written notice of the alleged violation of the program's rules or conditions; (2) a statement of the actual reason why the inmate's removal from work release is being considered; (3) a report or summary of the evidence against him or her; (4) an opportunity to be heard and to present evidence; (5) advance notice of a temporary release committee hearing; (6) the right to confront and cross-examine adverse witnesses; (7) a TRC composed of neutral decisionmakers; and (8) a post-hearing written account of the actual reason for removal and a summary of the evidence supporting that reason.

Quartararo v. Hoy, 113 F. Supp. 2d at 412; *see* Gutierrez v. Joy, 502 F. Supp. 2d 352, 358–59 (S.D.N.Y. 2007) (evidence that defendants did not provide notice of charges and excluded plaintiff from his own hearing by transferring him to another prison, so he was unable to call witnesses or produce evidence, supported a due process claim despite prison officials' claim of an emergency).

In *Anderson v. Recore*, 446 F.3d 324, 329–33 (2d Cir. 2006), the court held that due process would be satisfied by giving the prisoner a disciplinary hearing concerning the alleged violation of temporary release rules, and a hearing before the Temporary Release Committee on whether the facts established at the disciplinary hearing merited removal from temporary release. That seems to mean that the elements of *Morrissey* due process that are not included in *Wolff* process for disciplinary hearings—confrontation and cross-examination, absent a specific finding of good cause to disallow it—are left out of the fact-finding process, where they might be useful, and left in the proceeding to determine what sanction to impose, where they are not so useful.

supports the latter argument for release programs where the prisoner lives in the community. State law or regulations may entitle you to more procedural protections than the federal Constitution, and you may be able to enforce these rules in a state court proceeding.[914] Violation of state law protections that exceed federal due process requirements does not deny due process.[915]

Often, temporary release programs simply exclude certain categories of prisoners from eligibility. The courts have generally upheld the discretion of legislatures and of prison officials in making these decisions.[916] Courts also defer to

___

Prison disciplinary proceedings are discussed in § H.1 of this chapter; parole and probation revocation, in § H.6.c; administrative segregation, in § H.2.

[914]*See* Taylor v. Franzen, 93 Ill.App.3d 758, 48 Ill.Dec. 840, 417 N.E.2d 242, 245 (Ill.App. 1981), *supplemented*, 51 Ill.Dec. 645, 420 N.E.2d 1203 (1981); *see also In re* Head, 147 Cal.App.3d 1125, 195 Cal.Rptr. 593, 595–98 (1983) (for initial denial of work furlough, state constitution's due process clause required written notice that the prisoner would be excluded, access to the information the decision was based on, an opportunity for the prisoner to respond orally, and a written statement of the final decision).

[915]Domka v. Portage County, Wis., 523 F.3d 776, 784 (7th Cir. 2008); Holcomb v. Lykens, 337 F.3d 217, 224 (2d Cir. 2004).

[916]Lee v. Governor of State of New York, 87 F.3d 55, 58–59 (2d Cir. 1996) (persons convicted of certain categories of felony); Dominique v. Weld, 73 F.3d 1156, 1159-63 (1st Cir. 1996) (sex offenders who had not completed a treatment program); Karacsonyi v. Radloff, 885 F. Supp. 368, 370 (N.D.N.Y. 1995) (prisoners who refused to participate in Inmate Financial Responsibility Program); Mahfouz v. Lockhart, 826 F.2d 791, 794 (8th Cir. 1987) (sex offenders); Fuller v. Lane, 686 F. Supp. 686, 689–90 (C.D.Ill. 1988); Fernandez-Collado v. I.N.S., 644 F. Supp. 741, 744 (D.Conn. 1986) (prisoner subject to immigration detainer), *aff'd*, 857 F.2d 1461 (2d Cir. 1987); Luttrell v. Dep't of Corrections, 421 Mich. 93, 365 N.W.2d 74, 78–82 (Mich. 1984) (drug traffickers); Jansson v. Dep't of Corrections, 147 Mich.App. 774, 383 N.W.2d 152, 153–54 (Mich. App. 1985) (sex offenders); Jiminez v. Coughlin, 117 A.D.2d 1, 501 N.Y.S.2d 539, 542 (N.Y.App.Div. 1986) (deportable aliens), *appeal denied*, 68 N.Y.2d 606 (1986); *see* Baumann v. Arizona Dep't of Corrections, 754 F.2d 841, 843–45 (9th Cir. 1985) (white collar criminals) (suggesting that exclusion of white-collar criminals would be upheld as rationally related to public perceptions of fairness); Jamieson v. Robinson, 641 F.2d 138, 141–43 (3d Cir. 1981) (officials could offer work release at some prisons and not others). *But see In re* Head, 147 Cal.App.3d 1125, 195 Cal.Rptr. 593, 598 (1983) (striking down blanket exclusion of certain categories of prisoners on state law grounds).

There is a controversy in the federal system over assignment of prisoners to community confinement centers ("halfway houses"), now known as Residential Re-Entry Centers. *See* Miller v. Whitehead, 527 F.3d 752, 754 (8th Cir. 2008).

The Bureau of Prisons enacted a regulation, 28 C.F.R. §§ 570.20–21, providing that prisoners could be placed in these institutions only during the last six months of their sentences, and for no longer than six months. Several federal appeals courts held that this regulation is illegal because it conflicts with the federal statute that authorizes it, and one federal appeals court upheld the regulation. The case that upheld it, which discusses the other decisions

the decisions of temporary release officials about particular individuals, even if they appear inconsistent,[917] unless a decision is clearly based on some completely illegitimate factor.[918] Prison officials may impose conditions on admission to temporary release.[919] Changes in temporary release eligibility rules generally do not violate the constitutional prohibition on *ex post facto* laws.[920]

Federal courts have heard challenges to temporary release denial and revocation under the civil rights statutes, and have not required that they be pursued via petition for habeas corpus after exhaustion of state judicial remedies.[921] In state courts, the proper remedy will be dictated by the statutes and jurisdictional rules of each state.[922] Courts may order prisoners restored to temporary release and may award damages if they find that temporary release has been revoked unlawfully.[923]

7. Correcting Your File

There is a limited due process right to have erroneous and derogatory information expunged from a prisoner's parole or institutional file.[924] Courts have stressed that it is *not* a general right of prisoners to inspect their files[925] and have insisted that prisoners cannot obtain relief without establishing each of several elements: false factual information in the file,[926] official reliance on the misinformation,[927] an adverse result that is constitutionally significant,[928] and an

---

and the history of the dispute, is *Muniz v. Sabol*, 517 F.3d 29 (1st Cir. 2008), *cert. denied sub nom* Gonzalez v. Sabol, 129 S. Ct. 115 (2008). The dispute has continued since *Muniz*. *Compare* Rodriguez v. Smith, 541 F.3d 1180 (9th Cir. 2008) (rejecting *Muniz*) with Miller v. Whitehead, *supra* (agreeing with *Muniz*). Presumably this conflict will be resolved by the Supreme Court in another case.

[917]For example, in *Martino v. Gard*, 526 F. Supp. 958, 960–61 (E.D.N.Y. 1981), the plaintiff alleged that he had been treated differently from his brother, who had received the same sentence for the same criminal act and had a similar prison record. The court held that there was no constitutional violation. *Accord*, Dugar v. Coughlin, 613 F. Supp. 849, 857 (S.D.N.Y. 1985); Rowe v. Cuyler, 534 F. Supp. 297, 301 (E.D.Pa.), *aff'd*, 696 F.2d 985 (3d Cir. 1982); Young v. Hunt, 507 F. Supp. 785, 789 (N.D.Ind. 1981).

A complete failure to exercise discretion was struck down in *Ortiz v. Wilson*, 113 Misc.2d 226, 448 N.Y.S.2d 918 (N.Y.Sup. 1981), *aff'd*, 86 A.D.2d 987, 449 N.Y.S.2d 818 (N.Y.App.Div. 1982). In that case, the prison Temporary Release Committee "blindly adher[ed]" to a decision made 19 months earlier at another prison without considering the prisoner's more recent prison record.

[918]Friedl v. City of New York, 210 F.3d 79, 86 (2d Cir. 2000) (holding plaintiff who was removed from work release for applying for food stamps and administratively appealing the denial stated a claim for retaliation for exercise of First Amendment rights); Flaherty v. Coughlin, 713 F.2d 10 (2d Cir. 1983) (retaliation for lawsuits); Quartararo v. Hoy, 113 F. Supp. 2d 405, 415 (E.D.N.Y. 2000) (holding that notoriety of prisoner's offense and community opposition to his release were not evidence supporting revocation of release because the regulations did not make those factors reason for removal); Jones v. Coughlin, 696 F. Supp. 916, 922–23 (S.D.N.Y. 1988) (retaliation for lawsuits).

The New York courts have held that temporary release decisions will be overturned only for "irrationality bordering on impropriety." Gonzales v. Wilson, 106 A.D.2d 386, 482 N.Y.S.2d 302, 303 (N.Y.App.Div. 1984). Under this standard, one court struck down as irrational the denial of a furlough to a prisoner with AIDS; it was allegedly based on medical reasons, but the furlough was for one week and the prisoner was only medically examined every two weeks. Lopez v. Coughlin, 139 Misc.2d 851, 529 N.Y.S.2d 247, 249 (N.Y.Sup. 1988).

[919]*See, e.g.*, Ervin v. Blackwell, 733 F.2d 1282, 1285–86 (8th Cir. 1984) (prisoner could be required to contribute to his own maintenance on work release); Mastrian v. Schoen, 725 F.2d 1164 (8th Cir. 1984) (same).

[920]Lee v. Governor of State of New York, 87 F.3d 60, 60 (2d Cir. 1996); Dominique v. Weld, 73 F.3d 1156, 1161–63 (1st Cir. 1996). In *Plyler v. Moore*, 129 F.3d 728, 734 (4th Cir. 1997), the court held that a statute excluding prisoners convicted of certain crimes from pre-release "furloughs" granted to ease prison overcrowding was an *ex post facto* law. However, the "furloughs" occurred at the end of the prisoner's sentence and led to earlier release, making the case similar to the Supreme Court's decision *Lynce v. Mathis*, 519 U.S. 433, 117 S. Ct. 891 (1997), which held that a state statute which

retroactively cancelled provisional early release credits violated the Ex Post Facto Clause. *Plyler* really isn't a temporary release case despite the use of the word "furlough."

[921]*See* Ch. 8, § H.1.a, n.561.

[922]*See, e.g.*, Dorbolo v. Sullivan, 450 A.2d 1185, 1186 (Del. Super. 1982) (state court habeas corpus could not be used); Dougherty v. State, 323 N.W.2d 249, 250 (Iowa 1982) (state Administrative Procedures Act must be used); *In re* Head, 147 Cal. App.3d 1125, 195 Cal.Rptr. 593, 596 (1983) (state habeas corpus was proper).

[923]Quartararo v. Hoy, 113 F. Supp. 2d 405, 418–22 (E.D.N.Y. 2000) (directing restoration to work release, stating the plaintiff is entitled to damages for lost wages, emotional distress, and possibly for SHU placement after revocation; also directing that after restoration, he not be supervised by any of the defendants in this action and not be subjected to retaliation).

[924]Paine v. Baker, 595 F.2d 197, 201 (4th Cir. 1979); *accord*, Farinaro v. Coughlin, 642 F. Supp. 276, 281–82 (S.D.N.Y. 1986) and cases cited; Bukhari v. Hutto, 487 F. Supp. 1162, 1167–78 (E.D.Va. 1980). The question of parole denials based on false information is discussed in n.826, above.

[925]Bloodgood v. Garraghty, 783 F.2d 470, 473 (4th Cir. 1980); Paine v. Baker, 595 F.2d at 201.

[926]Jones v. Ray, 279 F.3d 944, 946 (11th Cir.2001); Hernandez v. Johnston, 833 F.2d 1316, 1318–19 (9th Cir. 1987) (holding opinions and evaluations were not factual and would not be expunged); Hill v. State, 594 So.2d 246, 248 (Ala.Cr.App. 1992) (holding prisoner failed to show that the information was false).

[927]Bloodgood v. Garraghty, 783 F.2d at 473; Reyes v. Supervisor of Drug Enforcement Agency, 647 F. Supp. 1509, 1513 (D.P.R. 1986), *aff'd in part and vacated in part*, 834 F.2d 1093 (1st Cir. 1987); Hill v. State, 594 So.2d at 248; Drennon v. Craven, 141 Idaho 34, 38, 105 P.3d 694, 698 (Idaho App. 2004) (all ruling against plaintiffs who did not show that the allegedly false information was relied upon).

[928]Hampton v. Mouser, 701 F.2d 766, 767 (8th Cir. 1983) (holding that prisoner was not specific enough about the information's effect on the "severity or terms of his confinement"); Robbins v. South, 595 F. Supp. 785, 791 (D.Mont. 1984) (holding

unsuccessful attempt to get the problem corrected administratively.[929] The requirement of a constitutionally significant adverse result may be especially hard to meet. Some courts have held that you must show that you were deprived of a liberty interest,[930] which is very difficult to do in light of the restrictive definition of liberty interests in *Sandin v. Conner.*[931] You must be sure to utilize any available statutory or administrative procedure before challenging the incorrect information under the Due Process Clause,[932] both because the due process law requires it and because of the administrative exhaustion requirement of the Prison Litigation Reform Act.[933] In fact, at least one federal circuit has held that the available administrative remedies provide all the process due to federal prisoners with respect to the accuracy of their files[934]—that is, once you've used them, win or lose, you have no basis for a lawsuit.

In a criminal proceeding, there is a right "not to be sentenced on the basis of information that is materially false, and that right is protected by affording the defendant notice of and an opportunity to respond to information on which the court intends to rely in imposing sentence."[935] Criminal proceedings are beyond the scope of this Manual.

Courts may direct the expungement of prison records of particular disciplinary proceedings as a remedy when

they find that the proceeding denied due process,[936] or that the information in the records otherwise results from a constitutional violation.[937]

There may be procedural or other obstacles to suits alleging reliance on false prison records. A suit alleging that you were denied parole or other form of release based on erroneous records may be barred by the rule that you can't challenge the fact or duration of confinement in a civil rights lawsuit without first exhausting state remedies and if necessary federal habeas corpus.[938] If the erroneous information originated in a probation report or other document prepared for or at the direction of a court, the people who prepared it may be protected from suit by judicial immunity;[939] in such a case your only remedy may be an injunction to correct the information.

The federal Privacy Act[940] provides limited rights to federal prisoners with respect to inaccurate files.[941] It requires federal executive agencies[942] to maintain records used in making determinations about individuals "with such accuracy . . . as is reasonably necessary to assure fairness

---

prisoner had failed to identify the consequences of having the information in his file).

[929]Hernandez v. Johnston, 833 F.2d 1316, 1318–19 (9th Cir. 1987) (noting that the prisoner had not used the formal state procedure); Bukhari v. Hutto, 487 F. Supp. at 1167–68 (holding prisoner had failed to request the removal of the information).

[930]Johnson v. Rodriguez, 110 F.3d 299, 308–309 n.13 (5th Cir.1997); Reffitt v. Nixon, 917 F. Supp. 409, 413–14 (E.D.Va. 1996) (right not to have parole release decisions based on false information exists only if there is a liberty interest in getting parole), *aff'd*, 121 F.3d 699 (4th Cir. 1997) (unpublished). *Contra*, Monroe v. Thigpen, 932 F.2d 1437, 1441–42 (11th Cir. 1991) (defendants admitted falsity of information); Paine v. Baker, 595 F.3d at 202 (noting that adverse decision on a non-constitutional matter "may have collateral consequences touching on the liberty interest"); *see* Adams v. Agniel, 405 F.3d 643, 645 (8th Cir. 2005) (per curiam) (if there is a claim based on false information in the absence of a liberty interest, it is limited to "extreme" cases such as arbitrary or knowing use of false information). The court in *Johnson v. Rodriguez, supra*, argues that both *Monroe* and *Paine v. Baker* have been undermined by later decisions.

[931]515 U.S. 472, 484, 115 S. Ct. 2293 (1995); *see* §§ A, B of this chapter.

[932]*See* Fendler v. U.S. Bureau of Prisons, 846 F.2d 550, 554 (9th Cir. 1988) (holding that federal Privacy Act provided a limited administrative remedy to federal prisoners); Hernandez v. Johnston, 833 F.2d at 1318–19 (noting that state law created a formal administrative procedure); *see also* Sellers v. Bureau of Prisons, 959 F.2d 307, 312 (D.C. Cir. 1992) (discussing prisoners' rights under federal Privacy Act).

[933]*See* Ch. 9, § D.

[934]Castaneda v. Henman, 914 F.2d 981, 985–86 (7th Cir. 1990).

[935]Hili v. Sciarrota, 140 F.3d 210, 215 (2d Cir. 1998).

[936]*See* § H.1.r.(5) of this chapter.

[937]Kerr v. Farrey, 95 F.3d 472, 476 (7th Cir. 1996) (plaintiff could seek expungement from prison records of his refusal to attend a program with explicit religious content); Spruytte v. Hoffner, 181 F. Supp. 2d 736, 745 (W.D.Mich. 2001) (directing expungement from records of "security threat" label insofar as it was based on an incident which involved retaliatory action by officials); Gaston v. Coughlin, 81 F. Supp. 2d 381, 392 (N.D.N.Y. 1999) (directing expungement of prison files of trumped-up allegations of a planned work stoppage made in retaliation for prisoner's exposure of illegal practices), *reconsideration denied*, 102 F. Supp. 2d 51 (N.D.N.Y. 2000); *see* Toolasprashad v. Bureau of Prisons, 286 F.3d 576, 586 (D.C. Cir. 2002) (holding that falsifying a transfer memorandum resulting in reclassification as a "special offender" and a transfer to a less desirable prison, in retaliation for filing grievances and contacting public officials, stated a constitutional claim).

[938]That is less likely to be the case than in the past, since the Supreme Court has now clarified that civil rights lawsuits are barred only if a decision for the plaintiff would "necessarily imply" the invalidity of the decision keeping her confined. If the plaintiff requests only that records be corrected, which may or may not result in release at a later time, the civil rights suit can go forward. Adams v. Agniel, 405 F.3d 643, 644–45 (8th Cir. 2005) (per curiam) (citing Wilkinson v. Dotson, 544 U.S. 74, 125 S. Ct. 1242 (2005)). These issues are discussed further at Ch. 8, § H.1.a.

[939]*See* Ch. 8, § L.2, n.790.

[940]5 U.S.C. § 552a. Other aspects of the Privacy Act are discussed in Ch. 3, § E.3, n.939; Ch. 10, § K.1, n.405.

[941]As the name suggests, the Privacy Act also has provisions limiting the disclosure and use of records by government agencies. *See, e.g.,* Maydak v. U.S., 363 F.3d 512, 515–16 (D.C. Cir. 2004) (describing provisions). These are discussed in Ch. 3, § E.3, n.939.

[942]The judicial branch is excluded from the terms of the Privacy Act, so courts and agencies that work for the court system are not subject to its requirements. *See, e.g.,* Callwood v. Dep't of Probation of the Virgin Islands, 982 F. Supp. 341, 343 (D.V.I. 1997) (holding federal Department of Probation exempt from the Privacy Act because it is an arm of the court).

to the individual in the determination,"[943] and to respond to requests to amend them.[944] These provisions may be enforced by civil suits to amend inaccurate records[945] or for damages for "intentional or willful" refusal to correct inaccurate information that then results in an adverse determination.[946] However, the federal Bureau of Prisons has exempted its inmate record systems and pre-sentence reports from the amendment provisions,[947] and the federal Parole Commission has done the same for its inmate records and pre-sentence reports,[948] though other BOP records, and other agency records, may be within their scope. You can still sue for damages for adverse determinations based on those records; such a claim requires the plaintiff to allege (and eventually to prove) "that an agency failed to maintain accurate records, that it did so intentionally or willfully, and consequently, that an 'adverse' 'determination [wa]s made' respecting the plaintiff."[949] The proper defendants in Privacy Act cases are federal agencies, not individual agency employees.[950] Privacy Act claims are governed by a two-year statute of limitations that runs from the time of the alleged violation or the plaintiff's discovery of it, not from subsequent decisions based on the inaccurate records.[951]

Privacy Act claims alleging the inaccuracy of records on which a prisoner's criminal conviction, sentence, or release date calculation is based may be barred by the rule that challenges to the fact or duration of confinement may not be challenged in a civil action until the relevant decision has been directly overturned or challenged through a habeas corpus proceeding.[952]

8. Property

Prison officials may substantially restrict the property inmates may possess.[953] "[B]ut when inmates are afforded the opportunity . . . to possess property, they enjoy a protected interest in that property that cannot be infringed without due process."[954] Because the Supreme Court's decision in *Sandin v. Conner* addressed deprivations of prisoners' liberty, it should not be applicable to deprivations of property.[955]

Property rights are also protected by the Fifth Amendment, which states: " . . . [N]or shall private property be taken for public use, without just compensation."[956] This provision has rarely been applied in prison cases.[957] Property restrictions or confiscations that are done for reasons of security or prison administration are considered to be exercises of the "police power," or similar to a statutory forfeiture, neither of which is considered a "taking" of property.[958]

---

[943]5 U.S.C. § 552a(e)(5); *see* Sellers v. Bureau of Prisons, 959 F.2d 307, 311–12 (D.C. Cir. 1992) (holding duty to maintain accurate records was not satisfied by noting the plaintiff's disagreement with the records in a case where the truth was easily ascertainable).

[944]5 U.S.C. § 552a(d)(2).

[945]5 U.S.C. §§ 552a(g)(1), 552(g)(2)(A).

[946]5 U.S.C. § 552a(g)(4); *see* Doe v. Chao, 540 U.S. 614, 124 S. Ct. 1204 (2004) (holding that plaintiff must prove "actual damages" in order to receive minimum damage award of $1000 for Privacy Act violation).

[947]White v. U.S. Probation Office, 148 F.3d 1124, 1125 (D.C. Cir. 1998) (per curiam); *see* Fendler v. U.S. Bureau of Prisons, 846 F.2d 550 (9th Cir. 1988) (discussing BOP's Privacy Act exemptions).

[948]Deters v. U.S. Parole Comm'n, 85 F.3d 655, 658 n.2 (D.C. Cir. 1996) (citing 28 C.F.R. §§ 16.85, 16.51(c)).

[949]Toolasprashad v. Bureau of Prisons, 286 F.3d 576, 583 (D.C. Cir. 2002); *accord,* Perry v. Bureau of Prisons, 371 F.3d 1304, 1305 (11th Cir. 2004) and cases cited; Deters v. U.S. Parole Comm'n, 85 F.3d 655, 657 (D.C. Cir. 1996) (holding that Privacy Act damage plaintiffs must show that they are aggrieved by an adverse determination; that the agency failed to maintain its records accurately enough to assure a fair determination; that reliance on inaccurate records was a proximate cause of the adverse determination; and that the agency acted intentionally or willfully in failing to maintain accurate records). In *Toolasprashad,* the court held that allegations that prison personnel fabricated and falsified records in retaliation for filing grievances would be "willful or intentional." 286 F.3d at 584.

[950]Perry v. Bureau of Prisons, 371 F.3d at 1305.

[951]5 U.S.C. § 552a(g)(5); *see* Harrell v. Fleming, 285 F.3d 1292, 1293–94 (10th Cir. 2002); Armstrong v. U.S. Bureau of Prisons, 976 F. Supp. 17, 21–22 (D.D.C. 1997), *aff'd,* 1998 WL 65543 (D.C. Cir., Jan. 30, 1998) (unpublished).

[952]*See* Razzoli v. Federal Bureau of Prisons, 230 F.3d 371, 375–76 (D.C. Cir. 2000); Jackson v. Federal Bureau of Prisons, 538 F. Supp. 2d 194, 198 (D.D.C. 2008). These issues are discussed further at Ch. 8, § H.1.a; *see also* Whitley v. Hunt, 158 F.3d 882, 889 (5th Cir. 1998) (holding that prisoners' claim that prison officials relied on inaccurate information about his sentence was essentially a claim that the sentence was improperly entered, and should have been resolved on direct appeal).

[953]*See* Ch. 3, § F for a discussion of rules limiting property.

[954]McCrae v. Hankins, 720 F.2d 863, 869 (5th Cir. 1983); *accord,* Bryant v. Barbara, 11 Kan.App.2d 165, 717 P.2d 522, 524 (Kan.App. 1986).

[955]Handberry v. Thompson, 446 F.3d 335, 353 n.6 (2d Cir. 2006); Bulger v. U.S. Bureau of Prisons, 65 F.3d 48, 50 (5th Cir. 1995); Arney v. Simmons, 923 F. Supp. 173, 177, n.4 (D.Kan. 1996); Wenzler v. Warden of G.R.C.C., 949 F. Supp. 399, 402, n.1 (E.D.Va. 1996); Jeffries v. Tennessee Dep't of Correction, 108 S.W.3d 862, 871–72 (Tenn.Ct.App. 2002). *Contra,* Cosco v. Uphoff, 195 F.3d 1221, 1223–24 (10th Cir. 1999).

[956]U.S. Const., Amend. V.

[957]There are a few exceptions. Some courts have held the confiscation of interest on inmates' funds violates the Fifth Amendment. *See* cases cited in § H.8.d of this chapter, n.1022; Howland v. State, 169 Ariz. 293, 818 P.2d 1169, 1171 n.3 (Ariz.App. 1991) (dictum) ("An allegation that prison employees unlawfully took a prisoner's private property raises an issue whether that conduct violates the just compensation clause.")

Before prosecuting a claim under the Takings Clause, you must seek and be denied "just compensation" through any available remedy provided by the responsible governmental body. Williamson County Regional Planning Comm'n v. Hamilton, 473 U.S. 172, 194-97, 105 S. Ct. 3108 (1985).

[958]Savko v. Rollins, 749 F. Supp. 1403, 1412–15 (D.Md. 1990); Cody v. Leapley, 476 N.W.2d 257, 260–61 (S.D. 1991).

Prisoners' due process rights are limited in property cases. Deprivations of property resulting from negligence, or "mere lack of due care," do not deny due process at all.[959] These must be redressed, if at all, through a tort damage action[960] or a grievance or other administrative remedy. Intentional deprivations of property that are "random and unauthorized" also do not deny due process as long as there is an adequate post-deprivation remedy, such as a tort suit or administrative procedure that can provide compensation.[961] Only if there is no such procedure or it is inadequate will you have a due process claim.[962]

As a practical matter, federal courts are not disposed to find state procedures inadequate without a very strong reason, and some federal judges are disposed to look for ways to dismiss prisoner property claims because they consider them trivial and beneath their dignity.[963] Unless you are certain that there is no adequate remedy in state court or state administrative procedure, you are well advised to use available state remedies before pursuing a federal civil rights suit for property loss (and of course you must exhaust the prison administrative process in any case).

If your property is unique or irreplaceable or if you need it immediately, you may want an order that it be returned to you now, as opposed to an award of damages sometime in the future. The federal courts have not agreed on whether a damages remedy provides due process when what you really need is the return of your property.[964]

Many prisoners are subject to actions for forfeiture of property allegedly related to their criminal behavior.[965] In general, criminal forfeiture is beyond the scope of this Manual, but we will mention a couple of points. There is a recurrent problem of prosecutors' failure to provide adequate notice of forfeiture proceedings to defendants who are in prison. The Supreme Court has held that notice need not actually be received by the prisoner as long as it is sent to the place where the prisoner is held.[966] However, courts continue to hold that notice of forfeiture is inadequate when it is sent somewhere the prisoner is *not* held.[967]

The federal forfeiture statute also provides that

> in no event shall a prisoner file a claim under a civil forfeiture statute or appeal a judgment in a civil action or proceeding based on a civil forfeiture statute if the prisoner has, on three or more prior occasions, while incarcerated or detained in any facility, brought an action or appeal in a court of the United States that was dismissed on the grounds that it is frivolous or malicious, unless the prisoner shows extraordinary and exceptional circumstances.[968]

This provision is modeled on the "three strikes" provision of the Prison Litigation Reform Act,[969] but is much more extreme; it bars most prisoners with three strikes from contesting forfeitures of property at all. This seems to us like a blatantly unconstitutional deprivation of property without due process of law. We can't find a single case where it has been applied, so maybe the courts think so too.

The Supreme Court has held that a young person's state law right to an education is a property interest, and

---

[959]Daniels v. Williams, 474 U.S. 327, 331–32, 106 S. Ct. 662 (1986). Previously, in *Parratt v. Taylor*, 451 U.S. 527, 101 S. Ct. 1908 (1981), the Supreme Court had held that under some circumstances negligent deprivation of property denies due process, but *Daniels v. Williams* overruled that part of *Parratt*.

[960]See § H.8.c of this chapter for a discussion of state court damage actions related to property.

[961]Hudson v. Palmer, 468 U.S. 517, 533–35, 104 S. Ct. 3194 (1984). The meaning of "random and unauthorized" and what constitutes an adequate post-deprivation remedy is discussed in § E of this chapter.

[962]See § F of this chapter for discussion of the adequacy of post-deprivation remedies. For federal prisoners, there is a question whether they have *any* remedy for intentional property deprivations under current law. This point is discussed in § H.8.c of this chapter.

[963]See, e.g., Harper v. Kemp, 677 F. Supp. 1213, 1215 (M.D.Ga. 1988); *see also* Smith v. Rose, 760 F.2d 102, 108 (6th Cir. 1985) (dissenting opinion) (accusing court majority of being more concerned with remedying caseload problems than due process violations). *But see* Lewis v. Woods, 848 F.2d 649, 650–51 (5th Cir. 1988) ("A violation of constitutional rights is never *de minimis*, a phrase meaning so small or trifling that the law takes no account of it.").

[964]Compare Bumgarner v. Bloodworth, 738 F.2d 966, 968 (8th Cir. 1984) (state remedy that did not provide for return of property was inadequate) *with* Shango v. Jurich, 681 F.2d 1091, 1105 (7th Cir. 1982) (loss of unique property did not constitute irreparable harm justifying an injunction).

In some states there are state law remedies by which you may obtain the return of property. See § H.8.c of this chapter.

[965]The federal asset forfeiture provisions are at 18 U.S.C. §§ 981–987. States may have their own forfeiture statutes.

[966]Dusenberry v. U.S., 534 U.S. 161, 169–70, 122 S. Ct. 694 (2002); *see* Chairez v. U.S., 355 F.3d 1099, 1101–02 (7th Cir. 2004) (applying *Dusenberry*, declining to inquire into operation of jail's internal mail delivery). *But see* Nunley v. Department of Justice, 425 F.3d 1132, 1137–38 (8th Cir. 2005) (rejecting Seventh Circuit's refusal to examine prison mail delivery, holding the plaintiff has the burden of proof of its inadequacy); Collette v. Drug Enforcement Administration, 386 F. Supp. 2d 1120, 1133 n.18 (D.Alaska 2005) (notice sent to a jail was not adequate in instances where there was no evidence any jail member signed the certified mail receipt or where the notice was returned marked "Returned to Sender, Unknown"), *aff'd in part, rev'd in part on other grounds, and remanded*, 247 Fed.Appx. 87 (9th Cir. 2007) (unpublished).

[967]Nunley v. Dep't of Justice, 425 F.3d 1132, 1136 (8th Cir. 2005) (notice to an outside address did not suffice where the prisoner was known to be in jail); U.S. v. Howell, 354 F.3d 693, 696 (7th Cir. 2004) (sending notice to two addresses, one of which was known to be vacant, resulting in both notices' being returned undelivered, while failing to send the notice to the address on the prisoner's driver's license or to the Minnesota jail where he was known to be held, was not adequate).

[968]18 U.S.C. § 983(h)(3).

[969]28 U.S.C. § 1915(g); *see* Ch. 9, § B.

some courts have held that prisoners retain this right at least to some degree.[970]

a. Authorized Deprivations and Established Procedures

Deprivations of property that are "authorized" or result from an "established procedure" may deny due process regardless of whether there is a post-deprivation remedy.[971] Searches and shakedowns conducted pursuant to regulations or to the orders of responsible officials are considered authorized or established even if they are new, emergency measures.[972] However, in an emergency situation, prison officials may take the property first and deal with your procedural rights later.[973] Courts will generally uphold prison officials' judgment in limiting the property prisoners may possess,[974] and officials may retract authorization to have certain property as long as prisoners are given the opportunity to send the property to someone outside the prison.[975]

Some older cases held that when prison officials intentionally seize property, they must give the prisoner a receipt for the seized property, a statement of reasons for the seizure, the right to be heard in opposition to the seizure, and a decision with reasons if the seizure is upheld,[976] the last of which may be afforded at a disciplinary hearing if the prisoner is charged with a contraband offense.[977] These procedures are designed to prevent improper deprivations of property rather than to remedy them later with damages. After *Hudson v. Palmer*,[978] these cases are clearly no longer good law with respect to "random and unauthorized" acts by staff, for which due process requires only a post-deprivation remedy. However, we believe that these procedural protections should apply to seizures of property that are done in connection with established procedures such as cell searches, inspection of incoming packages, etc. The courts have not to our knowledge addressed this issue since *Hudson* was decided.[979]

A Supreme Court case decided the same day as *Hudson* deals with a different due process question. In *Block v. Rutherford*, the Court held that due process does not require prison officials to permit pretrial detainees to watch searches of their cells.[980]

A few courts have held that if an item is contraband, a prisoner has no "property interest" in it, and it can therefore be taken without due process.[981] We think that holding is wrong because it misses the point: there should be an opportunity to be heard on the question whether the item is contraband.[982] However, if it is established, or there is no

---

[970]See Ch. 2, § I.1, nn.1246–1247.

[971]Logan v. Zimmerman Brush Co., 455 U.S. 422, 436, 102 S. Ct. 1148 (1982); *accord*, Allen v. Thomas, 388 F.3d 147, 149 (5th Cir. 2004) (confiscation of property under authority of a prison administrative directive was not random and unauthorized and *Parratt* did not apply); Farid v. Smith, 850 F.2d 917, 925 (2d Cir. 1988); Caldwell v. Miller, 790 F.2d 589, 608 (7th Cir. 1986); Piatt v. MacDougall, 773 F.2d 1032, 1035 (9th Cir. 1985) (en banc); Chavers v. Abrahamson, 803 F. Supp. 1512, 1515 (E.D.Wis. 1992); Harper v. Kemp, 677 F. Supp. 1213, 1217–18 (M.D.Ga. 1988); Artway v. Scheidemantel, 671 F. Supp. 330, 334 (D.N.J. 1987).

The meaning of these terms is discussed in more detail in § E of this chapter.

[972]Caldwell v. Miller, 790 F.2d 589, 608 (7th Cir. 1986).

[973]Beck v. Lynaugh, 842 F.2d 759, 761 (5th Cir. 1988) (immersion heaters that presented a fire hazard could be confiscated without a prior hearing); Caldwell v. Miller, 790 F.2d at 608–09; Shabazz v. Odum, 591 F. Supp. 1513, 1517 (M.D.Pa. 1984).

[974]Beck v. Lynaugh, 842 F.2d at 761; Lyon v. Farrier, 730 F.2d 525, 527 (8th Cir. 1984); *see also* Salahuddin v. Coughlin, 591 F. Supp. 353, 358 (S.D.N.Y. 1984) (limit on property that prison would pay to have transferred did not deny due process where prisoners had notice of it). *But see* Holloway v. Lockhart, 792 F.2d 760, 762 (8th Cir. 1986) (allegation that the right to possess a radio and carbon paper had been retracted for no reason stated a due process claim).

[975]Caldwell v. Miller, 790 F.2d at 609 (denial of right to send confiscated hardcover books to friends outside prison might have denied due process and did violate prison regulations); Lyon v. Farrier, 730 F.2d at 527 (where inmates could send property home, due process was not violated); Neal v. Lewis, 325 F. Supp. 2d 1231, 1238 (D.Kan. 2004) (destroying confiscated religious books without a hearing did not deny due process, since the defendants had given options for disposing of them and the prisoner refused to choose among them), *aff'd*, 414 F.3d 1244, 1248 (10th Cir. 2005); Sivak v. State, 111 Idaho 118, 721 P.2d 218, 221 (Idaho App. 1986); *see* Blum v. State, 171 Ariz. 201, 829 P.2d 1247, 1250–53 (Ariz.App. 1992) (requirement that prisoners dispose of or forfeit property they had previously been permitted violated a state statute).

[976]U.S. ex rel. Wolfish v. Levi, 428 F. Supp. 333, 342 (S.D.N.Y. 1977), *supplemented*, 439 F. Supp. 114, 151 (S.D.N.Y. 1977), *aff'd in pertinent part*, 573 F.2d 118, 131–32 n.29 (2d Cir. 1978), *rev'd on other grounds sub nom*. Bell v. Wolfish, 441 U.S. 520, 99 S. Ct. 1861 (1979); Steinberg v. Taylor, 500 F. Supp. 477, 479–80 (D.Conn. 1980). *But see* Thornton v. Redman, 435 F. Supp. 876, 881 (D.Del. 1977) (holding procedures not required during general shakedown).

[977]Stewart v. McGinnis, 5 F.3d 1031, 1037 (7th Cir. 1993).

[978]Hudson v. Palmer, 468 U.S. 517, 104 S. Ct. 3194 (1984).

[979]Two federal appeals courts have held that if the prison's policy calls for receipts for seized property, an officer's failure to provide one does not deny due process because it is a deviation from established procedure. See Stewart v. McGinnis, 5 F.3d 1031, 1036 (7th Cir. 1993); Watson v. Caton, 984 F.2d 537, 541 (1st Cir. 1993). We think this holding is wrong. If the officer is authorized to take prisoners' property, the deprivation of property is not "random and unauthorized." The failure to follow due process requirements does not make the deprivation "random and unauthorized" as those words are used in *Hudson*. An officer's seizure of property is only random and unauthorized if the officer is not authorized to make the seizure. This point is discussed in more detail in § E of this chapter.

[980]468 U.S. 576, 589–91, 104 S. Ct. 3227 (1984).

[981]Lyon v. Farrier, 730 F.2d 525, 527 (8th Cir. 1984); McWhorter v. Jones, 573 F. Supp. 33, 34–35 (E.D.Tenn. 1983); Bryant v. Barbara, 11 Kan.App. 2d 165, 717 P.2d 522, 524 (Kan.App. 1986).

[982]Stewart v. McGinnis, 5 F.3d 1031, 1037 (7th Cir. 1993); Farid v. Smith, 850 F.2d 917, 925 (2d Cir. 1988) (evidence that prison officials made prisoners send alleged contraband out immediately and routinely denied their subsequent grievances raised a factual question whether due process was violated); U.S. ex rel.

dispute, that the property is contraband under prison rules, its confiscation will not deny due process.[983]

b. Substantive Constitutional Rights Some deprivations of property infringe on constitutional rights such as religious freedom or access to the courts.[984] Under extreme circumstances, a property deprivation might constitute cruel and unusual punishment.[985] A claim based on one of these rights is not a procedural due process claim at all, so you can proceed with a civil rights suit about it regardless of whether there is an adequate post-deprivation remedy.[986]

Even if you have a clear-cut case of substantive constitutional violation, you will be required to exhaust any administrative remedies that might address the deprivation before filing a federal suit (and in most cases before a state suit). After you do that, if you do not get relief, it may be prudent to file suit in state court, rather than take the risk that a federal court will disagree about your federal claim and dismiss, leaving you to start over in state court. This is especially true if your main concern is getting compensation for the property.

c. Tort and State Law Remedies If you have suffered a property loss, determining your state law remedies should be your first priority, partly because of the above-described limitations on federal civil rights remedies[987] and partly because state remedies may be faster and simpler. Different states provide different kinds of remedies for infringement of property rights, and you will have to research your state's law to learn your options[988]—and do it quickly, since some property remedies have very short filing deadlines. Some states have tort claims statutes that permit suit against

state or local governments for their employees' acts.[989] Some have administrative claims procedures.[990] Others permit suit against the particular employee who was at fault.[991]

In many cases you will need only to assert that prison employees were negligent in losing or damaging your property.[992] One state court has held that prison officials' tort law duty is "to provide inmates adequate means of storing their property and the duty to conduct a prompt search when property is reported stolen."[993] In some cases—especially if you are complaining about an intentional act—you will need to invoke one of the old common law remedies for torts involving property.[994]

- An action for conversion alleges that the defendant has without authorization deprived the plaintiff of property, either permanently or indefinitely.[995]

Wolfish v. Levi, 439 F. Supp. 114, 151 (S.D.N.Y. 1977) (prisoners must have an opportunity to contest decision that an item is contraband), *aff'd in pertinent part*, 573 F.2d 118, 131–32 n.29 (2d Cir. 1978), *rev'd on other grounds sub nom.* Bell v. Wolfish, 441 U.S. 520, 99 S. Ct. 1861 (1979).

[983]*See* § H.8.d of this chapter concerning confiscation of money.

[984]*See* Ch. 3, §§ C.2.b, D.2.e.

[985]Hudson v. Palmer, 468 U.S. 517, 530, 104 S. Ct. 3194 (1984).

[986]*See, e.g.,* Collins v. Goord, 438 F. Supp. 2d 399, 418–19 (S.D.N.Y. 2006) (allegation that typewriter was destroyed in retaliation for lawsuits and grievances stated a First Amendment claim, separate from due process claim which was barred by existence of state tort remedies); *see also* § E of this chapter, nn.106–107.

[987]*See* Howard v. Pettus, 745 S.W.2d 821, 822 (Mo.App. 1988) (seizure of $20 worth of prison "coupon books" "failed to measure up to constitutional dimensions" but compensation was required under state law).

[988]This is true even if you are a federal prisoner. The Federal Tort Claims Act employs the tort law of the state in which the tort occurred. *See* Ch. 8, § C.2.a.

[989]*See, e.g.,* Parratt v. Taylor, 451 U.S. 527, 543–44, 101 S. Ct. 1908 (1981) (Nebraska tort claims procedure); Shorter v. Lawson, 403 F. Supp. 2d 703, 707 (N.D.Ind. 2005) (Indiana tort claims act); Balabin v. Scully, 606 F. Supp. 176, 182–83 (S.D.N.Y. 1985) (New York Court of Claims Act); Robbins v. South, 595 F. Supp. 785, 791 (D.Mont. 1984) (Montana Tort Claims Act); Thurman v. Rose, 575 F. Supp. 1488, 1489 (N.D.Ind. 1983) (Indiana Tort Claims Act); Cody v. Leapley, 476 N.W.2d 257, 260 (S.D. 1991) (state constitution and statutes provide for property claims against the state). *But see* Wheat v. Texas Dep't of Corrections, 715 S.W.2d 362, 363 (Tex. App. 1986) (state was immune under Tort Claims Act from property claim by prisoner).

[990]*See, e.g.,* Price v. Harris, 722 F.2d 427, 428 (8th Cir. 1983); Al-Mustafa Irshad v. Spann, 543 F. Supp. 922, 927 (E.D.Va. 1982).

[991]*See, e.g.,* Williams v. Morris, 697 F.2d 1349, 1351 (10th Cir. 1982) (Utah law).

[992]*See* Marshall v. Norwood, 741 F.2d 761, 763 (5th Cir. 1984) (Louisiana statute); Loftin v. Thomas, 681 F.2d 364, 365 (5th Cir. 1982) (Texas statute); Williams v. Morris, 697 F.2d at 1351 (Utah common law).

[993]Shackelford v. Marion Correctional Institution, 61 Ohio Misc.2d 201, 577 N.E.2d 138, 139 (Ohio Ct.Cl. 1988) (duty was met by providing a locker box and conducting a search after the theft).

[994]The following discussion is based in large part on information in W. Page Keeton et al., Prosser and Keeton on The Law of Torts § 11, at 47 (5th ed. 1984) and Black's Law Dictionary (5th ed. 1979).

[995]*See* Lindsey v. Storey, 936 F.2d 554, 561 (11th Cir. 1991) (conversion suits are authorized by Georgia statute); Brooks v. Dutton, 751 F.2d 197, 199 (6th Cir. 1985) (conversion suits can be brought under Tennessee tort claims procedure); Balabin v. Scully, 606 F. Supp. at 182 (conversion suits can be brought under state Court of Claims Act); Al-Mustafa Irshad v. Spann, 543 F. Supp. at 927 (common law conversion suit could be brought against individual prison employee); Howland v. State, 169 Ariz. 293, 818 P.2d 1169, 1172–73 (Ariz.App. 1991) (conversion suits are authorized by Arizona law); Grant v. Newsome, 201 Ga.App. 710, 411 S.E.2d 796, 798 (Ga.App. 1991) ("freezing" of inmate's account without following lawful procedures established a tort under state conversion statute).

- An action for detinue alleges that the defendant is in possession of the plaintiff's property; it seeks return of the property.[996]
- An action for replevin is similar to a detinue suit.[997]
- A suit on a bailment alleges that property has been turned over by the plaintiff to the defendant for a limited purpose and was to be returned or disposed of according to the plaintiff's instructions, and that the defendant has failed to carry out those terms.[998] Traditionally a bailment was considered a kind of contract, and some courts have held that prison officials do not create a bailment when they take possession of prisoners' property because the prisoner has no choice whether to give it up.[999]

Different states may have different rules governing these actions, and you should research the law of your state to determine which one, if any, fits the facts of your case.

It is not clear whether federal prisoners have any tort remedies for deprivations of property. The FTCA is their designated remedy for the torts of federal prison personnel. However, the FTCA bars recovery for "[a]ny claim arising in respect of . . . the detention of any goods, merchandise, or other property by any officer of customs or excise or any other law enforcement officer."[1000] The Supreme Court has recently held that Bureau of Prisons employees are "other law enforcement officers" under this provision, which means prisoners whose property is "detained" by federal prison staff can't sue about it,[1001] or sue about damage done to it while detained, under the FTCA.[1002] There is an administrative remedy for *negligent* deprivations of property by federal officials. The federal "Small Tort Claims Act" provides that agencies may settle claims for up to $1000 for damage or loss to private property caused by the negligence of federal officers or employees acting within the scope of their employment.[1003]

It remains to be seen whether federal prisoners who do not have a post-deprivation remedy under the FTCA for *intentional* deprivation of property will now be allowed to sue Bureau of Prisons personnel for denying them due process in such cases. As we have noted, the Supreme Court said that intentional deprivations of property by prison staff that are "random and unauthorized" do not deny due process as long as there is a post-deprivation remedy such as a tort suit.[1004] If the tort remedy is not available, one might think that such a deprivation *would* deny due process, and a

---

[996]Al-Mustafa Irshad v. Spann, 543 F. Supp. at 927 (common law detinue suit could be brought against individual prison employee).

[997]In *Herron v. Wyrick*, 686 S.W.2d 56, 57 (Mo.App. 1985), the court held that a prisoner had stated a claim for replevin against a prison official when he alleged that the defendant "willfully exerted control over [his] personal property in a manner inconsistent with [his] right to the property, and has refused to return the property on demand." The defendant had confiscated various tools that the plaintiff had bought while in prison and kept in the prison's hobby room; the plaintiff alleged that this was in violation of prison rules that permitted him to have the tools.

[998]*See* Fearon v. State of California Dep't of Corrections, 162 Cal. App.3d 1254, 209 Cal.Rptr. 309, 311 and n.1 (1984) (allegation that prison lost property taken from plaintiff for safekeeping on admission "indicate[s] the existence of a bailment contract"); Nitcher v. Thompson, 777 S.W.2d 626, 628 (Mo.App. 1989) (prison authorities created a bailment when they took possession of the plaintiff's property when moving him to another housing unit); People v. Natal, 75 N.Y.2d 379, 553 N.E.2d 239, 553 N.Y.S.2d 650, 651 (N.Y. 1990) (items taken by prison authorities "are held as bailments, to be safeguarded for the accused during incarceration"); Bacote v. Ohio Dep't of Rehabilitation and Correction, 61 Ohio Misc.2d 284, 578 N.E.2d 565, 566 (Ct.Cl. Ohio 1990) (officer created a bailment when he took the plaintiff's locker box to his desk).

The failure to return bailed property "gives rise to an inference of negligence, and shifts the burden to the bailee . . . to present sufficient evidence to counterbalance this inference." Bacote v. Ohio Dep't of Rehabilitation and Correction, 578 N.E.2d at 566.

[999]Spruytte v. Dep't of Corrections, 82 Mich.App. 145, 266 N.W.2d 482 (1978); Dep't of Corrections v. Board of Claims, 580 A.2d 923, 926 n.4 (Pa.Cmwlth. 1990). However, it has been suggested that this situation "appropriately would be classified as a gratuitous bailment for the sole benefit of the bailor." Marquez v. State, 754 P.2d 705, 707 (Wyo. 1988) (concurring opinion).

[1000]28 U.S.C. § 2680(c).

[1001]Ali v. Federal Bureau of Prisons, 552 U.S. 214, 128 S. Ct. 831 (2008).

[1002]*See* Kosak v. U.S., 465 U.S. 848, 862, 104 S. Ct. 1519 (1984) (§ 2680(h) bars suit for damage caused by negligent handling of property while detained).

The Supreme Court didn't rule on the meaning of "detention" of property in *Ali, see* 128 S. Ct. at 835 n.2 (the prisoner's claim in that case was that property had been removed from the plaintiff's bags during a transfer). The government will likely claim that any time prison staff deal with a prisoner's property, however briefly, it is a "detention." Some courts have distinguished between damage done during "seizure" of property (not covered by § 2680(c)) and during "detention" of property (which includes "post-seizure" events). *See, e.g.*, Hallock v. U.S., 253 F. Supp. 2d 361, 366–67 (N.D.N.Y. 2003). That distinction would mean that if staff damaged your property in the course of a search, you could seek damages under the FTCA, but if they just took your property and didn't give it back, or damaged or destroyed it after taking it away, you would not have a remedy under the FTCA. But other courts have held that § 2680(c) does apply to damage to property inflicted during the execution of a search warrant or other short-term inspection. *See* Endicott v. Bureau of Alcohol, Tobacco, Firearms and Explosives, 338 F. Supp. 2d 1183 (W.D.Wash. 2004); Locks v. Three Unidentified Customs Service Agents, 759 F. Supp. 1131, 1133 (E.D.Pa. 1990).

[1003]31 U.S.C. § 3723. To use this remedy, you would file a claim just as you would under the FTCA. Ali v. Federal Bureau of Prisons, 552 U.S. 214, 128 S. Ct. 831, 839 (2008) (citing 28 C.F.R. 543.31 *et seq.*). This section does not authorize lawsuits against the government, Bazuaye v. U.S., 83 F.3d 482, 486 n.3 (D.C. Cir. 1996), so if you can't bring an FTCA suit, you are stuck with what the government is willing to settle for.

[1004]Hudson v. Palmer, 468 U.S. 517, 533–35, 104 S. Ct. 3194 (1984).

federal prisoner could bring a *Bivens* suit about it.[1005] However, there is an administrative remedy that allows the Attorney General to settle claims for up to $50,000 for "damage to, or loss of, privately owned property, caused by an investigative or law enforcement officer as defined in section 2680(h) of title 28 who is employed by the Department of Justice acting within the scope of employment."[1006] Since the Bureau of Prisons is part of the Department of Justice, and since as we have noted Bureau of Prisons personnel are considered "law enforcement officers" under 28 U.S.C. § 2680(h), this provision may allow compensation for intentional damage or loss to property. If it does, courts may say that the existence of that remedy is sufficient to provide due process in place of the FTCA, so intentional property deprivations by federal prison staff still will not deny due process. The courts will have to sort these issues out in the next few years.

It is also possible that some federal prisoners may be able to seek compensation for property loss under the Tucker Act, which provides: "The United States Court of Federal Claims shall have jurisdiction to render judgment upon any claim against the United States founded either upon the Constitution, or any Act of Congress or any regulation of an executive department, or upon any express or implied contract with the United States, or for liquidated or unliquidated damages in cases *not sounding in tort*."[1007] Tucker Act liability for prisoners' property-related claims has not been explored fully by the courts.[1008]

d. Money Prisoners' money is property[1009] and, like other property, is protected by the Due Process Clauses and the Takings Clause of the Constitution. However, prison officials have substantial discretion in handling and regulating prisoners' money.[1010] Further, there are a number of situations in which the Constitution does permit prison officials to take prisoners' money.

Cash is contraband in most prisons, and most courts have held that cash found in prisoners' possession may be permanently confiscated.[1011] Some courts have held that a permanent forfeiture of cash denies due process unless it is authorized by statute,[1012] but others have either not required such authorization[1013] or have been willing to find it in very general statutes or regulations.[1014] You should assume that if you possess cash in jail or prison, you risk losing it.

There is no constitutional right to be paid for work done in prison.[1015] If state law, or federal statutes or regulations, create a right to be paid, that right is protected by due

---

[1005]*See* Ch. 8, § B.2.c.

[1006]31 U.S.C. § 3724. As with 18 U.S.C. § 3723, you must submit a claim as you would under the FTCA, and this section does not authorize a lawsuit if you do not like the government's offer.

[1007]28 U.S.C. § 1491(a)(1) (emphasis supplied). The "Little Tucker Act" contains a similar provision for claims not exceeding $10,000. Little Tucker Act claims can be brought either in the Court of Federal Claims or federal district court. 13 U.S.C. 1346(a). Tucker Act recovery is limited to claims based on a "source of substantive law" that could "fairly be interpreted as mandating compensation by the Federal Government for the damage sustained." U.S. v. Mitchell, 463 U.S. 206, 216–17, 103 S. Ct. 2961 (1983).

[1008]*See* U.S. v. Minor, 228 F.3d 352, 355 (4th Cir. 2000) (prisoner's challenge to forfeiture for which he received inadequate notice could not be pursued under the Tucker Act but was an equitable claim for the return of personal property improperly seized under the Fourth Amendment and Fifth Amendment); Blazavich v. U.S., 29 Fed.Cl. 371 (Fed.Cl. 1993) (claim for loss of property in mail was a tort claim which could not be pursued under the Tucker Act).

[1009]Higgins v. Beyer, 293 F.3d 683, 693 (3d Cir. 2002); Wright v. Riveland, 219 F.3d 905, 913 (9th Cir. 2000) (inmates have a protectable property interest in funds received from outside sources); Hampton v. Hobbs, 106 F.3d 1281, 1287 (6th Cir. 1997); Mahers v. Halford, 76 F.3d 951, 954 (8th Cir. 1996); Longmire v.

Guste, 921 F.2d 620, 624 n.3 (5th Cir. 1991); Alexanian v. New York State Urban Development Corp., 554 F.2d 15, 17 (2d Cir. 1977).

One federal circuit has held to the contrary. In *Steffey v. Orman*, 461 F.3d 1218 (10th Cir. 2006), the mother of a prisoner sent a $50 money order to another prisoner, and it was confiscated and not returned to the sender pursuant to a rule against prisoners' receiving money from other prisoners' family members. The court noted that it (unlike most other courts) had previously held that prisoners' property interests were governed by the "atypical and significant" standard of *Sandin v. Conner*, 515 U.S. 472, 484, 115 S. Ct. 2293 (1995), and said that the prisoner's interest in $50 was not atypical and significant (it was "an inchoate, unrealized expectation in a gift of contraband funds"), and the rule under which it had been seized was reasonable. Steffey v. Orman, 461 F.3d at 1222. Upholding the confiscation simply on the grounds that the rule was reasonable might be justified, in the same way that courts have permitted cash in prisoners' possession to be seized (see next paragraph). But to say that money can be seized without due process because its loss is not atypical and significant would mean that it is not property at all, and would allow prison officials to seize money coming to a prisoner under any circumstances. We find it hard to believe that the court meant to hold that, or that any court could adopt such a rule.

[1010]*See* Ch. 3, § F, n.980.

[1011]Baker v. Piggott, 833 F.2d 1539, 1540 (11th Cir. 1987); Harris v. Forsyth, 735 F.2d 1235, 1236 (11th Cir. 1984); Hanvey v. Blankenship, 631 F.2d 296, 297 (4th Cir. 1980); Sullivan v. Ford, 609 F.2d 197, 198 (5th Cir. 1980); Lowery v. Cuyler, 521 F. Supp. 430, 432–33 (E.D.Pa. 1981); Webb v. Lane, 222 Ill.App.3d 322, 164 Ill.Dec. 761, 583 N.E.2d 677, 681–86 (Ill.App. 1991); Petition of Smith, 82 N.C.App. 107, 345 S.E.2d 423, 425–26 (N.C.App. 1986). *But see* Exum v. Dugger, 591 So.2d 1088, 1089–90 (Fla.App. 1992) (cash found in incoming mail could not be confiscated under a rule prohibiting money to be "given directly or received by any inmate").

[1012]Sell v. Parratt, 548 F.2d 753, 758 (8th Cir. 1977); Balkcom v. Heptinstall, 263 S.E.2d 275, 276–77, 152 Ga.App. 539 (Ga.App. 1979).

[1013]Best v. State, 736 P.2d 171, 172 (Okla.App. 1987).

[1014]*See* Lowery v. Cuyler, 521 F. Supp. at 432–33 (statute permitting prison officials to promulgate rules, and rule defining money as contraband, were sufficient to permit forfeiture).

[1015]*See* Ch. 2, § I.2, n.1274.

process like any other entitlement.[1016] But the same law can also limit this right. For example, due process is not violated by a requirement that the prisoner pay part of her wages for subsistence or authorize deductions for other reasons,[1017] or by a "pay lag" procedure under which prisoners' pay is always delayed,[1018] if state law so provides.

Prison officials may require that at least part of prisoners' money be kept in non-interest-bearing accounts.[1019] Where prisoners' money does earn interest, courts have disagreed over whether the interest must be paid to the prisoners under the Takings Clause of the Fifth Amendment as well as the Due Process Clauses.[1020] The usual rule is that interest is the property of the person who owns the principal, and if public officials appropriate it, they violate the Fifth Amendment ban on taking of property for public use without just compensation.[1021] Some courts have applied this rule to prisoners' money.[1022] Others, however, have

avoided requiring payment of interest to prisoners on the ground that traditionally, prisoners did not have property rights in their wages, so the traditional "interest follows principal" rule does not apply to them; under these holdings, prisoners' right to interest would depend entirely on state law.[1023] Even if interest on prisoners' money is deemed to be their property, it need be paid only to prisoners whose individual funds generated interest in an amount larger than their share of the cost of administering the fund of prisoners' money.[1024]

Prison officials may not simply take money out of a prisoner's account without notice or hearing.[1025] The process due when money is taken from a prisoner's account may be different in different situations. Restitution may be employed as a disciplinary measure for prison misconduct,[1026] but only after a hearing that satisfies the usual disciplinary

---

[1016]Brooks v. George County, Miss., 84 F.3d 157, 164 (5th Cir. 1996) (prisoner who had not been convicted and who did work voluntarily on public property had a legitimate expectation under state law of wages for it); Gilbreath v. Cutter Biological, Inc., 931 F.2d 1320, 1327 (9th Cir. 1991); James v. Quinlan, 866 F.2d 627, 630 (3d Cir. 1989) (addressing federal regulation); Piatt v. MacDougall, 773 F.2d 1032, 1036 (9th Cir. 1985) (en banc); Flowers v. Fauver, 683 F. Supp. 981, 983–85 (D.N.J. 1988); Ingenito v. Department of Corrections, State of New Jersey, 568 F. Supp. 946, 953 (D.N.J. 1983).

[1017]James v. Quinlan, 866 F.2d 627, 630 (3d Cir. 1989) (regulation that required prisoners to assign half their money to pay court-ordered obligations or lose their prison industries jobs upheld); Hrbek v. Farrier, 787 F.2d 414, 416–17 (8th Cir. 1986); Turner v. Nevada Bd. of State Prison Comm'rs, 624 F. Supp. 318, 320–22 (D.Nev. 1985); Cumbey v. State, 699 P.2d 1094, 1097–98 (Okla. 1985).

[1018]Allen v. Cuomo, 100 F.3d 253 261 (2d Cir. 1996).

[1019]Foster v. Hughes, 979 F.2d 130, 132–33 (8th Cir. 1992) (upholding failure to provide for interest-bearing accounts; prisoners were allowed to buy savings bonds); Gray v. Lee, 486 F. Supp. 41, 46 (D.Md. 1980), aff'd, 661 F.2d 921 (4th Cir. 1981); Sahagian v. Dickey, 646 F. Supp. 1502, 1507 n.1 (W.D.Wis. 1986); Cumbey v. State, 699 P.2d 1094, 1098 (Okla. 1985).

[1020]See Vance v. Barrett, 345 F.3d 1083, 1088–89 (9th Cir. 2003) (explaining and distinguishing these clauses).

[1021]Webb's Fabulous Pharmacies, Inc. v. Beckwith, 449 U.S. 155, 164, 101 S. Ct. 446 (1980); see U.S.Const., Amend. V.

[1022]Vance v. Barrett, 345 F.3d at 1089–91 (9th Cir. 2003) (holding that prisoners' interest is their property; deprivations pursuant to statute present Takings Clause issues and deprivations without statutory authorization present due process questions); Blaisdell v. Dep't of Public Safety, 119 Hawai'i 275, 285–86, 196 P.3d 277 (2008); Douglas v. Ward, No. 77 Civ. 2559-CLB, Memorandum and Order (S.D.N.Y., Jan. 3, 1980); Fayerweather v. Wainwright, TCA 75-3 (N.D.Fla., Aug. 20, 1976) (quoted in Smith v. Robinson, 456 F. Supp. 449, 453–54 (E.D.Pa. 1978)); see also Eubanks v. McCotter, 802 F.2d 790, 791–93 (5th Cir. 1986) (allegation that interest was taken by prison officials was not frivolous). In the Eubanks case, the prisoners also argued that a state statute requiring that commissary profits be expended for inmate programs created a property interest for the inmates as a group, and that the use of

these profits for other purposes deprived them of their property without due process. The court held that this argument was not frivolous.

[1023]Givens v. Alabama Dep't of Corrections, 381 F.3d 1064, 1066–70 (11th Cir. 2004); Washlefske v. Winston, 234 F.3d 179, 185 (4th Cir. 2000); Young v. Wall, 359 F. Supp. 2d 84, 91–92 (D.R.I. 2005) (following Washlefske and Givens, but holding that prisoner might have a due process claim to interest based on state regulations). Both Givens and Washlefske address money paid to prisoners for their labor. Whether their rationale would extend to money from other sources is an open question. See Allen v. Cuomo, 100 F.3d 253, 262 (2d Cir. 1996) (holding that two-week "pay lag" did not violate Takings Clause based on impact on interest earnings).

[1024]Schneider v. California Dep't of Corrections, 345 F.3d 716, 721 (9th Cir. 2003); McIntyre v. Bayer, 339 F.3d 1097, 1099–1102 (9th Cir. 2003). Cf. Butler v. Michigan State Disbursement Unit, 275 Mich.App. 309, 738 N.W.2d 269 (Mich.App. 2007) (holding state could retain interest on child support payments it held and disbursed, since the cost of mailing a single disbursement exceeded a year's interest on the plaintiff's funds).

[1025]Artway v. Scheidemantel, 671 F. Supp. 330, 337 (D.N.J. 1987); State v. O'Connor, 171 Ariz. 19, 827 P.2d 480, 484–85 (Ariz. App. 1992) (hearing required before removing money from account pursuant to crime victim's restitution lien); Wojnicz v. Dep't of Corrections, 32 Mich.App. 121, 188 N.W.2d 251, 253–54 (1971); Randolph v. Dep't of Correctional Services, 205 Neb. 672, 289 N.W.2d 529, 531 (Neb. 1980); see also Burns v. Pa. Dep't of Correction, 544 F.3d 279, 291 (3d Cir. 2008) (assessment of prisoner account for restitution after disciplinary conviction was a deprivation of property requiring due process even though officials had never actually removed the money); Grant v. Newsome, 201 Ga.App. 710, 411 S.E.2d 796, 798 (Ga.App. 1991) (unauthorized "freezing" of inmate account was a tort under state conversion statute); Casteel v. Vaade, 481 N.W.2d 476, 478, 485 (Wis. 1992) (alleged refusal by authorities to credit inmate with check sent to him stated a due process claim). A court order to remove funds to pay court costs from a prisoner's account was held to be within the court's authority, but to deny due process where the court did not allow the prisoner an opportunity to be heard. Reed v. State, 269 S.W.3d 619, 624–27 (Tex.App. 2008).

[1026]See n.556, above.

due process requirements[1027] and addresses the relevant issues.[1028] Other non-routine deductions will generally require notice and a hearing.[1029] But if deductions are made in the ordinary course of prison business (other than disciplinary proceedings), due process may be satisfied simply by providing a complete account statement and an opportunity to challenge errors afterwards, through a grievance procedure or otherwise.[1030]

Some states' statutes permit the seizure of prisoners' funds or assets to pay the costs of their incarceration or the enforcement of debts such as court-ordered restitution or child support.[1031] These statutes have generally been upheld against due process challenges and other constitutional attacks.[1032] However, state law also places limits on the collection of debts; you should consult your state's law of debtors' rights and creditors' remedies to determine if any of these limits protect you. For example, in some states, there are minimum amounts of money that a debtor must be permitted to keep. Some states provide for the appointment of a trustee for a prisoner's estate, whose duty is to preserve the estate both for the inmate's benefit and for the benefit of persons like crime victims who may have claims against the inmate.[1033] Some federal benefits are protected by federal law from confiscation by state or local government.[1034]

The Eleventh Amendment forbids the federal courts to order retroactive payments of money that has been unlawfully withheld by state governments.[1035] For that reason, if you have a dispute with state prison officials over pay or other money issues, you either should get into federal court quickly and seek an injunction before your money is taken, or else explore the availability of a state remedy.[1036]

[1027]*See* n.286, above.

[1028]*See* n.558, above.

[1029]Wojnicz v. Dep't of Corrections, 188 N.W.2d at 253–54.

[1030]Sickles v. Campbell County, Kentucky, 501 F.3d 726, 731–32 (6th Cir. 2007) (due process was satisfied by opportunity to file a grievance and contest deductions pursuant to a statute charging jail prisoners for cost of incarceration); Jensen v. Klecker, 648 F.2d 1179, 1183 (8th Cir. 1981); Sahagian v. Dickey, 646 F. Supp. 1502, 1509 (W.D.Wis. 1986); *see also* Reynolds v. Wagner, 128 F.3d 166, 179–81 (3d Cir. 1997) (holding that due process was satisfied by notice of a policy of charging for medical appointments and providing a post-deduction grievance procedure); Scott v. Angelone, 771 F. Supp. 1064, 1067–68 (D.Nev. 1991) (where state regulations authorized deductions for non-emergency medical visits, due process was satisfied by notifying inmates of the billing system, requiring the inmate's authorization before treatment was given, and providing "accounting inquiry" and grievance procedures to correct mistakes), *aff'd*, 980 F.2d 738 (9th Cir. 1982); Smith v. Robinson, 456 F. Supp. 456, 455–56 (E.D.Pa. 1978) (incomplete statements could infringe First Amendment rights by interfering with correspondence).

[1031]Mahers v. Halford, 76 F.3d 951, 954–55 (8th Cir. 1996) (state law applying 20% of all money received to restitution obligations did not deny due process, because the plaintiff had already had due process in the criminal proceeding that led to the restitution order; statute did not deprive prisoners of the benefit of their money, because it lessened their debts; Abney v. Alameida, 334 F. Supp. 2d 1221, 1229 (S.D.Cal. 2004) (state law allowing deduction of 20% of funds received from outside prison to pay restitution orders did not violate the Takings Clause; restitution orders are civil judgments and the law merely provided a way to enforce them; it did not deny due process, since the deduction was authorized by state law as a result of his criminal conviction); *see* Ch. 3, § G.3, nn.1056–1059, concerning enforcement of child support orders. *But see* State v. Murray, 621 P.2d 334, 340–43 (Haw. 1981) (state statutes forbade garnishment, levy, or enforcement of restitution order against money earned by prisoners), *overruled on other grounds*, State v. Feliciano, 103 Hawai'i 269, 81 P.3d 1184 (Hawaii 2003).

In *Mahers v. Halford, supra*, the federal appeals court held that no individualized pre-deprivation hearing was needed to take money pursuant to the state statute at issue. *Mahers*, 76 F.3d at 955. The Iowa Supreme Court disagreed. Walters v. Grossheim, 554 N.W.2d 530, 531 & n.1 (Iowa 1996) (rejecting *Mahers* holding); Walters v. Grossheim, 525 N.W.2d 830, 832 (Iowa 1994) (hearing could be "an informal, nonadversarial review of [plaintiff's] written objections to the proposed withdrawal of funds").

[1032]Slade v. Hampton Roads Regional Jail, 407 F.3d 243, 251–55 (4th Cir. 2005) (upholding charge of $1.00 a day for pretrial detention, with refunds for those adjudicated not guilty); Owens v. Sebelius, 357 F. Supp. 2d 1281, 1286–1290 (D.Kan. 2005) ($25.00 monthly supervision fee for parolees, which the plaintiff had to pay off after his parole was revoked, did not violate the Eighth Amendment or the Ex Post Facto Clause, deny due process, or constitute an unlawful taking of property); Burns v. State, 303 Ark. 64, 793 S.W.2d 779, 780 (Ark. 1990) (upholding confiscation of prisoner's inheritance against due process, equal protection, and Ex Post Facto Clause challenges); State, Michigan State Treasurer v. Turner, 110 Mich.App. 228, 312 N.W.2d 418, 420–21 (Mich.App. 1981); *see* Abney v. Alameida, 334 F. Supp. 2d 1221, 1228 (S.D.Cal. 2004) ("administrative fee" of 2% of funds sent to prisoners did not violate the Takings Clause; reasonable user fees that reimburse the cost of government services are not takings); *see also* Sickles v. Campbell County, Kentucky, 501 F.3d 726, 730–33 (6th Cir. 2007) (upholding deductions without a pre-deprivation hearing under statute authorizing counties to charge up to $50.00 a day or the actual per diem cost of incarceration to all prisoners held in their jails, and collect by deducting 25% of all deposits to prisoners' account, even before prisoner is convicted; no challenge to charges themselves). *But see* State ex rel. Nixon v. Robinson, 269 S.W.3d 432, 434–35 (Mo.App. 2008) (state could not take bonds which were joint property of prisoner and wife under state Incarceration Reimbursement Act).

[1033]*See* Ch. 3, § C., n.410.

[1034]*See* Bennett v. Arkansas, 485 U.S. 395, 108 S. Ct. 1204 (1988) (Social Security benefits); Higgins v. Beyer, 293 F.3d 683, 692–94 (3d Cir. 2002) (prison officials could not take money from veterans' benefits to pay restitution); Nelson v. Hiss, 271 F.3d 891, 894–96 (9th Cir. 2001).

[1035]Edelman v. Jordan, 415 U.S. 651, 658, 94 S. Ct. 1374 (1974); *see* Ch. 8, § L.1, for a more detailed discussion of the Eleventh Amendment.

[1036]*See* State ex rel. Wiggins v. Barnes, 57 Ohio St.3d 45, 565 N.E.2d 598, 600 (Ohio 1991) (ordering increase in pay and back pay under state law).

9. Excessive Confinement[1037]

Prisoners have a liberty interest in being released on time, in conformity with the sentence imposed and with other relevant laws such as those providing for good time.[1038] Most courts have also held that the failure to obey a court order requiring a prisoner's release denies due process.[1039] Ordinary negligence that causes a prisoner to be held past release date—making a mistake in arithmetic, *e.g.*, or losing a file or document—will not deny due process.[1040] Most courts hold that due process is denied if a prisoner is not released on time as a result of deliberate indifference.[1041] Some courts

have also held that deliberate indifference resulting in excessive confinement constitutes cruel and unusual punishment.[1042]

> To establish deliberate indifference in an excessive confinement case, a plaintiff must first demonstrate that a prison official had knowledge of the prisoner's problem and thus of the risk that unwarranted punishment was being, or would be, inflicted. Second, the plaintiff must show that the official either failed to act or took only ineffectual action under the circumstances indicating that his or her response to the problem was a product of deliberate indifference to the prisoner's plight. Finally, the plaintiff must demonstrate a causal connection between the official's response to the problem and the infliction of the unjustified detention.[1043]

Prison officials cannot be held liable for excessive confinement if they don't know about it,[1044] so you must let them know if your sentence has been miscalculated, and do so early enough that they can correct the mistake in time.

The courts have not agreed on what process is due once prison officials are put on notice of an error in sentence calculation. One court has held that a hearing is required.[1045] However, most courts say that prison officials must investigate the merits of the prisoner's claim and respond to it.[1046]

[1037]This section deals only with failures by prison and jail staff to release prisoners when they are entitled to be released. Broader questions of legality in sentencing are beyond the scope of this Manual.

[1038]Sample v. Diecks, 885 F.2d 1099, 1114 (3d Cir. 1989); Bergen v. Spaulding, 881 F.2d 719, 721 (9th Cir. 1989); Toney-El v. Franzen, 777 F.2d 1224, 1226–27 (7th Cir. 1985); Haygood v. Younger, 769 F.2d 1350, 1354 (9th Cir. 1985) (en banc); McGann v. Cunningham, 315 F. Supp. 2d 150, 155 (D.N.H. 2004) ("Any continued detention after the state has lost its lawful authority to hold a prisoner deprives him of a liberty interest in freedom from restraint that is protected from unlawful state deprivation by the Due Process Clause of the Fourteenth Amendment." Defendants did not credit plaintiff properly with good time.); *see also* Oviatt by and through Waugh v. Pearce, 954 F.2d 1470, 1475 (9th Cir. 1992) (liberty interests were created by state statutes requiring release of detainees after 60 days without a trial and requiring arraignment of detainees within 30 days).

[1039]Davis v. Hall, 375 F.3d 703, 712–13 (8th Cir. 2004) (even a 30-minute detention after release order can deny due process); Slone v. Herman, 983 F.2d 107, 110 (8th Cir. 1993); Huddleston v. Shirley, 787 F. Supp. 109, 110–11 (N.D.Miss. 1992) and cases cited; Tasker v. Moore, 738 F. Supp. 1005, 1010 (S.D.W.Va. 1990); *see* Abiff v. Slaton, 806 F. Supp. 993, 998 (N.D.Ga. 1992) (allegation that the plaintiff had to wait 19 months for a bail hearing after his sentence was vacated stated a constitutional claim). *Contra*, Pacelli v. deVito, 972 F.2d 871, 876 (7th Cir. 1992). The *Pacelli* decision says that disobeying a state court's writ of habeas corpus ordering the petitioner's release does not violate the Constitution but merely constitutes contempt of court. We don't think that can be right; surely it is a deprivation of liberty without due process to continue to detain someone after the legal basis for detention has been removed. *Pacelli* has not been followed by other federal circuits as far as we can determine.

[1040]Golberg v. Hennepin County, 417 F.3d 808, 812 (8th Cir. 2005) (brief overdetention when plaintiff was "lost" in a new computer system was negligence at most); Wadhams v. Procunier, 772 F.2d 75, 77 (4th Cir. 1985); *see* Daniels v. Williams, 474 U.S. 327, 328, 106 S. Ct. 662 (1986).

[1041]Davis v. Hall, 375 F.3d 703, 718–19 (8th Cir. 2004); McCurry v. Moore, 242 F. Supp. 2d 1167, 1180 (N.D.Fla. 2002) (deliberate indifference standard governs both due process and Eighth Amendment claims); Brown v. Coughlin, 704 F. Supp. 41, 44 (S.D.N.Y. 1989); *see* Alexander v. Perrill, 916 F.2d 1392, 1395 (9th Cir. 1990) ("You [prison officials] can't just sit on your duff and not do anything."); Johnson v. Herman, 132 F. Supp. 2d 1130, 1139–40 (N.D.Ind. 2001) (waiting 18 days to make the first inquiry after plaintiff's complaint, and then relying on an unidentified

judicial staff person's statement that the person should remain in jail, could be found to be deliberate indifference); Campbell v. Illinois Dep't of Corrections, 907 F. Supp. 1173, 1180 (N.D.Ill. 1995) (magnitude of the error in plaintiff's sentence calculation, and the ease with which it could have been detected, supported deliberate indifference claim).

[1042]Campbell v. Peters, 256 F.3d 695, 700 (7th Cir. 2001); Sample v. Diecks, 885 F.2d at 1109–10; Haygood v. Younger, 769 F.2d 1350, 1354–55 (9th Cir.1985) (en banc); Plumb v. Prinslow, 847 F. Supp. 1509, 1521 (D.Or.1994). *Contra*, Jones v. City of Jackson, 203 F.3d 875, 880–881 (5th Cir.2000). *See* McCurry v. Moore, 242 F. Supp. 2d 1167, 1178–79 (N.D.Fla. 2002) (noting disagreements among courts over due process and Eighth Amendment bases for unjustified confinement claims).

[1043]Sample v. Diecks, 885 F.2d at 1108–09; *accord*, Campbell v. Illinois Dep't of Corrections, 907 F. Supp. 1173, 1181 (N.D.Ill. 1995) (noting that *Sample* is consistent with later Supreme Court deliberate indifference law).

[1044]Pacelli v. deVito, 972 F.2d at 875–76; Sample v. Diecks, 885 F.2d at 1110; Haygood v. Younger, 769 F.2d at 1359; Wadhams v. Procunier, 772 F.2d at 77 (recovery denied where the prisoner delayed informing officials of the problem); Brown v. Coughlin, 704 F. Supp. at 44. Similarly, in *Cousins v. Lockyer*, 568 F.3d 1063 (9th Cir. 2009), the plaintiff's conviction was invalidated when the statute under which he was convicted was held unconstitutional. However, the court held that there was no clearly established constitutional duty for state officials to personally check all state appellate decisions, apply them to every prisoner affected, and contact the sentencing court. *Cousins*, 568 F.3d at 1070.

[1045]Haygood v. Younger, 769 F.2d at 1359.

[1046]Toney-El v. Franzen, 777 F.2d 1224, 1229 (7th Cir. 1985) (mathematical calculation and opportunity to contest it in writing were sufficient); Royal v. Durison, 319 F. Supp. 2d 534, 539

One leading decision stated that "to the extent possible the inmate [must] be afforded predeprivation process"[1047] and that the responsible official must promptly hear the prisoner's complaint and promptly "refer doubtful issues to someone trained in the law and with authority to resolve the controversy."[1048]

You should do everything you can to get your sentence properly calculated before you are held past your release date. You should call the error to prison officials' attention at the earliest possible date, and if it does not appear that they are dealing with the problem, you should bring an appropriate action in court to force them to do so.[1049] As discussed in more detail elsewhere in this Manual,[1050] actions by state prisoners to obtain immediate or earlier release from prison must commence with exhaustion of state court remedies;[1051] if state remedies do not solve the problem, you must then proceed by writ of habeas corpus in federal court. If you are a federal prisoner, you must exhaust administrative remedies before seeking judicial relief from an erroneous sentence computation.[1052]

If your efforts are unsuccessful and you are not released on time, you should research the availability of a tort action for false imprisonment or negligence, as well as a damage claim for denial of due process. State prisoners may pursue tort cases in state court or, in some cases, under the pendent or supplemental jurisdiction of the federal courts.[1053]

The elements of the tort of false imprisonment are (1) detention or imprisonment that is (2) unlawful or not legally justifiable.[1054] The plaintiff can recover for false imprisonment as long as the defendant intended to confine the plaintiff, even if the ultimate cause of the confinement was negligent acts of the defendant.[1055] However, if prison officials act under an apparently valid order of commitment or other judicial order, they are not liable (for state law torts *or* constitutional violations) even if the order is later found to be mistaken or invalid.[1056]

Federal prisoners' remedy for torts by prison officials is the Federal Tort Claims Act (FTCA),[1057] but it is not clear whether or under what circumstances prisoners can sue for excessive confinement under the FTCA. The FTCA does not permit suit for false imprisonment *except* based on "acts or omissions of investigative or law enforcement officers of the United States Government."[1058] Bureau of Prisons employees are, by statute, "investigative or law enforcement officers,"[1059] but some courts have held or suggested that they are only to be treated as such for FTCA purposes when they are actually performing investigative or law enforcement duties, rather than prison administration.[1060]

(E.D.Pa. 2004) (due process requires "meaningful and expeditious consideration of claims that the term of prisoner's [sic] sentence has been miscalculated"), *aff'd on other grounds*, 254 Fed.Appx. 163 (3d Cir. 2007) (unpublished), *cert. denied*, 128 S. Ct. 2502 (2008); Brown v. Coughlin, 704 F. Supp. at 44 (prison official with actual notice of an error must "obtain the paperwork necessary to discern the correct release date"); Littlefield v. Caton, 679 F. Supp. 90, 94 (D.Me. 1988) (notice and explanation of sentence recalculation were adequate), *aff'd*, 856 F.2d 344 (1st Cir. 1988).

[1047]Sample v. Diecks, 885 F.2d at 1116; *see* Toney-El v. Franzen, 777 F.2d at 1228 (noting that administrative and judicial remedies were available in advance). Predeprivation process, in this context, would mean addressing the problem before the proper release date passed, assuming there was enough time from the point officials were notified of the problem.

[1048]Sample v. Diecks, 885 F.2d at 1115–16; *see also* Oviatt by and through Waugh v. Pearce, 954 F.2d 1470, 1478 (9th Cir. 1992) (due process required Sheriff to provide an internal procedure for keeping track of detainees' arraignment dates).

[1049]*See* Toney-El v. Franzen, 777 F.2d at 1228 (prisoner's ability to complain informally and to bring suit in state court over erroneous release date provided the process due; since he did not use them, he had no due process claim).

[1050]*See* Ch. 8, § H.1.a, and Ch. 9, § D.

[1051]*See, e.g.,* Toney-El v. Franzen, 777 F.2d at 1228 (writ of mandamus); Matter of Schaupp, 66 Wash.2d 45, 831 P.2d 156, 157 (Wash.App. 1992) (personal restraint petition).

[1052]U.S. v. Flanagan, 868 F.2d 1544, 1546–47 (11th Cir. 1989).

[1053]*See* Oviatt by and through Waugh v. Pearce, 954 F.2d 1470, 1481 (9th Cir. 1992) (affirming a federal court damage award for false imprisonment); Biberdorf v. Oregon, 243 F. Supp. 2d 1145, 1158–61 (D.Or. 2002) (entertaining supplemental false

imprisonment claim). Pendent and supplemental jurisdiction are discussed in Ch. 8, § F.1.

[1054]Hart v. Walker, 720 F.2d 1436, 1439 (5th Cir. 1983); Weisman v. LeLandais, 532 F.2d 308, 311 (2d Cir. 1976). Sometimes these elements are stated in a more elaborate form: the plaintiff must show that the defendant intended to confine her, the plaintiff was conscious of the confinement, she did not consent to the confinement, and the confinement was not legally privileged. Broughton v. State, 37 N.Y.2d 451, 456, 373 N.Y.S.2d 87, 335 N.E.2d 310 (N.Y. 1975).

Even if an initial confinement is valid, a claim for false imprisonment will lie if the plaintiff is further unreasonably detained. Gonzalez v. Bratton, 147 F. Supp. 2d 180, 201 (S.D.N.Y. 2001), *aff'd*, 48 Fed.Appx. 363 (2d Cir. 2002) (unpublished).

[1055]W. Page Keeton et al., *Prosser and Keeton on The Law of Torts* § 11, at 52–53 (5th ed. 1984).

[1056]Hernandez v. Sheahan, 455 F.3d 772, 776–77 (7th Cir. 2006); Scull v. New Mexico, 236 F.3d 588, 596–97 (10th Cir. 2000); Middleton v. State, 54 A.D.2d 450, 389 N.Y.S.2d 159, 160 (N.Y.App. Div. 1976), *aff'd*, 43 N.Y.2d 678 (N.Y. 1977).

[1057]*See* Ch. 4, § C.2.

[1058]28 U.S.C. § 2680(h).

[1059]The FTCA defines this term to include "any officer of the United States who is empowered by law to execute searches, to seize evidence or to make arrests for violations of federal law." 28 U.S.C. § 2680(h). Officers and employees of the Bureau of Prisons are empowered to make arrests for certain federal law violations. 18 U.S.C. § 3050. A number of courts have said that BOP personnel fall within these definitions. *See, e.g.,* Hernandez v. Lattimore, 612 F.2d 61, 74 (2d Cir. 1979); Sheppard v. U.S., 537 F. Supp. 2d 785, 791 (D.Md. 2008) and cases cited. The Supreme Court held that they were law enforcement officers in interpreting another section of the FTCA. Ali v. Federal Bureau of Prisons, 552 U.S. 214, 128 S. Ct. 831 (2008).

[1060]Puccini v. U.S., 978 F. Supp. 760, 761 (N.D.Ill. 1997); *see* Sheppard v. U.S., 537 F. Supp. 2d 785, 791–92 (D.Md. 2008)

This distinction is not supported by the statute, as other decisions have recognized.[1061] Under those decisions, false imprisonment or excessive confinement caused by a Bureau of Prisons employee who has law enforcement authority should be actionable under the FTCA regardless of whether the employee was using that authority at the time of the tort. Some courts have held that federal prisoners can pursue claims of unlawful confinement under the FTCA as claims of negligence rather than false imprisonment,[1062] but others have said that if the facts support a false imprisonment claim, the restriction on false imprisonment claims applies.[1063] Federal prisoners may also have a remedy for unjust conviction and imprisonment in the United States Court of Claims under limited circumstances.[1064]

State tort claims may be subject to different rules of immunity than those that apply in federal civil rights actions.[1065] However, judges, and persons who are acting under judicial supervision or implementing court orders, are generally immune from damage liability under both federal and state law.[1066]

In any lawsuit based on imprisonment past the proper release date, you must be sure you sue the right defendants.

Constitutional claims for unlawful confinement are governed by the same "personal involvement" requirement as other § 1983 and *Bivens* claims.[1067] If state law permits you to sue the state itself for false imprisonment, you may be able to avoid some of the problems of pinpointing who was at fault. Sometimes mistakes in release date computation are made because of a lack of communication between jurisdictions. Unless prison officials are actually aware of a mistake made in another jurisdiction, they are unlikely to be held liable for relying on it.[1068]

Excessive confinement can happen before a person is convicted, and such cases raise some different kinds of issues than those involving release at the end of a sentence. Confinement after a warrantless arrest while awaiting a probable cause hearing is governed by the Fourth Amendment, which requires a judicial determination of probable cause within 48 hours of arrest.[1069] State law may

---

(citing *Puccini*, not deciding question). One federal circuit, the Third, has taken an even narrower view, holding that the § 2680(h) exception for investigative and law enforcement officers applies only to acts committed during the course of a search, seizure, or arrest. Other courts have not followed this view. *Sheppard*, 537 F. Supp. 2d at 790 (citing Pooler v. U.S., 787 F.2d 868, 872 (3d Cir. 1986)).

[1061]Reynolds v. U.S., 549 F.3d 1108, 1114 (7th Cir. 2008); Sami v. U.S., 617 F.2d 755, 764–65 (D.C. Cir.1979); Ortiz v. Pearson, 88 F. Supp. 2d 151, 154–55 (S.D.N.Y. 2000). These cases all hold that the "investigative or law enforcement officer" exception to § 2680(h) is not limited to cases where the officers were performing particular duties.

[1062]Biberdorf v. Oregon, 243 F. Supp. 2d 1145, 1161 (D.Or. 2002); *see* Pate v. U.S., 328 F. Supp. 2d 62, 74–76 (D.D.C. 2004) (rejecting argument that negligence claims are barred by exemption for false imprisonment suits, but holding there is no FTCA claim for this plaintiff because the District of Columbia does not have an analogous claim against private persons for not following agency regulations).

[1063]Snow-Erlin v. U.S., 470 F.3d 804, 809 (9th Cir. 2006); Sheppard v. U.S., 537 F. Supp. 2d 785, 789 (D.Md. 2008). In *Snow-Erlin*, the question whether the investigative/law enforcement officer exception applies was not discussed.

[1064]*See* Ch. 8, § C.2.a, n.307.

[1065]*See, e.g.*, Cousins v. Lockyer, 568 F.3d 1063, 1068 (9th Cir. 2009) (holding prosecutor had absolute immunity and other defendants had qualified immunity from federal claims, but state prosecutorial immunity did not extend to false imprisonment claims and state courts do not extend qualified immunity to state civil rights claims); Biberdorf v. Oregon, 243 F. Supp. 2d 1145, 1158–59 (D.Or. 2002) (if plaintiff's over-detention resulted from a county policy, his false imprisonment claim is barred by discretionary immunity; if it resulted from employees' errors in applying policy, there is no immunity).

[1066]*See* Ch. 8, §§ L.2, L.5.

[1067]*See, e.g.*, Turner v. City of Taylor, 412 F.3d 629, 642 (6th Cir. 2005) (where prisoner was held for four days without being arraigned, shift supervisors at jail could be held liable if a magistrate was available for arraignment, and officer whose job it was to know what was in the jail log, which showed the length of plaintiff's incarceration, could also be held liable); Hayes v. Faulkner County, Ark., 388 F.3d 669, 673–74 (8th Cir. 2004) (jail administrator who knew of plaintiff's prolonged detention without court appearance could be held liable; municipality could be held liable where detention resulted from its policy of not taking prisoners to court until the court asked for them); Davis v. Hall, 375 F.3d 703, 716 (8th Cir. 2004) (prison staff who knew about a court order requiring prisoner's release could be liable for failing to act on it); Sample v. Diecks, 885 F.2d at 1112, 1115, 1118 (senior records officer held liable because he knew there was a problem and it was his job to solve it; the Commissioner was not liable because he had established procedures to deal with erroneous confinement claims).

[1068]Allen v. Lowder, 875 F.2d 82, 84–85 (4th Cir. 1989); Wadhams v. Procunier, 772 F.2d at 77; Middleton v. State, 54 A.D.2d 450, 389 N.Y.S.2d 159, 160 (N.Y.App.Div. 1976), *aff'd*, 43 N.Y.2d 678 (N.Y. 1977).

[1069]County of Riverside v. McLaughlin, 500 U.S. 44, 56, 111 S. Ct. 1661 (1991); Bryant v. City of New York, 404 F.3d 128, 136 (2d Cir. 2005); Alkire v. Irving, 330 F.3d 802, 815 (6th Cir. 2003) (policy of not holding court over weekends was a municipal policy which could violate the Constitution as applied to a plaintiff who spent 72 hours in jail before a probable cause hearing); Perez-Garcia v. Village of Mundelein, 396 F. Supp. 2d 907, 911 (N.D.Ill. 2005) ("Jailing a person for a period of time over his vigorous protest that he is the wrong person, without investigation or bringing him before a magistrate, can raise serious constitutional questions under the due process clause."); Blumel v. Mylander, 954 F. Supp. 1547, 1556–57 (M.D.Fla. 1997) (corporate policy of private jail operator not to release anyone without a judge's order, even if there has been no probable cause determination, was deliberately indifferent to constitutional rights). When an arrestee appears before a court and the court does *not* find probable cause, the arrestee cannot be detained any longer even if the court sets bail. Lingenfelter v. Board of County Comm'rs of Reno County, Kansas, 359 F. Supp. 2d 1163, 1170–72 (D.Kan. 2005).

In *Turner v. City of Taylor*, 412 F.3d 629 (6th Cir. 2005), the court upheld a policy of holding domestic violence arrestees for a

provide a higher standard than 48 hours, but if so you will have to enforce it in state court.[1070] When arrest is pursuant to warrant (meaning that there has been a probable cause determination), due process forbids extended detention without appearance before a court[1071] or without investigation if the arrestee protests that the arrest was erroneous or the continued detention is improper.[1072] Other forms of post-arrest confinement (*e.g.*, after a hearing when the arrestee is entitled to be released or to arrange for bail) are also governed by the Due Process Clause.[1073] (The 48-hour

period generally allowed before arraignment of persons arrested without warrants should not apply to persons who are past the stage of determining probable cause and have been ordered released by a court.[1074])

Recently a number of courts have held that compensatory damages for excessive or unlawful confinement are barred by the Prison Litigation Reform Act's provision barring recovery for mental or emotional injury without physical injury.[1075] We think that is completely wrong. Excessive or unlawful confinement represents a loss of liberty, which has long been recognized as a completely separate category of damages from mental or emotional injury.[1076]

10. Clemency and Pardons

The constitutional status of clemency and pardon proceedings is unclear. States are not required by the federal Constitution to have such processes,[1077] though most or all do. In *Ohio Adult Parole Authority v. Woodard*,[1078] four Supreme Court Justices joined in holding, in effect, that there are no due process protections in the clemency or pardon process, since these have traditionally been matters of grace committed to the authority of the executive.[1079] The other five Justices did not go that far, stating that

_____

minimum of 20 hours unless they were arraigned and released by a court; these arrestees were denied the local practice of having bail set by the police. However, it said that holding an arrestee for four days was presumptively unreasonable and unconstitutional. 412 F.3d 639–41.

[1070]*See* People ex rel. Maxian on behalf of Roundtree v. Brown, 77 N.Y.2d 422, 426–27, 570 N.E.2d 223 (1991) (holding pre-arraignment delay of more than 24 hours violates state law unless there is a reason why it is necessary).

[1071]Hayes v. Faulkner County, Ark., 388 F.3d 669, 673–75 (8th Cir. 2004) (affirming damage awards totalling $50,000 for 38 days in jail before a court appearance; policy of not producing warrant arrestees until the court asked for them was deliberate indifference); Armstrong v. Squadrito, 152 F.3d 564, 576–79 (7th Cir. 1998) (holding a warrant arrestee for 57 days without a court appearance despite his daily protests could constitute deliberate indifference and could shock the conscience).

[1072]Fairley v. Luman, 281 F.3d 913, 917 (9th Cir. 2002) ("Even detention pursuant to a valid warrant but in the face of repeated protests of innocence will, after a lapse of time, deprive the accused of a constitutional 'liberty.'"); Armstrong v. Squadrito, 152 F.3d 564, 579–80 (7th Cir. 1998) (refusal to take complaints of prisoners who said they were improperly confined could support liability); *see* Baker v. McCollan, 443 U.S. 137, 143–45, 99 S. Ct. 2689 (1979) (holding three days' erroneous post-arrest confinement pursuant to a facially valid warrant did not violate the Fourth Amendment; it might deprive the person of liberty without due process "after the lapse of a certain amount of time").

[1073]Berry v. Baca, 379 F.3d 764, 768–69, 772 (9th Cir. 2004) (allegation that arrestees were held 26–29 hours after court-authorized release because of municipal policies of deliberate indifference supported a due process claim); Powell v. Barrett, 376 F. Supp. 2d 1340, 1352 (N.D.Ga. 2005) (allegations that plaintiffs were held for one to ten days after they were ordered released stated a claim), *aff'd in part, rev'd in part, and remanded on other grounds*, 496 F.3d 1288 (11th Cir. 2007) *and* 246 Fed.Appx. 615 (11th Cir. 2007) (unpublished); Gaylor v. Does, 105 F.3d 572, 576–78 (10th Cir. 1997) (plaintiff obtained a liberty interest in release once bail was set, and failure to notify him of his bail amount could deny due process); Brooks v. George County, Miss., 84 F.3d 157, 166–67 (5th Cir. 1996) (claim of eight months' detention after charges were dismissed should have been pursued under the Due Process Clause, not the Fourth Amendment, since he was arrested with probable cause).

Some courts have held that excessive detention after a release order must "shock the conscience" to deny due process. *See, e.g.*, Golberg v. Hennepin County, 417 F.3d 808, 811 & n.3 (8th Cir. 2005); Luckes v. County of Hennepin, Minnesota, 415 F.3d 936, 939 (8th Cir. 2005). Some of them have referred to that standard as especially demanding. *Golberg*, 417 F.3d 811 n.3. However, the

Supreme Court said that in the "circumstances of normal pretrial custody," a showing of deliberate indifference is sufficient to meet the "shock the conscience" standard. It is only in emergency situations requiring "instant judgment" that a greater showing (*i.e.*, intent to do harm) is required. County of Sacramento v. Lewis, 523 U.S. 833, 849–53, 118 S. Ct. 1708 (1998); *accord*, Armstrong v. Squadrito, 152 F.3d 564, 576–77 (7th Cir. 1998) (holding deliberate indifference can satisfy the "shock the conscience" test in an excessive detention case).

[1074]Berry v. Baca, 379 F.3d 764 at 772.

[1075]*See* Ch. 9, § E.2.

[1076]Kerman v. City of New York, 374 F.3d 93, 125 (2d Cir. 2004) ("The damages recoverable for loss of liberty for the period spent in a wrongful confinement are separable from damages recoverable for such injuries as physical harm, embarrassment, or emotional suffering; even absent such other injuries, an award of several thousand dollars may be appropriate simply for several hours' loss of liberty."); *see* Randall v. Prince George's County, 302 F.3d 188, 209 (4th Cir. 2002) (false imprisonment plaintiff may claim "compensation for loss of time, for physical discomfort or inconvenience," as well as physical injury); Biberdorf v. Oregon, 243 F. Supp. 2d 1145, 1164 (D.Or. 2002) (claim for non-economic damages is not barred by state law limits on recovery for emotional distress because claim "is for loss of his liberty over several weeks and, therefore, is broader than 'mere' emotional distress").

[1077]Connecticut Bd. of Pardons v. Dumschat, 452 U.S. 458, 464, 101 S. Ct. 2460 (1981).

[1078]523 U.S. 272, 118 S. Ct. 1244 (1998).

[1079]Ohio Adult Parole Auth. v. Woodard, 523 U.S. 272, 276, 118 S. Ct. 1244 (1998); *see id.*, 523 U.S. at 285 ("Here, the executive's clemency authority would cease to be a matter of grace committed to the executive authority if it were constrained by the sort of procedural requirements that respondent urges."); *see also* Connecticut Bd. of Pardons v. Dumschat, 452 U.S. at 464 (". . . [P]ardon and commutation decisions have not traditionally

"some *minimal* procedural safeguards apply to clemency proceedings."[1080] However, even those Justices did not see a due process problem in giving a prisoner only three days' notice of a clemency interview and ten days' notice of a hearing, or in the fact that these proceedings occurred while post-conviction judicial proceedings were still pending, that counsel was excluded from the interview and restricted in participation in the hearing, and that the prisoner was not permitted to testify at the hearing.[1081] They suggested that due process scrutiny would be reserved for extreme circumstances.[1082] While at least one decision has found such circumstances,[1083] most have not.[1084] Courts have held that due process is not violated by a general policy of not granting clemency in capital cases.[1085]

Other legal issues may arise in connection with clemency or pardon proceedings.[1086] The Supreme Court held that a procedure which required an interview without counsel present, and permitted the authorities to make an adverse inference from the applicant's silence or to use her statements against her, did not violate the Fifth Amendment's privilege against self-incrimination, since the process and the interview were voluntary and not compelled.[1087] One lower court held that a change in voting requirements in clemency proceedings violated the Ex Post Facto Clause, though that ruling was later overturned on other grounds.[1088] Violation of state laws and regulations in clemency or pardon proceedings may be challenged in state court.

---

been the business of courts; as such, they are rarely, if ever, appropriate subjects for judicial review.").

[1080]*Woodard*, 523 U.S. at 289 (O'Connor, J., concurring in part and concurring in the judgment); *see id.*, 523 U.S. at 292–93 (Stevens, J., concurring in part and dissenting in part). These separate opinions give considerable weight to the fact that the prisoner in *Woodard* had been sentenced to death; it is possible that no due process rights would be found in a case involving a lesser penalty.

[1081]*Woodard*, 523 U.S. at 289 (O'Connor, J.).

[1082]Justice O'Connor stated: "Judicial intervention might, for example, be warranted in the face of a scheme whereby a state official flipped a coin to determine whether to grant clemency, or in a case where the State arbitrarily denied a prisoner any access to its clemency process." *Woodard*, 523 U.S. at 289.

[1083]*See* Young v. Hayes, 218 F.3d 850, 853 (8th Cir. 2000) (finding due process denial where prosecutor threatened an attorney with loss of employment if she provided information to the Governor relevant to a clemency proceeding; stay of execution granted), *appeal dismissed as moot*, 266 F.3d 791 (9th Cir. 2001); *see also* Wilson v. U.S. District Court for Northern District of California, 161 F.3d 1185, 1187 (9th Cir. 1998) (allegation that the state's communications about a clemency proceeding misled prisoner's counsel about the issues to be considered in the clemency proceeding stated a due process claim under *Woodard*).

[1084]*See* Bowens v. Quinn, 561 F.3d 671, 673–76 (7th Cir. 2009) (rejecting claim that due process requires prompt decisions of clemency petitions); Noel v. Norris, 336 F.3d 648, 649 (8th Cir. 2003) (due process was not violated by short deadline for clemency application and refusal to provide for brain scan of prisoner where prisoner filed 400-page clemency application with some evidence concerning his brain damage claim); Parker v. State Bd. of Pardons and Paroles, 275 F.3d 1032, 1036–37 (11th Cir. 2001) (affirming holding that chair of parole board was not so biased as to deny due process based on his three-year-old statement that no one on death row would ever get clemency from him, since he said at trial he now had an open mind); Gilreath v. State Bd. of Pardons and Paroles, 273 F.3d 932, 934 (11th Cir. 2001) (due process was not violated where two members of a five-member board were under investigation and a third had not attended the meeting at which favorable evidence was presented); Workman v. Bell, 245 F.3d 849, 852–53 (6th Cir. 2001) (allegation that false evidence was presented at commutation hearing did not raise a due process claim).

[1085]Anderson v. Davis, 279 F.3d 674, 676 (9th Cir. 2002).

[1086]Morales v. Willett, 417 F. Supp. 2d 1141, 1142–43 (C.D.Cal. 2006) (District Attorney would not be barred from clemency proceeding on the ground that the prisoner's former defense attorney worked for the DA's office, where there was no evidence that attorney had been or would be involved in the clemency proceeding or provide confidential or privileged information.).

[1087]Ohio Adult Parole Auth. v. Woodard, 523 U.S. at 286.

[1088]In *Pennsylvania Prison Society v. Rendell*, 419 F. Supp. 2d 651, 660–62 (M.D.Pa. 2006), *appeal dismissed and remanded*, 508 F.3d 156 (3d Cir. 2007), the court held that a new requirement of a unanimous vote by the Board of Pardons to recommend commutation for a life-sentenced prisoner violated the Ex Post Facto Clause. It also held that requiring inclusion of a crime victim on the Board of Pardons did not violate either the Due Process Clause or the Ex Post Facto Clause. 419 F. Supp. 2d at 656–60. The appeals court later held that none of the plaintiffs appeared to have standing to challenge the provisions, 508 F.3d at 162–69, and remanded for further consideration of that question. The suit was then dismissed. Pennsylvania Prison Soc. v. Rendell, 2008 WL 2227536 (M.D.Pa. 2008).

sex offender status,[25] or other factors,[26] or to pay inmates differently for similar work.[27] Decisions about classification and admission to prison programs are generally upheld under the rational basis test.[28]

Some courts have departed from standard equal protection principles and have held that prisoners' equal protection claims are generally governed by the "reasonable relationship" test of *Turner v. Safley*,[29] or have treated the rational basis standard as equivalent to the *Turner* standard in prison cases.[30] This can actually be to prisoners' advantage, since courts applying the *Turner* standard generally expect prison officials to come forward with the actual reasons for their policies and provide some evidence or at least experience in support of it,[31] while the rational basis test is less demanding, as discussed above.

Prisoners have been more successful in equal protection challenges to discrimination based on race. In *Johnson v. California*,[32] the Supreme Court held that prison racial discrimination is subject to strict scrutiny, and that government must prove that racial classifications "are narrowly tailored measures that further compelling governmental interests,"

even when prison officials claim they are necessary to control violence.[33] The Court said that the principle of deference to prison officials' judgment does not apply to cases involving racial discrimination.[34] Before *Johnson*, numerous decisions had held intentional racial segregation and discrimination unlawful in prison jobs and programs,[35] in discipline,[36] and in housing,[37] without always making clear

---

[25]Coughlin, 748 F.2d 783, 787–88 (2d Cir. 1984) (inmate sentenced to death for murdering a guard could be kept in closer security than others); Morris v. McCotter, 773 F. Supp. 969, 972–73 (E.D. Tex. 1991) (exclusion of convicted murderers from furlough program did not deny equal protection); Russell v. Eaves, 722 F. Supp. 558, 560 (E.D. Mo. 1989) (sex offenders could be required to complete a treatment program before becoming parole eligible); Fuller v. Lane, 686 F. Supp. 686, 689–91 (C.D. Ill. 1988) (exclusion of sex offenders from work release did not deny equal protection); *see also* Faheem-El v. Klincar, 841 F.2d 712, 727–29 (7th Cir. 1988) (en banc) (denial of bail to parolees, but not probationers, arrested for new crimes did not deny equal protection).

[25]Wirsching v. Colorado, 360 F.3d 1191, 1205 (10th Cir. 2004); Glauner v. Miller, 184 F.3d 1053, 1054 (9th Cir. 1999); Roe v. Marcotte, 193 F.3d 72, 82 (2d Cir. 1999).

[26]More v. Farrier, 984 F.2d 269, 271–72 (8th Cir. 1993) (officials could deny cable TV hookups to wheelchair-bound inmates based on the effort required to install it); Farmer v. Carlson, 685 F. Supp. 1335, 1344 (M.D. Pa. 1988) (placement of transsexual inmate in administrative segregation rather than high-security general population did not deny equal protection). *But see* Kelley v. Vaughn, 760 F. Supp. 161, 163–64 (W.D. Mo. 1991) (allegation that the plaintiff was denied equal protection by being fired from his bakery job for his homosexuality was not frivolous).

[27]*See* Ch. 2, § I.2, n.1276.

[28]*See* Ch. 2, § H, n.1210; § I.1, n.1235.

[29]*See* Taylor v. Johnson, 257 F.3d 470, 473–74 (5th Cir. 2001); Morrison v. Garraghty, 239 F.3d 648, 654–56 (4th Cir. 2001); DeHart v. Horn, 227 F.3d 47, 61 (3d Cir. 2000) (en banc); Allen v. Cuomo, 100 F.3d 253, 260–61 (2d Cir. 1996) (all applying *Turner* standard to equal protection claims. The *Turner* standard is discussed in Ch. 3, § A.

[30]*See, e.g.*, Gwinn v. Awmiller, 354 F.3d 1211, 1228–29 (10th Cir. 2004) (applying reasonable relationship standard); Prevard v. Fauver, 47 F. Supp. 2d 539, 543 (D.N.J. 1999), *aff'd*, 202 F.3d 254 (3d Cir. 1999) (unpublished).

[31]*See* Ch. 3, § A, for further discussion of this point.

[32]543 U.S. 499, 125 S. Ct. 1141 (2005).

[33]Johnson v. California, 543 U.S. at 506–07, 509–15. *Johnson* relied in part on *Lee v. Washington*, 390 U.S. 333, 88 S. Ct. 994 (1968), which struck down Alabama's prison racial segregation. Three Justices said in that case that "prison authorities have the right, acting in good faith and in *particularized circumstances*, to take into account racial tensions in maintaining security, discipline, and good order in prisons and jails." *Lee*, 390 U.S. at 334 (concurring opinion) (quoted in *Johnson*, 543 U.S. at 507). *See* Brand v. Motley, 526 F.3d 921, 924 (6th Cir. 2008) ("In prison housing, the Equal Protection Clause forbids racial classifications absent compelling justifications and a narrowly tailored plan."). *But see* Meggett v. Pennsylvania Dep't of Corrections, 892 A.2d 872, 887 (Pa.Cmwlth. 2006) (restrictions on "Afro hairstyles" were not subject to strict scrutiny because such styles denote a "cultural norm" and not race). *Cf.* Lindell v. Houser, 442 F.3d 1033, 1035–36 (7th Cir. 2006) (holding there is no right to be housed with "members of [one's] own race, culture, or temperament").

[34]Johnson v. California, 543 U.S. at 509–14.

[35]DeWalt v. Carter, 224 F.3d 607, 618 (7th Cir. 2000) (holding allegation of racially discriminatory removal from job stated a claim); La Bounty v. Adler, 933 F.2d 121, 123 (2d Cir. 1991); Black v. Lane, 824 F.2d 561, 562 (7th Cir. 1987); Foster v. Wyrick, 823 F.2d 218, 222 (8th Cir. 1987); Moore v. Clarke, 821 F.2d 518, 519 (8th Cir. 1987); Bentley v. Beck, 625 F.2d 70 (5th Cir. 1980); Finney v. Arkansas Board of Correction, 505 F.2d 194, 209–10 (8th Cir. 1974); Santiago v. Miles, 774 F. Supp. 775, 797–801 W.D.N.Y. 1991); Brown v. Sumner, 701 F. Supp. 762, 766 (D. Nev. 1988); Ramos v. Lamm, 485 F. Supp. 122, 164 (D. Colo. 1979), *aff'd in pertinent part*, 639 F.2d 559, 581 (10th Cir. 1980); Gates v. Collier, 349 F. Supp. 881, 887, 893 (N.D. Miss. 1972), *aff'd*, 501 F.2d 1291 (5th Cir. 1974); U.S. ex rel. Motley v. Rundle, 340 F. Supp. 807, 809 (E.D. Pa. 1972).

[36]Serrano v. Francis, 345 F.3d 1071, 1082–83 (9th Cir. 2003) (holding racial comments by hearing officer raised a factual issue as to his motivation in denying witnesses); Propst v. Leapley, 886 F.2d 1068, 1070 (8th Cir. 1989); Henard v. Parke, 5 F. Supp. 2d 641, 642–44 (N.D. Ind. 1998) (holding racial disparities in discipline reflected racial discrimination), *vacated as moot*, 191 F.3d 456 (7th Cir. 1999); Santiago v. Miles, 774 F. Supp. at 797–801; McCray v. Bennett, 467 F. Supp. 187, 195–96 (M.D. Ala. 1988); *see* Powells v. Minnehaha County Sheriff Dep't, 198 F.3d 711, 712 (8th Cir. 1999) (per curiam) (holding allegation that black prisoner was placed in solitary while a white prisoner who engaged in the same conduct was not stated an equal protection claim).

[37]Lee v. Washington, 390 U.S. 333, 88 S. Ct. 994 (1968); Harris v. Greer, 750 F.2d 617, 618 (7th Cir. 1984); Jones v. Diamond, 636 F.2d 1364, 1373 (5th Cir. 1981) (en banc); U.S. v. Wyandotte County, Kansas, 480 F.2d 969, 971–72 (10th Cir. 1973) (per curiam); Mason v. Schriro, 45 F. Supp. 2d 709, 713–15 (W.D. Mo. 1999); Santiago v. Miles, 774 F. Supp. at 797–801; Stewart v. Rhodes, 473 F. Supp. 1185, 1187–89 (S.D. Ohio 1979), *appeal dismissed*, 661 F.2d 934 (6th Cir. 1981); Mickens v. Winston, 462 F. Supp. 910, 911–13 (E.D. Va. 1978), *aff'd without opinion*, 609 F.2d 508 (4th Cir. 1979); Battle v. Anderson, 376 F. Supp. 402, 421 (E.D. Okla. 1974).

what legal standard they were applying. Prisoners may also be protected by Title VII of the federal Civil Rights Act,[38] which prohibits racial discrimination in employment, and which does not require a showing of intentional discrimination; proof of "disparate impact" is enough.[39] Courts have disagreed over whether Title VII applies to prisoners.[40]

Discrimination against aliens is also subjected to "strict scrutiny" in non-prison cases.[41] However, courts have generally applied the rational basis test to alien prisoners' equal protection claims, either because they say that standard generally applies in prison,[42] or because they find that the challenged actions are not really discrimination based on

alienage. Thus, one court held that placing Cuban inmates who were subject to deportation in administrative segregation, after other such inmates had been involved in riots in other prisons, was not really based on alienage, but on the plaintiff's "membership in a class of persons who faced potential deportation as a result of the agreement between the United States and Cuba."[43]

The equal protection standard for gender discrimination in prison is unsettled. In cases challenging lack of program opportunities for female prisoners, many courts have applied a "heightened" or "intermediate" scrutiny test that calls for "parity of treatment," which requires prison officials "to provide women inmates with treatment facilities that are substantially equivalent to those provided for men—i.e., equivalent in substance, if not in form—unless their actions. . . nonetheless bear a fair and substantial relationship to achievement of the State's correctional objectives."[44] Gender differences in security policies such as grooming

---

[38]42 U.S.C. § 2000e.

[39]Wards Cove Packing Co., Inc. v. Atonio, 490 U.S. 642, 645–46, 109 S. Ct. 2115 (1989). Title VII has a requirement of exhaustion of administrative remedies. Foster v. Wyrick, 823 F.2d 218, 221–22 (8th Cir. 1987). A prisoner would probably have to exhaust anti-discrimination remedies *and* the prison grievance process before filing suit under Title VII. *See* Ch. 9, § D for a discussion of the Prison Litigation Reform Act exhaustion requirement.

[40]*See* Vanskike v. Peters, 974 F.2d 806, 810 n.5 (7th Cir.1992) (dictum) ("Given the broad policies behind Title VII, there would appear to be no reason to withhold Title VII's protections from extending inside the prison walls."); Baker v. McNeil Island Correctional Center, 859 F.2d 124, 127–28 (9th Cir. 1988) (holding a prisoner's discrimination allegations stated a Title VII claim); *see also* Al-Zubaidy v. TEK Industries, Inc., 406 F.3d 1030, 1036–37 (8th Cir. 2005) (hearing prisoner's Title VII claim without reference to question of statute's applicability); Cleveland v. State, 2001 WL 888718 (Iowa Dist. 2001) (following *Baker* with respect to a similar state statute).

Other courts, however, have held that a prisoner is not an "employee" who can sue under Title VII. *See* Williams v. Meese, 926 F.2d 994, 997 (10th Cir. 1991); McCaslin v. Cornhusker State Industries, 952 F. Supp. 652, 655–58 (D. Neb. 1996) and cases cited. The federal Equal Employment Opportunity Commission has taken that view, holding that a prisoner working in the prison setting is not an employee under Title VII, though a prisoner who independently seeks work outside the prison and comes under the control of an independent employer may be an employee. E.E.O.C. Appeal No. 01964038, 1999 WL 146596, *4 & n.1 (March 2, 1999). Similarly, some courts have suggested that the *Baker* decision is limited to cases where the prisoner is working outside the prison for an employer other than the prison. *See* Coupar v. U.S. Dep't of Labor, 105 F.3d 1263, 1266 (9th Cir. 1997).

[41]*See* n.8 of this chapter.

[42]*See* Isaraphanic v. Coughlin, 716 F. Supp. 119, 120–21 (S.D.N.Y. 1989) (holding rational basis or reasonable relationship standard applied to alien prisoner with an immigration detainer who challenged the denial of temporary release and imposition of a higher security classification; upholding this treatment as rationally based on the prisoner's enhanced risk of escape). *Cf.* Delgado v. Federal Bureau of Prisons, 727 F. Supp. 24, 25, 27–28 (D.D.C. 1989) (holding placement of Cuban inmates in a separate unit because of "the uniqueness of their needs" and to expedite immigration paperwork, with no allegation that they were denied rights and privileges of other prisoners, did not deny equal protection), *reconsideration denied*, 1990 WL 20037 (D.D.C., Feb. 9, 1990).

[43]Vallina v. Meese, 704 F. Supp. 769, 772 (E.D. Mich. 1989); *see* McLean v. Crabtree, 173 F.3d 1176, 1185–86 (9th Cir. 1999) (holding that exclusion of prisoners with detainers from a sentence reduction program involving community-based drug treatment was not discrimination based on alienage, but discrimination based on detainers, which was rational because such prisoners would present a flight risk in community-based programs); Franklin v. Barry, 909 F. Supp. 21, 27–28 (D.D.C. 1995) (upholding exclusion of persons with detainers from minimum security classification based on same reasoning as *McLean*).

[44]Glover v. Johnson, 478 F. Supp. 1075, 1079 (E.D. Mich. 1979) (finding that vocational programs for men were more numerous and more likely to provide marketable skills than those for women); *accord*, Clarkson v. Coughlin, 898 F. Supp. 1019, 1043 (S.D.N.Y. 1995) (holding that provision of a Sensorially Disabled Unit for men but not women denied equal protection); West v. Virginia Dep't of Corrections, 847 F. Supp. 402, 407–09 (W.D. Va. 1994) (holding failure to provide boot camp programs for women as well as men denied equal protection); Casey v. Lewis, 834 F. Supp. 1477, 1550–51 (D. Ariz. 1993) (holding inequalities in mental health treatment denied equal protection); McCoy v. Nevada Dep't of Prisons, 776 F. Supp. 521, 523 (D. Nev. 1991); Glover v. Johnson, 721 F. Supp. 808, 848–49 (E.D. Mich. 1989) (explaining "parity" in more detail), *aff'd in part and rev'd in part on other grounds*, 934 F.2d 703 (6th Cir. 1991); Canterino v. Wilson, 546 F. Supp. 174, 210–12 (W.D. Ky. 1982), *vacated and remanded on other grounds*, 869 F.2d 948 (6th Cir. 1989); Dawson v. Kendrick, 527 F. Supp. 1252, 1317 (S.D. W.Va. 1981); McMurry v. Phelps, 533 F. Supp. 742, 767–68 (W.D. La. 1982); *see* Roubideaux v. North Dakota Dep't of Corrections and Rehabilitation, 570 F.3d 966, 974–75 (8th Cir. 2009) (applying heightened scrutiny, but upholding placement of some female prisoners, but no males, in county jails with more limited programming because the statutes "substantially relate to the important governmental objective of providing adequate segregated housing for women inmates"); Smith v. Bingham, 914 F.2d 740, 742 (5th Cir. 1990) (male prisoner working as a writ-writer at women's prison need not be permitted to enroll in women's vocational programs; separation of sexes had a "substantial relationship" to important security objectives).

rules have generally been upheld under the intermediate scrutiny standard.[45]

Some courts have tried to avoid or limit the intermediate scrutiny/parity of treatment approach by applying the Supreme Court's holding in *Turner v. Safley*, that restrictions on prisoners' constitutional rights need only bear a "reasonable relationship" to legitimate penological interests.[46] One court suggested that intermediate scrutiny applies to prison gender discrimination cases involving "general budgetary and policy choices," but that the rational basis test is applicable to gender discrimination in the daily management of prisons.[47] Another has held that parity of treatment is satisfied if there is a reasonable relationship under the *Turner* standard.[48] However, the Supreme Court's holding that racial discrimination cannot be justified by meeting the *Turner*

standard[49] would seem to support an argument that it is not suited to gender discrimination either.

Some more recent decisions have avoided any analysis of unequal program access for women by declaring that women are not "similarly situated"[50] to men—because, for example, the women's prison is smaller than the men's prisons, the length of stay for men is longer, the women's prison has a lower security classification than some of the men's prisons, and women prisoners have "special characteristics distinguishing them from male inmates, ranging from the fact that they are more likely to be single parents with primary responsibility for child rearing to the fact that they are more likely to be sexual or physical abuse victims."[51] Some of these decisions have assumed that once they find that women are not similarly situated to men, *no* standard of scrutiny is required, and prison officials need not justify

---

[45]*See* DeBlasio v. Johnson, 128 F. Supp. 2d 315, 327–28 (E.D. Va. 2000) (applying intermediate scrutiny; upholding ban on long hair for men but not women based on evidence that women are not as violent as men and not as prone to conceal weapons or escape), *aff'd*, 13 Fed.Appx. 158 (4th Cir. 2001) (unpublished); Ashann-Ra v. Commonwealth of Va., 112 F. Supp. 2d 559, 570–72 (W.D. Va. 2000) (similar to *DeBlasio*; holding that "parity of treatment" was satisfied because most grooming rules were the same for men and women, and the hair length difference was justified by men's greater propensities to violence, hiding contraband, and escape); Davie v. Wingard, 958 F. Supp. 1244, 1252–53 (S.D. Ohio 1997) (same); DuPont v. Commissioner of Correction, 448 Mass. 389, 402–03, 861 N.E.2d 744 (2007) (upholding use of department disciplinary unit (DDU) for male but not female prisoners because they were not similarly situated; there had been much more violence and disruption among the male than the female population). *But see* Ford v. City of Boston, 154 F. Supp. 2d 131, 150–51 (D. Mass. 2001) (applying intermediate scrutiny to strike down a practice of sending women arrestees to a jail where they were subjected to strip searches on intake, while male arrestees were sent to facilities which did not require such searches).

[46]Turner v. Safley, 482 U.S. 78, 89, 107 S. Ct. 2254 (1987); *see* Ch. 3, § A, concerning this standard.

[47]Pitts v. Thornburgh, 866 F.2d 1450, 1453–55 (D.C. Cir. 1989); *see* Pargo v. Elliott, 49 F.3d 1355, 1357 (8th Cir. 1995) (citing *Pitts* with apparent approval), *on remand*, 894 F. Supp. 1243, 1253–64 (S.D. Iowa 1995) (declining to apply heightened scrutiny absent a facial classification by gender, but examining the record for "invidious" discrimination), *aff'd*, 69 F.3d 80 (8th Cir. 1995) (per curiam).

The *Pitts* court suggested that distinctions based on gender are more likely to be upheld if they are not based on "traditional stereotyping or archaic notions of 'appropriate' gender roles." 866 F.2d at 1459. *Cf.* Dothard v. Rawlinson, 433 U.S. 321, 336–37, 97 S. Ct. 2720 (1977) (Title VII case upholding discrimination against women in hiring for inmate contact positions in extremely violent men's prisons).

[48]Glover v. Johnson, 35 F. Supp. 2d 1010, 1013–15 (E.D. Mich. 1999) (holding that "parity of treatment" is to be determined by *Turner v. Safley* reasonable relationship analysis), *aff'd*, 198 F.3d 557 (6th Cir. 1999) (not reaching the question); *see* Glover v. Johnson, 138 F.3d 229, 253 (6th Cir. 1997) (stating in dictum that no federal appeals court ever adopted the parity standard and finding of violation under it is of "dubious validity").

[49]Johnson v. California, 543 U.S. 499, 509–14 125 S. Ct. 1141 (2005).

[50]"Similarly situated" is not well defined. As one court stated:

Whether two groups of persons are similarly situated is not easily ascertained. "The test is whether a prudent person, looking objectively at the incidents, would think them roughly equivalent and the protagonists similarly situated.. . . [T]he 'relevant aspects' are those factual elements which determine whether reasoned analogy supports, or demands, a like result. Exact correlation is neither likely nor necessary.. . ."

DuPont v. Commissioner of Correction, 448 Mass. 389, 400, 861 N.E.2d 744 (2007) (citations omitted).

[51]Klinger v. Dep't of Corrections, 31 F.3d 727, 733 (8th Cir. 1994); *accord*, Women Prisoners of the District of Columbia Dep't of Corrections v. District of Columbia, 93 F.3d 910, 925–27 (D.C. Cir. 1996); Keevan v. Smith, 100 F.3d 644, 647–50 (8th Cir. 1996); Pargo v. Elliott, 894 F. Supp. 1243, 1258–62 (S.D. Iowa 1995), *aff'd*, 69 F.3d 280 (8th Cir. 1993) (per curiam); *see* Prince v. Endell, 78 F.3d 397, 398–99 (8th Cir. 1996) (per curiam) (holding prison officials were immune because they could have reasonably believed the genders were not similarly situated, since they lived in different types of prisons with different clothing policies and different violence levels, and officials).

In *Pargo*, the plaintiffs focused on differences in programs among prisoners of the same types of custody classification and sentence length, but the court still found that they were not similarly situated to men because women of all classifications were contained in a single institution, unlike men; women generally serve less time in prison because they are sentenced for fewer and less serious crimes and are often paroled earlier because they are considered lower risk than men; and "characteristics common to inmates at the women's institution are different from characteristics of inmates at men's institutions." These "rang[e] from the fact that they are more likely to be single parents with primary responsibility for child rearing to the fact that they are more likely to be sexual or physical abuse victims. Male inmates, in contrast, are more likely to be violent and predatory than female inmates." 894 F. Supp. at 1261.

In *Yates v. Stalder*, 217 F.3d 332 (5th Cir. 2000), the appeals court cautioned that lower courts cannot simply assume that prisons housing men and women are dissimilar, but must develop a record and analyze the facts.

unequal treatment at all, no matter how extreme it may be.[52] This approach was sharply, and we think correctly, criticized in one dissenting opinion, which stated:

> It is important not to lose sight of basic commonalities that justify similar treatment. All inmates, regardless of gender, are under the custody and control of the state as a result of their criminal behavior; all are subject to the same general departmental regulations and policies; and the incarceration in all cases shares common goals, including the reform and rehabilitation of individual offenders. These common characteristics provide a basis for the Department of Corrections to design a program that gives substantially equal opportunities to women and men for rehabilitative work while confined.[53]

Further, the Supreme Court has said in a non-prison case that even if the genders are not similarly situated, a court "still must determine whether the statutory classification is rationally related to a permissible state objective."[54] However, as stated above, prison officials almost always win under the rational basis test. Therefore, if you are faced with the "not similarly situated" argument, you should respond that male and female prisoners *are* similarly situated enough that the Equal Protection Clause is applicable, and that the heightened scrutiny standard should apply. The court can allow for differences in the size of prisons, length of stay, security classification, and "special characteristics" using heightened scrutiny, since that standard does not require identical treatment, but only "parity of treatment" or "substantially equivalent" treatment.[55]

Courts have also rejected gender discrimination claims on the ground that policies that resulted in unequal treatment were not intended to discriminate against women.[56]

Prisoners enjoy some protection under Title IX of the Education Amendments of 1972, which prohibits gender discrimination in any education program or activity receiving federal funds.[57] While the statute has several exceptions, prisons are not among them, and some courts have held that prisons are within Title IX's scope.[58] One court has held that Title IX requires equality, and not merely "parity," of treatment, unlike the Equal Protection Clause, though as a practical matter precise equality is not required.[59] Other courts have applied the same requirement that women prisoners be "similarly situated" to male prisoners, both in their personal characteristics and the size of their populations and the prisons they are held in, to Title IX claims as to equal protection claims.[60]

Discrimination against gay prisoners may deny equal protection if it is without rational basis.[61] Courts have generally accepted prison officials' arguments that for security reasons they must discourage homosexual activity and avoid having inmates identified to other inmates as gay,[62] though

---

[52]*See* Keevan v. Smith, 100 F.3d at 649 ("There can be no such meaningful comparison for equal protection purposes between two sets of inmates who are not similarly situated."); Klinger v. Dep't of Corrections, 31 F.3d at 731 ("Absent a threshold showing that she is similarly situated to those who allegedly receive favorable treatment, the plaintiff does not have a viable equal protection claim.").

[53]Keevan v. Smith, 100 F.3d at 652 (Heaney, J., dissenting).

[54]Parham v. Hughes, 441 U.S. 347, 357, 99 S. Ct. 1742 (1979); *see* Pargo v. Elliott, 894 F. Supp. at 1262–64 (applying *Parham* holding to prison discrimination case, finding rational basis for disparities).

[55]Glover v. Johnson, 478 F. Supp. at 1079; *accord,* Bukhari v. Hutto, 487 F. Supp. 1162, 1172 (E.D. Va. 1980).

[56]Keevan v. Smith, 100 F.3d 644, 651 (8th Cir. 1996); Pargo v. Elliott, 894 F. Supp. 1243, 1264, 1290 (S.D. Iowa 1995), *aff'd,* 69 F.3d 280 (8th Cir. 1995) (per curiam).

[57]20 U.S.C. §1681(a). Title IX does not require proof of discriminatory intent. Communities for Equity v. Michigan High School Athletic Ass'n., 459 F.3d 676, 696 (6th Cir. 2006), *cert.*

denied, 549 U.S. 1322 (2007). However, a showing of intent may be required to recover damages against a public agency. *See* Franklin v. Gwinnett County Public Schools, 503 U.S. 60, 74–75, 112 S. Ct. 1028 (1992).

[58]Roubideaux v. North Dakota Dep't of Corrections and Rehabilitation, 570 F.3d 966, 976–77 (8th Cir. 2009) ("A state's prison system as a whole qualifies as a program or activity within the meaning of Title IX."); Jeldness v. Pearce, 30 F.3d 1220, 1224–25 (9th Cir. 1994)

The *Roubideaux* court rejected the argument that the prison industries program was an educational program, but applied Title IX to vocational education. 570 F.3d at 977–78.

[59]Jeldness v. Pearce, 30 F.3d at 1226–28. Under that standard, "state prisons receiving federal funds are required by Title IX to make reasonable efforts to offer the same educational opportunities to women as to men. Although the programs need not be identical in number or content, women must have reasonable opportunities for similar studies and must have an equal opportunity to participate in programs of comparable quality." *Jeldness,* 30 F.3d at 1229. In *Jeldness,* the court held, among other things, that giving merit pay to men but not women for participating in the same vocational programs violated Title IX. *Id.,* 30 F.3d at 1230–31.

[60]Roubideaux, 570 F.3d at 978 (citing Klinger v. Department of Corrections, 107 F.3d 609, 616 (8th Cir. 1997)); Women Prisoners of the District of Columbia Dep't of Corrections v. District of Columbia, 93 F.3d 910, 925–27 (D.C. Cir. 1996).

[61]Johnson v. Johnson, 385 F.3d 503, 532 (5th Cir. 2004) (holding denial of protection of gay prisoner from assault would serve no legitimate purpose); Kelley v. Vaughn, 760 F. Supp. 161, 163–64 (W.D. Mo. 1991) (gay prisoner's claim that he was fired from his job because of his sexual orientation was not frivolous); Doe v. Sparks, 733 F. Supp. 227, 231, 233–34 (W.D.Pa. 1990) and cases cited.

In *Doe,* the court held that in general, gays are not protected by the Equal Protection Clause because certain kinds of homosexual conduct may be prohibited by law. 733 F. Supp. at 231–32 (citing Bowers v. Hardwick, 478 U.S. 186, 106 S. Ct. 2841 (1986)). Since *Bowers v. Hardwick* has now been overruled, *see* Lawrence v. Texas, 539 U.S. 558, 577–78, 123 S. Ct. 2472 (2003), that argument is no longer valid. *See also* Romer v. Evans, 517 U.S. 620, 116 S. Ct. 1620 (1996) (striking down class-based legislation directed at gays).

[62]Veney v. Wyche, 293 F.3d 726, 733–35 (4th Cir. 2002) (upholding exclusion of gay prisoners from double-celling); Brown

courts sometimes find that these concerns are not logically connected to the restrictions in a particular case.[63]

Age discrimination in prison may also deny equal protection[64] if it lacks a rational basis.[65] One court has held that the Federal Age Discrimination in Employment Act[66] does not apply to prisoners.[67]

Discrimination against disabled prisoners only denies equal protection if it lacks a rational basis; however, the disabled enjoy greater protection under the federal Americans with Disabilities Act and Rehabilitation Act.[68]

Claims of discrimination among different religious sects are addressed in another chapter.[69]

The failure to provide Spanish-language classes for non-English speaking prisoners has been held not to deny equal protection.[70]

Most equal protection claims involve an allegation that the plaintiff, because of his membership in some group or category, has been treated unequally compared to persons who belong to some other group or category. In such cases, the plaintiff must be clear about what the groups are that he says are treated differently.[71] However, under current law, a prisoner need not be a member of a group or class that is discriminated against in order to state an equal protection claim, contrary to some earlier decisions. The Supreme Court has held that an individual who claims he has been treated differently from others similarly situated, intentionally and without rational basis, states an equal protection claim as a "class of one."[72]

v. Johnson, 743 F.2d 408, 412–13 (6th Cir. 1984) (upholding censorship of publications that "condoned" homosexuality); *see* Star v. Gramley, 815 F. Supp. 276, 278–79 (C.D. Ill. 1993) (upholding denial to male inmate of the right to wear women's clothing and makeup). *But see* Harper v. Wallingford, 877 F.2d 728, 733 (9th Cir. 1989) ("Merely advocating homosexual activity is not a sufficient basis for a ban."). One court has held that segregating an intersexual (transgendered) prisoner throughout a long stay in jail for safety reasons did not deny equal protection. DiMarco v. Wyoming Dep't of Corrections, Division of Prisons, Wyoming Women's Center, 300 F. Supp. 2d 1183, 1197 (D. Wyo. 2004), *rev'd on other grounds*, 473 F.3d 1334 (10th Cir. 2007).

[63]*See* Phelps v. Dunn, 965 F.2d 93, 99–100 (6th Cir. 1992) (prison officials were not entitled to summary judgment for excluding gay inmate from religious services, since the warden and the chaplain agreed he presented no security risk); Espinoza v. Wilson, 814 F.2d 1093, 1098 (6th Cir. 1987) (rejecting the need to avoid identifying the plaintiffs as gay because they were already so identified); Doe v. Sparks, 733 F. Supp. at 233–34 (striking down prohibition on visits from same-sex "boy/girlfriends" because prison officials failed to show how the rule advanced their legitimate interests).

[64]Williams v. Meese, 926 F.2d 994, 998 (10th Cir. 1991).

[65]Gregory v. Ashcroft, 501 U.S. 452, 470, 111 S. Ct. 2395 (1991).

[66]29 U.S.C. §§ 621–34

[67]Williams v. Meese, 926 F.2d at 998.

[68]*See* Ch. 2, § F.4.h(2), concerning those statutes.

[69]*See* Ch. 3, § D.3.

[70]Pabon v. McIntosh, 546 F. Supp. 1328, 1341 (E.D. Pa. 1982); *see also* Bonner v. Lewis, 857 F.2d 559, 565 (9th Cir. 1988) (failure to provide a sign language interpreter to a deaf inmate did not deny equal protection; cost concerns could meet the rational basis test).

[71]Trujillo v. Williams, 465 F.3d 1210, 1228 (10th Cir. 2006).

[72]Village of Willowbrook v. Olech, 528 U.S. 562, 564–65, 120 S. Ct. 1073 (2000).

"Class of one" equal protection claims are evaluated under the rational basis test. Borzych v. Frank, 340 F. Supp. 2d 955, 970 (W.D. Wis. 2004), *reconsideration denied on other grounds*, 2004 WL 2491597 (W.D. Wis., Oct. 28, 2004). The plaintiff in such a case will be required to show, not only that he was badly treated, but also that persons similarly situated were not treated that way. Alicea v. Howell, 387 F. Supp. 2d 227, 236 (W.D.N.Y. 2005).

CHAPTER 6

Pretrial Detainees' Rights

Pretrial detainees occupy a different legal status from convicts, though that does not necessarily mean their rights are significantly different, as we explain in this chapter. There is some disagreement about when a person becomes a pretrial detainee[1] and ceases to be one.[2]

Under the Due Process Clause, pretrial detainees cannot be punished.[3] They can only be detained to ensure their presence at trial, and subjected to rules and restrictions that are reasonably related to jail management and security.[4]

Conditions and practices of pretrial detention may be unconstitutionally punitive if they are intended to punish detainees.[5] They may also constitute punishment if they are "arbitrary or purposeless" or "excessive" in relation to their purposes.[6] But if they are "reasonably related to a legitimate governmental objective," they are not considered punishment and do not deny due process.[7] Unless there is

---

[1]Some courts have held that the line between arrest (governed by the Fourth Amendment's objective reasonableness test) and pretrial detention (governed by due process) is the initial judicial probable cause hearing. These holdings occur most often in use of force cases, see Ch. 2, § G.2.a(3), but the Seventh Circuit has held that the conditions of confinement of an arrestee held for four days and nights before being brought before a judge are subject to Fourth Amendment scrutiny. Lopez v. City of Chicago, 464 F.3d 711, 718–20 (7th Cir. 2006); accord, Williams v. Rodriguez, 509 F.3d 392, 403 (7th Cir. 2007) (applying holding to medical care claim).

[2]Courts have disagreed whether persons already convicted but awaiting sentencing are to be treated like detainees or convicts. Compare Tilmon v. Prator, 368 F.3d 521, 523 (5th Cir. 2004) ("In our view, the adjudication of guilt, i.e., the conviction, and not the pronouncement of sentence, is the dispositive fact with regard to punishment in accordance with due process."); Berry v. City of Muskogee, 900 F.2d 1489, 1493 (10th Cir. 1990) ("The critical juncture is conviction. . . at which point the state acquires the power to punish and the Eight Amendment is implicated.") with Lewis v. Downey, 581 F.3d 467, 475 (7th Cir. 2009) (state does not acquire right to punish until sentencing); Fuentes v. Wagner, 206 F.3d 335, 341 (3d Cir. 2000) (the right to remain at liberty continues until sentencing); Benjamin v. Malcolm, 646 F. Supp. 1550, 1556, n.3 (S.D.N.Y. 1986) (convicted inmates not yet sentenced to prison should be treated as detainees since they may receive suspended sentences or some outcome other than a prison term).

There is a similar disagreement about the standard governing treatment of accused parole violators. Compare Datz v. Hudson, 806 F. Supp. 982, 988 n.8 (N.D. Ga. 1992) (applying Eighth Amendment to parole violator's claim), aff'd, 14 F.3d. 58 (11th Cir. 1994) with Benjamin v. Malcolm, 646 F. Supp. at 1556 n.3 (". . . [T]he alleged parole violators ought not to be treated differently from other detainees, since the charges of parole violation standing against them are unproven, and in many instances, involve the same charges as those for which they are substantively detained.") and Hamilton v. Lyons, 74 F.3d 99, 106 (5th Cir. 1996) ("[We] apply Bell's standard to detained parolees only to the extent that we recognize that a parolee arrested for a subsequent crime has a due process right to be free from punishment for the subsequent crime until convicted of the subsequent crime.").

[3]Bell v. Wolfish, 441 U.S. 520, 535, 99 S. Ct. 1861 (1979); accord, Block v. Rutherford, 468 U.S. 576, 585–86, 104 S. Ct. 3227 (1984); Magluta v. Samples, 375 F.3d 1269, 1273 (11th Cir. 2004).

[4]Bell v. Wolfish, 441 U.S. at 540.

[5]McMillian v. Johnson, 88 F.3d 1554, 1564 (11th Cir.) (holding evidence that a detainee in a capital case was placed on death row, contrary to state law and prison regulations, for punitive rather than security reasons supported due process claim, even if there could have been a legitimate alternative purpose), amended, 101 F.3d 1363 (11th Cir. 1996); accord, Magluta v. Samples, 375 F.3d 1269, 1274–75 (11th Cir. 2004) (holding allegations that jail officials fabricated escape allegations and kept plaintiff in segregation in retaliation for constitutionally protected conduct stated a claim of unconstitutional punishment); Gerakaris v. Champagne, 913 F. Supp. 646, 651 (D.Mass. 1996); D.B. v. Tewksbury, 545 F. Supp. 896, 905 (D.Or. 1982).

[6]Bell v. Wolfish, 441 U.S. at 538–39. If that is the case, "a court permissibly may infer that the purpose of the governmental action is punishment that may not constitutionally be inflicted upon detainees qua detainees." Bell, 441 U.S. at 539; see Miller v. Fairman, 872 F. Supp. 498, 504 (N.D. Ill. 1994) ("This court fails to see how having a pretrial detainee sleep in a flooded area on a wet mattress infested with insects and mice furthers any legitimate governmental interest in maintaining the detention facility.").

Earlier pretrial detention cases had held that because of the presumption of innocence, detainees could only be held under the least restrictive conditions possible; restrictions placed on them had to be justified by a "compelling necessity." See, e.g., Rhem v. Malcolm, 507 F.2d. 333, 336 (2d Cir. 1974); Brenneman v. Madigan, 343 F. Supp. 128, 136–38 (N.D. Cal. 1972). The Supreme Court overruled these cases in Bell v. Wolfish, holding that the presumption of innocence is a rule of evidence and does not govern jail conditions. Bell, 441 U.S. at 532–33.

[7]Bell, 441 U.S. at 538–39; accord, id. at 551, 554; see Hartline v. Gallo, 546 F.3d 95, 99 (2d Cir. 2008) (strip search of pretrial detainees pursuant to policy was reasonable); Roberts v. State of R.I., 239 F.3d 107, 110–13 (1st Cir. 2001) (holding strip search policies unconstitutional in part); Edwards v. Johnson, 209 F.3d

"substantial evidence in the record to indicate that the officials have exaggerated their response to these considerations, courts should ordinarily defer to their expert judgment in such matters."[8] However, courts have also made it clear that "due deference does not mean blind deference."[9]

At least one state court has held that the *Bell v. Wolfish* "punishment" analysis is too "one-sided." That court ruled that the State constitution requires a higher standard than the federal constitution, namely "a balancing of the harm to individuals resulting from the condition imposed against the benefit sought by the government through its enforcement."[10]

Applying the "punishment" analysis, the Supreme Court in *Bell v. Wolfish* upheld several practices in one federal jail, including the double bunking of inmates, a rule limiting the sources from which inmates could receive publications, a prohibition on receipt of packages, a refusal to let inmates watch their rooms being searched, and routine body-cavity inspections after contact visits.[11] The Supreme Court has also held that pretrial detainees have no constitutional right to contact visits.[12] The lower courts have reached

a variety of conclusions about what constitutes punishment[13] and what does not.[14]

The rights of convicts, like the rights of detainees, are also governed by a "reasonable relationship" standard, this one set out in the Supreme Court's decision in *Turner v. Safley*.[15] The Supreme Court has never spelled out how the *Turner* and *Bell* standards compare, though it has said that when security practices are at issue there is little basis for distinguishing between convicts and detainees.[16] The *Turner* standard cannot apply in its entirety to pretrial detainees,

---

772, 779 (5th Cir. 2000) (prohibition of unauthorized physical contact between detainees and the public was a reasonable response to safety and order concerns and did not violate First Amendment).

[8]*Bell*, 441 U.S. at 540 n.23 (quoting Pell v. Procunier, 417 U.S. 817, 827, 94 S. Ct. 2800 (1974)); Turner v. Safley, 482 U.S. 78, 86, 107 S.Ct. 2254 (1987) (quoting *Pell*).

[9]U.S. v. Gotti, 755 F. Supp. 1159, 1164 (E.D.N.Y. 1991); *accord*, Lock v. Jenkins, 641 F.2d 488, 498 (7th Cir. 1981) ("We do not read anything in *Wolfish* to require this court to grant automatic deference to ritual incantations of prison officials that their actions foster the goals of order and discipline."); Akey v. Haag, 2006 WL 3246146, *4 (D.Vt. 2006) (quoting U.S. v. Gotti, *supra*); U.S. v. Lopez, 327 F. Supp. 2d 138, 143 (D.P.R. 2004) ("While we do give deference to correction officials, we cannot turn a blind eye. Institutional policies must be reasoned."); *see* Rose v. Saginaw County, 353 F. Supp. 2d 900, 921 (E.D. Mich. 2005) (exaggerated response to remove all clothes from any inmate placed in segregation); Newkirk v. Sheers, 834 F. Supp. 772, 781–83 (E.D. Pa. 1993) (exaggerated response to require female detainees to sleep on mattresses on floor when cots were available).

[10]Cooper v. Morin, 49 N.Y.2d 69, 424 N.Y.S.2d. 168, 399 N.E.2d 1188, 1194 (1979).

[11]Bell v. Wolfish, 441 U.S. at 541–62.

[12]Block v. Rutherford, 468 U.S. 576, 585–89, 104 S. Ct. 3227 (1984).

One State court has held that the State constitution protects a right to non-conjugal contact visits with family members. Cooper v. Morin, 399 N.E.2d at 1193–96.

[13]*See, e.g.*, Iqbal v. Hasty, 490 F.3d 143, 168–9 (2d Cir. 2007) (allegations that jail staff "placed a detainee in solitary confinement, deliberately subjected him to extreme hot and cold temperatures, shackled him every time he left his cell, and repeatedly subjected him to strip and body-cavity searches, and that these conditions were intended to be, and were in fact, punitive" stated a substantive due process claim under *Bell*), *aff'd in part, rev'd in part, and remanded on other grounds sub nom.* Ashcroft v. Iqbal, ___ U.S. ___, 129 S. Ct. 1937 (2009); Snow ex rel. Snow v. City of Citronelle, AL, 420 F.3d 1262, 1268 (11th Cir. 2005) (failure to prevent attempt or suicide itself can inflict punishment); Blackmore v. Kalamazoo County, 390 F.3d 890, 384 (6th Cir.2004) (pretrial detainee complaining for more than 48 hours about severe, stabbing abdominal pains and only given antacid is punishment); Covino v. Vermont Dep't of Corrections, 933 F.2d 128, 130 (2d Cir. 1991) (nine-month confinement of a detainee in administrative segregation "smacks of punishment" and should be analyzed under *Bell*); U.S. v. Lopez, 327 F. Supp. 2d 138, 144 (D.P.R. 2004) (standard procedure of placing detainees facing death penalty in a segregated housing unit was not rationally related to preserving order and safety and was therefore punishment); U.S. v. Gotti, 755 F. Supp. at 1164 (placing detainee in administrative detention based on his criminal charges and witness tampering accusations, with no showing of misbehavior in jail constituted punishment); Gawreys v. D.C. General Hospital, 480 F. Supp. 853, 855 (D. D.C. 1979) (use of metal restraints, rather than cloth or leather restraints required by jail regulations, was punishment).

[14]*See, e.g.*, Inmates of Allegheny County Jail v. Pierce, 612 F.2d 754, 760–61 (3d Cir. 1979), *on remand*, 487 F. Supp. 638 (W.D. PA 1980) (refusal to continue methadone treatment for detainees who had received it before their arrest was not punishment); Washington v. Tinsley, 809 F. Supp. 504, 506–07 (S.D. Tex. 1992) (jail no-smoking policy was not punishment because it was reasonably related to legitimate purposes of protecting non-smokers' health, eliminating fire hazards, and reducing litter); Doughty v. Board of Commissioners for County of Weld, Colo., 731 F. Supp. 423, 425–28 (D. Colo. 1989) (similar to *Washington v. Tinsley*); Doss v. Rapone, 601 F. Supp. 935, 37 (E.D. Pa. 1985) (22-hour-a-day lockup based on high bail and pending charges of violent crimes was not "punishment"; purpose was to keep violent offenders away from the largely nonviolent population of the jail); Ford v. Nassau County Executive, 41 F. Supp. 2d 392 (E.D.N.Y. 1999) (giving a choice between distributing food to inmates or being segregated in "lock-in" is not punishment because the chore was not overly burdensome).

[15]482 U.S. 78, 107 S. Ct. 2254 (1987); *see* Ch. 3, § A, for discussion of this standard.

[16]Bell v. Wolfish, 441 U.S. at 546, n.28; *accord*, Covino v. Patrissi, 967 F.2d 73, 78 n.4 (2d Cir. 1992).

since the "penological interests" with which *Turner* was concerned include "interests that relate to the treatment (including punishment, deterrence, rehabilitation, etc. . . . .) of persons convicted of crimes."[17] As a practical matter, the application of the standards has been similar, and in some cases the courts have failed to make any distinction between them.[18]

The Eighth Amendment's ban on cruel and unusual punishments should not apply to detainees, since as noted above, detainees cannot be punished at all, regardless of whether it is cruel and unusual.[19] However, in practice, courts determining detainees' rights under the Due Process Clauses have often adopted the Eighth Amendment standards in detainee cases that raise issues that are governed by the Eighth Amendment when raised by convicts.

Most courts have held that detainees' due process claims involving medical care and protection from inmate-on-inmate assault are governed by the Eighth Amendment deliberate indifference standard, which requires the plaintiff to show that the defendants have disregarded a risk of which they have actual knowledge.[20] Several federal circuits have held or suggested that there is a different standard in detainee medical care cases.[21]

Courts have differed over whether use of force against detainees is governed by the same "malicious and sadistic" standard as for convicts.[22]

With respect to conditions of confinement, the Supreme Court said in *Bell v. Wolfish* that crowding and other living conditions constitute punishment of detainees if they inflict "genuine privations and hardship over an extended period of time."[23] Courts applying *Bell* have intervened in many cases of inhumane jail conditions.[24] Particularly oppressive conditions may constitute punishment even if imposed for short periods of time.[25] However, pretrial detention conditions that have been held unconstitutional generally resemble those that have also been held to violate the Eighth

---

[17]Benjamin v. Fraser, 264 F.3d 175, 187 n.10 (2d Cir. 2001); *see* Shain v. Ellison, 273 F.3d 56, 65–66 (2d Cir. 2001) (holding *Turner* applies to prisons and not jails). *But see* Iqbal v. Hasty, 490 F.3d 143, 172 (2d Cir. 2007) (holding the claim of a person held "in a prison-like environment" in a jail and charged with felonies is governed by the *Turner* reasonable relationship standard), *aff'd in part, rev'd in part, and remanded on other grounds sub nom.* Ashcroft v. Iqbal, ___ U.S. ___, 129 S. Ct. 1937 (2009).

[18]Thus, in *Mauro v. Arpaio*, 188 F.3d 1054 (9th Cir. 1999) (en banc), the court applied the *Turner* standard to censorship of publications in a jail housing both sentenced prisoners and detainees, though it acknowledged that the rehabilitative rationale relied on has no application to detainees. 188 F.3d at 1059 n.2. The majority ignored *Bell. Compare id.* at 1067 (dissenting opinion) (pointing out inappropriateness of *Turner* standard in detainee case). Subsequently, the same court has applied *Bell* and rejected *Turner* in a detainee case, ignoring *Mauro.* Demery v. Arpaio, 378 F.3d 1020, 1028–29 (9th Cir. 2004).

[19]City of Revere v. Massachusetts General Hospital, 463 U.S. 239, 244, 103 S. Ct. 2979 (1983); Bell v. Wolfish, 441 U.S. 520 535, 99 S. Ct. 1861 (1979).

[20]*See, e.g.,* Caiozzo v. Koreman, 581 F.3d 63, 72 (2d Cir. 2009); Ford v. County of Grand Traverse, 535 F.3d 483, 495 (6th Cir. 2008); Hartsfield v. Colburn, 491 F.3d 394, 396 (8th Cir. 2007), *cert. denied,* 128 S. Ct. 1745 (2008); Young v. City of Mt. Ranier, 238 F.3d 567, 576 (4th Cir. 2001). *See* Ch. 2, §§ A.2, G.1a concerning these standards.

[21]*See* Ch. 2, § F.1.a, nn.259–61.

[22]*See* Ch. 2, § G.2.a.(1) (convicts) and § G.2.a.(2) (pretrial detainees). Arrestees' use of force claims are governed by the Fourth Amendment reasonableness standard, though there is

disagreement about exactly where the line is between arrest and pretrial detention. *See* Ch. 2, § G.2.a(3).

[23]*Bell,* 441 U.S. at 542; Zolnowski v. County of Erie, 944 F. Supp 1096, 1111–12 (W.D.N.Y. 1996) (quoting LaReau v. Manson, 651 F.2d 96, 104 (2d Cir. 1981)). These living conditions issues are discussed in detail in Ch. 2.

[24]*See, e.g.,* Jones v. Diamond, 636 F.2d 1364, 1373–74 (5th Cir. 1979) (en banc); Zolnowski v. County of Erie, 944 F. Supp. at 1117–18; Newkirk v. Sheers, 834 F. Supp. 772, 782 (E.D. Pa. 1993); Carty v. Farrelly, 957 F. Supp. 727, 735 (D. V.I. 1997); Young v. Keohane, 809 F. Supp. 1185, 1195 (M.D. Pa. 1992); Carver v. Knox County, Tenn., 753 F. Supp. 1370, 1386–94 (E.D. Tenn. 1989), *remanded for reconsideration,* 887 F.2d 1287 (6th Cir. 1989), *adhered to on remand,* 753 F. Supp. 1398 (E.D. Tenn. 1990); Vazquez v. Carver, 729 F. Supp. 1063, 1068–1070 (E.D. Pa. 1989); Gilland v. Owens, 718 F. Supp. 665, 685–88 (W.D. Tenn. 1989); Inmates of Allegheny County v. Wecht, 699 F. Supp. 1137, 1143–47 (W.D. Pa. 1988), *aff'd,* 874 F.2d 147, 153–54 (3d Cir. 1989), *vacated and remanded on other grounds,* 110 S. Ct. 355 (1989), *vacated as moot,* 893 F.2d. (3d Cir. 1990); Fambro v. Fulton county, Ga., 713 F. Supp. 1426, 1430–32 (N.D. Ga. 1989); Albro v. Onondaga County, 681 F. Supp. 991, 994–997 (N.D.N.Y. 1988); Albro v. County of Onaondaga, N.Y., 627 F. Supp. 1280, 1285–87 (N.D.N.Y. 1986); Reece v. Gragg, 650 F. Supp. 1297, 1301–05 (D. Kan. 1986); McMurry v. Phelps, 533 F. Supp. 742, 761–63 (W.D. La. 1982); Dawson v. Kendrick, 527 F. Supp. 1252, 1287–1315 (S.D. W.Va. 1981); Hutchings v. Corum, 501 F. Supp. 1276, 1293–95 (W.D. Mo. 1980); Heitman v. Gabriel, 524 F. Supp. 622, 624–29 (W.D. Mo. 1981); *see also* Lyons v. Powell, 838 F.2d. 28, 31 (1st Cir. 1988) (excessive lock-in and sleeping on a floor mattress stated a claim of unlawful punishment as to a detainee held in a state prison); Lock v. Jenkins, 641 F.2d 488, 492–94 (7th Cir. 1981) (excessive lock-in times for detainees held in a state prison constituted punishment).

[25]Anela v. City of Wildwood, 790 F.2d. 1063, 1069 (3d Cir. 1986) (overnight confinement in jail without drinking water, food, or sleeping facilities of persons who had done nothing but play their radio too loud in their home constituted "punishment"); Goodson v. City of Atlanta, 763 F.2d 1381, 1387 (11th Cir. 1985) (upholding damage for three-day period of "inedible food, no blankets or bedding, no sanitation, inadequate medical care, no shelter from the elements other than a concrete cell with broken windows permitting the passage of cold air, together with such unsanitary conditions and deprivation of rights as to endanger his health"), *rehearing denied,* 770 F.2d 175 (11th Cir. 1985); Benjamin v. Sielaff, 752 F. Supp. 140, 141 n.3 (S.D.N.Y. 1990) (confining detainees in non-housing areas and in areas without toilets was unconstitutional); Willis v. Bell, 726 F. Supp. 1118, 1122 (N.D. Ill. 1989) (allegation of 12 hours without food or access to a washroom after arrest stated a claim under the punishment standard if done intentionally).

Amendment, under its prohibition of "unquestioned and serious deprivations of basic human needs" or of the "minimal civilized measure of life's necessities."[26] Some courts have simply said outright that the Eighth Amendment standard defines what is unlawful punishment of detainees.[27]

Other courts have held that there is a difference in standards between convicts and detainees,[28] but few courts have spelled out what the difference means in concrete terms.[29] The Second Circuit has said that inquiring into "punitiveness" is "of limited utility" in evaluating conditions which "were not affirmatively imposed" (in that case, physical conditions such as lack of sanitation and working ventilation), and that the "actual knowledge" requirement of Eighth Amendment deliberate indifference law does not apply in such cases. Therefore, it held, "in a challenge by pretrial detainees asserting a *protracted* failure to provide safe prison conditions, the deliberate indifference standard does not require the detainees to show anything more than actual or imminent substantial harm."[30] This holding seems to be limited to institutional living conditions. The same court has recently reaffirmed that in cases involving "a serious medical condition or other serious threat to the health or safety of *a person* in custody," the "actual knowledge" standard applied in Eighth Amendment cases should also govern detainee cases.[31]

The Fifth Circuit has made a slightly different distinction, holding that "general conditions, practices, rules, or restrictions of pretrial confinement" are subject to the *Bell v. Wolfish* "punishment" analysis, while jail officials' "episodic acts or omissions" are governed by the "actual knowledge" deliberate indifference standard.[32] Even this difference does not seem to make much of a difference; the court said that "a proper application of *Bell's* reasonable relationship test is functionally equivalent to a deliberate indifference inquiry."[33]

There are some areas of law where it does seem clear that different legal standards apply to certain claims by detainees and convicts.

With respect to prison work, the Thirteenth Amendment prohibits "slavery [and] involuntary servitude, except as a punishment for crime whereof the party shall have been

---

[26]Rhodes v. Chapman, 452 U.S. 337, 347, 101 S. Ct. 2392 (1981); *see* Ch. 2, § A.1, for discussion of this standard.

[27]*See, e.g.,* Butler v. Fletcher, 465 F.3d 340, 344–45 (8th Cir. 2006) (holding that detainees' claims concerning adequate food, clothing, shelter, medical care, and reasonable safety are not governed by the *Bell v. Wolfish* "no punishment" standard, but by "principles of safety and general well-being," which turn out to be the deliberate indifference standard), *cert. denied*, 550 U.S. 917 (2007); Spencer v. Bouchard, 449 F.3d 721, 727 (6th Cir. 2006); Surprenant v. Rivas, 424 F.3d 5, 18 (1st Cir. 2005) (holding that the "parameters" of detainees' rights concerning conditions of confinement are "coextensive" with Eighth Amendment protections); Hart v. Sheahan, 396 F.3d 887 (7th Cir. 2005) (". . . [W]hen the issue is whether brutal treatment should be assimilated to punishment, the interests of the prisoner is [sic] the same whether he is a convict or a pretrial detainee. In either case he (in this case she) has an interest in being free from gratuitously severe restraints and hazards, while the detention facility has an interest in protecting the safety of inmates and guards and preventing escapes."); Craig v. Eberly, 164 F.3d 490, 495 (10th Cir. 1998) ("Although the Due Process Clause governs a pretrial detainee's claim of unconstitutional conditions of confinement,. . . the Eighth Amendment standard provides the benchmark for such claims."); Cottrell v. Caldwell, 85 F.3d 1480, 1490 (11th Cir. 1996) (Under Eighth Amendment and Due Process Clause, "the applicable standard is the same, so decisional law involving prison inmates applies equally to cases involving arrestees or pretrial detainees."); Hamm v. DeKalb County, 774 F.2d 1567, 1574 (11th Cir. 1985) (standards must be the same because to hold otherwise "would require courts to evaluate the details of slight differences in conditions" and would get courts involved in "minutiae" in jails that house both convicts and detainees).

[28]*See, e.g.,* Hubbard v. Taylor, 399 F.3d 150, 165–66 (3d Cir. 2005) (remanding a jail crowding claim, asserting that the applicable due process standard is not the same as the Eighth Amendment standard used by the district court, with no explanation of what the difference is).

[29]One court has held that in an overcrowded jail, detainees could be double-celled for 15 days while convicts could be double-celled for 30 days. LaReau v. Manson, 651 F.2d 96, 105, 109 (2d Cir. 1981).

[30]Benjamin v. Horn, 343 F.3d 35, 31 (2d Cir. 2003). In a later case the Second Circuit characterized *Benjamin* as holding that deliberate indifference "could be presumed from an absence of reasonable care" in detainee cases. Iqbal v. Hasty, 490 F.3d 143, 169 (2d Cir. 2007), *aff'd in part, rev'd in part, and remanded on other grounds sub nom.* Ashcroft v. Iqbal, ___ U.S. ___, 129 S. Ct. 1937 (2009).

[31]Caiozzo v. Koreman, 581 F.3d 63, 72 (2d Cir. 2009) (emphasis supplied). The court seems to be distinguishing between cases involving long-standing conditions affecting a number of prisoners (which do not require a showing of actual knowledge under the above-cited *Benjamin* decision) and cases involving particular events affecting an individual (which do require showing actual knowledge). *See Caiozzo*, 580 F.3d at 70 (noting that *Benjamin* said that "[i]n other types of challenges—for example, when pretrial detainees challenge discrete judgments of state officials—meeting the deliberate indifference standard may require a further showing" (citation omitted)).

[32]Hare v. City of Corinth, Miss., 74 F.3d 633, 643 (5th Cir. 1996) (en banc). To invoke the *Bell* analysis, this court says, a detainee must show that a challenged act or omission "implement[s] a rule or restriction or otherwise demonstrate[s] the existence of an identifiable intended condition or practice," or else show that acts or omissions "were sufficiently extended or pervasive, or otherwise typical of extended or pervasive misconduct by other officials, to prove an intended condition or practice to which the *Bell* test can be meaningfully applied." *Hare*, 74 F.3d at 645. Under *Hare*, the *Bell* standard can apply to individual cases. *See* Shepherd v. Dallas County, 591 F.3d 445, 453 (5th Cir. 2009) (applying *Bell* where individual was harmed because "[t]he jail's evaluation, monitoring, and treatment of inmates with chronic illness was. . . grossly inadequate due to poor or non-existent procedures and understaffing of guards and medical personnel," not because of fault on the part of particular individuals").

[33]*Hare*, 74 F.3d at 643.

duly convicted. . . ."[34] Thus, pretrial detainees, unlike convicts, may not be forced to work, except for housekeeping chores in their living units.[35]

Unlike convicts, persons awaiting trial have a Sixth Amendment right to the assistance of counsel and to an unimpeded criminal defense, a right that is different from the more general right of access to courts and not subject to its limitations.[36] Detainees, like convicts, are also entitled to the right of access to the courts. However, small local jails may not need to maintain as extensive law libraries as large State prisons,[37] and some courts have held (incorrectly, in our view) that having a lawyer for one's pending criminal case is sufficient to guarantee court access even as to civil rights matters.[38]

Most courts have held that the procedural due process rights of detainees are more extensive than those of convicts. The Supreme Court has said that a valid *conviction* sufficiently deprives a person of liberty that she is entitled to due process protections only if placed under conditions that impose "atypical and significant hardship on the inmate in relation to the ordinary incidents of prison life."[39] Most, but not all, courts have held that this rule does not apply to pretrial detainees, though they do not all agree what the rule for detainees is.[40]

Most courts have held that persons newly arrested cannot be strip searched without some reason to believe they are concealing contraband, and at least one court has extended this rule to jails.[41] Some courts have held that detainees, unlike convicts, may be subjected to warrantless cell searches only for prison security purposes and not purely for law enforcement purposes.[42]

In our view, detainees should be entitled to more protection than convicts with respect to communicating with the outside world. Most cases requiring reasonable telephone access involve detainees in local jails,[43] as do most cases requiring improvement of visiting hours or conditions, either for attorneys or for social and family visiting.[44] There are two very practical reasons for such a distinction. First, detainees all have pending criminal cases, and a pending trial generally requires more direct contact with one's

attorney[45] and with others (such as investigators, or persons who might be defense witnesses or who help locate witnesses) than does an appeal or a post-conviction proceeding.

Second, detainees are in jail because of arrests that they and their families generally did not plan for. By contrast, people who are sentenced to prison generally have advance notice of what is coming and time to get ready for it. Detainees therefore have a much greater need for contact with families and friends to deal with unexpected crises—to get a lawyer, try to arrange bail, pay the rent, get children taken care of, communicate with employers, get the car keys into the family's possession, etc. The courts have not adopted this reasoning explicitly, but we think it may be persuasive in determining whether jail officials have "exaggerated their response"[46] with respect to visiting, telephone access, and other communication issues.

Some older decisions held that it denies equal protection to treat detainees in local jails, who have not been convicted of anything, more harshly than state prisoners convicted of violent crimes.[47] Other decisions, however, have held that the Constitution is not violated by harsher treatment of detainees if they are held by a different agency of government from state prisoners,[48] or that the length of stay or other aspects of confinement are sufficiently different to justify these differences in treatment.[49]

Courts have disagreed whether the Constitution requires detainees to be separated from convicts.[50]

---

[34]U.S. Const., Amend. XIII.

[35]Ch. 2, § I.2, nn.1254–1259.

[36]Benjamin v. Fraser, 264 F.3d 175, 184–88 (2d Cir. 2001). The differences are discussed in Ch. 3, §§ C.1.a(7) and C.3.

[37]*See* Ch. 3, § C.2.a, n.526.

[38]*See* Ch. 3, § C.1.a(7).

[39]Sandin v. Conner, 515 U.S. 472, 484, 115 S. Ct. 2293 (1995).

[40]*See* Ch. 4, § C, for further discussion of this question.

[41]*See* Ch. 3, § E.2, nn.885–889, 899.

[42]Willis v. Artuz, 301 F.3d 65, 69 (2d Cir. 2002) ("a convicted prisoner's loss of privacy rights can be justified on grounds other than institutional security," *i.e.*, retribution); *compare* U.S. v. Cohen, 796 F.2d 20, 24 (2d Cir. 1986); *see* Ch. 3, § E.1, nn.872–873.

[43]*See* Ch. 3, § B.8, n.370.

[44]*See* Ch. 3, § B.7.

[45]A few courts have held that transfers of detainees to places where they have difficulty communicating with counsel presents constitutional problems. *See* Ch. 3, § C.3, n.594, and Ch. 4, § H.4, n.753.

[46]Bell v. Wolfish, 441 U.S. 520 535, 548, 99 S. Ct. 1861 (1979).

[47]*See, e.g.*, Rhem v. Malcolm, 507 F.2d 333, 336; (2d Cir. 1974); Hamilton v. Love, 328 F. Supp. 1182, 1191 (E.D. Ark. 1971). One court has held that leaving convicts in local jails because of lack of space may deny them the equal protection of the laws. Hill v. Hutto, 537 F. Supp. 1185, 1189 (E.D. Va. 1982) (finding equal protection violation where state prisoners were backed up in local jail because of lack of state prison space). *See* Ch. 5 for a discussion of the Equal Protection Clause.

[48]Dawson v. Kendrick, 527 F. Supp. 1252, 1286 (S.D. W.Va. 1981). If convicts and detainees *are* held by the same agency of government, such differences may deny equal protection. Lock v. Jenkins, 641 F.2d 488, 497 (7th Cir. 1981); Young v. Keohane, 809 F. Supp. 1185, 1194. (M.D. Pa. 1992).

[49]Feeley v. Sampson, 570 F.2d 364, 371 (1st Cir. 1978).

[50]*See* Ch. 2, § H, n.1225.

PART II

Enforcing Your Rights

CHAPTER 7

The Legal System

The United States has a federal system of government. This means that both the central government and the state governments have some sovereign (ruling) power, and both state and federal governments have court systems.

To understand the court system, you must understand the concept of *jurisdiction*, which refers to the power of a court to hear a case. If the case can be brought in more than one court, those courts are said to have *concurrent jurisdiction*. If the case may be brought only in one court, that court has *exclusive jurisdiction* over the case. *Subject matter jurisdiction* refers to a court's power to hear a particular kind of case. *Personal jurisdiction* refers to a court's power to hear a case against particular parties (*e.g.*, to make a citizen of one state defend a lawsuit brought in the courts of another state). A related concept is *venue*, which refers to the geographical rules determining which court will hear a particular case.

In any court case, there are *parties*. The party bringing a case to court is generally called the *plaintiff* or *petitioner*, depending on the type of case. The party opposing a plaintiff is called a *defendant*, while the party opposing a petitioner is called a *respondent*. A plaintiff files a *complaint*, while a petitioner files a *petition*. To bring an action under the federal civil rights statutes, one ordinarily files a complaint. To seek habeas corpus relief, one files a petition.

In addition to courts, federal, state and local governments have administrative agencies, such as the Federal Bureau of Prisons, the Federal Trade Commission, or a state Department of Corrections. While administrative agencies are not courts, they often decide disputes and issue decisions or orders in a way that is similar to the activities of a court, although less formal. A prison grievance or disciplinary system is an example of this administrative adjudication.[1]

This chapter describes the federal and state court systems and their relationship to each other and to administrative agencies.

A. THE FEDERAL COURTS

1. United States District Courts

With very few exceptions, prosecutions and lawsuits in federal courts begin in a United States district court. Some states, such as Colorado, have a single district court, which covers the entire state. Other states, such as Florida, are divided into districts, each of which has a separate district court.[2]

The United States district courts have jurisdiction over prosecutions for violation of federal criminal statutes.[3] They also have jurisdiction over a variety of types of civil cases. The most important category is cases "arising under the Constitution, statutes or treaties of the United States."[4] This is often referred to as "federal question" jurisdiction, and it includes cases alleging civil rights violation. Federal courts also have "diversity" jurisdiction over cases between citizens of different states,[5] as well as jurisdiction over habeas corpus actions by state and federal prisoners,[6] tort claims against

---

[1] Prison grievance and disciplinary decisions are generally given less weight by courts than are the decisions of other kinds of administrative agencies. *See* Ch. 8, § M, nn.932–935. Inmates are required to exhaust all steps of any available prison grievance

system before filing suit in federal court. *See* Ch. 9, § D, for a discussion of the administrative exhaustion requirement of the Prison Litigation Reform Act.

[2] There are also specialized courts, such as the United States Court of Claim, the Court of International Trade, and the federal Bankruptcy Court. These will seldom be of concern to prisoners proceeding *pro se*.

[3] 18 U.S.C. § 3232.

[4] 28 U.S.C. § 1331(a). Federal question jurisdiction is discussed in Ch. 8, §§ B and B.2.

[5] 28 U.S.C. § 1332(a). Diversity jurisdiction is discussed in § F.2 below.

[6] 28 U.S.C. §§ 2241, 2254, 2255.

the federal government,[7] mandamus actions against federal officials,[8] bankruptcy proceedings,[9] and others.[10] The venue of federal courts is also governed by statute.[11]

In cases involving federal rights, federal courts generally apply federal law. Procedural and evidentiary questions in federal district courts are governed by the Federal Rules of Civil Procedure and the Federal Rules of Evidence.[12] Federal courts apply state law—usually the law of the state where the claim arose—in diversity cases, and in other cases where litigants are asserting state law claims in federal court.

There are several types of federal law:

a) The Constitution
b) Statutes enacted by Congress
c) Treaties
d) Administrative rules or regulations
e) Judicial decisions

The United States Constitution is the supreme law of the land and is always to be followed. It is written in broad and general language which allows a lot of room for interpretation by judges. Most prisoners' lawsuits involve the amendments to the Constitution, usually the First, Fourth, Fifth, Sixth, Eighth, and Fourteenth Amendments.[13]

Federal legislation is passed by the United State Congress. It is collected in the United States Code (U.S.C.) and is also found in the compilations called United State Code Annotated (U.S.C.A.) and United States Code Service (U.S.C.S.). Federal legislation is to be followed unless it conflicts with the Constitution, in which case it is said to be unconstitutional.

Treaties are equal in stature to statutes, but they cannot override the Constitution. Treaties are rarely an issue in prison cases except when there is a question involving extradition or deportation.

Administrative rules and regulations are issued by administrative agencies. Their issuance is generally governed by the Administrative Procedures Act (APA). Administrative rules are binding on the agency which enact them, except when they violate a federal statute, treaty, or the Constitution. Administrative rules are published in the Code of Federal Regulations (C.F.R.).[14]

Judicial decisions are where much of the law is found. Because constitutions, statutes, and regulations often do not spell out the answer to every question or situation that may come up, it is necessary for courts to construe them and to apply them to particular fact situations.

United States district courts are obligated to follow the decisions of the United States Supreme Court as well as the decisions of the United States Court of Appeals for the circuit in which the district court is located. Cases decided by other circuits' courts of appeals and by other federal district courts are persuasive authority but not binding authority on a district court. The same is true of decisions of state courts except in diversity or other cases in which the federal court must apply state law.

Orders and opinions of the United States district courts are sometimes published and sometimes not. Those that are published are usually found in the Federal Supplement, Second Series (F.Supp.2d). Some are published in the Federal Rules Decisions (F.R.D.). Many unpublished district court opinions are found in electronic databases such as Westlaw or Lexis.[15]

2. United States Courts of Appeals

Each United States district court is part of a federal judicial circuit presided over by a court of appeals. There are 13 circuits, each of which covers a region of several states except for the District of Columbia Circuit and the Federal Circuit, which handles patent and copyright cases and other specialized matters.[16]

Each federal court of appeals hears appeals from federal district courts within its circuit. These courts' jurisdiction is limited by statute mostly to appeals from final decisions of the district courts and from decisions granting or denying injunctions.[17] The courts of appeals also review certain decisions of federal administrative agencies.[18]

A federal court of appeals applies the same law as a district court. It is bound by decisions of the United States Supreme Court. Federal appeals courts generally hear cases in panels of three judges. Decisions of these three-judge panels are binding on other panels of the same court. Occasionally, when an issue is particularly important or when there is a conflict among the decisions of different three-judge panels, all the judges will hear an appeal together. This is called sitting *in banc* (sometimes spelled *en banc*).

Proceedings in the courts of appeals are governed by the Federal Rules of Appellate Procedure. Published decisions of courts of appeals are found in the Federal Reporter (F.) and the Federal Reporter, Second Series and Third Series (F.2d and F.3d). Decisions of the courts of appeals that are unpublished are only supposed to address the dispute between the parties, and are not supposed to have precedential effect. Most circuits used to have rules restricting citation of unpublished decisions, but such rules are

---

[7] 28 U.S.C. § 1346(b).

[8] 28 U.S.C. § 1361.

[9] 28 U.S.C. § 1334.

[10] The federal courts' jurisdiction is set out in 28 U.S.C. §§ 1330–1360.

[11] 28 USC. §§ 1391–1407.

[12] These are published as part of 28 U.S.C., as well as in various separate editions.

[13] These rights are discussed in Chs. 2, 3, 4, 5, and 6.

[14] The Federal Bureau of Prisons' rules are found at 28 C.F.R. §§ 501 *et seq*.

[15] These databases are discussed in Ch. 11, § C.7.a.

[16] 28 U.S.C. § 1295.

[17] Federal appellate jurisdiction is discussed in more detail in Ch. 10, § U.1.

[18] 28 U.S.C. § 2342.

now forbidden.[19] In the past, unpublished decisions were listed in tables in the Federal Reporter indicating whether the court affirmed, reversed, or made some other disposition of the lower court decision. Now, however, many "unpublished" decisions are actually printed in another reporter, the Federal Appendix, and many others appear in electronic databases.

3. United States Supreme Court

The United States Supreme Court is the highest court in the land. Once it has ruled, there is no other court to go to. However, adverse decisions of the Supreme Court can be changed by federal statute as long as they do not involve interpretation of the Constitution. The Supreme Court's constitutional decisions can be changed only by constitutional amendment or by the Supreme Court's changing its mind and overruling one of its own decisions.

The Supreme Court's jurisdiction is defined both in the Constitution[20] and by federal statute.[21] In rare cases, the Supreme Court has "original" jurisdiction over a case, bypassing the district court and circuit court.[22] However, most cases get to the Supreme Court by way of writ of certiorari, which the Court has discretion to grant or deny. The Supreme Court takes cases involving federal law issues both from the federal courts of appeals and from the states' highest courts. Proceedings in the Supreme Court are governed by the Rules of the United States Supreme Court, which are published in the U.S. Code and in compilations of federal court rules.

Decisions of the Supreme Court are reported in the United States Reports (U.S.), Supreme Court Reporter (S.Ct.), and the United States Reports, Lawyers Edition (L.Ed. and L.Ed.2d). Supreme Court practice is discussed further in another chapter. [23]

B. THE STATE COURTS

Each state has its own court system. The names and jurisdictions of state courts differ from state to state, so we can't provide a description that will cover them all.

A typical state court system is that of Michigan. There, the two lowest courts are district courts and probate courts. District courts handle misdemeanor prosecutions and preliminary examinations in felony cases, search and arrest warrants, and civil cases involving claims for relatively small sums of money.

Probate courts handle juvenile prosecutions. They also handle cases of parental abuse or neglect and child custody cases other than those arising out of divorce or paternity actions. Probate courts handle the affairs of children and

mental incompetents and often appoint guardians for them. Probate courts handle wills and the distribution of property of those who have died.

Cases from district court and probate court are appealed to the circuit court. Circuit courts also handle felony prosecutions, divorce, paternity actions, injunctions, mandamus, and civil cases involving claims over $25,000.

Cases from circuit courts are appealed to the state court of appeals, and from there to the Supreme Court of Michigan. Some cases may then be reviewed by the U.S. Supreme Court, if they involve a substantial federal question and meet the criteria for Supreme Court review.

In other states, there are various types of courts with different names, including Orphans Court, Prothonotary Court, Superior Court, etc. The jurisdiction of each depends on state law. Some states have courts known as police courts or justice of the peace courts which hear low-level cases, mostly criminal, but whose decisions are usually reviewable *de novo* by a higher court. *De novo* review means that the reviewing court ignores what happened in the lower court and hears the case over from the beginning.

In many states, damage claims against the state or its agencies must be brought in a special court, often called a court of claims.[24]

Traditionally, prisoners who go to court to sue someone have believed they would get a better break from a federal court than from a state court. However, the federal courts have grown less favorable to prisoner cases over the years. Almost any civil action which can be brought in federal court, including civil rights actions, can be brought in state court as well, and you may be entitled to a more favorable legal standard in state court. There are also many kinds of legal claims that can be brought only in state court. Before you decide which court to file in, be very sure you have thought through your options in state court.[25]

C. ADMINISTRATIVE AGENCIES

Government in the United States and in each state is divided into three branches: legislative, executive, and judicial. Administrative agencies are part of the executive branch, and are under the authority of the governor, mayor, or the President. However, administrative agencies usually act independently of the governor, mayor, or President in their day-to-day operations.

Administrative agencies are created by state, local, or federal statute. The statute defines the jurisdiction of the agency, what its powers are, and what it is supposed to do with those powers. In many cases, administrative agencies may be taken to court to force them to comply with the statutes that govern them.

---

[19]Rule 32.1, Fed.R.App.P.

[20]U.S. Const., Art. III.

[21]28 U.S.C. §§ 1251–1258.

[22]28 U.S.C. § 1251.

[23]*See* § U.2 of Chapter 10.

---

[24]*See, e.g.,* M.C.L.A. § 600.6419; M.S.A. § 27A.6419 (requiring claims against the State of Michigan to be brought in the state Court of Claims).

[25]Issues to consider in deciding between state and federal courts are discussed in Ch. 8, § H.

Agencies are generally required to issue, or promulgate, rules governing their own activities and the activities of the people they regulate. Procedures for enacting rules are often found in an Administrative Procedures Act (APA).[26] Administrative regulations can be obtained from the agency itself, or from books which publish the regulations. Federal regulations are found in the Code of Federal Regulations (C.F.R.). States often have an Administrative Code where rules are published. Agencies are generally required to follow their own rules, and courts will enforce that duty if a state's administrative law gives them the power to do so.

D. RELATIONSHIP BETWEEN STATE AND FEDERAL COURTS

As a general rule, the state and federal court systems are completely separate, except for the ultimate review by the U.S. Supreme Court of state court decisions involving federal questions and federal habeas corpus review of state criminal convictions.

Under the Supremacy Clause of the Constitution,[27] state courts may not give orders to federal courts or otherwise interfere in their business. Federal courts may interfere in the activities of state courts only in the most limited circumstances.[28] Federal courts will generally not enjoin a state criminal prosecution even if it allegedly violates the constitution; you must raise the constitutional issue in the criminal case.[29] This doctrine has been extended to many civil proceedings as well.[30] Federal courts are also extremely reluctant to enter class action injunctions governing the operations of state courts.[31]

Federal courts often decide issues of state law. They hear claims based on state law under their diversity jurisdiction and their supplemental jurisdiction.[32] Sometimes they must apply or interpret state law in some way in making decisions of federal law.[33] Federal courts usually consider themselves bound by state court decisions interpreting state law.

State courts may decide issues of federal law as well, except in areas where Congress has declared the federal courts to have exclusive jurisdiction. State courts can hear claims under the federal civil rights statutes; they also frequently hear constitutional claims that arise in criminal cases. The Supreme Court has emphasized that state courts are as competent as federal courts to interpret the United States Constitution.

The doctrines of *res judicata* and collateral estoppel operate between state and federal courts.[34] That means you cannot litigate an issue in one court system and then, if you don't like the outcome, litigate the same issue in the other court system. There is one exception to this: The federal habeas corpus statutes permit federal courts, within limits, to review state court criminal convictions if they raise federal constitutional issues.[35]

---

[26]The federal APA appears at 5 U.S.C. §§ 551 *et seq.* Many states have similar statutes.

[27]U.S. Const., Art. VI.

[28]*See* 28 U.S.C. § 2282 (prohibiting federal injunction against proceedings in state courts except where authorized by an act of Congress, or where the injunction is necessary in aid of jurisdiction or to effectuate the judgment of a circuit court).

[29]Younger v. Harris, 401 U.S. 37, 91 S. Ct. 746 (1971).

[30]Moore v. Sims, 442 U.S. 45, 99 S. Ct. 2371 (1979); Trainor v Hernandez, 431 U.S. 434, 97 S. Ct. 1911 (1977).

[31]*See* Ch. 8, § H.1.a.

[32]These types of jurisdiction are discussed in Ch. 8, §§ F.1, F.2.

[33]For example, federal courts must sometimes use state law to determine who is responsible for a civil rights violation that arises from someone's failure to act. *See* Chapter 8, § B.4.a(2). State law determines who is a municipal "decisionmaker" for purposes of deciding whether a municipality can be held liable for civil rights violations. *See* Ch. 8, § B.4.b.

[34]These doctrines are discussed in more detail in Ch. 8, § M.

[35]There is a limited discussion of federal habeas corpus in Ch. 8, § H.1.a.

CHAPTER 8

Actions, Defenses, and Relief

A. INTRODUCTION

This chapter discusses the kinds of civil lawsuits state and federal prisoners can bring,[1] the defenses prison officials can raise, and the remedies prisoners can obtain. We will focus mostly on actions in federal court because it is not practical to try to explain the law of all 50 states. But state and local prisoners should keep in mind that you might have more rights in state court under state law than you do in federal court. You should therefore be familiar with the remedies available in the courts of your state.

B. CIVIL RIGHTS ACTIONS

Several federal statutes provide for civil rights lawsuits against state and local officials or governments, and in some cases against private persons.[2] Federal courts have "federal question" jurisdiction over such cases.[3] State courts also

---

[1]Prisoners, like other private citizens, cannot bring criminal actions or force prosecutors to file criminal charges. Linda R.S. v. Richard D., 410 U.S. 614, 619, 93 S. Ct. 1146 (1973) ("a private citizen lacks a judicially cognizable interest in the prosecution or nonprosecution of another"); *accord*, Diamond v. Charles, 1704, 476 U.S. 54, 64, 106 S. Ct. 1697 (1986); U.S. v. Nixon, 418 U.S. 683, 693, 94 S. Ct. 3090 (1974) ("the Executive Branch has exclusive authority and absolute discretion to decide whether to prosecute").

---

[2]Some states have their own civil rights statutes.

[3]28 U.S.C. § 1331(a) provides for federal court jurisdiction of "all civil actions under the Constitution, law, or treaties of the

have jurisdiction to hear claims based on federal civil rights statutes[4] and must apply federal law in doing so.[5]

1. 42 U.S.C. § 1983: Civil Rights Actions Against State and Local Officials and Private Contractors

Most prisoner civil rights suits are brought under 42 U.S.C. § 1983, which provides:

> Every person who, under color of any statute, ordinance, regulation, custom, or usage, of any State or Territory or the District of Columbia, subjects, or causes to be subjected, any citizen of the United States or other person within the jurisdiction thereof to the deprivation of any rights, privileges, or immunities secured by the Constitution and laws, shall be liable to the party injured in an action at law, suit in equity, or other proper proceeding for redress, except that in any action brought against a judicial officer for an act or omission taken in such officer's judicial capacity, injunctive relief shall not be granted unless a declaratory decree was violated or declaratory relief was unavailable. For the purposes of this section, any Act of Congress applicable exclusively to the District of Columbia shall be considered to be a statute of the District of Columbia.[6]

In plain English, this means that anyone whose rights under the Constitution or federal statutes have been violated by state or local officials can sue those officials under § 1983. A plaintiff suing under § 1983 must allege two "elements":

"that some person has deprived him of a federal rights" and that "the person who has deprived him of that right acted under color of state or territorial law."[7]

a. Rights, Privileges, or Immunities Secured by Federal Law Section 1983 does not create any rights.[8] It serves to enforce rights that already exist in the Constitution or in other provisions of federal law. Federal statutes and regulations may be enforceable under § 1983 under limited circumstances.[9] We don't discuss this subject in detail because the main federal statutes that benefit prisoners in state or local facilities are the Religious Land Use and Institutionalized Persons Act (RLUIPA) and the disability statutes, which don't require § 1983 for enforcement because they have their own enforcement mechanisms.[10] The direct enforcement of federal statutes and regulations by prisoners in federal institutions is discussed elsewhere.[11]

Violations of state or local law or prison regulations cannot be remedied under § 1983 unless they also violate your federal law rights.[12]

b. Persons A defendant must be a "person" to be sued under § 1983. In most cases, "person" means the same thing under § 1983 as in ordinary use. However, a city or county government is also a person for purposes of § 1983,[13] though

---

United States." Older cases may refer to a $10,000 "amount in controversy"; this requirement has been repealed.

[4]*See, e.g.*, Maine v. Thibotout, 448 U.S. 1, 100 S. Ct. 2502 (1980) (42 U.S.C. § 1983).

"Virtually every state has expressly or by implication opened its courts to § 1983 actions and there are no state court systems that refuse to hear § 1983 actions." Howlett v. Rose, 496 U.S. 356, 378 n.20, 110 S. Ct. 2430 (1990); *see* Haywood v. Drown, ___ U.S. ___, 129 S. Ct. 2108, 2114 (2009) (citing "presumption of concurrency").

[5]Howlett v. Rose, 496 U.S. at 375–78 (state immunity rules do not apply in state court § 1983 action); Felder v. Casey, 487 U.S. 131, 151, 108 S. Ct. 2302 (1988) (state notice of claim requirement does not apply in state court § 1983 action).

[6]42 U.S.C. § 1983.

There are whole books devoted to § 1983. The best is probably by Martin A. Schwartz, John E. Kirklin, and George C. Pratt. This is now a six-volume set, regularly supplemented. You can order these volumes separately. The titles of the volumes are: Volumes 1, 1A and 1B: *Section 1983 Litigation: Claims and Defenses* (4th ed.); Volume 2: *Secton 1983 Litigation: Statutory Attorney's Fees* (3d ed.); Volume 3: *Section 1983 Litigation: Federal Evidence* (4th ed.); Volume 4: *Section 1983 Litigation: Jury Instructions* (3d ed.), published by Aspen Publishers. Also recommended is Sheldon H. Nahmod, *Civil Rights and Civil Liberties Litigation: The Law of Section 1983* (Thomson/West, 4th ed., Supp. 2008) (three volumes). These books are probably too large and expensive for an individual prisoner to obtain, but they are certainly suitable for prison law libraries.

[7]Gomez v. Toledo, 446, U.S. 635, 640, 100 S. Ct. 1920 (1980); *accord*, West v. Atkins, 487 U.S. 42, 48, 108 S. Ct. 2250 (1988).

[8]Chapman v. Houston Welfare Rights Organization, 441 U.S. 600, 617–19, 99 S. Ct. 1905 (1979); *accord*, Graham v. Connor, 490 U.S. 386, 393–94, 109 S. Ct. 1865 (1989).

[9]*See* Maine v. Thiboutot, 448 U.S. 1, 4–8, 100 S. Ct. 2502 (1980). In recent years the Supreme Court has restricted statutory enforcement to instances where Congress has expressed in "clear and unambiguous terms" the intent to create an enforceable statutory right. Gonzaga University v. Doe, 536 U.S. 273, 290, 122 S. Ct. 2268 (2002); *accord*, Suter v. Artist M., 503 U.S. 347, 363, 112 S. Ct. 1360 (1992). Enforcement of federal regulations under § 1983 also depends on congressional intent. *See* Wright v. Roanoke Redev. and Housing Auth., 479 U.S. 418, 423–24, 431, 107 S. Ct. 766 (1987).

[10]These statutes are discussed in other sections of this book. *See* Ch. 2, § F.4.h.2 (disability statutes) and Ch. 3. § D.1.b. (RLUIPA).

[11]*See* § B.2.a–b of this chapter.

[12]Paul v. Davis, 424 U.S. 693, 700, 96 S. Ct. 1155 (1976) ("'Violation of local law does not necessarily mean that federal rights have been invaded.'" (citation omitted)); Sunrise Corp. of Myrtle Beach v. City of Myrtle Beach, 420 F.3d 322, 328 (4th Cir. 2005) ("[A] violation of state law is not tantamount to a violation of a federal right." (citation omitted)); Zahra v. Town of Southold, 48 F.3d 674, 681–82 (2d Cir. 1995); Bulger v. U.S. Bureau of Prisons, 65 F.3d 48, 49 (5th Cir. 1995).

[13]Monell v. Dep't of Social Services, 436 U.S. 658, 690–91, 98 S. Ct. 2018 (1978).

City and county governments can only be held liable under § 1983 for their policies, or for actions taken pursuant to their policies. This issue is discussed in § B.4.b of this chapter.

subdepartments of those governments generally are not.[14] A state is not a person.[15] A prison or jail is not a person.[16] Corporations are persons; a private corporation operating a prison or providing services to prisoners is treated like a city or county government under § 1983; it can only be held liable under § 1983 for corporate policies, or for acts of its employees done pursuant to corporate policy.[17]

Only a person who "subjects, or causes to be subjected" another person to a civil rights violation can be held liable. This "causation" requirement is very important, and we deal with it in a separate section.[18]

In addition to being a "person," a defendant must have the capacity to be sued under state law.[19] Correction departments and police departments may generally not be sued under § 1983 because under state law they are usually not "legal entities" capable of being sued.[20]

c. Color of State Law and Suing Private Contractors

A defendant must act under color of state law to be sued

---

[14]Rhodes v. McDannel, 145 F.2d 117, 120 (6th Cir. 1991); Vance v. County of Santa Clara, 928 F. Supp. 993, 995 (N.D. Cal. 1996).

[15]Will v. Michigan Dep't of State Police, 491 U.S. 58, 71, 109 S. Ct. 2304 (1989) ("We hold that neither a State nor its officials acting in their official capacities are 'persons' under § 1983.").

If you bring suit under the federal disability statutes or the Religious Land Use and Institutionalized Persons Act, you can sue government agencies and/or defendants in their official capacities, unlike § 1983. See Ch. 2, § F.4.h.2 (disability statutes) and Ch. 3., § D.1.b.(4) (RLUIPA).

[16]See Pittman v. Kurtz, 165 F. Supp. 2d 1243, 1247 (D.Kan. 2001); Powell v. Cook County Jail, 814 F. Supp. 757, 758 (N.D. Ill. 1993).

[17]See the next section for further discussion.

[18]See § B.4.a of this chapter.

[19]Fed.R.Civ.P. 17(b).

[20]Generally, agencies and departments cannot be sued separately from the government they are part of. See Dean v. Barber, 951 F.2d 1210, 1214 (11th Cir. 1992) (dismissing claim against an Alabama sheriff's department because the department was not subject to suit); Darby v. Pasadena Police Dep't 939 F.2d 311, 313–14 (5th Cir. 1991). There may be exceptions depending on state law. See Streit v. County of Los Angeles, 236 F.3d 552, 565 (9th Cir. 2001) (holding California sheriff's department a separate suable entity). In most cases, however, if you wish to sue about the policies of local agencies, you must sue the local government itself. See § B.4.b of this chapter concerning suits against municipal governments. If you are not challenging a policy but the acts of individual employees, you must sue the employees themselves.

If the agency involved is a state agency, it is protected from federal court suit by the Eleventh Amendment, and you may only sue the individual state officials or employees involved. See § L.1 of this chapter concerning the Eleventh Amendment.

An unincorporated association can be sued for violations of federal law, regardless of its state law capacity to be sued, under Rule 17(b), Fed.R.Civ.P. Corrente v. State of R.I., Dep't of Corrections, 759 F. Supp. 73, 80 (D.R.I. 1991) (allowing unincorporated correctional officers' association to be sued under § 1983).

under § 1983. "[G]enerally, a public employee acts under color of state law while acting in his official capacity or while exercising his responsibilities pursuant to state law."[21] This is true even if the employee is abusing or exceeding her authority or violating the law.[22] The color of law requirement of § 1983 is generally the same as the requirement of "state action" that must be shown to prove a violation of the Fourteenth Amendment,[23] and the two terms are often used interchangeably.

City and county officials and employees are considered to act under color of state law.[24] Federal personnel generally act under color of federal and not state law.[25] Prison personnel clearly exercise official power in their dealings with prisoners, so color of law is rarely an issue in prison cases.[26]

---

[21]West v. Atkins, 487 U.S. 42, 50, 108 S. Ct. 2250 (1988) ("The traditional definition of acting under color of state law requires that the defendant . . . exercised power possessed by virtue of state law and made possible only because the wrongdoer is clothed with the authority of state law." (internal citation and quotation marks omitted)); accord, Monroe v. Pape, 365 U.S. 167, 184, 81 S. Ct. 473 (1961); see Zambrana-Marrero v. Suarez-Cruz, 172 F.3d 122, 126 (1st Cir. 1999) (conduct must be related in some meaningful way either to the actor's governmental status or to the performance of his duties to be under color of law).

[22]"Misuse of power, possessed by virtue of state law and made possible only because the wrongdoer is clothed with the authority of state law, is action take 'under color of state law." Monroe v. Pape, 365 U.S. at 184 (quoting U.S. v. Classic, 313 U.S. 299, 326, 61 S. Ct. 1031 (1941)); accord, West v. Atkins, 487 U.S. at 50; Dossett v. First State Bank, 399 F.3d 940, 949 (8th Cir. 2005); U.S. v. Walsh, 194 F.3d 37, 51 (2d Cir. 1999); Smith v. Cochran, 216 F. Supp. 2d 1286, 1295 (N.D.Okla. 2001) (drivers' license examiner who forced a work release prisoner to have sex with him acted under color of law, since he used his authority delegated by the Department of Correction), aff'd, 339 F.3d 1205 (10th Cir. 2003); Evicci v. Baker, 190 F. Supp. 2d 233, 239 (D.Mass. 2002) (officers who beat plaintiff acted under color of law because it was their authority as correction officers that allowed them to beat him); Gwynn v. Transcor America, Inc., 26 F. Supp. 2d 1256, 1265–66 (D.Colo. 1998) (similar to Smith; officers raped prisoner during transportation). The Supreme Court has also equated "color of law" with the "pretense" of law. Screws v. U.S., 325 U.S. 91, 111, 65 S. Ct. 1031 (1945); accord, Dossett v. First State Bank, 399 F.3d at 949.

[23]West v. Atkins, 487 U.S. at 49; Lugar v. Edmonson Oil Co., 457 U.S. 922, 935 n.18, 102 S. Ct. 2744 (1982). There are circumstances in which the two are not the same, but these are unlikely to arise in prison litigation.

[24]See, e.g., Monroe v. Pape, 365 U.S. at 172–87 (city police acted under color of state law).

[25]District of Columbia v. Carter, 409 U.S. 418, 424, 93 S. Ct. 602 (1973); Settles v. U.S. Parole Com'n, 429 F.3d 1098, 1104 (D.C. Cir. 2005) ("Section 1983 does not apply to federal officials acting under color of federal law." (citations omitted)).

There can be exceptional situations in which federal officials act under color of state law, and state officials act under color of federal law. See the next section, n.47.

[26]Law enforcement officers using their official powers generally act under color of state law even if they are off duty or acting out of personal motivation. See Rivera v. LaPorte, 896 F.2d 691, 696

One exception is that some courts have held that prison chaplains or religious functionaries do not act under color of state law, at least when performing "inherently ecclesiastical functions" as opposed to "administrative and managerial tasks";[27] others have disagreed, as do we.[28]

People who work in a state or municipal prison, or perform required services for their prisoners, under private contract generally act under color of state law. (Suits against private corporations or individuals serving *federal* prisoners present more difficult problems and are discussed elsewhere.[29]) The Supreme Court has held that a doctor providing medical services under contract acted under color of state law, since the state had delegated its constitutional obligation to provide medical care to him.[30] The lower courts have extended this holding to medical providers and their employees generally,[31] though they have disagreed about those who do not have a contract with the prison.[32] Courts have also held that non-medical contractors who operate prisons or programs within prisons, and their employees, act under color of state law, since operating prisons is a

---

[27]Montano v. Hedgepeth, 120 F.3d 844, 850–51 (8th Cir. 1997); *accord*, Orafan v. Goord, 411 F. Supp. 2d 153, 169 (N.D.N.Y. 2006) (refusing to help provide Shiite programs and services was administrative and chaplain was a state actor; refusing to allow a prayer in the Shiite manner during a prayer service was purely ecclesiastical), *vacated and remanded on other grounds*, 249 Fed. Appx. 217 (2d Cir. 2007) (unpublished); Shilling v. Crawford, 2006 WL 1663827, *5 (D.Nev. 2006); Tripp v. Donovan, 1998 WL 338090, *3 (S.D.N.Y. 1998).

Montano relied on the Supreme Court's decision in *Polk County v. Dodson*, 454 U.S. 312, 324, 102 S. Ct. 445 (1981), which held that a public defender did not act under color of state law in exercising independent professional judgment in a criminal proceeding. Even the *Polk County* decision is limited to the exercise of judgment in individual cases; a public defender does act under color of law in making administrative decisions such as allocating resources and making policies, *e.g.*, requiring all clients to take a polygraph examination. Miranda v. Clark County, Nev., 319 F.3d 465, 468–72 (9th Cir. 2003). *Cf.* Young v. McKune, 280 F. Supp. 2d 1250, 1254–55 (D.Kan. 2003) (employee of private corporation providing legal services to prisoners was not shown to act under color of state law based solely on receiving state funding), *aff'd*, 85 Fed.Appx. 723 (10th Cir. 2004) (unpublished). Consistently with these decisions, the court that decided *Montano* later held that a corporation operating a religious program acted under color of state law where the state delegated "its 24-hour power to incarcerate, treat, and discipline inmates." Americans United for Separation of Church and State v. Prison Fellowship Ministries, Inc., 509 F.3d 406, 422–23 (8th Cir. 2007).

Courts have not generally applied the *Polk County* decision more widely to other kinds of prison contractors. *See* Conner v. Donnelly, 42 F.3d 220, 223 (4th Cir. 1994) ("As a general rule, then, a professional employed by the state to fulfill the state's constitutional obligations acts under color of state law; the narrow exception for public defenders, whose professional obligations make them the adversaries of the state, does not apply to physicians, who act on the state's behalf.").

[28]*See* Phelps v. Dunn, 965 F.2d 93, 102 (6th Cir.1992) ("A volunteer chaplain functions as part of and within the institutional structure of chapel command. He is distinguished from guests and visitors by being given privileges granted only to [prison] employees, including special training and an institutional identification card."); *accord*, Stubbs v. DeRose, 2007 WL 776789, *5 (M.D.Pa., Mar. 12, 2007); Paz v. Weir, 137 F. Supp. 2d 782, 805 (S.D.Tex. 2001); Shepherd v. Cline, 162 P.3d 65, 2007 WL 2080448, *3–4 (Kan.App., July 20, 2007) (unpublished).

[29]*See* § B.2.d of this chapter.

[30]West v. Atkins, 487 U.S. 42, 54–57, 108 S. Ct. 2250 (1988). The Supreme Court has also stated generally that state prisoners "enjoy a right of action against private correctional providers under 42 U.S.C. § 1983." Correctional Services Corp. v. Malesko, 534 U.S. 61, 71 n.5, 122 S. Ct. 515 (2001). However, it earlier said it was leaving the question open whether officers in a private prison acted under color of state law. Richardson v. McKnight, 521 U.S. 399, 413, 117 S. Ct. 2100 (1997).

[31]Walker v. Horn, 385 F.3d 321, 332 n.4 (3d Cir. 2004) (employee of contract medical provider assisting in force-feeding a prisoner acted under color of law); Howell v. Evans, 922 F.2d 712, 723–24 (11th Cir.) (same conclusion as to corporation providing medical care), *vacated as settled*, 931 F.2d 711 (11th Cir. 1991); Mitchell v. Aluisi, 872 F.2d 577, 580 (4th Cir. 1989) (*West* holding applies "to any health care provider, such as Szabo, whose 'conduct is fairly attributable to the State'" (citation omitted)); Carswell v. Bay County, 854 F.2d 454, 456 (11th Cir. 1988); Lagoy v. Correctional Medical Services, 358 F. Supp. 2d 58, 64 (N.D.N.Y. 2005) (same as to CMS and its employees).

[32]In *Conner v. Donnelly*, 42 F.3d 220, 223 (4th Cir. 1994), the court stated:

Regardless of the physician's employment relationship with the state, any physician authorized by the state to provide medical care to a prisoner exercises power that is traditionally the exclusive prerogative of the state. If the physician abuses this power by demonstrating deliberate indifference to the prisoner's serious medical needs, the prisoner suffers a deprivation under color of state law—not because the state has employed a bad physician, but because the state has incarcerated the prisoner and denied him the possibility of obtaining medical care on his own.

Accord, Anglin v. City of Aspen, Colo., 552 F. Supp. 2d 1229, 1242–46 (D.Colo. 2008). *Contra*, Scott v. Ambani, 577 F.3d 642, 648–49 (6th Cir. 2009) (radiation oncologist who treated plaintiff just because she had staff privileges at a hospital and was on duty when plaintiff was brought in was not a state actor); Sykes v. McPhillips, 412 F. Supp. 2d 197, 203–04 (N.D.N.Y. 2006) (hospital was not a state actor simply because prison brought prisoners there, without a contract; nor was doctor who provided emergency treatment to a prisoner on a one-time basis).

(2d Cir. 1990) (corrections officer involved in a purely private dispute who made an arrest using his powers as a peace officer); Traver v. Meshriy, 627 F.2d 934, 938 (9th Cir. 1980) (officer showed police ID while working as bank guard); Layne v. Sampley, 627 F.2d 12, 13 (6th Cir. 1980) (off-duty officer shot citizen with service revolver). There are rare exceptions. *See* Townsend v. Moya, 291 F.3d 859, 862 (5th Cir. 2002) (officer who engaged in horseplay involving a "purely private aim" did not act under color of law even though he injured a prisoner he had authority over).

traditionally governmental function.[33] Persons who provide goods or services to prisons, but are not delegated responsibility for prison operations, may be found not to act under color of state law.[34]

_____

[33]Americans United for Separation of Church and State v. Prison Fellowship Ministries, Inc., 509 F.3d 406, 422–23 (8th Cir. 2007) (private corporations operating a religious program acted under color of state law where state delegated "its 24-hour power to incarcerate, treat, and discipline inmates"); Rosborough v. Management & Training Corp., 350 F.3d 459, 461 (5th Cir. 2003) (private prison companies and their employees are state actors because "confinement of wrongdoers—though sometimes delegated to private entities—is a fundamentally governmental function"); Flint v. Kentucky Department of Corrections, 270 F.3d 340, 352–53 (6th Cir. 2001) (Correctional Industries employee in charge of the print shop was a state actor because he "performed functions typically attributed to the State: housing and providing security" for prisoners); Street v. Corr. Corp. of Am., 102 F.3d 810, 814 (6th Cir. 1996) (private prison guards were performing "the 'traditional state function' of operating a prison"); Skelton v. Pri-Cor, Inc., 963 F.2d 100, 101–02 (6th Cir. 1991) (private corporation operating a prison was performing a public function); Rodriguez-Garcia v. Davila, 904 F.2d 90, 98 (1st Cir. 1990) (prisons are a public function despite privatization) (dicta); Bender v. General Services Admin., 539 F. Supp. 2d 702, 712 (S.D.N.Y. 2008) (private security guard hired by contractor to work at federal agency was acting under color of federal law); Stephens v. Correctional Services Corp., 428 F. Supp. 2d 580, 584 (E.D.Tex. 2006) ("The maintenance of a prison system is something 'traditionally reserved to the state.'" Suit was for failure to protect from assault); Herrera v. County of Santa Fe, 213 F. Supp. 2d 1288, 1290 (D. N.M. 2002) ("It is settled in this District that... the manager and operator of the detention center [] would be considered a state actor for purposes of § 1983."); Gabriel v. Corrections Corp. Of Am., 211 F. Supp. 2d 132, 137 (D.D.C. 2002) (finding that private prison "provide[d] services normally provided by municipalities"); Palm v. Marr, 174 F. Supp. 2d 484, 487 (N.D. Tex. 2001) (stating that "the maintenance of a prison system has traditionally [been] the exclusive prerogative of the state" Wackenhut and its employees act under color of law); Giron v. Corr. Corp. of America, 14 F. Supp. 2d 1245, 1248 (D. N.M. 1998) (private prison guard acted under color of state law for purposes of § 1983 suit); Woodall v. Partilla, 581 F. Supp. 1066, 1071, 1076 (N.D. Ill 1984) (employee of civilian contractor did not act under color of law in filing disciplinary report against inmate, since she was analogous to complainant in a criminal case, but the contractor performed state action in employing inmates); Rathbun v. Starr Commonwealth for Boys, 145 Mich.App. 303, 377 N.W.2d 872, 877 (1985) (private corporation holding boys committed to custody of Department of Social Services acted under color of law).

One court has held that a private corporation that employed prisoners inside the prison did not act under color of state law because the corporation did not care about the rehabilitation of inmates; it only cared about making money. Keeling v. Schaefer, 181 F. Supp. 2d 1206, 1230 (D.Kan. 2001). We think that is wrong; the question is not what the corporation's motive was, but what function the state had delegated to it—in that case, providing rehabilitative activity for the prisoners.

[34]Steading v. Thompson, 941 F.2d 498, 499 (7th Cir. 1991) (tobacco company that sold products to the prison was not a state actor); Lewis v. Mitchell, 416 F. Supp. 935, 947 (S.D.Cal. 2005)

Corporations operating private prisons or providing services to prisoners are treated like city and county governments under § 1983: they can only be held liable for their policies, or for acts taken pursuant to their policies.[35] If their employees violate the law in ways not resulting from policy, the employees must be sued individually.[36]

The defense of qualified immunity is not available to employees of a private corporation or other private defendants.[37] (That defense would not be available to the private corporation itself anyway, since corporations are treated like city and county governments, which are not entitled to qualified immunity.[38]) It is not clear how much difference this makes, since the Supreme Court has mentioned the possibility of a "good faith" defense (which is very similar to qualified immunity) for such employees, and some lower courts have allowed it.[39] Some courts have held that punitive damages may be recovered against private corporations, even though they cannot be recovered against municipalities under § 1983.[40]

_____

(regional sales manager of company that sold food to the prison did not act under color of state law, since the prison did not delegate its obligation to provide food services to the company, just bought food from it); White v. Cooper, 55 F. Supp. 2d 848, 860 (N.D.Ill. 1999) (a construction company that was hired to renovate certain areas of the prison did not act under color of law, because the state retained responsibility to maintain acceptable conditions or move the prisoners; construction work is not a function traditionally restricted to state authorities).

[35]See cases cited in Ch. 2, § F.1.a, n.338.

[36]Hicks v. Frey, 992 F.2d 1450, 1456–58 (6th Cir. 1993) (upholding judgment against employee and dismissal of claim against corporation).

[37]Richardson v. McKnight, 521 U.S. 399, 412, 117 S. Ct. 2100 (1997) (officers of private prison); Wyatt v. Cole, 504 U.S. 158, 167–68, 112 S. Ct. 1827 (1992) (private defendants sued under § 1983 for invoking state replevin, garnishment, or attachment procedures); Toussie v. Powell, 323 F.3d 178, 183 (2d Cir. 2003) (private parties sued for conspiring with government officials to violate federal rights); Hinson v. Edmond, 192 F.3d 1342, 1345–47 (11th Cir. 1999) (doctor working under contract), _amended on other grounds_, 205 F.3d 1264 (11th Cir. 2000).

[38]See Owens v. City of Independence, 445 U.S. 622, 100 S. Ct. 1398 (1980); see § L.4 of this chapter, n.806.

[39]See Clement v. City of Glendale, 518 F.3d 1090, 1097 (9th Cir. 2008) (allowing defense where company "did its best to follow the law and had no reason to suspect that there would be a constitutional challenge to its actions"; non-prison case); Jordan v. Rothschild, 20 F.3d 1250, 1276 (3d Cir.1994) (allowing defense; non-prison case); Hunsberger v. Wood, 564 F. Supp. 2d 559, 572 (W.D.Va. 2008) (private parties entitled to good faith defense unless they "act with malice or . . . knew or should have known their actions violated the Constitution"), _rev'd and remanded on other grounds_, 570 F.3d 546 (4th Cir. 2009).

[40]Segler v. Clark County, 142 F. Supp. 2d 1264, 1268–69 (D.Nev. 2001); Campbell v. City of Philadelphia, 1990 WL 102945, *6 (E.D. Pa., July 18, 1990) ("the policy behind prohibiting recovery of punitive damages against a municipality does not apply" to private corporations); _see_ Woodward v. Correctional Medical Services of Illinois, Inc., 368 F.3d 917, 930 (7th Cir. 2004)

You may wish to bring suit against private contractors under state law instead of or in addition to federal law, if their conduct violated both, as is often the case.[41] You may also be able to sue a private contractor for breach of contract, arguing that you are a "third-party beneficiary" of the contract. For example, the Virginia Supreme Court has held that a prisoner could sue a prison medical provider for inadequate medical care that also did not satisfy the terms of the contract between the provider and the state.[42] Other courts have rejected third-party beneficiary claims.[43] Sometimes third-party beneficiary theories have been used to enforce settlement agreements in litigation.[44]

People who do not work for the prison administration or other agencies of government, or in the prison pursuant to contract, generally do not act under color of state law even if their actions have some impact on prisoners.[45]

_____

(affirming punitive damages against "a corporation that had little regard for the inmates whose care it was charged with"). When the Supreme Court held that municipalities were not subject to punitive damages, it emphasized the presumption against punitive damages against public entities, not corporations, City of Newport v. Fact Concerts, Inc., 453 U.S. 247, 262–63, 101 S. Ct. 2748 (1981), suggesting that punitives may be available against corporations.

[41]For example, deliberate indifference to medical care is likely to constitute medical malpractice or negligence as well; excessive force that violate the Eighth Amendment is likely to constitute assault and battery. *See* Ch. 2, §§ F.5, G.2.e. In some cases the claims can be brought together in federal court; in others they would require separate state court and federal court suits; in most cases both claims could be brought in one suit in state court. *See* § F.1 of this chapter concerning federal courts' pendent or supplemental jurisdiction.

[42]Ogunde v. Prison Health Services, Inc., 645 S.E.2d 520, 526 (2007); *accord*, Miller v. Corrections Corp. of America, 239 Fed. Appx. 396, 397 (9th Cir. 2007) (unpublished); Murns v. City of New York, 2001 WL 515201, *5 (S.D.N.Y., May 15, 2001). Similarly, the Alaska Supreme Court held that a prisoner could sue a private prison contractor to enforce a contract prescribing rights in disciplinary proceedings. Rathke v. Corrections Corp. of America, 153 P.3d 303, 310–11 (2007).

[43]*See, e.g.*, Storts v. Hardee's Food Systems, Inc., 919 F. Supp. 1513, 1519 (D. Kan. 1996) (contract that failed to spell out third-party rights did not create any such rights under Kansas law); Moore v. Gaither, 767 A.2d 278, 282 (D.C. 2001) (contract that specifically excluded third-party rights did not create them); Walters v. Kautzky, 680 N.W.2d 1, 4 (Iowa 2004) (same as *Moore*); Sisney v. State, 754 N.W.2d 639, 643–45 (S.D. 2008) (similar to *Storts*); *see also* Rochell Bobroff and Harper Jean Tobin, Third-Party Beneficiary Claims, Clearinghouse Rev. J. of Poverty Law & Policy 99 (July–August 2008) (discussing variety of approaches courts have taken to third-party beneficiary claims).

Third-party beneficiary claims involving federal prisoners are discussed in the next section.

[44]*See, e.g.*, Sisney v. Reisch, 754 N.W.2d 813, 817–18 (S.D. 2008); *see* § G of this chapter, n.491, concerning third-party beneficiary enforcement of consent judgments and orders.

[45]Franklin v. Fox, 312 F.3d 423, 444–46 (9th Cir. 2002) (prisoner's daughter, who tried to elicit a confession for the prosecutor, did not act under color of state law); Proffitt v. Ridgway,

Private persons who conspire or act jointly with state officials may act under color of state law.[46]

2. "Federal Question," Administrative Procedures Act, and *Bivens* Damages Actions Against Federal Officials and Contractors

a. Injunctive Actions Federal officials generally act under color of federal, not state, law and therefore may not be sued under § 1983.[47] There is no statute like § 1983 providing for suits against federal officials who violate your rights under color of federal law.[48] However, the federal district courts

_____

279 F.3d 503, 508 (7th Cir. 2002) (bystander who assisted a police officer in subduing an arrestee did not act under color of state law); Thibodeaux v. Bordelos, 740 F.2d 329, 332–22 (5th Cir. 1984) (inmate who set fire did not act under color of law); Figalora v. Smith, 238 F. Supp. 2d 658, 661 (D.Del. 2002) (prisoner who committed assault did not act under color of law); Jones v. Warden of Stateville Correctional Center, 918 F. Supp. 1142, 1148 (N.D.Ill. 1995) (television reporters who interviewed the plaintiff did not act under color of state law).

[46]Tower v. Glover, 467 U.S. 914, 920, 104 S. Ct. 2820 (1984) (private person may be acting under color of state law when conspiring with state officials to violate others' constitutional rights). *See also* Swift v. Lewis, 901 F.2d 730, 732 n.5 (9th Cir. 1990) (religious functionary who acted jointly with prison officials in denying the plaintiff a religious classification acted under color of state law); Temple v. Albert, 719 F. Supp. 265, 267 (S.D.N.Y. 1989) (doctor who conspired with police officers would act under color of state law).

[47]There can be exceptions where federal personnel act jointly or conspire with state officials. *See, e.g.*, Strickland on Behalf of Strickland v. Shalala, 123 F.3d 863, 867 (6th Cir. 1997) ("courts finding that a federal official has acted under color of state law have done so only when there is evidence that federal and state officials engaged in a conspiracy or 'symbiotic' venture to violate a person's rights under the Constitution or federal law." (citations omitted)); Hampton v. Hanrahan, 600 F.2d 600, 623 (7th Cir. 1979) (federal law enforcement officials who conspired with state and local authorities acted under color of state law); Brown v. Stewart, 910 F. Supp. 1064, 1068–69 (W.D.Pa. 1994) (federal marshals who arrested plaintiff pursuant to a state arrest warrant for a violation of state law, in cooperation with state police, acted under color of state law). They may also act under color of state law if they are carrying out state law in a particular case. Terrell v. Petrie, 763 F. Supp. 1342, 1344 (E.D. Va. 1991), *aff'd*, 952 F.2d 397 (4th Cir. 1991); Brown v. Stewart, 910 F. Supp. at 1068–69.

Conversely, state and local officials can act under color of federal law if they are acting solely pursuant to federal authority. Courts have disagreed over where the line between state and federal authority is drawn. *Compare* Askew v. Bloemker, 548 F.2d 673, 677 (7th Cir. 1976) (city police assigned to a federal agency acted under color of federal law); Bordeaux v. Lynch, 958 F. Supp. 77, 84 (N.D.N.Y. 1997) (same) *with* Jones v. U.S. Drug Enforcement Admin., 801 F. Supp. 15, 21–22 (M.D.Tenn. 1992) (local police acting at the direction of federal agencies acted under color of *state* law because they possessed their authority based solely on state law).

[48]Some courts have held that a complaint against federal officials that erroneously relies on § 1983 should be construed as a

have jurisdiction over "all civil actions arising under the Constitution, laws, or treaties of the United States"[49] (this is called federal question jurisdiction). They have always assumed that they can grant equitable (injunctive) relief against federal officials for such violations,[50] and injunctions have been granted in a number of federal prison cases.[51] Now a federal statute authorizes injunctive claims against the government itself as well.[52]

b. Administrative Procedures Act and Mandamus The Administrative Procedures Act (APA) provides generally that "[a] person suffering legal wrong because of agency action, or adversely affected or aggrieved by agency action

---

federal question action, *see* Brown v. Smith, 828 F.2d 1493, 1494 (10th Cir. 1987); Perez v. Hawk, 302 F. Supp. 2d 9, 18 (E.D.N.Y. 2004), but others have not, *see* Mitchell v. Chapman, 343 F.3d 811, 825 (6th Cir. 2003), so get it right in your complaint or you may risk dismissal.

　[49]28 U.S.C. § 1331.

　[50]Bivens v. Six Unknown Named Agents of Federal Bureau of Narcotics, 403 U.S. 388, 404–05, 91 S. Ct. 1999 (1971) (Harlan, J., concurring in the judgment); Simmat v. U.S. Bureau of Prisons, 413 F.3d 1225, 1231–32 (10th Cir. 2005) (noting that the federal prisoner could seek "an injunction, based on the federal courts' equity jurisdiction, to enforce the dictates of the Eighth Amendment").

　[51]*See, e.g.*, Jordan v. Pugh, 504 F. Supp. 2d 1109, 1126 (D.Colo. 2007) (enjoining enforcement of regulation barring prisoners from publishing under a byline), *motion to amend denied, motion for findings granted*, 2007 WL 2908931 (D.Colo., Oct. 4, 2007); Gartrell v. Ashcroft, 191 F. Supp. 2d 23, 40–41 (D.D.C. 2002) (granting injunction under Religious Freedom Restoration Act), *appeal dismissed*, 2003 WL 1873847 (D.C. Cir., Apr. 11, 2003); Kane v. Winn, 319 F. Supp. 2d 162, 213 (D. Mass. 2004); Ashkenazi v. Attorney General of the U.S., 246 F. Supp. 2d 1 (D.D.C. 2003) (granting injunction to implement previously planned transfer of plaintiff to community corrections center), *vacated as moot*, 346 F.3d 191 (D.C. Cir. 2003); Howard v. U.S., 864 F. Supp. 1019 (D. Colo. 1994) (granting injuncting protecting Satanist religious practice).

　[52]5 U.S.C. § 702. This statute states in relevant part:

> An action in a court of the United States seeking relief other than money damages and stating a claim that an agency or an officer or employee thereof acted or failed to act in an official capacity or under color of legal authority shall not be dismissed nor relief therein be denied on the ground that it is against the United States or that the United States is an indispensable party. The United States may be named as a defendant in any such action, and a judgment or decree may be entered against the United States: Provided, That any mandatory or injunctive decree shall specify the Federal officer or officers (by name or by title), and their successors in office, personally responsible for compliance.

See Trudeau v. Federal Trade Comm'n, 456 F.3d 178, 186–87 (D.C. Cir. 2006) (stating that § 702 waives immunity for all equitable claims against federal agencies or officers in their official capacities); Simmat v. U.S. Bureau of Prisons, 413 F.3d at 1233 (discussing § 702's scope and waiver of sovereign immunity).

---

within the meaning of a relevant statute, is entitled to judicial review thereof."[53] Specifically, courts may require agencies to act if they have unlawfully or unreasonably refused to do so, and may strike down agency actions if they are "arbitrary, capricious, an abuse of discretion, or otherwise not in accordance with law"; if they violate the Constitution; if they are not authorized by the statutes that give the agency power; if they are done in violation of legally required procedure; and for other reasons described in the statute.[54] The main benefit of the APA is that it clearly allows enforcement of federal statutes and regulations as well as the Constitution. The APA does not provide for the award of damages.[55]

"Agency action" which may be reviewed by courts includes "the whole or a part of an agency rule, order, license, sanction, relief, or the equivalent or denial thereof, or failure to act."[56] A "final action"[57] of any federal agency is subject to judicial review unless a federal statute specifies otherwise, or the action is "committed to agency discretion by law."[58]

Under the APA, courts may review claims that an agency action violates the Constitution or federal statutes,[59] or that it violates the agency's own regulations[60] (though "program statements" and other internal agency guidelines

---

　[53]5 U.S.C. § 702. The APA is not a grant of jurisdiction to the federal courts; they have jurisdiction of APA claims under the general federal question jurisdiction of 28 U.S.C. § 1331. Kane v. Winn, 319 F. Supp. 2d 162, 210 (D.Mass. 2004) (citing Califano v. Sanders, 430 U.S. 99, 105, 97 S. Ct. 980 (1977)).

　The APA is found in 5 U.S.C. §§ 551–583, 701–706, 801–808, 3105, 3344, 6362, and 7562. Much of the APA and the case law decided under it has little relevance to prisoners.

　[54]5 U.S.C. § 706.

　[55]Bigbee v. U.S., 359 F. Supp. 2d 806, 810 (W.D.Wis. 2005).

　[56]5 U.S.C. § 551(13).

　[57]A "final" action is "a definitive statement of the agency's position with direct and imediate consequences." Fox v. Lappin, 441 F. Supp. 2d 203, 207 (D.Mass. 2005). In *Fox*, the court said that either initial classification as a sex offender or denial of administrative requests for relief could be considered final, given the prisoner's impending release. *See* Kane v. Winn, 319 F. Supp. 2d at 211 ("a decision to deny an inmate a course of treatment is necessarily a 'final action,' at least once administrative remedies have been exhausted"). Since you are required to exhaust administrative remedies in all prison conditions cases, *see* Ch. 9, § D, it should rarely be an issue whether you have received a final decision.

　[58]5 U.S.C. §§ 701–702, 704; *see* Japan Whaling Ass'n v. American Cetacean Soc'y, 478 U.S. 221, 230 n.4, 106 S. Ct. 2860 (1986) (noting that judicial review "is available absent some clear and convincing evidence of legislative intention to preclude review" (cited in Kane v. Winn, 319 F. Supp. 2d at 210)).

　[59]U.S. v. McAllister, 969 F. Supp. 1200, 1213 (D.Minn. 1997) (reviewing claim that involuntary medication decision violated Constitution).

　[60]Caldwell v. Miller, 790 F.2d 589, 609–10 (7th Cir. 1986) ("Where the rights of individuals are affected, it is incumbent upon agencies to follow their own procedures." (quoting Morton v. Ruiz, 415 U.S. 199, 235, 94 S. Ct. 1055 (1974)); U.S. v. McAllister, 969 F. Supp. at 1213 (reversing decision to medicate prisoner involuntarily based on violation of federal regulations).

may not be enforceable under the APA[61]). Courts may review claims that a regulation violates the statute that the regulation is supposed to implement[62] or that it is "arbitary and capricious."[63] They may review claims that the agency has adopted a policy without following the procedure for public notice and comment that the APA requires.[64] Judicial review under the APA is generally supposed to be "on the record," *i.e.*, the court is to consider only the information that was before the agency when it acted.[65]

The Federal Bureau of Prisons (BOP) is an "agency" that is generally subject to the APA.[66] However, the use of the APA in challenges to prison conditions and the actions of prison officials has not been fully explored. Certain kinds of BOP actions are exempted from APA review; a federal statute forbids application of the APA to "the making of any determination, decision, or order" under 18 U.S.C. §§ 3621–3626,[67] statutes which address subjects such as classification, transfers, and early release.[68] Courts have refused to engage in broad review of prison conditions under the APA on the ground that it specifically exempts from judicial review "agency action (which is) committed to agency discretion by law,"[69] and the statutes governing federal prison conditions vest broad discretion in the government.[70] Courts have disagreed over whether the APA permits judicial review of prison disciplinary determinations (we think it does).[71] Courts have suggested that BOP medical policies may be subject to APA review.[72] They have also held or suggested that APA review may be available of such individual actions or decisions as classification as a sex offender,[73] denial of a course of medical treatment,[74] unauthorized disposition of confiscated personal property,[75] and involuntary administration of psychiatric medications.[76] The APA has been used in challenges to BOP rules and policies concerning early release and good time credit.[77]

---

[61]*See* Bigbee v. U.S., 359 F. Supp. 2d 806, 810 (W.D.Wis. 2005) (program statements and institution supplements "are not in the nature of policy statements and therefore do not give rise to a cause of action"); Kane v. Winn, 319 F. Supp. 2d 162, 212 (D.Mass. 2004).

[62]*See, e.g.*, Davis v. Crabtree, 109 F.3d 566, 568–70 (9th Cir. 1997) (holding that a regulation defining certain firearms and drug trafficking convictions as "crimes of violence" and excluding prisoners from a drug treatment/early release program based on them was inconsistent with the federal statute that the Bureau of Prisons was supposed to be implementing); Kimberlin v. U.S. Dep't of Justice, 150 F. Supp. 2d 36, 49 (D.D.C. 2001), *aff'd on other grounds*, 318 F.3d 228 (D.C. Cir. 2003).

[63]Arrington v. Daniels, 516 F.3d 1106, 1114 (9th Cir. 2008) (APA requires agencies to state a rationale for their decisions, and failure to do so renders BOP regulation arbitrary and capricious.).

[64]Paulsen v. Daniels, 413 F.3d 999, 1004 (9th Cir. 2005).

These notice and comment provisions appear in 5 U.S.C. § 553. They apply only to "legislative rules" (rules which in effect make law) but not to "interpretive rules, general statements of policy, or rules of agency organization, procedure, or practice." 5 U.S.C. § 553(b)(A); *see* Dismas Charities, Inc. v. U.S. Dep't of Justice, 401 F.3d 666, 679–80 (6th Cir. 2005); Monahan v. Winn, 276 F. Supp. 2d 196, 212–15 (D.Mass. 2003) (distinguishing interpretive and legislative rules). BOP "program statements" are internal policies similar to interpretive rules, and do not require notice and comment. Gunderson v. Hood, 268 F.3d 1149, 1151, 1154 (9th Cir. 2001) (citing Reno v. Koray, 515 U.S. 50, 61, 115 S. Ct. 2021 (1995)).

[65]Florida Power & Light Co. v. Lorion, 470 U.S. 729, 743–44, 105 S. Ct. 1598 (1985).

[66]Simmat v. U.S. Bureau of Prisons, 413 F.3d 1225, 1239 (10th Cir. 2005) cases cited; Kane v. Winn, 319 F. Supp. 2d 162, 210–11 (D.Mass. 2004) (noting that the Supreme Court has assumed the APA to apply).

[67]18 U.S.C. § 3625.

[68]*See, e.g.*, Tanner v. Federal Bureau of Prisons, 433 F. Supp. 2d 117, 122 n.5 (D.D.C. 2006) (holding § 3625 exempts decisions dealing with transfers or place of imprisonment from APA review).

This rule prevents judicial review of decisions in individual cases. It does not prevent review of the validity of rules and policies concerning these subjects. Richmond v. Scibana, 387 F.3d 602, 605 (7th Cir. 2004).

[69]5 U.S.C. § 701(a)(2).

[70]Wolfish v. Levi, 573 F.2d 118 (2d Cir. 1978), *rev'd on other grounds*, 441 U.S. 520, 99 S. Ct. 1861 (1979). The court cited 18 U.S.C. § 4042, which merely requires the Attorney General to provide "suitable" quarters, safekeeping, care and subsistence for all inmates in his custody, and 18 U.S.C. § 4081, which provides for an "integrated system which will assure the proper classification and segregation of Federal prisoners [to provide] an individualized system of discipline, care, and treatment of the persons committed to such institutions." *Wolfish*, 573 F.2d at 125; *see* Rezaq v. Nalley, 2008 WL 5172363, *13–14 (D.Colo., Dec. 10, 2008) (holding § 4081 bars APA challenge to classification of a particular restrictive housing unit as general population); Harrison v. Federal Bureau of Prisons, 464 F. Supp. 2d 552, 557–58 (E.D.Va. 2006) (holding § 4042 bars APA challenge to telephone charges).

[71]In *Clardy v. Levi*, 545 F.2d 1241, 1244–46 (9th Cir.1976), the court held that the APA rules for hearings, contained in 5 U.S.C. § 554, do not apply to Bureau of Prisons disciplinary proceedings, and also suggested more broadly that the APA is not applicable to the BOP. In *White v. Henman*, 977 F.2d 292, 293 (7th Cir.1992), the court disagreed (correctly in our view), holding that the Bureau of Prisons is clearly an "agency" subject to the APA, and explaining that subjecting the Bureau of Prisons disciplinary process to judicial review under the APA does not mean also having to follow the APA's rules for administrative hearings, which provide more procedural protections than do most prison disciplinary systems. *See also* Triplett v. Federal Bureau of Prisons, 2009 WL 792799, *6 (N.D.Tex., Mar. 24, 2009) (following *White*, not *Clardy*).

[72]Glaus v. Anderson, 408 F.3d 382, 387 (7th Cir. 2005) (suggesting plaintiff's remedy might be a "challenge to the BOP guidelines on treatment for hepatitis C").

[73]Fox v. Lappin, 441 F. Supp. 2d 203, 207 (D.Mass. 2005).

[74]Kane v. Winn, 319 F. Supp. 2d 162, 211 (D.Mass. 2004).

[75]Caldwell v. Miller, 790 F.2d 589, 609–10 (7th Cir. 1986).

[76]U.S. v. McAllister, 969 F. Supp. 1200, 1213 (D.Minn. 1997).

[77]Tablada v. Thomas, 533 F.3d 800 (9th Cir. 2008) (upholding BOP method of calculating good time); Arrington v. Daniels, 516 F.3d 1106, 1116 (9th Cir. 2008) (striking down BOP regulation excluding certain prisoners from early release based on completion of drug treatment); Richmond v. Scibana, 387 F.3d 602 (7th Cir.

When federal prisoners challenge administrative actions affecting the fact or duration of their incarceration, they must proceed by writ of habeas corpus, as explained in another section.[78] However, they may assert claims under the APA in their habeas proceedings.[79]

Federal courts also may hear an "action in the nature of mandamus" if prison officials have violated a very specific duty that they are plainly obligated to carry out.[80]

c. *Bivens* Claims: Damages Actions Against Federal Personnel

The Supreme Court has held that federal courts may award damages for violation of the Constitution and other federal laws against federal officials and employees as part of their "federal question" jurisdiction.[81] Such damage actions are called "*Bivens* actions" after the case that first recognized them. They were authorized by the Supreme Court in prisoners' Eighth Amendment suits,[82] and since then courts have allowed *Bivens* actions generally for prisoners' constitutional claims against federal prison personnel.[83]

Bivens actions are generally regarded as similar to § 1983 damage actions, and most of the § 1983 rules and defenses are also applied to them,[84] including personal immunities,[85] the law of damages,[86] the requirement of personal responsibility of defendants,[87] and statutes of limitations.[88] They may only be brought against individual defendants (not federal agencies) in their individual, not official, capacities.[89] In *Bivens* actions, courts determine whether defendants acted under color of federal law or engaged in federal government action, similarly to the color of law/state action analysis of § 1983.[90] *Bivens* suits (and federal question actions for

---

2004) (holding APA was the proper vehicle for challenging restriction on placement in community correction centers).

[78]*See* § H.1.b of this chapter.

[79]*See, e.g.*, Tablada v. Thomas, 553 F.3d at 806–07; Arrington v. Daniels, 516 F.3d at 1116.

[80]28 U.S.C. § 1361. *See* Simmat v. U.S. Bureau of Prisons, 413 F.3d 1225, 1235 (10th Cir. 2005) (district court had mandamus jurisdiction to require prisoner to be examined by dentists and have their recommendations implemented); Byrd v. Moore, 252 F. Supp. 2d 293, 302 (W.D.N.C. 2003) (granting injunction in the nature of mandamus to follow terms of federal statute and consider plaintiff for a community correction center); Muhammad v. U.S. Bureau of Prisons, 789 F. Supp. 449, 450 (D.D.C. 1992); Stover v. Carlson, 413 F. Supp. 718, 721 (D. Conn. 1976). *But see* U.S. v. McAllister, 969 F. Supp. 1200, 1212 (D.Minn. 1997) (mandamus was inappropriate in connection with an order concerning medication because medical decisions are discretionary). It is not clear whether there is anything that you can obtain via mandamus that you could not also obtain through a federal question action for an injunction, and the standards for mandamus are harder to meet. The mandamus procedure is seldom used in prison cases.

[81]Bivens v. Six Unknown Named Agents of Federal Bureau of Narcotics, 403 U.S. 388, 392-97, 91 S. Ct. 1999 (1971) (Fourth Amendment case). The Court has said that "*Bivens* established that the victims of a constitutional violation by a federal agent have a right to recover damages against the official in federal court despite the absence of any statute conferring such a right." Hartman v. Moore, 547 U.S. 250, 254 n.2, 126 S. Ct. 1296 (2002) (quoting Carlson v. Green, 446 U.S. 14, 18, 100 S. Ct. 1468 (1980)).

Federal question jurisdiction is authorized by 28 U.S.C. § 1331(a), which gives the district courts "original jurisdiction of all civil actions under the Constitution, laws, or treaties of the United States."

[82]Carlson v. Green, 446 U.S. 14, 18–19, 100 S. Ct. 1468 (1980); *see* Farmer v. Brennan, 511 U.S. 825, 114 S. Ct. 1970 (1994) (prisoner–prisoner assault case). In *Carlson*, the Court held that the fact that the defendants are prison officials is not a "special factor counseling hesitation" in permitting a *Bivens* suit to go forward. 446 U.S. at 18–19; *accord*, McCarthy v. Madigan, 503 U.S. 140, 151–52, 112 S. Ct. 1081 (1992).

[83]*See, e.g.*, Cleavinger v. Saxner, 474 U.S. 193, 106 S. Ct. 496 (1985) (disciplinary due process); Young v. Quinlan, 960 F.2d 351, 360–64 (3d Cir. 1992) (exposure to danger of inmate assault and confinement in "dry cell"); Williams v. Meese, 926 F.2d 994, 998 (10th Cir. 1991) (racial discrimination); Cale v. Johnson, 861 F.2d 943, 946–47 (6th Cir. 1988) (disciplinary due process and retaliation for complaining); Sizemore v. Williford, 829 F.2d 608, 610–11 (7th Cir. 1987) (denial of publications).

Bivens does not provide a remedy for violation of federal statutes or regulations; a "private right of action" for violating them exists only if Congress says so explicitly. Alexander v. Sandoval, 532 U.S. 275, 287, 121 S. Ct. 1511 (2001).

[84]The Supreme Court has said that in general "a *Bivens* action is the federal analog to suits brought against state officials under . . . 42 U.S.C. § 1983." Hartman v. Moore, 547 U.S. 250, 254 n.2, 126 S. Ct. 1296 (2002); *accord*, Abella v. Rubino, 63 F.3d 1063, 1065 (11th Cir. 1995) (claims under 42 U.S.C. § 1983 and *Bivens* are similar, courts generally apply § 1983 law to *Bivens* cases). There are exceptions. *See* Carlson v. Green, 446 U.S. at 23–24 (*Bivens* suits are governed by uniform federal rules of survivorship, while § 1983 applies state law in some cases).

[85]Wilson v. Layne, 526 U.S. 603, 609, 119 S. Ct. 1692 (1999) (qualified immunity analysis is the same under § 1983 and in *Bivens* actions); Butz v. Economou, 438 U.S. 478, 500, 98 S. Ct. 2894 (1978) (standards for absolute immunity are the same unless Congress directs otherwise); Center for Bio-Ethical Reform, Inc. v. City of Springboro, 477 F.3d 807, 831 (6th Cir. 2007); Jones v. New York State Division of Military and Naval Affairs, 166 F.3d 45, 51 (2d Cir. 1999). *See* § L of this chapter for a discussion of immunities.

[86]Halperin v. Kissinger, 606 F.2d 1192, 1207 (D.C. Cir. 1979), *aff'd in part, dismissed in part*, 452 U.S. 713 (1981).

[87]Ashcroft v. Iqbal, ___ U.S. ___, 129 S. Ct. 1937, 1948 (2009); Buford v. Runyon, 160 F.3d 1199, 1203 n.7 (8th Cir. 1998); Del Raine v. Williford, 32 F.3d 1024, 1047 (7th Cir. 1994). *See* § B.4.a of this chapter concerning the personal involvement requirement.

[88]Kelly v. Serna, 87 F.3d 1235, 1238 (11th Cir. 1996) ("[A] *Bivens* action is governed by the same statute of limitations as would a § 1983 action in that court."); Aanchez v. U.S., 49 F.3d 1329, 1330 (8th Cir. 1995); Kurinsky v. U.S., 33 F.3d 594, 599 (6th Cir. 1994); Van Strum v. Lawn, 940 F.2d 406, 410 (9th Cir. 1991); Bieneman v. City of Chicago, 864 F.2d 463, 469 (7th Cir. 1988); Chin v. Bowen, 833 F.2d 21, 23–24 (2d Cir. 1987); Afanador v. U.S. Postal Service, 787 F. Supp. 261, 265 (D. P.R. 1991), *aff'd*, 976 F.2d 724 (1st Cir. 1992).

[89]Hatten v. White, 275 F.3d 1208, 1210 (10th Cir. 2002).

[90]*See, e.g.*, U.S. v. Temple, 447 F.3d 130, 137–38 (2d Cir. 2006) (noting that § 1983 cases are helpful in assessing color of federal law);

injunctive relief) are subject to the requirement of exhaustion of administrative remedies.[91]

d. *Bivens* Claims and Private Defendants One major difference between *Bivens* actions and § 1983 actions is that you cannot sue a private corporation contracting with the federal government under *Bivens*.[92] In so holding, the Supreme Court emphasized that "[t]he purpose of *Bivens* is to deter *individual* federal officers from committing constitutional violations."[93] There is now a conflict among federal circuits over whether prisoners can sue the *individual* employees of private corporations contracting with the federal government.[94]

One court has said that the actions of corporate employees are not "fairly attributable" to the federal government, since the corporation is private and the government has no stake in it other than contracting with it.[95] This is very close to saying that private incarceration of federal prisoners does not take place under color of federal law. This reasoning is inconsistent with that of *West v. Atkins* and all the other § 1983 cases that have held that persons who are delegated the authority for *state* prison operation or for providing state prisoners constitutionally required services act under color of state law.[96]

Decisions rejecting *Bivens* claims against corporate employees have emphasized that there are other remedies (usually state court tort remedies) available to the affected prisoners.[97] However, the mere existence of state law remedies, without more, should not preclude the *Bivens* remedy.[98] In reality, state tort remedies may not be legally or practically available to indigent prisoners.[99] If that is the case in your situation, you should explain the reasons to the court,[100] though some courts obviously do not care.[101] You should also remind the court that the Supreme Court has said that federal rights should not be subject to the "vagaries" of state law.[102]

The *Holly* decision also says that the fact that Congress has authorized private incarceration at all means that allowing *Bivens* actions against private contractors might "frustrate a clearly expressed congressional policy."[103] This makes no sense at all, since Congress was well aware of the existence of the *Bivens* remedy and the likelihood it would be extended to private contractors in light of *West v. Atkins*; if that prospect had concerned it, it could have prohibited *Bivens* actions against private contractor employees.[104] However, in those circuits that have already held that *Bivens* actions will not lie against employees of private contractors, you will be left only with state law remedies and will generally have to enforce them in state courts.

Morast v. Lance, 807 F.2d 926, 931 (11th Cir. 1987); Haley v. Walker, 751 F.2d 284, 285 (8th Cir. 1984).

[91]*See* Ch. 9, § D for discussion of the exhaustion requirement under the Prison Litigation Reform Act, and § K in this chapter for further discussion of exhaustion of remedies.

[92]Correctional Services Corp. v. Malesko, 534 U.S. 61, 70–74, 122 S. Ct. 515 (2001).

[93]*Malesko*, 534 U.S. at 70 (emphasis supplied).

[94]Three circuits have barred suits against employees of private contractors. Alba v. Montford, 517 F.3d 1249, 1254–55 (11th Cir. 2008), *cert. denied*, 129 S. Ct. 632 (2008); Holly v. Scott, 434 F.3d 287, 295–97 (4th Cir. 2006); Peoples v. CCA Detention Centers, 422 F.3d 1090, 1101–03 (10th Cir. 2005), *vacated in pertinent part on other grounds*, 449 F.3d 1097 (10th Cir. 2006). The Tenth Circuit holding in *Peoples* has no precedential effect because it has been vacated, but it is likely to be persuasive when the court considers the question again. *See* Lindsey v. Bowlin, 557 F. Supp. 2d 1225, 1229–30 (D.Kan. 2008) (adhering to *Peoples* analysis).

One circuit has held to the contrary, Pollard v. Geo Group, Inc., ___ F.3d ___, 2010 WL 2246418 (9th Cir. 2010), as have several district courts. Bender v. General Services Admin., 539 F. Supp. 2d 702, 707–12 (S.D.N.Y. 2008) (rejecting *Holly v. Scott* and *Peoples v. CCA* holdings in case concerning employees of a private security company); Jama v. U.S.I.N.S., 343 F. Supp. 2d 338, 363 (D.N.J. 2004); Sarro v. Cornell Corrections, Inc., 248 F. Supp. 2d 52, 60–61 (D.R.I. 2003).

[95]Holly v. Scott, 434 F.3d at 291–93.

[96]*See* Pollard v. Geo Group, Inc., 2010 WL 2246418, *5–6; Bromfield v. McBurney, 2008 WL 2746289, *6–9 (W.D. Wash. 2008); Sarro v. Cornell Corrections, Inc., 248 F. Supp. 2d at 61. The dissenting judge in the *Holly* case makes this point, 434 F.3d at 297–303, though she accepts the argument that the existence of a state tort remedy means that no *Bivens* remedy should be available. *Id.* at 303. This subject is discussed in § B.1.c, above.

The *Holly* decision also relies heavily on the Supreme Court's holding that correction officers in a private prison contracting with a state are not entitled to the defense of qualified immunity under § 1983. 434 F.3d at 293–94 (citing Richardson v. McKnight, 521

U.S. 399, 117 S. Ct. 2100 (1997)). The dissenting judge also explains why this reasoning makes no sense. 434 F.3d at 299, as does the Ninth Circuit. Pollard v. Geo Group, Inc. 2010 WL 2246418, *6–7.

[97]*Alba*, 517 F.3d at 1254–55; *Holly*, 434 F.3d at 296; *Peoples*, 422 F.3d at 1103. Private corporations contracting with the federal government generally may not be sued under the Federal Tort Claims Act. *See* § C.2, n.300, below.

[98]Pollard v. Geo Group, Inc., 2010 WL 2246418, *10 (holding "the mere availability of a state law remedy does not counsel against allowing a *Bivens* cause of action"; relegating plaintiffs to state tort remedies does not serve deference to Congress). *But see* Correctional Services Corp. v. Malesko, 534 U.S. at 69 (rejecting the argument that a *Bivens* remedy must be available solely because of the lack of another *federal* remedy) (cited in *Alba*, 517 F.3d at 1254).

[99]Thus, in *Pollard*, the court points out the difficulty of determing whether many federal constitutional claims actually have analogous tort claims, and whether those claims will be barred by tort law defenses. 2010 WL 2246418, *13–15. In *Alba*, the plaintiff pointed out that as an indigent prisoner, he could not realistically pursue a state court malpractice action because state law requires submission with the complaint of a supporting affidavit from a physician identifying the negligence. *Alba*, 517 F.3d at 1254; *accord*, *Pollard*, 2010 WL 2246418, *16 (noting that *pro se* prisoners are not in the "same shoes" as other litigants).

[100]Bromfield v. McBurney, 2008 WL 2746289, *13–15 (W.D. Wash. 2008) (holding that defendants failed to show that there were other remedies for all the plaintiff's claims).

[101]*Alba*, 517 F.3d at 1255.

[102]Carlson v. Green, 446 U.S. 14, 22, 100 S. Ct. 1468 (1980); *accord*, Pollard v. Geo Group, Inc., 2010 WL 2246418, *12.

[103]Holly v. Scott, 434 F.3d at 290.

[104]Sarro v. Cornell Corrections, Inc., 248 F. Supp. 2d at 61 (noting absence of any congressional intent to preclude *Bivens* actions); *accord*, Bender v. General Services Admin., 539 F. Supp. 2d 702, 709 (S.D.N.Y. 2008).

3. Other Civil Rights Statutes

There are several civil rights statutes besides § 1983 that are sometimes invoked by prisoners.

a. 42 U.S.C. §§ 1981 and 1982: Racial Discrimination Claims Section 1981 provides that all persons must have the same rights "to make and enforce contracts, to sue, be parties, give evidence, and to the full and equal benefit of all laws and proceedings for the security of persons and property as is enjoyed by white citizens, and shall be subject to like punishment, pains, penalties, taxes, licenses, and exactions of every kind, and to no other." It adds that "the term 'make and enforce contracts' includes the making, performance, modification, and termination of contracts, and the enjoyment of all benefits, privileges, terms, and conditions of the contractual relationship."[105] Unlike 42 U.S.C. § 1983, § 1981 applies to the conduct of private persons, in addition to persons acting under color of state law.[106]

This statute is rarely of use to prisoners because it is limited to claims involving racial discrimination in the making and enforcement of contracts,[107] and few prisoner claims are of this sort.[108] If you did have such a claim against prison personnel, you could pursue it under § 1983, which addresses any claim of racial discrimination done under color of state law. In general, anything a prisoner can get under § 1981 she can also get under § 1983.[109] The comments in this section generally also apply to 42 U.S.C. § 1982, which prohibits racial discrimination with respect to the right to "inherit, purchase, lease, sell, hold, and convey real and personal property," and which is interpreted similarly to § 1981.[110]

b. 42 U.S.C. §§ 1985, 1986: Civil Rights Conspiracy Claims Several kinds of conspiracies, some of which may be relevant to prisoners, are addressed in 42 U.S.C. § 1985.[111] Section 1985 is not limited to persons who act under color of law; it reaches private conduct that fits the terms of the statute.[112] Conspiracy claims under § 1985 (like all conspiracy claims) require that the plaintiff allege and prove that the defendants agreed on a course of conduct that violated the statute.[113]

Persons who "conspire to deter, by force, intimidation, or threat, any party or witness" from attending or from testifying freely and truthfully in federal court, or conspire to harm a party or witnesses for doing so, or to influence or injure federal court jurors, are liable under the first clause of 42 U.S.C. § 1985(2).[114] The scope of the statute is strictly limited to improprieties involving witnesses and jurors in federal court, and does not extend to other alleged misconduct,[115] or to conduct affecting bodies other than federal courts.[116]

Other parts of § 1985 are intended to protect individuals' equal protection rights. These provisions require the plaintiff to allege and show "some racial, or perhaps otherwise class-based, invidiously discriminatory animus behind the conspirators' action."[117] ("Class-based animus" is not required for claims under the first clause of § 1985(2), discussed in the previous paragraph.[118]) The second clause

---

[105]42 U.S.C. § 1981 (a), (b).

[106]42 U.S.C. § 1981(c); *see* Patterson v. McLean Credit Union, 491 U.S. 164, 177, 109 S. Ct. 2363 (1989).

[107]*See generally* CBOCS West, Inc. v. Humphries, 553 U.S. 442, 128 S. Ct. 1951 (2008) (discussing statute and its history); Evans v. Holiday Inns, Inc., 951 F. Supp. 85, 88 (D. Md. 1997) (discussing amendment that expanded the statute's scope). *CBOCS West* held that § 1981 covers claims for retaliation for complaining about racial discrimination with respect to contracts. 128 S. Ct. at 1958.

[108]*See, e.g.,* Hunnicutt v. Armstrong, 305 F. Supp. 2d 175, 189–90 (D.Conn. 2004), *aff'd in pertinent part*, 152 Fed.Appx. 34 (2d Cir. 2005) (unpublished).

[109]The Supreme Court held that damages claims for violations of § 1981 against persons acting under color of state law must be pursued under § 1983. Jett v. Dallas Independent School District, 491 U.S. 701, 731-33, 109 S. Ct. 2702 (1989). Since Congress amended § 1981 in the Civil Rights Act of 1991, courts have split as to whether there is now a private action directly under § 1981. *Compare* Bolden v. City of Topeka, Kan., 441 F.3d 1129, 1137 (10th Cir. 2006) ("amendments to § 1981 do not expressly provide a private cause of action") *with* Federation of African American Contractors v. City of Oakland, 96 F.3d 1204 (9th Cir. 1996) (private cause of action under § 1981). If you think you have a § 1981 claim, you should also plead a § 1983 claim.

[110]CBOCS West, Inc. v. Humphries, 128 S. Ct. at 1955.

[111]Kush v. Rutledge, 460 U.S. 719, 725–27, 103 S. Ct. 1483 (1983) (describing scope of statute).

Several parts of § 1985 have little relevance to prisoners and will not be discussed here. These include § 1985(1), concerning actions intended to prevent persons from holding a federal office or carrying out its duties, or harming them for doing so, and a portion of § 1985(3) concerning actions intended to prevent persons from voting for or supporting a candidate for federal office.

[112]Griffin v. Breckenridge, 403 U.S. 88, 96–101, 91 S. Ct. 1790 (1971); Brawer v. Horowitz, 535 F.2d 830, 839–40 (3d Cir.1976).

[113]*See, e.g.,* Hunnicutt v. Armstrong, 305 F. Supp. 2d 175, 185, 190 (D.Conn. 2004), *aff'd in pertinent part*, 152 Fed.Appx. 34 (2d Cir. 2005) (unpublished).

[114]42 U.S.C. § 1985(2); *see* Haddle v. Garrison, 525 U.S. 121, 125, 119 S. Ct. 489 (1998) (interference with witness's employment could violate § 1985(2); "the gist of the wrong at which § 1985(2) is directed is not deprivation of property but intimidation or retaliation against witnesses in federal court proceedings."); *accord*, Kinney v. Weaver, 367 F.3d 337, 353 (5th Cir. 2004).

[115]*See, e.g.,* Kimble v. D.J. McDuffy, Inc., 648 F.2d 340, 347–48 (5th Cir. 1981) (en banc) (filing of lawsuits did not constitute "attending" court within the meaning of the statute).

[116]Foster v. Pall Aeropower Corp., 111 F. Supp. 2d 1320, 1323 (M.D. Fla. 2000) (statute does not cover conspiracies as to obstruction of justice in regards to hearings of administrative agencies); Herrera v. Scully, 815 F. Supp. 713, 726–27 (S.D.N.Y. 1993) (filing papers in state court was not within the scope of § 1985(2)).

[117]Bray v. Alexandria Women's Health Clinic, 506 U.S. 263, 269–70, 113 S. Ct. 753 (1993) (quoting Griffin v. Breckenridge, 403 U.S. 88, 102, 91 S. Ct. 1790 (1971)).

[118]Kush v. Rutledge, 460 U.S. 719, 726–27, 103 S. Ct. 1483 (1983) ("[I]t is clear that Congress did not intend to impose a requirement of class-based animus on persons seeking to prove a

of § 1985(2) provides for actions against persons who conspire to obstruct "the due course of justice" in *state* courts with intent to deny any citizen the equal protection of the laws or to harm a citizen for enforcing or attempting to enforce the right to equal protection.[119] In addition, § 1985(3) provides for damage actions against persons who "conspire . . . for the purpose of depriving . . . any person or class of persons of the equal protections of laws, or of equal privileges and immunities under the laws."[120]

The next statutory section, 42 U.S.C. § 1986, provides for damage liability for anyone "who, having knowledge that [a § 1985 conspiracy] is about to be committed," does nothing about it.[121]

Like § 1981, these statutes generally add little to the remedies prisoners already have under § 1983. Conspiracy claims can be brought under § 1983.[122] Private persons who conspire with state or local government employees or officials are considered to act under color of law and may be sued under § 1983.[123] Most of the conspiracies covered by these statutes can probably be litigated under § 1983 as access to courts or equal protection claims.[124]

c. Title VII, Federal Civil Rights Act: Employment Discrimination Claims   Title VII prohibits discrimination in employment and is discussed in Ch. 5.

d. 42 U.S.C. § 1997: Civil Rights of Institutionalized Persons Act (CRIPA)   This statute permits the federal government to bring lawsuits on behalf of prisoners and persons in other institutions such as mental hospitals under

certain limited circumstances.[125] The prisoners or residents of the institution can bring their own lawsuit or intervene in the CRIPA action if they are concerned that the government is not actually protecting their rights.[126] However, CRIPA does not itself confer any rights on individual inmates.[127]

The statutory section that contains CRIPA also contains parts of the Prison Litigation Reform Act (PLRA), enacted in 1996. That statute provides many restrictions and barriers to prisoners seeking to file federal lawsuits and does not confer any rights on prisoners. The PLRA is discussed in Ch. 9.

e. Rehabilitation Act and Americans with Disabilities Act   These statutes, which provide significant legal protections to disabled persons, including prisoners, are discussed in detail in Ch. 2, § F.4.h.

f. Religious Freedom Restoration Act (RFRA)   This statute, which was enacted in 1993 and provides enhanced protections to religious freedom, is discussed in Ch. 3, § D. It only applies to the Federal Government.[128]

g. Religious Land Use and Institutionalized Persons Act (RLUIPA)   This statute, which was enacted in 2000, is discussed in Ch. 3, § D. RLUIPA is not applicable to federal prisoners, but protects the religious rights of state prisoners.

h. Racketeer Influenced and Corrupt Organizations Act (RICO)   The Racketeer Influenced and Corrupt Organizations Act (RICO) is not a civil rights statute, but some prisoners have tried to use it as one, usually without much success. RICO is mainly a criminal statute, and

---

violation of their rights under the first clause of § 1985(2)."); *see also* Kinney v. Weaver, 301 F.3d 253, 264 (5th Cir. 2002).

[119]42 U.S.C. § 1985(2); *see generally* Chavis v. Clayton County School Dist., 300 F.3d 1288, 1291–94 (11th Cir. 2002).

[120]42 U.S.C. § 1985(3); *In re* Bayside Prison Litigation, 190 F. Supp. 2d 755, 766–67 (D.N.J. 2002) (finding complaint sufficiently pled § 1985(3) conspiracy); *see generally* Griffin v. Breckenridge, 403 U.S. 88, 91 S. Ct. 1790 (1971).

[121]42 U.S.C. § 1986.

[122]*See* Farhat v. Jopke, 370 F.3d 580, 599 (6th Cir. 2004) ("Claims of [civil] conspiracy must be pled with some specificity: vague and conclusory allegations that are unsupported by material facts are not sufficient to state a § 1983 claim."); Memphis, Tennessee Area Local, Am. Postal Workers Union, AFL-CIO v. City of Memphis, 361 F.3d 898, 905–06 (6th Cir. 2004) (describing allegations of civil conspiracy that were sufficient to overcome a motion to dismiss); Hafner v. Brown, 983 F.2d 570, 577–78 (4th Cir. 1992) (officers who watched an illegal beating without interfering participated in a civil conspiracy actionable under § 1983); Haley v. Dormire, 845 F.2d 1488, 1490 (8th Cir. 1988) (allegation of conspiracy to retaliate against the plaintiff for lawsuits stated a claim); Bontkowski v. Jenkins, 661 F.Supp, 576, 577 (N.D. Ill, 1987) (allegation of conspiracy to deny medical care stated a claim), *aff'd*, 860 F.2d 1082 (7th Cir. 1988).

[123]*See* cases cited in § B.1.c of this chapter, n.46, above.

[124]*See* Ch. 3, § C, and Ch. 5 concerning these claims.

[125]42 U.S.C. § 1997(a–c). The Attorney General may bring suit only for equitable relief, not damages, and only to ensure the "minimum corrective measures" necessary to remediate "egregious or flagrant conditions" depriving institution's residents of federally protected rights "pursuant to a pattern or practice of resistance." 42 U.S.C. § 1997a.

[126]42 U.S.C. § 1997j ("The provisions of this subchapter shall in no way expand or restrict the authority of parties other than the United States to enforce the legal rights which they may have pursuant to existing law with regard to institutionalized persons."); *see* U.S. v. State of Oregon, 839 F.2d 635, 637–38 (9th Cir. 1988) (allowing intervention); Messier v. Southbury Training School, 916 F. Supp. 133, 137–39 (D.Conn. 1996) (CRIPA consent judgment was not *res judicata* and not binding on institution's residents), *But see* U.S. v. State of Michigan, 940 F.2d 143, 163–66 (6th Cir. 1991) (prisoners' rights organization should not have been given the status of "litigating *amicus curiae*" in case brought by government under CRIPA).

[127]Mann v. Adams, 846 F.2d 589, 590 (9th Cir. 1988); Bieros v. Nicola, 860 F. Supp. 226, 235 (E.D.Pa.1994); Cooper v. Sumner, 672 F. Supp. 1361, 1367 (D.Nev. 1987).

[128]*See* City of Boerne v. Flores, 521 U.S. 507, 117 S. Ct. 2157, (1997) (court held that the application to states of the RFRA was beyond Congress' legislative authority under § 5 of the 14th Amendment).

prisoners can't file criminal charges or demand criminal prosecution.[129]

However, there are also provisions (referred to as "civil RICO") which state: "Any person injured in his business or property by reason of a violation of section 1962 of this chapter may sue therefor in any appropriate United States district court and shall recover threefold the damages he sustains and the cost of the suit. . . ."[130] Courts also can grant injunctions against RICO violations.[131]

There are very specific requirements for civil RICO suits which plaintiffs in prison cases can only rarely meet. First, a plaintiff must show two or more "predicate acts" of "racketeering activity" by the defendants; if these acts do not meet the strict definitions specified by the statute, there is no RICO claim.[132] The plaintiff must show an actual RICO violation, which usually involves some sort of unlawful debt or debt collection activities or use of the funds obtained from them, or other "pattern of racketeering activity."[133] A civil RICO plaintiff must also show he was "injured in his business or property" by the RICO violation, which courts have held means a business or property injury recognized by state law.[134] Thus, one court held that a person who was falsely imprisoned as a result of a "pattern of racketeering," and was therefore unable to work or to seek employment, was subjected to "intentional interference with contract and interference with prospective business relations," torts recognized under state law.[135] Courts have not been willing to extend this idea to prison employment, which is generally not considered a property right.[136] Violations of rights that do not involve injury to business or property are not RICO violations.[137] If your RICO claim involves your criminal

conviction, the *Heck v. Humphrey*[138] requirement that the conviction have previously been overturned before filing of a civil suit is applicable.[139]

i. Privacy Act The federal Privacy Act requires federal agencies to keep accurate records concerning individuals and to respond to requests to correct errors, and provides for civil suits to enforce these requirements, or to recover damages for adverse determinations based on inaccurate records, under limited circumstances.[140]

4. Suing the Right Defendants in Civil Rights Actions

a. Individual Defendants: Causation and Personal Involvement Under § 1983, only a person who "subjects, or causes to be subjected" the plaintiff to a deprivation of rights can be held liable. The doctrine of *respondeat superior*, which makes an employer automatically responsible for the wrongdoing of employees, does not apply under § 1983.[141] That means the warden or superintendent or commissioner cannot be held liable for every illegal act that takes place in jail or prison. The plaintiff must show the personal involvement[142] of each defendant in causing a violation of her rights.[143] The personal involvement requirement applies in

---

[129]*See* n.1 of this chapter.

[130]18 U.S.C. § 1964(c).

[131]18 U.S.C. § 1964(a).

[132]Scheidler v. National Organization for Women, 537 U.S. 393, 123 S. Ct. 1057 (2003). Racketeering activity consists of any of a long list of acts, most of which involve violation of federal criminal law. These are listed in 18 U.S.C. § 1961(1).

The plaintiff also "must show that the racketeering predicates are related, and that they amount to or pose a threat of continued criminal activity." H.J. Inc. v. Northwestern Bell Telephone Co., 492 U.S. 229, 109 S. Ct. 2893 (1989).

[133]What RICO prohibits is set out much more precisely and in more detail in 18 U.S.C. § 1962. *See* Tapia-Ortiz v. Winter, 185 F.3d 8, 11 (2d Cir.1999) (vague and conclusory allegations of conspiracy failed to explain how defendants participated in a pattern of racketeering activity in violation of the RICO Act). A "pattern of racketeering activity" requires at least two acts of racketeering activity within a 10-year period. 18 U.S.C. § 1961(5).

[134]Doe v. Roe, 958 F.2d 763, 768 (7th Cir. 1992); Alley v. Angelone, 962 F. Supp. 827, 832–33 (E.D. Va. 1997).

[135]Diaz v. Gates, 420 F.3d 897 (9th Cir. 2006) (en banc); *accord*, Guerrero v. Gates, 442 F.3d 697, 707–08 (9th Cir. 2006).

[136]*See* Alley v. Angelone, 962 F. Supp. at 832–33 (E.D.Va. 1997).

[137]*See* Asad v. Bush, 170 Fed.Appx. 668, 673 (11th Cir. 2006) (unpublished) (prisoner's racial and religious claims did not constitute requisite injury to his "business or property").

[138]512 U.S. 477, 114 S. Ct. 2364 (1994); *see* § H.1 of this chapter concerning *Heck*.

[139]*See* Williams v. Hill, 878 F. Supp. 269, 270–73 (D.D.C. 1995) (*Heck v. Humphrey* applicable to civil "RICO" action filed by a federal prisoner against federal prosecutors and other officials), *aff'd*, 74 F.3d 1339 (4th Cir. 1996). *See also* Hermansen v. Chandler, 211 F.3d 1269, 2000 WL 553957, *2 (6th Cir. 2000) (unpublished) ("This court has consistently applied th[e] [*Heck*] princip[le] to civil actions under RICO. . . .").

[140]5 U.S.C. § 552a. This statute and its limits are discussed in Ch. 3, § E.3, n.939; Ch. 4, § H.7, nn.540–52; and Ch. 10, § K.1, n.405.

[141]Parratt v. Taylor, 451 U.S. 527, 537 n.3, 101 S. Ct. 1908 (1981); Monell v. New York City Dep't Of Social Services, 436 U.S. 658, 691–93, 98 S. Ct. 2018 (1978). There are some older cases holding that state *respondeat superior* doctrines could be used under § 1983. These cases have been overruled. *See* Baskin v. Parker, 602 F.2d 1205, 1207–08 (5th Cir. 1979).

[142]Duffield v. Jackson, 545 F.3d 1234, 1238 (10th Cir. 2008); Grinter v. Knight, 532 F.3d 567, 575 (6th Cir. 2008); Miller v. Calhoun County, 408 F.3d 803, 817 n.3 (6th Cir. 2005) ("Because § 1983 liability cannot be imposed under a theory of *respondeat superior*, proof of personal involvement is required for a supervisor to incur personal liability."); Beck v. LaFleur, 257 F.3d 764, 766 (8th Cir. 2001) (prisoner must allege defendant's personal involvement or responsibility for constitutional violations to state § 1983 claim); Armstrong v. Squadrito, 152 F.3d 564, 581 (7th Cir. 1998) ("individual wrongdoing" must be shown); Colon v. Coughlin, 58 F.3d 865, 873 (2d Cir.1995).

[143]There has been one important exception to the personal involvement requirement. Courts have allowed prisoners to keep high-level supervisors as defendants, even without evidence of personal involvement, for purposes of discovery to determine who the proper defendants are. *See, e.g.*, Satchell v. Dilworth, 745 F.2d

civil rights actions against federal officials ("*Bivens* actions") as well as in § 1983 actions.[144]

There are various ways personal involvement can be shown. One court has said that a § 1983 defendant can be held liable if

> (1) the defendant participated directly in the alleged constitutional violation, (2) the defendant, after being informed of the violation through a report or appeal, failed to remedy the wrong, (3) the defendant created a policy or custom under which unconstitutional practices occurred, or allowed the continuance of such a policy or custom, (4) the defendant was grossly negligent in supervising subordinates who committed the wrongful acts, or (5) the defendant exhibited deliberate indifference to the rights of inmates by failing to act on information indicating that unconstitutional acts were occurring.[145]

Other courts have made similar statements,[146] though there are also some differences among courts,[147] so you should be sure you look at your circuit's statements about the personal involvement requirement.

A recent Supreme Court decision may have significantly changed supervisory liability law. The Court said in *Ashcroft v. Iqbal*: "In a § 1983 suit or a *Bivens* action—where masters do not answer for the torts of their servants—the term 'supervisory liability' is a misnomer. Absent vicarious liability, each Government official, his or her title notwithstanding, is only liable for his or her own misconduct."[148] The plaintiff in that case alleged that he had been subject to intentional discrimination based on his race, religion, and nationality, and the Court went on to say that the plaintiff would have to show that the high-ranking officials that he sued intentionally discriminated against him, not just that they knew somebody else was doing it. We think this means that in addition to showing that a defendant was personally involved in the sense of helping to cause a civil rights violation, you may also have to show that the defendant acted intentionally, or with deliberate indifference, or with

---

781, 786 (2d Cir. 1984) (holding corrections and parole commissioners could be named as parties "at least for purposes of discovery aimed at identifying those of their subordinates who are personally responsible for the departmental actions complained of"). *See* Ch. 10, § K.2, n.414. There may be some dispute about this practice, since a recent Supreme Court decision seems to require more specific pleading against supervisors and also emphasizes the protection of high-level government officials from the burden of discovery. Ashcroft v. Iqbal, ___ U.S. ___, 129 S. Ct. 1937, 1950 (2009). (This decision is discussed later in this section.) *But see* Harvey v. LaValley, 2009 WL 5219027, *3 (N.D.N.Y., Dec. 31, 2009) (restating rule permitting discovery after *Iqbal*).

[144]Ruiz Rivera v. Riley, 209 F.3d 24, 28 (1st Cir. 2000); Cronn v. Buffington, 150 F.3d 538, 544 (5th Cir. 1998); Risley v. Hawk, 108 F.3d 1396, 1396–97 (D.C. Cir. 1997); Terrell v. Brewer, 935 F.2d 1015, 1018 (9th Cir. 1991) and cases cited; *see* § B.2 of this chapter concerning such actions.

[145]Colon v. Coughlin, 58 F.3d 865, 873 (2d Cir.1995). Some lower courts have held that after *Ashcroft v. Iqbal, supra,* only the first and third categories can still be used to establish supervisory liability. *See* Bellamy v. Mount Vernon Hosp., 2009 WL 1835939, *6 (S.D.N.Y., June 26, 2009). Other decisions, however, have continued to cite the *Colon v. Coughlin* holding as setting the standard for supervisory liability after *Iqbal. See* Dowdy v. Hercules, 2010 WL 169624, *3, *6 (E.D.N.Y., Jan. 15, 2010); Jean v. Barber, 2010 WL 144396, *3 & n.10 (N.D.N.Y., Jan. 11, 2010); Harvey v. LaValley, 2009 WL 5219027, *3 & n.10 (N.D.N.Y., Dec. 31, 2009); Garcia v. Watts, 2009 WL 2777085, *12–19 (S.D.N.Y., Sept. 1, 2009). Still others have said that *Iqbal*'s effect on supervisory liability is limited to discrimination claims, since *Iqbal* does say that intent to discriminate must be shown to hold supervisors liable. *See* Sash v. U.S., 674 F.Supp.2d 531, 544 (S.D.N.Y. 2009) ("Where the constitutional claim does not require a showing of discriminatory intent, but instead relies on the unreasonable conduct or deliberate indifference standards of the Fourth and Eighth Amendments, the personal involvement analysis set forth in *Colon v. Coughlin* may still apply."); Jackson v. Goord, 664 F. Supp.2d 307, 324 & n.7 (S.D.N.Y., Sept. 21, 2009) (holding *Colon* standard is unaffected by *Iqbal* in deliberate indifference cases). The Second Circuit has not ruled on the question as of early 2010.

[146]*See, e.g.,* Valdes v. Crosby, 450 F.3d 1231, 1237 (11th Cir. 2006) (necessary causal connection can be shown when "(1) a 'history of widespread abuse' puts the responsible supervisor on notice of the need to correct the alleged deprivation, and he or she fails to do so; 2) a supervisor's custom or policy results in deliberate indifference to constitutional rights; or 3) facts support an inference that the supervisor directed subordinates to act unlawfully or knew that subordinates would act unlawfully and failed to stop them from doing so."), *cert. dismissed,* 549 U.S. 1249 (2007); Hildebrandt v. Illinois Dep't of Natural Resources, 347 F.3d 1014, 1039 (7th Cir. 2003) ("[a]n official satisfies the personal responsibility requirement of section 1983 . . . if the conduct causing the constitutional deprivation occurs at [his] direction or with [his] knowledge and consent. That is, he must know about the conduct and facilitate it, approve it, condone it, or turn a blind eye. In short, some causal connection or affirmative link between the action complained about and the official sued is necessary for § 1983 recovery." (citation omitted)).

[147]As indicated, the Second Circuit in *Colon* said that defendants can be liable if they are grossly negligent in supervising subordinates. Most other courts have said that deliberate indifference is required. *See, e.g.,* Doe v. City of Roseville, 296 F.3d 431, 439 (6th Cir. 2002); Cozzo v. Tangipahoa Parish Council-President Gov't, 279 F.3d 273, 286–87 (5th Cir. 2001); Doe v. Gooden, 214 F.3d 952, 955 (8th Cir. 2000).

[148]Ashcroft v. Iqbal, ___ U.S. ___, 129 S. Ct. 1937, 1949 (2009). The analogy in an Eighth Amendment case would be that supervisory defendants would always have to be shown to have been deliberately indifferent, *i.e.,* to have had actual knowledge of a serious risk and to have failed to act reasonably to avert it. *See* Chao v. Ballista, 630 F.Supp.2d 170, 178 (D.Mass. 2009) ("Notably, the state of mind required to make out a supervisory claim under the Eighth Amendment—i.e., deliberate indifference—requires less than the discriminatory purpose or intent that *Iqbal* was required to allege in his suit against Ashcroft and Mueller."); *accord,* Jackson v. Goord, 664 F.Supp.2d at 324 & n.7; Sash v. U.S.,2009 WL 4824669, *11. *See* Ch. 2, § A.2. *Iqbal* is also discussed in Ch. 10, § B.1, concerning pleading.

malicious and sadistic intent, depending on the requirement of the particular legal claim.[149] Another way of saying this is that you probably have to plead and prove all the elements of the legal claim against supervisory defendants, as you do with line staff, in all cases. You can certainly expect defense lawyers to make this argument, or to argue more broadly that almost all liability of supervisors has been eliminated.

You will have to see how *Iqbal* is interpreted in your federal circuit and in later Supreme Court cases to know whether and how much the law of supervisory liability has been altered. As we update this point in February, 2010, it is too early to know for certain.[150] In the next several sections,

we present the existing law, with warnings where appropriate about the possible effect of *Iqbal*.

We will discuss the personal involvement requirement in more detail in the next several sections.

1) *Direct Participation* Defendants who directly participate in constitutional violations may be held liable for their own actions.[151] However, lower level staff who were directly involved have sometimes been held not liable because they were only following orders or carrying out their supervisors' policies.[152] A direct participant in a violation must know the facts that make the conduct illegal in order to be held liable for it.[153]

2) *Indirect Participation* A defendant may be held liable "if the defendant set in motion a series of events" that she knew or reasonably should have known would cause a constitutional violation, even if others actually performed the violation.[154]

---

[149]For example, most Eighth Amendment claims of cruel and unusual punishment require a plaintiff to prove that defendants who are directly involved in the violation are deliberately indifferent. In use of force cases, defendants who directly use force must be shown to have acted maliciously and sadistically. *See* Ch. 2, §§ A.2, G.2.a.1.

[150]Some lower court decisions assume that nothing much has changed. For example, one court applying *Iqbal* reasserted its pre-*Iqbal* formula for supervisory liability, stating:

> Supervisors can be held liable for the actions of their subordinates (1) for setting in motion a series of acts by others, or knowingly refusing to terminate a series of acts by others, which they knew or reasonably should have known would cause others to inflict constitutional injury; (2) for culpable action or inaction in training, supervision, or control of subordinates; (3) for acquiescence in the constitutional deprivation by subordinates; or (4) for conduct that shows a "reckless or callous indifference to the rights of others."

Al-Kidd v. Ashcroft, 580 F.3d 949, 964-65 (9th Cir. 2009). *Accord*, Garvey v. Martinez, 2010 WL 569852, * 6-8 (M.D.Pa., February 1, 2010) (citing pre-*Iqbal* supervisory liability standards); Wathen v. Schriro, 2009 WL 2632719, *1 (D.Ariz., Aug. 25, 2009) (interpreting *Iqbal* as consistent with earlier decisions finding liability where supervisors "knew of the violations and failed to act to prevent them," or for "their own culpable action or inaction in the training, supervision, or control of subordinates" (citations omitted)); Ray v. Caruso, 2009 WL 2230935, *3 (E.D.Mich., July 22, 2009) ("To state a claim against a supervisory official, the civil rights complainant must allege that the supervisory official personally participated in the constitutional deprivation or that the supervisory official was aware of widespread abuses and, with deliberate indifference to the inmate's constitutional rights, failed to take action to prevent further misconduct.").

Other courts have concluded that the law of supervisory liability has been altered. *See, e.g.*, Sanchez v. Pereira-Castillo, 590 F.3d 31, 49 (1st Cir. 2009) (the former standard for claim of supervisory liability, "'the-defendant-unlawfuly-harmed-me' allegation", was changed by *Iqbal*); Lopez-Jimenez v. Pereira, 2010 WL 500407, *4 (D.P.R., February 3, 2010) (under *Iqbal*, allegations of failure to "adequately deploy[] staff at the correctional institutions to oversee compliance with constitutional standards, implement practices and procedures which would ensure the physical safety of the deceased, and monitor[] the observance of such practices and procedures" did not state a claim for supervisory liability); *see also* Parrish v. Ball, 594 F.3d 993, 1001 n.1 (8th Cir. 2010) (". . . *Iqbal*

may further restrict the incidents in which the 'failure to supervise' will result in liability.").

Courts' different conclusions about the effect of *Iqbal* on the Second Circuit *Colon v. Coughlin* supervisory liability standard are discussed in n.145, above.

[151]*See, e.g.*, Cortes-Quinones v. Jiminez-Nettleship, 842 F.2d 556, 559–61 (1st Cir. 1988) (holding Director of Penal Institutions, Corrections Administrator and jail superintendent liable for their roles in placing a mentally ill inmate in general population where there was no psychiatric care); McClary v. Coughlin, 87 F. Supp. 2d 205, 215 (W.D.N.Y. 2000) (members of an Administrative Segregation Review Committee who engaged in sham reviews could be held liable, even though the ultimate decision was the Superintendent's. "Personal involvement does not hinge on who has the ultimate authority. . . . Rather, the proper focus is the defendant's direct participation in, and connection to, the constitutional deprivation."), *aff'd*, 237 F.3d 185 (2d Cir. 2001); Martin v. Lane, 766 F. Supp. 641, 649–50 (N.D. Ill. 1991) (an allegation that the warden ordered a lockdown and the departmental director approved it sufficiently alleged their personal involvement in the resulting constitutional deprivations).

[152]*See* cases cited in § B.4.a(2) of this chapter, nn.157–158.

[153]Provost v. City of Newburgh, 262 F.3d 146, 154–55 (2d Cir. 2001). For example, the court said, a police officer who arrests someone pursuant to a warrant that appears valid, but was in fact obtained through perjury by other officers, cannot be held liable if he didn't know about the perjury.

[154]Conner v. Reinhard, 847 F.2d 384, 397 (7th Cir. 1988); *accord*, Bruner v. Baker, 506 F.3d 1021, 1026 (10th Cir. 2007); Valdes v. Crosby, 450 F.3d 1231, 1239–43 (11th Cir. 2006) (warden could be held liable for beating of prisoner based on evidence he was placed on notice of a history of widespread abuse but weakened protective measures, *e.g.* ending the videotaping of cell extractions), *cert. dismissed*, 549 U.S. 1249 (2007); Wulf v. City of Wichita, 883 F.2d 842, 864 (10th Cir. 1989) (holding that personal liability under 1983 can be imputed if it can be shown that defendant caused the alleged violations of plaintiff's rights); Greason v. Kemp, 891 F.2d 829, 836 (11th Cir. 1990) (". . .[A] supervisor can be held liable under section 1983 when a reasonable person in the supervisor's position would have known that his conduct infringed the constitutional rights of the plaintiff, . . . and his conduct was

(This principle may be affected by the recent decision, discussed above, in *Ashcroft v. Iqbal*.[155]) Officials who set policy, write regulations, or give orders may be liable even if they are not directly involved in enforcing them against you.[156]

_____

causally related to the constitutional violation committed by his subordinate. . . ." (footnote and citations omitted)); *cf.* Hildebrandt v. Illinois Dep't of Natural Res., 347 F.3d 1014, 1040 (7th Cir. 2003) (holding that evidence of defendant's attendance and active participation in meeting where § 1983 violation allegedly occurred did not create triable issue of fact as to personal involvement).

[155] ___ U.S. ___, 129 S. Ct. 1937 (2009). This case may require plaintiffs to show that indirectly involved defendants such as supervisors actually violated the law themselves, as opposed to just knowing or being in a position where they should know that their actions would cause a violation. *Compare* Argueta v. U.S. Immigration and Customs Enforcement, 2010 WL 398839, *8 (D.N.J., Jan 27, 2010) (supervisors who "wrote the policy, implemented it, and monitored its progress" could be held liable under *Iqbal*) *with* Whitten v. Blaisdell, 2010 WL 376903, 5 (D.N.H.), Jan. 22, 2010) (supervisor is not liable "if he or she is alleged merely to have been present for, or otherwise obtains knowledge of, the wrongdoing of a subordinate, or if the supervisor promulgated a policy that does not direct or condone the wrongful conduct of subordinates." (citation omitted)). *See* n.148, above, for further explanation of this point.

[156] Brock v. Wright, 315 F.3d 158, 165–66 (2d Cir. 2003) (Chief Medical Officer could be held liable for policy denying treatment for painful keloid scars.); Redman v. County of San Diego, 942 F.2d 1435, 1446–49 (9th Cir. 1991) (en banc) (Sheriff who tolerated overcrowding and approved a dangerous classification policy could be held liable even though he did not know of the specific danger to the plaintiff; captain who wrote the policy could also be liable); Boswell v. Sherburne County, 849 F.2d 1117, 1123 (10th Cir. 1988) (sheriff and chief jailer could be held liable for policy of minimizing medical costs); Roland v. Johnson, 856 F.2d 764, 770 (6th Cir. 1988) (Director and Warden could be liable based on policy of discouraging reports of rape); Martin v. Sargent, 780 F.2d 1334, 1338 (8th Cir. 1985) ("A prison warden can be held liable for policy decisions which create unconstitutional conditions."); James. v. Aidala, 389 F. Supp. 2d 451, 453 (W.D.N.Y. 2005) (allegation that Commisioner and Director of Special Housing created policy or custom of affirming unconstitutional disciplinary findngs but then reversing them if the prisoner goes to court stated a claim against those defendants); Johnson v. Pearson, 316 F. Supp. 2d 307, 317–18 (E.D.Va. 2004) (officials responsible for policy of double-celling prisoners with smokers regardless of health risks could be liable); Barrett v. Coplan, 292 F. Supp. 2d 281, 286–87 (D.N.H. 2003) (allegation that defendants acted pursuant to a statewide policy sufficiently pled a claim against the Commissioner of Corrections); Sulton v. Wright, 265 F. Supp. 2d 292, 300–01 (S.D.N.Y. 2003) (chief medical officer of the prison system could be liable where he "adopted a utilization review mechanism for specialist consultation and surgery approval that used a contractual vendor whose goal, in practice, was to limit care as much as possible"); Williams v. Coughlin, 875 F. Supp. 1004, 1014 (W.D.N.Y. 1995) (holding superintendent could be liable for approving policy withholding food to prisoners who failed to return used trays); Hill v. Koon, 732 F. Supp. 1076, 1084 (D.Nev. 1990) (associate warden was liable for ordering unlawful digital rectal searches); Langley v. Coughlin, 709 F. Supp. 482, 485–86 (S.D.N.Y. 1989) (unit chief who established

In fact, when prison employees act pursuant to orders, policy or regulation, the order-giver or policymaker may be the only person who can be held liable.[157] (Other decisions say that "following orders" is not an excuse for violating the law.[158] In practice, it probably depends on what the orders are and how clear it should have been that they were unlawful.)

_____

procedures for mental health unit could be held liable), *appeal dismissed*, 888 F.2d 252 (2d Cir. 1989); Reutcke v. Dahm, 707 F. Supp. 1121, 1134 (D.Neb. 1988) (prison warden was "ultimately responsible" for an unconstitutional court access system; a subordinate who had "input" but no final authority over the policy was not liable); Hearn v. Morris, 526 F. Supp. 267, 268 n.3 (E.D.Cal. 1981) (warden who promulgated or acquiesced in unlawful correspondence rule could be held liable); *see* Jeffers v. Gomez, 267 F.3d 895, 910 (9th Cir. 2001) ("Defendants are entitled to qualified immunity for claims arising out of their policy decisions unless the policy is 'so deficient that the policy itself is a repudiation of constitutional rights and is the moving force of the constitutional violation.'").

[157] Jacobs v. West Feliciana Sheriff's Dep't, 228 F.3d 388, 398 (5th Cir. 2000) (inexperienced officer could not be held liable for placing suicidal prisoner in unsafe cell; since "the orders he received from his two superiors were not facially outrageous, Rabalais acted reasonably in following them" and could not be found deliberately indifferent); Redman v. County of San Diego, 942 F.2d at 1449 (jail lieutenant who only carried out an unconstitutional classification policy could not be held liable); Wanger v. Bonner 621 F.2d 675, 683 (5th Cir. 1980) (upholding jury verdict against sheriff who adopted policies, but exonerating deputies who carried them out); Hill v. Koon, 732 F. Supp. at 1084 (lower level correctional personnel were not liable for performing unlawful rectal searches ordered by an associate warden); Smallwood v. Renfro, 708 F. Supp. 182, 189–90 (N.D. Ill. 1989) (sergeant could not be held liable for obeying lieutenant's direct order not to send the plaintiff to the hospital); Salahuddin v. Harris, 684 F.Supp 1224, 1228 (S.D.N.Y. 1988) (defendant who merely filled out disciplinary forms at someone else's direction was not liable); *see* Lawrence v. Bowersox, 297 F.3d 727, 733 (8th Cir. 2002) (upholding verdict for officer who followed orders to use chemical agents without knowing what had happened to justify it and did not act maliciously and sadistically).

[158] Kyle v. Holina, 2009 WL 1867671, *2 (W.D.Wis., June 29, 2009) ("Generally, there is no 'just following orders' defense in cases brought under 42 U.S.C. § 1983."); Dugas v. Jefferson County, 931 F. Supp. 1315, 1319 (E.D.Tex. 1996) (". . . [I]t appears long established that public officers are not shielded from civil liability for illegal acts simply because they act upon direction of policy-making superiors."), *aff'd*, 127 F.3d 33 (5th Cir. 1997); Wahad v. F.B.I., 813 F. Supp. 224, 230 (S.D.N.Y. 1993) ("The fact that one violates the constitutional rights of another because of the orders of superiors will not allow that person to avoid liability for those violations."); *see* Ramirez v. Butte-Silver Bow County, 283 F.3d 985, 990 (9th Cir. 2002) (officers leading a team executing a warrant must satisfy themselves that the warrant is valid and they understand its limits; line officers may take their supervisors' word for it).

Sometimes defendants argue that following orders entitles them to qualified immunity. Decisions on this point are mixed. *See* § L.4 of this chapter, nn.838–841.

A policy need not be formal or written to serve as the basis for liability.[159] "Tacit authorization" may be sufficient,[160] and failure to take remedial action may also be evidence of a policy.[161]

Proper policies may provide a defense for supervisory officials. If they give orders or establish policies that, if followed, would prevent constitutional violations, they are not liable if their subordinates violate the orders or policy,[162] except in those rare instances when it is shown that the

violation results from the supervisors' failure to train or supervise.[163]

3) Failure to Act Prison personnel may be held liable for their failure to act if it results in a constitutional violation.[164] Officers or supervisors can be held liable if they are present but fail to intervene when a prisoner is subjected to brutality by staff or assault by other inmates.[165] Officials or employees who know, or reasonably should know,[166] that a prisoner is being treated unconstitutionally may be held liable if they fail to do anything about it.[167] (This kind of liability may be affected by the recent Supreme Court decision in *Ashcroft v. Iqbal*, which may require that you show that a defendant who failed to act on something they knew or should have known would result in a violation of rights did so in a manner that itself violated the Constitution—*i.e.*, that the defendant had discriminatory intent in a discrimination case, or was deliberately indifferent in an Eighth Amendment case.[168])

Prison officials can be informed sufficiently to hold them liable in several ways. One is failure to act on a "report or appeal" within the prison system,[169] including

---

[159]Leach v. Shelby County Sheriff, 891 F.2d 1241, 1246 (6th Cir. 1989) (evidence that Sheriff "implicitly authorized, approved, or knowingly acquiesced" in his subordinates' actions could support his liability); Williams v. Wilkinson, 132 F. Supp. 2d 601, 610 (S.D.Ohio 2001) (entering injunction against warden based on continuation of an unwritten policy); *see* Ruiz v. Estelle, 679 F.2d 1115, 1154–55 (5th Cir. 1982) (systemwide injunction against prison system's managers could be entered based on "prevalent" unlawful practices). The question of what qualifies as a policy comes up a lot in cases involving city and county governments, which are discussed in § B.4.b of this chapter, below.

[160]Fruit v. Norris, 905 F.2d 1147, 1151 (8th Cir. 1990); Leach v. Shelby County Sheriff, 891 F.2d 1241, 1246 (6th Cir. 1989) (holding that a Sheriff who "implicitly authorized, approved, or knowingly acquiesced" in his subordinates' actions could be held liable). *But see* Whitten v. Blaisdell, 2010 WL 376903, *5 (D.N.H., Jan. 22, 2010) (supervisor is not liable "if he or she is alleged merely to have been present for, or otherwise obtains knowledge of, the wrongdoing of a subordinate, or if the supervisor promulgated a policy that does not direct or condone the wrongful conduct of subordinates". (citation omitted)).

The Supreme Court recently held that knowledge and acquiescence in subordinates' discriminatory behavior is not enough to hold supervisors liable when the claim is for intentional discrimination. Ashcroft v. Iqbal, ___ U.S. ___, 129 S. Ct. 1937, 1949 (2009). We do not think that this holding applies to claims of deliberate indifference, the standard that governs most prisoner claims, since showing that a defendant knows of a serious risk and fails to take reasonable action to correct it does show deliberate indifference. *See* Ch. 2, § A.2.

[161]Gomez v. Vernon, 255 F.3d 1118, 1127 (9th Cir. 2001) ("The Department's failure to investigate or correct constitutional violations supports the district court's finding that there was a policy or custom that led to violation of the inmates' rights."); Grandstaff v. City of Borger, Texas, 767 F.2d 161, 171 (5th Cir.1985) ("[S]ubsequent acceptance of dangerous recklessness by policymaker tends to prove his preexisting disposition and policy.").

[162]Combs v. Wilkinson, 315 F.3d 548, 558 (6th Cir. 2002) (holding Director who approved a tactical plan that was not unconstitutional could not be held liable for unauthorized beatings when plan was implemented); Buffington v. Baltimore County, Md., 913 F.2d 113, 122–23 (4th Cir. 1990) (en banc) (police chief was not liable for jail suicide that resulted from an officer's violation of the suicide prevention policy); Fisher v. Washington Area Metropolitan Area Transit Authority, 690 F.2d 1133, 1143 (4th Cir. 1982); Vasquez v. Coughlin, 726 F. Supp. 466, 473–74 (S.D.N.Y. 1989) (supervisory defendants were not liable for due process denials in disciplinary hearing when there were policies in place intended to prevent such denials); Heine v. Receiving Area Personnel, 711 F. Supp. 178, 186–87 (D. Del. 1989) (warden was

not liable for inmate assault because he had drafted and tried to enforce proper procedures that officers violated).

[163]*See* Goka v. Bobbitt, 862 F.2d 646, 651–52 (7th Cir. 1988) (supervisors could be held liable for knowing failure to enforce prison tool control policy).

[164]Estelle v. Gamble, 429 U.S. 97, 106, 97 S. Ct. 285 (1976) (medical care claims may be based on "acts or omissions"); Davis v. Rennie, 264 F.3d 86, 114 (1st Cir. 2001); Alexander v. Perrill, 916 F.2d 1392, 1395 (9th Cir. 1990) (prison officials "can't just sit on your duff and not do anything" to prevent violations of rights); Lewis v. Mitchell, 416 F. Supp. 2d 935, 945 (S.D. Cal. 2005) (a person may be liable under § 1983 if he "omits to perform an act which he is legally required to do that causes the deprivation of which [the plaintiff complains]." (quoting Johnson v. Duffy, 588 F.2d 740, 743 (9th Cir.1978)).

[165]*See* Ch. 2, § G.1.e, concerning inmate–inmate assaults, and § G.2.d, concerning misuse of force by staff.

[166]Some courts have rejected "should know" as a basis for § 1983 liability and have held that supervisory liability must be based on actual knowledge; this point is discussed further at the end of this section.

[167]Greason v. Kemp, 891 F.2d 829, 839–40 (11th Cir. 1990) (warden who knew or should have known of inadequate psychiatric staffing could be held liable); Johnson v. Pearson, 316 F. Supp. 2d 307, 317–18 (E.D.Va. 2004) (officials who failed to act on second-hand smoke complaint could be held liable).

[168]Ashcroft v. Iqbal, ___ U.S. ___, 129 S. Ct. 1937 (2009). This case is discussed in § B.4.a of this chapter, above.

[169]Wright v. Smith, 21 F.3d 496, 502 (2d Cir. 1994) (quoting Williams v. Smith, 781 F.2d 319, 323–24 (2d Cir. 1986)); *see* Fruit v. Norris, 905 F.2d 1147, 1151 (8th Cir. 1990) (warden could be held liable for prisoners' exposure to human waste at prison job where he rejected their disciplinary appeals raising lack of protective clothing); Smith v. Rowe, 761 F.2d 360, 369 (7th Cir. 1985) (Director of Corrections held liable for his failure to remedy improper segregation of prisoner after receiving report from staff member); Marcotte v. Monroe Corrections Complex, 394 F. Supp. 2d 1289, 1297–98 (W.D.Wash. 2005) (holding that adverse health department

a grievance.[170] Other, non-official sources of information may also support liability if not acted upon.[171] This can

include complaints from prisoners. There are some cases that state broadly that "allegations that an official ignored a prisoner's letter are insufficient to establish liability."[172] However, a number of decisions have held that prisoners' letters and other complaints could be sufficient to give notice of constitutional violations.[173] In our view the right approach is that a prisoner's letters may support liability if "the communication, in its content and manner of transmission, gave the prison official sufficient notice to alert him or her" to a violation of law.[174] Of course, prison officials cannot be held liable for failing to act on a complaint, grievance, etc., unless they receive it at a time when they can do something about

---

reports could support liability of superintendent and medical director), *reconsideration denied*, 2005 WL 2978651 (W.D.Wash., Nov. 7, 2005); Jama v. U.S. Immigration and Naturalization Service, 343 F. Supp. 2d 338, 381 (D.N.J. 2004) (facility administrators could be held liable for conditions based on inmate complaints, guards' reports, INS complaints, inmate and staff meetings); Amaker v. Hakes, 919 F. Supp. 127, 131–32 (W.D.N.Y. 1996) (holding that information coming to the Commissioner through the prison grievance process may support liability); Roucchio v. Coughlin, 923 F. Supp. 360, 379 (S.D.N.Y. 1996) (holding that service of state court lawsuit on Commissioner could support liability); Madrid v. Gomez, 889 F. Supp. 1146, 1198 (N.D.Cal. 1995) (internal use of force reports to supervisors supported their liability for excessive force); Gabai v. Jacoby, 800 F. Supp. 1149, 1156 (S.D.N.Y. 1992) (holding allegation that a supervisor who reviewed a deficient disciplinary proceeding on appeal and did not overturn it sufficiently pled personal involvement); Langley v. Coughlin, 709 F. Supp. 482, 486 (S.D.N.Y.) (holding Commissioner could be held liable based on the complaint in the case and on a Correctional Association report), *appeal dismissed*, 888 F.2d 252 (2d Cir. 1989).

[170]Johnson v. Pearson, 316 F. Supp. 2d 307, 317–18, 321 n.8 (E.D.Va. 2004); Verser v. Elyea, 113 F. Supp. 2d 1211, 1215–16 (N.D.Ill. 2000); Mason v. Schriro, 45 F. Supp. 2d 709, 712 (W.D.Mo. 1999); McPherson v. Coombe, 29 F. Supp. 2d 141, 145 (W.D.N.Y. 1998); Amaker v. Hakes, 919 F. Supp. 127 (W.D.N.Y. 1996). *But see* Johnson v. Snyder, 444 F.3d 579, 584 (7th Cir. 2006) (holding Director could not be held liable where he did not review grievance appeals).

There is some question under what circumstances rejecting a grievance can support liability for the violation that the grievance is about. *See* McKenna v. Wright, 386 F.3d 432, 437–38 (2d Cir. 2004) (questioning whether merely adjudicating a grievance could make one liable for the conduct complained of, but noting that the deputy superintendent who was in charge of the prison medical program could be held liable where he rejected a grievance concerning medical care *and* took no action to correct the problem). The question is always whether a particular defendant *caused* the violation of rights. If a defendant is informed of a violation through a grievance, has the authority to correct it, and does not do so, then the defendant may be liable. However, low-level grievance staff who do not have authority to overturn prison policies cannot be held liable for failing to do so. Shidler v. Moore, 409 F. Supp. 1060, 1068 (N.D.Ind. 2006); Johnson v. Pearson, 316 F. Supp. 2d 307, 314 (E.D.Va. 2004). Grievance staff are also not liable for dismissing grievances pursuant to the grievance rules they are charged with enforcing. Burks v. Raemisch, 555 F.3d 592, 594–95 (7th Cir. 2009). *Cf.* George v. Smith, 507 F.3d 605, 609 (7th Cir. 2007) (grievance personnel are not entitled to absolute immunity).

[171]Colon v. Coughlin, 58 F.3d 865, 873 (2d Cir. 1995); Wright v. Smith, 21 F.3d 496, 501 (2d Cir. 1994) (both citing "failing to act on information indicating that unconstitutional practices are taking place" as a basis for liability separate from non-response to a "report or appeal"); Al-Jundi v. Mancusi, 926 F.2d 235, 240 (2d Cir. 1991) (holding that supervisor who either knew of staff brutality or purposefully avoided finding out about it could be held liable); Walker v. Godinez, 912 F. Supp. 307, 312–13 (N.D.Ill. 1993) (holding allegation that warden and housing unit supervisor were told of staff misconduct and did nothing could support claim

against them); Hall v. Artuz, 954 F. Supp. 90, 95 (S.D.N.Y. 1997) (holding letter from Legal Aid Society could put prison superintendent and regional health services administrator on sufficient notice).

[172]*See, e.g.*, Watson v. McGinnis, 964 F. Supp. 127, 130 (S.D.N.Y. 1997); *accord*, Liner v. Goord, 310 F. Supp. 2d 550, 555 (W.D.N.Y. 2004).

[173]Jett v. Penner, 439 F.3d 1091, 1098 (9th Cir. 2006) (Prison administrators "are liable for deliberate indifference when they knowingly fail to respond to an inmate's requests for help."); Richardson v. Goord, 347 F.3d 431, 435 (2d Cir. 2003) (per curiam) (prisoner's claim that he wrote to the Commissioner about his medication problems raised a factual issue of the Commissioner's deliberate indifference); Reed v. McBride, 178 F.3d 849, 854 (7th Cir. 1999) ("'[A] prison official's knowledge of prison conditions learned from an inmate's communication can . . . require the officer to exercise his authority and to take the needed action to investigate, and if necessary, to rectify the offending condition.'" (quoting Vance v. Peters, 97 F.3d 987, 993 (7th Cir. 1996)); Gentry v. Duckworth, 65 F.3d 555, 561 (7th Cir. 1995); Ziemba v. Thomas, 390 F. Supp. 2d 136, 151–52 (D.Conn. 2005) (communications from prisoner and his mother to warden could support warden's liability); Smith v. Michigan, 256 F. Supp. 2d 704, 710–11 (E.D.Mich. 2003) (prisoner's complaints of lack of medical care could support officials' liability); Lavender v. Lampert, 242 F. Supp. 2d 821, 840–41 (D.Or. 2002) (communications from prisoner to Superintendent and health services manager could support their liability); Merritt v. Hawk, 153 F. Supp. 2d 1216, 1227–28 (D.Colo. 2001) (plaintiff's allegations that he had informed various supervisory officials about his problems sufficiently pled their personal involvement); Oladipupo v. Austin, 104 F. Supp. 2d 654, 661–62 (W.D.La. 2000); Alexander v. Sheahan, 998 F. Supp. 899, 901 (N.D.Ill. 1998); Barry v. Ratelle, 985 F. Supp. 1235, 1239 (S.D.Cal. 1997) (holding prisoner's letters to prison medical director sufficient to allege liability); Mandala v. Coughlin, 920 F. Supp. 342, 351 (E.D.N.Y. 1996); Pacheco v. Commisse, 897 F. Supp. 671, 678 (N.D.N.Y. 1995); Boone v. Elrod, 706 F. Supp. 636, 638 (N.D.Ill. 1989) (holding prisoner's letters sufficient); Strachan v. Ashe, 548 F. Supp. 1193, 1204 (D.Mass. 1982) (holding letter from plaintiff's attorney sufficient). *But see* Johnson v. Snyder, 444 F.3d 579, 584 (7th Cir. 2006) (Director could not be liable based on prisoner letters without evidence that he personally read them).

[174]Vance v. Peters, 97 F.3d 987, 993 (7th Cir. 1996); *see* Colon v. Coughlin, 58 F.3d at 873 ("The contents of the letter are not specified; we do not know, therefore, whether the letter was one that reasonably should have prompted [defendant] to investigate").

it; they can't become liable for something that is over before they hear about it.[175]

None of this means that an official is automatically liable whenever you allege that your rights are being violated—especially higher level officials such as wardens and commisioners, who may receive dozens or hundreds of complaints each month. A supervisory official who establishes and follows a procedure for others to address allegations of constitutional violation may have taken sufficient action not to be deemed a cause of the violation.[176]

More broadly, correctional supervisors may be held liable for failing to correct unconstitutional conditions or practices within their areas of authority if they knew or should have known about them,[177] though isolated occurrences are

not sufficient to put officials on notice of unconstitutional conditions or practices.[178] Lower level prison staff may be held liable for known or obvious conditions in the areas that they supervise.[179] (As noted earlier, under a recent Supreme Court decision, you may need to show that the defendant not only knew about the condition, but that her failure to act itself violated the Constitution.[180])

Officials may be held liable for failure to make policy or to take action to prevent predictable violations of rights within their areas of responsibility.[181] If a supervisor has

---

[175]George v. Smith, 507 F.3d 605, 609 (7th Cir. 2007).

[176]High-ranking officials can't be expected to intervene personally in response to every inmate letter; "referring the matter for further investigation or taking similar administrative steps" was "a reasonable discharge of their duty to protect the inmates in their care." Johnson v. Johnson, 385 F.3d 503, 526 (5th Cir. 2004); *see* Vaughn v. Greene County, Ark., 438 F.3d 845, 851 (8th Cir. 2006) (Sheriff's practice of delegating reading mail and responding to communications about prisoners was not deliberate indifference); Sealey v. Giltner, 116 F.3d 47, 51 (2d Cir. 1997) (holding a prisoner's letter to Commissioner could not support Commissioner's liability where he had referred it to the official directly concerned for decision); Sample v. Diecks, 885 F.2d 1099, 1110 (3d Cir. 1989) (holding warden was not liable for failure to release prisoner on time since he had procedures in place calling for other staff members to resolve release date issues).

[177]Danley v. Allen, 540 F.3d 1298, 1315 (11th Cir. 2008) (allegations that defendants, through "force reports and similar documents, inmate complaints, jailer complaints, attorney complaints, judicial officer complaints, and personal observation" knew that jailers "regularly used pepper spray excessively as a means of punishment and not for legitimate reasons" adequately stated supervisory liability claim); Valdes v. Crosby, 450 F.3d 1231, 1244 (11th Cir. 2006) (evidence that warden was placed on notice of a history of widespread abuse presented a jury question as to his liability for a prisoner's beating), *cert. dismissed*, 549 U.S. 1249 (2007); Turner v. City of Taylor, 412 F.3d 629, 642 (6th Cir. 2005) (jail shift supervisors could be liable for failure to produce arrestee in court for four days); Johnson v. Johnson, 385 F.3d 503, 526–27 (5th Cir. 2004) (members of a Classification Committee who did nothing in response to reports that a prisoner was being sexually assaulted could be found liable); Miller v. King, 384 F.3d 1248, 1263 (11th Cir. 2004) (prison supervisor can be liable when he knows prison medical staff, guards, or other prison officials are unlawfully delaying or denying an inmate's medical care, and the prison supervisor fails to correct the unlawful activity), *vacated and superseded on other grounds*, 449 F.3d 1149 (11th Cir. 2006); Taylor v. Michigan Dep't of Corrections, 69 F.3d 76, 81 (6th Cir. 1995) (warden could be liable for rape of prisoner based on failure to act on his knowledge of a breakdown in classification procedures and of the vulnerability of small, young prisoners as a class); Black v. Lane, 22 F.3d 1395, 1401 (7th Cir. 1994) (failure to act on conciliation agreement with Department of Justice concerning racial discrimination supported liability of Director of Corrections); LaMarca v. Turner, 995 F.2d 1526, 1538 (11th Cir. 1993)

(superintendent could be held liable for pattern of assault he knew about and was in a position to remedy); Howard v. Adkison, 887 F.2d 134, 138 (8th Cir. 1989) (housing unit supervisors could be held liable for protracted unsanitary conditions); Santiago v. Miles, 774 F. Supp. 775, 790–91 (W.D.N.Y. 1991) (holding that superintendent and deputy superintendent of prison had actual or constructive notice of race discrimination between white and black prisoners in housing, job assignments, and discipline, but failed to adequately eliminate such violations; therefore, they had sufficient personal involvement to be held liable); *see* Kitt v. Ferguson, 750 F. Supp. 1014, 1019 (D.Neb. 1990) ("a superintendent or warden, with policy-making authority, can be held liable for operating a prison with unsanitary and inhumane conditions"), *aff'd*, 950 F.2d 725 (8th Cir. 1991).

[178]Maldonado-Denis v. Castillo-Rodriguez, 23 F.3d 576, 582 (1st Cir. 1994); Brown v. Crawford, 906 F.2d 667, 671 (11th Cir. 1990) ("history of widespread abuse" is necessary to place supervisors on notice of need for action); Ross v. Reed, 719 F.2d 689, 699 (4th Cir. 1983) (prison officials could not be held liable for conditions that were "sporadic").

[179]Spencer v. Bouchard, 449 F.3d 721, 729–30 (6th Cir. 2006) (captain and lieutenant could be held liable for failing to act to correct cold and wet conditions in area they supervised); Clark-Murphy v. Foreback, 439 F.3d 280, 289 (6th Cir. 2006) (staff on housing unit where prisoner was locked into his cell with water turned off during heat alert, and died of thirst, could be liable); Turner v. City of Taylor, 412 F.3d 629, 642 (6th Cir. 2005) (officer could be liable for not getting arrestee to court, where police policy charged him with information contained in the jail log).

[180]*See* Ashcroft v. Iqbal, ___ U.S. ___, 129 S. Ct. 1937 (2009), discussed in § B.4.a of this chapter, above.

[181]Valdes v. Crosby, 450 F.3d 1231, 1239–43 (11th Cir. 2006) (warden could be held liable for beating of prisoner based on inaction and weakening of protective measures in the face of information suggesting widespread abuse), *cert. dismissed*, 549 U.S. 1249 (2007); Sulton v. Wright, 265 F. Supp. 2d 292, 300–01 (S.D.N.Y. 2003) (chief medical officer of the prison system could be liable where he failed to correct the failures of the medical tracking system which resulted in surgery having to be re-approved after transfers; and failed to correct the failure of medical holds and coordination of patient work-up between prisons); Bausch v. Sumiec, 139 F. Supp. 2d 1029, 1038 (E.D.Wis. 2001) (Secretary of Correction could be held liable for failing for three years to issue a policy to implement a court decision); Jackson v. Johnson, 118 F. Supp. 2d 278, (N.D.N.Y. 2000) (Director of Division for Youth could be held liable for failure to change policy concerning restraint techniques after risk of using them became known), *affirmed in part, dismissed in part on othe grounds*, 13 Fed.Appx. 51 (2d Cir. 2001) (unpublished).

delegated responsibility for a particular task to a subordinate, the supervisor is probably not liable for failure to perform the task, unless you can show that the supervisor knew or should have known that it was not getting done.[182]

The failure of higher officials to train or supervise their subordinates may establish the higher-ups' liability. This can take the form of failure to promulgate policies to guide subordinates' conduct,[183] failure to train,[184] failure to instruct or supervise subordinates,[185] or failure to respond to evidence of misconduct by subordinates.[186] A failure to train or supervise must be so serious as to constitute "deliberate indifference" before supervisors will be held liable on this basis.[187] When supervisors delegate authority, they are not liable

---

[182]*Compare* Sample v. Diecks, 885 F.2d 1099, 1110 (3d Cir. 1989) (warden is not liable for failure to release a prisoner on time if there are procedures in place calling for others to handle the problem) *with* Taylor v. Michigan Dep't of Corrections, 69 F.3d 76, 81 (6th Cir. 1995) (superintendent who knew his delegated authority was being re-delegated to lower level personnel, and had no means of learning whether authority was being abused, could be held liable) *and* LaMarca v. Turner, 995 F.2d at 1537–38 (superintendent could be held liable in part because he failed to ensure that his direct subordinates carried out his policies).

[183]Taylor v. Michigan Dep't of Corrections, 69 F.3d 76, 81 (6th Cir. 1995) (holding supervisor could be held liable for not adopting a policy requiring prisoners' files to be reviewed before transfer in order to avoid placing prisoners at risk of rape); Roland v. Johnson, 856 F.2d 764, 767, 770 (6th Cir. 1988) (holding that failure to adopt policies to respond to pattern of violence and sexual assaults could support prison supervisors' liability); Martin v. White, 742 F.2d 469, 475–76 (8th Cir. 1984) (similar to *Roland*); Horne v. Coughlin, 795 F. Supp. 72, 74–75 (N.D.N.Y. 1991) (holding that Commissioner could be held liable for lack of a policy requiring appointment of counsel substitute for a mentally retarded prisoner facing disciplinary charges); Sharpe v. City of Lewisburg, Tenn., 677 F. Supp. 1362, 1368 (M.D.Tenn. 1988) (holding failure to train officers to deal with the predictable problems of the mentally ill supported supervisory liability); Ferola v. Moran, 622 F. Supp. 814, 823 (D.R.I. 1985) (holding Director could be held liable for failure to promulgate policies sufficient to safeguard shackled inmates); Bryant v. McGinnis, 463 F. Supp. 373, 387 (W.D.N.Y. 1978) (holding Commissioner could be held liable for failure to promulgate regulations protecting Muslims' religious rights).

[184]Roberts v. City of Shreveport, 397 F.3d 287, 293 (5th Cir. 2005) ("for a supervisor to be liable for failure to train, 'the focus must be on the adequacy of the training program in relation to the tasks the particular officers must perform.'"); Wever v. Lincoln County, Nebraska, 388 F.3d 601, 607–08 (8th Cir. 2004) (two jail suicides may put Sheriff on notice that suicide prevention training is inadequate); Gilbert v. Selsky, 867 F. Supp. 159, 166 (S.D.N.Y. 1994) (holding that Director of Special Housing and Inmate Discipline could be held liable based on lack of formal training manual and requirement of training sessions for hearing officers); Allman v. Coughlin, 577 F. Supp. 1440, 1448 (S.D.N.Y. 1984) (holding systematic failures in training of emergency team could support liability of Commissioner); Sharpe v. City of Lewisburg, Tenn., 677 F. Supp. 1362, 1368 (M.D.Tenn. 1988) (holding county liable for failure to train police officers to deal with predictable problems with mentally ill persons); *see* Board of County Commissioners of Bryan County, Oklahoma v. Brown, 520 U.S. 397, 117 S. Ct. 1382 (1997) (noting that claims based on an inadequate program of training present more plausible causation scenarios than claims of failure to screen; municipal liability case).

[185]Taylor v. Michigan Dep't of Corrections, 69 F.3d 76, 80–81 (6th Cir. 1995) (holding that warden's failure to ensure that subordinates carried out transfer policy, with knowledge that there was a breakdown in proper workings of department, could support liability); Combs v. Wilkinson, 315 F.3d 548, 559 (6th Cir. 2002) (evidence that lieutenant did not maintain control of tactical operation and "questionable force" was used could support liability); Meriwether v. Coughlin, 879 F.2d 1037, 1048 (2d Cir. 1989) (warden and commissioner could be held liable for foreseeable retaliatory beatings by officers); Bolin v. Black, 875 F.2d 1343, 1347–48 (8th Cir. 1989) (similar to *Meriwether*); Kesler v. King, 29 F. Supp. 2d 356, 368 (S.D.Tex. 1998) (Sheriff who authorized use of emergency response team without giving it instructions, and then left the scene, could be liable for the results); Allman v. Coughlin, 577 F. Supp. 1440, 1448 (S.D.N.Y. 1984) (holding systematic failures in supervision of emergency team could support liability of Commissioner). *But see* Steidl v. Gramley, 151 F.3d 739, 741 (7th Cir. 1998) ("A warden is not liable for an isolated failure of his subordinates to carry out prison policies, however—unless the subordinates are acting (or failing to act) on the warden's instructions.").

[186]Valdes v. Crosby, 450 F.3d 1231, 1239–43 (11th Cir. 2006) (warden could be held liable for beating of prisoner based on evidence that he failed to act on information that certain guards abused prisoners and that he weakened protective measures), *cert. dismissed*, 549 U.S. 1249 (2007); Riley v. Olk-Long, 282 F.3d 592, 596–97 (8th Cir. 2002) (upholding jury verdict against warden and security director in sexual abuse case where they had evidence of officer's prior misconduct; guards' union contract was no defense); Estate of Davis by Ostenfeld v. Delo, 115 F.3d 1388, 1396 (8th Cir. 1997) (affirming damage award against prison superintendent based on evidence that he knew of an officer's propensity to use excessive force based on several prior incidents); Aponte Matos v. Toledo Dávila, 135 F.3d 182, 192 (1st Cir. 1998) (noting that a supervisor may be held liable for failure to discipline a "miscreant officer"); Gallardo v. DiCarlo, 203 F. Supp. 2d 1160, 1166 (C.D.Cal. 2002) (allegation of warden's failure to discipline, prosecute, or otherwise deal with known excessive force, refusal to investigate complaints, encouragement of excessive force by inaction and cover-up, etc., stated a claim against her); Kesler v. King, 29 F. Supp. 2d 356, 370 (S.D.Tex. 1998).

[187]Curry v. Scott, 249 F.3d 493, 508 (6th Cir. 2001); Thompson v. Upshur County, Texas, 245 F.3d 447, 459 (5th Cir. 2001) ("A sheriff not personally involved in the acts that deprived the plaintiff of his constitutional rights is liable under section 1983 if: 1) the sheriff failed to train or supervise the officers involved; 2) there is a causal connection between the alleged failure to supervise or train and the alleged violation of the plaintiff's rights; and 3) the failure to train or supervise constituted deliberate indifference to the plaintiff's constitutional rights. . . ."); Camilo-Robles v. Zapata, 175 F.3d 41, 44 (1st Cir. 1999); Aswegan v. Bruhl, 965 F.2d 676, 677 (8th Cir. 1992); Walker v. Norris, 917 F.2d 1449, 1456 (6th Cir. 1990); Greason v. Kemp, 891 F.2d 829, 837 (11th Cir. 1990); Sample v. Diecks, 885 F.2d 1099, 1117–18 (3d Cir. 1989); Jones v. City of Chicago, 856 F.2d 985, 992–93 (7th Cir. 1988).

every time someone abuses it.[188] The fact that prison guards have violated your rights does not by itself prove that their superiors failed to train or supervise them.

Defendants can be held liable for failing to act only if they had the power to correct the violation and the duty to act. No one can be held liable for events they have no control over,[189] though courts will look critically at officials' claims that they were powerless to act.[190] Defendants will also not be held liable for failure to do someone else's job.[191]

Sometimes you must look to state statutes or prison regulations to determine whose job it was to prevent a constitutional deprivation. Failure to perform a duty imposed by statute or regulation may make a defendant liable even if she does not know about the particular constitutional violation that results.[192] (This does *not* mean that violating a statute or regulation violates the Constitution. It just identifies who can be held liable once you have shown that the Constitution has been violated.)

Courts are reluctant to impose liability against high-level supervisors based on statutes or regulations that are extremely general.[193] If a statute or regulation imposes liability on one person, the result may be to excuse others from liability.[194]

---

[188]Al-Jundi v. Estate of Rockefeller, 885 F.2d 1060, 1065-66 (2d Cir. 1989); Sample v. Diecks, 885 F.2d 1099, 1117-18 (3d Cir. 1989).

[189]Pinto v. Nettleship, 737 F.2d 130, 132-33 (1st Cir. 1984); Williams v. Bennett, 689 F.2d 1370, 1388 (11th Cir. 1982); Johnson v. Pearson, 316 F. Supp. 2d 307, 315 (E.D.Va. 2004) (prison employee without power to make transfers was not liable for failing to act on prisoner's request); Morris v. Eversley, 282 F. Supp. 2d 196, 205 (S.D.N.Y. 2003) (superintendent could not be liable for failure to investigate claim of sexual abuse or remove officer from his position when those tasks were under the authority of Inspector General and Bureau of Labor Relations); see also Youngberg v. Romeo, 457 U.S. 307, 323, 102 S. Ct. 2452 (1981) (holding that a defendant unable to satisfy the constitutional standard because of budgetary constraints would be entitled to "good-faith immunity"). Compare Valdes v. Crosby, 450 F.3d 1231, 1243 (11th Cir. 2006) (warden could be held liable based on evidence of steps within his power to reduce violence in prison), cert. dismissed, 549 U.S. 1249 (2007).

[190]LaMarca v. Turner, 995 F.2d 1526, 1537-38 (11th Cir. 1993) (rejecting prison superintendent's defense that budget problems kept him from controlling violence where the record showed steps he could have taken to reduce violence); Masonoff v. DuBois, 336 F. Supp. 2d 54, 60-61 (D.Mass. 2004) (rejecting claim that prison officials lacked budget authority to replace chemical toilets, since they did have authority to maintain those toilets and other fixtures to address sanitation problems); Brown v. Mitchell, 327 F. Supp. 2d 615, 646 (E.D.Va. 2004) (holding there was a triable issue wherher Sheriff "knowingly maintained a dangerously overcrowded facility" where she claimed lack of power over crowding, but did not take advantage of state law provisions allowing a sheriff to notify a state court that a jail is overcrowded or unsuitable so the court can take remedial action).

[191]Burks v. Raemisch, 555 F.3d 592, 594-95 (7th Cir. 2009) ("Bureaucracies divide tasks; no prisoner is entitled to insist that one employee do another's job."); Serna v. Colorado Dep't of Corrections, 455 F.3d 1146, 1154 (10th Cir. 2006) (departmental Director could not be held liable for inadequate direct supervision of "SORT team" where direct supervision was the job of an on-side commander); Cuoco v. Moritsugu, 222 F.3d 99, 111 (2d Cir. 2000) (prison doctor could not be held liable for failing to intercede in the treatment of a patient assigned to another doctor); Scott v. Coughlin, 78 F. Supp. 2d 299, 312 (S.D.N.Y. 2000) (where Director of Special Housing was designated to review disciplinary appeals, other officials were not liable even if told of due process violations); Crawford v. Coughlin, 43 F. Supp. 2d 319, 324 (W.D.N.Y. 1999) (prison workplace quality control supervisor could not be held liable for dangerous working conditions where workplace safety was not his responsibility). Compare Taylor v. Michigan Dep't of Corrections, 69 F.3d 76, 81-82 (6th Cir. 1995) (warden can be liable for rape of vulnerable prisoner where he was responsible

"both for transfers and for adopting reasonable transfer procedures" and failed to do either; jury could find that he "personally had a job to do, and that he did not do it").

[192]Alexander v. Perrill, 916 F.2d 1392, 1398 (9th Cir. 1990) (failure to follow federal prison system's regulations and policies could support liability for failure to release prisoner on time); Lewis v. Smith, 855 F.2d 736, 738 (11th Cir. 1988) (state regulations made disciplinary board chair and director of work-release center responsible for ensuring that due process was followed); McQueen v. Tabah, 839 F.2d 1525, 1529-30 (11th Cir. 1988) (complaint of due process violation in "close management" placement stated a claim against the members of the classification team, who play a role under state regulations in the review process); Johnson-El v. Schoemehl, 878 F.2d 1043, 1049 (8th Cir. 1989) (liability may be based on "the breach of a legal duty that proximately causes the injury"); Slakan v. Porter, 737 F.2d 368, 373 (4th Cir. 1984) ("state statutes fixing the administrator's legal duties provide a useful guide in determining who had the responsibility and capability to end the offensive practices"); Smart v. Goord, 441 F. Supp. 2d 631, 644 (S.D.N.Y. 2006) (relying on regulation specifying superintendent's responsibility for certain decisions), on reconsideration on other grounds, 2008 WL 591230 (S.D.N.Y. 2008); Jones v. Lopez, 262 F. Supp. 2d 701, 709-18 (W.D.Tex. 2001) (holding state statutes imposed a duty on Sheriff to adopt reasonable procedures to ensure that no one is incarcerated without legal authority); Horne v. Coughlin, 795 F. Supp. 72, 74-75 (N.D.N.Y. 1991) (relying on statute delineating Commissioner's obligation to created policies and procedures for disciplinary process); Langley v. Coughlin, 709 F. Supp. 482, 486 (S.D.N.Y.) (relying on Commissioner's statutory duty to develop appropriate treatment for inmates needing psychiatric care), appeal dismissed, 888 F.2d 252 (2d Cir. 1989); see Abney v. Alameida, 334 F. Supp. 2d 1221, 1227 (S.D.Cal. 2004) (citing Director's statutory duties with respect to prisoner trust accounts and the resulting trustee relationship in allowing claim about deductions from account to go forward against Director).

The use of state law in this fashion to help determine who is liable for a federal law violation does not violate the Eleventh Amendment. See § F.1 of this chapter, n.462.

[193]Johnson-El v. Schoemehl, 878 F.2d at 1050 (Mayor could not be held liable for jail conditions based only on an "affirmative duty of supervision" in city charter).

[194]Willis v. Barksdale, 625 F. Supp. 411, 417 (W.D. Tenn. 1985) (custodial personnel were not liable for death of inmate because state statutes placed responsibility on medical department for

Prison wardens and other correctional supervisors are generally not liable for inadequate medical care when they rely on the judgment or competence of qualified medical personnel.[195] But they may be held liable for medical care deprivations if they fail to take steps to provide an adequate medical care system,[196] or if they fail to perform duties assigned to them with respect to medical care.[197]

In disciplinary cases, supervisory officials may be held liable on several grounds. Officials who know that a prison is utilizing unconstitutional procedures may be held liable if they fail to correct the violation.[198] Officials who review individual disciplinary proceedings may be held liable if they do not correct due process violations of which they have notice.[199] Officials may also be liable if they are informed of due process violations in other ways and fail to act on them.[200] Staff members who are involved in some way in disciplinary proceedings but do not participate in the hearing or in subsequent appeals or reviews of the hearing cannot be held liable for due process violations committed by the hearing officer or committee.[201] Where discipline is unconstitutional for substantive reasons and not due process denial (e.g., where a prisoner is disciplined for conduct that is constitutionally protected), all those who review and approve the discipline may be liable.[202]

Several times, we have referred to liability based on what officials knew, or should have known. Some courts have held that supervisors can be held liable for failing to remedy constitutional violations that they should have known about.[203] Others have rejected "should know" as a

---

prisoners with special needs); Polk v. Montgomery County, Md., 548 F. Supp. 613, 615 (D. Md. 1982) (state and county law made correction director, not Sheriff, responsible for treatment of prisoners), rev'd on other grounds, 782 F.2d 1196 (4th Cir. 1986); cf. Leach v. Shelby County Sheriff, 891 F.2d 1241, 1248 (6th Cir. 1989) (sheriff can be liable as policymaker of county for failure to ensure adequate medical care even though statute places responsibility on medical providers).

[195]See Ch. 2, § F.1.a, n.331.

The opposite is also true. Medical personnel are generally not responsible for the acts and judgments of correctional personnel, even if the medical personnel have some involvement with the relevant events. See Lair v. Oglesby, 859 F.2d 605, 606 (8th Cir. 1988) (doctor who prescribed medication could not be held liable for excessive force by officers who administered it); Hill v. Koon, 732 F. Supp. 1076, 1084 (D. Nev. 1990) (when correctional staff ordered digital rectal searches without justification, physician's assistants who performed them were not liable for the Fourth Amendment violation).

[196]Alsina-Ortiz v. LaBoy, 400 F.3d 77, 81 (1st Cir. 2005) (high-ranking officials could be held liable for deprivation of medical care if they knew of a pattern of staff failure to refer prisoners to health providers and did not make reasonable efforts to correct the problem; officer who did not report obviously ill prisoner to medical personnel could be held liable); McKenna v. Wright, 386 F.3d 432, 437–38 (2d Cir. 2004) (prison superintendents who were responsible for policies that resulted in deprivation of medical care could be held liable); Miller v. King, 384 F.3d 1248, 1263 (11th Cir. 2004) (prison supervisor could be liable for failing to act if on knowledge that prison staff are unlawfully delaying or denying medical care), vacated and superseded on other grounds, 449 F.3d 1149 (11th Cir. 2006); Greason v. Kemp, 891 F.2d 829, 839–40 (11th Cir. 1990) (warden was "responsible for ensuring that all services . . . were properly provided" and should have known about the inadequacy of psychiatric staffing"); see also Ch. 2, § F.1.a, nn.332–336.

[197]Hill v. Marshall, 962 F.2d 1209, 1213 (6th Cir. 1992) (Deputy Superintendent of Treatment could be held liable for failing to respond to prisoners' medical complaints when that was his assigned responsibility).

[198]Williams v. Smith, 781 F.2d 319, 324 (2d Cir. 1986) (warden could be liable if he accepted a policy or custom of due process denials in disciplinary hearings).

[199]Lewis v. Smith, 855 F.2d 736, 738 (11th Cir. 1988); King v. Higgins, 702 F.2d 18, 21 (1st Cir. 1983) (Superintendent who was designated to hear disciplinary appeals had a duty to conduct at least a "minimal investigation" and could be held liable for failure to do so upon receiving reports giving notice of due process violations); Johnson v. Coombe, 156 F. Supp. 2d 273, 278 (S.D.N.Y. 2000); Gabai v. Jacoby, 800 F. Supp. 1149, 1156 (S.D.N.Y. 1992).

[200]Wright v. Smith, 21 F.3d 496, 502 (2d Cir. 1994) (superintendent who was informed of due process denial through a habeas petition and failed to remedy it could be liable); Smith v. Rowe, 761 F.2d 360, 369 (7th Cir. 1985) (Director of Corrections held liable for his knowing failure to remedy improper segregation of prisoner); Rouccchio v. Coughlin, 923 F. Supp. 360, 379 (S.D.N.Y. 1996) (similar to Wright v. Smith); Pino v. Dalsheim, 605 F. Supp. 1305, 1319 (S.D.N.Y. 1985) (Commissioner held liable based on actual knowledge of unconstitutional disciplinary proceeding). But see Wright v. Collins, 766 F.2d 841, 850 (4th Cir. 1985) (warden was not liable for unlawful disciplinary proceeding based on inmate's letter that was too late for the warden to do anything); Garrido v. Coughlin, 716 F. Supp. 98, 100 (S.D.N.Y. 1988) (defendant who filled out disciplinary forms at someone else's direction was not liable).

[201]Baker v. Lyles, 904 F.2d 925, 929 (4th Cir. 1990) (staff members who investigated the incident were not liable for due process violations at the subsequent hearing); Cook v. Lehman, 863 F. Supp. 207, 211 (E.D. Pa. 1994) (same); Cepeda v. Coughlin, 785 F. Supp. 385, 391 (S.D.N.Y. 1992) (officer who prepared a misbehavior report was not liable for due process violations at the hearing); Salahuddin v. Harris, 684 F. Supp. 1224, 1228 (S.D.N.Y. 1988) (defendant who filled out disciplinary forms at someone else's direction was not liable); see Smart v. Goord, 441 F. Supp. 2d 631, 644 (S.D.N.Y. 2006) (lieutenant who wrote involuntary protective custody recommendation could not be held liable for hearing decision), on reconsideration on other grounds, 2008 WL 591230 (S.D.N.Y., Mar. 3, 2008).

[202]Williams v. Bitner, 359 F. Supp. 2d 370, 377 (M.D.Pa. 2005), aff'd in part, remanded in part, 455 F.3d 186 (3d Cir. 2006).

[203]See, e.g., Randall v. Prince Georges County, 302 F.3d 188, 207 (4th Cir. 2002) (actual or constructive knowledge may support supervisory liability); Poe v. Leonard, 282 F.3d 123, 143–44 (2d Cir. 2002) and cases cited; Camilo-Robles v. Hoyos, 151 F.3d 1, 7 (1st Cir. 1998) (". . . [S]upervisory liability does not require a showing that the supervisor had actual knowledge of the offending behavior; he 'may be liable for the foreseeable consequences of such conduct if he would have known of it but for his deliberate indifference or willful blindness.'" (citation omitted)).

basis for § 1983 liability and have held that supervisory liability must be based on actual knowledge.[204] Be sure that you know what your federal circuit has said on that point. More importantly, be aware of a recent Supreme Court decision that states that supervisory liability requires the plaintiff to show that the supervisor's actions actually violated the law.[205] This holding may require that the supervisor's failure to act be shown, *e.g.*, to be deliberately indifferent (for an Eighth Amendment claim) or involve intentional discrimination (for a claim of discriminatory treatment); if so, "should have known" would not be sufficient to hold that defendant liable.

4) *Injunctive Claims* The foregoing principles apply both to damage cases and to injunctive cases.[206] However, in injunctive cases courts are a little less strict about identifying exactly who was responsible for what. The inquiry is "broader and more generalized" and the focus is on "the combined acts or omissions" of the officials responsible for operating prisons.[207] One reason for the distinction is that injunctive cases are considered to be official capacity suits, and therefore are for practical purposes equivalent to suit against the governmental entity.[208]

The courts are mainly concerned that the defendants who are named in an injunctive case have the ability to end the constitutional violation if so ordered.[209] In damages cases, by contrast, the courts will look very closely at whether the plaintiff has alleged and proved an adequate basis of personal liability for each individual defendant.

5) *Pleading Personal Involvement* When you bring a civil rights action, you may not know at first exactly who was at fault. You must observe two principles in deciding whom to include as a defendant. First, you should include those people up and down the chain of command who can reasonably be said to have "caused you to be subjected" to a violation of law. Second, your inclusion of a defendant must be "well grounded in fact and . . . warranted by . . . law."[210]

This means you should be able truthfully to state in your complaint a rational basis for including each defendant that would permit you to obtain a judgment against her if you proved your allegations. However, this standard can be met by a reasonable expectation that evidence to that effect will be obtained in discovery.[211]

---

[204]*See, e.g.*, A.M. ex rel. J.M.K. v. Luzerne County Juvenile Detention Center, 372 F.3d 572, 586 (3d Cir. 2004) (citing Baker v. Monroe Township, 50 F.3d 1186, 1194 & n.3 (3d Cir. 1995)); Barry v. Ratelle, 985 F. Supp. 1235, 1239 (S.D.Cal. 1997).

[205]*See* Ashcroft v. Iqbal, ___ U.S. ___, 129 S. Ct. 1937 (2009), discussed in § B.4.a of this chapter, above.

[206]There are a few cases that say that *respondeat superior* applies in injunctive cases. *See, e.g.*, Malik v. Tanner, 697 F. Supp. 1294, 1304 (S.D.N.Y. 1988). Don't rely on them.

[207]Leer v. Murphy, 844 F.2d 628, 633 (9th Cir. 1988); *accord*, Tyson v. Ratelle, 166 F.R.D. 442, 446 (C.D. Cal. 1996).

[208]Houston v. Sheahan, 62 F.3d 902, 903 (7th Cir. 1995) (describing Sheriff and Warden as "stand-ins for the political body they serve" in an official capacity action seeking an injunction) (dictum); LaMarca v. Turner, 995 F.2d 1526, 1537–38 (11th Cir. 1993) (holding that injunctive Eighth Amendment claim focuses on "institution's historical indifference" rather than new superintendent's personal performance); Alberti v. Sheriff of Harris County, Texas, 937 F.2d 984, 999 (5th Cir. 1991) (citing knowledge by unnamed "relevant state officials" of local jail conditions and choice by "state" to leave prisoners in them as basis for injunctive relief); Hoptowit v. Spellman, 753 F.2d 779, 782 (9th Cir. 1985) (declining to reevaluate liability based on turnover in prison administration because the "personal conduct of the principal named defendants" was not the focus of the case); Williams v. Wilkinson, 132 F. Supp. 2d 601, 609 (S.D.Ohio 2001) (similar to *Hoptowit*). *Compare* Mayor v. Educational Equality League, 415 U.S. 605 (1974) (barring an injunction based on conduct that was limited to the tenure of a single departed official).

[209]Koehl v. Dalsheim, 85 F.3d 86, 89 (2d Cir. 1996) (affirming dismissal of damage claim against Superintendent for deprivation of prescription eyeglasses, but reversing dismissal of injunctive

claim, since Superintendent "had overall responsibility to ensure that prisoners' basic needs were met"); Luckey v. Harris, 860 F.2d 1012, 1015–16 (11th Cir. 1988); Woods v. Carey, 2006 WL 548190, *5 (E.D. Cal. 2006) ("[I]t follows that it is not necessary to allege the personal involvement of a state official when plaintiffs are attacking a state procedure on federal grounds that relates in some way to the job duties of the named defendant. All that is required is that the complaint name an official who could appropriately respond to a court order on injunctive relief should one ever be issued."); Torrence v. Pelkey, 164 F. Supp. 2d 264, 273 (D.Conn. 2001); Davidson v. Scully, 148 F. Supp. 2d 249, 254 (S.D.N.Y. 2001) and cases cited; Hobbs v. Pennell, 754 F. Supp. 1040, 1041 n.6 (D.Del. 1991) (prison chaplain was a proper defendant in an injunctive case against a rule about religious services, even though he did not institute the policy, because he was responsible for its enforcement and operation); Libby v. Marshall, 653 F. Supp. 359, 364 (D.Mass. 1986) (holding state officials could be joined in jail conditions case based on failure to provide funds; "those parties whose actions are necessary to a solution become part of the problem if they do not take such actions"), *appeal dismissed*, 833 F.2d 402 (1st Cir. 1987); *see* Clarkson v. Coughlin, 145 F.R.D. 339, 346 (S.D.N.Y. 1993) (there was "sufficient nexus" between superintendents' activities and the relief sought to justify joining them as defendants). *But see* Women's Emergency Network v. Bush, 323 F.3d 937, 949 (11th Cir. 2003) (Governor not subject to injunction where his relationship to enforcement of a challenged statute was "attenuated.").

[210]Rule 11, Fed.R.Civ.P. *See* Ch. 10, § W, for further discussion of Rule 11; *compare* Harden v. Peck, 686 F. Supp. 1254, 1263 (N.D. Ill. 1988) (Rule 11 sanctions imposed against plaintiff who "grab[bed] as many defendants as possible") *with* Costello v. Daddario, 710 F. Supp. 1035, 1037–38 (E.D. Pa. 1989) (plaintiffs' counsel did not violate Rule 11 by naming all officers present at beating as defendants where his client could not specifically identify any of them and the statute of limitations was about to run); *see* Brubaker v. City of Richmond, 943 F.2d 1363, 1373 (4th Cir. 1991) (a legal position violates Rule 11 if it "has 'absolutely no chance of success under the existing precedent.'" (citation omitted)).

[211]Bell Atlantic Corp. v. Twombly, 550 U.S. 544, 545, 127 S. Ct. 1955 (2007). Further, courts have held that supervisory officials

b. Suing Local Governments: The "Policy" Requirement

Under 42 U.S.C. § 1983, you can bring civil rights actions for damages against city and county governments (municipalities) *if* the constitutional violation resulted from a municipal policy or custom. This rule applies to most, but not all, local jails; in some states, jails are a state responsibility in whole or in part,[212] and you cannot sue state governments under § 1983, though you can sue state officials individually.[213]

The policy or custom requirement means that a city or county government is not liable under § 1983 just because one of its employees commits a constitutional violation; *respondeat superior* does not apply.[214] If the violation was not done pursuant to a policy or custom, you must sue the person or persons who committed it in their individual capacities.[215] (You may be able to pursue a *respondeat superior* tort claim under state law, and you may be able to join it with your § 1983 claim.[216])

To establish municipal liability you must show that the policy you identify actually caused the injury you are suing about—that is, that the policy was the "moving force" behind the injury.[217] In addition, you must show "fault" on the part of the municipality. Some policies are unconstitutional on

their face,[218] which satisfies the fault requirement.[219] Others, however, are not facially unconstitutional, but can be shown to result in constitutional violations.[220] In such cases, the plaintiff must show that the policy amounts to deliberate indifference on the part of the municipality.[221]

Municipalities may be liable for constitutional violations caused by "a policy statement, ordinance, regulation or decision officially adapted and promulgated by that body's officers."[222] Municipalities may also be liable for the lack of

---

may be retained as defendants for purposes of discovery to identify culpable staff members. *See* Ch. 10, § K.2, n.414. However, the naming of supervisory defendants, for this or any other purpose, will probably be hotly contested in light of the decision in *Ashcroft v. Iqbal*, ___ U.S. ___, 129 S. Ct. 1937, 1950 (2009). This decision is discussed in the preceding several sections.

[212]For example, in Alabama, county governments have no responsibility for jail operations, but are responsible for building and maintaining jails, so the counties can be responsible for violations resulting from physical conditions. Marsh v. Butler County, Ala., 268 F.3d 1014, 1027 (11th Cir. 2001) (en banc).

[213]That is because of states' Eleventh Amendment immunity, *see* § L.1 of this chapter, and because they are not considered "persons" under the statute. Will v. Michigan Dep't of State Police, 491 U.S. 58, 71, 109 S. Ct. 2304 (1989).

[214]Monell v. New York City Dep't of Social Services, 436 U.S. 658, 691–94, 98 S. Ct. 2304 (1989).

[215]Naming a defendant in her official capacity is the same as suing the municipality itself. Monell v. New York City Dep't of Social Services, 436 U.S. at 690 n.55. An official capacity claim will be dismissed if you fail to establish that the official acted pursuant to policy or custom.

[216]*See* § C of this chapter concerning tort claims, and § F.1 of this chapter concerning federal courts' supplemental or pendent jurisdiction over state law claims.

[217]Board of County Comm'rs v. Brown, 520 U.S. 397, 404, 117 S. Ct. 1382 (1997); *see* Ware v. Jackson County, Mo., 150 F.3d 873, 885 (8th Cir. 1998) (failure to discipline staff for sexual abuse was the moving force behind rape of plaintiff; "It is axiomatic that unpunished crimes tend to breed more criminal activity."). *But see* Jones v. Wellham, 104 F.3d 620, 627 (4th Cir. 1997) (decision to retain police officer who had been accused of rape was not the "moving force" behind the rape of the plaintiff 10 years later).

[218]*See, e.g.*, Cabrales v. County of Los Angeles, 886 F.2d 235, 236 (9th Cir. 1989) (policy of understaffing of mental health personnel); Weber v. Dell, 804 F.2d 796, 802–03 (2d Cir. 1986) (unconstitutional strip search policy).

[219]Board of County Comm'rs v. Brown, 520 U.S. 397, 404–05, 117 S. Ct. 1382 (1997).

[220]*See, e.g.*, Gibson v. County of Washoe, Nev., 290 F.3d 1175, 1189–91 (9th Cir. 2002) (holding county could be liable based on policy of delay in medical attention for combative, uncooperative, or intoxicated detainees, and policy of taking medications from newly admitted prisoners and not using them for immediate needs, if they caused the death of a mentally ill prisoner who received no medical attention or medication); Lawson v. Dallas County, 286 F.3d 257, 263–64 (5th Cir. 2002) (injuries to paraplegic prisoner were caused by official policies restricting nurses' ability to provide care, including limit on dressing changes, ban on foam mattresses, ban on nurses' entering prisoners' cells, etc.).

[221]Board of County Comm'rs v. Brown, 520 U.S. 397, 407, 117 S. Ct. 1382 (1997) (quoting Canton v. Harris, 489 U.S. 378, 388, 109 S. Ct. 1197 (1989)); Gregory v. City of Louisville, 444 F.3d 725, 752 (6th Cir. 2006); Berry v. Baca, 379 F.3d 764, 768–69 (9th Cir. 2004) (inefficient implementation of policies concerning timely release of prisoners could amount to a policy of deliberate indifference); Hayes v. Faulkner County, Ark., 388 F.3d 669, 674 (8th Cir. 2004) (jail policy of producing prisoners only when the court asked for them was a policy of deliberate indifference with respect to persons who were never called by the court); Ware v. Unified Sch. Dist. No. 492, 902 F.2d 815, 819–20 (10th Cir. 1990).

A claim of municipal policy of deliberate indifference generally requires only that the risk of violation of constitutional rights have been "obvious." Canton v. Harris, 489 U.S. at 390. This is equivalent to finding deliberate indifference based on risks that the official "should have known" about. However, individual defendants alleged to have violated the Eighth Amendment must be shown to have had actual knowledge of the risk. Farmer v. Brennan, 511 U.S. 825, 114 S. Ct. 1970 (1994); *see* Ch. 2, § A, on this point. Some courts have held that in an Eighth Amendment case, the more demanding "actual knowledge" standard of *Farmer* must be met to establish municipal liability. *See, e.g.*, Gibson v. County of Washoe, Nev., 290 F.3d 1175, 1192 (9th Cir. 2002). We think that is wrong. The *Canton* municipal liability standard is based on interpretation of the statute, 42 U.S.C. § 1983, and not on the Eighth Amendment. If there is an Eighth Amendment violation in the first place, then determining whether the municipality can be held liable for it should be governed by § 1983 law. Lawson v. Dallas County, 286 F.3d 257, 264 (5th Cir. 2002) (noting that the *Canton* standard applies to municipal liability even where *Farmer* governs claims against individuals).

[222]Monell v. New York City Dep't of Social Services, 436 U.S. 658, 690, 98 S. Ct. 2304 (1989).

adequate policies if their absence amounts to deliberate indifference.[223]

Policies need not be formal to support municipal liability. Cities and counties may be liable for constitutional violations caused by a "custom or usage" that is "so permanent and well settled" as to have "the force of law."[224] A practice may constitute such a custom or usage if it is "persistent and widespread,"[225] "long-standing,"[226] or "deeply embedded."[227] An informal custom or usage can be proven either by a large number of instances or by other evidence that it is routine practice.[228] Many courts have held that municipalities can be held liable for customs even if their policymakers do not have actual knowledge of them.[229]

A custom or usage can constitute municipal policy even if it is contrary to written policy or to law.[230] However, violations of formal policy will not make the municipality liable unless there is evidence of a custom of violating the written policy, or a systematic failure to enforce the written policy.[231]

---

[223]Conn v. City of Reno, 572 F.3d 1047, 1064 (9th Cir. 2009) (absence of a policy on reporting suicide threats could constitute municipal deliberate indifference); Long v. County of Los Angeles, 442 F.3d 1178, 1189–90 (9th Cir. 2006) (lack of adequate policies for transfer of patients who become medically unstable and for notification of a doctor when a patient falls or refuses essential medical treatment could support municipal liability); Calhoun v. Ramsey, 408 F.3d 375, 380 (7th Cir. 2005) (allegations of policies of omission require more evidence than a single incident); Blackmore v. Kalamazoo County, 390 F.3d 890, 900 (6th Cir. 2004) (lack of a written policy on dealing with prisoner illnesses could support municipal liability); Berg v. County of Allegheny, 219 F.3d 261, 275–76 (3d Cir. 2000) (lack of safeguards against data entry errors in procedure for issuing warrants could constitute a policy of deliberate indifference).

[224]Monell v. New York City Dep't of Social Services, 436 U.S. at 690–91.

[225]St. Louis v. Praprotnik, 485 U.S. 112, 127, 108 S. Ct. 915 (1988) (plurality opinion); Garretson v. City of Madison Heights, 407 F.3d 789 (6th Cir. 2005) (plaintiff must show "(1) a clear and persistent pattern of mishandled medical emergencies for pre-arraignment detainees; (2) notice, or constructive notice of such pattern, to [municipality]; (3) tacit approval of the deliberate indifference and failure to act amounting to an official policy of inaction; and (4) that the custom or policy of inaction was the 'moving force,' or direct causal link, behind the constitutional injury"); Church v. City of Huntsville, 30 F.3d 1332, 1345 (11th Cir.1994) (to demonstrate a policy or custom, it is "generally necessary to show a persistent and wide-spread practice."); Sorlucco v. New York City Police Dep't, 971 F.2d 864, 870 (2d Cir. 1992); Spell v. McDaniel, 824 F.2d 1380, 1391 (4th Cir. 1987).

[226]Anela v. City of Wildwood, 790 F.2d 1063, 1069 (3d Cir. 1986) (long-standing jail conditions constituted a municipal custom or usage).

[227]Doe v. Claiborne County, 103 F.3d 495, 507 (6th Cir. 1996) ("[F]or the purposes of Monell liability must be so permanent and well settled as to constitute a custom or usage with the force of law. In turn, the notion of 'law' includes deeply embedded traditional ways of carrying out state policy. It must reflect a course of action deliberately chosen from among various alternatives. In short, a 'custom' is a 'legal institution' not memorialized by written law." (citations and quotations omitted)); Fundiller v. City of Cooper City, 777 F.2d 1436, 1442 (11th Cir. 1985).

[228]See Davis v. Carter, 452 F.3d 686, 692–94 (7th Cir. 2006) (plaintiff proved a municipal policy of excessive delay in providing methadone treatment, submitting evidence that administrative practices made delays inevitable and staff testimony that they were widespread; he was not required to cite other individuals who suffered from the delays); Baron v. Suffolk County Sheriff's Dep't, 402 F.3d 225, 237–38 (1st Cir. 2005) (plaintiff correction officer proved a municipal custom of condoning harassment to enforce the "code of silence" about staff misconduct with his testimony about several incidents and a deputy superintendent's testimony that officers were reluctant to report certain things, that a code of silence existed, and that the plaintiff had violated it and consequences were likely); Wood v. Hancock County Sheriff's Dep't, 354 F.3d 57, 66 (1st Cir. 2003) (jury finding that strip search was pursuant to policy was supported by plaintiff's testimony that he was told it was "routine procedure," staff member testified that it was a "routine search," and it happened to the plaintiff twice at the hands of different officers); Nicholson v. Scoppetta, 344 F.3d 154, 165–66 (2d Cir. 2003) (citing testimony as well as an audit in support of finding that a municipal policy of deliberate indifference existed); Palmer v. Marion County, 327 F.3d 588, 595–96 (7th Cir. 2003) (isolated acts of misconduct do not prove a widespread practice).

[229]Baron v. Suffolk County Sheriff's Dep't, 402 F.3d 225, 236–237 (1st Cir. 2005) (Municipality is liable if custom is "so well settled and widespread that the policymaking officials of the municipality can be said to have either actual or constructive knowledge of it yet did nothing to end the practice." (citation omitted)); Baker v. District of Columbia, 326 F.3d 1302, 1306 (D.C. Cir. 2003); Piotrowski v. City of Houston, 237 F.3d 567, 578 (5th Cir. 2001) ("Actual or constructive knowledge of [a] custom must be attributable to the governing body of the municipality or to an official to whom that body has delegated policy-making authority." (citation omitted)); Thompson v. City of Los Angeles, 885 F.2d 1439, 1444 (9th Cir. 1989); Spell v. McDaniel, 824 F.2d at 1391 (liability may be based on "constructive knowledge," which "may be inferred from the widespread extent of the practices, general knowledge of their existence, manifest opportunities and official duty of responsible policymakers to be informed, or combinations of these"). But see Memphis, Tenn. Area Local, Am. Postal Workers Union v. City of Memphis, 361 F.3d 898, 902 (6th Cir. 2004) ("A municipal 'custom' may be established by proof of the knowledge of policymaking officials and their acquiescence in the established practice.").

[230]Redman v. County of San Diego, 942 F.2d 1435, 1445 (9th Cir. 1991) (en banc) (routine failure to follow written policy can be a "custom" supporting municipal liability); Garcia v. Salt Lake County, 768 F.2d 303 (10th Cir.1985) (county liable where jail personnel established unconstitutional jail customs contrary to written policy); Anela v. City of Wildwood, 790 F.2d at 1066–67; Martin v. Ezeagu, 816 F. Supp. 20, 25 (D.D.C. 1993).

[231]Thomas v. Cook County Sheriff's Dep't, 588 F.3d 445, 456 (7th Cir. 2009) (affirming municipal liability for injuries cause by "well-documented breakdowns in the County's policies for retrieving medical request forms"); Bradich v. City of Chicago, 413 F.3d 688, 690 (7th Cir. 2005) (failure to enforce written policy that was not systematic did not itself amount to a policy); Daskalea v.

For a municipality to be held liable, a policy must have been made by a municipal "policymaker," *i.e.*, someone who has the authority under state law[232] (which may include "custom or usage"[233]) to make final policy for the city or county concerning the subject of the litigation.[234] (This requirement is what distinguishes municipal liability from supervisory liability, discussed in the previous section—you don't have to show that a supervisor is the final policymaker for the municipality in order to establish that person's individual liability.) Lower-level staff may be municipal policymakers in a particular area if they exercise final authority without supervision or review.[235] Single acts or decisions may constitute municipal policy if they are made by policymakers.[236] The same is true of failures to act that amount to

deliberate indifference.[237] As a practical matter, in most cases the policymaker will be the person in charge of an agency—a sheriff, chief of police, head of a local correction department, etc. In some states, the sheriff is considered a state policymaker, rather than a county policymaker, so the county cannot be held liable for the sheriff's policies.[238]

Applying these principles, a number of courts have found that the failure to provide adequate facilities or funds to operate jails in a constitutional manner was a municipal policy or custom for which damages could be recovered against the city or government.[239] Prisoners have also

District of Columbia, 227 F.3d 433, 442 (D.C. Cir. 2000) (" . . . [A] 'paper' policy cannot insulate a municipality from liability where there is evidence, as there was here, that the municipality was deliberately indifferent to the policy's violation."); Ware v. Jackson County, Mo., 150 F.3d 873, 882 (8th Cir. 1998) (written policies prohibiting misconduct "are of no moment in the face of evidence that such policies are neither followed nor enforced").

[232]Jett v. Dallas Independent School District, 491 U.S. 701, 736–38, 109 S. Ct. 2702 (1989); *see* Jeffes v. Barnes, 208 F.3d 49, 56 (2d Cir. 2000) (under New York law, the county sheriff is final policymaker with respect to conduct of staff members toward fellow officers); Rivera v. Houston Independent School Dist., 349 F.3d 244, 247 (5th Cir. 2003) (state law gives Board of Trustees "the exclusive power and duty to govern and oversee the management of the public schools of the district."); Lytle v. Doyle, 326 F.3d 463, 471–72 (4th Cir. 2003) (City Manager is final policymaker over police department); Dotson v. Chester, 937 F.2d 920, 925–30 (4th Cir. 1991) (Sheriff had final policymaking authority over jail conditions). *Compare* Bennett v. City of Eastpointe, 410 F.3d 810, 819 (6th Cir. 2005) (instructions given by Chief of Police when he was a lieutenant was not a municipal policy because lieutenant was not a policymaker); Johnson v. Hardin County, Ky., 908 F.2d 1280, 1287 (6th Cir. 1990) (Sheriff was not shown to be jail policymaker with respect to medical care because state law gave authority to "fiscal court").

[233]St. Louis v. Praprotnik, 485 U.S. 112, 124 n.1, 108 S. Ct. 915 (1988) (plurality opinion); O'Brien v. City of Grand Rapids, 23 F.3d 990, 992 (6th Cir. 1994).

[234]An official may be a policymaker for some purposes but not others. Jeffes v. Barnes, 208 F.3d 49, 57 (2d Cir. 2000) and cases cited.

[235]Chew v. Gates, 27 F.3d 1432, 1445 (9th Cir. 1994); Mandel v. Doe, 888 F.2d 783, 794 (11th Cir. 1989) (physician's assistant made policy concerning medical care at road camp).

This does not mean that anybody who exercises discretion is a policymaker for municipal liability purposes. "[T]he delegation must be such that the subordinate's discretionary decisions are not constrained by official policies and are not subject to review." Mandel v. Doe, 888 F.2d at 792; *accord*, Miller v. Calhoun County, 408 F.3d 803, 814, 818 (6th Cir. 2005); Mejia v. City of New York, 228 F. Supp. 2d 234, 251–52 (E.D.N.Y. 2002).

[236]Pembaur v. City of Cincinnati, 475 U.S. 469, 480, 106 S. Ct. 1292 (1986) (plurality opinion); *see* Hampton Co. Nat. Sur., LLC v. Tunica County, Miss., 543 F.3d 221 (5th Cir. 2008); Williams v. Kaufman County, 352 F.3d 994, 1013–14 (5th Cir. 2003) (county

could be held liable for mass detention and strip searches where the Sheriff, the relevant policymaker, authorized them and testified they were consistent with policy). The Supreme Court has cautioned that a single decision will support municipal liability only "where the evidence that the municipality had acted and that the plaintiff had suffered a deprivation of federal rights also proved fault and causation." Board of County Comm'rs v. Brown, 520 U.S. 397, 404, 117 S. Ct. 1382 (1997).

[237]Amnesty America v. Town of West Hartford, 361 F.3d 113, 126–28 (2d Cir. 2004) (holding allegation that Chief of Police observed excessive force and failed to intervene stated a municipal liability claim); Brown v. Bryan County, OK, 219 F.3d 450, 459–62 (5th Cir. 2000) (single failure to train could result in municipal liability).

[238]In Alabama, authority over jail prisoners, employees, and the jail itself rests with the Sheriff, who is considered a state official. Marsh v. Butler County, Ala., 268 F.3d 1014, 1028 (11th Cir. 2001) (en banc); *see* Powell v. Barrett, 496 F.3d 1288, 1305–08 (11th Cir. 2007) (in Georgia, sheriffs function as agents of the state, not the county, with respect to policies and procedures governing jail conditions), *on rehearing on other grounds*, 541 F.3d 1298 (11th Cir. 2008) (en banc). In other states, sheriffs are county policymakers, at least for purposes of jail management. *See* Cortez v. Los Angeles, 294 F.3d 1186, 1189–90 (9th Cir. 2002) (California sheriff); DeGenova v. Sheriff of Du Page County, 209 F.3d 973, 975–77 (7th Cir. 2000) (Illinois sheriff). Whether the Sheriff is a state or local official depends on state law. McMillian v. Monroe County, Ala., 520 U.S. 781, 117 S. Ct. 1734 (1997); *see id.*, 520 U.S. at 795 & n.10 (noting variations among states). Whether a sheriff is a county or state official also determines whether she is protected by the Eleventh Amendment. *See* § L.1.a of this chapter, n.742.

[239]Surprenant v. Rivas, 424 F.3d 5, 20–21 (1st Cir. 2005) (affirming jury verdict against municipality based on Sheriff's failure to remedy obvious unsafe conditions); Redman v. County of San Diego, 942 F.2d 1435, 1444-45 (9th Cir. 1991) (en banc) (policies of overcrowding and inadequate classification supported municipal liability); Moore v. Morgan, 922 F.2d 1553, 1557 (11th Cir. 1991) (damages awarded based on a policy of delaying paying for a new jail); Thompson v. City of Los Angeles, 885 F.2d 1439, 1448–49 (9th Cir. 1989) (custom of providing inadequate bed space in jail could support municipal liability); Anela v. City of Wildwood, 790 F.2d 1063, 1069 (3d Cir. 1986) ("long-standing" unconstitutional jail conditions amounted to a municipal policy); Goodson v. City of Atlanta, 763 F.2d 1381, 1387–88 (11th Cir.) (inhumane jail conditions that had been called to the City Council's attention without action supported municipal liability), *rehearing denied*, 770 F.2d 175 (11th Cir. 1985); *see* Lopez v. LeMaster, 172 F.3d 756, 762–64 (10th Cir. 1999) (Sheriff's failure to provide

recovered damages in cases where municipal policies resulted in inadequate medical care or in the failure to provide adequate protection against assault by other inmates.[240] The same is true of police or jail procedures that were inadequate to prevent predictable constitutional violations.[241]

Inadequate training, supervision, or discipline of law enforcement personnel may support municipal liability if it is found to be so deficient as to constitute a policy of deliberate indifference,[242] either in jails and prisons[243] or in police departments.[244] There must be evidence about deficiencies

in training or supervision; courts will not assume that if prison staff violate your rights, they must have been inadequately trained or supervised.[245] Mere failure to respond to a few complaints or to give all the training that could have been provided will not make the local government liable.[246] If the municipality has training or procedures in place to deal with a particular problem, the fact that they occasionally fail to work or that employees sometimes disregard them does not make the municipality liable.[247] It is possible

_____

adequate staffing and surveillance and county government's failure to provide adequate funding could be policies of deliberate indifference in inmate–inmate assault case).

[240]See Ch. 2, § F.1.a, concerning medical care cases, and § G.1.e, concerning inmate assault cases.

[241]Oviatt by and through Waugh v. Pearce, 954 F.2d 1470, 1478 (9th Cir. 1992) (lack of procedures for avoiding detention without arraignment); Rivas v. Freeman, 940 F.2d 1491, 1495–96 (11th Cir. 1991) (inadequate procedures for identifying arrestees); DiLoreto v. Borough of Oaklyn, 744 F. Supp. 610, 623–24 (D.N.J. 1990) (lack of policy concerning bathroom visits by detainees); Watson v. McGee, 527 F. Supp. 234, 242 (S.D.Ohio 1981) (inadequate fire safety procedures in jail).

[242]Board of County Commissioners v. Brown, 520 U.S. 397, 407–08, 117 S. Ct. 1382 (1997); Canton v. Harris, 489 U.S. 378, 390, 109 S. Ct. 1197 (1989) ("[I]t may happen that in light of the duties assigned to specific officers or employees the need for more or different training is so obvious . . . that the policymakers of the city can reasonably be said to have been deliberately indifferent to the need."); see Conn v. City of Reno, 572 F.3d 1047, 1063 (9th Cir. 2009) (failure to train officers in suicide prevention and recognition of suicide risks could be found deliberately indifferent in light of predictability of police encounters with suicidal persons).

[243]Long v. County of Los Angeles, 442 F.3d 1178, 1187–88 (9th Cir. 2006) (inadequate training for nurses in monitoring, documenting, and assessing acute medical conditions in a jail with limited medical services where medically unstable prisoners needed to be transferred to a hospital); Olsen v. Layton Hills Mall, 312 F.3d 1304, 1319–20 (10th Cir. 2002) (evidence of failure to train jail's prebooking officers to recognize obsessive-compulsive disorder and to know what to do about it presented a jury question of deliberate indifference); Ware v. Jackson County, Mo., 150 F.3d 873, 885 (8th Cir. 1998) (holding failure to discipline officers for rape and sexual abuse could support municipal liability; where close supervision is needed but not provided, "the inevitable result is a continuation of the misconduct"); Young v. City of Augusta, Georgia, 59 F.3d 1160, 1171–72 (11th Cir. 1995) (holding evidence of lack of training to recognize the need for mental health treatment raised a triable question of municipal liability); Leach v. Shelby County Sheriff, 891 F.2d 1241 (6th Cir. 1989) (evidence of sheriff's failure to supervise and discipline staff with respect to the treatment of paraplegic inmates supported county liability).

[244]Gregory v. City of Louisville, 444 F.3d 725, 753–54 (6th Cir. 2006) (inadequate training or supervision as to duty to disclose exculpatory material stated a claim against city); Cruz v. City of Laramie, Wyo., 239 F.3d 1183, 1191 (10th Cir. 2001) (failure to train police officers in the use of hobble restraints, which were provided in police cars and which officials knew carried a risk of positional asphyxia, presented a material factual question as to municipal deliberate indifference); Brown v. Bryant County,

Oklahoma, 219 F.3d 450, 463 (5th Cir. 2000) (finding municipal liability based on Sheriff's failure to train an inexperienced officer with a questionable record); Mettler v. Whitledge, 165 F.3d 1197, 1205 (8th Cir. 1999) ("Evidence that a police department has failed to investigate previous incidents similar to the incident in question may support a finding that a municipal custom exists, and that such a custom encourages or allows officers to use excessive force without concern for punishment."); Robles v. City of Fort Wayne, 113 F.3d 732, 735 (7th Cir. 1997); Beck v. City of Pittsburgh, 89 F.3d 966, 975 (3d Cir. 1996) (evidence of lack of system for tracking civilian complaints against police raised a jury question of municipal liability); Parrish v. Luckie, 963 F.2d 201, 203–05 (8th Cir. 1992); Russo v. City of Cincinnati, 953 F.2d 1036, 1047–48 (6th Cir. 1992) (evidence of inadequate training in use of force against mentally ill persons supported a deliberate indifference claim); Ricciuti v. New York City Transit Authority, 941 F.2d 119, 123 (2d Cir. 1991) (municipal policy of deliberate indifference may be shown by "evidence that the municipality had notice of but repeatedly failed to make any meaningful investigation into charges that police officers had used excessive force"); Hammer v. Gross, 932 F.2d 842, 850 (9th Cir. 1991) (leaving option of forcible blood extraction to officers' discretion was evidence of a city policy permitting unreasonable force); Gentile v. County of Suffolk, 926 F.2d 142, 152–53 (2d Cir. 1991); Sharpe v. City of Lewisburg, Tenn., 677 F. Supp. 1362, 1368 (M.D.Tenn. 1988) (county held liable based on failure to train police officers to deal with predictable problems with mentally ill persons). Additional cases concerning municipal liability for police misconduct are cited in Ch. 2, § G.2.d, nn.1128–1129.

[245]Woloszyn v. County of Lawrence, 396 F.3d 314, 325–26 (3d Cir. 2005); Amnesty America v. Town of West Hartford, 361 F.3d 113, 130 (2d Cir. 2004) (plaintiff must show "more than the mere fact that the misconduct occurred in the first place"); Lopez v. LeMaster, 172 F.3d 756, 760 (10th Cir. 1999) (plaintiff "must identify a specific deficiency in the county's training program closely related to his ultimate injury, and must prove that the deficiency in training actually caused his jailer to act with deliberate indifference").

[246]Colburn v. Upper Darby Township, 946 F.2d 1017, 1029–30 (3d Cir. 1991) (plaintiffs could not prevail on claim of inadequate training without evidence of specific training that could reasonably be expected to prevent the constitutional violation); Mateyko v. Felix, 924 F.2d 824, 826 (9th Cir. 1990) (limitations on police training in use of taser guns did not amount to deliberate indifference).

[247]Johnson v. Blaukat, 453 F.3d 1108, 1114 (8th Cir. 2006) (violations of municipal policy do not state a claim against the municipality); Holmes v. Sheahan, 930 F.2d 1196, 1201–02 (7th Cir. 1991) (where county jail had procedures to ensure delivery of medical care, the fact that plaintiff "[fell] through the cracks" did not establish municipal liability); Wedemeier v. City of Ballwin,

to establish municipal liability for hiring decisions, but such claims are more difficult to prove than training claims.[248]

Some cases have held that if individual officers or employees are not found to have violated the Constitution, the municipality cannot be held liable either.[249] We think that depends on the circumstances. If a ruling on the individuals' conduct establishes that there was *no* constitutional violation, there is nothing for the city or county to be liable for. But often it is not that simple.

Courts have identified several situations where municipal liability can be found without individual liability. The combined conduct of several municipal employees acting pursuant to municipal policy may add up to a constitutional violation even if none of the named defendants individually violated the Constitution.[250] A municipality's failure to provide adequate jail funding, staffing, or procedures may cause a constitutional violation even if the individual staff members involved are doing the best they can in a bad situation.[251]

A municipality may be liable where the plaintiff's injury results from improper training or procedure even if the individual officer is exonerated.[252] Individual defendants may be entitled to qualified immunity for violating the Constitution, leaving the municipality as the only non-immune defendant.[253] A plaintiff may fail to name the correct individual defendants, or any individual defendants, but could still recover against the municipality if injured by a municipal policy.[254]

Where both a municipality and individual defendants are sued, defendants often ask the court to bifurcate (divide) the trial, first trying the claims against the individuals and then trying the claims against the municipality if necessary. Whether to grant such a motion is within the discretion of the district court.[255] Reasons favoring bifurcation include the possibility that a ruling in favor of individual defendants may mean that no trial is needed against the municipality, or that evidence that would come in against the municipality might be prejudicial to the individual defendants.[256] However, many courts have refused requests to bifurcate.[257]

---

931 F.2d 24, 26 (8th Cir. 1991) ("a single deviation from a written, official policy does not prove a conflicting custom or usage").

[248]Board of County Commissioners of Bryan County v. Brown, 520 U.S. 397, 409–10, 117 S. Ct. 1382 (1997) (noting that it is more difficult to predict the consequences of a bad hiring decision than those of a failure to train a staff member concerning a required skill); Wassum v. City of Bellaire, Texas, 861 F.2d 453, 456 (5th Cir. 1988) (minor departures from screening guidelines for police officers did not establish deliberate indifference).

[249]*See* Los Angeles v. Heller, 475 U.S. 796, 799, 106 S. Ct. 1571 (1986) (per curiam) (". . . [N]either *Monell* [citation omitted] nor any other of our cases authorizes the award of damages against a municipal corporation based on the actions of one of its officers when in fact the jury has concluded that the officer inflicted no constitution harm."); Ewolski v. City of Brunswick, 287 F.3d 492, 510 (6th Cir. 2002) ("Where . . . a municipality's liability is alleged on the basis of the unconstitutional actions of its employees, it is necessary to show that the employees inflicted a constitutional harm." (citation omitted)); Watkins v. City of Battle Creek, 273 F.3d 682, 687 (6th Cir. 2001) (if individual defendants are not found to have violated the Constitution, the city could not be held liable for inadequate training); Trigalet v. City of Tulsa, 239 F.3d 1150, 1155 (10th Cir.2001).

[250]Barrett v. Orange County Human Rights Com'n, 194 F.3d 341, 350 (2d Cir. 1999) ("[U]nder *Monell* municipal liability for constitutional injuries may be found to exist even in the absence of individual liability, at least so long as the injuries complained of are not solely attributable to the actions of named individual defendants."); Garcia v. Salt Lake County, 768 F.2d 303, 310 (10th Cir. 1985).

[251]Thomas v. Cook County Sheriff's Dep't, 588 F.3d 445, 455 (7th Cir. 2009) (finding municipal deliberate indifference, but not individual defendants' deliberate indifference, where known breakdown in procedures made it impossible for medical staff to respond adequately); Blackmore v. Kalamazoo County, 390 F.3d 890, 900 (6th Cir. 2004) (failure to provide substitute nurse when jail nurse was absent could support municipal liability); Anderson v. City of Atlanta, 778 F.2d 678, 686 (11th Cir. 1985). *But see* McDowell v. Brown, 392 F.3d 1283, 1290–92 (11th Cir. 2004) (inadequate staffing of "field division," resulting in delay in getting plaintiff to the hospital, did not support municipal liability where

understaffing was not shown to be intended to affect field division and plaintiff failed to show numerous incidents of delay; distinguishing *Anderson*).

[252]Fairley v. Luman, 281 F.3d 913, 916–18 (9th Cir. 2002) (improper arrest and detention resulted from "the collective inaction of the Long Beach Police Department"); Hopkins v. Andaya, 958 F.2d 881, 888 (9th Cir. 1992) (city could be liable for improper training/procedure even if the officer was found not liable for excessive use of force); Rivas v. Freeman, 940 F.2d 1491 (11th Cir. 1991) (county held liable for lack of policies, procedures, and training, but arresting officers were merely negligent and their acts flowed from the lack of policies).

[253]Chew v. Gates, 27 F.3d 1432, 1438–39 (9th Cir.1994); Newcomb v. City of Troy, 719 F. Supp. 1408, 1416–17 (E.D. Mich. 1989); *see* Owen v. City of Independence, 445 U.S. 622, 652, 100 S. Ct. 1398 (1980) (a "'systemic' injury" may "result not so much from the conduct of any single individual, but from the interactive behavior of several government officials, each of whom may be acting in good faith." (citation omitted)).

[254]Wilson v. Town of Mendon, 294 F.3d 1, 7 (1st Cir. 2002).

[255]Amato v. City of Saratoga Springs, 170 F.3d 311, 316 (2d Cir. 1999) (affirming grant of bifurcation). Bifurcation is authorized by Rule 42(b) of the Federal Rules of Civil Procedure, which gives the district court discretion to order separate trials to further convenience, avoid prejudice, or promote efficiency.

[256]Amato v. City of Saratoga Springs, 170 F.3d at 316.

[257]Jeanty v. County of Orange, 379 F. Supp. 2d 533, 549–50 (S.D.N.Y. 2005) ("the presumption is that all claims in a case will be resolved in a single trial, and 'it is only in exceptional circumstances where there are special and persuasive reasons for departing from this practice that distinct causes of action asserted in the same case may be made the subject of separate trials'"; holding "use of a special verdict form, a well-adapted jury charge, and carefully crafted limiting [jury] instructions" is preferable to possibly holding two trials (citation omitted)); Green v. Baca, 226 F.R.D. 624, 633 (C.D.Cal. 2005) (denying bifurcation where no individual defendants were sued); Estate of Owensby v. City of Cincinnati, 385 F. Supp. 2d 626, 666–67 (S.D.Ohio 2004) (denying bifurcation), *aff'd and remanded on other grounds*, 414 F.3d 596 (6th Cir. 2005);

If you have a state law *respondeat superior* tort claim against the municipality, be sure to point out to the court that that claim requires no additional discovery or evidence, so it should be tried with the individual claims if the case is bifurcated.[258]

The Supreme Court has said that in your complaint, you do not need to describe the municipal policy you challenge in any great detail, because such claims are subject to the same "notice pleading" requirement that applies generally to complaints in federal court.[259] However, a recent Supreme Court decision seems to make the federal pleading standard more demanding,[260] and that decision may apply to municipal policy claims.[261] You should at a minimum state what the policy is, and how you believe it caused your injury (*e.g.*, in a use of force case, you might allege that you were assaulted by staff as a result of a policy of biased investigations and refusal to discipline staff members who use excessive force, which leaves staff free to commit assaults knowing that they will not be held accountable, if you have a basis to believe that that is true).[262]

Local governments sued under § 1983 (and officials sued in their official capacities, which amounts to the same thing)

are not entitled to immunity defenses,[263] nor may punitive damages be assessed against them.[264]

c. Capacity   When you sue prison officials or other employees of a government agency, you should indicate whether you are naming them in their individual or their official capacities. This term refers to the capacity in which you sue them, not the capacity in which they acted during the events you sue about.[265] In a § 1983 case, each defendant against whom you seek damages should be named in her individual capacity in your complaint. Each defendant against whom you seek an injunction should be named in her official capacity. If you seek both kinds of relief against a defendant, name her in both capacities. The rules are a little different for cases brought under the federal disability statutes or the statutes that protect religious freedom, as explained in the sections on those statutes.[266]

If you wish to sue for damages for injuries resulting from a city or county policy, as explained in the previous section, you are allowed to name the officials responsible in their official capacities, because this amounts to the same thing as suing the city or county. However, it will probably be less confusing to name the city or county itself, and only name those officials whom you wish to sue in their individual capacities.

The reasons underlying these rules are discussed in more detail in other sections of this chapter.[267]

C. TORT ACTIONS

A tort is a personal injury caused by the wrongful or negligent act of another person. Most torts fall into two broad categories: intentional torts and negligence.

Medina v. City of Chicago, 100 F. Supp. 2d 893, 896 (N.D.Ill. 2000).

[258]Estate of Owensby v. City of Cincinnati, 385 F. Supp. 2d 626, 666 (S.D.Ohio 2004).

[259]Leatherman v. Tarrant County Narcotics Intelligence & Coordination Unit, 507 U.S. 163, 168, 113 S. Ct. 1160 (1993). There was some disagreement in lower courts as to what *Leatherman* required. *Compare* Galbraith v. County of Santa Clara, 307 F.3d 1119, 1127 (9th Cir. 2002) (holding "nothing more than a bare allegation that the individual officers' conduct conformed to official policy, custom, or practice" is required); Lanigan v. Village of East Hazel Crest, Ill., 110 F.3d 467, 480 (7th Cir. 1997) (holding general allegation of policy of inadequate police training or supervision was sufficient) *with* Spiller v. City of Texas City, Police Dep't, 130 F.3d 162, 167 (5th Cir. 1997) (requiring description of policy and its relationship to the underlying constitutional violation to "contain specific facts").

[260]*See* Ashcroft v. Iqbal, ___ U.S. ___, 129 S. Ct. 1937, 1949 (2009). The *Iqbal* holding is discussed in Ch. 9, § B.1, concerning pleading of complaints, and § B.4.a of this chapter, concerning supervisory liability.

[261]*See* McClelland v. City of Modesto, 2009 WL 2941480, *8 (E.D.Cal., Sept. 10, 2009) (allegations of municipal policy dismissed as conclusory); 5 Borough Pawn, LLC v. City of New York, 640 F. Supp. 2d 268, 299-300 (S.D.N.Y. 2009) (allegation that police misconduct resulted from municipal policy was implausible because plaintiff did not identify other officers who acted similarly; it was more plausible that the defendant "was a rogue officer who disobeyed City policy").

[262]*See* Ch. 2, § G.2.d, nn.1128–1129.

[263]Leatherman v. Tarrant County Narcotics Intelligence and Coordination Unit, 507 U.S. 163, 166, 113 S. Ct. 1160 (1993); Owen v. City of Independence, 445 U.S. 622, 100 S. Ct. 1398 (1980) (concerning qualified immunity); *see* § L of this chapter for a discussion of immunity.

[264]Cook County v. U.S. ex rel. Chandler, 538 U.S. 119, 123 S. Ct. 1239 (2003) ("Since municipalities' common law resistance to punitive damages still obtains, '[t]he general rule today is that no punitive damages are allowed unless expressly authorized by statute.'" (quoting Newport v. Fact Concerts, Inc., 453 U.S. 247, 260 n.21, 101 S. Ct. 2748 (1981)); *see* § O.1.d of this chapter for a discussion of punitive damages.

[265]Hafer v. Melo, 502 U.S. 21, 25, 112 S. Ct. 358 (1991); *see* Will v. Michigan Dep't of State Police, 491 U.S. 58, 71, 109 S. Ct. 2304 (1989) ("[A] suit against a state official in his or her official capacity is not a suit against the official but rather is a suit against the official's office.").

[266]*See* Ch. 2, § F.4.h(2), concerning the disability statutes, and Ch. 3, § D.1.b, concerning the religion statutes.

[267]Capacity issues involving state officials are discussed in § L.1 of this chapter. Damage cases against city and county officials are discussed in section § B.4.b of this chapter.

The intentional torts with which prisoners are most likely to be concerned include assault and battery,[268] false arrest or imprisonment,[269] malicious prosecution,[270] invasion of privacy,[271] and various torts involving deprivation of property,[272] all of which are discussed elsewhere in this Manual. There is also a tort of intentional infliction of mental or emotional distress (sometimes called "outrage"), which requires proof of (1) extreme and outrageous conduct (2) that intentionally or recklessly (3) causes emotional distress (4) which must be severe.[273] Such claims have been upheld in a number of prisoner cases where the conduct at issue was extreme enough.[274] However, the threshold for this tort seems to vary from court to court, with many claims that seem outrageous to us dismissed in some courts but allowed to go forward in others.[275]

Negligence is defined as "the failure to use such care as a reasonably prudent and careful person would use under similar circumstances,"[276] and it can include a broad range of acts or failures to act that result in injury. Prisoners have successfully pursued negligence claims based on accidents at work or elsewhere,[277] assaults by other prisoners,[278] loss of property,[279] medical malpractice or other forms of negligence related to medical care,[280] and negligent supervision or training resulting in injury,[281] among others.[282]

---

[268]Assault and battery are discussed in Ch. 2, § G.2.e.

[269]These torts amount to the same thing. W. Page Keeton *et al, Prosser and Keeton on the Law of Torts* § 11, at 47 (5th ed. 1984). *See* Ch. 4, § D.1.r(4), for a definition of false imprisonment.

[270]Malicious prosecution is "the groundless institution of criminal proceedings against the plaintiff." Prosser and Keeton, § 11 at 54. The elements of malicious prosecution are described in Ch. 4, § H.1.r(4). The United States Supreme Court recently held that a plaintiff is required to show a "lack of probable cause" in a claim of retaliatory prosecution. Hartman v. Moore, 547 U.S. 250, 265, 126 S. Ct. 1695 (2006).

[271]Invasion of privacy is discussed in Ch. 3, § E.3.

[272]These are discussed in Ch. 4, § H.8.c.

[273]White v. Ottinger, 442 F. Supp. 2d 236, 251 (E.D.Pa. 2006); *accord*, Estate of Trentadue ex rel. Aguilar v. U.S., 397 F.3d 840, 855–56 (10th Cir. 2005) (Oklahoma law); Doe v. Mills, 212 Mich. App. 73, 91, 536 N.W.2d 824 (1995); *see* Prosser and Keeton, § 12 at 57 (stating this tort requires the plaintiff to prove "infliction of mental suffering by conduct of a flagrant character, the enormity of which adds especial weight to the plaintiff's claim"); *accord*, Doe v. Mills, 212 Mich.App. at 91(conduct must be more than mere insulting, malicious, or aggravating; it must be "atrocious" and "utterly intolerable in a civilized community"). Courts have held that sexual abuse may constitute the intentional infliction of emotional distress, *see* Ch. 2, § G.2.c(4), n.1109, and at least one court has held that excessive force may be also. *See* Ch. 2, § G.2.e, n.1135.

Some states also recognize the tort of negligent infliction of emotional distress. *See, e.g.*, Bernstein v. Roberts, 405 F. Supp. 2d 34, 41–42 (D.D.C. 2005) (plaintiff must show (1) that Defendants acted negligently, (2) that Plaintiff suffered either a physical impact or was within the "zone of danger" of the defendants' actions, and (3) that Plaintiff suffered emotional distress that was "serious and verifiable"); Brown v. Youth Services Intern. of South Dakota, Inc., 89 F. Supp. 2d 1095, 1104–05 (D.S.D. 2000) (physical injury required for a negligent infliction of emotional distress claim).

[274]*See, e.g.*, Orwat v. Maloney, 360 F. Supp. 2d 146, 165 (D.Mass. 2005) ("falsely testifying against an inmate, knowing that the testimony would result in [disciplinary] confinement"); Bunyon v. Burke County, 306 F. Supp. 2d 1240, 1262 (S.D.Ga. 2004) (evidence of prolonged medical neglect resulting in paralysis supported outrage claim as well as medical negligence), *aff'd*, 116 Fed.Appx. 249 (11th Cir. 2004) (unpublished); Schmidt v. Odell, 64 F. Supp. 2d 1014, 1032 (D.Kan. 1999) (failure to accommodate double amputee's disability, so he had to move around on his knees); Kesler v. King, 29 F. Supp. 2d 356, 375 (S.D.Tex. 1998) (forcing prisoners to crawl on the floor while they were menaced and bitten by dogs,

resulting from inadequate supervision); Medley v. Turner, 869 F. Supp. 567, 578 (N.D.Ill. 1994) (failure to intervene in assault by another state trooper), *amended on other grounds*, 1995 WL 23522 (N.D.Ill., Jan. 14, 1995).

[275]*See, e.g.*, Garretson v. City of Madison Heights, 407 F.3d 789, 799 (6th Cir. 2005) (neglecting symptoms of diabetic crisis did not establish claim, because it had happened before and plaintiff wasn't seriously distressed; courts must distinguish between the outrageous and mere "petty oppression"); Austin v. Terhune, 367 F.3d 1167, 1172 (9th Cir. 2004) (allegation that a correction officer exposed his genitalia and made offensive statements to plaintiff and then filed a false disciplinary report when he complained did not state an outrage claim; the conduct was outrageous but there was no evidence of severe emotional distress); Jean-Laurent v. Wilkerson, 438 F. Supp. 2d 318, 328 (S.D.N.Y. 2006) (claim of excessive force does not sufficiently plead claim where plaintiff did not allege severe emotional distress); Jordan v. Delaware by and through the Delaware Dep't of Corrections, 433 F. Supp. 2d 433, 444 (D.Del. 2006) (denial of liver biopsy recommended by outside doctor was not extreme, outrageous, and/or exceeding "all possible bounds of decency"); Coppage v. Mann, 906 F. Supp. 1025, 1049–50 (E.D.Va. 1995) (medical neglect leading to paralysis, and failure to provide assistance after paralysis, was not outrageous enough).

[276]*Black's Law Dictionary* at 930 (8th ed. 1998).

[277]*See* Ch. 2, § G.3.d.

[278]*See* Ch. 2, § G.1.f.

[279]See Ch. 4, § H.8.c.

[280]*See* Ch. 2, § F.5.

[281]*See, e.g.*, Daskalea v. District of Columbia, 227 F.3d 433, 445 (D.C. Cir. 2000) (negligent supervision leading to sexual abuse); Pizzuto v. County of Nassau, 239 F. Supp. 2d 301, 312 (E.D.N.Y. 2003) (supervisor found grossly negligent in supervision of staff who beat a prisoner); Brown v. Youth Services Intern. of South Dakota, Inc., 89 F. Supp. 2d 1095, 1102–04 (D.S.D. 2000) (negligent hiring, retention, and supervision resulting in sexual abuse by staff); Kesler v. King, 29 F. Supp. 2d 356, 376–77 (S.D.Tex. 1998) (negligent hiring, training, and supervision).

[282]*See, e.g.*, Hott v. Hennepin County, Minn., 260 F.3d 901, 908–09 (8th Cir. 2001) (officer's failure to check on condition of suicidal prisoner as required by jail policy raised a factual issue as to his negligence); Downey v. Denton County, Texas, 119 F.3d 381, 387–88 (5th Cir. 1997) (leaving a female prisoner alone with an employee who sexually assaulted her was negligent); Jean-Laurent v. Wilkerson, 438 F. Supp. 2d 318, 327–28 (S.D.N.Y. 2006) (failure to intervene in an assault, authorizing the use of excessive force, and failing to intervene in an abusive strip search would constitute negligence if proven).

To constitute negligence, an act must violate a "duty of care" owed to the injured person,[283] and it must cause harm that is "within the class of reasonably foreseeable hazards that the duty exists to prevent."[284]

1. State Court Tort Actions

Torts are matters of state law and, with some exceptions,[285] you must bring tort cases in state court. Different states have different rules concerning torts committed by state, city, and county employees, including prison personnel. In many states, you can bring tort claims about injuries you sustain in prison against the state or local government that runs the prison, rather than individual prison employees, under the doctrine of *respondeat superior*.[286] In some cases you *must* bring suits about the torts of state employees against the state itself, often in a special court.[287] In other states, you must sue the individual employee.[288]

Many states require that you file a notice of claim or intent to sue within a very short time (often 90 days) after the injury. Some states limit the availability of punitive damages or of trial by jury in tort actions against governmental bodies. States have rules of immunity in tort cases that vary from state to state and are also different from the immunities available under § 1983.[289]

Some states have rules restricting or banning certain kinds of tort suits by prisoners. For example, some do not permit suits by prisoners against public employees or state or local agencies based on injuries inflicted by other prisoners.[290] In those states, you may have no remedy for an

---

[283]In general, prison officials owe prisoners a duty of care to protect them from risks that, as prisoners, they have diminished ability to protect themselves from. *See, e.g.*, Sanchez v. State of New York, 99 N.Y.2d 247, 252, 784 N.E.2d 675, 754 N.Y.S.2d 621 (N.Y. 2002) (duty to protect against assault by other prisoners); Joseph v. State, 26 P.3d 459, 467 (Alaska 2001) (duty to protect against self-harm); Moralli v. Lake County, Mont., 255 Mont. 23, 28, 839 P.2d 1287 (Mont. 1992) (duty to provide a "reasonably safe accommodation"; affirming liability for unsafe bathroom floor conditions). Prison officials have a duty to provide medical care, *see* Heumphreus v. State, 334 N.W.2d 757, 759 (Iowa 1983) ("reasonable diligence with reference to the care of injured, ill, or diseased inmates"), and medical personnel owe the same duty of care to prisoner-patients as they do to "free world" patients. *See* Ch. 2, § F.5, n.794.

[284]Sanchez v. State of New York, 99 N.Y.2d at 252; *see* Palay v. U.S., 349 F.3d 418, 433–34 (7th Cir. 2003) (discussing foreseeability); Downey v. Denton County, Texas, 119 F.3d 381, 387–88 (5th Cir. 1997) (same).

[285]As discussed in the next section, federal employees are absolutely immune from personal liability for torts committed within the scope of their employment. These may be redressed in federal court under the Federal Tort Claims Act.

If you have a federal law claim against state or local government personnel that belongs in federal court, you may be able to include a state law tort claim arising from the same facts in the case under the supplemental (pendent) jurisdiction of the federal courts. *See* § F.1 of this chapter. If the person who committed the tort is a citizen of a different state from you, you can bring a tort suit under the diversity jurisdiction of the federal courts. *See* § F.2 of this chapter.

[286]*See, e.g.*, 55 ILCS 5/3-6016 ("The sheriff shall be liable for any neglect or omission of the duties of his or her office, when occasioned by a deputy or auxiliary deputy, in the same manner as for his or her own personal neglect or omission."); Longin by Longin v. Kelly, 875 F. Supp. 196, 201–02 (S.D.N.Y. 1995) (state *respondeat superior* rule making employers responsible for employees' torts committed within the scope of employment applied to city government employees).

[287]For example, in Michigan all tort claims against employees of a State agency for acts within the scope of their employment (official capacity) must be brought against the state in the Court of Claims. Mich. Compiled Laws § 600.6419. However, "[c]ertain governmental instrumentalities are never within the jurisdiction of the Court of Claims. These include: counties, cities, villages, townships and school districts." *See* Doan v. Kellogg Community College, 80 Mich.App 316, 320; 263 NW2d 357 (1977) (citing MCL 691.1401(b) – (d)). Other states have similar schemes. *See* Fla. Stat. Ann. § 768.28 (providing for *respondeat superior* liability for the state and its subdivisions, providing immunity for individual employees).

The Supreme Court has recently struck down part of the New York State tort claim scheme, which not only directs tort claims against state employees to a special court, but also prohibits any individual capacity claims against correctional personnel—including § 1983 suits asserting federal claims—to be heard in its courts. The Court held that barring certain types of federal law claims from state courts, while allowing similar state law claims to go forward, discriminated against federal claims in violation of the Supremacy Clause of the Constitution. Haywood v. Drown, ___ U.S. ___, 129 S. Ct. 2108 (2009).

[288]For example, in California "public entities" are not liable for injuries caused by or to prisoners, Cal. Govt. Code § 844.6, except for certain limited categories including Interference with the right of prisoners to seek judicial review of the legality of their confinement, Cal. Govt. Code § 845.4, and failure to summon medical care for prisoner in need of immediate medical care. Cal. Govt. Code § 845.6. *See, e.g.*, Wright v. State, 122 Cal.App.4th 659, 672, 19 Cal.Rptr.3d 92 (Cal. App. 3 Dist. 2004) (state immunity from liability to prisoner); Teter v. City of Newport Beach, 30 Cal.4th 446, 451, 133 Cal.Rptr.2d 139 (2003) (city immunity from liability for injury to prisoner). Most prisoner tort suits must therefore be brought against the individual employees.

[289]*See* § L.5 of this chapter for a discussion of tort immunity rules; *see also* Ch. 2, § G.1.f, concerning their operation in inmate assault cases, and § F.5, n.810, concerning medical malpractice cases.

[290]N.J.S.A. 59:5-2(b)(4) (cited in Davidson v. Cannon, 474 U.S. 344, 346, 106 S. Ct. 668 (1986)); Bona v. Wynn, 311 N.J.Super. 257, 260, 709 A.2d 837 (1997) (applying statute to bar claim). Such prohibitions amount to immunity rules, and they are discussed further in § L.5 of this chapter.

assault by another inmate except for a civil rights suit alleging a constitutional violation.[291]

For all the foregoing reasons, you must review the tort law of your state—and in particular the relevant statutes—in order to determine if the injury you have suffered can be pursued successfully as a tort claim.

2. Federal Tort Claims Act

The Federal Tort Claims Act (FTCA)[292] allows suit against the federal government for torts committed by its employees,[293] with several important exceptions. The FTCA is the *only* remedy for most torts committed by federal employees within the scope of their employment. Federal employees are absolutely immune as individuals from suit for such torts.[294] The only proper defendant in an FTCA case is the United States.[295] If you file a tort suit against a federal employee individually, the Attorney General will certify that the employee was acting within the scope of her office or employment, the employee will be dismissed from the action, and the United States will be substituted as the defendant. If the case was filed in state court, it will be removed to federal court and will be treated as a suit against the United States under the FTCA.[296] These provisions do not apply to constitutional claims asserted against federal employees.[297] If a particular set of facts constitutes both a tort and a constitutional violation, you can pursue both an FTCA tort claim against the United States and a constitutional "*Bivens* claim" against the individuals.[298] The consequences of doing so, or of pursuing either remedy by itself, are discussed in another section.[299]

The government is generally not liable under the FTCA for the torts of private contractors.[300]

There is no right to a jury trial under the FTCA.[301]

As discussed below, the FTCA does not provide a remedy for all torts. If your suit alleges a tort that the FTCA does not cover, you may be left without any tort remedy.[302]

a. Liability Under the FTCA The FTCA permits suit in federal court for damages

> for injury or loss of property, or personal injury or death caused by the negligent or wrongful act or omission of any employee of the Government while acting within the scope of his office or employment, under circumstances where the United States, if a private person, would be liable to the claimant in accordance with the law of the place where the act or omission occurred.[303]

The FTCA makes the government liable under the doctrine of *respondeat superior* for many acts that would be common law torts in the state where they occurred.[304]

The FTCA provides a remedy only for tort claims,[305] and not for all of those. It excludes from its coverage certain intentional torts.[306] Others, including assault, battery, false imprisonment, false arrest, abuse of process, and malicious prosecution, are not actionable under the FTCA unless they are committed by federal investigative or law enforcement officers[307]—a category which includes federal

---

[291]*See* Ch. 2, § G.1, for a discussion of the constitutional law of inmate assault cases.

[292]28 U.S.C. §§ 1346(b), 2671–80.

[293]The United States Government can only be sued if it has specifically consented to be sued and has waived its sovereign immunity. *See* § L.1.b of this chapter for a discussion of federal sovereign immunity.

[294]28 U.S.C. § 2679(b)(1); Gutierrez de Martinez v. Lamagno, 515 U.S. 417, 425–26, 115 S. Ct. 2227 (1995).

[295]Jackson v. Kotter, 541 F.3d 688, 693 (7th Cir. 2008).

[296]28 U.S.C. § 2679 (d)(1)–(2). This statute is called the Federal Employees Liability Reform and Tort Compensation Act of 1988, or the Westfall Act. Its operation is discussed further in *Osborn v. Haley*, 549 U.S. 225, 127 S. Ct. 881 (2007).

[297]28 U.S.C. § 2679(b)(2)(A).

[298]*Bivens* claims are discussed in § B.2 of this chapter.

[299]*See* § H.2.b of this chapter.

[300]28 U.S.C. § 2671; *see* Alinsky v. U.S., 415 F.3d 639, 644 (7th Cir. 2005). A contractor may be deemed a federal employee whose acts subject the government to suit under the FTCA if the government exercises "day-to-day" control over the contractor's actions, but evidence of such control may be overcome by contract language or other facts designating the contractor as an independent contractor. Woodruff v. Covington, 389 F.3d 1117, 1127–28

(10th Cir. 2004). We would expect that most federal prison contracts would explicitly designate contractors as independent.

[301]28 U.S.C. § 2402; *see* § H.2.b of this chapter for further discussion.

[302]*See, e.g.*, B & A Marine Co., Inc. v. American Foreign Shipping Co., Inc., 23 F.3d 709, 714 (2d Cir. 1994) (citing U.S. v. Smith, 499 U.S. 160, 111 S. Ct. 1180 (1991)).

[303]28 U.S.C. § 1346(b).

[304]*See* U.S. v. Olson, 546 U.S. 43, 126 S. Ct. 510 (2005) (holding the government is liable under circumstances where a private person—not a state or local government—would be liable; circumstances need not be identical, only similar, to private liability for FTCA to provide a remedy).

[305]Paul v. U.S., 929 F.2d 1202, 1204 (7th Cir. 1991) (claim based on a plea bargain invokes contract, not tort, and is not actionable under the FTCA); City National Bank v. U.S., 907 F.2d 536, 546 (5th Cir. 1990) (grossly negligent breach of contractual duty excluded from FTCA as contract claim).

[306]Libel, slander, misrepresentation, deceit, and interference with contract rights are not actionable under the FTCA. 28 U.S.C. § 2680(h).

[307]28 U.S.C. § 2680(h).

Claims for unjust conviction and imprisonment may also be brought in the U.S. Court of Claims under the Unjust Conviction Statute for damages up to $100,000 for each 12-month period of incarceration for any plaintiff who was unjustly sentenced to death and $50,000 for each 12-month period of incarceration for any other plaintiff. 28 U.S.C. §§ 1495, 2513. To prevail, however, you have to get your conviction reversed or get pardoned on the ground that you were innocent and you must obtain a certificate of the court stating that you were innocent. These requirements are strictly applied. *See* Vincin v. U.S., 468 F.2d 930, 933 (Ct.Cl. 1972); Dethlefs v. U.S., 60 Fed.Cl. 810, 814 (2004) (dismissing a § 1495 claim, which

correctional officers.[308] Other intentional torts not mentioned in the statute may also be pursued under the FTCA.[309]

The FTCA generally does not allow suits for "constitutional torts" or other constitutional violations,[310] or for violations of federal statutes or regulations,[311] though if a state law tort is *also* a violation of federal constitution, statute, or regulations, that does not keep you from suing about the tort under the FTCA. If there is a state tort law duty of care, violation of a state or federal statute may support liability for negligence under the FTCA if violation of it would constitute negligence *per se* under state law.[312]

The FTCA extends to torts committed by federal employees within the "scope of [their] office or employment."[313] Whether a tort occurred within the scope of office or employment is governed by the law of the state where the tort occurred.[314] While definitions of scope of employment vary from state to state,[315] actions that have some relationship to the employee's job may be within the scope of employment even if they are unauthorized or even involve outright misconduct.[316] For federal law enforcement officers (which, as noted above, includes federal correctional officers), FTCA liability for certain intentional torts extends to those commited "within the scope of their authority *or* under color of Federal law,"[317] and the actions of prison and jail staff concerning prisoners will almost always be under color of federal law.[318] The Attorney General's certification that the defendant was acting within the scope of his employment is subject to judicial review.[319]

---

lacked an allegation that the conviction had been set aside, for failure to state a claim, rather than for lack of jurisdiction).

[308]McCarthy v. Madigan, 503 U.S.140, 155 n.6, 112 S. Ct. 1081 (1992) (noting government's concession); Hernandez v. Lattimore, 612 F.2d 61, 64 (2d Cir.1979); Sheppard v. U.S., 537 F. Supp. 2d 785, 791 (D.Md. 2008). One federal circuit has held that the exception for federal law enforcement officers applies only to actions performed in the course of a search, seizure, or arrest. Pooler v. U.S., 787 F.2d 868 (3d Cir. 1986). Most federal courts have rejected this interpretation. *See* Reynolds v. U.S., 549 F.3d 1108, 1114 (7th Cir. 2008); Ortiz v. Pearson, 88 F. Supp. 2d 151, 154–55 (S.D.N.Y. 2000).

This dispute over the law enforcement exception is an issue with respect to FTCA claims for false imprisonment. This subject is discussed in Ch. 4, § H.9, nn.1057–1063.

[309]*See, e.g.*, Raz v. U.S., 343 F.3d 945, 948 (8th Cir. 2003) and cases cited (invasion of privacy and trespass); Lhotka v. U.S., 114 F.3d 751, 753 (8th Cir. 1997) (trespass and nuisance).

[310]FDIC v. Meyer, 510 U.S. 471, 478, 114 S. Ct. 996 (1994) (FTCA's "reference to the 'law of the place' means law of the State— the source of substantive liability under the FTCA"); Carlson v. Green, 446 U.S. 14, 23, 100 S. Ct. 1468 (1980); Couden v. Duffy, 446 F.3d 483, 499 (3d Cir. 2006) and cases cited. You can bring an FTCA claim against the government and a constitutional claim against individual federal officials in the same case. *See* § H.2.b of this chapter for a more detailed discussion.

[311]Love v. U.S., 60 F.3d 642, 644 (9th Cir. 1995) ("The breach of a duty created by federal law is not, by itself, actionable under the FTCA."). An important exception is discussed below at nn.321–322.

[312]*See, e.g.*, Myers v. U.S., 17 F.3d 890, 899 (6th Cir. 1994) (there must be a tort duty under state law in order for federal regulations to define the standard of conduct under that duty); Lutz v. U.S., 685 F.2d 1178, 1184 (9th Cir. 1982) (same); American Exchange Bank of Madison, Wis. v. U.S., 257 F.2d 938, 942–53 (7th Cir. 1958) (state Safe Place Statute created duty of care; order of state Industrial Commission requiring handrails should be considered in determining whether duty was violated).

Negligence *per se* refers to violation of a regulation that causes the type of harm that the regulation was intended to prevent and that injures a member of the class of persons intended to be protected by the regulation. Swoboda v. U.S., 662 F.2d 326, 329 (5th Cir. 1981).

[313]28 U.S.C. § 1346(b)(1).

[314]McIntyre ex rel. Estate of McIntyre v. U.S., 545 F.3d 27, 38 (1st Cir. 2008); Johnson v. U.S., 534 F.3d 958, 963 (8th Cir. 2008); Harbury v. Hayden, 522 F.3d 413, 417 (D.C. Cir. 2008).

[315]McIntyre ex rel. Estate of McIntyre v. U.S., 545 F.3d at 38 (citing Massachusetts law that an employee's conduct is within the scope of his or her employment if (1) it is of the kind the employee was hired to perform, (2) it occurs within "authorized time and space limits," and (3) " 'it is motivated, at least in part, by a purpose to serve the employer.'" (citations omitted)); Johnson v. U.S., 534 F.3d at 963 (citing South Dakota law weighing "(1) whether the act is commonly done in the course of business; (2) the time, place, and purpose of the act; (3) whether the act is within the enterprise of the master; the similarity of the act done to the act authorized; (4) whether the means of doing harm has been furnished by the master; and (5) the extent of departure from the normal method of accomplishing an authorized result").

[316]McIntyre ex rel. Estate of McIntyre v. U.S., 545 F.3d at 38–47 (an FBI agent who leaked an informant's identity, resulting in his murder, acted within the scope of employment); Barry v. Whalen, 796 F. Supp. 885, 891–92 (E.D.Va. 1992). Scope of employment is discussed further in Ch. 2, § G.2.e, n.1148.

[317]28 U.S.C. § 2680(h) (emphasis supplied) (providing for liability for assault, battery, false imprisonment, false arrest, abuse of process, and malicious prosecution by federal law enforcement officers).

[318]*See* Bolton v. U.S., 347 F. Supp. 2d 1218, 1222–23 (N.D.Fla. 2004) (holding liability could extend to sexual battery by prison staff).

[319]Gutierrez de Martinez v. Lamagno, 515 U.S. 417, 115 S. Ct. 2227 (1995).

In most cases, torts committed by prison staff that harm prisoners will be within the scope of employment. In a borderline case, it will usually be in your interest to have the defendant certified as having acted within the scope of employment, because that way you are assured that the government will pay any judgment you recover. However, if your case involves a tort that the FTCA does not cover, a finding that the employee acted within the scope of employment means your lawsuit will be dismissed. In that kind of case, you might wish to contest the scope of employment determination, and argue that you should be able to proceed against the employee individually rather than the government. *See* Stokes v. Cross, 327 F.3d 1210, 1214 (D.C. Cir. 2003) ("[A] plaintiff challenging the government's scope of employment certification bears the burden of coming forward with specific facts rebutting the certification." (internal quotation marks and citation omitted)).

Substantive issues in an FTCA case are usually governed by state law,[320] with a very important exception. The Bureau of Prisons has a duty of care under federal statute to

> (2) provide suitable quarters and provide for the safekeeping, care, and subsistence of all persons charged with or convicted of offenses against the United States, or held as witnesses or otherwise;
>
> (3) provide for the protection, instruction, and discipline of all persons charged with or convicted of offenses against the United States . . . [321]

Negligent or intentional violations of this duty are actionable under the FTCA even if state law would not permit the suit.[322]

A wide variety of federal prisoner claims have been allowed to proceed under the FTCA, including assault by other prisoners,[323] assault and battery by staff,[324] medical malpractice,[325] and intentional infliction of emotional distress.[326]

Despite the statute's reference to loss of property, under current law, the FTCA does *not* generally provide a remedy for prisoners' lost property. The FTCA bars recovery for "[a]ny claim arising in respect of . . . the detention of any goods, merchandise, or other property by any officer of customs or excise or any other law enforcement officer."[327] Bureau of Prisons employees are "other law enforcement officers" under this provision, which means prisoners have no FTCA remedy when their property is "detained" by federal prison staff.[328] This decision, and other possible remedies for federal prisoners for property loss or damage, are discussed in another section.[329]

Accidents caused by prison staff's negligence are actionable under the FTCA as long as they are not work-related. The Inmate Accident Compensation system provides the only remedy for work accidents affecting prisoners.[330] Federal prosecutors are not considered law enforcement officers and cannot be sued under the FTCA, such as for malicious prosecution or abuse of process.[331]

You may be able to recover for injuries sustained in a local jail or private facility if you are placed in it by federal officials. The United States has a duty to use reasonable care in providing for the safety of federal prisoners confined in nonfederal institutions, and you can recover if they are negligent in doing so.[332] (This may be hard to prove, so it may be wise also to file a § 1983 claim or state law tort suit against any jail officials who were directly responsible for your injury.[333]) The government is not liable for the negligence of

---

[320]Molzof v. U.S., 502 U.S. 301, 303–07, 112 S. Ct. 711 (1992); Franklin v. U.S., 992 F.2d 1492, 1495 (10th Cir. 1993) (questions of liability under the FTCA are resolved in accordance with the law of the state where the alleged tortious activity took place).

[321]18 U.S.C. § 4042(a).

[322]U.S. v. Muniz, 374 U.S. 150, 165, 83 S. Ct. 1850 (1963) (inmate assault claim could be brought under the FTCA even though state tort law forbade such claims); Jones v. U.S., 91 F.3d 623, 624 (3d Cir. 1996).

[323]U.S. v. Muniz, 374 U.S. 150, 165, 83 S. Ct. 1850 (1973) (inmate assault claim could be brought under the FTCA even though state tort law forbade such claims); Jackson v. Kotter, 541 F.3d 688, 636–37 (7th Cir. 2008); Palay v. U.S., 349 F.3d 418, 427–31 (7th Cir. 2003); Sandoval v. U.S., 980 F.2d 1057, 1059 (5th Cir. 1993). Tort claims for prisoner assault, including FTCA claims, are discussed in more detail in Ch. 2, § G.1.f.

[324]Bolton v. U.S., 347 F. Supp. 2d 1218, 1222 (N.D.Fla. 2004) (allegation of sexual coercion could be pursued as a battery claim); Ortiz v. Peterson, 88 F. Supp. 2d 151 (S.D.N.Y. 2000); Harris v. U.S., 677 F. Supp. 403, 405–06 (W.D.N.C. 1988); *see* Ting v. U.S., 927 F.2d 1504, 1514 (9th Cir. 1991) (police shooting case). Tort suits for assault and battery are discussed in Ch. 2, § G.2.e.

[325]Gil v. Reed, 381 F.3d 649, 658–61 (7th Cir. 2004); Serra v. Pichardo, 786 F.2d 237 (6th Cir. 1986); *see* Gil v. Reed, 535 F.3d 551, 557–58 (7th Cir. 2008). Medical malpractice is discussed in Ch. 2, § F.5.

[326]Ross v. U.S., 641 F. Supp. 368, 377 (D.D.C. 1986); *see* Tekle ex rel. Tekle v. U.S., 511 F.3d 839, 856 (9th Cir. 2007) (police misconduct case). Under the Prison Litigation Reform Act, prisoners cannot recover damages for mental or emotional injury without showing physical injury as well, 28 U.S.C. § 1346(b)(2), so a claim for infliction of emotional distress cannot succeed unless it arises from circumstances that also involve physical injury, such as assault and battery or medical malpractice. *See* Ch. 9, § E, concerning this PLRA provision.

[327]28 U.S.C. § 2680(c).

[328]Ali v. Federal Bureau of Prisons, 552 U.S. 214, 128 S. Ct. 831 (2008).

[329]*See* Ch. 4, § H.8.c.

[330]*See* § E.2 of this chapter.

[331]Bernard v. U.S., 25 F.3d 98, 104–05 (2d Cir. 1994) (FTCA does not authorize suit with respect to the actions of federal prosecutors); Gray v. Bell, 542 F. Supp. 927, 933 (D.D.C.1982), *aff'd*, 712 F.2d 490 (D.C. Cir. 1983).

[332]Logue v. U.S., 412 U.S. 521, 532–33, 93 S. Ct. 2215 (1973) (U.S. Marshal allegedly failed to act on danger of inmate suicide); Sandoval v. U.S., 980 F.2d 1057, 1059 (5th Cir. 1993) (government could be liable for negligent placement in private facility); Cline v. U.S. Dep't of Justice, 525 F. Supp. 825, 831 (D. S.D. 1981); Brown v. U.S., 374 F. Supp. 723, 728–29 (E.D.Ark. 1974) (government negligently placed prisoner in dangerous local jail).

[333]There is another possible basis for suit by federal prisoners injured in local jails. Such prisoners may be third-party beneficiaries of the contract between the federal government and the local government if that contract requires that the jail or prison authorities provide for your safety. If so, you might be entitled to sue either the jail officials for failing to carry out the contract or the federal officials or government for failing to inspect and make sure that the contract was being honored. *See* Owens v. Haas, 601 F.2d 1242, 1247–51 (2d Cir. 1979); Hampton v. Holmesburg Prison Officials, 546 F.2d 1077, 1082 (3d Cir. 1976); Hook v. State of Ariz., Dep't of Corrections, 972 F.2d 1012, 1014 (9th Cir. 1992). Third-party beneficiary theories are discussed further in § B.1.c of this chapter, nn.42–44.

Breach of contract claims against the federal government must generally be brought in the Federal Court of Claims under the Tucker Act. 28 U.S.C. § 1345(a)(2). Claims for "tortious" breach of contract, however, must be brought in the Court of Claims under the Tucker Act and not under the FTCA. *See* U.S. v. Huff,

nonfederal jail personnel, and it generally has no duty to inspect or supervise local jails.[334]

The biggest problem for prisoner plaintiffs with the FTCA is the rule that the Government is not liable for government employees' performance (or non-performance) of a "discretionary function or duty."[335] That exception applies to "acts that are discretionary in nature, acts that 'involv[e] an element of judgment or choice.'"[336] It does not apply if a "federal statute, regulation, or policy specifically prescribes a course of action for an employee to follow," because "the employee has no rightful option but to adhere to the directive."[337] Courts have also held that constitutional violations are not protected by the exception, since no one has discretion to violate the Constitution.[338] Even if the

challenged conduct does involve "an element of judgment," the claim will be barred only if it is the kind of judgment that the discretionary function exception was designed to shield, i.e., "governmental actions and decisions based on considerations of public policy."[339]

In practice, the discretionary function exception has been interpreted very broadly by many courts.[340] Previously, courts had understood that the discretionary function exception barred liability only for actions at the "planning" level and not at the "operational" level, but the Supreme Court did away with that distinction.[341] As a result, courts have often held that decisions or actions by line prison staff are discretionary and not subject to FTCA liability.[342]

---

165 F.2d 720, 725 (5th Cir. 1948); Jeppesen Sanderson, Inc. v. U.S., 19 Cl.Ct. 233, 237 (Cl. Ct. 1990).

[334]See 28 U.S.C. § 2671; Logue v. U.S., 412 U.S. 521, 529, 93 S. Ct. 2215 (1973); Harper v. U.S., 515 F.2d 576, 578–79 (5th Cir. 1975).

[335]28 U.S.C. § 2680(a).

Immunity from tort liability for discretionary acts exists in many states, as well, but the rules are not always the same as under the FTCA. See § L.5 of this chapter for further discussion. This immunity is often at issue in prisoner assault cases. See Ch. 2, § G.1.f, for further discussion of such cases and the discretionary immunity under both state and federal law.

[336]U.S. v. Gaubert, 499 U.S. 315, 322–23, 111 S. Ct. 1267 (1991) (citations omitted).

[337]Id.; accord, Berkovitz v. U.S., 486 U.S. 531, 536, 537, 108 S. Ct. 1945 (1988); see, e.g., Lopez v. U.S., 376 F.3d 1055, 1058 (10th Cir. 2004) (stating that a United States Postal Service regulation requiring mailboxes to be "placed to conform to state laws" is a nondiscretionary mandate for the United States Postal Service to relocate mailboxes that are placed in violation of state law).

Another example of this distinction is Payton v. U.S., 679 F.2d 475 (5th Cir. 1982), in which the Government was sued because a federal prisoner murdered three people after being released on parole. The court held that the decision to parole him without requiring continued treatment or supervision was discretionary because the parole statute permitted parole release "in [the Board's] discretion" and "upon such terms and conditions . . . as the board shall prescribe . . ." Payton, 679 F.2d at 480–81 (citing 18 U.S.C. § 4203(a) (repealed)). But the actions of the Bureau of Prisons, which had failed to provide the parole board with the prisoner's records, were not discretionary because a federal statute required it to provide these records. Id. at 482 (citing 18 U.S.C. § 4208(c) (repealed)).

[338]Castro v. U.S., 560 F.3d 381, 388–89 (5th Cir. 2009); Thames Shipyard & Repair Co. v. U.S., 350 F.3d 247, 254 (1st Cir. 2003) ("[C]ourts have read the Supreme Court's discretionary function cases as denying protection to actions that are unauthorized because they are unconstitutional. . . ." (citing cases)); Raz v. U.S., 343 F.3d 945, 948 (8th Cir. 2003); Medina v. U.S., 259 F.3d 220, 225 (4th Cir. 2001) (noting that in determining the bounds of the discretionary function exception, "we begin with the principle that federal officials do not possess discretion to violate constitutional rights or federal statutes" (internal quotation marks and citations omitted)); Nurse v. U.S., 226 F.3d 996, 999, 1002 (9th Cir. 2000); Pooler v. U.S., 787 F.2d 868, 871 (3d Cir.1986) ("[I]f the complaint

were that agents of the government in the course of an investigation had violated constitutional rights or federal statutes, . . . federal officials do not possess discretion to commit such violations."); Myers & Myers, Inc. v. U.S. Postal Serv., 527 F.2d 1252, 1261 (2d Cir.1975) ("It is, of course, a tautology that a federal official cannot have discretion to behave unconstitutionally. . . ."); Wormley v. U.S., 601 F. Supp. 2d 27, 42–43 (D.D.C. 2009).

This does not mean that constitutional violations are actionable under the FTCA. It means that if you sue about a tort that also violates the Constitution, such as an assault and battery that is also excessive force under the Eighth Amendment, the government should not be entitled to the discretionary function exception.

[339]U.S. v. Gaubert, 499 U.S. at 322–23; Berkovitz v. U.S., 486 U.S. 531, 537, 108 S. Ct. 1945 (1988) (exception protects only the exercise of "policy judgment"); see U.S. v. Articles of Drug, 825 F.2d 1238, 1249 (8th Cir. 1987) (discretionary function exception applies only where action required consideration of policy); Jackson v. Kelly, 557 F.2d 735, 738 (10th Cir. 1977) (en banc) (holding that a doctor's exercise of medical judgment does not necessarily involve "governmental discretion").

[340]One federal judge has said that "the discretionary function exception has swallowed, digested and excreted the liability-creating sections of the Federal Tort Claims Act." Rosebush v. U.S., 119 F.3d 438, 444 (6th Cir.1997) (Merritt, C.J., dissenting). Another said that the FTCA "is largely a false promise in all but 'fender benders' and perhaps some cases involving medical malpractice by government doctors." Allen v. U.S., 816 F.2d 1417, 1424–25 (10th Cir.1987) (McKay, C.J., concurring).

[341]U.S. v. Gaubert, 499 U.S. at 325–26.

[342]See Santana-Rosa v. U.S., 335 F.3d 39, 43–44 (1st Cir. 2003) (holding that assignment of prisoners to jobs, and even failure to secure a scrub brush used in an assault, must be viewed as falling within the discretionary function exception); Cohen v. U.S., 151 F.3d 1338, 1342 (11th Cir. 1998) ("[E]ven if §§ 4042 imposes on the BOP a general duty of care to safeguard prisoners, the BOP retains sufficient discretion in the means it may use to fulfill that duty to trigger the discretionary function exception." The requirement to classify prisoners left the government with discretion about how to classify and place them.); Dykstra v. U.S. Bureau of Prisons, 140 F.3d 791, 795–97 (8th Cir. 1998) (no claim under the FTCA for BOP's alleged negligence in failing to protect an inmate from assault by another inmate because decisions whether to place an inmate in protective custody are the exercise of a discretionary function); Calderon v. U.S., 123 F.3d 947, 949–50 (7th Cir. 1997) (no claim under the FTCA based on the BOP's alleged negligence in failing to protect an inmate from attack by another inmate,

They are generally found non-discretionary only if they directly contradict some very specific rule.[343]

Most courts have held that the defense of qualified immunity is not applicable in an FTCA suit.[344] Qualified immunity has been tailored specifically for constitutional claims, which are not litigated under the FTCA, and to protect government officials' ability to act without fear of personal liability, which is also not an issue under the FTCA.[345]

The FTCA provides only for the recovery of compensatory damages.[346] You cannot use it to get punitive damages,[347] an injunction,[348] or expungement of prison records.[349]

b. Procedures Under the FTCA Before you can sue under the FTCA, you must exhaust administrative remedies by filing a claim with the governmental agency responsible for the tort.[350] Exhausting the prison grievance system does not satisfy the FTCA requirement, and filing a claim under the FTCA does not exhaust non-FTCA claims.[351] The claim must be filed within two years after the claim accrues.[352] (A claim "accrues" when the injured party knows, or should know, if she is exercising diligence, that the injury occurred and what caused it.[353])

Administrative exhaustion is an absolute requirement under the FTCA. If you fail to do it, or do not do it correctly, your case will be dismissed.[354] Filing your lawsuit within the time limit for the administrative claim does not substitute for the claim or extend the deadline for filing the claim.[355]

---

because decision whether to take disciplinary action against other inmate was the exercise of a discretionary function); Baum v. U.S., 986 F.2d 716, 720–21 (4th Cir. 1993) ("a reviewing court in the usual case is to look to the nature of the challenged decision in an objective, or general sense, and ask whether that decision is one which we would expect inherently to be grounded in considerations of policy."); Buchanan v. U.S., 915 F.2d 969, 971–72 (5th Cir. 1990) (holding that the discretionary function exception shielded prison officials' minute-to-minute decision making during a riot because such a situation clearly called for discretionary action); *see also* Barton v. U.S., 609 F.2d 977, 979 (10th Cir. 1979) (existence of a "fixed or readily ascertainable standard" of conduct means that the official's actions are not discretionary).

[343]*See, e.g.*, Parrott v. U.S., 536 F.3d 629, 638 (7th Cir. 2008) (violation of a separation order was not covered by the discretionary function exception; "As long as a valid separation order is in effect, there is no discretion left to operate on that narrow question."); Ashford v. U.S., 511 F.3d 501, 505 (5th Cir. 2007) (where there was evidence of a specific prison policy requiring separation of inmates based on certain kinds of risk or threat, inmate assault claim was not barred by the discretionary function exception).

The discretionary function exception is very frequently at issue in cases involving assaults by other prisoners. It, and tort suits for inmate assault in general, are discussed further in Ch. 2, § G.1.e.

[344]Castro v. U.S., 34 F.3d 106, 111 (2d Cir. 1994) ("qualified immunity will not immunize the United States from liability"); Ruffalo v. U.S., 590 F. Supp. 706, 710 (E.D. Mo. 1984); Arnsberg v. U.S., 549 F. Supp. 55, 57 (D.Ore. 1982), *rev'd on other grounds*, 757 F.2d 971 (9th Cir. 1985); Townsend v. Carmel, 494 F. Supp. 30, 36–37 (D.D.C. 1980); Picariello v. Fenton, 491 F. Supp. 1026, 1040–1042 (M.D.Pa. 1980); Crain v. Krehbiel, 443 F. Supp. 202, 216 (N.D. Cal. 1977). *Contra*, Norton v. U.S., 581 F.2d 390, 393–96 (4th Cir. 1978) (stating the United States is entitled to avail itself of any defenses its agents could raise in their individual capacities for intentional torts).

[345]Qualified immunity is discussed in detail in § L.4 of this chapter.

[346]28 U.S.C. § 1346(b); St. John v. U.S., 240 F.3d 671, 679 (8th Cir. 2001).

[347]28 U.S.C. § 2674; *see* Dolan v. U.S. Postal Service, 546 U.S. 481, 484–85, 126 S. Ct. 1252 (2006); Molzof v. U.S., 502 U.S. 301, 305, 112 S. Ct. 711 (1992).

[348]Redland Soccer Club, Inc. v. Department of Army of U.S., 55 F.3d 827, 848 (3d Cir. 1995).

[349]Walker v. U.S., 116 F.R.D. 149, 152 (S.D.N.Y. 1987).

[350]28 U.S.C. § 2675(a); McNeil v. U.S., 508 U.S. 106, 112, 113 S. Ct. 1980 (1993) ("Congress [in enacting FTCA] intended to require complete exhaustion of Executive remedies before invocation of the judicial process.").

[351]*See* Ch. 9, § D.1, nn.271–272.

[352]28 U.S.C. § 2401(b).

If you file on time but send your claim to the wrong agency, that agency is supposed to transfer it to the right agency or send it back to you. 28 C.F.R. § 14.2(b)(1). If it doesn't, the claim may be deemed properly filed *if* you have not waited until the last day or so to file. *Compare* Greene v. U.S., 872 F.2d 236, 237 (8th Cir. 1989); Bukala v. U.S., 854 F.2d 201, 202–04 (7th Cir. 1988) (claims timely filed with the wrong agency satisfied requirement) *with* Hart v. Dep't of Labor, 116 F.3d 1338, 1341 (10th Cir. 1997). However, if your claim is transferred to the right agency but arrives there after the two-year period has expired, your claim may be barred. *See* Lotrionte v. U.S., 560 F. Supp. 41, 43 (S.D.N.Y.), *aff'd*, 742 F.2d 1436 (2d Cir. 1983) (claim barred); Cronauer v. U.S., 394 F. Supp. 2d 93, 100 (D.D.C. 2005) (". . . [C]ourts do not consider claims filed with the wrong agency at the *last minute* to be timely filed pursuant to §§ 2401(b)." (emphasis in original)) and cases cited.

[353]U.S. v. Kubrick, 444 U.S. 111, 122, 100 S. Ct. 352 (1979). The limitations period generally runs from the point of injury, even if the plaintiff does not know that the injury violated her legal rights. U.S. v. Kubrick, 444 U.S. at 122; Callahan v. U.S., 426 F.3d 444, 452–53 (1st Cir. 2005) (plaintiffs may be charged with knowledge of events that receive widespread publicity); Diaz v. U.S., 165 F.3d 1337, 1339 (11th Cir. 1999) ("The general rule is that a claim under the FTCA accrues at the time of injury."). In medical malpractice cases, the claim generally accrues when the plaintiff has the information necessary to discover both his injury and its cause. Johnson v. U.S., 460 F.3d 616, 620–21 (5th Cir. 2006).

[354]McNeil v. U.S., 508 U.S. 106, 113, 113 S. Ct. 1980 (1993); Acosta v. U.S. Marshals Service, 445 F.3d 509, 513–14 (1st Cir. 2006) (completing administrative process is a non-waivable jurisdictional requirement; if alleging torts by employees of two federal agencies, plaintiff must file claims with both); Celestine v. Mount Vernon Neighborhood Health Center, 403 F.3d 76, 82 (2d Cir. 2005) (FTCA exhaustion requirement applies to claims removed from state courts.).

[355]Garrett v. U.S., 640 F.2d 24, 26 (6th Cir. 1981).

For federal prisoners, the responsible agency will usually be the Federal Bureau of Prisons (BOP).[356] You must file the claim with the regional office of the Bureau in the region where the tort happened[357] within two years after the claim accrues.[358] Settlements of up to $25,000 require approval of a "legal officer of the agency." Anything higher than $2500 requires approval by the Attorney General.[359]

If the BOP denies your claim, you must file your lawsuit within six months of the date of mailing of the notice of denial,[360] even if the six months expires before the two-year limitation period for filing the claim.[361] This deadline is enforced strictly.[362] Be sure to notify the BOP of any changes in your whereabouts so you will receive their notice of denial.[363]

The notice of denial must be sent to you by registered or certified mail; if it is not, the six-month time limit will not begin to run.[364] If the BOP has not acted on your claim within six months after you filed it, you are free to treat their inaction as a final denial and bring a lawsuit any time.[365]

You may not file a suit before you have exhausted administrative remedies; if you do, your case will be dismissed.[366] If you make this mistake and file a premature suit, you must file a new suit within the proper time frame.[367]

You should file your claim on the form provided by the BOP.[368] In theory, you can get these from the prison staff.[369] If you can't get the form, you can present "other written notification," such as a letter.[370] The letter should contain all the information called for by the form.[371] If someone else

---

[356]If you sustained your injury in a local jail, the appropriate federal agency may be the United States Marshals' Service of the Department of Justice.

[357]28 C.F.R. § 543.31(c).

[358]28 U.S.C. § 2401(b).

[359]28 U.S.C. § 2672; 28 C.F.R. § 14.6 (claims exceeding $25,000); 28 C.F.R. §§ 14.5 (claims exceeding $5,000).

[360]28 U.S.C. §§ 2401(b).

The agency can send the denial either to you or to your lawyer, if you have one, and any resulting confusion is not accepted as an excuse for missing the deadline. Shoff v. U.S., 245 F.3d 1266 (11th Cir. 2001) (letter sent to prisoner, rather than his attorney, was sufficient notice of denial of claim; separate letter to attorney not required).

[361]Childers v. U.S., 442 F.2d 1299, 1301 (5th Cir. 1971).

[362]See McDuffee v. U.S., 769 F.2d 492, 493–94 (8th Cir. 1985) (suit barred because it was filed one day late). *But see* Jackson v. Kotter, 541 F.3d 688, 694–97 (7th Cir. 2008) (where plaintiff filed suit within six months but did not name United States until later, amendment related back to filing of original complaint under Rule 15(c), Fed.R.Civ.P., and was timely).

[363]A notice that is sent to the wrong place does not start the six-month period. Matos v. U.S., 380 F. Supp. 2d 36, 39–40 (D. P.R. 2005) (time for filing lawsuit did not start from date of mailing of rejection of claim letter which was returned to agency as "undeliverable."). If for some other reason that is not your fault you don't receive the notice of denial until more than six months have passed, file your lawsuit as quickly as you can and point out to the court the actual date you received the notice of denial, and the reasons for the delay, if you know them. We haven't found a case presenting this situation and don't know how a court would rule on it.

[364]28 U.S.C. § 2401 (b); 28 C.F.R. §§ 14.9 ("Final denial of an administrative claim shall be in writing and sent to the claimant, his attorney, or legal representative by certified or registered mail.").

Some courts have excused non-compliance by the government with this requirement where the prisoner did receive the notice. See Pipkin v. U.S. Postal Serv., 951 F.2d 272, 274 (10th Cir. 1991) (failure to use registered or certified mail excused where plaintiff received the notice and was not prejudiced); Bryant v. Carlson, 652 F. Supp. 1286, 1287 n.2 (D.D.C. 1987) (sending notice certified to warden, rather than prisoner, excused where the notice was delivered to the prisoner, who signed for it).

[365]28 U.S.C. § 2675(a). Some courts have held, in effect, that if the agency fails to act within six months, there is no time limit on bringing suit. Pascale v. U.S., 998 F.2d 186, 192–93 (3d Cir. 1993) (if the agency does not formally deny the claim, and has not finally disposed of the claim within six months after it was filed, "the claimant may wait indefinitely before filing suit."); Taumby v. U.S., 919 F.2d 69, 70 (8th Cir. 1998) (confirming this interpretation). Others have held that suit must at least be filed within six months of whatever time the agency does deny the claim. Ellison v. U.S., 531 F.3d 359, 363 (6th Cir. 2008).

[366]McNeil v. U.S., 508 U.S. 106, 110–13, 113 S. Ct. 1980 (1993); Kaba v. Stepp, 458 F.3d 678, 688 (7th Cir 2006). A dismissal on these grounds does not toll the statute of limitations, so if it occurs after the limitations period has run, you will not be able to refile. Laroque v. U.S., 750 F. Supp. 181, 182–04 (E.D. N.C. 1990), *aff'd*, 917 F.2d 557 (4th Cir. 1990).

[367]McNeil v. U.S., 964 F.2d 647, 649 (7th Cir. 1992), *aff'd*, 508 U.S. 106, 113 S. Ct. 1980 (1993). You generally cannot get around this problem just by filing an amended complaint. See Duplan v. Harper, 188 F.3d 1195, 1199–1200 (10th Cir. 1999). (In *DuPlan* the court did treat an amended complaint as a new action, but that is because the government had agreed to do so.).

[368]See Appendix C, Form 16.

[369]28 C.F.R. § 543.31(b) ("Where do I obtain a form for filing a claim? You may obtain a form from staff in the Central Office, Regional Offices, Bureau institutions, or staff training centers.").

[370]28 C.F.R. § 14.2(a) (". . . [A] claim shall be deemed to have been presented when a Federal agency receives from a claimant, his duly authorized agent or legal representative, an executed Standard Form 95 or other written notification of an incident, accompanied by a claim for money damages in a sum certain for injury to or loss of property, personal injury, or death alleged to have occurred by reason of the incident; and the title or legal capacity of the person signing, and is accompanied by evidence of his authority to present a claim on behalf of the claimant as agent, executor, administrator, parent, guardian, or other representative."). One court held that plaintiff's sworn statement of the incident and his injuries satisfied the claim requirement where prison officials also had the benefit of full investigations. Blue v. U.S., 567 F. Supp. 394, 397–98 (D.Conn. 1983). However, it is not wise to rely on decisions like this, which are rare. Follow the rules or you risk dismissal of your claim.

[371]In general, the claim requirement is satisfied when the agency is given sufficient written notice of the circumstances to investigate and respond. Burchfield v. U.S., 168 F.3d 1252 (11th Cir. 1999) (inmate not required to identify each and every legal theory

submits the claim for you, it should contain evidence of that person's authority to act on your behalf.[372]

When you file your claim, the prison where the alleged tort occurred is supposed to investigate it.[373] The BOP may request additional information about your claim.[374] You should respond to such a request. If you don't, your failure to do so may be construed as a failure to file a proper claim, and may result in your lawsuit being dismissed.[375]

Once the investigation is complete, it is reviewed by the regional counsel.[376]

Your administrative claim must request a "sum certain" in money damages.[377] Failure to state a sum certain may result in dismissal of your lawsuit.[378] The amount you request in your claim is generally the upper limit on what you can receive in a subsequent lawsuit, unless an increased amount in damages is based upon new evidence that was not reasonably discoverable when you presented your administrative claim, or upon events that occurred after you filed your claim.[379]

Once you have filed your administrative claim, you may amend it before a final decision is made on it.[380] If your claim is denied, you may request reconsideration within the six-month period after denial, rather than filing a lawsuit at that time.[381] A request for reconsideration will toll (suspend) the time limit for filing your lawsuit. Once the BOP has

denied your request for reconsideration, you have another six-month period in which to file your lawsuit, starting with the date of the second denial letter.[382]

If you sue, your complaint should state the facts concerning submission of your administrative claim and the agency's denial or failure to act on it.[383] Suits under the FTCA must be filed in the federal judicial district "where the plaintiff resides or wherein the act or omission complained of occurred."[384] In most cases, the latter will be the district in which you were incarcerated at the time of the tort. However, if there are facts showing that the impetus for the tort came from somewhere else (e.g., the BOP headquarters in Washington D.C.), your suit may be filed in that district.[385]

Class actions may be allowed in theory under the FTCA, but they are nearly impossible in practice, because each class member must have filed, or authorized filing, a proper administrative claim stating a sum certain in damages.[386]

D. OTHER STATE COURT REMEDIES

Many states provide state court remedies for unlawful acts by prison personnel in addition to tort actions and state court § 1983 actions. These remedies may permit you to challenge violations of state or local law or prison regulations, which may provide greater rights than the federal Constitution, but which cannot be enforced against state officials under § 1983.[387] Sometimes these state remedies are faster and simpler than federal civil rights actions.

---

planned to pursue as long as presented sufficient facts to permit the Government to investigate the claim); Farmers State Saving Bank v. Farmers Home Admin., 866 F.2d 276, 277 (8th Cir. 1989).

[372]28 C.F.R. § 14.2(a).

[373]28 C.F.R. §§ 543.32(c)–(d).

[374]28 C.F.R. § 543.32(c).

[375]Most courts have held that this is not a basis for dismissal. See Santiago-Ramirez v. Secretary of Dep't of Defense, 984 F.2d 16 18–19 (1st Cir. 1993); Charlton v. U.S., 743 F.2d 557, 560–61 (7th Cir. 1984) (failure to respond to requests for further information does not require dismissal of FTCA action) and cases cited; Surratt v. U.S., 582 F. Supp. 692, 696–99 (N.D. Ill. 1984) and cases cited. However, you should respond to requests for information to be safe.

[376]28 C.F.R. § 543.32(d).

[377]28 C.F.R. § 14.2(a).

[378]See Dalrymple v. U.S., 460 F.3d 1318, 1325 (11th Cir. 2006) (noting that plaintiff may also provide documentation permitting calculation of damages); Glarner v. U.S., Dep't of Veterans Admin., 30 F.3d 697, 700 (6th Cir. 1994); Charlton v. U.S., 743 F.2d 557, 559–560 (7th Cir. 1984); Weaver v. Bratt, 421 F. Supp. 2d 25, 42 (D.D.C. 2006). But see Blue v. U.S., 567 F. Supp. 394, 397–98 (D.Conn. 1983) (excusing sum certain requirement under the circumstances).

[379]28 U.S.C. § 2675(b); see Hoehn v. U.S., 217 F. Supp. 2d 39, 43–44 (D.D.C. 2002) (rejecting demand for more damages than sought in administrative claim).

[380]28 C.F.R. § 14.2(c) ("Upon the timely filing of an amendment to a pending claim, the agency shall have six months in which to make a final disposition of the claim as amended and the claimant's option under 28 U.S.C. 2675(a) shall not accrue until six months after the filing of an amendment.").

[381]28 C.F.R. § 14.9(b).

[382]28 C.F.R. § 14.9(b) ("Upon the timely filing of a request for reconsideration the agency shall have 6 months from the date of filing in which to make a final disposition of the claim and the claimant's option under 28 U.S.C. 2675(a) shall not accrue until 6 months after the filing of a request for reconsideration.").

[383]Gillespie v. Civiletti, 629 F.2d 637, 640 (9th Cir. 1980) (timely filing and denial of administrative claim in proper agency is jurisdictional prerequisite to bringing suit under FTCA and should be alleged in the complaint).

[384]28 U.S.C. § 1402(b); see Zakiya v. U.S., 267 F. Supp. 2d 47, 58 (D.D.C. 2003) (some courts have construed Section 1402(b) broadly to allow venue "if sufficient activity giving rise to the plaintiff's cause of action took place here.").

[385]Kimberlin v. Quinlan, 774 F. Supp. 1, 9–10 (D.D.C. 1991), rev'd on other grounds, 6 F.3d 789 (D.C. Cir. 1993), remanded, 515 U.S. 321 (1995).

[386]Gollehon Farming v. U.S., 17 F. Supp. 2d 1145, 1161 (D. Mont. 1998) ("Because the jurisdictional requirements of the FTCA require each claimant to submit an individual claim, the court is compelled to conclude the named plaintiffs are barred from prosecuting a class action for damages under the Federal Tort Claims Act."), aff'd, 207 F.3d 1373 (Fed. Cir. 2000); Founding Church of Scientology v. Director, Federal Bureau of Investigation, 459 F. Supp. 748, 755–56 (D.D.C. 1978); Miles v. Bell, 621 F. Supp. 51, 70 (D. Conn. 1985).

[387]Sometimes claims based on state or local law or regulations may be included in the same case as a federal court § 1983 claim under the doctrine of pendent or supplemental jurisdiction. See § F.1 of this chapter.

State court remedies vary widely from state to state and we cannot review the law of all 50 states. However, we will try to give you an idea of what to look for.[388]

1. State Habeas Corpus or Post-Conviction Remedies

In some states, habeas corpus or a post-conviction remedy proceeding may be used to challenge violations of constitutional rights, statutes, or administrative rules by prison officials.[389] In other states, these remedies may not be used for such claims.[390]

2. Judicial Review of Administrative Action

Many states provide for judicial review of the actions of state or local agencies.

Sometimes this is done through writs of mandamus, certiorari, or prohibition, or some variation of these.[391]

These state procedures vary widely in scope and flexibility, and sometimes in name. For example, New York has combined mandamus, certiorari, and prohibition into a single writ commonly referred to as an "Article 78 proceeding," under which prisoners have been permitted to challenge sentence calculations, parole decisions, transfers and the denial of transfers, classification decisions, facility rules, and disciplinary decisions.[392] Prisoners can raise constitutional claims as well as claims based on state law and regulations in an Article 78 proceeding. Other states' remedies may be more restrictive.[393]

In some states, an administrative procedures act (APA) provides for judicial review of prison rules[394] and prison officials' actions.[395] The scope of these statutes varies from state to state, and in some cases prisoners have been excluded

---

[388]Factors you should consider in deciding whether to use these remedies or others are discussed in § H.3 of this chapter.

[389]*See In re* Head, 42 Cal.3d 223, 228 Cal. Rptr. 184, 721 P.2d 65 (1986) (challenge to work release procedure brought pursuant to habeas statute); *In re* Harrell, 2 Cal.3d 675, 87 Cal.Rptr. 504, 470 P.2d 640 (1970) ("The writ of habeas corpus may be sought by one lawfully in custody for the purpose of vindicating rights to which he is entitled even in confinement."); *In re* Bittaker, 55 Cal.App.4th 1004, 64 Cal.Rptr.2d 679, 682 (Cal. App. 1 Dist. 1997) (habeas used to challenge court imposed restriction on filing of lawsuits); Bradley v. State, 473 N.W.2d 224 (Iowa Ct.App.1991) (*Miranda* issues addressed in prison discipline post-conviction case); Wycoff v. Iowa Dist. Court For Lee County, 580 N.W.2d 786, 787 (Iowa 1998) (post-conviction proceedings used "where the prison discipline results in a substantial deprivation of the inmate's liberty or property interests." (citation omitted)); Schuyler v. Roberts, 36 Kan.App.2d 388, 139 P.3d 781, 782–83 (Kan. App. 2006) (classification of inmate as sex offender could be challenged by habeas), *aff'd*, 285 Kan. 677, 175 P.3d 259, 261 (2008); Wickham v. Fisher, 629 P.2d 896, 900 (Utah 1981) (state habeas could be used to challenge unconstitutional conditions of confinement; Burlett v. Holden, 835 P.2d 989, 991 (Utah App. 1992) (disciplinary sanction of restitution reviewed by habeas).

[390]*See, e.g.,* Dorbolo v. Sullivan, 450 A.2d 1185, 1186 (Del.1982) (state habeas is limited to review of confinement, and may not be used to review classification issues such as work release participation); State ex rel. Guth v. Fabian, 716 N.W.2d 23, 26–29 (Minn. App. 2006) (state habeas cannot be used to review non-constitutional classification issues, though court notes habeas can be used to challenge unconstitutional conditions of confinement); Al-Shabazz v. State, 338 S.C. 354, 369–70, 527 S.E.2d 742 (S.C. 2000) (post-conviction review limited to validity of confinement; all other matters must go through the prison remedy system with judicial review of final decisions).

[391]*See, e.g., In re* Head, 42 Cal.3d 223, 227–28, 228 Cal. Rptr. 184, 721 P.2d 65 (1986) (mandamus as well as habeas could be used to challenge denial of a work furlough); Murphy v. Superintendent, M.C.I., Cedar Junction, 396 Mass. 830, 489 N.E.2d 661, 663 (Mass. 1986) (holding state certiorari to be the only state remedy for challenges to disciplinary proceedings); Jordan v. Superintendent,

Massachusetts Correctional Inst., Cedar Junction, 53 Mass.App.Ct. 584, 587, 760 N.E.2d 807, 809 (Mass. App. Ct. 2002) (prison misconduct challenges brought pursuant to certiorari); State ex rel. L'Minggio v. Gamble, 263 Wis.2d 55, 68, 667 N.W.2d 1, 7 (Wis. 2003) (certiorari is the "well-established mode of judicial review" for prison disciplinary decisions).

[392]In an Article 78 proceeding, a court may determine:

1. Whether the body or officer failed to perform a duty enjoined upon it by law;
2. Whether the body or officer proceeded, is proceeding, or is about to proceed without or in excess of jurisdiction; or
3. Whether a determination was made in violation of lawful procedure, was affected by an error of law or was arbitrary and capricious or an abuse of discretion;
4. Whether a determination made as a result of a hearing held, and at which evidence was taken . . . is, on the entire record, supported by substantial evidence.

N.Y.C.P.L.R. § 7803.

Similar rules apply in some other states. *See* Vondra v. Colorado Dep't of Corrections, 226 P.3d 1165, 1167 (Colo.App. 2009), *cert. denied*, 2010 WL 983881 (Colo., Mar. 15, 2010) (holding designation as a sex offender is a quasi-judicial determination subject to judicial review under state statute).

[393]*See, e.g.,* Hargrove v. Dep't of Corrections, 601 So.2d 623 (Fla.App., 1 Dist.,1992) (only means of challenging prison officials' interpretation of their rules is the grievance system).

[394]Matter of Rules Adoption Regarding Inmate-Therapist Confidentiality, 224 N.J.Super. 252, 540 A.2d 212, 216–18 (Super. Ct. App. Div. 1988) (policies requiring disclosure by prison psychotherapists struck down); *see* Walen v. Dep't of Corrections, 443 Mich. 240, 505 N.W.2d 519, 521–22 (1993) (prison disciplinary proceedings were "contested cases" subject to APA procedural requirements, which are more favorable than constitutional requirements, and to state freedom of information law).

[395]*In re* Wilson, 202 Cal.App.3d 661, 249 Cal.Rptr. 36, 40–42 (1988) (classification decision reviewed under state APA but upheld under a "some evidence" standard); Dougherty v. State, 323 N.W. 2d 249, 250 (Iowa 1982) (work release revocation could be challenged under the state APA); DeWalt v. Warden, Marquette Prison, 112 Mich.App. 313, 315 N.W. 2d 584 (1982) (transfer reviewed, but upheld, under state APA).

partly or completely from their benefits.[396] In some states, prison grievance decisions are subject to judicial review, under the state APA or otherwise.[397] Administrative procedure acts generally have procedural requirements for rule-making, and prison rules and regulations have sometimes been struck down for failure to comply with them.[398]

The rules governing these proceedings vary from state to state, but there are certain things you should look for in assessing a state judicial review proceeding.

Exhaustion requirements. Typically, you will be required to exhaust your administrative remedies before going to court.[399] (Nowadays, of course, you must do this before going to federal court as well.[400])

Summary procedures and restricted evidence. Often, courts in administrative review proceedings proceed quickly, with little or no discovery and sometimes without holding a hearing. Often they are restricted to the evidence in the record made in an administrative proceeding, such as a grievance or disciplinary hearing.[401]

Short statutes of limitations. In some cases you must file your case within a few months of the act or decision you are complaining about.[402]

Limited relief. Often, these procedures will not provide all the relief that is available in a § 1983 action—especially damages.[403]

---

[396]*See, e.g.,* Wilkinson v. State, 172 Ariz. 597, 838 P.2d 1358, 1359–60 (Ariz. App. 1992) (amendment exempting rules "concerning only inmates" from APA review did not apply to rules concerning religious visitors, since they were not inmates); Clinton v. Bonds, 306 Ark. 554, 816 S.W.2d 169, 171 (Ark. 1991) (statute excluding prisoners from APA coverage entirely was not valid as applied to constitutional claims, upheld otherwise); Lono v. Ariyoshi, 63 Haw. 138, 621 P.2d 967, 981 (classification decision not reviewable under state APA because it was not a "contested case" requiring a hearing); Walen v. Dep't of Corrections, 443 Mich. 240, 505 N.W.2d 519, 521–22 (1993) (explaining legislature exempted prison system from some, but not all, APA provisions after appellate court held disciplinary proceedings were contested cases under the APA); Zeltner v. N.J. Dep't of Corrections, 201 N.J. Super. 195, 492 A.2d 1084 (App. Div. 1985) (APA review of prison decisions limited to disciplinary proceedings resulting in loss of a year's good time or more), *certification denied,* 102 N.J. 299 (1985); Canady v. Reynolds, 880 P.2d 391, 398 (Okla. Crim. App. 1994) (prison system's calculation of sentencing credits exempted from APA review).

In a number of states, prisoners may not seek judicial review of disciplinary proceedings under the state APA. *See* Rose v. Arizona Dep't of Corrections, 167 Ariz. 116, 804 P.2d 845, 848–49 (Ct. App. 1991) (may obtain review by "special action" instead); Wycoff v. Iowa District Court for Lee County, 580 N.W.2d 786 (Iowa 1998) (may use post-conviction relief proceeding instead); L'Heureux v. State Dep't of Corrections, 708 A.2d 549, 551–53 (R.I. 1998) (classification proceedings and rule-making also excluded); Dawson v. Hearing Comm., 92 Wash.2d 391, 597 P.2d 1353 (1979) (en banc); *see* Ch. 4, § H.1.r, for additional discussion of state remedies in disciplinary cases.

[397]Jenkins v. Morton, 148 F.3d 257, 259–60 (3d Cir. 1998) (noting New Jersey grievances can be appealed to state appellate court); Holsey v. Inmate Grievance Com'n, 296 Md. 601, 464 A.2d 1017 (Md. 1983); Al-Shabazz v. State, 338 S.C. 354, 369–70, 527 S.E.2d 742 (S.C. 2000) (holding final grievance decisions reviewable under APA).

[398]Morales v. California Dep't of Corrections and Rehabilitation, 168 Cal.App.4th 729, 735–41, 85 Cal.Rptr.3d 724 (Cal.App., 1st Dist. 2008) (holding lethal injection protocol was subject to state APA; noting state APA has an exception for rules affecting only one prison); Massey v. Secretary, Dep't of Public Safety and Correctional Services, 389 Md. 496, 517–19, 886 A.2d 585, 600 (Md. 2005) (prison disciplinary rules must be enacted in compliance with APA, since they affect fundamental rights and not just internal management); Martin v. Dep't of Corrections, 424 Mich. 553, 562–65, 384 N.W.2d 392 (1986) (disciplinary rules must be promulgated through APA, since inmates are part of the public); Hampton v. Dep't of Corrections, 336 N.J.Super. 520, 765 A.2d 286, 291 (N.J. Super. A.D.2001) (classification standard invalid since not promulgated pursuant to APA); Dep't of Correction v. McNeil, 209 N.J.Super. 120, 506 A.2d 1291 (N.J. Super. App. Div. 1986) (disciplinary rules must be issued consistently with state APA; court refused to overturn past convictions); Jones v. Smith, 64

N.Y.2d 1003, 1005–06, 478 N.E.2d 1191, 466 N.Y.S.2d 175 (N.Y. 1985) (disciplinary rules not filed with Secretary of State could not be enforced).

[399]*See, e.g.,* Johnson v. Illinois Dep't of Corrections, 857 N.E.2d 282, 285 (Ill. App. 4 Dist. 2006) (inmate required under general state administrative law to exhaust grievance process to challenge denial of good time); Anderson v. Myers, 268 Mich.App. 713, 709 N.W.2d 171, 173–74 (2005) (lawsuit against parole officer required exhaustion pursuant to state Prison Litigation Reform Act).

[400]*See* Ch. 9, § D, concerning the exhaustion requirement of the federal Prison Litigation Reform Act.

[401]*See, e.g.,* Holsey v. Inmate Grievance Comm'n, 296 Md. 601, 464 A.2d 1017, 1019 (Ct.App. 1983) (judicial review of grievance proceeding limited to the grievance record); State ex rel. L'Minggio v. Gamble, 263 Wis.2d 55, 68, 667 N.W.2d 1, 7 (Wis. 2003) ("A certiorari court is limited to reviewing the record and cannot consider additional facts outside of the record."); *see also* Smith v. Dep't of Corrections, 219 Or.App. 192, 194, 198, 182 P.3d 250 (2008) (judicial review of prison rules may be based only on "the face of the rule and the law pertinent to it"; claim that would require an evidentiary record could not be heard).

[402]*See, e.g.,* Glastonbuly Volunteer Ambulance Assn. v. FOIC, 227 Conn. 848, 852–54, 633 A.2d 305 (1993) (45-day filing requirement for administrative appeal was mandatory); *see also* Duffy v. Mass. Dep't of Corrections, 746 F. Supp. 232, 233 (D. Mass. 1990) (state certiorari proceedings governed by 60-day limitations period); Purcell v. Dennison, 29 A.D.3d 1128, 814 N.Y.S.2d 787 (2006) (petitioner missed four-month statute of limitations for commencing Article 78 proceeding; time began to run when he received notice of denial of administrative appeal).

[403]You may be able to bring a state proceeding that does not have jurisdiction to award damages, and later sue for damages under § 1983. *See* § M of this chapter.

Limited scope. Some administrative actions or rules may not be reviewable.[404] Some state remedies are limited to federal constitutional claims.[405]

E. WORKERS' COMPENSATION

In some states and in the federal prison system, prisoners are eligible for a form of workers' compensation for work accidents, and are barred from bringing tort suits about them.[406] Workers' compensation provides for payments to injured workers, generally based on their lost earning capacity. Compensation cases are usually decided through an administrative procedure governed by state statutes and regulations; judicial review may be provided in the state courts.

1. State Workers' Compensation Laws

Most states do not provide workers' compensation to prisoners, either because their statutes explicitly exclude prisoners[407] or because court decisions make prisoners ineligible.[408] In a few states, prisoners are generally eligible

---

[404]For example, one state court held that its jurisdiction in a certiorari proceeding did not extend to a claim of deprivation of privileges in retaliation for exercise of constitutional rights, Ennis v. Schuetzle, 488 N.W.2d 867, 872 (N.D. 1992), a claim that would clearly have been actionable in a § 1983 action in state or federal court. *See also* Smith v. Oregon State Penitentiary, 113 Or.App. 386, 387, 832 P.2d 1270 (1992) (APA review of prison rules limited to those that prisoners can be disciplined for violating).

[405]*See, e.g.*, Clinton v. Bonds, 306 Ark. 554, 816 S.W.2d 169, 171 (1991).

[406]Jennifer v. State, Dep't of Public Safety and Correctional Services, 176 Md.App. 211, 932 A.2d 1213 (Md.App. 2007) (holding prisoner's tort claim for work-related injury barred by provision for workers' compensation); Richardson v. N.C. Dep't of Correction, 118 N.C.App. 704, 705–06, 457 S.E.2d 325 (1995) (prisoner injured in accident who could pursue workers' compensation after release was barred from filing a tort suit), *aff'd*, 345 N.C. 128, 478 S.E.2d 501 (1996).

[407]*See, e.g.*, Fla.Stat. § 946.002(5) (prisoner is not considered an employee of the state; nor does a prisoner come within any other provision of the Workmen's Compensation Act); W.Va.Code § 23-4-1e(b) (no prisoner who suffers injury during work which is imposed upon him during incarceration is compensable).

[408]These decisions usually hold that a prisoner is not an "employee" because there is no voluntary contract of hire or because the inmate does not receive substantial pay.

> Convicts and prisoners have usually been denied compensation for injuries sustained in connection with work done within the prison, even when some kind of reward attended their exertions. The reason given is that such a convict cannot and does not make a true contract of hire with the authorities by whom he is confined. The inducements which might be held out to him, in the form of extra food or even money, are in no sense consideration for an enforceable contract of hire.

Larson, *The Law of Workmen's Compensation*, § 47.31 (1993); *see, e.g.*, Lanford v. City of Sheffield, 689 So.2d 176, 179 (Ala. Civ. App.

---

for workers' compensation.[409] In some states, courts have held that prisoners may be eligible for compensation when employed by a private employer, on work release or otherwise.[410] A prisoner may also be considered an employee for compensation purposes in a prison work situation that is designed to resemble free-world employment.[411]

In those states that do provide compensation to prisoners, there are often strict limits on eligibility,[412] and the

---

1997); Porter v. Dep't of Corrections, 876 S.W.2d 646, 647–48 (Mo. App. 1994) (citing absence of "genuine employment relationship"); Commonwealth v. Woodward, 249 Va. 21, 452 S.E.2d 656, 658 (1995) (denying benefits to a prisoner because prisoners "not on a work release program" are incapable of making "a true contract of hire with the authorities by whom he is confined.").

[409]*See* Or. Rev. Stat. § 655.510; Rowland v. County of Sonoma, 220 Cal.App.3d 331, 334 (1990) (under certain circumstances, a county inmate may be an employee for purposes of recovering workers' compensation benefits); Morales v. Workers' Comp. Appeals Bd., 186 Cal.App.3d 283, 288–289 (1986) (county work release prisoner was an employee).

[410]*See, e.g.*, Benavidez v. Sierra Blanca Motors, 122 N.M. 209, 922 P.2d 1205, 1211 (1996) (holding that claimant's "status as an inmate does not preclude the existence of an employer–employee relationship for the purpose of receiving workers' compensation benefits"); Courtesy Construction Corp. v. Derscha, 431 So.2d 232, 232–33 (Fla. Dist. Ct. App. 1983) (holding that "[w]ork-released prisoners engaged to work in private enterprise, for compensation paid them by private businesses that are 'employers' in every practical sense of the word, are not excluded from [the Workers' Compensation Act]"); Hamilton v. Daniel International Corp., 273 S.C. 409, 257 S.E.2d 157, 158 (S.C. 1979) (holding that defendant required to provide workers' compensation benefits due to the existence of an employer–employee relationship and that "[claimant] transcended his prisoner status and became a private employee entitled to workmen's compensation benefits"); *see also* 1B Arthur Larson, *The Law of Workmen's Compensation*, §§ 47.31(d) (1995) ("There has been a greater inclination to find employee status for prisoners when, instead of merely working within the prison, they have been lent to other state agencies or even private employers.").

[411]*See* Barnard v. State, 642 A.2d 808, 819 (Del. Super. 1992) ("when an inmate voluntarily applies for a job outside the prison grounds, when the employer chooses to hire him, pays his wages, offers him work at considerable risk to himself, and benefits substantially from his services, that inmate is an employee" under state compensation law), *aff'd*, 637 A.2d 829 (Del. 1994). *But see* Graves v. Workmen's Compensation Appeal Board, 668 A.2d 606 (Pa. Cmwlth. 1995) (an escaped prisoner who was injured while employed was not entitled to workers' compensation benefits).

[412]*See* Iowa Code § 85.62 (county jail prisoners only); Md. Code, Labor and Employment, § 9-221 (a) (county jail prisoners with permanent disabilities, or after death; prisoners working in Maryland Correctional Enterprises); Neb. Rev. St. § 48-115(a) (prisoners employed by private corporations); S.C. Code 1976 § 42-1-480 (prisoners eligible for benefits only after release); Rev. Code Wash. § 72.60.102 (prisoners eligible only after release); Wis. Stat. Ann. § 303.21(b) (eligibility limited to prisoners injured in "structured work program" off prison grounds or "secure work program," not prison industry or work release; prisoners working for private employers are eligible under a different statute).

benefits paid may be less than in "free world" compensation cases.[413] Some of the states that will not provide workers' compensation to a prisoner when confined will provide such compensation if the disabling injury has a continuing effect after the release of the prisoner or the prisoner suffers an accidental death.[414]

Many states suspend workers' compensation benefits previously awarded when the recipient is incarcerated.[415]

2. Compensation for Federal Prisoners and Pretrial Detainees

Federal prisoners injured in work-related accidents must seek compensation under the Inmate Accident Compensation Act (IACA), which compensates federal prisoners and federal pretrial detainees for "injuries suffered in any industry or in any work activity in connection with the maintenance or operation of the institution in which the inmates are confined."[416] Work-related injuries include "any injury, including occupational disease or illness, proximately caused by the actual performance of the inmate's work assignment."[417]

The IACA is also your only remedy for medical treatment for a work-related injury that is inadequate or aggravates the injury.[418]

The compensation system is the exclusive remedy *against the government* for federal prisoners' work injuries; the FTCA may not be used.[419] The system does not prevent you from seeking other remedies against parties other than the government, such as a *Bivens* suit against individual prison officials who may have committed a constitutional violation leading to your injury.[420]

This system does not provide compensation until you are released from prison or jail.[421] While you are still confined, your compensation is limited to lost prison wages. To seek "lost-time wages," you must inform the institutional safety manager of your "lost time" and that person will submit a BP-140 Injury Report form to the Institutional Safety Committee at its next meeting.[422] You must be off work for three consecutive work day to receive "lost-time wages" and these wages are limited to 75% of your work assignment rate at the time of the injury.[423] The Committee's decision may be appealed through the Bureau of Prisons' Administrative Remedy Procedure.[424]

Apart from lost prison wages, compensation is based solely on the degree of impairment you suffer at the time you are released from confinement.[425] There is no provision for awards for pain and suffering. The amount of compensation is based on the federal minimum wage.[426] The provisions of the Federal Employees' Compensation Act[427]

---

[413]N.C.Gen. Stat. Ann. § 97-13 (compensation limited to $30.00 a week and to cases of death or permanent disability); Wis. Stat. Ann. § 303.21 (limiting total benefits to $10,000 for prisoners).

[414]*See, e.g.*, N.C. Gen. Stat. § 97-13 (paying benefits only upon release or in case of death); Wyo. Stat. 1977 § 27-14-404 (denying benefits during incarceration, paying any remaining benefits after release).

[415]Some statutes simply deny benefits during incarceration. *See, e.g.*, Mich.Comp.Laws § 418.361(1). Others suspend benefits unless the employee has dependents, in which case the benefits continue for them. *See* La. Rev. Stat. Ann. § 23:1201.4; N.D. Cent. Code § 65-05-08.2; *see also* Wood v. Beatrice Foods Co., 813 P.2d 821 (Colo. App. 1991) (upholding statute that suspended all benefits to prisoners following conviction except for permanent disability benefits which had been assigned to prisoner's spouse or minor children). One state court has struck down as unconstitutional a law suspending workers' compensation benefits for prisoners without dependents or ineligible for release. Willoughby v. Dep't of Labor and Industries of the State of Wash., 147 Wash.2d 725, 57 P.3d 611 (2002).

Decisions are divided on whether incarceration requires termination of previously obtained benefits where the statute does not address the question. *See* Hardin's Bakery v. Taylor, 631 So.2d 201, 206–10 (Miss. 1994) (holding benefits should continue) and cases cited; *see also* Deaton, Inc. v. McPherson, 655 So.2d 991, 994 (Ala. Civ. App. 1994) (partial disability benefits should continue upon incarceration where statute only said that total disability payments should cease; noting statute also provided that total disability payments should continue for the benefit of anyone dependent on the disabled employee).

[416]18 U.S.C. § 4126(c)(4); *see* Paschal v. U.S., 302 F.3d 768, 769 (7th Cir. 2002) (IACA applies to pretrial detainees).

[417]28 C.F.R. [Code of Federal Regulations] § 301.102(a). This includes injuries resulting from voluntary work approved by staff in the maintenance or operation of the prison. It does not include injuries received going to or leaving work, or going to or coming from lunch, or participating in institutional programs, or injuries

resulting from willful violations of rules and regulations governing a job assignment. 28 C.F.R. §§ 301.301(b), (d).

[418]28 C.F.R. § 301.301(b); Vander v. U.S. Dep't of Justice, 268 F.3d 661, 663 (9th Cir. 2001). The IACA is also the exclusive remedy when a work-related injury stems from a negligent job assignment or when a pre-existing injury or condition is aggravated by a work assignment. Wooten v. U.S., 825 F.2d 1039, 1044–45 (6th Cir. 1987).

[419]28 C.F.R. § 301.319; U.S. v. Demko, 385 U.S. 149, 152–53, 87 S. Ct. 382 (1966); Vander v. U.S. Dep't of Justice, 268 F.3d at 663.

[420]Smith v. U.S., 561 F.3d 1090, 1101–03 (10th Cir. 2009); Bagola v. Kindt, 131 F.3d 632, 642–45 (7th Cir. 1997); Byrd v. Warden, 376 F. Supp. 37, 41 (S.D.N.Y. 1974).

[421]28 C.F.R. § 301.301(a) ("No compensation for work-related injuries resulting in physical impairment shall be paid prior to an inmate's release.").

[422]28 C.F.R. § 301.202(a). The Safety Committee is to provide the inmate with a copy of its determination. *Id.* The Safety Committee's lost-time wages determination does not confirm the validity of any future claim to recover for work-related physical impairment or death. 28 C.F.R. § 301.202(b).

[423]28 C.F.R. § 301.203. If you are approved for "lost-time wages," these wages will only continue as long as you are available to work even though you cannot work due to your injuries. *See* 28 C.F.R. § 301.204.

[424]28 C.F.R. § 301.205.

[425]28 C.F.R. § 301.314(a).

[426]28 C.F.R. § 301.314(c).

[427]18 U.S.C. 4121 *et seq.*

will be followed when practicable in determining disability and payment.[428]

To obtain compensation, you must take the following steps.

Report the injury immediately. If you don't, you may be denied compensation.[429] Your supervisor should submit to the institutional safety manager a BP-140 form containing a signed statement by you about how the injury occurred as well as witness names and statements and other information.[430]

Between 45 and 15 days before your release date, you should submit a Federal Prison Industries Form 43 (Inmate Claim for Compensation on Account of Work Injury). You are entitled to assistance in filling out the form if needed.[431] If "circumstances preclude submission" of the form in accordance with these rules, you may submit a claim up to 60 days after your release; if you have "good cause," you may submit it up to a year after release.[432] A dependent may submit a claim up to one year after the inmate work-related death.[433]

If you complete the form while you are still in prison, you should submit it to the Institution Safety Manager.[434] You will be given a physical examination, which is mandatory.[435] If you submit your form after your release, you should send it directly to the Claims Examiner, Federal Bureau of Prisons, 320 First Street N.W., Washington, D.C. 20534.[436] You must keep the Claims Examiner informed of your address.[437]

Your compensation claim will be decided by a Bureau of Prison Claims Examiner and you will be given notice of the determination.[438] You may appeal to the Inmate Accident Compensation Committee of the Federal Bureau of Prisons within 30 days of the decision and request either an in-person hearing or "reconsideration," which means review of the record. (Your request may be made up to 30 days later for "good cause shown.") The Committee will send you a copy of the information on which the Claims Examiner based the decision.[439] You may present additional evidence at a hearing or submit additional documentary evidence if your request is for reconsideration.[440]

The hearing or reconsideration is ordinarily held within 60 days of your request. You will be given notice of the hearing, which will be conducted at the Central Office of the Bureau of Prisons in Washington, D.C.[441] If you don't show up for a hearing or show "good cause" for non-appearance within 10 days afterward, your claim will be deemed abandoned.[442]

You may be represented at the hearing by the non-incarcerated person of your choice if you give prior written notice that you have appointed that person as your representative.[443] You may present non-incarcerated witnesses if you give the Committee 10 days' notice of their identities and an outline of their testimony; testimony of witnesses in prison may be submitted in writing.[444] You can get a copy of the hearing recording or transcript by requesting it within 90 days.[445] Decision is usually rendered within 30 days.[446]

The Committee's decision can be appealed within 90 days to the Chief Operating Officer of the Federal Prison Industries, Inc., 320 First Street NW., Washington, DC 20534. The officer should affirm, reverse, or amend the decision within 90 days of the appeal.[447]

You may be able to obtain additional medical treatment at the government's expense after your release from prison if it will reduce the degree of your impairment. You *must* obtain the claims examiner's prior approval for such treatment.[448] If you are awarded a monthly payment because of your work-related injuries, this amount will be suspended if you become incarcerated again.[449]

F. Bringing State Law Claims in Federal Court

In general, claims based on state law do not belong in federal court and will be dismissed at the earliest opportunity. However, there are some exceptions. The FTCA, discussed in § C.2 of this chapter, provides for certain state law claims to be heard against the federal government in federal court. The other important exceptions are discussed below.

1. Supplemental or Pendent Jurisdiction

If you have a federal law claim that is properly in federal court, such as a civil rights claim under § 1983, the federal court may also hear state law claims arising from the same facts.[450] This doctrine used to be called "pendent"

---

[428]28 C.F.R. § 301.314(b).

[429]28 C.F.R. § 301.104.

[430]28 C.F.R. § 301.105.

[431]28 C.F.R. § 301.303(a).

[432]28 C.F.R. § 301.303(f).

[433]28 C.F.R. § 301.302.

[434]28 C.F.R. § 301.303(a).

[435]28 C.F.R. § 301.303(c).

[436]28 C.F.R. § 301.303(f).

[437]28 C.F.R. § 301.303(e).

[438]28 C.F.R. § 301.305.

[439]28 C.F.R. § 301.306.

[440]28 C.F.R. §§ 301.308, 301.309(b).

---

[441]28 C.F.R. § 301.307.

[442]28 C.F.R. § 301.309(a).

[443]28 C.F.R. § 301.304(a).

[444]28 C.F.R. § 301.310.

[445]28 C.F.R. § 301.309(g). It is up to the Committee whether you get a recording or a transcript.

[446]28 C.F.R. § 301.312.

[447]28 C.F.R. § 301.313.

[448]28 C.F.R. § 301.317.

[449]28 C.F.R. § 301.316.

[450]For example, an assault by staff that violates the Constitution is probably also an assault and battery under most states' tort law. *See* Ch. 2, § G.2, concerning use of force claims.

jurisdiction by the courts.[451] It is now codified in a statute that calls it "supplemental" jurisdiction.[452] Courts have discretion whether to exercise supplemental jurisdiction,[453] and the statute sets out several factors that may weigh against exercising it:

(1) the [state] claim raises a novel or complex issue of State law,[454]

(2) the [state] claim substantially predominates over the [federal] claim or claims over which the district court had original jurisdiction,

(3) the district court has dismissed all [federal] claims over which it has original jurisdiction,[455] or

(4) in exceptional circumstances, there are other compelling reasons for declining jurisdiction.[456]

This statute permits a supplemental state law claim to be brought against a party even if there is no federal law claim against that party.[457] For example, if a city jail officer uses unconstitutional excessive force against you, but her actions are not caused by a city policy, you have a federal law claim only against the officer and not against the city.[458] This statute permits you to join a state law *respondeat superior* claim against the city (if state law provides for one) in the federal lawsuit, even though there is no federal law claim against the city, if that claim is based upon the same facts as the federal claim.

There are some important limitations on supplemental jurisdiction. If you are seeking an injunction concerning your treatment in prison, your claim is governed by the Prison Litigation Reform Act's "prospective relief" provisions, which allow relief only for violations of "Federal right[s]."[459] That means you cannot obtain an injunction about prison conditions in federal court based on a supplemental state law claim.[460]

The Eleventh Amendment also limits supplemental jurisdiction. That Amendment prevents federal courts from hearing claims against state governments unless Congress specifically says they can.[461] The Supreme Court has held that it also prohibits federal courts from hearing supplemental state law claims against state officials if they are being sued in their official capacity.[462] That means you must pursue state law official capacity claims against state officials (which includes injunctive claims) in state court.[463]

---

[451]Hagans v. Lavine, 415 U.S. 528, 545–46, 94 S. Ct. 1372 (1974); United Mine Workers v. Gibbs, 383 U.S. 715, 725–26, 86 S. Ct. 1130 (1966).

[452]28 U.S.C. § 1367.

[453]City of Chicago v. International College of Surgeons, 522 U.S. 156, 173–74, 118 S. Ct. 523 (1997).

[454]See, e.g., Key v. Grayson, 163 F. Supp. 2d 697, 705 (E.D.Mich. 2001) (retroactivity of a state disability right statute is a novel and complex issue and court would not exercise supplemental jurisdiction); Roe v. City of Milwaukee, 26 F. Supp. 2d 1119, 1123 (E.D.Wis. 1998) (applicability of state HIV privacy law to facts of case was a novel question and court declined supplemental jurisdiction).

[455]Federal courts have discretion to retain jurisdiction of state law claims even if the federal claims are disposed of. Osborn v. Haley, 549 U.S. 225, 127 S. Ct. 881 (2007). Courts rarely do so, especially if the federal claims drop out early in the case. See Carnegie-Mellon Univ. v. Cohill, 484 U.S. 343, 350, 108 S. Ct. 614 (1988) ("When the balance of these factors indicates that a case properly belongs in state court, as when the federal-law claims have dropped out of the lawsuit in its early stages and only state-law claims remain, the federal court should decline the exercise of jurisdiction. . . ." (footnote and internal citation omitted)); Gibson v. Weber, 433 F.3d 642, 647 (8th Cir. 2006). But see Motorola Credit Corp. v. Uzan, 388 F.3d 39, 56 (2d Cir. 2004) (in general, if all federal claims are dismissed after trial, state claims should be dismissed as well; but if the federal claims are dismissed late in the action, after substantial time, effort, and money has been spent in preparing the state claims, dismissing the state claims may not be fair and is not necessary); Coppage v. Mann, 906 F. Supp. 1025, 1046–47 (E.D.Va. 1995) (retaining jurisdiction over state law medical care claims after dismissal of federal claims because state claims were nearly ready for trial).

[456]28 U.S.C. § 1367(c). A good discussion of these four factors are found in Parker v. Scrap Metal Processors, Inc., 468 F.3d 733, 743–47 (11th Cir. 2006). See also Carnegie-Mellon Univ. v. Cohill, 484 U.S. 343, 349–52, 108 S. Ct. 614 (1988); Itar-Tass Russian News Agency v. Russian Kurier, Inc., 140 F.3d 442, 447–48 (2d Cir. 1998).

[457]28 U.S.C. § 1367(a).

[458]See § B.4.b of this chapter.

[459]18 U.S.C. 3626(a)(1); see Ch. 9, § K, for further discussion of these provisions.

[460]Handberry v. Thompson, 446 F.3d 335, 344–46 (2d Cir. 2006) (PLRA overrides supplemental jurisdiction in prison cases).

[461]See § L.1 of this chapter for a discussion of the Eleventh Amendment.

[462]Pennhurst State School & Hospital v. Halderman, 465 U.S. 89, 107, 109 n.17, 114 n.25, 121, 104 S. Ct. 900 (1984); accord, Ashker v. California Dep't of Corrections, 112 F.3d 392, 394 (9th Cir. 1997); Hales v. City of Montgomery, 347 F. Supp. 2d 1167, 1173 (M.D. Ala. 2004). This rule was not changed by the later enactment of the supplemental jurisdiction statute. Raygor v. Regents of Univ. of Minnesota, 534 U.S. 533, 543, 122 S. Ct. 999 (2002).

Even under Pennhurst, federal courts may enforce state law when doing so is necessary to protect constitutional rights. Alberti v. Sheriff of Harris County, Texas, 937 F.2d 984, 1001 (5th Cir. 1991); Benjamin v. Malcolm, 803 F.2d 46, 50–52 (2d Cir. 1986); U.S. v. State of Michigan, 680 F. Supp. 928, 998 (W.D. Mich. 1987) (court can order state to comply with state law "when noncompliance with state law implicates the constitutional rights of the inmates at the subject institutions, and . . . when compliance with state law is the most effective remedy for any specific unconstitutional conditions").

Under Pennhurst, federal courts may also use state law to help determine what party is responsible for a federal law violation, Henrietta D. v. Bloomberg, 331 F.3d 261, 289–90 (2d Cir. 2003); Venters v. City of Delphi, 123 F.3d 956, 966 (7th Cir. 1997); Doe v. Rains County Independent School Dist., 66 F.3d 1402, 1407 (5th Cir. 1995); see Komyatti v. Bayh, 96 F.3d 955, 960 (7th Cir. 1996) (federal courts may use the terms of state statutes in formulating remedies for federal law violations); see § B.4.a of this chapter, and whether state law creates a liberty interest protected by due process. See Ch. 4, § A.2.

[463]You may file your state law claim in state court and file your federal law claim separately in federal court (i.e., "bifurcate" your claim).

Most lower courts have held that *Pennhurst* does not bar supplemental state law damage claims against individual state officials in their individual capacities.[464] That means, for example, you can bring both a constitutional "deliberate indifference" claim and a state law malpractice claim in the same federal court suit against state prison medical staff,[465] assuming state law would allow such a claim against individuals.

The *Pennhurst* decision only affects suits against state officials and employees. It has no application at all to suits against city or county governments or their personnel.[466] It is also limited to claims based on state law; it does not limit federal law claims against anyone.

The supplemental jurisdiction statute provides that the statute of limitations for supplemental state law claims is tolled while the claims are pending in federal court, and for 30 days after they are dismissed, unless state law provides for a longer tolling period.[467] This means that if your state law claim is dismissed by the federal court for some reason, and the state statute of limitations has run, you still get 30 days after dismissal to file your claim in state court. This provision does *not* toll the limitations period for state law claims against states.[468] If you have such a claim, you should

file it in state court within the limitations period, and not federal court, or you may lose it.

When you bring a state law claim under the federal court's supplemental jurisdiction, that claim is governed by state rules of law, just as if it had been brought in a state court.[469] Thus, there may be defenses or other problems with a state law claim that do not apply to a § 1983 claim.[470] However, several federal courts have held that even if state law provides that a case must be heard in a particular state court, the federal court may still exercise supplemental jurisdiction over it.[471]

Pennhurst State School & Hospital v. Halderman, 465 U.S. at 122. However, if the state case is decided first, and you could have raised your federal law claim in the state proceeding, the doctrine of *res judicata* or preclusion may bar the federal suit. San Remo Hotel, L.P. v. City and County of San Francisco, Cal., 545 U.S. 323, 341, 125 S. Ct. 2491 (2005); Migra v. Warren City School Dist. Bd. of Education, 565 U.S. 75, 80–85, 104 S. Ct. 92 (1984). *Res judicata* is discussed in § M of this chapter.

[464]Bad Frog Brewery, Inc. v. New York State Liquor Authority, 134 F.3d 87, 102 (2d Cir. 1998); Han v. U.S. Dep't of Justice, 45 F.3d 333, 338 (9th Cir. 1995) ("The Eleventh Amendment does not bar a suit seeking damages against a state official in his individual capacity."); Williams v. Com. of Ky., 24 F.3d 1526, 1543 (6th Cir. 1994); Wilson v. UT Health Ctr., 973 F.2d 1263, 1271 (5th Cir. 1992) ("'*Pennhurst* and the Eleventh Amendment do not deprive federal courts of jurisdiction over state law claims against state officials strictly in their individual capacities.'"); Rosado v. Zayas, 813 F.2d 1263, 1272 (1st Cir. 1987); *see also* Deakins v. Monaghan, 484 U.S. 193, 203–04, 108 S. Ct. 523 (1988) (noting Supreme Court has not decided the question). *But see* Hughes v. Savell, 902 F.2d 376, 378–79 (5th Cir. 1990) (tort claims barred where state law made the state liable for its employees' negligence); Colon v. Schneider, 899 F.2d 660, 672 (7th Cir. 1990) (damage claim based on violation of prison regulations barred); Beehler v. Jeffes, 664 F. Supp. 932, 941–42 (M.D. Pa. 1986) (tort claims barred).

[465]*See, e.g.*, Ashker v. California Dep't of Corrections, 112 F.3d 392 (9th Cir. 1997).

[466]Charter Tp. of Muskegon v. City of Muskegon, 303 F.3d 755, 763 (6th Cir. 2002).

[467]28 U.S.C. § 1367(d); *see* Jinks v. Richland County, 538 U.S. 456, 123 S. Ct. 1667 (2003) (upholding provision's constitutionality in general and as applied to claims against county governments).

[468]Raygor v. Regents of Univ. of Minnesota, 534 U.S. 533, 543–46, 122 S. Ct. 999 (2002). This too is said to be a result of the states' Eleventh Amendment immunity.

[469]Baker v. Coughlin, 77 F.3d 12, 15 (2d Cir. 1996) ("a federal court acts essentially as a state court in addressing pendent state law claims").

[470]*See, e.g.*, Brown v. Harris, 240 F.3d 383, 386 (4th Cir. 1997) (state law jail suicide claim was barred by state rule barring wrongful death suits arising from illegal acts by the decedent); Quezada v. County of Bernalillo, 944 F.2d 710, 721 (10th Cir. 1991) (plaintiff's damages for negligence were reduced under state's comparative fault rule, not applicable to § 1983 claim); Buffington v. Baltimore County, Md., 913 F.2d 113, 125–26 (4th Cir. 1990) (pendent negligence claims barred by state law immunity rules in jail suicide case); Hamilton v. Roth, 624 F.2d 1204, 1208–12 (3d Cir. 1980) (pendent malpractice claim subject to state requirement of submission to arbitration board).

[471]*See* Davet v. City of Cleveland, 456 F.3d 549, 554–55 (6th Cir. 2006); Thompkins v. Stuttgart School Dist., 787 F.2d 439, 441 (8th Cir. 1986); Goka v. Bobbitt, 625 F. Supp. 319, 324 (N.D. Ill. 1985); Wojciechowski v. Harriman, 607 F. Supp. 631, 633 (D. N.M. 1985) (state statute granting exclusive jurisdiction to state courts over certain tort claims was unconstitutional insofar as it limited federal courts' pendent jurisdiction); *see also* Jones v. Coughlin, 665 F. Supp. 1040, 1046–47 (S.D.N.Y. 1987) (pendent claims for "deliberate, systematic and grossly unlawful violations of civil rights" are not governed by statute relegating tort claims to state court of claims). *Contra*, Turner v. Miller, 301 F.3d 599, 602 (7th Cir. 2002) (federal court jurisdiction over tort claim against state employee was barred because of sovereign immunity where state law directed hearing such cases in state Court of Claims); Cartagena v. City of New York, 257 F. Supp. 2d 708, 710 (S.D.N.Y. 2003) (court could not exercise supplemental jurisdiction over state "Article 78" proceeding).

The holdings of *Davet* and the other cases cited appears to be supported by *Marshall v. Marshall*, 547 U.S. 293, 312–14, 126 S. Ct. 1735 (2006), which holds that federal courts may hear cases under their diversity jurisdiction even if state law places exclusive jurisdiction in a state court. Since both supplemental and diversity jurisdiction involve federal courts hearing state law claims, it is hard to see why the rules should be different for supplemental jurisdiction.

The *Marshall* decision does not prevent federal courts from refusing to exercise supplemental jurisdiction in that situation as a matter of discretion. *See* Gregory v. Shelby County, Tennessee, 220 F.3d 433, 446 (6th Cir. 2000) (stating, "In this instance, the Tennessee legislature expressed a clear preference that TGTLA claims be handled by its own state courts. This unequivocal preference of the Tennessee legislature is an exceptional circumstance for declining jurisdiction.").

Federal courts have exercised supplemental jurisdiction in prison cases over a wide variety of state law claims including state law torts,[472] violation of state statutes or administrative law,[473] and state constitutional violations.[474] Violation of state statutory, administrative, or constitutional law does not necessarily give rise to a claim for damages; this will be determined by state law even if you are litigating in federal court.[475]

Marshall and the other cases cited also do not address the situation where state law says that a claim against a state employee or official must be brought as a case against the state, over which the federal courts under *Pennhurst* cannot exercise supplemental jurisdiction because of the Eleventh Amendment. Baker v. Coughlin, 77 F.3d 12, 15–16 & n.3 (2d Cir. 1996); Smith v. Ozmint, 394 F. Supp. 2d 787, 791–92 (D.S.C. 2005); Doran by and through Doran v. Condon, 983 F. Supp. 886, 890 (D.Neb. 1997).

[472]Wilson v. Lawrence County, Mo., 154 F.3d 757, 761 (8th Cir 1998) (district court should have exercised jurisdiction over state law claim of false imprisonment); Daskalea v. District of Columbia, 227 F.3d 433, 444–46 (D.C. Cir. 2000) (negligent supervision resulting in sexual abuse); Green v. Johnson, 977 F.2d 1383, 1388 (10th Cir. 1992) (intentional infliction of emotional distress); Oviatt by and through Waugh v. Pearce, 954 F.2d 1470, 1479–80 (9th Cir. 1992) (false imprisonment); Miller v. Lovett, 879 F.2d 1066, 1072–73 (2d Cir. 1989) (assault and battery); Chambers v. Ingram, 858 F.2d 351, 355–61 (7th Cir. 1988) (malpractice); Molton v. City of Cleveland, 839 F.2d 240, 247–48 (6th Cir. 1988) (tort claim in jail suicide case); Duckworth v. Franzen, 780 F.2d 645, 656 (7th Cir. 1985) (court should consider exercising pendent jurisdiction over negligence claim in prison bus fire case); Jean-Laurent v. Wilkerson, 438 F. Supp. 2d 318, 327–28 (S.D.N.Y. 2006) (negligence claims for failure to intervene in an assault, authorizing the use of excessive force, and failing to intervene in an abusive strip search); Smith v. Jordan, 527 F. Supp. 167, 173 (S.D. Ohio 1981) (state law privacy claims).

[473]Ramsey v. Schauble, 141 F. Supp. 2d 584, 591–92 (W.D.N.C. 2001) (claim under state statute providing damage remedy for injuries in jail); Shabazz v. Cole, 69 F. Supp. 2d 210, 219 (D.Mass. 1999) (state certiorari claim to review disciplinary proceeding); Nolley v. County of Erie, 776 F. Supp. 715, 725–28 (W.D.N.Y. 1991) (state HIV confidentiality law).

[474]Marcera v. Chinlund, 91 F.R.D. 579, 581–82 (W.D.N.Y. 1981) (state constitutional requirement of contact visits for pretrial detainees); *see* Bahrampour v. Lampert, 356 F.3d 969, 978–79 (9th Cir. 2004) (district court directed to consider supplemental jurisdiction over Oregon Constitution claim).

[475]*See, e.g.,* Giraldo v. California Dep't of Corrections and Rehabilitation, 168 Cal.App.4th 231, 253–57, 85 Cal.Rptr.3d 371 (2008) (finding no damages remedy for violation of state constitution cruel and unusual punishments clause where other damage remedies were available); Gates v. Superior Court, 32 Cal. App.4th 481, 516–25, 38 Cal.Rptr.2d 489 (Cal.App. 1995) (whether damages are available for violations of the California Constitution depends on the voters' intent in adopting the particular section under which damages are sought); Binette v. Sabo, 244 Conn. 23, 45–48, 710 A.2d 688 (Conn. 1998) (recognizing a damages remedy for searches and seizures in violation of the state constitution, but warning that the question of damages for other state constitutional violations must be determined case by case); Jones v. Powell, 462 Mich. 329, 337, 612 N.W.2d 423 (2000) (damage remedy for state

If you intend to invoke a federal court's supplemental jurisdiction, be sure to say so in the jurisdictional paragraph of your complaint. Also be sure to explain exactly what the state law claims are. If you don't do this, you are asking for trouble later.[476]

2. Diversity Jurisdiction

Plaintiffs may pursue state law claims in federal court when the plaintiff and defendant are citizens of different states[477] and when the "matter in controversy" is greater that $75,000 for an individual plaintiff[478] or $5,000,000 if the case is brought as a class action.[479] Such cases are called "diversity of citizenship" cases. The federal courts have jurisdiction only when diversity is "complete"—that is, when no plaintiff is a citizen of the same state as any of the defendants.[480] If a case

---

constitutional violations is not available where there is any other remedy, such as a § 1983 suit or tort claim against municipality or individual defendant); City of Beaumont v. Bouillion, 896 S.W.2d 143, 149 (Texas 1995) (no damage remedy under Texas Constitution); *see also* Lopez v. Smiley, 375 F. Supp. 2d 19, 24–26 (D.Conn. 2005); Smith v. Michigan, 256 F. Supp. 2d 704 (E.D.Mich. 2003). Federal courts are reluctant to exercise supplemental jurisdiction where state law is unsettled as to whether there is a damage claim or not. Lopez v. Smiley, 375 F. Supp. 2d 19, 24–26 (D.Conn. 2005) (citing *Binette* decision in declining to exercise supplemental jurisdiction over various Connecticut constitutional claims because the Connecticut courts had not yet determined that there should be a damage remedy for them).

[476]Several courts have held that supplemental claims should not be considered if they are not formally raised in a timely manner. *See, e.g.,* Rodriguez v. Doral Mortg. Corp., 57 F.3d 1168, 1174 (1st Cir. 1995) and cases cited; Greene v. Town of Blooming Grove, 935 F.2d 507, 510–11 (2d Cir. 1991) (reversing exercise of jurisdiction over pendent claim that was neither pleaded nor discretely raised during the litigation).

[477]28 U.S.C. § 1332(a)(1). "States" include the Territories, the District of Columbia, and Puerto Rico. 28 U.S.C. § 1332(e). A state itself is not a "citizen" under this statute, nor are most state agencies. Moor v. County of Alameda, 411 U.S. 693, 717, 93 S. Ct. 1785 (1973); Jakoubek v. Fortis Benefits Ins. Co., 301 F. Supp. 2d 1045, 1048 (D. Neb. 2003). A city or county government may be a "citizen" of a state. Moor v. County of Alameda, 411 U.S. at 717–21.

[478]28 U.S.C. § 1332(a). This amount used to be $50,000 but was raised in 1996. For discussion of the meaning of "matter in controversy," *see* Exxon Mobil Corp. v. Allapattah Servs., 545 U.S. 546, 125 S. Ct. 2611 (2005); Everett v. Verizon Wireless, Inc., 460 F.3d 818, 822–24 (6th Cir. 2006).

[479]28 U.S.C. § 1332(d)(6). *See* Blockbuster, Inc. v. Galeno, 472 F.3d 53 (2d Cir. 2006) (discussing class action amount requirement).

[480]*See* Wisconsin Dep't of Corrections v. Schacht, 524 U.S. 381, 388, 118 S. Ct. 2047 (1998) and cases cited (diversity of citizenship among the parties is complete only if no plaintiff and no defendant are citizens of same state).

in state court satisfies the requirements for diversity jurisdiction, defendants can remove it to federal court.[481]

A prisoner's residence or "domicile" is presumed to be the state she lived in before being imprisoned.[482] Thus, if you are imprisoned outside your home state, you may be able to bring state law suits in federal court under diversity jurisdiction against personnel of the prison where you are held, since you are a citizen of a different state.

You may bring almost any kind of civil suit under the federal courts' diversity jurisdiction that you could bring in state court. The courts have created two exceptions. They will not hear domestic relations cases (marriage, divorce, child custody, etc.) based on diversity,[483] nor will they hear probate cases (wills and estates).[484] However, prisoners have invoked diversity jurisdiction to bring tort suits in federal court against prison personnel[485] as well as claims against private persons or corporations.[486]

Although diversity cases are heard in federal court under the federal courts' procedural rules, they are governed in most other respects by state law.[487] They are exempt from some provisions of the Prison Litigation Reform Act.[488]

G. RIGHTS BASED ON COURT ORDERS

Some jails and prisons are subject to court orders in prisoners' civil rights class actions. Class action judgments are supposed to determine the rights of class members,[489] whether they are entered as a result of a court decision or by agreement of the parties approved by the court,[490] so if your problem is covered by the judgment or order, your remedy

---

[481]*See, e.g.*, Mitchell v. Brown & Williamson Tobacco Corp., 294 F.3d 1309, 1314–15 (11th Cir. 2002).

[482]Sullivan v. Freeman, 944 F.2d 334, 337 (7th Cir. 1991) and cases cited.

Several courts have held that if a prisoner has formed an intention of living in another state after her release, that state may be considered to be her domicile. Smith v. Cummings, 445 F.3d 1254, 1260 (10th Cir. 2006) and cases cited; *see* Jones v. St. Tammany Parish Jail, 4 F. Supp. 2d 606, 609 (E.D.La. 1998) (plaintiff injured in Louisiana jail who remained in Louisiana because of his injuries but intended to return to California was domiciled in California for diversity purposes).

[483]Ankenbrandt v. Richards, 504 U.S. 689, 112 S. Ct. 2206 (1992); Vaughan v. Smithson, 883 F.2d 63, 64–65 (10th Cir. 1989).

The federal courts will only hear domestic relations matters when there is a substantial federal law question involved, such as a prisoner's inability to gain access to state court to litigate a domestic relations question, *see* Lynk v. LaPorte Superior Court No. 2, 789 F.2d 554, 558 (7th Cir. 1986), or a claim that state procedures for resolving these questions are unconstitutional. *See* Ch. 3, § G.

[484]Marshall v. Marshall, 547 U.S. 293, 308–09, 126 S. Ct. 1735 (2006); Georges v. Glick, 856 F.2d 971, 973–74 (7th Cir. 1988).

[485]Hazen v. Pasley, 768 F.2d 226, 228–29 (8th Cir. 1985) (state law property claim); Snyder v. Baumecker, 708 F. Supp. 1451, 1461 (D. N.J. 1989) (negligence claim based on inmate suicide).

[486]Mitchell v. Brown & Williamson Tobacco Corp., 294 F.3d 1309, 1314–15 (11th Cir. 2002) (tort claim against tobacco companies); Richard v. Ray, 290 F.3d 810, 812 (6th Cir. 2002) (malpractice claim against private doctor and hospital); Romandette v. Weetabix Co., Inc., 807 F.2d 309 (2d Cir. 1986) (products liability case).

[487]*See* IDX Sys. Corp. v. Epic Sys. Corp., 285 F.3d 581, 586 (7th Cir. 2002) (noting that "our task is to implement state law as state courts would implement it"). This would mean that if your state has a comparative negligence statute or rule, the jury will be instructed to determine what percentage, if any, that you were responsible for the injuries that occurred to you. *See* Reginald Martin Agency, Inc. v. Conseco Medical Ins. Co., 460 F. Supp. 2d 915 (S.D. Ind. 2006) (attorney–client privilege determined by state law); Quintana v. Baca, 233 F.R.D. 562, 566 (C.D. Cal. 2005) (damages for state law tort claim governed by state comparative negligence rule); Damron v. Smith, 616 F. Supp. 424, 426 (E.D. Pa. 1985) (in diversity action based on inmate assault, all the defendants were immune under state law).

[488]*See, e.g.*, Mitchell v. Brown & Williamson Tobacco Group, 294 F.3d at 1317 (PLRA prohibition on damages for mental or emotional injury without physical injury "does not apply to prisoner lawsuits unrelated to prison conditions filed in state court based solely on state law and removed by defendants to federal court based on diversity jurisdiction.").

[489]Martin v. Davies, 917 F.2d 336, 339 (7th Cir. 1990); Daniel B. v. O'Bannon, 588 F. Supp. 1095, 1099–1100 (E.D. Pa. 1984) (all class members are bound by final judgment in a class action).

Court decisions in class actions may determine certain facts for purposes of later actions, but they generally do not determine the liability of particular individual defendants. Class action decisions concerning general conditions may not determine the rights of prisoners asserting particular needs or circumstances. *See* § M of this chapter concerning *res judicata* and collateral estoppel.

[490]*See* Rufo v. Inmates of Suffolk County Jail, 502 U.S.367, 387, 112 S. Ct. 748 (1992) (holding consent decrees enforceable and "subject to the rules generally applicable to other judgments and decrees"); Kaufman v. McCaughtry, 419 F.3d 678, 685 (7th Cir. 2005) (plaintiff is bound by class action settlement agreement defining what publications prisoners can receive); Smith v. City of Chicago, 769 F.2d 408, 411 (7th Cir. 1985) (consent decree "defines and shapes the rights in question").

The fact that an order is old does not mean a court should not enforce it, if it is still in effect. Florida Association for Retarded Citizens, Inc. v. Bush, 246 F.3d 1296, 1298 (11th Cir. 2001) (stating "a district court should enforce an injunction until either the injunction expires by its terms or the court determines that the injunction should be modified or dissolved. . . . Designating a case 'closed' does not prevent the court from reactivating a case either of its own acord or at the request of the parties."). However, defendants may respond to an enforcement attempt by moving to terminate the order. *See* Imprisoned Citizens Union v. Ridge, 169 F.3d 178, 190 (3d Cir. 1999) (terminating order under Prison Litigation Reform Act despite allegations of noncompliance with the order).

is probably to try to enforce it. Some courts have held that prisoners can enforce prior judgments in cases that were *not* class actions,[491] though prisoners cannot be bound by judgments in cases where they were not parties and no class was certified.[492]

If a class action order has resolved a constitutional issue, the courts will generally not hear a separate constitutional claim about it; the order is the measure of class members' rights. However, violation of an injunctive order does not by itself form the basis of a § 1983 suit.[493] You should file a motion in the case where the order was entered seeking a finding of contempt[494] or a supplementary order.[495] Courts have held that a motion to enforce an order in a pre-existing case is not a new "action" and therefore does not require exhaustion of administrative remedies under the Prison Litigation Reform Act.[496]

An order that has been vacated or terminated under the Prison Litigation Reform Act[497] or for other reasons[498] can no longer be enforced.[499] (On the other hand, an order that is no longer in effect cannot limit the ability of plaintiffs to pursue a new lawsuit if officials are violating the law.[500]) Some consent judgments cannot be enforced by individual prisoners because they contain provisions prohibiting individual enforcement. Some federal court cases are resolved with "private settlement agreements" which are not enforceable as court orders; they are enforceable, if at all, only as contracts between the parties in state court.[501]

If you are seeking a further order enforcing or changing the terms of an injunction, you must do so in the court in which the injunction was entered, usually through counsel for the class.[502] If you cannot get help from class counsel, you may seek to intervene in the class action or to have counsel replaced.[503] If the subject of your suit is not covered by the class action, you need not proceed via the class action.[504]

---

[491]Several decisions have held that prisoners who are "intended third-party beneficiaries" of an order or consent decree can enforce it even if the case was not a class action. *See* Floyd v. Ortiz, 300 F.3d 1223, 1226 (10th Cir. 2002) and cases cited; Hook v. State of Ariz. Dep't of Corrections, 972 F.2d 1012, 1014 (9th Cir. 1992); South v. Rowe, 759 F.2d 610, 612 (7th Cir. 1985). *But see* Aiken v. City of Memphis, 37 F.3d 1155, 1168 (6th Cir.1994) (citing Blue Chip Stamps v. Manor Drug Stores, 421 U.S. 723, 750, 95 S. Ct. 1917 (1975)) (rejecting third-party enforcement). *Cf.* Pure Country, Inc. v. Sigma Chi Fraternity, 312 F.3d 952, 958 (8th Cir. 2002) (consent decree enforceable by a third party only if the parties "intended to give that third party a legally binding and enforceable right to that benefit").

[492]Gonzalez v. Litscher, 230 F. Supp. 2d 950, 956–59 (W.D.Wis. 2002), *aff'd on other grounds*, 79 Fed.Appx. 215 (7th Cir. 2003) (unpublished).

[493]Floyd v. Ortiz, 300 F.3d 1223, 1226 (10th Cir. 2002); DeGidio v. Pung, 920 F.2d 525, 534 (8th Cir. 1990) (consent decree may not be enforced through § 1983 action); Green v. McKaskle, 788 F.2d 1116, 1123 (5th Cir. 1986) (consent judgment is not a "law" enforceable under § 1983); Batista v. Rodriguez, 702 F.2d 393, 398 (2d Cir. 1983).

[494]Cagle v. Sutherland, 334 F.3d 980, 987 n.9 (11th Cir. 2003) ("Because consent decrees are enforceable through contempt, little need exists to allow suits under section 1983."); Welch v. Spangler, 939 F.2d 570, 572 (8th Cir. 1991); Ross-Simons of Warwick, Inc. v. Baccarat, Inc., 182 F.R.D. 386, 399 (D. R.I. 1998) (violation of injunction does not create separate cause of action; only remedy for violation of contempt).

If you are seeking contempt, make that clear in your papers. Otherwise the court may dismiss your case if it looks like an improper attempt to base a separate § 1983 claim on an order or consent decree.

Contempt is discussed in more detail in Ch. 10, § T.2.b.1.

[495]Cook v. City of Chicago, 192 F.3d 693, 695 (7th Cir. 1999) (supplementary order may be "preferred as less condemnatory than a judgment of contempt" but still be "designed to make the party whole for his or her loss"). At least one federal court holds that contempt is the *only* permissible means of enforcing a prior order. *See* Reynolds v. Roberts, 207 F.3d 1288, 1298 (11th Cir. 2000).

[496]*See* Ch. 9, § D, n.228.

[497]*See* Ch. 9, § K.4, concerning termination of court orders under the PLRA.

[498]Some court orders provide for their own termination. *See, e.g.,* Joseph A. by Wolfe v. New Mexico Dep't of Human Services, 69 F.3d 1080, 1083 (10th Cir. 1995) (order was to terminate after "substantial and continuous compliance" for 12 consecutive months); J.G. v. Board of Educ. of Rochester City Sch. Dist., 193 F. Supp. 2d 693, 700 (W.D.N.Y. 2002).

[499]J.G. v. Board of Educ. of Rochester City Sch. Dist., 193 F. Supp. 2d at 701.

[500]*See* Goff v. Harper, 235 F.3d 410, 413 (8th Cir. 2000) (prior consent decree that was terminated did not limit court's ability to grant relief in a new lawsuit).

[501]A federal court settlement agreement is enforceable in federal court only if the order resolving the case says the court may enforce it, or if the court's order embodies or adopts the actual terms of the settlement. Scelsa v. City University of New York, 76 F.3d 37, 40 (2d Cir.1996) (citing Kokkonen v. Guardian Life Ins. Co., 511 U.S. 375, 381, 114 S. Ct. 1673 (1994)). If the agreement does not meet one of these requirements for enforceability, it is a contract enforceable only in state court. Kokkonen v. Guardian Life Ins. Co., 511 U.S. at 381–82. The Prison Litigation Reform Act provides specifically for private settlement agreements in prison cases. 18 U.S.C. § 3626(c)(2).

[502]McNeil v. Guthrie, 945 F.2d 1163, 1166 (10th Cir. 1991); Long v. Collins, 917 F.2d 3, 4–5 (5th Cir. 1990); Gillespie v. Crawford, 858 F.2d 1101, 1103 (5th Cir. 1988) (en banc) (class members must enforce rights "by urging further action through the class representative and attorney, including contempt proceedings, or by intervention in the class action"); Jacobson v. Schwarzenegger, 357 F. Supp. 2d 1198, 1209 (C.D. Cal. 2004); Bolden v. Stroger, 306 F. Supp. 2d 792, 793 (N.D.Ill. 2004) (challenge based on disability statutes to programs created by consent judgment should be raised in the court that entered the consent judgment).

[503]*See* § J.2 of this chapter.

[504]McNeil v. Guthrie, 945 F.2d 1163, 1166–67 & n.4 (10th Cir. 1991); Hooten v. Jenne, 786 F.2d 692, 695 (5th Cir. 1986). *But see* Facteau v. Sullivan, 843 F.2d 1318, at 1319 (10th Cir. 1988) (case transferred to the class action court to determine if the plaintiff's claims were within the scope of the class action).

The courts take a similar approach when there is a pending, unresolved class action: they do not want to hear individual injunctive complaints separately.[505] You should be prepared to explain why you need special treatment and cannot wait for the class action to be resolved. For example, if you need surgery or other treatment promptly for a painful or dangerous condition, the existence of a pending class action that may reform the medical care system sometime in the future does not help you. If the class action does not deal with the subject matter you wish to raise, you should make that fact clear.

The courts have been less consistent in handling damage claims that involve violations of class action injunctions.[506] It is clear that damages may be awarded in a proceeding for contempt of a class action order.[507] However, in some cases courts have heard independent § 1983 claims alongside the claim of violation of the order.[508] In others, they have treated the terms of the order as defining the plaintiff's constitutional rights in a separate § 1983 claim[509] or have applied the order's terms in some other way.[510] Some courts have held

that damage claims arising from prior class judgments should be pursued before the court that entered the judgment.[511] If you raise a claim that is not actually addressed in a court order, the order does not bar your claim.[512]

If there is a pending class action for injunctive relief, a class member is not barred from pursuing a separate suit for damages,[513] though a named plaintiff is barred.[514]

H. Choosing a Remedy

1. Civil Rights and Other Civil Actions vs. Federal Habeas Corpus, Appeal, and Post-Conviction Remedies

a. State Prisoners and the *Preiser/Heck* Rule   State prisoners challenging their treatment in prison should use 42 U.S.C. § 1983, rather than a petition for a federal court writ of habeas corpus; habeas is for challenges to your confinement itself, or to its length.[515] Courts have generally held

---

[505]Jacobson v. Schwarzenegger, 357 F. Supp. 2d 1198, 1209 (C.D. Cal. 2004) ("Individual lawsuits for injunctive and declaratory relief may not be brought if there is a class action pending involving the same subject matter."); Dotson v. Maschner, 764 F. Supp. 163, 167 (D. Kan. 1991).

[506]They have rejected the view that an injunctive class action judgment prevents future damage claims by class members. Hiser v. Franklin, 94 F.3d 1287, 1291 (9th Cir. 1996) and cases cited; Fortner v. Thomas, 983 F.2d 1024, 1031 (11th Cir. 1993); Gates v. Towery, 456 F. Supp. 2d 953, 963 (N.D. Ill. 2006); Coleman v. General Motors Acceptance Corp., 220 F.R.D. 64, 81 (M.D. Tenn. 2004); Gonzalez v. Litscher, 230 F. Supp. 2d 950, 959–60 (W.D.Wis. 2002) (citing Crowder v. Lash, 687 F.2d 996, 1008–09 (7th Cir.1982)).

[507]See Ch. 10, § T.2.b.1, nn.1083–87.

[508]Williams v. Lane, 851 F.2d 867, 873–74 (7th Cir. 1988) (both judgment violations and independent constitutional violations found); Weeks v. Benton, 649 F. Supp. 1297, 1302, 1309–10 (S.D. Ala. 1986) (both § 1983 claim and contempt claim permitted to go forward); Adams v. Wolff, 624 F. Supp. 1036, 1039 (D. Nev. 1985) (denial of recreation found to violate both consent judgment and Constitution).

[509]Malik v. Miller, 679 F. Supp. 268, 269–70 (W.D.N.Y. 1978) (consent decree violations supported plaintiff's claim of unconstitutional strip search). *Contra*, Kaminsky v. Rosenblum, 737 F. Supp. 1309, 1317 n.6 (S.D.N.Y. 1990) (consent decree violations did not support claim of unconstitutional medical care), *appeal dismissed*, 929 F.2d 922 (2d Cir. 1991).

[510]Ryan v. Burlington County, N.J., 889 F.2d 1286, 1293–94 (3d Cir. 1989) (failure to remedy known consent judgment violations may establish liability of supervisors for consequences); Wilson v. Harper, 949 F. Supp. 714, 724 n.19 (S.D.Iowa 1996) (consent decree that incorporated basic legal standards could be relevant to claim of qualified immunity); *see* Smith v. Sumner, 994 F.2d 1401, 1406 (9th Cir. 1993) (holding that a consent decree may create a liberty interest protected by due process).

Several courts have held that violation of a consent decree may be relevant to whether the defendants were deliberately indifferent. Cagle v. Sutherland, 334 F.3d 980, 987 (11th Cir. 2003)

(medical care case); DeGidio v. Pung, 920 F.2d 525, 531 (10th Cir. 1990) (medical care); Cortes-Quinones v. Jiminez-Nettleship, 842 F.2d 556, 560–61 (1st Cir. 1988) (consent decree violations were evidence of deliberate indifference in inmate murder case).

[511]Klett v. Pim, 965 F.2d 587, 590–91 (8th Cir. 1992) (contempt motion for damages); Spears v. Johnson, 859 F.2d 853, 855 (11th Cir. 1988) (§ 1983 damages claim transferred to district of class action court), *vacated in part on other grounds*, 876 F.2d 1485 (11th Cir. 1989); Atkins v. County of Orange, 251 F. Supp. 2d 1225, 1233 n.6 (S.D.N.Y. 2003); *see* Fortner v. Thomas, 983 F.2d 1024, 1031 (11th Cir. 1993) (holding it "may" be proper to consolidate such claims with the class action or refer them to class counsel); Pidge v. Superintendent, Mass. Correctional Institution, Cedar Junction, 32 Mass.App. 14, 584 N.E.2d 1145, 1148 (Mass. App. 1992) (state court lacked jurisdiction over claim of contempt of federal court order).

Damage claims that deal with the same subject matter as a class action that has been settled need not be brought by class counsel. Harper v. Thomas, 988 F.2d 101, 104 (11th Cir. 1993).

[512]Krug v. Lutz, 329 F.3d 692, 695 (9th Cir. 2003); Watts v. Ramos, 948 F. Supp. 739, 742 (N.D.Ill. 1996) (class injunction requiring one hour of recreation five days a week with "reasonable exceptions" for "fractious inmates" did not bar claim that plaintiff was denied recreation for 4 consecutive 90-day periods).

[513]Kidd v. Andrews, 340 F. Supp. 2d 333, 337 (W.D.N.Y. 2004) and cases cited; *see* McDuffie v. Hopper, 982 F. Supp. 817, 829–30 (M.D.Ala. 1997) (estate of prisoner who committed suicide could seek damages despite pendency of class action concerning mental health treatment).

[514]Kidd v. Andrews, 340 F. Supp. 2d at 337.

[515]Muhammad v. Close, 540 U.S. 749, 750, 124 S. Ct. 1256 (2004) (per curiam) ("Challenges to the validity of any confinement or to particulars affecting its duration are the province of habeas corpus; requests for relief turning on circumstances of confinement may be presented in a § 1983 action."); *accord*, Nelson v. Campbell, 541 U.S. 637, 643, 124 S. Ct. 2117 (2004) (stating that "constitutional claims that merely challenge the conditions of a prisoner's confinement, whether the inmate seeks monetary or injunctive relief, fall outside that core [of habeas corpus] and may be brought pursuant to § 1983 in the first instance.").

that you cannot challenge conditions of confinement by writ of federal habeas corpus.[516] In particular, you cannot obtain release from confinement via habeas corpus on the grounds of unconstitutional treatment in prison. The proper remedy is a suit to change the conditions.[517] There is still some disagreement, however, over where the line is drawn between challenging conditions of confinement and challenging the confinement itself.[518]

You cannot use § 1983 to challenge your criminal conviction or sentence. When a state prisoner challenges "the very fact or duration of his physical imprisonment, and the relief he seeks is a determination that he is entitled to immediate release or a speedier release from that imprisonment, his sole remedy is a writ of habeas corpus."[519]

Challenges to criminal convictions and sentences are beyond the scope of this Manual, but here are some of the basics you should know. The law governing federal habeas corpus is set out in the United States Code,[520] and in two sets of court rules.[521] State prisoners who are in custody pursuant to a state court judgment must proceed under 28 U.S.C. § 2254; prisoners who are not convicted (e.g., pretrial detainees, persons awaiting extradition, etc.) should use 28 U.S.C. § 2241.[522]

In 1996, Congress enacted the Antiterrorism and Effective Death Penalty Act of 1996 (AEDPA), which amended the habeas statutes to impose severe restrictions on the filing of habeas petitions. For example, prisoners must file the writ within one year from the date the criminal judgment becomes final, which usually means the point where you have exhausted your state court remedies.[523] In order to file a second or successive habeas petition, you must seek and obtain authorization from the federal Court of Appeals.[524] A court cannot grant habeas relief unless the state court decision is "contrary to, or involved an unreasonable application of, clearly established Federal law, as determined by the Supreme Court of the United States"[525]—meaning that if you raise an issue that the Supreme Court has not yet addressed, you cannot win even if you are right.

The rule restricting challenges to criminal convictions, or anything else affecting the fact or duration of a prisoner's custody, to habeas corpus is designed to prevent prisoners from circumventing the habeas requirement to exhaust state judicial remedies before bringing such claims into federal court.[526] Exhaustion means presenting all your arguments to the state courts and appealing them as far as you can in the state court system.

You cannot use a § 1983 civil action[527] to get around the habeas exhaustion requirement, even if you only ask for damages or some other form of relief, rather than release from custody. In *Heck v. Humphrey*, the Supreme Court held that actions challenging the legality of state criminal convictions or sentences must await the exhaustion of state remedies no matter what relief you ask for, *and* you must get the conviction or sentence struck down, either in state court or via federal habeas corpus, before you can seek damages for it.[528] (This "favorable termination" rule has also been applied to prison disciplinary proceedings involving lost good time, as discussed below.) In *Heck*, the Court said that a § 1983 claim about a criminal conviction does not accrue (come into existence) until the conviction is overturned.[529]

---

[516]Muhammad v. Close, 540 U.S. at 751 n.1 (noting Supreme Court has never followed prior "speculation" that habeas could be used to remedy "additional and unconstitutional restraint" in prison); Glaus v. Anderson, 408 F.3d 382, 386–88 (7th Cir. 2005); Rael v. Williams, 223 F.3d 1153, 1154 (10th Cir. 2000).

[517]Glaus v. Anderson, 408 F.3d 382, 387 (7th Cir. 2005) and cases cited; Fielding v. LeFevre, 548 F.2d 1102, 1108–09 (2d Cir. 1977).

[518]*See* n.556, below.

[519]Preiser v. Rodriguez, 411 U.S. 475, 500, 93 S. Ct. 1827 (1973).

[520]*See* 28 U.S.C. §§ 2241 through 2255; there are additional provisions for capital cases in 28 U.S.C. §§ 2261–2266.

[521]*See* Rules Governing Section 2254 Cases in the United States District Courts (for challenges to state court convictions and sentences); Rules Governing Section 2255 Proceedings for the United States District Courts (federal convictions and sentences).

[522]White v. Lambert, 370 F.3d 1002, 1008–09 (9th Cir. 2004). One federal circuit has held that state prisoners can rely on either § 2254 or § 2241. *See* Montez v. McKinna, 208 F.3d 862, 865 (10th Cir.2000).

[523]28 U.S.C. § 2241(d)(1) (state prisoners); 28 U.S.C. § 2255(f) (federal prisoners); *see* Day v. McDonough, 547 U.S. 198, 208–210, 126 S. Ct. 1675 (2006) (discussing habeas one-year time limit).

[524]28 U.S.C. § 2241(d)(3) (state prisoners); 28 U.S.C. § 2255(h) (federal prisoners); *see* Gonzalez v. Crosby, 545 U.S. 524, 530–32, 125 S. Ct. 2641 (2005) (discussing second and successive petition rule).

[525]28 U.S.C. § 2254(d)(1).

[526]Nelson v. Campbell, 541 U.S. 637, 643, 124 S. Ct. 2117 (2004) (citing Preiser v. Rodriguez, 411 U.S. 475, 489, 93 S. Ct. 1827 (1973)); *see* 28 U.S.C. §§ 2254(b)–(c); *see also* Rhines v. Weber, 544 U.S. 269, 125 S. Ct. 1528 (2005) (holding court can stay a habeas petition to allow the petitioner to present any unexhausted claims to the state court and then return to federal court to proceed with the petition).

[527]The rules under discussion also apply to other civil actions, including claims under 42 U.S.C. §§ 1981, 1985, and 1986. Amaker v. Weiner, 179 F.3d 48, 51–52 (2d Cir. 1999).

[528]Heck v. Humphrey, 512 U.S. 477, 486–87, 114 S. Ct. 2364 (1994) ("[I]n order to recover damages for allegedly unconstitutional conviction or imprisonment, or for other harm caused by actions whose unlawfulness would render a conviction or sentence invalid, a § 1983 plaintiff must prove that the conviction or sentence has been reversed on direct appeal, expunged by executive order, declared invalid by a state tribunal authorized to make such determination, or called into question by a federal court's issuance of a writ of habeas corpus. . . ."). *See, e.g.*, Amaker v. Weiner, 179 F.3d 48, 51 (2d Cir. 1999) (claim of withholding of exculpatory evidence at criminal trial was barred by *Heck*); Hamilton v. Lyons, 74 F.3d 99, 103 (5th Cir. 1996) (claims that law enforcement personnel coerced self-incriminating statements and altered and destroyed material evidence were barred by *Heck*).

[529]*Heck*, 512 U.S. at 489–90.

That means that the statute of limitations on a claim that is subject to the *Heck* rule does not even start to run until you get the conviction or sentence overturned.[530]

This does not mean that everything connected with your criminal case requires exhaustion of state judicial remedies. The question under *Heck* is "whether a judgment in favor of the plaintiff would *necessarily* imply the invalidity of his conviction or sentence"; if not, the action may proceed.[531] For example, courts have held that a § 1983 action to compel release of DNA evidence is not subject to *Preiser* and *Heck* because a favorable ruling would not "necessarily imply" the invalidity of the plaintiff's conviction; the conviction *might* be overturned later, but only after the DNA was tested and after further proceedings in the state courts.[532] Determining whether a claim can go forward despite *Heck* often requires a close examination of exactly what legal and factual claims are asserted in the § 1983 action and whether they are really incompatible with the elements of the criminal conviction

and the facts proven in the criminal case.[533] You may also be able to litigate issues under § 1983 that are related to criminal charges that never resulted in conviction.[534]

There are other rules, in addition to the exhaustion requirement, that make it difficult to win § 1983 cases arising from criminal proceedings. As long as the criminal judgment stands, it may bar your damage claim under the doctrine of *res judicata*. If the criminal court decided an issue against you, such as the validity of a search, the principle of collateral estoppel will probably prevent you from relitigating the issue in a federal civil suit unless you first get the criminal court decision overturned.[535]

If your state criminal proceedings (trial or appeal) are still going on, the court may dismiss your civil case under the abstention doctrine.[536] The judge, prosecutor, and witnesses in your criminal case are generally immune from damages under § 1983.[537] Also keep in mind that even if you get your conviction reversed in state court, you will not have the basis for a civil rights suit unless you can show a violation of your rights under the United States Constitution and not just state law.[538]

---

[530]Unfortunately, this can get complicated if the claim is one that arises *before* there is a conviction (*e.g.*, if the claim is for false arrest). In that kind of case, the statute of limitations starts running immediately, meaning that you may have to bring your § 1983 claim before you get any conviction reversed or set aside, or even before the charges are disposed of. Wallace v. Kato, 549 U.S. 384, 391, 127 S. Ct. 1091 (2007); *accord*, Watts v. Epps, 475 F. Supp. 2d 1367, 1368–69 (N.D. Ga. 2007). The court hearing your civil case can stay it until the criminal issue has been resolved. *Wallace*, 549 U.S. at 393–94. If you are then convicted, the limitations period stops running, and your civil rights suit is subject to dismissal under *Heck* until such time as you get the conviction reversed, at which time the limitations period will begin to run again. *Id.* at 397.

[531]Heck v. Humphrey, 512 U.S. at 487 (emphasis supplied); *accord*, Muhammad v. Close, 540 U.S. 749, 751–752, 124 S. Ct. 1256 (2004) (per curiam).

For example, in *Heck* the Court said that a suit over an unreasonable search might not be barred, since doctrines like independent source, inevitable discovery, and especially harmless error meant that proving the search was illegal would not *necessarily* imply that the conviction was unlawful. *Heck*, 512 U.S. at 487 n.7; *cf., e.g.*, Ballenger v. Owens, 352 F.3d 842, 845–47 (4th Cir. 2003) (illegal search claim barred by *Heck* rule because on these facts, holding the search was illegal would invalidate the use of essential evidence underlying the plaintiff's conviction); Hughes v. Lott, 350 F.3d 1157, 1160–61 (11th Cir. 2003) (permitting § 1983 action alleging Fourth Amendment violation to proceed, since facts surrounding conviction were not yet known and court could not tell whether decision for plaintiff would invalidate conviction). However, the Court in *Heck* cautioned that if a § 1983 plaintiff argues that her claim will not invalidate a criminal conviction, she will need to show some concrete injury other than the conviction and resulting imprisonment or other sentence if it has not been overturned. *Heck*, 512 U.S. at 487 n.7.

[532]Osborne v. District Attorney's Office for the Third Judicial District, 423 F.3d 1050, 1055 (9th Cir. 2005); Bradley v. Pryor, 305 F.3d 1287, 1290 (11th Cir. 2002) (permitting 1983 action to be used to obtain DNA evidence because that evidence by itself does not "necessarily demonstrate[] or even impl[y] that his conviction is invalid.").

---

[533]*See, e.g.*, McCann v. Neilsen, 466 F.3d 619, 621–22 (7th Cir. 2006) (arrestee's excessive force claim against arresting officer could be brought as § 1983 action); Young v. Nickols, 413 F.3d 416, 418–19 (4th Cir. 2005) (prisoner's allegations that officers illegally extradited him were sufficient to state civil rights claim under § 1983); Smith v. City of Hemet, 394 F.3d 698, 696–99 (9th Cir. 2005) (en banc) (conviction for obstructing a police officer did not bar excessive force claim under *Heck* because the officer could have used excessive force even if the plaintiff was guilty as charged); Cole v. Doe 1 thru 2 Officers of the City of Emeryville Police Dep't, 387 F. Supp. 2d 1084, 1090 (N.D.Cal. 2005) (where plaintiff alleged his traffic conviction was based on a stop and arrest based on racial profiling, his claim about the arrest was subject to *Heck/Preiser*, but his claim of unreasonable detention and search were not because they were not inconsistent with the conviction); *see also* Gerstein v. Pugh, 420 U.S. 103, 107 n.6, 95 S. Ct. 854 (1975) (challenge to lack of probable cause hearings in state court could be pursued under § 1983 because the plaintiffs did not seek release); Lee v. Winston, 717 F.2d 888, 891–93 (4th Cir. 1983) (injunction to bar surgical removal of bullet from prisoner's chest could be obtained under § 1983), *aff'd on other grounds*, 470 U.S. 753, 105 S. Ct. 1611 (1985).

[534]*See, e.g.*, Parker v. Fort Worth Police Dep't, 980 F.2d 1023, 1025 (5th Cir. 1993).

[535]Allen v. McCurry, 449 U.S. 90, 102–05, 101 S. Ct. 441 (1980). Collateral estoppel and res judicata are discussed in more detail in § M of this chapter.

[536]*See* Younger v. Harris, 401 U.S. 37, 91 S. Ct. 746 (1971).

[537]These immunities are discussed in § L.2 of this chapter.

[538]*See, e.g.*, Albright v. Oliver, 510 U.S. 266, 114 S. Ct. 807 (1994) (plurality opinion) (holding that a criminal prosecution without probable cause, in which the defendant was not arrested, does not deny substantive due process; question of Fourth Amendment violation not reached).

In general, civil lawsuits arising from criminal prosecutions are beyond the scope of this Manual. Other books that may be helpful on this subject are listed in Ch. 1, n.1, and in Appendix D.

For these reasons you should never delay or bypass pursuing your state court appeal, state habeas corpus, or other state post-conviction remedy while you bring a § 1983 case about it. You will not be able to get your conviction invalidated under § 1983, and if you miss a statute of limitations or other time deadline on the state remedy, you may be left without any avenue of relief even if your claim is valid.

The habeas exhaustion rule is not limited to challenges to criminal convictions and sentences. The Supreme Court held in *Preiser v. Rodriguez* (a case involving good time lost in a disciplinary proceeding) that any action challenging the "fact or duration" of imprisonment and seeking "immediate" or "speedier" release is subject to the habeas exhaustion requirement,[539] since anything affecting a prisoner's custody is part of the "core of habeas corpus."[540] Later, it held in *Edwards v. Balisok* that the "favorable termination" rule of *Heck v. Humphrey* also applies to disciplinary proceedings that affect the length of confinement by taking away good time.[541] That means you must get the decision you are challenging overturned, through a state administrative or judicial proceeding or a federal administrative or habeas proceeding, before you can bring a federal civil rights action about it.

The *Preiser/Heck* rules extend to any other claim that may directly affect whether you are incarcerated, or for how long, such as claims about the grant or revocation of probation and parole[542] or errors in calculating release or parole eligibility dates.[543] Several courts have also held that *Preiser* and *Heck* apply to civil confinement such as commitment under a sex offender statute.[544]

In some cases, prisoners cannot exhaust state judicial remedies concerning disciplinary, parole, or other administrative decisions because the state provides no judicial review of them. In such cases, exhausting available administrative remedies will satisfy the habeas exhaustion requirement.[545] The majority of courts has held that the one-year limitations period of AEDPA applies to state prisoners'

habeas petitions about administrative decisions as well as challenges to criminal convictions and sentences.[546] That period begins to run when the administrative action becomes final after administrative appeals are concluded.[547] Courts have disagreed over whether administrative decisions are governed by the provision that habeas relief is barred unless the state court decision is "contrary to, or involved an unreasonable application of, clearly established Federal law, as determined by the Supreme Court of the United States,"[548] which means you cannot rely on law established only in the lower courts.

The Supreme Court has recently clarified the scope of the *Preiser/Heck* rules by emphasizing that they apply only in cases where "success in [the federal] action would *necessarily* demonstrate the invalidity of confinement or its duration."[549] Challenges to state laws, procedures, or standards that would not *necessarily* invalidate the confinement or its duration are unaffected. Thus, prisoners who challenge procedures for denial of parole eligibility or procedures for parole release decisions, without actually challenging the decisions about their own parole status, can proceed directly under § 1983. That is because success in their suits would not *necessarily* result in their earlier release, but only in new proceedings which *might* hasten their release.[550]

---

539 Preiser v. Rodriguez, 411 U.S. 475, 500, 93 S. Ct. 1827 (1973); *accord*, Wilkinson v. Dotson, 544 U.S. 74, 86, 125 S. Ct. 1242 (2005).

540 *Preiser*, 411 U.S. at 488–89.

541 Edwards v. Balisok, 520 U.S. 641, 117 S. Ct. 1584 (1997) (inmate cannot bring § 1983 challenging disciplinary conviction if he has lost good time or the length of his confinement has been extended until the conviction has been reversed or invalidated).

542 Preiser v. Rodriguez, 411 U.S. at 486; Butterfield v. Bail, 120 F.3d 1023 (9th Cir. 1997) (challenge to parole revocation); Lindsey v. Wells, 901 F.2d 96, 97 (8th Cir. 1990) (challenge to parole denial).

543 Campbell v. Williamson, 783 F. Supp. 1161, 1164 (C.D.Ill. 1992).

544 Huftile v. Miccio-Fonseca, 410 F.3d 1136, 1139–40 (9th Cir. 2005); Hubbs v. County of San Bernardino, CA, 538 F. Supp. 2d 1254, 1263–64 (C.D.Cal. 2008); Rogers v. Ill. Dep't of Corr. Special Eval. Unit, 160 F. Supp. 2d 972, 977–78 (N.D.Ill.2001).

545 Wilson v. Jones, 430 F.3d 1113, 1118 (10th Cir. 2005); Moffatt v. Director, TDCJ-CJID, 390 F. Supp. 2d 560, 561 (E.D.Tex.

2005), *subsequent determination*, 2005 WL 3068796 (E.D.Tex. Nov. 14, 2005).

546 Dulworth v. Evans, 442 F.3d 1265, 1267–68 (10th Cir. 2006); Shelby v. Bartlett, 391 F.3d 1061, 1064–65 (9th Cir. 2004); Wade v. Robinson, 327 F.3d 328, 330–31 (4th Cir. 2003); Cook v. New York State Div. of Parole, 321 F.3d 274, 279–80 (2d Cir. 2003); Kimbrell v. Cockrell, 311 F.3d 361, 363 (5th Cir. 2002). One federal appeals court has held that this one-year limitations period is inapplicable where the challenge is to an administrative decision. Cox v. McBride, 279 F.3d 492, 493–94 (7th Cir. 2002).

547 Shelby v. Bartlett, 391 F.3d at 1066.

548 28 U.S.C. § 2254(d)(1). *Compare* Brown v. Braxton, 373 F.3d 501, 509 (4th Cir. 2004) (applying statute to prison disciplinary proceeding) *with* White v. Indiana Parole Bd., 266 F.3d 759, 763–66 (7th Cir. 2001) (holding statute does not apply to disciplinary decision because it is not the action of a court). We think the *White* case is correct, since the statute refers to claims "adjudicated on the merits in State *court* proceedings," and a prison disciplinary board is not a "court." However, if your state provides judicial review of disciplinary or other administrative decisions, you must pursue those judicial remedies to satisfy the habeas exhaustion requirement, and at that point you will be subject to § 2254(d)(1) because your claim will have been adjudicated on the merits in a state court. *See* Gomez v. Graves, 323 F.3d 610, 612 (8th Cir. 2003).

549 Wilkinson v. Dotson, 544 U.S. 74, 82, 125 S. Ct. 1242 (2005) (emphasis supplied).

550 *Wilkinson*, 544 U.S. at 81 (". . . [T]he prisoner's claim for an injunction barring *future* unconstitutional procedures did *not* fall within habeas' exclusive domain. That is because '[o]rdinarily, a prayer for such prospective relief will not "necessarily imply" the invalidity of a previous loss of good-time credits.'" (citation omitted)); Thomas v. Eby, 481 F.3d 434, 439–40 (6th Cir. 2007) (challenge to deprivation of "disciplinary credits" was not barred by *Preiser/Heck* because those credits only affected parole eligibility

The Supreme Court has also clarified in *Muhammad v. Close* that prison sanctions which do not affect a prisoner's release date, such as disciplinary segregation, are not governed by the *Preiser/Heck* rule.[551] The same is true of requirements for sex offender registration,[552] placement in administrative segregation,[553] or other actions by prison officials or other administrative personnel that do not affect the length of confinement.[554] In such cases, you can sue under § 1983 without having to get a favorable termination through exhausting state judicial remedies or a federal habeas corpus proceeding. (You do have to exhaust administrative remedies as required by the Prison Litigation Reform Act (PLRA) if the action affects your treatment in prison.) One federal appeals court has held that even when a prisoner has lost good time, if she abandons forever any challenge to that loss of good time or other sanction affecting the length of confinement, the *Preiser/Heck* rules do not apply, and a § 1983 challenge to other sanctions such as segregated confinement may go forward without habeas exhaustion and favorable termination.[555]

There is still some disagreement about the exact dividing line between habeas and § 1983; some courts have held that challenges to the *place* of confinement, including both placement in segregated confinement or in a particular facility, can be pursued via habeas,[556] though it may be that

Muhammad v. Close will be found to have overruled those decisions. Courts have disagreed over whether challenges to conditions of parole or probation are part of the "core of habeas corpus" and therefore subject to the rules of *Preiser* and *Heck*.[557]

In some instances, depending on the law of the federal jurisdiction you are in, you may have a choice of proceeding via habeas or § 1983.[558] In making that choice, keep in mind that:

- you cannot get damages through habeas corpus;
- § 1983 may require exhaustion of administrative remedies, but habeas will require exhaustion of *judicial* remedies if there are any, probably in addition to administrative remedies;
- § 1983 will require you to identify which individual is personally responsible for your treatment,[559] while habeas requires only that you name the person who has you in custody;[560]
- habeas corpus will probably subject you to the various restrictive rules of AEDPA discussed earlier in this section.

The *Preiser/Heck* rules do not apply to cases involving temporary release programs because admission to such programs generally does not shorten a prisoner's incarceration. Temporary release cases can therefore be brought immediately under § 1983.[561]

---

date, leaving discretion to grant or deny parole); Young v. Nickols, 413 F.3d 416, 419 (4th Cir. 2005) (claim for illegal extradition did not necessarily imply that revocation of probation leading to confinement was invalid); Adams v. Agniel, 405 F.3d 643, 644–45 (8th Cir. 2005) (per curiam) (request to correct allegedly erroneous information in parole record was not barred, since plaintiff still might not get paroled even if the information was corrected). *Compare* Williams v. Consovoy, 453 F.3d 173, 177–78 (3d Cir. 2006) (claim that revocation of parole was unconstitutional was barred by *Preiser/Heck* since it would imply that confinement was invalid).

[551]Muhammad v. Close, 540 U.S. 709, 124 S. Ct. 1256 (2004) (per curiam).

[552]*See* Neal v. Shimoda, 131 F.3d 818, 823–24 (9th Cir. 1997) (noting that success on the merits for the inmate would not call into question the validity of their confinement; it would merely remove them from the sex offender list and registration program requirements).

[553]*See* Brown v. Plaut, 131 F.3d 163, 167–68 (D.C. Cir. 1997).

[554]*See, e.g.*, Docken v. Chase, 393 F.3d 1024, 1026–28 (9th Cir. 2004).

[555]Peralta v. Vasquez, 467 F.3d 98, 104–06 (2d Cir. 2006), *cert. denied*, 551 U.S. 1145 (2007).

[556]Medberry v. Crosby, 351 F.3d 1049, 1053 (11th Cir. 2003); Abdul-Hakeem v. Koehler, 910 F.2d 66, 69–70 (2d Cir. 1990); Krist v. Ricketts, 504 F.2d 887, 887–88 (5th Cir. 1974) (per curiam); Kane v. Winn, 319 F. Supp. 2d 162, 215 (D.Mass. 2004) (habeas might be used in "extreme cases where transfer or release might be a necessary remedy"). *Contra*, Montgomery v. Anderson, 262 F.3d 641, 643–44 (7th Cir. 2001) ("Disciplinary segregation affects the severity rather than duration of custody. More-restrictive custody must be challenged under § 1983, in the uncommon circumstances when it can be challenged at all."); Brown v. Plaut, 131 F.3d 163,

167–68 (D.C. Cir. 1997); Toussaint v. McCarthy, 801 F.2d 1080, 1102–03 (9th Cir. 1986).

[557]*Compare* Williams v. Wisconsin, 336 F.3d 576, 579–80 (7th Cir. 2003) (explaining that conditions of parole "'define the perimeters of'" confinement and thus challenges to particular conditions must be brought as habeas corpus petitions and not as civil suits under § 1983 (quoting Drollinger v. Milligan, 552 F.2d 1220, 1224–25 (7th Cir.1977)); Cordell v. Tilton, 515 F. Supp. 2d 1114, 1132 (S.D.Cal. 2007) *with* Yahweh v. U.S. Parole Comm'n, 158 F. Supp. 2d 1332, 1338–40 (S.D.Fla. 2001).

Some recent decisions hold that the decision in *Wilkinson v. Dotson*, discussed above, undermines the Seventh Circuit decisions in *Drollinger* and *Williams*. *See* Lee v. Jones, 2006 WL 44188, *4 (D.Or., Jan. 9, 2006); *accord*, Loritz v. Dumanis, 2007 WL 1892109, *3–4 (D.Nev., June 27, 2007). We think that is correct.

[558]*See, e.g.*, Terrell v. U.S., 565 F.3d 442, 446–47 (6th Cir. 2009) (challenge to use of videoconferencing at parole proceedings could proceed under habeas or § 1983); Docken v. Chase, 393 F.3d 1024, 1026–28 (9th Cir. 2004) (challenge to change in frequency of parole consideration could be brought via habeas or § 1983); Abdul-Hakeem v. Koehler, 910 F.2d 66, 69–70 (2d Cir. 1990) (either habeas or § 1983 may be used to challenge the place of confinement, including segregation).

[559]*See* § B.4.a of this chapter.

[560]Rule 2, Rules Governing Section 2254 Cases in the United States District Courts ("If the petitioner is currently in custody under a state-court judgment, the petition must name as respondent the state officer who has custody.").

[561]Anderson v. Recore, 446 F.3d 324, 334 (2d Cir. 2006); Kim v. Hurston, 182 F.3d 113, 118 n.3 (2d Cir. 1999) (holding that temporary release revocation claim is about "conditions of

In some cases involving administrative decisions that are subject to the *Heck/Preiser* rules, you may be unable to use federal habeas corpus because by the time you complete the necessary exhaustion, you have been released and your habeas claim is moot.[562] If you haven't gotten the adverse decision overturned and you can't use federal habeas, then you can't satisfy the *Heck v. Humphrey* rule and move on to pursue damages under § 1983. Several federal circuits have held that under those circumstances, if you had no opportunity to pursue federal habeas corpus, you can go ahead under § 1983 anyway.[563]

b. Federal Prisoners Federal prisoners' civil rights actions, habeas petitions, appeals, and post-conviction remedies are governed by rules similar to those described for state prisoners, except that post-appeal challenges to a criminal conviction or sentence should be presented by motion to vacate, set aside, or correct the sentence pursuant to 28 U.S.C. § 2255, filed in the court where the sentence and conviction were obtained, at the earliest opportunity.[564]

For federal prisoners, § 2255 plays the role that habeas corpus under 28 U.S.C. § 2254 plays for state prisoners.[565] Section 2255 is *not* a substitute for a direct appeal. You must raise all issues in your direct appeal that are supported by the trial record, or you may lose the right to present them later. Issues that do not appear in the trial record (*e.g.*, claims of ineffective assistance of counsel, or of newly discovered evidence) can be raised under § 2255.[566] Rule 35(a) of the Federal Rules of Criminal Procedure provides for correction of sentences resulting from "arithmetical, technical, or other clear error" upon motion made within seven days of the sentence.[567] Other claims that sentences are illegal or defective must be raised under 28 U.S.C. § 2255.

Federal prisoners may petition for a writ of habeas corpus under 28 U.S.C. § 2241, but for federal prisoners, habeas is reserved for challenges to the way your sentence is being carried out, which generally means matters such as parole procedures, sentence computation, or loss of good time.[568] The Prison Litigation Reform Act (PLRA) administrative exhaustion requirement does not apply to habeas proceedings,[569] but prisoners must still exhaust administrative remedies before pursuing a § 2241 petition.[570] The habeas exhaustion requirement, unlike the PLRA, has an

---

confinement" and need not be pursued via habeas corpus); Nelson v. Murphy, 44 F.3d 497, 499 (7th Cir. 1995) (same as *Kim*); Graham v. Broglin, 922 F.2d 379, 381–82 (7th Cir. 1991); Gwin v. Snow, 870 F.2d 616, 624 (11th Cir. 1989); Hake v. Gunter, 824 F.2d 610, 611 (8th Cir. 1987); Jamieson v. Robinson, 641 F.2d 138, 141 (3d Cir. 1981); Wright v. Cuyler, 624 F.2d 455, 457–59 (3d Cir. 1980); Morris v. McCotter, 773 F. Supp. 969, 971 (E.D.Tex. 1991); *see* Taylor v. U.S. Probation Office, 409 F.3d 426 (D.C. Cir. 2005) (holding § 1983 action proper to challenge inmate's placement in a detention facility rather than in a halfway house).

One court has held that habeas may be used to challenge revocation of work release when the program is "closely connected to a prisoner's impending release," but did not hold that § 1983 was unavailable. Brennan v. Cunningham, 813 F.2d 1, 4–5 (1st Cir. 1987).

[562]This is a problem only if you are challenging parole revocation or another administrative determination. If you are challenging your criminal conviction itself, your claim is presumed not to be moot because of the ongoing "collateral consequences" of a criminal conviction. However, administrative decisions such as parole revocation are not presumed to have such consequences; you have to show there is some ongoing detriment to you from the adverse determination. *See* Spencer v. Kemna, 523 U.S. 1, 8–9, 118 S. Ct. 978 (1998). This is hard to do if you have been released. The desire to recover damages does not save your habeas claim from mootness.

[563]Huang v. Johnson, 251 F.3d 65, 74 (2d Cir. 2001); *accord*, Nonnette v. Small, 316 F.3d 872, 875–76 (9th Cir. 2002). Other circuits have held to the contrary, which means you have no remedy if, for example, you spend significant time in prison because you lose good time or your parole is revoked, but by the time you finish exhausting state judicial remedies you have been released. *See* Entzi v. Redmann, 485 F.3d 998, 1003 (8th Cir. 2007), *cert. denied*, 128 S. Ct. 1714 (2008); Gilles v. Davis, 427 F.3d 197, 210 (3d Cir. 2005).

[564]Motions under § 2255 are governed by a one-year statute of limitations, running from the date on which the judgment of conviction became final, the date on which any government-created impediment to filing was removed, the date on which the right asserted was first recognized by the Supreme Court if made

retroactive, or the date on which the facts supporting the claims could have been discovered through due diligence. 18 U.S.C. § 2255(f); *see* Johnson v. U.S., 544 U.S. 295, 125 S. Ct. 1571 (2005) (vacatur of prior conviction on which enhanced sentence was based was a fact starting a new one-year time period); Akins v. U.S., 204 F.3d 1086, 1089–90 (11th Cir. 2000) (refusing to toll limitations period based on prison lockdowns and temporary loss of legal papers where prisoner had plenty of time to get his motion in anyway).

[565]*See* U.S. v. Hayman, 342 U.S. 205, 72 S. Ct. 263 (1952) (explaining role of § 2255).

[566]Massaro v. U.S., 538 U.S. 500, 123 S. Ct. 1690 (2003) (ineffective counsel claims can be raised under § 2255).

[567]Saturdays, Sundays, and holidays are excluded from this period under Rule 45(a)(2), Fed.R.Crim.P. *See* U.S. v. Lett, 483 F.3d 782, 787–90 (11th Cir. 2007) (discussing Rule 35(a) authority), *cert. denied*, 129 S. Ct. 31 (2008).

Rule 35(b) provides for sentence reductions requested by the government. *See* U.S. v. Haskins, 479 F.3d 955, 957 (8th Cir. 2007) (per curiam); U.S. v. Coppedge, 135 F.3d 598, 599 (8th Cir. 1998) (per curiam) (discussing application of Rule 35(b)).

[568]Carmona v. U.S. Bureau of Prisons, 243 F.3d 629, 632 (2d Cir. 2001) (habeas appropriate for challenge to disciplinary sanctions including loss of good time); Chambers v. U.S., 106 F.3d 472, 474–75 (2d Cir. 1997) (sentence calculation properly challenged by habeas); Green v. Nelson, 442 F. Supp. 1047, 1059–60 (D. Conn. 1977) (challenge to parole rescission procedures heard via habeas). *But see* Morales v. U.S., 353 F. Supp. 2d 204 (D.Mass. 2005) (§ 2241 provides no authority for modifying a valid sentence based on medical concerns). The scope of § 2241 jurisdiction is discussed further below at nn.578–579, below.

[569]*See* Ch. 9, § D, concerning the PLRA exhaustion requirement.

[570]Carmona v. U.S. Bureau of Prisons, 243 F.3d 629, 634 (2d Cir. 2001); Moreland v. Federal Bureau of Prisons, 363 F. Supp. 2d

exception for cases where exhaustion would be futile or irreparable harm might be suffered if exhaustion were required.[571]

The *Heck/Preiser* rules[572] apply to federal prisoners as well as state prisoners; they may not bypass the criminal appeals process and the review available under § 2241 and § 2255 by bringing a *Bivens* damages action or other civil action to litigate issues related to their criminal convictions or sentences, or matters affecting release dates.[573] You must get your conviction reversed or vacated through these procedures before a civil action based on the conviction has any chance of success, though—as with state prisoners— challenges that would not actually invalidate the criminal conviction or sentence can go forward without exhausting the §§ 2241 and 2255 remedies.

A federal prisoner challenging prison conditions or mistreatment by prison personnel should generally bring a civil action: for damages, a federal question (*Bivens*) action[574] or a Federal Tort Claims Act (FTCA)[575] case, and for an injunction, a federal question injunctive action[576] or an APA or mandamus proceeding,[577] depending on the facts involved. As with state prisoners, it is not completely clear where the line is drawn between custody-related matters that must be raised through habeas and § 2255, and conditions issues that must be raised in a civil action. One federal court has broadly stated that federal prisoners may proceed under 28 U.S.C. § 2241 in challenges to the execution (rather than the imposition) of sentence, a category it says "includes matters such as 'the administration of parole, computation of a prisoner's sentence by prison officials, prison disciplinary actions, prison transfers,

type of detention and prison conditions."[578] Other courts have taken narrower views.[579] For example, courts have disagreed whether disputes over placement in a community correction center (now called "residential reentry centers"), as opposed to a regular prison, should be addressed under § 2241 or under the Administrative Procedures Act.[580] Federal prisoners cannot obtain release from prison through § 2241 or § 2255 based on their treatment in prison.[581]

2. Civil Rights Actions vs. Tort Actions

a. State Prisoners: § 1983 vs. State Court Tort Actions The most important consideration in deciding between a § 1983 action and a tort action is: Do you have a valid federal law claim? If you don't, your § 1983 lawsuit filed in federal court will be dismissed.

Many valid constitutional claims are also torts: malicious misuse of force will usually constitute assault and battery, deliberate indifference to medical needs may constitute medical malpractice or negligence, deliberate indifference to prisoners' safety may also be negligence. If you do have both a constitutional claim and a tort claim arising from the same facts, bear in mind that you may not have to choose between them.

You can join a tort claim against a local government or its employees with a § 1983 claim under the federal courts' supplemental jurisdiction. You may be able to join a tort claim against state officials—but not the state itself—in a federal court § 1983 suit.[582] You may also be able to join a

---

882, 885 (S.D.Tex. 2005), *reversed on other grounds*, 431 F.3d 180 (5th Cir. 2005).

[571]Pimentel v. Gonzales, 367 F. Supp. 2d 365, 371–72 (E.D.N.Y. 2005) (§ 2241 requirement is "prudential, not statutory"); Moreland v. Federal Bureau of Prisons, 363 F. Supp. 2d at 885.

Exhaustion may also be excused under the habeas "cause and prejudice" standard when "legitimate circumstances beyond the prisoner's control preclude him from fully pursuing his administrative remedies." Carmona v. U.S. Bureau of Prisons, 243 F.3d 629,at 634 (2d Cir. 2001); *see* Moscato v. Federal Bureau of Prisons, 98 F.3d 757, 761 (3d Cir. 1996) (adopting cause and prejudice standard).

[572]These rules are discussed in the preceding section.

[573]Glaus v. Anderson, 408 F.3d 382, 386 (7th Cir. 2005); Taylor v. U.S. Probation Office, 409 F.3d 426, 430–31 (D.C. Cir. 2005) (complaint that prisoner was placed in a detention center despite a court order to confine him at a halfway house was not governed by *Heck* favorable termination rule because it challenged the place of confinement rather than the confinement itself); Marchetti v. Bitterolf, 968 F.2d 963, 966–67 (9th Cir. 1992); Greene v. Meese, 875 F.2d 639, 641–42 (7th Cir. 1989); Zolicoffer v. Federal Bureau of Investigation, 884 F. Supp. 173, 175–76 (M.D.Pa. 1995).

[574]These actions are described in § B.2.c–d of this chapter.

[575]The FTCA is discussed in § C.2 of this chapter.

[576]These actions are discussed in § B.2.a of this chapter.

[577]These two remedies are discussed in § B.2.b of this chapter.

[578]*See* Levine v. Apker, 455 F.3d 71, 78 (2d Cir. 2006) (quoting Jiminian v. Nash, 245 F.3d 144, 146 (2d Cir. 2001)); *accord*, Bostic v. Carlson, 884 F.2d 1267, 1269 (9th Cir. 1989) (habeas may be used to obtain release from disciplinary segregation and expungement of disciplinary records); Boudin v. Thomas, 732 F.2d 1107, 1111 (2d Cir.) (habeas may be used to obtain release from segregation), *reh'g denied*, 737 F.2d 261, 262 (2d Cir. 1984); Venable v. Thornburgh, 766 F. Supp. 1012, 1013 (D.Kan. 1991) (challenge to transfer of D.C. prisoner to federal custody heard via habeas corpus).

[579]*See* U.S. v. Garcia, 470 F.3d 1001, 1002–03 (10th Cir. 2006) (challenges to place of confinement within a particular prison system must proceed as a civil action and not under § 2241 (citing Boyce v. Ashcroft, 251 F.3d 911, 917–18 (Cir. 2001), *vacated as moot*, 268 F.3d 953 (10th Cir. 2001))).

The same questions about the scope of habeas corpus arise under 42 U.S.C. § 1983 for state prisoners. *See* § H.1.a of this chapter, nn. 515-516, 556-557, above.

[580]*Compare* Muniz v. Sabol, 517 F.3d 29, 34 (1st Cir. 2008), *cert. denied*, 129 S. Ct. 115 (2008); Levine v. Apker, 455 F.3d 71, 78 (2d Cir. 2006); Woodall v. Federal Bureau of Prisons, 432 F.3d 235, 241–44 (3d Cir. 2005) (all holding § 2241 an appropriate remedy) and cases cited *with* Richmond v. Scibana, 387 F.3d 602, 605–06 (7th Cir. 2004) (APA was the proper means of challenging rule restricting community correction center placement).

[581]Glaus v. Anderson, 408 F.3d 382, 387 (7th Cir. 2005).

[582]*See* § F.1 of this chapter, concerning pendent and supplemental jurisdiction.

§ 1983 claim with a tort claim in state court, depending on state law. (Whether bringing both claims is to your advantage or just makes the case more complicated is a judgment you will have to make.)

In deciding which kind of case to file, you should consider the following factors:

Defendants. Under § 1983, you must pinpoint which individuals caused your constitutional deprivation, or else prove the existence of a local government policy that caused it.[583] In some states, you can bring a tort suit against the state or local government under the doctrine of *respondeat superior.* This may be to your advantage if you can't precisely identify which employee was responsible for your injury.

Jury trial. Under § 1983, you have the right to a jury trial. In some state civil actions (often, those that are brought against the state or local government under *respondeat superior*), there is no right to a jury trial. The factors you should consider in deciding whether you want a jury trial are discussed elsewhere in this Manual.[584]

If you do want a jury trial, the area from which the jury will be drawn is also a consideration. Federal judicial districts are generally larger than state judicial districts. If you were injured in a city jail, a state court jury might be drawn entirely from the city, which might mean a more liberal-minded and racially balanced jury pool; a federal court jury might be drawn both from the urban area and the surrounding suburbs, where the population tends to be more predominantly white and conservative. On the other hand, a state court jury in a rural county where the prison is a major employer may be more hostile to prisoners than a jury drawn from the corresponding federal judicial district.

Damages. Under § 1983, you can recover damages. However, the Prison Litigation Reform Act (PLRA) provides that you cannot recover compensatory damages for mental and emotional anguish suffered in custody unless you have also suffered a physical injury, though most federal courts will allow recovery of nominal and punitive damages even in the absence of physical injury.[585] In some state court actions (again, they tend to be those brought directly against the state or local government), you can only recover compensatory damages. Thus, if you were treated in an outrageous way, but your injury is not easy to measure in dollars and cents (*e.g.*, an abusively conducted strip search), a remedy that permits punitive damages may be more appropriate.[586] On the other hand, if you did not suffer any physical injury and do not have a strong case for punitive damages, a state court tort suit that is not subject to the PLRA may be a better choice (at least in those states that do not have damage restrictions similar to the PLRA).

Exhaustion of remedies. Under § 1983, prisoners are required to exhaust administrative remedies before filing suit.[587] Many states impose such requirements too, or require filing a "notice of claim" as a precondition for all tort suits against state or local government.[588] Your choice of which suit to file may be determined by which administrative filing rule you have complied with.

You should always file the state notice of claim, or take any other steps state law requires as a prerequisite to filing a tort claim, even if you have already decided to proceed under § 1983. You might change your mind, and even if you don't, the court might change it for you by dismissing your § 1983 claim. Keep your options open.

Statutes of limitations. If the statute of limitations has run on either the § 1983 or the tort claim, obviously you will have to file the one that is not time-barred.[589]

Assignment of counsel. The federal courts have the authority to request (not order) a lawyer to represent you in a § 1983 case.[590] You should find out whether the state courts in your jurisdiction have that authority. You should also try to find out if either court system actually does appoint counsel with any frequency. Some courts have very good counsel appointment programs and others do not.

Immunity rules. You cannot win a damage lawsuit if the defendants are immune. Tort law immunities are generally very different from § 1983 immunities. They also differ from state to state. Depending on the facts of your case and who the defendants are, your case may be barred by immunity under tort law but not under § 1983, or vice versa.[591]

Attorneys' fees. The court may award attorneys' fees to the plaintiff in a § 1983 case.[592] This is not the case with tort cases in most states; you will have to pay a lawyer out of your pocket or out of your damages, if any. It may be easier to persuade a lawyer to take your case if there is the possibility of court-ordered attorneys' fees—especially if the case is one that may not yield a large award of damages.

b. Federal Prisoners: Federal Question (*Bivens*) Actions vs. the Federal Tort Claims Act In deciding whether to bring a *Bivens* action or an FTCA action, you should keep in mind the differences between them. You should also remember that you can bring both claims, and even join them in the same lawsuit, subject to the rules described below.[593]

---

[583]*See* § B.4 of this chapter concerning the personal involvement requirement and suits based on local government policies.

[584]*See* Ch. 10, § R.2.

[585]*See* Ch. 9, § E, for a discussion of the physical injury requirement of the PLRA.

[586]*See* § O.1 of this chapter for a discussion of damages.

[587]*See* Ch. 9, § D, concerning exhaustion of remedies under the Prison Litigation Reform Act.

[588]*See* § K of this chapter concerning exhaustion of remedies generally.

[589]*See* § N of this chapter for a discussion of statutes of limitations.

[590]*See* Ch. 10, § C.5, concerning assignment of counsel.

[591]*See* § L of this chapter concerning immunity rules.

[592]42 U.S.C. § 1988; *see also* Ch. 10, § Y for a discussion of attorney's fees.

[593]There is one exception. The Supreme Court has held that 42 U.S.C. § 233(a) makes the FTCA the only remedy for injuries caused by actions of United States Public Health Service physicians

- The FTCA provides a remedy only for common-law torts; a *Bivens* action can be brought for constitutional violations.[594]
- In an FTCA action, there is no right to a jury trial; in a *Bivens* action, either plaintiff or defendant can demand a jury trial.[595]
- An FTCA judgment bars any recovery against individual employees concerning the same subject matter.[596] If you win a *Bivens* action, you can in theory proceed on your FTCA claim and recover against the government if you are unable to collect on the judgment against the individuals, though you would have to have filed your FTCA action before the statute of limitations ran and then persuaded the court to delay the FTCA trial until after the *Bivens* trial.
- Under the FTCA, you can recover only compensatory damages; in a *Bivens* action, you can also obtain punitive damages.[597]
- Under the FTCA, officials are immune if they were performing discretionary functions or acting pursuant to a statute or regulation.[598] In a *Bivens* action, most officials are entitled only to qualified immunity.[599]

3. Civil Rights Actions vs. Other State Court Remedies

Many state courts hear challenges to prison rules and official actions, either by state habeas corpus or post-conviction proceedings or by a proceeding for judicial review of administrative action.[600] Questions you should ask about these state remedies include the following.

Can you get a better legal standard? Sometimes state law or prison regulations provide more rights than the federal Constitution; if so, be sure the law or regulation is actually enforceable in the state proceeding.

Does your case fit the remedy? Often there are technical rules about what kinds of acts or decisions can be challenged in a state proceeding.

Is the state proceeding faster? Sometimes state administrative review proceedings are designed to be quicker and simpler than § 1983 actions.

What relief do you need, and does the state proceeding provide it? For example, sometimes state remedies, unlike § 1983, do not provide for damages; you must determine how important damages are compared to the benefits of the state court action. If you are serving a year in segregation, a state remedy that might get you out faster could be preferable. If you are serving a month in segregation, even the quickest remedy will probably not get you out earlier, so you might be more concerned about damages.[601]

What kind of hearing or discovery do you need? Many state remedies are restricted to the record made in an administrative proceeding. If you need to present "extrinsic" evidence (*e.g.*, testimony that witnesses were threatened off the record in a disciplinary hearing), the state proceeding may not provide this opportunity.

I. JUSTICIABILITY

The Constitution provides that the federal courts may only resolve "cases" or "controversies."[602] This means that courts will only consider actual, concrete disputes and not abstract, hypothetical issues. This doctrine is generally termed "justiciability."[603]

---

within the scope of their duties. Hui v. Castaneda, ___ S.Ct. ___, 2010 WL 1740524 (2010).

[594]*See* §§ B.2.c, C.2.a of this chapter.

[595]*Compare* Carlson v. Green, 446 U.S. 14, 22–23, 100 S. Ct. 1468 (1980) *with* 28 U.S.C. § 2402. Courts sometimes use an advisory jury on FTCA claims, especially if they already have a jury hearing the constitutional claims at the same time. *See* Rule 39(c), Fed.R.Civ.P ("the court upon motion or of its own initiative may try an issue with an advisory jury"); Kaniff v. U.S., 351 F.3d 780, 784 (7th Cir. 2003) (court disregarded advisory jury findings); Serra v. Pichardo, 786 F.2d 237, 241–42 (6th Cir. 1986) (court used *Bivens* claim jury as advisory jury on FTCA claim and adopted findings).

[596]28 U.S.C. § 2676. This rule applies even if the two cases are tried at the same time, and regardless of whether the *Bivens* claim judgment is entered first. Manning v. U.S., 546 F.3d 430, 437 (7th Cir. 2008), *cert. denied*, 130 S. Ct. 552 (2009); Harris v. U.S. 422 F.3d 322, 333–34 (6th Cir. 2005) (citing Serra v. Pichardo, 786 F.2d, 237, 241–42 (6th Cir. 1986)); Estate of Trentadue ex rel. Aguilar v. U.S., 397 F.3d 840, 859 (10th Cir. 2005). It also applies regardless of whether the FTCA judgment is in favor of the government or the plaintiff. *Harris*, 422 F.3d at 334–35; *Trentadue*, 397 F.3d at 858. *Contra*, Kreines v. U.S., 959 F.2d 834, 838 (9th Cir.1992) (judgment favorable to the government does not bar a *Bivens* judgment entered at the same time).

[597]*Compare* Carlson v. Green, 446 U.S. 14, 21–22, 100 S. Ct. 1468 (1980) *with* 28 U.S.C. § 2674.

[598]*See* § C.2.a of this chapter.

[599]Butz v. Economou, 438 U.S. 478, 498–504, 98 S. Ct. 2894 (1978).

[600]*See* § D of this chapter.

[601]In some states you can obtain relief in a state proceeding that does not provide damages, and then sue for damages under § 1983. *See* § M of this chapter.

[602]U.S. Const., Art. III, § 2.

[603]Renne v. Geary, 501 U.S. 312, 315–16, 111 S. Ct. 2331 (1991); Flast v. Cohen, 392 U.S. 83, 94–97, 88 S. Ct. 1942 (1968). The justiciability doctrines discussed in this section apply to federal courts. The rules in state court may be different. Virginia v. Hicks, 539 U.S. 113, 120, 123 S. Ct. 2191 (2003); *see* Jennifer Friesen, 1 *State Constitutional Law: Litigating Individual Rights, Claims and Defenses* at § 7.09[2] (LexisNexis Matthew Bender ed. 2006).

Justiciability has several sub-categories. The ones that most often arise in prison cases are standing, ripeness, and mootness. These doctrines affect prisoners' ability to seek injunctive or declaratory relief, but not damages. If you have suffered a compensable injury, you are entitled to seek damages, but having a past injury does not by itself allow you to seek injunctive or declaratory relief, as discussed below.

These doctrines can get complicated, but in prison cases, justiciability issues tend to be fairly simple and repetitive. Therefore, when you research a justiciability issue, you should focus on prison cases with facts similar to your situation.

1. Standing

A plaintiff has standing to sue only if the defendants' conduct has caused her some actual injury or threatens to do so, and if a favorable court decision is likely to redress the injury.[604] Therefore, prisoners cannot challenge conditions or practices that have not harmed or threatened to harm them personally.[605] The harm need not be physical or economic.[606]

---

[604]Sprint Communications Co., L.P. v. APCC Services, Inc., ___ U.S. ___, 128 S. Ct. 2531, 2535 (2008); Allen v. Wright, 468 U.S. 737, 751, 104 S. Ct. 3315 (1984); Valley Forge Christian College v. Americans United for Separation of Church and State, 454 U.S. 464, 472, 102 S. Ct. 752 (1982); Tarnsey v. O'Keefe, 225 F.3d 929, 934 (8th Cir. 2000).

[605]Pennsylvania Prison Soc. v. Cortes, 508 F.3d 156, 165–66 (3d Cir. 2007) (prisoners lacked standing to challenge clemency procedures where none of them had filed clemency applications and they could not show that the procedures would disadvantage them); Williams v. District of Columbia, 530 F. Supp. 2d 119, 127 (D.D.C. 2008) (to have standing to challenge environmental tobacco smoke, inmate must show that he personally will suffer from being subjected to it).

Courts have held that prisoners seeking religious accommodations must request those accommodations, unless it is clearly futile to do so, in order to have standing to challenge the failure to accommodate. Resnick v. Adams, 348 F.3d 763, 767–68 (9th Cir. 2003); Jackson-Bey v. Hanslmaier, 115 F.3d 1091, 1096–98 (2d Cir. 1997).

Courts have disagreed whether being required to pay a fee that the prisoner is capable of paying, but that others do not have to pay, confers standing. *Compare* Lyons v. Krol, 127 F.3d 763, 765 (8th Cir. 1997) (finding no standing) *with* Lewis v. Sullivan, 135 F. Supp. 2d 954, 958 (W.D.Wis. 2001) (rejecting *Krol*, finding standing), *rev'd on other grounds*, 279 F.3d 526 (7th Cir. 2002).

[606]*See, e.g.*, Americans United for Separation of Church and State v. Prison Fellowship Ministries, Inc., 509 F.3d 406, 419 (8th Cir. 2007) (inmates who alleged that they had "altered their behavior and had direct, offensive, and alienating contact" with a religious program had standing to challenge it as an establishment of religion); Paulsen v. Daniels, 413 F.3d 999, 1005 (9th Cir. 2005) (prisoners had standing to challenge a rule made without following the usual public rulemaking process; this failure deprived them of the "concrete interest to have the public participate in the rulemaking that made them ineligible for a sentence reduction"); Sweet v. McDonough,

The deprivation of a statutory right can confer standing.[607] In cases about the right of access to courts, the "actual injury" that prisoners are required to show is that "a non-frivolous legal claim had been frustrated or was being impeded."[608]

A plaintiff cannot challenge the violation of someone else's rights,[609] except in cases where the violation of the other person's rights can be shown to cause injury to the plaintiff herself.[610] The Supreme Court has held that the

---

2007 WL 567289, *3 (N.D.Fla., Feb. 16, 2007) (prisoner had standing to challenge vague disciplinary rule; "Injury in this context is having to restrain one's everyday behavior without knowing what will trigger a disciplinary action. Injury in this context is being daily subjected to the threat of retaliatory or arbitrary construction of the rule for doing nothing more than living what is otherwise the normal life of a person serving a life sentence.").

[607]Duffy v. Riveland, 98 F.3d 447, 453 (9th Cir. 1996) (prisoner denied sign language interpreter at disciplinary and classification hearings had standing under Americans with Disabilities Act to challenge the denial regardless of whether he attended the hearings).

[608]Lewis v. Casey, 518 U.S. 343, 351–53, 116 S. Ct. 2174 (1996). This rule is discussed in more detail in Ch. 2, § C.1.a(1).

[609]Ziemba v. Rell, 409 F.3d 553, 555 (2d Cir. 2005) (Order) (prisoners did not have standing to challenge another prisoner's execution based on their claim that it might cause them to act suicidally; the link between execution and plaintiffs' actions was "too attenuated"); Massey v. Wheeler, 221 F.3d 1030, 1035 (7th Cir. 2000) (attorney did not have standing to bring litigation on behalf of inmate to avoid exhaustion requirement of Prison Litigation Reform Act); Purvis v. Ponte, 929 F.2d 822, 825 n.6 (1st Cir. 1991); Murphy v. Morris, 849 F.2d 1101, 1105–06 (8th Cir. 1988) (the plaintiff lacked standing to complain of the seizure of a letter from a non-prisoner to another inmate); Martin v. Sargent, 780 F.2d 1334, 1337 (8th Cir. 1985) (prisoner lacked standing to seek an injunction against mistreatment of other prisoners); Booth v. King, 346 F. Supp. 2d 751, 761 (E.D.Pa. 2004) (plaintiff lacked standing to complain about confiscation of *kufis* where his book had not been taken); McCloud v. Delaney, 677 F. Supp. 230, 232 (S.D.N.Y. 1988) (plaintiff's relatives could not bring suit to complain of his medical treatment).

Prisoners who are class members in class actions have standing to assert rights based on court orders in those actions, *see, e.g.*, Glover v. Johnson, 931 F. Supp. 1360, 1371 (E.D.Mich. 1996), *aff'd in part, rev'd in part on other grounds, and remanded*, 138 F.3d 229 (6th Cir. 1998), and also have standing as third-party beneficiaries to enforce orders in non-class actions to which they were not parties, if they are part of a group the order was entered to benefit. Hook v. State of Arizona Dep't of Corrections, 972 F.2d 1012, 1014–15 (9th Cir. 1992); *see* § G for further discussion of third-party beneficiary enforcement of orders.

[610]Hassine v. Jeffes, 846 F.2d 169, 178 n.5 (3d Cir. 1988) (plaintiffs could challenge the failure to provide mental health services to other inmates when that failure had effects on the plaintiffs' safety).

Courts have disagreed whether prisoners have standing to assert the First Amendment rights of prison staff in challenging restrictions on staff's communications with authorities in favor of parole or clemency. *Compare* Shimer v. Washington, 100 F.3d 506,

rights of prisoners and their outside correspondents to communicate with each other are "inextricably meshed" so that a prisoner's challenge to correspondence rules could be decided based on the rights of the outside correspondent.[611]

A plaintiff does not have standing to seek relief that will not benefit her personally.[612] Thus, a person injured by a past violation of law does not have standing to seek an injunction unless the past violation has continuing effects[613] or the violation is likely to be repeated in the future.[614] Plaintiffs can

show a likelihood of future violation by showing that the conduct or actions they wish to challenge are sanctioned by a written policy or are part of a pattern of officially sanctioned behavior,[615] or that conditions otherwise present an imminent threat of harm.[616] Courts have also recognized that the likelihood of recurrence of violations against a particular person is greater in prison than in civilian life.[617] Prisoners generally do not have standing to seek injunctions against prison conditions or practices after they are released;[618] courts are not willing to assume that they will violate the law and be imprisoned again.[619] Similarly, prisoners lack standing to challenge conditions in particular

---

508 (7th Cir. 1996) (prisoners have standing) *with* Harris v. Evans, 20 F.3d 1118, 1122–25 (11th Cir. 1994) (prisoners lack standing).

[611]Procunier v. Martinez, 416 U.S. 396, 409, 94 S. Ct. 1800 (1974). The opposite is true too. Canadian Coalition against the Death Penalty v. Ryan, 269 F. Supp. 2d 1199, 1201 (D.Ariz. 2003) (organization that communicated with prisoners had standing to challenge prison restrictions that restricted the circulation of its message). This subject is discussed further in Ch. 3, § B.1.a, n.65.

By the reasoning of *Procunier*, both prisoners and non-prisoners should be able to challenge all restrictions that affect their ability to communicate or visit with each other. The courts have not always accepted this view. *See* Mendoza v. Blodgett, 960 F.2d 1425, 1433 (9th Cir. 1992) (prisoner could not assert his wife's right to visit); U.S. v. Vasta, 649 F. Supp. 974, 991–92 (S.D.N.Y. 1986) (prisoners whose telephone conversation were recorded did not have standing to raise the rights of the non-prisoners at the other end of the telephone lines). We think these cases are mistaken on this point in view of *Procunier*. Decisions under the federal disability statutes have been more favorable in this regard. *See* Fulton v. Goord, 591 F.3d 37, 42-43 (2d Cir. 2009) (prisoner's wife had standing to challenge prisons' failure to accommodate her disability so she could visit him); Niece v. Fitzner, 922 F.Supp. 1208 (E.D.Mich. 1996) (holding both prisoner and his deaf fianceé had standing to challenge the prison's failure to provide a Telecommunications Device for the Deaf so they could communicate). Courts have disagreed whether inmate law clerks or "jailhouse lawyers" have standing to assert the rights of other inmates to their services. *See* cases cited in Ch. 3, § C.2.c., n.557.

[612]O'Connor v. Jones, 946 F.2d 1395, 1400 (8th Cir. 1991) (prisoner lacked standing to challenge state's practice of hiring private law firms to defend prisoner lawsuits); Newsom v. Norris, 888 F.2d 371, 380–82 (6th Cir. 1989) (inmate "advisors," who assisted other inmates in disciplinary proceedings, lacked standing to seek an order requiring better training for newly appointed advisors); Rial v. Burmila, 782 F. Supp. 1291, 1292–93 (N.D. Ill. 1992) (prisoner lacked standing to demand the criminal prosecution of officers who allegedly beat him); Martin v. Lane, 766 F. Supp. 641, 644–45 (N.D. Ill. 1991) (prisoner lacked standing to complain of alleged racial discrimination against staff and of failure to deposit inmate funds in minority-owned banks).

[613]Kerr v. Farrey, 95 F.3d 472 (7th Cir. 1996) (plaintiff released on parole had standing to pursue expungement of disciplinary proceeding because it might have a continuing adverse effect on him).

[614]Los Angeles v. Lyons, 461 U.S. 95, 102, 103 S. Ct. 1660 (1983); Shain v. Ellison, 356 F.3d 211, 215–16 (2d Cir. 2004) (plaintiff who had been arrested and strip searched, then released, did not have standing to challenge strip search practice where there was only a "speculative and conjectural" likelihood it would happen to him again); Butler v. Dowd, 979 F.2d 661, 674 (8th Cir. 1992); Lynch v. Baxley, 744 F.2d 1452, 1457 (11th Cir. 1984) (plaintiff had

standing to challenge the use of jails for persons awaiting civil commitment hearings, since he had been detained for this purpose more than once).

[615]Armstrong v. Davis, 275 F.3d 849, 861 (9th Cir. 2001); *see* Goff v. Nix, 803 F.2d 358, 361 n.6 (8th Cir. 1986) (inmates had standing to challenge entire strip search policy even though each inmate might not be subjected to each type of search mentioned in policy); Mayweathers v. Terhune, 328 F. Supp. 2d 1086, 1094 (E.D.Cal. 2004) (plaintiffs had standing to challenge rule requiring work on Jumu'ah, even though they had not been disciplined because they were protected by a preliminary injunction); Cohen v. Coahoma County, Miss., 805 F. Supp. 398, 405 (N.D. Miss. 1992) (prisoner had standing to challenge misuse of force based on the beatings of other inmates because the Sheriff said he would use force in the same way in the future); Jensen v. Lick, 589 F. Supp. 35, 37 (D. N.D. 1984) (plaintiff whose punishment for refusing a drug test had been administratively overturned had standing to challenge use of test, since he was still subject to testing program involving random selection).

[616]Smith v. Arkansas Dep't of Correction, 103 F.3d 637, 644 (8th Cir. 1996) (prisoner who had not yet been assaulted had standing to challenge conditions that presented a serious risk of assault).

[617]Ingles v. City of New York, 2003 WL 402565, *9 (S.D.N.Y., Feb. 20, 2003) (noting that prisoners complaining of excessive force are "subject to the continual control of DOC staff" and are therefore "members of an identified class of 'targeted individuals'"); Williams v. Wilkinson, 132 F. Supp. 2d 601, 606 (S.D.Ohio 2001) ("By virtue of his confinement, Mr. Williams is in continual contact with correction officers whose job it is to scrutinize closely his behavior for possible rule infractions."); *see* Smith v. Zachary, 255 F.3d 446, 450 (7th Cir. 2001) ("In the context of prisons, harassment from correctional officers or government officials is not equivalent to an unsolicited attack on the street; rather, the harassment is made possible by the correction environment.").

[618]Nelsen v. King County, 895 F.2d 1248, 1250–54 (9th Cir. 1990); Powell v. Barrett, 376 F. Supp. 2d 1340, 1358 (N.D.Ga. 2005) (". . . Plaintiffs have directed the Court to no authority actually holding that a civilian claimant's potential for recidivism was so high that it took his future arrest and detainment out of the realm of the hypothetical, laying the foundation for equitable standing."), *aff'd in part and remanded on other grounds*, 541 F.3d 1298 (11th Cir. 2008) (en banc); Kritenbrink v. Crawford, 313 F. Supp. 2d 1043, 1053 (D.Nev. 2004).

[619]*But see* R.G. v. Koller, 415 F. Supp. 2d 1129, 1136–37 (D. Haw. 2006) (released juvenile prisoners had standing to challenge conditions where they had already been returned to the institution

prisons or units once they are transferred out of them,[620] unless of course the same conditions exist at the place to which they are transferred.[621]

These concerns about likelihood of recurrence only apply to claims for injunctive or declaratory relief; prisoners can seek damages for past injuries even if they are not likely to recur.[622]

Prisoners and other private citizens do not have standing to bring criminal prosecutions, or to demand that prosecutors do so; that decision is up to the prosecutors.[623]

If you are seeking declaratory or injunctive relief, you should plead in your complaint the facts that give you standing,[624] i.e., the reason you continue to be harmed by the challenged rule or practice, or the reason that you expect the harm to recur.

2. Mootness

A case is moot when the legal dispute between the plaintiff and the defendants has been resolved for practical purposes or has ceased to exist—i.e., when there is no longer a "live" case or controversy. Mootness is established only if "(1) it can be said with assurance that 'there is no reasonable expectation . . . ' that the alleged violation will reoccur . . . and (2) interim relief or events have completely and irrevocably eradicated the effects of the alleged violation."[625] If there is a

concrete reason to believe the violation is likely to recur, the case is not moot.[626] The party claiming mootness has the burden of showing that the case is actually moot.[627]

The law of mootness is very similar in many respects to the law of standing. Standing is assessed based on the facts as of the time of filing of the complaint, while mootness reflects events that occurred after the complaint was filed.[628] Like standing, mootness is an issue for claims for injunctive or declaratory relief; once you are injured, your claim for damages does not become moot.[629]

A case can be moot at the time it is filed, or it can become moot while it is in progress, even on appeal. When a case becomes moot at any stage, it must be dismissed.[630] There is an exception for class actions,[631] but since pro se litigants are not allowed to represent a class, we do not discuss it in detail.[632]

Short-lived legal violations that are over with before they can be challenged in court are not considered moot if they are "capable of repetition, yet evading [judicial] review" and if there is a "reasonable likelihood" that they will happen again to the same plaintiff.[633]

---

multiple times and where most offenders were returned, and they need not break the criminal law to be returned).

[620]Meuir v. Greene County Jail Employees, 487 F.3d 1115, 1119–20 (8th Cir. 2007) (prisoner transferred to state prison lacked standing to seek an injunction about dental care at a county jail); Westefer v. Snyder, 422 F.3d 570, 573 n.2 (7th Cir. 2005); Martin v. Sargent, 780 F.2d 1334, 1337 (8th Cir. 1985); Stewart v. McGinnis, 800 F. Supp. 604, 607 (N.D. Ill. 1992), aff'd, 5 F.3d 1031 (7th Cir. 1993); Knox v. McGinnis, 783 F. Supp. 349, 352–53 (N.D. Ill. 1991) ("we must assume that Knox will abide by prison rules and thereby avoid a return to segregation status"); see Bennett v. Westfall, 640 F. Supp. 169, 170 (S.D. W.Va. 1986) (plaintiff who had been transferred could not represent a class of inmates at the sending institution and could not seek injunctive relief), aff'd, 836 F.2d 1342 (4th Cir. 1988).

[621]Lehn v. Holmes, 364 F.3d 862, 871 (7th Cir. 2004) (transfers did not deprive prisoner of standing where he challenged a statewide policy).

[622]See Hodgers-Durgin v. de la Vina, 199 F.3d 1037, 1041 n.1 (9th Cir. 1999) (a plaintiff may have standing to seek damages without having standing to seek an injunction), overruling Nava v. City of Dublin, 121 F.3d 453 (9th Cir. 1997).

[623]See cases cited in n.1 of this chapter.

[624]Allen v. Wright, 468 U.S. 737, 751, 104 S. Ct. 3315 (1984) ("A plaintiff must allege personal injury fairly traceable to the defendant's allegedly unlawful conduct and likely to be redressed by the requested relief." (emphasis supplied)).

[625]County of Los Angeles v. Davis, 440 U.S. 625, 631, 99 S. Ct. 1379 (1979) (citations omitted); accord, Parents Involved in Community Schools v. Seattle Sch. Dist. No. 1, 551 U.S. 701, 719, 127 S. Ct. 2738 (2007); Holland v. New Jersey Dep't of Corrections, 246 F.3d 267, 274 (3d Cir. 2001) (". . . [A] case is not moot, even if

the [appellant's] primary injury is resolved, so long as the [appellant] continues to suffer some harm that a favorable court decision would remedy." (citation omitted)).

[626]See Washington v. Harper, 494 U.S. 210, 218–19, 110 S. Ct. 1028 (1990) (holding that cessation of administering antipsychotic drugs to inmate did not moot case since inmate was still suffering from mental illness).

[627]Friends of the Earth, Inc. v. Laidlaw Environmental Services (TOC), Inc., 528 U.S. 167, 189, 120 S. Ct. 693 (2000) (referring to "heavy burden" of establishing mootness); Firefighters Local 1784 v. Stotts, 467 U.S. 561, 569–70, 104 S. Ct. 2576 (1984).

[628]See County of Riverside v. McLaughlin, 500 U.S. 44, 51, 111 S. Ct. 1661 (1991); U.S. Parole Comm'n v. Geraghty, 445 U.S. 388, 397, 100 S. Ct. 1202 (1980) (stating that mootness is "the doctrine of standing set in a time frame: The requisite personal interest that must exist at the commencement of the litigation (standing) must continue throughout its existence." (citation and internal quotation marks omitted)).

[629]Boag v. MacDougall, 454 U.S. 364, 364, 102 S. Ct. 700 (1982) (transfer to another prison did not moot prisoner's damages claim arising from placement in earlier prison); Utah Animal Rights Coalition v. Salt Lake City Corp., 371 F.3d 1248, 1257 (10th Cir. 2004) (though injunctive claim was moot, nominal damages claim was not).

[630]City of Mesquite v. Aladdin's Castle, Inc., 455 U.S. 283, 288 n.9, 102 S. Ct. 1070 (1982).

[631]Sosna v. Iowa, 419 U.S. 393, 399, 402, 95 S. Ct. 553 (1975) (holding that a certified class "acquires a legal status separate from" that of the named plaintiff, and the requisite continuing case or controversy may be between class members and defendant); see County of Riverside v. McLaughlin, 500 U.S. 44, 51–52, 111 S. Ct. 1661 (1991) (class certification may "relate back" to time of filing of complaint where claims are quickly mooted).

[632]See § J of this chapter concerning class actions.

[633]Spencer v. Kemna, 523 U.S. 1, 17–18, 118 S. Ct. 978 (1998) ("The capable-of-repetition-doctrine applies only . . . [when] . . . two circumstances [are] simultaneously present: (1) the challenged action is in its duration too short to be fully litigated prior to

A prisoner's claim for injunctive relief from prison conditions or practices generally becomes moot if the plaintiff is released from prison.[634] Courts are reluctant to assume that a plaintiff will again be arrested or convicted of a crime and be subject to prison conditions again,[635] though they will do so if the facts indicate that re-incarceration is likely.[636] A challenge to a condition or practice at a particular prison or unit is generally moot if the plaintiff is transferred,[637] unless there is some factual basis to expect the plaintiff to be subjected to the violation again,[638] or the plaintiff has challenged a system-wide policy that will still apply after transfer.[639]

Transfer or release will also not moot a case if the action that the plaintiff has challenged has a continuing effect after the transfer or release.[640]

A case can become moot as a result of actions by the defendants. If officials give the plaintiff all the relief she seeks, the case may be moot.[641] Prison officials sometimes claim that a case is moot because they have changed the policy or practice that is under attack. However, reforms undertaken under pressure of litigation generally do not moot injunctive claims[642] unless they involve amendment of

---

cessation or expiration, and (2) there is a reasonable expectation that the same complaining party [will] be subject to the same action again." (citations omitted)); *accord*, Honig v. Doe, 484 U.S. 305, 318, 108 S. Ct. 592 (1988); *see also* Bowens v. Quinn, 561 F.3d 671, 673 (7th Cir. 2009) (denial of pardon applications did not moot complaints about delay in deciding them, since the delay could recur if the plaintiffs applied again); Clark v. Brewer, 776 F.3d 226, 229 (8th Cir. 1985) (release from "close management" did not moot case because there was a "virtual certainty" that the plaintiff would be returned there); Lynch v. Baxley, 744 F.2d 1452, 1457 (11th Cir. 1984) (plaintiff's challenge the use of jails for persons awaiting civil commitment hearing was not moot, since he had been detained for this purpose more than once).

[634]Koch v. Schriro, 399 F.3d 1099, 1100–01 (9th Cir. 2005); McAlpine v. Thompson, 187 F.3d 1213, 1215–16 (10th Cir. 1999); Reimers v. State of Oregon, 863 F.2d 630, 632 (9th Cir. 1988).

[635]Spencer v. Kemna, 523 U.S. 1, 15, 118 S. Ct. 978 (1998); Slade v. Hampton Roads Regional Jail, 407 F.3d 243, 249 (4th Cir. 2005).

[636]*See* Demery v. Arpaio, 378 F.3d 1020, 1027 (9th Cir. 2004) (challenge to jail practice was not moot where some released plaintiffs had been jailed repeatedly); Lynch v. Baxley, 744 F.2d 1452, 1457 (11th Cir. 1984) (plaintiff's challenge to the use of jails for persons awaiting civil commitment hearing was not moot, since he had been detained for this purpose more than once).

[637]Higgason v. Farley, 83 F.3d 807, 811 (7th Cir. 1996) (per curiam) (because prisoner claiming retaliatory transfer had been transferred yet again, claims for injunctive and declaratory relief were moot); Smith v. Hundley, 190 F.3d 852, 855 (8th Cir. 1999) (mere possibility of being returned to sending prison did not save case from mootness); Moore v. Thieret, 862 F.2d 148, 150 (7th Cir. 1988) (injunctive claim was mooted by transfer but could be reinstated if the defendants tried to return the plaintiff).

[638]*See* Davis v. New York, 316 F.3d 93, 99 (2d Cir. 2002) (challenge to second-hand smoke exposure was not mooted by transfer where plaintiff alleged the problem persisted at the new prison); Clark v. Brewer, 776 F.2d 226, 229 (8th Cir. 1985) (release from "close management" did not moot case because there was a "virtual certainty" that the plaintiff would be returned there); Spellman v. Hopper, 142 F. Supp. 2d 1323, 1325 n.1 (M.D. Ala. 2000) (challenge to segregation rule was not moot where plaintiff had spent most of his life sentence in segregation unit and would probably return); Mitchell v. Angelone, 82 F. Supp. 2d 485, 490 (E.D. Va. 1999) (holding that plaintiff had been transferred so frequently that there was a reasonable expectation he would be returned to prison sued about).

[639]Lehn v. Holmes, 364 F.3d 862, 871–72 (7th Cir. 2004) (transfer of prisoner does not moot claim of exposure to

environmental tobacco smoke where it results from a system-wide policy to house non-smoking with smoking prisoners); Nelson v. Heiss, 271 F.3d 891, 897 (9th Cir. 2001) (transfer mooted claim against officials at sending prison, but not claim against Director of prison system, for system-wide rule); Randolph v. Rodgers, 170 F.3d 850, 856–57 (8th Cir. 1999) (inmate suing Missouri Department of Corrections and various officials for denying him sign-language interpreter at disciplinary hearings was entitled to injunction against MDOC despite his transfer to new facility during course of lawsuit; inmate remained under control of MDOC, which controlled both facilities and funding necessary to provide sign language interpreter).

[640]Vitek v. Jones, 445 U.S. 480, 486–87, 100 S. Ct. 1254 (1980) (release on parole does not moot challenge to involuntary subjection to mental treatment when such treatment is also a condition of parole); Mujahid v. Daniels, 413 F.3d 991, 994–95 (9th Cir. 2005) (challenge to calculation of good time was not mooted by commencement of supervised release, since a favorable decision might reduce the length of supervised release); Thompson v. Carter, 284 F.3d 411, 415 (2d Cir. 2002) (demand for return of confiscated medication was not mooted by transfer); Washington v. James, 782 F.2d 1134, 1137 (2d Cir. 1986) (transfer did not moot claim for expungement of record); Chapman v. Pickett, 586 F.2d 22, 26–27 (7th Cir. 1978) (release from prison did not moot claim for expungement of disciplinary record).

[641]Alston v. Robinson, 791 F. Supp. 569, 578 (D. Md. 1992) (reinstatement to work release mooted claim of improper removal from work release); Holtz v. Richards, 779 F. Supp. 111, 113 (N.D. Ind. 1991) (habeas corpus petition seeking return of good time was mooted when officials restored the good time).

Granting part of the relief sought does not moot the case. Gates v. Towery, 430 F.3d 429, 432 (7th Cir. 2005) ("To eliminate the controversy and make a suit moot, the defendant must satisfy the plaintiffs' *demands*; only then does no dispute remain between the parties.").

[642]Parents Involved in Community Schools v. Seattle Sch. Dist. No. 1, 551 U.S. 701, 719, 127 S. Ct. 2738 (2007) ("Voluntary cessation does not moot a case or controversy unless 'subsequent events ma[ke] it absolutely clear that the allegedly wrongful behavior could not reasonably be expected to recur.' . . ." (citations omitted)); City of Mesquite v. Aladdin's Castle, 455 U.S. 283, 289, 102 S. Ct. 1070 (1982); Akers v. McGinnis, 352 F.3d 1030, 1035 (6th Cir. 2003); Kellogg v. Shoemaker, 46 F.3d 503, 507 (6th Cir. 1995) (changes in parole procedure "on the eve of adjudication" did not moot challenge to *new* parole procedures, brought by plaintiffs who previously had their parole revoked); *see* Sutton v. Rasheed, 323 F.3d 236, 248 (3d Cir. 2003) (finding mootness, but warning that where prison authorities have undertaken to voluntarily change a policy, "a claim will not be rendered moot if there remains

relevant statutes or some other very convincing indication that the change of position is permanent.[643] In some cases, where the defendants have changed their policies in response to a lawsuit, the court has simply enjoined them to conform to their own new policies.[644]

In addition, policy changes do not moot a case if they fail to address all aspects of the dispute between the parties[645] or if there is no assurance that they have eliminated or will eliminate the legal violations.[646] Changes in personnel in the prison administration do not moot an injunctive claim unless the claim is against a policy or conduct that is "personal" to particular officials.[647]

There is a special mootness rule in habeas corpus proceedings. A habeas petition challenging a criminal conviction does not become moot when the prisoner is released because the conviction may have continuing "collateral consequences" such as limited employment prospects or enhancement of future criminal sentences. However, that rule does not apply to a habeas challenge to parole revocation (or presumably to matters such as sentence calculation and loss of good time), because these decisions are not likely to have such collateral consequences in themselves.[648] In cases that require you to fulfill the habeas corpus exhaustion requirement before you can bring a § 1983 action for damages, you might be left without a remedy if your habeas petition is held moot. Courts are divided on that question.[649]

3. Ripeness

Ripeness is a justiciability doctrine designed to avoid premature decisions.[650] Whether a dispute is ripe for judicial review depends on "(1) the fitness of the issues for judicial decision and (2) the hardship to the parties of withholding court consideration."[651] A claim is not ripe for judicial

---

the possibility that plaintiffs will be disadvantaged in the same fundamental way." (internal quotation marks omitted)).

[643]White v. Lee, 227 F.3d 1214, 1243 (9th Cir. 2000) (change in policy that was permanent, addressed entirety of plaintiffs' complaint, and had been in effect without backsliding for several years satisfied "heavy burden" of showing mootness); Valero Terrestrial Corp. v. Paige, 211 F.3d 112, 116 (4th Cir. 2000) (statutory changes that discontinue a challenged practice are usually enough to moot a case). *Compare* Tsombanidis v. West Haven Fire Dep't, 352 F.3d 565, 574 (2d Cir. 2003) (change in agency's interpretation of fire code did not moot the case, since it might change its interpretation back); Sasnett v. Litscher, 197 F.3d 290, 291 (7th Cir. 1999) (rule change did not moot case where prison officials said they had no intention of going back to the old rule, but continued to argue that it was lawful).

[644]*See* I.Appel Corp. v. Munsingwear, Inc., 646 F. Supp. 685, 687 (S.D.N.Y. 1995); *see also* Main Road v. Aytch, 565 F.2d 54, 59 (3d Cir. 1977) (where defendants had promulgated an acceptable policy, the plaintiffs were entitled to a declaratory judgment that the old policy was unconstitutional).

[645]Longstreth v. Maynard, 961 F.2d 895, 900 (10th Cir. 1992); Gluth v. Kangas, 951 F.2d 1504, 1507 (9th Cir. 1991); Williams v. Lane, 646 F. Supp. 1379, 1409 (N.D. Ill. 1986), *aff'd*, 851 F.2d 867 (7th Cir. 1987); Jones v. Wittenberg, 73 F.R.D. 82, 84 (N.D. Ohio 1976).

[646]Gates v. Cook, 376 F.3d 323, 337, 342–43 (5th Cir. 2004) (officials' assurance that they would comply with certain standards did not moot a case where unlawful conditions were long-standing); Davis v. New York, 316 F.3d 93, 99 (2d Cir. 2002) (new smoking policy did not moot second-hand smoke case where plaintiff alleged that the policy was not enforced); Ginest v. Board of County Com'rs. of Carbon County, 333 F. Supp. 1190, 1209 (D.Wyo. 2004) (case was not mooted by policy changes that were "expected to remedy" constitutional violations); Skinner v. Uphoff, 234 F. Supp. 2d 1208, 1215 (D.Wyo. 2002) ("New and improved policies are meaningless if they are not followed."); Fisher v. Koehler, 692 F. Supp. 1519, 1566 (S.D.N.Y. 1988) (" . . . [T]he depressing reality is that while commissioners come and go, problems linger on, and present and future inmates are entitled to the assurance that these problems will be, and remain, redressed."); Lawson v. Wainwright, 641 F. Supp. 312, 330 (S.D. Fla. 1986), *aff'd in part and remanded on other grounds*, 840 F.2d 781 (11th Cir. 1987), *vacated and remanded on other grounds*, 490 U.S. 1078 (1989); Green v. McCall, 636 F. Supp. 101, 106 (D. Conn. 1986), *aff'd*, 822 F.2d 284 (2d Cir. 1987).

[647]*See* Santiago v. Miles, 774 F. Supp. 775 (W.D.N.Y. 1991) (changes in the prison administration did not obviate the need for injunctive relief against a long-standing pattern of racial

---

discrimination). *But see* Munir v. Scott, 792 F. Supp. 1472, 1476 (E.D. Mich. 1992) (warden's retirement mooted an injunctive claim against a policy that had not been supported by anyone else in the prison system), *rev'd on other grounds*, 12 F.3d 213, 1993 WL 465162 (6th Cir. 1993).

[648]Spencer v. Kemna, 523 U.S. 1, 118 S. Ct. 978 (1998); Wilson v. Terhune, 319 F.3d 477, 481 (9th Cir. 2003) (holding that collateral consequences are not presumed from prison disciplinary proceedings).

[649]*See* § H.1.a of this chapter, n.563.

[650]National Park Hospitality Ass'n v. Dep't of Interior, 538 U.S. 803, 807–08, 123 S. Ct. 2026 (2003) (ripeness rules serve "to prevent the courts, through avoidance of premature adjudication, from entangling themselves in abstract disagreements over administrative policies, and also to protect the agencies from judicial interference until an administrative decision has been formalized and its effects felt in a concrete way by the challenging parties" (quoting Abbott Laboratories v. Gardner, 387 U.S. 136, 148–149, 87 S. Ct. 1507 (1967)).

[651]*National Park Hospitality Ass'n*, 538 U.S. at 808. Thus, in *U.S. v. Loy*, 237 F.3d 251 (3d Cir. 2001), a person convicted of possessing child pornography challenged a condition of supervised release that he could not possess any sort of pornography. The court held that his claim was ripe and he did not have to wait until the government tried to revoke his supervised release because the condition required the defendant immediately to change his behavior, it presented a pure question of law amenable to immediate judicial review, and it appeared that Congress intended for such conditions to be reviewed earlier rather than later. *Loy*, 237 F.3d at 257–58; *compare* Kirby v. Siegelman, 195 F.3d 1285, 1290 (11th Cir. 1999) (challenge to community notification requirement of sex offender law was not ripe because prisoner would not be affected until his release in six years, the statute might be repealed or amended by then, and he would suffer no hardship from the lack of an immediate ruling).

decision if it involves future events that may not occur[652] or questions that have not yet become factually concrete enough for a court to decide.[653]

J. CLASS ACTIONS

In a class action, the persons who bring the suit (the "representative parties" or "named plaintiffs") attempt to vindicate both their own legal rights and the rights of others who are similarly situated ("absent" or "unnamed" class members). Class actions in federal court are governed by Rule 23 of the Federal Rules of Civil Procedure; many district courts have their own local rules supplementing Rule 23.[654] State courts have their own class action rules and procedures. Class actions may be brought on behalf of all inmates in a prison system, in one or more individual prisons, in particular housing units, or in a particular status or category.[655]

Federal court suits to reform prison conditions are typically brought as class actions.[656]

To pursue a class action for injunctive relief against prison conditions, a prisoner must be subject to or threatened with those conditions at the time the case is filed[657]—i.e., she must have standing and her claim must not be moot, just like an individual filing suit for an injunction. Once the case is certified as a class action, it can continue even if the named plaintiffs are released or transferred.[658] If the named plaintiffs' claim becomes moot before the class is certified, the court should permit other class members to intervene and continue the litigation rather than immediately dismiss the case.[659]

---

[652]*See, e.g.*, Askins v. District of Columbia, 877 F.2d 94, 97–99 (D.C. Cir. 1989) (challenge to proposed transfer was not ripe because no final decision to transfer had been made); Murphy v. Missouri Dep't of Corrections, 814 F.2d 1252, 1257 (8th Cir. 1987) (claim that Aryan Nations should be recognized as a religion was not ripe because prison officials had not been asked to recognize it); Lindell v. Casperson, 360 F. Supp. 2d 932 (W.D.Wis. 2005) (complaint that prison offered Bible Anger Management but not Wotan Anger Management was not ripe because the plaintiff had not reached the classification level where he would be eligible for such a program), *aff'd*, 169 Fed.Appx. 999 (7th Cir. 2006) (unpublished); Abraham v. Marist College, 706 F. Supp. 294, 295–96 (S.D.N.Y. 1989). *But see* St. Paul Area Chamber of Commerce v. Gaertner, 439 F.3d 481, 487 (8th Cir. 2006) (ripeness was demonstrated by a specific intent to pursue conduct in violation of a challenged statute).

[653]18 Unnamed "John Smith" Prisoners v. Meese, 871 F.2d 881, 883 (9th Cir. 1989) (challenge to proposed double-celling of protected witnesses was unripe because the effects of double celling were speculative); Kines v. Day, 754 F.2d 28, 31 (1st Cir. 1985) (challenge to application of rule restricting receipt of publications was not ripe without a showing of its application to particular publications).

[654]*See, e.g.*, Local Practice Rules, U.S. District Court for the Northern District of New York, Rules 23.1 (requiring the words "class action" to appear next to the caption of the complaint if the plaintiff seeks to maintain a class action), 23.2 (requiring class certification motion to be brought "[a]s soon as practicable" after suit is filed).

There is also a Class Action Fairness Act (CAFA), Pub. L. No. 109-2, 119 Stat. 4 (Feb. 18, 2005), which expands federal diversity jurisdiction over interstate class actions, establishes procedures for providing notice of settlements to "appropriate" federal and state officials, and limits attorneys' fee awards in "coupon" settlements. William B. Rubenstein *et al.*, *Newberg on Class Actions* § 1.1 at 17 (Thomson West 4th ed., Supp. 2008). As far as we can tell, CAFA has little relevance to prison conditions litigation.

[655]*See, e.g.*, Rouse v. Plantier, 182 F.3d 192, 194 (3d Cir. 1999) (noting certification of class of diabetics at a prison medical center); Barnes v. District of Columbia, 242 F.R.D. 113, 124–25 (D.D.C. 2007) (class certified challenging overdetention and strip searches throughout D.C. Department of Corrections); Hilton v. Wright,

235 F.R.D. 40, 51, 54–55 (N.D.N.Y. 2006) (certifying statewide class of prisoners challenging denial of Hepatitis C treatment to prisoners who had not completed substance abuse treatment); Austin v. Wilkinson, 189 F. Supp. 2d 719, 721–22 (N.D. Ohio. 2002) (class action on behalf of prisoners at one "supermax" prison challenging procedural protections for placement there), *aff'd in part, rev'd in part, and remanded*, 372 F.3d 346 (6th Cir. 2004), *aff'd in part, rev'd in part*, 545 U.S. 209, 125 S. Ct. 2384 (2005); Bradley v. Harrelson, 151 F.R.D. 422, 425–28 (M.D. Ala. 1993) (certifying class of seriously mentally ill prisoners at one prison to challenge adequacy of mental health services); Dean v. Coughlin, 107 F.R.D. 331, 332–35 (S.D.N.Y. 1985) (certifying class of "all persons who are or will be inmates" at one prison to challenge inadequate dental care).

[656]Hassine v. Jeffes, 846 F.2d 169, 180 (3d Cir. 1988) (class certification "is an especially appropriate vehicle for actions seeking prison reform") (citing Coley v. Clinton, 635 F.2d 1364 (8th Cir. 1980)); Clarkson v. Coughlin, 783 F. Supp. 789, 797 (S.D.N.Y. 1992) (class actions "generally tend to be the norm" in prison conditions cases). Class actions for damages are much less frequent, though not unknown, in prison litigation.

In some cases, habeas corpus proceedings about issues that affect a large number of people have been brought as class actions, using Rule 23 as an "analogue" since it does not directly govern habeas proceedings. *See* Ali v. Ashcroft, 346 F.3d 873, 888–91 (9th Cir. 2003) and cases cited, *withdrawn on other grounds*, 421 F.3d 795 (9th Cir. 2005).

[657]Johnson v. Duffy, 588 F.2d 740, 745 (9th Cir. 1978). *See* § J.1, J.2, of this chapter concerning standing and mootness.

[658]Zablocki v. Redhail, 434 U.S. 374, 382 n.9, 98 S. Ct. 673 (1978); Sosna v. Iowa, 419 U.S. 393, 399–402, 95 S. Ct. 553 (1975); Wilson v. Sullivan, 709 F. Supp. 1351, 1355–56 (D. N.J. 1989).

[659]Birmingham Steel Corp. v. Tennessee Valley Authority, 353 F.3d 1331, 1339 (11th Cir. 2003) (while a loss of standing might justify dismissal of the named plaintiff as a representative, it does not necessarily call for the simultaneous dismissal of the class action, if members of that class might still have live claims); Wade v. Kirkland, 118 F.3d 667, 670 (9th Cir. 1997); Cotterall v. Paul, 755 F.2d 777, 780 (11th Cir. 1985).

In some cases involving claims that are "inherently transitory," the courts have permitted named plaintiffs to continue to represent the class even after their claims were moot. County of Riverside v. McLaughlin, 500 U.S. 44, 111 S. Ct. 1661, 1667 (1991) and cases cited; Goetz v. Crosson, 728 F. Supp. 995, 1000–01 (S.D.N.Y. 1990). This treatment will not be granted automatically; the plaintiff must show that it is necessary in order for the claim

1. Bringing a Class Action

The most important thing for a *pro se* litigant to know about class actions is that *pro se* prisoners are generally not permitted to represent classes.[660] However, you may wish to plead a class action and ask the court to appoint counsel,[661] so we will describe the basic rules governing class actions.

For a case to be treated as a class action, you must include "class action allegations"[662] in the complaint. You must also file a motion for certification of the class[663] and persuade the court to grant it.[664] The district court is supposed to decide class certification motions "[a]t an early practicable time,"[665] and if it grants the motion, issue an order defining the class and the class claims issues, or defenses, and name class counsel.[666] Decisions granting or denying class certification can only be appealed by permission of the federal appeals court.[667]

To be eligible for class action certification, a lawsuit must meet several basic requirements. One requirement that is not mentioned in Rule 23 is "ascertainability," which means that the class must be defined in a way that permits the court to determine who is a class member and who is not.[668] Other prerequisits for a class action are listed in Rule 23(a), Fed.R.Civ.P. Your complaint or class certification

motion should show that the case meets each one of them.[669]

1. The class must be so numerous that joinder of all class members is impracticable.[670] To meet this requirement, the class need not be enormous in number.[671] It is not necessary to prove the size of the class with precision as long as there is some basis for a reasonable estimate.[672] The court will consider other factors that may make individual joinder of all class members impractical,[673] including that class members are unlikely to bring their own suits because of poverty, illitreacy or language barriers, lack of education, limited access to legal representation, etc.[674] The fact that a

---

[660] *See* n.692 of this section.

[661] *See* Hagan v. Rogers, 570 F.3d 146, 159 (3d Cir. 2009) (holding district court abused its discretion in denying class certification to *pro se* plaintiffs without ruling on their request for appointment of counsel).

[662] These are allegations that the case meets the requirements of the rules for certification of class actions, discussed below.

[663] Some federal district courts have local rules requiring the plaintiff to file a class certification motion promptly. *See, e.g.*, Rule 23.2, Local Rules of Practice, United States District Court for the Northern District of New York (requiring a class motion to be filed "as soon as practicable" after the complaint is filed).

[664] Newsom v. Norris, 888 F.2d 371, 381–82 (6th Cir. 1989) (court cannot grant class certification where it has not been requested).

[665] Rule 23(c)(1)(A), Fed.R.Civ.P. Excessive delay in deciding class certification motions can cause great confusion and has been strongly disapproved by appellate courts. *See, e.g.*, Nelson v. Murphy, 44 F.3d 497, 500 (7th Cir. 1995); Henry v. Gross, 803 F.2d 757, 769 (2d Cir. 1986).

[666] Rule 23(c)(1)(B), Fed.R.Civ.P.

[667] Rule 23(f), Fed.R.Civ.P. Courts are reluctant to accept such appeals. *See, e.g.*, Sumitomo Copper Litigation v. Credit Lyonnais Rouse, Ltd., 262 F.3d 134, 139 (2d Cir. 2001) (holding parties seeking to appeal a class certification decision "must demonstrate either (1) that the certification order will effectively terminate the litigation and there has been a substantial showing that the district court's decision is questionable, or (2) that the certification order implicates a legal question about which there is a compelling need for immediate resolution").

[668] John v. National Sec. Fire and Cas. Co., 501 F.3d 443, 445 (5th Cir. 2007); McBean v. City of New York, 228 F.R.D. 487, 492 (S.D.N.Y. 2005) ("A class is ascertainable when defined by objective

ever to be litigated. Inmates of Lincoln Intake and Detention Facility v. Boosalis, 705 F.2d 1021, 1024 (8th Cir. 1983).

---

criteria that are administratively feasible, without a subjective determination.").

[669] These are set out in Rule 23(a), Fed.R.Civ.P. *See also* Stout v. J.D. Byrider, 228 F.3d 709, 717 (6th Cir. 2000) (requiring "rigorous analysis" under Rule 23(a) standards).

[670] Rule 23(a)(1), Fed.R.Civ.P.

[671] Stewart v. Abraham, 275 F.3d 220, 226–27 (3d Cir. 2001) ("No minimum number of plaintiffs is required to maintain a suit as a class action, but generally if the named plaintiff demonstrates that the potential number of plaintiffs exceeds 40, the first prong of Rule 23(a) has been met."); Cypress v. Newport News General & Nonsectarian Hospital Assn., 375 F.2d 648, 653 (4th Cir. 1976) (class of 18); Amone v. Aveiro, 226 F.R.D. 677, 684 (D.Haw. 2005) (class of 40); Clarkson v. Coughlin, 145 F.R.D. 339, 347–48 (S.D.N.Y. 1993) (certifying class of deaf prisoners with male subclass of 49 and female subclass of at least seven); Ikonen v. Hartz Mountain Corp., 122 F.R.D. 258, 262 (S.D. Cal 1988) ("As a general rule, classes of 20 are too small, classes of 20–40 may or may not be big enough . . . and classes of 40 or more are numerous enough").

[672] Evans v. U.S. Pipe & Foundry Col, 696 F.2d 925, 930 (11th Cir. 1983); Fox v. Cheminova, 213 F.R.D. 113, 122 (E.D.N.Y. 2003); Martinez v. Mecca Farms, Inc., 213 F.R.D. 601, 605 (S.D.Fla. 2002) ("The court may make commonsense assumptions in order to find support for numerosity."); Daniels v. City of New York, 198 F.R.D. 409, 417 (S.D.N.Y. 2001) (similar to *Martinez*), *reconsideration denied*, 199 F.R.D. 513 (S.D.N.Y. 2001); Perez-Funez v. INS, 611 F. Supp. 990, 995 (C.D.Cal.1984).

[673] *See, e.g.*, Grant v. Sullivan, 131 F.R.D. 436, 446 (M.D. Pa. 1990) (the fact that many class members' identities could only be determined from defendants' records supported certification); Doe v. Coughlin, 697 F. Supp. 1234, 1236 n.4 (N.D.N.Y. 1988) (class members' need for anonymity supported certification); Patrykus v. Gomilla, 121 F.R.D. 357, 361 (N.D. Ill. 1988) (similar to *Doe*).

[674] Cortigiano v. Oceanview Manor Home for Adults, 227 F.R.D. 194, 204–05 (E.D.N.Y. 2005) (citing class members' fear of reprisals, mental disabilities, and lack of resources to prosecute their own claims in certifying class in group residence case); Amone v. Aveiro, 226 F.R.D. 677, 684 (D.Haw. 2005) (class certified of individuals "whose financial circumstances may prevent them from pursuing individual litigation, who are unlikely to know that a cause of action exists, and whose individual claims are likely to be too small to make individual litigation feasible"); Fox v. Cheminova, 213 F.R.D. 113, 122 (E.D.N.Y. 2003) ("Factors in determining impracticality of joinder include: judicial economy achieved from the avoidance of multiple concurrent actions; the geographic dispersion of members of the class; the relative financial resources of the class members; the ability of claimants to institute individual

class is "fluid"—*i.e.*, that its membership changes, as is true of most prison and jail populations—weighs in favor of class certification in cases seeking injunctive relief.[675]

2. *There must be questions of law or fact common to the class members and you.*[676] This requirement is met if there is one or more common issues of law or fact as to all or most of the class members.[677] The existence of some factual variations does not defeat class certification.[678] Thus, if you

___

actions; and any requests for prospective or injunctive relief affecting future class members."); Saur v. Snappy Apple Farms, Inc., 203 F.R.D. 281, 286 (W.D.Mich. 2001) (noting that most class members are not native English speakers and "will have difficulty in understanding English and utilizing court systems in the United States of America," that they "are likely to lack financial resources," and individuals' claims are small enough that individual suits are unlikely); Hernandez v. Alexander, 152 F.R.D. 192, 194 (D. Nev. 1993) ("Apart from class size, factors relevant to the joinder impracticability issue include judicial economy arising from avoidance of a multiplicity of actions, geographic dispersement of class members, sized of individual claims, financial resources of class members, the ability of claimants to institute individual suits, and requests for prospective injunctive relief which would involve future class members." (citation omitted)); *see* U.S. *ex rel.* Sero v. Preiser, 506 F.2d 1115, 1126 (2d Cir. 1974) ("Because many of those serving reformatory sentences are likely to be illiterate or poorly educated, and since most would not have the benefit of counsel to prepare habeas corpus petitions, it is not improbable that more than a few would otherwise never receive the relief here sought on their behalf.").

[675]Skinner v. Uphoff, 209 F.R.D. 484, 488 (D.Wyo. 2002); Nicholson v. Williams, 205 F.R.D. 92, 98 (E.D.N.Y. 2001); Christina A. *ex rel.* Jennifer A. v. Bloomberg, 197 F.R.D. 664, 667 (D.S.D. 2000); San Antonio Hispanic Police Officers' Organization v. City of San Antonio, 188 F.R.D. 433, 442 (W.D.Tex. 1999); Dean v. Coughlin, 107 F.R.D. 331, 331 (S.D.N.Y. 1985); Arrango v. Ward, 103 F.R.D 638, 640 (S.D.N.Y. 1984); Powell v. Ward, 487 F. Supp. 917, 921–22 (S.D.N.Y. 1980), *aff'd as modified*, 643 F.2d 924 (2d Cir. 1981); *see* Gerstein v. Pugh, 420 U.S. 103, 110–11 n.11, 95 S. Ct. 854 (1975).

In cases involving fluid classes, the class often is certified to include future as well as present members. *See, e.g.,* Neiberger v. Hawkins, 208 F.R.D. 301, 318–19 (D.Colo. 2002); Jones'El v. Berge, 172 F. Supp. 2d 1128, 1131 (W.D.Wis. 2001); Dean v. Coughlin, 107 F.3d at 335; Arrango v. Ward, 103 F.3d at 639. Even if future class members are not included in the class definition, those individuals will benefit from any relief that is granted when they become class members. Bremiller v. Cleveland Psychiatric Institute, 898 F. Supp. 572, 579 (N.D.Ohio 1995).

[676]Rule 23(a)(2), Fed.R.Civ.P.

[677]Smith v. Texaco, Inc., 263 F.3d 394. 405 (5th Cir. 2001); Baby Neal for and by Kanter v. Casey, 43 F.3d 48, 56 (3d Cir. 1994); Dunn v. City of Chicago, 231 F.R.D. 367, 372 (N.D.Ill. 2005), *amended on other grounds*, 2005 WL 3299391 (N.D.Ill., Nov. 30, 2005).

[678]*See* Armstrong v. Davis, 275 F.3d 849, 868 (9th Cir. 2001) (alleged system-wide failure to accommodate disabled prisoners and parolees is a common issue despite differences in class members' disabilities); Baby Neal v. Casey, 43 F.3d 48, 57 (3d Cir. 1994) ("Indeed, (b)(2) classes have been certified in a legion of civil rights cases where commonality findings were based primarily on

challenge a prison's failure to provide adequate medical care, which affects all prisoners, the fact that different prisoners have different medical problems will not defeat class certification.[679]

3. *The claims or defenses of the representative parties must be typical of the claims or defenses of the other class members.*[680] The "typicality" requirement means only that the named plaintiff's claims involve a "common element of fact or law"[681] or "the same legal or remedial theory" as the other class members' claims.[682] The fact that some class members might choose not to assert their rights does not mean that the named plaintiffs' claims are not typical,[683] nor does the existence of other factual variations.[684]

4. *The representative parties must fairly and adequately protect the interest of the class.*[685] This requirement means that "the class representative has common interests with unnamed class members and will vigorously prosecute the

___

the fact that defendant's conduct is central to the claims of all class members irrespective of their individual circumstances and the disparate effects of the conduct."); Amone v. Aveiro, 226 F.R.D. 677, 684–85 (D.Haw. 2005) (where plaintiffs challenge a policy or practice affecting the whole class, factual variations among class members do not defeat class certification); Marisol A. by Forbes v. Giuliani, 929 F. Supp. 662, 690 (S.D.N.Y. 1996) (commonality found despite "differences among the questions raised by individual members." (citation omitted)), *aff'd*, 126 F.3d 372 (2d Cir. 1997).

[679]Bradley v. Harrelson, 151 F.R.D. 422, 426 (M.D. Ala. 1993); Dean v. Coughlin, 107 F.R.D. at 333; Gorton v. Johnson, 100 F.R.D. 801, 802 (E.D. Mich. 1981).

[680]Rule 23(a)(3), Fed.R.Civ.P.

[681]Beattie v. CenturyTel, Inc., 511 F.3d 554, 561 (6th Cir. 2007), (citing Senter v. General Motors Corp., 532 F.2d 511, 525 n.31 (6th Cir. 1976), *cert. denied*, 129 S. Ct. 608 (2008)); *see* Skinner v. Uphoff, 209 F.R.D. 484, 488 (D.Wyo. 2002); Nicholson v. Williams, 205 F.R.D. 92, 98 (E.D.N.Y. 2001) ("Typicality is satisfied where the claims of the named plaintiffs arise from the same practice or course of conduct that gives rise to the claims of the proposed class members.").

[682]J.B. ex rel. Hart v. Valdez, 186 F.3d 1280, 1299 (10th Cir. 1999); *see* DeHoyos v. Allstate Corp., 240 F.R.D. 269, 282 (W.D. Tex. 2007) ("The test is simply whether the defendant discriminated 'in the same general fashion against the class representatives and the other members of the class.'" (citation omitted)).

[683]Wilder v. Bernstein, 499 F. Supp. 980, 993 (S.D.N.Y. 1990); Cicero v. Olgiati, 410 F. Supp. 1080, 1098 (S.D.N.Y. 1976).

[684]Armstrong v. Davis, 275 F.3d 849, 868 (9th Cir. 2001) (claims of prisoners complaining of prison and parole authorities' failure to accommodate their disabilities were typical even though they had different disabilities); Baby Neal v. Casey 43 F.3d 48, 58 (3d Cir. 1994) (". . . [C]ases challenging the same unlawful conduct which affects both the named plaintiffs and the putative class usually satisfy the typicality requirement irrespective of the varying fact patterns underlying the individual claims."); Hassine v. Jeffes, 846 F.2d 169, 177 (3d Cir. 1988) (named plaintiffs could have "typical" claims without asserting "precisely the same" injuries as other class members); Berry v. Baca, 226 F.R.D. 398, 404–05 (C.D.Cal. 2005); Bullock v. Sheahan, 225 F.R.D. 227, 230 (N.D.Ill. 2004); Dean v. Coughlin, 107 F.R.D. at 334.

[685]Rule 23(a)(4), Fed.R.Civ.P.

interests of the class through qualified counsel."[686] The "common interests" prong means that the court will consider whether you have any conflicts of interest with other class members that would prevent you from being able to represent them fairly.[687] Mere differences of opinion among class members will not defeat certification.[688] Sometimes defendants argue that named plaintiffs in prison and other kinds of civil rights litigation are not adequate representatives because they have criminal records, suffer from mental illness, etc. Courts have rejected this argument, pointing out that if they accepted it, whole classes of plaintiffs would be barred from class action litigation.[689]

The "qualified counsel" requirement has generally been construed to mean that counsel must have a reasonable amount of experience relevant to the proposed class action.[690] The rules now spell this out: courts are supposed to appoint (*i.e.*, approve) class counsel, based on the work they have done in investigating the case; their experience in handling class actions, other complex litigation, and the types of claims in the case; their knowledge of the applicable law; the resources they will commit to representing the class; and any other factors relevant to their ability to fairly and adequately represent the class.[691]

The qualified counsel requirement also means that if you are proceeding *pro se*, you don't meet it. Courts are generally unwilling to assume that a *pro se* prisoner is capable of representing other prisoners' interests as well as her own.[692]

If you want to pursue a class action and do not have a lawyer, be sure you ask the court to appoint counsel. You should argue that if class actions are too complex for a *pro se* prisoner to handle, that complexity ought to support appointment of counsel.[693]

In addition to the requirements of Rule 23(a), a class action must satisfy one of the requirements in Rule 23(b). Cases seeking injunctive relief are generally certified under Rule 23(b)(2), which requires you to show that "the party opposing the class has acted or refused to act on grounds that apply generally to the class, so that final injunctive relief or corresponding declaratory relief is appropriate respecting the class as a whole."[694] Courts have said that Rule 23(b)(2) certification is "particularly appropriate in the prison litigation context where only injunctive and declaratory relief are sought."[695]

When damages are sought for a class, the case generally must be certified under Rule 23(b)(3), which requires the court to find that common questions "predominate" over questions affecting only individuals and that a class action is "superior" to other methods of handling the controversy.[696]

---

[686]Piazza v. Ebsco Industries, Inc., 273 F.3d 1341, 1346 (11th Cir. 2001); *accord*, Longden v. Sunderman, 123 F.R.D. 547, 557 (N.D.Tex. 1988); Kuck v. Berkey Photo, Inc., 81 F.R.D. 736, 740 (S.D.N.Y. 1979) (plaintiff must show "that plaintiffs' counsel is competent, and that the interests of the named plaintiffs are not adverse to those of the class").

[687]Valley Drug Co. v. Geneva Pharm., Inc., 350 F.3d 1181, 1189 (11th Cir. 2003) (where *fundamental* conflicts of interest exist within a class, class certification is inappropriate); Knop v. Johnson, 667 F. Supp. 467, 500 (W.D. Mich. 1987) (decertifying class as to one issue where conflict became apparent), *aff'd in pertinent part*, 977 F.2d 996 (6th Cir. 1992).

The court may remove a named plaintiff from her representative role and substitute someone else if it believes the named plaintiff is not fairly representing the class. Heit v. van Ochten, 126 F. Supp. 2d 487, 494–95 (W.D.Mich. 2001).

[688]Horton v. Goose Creek Independent Sch. Dist., 690 F.2d 470, 484–88 (7th Cir. 1982); Williams v. Lane, 96 F.R.D. 383, 386 (N.D.Ill. 1982).

[689]Ingles v. City of New York, 2003 WL 402565, *6–7 (S.D.N.Y., Feb. 20, 2003); Daniels v. City of New York, 198 F.R.D. 409, 418–19 (S.D.N.Y. 2001) (citing Jane B. by Martin v. New York City Dep't of Soc. Servs., 117 F.R.D. 64, 71 (S.D.N.Y.1987)); Neiberger v. Hawkins, 208 F.R.D. 301 (D.Colo. 2002).

[690]*See* Bynum v. District of Columbia, 217 F.R.D. 43, 47 (D.D.C. 2003); Daniels v. City of New York, 198 F.R.D. 409, 418 (S.D.N.Y. 2001).

[691]Rule 23(g)(1), Fed.R.Civ.P.

[692]Graham v. Perez, 121 F. Supp. 2d 317, 321 (S.D.N.Y. 2000) ("[i]t is well settled in this circuit that *pro se* plaintiffs cannot act as class representatives" because they do not satisfy the requirements

of Rule 23(a)(4) (citation omitted)); Maldonado v. Terhune, 28 F. Supp. 2d 284, 288 (D. N.J. 1998) (holding that *pro se* prisoners are "inadequate to represent the interests of his fellow inmates in a class action"); Allnew v. City of Duluth, 983 F. Supp. 825, 830 (D. Minn. 1997) and cases cited.

For rare exceptions in which *pro se* prisoners have obtained class certification, *see* Dorrough v. Hogan, 563 F.2d 1259, 1261 (5th Cir. 1977) (noting the defendants did not object to certification); Balla v. Idaho State Board of Corrections, 595 F. Supp.1558, 1561 (D. Idaho 1984).

[693]*See* Nilsson v. Coughlin, 670 F. Supp. 1186, 1191 (S.D.N.Y. 1987). Appointment of counsel is discussed in Ch. 10, § C.5.

You should understand that if you start a class action and a lawyer is appointed, she will be responsible not only to you but also to all other class members. Rule 23(g)(4), Fed.R.Civ.P. ("Class counsel must fairly and adequately represent the interests of the class.") That means she might have to disregard your wishes if in her professional judgment the interests of the class as a whole required it. *See, e.g.*, Laskey v. International Union, UAW, 638 F.2d 954, 957 (6th Cir. 1981) ("That the class counsel proposed a settlement which the named representatives opposed does not prove that the interests of the class were not protected."); Heit v. van Ochten, 126 F. Supp. 2d 487, 494–95 (W.D.Mich. 2001) (relieving counsel from representing named plaintiff, appointing new class representative on ground that original named plaintiff was not representing class's interests). On balance, we think that the benefits of getting a competent lawyer to pursue a class action will usually outweigh the risks that the named plaintiff will lose control of the case.

[694]*See* Zinser v. Accufix Research, 253 F.3d 1180, 1195 (9th Cir. 2001) ("Class certification under Rule 23(b)(2) is appropriate only where the primary relief sought is declaratory or injunctive."), *amended*, 273 F.3d 1266 (9th Cir. 2001).

[695]Hawker v. Consovoy, 198 F.R.D. 619, 626 (D.N.J. 2001) (citing Austin v. Hopper, 15 F. Supp. 2d 1210, 1229 (M.D.Ala.1998)).

[696]Rule 23(b)(3), Fed.R.Civ.P.; *see* Kerr v. City of West Palm Beach, 875 F.2d 1546, 1557–58 (11th Cir. 1989) (upholding denial

Some decisions have held that some class damages can be awarded in a Rule 23(b)(2) class action, though they have not agreed on the details.[697] Others have avoided the question by certifying the injunctive claims under Rule 23(b)(2) and the damages claims under rule 23(b)(3).[698]

Class actions may also be certified under Rule 23(b)(1), which provides for certification if permitting separate actions involving class members would risk "inconsistent or varying adjudications" or decisions that would impair the rights of other class members.[699] This rule has been used in both injunctive and damages cases.[700]

It is harder to get class certification for damage claims than for injunctive claims because damages typically have to be tailored to the injury suffered by each individual. Courts have come up with various ways of managing this process.[701]

In some cases, class damage awards have simply been standardized.[702]

These problems do not arise when the action seeks injunctive or declaratory relief for the class and damages are sought only for the named plaintiffs as individuals. Only the injunctive claims require class certification, and this can be done under Rule 23(b)(2).

Some courts have held that class certification is unnecessary in cases against prison officials or other government officials, reasoning that any declaratory or injunctive relief granted will benefit all affected persons even without class certification.[703] Other courts have either rejected this approach entirely[704] or have recognized that it is often not practical to apply it to prison and other civil rights cases, since without class certification the case could become moot if the named plaintiff were transferred or released.[705] In particular, cases that require "affirmative steps to remedy existing unconstitutional conditions," rather than just striking down a statute or regulation, are appropriate for class certification.[706]

---

of class certification in police misconduct damages case); McBean v. City of New York, 228 F.R.D. 487, 503 (S.D.N.Y. 2005) (finding class action superior method of handling class action about strip searches of arrestees).

[697]*Compare* Robinson v. Metro-North Commuter Railroad Co., 267 F.3d 147, 165 (2d Cir. 2001) (taking *ad hoc* approach to question whether 23(b)(2) certification should be allowed where there are injunctive and damages claims; rejecting "incidental damages" rule) *with* Allison v. Citgo Petroleum Crop., 151 F.3d 402, 415–17 (5th Cir. 1998) (only incidental damages can be recovered in a 23(b)(2) action); *see* Williams v. Lane, 129 F.R.D. 636 (N.D. Ill. 1990) (holding prisoners who had obtained an injunction in a Rule 23(b)(2) class action could subsequently recover damages as well).

[698]*See, e.g.*, Marriott v. County of Montgomery, 227 F.R.D. 159, 172–73 (N.D.N.Y. 2005), *aff'd*, 2005 WL 3117194 (2d Cir., Nov. 22, 2005) (unpublished); Bynum v. District of Columbia, 217 F.R.D. 43, 51–52 (D.D.C. 2003); Anderson v. Cornejo, 199 F.R.D. 228, 242–44 (N.D.Ill. 2000).

[699]Rule 23(b)(1), Fed.R.Civ.P.

[700]Ingles v. City of New York, 2003 WL 402565, *7 (S.D.N.Y., Feb. 20, 2003); Berry v. Baca, 226 F.R.D. 398, 406 (C.D.Cal. 2005); Chang v. U.S., 217 F.R.D. 262, 273 n.5 (D.D.C. 2003). *But see* Jones v. American General Life and Accident Ins. Co., 213 F.R.D. 689, 697 (S.D.Ga. 2002) (stating Rule 23(b)(1) applies only where party could be in a position where it could not obey one court order without violating another).

[701]*See In re* Visa Check, 280 F.3d 124,141 (2d Cir. 2001) (citations omitted):

> There are a number of management tools available to a district court to address any individualized damages issues that might arise in a class action, including: (1) bifurcating liability and damage trials with the same or different juries; (2) appointing a magistrate judge or special master to preside over individual damages proceedings; (3) decertifying the class after the liability trial and providing notice to class members concerning how they may proceed to prove damages; (4) creating subclasses; or (5) altering or amending the class.

Accord, Zuccarini v. Hoechst, 200 F.R.D. 326, 349 (E.D. Mich. 2001); Bertulli v. Indep. Ass'n of Cont'l Pilots, 242 F.3d 290, 298 (5th Cir. 2001) (affirming district court's determination that common issues predominated because "[a]lthough calculating damages will require some individualized determinations, it

appears that virtually every issue prior to damages is a common issue").

[702]Dellums v. Powell, 566 F.2d 216, 227–28 (D.C. Cir. 1977) (endorsing standardized awards for subclasses); Allman v. Coughlin, 577 F. Supp. 1440, 1444 (S.D.N.Y. 1984) (class certified for abuses inflicted after jail disturbance; plaintiffs sought standardized awards); *see* Al-Jundi v. Mancusi, 113 F. Supp. 2d 441 (W.D.N.Y. 2000) (describing standardized awards in settlement of Attica disturbance litigation); *In re* Jackson Lockdown/MCO Cases, 107 F.R.D. 703 (E.D. Mich. 1985) (approving consent judgment in prison disturbance case providing for standardized damage awards for 48 named plaintiffs in consolidated cases, one fund for benefit of class members suffering injury, and another fund for benefit of class as whole).

[703]*See, e.g.*, Lent v. Lopes, 107 F.R.D. 62, 63 (D. Conn. 1985).

[704]*See, e.g.*, Penland v. Warren County Jail, 797 F.2d 332, 334–35 (6th Cir. 1986); Brown v. Scott, 602 F.2d 791, 795 (7th Cir. 1979), *aff'd on other grounds sub nom.* Carey v. Brown 447 U.S. 455, 100 S. Ct. 2286 (1980); Matyasovsky v. Housing Auth. of the City of Bridgeport, 226 F.R.D. 35, 43 (D.Conn. 2005) (proposed class representative has a right to certification if the requirements of Rule 23 are met); Daniels v. City of New York, 199 F.R.D. 513, 514–15 (S.D.N.Y. 2001) (stating a variety of reasons supporting class certification); Hill v. Butterworth, 170 F.R.D. 509, 518–19 (N.D.Fla. 1997), *vacated on other grounds*, 147 F.3d 1333 (11th Cir. 1998); Communities for Equity v. Michigan High School Athletic Ass'n, 192 F.R.D. 568, 575 (W.D. Mich. 1999) (citing *Penland*).

[705]*See* Lasky v. Quinlan, 558 F.2d 1133, 1136 (2d Cir. 1977); Kapps v. Wing, 283 F. Supp. 2d 866, 873 (E.D.N.Y. 2003), *aff'd in part and vacated in part on other grounds* 404 F.3d 105 (2d Cir. 2005); Neiberger v. Hawkins, 208 F.R.D. 301, 318 (D.Colo. 2002); Gluckenberger v. Boston University, 957 F. Supp. 306, 326–27 (D.Mass. 1997); Kutschbach v. Davies, 885 F. Supp. 1079, 1086 (S.D.Ohio 1995).

[706]Jane B. v. New York City Dep't of Social Services, 117 F.R.D. 64, 72 (S.D.N.Y. 1987); *accord*, Karen L. v. Physicians Health Services, 202 F.R.D. 94, 103–05 (D.Conn. 2001); Lucas v. Wasser, 73 F.R.D. 361, 363 (S.D.N.Y. 1976); *see* Matyasovsky v. Housing Auth. of the City of Bridgeport, 226 F.R.D. at 43 (where defendants

2. Your Rights as a Class Member

When a court certifies a class, it generally orders notice to the class. In damage cases certified under Rule 23(b)(3), class members should each receive "the best notice that is practicable under the circumstances, including individual notice to all members who can be identified through reasonable effort," and individuals have the right to "opt out" (be excluded) from the class so they can pursue separate actions.[707] In class actions under Rule 23(b)(2) for declaratory or injunctive relief, whether and how notice is given is within the discretion of the district court,[708] and there is generally no right to opt out.[709]

Courts generally require some form of notice in Rule 23(b)(2) class actions about prison conditions, such as distribution to all class members or to all incoming inmates, or posting the notice in housing areas, law libraries, and other areas of the prison.[710] A class notice should provide that you can obtain a copy of the complaint from class counsel.[711]

Once a class is certified, class counsel is obligated to represent the interests of the entire class.[712] This does not mean they have to deal with every individual class member's individual problems, though some class counsel might try. However, courts are extremely reluctant to hear individual prisoners' problems when there is a class action on the same subject.[713]

If you are in this position—*e.g.*, if a class action has been brought to reform the medical care system someday, but you need particular treatment now—you should first ask class counsel to help you. If they can't or won't, and you decide to sue, explain in your papers that you have tried to get help from class counsel, and explain why you need individual relief now rather than waiting for the final judgment in the class action.

As an unnamed class member, you are generally not obligated to do anything.[714] But you can help class counsel win the case by providing them with information you have that is relevant to the complaint's allegations, by letting them know if notices are not properly posted, and by agreeing to testify if asked (which will probably also mean submitting to discovery; it is common practice to take depositions of class members who will testify at trial).

If you disagree with the way class counsel is handling the case, or do not understand it, you are free to express your views or to ask for an explanation from counsel. Rule 23(d) also authorizes the court to permit class members "to intervene and present claims or defenses, or otherwise to come into the action." In addition, class members may move to replace class counsel.[715] However, courts are unlikely to take any action based on a disagreement between counsel and some class members as long as it appears that counsel is making an effort to represent the class's interests.[716]

---

were alleged to have disobeyed the law for years, court declined to withhold class certification).

[707]Rule 23(c)(2)(B), Fed.R.Civ.P.; Reeb v. Ohio Dep't of Rehabilitation and Correction, 435 F.3d 639, 645–46 (6th Cir. 2006); *In re* Veneman, 309 F.3d 789, 792 (D.C. Cir. 2002).

[708]Rule 23(d)(2)(A), Fed.R.Civ.P. ("the court may direct appropriate notice to the class"); *see, e.g.*, Wyandotte Nation v. City of Kansas City, Kansas, 214 F.R.D. 656, 664 (D. Kan. 2003) (ordering notice). In Rule 23(b)(2) class actions where "incidental" money damages are at issue, some courts have held that notice is required, *In re* Monumental Life Ins. Co., 365 F.3d 408, 416–17 (5th Cir. 2004) (also allowing opt-out in court's discretion), and others have directed it as a matter of discretion. *See* Ellis v. Costco Wholesale Corp., 240 F.R.D. 627, 644 (N.D. Cal. 2007) (exercising discretion to order notice in 23(b)(2) class when "incidental" money damages involved).

[709]However, some courts have allowed class members to opt out in those situations. *In re* Monumental Life Ins. Co., 365 F.3d at 417; Ellis v. Costco Wholesale Corp., 240 F.R.D. at 644.

[710]*See, e.g.*, Dean v. Coughlin, 107 F.R.D. 331, 335 (S.D.N.Y. 1985) (requiring individual notice to all class members and posting in prison's common areas); Arrango v. Ward 103 F.R.D. 638, 640–41 (S.D.N.Y. 1984) (requiring posting of notice in common areas of maximum security unit).

[711]Allen v. Isaac, 100 F.R.D. 373, 375 (D.C. Ill. 1983).

[712]Rule 23(g)(4), Fed.R.Civ.P.

[713]*See* § G of this chapter.

[714]Unnamed class members may be subject to discovery in the court's discretion, but such discovery is not favored and there must generally be a good reason for it, such as inability to obtain the information from the named plaintiffs or class counsel. *See, e.g.*, Mehl v. Canadian Pacific Ry., 216 F.R.D. 627, 631–32 (D. N.D. 2003) (denying discovery request of unnamed plaintiffs; "such discovery is not generally encouraged due to its potential for harassment and due to concerns regarding its practicality"); Schwartz v. Celestial Seasonings, 185 F.R.D. 313, 316–18 (D. Colo. 1999) (allowing limited discovery of unnamed class members). Some courts have held that to obtain discovery of unnamed class members defendant must show that it needs the discovery for trial of the issues common to the class, it is not seeking discovery with the purpose or effect of harassing absent class members or altering the membership of the class, and that the discovery is directly relevant to the issues to be tried concerning the class action aspects of the case. *See* Krueger v. New York Tel. Co., 163 F.R.D. 446, 450–51 (S.D.N.Y. 1995) (citing U.S. v. Trucking Employers, Inc., 72 F.R.D. 101, 104 (D.D.C. 1976)).

[715]*See* Gates v. Cook, 234 F.3d 221, 228–30 (5th Cir. 2000) (holding substitution of class counsel was warranted in light of present counsel's poor performance and poor relationship with class members); McNeil v. Guthrie, 945 F.2d 1130, 1166–67 (10th Cir. 1991); U.S. v. City of Montgomery, Ala., 162 F.R.D. 362, 364 (M.D. Ala. 1995) (non-party request to remove counsel denied since the requestor did not seek to intervene or request findings pursuant to Rule 23).

[716]*See, e.g.*, Kincade v. General Tire & Rubber Co., 635 F.2d 501, 508 (5th Cir. 1981) ("Because the 'client' in a class action consists of numerous unnamed class members as well as the class representatives, and because '[t]he class itself often speaks in several voices . . ., it may be impossible for the class attorney to do more than act in what he believes to be the best interests of the class as a whole. . . .'" (citation omitted) (alteration and omissions in original)); Maywalt v. Parker & Parsley Petroleum Co., 155 F.R.D. 494, 497 (S.D.N.Y. 1994) ("In the absence of concretely alleged acts of impropriety by the duly certified Class Counsel, or a showing of abridgment of a significant minority of the Class' rights,

When counsel proposes to settle a class action by making an agreement with the defendants, the rules require that the court "direct notice in a reasonable manner to all class members who would be bound by the proposal."[717] The way in which notice is given is within the court's discretion,[718] at least in injunctive cases.[719] In prison conditions case settlements, a written notice is generally provided to class members, describing the terms of the settlement and telling prisoners how they can submit comments or objections to counsel or the court.[720] In our experience, the notice

generally provides that class members can obtain an actual copy of the settlement from class counsel, or otherwise.[721] In any case, a notice should "'fairly apprise' the class members of the terms of the proposed settlement and of their options."[722]

We think it is good practice for class counsel to arrange to meet with class members in the prison to explain the settlement and to answer questions.[723] Class members who do not like a proposed settlement should make their views known during this process; if they do not receive a satisfactory explanation or changes in the settlement, they can file objections with the court.

If a proposed settlement will bind class members, the court "may approve it only after a hearing and on finding that it is fair, reasonable, and adequate."[724] In making that decision, the court should consider the comments of class

---

this Court will not grant the hasty application of the Moving Representative Plaintiffs to replace Class Counsel on the eve of the Settlement Hearing."), aff'd, 67 F.3d 1072, 1079 (2d Cir. 1995); Arney v. Finney, 766 F. Supp. 934, 940–41 (D.Kan. 1991) (refusing to replace class counsel, denying intervention), aff'd, 967 F.2d 418, 422 (10th Cir. 1992); see McNeil v. Guthrie, 945 F.2d 1163, 1167 (10th Cir. 1989) ("All of class counsel's judgments cannot be challenged in court.").

[717]Rule 23(e)(1), Fed.R.Civ.P.; see In re Integra Realty Res., Inc., 262 F.3d 1089, 1110–11 (10th Cir. 2001) (holding Rule 23 and due process requisites satisfied where the record indicated that only 77% of class members actually received notice of the settlement).

[718]Wolfert ex rel. Estate of Wolfert v. Transamerica Home First, Inc. 439 F.3d 165, 176 (2d Cir. 2006) (notice by first class mail, not certified, was sufficient); DeJulius v. New England Health Care Employees Pension Fund, 429 F.3d 935, 944 (10th Cir. 2005) (mailed individual notice may be required where class members must file claims to collect from a settlement); Mirfasihi v. Fleet Mortg. Corp. 356 F.3d 781, 786 (7th Cir. 2004) ("When individual notice is infeasible, notice by publication in a newspaper of national circulation (here *USA Weekend*, a magazine that is included in hundreds of Sunday newspapers) is an acceptable substitute.").

[719]Rule 23(c)(2)(B), Fed.R.Civ.P., requires that courts certifying a Rule 23(b)(3) class action for damages give "the best notice [of the certification] that is practicable under the circumstances, including individual notice to all members who can be identified through reasonable effort." Some courts have applied this more demanding standard to notice of settlement as well as notice of class certification. *See, e.g.,* Fidel v. Farley, 534 F.3d 508, 513 (6th Cir. 2008).

[720]*See* Isby v. Bayh, 75 F.3d 1191, 1195 n.2 (7th Cir. 1996) (approving notice by distribution of the proposed judgment to all 200 inmates on a particular date, without posting in common areas, in a "Supermax" prison); Van Horn v. Trickey, 840 F.2d 604, 606 (8th Cir. 1998) (holding individual notice to named plaintiffs and flyers posted in the jail gave sufficient notice); Ruiz v. McCaskle, 724 F.2d 1149, 1152 (5th Cir. 1984) (approving notice made available in prison "writ rooms," published in prison newspaper, and posted in housing areas); Laube v. Campbell, 333 F. Supp. 2d 1234, 1241 (M.D.Ala. 2004) (court-approved notice was posted, copies of a court-approved comment form and drop boxes for the forms were provided); Gaddis v. Campbell, 301 F. Supp. 2d 1310, 1314 (M.D.Ala. 2004) (court-approved notice was conspicuously posted on community bulletin boards in every Corrections Department dormitory, as well as law libraries and dining areas, and was served individually on each inmate in segregation); Cody v. Hillard, 88 F. Supp. 2d 1049, 1051–52 (D. S.D. 2000) (court "directed counsel to post the Notice in the housing units of the SDSP, to give individual notice to inmates in the Special Housing

Units or in other segregated confinement, to have the Notice read to inmates classified as illiterate, and to have the notice read by interpreters to non-English speaking inmates"); Austin v. Hopper, 28 F. Supp. 2d 1231, 1236 (M.D. Ala. 1998) (court-approved notice was posted on dormitory bulletin boards and in law libraries and dining areas of each prison and was also sent to county jails; notice described settlement and the right to object; inmates were provided with objection forms); In re Southern Ohio Correctional Facility, 173 F.R.D. 205, 211 (S.D.Ohio 1997) (notice mailed to all prisoners who had been at the prison at the pertinent time, and posted in all cellblocks; notice and the settlement itself placed in every prison library); Austin v. Pennsylvania Dep't of Corrections, 876 F. Supp. 1437, 1455–56 (E.D.Pa. 1995) (notice given by posting in all common areas on three occasions); *see also* McBean v. City of New York, 233 F.R.D. 377, 382 (S.D.N.Y. 2006) (notice given to class members, who included present and former jail prisoners, by publishing notices in newspapers, posting notices in prison facilities, and contacting the Department of Homeless Services).

[721]Cody v. Hillard, 88 F. Supp. 2d at 1052; In re Southern Ohio Correctional Facility, 173 F.R.D. 205, 211 (S.D.Ohio 1997) (settlement placed in all prison law libraries).

[722]*In re* Integra Realty Resources, Inc., 262 F.3d 1089, 1111 (10th Cir. 2001); *see* Ruiz v. McCaskle, 724 F.2d at 1153 (notice gave "fair recital" of agreement's terms); Austin v. Hopper, 28 F. Supp. 2d at 1236 (notice told inmates about nature of settlement, its advantages and disadvantages).

[723]*See* Laube v. Campbell, 333 F. Supp. 2d 1234, 1240–41 (M.D.Ala. 2004) (noting counsel's visits to prisons involved, including segregation and death row units); In re Southern Ohio Correctional Facility, 173 F.R.D. 205, 211 (S.D.Ohio 1997) (class counsel visited class members at seven prisons); Diaz v. Romer, 801 F. Supp. 405, 410 (D.Colo. 1992), aff'd, 9 F.3d 116 (10th Cir. 1993) (unpublished); Costello v. Wainwright, 489 F. Supp. 1100, 1101 (M.D.Fla. 1980); *see also* Watson v. Ray, 90 F.R.D. 143, 145 (S.D. Iowa 1981) (noting judge met with inmate group to discuss class settlement).

[724]Rule 23(e)(2), Fed.R.Civ.P.; *see* Churchill Village v. General Electric, 361 F.3d 566, 575–77 (9th Cir. 2004) (discussing factors court should consider in determining if settlement is "fair, reasonable and adequate"); Ingles v. Toro, 438 F. Supp. 2d 203 (S.D.N.Y. 2006) (approving settlement in class action about excessive force); Heit v. van Ochten, 126 F. Supp. 2d 487 (W.D.Mich. 2001) (approving settlement in disciplinary procedures case).

members, but it need not follow them.[725] In most cases, the court will accept the judgment of class counsel that the settlement should be approved. However, if it appears that counsel has not thought matters through or has otherwise not done their homework, the settlement will not be approved.[726]

In cases about prison conditions, courts must determine whether the settlement complies with the relevant portions of the Prison Litigation Reform Act (PLRA).[727]

Class members who oppose entry of a settlement may appeal *if* they have filed objections with the court to approval of the settlement; they need not have actually intervened.[728] Once a class action is decided, either by court decision or by settlement, the judgment determines the rights of all class members with respect to the matters at issue in the class action.[729]

K. Exhaustion of Remedies

The law often requires that before you sue, you first present your problem to another court or to an administrative agency or a grievance system and then follow that process as far as you can. This process is called the "exhaustion" of judicial or administrative remedies.[730] Exhaustion requirements vary according to the kind of case you wish to pursue and the court you will pursue it in.

State prisoners seeking to file petitions for a writ of habeas corpus in federal court must first exhaust their state judicial remedies. To exhaust a challenge to a criminal conviction or sentence, the petitioner must present her claims through the entire state criminal appellate process (including discretionary appeals), or through one complete round of the state's post-conviction process.[731] To exhaust a challenge to an administrative decision affecting the fact or duration of incarceration, such as a denial of parole or a loss of good time in a disciplinary proceeding, the petitioner must have used whatever remedies the state makes available for the claim, whether administrative or judicial.

Federal prisoners seeking to challenge their criminal convictions or sentences must proceed under 28 U.S.C. § 2255 after exhausting direct appeal proceedings. Federal prisoners challenging administrative decisions that affect the fact or duration of their confinement must proceed via habeas corpus under 28 U.S.C. § 2241 after exhaustion of any administrative remedies available to them.[732]

All prisoners, state or federal, must exhaust their available administrative remedies (usually, but not always, the prison grievance system) under the Prison Litigation Reform Act (PLRA) before filing a civil action about prison conditions under 42 U.S.C. § 1983 or any other federal law—regardless of whether you file in state or federal court.[733] You also may have to exhaust administrative remedies before filing a purely state law case in state court, since many states have enacted laws similar to the federal PLRA. You will have to check the laws of your state to find out for certain.

---

[725]Ball v. AMC Entertainment, Inc., 315 F. Supp. 2d 120, 129 (D.D.C. 2004); *see also* Van Horn v. Trickey, 840 F.2d 604, 606–08 (8th Cir. 1988) (approving settlement even though 180 of 400 inmates objected).

In our experience, prisoners sometimes object to settlements that do not contain everything the prisoners want without understanding that there is a substantial risk of losing the whole case or getting a less favorable result by going to trial. *See, e.g.,* Gaddis v. Campbell, 301 F. Supp. 2d 1310, 1314 (M.D.Ala. 2004). These are factors that the court must consider and that class counsel should explain to the members if they object. *See* Harris v. Reeves, 761 F. Supp 382, 394–95 (E.D.Pa. 1991) (noting that many class members dropped their objections based on counsel's explanation); *see also* Ingles v. Toro, 438 F. Supp. at 212–16 (reviewing factors supporting adequacy of settlement).

[726]*See, e.g.,* Wyatt by and through Rawlins v. Horsley, 793 F. Supp. 1053 (M.D.Ala. 1991).

Strictly speaking, the court has no ability to modify particular provisions, but only to approve or disapprove the whole agreement. Evans v. Jeff D., 475 U.S. 717, 727, 106 S. Ct. 1531 (1986). However, courts sometimes tell the parties which portions they have problems with, and the parties renegotiate those provisions rather than have the whole agreement disapproved. *See* Valley Disposal, Inc. v. Central Vermont Solid Waste Management Dist., 71 F.3d 1053, 1059 n.5 (2d Cir. 1995) ("A district court certainly has the power to approve or disapprove a settlement agreement conditionally—thereby giving the parties an opportunity to insert a provision that the court believes necessary or to remove a provision to which it objects."); Williams v. Vukovich, 720 F.2d 909, 921 (6th Cir. 1983) ("If the court determines that the decree is problematic, it should inform the parties of its precise concerns and give them an opportunity to reach a reasonable accommodation."); Reid v. State of New York, 570 F. Supp. 1003, 1007 (S.D.N.Y. 1983) (disapproving decree unless two modifications are made); Morales v. Turman, 569 F.Supp 332, 338–39 (E.D.Tex. 1983) (stating steps that must be taken before decree will be approved).

[727]Laube v. Campbell, 333 F. Supp. 2d 1234, 1238–39 (M.D.Ala. 2004). A "private settlement agreement" need not comply with the PLRA, but it also cannot be enforced in federal court. *See* Ingles v. Toro, 438 F. Supp. 203, 214–16 (S.D.N.Y. 2006); *see* Ch. 9, § K.6, for further discussion of the relevant PLRA provisions.

[728]Devlin v. Scardelletti, 536 U.S. 1, 122 S. Ct. 2005 (2002).

[729]*See* § G of this chapter concerning rights based on court orders and § M of this chapter concerning rules of *res judicata* and collateral estoppel.

[730]Exhaustion of remedies is not to be confused with the rule that in certain situations, due procss is satisfied by the existence of post-deprivation remedies. This rule is discussed in Ch. 4, § E.

[731]Randy Hertz and James S. Liebman, 2 *Federal Habeas Corpus Practice and Procedure* § 23.3b (Matthew Bender, 5th ed. 2005). Habeas exhaustion in criminal cases is a complicated subject that is beyond the scope of this Manual. There is a brief discussion of federal habeas for state prisoners in § H.1.a of this chapter.

[732]*See* § H.1.b of this chapter for further discussion of these statutes.

[733]42 U.S.C. § 1997e(a). The PLRA exhaustion requirement is discussed in Ch. 9, § D.

Judicial proceedings to review administrative action, whether under state law or under the federal Administrative Procedures Act,[734] will generally require exhaustion of administrative remedies.

Tort claims against governmental bodies generally require filing a document often called a claim or notice of claim, usually within a relatively short period of time like 90 or 120 days, before filing a lawsuit against the government. This is true both of the Federal Tort Claims Act (FTCA)[735] and in most cases of state and local governmental tort liability.[736]

If you are injured in prison and think you may wish to bring suit about it, you should always file both the claim or notice of claim *and* pursue a grievance so you will keep all your possible remedies available. If you decide to pursue a state tort or FTCA suit, having filed a prison grievance will not satisfy a requirement to file a claim or notice of claim. If you decide to pursue a civil rights claim under 42 U.S.C. § 1983 or *Bivens*, having filed a claim or notice of claim will not satisfy the PLRA.[737]

L. Immunities

Immunities are rules that prevent courts from granting relief even in cases where someone's rights have been violated. You have to know immunity rules to know whether you have a winnable case. In addition, because state law and federal law immunities are often different, immunity rules may determine which court you file in and which legal claims you raise.

1. The Eleventh Amendment and Sovereign Immunity

a. Immunity of State Governments and Agencies in Federal Court The Eleventh Amendment states that the federal courts cannot hear suits against a state by citizens of a different state.[738] The federal courts have held that it also bars suits against states by their own citizens, consistently with the ancient doctrine of sovereign immunity.[739]

The Eleventh Amendment does not forbid suing state *officials* for damages in their individual capacities, and for declaratory or injunctive relief in their official capacities. Local governments and their agencies are not protected by the Eleventh Amendment even in damages suits[740] unless they function as "arm[s] of the state."[741] Whether or not a county sheriff sued for damages in her official capacity is a state official protected by Eleventh Amendment immunity, or a local official who is not, depends on state law, and the answer may also depend on what function the sheriff is being sued about.[742]

Eleventh Amendment law has become so confusing over the years that even the courts admitted long ago that it doesn't make much sense.[743] However, if you stick to the following rules, you should be able to stay out of Eleventh Amendment trouble in cases brought under 42 U.S.C. § 1983.[744]

(1) You can't name the state as a defendant in federal court under § 1983.[745] Nor can you name the state Department of Correction or any other state governmental agency.[746]

---

[734]The federal APA is discussed in § B.2.b of this chapter. State judicial review is discussed in § D.2.

[735]The FTCA is discussed in § C.2 of this chapter.

[736]State tort actions are discussed in § C.1 of this chapter.

[737]*See* Ch. 9, § D.1, nn.271–272.

[738]U.S.Const., Amend. XI. The actual language of the amendment is: "The judicial power of the United States shall not be construed to extend to any suit in law or equity, commenced or prosecuted against one of the United States by citizens of another state, or by citizens or subjects of any foreign state."

[739]Edelman v. Jordan, 415 U.S. 651, 662–63, 94 S. Ct. 1374 (1974). The exact relationship between the Eleventh Amendment and sovereign immunity is a bit murky. You can assume that they amount more or less to the same thing.

State and local governments may also enjoy sovereign immunity under state law. *See* § L.5 of this chapter.

[740]Monell v. New York City Dep't of Social Services, 436 U.S. 658, 690 n.54, 98 S. Ct. 2018 (1978).

[741]Northern Ins. Co. of New York v. Chatham County, Georgia, 547 U.S. 189, 194, 126 S. Ct. 1689 (2006).

[742]*See, e.g.*, Abusaid v. Hillsborough County Bd. of County Com'rs, 405 F.3d 1298, 1305–13 (11th Cir. 2005) (Florida sheriff was a county official not protected by the Eleventh Amendment when enforcing a county ordinance); Huminski v. Corsones, 396 F.3d 53, 75 (2d Cir. 2005) (Vermont sheriff was a state official when enforcing state law); Manders v. Lee, 338 F.3d 1304, 1319–28 (11th Cir. 2003) (holding Georgia sheriffs are state officials protected in their official capacities by the Eleventh Amendment with regard to making use of force policy and training and disciplining deputies concerning it); Alkire v. Irving, 330 F.3d 802, 811 (6th Cir. 2003) (Ohio sheriff was not an "arm of the state" for Eleventh Amendment purposes); Gottfried v. Medical Planning Services, Inc., 280 F.3d 684, 692 (6th Cir. 2002) (Ohio sheriff was an "arm of the state" protected by the Eleventh Amendment in enforcing a state court injunction). Whether a sheriff is a state or local official is also important for determining whether a county can be held liable for the sheriff's actions. *See* § B.4.b of this chapter, n.238.

[743]*See, e.g.*, Eng v. Coughlin, 858 F.2d 889, 897 (2d Cir. 1988) ("not . . . a model of logical symmetry, but marked rather by a baffling complexity"); Spicer v. Hilton, 618 F.2d 232, 235 (3d Cir. 1980) ("Any step through the looking glass of the Eleventh Amendment leads to a wonderland of judicially created and perpetuated fiction and paradox.").

[744]We are focusing on § 1983 in this discussion because most state prisoner suits are brought under it. The rules are different under the federal disability statutes and the Religious Land Use and Institutionalized Persons Act, discussed later in this section.

[745]Alabama v. Pugh, 438 U.S. 781, 782, 98 S. Ct. 3057 (1978).

[746]Pennhurst State School & Hospital v. Halderman, 465 U.S. 89, 100, 104 S. Ct. 900 (1984) (the Eleventh Amendment bars a federal court suit naming "the State or one of its agencies or departments" as defendant"); Callahan v. City of Philadelphia, 207 F.3d 668, 670 (3d Cir. 2000).

(2) You can't sue a state official for damages in her official capacity in federal court under § 1983. This is deemed to be the same as suing the state.[747] To get damages from state officials, you must name the defendants in their individual or personal capacities.[748] Most courts hold that if the complaint doesn't specifically state in what capacity the defendants are sued, they will look to the "course of proceedings" to figure it out.[749] However, at least one federal appeals court says that if the plaintiff doesn't clearly state that she is suing defendants in their official capacities, courts should assume that they are sued in their official capacities.[750] To avoid problems, spell it out.

(3) Though you can get compensatory and punitive damages from a state official in her individual capacity, you can't get a payment of money improperly withheld by the state (*e.g.*, back wages) regardless of how you designate the defendants' capacity.[751]

(4) You can sue a state official—but not the state itself—for an injunction in her official capacity.[752] This is true even if the state will have to spend money to comply with the injunction.[753]

(5) Injunctive claims based only on state law may not be brought in federal court against state officials in any capacity.[754] Most courts have held that this rule does not apply to individual capacity damage claims.[755]

Prison officials may claim that they are protected by the Eleventh Amendment because they were *acting* in their official capacities even if you sued them in their individual capacities. The Supreme Court has rejected this argument.[756]

There are two major exceptions to the states' sovereign immunity. Congress can abrogate (take away) the states' Eleventh Amendment protection by statute, relying on the power conveyed in part of the Fourteenth Amendment.[757] States can also consent to be sued in federal court and thereby waive their Eleventh Amendment immunity.[758]

A state agency may not be protected by the Eleventh Amendment if it is sufficiently financially separate from the state. *See, e.g.*, Harter v. Vernon, 101 F.3d 334, 337 (4th Cir. 1996); *see also* Hess v. Port Auth. Trans-Hudson, 513 U.S. 30, 38, 115 S. Ct. 394 (1994) (Eleventh Amendment inquiries should be guided by its two reasons for being: preventing judgments from depleting state treasuries, and maintaining "the integrity retained by each State in our federal system.").

[747]Kentucky v. Graham, 473 U.S. 159, 169, 105 S. Ct. 3099 (1985); Ruiz v. McDonnell, 299 F.3d 1173, 1180 (10th Cir. 2002).

[748]Hafer v. Melo, 502 U.S. 21, 25, 112 S. Ct. 358 (1991); Scheuer v. Rhodes, 416 U.S. 232, 238, 94 S. Ct. 1683 (1974); Cornforth v. Univ. of Okla. Bd. of Regents, 263 F.3d 1129, 1132–33 (10th Cir. 2001).

Some states have indemnification statutes that make the state pay damages that are awarded against state officials. An indemnification law does not turn your lawsuit into a suit against the state that is barred by the Eleventh Amendment. *Cornforth*, 263 F.3d at 1133; Okruhlik v. University of Arkansas ex rel. May, 255 F.3d 615, 627 (8th Cir. 2001); Hudson v. City of New Orleans, 174 F.3d 677, 687 n.7 (5th Cir. 1999); Berman Enters., Inc. v. Jorling, 3 F.3d 602, 606 (2d Cir. 1993).

If the state agrees to pay damages that are awarded against individual defendants, it cannot then refuse to pay and claim Eleventh Amendment immunity. *See* Ch. 10, § T.2.a.

[749]*See, e.g.*, Moore v. City of Harriman, 272 F.3d 769, 773 (6th Cir. 2001) (en banc) and cases cited. The course of proceedings test is intended to determine whether the defendants had sufficient notice that they were being sued individually. It "considers such factors as the nature of the plaintiff's claims, requests for compensatory or punitive damages, and the nature of any defenses raised in response to the complaint, particularly claims of qualified immunity, to determine whether the defendant had actual knowledge of the potential for individual liability. . . . The test also considers whether subsequent pleadings put the defendant on notice of the capacity in which he or she is sued." *Moore*, 272 F.3d at 772 n.1.

[750]*See* Baker v. Chisom, 501 F.3d 920, 924 (8th Cir. 2007), *cert. denied*, 128 S. Ct. 2932 (2008). One circuit makes the opposite assumption. Romano v. Bible, 169 F.3d 1182, 1186 (9th Cir. 1999) ("We also have presumed that officials necessarily are sued in their personal capacities where those officials are named in a complaint, even if the complaint does not explicitly mention the capacity in which they are sued.").

[751]Edelman v. Jordan, 415 U.S. 651, 668, 94 S. Ct. 1374 (1974); Luder v. Endicott, 253 F.3d 1020, 1024 (7th Cir. 2001) (prison employees could not get back wages by naming officials in their personal capacity).

[752]Kentucky v. Graham, 473 U.S. at 167 n.14.

[753]Edelman v. Jordan, 415 U.S. at 667–68.

[754]Pennhurst State School & Hospital v. Halderman, 465 U.S. 89, 121, 104 S. Ct. 900 (1984); *see* § F of this chapter for further discussion of state law claims in federal court.

[755]*See* § F of this chapter, n.464.

[756]Hafer v. Melo, 502 U.S. 21, 27-28, 112 S. Ct. 358 (1991).

[757]Nevada Dep't of Human Resources, 538 U.S. 721, 726, 123 S. Ct. 1972 (2003).

[758]College Sav. Bank v. Florida Prepaid Postsecondary Expense Bd., 527 U.S. 666, 675, 119 S. Ct. 2219 (1999). One state (Rhode Island) has done so. Ducally v. Rhode Island Dep't of Corrections, 160 F. Supp. 2d 220, 225 (D. R.I. 2001).

The legal test for finding that a state has waived its Eleventh Amendment protections is "a stringent one. . . . [A] State does not consent to suit in federal court merely by consenting to suit in the courts of its own creation. . . . Nor does it consent to suit in federal court merely by stating its intention to sue and be sued, . . . or even by authorizing suits against it in any court of competent jurisdiction." College Sav. Bank v. Florida Prepaid Postsecondary Expense Bd., 527 U.S. at 675–76 (citations and internal quotation marks omitted).

If a state or "arm of the state" voluntarily invokes federal court jurisdiction, it waives its Eleventh Amendment defense. For example, if the state removes a case from state to federal court, and the case includes claims as to which the state had waived sovereign immunity in *state* court, the defendant waives any Eleventh Amendment defense in *federal* court. Lapides v. Board of Regents of the University System of Georgia, 535 U.S. 613, 624, 122 S. Ct. 1640 (2002). Some federal courts have extended this rule to hold that the state's removal of a case waives its Eleventh Amendment immunity from federal claims as well, *see* Meyers v. Texas, 410 F.3d

Neither of these points is relevant to suits under 42 U.S.C. § 1983, since Congress did not abrogate Eleventh Amendment immunity in enacting § 1983,[759] and since a state is not a "person" who can be sued under § 1983 anyway.[760]

Congress has abrogated the states' Eleventh Amendment immunity, at least in part, in the Americans with Disabilities Act (ADA), and you can obtain declaratory and injunctive relief against states under it. The Supreme Court has held that prisoners can recover damages for ADA violations that are also violations of the Constitution,[761] but it is not yet settled whether damages can be recovered for wrongs that violate the ADA but do not also violate the Constitution.[762]

This issue does not arise under the Rehabilitation Act, since ongoing acceptance of federal funds waives the Eleventh Amendment defense to Rehabilitation Act claims, and virtually every correction department, sheriff's office, etc., accepts some federal funds. These issues are discussed in more detail elsewhere in this Manual.[763]

Congress has also abrogated states' sovereign immunity in the Religious Land Use and Institutionalized Persons Act (RLUIPA), which allows relief against a "government," defined to include State, county, city, and other governments and branches and agencies of governments as well as individuals, for infringements of religious freedom.[764] Congress relied on its powers under the Spending Clause and the Commerce Clause of the Constitution, and not on §5 of the Fourteenth Amendment, in enacting RLUIPA.[765] You can clearly get an injunction against religious restrictions that violate RLUIPA, and some courts have held that RLUIPA also overrides the states' Eleventh Amendment sovereign immunity against damages in federal court, so you can get

damages against state governments or state officials in their official capacity. Others have disagreed, holding damages can only be recovered against state officials in their individual capacities, as under § 1983, or not at all. The issue is not settled, and we discuss it in more detail elsewhere.[766]

States may have their own law of sovereign immunity applicable in state courts; this subject is discussed in § L.5 of this chapter.

b. Federal Government Sovereign Immunity The federal government is not protected by the Eleventh Amendment, but the doctrine of sovereign immunity bars any suit against the government or its agencies except when the government gives its consent.[767] The government has consented to be sued for various torts in the FTCA,[768] but has not consented to be sued for damages for constitutional violations.[769]

Constitutional damages suits must therefore be brought against federal government officials in their individual capacities.[770] With respect to injunctive claims, sovereign immunity has been waived by a federal statute, and such claims may be brought against the United States, against federal agencies, or against federal officials in their official capacities.[771]

2. Absolute Immunity of Judges, Prosecutors, Witnesses, and Legislators

Judges are absolutely immune from damage awards in civil rights cases for acts taken in their judicial capacities.[772] Only if they act in the "clear absence of all jurisdiction" can they be held liable.[773] Showing that the judge was wrong is not enough; you must show a complete departure from the

---

236, 247–50 (5th Cir. 2005), *cert. denied*, 550 U.S. 917 (2007), including claims asserted *after* the case is removed. *See* Embury v. King, 361 F.3d 562, 564–66 (9th Cir. 2004). *Contra*, Stewart v. North Carolina, 393 F.3d 484 (4th Cir. 2005) (removal to federal court waives Eleventh Amendment immunity only where state has waived its immunity to suit in state court, as was the case in *Lapides*).

[759]Quern v. Jordan, 440 U.S. 332, 341, 99 S. Ct. 1139 (1979).

[760]Will v. Michigan Dep't of State Police, 491 U.S. 58, 71, 109 S. Ct. 2304 (1989); *see* Callahan v. City of Philadelphia, 207 F.3d 668, 670 (3d Cir. 2000) (state court Warrant Division and Eviction Unit is a state agency and not a person under § 1983); Ducally v. Rhode Island Dep't of Corrections, 160 F. Supp. 2d at 228 (dismissing claim against state agency because it is not a person suable under § 1983).

[761]U.S. v. Georgia, 546 U.S. 151, 155–60, 126 S. Ct. 877 (2006).

[762]*See* Ch. 2, § F.4.h(2), nn.734–738.

[763]*See* Ch. 2, § F.4.h(2), n.739.

[764]42 U.S.C. § 2000cc-5(4)(A).

[765]Cutter v. Wilkinson, 544 U.S. 709, 715, 125 S. Ct. 2113 (2005). RLUIPA was enacted after the much broader Religious Freedom Restoration Act, which relied on Congress's Fourteenth Amendment authority, was struck down insofar as it applied to state government on the ground that it exceeded that authority. *Cutter*, 544 U.S. at 714–15 (citing City of Boerne v. Flores, 521 U.S. 507, 532–36, 117 S. Ct. 2157 (1997)).

[766]*See* Ch. 3, § D.1.b(3).

[767]F.D.I.C. v. Meyer, 510 U.S. 471, 475, 114 S. Ct. 996 (1994); U.S. v. Testan, 424 U.S. 392, 399, 96 S. Ct. 948 (1976); *see* Gomez-Perez v. Potter, ___ U.S. ___, 128 S. Ct. 1931, 1942–43 (2008) (any waiver of federal sovereign immunity must be stated explicitly in a statute and must be construed strictly by the courts).

[768]*See* § C.2 of this chapter.

[769]McLean v. U.S., 566 F.3d 391, 401 (4th Cir. 2009); McCloskey v. Mueller, 446 F.3d 262, 271 (1st Cir. 2006); Dorman v. Simpson, 893 F. Supp. 1073, 1078 (N.D. Ga. 1995); Deutsch v. Federal Bureau of Prisons, 737 F. Supp. 261, 265 (S.D.N.Y.) and cases cited, *aff'd*, 930 F.2d 909 (2d Cir. 1991).

[770]Carlson v. Green, 446 U.S. 14, 100 S. Ct. 1468 (1980); McCloskey v. Mueller, 446 F.3d at 271–72 (1st Cir. 2006) ("The *Bivens* doctrine allows constitutional claims against federal officials, in their individual capacities, for actions taken under color of *federal* law."). These actions are discussed in § B.2.c of this chapter.

[771]5 U.S.C. § 702; *see* § B.2.a of this chapter for further Discussion of injunctive actions against the federal government or its officials.

[772]Stump v. Sparkman, 435 U.S. 349, 98 S. Ct. 1099 (1978).

[773]Stump v. Sparkman, 435 U.S at 356–57 (judge was immune for entering an illegal sterilization order in a case over which he had jurisdiction); *see* Bradley v. Fisher, 80 U.S. (13 Wall.) 335, 352 (1871) (probate court judge who tried a criminal case would act in the absence of all jurisdiction and lose immunity).

judicial role,[774] and the courts define the judicial role very broadly.[775]

Judges are entitled only to qualified immunity for the performance of non-judicial (*i.e.*, executive or administrative) functions.[776] Judges are not absolutely immune from injunctive relief,[777] though a federal statute limits such relief to cases where a declaratory judgment has been obtained and violated or declaratory relief is not available.[778] Judicial immunity extends to officials and employees who act under

the direct orders or supervision of judges,[779] though not to court reporters, since they do not exercise enough discretion to merit immunity.[780]

Similarly, prosecutors are absolutely immune for all their actions in "initiating a prosecution and presenting the state's case,"[781] even if the defendant is later found to have

---

[774]Mireles v. Waco, 502 U.S. 9, 11–13, 112 S. Ct. 286 (1992) (judge who allegedly directed police officers to seize a lawyer and bring him into his courtroom was not acting in the absence of jurisdiction even if he directed the use of excessive force); Barrett v. Harrington, 130 F.3d 246, 262 (6th Cir. 1997) (statements to news media by judge were not judicial acts). For examples of the extreme behavior required before damages will be awarded against a judge, *see* Harper v. Merckle, 638 F.2d 848, 851–52 (5th Cir. 1982) (finding that when plaintiff went to judge's chambers for information, judge demanded that he be sworn, chased him down the hall, had him pursued and arrested, and held him in contempt without an attorney); Harris v. Harvey, 605 F.2d 330, 336 (7th Cir. 1979) (judge engaged in campaign of racially motivated vilification of a police official done outside the courtroom and not part of his judicial functions); Zarcone v. Perry, 572 F.2d 52, 53 (2d Cir. 1978) (judge had coffee vendor brought into chambers in handcuffs to abuse him for the low quality of his coffee).

[775]*See* Brookings v. Clunk, 389 F.3d 614, 622 (6th Cir. 2004) (holding that state judge "was engaged in a judicial act" in swearing out a criminal complaint against a person he believed had committed a crime in his court, and was entitled to immunity even if he "twisted the arms of the prosecutor to get the case prosecuted"); Barrett v. Harrington, 130 F.3d 246, 260 (6th Cir. 1997) (holding that "a judge instigating a criminal investigation against a disgruntled litigant who has harassed her is a judicial act" entitled to immunity); Johnson v. Kegans, 870 F.2d 992, 997–98 (5th Cir. 1989) (judge was immune for letter to parole board recommending denial of parole); Ashelman v. Pope, 793 F.2d 1072, 1078 (9th Cir. 1986) (en banc) (judge was immune for conspiring with prosecutor concerning how to decide a case); Figueroa v. Kapelman, 526 F. Supp. 681, 683–84 (S.D.N.Y. 1981) (judge was immune for order to transfer an inmate to prevent a boycott of courts).

[776]Forrester v. White, 484 U.S. 219, 229–30, 108 S. Ct. 538 (1988) (employment decision concerning probation officer); Morrison v. Lipscomb, 877 F.2d 463, 465–66 (6th Cir. 1989) (order imposing two-week moratorium on certain writs during holiday season; "Any time an action taken by a judge is not an adjudication between parties, it is less likely that the act is a judicial one."); Santiago v. City of Philadelphia, 435 F. Supp. 136, 146 (E.D. Pa. 1977) (administration of juvenile detention center). *But see* Davis v. Tarrant County, Tex., 565 F.3d 214, 227 (5th Cir. 2009) (decision of which attorneys are eligible for court appointments "is inextricably linked to and cannot be separated from the act of appointing counsel in a particular case, which is clearly a judicial act"); *accord*, Roth v. King, 449 F.3d 1272, 1286–87 (D.C. Cir. 2006), *cert. denied*, 549 U.S. 1210 (2007).

[777]Pulliam v. Allen, 466 U.S. 522, 541–43, 104 S. Ct. 1970 (1984).

[778]42 U.S.C. § 1983. In *Roth v. King*, 449 F.3d 1272, 1286–87 (D.C. Cir. 2006), *cert. denied*, 549 U.S. 1210 (2007), the court characterized § 1983 as immunizing judges. We think it does not

immunize them but just sets a precondition for obtaining relief against them.

[779]*See, e.g.,* Whitesel v. Sengenberger, 222 F.3d 861, 867 (10th Cir. 2000) (court's pretrial officers were immune for assisting in bond-setting and issuing form temporary restraining orders in domestic violence cases; "[A]bsolute judicial immunity has been extended to non-judicial officers where their duties had an integral relationship with the judicial process.") (internal quotation marks omitted); McArdle v. Tronetti, 961 F.2d 1083, 1085 (3d Cir. 1992) (prison physician and prison counselor were absolutely immune as to their testimony in court and psychiatric reports to the judge, as that was an "integral part of the judicial process"); Turney v. O'Toole, 898 F.2d 1470, 1472 (10th Cir.1990) (state prison superintendent and psychologist were entitled to absolute immunity when they transferred the defendant to the facility pursuant to a facially valid court order (quotations and citations omitted) (alteration in the original)); Valdez v. City of Denver, 878 F.2d 1285, 1288–90 (10th Cir. 1989) (deputy sheriffs executing a facially valid court order were immune); *see also* Roth v. King, 449 F.3d 1272, 1287 (D.C. Cir. 2006) (director of public defender service was immune from § 1983 suit for injunctive relief for administrative role in indigent defense system), *cert. denied*, 549 U.S. 1210 (2007).

Court clerks are generally absolutely immune for their performance of discretionary functions that are closely related to the judicial process. *See, e.g.,* Kincaid v. Vail, 969 F.2d 594, 601 (7th Cir. 1992) (court clerks were immune for returning complaint and filing fee and telling the plaintiff to go to small claims court at a judge's direction). Courts have disagreed whether clerks are entitled to absolutely immune for ministerial actions (those involving no discretion) done at a judge's direction. *Compare* McCaw v. Winter, 745 F.2d 533, 534 (4th Cir. 1984) (clerk was absolutely immune for actions with respect to jury selection done per judge's orders) *with* Morrison v. Lipscomb, 877 F.2d 463, 468 (6th Cir. 1989) (no immunity at all for actions dictated by court order and leaving no discretion).

[780]Antoine v. Byers & Anderson, Inc., 508 U.S. 429, 434–36, 113 S. Ct. 2167 (1993).

[781]Imbler v. Pachtman, 424 U.S. 409, 431, 96 S. Ct. 984 (1975); *accord*, Kalina v. Fletcher, 522 U.S. 118, 129 118 S. Ct. 502 (1997) (prosecutor was absolutely immune for preparation and filing of information and motion for an arrest warrant); Buckley v. Fitzsimmons, 509 U.S. 259, 273, 113 S. Ct. 2606 (1993) (prosecutors were entitled to absolute immunity for acts associated with the initiation of judicial proceedings, including "professional evaluation of the evidence assembled by the police and appropriate preparation for its presentation at trial or before a grand jury after a decision to seek an indictment has been made"); Burns v. Reed, 500 U.S. 478, 487–89, 111 S. Ct. 1934 (1991) (prosecutor was absolutely immune for court appearance at probable cause hearing); Broam v. Bogan, 320 F.3d 1023, 1030 (9th Cir. 2003) (prosecutor's failure to comply with *Brady* rule involves "an exercise of the prosecutorial function and entitles [him] to absolute immunity from a civil suit for damages"). In *Cousins v. Lockyer*, 568 F.3d 1063 (9th Cir. 2009), the

been wrongfully convicted.[782] However, they are not absolutely immune for actions not directly related to presenting cases in court.[783] Absolute immunity does protect some administrative actions by prosecutors that have a close relationship to presenting cases in court.[784] Police officers and other witnesses enjoy absolute immunity from damages under § 1983 for their testimony and other participation in judicial proceedings,[785] though this absolute immunity does not necessarily extend to testimony or participation in *ex parte* (non-adversary) proceedings.[786]

Officials involved in "quasi-judicial" proceedings may have absolute immunity as do judges and prosecutors involved in judicial proceedings. This generally does *not* include prison officials involved in prosecuting or deciding disciplinary charges. They are entitled only to qualified immunity, not absolute immunity, because prison disciplinary proceedings lack most of the procedural safeguards of court proceedings and of non-prison administrative proceedings.[787] The same is true of grievance personnel.[788]

Parole and probation officials and employees, like judges, prosecutors, and those who work under them, are entitled to absolute immunity for decisions to grant or revoke parole and for the conduct of parole and probation hearings.[789] They also enjoy absolute immunity for matters involving the judicial sentencing process.[790] They are entitled only to qualified immunity when they perform administrative

---

court held that the state Attorney General was immune from suit for the plaintiff's continued imprisonment under a statute that had been held unconstitutional by the state courts, since the Attorney General would have had to petition the court for the plaintiff's release, which would involve "his role as an advocate for the State." *Cousins*, 568 F.3d at 1068.

[782]Van de Kamp v. Goldstein, ___ U.S. ___, 129 S. Ct. 855, 860–61 (2009).

[783]Kalina v. Fletcher, 522 U.S. 118, 131, 118 S. Ct. 502 (1997) (prosecutor was not absolutely immune for swearing to a probable cause certificate, since she was acting as a witness and not an advocate); Buckley v. Fitzsimmons, 509 U.S. at 268–69 (prosecutor was not absolutely immune for fabricating evidence during preliminary investigation and for public statements); Burns v. Reed, 509 U.S. at 492–95 (prosecutor was entitled only to qualified immunity for advice to police during an investigation); Mink v. Suthers, 482 F.3d 1244, 1263 (10th Cir. 2007) (absolute immunity not available to prosecutor for review of search warrant before court proceedings began), *cert. denied*, 128 S. Ct. 1122 (2008); Smith v. Power, 346 F.3d 740, 742 (7th Cir. 2003) (city attorney who gave notice of demolition of unsafe building as first step in civil proceedings to demolish it was entitled to absolute immunity); Price v. Moody, 677 F.2d 676, 677–78 (8th Cir. 1981) (ordering prisoner's confinement under unlawful conditions); Henderson v. Fisher, 631 F.2d 1115, 1120 (3d Cir. 1980) (preservation of evidence); Leibowitz v. U.S. Dep't of Justice, 729 F. Supp. 556, 561–62 (E.D. Mich. 1989) (requesting a prisoner's segregation), *aff'd*, 914 F.2d 256 (6th Cir. 1990).

[784]Van de Kamp v. Goldstein, 129 S. Ct. at 861–62, 864 (holding district attorney and chief assistant were absolutely immune for alleged failure to train and supervise deputies in turning over impeachment-related information to the defense, and for failure to create an information management system concerning jailhouse informants); Cousins v. Lockyer, 568 F.3d at 1069 (holding Attorney General immune for failing to maintain a tracking system for appellate decisions with implications for individual prisoners' convictions).

[785]Briscoe v. LaHue, 460 U.S. 325, 103 S. Ct. 1108 (1983); Dornheim v. Sholes, 430 F.3d 919, 925 (8th Cir. 2005) (guardian *ad litem* and court-appointed medical experts granted absolute immunity as to testimony); Morstad v. Dep't of Corr. and Rehab., 147 F.3d 741, 744 (8th Cir. 1998) (court-appointed psychiatrist "enjoyed absolute immunity for the testimony and reports . . . submitted to the court").

[786]Kalina v. Fletcher, 522 U.S. 118, 131, 118 S. Ct. 502 (1997) (prosecutor was not immune for executing certification for *ex parte* determination of probable cause); Cruz v. Kauai County, 279 F.3d 1064, 1067–68 (9th Cir. 2002) (prosecutor was not immune for swearing to alleged facts in support of *ex parte* bail revocation motion; "he stepped outside of his prosecutorial role, and into the

role of witness, when he personally attested to the truth of facts in the affidavit"). *But see* Todd v. Weltman, Weinberg & Reis Co., L.P.A., 434 F.3d 432, 439–47 (6th Cir. 2006) (rejecting reasoning of *Cruz* and similar cases, noting that grand jury testimony is generally covered by immunity even though *ex parte*, but concluding that a witness supplying self-interested testimony in a garnishment proceeding is not immune).

[787]Cleavinger v. Saxner, 474 U.S. 193, 202, 106 S. Ct. 496 (1985); *see* Ch. 4, § D.1.r(4), for further discussion of this subject.

[788]Burks v. Raemisch, 555 F.3d 592, 595–96 (7th Cir. 2009) (inmate complaint examiner entitled to qualified immunity (citing Cleavinger v. Saxner, *supra*)); Ferreiras v. York County, Pa., 2006 WL 508048, *3 (M.D.Pa., Mar. 1, 2006); Lindell v. O'Donnell, 2005 WL 2740999, *14–15 (W.D.Wis., Oct. 21, 2005) (repudiating earlier decision finding absolute immunity for complaint examiners). *Cf.* Hamilton v. Leavy, 322 F.3d 776, 777–86 (3d Cir. 2003) (district court should have assessed degree of independence of Classification Committee and the procedural protections of its process before rejecting members' claim to absolute immunity).

[789]Williams v. Consovoy, 453 F.3d 173, 178–79 (3d Cir. 2006) (private psychologist who contracted with state to perform evaluation and present his findings to parole board enjoyed absolute immunity from inmate's § 1983 action alleging wrongful denial of parole based upon his report); Figg v. Russell, 433 F.3d 593, 597–99 & n.1 (8th Cir. 2006) (parole board members, parole agent, and prison staffers were immune from damages for revocation of suspended sentence and incarceration); Scotto v. Almenas, 143 F.3d 105, 111 (2d Cir. 1998) ("[A] parole board official is absolutely immune from liability for damages when he decides to grant, deny, or revoke parole, because this task is functionally comparable to that of a judge." (internal quotation marks omitted)); Wilson v. Kelkhoff, 86 F.3d 1438, 1444 (7th Cir. 1996) (parole board members were entitled to absolute immunity for parole revocation).

Some courts have extended this immunity very broadly to all matters connected with parole decisions. *See* Thompson v. Duke, 882 F.2d 1180, 1183–85 (7th Cir. 1989) (scheduling of hearings).

[790]Peay v. Ajello, 470 F.3d 65, 70 (2d Cir. 2006) (probation officer had absolute immunity for preparation and submission of presentence report); Hili v. Sciarrota, 140 F.3d 210, 213–17 (2d Cir. 1998); Turner v. Barry, 856 F.2d 1539, 1540–41 (D.C. Cir. 1988) and cases cited (probation officer was immune for allegedly false pre-sentencing report).

or executive functions[791] and investigating violations and initiating revocation proceedings.[792] At least one court has held that a state governor's extradition officer performs quasi-judicial duties and is therefore immune.[793]

Legislators, whether state, local, or regional,[794] are generally held to be immune for their legislative acts,[795]

---

[791]King v. Simpson, 189 F.3d 284, 288 (2d Cir. 1999) (allegation that parole commissioner delayed plaintiff's release for months should not have been dismissed on absolute immunity grounds without a record showing whether his actions were quasi-adjudicative or merely administrative); Anton v. Getty, 78 F.3d 393, 396 (8th Cir. 1996) (scheduling pre-parole placement in community corrections center was "logistical" and not protected by absolute immunity).

[792]Trask v. Franco, 446 F.3d 1036, 1039, 1044–45 (10th Cir. 2006) (probation officer only entitled to qualified immunity for unlawful residential search); O'Rourke v. Hayes, 378 F.3d 1201, 1209–10 (11th Cir. 2004) (probation officer entitled only to qualified immunity for search of parolee's work office); Swift v. California, 384 F.3d 1184, 1191–92 (9th Cir. 2004) (parole agent entitled only to qualified immunity as to investigating parole violation, ordering issuance of parole hold and arrest of parolee); Wilson v. Kelkhoff, 86 F.3d 1438, 1445–46 (7th Cir. 1996) (employee who prepared and filed parole revocation charges was not entitled to absolute immunity); Jones v. Moore, 986 F.2d 251, 253 (8th Cir. 1993) (issuance of parole violation report); Harper v. Jeffries, 808 F.2d 281, 284 (3d Cir. 1986) (initiation of charges and presentation of evidence at revocation hearing by probation officer); Ray v. Pickett, 734 F.2d 370, 373–74 (8th Cir. 1984) (filing of violation report by probation officer); see Dawson v. Newman, 419 F.3d 656, 662 (7th Cir. 2005) (parole officials were not entitled to absolute immunity where they refused to investigate plaintiff's (correct) claim that he was entitled to release from supervision).

The Supreme Court adopted a "functional" test for assessing the immunity of non-judicial officials. Antoine v. Byers & Anderson, Inc., 508 U.S. 429, 434–36, 113 S. Ct. 2167 (1993). This decision narrowed the scope of absolute immunity that some lower courts had recognized, so earlier decisions on this subject may not be reliable. See Swift v. California, 384 F.3d 1184 at 1190 (recognizing the partial overruling of Anderson v. Boyd, 714 F.2d 906 (9th Cir. 1983), which had immunized any action "related to" the grant, revocation, or denial of parole).

[793]White v. Armontrout, 29 F.3d 357, 360 (8th Cir. 1994).

[794]Federal legislators are protected from liability for their legislative acts by the Speech and Debate Clause, U.S. Const., Art. I, § 6. Bastien v. Office of Senator Ben Nighthorse Campbell, 390 F.3d 1301, 1305–15 (10th Cir. 2004) and cases cited.

[795]Bogan v. Scott-Harris, 523 U.S. 44, 51–53, 118 S. Ct. 966 (1998); Supreme Court of Virginia v. Consumers Union, 446 U.S. 719, 732, 100 S. Ct. 1967 (1980); Shoultes v. Laidlaw, 886 F.2d 114, 117 (6th Cir. 1989) and cases cited; see Mitchell v. Kirk, 20 F.3d 936 (8th Cir. 1994) (state legislator who wrote to prison officials questioning a prisoner's privileges was performing a legislative function).

Legislative immunity extends to injunctive relief as well as damage suits. Supreme Court of Virginia v. Consumers Union, 446 U.S. at 733. It also extends to non-legislative officials when they perform functions that are part of the legislative process, such as introducing a budget or signing an ordinance into law. Bogan v. Scott-Harris, 523 U.S. 44, 55, 118 S. Ct. 966 (1998).

but not for their administrative or managerial actions.[796] However, this immunity does not protect local governments themselves, which are often liable under § 1983 for acts of their legislative bodies.[797]

3. Immunity of Federal Officials for Common-Law Torts

By statute, federal employees are immune from liability for all torts committed within the scope of their employment; the FTCA is the exclusive remedy for such torts.[798]

The statute's coverage is limited to state law torts, so you can still bring *Bivens* claims against federal officials to remedy constitutional violations.[799] In cases alleging constitutional violations, federal officials are generally entitled to the same personal immunities as state officials.[800]

4. Qualified Immunity

Qualified immunity means that an official must have fair notice of the law before being subject to suit for damages for violating it.[801] Qualified immunity protects officials from damage liability in federal civil rights cases[802] unless they

---

[796]An action is protected by legislative immunity if it is legislative in form (*e.g.*, voting for an ordinance, or submitting legislation for action, or signing it into law) and in substance (*i.e.*, "a discretionary, policymaking decision"). Bogan v. Scott-Harris, 523 U.S. at 55. *Compare* Kamplain v. Curry County Bd. of Com'rs, 159 F.3d 1248, 1252 (10th Cir. 1998) (banning an individual from speaking at county legislature's meetings was administrative and not legislative); Ryan v. Burlington County, 889 F.2d 1286, 1290–91 (3d Cir. 1989) (county freeholders were not immune for "managerial" decisions concerning daily operations of a jail); Hernandez v. Gates, 100 F. Supp. 2d 1209, 1212 (C.D.Cal. 2000) (city council decisions to indemnify police officers for punitive damages were administrative, not legislative); *see* Bastien v. Office of Senator Ben Nighthorse Campbell, 390 F.3d 1301 (10th Cir. 2004) (U.S. Senator not immune under Speech and Debate Clause for employment and retaliation claim).

[797]Board of County Comm'rs v. Umbehr, 518 U.S. 668, 677 n.*, 116 S. Ct. 2342 (1996) (legislative immunity applies only to legislators in their individual capacities); *see* § B.4.b of this chapter concerning municipal liability.

[798]28 U.S.C. § 2679(b)(1); *see* § C.2 of this chapter for discussion of the FTCA and the operation of this statutory immunity.

[799]*See* § B.2.c of this chapter concerning *Bivens* actions.

[800]*See* cases cited in § B.2.c of this chapter, n.85. The federal government itself enjoys sovereign immunity except in those circumstances where it has consented to suit. See § L.1.b of this chapter.

[801]Hope v. Pelzer, 536 U.S. 730, 739–40, 122 S. Ct. 2508 (2002).

[802]Qualified immunity applies to state law claims only if state law provides for it. Cousins v. Lockyer, 568 F.3d 1063, 1072 (9th Cir. 2009) (California qualified immunity does not apply to tort claims or state civil rights claims); Napolitano v. Flynn, 949 F.2d 617, 620–21 (2d Cir. 1991) (cited in Kerman v. City of New York, 374 F.3d 93, 116 (2d Cir. 2004)); Lee v. Cline, 384 Md. 245, 258–59, 863 A.2d 297 (Md. 2004) (Maryland courts have rejected qualified

violate "clearly established statutory or constitutional rights of which a reasonable person would have known."[803] It focuses on "the objective reasonableness of an official's conduct, as measured by reference to clearly established law," rather than their motives or other aspects of their state of mind.[804] Under this objective standard, it is not a defense that officials did not actually know what the law required.[805]

Qualified immunity only applies to officials sued in their individual capacities for money damages. It does not protect municipalities or officials sued in their official capacities,[806] and it does not apply to claims for injunctive relief.[807] Employees of private prisons, and other private parties who act under color of state law, are not protected by qualified immunity,[808] though they may possess a similar "good faith" defense.[809]

The Supreme Court has described qualified immunity as extending to "officials performing discretionary functions."[810] Some courts have held that officials who exceed their discretion are not entitled to immunity.[811] Other courts have rejected or questioned this distinction.[812]

The Supreme Court used to say that courts deciding qualified immunity claims should first decide whether the plaintiff had alleged or shown a violation of law at all, and then decide whether that law was clearly established. It has now changed its mind and said that lower courts can, if they prefer, decide the "clearly established" question first.[813] That means that, if the law is not established, the claims may be dismissed without a decision as to whether the challenged conduct violates the law.

When an official claims qualified immunity, the court must generally determine whether the law was clearly established at the time the defendant committed the allegedly illegal acts.[814]

Law can be clearly established in several ways. If the defendants directly violate a court judgment or order, they have of course violated clearly established law.[815] Law can also be clearly established by decisions of the Supreme Court or of the state or federal courts in the jurisdiction where the acts occurred.[816] Some courts also hold that decisions from

---

immunity for state constitutional violations and most intentional torts, but state Tort Claims Act provides immunity for employees and a separate remedy against the State for torts committed within the scope of employment). Most courts have held that qualified immunity is not available under the FTCA. *See* § C.2.a of this chapter.

[803]Harlow v. Fitzgerald, 457 U.S. 800, 817–18, 102 S. Ct. 2727 (1982). The question has also been stated as "whether a reasonable officer could have believed [her actions] to be lawful, in light of clearly established law and the information the [defendant] possessed." Anderson v. Creighton, 483 U.S. 635, 641, 107 S. Ct. 3034 (1987).

[804]*Harlow*, 457 U.S. at 818.

The defendants' state of mind is often relevant to the question whether they violated the law at all, since some constitutional claims require proof of malice, deliberate indifference, or other subjective element. *See* Ch. 2, §§ A.2, F.1, G.1.a, G.2.

[805]Chandler v. Baird, 926 F.2d 1057, 1060 (11th Cir. 1991) (fact that neither defendant "understood" that their actions were illegal did not establish qualified immunity).

[806]Leatherman v. Tarrant County Narcotics Intelligence and Coordination Unit, 507 U.S. 163, 166–67, 113 S. Ct. 1160 (1993) (citing Owens v. City of Independence, 445 U.S. 622, 100 S. Ct. 1398 (1980)); P.C. v. McLaughlin, 913 F.2d 1033, 1039 (2d Cir. 1990).

This is true even if the defendants are immune in their individual capacities. *See, e.g.,* Clark v. Tinnin, 731 F. Supp. 998, 1007 (D. Colo. 1990).

[807]South Carolina St. Board of Dentistry v. F.T.C., 455 F.3d 436, 446–47 (4th Cir. 2006); American Fire, Theft & Collision Managers, Inc. v. Gillespie, 932 F.2d 816, 818 (9th Cir. 1991).

[808]*See* § B.1.c of this chapter, nn.37–38.

[809]*See* § B.1.c, n.39.

[810]Harlow v. Fitzgerald, 457 U.S. 800, 818, 102 S. Ct. 2727 (1982).

[811]Harbert Intern., Inc. v. James, 157 F.3d 1271, 1281 (11th Cir. 1998); *In re* Allen, 106 F.3d 582, 592–97 (4th Cir. 1997) (official who acts completely outside the scope of her authority as clearly limited by statutes and regulations is not entitled to immunity); Boretti v. Wiscomb, 930 F.2d 1150, 1156 (6th Cir. 1991) (prison pharmacist who refused to fill a prescription was not immune because he lacked discretion to refuse a doctor's order); Howard v. Adkison, 887 F.2d 134, 140 (8th Cir. 1989) (defendants who acted in violation of prison policies were not immune); Woods v. White, 689 F. Supp. 874, 877 (W.D.Wis. 1988) (disclosing medical information about a prisoner was not within prison officials' discretion), *aff'd*, 899 F.2d 17 (7th Cir. 1990).

[812]*See, e.g.,* McIntosh v. Weinberger, 810 F.2d 1411, 1432 (8th Cir. 1987), *vacated on other grounds*, 487 U.S 1212, 108 S. Ct. 2861 (1988); Gagne v. City of Galveston, 805 F.2d 558, 559–60 (5th Cir. 1986).

[813]Pearson v. Callahan, ___ U.S. ___, 129 S. Ct. 808, 818 (2009).

[814]Harlow v. Fitzgerald, 457 U.S. at 818.

[815]Davis v. Hall, 375 F.3d 703, 713–14 (8th Cir. 2004); Slone v. Herman, 983 F.2d 107, 109–10 (8th Cir. 1993); Cortes-Quinones v. Jiminez-Nettleship, 842 F.2d 556, 561–62 (1st Cir. 1988); Dzana v. Foti, 829 F.2d 558, 562 (5th Cir. 1987); Williams v. Bennett, 689 F.2d 1370, 1385–86 (11th Cir. 1982); Tasker v. Moore, 738 F. Supp. 1005, 1011 (S.D. W.Va. 1990); *see* Kaminsky v. Rosenblum, 737 F. Supp. 1309, 1319 (S.D.N.Y. 1990) (federal court consent judgment may serve to make officials "particularly aware of the legal requirements"), *appeal dismissed*, 929 F.2d 922 (2d Cir. 1991). However, prison officials may be entitled to qualified immunity for violations of court orders so long and complicated that they cannot be expected to know all their terms. Green v. McKaskle, 788 F.2d 1116, 1124 (5th Cir. 1986).

[816]*See, e.g.,* Jenkins by Hall v. Talladega City Bd. of Educ., 115 F.3d 821, 826 n.4 (11th Cir. 1997) ("In this circuit, the law can be clearly established for qualified immunity purposes only by decisions of the U.S. Supreme Court, Eleventh Circuit Court of Appeals, or the highest court of the state where the case arose." (internal quotations omitted)).

other jurisdictions may establish the law.[817] If court rulings are inconsistent or contradictory, or there are only a few of them from lower courts or other jurisdictions, defendants are likely to be held immune.[818] Once the law is established, defendants are not entitled to immunity based on speculations that the law might change.[819]

State law and prison regulations are not "clearly established law" for qualified immunity purposes; officials do not automatically lose their federal law qualified immunity by violating them.[820] However, state law or regulations that conform to the Constitution may help show how well established the constitutional right is.[821] State law or regulations may also identify the officials who clearly had the duty to correct particular kinds of constitutional violations.[822]

Some courts have held that officials who violate regulations or state law may lose their immunity because they are no longer performing discretionary functions.[823]

On the other hand, officials may be entitled to qualified immunity if they act in reliance on statutes or regulations that have not previously been held unconstitutional.[824] However, reliance on statutes and regulations is not a defense if officials engage in clearly unconstitutional conduct.[825] (This issue is similar to the "following orders" defense discussed later in this section.[826])

You should consult Chapters 2 through 6 of this Manual to find out what law was clearly established at what time. We have cited as many cases as we could fit in, in part to help you deal with the qualified immunity defense.

Even if the law is clearly established in some general way, the defendants are immune unless it is "apparent" that their particular actions violated that law. That does not mean you have to find a prior case holding the defendants' exact actions unconstitutional.[827] A case must have "some but not precise factual correspondence with precedents" to give officials notice; they must apply "general, well-developed legal

---

[817]Novitsky v. City of Aurora, 491 F.3d 1244, 1255–56 (10th Cir. 2007) (finding law is clearly established if plaintiff presents law from "other circuits that is 'on point.'"); Tekle ex rel. Tekle v. U.S., 511 F.3d 839, 847 (9th Cir. 2007) (holding that "in the absence of binding precedent, we 'look to whatever decisional law is available to ascertain whether the law is clearly established for qualified immunity purposes, including decisions of state courts, other circuits, and district courts.'" (citations omitted)).

[818]Lee v. Dugger, 902 F.2d 822, 824 (11th Cir. 1990) (single decision of state intermediate appellate court did not establish the law); Hensley v. Wilson, 850 F.2d 269, 275 (6th Cir. 1988) (a single decision from another circuit cannot clearly establish the law); Doyle v. Camelot Care Centers, Inc., 160 F. Supp. 2d 891, 911 (N.D. Ill. 2001) (single decison from state appellate court not sufficient to clearly establish the law), aff'd, 305 F.3d 603 (7th Cir. 2002).

[819]Anderson v. Recore, 317 F.3d 194, 200–01 (2d Cir. 2003); Thompson v. County of Franklin, 987 F. Supp. 111, 119 (N.D.N.Y. 1997), motion granted on other grounds, 127 F. Supp. 2d 145 (N.D.N.Y. 2000), aff'd, 314 F.3d 79 (2d Cir. 2002); Bass v. Coughlin, 800 F.Supp 1066, 1071 (N.D.N.Y. 1991), aff'd, 976 F.2d 98 (2d Cir. 1992).

[820]Davis v. Scherer, 468 U.S. 183, 195–97, 104 S. Ct. 3012 (1984) (holding that an official's clear violation of a state administrative regulation does not overcome qualified immunity); Doe v. Delie, 257 F.3d 309, 318–19 (3d Cir. 2001).

[821]Sepulveda v. Ramirez, 967 F.2d 1413, 1416 (9th Cir. 1992); Diercks v. Durham, 959 F.2d 710, 713 (8th Cir. 1992); Chalkboard, Inc. v. Brandt, 902 F.2d 1375, 1382 (9th Cir. 1989); Walters v. Western State Hospital, 864 F.2d 695, 699–700 (10th Cir. 1988); Young v. Keohane, 809 F.Supp 1185, 1197 (M.D. Pa. 1992); Valdez v. Farmon, 766 F. Supp. 1529, 1538–39 (E.D. Cal. 1991); O'Brien v. Borough of Woodbury Heights, 679 F. Supp. 429, 435–36 (D.N.J. 1988) (amendment of state statute limiting strip searches of arrestees helped overcome qualified immunity); see also Green v. Bauvi, 792 F. Supp. 928, 940 (S.D.N.Y. 1992) (where due process required a hearing within a "reasonable" time, defendants could not have reasonably believed that exceeding the time limit set by their own regulations was reasonable); cf. Hope v. Pelzer, 536 U.S. 730, 742–45, 122 S. Ct. 2508 (2002) (defendants' disregard of regulations mitigating the harshness of "hitching post" practice supports conclusion that defendants knew their conduct was wrongful).

[822]Alexander v. Perrill, 916 F.2d 1392, 1398 (9th Cir. 1990) (Federal Bureau of Prisons regulations and policies helped establish an officials' duty to investigate claim that prisoner was kept past his

release date); Feagin v. Broglin, 693 F. Supp. 736, 739 (N.D.Ind. 1988) (state regulations could defeat superintendent's claim to qualified immunity by indicating that he was responsible for reviewing disciplinary proceedings).

[823]See nn.811–812 of this section, above.

[824]Roska v. Peterson, 328 F.3d 1230, 1251 (10th Cir. 2003) (reliance on advice of counsel or on a statute can constitute "extraordinary circumstances" making actions objectively reasonable even if they violate established law); Bahrampour v. Lampert, 356 F.3d 969, 977 (9th Cir. 2004) (officials could reasonably rely on regulations that had been upheld by some courts); Wolfel v. Morris, 972 F.2d 712, 720 (6th Cir. 1992).

[825]Guillemard-Ginorio v. Contreras-Gomez, 490 F.3d 31, 40 (1st Cir. 2007) (reliance on "patently unconstitutional" statute did not confer immunity); Lawrence v. Reed, 406 F.3d 1224, 1232 (10th Cir. 2005) (" . . . [T]the overarching inquiry is whether, in spite of the existence of the statute, a reasonable officer should have known that his conduct was unlawful.").

[826]See nn.837–841, below.

[827]Anderson v. Creighton, 483 U.S. 635, 640, 107 S. Ct. 3034 (1987); see also Hope v. Pelzer, 536 U.S. 730, 739–40, 122 S. Ct. 2508 (2002) (officials can be on notice that their conduct violates established law even in "novel circumstances"; courts need not have held that "fundamentally similar" conduct was unlawful to defeat qualified immunity).

principles" to the varying situations they face.[828] They cannot escape liability by making fine distinctions.[829]

Officials are expected to use common sense in assessing their legal obligations.[830] If an infringement of rights is extreme, sweeping, or obvious, those responsible for it are not immune even if there is no prior factually similar case.[831]

Similarly, if defendants offer no reasonable correctional justification for their conduct, the lack of a prior "case in point" will not make them immune.[832]

A defendant may be entitled to qualified immunity even where the law was clearly established if she lacked enough information about the facts to know that her actions

---

[828]Sparr v. Warden, 306 F.3d 589, 593 (8th Cir. 2002) (citation omitted); McMillian v. Johnson, 88 F.3d 1554, 1565 (11th Cir. 1996) (where punishment of pretrial detainees was generally forbidden, transferring a detainee to death row for punitive reasons was not protected by immunity despite lack of a prior case in point); Eastwood v. Department of Corrections of State of Oklahoma, 846 F.2d 627, 630 (10th Cir. 1988) ("some but not precise factual correspondence" to previous case law is required to defeat qualified immunity); Brooks v. Berg, 270 F. Supp. 2d 302, 311 (N.D.N.Y. 2003) (where the general right of prisoners to receive medical care was established, defendants were not entitled to qualified immunity for denying care for transsexualism), *vacated in part on other grounds*, 289 F. Supp. 2d 286 (N.D.N.Y., Oct. 29, 2003); *see* U.S. v. Lanier, 520 U.S. 259, 271, 117 S. Ct. 1219 (1997) (adopting same standard in criminal case).

[829]For example, one court denied immunity to a pharmacist who allegedly refused to fill a prisoner's prescription. Even though there was no prior law spelling out prison pharmacists' constitutional duties, it was clearly established that, in general, intentional interference with treatment prescribed by a doctor is unlawful. Johnson v. Hay, 931 F.2d 456, 460–61 (8th Cir. 1991) (citing Estelle v. Gamble, 429 U.S. 97, 105, 97 S. Ct. 285 (1976)); *see* Hope v. Pelzer, 536 U.S. 730, 742–43, 122 S. Ct. 2508 (2002) (where prior law prohibited handcuffing inmates to a fence for long periods, officials were not immune for handcuffing them to a "hitching post"); Clement v. Gomez, 298 F.3d 898, 906 (9th Cir. 2002) (where it was clearly established that interference with access to medical care is unconstitutional, officers who prevented prisoners exposed to pepper spray from being decontaminated were not entitled to immunity despite lack of a case in point); Henderson v. DeRobertis, 940 F.2d 1055, 1059 (7th Cir. 1991) (since the right to adequate heat and shelter was clearly established, officials were liable for failing to provide extra clothing or blankets when the prison heat failed in sub-zero weather even though there was no case law concerning these abnormal conditions); Powell v. Lennon, 914 F.2d 1459, 1464 (11th Cir. 1990) (unlawfulness of exposing prisoner to asbestos hazard "should have been apparent" in light of law forbidding deliberate indifference to medical needs); Greason v. Kemp, 891 F.2d 829, 833–35 (11th Cir. 1990) (the right to psychiatric care was clearly established; no precedent was needed that abruptly discontinuing medication without examining the patient's record or conducting a mental status examination denied that right).

[830]Giebel v. Sylvester, 244 F.3d 1182, 1189 (9th Cir. 2001) (holding that "even if there is no closely analogous case law, a right can be clearly established on the basis of 'common sense.'"); Sepulveda v. Ramirez, 967 F.2d 1413, 1416 (9th Cir. 1992) (officer was not immune for conduct that "runs contrary to common sense, decency," and state regulations); Howard v. Adkison, 887 F.2d 134, 140 (8th Cir. 1989) (illegality of filthy conditions was apparent; "common sense is sometimes helpful"); Walters v. Western State Hosp., 864 F.2d 695, 699 (10th Cir. 1988).

[831]Brosseau v. Haugen, 543 U.S. 194, 198, 125 S. Ct. 596 (2004) ("in an obvious case, [general] standards can 'clearly establish'

[a right] . . . even without a body of relevant case law."); *see* Tekle ex rel. Tekle v. U.S., 511 F.3d 839, 848 (9th Cir. 2006) (where 20 officers were present for an arrest, handcuffing and pointing guns at an 11-year old who posed no threat was obviously unreasonable); Austin v. Johnson, 328 F.3d 204, 210 (5th Cir. 2003) (waiting two hours to call an ambulance after a prisoner had lost consciousness from the heat was obviously unlawful); McDonald v. Haskins, 966 F.2d 292, 295 (7th Cir. 1992) (stating "[i]t should have been obvious" that threatening to shoot a nine-year-old child was unlawful); Martin v. Board of County Commissioners of Pueblo County, 909 F.2d 402, 407 (10th Cir. 1990) (unlawfulness of removing an arrestee with a broken neck from the hospital violated clearly established law regarding unreasonable seizures); Jackson v. Elrod, 881 F.2d 441, 446 (7th Cir. 1989) (defendants were not immune for imposing a complete ban on hardcover books, even with covers removed); Parker v. Williams, 862 F.2d 1471, 1477 (11th Cir. 1989) (sheriff who hired a deputy who had a history of indecent exposure, mental problems, and drug use was not entitled to qualified immunity for violating the "Fourteenth Amendment right to be free from arbitrary risks of serious personal injury during pre-trial detainment"); Hammond v. Gordon County, 316 F. Supp. 2d 1262, 1286 (N.D.Ga. 2002) (sexual harassment and abuse of prisoners was obviously unconstitutional regardless of lack of case law); Landman v. Royster, 354 F. Supp. 1292, 1318 (E.D.Va. 1973) (qualified immunity denied when violations were "of such a shocking nature that no reasonable man could have believed that they were constitutional").

One federal circuit has held that in Eighth or Fourteenth Amendment use of force cases, which require showing an "extreme" subjective element of malicious and sadistic intent, qualified immunity is not available once that showing has been made. Johnson v. Breeden, 280 F.3d 1308, 1321 (11th Cir. 2002); *accord*, Fennell v. Gilstrap, 559 F.3d 1212, 1216–17 (11th Cir. 2009).

[832]Quinn v. Nix, 983 F.2d 115, 119 (8th Cir. 1993) (officials who forced inmates to cut their hair without a legitimate penological reason were not immune); Allen v. Higgins, 902 F.2d 682, 684 (8th Cir. 1990) (official who censored catalog without examining it was not immune); Williams v. Lane, 851 F.2d 867, 882–83 (7th Cir. 1988) (lack of a rational basis for various restriction in protective custody defeated qualified immunity); Van Poyck v. Dugger, 779 F. Supp. 571, 577 (M.D.Fla. 1991); Hill v. Koon, 732 F. Supp. 1076, 1083 (D.Nev. 1990) (officials were not immune for intrusive rectal searches when jury found no rational relationship to legitimate penological purposes); *see also* Marriott by and through Marriott v. Smith, 931 F.2d 517, 520–21 (8th Cir. 1991) (defendants who failed to get a warrant to search a visitor after her visit, when she had no further opportunity to smuggle contraband, could not rely on the "prison visitor exception" to the warrant requirement, and were not entitled to qualified immunity); Griffin v. Lombardi, 946 F.2d 604, 607–08 (8th Cir. 1991) (officials who presented rational justification for rule were not entitled to immunity when there was evidence that they did not follow their own rule in dealing with other inmates).

violated that law[833]—though defendants will be liable if they *should* have reasonably obtained more information.[834] A defendant may also be immune for clear constitutional violations if they were beyond her power to prevent.[835]

Even if a defendant's actions violated clearly established law, she may still be immune based on "extraordinary circumstances."[836] For example, a defendant's claim that she acted on the legal advice of counsel may establish the immunity defense, though only under limited circumstances.[837]

Whether following the orders of superiors or the rules and policies of employers supports a qualified immunity defense,[838] or not,[839] seems to turn on the court's view of the particular circumstances of the case. Where the "followers" had no reason to know that the orders were unlawful, or where they were acting pursuant to long-established institutional policy, they are more likely to be granted immunity.[840]

---

[833]Anderson v. Creighton, 483 U.S. 635, 641, 107 S. Ct. 3034 (1987) (qualified immunity is assessed "in light of . . . the information the [defendants] possessed"); Cannon v. City & County of Denver, 998 F.2d 867, 874 (10th Cir. 1993) ("The circumstances must be such that the defendant was so 'prevented' from knowing that his actions were unconstitutional that he should not be imputed with knowledge of a clearly established right." (citation and footnote omitted)); Floyd v. Laws, 929 F.2d 1390, 1393–94 (9th Cir. 1991); Foster v. Basham 932 F.2d 732, 735 (8th Cir. 1991); Moore v. Dowd, 731 F. Supp. 921, 924 (E.D.Mo. 1990).

In a prison mental health care case, the court stated that the question is "whether a reasonable doctor in the same circumstances and possessing the same knowledge as [the defendants] could have concluded that his actions were lawful." Waldrop v. Evans, 871 F.2d 1030, 1034 (11th Cir. 1989).

[834]Jones v. Wilhelm, 425 F.3d 455, 461 (7th Cir. 2005) (requiring actual knowledge of relevant facts to overcome immunity in all cases would allow state actors to "trample on the constitutional rights of citizens by maintaining willful ignorance").

[835]McCord v. Maggio, 927 F.2d 844, 848 (5th Cir. 1991) ("extraordinary circumstances" such as budgetary constraints and lack of feasible alternatives might support immunity); Birrell v. Brown, 867 F.2d 956, 959 (6th Cir. 1989) (prison officials were immune for unconstitutional conditions caused by budgetary restraints); see also Dean v. Thomas, 933 F. Supp. 600, 607–609 (S.D.Miss. 1996) (acknowledging principle, finding these defendants not immune).

[836]Harlow v. Fitzgerald, 457 U.S. 800, 818–19, 102 S. Ct. 2727 (1982).

[837]Courts are aware of the danger that officials could be immunized from liability "via the simple expedient of consulting counsel," Melton v. Oklahoma City, 879 F.2d 706, 731 (10th Cir. 1989), and have proceeded cautiously in recognizing such a defense. See Lawrence v. Reed, 406 F.3d 1224, 1230–31 (10th Cir. 2005) (holding that legal consultation will lead to qualified immunity if "the consultation so 'prevented' [the official] from knowing that his actions were unconstitutional that he should not be imputed with knowledge of a clearly established right." (citing Roska ex rel. Roska v. Peterson, 328 F.3d 1230, 1251 (10th Cir. 2003))); Dixon v. Wallowa County, 336 F.3d 1013, 1019 (9th Cir. 2003) (whether counsel's advice can establish qualified immunity depends on whether counsel was independent, whether advice concerned constitutionality of the conduct in question, whether counsel was aware of all relevant facts, and whether advice was sought before the defendant acted). Compare Woodwind Estates v. Gretkowski, 205 F.3d 118, 125 (3d Cir. 2000) (qualified immunity claim rejected where legal advice was not reasonable and law was not unclear); Buonocore v. Harris, 134 F.3d 245, 252–53 (4th Cir. 1998) (reliance on legal advice does not establish qualified immunity if the defendant did not follow the advice); Walters v. Grossheim, 990 F.2d 381, 384 (8th Cir. 1993) (defendants who

disobeyed a court order to release a prisoner were not immune based on legal advice that the order was not lawful); Naugle v. Witney, 755 F. Supp. 1504, 1518 (D. Utah 1990) (holding that officials who give legal advice contrary to clearly established law maybe held liable).

If defendants claim that they relied on the advice of counsel, they may waive their attorney–client privilege and you may be entitled to discovery concerning their communications with their lawyers. Mitzner v. Sobol, 136 F.R.D. 359, 361–62 (S.D.N.Y. 1991); Hearn v. Rhay, 68 F.R.D. 574, 581 (E.D.Wash.1975). But see Ross v. City of Memphis, 423 F.3d 596, 603–05 (6th Cir. 2005) (individual defendant's assertion of qualified immunity did not waive City's privilege with respect to defendant's conversations with City attorney).

[838]Lauro v. Charles, 219 F.3d 202, 216 n.10 (2d Cir. 2000) (following orders was one factor supporting immunity); DeToledo v. County of Suffolk, 379 F. Supp. 2d 138, 149 (D.Mass. 2005) ("That the defendants are excused from liability by virtue of 'following orders' is not intuitively appealing, but also not shocking in a correctional environment strongly influenced by military values of hierarchy and obedience to orders." A contrary rule "would appear neither constitutionally wise nor institutionally desirable," nor fair to rank and file staff.).

[839]O'Rourke v. Hayes, 378 F.3d 1201, 1210 n.5 (11th Cir. 2004) (stating "since World War II, the 'just following orders' defense has not occupied a respected position in our jurisprudence"); Thaddeus-X v. Blatter, 175 F.3d 378, 393 (6th Cir. 1999) ("Reliance on a superior's orders does not in itself dissipate all liability."); Patzner v. Burkett, 779 F.2d 1363, 1371 (8th Cir. 1985) (acting pursuant to orders "does not provide a basis for broader immunity").

[840]Bilida v. McCleod, 211 F.3d 166, 174–75 (1st Cir. 2000) ("Plausible instructions from a superior or fellow officer support qualified immunity where, viewed objectively in light of the surrounding circumstances, they could lead a reasonable officer to conclude that the necessary legal justification for his actions exists."); Hartsfield v. Lemacks, 50 F.3d 950, 956 (11th Cir. 1995) (officers who had no reason to know they were searching the wrong house were immune, although the deputy who led them to it and did nothing to make sure it was the right house was not immune); Vela v. White, 703 F.2d 147, 152 (5th Cir. 1983) (officer who made arrest without probable cause at superior's instruction, but had not been present during the whole incident and had only been on the job a year, was immune); Williams v. Goord, 142 F. Supp. 2d 416, 430 (S.D.N.Y. 2001) ("Higher ranking officials are held to a higher standard of legal knowledge than their subordinates. . . . As these officers had no input into the development and implementation of the restraint policy and were merely following what they believed to be lawful orders, they are entitled to qualified immunity."); Smallwood v. Renfro, 708 F. Supp. 182, 191 (N.D. Ill. 1989) (sergeant was entitled to qualified immunity for relying on his superior's evaluation of the facts).

Where their actions are more clearly contrary to established law, immunity is more likely to be denied.[841]

Procedurally, qualified immunity is an affirmative defense that the defendants have the burden of pleading[842] (though of course the plaintiff must plead a violation of clearly established federal law in the first place[843]). Ordinarily, affirmative defenses are waived if not pled or not pursued promptly during the litigation.[844] However, courts have been extremely lenient in allowing defendants to raise the defense late—even at trial, or afterward—rather than hold that defendants waived it.[845]

Courts have disagreed over who has the burden of persuasion on qualified immunity.[846]

Qualified immunity is not just a protection from liability, but also "an entitlement not to stand trial or face the other burdens of litigation," such as discovery.[847] For that reason, courts have made special procedural rules for qualified immunity so it can be addressed early in a case. Defendants who raise a qualified immunity defense can file a motion to dismiss or for judgment on the pleadings, or a motion for summary judgment based on qualified immunity.[848] If they lose, they can raise it again at the next stage of the case.[849] If they lose a motion to dismiss or for summary judgment on qualified immunity, they are entitled to an immediate ("interlocutory") appeal if the qualified immunity issue is one of law (whether the defendants' actions violated clearly established law) and is not based solely on a factual dispute.[850] In practice, often qualified immunity appeals focus on whether the law was violated at all, not whether it was clearly established or extraordinary circumstances excused its violation.[851]

That means if the defendants simply deny doing what you accuse them of, they are not entitled to an

---

[841]California Attorneys for Criminal Justice v. Butts, 195 F.3d 1039, 1049–50 (9th Cir. 1999) (denying qualified immunity to police officers who intentionally violated *Miranda* rules and said they relied on the city's police training; "The fact that Los Angeles and Santa Monica may have trained their police to violate the rights of individuals does not provide any defense for these officers." Further, officers' training did not *require* them to violate *Miranda*.); J.H.H. v. O'Hara, 878 F.2d 240, 244 n.4 (8th Cir. 1989) ("Following orders does not constitute a 'good faith' defense against invidious racial discrimination."); Walters v. Western State Hospital, 864 F.2d 695, 700 (10th Cir. 1988) (policy of holding all newly admitted patients incommunicado for seven to ten days was clearly unlawful and defendants were not immune); Walsh v. Franco, 849 F.2d 66, 69–70 (2d Cir.1988) (denying qualified immunity for following jail strip search policy where that kind of policy had previously been held unconstitutional); Brooks v. Berg, 270 F. Supp. 2d 302, 312 (N.D.N.Y. 2003) ("Prison officials cannot deny transsexual inmates all medical treatment simply by referring to a prison policy which makes a seemingly arbitrary distinction between inmates who were and were not diagnosed with GID prior to incarceration." It is clearly established that officials must provide care for medical needs that arose before incarceration.), *vacated in part on other grounds*, Brooks v. Berg, 289 F. Supp. 2d 286 (N.D.N.Y. 2003).

[842]Crawford-El v. Britton, 523 U.S. 574, 587, 118 S. Ct. 1584 (1998) (citing Gomez v. Toledo, 446 U.S. 635, 639–641, 100 S. Ct. 1920 (1980)); Thomas v. Independence Tp., 463 F.3d 285, 293–94 (3d Cir. 2006). This means that defendants should raise qualified immunity in their answer, or in a motion to dismiss the complaint.

[843]Mitchell v. Forsyth, 472 U.S. 511, 526, 105 S. Ct. 2806 (1985).

[844]*See* McCardle v. Haddad, 131 F.3d 43, 51 (2d Cir. 1997) (holding that qualified immunity defense can be waived "either by failure to raise it in a timely fashion . . . or by failure to raise it with sufficient particularity"); *see* Sales v. Grant, 224 F.3d 293, 296 (4th Cir. 2000) (recognizing that qualified immunity, even if pled, can be waived on appeal if not "squarely presented" to district court).

[845]*See, e.g.*, Ridpath v. Board of Governors Marshall University, 447 F.3d 292, 305–06 (4th Cir. 2006) (a court may choose to address qualified immunity if not properly asserted so long as the plaintiff is not "prejudiced"); Hill v. McKinley, 311 F.3d 899, 902 (8th Cir. 2002) (qualified immunity defense not waived when first reasserted in post-trial motion); Rakovich v. Wade, 850 F.2d 1180, 1204 (7th Cir. 1988) (en banc) (defense could be raised during trial); Kelson v. City of Springfield, 767 F.2d 651, 657 (9th Cir. 1985) (defense could be raised in an amended answer filed after an appeal).

[846]*Compare* Kopec v. Tate, 361 F.3d 772, 776 (3d Cir. 2004); Wilson v. Kittner, 337 F.3d 392, 397 (4th Cir. 2003); Lee v. Sandberg, 136 F.3d 94, 101 (2d Cir. 1997); Burnham v. Ianni, 119 F.3d 668, 674 (8th Cir. 1997) (holding burden is on defendants) *with* Jewett v. Anders, 521 F.3d 818, 823 (7th Cir. 2008); Verdecia v. Adams, 327 F.3d 1171, 1174 (10th Cir. 2003); Bazan v. Hidalgo County, 246 F.3d 481, 490 (5th Cir. 2001) (holding burden is on plaintiffs) *and* Epps v. Watson, 492 F.3d 1240, 1243 (11th Cir. 2007); Humphrey v. Marby, 482 F.3d 840, 846 (6th Cir. 2007) (both holding defendant must show she was engaged in a discretionary function, and plaintiff must show deprivation of a constitutional right and that the right was clearly established); *see* Houghton v. South, 965 F.2d 1532 (9th Cir. 1992) (plaintiff has burden of showing rights were clearly established, defendants have burden of proving defense).

[847]Saucier v. Katz, 533 U.S. 194, 199–200, 121 S. Ct. 2151 (2001) (quoting Mitchell v. Forsyth, 472 U.S. 511, 526, 105 S. Ct. 2806 (1985)).

[848]These motions are discussed in Ch. 9, §§ I and L, respectively.

[849]*See* Johnson v. Breeden, 280 F.3d 1308, 1317 (11th Cir. 2002) ("Defendants who are not successful with their qualified immunity defense before trial can re-assert it at the end of the plaintiff's case in a Rule 50(a) motion.").

[850]Johnson v. Frankell, 520 U.S. 911, 915, 117 S. Ct. 1800 (1997); Johnson v. Jones, 515 U.S. 304, 317, 115 S. Ct. 2151 (1995) (A denial of a claim of qualified immunity is immediately appealable only if the appeal is premised not on a factual dispute, but rather on "neat abstract issues of law." (citations and quotation marks omitted)).

In state courts, whether there is an interlocutory appeal of the denial of a qualified immunity motion is determined by state law; state courts do not have to follow the federal appeal rules. Johnson v. Frankell, 520 U.S. at 516.

[851]Siegert v. Gilley, 500 U.S. 226, 232, 111 S. Ct. 1789 (1991).

immediate appeal.[852] However, if defendants argue that even under your version of the facts, there was no violation of clearly established law, they are entitled to appeal, even if there is also a factual dispute.[853] Discovery is to be stayed until the immunity issue is decided, except to the extent that discovery is necessary to present the immunity question.[854]

What you must plead in a case with a qualified immunity defense is not entirely clear. Some courts have held that plaintiffs must meet a "heightened pleading" standard to make it easier to decide qualified immunity on a motion to dismiss. That would mean that the plaintiff must plead the facts of defendants' alleged conduct "with some specificity" and not rely on "vague and conclusory" allegations.[855] The Supreme Court has generally disapproved of heightened pleading standards in recent years,[856] and many courts have held that there can be no heightened pleading requirement in light of these decisions.[857] However, a more recent Supreme Court case says that a complaint must "contain sufficient factual matter . . . to 'state a claim to relief that is plausible on its face,'" which is accomplished "when the plaintiff pleads factual content that allows the court to draw the reasonable inferences that the defendant is liable for the misconduct alleged."[858] Whether this decision imposes a heightened pleading requirement remains to be seen. In any case, you should make it clear in your complaint just what each defendant did or failed to do that you believe violated your rights.[859]

Entitlement to qualified immunity "ordinarily should be decided by the court long before trial"[860] on a motion to dismiss or for summary judgment. That is not possible if there are disputed facts that must be resolved in order to decide qualified immunity,[861] and if one of the parties has requested a jury trial. In that situation, most courts will submit the factual issues to the jury and then decide qualified immunity based on the jury's factual findings.[862]

5. State Tort Law Immunities

Under state law, prison personnel and state and local governments may be immune from some or all suits for damages. These immunities vary from state to state and we can only give a broad description of the kinds of immunities that you may encounter. You will have to research state statutes and case law to find out more about them. (Keep in mind

---

[852]*See* Livermore v. Lubelan, 476 F.3d 397, 403 (6th Cir. 2007); Doe v. Groody, 361 F.3d 232, 237 (3d Cir. 2004) (appeal of an interlocutory order as a "denial of qualified immunity that turns on an issue of law—rather than a factual dispute—is appealable as a collateral order under 28 U.S.C. §§ 1291.").

[853]Nolan v. Jackson, 102 F.3d 1187, 1190 (11th Cir. 1997).

[854]Crawford-El v. Britton, 523 U.S. 574, 598, 118 S. Ct. 184 (1998); *see* Castro v. U.S., 34 F.3d 106, 112 (2d Cir. 1994) ("Where the claimant's description of the events suggests that the defendants' conduct was unreasonable, and the facts that the defendants claim are dispositive are solely within the knowledge of the defendants and their collaborators, summary judgment can rarely be granted without allowing the plaintiff an opportunity for discovery as to the questions bearing on the defendants' claims of immunity."); Estate of Sorrells v. City of Dallas, 192 F.R.D. 203, 209 (N.D.Tex. 2000) (noting that it was unfair for the defendants to "hide behind the shield of qualified immunity to deny access to evidence solely within their control while using that same evidence against plaintiffs.").

[855]*See* Epps v. Watson, 492 F.3d 1240, 1242–43 (11th Cir. 2007) (citations omitted); *accord*, Nunez v. Simms, 341 F.3d 385, 388 (5th Cir. 2003) ("Heightened pleading in qualified immunity cases requires that plaintiffs rest their complaint on more than conclusions alone and plead their case with precision and factual specificity.").

[856]*See* Swierkiewicz v. Sorema, 534 U.S. 506, 512–13, 122 S. Ct. 992 (2002) (rejecting heightened pleading requirement in employment discrimination cases); Leatherman v. Tarrant County Narcotics Intelligence & Coordination Unit, 507 U.S. 163, 168, 113 S. Ct. 1160 (1993) (rejecting heightened pleading in cases asserting municipal liability). In *Crawford-El v. Britton*, 523 U.S. 574, 118 S. Ct. 1584 (1998), the Court rejected special requirements for summary judgment motions in qualified immunity cases, but also said that a court concerned with protecting defendants' ability to raise the qualified immunity defense at an early point could take such measures as directing the plaintiff to file a reply to the defendants' answer under Rule 7(a), Fed.R.Civ.P., or grant a motion by defendants for a more definite statement under Rule 12(e). *Crawford-El*, 523 U.S. at 598.

[857]*See, e.g.*, Thomas v. Independence Twp., 463 F.3d 285, 294–95 (3d Cir. 2006); Doe v. Cassel, 403 F.3d 986, 989 (8th Cir. 2005); Trulock v. Freeh, 275 F.3d 391, 405 (4th Cir. 2005);

Educadores Puertorriquenos en Accion v. Hernandez, 367 F.3d 61, 66–67 (1st Cir. 2004); Phelps v. Kapnolas, 308 F.3d 180, 186–87 & n.6 (2d Cir. 2002); Galbraith v. County of Santa Clara, 307 F.3d 1119, 1125–26 (9th Cir. 2002); Goad v. Mitchell, 297 F.3d 497, 501–03 (6th Cir. 2002); Currier v. Doran, 242 F.3d 905, 915–16 (10th Cir. 2001); Harbury v. Deutch, 233 F.3d 596, 611 (D.C. Cir. 2000), *rev'd on other grounds sub nom.* Christopher v. Harbury, 536 U.S. 403, 122 S. Ct. 2179 (2002); Nance v. Vieregge, 147 F.3d 589, 590–91 (7th Cir. 1998). Pleading requirements are discussed further in Ch. 9, § B.1.

[858]Ashcroft v. Iqbal, ___ U.S. ___, 129 S. Ct. 1937, 1949 (2009).

[859]*See* Ch. 10, § B.1, for further discussion of drafting complaints, and § B.4.a of this chapter for further discussion of the *Iqbal* decision.

[860]Hunter v. Bryant, 502 U.S. 224, 228, 112 S. Ct. 534 (1991) (per curiam).

[861]This generally means that if the plaintiff's allegations about the defendants' actions are true, they violated clearly established law, but if they are not true, they did not violate established law.

[862]*See, e.g.*, Curley v. Klem, 499 F.3d 199, 211 (3d Cir. 2007); Willingham v. Crooke, 412 F.3d 553, 559–60 (4th Cir. 2005); Littrell v. Franklin, 388 F.3d 578, 584–85 (8th Cir. 2004). The court can pose questions to the jury to obtain specific factual findings from it. *Littrell, id.; see* Rule 49, Fed.R.Civ.P. Some courts have said that in a factually contested case going to a jury, the question of qualified immunity should be decided by the jury. *See, e.g.*, McCoy v. Hernandez, 203 F.3d 371, 376 (5th Cir. 2000); *see also* Keylon v. City of Albuquerque, 535 F.3d 1210, 1217–18 (10th Cir. 2008) (qualified immunity may be for the jury in "exceptional circumstances").

while doing so that private corporations operating prisons or providing services, and their employees, may not be entitled to all state law immunities.[863]) We do discuss state law immunities further in other sections of this Manual in connection with specific kinds of state law claims.[864]

The most common types of immunity you will encounter in litigating state law damages claims include the following.[865]

Sovereign immunity.[866] States and state agencies are immune from suit under state law unless the state has waived or abolished its immunity. Most states have done this to some extent, either by statute or court decision. Often states place conditions on their waiver of immunity by requiring you to sue in a special court or administrative agency, by limiting the damages that are available, or by prohibiting jury trial.[867] In many states, the immunity of local government has also been abolished; in others, it still exists. Individual employees may or may not be protected by government's sovereign immunity; this will vary from state to state.

In some states, state and local governments are immune from suits based on "governmental" but not "proprietary" (commercial) activities. This distinction is poorly defined, but most aspects of operating prisons and jails are likely to be considered governmental in nature.[868]

---

[863]*See* Brown v. Youth Services Intern. of South Dakota, Inc., 89 F. Supp. 2d 1095, 1102 (D.S.D. 2000) (citing SDCL § 3-21-8: a state law immunizing persons, political subdivisions, and the state from liability for failure to provide a prison or jail or for failure to provide sufficient equipment, personnel, programs, facilities, or services in one, did not apply to the defendant private corporation); Giron v. Correction Corp. of America, 14 F. Supp. 2d 1245, 1252 (D.N.M. 1998) (private prison employee was not immune under state tort claims act).

[864]*See* Ch. 2, § II.F.5, concerning medical negligence and malpractice cases; § G.1.f on tort claims for inmate assaults; § G.2.e on tort claims for assault and battery by staff; Ch. 4, § D.1.r.4 on remedies for improper disciplinary proceedings; § H.8.d on remedies for loss of property.

[865]This discussion draws on W. Page Keeton et al., *Prosser and Keeton on the Law of Torts* § 131–32 (5th ed. 1984).

[866]Federal government sovereign immunity is discussed in § L.1.b of this chapter. The sovereign immunity of states under federal law is discussed in § L.1.a.

[867]For example, New York does all these things by requiring suits against state prison personnel to be brought in the Court of Claims, where the State is the defendant, there is no jury trial, and punitive damages are not allowed. N.Y. Correction Law § 24; *see* Sharpata v. Town of Islip, 56 N.Y.2d 332, 452 N.Y.S.2d 347 (N.Y. 1982) (no punitive damages); Page v. La Buzzetta, 466 N.Y.S.2d 769, 771, 96 A.D.2d 694 (N.Y.App.Div. 1983) (no jury trial). This statute was recently held unconstitutional as applied to the exclusion of federal § 1983 claims against prison staff from state courts, *see* Haywood v. Drown, ___ U.S. ___, 129 S. Ct. 210 (2009), but it will probably remain applicable to state law claims in state court.

[868]*See, e.g.*, Brown v. Mitchell, 308 F. Supp. 2d 682, 691 (E.D.Va. 2004) (operating a jail is a governmental function under Virginia law).

Discretionary or policy immunity. State and local governments and their personnel are frequently immune from suit for "discretionary" actions but not "ministerial" ones. This is another murky distinction, and one that varies from state to state. Essentially, discretionary actions are those that require the actor to make a decision, and ministerial ones are those that involve only following instructions.[869] (Some courts make it more complicated.[870]) Some state courts make a distinction between the planning level (where defendants are immune) and the operational functions of government (where they are not immune).[871] Note that state law that

---

[869]One state court has held that "an official duty is ministerial when it is absolute, certain and imperative, involving merely execution of a specific duty arising from fixed and designated facts. Discretionary or judicial duties are such as necessarily require the exercise of reason in the adaptation of the means to an end, and discretion in determining how or whether the act shall be done or the course pursued." Travis v. Pinto, 87 N.J.Super. 263, 208 A.2d 828, 831 (1965); *accord*, Lodl v. Progressive N. Ins. Co., 253 Wis.2d 323, 646 N.W.2d 314, 321 (2002) ("a duty is regarded as ministerial when it has been 'positively imposed by law, and its performance required at a time and in a manner, or upon conditions which are specifically designated. . . .'" (emphasis added) (citations omitted)). *Cf.* Perrin v. Gentner, 177 F. Supp. 2d 1115, 1125–26 (D.Nev. 2001) (police decision to stop a person on the street may have been discretionary, but shooting him was operational); Jackson v. Johnson, 118 F. Supp. 2d 278, 295 (N.D.N.Y. 2000) (use of restraint holds was not discretionary, since policy prescribed the reasons they could be used and the way in which they were to be applied), *aff'd in part, dismissed in part on other grounds*, 13 Fed.Appx. 51 (2d Cir. 2001) (unpublished). *But see* Martin v. Somerset County, 387 F. Supp. 2d 65, 82–83 (D.Me. 2005) (noting Maine discretionary immunity has been construed by state courts to be equivalent to federal law qualified immunity).

There is a similar "discretionary function exception" under the FTCA which is governed by federal law standards, which may differ from state law. *See* § C.2.a of this chapter.

[870]*See* District of Columbia v. Jones, 919 A.2d 604, 608 (D.C. 2007) (the court must "balance the contending interests and determine whether society's concern to shield the particular government function at issue from the disruptive effects of civil litigation requires subordinating the vindication of private injuries otherwise compensable at law"; courts may consider "(1) the nature of the injury, (2) the availability of alternative remedies, (3) the ability of the courts to judge fault without unduly invading the executive's function, and (4) the importance of protecting particular kinds of acts. . . . [A] court may use other factors it deems relevant.").

[871]*See, e.g.*, Gillan v. City of San Marino, 147 Cal. App.4th 1033, 55 Cal.Rptr. 3d 158, 173 (Cal.App. 2dDist. 2007); *accord*, Unzen v. City of Duluth, 683 N.W.2d 875, 882 (Minn.App. 2004), (planning-level functions "require evaluating such factors as the financial, political, economic, and social effects of a given plan"; operational functions "are those actions involving the ordinary, day-to-day operations of the government"); *see also* Smith v. Franklin County, 227 F. Supp. 2d 667, 680–81 (E.D.Ky. 2002) (hiring staff is a discretionary function, but administering medical care is a ministerial function unprotected by immunity); Taylor v. Buff, 172 Cal.App.3d 384, 389, 218 Cal.Rptr. 249, 252 (Cal.App. 3d

immunizes governmental bodies for their policy decisions has the opposite effect from federal law, which requires a showing of governmental policy to recover against a local government under § 1983.[872]

In practice, many courts apply discretionary immunity to ordinary day-to-day decisions of prison officials.[873] In some states discretionary immunity applies to ordinary negligence, but not to grossly or wantonly negligent acts,[874] or those based on corrupt or malicious motives.[875]

Judicial and legislative immunities. Both governmental units and individual defendants are generally immune for legislative and judicial actions. Judicial immunity extends to prosecutors, grand juries, and other persons and activities closely related to the judicial process.[876]

Special rules for prisoner cases. Some states have statutes or rules governing prisoner cases that have the same effect as immunity rules, even if they don't use that term. Some states forbid or severely limit suits based on inmate–inmate assaults,[877] and others have different restrictions on prisoner suits.[878] In some states and in the federal prison system, prisoners may not sue for work accidents because they are entitled to a limited form of workers' compensation.[879]

Dist. 1985) (where Sheriff lacked funds to repair malfunctioning locking system, decision that it was less dangerous to leave cells unlocked than to chain and padlock them was discretionary); Ferguson v. Perry, 593 So.2d 273, 277–78 (Fla.App. 1992) (inmate classification is discretionary but providing medical care is operational); Erskine v. Commissioner of Corrections, 682 A.2d 681, 685 (Me. 1996) (claim that defendants negligently promulgated policies, failed to appropriately train the staff, and failed to take precautions to protect prisoners against assault was barred by discretionary immunity); Lyons v. State by Humphrey by Pung, 366 N.W.2d 621, 623 (Minn.App. 1985) (where prisoner was assaulted with a laundry pin fastener in a recreation area, State was immune for discretionary decision to allow use of laundry pins).

[872]*See* Biberdorf v. Oregon, 243 F. Supp. 2d 1145, 1158–59 (D. Or. 2002) (if the plaintiff's over-detention resulted from policy, his state law false imprisonment claim was barred by immunity, but his § 1983 claim against the county could go forward).

[873]*See, e.g.,* Dowty v. Tarrell, 368 F. Supp. 2d 1024, 1027–28 (D.S.D. 2005) (claims of slip and fall in shower and failure to provide medical care were barred by immunity designed to protect discretionary decisions); Richards v. Southeast Alabama Youth Services Detention Center, 105 F. Supp. 2d 1268, 1281–82 (M.D.Ala. 2000) (failure to conduct an adequate search, allowing arrestee to bring a gun into the facility and kill himself, was discretionary); Texas Dep't of Criminal Justice v. Watt, 949 S.W.2d 561, 565–66 (Tex.App.-Waco 1997) (use of force to remove prisoner from cell was discretionary); Alford v. Osei-Kwasi, 203 Ga.App. 716, 418 S.E.2d 79, 85 (Ga.App. 1992) (use of force case was governed by immunity for discretionary acts); Hann v. State, 137 Misc.2d 605, 521 N.Y.S.2d 973, 977 (N.Y.Ct.Cl. 1987) (early return of segregation inmate to general population based on psychiatric discharge was discretionary).

[874]*See, e.g.,* Barrett ex rel Barrett v. Unified School Dist. No. 259, 272 Kan. 250, 32 P.3d 1156, 1167 (2001); Jackson v. Dep't Of Corrections, 390 S.E.2d 467, 469 (S.C.App. 1989), *aff'd,* 302 S.C. 519 (1990); *see also* Oviatt by and through Waugh v. Pearce, 954 F.2d 1470, 1480–81 (9th Cir. 1992) (Oregon Tort Claims Act "discretionary function" exception does not immunize intentional or deliberately indifferent acts but does immunize gross negligence); Peterson v. Traill County, 601 N.W.2d 268, 275 (N.D. 1999) (employees are immune for ordinary negligence, though governmental bodies are not).

[875]*See, e.g.,* Hyatt v. Anoka Police Dep't, 700 N.W.2d 502, 508–09 (Minn.App. 2005) (no immunity for malicious act); Autry v. Western Ky. University, 219 S.W.3d 713, 717 (Ky. 2007) (no immunity for act "done willfully or maliciously with intent to harm, or if it is committed with a corrupt motive or in bad faith").

---

[876]W. Page Keeton *et al., Prosser and Keeton on the Law of Torts* at 1046, 1057–59 (5th ed. 1984). *But see* Brunsvold v. State, 250 Mont. 500, 820 P.2d 732, 735 (1991) (probation officer who miscalculated good time on prisoner's sentence was not an agent of the judiciary and was not immune); *see also* Hudgins v. McAtee, 596 N.E.2d 286, 288 (Ind.App. 1992) (statutory immunity for law enforcement activities did not extend to jail administration). The scope of this immunity may vary from state to state and may differ from federal judicial immunity. *See* Cousins v. Lockyer, 568 F.3d 1063, 1071 (9th Cir. 2009) (noting that California prosecutorial immunity did not extend to suits for false imprisonment).

[877]New Jersey does not permit tort suits against public employers or governmental bodies based on "any injury caused by ... a prisoner to any other prisoner." N.J.S.A. 59:5–2(b)(4) (cited in Davidson v. Cannon, 474 U.S. 344, 346, 106 S. Ct. 668 (1986)). South Dakota has a similar immunity statute. *See* Webb v. Lawrence County, 144 F.3d 1131, 1139–40 (8th Cir. 1998) (finding immunity under statute providing that "[n]o person [or] political subdivision ... is liable ... for any injury caused by or resulting from ... a prisoner to any other prisoner" (citing S.D.Codified Laws § 3-21-9)).

[878]*See* Phillips v. Monroe County, Miss., 311 F.3d 369, 375 (5th Cir. 2002) (citing Miss.Code Ann. § 11-46-9(1)(m); noting that Mississippi excluded prisoners from its waiver of sovereign immunity, barring tort claims); Sealock v. Colorado, 218 F.3d 1205, 1212 (10th Cir. 2000) (noting that Colorado excluded prisoners from its waiver of sovereign immunity; upholding constitutionality of exclusion); Simmons v. City of Philadelphia, 947 F.2d 1042, 1078 (3d Cir. 1991) (noting that local governments are immune under state Tort Claims Act for injuries resulting from jail conditions); Cooper v. Office of the Sheriff of Will County, 333 F. Supp. 2d 728 (N.D.Ill. 2004) (citing Illinois Tort Immunity Act which bars liability for failure to furnish or obtain medical care except where the employee knows from observation that the prisoner is in need of immediate attention and through willful and wanton conduct doesn't take reasonable action to get it); Teter v. City of Newport Beach, 30 Cal.4th 446, 448, 133 Cal.Rptr.2d 139 (Cal. 2003) (citing Cal. Government Code § 844.6) (noting that a public entity is not liable for an "injury to any prisoner" with some exceptions); Bollinger v. Schneider, 64 Ill.App.3d 758, 21 Ill. Dec. 522, 381 N.E.2d 849, 851–54 (1978) (citing Ill.Rev.Stat. 1975, ch. 85, §§ 4-103, 9-103) (public entities and employees are immune from liability for "failure to provide sufficient equipment, personnel or facilities" in jails and prisons, but this immunity is waived if the public entity purchases insurance).

[879]*See* § E of this chapter.

M. Res Judicata and Collateral Estoppel

Once a case is decided, the courts prefer that it remain decided. The doctrines of *res judicata* ("claim preclusion") and collateral estoppel ("issue preclusion") are designed to accomplish this purpose.[880]

If you lose a case, you may have the right to appeal or to move to modify, amend or vacate the judgment, but you cannot simply bring another suit and re-litigate the claim that you have previously lost, even if you go to a different court or bring a different type of lawsuit.[881] If you bring litigation that is clearly repetitive, you may be sanctioned by the court.[882]

This means that if you bring a lawsuit and then for some reason you cannot pursue it at that time, you should consider taking a voluntary dismissal, which generally does not bar you from bringing the suit at a later time.[883] Otherwise, if the defendants get the case dismissed because you failed to respond to a motion, the decision will be final, and you will be precluded from re-filing the case at a later time.

Rules concerning *res judicata* and collateral estoppel vary from state to state. Federal courts apply state court rules of preclusion to state court decisions under the "full faith and credit" doctrine.[884] If the prior decision is federal, then federal preclusion rules will apply.[885] In this section, we discuss the general outlines of *res judicata* and collateral estoppel without much exploration of state-by-state variations. Be sure you research your state's law if you have an issue involving claim or issue preclusion arising from a state court decision.

Res judicata (Latin for "thing decided") generally means that you cannot bring a lawsuit if there has already been a judgment on the merits of the same cause of action by a court of competent jurisdiction in a prior suit involving the same parties or their privies.[886] This is true even if the first lawsuit was decided in your favor.[887]

A "judgment on the merits" is one that decides whether or not the plaintiff's legal rights were violated by the defendants.[888] A judgment is generally not on the merits if the court holds that it lacks jurisdiction,[889] that the case is moot, that the plaintiff failed to exhaust administrative remedies,[890] or some other reason unrelated to the legal claim that you are suing about.[891] However, a default judgment is generally

---

[880]These terms are discussed in *Migra v. Warren City School Dist. Bd. of Educ.*, 565 U.S. 75, 77 n.1, 104 S. Ct. 92 (1984).

[881]Robbins v. Clarke, 946 F.2d 1331, 1334 (8th Cir. 1991) (prisoner barred from litigating the "same claim repackaged").

[882]*See, e.g.,* Cromer v. Kraft Foods North America, Inc., 390 F.3d 812, 818 (4th Cir. 2004) ("meritless and repetitive actions" justified an injunction limiting future filings); Kurkowski v. Volcker, 819 F.2d 201, 203–04 (8th Cir. 1987) (requiring payment of attorney's fees of $5400 for filing same claims a second time); Anderson v. D.C. Public Defender Service, 881 F. Supp. 663, 667–71 (D.D.C. 1995) (injunction held appropriate against plaintiff who filed repetitive litigation); Williams v. Duckworth, 617 F. Supp. 597, 599–602 (N.D.Ind. 1985) (imposing $100 fine on prisoner for repetitive litigation and requiring payment of $200 in attorney's fees).

[883]*See* Rule 41(a)(1), Fed.R.Civ.P. Under this rule, a voluntary dismissal that you accomplish by notice or stipulation is "without prejudice," which means it does not bar a later suit, as long as you file the notice or stipulation before the complaint is answered or a motion for summary judgment is filed, and if you have not already dismissed the same case previously. If the answer or a summary judgment motion has been filed, Rule 41(a)(2) requires that you get the court to enter an order saying that the dismissal is without prejudice, or it will be with prejudice. *See* Ch. 10, § I, nn.364–368.

If you voluntarily dismiss, you do have to re-file the case within the limitations period. *See* § N of this chapter concerning statutes of limitations.

[884]Migra v. Warren City School Dist. Bd. of Educ., 565 U.S. 75, 81, 104 S. Ct. 92 (1984). The Full Faith and Credit Clause of the Constitution, U.S. Const., Art. IV, § 1, applies only to the states. However, Congress has enacted a statute that requires federal courts as well to honor state court judgments. 28 U.S.C. § 1738.

[885]Marvel Characters, Inc. v. Simon, 310 F.3d 280, 286 (2d Cir. 2002).

[886]St. Paul Fire and Marine Ins. Co. v. Compaq Computer Corp., 457 F.3d 766, 770 (8th Cir. 2006); Jones v. S.E.C., 115 F.3d 1173, 1178 (4th Cir. 1997); Fox v. Maulding, 112 F.3d 453, 456 (10th Cir. 1997).

[887]Murphy v. Jones, 877 F.2d 682, 686 (8th Cir. 1989) (after settlement, cannot bring a second claim arising from "the same transaction or series of transactions"); Hunnicutt v. Armstrong, 305 F. Supp. 2d 175 (D.Conn. 2004), *aff'd in part, vacated in part, and remanded on other grounds,* 152 Fed.Appx. 34 (2d Cir. 2005) (unpublished).

[888]The "merits" have traditionally been defined as "'the real or substantial grounds of action or defense as distinguished from matters of practice, procedure, jurisdiction or form.'" Morgan v. City of Rawlins, 792 F.2d 975, 979 (10th Cir. 1986) (quoting Clegg v. U.S., 112 F.2d 886 (10th Cir.1940)); *accord,* City of Painesville, Ohio v. First Montauk Financial Corp., 178 F.R.D. 180, 185 (N.D. Ohio 1998).

Thus, a dismissal for failure to state a claim is generally on the merits, Federated Dep't Stores, Inc. v. Moitie, 452 U.S. 394, 399 n.3 (1981), unless the court says otherwise (*i.e.,* dismisses without prejudice). A dismissal for failure to state a claim means that your allegations if proved would not establish a violation of law by the defendants. A dismissal without prejudice, however, is not considered to be on the merits.

[889]Rule 41(b), Fed.R.Civ.P.

[890]Heath v. Cleary, 708 F.2d 1376, 1380 n.4 (9th Cir. 1983).

[891]*See, e.g.,* Sterling v. U.S., 85 F.3d 1225, 1228 (7th Cir. 1996) (dismissal under "fugitive disentitlement" rule because plaintiff had escaped was not on the merits); Skinner v. Chapman, 489 F. Supp. 2d 298, 302–03 (W.D.N.Y. 2007) (dismissal of lawsuit under *Heck-Balisok* rule because criminal conviction had not yet been reversed does not preclude later filing of civil rights action after reversal of conviction); D'Angelo v. City of New York, 929 F. Supp. 129, 134 (S.D.N.Y. 1996) (dismissals for failure to file a tort notice of claim were not on the merits).

There may be some variation from state to state about what constitutes the merits. *Compare* Wade v. City of Philadelphia, 765 F.2d 405, 410–11 (3d Cir. 1985) (ruling on state law immunity

considered to be on the merits,[892] as is dismissal resulting from a settlement.[893] Voluntary dismissal can be on the merits, or not, as prescribed in the Federal Rules of Civil Procedure.[894] Dismissal for failure to prosecute is on the merits unless the court states otherwise.[895]

A "court of competent jurisdiction" is one that has jurisdiction over the relevant parties and the subject matter.[896] *Res judicata* may not apply where the first court "did not have the power to award the full measure of relief sought in the later litigation."[897] Thus, several decisions have held that a decision in a proceeding that could not award damages is not *res judicata* in a later § 1983 suit seeking damages.[898]

The "relevant parties" means what it sounds like—the same plaintiff and defendants. "Privies" refers to the old and poorly defined legal concept of "privity,"[899] which is rarely an issue in prison cases.[900]

The "same cause of action" means that the earlier case and the current case arise from the same set of facts.[901] If the second suit arises from significantly different facts—even if there is some factual overlap—*res judicata* will not apply.[902] For example, if you are beaten up on two occasions, you should be able to bring two lawsuits even if the same officers are involved. However, different legal claims arising out of the same facts may amount to the same cause of action.[903] Claims that could have been brought on the same facts in the first action, but were not brought, are barred.[904]

---

questions was not "on the merits" for purposes of a later § 1983 action to which state law immunities did not apply) *with* Lommen v. City of East Grand Forks, 97 F.3d 272, 275 (8th Cir. 1996) (holding immunity question was on the merits under a different state's law).

[892]Morris v. Jones, 329 U.S. 545, 550–51, 67 S. Ct. 451 (1947) (default judgment is *res judicata* in the absence of fraud or collusion).

[893]U.S. v. Southern Ute Tribe or Band of Indians, 402 U.S. 159, 174, 91 S. Ct. 1336 (1971).

[894]Rule 41(a), Fed.R.Civ.P.; *see* n.883, above, on this subject.

[895]Rule 41(b), Fed.R.Civ.P.

[896]Dowell v. Applegate, 152 U.S. 327, 343, 14 S. Ct. 611 (1894).

[897]Brody v. Village of Port Chester, 345 F.3d 103, 114 (2d Cir. 2003) (citation omitted); *accord*, Pack v. Artuz, 348 F. Supp. 2d 63, 69 (S.D.N.Y. 2004) (state Court of Claims lacked jurisdiction to hear individual capacity claims against prison officials, so decision on claim against the State was not *res judicata* as to individuals). *Contra*, Livingston v. Goord, 225 F. Supp. 2d 321 (W.D.N.Y. 2002) (plaintiff who won damages for assault and battery in state Court of Claims against state government could not bring a federal court § 1983 suit about the same event to obtain relief barred in the state court), *aff'd in part, vacated in part on other grounds*, 153 Fed. Appx. 769 (2d Cir. 2005) (unpublished).

[898]Reed v. McKune, 298 F.3d 946, 951 (10th 2002) (prior habeas proceeding was not *res judicata* in subsequent § 1983 action); Burgos v. Hopkins, 14 F.3d 787, 791–92 (2d Cir. 1994); Bates v. Dep't of Corrections, 774 F. Supp. 536, 539 (E.D. Wis. 1991); Catten v. Coughlin, 644 F. Supp. 1228, 1229 (S.D.N.Y. 1986) ("Article 78" proceeding that could not grant damages did not preclude later § 1983 damages action) (citing Davidson v. Capuano, 792 F.2d 275, 278 (2d Cir. 1986)). *Contra*, Rodziewicz v. Beyer, 809 F. Supp. 1164, 1167–70 (D. N.J. 1992) (rejecting *Davidson v. Capuano* holding).

Even if the entire claim is not barred by *res judicata*, particular issues that were decided in the prior litigation may collaterally estop the plaintiff as to those issues in a subsequent § 1983 case. Reed v. McKune, 298 F.3d 946, 951 (10th Cir. 2002); Giakoumelos v. Coughlin, 88 F.3d 56, 61 (2d Cir. 1996); Burgos v. Hopkins, 14 F.3d at 792–93. Collateral estoppel is discussed later in this chapter.

[899]Privity refers to any of a number of close legal relationships that may cause courts to deem it fair to hold that an earlier judgment involving one party should bind another party in later litigation. Factors supporting privity can include a contractual relationship, a fiduciary duty, representation by the same counsel, a family relationship, or a customer–provider relationship, among others. *See* Ferris v. Cuevas, 118 F.3d 122, 127–29 (2d Cir. 1997).

[900]*But see* White v. Kelsey, 935 F.2d 968, 969–70 (8th Cir. 1991) (doctor who provided post-traumatic care was not in privity with another doctor who provided traumatic care for the same injury); Lawson v. Toney, 169 F. Supp. 2d 456, 465 (M.D.N.C. 2001) (claims against Sheriff dismissed in state court were *res judicata* against later-filed claims against Sheriff's insurance company, since Sheriff and insuror were in privity); Jones v. McAndrew, 996 F. Supp. 1439, 1448 (N.D.Fla. 1998) (prisoner co-plaintiffs in a challenge to execution procedures were not in privity, so a prior decision against one did not bar the claims of the others).

[901]O'Connor v. Pierson, 586 F.3d 64, 69–70 (2d Cir. 2009) (claims arising "out of the same transaction, or series of connected transactions" are the same claim for *res judicata* purposes; decision on claim of intentional infliction of emotional distress was *res judicata* as to late due process claim because the facts underlying the two claims were so similar); Murphy v. Jones, 877 F.2d 682, 684–85 (8th Cir. 1989) (case arising "from the same nucleus of operative fact or one based upon the same factual predicate" involves the same cause of action).

[902]Thomas v. Evans, 880 F.2d 1235, 1240–41 (11th Cir. 1989); *see* Baker Group, L.C. v. Burlington N. & Santa Fe Ry. Co., 228 F.3d 883, 886 (8th Cir. 2000) (claim preclusion does not apply to claim of breach of contract that had not occurred at the time the first suit was decided, even though the same contract was involved).

[903]Hernandez v. Cunningham, 914 F. Supp. 72, 75 (S.D.N.Y. 1996) (Title VII claim was barred by prior § 1983 action; they constituted same cause of action because same factual predicate was involved).

[904]Lundquist v. Rice Mem. Hosp., 238 F.3d 975, 977 (8th Cir. 2001) ("'If the three elements are met, the parties are thereafter bound "not only as to every matter which was offered and received to sustain or defeat the claim or demand, but as to any other admissible matter which might have been offered for that purpose."'" (citation omitted)); Fox v. Maulding, 112 F.3d 453, 456 n.6 (10th Cir. 1997); Klein v. Zavaras, 80 F.3d 432, 435 (10th Cir. 1996) (where plaintiff brought due process claim in state court and lost, equal protection claims arising from the same facts were barred by *res judicata*); Landrigan v. City of Warwick, 628 F.2d 736, 740 (1st Cir. 1980) (plaintiff who won an assault and battery case could not then pursue a § 1983 case against the same officer arising

Courts must determine exactly what was at issue in an earlier case when applying *res judicata* to a subsequent case.[905]

Collateral estoppel is the principle that a party cannot relitigate particular factual or legal issues which were litigated and decided in a prior suit involving that party, regardless of whether the cause of action was the same.[906]

Collateral estoppel applies in civil actions even if the earlier case was a criminal prosecution.[907] Although the criminal case and a civil suit are not the same cause of action, the factual and legal issues may be the same. For example, if the court in your criminal case decided in a suppression motion that a search of your person, house, or car did not violate the Fourth Amendment, you will probably be collaterally estopped from later bringing a damage action claiming that the search was unconstitutional.[908] In most states, the same principle applies to other issues in a criminal prosecution.[909] (Unfortunately this only goes one way; if

you win a suppression motion or other issue in your criminal case, and then bring suit against police officers involved in the violation of your rights, they are not collaterally estopped because they are not considered to have been parties to the State's prosecution of you.[910]) If your conviction is reversed or vacated, findings made in that proceeding cease to have any preclusive effect.[911]

An earlier suit will not bar a later suit if the factual and legal issues were not the same, even if both suits arise from the same occurrence.[912] For example, the fact that you were convicted of a crime does not necessarily determine whether excessive force was used against you; depending on the facts underlying your criminal conviction, both the crime and the excessive force may have occurred.[913]

---

from the same beating). *But see* Marvel Characters, Inc. v. Simon, 310 F.3d 280, 288 (2d Cir. 2002) (claim that did not exist at the time of the first action could not have been brought in that action and was not barred in a later action).

[905]Thomas v. Evans, 880 F.2d at 1241; *see* Exxon Mobil Corp. v. Saudi Basic Indus. Corp., 544 U.S. 280, 293, 125 S. Ct. 1517 (2005) (federal court does not lose jurisdiction when a state court enters judgment on the same subject matter, but must determine extent of preclusive effect of state court judgment).

[906]Kremer v. Chemical Construction Corp., 456 U.S 461, 466 n.6, 102 S. Ct. 1883 (1982); Latino Officers Ass'n v. City of New York. 253 F. Supp. 2d 771, 782 (S.D.N.Y. 2003); Washington v. Chrans, 769 F. Supp. 1045, 1049 (C.D.Ill. 1991).

[907]The rules for habeas corpus proceedings are different. In the past, courts held that the doctrine of collateral estoppel did not apply to the factual findings of state criminal prosecutions when they were challenged in federal habeas corpus petitions. *See* Washington v. Chrans, 769 F. Supp. 1045, 1049 (C.D.Ill. 1991) (citing Preiser v. Rodriguez, 411 U.S. 475, 496, 92 S. Ct. 1825 (1973)). In the Anti-Terrorism and Effective Death Penalty Act, which amended the federal habeas corpus statutes, Congress changed the law to provide that the writ should not be granted on factual grounds unless the state court conviction "was based on an unreasonable determination of the facts in light of the evidence presented in the State court proceeding." 28 U.S.C. § 2254(d)(2). While collateral estoppel still doesn't strictly apply, the standard for overturning a state court factual finding is now very high.

[908]Allen v. McCurry, 449 U.S. 90, 101 S. Ct. 411 (1980). By contrast, if there was no decision in the criminal case on the legality of the search or arrest, your criminal conviction will generally not estop you from suing for the constitutional violation. Haring v. Prosise, 462 U.S. 306, 316, 103 S. Ct. 2368 (1983).

The collateral estoppel effect of matters decided in your criminal conviction is one reason that you cannot challenge your criminal conviction in a civil lawsuit or bring a § 1983 suit for damages based on matters that were determined adversely to you in the criminal case. First, you have to get your conviction reversed, either through the appellate process or through habeas corpus or another post-conviction remedy. The *Preiser/Heck* rule also leads to this conclusion. *See* § H.1.a of this chapter.

[909]*See, e.g.,* Wheeler v. Nieves, 762 F. Supp. 617, 626–27 (D.N.J. 1991) (guilty verdict by jury precluded civil action challenging

criminal trial evidence; criminal court rulings precluded challenge to identification procedures); Sibert v. Phelan, 901 F. Supp. 183, 187 (D.N.J. 1995) (judge's decision of issues on suppression motion could collaterally estop plaintiff in later civil action before jury). However, as with other preclusion issues, the rules on this point may vary from state to state. *See, e.g.,* Kane v. Hargis, 987 F.2d 1005, 1008 (4th Cir. 1993) (facts underlying a criminal conviction are not given preclusive effect in a civil action); Johnson v. City of Chicago, 712 F. Supp. 1311, 1314 (N.D.Ill. 1989) (same).

[910]*See* Hardesty v. Hamburg Tp., 461 F.3d 646, 651 (6th Cir. 2006); Morgan v. Gertz, 166 F.3d 1307, 1309 (10th Cir. 1999); Tierney v. Davidson, 133 F.3d 189, 195 (2d Cir. 1998).

[911]Aguillard v. McGowen, 207 F.3d 226, 229 (5th Cir. 2000); Dodrill v. Ludt, 764 F.2d 442, 443 (6th Cir. 1985).

In a criminal proceeding, the government may not use collateral estoppel to establish an element of a criminal offense or to conclusively rebut an affirmative defense on which the Government bears the burden of proof beyond a reasonable doubt. U.S. v. Arnett, 353 F.3d 765, 766 (9th Cir. 2003) (en banc) (per curiam).

[912]Pack v. Artuz, 348 F. Supp. 2d 63, 71–73 (S.D.N.Y. 2004) (decision on state tort claim finding that plaintiff did not suffer from an ailment resulting from prison asbestos exposure did not estop plaintiff in later federal action under Eighth Amendment asserting that plaintiff had been exposed to an unreasonable risk and defendants were deliberately indifferent to it); *see* Matosantos Commercial Corp. v. Applebee's Int'l., Inc., 245 F.3d 1203, 1212 (10th Cir. 2001) (noting that "[c]ollateral estoppel is also not appropriate when a party in a subsequent suit faces a less demanding burden of proof than the burden of proof in the prior litigation").

[913]*See* Ballard v. Burton, 444 F.3d 391, 401 (5th Cir. 2006) (simple assault conviction did not preclude an excessive force claim); Curry v. City of Syracuse, 316 F.3d 324, 332 (2d Cir. 2003) (finding at parole revocation proceeding that plaintiff had struck a police officer did not estop plaintiff's claim that the officer had used excessive force); Willingham v. Loughman, 261 F.3d 1178, 1183 (11th Cir. 2001) (conviction for attempted murder did not estop plaintiff's claim police used excessive force, though trial transcript showed that jury must have determined plaintiff threw a knife, and that factual determination was binding), *vacated on other grounds,* 537 U.S. 801 (2002); Martinez v. City of Albuquerque, 184 F.3d 1123, 1127 (10th Cir. 1999) (conviction for resisting arrest did not estop excessive force claim, since trial court record showed conviction was based on fleeing the scene and not on later incident for which he claimed excessive force); Perrin v. Daggy, 776 F. Supp. 1345, 1346–48 (N.D.Ind. 1991) (convictions for resisting arrest

If an issue was presented in an earlier case but not actually decided, you generally will not be collaterally estopped.[914] For estoppel to apply, some courts hold it must be proven that the issue was essential to the decision in the earlier case.[915] If it is impossible to tell what was litigated and decided in the prior action, collateral estoppel cannot apply.[916] The burden of proving collateral estoppel—*i.e.*, proving what was decided in the prior action—lies with the party who would benefit from the preclusion.[917]

For collateral estoppel to apply, the party being estopped must have had a full and fair opportunity to litigate in the prior case.[918] This requirement may be violated by lack of competent representation,[919] unfair limits on what issues could be pursued or what evidence could be presented,[920] inadequate notice and preparation time,[921] or the lack of opportunity to appeal.[922]

A class action judgment for injunctive relief in favor of a class of prisoners does not bar later damage actions by individual class members based on the same constitutional violations.[923] A ruling *against* the plaintiff class would bar such actions unless the individual plaintiff could show that she was treated differently from the rest of the class, that conditions had changed since the class action ruling,[924] or that the legal claim she raised had not been adequately presented in the class action.[925]

---

and disorderly conduct did not preclude excessive force claim but could be used to establish that he had committed those crimes). *But see* Morgan v. Ward, 699 F. Supp. 1025, 1047–48 (N.D.N.Y. 1988) (prisoner's guilty plea to attempted assault estopped him from denying that he instigated the incident in question). *Cf.* Darrah v. City of Oak Park, 255 F.3d 301, 311 (6th Cir. 2001) (holding that a state court's determination of probable cause at the preliminary hearing does not preclude a subsequent civil action from litigating the issue of whether the officers made materially false statements to establish probable cause). *But see* Hinchman v. Moore, 312 F.3d 198, 203 (6th Cir. 2002) (questioning *Darrah*).

[914]Haring v. Prosise, 462 U.S. 306, 315, 103 S. Ct. 2368 (1983); Cepeda v. Coughlin, 785 F. Supp. 385, 387–90 (S.D.N.Y. 1992) (dismissal of state court challenge to disciplinary conviction on statute of limitations grounds did not preclude § 1983 action because the legality of the disciplinary proceeding had not actually been decided).

[915]Haring v. Prosise, 462 U.S. at 315 (applying Virginia law); Curry v. City of Syracuse, 316 F.3d 324, 331 (2d Cir. 2003) (under New York law, issue must be "decisive" in the second action for collateral estoppel to apply).

[916]Haring v. Prosise, 462 U.S. at 313.

[917]U.S. v. Dominguez, 359 F.3d 839, 842 (6th Cir. 2004); Havoco of Am., Ltd. v. Freeman, Atkins & Coleman, Ltd., 58 F.3d 303, 308 (7th Cir. 1995).

[918]Allen v. McCurry, 449 U.S. 90, 101, 101 S. Ct. 411 (1980).

[919]Curry v. City of Syracuse, 316 F.3d 324, 332 (2d Cir. 2003) (examining "the competence and experience of counsel"; applying collateral estoppel where prisoner in parole revocation hearing was capably represented and had an incentive to litigate the issue); Pack v. Artuz, 348 F. Supp. 2d 63, 75 (S.D.N.Y. 2004) (lack of counsel is "relevant factor" in determining fairness of proceeding); Vega v. State University of New York Bd. of Trustees, 67 F. Supp. 2d 324, 337 (S.D.N.Y. 1999); Cerbone v. County of Westchester, 508 F. Supp. 780, 785 (S.D.N.Y. 1981).

[920]Awabdy v. City of Adelanto, 368 F.3d 1062, 1068 (9th Cir. 2004) (". . . [C]ollateral estoppel does not apply when the decision to hold a defendant to answer was made on the basis of fabricated evidence presented at the preliminary hearing or as the result of other wrongful conduct by state or local officials."); Bailey v. Andrews, 811 F.2d 366, 369–70 (7th Cir. 1987) (preliminary hearing with no opportunity to cross-examine police officer was not preclusive as to probable cause for arrest); Sprecher v. Graber, 716 F.2d 968, 972 (2d Cir. 1983) (lack of opportunity for discovery and difference in burden of proof prevented summary subpoena

enforcement proceeding from having preclusive effect); Pack v. Artuz, 348 F. Supp. 2d 63, 75–77 (S.D.N.Y. 2004) (hasty dismissal of state court tort claim based on admission of lack of medical evidence concerning asbestos exposure, with no opportunity to submit documentary evidence concerning his exposure and its consequences, denied plaintiff a full and fair opportunity to be heard); Henry v. Ryan, 775 F. Supp. 247, 252 (N.D.Ill. 1991) (lack of evidentiary hearing deprived proceeding to quash subpoena of collateral estoppel effect).

[921]Richards v. Jefferson County, Ala., 517 U.S. 793, 800–01, 116 S. Ct. 1761 (1996) (setting forth due process requirements for granting prior judgment preclusive effect); Abdulhay v. Bethlehem Medical Arts, L.P., 425 F. Supp. 2d 646, 656 (E.D.Pa. 2006); Lee v. Winston, 717 F.2d 888, 895–96 (4th Cir. 1983), *aff'd on other grounds*, 470 U.S. 753, 105 S. Ct. 1611 (1985).

[922]Locurto v. Giuliani, 447 F.3d 159, 171 (2d Cir. 2006); Dixon v. Richer, 922 F.2d 1456, 1459 (10th Cir. 1991) (an indispensable prerequisite to the application of collateral estoppel, includes the opportunity to appeal an adverse ruling-an opportunity denied to acquitted defendants); Johnson v. Watkins, 101 F.3d 792, 796 (2d Cir. 1996) (finding no collateral estoppel because a § 1983 plaintiff, who had been acquitted in state court, had no opportunity to appeal the state court's adverse finding that, although he was not guilty, the police did have probable cause to arrest him).

[923]*See* § G of this chapter.

[924]Cameron v. Tomes, 990 F.2d 14, 17–18 (1st Cir. 1993) (in rejecting argument that individual claim was barred by *res judicata* effect of class action, court stated that "a class action judgment . . . binds the class members as to matters actually litigated but does not resolve any claim based on individual circumstances that was not addressed in the class action. . . . [C]lass action institutional litigation often addresses general circumstances, not the distinctive plight of someone claiming special needs or status."); Jones v. Sargent, 737 F.2d 766, 767 (8th Cir. 1984) (class action judgment was not *res judicata* when the plaintiff alleged that the facts had changed after judgment was entered); Tunnell v. Office of the Public Defender, 583 F. Supp. 762, 765–66 (E.D.Pa. 1984).

[925]Cameron v. Tomes, 990 F.2d at 17; Ferguson v. Dep't Of Corrections, 816 P.2d 134, 138–39 (Alaska 1991) (prisoner could challenge drug testing procedure because the constitutional questions had not been adequately presented in a class action). *See also* Dumas v. Major League Baseball Properties, Inc., 52 F. Supp. 2d 1183, 1192 (S.D.Cal. 1999) ("prior to certification of a class, an individual plaintiff will not be barred by principles of res judicata or collateral estoppel by a dismissal in another action").

Res judicata and collateral estoppel can work to a plaintiff's advantage.[926] If in a prior lawsuit it was established that particular conditions or practices were unlawful, prison officials may be barred from relitigating them in your present lawsuit.[927] However, to recover damages against particular officials you still have to prove that they were responsible for subjecting you to those conditions or causing you to be injured by them.[928]

Winning a habeas corpus proceeding or getting a disciplinary conviction thrown out in state court may not be preclusive in a later § 1983 damage suit, because the parties or the issues may be different.[929] You will generally not be able to use collateral estoppel based on favorable findings in a criminal prosecution, since the defendants you would have to sue about police or other investigative misconduct would not have been parties, or considered to be in privity, with the state that prosecuted you.[930] For similar reasons, getting a criminal case dismissed or a conviction reversed may not be preclusive in a § 1983 suit against officials responsible for the prosecution.[931]

Defendants may argue that if you were disciplined for some occurrence in prison, the findings of the prison disciplinary body should collaterally estop you from suing about the same occurrence. It is true that the factual findings of administrative agencies may be binding in later litigation if the agency acted in a judicial capacity and resolved disputed issues of fact that the parties had an adequate opportunity to litigate.[932] However, courts have generally not given preclusive effects to the findings of prison disciplinary bodies, since they are not considered preclusive under their respective states' law.[933] It is doubtful whether a prison disciplinary proceeding ever provides a full and fair opportunity to litigate a constitutional claim, since the due process requirements for such hearings are limited for reasons of prison security.[934] Both state and federal courts have questioned

---

[926]Collateral estoppel used by a plaintiff is called "offensive" collateral estoppel. Parklane Hosiery Co. v. Shore, 439 U.S. 322, 326 n.4, 99 S. Ct. 645 (1979). Its elements are the same as those of a defendant's claim of collateral estoppel: an issue must have been actually litigated and decided in a final judgment, there must have been a full and fair opportunity to litigate it, and the person against whom it is asserted in the second action must have been a party or in privity within a party in the first action. *Parklane Hosiery*, 439 U.S. at 329.

As with all preclusion questions where the first decision is from a state court, state preclusion law must be applied, and there are some variations from state to state. *See, e.g.*, Hardesty v. Hamburg Tp., 461 F.3d 646, 651 (6th Cir. 2006) (In Michigan, "collateral estoppel cannot be used offensively to preclude the litigation of an issue addressed in an associated criminal case.").

[927]McDuffie v. Estelle, 935 F.2d 682, 685–86 (5th Cir. 1991); Benjamin v. Coughlin, 905 F.2d 571, 575–76 (2d Cir. 1990) (state court decision that religious restrictions were unconstitutional estopped the state from defending them in federal court); Rourke v. New York State Dep't of Correctional Services, 915 F. Supp. 525 (N.D.N.Y. 1995) (correction officials who lost state court proceeding which granted reinstatement and back pay to correction officer on grounds of religious freedom violation were estopped from disputing the sincerity of his religious beliefs in a later federal court Title VII suit). *But see* Borst v. Chevron Corp., 36 F.3d 1308, 1314 n.11 (5th Cir. 1994) (noting that because the appellate court did not consider an issue, "the district court's ruling on that issue is not conclusive between the parties").

[928]McDuffie v. Estelle, 935 F.2d at 690 n.17; Williams v. Bennett, 689 F.2d 1370, 1383 (11th Cir. 1982); *see* § B.4.a of this chapter concerning the § 1983 personal involvement requirement.

[929]Fox v. Coughlin, 893 F.2d 475, 478 (2d Cir. 1990) (decision that a hearing officer abused his discretion under state law did not establish that the hearing officer denied due process); Gutierrez v. Coughlin, 841 F.2d 484, 486 (2d Cir. 1986) (prisoner's victory in state court challenge to disciplinary proceeding was not preclusive in a suit for damages against prison personnel in their individual capacities.); Garza v. Henderson, 779 F.2d 390, 394 (7th Cir. 1985) (habeas corpus decision was not binding on disciplinary committee members who were not parties in the habeas action); Zavaro v. Coughlin, 775 F. Supp. 84, 87–88 (W.D.N.Y. 1991) (state court reversal of a disciplinary conviction was not preclusive against the Commissioner because it was brought in his official and not his personal capacity, and was not preclusive against the hearing officer because he was not a party to the prior case), *aff'd*, 970 F.2d 1148 (2d Cir. 1992); *see generally* Matosantos Commercial Corp. v.

Applebee's Int'l., Inc., 245 F.3d 1203, 1212 (10th Cir. 2001) (noting that "[c]ollateral estoppel is also not appropriate when a party in a subsequent suit faces a less demanding burden of proof than the burden of proof in the prior litigation").

[930]*See* n.910, above.

[931]Aguillard v. McGowen, 207 F.3d 226, 229 (5th Cir. 2000) ("A conviction overturned on appeal cannot constitute a final judgment for purposes of collateral estoppel."); Dodrill v. Ludt, 764 F.2d 442, 443 (6th Cir. 1985) (". . . [A] judgment which is vacated, for whatever reason, is deprived of its conclusive effect" and thus all "factual determinations [are] vacated . . . and their preclusive effect surrendered."); *see also* U.S. v. Arnett, 353 F.3d 765, 766 (9th Cir. 2003) (en banc) (per curiam order) (government may not use offensive collateral estoppel to establish an element of a criminal offense or to conclusively rebut an affirmative defense on which the Government bears the burden of proof beyond a reasonable doubt).

[932]University of Tennessee v. Elliott, 478 U.S. 788, 799, 106 S. Ct. 3220 (1986).

[933]Simpson v. Nickel, 450 F.3d 303, 306 (7th Cir. 2006); Johnson v. Freeburn, 144 F. Supp. 2d 817, 823 (E.D.Mich. 2001); Marquez v. Gutierrez, 51 F. Supp. 2d 1020 (E.D.Cal. 1999); Riley v. Kurtz, 893 F. Supp. 709, 720–21 (E.D.Mich. 1995). *Simpson* also says that a contrary ruling would mean that "prison disciplinary boards could immunize guards who violate prisoners' rights, and the act of penalizing speech would be self-vindicating," *Simpson*, 450 F.3d at 308, suggesting that the First Amendment itself would bar giving disciplinary findings preclusive effect. *See also* Johnson v. Freeburn, 144 F. Supp. 2d at 823 (noting that allowing disciplinary hearings to preclude litigation of retaliation claims would put pressure on hearing officers to avoid dismissing marginal disciplinary charges to protect officers from litigation).

[934]Johnson v. Freeburn, 144 F. Supp. 2d at 823 (noting that prisoners can be convicted at disciplinary hearings on hearsay from confidential informants); *see* Gwinn v. Awmiller, 354 F.3d

whether such hearings are judicial in nature and whether they are likely to provide an impartial forum for resolution of disputes between prisoners and prison staff.[935]

N. Statutes of Limitations

Statutes of limitations are time limits on filing a lawsuit. If you wait too long, your suit will be "time-barred" and there is nothing you can do to revive it. For this reason, when you plan to file a suit, find out what the statute of limitations is, and don't put things off until the last minute. If you make a mistake or have a problem with prison procedures that delays your filing, you could lose your right to sue.

The statute of limitations is an affirmative defense, which means that the defendants have the burden of pleading it in their answer and proving that the claim is time-barred.[936]

Different kinds of lawsuits involve different statutes of limitations. Statutes of limitations generally apply to damage claims, but some states also have limitations for other kinds of actions.[937] Equitable (injunctive) claims generally are not subject to statutes of limitations,[938] though they may be subject to the equitable doctrine of laches.[939]

State law suits are governed by state statutes of limitations, and different state statutes may apply to different kinds of cases.[940] Federal civil rights actions do not have their own statutes of limitations, and are also governed by state statutes, but the Supreme Court has ruled that in each state, all § 1983 claims are governed by one state statute, the state's "general or residual statute for personal injury actions."[941] The same rule applies to *Bivens* civil rights actions against

---

1211, 1219 n.3 (10th Cir. 2004) (noting prison sex offender hearing would not be preclusive in later non-prison proceedings); Colon v. Coughlin, 58 F.3d 865, 869 (2d Cir. 1995) ("We think there is a substantial question as to whether, under New York law, collateral estoppel should ever apply to fact issues determined in a prison disciplinary hearing and reviewed for substantial evidence in an Article 78 proceeding, given the 'procedural laxity' of such prison hearings, . . . and the limited nature of substantial-evidence review." (dictum)); *see generally* Wolff v. McDonnell, 418 U.S. 539, 94 S. Ct. 2963 (1974) (denying prisoners right of confrontation and cross-examination; holding the right to call witnesses and present documentary evidence limited by "institutional safety [and] correctional goals"; denying right to counsel). The Supreme Court cited similar considerations in denying federal prison disciplinary hearing officers absolute immunity. Cleavinger v. Saxner, 474 U.S. 193, 206, 106 S. Ct. 496 (1985) ("The prisoner was to be afforded neither a lawyer nor an independent nonstaff representative. There was no right to compel the attendance of witnesses or to cross-examine. There was no right to discovery. There was no cognizable burden of proof. No verbatim transcript was afforded. Information presented often was hearsay or self-serving. The committee members were not truly independent. In sum, the members had no identification with the judicial process of the kind and depth that has occasioned absolute immunity.").

[935]Johnson v. Freeburn, 144 F. Supp. 2d at 823 (noting that a preclusion rule would result in pressure on hearing officers not to dismiss disciplinary charges); Marquez v. Gutierrez, 51 F. Supp. 2d at 1027 (noting state courts' holding that a disciplinary hearing is not a "judicial-type adversary proceeding" and is not conducted by a "detached and neutral judicial officer acting in a judicial capacity"). The Supreme Court made similar observations in holding that prison disciplinary hearing officers are entitled only to qualified immunity and not absolute quasi-judicial immunity. Cleavinger v. Saxner, 474 U.S. at 203–04. While these comments do not directly concern preclusion, they should be called to the court's attention if defendants suggest your disciplinary conviction should have preclusive effect in your lawsuit.

[936]Tello v. Dean Witter Reynolds, Inc., 494 F.3d 956, 974 (11th Cir. 2007); Cooey v. Strickland, 479 F.3d 412, 416 (6th Cir. 2007), *cert. denied*, 128 S. Ct. 2047 (2008); Fratus v. Deland, 49 F.3d 673, 675 (10th Cir. 1995).

If you claim that you are entitled to an exception to the statute of limitations, you will have the burden of proof on that point. Firstcom, Inc. v. Qwest Corp., 555 F.3d 669, 675 (8th Cir. 2009).

[937]Actions seeking judicial review of administrative action may have statutes of limitations. *See* § D.2 of this chapter.

[938]*See* Holmberg v. Armbrecht, 327 U.S. 392, 396, 66 S. Ct. 582 (1946).

Recently, several courts have held that § 1983 challenges to methods of execution are subject to the statute of limitations governing § 1983 cases. Walker v. Epps, 550 F.3d 407, 411–12 (5th Cir. 2008), *cert. denied*, 130 S. Ct. 57 (2009); Cooey v. Strickland, 479 F.3d 412 (6th Cir. 2007), *cert. denied*, 128 S. Ct. 2047 (2008).

[939]Laches is "an equitable defense that applies where there is '(1) lack of diligence by the party against whom the defense is asserted, and (2) prejudice to the party asserting the defense'" resulting from the delay in bringing suit. Nat'l R.R. Passenger Corp. v. Morgan, 536 U.S. 101, 121–22, 122 S. Ct. 2061 (2002) (internal quotation marks omitted). As far as we know, this doctrine is rarely used in prisoner injunctive litigation.

[940]For example, many states have separate statutes of limitations for intentional torts, non-intentional torts, medical malpractice, tort suits against state or local government, and suits against sheriffs.

The FTCA, which permits federal prisoners to bring tort suits under state law against the federal government, has its own limitations provisions, discussed in § C.2.b of this chapter.

[941]Owens v. Okure, 488 U.S. 235, 243–50, 109 S. Ct. 573 (1989) (rejecting the use of the statute of limitations for intentional torts); *see* Farrell v. McDonough, 966 F.2d 279, 280–82 (7th Cir. 1992) (applying the state's most general personal injury statute rather than a residual statute that included non-tort claims); Duffy v. Mass. Dep't of Corrections, 746 F. Supp. 232, 233 (D.Mass. 1990) (statute of limitations for state certiorari proceedings did not apply to § 1983 actions).

A "general" personal injury statute of limitations is one which applies to all personal injury actions except for certain specific exceptions. A "residual" statute of limitations is one which applies to all kinds of lawsuits, including personal injury actions, not specifically provided for by another statute of limitations. You should first determine if your state has a general personal injury statute. You should look for a residual statute only if there is no general personal injury statute. Owens v. Okure, 488 U.S. at 250–51 n.12; Moore v. Liberty Nat'l Life Ins. Co., 267 F.3d 1209, 1219 (11th Cir. 2001) (Alabama residual statute is two years).

federal prison personnel.[942] If a state passes a special short statute of limitations for federal civil rights actions or for prisoner actions, it will not be applied in § 1983 or *Bivens* actions.[943]

Suits under some federal statutes are governed by the Uniform Statute of Limitations on Federal Claims, which provides a four-year statute of limitation for any cause of action or claim that is created by Congress after December 1, 1990.[944] That four-year limitations period applies to claims under the Religious Freedom Restoration Act (RFRA), enacted in 1993,[945] and the Religious Land Use and Institutionalized Person Act (RLUIPA), enacted in 2000.[946] Claims under Title II of the Americans with Disabilities Act (ADA), which was enacted before December 1, 1990, are governed by the state limitations period, like § 1983 suits.[947]

This means that state and federal legal claims arising from the same set of facts may be subject to different limitations periods, even if you bring them in the same case. For example, a § 1983 claim based on a beating by officers will be governed by the "general or residual" personal injury statute, while the state law assault and battery claim arising from the same incident may be governed by a separate statute specifically for assault cases or for intentional torts.

If the incident involved interference with religious practice, a RLUIPA or RFRA claim would be governed by the four-year period for federal statutory claims, and a state law religious rights claim might be governed by yet another statute of limitations.

State statutes of limitations applicable to § 1983 claims range from six years to as short as one year, with most in the range of two to three years.[948] (The Supreme Court has held that a six-month limitations period is too short for § 1983 cases.[949]) Since state legislatures can change statutes of limitations whenever they want, you should always check the current statutes to make sure you know what the time limit is.

In federal court, the statute of limitations generally starts to run when the claim "accrues," *i.e.*, when the plaintiff knows or has reason to know of the wrong upon which the action is based.[950] There is an exception to this rule for actions that, if successful, would demonstrate that a prisoner's criminal conviction or sentence or continuing confinement is invalid. Such claims do not accrue until and unless the prisoner gets the relevant decision (which may be a criminal conviction or sentence, or a loss of good time, a parole revocation, or a miscalculation of sentence) overturned administratively or judicially.[951] The limitations period would start to run on the date that the challenged decision is overturned.

If a violation of rights takes place over a period of time, it may be considered to be a "continuing wrong" (or continuing harm, violation, etc.). That means the statute of limitations may not start to run until the end of that period,[952]

---

[942]*See* § B.2 of this chapter, n.88.

[943]Arnold v. Duchesne County, 26 F.3d 982, 987–88 (10th Cir. 1994); Johnson v. Davis, 582 F.2d 1316, 1317–19 (4th Cir. 1978); Shelton v. Angelone, 148 F. Supp. 2d 670, 677 (W.D.Va. 2001) (declining to apply a state statute providing that prisoner claims about conditions of confinement must be brought in one year, or six months after exhaustion of administrative remedies, in § 1983 case), *aff'd*, 49 Fed.Appx. 451 (4th Cir. 2002) (unpublished); Larson v. Snow College, 189 F. Supp. 2d 1286, 1292–97 (D.Utah 2000).

[944]28 U.S.C.A. § 1658(a) ("Except as otherwise provided by law, a civil action arising under an Act of Congress enacted after the date of the enactment of this section may not be commenced later than 4 years after the cause of action accrues.").

[945]Pineda-Morales v. De Rosa, 2005 WL 1607276, *8 (D.N.J., July 6, 2005) (citing Jama v. U.S. INS, 343 F. Supp. 2d 338, 365 (D.N.J. 2004)).

[946]Couch v. Jabe, 479 F. Supp. 2d 569, 577 (W.D.Va. 2006); U.S. v. Maui County, 298 F. Supp. 2d 1010, 1012–1013 (D.Haw. 2003).

[947]*See, e.g.*, Foster v. Morris, 208 Fed.Appx. 174, 178 (3d Cir. 2006) (unpublished); Gaona v. Town & Country Credit, 324 F.3d 1050, 1055–56 (8th Cir. 2003); Pickern v. Holiday Quality Foods Inc., 293 F.3d 1133, 1137 n.3 (9th Cir. 2002).

One court suggested that the four-year period of the Uniform Statute of Limitations on Federal Claims might apply to the ADA because parts of the ADA did not actually go into effect until 1992. Holmes v. Texas A & M University, 145 F.3d 681, 686 (5th Cir. 1998). However, later decisions have rejected that idea. Coker v. Dallas County Jail, 2008 WL 763167, *3–4 (N.D.Tex. 2008), *accepted in part, rejected in part on other grounds*, 2008 WL 763166 (N.D.Tex., Mar. 19, 2008); Chisholm v. United of Omaha Life Ins. Co., 514 F. Supp. 2d 318, 326 (D.Conn. 2007) and cases cited; Duprey v. Conn. DMV, 191 F.R.D. 329, 341 (D.Conn. 2000); Doukas v. Metropolitan Life Ins. Co., 882 F. Supp. 1197, 1200 n.4 (D.N.H.1995).

[948]Martin A. Schwartz, 1B *Section 1983 Litigation: Claims and Defenses* at § 1202[B] (Supp. 2009). At present, one-year statutes of limitations apply to civil rights actions in several states: Kentucky, *see* Dixon v. Clem, 492 F.3d 665 (6th Cir. 2007); Collard v. Board of Nursing, 896 F.2d at 181–82 (citing Ky.Rev.Stat.Ann. § 413.140(1) (a)); Louisiana, *see* Bourdais v. New Orleans, 485 F.3d 294 (5th Cir. 2007); Elzy v. Roberson, 868 F.2d 793, 794 (5th Cir. 1989) (citing La.Ev.Code Ann., tit. 3492); Puerto Rico, *see* Lopez-Gonzalez v. Municipality of Camero, 404 F.3d 548 (1st Cir. 2005); Rodriguez Narvaez v. Nazario, 895 F.2d 38, 42 (1st Cir. 1990) (citing P.R.Laws Ann., tit. 31, § 5298(2)); Tennessee, *see* Eidson v. Tennessee Dep't of Children's Servs., 510 F.3d 631 (6th Cir. 2007); Collard v. Board of Nursing, 896 F.2d at 183 n.4.

[949]Burnett v. Grattan, 468 U.S. 42, 50–53, 104 S. Ct. 2924 (1984).

[950]Marrero-Gutierrez v. Molina, 491 F.3d 1, 5–6 (1st Cir. 2007); Brown v. Ga. Bd. of Pardons & Paroles, 335 F.3d 1259, 1261 (11th Cir. 2003). Different rules may apply in state courts.

[951]This rule is discussed in § H.1 of this chapter.

[952]*See* Heard v. Sheahan, 253 F.3d 316, 320 (7th Cir. 2001) (adopting continuing wrongs rule for § 1983 suits) and cases cited; *accord*, Shomo v. City of New York, 579 F.3d 176, 181 (2d Cir. 2009) (following *Heard v. Sheahan*); Hensley v. City of Columbus, 557 F.3d 693, 697 (6th Cir. 2009) ("continuous violation" exists if "(1) the defendants engage in continuing wrongful conduct; (2) injury to the plaintiffs accrues continuously; and (3) had the defendants at any time ceased their wrongful conduct, further injury would have been avoided"); *see* Tiberi v. Cigna Corp., 89 F.3d 1423,

and a plaintiff can recover for the whole course of conduct even if it started outside the limitations period.[953] The continuing wrong rule is applicable to continuing wrongful action, *not* to continuing injury accruing from an earlier wrong.[954] However, when the basis of the complaint is an ongoing failure to treat an ongoing harm, the continuing wrong rule may be applicable.[955]

Do not rely on the continuing wrong rule if you don't have to. Courts often decline to apply it, especially if they think the plaintiff should have been able to bring suit earlier.[956] The continuing wrong doctrine does not apply to a series of discrete actions,[957] and it can be hard to know where the line is drawn between continuing and discrete. A series of events that are related but of different types will probably not be treated as a continuing wrong.[958] Courts have disagreed whether a term in segregation is a continuing violation which accrues only upon release.[959] You should therefore play it safe and try to bring your suit early enough so that everything that you want to recover for is within the limitations period, and you don't have to rely on the continuing violation rule.

In federal court, to satisfy the statute of limitations, you need only file your complaint before the limitations period has run.[960] (State law may differ; some states require you to file *and* serve the complaint within the limitations period, though this law will not be applied in federal court.[961]) Ordinarily, a complaint is considered filed for limitations

---

1430–31 (10th Cir. 1996) (applying New Mexico law and holding claim accrues, and limitations period runs, from date of last injury or when "the wrong is over and done with").

[953]Heard v. Sheahan, 253 F.3d at 318 ("A violation is called 'continuing,' signifying that a plaintiff can reach back to its beginning even if that beginning lies outside the statutory limitations period, when it would be unreasonable to require or even permit him to sue separately over every incident of the defendant's unlawful conduct."); Taylor v. Meirick, 712 F.2d 1112, 1118–19 (7th Cir. 1983); Ingalls v. Florio, 968 F. Supp. 193, 200–01 (D.N.J. 1997) (claims of denial of medical care were continuing violations); Little v. Lycoming County, 912 F. Supp. 809, 815 (M.D.Pa. 1996) (claims of failure to accommodate disability and of exposure to second-hand smoke were continuing violations), *aff'd*, 101 F.3d 691(3d Cir. 1996).

[954]Delaware State College v. Ricks, 449 U.S. 250, 258, 101 S. Ct. 487 (1980).

[955]Shomo v. City of New York, 579 F.3d at 181 (plaintiff must allege ongoing policy of deliberate indifference to medical needs and some acts in furtherance of the policy within the limitations period); Heard v. Sheahan, 253 F.3d at 318 (ongoing failure to treat a painful medical condition was a continuing violation for limitations purposes).

[956]Wilson v. Giesen, 956 F.2d 738, 743 (7th Cir. 1992) (continuing wrong rule does not apply to cases where the harm was "definite and discoverable" and redress could have been sought at an earlier date); Anderson v. City of Chicago, 803 F. Supp. 1327, 1329 (N.D.Ill. 1992) (false arrest claim accrues on the date of arrest even if it results in imprisonment after arrest).

Though the continuing wrong rule is often invoked in medical care cases, courts often find reasons not to apply it. *See, e.g.,* Shell v. Brzezniak, 365 F. Supp. 2d 362, 368 (W.D.N.Y. 2005) (continuing wrong rule did not apply where the defendants involved in the older parts of the claim were not involved in any actions within the limitations period); Lopez v. U.S., 349 F. Supp. 2d 179, 185 (D. Mass. 2004) ("The doctrine permits a patient to repose trust in the treating doctor, and excuses a patient from challenging the quality of care by filing suit until the doctor–patient relationship has ended." The plaintiff was not entitled to the benefit of the continuing wrong rule for events that happened after he retained a lawyer, which disrupted the doctor–patient relationship.).

[957]Scott v. Garcia, 370 F. Supp. 2d 1056, 1065 (S.D.Cal. 2005) (continuing treatment rule not applicable to discrete acts such as decisions to transfer or to delay treatment; plaintiff failed to show a "systemic policy or practice" underlying those acts); Jama v. U.S. Immigration and Naturalization Service, 343 F. Supp. 2d 338, 364 (D.N.J. 2004) (allegations of beatings, thefts, sexual misconduct

may be discrete acts not treated as continuing violations); Konigsberg v. LeFevre, 267 F. Supp. 2d 255, 262–63 (N.D.N.Y. 2003).

In some cases, courts have held that a series of discrete acts that stem from an event earlier than the limitations period is a continuing violation, so the whole series is not time-barred based on the date of the initial event, but those particular acts that occurred earlier than the limitations period *are* time-barred. *See, e.g.,* Wells v. U.S., 420 F.3d 1343, 1346–47 (Fed.Cir. 2005) (challenge to deductions from prison account was not time-barred because they were continuing, but prisoner could only challenge those deductions made within the limitations period).

[958]For example, if you are beaten, given an unconstitutional disciplinary hearing, and then subjected to unlawful conditions in segregation for a year, the court is likely to hold that these are separate claims; if you wait too long, you may be able to sue only about the segregation conditions but not the beating or the hearing.

[959]*Compare* Edmonson v. Coughlin, 21 F. Supp. 2d 242, 246 (W.D.N.Y. 1998) (yes) *with* Love v. Cook County, 82 F. Supp. 2d 911, 914–15 (N.D.Ill. 2000) (no). The *Edmonson* decision is consistent with law holding that claims for failure to release on time and for false imprisonment accrue at the time of release. *See* Abiff v. Slaton, 806 F. Supp. 993, 996 (N.D.Ga. 1992), *aff'd,* 3 F.3d 443 (11th Cir. 1993) (citing Donaldson v. O'Connor, 493 F.2d 507, 529 (5th Cir.1974), *vacated on other grounds,* 422 U.S. 563, 95 S. Ct. 2486 (1975)). *But see* Savory v. Lyons, 469 F.3d 667, 672–73 (7th Cir. 2006) (refusing to apply continuing violation rule to ongoing imprisonment resulting from denial of access to DNA evidence where plaintiff said he was not challenging the fact or duration of confinement; plaintiff knew of the violation of rights as of the denial). Consistently with *Savory,* it might be that a period of segregation that results from a single wrongful act (*e.g.,* an unlawful disciplinary proceeding) is not a continuing violation, but a case in which prison officials review and continue the segregation on an ongoing basis is a continuing violation.

[960]*See, e.g.,* West v. Conrail, 481 U.S. 35, 39, 107 S. Ct. 1538 (1987); Henderson v. U.S., 517 U.S. 654, 657 n.2, 116 S. Ct. 1658 (1996) ("In a suit on a right created by federal law, filing a complaint suffices to satisfy the statute of limitations."); *cf.* Houston v. Lack, 487 U.S. 266, 108 S. Ct. 2379 (1988).

[961]McGuire v. Turnbo, 137 F.3d 321, 323–24 (5th Cir. 1998).

purposes when the clerk receives it.[962] Since prisoners are usually dependent on prison staff to send their mail, the federal courts have held that a prisoner's complaint or other document is filed as of the time the prisoner gives it to prison staff or places it in the prison mailbox consistently with prison procedure for legal mail. (State courts do not all follow the mailbox rule; be sure you know what your state law requires.[963]) If a complaint is otherwise timely, it will not become time-barred just because the actual filing in the clerk's office is delayed by clerical errors or screening or processing procedures, or even the plaintiff's failure to comply with all rules.[964]

Sometimes a statute of limitations is "tolled" (suspended). Federal courts which "borrow" state statutes of limitations also borrow their tolling rules.[965] Limitations periods may be tolled by statute when a person is mentally ill or otherwise incapacitated,[966] a minor,[967] or for other reasons. Courts have mostly held that the limitations period is tolled while a prisoner is exhausting administrative remedies as required by the Prison Litigation Reform Act.[968] Some state statutes provide that the limitations period is tolled while a person is incarcerated.[969] These statutes can present technical issues of interpretation,[970] so it is not wise to rely on them unless you are absolutely sure of how the courts have applied them. In addition, there has been a trend to get rid of special tolling rules for prisoners.[971] Be sure you have the current version of the relevant state statute before you rely on it.

Tolling rules that discriminate against federal civil rights claims, or against certain kinds of them, are inconsistent with the policy of § 1983 and will not be applied in § 1983 cases.[972] When statutes of limitations are shortened by state legislatures, persons affected must be allowed a reasonable time to get their claims in.[973]

If your case is dismissed without prejudice, but the statute of limitations has run, ordinarily it will be time-barred.[974] Some states have statutes that toll the limitations period, or provide a set period of time in which to re-file, where a case that was timely filed is dismissed for reasons other than the

---

[962]Rule 5(d)(2), Fed.R.Civ.P. ("A paper is filed by delivering it . . . to the clerk. . . .").

[963]*See* Ch. 10, § H., for a further discussion of the prison mailbox rule.

[964]Complaints presented to the clerk within the limitations period have been deemed timely even though their formal filing was delayed by the failure to provide the necessary prison account statement, Garrett v. Clarke, 147 F.3d 745 (8th Cir. 1998); the need to process an *in forma pauperis* application, Toliver v. Sullivan County, 841 F.2d 41, 42 (2d Cir. 1988); errors in the clerk's office, Owens-El v. U.S. Attorney General, 759 F.2d 349, 350 (4th Cir. 1985); and the plaintiff's errors. Robinson v. Doe, 272 F.3d 921, 922–23 (7th Cir. 2001) (complaint was deemed filed when received, even though it was returned to plaintiff because he failed to enclose filing fee or *in forma pauperis* motion). The *Robinson* case cites the rule that the clerk "shall not refuse to accept for filing any paper presented for that purpose solely because it is not presented in proper form as required by these rules or any local rules." Rule 5(d) (4), Fed.R.Civ.P. (formerly Rule 5(e)).

[965]Board of Regents v. Tomanio, 446 U.S. 478, 483–86, 100 S. Ct. 1790 (1980). *But see* Dixon v. Chrans, 986 F.2d 201, 205–06 (7th Cir. 1993) (tolling provision that singled out prisoner suits against prison personnel would not be applied because it unduly burdened the § 1983 remedy).

[966]*See* Fratus v. Deland, 49 F.3d 673, 675 (10th Cir. 1995); Neiberger v. Hawkins, 208 F.R.D. 301, 311 (D.Colo. 2002) (state statute tolling limitations during disability, and giving unrepresented persons an additional two years, applied to persons committed as not guilty by reason of insanity). *But see* Douglas v. York County, 433 F.3d 143, 152–53 (1st Cir. 2005) (plaintiff denied tolling on grounds of mental illness where she had been able to function in society during the relevant period); Bradley v. Macomb County, 370 F. Supp. 2d 607, 611 (E.D.Mich. 2005) (plaintiff denied tolling on grounds of mental illness where he was able to comprehend his rights).

[967]Papa v. U.S., 281 F.3d 1004, 1009 (9th Cir. 2002) (claims of minor children are tolled until they reach the age of majority unless they file suit earlier under California law); Paige v. Police Dep't of City of Schenectady, 264 F.3d 197, 199–200 (2d Cir. 2001) (minor's claims accrued at age of majority, and she was obliged to sue within the limitations period after she became an adult).

[968]*See* Ch. 9, § D.9. Some courts have held that this depends on state law, so be sure you know what courts in your jurisdiction have said about this point.

[969]Hardin v. Straub, 490 U.S. 536, 540 n.8, 109 S. Ct. 1998 (1989) (listing states with such statutes as of 1989).

[970]*See, e.g.,* Bianchi v. Bellingham Police Dep't, 909 F.2d 1316, 1318 (9th Cir. 1990) (statute applies only to "actual, uninterrupted incarceration"); Jones v. City of Hamtramck, 905 F.2d 908, 909 (6th Cir. 1990) (law tolling statute of limitations for imprisoned persons did not apply to pretrial detainees); Arnold v. District of Columbia, 211 F. Supp. 2d 144, 147–48 (D.D.C. 2002) (local statute of limitations may be tolled when the complainant is imprisoned at the time the right of action accrues, but if the complainant is subsequently released, the statute of limitations begins running immediately and is not again tolled if the plaintiff is reincarcerated on separate charges; *see* Gausvik v. Perez, 239 F. Supp. 2d 1108, 1123–24 (E.D.Wash. 2002) (upholding statute tolling limitations during pre-sentencing incarceration but not after sentencing), *rev'd in part on other grounds,* 345 F.3d 813 (9th Cir. 2003).

[971]*See* Delgado-Brunet v. Clark, 93 F.3d 339, 342 (7th Cir. 1996) (Illinois); Brown v. Wigginton, 981 F.2d 913, 914 (6th Cir. 1992) (Kentucky); Wilson v. Giesen, 956 F.2d 738, 741 (7th Cir. 1992) (Illinois); Street v. Vose, 936 F.2d 38, 40 (1st Cir. 1991) (Massachusetts); Burrell v. Newsome, 883 F.2d 416, 419 (5th Cir. 1989) (Texas); *see also* Jones v. Blanas, 393 F.3d 918, 927–28 (9th Cir. 2004) (noting California's two-year tolling for incarceration).

[972]Dixon v. Chrans, 986 F.2d 201, 205 (7th Cir. 1993) (statute tolling limitations period for imprisoned persons except for claims against prison system or its officials); Hughes v. Sheriff, 814 F.2d 532, 535 (8th Cir. 1987) (state law that tolled the limitations period for imprisoned persons, but excluded federal civil rights actions from tolling), *appeal dismissed and cert. denied,* 484 U.S. 802 (1987).

[973]Delgado-Brunet v. Clark, 93 F.3d 339, 342 (7th Cir. 1996).

[974]Long v. Simmons, 77 F.3d 878, 880 (5th Cir. 1996); McCoy v. Goord, 255 F. Supp. 2d 233, 252 (S.D.N.Y. 2003).

merits.[975] These "savings statutes" may apply where your case is dismissed for filing in the wrong court, *e.g.*, if you file your state law claim in federal court and it is dismissed.[976] The details of these statutes vary from state to state.[977] There is a federal savings statute for state law claims that are filed in federal court under their supplemental (pendent) jurisdiction; the state limitations period is tolled while the case is in federal court and for 30 days after dismissal, unless state law provides for a longer tolling period.[978]

If you were prevented by circumstances outside your control from filing suit within the statute of limitations, you may be able to proceed anyway. The doctrine of equitable tolling provides that in some circumstances, a plaintiff who has exercised due diligence but has not been able to file suit within the limitations period still be allowed to go forward, whether or not the defendants are responsible for the plaintiff's failure.[979] Courts have held that inability to file timely caused by the restrictions of imprisonment, and especially by those of segregated housing, may support an argument of equitable tolling.[980] Some courts have held that

"extraordinary circumstances" must be shown to merit equitable tolling,[981] especially in cases involving the one-year time limit for habeas corpus petitions of the Antiterrorism and Effective Death Penalty Act.[982] If you miss the deadline in part because you waited until the last minute to file, courts are not likely to give you the benefit of equitable tolling.[983] If you did not exercise diligence in trying to file timely, your case will not be equitably tolled.[984]

The doctrine of equitable estoppel tolls the limitations period in cases where defendants engaged in misrepresentation or concealment or other misconduct, and the plaintiff delayed bringing suit in reliance on it.[985] Equitable estoppel

---

[975]*See, e.g.*, Miller v. Norris, 247 F.3d 736, 740 (8th Cir. 2001) (Arkansas law gave plaintiff a year to reinstate his suit after a dismissal for failure to exhaust administrative remedies).

[976]*See, e.g.*, Delgado v. New York City Dep't of Correction, 797 F. Supp. 327, 329 (S.D.N.Y. 1992).

[977]*Compare* Thomas v. Timko, 428 F. Supp. 2d 855, 856–57 (N.D.Ind. 2006) (where case was dismissed for non-exhaustion, limitations period was not tolled because state statute applied only if dismissal did not result from negligence in prosecution, and failure to exhaust was negligence) *with* Allaway v. McGinnis, 362 F. Supp. 2d 390, 393–96 (W.D.N.Y. 2005) (holding dismissal for non-exhaustion is within scope of state statute providing that actions timely commenced and terminated otherwise than a voluntary discontinuance, lack of personal jurisdiction, failure to prosecute, or final judgment on the merits may be refiled within six months).

[978]28 U.S.C. § 1367(d); *see* § F.1 of this chapter, nn.467–468.

[979]Shropshear v. Corporation Counsel of Chicago, 275 F.3d 593, 595 (7th Cir. 2001); *see* Donald v. Cook County Sheriff's Dep't, 95 F.3d 548, 562 (7th Cir. 1996) (plaintiff may be entitled to equitable tolling because of the plaintiff's inability to identify the people who injured him without discovery or the assistance of the court and the court's delay and ultimate denial of his motion for appointment of counsel, combined with lack of notice that the plaintiff had sued the wrong defendants); Wisenbaker v. Farwell, 341 F. Supp. 2d 1160, 1165–68 (D.Nev. 2004) (citing plaintiff's diligence in pursuing his claim and his *pro se* status and probable lack of understanding of the consequences of filing an earlier suit before exhaustion was completed; noting lack of prejudice to defendants); White v. Cooper, 55 F. Supp. 2d 848, 856–57 (N.D.Ill. 1999) (equitable tolling applied where prisoner sought discovery timely but defendants did not respond and court did not enforce requests promptly; equitable tolling "does not depend on the fault of any particular defendant, but rather on a plaintiff's inability, despite due diligence, to obtain information vital to bringing a claim").

[980]Fogle v. Pierson, 435 F.3d 1252, 1258–59 (10th Cir. 2006); Jones v. Blanas, 393 F.3d 918, 929 (9th Cir. 2004) (to deny tolling would "effectively insulate from legal challenge the very confinement that may unconstitutionally restrict a detainee's access to justice in

the first place"). *But see* Roberts v. Barreras, 484 F.3d 1236, 1241–42 (10th Cir. 2007) (under New Mexico law, *Bivens* action not tolled due to alleged denial of law library access to learn the proper statute of limitations).

[981]Fogle v. Pierson, 435 F.3d at 1258–59; Walker v. Jastremski, 430 F.3d 560, 564 (2d Cir. 2005) (exceptional circumstances must be beyond the party's control); Moody v. Kearney, 380 F. Supp. 2d 393, 397–98 (D.Del. 2005) (claim that action about which prisoner was complaining injured him so badly that he could not pursue a remedy timely appeared to meet extraordinary circumstances standard); Langella v. Bush, 306 F. Supp. 2d 459, 467 (S.D.N.Y. 2004) (plaintiff met requirement of "exceptional circumstances" and diligence where he was *pro se* and he missed the deadline by only three days).

[982]*See* Ch. 3, § C, nn.411–416.

[983]Wayne v. Jarvis, 197 F.3d 1098, 1104 (11th Cir. 1999) (plaintiff waited until 16 days before the end of the limitations period to file); U.S. ex rel. Santiago v. Hinsley, 297 F. Supp. 2d 1065, 1067–68 (N.D.Ill. 2003).

[984]Paige v. Police Dep't of City of Schenectady, 264 F.3d 197, 199–200 (2d Cir. 2001) (where plaintiff had enough information to sue timely, equitable tolling did not apply despite police cover-up); Pompey v. Lumpkin, 321 F. Supp. 2d 1254, 1265–66 (M.D.Ala. 2004) ("Equitable tolling is not appropriate when the plaintiff could have, through due diligence, discovered the correct defendant's name within the limitations period."), *aff'd*, 127 Fed.Appx. 473 (11th Cir. 2005) (unpublished); Howze v. Zon, 319 F. Supp. 2d 344, 346–47 (W.D.N.Y. 2004).

[985]Guerrero v. Gates, 442 F.3d 697, 706–07 (9th Cir. 2006) (estoppel denied where plaintiff did not rely on defendants' misrepresentation); Bell v. City of Milwaukee, 746 F.2d 1205, 1229–31 (7th Cir. 1984), *overruled on other grounds*, Russ v. Watts, 414 F.3d 783 (7th Cir. 2005); Doe v. Thompson, 332 F. Supp. 2d 124, 134 (D.D.C. 2004) (limitations period not tolled absent "materially and willfully misrepresent[ation]" of relevant information); Howard v. Mendez, 304 F. Supp. 2d 632, 636 (M.D.Pa. 2004) (holding Pennsylvania estoppel rule is not limited to "fraud 'in the strictest sense,' but also extends to a defendant's conduct that is even unintentionally an act of fraud of concealment that leads the plaintiff not to file within the limitations period"); Ovando v. City of Los Angeles, 92 F. Supp. 2d 1011, 1024 (C.D.Cal. 2000) ("A public entity may be estopped from asserting non-compliance with [the state tort claim act's limitations period] when affirmative acts of its agents, especially authority figures, deterred the filing of a timely claim." Here, police officers testified falsely to cover up their misconduct.).

is sometimes also called fraudulent concealment.[986] The courts are not always consistent in using these terms, and the details of these doctrines vary among states and the federal government,[987] so be sure to look at the law from the jurisdiction where you will be litigating.

You should never count on getting the benefit of any of these rules; do everything you can to file your complaint timely. If there is something you think you need for your complaint, but you can't get it in time, you are probably better off filing your incomplete complaint timely and then seeking to amend it later.

Your suit must be commenced within the statute of limitations against each defendant in order to keep that defendant in the case. You can amend your complaint after the limitations period has expired if "the amendment asserts a claim or defense that arose out of the conduct, transaction, or occurrence set out—or attempted to be set out—in the original pleading,"[988] which basically means if the amendment deals with the same subject matter. However, you can't name new defendants after the limitations period has expired, unless you can satisfy the "same subject matter" rule *and* unless, within the time permitted for service of process,[989] the new defendants received adequate notice of the action, and they knew or should have known that they would have been sued "but for a mistake concerning the proper party's identity."[990]

Rule 15(c)'s requirement of a "mistake" concerning a defendant's identity is applied strictly. It covers situations where you sued the wrong person.[991] It also applies where the plaintiff sued the wrong *kind* of defendant, *e.g.*, she sued a municipality where only individual liability was appropriate, and later sought to add individual defendants; this is a mistake of law.[992] However, most courts hold that it *does not* cover situations where you simply didn't know who the proper defendant was. That means if you learn only after filing your complaint that a particular person was involved in violating your rights, or if you name "John Doe" defendants because you know what they did but you don't know their names, you probably cannot add those persons once you know their identity unless you do it within the limitations period.[993] Some decisions do treat lack of knowledge as a mistake for purposes of this rule, but they are a minority.[994]

Even in cases that do involve a "mistake" within the meaning of Rule 15(c), you must also satisfy the notice requirements of the rule.[995]

For these reasons, you should make every effort to identify and name all the proper defendants before the statute of limitations has run, *e.g.*, by taking the necessary discovery

---

[986]Guerrero v. Gates, 442 F.3d 697, 706 (5th Cir. 2006); Williams v. Hartje, 827 F.2d 1203, 1205–06 (8th Cir. 1987).

[987]*See, e.g.*, Garrett v. Fleming, 362 F.3d 692, 697 (10th Cir. 2004) (holding plaintiff was not entitled to equitable tolling because he did not show fraudulent concealment as required by Colorado law).

[988]Rule 15(c)(1)(B), Fed.R.Civ.P.

[989]This is 120 days after the complaint is filed, unless the court extends the time. Rule 4(m), Fed.R.Civ.P.

[990]Rule 15(c)(1)(C), Fed.R.Civ.P.; *see* Jackson v. Kotter, 541 F.3d 688, 696 (7th Cir. 2008) (plaintiff's error in naming individual defendants, rather than the United States, in a FTCA suit was the kind of mistake that Rule 15(c) allows to be corrected; the Attorney General and U.S. Attorney received sufficient notice of the suit and should have known the United States was the proper defendant); Moore v. City of Harriman, 272 F.3d 769, 774 (6th Cir. 2001) (allowing amendment to sue parties in individual capacity rather than official capacity where they had notice of the suit by being served in their official capacities); Soto v. Brooklyn Correctional Facility, 80 F.3d 34, 36 (2d Cir. 1996) (where plaintiff sued the jail but not individual officers, the officers, who are presumed to know the law, would know that they would have been sued if they heard about the lawsuit); Lacedra v. Donald W. Wyatt Detention Facility, 334 F. Supp. 2d 114, 130–32 (D.R.I. 2004) (where plaintiff named the detention facility as defendant, made it clear he was trying to sue whoever was in charge, and the administration and the private medical provider had the same lawyer, the private provider had sufficient notice it would be sued and the claim related back).

[991]*See, e.g.*, Bradley v. Macomb County, 370 F. Supp. 2d 607, 611–13 (E.D.Mich. 2005).

[992]Hayes v. Faulkner County, Ark., 388 F.3d 669, 675–76 (8th Cir. 2004) (claim against jail administrator related back where county was sued and administrator had notice); Mosley v. Jablonsky, 209 F.R.D. 48, 51–53 (E.D.N.Y. 2002) (where plaintiff sued municipal agencies but did not allege a municipal policy, failure to name individuals was a mistake of law, and amendment to add individual defendants related back); *see also* cases cited in n.990, above.

[993]*See, e.g.*, Garrett v. Fleming, 362 F.3d 692, 696 (10th Cir. 2004); Wayne v. Jarvis, 197 F.3d 1098, 1103–04 (11th Cir. 1999) and cases cited, *overruled on other grounds*, Manders v. Lee, 338 F.3d 1304, 1328 n.52 (11th Cir. 2003); Jacobsen v. Osborne, 133 F.3d 315, 321 (5th Cir. 1998); King v. One Unknown Federal Correctional Officer, 201 F.3d 910, 914 (7th Cir. 2000); Baskin v. City of Des Plaines, 138 F.3d 701, 704 (7th Cir. 1998); Broner v. Flynn, 311 F. Supp. 2d 227, 235 n.8 (D.Mass. 2004).

[994]As far as we can tell, only two federal circuits allow treating lack of knowledge of a defendant's identity as a mistake under rule 15(c). *See* Goodman v. Praxair, Inc., 494 F.3d 458, 470–73 (4th Cir. 2007); Arthur v. Maersk, Inc., 434 F.3d 196, 208 (3d Cir. 2006).

[995]Ayala Serrano v. Lebron Gonzales, 909 F.2d 9, 12 (1st Cir. 1990) (since the defendant officer's superiors had been served and he had been present at the incident, the claim related back); Bradley v. Macomb County, 370 F. Supp. 2d 607, 611–13 (E.D.Mich. 2005) (claim related back where plaintiff named the wrong officer, the same lawyer represented him and the right officer too, and submitted papers denying that the wrong officer was responsible); Daily v. Monte, 26 F. Supp. 2d 984, 987–88 (E.D.Mich. 1998) (where county attorney represented both old and new defendants and appeared to have investigated incident fully, court concludes new defendants had sufficient notice); *see* cases cited in n.990, above. *But see* Singletary v. Pennsylvania Dep't of Correction, 266 F.3d 186, 196 (3d Cir. 2001) (declining to allow relation back based on "shared attorney" theory because the attorney did not represent both old and new defendants during the relevant time period).

well in advance of that date. If you do your best to take discovery promptly, but defendants do not provide the information, you may be entitled to equitable tolling if you miss the limitations deadline.[996]

You may be able to avoid the strict requirements of Rule 15(c) by relying on state law. The rule provides that a claim will relate back if "the law that provides the applicable statute of limitations" would permit it to relate back.[997] Since § 1983 actions use state statutes of limitations, state "relation back" law can be applied, and sometimes it is more favorable to the plaintiff than the federal rule.[998]

O. RELIEF

1. Damages[999]

There are three kinds of damages: compensatory, nominal, and punitive. All of these can be awarded in federal civil rights actions if the evidence supports them. The law of damages is generally similar in federal civil rights actions and in state tort actions. Some states have more restrictive damage rules, but these will not be applied in federal civil rights actions if they are inconsistent with the purposes of the civil rights laws.[1000]

The Prison Litigation Reform Act (PLRA) has drastically limited the damages prisoners can recover in some cases by providing that "[n]o Federal civil action may be brought by a prisoner . . . for mental or emotional injury suffered while in custody without a prior showing of physical injury."[1001] This provision is discussed in detail elsewhere in this Manual.[1002] In a nutshell, most courts have held that it means that prisoners cannot recover compensatory damages for mental or emotional injury without physical injury; some have said that prisoners also cannot recover punitive damages in such cases. Most courts have also held or assumed (incorrectly, in our opinion) that non-physical injuries such as deprivations of religious freedom or free speech rights, or wrongful confinement in segregation or under grossly unconstitutional conditions, are no more than "mental or emotional injury" for which damages cannot be awarded without physical injury.

For these reasons, if you have a case involving a non-physical injury which you believe merits an award of damages, and if it is possible for you to wait until you are out of prison before filing it while still complying with the relevant statute of limitations,[1003] it may be wise to do so. If you file after you are released, the case will not be an action "brought by a prisoner" and will not be subject to this PLRA provision.[1004] You should also consider whether state court remedies not subject to the PLRA might be more to your advantage than a federal civil rights action.

a. Compensatory Damages Compensatory damages represent the money value of the harm or injury caused by a violation of the plaintiff's rights. They are not discretionary;

---

[996]See Murphy v. West, 533 F. Supp. 2d 312, 316–17 (W.D.N.Y. 2008) (following *Byrd v. Abate*, below); White v. Cooper, 55 F. Supp. 2d 848, 857 (N.D.Ill. 1999) (the plaintiff is entitled to equitable tolling because he timely sought discovery but the defendants did not comply and the court declined to make them until after court-appointed counsel had appeared); Cunningham v. Eyman, 11 F. Supp. 2d 969, 973–74 (N.D.Ill. 1998) (noting that court had tolled the statute of limitations until a reasonable time after U.S. Marshals provided information plaintiff had sought promptly to identify proper defendants); Byrd v. Abate, 964 F. Supp. 140, 145 (S.D.N.Y. 1997) (allowing late amendment naming former John Doe defendant to relate back under Rule 15(c), contrary to the usual rule, because defense counsel delayed identifying him until after the statute of limitations had run; to hold otherwise "would permit defense counsel to eliminate claims against any John Doe defendants merely by resisting discovery until the statute of limitations has ended").

[997]Rule 15(c)(1)(A), Fed.R.Civ.P.

[998]See, e.g., Merritt v. County of Los Angeles, 875 F.2d 765, 768 (9th Cir. 1989) (relation back does not require timely notice to the new defendants under California law); Rivera v. Alvarado, 240 F. Supp. 2d 136, 141–42 (D.P.R. 2003) (Puerto Rico law tolls the limitations period against joint tortfeasors when a complaint is filed against any of them); Wilson v. City of Atlantic City, 142 F.R.D. 603, 606 (D.N.J. 1992).

[999]This section deals with the law governing different types of damages and the typical range of damage awards in prison cases. There are many issues relevant to damage claims that are addressed elsewhere in this Manual, such as immunity from damages, *see* § L of this chapter; the impact of the Prison Litigation Reform Act on damages, *see* Ch. 9, § E, and the availability of damages under the federal disability statutes, *see* Ch. 2, § F.4.h.2; the federal religious rights statutes, *see* Ch. 3, § D.1.b.4; and state tort actions and the FTCA. *See* § C of this chapter.

[1000]Berry v. City of Muskogee, 900 F.2d 1489, 1503–07 (10th Cir. 1990) (state law limits on wrongful death damages would not be applied under § 1983); McFadden v. Sanchez, 710 F.2d 907, 911 (2d Cir. 1983) (similar to *Berry*); Garrick v. City and County of Denver, 652 F.2d 969, 971 (10th Cir. 1981) (federal law governs availability and computation of punitive damages regardless of state law limitations); Hegarty v. Somerset County, 848 F. Supp. 257, 268–69 (D.Me. 1994) (similar to *Berry* and *McFadden*), *aff'd in part on other grounds and remanded*, 53 F.3d 1367 (1st Cir. 1995); *see* Hankins v. Finnel, 759 F. Supp. 569, 573 (W.D.Mo. 1991) (state could not use law permitting forfeiture of prisoner's assets to avoid paying federal court damage judgment), *aff'd*, 964 F.2d 853 (8th Cir. 1992).

[1001]42 U.S.C. § 1997e(e).

[1002]See Ch. 9, § E.

[1003]Statutes of limitations are discussed in the previous section.

[1004]See Ch. 9, § E, n.542; *see also* Ch. 9, nn.3–21, concerning the meaning of "prisoner" in the PLRA.

if an individual proves that a violation of his rights caused injury,[1005] compensatory damages must be awarded.[1006]

Compensable injuries include actual monetary losses like lost wages or the value of destroyed or confiscated property.[1007] They also include physical pain and injury,[1008] psychological damage including personal humiliation and mental anguish,[1009] loss of liberty,[1010] and injuries to the

quality of an individual's life, such as placement in segregation or disgusting conditions, or deprivation of privileges,[1011] or failure to accommodate serious disabilities.[1012] However, as explained above, in cases "brought by a prisoner," the Prison Litigation Reform Act (PLRA) forbids recovery of compensatory damages for mental or emotional injury without physical injury, and most courts apply that rule to quality-of-life cases as well (though most courts allow recovery of punitive damages even if compensatory damages are barred).[1013]

The PLRA will not be an issue if you file your case when you are not a prisoner, if you persuade the court your injury was not "mental or emotional," or if you had a physical injury along with any other injury you may claim. However, there may still be problems in recovering damages for non-physical injuries. The Supreme Court has said that damages cannot be awarded for the abstract value of constitutional rights,[1014] and courts and juries have had a hard time

---

[1005]The violation must have been the "proximate cause" of the injury, which means that "except for the constitutional tort, such injuries and damages would not have occurred and further that such injuries and damages were the reasonably foreseeable consequences of the acts or omissions in issue." Jackson v. Sauls, 206 F.3d 1156, 1168 (11th Cir. 2000).

[1006]Smith v. Wade, 461 U.S. 30, 52, 103 S. Ct. 1625 (1983); H.C. by Hewett v. Jarrard, 786 F.2d 1080, 1088 (11th Cir. 1986).

[1007]See, e.g., Thompson v. Carter, 284 F.3d 411, 418 (2d Cir. 2002) (value of seized property could be recovered if proved); Morgan v. Farrier, 924 F.2d 134, 136 (8th Cir. 1991) (lost wages included in damages for improper segregation); Spruytte v. Hoffner, 181 F. Supp. 2d 736, 744–45 (W.D.Mich. 2001) (lost wages included in damages for retaliatory transfer); Broulette v. Starns, 161 F. Supp. 2d 1021, 1027 (D.Ariz. 2001) (awarding replacement cost of confiscated magazines); Gaston v. Coughlin, 81 F. Supp. 2d 381, 392 (N.D.N.Y. 1999) (awarding lost wages and extra educational costs resulting from retaliatory job loss and transfer), reconsideration denied, 102 F. Supp. 2d 81 (N.D.N.Y. 2000); Castle v. Clymer, 15 F. Supp. 2d 640, 668 (E.D.Pa. 1998) (plaintiff could recover difference between higher paying job he lost and the lower paying job he had after a retaliatory transfer); Soto v. Lord, 693 F. Supp. 8, 22 (S.D.N.Y. 1988) (similar to Morgan); Adams v. Wolff, 624 F. Supp. 1036, 1040 (D.Nev. 1985) (similar to Morgan and Soto).

[1008]Champion v. Outlook Nashville, Inc., 380 F.3d 893, 906–07 (6th Cir. 2004) (affirming $900,000 for pain and suffering during police abuse that caused death); Rangolan v. County of Nassau, 370 F.3d 239, 245–47 (2d Cir. 2004) (affirming $300,000 for past pain and suffering, requiring reduction of award for future pain and suffering, for prisoner seriously injured in assault); Consolo v. George, 58 F.3d 791 (1st Cir. 1995) (affirming damages for pain and suffering resulting from denial of medical treatment); Boretti v. Wiscomb, 930 F.2d 1150, 1155 (6th Cir. 1991) (damages for deprivation of medical care case can be awarded for pain and mental anguish even if there is no permanent injury).

[1009]Memphis Community Sch. Dist. v. Stachura, 477 U.S. 299, 307, 106 S. Ct. 2537 (1986); Jolivet v. Deland, 966 F.2d 573, 576–77 (10th Cir. 1992) (award for emotional harm from disclosure of private correspondence); Hill v. Marshall, 962 F.2d 1209, 1215 (6th Cir. 1992) (citing mental anguish from increased risk of tuberculosis infection); Wright v. Sheppard, 919 F.2d 665, 669–70 (11th Cir. 1990) (in computing damages, court should consider evidence of pain, humiliation, emotional distress, mental anguish, physical injuries that limited the plaintiff's ability to work, nightmares, and loss of his house, his job, and his wife).

[1010]Kerman v. City of New York, 374 F.3d 93, 125 (2d Cir. 2004) ("The damages recoverable for loss of liberty for the period spent in a wrongful confinement are separable from damages recoverable for such injuries as physical harm, embarrassment, or emotional suffering; even absent such other injuries, an award of several thousand dollars may be appropriate simply for several hours' loss of liberty."); Biberdorf v. Oregon, 243 F. Supp. 2d 1145, 1164 (D.Or. 2002) (loss of liberty is "broader than 'mere' emotional distress").

[1011]Trobaugh v. Hall, 176 F.3d 1087, 1089 (8th Cir. 1999) (damages should have been awarded for retaliatory placement in segregation); Goff v. Burton, 91 F.3d 1188, 1192 (8th Cir. 1996) (affirming $2250 award at $10 a day for lost privileges resulting from a retaliatory transfer to a higher security prison); Walters v. Grossheim, 990 F.2d 381, 385 (8th Cir. 1993) (damage award was properly based on a "careful assessment of the loss of privileges" resulting from improper retention in a restrictive classification status); Howard v. Adkison, 887 F.2d 134, 139 (8th Cir. 1989) (compensatory damages were proper for filthy cell conditions there was no "formal evidence of actual damage, but such harm can be inferred from the circumstances as well as established by the testimony" (citation omitted)); Ustrak v. Fairman, 781 F.2d 573, 578–79 (7th Cir. 1986) (in case involving unlawful transfer, evidence of "[h]ow much nicer" the other prison was—e.g., differences in cell sizes, daily routines, diet, or incidents of violence—could support a damage award); Caldwell v. District of Columbia, 201 F. Supp. 2d 27, 33 (D.D.C. 2001) (damages awarded for "feces in his cell, small cells and beds, lack of outdoor recreation, general lack of cleanliness, poor ventilation, smoke and mace in the air, flooding in the cellblocks, noise and odors in the cell blocks, foul water dripping in his cell and poor temperature regulation"); Adams v. Wolff, 624 F. Supp. at 1039–40 (damages awarded for denial of recreation to protective custody inmate).

[1012]Simmons v. Cook, 154 F.3d 805, 809 (8th Cir. 1998) (upholding award of $2000 for paraplegic prisoners placed in inaccessible segregation cells); Love v. Westville Correctional Center, 103 F.3d 558, 559, 561 (7th Cir. 1996) (upholding award of $31,000 to quadriplegic prisoner held for a year and unable to use recreational, dining, and visiting facilities and unable to participate in prison programs).

[1013]See Ch. 9, § E, concerning the PLRA provision affecting damages.

[1014]Memphis Community School District v. Stachura. 477 U.S. 299, 310, 106 S. Ct. 2537 (1986); Brown v. Bryan County, OK., 219 F.3d 450, 465, 467–68 (5th Cir. 2000) (damages awarded for injuries; separate award for constitutional violation vacated).

For this reason, you are only entitled to one award of damages for a single injury, even if it resulted from violations of more than one of your legal rights. Gilmere v. City of Atlanta, Ga., 864 F.2d 734, 740 (11th Cir. 1989) (there was no basis for separate awards

translating constitutional violations into dollar amounts. The result has been inconsistent decisions and many cases in which prisoners proved constitutional violations but received only nominal damages (which are discussed in the next section),[1015] though other courts have made compensatory awards for equally intangible violations.[1016]

To keep this from happening to you, you should present the constitutional violation in as concrete a form as possible.[1017] For example, if prison officials violated your First Amendment rights by withholding a newspaper you subscribed to, the issue would not be how much the First Amendment is worth, but how much the ability to read the newspaper for a particular period of time is worth.[1018] You do not have to prove the precise dollar value of constitutional violations,[1019] but you must provide an evidentiary basis for the court or jury to work from.

Your testimony, or that of persons who know you, may be sufficient evidence to show that you suffered actual harm from deprivations such as not being able to read the newspaper. In cases involving the conditions of confinement, it may be enough just to describe the conditions, and compare them to the normal conditions of confinement if there is a difference.[1020] The point is to give as complete a factual picture as you can of what happened to you and how significant it was.[1021] In cases where you are able to recover damages for mental or emotional injury (either because the PLRA is inapplicable, or because you also suffered physical injury), your testimony, or that of persons who know you, may be sufficient evidence of such injury if it is reasonably detailed, or the injury may be inferred from the circumstances.[1022]

---

for due process and Fourth Amendment violations that caused the same injury); U.S. Industries, Inc. v. Touche Ross & Co., 854 F.2d 1223, 1261–1262 (10th Cir. 1988) ("Where a single injury gives rise to more than one claim for relief, a plaintiff may recover his damages under any claim, but he may recover them only once.").

[1015]*See, e.g.,* Williams v. Brimeyer, 116 F.3d 351, 352 (8th Cir. 1997) (refusal to allow receipt of constitutionally protected religious publications); Sockwell v. Phelps, 20 F.3d 187 (5th Cir. 1994) (racial segregation); Allen v. Higgins, 902 F.2d 682, 684 (8th Cir. 1990) (denial of right to receive a catalog); Archie v. Christian, 812 F.2d 250, 252 (5th Cir. 1987) (court access denial); Kincaid v. Rusk, 670 F.2d 737, 745–46 (7th Cir. 1982); McNamara v. Moody, 606 F.2d 621, 626 (5th Cir. 1979); Nolley v. County of Erie, 802 F. Supp. 898, 909 (W.D.N.Y. 1992) (denial of law library access); Faulkner v. McLocklin, 727 F. Supp. 486, 492 (N. D.Ind. 1989) (opening of privileged mail); Reutcke v. Dahm, 707 F. Supp. 1121, 1135–36 (D. Neb. 1988) (denial of court access); *see also* Cowans v. Wyrick, 862 F.2d 697, 699 (8th Cir. 1988) (a jury must award nominal damages if it has found cruel and unusual punishment but cannot convert the injury into a monetary amount).

When there is evidence of a compensable injury caused by a violation of the plaintiff's rights, compensation must be awarded. For example, it is possible for a jury or court to find liability for excessive force but not to award compensatory damages, but only under very limited circumstances: if there had been both justifiable and unjustifiable force, and injuries resulted from justifiable force; or if there was no credible evidence of injury; or if the injuries were of no monetary value. Briggs v. Marshall, 93 F.3d 355, 360 (7th Cir.1996); Westcott v. Crinklaw, 133 F.3d 658, 661–63 (8th Cir. 1998).

[1016]*See, e.g.,* Sallier v. Brooks, 343 F.3d 868, 880 (6th Cir. 2003) (affirming jury award of $750 in compensatory damages for each instance of unlawful opening of legal mail and $250 punitive damages); Lowrance v. Coughlin, 862 F. Supp. 1090, 1120 (S.D.N.Y. 1994) (awarding significant damages for repeated retaliatory prison transfers, segregation, cell searches); Vanscoy v. Hicks, 691 F. Supp. 1336 (M.D.Ala. 1988) (awarding $50 for pretextual exclusion from religious service, without evidence of mental anguish or suffering); *see also* Carr v. Whittenburg, 2006 WL 1207286, *3 (S.D.Ill., Apr. 28, 2006) (stating that specific First Amendment violations may be compensable through "general damages" or "presumed damages" even without proof of injury, though damages cannot be recovered based on the abstract value or importance of the right).

[1017]*See* Kerman v. City of New York, 374 F.3d 93, 130 (2d Cir. 2004) (holding claim of unlawful detention "does not involve either procedural due process or an attempt to vindicate an abstract societal interest. Rather, it involves an anything-but-abstract physical detention." Such loss of liberty may be compensated in damages.).

[1018]*See* Vanscoy v. Hicks, 691 F. Supp. 1336, 1338 (M.D.Ala. 1988) (awarding small amount of compensatory damages for guard's misconduct that resulted in plaintiff's missing one religious service).

[1019]Sample v. Diecks, 885 F.2d 1099, 1112 (3d Cir. 1989) ("Surely, if we required an accountant's methodology to be applied in such matters, no price could be fixed and constitutional wrongs would go uncompensated entirely, as well as undeterred"); Benjamin v. Sielaff, 752 F. Supp. 140, 149 n.27 (S.D.N.Y. 1990) (citing *Sample*).

[1020]*See* cases cited in n.1011, above.

[1021]*See* Levka v. City of Chicago, 748 F.2d 421, 424–27 (7th Cir. 1984) (relating variations in damage awards in strip search cases to differences in the facts of the cases). An example of how to argue such a point in closing argument appears in Ch. 10, § R.12.

[1022]Poy v. Boutselis, 352 F.3d 479, 485–86 (1st Cir. 2003) (jury award of $5000 for severe emotional stress in police beating case upheld without medical or psychiatric evidence; "A jury could reasonably infer from such humiliation, long continued pain, and facial disfigurement a condition of severe emotional stress."); Denius v. Dunlap, 330 F.3d 919, 929 (7th Cir. 2003) (plaintiff's statement that he was "embarrassed and humiliated" was insufficient; "when the injured party's own testimony is the only proof of emotional damages, he must explain the circumstances of his injury in reasonable detail; he cannot rely on mere conclusory statements . . . unless the facts underlying the case are so inherently degrading that it would be reasonable to infer that a person would suffer emotional distress from the defendant's action."); Robles v. Prince George's County, Md., 302 F.3d 262, 270 (4th Cir. 2002) (where police handcuffed arrestee to a pole and left him, his testimony about fear, humiliation, and sleeplessness supported damages; "any reasonable person would have been upset by what happened here"); Makin v. Colorado Dep't of Corrections, 183 F.3d 1205, 1215 (10th Cir. 1999) (plaintiff's testimony in religious rights case "provides some evidence that he suffered mental or emotional distress as a result of defendants' actions for which he may recover"); Bolden v. SEPTA, 21 F.3d 29, 34 n.3 (3d Cir. 1994); Hill v. Marshall, 962 F.2d 1209, 1215 (6th Cir. 1992); H.C. by Jewett v. Garrard, 786 F.2d 1080, 1088 (11th Cir. 1986); King v. Wells, 760

The Supreme Court has held that something called "presumed damages" "may possibly" be appropriate as a substitute for compensatory damages in cases where the plaintiff's injury is impossible to measure.[1023] The Court has not spelled out how this concept can be used, though it has said that it requires more than just showing that you were deprived of a procedural right.[1024] Some courts have suggested that presumed damages are particularly appropriate in First Amendment cases.[1025] One court has said that presumed damages are appropriate in connection with unlawful detention, noting that such detention causes the injury of loss of liberty regardless of whether there is further evidence of injury.[1026] (This idea would seem to be applicable to cases involving unlawful placement in segregation.) However, at least one court has also held that presumed damages cannot be awarded for an injury that is not compensable under the PLRA's provision concerning mental or emotional injury.[1027]

Given how poorly developed the presumed damages idea is, you should probably not ask for presumed damages instead of compensatory damages. As we suggested above, you should provide as much detail as possible about the constitutional violation you suffered and its results, and argue that your injury is concrete enough that compensatory damages can be awarded.[1028] You may wish to ask for presumed damages in the alternative.

There are special problems in proving injury in procedural due process cases.[1029] For example, if you show that you were put in segregation without adequate notice and a hearing, the defendants will probably claim that you would have been found guilty and sent to segregation even with a proper hearing. To get damages for the segregation time, you have to convince the court that a proper hearing would have kept you out of segregation or shortened your sentence.[1030] The violation of a procedural right, without some proof of injury, is not compensable.[1031] While procedural violations may result in compensable emotional injury,[1032] you cannot recover mental or emotional injury damages if your case is subject to the PLRA.

Compensatory damages are usually "joint and several." That means you are awarded a single sum of money for a single injury, regardless of how many defendants are involved, and you can try to collect the judgment against any of the defendants who are held liable.[1033] However, compensatory damages may be assessed separately against different defendants if the evidence shows that they were responsible for different injuries.[1034]

b. Nominal Damages If you prove that your rights were violated but do not prove any injury, you can recover "nominal" damages.[1035] Courts have disagreed whether nominal

---

F.2d 89, 94 (6th Cir. 1985); *see also* Whitley v. Seibel, 676 F.2d 245, 252 (7th Cir. 1982) (testimony of plaintiff's acquaintances supported damage award).

[1023]Memphis Community School District v. Stachura, 477 U.S. 299, 310, 316, 106 S. Ct. 2537 (1986) (presumed damages are designed to "roughly approximate the harm that the plaintiff suffered and thereby compensate for harms that may be impossible to measure.").

Presumed damages are not appropriate where compensatory damages can be readily measured. Norwood v. Bain, 143 F.3d 843, 856 (4th Cir. 1998), *aff'd by equally divided court*, 166 F.3d 243 (4th Cir. 1999) (en banc); Trevino v. Gates, 99 F.3d 911, 921–22 (9th Cir. 1996); Turner v. Chicago Housing Authority, 969 F.2d 461, 463 (7th Cir. 1992); Lewis v. Harrison School Dist. No. 1, 805 F.2d 310, 317 (8th Cir. 1986); Klinger v. Nebraska Dep't of Correctional Services, 902 F. Supp. 1036, 1042 (D.Neb. 1995), *rev'd on other grounds*, 107 F.3d 609 (8th Cir. 1997).

[1024]Carey v. Piphus, 435 U.S. 247, 264–65 and n.22, 98 S. Ct. 1042 (1978).

[1025]Walje v. City of Winchester, Ky., 827 F.2d 10, 12–13 (6th Cir. 1987); *see also* Hessel v. O'Hearn, 977 F.2d 299, 301 (7th Cir. 1992) (presumed damages may be available for free speech or search and seizure violations); Nolley v. County of Erie, 802 F. Supp. 898, 905 (W.D.N.Y. 1992) ($10 a day presumed damages awarded for invasion of privacy).

[1026]Kerman v. City of New York, 374 F.3d 93, 130 (2d Cir. 2004) (unlawful detention is appropriate for a presumed damages award, since the injury of loss of liberty is inherent in it).

[1027]Allah v. Al-Hafeez, 226 F.3d 247, 251 (3d Cir. 2000).

[1028]That is definitely our suggestion with respect to federal civil rights actions. State courts hearing tort cases may be more

comfortable with the idea of presumed damages. *See, e.g.*, Allard v. Church of Scientology of California, 58 Cal.App.3d 439, 129 Cal. Rptr. 797, 804 (Cal.App. 1976) (malicious prosecution). If you bring suit in state court, you should research the state's law of damages to determine the best way to present the issue. However, we doubt that you can go too far wrong in any court by spelling out the nature of your injury as much as possible.

[1029]This subject is discussed in more detail in Ch. 4, § H.1.r(4).

[1030]Shango v. Jurich, 965 F.2d 289, 294–95 (7th Cir. 1992); *see* Long v. Shillinger, 927 F.2d 525, 527–28 (10th Cir. 1991) (due process was denied in extradition hearing but the outcome would have been the same if due process had been followed, so compensatory damages are denied).

[1031]Carey v. Piphus, 435 U.S. 247, 261, 98 S. Ct. 1042 (1978).

[1032]*Carey*, 435 U.S. at 263–64.

[1033]Tilcon Capaldi, Inc. v. Feldman, 249 F.3d 54, 62 (1st Cir. 2001) (defining joint and several liability to mean "that damages are a single sum specified in the judgment, that each wrongdoer is liable for the full amount, but the wronged party cannot collect under the judgment *more* than the single sum"); Weeks v. Chaboudy, 984 F.2d 185, 189 (6th Cir. 1993).

[1034]Watts v. Laurent, 774 F.2d 168, 179–81 (7th Cir. 1985).

[1035]Carey v. Piphus, 435 U.S. at 267 (holding nominal damage award required upon proof of procedural due process violation without proof of injury). Courts have so held in cases involving other constitutional rights without proof of injury. Risdal v. Halford, 209 F.3d 1071, 1072 (8th Cir. 2000); LeBlanc-Sternberg v. Fletcher, 67 F.3d 412, 431 (2d Cir. 1995); Floyd v. Laws, 929 F.2d 1390, 1402 (9th Cir. 1991); Lewis v. Woods, 848 F.2d 649, 651 (5th Cir. 1988).

damages are limited to $1.00,[1036] or whether larger amounts can be awarded.[1037] Nominal damages are not appropriate where the court or jury finds liability and the evidence clearly shows injury.[1038] If you recover nominal damages, you may also be able to recover punitive damages.[1039] If you have a lawyer, recovering nominal damages makes you a prevailing party who may recover attorneys' fees, but the court in its discretion may reduce the fee or deny it based on limited success.[1040] The Prison Litigation Reform Act does not bar recovery of nominal damages in mental/emotional injury cases.[1041]

c. Punitive Damages Punitive or exemplary damages are intended to punish the defendants for their conduct and deter them and others from committing similar acts in the future.[1042] If your rights have been violated, you can get punitive damages without proving actual injury or being awarded compensatory damages.[1043] However, you must show that the defendants acted with reckless indifference to your rights, ill will, a desire to injure, or malice.[1044]

Under 42 U.S.C. § 1983, punitive damages can only be awarded against individuals, not against city or county governments.[1045] They cannot be awarded at all under the Federal Tort Claims Act[1046] or the federal disability statutes.[1047] Many states have additional restrictions on punitive damages, though these restrictions are generally not applied in federal civil rights actions.[1048] Some federal courts have held that punitive damages are restricted by the Prison Litigation Reform Act (PLRA).[1049]

Punitive damages are discretionary; the judge or jury is not required to award them.[1050] Punitive damages may be denied if the plaintiff as well as the defendants committed

---

[1036]Carey v. Piphus, 435 U.S. at 267 ("not to exceed one dollar"); Corpus v. Bennett, 430 F.3d 912, 916 (8th Cir. 2005) (affirming reduction of $75,000 nominal award to $1.00); Wiggins v. Rushen, 760 F.2d 10009, 1012 (9th Cir. 1985) ($250 was not nominal).

[1037]See Fegans v. Norris, 537 F.3d 897, 908 (8th Cir. 2008) (affirming $1500 nominal award for protracted denial of religious diet, noting it amounted to $1.44 a meal); Williams v. Kaufman County, 352 F.3d 994, 1014–15 & n.70 (5th Cir. 2003) (affirming nominal awards of $100 to persons unlawfully searched, noting other awards in the hundreds and low thousands of dollars); Romano v. U-Haul Intern., 233 F.3d 655, 671 (1st Cir. 2000) (nominal damages not limited to $1.00, but $500 was too much).

[1038]Westcott v. Crinklaw, 133 F.3d 658, 661–63 (8th Cir. 1998) (jury verdict of nominal damages in fatal police shooting case set aside, new trial granted; nominal damages would be appropriate only if there had been both justifiable and unjustifiable force, and injuries resulted from justifiable force; or if there was no credible evidence of injury; or if the injuries were of no monetary value); Atkins v. New York City, 143 F.3d 100, 104 (2d Cir. 1998).

[1039]See n.1043, below.

[1040]Farrar v. Hobby, 506 U.S. 103, 574–75, 113 S. Ct. 566 (1992) (even though plaintiff was prevailing party, no fees awarded since plaintiff had requested $17 million and got only $1.00); Maul v. Constan, 23 F.3d 143 (7th Cir. 1994). A number of courts have made substantial fee awards in cases yielding only nominal damages where a decision for the plaintiff brought some other benefit, such as a declaratory judgment, a change in policy, or reduced likelihood of future violations. Lippoldt v. Cole, 468 F.3d 1204, 1223–24 (10th Cir. 2006); Muhammad v. Lockhart, 104 F.3d 1069, 1070 (8th Cir. 1997); Wilcox v. City of Reno, 42 F.3d 550, 555 (9th Cir. 1994) ("[i]f the lawsuit achieved other tangible results—such as sparking a change in policy or establishing a finding of fact with potential collateral estoppel effects—such results will, in combination with an enforceable judgment for a nominal sum, support an award of fees."); Jones v. Lockhart, 29 F.3d 422 (8th Cir. 1994).

[1041]See Ch. 9, § E.1.

[1042]Smith v. Wade, 461 U.S. 30, 49–51, 103 S. Ct. 1625 (1983); Royal v. Kautzky, 375 F.3d 720, 724 (8th Cir. 2004).

[1043]Williams v. Kaufman County, 352 F.3d 994, 1015 (5th Cir. 2003) ("Just as nominal damages are allowed without proof of injury, 'a punitive award may stand in the absence of actual damages where there has been a constitutional violation.'"); accord, Walker v. Bain, 257 F.3d 660, 674 (6th Cir. 2001); Robinson v. Cattaraugus County, 147 F.3d 153, 161 (2d Cir. 1998).

This is the rule under § 1983 and under the law of some states. In other states, you cannot receive punitive damages unless you also receive compensatory damages, a view that has been disapproved by the leading treatise on torts. W. Page Keeton *et al., Prosser and Keeton on the Law of Torts* at 14 (5th ed. 1984).

[1044]Smith v. Wade, 461 U.S. at 46–52; see Royal v. Kautzky, 375 F.3d 720, 725 (8th Cir. 2004) (affirming denial of punitive damages for retaliatory discipline based on lower court's finding of no evil motive); Hill v. Marshall, 962 F.2d 1209, 1217 (6th Cir. 1992).

[1045]City of Newport v. Fact Concerts, Inc., 453 U.S. 247, 269–70, 101 S. Ct. 2748 (1981).

[1046]See § C.2.a of this chapter.

[1047]Barnes v. Gorman, 536 U.S. 181, 186–89, 122 S. Ct. 2097 (2002).

[1048]See, e.g., Garrick v. City and County of Denver, 652 F.2d 969, 971 (10th Cir. 1981) (federal law governs availability and computation of punitive damages regardless of state law limitations); Bird v. Figel, 725 F. Supp. 406, 412 (N.D.Ind. 1989) (refusing to apply state law requiring that punitive damages be proved by clear and convincing evidence).

Punitive damages are often not permitted in state court suits against state or local governments.

[1049]Some federal courts have held that punitive damages may not be awarded to prisoners who show mental or emotional injury without physical injury. See Ch. 9, § E.1, n.553. Some have also held that punitive damages are restricted by the PLRA's "prospective relief" provisions. See Ch. 9, § K, n.644.

[1050]Smith v. Wade, 461 U.S. 30, 52, 103 S. Ct. 1625 (1983); Fairley v. Jones, 824 F.2d 440, 444 (5th Cir. 1987). But see Webb v. Arresting Officers, 749 F.2d 500, 502 (8th Cir. 1984) (judge who denies punitive damages after a bench trial must explain why).

Occasionally an appellate court will direct a punitive award in a case that was tried by the judge and not by a jury. Wright v. Sheppard, 919 F.2d 665, 671 (11th Cir. 1990); H.C. by Hewett v. Jarrard, 786 F.2d 1080, 1089 (11th Cir. 1986).

misconduct.[1051] The Supreme Court has held that punitive damages should reflect (1) the "reprehensibility" of the defendant's conduct, (2) a "reasonable relationship" to the harm the plaintiff (or related victim) suffered, and (3) the presence (or absence) of "sanctions," e.g., criminal penalties, that state law provided for comparable conduct.[1052] In general, it has said, punitive damages should be no more than nine times as large as compensatory damages, though larger punitive awards may be permissible where "a particularly egregious act has resulted in only a small amount of economic damages."[1053] Several courts have applied this last point to civil rights cases, which often result in small compensatory or nominal awards.[1054]

Punitive damages are usually not joint and several, but are awarded separately against each defendant based on that individual's actions.[1055] If substantial punitive damages are sought, evidence relating to the defendant's income or net worth may be admissible.[1056]

[1051]Guerra v. Drake, 371 F.3d 404, 405 (8th Cir. 2004) (per curiam); Green v. Johnson, 977 F.2d 1383, 1389 (10th Cir. 1992). The plaintiff's misconduct does not have to result in the denial of punitive damages. Bogan v. Stroud, 958 F.2d 180, 186 (7th Cir. 1992) (upholding punitive damages to inmate who was beaten, even though he had stabbed an officer).

[1052]BMW of North America, Inc. v. Gore, 517 U.S. 559, 585–85, 116 S. Ct. 1589 (1996); see DiSorbo v. Hoy, 343 F.3d 172, 186 (2d Cir. 2003) (holding punitive damages excessive under Gore in police abuse case).

[1053]State Farm Mutual Automobile Ins. Co. v. Campbell, 538 U.S. 408, 425, 123 S. Ct. 1513 (2003). The Court also said when compensatory damages are substantial, then a smaller ratio of punitive damages, "perhaps only equal to compensatory damages," may be permissible. Id.

[1054]Williams v. Kaufman County, 352 F.3d 994, 1016 (5th Cir. 2003) ("Because actions seeking vindication of constitutional rights are more likely to result only in nominal damages, strict proportionality would defeat the ability to award punitive damages at all."); Sherman v. Kasotakis, 314 F. Supp. 2d 843, 874–75 (N.D.Iowa 2004).

[1055]Loughman v. Consol-Pennsylvania Coal Co., 6 F.3d 88, 100–01 & n.7 (3d Cir. 1993) (". . . [W]e note that there are strong policy arguments against permitting the entry of joint and several liability on punitive damages."); Rodick v. City of Schenectady, 1 F.3d 1341, 1349 (2d Cir. 1993); McFadden v. Sanchez, 710 F.2d 907, 914 (2d Cir. 1983); see Larez v. City of Los Angeles, 946 F.2d 630, 639 (9th Cir. 1991) (awarding punitive damages separately against various police officers).

Sometimes punitive damages are awarded jointly and severally against defendants who have acted in concert. Tolbert v. Queens College, 242 F.3d 58, 77–78 (2d Cir. 2001); Chase v. Cohen, 519 F. Supp. 2d 267 (D.Conn. 2007) (no public policy against awarding joint and several liability for punitive damages when parties have acted in concert).

[1056]White v. Ford Motor Co., 500 F.3d 963, 976 (9th Cir. 2007) ("A punitive damages award is supposed to sting so as to deter a defendant's reprehensible conduct, and juries have traditionally been permitted to consider a defendant's assets in determining an award that will carry the right degree of sting." (citation omitted)); Patterson v. Balsamico, 440 F.3d 104, 122 (2d Cir. 2006) (holding

Punitive damages have been awarded in a wide variety of prison cases.[1057]

d. Amounts of Damages In deciding what amount of damages to request, you should remember that most damage awards in prison cases are fairly small. Large awards tend to be made only in cases involving serious bodily harm or shockingly bad treatment,[1058] including medical neglect and

---

punitive award excessive in light of defendant's financial situation); Tasker v. Moore, 738 F. Supp. 1005, 1015–16 (S.D.W.Va. 1990) (punitive damages of $200,000 against former governor reduced to $20,000).

The defendant has the burden of proving lack of financial resources. Provost v. City of Newburgh, 262 F.3d 146, 163 (2d Cir. 2001); Mason v. Oklahoma Turnpike Authority, 182 F.3d 1212, 1214 (10th Cir. 1999); Kemezy v. Peters, 79 F.3d 33, 34–36 (7th Cir.1996) (rejecting a claim that the plaintiff is required to show evidence of net worth and placing the burden of producing such evidence on the defendant). But see Gordon v. Norman, 788 F.2d 1194, 1199–1200 (6th Cir. 1986) (punitive damages against police officers reduced on the assumption that they do not make much money). If the defendants put in information about their financial situation, but the state or local government will actually be paying any judgment, the plaintiff may be able to put that fact into evidence, though ordinarily it is not allowed. See Lawson v. Trowbridge, 153 F.3d 368, 379–80 (7th Cir. 1998).

[1057]See, e.g., Surprenant v. Rivas, 424 F.3d 5, 12 (1st Cir. 2005) (noting jury award of punitive damages of $5500 for accusing officer and $15,000 for hearing officer in case of trumped-up disciplinary charges); Reilly v. Grayson, 310 F.3d 519, 521 (6th Cir. 2002) (upholding punitive damages for exposure of an asthmatic prisoner to second-hand smoke contrary to medical recommendations); Gregory v. Shelby County, Tenn., 220 F.3d 433, 444–45 (6th Cir. 2000) (upholding an award of $2.2 million for punitive damages based upon reprehensible conduct of guard that result in the death of the inmate); Flowers v. Phelps, 956 F.2d 488, 489 (5th Cir. 1992) ($25,000 against officers who beat a handcuffed prisoner); Walker v. Norris, 917 F.2d 1449, 1459 (6th Cir. 1990) ($2000 and $2500 against guards who watched an inmate being stabbed to death); Wright v. Jones, 907 F.2d 848, 850 (8th Cir. 1990) ($225 against each guard in inmate assault case); McHenry v. Chadwick, 896 F.2d 184, 186 (6th Cir. 1990) ($2600 in punitive damages awarded in use of force case); Glaspy v. Malicoat, 234 F. Supp. 2d 890, 897 (W.D. Mich. 2001) (awarding $5000 in punitive damages where officer refused to allow prison visitor to use the rest room, causing him to urinate on himself); Williams v. Patel, 104 F. Supp. 2d 984, 998 (C.D.Ill. 2000) (medical neglect of prisoner with an eye injury resulting in loss of the eye); Mathie v. Fries, 935 F. Supp. 1284, 1307 (E.D.N.Y. 1996) (awarding punitive damages of $500,000 to inmate who was sexually assaulted by staff), aff'd, 121 F.3d 808 (2d Cir. 1997).

[1058]See Hanig v. Lee, 415 F.3d 822, 824 (8th Cir. 2005) (affirming $153,000 for excessively tight handcuffing, based on expert testimony about permanent injury and loss of earning capacity); Robles v. Prince George's County, Maryland, 302 F.3d 262, 272 (4th Cir. 2002) ($25,000 in compensatory damages and $15,000 in punitives for being handcuffed to pole in parking lot and left there by police for 10 minutes); Cantu v. Jones, 293 F.3d 839, 844 (5th Cir. 2002) ($22,500 for inmate–inmate razor blade assault resulting in 52 sutures); Gregory v. Shelby County, Tenn., 220 F.3d

failure to accommodate disabilities.[1059] Awards for physical abuse not involving serious or permanent injury are usually much lower.[1060] Awards in sexual abuse cases vary widely.[1061]

Damages for improper confinement in segregation have been awarded by some courts on the basis of a daily

---

433, 444–45 (6th Cir. 2000) (compensatory damages of $778,000 and punitives of $2.2 million were not excessive based upon reprehensible conduct of guard that result in the death of a prisoner); Cooper v. Casey, 97 F.3d 914, 919–20 (7th Cir. 1996) (affirming jury verdict of $5000 compensatory and $60,000 punitive to each of two prisoners beaten by guards); Blissett v. Coughlin, 66 F.3d 531, 536 (2d Cir. 1995) ($75,000 plus punitive damages for beating and placement in feces-smeared strip cell for eight days); Flowers v. Phelps, 956 F.2d 488, 491 (5th Cir. 1992) (affirming award of $3000 in actual and $25,000 in punitive damages for beating received by inmate); Walker v. Norris, 917 F.2d 1449, 1459 (6th Cir. 1990) ($175,000 to estate of inmate who was stabbed to death while guards looked on and did nothing); Blackburn v. Snow, 771 F.2d 556, 572–73 (1st Cir. 1985) ($177,040 for improper strip search of visitor upheld based on substantial record of psychological injury); Spell v. McDaniel, 824 F.2d 1380 (4th Cir. 1987) ($900,000 for beating resulting in the loss of one testicle); Ziemba v. Armstrong, 433 F. Supp. 2d 248, 252–56 (D. Conn. 2006) (upholding $100,000 compensatory and $150,000 punitive where prisoner was restrained face down for 22 1/2 hours and physically abused by staff); Jackson v. Austin, 241 F. Supp. 2d 1313, 1319, 1323 (D.Kan. 2003) (awarding $15,000 in compensatory damages and $30,000 in punitives to prisoner who was grabbed by three officers, pushed to the floor, handcuffed, and dragged 50 yards on the floor, causing a contusion, swelling of his knee, shoulder and wrists and "severe and excruciating pain"); Miller v. Shelby County, 93 F. Supp. 2d 892, 902 (W.D.Tenn. 2000) ($40,000 for inmate assault resulting in permanent shoulder injury among others); McCullough v. Cady, 640 F. Supp. 1012, 1014 (E.D.Mich. 1986) ($60,000 for prisoner shot in the knee).

[1059]Consolo v. George, 58 F.3d 791, 795 (1st Cir. 1995) ($90,000 for denial of medical care to arrestee who had sustained a fractured pelvis); Hill v. Marshall, 962 F.2d 1209, 1215 (6th Cir. 1992) ($95,000 for failure to provide tuberculosis medication); Mandel v. Doe, 888 F.2d 783, 787 (11th Cir. 1989) ($500,000 for medical neglect resulting in complete hip replacement); Serra v. Pichardo, 786 F.2d 237, 239 (6th Cir. 1986) ($625,000 for loss of leg); Berman v. U.S., 205 F. Supp. 2d 362, 375 (M.D.Pa. 2002) ($178,294 under FTCA for failure to provide for post-ileostomy care resulting in need for more surgery); Lawson v. Dallas County, 112 F. Supp. 2d 616, 637 (N.D.Tex. 2000) ($250,000 for neglect of incontinent paraplegic prisoner resulting in extensive bedsores requiring surgery), aff'd, 286 F.3d 257 (5th Cir. 2002); Williams v. Patel, 104 F. Supp. 2d 984, 997–98 (C.D.Ill. 2000) ($750,000 compensatory and $100,000 punitive for medical neglect resulting in loss of an eye); Muhammad v. U.S., 6 F. Supp. 2d 582, 593–94 (N.D.Tex. 1998) ($45,000 under FTCA for prisoner with back and leg injuries and neurological problem who against medical recommendations was kept for 20 months in prisons where he had to walk long distances and climb stairs); Williams v. U.S., 747 F. Supp. 967, 1014 (S.D.N.Y. 1990) ($500,000 awarded under FTCA to prisoner whose leg had to be amputated as a result of medical malpractice).

[1060]Guerra v. Drake, 371 F.3d 404, 405 (8th Cir. 2004) (per curiam) ($1500 for long stay in a restraint chair and $500 for excessive force); Lawrence v. Bowersox, 297 F.3d 727, 730–31 (8th Cir. 2002) (affirming $1.00 nominal award and $10,000 punitive for unnecessary pepper-spraying); Estate of Davis by Ostenfeld v. Delo, 115 F.3d 1388, 1393 (8th Cir. 1997) ($10,000 compensatory and $5000 punitive against each of two defendants for a beating leaving numerous contusions and lacerations requiring sutures); Burgin v. Iowa Dep't Of Corrections, 923 F.2d 637, 639 (8th Cir. 1991) ($1250 awarded for beating resulting in multiple abrasions and contusions, a swollen and bleeding nose and a tender left clavicle); McHenry v. Chadwick, 896 F.2d 184, 186 (6th Cir. 1990) ($150 compensatory and $2600 in punitive damages for beating that did not result in serious injury); Hay v. City of Irving, Texas, 893 F.2d 796, 798, 800 (5th Cir. 1990) ($325 compensatory and $750 punitive damages for beating resulting in "severe" and painful bruises); Campbell v. Grammar, 889 F.2d 797, 802 (8th Cir. 1989) (inmates sprayed with a fire hose awarded $750 for several months' back pain, $100 for temporary blurred vision, and $50 for a day's pain in ribs and thighs); Meriwether v. Coughlin, 879 F.2d 1037, 1047–8 (2d Cir. 1989) ($500 to $5025 for unjustified beatings); Taylor v. Green, 868 F.2d 162 163 (5th Cir. 1989) (affirming award of $1 nominal and $200 in punitive damages from each defendant for beating); Romaine v. Rawson, 140 F. Supp. 2d 204, 214 (N.D.N.Y. 2001) ($100 for "minor" physical injury, $900 for mental and emotional injury, and $500 in punitives for being struck several times in the face); Jones v. Huff, 789 F. Supp. 526, 537 (N.D.N.Y. 1992) ($6000, $3000, and $500 for beatings); Oses v. Fair, 739 F. Supp. 707, 710 (D.Mass. 1990) ($1000 for humiliating beating and threats at gunpoint); Ferola v. Moran, 622 F. Supp. 814, 823–24 (D.R.I. 1985) ($1000 for protracted physical restraint under harsh conditions); but see Hutchinson v. Stuckey, 952 F.2d 1418, 1422 (D.C. Cir. 1992) ($50,000 was excessive for a use of force with minor injuries).

[1061]Riley v. Olk-Long, 282 F.3d 592, 594 (8th Cir. 2002) (noting $15,000 compensatory and $30,000 in punitive damages for course of sexual abuse); Beers-Capitol v. Whetzel, 256 F.3d 120, 125 (3d Cir. 2001) (noting award of $200,000 for sexual assaults against two residents of female juvenile detention facility); Berry v. Oswalt, 143 F.3d 1127, 1129–30 (8th Cir. 1998) ($65,000 compensatory and $15,000 against rapist, $40,000 total against sexual harasser); Mathie v. Fries, 121 F.3d 808, 813–17 (2d Cir. 1997) ($250,000 compensatory and $200,000 punitive damages for course of sexual abuse by jail official); Morris v. Eversley, 343 F. Supp. 2d 234, 248 (S.D.N.Y. 2004) (noting $500 award for sexual assault from one jury, followed by $1000 award at new trial by second jury).

amount[1062] and by others on a "lump sum" basis.[1063] Larger awards have been made for confinement under particularly bad conditions.[1064] Damages for other kinds of violations are often modest.[1065] Further, as previously noted, many courts

have held that under the Prison Litigation Reform Act, prisoners may not receive compensatory (and in some court, punitive) damages for conditions of confinement unless they show resulting physical injury.

You should be realistic in the amount of damages you request in your complaint. Demanding enormous sums of money may satisfy your anger, but it will not help win your case, and in fact it may hurt it. Judges may be antagonized or refuse to take you seriously,[1066] and defendants may be unwilling to discuss settlement if they think you are totally unreasonable.

The amount of damages you request in your complaint does not limit the amount you may be awarded at trial.[1067]

[1062]Stevens v. McHan, 3 F.3d 1204, 1207 (8th Cir. 1993) (citing awards from $25 to $129 a day); Nolley v. County of Erie, 802 F. Supp. 898, 907–08 (W.D.N.Y. 1992) ($125 a day for confinement among psychotics); Charron v. Medium Security Institution, 730 F. Supp. 987, 997 (E.D.Mo. 1989) ($100 a day); Soto v. Lord, 693 F. Supp. 8, 21–22 (S.D.N.Y. 1988) ($50 a day; citing earlier cases awarding $25 to $40 a day); Adams v. Wolff, 624 F. Supp. 1036 (D. Nev. 1985) ($16 a week for denial of recreation in protective custody, $40 a day for wrongful confinement in punitive segregation); Riley v. Johnson, 528 F. Supp. 333, 343 (E.D.Mich. 1981) ($25 a day). *But see* Sourbeer v. Robinson, 791 F.2d 1094, 1105 (3d Cir. 1986) (award limited to $10 a day).

[1063]Dannenberg v. Valadez, 338 F.3d 1070, 1072 (9th Cir. 2003) (noting jury verdict of $6500 compensatory and $2500 punitive for 34 days' retaliatory segregation and deprivation of legal papers); Diercks v. Durham, 959 F.2d 710, 711–12 (8th Cir. 1992) ($3600 for 39 days' segregation and 102-day delay in transfer to pre-release center); Chapman v. Pickett, 801 F.2d 912, 916–7 (7th Cir. 1986) ($7000 for nine months' segregation, or about $25 a day), *vacated*, 484 U.S. 807, 108 S. Ct. 54 (1987), *remanded*, 840 F.2d 20 (7th Cir. 1988); Larkins v. Oswald, 510 F.2d 583, 589–90 (2d Cir. 1975) ($1000 for 12 days in segregation); McClary v. Coughlin, 87 F. Supp. 2d 205, 218–19 (W.D.N.Y. 2000) (reducing $660,000 jury verdict for four years in administrative segregation to $237,000, about $175 a day), *aff'd*, 237 F.3d 185 (2d Cir. 2001); Maurer v. Patterson, 197 F.R.D. 244, 249 (S.D.N.Y. 2000) ($25,000 for a month's segregation plus removal from inmate grievance committee and possible effect on parole); Morgan v. Ward, 699 F. Supp. 1025, 1045 (N.D.N.Y. 1988) ($750 awarded for about nine weeks in punitive segregation in the early 1970s).

[1064]Simmons v. Cook, 154 F.3d 805, 809 (8th Cir. 1998) ($2000 upheld for paraplegic prisoners held in segregation for 32 hours, denied their prescribed mattresses, and denied food and toilet access); Goodson v. City of Atlanta, 763 F.2d 1381, 1383, 1387 (11th Cir.) ($45,000 in compensatory damages and $5000 in punitive damages for three days under unconstitutional conditions), *rehearing denied*, 770 F.2d 175 (11th Cir. 1985); Smith v. Rowe, 761 F.2d 360, 368–9 (7th Cir. 1985) (award of $80,770 upheld where plaintiff spent almost two years in segregation, lacked adequate clean clothing, had to put a blanket over the window to keep out the cold, lost over 30 pounds, etc.); Saxner v. Benson, 727 F.2d 669, 672–3 (7th Cir. 1984) ($4500 for 35 days confinement under "extremely unsanitary and repulsive conditions"), *aff'd sub nom.* Cleavinger v. Saxner, 474 U.S. 193, 106 S. Ct. 496 (1985); Maxwell v. Mason, 668 F.2d 361, 366 (8th Cir. 1981) ($1400 for 14 days in strip cell); Benjamin v. Sielaff, 752 F. Supp. 140, 148 (S.D.N.Y. 1990) ($150 a day awarded for inmates held for more than 24 hours in receiving rooms and other non-housing areas); O'Connor v. Keller, 510 F. Supp. 1359, 1375 (D. Md. 1981) ($100 a day for strip cell confinement). *But see* Howard v. Adkison, 887 F.2d 134, 136, 139 (8th Cir. 1989) ($500 in compensatory damages plus substantial punitive award for five months' confinement under filthy conditions in protective custody).

[1065]Walker v. Bain, 257 F.3d 660, 663–64 (6th Cir. 2001) ($300 and $125 for a retaliatory cell search and confiscation of documents and property, and delaying providing grievance forms); Walters v.

Grossheim, 990 F.2d 381, 385 (8th Cir. 1993) ($4.00 a day for improper retention in a lower classification grade); Gordon v. Faber, 973 F.2d 686, 687 (8th Cir. 1992) ($75.00 for several hours' exposure to sub-freezing weather without hats or gloves); Aswegan v. Bruhl, 965 F.2d 676, 677 (8th Cir. 1992) ($500 compensatory and $1500 punitive for medical neglect); Green v. Johnson, 977 F.2d 1383, 1388–89 (10th Cir. 1992) ($15,000 for inmate assault, staff abuse, and strip cell confinement); Jolivet v. Deland, 966 F.2d 573, 576–7 (10th Cir. 1992) ($250 for disclosure of private correspondence); Smith v. Galley, 919 F.2d 893, 894 (4th Cir. 1990) ($15,000 for denial of a wheelchair to an inmate who could not walk), *rev'd on other grounds sub nom.* Smith v. Barry, 502 U.S. 244 (1992); Toombs v. Bell, 915 F.2d 345, 349 (8th Cir. 1990) ($7500 for medical neglect); Bee v. Greaves, 910 F.2d 686, 687 n.1 (10th Cir. 1990) ($100 compensatory and $300 punitive damages for forcible administration of thorazine); Wright v. Jones, 907 F.2d 848, 850 (8th Cir. 1990) ($1000 in compensatory and $225 from each guard in punitive damages for inmate assault); Sample v. Diecks, 885 F.2d 1099, 1112 (3d Cir. 1989) ($20 a day for prisoner who was held in prison for nine months past his release date); Mayberry v. Walters, 862 F.2d 1040, 1041–2 (3d Cir. 1988) ($500 compensatory and $500 punitive damages for inmate assault); Straub v. Monge, 815 F.2d 1467, 1468 (11th Cir. 1987) ($3000 for denial of law library to prisoner defending a civil forfeiture action); Lewis v. Cooper, 771 F.2d 334, 335 (7th Cir. 1985) ($2000 in compensatory damages and $3500 in punitive damages for denial of medical attention); Nolley v. County of Erie, 802 F. Supp. 898, 905, 910 (W.D.N.Y. 1992) ($30 a day for invasion of medical privacy, $10 a week for exclusion from religious services); Hill v. Koon, 732 F. Supp. 1076, 1083 (D.Nev. 1990) (compensatory damages of $1000 and punitive damages of $3000 for unjustified digital rectal searches), *rev'd on other grounds sub nom.* 977 F.2d 589 (9th Cir. 1992); Vanscoy v. Hicks, 691 F. Supp. 1336, 1338 (M.D.Ala. 1988) ($50 awarded for a single instance of refusing to let the plaintiff go to religious services); Campbell v. Thornton, 644 F. Supp. 103, 106 (W.D.Mo. 1986) ($5000 awarded for religious freedom violation, $1000 for mail censorship, $2000 for forced sex).

[1066]*See, e.g.,* Moore v. Pemberton, 110 F.3d 22, 23 (7th Cir. 1997) (per curiam) (court concludes suit is malicious, as well as frivolous, because the plaintiff demanded $3.5 million in damages for a minor disciplinary sanction); Sloan v. Southampton Correctional Center, 476 F. Supp. 196, 197 (E.D.Va. 1979).

[1067]Steinmetz v. Bradbury Co., Inc., 618 F.2d 21, 24 (8th Cir. 1980); Paul v. Gomez, 190 F.R.D. 402, 403 (W.D.Va. 2000) ("Under federal procedure, an *ad damnum* serves no practical purpose in a contested case, since the court must award the full relief to which

In federal court, the rules do not require you to state a definite dollar amount at all,[1068] and it may be to your advantage not to do so.[1069]

2. Injunctions

An injunction is a court order requiring a party to perform some action (a "mandatory" injunction) or to refrain from performing some action (a "prohibitory" injunction).[1070] Procedurally, there are several kinds of injunctions.

A permanent injunction is granted only after there has been a final decision on the merits of the case.[1071]

A preliminary injunction is granted to prevent a party from suffering irreparable harm while she awaits the final disposition of the case. A temporary restraining order (TRO) is granted, sometimes without notice to the other side, only to prevent immediate and irreparable injury and only until the court has time to schedule a hearing to determine whether a preliminary injunction is justified.[1072]

The Prison Litigation Reform Act (PLRA) restricts prisoners' ability to get an injunction and keep it in effect.[1073] These PLRA provisions are discussed elsewhere in this Manual.[1074] In a nutshell, injunctions in prisoner cases are supposed to go no further than necessary to correct a violation of federal law (which is not really much different from the law governing federal court injunctions generally); that restriction applies to settlements; and injunctions may be terminated on defendants' request after two years unless the

court finds that there is a continuing and ongoing federal law violation.

To get an injunction,[1075] you must generally show that you do not have an "adequate remedy at law," which means that an award of damages or other relief will not adequately protect you.[1076] You must also show that there is an actual danger of future violation of your rights. Past violations, by themselves, will not entitle you to an injunction,[1077] though past misconduct may be evidence that future misconduct is likely.[1078] Changes in policy under pressure of litigation do not necessarily defeat an injunctive claim.[1079]

The risk of future harm must affect you personally; you generally cannot get an injunction solely to protect other prisoners unless your case has been certified as a class action.[1080] In some cases, courts have been willing to grant an injunction striking down a prison policy, without restricting its effect to the particular plaintiff and without certifying a class,[1081] but a court is unlikely to do this if the plaintiff is

---

the plaintiff is entitled, regardless of the state of the pleadings." (footnote omitted)); Bergeson v. Dilworth, 738 F. Supp. 1361, 1364 (D.Kan. 1990) and cases cited, aff'd, 959 F.2d 245 (10th Cir. 1992) (unpublished).

[1068]CNW Corp. v. Japonica Partners, L.P., 776 F. Supp. 864, 869 (D.Del. 1990); R.S.E., Inc. V. Pennsy Supply, Inc., 77 F.R.D. 702, 703 (M.D.Pa. 1977) (federal rules require only a statement of the "*type of relief*" requested) (emphasis supplied).

[1069]In determining whether a civil rights plaintiff is entitled to attorneys' fees, the courts often compare the amount of damages awarded to the amount claimed in the complaint. *See* Farrar v. Hobby, 506 U.S. 103, 113 S. Ct. 566 (1992). If you have an attorney, or are hoping to obtain one, it may be better to avoid stating a precise amount in the complaint in case you are awarded a small amount of damages.

[1070]Louis Vuitton Malletier v. Dooney & Bourke, Inc., 454 F.3d 108, 114 (2d Cir. 2006) (citations omitted).

[1071]Marriott v. County of Montgomery, 426 F. Supp. 2d 1, 11 (N.D.N.Y. 2006) ("The standard for a permanent injunction is essentially the same as the standard for a preliminary injunction, except that the moving party, instead of showing a likelihood of success on the merits must show actual success on the merits." (citing Amoco Prod. Co. v. Village of Gambell, 480 U.S. 531, 546 n.12, 107 S. Ct. 1396 (1987)); *see* AmeriSteel Corp. v. International Brotherhood of Teamsters, 267 F.3d 264, 267 (3d Cir. 2001) (permanent injunction is a final order and appealable).

[1072]Rule 65(b), Fed.R.Civ.P.

[1073]*See* 18 U.S.C. § 3626.

[1074]*See* Ch. 9, § K.

[1075]This discussion is based on federal law. State courts may have different standards.

[1076]Morales v. Trans World Airlines, Inc., 504 U.S. 374, 381, 112 S. Ct. 2031 (1992). *But see* Register.com, Inc. v. Verio, Inc. 356 F.3d 393, 404 (2d Cir. 2004) (injunctive relief is appropriate where damages would be "very difficult to calculate").

[1077]Farmer v. Brennan, 511 U.S. 825, 846, 114 S. Ct. 1970 (1994); Wessel v. City of Albuquerque, 299 F.3d 1186, 1194 (10th Cir. 2002); Belk v. Charlotte-Mecklenburg Bd. of Educ., 269 F.3d 305, 347 (4th Cir. 2001); Young v. Lane, 922, F.2d 370, 374 (7th Cir. 1991) (prisoner who had been transferred out of the prison where his rights were violated was not entitled to an injunction unless he could show it was likely he would be transferred back); O.K. v. Bush, 377 F. Supp. 2d 102, 113 (D.D.C. 2005).

[1078]Orantes-Hernandez v. Thornburgh, 919 F.2d 549, 564 (9th Cir. 1990); Lopez v. Garriga, 917 F.2d 63, 67 (1st Cir. 1990) (requiring "likelihood of future unlawful conduct on the defendant's part"); Commodity Futures Trading Com'n v. Wall Street Underground, Inc., 281 F. Supp. 2d 1260, 1273 (D.Kan. 2003) ("In drawing the inference from past violations that future violations may occur, the court should look at the 'totality of circumstances, and factors suggesting that the infraction might not have been an isolated occurrence are always relevant.'" (citation omitted)).

[1079]City of Mesquite v. Aladdin's Castle, 455 U.S. 283, 289, 102 S. Ct. 1070 (1982); U.S. v. Oregon State Medical Society, 343 U.S. 326, 333, 81 S. Ct. 1278 (1952); Eng v. Smith, 849 F.2d 80, 83 (2d Cir. 1988). For discussion of similar issues, *see* § I.2 of this chapter concerning mootness.

[1080]Young v. Lane, 922 F.2d at 373–74 n.9; *see* §§ I.1 and I.2 of this chapter concerning standing and mootness.

[1081]*See* Clement v. California Dep't of Corrections, 364 F.3d 1148, 1152–53 (9th Cir. 2004) (single plaintiff obtained statewide injunction against banning of internet materials); Ashker v. California Dep't of Corrections, 350 F.3d 917, 924 (9th Cir. 2003) (statewide injunction issued based on claim by one inmate); Jordan v. Pugh, 2007 WL 2908931, *4 (D.Colo., Oct. 4, 2007) (holding a nationwide injunction appropriate where a rule was found facially overbroad under the First Amendment); Riley v. Brown, 2006 WL 1722622, *14 (D.N.J., June 21, 2006) (entering injunction to protect all prisoners from sex offender facility from assault notwithstanding lack of class certification since the record shows that all of them

no longer affected by the policy. Courts have disagreed whether the PLRA limits the scope of injunctions in non-class actions to the individual plaintiffs.[1082]

In general, there is no right to a jury trial in injunctive cases.[1083] However, if you bring both injunctive and damage claims, there is a right to a jury on the damage claims, and the court must handle the case so as to preserve that right. This usually means hearing the damage claims first,[1084] though this rule does not prevent a court from granting

temporary (preliminary) injunctive relief pending a final disposition of all claims.[1085] An adverse jury verdict on damages for past conduct does not necessarily prevent the court from granting an injunction.[1086]

a. Preliminary Injunctions and Temporary Restraining Orders

To get a preliminary injunction, you must show some combination of the following things:[1087]

(1) You will suffer "irreparable injury" without an injunction. A showing that your constitutional rights are likely to be violated is usually enough to meet the irreparable harm requirement.[1088]

(2) You will suffer more without an injunction than prison officials will suffer if the injunction is granted. This is called the "balance of hardships."[1089]

---

were at risk because of their status; stating the injunction "is not overly broad because it applies to a particular group of inmates who are likely to be targeted by other state inmates and it does not apply to any inmates that are unlikely to be targeted."); Doe 1 v. Rumsfeld, 341 F. Supp. 2d 1, 16–19 (D.D.C. 2004) (invalidating regulation nationally and cases cited, *remanded as moot*, 172 Fed. Appx. 327 (D.C. Cir. 2006) (unpublished); Williams v. Wilkinson, 132 F. Supp. 2d 601, 604, 608–09, 611–12 (S.D.Ohio 2001) (finding an informal policy of refusing to call witnesses in disciplinary hearings, directing defendants to promulgate a new policy); Mujahid v. Sumner, 807 F. Supp. 1505, 1513 (D.Haw. 1992), *aff'd*, 996 F.2d 1226 (9th Cir. 1993); McCargo v. Vaughn, 778 F. Supp. 1341, 1342 (E.D.Pa. 1991); *see* Sharif by Salahuddin v. New York State Education Department, 709 F. Supp. 345, 359 (S.D.N.Y. 1989) (non-prison case) and cases cited. *But see* Sharpe v. Cureton, 319 F.3d 259, 273 (6th Cir. 2003) ("While district courts are not categorically prohibited from granting injunctive relief benefitting an entire class in an individual suit, such broad relief is rarely justified because injunctive relief should be no more burdensome to the defendant than necessary to provide complete relief to the plaintiffs."); Easyriders Freedom F.I.G.H.T. v. Hannigan, 92 F.3d 1486, 1501–02 (9th Cir. 1996) (injunction can extend beyond individual plaintiffs "if such breadth is necessary to give prevailing parties the relief to which they are entitled"); Hernandez v. Reno, 91 F.3d 776, 781 (5th Cir. 1996) ("Class-wide relief may be appropriate in an individual action if such is necessary to give the prevailing party the relief to which he or she is entitled."). *Contra*, Tesmer v. Granholm, 333 F.3d 683, 702 (6th Cir. 2003) (en banc) ("Declaratory judgment is effective as to only the plaintiffs who obtained it. . . . When a class has not been certified, the only interests of concern are those of the named plaintiffs."), *rev'd on other grounds*, 543 U.S. 125 (2004); McKenzie v. City of Chicago, 118 F.3d 552, 555 (7th Cir. 1997) ("[b]ecause a class has not been certified, the only interests at stake are those of the named plaintiffs").

Courts have also held that prisoners who are not named parties may be third-party beneficiaries of orders or judgments and may be able to enforce them. *See* § G of this chapter, n.491.

[1082]Lindell v. Frank, 377 F.3d 655, 660 (7th Cir. 2004) (yes); Clement v. California Dep't of Corrections, 364 F.3d at 1152–53 (no); Williams v. Wilkinson, 132 F. Supp. 2d 601, 604, 608–09, 611–12 (S.D.Ohio 2001) (no); *see also* Gomez v. Vernon, 255 F.3d 1118, 1130–31 (9th Cir. 2001) (holding restriction of relief to individuals helped meet PLRA limits).

[1083]City of Monterey v. Del Monte Dunes at Monterey, Ltd., 526 U.S. 687, 719, 119 S. Ct. 1624 (1999); *see* Ch. 10, § R.2, concerning the right to a jury trial.

[1084]Beacon Theaters v. Westover, 359 U.S. 500, 510–11, 79 S. Ct. 948 (1959); Perez-Serrano v. DeLeon-Velez, 868 F.2d 30, 32–33 (1st Cir. 1989). *Cf. City of Monterey*, id., at 730 ("The right of jury trial is not eliminated, of course, by virtue of the fact that, under

our modern unified system, the equitable relief of an injunction is also sought." (Scalia, J., concurring)).

The reason this is an issue is that a final determination of the injunctive claim by the court would constitute *res judicata* or collateral estoppel as to a later jury determination of damage issues, and thereby infringe on the Seventh Amendment right to have the facts decided by a jury. Beacon Theaters v. Westover, 359 U.S. at 503–04.

[1085]Dairy Queen v. Wood, 369 U.S. 469, 479 n.20, 82 S. Ct. 894 (1962).

[1086]Burton v. Armontrout, 975 F.2d 543, 544–45 (8th Cir. 1992) (noting court may rely on evidence not available to jury, and jury's factual findings may be inconclusive, especially if there is a general verdict); Johnson v. Bowers, 884 F.2d 1053, 1057 (8th Cir. 1989) (noting additional time prisoner had waited for medical treatment since time of jury trial).

[1087]All federal courts use some combination of these factors. *See* Winter v. Natural Resources Defense Council, Inc., ___ U.S. ___, 129 S. Ct. 365, 374 (2008). Be sure you find out how the appeals court in your federal circuit has phrased the standard. *See, e.g.*, Lambert v. Buss, 498 F.3d 446, 451 (7th Cir. 2007); Schrier v. University of Colorado, 427 F.3d 1253, 1258 (10th Cir. 2005); Overstreet v. United Broth. of Carpenters and Joiners of America, Local Union No. 1506, 409 F.3d 1199, 1207 (9th Cir. 2005).

[1088]Winter v. Natural Resources Defense Council, Inc., 129 S. Ct. at 375 (party seeking injunction must show likelihood, not mere possibility, of irreparable harm); Elrod v. Burns, 427 U.S. 347, 373, 96 S. Ct. 2673 (1976); American Trucking Associations, Inc. v. City of Los Angeles, 559 F.3d 1046, 1058–59 (9th Cir. 2009); Campbell v. Miller, 373 F.3d 834, 840 (7th Cir. 2004); Connecticut Dep't of Environmental Protection v. O.S.H.A., 356 F.3d 226, 231 (2d Cir. 2004); Newsom v. Norris, 888 F.2d 371, 378 (6th Cir. 1989).

[1089]*See, e.g.*, Lambert v. Buss, 498 F.3d 446, 452–53 (7th Cir. 2007); Mitchell v. Cuomo, 748 F.2d 804, 808 (2d Cir. 1984) (holding that dangers posed by prison crowding outweighed state's financial and administrative concerns); Duran v. Anaya, 642 F. Supp. 510, 527 (D.N.M. 1986) (holding that prisoners' interest in safety and medical care outweighed state's interest in saving money by cutting staff).

(3) You are likely to succeed on the merits—*i.e.*, you will probably win your case in the end.[1090] Some courts have held that if you make a strong showing that the balance of hardships favors you, you need only show a "fair ground for litigation" and not a likelihood of success in order to obtain a preliminary injunction.[1091] Courts have disagreed whether mandatory and prohibitory injunctive relief are governed by different standards for granting preliminary injunctions.[1092]

(4) It is in the public interest to grant the injunction. Your argument will generally be that it is always in the public interest for government officials, including prison personnel, to obey the Constitution and other laws.[1093]

Preliminary injunctions in prison cases must also satisfy the requirements of the Prison Litigation Reform Act (PLRA) for prospective relief, and they are limited to 90 days, though consecutive injunctions can be granted if necessary.[1094] Most courts have held that you have to exhaust administrative remedies under the PLRA before you can get preliminary relief.[1095]

Prisoners have been granted preliminary injunctions in a variety of cases.[1096]

[1090]*See, e.g.,* Gonzales v. O Centro Espirita Beneficente Uniao do Vegetal, 546 U.S. 418, 428, 126 S. Ct. 1211 (2006); New Comm Wireless Servs., Inc. v. Sprint Com, Inc., 287 F.3d 1, 9 (1st Cir. 2002) ("[I]f the moving party cannot demonstrate that he is likely to succeed in his quest, the remaining factors become matters of idle curiosity."). Courts may differ about exactly what likelihood of success means, so you should look at the most recent preliminary injunction law from the circuit and the district you will be filing in. *Compare* Cooper v. Salazar, 196 F.3d 809, 813 (7th Cir. 1999) (likelihood of success means "better than negligible chance of succeeding") *with* Marriott v. County of Montgomery, 227 F.R.D. 159, 174 (N.D.N.Y. 2005) (likelihood of success means more than a 50% chance (citing Abdul Wali v. Coughlin, 754 F.2d 1015, 1025 (2d Cir.1985)), *aff'd*, 2005 WL 3117194 (2d Cir. 2005) (unpublished).

[1091]Bronx Household of Faith v. Board of Educ. of the City of New York, 331 F.3d 342, 349 (2d Cir. 2003); Six Clinics Holding Corp. v. Cafcomp Sys., Inc., 119 F.3d 393, 402 (6th Cir. 1997); *see also* Warsoldier v. Woodford, 418 F.3d 989, 993–94 (9th Cir. 2005) (plaintiff must show "either (1) a likelihood of success on the merits and the possibility of irreparable injury or (2) the existence of serious questions going to the merits and the balance of hardships tipping in [his] favor.").

Courts that apply this lower standard sometimes also hold that it does not apply to "government action taken in the public interest pursuant to a statutory or regulatory scheme," and that likelihood of success must still be shown in that kind of case. *See* Planned Parenthood Minnesota, North Dakota, South Dakota v. Rounds, 530 F.3d 724, 731–32 (8th Cir. 2008); Jolly v. Coughlin, 76 F.3d 468, 473 (2d Cir. 1996). This rule does not apply to action taken by individual officials that is not done pursuant to statutes or regulations. Piscottano v. Murphy, 317 F. Supp. 2d 97, 104 (D.Conn. 2004).

[1092]*Compare* United Food and Commercial Workers Union, Local 1099 v. SW. Ohio Regional Transit Auth., 163 F.3d 341, 348 (6th Cir. 1998) (no difference) *with* Louis Vuitton Malletier v. Dooney & Bourke, Inc., 454 F.3d 108, 114 (2d Cir. 2006) (plaintiff must show "clear" or "substantial" likelihood of success to obtain mandatory injunction).

[1093]Phelps-Roper v. Nixon, 545 F.3d 685, 690 (8th Cir. 2008) (" . . . [I]t is always in the public interest to protect constitutional rights."); Mayweathers v. Newland, 258 F.3d 930, 938 (9th Cir. 2001) (" . . . [T]he free exercise of religion in prisons is obviously in the public interest."); Washington v. Reno, 35 F.3d 1093, 1103

(6th Cir. 1994); R.G. v. Koller, 415 F. Supp. 2d 1129, 1162 (D.Haw. 2006) (" . . . [P]rotection of constitutional rights is a compelling public interest."); Roe v. Crawford, 396 F. Supp. 2d 1041, 1045 (W.D.Mo. 2005) (abortion rights case), *stay denied*, 546 U.S. 959 (2005); Laube v. Haley, 234 F. Supp. 2d 1227, 1252 (M.D.Ala. 2002); McClendon v. City of Albuquerque, 272 F. Supp. 2d 1250, 1259 (D.N.M. 2003) ("The public has an interest in the City's and the County's maintenance of prison facilities that provide the minimal conditions of confinement required by the Constitution and federal law."); Forchion v. Intensive Supervised Parole, 240 F. Supp. 2d 302, 310 (D.N.J. 2003); Howard v. U.S., 864 F. Supp. 1019, 1029 (D.Colo. 1994) ("Enforcement of [constitutional] rights is clearly very much in the public interest."); ILQ Investments, Inc., v. City of Rochester, 816 F. Supp. 516, 527 (D.Minn. 1993) ("Upholding constitutionally guaranteed rights is in the public interest."), *rev'd on other grounds*, 25 F.3d 1413 (8th Cir. 1994); Doe v. Barron, 92 F. Supp. 2d 694, 697 (S.D.Ohio 1999) ("It is in the public's interest to uphold that right [to terminate pregnancy] when it is being arbitrarily denied by prison officials absent medical or other legitimate concerns."); Duran v. Anaya, 642 F. Supp. at 527 ("Respect for law, particularly by officials responsible for the administration of the [City's] correctional system, is in itself a matter of the highest public interest."); Llewelyn v. Oakland County Prosecutor's Office, 402 F. Supp. 1379, 1393 (E.D.Mich. 1975) ("The Constitution is the ultimate expression of the public interest."); *see also* City of Los Angeles v. Lyons, 461 U.S. 95, 136, 103 S. Ct. 1660 (1983) ("Courts of equity have much greater latitude in granting injunctive relief 'in furtherance of the public interest . . . than when only private interests are involved.'").

[1094]*See* Ch. 9, § K.2.

[1095]*See* Ch. 9, § D, nn.234–237 (suggesting ways to argue to the contrary).

[1096]*See, e.g.,* Jones v. Caruso, 569 F.3d 258, 278–79 (6th Cir. 2009) (affirming injunction against broad prohibition of material related to Uniform Commercial Code); Bear v. Kautzky, 305 F.3d 802, 805–06 (8th Cir. 2002) (affirming injunction against prison policy that precluded inmate from communication with other prisoners who were jailhouse lawyers); Stringer-El v. Nix, 945 F.2d 1015 (8th Cir. 1991) (requiring release from unlawful segregation); Diamontiney v. Borg, 918 F.2d 793 (9th Cir. 1990) (requiring delivery of legal mail); Newsom v. Norris, 888 F.2d 371 (6th Cir. 1989) (reinstating inmate clerks unlawfully fired from their jobs); Monmouth County Correctional Institutional Inmates v. Lanzaro, 834 F.2d 326 (3d Cir. 1987) (protecting abortion rights); Johnson v. Sullivan, 2008 WL 5396614, *7 (E.D.Cal., Dec. 23, 2008) (allowing access to counsel), *reconsideration denied*, 2009 WL 160250 (E.D.Cal., Jan. 21, 2009); Farnam v. Walker, 593 F. Supp. 2d 1000, 1011–19 (C.D.Ill. 2009) (requiring specialist care for cystic fibrosis); Gammett v. Idaho State Bd. of Corrections, 2007 WL 2186896, *12–17 (D.Idaho, July 27, 2007) (requiring hormone and psychotherapeutic treatment for gender identity disorder),

Temporary restraining orders are extremely difficult to get. The factors courts consider are the same as for a preliminary injunction, but courts generally require a stronger showing. In prison cases, courts are likely to grant a TRO only to prevent immediate and irreparable deprivations of constitutional rights.[1097]

Temporary restraining orders are also difficult to seek procedurally. Usually, a litigant seeking a TRO rushes to court, persuades the judge to sign the order and schedule a hearing, and immediately serves the order personally on the adverse party. This is difficult to manage *pro se* if you are

---

reconsideration denied, 2007 WL 2684750 (D.Idaho, Sept. 7, 2007); Stringham v. Bick, 2007 WL 60996 (E.D.Cal., Jan. 8, 2007) (directing placement of plaintiff in cell with tinted windows because of his medical problems), *report and recommendation adopted*, 2007 WL 806619 (E.D.Cal., Mar. 15, 2007); Bowers v. City of Philadelphia, 2007 WL 219651 (E.D.Pa., Jan. 25, 2007) (relieving conditions in intake units and police lockups); Riley v. Brown, 2006 WL 1722622, *14 (D.N.J., June 21, 2006) (protecting safety of sex offenders); Jones'El v. Berge, 164 F. Supp. 2d 1096, 1116–25 (W.D.Wis. 2001) (requiring removal of seriously mentally ill prisoners from "supermax" prison); Castellini v. Lappin, 365 F. Supp. 197, 206 (D.Mass. 2005) (requiring Bureau of Prisons to continue "shock incarceration" program until it complies with APA requirements for notice and comment); Cohen v. Coahoma County, Miss., 805 F. Supp. 398, 400, 406 (N.D.Miss. 1992) (enjoining the use of physical pain to coerce information); Pratt v. Rowland, 770 F. Supp. 1399 (N.D.Calif. 1991) (forbidding threats, harassment, and punishment because of political beliefs or media attention); Martyr v. Bachik, 770 F. Supp. 1406 (D.Or. 1991) (protecting correspondence rights); Madden v. Kemna, 739 F. Supp. 1358 (W.D.Mo. 1990) (ameliorating protective custody conditions); Yarbaugh v. Roach, 736 F. Supp. 318 (D.D.C. 1990) (requiring medical treatment); Phillips v. Michigan Dep't of Corrections, 731 F. Supp. 792 (W.D.Mich. 1990) (continuing transsexual's estrogen treatment), *aff'd*, 932 F.2d 969 (6th Cir. 1991); Berrios-Berrios v. Thornburg, 716 F. Supp. 987 (E.D.Ky. 1989) (permitting prisoner to breast-feed her child in the visiting room); Czajka v. Moore, 708 F. Supp. 253 (E.D.Mo. 1989) (barring due process violations).

[1097]*See, e.g.*, Jackson v. District of Columbia, 254 F.3d 262, 265 (D.C. Cir. 2001) (noting grant of TRO against imposition of grooming policy on prisoners with religious objections); Washington v. Reno, 35 F.3d 1093, 1096–97 (6th Cir. 1994) (noting grant of TRO against restrictive changes in prison telephone system); Webster v. Sowders, 846 F.2d 1032, 1034 (6th Cir. 1988) (noting that the lower court granted a TRO to plaintiffs who were assigned to perform asbestos removal under unsafe conditions); Rosado v. Alameida, 349 F. Supp. 2d 1340, 1342 (S.D.Cal. 2004) (noting grant of TRO requiring immediate medical attention for prisoner with Hepatitis C and cirrhosis); Goodman v. Money, 180 F. Supp. 2d 946, 947–48 (N.D.Ohio 2001) (granting TRO to prevent immediate deprivation of religious rights); Doe v. Barron, 92 F. Supp. 2d 694, 696–97 (S.D.Ohio 1999) (granting TRO to pregnant prisoner to obtain an abortion); U.S. v. State of Michigan, 680 F. Supp. 928, 1045–47 (W.D.Mich. 1987) (granting TRO because crowding in reception center posed fire, sanitation, and safety risks); James v. Edwards, 683 F. Supp. 157, 159–60 (E.D.La. 1987) (granting TRO to prisoner who was scheduled for execution before his time to seek Supreme Court review had expired).

locked up. If you seek a TRO by mailing papers to the court, the court will probably not grant the TRO; more likely, if it believes your situation is genuinely urgent, it will simply schedule a preliminary injunction hearing quickly.

Litigants who obtain a preliminary injunction or TRO are usually asked to post security.[1098] However, this rule is not supposed to be applied so as to deny judicial review,[1099] and courts have not required impoverished litigants to post security.[1100] Security is not required if the relief you are seeking will not impose monetary loss on the defendants.[1101]

b. Papers to File When Seeking a Preliminary Injunction or TRO

If your case has already been filed and you have been granted *in forma pauperis* status, you need only file a motion for a temporary restraining order and/or a preliminary injunction.[1102] If you are seeking a TRO, you should also submit a proposed order granting you the relief you request. Orders granting a TRO are generally presented as orders to show cause.[1103] If you seek a TRO, you must also ask for a preliminary injunction, since TROs are only granted for a long enough period to permit the court to schedule a preliminary injunction hearing.

Examples of TRO papers are included in the Appendices.[1104] A motion for a TRO or a preliminary injunction must be supported by an affidavit or declaration setting out the facts—at a minimum, your own sworn statement. If you can get affidavits or declarations from others with personal knowledge, or if you can attach documents that support your claim, they may also be helpful. You should

---

[1098]Rule 65(c), Fed.R.Civ.P.; *see* Curtis 1000, Inc. v. Yougblade, 878 F. Supp. 1224, 1275–82 (N.D.Iowa 1995) (describing bond requirement). *But see* University Books & Videos, Inc. v. Metropolitan Dade County, 33 F. Supp. 2d 1364, 1374 (S.D.Fla. 1999) (requiring a bond is discretionary, and has been waived "(1) when the party seeking the injunction has a high probability of succeeding on the merits of its claim, . . .; (2) when the party to be enjoined is a municipality or county government that likely would not incur any significant cost or monetary damages from the issuance of the injunction, . . .; (3) when demanding a bond from the party seeking the injunction would injure the constitutional rights of the party or the public. . . .").

[1099]People of State of Cal. ex. rel. van de Kamp v. Tahoe Regional Planning Agency, 766 F.2d 1319, 1325–26 (9th Cir. 1985).

[1100]*See, e.g.*, Johnson v. Board of Police Commissioners, 351 F. Supp. 2d 929, 952 (E.D.Mo. 2004) (district court has discretion to waive security, "especially when doing so would function to bar poor people from obtaining judicial redress" and cases cited); Noble v. Tooley, 125 F. Supp. 2d 481, 486 (M.D.Fla. 2000); J.L. v. Parham, 412 F. Supp. 112, 140 (M.D.Ga. 1976) (holding that *in forma pauperis* litigant should not be required to post security), *rev'd on other grounds*, 442 U.S. 584, 99 S. Ct. 2493 (1979).

[1101]Noble v. Tooley, 125 F. Supp. 2d at 486; Cohen v. Coahoma County, Miss., 805 F. Supp. 398, 408 (N.D.Miss. 1992).

[1102]Motion practice generally is discussed in Ch. 10, § F. The form of motion papers is discussed in Ch. 10, § D.

[1103]*See* Ch. 10, § F, for a discussion of such orders.

[1104]Appendix C, Form 11.

submit a brief explaining why your case meets the legal criteria for granting a TRO or preliminary injunction. You should also include proof of service or of your attempts to serve the defendants.[1105]

If your case has not already been filed, you must file a complaint in order to seek a TRO or preliminary injunction, along with an *in forma pauperis* motion if you cannot pay the fees. You may also wish to file a motion for the appointment of counsel, although if you are seeking emergency relief it is doubtful if the court could find an attorney for you in time to be helpful.

3. Declaratory Judgments

A declaratory judgment is a binding statement of your legal rights from a court, but it does not actually order anyone to do anything. The federal Declaratory Judgments Act provides that a federal court "may declare the rights and other legal relations of any interested party seeking such declaration, whether or not further relief is or could be sought."[1106] A declaratory judgment is a form of prospective relief,[1107] and therefore is subject to the Prison Litigation Reform Act provisions governing such relief.

You need not show irreparable harm or inadequate remedies at law to get a declaratory judgment.[1108] However, there must be an "actual controversy" between you and the defendants for a declaratory judgment to issue.[1109] You generally may not obtain a federal court declaratory judgment regarding the legality or the length of your incarceration, since habeas corpus is the exclusive remedy in such cases.[1110]

A court may prefer to grant a declaratory judgment rather than an injunction in a case in which it expects prison officials to comply without resistance and in which the issues are very clear-cut—*e.g.*, the constitutionality of a statute, regulation, or well-established administrative practice.[1111]

If you obtain a declaratory judgment and prison officials do not follow it, the court has the power to grant an injunction ordering them to do so.[1112]

You may ask for a declaratory judgment along with other forms of relief such as damages or an injunction. This request should be made in the relief section of the complaint.

[1105]Rule 65(b), Fed.R.Civ.P., requires the applicant's attorney to certify in writing "any efforts made to give notice and the reasons why it should not be required." This requirement will undoubtedly be applied to *pro se* litigants as well.

[1106]28 U.S.C. § 2201.

State courts may have different rules concerning declaratory judgments. These will generally appear in the state's statutes or court rules and there will probably be state court case law interpreting the rules.

[1107]Ellis v. Dyson, 421 U.S. 426, 443–44, 95 S. Ct. 1691 (1975); Canadian Lumber Trade Alliance v. U.S., 517 F.3d 1319, 1338 (Fed. Cir. 2008).

[1108]Rule 57, Fed.R.Civ.P.; *see* PGBA, LLC v. U.S., 389 F.3d 1219, 1228 n.6 (Fed. Cir. 2004) and cases cited.

[1109]28 U.S.C. § 2201; *see* Lafaut v. Smith, 834 F.2d 389, 394–95 (4th Cir. 1987) (declaratory judgment could not be granted to prisoner who had been released); Ramos v. Puerto Rico Medical Examining Bd., 491 F. Supp. 2d 238, 242 (D.P.R. 2007) (declaratory judgment is governed by same standing requirements as other actions).

[1110]*See* § H.1.a of this chapter.

[1111]*See., e.g.*, Gittens v. LeFevre, 891 F.2d 38, 43 (2d Cir. 1989) (declaring pre-hearing disciplinary confinement rules unconstitutional); Karr v. Bay, 413 F. Supp. 579, 585 (N.D.Ohio 1976) (granting declaration regarding incarceration of indigents for non-payment of fines); Morris v. Travisono, 373 F. Supp. 177, 182 (D.R.I. 1974), *aff'd*, 509 F.2d 1358 (1st Cir. 1975) (granting declaratory judgment regarding prison disciplinary rules).

[1112]28 U.S.C. § 2202 (authorizing "further necessary or proper relief"); *see* Powell v. McCormack, 395 U.S. 486, 499, 89 S. Ct. 1944 (1969); Morris v. Travisono, 373 F. Supp. at 182.

CHAPTER 9

The Prison Litigation Reform Act

The Prison Litigation Reform Act ("PLRA") is a federal statute that makes it more difficult for prisoners to pursue legal claims in federal court and to get meaningful relief if they do pursue them. The PLRA requires indigent prisoners, unlike other indigent litigants, to pay filing fees in installments; it bars prisoners from using the *in forma pauperis* (IFP) procedures at all under some circumstances; it limits the damages prisoners can receive for certain kinds of constitutional violations; it requires prisoners to exhaust administrative remedies before filing suit. Its various provisions have been upheld against all constitutional challenges to date.[1]

The PLRA makes it extremely important to be sure your legal claim is well founded before you file it, since you will have to pay the $350 filing fee for any case you file in federal court (appeals cost $450), and if your case is dismissed, you may incur a "strike," three of which will disqualify you from IFP status in the future. The PLRA's administrative exhaustion requirement means that you *must* pursue *and complete* the prison grievance process, or other administrative remedy applicable to your problem, before you file suit, or your suit will be dismissed. These and the other PLRA provisions, and how the courts have applied them, are discussed in detail in the rest of this chapter.

Most of the important PLRA provisions apply to actions "brought" by "prisoners." Most courts have held that an action is "brought" for PLRA purposes when the prisoner tenders the complaint to court, and not at the later point when the court finishes screening the case and deciding whether to grant IFP status and then formally files the complaint.[2]

A "prisoner" for PLRA purposes is "any person incarcerated or detained in any facility who is accused of, convicted of, sentenced for, or adjudicated delinquent for, violations of criminal law or the terms and conditions of parole, probation, pretrial release, or diversionary

program."[3] This category includes military prisoners[4] and persons held in privately operated prisons and jails,[5] juvenile facilities,[6] or "halfway houses" or drug treatment programs that the person is confined in as a result of a criminal charge or conviction.[7]

Persons who are civilly committed are generally not prisoners, even if their commitment has its origins in past criminal charges or sentences.[8] But if their criminal proceedings

---

[1]*See, e.g.*, Rodriguez v. Cook, 169 F.3d 1176, 1178–82 (9th Cir. 1999) (upholding "three strikes" requirement barring some prisoners from *in forma pauperis* status); Martin v. Scott, 156 F.3d 578, 580 n.2 (5th Cir. 1988) (upholding initial screening of prisoner cases); Zehner v. Trigg, 133 F.3d 459, 461–63 (7th Cir. 1997) (upholding limits on damages); Nicholas v. Tucker, 114 F.3d 17, 21 (2d Cir. 1997) (upholding filing fees requirement).

[2]O'Neal v. Price, 531 F.3d 1146, 1151–52 (9th Cir. 2008); Vaden v. Summerhill, 449 F.3d 1045, 1050 (9th Cir. 2006); Ford v. Johnson, 362 F.3d 395, 399–400 (7th Cir. 2004). *Contra*, Ellis v. Guarino, 2004 WL 1879834, *6 (S.D.N.Y., Aug. 24, 2004).

Under the "prison mailbox" rule, a prisoner's complaint would be deemed filed when it is delivered to prison officials for mailing. Schoenlein v. Halawa Correctional Facility, 2008 WL 4761791, *3–5 (D.Haw., Oct. 29, 2008); Gilliam v. Holt, 2008 WL 906479, *6 (M.D.Pa., Mar. 31, 2008) (case was brought by a prisoner where it was delivered to prison officials for mailing before prisoner's release but arrived at court after release). *See* Ch. 10, § H, for discussion of the prison mailbox rule.

[3]42 U.S.C. § 1997e(h); 28 U.S.C. § 1915(h); 28 U.S.C. § 1915A(c) (emphasis supplied). The administrative exhaustion requirement is said to apply to "a prisoner confined in any jail, prison, or other correctional facility," 42 U.S.C. § 1997e(a); the difference in phraseology does not seem to make a substantive difference.

[4]Marrie v. Nickels, 70 F. Supp. 2d 1252, 1262 (D.Kan. 1999).

[5]*See* Roles v. Maddox, 439 F.3d 1016, 1017–18 (9th Cir. 2006); Boyd v. Corrections Corporation of America, 380 F.3d 989, 993–94 (6th Cir. 2004); Ross v. County of Bernalillo, 365 F.3d 1181, 1184 (10th Cir. 2004); Lodholz v. Puckett, 2003 WL 23220723, *4–5 (W.D.Wis., Nov. 24, 2003), *reconsideration denied in part*, 2004 WL 67573 (W.D.Wis., Jan. 13, 2004) (all holding the PLRA exhaustion requirement applicable to persons held in private prisons).

[6]Christina A. ex rel. Jennifer A. v. Bloomberg, 315 F.3d 990, 994–95 (8th Cir. 2003) (holding attorneys' fees provisions apply to juveniles); Alexander S. v. Boyd, 113 F.3d 1373, 1383–85 (4th Cir. 1997) (same); Lewis v. Gagne, 281 F. Supp. 2d 429, 433 (N.D.N.Y. 2003) (holding exhaustion requirement applies to juveniles).

[7]Jackson v. Johnson, 475 F.3d 261, 266–67 (5th Cir. 2007) (holding that parolee in a halfway house, which he could not leave without permission, as a result of his criminal conviction was a prisoner); Ruggiero v. County of Orange, 467 F.3d 170, 174–75 (2d Cir. 2006) (holding "drug treatment campus" was a "jail, prison, or other correctional facility" under 42 U.S.C. § 1997e(a) even though state law said it wasn't a correctional facility; that term "includes within its ambit all facilities in which prisoners are held involuntarily as a result of violating the criminal law"); Witzke v. Femal, 376 F.3d 744, 752–53 (7th Cir. 2004) (holding "intensive drug rehabilitation halfway house" was an "other correctional facility" under the PLRA); Fernandez v. Morris, 2008 WL 2775638, *2 (S.D.Cal., July 16, 2008); Clemens v. SCI-Albion, 2006 WL 3759740, *5 (W.D.Pa., Dec. 19, 2006) (holding halfway house with random urine tests, limited visiting was an "other correctional facility"); *see* Miller v. Wayback House, 2006 WL 297769, *4 (N.D.Tex., Feb. 1, 2006) (assuming plaintiff, released on parole to halfway house, was a prisoner, without much analysis whether facility was a correctional facility under the statute), *aff'd*, 253 Fed.Appx. 399 (5th Cir. 2007) (unpublished).

[8]The largest categories of such persons include those civilly detained pursuant to sexually violent predator statutes, *see* Merryfield v. Jordan, 584 F.3d 923, 927 (8th Cir. 2009); Michau v. Charleston County, S.C., 434 F.3d 725, 727–28 (4th Cir. 2006); Troville v. Venz, 303 F.3d 1256, 1260 (11th Cir. 2002); Page v. Torrey, 201 F.3d 1136, 1139–40 (9th Cir. 2000); Esparza v. Baca, 2008 WL 4500673, *4 (C.D.Cal., Sept. 30, 2008) (holding civilly committed sex offender was not a prisoner even if he remained in prison awaiting a hearing); McClam v. McDonald, 2008 WL 4177217, *3 (D.S.C., Sept. 8, 2008), and persons detained in connection with immigration-related proceedings. *See* Andrews v.

are still pending, they remain pretrial detainees, and are therefore prisoners.[9] Thus, criminal defendants held in mental hospitals as incompetent to assist in their defense are prisoners, since the charges remain pending as long as there is some prospect that they may become competent,[10] but defendants psychiatrically confined after a finding of not guilty by reason of insanity are not prisoners, since their criminal charges are disposed of.[11]

Prisoners cease to be prisoners for PLRA purposes when they are released from prison, whether on parole or otherwise.[12] There is an important exception: persons released on parole to residential facilities they are not free to leave are still prisoners, because they are still "confined" to institutions that fit the definition of "correctional facilities."[13] Most courts have held that release from prison does not affect the status of cases filed before the plaintiff's release; they were still "brought by a prisoner" and remain subject to the PLRA.[14] A few courts have held that filing an amended complaint after release means that the case is no longer "brought by a prisoner."[15] In cases where persons are released

---

King, 398 F.3d 1113, 1121–22 (9th Cir. 2005) (stating that PLRA "three strikes" provision did not apply to dismissals of actions brought while a plaintiff was in INS custody "so long as the detainee did not also face criminal charges"); Agyeman v. I.N.S., 296 F.3d 871, 885–86 (9th Cir. 2002); LaFontant v. INS, 135 F.3d 158 (D.C. Cir. 1998); Mohamed v. Lowe, 2008 WL 5244935, *1 (M.D.Pa., Dec. 16, 2008); Bromfield v. McBurney, 2008 WL 4426827, *2 (W.D.Wash., Sept. 26, 2008); Gashi v. County of Westchester, 2005 WL 195517, *1 (S.D.N.Y., Jan. 27, 2005). *See also* Perkins v. Hedricks, 340 F.3d 582, 583 (8th Cir. 2003) (person civilly detained in prison Federal Medical Center). *Contra*, Willis v. Smith, 2005 WL 550528, *10 (N.D.Iowa, Feb. 28, 2005) (holding that a person civilly committed as a sexually violent predator after completion of his sentence was a prisoner for PLRA purposes).

[9]Kalinowski v. Bond, 358 F.3d 978, 979 (7th Cir. 2004) (holding that persons held under the Illinois Sexually Dangerous Persons Act are prisoners for PLRA purposes).

[10]Ruston v. Church of Jesus Christ of Latter-Day Saints, 2007 WL 2332393, *1 (D.Utah, Aug. 13, 2007); *In re* Rosenbalm, 2007 WL 1593207, *2 (N.D.Cal., June 1, 2007) (noting that such hospitalization is part of the criminal proceeding under state law); Gibson v. Commissioner of Mental Health, 2006 WL 1234971, *6 (S.D.N.Y., May 8, 2006) (applying "three strikes" provision to a criminal defendant hospitalized as incompetent to stand trial), *relief from judgment denied*, 2006 WL 2192865 (S.D.N.Y., Aug. 2, 2006).

[11]Koloctronis v. Morgan, 247 F.3d 726, 728 (8th Cir. 2001); Mullen v. Surtshin, 590 F. Supp. 2d 1233, 1240 (N.D.Cal. 2008); Phelps v. Winn, 2007 WL 2872465, *1 (D.Mass., Sept. 27, 2007) (so holding, notwithstanding that the plaintiff is held by the Bureau of Prisons).

A person who is psychiatrically committed pursuant to statutory requirement after being found "guilty but insane," in states whose law provides for such a verdict, is a prisoner under the PLRA because the basis for confinement is a criminal conviction. Magnuson v. Arizona State Hosp., 2010 WL 283128, *1 n.5, *2 (D.Ariz., Jan. 20, 2010).

[12]Talamantes v. Leyva, 575 F.3d 1021, 1023–24 (9th Cir. 2009); Jackson v. Johnson, 475 F.3d 261, 266–67 (5th Cir. 2007) (parolees released into the general public are not prisoners); Norton v. The City Of Marietta, OK, 432 F.3d 1145, 1150 (10th Cir. 2005); Nerness v. Johnson, 401 F.3d 874, 876 (8th Cir. 2005) (per curiam); Ahmed v. Dragovich, 297 F.3d 201, 210 n.10 (3d Cir. 2002) and cases cited; Janes v. Hernandez, 215 F.3d 541, 543 (5th Cir. 2000); Greig v. Goord, 169 F.3d 165, 167 (2d Cir. 1999); Kerr v. Puckett, 138 F.3d 321, 322 (7th Cir. 1998); Wormley v. U.S., 601 F. Supp. 2d 27, 44 (D.D.C. 2009); Mabry v. Freeman, 489 F. Supp. 2d 782, 785–86 (E.D.Mich. 2007); Bisgeier v. Michael [*sic*] Dep't of Corrections,

2008 WL 227858, *4 (E.D.Mich., Jan. 25, 2008) ("While there may be certain conditions imposed upon Plaintiff as a parolee, there can be no doubt that he is neither 'confined,' 'incarcerated,' nor 'detained in' any jail, prison, or other correctional facility."); Hoffman v. Tuten, 446 F. Supp. 2d 455, 468 (D.S.C. 2006); Keel v. CDCR, 2006 WL 2402100, *2 (E.D.Cal., Aug. 18, 2006) (holding parolee was not a prisoner); Lake v. Schoharie County Com'r of Social Services, 2006 WL 1891141, *4 (N.D.N.Y., May 16, 2006) (rejecting argument that the PLRA's "underlying policy considerations" supported applying the attorneys' fees limits to a released prisoner); Rose v. Saginaw County, 232 F.R.D. 267, 275–77 (E.D.Mich. 2005); Wilson v. Hampton County, 2005 WL 2877725, *3 (D.S.C., Oct. 31, 2005) (relying on Greig v. Goord); Black v. Franklin County, Kentucky, 2005 WL 1993445, *4–5 (E.D.Ky., Aug. 16, 2005).

A couple of cases hold that the prohibition on actions for mental or emotional injury without physical injury, 42 U.S.C. § 1997e(e), applies to cases filed after release. We think they are wrong. *See* § E of this chapter, n.542.

[13]Jackson v. Johnson, 475 F.3d at 265–67; Clemens v. SCI-Albion, 2006 WL 3759740, *5 (W.D.Pa., Dec. 19, 2006) (holding halfway house with random urine tests, limited visiting was an "other correctional facility").

[14]*See* Williams v. Henagan, 595 F.3d 610, 618–19 (5th Cir. 2010) (exhaustion requirement); Cox v. Mayer, 332 F.3d 422, 425–27 (6th Cir. 2003) (exhaustion requirement); Harris v. Garner, 216 F.3d 970, 973–76 (11th Cir. 2000) (en banc) (physical injury requirement); Ross v. Felstead, 2006 WL 2707344, *7 n.6 (D.Minn., Sept. 19, 2006) (exhaustion requirement); Collins v. Goord, 438 F. Supp. 2d 399, 408–09 (S.D.N.Y. 2006) (exhaustion requirement; stating the statutory language "brought" requires a focus on the plaintiff's status at the time of filing); Becker v. Vargo, 2004 WL 1068779, *3 (D.Or., Feb. 17, 2004) (exhaustion requirement), *report and recommendation adopted*, 2004 WL 1071067 (D.Or., Mar. 12, 2004) *and* 2004 WL 1179332 (D.Or., May 27, 2004); Richardson v. Romano, 2003 WL 1877955, *2 (N.D.N.Y., Mar. 31, 2003) (exhaustion requirement). *Contra*, Stevens v. Goord, 2003 WL 21396665, *4 (S.D.N.Y., June 16, 2003), *on reargument*, 2003 WL 22052978 (S.D.N.Y., Sept. 3, 2003); Morris v. Eversley, 205 F. Supp. 2d 234, 241 (S.D.N.Y. 2002); Dennison v. Prison Health Services, 2001 WL 761218, *2–3 (D.Me., July 6, 2001); Ovens v. State of Alaska, Dep't of Corrections, 2000 WL 34514101, *3 (D.Alaska, Mar. 13, 2000).

Courts have disagreed whether prisoners proceeding *in forma pauperis* who are released after filing remain obliged to pay the filing fee in installments. *See* § A, nn.72–74, below.

[15]Minix v. Pazera, 2007 WL 4233455, *2–3 (N.D.Ind., Nov. 28, 2007) (holding that filing of amended complaint after release was equivalent to filing a new complaint, and ex-prisoner need not have met the exhaustion requirement; amendment reasserted a federal claim that had been dismissed); Gibson v. Commissioner of

and reincarcerated, whether the plaintiff was incarcerated at the time the suit was filed determines whether he is a prisoner for PLRA purposes.[16] So if you expect to be released from prison early enough that you can still file as a nonprisoner within the statute of limitations *and* have time to do any discovery necessary to identify all the correct parties, you would be wise to do so—and to be sure you file promptly after release, since if you are reincarcerated before you can file, you will again be stuck with the PLRA. If you do file and then are released, you can voluntarily dismiss your action

and refile it to avoid the PLRA's requirements as long as the limitations period has not expired.[17]

Persons who join a previously filed case are prisoners if they are incarcerated as of the date they join the case, not as of the date the case was first filed.[18]

Persons who are not lawfully subject to detention are not prisoners.[19] Prospective prisoners are not prisoners; an arrestee is not a prisoner even if he is subsequently jailed.[20] Someone who has been sentenced to prison but has not yet surrendered is not "confined" in a correctional facility even though he may be within the prison system's legal custody.[21]

Several important PLRA provisions apply only to civil actions or appeals.[22] Legitimate habeas corpus and other

---

Mental Health, 2006 WL 1234971, *6 (S.D.N.Y., May 8, 2006) (rejecting as "victory of form over substance" dismissal for nonpayment of filing fee under PLRA where the prisoner had been released and his amended complaint was offered when he was no longer a prisoner), *relief from judgment denied*, 2006 WL 2192865 (S.D.N.Y., Aug. 2, 2006); Prendergast v. Janecka, 2001 WL 793251, *1 (E.D.Pa., July 10, 2001) (holding that the PLRA ceases to apply when a post-release amended complaint is filed); *see also* Segalow v. County of Bucks, 2004 WL 1427137 (E.D.Pa., June 24, 2004). *Contra*, Harris v. Garner, 216 F.3d at 973–76 (holding that filing of amended complaint does not change plaintiffs' status); Barrett v. Maricopa County Sheriff's Office, 2010 WL 46786, *4 (D.Ariz., Jan. 4, 2010) (same); Barnhardt v. Tilton, 2009 WL 3300090, *3 (E.D.Cal., Oct. 14, 2009) (same)

[16]*Compare* Lopez v. City of New York, 2009 WL 229956, *3–4 (S.D.N.Y., Jan. 30, 2009) (plaintiff jailed repeatedly need not have exhausted where she filed when out of jail); Segalow v. County of Bucks, 2004 WL 1427137, *1 (holding that a prisoner who was released, filed his complaint, was reincarcerated, was released again, and filed an amended complaint naming a new party was not a prisoner for PLRA purposes); Dolberry v. Levine, 567 F. Supp. 2d 413, 422 (W.D.N.Y. 2008) (claim filed while plaintiff was out of prison was not governed by "three strikes" provision) *with* Shembo v. Bailey, 2009 WL 129974, *2–3 (W.D.N.C., Jan. 20, 2009); Soto v. Erickson, 2007 WL 1430201, *4 & n.4 (E.D.Wis., May 11, 2007), *relief from judgment denied*, 2007 WL 2209257 (E.D.Wis., July 27, 2007); Colby v. Sarpy County, 2006 WL 519396, *1 (D. Neb., Mar. 1, 2006); Gibson v. Brooks, 335 F. Supp. 2d 325, 330–31 (D.Conn. 2004) (holding the exhaustion requirement applied to a prisoner who was released after the incident sued about, but did not file suit until he had been reincarcerated); *see* George v. Hogan, 2008 WL 906523, *6 (M.D.Pa., Mar. 31, 2008) (holding plaintiff who was an ICE detainee at the time of the relevant events but was criminally committed when he filed suit was required to exhaust). Under the latter holdings, a prisoner who was released after the claim arose and then reincarcerated before filing would be obliged to try to exhaust upon reincarceration, relying on any provision allowing late filings for good cause. Soto v. Erickson, 2007 WL 1430201, *4 & n.4; *see* Duvall v. Dallas County, Tex., 2006 WL 3487024, *4 (N.D.Tex., Dec. 1, 2006) (directing defendants to submit proof of their claim that the plaintiff was a prisoner at filing and subject to the PLRA); Lopez v. City of New York, 2009 WL 229956, *3–4 (S.D.N.Y., Jan. 30, 2009) (suggesting that prisoner who was repeatedly jailed, but never for long enough to complete the grievance process, would not be required to exhaust); Almond v. Tarver, 468 F. Supp. 2d 886, 896–97 (E.D.Tex. 2006) (holding that a prisoner who pursued the grievance process but was released before it concluded, then was reincarcerated in a different system and filed suit while there, could not practicably be required to resume the grievance process and had sufficiently exhausted).

[17]Dixon v. Page, 291 F.3d 485, 488 n.1 (7th Cir. 2002); Ahmed v. Dragovich, 297 F.3d 201, 210 (3d Cir. 2002); Ladd v. Dietz, 2007 WL 160762, *1 (D.Neb., Jan. 17, 2007). Voluntary dismissal is discussed in Ch. 10, § I, nn.364–69.

[18]Turner v. Grant County Detention Center, 2008 WL 821895, *5 (E.D.Ky., Mar. 26, 2008); *In re* Bayside Prison Litigation, 2007 WL 327519, *4 (D.N.J., Jan. 30, 2007).

In the *Bayside* case, one of the numerous plaintiffs alleging abuse by prison staff had joined the action only after he was released. Prison officials argued that his claim should be deemed to "relate back" to the filing of the original complaint under Rule 15(c), Fed.R.Civ.P., when he was still in prison, so it would be barred. The court held that that Rule did not apply, since it was intended for a completely different purpose (to mitigate the effect of statutes of limitations). The court pointed out that the plaintiff would have been free to file a separate suit after release in any case.

[19]Lee v. State Dep't of Correctional Services, 1999 WL 673339, *4 (S.D.N.Y., Aug. 30, 1999) (holding that a mentally retarded person imprisoned based on mistaken identity was not a prisoner because he had not actually been accused or convicted of any crime); Williams v. Block, 1999 WL 33542996, *6 (C.D.Cal., Aug. 11, 1999) (holding that persons held after they were entitled to be released were not prisoners); Watson v. Sheahan, 1998 WL 708803, *2 (N.D.Ill., Sept. 30, 1998) (holding that persons detained for 10 hours after they were legally entitled to be released were not prisoners during that period).

[20]Brewer v. Philson, 2007 WL 87625, *2 (W.D.Ark., Jan. 10, 2007) (holding plaintiff was not a prisoner for purposes of excessive force on arrest, though he was for purposes of excessive force in a jail holding cell); Lofton v. Cleveland City Jail Institution Guard Badge No. 3701, 2006 WL 3022989, *2 (N.D.Ohio, Oct. 23, 2006) (same). *But see* Roach v. Bandera County, 2004 WL 1304952, *5 (W.D.Tex., June 9, 2004) (holding that a person beaten in jail was not a prisoner because he had not yet been brought before a judicial officer). *Roach* relied on Circuit law holding that the line between arrest and detention or incarceration is drawn after arrest, processing, and significant periods of time in detention. The purpose of that line is to determine whether the Fourth Amendment or the Due Process Clause applies to excessive force claims, and it is doubtful whether that analysis makes sense for PLRA purposes. *Id.*

[21]Jasperson v. Federal Bureau of Prisons, 460 F. Supp. 2d 76, 87 (D.D.C. 2006).

[22]These include the provisions concerning prospective relief, 18 U.S.C. § 3626(b); the physical injury requirement, 42 U.S.C.

post-judgment proceedings generally are not considered civil actions subject to the PLRA.[23] Motions to vacate a criminal sentence under 28 U.S.C. § 2255 also generally are not considered civil actions.[24] Writs of mandamus (commanding a public official to perform his or her duty) and other extraordinary writs are considered civil actions—and are thus subject to the PLRA—when the relief sought is similar to that in a civil action but not when the writ is directed to criminal matters.[25]

Bankruptcy cases and challenges to seizures of property related to criminal proceedings have been treated as civil actions subject to the filing fees provisions.[26] Courts have disagreed over whether motions made under the caption of a criminal prosecution, addressing conditions of confinement related to the prosecution, are civil actions.[27]

---

§ 1997e(e); the filing fees provisions, 28 U.S.C. § 1915(b); the "three strikes" provision, 28 U.S.C. § 1915(g), and the provision for revocation of earned release credit. 28 U.S.C. § 1932. The requirement of exhaustion of administrative remedies, 42 U.S.C. § 1997e(a), is not limited to civil actions.

[23]See Garza v. Thaler, 585 F.3d 888, 889-90 (5th Cir. 2009) (holding PLRA filing fees provision did not apply to habeas corpus appeal and district court could not impose them as a matter of discretion); Skinner v. Wiley, 355 F.3d 1293, 1293 (11th Cir. 2004) (holding PLRA inapplicable to habeas arising from prison disciplinary proceeding); Malave v. Hedrick, 271 F.3d 1139, 1140 (8th Cir. 2001) (holding PLRA does not apply to challenge to delayed parole revocation hearing); Carmona v. U.S. Bureau of Prisons, 243 F.3d 629, 634 (2d Cir. 2001) (stating that the PLRA does not apply to 18 U.S.C. § 2241 petitions); Walker v. O'Brien, 216 F.3d 626, 633-36 (7th Cir. 2000) (holding proper habeas actions under § 2241 and § 2254 are not civil actions under the PLRA regardless of subject matter); Jennings v. Natrona County Det. Ctr. Med. Facility, 175 F.3d 775, 779 (10th Cir. 1999); Blair-Bey v. Quick, 151 F.3d 1036, 1039-41 (D.C. Cir. 1998), on reh'g, 159 F.3d 591 (D.C. Cir. 1998); Davis v. Fechtel, 150 F.3d 486, 488-90 (5th Cir. 1998); McIntosh v. U.S.Parole Comm'n, 115 F.3d 809, 811-12 (10th Cir. 1997); Carson v. Johnson, 112 F.3d 818, 821 (5th Cir. 1997); Anderson v. Singletary, 111 F.3d 801, 805 (11th Cir. 1997); Santana v. U.S., 98 F.3d 752, 757 (3d Cir. 1996). But see Kincade v. Sparkman, 117 F.3d 949, 952 (6th Cir. 1997) (prisoners may not "cloak" civil actions in habeas/post-conviction guise).

By "legitimate" habeas proceedings, we mean those that challenge your custody in some fashion. Most courts hold that you cannot challenge prison conditions via federal habeas corpus. See, e.g., Beardslee v. Woodford, 395 F.3d 1064, 1068-69 (9th Cir. 2005). The main exceptions to this rule involve confinement to segregation and disciplinary proceedings. Some courts have held that getting out of segregation, like getting out of prison entirely, may be pursued by habeas corpus. See, e.g., Medberry v. Crosby, 351 F.3d 1049, 1053 (11th Cir. 2003). Others have held that it cannot. See, e.g., Montgomery v. Anderson, 262 F.3d 641, 643-44 (7th Cir. 2001). In addition, disciplinary proceedings that result in loss of good time instead of or in addition to placement in segregation must be challenged via habeas corpus. Edwards v. Balisok, 520 U.S. 641, 117 S. Ct. 1584 (1997). See Ch. 4, § H.r(2), and Ch. 8, § H.1.a, for further discussion of these points.

[24]Kincade v. Sparkman, 117 F.3d 949, 950 (6th Cir. 1997); U.S. v. Cole, 101 F.3d 1076, 1077 (5th Cir. 1996).

[25]In re Crittenden, 143 F.3d 919, 920 (5th Cir. 1998); Santee v. Quinlan, 115 F.3d 355, 357 (5th Cir. 1997) (finding writ of mandamus filed by prisoner essentially civil, and therefore covered by PLRA); In re Smith, 114 F.3d 1247, 1250 (D.C. Cir. 1997) (holding writ of prohibition in question was within scope of PLRA because it contained "underlying claims that are civil in nature"); In re Tyler, 110 F.3d 528, 529 (8th Cir. 1997) ("[A] mandamus

petition arising from an ongoing civil rights lawsuit falls within the scope of the PLRA."); In re Washington, 122 F.3d 1345, 1345 (10th Cir. 1997) (determining that petitions for writs of mandamus are civil actions under PLRA); Green v. Nottingham, 90 F.3d 415, 418 (10th Cir. 1996) ("[W]e conclude that petitions for a writ of mandamus are included within the meaning of the term 'civil action' as used in § 1915."). Contra, Madden v. Myers, 102 F.3d 74, 76 (3d Cir. 1996) (finding "a writ of mandamus is by its very nature outside the ambit of [PLRA]"); Martin v. U.S., 96 F.3d 853, 854 (7th Cir. 1996) (holding that "a petition for mandamus in a criminal proceeding is not a form of prisoner litigation" and thus is not covered by PLRA); In re Nagy, 89 F.3d 115, 116 (2d Cir. 1996) (denying PLRA coverage "to writs directed at judges conducting criminal trials").

[26]U.S. v. Howell, 354 F.3d 693, 695-96 (7th Cir. 2004) (holding that prisoners challenging administrative forfeiture are required to abide by the limitations imposed by PLRA); U.S. v. Minor, 228 F.3d 352 (4th Cir. 2000) (holding that an equitable challenge to a completed forfeiture is a civil action); U.S. v. Jones, 215 F.3d 467, 469 (4th Cir. 2000) (holding that a motion under Federal Rule of Criminal Procedure 41(e) for the return of seized property is a civil action); Lefkowitz v. Citi-Equity Group, Inc., 146 F.3d 609, 612 (8th Cir. 1998) ("[W]e conclude that, under the plain language of [PLRA], the phrase 'civil action or appeal' is not limited to challenges to conditions of confinement, and encompasses the instant commercial litigation."); Pena v. U.S., 122 F.3d 3, 4 (5th Cir. 1997) (holding that a motion under Federal Rule of Criminal Procedure 41(e) for the return of seized property is a "civil action" subject to the PLRA filing fee requirements).

[27]In U.S. v. Lopez, 327 F. Supp. 2d 138, 140-42 (D.P.R. 2004), the court held that a motion challenging placement in administrative segregation after the government decided to seek the death penalty against the defendant was not a civil action, and granted relief. In another case raising the same issue, the court made a similar statement but ultimately disposed of the matter by holding that the motion was properly treated as a habeas corpus proceeding to which the PLRA is inapplicable. U.S. v. Catalan-Roman, 329 F. Supp. 2d 240, 250-51 (D.P.R. 2004). In U.S. v. Hashmi, 2008 WL 216936, *6-7 (S.D.N.Y., Jan. 16, 2008), the court held that a motion in a criminal case contesting "Special Administrative Measures" affecting communication between the defendant and his counsel was not an "action," a term which it defined to mean a separate proceeding, and plaintiff need not exhaust administrative remedies. Other decisions are to the contrary, holding that motions challenging SAMs or other pretrial jail restrictions must be exhausted. See U.S. v. Khan, 540 F. Supp. 2d 344, 349-52 (E.D.N.Y. 2007) (this court seems to confuse PLRA and habeas exhaustion requirements); U.S. v. Ali, 396 F. Supp. 2d 703, 705-77 (E.D.Va. 2005). An appellate decision holds that a motion in a long-completed criminal case challenging a prison policy forbidding prisoners from retaining possession of pre-sentence reports should have been treated as a separate civil action and that it required exhaustion. U.S. v. Antonelli, 371 F.3d 360, 361 (7th Cir. 2004).

Motions made in a civil action that has already been "brought" are not separate actions for purposes of the PLRA.[28]

Unfortunately, many important PLRA decisions are not reported, so we have had to include many more Westlaw citations to decisions not available in the printed case reporters than in other parts of this Manual.

A. FILING FEES

The PLRA requires indigent prisoners who are granted *in forma pauperis* (IFP) status in federal court civil actions to pay the filing fee in full, over time, as they have money in their prison accounts. Prisoners may ask why they should bother seeking IFP status if they will have to pay the filing fees anyway. If you do not proceed IFP, you will have to pay the entire fee *up front* (before you can file the case). Also, IFP litigants are eligible to have their summons and complaints served by the U.S. Marshals Service[29] and to be excused from payment of some costs (though not filing fees) on appeal.[30] Without IFP status, you will have to take care of service and pay appeal costs yourself.[31]

Prisoners seeking IFP status must submit *certified* statements[32] of their prison accounts for the preceding six months.[33] This requires prison officials' cooperation. However, your case should not be dismissed because prison officials don't submit the information promptly.[34] If they fail

or refuse to provide a certified statement, the court can order them to do so.[35] District courts have different procedures for acquiring the certified statements; in some courts prisoners must get them from prison officials, but in others the court directs officials to submit the information. Prisoners should obtain the necessary forms and instructions from the clerk of the court in which they intend to bring suit.[36]

Prisoners who are granted IFP status now must pay the *entire* fee for filing either a complaint or an appeal[37] in installments according to the following formula:

> (1) . . . The court shall assess and, when funds exist, collect, as a partial payment of any court fees required by law, an initial partial filing fee of 20 percent of the greater of—
>   (A) the average monthly deposits to the prisoner's account; or
>   (B) the average monthly balance in the prisoner's account for the 6-month period immediately preceding the filing of the complaint or notice of appeal.
> (2) After payment of the initial partial filing fee, the prisoner shall be required to make monthly payments of 20 percent of the preceding month's income credited to the prisoner's account. The agency having custody of the prisoner shall forward payments from the prisoner's account to the clerk of the court each time the amount in the account exceeds $10 until the filing fees are paid.[38]

Your case should not be dismissed if you cannot pay the initial fee. The statute says that the initial fee is to be collected "when funds exist," and it adds that prisoners shall not be prohibited from bringing suit or appealing a judgment because they cannot pay.[39] A case should not be dismissed for nonpayment without first determining if the

---

[28]*See* § D of this Chapter, n.228.

[29]28 U.S.C. § 1915(d).

[30]28 U.S.C. § 1915(c).

[31]*See* Ch. 10, § C.3, for additional information on *in forma pauperis* status; § C.4, concerning service of process; and § U, concerning appeals.

[32]28 U.S.C. § 1915(a)(2).

[33]*See* Spaight v. Makowski, 252 F.3d 78, 79 (2d Cir. 2001) (holding that the relevant time period on appeal is six months before filing the notice of appeal, not six months before moving for *in forma pauperis* status); McGore v. Wrigglesworth, 114 F.3d 601, 605 (6th Cir. 1997) (warning that failure to pay fee or to provide necessary affidavit of indigency or trust account statement may eventually result in dismissal of case).

As a practical matter, courts have sometimes accepted information supplied by prison officials that was a little out of date. *See* Jackson v. Wright, 1999 WL 160782, *1 n.2 (N.D. Ill., Mar. 10, 1999) (accepting statement ending the month before the complaint was filed in light of the small amounts involved); Lam v. Clark, 1999 WL 90635, *1 (N.D. Ill., Feb. 10, 1999) (accepting account information ending three and a half weeks before the filing of the complaint, since there is a consistent pattern for the six months covered).

[34]*See* Lawton v. Ortiz, 2006 WL 2689508, *1 (D.N.J., Sept. 19, 2006) (granting IFP status where prisoner said officials didn't respond to plaintiff's requests for an account statement and other evidence showed he was indigent); Gant v. Dane County Sheriff Office, 2000 WL 34227527, *1 (W.D. Wis., Aug. 23, 2000) (requesting that sheriff provide a copy of the procedure for obtaining an account statement and ask jail officials to provide a statement, where prisoner said his repeated efforts had been unavailing).

Delay in submitting the financial information will not cause prisoners to miss the statute of limitations as long as the complaint itself is submitted in time. *See* Garrett v. Clarke, 147 F.3d 745, 746 (8th Cir. 1998) ("For purposes of the statute of limitations, the filing of a complaint commences a federal cause of action. . . . [T]he prisoner should be allowed to file the complaint, and then supply a prison account statement within a reasonable time." (citations omitted)).

[35]*See* Stinnett v. Cook County Med. Staff, 1999 WL 169327, *1 (N.D. Ill., Mar. 19, 1999) (requiring prison officials to send a certified copy of prisoner's financial statement to the court).

[36]The addresses of the federal district courts, organized by Circuit, are provided in Appendix A.

[37]The fee for filing a federal court civil complaint is $350.00. 28 U.S.C. § 1914(a). For appeals, there is a $450.00 filing fee. *See* U.S. Courts, Federal Court Fees, *available at* http://www.uscourts.gov/fedcourtfees/courtappealsfee_January2007.pdf (last visited Feb. 16, 2007).

[38]28 U.S.C. §§ 1915(b)(1)–(2).

[39]28 U.S.C. § 1915(b)(4); *see* Taylor v. Delatoor, 281 F.3d 844, 850–51 (9th Cir. 2002) (a prisoner who cannot pay the initial fee must be allowed to proceed with his case and not merely be granted more time to pay).

prisoner has had the opportunity to pay and has taken the steps within his own control to make the payment.[40] However, if you intentionally do not pay, or if you fail to take the necessary steps to pay (*e.g.*, by spending all your money on something else), your case is likely to be dismissed.[41]

Prisoners generally may not be prohibited from bringing an action because they owe fees from a prior action.[42] However, one federal circuit has held that prisoners who seek dishonestly to evade payment of filing fees, or fail to pay fees that they incur because they are subject to the "three strikes" provision,[43] can be denied *in forma pauperis* status or barred outright from filing.[44]

If you lose a case, a federal court may decide to charge you for the costs of the lawsuit.[45] Courts are not required to make awards of costs against indigent prisoners; instead they have discretion to assess or refrain from assessing costs.[46] But if a court decides to assess costs, you cannot appeal that decision.[47] Costs are to be collected in installments the same way as filing fees.[48]

There are no exceptions to the fee requirement,[49] and the court has no authority to defer payment until after your release.[50] Once you file the suit or appeal, you are on the hook for the fee,[51] and you cannot get it back or be excused from it by voluntarily withdrawing the complaint or appeal.[52] Prison officials must keep collecting the fees if you remain within their legal custody, even if you are transferred to

---

[40]Redmond v. Gill, 352 F.3d 801, 804 (3d Cir. 2003) (holding that district court abused its discretion in dismissing a case when plaintiff failed to return an authorization form for payment of fees within 20 days; requiring that plaintiff be given more time); Wilson v. Sargent, 313 F.3d 1315, 1321 (11th Cir. 2002) ("... The [d]istrict court must take reasonable steps ... to determine whether the prisoner complied with the order by authorizing payment by prison officials." Steps may include issuing a show-cause order, allowing objections to the magistrate's report, communicating by telephone, fax, or email with officials of the custodial institution, and issuing an order to the custodial institution." (citation omitted)); Hatchett v. Nettles, 201 F.3d 651, 652 (5th Cir. 2000) ("... [I]t is an abuse of discretion for a district court to dismiss an action for failure to comply with an initial partial filing fee order without making some inquiry regarding whether the prisoner has complied with the order by submitting any required consent forms within the time allowed for compliance."); McGore v. Wrigglesworth, 114 F.3d 601, 607–08 (6th Cir. 1997) ("... [A] case may not be dismissed when the payment of an assessment has been delayed by prison officials. A prisoner cannot be penalized when prison officials fail to promptly pay an assessment."); *see* Beyer v. Cormier, 235 F.3d 1039, 1041 (7th Cir. 2000) (holding that court should have communicated with prison officials or granted an extension of payment deadline). *But see* Cosmo v. Meadors, 351 F.3d 1324, 1332 (10th Cir. 2003) (holding that a court which issued repeated orders to show cause with opportunities for plaintiff to document that he had tried to pay had done enough and no hearing was necessary before dismissal).

[41]*See* Cosmo v. Meadors, 351 F.3d at 1332 (affirming dismissal of case where plaintiff said he couldn't pay the fees but had spent his money on other items); *In re* Smith, 114 F.3d 1247, 1251 (D.C. Cir. 1997) (holding that failure to submit required documentation or make payments "may result in dismissal of a prisoner's action"); Jackson v. N.P. Dodge Realty Co., 173 F. Supp. 2d 951, 952 (D. Neb. 2001) (rejecting prisoner's claim where he was clearly able to pay).

[42]Walp v. Scott, 115 F.3d 308, 309–10 (5th Cir. 1997).

[43]28 U.S.C. § 1915(g); *see* next section for further discussion of this provision.

[44]Campbell v. Clarke, 481 F.3d 967, 969–70 (7th Cir. 2007); Sloan v. Lesza, 181 F.3d 857, 859 (7th Cir. 1999). However, another court has held that a prisoner who is subject to the "three strikes" provision of the PLRA and who has not paid filing fees owed from prior suits cannot be barred from filing under the "imminent danger of serious physical injury" exception to that provision. Miller v. Donald, 541 F.3d 1091, 1099 (11th Cir. 2008). This exception is discussed further in the next section.

[45]28 U.S.C. § 1915(f)(2). Costs are discussed further in Ch. 10, § V.

[46]Feliciano v. Selsky, 205 F.3d 568, 572 (2d Cir. 2000) (noting "the ability of a court to require, as a matter of discretion, that the indigent prisoner pay the costs, or some part of them").

[47]Whitfield v. Scully, 241 F.3d 264, 272–73 (2d Cir. 2001) ("[T]he 1996 amendments to § 1915 have undercut the ability of prisoners to appeal an award of costs on the ground of indigency.").

[48]Skinner v. Govorchin, 463 F.3d 518, 523–24 (6th Cir. 2006) (recovery of costs limited to 20% of funds a month).

[49]*See* Porter v. Dep't of the Treasury, 564 F.3d 176, 180 (3d Cir. 2009) (court had no authority to waive appellate filing fee in case governed by PLRA); Lebron v. Russo, 263 F.3d 38, 42 (2d Cir. 2001) (refusing to grant an exception to filing fee requirement even where plaintiff had to re-file due to a judicial error in the first filing).

[50]Ippolito v. Buss, 293 F. Supp. 2d 881, 883 (N.D. Ind. 2003).

[51]*See* Porter v. Dep't of the Treasury, 564 F.3d at 180 n.4 (once court grants IFP status on appeal, prisoner is obliged to pay the fee in full); McGore v. Wrigglesworth, 114 F.3d 601, 607 (6th Cir. 1997); Robbins v. Switzer, 104 F.3d 895, 897–98 (7th Cir. 1997); Leonard v. Lacy, 88 F.3d 181, 184–85 (2d Cir. 1996) ("... [W]e will apply the PLRA to impose any required obligation for filing fees (subject to installment payments) upon all prisoners who seek to appeal civil judgments without prepayment of fees. That obligation will be imposed prior to any assessment of the frivolousness of the appeal.").

[52]Goins v. Decaro, 241 F.3d 260, 261–62 (2d Cir. 2001) ("The PLRA makes no provision for return of fees partially paid or for cancellation of the remaining indebtedness in the event that an appeal is withdrawn."); McGore v. Wrigglesworth, 114 F.3d 601, 607 (6th Cir. 1997)

There are exceptions in some district courts related to the way they handle the filing of prisoner complaints. In some courts, after you submit the complaint, it is not actually filed until you complete some further paperwork, so if you change your mind and don't submit the paperwork, you may not be charged. In at least one district, the court "administratively terminates" meritless cases without filing them, and does not file the complaint or impose a filing fee unless the prisoner asks to reopen the case. *See, e.g.*, Parker v. Hess, 2008 WL 4424808, *1–2 (D.N.J., Sept. 25, 2008). These are rare exceptions. In most courts, you should assume that when you send in the complaint or notice of appeal, you owe the filing fee.

another jurisdiction.[53] They are required to give these fees priority over other deductions.[54]

Filing fee payments are to be calculated based on all money the prisoner receives (not just prison wages), and deductions may not be made for money spent on legal copies and postage.[55] The 20% monthly payment is to be computed separately for each case. Some courts have held that only one fee can be collected at a time, limiting fee collection to 20% of a prisoner's income,[56] or that only one fee and one award of costs can be collected at once, limiting payment to 40% of income.[57] Other courts have held that all fees are to be collected at the same time.[58]

In class actions, only the prisoners who signed the complaint or notice of appeal are responsible for payment of fees.[59] In cases involving multiple plaintiffs, the courts have disagreed about payment of filing fees. One federal appeals court held that "each prisoner should be proportionally liable for any fees and costs that may be assessed. Thus, any fees and costs that the district court . . . may impose shall be equally divided among all the prisoners."[60] Another appeals court has held that multiple prisoners joining similar claims not only must each pay a filing fee, but also must each file a separate complaint.[61] More recently, other federal appeals courts have agreed that each prisoner plaintiff must

---

[53]Beese v. Liebe, 153 F. Supp. 2d 967, 969–70 (E.D. Wis. 2001) (holding state officials obligated "to put into place procedures for continuing the collection of the filing fees. . . . The payments do not stop, nor are they even temporarily placed on hold, just because the Secretary has chosen to send [prisoners] out-of-state." (citation omitted)). *See generally* Hall v. Stone, 170 F.3d 706, 708 (7th Cir. 1999) ("Custodians must remit as ordered under § 1915 without regard to the prisoner's wishes.").

[54]Smith v. Huibregtse, 151 F. Supp. 2d 1040, 1043 (E.D. Wis. 2001) (finding "funds exist within the meaning of the PLRA whenever a prisoner has funds or receives income and prison officials must give payment of federal court filing fees priority").

[55]Rutledge v. Romero, 1999 WL 412778, *1–2 (N.D. Ill., June 3, 1999) (establishing that funds calculation is based on all money in account, including money from third parties and money intended for legal communication). Courts have disagreed whether money that is withheld from a prisoner's income and held until release should be counted in calculating the fees and used to pay the fees. *Compare* Cardew v. Gord, 26 Fed.Appx. 48, 50 (2d Cir. 2001) (unpublished) (noting district court decision that "lag pay" should not be used for filing fees) *with* Spence v. McCaughtrey, 46 F. Supp. 2d 861, 862–63 (E.D. Wis. 1999) (holding that prisoner's "release account" was a "prisoner's account" under the statute and should be used for filing fees purposes).

[56]Tucker v. Branker, 142 F.3d 1294, 1298 (D.C. Cir. 1998) (holding "the payment requirement of the PLRA never exacts more than 20% of an indigent prisoner's assets or income").

[57]Whitfield v. Scully, 241 F.3d 264, 276–78 (2d Cir. 2001) ("28 U.S.C. § 1915(b)(2) permits the recoupment of up to 40% of a prisoner's monthly income at any given time—20% for filing fees under § 1915(b) and an additional 20% for costs under § 1915(f)."); *see also* Lafauci v. Cunningham, 139 F. Supp. 2d 144, 147 (D. Mass. 2001) (stating that simultaneous collection of fees depriving prisoners of all resources could "raise serious constitutional concerns").

[58]Atchison v. Collins, 288 F.3d 177, 180–81 (5th Cir. 2002) (applies "per case" and not "per prisoner" analysis in determining that 1915(b)(2) requires 20% payment as to each lawsuit); Lefkowitz v. Citi-Equity Group, Inc., 146 F.3d 609, 612 (8th Cir. 1998) (holding 20% assessment rate applies in every case); Newlin v. Helman, 123 F.3d 429, 436 (7th Cir. 1997) (same), *overruled on other grounds by* Walker v. O'Brien, 216 F.3d 626 (7th Cir. 2000); *see* Miller v. Lincoln County, 171 F.3d 595, 596 (8th Cir. 1999) (declining to reduce monthly payments for prisoner with multiple cases); Henderson v. Brush, 2007 WL 5448217, *1 (W.D.Wis., May 7, 2007) (initial fee for new case takes priority over installments for

earlier fees where 100% of prisoner's regular income was being collected for them).

[59]Talley-Bey v. Knebl, 168 F.3d 884, 887 (6th Cir. 1999) ("[I]n cases involving class actions, . . . the responsibility of paying the required fees and costs rests with the prisoner or prisoners who signed the complaint. . . . [O]n appeal, the prisoner or prisoners signing the notice of appeal are obligated to pay all appellate fees and costs."); *In re* Prison Litigation Reform Act, 105 F.3d 1131, 1138 (6th Cir. 1997) (same).

[60]*In re* Prison Litigation Reform Act, 105 F.3d 1131, 1138 (6th Cir. 1997).

One lower court has taken a different approach to dividing the filing fee, holding that "the filing fee obligation is joint and several. If the parties pay the entire fee, they may divide it up between them as they see fit and it is of no concern to the court. When the parties don't pay the entire fee, all are obligated for the entire amount of the filing fee until it has been paid in full, even if the burden falls on a few of them unequally." Alcala v. Woodford, 2002 WL 1034080, *1 (N.D. Cal., May 21, 2002). Consistently with this view, another court held in a multi-plaintiff action that the lead plaintiff, who had three strikes, was liable for the $350 filing fee up front, but observed that the other plaintiffs didn't file IFP applications and presumably could pool their resources and pay the fees. Hartsfield v. Iowa Dep't of Corrections, 2007 WL 61858, *1 (N.D.Iowa, Jan. 3, 2007); see Stewart v. Missouri Dep't of Corrections, 2007 WL 2782529, *5 (W.D.Mo., Sept. 21, 2007) (assessing initial fees against each of multiple plaintiffs, noting that payment of those amounts would exceed the full amount of the filing fee, and directing payment of the full fee within 30 days).

[61]Hubbard v. Haley, 262 F.3d 1194, 1197 (11th Cir. 2001). *Hubbard* said that the clear language of the PLRA requires each prisoner to bring a separate suit. We can't find anything in the PLRA that says that. However, a number of other courts have adopted *Hubbard's* holding. *See* Banks v. Bradshaw, 2008 WL 4145218, *1 (S.D.Miss., Sept. 5, 2008); Caputo v. Belmar Municipality & County, 2008 WL 1995149, *2–3 (D.N.J., May 2, 2008); Kron v. Cook, 2008 WL 194367, *1 (S.D.Tex., Jan. 23, 2008); Worthen v. Oklahoma Dep't of Corrections, 2007 WL 4563665, *3 (W.D.Okla., Dec. 7, 2007) (citing individualized issues concerning administrative exhaustion), *report and recommendation adopted in part*, 2007 WL 4563644 (W.D.Okla., Dec. 20, 2007); Lilly v. Ozmint, 2007 WL 2022190, *1 (D.S.C., July 11, 2007); Osterloth v. Hopwood, 2006 WL 3337505, *2–5 (D.Mont., Nov. 15, 2006); Ray v. Evercom Systems, Inc., 2006 WL 2475264, *5–6 (D.S.C., Aug. 25, 2006) (extending holding to a fee-paid case); Amir Sharif v. Dallas County, 2006 WL 2860552, *3–4 (N.D.Tex. Oct. 5, 2006); Swenson v. MacDonald, 2006 WL 240233, *3–4 (D.Mont. Jan. 30, 2006).

separately pay the full filing fee, but need not file a separate complaint.[62]

These latter two holdings appear contrary to the recent Supreme Court decision in *Jones v. Bock*,[63] which held that courts should not interpret the PLRA to depart from the usual procedural practices, except to the extent that the PLRA actually says to do so.[64] The usual procedural practice is to allow plaintiffs to file joint complaints under Rule 20 of the Federal Rules of Civil Procedure, and to our knowledge, only one filing fee is usually required when multiple plaintiffs join in the same complaint.[65]

The joinder rules also permit plaintiffs to sue multiple defendants and bring multiple claims in the same lawsuit, but only as long as the injuries all arise out of the same "transaction, occurrence, or series of transactions or occurrences" and when there is "any question of law or fact common to all plaintiffs."[66] Those rules have not always been enforced in the past. Because of the PLRA filing fee requirement, some courts are now scrupulously enforcing the joinder rules against prisoners so they can't pay a single filing fee to litigate claims that, strictly speaking, call for separate complaints and fees.[67]

Constitutional challenges to the filing fees provisions have been unsuccessful. The provisions have been held not to violate the right of access to courts, the First Amendment, the Equal Protection Clause, the Due Process Clause, and other constitutional provisions.[68] In upholding the statute, courts have emphasized the fact that it does not actually bar anyone from bringing suit.[69]

The filing fees provisions of the PLRA are written to govern proceedings in federal court, and presumably have no application in state court.[70] However, many states have statutes governing prisoner filing fees, and you must abide by those if you file suit in state court.

The filing fees provisions (like most other PLRA provisions) apply only to cases brought by persons who are prisoners at the time of filing.[71] Although a person who has been released is no longer a prisoner, courts have disagreed about the obligations of persons released *after* filing a complaint or notice. Some courts say the obligation to pay ends on the prisoner's release.[72] Others say a released prisoner must pay any fees that were due before release.[73] One court has said that a released prisoner must continue to pay until the full filing fee is paid, but does not explain how payments are to

---

[62]Hagan v. Rogers, 570 F.3d 146, 154–56 (3d Cir. 2009); Boriboune v. Berge, 391 F.3d 852, 854–56 (7th Cir. 2004); *see* Suarez v. A1, 2006 WL 3694598, *4 (D.N.J., Dec. 13, 2006) (acknowledging the difficulties of joint litigation, but holding that different plaintiffs who sought the same remedy could proceed jointly though they each had to pay a filing fee).

[63]Jones v. Bock, 549 U.S. 199, 127 S. Ct. 910 (2007).

[64]Jones v. Bock, 549 U.S. at 212–13. *Jones* addressed the PLRA's exhaustion requirement, but its holding seems equally applicable to other PLRA provisions. *See* Miller v. Donald, 541 F.3d 1091, 1099 (11th Cir. 2008) (same holding as to PLRA "three strikes" provision).

[65]The relevant statute says: "The clerk of each district court shall require the *parties* instituting any civil action, suit or proceeding in such court, whether by original process, removal or otherwise, to pay *a* filing fee of $350. . . ." 28 U.S.C. § 1914(a) (emphasis supplied). That language certainly suggests that a single filing fee is required even if there are multiple plaintiffs. The statute continues: "The clerk shall collect from the parties such additional fees only as are prescribed by the Judicial Conference of the United States." 28 U.S.C. § 1914(b). That language, in addition to *Jones v. Bock*, seems to forbid courts to require multiple fees based on their interpretation of the PLRA.

[66]Rule 20(a), Fed.R.Civ.P. (joinder of defendants). With respect to a single defendant, a plaintiff may join "as many claims as it has against an opposing party." Rule 18(a), Fed.R.Civ.P. (joinder of claims).

[67]*See* George v. Smith, 507 F.3d 605, 607–08 (7th Cir. 2007); Valdez v. Dretke, 2007 WL 2177007, *8–9 (S.D.Tex., July 26, 2007); Vasquez v. Schueler, 2007 WL 5431016, *2 (W.D.Wis., Nov. 29, 2007); *see also* Pope v. Miller, 2007 WL 2427978, *4–5 (W.D.Okla., Aug. 21, 2007) (holding claims of two plaintiffs were misjoined under Federal Rules where they involved distinct factual issues as to exhaustion and merits). This issue is discussed in more detail in Ch. 10, § B.2.

[68]Murray v. Dosal, 150 F.3d 814, 818 (8th Cir. 1998) (holding filing fee provision withstands constitutional challenges); Lefkowitz v. Citi-Equity Group, Inc., 146 F.3d 609, 612 (8th Cir. 1998) (rejecting equal protection claim and holding filing fee provision does not unconstitutionally impede access to courts); Tucker v. Branker, 142 F.3d 1294, 1301 (D.C. Cir. 1998) (same); Lucien v. DeTella, 141 F.3d 773, 775–76 (7th Cir. 1998) (finding statute does not violate prisoners' due process rights); Shabazz v. Parsons, 127 F.3d 1246, 1248 (10th Cir. 1997) (holding the provisions "pass constitutional muster"); Norton v. Dimazana, 122 F.3d 286, 291 (5th Cir. 1997) (finding provisions do not violate prisoners' right to access courts); Mitchell v. Farcass, 112 F.3d 1483, 1490 (11th Cir. 1997) (finding no equal protection violation); Nicholas v. Tucker, 114 F.3d 17, 21 (2d Cir. 1997) (holding the provisions constitutional both on their face and as applied to prisoner); Hampton v. Hobbs, 106 F.3d 1281, 1288 (6th Cir. 1997) ("[W]e find that the fee provisions of the PLRA violate neither a prisoner's constitutional right of access to the courts, nor his rights under the First Amendment, the Due Process Clause, the Equal Protection Clause, or the Double Jeopardy Clause of the United States Constitution."); Roller v. Gunn, 107 F.3d 227 (4th Cir. 1997). *But see* Murray v. Dosal, 150 F.3d 814, 820–21 (Heaney, J., dissenting) (arguing that filing fee provisions are unconstitutional).

[69]*See, e.g.,* Nicholas v. Tucker, 114 F.3d at 21 (citing 28 U.S.C. § 1915(b)(4)).

[70]*See* Gomez v. Evangelista, 185 Misc.2d 816, 714 N.Y.S.2d 636, 638–39 (N.Y.Sup. 2000) (holding federal PLRA inapplicable to state court proceedings), *rev'd on other grounds*, 290 A.D.2d 351, 736 N.Y.S.2d 365 (App.Div. 2002).

[71]*See* n.12 of this chapter.

[72]*See, e.g.,* DeBlasio v. Gilmore, 315 F.3d 396, 398–99 (4th Cir. 2003) and cases cited (holding released prisoner need not pay fees due before release because "[a] released prisoner should not have to shoulder a more difficult financial burden than the average indigent plaintiff in order to continue his lawsuit"); McGann v. Comm'r, Soc. Sec. Admin., 96 F.3d 28, 29–30 (2d Cir.1996).

[73]*See, e.g.,* In re Smith, 114 F.3d 1247, 1251–52 (D.C. Cir. 1997); Robbins v. Switzer, 104 F.3d 895, 898–99 (7th Cir. 1997).

be assessed against a released prisoner who cannot pay the entire balance at once but no longer has a prison account.[74]

B. THE "THREE STRIKES" PROVISION

Filing fees are also addressed by the "three strikes" provision, one of the most damaging parts of the PLRA, which provides:

> In no event shall a prisoner bring a civil action or appeal a judgment in a civil action or proceeding under this section [*i.e.*, proceed *in forma pauperis*] if the prisoner has, on 3 or more prior occasions, while incarcerated or detained in any facility, brought an action or appeal in a court of the United States that was dismissed on the grounds that it is frivolous, malicious, or fails to state a claim upon which relief may be granted, unless the prisoner is under imminent danger of serious physical injury.[75]

This provision means that if you have had three complaints or appeals dismissed as frivolous, malicious, or failing to state a claim, you cannot proceed *in forma pauperis* unless you can show you are in imminent danger of serious injury.[76] Thus, you have to pay the entire filing fee *up front*, or your case will be dismissed,[77] and you will still have to pay the fee in installments even though you won't get anything for it.[78] If you haven't paid the fee, and the court rules that

you are subject to the three strikes provision, most courts say you should have an opportunity to pay in order to avoid dismissal.[79] One court, however, has said that a prisoner, who sought IFP status, even though he had already been found to have three strikes, had committed "a fraud on the federal judiciary," and it dismissed his appeal.[80] That court has also held that a litigant with three strikes can be barred from filing any further papers in court until all previously incurred fees have been paid.[81] However, that rule cannot be extended to bar *in forma pauperis* filings by prisoners whose cases satisfy the "imminent danger of serious physical injury" exception to § 1915(g).[82]

Some courts have held that the three strikes provision bars courts from appointing counsel for prisoners with three strikes.[83] We think that is wrong, for reasons we explain elsewhere.[84]

The three strikes provision makes it that much more important to be sure that any complaint you file is based on facts, asserted in the complaint, that amount to a violation of law. If you file lawsuits based just on your general feeling that someone has mistreated you, you will probably be assessed strikes and may not be able to proceed *in forma pauperis* in the future when you need to.

The three strikes provision, like the filing fees provisions, applies to "prisoners"—*i.e.*, people who are incarcerated when they file suit.[85] It applies to civil actions or appeals, categories that generally do not include habeas corpus or other challenges to criminal convictions or sentences.[86] Most courts have held that the three strikes provision does not apply retroactively to prohibit or revoke *in forma pauperis*

---

[74]*See* Gay v. Tex. Dep't of Corr. State Jail Div., 117 F.3d 240, 242 (5th Cir. 1997).

[75]28 U.S.C. § 1915(g). As with the filing fees provisions discussed in the previous section, this provision does not apply to a person who is not a prisoner when he or she files suit. *See* Kolocotronis v. Morgan, 247 F.3d 726, 728 (8th Cir. 2001) (holding provision does not apply to person committed after finding of not guilty by reason of insanity).

[76]One court has held that a prisoner with three strikes is barred from intervening in an already filed civil action. Holloway v. Magness, 2008 WL 2367235, *9 (E.D.Ark., June 6, 2008). We don't think the statute supports the court's interpretation of it. The court does not explain how it gets from the the statutory language, "bring a civil action or appeal a judgment in a civil action or proceeding," to intervention, which is neither bringing a civil action nor appealing a judgment.

[77]*See* Jones v. Federal Bureau of Prisons, 2008 WL 2512919, *1–2 (E.D.Tex., June 19, 2008) (rejecting request for a "payment plan," since that would amount to proceeding *in forma pauperis*). One decision does state that district courts have the discretion to allow a litigant with three strikes to pay fees over time. Dudley v. U.S., 61 Fed.Cl. 685, 688 (Fed.Cl. 2004). In addition, a timely notice of appeal confers appellate jurisdiction even if the filing fee is not tendered timely. Daly v. U.S., 2004 WL 1701062, *2 (10th Cir., July 30, 2004) (unpublished) and cases cited. That may mean that if you don't have the filing fee within the 30 days during which a notice of appeal must be filed, you will have some additional time to pay the filing fee after you file the notice of appeal. This question has not to our knowledge been explored.

[78]Schultz v. Wallace, 2006 WL 6000792, *2 (W.D.Wis., Feb. 28, 2006).

[79]*See* Smith v. District of Columbia, 182 F.3d 25, 29–30 (D.C. Cir. 1999) (person barred from filing as a poor person has 14 days to pay filing fee so that his suit may proceed); Greene v. C.D.C. 2006 WL 2385150, *1 n.1 (E.D.Cal., Aug. 17, 2006) (noting that the statute says only that prisoners can't proceed "under this section"— *i.e.*, 28 U.S.C. § 1915, the *in forma pauperis* statute—if they have three strikes, while other provisions of § 1915 explicitly provide for dismissal). *Contra*, Dupree v. Palmer, 284 F.3d 1234, 1236 (11th Cir. 2002) (holding suit must be dismissed without prejudice and refiled, since statute says fee is to be paid at the initiation of suit).

[80]Sloan v. Lesza, 181 F.3d 857, 859 (7th Cir. 1999) ("Litigants to whom [the three strikes provision] applies take heed! An effort to bamboozle the court by seeking permission to proceed *in forma pauperis* after a federal judge has held that § 1915(g) applies to a particular litigant will lead to immediate termination of the suit. Moreover, the fee remains due. . . .").

[81]Sloan v. Lesza, 181 F.3d 857, 859 (7th Cir. 1999).

[82]Miller v. Donald, 541 F.3d 1091, 1099 (11th Cir. 2008). That exception is discussed in § B.2, below.

[83]Hairston v. Blackburn, 2010 WL 145793, *10 (S.D.Ill., Jan. 12, 2010); Ammons v. Gerlinger, 2007 WL 5595899, *1 (W.D.Wis., May 1, 2007).

[84]*See* Ch. 10, § C.5, n.233.

[85]*See* nn.3–21 of this chapter concerning who is a "prisoner" for PLRA purposes.

[86]*See* nn.23–27 of this chapter concerning the meaning of "civil action."

status for complaints filed (or appeals begun) before the provision went into effect.[87]

You cannot dispute the correctness of prior dismissals that are counted as strikes under § 1915(g).[88] However, you should be able to dispute whether a dismissal is properly classified as a strike. This is important because in the past, some courts held that dismissal for failure to exhaust remedies is a strike, but many of those decisions are now invalid under a later Supreme Court decision.[89] You can argue that a prior dismissal was not really a strike when you file a new case and the court considers how many strikes you have. If the court declared your earlier case a strike at the time of dismissal, and that classification is now invalid, you may also be able to get relief under Rule 60(b) of the Federal Rules of Civil Procedure.[90]

Federal courts have not resolved whether the three strikes provision applies when a prisoner with three strikes files a case in *state* court and the *defendants* then remove the case to federal court.[91] The statute says: "In no event shall a prisoner bring a civil action or appeal a judgment in a civil action or proceeding *under this section*" (*i.e.*, under the federal *in forma pauperis* statute) if the prisoner has three strikes.[92] Since a case filed in state court is not "brought" under the federal *in forma pauperis* provisions, but under the rules of the state court, the three strikes provision should have no application in state court.[93] A prisoner with three

strikes who can't pay the federal filing fee may prefer to file in state court if the state law *in forma pauperis* provisions permit. If the defendants then remove it, they are responsible for paying the federal filing fee.[94] One federal appeals court has explicitly held that prisoners can "seek relief in state court, where limitations on filing I.F.P. may not be as strict," as one of the grounds for upholding the constitutionality of § 1915(g).[95] However, other courts have suggested that it is inappropriate, or even sanctionable, for prisoners to do this, since they would be evading various PLRA provisions.[96] This view seems wrong to us. If Congress had wished to forbid state court filings by prisoners with three strikes, it could have said so (though there would be questions about its power to do so). If it did not wish for such cases to be removed to federal court, it could have said that too. Prisoner plaintiffs should hardly be penalized for the actions of defendants in removing cases, or for reading statutes the way they are written, especially in view of the Supreme Court's warning that courts should not expand the PLRA's requirements according to their own policy views.[97]

1. What Is a Strike?

The PLRA is very specific about what dismissals count as strikes: dismissals for frivolousness, maliciousness, or failure to state a claim. Failure to state a claim means that even if all the facts in your complaint are true, they could not possibly establish a violation of law that the court could remedy.[98] A legally frivolous suit is one that fails to raise an "arguable question of law"[99] or is based on an "indisputably meritless legal theory,"[100] or one in which the complaint itself makes clear that the case is barred by a defense such as the

[87]Gibbs v. Ryan, 160 F.3d 160, 162–64 (3d Cir. 1998); Chandler v. D.C. Dep't of Corr., 145 F.3d 1355, 1358 (D.C. Cir. 1998); Canell v. Lightner, 143 F.3d 1210, 1212–13 (9th Cir. 1998). *Contra*, Adepegba v. Hammons, 103 F.3d 383, 385–87 (5th Cir. 1996).

[88]*See, e.g.*, Brown v. Gallegos, 2008 WL 782533, *1 (N.D.Cal., Mar. 24, 2008).

[89]*See* Feathers v. McFaul, 274 Fed.Appx. 467, 469 (6th Cir. 2008) (unpublished) (holding two prior dismissals were for failure to plead exhaustion and were not strikes). This issue is discussed in the next subsection at nn.111–118, below.

[90]In *Dalvin v. Beshears*, 943 F. Supp. 578, 579 (D.Md. 1996), the court granted relief under Fed.R.Civ.P. 60(b)(6), which refers to "any other reason that justifies relief" from a prior judgment," on the ground that under the unique circumstances of that case it was excessively harsh to charge the plaintiff a strike. If you are basing your request on a change in the law governing strikes, Rule 60(b)(5), which authorizes relief when "applying [the judgment] prospectively is no longer equitable," may be more appropriate.

[91]A defendant may remove a state court case to federal court if it is a case that could have been filed in federal court initially, 28 U.S.C. § 1441, or if it is against federal officers or agencies. 28 U.S.C. § 1442.

[92]28 U.S.C. § 1915(g).

[93]*See* Lakes v. State, 333 S.C. 382, 387, 510 S.E.2d 228 (S.C.Ct. App. 1998) (holding prisoner could proceed IFP, since South Carolina has no analogy to PLRA's three strikes provision).

A case filed in state court, removed to federal court, and then dismissed as frivolous, malicious, or not stating a claim should also not be a strike for purposes of future proceedings in federal court, in our view, since a strike, too, is defined as an action "brought . . . in a court of the United States" by the prisoner. However, case law does not support our view. *See* nn.127–128, below.

[94]28 U.S.C. § 1914(a) ("The clerk of each district court shall require the parties instituting any civil action, suit or proceeding in such court, whether by original process, removal or otherwise, to pay a filing fee of $350. . . ."); *see* Hairston v. Blackburn, 2010 WL 145793, *1 (S.D.Ill., Jan. 12, 2010).

[95]Abdul-Akbar v. McKelvie, 239 F.3d 307, 314–15 (3d Cir. 2001).

[96]Crooker v. Burns, 544 F. Supp. 2d 59, 62 (D.Mass. 2008) (citing prior unpublished opinion).

Another court has balanced the concern about evading the PLRA and the concern about preserving access to the courts expressed in *Abdul-Akbar v. McKelvie* by remanding the removed case from federal court back to state court. Bartelli v. Beard, 2008 WL 4363645, *1–2 (M.D.Pa., Sept. 24, 2008). The problem with this solution is that it deprives defendants of their statutory right to remove certain cases to federal court.

[97]Jones v. Bock, 549 U.S. 199, 212–13, 221–24, 127 S. Ct. 910 (2007); *see* Miller v. Donald, 541 F.3d 1091, 1099 (11th Cir. 2008) (applying *Jones* prohibition on judicial supplementation of PLRA to three strikes provision).

[98]Jones v. Bock, 549 U.S. at 213–17; *see* Ch. 10, § B.1 for further discussion.

[99]Neitzke v. Williams, 490 U.S. 319, 328, 109 S. Ct. 1827 (1989).

[100]Neitzke v. Williams, 490 U.S. at 327.

statute of limitations.[101] A factually frivolous suit is one that alleges "fantastic or delusional scenarios."[102] A malicious suit is one that is filed for an improper purpose or amounts to an abuse of the legal system.[103]

A case dismissed for any reason other than frivolousness, maliciousness, or failure to state a claim is *not* a strike.[104] Dismissal for suing an immune defendant is not a strike, since that reason does not appear in § 1915(g), even though it appears in other PLRA sections pertaining to *in forma pauperis* proceedings.[105] Dismissals are not strikes if they are on grounds such as lack of prosecution,[106] lack of jurisdiction,[107] or expiration of the statute of limitations.[108]

———————

[101]*Neitzke*, 490 U.S. at 327–28; Street v. Vose, 936 F.2d 38, 39 (1st Cir. 1991) (upholding dismissal of claim as frivolous where statute of limitations had expired).

[102]Neitzke v. Williams, 490 U.S. at 328. The meaning of frivolous is discussed further in Ch. 10, § C.3.b.

[103]*See* Ch. 10, § C.3.b, n.135.

[104]*See* Tafari v. Hues, 473 F.3d 440, 443 (2d Cir. 2007) (refusing to treat an appeal dismissed as premature as a strike, stating the PLRA "was designed to stem the tide of egregiously meritless lawsuits, not those temporarily infected with remediable procedural or jurisdictional flaws"); Andrews v. King, 398 F.3d 1113, 1120 (9th Cir. 2005); Fortson v. Kern, 2005 WL 3465843, *2 (E.D. Mich., Dec. 19, 2005) (holding dismissal for failure to pay initial filing fee is not a strike); Maree-Bey v. Williams, 2005 WL 3276276, *2 (D.D.C. Aug. 1, 2005) (holding dismissal under Rule 8 of the Federal Rules of Civil Procedure is not a strike).

One federal court has recently held that courts have discretion to deny *in forma pauperis* status to a prisoner if there is a "pattern of abusing the IFP privilege in his litigation history," even if that history does not satisfy the three strikes provision, Mitchell v. Federal Bureau of Prisons, 587 F.3d 415, 420 (D.C. Cir. 2009).

[105]Muqit v. Kitchens, 2009 WL 87429, *1 n.1 (D.S.C., Jan. 13, 2009); Searcy v. Federal Bureau of Prisons, 2007 WL 4322152, *5 (D.S.C., Dec. 6, 2007).

[106]Butler v. Department of Justice, 492 F.3d 440, 443–45 (D.C. Cir. 2007); Harden v. Harden, 2007 WL 2257327, *1 (D.Neb., Aug. 3, 2007); Green v. Dewitt, 2006 WL 1074983, *1 (D.S.C., Apr. 20, 2006). A recent decision holding that "[a] history of failure to prosecute is akin to the filing of a frivolous claim" and is a strike, Gill v. Pidlypchak, 2006 WL 3751340, *4 n.7 (N.D.N.Y., Dec. 19, 2006), appears to be wrong, since the statute does not refer to claims that are "akin" to frivolous claims.

[107]Thompson v. Drug Enforcement Admin., 492 F.3d 428, 437 (D.C. Cir. 2007); Daniels v. Woodford, 2008 WL 2079010, *6, 8 (C.D.Cal., May 13, 2008); Ray v. Seventh Ave. Co., 2007 WL 5303981, *1 (W.D.Wis., July 11, 2007); Fitts v. Burt, 2008 WL 842705, *5 (E.D.Mich., Jan. 24, 2008), *report and recommendation adopted*, 2008 WL 878522 (E.D.Mich., Mar. 28, 2008), *reconsideration denied*, 2008 WL 2357739 (E.D.Mich., June 10, 2008); Harden v. Harden, 2007 WL 2257327, *1 (D.Neb., Aug. 3, 2007).

[108]Myles v. U.S., 416 F.3d 551, 553 (7th Cir. 2005) (noting that dismissal based on limitations is not a strike since it is based on an affirmative defense); Daniels v. Woodford, 2008 WL 2079010, *6, 8 (C.D.Cal., May 13, 2008).

A grant of summary judgment—which is based on the absence of material issues of fact—on part or all of a case is generally not a strike.[109] Defendants sometimes make motions that raise factual issues properly raised by summary judgment, but call them motions to dismiss. The court should either exclude all factual materials submitted with such a motion, or should convert the motion to one for summary judgment. You should be sure to flag this issue for the court so if it decides the motion against you, the decision will be a grant of summary judgment and not a dismissal for failure to state a claim, since the latter will count as a strike.[110]

Failure to exhaust administrative remedies is not a failure to state a claim unless non-exhaustion is apparent on the face of the complaint.[111] That means dismissal for non-exhaustion should generally not be a strike.[112] Before *Jones v. Bock*, one federal circuit held that "[a] claim that fails to allege the requisite exhaustion of remedies is tantamount to one that fails to state a claim upon which relief may be granted" and therefore was a strike.[113] That is wrong under *Jones*, since that case holds that plaintiffs need not allege exhaustion,[114] and we think it is also wrong because the three strikes provision doesn't authorize charging a strike for anything "tantamount to" failing to state a claim.[115] Other courts,

———————

[109]*See* Stallings v. Kempker, 109 Fed.Appx. 832 (8th Cir. 2004) (unpublished); Page v. Reynolds, 2008 WL 4427324, *1 n.* (D.S.C., Sept. 29, 2008) (citing Pressley v. Rutledge, 82 Fed.Appx. 857, 858 (4th Cir. 2003) (unpublished)); Daniels v. Woodford, 2008 WL 2079010, *6 (C.D.Cal., May 13, 2008); Chavis v. Curlee, 2008 WL 508694, *4 (N.D.N.Y., Feb. 21, 2008); Ramsey v. Goord, 2007 WL 1199573, *2 (W.D.N.Y., Apr. 19, 2007); Chappell v. Pliler, 2006 WL 3780914, *3 (E.D.Cal., Dec. 21, 2006) ("The granting of summary judgment on some claims precludes a determination that the case was dismissed for failure to state a claim on which relief could be granted."); Johnson v. Sheahan, 2005 WL 2739183, *4 (N.D.Ill. Oct. 24, 2005); Walker v. Kidney Doctor, 1997 WL 698190, *2 (S.D.N.Y., Nov. 7, 1997) (noting earlier grant of summary judgment against plaintiff did not count as a strike). *But see* Davis v. Kakani, 2007 WL 2221402, *2 (E.D.Mich., July 31, 2007) (holding summary judgment can be a strike if the decision says no claim was stated).

[110]Summary judgment, including conversion of motions to dismiss, is discussed in Ch. 10, § L.

[111]Jones v. Bock, 549 U.S. 199, 214–15, 127 S. Ct. 910 (2007).

[112]Before *Jones v. Bock*, a number of courts had already so held. *See* Snider v. Melindez, 199 F.3d 108, 111 (2d Cir. 1999) (holding non-exhaustion is not failure to state a claim and is not a strike); Green v. Young, 454 F.3d 405, 408–09 (4th Cir. 2006) (same); Smith v. Duke, 296 F. Supp. 2d 965, 965–66 (E.D.Ark. 2003); Henry v. Med. Dep't at SCI-Dallas, 153 F. Supp. 2d 553, 556 (M.D.Pa. 2001).

[113]Rivera v. Allin, 144 F.3d 719, 731 (11th Cir. 1998).

[114]Hernandez v. Florida Dep't of Corrections, 281 Fed.Appx. 862, 867 (11th Cir. 2008) (unpublished) (acknowledging *Rivera v. Allin* is overruled by *Jones v. Bock*); Adamson v. De Poorter, 2008 WL 4382815, *4 (N.D.Fla., Sept. 25, 2008) (same).

[115]This kind of expansion of PLRA provisions beyond the language of the statute was condemned by the Supreme Court in *Jones v. Bock*, 549 U.S. 199, 212–13, 221–24, 127 S. Ct. 910 (2007),

chiefly within the Fifth Circuit, have held that a case dismissed for non-exhaustion is a strike because it seeks "relief to which [the plaintiff] is not entitled" and is therefore frivolous.[116] We think that is wrong too, since an unexhausted case does not necessarily fail to raise "an arguable question of law" or rest on an "indisputably meritless legal theory," which as discussed above is what "frivolous" means.[117] Certainly, if there was an argument that what you did should have satisfied the exhaustion requirement, or that no administrative remedy was really available to you, your case should not be viewed as frivolous and treated as a strike even if the court ultimately ruled that you had failed to exhaust.[118]

Most courts have held that a partial dismissal—i.e., an order that throws out some claims or some defendants, but lets the rest of the case go forward—is not a strike,[119] nor is a case where some claims are dismissed on grounds specified in § 1915(g), but other claims are dismissed on other grounds.[120] However, there are some recent decisions to the contrary. The federal appeals court for the Seventh Circuit has held that if *any* claim is dismissed as on the § 1915(g)

grounds, the prisoner is charged a strike.[121] We see no basis for this holding, since Congress's purpose was to cut down on "egregiously meritless lawsuits,"[122] and the Seventh Circuit rule would penalize prisoners who file meritorious cases but make even a single mistake such as suing a wrong parties or citing a wrong legal theory. Another circuit has held that if part of the case is dismissed on "three strikes" grounds but the rest of it is dismissed for failure to exhaust, the prisoner is charged a strike.[123]

A case that is voluntarily withdrawn is not a strike.[124] An action that was never accepted for filing cannot be a strike.[125] Only *federal* court dismissals count as strikes, since a state court is not a "court of the United States" under the statute.[126] Some courts have charged the plaintiff a strike in a case filed in state court and removed to federal court by the defendants.[127] This appears to be wrong, since § 1915(g) applies to those who on three occasions "brought an action or appeal in a court of the United States" that was dismissed as frivolous, malicious, or failing to state a claim. A prisoner who files in state court does not "bring" the action "in a court of the United States."[128]

with respect to the exhaustion requirement, and has been applied to the three strikes provision as well. *See* Miller v. Donald, 541 F.3d 1091, 1099 (11th Cir. 2008). Further, as one court observed about the three strikes provision: "A provision barring access to the courts such as section 1915(g) must be construed narrowly."

[116]*See, e.g.*, Wallmark v. Johnson, 2003 WL 21488141, *1 (N.D. Tex., Apr. 28, 2003).

[117]One court interpreting the three strikes provision has said that the PLRA "was designed to stem the tide of egregiously meritless lawsuits, not those temporarily infected with remediable procedural or jurisdictional flaws" such as failure to exhaust. Tafari v. Hues, 473 F.3d 440, 443 (2d Cir. 2007).

[118]One recent decision held that an unexhausted claim may be found frivolous and charged as a strike if brought "with full knowledge that it is subject to dismissal for failure to exhaust," but that a case involving even a "debatable" argument that it was exhausted should not be treated as a strike. Adamson v. De Poorter, 2008 WL 4382815, *4 (N.D.Fla., Sept. 25, 2008).

[119]Thompson v. Drug Enforcement Admin., 492 F.3d 428, 432 (D.C. Cir. 2007) (statute does not apply to actions "containing at least one claim falling within none of the three strike categories"); Tafari v. Hues, 539 F. Supp. 2d 694, 701–02 (S.D.N.Y. 2008) (extensive discussion and review of case law); Maree-Bey v. Williams, 2006 WL 463259, *1 (D.D.C., Feb. 24, 2006) ("Under the plain language of the statute, the dismissal of a claim in a pending action cannot possibly trigger the so-called three-strikes bar."); Barela v. Variz, 36 F. Supp. 2d 1254, 1259 (S.D.Cal. 1999) ("Since the Court in that case reached Plaintiff's claims on the merits as to some of the defendants, this Court finds it unfair to penalize Plaintiff for including a defendant against whom he could not state a cause of action.").

[120]*See* Fortson v. Kern, 2005 WL 3465843, *2 (E.D.Mich., Dec. 19, 2005) (holding that case deemed frivolous as to one defendant and otherwise dismissed for failure to pay the filing fee was not a strike); Barela v. Variz, 36 F. Supp. 2d 1254, 1259 (S.D.Cal. 1999) (holding a case was not a strike where some claims were dismissed for failure to state a claim and defendants were granted summary judgment in others).

[121]George v. Smith, 507 F.3d 605, 607–08 (7th Cir. 2007). That court has also held that in cases involving multiple plaintiffs, *every* plaintiff is charged a strike if a claim involving *any one* of the plaintiffs is a strike. Boriboune v. Berge, 391 F.3d 852, 855–56 (7th Cir. 2004). The court did not cite any authority for this holding and did not engage in any substantial statutory analysis, and we think it is wrong. However, unless the Supreme Court rules otherwise, you are stuck with these rules if you are litigating in the Seventh Circuit.

[122]Tafari v. Hues, 473 F.3d 440, 443 (2d Cir. 2007).

[123]Pointer v. Wilkinson, 502 F.3d 369, 376 (6th Cir. 2007).

[124]Armentrout v. Tyra, 175 F.3d 1023, 1999 WL 86355, *1 (8th Cir., Feb. 9, 1999) (unpublished); Daniels v. Woodford, 2008 WL 2079010, *5 (C.D.Cal., May 13, 2008); Voyles v. State of Alaska, 2005 WL 1172430, *3 n.39 (D.Alaska, May 11, 2005). Decisions in one court have held that a prisoner who receives a magistrate judge's recommendation for dismissal cannot avoid a strike by dismissing voluntarily afterward. *See* Johnson v. Edlow, 37 F. Supp. 2d 775, 776–78 (E.D.Va. 1999) (citing prior pattern of seeking voluntary dismissal after court and defendants have expended substantial resources on the case; dismissing as malicious); Sumner v. Tucker, 9 F. Supp. 2d 641, 644 (E.D.Va. 1998). *Contra*, Williams v. Grannis, 2008 WL 4078664, *3–4 (E.D.Cal., Aug 29, 2008) (voluntary dismissal following dismissal without prejudice for failure to state a claim, with leave to file an amended complaint, is not a strike).

[125]Wilson v. Yaklich, 148 F.3d 596, 603 (6th Cir. 1998).

[126]Elliott v. Beard, 2006 WL 4404771, *3 (W.D.Pa., Sept. 27, 2006); Miller v. John Doe, 2005 WL 1308408, *1 (E.D.Wis. May 31, 2005); Freeman v. Lee, 30 F. Supp. 2d 52, 54 (D.D.C. 1998).

[127]*See* Olmsted v. Frank, 2008 WL 4104009, *1, 6 (W.D.Wis., Sept. 3, 2008); Olmsted v. Sherman, 2008 WL 3455300, *1 (W.D.Wis., Aug. 12, 2008); Farnsworth v. Washington State Department of Corrections, 2007 WL 1101497, *1–2 (W.D.Wash., Apr. 9, 2007).

[128]There is a similar question whether a case brought in state court by a plaintiff with three strikes, then removed to federal

Denial of a motion filed in an already filed case is not a strike.[129]

One recent decision holds that dismissal without prejudice for failure to state a claim is not a strike, since such dismissals include perfectly meritorious cases that were inadequately pled, though dismissal as frivolous is always a strike.[130]

A dismissal cannot be a strike if it is impossible to tell what the cause for dismissal was.[131] Some decisions have held that prisoners should not be given a strike based on law that was unclear or that changed after they filed.[132] Dismissals may be strikes even if they were not *in forma pauperis* cases.[133] Cases filed or dismissed before the PLRA was enacted are counted as strikes.[134]

A dismissal in a habeas corpus action is not a strike.[135] Courts have disagreed over whether actions dismissed because they were mistakenly filed under 42 U.S.C. § 1983, but should have been filed as habeas petitions, count as strikes.[136] A case that should have been filed under § 1983,

but was filed as a habeas petition to avoid the three strikes provision may be counted as a strike.[137] In the past, courts have sometimes just treated habeas petitions that should have been filed under § 1983 as § 1983 cases, and gone forward with them,[138] but several courts have cautioned that this should not automatically be done under the PLRA; since prisoners could end up being charged a strike, they ought to have a chance to think it over before proceeding.[139]

In a class action, only the named plaintiffs are subject to the three strikes provision.[140]

One court has held that a dismissal counts as a strike even if the case was filed by an ex-prisoner after release, if the plaintiff later returns to prison.[141] However, this holding seems contrary to the statutory language, which says that prior actions brought "while incarcerated or detained" are considered strikes.[142]

Appeals count as strikes under § 1915(g) only if they are "dismissed . . . [as] frivolous, malicious, or fail[ing] to state a claim upon which relief may be granted."[143] If the appeals court merely affirms a district court decision that was dismissed for one of the reasons stated in § 1915(g), the appeal is not a separate strike.[144] An appeal that is dismissed

---

court, must be dismissed under § 1915(g). This question is discussed above at nn.93–97.

[129]Belton v. U.S., 2008 WL 2273272, *10 (E.D.Wis., June 2, 2008) (motion under Rule 60(b) is not a strike; statute "does not apply to motions, only 'actions' or 'appeals'").

[130]McLean v. U.S., 566 F.3d 391, 396–99 (4th Cir. 2009). Other courts have disagreed. *See* O'Neal v. Price, 531 F.3d 1146, 1154–55 (9th Cir. 2008).

[131]*See* Andrews v. King, 398 F.3d 1113, 1120 (9th Cir. 2005); Freeman v. Lee, 30 F. Supp. 2d 52, 54 (D.D.C. 1998).

[132]*See* Clemente v. Allen, 120 F.3d 703, 705 n.1 (7th Cir. 1997) (holding that appeal was not a strike in the absence of published law on the question before the court ruled); Hairston v. Falano, 1999 WL 412440, *1–2 (N.D.Ill. May 28, 1999) (holding that dismissal was not a strike where plaintiff's claim, valid when filed, was dismissed based on a change in the law).

[133]Duvall v. Miller, 122 F.3d 489, 490 (7th Cir. 1997).

[134]Welch v. Galie, 207 F.3d 130, 131 (2d Cir. 2000); Rivera v. Allin, 144 F.3d 719, 729–31 (11th Cir. 1998); Wilson v. Yaklich, 148 F.3d 596, 603–04 (6th Cir. 1998); Keener v. Pa. Bd. of Prob. & Parole, 128 F.3d 143, 144 (3d Cir. 1997); Tierney v. Kupers, 128 F.3d 1310, 1312 (9th Cir. 1997); Adepegba v. Hammons, 103 F.3d 383, 387 (5th Cir. 1996) (holding strikes provision can apply retroactively); Green v. Nottingham, 90 F.3d 415, 420 (10th Cir. 1996); Abdul-Wadood v. Nathan, 91 F.3d 1023, 1025 (7th Cir. 1996).

[135]Andrews v. King, 398 F.3d 1113, 1122–23 & n.12 (9th Cir. 2005) and cases cited.

[136]*Compare* Bure v. Miami-Dade Police Dep't, 2008 WL 2374149, *3 (S.D.Fla., June 6, 2008) (mistakenly filed § 1983 is a strike); Grant v. Sotelo, 1998 WL 740826, *1 (N.D.Tex. Oct. 17, 1998) (holding § 1983 case that should have been filed under habeas corpus is frivolous); and cases cited, *with* Whitfield v. Lawrence Correctional Center, 2008 WL 3874718, *3–4 (S.D.Ill., Aug. 18, 2008); Rogers v. Wis. Dep't of Corr., 2005 WL 300291, *3 (W.D.Wis., Feb. 3, 2005) (holding that dismissal of a § 1983 action that should have been filed as a habeas petition is not a strike because "dismissal . . . for failure to use the proper avenue for relief" is not a ground listed in the statute); *see* Patton v. Jefferson Corr. Ctr., 136 F.3d 458, 464 (5th Cir. 1998) (holding that § 1983 actions

that should have been filed as habeas petitions but would have been frivolous as such were strikes).

[137]Andrews v. King, 398 F.3d 1113, 1123 n.12 (9th Cir. 2005).

[138]*See* Carson v. Johnson, 112 F.3d 818, 819 (5th Cir. 1997) (construing habeas corpus petition as a § 1983 case).

[139]Pischke v. Litscher, 178 F.3d 497, 500 (7th Cir. 1999) (dismissing habeas corpus actions and indicating plaintiffs may re-file complaints as civil rights claims); Brown v. Woodring, 2009 WL 4040067, *3 (C.D.Cal., Nov. 17, 2009) (citing PLRA filing fee and initial screening requirements, three strikes provision, and fact that plaintiff did not seem to have exhausted administrative remedies as reasons not to convert habeas to § 1983 action).

[140]Meisberger v. Donahue, 245 F.R.D. 627, 630 (S.D.Ind. 2007).

[141]*See* Robbins v. Switzer, 104 F.3d 895, 897 (7th Cir. 1997) (holding dismissal would count as strike if released petitioner ever returns to prison).

[142]28 U.S.C. § 1915(g); *see* Arvie v. Lastrapes, 106 F.3d 1230, 1232 (5th Cir. 1997) (per curiam) (remanding to determine whether the plaintiff was a prisoner when he filed his previous actions).

[143]28 U.S.C. § 1915(g); *see* Andrews v. King, 398 F.3d 1113, 1120–21 (9th Cir. 2005) (holding that an appeal dismissed for lack of jurisdiction is not a strike); Newlin v. Helman, 123 F.3d 429, 433 (7th Cir. 1997) (holding that frivolous appeal of a dismissed claim counts as a second strike).

[144]Jennings v. Natrona County Det. Ctr. Med. Facility, 175 F.3d 775, 780 (10th Cir. 1999) ("Under the plain language of the statute, only a dismissal may count as strike, not the affirmance of an earlier decision to dismiss."); Adepegba v. Hammons, 103 F.3d 383, 387 (5th Cir. 1996) ("It is straightforward that affirmance of a district court dismissal as frivolous counts as a single 'strike.'"); Barela v. Variz, 36 F. Supp. 2d 1254, 1258 (S.D. Cal. 1999); Freeman v. Lee, 30 F. Supp. 2d 52, 54 & n.3 (D.D.C. 1998); *see also* Henderson v.

on grounds other than those stated in § 1915(g) cannot be a separate strike even if the district court decision counts as a strike.[145]

Some courts have held that "[a] dismissal should not count against a petitioner until he has exhausted or waived his appeals."[146] Thus, if you receive a third strike in a district court decision, you should still be able to appeal that decision *in forma pauperis* without being barred by the three strikes provision.[147] The Seventh Circuit Court of Appeals, however, has made matters more complicated, holding that a prisoner cannot directly appeal a decision that counts as a third strike. Instead, the prisoner must apply to the appeals court for *in forma pauperis* status. The appeals court will then decide whether the lower court was correct in issuing the third strike to the prisoner, or whether the lower court was incorrect and should not have issued the third strike.[148] If an appeals court finds that your claim was not frivolous or malicious and did not fail to state a claim, the strike will be eliminated and your appeal can go forward.[149]

The defendants bear the burden of producing sufficient evidence to show that a prisoner has three strikes; if they do, the burden shifts to the prisoner to show that is not the case.[150] Defendants do not meet their burden just by showing that cases were dismissed; they must show that the reasons for the dismissals are those specified by the three strikes provision.[151] A court must, when applying the three strikes provision, clearly identify each case relied on.[152]

The three strikes provision cannot be used to revoke *in forma pauperis* status in a case filed before the plaintiff had three strikes, since the statute restricts prisoners' ability to "bring" suit if they have three strikes, not their ability to maintain suits previously brought.[153] (A case is "brought" for these purposes when the plaintiff tenders the complaint to the court, even if there is a significant time lag caused by the *in forma pauperis* and merits screening before it is filed.[154]) Nor does it prevent a plaintiff from filing an amended complaint in a suit filed before he had three strikes.[155]

One court has held that when multiple plaintiffs join in one lawsuit, each plaintiff's claims must be treated as a separate "action," and each plaintiff must be charged a strike for every plaintiff whose "action" is dismissed in its entirety.[156] This decision appears contrary to the statute, which seems

---

Norris, 129 F.3d 481, 485 n.4 (8th Cir. 1997) (recognizing that appeals of claims found to be frivolous are not automatically also frivolous).

Courts are not always careful in dealing with this issue. *See* Montanez v. DeTella, 172 F.3d 53, 1999 WL 38089, *2 (7th Cir., Jan. 14, 1999) (unpublished) (stating that affirmance of appeal from dismissal is itself a second strike, without discussing contrary authority). If you get a decision like this, be sure to ask the court to reconsider charging you with the second strike.

[145]Tafari v. Hues, 473 F.3d 440, 442–44 (2d Cir. 2007) (holding an appeal dismissed as premature was not a strike); Cosby v. Knowles, 145 F.3d 1345, 1998 WL 196596, *1 (10th Cir., Apr. 23, 1998) (unpublished) (noting that dismissal based on denial of *in forma pauperis* status, not the merits, is not a strike even though merits were frivolous).

[146]Adepegba v. Hammons, 103 F.3d 383, 387 (5th Cir. 1996); *accord*, Thompson v. Drug Enforcement Admin., 492 F.3d 428, 432 (D.C. Cir. 2007) ("A contrary rule would, within those narrow set of cases in which the third strike is appealed, effectively eliminate our appellate function. Had Congress intended such an unusual result, we expect it would have clearly said so."); Campbell v. Davenport Police Dep't, 471 F.3d 952, 953 (8th Cir. 2006). Some courts disagree. *See* Meador v. Alvidrez, 2009 WL 1929449, *2 (E.D.Cal., July 2, 2009). Once the time for appeal has passed, filing a late notice of appeal will not keep the dismissal from being a strike. Smith v. District of Columbia, 182 F.3d 25, 27–28 (D.C. Cir. 1999).

[147]Jennings v. Natrona County Det. Ctr. Med. Facility, 175 F.3d 775, 780 (10th Cir. 1999); Adepegba v. Hammons, 103 F.3d 383, 387 (5th Cir. 1996).

[148]Robinson v. Powell, 297 F.3d 540, 541 (7th Cir. 2002); *see* Boriboune v. Berge, 2005 WL 1378930 (W.D.Wis., June 9, 2005) (instructing plaintiff in how to use the prescribed procedure).

[149]Jennings v. Natrona County Det. Ctr. Med. Facility, 175 F.3d 775, 780 (10th Cir. 1999); Adepegba v. Hammons, 103 F.3d 383, 387 (5th Cir. 1996).

[150]Andrews v. King, 398 F.3d 1113, 1116, 1120 (9th Cir. 2005); *accord*, Thompson v. Drug Enforcement Admin., 492 F.3d 428, 435–36 (D.C. Cir. 2007); Green v. Morse, 2006 WL 2128609, *2–3 (W.D.N.Y., May 26, 2006). In practice, the three strikes provision is often raised by courts themselves at initial screening. *See* Owens-El v. U.S., 2006 WL 2252845, *1 n.3 (W.D.Okla., Aug. 7, 2006).

[151]Andrews v. King, 398 F.3d at 1120; *see* Thompson v. Drug Enforcement Admin., 492 F.3d at 436; Green v. Morse, 2006 WL 2927871, *4 (W.D.N.Y., Oct. 12, 2006) (both applying *Andrews* holding, finding docket entries sufficient to establish strikes).

[152]*See* Evans v. Ill. Dep't of Corr., 150 F.3d 810, 812 (7th Cir. 1998) ("[I]n the order denying leave to proceed *in forma pauperis* the district court must cite specifically the case names, case docket numbers, districts in which the actions were filed, and the dates of the orders dismissing the actions."); *accord*, Jennings v. Dist. Ct. for Seventh Judicial Dist., 172 F.3d 879, 1999 WL 72221, *1 (10th Cir., Feb. 16, 1999) (unpublished) (remanding because district court did not specify which prior actions or appeals were frivolous).

[153]Nicholas v. American Detective Agency, 254 Fed.Appx. 116, 117 (3d Cir. 2007) (unpublished); Mills v. White, 2006 WL 1458312, *1 (8th Cir., May 30, 2006) (unpublished); Nali v. Caruso, 2008 WL 718155, *2 (E.D.Mich., Mar. 14, 2008); Ali v. County of Sacramento, 2008 WL 449660, *1 (E.D.Cal., Feb. 15, 2008), *report and recommendation adopted*, 2008 WL 2477587 (E.D.Cal., June 17, 2008); Cruz v. Marcial, 2002 WL 655520 (D.Conn., Apr. 18, 2002). *Contra*, Nichols v. Rich, 2004 WL 743938, *2 (N.D.Tex., Apr. 7, 2004) (citing goals of the statute but not addressing its actual language), *report and recommendation adopted*, 2004 WL 1119689 (N.D.Tex., May 18, 2004).

[154]*See* n.2 of this chapter.

[155]Elkins v. Schrubbe, 2005 WL 1154273, *1 (E.D.Wis., Apr 20, 2005).

[156]Boriboune v. Berge, 2005 WL 1320345, *4–8 (W.D.Wis., June 1, 2005) (declaring that several plaintiffs received three strikes from this single multi-plaintiff lawsuit). The court does not claim to find the basis for its holding in the statutory language; rather, it says it is interpreting a Seventh Circuit opinion remanding the case, and expresses hope that the court of appeals will clarify the matter. That has not happened.

intended to hold prisoners responsible for their own legal claims, but not for those of other persons.[157] So far, other courts have not adopted this view.

2. The "Imminent Danger of Serious Physical Injury" Exception

The three strikes provision does not bar a prisoner from proceeding *in forma pauperis* if he is in "imminent danger of serious physical injury."[158] The existence of such a danger is assessed as of the time of filing suit or at the time the prisoner makes an *in forma pauperis* application in the district court or on appeal.[159] In fact, some courts have said that a danger that arose after the case was filed, and is ongoing, does not qualify for the exception.[160]

The "imminent danger" requirement has been held to be satisfied by allegations that prison staff refused protective custody to a prisoner targeted by gangs,[161] disclosed a

---

[157]*See* Swenson v. McDonald, 2006 WL 240233, *3–4 (D. Mont., Jan. 30, 2006) (criticizing logic of *Boriboune*). *Swenson* points out that *Boriboune's* imposition of strikes based on the separate claims of individual plaintiffs contradicts the statute's reference to "action[s]" rather than claims; that its view that each prisoner litigant is responsible under Rule 11 for statements made by other plaintiffs is inconsistent with the lack of authority of *pro se* litigants to make representations on behalf of anyone other than themselves and with *pro se* prisoners' limited ability to investigate the merits of others' claims; and that the practical difficulties of multi-plaintiff prisoner litigation do not support imposing on each litigant responsibility for other prisoners' claims in such litigation.

[158]28 U.S.C. § 1915(g); *see* Miller v. Donald, 541 F.3d 1091, 1099 (11th Cir. 2008) (rejecting district court practice of barring prisoners with three strikes from filing under "imminent danger of serious physical injury" exception if they have not paid filing fees owed from previous cases).

[159]Polanco v. Hopkins, 510 F.3d 152, 156 (2d Cir. 2007) (rejecting argument that time-of-filing rule denies court access to those who can't get their claims in during the time they are in danger); Ibrahim v. District of Columbia, 463 F.3d 3, 6–7 (D.C. Cir. 2006); Heimermann v. Litscher, 337 F.3d 781, 782 (7th Cir. 2003); Martin v. Shelton, 319 F.3d 1048, 1050 (8th Cir. 2003); Malik v. McGinnis, 293 F.3d 559, 562–63 (2d Cir. 2002); Abdul-Akbar v. McKelvie, 239 F.3d 307, 312–16 (3d Cir. 2001) (en banc); Ashley v. Dilworth, 147 F.3d 715, 717 (8th Cir. 1998) (all holding danger must exist at the time of filing the complaint); *see also* Medberry v. Butler, 185 F.3d 1189, 1192–93 (11th Cir. 1999) (rejecting idea that imminent danger is measured at time of incident, but not deciding whether time of filing or IFP motion is appropriate rule); Banos v. O'Guin, 144 F.3d 883, 884–85 (5th Cir. 1998) (per curiam) (holding danger must exist at time of filing or time of IFP motion).

[160]Trice v. Vazquez, 2006 WL 3191175, *2 (S.D.Ga. Nov. 1, 2006); *see* Peterson v. Perdue, 2008 WL 3887630, *1 n.1, *3 (S.D.Ga., Aug. 21, 2008) (magistrate judge held that alleged threat of sexual assault did not meet standard because plaintiff had not been assaulted or injured; district judge held that even though he was sexually assaulted after that decision, the assault did not satisfy the statute because it occurred after filing).

[161]Cain v. Jackson, 2007 WL 2787979, *2 (S.D.Tex., Sept. 24, 2007) (allegation that plaintiff had been assaulted repeatedly by

---

prisoner's history as an informant, resulting in threats and assaults,[162] or repeatedly placed or retained a prisoner near known enemies.[163] Courts have also found imminent danger where the plaintiff was denied treatment for an ongoing serious medical problem[164] or disability,[165] or subjected to environmental conditions that caused or aggravated such

---

gang members and denied protective custody met the standard).

[162]*See* Gibbs v. Roman, 116 F.3d 83, 84–86 (3d. Cir. 1997); Malik v. McGinnis, 293 F.3d 559, 562 (2d Cir. 2002); *see* Matthews v. U.S., 72 Fed.Cl. 274, 278 (Fed.Cl. 2006) (allegation that prison officials defamed plaintiff, resulting in threats and violence from other prisoners, met the standard), *reconsideration denied*, 73 Fed. Cl. 524 (Fed.Cl. 2006).

[163]*See* Ashley v. Dilworth, 147 F.3d 715, 717 (8th Cir. 1998); Norwood v. Radtke, 2007 WL 5541973, *3 (W.D.Wis., Aug. 22, 2007) (gay plaintiff's allegation that he was double-celled with a prisoner who didn't like gays met the standard), *motion to amend denied*, 2007 WL 5527749 (W.D.Wis., Sept. 4, 2007).

[164]*See* Ibrahim v. District of Columbia, 463 F.3d 3, 6–7 (D.C. Cir. 2006) (holding that deterioration from lack of treatment for Hepatitis C sufficiently pleaded imminent danger of serious physical injury); Brown v. Johnson, 387 F.3d 1344, 1350 (11th Cir. 2004) (holding that a prisoner who alleged that lack of treatment was worsening his illnesses sufficiently pleaded imminent danger of serious physical injury); McAlphin v. Toney, 281 F.3d 709, 711 (8th Cir. 2002) (prisoner's complaint alleging denial of treatment for medical/dental condition posed imminent danger was sufficient to permit him to proceed *in forma pauperis* despite the fact that he had three strikes); Almond v. Wisconsin, 2008 WL 2903574, *1 (E.D.Wis. Jul. 24, 2008) (allegation of untreated infection satisfied requirement); Grissom v. Pininski, 2008 WL 2218262, *1–2 (W.D.Wis., May 23, 2008) (allegation of denial of medical care for apparent broken wrist met the imminent danger standard); Jensen v. Knowles, 2008 WL 744726, *2 (E.D.Cal., Mar. 18, 2008) (holding complaint of failure to provide diabetic diet met the standard, noting need "to avoid overly detailed inquiries into what dangers are serious enough"); Harris v. Beard, 2007 WL 404042, *2 (M.D.Pa., Feb. 1, 2007) (holding complaint of inadequate medical care for chronic back injury, plus deprivation of cane despite need to walk long distances and climb stairs, and deprivation of lower bunk status, met imminent danger standard); Bacon v. Epps, 2006 WL 1382314, *2 (W.D.Mo. May 17, 2006) (allowing claim to go forward under imminent danger standard that a dentist's drill bit came loose, was lost inside plaintiff, and he did not receive treatment even after passing blood); Voth v. Lytle, 2005 WL 3358909, *1 (D.Or., Dec. 8, 2005) (holding plaintiff's claim of severe pain and rectal bleeding and overruling of recommendations for surgery satisfy the "imminent danger of serious physical injury" standard notwithstanding defendants' claim that the condition is "relatively stable and long-standing").

[165]Fuller v. Wilcox, 2008 WL 2961388, *1 (10th Cir., Aug. 4, 2008) (unpublished) (denial of a wheelchair, meaning that plaintiff must crawl, and could not walk to the shower or lift himself to his bed, "could result in a number of serious physical injuries"); Miller v. Meadows, 2005 WL 1983838, *4 (M.D.Ga., Aug. 11, 2005) (paraplegic who alleged he was denied physical therapy and necessary medical devices and/or treatments and that this denial is "resulting in bed sores, serious atrophy, and deterioration of his spinal condition" sufficiently alleged imminent danger of serious physical injury).

problems.[166] To meet the "serious physical injury" requirement, the threatened injury need not be as serious as to be an Eighth Amendment violation in and of itself,[167] though in many cases the alleged risk has been rejected as not serious enough.[168]

On its face, a credible allegation of imminent danger of serious physical injury meets the statutory requirement.[169]

The risk of future injury can be sufficient,[170] though many such allegations have been dismissed as incredible or speculative.[171] If serious allegations of imminent danger are disputed, the court may hold a hearing or rely on affidavits, depositions, or records to resolve the question.[172] Some courts,

---

[166]Gibbs v. Cross, 160 F.3d 962, 966–67 (3d Cir. 1998); see Rankins v. Rowland, 2006 WL 1836671, *1 n.1 (4th Cir., June 27, 2006) (unpublished) (holding that an allegation that a poor ventilation system caused the plaintiff bodily harm and he was denied medical treatment for his symptoms made a "colorable showing" of imminent danger); Smith v. Ozmint, 2008 WL 1883200, *4 (D.S.C., Apr. 23, 2008) (imminent danger standard met by allegations of use of hazardous Chinese products, 24-hour illumination in cells, exposure to deranged behavior and unsanitary conditions from mentally ill prisoners in the segregation unit, deprivation of sunlight, and exposure to mold).

[167]See Ciarpaglini v. Saini, 352 F.3d 328, 330–31 (7th Cir. 2003) (holding allegations that termination of psychiatric medication resulted in panic attacks which caused "heart palpitations, chest pains, labored breathing, choking sensations, and paralysis in his legs and back" met the imminent danger standard); Gibbs v. Cross, 160 F.3d 962, 964 (3d Cir. 1998) (holding allegation that plaintiff was subjected to "dust, lint and shower odor" via cell vent, resulting in severe headaches, change in voice, mucus full of dust and lint, and watery eyes sufficiently alleged imminent danger of serious injury).

[168]See, e.g., Burghart v. Corrections Corp. of America, 2008 WL 619308, *1 (W.D.Okla., Mar. 4, 2008) (complaints of migraine headaches, fatigue, depression, weight gain and sleeping disorders did not meet standard); Johnson v. Alabama Dep't Of Corrections, 2008 WL 276577, *1 (M.D.Ala., Jan. 29, 2008) (discontinuance of hormone treatment for gender identity disorder, allegedly causing "excessive weight gain, complete body fat redistribution, dizzy spells, fainting spells, headaches, hot-flashes, anxiety, severe depression, more depression than usual, . . . [and] the growth of first time facial hair," did not meet the imminent danger standard); Oluwa v. Bliesner, 2007 WL 2457510, *1 (N.D.Cal., Aug. 27, 2007) (lack of a Rastafarian diet did not meet the standard).

[169]See Jackson v. Jackson, 2009 WL 1587830, *1 (11th Cir. 2009) (plaintiff "claims that he has a hernia that causes him to suffer from severe pain in his testicles and abdomen, blood in his urine, nausea, and weight loss. Jackson contends that without surgery, which the defendant prison officials will not approve, he will continue to suffer from those injuries and may even face tissue death, gangrene, and internal bleeding. Based on these allegations, which we must construe liberally, accept as true, and view as a whole, . . . we conclude that Jackson has sufficiently demonstrated that he was in imminent danger of serious physical injury when he filed suit."); Ciarpaglini v. Saini, 352 F.3d 328, 330–31 (7th Cir. 2003) (holding allegations of panic attacks leading to heart palpitations, chest pains, labored breathing, choking sensations, and paralysis meet the imminent danger standard; disapproving extensive inquiry into seriousness of allegations at pleading stage); White v. Colorado, 157 F.3d 1226, 1232 (10th Cir. 1998) (rejecting claim because plaintiff failed to raise a credible allegation of imminent danger of serious physical harm); see also Andrews v. Cervantes, 493 F.3d 1047, 1050 (9th Cir. 2007) ("the three-strikes rule is a screening device that does not judge the merits of prisoners'

lawsuits"); Lewis v. Sullivan, 279 F.3d 526, 531 (7th Cir. 2002) (stating that the exception applies "[w]hen a threat or prison condition is real and proximate, and when the potential consequence is 'serious physical injury'").

[170]Gibbs v. Cross, 160 F.3d 962, 966–67 (3d Cir. 1998) (relying on alleged environmental hazards in prison); see Ibrahim v. District of Columbia, 463 F.3d 3, 6–7 (D.C. Cir. 2006) (holding that deterioration from lack of treatment for Hepatitis C sufficiently pled imminent danger of serious physical injury); Brown v. Johnson, 387 F.3d 1344, 1350 (11th Cir. 2004) (similar to Ibrahim); McAlphin v. Toney, 281 F.3d 709, 711 (8th Cir. 2002) (holding that a prisoner who alleged that he was transferred to a prison without adequate dental facilities while in the midst of a course of dental treatment, and dental infection was spreading in his mouth, sufficiently pled imminent danger). But see Brown v. Beard, 492 F. Supp. 2d 474, 479 (E.D.Pa. 2007) (risk factors for heart disease were not sufficiently "imminent" to meet the requirement).

[171]See, e.g., Mathis v. Smith, 2006 WL 1342840, *1 (11th Cir., May 17, 2006) (unpublished) (affirming rejection on credibility grounds of claim of ongoing threats to life by guard because of prisoner's prior false representations, history of frivolous litigation, and unrelated allegations in his complaint); Robinson v. Mawer, 2008 WL 1986239, *2–3 (W.D.Mich., May 2, 2008) (holding claim that prisoner's hand was broken and he couldn't defend himself against assault did not allege imminent danger because there was no showing that he would imminently be assaulted); Althouse v. Roe, 542 F. Supp. 2d 543, 546 (E.D.Tex. 2008) (holding claim that attention deficit hyperactivity disorder might lead the plaintiff impulsively to put himself in danger was too speculative to show imminent danger); Tucker v. Dawkins, 2008 WL 510199, *2 (W.D.N.C., Feb. 22, 2008) (broad and unsupported allegation that superintendent had solicited prisoners to murder plaintiff does not meet imminent danger standard); Leach v. Brownlee, 2007 WL 3025092, *2 (E.D.Ark., Oct. 15, 2007) (holding that prospect of being sent to a sex offender program and being housed with sex offenders who, the plaintiff said, might cut his throat was not specific enough to show imminent danger); Spencer v. Missouri Dep't of Corrections, 2007 WL 781210, *1 (E.D.Mo., Mar. 9, 2007) (holding claim that 17 months of tooth pain means "it is only a matter of time" before plaintiff gets an infection or "something worse" happens did not satisfy imminent danger standard), reconsideration denied, 2007 WL 1049339 (E.D.Mo., Apr. 5, 2007); Rodriguez v. Texas Dep't of Public Safety, 2007 WL 162830, *2–3 (E.D.Tex., Jan 22, 2007) (stating, after a hearing where plaintiff reported a three-month-old threat to "bash his brains in" and his cell door having been left open on the night of a homicide, that plaintiff's "subjective belie[f]" in danger was not supported by objective evidence); Johnson v. Barney, 2005 WL 2173950, *1 (S.D.N.Y., Sept. 6, 2005) (holding a prisoner who had been beaten once at a particular prison did not face an "imminent danger" because he might be at that prison again in the future).

[172]Gibbs v. Roman, 116 F.3d 83, 86 (3d Cir. 1997); see White v. Colorado, 157 F.3d 1226, 1232 (10th Cir. 1998) (refusing to credit allegations of inadequate medical care based on magistrate judge's examination of medical records and failure to specify the nature of

however, seem just to have made their own judgments about the credibility of the prisoner's claim based on no more than the *pro se* complaint's allegations, sometimes supplemented by the prisoner's response to an order to show cause, or objections to a magistrate judge's report.[173] Some courts have rejected seemingly substantial allegations of threat of injury.[174] Some decisions have rejected imminent danger

claims based on evidence that prison officials had made some response to the threat, without looking closely at the adequacy of that response.[175]

Alleging imminent danger of serious physical injury does not authorize a prisoner with three strikes to bring suits unrelated to the danger. There must be some "nexus" between the complaint's allegations and the danger of injury. One court has held: "In deciding whether such a nexus exists, we will consider (1) whether the imminent danger of serious physical injury that a three-strikes litigant alleges is *fairly traceable* to unlawful conduct asserted in the complaint and (2) whether a favorable judicial outcome would

---

the imminent injury); Norwood v. Radtke, 2007 WL 5431018, *1 (W.D.Wis., Dec. 2, 2007) (allowing case to proceed based on alleged risk of assault by other prisoners, setting evidentiary hearing expecting either to grant preliminary relief or revoke *in forma pauperis* status); James v. Dormire, 2008 WL 625027, *2–3 (W.D.Mo., Mar. 4, 2008) (court allowed claim to go forward based on allegations that sharing electric razors presented a danger of spreading infection, then found no imminent danger after a hearing because officials said they cleaned the razors between uses and wiped them down with Barbicide); Baptiste v. Harper, 2007 WL 4224727, *1 (M.D.Ga., Nov. 27, 2007) (holding claim of risk of assault because the plaintiff had been labelled a snitch did not meet the standard where he had never asked for protective custody and had not been assaulted in months in general population); Williams v. Goord, 2007 WL 952053, *6 (N.D.N.Y., Mar. 29, 2007) (holding complications of a knee injury did not meet the standard where plaintiff's exhibits show he had received a lot of medical treatment); Thomas v. Woodford, 2006 WL 3437525, *2 (E.D. Cal. Nov. 27, 2006) (rejecting claim of imminent danger based on allegedly inadequate medical care for blurry vision, gum disease, and HIV with risk of nerve damage; court reviewed medical records and said plaintiff was getting ongoing care).

[173]*See, e.g.*, Jones v. Epps, 2008 WL 907663, *1 (S.D.Miss., Apr. 2, 2008) (rejecting claim of imminent danger based on exposure to second-hand smoke and resulting asthma), *certificate of appealability denied*, 2008 WL 1932402 (S.D.Miss., Apr. 28, 2008); Pruden v. Mayer, 2008 WL 919554, *3 (M.D.Pa., Apr. 2, 2008) (concluding that prisoner's medical care claims did not pose imminent danger because they had occurred over a long period of time); Porter v. Barfield, 2007 WL 4365449, *1 (M.D.Fla., Dec. 10, 2007) (rejecting claim of imminent danger based on alleged death threats by guards, on the ground that none of those guards were defendants, plaintiff had filed still-pending grievances concerning them, and he did not seek injunctive relief); Hickmon v. Florida Dep't of Corrections, 2007 WL 3023990, *2 (N.D.Fla., Oct. 16, 2007) (holding that prisoner's complaint lacked sufficient detail to demonstrate imminent danger, and the fact that he had been placed in protective custody and then waited two months to file showed it was not imminent); Martinez v. Cosner, 2007 WL 2962733, *1 (D.Colo., Oct. 9, 2007) (holding that claim of gang attack did not meet standard where plaintiff had been placed in protective custody and did not say he was housed with gang members; claim of suicide risk did not meet standard because he waited almost a month before presenting his claims and did not seek injunctive relief); Gilmore v. Wright, 2007 WL 2564702, *2–3 (D.S.C., Aug. 14, 2007) (assuming complaint of inability to see an "HIV doctor" reflects only a desire to see a doctor of plaintiff's choice, holding internal bleeding does not pose imminent danger because it seems to have been a problem for two years), *report and recommendation adopted*, 2007 WL 2493569 (D.S.C., Aug. 29, 2007).

[174]*See* Palmer v. N.Y.S. Dep't of Correction Greenhaven, 2007 WL 4258230, *3 (S.D.N.Y., Dec. 4, 2007) (finding frivolous a prisoner's allegation of imminent danger in that his toenails were

turning black, yellow, and green from an infection, and his fingernails were becoming swollen, and he was going to lose six toenails and a fingernail as a result), *aff'd*, 2009 WL 2243706 (2d Cir., July 28, 2009); Censke v. Smith, 2007 WL 2594539, *2 (W.D.Mich., Sept. 4, 2007) (holding that a prisoner who alleged that he was routinely exposed to raw sewage flooding his cell and leaking from the ceiling, and who said he had experienced various illnesses as a result, did not meet the standard), *reconsideration denied*, 2007 WL 2904047 (W.D.Mich., Oct. 3, 2007); Fuller v. Johnson County Bd. of County Com'rs, 2007 WL 2316926, *1 n.3 (D.Kan., Aug. 8, 2007) (holding plaintiff's claim that "emission of dust, lint, shower odor, and dead human skin caused him to suffer headaches, watery eyes, a change in voice, and increased mucus" did not satisfy the exception because he "did not as directly complain of breathing difficulties" as did a prisoner in another case); Owens v. Filsinger, 2007 WL 844827, *2 (W.D.Mich., Mar. 19, 2007) (holding plaintiff complaining of lack of Hepatitis C treatment for years did not allege imminent danger absent non-conclusory claim of serious injury); Watley v. Collins, 2006 WL 3422996, *1–2 (S.D.Ohio, Nov. 28, 2006) (holding plaintiff failed to meet imminent danger standard despite allegations that he is mentally ill and has been placed in supermax conditions as a result of his misbehavior, which aggravates his mental illness and therefore his misbehavior; has attempted suicide; engages in deranged behavior disturbing other inmates, who throw urine and feces at him; and has been maced); Hamilton v. Blunt, 2006 WL 2714910, *1–2 (W.D.Mo., Sept. 22, 2006) (holding allegation that environmental tobacco smoke aggravated plaintiff's preexisting asthma did not meet imminent danger standard); Jones v. Large, 2005 WL 2218420, *1 (W.D.Va., Sept. 13, 2005) (holding exception inapplicable despite prisoner's allegation of verbal threats by staff, including to "whupp his ass" and to kill him).

[175]*See, e.g.*, Skillern v. Georgia Dep't of Corrections, 2006 WL 1843561, *3 (11th Cir., July 6, 2006) (unpublished) (holding that allegation of repeated transfers of prisoner with diagnosed cardiac condition did not meet the standard since defendants hospitalized him after each transfer to treat his dehydration, fatigue, angina pectoris, and syncope (fainting) episodes); Gillilan v. Walkins, 2007 WL 2904129, *2 (S.D.Ga., Oct. 1, 2007) (holding plaintiff's claim of suicide risk arising from his mental health problems did not present an imminent risk because he had a new mental health counselor); Reeves v. Alexander, 2007 WL 2792222, *2 n.1 (W.D.Mich., Sept. 24, 2007) (holding allegation that unsanitary environment causes asthmatic breathing difficulties, bleeding, and headaches as a result of allergies does not meet imminent danger standard, since plaintiff has been taken to the hospital by ambulance as needed).

redress that injury."[176] That does not mean the case will be restricted to the precise defendants and allegations currently responsible for the danger, or to relief that will abate it.[177] A claim of imminent danger does not excuse the prisoner from the PLRA's administrative exhaustion requirement.[178]

One court has held that self-inflicted injury cannot meet the imminent danger standard because "[e]very prisoner would then avoid the three strikes provision by threatening suicide."[179] We think this statement is extreme and unwarranted. Many prison suicides and attempted suicides result directly from serious mental illness,[180] and it would be cruel and dangerous to prevent prisoners with mental illness from going to court to seek treatment or to seek other help to reduce the effects of their illness.

3. Constitutional Challenges to the Three Strikes Provision

So far, the federal courts have upheld § 1915(g).[181] Several district courts held the provision unconstitutional, but those decisions are now overruled.[182]

We think the three strikes provision is unconstitutional for reasons that have not yet been addressed by the courts. The right of access to courts "is part of the right of petition protected by the First Amendment."[183] As such, it is "generally subject to the same constitutional analysis" as is the right to free speech.[184] Because the three strikes provision addresses the conduct of litigation in court and not the internal operations of prisons, it is governed by the same First Amendment standards as other "free world" free

[176]Pettus v. Morgenthau, 554 F.3d 293, 299 (2d Cir. 2009); *see* Fuller v. Johnson County Bd. of County Com'rs, 2007 WL 2316926, *1 (D.Kan., Aug. 8, 2007) (complaints about the ventilation system did not meet the imminent danger standard where the plaintiff's claim addressed accessibility for the disabled); Barber v. Ohio University, 2007 WL 1831099, *2 (S.D.Ohio, June 25, 2007) (claim that plaintiff was in danger from retaliation for filing this lawsuit was not closely enough related to claims in complaint to invoke imminent danger exception).

[177]*See* Andrews v. Cervantes, 493 F.3d 1047, 1052 (9th Cir. 2007) (". . . [Q]ualifying prisoners can file their entire complaint IFP; the exception does not operate on a claim-by-claim basis or apply to only certain types of relief."); Ciarpiaglini v. Saini, 352 F.3d 328, 330 (7th Cir. 2003) (holding damages claim could go forward even though injunctive claim on which "imminent danger" allegation was based was moot); Nelson v. Moncrief, 2006 WL 3690933, *2–3 (E.D.Ark., Dec. 13, 2006) (rejecting argument that damages claims should not go forward because they don't serve the purpose of the imminent danger exception); Bond v. Aguinaldo, 228 F. Supp. 2d 918, 919 (N.D. Ill. 2002) (allowing claim against defendants responsible for medical care at prisons from which plaintiff had been transferred). *But see* McAlphin v. Toney, 375 F.3d 753 (8th Cir. 2004) (holding that a complaint that satisfies the imminent danger exception cannot be amended to include claims that don't involve imminent danger); Miller v. Meadows, 2005 WL 1983838, *5 (M.D.Ga. Aug. 11, 2005) (allowing only those claims to go forward that presented an imminent danger).

[178]McAlphin v. Toney, 375 F.3d 753, 755 (8th Cir. 2004).

[179]Wallace v. Cockrell, 2003 WL 21418639, *3 (N.D.Tex., Mar. 10, 2003), *approved as supplemented*, 2003 WL 21447831 (N.D.Tex., Mar. 27, 2003). *Contra*, Gilbert-Mitchell v. Lappin, 2008 WL 4545343, *3 (S.D.Ill., Oct. 10, 2008) (allegation that discontinuation of psychotropic medications caused plaintiff to injure himself could mean that he was in imminent danger of self-injury without them).

[180]*See* Sanville v. McCaughtry, 266 F.3d 724, 728 (7th Cir. 2001) (alleging that prison officials' failure to medicate mentally ill prisoner resulted in prisoner's suicide); Eng v. Smith, 849 F.2d 80 (2d Cir. 1988) (affirming injunction based on findings that state prison's policies for the treatment of mentally ill prisoners were insufficient for prisoners' protection).

[181]*See* Polanco v. Hopkins, 510 F.3d 152, 156 (2d Cir. 2007); Lewis v. Sullivan, 279 F.3d 526, 528 (7th Cir. 2002) (rejecting access to courts claim); Higgins v. Carpenter, 258 F.3d 797, 799–801 (8th Cir. 2001) (rejecting equal protection and access to courts arguments); Medberry v. Butler, 185 F.3d 1189, 1193 (11th Cir. 1999) (rejecting Ex Post Facto Clause argument); Rodriguez v. Cook, 169 F.3d 1176, 1178–82 (9th Cir. 1999) (rejecting due process, equal protection, access to courts, Ex Post Facto Clause, and separation of powers arguments); White v. Colorado, 157 F.3d 1226, 1233–34 (10th Cir. 1998) (rejecting access to courts and equal protection challenges); Wilson v. Yaklich, 148 F.3d 596, 604–06 (6th Cir. 1998) (rejecting equal protection, due process, and other challenges); Rivera v. Allin, 144 F.3d 719, 723–29 (11th Cir. 1998) (stating IFP status is "a privilege, not a right"; upholding provision against First Amendment, access to courts, separation of powers, due process, and equal protection challenges); Carson v. Johnson, 112 F.3d 818, 821 (5th Cir. 1997) (stating that the plaintiff "still has the right to file suits if he pays the full filing fees in advance, just like everyone else"; holding that the Constitution requires waiver of filing fees only in connection with "fundamental" interests, which court equates with the "atypical and significant" standard of *Sandin v. Conner*, 515 U.S. 472, 115 S. Ct. 2293 (1995)).

[182]Lewis v. Sullivan, 135 F. Supp. 2d 954, 969 (W.D.Wis. 2001) (striking statute down), *rev'd*, 279 F.3d 526 (7th Cir. 2001); Ayers v. Norris, 43 F. Supp. 2d 1039, 1050–51 (E.D.Ark. 1999) (same), *rev'd sub nom* Higgins v. Carpenter, 258 F.3d 797 (8th Cir. 2001); Lyon v. Krol, 940 F. Supp. 1433, 1439 (S.D.Iowa 1996) (same), *appeal dismissed and remanded*, 127 F.3d 763, 765 (8th Cir. 1997).

One state court has held a state law three strikes provision unconstitutional under the Open Courts Clause of the state constitution. Smith v. Indiana Dep't of Correction, 883 N.E.2d 802 (Ind. 2008). That statute, Indiana Code § 34-58-2-1, barred prisoners from filing suit at all if they had three strikes, unless they were in immediate danger of serious bodily injury. It did not address whether excluding prisoners from *in forma pauperis* status would violate the state constitution.

[183]Cal. Motor Transp. Co. v. Trucking Unlimited, 404 U.S. 508, 513, 92 S. Ct. 609 (1972).

[184]Wayte v. U.S., 470 U.S. 598, 610 n.11, 105 S. Ct. 1524 (1985). Indeed, the Supreme Court has simply stated that advocacy in litigation *is* speech. Legal Servs. Corp. v. Velazquez, 531 U.S. 533, 542–43, 121 S. Ct. 1043 (2001) (holding legal representation is speech).

speech claims.[185] This body of law requires that restrictions on expression be narrowly tailored to the problem they are supposed to solve.[186] Applying that principle, the Supreme Court has said that public officials could not recover damages for defamation unless the statements they sued about were knowingly false or made with reckless disregard for their truth; the First Amendment requires "breathing space," and a margin for error is required for inadvertently false speech, or true speech will be deterred.[187] This principle has been applied in cases where the government has sought to impose sanctions for litigation because it allegedly violates antitrust[188] or labor law.[189] The Supreme Court has said that sanctions may not be imposed against persons who bring litigation unless the litigation is both objectively and subjectively without basis.[190]

Applied to the three strikes provision, the "breathing space" principle would mean that prisoners could only be sanctioned for lawsuits that were not only objectively without merit, but were also known by the plaintiff to be meritless, or were intentional abuses of the judicial system. The three strikes provision sweeps far more broadly than that. It imposes a penalty on lay persons proceeding *pro se*, which in some cases results in barring them from court, for honest mistakes of law as well as for abuses of the legal system. Such a system risks deterring prisoners from filing meritorious claims, just as an overbroad law of defamation could deter true speech about public officials. The three strikes provision should therefore be found unconstitutional unless it is interpreted consistently with the "breathing space" principle, *i.e.*, by limiting its application to malicious actions, or those that are clearly intentional abuses of the judicial system, as opposed to honest mistakes. The three strikes provision also appears unconstitutional under the legal principles that had been developed before the PLRA governing restrictions on prisoners' litigation and their use of the *in forma pauperis* provisions.[191]

C. Screening and Dismissal of Prisoner Cases

The PLRA requires federal courts to screen all suits by prisoners against government employees, *and* all *in forma pauperis* cases, and to dismiss cases that are frivolous or malicious, that fail to state a claim on which relief may be granted,[192] or that seek damages from a defendant who is immune from damage claims.[193] If a court does not immediately dismiss such claims, it must dismiss them as soon afterward as is feasible. Cases filed in state court and then removed to federal court by the defendants are subject to screening.[194]

This power of dismissal, which used to be limited to *in forma pauperis* cases, now extends to *all* prisoner cases.[195] The courts' ability to dismiss cases *sua sponte* (without a motion by the defendant) used to be limited to frivolous and malicious cases, but has now been extended to cases failing to state a claim and cases suing immune defendants. Such dismissals may be done without prior notice or an opportunity to respond first,[196] but one federal circuit has cautioned that this ought to be done only where "it is unmistakably clear that the court lacks jurisdiction, or that the complaint lacks merit or is otherwise defective."[197]

Most courts have held that under the PLRA, as under prior law, *pro se* litigants are allowed an opportunity to amend deficient complaints before the court finally dismisses them.[198] One federal circuit has held that the PLRA

---

[185]Thornburgh v. Abbott, 490 U.S. 401, 403, 109 S. Ct. 1874 (1989) (distinguishing between regulations of material sent into prison and material sent out of prison for purposes of First Amendment).

[186]NAACP v. Button, 371 U.S. 415, 438, 83 S. Ct. 328 (1963) ("Precision of regulation must be the touchstone in an area so closely touching our most precious freedoms.").

[187]N.Y. Times Co. v. Sullivan, 376 U.S. 254, 272, 84 S. Ct. 710 (1964).

[188]Cal. Motor Transp. Co. v. Trucking Unlimited, 404 U.S. 508, 511, 92 S. Ct. 609 (1972) (applying rule in antitrust context).

[189]Bill Johnson's Rests., Inc. v. NLRB, 461 U.S. 731, 741, 103 S. Ct. 2161 (1983) (applying rule in labor context).

[190]Prof'l Real Estate Investors, Inc. v. Columbia Pictures Indus., Inc., 508 U.S. 49, 60–61, 113 S. Ct. 1920 (1993) (requiring both subjective and objective intent).

[191]See Ch. 10, § X for further discussion.

[192]The meaning of these terms is discussed in Ch. 10, § C.3.b.

[193]These requirements appear in three overlapping statutory provisions: 28 U.S.C. § 1915(e)(2); 28 U.S.C. § 1915A; and 42 U.S.C. § 1997e(c)(1). The screening process is discussed further in Ch. 10, § C.3.b.

Failure to exhaust administrative remedies is generally not a failure to state a claim and therefore will seldom be a basis for dismissal at the screening stage. See Jones v. Bock, 549 U.S. 199, 214–15, 127 S. Ct. 910 (2007); this issue is discussed further at nn.111–112 in this chapter.

[194]Crooker v. Burns, 544 F. Supp. 2d 59, 67 (D.Mass. 2008) and cases cited.

[195]Plunk v. Givens, 234 F.3d 1128, 1129 (10th Cir. 2000); Ray v. Evercom Systems, Inc., 2006 WL 2475264, *3–4 (D.S.C., Aug. 25, 2006) (holding fee-paid prisoner case raising antitrust claims rather than prison conditions, and joining governmental defendants, is subject to § 1915A screening).

[196]Plunk v. Givens, 234 F.3d at 1129 (upholding lower court *sua sponte* dismissal where no hearing was provided); Carr v. Dvorin, 171 F.3d 115, 116 (2d Cir. 1999) (per curiam) ("The statute clearly does not require that process be served or that the plaintiff be provided an opportunity to respond before dismissal.").

[197]Giano v. Goord, 250 F.3d 146, 151 (2d Cir. 2001) (quoting Carr v. Dvorin, 171 F.3d 115, 116 (2d Cir. 1999)).

[198]Gomez v. USAA Fed. Sav. Bank, 171 F.3d 794, 795–96 (2d Cir. 1999) (holding that dismissal of a *pro se* complaint under § 1915(e)(2)(B) should be done with leave to amend "unless the court can rule out any possibility, however unlikely it might be, that an amended complaint would succeed in stating a claim"); *accord*, Brown v. Johnson, 387 F.3d 1344, 1348–49 (11th Cir. 2004);

prohibits this opportunity to amend, but in our view that holding is undermined by a later Supreme Court decision.[199] The PLRA screening provisions do not affect the rule that a court reviewing a complaint must accept as true all allegations of material fact and construe them in the light most favorable to the plaintiff, or the rule that courts must construe *pro se* pleadings liberally.[200]

Before the PLRA, dismissal as frivolous or malicious under the IFP statutes was within the district courts' discretion. The PLRA has expanded the grounds for dismissal to include failure to state a claim and seeking damages from a party who is immune from damages, and has made dismissal *mandatory* rather than discretionary. The way in which appeals courts review PLRA dismissals has not been fully settled. Some courts have held that dismissal under the PLRA is subject to *de novo* review, which means that the appeals court may decide the matter however it thinks best.[201] Some courts have held that dismissals for failure to state a claim are reviewed *de novo*, but dismissals as

frivolous or malicious remain subject to an "abuse of discretion" standard (which means that the appeals court will not overrule the district court's decision unless it thinks the district court made a very big mistake).[202] Other courts have not fully addressed the question.[203]

Delays in the PLRA-dictated screening process are generally good cause for extending the 120-day time period for serving process.[204]

The screening provisions have been held not to deny due process,[205] equal protection,[206] or the right of access to courts.[207]

Grayson v. Mayview State Hosp., 293 F.3d 103, 109–14 (3d Cir. 2002); Shane v. Fauver, 213 F.3d 113, 117 (3d Cir. 2000) (adhering to pre-PLRA practice); Lopez v. Smith, 203 F.3d 1122, 1124 (9th Cir. 2000) (en banc) (same); *see also* Bazrowx v. Scott, 136 F.3d 1053, 1054 (5th Cir. 1998) (holding under 42 U.S.C. § 1997e(c) that dismissing a *pro se* complaint for failure to state a claim without giving the plaintiff an opportunity to amend is generally error; however, it is harmless error to dismiss without prejudice); Ragins v. Gilmore, 48 F. Supp. 2d 566, 568 (E.D.Va. 1999) ("Finally, where a *pro se* complaint contains a potentially cognizable claim, plaintiff should be allowed to particularize the claim.").

[199]In *McGore v Wrigglesworth*, 114 F.3d 601, 612 (6th Cir. 1997), the court said: "Under the Prison Litigation Act, courts have no discretion in permitting a plaintiff to amend a complaint to avoid a *sua sponte* dismissal." *Accord*, Baxter v. Rose, 305 F.3d 486, 489 (6th Cir. 2002) ("a plaintiff in a case covered by the PLRA may not amend his complaint to avoid a *sua sponte* dismissal."). However, the Supreme Court has held, in connection with the PLRA's administrative exhaustion requirement, that the screening requirement "does not—explicitly or implicitly—justify deviating from the usual procedural practice beyond the departures specified by the PLRA itself." Jones v. Bock, 549 U.S. 199, 214, 127 S. Ct. 910 (2007). Since a plaintiff's ability to amend the complaint freely is part of the "usual procedural practice," *see* Rule 15(a)(2), Fed. R. Civ. P., it would appear that the basis for the Sixth Circuit's holding has been undermined. However, the Sixth Circuit has not acknowledged this point. *But see* Conway v. Wilkinson, 2007 WL 901531, *2 (S.D.Ohio, Mar. 26, 2007) (holding amendment to address exhaustion is permitted in light of *Jones* since it is no longer an attempt to cure a deficiency).

[200]*See* Resnick v. Hayes, 213 F.3d 443, 446 (9th Cir. 2000) (agreeing with district court's liberal construction of *pro se* pleading); Gomez v. USAA Fed. Sav. Bank, 171 F.3d 794, 795–96 (2d Cir. 1999) (per curiam) (noting that *pro se* complaints must be read liberally).

[201]*See* Liner v. Goord, 196 F.3d 132, 134 (2d Cir. 1999) (holding that "28 U.S.C. § 1915A and 42 U.S.C. § 1999e(c)(2) dismissals are subject to *de novo* review"); Barren v. Harrington, 152 F.3d 1193, 1194 (9th Cir. 1998) (holding that dismissals for failure to state a claim are reviewed *de novo*); McGore v. Wrigglesworth, 114 F.3d

601, 604 (6th Cir. 1997) (concluding that provision requires *de novo* review).

[202]*See* Bilal v. Driver, 251 F.3d 1346, 1348–49 (11th Cir. 2001) (holding that abuse of discretion standard was proper for review of dismissal based on frivolity); Jackson v. Ward, 185 F.3d 874, 1999 WL 498491, *1 (10th Cir., July 15, 1999) (unpublished) (dismissals under § 1915(e)(2)(B)(i) as frivolous or malicious are reviewed for abuse of discretion; court should "consider, *inter alia*, whether the plaintiff is proceeding *pro se* and whether the district court inappropriately resolved genuine issues of material fact"); Harper v. Showers, 174 F.3d 716, 718 n.3 (5th Cir. 1998) (stating that *de novo* review is only appropriate for dismissals for failure to state a claim on which relief may be granted).

[203]*See* Mathis v. N.Y. Life Ins. Co., 133 F.3d 546, 547 (7th Cir. 1998) (not deciding question); McWilliams v. Colorado, 121 F.3d 573, 574–75 (10th Cir. 1997) (stating that § 1915(e)(2) dismissals are reviewed for abuse of discretion; case before court was frivolous). Fitzgerald v. First E. Seventh St. Tenants Corp., 221 F.3d 362, 364 n.2 (2d Cir. 2000) (indicating the standard of review for § 1915(e) is unsettled law).

[204]Shabazz v. Franklin, 380 F. Supp. 2d 793, 799–800 (N.D.Tex. 2005).

[205]Vanderberg v. Donaldson, 259 F.3d 1321, 1324 (11th Cir. 2001) ("The complained of procedure did not deny Plaintiff due process."); Curley v. Perry, 246 F.3d 1278, 1283–84 (10th Cir. 2001) (finding no due process violation).

[206]Vanderberg v. Donaldson, 259 F.3d 1321, 1324 (11th Cir. 2001) ("[S]ection 1915(e)(2)(B)(ii) is rationally related to the government's legitimate interests in deterring meritless claims and conserving judicial resources and, therefore, does not violate the Equal Protection Clause."); Curley v. Perry, 246 F.3d 1278, 1285 (10th Cir. 2001), (addressing 28 U.S.C. § 1915(e)(ii)(B)(ii) and finding no equal protection violation, but not addressing 18 U.S.C. § 1915A); Christiansen v. Clarke, 147 F.3d 655, 657–58 (8th Cir. 1998) (finding statute survives equal protection challenge); Hanley v. Stewart, 21 F. Supp. 2d 1088, 1093 (D.Ariz. 1998) (same).

[207]Martin v. Scott, 156 F.3d 578, 580 n.2 (5th Cir. 1998) (finding provision does not unconstitutionally restrict access to federal courts). *But see* Mitchell v. Farcass, 112 F.3d 1483, 1490–93 (11th Cir. 1997) (Lay, J., concurring) (arguing that the screening provisions do violate equal protection and the right of access to courts). A concurring opinion is one filed by a judge or judges in which they agree with the result of the opinion of the court filed in the case, although they disagree with the reasoning and state separately their reasoning. This means that you cannot solely rely on a concurring opinion in arguing your point because the opinion of the majority of the court, not the concurring opinion, is law.

D. EXHAUSTION OF ADMINISTRATIVE REMEDIES

The PLRA exhaustion requirement says:

No action shall be brought with respect to prison conditions under [42 U.S.C. § 1983] . . . or any other Federal law, by a prisoner confined in any jail, prison, or other correctional facility until such administrative remedies as are available are exhausted.[208]

This means you have to take your problem to the prison grievance system, or whatever other complaint or appeal system applies, before you bring suit—and you have to do it right and pursue the process all the way to the end. More prisoners lose their cases because of failure to exhaust administrative remedies, or to exhaust correctly, than from any other part of the PLRA.

Here is the bottom line: If something happens to you that you may want to bring suit about:

- Find out what remedies are available right away. Better yet, know your prison's grievance system and other remedies *before* you have a problem. Time deadlines are often very short. If you wait until you have a problem and have firmly decided whether to sue, it may be too late to exhaust.
- Always use the prison grievance system or any other available remedy, such as a disciplinary appeal.
- If you think there's a reason why you shouldn't have to exhaust, forget it. Exhaust anyway.
- Take all the available appeals, even if you get what you think is a favorable decision at an earlier point.
- If you don't get an answer to a grievance, try to appeal anyway. Many grievance systems say that if a certain amount of time passes and there's no decision, you can treat the non-response as a denial of the grievance, and appeal—and if you don't, a court may say you didn't exhaust.
- Be sure you use the right remedy if there is more than one possibility (*e.g.*, grievance versus disciplinary appeal). If you're not sure which remedy to use, try both.
- If prison employees tell you an issue is not grievable but you think it is, request that they process your grievance anyway so you will have a record of it. (And if there is a way to appeal or grieve a decision that something isn't grievable, do it!)
- If prison employees tell you something will be taken care of and you don't need to file a grievance, exhaust anyway if you think there is any chance you may wish to file suit.

- Follow the rules of the grievance system or other remedy as best you can.
- If the people running the grievance system or other remedy tell you that you did it wrong and you need to do something differently to fix it, follow the instructions even if you think they are wrong, and make a record of what you were told.
- If you make a mistake, like missing a time deadline, don't give up; file the grievance or appeal anyway, explain the reasons you made the mistake, ask that your grievance be considered despite your mistake, and appeal as far as you can if you lose.

The reason for all of this is that once you file suit, prison officials and their lawyers will look for any possible basis to say that you did not exhaust correctly and shouldn't be allowed to sue. You should be able to show the court that you did everything you could to comply with the exhaustion requirement, which requires following the prison's rules for grievances and other complaints or appeals.

The PLRA makes exhaustion of the grievance system *mandatory*.[209] That is true even if you are suing for damages and the grievance system doesn't provide damages.[210] You must exhaust *before* you file suit, not afterward.[211]

---

[208]42 U.S.C. § 1997e(a).

[209]Porter v. Nussle, 534 U.S. 516, 524, 122 S. Ct. 983 (2002) (requiring exhaustion). Though mandatory, exhaustion is not jurisdictional. Woodford v. Ngo, 548 U.S. 81, 101, 126 S. Ct. 2378 (2006). That means if you didn't exhaust and you think you have a good enough reason, the court at least has the power to consider your argument—though such arguments will seldom be successful, as discussed throughout this chapter.

Exhaustion is mandatory for *each* prisoner individually. Doss v. Gilkey, 649 F.Supp.2d 905, 913 (S.D.Ill. 2009) (holding imprisoned husband's grievance did not exhaust incarcerated wife's complaint about inability to correspond with him). "Vicarious" exhaustion is not permitted, except in class actions. Hattie v. Hallock, 8 F. Supp. 2d 685, 689 (N.D.Ohio), *judgment amended*, 16 F. Supp. 2d 834 (N.D.Ohio 1998). Some prison systems do provide for "group grievances," and a group grievance that complies with prison rules will exhaust. *See* Shirley v. Tuggle, 331 Fed.Appx. 484, 485 (9th Cir. 2009) (defendants failed to establish non-exhaustion where it appeared grievance had been treated as a group grievance) (unpublished). In class actions, generally only the named plaintiffs are required to exhaust, and exhaustion by a single class member is sufficient to exhaust the class's claims. *See* Chandler v. Crosby, 379 F.3d 1278, 1287 (11th Cir. 2004); Gates v. Cook, 376 F.3d 323, 329 (5th Cir. 2004); Jackson v. District of Columbia, 254 F.3d 262, 268-69 (D.C. Cir. 2001) (citing Foster v. Gueory, 655 F.2d 1319, 1321-22 (D.C. Cir. 1981)); Jones'El v. Berge, 172 F.Supp.2d 1128, 1131-33 (W.D.Wis. 2001).

[210]Booth v. Churner, 532 U.S. 731, 738, 121 S. Ct. 1819 (2001).

[211]Neal v. Goord, 267 F.3d 116, 121–23 (2d Cir. 2001); Jackson v. District of Columbia, 254 F.3d 262, 269 (D.C. Cir. 2001); Perez v. Wis. Dep't of Corr., 182 F.3d 532, 534–35 (7th Cir. 1999); Freeman v. Francis, 196 F.3d 641, 644 (6th Cir. 1999); Wendell v. Asher, 162 F.3d 887, 890 (5th Cir. 1998). *But see* Curry v. Scott, 249 F.3d 493,

If you have not exhausted, your case will be *dismissed* rather than stayed.[212] (A recent Supreme Court decision supports an argument that that rule is not necessarily valid in every case,[213] but it's safer to comply with the rule than be a test case for that argument.)

Most courts have held that dismissal for non-exhaustion is supposed to be "without prejudice,"[214] meaning in theory that you can re-file your case after you pursue your grievance. In reality, your grievance will almost certainly be late by that time,[215] and it will be up to prison officials to decide whether to allow you to pursue a late grievance.[216] If the statute of limitations has run on your claim at the time it is dismissed, your case may be permanently time-barred.[217] So it is very important to get exhaustion right the first time, since realistically you may not get a second chance.

One circuit has held that dismissal for non-exhaustion may be with prejudice with regard to the prisoner's ability to proceed *in forma pauperis*, meaning that if you were able to exhaust after dismissal, and then brought suit again, you would have to pay the full filing fee up front. That court stated that a prisoner who filed without exhaustion "sought relief to which he was not entitled—that is, federal court intervention in prison affairs prior to the prison having had the opportunity to address the complaint within its grievance procedures."[218] We think this rule is an excessively punitive response to what may be only the blunder of a *pro se* litigant; worse, it is also an outright denial of access to courts if the prisoner is indigent and unable to pay the filing fee up front. This rule has not been reexamined after *Jones v. Bock*.[219] We think it is invalid under *Jones*. In that case, the Supreme Court held that PLRA provisions should not be read to overturn the ordinary practices of litigation (referring both to the Federal Rules of Civil Procedure, and to practices not governed by those Rules) without a clear statement by Congress.[220] There seems no apparent reason

---

502 (6th Cir. 2001) (stating that pre-filing exhaustion is "the preferred practice," but allowing exhaustion prior to filing an *amended* complaint in a case filed shortly after the PLRA's enactment that involved some pre-PLRA conduct).

[212]Neal v. Goord, 267 F.3d 116, 121–23 (2d Cir. 2001); Perez v. Wis. Dep't of Corr., 182 F.3d 532, 534–35 (7th Cir. 1999).

A few decisions have granted stays pending exhaustion under unusual circumstances. *See* Hause v. Smith, 2006 WL 2135537, *1–2 (W.D.Mo. July 31, 2006) (directing that the plaintiff be allowed to file a grievance and that its processing be expedited and the results submitted to the court where the prisoner said his exhaustion efforts had been "significantly thwarted" by staff); Campbell v. Chaves, 402 F. Supp. 2d 1101, 1108–09 (D.Ariz. 2005) (staying litigation and directing the prison system to consider a grievance where the prisoner had filed a tort claim rather than a grievance at staff direction, the tort claim had been rejected for jurisdictional reasons, and meanwhile the grievance system rules had been changed so the matter would have been grievable); McCaffery v. Winn, 2005 WL 2994370, *1 (D.Mass., Nov. 8, 2005); Kennedy v. Mendez, 2004 WL 2280225, *1–2 (M.D.Pa., Oct. 7, 2004) (stating a stay was appropriate because exhaustion was raised when the litigation was at an advanced state). Similarly, in *Ouellette v. Maine State Prison*, 2006 WL 173639 (D.Me., Jan. 23, 2006), *aff'd*, 2006 WL 348315 (D.Me., Feb. 14, 2006), where the plaintiff did not complete exhaustion because of actions by grievance staff suggesting no further remedies were available to him, the court stated: "Given that the spirit of § 1997e(a) is to allow the correctional institution an opportunity to address allegations of civil rights abuses, if the defendants wish to file a motion to stay this action to allow the parties to funnel Ouellette's grievance through the second and third stages of the grievance procedure, such a request would deserve consideration." *Id.*, *4; *see also* Nieves v. Ortiz, 2007 WL 1791256, *6 (D.N.J., June 19, 2007) (staying defendants' motion for summary judgment pending exhaustion, no reference to contrary case law).

[213]In *Jones v. Bock*, 549 U.S. 199, 214–17, 127 S. Ct. 910 (2007), the Supreme Court held that the PLRA did not overturn usual litigation practices except to the extent it said so. The discretion to grant a stay is part of usual litigation practice. Congress did not say anything in the PLRA about stays pending exhaustion—it just removed the prior provision requiring a stay when a court thought exhaustion should be required—so it can be argued that courts retain their discretion in this regard. *See* Cruz v. Jordan, 80 F. Supp. 2d 109, 124 (S.D.N.Y. 1999) ("There is simply no evidence that Congress intended by Section 1997e(a) to remove every aspect of the district court's traditional equity jurisdiction."). Even if a court was persuaded by this argument, we would expect it would only grant a stay if the prisoner had a pretty good reason for not having exhausted before filing, as in the cases in the previous footnote.

[214]Gallagher v. Shelton, 587 F.3d 1063, 1068 (10th Cir. 2009); Bryant v. Rich, 530 F.3d 1368, 1379 (11th Cir. 2008), *cert. denied*, 129 S.Ct. 733 (2008); O'Guinn v. Lovelock Correctional Center, 502 F.3d 1056, 1059 (9th Cir. 2007); Boyd v. Corr. Corp. of Am.,

---

380 F.3d 989, 994 (6th Cir. 2004), *cert. denied*, 544 U.S. 920 (2005).

There are some variations on this idea. Some courts have held that dismissal may be with prejudice if it is clear that you cannot at that point exhaust and then re-file. Berry v. Kerik, 366 F.3d 85, 87–88 (2d Cir. 2004); Steele v. Federal Bureau of Prisons, 355 F.3d 1204, 1213 (10th Cir. 2003). However, another federal appeals court has held (correctly, in our view) that all dismissals for non-exhaustion should be without prejudice, since states may allow litigants to cure failure to exhaust, or plaintiffs may be able to proceed without exhaustion in state court, and defenses to a new suit should be addressed directly in that suit. Ford v. Johnson, 362 F.3d 395, 401 (7th Cir. 2004).

[215]Regan v. Frank, 2007 WL 106537, *4–5 (D.Haw., Jan. 9, 2007).

[216]*See* § D.6 of this chapter for more discussion of time limits.

[217]Or it may not be. There may be "tolling" provisions of state law that suspend the operation of the statute of limitations when you bring a suit, it is dismissed, and you have to re-file it. *See* § D.6 of this chapter for more information about tolling provisions.

[218]Underwood v. Wilson, 151 F.3d 292, 296 (5th Cir. 1998). At least one district court has held that this disposition is appropriate only if the whole case is not exhausted. Cantoral v. Dretke, 2005 WL 2297222, *4 (E.D.Tex., Sept. 19, 2005).

[219]*See* Barnes v. Brownlow, 2008 WL 2704868, *3 (E.D.Tex., July 7, 2008); McGrew v. Teer, 2008 WL 2277818, *2 (M.D.La., June 3, 2008); Johns v. Edwards, 2007 WL 1958962, *3 (E.D.La., June 28, 2007) (all following *Underwood* after the decision in *Jones*).

[220]Jones v. Bock, 549 U.S. 199, 220–21, 224, 127 S. Ct. 910 (2007).

why the PLRA should require abandonment of the usual practice under the *in forma pauperis* statutes, which does not restrict prisoners' ability to re-file dismissed cases, since the PLRA doesn't say anything about that subject.

Courts have not settled whether you must pay a second filing fee if your case is dismissed for non-exhaustion and you then are able to exhaust and refile it. The only federal appeals court to consider the question held that a plaintiff need not pay a new filing fee when re-filing a claim that was previously dismissed for non-exhaustion.[221] Other courts have generally said that a new case must be filed after a dismissal for non-exhaustion, rather than reopening the dismissed case.[222] Ordinarily this would require a new filing fee. However, in most cases you should not be charged a "strike" for a dismissal for non-exhaustion unless the failure to exhaust was apparent on the face of the complaint.[223]

The exhaustion provision of the PLRA applies to any case brought by "a prisoner confined in any jail, prison, or other correctional facility" about prison conditions under federal law.[224] A case is "brought by a prisoner" if the plaintiff is a prisoner at the time of filing; if not, the plaintiff need

not have exhausted.[225] PLRA exhaustion does not apply to petitions for habeas corpus,[226] though habeas has its own exhaustion requirement.[227] A motion to enforce an order or to obtain further relief in a pre-existing case is not a new "action" and does not require PLRA exhaustion.[228]

The PLRA exhaustion requirement applies to § 1983 actions filed in state court, including those later removed to federal court.[229] State court actions *not* brought under § 1983, or other federal law, such as tort suits or administrative law proceedings, may have their own exhaustion requirements, which may or may not be similar to the PLRA provision.[230] Actions or claims in federal court that are based

---

[221]Owens v. Keeling, 461 F.3d 763, 772–74 (6th Cir. 2006). The court explained that the filing fee is required of parties "instituting" a civil action, 28 U.S.C. § 1914(a), and that re-filing a now-exhausted claim is not "instituting" suit but merely following the court-prescribed procedure for curing the initial complaint's deficiency. *Accord*, Goodson v. Cortney, 2006 WL 3314537, *1 (D. Kan., Oct. 24, 2006) (adopting *Owens* holding).

[222]*See* Williams v. Ramirez, 2006 WL 2475339, *2 (E.D.Cal., Aug. 28, 2006) (advising plaintiff that a new post-exhaustion complaint should not bear the docket number of the dismissed action; a new *in forma pauperis* application is required); Baggett v. Smith, 2006 WL 1851221, *1 (W.D.Mich., June 29, 2006); Okoro v. Krueger, 2006 WL 1494967, *1–2 (E.D.Mich., May 30, 2006).

[223]*See* § B.1 of this chapter, nn.111–118, concerning this issue.

[224]42 U.S.C. § 1997e(a).

The statute does not apply to any cases still pending that were filed before the PLRA was enacted. Scott v. Coughlin, 344 F.3d 282, 290 (2d Cir. 2003); Salahuddin v. Mead, 174 F.3d 271, 274 (2d Cir. 1999); Tyree v. Weld, 2010 WL 145882, *9 n.11 (D.Mass., Jan. 11, 2010); *see* Caruso v. Zenon, 2005 WL 5957978, *7–8 (D.Colo., July 25, 2005) (holding that filing of amended complaint in pre-PLRA case does not require exhaustion where it merely clarifies already filed allegations). It does apply to cases filed after enactment of the PLRA even if the allegations are about events before the PLRA. White v. McGinnis, 131 F.3d 593, 595 (6th Cir. 1997); Garrett v. Hawk, 127 F.3d 1263, 1266 (10th Cir. 1998). However, if the time limit on the administrative remedy had passed when the exhaustion requirement was enacted, so the prisoner never had a chance to comply with it, exhaustion is not required. Wyatt v. Leonard, 193 F.3d 876, 879 (6th Cir. 1999). A post-PLRA amended complaint in a pre-PLRA case need not have been exhausted if it merely clarifies existing allegations, but if it adds new claims, those claims must be exhausted. Shariff v. Coombe, 655 F.Supp.2d 274, 284 (S.D.N.Y. 2009). A post-PLRA motion to enforce a judgment in a pre-PLRA case need not be exhausted. Clarkson v. Coughlin, 2006 WL 587345, *3 (S.D.N.Y., Mar. 10, 2006).

[225]*See* § A of this chapter, nn.2–21, for discussion of the "brought by a prisoner" requirement.

[226]Carmona v. U.S. Bureau of Prisons, 243 F.3d 629, 632–34 (2d Cir. 2001); Lewis v. Whitehead, 2006 WL 3359639, *2 (D.S.D., Nov. 15, 2006); Monahan v. Winn, 276 F. Supp. 2d 196, 204 (D. Mass. 2003).

[227]The habeas exhaustion requirement is discussed in Ch. 8, § H.1. It requires state prisoners to exhaust *judicial* remedies. Federal prisoners challenging administrative decisions must exhaust administrative remedies, and the habeas exhaustion requirement is slightly different from the PLRA exhaustion requirement, allowing certain exceptions not permitted under the PLRA. *See* U.S. v. McGriff, 468 F. Supp. 2d 445, 447 (E.D.N.Y. 2007) (noting that habeas exhaustion requirement can be dispensed with on grounds of futility or prevention of irreparable harm, unlike the PLRA requirement); Putnam v. Winn, 441 F. Supp. 2d 253, 255–56 (D.Mass. 2006) (noting that habeas exhaustion could be waived by court); Perez v. Zenk, 2005 WL 990696, *2 (E.D.N.Y., Apr. 11, 2005).

[228]Coleman v. Schwarzenegger, 2008 WL 4813371, *2 (E.D.Cal., Nov. 3, 2008); Ayyad v. Gonzales, 2008 WL 2955964, *2 (D.Colo., July 31, 2008); Arce v. O'Connell, 427 F. Supp. 2d 435, 440–41 (S.D.N.Y. 2006); Clarkson v. Coughlin, 2006 WL 587345, *3 (S.D.N.Y., Mar. 10, 2006); *compare* Smith v. Federal Bureau of Prisons, 300 F.3d 721, 723 (6th Cir. 2002) (separate action to enforce a settlement agreement requires PLRA exhaustion, even though the settlement agreement itself includes a different exhaustion requirement).

[229]*See* Johnson v. State of La. *ex rel.* Dep't of Public Safety & Corr., 468 F.3d 278, 280 (5th Cir. 2006) ("The PLRA's exhaustion requirement applies to all Section 1983 claims regardless of whether the inmate files his claim in state or federal court."); Blakely v. Ozmint, 2006 WL 2850545, *2 (D.S.C., Sept. 29, 2006) (applying exhaustion requirement in § 1983 action removed from state court based on federal question); King v. Peoples, 1998 WL 191839 (OhioCt.App. Mar. 31, 1998) (applying PLRA's exhaustion requirement to § 1983 claim brought in Ohio state court); Knowlin v. Dir., 570 N.W.2d 253, 1997 WL 528225 (Wis.Ct.App., Aug. 28, 1997) (unpublished) (applying PLRA's exhaustion requirements to § 1983 claim brought in Wisconsin state court).

[230]Some states have enacted statutes with exhaustion requirements modelled on the PLRA. *See, e.g.,* Mich. Compiled Law § 600.5503. Many states and municipalities have "notice of claim" rules that require you to file a statement of your claim with a government agency before you can file a tort suit; these must often be filed within short time periods, such as 90 days. Administrative law challenges to government actions generally

on state law need not satisfy the PLRA exhaustion requirement, but they must satisfy any state law exhaustion requirement.[231]

Most courts have held that there is no emergency exception to the exhaustion requirement.[232] There are a few decisions that have allowed cases to go forward without exhaustion to avoid irreparable harm,[233] but they mostly do

not provide much legal justification for bypassing the exhaustion requirement. The strongest basis for requesting court intervention without waiting for exhaustion is a decision stating that there is no irreparable harm exception, but that under the PLRA, courts retain their traditional equitable discretion to grant temporary relief to maintain the status quo *pending* exhaustion.[234] We have found only one instance of a prisoner actually obtaining relief on that basis,[235] but the argument may have been strengthened by the recent Supreme Court decision which held that unless the PLRA explicitly says so, it does not overturn the usual practices of litigation,[236] which arguably include the discretion to grant relief pending exhaustion. This argument is

---

require exhaustion of administrative remedies. *See* Ch. 8, § K, on exhaustion generally.

[231]Artis-Bey v. District of Columbia, 884 A.2d 626, 631 (D.C. 2005); Shaheed Muhammad v. Dipaolo, 393 F. Supp. 2d 80, 92 n.5 (D.Mass. 2005); Torres v. Corrections Corp. of America, 372 F. Supp. 2d 1258, 1262 (N.D.Okla. 2005).

[232]Horacek v. Caruso, 2009 WL 125398, *3 (W.D.Mich., Jan. 15, 2009); Sanders v. Norris, 2008 WL 2926198, *2 n.8 (E.D.Ark., July 24, 2008) ("Recognizing an exception for 'urgent medical needs' would defeat the purpose of the exhaustion requirement, which is to give prison officials the first opportunity to promptly remedy a situation within the prison system."); Shendock v. Green Rock Correctional Center, 2008 WL 2038794, *1–2 (W.D.Va., May 12, 2008) (prisoner must pursue grievance even if the harm is done before exhaustion can be completed); Griffin v. Samuels, 2008 WL 961241, *3 (D.N.J., Apr. 8, 2008); Cochran v. Caruso, 2008 WL 397597, *3 (W.D.Mich., Feb. 11, 2008) (plaintiff's allegation of urgent need for medical intervention did not justify failure to exhaust before filing); Rendelman v. Galley, 2007 WL 2900460, *2 (D.Md., Feb. 15, 2007) (dismissing despite plaintiff's claim of imminent danger and request for a "protective order" pending exhaustion), *aff'd*, 230 Fed.Appx. 314 (4th Cir. 2007) (unpublished); Williams v. CDCR, 2007 WL 2384510, *4 (E.D.Cal., Aug. 17, 2007) ("The presence of exigent circumstances does not relieve a plaintiff from fulfilling this requirement."), *report and recommendation adopted*, 2007 WL 2793117 (E.D.Cal., Sept. 26, 2007); Ford v. Smith, 2007 WL 1192298, *2 (E.D.Tex., Apr. 23, 2007) (dismissing where plaintiff said his safety was in danger and he sought a continuance until exhaustion was completed); Patterson v. La. Corr. Servs., Inc., 2006 WL 3845017, *6 (W.D.La., Oct. 20, 2006); Dartson v. Kastner, 2006 WL 3702634, *2 (E.D.Tex., Dec. 13, 2006); Aburomi v. U.S., 2006 WL 2990362, *1 (D.N.J., Oct. 17, 2006) ("It is understandable that Plaintiff would want immediate treatment for a perceived recurrence of cancer, but the administrative remedy program is mandatory regardless of the nature of the relief sought."); Bovarie v. Giurbino, 421 F. Supp. 2d 1309, 1314 (S.D.Cal. 2006); Jones v. Oaks Corr. Facility Health Servs., 2005 WL 3312562, *2 (W.D.Mich., Dec. 7, 2005); Calderon v. Anderson, 2005 WL 2277398, *5 (S.D.W.Va., Sept. 19, 2005); Drabovskiy v. U.S., 2005 WL 1322550, *2 (E.D.Ky., June 2, 2005); Joseph v. Jocson, 2004 WL 2203298, *1 (D.Or., Sept. 29, 2004); Kane v. Winn, 319 F. Supp. 2d 162, 223 (D.Mass. 2004) (rejecting "grave harm" argument while noting that the administrative process takes less than four months and the plaintiff was complaining about lack of treatment for a slowly progressing case of Hepatitis C); *see also* Jones v. Sandy, 2006 WL 355136, *10 & n.3 (E.D.Cal., Feb. 14, 2006) (stating there is no emergency exception to exhaustion, but the court might reconsider that conclusion if it learned there was no emergency grievance procedure), *report and recommendation adopted*, 2006 WL 708346 (E.D.Cal., Mar. 20, 2006).

[233]*See* Evans v. Saar, 412 F. Supp. 2d 519, 527 (D.Md. 2006) (declining to dismiss for non-exhaustion, given "shortness of time," where plaintiff challenged the protocol for his impending execution

and the grievance process was not complete); Howard v. Ashcroft, 248 F. Supp. 2d 518, 533–34 (M.D.La. 2003) (holding that prisoner fighting transfer from community corrections to a prison need not exhaust where appeal would take months and prison officials wanted to transfer her despite any pending appeal); Ferguson v. Ashcroft, 248 F. Supp. 2d 547, 563–64 (M.D.La. 2003) (same as *Howard*); Borgetti v. Bureau of Prisons, 2003 WL 743936, *2 n.2 (N.D.Ill., Feb. 14, 2003) (holding that "the court's jurisdiction is secure" to decide a case in which the prisoner sought immediate injunctive relief and exhaustion would almost certainly take longer than the remainder of his sentence). One court has said that these decisions really reflect that the claims would be moot before exhaustion was completed, so there was no remedy actually available. Ung v. Lappin, 2007 WL 5465992, *4 (W.D.Wis., Jan. 29, 2007), *reconsideration denied*, 2007 WL 5490150 (W.D.Wis., Mar. 12, 2007).

The Second Circuit once said the question was open whether there was an irreparable harm exception to PLRA exhaustion. *See* Marvin v. Goord, 255 F.3d 40, 43 (2d Cir. 2001). However, no lower court has granted relief based on that statement, and courts have questioned whether it is consistent with Supreme Court decisions. *See* Rivera v. Pataki, 2003 WL 21511939, *6 (S.D.N.Y., July 1, 2003).

[234]Jackson v. District of Columbia, 254 F.3d 262, 267–68 (D.C. Cir. 2001).

[235]Stringham v. Bick, 2008 WL 4145473, *4 (E.D.Cal., Sept. 3, 2008) (noting preliminary injunction requiring prisoner to be housed consistently with his medical condition), *report and recommendation adopted*, 2008 WL 4472954 (E.D.Cal., Sept. 30, 2008). In another case, the court indicated relief appeared warranted, and jail officials hastily addressed the problem, so relief was not necessary. Tvelia v. Dep't of Corr., 2004 WL 298100, *2 (D.N.H. Feb. 13, 2004).

Several courts have rejected the idea of granting relief pending exhaustion, but they did not seem to be aware of the *Jackson* decision. *See* Blain v. Bassett, 2007 WL 4190937, *2 (W.D.Va., Nov. 21, 2007) (refusing to direct delay of new prison rule pending plaintiff's completion of exhaustion, dismissing action; *Jackson* not cited); McCauley v. Bassett, 2007 WL 4125375, *2 (W.D.Va., Nov. 20, 2007) (same); Glick v. Montana Dep't of Corrections, 2007 WL 2359776, *2 (D.Mont., Aug. 14, 2007) (dismissing for non-exhaustion, ignoring plaintiff's claim that he was seeking preliminary relief to avoid irreparable harm pending exhaustion; *Jackson* not cited).

[236]Jones v. Bock, 549 U.S. 199, 214–17, 220–22, 127 S. Ct. 910 (2007). The Court specifically referred to the usual practice under the Federal Rules of Civil Procedure. Injunctions including

most likely to succeed where you have a very strong case of irreparable harm if you do not get temporary relief, and if you are arguing for relief "pending" exhaustion, you had better have the grievance process under way when you make that argument.[237]

1. What Is Exhaustion?

Exhaustion under the PLRA means "proper exhaustion," *i.e.*, "compliance with an agency's deadlines and other critical procedural rules."[238] Exhaustion also means taking your complaint all the way to the top of the internal complaint process that applies to your problem, whatever that process may be (usually the grievance system). You must take every appeal that is available to you,[239] and finish the process *before* you bring the suit.[240] (For exhaustion purposes, most courts say that the date you are considered to have brought suit is the date when the complaint is first tendered to the clerk's office, not when the formalities of filing and the processing of any *in forma pauperis* application are completed.[241])

Some courts have taken this idea to an extreme and have held that prisoners cannot amend their complaints to add additional claims unless the new claims were exhausted

___

preliminary injunctions are addressed in Rule 65 of the Federal Rules.

[237]In *Stringham v. Bick*, where relief pending exhaustion was granted, the court said that when exhaustion is completed, the case must be dismissed and re-filed, since it was initially filed before exhaustion. 2008 WL 4145473, *9. This seems to us like an absurd waste of effort that serves no useful purpose. However, if the plaintiff does *not* complete exhaustion after obtaining relief, it seems likely that the case will be dismissed for non-exhaustion and the plaintiff will be barred from reinstating the litigation and will lose the relief previously granted. So be sure you finish the job!

[238]Woodford v. Ngo, 548 U.S. 81, 90–91, 126 S. Ct. 2378 (2006). The "proper exhaustion" rule is discussed further in § D.5 of this chapter.

[239]See Wright v. Hollingsworth, 260 F.3d 357, 358 (5th Cir. 2001); White v. McGinnis, 131 F.3d 593, 595 (6th Cir. 1997) (affirming dismissal for failing to appeal denial of grievance); Lopez v. Smiley, 2003 WL 22217109, *2 (D.Conn., Sept. 22, 2003) (holding that a prisoner who appealed, but whose appeal was not received and was told it was too late to file another, had exhausted).

[240]Johnson v. Jones, 340 F.3d 624, 627–28 (8th Cir. 2003); Neal v. Goord, 267 F.3d 116, 122 (2d Cir. 2001). *But see* Plaster v. Kneal, 2008 WL 4090790, *3–4 (M.D.Pa., Aug. 29, 2008) (holding plaintiff exhausted where his grievance was filed after the initial complaint but before the amended complaint).

[241]See Vaden v. Summerhill, 449 F.3d 1047, 1050–51 (9th Cir. 2006); Ford v. Johnson, 362 F.3d 395, 399–400 (7th Cir. 2004); Gillet v. Anderson, 577 F. Supp. 2d 828, 833–34 (W.D.La., Aug. 3, 2008) (case was "brought" for exhaustion purposes when complaint was first submitted, even though it was returned to plaintiff for submission on a required form). *Contra*, Ellis v. Guarino, 2004 WL 1879834, *6 (S.D.N.Y., Aug. 24, 2004) (holding the plaintiff exhausted where the final step in the grievance process took place during the 11 months between submission of the complaint and the completion of processing in the *pro se* office; citing contrary cases).

before the initial complaint was filed.[242] Most courts, however, have said that as long as the new issues are exhausted before you try to add them to the case, you can amend your complaint to add them.[243] That view appears correct. Suppose a prisoner exhausts claim A, then files suit about it, and then exhausts claim B, and then amends his complaint to add claim B. He has not at any point brought an action without exhaustion, which is what § 1997e(a) forbids. That view is also consistent with the Supreme Court's recent holding that the PLRA does not require deviating from ordinary federal procedural practice unless it says so explicitly.[244] The free amendment of complaints is part of ordinary federal procedural practice.[245]

Once the deadline for final decision of your last appeal has passed, you can file suit.[246] (If a prisoner files suit after

___

[242]See, e.g., Harbin-Bey v. Rutter, 420 F.3d 571, 580 (6th Cir. 2005) (holding that claims post-dating the original complaint and exhausted after its filing could not be added); *accord*, Sua v. Espinda, 2010 WL 184314, *2 (D.Haw., Jan. 19, 2010); Ellenburg v. Mahoney, 2008 WL 1992162, *5 (D.Mont., May 7, 2008); Chalif v. Spitzer, 2008 WL 1848650, *13 (N.D.N.Y., Apr. 23, 2008); Holley v. Cal. Dep't of Corr., 2006 WL 1581907, *2 (E.D.Cal., June 6, 2006) (holding that claims dismissed for non-exhaustion cannot be reinstated by amendment after exhaustion), *report and recommendation adopted*, 2006 WL 1991837 (E.D.Cal., July 14, 2006); Coltar v. Jacinto, 2007 WL 184808, *4 (E.D.Cal., Jan. 19, 2007).

[243]See Cannon v. Washington, 418 F.3d 714, 719–20 (7th Cir. 2005) (rejecting defendants' argument that new claims could not be added by amendment even if they had been exhausted); Barnes v. Briley, 420 F.3d 673, 677–78 (7th Cir. 2005); Lawson v. McDonough, 2006 WL 3844474, *22 (N.D.Fla., Dec. 27, 2006); Ajaj v. U.S., 2006 WL 1305198, *7 (D.Colo., May 11, 2006); Anthony Smith v. Worsham, 2005 WL 2239925, *3–4 (D.Colo. Sept. 14, 2005); Amador v. Superintendents of Dep't. of Corr. Servs., 2005 WL 2234050, *8 n.9 (S.D.N.Y., Sept. 13, 2005); Carter v. Wright, 211 F.R.D. 549, 551 (E.D.Mich. 2003); Madison v. Mazzuca, 2004 WL 3037730, *14 (S.D.N.Y. Dec. 30, 2004); Cline v. Fox, 266 F. Supp. 2d 489, 493 (N.D.W.Va. 2003), *reconsideration granted*, 282 F. Supp. 2d 490 (N.D.W.Va. 2003) (dismissing unexhausted claim, then allowing it to be reinstated after exhaustion).

[244]Jones v. Bock, 549 U.S. 199, 214–17, 220–22, 127 S. Ct. 910 (2007) concerning situations that § 1997e(a) does not explicitly address.

Some of the cases barring amendment to add claims say that the terms of Rule 15, Fed.R.Civ.P., concerning amendment of complaints cannot prevail over the substantive requirements of § 1997e(a). *See, e.g.*, Jeffery v. Bennge, 2008 WL 2131562, *5 (E.D.Cal., May 21, 2008), *report and recommendation adopted*, 2008 WL 2543954 (E.D.Cal., June 23, 2008). That is just the opposite of what *Jones v. Bock* held.

[245]See Fed. R. Civ. P. Rule 15(a) (providing for amendments to complaints); *see also* Ch. 10, § J, concerning amending complaints.

[246]Whitington v. Ortiz, 472 F.3d 804, 807–08 (10th Cir. 2007); Powe v. Ennis, 177 F.3d 393, 394 (5th Cir. 1999) ("A prisoner's administrative remedies are deemed exhausted when a valid grievance has been filed and the state's time for responding thereto has expired."); Williams v. Cornell Corrections of Georgia, 2007 WL 2317633, *3 (S.D.Ga., Aug. 10, 2007) (noting grievance rules required nothing more of prisoner than filing the final appeal and

the time limit for decision has passed, and then grievance authorities issue a late decision, the prisoner has exhausted.[247]) It is not clear how long you have to wait if the system has no deadline for deciding your final appeal.[248]

A number of decisions have said that if you don't get a response to your initial grievance, you have exhausted.[249] However, other courts have said that if the grievance system allows you to treat a non-response as a denial of your grievance and appeal it, you must do so.[250] When in doubt, try to

---

waiting 90 days); Mattress v. Taylor, 487 F. Supp. 2d 665, 670–62 (D.S.C. 2007) (holding plaintiff had exhausted where the deadline for final decision was 180 days and the plaintiff had waited 11 months to file); Jones v. DeTella, 12 F. Supp. 2d 824, 826 (N.D.Ill. 1998); Barry v. Ratelle, 985 F. Supp. 1235, 1238 (S.D.Cal. 1997).

[247]Magee v. Chavez, 2008 WL 2283133, *3 (E.D.Cal., May 30, 2008), *report and recommendaton vacated on other grounds*, 2008 WL 2858198 (E.D.Cal., July 24, 2008); Curtis v. Buckley, 2008 WL 1970812, *2 (E.D.Cal., May 2, 2008); Stornes v. Guild, 2008 WL 828790, *4–5 (W.D.Mich., Mar. 27, 2008); Eberle v. Wilkinson, 2007 WL 1666229, *1–2 (S.D.Ohio, June 4, 2007); DeJesus v. Williams, 2007 WL 1201599, *3 (D.Del., Apr. 23, 2007) (declining to dismiss for non-exhaustion where plaintiff's grievance took seven months to get to the medical unit and he had filed suit before it was decided); Arreola v. Hickman, 2006 WL 2590890, *2 (E.D.Cal., Sept. 8, 2006); Christian v. Goord, 2006 WL 1459805, *6 (N.D.N.Y., May 22, 2006); Thompson v. Koneny, 2005 WL 1378832, *5 (E.D.Mich., May 4, 2005); Dimick v. Baruffo, 2003 WL 660826, *4 (S.D.N.Y., Feb. 28, 2003); *see* Cooper v. Beard, 2007 WL 1959300, *5 (M.D.Pa., July 2, 2007) (where Request for Religious Accommodation was a prerequisite for a grievance, and plaintiff did not get a timely response and went forward with a grievance before receiving a late response, he exhausted); Daker v. Ferrero, 2004 WL 5459957, *2 (N.D.Ga., Nov. 24, 2004) (prisoner who was prevented from appealing lack of decision at intermediate stage, filed suit, and was later afforded an opportunity to appeal had exhausted when he was prevented from appealing). *But see* Morris v. McGrath, 2006 WL 2228944, *4 (N.D.Cal., July 31, 2006) (dismissing for non-exhaustion where the final grievance decision was late, but the authorities had been in touch with the plaintiff for more information and he knew they were working on his grievance). In *Alex v. Stalder*, 2007 WL 4919781 (W.D.La., Dec. 3, 2007), the plaintiff did not receive a timely decision, filed suit, and then received a notice that grievance officials had given themselves more time. The court held that the plaintiff should have dismissed his complaint without prejudice and refiled it after the process was completed. The court said: "This may seem a bit harsh, considering the circumstances, but this court is besieged with unexhausted prisoner complaints." 2007 WL 4919781, *4.

[248]*See* Olmsted v. Cooney, 2005 WL 233817, *2 (D.Or., Jan. 31, 2005) (holding that prisoner who waited seven weeks after filing last appeal did not fail to exhaust); Thompson v. Koneny, 2005 WL 1378832, *5 (E.D.Mich., May 4, 2005) (holding that a decision delayed six and a half months was not "timely" and case could not be dismissed for non-exhaustion where prisoner filed after five and a half months); McNeal v. Cook County Sheriff's Dep't, 282 F. Supp. 2d 865, 868 n.3 (N.D.Ill. 2003) (holding 11 months is long enough to wait, citing cases holding that seven months is long enough and one month is not). However, the Seventh Circuit said, in connection with a grievance system that called for appeal decisions within 60 days "whenever possible," that the remedy did not become "unavailable" and allow the prisoner to bring suit because it took six months to get a decision. "Even six months is prompt compared with the time often required to exhaust appellate remedies from a conviction." Ford v. Johnson, 362 F.3d 395, 400 (7th Cir. 2004). We think this comparison is inappropriate, since administrative remedies are supposed to be faster than judicial ones.

[249]*See, e.g.*, Brengettcy v. Horton, 423 F.3d 674, 682 (7th Cir. 2005) (holding prisoner who received no decision had exhausted where the grievance policy did not say what to do absent a decision); Boyd v. Corr. Corp. of Am., 380 F.3d 989, 996 (6th Cir. 2004) (holding that "administrative remedies are exhausted when prison officials fail to timely respond to a properly filed grievance," though distinguishing a case where the prisoner could proceed without a decision); Lewis v. Washington, 300 F.3d 829, 833 (7th Cir. 2003) (non-response made remedy unavailable); Hill v. Truelove, 2010 WL 56144, *10 (W.D.Okla., Jan. 6, 2010); Hambrick v. Morton, 2009 WL 1759564, *1, 3 (S.D.Ga., June 19, 2009) (allegation that prisoner whose grievance remained pending after a year and who was denied an appeal form sufficiently alleged exhaustion of available remedies); Moro v. Winsor, 2008 WL 718687, *4–5 (S.D.Ill., Mar. 14, 2008) (holding remedy unavailable to prisoner whose appeal was untimely because he could not get a timely answer at the first level in a system that required a response in order to appeal); Cooper v. Rothstein, 2007 WL 1452989, *2 (N.D.Ill., May 17, 2007) (following *Brengettcy*); Woulard v. Food Service, 294 F. Supp. 2d 596, 602 (D.Del., 2003); Green v. Hartman, 2006 WL 2699336, *3 (N.D.Ill., Sept. 18, 2006) (refusing to dismiss where plaintiff received no decision from which he could appeal and waited 60 days to file though the decision deadline was 30 days); Brookins v. Vogel, 2006 WL 3437482, *3 (E.D.Cal. Nov. 28, 2006) (holding that a prisoner who filed a grievance, got no response, and was told it had never been received, and whose subsequent attempts were rejected as untimely, had exhausted because he was "prevented from complying with the exhaustion requirement"); Palmer v. Goss, 2003 WL 22327110, *5 (S.D.N.Y., Oct. 10, 2003) (prisoner who filed a grievance, but did not pursue it when he learned that the crucial evidence had been destroyed, had made a sufficiently reasonable attempt to exhaust), *reconsideration denied*, 2003 WL 22519446 (S.D.N.Y., Nov. 5, 2003), *aff'd on other grounds*, 364 F.3d 60 (2d Cir. 2004); Lane v. Doan, 207 F. Supp. 2d 212 (W.D.N.Y. 2003) (prisoner who made "reasonable attempts" to file and prosecute grievances, but had many of his grievances and inquiries ignored, had exhausted); Sweet v. Wende Corr. Facility, 253 F. Supp. 2d 492, 495 (W.D.N.Y. 2003); Martin v. Snyder, 2002 WL 484911, *3 (N.D.Ill., Mar. 28, 2002) (rejecting argument that plaintiff "should have filed even more grievances about defendants' failure to respond"); Armstrong v. Drahos, 2002 WL 187502, *1 (N.D.Ill., Feb. 6, 2002) ("If [plaintiff] received no response, there was nothing to appeal.").

[250]*See* Turner v. Burnside, 541 F.3d 1077, 1084–85 (11th Cir. 2008) (where prisoner alleged that the warden tore up his grievance, he would have been obliged to file an appeal from the lack of a decision, except that the warden also threatened him); Cox v. Mayer, 332 F.3d 422, 425 n.2 (6th Cir. 2003); Williams v. Lewis, 2008 WL 860113, *3 (N.D.Cal., Mar 28, 2008) (prisoner who got no response at the "informal level" did not exhaust because he failed to ask the Appeals Coordinator to waive the informal level requirement as the rules permitted); Clarke v. Thornton, 515 F. Supp. 2d 435, 438–41 (S.D.N.Y. 2007); Williams v. Arpaio, 2007 WL 2903025, *3 (D.Ariz., Sept. 28, 2007); Walker v. Seal, 2007 WL 1169364, *2 (E.D.La., Apr. 19, 2007); Rockwell ex rel. Gill v. State

appeal, even if officials have failed to respond. Prison officials cannot keep you out of court by simply ignoring your grievances,[251] but once you bring suit, they may argue that you did not try hard enough to exhaust.

Courts have said that if you *win* your grievance before the final stage and don't appeal, you have exhausted, since it makes no sense to appeal if you have won.[252] That is very

sensible, but it may be wisest not to rely on it, because courts have also held that if you don't win all possible relief in the grievance, you haven't exhausted all available remedies.[253] In hindsight, prison officials and their lawyers will always be

---

Oregon, 2007 WL 1039521, *4 (D.Or., Apr. 3, 2007) (noting rules permitted filing a new grievance about the lack of response to an earlier grievance); Martinez v. Dr. Williams R., 186 F. Supp 2d 353, 357 (S.D.N.Y. 2002); Smith v. Stubblefield, 30 F. Supp. 2d 1168, 1174 (E.D.Mo. 1998).

[251]*See* Duke v. Hardin County, 2008 WL 918136, *2 (W.D.Ky., Mar. 31, 2008) (holding prisoner exhausted where he received a response stating the matter had been investigated and turned over to the Jailer, and the Jailer never responded); Levi v. Briley, 2006 WL 2161788, *3 (N.D. Ill., July 28, 2006) (declining to dismiss where the prisoner had waited two years for a final decision); Brown v. Koenigsmann, 2003 WL 22232884, *4 (S.D.N.Y., Sept. 29, 2003); Casarez v. Mars, 2003 WL 21369255, *6 (E.D.Mich., June 11, 2003); John v. N.Y.C. Dep't of Corr., 183 F. Supp. 2d 619, 625 (S.D.N.Y. 2002) (rejecting argument that after three years, prisoner must continue waiting for a decision); *see* Maraglia v. Maloney, 499 F. Supp. 2d 93, 97 (D.Mass. 2007) (holding that prisoner was not required to file a grievance about the failure to respond to a grievance absent a regulation to that effect). In *Dole v. Chandler*, 438 F.3d 804, 811–12 (7th Cir. 2006), the court held a prisoner had exhausted when he did everything necessary to exhaust but his grievance simply disappeared, and he received no instructions as to what if anything to do about it. *Accord*, Wilkerson v. Jenkins, 2010 WL 384737, *3 (D.Md., Jan. 27, 2010) (similar to *Dole*); Franklin v. Butler, 2008 WL 4078797, *3 (E.D.Cal., Aug. 29, 2008) (noting rules contained no instructions what to do when a grievance was apparently lost), *report and recommendation adopted*, 2008 WL 4601081 (E.D.Cal., Oct. 15, 2008).

[252]*See* Brown v. Valoff, 422 F.3d 926, 935 (9th Cir. 2005) (holding "a prisoner need not press on to exhaust further levels of review once he has either received all 'available' remedies at an intermediate level of review or been reliably informed by an administrator that no remedies are available"); Abney v. McGinnis, 380 F.3d 663, 669 (2d Cir. 2004) (holding a prisoner who repeatedly got favorable decisions that later were not carried out had exhausted despite failure to appeal the favorable decisions); Patch v. Arpaio, 2010 WL 432354, *7-10 (D.Ariz., Feb. 2, 2010) (plaintiff who complained of spoiled food exhausted where jail authorities apologized, replaced the food, and gave instructions to prevent any recurrence); Barrett v. Maricopa County Sheriff's Office, 2010 WL 46786, *4-5 (D.Ariz., Jan. 4, 2010) (prisoner who got his medication, which was all he sought, through the pre-grievance informal process had exhausted); Henderson v. Moore, 2008 WL 2704674, *4 (S.D.Tex., July 2, 2008); Henderson v. Bettus, 2008 WL 899251, *4 (M.D.Fla., Mar. 31, 2008) (holding favorable decision completed exhaustion where policy did not require appealing a grievance that was satisfactorily resolved); Redden v. Kearney, 2008 WL 440370, *7-8 (D.Del., Feb. 15, 2008) (plaintiff who received the relief sought exhausted; grievance rules said resolution at the first level ends the grievance process); Lay v. Hall, 2007 WL 137155, *6 (E.D.Cal., Jan. 17, 2007) (holding that a prisoner who grieved the failure to provide surgery and got a decision stating that a request for surgery had been made as a result sufficed to exhaust); Mocnik v. Williams,

2006 WL 3538989, *5 (W.D.Wis., Dec. 6, 2006) (holding prisoner who got a grievance response that his complaint would be investigated had exhausted where prison officials admitted there was no more relief he could get); Bolton v. U.S., 347 F. Supp. 2d 1218, 1220 (N.D.Fla. 2004) (holding a prisoner exhausted when she complained informally, the first step of the Federal Bureau of Prisons remedy, and the offending officer resigned when confronted; "When a prisoner wins in the administrative process, he or she need not continue to appeal the favorable ruling."); Cotton v. Kingston, 2004 WL 2325053, *4 (W.D.Wis., Sept. 4, 2004) (holding a favorable decision need not be appealed unless grievance policy explicitly requires it); Gibson v. Brooks, 335 F. Supp. 2d 325, 327, 333 (D.Conn. Sept. 16, 2004) (holding that a prisoner who said he complained about an assault he had given warning about, and received an apology, sufficiently alleged a favorable informal resolution); Sulton v. Wright, 265 F. Supp. 2d 292, 298–99 (S.D.N.Y. 2003); Dixon v. Goord, 224 F. Supp. 2d 739, 749 (S.D.N.Y. 2002) ("The exhaustion requirement is satisfied by resolution of the matter, *i.e.*, an inmate is not required to continue to complain after his grievances have been addressed."); Brady v. Attygala, 196 F. Supp. 2d 1016, 1020 (C.D.Cal. 2002) (holding plaintiff had exhausted where he grieved to see an ophthalmologist and was taken to see an ophthalmologist before the grievance process was completed); Gomez v. Winslow, 177 F. Supp. 2d 977, 985 (N.D.Cal. 2001) (allowing damage claim to go forward where prisoner had stopped pursuing grievance process when he received all the relief it could give him); McGrath v. Johnson, 67 F. Supp. 2d 499, 510 (E.D.Pa. 1999) (allowing suit to go forward for failure to carry out favorable grievance decision); *see also* Marvin v. Goord, 255 F.3d 40, 43 n.3 (2d Cir. 2001) (holding that succeeding through informal channels met the exhaustion requirement, since the grievance procedure states that it is "intended to supplement, not replace, existing formal or informal channels of problem resolution"). *But see* Glenn v. Thompson, 2008 WL 4107800, *5–6 (E.D.Tex., Sept. 3, 2008) (holding prisoner must appeal even after receiving a response stating that an investigation will be conducted, where that is all the relief available).

[253]*See* Ross v. County of Bernalillo, 365 F.3d 1181, 1186–87 (10th Cir. 2004) ("When there is *no possibility of any further relief*, the prisoner's duty to exhaust available administrative remedies is complete." (emphasis added)); *see also* Coleman v. Los Angeles, 2008 WL 4449598, *3 (C.D.Cal., Sept. 30, 2008) (plaintiff who requested two consecutive hours of law library time each week, received only a vague commitment to try to provide more time, and did not appeal did not exhaust); Garcia v. Kirkland, 2006 WL 3533044, *4 (N.D.Cal., Dec. 7, 2006) (holding grievance only partially granted left the prisoner with available remedies because he could appeal); Green v. Cahal, 2004 WL 1078988, *2–3 (D.Or., May 11, 2004) (holding that a prisoner whose complaint of medical care delay resulted in a decision that treatment was forthcoming should nonetheless have appealed); Rivera v. Pataki, 2003 WL 21511939, *7 (S.D.N.Y., July 1, 2003) (noting it "made sense" for a prisoner to appeal where an intermediate decision granted him some relief but did not change the challenged policy).

able to think of some relief you could theoretically have obtained, and the court may accept their arguments.[254]

Courts have held that if you have been "reliably informed by an administrator that no remedies are available," you are not required to pursue the process any further.[255] Similarly, courts have held that if a prisoner's grievance is rejected on the ground that the prisoner has already received the relief sought, he has exhausted.[256] If you do not have such a statement from prison officials, and you want to bring suit, it is probably wise to appeal any decision all the way up, no matter what. If you have to explain why you are appealing in these circumstances, you should probably say something like "to exhaust my administrative remedies by calling this problem to the attention of high-level officials so they can take whatever action is necessary to make sure it never happens again."[257]

Exhaustion means using whatever formal complaint procedure is available, usually a grievance system or administrative appeal. "Proper exhaustion" is required—that is, you must follow the rules of the prison procedure.[258]

If you do that, courts cannot require you to do more.[259] Letters and other informal means of complaint, such as cooperating in an internal affairs or inspector general's investigation, generally will not suffice to exhaust[260] unless the prison rules identify them as an alternative means of complaint,[261] or unless there are circumstances justifying your failure to exhaust properly.[262] In a few cases, courts have held that non-grievance complaints that were in fact reviewed at the highest levels of the agency satisfied the exhaustion requirement in the particular circumstances of

---

[254]*See, e.g.*, Braham v. Clancy, 425 F.3d 177, 182–83 (2d Cir. 2005) (holding that a prisoner who asked for a cell change through an informal process, and got it, failed to exhaust because he did not go on to file a formal grievance, which could have granted further relief such as changes in policy or discipline of staff); *accord*, Ruggiero v. County of Orange, 467 F.3d 170, 178 (2d Cir. 2006) (holding that prisoner who prevailed informally was required to exhaust the grievance process because of "the larger interests at stake"). Another circuit has rejected this idea (correctly in our view), stating that "we do not think it [the prisoner's] responsibility to notify persons higher in the chain when this notification would be solely for the benefit of the prison administration." Thornton v. Snyder, 428 F.3d 690, 696–97 (7th Cir. 2005).

[255]Brown v. Valoff, 422 F.3d 926, 935 (9th Cir. 2005); *accord*, Hendon v. Ramsey, 2007 WL 1120375, *9–10 (S.D.Cal., Apr. 12, 2007) (holding plaintiff had exhausted where his appeal was partly granted and he was told that it was being referred for investigation and any finding of staff misconduct would be confidential and he would not be informed of it); Cahill v. Arpaio, 2006 WL 3201018, *3 (D.Ariz., Nov. 2, 2006) (holding plaintiff reasonably relied on grievance hearing officer telling him that "(1) the matter was under investigation and he would not be notified of the results, (2) he could not appeal and would not be given a form, and (3) he should proceed to federal court," notwithstanding that the preprinted decision form said it could be appealed); Candler v. Woodford, 2007 WL 3232435, *4–5 (N.D.Cal., Nov. 1, 2007) (similar to *Hendon* and *Cahill*).

[256]James v. Davis, 2006 WL 2171082, *17 (D.S.C., July 31, 2006); Elkins v. Schrubbe, 2006 WL 1663779, *55 (E.D.Wis., June 15, 2006).

[257]*See* Ruggiero v. County of Orange, 467 F.3d 170, 177 (2d Cir. 2006) (holding prisoner who obtained what he wanted informally was still required to exhaust because a grievance "still would have allowed prison officials to reconsider their policies and discipline any officer who had failed to follow existing policies").

[258]Woodford v. Ngo, 548 U.S. 81, 106, 126 S. Ct. 2378 (2006); *see* § D.5 of this chapter for further discussion of the "proper exhaustion" rule and possible exceptions to it.

[259]Jones v. Bock, 549 U.S. 199, 218, 127 S. Ct. 910 (2007) ("Compliance with prison grievance procedures . . . is all that is required by the PLRA to 'properly exhaust.'")

[260]*See* Ruggiero v. County of Orange, 467 F.3d 170, 177 (2d Cir. 2006) (holding that talking with Sheriff's Department investigators rather than filing a jail grievance did not satisfy the exhaustion requirement); Panaro v. City of North Las Vegas, 423 F.3d 949, 953 (9th Cir. 2005) (holding that participation in an internal affairs investigation did not exhaust because it did not provide a remedy for the prisoner, even though the officer was disciplined); Yousef v. Reno, 254 F.3d 1214, 1221–22 (10th Cir. 2001) (holding that a letter to the Attorney General was insufficient to exhaust as to actions that had been authorized by the Attorney General, despite the government's lack of clarity as to what authority the administrative remedy procedure might have over the Attorney General's decisions); Chelette v. Harris, 229 F.3d 684, 688 (8th Cir. 2000) (telling the warden about the problem did not exhaust even though the warden said he would "take care" of it); Freeman v. Francis, 196 F.3d 641, 644 (6th Cir. 1999) (prompting a use of force investigation did not substitute for filing a grievance); Scott v. Gardner. 287 F. Supp. 2d 477, 488 (S.D.N.Y. 2003) (letters of complaint are not part of the grievance process and do not exhaust); Onapolis v. Lamanna, 70 F. Supp. 2d 809, 813 (N.D.Ohio 1999) (letters and telephone calls did not satisfy the exhaustion requirement).

[261]In *Pavey v. Conley*, 170 Fed.Appx. 4, 8 (7th Cir. 2006) (unpublished), the plaintiff alleged that prison staff had broken his arm and he couldn't write, and the grievance rules said that prisoners who couldn't write could be assisted by staff. The court held that any memorialization of his complaint by investigating prison staff might qualify as a grievance—and even if they did not write it down, he might have "reasonably believed that he had done all that was necessary to comply with" the policy. *See also* Carter v. Symmes, 2008 WL 341640, *3 (D.Mass., Feb. 4, 2008) (timely letter from counsel served to exhaust where grievance rules did not specify use of a form; the letter was considered as part of prisoner's grievance raising other issues); Rand v. Simonds, 422 F. Supp. 2d 318, 326 (D.N.H. 2006) (holding that a policy stating prisoners have the "right and opportunity" to file grievances "did not fairly suggest that the grievance procedure was the only way, or even the correct way, for inmates to complain about their treatment"); Carter v. Klaus, 2006 WL 3791342, *3 (M.D.Pa., Dec. 22, 2006) (noting that prison policy allowed physical abuse complaints to be pursued as grievances or as complaints to the Office of Professional Responsibility); Shaheed-Muhammad v. Dipaolo, 393 F. Supp. 2d 80, 96–97 (D.Mass. 2005) (concluding that letters to officials are considered grievances under state law).

[262]*See* § D.5 of this chapter for a discussion of circumstances that may justify failure to exhaust properly.

those cases,[263] though it is not clear whether these cases are good law after the *Woodford v. Ngo* "proper exhaustion" holding. It is also questionable whether cases holding that "informal" exhaustion will satisfy the PLRA are still good law; don't rely on them unless you have to.[264]

One federal appeals court, the Second Circuit, has held that if a prisoner uses the wrong remedy through a reasonable misunderstanding of the rules, the prisoner is justified in failing to exhaust correctly; if the correct administrative remedy is still available, the prisoner must try to use it, but if it is no longer available, the prisoner's case may go forward without exhaustion.[265] A prisoner may also be justified in failing to exhaust the correct procedures because of threats or intimidation by prison staff.[266] These rules appear still to be good law after the *Woodford* "proper exhaustion" ruling, since they address fact situations that were not before the Supreme Court in *Woodford*, but the Second Circuit has not ruled on that question yet.[267]

The exhaustion requirement refers only to administrative remedies, so you do not have to exhaust judicial remedies (*i.e.*, go to state court) before you go to federal court.[268]

---

[263]*See* Camp v. Brennan, 219 F.3d 279, 280 (3d Cir. 2000) (holding that use of force allegation reportedly investigated and rejected by Secretary of Correction's office needed no further exhaustion); Franklin v. Oneida Correctional Facility, 2008 WL 2690243, *7 (N.D.N.Y., July 1, 2008) (denying summary judgment where prisoner's letter to Commissioner prompted an investigation that might have made a grievance redundant); Roland v. Murphy, 289 F. Supp. 2d 321, 324 (E.D.N.Y. 2003) (complaints to Sheriff's Department Internal Affairs unit and District Attorney's office gave "ample opportunity" to address complaint internally); Noguera v. Hasty, 2000 WL 1011563, *11 (S.D.N.Y., July 21, 2000) (exhaustion requirement satisfied in unusual case where the prisoner's informal complaint of rape resulted in an Internal Affairs investigation), *report and recommendation adopted in part*, 2001 WL 243535 (S.D.N.Y., Mar. 12, 2001). These cases are unusual and you should not bypass the grievance system and count on getting such a decision. However, if you are in the position where you must argue that another kind of complaint meets the exhaustion requirement, be sure to remind the court that the Supreme Court, in discussing Congress' purpose in requiring exhaustion, said that "Congress afforded corrections officials time and opportunity to address complaints internally before allowing the initiation of a federal case." Porter v. Nussle, 534 U.S. 516, 525, 122 S. Ct. 983 (2002). You can then argue that if prison officials actually reviewed your complaint, they had the opportunity to address the complaint internally, and the exhaustion requirement was therefore satisfied. The likelihood of success of this argument is not high. *See, e.g.*, Macias v. Zenk, 495 F.3d 37, 43–44 (2d Cir. 2007) (holding "after *Woodford* notice alone is insufficient"; the PLRA requires both "substantive exhaustion" (notice to officials) and "procedural exhaustion" (following the rules)).

[264]The Second Circuit held that a prisoner who succeeded in resolving his complaint through informal channels met the New York State exhaustion requirement, since the grievance procedure states that it is "intended to supplement, not replace, existing formal or informal channels of problem resolution." Marvin v. Goord, 255 F.3d 40, 43 n.3 (2d Cir. 2001); *see* Gibson v. Brooks, 335 F. Supp. 2d 325, 331–34 (D. Conn. 2004) (holding that a prisoner who said he complained informally about an assault he had warned prison staff about, and who had received an apology, had sufficiently alleged a favorable resolution). That holding applied only to prisoners who succeeded in resolving their complaint informally; if they failed, they had to go through the grievance system to exhaust. *See* Ortiz v. McBride, 380 F.3d 649, 653–54 (2d Cir. 2004); Stephenson v. Dunford, 320 F. Supp. 2d 44, 51 (W.D.N.Y. 2004); Thomas v. Cassleberry, 315 F. Supp. 2d 301, 304 (W.D.N.Y. 2004) (holding a complaint to the Inspector General exhausts informally only if the resolution is favorable).

In later decisions, however, the Second Circuit called the whole idea of informal exhaustion into question by holding that a prisoner who got what he asked for in an informal process should have filed a formal grievance anyway because that process could have provided other relief, such as changes in policy or discipline of staff. Braham v. Clancy, 425 F.3d 177, 183 (2d Cir. 2005); *accord*, Ruggiero v. County of Orange, 467 F.3d 170, 177 (2d Cir. 2006)

(holding prisoner beaten in jail, who talked to Sheriff's Department investigators and then was transferred, did not exhaust). *Ruggiero* says that *Marvin v. Goord* "does not imply that a prisoner has exhausted his administrative remedies every time he receives his desired relief through informal channels." So, if you solve your problem informally but still want to bring suit about what happened, you should still file a grievance and pursue it all the way to the top, stating, for example, that you want "prison officials to reconsider their policies and discipline any officer who had failed to follow existing policies." Ruggiero v. County of Orange, 467 F.3d 170, 177 (2d Cir. 2006).

[265]Giano v. Goord, 380 F.3d 670, 678–80 (2d Cir. 2004) (holding that prisoner who used a disciplinary appeal rather than a grievance for his issues did so reasonably); *accord*, Hemphill v. New York, 380 F.3d 680, 689–90 (2d Cir. 2004); Larkins v. Selsky, 2006 WL 3548959, *9 (S.D.N.Y., Dec. 6, 2006) (holding that a prisoner who used a grievance rather than a disciplinary appeal did so reasonably); *see also* Warren v. Purcell, 2004 WL 1970642, *6 (S.D.N.Y., Sept. 3, 2004) (holding that a "baffling" grievance response that left the prisoner with no clue what to do next was a special circumstance justifying failure to exhaust).

[266]Hemphill v. New York, 380 F.3d 680, 690 (2d Cir. 2004) (noting that a prisoner may well be deterred from filing an internal grievance but not from "appealing directly to individuals in positions of greater authority within the prison system, or to external structures of authority such as state or federal courts").

[267]Other courts have endorsed the *Hemphill* holding after the decision in *Woodford*. *See* Turner v. Burnside, 541 F.3d 1077, 1085 (11th Cir. 2008); Kaba v. Stepp, 458 F.3d 678, 684–85 (7th Cir. 2006); Hernandez v. Schriro, 2006 WL 2989030, *4 (D.Ariz., Oct. 18, 2006); James v. Davis, 2006 WL 2171082, *16–17 (D.S.C. July 31, 2006); Stanley v. Rich, 2006 WL 1549114, *2 (S.D.Ga., June 1, 2006) (stating "threats of violent reprisal may, in some circumstances, render administrative remedies 'unavailable' or otherwise justify an inmate's failure to pursue them").

[268]You must exhaust state judicial remedies before you can bring a case in federal court challenging a decision that affects your release from incarceration, such as a disciplinary proceeding at which you lost good time credits. *See* Edwards v. Balisok, 520 U.S. 641, 117 S. Ct. 1584 (1997) (holding that a state prisoner's claim for damages for violation of his due process rights cannot be recognized in federal court if a verdict in his favor would imply the invalidity

That means that in states that allow final grievance decisions to be appealed to the state courts, you don't have to take that appeal as long as you completed the final administrative steps.[269]

The administrative remedies Congress had in mind when it enacted the PLRA are internal prison grievance procedures.[270] A prisoner is not required to exhaust state or federal tort claim procedures, unless the prisoner wishes to sue under the tort claims system.[271] For federal prisoners, Federal Tort Claims Act (FTCA) claims must be exhausted through the tort claims procedure, but other claims arising from federal prisons must be exhausted through the federal Administrative Remedy Procedure.[272] Several New York

federal courts have held that prisoners making disability-related complaints must exhaust the U.S. Department of Justice's disability complaint procedure in addition to the prison grievance procedure.[273] Others have disagreed,[274] and we agree that the argument is wrong, since as noted Congress was concerned about internal prison procedures.[275]

2. What Are Prison Conditions?

The exhaustion requirement applies to cases filed by prisoners about "prison conditions." The Supreme Court has said that phrase applies "to all inmate suits about prison life, whether they involve general circumstances or particular episodes, and whether they allege excessive force or some other wrong."[276] In other words, if it happened to you in

---

of his sentence, unless that sentence has already been invalidated). This rule has nothing to do with the PLRA.

[269]See Jenkins v. Morton, 148 F.3d 257, 259–60 (3d Cir. 1998) (finding prisoner not required to exhaust his state judicial remedies prior to bringing an action covered by PLRA); Mullins v. Smith, 14 F. Supp. 2d 1009, 1012 (E.D.Mich. 1998) (court dismissed plaintiff's claim as frivolous, but noted that plaintiff had exhausted his administrative remedies).

There are some decisions in one federal district court requiring use of a judicial appeal procedure from grievance decisions. See, e.g., Williams v. Harris, 2007 WL 2156669, *6–7 (D.S.C., July 26, 2007). However, most decisions, and the more recent ones, hold that judicial appeals are not required to exhaust. See, e.g., Johnson v. Ozmint, 567 F. Supp. 2d 806, 820 n.5 (D.S.C. 2008); Charles v. Ozmint, 2006 WL 1341267, *4 n.3 (D.S.C., May 15, 2006) (holding that appeal to an administrative law judge under state Administrative Procedures Act "would invoke state judicial remedies" and is not required by the PLRA).

[270]See Jones v. Bock, 549 U.S. 199, 218, 127 S. Ct. 910 (2007) ("Compliance with *prison grievance procedures*, therefore, is all that is required by the PLRA to 'properly exhaust.'" (emphasis supplied)); Porter v. Nussle, 534 U.S. 516, 524–25, 122 S. Ct. 983 (2002) (stating that the exhaustion requirement was intended to give *corrections officials* the opportunity to solve problems before suit was filed). In *Rumbles v. Hill*, 182 F.3d 1064, 1069–70 (9th Cir. 1999), the court pointed out that the legislative history of the PLRA and of its predecessor statutes showed that Congress used the term "administrative remedies" to refer to prison grievance procedures. See also Massey v. Helman, 196 F.3d 727, 733–34 (7th Cir. 1999) (holding that the PLRA requires exhaustion of internal prison remedies); Alexander v. Hawk, 159 F.3d 1321, 1326 (11th Cir. 1998) (same); Aiello v. Litscher, 104 F. Supp. 2d 1068, 1074 (W.D. Wis. 2000) (prisoners who had exhausted the grievance system were not required also to exhaust a procedure providing for declaratory rulings by agencies).

[271]See Macias v. Zenk, 495 F.3d 37, 42–44 (2d Cir. 2007); Rumbles v. Hill, 182 F.3d 1064, 1069–70 (9th Cir. 1999); Blas v. Endicott, 31 F. Supp. 2d 1131, 1132–34 (E.D. Wis. 1999).

[272]Garrett v. Hawk, 127 F.3d 1263, 1266 (10th Cir. 1998) (holding that FTCA administrative filing is not "available" to prisoner pursuing *Bivens* claim against individual prison staff); Crum v. Dupell, 2008 WL 902177, *3 (N.D.N.Y., Mar. 31, 2008) (". . . [T]he exhaustion procedures under the FTCA and under the PLRA for *Bivens* claims differ, and fulfillment of one does not constitute satisfaction of the other."); James v. Superior Court of New Jersey Bergen County, 2007 WL 3071794, *10 (D.N.J., Oct. 19, 2007)

(holding tort claims require exhaustion of the tort claim procedure), *vacated on other grounds*, 287 Fed.Appx. 140 (3d Cir. 2008) (unpublished); Richard v. Capps, 2007 WL 2428928, *3–4 (N.D.Tex., Aug. 28, 2007) (noting no need to canvass ARP exhaustion for a FTCA claim. "The exhaustion requirements for a *Bivens* claim are separate and distinct from the exhaustion requirements under the FTCA."); Davis v. Miner, 2007 WL 1237924, *5 (M.D.Pa., Apr. 26, 2007) (dismissing *Bivens* claim for failure to exhaust administrative remedy, noting plaintiff can still file tort claim and proceed under FTCA); McClenton v. Menifee, 2006 WL 2474872, *16 (S.D.N.Y., Aug. 22, 2006); Hartman v. Holder, 2005 WL 2002455, *6–8 (E.D.N.Y., Aug. 21, 2005); Taveras v. Hasty, 2005 WL 1594330, *2–3 (E.D.N.Y., July 7, 2005); Williams v. U.S., 2005 WL 44533, *1 (D.Kan., Jan. 7, 2005); Bolton v. U.S., 347 F. Supp. 2d 1218, 1221 (N.D.Fla. 2004) (holding prisoner seeking damages properly followed the "appropriate statutorily-mandated procedure" by filing an FTCA claim).

[273]William G. v. Pataki, 2005 WL 1949509, *5–6 (S.D.N.Y., Aug. 12, 2005); Scott v. Goord, 2004 WL 2403853, *7 (S.D.N.Y., Oct. 27, 2004); Burgess v. Garvin, 2003 WL 21983006, *3 (S.D.N.Y., Aug. 19, 2003), *on reconsideration*, 2004 WL 527053 (S.D.N.Y., March 16, 2004).

[274]Degrafinreid v. Ricks, 2004 WL 2793168, *14 n.10 (S.D.N.Y., Dec. 6, 2004); Veloz v. State of New York, 2004 WL 2274777, *8 (S.D.N.Y., Sept. 30, 2004), *aff'd*, 178 Fed.Appx. 39, (2d Cir. 2006) (unpublished); Shariff v. Artuz, 2000 WL 1219381 (S.D.N.Y. Aug. 28, 2000); Singleton v. Perilli, 2004 WL 74238, *4 (S.D.N.Y., Jan 16, 2004) (dictum).

New York's prison system has repudiated the argument that prisoners must exhaust the Department of Justice procedures, *see* Rosario v. Goord, 400 F.3d 108 (2d Cir. 2005) (per curiam) though it continues to be asserted by other state agencies. *See* William G. v. Pataki, 2005 WL 1949509 (S.D.N.Y., Aug. 12, 2005) (accepting argument in action defended by state Division of Parole and Office of Mental Health).

[275]This view is supported by a recent decision holding that exhausting the Department of Justice procedure does not satisfy the PLRA. *See* O'Guinn v. Lovelock Correctional Center, 502 F.3d 1056, 1062–63 (9th Cir. 2007). This decision further confirms that the DOJ procedure is not what Congress had in mind in the PLRA exhaustion requirement.

[276]Porter v. Nussle, 534 U.S. 516, 532, 122 S. Ct. 983 (2002). Even if state law or grievance rules say you are not *required* to exhaust a particular type of claim, you are probably required to do

prison, it is probably covered by the exhaustion requirement.[277] Older decisions holding that use of force cases are not about "prison conditions" and need not be exhausted are no longer good law.

Actions of persons or agencies outside the prison system are generally not prison conditions,[278] though actions taken in prison based on them probably are.[279] Occurrences or

conditions in police custody are generally not considered prison conditions.[280] The same should be true of medical facilities outside the prison system, but the cases are divided on the question.[281] If you have a problem caused by an agency or facility outside the prison system, you should not rely exclusively on the "not prison conditions" argument. To be safe, if the outside agency or facility has a complaint procedure, you should try to use it, and you should also probably file a grievance within the prison system about your problem unless it is absolutely clear from the grievance policy that it does not cover your complaint.[282]

Disputes over whether you should be in prison at all are not about prison conditions.[283] Courts have reached differing decisions on matters related to parole release

---

so under the PLRA if you *can* get some relief from the grievance system. *See* Short v. Greene, 577 F. Supp. 2d 790, 791–93 (2008). If state law or grievance rules say you cannot get relief for a particular kind of claim, then the remedy is not "available" and you don't have to exhaust it. This issue is discussed further in the next section.

[277]*See, e.g.*, Krilich v. Fed. Bureau of Prisons, 346 F.3d 157, 159 (6th Cir. 2003) (holding that intrusions on attorney–client correspondence and telephone conversations are prison conditions notwithstanding argument that attorney–client relationship "transcends the conditions of time and place"); U.S. v. Carmichael, 343 F.3d 756, 759–60 (5th Cir. 2003) (holding that statutorily required DNA collection is a prison condition); Castano v. Neb. Dep't of Corr., 201 F.3d 1023 (8th Cir. 2000) (failure to provide interpreters for Spanish-speaking prisoners is a prison condition); Brewer v. Philson, 2007 WL 87625, *2 (W.D.Ark., Jan. 10, 2007) (holding that excessive force on arrest does not require exhaustion, but excessive force after arrest in a jail holding cell does); Ray v. Evercom Systems, Inc., 2006 WL 2475264, *5 (D.S.C., Aug. 25, 2006) (holding antitrust suit about telephone service charges was about prison conditions); Dennis v. Taft, 2004 WL 4506891, *4 (S.D.Ohio, Sept. 24, 2004) (holding challenge to execution procedures is about "prison conditions"; it involves "the effects of actions by government officials on the lives of persons confined in prison."); Johnson v. Luttrell, 2005 WL 1972579, *3 (W.D.Tenn., Aug. 11, 2005) ("Plaintiff's inability to obtain an application for an absentee ballot in a timely manner is a 'prison conditions claim.'").

A rare exception to this rule of thumb is Ayyad v. Gonzales, 2008 WL 203420, *3 (D.Colo., Jan. 17, 2008), *vacated on reconsideration on other grounds*, 2008 WL 2955964 (D.Colo., July 31, 2008), which holds that denial of a prisoner's ability to meet with clinical law students was not a matter of prison conditions, in part because the administrative dictates were made by the Attorney General and the Bureau of Prisons had no authority to remove or amend them.

[278]Boyd v. Driver, 579 F.3d 513, 514 n.2 (5th Cir. 2009) (per curiam) (allegation of misconduct in criminal prosecution arising from altercation in prison was not about prison conditions).

[279]For example, one court held that the Department of Homeland Security's placement of a prisoner on a "watch list" was not a prison condition requiring exhaustion; however, the prison's actions in placing him in segregation or depriving him of telephone privileges did require exhaustion. Almahdi v. Ridge, 2006 WL 3051791, *2 (3d Cir., Oct. 27, 2006) (unpublished). Another has held that a prisoner's claim that prosecutors and investigators conspired to harm him in jail because he had information about official corruption was not a prison conditions claim, even though it had an impact on prison conditions, and the exhaustion requirement did not apply. Johnson v. Quinn, 1999 WL 116222, *3 (N.D.Ill., Feb. 26, 1999); *see* Holtz v. Monsanto, Inc., 2006 WL 1596830, *1 (S.D.Ill., June 6, 2006) (holding prisoner's claim of "negligence, strict products liability, 'deceit and misrepresentation,' and breach of express or implied warranties arising out of Defendants' involvement with the product Aspartame," was not

about prison conditions). *Compare* Reid v. Fed. Bureau of Prisons, 2005 WL 1699425, *3 (D.D.C., July 20, 2005) (holding Privacy Act claim about inaccuracy in prison records affecting classification was about prison conditions) *with* Lee v. U.S. Dep't of Justice, 235 F.R.D. 274, 290 (W.D.Pa. 2006) (holding alleged violation of Privacy Act resulting in plaintiff's and his agents' being unable to access his outside bank accounts for a year "did not relate to prison life" and need not be exhausted).

[280]*See* Brewer v. Philson, 2007 WL 87625, *2 (W.D.Ark., Jan. 10, 2007); Bowers v. City of Philadelphia, 2007 WL 219651, *34 n.40 (E.D.Pa., Jan. 25, 2007) (holding that police holding cells were not prisons for purpose of prisoner release provisions of PLRA); *see* Battle v. Whetsel, 2006 WL 2010766, *3 n.4 (W.D.Okla., July 17, 2006) (holding police interrogation and refusal to allow call to lawyer were not prison conditions even though they occurred in the jail).

[281]In *Borges v. Adm'r for Strong Mem. Hosp.*, 2002 WL 31194558, *3 (W.D.N.Y., Sept. 30, 2002), the court expressed doubt that a claim made by prisoners injured by dentists at an outside hospital involved prison conditions, since the grievance system probably could not take any action against defendants. The court reached the opposite conclusion in *Abdur-Raqiyb v. Erie County Medical Center*, 536 F. Supp. 2d 299, 304 (W.D.N.Y. 2008), on the ground that the statute is supposed to be read broadly and the plaintiff was clearly a prisoner. However, the court did not explain what action the grievance system could take, or what remedy was available to the prisoner that actually had any authority over his complaint.

[282]If the grievance rules exclude your problem from consideration, or if you get a decision stating that the system will not hear your complaint, then you will have proof that the grievance system is not an available remedy under the PLRA. See § D.3, below, concerning available remedies.

[283]White v. Thompson, 2007 WL 628121, *2–3 (S.D.Ga., Feb. 26, 2007) (holding false imprisonment claims not about prison conditions); Bost v. Adams, 2006 WL 1674485, *5 (S.D.W.Va., June 12, 2006) (holding challenge to a restriction on the time a prisoner could serve in a community corrections center was not about prison conditions); Fuller v. Kansas, 2005 WL 1936007, *2 (D.Kan., Aug. 8, 2005) (holding claims of false arrest and imprisonment are not prison conditions claims under the statute), *aff'd*, 175 Fed. Appx. 234 (10th Cir. 2006) (unpublished); Wishorn v. Hill, 2004 WL 303571, *11 (D.Kan., Feb. 13, 2004) (holding detention without probable cause is not a prison condition); Monahan v. Winn, 276 F. Supp. 2d 196, 204 (D.Mass. 2003) (holding that a Bureau of Prisons rule revision that abolished its discretion to designate certain

or revocation.[284] Complaints from halfway houses or residential treatment programs are about prison conditions if you are there because of a criminal conviction or charge and you are not free to leave.[285] However, courts have held that issues about placement in or removal from such programs are not about prison conditions.[286] One court has held that a

claim that prisoners with mental illness were discharged without receiving psychiatric medication and referrals is not about prison conditions.[287]

3. What Are "Available" Remedies?

The PLRA says you must exhaust remedies that are "available." If remedies were *not* available at the time you needed to exhaust, you can proceed with your case without exhaustion.[288]

A remedy is "available" if it has any "authority to provide any relief or to take any action whatsoever in response to a complaint."[289] That means if it's there and will address your problem, you must use it.[290] A remedy that does not provide for damages is available, and you must exhaust it, even if all you are seeking is damages.[291] You may believe that the grievance system in your prison is unfair, futile, and a waste of time, but even if you are right, you have to

_____

offenders to community confinement facilities did not involve prison conditions).

[284]*Compare* Hernandez-Vazquez v. Ortiz-Martinez, 2010 WL 132343, *4 (D.P.R., Jan. 8, 2010) (delayed parole hearing is not a prison condition); L.H. v. Schwarzenegger, 519 F. Supp. 2d 1072, 1081 n.9 (E.D.Cal. 2007) (holding parole violation procedures are not prison conditions); Swimp v. Rubitschun, 2006 WL 3370876, *6 n.1 (W.D.Mich., Nov. 20, 2006) (holding challenge to a parole decision was not about prison conditions); Valdivia v. Davis, 206 F. Supp. 2d 1068, 1074 n.12 (E.D.Cal. 2002) (holding that a challenge to parole revocation procedures was not a "civil action with respect to prison conditions" under 18 U.S.C. § 3626(g)(2)) *with* Morgan v. Messenger, 2003 WL 22023108 (D.N.H., Aug. 27, 2003) (holding that sex offender treatment director's disclosure of private information from plaintiff's treatment file to parole authorities and prosecutor involved prison conditions, since the director was a prison employee and the action affected the duration of his prison confinement); Salaam v. Consovoy, 2000 WL 33679670, *4 (D.N.J., Apr. 14, 2000) (holding that the failure to provide proper parole release hearings is a prison condition). *Salaam* may be distinguishable from *Valdivia* on the ground that parole release hearings involve a process commenced in prison, while parole revocation proceedings are commenced and are based on events that took place outside prison. *See also* Farnworth v. Craven, 2007 WL 793397, *2–3 (D.Idaho, Mar. 14, 2007) (holding demand for new parole hearing was about "prison conditions" because it need not be pursued via habeas corpus, but grievance system was not available for it because it had no authority over the Parole Commission).

[285]Ruggiero v. County of Orange, 467 F.3d 170, 174–75 (2d Cir. 2006) (holding "drug treatment campus" was a "jail, prison, or other correctional facility"; that term "includes within its ambit all facilities in which prisoners are held involuntarily as a result of violating the criminal law"); Witzke v. Femal, 376 F.3d 744, 752–53 (7th Cir. 2004) (complaint about "intensive drug rehabilitation halfway house" addressed prison conditions); Clemens v. SCI-Albion, 2006 WL 3759740, *5 (W.D. Pa., Dec. 19, 2006) (complaint about halfway house with random urine tests, limited visiting was about prison conditions); William G. v. Pataki, 2005 WL 1949509, *2–3 (S.D.N.Y., Aug. 12, 2005) (question whether persons incarcerated pending parole revocation proceedings were entitled to be placed in less restrictive residential treatment programs for mental illness and chemical addition involved prison conditions).

[286]*See* Bost v. Adams, 2006 WL 1674485, *5 (S.D.W.Va., June 12, 2006) (holding challenge to a restriction on the time a prisoner could serve in a community corrections center was not about prison conditions); Belk v. Federal Bureau of Prisons, 2004 WL 5352260, *14 (W.D.Wis., Oct. 15, 2004) (challenge to transfer from prison camp to halfway house involved a "quantum change" in level of custody and was not about prison conditions); Tristano v. Federal Bureau of Prisons, 2004 WL 5284511, *12 (W.D.Wis., Oct. 15, 2004) (same as *Belk*); Monahan v. Winn, 276 F. Supp. 2d 196, 204 (D.Mass. 2003) (holding that a Bureau of Prisons rule revision that abolished its discretion to designate certain offenders to

community confinement facilities did not involve prison conditions).

[287]Bolden v. Stroger, 2005 WL 283419, *1 (N.D.Ill., Feb. 1, 2005). However, the court held that a claim of exclusion of persons with mental illness from pre-release programs was about prison conditions. *Id.*, *2.

[288]*See, e.g.*, Abney v. McGinnis, 380 F.3d 663, 667 (2d Cir. 2004).

One recent decision by the Seventh Circuit Court of Appeals takes a slightly different approach, holding that if a failure to exhaust was "innocent"—which is the case if remedies were not available—the prisoner "must be given another chance to exhaust (provided that there exist remedies that he will be permitted by the prison authorities to exhaust, so that he's not just being given a runaround)." Pavey v. Conley, 544 F.3d 739, 742 (7th Cir. 2008), *cert. denied*, 129 S. Ct. 1620 (2009). We think this is wrong. The statute says that "[n]o action shall be brought" without exhaustion of available remedies. 42 U.S.C. § 1997e(a). That language indicates that it is at the point at which the action is "brought" that exhaustion and availability are to be assessed. The fact that defendants make a remedy available after the case is "brought" should not mean you have to start over.

One other circuit has a "do-over" rule, but it is different from this Seventh Circuit rule. In the Second Circuit, if remedies are unavailable, the plaintiff need not exhaust. Abney v. McGinnis, *supra*. However, even if remedies are available, that court holds that there can be "special circumstances" that excuse exhaustion, but in those cases, the prisoner must try again if remedies are still available. Hemphill v. New York, 380 F.3d 680, 690–91 (2d Cir. 2004); *see* Brownell v. Krom, 446 F.3d 305, 312–13 (2d Cir. 2006) (finding special circumstances, noting the plaintiff had already tried again but was not allowed to grieve).

[289]Booth v. Churner, 532 U.S. 731, 738, 121 S. Ct. 1819 (2001).

[290]A system that is *not* there—*i.e.*, that exists only on paper—need not be exhausted. Martin v. Sizemore, 2005 WL 1491210, *1, *3 (E.D.Ky., June 22, 2005) (where it was alleged that "[t]here is no grievance committee here, your grievances are simply turned over to the person you file on and you get threatened," the court could not dismiss for non-exhaustion).

[291]Booth v. Churner, 532 U.S. at 740–41.

exhaust anyway.[292] The requirement of pre-PLRA law that remedies be "plain, speedy and effective" has been repealed.

A remedy need not have any particular legal status or degree of formality to be available and to require exhaustion.[293] In a very few cases, courts have not required exhaustion of processes that do not appear organized or empowered to provide actual solutions to individual prisoners' complaints. Though they may be available, in effect, they are not remedies (though the courts don't put it in those terms).[294] Courts will probably be reluctant to find that a prison

remedy falls into that category, so we don't recommend that you rely on these decisions if you don't have to; it is wiser to try the remedy first so exhaustion will not be an issue in your case.

The "available" remedy you must exhaust will usually be the prison grievance procedure.[295] However, if an issue is not "grievable" under the grievance rules, you do not have to exhaust the grievance system, because it is not available for your problem.[296] Each prison or jail system will have its own set of non-grievable issues, and they vary widely from

---

[292]Booth v. Churner, 532 U.S. at 738 n.6 ("[W]e will not read futility or other exceptions into statutory exhaustion requirements where Congress has provided otherwise." (citation omitted)); see Boyd v. Corrections Corporation of America, 380 F.3d 989, 998 (6th Cir. 2004) and cases cited (holding that prisoners' subjective belief the process will be unresponsive does not excuse exhaustion); Alexander v. Tippah County, Miss., 351 F.3d 626, 630 (5th Cir. 2003) (holding that allegations of the grievance system's inadequacy did not excuse failure to exhaust). But see Westefer v. Snyder, 422 F.3d 570, 579 (7th Cir. 2005) (holding a "transfer review" process failed to afford a remedy in part because it was not "effective" for prisoners not informed of the reasons for their transfer).

This means, e.g., that if another prisoner has just grieved the same issue and lost, you still need to grieve it yourself, even though you are certain that it is futile because you will get the same ruling. See King v. Caruso, 2008 WL 4534076, *1 (W.D.Mich., Sept. 30, 2008); see also Hattie v. Hallock, 8 F. Supp. 2d 685, 689 (N.D.Ohio) (stating that "vicarious" exhaustion is not permitted, except in class actions), judgment amended, 16 F. Supp. 2d 834 (N.D.Ohio 1998).

[293]Ferrington v. Lousiana Dep't of Corrections, 315 F.3d 529, 531–32 (5th Cir. 2002) (holding grievance system that had been held unconstitutional under state constitution insofar as it divested the state courts of original jurisdiction over tort cases, but continued in operation, remained "available" for purposes of PLRA exhaustion); Concepcion v. Morton, 306 F.3d 1347, 1353–54 (3d Cir. 2002) (holding that a grievance procedure described in an inmate handbook but not formally adopted by a state agency was an available remedy to be exhausted).

[294]One court has held that a process that has no authority over anything except to "'make recommendations for change' to administrative officials" need not be exhausted because that is not the type of "responsive action" envisioned in Booth. In re Bayside Prison Litigation, 190 F. Supp. 2d 755, 771–72 (D.N.J. 2002) (ruling on prison complaint and Ombudsman procedures); see Freeman v. Snyder, 2001 WL 515258, *7 (D.Del., Apr. 10, 2001) (holding the "vague, informal process described by the defendants is 'hardly a grievance procedure'").

Courts have held that a "Warden's Forum," a body consisting of elected inmate representatives who alone have the right to raise issues there, was not an available remedy because the plaintiff did not have a "personal, direct right" to pursue a complaint before that body. Jones v. Michigan Dep't of Corrections, 2008 WL 762241, *4–5 (W.D.Mich., Mar. 18, 2008); Mitchell v. Caruso, 2008 WL 4057913, *6 (W.D.Mich., Aug. 28, 2008). Other decisions have held to the contrary about the Warden's Forum, but without considering the concerns raised in Jones. See Berryman v. Granholm, 2007 WL 2259334, *10–11 (E.D.Mich., Aug. 3, 2007) (noting that issues regarding the content of a policy or procedure are properly raised via the Warden's Forum and not the grievance system); Jackson v. Caruso, 2008 WL 828118, *4 (W.D.Mich., Feb. 12, 2008) (same),

report and recommendation adopted as modified on other grounds, 2008 WL 828116 (W.D.Mich., Mar. 26, 2008).

Another court has held that a "Self-Initiated Progress Report" process, which permitted prisoners denied parole to seek reconsideration six months or more later and show that circumstances have changed, was not equivalent to a grievance system and need not be exhausted. Armstrong v. Beauclair, 2007 WL 1381790, *8–9 (D. Idaho, Mar. 29, 2007) ("It is clear that the SIPR is not a problem-solving mechanism. . . .").

[295]See cases cited in n.270, above.

The prisoner must use the administrative procedure of the institution or system where his or her problem arose. Acosta v. U.S. Marshals Service, 445 F.3d 509, 512–13 (1st Cir. 2006) (holding that a prisoner who was placed by the Marshals Service in several county jails and two federal prisons, but only used the Marshals' complaint system, failed to exhaust either as to the jails or as to the Bureau of Prisons institutions).

[296]See Owens v. Keeling, 461 F.3d 763, 769 (6th Cir. 2006) (holding grievance system was not an available remedy for classification complaint where prison required use of a separate classification appeal procedure); Mojias v. Johnson, 351 F.3d 606, 610 (2d Cir. 2003) (courts must establish that the prisoner's claim does not fall into an exception to the administrative remedy); Snider v. Melindez, 199 F.3d 108, 114 (2d Cir. 1999) ("[T]he provision clearly does not require a prisoner to exhaust administrative remedies that do not address the subject matter of his complaint."); Mitchell v. Caruso, 2006 WL 3825077, *2 (E.D. Mich., Dec. 26, 2006) (noting that grievance policy made "the content of a policy or procedure" non-grievable); Davis v. Frazier, 1999 WL 395414, *4 (S.D.N.Y., June 15, 1999) (noting allegation that New York City prisoners are told at orientation that "a grievance cannot be brought against Officers or Staff" could estop defendants from claiming a failure to exhaust); McGrath v. Johnson, 67 F. Supp. 2d 499, 510–11 (E.D. Pa. 1999) (holding prisoner not required to file a grievance on a matter the inmate grievance procedure would not address); Rizzuto v. City of New York, 2003 WL 1212758, *4 (S.D.N.Y., Mar. 17, 2003) (noting that claims of assault, verbal harassment, or matters under Inspector General investigation are non-grievable).

One court has recently stated that exhaustion is required "even if a prisoner 'understood that the claims put forth in [his] complaint were "non-grievable" under prison policy.'" Steele v. Fed. Bureau of Prisons, 355 F.3d 1204, 1214 (10th Cir. 2003) (quoting Beaudry v. Corr. Corp. of Am., 331 F.3d 1164, 1166 (10th Cir. 2003)). The court referred to situations where a prisoner thought a claim was non-grievable, but was wrong. If there is any question whether your claim is grievable, you should exhaust.

system to system,[297] so you must study the policies at your institution to see whether the grievance system or another remedy is available for your problem.[298]

Courts have held that issues over which the grievance system has no actual authority need not be exhausted, even if they are not listed as non-grievable.[299] Also, an issue may be grievable on paper but non-grievable in fact, and therefore the remedy will not be available, because of the way the grievance system actually operates.[300] It is wise to try to

exhaust anyway in these situations, since otherwise it may be hard to prove that the grievance system does not operate according to the rules on paper.

Often, prisons have separate, specialized remedies for non-grievable issues. These are available remedies and you must use them for the problems they have authority over.[301] This issue arises most frequently with disciplinary proceedings and issues related to them: to satisfy the "proper exhaustion" requirement,[302] you must choose correctly between appealing a disciplinary action and filing a separate grievance—and sometimes you may need to do both. In most systems, it appears, a suit that attacks the conduct of the disciplinary hearing itself is exhausted by a disciplinary appeal.[303] A suit about the events underlying the disciplinary

---

[297]See, e.g., Owens v. Keeling, 461 F.3d 763, 769–70 (6th Cir. 2006) (noting classification matters are excluded from Tennessee grievance system); Figel v. Bochard, 89 Fed.Appx. 970, 971 (6th Cir. 2004) (unpublished) (noting that Michigan system makes non-grievable issues that "involve a significant number of prisoners"); Mitchell v. Caruso, 2006 WL 3825077, *2 (E.D.Mich., Dec. 26, 2006) (noting that "the content of a policy or procedure" is not grievable in Michigan); Cordero v. Bureau of Prisons, 2005 WL 1205808, *1 (M.D.Pa., Apr. 27, 2005) (noting that Privacy Act and Freedom of Information Act matters are excluded from the federal Administrative Remedy Program); Richards v. Massachusetts Dep't of Correction, 2005 WL 283203, *1 (D.Mass., Feb. 7, 2005) (noting that Massachusetts system allows grievances about "matters concerning access to medical or mental health care" but not "medical or clinical decisions related to an inmate's physical or mental condition").

In some instances, the complaints of particular categories of prisoners are non-grievable. See n.331 of this section, below.

[298]State law or grievance rules that say you are not required to exhaust particular issues do not excuse you from exhausting under the PLRA, which is federal law. Short v. Greene, 577 F. Supp. 2d 790, 791–93 (S.D.W.Va. 2008). Only if the remedy is not available for particular issues—i.e., you cannot get any relief for those issues through it—are you excused from using the remedy.

[299]See Nooner v. Norris, 2006 WL 4958988, *3 (E.D.Ark., June 19, 2006) (holding that prisoner challenging lethal injection protocol need not exhaust the grievance process because it had no authority, since state law placed the subject entirely in the Director's authority); Farnworth v. Craven, 2007 WL 793397, *5 (D.Idaho, Mar. 14, 2007) (holding prisoner seeking a new parole hearing need not exhaust the grievance system because it had no authority over the Parole Commission); Stevens v. Goord, 2003 WL 21396665, *5 (S.D.N.Y., June 16, 2003) (private prison medical provider failed to show that the prison grievance procedure would actually have authority over claims against it), adhered to on reargument, 2003 WL 22052978 (S.D.N.Y., Sept. 3, 2003); Handberry v. Thompson, 92 F. Supp. 2d 244, 247 (S.D.N.Y. 2000) (holding that prisoners need not grieve failure to deliver educational services because the issues were out of the control of the Department of Corrections). But see Arsberry v. Illinios, 244 F.3d 558, 562 (7th Cir. 2001) ("[P]laintiffs say they have no such remedies against exorbitant phone bills, but the cases we have cited reject a 'futility' exception to the requirement of exhaustion."). The Arsberry court seems to have overlooked the distinction between an allegedly futile remedy and one that is not available. Its holding appears inconsistent with the Supreme Court's statement in Booth v. Churner, see n.289, above, about the meaning of "available."

[300]See Marshall v. Knight, 2006 WL 3354700, *4 (N.D.Ind., Nov. 17, 2006) (instructions to grievance personnel to respond to grievances about law library hours only by sending prisoners a copy of a memo deprived grievance staff of authority to act on

those grievances and made the remedy unavailable); Wigfall v. Duval, 2006 WL 2381285, *8 (D.Mass., Aug. 15, 2006) (citing evidence that use of force claims were not treated as grievances); Scott v. Gardner, 287 F. Supp. 2d 477, 491 (S.D.N.Y. 2003) (holding that allegations that grievance staff refused to process and file grievances about occurrences at other prisons, claiming they were not grievable, sufficiently alleged lack of an available remedy); Casanova v. Dubois, 2002 WL 1613715, *6 (D.Mass., July 22, 2002) (finding that, contrary to written policy, practice was "to treat complaints of alleged civil rights abuses by staff as 'not grievable'"), remanded on other grounds, 304 F.3d 75 (1st Cir. 2002); Livingston v. Piskor, 215 F.R.D. 84, 86–87 (W.D.N.Y. 2003) (citing evidence that grievance personnel refused to process grievances where a disciplinary report had been filed covering the same events); Davis v. Frazier, 1999 WL 395414, *4 (S.D.N.Y., June 15, 1999) (if prisoners are told at orientation that "a grievance cannot be brought against Officers or Staff," prisoners would be excused from exhausting such claims); see Marr v. Fields, 2008 WL 828788, *6 (W.D.Mich., Mar. 27, 2008) (evidence that hearing officers interpreted grievance policy broadly to exclude all grievances with any relationship to a disciplinary charges could excuse failure to exhaust).

[301]See Owens v. Keeling, 461 F.3d 763, 769–72 (6th Cir. 2006) (holding prisoner who filed classification appeal exhausted, notwithstanding failure to complete inapplicable grievance procedure); Jenkins v. Haubert, 179 F.3d 19, 23 n.1 (2d Cir. 1999) (appeal of disciplinary conviction satisfied the exhaustion requirement); Timley v. Nelson, 2001 WL 309120, *1 (D.Kan., Feb. 16, 2001) (prisoner's failure to pursue "religious accommodation" exception procedure meant that administrative remedies were not exhausted); Mullins v. Smith, 14 F. Supp. 2d 1009, 1012 (E.D.Mich. 1998) (prisoner exhausted state administrative remedies by submitting a request for a rehearing).

[302]This rule is discussed in § D.5 of this chapter.

[303]Davis v. Barrett, 575 F.3d 129, 133 (2d Cir. 2009) (disciplinary appeal exhausted due process claim; plaintiff's argument that SHU conditions were atypical and significant so as to require due process did not require a separate grievance); Jenkins v. Haubert, 179 F.3d 19, 23 n.1 (2d Cir. 1999) (holding that disciplinary appeals exhausted plaintiff's challenge to the resulting disciplinary sanctions); Portley-El v. Steinbeck, 2008 WL 697383, *10 (D.Colo., Mar. 14, 2008) (holding that a disciplinary appeal exhausted due process claims under rule stating grievance procedure may not be used to seek review of disciplinary convictions; rejecting defendants' argument that constitutional claims could be grieved); Rivera v.

charges (*e.g.*, a claim that the charges were retaliatory, or the incident really involved staff misconduct rather than prisoner misconduct) will generally not be exhausted by a disciplinary appeal and will require a separate grievance,[304] though some courts have held otherwise.[305] In all cases it is

the prison's rules governing grievances and appeals that will determine which remedy is the correct one,[306] so assume nothing and read the rules carefully. The problem is that prison rules are often unclear, to the point where even prison officials can't keep them straight.[307] This sort of confusion about the scope of disciplinary appeals and grievances is common.[308] In some cases, grievance bodies have

_____

Goord, 2003 WL 1700518, *10 (S.D.N.Y., Mar. 28, 2003) (holding that a claim of hearing officer misconduct was exhausted by a disciplinary appeal); Muhammad v. Pico, 2003 WL 21792158, *8 n.22 (S.D.N.Y., Aug. 5, 2003) (holding due process claims exhausted by disciplinary appeal); Sweet v. Wende Correctional Facility, 253 F. Supp. 2d 492, 496 (W.D.N.Y. 2003) (holding an appeal from a disciplinary hearing may exhaust if it raises the same issues as the subsequent federal complaint). *But see* Rivera v. Nelson, 2006 WL 2038393, *1 (D.Colo., July 17, 2006) (holding that disciplinary appeals exclusively addressed only "the *conviction* that resulted from the disciplinary hearing and the *placement* that resulted from the administrative segregation hearing," and due process claims should have been the subject of separate grievances); *accord*, Ross v. Gibson, 2006 WL 2567853, *2 (D.Colo., Aug. 8, 2006).

[304]*See* Farid v. Ellen, 593 F.3d 233, 2010 WL 308971, 248 (2d Cir. 2010) (disciplinary appeal of contraband and smuggling charges did not exhaust claim of confiscation of papers and personal effects where confiscation was not a "constituent element of the disciplinary hearing"); Terrase v. Cain, 2008 WL 717737, *2 (M.D.La., Mar. 17, 2008) (a disciplinary appeal did not exhaust a claim of failure to protect, since it did not give officials adequate notice of that claim); Chavis v. Goord, 2007 WL 2903950, *9–10 (N.D.N.Y., Oct. 1, 2007) (holding disciplinary appeal did not exhaust plaintiff's claim for retaliation and interference with religious exercise; noting case is "readily distinguishable" from due process challenges to hearing); Webster v. Kurtz, 2006 WL 893606, *2 (D.Colo., Mar. 31, 2006) (holding that successful disciplinary appeal did not exhaust claims of subsequent retaliation and refusal to reinstate visiting privileges; these should have been grieved notwithstanding rule prohibiting grieving disciplinary convictions); Belton v. Robinson, 2006 WL 231608, *3–4 (D.N.J., Jan. 30, 2006) (holding that an appeal of a disciplinary conviction did not exhaust a claim that the officer injured the plaintiff during the incident); Rodney v. Goord, 2003 WL 21108353, *6 (S.D.N.Y., May 15, 2003) (holding an allegation of false disciplinary charges had to be grieved in addition to appealing the disciplinary conviction); Tookes v. Artuz, 2002 WL 1484391, *4 (S.D.N.Y., July 11, 2002) (holding that appeal of disciplinary conviction did not exhaust as to claim against officer who allegedly wrote a false disciplinary report); Cherry v. Selsky, 2000 WL 943436, *7 (S.D.N.Y., July 7, 2000) (same as *Tookes*).

[305]*See* Mitchell v. Horn, 318 F.3d 523, 531 (3d Cir. 2003) (holding that a prisoner who claimed retaliatory discipline exhausted by appealing the disciplinary decision to the highest level); Harper v. Harmonn, 2006 WL 2522409, *3–4 (E.D.Cal., Aug. 29, 2006) (holding that a disciplinary appeal exhausted the plaintiff's claim that staff members falsified the charges against him); Samuels v. Selsky, 2002 WL 31040370, *8 (S.D.N.Y., Sept. 12, 2002) (holding that propriety of confiscation of religious materials had been exhausted via a disciplinary appeal from the resulting contraband and "demonstration" charges; "issues directly tied to the disciplinary hearing which have been directly appealed need not be appealed again collaterally through the Inmate Grievance Program"); *see also* Hopkins v. Coplan, 2005 WL 615746, *2 (D.N.H., Mar. 16, 2005) (holding that a disciplinary appeal did not

exhaust a claim of a staff-prompted inmate assault, which it did not focus on or set out in detail; stating in dictum that if the appeal had set out the claim in detail and identified the relevant parties and their wrongful conduct, the court might treat it as "the functional equivalent of an exhausted grievance").

[306]Woodford v. Ngo, 548 U.S. 81 (2006); *see* Fortney v. Schultz, 2010 WL 376932, *2 (W.D.Wis., Jan. 27, 2010) (noting that disciplinary appeals in this prison system exhaust as to sufficiency of the evidence, but procedural errors must be challenged through a subsequent grievance); Madyun v. Cook, 2008 WL 4330896, *3 (W.D.Wis., May 23, 2008); Keal v. Washington, 2007 WL 1977155, *2 (W.D.Wash., July 3, 2007) (noting disciplinary appeal must be used to challenge infraction or sanction for infraction, but staff misconduct grievance was the remedy for use of force complaint).

If the designated remedy is a disciplinary appeal, but the prisoner cannot appeal because he pled guilty to the offense, the remedy is not available. Marr v. Fields, 2008 WL 828788, *5–7 (W.D.Mich., Mar. 27, 2008).

[307]For example, in one New York State case, prison officials argued that a prisoner claiming retaliatory fabrication of evidence in a disciplinary proceeding should have filed a separate grievance, not a disciplinary appeal, to exhaust that issue. The court said dismissal for non-exhaustion was inappropriate because the rule was unclear and the prisoner had a reasonable belief that his complaint could only be pursued in an appeal. Giano v. Goord, 380 F.3d 670, 679 (2d Cir. 2004). Prison officials never clarified the rule, and a few years later they made the exact opposite argument, saying that the prisoner had filed a grievance about retaliatory false discipline, and he should have pursued a disciplinary appeal instead. Larkins v. Selsky, 2006 WL 3548959, *9 (S.D.N.Y., Dec. 6, 2006). The court ruled against them in that case too, since the rule was still confusing.

[308]*See* Johnson v. Testman, 380 F.3d 691, 696–97 (2d Cir. 2004) (remanding for consideration of claim that "because under BOP regulations the appellate process for disciplinary rulings and for grievances was one and the same, [plaintiff] reasonably believed that raising his complaints during his disciplinary appeal sufficed to exhaust his available administrative remedies"); Woods v. Lozer, 2007 WL 173704, *3 (M.D.Tenn., Jan. 18, 2007) (where a grievance decision found a use of force claim was not grievable because it was erroneously said to seek review of disciplinary procedures and punishments, the prisoner exhausted when he appealed that decision); Cahill v. Arpaio, 2006 WL 3201018, *2 (D.Ariz., Nov. 2, 2006) (stating jail rules concerning what aspects of a disciplinary incident can be grieved are "sufficiently confusing such that Plaintiff's interpretation that he could not grieve his excessive force claim is reasonable"); Branch v. Goord, 2006 WL 2807168, *3 (S.D.N.Y., Sept. 28, 2006) (finding plaintiff's misunderstanding that all matters concerning disciplinary hearings were exempt from grievance process was "reasonable" under *Giano*, cited in previous note); *see* Ray v. Kertes, 130 Fed.Appx. 541, 544 (3d Cir. 2005) (unpublished) (citing *Giano*); Parish v. Lee, 2004 WL 877103, *4 (E.D.La., Apr. 22, 2004) ("The inmates must be given the benefit

Exhaustion of Administrative Remedies 577

misapplied their own rules and have erroneously rejected grievances that had anything to do with incidents that resulted in discipline.[309] In some prison systems, however, the rules *do* bar grievances that have any relationship to a disciplinary incident.[310] The bottom line is that you must read the rules very carefully to determine whether a particular issue (the actions of the hearing officer, the bringing of charges, or the evidence behind them, or the underlying incident) calls for a grievance or a disciplinary appeal. In some cases both will be required if you wish to raise multiple issues.[311] If the rules are not absolutely clear, it may be wise to file both to protect yourself from an argument later that whatever you did was wrong. If prison officials reject your attempt to use a particular remedy, it is harder for them to argue later that you should have used it.

A remedy may not be available because of circumstances peculiar to a particular case. For example, a prisoner

---

of the doubt based on what appears to be the written policy to which they are bound."); *see also* Vasquez v. Hilbert, 2008 WL 2224394, *4 (W.D.Wis., May 28, 2008) (declining to dismiss where plaintiff exhausted his medical claim late because medical treatment was mentioned in a disciplinary report and the rules said a grievance raising "any issue related to the conduct report" must await completion of the disciplinary process; plaintiff acted reasonably in waiting).

[309]Woods v. Lozer, 2007 WL 173704, *3 (M.D.Tenn., Jan. 18, 2007) (holding a prisoner exhausted when he appealed a grievance decision stating that his use of force claim was not grievable because it was mistakenly said to seek review of disciplinary procedures and punishments); Livingston v. Piskor, 215 F.R.D. 84, 86–87 (W.D.N.Y. 2003) (evidence that grievance personnel refused to process grievances where a disciplinary report had been filed covering the same events precluded dismissal for non-exhaustion).

[310]*See* Vasquez v. Hilbert, 2008 WL 2224394, *4 (W.D.Wis., May 28, 2008) (citing rule that a grievance raising "any issue related to the conduct report" must await completion of the disciplinary process); James v. McCall, 2007 WL 752161, *5 (D.S.C., Mar. 8, 2007) (citing rule stating "[w]hen an inmate is involved in an incident that results in a disciplinary, that issue/complaint becomes non-grievable"); Lindell v. O'Donnell, 2005 WL 2740999, *27, 31 (W.D.Wis., Oct. 21, 2005) (rejecting argument that plaintiff should have filed an inmate complaint where the relevant policy forbade using inmate complaints for "any issue related to a conduct report.").

[311]For example, in some prison systems, appealing a disciplinary conviction and challenging the rule under which you were convicted require, respectively, a disciplinary appeal and a separate grievance. *See* Singh v. Goord, 520 F. Supp. 2d 487, 497–98 (S.D.N.Y. 2007) (holding successful disciplinary appeal challenging discipline for refusing work contrary to religious beliefs did not exhaust plaintiff's challenge to the underlying disciplinary rule; a separate grievance was required); Hattie v. Hallock, 8 F. Supp. 2d 685, 689 (N.D.Ohio 1998) (holding that in order to challenge a prison rule, the prisoner must not only appeal from the disciplinary conviction for breaking it, but must also grieve the validity of the rule), *judgment amended*, 16 F. Supp. 2d 834 (N.D.Ohio 1998). Other examples of issues not exhausted by a disciplinary appeal are cited in n.304, above.

may be unable to file a grievance because of a medical condition.[312] Courts have made a number of decisions concerning mental illness or retardation, some favoring prisoners[313] and some favoring prison officials,[314] without settling on any

---

[312]Days v. Johnson, 322 F.3d 863, 867 (5th Cir. 2003) (noting that "one's personal ability to access the grievance system could render the system unavailable"); Macahilas v. Taylor, 2008 WL 220364, *4 (E.D.Cal., Jan. 25, 2008) (denying summary judgment to defendants where prisoner said "his mind was too clouded" by a physical illness to grieve timely), *report and recommendation adopted*, 2008 WL 506109 (E.D.Cal., Feb. 22, 2008); Ricketts v. AW of Unicor, 2008 WL 1990897, *6 (M.D.Pa., May 6, 2008) (denying dismissal for non-exhaustion where prisoner said he was in the hospital paralyzed throughout the period for filing a grievance); Holcomb v. Director of Corr., 2006 WL 3302436, *6–7 (N.D.Cal., Nov. 14, 2006) (holding a prisoner rendered quadriplegic and never returned to prison after his injury did not have an opportunity to file timely). *But see* Ferrington v. La. Dep't of Corr., 315 F.3d 529, 532 (5th Cir. 2002) (holding plaintiff's near blindness did not exempt him from exhausting, since he had managed to file the lawsuit).

[313]*See* Cole v. Sobina, 2007 WL 4460617, *7 (W.D.Pa., Dec. 19, 2007) (refusing to dismiss for non-exhaustion where plaintiff alleged mental disabilities which could account for his noncompliance with grievance procedures); Whitington v. Sokol, 491 F. Supp. 2d 1012, 1019 (D.Colo. 2007) (refusing to dismiss for non-exhaustion where plaintiff alleged he had no remedies because he was mentally incapacitated and was transferred to a mental institution shortly after the incident he sued about); Petty v. Goord, 2007 WL 724648, *8 (S.D.N.Y., Mar. 5, 2007) (refusing to dismiss for non-exhaustion where prisoner was transferred to a mental hospital after filing a grievance and missed the final deadline; the court notes there is no evidence before it of his mental state at the time, and holds that two months plus in a mental hospital constituted special circumstances); LaMarche v. Bell, 2005 WL 2998614, *3 (D.N.H., Nov. 8, 2005) (acknowledging that evidence of mental illness might support argument that late grievance should be deemed effective); Ullrich v. Idaho, 2006 WL 288384, *3 (D.Idaho, Feb. 6, 2006) (dismissing for non-exhaustion, but directing prison officials to appoint someone to assist the plaintiff, who alleged mental illness and denial of psychiatric treatment); *see also* Macahilas v. Taylor, 2008 WL 220364, *4 (E.D.Cal., Jan. 25, 2008) (denying summary judgment to defendants based on alleged psychological effects of a serious physical illness), *report and recommendation adopted*, 2008 WL 506109 (E.D.Cal., Feb. 22, 2008). In *Johnson-Ester v. Elyea*, 2007 WL 3046155, *2 (N.D.Ill., Oct. 10, 2007), the mother of a mentally incompetent prisoner said she had made repeated complaints about his medical care without success; the court rejected defendants' argument that the case should be dismissed for non-exhaustion, citing the mother's assertions that "she did what she could do" to solve the problem administratively, but it did not clarify what it thought the PLRA requires or permits in this sort of situation.

[314]*See* Braswell v. Corrections Corp. of America, 2009 WL 2447614, *8 (M.D.Tenn., Aug. 10, 2009) (holding that mental illness excuses non-exhaustion only insofar as "an inmate's mental incapacity rendered him unable to communicate in any intelligible form for a particular period"); Gomez v. Swanson, 2009 WL 1085274, *4 (E.D.Cal., Apr. 22, 2009) ("He has neither come forward with evidence illustrating the nature and severity of those problems, nor has he alleged facts showing precisely how his mental status was an issue in failing to exhaust."); Rigsby v. Schriro, 2008

clear standard for such cases. Courts have also not taken any consistent position concerning prisoners who may

be unable to use the grievance system properly because of other disabilities,[315] illiteracy or lack of education,[316]

WL 2705376, *3 (D.Ariz., July 9, 2008) (dismissing for non-exhaustion where plaintiff said that in 2007 he had been the victim of assaults in 2004 that resulted in brain swelling, partial memory loss, depression, and PTSD; plaintiff "provides no specific information about how these injuries prevented him from initiating, much less completing, the inmate grievance process"); Fleming v. Dettloff, 2008 WL 2558021, *2 (E.D.Mich., June 24, 2008) (dismissing for non-exhaustion despite plaintiff's allegation of mental incompetence and his participation in the prison Mental Health Program, since he presented "no evidence of mental incompetency beyond allegations and conclusory statements in the pleadings"); Lawson v. Davis, 2008 WL 1885813, *2 (W.D.Va., Apr. 28, 2008) (dismissing challenge to 90-day waiting period for psychiatric medications since the plaintiff did not allege facts indicating his mental problems prevented him from understanding or using the grievance procedures), aff'd, 285 Fed.Appx. 77 (4th Cir. 2008) (unpublished); Baker v. Schriro, 2008 WL 622020, *5–6 (D.Ariz., Mar. 4, 2008) (rejecting claim of inability to follow grievance procedure where plaintiff was representing himself in three criminal appeals and initating three civil rights actions during the same time period), review denied, 2008 WL 2003757 (D.Ariz., May 8, 2008); Saggese v. Corrente, 2008 WL 474110, *5 & n.5 (D.N.J., Feb. 15, 2008) (rejecting prisoner's claim that he was mentally ill and "in a blur" since his claims of overmedication and injury only cover two weeks and he could have exhausted after that); Williams v. Pettiford, 2007 WL 3119548, *2–3 (D.S.C., Oct. 22, 2007) (rejecting argument that prisoner who was dyslexic and mentally ill was not required to exhaust), aff'd, 272 Fed.Appx. 311 (4th Cir. 2008) (unpublished); Yorkey v. Pettiford, 2007 WL 2750068, *4–5 (D.S.C., Sept. 20, 2007) (stating Woodford v. Ngo "appears to have foreclosed" argument that mental illness excused plaintiff from exhausting), aff'd, 271 Fed.Appx. 337 (4th Cir. 2008) (unpublished); Evans v. McWilliams, 2007 WL 2410370, *2 (D.Ariz., Aug. 21, 2007) (refusing to exempt prisoner from exhaustion requirement based on claim of mental illness since there is no "extenuating circumstances" exception, he provided no evidence of his illness, and he had made complaints to authorities), subsequent determination, 2007 WL 2949007 (D.Ariz., Oct. 10, 2007); Bester v. Dixion, 2007 WL 951558, *10 (N.D.N.Y., Mar. 27, 2007) (noting initial concern that prisoner had been transferred to a psychiatric hospital because of a mental condition, but dismissing since he had written complaints and spoken to investigators); Hall v. Cheshire County Dep't of Corrections, 2007 WL 951657, *1–2 (D.N.H., Mar. 27, 2007) (dismissing for non-exhaustion even though plaintiff's claim was failure to treat his mental illness resulting in conduct such as cutting himself repeatedly and swallowing glass; no inquiry into whether his mental condition could have affected his ability to exhaust); LaMarche v. Bell, 2006 WL 2927242, *5 (D.N.H., Oct. 13, 2006), on reconsideration in part, 2006 WL 3359022 (D.N.H., Nov. 17, 2006); Williams v. Kennedy, 2006 WL 18314, *2 (S.D.Tex., Jan. 4, 2006) (dismissing despite prisoner's claim he didn't know of the exhaustion requirement and a prior brain injury made it difficult for him to remember things); Bakker v. Kuhnes, 2004 WL 1092287 (N.D.Iowa, May 14, 2004) (rejecting plaintiff's argument that his medication doses were so high they "prohibited him from being of sound mind to draft a grievance"; noting that he failed to submit a grievance after his medication was corrected, and he filed other grievances during the relevant period).

[315]Williams v. Hayman, 657 F.Supp.2d 488, 495-97 (D.N.J. 2008) (evidence of the deaf plaintiff's inability to communicate in writing or with his counselor raised a factual issue concerning availability to him of the grievance remedy); Johnson-Ester v. Elyea, 2009 WL 632250, *6-8 (N.D.Ill., Mar. 9, 2009) (where prisoner could not write, ambulate, or make himself understood, and may have been irrational or delusional at times, he was not capable of pursuing a grievance; letters from his mother and lawyer about his condition put officials on sufficient notice they should have assisted him in filing a grievance; grievance system made no provision for outside persons to use it); Kuhajda v. Ill. Dep't of Corr., 2006 WL 1662941, *1 (C.D.Ill., June 8, 2006) (holding that a prisoner who is hearing-impaired and has limited ability to read and write, and who did not have the assistance of a sign language interpreter, raised a factual issue concerning availability of remedies); see Elliott v. Monroe Correctional Complex, 2007 WL 208422, *3 (W.D.Wash., Jan. 23, 2007) (dismissing for non-exhaustion where plaintiff with cerebral palsy was provided with assistance and had filed numerous grievances, though he hadn't actually exhausted any).

[316]Robertson v. Dart, 2009 WL 2382527, *3 (N.D.Ill., Aug. 3, 2009) (denying summary judgment on exhaustion where the illiterate plaintiff alleged that a staff member gave him wrong information about how to mark a form to appeal his grievance decision); Cook v. LaPonsie, 2008 WL 4425589, *5 (W.D.Mich., Sept. 26, 2008) (excusing plaintiff's mis-description of incident in his grievance where he was illiterate and someone else had written the grievance for him); Langford v. Ifediora, 2007 WL 1427423, *3–4 (E.D.Ark., May 11, 2007) (holding plaintiff's age, deteriorating health, and lack of general education, combined with failure to provide him assistance in preparing grievances, raised a factual issue concerning the availability of the remedy to him); Kuhajda v. Ill. Dep't of Corr., 2006 WL 1662941, *1 (C.D.Ill., June 8, 2006) (citing hearing-impaired prisoner's limited ability to read and write, and lack of a sign language interpreter, raised a factual issue concerning availability of remedies). In the unreported decision in Davis v. Corr. Corp. of Am., 131 Fed.Appx. 127, 128–29 (10th Cir. 2005) (unpublished), the court rejected the argument that the plaintiff's educational deficiencies (he said he was a "slow learner and thinker" still working to obtain a G.E.D.) should excuse his failure to exhaust, noting that his papers "did not describe insurmountable barriers to his filing of grievances and did not show that prison officials had effectively foreclosed his efforts." See also Ramos v. Smith, 187 Fed.Appx. 152, 154 (3d Cir. 2006) (unpublished) (rejecting claim of illiteracy, since federal regulations require assistance to illiterate prisoners, and he did not alleged that he asked for such assistance); Georgacarakos v. Watts, 147 Fed. Appx. 12, 14–15 (10th Cir. 2005) (unpublished) (ignoring litigant's plea to appoint counsel if his exhaustion presentation was inadequate, in light of his lack of "means and sophistication").

inability to speak or write English,[317] or youth.[318]

A remedy may be unavailable because the prisoner has been transferred out of the particular prison or jail system.[319]

However, the remedy *is* available if the system provides a way to pursue grievances after transfer.[320] Also, if a prisoner had time to file a grievance before transfer and failed to do so, he will probably be deemed to have failed to exhaust.[321] Be careful with this issue. Courts sometimes assume that a remedy remains available after transfer whether or not there

---

[317]Several courts have refused to find non-exhaustion where a monolingual Spanish-speaking plaintiff alleged he could not understand or follow the grievance procedures because he could not get them, or get help with them, in Spanish. *See* Bojorquez v. Fitzsimmons, 2009 WL 790950, *4–5 (C.D.Ill., Mar. 23, 2009); Abel v. Pierson, 2008 WL 509466, *4 (S.D.Ill., Feb. 13, 2008); Ramos v. Rosevthal, 2007 WL 1464436, *1 n.1 (D.Neb., May 17, 2007); Gonzalez v. Lantz, 2005 WL 1711968, *3 (D. Conn., July 20, 2005). *Contra*, Benavidez v. Stansberry, 2008 WL 4279559, *4 (N.D.Ohio, Sept. 12, 2008) (holding there is no exception to the exhaustion requirement for persons who do not get the grievance procedures in a language they can read).

[318]One appeals court has rejected the argument that a juvenile jail inmate complaining of excessive force should be excused from failure to use the grievance process in part because he was a juvenile. Brock v. Kenyon County, Ky., 93 Fed.Appx. 792, 798 (6th Cir. 2004) (unpublished); *see also* Minix v. Pazera, 2005 WL 1799538, *4 (N.D.Ind., July 27, 2005) (holding that a juvenile's mother's repeated complaints to numerous officials did not exhaust her son's complaint of being beaten and raped). By contrast, in *Lewis v. Gagne*, 281 F. Supp. 2d 429, 433–35 (N.D.N.Y., 2003), the court held that a juvenile detainee's mother, who had complained to facility staff and contacted an attorney, family court, and the state Child Abuse and Maltreatment Register, and whose complaints were known to the facility director and agency counsel, had made sufficient "reasonable efforts" to exhaust, without explicitly commenting on the juvenile detainee's own status or capacity to follow administrative procedures.

[319]Rodriguez v. Westchester County Jail Corr. Dep't, 372 F.3d 485, 488 (2d Cir. 2004); Gomez v. Ficket, 2008 WL 4279596, *3 (W.D.Wash., Sept. 16, 2008) (declining to dismiss where plaintiff's claim based on jail staff's actions did not arise until he had been transferred to state prison, and defendants submitted no evidence of an available remedy); Ammouri v. Adappt House, Inc., 2008 WL 2405762, *3 (E.D.Pa., June 12, 2008) (noting that plaintiff was repeatedly told he could not grieve matters from his previous institution); Davis v. Kirk, 2007 WL 4353798, *7 (S.D.Tex., Dec. 11, 2007) (holding prisoner's grievance appeal was moot on transfer); Thomas v. Maricopa County Bd. of Supervisors, 2007 WL 2995634, *4 (D.Ariz., Oct. 12, 2007) (declining to dismiss where the prisoner did not have knowledge of the violation until after his release and the grievance policy did not provide for grievances after release); Ray v. Hogg, 2007 WL 2713902, *12 (E.D.Mich., Sept. 18, 2007) (holding prisoner transferred out of jail had no access to jail grievance process); Basham v. Correctional Medical Services, Inc., 2007 WL 2481338, *5 (S.D.W.Va., Aug. 29, 2007) (holding defendants failed to show a grievance appeal was available to a hospitalized prisoner separated from his grievance documents); Knight v. Dutcher, 2007 WL 2407034, *12 (D.Neb., Aug. 20, 2007) (declining to dismiss where plaintiff was transferred before he could grieve and defendants did not meet their burden of showing the remedy was available after transfer); Goldwater v. Arpaio, 2007 WL 1577891, *2 (D.Ariz., May 31, 2007) (declining to dismiss for non-exhaustion where prisoner was transferred and grievance policy did not provide for post-transfer grievances); Mellender v. Dane County, 2006 WL 3113212, *3 (W.D.Wis., Oct. 27, 2006) (refusing to dismiss for non-exhaustion where prisoner transferred

from jail to prison tried to mail a grievance to the jail and then tried to use the prison's grievance system to complain about the jail); Szkup v. Arpaio, 2006 WL 2821685, *2 (D.Ariz., Sept. 29, 2006) (declining to dismiss for non-exhaustion where jail policy didn't say and defendants submitted no evidence it was available after transfer); Bradley v. Washington, 441 F. Supp. 2d 97, 102–03 (D.D.C. Aug. 2, 2006) (holding D.C. remedies became unavailable upon prisoner's transfer to federal medical facility, since D.C. procedures say they apply to facilities under authority, jurisdiction, or contract with D.C.); Barnard v. District of Columbia, 223 F. Supp. 2d 211, 214 (D.D.C. 2002) (holding that a prisoner who was first hospitalized, then involved in hearings, then transferred during the 15 days he had to file a grievance may not have had a grievance remedy available); Mitchell v. Angelone, 82 F. Supp. 2d 485, 490 (E.D.Va. 1999) (excusing exhaustion by prisoner who had been transferred so frequently he had never had time to exhaust); *see* Miller v. Norris, 247 F.3d 736, 740 (8th Cir. 2001) (holding that a transferred prisoner who alleged he could not get grievance forms for the transferring prison system sufficiently alleged exhaustion of available remedies).

[320]*In re* Bayside Prison Litigation, 2008 WL 2387324, *5 (D.N.J., May 19, 2008) (prisoner transferred within New Jersey prison system could still use the grievance system); Cohea v. Jones, 2008 WL 114956, *5 (E.D.Cal., Jan. 11, 2008) (same for California), *report and recommendation adopted*, 2008 WL 496143 (E.D.Cal., Feb. 21, 2008), *aff'd*, 331 Fed.Appx. 475 (9th Cir. 2009) (unpublished); Jackson v. Walker, 2007 WL 2344938, *5 (E.D.Ky., Aug. 14, 2007) (holding transfer did not excuse non-exhaustion because the process can be completed by mail), *amended on reconsideration in part*, 2007 WL 2702325 (E.D.Ky., Sept. 12, 2007), *amended in part*, 2007 WL 3145957 (E.D.Ky., Oct. 25, 2007); Lawrence v. Washington, 2006 WL 1071510, *2 (D.D.C. Apr. 21, 2006) (holding transfer within system did not excuse failure to exhaust where regulations permit grievances after transfer), *aff'd*, 204 Fed.Appx. 27 (D.C. Cir. 2006) (unpublished); Soto v. Belcher, 339 F. Supp. 2d 592, 595 (S.D.N.Y. 2004) (holding transfer did not excuse exhaustion since regulations permit grievances after transfer); Delio v. Morgan, 2003 WL 21373168, *3 (S.D.N.Y., June 13, 2003).

In *Brownell v. Krom*, 446 F.3d 305, 312–13 (2d Cir. 2006), the court found special circumstances justifying the plaintiff's failure to exhaust correctly where grievance regulations did prescribe the handling of grievances following a transfer, but prison staff did not follow their own rules.

[321]James v. Williams, 2005 WL 4859251, *2 (W.D.N.C., May 24, 2005) (noting that the prisoner had 11 days to file a new grievance after his first one was rejected and that under the grievance policy he could have filed it at the new prison as well); Timmons v. Pereiro, 2003 WL 179769, *2 (S.D.N.Y., Jan. 27, 2003) (holding that transfer out of state did not excuse failure to exhaust where there was time to file before the plaintiff was moved and in any case the system permits grievances to be pursued after transfer), *aff'd in part, vacated in part, and remanded*, 88 Fed.Appx. 447 (2d Cir. 2004) (unpublished).

is any evidence to that effect.[322] If you get transferred before you can file a grievance, or while a grievance is pending, you should do your best to pursue the grievance. Maybe you will succeed, but if you don't, you will be able to demonstrate that the remedy was not available to you. [323] In any case, you may need to show the court good reasons why you couldn't exhaust after a transfer.

A remedy may be made unavailable by the acts or omissions of prison personnel. Most courts have held that threats or assaults directed at preventing prisoners from complaining may make remedies unavailable in fact, even if they are available in theory.[324] Courts ask "would 'a similarly situated individual of ordinary firmness' have deemed [the remedy] available,"[325]

which is essentially the same standard as applied in First Amendment retaliation cases.[326]

Remedies may be made unavailable by other forms of obstruction by prison staff, intentional[327]

---

reprisal may, in some circumstances, render administrative remedies 'unavailable' or otherwise justify a prisoner's failure to pursue them" (citing *Hemphill*)); Larry v. Byno, 2006 WL 1313344, *4 (N.D.N.Y. May 11, 2006) (applying *Hemphill*); Orraca v. McCreery, 2006 WL 1133254, *5 (N.D.N.Y., Apr. 25, 2006) (applying *Hemphill*); Holiday v. Giusto, 2005 WL 3244329, *2–3 (D.Or., Nov. 30, 2005) (adopting *Hemphill* analysis).

Hemphill noted that threats or intimidation "may well deter a prisoner of 'ordinary firmness' from filing an internal grievance, but not from appealing directly to individuals in positions of greater authority within the prison system, or to external structures of authority such as state or federal courts." *Accord*, Turner v. Burnside, 541 F.3d at 1085–86. Thus the fact that a prisoner has, for example, written a letter of complaint to the Superintendent (as in *Hemphill*) does not establish that he was not deterred from filing an ordinary grievance.

One court has held that remedies were unavailable to a prisoner who was told by staff that his safety would be protected by a transfer only if he withdrew his grievance (which he did). Paynes v. Runnels, 2008 WL 4078740, *6 (E.D.Cal., Aug. 29, 2008) ("Practically speaking, this offer took the grievance outside the established procedures and rendered the grievance process unavailable."), *report and recommendation adopted*, 2008 WL 4464828 (E.D.Cal., Sept. 30, 2008). In *Payne*, the plaintiff, a transsexual prisoner who had been assaulted, was promised a transfer, placed in segregation instead, and his subsequent grievance dismissed as untimely.

[326]*See* Ch. 3, § B.1.6, concerning First Amendment retaliation.

[327]Dole v. Chandler, 438 F.3d 804, 809, 812 (7th Cir. 2006) ("Prison officials may not take unfair advantage of the exhaustion requirement, . . . and a remedy becomes 'unavailable' if prison employees do not respond to a properly filed grievance or otherwise use affirmative misconduct to prevent a prisoner from exhausting"; prisoner whose properly filed grievance simply vanished, and who received no instructions what to do about it, did "all that was reasonable to exhaust."); Miller v. Norris, 247 F.3d 736, 740 (8th Cir. 2001) ("We believe that a remedy that prison officials prevent a prisoner from 'utiliz[ing]' is not an 'available' remedy under § 1997e(a) . . ."); Miller v. Catlett, 2010 WL 444734, *3 (S.D.Cal., Feb. 1, 2010) (where prisoner's staff complaint was rejected on the ground it was really a disciplinary appeal, with no instruction as to what to do to file a staff complaint, plaintiff did not fail to exhaust); Franklin v. Butler, 2008 WL 4078797, *3 (E.D.Cal., Aug. 29, 2008) (refusing to dismiss where grievance was apparently lost and the rules contained no instructions for what to do if that happened), *report and recommendation adopted*, 2008 WL 4601081 (E.D.Cal., Oct. 15, 2008); Ponton v. Bailey, 2006 WL 3498309, *4 (W.D. Pa., Dec. 4, 2006) (same as *Dole v. Chandler*); Alwood v. Randt, 2006 WL 2639887, *2 (N.D.Ind., Sept. 12, 2006) (denying summary judgment where prisoner's sworn statement said that a prison official came to his cell and "ripped up his grievance, thereby refusing to allow it to be processed"); Hause v. Smith, 2006 WL 2135537, *1–2 (W.D.Mo., July 31, 2006) (holding allegations that attempts to file grievances were "significantly thwarted" suffice at the pleading stage; court notes it directed that the plaintiff be

---

[322]Blakey v. Beckstrom, 2007 WL 204005, *2 (E.D.Ky., Jan. 24, 2007) (holding without record support that transfer did not make grievance procedures unavailable); Mills v. U.S., 2006 WL 3314644, *3 (E.D.N.Y., Nov. 14, 2006) (holding transfer "does not relieve [prisoner] of the obligation to pursue the grievance procedures available in the facility where the conduct occurred"); Hemingway v. Lantz, 2006 WL 1237010, *2 (D.N.H., May 5, 2006) (holding prisoner who said he didn't exhaust for fear of retaliation should have filed a grievance after his transfer to the "safety" of another state, without inquiring whether an out-of-state grievance would have been processed); Crump v. May, 2006 WL 626915, *3 (D.Del., Mar. 14, 2006) (asserting that a prisoner who was transferred after an incident still had five days of the seven-day time limit when he arrived at the new prison, without inquiring whether he could have filed a grievance at the new prison about events at the old prison).

[323]*See* Mellender v. Dane County, 2006 WL 3113212, *3 (W.D.Wis., Oct. 27, 2006) (noting that after transfer from jail to prison, plaintiff tried to mail a grievance to the jail and then to use the prison's grievance system to complain about the jail).

[324]A few lower courts have rejected the idea that threats or fear can excuse non-exhaustion. *See, e.g.,* Glick v. Montana Dep't of Corrections, 2007 WL 2359776, *2 n.3 (D.Mont., Aug. 14, 2007) (holding fear of retaliation cannot excuse non-exhaustion since retaliation is illegal); Ware v. Tappin, 2006 WL 3533116, *6–7 (W.D.La., Nov. 3, 2006) (holding fear of retaliation is "no valid defense for failing to exhaust"); Broom v. Engler, 2005 WL 3454657, *3 (W.D.Mich., Dec. 16, 2005) (stating "[t]he PLRA does not excuse exhaustion for a prisoner . . . who is afraid to complain").

[325]Hemphill v. New York, 380 F.3d 680, 688 (2d Cir. 2004); *accord*, Turner v. Burnside, 541 F.3d 1077, 1084 (11th Cir. 2008) ("Remedies that rational inmates cannot be expected to use are not capable of accomplishing their purposes, and so are not available." (following *Hemphill* and *Kaba*)); Kaba v. Stepp, 458 F.3d 678, 684–85 (7th Cir. 2006) (adopting *Hemphill* analysis); Baker v. Schriro, 2008 WL 622020, *8 (D.Ariz., Mar. 4, 2008) (holding plaintiffs' allegations of threats by staff and of practice of requiring grievances to be screened by gang members satisfied "ordinary firmness" standard), *review denied*, 2008 WL 2003757 (D.Ariz., May 8, 2008); Mitchell v. Adams, 2008 WL 314129, *9–13 (E.D.Cal., Feb. 4, 2008) (citing course of threatening conduct affecting multiple grievances), *report and recommendation adopted*, 2008 WL 595922 (E.D.Cal., Mar. 3, 2008); Harcum v. Shaffer, 2007 WL 4190688, *5 (E.D.Pa., Nov. 21, 2007) (holding that threats causing the prisoner to withdraw his grievance "removed the availability of further administrative remedies"); Stanley v. Rich, 2006 WL 1549114, *2 (S.D.Ga., June 1, 2006) (stating "threats of violent

or otherwise.[328] For example, a rule denying postage to indigents to mail a grievance appeal may make the appeal unavailable,[329] as may deprivation of writing materials or

documentation to prisoners in a segregation unit.[330] Sometimes prisoners in a particular status or situation are simply excluded from using the grievance system.[331] Rules specifically designed to limit prisoners' use of the grievance system may make the remedy unavailable for some prisoners. Rules limiting prisoners to a certain number of grievances may make the remedy unavailable for prisoners who are over the limit, depending on the limit's severity.[332]

---

allowed to file a grievance and that its processing be expedited); Labounty v. Johnson, 253 F. Supp. 2d 496, 502–04 (W.D.N.Y. 2003) (holding that grievance supervisor's alleged failure to follow procedures, preventing plaintiff's appeal, barred summary judgment for non-exhaustion); Liggins v. Barnett, 2001 WL 737551 *14–15 (S.D.Iowa, May 15, 2001) (holding allegation that plaintiff filed grievances and prison staff destroyed them supported claim of substantial compliance; allegation that grievances were destroyed and grievance committee given a false report by staff member raised an inference that filing a grievance was an unavailable remedy); Johnson v. True, 125 F. Supp. 2d 186, 188–89 (W.D.Va., 2000) (holding allegation that efforts to exhaust were frustrated by prison officials raised an issue of material fact whether plaintiff exhausted "available" remedies), *appeal dismissed*, 32 Fed.Appx. 692 (4th Cir. 2002) (unpublished); Bullock v. Horn, 2000 WL 1839171, *2 (M.D.Pa., Oct. 31, 2000) (holding allegation that prison officials returned grievances unprocessed, without grievance numbers, making appeal impossible was sufficient to defeat a motion to dismiss).

[328]Frost v. McCaughtry, 215 F.3d 1329, 1329 (7th Cir. 2000) (unpublished) (holding allegation that no grievance appeal was available to plaintiff because of ongoing administrative changes during the relevant time period raised a factual question as to availability); Brookins v. Vogel, 2006 WL 3437482, *3 (E.D.Cal., Nov. 28, 2006) (holding that a prisoner who filed a grievance, got no response, and was told it had never been received, and whose subsequent attempts were rejected as untimely, had exhausted); Cahill v. Arpaio, 2006 WL 3201018, *3 (D.Ariz., Nov. 2, 2006) (holding grievance process became unavailable when hearing officer stated the matter was under investigation and the plaintiff would not be informed of the results, he could not appeal and he would not be given a form, and he should proceed to federal court); Bennett v. Douglas County, 2006 WL 1867031, *2 (D.Neb., June 30, 2006) (declining to dismiss for failure to appeal to the Chief Deputy of the jail where there was no Chief Deputy); Howard v. City of New York, 2006 WL 2597857, *7 (S.D.N.Y., Sept. 6, 2006) (holding allegations that plaintiff asked to see the grievance officer but was never called, and when transferred was told he could not grieve a matter from the previous facility, did not support dismissal of the complaint); Kinzey v. Beard, 2006 WL 2829000, *10 (M.D.Pa., Sept. 1, 2006) (refusing to dismiss for non-exhaustion where the failure to exhaust was caused by prison officials' failure to follow their own rules); Williams v. Hagen, 2005 WL 1204324, *2 (D.Neb., May 11, 2005) (declining to dismiss in light of plaintiff's allegation of "total disarray . . . with regard to the grievance process"); Labounty v. Johnson, 253 F. Supp. 2d 496, 504–06 (W.D.N.Y. 2003) (holding that prisoner's factually supported claim that his grievance was consolidated with another prisoner's, and the decision did not mention the issue he was concerned about, presented a factual issue whether it was "reasonable for plaintiff to be confused under such circumstances").

[329]Bey v. Caruso, 2007 WL 2875196, *1 (E.D.Mich., Sept. 28, 2007) (noting that denial of "postal loan" was based on plaintiff's using his religious name suffix on the relevant form, contrary to the policy he was trying to challenge; "the procedural question of exhaustion is inextricably intertwined with the merits of this case"); Cordova v. Frank, 2007 WL 2188587, *6 (W.D.Wis., July 26, 2007);

Kaufman v. Schneiter, 474 F. Supp. 2d 1014, 1032 (W.D.Wis. 2007) (dictum).

[330]Weighall v. Pea, 2007 WL 4111376, *4 (W.D.Wash., Nov. 16, 2007); Woods v. Carey, 2007 WL 2688819, *1–2 (E.D.Cal., Sept. 13, 2007) (refusing to dismiss for non-exhaustion pending inquiry into plaintiff's access to his legal property, lack of which he said impeded his timely appeal).

[331]See Sease v. Phillips, 2008 WL 2901966, *5 (S.D.N.Y., July 24, 2008) (summary judgment based on non-exhaustion denied where prisoner in "transient status" was told his grievance could not be processed, and it wasn't); Muhammad v. U.S. Marshall Service, 2008 WL 2367302, *5 (W.D.Pa., June 10, 2008) (refusing to dismiss where plaintiff alleged that because of his status as a federal detainee, the jail grievance system was not made known to him); Marr v. Fields, 2008 WL 828788, *5–7 (W.D.Mich., Mar. 27, 2008) (holding exclusion of prisoners who pled guilty from disciplinary appeal process made the remedy unavailable); Murphy v. Colorado Dep't of Corrections (CDOC), 2008 WL 608583, *5 (D.Colo., Mar. 4, 2008) (noting prisoners transferred under Interstate Corrections Compact were excluded from grievance system, which was therefore unavailable to them); Daker v. Ferrero, 2004 WL 5459957, *2–3 (N.D.Ga., Nov. 24, 2004) (prisoner lacked an available remedy when he was placed in "sleeper" status, meaning he remained officially assigned to another prison and was not allowed to file grievances where he was actually located).

[332]Rhodan v. Schofield, 2007 WL 1810147, *6 (N.D.Ga., June 19, 2007) (holding prisoner who said he was told he could not have two grievances pending at once raised a factual issue as to availability of remedies); Wood v. Idaho Dep't of Corrections, 2006 WL 694654, *6 (D.Idaho, Mar. 16, 2006) (holding that a prisoner whose grievance was returned because he was only allowed to have three pending at one time had exhausted, since he had done what he could do to exhaust). *But see* Moore v. Bennette, 517 F.3d 717, 729–30 (4th Cir. 2008) (where rules allowed only one grievance at a time except for emergencies, and plaintiff labelled his second grievance an emergency but it did not meet the criteria in the grievance rules for an emergency and was dismissed, plaintiff's failure to resubmit it when his first grievance was decided was a failure to exhaust); West v. Endicott, 2008 WL 906225, *3 (E.D.Wis., Mar. 31, 2008) (holding a system that allowed two grievances a week did not prevent the plaintiff from exhausting), *reconsideration denied*, 2008 WL 2035474 (E.D.Wis., May 12, 2008); Williams v. Washington, 2008 WL 2078124, *4 (W.D.Wash., Feb. 21, 2008) (prisoner whose grievance was rejected because he was not allowed to have more than five grievances "active" at one time, and who did not withdraw a grievance so he could file the new one, failed to exhaust), *report and recommendation adopted*, 2008 WL 2078123 (W.D.Wash., May 14, 2008); McGrew v. Teer, 2008 WL 516547, *2 (M.D.La., Jan. 23, 2008) (dismissing for non-exhaustion where plaintiff's grievance was not decided but was "placed on backlog" pending exhaustion of other previously filed grievances; he filed suit three and a half months after filing his grievance); Oestricher

A system of "modified grievance access," which requires prior permission to file a grievance, makes the remedy unavailable if permission is not granted.[333] Remedies may also be made unavailable by actions of supervisors or grievance staff with respect to particular grievances or grievants,[334]

by purposeful staff misconduct,[335] by neglect or accident,[336]

---

v. Wallace, 2007 WL 4224929, *3 n.7 (E.D.La., Nov. 27, 2007) (dictum) (stating that a "backlog system" that deferred multiple grievances from the same prisoner is constitutionally permissible and does not excuse failure to exhaust); Edmond v. Lindsey, 2006 WL 3203755, *2 (S.D.Miss., Nov. 3, 2006) (holding that officials' refusal to process grievances based on a rule allowing only 10 grievances to be pending at once did not excuse the plaintiff's failure to exhaust); *see also* Riley v. Crawford, 2007 WL 4468701, *3 (W.D.Mo., Dec. 17, 2007) (expressing concern that "one grievance a week" policy could deny access for legitimate complaints, but holding that it did not make remedies unavailable for problems that occurred over a period of months).

[333]Bagetta v. Caruso, 2008 WL 723546, *4–5 (W.D.Mich., Mar. 12, 2008); Dawson v. Norwood, 2007 WL 3302102, *9 (W.D.Mich., Nov. 6, 2007) ("If a prisoner has been placed on modified access to the grievance procedure and attempts to file a grievance which is deemed to be non-meritorious, he has exhausted his 'available' administrative remedies as required by § 1997e(a)." (citation omitted)); Hahn v. Tarnow, 2006 WL 1705128, *2 n.4 (W.D.Mich., June 16, 2006) (holding that a plaintiff on "modified grievance restriction" who was denied grievance forms did not have an available remedy). A rule requiring prisoners on modified grievance status to submit a notarized affidavit with a grievance may make the remedy unavailable if the prisoner cannot get access to a notary. Thomas v. Guffy, 2008 WL 2884368, *2–3 (W.D.Okla., July 25, 2008).

[334]Howard v. Hill, 156 Fed.Appx. 886, 886 (9th Cir. 2005) (unpublished) (holding that a prisoner who had been told he would not receive responses to his grievances had no remedy available); Woods v. Carey, 2008 WL 447553 (E.D.Cal., Feb. 15, 2008) (where grievance official directed plaintiff to the medical appeals analyst, but that person said plaintiff's grievance must first be processed by the grievance office, plaintiff had exhausted; court refers to "runaround"); Bradley v. McVay, 2008 WL 495732, *3 (E.D.Cal., Feb. 21, 2008) (if prison officials required plaintiff to go to an interview room for an investigation, and he could not do so without the cane he had been deprived of, the grievance process would not be available to him), *report and recommendation adopted*, 2008 WL 669858 (E.D.Cal., Mar. 7, 2008); Baylis v. Taylor, 475 F. Supp. 2d 484, 488 (D.Del. 2007) (holding officials' withdrawal of plaintiff's grievances because of litigation meant that he had exhausted, since no further remedies were available); Ray v. Jones, 2007 WL 397084, *2 (W.D.Okla., Feb. 1, 2007) (holding grievance process was not an available remedy because of ongoing internal affairs investigation); Marshall v. Knight, 2006 WL 3354700, *4 (N.D.Ind., Nov. 17, 2006) (holding that instructions to grievance personnel to respond to grievances about law library hours only by sending prisoners a copy of a memo deprived grievance staff of authority to act on those grievances and made the remedy unavailable); James v. Davis, 2006 WL 2171082, *17 (D.S.C., July 31, 2006) (holding that return of grievances unprocessed, on the ground that the problems were taken care of and that damages claims could not be grieved, thwarted plaintiff's ability to exhaust). *But see* Howard v. Smith, 2008 WL 816685 (S.D.Ga., Feb. 28, 2008), *report and recommendation rejected in pertinent part*, 2008 WL 816684

(S.D.Ga., Mar. 26, 2008), *on reconsideration on other grounds*, 2008 WL 2316718 (S.D.Ga., June 4, 2008). In *Howard*, the prison system introduced a rule newly requiring an additional "informal" step in the grievance process, and plaintiff's pending grievances were all canceled; the magistrate judge said he was deemed to have exhausted his claims, but the district judge rejected that conclusion without explanation.

[335]Allen v. City of Saint Louis, 2008 WL 695393, *4–5 (E.D.Mo., Mar. 12, 2008) (finding remedies unavailable where plaintiff's requests for forms and information about how to file were ignored, denied, or "pacified with promises" of an investigation, and he was improperly segregated to prevent access to the grievance procedure and third parties); Miller v. Berkebile, 2008 WL 635552, *7–9 (N.D.Tex., Mar. 10, 2008) (where official refused to process first-stage grievances contrary to policy, remedy was unavailable; prisoners need not take steps not prescribed in the policy to get around him; PLRA law applied in § 2241 case); Smith v. Westchester County Dep't of Corrections, 2008 WL 361130, *3 (S.D.N.Y., Feb. 7, 2008) (remedies were unavailable if supervisors refused to accept plaintiff's grievance); Crawford v. Berkebile, 2008 WL 323155, *7–8 (N.D.Tex., Feb. 6, 2008) (counselor's refusal to accept grievance forms made the remedy unavailable; prisoners were not required to go to other officials where it was the counselor's job to receive grievances); Barndt v. Pucci, 2007 WL 1031509, *2–3 (M.D.Pa., Mar. 30, 2007) (denying summary judgment where prisoner alleged he could not grieve because he was deprived of writing materials and legal paperwork for four months); Alwood v. Randt, 2006 WL 2639887, *2 (N.D.Ind., Sept. 12, 2006) (denying summary judgment where prisoner's sworn statement said that a prison official came to his cell and "ripped up his grievance, thereby refusing to allow it to be processed"); Collins v. Goord, 438 F. Supp. 2d 399, 415 (S.D.N.Y. 2006) (holding allegations that facility personnel invented a screening procedure and did not allow him to file his grievance raised a material issue under "an exception to the PLRA's exhaustion requirement where prison authorities actively obstruct an inmate's ability to 'properly' file a prison grievance"); Blount v. Fleming, 2006 WL 1805853, *2–4 (W.D.Va., June 29, 2006) (stating "when prison officials prevent an inmate from access to or use of a prison inmate's grievance system, an inmate's failure to exhaust is excused because he had no 'available' administrative remedy"; finding *inter alia* that defendants falsely claimed not to have received plaintiff's grievances); Carter v. Newland, 441 F. Supp. 2d 208, 211 (D.Mass. 2006) (declining to dismiss for non-exhaustion in view of allegations that a prison counselor tore up the plaintiff's grievances).

[336]Pavey v. Conley, 170 Fed.Appx. 4, 9 (7th Cir. 2006) (unpublished) (holding that isolating and failing to assist a prisoner who couldn't write could render the remedy unavailable); Monroe v. Beard, 2007 WL 2359833, *12–13 (E.D.Pa., Aug. 16, 2007) (holding the grievance process unavailable where prisoners were told to object to certain searches through an Unacceptable Correspondence Form, and they would be notified of the results of an investigation and then could file a grievance, but were not so notified), *aff'd*, 536 F.3d 198, 204 n.6 (3d Cir. 2008); Warren v. Purcell, 2004 WL 1970642, *6 (S.D.N.Y., Sept. 3, 2004) (holding "baffling" grievance response that left prisoner with no clue what to do next estopped defendants from claiming the defense and constituted special circumstances justifying failure to exhaust).

or by events that are merely unexplained.[337] However, courts are unlikely to credit vague or conclusory claims of obstruction,[338] so if you make a claim of this nature, you had better be prepared to back it up with facts. Numerous courts have held that allegations of the denial of necessary grievance forms are sufficient to prevent dismissal for non-exhaustion,[339] though (as with all obstruction claims) courts are suspicious of such claims if they are unsupported by factual detail or evidence of efforts to get the forms,[340] or if the prisoner filed other grievances around the same time.[341]

In *Ouellette v. Maine State Prison*, 2006 WL 173639, *3–4 (D. Me., Jan. 23, 2006), *aff'd*, 2006 WL 348315 (D.Me., Feb. 14, 2006), the plaintiff wrote a letter of complaint and filed a formal grievance, and received a response to the letter but not to the grievance; he requested a formal response (by then overdue) to his grievance and filed suit when he did not promptly receive it. The court rejected the argument that he should have filed a grievance appeal treating the response to his letter as the grievance response, stating that on these facts he could have believed that he had no further remedies available, and expressing concern that the defendants insisted on strict compliance with procedure while staff were not strictly complying with their part of the rules.

[337]Dole v. Chandler, 438 F.3d 804, 809, 812 (7th Cir. 2006) (holding prisoner whose properly filed grievance simply vanished, and who received no instructions what to do about it, did "all that was reasonable to exhaust"); Franklin v. Butler, 2008 WL 4078797, *3 (E.D.Cal., Aug. 29, 2008) (similar to *Dole*), *report and recommendation adopted*, 2008 WL 4601081 (E.D.Cal., Oct. 15, 2008); Johnson v. Tedford, 2007 WL 4118284, *3 (N.D.N.Y., Nov. 16, 2007) (holding a prisoner whose grievance is not recorded or given a grievance number, so the lack of response cannot be appealed, may have exhausted) and cases cited, *report and recommendation adopted in pertinent part, rejected in part*, 616 F. Supp. 2d 321, 326 (N.D.N.Y. 2007); Burrows v. Gifford, 2007 WL 2827779, *2 (E.D.Cal., Sept. 27, 2007) (holding remedies would be unavailable to a prisoner who received a grievance decision too late to appeal it).

[338]See, e.g., Stine v. Wiley, 2007 WL 121822, *1–2 (D.Colo., Jan. 10, 2007); Djukic v. Arpaio, 2006 WL 2850060, *3 (D.Ariz., Sept. 26, 2006).

[339]Dale v. Lappin, 376 F.3d 652, 654–56 (7th Cir. 2004) (per curiam); Mitchell v. Horn, 318 F.3d 523, 529 (3d Cir.3d Cir. 2003); Miller v. Norris, 247 F.3d 736, 740 (8th Cir. 2001); Bertres v. Byers, 2007 WL 4224389, *8 (M.D.Pa., Nov. 28, 2007) (". . . [P]laintiff's statements under penalty of perjury in his complaint that he was not provided a grievance form are adequate to establish that it is in dispute whether he was reasonably able to exhaust."); Chatham v. Adcock, 2007 WL 2904117, *14 (N.D.Ga., Sept. 28, 2007) ("It would be an anomalous result, indeed, if prison officials could foreclose prison inmates from filing civil rights lawsuits in federal court simply by depriving them of the means to fulfill a mandatory prerequisite to doing so."), *aff'd*, 334 Fed.Appx. 281 (11th Cir. 2009) (unpublished); Hedgespeth v. Hendricks, 2007 WL 2769627, *5 (D.N.J., Sept. 21, 2007) (refusing to dismiss where plaintiff alleged that he was told by housing officers there were no grievance forms, and inmate handbook said housing officers were the source of forms); Cody v. White, 2007 WL 1726583, *2 (D.N.D., June 13, 2007) (denying summary judgment where segregation prisoner said he couldn't get forms from staff and rules did not seem to allow him to go to grievance office); Tabarez v. Butler, 2007 WL 988040, *2–3 (E.D.Cal., Mar. 30, 2007) (holding defendants' claim that prisoners "customarily" have access to grievance forms did not mean this plaintiff did, especially since he said only those who were "on good terms" with the guards could get forms), *report and recommendation adopted*, 2007 WL 1804968 (E.D.Cal., June 21, 2007); Bowers v. City of Philadelphia, 2007 WL 219651, *16 (E.D.Pa., Jan. 25, 2007) (holding grievance process unavailable where forms were not provided in police custody or jail intake area); Allen v. McMorris, 2007 WL 172564, *2 (E.D.Mo., Jan. 19, 2007) (holding allegation that prisoner could not get grievance policy or forms barred summary judgment for defendants); Wallace v. Williams, 2006 WL 3091435, *3 (S.D.Ga., Oct. 30, 2006) (three unsuccessful requests for grievance forms were enough; "While a prisoner must make a diligent effort to exhaust his available remedies, his required persistence is constrained by the bounds of reasonableness."); Enigwe v. Zenk, 2006 WL 2654985, *4 (E.D.N.Y., Sept. 15, 2006) (denying summary judgment to defendants where plaintiff asserted his repeated efforts to obtain forms were fruitless); Montgomery v. Johnson, 2006 WL 2403305, *11 (W.D.Va., Aug. 18, 2006) (crediting evidence that policies and practices were not followed and plaintiff was unable to obtain forms), *report and recommendation adopted*, 2006 WL 3099651 (W.D.Va., Oct. 30, 2006); Abney v. County of Nassau, 237 F. Supp. 2d 278, 282 (E.D.N.Y. 2002) (holding that prisoner who could not get grievance forms and wrote grievance on plain paper, but never got a response had exhausted); Kendall v. Kittles, 2003 WL 22127135, *4 (S.D.N.Y., Sept. 15, 2003) (declining to dismiss where prisoner said he could not get grievance forms; the fact that he filed grievances at other times showed only that forms were available on the dates those grievances were filed, and not that such forms were always available); *see* Goebert v. Lee County, 510 F.3d 1312, 1324–25 (11th Cir. 2007) (rejecting argument that plaintiff didn't exhaust because she used the wrong form, since there was no evidence that the right form even existed, much less that she had or knew about it).

[340]See, e.g., Lomas v. U.S., 2008 WL 819459, *3 (W.D.Okla., Mar. 25, 2008) (citing plaintiff's failure to state "to whom or when the requests were made or to explain his access to certain forms and not others"); Dye v. Bartow, 2007 WL 3306771, *6 (E.D.Wis., Nov. 6, 2007) (citing plaintiff's failure to identify the forms he requested and the date of request, to supply a copy of his request, or to submit evidence detailing officials' response to his requests), *aff'd*, 282 Fed.Appx. 434 (7th Cir. 2008) (unpublished); Beasley v. Kontek, 2007 WL 3306637, *2 (N.D.Ohio, Nov. 5, 2007) ("A prisoner may not be excused from exhausting internal remedies if his failure resulted from a form not being provided to him, unless he alleges that there was no other source for the form or that he can prove that he made other attempts to 'obtain a form or file a grievance.'" (quoting Jones v. Smith, 266 F.3d 399, 400 (6th Cir.2001)).

[341]See, e.g., Guel v. Larkin, 2008 WL 1994942, *5–6 (W.D.Ark., May 6, 2008).

The failure to inform prisoners about the existence of remedies,[342] or about the rules for using them,[343] or misinforming prisoners about their availability or operation, may make remedies unavailable.[344] A number of decisions have

---

[342]Goebert v. Lee County, 510 F.3d 1312, 1322–23 (11th Cir. 2007) (holding that an appeal procedure not described in the inmate handbook, but only in the operating procedures the inmates did not have access to, was not an available remedy); Westefer v. Snyder, 422 F.3d 570, 580 (7th Cir. 2005) (holding that defendants did not show remedies were available where there was no "clear route" for challenging certain decisions); Russell v. Unknown Cook County, Sheriff's Officers, 2004 WL 2997503, *4–5 (N.D.Ill., Dec. 27, 2004) (holding where plaintiff alleged ignorance of the remedy, defendants must establish that they gave actual notice of it); Sadler v. Rowland, 2004 WL 2061518, *7 (D.Conn., Sept. 13, 2004) (refusing to dismiss claim of Connecticut prisoner transferred to Virginia who attempted to grieve in Virginia and was not told to file separate grievances in Connecticut); Burgess v. Garvin, 2004 WL 527053, *5 (S.D.N.Y., Mar. 16, 2004) (holding that "procedural channels . . . not made known to prisoners . . . are not an 'available' remedy in any meaningful sense. . . . [Congress] cannot have meant that prisoners would be expected to exhaust remedies of which they were kept entirely ignorant."); Arnold v. Goetz, 2003 WL 256777, *6–7 (S.D.N.Y., Feb. 4, 2003) (holding defendants required to make a "reasonable, good faith effort to make the grievance procedure available to inmates"); Hall v. Sheahan, 2001 WL 111019, *2 (N.D.Ill., Feb. 2, 2001) (holding that an institution cannot keep prisoners in ignorance of the grievance procedure and then fault them for not using it. "A grievance procedure that is not made known to inmates is not an 'available' administrative remedy."); Alvarez v. U.S., 2000 WL 557328, *2 (S.D.N.Y., May 8, 2000) (stating that a showing that prisoner was not "meaningfully informed" about administrative remedies could establish that they were not available), on reconsideration, 2000 WL 679009 (S.D.N.Y., May 24, 2000).

In Davis v. Milwaukee County, 225 F. Supp. 2d 967, 975–76 (E.D. Wis. 2002), the court held that the plaintiff had been denied access to the courts by defendants' hindering his ability to exhaust, inter alia, by failing to make available materials concerning the grievance procedure.

[343]Jackson v. Ivens, 244 Fed.Appx. 508, 513 (3d Cir. 2007) (unpublished) ("We will not condition exhaustion on unwritten or 'implied' requirements." (citing Spruill v. Gillis, 372 F.3d 218, 234 (3d Cir. 2004)); Sims v. Rewerts, 2008 WL 2224132, *5–6 (E.D.Mich., May 29, 2008) (declining to dismiss where plaintiff failed to comply with a time limit that had been changed without notice); Cabrera v. LeVierge, 2008 WL 215720, *6 (D.N.H., Jan. 24, 2008) ("inmates cannot be expected to meet procedural requirements that are undisclosed"); Lampkins v. Roberts, 2007 WL 924746, *3 (S.D.Ind., Mar. 27, 2007) (refusing to dismiss for missing a five-day time deadline which was not made known in the materials made available to prisoners).

[344]Marella v. Terhune, 568 F.3d 1024, 1027 (9th Cir. 2009) (where appeal was screened out with a form stating the decision was not appealable, prisoner was not required to appeal further); Pavey v. Conley, 170 Fed.Appx. 4, 8–9 (7th Cir. 2006) (unpublished) (stating that "inmates may rely on the assurances of prison officials when they are led to believe that satisfactory steps have been taken to exhaust administrative remedies. . . . [P]rison officials will be bound by their oral representations to inmates concerning

compliance with the grievance process"; plaintiff, who could not write, could reasonably rely on assurances that his oral complaint would be investigated.); Brown v. Croak, 312 F.3d 109, 112–13 (3d Cir. 2002) (holding that if security officials told the plaintiff to wait for completion of an investigation before grieving, and then never informed him of its completion, the grievance system was unavailable to him); Miller v. Tanner, 196 F.3d 1190 (11th Cir. 1999) (holding that grievance decision that stated it was non-appealable need not have been appealed); Plaster v. Kneal, 2008 WL 4090790, *3–4 (M.D.Pa., Aug. 29, 2008) (refusing to dismiss where grievance appeal was late because plaintiff followed staff's incorrect instructions on where to send it); Born v. Monmouth County Correctional Inst., 2008 WL 4056313, *4 (D.N.J., Aug. 28, 2008) (officer's instruction that complaint of staff sexual abuse should be made to Internal Affairs rather than grievance process might excuse failure to use grievance process); Chinnici v. Edwards, 2008 WL 3851294, *5 (D.Vt., Aug. 12, 2008) (supervisor's statement that sex abuse complaint did not require completing the grievance process could constitute estoppel or special circumstances excusing non-exhaustion); Spinney v. U.S., 2008 WL 1859810, *6 (W.D.Pa., Apr. 23, 2008) (if plaintiff delayed one grievance on advice of counselor, remedy may not have been available to him); Tinsley v. Giorla, 2008 WL 901697, *5 (E.D.Pa., Apr. 1, 2008) (if a prison official told a prisoner a decision could not be appealed, contrary to written grievance policy, the grievance procedure could be found unavailable); Kelley v. Roberts, 2008 WL 714097, *2 (W.D.Wash., Mar. 14, 2008) (declining to dismiss claim of plaintiff who was advised through an "initial grievance" that his issue should be addressed through the classification process and not the grievance process, and did so); Bryant v. Sacramento County Jail, 2008 WL 410608, *5–6 (E.D.Cal., Feb. 12, 2008) (denying summary judgment where prisoner was directed to "citizen complaint" procedure rather than jail grievance procedure), report and recommendation adopted, 2008 WL 780704 (E.D.Cal., Mar. 21, 2008); Flory v. Claussen, 2006 WL 3404779, *3 (W.D.Wash., Nov. 21, 2006) (holding prisoner who followed officials' instruction to file an "appeal" to the Facility Risk Management Team about removal from his job, rather than a grievance, exhausted); Scott v. Cal. Supreme Court, 2006 WL 2460737, *7 (E.D.Cal., Aug. 23, 2006) (holding that a prisoner who had relied on officials' misinformation and sought relief in state court had exhausted, notwithstanding officials' subsequent issuance of an untimely decision which he did not appeal); Beltran v. O'Mara, 405 F. Supp. 2d 140, 154 (D.N.H. 2005) (holding, where a grievance was rejected on the ground that incidents which were the subject of disciplinary proceedings could not be grieved, "a reasonable inmate in [the plaintiff's] position" would believe the grievance process was not an available remedy and his claims should be raised in the disciplinary process), on reconsideration, 2006 WL 240558 (D.N.H., Jan. 31, 2006); Wheeler v. Goord, 2005 WL 2180451, *6 (N.D.N.Y., Aug. 29, 2005) (holding prisoner who was erroneously told to "write to Sergeant Coffee" to grieve raised an issue whether remedies were available); Willis v. Smith, 2005 WL 550528, *13 (N.D.Iowa, Feb. 28, 2005) (declining to dismiss where plaintiff relied on the statement of a prison official that the written grievance policy was unavailable); Croswell v. McCoy, 2003 WL 962534, *4 (N.D.N.Y., Mar. 11, 2003) (holding that a prisoner who relies on prison officials' representations as to correct procedure has exhausted); O'Connor v. Featherston, 2003 WL 554752, *2–3 (S.D.N.Y., Feb. 27, 2003) (holding allegation that prison

refused to dismiss for non-exhaustion where prisoners had relied on prison personnel's representations that an issue was non-grievable,[345] though such claims must be factually

specific (*i.e.*, who told you what on what date, at a minimum); vague allegations to that effect will not excuse non-exhaustion.[346] Further, prisoners' ignorance of the remedy does not excuse them from using it if it has been made known to them, for example, in an inmate orientation handbook.[347] You must pay attention to the information that is made available to you. Prison officials' statements that do not directly misrepresent the operation of the grievance system generally are not held to excuse the failure to exhaust, even if a prisoner relies on them.[348] Actions that intimidate

---

Superintendent told a prisoner to complain via the Inspector General rather than the grievance procedure presented triable factual issues); Heath v. Saddlemire, 2002 WL 31242204, *5 (N.D.N.Y., Oct. 7, 2002) (holding that a prisoner who was told by the Commission of Correction that notifying the Inspector General was the correct procedure was entitled to rely on that statement); Thomas v. N.Y. State Dep't of Corr. Servs., 2002 WL 31164546, *3 (S.D.N.Y., Sept. 30, 2002) (holding that a prisoner's allegation that an officer told him he didn't need to grieve because other prisoners had done so was sufficient to defeat summary judgment for non-exhaustion); Lee v. Walker, 2002 WL 980764, *2 (D.Kan., May 6, 2002) (holding that prisoner who sent his grievance appeal to the wrong place would be entitled to reconsideration of dismissal if he showed that the prison handbook said it was the right place); Feliz v. Taylor, 2000 WL 1923506, *2–3 (E.D.Mich., Dec. 29, 2000) (holding that a plaintiff who was told his grievance was being investigated, then when he tried to appeal later was told it was untimely, had exhausted, since he had no reason to believe he had to appeal initially).

In *Davis v. Milwaukee County,* 225 F. Supp. 2d 967, 976 (E.D.Wis. 2002), the court held that the plaintiff had been denied access to courts by defendants' hindering his ability to exhaust, inter alia, by telling him that his complaint was "not a grievable situation."

[345]Marr v. Fields, 2008 WL 828788, *6 (W.D.Mich., Mar. 27, 2008) (where prisoner was told by staff his disciplinary retaliation claim could not be grieved, dismissal for non-exhaustion was denied); Greene v. C.D.C., 2008 WL 413750, *2 (E.D.Cal., Feb. 8, 2008) (plaintiff exhausted without completing the grievance process where the response to his grievance said it was an abuse of the process and plaintiff should instead use a form for requesting an interview instead), *report and recommendation adopted,* 2008 WL 683551 (E.D.Cal., Mar. 13, 2008); Smith v. Westchester County Dep't of Corrections, 2008 WL 361130, *3 (S.D.N.Y., Feb. 7, 2008) (plaintiff reasonably believed his claim was not grievable where a Sergeant told him so); Riley v. Hawaii Dep't of Public Safety, 2007 WL 3072777, *4–6 (D.Haw., Oct. 17, 2007) (holding sexual assault victims who completed the emergency grievance process as instructed, rather than the regular grievance process, had exhausted); Rasmussen v. Richards, 2007 WL 2677129, *2 (W.D.Wash., Sept. 7, 2007) (declining to dismiss for non-exhaustion where prisoner challenging failure to release him on the proper date was told he could not file a grievance concerning his sentence); Lewis v. Cunningham, 2007 WL 2412258, *2 (S.D.N.Y., Aug. 23, 2007) (holding prisoner who was told by grievance official that his medical complaint should go to the Chief Medical Officer rather than the grievance system showed special circumstances excusing lack of proper exhaustion); Lane v. Doan, 287 F. Supp. 2d 210, 212 (W.D.N.Y. 2003) (holding that exhaustion is excused where the plaintiff is led to believe the complaint is not a grievance matter or would otherwise be investigated, or that administrative remedies are unavailable); Simpson v. Gallant, 231 F. Supp. 2d 341, 350 (D.Me. 2002) (holding a prisoner who had been told the issue was not grievable had sufficiently exhausted); Boomer v. Lanigan, 2002 WL 31413804, *8 (S.D.N.Y., Oct. 25, 2002) (holding that an allegation that prison staff returned plaintiff's grievance and told him the matter was not handled by the grievance process raised a

factual issue barring summary judgment); Boomer v. Lanigan, 2001 WL 1646725 (S.D.N.Y., Dec. 17, 2001) (holding that a prisoner who was told by grievance staff that his grievance could not be handled sufficiently alleged exhaustion); Freeman v. Snyder, 2001 WL 515258, *7–8 (D.Del., Apr. 10, 2001) (holding prisoner not obliged to exhaust where prison staff told him he could not grieve the issue and he should take other steps instead); *see also* Matthews v. Thornhill, 2008 WL 2740323, *4 (W.D.Wash., May 21, 2008) (it is "disingenous" for defendants to rely on published policies stating what is grievable when they have already rejected plaintiff's grievances as raising non-grievable issues). *Contra,* Herron v. Elkins, 2006 WL 3803946, *3 (E.D.Mo., Nov. 7, 2006) (dismissing where staff told plaintiff his claim was not grievable; his "subjective belief" based on those statements did not excuse non-exhaustion); Overton v. Davis, 460 F. Supp. 2d 1008, 1010–11 (S.D.Iowa, 2006) (holding prisoner failed to exhaust where he said he was told his property confiscation was non-grievable but the written policy said it was and also that written notice is given when a complaint is non-grievable); Owens v. Maricopa County Sheriff's Office, 2006 WL 997205, *1 (D.Ariz., Apr. 14, 2006) (holding prisoner must appeal "non-grievable" determination, especially where policy does not support it); Mendez v. Herring, 2005 WL 3273555, *2 (D.Ariz., Nov. 29, 2005) (dismissing claim of a prisoner who said staff told him his rape complaint was not grievable, since futility is not an excuse).

[346]*See* Fuentes-Ramos v. Arpaio, 2007 WL 1670142, *2 (D. Ariz., June 8, 2007) (refusing to credit "generalized allegations" that officers told plaintiff his issues were non-grievable).

[347]Gibson v. Weber, 431 F.3d 339, 341 (8th Cir. 2005) (holding that prisoners who admitted receiving guide that explained the grievance procedure were not excused from using it by their allegations that prison personnel had "made it clear" that they should instead voice complaints informally to medical personnel); Boyd v. Corr. Corp. of Am., 380 F.3d 989 (6th Cir. 2004); Francisco v. Reese, 2009 WL 77458, *4 (S.D.Miss., Jan. 9, 2009) (claim of ignorance of remedy discounted where plaintiff had signed for receipt of information about it); Edwards v. Ala. Dep't of Corr., 81 F. Supp. 2d 1242, 1256–57 (M.D.Ala., 2000); Rizzuto v. City of New York, 2003 WL 1212758, *5 (S.D.N.Y., Mar. 17, 2003) (refusing to credit prisoner's claim that he never received information about the grievance system in light of signed receipt for rule book); Carter v. Woodbury County Jail, 2003 WL 1342934 (N.D.Iowa, Mar. 18, 2003) (similar to *Rizzuto*).

[348]Gibson v. Weber, 431 F.3d 339, 341 (8th Cir. 2005) (holding that general allegation that prison personnel "made it clear" they should make medical complaints informally did not excuse prisoners from using a grievance procedure they admitted having been informed of); Lyon v. Vande Krol, 305 F.3d 806, 809 (8th Cir. 2002) (holding that warden's statement that a decision about religious matters rested in the hands of "Jewish experts" did not

or mislead a prisoner into not exhausting, or not exhausting correctly, may be deemed to estop (*i.e.*, prevent) prison personnel from claiming non-exhaustion, in addition to or instead of making the remedy unavailable.[349]

If there is some reason outside your control that you cannot exhaust in a timely and procedurally correct fashion, you might think this means that the remedy is not available to you and you don't have to exhaust. Don't assume this. A number of courts have held, for example, that if prisoners are prevented from filing grievances at the correct time, they must file them whenever they can, even if the grievances will be denied as untimely.[350] This makes no sense under the "proper exhaustion" rule, but courts do it anyway, so don't fall into the trap. File the grievance as soon as you can, explain why it is late and ask that the lateness be excused, and appeal all the way to the top. Do the same in any other

_____

excuse non-exhaustion, but was at most a prediction that the plaintiff would lose; courts will not consider prisoners' subjective beliefs in determining whether procedures are "available"); Jackson v. District of Columbia, 254 F.3d 262, 269–70 (D.C. Cir. 2001) (holding that a plaintiff who complained to three prison officials and was told by the warden to "file it in the court" had not exhausted); Yousef v. Reno, 254 F.3d 1214, 1221–22 (10th Cir. 2001) (holding that plaintiff who was confused by prison officials' erroneous representations about the powers of the grievance system was still required to exhaust); Chelette v. Harris, 229 F.3d 684, 688 (8th Cir. 2000) (holding that a plaintiff who complained to the warden and was told the warden would take care of his problem, was not excused from exhausting the grievance system); Singh v. Goord, 520 F. Supp. 2d 487, 496 (S.D.N.Y. 2007) (officials' designating a particular staff member to deal with plaintiff's concerns did not excuse non-exhaustion where he was not instructed not to file grievances); Thomas v. N.Y. State Dep't of Corr. Servs., 2003 WL 22671540, *3–4 (S.D.N.Y., Nov. 10, 2003) (dismissing case where prison staff told the prisoner a grievance was not necessary; this was "bad advice, not prevention or obstruction," and the prisoner did not make sufficient efforts to exhaust).

[349]Assaults or threats can estop defendants from claiming exhaustion. Hemphill v. New York, 380 F.3d 680, 688–89 (2d Cir. 2004); Ziemba v. Wezner, 366 F.3d 161, 162–63 (2d Cir. 2004); Messa v. LeClaire, 2007 WL 2292975, *4 (N.D.N.Y., Feb. 26, 2007) (holding threats by unidentified prison staff could estop the named defendants), *report and recommendation adopted*, 2007 WL 2288106 (N.D.N.Y., Aug. 6, 2007); Larry v. Byno, 2006 WL 1313344, *4 (N.D.N.Y., May 11, 2006). Misstatements or withholding of essential information by prison personnel about the operation of the grievance system can also support an estoppel argument. *See* Pacheco v. Drown, 2010 WL 144400, *21 (N.D.N.Y., Jan. 11, 2010) (citing erroneous ruling that plaintiff's grievance was non-grievable); Chinnici v. Edwards, 2008 WL 3851294, *5 (D.Vt., Aug. 12, 2008) (citing supervisor's statement that sex abuse complaint did not require completing the grievance process); Cabrera v. LeVierge, 2008 WL 215720, *6 (D.N.H., Jan. 24, 2008) ("Defendants' reliance upon undisclosed rules to reject plaintiff's grievance form necessarily estops them from relying upon plaintiff's failure to exhaust those remedies as a defense."); Tweed v. Schuetzle, 2007 WL 2050782, *8 (D.N.D., July 12, 2007) (citing officials' advice to plaintiffs that the grievance system was the wrong remedy for them); Snyder v. Goord, 2007 WL 957530, *10 (N.D.N.Y., Mar. 29, 2007); Warren v. Purcell, 2004 WL 1970642, *6 (S.D.N.Y., Sept. 3, 2004) (citing "baffling" grievance response that left prisoner with no clue what to do next); Rivera v. Goord, 2003 WL 1700518, *7 (S.D.N.Y., Mar. 28, 2003) (officials said plaintiff's complaint is not a "grievance matter"); Heath v. Saddlemire, 2002 WL 31242204, *5 (N.D.N.Y., Oct. 7, 2002) (similar to *Rivera*); Simpson v. Gallant, 223 F. Supp. 2d 286, 292 (D. Me. 2002) (same), *aff'd*, 62 Fed.Appx. 368 (1st Cir. 2003) (unpublished); Davis v. Frazier, 1999 WL 395414, *4 (S.D.N.Y., June 15, 1999) (prisoners allegedly told that "a grievance cannot be brought against Officers or Staff"). Estoppel has been invoked in a variety of other circumstances as well. *See* Lawyer v. Gatto, 2007 WL 549440, *7 (S.D.N.Y., Feb. 21, 2007)

(holding defendants estopped from arguing plaintiff should have refiled his grievance citing mitigating circumstances for its lateness where the grievance supervisor had already rejected his mitigating circumstances); Gay v. Correctional Medical Services, 2007 WL 495241, *3 (D.Vt., Feb. 9, 2007) (holding officer's admission that she received and signed the plaintiff's grievance but then returned it to him rather than forwarding it as required may estop the defendants); Martin v. Sizemore, 2005 WL 1491210, *3 (E.D., Ky. June 22, 2005) (holding defendants estopped where they "designed their 'complaint' system so that inmates were often allegedly dependent upon the very persons against whom they were registering a complaint to transport the complaint to the front office or to personally and independently of a committee resolve the matter"); Hall v. Sheahan, 2001 WL 111019, *2 (N.D.Ill., Feb. 2, 2001) (holding that a prison official's statement to the prisoner that she would have the toilet fixed, and he should stop asking her about it, might prevent defendants from claiming that the prisoner had failed to exhaust).

The circumstances that support an estoppel argument will generally also support an argument that the remedy was unavailable, and you should make that argument as well. *See* Abney v. McGinnis, 380 F.3d 663, 667 (2d Cir. 2004) (suggesting courts consider availability first). Estoppel arguments can be problematical. Some courts have held that estoppel requires a showing of affirmative deceit or other misconduct by the defendants, not just mistakes. *See, e.g.*, Lewis v. Washington, 300 F.3d 829, 834–35 (7th Cir. 2002) (declining to apply equitable estoppel where the defendants did not affirmatively mislead the plaintiff, but merely failed to respond to grievances); Wolfe v. Alameida, 2008 WL 4454053, *2–3 (E.D.Cal., Sept. 29, 2008) (holding estoppel against government requires a showing of "affirmative misconduct going beyond mere negligence," of serious injustice, and no harm to the public interest from imposing estoppel). Also, some courts have held or suggested that estoppel can only be found if the actions supporting estoppel were done by the defendants in the case, as opposed to, *e.g.*, grievance personnel who are not parties. *See, e.g.* Dillon v. Rogers, 596 F.3d 260, 270 (5th Cir. 2010); Collins v. Goord, 438 F. Supp.2d 399, 415 n.16 (S.D.N.Y. 2006). Others have disagreed. *See* Snyder v. Goord, 2007 WL 957530, *10 (N.D.N.Y., Mar. 29, 2007) (holding misleading advice from grievance supervisor could estop named defendant); Messa v. LeClaire, 2007 WL 2292975, *4 (N.D.N.Y., Feb. 26, 2007) (holding threats by unidentified prison staff could estop the named defendants), *report and recommendation adopted*, 2007 WL 2288106 (N.D.N.Y., Aug. 6, 2007). The issue remains unresolved.

[350]*See* cases cited in n.462, below. For more information about time limits, see § D.6 of this chapter.

case where your grievance is rejected for not following the rules, but you were prevented in some fashion from following the rules.

Some courts have held that if your grievance or appeal simply "disappears," it's not enough just to say that when you go to court; you must take some action to follow up on the missing grievance.[351] One federal appeals court has recently held that if the failure to exhaust was "innocent," the prisoner "must be given another chance to exhaust (provided that there exist remedies that he will be permitted by the prison authorities to exhaust, so that he's not just being given a runaround)."[352]

Courts may be very skeptical of claims that you have exhausted your remedies when there is no record of your actions, or of claims that you were not informed or misinformed about the grievance process.[353] It is therefore prudent to do everything you can to exhaust even if you know the effort is going to fail—and keep your own records to help you prove you tried. For example, if prison staff refuses to provide you with grievance forms, you might write your grievance on a sheet of paper, explain that you can't get the forms, and appeal if they reject the grievance for not being on the right form.[354] If prison staff tells you that you don't need to file a grievance, file it anyway; if they tell you that the issue is not "grievable"—i.e., that the grievance system is not available to you for that issue—try to file the grievance anyway, so that you will get a decision in writing telling you that it isn't grievable. If they refuse to accept your grievance, write to the Warden or Superintendent, tell him or her that you were not allowed to file your grievance, and ask that it either be investigated as a non-grievance complaint or

treated as a grievance in case you were misinformed by the lower level staff. It may also be worthwhile (and in some cases the grievance rules may provide for it) to file a grievance about the refusal to accept your grievance. Keep copies of everything.

4. What Must You Put in Your Grievance or Administrative Appeal?

Your grievance or other administrative complaint must include all the issues you wish to sue about; issues not raised administratively cannot be litigated.[355] Sometimes you have to use more than one remedy to exhaust all your issues.[356]

How specific and detailed must you be in a grievance or appeal to satisfy the exhaustion requirement? The Supreme Court has said that the prison's rules govern: "The level of detail necessary in a grievance to comply with the grievance procedures will vary from system to system and claim to claim, but it is the prison's requirements, and not the PLRA, that define the boundaries of proper exhaustion."[357] In that case, the Court said that Michigan prisoners did not have to

---

[351]Boyer v. Farlin, 2006 WL 3590174, *3 (C.D.Ill., Dec. 8, 2006) (holding prisoner didn't exhaust because he failed to explain why he didn't take any action for two months when he didn't receive a notice that his appeal had been received). For more information on what to do if your grievance is taken from you or ignored, see nn.249–251 of this chapter. The Seventh Circuit has held that a remedy becomes "unavailable" if prison employees try to take unfair advantage of the exhaustion requirement by not responding to a grievance or otherwise preventing a prisoner from exhausting. In that case, the court ruled that a prisoner whose properly filed grievance had simply vanished did "all that was reasonable to exhaust." Dole v. Chandler, 438 F.3d 804, 809, 812 (7th Cir. 2006).

[352]Pavey v. Conley, 544 F.3d 739, 742 (7th Cir. 2008), cert. denied, 129 S. Ct. 1620 (2009).

[353]See, e.g., Perez v. Arpaio, 2006 WL 3421770, *2 (D.Ariz., Nov. 21, 2006) (rejecting claim that some unidentified person told the plaintiff his issues were not grievable); Gaughan v. U.S. Bureau of Prisons, 2003 WL 23139359, *2–3 (N.D.Ill., Dec. 30, 2003) (rejecting claim that prisoner had exhausted but defendants had not made a record of it); Thomas v. N.Y. State Dep't of Corr. Serv., 2003 WL 22671540, *3–4 (S.D.N.Y., Nov. 10, 2003) (dismissing case where prison staff allegedly told the prisoner a grievance was not necessary for failure to exhaust).

[354]See Abney v. County of Nassau, 237 F. Supp. 2d 278, 282 (E.D.N.Y. 2002) (holding that prisoner who could not get grievance forms and wrote grievance on plain paper, but never got a response, had exhausted).

[355]Jones v. Bock, 549 U.S. 199, 219–20, 127 S. Ct. 910 (2007); see Johnson v. Johnson, 385 F.3d 503, 517–19 (5th Cir. 2004) (holding that a prisoner who complained of sexual assault and referred to his sexual orientation in his grievance, but said nothing about his race, did not exhaust his racial discrimination claim); Black v. Goord, 2007 WL 3076998, *4 (W.D.N.Y., Oct. 19, 2007) (holding grievances about the length of time the plaintiff was held in full restraints did not exhaust his complaint about pain and inability to exercise or about lack of due process in renewing the restraint orders); Lilly v. Smith, 2007 WL 1832040, *2 (C.D.Ill., June 25, 2007) (dismissing claim about placement in restraint chair which was not mentioned in plaintiff's use of force grievance); Malik v. Sabree, 2007 WL 781640, *4 (D.S.C., Mar. 13, 2007) (holding grievance about Muslim feasts did not exhaust a claim about Muslim fasts); Beltran v. O'Mara, 405 F. Supp. 2d 140, 152 (D.N.H. 2005) (holding that complaints about specific segregation conditions, such as lack of toilet paper, did not exhaust as to conditions in general or conditions not mentioned in the grievances), on reconsideration, 2006 WL 240558 (D.N.H., Jan. 31, 2006); Page v. Breslin, 2004 WL 2713266, *3 (E.D.N.Y., Nov. 29, 2004) (holding that a grievance about harassing conduct exhausted only as to those incidents mentioned in the grievance); Cooper v. Garcia, 55 F. Supp. 2d 1090, 1094–95 (S.D.Cal. 1999) (plaintiff exhausted his claim about his status as a sex offender but not his Eighth Amendment claim).

[356]This is most often the case in connection with disciplinary proceedings. See nn.304–311, above.

[357]Jones v. Bock, 549 U.S. 199, 219, 127 S. Ct. 910 (2007) (holding prisoners could not be required to name in their grievance all the defendants they later sue where the grievance rules did not so require).

One circuit has said that "no administrative system may demand that the prisoner specify each remedy later sought in litigation—for Booth v. Churner . . . holds that [§] 1997e(a) requires each prisoner to exhaust a process and not a remedy." Strong v. David, 297 F.3d 646, 649–50 (7th Cir. 2002).

name in their grievances all the people they later sued, since the grievance rules at that time did not so require.[358]

At present, most grievance systems do not spell out the level of detail required. Either they say nothing about the level of detail required in grievances, or the requirement is very general.[359] Several courts have taken the view that if the policy doesn't have more specific requirements, a "grievance suffices if it alerts the prison to the nature of the wrong for which redress is sought. As in a notice pleading system, the grievant need not lay out the facts, articulate legal theories, or demand particular relief. All the grievant need do is object intelligibly to some asserted shortcoming."[360] Courts have adopted that standard because it is sufficient to give prison officials time and opportunity to resolve problems before they turn into lawsuits, which is the purpose of the PLRA exhaustion requirement, and it makes no sense to demand more detail at the administrative stage than is required for complaints in federal court.[361] An example of a grievance that meets the "object intelligibly" standard (though just barely) is one in a sexual assault case where the prisoner said only: "[T]he administration don't do there job. [A sexual assault] should've never happen again," and requested that the assailant be criminally prosecuted.[362]

Even courts that do not cite the "object intelligibly" standard have generally not required a great deal of specificity and detail in grievances where the grievance policy did not require it, and have not accepted hypertechnical arguments by prison officials that grievances were inadequate.[363]

---

[358]Jones v. Bock, 549 U.S. at 218. Some systems do have such "name the defendant" policies, and Michigan has now adopted one too; these are discussed below at nn.374–389.

[359]For example, the New York State grievance system requires only that prisoners include a "concise, specific description of the problem and the action requested and indicate what actions the grievant has taken to resolve the complaint, *i.e.*, specific persons/areas contacted and responses received." 7 New York Code of Rules & Regulations § 701.5(a)(2). The courts have held that this requirement is not sufficient to instruct prisoners that they need to name the individuals who later become defendants in a lawsuit. Espinal v. Goord, 558 F.3d 119, 126 (2d Cir. 2009).

[360]Strong v. David, 297 F.3d 646, 650 (7th Cir. 2002); *accord*, Griffin v. Arpaio, 557 F.3d 1117, 1120 (9th Cir. 2009) ("A grievance need not include legal terminology or legal theories unless they are in some way needed to provide notice of the harm being grieved. A grievance also need not contain every fact necessary to prove each element of an eventual legal claim. The primary purpose of a grievance is to alert the prison to a problem and facilitate its resolution, not to lay groundwork for litigation."); Kikumura v. Osagie, 461 F.3d 1269, 1283 (10th Cir. 2006); Johnson v. Testman, 380 F.3d 691, 697 (2d Cir. 2004); Milan v. Chen, 2008 WL 2229215, *5 (C.D.Cal., Feb. 5, 2008), *report and recommendation adopted*, 2008 WL 2116930 (C.D.Cal., May 14, 2008) *and* 2008 WL 2116959 (C.D.Cal., May 14, 2008); *see* Wine v. Pollard, 2008 WL 4379236, *3 (W.D.Wis., Sept. 23, 2008) (requiring prisoners to identify every possible legal theory in a grievance "would be unfair and possibly invalid"); Jones 'El v. Berge, 172 F. Supp. 2d 1128, 1134 (W.D.Wis. 2001) (holding that once a claim is exhausted, "[a]ny claim for relief that is within the scope of the pleadings" may be litigated without further exhaustion).

[361]Johnson v. Testman, 380 F.3d at 697.

[362]Riccardo v. Rausch, 375 F.3d 521, 524 (7th Cir. 2004); *see* Westefer v. Snyder, 422 F.3d 570, 580–81 (7th Cir. 2005) (holding that plaintiffs sufficiently exhausted complaints about transfers to a

high-security prison by listing "Transfer from Tamms" as a requested remedy, or by expressing concern about not being given a reason for the transfer, in grievances about the conditions at that prison); Barnes v. Briley, 420 F.3d 673, 678–79 (7th Cir. 2005) (holding a grievance "in regards to a request for [sic] for medical test and treatment. I have requested several times to be tested for Tuberculosis, H.I.V., Hepatitis, etc. for the past few years" exhausted as to the past failure to respond to such requests by a doctor not named in the grievance and no longer employed at the prison).

[363]*See, e.g.*, McAlphin v. Toney, 375 F.3d 753, 755 (8th Cir. 2004) (per curiam) (treating claim that two defendants failed to treat plaintiff's dental grievances as emergency matters, and that others refused to escort him to the infirmary for emergency treatment as both part of a single exhausted claim of denial of emergency dental treatment); Kikumura v. Hurley, 242 F.3d 950, 956 (10th Cir. 2001) (holding complaint sufficient to meet the exhaustion requirement where the plaintiff said that he was denied Christian pastoral visits, though the defendants said his claim should be dismissed because he had not stated in the grievance process that his religious beliefs include elements of both the Buddhist and Christian religions); Carter v. Symmes, 2008 WL 341640, *4 (D.Mass., Feb. 4, 2008) (adopting administrative law rule that "claims not enumerated in an initial grievance are allowed notwithstanding the exhaustion requirement if they 'are like or reasonably related to the substance of charges timely brought before [the agency]'"); Crawford v. Dretke, 2007 WL 172628, *7 (S.D.Tex., Jan. 11, 2007) (holding that a generalized statement sufficed to exhaust where the alleged violations were repetitive and involved the same defendants), *report and recommendation adopted*, 2007 WL 784343 (S.D.Tex., Mar. 12, 2007), *appeal dismissed on other grounds*, 265 Fed.Appx. 296 (5th Cir. 2008) (unpublished); Grant v. Cathel, 2007 WL 119158, *5 (D.N.J. Jan. 10, 2007) (holding that a prisoner's complaint that he was not receiving prescribed cancer treatment and medication and was in great pain care sufficiently exhausted a claim that defendants failed to provide an escort to get him to his medical appointments and defendants failed to supervise his medical care; plaintiff's grievance "discuss[ed] the primary grievance underlying his claims, his allegedly inadequate medical treatment"); Underwood v. Mendez, 2006 WL 860142, *5 (M.D.Pa., Mar. 31, 2006) (holding that a prisoner who complained of a retaliatory transfer need not also have mentioned in his grievance a falsified progress report and a conspiracy, since these were just factual allegations supporting his retaliation claim); Hoffenberg v. Fed. Bureau of Prisons, 2004 WL 2203479, *12 (D.Mass., Sept. 14, 2004) (holding that a prisoner's complaint that restrictions on his legal telephone calls interfered with his efforts to pursue litigation to collect money owed him, so he could satisfy his restitution obligation, "comprehended" his access to courts claim, notwithstanding defendants' "overly technical" argument to the contrary); Mester v. Kim, 2005 WL 3507975, *2 (E.D.Cal., Dec. 22, 2005) (holding that a grievance asserting that the plaintiff had a hernia and had not received necessary surgery sufficiently exhausted without detailing the acts or omissions of individual defendants), *report and recommendation adopted*, 2006 WL 354654 (E.D.Cal., Feb. 15,

Their concern is whether the grievance provides enough information for prison officials to be able to investigate the prisoner's problem.[364] Thus, grievances do not satisfy the exhaustion requirement when they are so vague or incomplete that prison officials cannot reasonably be expected to understand what the prisoner was complaining about.[365] But courts have emphasized that grievances are not required to rehearse the legal arguments and claims later asserted in a lawsuit.[366]

Despite all these decisions, some courts have held grievances inadequate when they failed specifically to mention claims of denial of First Amendment rights,[367] unlawful retaliation,[368] discrimination contrary to the Equal Protection Clause,[369] or conspiracy that prisoners later asserted in their

---

2006); Pineda-Morales v. De Rosa, 2005 WL 1607276, *6 (D.N.J., July 6, 2005) (holding that a complaint seeking increased accommodation for prisoner's religion, and stating that it could not be accommodated by existing Protestant services and that their doctrines were incompatible, sufficiently exhausted his claim for official recognition of his Apostolic sect even though it did not mention the Religious Freedom Restoration Act or specifically request recognition); Lyerly v. Phillips, 2005 WL 1802972, *2 (S.D.N.Y., July 29, 2005) (holding that complaint of exposure to second-hand smoke sufficiently exhausted without detail of the plaintiff's medical condition, the relief sought, or the names of the culprits); Davis v. Stanford, 382 F. Supp. 2d 814, 819 (E.D.Va. 2004) (holding a claim of inadequate medical care, "liberally construed," was encompassed by a grievance concerning inadequate treatment for the resulting pain), aff'd, 127 Fed.Appx. 680 (4th Cir. 2005) (unpublished); Cassels v. Stalder, 342 F. Supp. 2d 555, 560 (M.D.La. 2004) (holding that disciplinary appeal from conviction for "spreading rumors," in which the prisoner stated that he had placed an advertisement "in seek of legal help" and was "being retaliated against," sufficiently exhausted his claims of denial of access to courts and the right to seek counsel, retaliation, and vagueness and overbreadth of the disciplinary rule).

There are exceptions. See Davis v. Knowles, 2007 WL 214598, *3 (E.D.Cal., Jan. 25, 2007) (holding prisoner who grieved that he had been denied treatment for his injured finger at every prison he had been at should have spelled out that he was denied access to an orthopedic surgeon around a particular date, then transferred two months later and denied medical care), report and recommendation adopted, 2007 WL 1141583 (E.D.Cal., Apr. 17, 2007).

[364]Tillis v. Lamarque, 2006 WL 644876, *7 (N.D.Cal., Mar. 9, 2006) ("In determining whether a claim has been exhausted, a court must consider whether a reasonable investigation of the complaint would have uncovered the allegations now before it.").

[365]See, e.g., Thompson v. Stalder, 2008 WL 874138, *4 (M.D.La., Apr. 1, 2008) (holding a general statement that plaintiff was "unable to practice [his] religious beliefs" did not exhaust his specific claims to a meat-free diet and Rastafarian services and literature; it did not provide a fair opportunity to address the claims later asserted in his suit; Beltran v. O'Mara, 405 F. Supp. 2d 140, 152 (D.N.H. 2005) (holding that allegations the plaintiff was "being punished for no reason" and isolated from other prisoners were "too vague" to allow officials to make any response), on reconsideration, 2006 WL 240558 (D.N.H., Jan. 31, 2006); Aguirre v. Feinerman, 2005 WL 1277860, *6 (S.D.Ill., May 10, 2005) (holding that a grievance that specifically mentioned physical therapy, but mentioned other medical care only generally, did not exhaust as to the failure to diagnose the plaintiff's congestive heart failure; "While specifically identifying the ailment would not be required, there must be some indication as to what medical issues the plaintiff was complaining about."); Ball v. McCaughtry, 2004 WL 1013362, *2 (W.D.Wis., May 6, 2004) (holding that a prisoner who complained about seized papers that he identified only as "gay materials," even when asked for more information, was insufficiently specific to satisfy a

grievance policy calling for sufficient facts to allow an examiner to investigate the complaint).

[366]See Griffin v. Arpaio, 557 F.3d 1117, 1120 (9th Cir. 2009) ("A grievance need not include legal terminology or legal theories unless they are in some way needed to provide notice of the harm being grieved. A grievance also need not contain every fact necessary to prove each element of an eventual legal claim. The primary purpose of a grievance is to alert the prison to a problem and facilitate its resolution, not to lay groundwork for litigation."); Johnson v. Johnson, 385 F.3d 503, 517–18 (5th Cir. 2004) (agreeing that legal theories need not be presented in grievances; holding that a prisoner who complained of sexual assault, made repeated reference to his sexual orientation, and said nothing about his race had exhausted his sexual orientation discrimination claim but not his racial discrimination claim); Burton v. Jones, 321 F.3d 569, 575 (6th Cir. 2003) (holding grievance need not "allege a specific legal theory or facts that correspond to all the required elements of a particular legal theory"); Parker v. Robinson, 2008 WL 2222040, *7 (D.Me., May 22, 2008) (point of exhaustion requirement "is not to make sure prisoners identify their potential litigable civil rights claims early on but it is to give the correctional institution the opportunity to address (and hopefully resolve) the grieved-of conduct/condition before the dispute moves to litigation. The administrative grievance process is not a dress-rehearsal hurdle to civil litigation . . ."); Hooks v. Rich, 2006 WL 565909, *5 (S.D.Ga., Mar. 7, 2006) ("Section 1997e(a) is not intended to result in 'fact-intensive litigation' over whether every fact relevant to the cause of action was included in the grievance."); Williams v. Wilkinson, 122 F. Supp. 2d 894, 899 (S.D.Ohio 2000) (rejecting an argument by defendants that "each claim at each stage [of the grievance process] must parallel each and every claim in the federal complaint").

[367]See Dye v. Kingston, 130 Fed.Appx. 52, 56 (7th Cir. 2005) (unpublished) (holding that a prisoner who complained in his grievance of missing property items, including his Bibles, failed to exhaust his First Amendment claim by failing to state that the Bibles' loss was "infringing on his religious practice").

[368]Brownell v. Krom, 446 F.3d 305, 311 (2d Cir. 2006) (claim of lost property "does not trigger the level of investigation that a grievance suggesting retaliation would trigger"); Griffin v. Miner, 2006 WL 3169644, *1–2 (N.D.Ohio, Nov. 1, 2006) (plaintiff who didn't mention his retaliation theory in his grievance did not exhaust with respect to retaliation); Robins v. Atchue, 2006 WL 1283470, *4 (E.D.Cal., May 10, 2006) (holding disciplinary appeal that did not mention retaliation could not exhaust a retaliation claim), report and recommendation adopted, 2006 WL 1882940 (E.D.Cal., July 7, 2006); Lindell v. Casperson, 360 F. Supp. 2d 932, 949 (W.D.Wis. 2005), aff'd, 169 Fed.Appx. 999 (7th Cir. 2006) (unpublished).

[369]Johnson v. Johnson, 385 F.3d 503, 518 (5th Cir. 2004) (holding that a prisoner who complained of sexual assault, made repeated reference to his sexual orientation, but said nothing about his race had exhausted his sexual orientation discrimination claim but not his racial discrimination claim); Goldsmith v. White, 357 F.

lawsuits, even if they fully stated the underlying facts in their grievances.[370] We think some of these decisions are inconsistent with the many decisions cited above (sometimes from the same courts) that say prisoners don't have to plead legal theories or spell out the elements of legal claims in their grievances. A number of recent decisions support our view, holding that as long as the facts are in the grievance, prisoners need not have specifically grieved claims of discrimination,[371] conspiracy,[372] or retaliation.[373]

As a practical matter, if you think that something you are grieving resulted from retaliation, involved conspiracy, etc., you should probably say so in the grievance. If you have only suspicion, but no concrete facts to go on, you may wish to say, for example, that you do not know whether there was any discrimination, conspiracy, or retaliatory motive, but those possibilities should be investigated.

As noted above, some prison systems do require naming the responsible employees in grievances;[374] some have added this requirement recently.[375] Such policies must be made explicit to be binding; courts will not infer a requirement of

---

Supp. 2d 1336, 1338–41 (N.D.Fla. 2005); Young v. Goord, 2002 WL 31102670, *4 (E.D.N.Y., Sept. 3, 2002) (holding that a prisoner who alleged in his grievance only that he had been disciplined for conduct that did not violate the rules could not litigate an equal protection claim that he was disciplined for discriminatory reasons), *aff'd in part, vacated in part on other grounds*, 67 Fed. Appx. 638 (2d Cir. 2003) (unpublished).

[370]Means v. Lambert, 2007 WL 4591251, *3 (W.D.Okla., Dec. 28, 2007) (dismissing conspiracy claim for failure to allege an agreement in the grievance); Sisney v. Reisch, 2007 WL 951858, *6 (D.S.D., Mar. 26, 2007) (same); Lindell v. Frank, 2005 WL 2339145 (W.D.Wis., Sept. 23, 2005) (holding failure to mention conspiracy allegations in grievance appeal meant that claim was not exhausted). *But see* Ketzner v. Williams, 2008 WL 4534020, *17 (W.D.Mich., Sept. 30, 2008) (allusion to "combined effort" arguably exhausted conspiracy claim); Teague v. Wadas, 2008 WL 4371926, *4 (D. Colo., Sept. 22, 2008) (conspiracy allegation can be inferred from grievances; "the language and assertions in Plaintiff's grievances must be considered in their entirety, rather than piecemeal").

[371]*See* Rowe v. Bergh, 2008 WL 4425547, *5 (W.D.Mich., Sept. 26, 2008) (where grievance policy required only facts, not legal theories, plaintiff's failure to assert that his problems were caused by racial discrimination was not a failure to exhaust).

[372]Espinal v. Goord, 558 F.3d 119, 127–28 (2d Cir. 2009) (conspiracy is a legal theory which need not be asserted in a grievance to exhaust); Ramos v. Monteiro, 2008 WL 4184644, *11 (C.D.Cal., Sept. 8, 2008) (similar to *Espinal*); Kitchen-Bey v. Hoskins, 2006 WL 3370873, *4 (W.D. Mich., Nov. 20, 2006) (similar to *Espinal*), *amended and superseded on other grounds*, 2006 WL 3500617 (W.D.Mich., Dec. 4, 2006).

[373]Mitchell v. Horn, 318 F.3d 523, 531 (3d Cir. 2003) (holding that a prisoner who claimed retaliatory discipline exhausted by appealing the disciplinary decision to the highest level); Lugo v. Van Orden, 2008 WL 2884925, *2 (N.D.N.Y., July 23, 2008) (plaintiff exhausted despite not specifically mentioning retaliation where he "raised the identical fact pattern" in grievance and lawsuit); Cromer v. Braman, 2008 WL 907468, *13 (W.D.Mich., Mar. 31, 2008) (grievance alleging harassment that was considered on the merits need not have also alleged retaliation); Daher v. Kasper, 2008 WL 553644, *4 (N.D.Ind., Feb. 26, 2008); El-Shaddai v. Wheeler, 2008 WL 410711, *5 (E.D.Cal., Feb. 12, 2008) (where the grievance form merely directs prisoners to "describe the problem and the action requested," the prisoner need not specify legal theories including whether the motive was retaliatory), *report and recommendation adopted*, 2008 WL 892900 (E.D.Cal., Mar. 31, 2008); Reeder v. Doe 5, 507 F. Supp. 2d 468, 482 n.16 (D.Del. 2007) (rejecting argument that "plaintiff must submit a specific grievance complaining of retaliation. . . . There need be only a shared factual basis, not perfect overlap, between a grievance and the complaint."), *reconsideration denied*, 2008 WL 4368631 (D.Del., Sept. 18, 2008); Davison v. MacLean, 2007 WL 1520892, *6 (E.D.Mich., May 22,

2007) (holding prisoner should include "known and obviously material facts" such as officer's stated religious bias, but cannot be required to present information he does not have at the time), *reconsideration denied*, 2007 WL 1806204 (E.D.Mich., June 21, 2007); Varela v. Demmon, 491 F. Supp. 2d 442, 448 (S.D.N.Y. 2007) (holding grievance need not include the word "retaliation" if it states facts from which retaliation can be inferred); Jennings v. Huizar, 2007 WL 2081200, *4 (D.Ariz., July 19, 2007) (holding prisoner need not have alleged retaliation in his grievance; alleging that act was done for an improper purpose was sufficient; plaintiff "not required to specifically identify . . . theories of recovery in his inmate grievance"), *aff'd*, 315 Fed.Appx. 633 (9th Cir. 2009) (unpublished); Underwood v. Mendez, 2006 WL 860142, *5 (M.D.Pa., Mar. 31, 2006) (holding that a prisoner who complained of a retaliatory transfer need not also have mentioned in his grievance a falsified progress report and a conspiracy, since these were just factual allegations supporting his retaliation claim).

[374]*See, e.g.,* Talley v. Johnson, 2008 WL 2223259, *2 (M.D.Ga., May 1, 2008) (noting requirement to "state fully the time, date, names of facility staff and inmates involved, witnesses, and a narrative of the event"), *report and recommendation adopted*, 2008 WL 2223258 (M.D.Ga., May 23, 2008); Olney v. Hartwig, 2007 WL 438781, *1 (D.Or., Feb. 6, 2007) (citing Oregon policy requiring a separate grievance against each responsible staff member); Jones v. Courtney, 2006 WL 3306850, *4 (D.Kan., Nov. 13, 2006) (noting that Kansas grievance policy requires stating "who is the subject of the complaint" and "what effect the . . . person is having on the grievant"); Lane v. Harris County Jail Medical Dep't, 2006 WL 2868944, *5 (S.D.Tex., Oct. 5, 2006) (noting that jail policy demands a written statement that "fully and truthfully explains the incident that occurred," along with the "date, time and location of the incident," and the "names of any Deputies, Staff Members or inmates who were involved or are witnesses").

[375]Michigan has changed its policy, which formerly required prisoners only to "be as specific as possible" but to "[b]e brief and concise," to require inclusion of "[d]ates, times, places and names of all those involved in the issue being grieved." Mich. Dep't of Corr. Policy Dir. No. 03.02.130 (Dec. 19, 2003). In Illinois, after the Seventh Circuit observed that there was no specificity requirement in the grievance policy, *Strong v. David*, 297 F.3d 646, 650 (7th Cir. 2002), the prison system revised its policy to require "factual details regarding each aspect of the offender's complaint, including what happened, when, where, and the name of each person who is the subject of or who is otherwise involved in the complaint. This provision does not preclude an offender from filing a grievance when the names of individuals are not known, but the offender must include as much descriptive information about the individual as possible." 20 Ill.Admin. Code § 504.810(b).

naming defendants from more general requirements in a grievance policy.[376] If there is such a policy, some courts assume that any defendant not named in the grievance must be dismissed from the subsequent lawsuit.[377] (Since the Supreme Court has rejected the "total exhaustion" rule, the failure to name some defendants will not require dismissal of the entire case under a name-the-defendant rule.[378]) However, courts have also acknowledged that even under such a rule, prisoners cannot be required to provide information they do not possess.[379] Some courts have held that a

description of the defendant's position or conduct,[380] or even a general identification of the relevant unit or body, [381]

[376]Espinal v. Goord, 558 F.3d 119, 126 (2d Cir. 2009) (naming defendants not required by New York State grievance policy that called for a "concise, specific description of the problem and the action requested" and what the grievant had done to resolve the problem; rule that accused staff member is "direct party" to the grievance who has the right to be heard and to appeal is not an identification requirement); Holloway v. Correctional Medical Services, 2007 WL 1445701, *3 (E.D.Mo., May 11, 2007) (grievance policy said "the offender should provide whatever material/information is available to her/him"); Skinner v. Schriro, 2007 WL 2177326, *3 (D.Ariz., July 27, 2007) (grievance policy said "state briefly but completely the problem on which you desire assistance. Provide as many details as possible.").

[377]See, e.g., Walker v. Hofbauer, 2007 WL 2710823, *4 (W.D.Mich., Sept. 13, 2007) (holding defendants not named must be dismissed given Michigan's revised grievance policy). This approach has led to some particularly harsh and absurd results.

There may also be a question of what it means to name the defendants. In McKinney v. Kelchner, 2007 WL 2852373, *4 (M.D.Pa., Sept. 27, 2007), the court held that a grievance stating it was "on" two staff members in a use of force case, but also named other involved staff, sufficiently identified the latter that they could be sued; the grievance system's failure to acknowledge and decide the culpability of those persons was not a failure by the plaintiff to exhaust. In Spearman v. Smith, 2007 WL 2710097, *4 (E.D.Mich., Aug. 31, 2007), the court held that the plaintiff exhausted against L. Smith, notwithstanding misidentifying her as S. Smith, since the grievance process ruled on the merits of the claim.

[378]See Jones v. Bock, 549 U.S. 199, 219–24, 127 S. Ct. 910 (2007).

[379]Brown v. Sikes, 212 F.3d 1205, 1207–08 (11th Cir. 2000); accord, Sanks v. Franklin, 2010 WL 234785, *6 (M.D.Ga., Jan. 13, 2010) (question is "whether Plaintiff knew or reasonably should have known who was responsible" for the alleged deprivation"); Nelson v. Madan, 2005 WL 2416036, *2 (M.D.Fla., Sept. 30, 2005). In Contor v. Caruso, 2008 WL 878665, *3 (W.D.Mich., Mar. 28, 2008), the plaintiff said he did not know who denied his requests for medical care, and asked in his grievance for that person's name. The court held that his grievance sufficiently put defendants on notice of his claim against a medical provider employee. Similarly, in Robinson v. Johnson, 343 Fed.Appx. 778, 781-82 (3d Cir. 2009) (unpublished), the court declined to dismiss claims against the commissioner and superintendent not named in a grievance where the policies they were responsible for and the persons responsible for them were not made known to prisoners, and where grievance response addressed policies anyway. One court has said that a strict name-the-defendant policy would require prison officials to make provision for discovery in the grievance process, or else the requirement would be invalid because in conflict with the federal policies underlying the civil rights statutes. Freeman v. Berge, 2004

WL 1774737, *3-4 (W.D.Wis., July 28, 2004); accord, Czapiewski v. Bartow, 2008 WL 2622862, *1-2 (W.D.Wis., July 1, 2008) (reiterating point after Woodford v. Ngo and Jones v. Bock).

[380]See Jackson v. Hornick, 2006 WL 1766839, *2 (W.D.Mich., June 21, 2006) (holding a plaintiff who identified the defendant by the initials of his position (A.DDW of SCC) had exhausted); Iacovone v. Wilkinson, 2005 WL 3299032, *5 (S.D.Ohio, Dec. 2, 2005) (holding that failure to name defendants was not a failure to exhaust where the plaintiff's detailed description of his complaint permitted their identification and he did not know their correct identities), report and recommendation adopted as modified, 2006 WL 689102 (S.D.Ohio, Mar. 14, 2006); Gibson v. Shabaaz, 2005 WL 1515396, *7 (S.D.Tex., June 23, 2005) (holding reference to nurse and optometrist were sufficient to exhaust; defendants could have reviewed plaintiff's medical records and learned their identities); Blackshear v. Messer, 2003 WL 21508190, *2 (N.D.Ill., June 30, 2003) (holding that prisoner who failed to identify the nurse he was complaining about had exhausted, since that person could be identified from other information in his grievance "with a little follow-up investigation by the Jail").

[381]See Johnson v. Johnson, 385 F.3d 503, 523 (5th Cir. 2004) (holding identification of Unit Classification Committees was sufficient to exhaust as to their members); Cutler v. Correctional Medical Services, 2010 WL 339760, *5 (D.Idaho, Jan. 22, 2010) (complaint about inadequate medical care sufficiently notified private medical provider and its supervisory personnel of allegation that provider was not performing its duty); Downing v. Correction Medical Services Inc., 2009 WL 511849, *7 (W.D.Mich., Feb. 26, 2009) (naming some individuals plus all Bureau of Health Care personnel who had treated plaintiff over the last six months sufficed); Young v. Good, 2008 WL 4816474, *4 (W.D.Pa., Nov. 4, 2008) (grievance identifying "food services" sufficiently identified Food Services Supervisor, Cook Supervisor, and Deputy Warden who supervised food services); Austin v. Correctional Medical Services, Inc., 2008 WL 4426342, *5 (W.D.Mich., Sept. 26, 2008) (grievance against "the Medical Service Department" held "more than sufficient to put on notice any and all individuals and entities involved with providing health care to prisoners at MCF"); Binion v. Glover, 2008 WL 4097407, *4 (E.D.Mich., Aug. 29, 2008) (holding "failure to identify a person by name does not preclude exhaustion . . . as long as the prisoner identifies a defendant based on the factual allegations"; complaint about dialysis unit's failure to follow prison policies regarding needle disposal exhausted against both medical defendants who violated the policies and correctional defendants who failed to enforce them); Stevenson v. Michigan Dep't of Corrections, 2008 WL 623783, *11 (W.D.Mich., Mar. 4, 2008) (a policy requiring plaintiff to provide "the facts" including "who" did not require naming all defendants; naming "health care" exhausted against the private provider of medical care, and naming TriCounty Orthopedic was sufficient to exhaust against a doctor employed by it; naming some defendants at the second grievance stage exhausted against them); Jackson v. Caruso, 2008 WL 828118, *4 (W.D.Mich., Feb. 12, 2008) ("library staff" sufficed to exhaust against individual members of the library staff), report and recommendation adopted as modified on other grounds, 2008 WL 828116 (W.D.Mich., Mar. 26, 2008). Contra, Harris v. LePlante, 2008 WL 822146, *3 (W.D.Mich., Mar. 26, 2008) (naming "unit staff" does not exhaust under a name the defendant rule); Peterson v. Riverside Correctional

will suffice, or that a name-the-defendant rule is satisfied if the defendant was identified by prison officials in the *response* to the prisoner's grievance,[382] or by the prisoner in an appeal from the initial grievance.[383] Some courts have also held that naming of defendants was not required where the prisoner's complaint concerned an official decision or policy and not the unauthorized conduct of staff,[384] or where the prisoner's complaint of a long history of abusing prisoners sufficiently alerted officials to problems of supervision and management without actually naming the supervisors in the grievance.[385]

If your prison has a name-the-defendant grievance rule, and you aren't sure you know who all the potential

defendants are, make that very clear in your grievance. For example, if you were beaten by several officers while others looked on and did not intervene, you might write that your grievance is against "Officers Smith and Jones, who beat me, along with the other officers present who beat me or who stood by and did not intervene to stop the beating, and whose names I do not know." If you think there is a practice of beating prisoners that higher ups in the prison are responsible for, you might add something like "Sergeant Black, Lieutenant White, Deputy Superintendent Green and Superintendent Redd, and any other supervisors unknown to me who fail to train and supervise the security staff and keep them from using excessive and unnecessary force." Another example: If you are denied a book you have ordered by the mail room officer who tells you only "it's not allowed," your grievance might say it was against "Officer Jones in the mail room, and any other person unknown to me who made the decision or policy (if any) resulting in this book being denied to me, or if there is no such decision or policy, the supervisor of the mail room operation, unknown to me, who allows mail room staff to deny books to prisoners in the absence of a policy permitting it."

On this point, like everything else connected with exhaustion, you must always start by learning what the grievance rules require and do your best to comply with them. The foregoing comments are for situations where the grievance rules about naming defendants are not clear or where you are unable to comply with them fully because you do not have the necessary information.

Even if there is no name-the-defendant rule, you should think about the different events and policies that are or might be involved in the problem you are grieving, and mention them. A number of courts have held that if the *conduct* of particular defendants is not mentioned in the grievance, you may not have exhausted your claim. This can be a particular problem when you wish to bring claims of supervisory liability; a number of courts have held that prisoners who exhausted an underlying incident failed to exhaust their claims that higher level officials were responsible for it.[386] We think this is wrong, and that if your grievance gives notice of what happened to you, it is prison officials' job to

---

Facility, 2006 WL 753126, *2 (W.D.Mich., Mar. 23, 2006) (holding grievance referring to "kitchen staff [and] officers," "food service," and the "inspector's office" did not sufficiently identify parties).

[382]Spruill v. Gillis, 372 F.3d 218, 234 (3d Cir. 2004); *accord*, Williams v. Beard, 482 F.3d 637, 639–40 (3d Cir. 2007) (where the defendant not named in the grievance was the person who received the grievance, and his response showed his knowledge and involvement, plaintiff exhausted); Sisney v. Reisch, 2007 WL 951858, *5 (D.S.D., Mar. 26, 2007) (similar to *Williams*); Sides v. Cherry, 2007 WL 1411841, *3 (W.D.Pa., May 10, 2007) (holding policy satisfied where grievance response said "[a]ll staff involved were interviewed regarding your claims" and the defendants were specifically named in the response); Reaves v. Caruso, 2006 WL 2077589, *3 (E.D.Mich., July 24, 2006).

[383]Stevenson v. Michigan Dep't of Corrections, 2008 WL 623783, *11 (W.D.Mich., Mar. 4, 2008); Marshall v. Hubbard, 2007 WL 1627534, *4 (E.D.Ark., June 4, 2007) (plaintiff exhausted against a doctor whom he had not seen when he filed his original grievance but referred to in his appeals of the initial grievance).

[384]In *Chimenti v. Mohadjerin*, 2008 WL 2551603, *4–5 (M.D.Pa., June 24, 2008), the plaintiff failed to name the Secretary of Corrections because he did not know of the Secretary's involvement, but he named the Department of Corrections as an entity and challenged a departmental policy of inaction; the court held that officials received adequate notice and it was not "practicable" for plaintiff to name the Secretary. *See* Harris v. Moore, 2005 WL 1876126, *2 (E.D.Mo., Aug. 8, 2005); Smeltzer v. Hook, 235 F. Supp. 2d 736, 741–42 (W.D.Mich. 2002) (declining to apply rule to policy challenge, since failure to name individuals did not hamper the defendants' investigation). In *Pickelhaupt v. Jackson*, 2008 WL 4457823 (E.D.Mich., July 22, 2008), *report and recommendation adopted in part, rejected in part on other grounds*, 2008 WL 4457807 (E.D.Mich., Sept. 30, 2008), the prisoner complained that he was paid at the wrong rate, and the court declined to dismiss for non-exhaustion, saying "his naming of, or failure to name, any particular individual did not in any way interfere with the ability of corrections officials to conduct an investigation." 2008 WL 4457823, *12. In *Robinson v. Johnson*, 343 Fed.Appx. 778, 781-82 (3d Cir. 2009) (unpublished), the court declined to dismiss claims against the commissioner and superintendent who were not named in a grievance where the policies they were responsible for and the fact that they were responsible for them were not made known to prisoners, and where the grievance response addressed the policies anyway.

[385]*See* Hooks v. Rich, 2006 WL 595909, *6 (S.D.Ga., Mar. 7, 2006).

[386]*See* Kozohorsky v. Harmon, 332 F.3d 1141, 1143 (8th Cir. 2003) (dismissing claims against supervisor for failure to control officers who abused the plaintiff because the supervisor was not named in the grievance); Williams v. Forrest, 2005 WL 820551 (N.D.Tex., Apr. 6, 2005) (holding plaintiff was required to name supervisors of staff members who carried out a retaliatory transfer in order to sue the supervisors), *report and recommendation adopted*, 2005 WL 1163301 (N.D.Tex., May 9, 2005); *see also* Evans v. Correctional Medical Services, 2008 WL 1805375, *4 (E.D.Ark., Apr. 18, 2008) (holding prisoner did not exhaust his otherwise exhausted claim against a private medical provider because his grievances failed to "allege any facts that CMS directly participated in a constitutional violation, learned of an alleged constitutional violation and failed to act, created a policy or custom allowing or encouraging illegal acts, or managed its employees in a way that was grossly negligent").

figure out why it happened and who besides the immediate participants might be at fault.[387] However, courts may not accept that argument, and you should try to protect yourself in writing your grievances.

For instance, in the use of force example above, even if the grievance policy doesn't say anything about naming the responsible individuals, you might say: "I was beaten without justification by Officers Smith and Jones and others, while other officers stood by and did not intervene, and I am also complaining about the lack of training and supervision that allows security staff to use excessive and unnecessary force and get away with it."[388] In the book seizure example, you might say: "I was denied the book *A Time to Die* about the 1971 Attica disturbance, and I am also complaining about the policies and practices that allow the denial to prisoners of books without good reason and without clear written criteria and procedures." (Or, if they do have clear criteria and procedures but you wish to challenge them, mention those in the grievance too.)

If there *is* a name-the-defendants rule, to preserve your supervisory liability claim, you would add the identities of those persons whom you believe to be responsible for the lack of training and supervision and for the inadequate policies and procedures, if you know any of them. You would state that your grievance is also against any other person whose identity you don't know who is responsible for the lack of training and supervision, the inadequate policies, or whatever you think may be the problem underlying what happened to you. If you are dealing with employees of a private corporation, such as a medical provider or private prison operator, you should mention both the individual employees involved *and* the corporation they work for.[389] If your claim arises in a city or county jail and you may wish to sue the city or county over a municipal policy, or if your claim would be filed under the disability statutes that provide for liability of a government agency rather than individuals, it is wise to mention in your grievance the government or agency and any policy you think may have caused your problem.

Similarly, if you get more information about a problem after you have filed a grievance about it (or more information about the people responsible, if the system requires that), you should consider filing a separate grievance reflecting the new information. (It might make more sense to amend your existing grievance or add the new allegations to an appeal from it, but that will only work if the grievance rules allow for it, and our impression is that few grievance systems do.[390] As always, read the grievance rules closely.)

In *Kikumura v. Osagie*, 461 F.3d 1269, 1285–86 (10th Cir. 2006), the court held that the plaintiff's claim of supervisory liability for correctional staff's failure to get him timely medical care was not exhausted because his grievance requesting action to discipline persons who violated agency policy or to "introduce new policy so that the same wrong-doing won't happen again" did not sufficiently alert prison officials that the injuries might have been caused by inadequate training and disciplinary programs.

[387]As one court pointed out, in declining to dismiss a claim of inadequate training for non-exhaustion: "Basic notions of fairness support the conclusion that an inmate need not identify responsible individuals or legal theories related to an incident in every case." Grievances that placed defendants on notice of line officers' conduct "identified the core issue; from them, defendants could have discovered any possible wrongdoing related to [them], including their supervisor's failure to train them." Czapiewski v. Bartow, 2008 WL 2622862, *1–2 (W.D.Wis., July 1, 2008); *accord*, Cutler v. Correctional Medical Services, 2010 WL 339760, *6 (D.Idaho, Jan. 22, 2010) ("The simple and more prudent way to interpret the grievance process is that once an inmate has availed himself of all of the grievance procedures as to his problem, he is free to sue any state actor who could have liability under the provision of law governing his cause of action."); Davis v. Rhoomes, 2009 WL 415628, *5, 6 (S.D.N.Y., Feb. 12, 2009) (plaintiff who exhausted underlying allegations of misconduct was not barred from pursuing supervisory liability against another defendant); Brown v. Runnels, 2006 WL 2849871, *4 (E.D.Cal., Oct. 3, 2006) (declining to dismiss for non-exhaustion based on failure specifically to grieve that supervisory defendants failed to rectify the problem). Similarly, in *Sacred Feather v. Merrill*, 2008 WL 2510100, *3 n.7 (D.Me., June 19, 2008), the court stated:

> ... [I]t would be ludicrous to argue that the failure to name a warden (or a commissioner) in the grievance itself could defeat a claim against them vis-à-vis the issue complained of; it would basically require an inmate to anticipate that he was not going to get any relief through the grievance process and that a 42 U.S.C. § 1983 action was inevitable. That is not in keeping with the stated purpose of the prison's grievance policy or the 42 U.S.C. § 1997e(a) exhaustion requirement, which is meant to assure that the prison officials get the first crack at rectifying an alleged wrong.

Accord, Czapiewski v. Bartow, 2008 WL 2622862, *1–2 ("In most instances, it is not necessary to identify the responsible parties in an inmate complaint to achieve the purpose of administrative exhaustion, which is to give prison officials a chance to resolve the complaint without judicial intervention."); *see* Robinson v. Johnson, 343 Fed.Appx. 778, 781–82 (3d Cir. 2009) (unpublished) (declining to dismiss claims against commissioner and superintendent not named in grievance where policies they were responsible for and persons responsible for them were not made known to prisoners, and where grievance response addressed policies anyway).

[388]*See* Kozohorsky v. Harmon, 332 F.3d 1141, 1143 (8th Cir. 2003) (holding that a grievance complaining of excessive force by line staff did not exhaust the plaintiff's claim that a supervisor failed to supervise and take action against them).

[389]*See* Basat v. Caruso, 2008 WL 275679, *4 (E.D.Mich., Jan. 31, 2008) (plaintiff could not name the Department of Correction in his disability suit because he didn't name it in his grievance, even though he had named the individual department employees); Vandiver v. Martin, 304 F. Supp. 2d 934, 943–44 (E.D.Mich. 2004) (holding plaintiff failed to exhaust against the corporate medical provider, even though he named individual medical practitioners employed by the provider, because his grievance said only that the provider would be liable if his foot was amputated).

[390]*See, e.g.*, Johnson v. Rowley, 569 F.3d 40, 45 (2d Cir. 2009) (holding issue raised on appeal was not exhausted where regulations prohibited amending grievance on appeal). *But see* Bouman v. Robinson, 2008 WL 2595180, *2 (W.D.Wis., June 27, 2008) (allowing consideration of issue raised on appeal where no rule

If a new grievance is past the grievance deadline, explain that you couldn't file it within the deadline because you didn't have the information. For example, if you file a grievance stating that you have been denied certain medical care by the prison's medical director, and then later on you learn that your care was denied by a "utilization review" process in the prison system's central office, you might wish to file and exhaust a new grievance about the utilization review decision and those responsible for it. The grievance system may or may not accept such grievances, but filing them may be the best way to protect yourself when you have already filed a grievance but then you learn new information that will be reflected in your lawsuit.[391] If your second grievance

is rejected, that will help show that the remedy was not available.

The point of this discussion is that prison officials and their lawyers have strong incentives to try to get cases thrown out for non-exhaustion rather than have to face the merits, and judges may be receptive to their arguments. So you should try to make your grievance reflect all aspects of the problem that you may wish to bring suit about, so the judge will see that you did your best to bring everything to prison officials' attention in compliance with the grievance system's rules before you filed suit.

If the grievance system actually investigates and addresses your complaint on the merits, rather than throwing it out for not being specific or detailed enough, you should be deemed to have exhausted, even if the defendants' lawyers later claim that you should have said more in the grievance.[392] This rule has been applied to failure to name

---

was cited barring amending a grievance appeal and officials considered the issue); Morris v. Hickison, 2008 WL 2261431, *3 (E.D.Cal., June 2, 2008) (holding prisoner complaining of retaliation for filing of grievance could raise that claim in an appeal of the initial grievance), *report and recommendation adopted*, 2008 WL 3976924 (E.D.Cal., Aug. 20, 2008); Edwards v. Hook, 2007 WL 1756347, *4–5 (E.D.Cal., June 18, 2007) (holding plaintiff who grieved an officer's conduct and complained about the lack of a thorough investigation of it in his grievance appeals had exhausted all of the claims; neither the PLRA nor grievance rules required him to "re-start the grievance process" when a new related claim emerges during the process), *report and recommendation adopted*, 2007 WL 2225993 (E.D.Cal., Aug. 2, 2007); Marshall v. Hubbard, 2007 WL 1627534, *4 (E.D.Ark., June 4, 2007) (similar holding in medical care case where post-grievance events were raised in grievance appeals).

[391]Courts have not resolved this issue. In the Michigan grievance system, officials at one point took the position that a new grievance was required to add new defendants; however, they abandoned this position when their system was reviewed by the Supreme Court. Jones v. Bock, 549 U.S. 199, 217 n.7, 127 S. Ct. 910 (2007). Since then, some courts have continued to hold that a new grievance is required when a prisoner learns new information that may be reflected in a lawsuit. *See* Parker v. Mulvaney, 2008 WL 4425579, *4 (W.D.Mich., Sept. 26, 2008) (stating plaintiff who learns the identity of persons not identified in a step 1 grievance should file a new step 1 grievance identifying them); Fulgham v. Snyder, 2008 WL 785524, *3 (W.D.Mich., Mar. 21, 2008) (same). However, when prisoners file new grievances about previously grieved matters adding new information or defendants, the new grievances are often dismissed as duplicative of the prior grievance. A number of decisions have held that such rejection is improper, or that it shows that the earlier grievance was sufficient to exhaust. *See* Bey v. Luoma, 2008 WL 4534427, *4 (W.D.Mich., Sept. 30, 2008) (holding dismissal of grievance naming new defendants as duplicative implied they had been exhausted in an earlier grievance); Torrez v. McKee, 2008 WL 4534126, *9 (W.D.Mich., Sept. 30, 2008) (holding a grievance that named new defendants was not duplicative); Cromer v. Chaney, 2008 WL 4056314, *8 (W.D.Mich., Aug. 27, 2008) (if prisoners are required to name defendants in their grievances, a second grievance naming additional defendants cannot be found duplicative); Sullivan v. Caruso, 2008 WL 356878, *10 (W.D.Mich., Feb. 7, 2008). *Contra,* Laster v. Pramstaller, 2008 WL 474146, *5 (E.D.Mich., Feb. 15, 2008) (a grievance naming a defendant that is dismissed as duplicative of an earlier grievance not naming that defendant fails

to exhaust). We think *Laster* is wrong. Prison officials should not be able to have it both ways by requiring prisoners to provide information in grievances that it takes time to find out, and then refusing to let them provide it when they get it.

This issue has not been much explored yet in other systems. *See* Brownell v. Krom, 446 F.3d 305, 313 (2d Cir. 2006) (refusing to dismiss where plaintiff's initial grievance did not contain essential information, but there was no procedure apparent for supplementing their grievances or bringing new ones); Dunbar v. Jones, 2007 WL 2022083, *8 (M.D.Pa., July 9, 2007) (rejecting the argument that the plaintiff should have amended his grievance to name a defendant whose identity he did not initially know, since the rules did not provide for such amended grievances, but dismissing the claim against that defendant because the plaintiff didn't add her name in his grievance appeals—without citing anything in the grievance policy that permits adding new material in grievance appeals).

[392]Espinal v. Goord, 558 F.3d 119 (2d Cir. 2009) (medical care complaint not raised explicitly in grievance was exhausted where grievance decision addressed it; medical care complaint stated in very general terms was exhausted where grievance decision addressed plaintiff's care with specificity); Monger v. Tilton, 2008 WL 3863696, *4–5 (E.D.Cal., Aug. 18, 2008) (statements made by plaintiff during grievance interviews and acknowledged in the response to his grievance helped show what was grieved); Freeman v. Salopek, 2008 WL 743952, *4 (M.D.Fla., Mar. 19, 2008) (rejecting claim that grievance was "undated, unclear, and vague" where final decisionmaker gave response addressing the precise issue raised in the grievance); Carter v. Symmes, 2008 WL 341640, *5 (D.Mass., Feb. 4, 2008) (issue not raised in the grievance, but spelled out in a timely letter from counsel, and actually investigated by defendants, was exhausted); Holley v. California Dep't of Corrections, 2007 WL 586907, *6–8 (E.D.Cal., Feb. 23, 2007) (holding prisoner who complained about being required to cut his hair, asserting religious discrimination at the first stage and gender discrimination at the last, and received a decision on the merits, exhausted), *report and recommendation adopted*, 2007 WL 869956 (E.D.Cal., Mar. 22, 2007); Ambriz v. Kernan, 2007 WL 214594, *6 (E.D.Cal., Jan. 25, 2007) (noting that the "responses of the reviewers flesh out the circumstances of which plaintiff was complaining," finding exhaustion), *report and recommendation adopted*, 2007 WL 869732 (E.D.Cal., Mar. 21, 2007); Baskerville v. Blot, 224 F. Supp. 2d 723,

persons in a grievance who were later named as defendants in lawsuits.[393]

5. Doing It Right: The "Proper Exhaustion" Rule

Prisoners not only must exhaust, they must also do it right. The Supreme Court has held that "the PLRA exhaustion requirement requires proper exhaustion,"[394] which "demands compliance with an agency's deadlines and other critical procedural rules because no adjudicative system can function effectively without imposing some orderly structure on the course of its proceedings."[395] If your administrative complaint is rejected because you did not follow the procedures,

your lawsuit most likely will be barred for non-exhaustion.[396]

This does *not* mean that if you violate a procedural rule, you should just give up. You should pursue your grievance, request that your error be excused or that you be permitted to re-file your grievance and start over, and explain any circumstances that might have caused you to make a mistake. Sometimes grievance systems allow prisoners to correct and re-file their grievances (in fact, sometimes they instruct prisoners to do so[397]). Also, sometimes grievance systems simply overlook procedural mistakes, and courts have held that if prison officials decide the merits of a grievance rather than rejecting it for procedural noncompliance, they cannot later claim non-exhaustion based on a procedural flaw that they let pass earlier.[398] In any case, the harder you have tried to exhaust, the more likely the court is to rule in your favor in a close case.

There is also a potential trap in the proper exhaustion rule. Sometimes prisoners are not able to follow the rules for reasons outside their control—*e.g.*, they miss a deadline because they are out of the institution and have no access to the grievance process, or they have a medical problem that prevents them from filing. One would think that in those circumstances, the administrative remedy was not available, and the affected prisoner is excused from exhausting. However, a number of courts have held that prisoners who are prevented from exhausting properly must try to exhaust improperly—*e.g.*, if they can't file a timely grievance, they should file a late grievance when they can, or else their cases may be dismissed for non-exhaustion.[399] This doesn't make any sense in light of the "proper exhaustion" rule, but courts do it, so you should act to protect yourself against such a dismissal by filing and pursuing the late or otherwise improper grievance.

It isn't clear how inflexible this proper exhaustion rule is. The *Woodford* Court said it was not ruling on the possibility that prisons might "create procedural requirements for the purpose of tripping up all but the most skillful prisoners," since the case did not present that situation.[400]

730 (S.D.N.Y. 2002) (holding that where the plaintiff's issues were actually investigated as a result of his grievance, the purposes of the exhaustion requirement had been served and the plaintiff had therefore exhausted); *see* J.P. v. Taft, 439 F. Supp. 2d 793, 826 (S.D.Ohio 2006) (holding defendants who said they "consistently tried" to satisfy the juvenile plaintiff's request for an attorney could not be heard to claim they were not sufficiently on notice from his grievance of his request for an attorney. "Defendants cannot have it both ways."). This is related to the more general principle that if the administrative system decides the merits of your complaint rather than throwing it out for procedural defects, those procedural defects are waived and the defendants can't rely on them in court. *See* nn.434–436 of this chapter, below.

[393]Robinson v. Johnson, 343 Fed.Appx. 778, 781-82 (3d Cir. 2009) (unpublished) (declining to dismiss claims against commissioner and superintendent not named in grievance where the grievance response addressed their policies anyway); Austin v. Correctional Medical Services, Inc., 2008 WL 4426342, *5 (W.D.Mich., Sept. 26, 2008); Fitts v. Burt, 2008 WL 878532, *8 (E.D.Mich., Jan. 24, 2008), *report and recommendation adopted*, 2008 WL 878522 (E.D.Mich., Mar. 28, 2008), *reconsideration denied*, 2008 WL 2357739 (E.D.Mich., June 10, 2008); Baker v. Vanderark, 2007 WL 3244075, *7-8 (W.D.Mich., Nov. 1, 2007). Some defendants have objected that this is unfair because they have no way of knowing who will eventually be sued if they are not named in the grievance, and some courts have accepted this argument. *See, e.g.,* Basat v. Caruso, 2008 WL 4457828, *15 (E.D.Mich., Sept. 30, 2008). However, the purpose of the exhaustion requirement is to give prison officials notice of problems, not to give notice of who will be sued. Jones v. Bock, 549 U.S. 199, 219, 127 S. Ct. 910 (2007). If defendants need additional information about the incident in order to address the problem, they can reject the grievance as not specific enough, or they can investigate the grievance and interview the complainant, as grievance rules generally provide. *See* Calhoun v. Hill, 2008 WL 4344622, *11 (E.D.Mich., Aug. 19, 2008), *report and recommendation adopted in part, rejected in part on other grounds*, 2008 WL 4277171 (E.D.Mich., Sept. 17, 2008).

[394]Woodford v. Ngo, 548 U.S. 81, 106, 126 S. Ct. 2378 (2006).

[395]*Woodford*, 548 U.S. at 90–91; *accord*, Jones v. Bock, 549 U.S. 199, 218, 127 S. Ct. 910 (2007) ("Compliance with prison grievance procedures . . . is all that is required by the PLRA to properly exhaust.").

[396]*Woodford*, 548 U.S. at 90-91; Pozo v. McCaughtry, 286 F.3d 1022, 1023–24 (7th Cir. 2002).

[397]If they do, you should follow the directions even if you disagree with them. *See* n.449, below.

[398]*See* cases cited in nn.435–436, below. Courts have disagreed over whether a grievance exhausts if it is rejected both on the merits and for procedural reasons. *See* cases cited in n.438, below.

[399]*See* cases cited in n.462, below.

[400]Woodford v. Ngo, 548 U.S. at 102. This is a concern that has been expressed by numerous courts. *See, e.g.,* Hooks v. Rich, 2006 WL 565909, *5 (S.D.Ga., Mar. 7, 2006) ("The exhaustion requirement is a gatekeeper, not a 'gotcha' meant to trap unsophisticated prisoners who must navigate the administrative process pro se."); Ouellette v. Maine State Prison, 2006 WL 173639, *3 n.2 (D.Me., Jan. 23, 2006) (noting that once suit is filed, "the defendants in hindsight can use any deviation by the prisoner to argue that he or she has not complied with 42 U.S.C. § 1997e(a) responsibilities"), *aff'd*, 2006 WL 348315 (D.Me., Feb. 14, 2006);

Several post-*Woodford* decisions have cited that statement in holding that prisoners who didn't fully comply with procedural requirements, but who were arguably "tripped up" by them, should not have their cases dismissed for non-exhaustion.[401] The *Woodford* Court also said that it was relying for its proper exhaustion rule on exhaustion law from administrative law and habeas corpus. In response, Justice Breyer, in a separate opinion, observed that administrative law "contains well established exceptions to exhaustion" (citing exceptions for constitutional claims, futility of exhaustion, and hardship), and so does habeas corpus (citing exceptions for procedural rules that are "not firmly established and regularly followed," cases where the petitioner shows "cause and prejudice" to overcome a procedural default, and cases where a "miscarriage of justice" would result from enforcing the procedural default).[402] Several decisions have cited Justice Breyer's comments in allowing claims to go forward despite failures to comply completely with grievance rules.[403]

Both before and after *Woodford*, the lower courts have generally accepted that there are some circumstances where failure to exhaust or to do so according to the prison rules will not result in dismissal. The Second Circuit has gone furthest in describing these circumstances, stating:

> First, the court must ask: whether administrative remedies were in fact "available" to the prisoner. [Second], [t]he court should also inquire . . . whether the defendants' own actions inhibiting the inmate's exhaustion of remedies may estop one or more of the defendants from raising the plaintiff's failure to exhaust as a defense. [Third], [i]f the court finds that administrative remedies were available to the plaintiff, and that the defendants are not estopped and have not forfeited their non-exhaustion defense, but that the plaintiff nevertheless did not exhaust available remedies, the court should consider whether special circumstances have been plausibly alleged that justify the prisoner's failure to comply with administrative procedural requirements. . . .
>
> . . . What constitutes justification in the PLRA context "must be determined by looking at the circumstances which might understandably lead usually uncounselled prisoners to fail to grieve in the normally required way."[404]

The court first said this before *Woodford*, but post-*Woodford* decisions indicate that this analysis remains good

---

Campbell v. Chaves, 402 F. Supp. 2d 1101, 1106 n.3 (D.Ariz. 2005) (noting danger that grievance systems might become "a series of stalling tactics, and dead-ends without resolution"); LaFauci v. N.H. Dep't of Corr., 2005 WL 419691, *14 (D.N.H., Feb. 23, 2005) ("While proper compliance with the grievance system makes sound administrative sense, the procedures themselves, and the directions given to inmates seeking to follow those procedures, should not be traps designed to hamstring legitimate grievances."); Rhames v. Fed. Bureau of Prisons, 2002 WL 1268005, *5 (S.D.N.Y., June 6, 2002) ("While it is important that prisoners comply with administrative procedures designed by the Bureau of Prisons, rather than using any they might think sufficient, . . . it is equally important that form not create a snare of forfeiture for a prisoner seeking redress for perceived violations of his constitutional rights.").

[401]Timberlake v. Buss, 2007 WL 1280659, *2–3 (S.D.Ind., May 1, 2007) (declining to dismiss challenge to execution protocols where they were not disclosed to plaintiff and he had no reason to have known about them); Lampkins v. Roberts, 2007 WL 924746, *2–3 (S.D.Ind., Mar. 27, 2007) (declining to dismiss for missing a five-day deadline that was not shown to have been made known to prisoners); Brookins v. Vogel, 2006 WL 3437482, *3 (E.D.Cal., Nov. 28, 2006) (holding that a prisoner who filed a grievance, got no response, and was told it had never been received, and whose subsequent attempts were rejected as untimely, had exhausted under the pre-*Woodford* rule that exhaustion occurs when prison officials fail to respond to a grievance within the policy time limits; stating prisoner asserted without contradiction that he was "prevented from complying with the exhaustion requirement"), *report and recommendation adopted*, 2007 WL 433155 (E.D.Cal., Feb. 8, 2007); Flory v. Claussen, 2006 WL 3404779, *3–4 (W.D.Wash., Nov. 21, 2006) (holding prisoner who followed officials' advice and filed an appeal to the Facility Risk Management Team rather than a grievance exhausted); Parker v. Robinson, 2006 WL 2904780, *7–12 (D.Me., Oct. 10, 2006) (refusing to dismiss where the prisoner sent his appeal to the Commissioner who was supposed to decide it, not the person who was supposed to forward it to the Commissioner under the rules); Thomas v. Hickman, 2006 WL 2868967, *9 (E.D.Cal., Oct. 6, 2006) (declining to dismiss where the prisoner's grievance was untimely but the prisoner did not know about the violation until long after the deadline had passed).

[402]Woodford v. Ngo, 548 U.S. 81, 103–04, 126 S. Ct. 2378 (2006) (concurring opinion). Justice Breyer's assertions seem contrary at least in part to the Court's earlier observation in *Booth v. Churner* that the PLRA rendered inapplicable "traditional doctrines of administrative exhaustion, under which a litigant need not apply to an agency that has 'no power to decree . . . relief,' or need not exhaust where doing so would otherwise be futile." Booth v. Churner, 532 U.S. 731, 741 n.6, 121 S. Ct. 1819 (2001); *see* Ngo v. Woodford, 539 F.3d 1108, 1110 (9th Cir. 2008) (stating after Supreme Court decision: "It is unclear whether we can read exceptions into the PLRA's exhaustion requirement."); Wigfall v. Duval, 2006 WL 2381285, *2–3 (D.Mass., Aug. 15, 2006) (acknowledging tension between the Breyer opinion and *Booth*, indicating its view that estoppel is applicable notwithstanding *Woodford*). On the other hand, the *Woodford* majority's assertion that exhaustion means the same thing under the PLRA that it does in administrative law appears equally inconsistent with the *Booth* observation.

[403]Brookins v. Vogel, 2006 WL 3437482, *3 (E.D.Cal., Nov. 28, 2006), *report and recommendation adopted*, 2007 WL 433155 (E.D.Cal., Feb. 8, 2007); Parker v. Robinson, 2006 WL 2904780, *8, 11 (D.Me., Oct. 10, 2006); Thomas v. Hickman, 2006 WL 2868967, *9 (E.D.Cal., Oct. 6, 2006); Collins v. Goord, 438 F. Supp. 2d 399, 411 n.13 (S.D.N.Y. 2006).

[404]Brownell v. Krom, 446 F.3d 305, 311–12 (2d Cir. 2006) (quoting Hemphill v. New York, 380 F.3d 680, 686 (2d Cir. 2004)); Giano v. Goord, 380 F.3d 670, 686 (2d Cir. 2004)).

law, though some decisions applying it may be overruled.[405] Other courts have relied on the Second Circuit analysis after *Woodford*.[406] The Second Circuit has held that after *Woodford*, it is not enough that a prisoner's informal complaints gave prison officials enough notice to investigate a problem. It stated that the PLRA requires both "substantive exhaustion" (notice to officials) and "procedural exhaustion" (following the rules), and that "after *Woodford* notice alone is insufficient."[407] However, it has not backed off its earlier holding that special circumstances such as a prisoner's reasonable interpretation of confusing grievance rules may justify the failure to follow procedural rules correctly.[408]

More specific questions remaining after *Woodford* include the following:

(a) What If Procedural Requirements Are Not Clear? The Second Circuit had held before *Woodford* that a prisoner who acted reasonably when the rules were not clear presented special circumstances justifying his failure to exhaust properly, even if he turned out to be wrong,[409] and other

---

[405]Collins v. Goord, 438 F. Supp. 2d 399, 411 n.13 (S.D.N.Y. 2006) (*Woodford* "appears to leave open the question of whether exhaustion applies in situations . . . where, for example, administrative remedies are not 'available' to the prisoner at the time of the grievable incident or where prison authorities actively interfere with an inmate's ability to invoke such remedies"); *accord*, Withrow v. Taylor, 2007 WL 3274858, *6 (N.D.N.Y., Nov. 5, 2007) (citing Justice Breyer's favorable citation of Giano v. Goord, 380 F.3d 670, 677–78 (2d Cir. 2004)); Bester v. Dixion, 2007 WL 951558, *7–8 (N.D.N.Y., Mar. 27, 2007); Shomo v. Goord, 2007 WL 2693526, *6 (N.D.N.Y., Sept. 11, 2007); Hairston v. LaMarche, 2006 WL 2309592, *6 n.9 (S.D.N.Y. Aug. 10, 2006). The *Collins* court specifically noted that Justice Breyer cited with approval *Giano v. Goord*, which held that exhaustion is "mandatory" but subject to the "caveats" outlined in *Hemphill*. 380 F.3d at 677–78. Justice Breyer urged district courts to continue to consider "any challenges that [the prisoner] may have concerning whether his case falls into a traditional exception that the [PLRA] implicitly incorporates." Woodford v. Ngo, 548 U.S. 81, 104, 126 S. Ct. 2378 (2006) (Breyer, J., concurring in judgment). *See* Hernandez v. Schriro, 2006 WL 2989030, *4 (D.Ariz., Oct. 18, 2006) (applying *Hemphill* analysis after *Woodford*); James v. Davis, 2006 WL 2171082, *16–17 (D.S.C., July 31, 2006) (same).

In *Hairston v. LaMarche*, 2006 WL 2309592, *8, 11 (S.D.N.Y., Aug. 10, 2006), the court distinguished *Woodford* on the ground that Mr. Hairston, unlike the *Woodford* plaintiff, had not "bypass[ed] prison grievance procedures" or "attempt[ed] to circumvent the exhaustion requirements." Rather, he had tried hard and in multiple ways to bring his complaint to the attention of responsible officials. "[A]lthough each of his efforts, alone, may not have fully complied, together his efforts sufficiently informed prison officials of his grievance and led to a thorough investigation of the grievance as to satisfy the purpose of the PLRA or to constitute 'special circumstances' [to] justify any failure to fully comply with DOCS' exhaustion requirements." *Hairston, id.,* *8; *see* Parker v. Robinson, 2006 WL 2904780, *7–12 (D.Me., Oct. 10, 2006) (declining to dismiss for non-exhaustion where plaintiff sent his appeal directly to the Commissioner, rather than sending it to the Grievance Review Officer to forward to the Commissioner); Rainge-El v. Moschetti, 2006 WL 1980287, *1 (D.Colo., July 12, 2006) (questioning *Woodford*'s applicability where the plaintiff "did not entirely ignore the prison's administrative grievance machinery").

[406]For example, other circuits have adopted the Second Circuit framework for determining when prison officials' threats or intimidation make remedies "unavailable." *See* Turner v. Burnside, 541 F.3d 1077, 1084–86 (11th Cir. 2008); Kaba v. Stepp, 458 F.3d 678, 684–86 (7th Cir. 2006). The Ninth Circuit, citing Second, Seventh and Eleventh Circuit decisions, has held that a litigant's failure to exhaust timely was excused because he took "reasonable and appropriate steps to exhaust . . . and was precluded from exhausting, not through his own fault but by the Warden's mistake." Nunez v. Duncan, 591 F.3d 1217, 1224 (9th Cir. 2010). Conversely, another recent decision rejected the "special circumstances" prong of the Second Circuit framework, focusing instead on the question whether remedies were available. Dillon v. Rogers, 596 F.3d 260, 270 (5th Cir. 2010) (holding that "reprehensible" circumstances do

not "grant[] us license to carve out new exceptions to the PLRA's exhaustion requirement").

[407]Macias v. Zenk, 495 F.3d 37, 43–44 (2d Cir. 2007). In saying this, it overruled its own pre-*Woodford* statements in *Braham v. Clancy*, 425 F.3d 177, 183 (2d Cir. 2004), that suggested notice might be sufficient by itself to satisfy the exhaustion requirement.

[408] Macias v. Zenk, 495 F.3d at 43 n.1 (citing Hemphill v. New York, 380 F.3d 680, 690 (2d Cir. 2004)); *see* Benjamin v. Commissioner, N.Y. State Dep't of Correctional Services, 2007 WL 2319126, *14 (S.D.N.Y., Aug. 10, 2007) (*following Macias,* noting that plaintiff could not have believed a disciplinary appeal was his only remedy for a use of force complaint), *vacated and remanded on other grounds,* 293 Fed.Appx. 69 (2d Cir. 2008) (unpublished).

[409]Giano v. Goord, 380 F.3d 670 (2d Cir. 2004). The *Giano* court said that prison rules "do not differentiate clearly between grievable matters relating to disciplinary proceedings, and non-grievable issues concerning the 'decisions or dispositions' of such proceedings," and that a "learned" district judge had recently interpreted the prison administrative rules in the same way as the plaintiff; *accord,* Brownell v. Krom, 446 F.3d 305, 312 (2d Cir. 2006) (holding prisoner who was given erroneous advice as to which prison to complain to about property lost in transfer, which resulted in a failure to investigate, and who was given erroneous advice by staff to abandon the property claim and pursue a grievance instead, showed special circumstances excusing his failure to exhaust correctly); Abney v. McGinnis, 380 F.3d 663, 668–69 (2d Cir. 2004) (noting the lack of instruction in the grievance rules for instances where a favorable grievance decision is not carried out); Johnson v. Testman, 380 F.3d 691, 696–97 (2d Cir. 2004) (holding that a federal prisoner's argument that he adequately raised his prisoner-prisoner assault claim through an appeal of the disciplinary proceeding that arose from the incident should be considered by the district court); Hemphill v. New York, 380 F.3d 680, 689–90 (2d Cir. 2004) (holding that plaintiff's arguments that lack of clarity in grievance regulations supported the reasonableness of his belief that he could exhaust by writing directly to the Superintendent); Barad v. Comstock, 2005 WL 1579794, *7–8 (W.D.N.Y., June 30, 2005) (holding allegation that prison staff told plaintiff erroneously that his time to commence a grievance had lapsed while he was hospitalized and bedridden constituted special circumstances); Roque v. Armstrong, 392 F. Supp. 2d 382, 391 (D. Conn. 2005) (denying summary judgment to defendants where it appeared that neither the prisoner nor the grievance system entirely followed the

courts have agreed or have held remedies unavailable under those circumstances.[410] Since *Woodford*, courts have continued to hold that prisoners' cases cannot be dismissed for non-exhaustion where it was unclear what they had to do to exhaust, either because the rules were not clear,[411] or because

the actions or instructions of officials (often in violation of their own rules) created confusion in a particular case,[412]

___

rules but the prisoner had received a response from the Commissioner, the final grievance authority); Warren v. Purcell, 2004 WL 1970642, *6 (S.D.N.Y., Sept. 3, 2004) (holding "baffling" grievance response that left prisoner with no clue as to what to do next was a special circumstance).

[410]*See* Dole v. Chandler, 438 F.3d 804, 811–12 (7th Cir. 2006) (holding a prisoner had exhausted when he did everything necessary to exhaust but his grievance simply disappeared, and he received no instructions as to what if anything to do about it); Westefer v. Snyder, 422 F.3d 570, 580 (7th Cir. 2005) (holding prison officials did not establish a failure to exhaust available remedies where their policies did not "clearly identif[y]" the proper remedy and there was no "clear route" for prisoners to challenge certain decisions); Ouellette v. Maine State Prison, 2006 WL 173639, *3–4 (D.Me., Jan. 23, 2006) (denying summary judgment to defendants where plaintiff's failure to exhaust was attributable to grievance staff's procedural deviations), *aff'd*, 2006 WL 348315 (D.Me., Feb. 14, 2006); Dunmire v. DePasqual, 2005 WL 4050175, *1 (W.D.Pa., Oct. 21, 2005) (denying motion to dismiss for non-exhaustion in light of plaintiff's objections that prison officials had failed to comply with their own procedures); Shaheed-Muhammad v. Dipaolo, 393 F. Supp. 2d 80, 97 (D.Mass. 2005) ("Having failed to abide by the strictures of their own regulations, defendants should not be allowed to claim plaintiff's noncompliance as a bar.").

[411]Malik v. District of Columbia, 574 F.3d 781, 785–86 (D.C. Cir. 2009) (declining to find non-exhaustion where transfers were non-grievable and policy did not say whether claim of retaliation would make the transfer grievable); Cutler v. Correctional Medical Services, 2010 WL 339760, *5 (D.Idaho, Jan. 22, 2010) (noting that requirement to identify responsible staff members is listed in only one of four documents addressing grievance policy); Woodard v. O'Brien, 2010 WL 148301, *15 (N.D.Iowa, Jan. 14, 2010) (finding plaintiff complied with procedure "to the best of his ability to understand it," citing ambiguous appeal rule, the grievance officer's failure to recognize his attempts at informal resolution, and officer's failure to advise him what more he needed to do); Bellamy v. Mount Vernon Hosp., 2008 WL 3152963, *5 (S.D.N.Y., Aug. 5, 2008) (where allowance for late grievances was limited to 45 days after an "alleged occurrence," and the plaintiff thought the "occurrence" was his surgery and not his knowledge of its side-effects, he reasonably believed no remedy remained available to him); Vasquez v. Hilbert, 2008 WL 2224394, *4 (W.D.Wis., May 28, 2008) (holding plaintiff exhausted when he grieved his medical claim late because medical treatment was mentioned in a disciplinary report, and the rules said a grievance raising "any issue related to the conduct report" must await completion of the disciplinary process; plaintiff acted reasonably in waiting. "... [W]hen prison officials fail to 'clearly identif[y]' the proper route for exhaustion, they cannot later fault the prisoner for failing to predict the correct choice. . . . The burden is on the Department of Corrections to make grievance procedures clear and easy to follow."); Wilson v. Budgeon, 2007 WL 464700, *5 (M.D.Pa., Feb. 13, 2007) (declining to dismiss for non-exhaustion where rules did not clearly instruct the prisoner whether to raise his retaliation claim in a disciplinary appeal or a grievance), *appeal dismissed*, 248

Fed.Appx. 348 (3d Cir. 2007) (unpublished). *Cf.* Ngo v. Woodford, 539 F.3d 1108, 1112 (9th Cir. 2008) (concurring opinion) (discussing lack of clarity in California grievance regulations).

[412]Monroe v. Beard, 2007 WL 2359833, *12–13 (E.D.Pa., Aug. 16, 2007) (holding the grievance process unavailable where prisoners were told to object to certain searches through an Unacceptable Correspondence Form, and they would be notified of the results of an investigation and then could file a grievance, but were not so notified), *aff'd*, 536 F.3d 198, 204 n.6 (3d Cir. 2008); Woods v. Carey, 2007 WL 2254428, *3 (E.D.Cal., Aug. 3, 2007) (holding plaintiff exhausted where he could not complete the process because prison officials rejected his appeal on procedurally improper grounds), *vacated on other grounds*, 2007 WL 2688819 (E.D.Cal., Sept. 13, 2007); Lawyer v. Gatto, 2007 WL 549440, *8 (S.D.N.Y., Feb. 21, 2007) (holding prisoner whose grievance was referred to the Inspector General's office was not obliged to wait until the IG's investigation was concluded since the rules did not say otherwise; it was the prison system's responsibility to make such a requirement clear); Partee v. Grood, 2007 WL 2164529, *4 (S.D.N.Y., July 25, 2007) (declining to dismiss where prisoner was told his issue was "beyond the purview" of the grievance program; analogizing to the unclear rule in *Giano*), *aff'd*, 2009 WL 1582927 (2d Cir. 2009); Cooper v. Beard, 2007 WL 1959300, *5 (M.D.Pa., July 2, 2007) (where Request for Religious Accommodation was a prerequisite for a grievance, and plaintiff did not get a timely response and had moved on to the grievance process by the time he received a late response, court excuses plaintiff's procedural non-compliance in light of defendants' noncompliance); Ray v. Jones, 2007 WL 397084, *10 (W.D.Okla., Feb. 1, 2007) (holding plaintiff exhausted where in response to his complaint he was repeatedly told that the matter had been turned over to Internal Affairs and where relief was granted in that process); Woods v. Lozer, 2007 WL 173704, *3 (M.D.Tenn., Jan. 18, 2007) (holding a prisoner exhausted when he appealed a decision that his use of force claim was not grievable because it was mistakenly said to seek review of disciplinary procedures and punishments); Martinez v. Weir, 2006 WL 2884775, *2 (D.Conn., Oct. 10, 2006) (refusing to dismiss, noting that the plaintiff had exhausted twice in the face of a disappearing grievance and prison officials' own procedural mistakes); Hernandez v. Schriro, 2006 WL 2989030, *4 (D.Ariz., Oct. 18, 2006) (finding special circumstances justifying failure to appeal rejection of grievance where it was returned unprocessed because defendants mischaracterized it); Kinzey v. Beard, 2006 WL 2829000, *10 (M.D.Pa., Sept. 1, 2006) (refusing to dismiss for non-exhaustion where the failure to exhaust was caused by prison officials' failure to follow their own rules); Brady v. Halawa Corr. Facility Medical Unit Staff, 2006 WL 2520607, *17–18 (D.Haw., Aug. 29, 2006) (holding prisoner transferred while his grievance was pending exhausted where he "was inadvertently thwarted by the two prisons' confusion over the matter"), *aff'd*, 285 Fed.Appx. 424 (9th Cir. 2008) (unpublished); Scott v. Cal. Supreme Ct., 2006 WL 2460737, *7 (E.D.Cal., Aug. 23, 2006) (holding that a prisoner who had relied on officials' misinformation and sought relief in state court had exhausted, notwithstanding officials' subsequent issuance of an untimely decision which he did not appeal; "Prison officials cannot effectively thwart an inmate's attempt to exhaust a claim by failing to follow their own regulations and then later require him to begin the exhaustion process again once they decide

or both[413] (though some courts have ruled against prisoners in situations where they simply guessed wrong in a confusing situation[414]). There are cases where the court has declined to dismiss for non-exhaustion because the prisoner lacked sufficient knowledge of the facts to comply with the grievance rules.[415] In some cases an unsettled legal

situation concerning the exhaustion requirement itself has been held to constitute special circumstances justifying failure to exhaust correctly.[416] Since *Woodford* does not address situations where the rules do not possess "relative simplicity," and it does not say anything about the meaning of "available," we think it is still valid law that prisoners' cases need not be dismissed where there are "special circumstances" justifying the failure to exhaust or where the grievance rules are so unclear as to make the remedy unavailable.

Frequently the actual practice in prison grievance systems diverges from the formal written procedure. Courts have held that a prisoner who complies with the informal practice has satisfied the exhaustion requirement,[417] and have refused to enforce compliance with supposed grievance rules that do not appear in the written policy.[418]

---

[413]Turner v. Burnside, 541 F.3d 1077, 1083 (11th Cir. 2008) (holding a prisoner whose grievance was torn up by the warden was not required to file another one or grieve the warden's action; "[n]othing in [the rules] requires an inmate to grieve a breakdown in the grievance process"); Miller v. Berkebile, 2008 WL 635552, *7–9 (N.D.Tex., Mar. 10, 2008) (unjustified refusal to process initial grievances made remedy unavailable; court rejects argument that prisoners should have taken other steps not specified in the policy to get around the grievance officer's misconduct; PLRA law applied in § 2241 case); Crawford v. Berkebile, 2008 WL 323155, *7–8 (N.D.Tex., Feb. 6, 2008) (same).

[414]Thus, in *Marshall v. Knight*, 2006 WL 3714713 (N.D.Ind., Dec. 14, 2006), a prisoner alleged that he had been retaliated against in classification and disciplinary matters did not file a grievance because classification and disciplinary matters are excluded from the grievance system. The court held that he had failed to exhaust because retaliation claims might be grievable. 2006 WL 3714713, *1. The decision gave no consideration to the reasonableness of Mr. Marshall's interpretation of the rules. The court took a more reasonable approach to this situation in *Malik v. District of Columbia*, 574 F.3d 781, 785–86 (D.C. Cir. 2009), in which the grievance policy said transfers are not grievable, and the plaintiff complained of a retaliatory transfer: the court declined to find non-exhaustion, stating: "The policy simply does not make clear the status of a claim for reprisal (a covered subject) that took place during an institutional transfer (a non-covered event)."

Similarly to *Marshall v. Knight*, in *Williams v. McGrath*, 2007 WL 3010577, *6 (N.D.Cal., Oct. 12, 2007), aff'd, 320 Fed.Appx. 728 (9th Cir. 2009) (unpublished), the court held that a prisoner whose grievance was rejected for failure to provide necessary documentation, and who was then denied access to the documentation, should have resubmitted his appeal without the documentation, or should have filed a new grievance, despite the prisoner's concerns that his grievance had already been rejected once for lack of the documentation and that if he filed a second grievance he would be in violation of the rule against duplicative grievances.

[415]Thomas v. Hickman, 2006 WL 2868967, *9 (E.D.Cal., Oct. 6, 2006) (declining to dismiss where the prisoner's grievance was untimely but the prisoner did not know about the violation until long after the deadline had passed); Borges v. Piatkowski, 337 F. Supp. 2d 424, 427 n.3 (W.D.N.Y. 2004) (holding that a prisoner who did not have reason to know he had a medical care claim until he had been transferred to another prison and the 14-day deadline had long expired was justified by special circumstances in not exhausting); see Brownell v. Krom, 446 F.3d 305, 312 (2d Cir. 2006) (citing system's lack of provision for supplementing or re-filing existing grievances to reflect new information).

[416]In *Rodriguez v. Westchester County Jail Correctional Dep't*, 372 F.3d 485, 487 (2d Cir. 2004), the court held that the plaintiff's belief that he did not have to exhaust an excessive force claim was reasonable, since the court had adopted the same view until reversed by the Supreme Court in *Porter v. Nussle*, 534 U.S. 516, 122 S. Ct. 983 (2002). *Accord*, Wilkinson v. Banks, 2007 WL 2693636, *6 (W.D.N.Y., Sept. 10, 2007) (holding grievance filed a few weeks after *Booth v. Churner* held damages claims must be exhausted satisfied the requirement); Barad v. Comstock, 2005 WL 1579794, *7 (W.D.N.Y., June 30, 2005) ((". . . [T]he question here for special circumstances is not the *actual* state of the law (or the retroactive application of new decisional law . . .), but the *inmate's* belief of what the law was when he should have grieved the matter and whether that belief is reasonable."); Rivera v. Pataki, 2005 WL 407710, *12 (S.D.N.Y., Feb. 7, 2005) ("Rivera did the best he could to follow DOCS regulations while responding to an evolving legal framework"; noting he had filed at a time when it appeared that his claim need not be exhausted, and had tried to exhaust after dismissal for non-exhaustion mandated by a subsequent Supreme Court decision).

[417]Curtis v. Timberlake, 436 F.3d 709, 712 (7th Cir. 2005); see Marr v. Fields, 2008 WL 828788, *6 (W.D.Mich., Mar. 27, 2008) (if policy requiring administrative appeals rather than grievances in disciplinary cases was applied broadly in practice to related matters such as claims of retaliatory discipline, grievance process was not an available remedy for such complaints).

[418]Jackson v. Ivens, 244 Fed.Appx. 508, 513 (3d Cir. 2007) (unpublished) ("We will not condition exhaustion on unwritten or 'implied' requirements." (*citing* Spruill v. Gillis, 372 F.3d 218, 234 (3d Cir. 2004)); *see* Goebert v. Lee County, 510 F.3d 1312, 1322–23 (11th Cir. 2007) (holding grievance appeal was not an available remedy where prisoners were not informed of its existence and had no way to find out); Sims v. Rewerts, 2008 WL 2224132, *5–6 (E.D.Mich., May 29, 2008) (declining to dismiss where plaintiff failed to comply with a time limit that had been changed without notice); Cabrera v. LeVierge, 2008 WL 215720, *5–6 (D.N.H., Jan. 24, 2008) (refusing to hold prisoners to rules and procedures not described in inmate handbook); Lampkins v. Roberts, 2007 WL 924746, *3 (S.D.Ind., Mar. 27, 2007) (refusing to dismiss for missing a five-day time deadline which was not made known in the materials made available to prisoners). *Cf.* Turner v. Burnside, 541 F.3d 1077, 1083–84 (11th Cir. 2008) (where warden tore up prisoner's grievance, he was not required to re-file his grievance or grieve the warden's action, neither of which were prescribed by

to follow the regulations."); Fuller v. Cal. Dep't of Corr., 2006 WL 2385177, *3 (E.D.Cal., Aug. 17, 2006) (holding that a prisoner whose intermediate appeal was rejected for "excessive verbiage" and failure to complete documents correctly was not shown to have further available remedies because officials did not instruct him whether to resubmit a corrected appeal or appeal to the next level if he wished to pursue the matter).

(b) What If the Prisoner Is Misled or His Exhaustion Efforts Obstructed by Prison Staff? Numerous cases hold that non-exhaustion caused by such actions by prison staff does not bar the prisoner from proceeding with a subsequent lawsuit.[419] No such fact pattern was before the Court in *Woodford*, and it did not purport to address the question. These decisions are still valid after *Woodford*, especially since many of them hold that under the circumstances, administrative remedies were not "available," a statutory term *Woodford* did not address.

(c) What If the Prisoner Is Threatened or Intimidated by Prison Staff into Not Following the Grievance Procedure? Courts have held that threats or other intimidating conduct may make administrative remedies in general, or the usual grievance remedy in particular, unavailable to a prisoner, both before *Woodford* and afterward.[420] These courts have specifically observed that threats or other intimidation might deter prisoners from filing an internal grievance, but not from appealing directly to persons in higher authority, in the prison system or to external authority such as state or federal courts, so the grievance system would be unavailable but other remedies might be available.[421] *Woodford* did not address this issue.

(d) Is There Any Limit to the Procedural Rules That Can Be Enforced by a "Proper Exhaustion" Rule? *Woodford* declined to address the possibility that prisons might "create procedural requirements for the purpose of tripping up all but the most skillful prisoners,"[422] but the concern is a real one that has been expressed by

grievance rules); Miller v. Berkebile, 2008 WL 635552, *7–9 (N.D.Tex., Mar. 10, 2008) (where official refused to process grievances contrary to policy, prisoners were not required to take steps not prescribed in the policy to get around him; PLRA law applied in § 2241 case); Crawford v. Berkebile, 2008 WL 323155, *7–8 (N.D.Tex., Feb. 6, 2008) (same).

[419]See nn.327–349 of this chapter and the corresponding text for more information.

[420]See Hemphill v. New York, 380 F.3d 680, 686–90 (2d Cir. 2004); *accord*, Kaba v. Stepp, 458 F.3d 678, 684–86 (7th Cir. 2006) (adopting *Hemphill* analysis after *Woodford*); *see* cases cited in § D.3 of this chapter, nn.325–326.

In *Hemphill*, the plaintiff, who alleged he was threatened and physically assaulted to prevent him from complaining, wrote a letter to the Superintendent rather than filing a grievance. The *Hemphill* decision also holds that such conduct by prison staff may estop the defendants from asserting the exhaustion defense, or may constitute special circumstances justifying failure to exhaust, or failure to do so consistently with the grievance rules.

[421]Hemphill v. New York, 380 F.3d at 688, 690; *accord*, Turner v. Burnside, 541 F.3d 1077, 1085–86 (11th Cir. 2008); Kaba v. Stepp, 458 F.3d at 684–85; *see* Ziemba v. Wezner, 366 F.3d 161, 164 (2d Cir. 2003) (directing district court to consider whether a complaint to the FBI and subsequent investigation could amount to exhaustion by a plaintiff subjected within the prison to threats, beatings, and denial of writing implements and grievance forms).

[422]Woodford v. Ngo, 548 U.S. 81, 102, 126 S. Ct. 2378 (2006).

many courts.[423] Many prisoners' grievances have been rejected by prison officials for the most trivial of rules violations,[424]

[423]*See* cases cited in n.400, above.

[424]For example, grievances have been rejected by prison officials for "writing outside the boundaries of the form," Elliott v. Jones, 2008 WL 420051, *4 (N.D.Fla., Feb. 12, 2008), or signing in the wrong color of ink or writing in pencil rather than pen. Ramsey v. McGee, 2007 WL 2744272, *2 (E.D.Okla., Sept. 19, 2007). In those cases, the federal court did not dismiss the lawsuits based on those violations. But in many other cases, federal courts have dismissed prisoners' suits based on trivial procedural mistakes. *See* Whitener v. Buss, 268 Fed.Appx. 477, 478–79 (7th Cir. 2008) (unpublished) (dismissing claim of prisoner who missed a 48-hour grievance deadline because he needed the relevant officers' names and it took a week to get them, and he didn't ask for waiver of the time limit); Thomas v. Parker, 2008 WL 2894842, *12 (W.D.Okla., July 25, 2008) (dismissing because prisoner submitted a "Statement under Penalty of Perjury" pursuant to state law rather than the notarized affidavit required by grievance policy); Whitney v. Simonson, 2007 WL 3274373, *2 (E.D.Cal., Nov. 5, 2007) (dismissing because plaintiff filed a new grievance rather than seeking reinstatement of his existing grievance; court admits defendants' approach is "hyper-technical" but holds *Woodford* requires dismissal), *report and recommendation adopted*, 2007 WL 4591593 (E.D.Cal., Dec. 28, 2007), *aff'd*, 317 Fed.Appx. 690 (9th Cir. 2009) (unpublished); Cadogan v. Vittitow, 2007 WL 2875464, *2–3 (E.D.Mich., Sept. 30, 2007) (dismissing where grievance was rejected for "including extraneous information, going beyond the scope of the issue being grieved"—by attaching seven pages of information relating to requests for dental care, medical information, and dental care standards, apparently relevant to claim); Cordova v. Frank, 2007 WL 2188587, *6 (W.D.Wis., July 26, 2007) (holding that a prisoner who clearly had good cause for his late grievance failed to exhaust because he didn't explain the reason so officials could consider whether to excuse his lateness); Chatman v. Johnson, 2007 WL 2023544, *6 (E.D.Cal., July 11, 2007) (prisoner re-submitted his appeal to Inmate Appeals Branch rather than to the appeals coordinator as directed), *report and recommendation adopted*, 2007 WL 2796575 (E.D.Cal., Sept. 25, 2007); Scarborough v. Cohen, 2007 WL 934594, *6 (N.D.Fla., Mar. 26, 2007) (dismissing for non-exhaustion where plaintiff had filed an "inmate request form" rather than an "informal grievance" before formally grieving); Hashiyah v. Wisconsin Dep't of Corrections, 2006 WL 2845701, *10 (E.D.Wis., Sept. 29, 2006) (dismissing for non-exhaustion where grievance was dismissed because plaintiff added his religious name as well as his "incarcerated name"); McNeal v. Cabana, 2006 WL 2794337, *1 (N.D.Miss., Jan. 23, 2006) (dismissing for non-exhaustion because the plaintiff mailed his appeal directly to the appeal body rather than using a request for services form); *see also* Rollings-Pleasant v. Deuel Vocational Ins., 2007 WL 2177832, *6 (E.D.Cal., July 27, 2007) (dismissing for non-exhaustion where grievance was "cancelled" for non-cooperation with investigation after prisoner argued about needing to make a phone call and asked about a different grievance; no finding that he refused to answer questions about the grievance at issue), *report and recommendation adopted*, 2007 WL 2900459 (E.D.Cal., Sept. 28, 2007). *Cf.* Love v. Pullman, 404 U.S. 522, 526, 92 S. Ct. 616 (1972) (stating "technicalities are particularly inappropriate in a statutory scheme in which laymen, unassisted by trained lawyers initiate the process").

and some rules do seem designed to trip prisoners up,[425] or have that effect.[426]

A few courts have suggested limits on the kinds of rules prisons can require prisoners to comply with, under penalty of having their cases dismissed for non-exhaustion. As discussed earlier, rules that make it impossible for a prisoner to comply may make the remedy unavailable on the facts of a particular case.[427] Some courts have said that "procedural requirements must . . . not be imposed in a way that offends the Federal Constitution or the federal policy embodied in § 1997e(a)."[428] One recent decision suggested that excessively technical grievance rules could make the administrative remedy unavailable, citing the Supreme Court's long-ago statement that "the creation of an additional procedural technicality . . . [is] particularly inappropriate in a statutory scheme in which laymen, unassisted by trained lawyers, initiate the process."[429] The court also held that a grievance rule that unreasonably limited prisoners' right of access to courts might be unconstitutional under the *Turner v. Safley* standard, which requires restrictions on prisoners' constitutional rights to be reasonably related to legitimate

penological purposes.[430] Though it upheld the grievance rule at issue,[431] the decision lays a foundation for striking down extreme grievance rules that cause great difficulties in complying without serving a useful and legitimate purpose.

Woodford itself said that "[p]roper exhaustion demands compliance with an agency's deadlines and other critical procedural rules."[432] This implies that there are some procedural rules that are not "critical" and whose violation does not threaten the system's functioning. That in turn would imply that a failure to follow such rules would not be a failure to exhaust (though it is not wise to test that proposition if you don't have to—do your best to follow *all* the grievance rules.) *Woodford* did not say how to determine if a rule is critical, and the lower courts have not said much about that either,[433] though one district court has suggested that if the

---

[425]A recent example of a rule that appears designed to trip prisoners up is Oklahoma's rule that prisoners on "grievance restriction" must list in any grievance all their other grievances within the preceding calendar year, by grievance number, date, description, and disposition at each level. One prisoner's complaint that he did not have that information, and that officials refused to provide him a copy of the grievance log so he could obtain it, was brushed off by the court. Tigert v. Jones, 2008 WL 2853625, *7–8 (W.D.Okla., July 21, 2008).

[426]A recent decision upheld the application of the Bureau of Prisons' regulation defining a grievance appeal as filed when it is logged as received, holding that even if the plaintiff's assertion that he mailed his appeal and it never arrived was true, he failed to exhaust. Williams v. Burgos, 2007 WL 2331794, *3 (S.D.Ga., Aug. 13, 2007). *Contra*, Crum v. U.S., 2008 WL 744727, *8 (W.D.Pa., Mar. 18, 2008) (where plaintiff showed that he submitted his appeal for mailing six weeks before it was received, there was a genuine issue of material fact whether plaintiff was prevented from filing a timely appeal so as to excuse failure to exhaust).

[427]*See* § D.3 of this chapter concerning "available" remedies.

[428]Spruill v. Gillis, 372 F.3d 218, 232 (3d Cir. 2004); *accord*, Strong v. David, 297 F.3d 646, 649–50 (7th Cir. 2002) ("The only constraint is that no prison system may establish a requirement inconsistent with the federal policy underlying Section 1983 and Section 1997e(a).").

[429]Lafountain v. Martin, 2008 WL 1923262, *15 (W.D.Mich., Apr. 28, 2008), *vacated and remanded on other grounds*, 334 Fed. Appx. 738 (6th Cir. 2009) (quoting Love v. Pullman Co., 404 U.S. 522, 526–27, 92 S. Ct. 616 (1972), as quoted in Kikimura v. Osagie, 461 F.3d 1269, 1283–84 (10th Cir. 2006)); *see Lafountain*, 2008 WL 1923262, *19 (referring to "existing federal precedent limiting procedural requirements for exhaustion in the civil administrative context, *see Love* . . . (barring creation of excessive procedural technicalities in statutory schemes in which laymen initiate the process)").

[430]*See* Turner v. Safley, 482 U.S. 78, 107 S. Ct. 2254 (1987). *LaFountain* said:

> Rubber-stamping unlimited administrative restrictions would permit state prisons to adopt grievance procedures solely for the purpose of requiring impossible compliance in order to terminate prisoners' access to the courts, in violation of the first prong of the *Turner* test . . . (requiring the governmental objective to be both legitimate and neutral). Such uncritical acceptance of prison restrictions also would permit prisons to effectively eliminate all means for prisoners to exercise their rights to challenge prison conditions, in violation of the second prong of *Turner* . . . (requiring that prison limitations on constitutional rights leave "alternative means of exercising the right [] open to prison inmates").

2008 WL 1923262, *19.

[431]The court held that the "no multiple issues" rule was not unconstitutional as applied to the plaintiff's grievance, which addressed incidents occurring over a six-month time period; he had ample opportunity to grieve each of the incidents separately, and the rule served a useful purpose in simplifying the claims addressed in any given grievance proceeding. *Lafountain*, 2008 WL 1923262, *15 ("the requirements that grievances be submitted timely, raising one issue in sufficient detail, and not duplicate issues previously grieved are rationally related to legitimate penological interests." On appeal, the appellate court did not reach this issue, holding that the plaintiff did not actually raise multiple issues, since the various incidents were all part of a single retaliation claim. LaFountain v. Martin, 334 Fed.Appx. 738, 741 (6th Cir. 2009)) However, a "no multiple issues" rule can be applied so as to make remedies unavailable. *See* n.441, below, concerning this point.

[432]Woodford v. Ngo, 548 U.S. 81, 90–91, 126 S. Ct. 2378 (2006).

[433]One district court has said that a policy as to what issues were suitable for the grievance system must not be critical, since the determination of non-grievability is itself appealable. However, in that case the prisoner was following the rules as written and prison officials seemed to be misinterpreting their own rules or using unwritten rules at variance from those the prisoners relied on. *See* Woods v. Lozer, 2007 WL 173704, *3 (M.D.Tenn., Jan. 18, 2007). Another court, without using the word "critical," excused a prisoner's sending of his appeal directly to the appellate decision-maker rather than sending it via the designated recipient, noting that the latter received the appeal and had an opportunity to

administrative body reaches the merits despite the violation of a procedural rule, it must not have been critical, at least in that case.[434] That view is consistent with many other decisions, both before[435] and after *Woodford*,[436] holding that

---

address the problem. Parker v. Robinson, 2006 WL 2904780, *11–12 (D.Me., Oct. 10, 2006).

An example of a rule that appears to us to be non-critical is found in *Lugo v. Ryan*, 2006 WL 163534, *1 (D.Ariz., Jan. 19, 2006), which cites a rule requiring the grievance process to be commenced with an "informal inmate letter" that must begin with the formula "I am attempting to informally resolve the following problem." We would think that omitting that recitation could not be treated as a procedural default.

[434]Jones v. Stewart, 457 F. Supp. 2d 1131, 1136 (D.Nev. 2006).

[435]Gates v. Cook, 376 F.3d 323, 331 n.6 (5th Cir. 2004) (noting that the plaintiff sent a form to the Commissioner rather than the Legal Adjudicator but defendants did not reject it for noncompliance; in addition, the grievance was submitted by the prisoner's lawyer and not by the prisoner as the rules specify); Spruill v. Gillis, 372 F.3d 218, 234 (3d Cir. 2004); Ross v. County of Bernalillo, 365 F.3d 1181, 1186 (10th Cir. 2004); Pozo v. McCaughtry, 286 F.3d 1022, 1025 (7th Cir. 2002); *see* Barnes v. Briley, 420 F.3d 673, 679 (7th Cir. 2005) (holding claim was not procedurally defaulted where an initial grievance was rejected as untimely but plaintiff later "restarted" the grievance process and received a decision on the merits); Gregory v. Ayers, 2006 WL 548444, *2–3 (E.D.Cal., Mar. 3, 2006) (holding that matters not initially exhausted which were addressed in a later grievance about threats arising from the first grievance were exhausted by the later grievance), *report and recommendation adopted*, 2006 WL 845846 (E.D.Cal., Mar. 31, 2006); Simpson v. Nickel, 2005 WL 2429805, *3 (W.D.Wis., Sept. 29, 2005) (holding that state law stating "a prisoner's failure to raise an issue at an initial disciplinary hearing constitutes waiver of the issue on appeal" did not govern the federal question of compliance with § 1997e(a)); Shaheen v. Hollins, 2005 WL 2179400, *4 (N.D.N.Y., Sept. 7, 2005) (declining to dismiss where prisoner was told his complaint was non-grievable, appealed, and had his complaint referred to the correct decision-maker on appeal), *report and recommendation adopted*, 2005 WL 2334387 (N.D.N.Y., Sept. 23, 2005); *see also* Tweed v. Schuetzle, 2007 WL 2050782, *7–8 (D.N.D., July 12, 2007) (holding warden's response to plaintiffs' non-grievance letter, addressing their claim and making no reference to procedural issues in the grievance, might waive such issues, especially in light of uncertainty whether the grievance system was available).

[436]Robinson v. Johnson, 343 Fed.Appx. 778, 781-82 (3d Cir. 2009) (unpublished) (declining to dismiss claims against commissioner and superintendent not named in grievance where grievance response addressed policies they were responsible for); Subil v. U.S. Marshal, 2008 WL 835712, *5 (N.D.Ind., Mar. 24, 2008) (declining to dismiss for non-exhaustion where grievance was not filed in the normal channels, but the final reviewing authority accepted and responded to it); Broder v. Correctional Medical Services, Inc., 2008 WL 704229, *2 (E.D.Mich., Mar. 14, 2008); Pierce v. Hillsborough County Dep't of Corrections, 2008 WL 215716, *6 (D.N.H., Jan. 24, 2008); Furnace v. Evans, 2008 WL 160968, *3-4 (N.D.Cal., Jan. 15, 2008); Trenton v. Arizona Dep't of Corrections, 2008 WL 169642, *4 (D.Ariz., Jan. 14, 2008); Baker v. Vanderark, 2007 WL 3244075, *7-8 (W.D.Mich., Nov. 1, 2007) (citing *Woodford* "proper exhaustion" holding as requiring officials

prison officials cannot rely on a prisoner's noncompliance with rules if they addressed the merits of the complaint in the grievance process rather than throwing the grievance out based on that noncompliance. If your grievance is rejected for petty procedural reasons *without* reaching the merits, you can certainly argue that the rule you violated was not "critical," but at present there is little support in the case law for that argument.[437]

Courts have disagreed over whether a grievance exhausts if it is rejected both on the merits and for procedural reasons.[438] If the purpose of the "proper exhaustion"

---

to raise procedural defects timely); Riley v. Hawaii Dep't of Public Safety, 2007 WL 3072777, *4–6 (D.Haw., Oct. 17, 2007) (holding prisoners complaining of sexual assault who completed the emergency grievance procedure as instructed, and whose complaints were processed through it, had exhausted despite not also completing the standard grievance process); Odighizuwa v. Strouth, 2007 WL 1170640, *4 (W.D.Va., Apr. 17, 2007), *aff'd*, 261 Fed.Appx. 498 (4th Cir. 2008) (unpublished); Ellis v. Albonico, 2007 WL 809804, *4 (E.D.Cal., Mar. 15, 2007) (where defendants couldn't locate plaintiff's alleged first level grievance, but the warden said his complaint would be investigated regardless, the requirement to submit a first level grievance was waived), *report and recommendation adopted*, 2007 WL 954727 (E.D.Cal., Mar. 29, 2007); Strope v. Collins, 2006 WL 3390393, *3 (D.Kan., Nov. 22, 2006); Jones v. Stewart, 457 F. Supp. 2d 1131, 1134–37 (D.Nev., 2006); Kretchmar v. Beard, 2006 WL 2038687, *5 (E.D.Pa., July 18, 2006) ("When the merits of a prisoner's claim have been fully examined and ruled upon by the ultimate administrative authority, prison officials can no longer assert the defense of failure to exhaust, even if the inmate did not follow proper administrative procedure."). *Jones v. Stewart, id.*, argues that the *Woodford* opinion sets out a "merits test" (did the agency address the merits up to the highest level?) and a "compliance test" (did the plaintiff follow the rules?), and "proper exhaustion" is satisfied by compliance with either. *Accord*, Cohen v. Baca, 2007 WL 1575245, *5 (D.Nev., May 30, 2007).

[437]What little we have come up with is in n.433, above. Remember that in *Woodford v. Ngo*, grievance time limits were treated as critical. *Woodford*, 548 U.S. at 90-91.

One of the considerations in assessing procedural default in habeas corpus is whether the state courts "actually enforced the state procedural rule so as to bar that claim." Lafountain v. Martin, 2008 WL 1923262, *16 (W.D.Mich., Apr. 28, 2008), *vacated and remanded on other grounds*, 334 Fed.Appx. 738 (6th Cir. 2009) and cases cited. That question is similar to whether a grievance body actually relied on a procedural rule in dismissing a grievance.

[438]*Compare* Grear v. Gelabert, 2008 WL 474098, *2 n.1 (W.D.Mich., Feb. 15, 2008); Cobb v. Berghuis, 2007 WL 4557856, *1 (W.D.Mich., Dec. 21, 2007) (holding that a grievance rejected for both reasons does not exhaust) *with* Kelley v. DeMasi, 2008 WL 4298475, *4 n.10 (E.D.Mich., Sept. 18, 2008); McCarroll v. Sigman, 2008 WL 659514, *4 (W.D.Mich., Mar. 6, 2008) (finding exhaustion on those facts), *reconsideration granted on other grounds*, 2008 WL 2064796 (W.D.Mich., May 13, 2008); *see* Lee v. Smith, 2010 WL 114876, *3 (S.D.Ga., Jan. 12, 2010) (declining to dismiss where plaintiff's grievance was decided on the merits at the first level, and the rules did not appear to authorize rejection for procedural defects on appeal); Harris v. West, 2008 WL 695404, *3 (W.D.Mich.,

rule is to preserve the system's ability to "function effectively,"[439] it would seem that a decision on the merits is a good indication that the system *has* functioned effectively, and dismissal serves no useful purpose.

Only a few courts have actually said what kind of grievance rule might be inconsistent with federal policy, so a violation of it would not require dismissal for non-exhaustion. One circuit has said that "no administrative system may demand that the prisoner specify each remedy later sought in litigation—for *Booth v. Churner* . . . holds that [§] 1997e(a) requires each prisoner to exhaust a process and not a remedy."[440] Another circuit held that a "no multiple issues" rule could not be enforced in a case where it was impossible for the prisoner to frame the claims that he wished to litigate without referring to multiple incidents in his grievance.[441]

Mar. 11, 2008) (finding exhaustion where prisoner's step II grievance was rejected as untimely but his final appeal was addressed on the merits). *Contra,* Scott v. Ambani, 2008 WL 597833, *2 (E.D.Mich., Feb. 29, 2008) (finding non-exhaustion where intermediate appeal reached the merits but final appeal did not).

[439]Woodford v. Ngo, 548 U.S. at 90.

[440]Strong v. David, 297 F.3d 646, 649–50 (7th Cir. 2002). Courts have enforced grievance rules requiring prisoners to demand *some* relief in their grievances. Edwards v. Rainey, 2009 WL 742165, *2 (E.D.Okla., Mar. 20, 2009) (dismissing for non-exhaustion where policy required a request for relief but plaintiff's grievances said only that he wanted to exhaust his administrative remedies).

[441]In *Moore v. Bennette,* 517 F.3d 717, 722, 730 (4th Cir. 2008), the court held that the plaintiff had properly exhausted, even though his grievance was rejected for including "more than one issue," because his complaint was about "being punished in various ways for conduct he had never been informed of or charged with. Under these circumstances, requiring Moore to grieve each of the alleged components of his punishment separately would have prevented him from fairly presenting his claim in its entirety." The court upheld the dismissal of other claims for which his grievance was dismissed for including more than one issue, despite the plaintiff's claim that both issues were examples of a pattern of inadequate medical care. *Moore,* 517 F.3d at 729. In *Simpson v. Greenwood,* 2007 WL 5445538, *5 (W.D.Wis., Apr. 6, 2007), the court said that it might have refused to enforce such a rule because the term "issue" is too vague to understand, but under the prison's rules the prisoner was given instructions how to comply and allowed another chance to grieve.

"No multiple issues" rules are especially subject to manipulation, since what constitutes an "issue" may be a matter of interpretation. *See* Starks v. Lewis, 2008 WL 2570960, *5 (W.D.Okla., June 24, 2008) (plaintiff said he raised one issue, "Mr. Lewis calling me a snitch, placing my life in danger"; grievance staff said issues raised included "fired from OCI; inmate typing responses and inmates read response, placing life in danger," even though plaintiff disclaimed any request to get his job back; dismissed for non-exhaustion), *aff'd,* 313 Fed.Appx. 163 (10th Cir. 2009) (unpublished); Lafountain v. Martin, 2008 WL 1923262, *19 (W.D.Mich., Apr. 28, 2008) (upholding application of multiple issues prohibition), *vacated and remanded,* 334 Fed.Appx. 738 (6th Cir. 2009) (unpublished) (holding that grievance did not in fact raise multiple issues) .

(e) Can Federal Courts Overrule a Grievance System's Procedural Rejection of a Grievance? Some courts have said that they cannot re-examine prison officials' decisions rejecting grievances for procedural reasons, an approach which has led to grossly unfair results in some cases.[442] Other federal courts have assumed that they do have the power to review such conclusions, both before and after *Woodford,* though they usually don't explain why they think they can do so.[443] One federal circuit has held that a procedural decision

---

[442]In *Lindell v. O'Donnell,* 2005 WL 2740999, *18, *22, *26 (W.D. Wis. Oct. 21, 2005), the plaintiff alleged that he had not received notice that a letter had been confiscated until almost a year afterward; when he tried to grieve, his grievance was dismissed as time-barred, even though it was impossible for him to file timely because of the lack of notice. The court said that it could not review the administrative determination, and found additional claims defaulted. That court said later that prison officials' application of grievance rules were not "unreviewable"; "the question is whether the prisoner had 'a meaningful opportunity' to present his grievance. . . . [C]ourts need not defer to interpretations that are clearly erroneous or inconsistent with the language of the regulation." Simpson v. Greenwood, 2007 WL 5445538, *4 (W.D.Wis., Apr. 6, 2007) (citation omitted). The appeals court for that circuit has subsequently stated, in an unpublished opinion: "As long as the state's application of its own procedural rules is not arbitrary or capricious, we will not substitute our judgment for the state's." Hoeft v. Wisher, 181 Fed.Appx. 549, 551 (7th Cir. 2006) (unpublished); *see* Starks v. Lewis, 2008 WL 2570960, *5 (W.D.Okla., June 24, 2008) ("Even when prison authorities are incorrect about the existence of the perceived deficiency, the inmate must follow the prescribed steps to cure it. . . . An inmate's disagreement with prison officials as to the appropriateness of a particular procedure under the circumstances, or his belief that he should not have to correct a procedural deficiency does not excuse his obligation to comply with the available process. . . ."), *aff'd,* 313 Fed.Appx. 163 (10th Cir. 2009) (unpublished); Williams v. Burgos, 2007 WL 2331794, *3 (S.D.Ga., Aug. 13, 2007) (holding Bureau of Prisons regulation defining an appeal as filed only when it is logged as received would apply even if plaintiff's assertion that he mailed his appeal was true).

[443]*See* Price v. Kozak, 569 F. Supp. 2d 398, 407 (D.Del. 2008) (holding plaintiff's grievances timely despite their rejection as late); Fosselman v. Evans, 2008 WL 4369984, *2 (N.D.Cal., Sept. 24, 2008) (rejecting "erroneous" decision screening out plaintiff's grievance; decision said he had not showed an adverse effect on his welfare but he produced a memo showing his privileges had been restricted); Moton v. Cowart, 2008 WL 2117120, *6 (M.D.Fla., May 19, 2008) (rejecting decision that plaintiff's complaint was not grievable, and an appeal decision that it must be re-commenced at the facility, as contrary to prison system's own policy); Shoucair v. Warren, 2008 WL 2033714, *7–8 (E.D.Mich., May 9, 2008) (rejecting decision that grievance failed to identify a policy violation, since the grievance rules did not require it, and that decision was vague, since it set forth basic facts and defendants failed to follow their rules requiring investigation of such complaints); Johnson v. Correctional Medical Services, Inc., 2008 WL 878767, *5 (W.D.Mich., Mar. 3, 2008) (rejecting officials' decision that grievance was duplicative); Elliott v. Jones, 2008 WL 420051, *4–5 (N.D.Fla., Feb. 12, 2008) (refusing to dismiss where defendants rejected plaintiff's emergency grievance, which the

that prevented the prisoner "from fairly presenting his claim in its entirety" need not be followed by the federal court.[444] Another recent decision noted that *Woodford* relied on the habeas corpus doctrine of procedural default in adopting its "proper exhaustion" rule, and said that "the contours of the procedural default doctrine would require the Court to consider whether the last administrative decisionmaker relied on an established procedural rule and whether a reasonable reviewer could have determined that the prisoner actually violated the established rule."[445] We think that is correct, and that the PLRA clearly calls for an independent judgment by the court as to whether the plaintiff has properly exhausted, though courts' willingness to overrule grievance bodies' procedural rulings will probably be limited to extreme cases.[446]

Several decisions have refused to dismiss for non-exhaustion where a prisoner's grievance had been rejected as duplicative of an earlier grievance.[447] This issue sometimes arises when prisoners subject to a "name the defendant" grievance policy file a second grievance in order to exhaust against additional potential defendants not known to them initially.[448]

(f) What If the Prisoner Fails to Comply with Directions from Prison Staff with Respect to a Particular Grievance? Numerous decisions have held that a prisoner who disregards instructions by grievance personnel as to how to proceed fails to exhaust.[449] However, some courts have refused

---

court concludes met the standards, and then rejected his regular grievance for no apparent reason, and rejected his appeal for writing outside the lines); George v. Smith, 2006 WL 3751407, *5–6 (W.D.Wis., Dec. 12, 2006) (holding that timeliness of grievance appeals must be assessed based on when they were sent, not when they arrived, despite grievance body's contrary interpretation of its own rule), aff'd, 507 F.3d 605 (7th Cir. 2007); Thomas v. Hickman, 2006 WL 2868967, *9–10 (E.D.Cal., Oct. 6, 2006) (allowing case to go forward even though grievance was untimely, since the prisoner did not know of her injury until long after the grievance deadline had passed); O'Connor v. Featherston, 2002 WL 818085, *2 (S.D.N.Y., Apr. 29, 2002) (refusing to be bound by rejection of request to file a late grievance where the plaintiff had been kept in medical restriction for the 14 days in which he was required to file a timely grievance); Graham v. Perez, 121 F. Supp. 2d 317, 322 and n.9 (S.D.N.Y. 2000) (holding that the court will independently determine whether a prisoner has presented "mitigating circumstances" under grievance rules for late grievance).

In *Vasquez v. Hilbert*, 2008 WL 2224394 (W.D.Wis., May 28, 2008), the defendants agreed that grievance officials had interpreted their own rules erroneously, but argued that the plaintiff failed to exhaust because he should have done a better job of showing the officials that they were wrong. The court didn't buy it. Vasquez, 2008 WL 2224394, *3 (holding argument "unreasonable, unfair and inconsistent with circuit precedent").

[444]Moore v. Bennette, 517 F.3d 717, 730 (4th Cir. 2008). In *Moore*, the court rejected a finding of non-exhaustion under a rule against complaining about more than one incident in a grievance where the prisoner's claim was about multiple different punishments for conduct that he had never been informed of or charged with. The court approved dismissal of other claims for non-exhaustion under the same rule because in those instances the rule didn't prevent the prisoner from presenting his claim. *Moore*, 517 F.3d at 722, 729. See n.441, above, for further discussion of this case.

[445]Lafountain v. Martin, 2008 WL 1923262, *16 (W.D.Mich., Apr. 28, 2008), *vacated and remanded on other grounds*, 334 Fed. Appx. 738 (6th Cir. 2009). The court further observed that instructions by grievance officials that are contrary to the relevant state regulations may make the remedy unavailable. *Id.*

[446]*Lafountain* essentially requires that the grievance body's decision be not only wrong, but unreasonable. An even stronger statement appears in *Muniz v. Kaspar*, 2008 WL 3539270, *4–5 (D.Colo., Aug. 12, 2008), where the plaintiff sought to exhaust his

administrative remedies he could bring a damages suit, even though his second-level appeal was rejected on the ground that it did not state the relief requested, nor did the grievance system provide for damages. The court rejected these "spurious procedural grounds," but warned: "Only where the 'procedural' defect cited by the prison is so transparently without merit as to be arbitrary and capricious on its face, coupled with a grievance procedure that does not provide a reasonable opportunity for refiling of a procedurally compliant grievance in the event of a procedural denial, will the Court consider whether the grievance procedure has been rendered unavailable." 2008 WL 3539270, *5 n.5.

[447]Some decisions have held that dismissal of a grievance as duplicative did not mean that the plaintiff had not exhausted properly, but suggested that he exhausted in an earlier grievance. Neal v. Butts, 2008 WL 2704663, *5 (E.D.Mich., July 9, 2008); Broyles v. Correctional Medical Services, Inc., 2008 WL 1745554, *6 (W.D.Mich., Apr. 14, 2008); Houston v. Riley, 2008 WL 762114, *3 (W.D.Mich., Feb. 25, 2008); Doyle v. Jones, 2007 WL 4052032, *8–9 (W.D.Mich., Nov. 15, 2007). In *Gabby v. Luy*, 2006 WL 167673, *4 (E.D.Wis., Jan. 23, 2006), the prisoner had filed one grievance and failed to appeal, then filed a second grievance which was rejected on the ground that the issue had been raised in the previous grievance. The court found exhaustion, implicitly rejecting defendants' argument that if a prisoner tries to exhaust an issue and makes a procedural mistake, he is barred from trying again and doing it right even if the later grievance is otherwise proper. In *Gatlin v. Nichols*, 2007 WL 4219170, *2 (E.D.Cal., Nov. 29, 2007), *report and recommendation adopted*, 2008 WL 191989 (E.D.Cal., Jan. 23, 2008), the plaintiff filed a grievance about a non-functioning wheelchair, then later filed a grievance about not getting a replacement wheelchair when the prison took his wheelchair away to get it repaired, and the court simply found that grievance officials were wrong in finding the second one duplicative.

[448]*See* § D.4 of this chapter, n.391.

[449]*See* Cannon v. Washington, 418 F.3d 713, 718 (7th Cir. 2005); Carroll v. Yates, 362 F.3d 984, 985 (7th Cir. 2004); Ford v. Johnson, 362 F.3d 395, 397 (7th Cir. 2004) ("Just as courts may dismiss suits for failure to cooperate, so administrative bodies may dismiss grievances for lack of cooperation; in either case this procedural default blocks later attempts to litigate the merits."); Jernigan v. Stuchell, 304 F.3d 1030, 1032–33 (10th Cir. 2002) (holding that a prisoner who received no response to a grievance and refused the appeals body's direction to try to get one had failed to exhaust); Lee v. Smith, 2010 WL 114876, *3 (S.D.Ga., Jan. 12, 2010) (declining to dismiss where plaintiff's grievance was decided on the merits at the first level, and the rules did not appear to

to find non-exhaustion where the instructions or the grievance body's dismissal were not supported by the written grievance policy.[450] We suggest following the directions,

rather than setting the stage for an argument about whether you were required to follow them. If you question whether the directions are correct, you can add a note to the grievance or appeal that you are proceeding as instructed by staff, and include the date of the instructions and the name of the person who gave them.

6. Time Limits

The "proper exhaustion" rule, discussed in the previous section, requires compliance with time limits,[451] despite the very short deadlines of most prison grievance systems.[152] Cases will usually be dismissed for non-exhaustion if the prisoner's grievance was rejected as untimely.[453] As with other procedural errors, some cases are allowed to go forward despite untimely exhaustion because of factors such as misunderstanding of the exhaustion requirement,[454] unclear

---

authorize rejection for procedural defects on appeal); Abdulhaseeb v. Calbone, 2008 WL 904661, *15 (W.D.Okla., Apr. 2, 2008) (holding prisoner failed to exhaust when he did not comply with demand to supplement his grievance with information about additional grievances he had filed after the one in question, despite his belief that the demand was unreasonable); Skipper v. South Carolina Dep't of Corrections, 2008 WL 608575, *4 (D.S.C., Mar. 4, 2008); Keeton v. Forsythe, 2008 WL 436945, *2 (E.D.Cal., Feb. 14, 2008) (plaintiff failed to exhaust when he did not comply with instruction to resubmit his grievance because his writing was too small to read), *report and recommendation adopted*, 2008 WL 780700 (E.D.Cal., Mar. 20, 2008); Whitney v. Simonson, 2007 WL 3274373, *2 (E.D.Cal., Nov. 5, 2007) (dismissing claim of prisoner who filed a new grievance rather than trying to reinstate the old one as instructed; court concedes this approach is "hyper-technical" but required by *Woodford v. Ngo*), *report and recommendation adopted*, 2007 WL 4591593 (E.D.Cal., Dec. 28, 2007), *aff'd*, 317 Fed.Appx. 690 (9th Cir. 2009) (unpublished); Richardson v. Llamas, 2007 WL 2389835, *3 (E.D.Cal., Aug. 20, 2007) (holding plaintiff did not exhaust where he failed to cooperate with an interview concerning his complaint of sexual abuse), *report and recommendation adopted*, 2007 WL 2904087 (E.D.Cal., Oct. 1, 2007); *contra*, Vega v. Alameida (next footnote); Cyrus v. Shepard, 2007 WL 2155527, *7–8 (M.D.Pa., July 26, 2007) (holding a plaintiff who used a "sensitive grievance" procedure, was told to use the regular procedure, and didn't, failed to exhaust); Walton v. Ayon, 2007 WL 1792309, *2 (E.D.Cal., June 19, 2007), *report and recommendation adopted*, 2007 WL 3170679 (E.D.Cal., Oct. 26, 2007); Fleming v. Geo Group, Inc., 2007 WL 162535, *2 (W.D.Okla., Jan. 18, 2007) (dismissing for non-exhaustion where prisoner ignored instructions to submit a legible copy of his grievance and appealed twice instead); Faysom v. Timm, 2005 WL 3050627, *2–3 (N.D.Ill., Nov. 9, 2005) (holding plaintiff who did not respond to Administrative Review Board's request for more information and clarification failed to exhaust); Jones v. Doty, 2005 WL 2860971, *2 (E.D.Tex., Oct. 28, 2005) (holding a prisoner who used the "sensitive grievance" procedure and was told he should use the regular grievance procedure, but did not, failed to exhaust, even though he appealed the denial of the "sensitive grievance"); Robinson v. Shannon, 2005 WL 2416116, *5 (M.D.Pa., Sept. 30, 2005) (holding that prisoner who was instructed on appeal to attach the Superintendent's response did not exhaust where he failed to respond and say there was no response); Hazleton v. Alameida, 358 F. Supp. 2d 926, 935 (C.D.Cal. 2005) (holding prisoner who failed to follow instructions did not exhaust).

[450]*See* Young v. Hightower, 395 F. Supp. 2d 583, 586–87 (E.D.Mich. 2005) (holding plaintiff's alleged failure to supply requested documents was not a failure to exhaust where the grievance policy said grievances should not be denied for failure to provide documentation); Vega v. Alameida, 2005 WL 1501531 (E.D Cal., June 20, 2005) (declining to dismiss where a prisoner's grievance and appeal were "cancelled" because he was "incorporative," citing defendants' failure to provide facts supporting the cancellation of the grievance), *report and recommendation adopted*, 2007 WL 2904087 (E.D.Cal., Oct. 1, 2007); Griffen v. Cook, 2005 WL 1113830, *7–8 (D.Or., May 10, 2005) (declining to dismiss for non-exhaustion where plaintiff's

grievances were returned unprocessed with instructions, but the grievance policy made no provision for returning grievances unprocessed), *report and recommendation adopted as modified*, 2005 WL 2314124 (D.Or., Sept. 21, 2005).

One court has been remarkably vociferous concerning the prisoner's obligation to follow erroneous instructions. Starks v. Lewis, 2008 WL 2570960, *5 (W.D.Okla., June 24, 2008) ("Even when prison authorities are incorrect about the existence of the perceived deficiency, the inmate must follow the prescribed steps to cure it. . . . An inmate's disagreement with prison officials as to the appropriateness of a particular procedure under the circumstances, or his belief that he should not have to correct a procedural deficiency does not excuse his obligation to comply with the available process. . . ."), *aff'd*, 313 Fed.Appx. 163 (10th Cir. 2009) (unpublished). *Contra*, Lafountain v. Martin, 2008 WL 1923262, *16 (W.D.Mich., Apr. 28, 2008) (suggesting that instructions by grievance personnel contrary to state regulations may make the remedy unavailable), *vacated and remanded on other grounds*, 334 Fed.Appx. 738 (6th Cir. 2009).

[451]Woodford v. Ngo, 548 U.S. 81, 90–91, 126 S. Ct. 2378 (2006).

[452]The plaintiff in *Woodford* had missed a 15-day deadline, and the Court noted that such deadlines are typically 14–30 days according to the United States and even shorter according to the plaintiff. 548 U.S. at 95–96. Some are as short as 24 hours. *See* Franklin v. Beth, 2008 WL 4131629, *4 (E.D.Wis., Sept. 4, 2008).

[453]*See, e.g.*, Scott v. Ambani, 577 F.3d 642, 647 (6th Cir. 2009); Williams v. Comstock, 425 F.3d 175, 176–77 (2d Cir. 2005) (per curiam).

[454]Williams v. Comstock, 425 F.3d 175, 177 (2d Cir. 2005) (citing Rodriguez v. Westchester County Jail Corr. Dep't, 372 F.3d 485 (2d Cir. 2004)).

rules,[455] threats or intimidation,[456] or other factors interfering with a prisoner's ability to exhaust timely.[457] Prisoners'

<hr>

[455]Williams v. Comstock, 425 F.3d 175, 177 (2d Cir. 2005) (citing Giano v Goord, 380 F.3d 670, 677 (2d Cir. 2004)); Plaster v. Kneal, 2008 WL 4090790, *3–4 (M.D.Pa., Aug. 29, 2008) (declining to dismiss where grievance appeal was late because prison officials told plaintiff to send it to the wrong place); Bellamy v. Mount Vernon Hosp., 2008 WL 3152963, *5 (S.D.N.Y., Aug. 5, 2008) (declining to dismiss where prisoner reasonably believed his claim was time-barred before he had an opportunity to grieve).

A reasonable if mistaken appreciation of the facts may also justify lack of timely exhaustion or result in a holding that the remedy was unavailable. In *Borges v. Piatkowski*, 337 F. Supp. 2d 424, 427 & n.3 (W.D.N.Y. 2004), the prisoner missed the 14-day grievance deadline because he had no reason to know he had a medical problem until after the time had expired and he had been transferred to another prison. The court did not dismiss his suit for lack of timely exhaustion; it held that he had no available remedy, or alternatively that he was justified by special circumstances in not exhausting.

[456]*See, e.g.*, Hemphill v. New York, 380 F.3d 680, 690–91 (2d Cir. 2004). Following *Hemphill*, several decisions have held that prisoners who did not exhaust because of assaults and/or threats until after they had been transferred were justified in failing to exhaust timely. Lunney v. Brureton, 2007 WL 1544629, *9–10 (S.D.N.Y., May 29, 2007), *objections overruled*, 2007 WL 2050301 (S.D.N.Y., July 18, 2007); Thomas v. Cassleberry, 2007 WL 1231485, *2 (W.D.N.Y., Apr. 24, 2007); *see* Cotton-Schrichte v. Peate, 2008 WL 3200775, *4 (W.D.Mo., Aug. 5, 2008) (declining to dismiss case of prisoner who was raped by a staff member and threatened into silence). *But see* n.462, below, noting cases holding that prisoners must file untimely grievances after transfer.

[457]Days v. Johnson, 322 F.3d 863, 867–68 (5th Cir. 2003); Moro v. Winsor, 2008 WL 718687, *4–5 (S.D.Ill., Mar. 14, 2008) (holding remedy unavailable to prisoner whose appeal was untimely because he could not get a timely answer at the first level in a system that required a response in order to appeal); McManus v. Schilling, 2008 WL 682577, *8 (E.D.Va., Mar. 7, 2008) (holding prisoner whose appeal deadlines passed because grievance responses were not delivered to him timely had no available remedy); Thorns v. Ryan, 2008 WL 544398, *3–4 (S.D.Cal., Feb. 26, 2008) (refusing to dismiss where grievance appeal was untimely because of delay in receiving the decision; appeal was timely measured from when plaintiff received it); Sanchez v. Penner, 2008 WL 544591, *6 (E.D.Cal., Feb. 26, 2008) (same as *Thorns*), *report and recommendation adopted*, 2008 WL 892760 (E.D.Cal., Mar. 31, 2008); Macahilas v. Taylor, 2008 WL 220364, *4 (E.D.Cal., Jan. 25, 2008) (denying summary judgment where prisoner said "his mind was too clouded" by illness even to know he had a claim within the time limit), *report and recommendation adopted*, 2008 WL 506109 (E.D.Cal., Feb. 22, 2008); Cordova v. Frank, 2007 WL 2188587, *6 (W.D.Wis., July 26, 2007) (holding remedy unavailable where a prisoner's appeal was late because he was indigent and prison rules forbade advancing him the postage to mail it); Kaufman v. Schneiter, 474 F. Supp. 2d 1014, 1032 (W.D.Wis. 2007) (stating same view as *Cordova*); Williams v. Hurley, 2007 WL 1202723, *6 (S.D.Ohio, Apr. 23, 2007) (holding that a prisoner whose cancer was not diagnosed until long after the 14-day grievance deadline had passed had no available remedy; no reference to any provision for filing untimely); Cruz v. Jordan, 80 F. Supp. 2d 109, 124 (S.D.N.Y. 1999) (holding remedies

<hr>

suits cannot be dismissed for non-exhaustion based on violation of time limits that are not made known to the prisoners.[458]

If a grievance concerns an ongoing condition, most courts assume that it must be timely,[459] though there may be disagreements about what is ongoing,[460] and when a

<hr>

were not available to a prisoner who was unconscious and hospitalized during the time period for filing a grievance, where prison officials had said his grievance was time-barred).

[458]*See* Sims v. Rewerts, 2008 WL 2224132, *5–6 (E.D.Mich., May 29, 2008) (declining to dismiss where plaintiff failed to comply with a time limit that had been changed without notice); Lampkins v. Roberts, 2007 WL 924746, *3 (S.D.Ind., Mar. 27, 2007) (refusing to dismiss for missing a five-day time deadline which was not made known in the materials made available to prisoners).

[459]Hagopian v. Smith, 2008 WL 3539251, *4 (E.D.Mich., Jan. 31, 2008); Rollins v. Magnusson, 2007 WL 2302141, *5 (D.Me., Aug. 9, 2007) (declining to credit dismissal as untimely, since the plaintiff was "clearly grieving the continued confiscation of his legal material"); Holloway v. Correctional Medical Services, 2007 WL 1445701, *5 (E.D.Mo., May 11, 2007) (holding grievance timely since plaintiff was grieving "the continual denial of information and treatment" that "continued to occur" when he filed his grievance and afterward); Simpson v. Greenwood, 2007 WL 5445538, *6 (W.D.Wis., Apr. 6, 2007); Abuhoran v. Morrison, 2005 WL 2140537, *6 (E.D.Pa., Sept. 1, 2005) (noting that finding of procedural default did not prevent plaintiffs from filing a new grievance challenging ongoing policy "at any time"); *see also* Wilkerson v. Beitzel, 2005 WL 5280675, *3 n.4 (D.Md., Nov. 10, 2005) (holding plaintiff had exhausted, notwithstanding dismissal under rule that any complaint concerning a prison policy must be raised within 30 days of arrival at the prison, regardless of whether complaint is ongoing; court says policy "borders on sophistry"), *aff'd*, 184 Fed.Appx. 316 (4th Cir. 2006) (unpublished). *But see* Andrade v. Maloney, 2006 WL 2381429, *6 (D.Mass., Aug. 16, 2006) ("I will not toll the filing deadline because the generalized complaint was somehow a continuing violation. To do so 'would undermine the very purpose of the deadline, which is to limit the time to file a claim.' . . . It would also be inconsistent with the policy judgments underlying the Supreme Court's decision in *[Woodford v.] Ngo*." (citation omitted)); Wallace v. Burbury, 2003 WL 21302947, *5 (N.D.Ohio, June 5, 2003) (declining to extend a 14-day deadline to reflect the five days of Passover when the grievant was religiously prohibited from working; declining to treat religious infringement as a continuing violation extending through Passover).

[460]One court held that a complaint about the treatment of a chronic medical condition is "'ongoing,' and a grievance that identifies the persistent failure to address that condition must be considered timely as long as the prison officials retain the power to do something about it." Ellis v. Vadlamudi, 568 F. Supp. 2d 778, 783–84 (E.D.Mich. 2008). The court distinguished these facts from those in *Johnson v. Johnson*, 385 F.3d 503, 519 (5th Cir. 2004), which held that a prisoner complaining of a series of sexual assaults could only sue about those that had occurred within the period encompassed by the grievance time limit. The *Ellis* court said *Johnson* addressed a series of discrete events, while complaints about the treatment of chronic medical problems were more similar to "continuing violations" for which the statute of limitations does not begin to run until they are over. *Ellis*, 568 F. Supp. 2d at

problem stops being ongoing so the time limit starts to run.[461]

Under the "proper exhaustion" rule, you might think that if something outside your control prevents you from exhausting timely, you can forget about exhausting on the ground that the remedy was not available to you. However, many decisions have said that under those circumstances, you must file a grievance as soon as you are no longer subject to whatever obstacle kept you from exhausting.[462]

Some courts have disagreed,[463] but to be safe you should try

---

784–85; see Ch. 8, § N, concerning continuing violations and statutes of limitations.

[461]One court held that a prisoner who said he had been promised a motion for sentence reduction in return for his cooperation with an investigation of staff corruption had failed to exhaust because he did not file a grievance within 20 days of the time the defendants' inaction became "manifest." Johnson v. Townsend, 2007 WL 2407267, *3 (E.D.Ky., Aug. 20, 2007). The court did not explain how a prisoner is supposed to know when prosecutorial inaction becomes "manifest." See also Hoye v. Nelson, 2007 WL 5062014, *7 (W.D.Mich., Oct. 18, 2007) (holding timeliness for a medical grievance must be measured from the date of denial of care, not from the beginning of the medical problem, if there is a deadline measured in days), report and recommendation adopted in part and remanded on other grounds, 2008 WL 907453 (W.D.Mich., Mar. 28, 2008).

In Velez v. Guldan, 2008 WL 4443269 (N.D.N.Y., Sept. 26, 2008), the plaintiff complained about protracted delay in dental care, and filed his grievance after about two years, while the problem was ongoing. The defendants argued that because he filed his grievance "after the fact," he did not give the defendants sufficient opportunity to correct the problem. The court rejected this argument, noting that the grievance policy encourages prisoners to try to solve problems informally before filing a grievance, which the plaintiff seemed to have done, and that the grievance rules did not require him to act differently. Even if he had received an extraction before he filed his grievance, he could still complaint about "the delay, the effect of the delay, or about the care itself." 2008 WL 4443269, *8.

[462]Bryant v. Rich, 530 F.3d 1368, 1379 (11th Cir. 2008) (holding prisoner who said he didn't grieve for fear of assault should have exhausted after transfer), cert. denied, 129 S. Ct. 733 (2008); Mayhew v. Gardner, 2008 WL 4093130, *4–5 (M.D.Tenn., Aug. 22, 2008) (prisoner segregated without writing materials should have filed grievance after release even though the deadline had passed); Ory v. McHugh, 2008 WL 2756463, *4 (N.D.Fla., July 14, 2008); In re Bayside Prison Litigation, 2008 WL 2387324, *5 (D.N.J., May 19, 2008); Chavez v. Thorton, 2008 WL 2020319, *4–5 (D.Colo., May 9, 2008); Williams v. Marshall, 2008 WL 717818, *6–7 (S.D.Ga., Mar. 17, 2008); Campbell v. Oklahoma County Detention Center, 2008 WL 490619, *5 (W.D.Okla. Feb. 21, 2008) (prisoner who alleged threats should have filed a grievance after transfer); Green v. McBride, 2007 WL 2815444, *3 (S.D.W.Va., Sept. 25, 2007) (holding prisoner who was kept on suicide watch without necessary materials until past the grievance deadline should have filed a late grievance); Poole v. Rich, 2007 WL 2238831, *3–4 (S.D.Ga., Aug. 1, 2007) (same as Bryant v. Rich), aff'd, 312 Fed.Appx. 165 (11th Cir. 2008) (unpublished), cert. denied, 129 S. Ct. 119 (2008); Stephens v. Howerton, 2007 WL 1810242, *4 (S.D.Ga., June 21, 2007) (holding injured prisoner should have filed a grievance when he was able to write), aff'd, 270 Fed.Appx. 750 (11th Cir. 2008) (unpublished), cert. denied, 129 S. Ct. 119 (2008); Calloway v. Contra Costa County

Jail Corr. Officers, 2007 WL 134581, *28 (N.D.Cal., Jan. 16, 2007) (holding prisoner removed from jail to prison and then returned to jail where claim arose should have filed a grievance upon return to jail), aff'd, 243 Fed.Appx. 320 (9th Cir. 2007) (unpublished); Benfield v. Rushton, 2007 WL 30287, *4 (D.S.C., Jan. 4, 2007) (holding a hospitalized prisoner should have filed a grievance upon release from the hospital); Duvall v. Dallas County, Tex. 2006 WL 3487024, *4–5 (N.D.Tex., Dec. 1, 2006) (similar to Benfield); Bradley v. Washington, 441 F. Supp. 2d 97, 101 (D.D.C. 2006) (holding a week's deprivation of writing materials did not make remedies unavailable where the plaintiff had 15 days to file a grievance); Stanley v. Rich, 2006 WL 1549114, *3 (S.D.Ga., June 1, 2006) (holding a prisoner who complained of threats of retaliation should have filed a grievance when conditions changed, i.e., the administration was replaced and several officers were suspended and eventually terminated); Langford v. Rich, 2006 WL 1549120, *2 (S.D.Ga., June 1, 2006) (holding a prisoner who complained of threats of retaliation at one prison should have filed a grievance upon being transferred); Hemingway v. Lantz, 2006 WL 1237010, *2 (D.N.H., May 5, 2006) (holding a prisoner who said he did not grieve for fear of staff retribution should have done so once transferred to the "safety" of another state); Haroon v. Cal. Dep't of Corr. and Rehabilitation, 2006 WL 1097444, *3 (E.D.Cal., Apr. 26, 2006) (holding that a prisoner who was in a coma during the usual time limit should have filed afterwards), report and recommendation adopted, 2006 WL 1629123 (E.D.Cal. June 9, 2006); Isaac v. Nix, 2006 WL 861642, *4 (N.D.Ga., Mar. 30, 2006) (holding prisoner who said he couldn't get grievance forms within a five-day time limit should have filed a grievance within five days of getting the forms); Winstead v. Castellaw, 2005 WL 1081353, *2 (E.D.Va., May 6, 2005) (dismissing for non-exhaustion where prisoner claimed he could not get grievance forms in segregation but did not file a grievance once released from segregation); Goldenberg v. St. Barnabas Hosp., 2005 WL 426701, *5 (S.D.N.Y., Feb. 23, 2005) (stating prisoner who was physically and mentally incapable of filing a grievance after the challenged conduct failed to explain why he didn't exhaust later); Patterson v. Goord, 2002 WL 31640585, *1 (S.D.N.Y., Nov. 21, 2002) (holding allegations of staff threats insufficient to justify late grievance where prisoner failed to submit grievance promptly upon transfer from prison where he was being threatened).

[463]See Cotton-Schrichte v. Peate, 2008 WL 3200775, *4 (W.D.Mo., Aug. 5, 2008) (prisoner who was raped by a staff member and threatened into silence "was not required to file a grievance after the threats were removed and outside of the time allowed for filing it, on the hope that an administrator would exercise discretion and process the grievance. For the court to dismiss a case for failure to exhaust under these circumstances would be inherently unjust."); Bellamy v. Mount Vernon Hosp., 2008 WL 3152963, *5 (S.D.N.Y., Aug. 5, 2008) (declining to dismiss where prisoner reasonably believed his claim was time-barred before he had an opportunity to grieve); Rivera v. Management & Training Corp., 2008 WL 2397418, *3 (D.Ariz., June 10, 2008) (holding prisoner who could not initially grieve because he was transferred out of the prison system was not required to file an untimely grievance when he was returned months later); McManus v. Schilling, 2008 WL 682577, *8 (E.D.Va., Mar. 7, 2008) (holding prisoner whose appeal deadlines passed because grievances responses were not delivered to him untimely had no available remedy); Williams v. Hurley, 2007 WL

to exhaust as quickly as you can even if you have blown the grievance deadline.

Many grievance systems allow late grievances under certain circumstances.[464] In order to take advantage of such a provision, you have to ask for it—you can't just argue later in court that your grievance was not untimely because they *could* have given you an extension.[465]

As with other procedural violations, it is not clear to what extent federal courts are free to re-examine administrative determinations that a grievance is untimely[466] or that a late grievance should not be allowed.[467]

1202723, *6 (S.D.Ohio, Apr. 23, 2007) (holding that a prisoner whose cancer was not diagnosed until long after the 14-day grievance deadline had passed had no available remedy; no reference to any provision for filing untimely).

[464]For example, the New York State grievance system permits late grievances for "mitigating circumstances," Graham v. Perez, 121 F. Supp. 2d 317, 322 (S.D.N.Y. 2000) (quoting regulation), which include "*e.g.,* timely attempts to resolve informally by the inmate." 7 New York Code of Rules & Regulations § 701.6(g)(1)(i)(a). This rule also provides: "An exception to the time limit may not be granted if the request was made more than 45 days after an alleged occurrence." *Id.*

[465]Patel v. Fleming, 415 F.3d 1105, 1110–11 (10th Cir. 2005) (holding that the existence of provisions for time extensions did not save the untimely grievance of a prisoner who never sought one); Pozo v. McCaughtry, 286 F.3d 1022, 1025 (7th Cir. 2002) (same as *Patel*); Harper v. Jenkin, 179 F.3d 1311, 1312 (11th Cir. 1999) (holding that a prisoner whose grievance was dismissed as untimely was obliged to appeal, since the system provided for waiver of time limits for "good cause"); Tafari v. Stein, 2008 WL 1991039, *6 (W.D.N.Y., May 5, 2008), *reconsideration denied,* 2008 WL 3852150 (W.D.N.Y., Aug. 15, 2008); Cordova v. Frank, 2007 WL 2188587, *6 (W.D.Wis., July 26, 2007) (holding that a prisoner who clearly had good cause for his late grievance failed to exhaust because he didn't explain the reason so officials could consider whether to excuse his lateness); Soto v. Belcher, 339 F. Supp. 2d 592, 596 (S.D.N.Y. 2004) (holding that a prisoner who learned of his problem after the deadline passed should have sought to file a late grievance); Kaiser v. Bailey, 2003 WL 21500339, *6 (D.N.J., July 1, 2003) (holding that a prisoner who did not follow instructions to obtain verification that untimeliness was not his fault failed to exhaust); Roa v. Fowler, 2003 WL 21383264 (W.D.N.Y., Apr. 16, 2003); Steele v. N.Y. State Dep't of Corr. Servs., 2000 WL 777931 (S.D.N.Y., June 19, 2000), *motion to vacate denied,* 2000 WL 1731337 (S.D.N.Y., Nov. 21, 2000); *see* Whitener v. Buss, 268 Fed. Appx. 477, 478–79 (7th Cir. 2008) (unpublished) (dismissing claim of prisoner who missed a 48-hour grievance deadline because he needed the relevant officers' names and it took a week to get them, and he didn't ask for waiver of the time limit).

[466]For examples of decisions where courts refused to re-examine questionable prison timeliness decisions, *see* Wall v. Holt, 2007 WL 89000, *3–4 (M.D.Pa., Jan. 9, 2007) (holding timeliness is measured by when grievance appeal arrives under Bureau of Prisons' regulation, notwithstanding "prison mailbox" rule and claim that the appeal was mailed in plenty of time); Lindell v. O'Donnell, 2005 WL 2740999, *18 (W.D.Wis., Oct. 21, 2005) (holding that the court could not review an administrative finding of untimeliness even though, the plaintiff alleged that he had not received notice that a letter had been confiscated until almost a year afterward, and it was impossible for him to file timely because of the lack of notice).

For decisions where courts exercised independent judgment about timeliness, *see* Price v. Kozak, 569 F. Supp. 2d 398, 407 (D. Del. 2008) (holding plaintiff's grievances timely despite their inexplicable rejection as late); Fosselman v. Evans, 2008 WL 4369984, *2 (N.D.Cal., Sept. 24, 2008) (holding finding of untimeliness "erroneous" based on court's time calculation); Paynes v. Runnels, 2008 WL 4078740, *6 (E.D.Cal., Aug. 29, 2008) (holding that where first level decided the merits, dismissal at the second level for untimeliness was not authorized by the grievance rules), *report and recommendation adopted,* 2008 WL 4464828 (E.D.Cal., Sept. 30, 2008); Ashker v. Schwarzenegger, 2007 WL 1725417, *6 (N.D.Cal., June 14, 2007) (denying summary judgment where defendants said plaintiff's grievance was untimely but plaintiff said it was timely measured from his receipt of the decision at issue), *amended on reconsideration on other grounds,* 2007 WL 2781273 (N.D.Cal., Sept. 20, 2007); George v. Smith, 2006 WL 3751407, *5–6 (W.D.Wis., Dec. 12, 2006) (holding that timeliness of grievance appeals must be assessed based on when they were sent, not when they arrived, citing "prison mailbox" rule, despite grievance body's contrary interpretation of its own rule), *aff'd on other grounds,* 507 F.3d 605 (7th Cir. 2007); Thomas v. Hickman, 2006 WL 2868967, *9–10 (E.D.Cal., Oct. 6, 2006) (holding that a prisoner had no available remedy where she did not know of the wrong within the 15-day time limit and officials dismissed her grievances as untimely); *see also* Marella v. Terhune, 568 F.3d 1024, 1027 (9th Cir. 2009) (holding district court should have determined whether plaintiff's grievance fell into an exception to the time limits, even though state officials had rejected it as untimely); Armitige v. Cherry, 2007 WL 1751738, *5 (S.D.Tex., May 30, 2007) (stating in dictum that a grievance's timeliness is determined in the same way as courts determine when a claim accrues, based on when the prisoner should have known he had a claim (in this case that his broken leg had been misdiagnosed). In *Merlino v. Westwood,* 2007 WL 4326803, *4–5 (E.D.Mich., Dec. 10, 2007), the court rejected defendants' claim of untimeliness based on its own time calculation under defendants' rules, but it is not clear whether the grievance was actually rejected as untimely.

One court has held that a grievance rule stating that a prisoner "should" file within 15 days, not that he "must" file within 15 days, is not a mandatory rule and failing to meet it does not render a grievance untimely. Edwards v. Dwyer, 2008 WL 243943, *8 (E.D.Mo., Jan. 25, 2008). Don't rely on this; we would expect most courts to say that prisoners are required to do what the policy says they "should" do.

[467]Moore v. La. Dep't of Public Safety & Corr., 2002 WL 1791996, *4 (E.D.La., Aug. 5, 2002) (declining to enforce 30-day

When a claim is dismissed for non-exhaustion, the deadline for administrative proceedings will almost always have passed. In some cases, prisoners may be allowed to exhaust at that point if there is a grievance rule providing for late grievances, but that will be up to grievance officials to decide.[468] Some courts have held that under some circumstances, where prisoners had justifiable reasons for failure to exhaust, their cases should not be dismissed unless they have a chance to try again.[469] Others have directed that grievance officials consider particular grievances on their merits after dismissal for non-exhaustion.[470] The doctrine of equitable tolling,[471] which is usually applied to statutes of limitations, may also excuse late grievance filings under some circumstances.[472]

As with other procedural errors, untimely filing can be waived by prison officials in the administrative process: if the grievance is late but they decide the merits anyway, you have satisfied the exhaustion requirement.[473]

_____

time limit; declaring 30-day delay in filing complaint "not unreasonable" given that the plaintiff was a juvenile in state custody); O'Connor v. Featherston, 2002 WL 818085, *2 (S.D.N.Y., Apr. 29, 2002) (refusing to be bound by rejection of request to file a late grievance where the plaintiff had been kept in medical restriction for the 14 days in which he was required to file a timely grievance); Graham v. Perez, 121 F. Supp. 2d 317, 322 n.9 (S.D.N.Y. 2000) (holding court will decide whether late exhaustion is excused by mitigating circumstances such as transfer to another facility or the unavailability of grievance representatives to prisoners in a segregated unit); *see also* Lawyer v. Gatto, 2007 WL 549440, *7 (S.D.N.Y., Feb. 21, 2007) (holding that grievance supervisor's rejection of claimed mitigating circumstances rendered the remedy unavailable, where earlier grievances had disappeared). *But see* Cole v. Miraflor, 2006 WL 457817, *4 (S.D.N.Y., Feb. 23, 2006) (stating that prison officials' determination regarding mitigating circumstances "is conclusive on the issue of exhaustion"); Patterson v. Goord, 2002 WL 31640585, *1 (S.D.N.Y., Nov. 21, 2002) (refusing to disturb finding of no mitigating circumstances where prisoner had waited six months after dismissal for non-exhaustion before filing a grievance).

[468]In *Brownell v. Krom*, 446 F.3d 305 (2d Cir. 2006), a prisoner attempted to exhaust his claim after dismissal for non-exhaustion in the district court, but his grievance was dismissed as untimely, despite facts that led the Second Circuit to find special circumstances justifying his initial failure to exhaust correctly.

[469]The Second Circuit has held that if remedies are not available, or if the defendants are estopped from claiming non-exhaustion, the prisoner is not required to exhaust. But on a lesser showing of "special circumstances" justifying failure to exhaust or to exhaust correctly, the prisoner will be expected to try to exhaust again if remedies remain available. Brownell v. Krom, 446 F.3d 305, 313 (2d Cir. 2006); Giano v. Goord, 380 F.3d 670, 679–80 (2d Cir. 2004); Hemphill v. New York, 380 F.3d 680, 690–91 (2d Cir. 2004). The Seventh Circuit has held more broadly that whenever a failure to exhaust is "innocent," the prisoner "must be given another chance to exhaust (provided that there exist remedies that he will be permitted by the prison authorities to exhaust, so that he's not just being given a runaround)." Pavey v. Conley, 544 F.3d 739, 742 (7th Cir. 2008), *cert. denied*, 129 S. Ct. 1620 (2009).

[470]George v. Morrison-Warden, 2007 WL 1686321, *4 (S.D.N.Y., June 11, 2007) (dismissing for failure to appeal, holding plaintiff's efforts had "earned him a response," directing officials to treat a renewed appeal as timely and respond to it); Hill v. Chalanor, 419 F. Supp. 2d 255, 259 (N.D.N.Y. 2006) (finding appeal was "technically available," failure to appeal resulted from "confusion or mis-communication" and not official misconduct, directing that plaintiff's renewed grievance appeal "shall be deemed timely" and directing prison officials to make sure it reached its destination); Burgess v. Morse, 259 F. Supp. 2d 240, 247 (W.D.N.Y. 2003) (directing "that the IGRC Supervisor consider referral from this Court as a mitigating circumstance" for the plaintiff's untimely filing); Cardona v. Winn, 170 F. Supp. 2d 131 (D.Mass. 2001) (holding that the grievance appeal deadline should be extended because the prisoner may have missed it out of "excusable neglect"); *see* Coronado v. Goord, 2000 WL 52488 (S.D.N.Y., Jan. 24, 2000) (dismissing case, suggesting that a time extension for the grievance should be granted).

[471]*See* nn.530–531 of this chapter and the corresponding text, and Ch. 8, § N, for more information about the doctrine of equitable tolling.

One court has held that that equitable tolling does not apply to grievance proceedings. Diaz v. Rutter, 2007 WL 2683532, *7 (W.D.Mich., Sept. 7, 2007) (holding equitable tolling applies to statutes of limitations but not grievance proceedings). Others disagree, as cited in this section.

[472]In one case, a prisoner's claim was not subject to the exhaustion requirement under his circuit's law at the relevant time. Then a Supreme Court decision made it clear that the claim *did* have to be exhausted. The plaintiff then promptly filed a grievance, which was dismissed as untimely. The court held that the plaintiff, who "promptly and consistently made good faith efforts" to pursue his claims and was victimized by extraordinary circumstances, should have the benefit of equitable tolling, with the deadline for filing a grievance extended to 20 days (the grievance time limit) after he received the court's decision dismissing his case. Gambina v. Dever, 2006 WL 894900, *3–4 (D.Colo., Mar. 31, 2006). Similarly, in *Rivera v. Goord*, 253 F. Supp. 2d 735, 753 (S.D.N.Y. 2003), the defendants raised the exhaustion defense only after a Supreme Court decision made the requirement applicable; the court said defendants had waived the defense, and it would permit them to assert it based on a change in the law only if they gave the prisoner a chance to exhaust. ("In other words, DOCS cannot have it both ways.") When defendants then rejected his grievances as untimely, the court held that defendants were estopped from raising exhaustion under those circumstances and that the plaintiff showed special circumstances justifying his failure to exhaust. Rivera v. Pataki, 2005 WL 407710, *11–13 (S.D.N.Y. Feb., 7, 2005) (noting that "Rivera did the best he could to follow DOCS regulations while responding to an evolving legal framework"). *See also* Kelley v. DeMasi, 2008 WL 4298475, *4 & n.9 (E.D.Mich., Sept. 18, 2008) (grievance deadline tolled where prisoner had severe medical problems leading to hospitalization during the time he should have appealed the grievance); *see* Anthony v. Gilman, 2008 WL 115531, *2 (W.D.Mich., Jan. 10, 2008) (applying equitable tolling to grievance deadline, but ruling against prisoner on the merits).

[473]Riccardo v. Rausch, 375 F.3d 521, 524 (7th Cir. 2004); Ross v. County of Bernalillo, 365 F.3d 1181, 1186 (10th Cir. 2004); Pozo v. McCaughtry, 286 F.3d 1022, 1025 (7th Cir. 2002); Ellis v. Vadlamudi, 568 F. Supp. 2d 778, 785–86 (E.D.Mich. 2008) (citing *Woodford v. Ngo*'s analogy to the habeas corpus procedural default

If a grievance system has no time limit, delay in filing cannot bar a prisoner's claim for non-exhaustion.[474] An unexhausted claim should be dismissed without prejudice, and the litigant will have the opportunity to seek to exhaust.[475]

Here is the practical bottom line about time limits. Obviously, you should learn the rules and be sure you meet the deadlines. But if you miss a grievance deadline, don't give up. Proceed with your grievance anyway, as quickly as you can. Request permission to file a late grievance if the rules provide for such a request. Explain why you were late, and cite any relevant part of the grievance rules.[476] Take all the available appeals if the grievance officials reject your grievance for lateness anyway. If they deal with the merits of your grievance, then its lateness won't matter. If they don't, you may still be able to argue in court either that you were justified by special circumstances in failing to file a grievance on time, or that circumstances prevented you from filing on time and the remedy was therefore unavailable. If you do not complete the grievance process, or take it as far as you are allowed, you will not be able to do this.

7. "Total Exhaustion"

Some courts adopted the "total exhaustion" rule, which said that if a prisoner includes any unexhausted claims in a complaint, the whole case had to be dismissed.[477] However, that rule is history; the Supreme Court has held that it is not required by the PLRA.[478] If part of your case is not exhausted, then only that part should be dismissed for non-exhaustion.

8. How Exhaustion Is Litigated

Exhaustion is an "affirmative defense," so you don't have to plead it in your complaint—the defendants must raise it.[479] If you have in fact properly exhausted, it may be good practice to put it in the complaint anyway. Then if the defendants make a motion to dismiss, you can simply refer to the relevant paragraph of your complaint in response, since on such a motion the court must assume that the facts you allege in your complaint are true.[480] If you did *not* properly exhaust,

---

rule, and pointing out that in habeas, if a state court decides the merits, procedural default is excused); Harris v. West, 2008 WL 695404, *3 (W.D.Mich., Mar. 11, 2008); Stevenson v. Michigan Dep't of Corrections, 2008 WL 623783, *12 (W.D.Mich., Mar. 4, 2008); Shaw v. Frank, 2008 WL 283007, *8 (E.D.Wis., Jan. 31, 2008) (grievance untimely by five years), *aff'd*, 288 Fed.Appx. 299 (7th Cir. 2008) (unpublished); Johnson v. Beardslee, 2007 WL 2302378, *3 (W.D.Mich., Aug. 8, 2007); Jenkins v. Baumler, 2007 WL 2023538, *3 (E.D.Cal., July 11, 2007), *report and recommendation adopted*, 2007 WL 2782875 (E.D.Cal., Sept. 25, 2007); Coronado v. Schriro, 2007 WL 1687604, *5 (D.Ariz., June 8, 2007); Armitige v. Cherry, 2007 WL 1751738, *6 (S.D.Tex., May 30, 2007); Maraglia v. Maloney, 2006 WL 3741927, *7 (D.Mass., Dec. 18, 2006); Harris v. Aidala, 2006 WL 2583256, *2 (W.D.N.Y. Sept. 6, 2006); Griswold v. Morgan, 317 F. Supp. 2d 226, 229–30 (W.D.N.Y. 2004); *see* Barnes v. Briley, 420 F.3d 673, 679 (7th Cir. 2005) (holding claim was not procedurally defaulted where an initial grievance was rejected as untimely but plaintiff later "restarted" the grievance process and received a decision on the merits); Conyers v. Abitz, 416 F.3d 580, 585 (7th Cir. 2005) (holding claim exhausted where grievance was "principally rejected on the merits with an ambiguous secondary observation that it was untimely"). In *Conyers*, the court in dictum said that a claim "may" be procedurally barred if the grievance was rejected both on the merits and for untimeliness. *Accord*, Cobb v. Berghuis, 2007 WL 4557856, *1 (W.D.Mich., Dec. 21, 2007). *But see* Scott v. Ambani, 2008 WL 597833, *2 (E.D.Mich., Feb. 29, 2008) (untimeliness was not waived where the merits were decided only at intermediate stages); Cole v. Litscher, 343 F. Supp. 2d 733, 741 (W.D.Wis. 2004) (holding that a grievance rejected on both grounds suffices to exhaust, since when the grievance process rules on an issue, the purpose of the exhaustion requirement is satisfied; the habeas rule is different because the purpose of habeas exhaustion is different), *reconsideration denied*, 2005 WL 318819 (W.D.Wis., Feb. 1, 2005).

[474]Schonarth v. Robinson, 2008 WL 510193, *3–4 (D.N.H., Feb. 22, 2008) (grievance filed two years after the jail was demolished, but otherwise complying with grievance rules, exhausted); *accord*, Cabrera v. LeVierge, 2008 WL 215720, *5–6 (D.N.H., Jan. 24, 2008); Owens v. County of Ingham, 2008 WL 324292, *2 (W.D.Mich., Jan. 7, 2008). *But see* Hopkins v. Coplan, 2007 WL 2264597, *3–4 (D.N.H., Aug. 6, 2007) (holding that where there was *no* time limit when the plaintiff's claim arose, but one was instituted later, the plaintiff was obliged to comply with that time limit as measured from the date it was promulgated).

[475]Alexander v. Dickerson, 2008 WL 1827609, *6 (E.D.Tex., Apr. 22, 2008).

[476]For example, under the New York State regulation cited above with its "mitigating circumstances" exception, you should explain why you didn't file timely and why those reasons ought to be considered mitigating circumstances.

[477]*See, e.g.*, Ross v. County of Bernalillo, 365 F.3d 1181, 1188–90 (10th Cir. 2004).

[478]Jones v. Bock, 549 U.S. 199, 219–24, 127 S. Ct. 910 (2007).

Before *Jones v. Bock*, the Ninth Circuit had held that when claims were "closely related and difficult to untangle," the presence of unexhausted claims among them supported dismissal of the entire complaint, but otherwise rejected total exhaustion. Lira v. Herrera, 427 F.3d 1164, 1175-76 (9th Cir. 2005), *cert. denied*, 127 S.Ct. 1212 (2007). Some district courts have continued to use that analysis. *See* Candler v. Woodford, 2007 WL 3232435, *3–4 & n.2 (N.D.Cal., Nov. 1, 2007); Taylor v. Calipatria, 2007 WL 2712225, *6 & n.4 (S.D.Cal., Sept. 13, 2007) (stating "*Lira* is consistent with *Jones*, although *Lira* provides more detailed analysis"). Since *Jones v. Bock* rejected the total exhaustion rule entirely without mentioning any exceptions, we don't see any basis for continuing to apply the *Lira* exception.

[479]Jones v. Bock, 549 U.S. 199, 212–17, 127 S. Ct. 910 (2007). This could change. The Court suggested there might be reasons to amend the Federal Rules of Civil Procedure to make exhaustion a pleading requirement, so be sure you have the current rules (the pleading rule is Fed. R. Civ. P. 8).

[480]*See* Amaker v. Goord, 1999 WL 511990, *4–5 (S.D.N.Y., July 20, 1999) (holding that a general assertion of exhaustion in

but you think you have a good argument that administrative remedies were not available to you, or that there are special circumstances that justify your failure to exhaust, it is probably better to leave exhaustion out of the complaint entirely, since the court might think it could dismiss your complaint on the ground that on its face it shows failure to exhaust.[481] If you leave exhaustion out of the complaint and the defendants then make a motion claiming non-exhaustion, at that point you will have the opportunity to provide a fuller explanation. Here's the rule of thumb: if you can truthfully write in your complaint, "Plaintiff has exhausted all available administrative remedies for his claims," without further explanation, you may as well do it. If it's more complicated than that, leave it out.

Leaving exhaustion out of the complaint may not be possible in some cases, since the court may require prisoners to use a form complaint that asks about exhaustion.[482] That practice appears to be invalid after *Jones v. Bock*, since it in effect requires prisoners to plead exhaustion in the complaint, contrary to *Jones*.[483] (Refusing to answer the question on that ground is not a good idea, since litigants are expected to obey court rules and court orders, and refusal might result in delay in processing your case, or even in dismissal if the court didn't agree with you.) Some form complaints call for limited information, or just ask the

prisoner to check boxes. In such cases, you should be sure that if you didn't exhaust, you put enough information on the form for the court to understand why you didn't—*e.g.*, if the issue was not grievable, or if you were denied the necessary forms or threatened with harm if you filed a grievance. For example, if the form asks whether you exhausted at the prison you are held at, but you exhausted at another prison and then were transferred, don't just write "No"—explain that you did exhaust at another location.

Since exhaustion is not a pleading requirement, it cannot be addressed at initial screening or by motion under Fed.R.Civ.P. 12(b)(6) to dismiss for failure to state a claim, except in those cases where non-exhaustion is clear on the face of the complaint.[484] (In our view, almost the only situations in which non-exhaustion can legitimately be said to be clear on the face of the complaint are those in which the complaint indicates that the prisoner did not exhaust, or abandoned the process, for reasons that are not legitimate as a matter of law, such as a belief that it is futile or that it cannot provide a particular remedy, or the complaint indicates that the prisoner began the process but it is not completed yet.) Nor can exhaustion be addressed on a motions under Rule 12(b)(1), Fed.R.Civ.P., to dismiss for lack of

---

response to a motion to dismiss was sufficient in the absence of a record indicating what grievances the plaintiff had filed and what had happened to them); Wright v. Dee, 54 F. Supp. 2d 199, 206 (S.D.N.Y. 1999) (holding assertion of exhaustion made in response to motion to dismiss was sufficient); *see also* Robinson v. Dep't of Corr., 1998 WL 883301, *4 (S.D.N.Y., Dec. 17, 1998) (holding allegation of lack of remedies was sufficient at screening stage).

[481]*See* Jones v. Bock, 549 U.S. 199, 214–15, 127 S. Ct. 910 (2007).

[482]*See, e.g.*, Edwards v. Haws, 2008 WL 5377995, *2 (C.D.Cal., Dec. 23, 2008); Harvey v. Ponder, 2008 WL 5071131, *3 (N.D.Cal., Nov. 26, 2008); *see* n.506, below, concerning courts' practice of relying on check marks or brief answers in form complaints to dismiss for non-exhaustion.

[483]One federal circuit has so held, though unfortunately in an unpublished opinion. In *Torns v. Mississippi Dep't of Corrections*, 301 Fed. Appx. 386 (5th Cir. 2008) (unpublished), the district court dismissed for non-exhaustion based on the prisoner's answers to questions on the form. The appeals court said "the district court erred by using Question 7 of the prisoner's form complaint to prompt Torns for information about his exhaustion of administrative remedies and by relying on the elicited information." 301 Fed.Appx. at 389. The court relied on *Carbe v. Lappin*, 492 F.3d 325 (5th Cir. 2007), which holds that "a district court cannot by local rule sidestep *Jones* by requiring inmates to affirmatively plead exhaustion." 492 F.3d at 328. In order to dismiss for non-exhaustion, *Torns* said, the court must find non-exhaustion apparent on the face of the *other* parts of the complaint. 301 Fed.Appx. at 389. *See also* Randolph v. City of New York Dep't of Correction, 2007 WL 2660282, *7–8 (S.D.N.Y., Sept. 7, 2007) (holding that interpreting brief and ambiguous information on a complaint form to show non-exhaustion is inconsistent with *Jones v. Bock*'s holding that exhaustion is an affirmative defense).

[484]Jones v. Bock, 549 U.S. at 214-15.

It is rare for exhaustion to be genuinely apparent on the face of the complaint since there are so many circumstances under which a prisoner might not be required to exhaust, as we explain in other sections. We explain later in this section what must be shown to establish non-exhaustion. Courts must "ensure that any defects in exhaustion were not procured from the action or inaction of prison officials" and that the prisoner is "without valid excuse" for non-exhaustion. Aquilar Avellaveda v. Terrell, 478 F.3d 1223, 1225 (10th Cir. 2007); *accord*, Meador v. Pleasant Valley State Prison, 333 Fed.Appx. 177, 178 (9th Cir. 2009) (unpublished) (concession that grievance was untimely did not establish non-exhaustion, since the grievance rules allow late exhaustion under some circumstances, and plaintiff also alleged reasons he was unable to file timely); Anderson v. XYZ Correctional Health Services, Inc., 407 F.3d at 682 & n.5 ("To determine whether an inmate has exhausted his administrative remedies requires an understanding of the remedies available and thus likely would require information from the defendant as well as the inmate."); Stewart v. Central Arizona Correction Facility, 2009 WL 3756504, *3 (D.Ariz., Nov. 9, 2009) (admission of non-exhaustion on the face of the complaint did not warrant dismissal where other allegations would support an argument that remedies were unavailable), *reconsideration denied*, 2009 WL 5184466 (D.Ariz., Dec. 22, 2009).

Courts have rejected the idea that non-exhaustion is apparent if you provide any information about exhaustion in your complaint, and it doesn't completely establish that you have exhausted. *See, e.g.*, Carson v. Monroe, 2008 WL 822150, *4 (W.D.Mich., Mar. 26, 2008) ("The fact that Plaintiff attaches grievances to his complaint or to other pleadings that may not show exhaustion of every issue presented is of no consequence, because Plaintiff has no duty to show exhaustion. The burden lies solely with a defendant to show that Plaintiff failed to exhaust grievance remedies.")

subject matter jurisdiction, since failure to exhaust is not jurisdictional.[485]

In most courts, defendants who claim you didn't exhaust will have to raise that claim in a motion for summary judgment, which requires them to submit admissible factual evidence showing that you didn't exhaust.[486] Sometimes defendants say they are moving to dismiss the complaint under Rule 12(b)(6) of the Federal Rules of Civil Procedure, but include factual materials like documents or affidavits, which cannot be considered on a motion to dismiss. The court may then convert the motion to one for summary judgment,[487] though it is not required to—it can just deny the motion to dismiss.[488] If you are faced with a summary judgment motion, you will have to respond to defendants' factual presentation with your own admissible evidence.[489] This evidence can consist of your declaration or sworn affidavit (not just a statement in a brief or a letter to the court) establishing that you exhausted, or were unable to exhaust for some legitimate reason, and/or documentary evidence such as a final grievance decision showing you exhausted, or a grievance policy showing that your problem is not grievable. You should also look critically at the defendants' evidence and, if it doesn't really show that you failed to exhaust, explain why to the court.[490] If the defendants do not show that it is *undisputed* that you have failed to exhaust and you don't have an adequate excuse or explanation, summary judgment should be denied. That usually means that the issue of exhaustion will be determined at trial, by the jury if it is a jury trial.[491]

Some courts have taken different approaches to litigating exhaustion.[492] The Ninth Circuit has held that failure to exhaust is "a matter in abatement, which is subject to an unenumerated Rule 12(b) motion, rather than a motion for summary judgment."[493] The difference that makes is that courts (not juries) can decide disputed factual issues based on documents, without holding a hearing, under this procedure, rather than leaving factual disputes for the trial.[494]

---

[485]See Woodford v. Ngo, 548 U.S. 81, 101, 126 S. Ct. 2378 (2006).

[486]See Rule 56, Fed.R.Civ.P. Most federal courts have routinely addressed exhaustion disputes under the summary judgment rule. *See, e.g.*, Brownell v. Krom, 446 F.3d 305, 310 (2d Cir. 2006); Brown v. Croak, 312 F.3d 109, 111–12 (3d Cir. 2002); Fields v. Oklahoma State Penitentiary, 511 F.3d 1109, 1111–12 (10th Cir. 2007).

[487]McCoy v. Goord, 255 F. Supp. 2d 233, 251 (S.D.N.Y. 2003).

[488]See, e.g., Dowdy v. Hercules, 2010 WL 169624, *4 (E.D.N.Y., Jan. 15, 2010) (because of "plaintiff's incarceration, his *pro se* status, and the lack of any discovery, the Court declines to convert defendants' motion"); Perez v. Westchester County Dep't of Corrections, 2007 WL 1288579, *3 n.6 (S.D.N.Y., Apr. 30, 2007); Doe v. Torres, 2006 WL 290480, *8 (S.D.N.Y., Feb. 8, 2006). We are not sure why more courts don't just deny the motions to dismiss and leave it to the defendants to make a proper summary judgment motion.

[489]See Ch. 10, § L, concerning summary judgment procedures.

[490]See nn.509–513, below, for cases in which courts have found that defendants' evidence failed to show that prisoners did not exhaust.

[491]Blount v. Johnson, 373 F. Supp. 615, 619 (W.D.Va. 2005) (stating a factual dispute concerning exhaustion "is appropriately submitted to the trier of fact for resolution"), *vacated on other grounds*, 2005 WL 2246558 (W.D.Va., Sept. 15, 2005); Donahue v. Bennett, 2004 WL 1875019, *6 (W.D.N.Y. Aug. 17, 2004); Kendall v. Kittles, 2004 WL 1752818, *5 (S.D.N.Y., Aug. 4, 2004) (holding credibility issues about access to grievance forms and whether the

plaintiff was told his claim was nongrievable "are properly for a jury."); Branch v. Brown, 2003 WL 21730709, *12 (S.D.N.Y. July 25, 2003) (holding that "defendants must show that no reasonable jury could fail to find in their favor on this issue" to obtain dismissal for non-exhaustion), *judgment granted on other grounds*, 2003 WL 22439780 (S.D.N.Y., Oct. 28, 2003); Williams v. MacNamara, 2002 WL 654096, *4 (N.D.Cal., Apr. 17, 2002); *see also* Foulk v. Charrier, 262 F.3d 687, 697–98 (8th Cir. 2001) (resolving exhaustion claim on appeal based on trial evidence); Moody v. Pickles, 2006 WL 2645124, *5 n.15 (N.D.N.Y., Sept. 13, 2006) (resolving exhaustion claim after judgment based on trial evidence).

[492]Some have simply held evidentiary hearings to determine factual disputes about exhaustion, without much discussion of why it is appropriate to proceed in that way. Sease v. Phillips, 2008 WL 2901966, *6 (S.D.N.Y., July 24, 2008); Peterson v. Roe, 2007 WL 432962, *1 (D.N.H., Feb. 2, 2007) (finding officials credible as to failing to receive appeal, plaintiff credible as to mailing it and as to the unreliability of the internal mail); Parker v. Robinson, 2006 WL 2583730, *1 (D.Me., Sept. 6, 2006) (noting plaintiff had objected to hearing in light of finding that factual disputes precluded summary judgment); Montgomery v. Johnson, 2006 WL 2403305, *1 (W.D.Va., Aug. 18, 2006), *report and recommendation adopted*, 2006 WL 3099651 (W.D.Va., Oct. 30, 2006) (holding that evidentiary hearing with disputed evidence established only that summary judgment should be denied); *see also* Johnson v. Garraghty, 57 F. Supp. 2d 321, 329 (E.D.Va. 1999) (holding that disputed claim that defendants obstructed exhaustion merits an evidentiary hearing). *But see* Mitchell v. Adams, 2008 WL 314129, *14 (E.D.Cal., Feb. 4, 2008) (reserving factual dispute for trial because the court lacks time and resources for an evidentiary hearing), *report and recommendation adopted*, 2008 WL 595922 (E.D.Cal., Mar. 3, 2008).

[493]Wyatt v. Terhune, 315 F.3d 1108, 1119 (9th Cir. 2003). *But see* Arias v. Bell, 2008 WL 4369309, *1 (S.D.Cal., Sept. 23, 2008) (where plaintiff alleged he was misled about grievance procedure by a staff member, defendants failed to substantiate their non-exhaustion defense when they failed to present a declaration from that staff member).

[494]Ritza v. Int'l Longshoremen's & Warehousemen's Union, 837 F.2d 365, 369 (9th Cir. 1988) (per curiam) (cited in Wyatt v. Terhune, 315 F.3d 1108, 1119–20 (9th Cir. 2003)).

A number of recent decisions have emphasized the similarity of the "matter in abatement" procedure to summary judgment, stating that credibility issues cannot be decided on motion. *See, e.g.*, Fahie v. Tyson, 2007 WL 3046016, *2–3 (E.D.Cal., Oct. 18, 2007); Williams v. CDCR, 2007 WL 2384510, *1 (E.D.Cal., Aug. 17, 2007), *report and recommendation adopted*, 2007 WL 2793117 (E.D.Cal., Sept. 26, 2007); *see also* Norton v. Contra Costa County Sheriff's Dep't, 2008 WL 4279473, *1 n.1 (N.D.Cal., Sept. 11, 2008) (holding court that looks beyond the pleadings must give the prisoner fair notice of opportunity to develop a record, as in summary judgment proceedings).

Recently, the Eleventh Circuit has adopted this approach too.[495] If you are faced with such a motion in a district court in the Ninth or Eleventh Circuit, you should respond to it the same way you would respond to a summary judgment motion, with declarations or sworn affidavits stating relevant facts within your knowledge, and with documents showing relevant facts, such as the prison grievance policy, grievances you filed, decisions or other documents you received in response, etc.

The Seventh Circuit, by contrast, has rejected the matter in abatement approach and has held that whenever exhaustion "is contested," the district court should conduct a hearing on exhaustion, allowing discovery which will usually be limited to exhaustion, and decide the exhaustion question. Ordinarily, only if the court finds the plaintiff has exhausted will the case proceed to discovery on the merits.[496] The court did not explain whether "contested" means raised as a defense in the answer, raised by motion, or turning on a material issue of fact and therefore not susceptible to summary judgment. The court's expressed concern was to avoid presentation of exhaustion to the jury; it stated that "juries do not decide what forum a dispute is to be resolved in. . . . Until the issue of exhaustion is resolved, the court cannot know whether it is to decide the case or the prison authorities are to."[497]

The Seventh Circuit approach appears to be contrary to *Jones v. Bock*,[498] which held that the PLRA exhaustion requirement does not allow judges to make up new rules based on their policy views. The PLRA does not alter ordinary litigation practices governed by the Federal Rules of Civil Procedure or by general practice unless it says so[499]— and on this point, the PLRA doesn't say anything. As stated above, exhaustion is an affirmative defense, and ordinarily, affirmative defenses are tried along with the merits, by a jury if a jury trial has been requested.[500] A rule permitting only

exhaustion-related discovery until exhaustion is resolved is not consistent with the Federal Rules' discovery procedures.[501] Further, the decision invents a seemingly unprecedented (at least it cites no precedent) means of addressing facts that are essential to the exhaustion decision but are also relevant to the merits of the plaintiff's claim: the jury will find the merits facts "without being bound by (or even informed of)" the district court's determinations.[502] This notion of having a court make factual findings, and then ignoring them in the remainder of the case, is not a usual litigation practice as far as we know. Of course if you are in a court in the Seventh Circuit, you will be bound by these rules. In other courts, the foregoing arguments may help persuade a court not to adopt the Seventh Circuit approach. These procedural issues will eventually have to be resolved by the Supreme Court.

Since exhaustion is an affirmative defense, the defendants will have the burden of proving non-exhaustion as well as pleading it.[503] Establishing non-exhaustion requires three things:

(1) evidence that there actually was an available administrative remedy for your problem.[504]

[495]Bryant v. Rich, 530 F.3d 1368 (11th Cir. 2008), *cert. denied*, 129 S. Ct. 733 (2008). The dissenting opinion in *Bryant* presents arguments why this approach is incorrect. Bryant, 530 F.3d at 1379–82. The court in *Pavey v. Conley*, 544 F.3d 739, 741 (7th Cir. 2008), *cert. denied*, 129 S. Ct. 1620 (2009), rejects it also, as does the district court in *Benavidez v. Stansberry*, 2008 WL 4279559, *6–7 (N.D.Ohio, Sept. 12, 2008) (holding that there is "no such thing as an 'unenumerated 12(b) motion'").

[496]Pavey v. Conley, 544 F.3d 739, 742 (7th Cir. 2008), *cert. denied*, 129 S. Ct. 1620 (2009).

[497]Pavey v. Conley, 544 F.3d at 741.

The Fifth Circuit has very recently adopted a variation of this rule, holding that exhaustion should ordinarily be addressed by summary judgment motion, but if summary judgment is denied, "the judge may resolve disputed facts concerning exhaustion, holding an evidentiary hearing if necessary." Dillon v. Rogers, 596 F.3d 260, 273 (5th Cir. 2010).

[498]549 U.S. 199, 127 S. Ct. 910 (2007).

[499]*Jones*, 549 U.S. at 212–13, 221–24.

[500]*See* Fowler v. Land Management Groupe, Inc., 978 F.2d 158, 162 (4th Cir. 1992); Fireman's Fund Ins. Co. v. Murchison, 937 F.2d 204, 210 (5th Cir. 1991); Katz v. Goodyear Tire & Rubber Co., 737

F.2d 238, 243 n.2 (2d Cir.1984); Maraglia v. Maloney, 499 F. Supp. 2d 93, 94–95 (D.Mass. 2007) (noting that *Jones v. Bock* said to treat exhaustion like other affirmative defenses, and that these are usually jury issues); Lunney v. Brureton, 2007 WL 1544629, *10 n.4 (S.D.N.Y., May 29, 2007) (same), *objections overruled*, 2007 WL 2050301 (S.D.N.Y., July 18, 2007).

[501]The court qualified this holding to say that "in the ordinary case" discovery on the merits should be put off until exhaustion is resolved, but that "there may be exceptional cases in which expeditious resolution of the litigation" calls for allowing some merits-related discovery before exhaustion is decided. *Pavey*, 544 F.3d at 742.

[502]Pavey v. Conley, 544 F.3d at 742.

[503]Roberts v. Barreras, 484 F.3d 1236, 1240–41 (10th Cir. 2007) (citing established rules that the burden of proving affirmative defenses is on the defendant and that burden of proof follows burden of pleading); Anderson v. XYZ Correctional Health Services, Inc., 407 F.3d 674, 683 (4th Cir.2005); Nerness v. Johnson, 401 F.3d 874, 876 (8th Cir. 2005) (per curiam); Wyatt v. Terhune, 315 F.3d 1108, 1117–18 (9th Cir. 2003) (2003) and cases cited; Turner v. Grant County Detention Center, 2008 WL 821895, *5 (E.D.Ky., Mar. 26, 2008).

[504]*See* Brown v. Valoff, 422 F.3d 926, 940 (9th Cir. 2005) ("Establishing, as an affirmative defense, the existence of further 'available' administrative remedies requires evidence, not imagination."); Fernandez v. Morris, 2008 WL 2775638, *3 (S.D.Cal., July 16, 2008) (defendants who failed to show availability of remedies in segregation were not entitled to dismissal for non-exhaustion); Ayala v. C.M.S., 2008 WL 2676602, *3 (D.N.J., July 2, 2008) (defendants who failed to specify what procedures were available were not entitled to dismissal for non-exhaustion); Ammouri v. Adappt House, Inc., 2008 WL 2405762, *3 (E.D.Pa., June 12, 2008) (defendants who provided only "minimal explanation or proof" concerning the relevant grievance procedures did not establish non-exhaustion); Bryant v. Sacramento County Jail, 2008 WL 410608, *4–5 (E.D.Cal., Feb. 12, 2008) (defendants

One federal circuit has held that prisoner complaints should not be dismissed for non-exhaustion without the court having "establish[ed] the availability of an administrative remedy from a legally sufficient source."[505] To do that, the court must examine

whether the remedy actually will address the kind of claim the prisoner raises, and must look at any exceptions to the remedy to be sure the claim doesn't fall into one of them.[506] Defendants must also show what prisoners are required to do in order to exhaust.[507]

(2) evidence that you were a prisoner, and therefore required to exhaust, when you filed your complaint.[508]

(3) evidence that you didn't exhaust. Several courts have found prison officials' affidavits and documentation asserting that a prisoner didn't exhaust to be insufficient or even inadmissible into evidence because they were completely conclusory,[509] failed to set out how records

---

who showed there was a grievance system and plaintiff didn't use it, but failed to show the plaintiff was notified of the grievance system, did not meet their burden on summary judgment), *report and recommendation adopted*, 2008 WL 780704 (E.D.Cal., Mar. 21, 2008); Martino v. Westchester County Dep't of Corrections, 2008 WL 144827, *2 (S.D.N.Y., Jan. 15, 2008) (defendants who failed to identify available remedies or show that they were available to the plaintiff did not establish non-exhaustion); McCray v. Peachey, 2007 WL 3274872, *4–5 (E.D.La., Nov. 6, 2007) (holding defendants failed to show that the grievance policy they relied on was in effect at the relevant time and the plaintiff was advised of it); Farrell v. Hunter, 2006 WL 4756454, *4 (M.D.Fla., Oct. 27, 2006) (holding defendants who failed to place their administrative procedures in the record had not met their burden of showing lack of exhaustion); Haggenmiller v. Klang, 2006 WL 2917177, *3 (D.Minn., Oct. 11, 2006) ("defendant has not established that an administrative complaint procedure exists" at the jail); Conner v. Martinez, 2006 WL 2668977, *2 (D.Ariz., Sept. 14, 2006) ("Defendant bears the burden of specifying what remedies were 'available' to Plaintiff."); Rahim v. Sheahan, 2001 WL 1263493, *6–7 and n.3 (N.D.Ill., Oct. 19, 2001) (holding defendants have the burden of "proving that there is an administrative process that would be able to take action in response to [the specific] complaints—action, that is, other than saying, 'Sorry, we can't do anything about it.'"); Raines v. Pickman, 103 F. Supp. 2d 552, 555 (N.D.N.Y. 2000) (holding "it is [defendants'] burden to come forward to show that an administrative remedy exists for plaintiff to pursue in reference to his claims of excessive force").

[505]Snider v. Melindez, 199 F.3d 108, 114 (2d Cir. 1999); *accord*, Brown v. Valoff, 422 F.3d 926, 940 (9th Cir. 2005) ("Establishing, as an affirmative defense, the existence of further 'available' administrative remedies requires evidence, not imagination."); Haggenmiller v. Klang, 2006 WL 2917177, *3 (D.Minn., Oct. 11, 2006) (noting "the defendant has not established that an administrative complaint procedure exists"); Conner v. Martinez, 2006 WL 2668977, *2 (D.Ariz., Sept. 14, 2006) ("Defendant bears the burden of specifying what remedies were 'available' to Plaintiff."); Baker v. Allen, 2006 WL 1128712, *9 (D.N.J., Apr. 24, 2006) (denying motion to dismiss because medical provider failed to describe grievance procedures existed for its program), *amended on reconsideration*, 2006 WL 2226351 (D.N.J., Aug. 3, 2006); Monroe v. Fletcher, 2006 WL 1699701, *2 (W.D.Va., June 12, 2006) (holding defendants did not show the existence of a "specific, available remedy" against the U.S. Marshals Service); Worthy v. Dep't of Corr., 2006 WL 776791, *4–5 (D.N.J., Mar. 27, 2006) (holding that defendants' submissions did not sufficiently establish available administrative remedies); Jordan v. Linn County Jail, 2006 WL 581254, *3 (N.D.Iowa, Mar. 10, 2006) (rejecting defendants' argument that the plaintiff failed to appeal on the ground that the record did not establish the existence of an appeals process), *report and recommendation adopted*, 2006 WL 1071758 (N.D.Iowa, Apr. 20, 2006); Clavier v. Goodson, 2005 WL 3213914, *3 (E.D.Mo., Nov. 30, 2005) (holding that defendants seeking summary judgment must submit evidence establishing what

grievance procedure was available); Bafford v. Simmons, 2001 WL 1677574, *4 (D.Kan., Nov. 7, 2001) (holding that defendants moving for summary judgment "must identify the specific remedies and provide evidence that they were not exhausted").

[506]Mojias v. Johnson, 351 F.3d 606, 610 (2d Cir. 2003); *accord*, Anderson v. XYZ Correctional Health Services, 407 F.3d 674, 683 n.5 (4th Cir. 2005).

In *Mojias*, the court criticized the lower court for relying on check marks and questionnaire answers on a form complaint to determine exhaustion. 351 F.3d at 609–10. That pernicious practice persists in some jurisdictions. *See* Winfield v. Soloman, 2008 WL 2169521, *1–2 (E.D.Cal., May 23, 2008); White v. Director of Corrections, 2007 WL 4210405, *1 (E.D.Cal., Nov. 28, 2007), *report and recommendation adopted*, 2008 WL 732783 (E.D.Cal., Mar. 17, 2008); Brisbane v. Dewitt, 2006 WL 3541858, *2 (D.S.C., Dec. 7, 2006); Williams v. Uy, 2004 WL 937598, *1 (N.D.Tex., Apr. 30, 2004), *appeal dismissed*, 111 Fed.Appx. 310 (5th Cir. 2004) (unpublished). In *Randolph v. City of New York Dep't of Correction*, 2007 WL 2660282, *7–8 (S.D.N.Y., Sept. 7, 2007), the court points out that reading such brief and ambiguous information to show non-exhaustion is inconsistent with the Supreme Court's holding in Jones v. Bock that exhaustion is an affirmative defense, as well as with the "case-specific" Second Circuit analysis of exhaustion questions, which requires a factual record.

[507]Woodson v. Oklahoma State Dep't of Health, 2008 WL 4365051, *11–13 (W.D.Okla., Sept. 17, 2008) (where defendants failed to show that their revised appeal policy was in place and plaintiff was on notice of it, they failed to show non-exhaustion from his failure to use it); Ayala v. C.M.S., 2008 WL 2676602, *3 (D.N.J., July 2, 2008) (where plaintiff said he was unable to pursue administrative remedies, defendants' failure to establish their policy's requirements made it impossible for the court to assess plaintiff's claim).

[508]Abner v. County of Saginaw County, 496 F. Supp. 2d 810, 823 (E.D.Mich. 2007), *vacated in part on reconsideration on other grounds*, 2007 WL 4322167 (E.D.Mich., Nov. 28, 2007); Duvall v. Dallas County, Tex., 2006 WL 3487024, *4 (N.D.Tex., Dec. 1, 2006); Dutcher v. County of LaCrosse, WI, 2005 WL 2100979, *2 (W.D.Wis., Aug. 30, 2005); Moore v. Baca, 2002 WL 31870541, *2 (C.D.Cal., Dec. 11, 2002).

[509]*See* Ray v. Kertes, 130 Fed.Appx. 541, 543 (3d Cir. 2005) (unpublished) (holding "conclusory statement" that "does not constitute a factual report describing the steps Ray did or did not take to exhaust his grievances" did not meet defendants' burden);

were searched,[510] rested on hearsay,[511] or otherwise failed to establish a failure to exhaust.[512]

In a number of cases, plaintiffs have produced documentation of grievances that prison officials had claimed did not exist.[513]

Owens v. Campbell, 2007 WL 2128244, *4 n.3 (D.S.C., Mar 26, 2007) (where plaintiff alleged he never received a response to his grievance, defendants failed to meet their burden when they provided no evidence about their procedure or what happened to his grievance), *report and recommendation adopted in part*, 2007 WL 2128287 (D.S.C., July 25, 2007); Laws v. Walsh, 2003 WL 21730714, *3 n.3 (W.D.N.Y., June 27, 2003) (holding conclusory affidavit about records search and lack of appeals inadmissible).

[510]Ortiz v. Kilquist, 2006 WL 2583714, *2 (S.D.Ill., Aug. 3, 2006) (noting defendants' failure to disclose record-keeping practices in denying summary judgment); Livingston v. Piskor, 215 F.R.D. 84, 85–86 (W.D.N.Y. 2003) (holding that defendants' affidavits that they had no record of grievances and appeals by the plaintiff were inadequate where they did not respond to his allegations that his grievances were not processed as policy required, and where they gave no detail as to "the nature of the searches . . ., their offices' record retention policies, or other facts indicating just how reliable or conclusive the results of those searches are"); Thomas v. N.Y. State Dep't of Corr. Servs., 2002 WL 31164546 (S.D.N.Y., Sept. 30, 2003) (similar to *Livingston*).

[511]Donahue v. Bennett, 2003 WL 21730698, *4 (W.D.N.Y., June 23, 2003) (holding counsel's hearsay affirmation about a telephone call with grievance officials did not properly support their motion); *see* Mandeville v. Anderson, 2007 WL 4287724, *3–4 (D.N.H., Dec. 4, 2007) (declining to dismiss based on a prison official's characterization of plaintiff's complaints where the actual complaints were not submitted to court).

In *Collins v. McCaughtry*, 2005 WL 503818, *2 (W.D.Wis., Feb. 28, 2005), the court held that a declaration summarizing the contents of the plaintiff's grievances was admissible under Fed.R.Evid. 1006, which allows admission of summaries of voluminous writings, etc., that cannot conveniently be examined in court. The plaintiff disputed defendants' claim that he had failed to exhaust and stated that certain of his grievances did raise the issues he was suing about. The court held that his declaration was not sufficient to establish the content of his grievances, but since the defendants had the burden of proof, they would have to submit copies of the disputed grievances. *See also* Zarco v. Burt, 355 F. Supp. 2d 1168, 1174 (S.D.Cal. 2004) (holding grievance records summary admissible under Fed.R.Evid. 803(7) and 901).

[512]*See* Wyatt v. Terhune, 315 F.3d 1108, 1120 (9th Cir. 2003) (noting that defendants' affidavit does not state whether the plaintiff exhausted his appeals; their "Appeal Record" lacks a foundation and is not shown to be complete); Romeo v. Marshall, 2008 WL 4375776, *3 (C.D.Cal., Aug. 25, 2008) (holding defendants failed to show plaintiff's appeal was late where the time limit was triggered by receipt of the lower level decision and they did not show when plaintiff received it); Franklin v. Butler, 2008 WL 4078797, *2 (E.D.Cal., Aug. 29, 2008) (rejecting claims by an official at one prison without a showing that he had access to information from the prison where the grievance was filed, and claims that no appeal was recorded where the grievance would have been treated through the separate "staff complaint" process under the grievance rules), *report and recommendation adopted*, 2008 WL 4601081 (E.D.Cal., Oct. 15, 2008); Davis v. Michigan Dep't of Corrections, 2008 WL 1820926, *1–2 (W.D.Mich., Apr. 4, 2008) (unauthenticated documents could not be considered on a summary judgment motion); Deemer v. Stalder, 2007 WL 4589799, *2 (W.D.La., Nov.

27, 2007) (declining to dismiss where defendants' affidavit failed to explain source of much information); Davis v. Barton, 2007 WL 2782366, *6 (E.D.Mo., Sept. 21, 2007) and 2007 WL 2782369, *3–4 (E.D.Mo., Sept. 21, 2007) (holding evidence that there was no record of plaintiff's grievance was unresponsive to his allegation that officials refused to process it); DeFranco v. Wolfe, 2007 WL 1704770, *4–5 (W.D.Pa., June 12, 2007) (holding declaration that showed only that the declarant had searched records in her own office did not show that plaintiff had failed to file a grievance), *reconsideration denied on other grounds*, 2007 WL 1810722 (W.D.Pa., June 21, 2007), *vacated on other grounds*, 2007 WL 1830770 (W.D.Pa., June 22, 2007); Thixton v. Berge, 2006 WL 3761342, *3 (W.D.Wis., Dec. 19, 2006) (noting that the absence of an appeal about lack of a working toilet and sink did not establish non-exhaustion, since if he prevailed at the first stage he would have exhausted without an appeal, and he might have filed an appeal about conditions in general including the sink and toilet issue); Ortiz v. Kilquist, 2006 WL 2583714, *2 (S.D.Ill., Aug. 3, 2006) (noting that while defendants said they had no record of plaintiff's grievances, his medical records indicated he was seen because of a grievance); Wigfall v. Duval, 2006 WL 2381285 (D. Mass., Aug. 15, 2006) (citing "unacceptable lack of candor and completeness" in defendants' presentation of evidence regarding exhaustion; they claimed to log all grievances, but evidence suggested use of force claims were not considered grievances); Montgomery v. Johnson, 2006 WL 2403305, *11 (W.D.Va., Aug. 18, 2006) (crediting evidence that policies and practices were not followed and remedies were not in fact available to the plaintiff during the relevant time period), *report and recommendation adopted*, 2006 WL 3099651 (W.D.Va., Oct. 30, 2006); Blount v. Fleming, 2006 WL 1805853, *2–4 (W.D.Va., June 29, 2006) (finding that officials' representation concerning non-exhaustion of certain claims was false); Woods v. Arpaio, 2006 WL 197149, *3 (D.Ariz., Jan. 24, 2006) (noting that affidavit concerning search of grievance records showed that affiant had searched under the wrong inmate number); Simpson v. Nickel, 2005 WL 2429805, *3 (W.D.Wis., Sept. 29, 2005) (holding that defendants did not establish plaintiff's failure to raise an issue in his disciplinary hearing where they failed to submit the statement of his advocate at the hearing); Paez v. Cambra, 2005 WL 1342843, *2 (E.D.Cal., May 27, 2005) (holding the lack of a record of a final level grievance did not establish non-exhaustion since the grant of relief at a lower level may mean no further appeal is required); Perkins v. Obey, 2005 WL 433580, *4 (S.D.N.Y., Feb. 23, 2005) (holding the absence of a computer record did not establish non-exhaustion, since it could reflect the failure to make a record).

[513]Baker v. Schriro, 2008 WL 3877973, *5 (D.Ariz., Aug. 20, 2008); Menteer v. Applebee, 2008 WL 2649504, *6 (D.Kan., June 27, 2008) (finding material issue of fact where defendants said plaintiff filed no grievances but plaintiff produced copies of the grievances and the decisions on them); Marlin v. Dube-Gilley, 2008 WL 2952072, *2 (E.D.Ark., June 24, 2008) (plaintiff produced the grievance form that defendants said they could not find), *report and recommendation adopted*, 2008 WL 2952113 (E.D.Ark., Jul. 29, 2008), *reconsideration denied*, 2008 WL 3992232 (E.D.Ark., Aug. 20, 2008); Hattrick v. FMC-Devens Staff, 2008 WL 687410, *5 (D.Mass., Mar. 5, 2008) (refusing to dismiss where defendants said

Like other affirmative defenses, the exhaustion defense can be waived by failure of the defendants to raise it, or to do so timely.[514] Your claim that defendants have waived

exhaustion will be much stronger if you can show that their failure to raise it timely has prejudiced you in some way.[515] The exhaustion defense, even if it has been technically waived, may be revived procedurally[516] or in the exercise of

they had no record of plaintiff's grievance but he produced other grievances not listed in their database); Bennett v. Douglas County, 2006 WL 1867031, *3 n.2 (D.Neb., June 30, 2006) (noting cases where jail officials had asserted they were "unable to locate" grievances but the prisoners produced them); Lodato v. Ortiz, 314 F. Supp. 2d 379, 385 (D.N.J. 2004) (denying summary judgment where defendants said they had no record of plaintiff's grievance, but they also had no record of other grievances which were undisputably filed).

[514]See Handberry v. Thompson, 446 F.3d 335, 342–43 (2d Cir. 2006) and cases cited (finding waiver); Anderson v. XYZ Correctional Health Services, Inc., 407 F.3d 674, 679–80 (4th Cir.2005); Johnson v. Testman, 380 F.3d 691, 695–96 (2d Cir. 2004) (holding the defense was waived by failure to assert it in the district court); Randolph v. Rodgers, 253 F.3d 342, 348 n.11 (8th Cir. 2001) (finding defendants "waived [PLRA exhaustion] argument on appeal" because it was not raised in the District Court); Smith v. Mensinger, 293 F.3d 641, 647 n.3 (3d Cir. 2002); Dalluge v. Coates, 2008 WL 678647, *3 (E.D.Wash., Mar. 7, 2008) (admission in answer that "the grievance process is completed" waived the defense), reconsideration denied, 2008 WL 828261 (E.D.Wash., Mar. 25, 2008), aff'd, 341 Fed.Appx. 310 (9th Cir. 2009) (unpublished); Mendez v. Kham, 2008 WL 821968, *4 (W.D.N.Y., Mar. 26, 2008) (omission from answer waived exhaustion defense); Becker v. Indiana State Prison/Indiana Dep't of Correction, 2007 WL 2710474, *3–4 (N.D.Ind., Sept. 12, 2007) (denying defendants' request to amend answer to assert non-exhaustion because it was not filed until summary judgment motion was fully briefed); Brown v. Kirk, 2007 WL 1377650, *8 (D.S.C., May 8, 2007) (holding failure to plead exhaustion in answer waived the defense); Webb v. Fox, 2007 WL 1219402, *4 (D.S.C., Apr. 24, 2007) (holding failure to plead exhaustion or argue it in their summary judgment motion waived it); Walton v. Breeyear, 2007 WL 446010, *8 (N.D.N.Y., Feb. 8, 2007) (finding waiver based on failure to plead); Ludy v. Sherman, 2007 WL 320831, *7 (W.D.Pa., Jan. 30, 2007) (holding that court "is compelled to address the merits" of a claim as to which defendants disavowed an exhaustion defense); Holland v. Goord, 2006 WL 1983382, *4 n.2 (W.D.N.Y., July 13, 2006) ("Defendants have not raised [exhaustion] by way of a motion to dismiss, or in their answer, or by the summary judgment motion now before the Court. Thus, the Court finds defendants have waived the exhaustion requirement."); Wright v. Goord, 2006 WL 839532, *5 (N.D.N.Y., Mar. 27, 2006) (holding otherwise well-taken non-exhaustion defense, raised on a summary judgment motion, was waived by failure to plead it or raise it by motion to dismiss); Jones v. Gardels, 2006 WL 37039, *3 (D.Del., Jan. 6, 2006) (holding failure to raise exhaustion before the close of discovery waived it); Markay v. Yee, 2005 WL 3555473, *8 (E.D.Cal., Dec. 23, 2005) (holding defense waived where defendants did not include non-exhaustion in their motion to dismiss), report and recommendation adopted, 2006 WL 403919 (E.D.Cal., Feb. 17, 2006); Wilson v. Hendel, 2005 WL 775902, *3–4 (W.D.N.Y., Apr. 6, 2005) (holding defense waived where it was not asserted after Porter v. Nussle and defendants did not respond to plaintiffs' waiver argument); Leybinsky v. Milich, 2004 WL 2202577, *2 (W.D.N.Y., Sept. 29, 2004) (holding exhaustion defense not pleaded in answer and not raised until discovery was over and case was trial ready was waived); Rahim v.

Sheahan, 2001 WL 1263493, *6–*7 and n.3 (N.D., Ill., Oct. 19, 2001) (holding the PLRA exhaustion requirement is a "non-jurisdictional prerequisite to suit that can be waived where the defendants do not raise the defense in a timely manner," here, two and one-half years); Orange v. Strain, 2000 WL 158328, *10–11 (E.D.La., Feb. 10, 2000) (finding defendant waived the PLRA exhaustion requirement because it was not raised in a timely manner], here, two years), aff'd, 252 F.3d 436 (5th Cir. 2001) (unpublished); Williams v. Ill. Dep't of Corr., 1999 WL 1068669, *3–4 (N.D.Ill., Nov. 17, 1999) (finding that defendant had waived the affirmative defense of plaintiff's failure to exhaust administrative remedies because it had not pleaded the defense and raised the defense for the first time at the summary judgment stage). But see Massey v. Helman, 196 F.3d 727, 735 (7th Cir. 1999) (holding that the filing of an amended complaint by plaintiff revived defendants' right to raise exhaustion and other defenses); Chase v. Peay, 286 F. Supp. 2d 523, 531 (D.Md. 2003) (noting that in the Fourth Circuit affirmative defenses are not waived except for unfair surprise or prejudice), aff'd, 98 Fed.Appx. 253 (4th Cir. 2004) (unpublished).

One federal court had held that exhaustion cannot be waived, and concluded it must be a pleading requirement and not an affirmative defense. Steele v. Fed. Bureau of Prisons, 355 F.3d 1204, 1209 (10th Cir. 2003). This decision is overruled by Jones v. Bock, which as discussed earlier holds that non-exhaustion is an affirmative defense.

[515]See Handberry v. Thompson, 446 F.3d 335, 343 (2d Cir. 2006) (noting that plaintiffs could have timely exhausted and returned to court had the defense been timely raised); Bonilla v. Janovick, 2005 WL 61505, *2 (E.D.N.Y., Jan. 7, 2005) (holding defense waived where it was not asserted for two years and eight months, plaintiff would have to expend additional resources and his long-pending case would be delayed, and further discovery and additional dispositions would be needed to determine whether special circumstances excusing failure to exhaust were present); Thomas v. Keyser, 2004 WL 1594865, *2 (S.D.N.Y., July 16, 2004) (declining to allow assertion of non-exhaustion after 21 months of delay, where plaintiff would be prejudiced by having to re-file after investing time and effort in completing discovery); Hightower v. Nassau County Sheriff's Dep't, 325 F. Supp. 2d 199, 205 (E.D.N.Y. 2004) (holding defense waived where raised only after trial, after 23 months' delay and plaintiffs' loss of opportunity to take discovery), vacated in part on other grounds, 343 F. Supp. 2d 191 (E.D.N.Y., Nov. 1, 2004); Rahim v. Sheahan, 2001 WL 1263493, *6–7 and n.3 (N.D.Ill., Oct. 19, 2001) (noting that one defendant was deceased and would not be able to exhaust and re-file); Orange v. Strain, 2000 WL 158328 (E.D.La., Feb. 10, 2000) (finding waiver where the defense was asserted after the passage of two years and the plaintiff's transfer out of the county jail at issue, presenting "myriad logistical difficulties" to his exhausting), aff'd, 252 F.3d 436 (5th Cir. 2001) (unpublished). Some courts require a showing of prejudice for waiver. See Curtis v. Timberlake, 463 F.3d 709, 711 (7th Cir. 2005); Panaro v. City of North Las Vegas, 432 F.3d 949, 952 (9th Cir. 2005).

[516]If the plaintiff files an amended complaint, the defendants must generally file an amended answer, and they can add an exhaustion defense at that time. Massey v. Helman, 196 F.3d 727

the court's discretion.[517] However, in one case where the defendants sought relief from waiver on the ground that the law had changed to bring the claim within the exhaustion requirement, the court conditioned the relief on prison officials' permitting the prisoner to exhaust late, since the prisoner, too, had relied on prior law.[518]

If a court refuses to dismiss your case for non-exhaustion, prison officials cannot appeal immediately; they have to wait until the end of the case[519] unless the court allows an interlocutory appeal under 28 U.S.C. § 1292(b).[520]

9. Exhaustion and Statutes of Limitations

Courts have generally held that the statute of limitations is tolled (suspended) while you are exhausting administrative remedies, meaning the time does not start to run until you get a final administrative decision. However, courts have not agreed on the reason for this conclusion. Some courts have applied state tolling rules.[521] Some have said that the PLRA itself requires tolling during exhaustion.[522] Some don't make clear why they conclude that exhaustion tolls the limitations period.[523] Since it is possible that a state tolling rule might not protect you, or that a judge might take a different view in a court where the issue is not settled,[524] it is wise to plan on

---

(7th Cir. 1999); Howard v. City of New York, 2006 WL 2597857, *6 (S.D.N.Y., Sept. 6, 2006). One court has held that it was not an abuse of discretion to construe a "notice" by one party that it would rely on another party's exhaustion defense as an amended answer properly raising the defense. Jackson v. District of Columbia, 254 F.3d 262, 267 (D.C. Cir. 2001).

[517]Defendants may move to file an amended answer under Rule 15(a)(2), Fed.R.Civ.P., which says courts "should freely give leave when justice so requires." *See* Stephenson v. Dunford, 320 F. Supp. 2d 44, 48–49 (W.D.N.Y. 2004) (allowing amendment of answer to assert exhaustion 22 months after Supreme Court decision showed the defense was available), *vacated and remanded on other grounds*, 2005 WL 1692703 (2d Cir., July 13, 2005); Stevens v. Goord, 2003 WL 21396665, *4 (S.D.N.Y., June 16, 2003) (allowing revival of waived exhaustion defense), *on reargument*, 2003 WL 22052978 (S.D.N.Y., Sept. 3, 2003). *But see* Mendez v. Barlow, 2008 WL 2039499, *2 (W.D.N.Y., May 12, 2008) (where the court has set a cut-off date for such motions, the liberal standard for amendment of pleadings is inapplicable; waiver enforced based on "undue delay"); Abdullah v. Washington, 530 F. Supp. 2d 112, 115 (D.D.C. 2008) (denying amendment to answer asserting exhaustion defense five years after filing; plaintiff would be prejudiced because discovery was closed and plaintiff might have formulated discovery differently if exhaustion had been asserted); Thomas v. Keyser, 2004 WL 1594865, *2 (S.D.N.Y., July 16, 2004) (declining to allow revival of defense); Hightower v. Nassau County Sheriff's Dep't, 325 F. Supp. 2d 199, 205 (E.D.N.Y. 2004) (same), *vacated in part on other grounds*, 343 F. Supp. 2d 191 (E.D.N.Y. 2004).

In *Panaro v. City of North Las Vegas*, 423 F.3d 949, 952 (9th Cir. 2005), the court held that exhaustion can be raised at the summary judgment stage, even if not pled, as long as the adverse party is not prejudiced. *Accord*, Tyner v. Donald, 2007 WL 842131, *2 n.1 (M.D.Ga., Mar. 16, 2007) (holding defense may be raised at a "pragmatically sufficient" time if there is no prejudice to the plaintiff). Contra, Wright v. Goord, 2006 WL 839532, *5 (N.D.N.Y., Mar. 27, 2006); Mayoral v. Illinois Dep't Of Corrections, 2002 WL 31324070, *1 (N.D.Ill., Oct. 17, 2002).

[518]Rivera v. Goord, 2003 WL 1700518, *13 (S.D.N.Y., Mar. 28, 2003) (stating "In other words, DOCS cannot have it both ways."). The change in law was the Supreme Court's decision in *Porter v. Nussle*, 534 U.S. 516, 122 S. Ct. 983 (2002), reversing the Second Circuit's holding that use of force claims were not subject to the exhaustion requirement.

[519]Davis v. Streekstra, 227 F.3d 759, 762–63 (7th Cir. 2000).

[520]That statute is discussed in Ch. 10, § U.1.c, n.1158.

[521]Roberts v. Barreras, 484 F.3d 1236, 1240 (10th Cir. 2007); Leal v. Georgia Dep't of Corrections, 254 F.3d 1276, 1280 (11th Cir. 2001) (assuming that state law provides the tolling rule); Harris v. Hegmann, 198 F.3d 153, 157–58 (5th Cir. 1999); Hall v. Corrections Corp. of America, 2007 WL 2688880, *1 (D.Kan., Sept. 13, 2007) (stating Kansas tolling law governed even in a *Bivens* action), *subsequent determination*, 2008 WL 53666 (D.Kan., Jan. 3, 2008); Wisenbaker v. Farwell, 341 F. Supp. 2d 1160 (D.Nev. 2004); Howard v. Mendez, 304 F. Supp. 2d 632, 636 (M.D.Pa. 2004) (applying state tolling rules to a case involving a federal prisoner).

[522]Brandon v. Bergh, 2009 WL 4646954, *3 (W.D.Mich., Dec. 8, 2009); Bourguignon v. Armstrong, 2007 WL 2495230, *2–4 (D. Conn., Aug. 28, 2007) and cases cited; Wright v. O'Hara, 2004 WL 1793018, *6 (E.D.Pa., Aug. 11, 2004). The *Brandon* decision states:

> [§ 1997e(a)] unambiguously requires exhaustion as a mandatory threshold requirement in prison litigation. Prisoners are therefore prevented from bringing suit in federal court for the period of time required to exhaust "such administrative remedies as are available." For this reason, the statute of limitations which applied to Plaintiff's civil rights action was tolled for the period during which his available state remedies were being exhausted.

2009 WL 4646954, *3.

[523]Brown v. Valoff, 422 F.3d 926, 943 (9th Cir. 2005); Johnson v. Rivera, 272 F.3d 519, 521 (7th Cir. 2001); Brown v. Morgan, 209 F.3d 595, 596 (6th Cir. 2000) (not referring to state law, but relying on *Harris v. Hegmann*, which did); Drain v. McLeod, 2007 WL 172349, *5 (E.D.Pa., Jan. 19, 2007) ("courts have uniformly held that the statute of limitations on a § 1983 claim is tolled while a prisoner exhausts his available administrative remedies"); Pratt v. New Hampshire Dep't of Corrections, 2006 WL 995121, *6 (D.N.H., Mar. 31, 2006).

[524]In some states, the state tolling rules will *not* toll the limitations period during exhaustion. *See* Braxton v. Zavaras, 2009 WL 5743217, *4-5 (D.Colo., Dec. 11, 2009) (no tolling where plaintiffs did not allege legal disability or mental incompetence; denying equitable tolling as well where plaintiff still had substantial time under the limitations period when he finished exhausting), *report and recommendation adopted*, 2010 WL 420035 (D.Colo., Feb. 1, 2010); Smith v. Wilson, 2009 WL 3444662, *3-4 (N.D.Ind., Oct. 22, 2009) (where state law limited statutory tolling to persons less than eighteen years of age, mentally incompetent, or out of the United States, plaintiff was not entitled to tolling while he exhausted administrative remedies).

There are a very few cases that simply reject the idea of tolling during exhaustion. In *Thomas v. Henry*, 2002 WL 922388, *2 (S.D.N.Y., May 7, 2002), the court relied on a statement in a Supreme

getting your complaint in within the usual time limitation if you can.

If your case is dismissed for non-exhaustion and you want to try to exhaust and re-file it,[525] the statute of limitations may have run by then. Ordinarily your case would be time-barred. However, some states have statutes that toll the statute of limitations for various reasons, including dismissals for reasons not involving the merits of the case. (State tolling rules are applied by federal courts in civil rights actions.[526]) For example, a New York statute says that if an action was timely commenced but was "terminated in any other manner than by a voluntary discontinuance, a failure to obtain personal jurisdiction over the defendant, a dismissal of the complaint for neglect to prosecute the action, or a final judgment on the merits," a description that seems to include dismissal for non-exhaustion, the plaintiff has six months to file a new lawsuit about the subject matter of the dismissed lawsuit.[527] New York state law also tolls the statute of limitations "[w]here the commencement of an action has been stayed . . . by statutory prohibition," which seems to apply to the PLRA's requirement that administrative remedies be exhausted before filing suit.[528] Tolling rules vary from state to state and will not always be helpful in cases

involving exhaustion.[529] In addition to statutory tolling, some courts have applied the courts' own doctrine of equitable tolling,[530] so that time you spend prosecuting an action that is dismissed for non-exhaustion, and further time spent in exhausting administrative remedies after the dismissal, will not count against the statute of limitations.[531]

A court could also grant a stay pending exhaustion in a case that would be time-barred if it were dismissed for non-exhaustion, but most courts have held that stays are no longer permitted under the PLRA and that unexhausted claims must instead be dismissed.[532] However, the courts have not explicitly ruled out the possibility of an exception to the dismissal rule in order to save the meritorious claim of a plaintiff who has some excuse for not having exhausted.[533]

Another approach is for the plaintiff, after dismissal and subsequent exhaustion, to file a motion for relief from the judgment of dismissal under Rule 60(b) of the Federal Rules of Civil Procedure, rather than to file a

---

Court case that "the pendency of a grievance . . . does not toll the running of the limitations periods." Delaware State College v. Ricks, 449 U.S. 250, 261, 101 S.Ct. 498 (1980). But the employment grievance at issue in *Ricks* was not one which had to be exhausted before suit could be brought, so *Ricks* is not relevant to the question of tolling during exhaustion under the PLRA. In *Bond v. Rhodes*, 2007 WL 2752340, *4 (W.D.Pa., Sept. 19, 2007), the court rejected the argument that the plaintiff's claim accrued only upon completion of exhaustion, but failed to note the large body of law concerning tolling. Similarly, the court in *Vantassel v. Rozum*, 2009 WL 1833601, *2 (W.D.Pa., June 25, 2009), asserted that exhaustion does not toll the limitations period, while ignoring all contrary authority.

[525]You may not be allowed to do this because your grievance, too, may be time-barred, unless you persuade prison officials that there is a reason they should hear your late grievance. *See* § D.6 of this chapter, nn.468–470, for more information on this point.

[526]Bd. of Regents v. Tomanio, 446 U.S. 478, 483–86, 100 S. Ct. 1790 (1980).

[527]N.Y. C.P.L.R. 205(a); *see* Villante v. Vandyke, 93 Fed.Appx. 307, 309 (2d Cir. 2004) (unpublished) (noting prison officials' statement that the statute applied to dismissal for non-exhaustion under the PLRA); Rivera v. Pataki, 2003 WL 21511939, *9 and n.13 (S.D.N.Y., July 1, 2003); Richardson v. Romano, 2003 WL 1877955, *2 n.1 (N.D.N.Y., Mar. 31, 2003).

That statute also requires that service of process be completed within the six-month period. However, courts have held that this service requirement is not binding in federal court, since state law governing the method or timing of service of process is not borrowed along with the statute of limitations for federal claims. Allaway v. McGinnis, 362 F. Supp. 2d 390, 395 (W.D.N.Y. 2005); Gashi v. County of Westchester, 2005 WL 195517, *9 (S.D.N.Y., Jan. 27, 2005); *see also* Miller v. Norris, 247 F.3d 736, 740 (8th Cir. 2001) (applying similar statute).

[528]N.Y. C.P.L.R. 204(a).

[529]For example, the relevant Indiana tolling statute applies only if the case is dismissed for reasons other than negligence in prosecuting it. One court has held that failure to exhaust constitutes negligence, so the statute was not tolled and the claim was time-barred in that case. Thomas v. Timko, 428 F. Supp. 2d 855, 857 (N.D.Ind. 2006).

[530]Equitable tolling is a doctrine that "permits a party to sue after the passing of the statute of limitations if the party has acted with reasonable care and diligence." Bridgeway Corp. v. Citibank, N.A., 132 F. Supp. 2d 297, 303 (S.D.N.Y. 2001); *see* Walker v. Jastremski, 430 F.3d 560, 564 (2d Cir. 2005) (tolling may apply where "extraordinary circumstances" prevented a party acting with reasonable diligence from complying with a time limit). Equitable tolling is discussed further in Ch. 8, § N, nn.979–984.

Some courts have applied equitable tolling to the filing of a late grievance. *See n.472* of this chapter.

[531]Wright v. Hollingsworth, 260 F.3d 357, 359 (5th Cir. 2001); Clifford v. Gibbs, 298 F.3d 328, 333 (5th Cir. 2002); Wisenbaker v. Farwell, 341 F. Supp. 2d 1160, 1166–68 (D.Nev. 2004); McCoy v. Goord, 255 F. Supp. 2d 233, 253 (S.D.N.Y. 2003) ("Courts may combine a dismissal without prejudice with equitable tolling, when a judicial stay is not available, to extend the statute of limitations 'as a matter of fairness where a plaintiff has . . . asserted his rights in the wrong forum.'"; suggesting in dictum that time spent in federal court may also be tolled (citation omitted)). Courts are more likely to apply equitable tolling if there is some reason it would be unfair to dismiss your case as time-barred, such as your having made a technical mistake the first time you tried to exhaust. *Contra*, Crump v. Darling, 2007 WL 851750, *13–14 (W.D.Mich., Mar. 21, 2007) (denying equitable tolling to prisoner whose case was dismissed for non-exhaustion).

[532]*See* Neal v. Goord, 267 F.3d 116, 122 (2d Cir. 2001); *see* nn.211–212, above. There is an argument that this holding is wrong under a recent Supreme Court decision. *See* n.213, above.

[533]*See* Cruz v. Jordan, 80 F. Supp. 2d 109, 124 (S.D.N.Y. 1999) ("There is simply no evidence that Congress intended by section 1997e(a) to remove every aspect of the district court's traditional equity jurisdiction" to grant stays.). *But see* McCoy v. Goord, 255 F. Supp. 2d 233, 254 (S.D.N.Y. 2003) (holding that the PLRA removed courts' authority to grant stays even to avoid limitations problems).

new complaint.[534] Rule 60(b) has been used to permit litigants who timely filed and diligently pursued their cases to revive suits that had become time-barred after dismissal in circumstances including those in which the plaintiff was victimized by a change or lack of clarity in the law[535] or simply made an error of law.[536] The fact that a case has not yet been heard on the merits weighs heavily in favor of granting such relief.[537] Although several courts in different circumstances have held that Rule 60(b) cannot be used to reinstate cases after a dismissal for non-exhaustion,[538] they appear not to have addressed whether a plaintiff who has proceeded diligently can use it to avoid being time-barred.

It also would seem logical that a prisoner who has filed an action that will likely be dismissed for failure to exhaust or to exhaust properly could file a second action after non-exhaustion is cured, but before the limitations period

has run, and then move to voluntarily dismiss the first action.[539]

E. Mental or Emotional Injury

The PLRA provides:

> No Federal civil action may be brought by a prisoner confined in a jail, prison, or other correctional facility, for mental or emotional injury suffered while in custody without a prior showing of physical injury.[540]

A similar requirement was added by the PLRA to the Federal Tort Claims Act ("FTCA"):

> No person convicted of a felony who is incarcerated while awaiting sentencing or while serving a sentence may bring a civil action against the United States or an agency, officer, or employee of the Government, for mental or emotional injury suffered while in custody without a prior showing of physical injury.[541]

Note that this FTCA section applies only to convicted felons and not to pretrial detainees or misdemeanants, unlike 42 U.S.C. § 1997e(e).

The statute applies to cases "brought by a prisoner," not those filed after release.[542] Courts are divided over whether

---

[534]That Rule permits relief based *inter alia* upon "mistake, inadvertence, surprise, or excusable neglect," an argument that "applying [the judgment] prospectively is no longer equitable," or "any other reason that justifies relief from the operation of the judgment." Rule 60(b)(1),(5),(6), Fed.R.Civ.P.

[535]*See* North Carolina Alliance for Transp. Reform, Inc. v. U.S. Dep't of Transportation, 104 F. Supp. 2d 599, 605–06 (M.D.N.C. 2000) (granting relief from judgment under Rule 60(b)(6) "catchall" provision so a plaintiff could file a timely attorneys' fees motion after being misled by local rules about the time limit; in the alternative, equitably tolling the statutory limitations period); Allen v. Shalala, 835 F. Supp. 462, 464–65 (N.D.Ill. 1993) (granting relief from judgment under Rule 60(b)(6) to permit timely filing of fees motion rendered untimely by a change in the law); *see also* Bridgeway Corp. v. Citibank, N.A., 132 F. Supp. 2d 297, 300–01, 303 (S.D.N.Y. 2001) (granting relief under Rule 60(b)(6) to reinstate claims of litigant whose foreign judgment on the same subject matter was ruled unenforceable; equitable tolling applied; "Equitable tolling permits a party to sue after the passing of the statute of limitations if the party has acted with reasonable care and diligence.").

[536]*See* Scott v. U.S. Environmental Protection Agency, 185 F.R.D. 202, 204–06 (E.D.Pa. 1999) (relieving plaintiff from voluntary dismissal based on erroneous belief that she could pursue her FTCA claim with other claims in state court; citing excusable neglect provision of rule), *reconsideration denied*, 1999 WL 358918 (E.D.Pa., June 2, 1999); Balik v. Apfel, 37 F. Supp. 2d 1009, 1010 (S.D.Ohio 1999) (granting relief under excusable neglect and "catchall" provisions to re-enter judgment so mentally impaired plaintiff could appeal timely), *aff'd*, 210 F.3d 371 (6th Cir. 2000) (unpublished).

[537]*See* Bridgeway Corp. v. Citibank, N.A., 132 F. Supp. 2d at 301; Scott v. U.S. Environmental Protection Agency, 185 F.R.D. at 206.

[538]Baggett v. Smith, 2006 WL 1851221, *1 (W.D.Mich., June 29, 2006); Okoro v. Krueger, 2006 WL 1494637, *2 (E.D.Mich., May 30, 2006) (refusing to reinstate action after dismissal for non-exhaustion once exhaustion was completed). *But see* Siddiq v. Champion, 2006 WL 958584, *3 (W.D.Mich., Apr. 10, 2006) (allowing supplementation of record so plaintiff could show that he had in fact exhausted).

[539]*See* Rule 41(a), Fed.R.Civ.P., concerning voluntary dismissals. While it would be preferable from the prisoner's point of view just to file an amended or supplemental complaint after exhaustion, most courts have held that exhaustion must be completed before the initial complaint is filed, *see* Johnson v. Jones, 340 F.3d 624, 627–28 (8th Cir. 2003) and cases cited (overruling prior authority), and some have explicitly held that an initial failure to exhaust cannot be cured by filing a new complaint in the same case after exhaustion. See Cox v. Mayer, 332 F.3d 422, 428 (6th Cir. 2003).

[540]42 U.S.C. § 1997e(e).

[541]28 U.S.C. § 1346(b)(2). The FTCA is discussed in Ch. 8, § C.2.

[542]Harris v. Garner, 216 F.3d 970, 976–80 (11th Cir. 2000) (en banc); Kerr v. Puckett, 138 F.3d 321, 323 (7th Cir. 1998); Trevino v. Bandera County, Tex., 2008 WL 4239842, *3 (W.D.Tex., Sept. 15, 2008); Lombard v. Gusman, 2008 WL 2704527, *3 (E.D.La., July 3, 2008); Rose v. Saginaw County, 232 F.R.D. 267, 277 (E.D.Mich. 2005); Black v. Franklin County, Kentucky, 2005 WL 1993445, *4–5 (E.D.Ky., Aug. 16, 2005); Billingsley v. Shelby County Dep't of Correction, 2004 WL 2757915, *7 n.4 (W.D.Tenn., Nov. 24, 2004); Dill v. Oslick, 1999 WL 508675, *5 (E.D.Pa., July 19, 1999); Harris v. Zappan, 1999 WL 391490, *2 (E.D.Pa., May 28, 1999).

A couple of decisions have held that, unlike other parts of the PLRA, this provision does apply to cases filed by released prisoners, because that result is more consistent with Congress's purpose in enacting it. *See* Cox v. Malone, 199 F. Supp. 2d 135, 140 (S.D.N.Y. 2002), *aff'd*, 56 Fed.Appx. 43 (2d Cir. 2002) (unpublished); Lipton v. County of Orange, NY, 315 F. Supp. 2d 434, 456–57 (S.D.N.Y. 2004). However, that is not the way Congress wrote the statute. *See* Kerr v. Puckett, 138 F.3d at 322 ("The statutory language does not leave wriggle room; a convict out on parole is not a 'person incarcerated or detained in any facility who is . . . adjudicated delinquent for, violations of . . . the terms and conditions of parole.").

the provision continues to apply to a person who sues while in prison and files an amended complaint after release.[543] If a case is dismissed because of this statute, dismissal should be without prejudice to refiling once the prisoner is no longer incarcerated.[544]

One federal circuit has held that the statute applies to a claim that arose before, and was unrelated to, the plaintiff's present incarceration, but was filed after incarceration.[545] The same circuit has held that in a case removed from state court, § 1997e(e) does not apply to claims based solely on state law—implying, but not holding, that federal claims originally filed in state court are governed by the statute.[546] We think that is wrong. The statute says that "no Federal civil action may be brought"[547] for mental or emotional injury without physical injury. The term "Federal civil action" is not defined, but we think this phrase refers to a civil action that is brought in federal *court*. If Congress had meant this statute to refer to all claims based on federal *law*, in state as well as federal courts, it presumably would have said so, by using a phrase like "action . . . under section 1983 of this title, or any other Federal law," as it did in the exhaustion requirement.[548] Further, courts have held that the phrase "may be brought" ties the statute's applicability to the time when the case is "brought," *i.e.*, filed.[549] If that is the case, a suit filed in state court is not a "Federal civil action" when brought, so § 1997e(e) should not be applicable to it under any circumstances, even if the case is later removed to

federal court by the defendants. We are not aware of decisions on this precise point.

So far, the courts have upheld the constitutionality of the mental/emotional injury provision, at least as limited to damage claims.[550]

1. What Does the Statute Do?

Section 1997e(e) prohibits "action[s] . . . for mental or emotional injury" without physical injury, but courts have not interpreted it as a ban on entire actions. If you have one claim for mental or emotional injury, and another claim for something else entirely, like loss or damage to property, the other claim is not affected.[551] Also, courts have interpreted the statute to prohibit only awards of damages for mental or emotional injury, and most courts have held it is only a prohibition on compensatory damages. That means you could still get nominal or punitive damages, or an injunction, for mental or emotional injury.[552] (A minority of

---

Other decisions have explicitly rejected this reasoning of *Cox v. Malone. See* Kelsey v. County of Schoharie, 2005 WL 1972557, *1–3 (N.D.N.Y., Aug. 5, 2005) (citing *Kerr*); Rose v. Saginaw County, 232 F. Supp. 2d 267, 277 (E.D.Mich. 2005); Sutton v. Hopkins County, Ky., 2005 WL 3478152, *3–4 (W.D.Ky., Dec. 19, 2005) (following *Rose*). Although *Cox* was affirmed on appeal, the appellate decision in Cox is unpublished and non-precedential.

[543]*Compare* Harris v. Garner, 216 F.3d 970, 973–76 (11th Cir. 2000) (en banc) (holding that released plaintiffs remain prisoners for purposes of § 1997e(e)), *with* Prendergast v. Janecka, 2001 WL 793251, *1 (E.D.Pa., July 10, 2001) (holding that the provision ceases to apply when a post-release amended complaint is filed).

[544]Douglas v. Yates, 535 F.3d 1316, 1320 (11th Cir. 2008) (citing Harris v. Garner, 216 F.3d 970, 985 (11th Cir. 2000) (en banc)). As explained in the next section, dismissal of the entire action may not be appropriate, since some courts hold that the statute restricts only compensatory damages.

[545]Napier v. Preslicka, 314 F.3d 528, 532–34 (11th Cir. 2002), *rehearing denied*, 331 F.3d 1189 (11th Cir. 2003). This interpretation sharply divided both the panel and the court as a whole. *Napier.*, 314 F.3d at 534–37; 331 F.3d at 1190–96.

[546]Mitchell v. Brown & Williamson Tobacco Corp., 294 F.3d 1309, 1315 (11th Cir. 2002). At least one court, however, has applied the statute to a state law claim brought under the court's supplemental jurisdiction. Hines v. Oklahoma, 2007 WL 3046458, *6 (W.D.Okla., Oct. 17, 2007).

[547]42 U.S.C. § 1997e(e).

[548]42 U.S.C. § 1997e(a).

[549]*See* Craig v. Eberly, 164 F.3d 490, 494–95 (10th Cir. 1998); Swan v. Banks, 160 F.3d 1258, 1259 (9th Cir. 1998).

[550]*See* Davis v. District of Columbia, 158 F.3d 1342, 1347 (D.C. Cir. 1998) (holding that curtailment of damage remedies does not "directly and substantially" interfere with the constitutional right the plaintiff seeks to enforce and survives rational basis equal protection scrutiny); Zehner v. Trigg, 133 F.3d 459, 461–63 (7th Cir. 1997). *But see* Oliver v. Scott, 276 F.3d 736, 747 n.20 (5th Cir. 2002) (noting "difficult" constitutional question whether Congress can eliminate nominal and punitive damages for mental or emotional injury).

One circuit has held that the statute would be an unconstitutional limitation on judicial remedies for constitutional violations if it did not allow for injunctive relief and contempt sanctions. Zehner v. Trigg, 133 F.3d at 461–63. Other courts have held that injunctive and declaratory relief remain available without addressing so explicitly whether they are constitutionally required. *See* Harris v. Garner, 190 F.3d 1279, 1288–89 (11th Cir. 1999), *reinstated in pertinent part*, 216 F.3d 970, 972 (11th Cir. 2000) (en banc); Davis v. District of Columbia, 158 F.3d 1342, 1347 (D.C. Cir. 1998).

[551]Jones v. Bock, 549 U.S. 199, 222–23, 127 S. Ct. 910 (2007); Robinson v. Page, 170 F.3d 747, 749 (7th Cir. 1999).

[552]Hutchins v. McDaniels, 512 F.3d 193, 196–98 (5th Cir. 2007); Thompson v. Carter, 284 F.3d 411, 418 (2d Cir. 2002) and cases cited; Royal v. Kautzky, 375 F.3d 720, 723 (8th Cir. 2004); Calhoun v. DeTella, 319 F.3d 936, 941 (7th Cir. 2003); Mitchell v. Horn, 318 F.3d 523, 533 (3d Cir. 2003); Searles v. Van Bebber, 251 F.3d 869, 879–81 (10th Cir. 2001); Allah v. Al-Hafeez, 226 F.3d 247, 252 (3d Cir. 2000); Haynes v. Stephenson, 2008 WL 4368994, *19 (E.D.Ark., Sep 19, 2008) ($2500 in punitive and $1.00 in nominal damages awarded where plaintiff spent five days in isolation as a result of unconstitutional retaliation), *report and recommendation adopted*, 2008 WL 4808848 (E.D.Ark., Oct. 30, 2008); Green v. Padula, 2007 WL 4124830, *3 (D.S.C., Sept. 25, 2007), *report and recommendation rejected in part on other grounds*, 2007 WL 4124663 (D.S.C., Nov. 19, 2007); Williams v. Sharrett, 2007 WL 2406960, *4 (W.D.Mich., Aug. 20, 2007); Donovan v. Magnusson, 2005 WL 757585, *16 (D.Me., Mar. 11, 2005); *see* Calhoun v. DeTella, 319 F.3d at 943 (noting that nominal damages "are awarded to vindicate rights, not to compensate for resulting injuries," and that punitive damages "are designed to punish and deter wrongdoers

courts have said you can't get punitive damages for such injury.[553])

This statute is typically addressed on motions to dismiss and for summary judgment and on initial screening of the complaint, though a few courts have held that it presents an issue for trial.[554] The only federal appeals court to decide the question so far held that the provision creates an affirmative defense rather than a jurisdictional requirement, by analogy with the administrative exhaustion requirement of the PLRA.[555] If the statute creates an affirmative defense, you should not have to plead the existence of a physical injury in your complaint, but the district court should be free to dismiss if the complaint on its face shows that you are a prisoner seeking damages for mental or emotional injury without physical injury.[556] However, courts should not be able to apply § 1997e(e) where the plaintiff simply fails to plead a physical injury without otherwise characterizing his injury. Despite this reasoning, many courts do exactly that.[557] For this reason, if you have suffered physical injury, or another injury that is not mental or emotional, you should probably plead it in your complaint, unless the law becomes clear that you don't need to do so.[558]

_____

for deprivations of constitutional rights, they are not compensation for emotional and mental injury.").

The Supreme Court has held that punitive damages are generally supposed to be reasonably proportional to compensatory damages, though larger punitive awards may be allowed where particularly egregious acts lead only to small compensatory awards. *See* Ch. 8, § O.1.c, nn.554-555. That point would seem to be applicable to cases where the PLRA bars a compensatory award. Tate v. Dragovich, 2003 WL 21978141, *9 (E.D.Pa., Aug. 14, 2003).

[553]*See* Smith v. Allen, 502 F.3d 1255, 1271–72 (11th Cir. 2007); Davis v. District of Columbia, 158 F.3d 1342, 1348 (D.C. Cir. 1998); Page v. Kirby, 314 F. Supp. 3d 619, 622 (N.D.W.Va. 2004).

[554]Thomas v. Thomas, 2007 WL 2177066, *6 (S.D.Ga., July 25, 2007) ("The amount of damages Plaintiff may be entitled to recover is a determination reserved for the trier of fact, not the Court on a summary judgment motion."); *accord*, Johnson v. Raemisch, 557 F. Supp. 2d 964, 975 (W.D.Wis. 2008) (stating that question of damages for censorship of newspaper was for trial, questioning whether substantial damages could be shown); Thompson v. Caruso, 2008 WL 559655, *1–2 (W.D.Mich., Feb. 27, 2008) (plaintiff in First Amendment case would be allowed to present proof and argue for recovery of nominal, compensatory, and punitive damages for all injuries except mental and emotional ones).

[555]Douglas v. Yates, 535 F.3d 1316, 1320 (11th Cir. 2008); *see* § D.8 of this chapter concerning this aspect of the exhaustion requirement.

[556]*Douglas*, 535 F.3d at 1321. *But see* Johnson v. Crawson, 2008 WL 4382810, *3 (N.D.Fla., Sept. 25, 2008) (citing *Douglas*, but holding that "plaintiff neither claims nor alleges facts to remotely suggest a physical injury arising from defendants' conduct").

[557]*See, e.g.*, Oliver v. Wolfenbarger, 2008 WL 4387210, *10 (E.D.Mich., Sept. 24, 2008) (holding plaintiff cannot recover for mental or emotional injuries because he did not allege physical injury in his complaint).

[558]Pleading injuries that are neither physical nor mental/ emotional is discussed in the next section.

2. What Is Mental or Emotional Injury?

The courts have not completely worked out the meaning of "mental or emotional injury." Some courts have interpreted it narrowly, *e.g.*: "The term 'mental or emotional injury' has a well understood meaning as referring to such things as stress, fear, and depression, and other psychological impacts."[559] Courts have also recognized a variety of constitutional injuries that are neither physical nor mental or emotional, and therefore are not affected by the statute.[560]

Other courts, however, seem to assume that any violation of constitutional rights that doesn't result in physical injury or loss or damage to property amounts only to mental or emotional injury.[561] For example, in *Allah v. Al-Hafeez*,[562] the prisoner complained that prison policies prevented him from attending services of his religion, and the court said he couldn't pursue compensatory damages because the injury for which he sought compensation must be a mental or emotional one.[563] Is not being able to go to

_____

[559]Amaker v. Haponik, 1999 WL 76798, *7 (S.D.N.Y., Feb. 17, 1999) (also noting that requiring physical injury in all cases would make the term "mental or emotional injury" superfluous); *see* Robinson v. Page, 170 F.3d 747, 748 (7th Cir. 1999) (restricting the domain of the statute to suits in which mental or emotional injury is claimed).

[560]Courts have acknowledged that § 1997e(e) does not bar compensatory damages for loss of property. Thompson v. Carter, 284 F.3d 411, 418 (2d Cir. 2002); Robinson v. Page, 170 F.3d 747, 748 (7th Cir. 1999). Other such interests that at least some courts have acknowledged are neither physical nor emotional in nature include First Amendment rights, and a claim of exclusion from an alcohol treatment program in violation of the disability statutes, Parker v. Mich. Dep't of Corr., 2001 WL 1736637, *2 (W.D.Mich., Nov. 9, 2001); Fourth Amendment bodily privacy claim and Eighth Amendment conditions of confinement and medical care claims, *see* Waters v. Andrews, 2000 WL 1611126, *4 (W.D.N.Y., Oct. 16, 2000); and freedom from racial discrimination, see Mason v. Schriro, 45 F. Supp. 2d 709, 716–20 (W.D.Mo. 1999). *See also* Lewis v. Sheahan, 35 F. Supp. 2d 633, 637 n.3 (N.D.Ill.1999) (acknowledging right to access the courts); Friedland v. Fauver, 6 F. Supp. 2d 292, 310 (D.N.J. 1998) (acknowledging right to freedom from arrest and incarceration without probable cause).

[561]Worse, some courts just say, *e.g.*: ". . . [A] prisoner may not maintain an action for monetary damages against state officials based on an alleged constitutional violation absent some showing of a physical injury." Charles v. Nance, 186 Fed.Appx. 494, 495 (5th Cir. 2006) (unpublished); *accord, e.g.*, Nelis v. Kingston, 2007 WL 4171517, *6 (E.D.Wis., Nov. 20, 2007) (". . . [U]nder the [PLRA], recovery in prisoner lawsuits is limited where, as here, there is no showing of physical injury."); Wimble v. Cotton, 2007 WL 756597, *3 (D.Vt., Mar. 8, 2007) ("It is well established that a prisoner may not collect compensatory damages for a constitutional violation without showing that he has suffered a physical injury."); Bownes v. MDOC Employees, 2006 WL 3690743, *1 (N.D.Miss., Dec. 12, 2006) (stating "the Plaintiff has not alleged the requisite physical injury that must accompany any § 1983 claim for damages").

[562]Allah v. al-Hafeez, 226 F.3d 247 (3d Cir. 2000).

[563]Allah v. Al-Hafeez, 226 F.3d 247, 250 (3d Cir. 2000) ("Allah seeks substantial damages for the harm he suffered as a

church a mental or emotional injury? It seems to us that freedom of religion is an issue of liberty, not just a matter of mental or emotional injury. Nevertheless, many courts have assumed that infringement on religious freedom as well as other sorts of deprivations of liberty inflict only mental or emotional injury, including claims of unlawful

---

result of defendants' alleged violation of his First Amendment right to free exercise of religion. As we read his complaint, the only actual injury that could form the basis for the award he seeks would be mental and/or emotional injury."). At this point there is a very long list of decisions holding that deprivations of religious rights amount only to mental or emotional injury. *See, e.g.,* Fegans v. Norris, 537 F.3d 897, 908 (8th Cir. 2008) (applying § 1997e(e) to deprivation of religious diet, but affirming "nominal" award of $1500 ($1.44 per affected meal)); Mayfield v. Texas Dep't of Criminal Justice, 529 F.3d 599, 605–06 (5th Cir. 2008) (applying § 1997e(e) to claims of restricted religious exercise); Hendrickson v. Caruso, 2008 WL 623788, *10 n.7 (W.D.Mich., Mar. 4, 2008) (applying § 1997e(e) to deprivation of Satanist texts); Van Wyhe v. Reisch, 536 F. Supp. 2d 1110, 1126 (D.S.D. 2008) (applying § 1997e(e) to removal from religious diet, *aff'd in part, rev'd in part on other grounds,* 581 F.3d 639 (8th Cir. 2009)), *petition for cert. filed,* 78 U.S.L.W. 3439 (January 8, 2010); Sisney v. Reisch, 533 F. Supp. 2d 952, 973–74 (D.S.D. 2008) (applying § 1997e(e) to various religious deprivations), *aff'd in part on other grounds, rev'd in part on other grounds sub nom.* Van Wyhe v. Reisch, 581 F.3d 639 (8th Cir. 2009), *petition for cert. filed,* 78 U.S.L.W. 3439 (January 8, 2010); Nelis v. Kingston, 2007 WL 4171517, *6 (E.D.Wis., Nov. 20, 2007) (applying § 1997e(e) to claim of exclusion from religious exercises); Priest v. Dep't of Corrections, 2007 WL 2728354, *1–2 (N.D.Fla., Sept. 14, 2007) (applying § 1997e(e) to Muslim prisoner's claim of subjection to blasphemy in 12-step addiction program); Gill v. Hoadley, 2007 WL 1341468, *4 (N.D.N.Y., May 4, 2007) (applying § 1997e(e) to deprivation of religious exercise); Perez v. Frank, 2007 WL 1101285, *17 (W.D.Wis., Apr. 11, 2007) (holding plaintiff asserting various religious violations "will not be entitled to compensation for any emotional or spiritual distress he may have suffered"); Quin'ley v. Corrections Corporation of America, 2007 WL 624539, *1 (N.D.Miss., Feb. 23, 2007) (applying mental/emotional injury provision to failure to provide Asaru religious services, refusing to credit claim that migraines, insomnia, cramps and nervous problems resulted); Scott v. Ozmint, 467 F. Supp. 2d 564, 569 (D.S.C. 2006) (holding claim of refusal to recognize religion barred absent physical injury); Massingill v. Livingston, 2006 WL 2571366, *2–3 (E.D.Tex., Sept. 1, 2006) (holding claims asserting various religious restrictions were subject to mental/emotional injury provision); Daniels v. Waller, 2006 WL 763115, *2 (S.D.Miss., Mar. 24, 2006) (holding claim of refusal to acknowledge Muslim name was one for mental or emotional injury).

---

arrest and confinement[564] and racial discrimination[565] among many others.[566]

Many courts have also held that complaints of exposure to unconstitutional prison living conditions—those that deny the "minimal civilized measure of life's necessities"[567]—are claims of mental or emotional injury barred by § 1997e(e) unless there are also allegations of physical injury.[568]

---

[564]Brown v. Sudduth, 255 Fed.Appx. 803, 808 (5th Cir. 2007) (unpublished) (applying § 1997e(e) to claim of false arrest; plaintiff "sought compensatory damages for the sole alleged injury of liberty deprivation. Having not alleged a physical injury, the district court correctly concluded that Brown's claim for compensatory damages must fail."); Scott v. Denzer, 2008 WL 694717, *8 (W.D.Ark., Mar. 12, 2008) (claim of wrongful detention before delayed initial court appearance); Brumett v. Santa Rosa County, 2007 WL 4287558, *2 (N.D.Fla., Dec. 4, 2007) (claim of six months' illegal detention); Layne v. McDonough, 2007 WL 2254959, *4 (N.D.Fla., Aug. 6, 2007) (claim of 25 days' wrongful incarceration); Watts v. Smith, 2007 WL 2257601, *3–4 (N.D.Fla., Aug. 6, 2007) (false arrest), *subsequent determination,* 2007 WL 2462012, *2–3 (N.D.Fla., Aug. 28, 2007); Scott v. Belin, 2007 WL 2390383, *4 (W.D.Ark., Aug. 2, 2007) (detention for 76 days without being brought before a court), *report and recommendation adopted,* 2007 WL 2416408 (W.D.Ark., Aug. 20, 2007); Campbell v. Johnson, 2006 WL 3408177, *1 (N.D.Fla., Nov. 27, 2006) (refusal to accept paperwork and collateral for release on bond).

[565]Jones v. Pancake, 2007 WL 2407271, *3 (W.D.Ky., Nov. 15, 2007) (racial discrimination claim).

[566]Marshall v. Graham, 2009 WL 151693, *3 (W.D.Ky., Jan. 21, 2009) (rough and humiliating searches); Lopeztegui v. Wendt, 2008 WL 1869097, *2 (N.D.W.Va., Apr. 24, 2008) (mishandled mail); Jordan v. Corrections Corp. of America, 2008 WL 687329, *2 (M.D.Ga., Mar. 11, 2008) (confiscation of mail); Jones v. Corley, 2008 WL 616114, *2–3 (N.D.Fla., Mar. 3, 2008) (*Miranda* violation and forced consent to search); Lattanzio v. Holt, 2008 WL 553703, *2 (M.D.Pa., Feb. 27, 2008) (interference with visiting); Johnson v. Georgia, 2007 WL 2684985, *2–3 (M.D.Ga., Sept. 7, 2007) (violation of attorney–client privilege); Johnson v. Burkette, 2007 WL 2406988, *3 (N.D.Fla., Aug. 21, 2007) (claim that defendants' actions destroyed plaintiff's marriage and left him homeless on release); Charest v. Montgomery, 2007 WL 2069927, *6 n.6 (S.D.Ala., July 17, 2007) (strip search in presence of an opposite sex prisoner); Robinson v. Dep't of Corrections, 2007 WL 2107172, *5 (N.D.Fla., July 13, 2007) (stopping of mail and delaying filing of lawsuits as well as deprivation of religious materials), *report and recommendation adopted,* 2007 WL 3010790 (N.D.Fla., Oct. 12, 2007); Ivy v. New Albany City Police Dep't, 2006 WL 3103138(N.D.Miss., Oct. 31, 2006) (being held naked in an isolation cell); Caudell v. Rose, 2005 WL 1278543, *3 (W.D.Va., May 27, 2005) (seizure of legal papers), *report and recommendation adopted,* 378 F. Supp. 2d 725 (W.D.Va. 2005); Ashann Ra v. Com. of Va., 112 F. Supp. 2d 559, 566 (E.D.Va. 2000) (holding that a complaint that a prisoner was routinely viewed in the nude by opposite-sex staff stated a constitutional claim sufficiently clearly established to defeat qualified immunity, but was not actionable because of the mental/emotional injury provision).

[567]Rhodes v. Chapman, 452 U.S. 337, 347, 101 S. Ct. 2392 (1981).

[568]*See, e.g.,* Harden-Bey v. Rutter, 524 F.3d 789, 795 (6th Cir. 2008) (barring damages for three years in segregation); Harper v. Showers, 174 F.3d 716, 719–20 (5th Cir. 1999) (barring damage

Such holdings appear inconsistent with the Supreme Court's statements that it is the objective seriousness of the

conditions, and not their effect on the prisoner, that determines their lawfulness.[569] It is questionable whether a claim alleging conditions that are objectively intolerable is an "action for mental or emotional injury," even if the conditions also (not surprisingly) lead to such an injury.[570]

We think the right approach is that of the minority of courts who say that "the violation of a constitutional right is an independent injury that is immediately cognizable and outside the purview of § 1997e(e),"[571] completely apart from

---

claims for placement in filthy cells formerly occupied by psychiatric patients and exposure to deranged behavior of those patients); Bryant v. Moore, 2008 WL 190462, *2–3 (E.D.Ark., Jan. 18, 2008) (deprivation of food, water, and restroom during trip to hospital); Stainbrook v. Houston, 2007 WL 3244086, *1 (D.Neb., Nov. 1, 2007) (deaf prisoner's complaint of lack of visual alarm system and assistive communications devices); Norman v. TDCJ-ID, 2007 WL 3037129, *6 (E.D.Tex., Oct. 18, 2007) (applying § 1997e(e) to claim of failure to accommodate disability); Jones v. Stadler, 2007 WL 2900495, *1–2 (M.D.La., Oct. 2, 2007) (allegation that bilateral amputee was deprived of his prosthesis, requiring him to scoot across the floor to get to the toilet); Lopez v. S.C.D.C., 2007 WL 2021875, *3 (D.S.C., July 6, 2007) (confinement for seven days without toilet, sink, bed, mattress, soap, toothbrush, running water, so plaintiff had to urinate and defecate on the floor or in trays or cups and was unable to shower); Ashe v. Smith, 2007 WL 1423730, *1–2 (D.S.C., May 10, 2007) (exposure to human waste during cell block floods); Meyers v. Arpaio, 2007 WL 1302746, *5 (D.Ariz., May 3, 2007) (crowding and resulting violent conditions, where plaintiff was not himself injured); Lloyd v. Briley, 2007 WL 917385, *5 (N.D.Ill., Mar. 23, 2007) (confinement in strip cell with no light and no running water); Henderson v. Johnson, 2007 WL 781767, *6–7 (C.D.Ill., Mar. 12, 2007) (setting aside $300 jury award for segregation where plaintiff submitted no evidence of physical injury; reducing punitive damages from $5000 to $500); Ellis v. ABL Food Serv., 2007 WL 196860, *1–2 (M.D.Ga., Jan. 23, 2007) (rusty pipes and chipping ceiling paint in the cooking area, resulting in rust and paint chips in the food); Jones v. Epps, 2006 WL 3196460, *1 (S.D.Miss., Nov. 3, 2006) (exposure to human waste from defective toilets), *certificate of appealability denied*, 2008 WL 1932402 (S.D.Miss., Apr. 28, 2008); Pearson v. Strain, 2006 WL 3858737, *11 (E.D.La., Oct. 30, 2006) (holding thirst, hunger pains, and brief nausea from the smell of feces and urine in the aftermath of Hurricane Katrina did not satisfy § 1997e(e); Stames v. Gillespie, 2004 WL 1003358, *9 (D.Kan., Mar. 29, 2004) (holding allegation that segregated prisoner was denied showers, drinking water, and water for cleaning and personal hygiene and prevented from communicating with lawyer and family barred by § 1997e(e)); Gibson v. Ramsey, 2004 WL 407025 (N.D.Ill., Jan. 29, 2004) (holding allegations of crowding, noise, bad water, and lack of ventilation, unsupported by evidence of physical injury, not to meet the requirements of the mental/emotional injury provision); Hammond v. Briley, 2004 WL 413293, *5 (N.D.Ill., Jan. 29, 2004) (holding that lack of a working light in plaintiff's cell required proof of physical injury to be actionable); Adnan v. Santa Clara County Dep't of Corr., 2002 WL 32058464, *3 (N.D.Cal., Aug. 15, 2002) (holding that prisoner who complained that he was kept in solitary confinement, his hands and feet were shackled, and he was subjected to body cavity strip searches and allowed out of his cell only three hours a week could not seek compensatory damages because he did not allege physical injury); Lynch v. Robinson, 2002 WL 1949731, *2 (N.D.Ill., Aug. 22, 2002) (holding restrictions of segregated confinement not actionable without allegation of physical injury; *see* Jackson v. Carey, 353 F.3d 750, 758 (9th Cir. 2003) (holding that an allegation of placement in segregation without due process might be saved from the mental/emotional injury bar by allegations of inadequate medical care in the segregation unit).

[569]Wilson v. Seiter, 501 U.S. 294, 303, 111 S. Ct. 2321 (1991); *see* Helling v. McKinney, 509 U.S. 25, 35–37, 113 S. Ct. 2475 (1993) (instructing as to objective assessment of environmental tobacco smoke exposure); *see also* Fields v. Ruiz, 2007 WL 1821469, *7 (E.D.Cal., June 25, 2007) (for Eighth Amendment claims, "the issue is the nature of the deprivation, not the injury"), *report and recommendation adopted*, 2007 WL 2688453 (E.D.Cal., Sept. 10, 2007); Armstrong v. Drahos, 2002 WL 187502, *2 (N.D.Ill., Feb. 6, 2002) ("Because the Eighth Amendment is understood to protect not only the individual, but the standards of society, the Eighth Amendment can be violated even when no pain is inflicted, if the punishment offends basic standards of human dignity.").

[570]A few decisions make this sort of distinction. In *Nelson v. CA Dept of Corrections*, 2004 WL 569529 (N.D.Cal., Mar. 18, 2004), *aff'd*, 131 Fed.Appx. 549 (9th Cir. 2005) (unpublished), the plaintiff complained of being provided only boxer shorts and a T-shirt for outdoor exercise in cold weather. The court said: "Even if Nelson's complaint does include a request for damages for mental and emotional injury, it also includes a claim for an Eighth Amendment violation as to which the § 1997e(e) requirement does not apply. In other words, damages would be available for a violation of his Eighth Amendment rights without regard to his ability to show physical injury." Id., *7; *see* Pippin v. Frank, 2005 WL 756155, *1 (W.D.Wis., Mar. 30, 2005) (stating that § 1997e(e) precludes claims for mental or emotional injury but not a claim that plaintiff was "falsely confined" in segregation as a result of constitutional violations); *see also* Aldridge v. 4 John Does, 2005 WL 2428761, *3 (W.D.Ky., Sept. 30, 2005) (stating generally that "damages resulting from constitutional violations" are "separate categories of damages" from physical or mental injuries in case where plaintiff alleged medical deprivations, protracted segregation, and denial of access to courts).

[571]Shaheed-Muhammad v. Dipaolo, 393 F. Supp. 2d 80, 108 (D.Mass. 2005); *accord*, Rowe v. Shake, 196 F.3d 778, 781–82 (7th Cir. 1999) ("A prisoner is entitled to judicial relief for a violation of his First Amendment rights aside from any physical, mental, or emotional injury he may have sustained."); Canell v. Lightner, 143 F.3d 1210, 1213 (9th Cir. 1998); Lira v. Director of Corrections, 2008 WL 619017, *12 (N.D.Cal., Mar. 4, 2008) (allowing claim of eight-year SHU confinement leading to PTSD to go forward); Carr v. Whittenburg, 2006 WL 1207286, *3 (S.D.Ill., Apr. 28, 2006) (stating that specific First Amendment violations may be compensable through "general damages" or "presumed damages" even without proof of injury, though damages cannot be recovered based on the abstract value or importance of the right); Lipton v. County of Orange, NY, 315 F. Supp. 2d 434, 457 (S.D.N.Y. 2004) ("Although § 1997e(e) applies to plaintiff's First Amendment retaliation claim, a First Amendment deprivation presents a cognizable injury standing alone and the PLRA 'does not bar a separate award of damages to compensate the plaintiff for the First Amendment violation in and of itself.'" (quoting Ford v. McGinnis,

any mental or emotional injury. Some courts have said the same thing—that "damages resulting from constitutional violations" are "separate categories of damages" from physical or mental injuries—in cases about unconstitutional conditions of confinement or restrictive confinement without due process.[572]

That approach is consistent with tort law, which is supposed to be the basis of the law of damages under 42 U.S.C. § 1983,[573] but which courts seem mostly to have ignored in PLRA cases. Historically, tort law divided damages into six categories: injury to property; physical injuries; mental injuries; injuries to family relations; injuries to personal liberty; and injuries to reputation.[574] Under that categorization, deprivation of religious freedom or placement in segregation without due process would inflict injury to personal liberty. They might inflict mental or emotional injury too, but that injury would be separate and in addition to the deprivation of liberty, which in itself would be a compensable injury.[575]

You may not be able to get a court to look at your case this way. Some courts have rejected this approach outright.[576] Others, however, don't seem to have recognized the issue. If you are bringing a case about something that did not cause you physical injury, you should make it very clear that you are seeking damages for something other than mental or emotional injury. For example, if you are suing for being placed in segregation without due process for a long period, and you were not physically injured as a result, do not write in your complaint that "plaintiff seeks damages for mental

---

198 F. Supp. 2d 363, 366 (S.D.N.Y. 2001)); Cancel v. Mazzuca, 205 F. Supp. 2d 128, 138 (S.D.N.Y. 2002) (noting that plaintiff "brought this action, inter alia, for alleged violations of his First Amendment rights, rather than 'for mental or emotional injury'").

[572]Aldridge v. 4 John Does, 2005 WL 2428761, *3 (W.D.Ky., Sept. 30, 2005) (ruling in case involving medical deprivations, protracted segregation, and denial of access to courts); *accord*, Mitchell v. Horn, 318 F.3d 523, 534 (3d Cir. 2003) (stating that requests for damages for loss of "status, custody level and any chance at commutation" resulting from a disciplinary hearing were "unrelated to mental injury" and "not affected by § 1997e(e)'s requirements."); Benge v. Scalzo, 2008 WL 2157024, *10 (D.Ariz., May 21, 2008) (allegation of psychiatric neglect were not subject to § 1997e(e)); Wittkamper v. Arpaio, 2008 WL 1994908, *1–2 (D.Ariz., May 6, 2008) (allegations of unsanitary conditions were not subject to § 1997e(e)); Davis v. Arpaio, 2008 WL 1840732, *2–3 (D.Ariz., Apr. 23, 2008) (holding allegations of denial of rights with respect to clothing, hygiene, legal calls, recreation, library access, medical problems, sleep deprivation, etc., were not subject to § 1997e(e)); Cockcroft v. Kirkland, 2008 WL 683446, *7 (N.D.Cal., Mar. 10, 2008) ("the violation of a constitutional right has a compensatory value regardless of what the physical/emotional injuries are"; plaintiff alleged exposure to waste from back-flushing toilet); Harris v. Arpaio, 2008 WL 190399, *8 (D.Ariz., Jan. 18, 2008) (plaintiff could seek compensatory and other damages for delay in medical diet), reconsideration denied, 2008 WL 508651 (D.Ariz., Feb. 21, 2008); Fields v. Ruiz, 2007 WL 1821469, *7 (E.D.Cal., June 25, 2007) (holding prisoner alleging he was confined in a cell with an overflowing toilet for 28 days was not "seeking compensatory damages for mental or emotional injuries"; for Eighth Amendment claims, "the issue is the nature of the deprivation, not the injury"), *report and recommendation adopted*, 2007 WL 2688453 (E.D.Cal., Sept. 10, 2007); Hill v. Arpaio, 2007 WL 1120305, *3 (D.Ariz., Apr. 11, 2007) (holding plaintiff could not recover for mental stress caused by crowding, but could recover for violation of the Fourteenth Amendment); Pippin v. Frank, 2005 WL 756155, *1 (W.D.Wis., Mar. 30, 2005) (stating that § 1997e(e) precludes claims for mental or emotional injury but not a claim that plaintiff was "falsely confined" in segregation as a result of constitutional violations); Nelson v. Cal. Dep't of Corr., 2004 WL 569529, *7 (N.D.Cal., Mar. 18, 2004), aff'd, 131 Fed.Appx. 549 (9th Cir. 2005) (unpublished) (stating, in case involving inadequate clothing for outdoor exercise in cold weather: "Even if Nelson's complaint does include a request for damages for mental and emotional injury, it also includes a claim for an Eighth Amendment violation as to which the § 1997e(e) requirement does not apply. In other words, damages would be available for a violation of his Eighth Amendment rights without regard to his ability to show physical injury.").

[573]Smith v. Wade, 461 U.S. 30, 34, 103 S. Ct. 1625 (1983); Carey v. Piphus, 435 U.S. 247, 257–58, 98 S. Ct. 1042 (1978).

[574]Arthur G. Sedgwick & Joseph H. Beale, Jr., 1 Sedgwick's Treatise on Damages 50–51 (8th ed. 1891).

[575]This idea is illustrated by a non-prison case, *Kerman v. City of New York*, 374 F.3d 93 (2d Cir. 2004). The plaintiff, who had been involuntarily placed in a mental hospital, brought both a Fourth Amendment unreasonable seizure claim and a tort claim for false imprisonment. The court said: "The damages recoverable for loss of liberty for the period spent in a wrongful confinement are separable from damages recoverable for such injuries as physical harm, embarrassment, or emotional suffering; even absent such other injuries, an award of several thousand dollars may be appropriate simply for several hours' loss of liberty." *Kerman*, 374 F.3d at 125. Similarly, in a pre-PLRA prison case about unconstitutional placement in segregation, the plaintiff claimed "distress flowing from the fact of punitive segregation," but didn't submit any actual evidence of distress. The court therefore awarded only $1.00 for distress, but it separately awarded damages of $50.00 a day for the confinement itself, again illustrating the distinction between a deprivation of liberty and the emotional injury that can result from such a deprivation. Soto v. Lord, 693 F. Supp. 8, 22–23 (S.D.N.Y. 1988).

[576]Pearson v. Welborn, 471 F.3d 732, 744–45 (7th Cir. 2006); Royal v. Kautzky, 375 F.3d 720, 724 (8th Cir. 2004) (declining to award a prisoner who spent 60 days in segregation "some indescribable and indefinite damage allegedly arising from a violation of his constitutional rights"). The Seventh Circuit had held before the PLRA was enacted that "[t]he loss of amenities within prison is a recoverable item of damages," which can be proven by testimony concerning differences in physical conditions, daily routine, etc. Ustrak v. Fairman, 781 F.2d 573, 578 (7th Cir. 1986). *Ustrak* seemed to suggest that being subjected to restrictive or unlawful prison conditions is not merely a mental or emotional injury, and is consistent with the argument we are suggesting. However, when this point was raised after the PLRA, the same court said that *Ustrak* did not support that argument. Pearson v. Welborn, 471 F.3d at 744–45.

anguish and psychological torture." You will probably be better off with something like this:

> Plaintiff seeks compensatory damages for the loss of privileges and quality of life in his prison living conditions, and loss of the limited liberty enjoyed by prisoners, resulting from his segregated confinement, in that he was confined for 23 hours a day in a cell roughly 60 feet square, and deprived of most of his personal property as well as the ability to work, attend educational and vocational programs, watch television, associate with other prisoners, attend outdoor recreation in a congregate setting with the ability to engage in sports and other congregate recreational activities, attend meals with other prisoners, attend religious services [and whatever other privileges you may have lost].
>
> Plaintiff does not seek compensatory damages for mental or emotional distress.
>
> Plaintiff seeks punitive damages against defendant(s) [state names] for their willful and malicious conduct in confining the plaintiff to segregation after a hearing in which he was denied basic rights to due process of law.[577]

If you did suffer some physical injury from being kept in segregation, you should still protect yourself (in case the court doesn't find your injury serious enough to satisfy the statute) with a damages demand, similar to the above, that distinguishes mental and emotional injury from other injury. After stating that you sought damages for your physical injury, you would use the same kind of damages demand as above. Just substitute "Plaintiff separately and in addition seeks compensatory damages for the mental or emotional distress resulting from his prolonged confinement in segregation without due process of law" for the second paragraph in the above example. You will thus make it clear that you are seeking compensation for three separate injuries: physical injury; loss of liberty; and mental or emotional injury.

You would take a similar approach in demanding damages for any other kind of constitutional violation that didn't inflict physical injury, like deprivations of religious freedom, freedom of speech, placement in filthy and disgusting physical conditions, etc. There will still be some violations—*e.g.*, the deprivation of psychiatric treatment not resulting in suicide or self-mutilation[578]—that you will not be able to describe as deprivations of personal liberty or of "the minimal civilized measure of life's necessities,"[579] because they really are about mental or emotional injury.

There is no guarantee of success if you do as we suggest. Additionally, even apart from the PLRA, intangible

constitutional rights are very hard to place a dollar value on (meaning that courts will often give up and just award nominal damages[580]), and the Supreme Court has cautioned that damage awards cannot be based on the "abstract 'importance' of a constitutional right."[581] However, courts have made compensatory awards for violations of First Amendment and other intangible rights based on their particular circumstances and without reference to mental or emotional injury,[582] and you should call this fact to the court's attention if prison officials argue that you can only recover nominal damages.

3. What Is Physical Injury?

Prisoners must show physical injury in order to recover damages for mental or emotional injury, but courts have not fully explained what it takes to satisfy that requirement. They have said that an injury "must be more than *de minimis*, but need not be significant."[583] However, courts disagree over where the *de minimis* line is drawn. One appeals court has said that injury need not be observable or diagnosable, or require treatment by a medical care professional, to meet the § 1997e(e) standard.[584] But a much-cited district court

---

[577]In Ch. 10, § R.12, right after n.859, we make a similar suggestion for closing argument at trial. We present a damages demand reflecting these ideas at the end of the model complaint in Appendix 1a.

[578]*See, e.g.*, Hunnicutt v. Armstrong, 305 F. Supp. 2d 175, 186 (D.Conn. 2004).

[579]Rhodes v. Chapman, 452 U.S. 337, 347, 101 S. Ct. 2392 (1981).

[580]Williams v. Kaufman County, 352 F.3d 994, 1012 (5th Cir. 2003) (noting the frequency of nominal awards under § 1983); *see also* Carlo v. City of Chino, 105 F.3d 493 (9th Cir. 1997) (noting nominal award for denial of telephone access to overnight detainee); Sockwell v. Phelps, 20 F.3d 187 (5th Cir. 1994) (noting nominal award for racial segregation). Usually, nominal damages are $1.00. However, there are some cases that have awarded higher sums and still called them nominal. *See* Ch. 8, § O.1.b, concerning nominal damages.

[581]Memphis Community Sch. Dist. v. Stachura, 477 U.S. 299, 310, 106 S. Ct. 2537 (1986).

[582]*See, e.g.*, Sallier v. Brooks, 343 F.3d 868, 880 (6th Cir. 2003) (affirming jury award of $750 in compensatory damages for each instance of unlawful opening of legal mail); Goff v. Burton, 91 F.3d 1188, 1192 (8th Cir. 1996) (affirming $2250 award at $10 a day for lost privileges resulting from a retaliatory transfer to a higher security prison); Lowrance v. Coughlin, 862 F. Supp. 1090, 1120 (S.D.N.Y. 1994) (awarding significant damages for repeated retaliatory prison transfers, segregation, cell searches); Vanscoy v. Hicks, 691 F. Supp. 1336 (M.D. Ala. 1988) (awarding $50 for pretextual exclusion from religious service, without evidence of mental anguish or suffering); *see also* Carr v. Whittenburg, 2006 WL 1207286, *3 (S.D.Ill., Apr. 28, 2006) (stating that specific First Amendment violations may be compensable through "general damages" or "presumed damages" even without proof of injury, though damages cannot be recovered based on the abstract value or importance of the right).

[583]Siglar v. Hightower, 112 F.3d 191, 193 (5th Cir. 1997).

[584]Oliver v. Keller, 289 F.3d 623, 628 (9th Cir. 2002); *accord*, Mansoori v. Shaw, 2002 WL 1400300, *4 (N.D.Ill., June 28, 2002) (stating that injury need not be shown by objective evidence). Another court has rejected an effort to read "long-term" into the physical injury requirement. Glenn v. Copeland, 2006 WL 1662921, *4 (N.D.Fla., June 9, 2006) ("Presumably . . . any physical injury, even if short-term, is sufficient" to meet the statutory threshold.). *But see* Brown v. Simmons, 2007 WL 654920, *6 (S.D.Tex., Feb. 23,

decision held in an assault case that under § 1997e(e) and the *de minimis* standard:

> A physical injury is an observable or diagnosable medical condition requiring treatment by a medical care professional. It is not a sore muscle, an aching back, a scratch, an abrasion, a bruise, etc., which lasts even up to two or three weeks.... [It is] more than the types and kinds of bruises and abrasions about which the Plaintiff complains. Injuries treatable at home and with over-the-counter drugs, heating pads, rest, etc., do not fall within the parameters of 1997e(e).[585]

A number of courts have dismissed identifiable traumatic injuries as *de minimis*.[586] Others, however, have held that relatively superficial traumatic injuries are actionable under § 1997e(e).[587]

_____

2007) (holding burns on face that "healed well" and "had no lasting effect" did not satisfy the statute).

[585]Luong v. Hatt, 979 F. Supp. 481, 485–86 (N.D.Tex. 1997). *But see* Pierce v. County of Orange, 526 F.3d 1190, 1224 (9th Cir. 2008) ("Our court has rejected as overly restrictive the standard for *de minimis* injuries espoused by the Northern District of Texas in *Luong v. Hatt....*"; noting that bedsores and bladder infections resulting from inadequate accommodation of paraplegic's disabilities met *Luong* standard), *cert. denied*, 129 S. Ct. 597 (2008).

[586]*See, e.g.*, Carr v. Horton, 2008 WL 4391156, *1 (N.D.Tex., Sept. 29, 2008) (plaintiff alleged lacerations on two fingers, permanent scarring, and the loss of two fingernails; medical records listed a small superficial laceration; court calls injury *de minimis*); Griggs v. Horton, 2008 WL 833091, *1 (N.D.Tex., Mar. 28, 2008) (wrist abrasion, tenderness to rib cage were *de minimis*); Diggs v. Emfinger, 2008 WL 544293, *4 (W.D.La., Jan. 10, 2008) (allegation of an "open wound" causing "severe pain" did not exceed the *de minimis* threshold), *report and recommendation rejected on other grounds*, 2008 WL 516378 (W.D.La., Feb. 25, 2008); Lyons v. Leonhardt, 2007 WL 2875134, *11 (D.Nev., Sept. 27, 2007) (holding loss of circulation in hands, brief pain in shoulder, and three-day pain in pelvis from use of force was *de minimis*); Brown v. Simmons, 2007 WL 654920, *6 (S.D.Tex., Feb. 23, 2007) (holding facial burns that "healed well" and "had no lasting effect" did not satisfy statutory threshold); Hejny v. Dallas County Jail, 2007 WL 426228, *2 (N.D.Tex., Feb. 5, 2007) (holding bruises, deep scratches, and sore neck from being slammed to the ground were *de minimis*); Green v. McBride, 2007 WL 295592, *4 (D.S.C., Jan. 29, 2007) (holding plaintiff who alleged that he was punched in the face and thrown on his face on the floor and sustained a bruised, swollen, and scraped cheek had only *de minimis* injuries).

[587]*See, e.g.*, Law v. McDaniel, 2008 WL 4371771, *2–3 (D.Nev., Aug. 20, 2008) (bruises from kick to the stomach met physical injury requirement); Jackson v. Armstrong, 2008 WL 3876604, *5–6 (S.D.Ohio, Aug. 20, 2008) (edema of forearm and pain from repeated baton blows were "palpable physical injury" satisfying § 1997e(e)); Sanders v. Day, 2008 WL 748170, *2 (M.D.Ga., Mar. 19, 2008) (holding allegation of kicking and using pepper spray on a handcuffed suspect was not *de minimis*; no details stated); Lathon v. Washbourne, 2007 WL 2710429, *8 (W.D.Ark., Sept. 13, 2007) (holding a bleeding leg, swollen testicles, and injuries to back and

Several courts have held that the physical results of emotional distress are not physical injury for purposes of this provision,[588] which seems wrong: the statutory language implies that mental or emotional injury *with* physical injury should be actionable. Decisions are split on the question whether the risk of future injury meets the § 1997e(e) standard,[589] and also over how closely physical injury must

_____

neck satisfied the physical injury requirement); Edwards v. Miller, 2007 WL 951696, *1–2 (D.Colo., Mar. 28, 2007) (allegation of being punched in the face and bitten on the arm over a 10-minute period, causing damage to forehead and facial injuries, and leaving a lasting effect in the form of severe headaches, is more than *de minimis*); Cotney v. Bowers, 2006 WL 2772775, *7 (M.D.Ala., Sept. 26, 2006) (holding bruised ribs that took weeks to heal could be found not *de minimis*); Oliver v. Gaston, 2006 WL 2805343, *6 (S.D.Miss., Sept. 7, 2006) (holding "numerous swollen spots, bruises and abrasions to the face and scalp" were more than *de minimis*); Evans v. Alameida, 2006 WL 618298, *1 (E.D.Cal., Mar. 10, 2006) (noting prior decision that "abrasions and bleeding" met the standard), *report and recommendation adopted*, 2006 WL 1774875 (E.D.Cal., June 26, 2006); Hardin v. Fullenkamp, 2001 WL 35816398, *7 (S.D.Iowa, June 22, 2001) (holding evidence prisoner was cut and bruised and other inmates' affidavits that they saw him beaten and later limping met the standard).

[588]Davis v. District of Columbia, 158 F.3d 1342, 1349 (D.C. Cir. 1998); Hughes v. Colorado Dep't of Corrections, 594 F. Supp. 2d 1226, 1238–39 (D.Colo. 2009); Darvie v. Countryman, 2008 WL 2725071, *7 n.12 (N.D.N.Y., July 10, 2008) (characterizing "anxiety, depression, stress, nausea, hyperventilation, headaches, insomnia, dizziness, appetite loss, weight loss, etc.," as "essentially emotional in nature"), *report and recommendation adopted*, 2008 WL 3286250 (N.D.N.Y., Aug. 7, 2008); McCloud v. Tureglio, 2008 WL 1772305, *9 (N.D.N.Y., Apr. 15, 2008); Martin v. Vt. Dep't of Corr., 2005 WL 1278119 (D.Vt., May 25, 2005) (stating that "physical manifestations of stress are insufficient to establish physical injury under the PLRA"), *report and recommendation adopted*, 2005 WL 2001749 (D.Vt., Aug. 19, 2005); Minifield v. Butikofer, 298 F. Supp. 2d 900, 905 (N.D.Cal. 2004) ("Physical symptoms that are not sufficiently distinct from a plaintiff's allegations of emotional distress do not qualify as a prior showing of physical injury."); Todd v. Graves, 217 F. Supp. 2d 958, 960 (S.D.Iowa 2002) (holding that allegations of stress-related aggravation of hypertension, dizziness, insomnia and loss of appetite were not actionable); Cannon v. Burkybile, 2002 WL 448988, *4 (N.D.Ill., Mar. 22, 2002); McGrath v. Johnson, 67 F. Supp. 2d 499, 508 (E.D.Pa. 1999). *But see* Montemayor v. Fed. Bureau of Prisons, 2005 WL 3274508, *5 (D.D.C., Aug. 25, 2005) (holding that a heart attack resulting from physical and emotional stress caused by treatment in prison would meet the physical injury requirement); Perkins v. Ark. Dep't of Corr., 165 F.3d 803, 807–08 (8th Cir. 1999) (remanding question whether an allegation of mental anguish so severe that it caused physical deterioration and would shorten plaintiff's life was sufficient under § 1997e(e)).

[589]*Compare* Zehner v. Trigg, 133 F.3d 459 (7th Cir. 1997) (holding exposure to asbestos without claim of damages for physical injury is not actionable); Smith v. U.S., 2007 WL 2155651, *4 (D.Kan., July 26, 2007) (same as *Zehner*), *reconsideration denied*, 2007 WL 4570888 (D.Kan., Dec. 27, 2007), *motion to amend denied*, 2008 WL 1735190 (D.Kan., Apr. 10, 2008); Kutch v. Valdez, 2006 WL 3487657, *4 (N.D.Tex., Dec. 4, 2006) (holding potential future complications of untreated high blood pressure are not physical

be connected to mental or emotional injury for the latter to be actionable.[590] Self-inflicted injuries may satisfy the § 1997e(e) requirement.[591]

A variety of injuries short of visible damage to body parts have been held to satisfy the physical injury requirement. Most courts, but not all, have held that sexual assault is a physical injury.[592] Other injuries that at least some courts have held satisfy the physical injury requirement include:

- loss of consciousness[593]
- bodily disturbances resulting from medication withdrawal, overdose or error[594]

---

[590]*Compare* Phillips v. Steinbeck, 2008 WL 821789, *21 (D.Colo., Mar. 26, 2008) (plaintiff who alleged he was labelled an informant by staff and assaulted by inmates in retaliation for complaints about staff could seek damages for both Eighth Amendment and access to courts claims based on injuries from assault); Root v. Watkins, 2007 WL 5029118, *8 (D.Colo., Aug. 28, 2007) (plaintiff alleged that one defendant refused to do anything about loud prisoner conduct, and when he complained to another defendant, he was labelled a snitch and then attacked by other prisoners; he could seek damages against both defendants), *objections overruled*, 2008 WL 793513 (D.Colo., Mar. 19, 2008); Fogle v. Pierson, 2008 WL 821803, *9 (D.Colo., Mar. 26, 2008) (prisoner complaining of injury from protracted segregation could seek damages both for due process claim for segregation placement and claim of denial of access to courts which arguably prolonged the confinement); Noguera v. Hasty, 2001 WL 243535 (S.D.N.Y., Mar. 12, 2001) (holding that allegations of retaliation for reporting a rape by an officer were closely enough related to the rape that a separate physical injury need not be shown), *with* Purvis v. Johnson, 78 Fed.Appx. 377 (5th Cir. 2003) (unpublished) (holding that a prisoner alleging assault by a staff member could not also pursue a claim for obstruction of the post-assault investigation); Johnson v. Dallas County Sheriff Dep't, 2008 WL 2378269, *3 (N.D.Tex., June 6, 2008) (alleged sexual assault was a physical injury, but conduct of officials after the assault did not inflict injury and was not actionable); Slusher v. Samu, 2006 WL 3371636, *13 (D.Colo., Nov. 21, 2006) (holding that a prisoner with multiple claims could only recover damages for the one claim as to which he alleged physical injury).

In *Tate v. Alamance County Jail*, 2007 WL 2156319 (M.D.N.C., July 26, 2007), the plaintiff alleged that defendants had denied him pain medication after surgery. The court rejected defendants' argument that the plaintiff "must allege that there was a physical injury which resulted from the failure to provide requested medication. However, the clear words of the statute only state that the mental or emotional injury must have a prior physical injury component to it, not that the mental or emotional injury resulted in a physical injury." Here the "prior physical injury component" was the surgery. 2007 WL 2156319, *1.

[591]Scarver v. Litscher, 371 F. Supp. 2d 986, 997–98 (W.D.Wis. 2005) (citing self-inflicted overdose of Thorazine and self-inflicted razor cut in holding prisoner with mental illness had alleged

---

injury under statute) *with* West v. Walker, 2007 WL 2608789, *6 (N.D.Ill., Sept. 4, 2007) (holding prisoner may pursue claim of "documentably increased likelihood of future harm" from second-hand smoke); Pack v. Artuz, 348 F. Supp. 2d 63, 74 n.12 (S.D.N.Y. 2004) (holding proof of asbestos exposure posing a serious risk of harm would establish an Eighth Amendment violation entitling the plaintiff to nominal damages regardless of present injury); Crawford v. Artuz, 1999 WL 435155 (S.D.N.Y., June 24, 1999) (holding that a claim for asbestos exposure without present physical injury was not barred by the statute because it did not assert mental or emotional injury); *see also* Robinson v. Page, 170 F.3d 747, 749 (7th Cir. 1999) (leaving open question whether required physical injury "must be a palpable, current injury (such as lead poisoning) or a present condition not injurious in itself but likely to ripen eventually into a palpable physical injury").

---

physical injury), *aff'd on other grounds*, 434 F.3d 972 (7th Cir. 2006).

[592]*See* Liner v. Goord, 196 F.3d 132, 135 (2d Cir. 1999) (holding that "alleged sexual assaults," also described as "intrusive body searches," "qualify as physical injuries as a matter of common sense" and "would constitute more than *de minimis* injury"); Duncan v. Magelessen, 2008 WL 2783487, *2 (D.Colo., July 15, 2008) ("unwanted sexual contact, alone, is a physical injury for which there may be compensation"); Kemner v. Hemphill, 199 F. Supp. 2d 1264, 1270 (N.D.Fla. 2002) (holding that sexual assault, "even if considered to be *de minimis* from a purely physical perspective, is plainly 'repugnant to the conscience of mankind.' Surely Congress intended the concept of 'physical injury' in § 1997e(e) to cover such a repugnant use of physical force."); Nunn v. Mich. Dep't of Corr., 1997 WL 33559323, *4 (E.D.Mich., 1997); *see also* Boxer X v. Harris, 2007 WL 1731436, *2 (S.D.Ga., June 4, 2007) (declining to dismiss claim that officer required prisoner to masturbate for her, citing his argument that "masturbation can be painful when performed unwillingly"), *referred*, 2007 WL 1812631, *2 (S.D.Ga., June 18, 2007); Knight v. Simpson, 2008 WL 1968770, *3 n.6 (M.D.Pa., Apr. 3, 2008) (stating sexual assault plaintiff alleged physical injury; no explanation), *report and recommendation adopted in pertinent part*, 2008 WL 1968762 (M.D.Pa., May 2, 2008); Ogden v. Chesney, 2003 WL 22225763 (E.D.Pa., Sept. 17, 2003) (holding plaintiff's allegation that "prison officials allowed a drug dog to sniff and lick his genitals during a strip search" was sufficient to withstand summary judgment). *But see* Jones v. Gudmundson, 2008 WL 651994, *3 (D.Minn., Mar. 7, 2008) (holding male prisoner's complaint of sexual relationship with female employee was precluded absent physical injury; nothing indicates the relationship was nonconsensual or the plaintiff suffered any non-physical harm); Cobb v. Kelly, 2007 WL 2159315, *1 (N.D.Miss., July 26, 2007) (holding male prisoner's allegation that female officer "reached her hand between his legs and rubbed his genitals" was not a physical injury under § 1997e(e)); Smith v. Shady, 2006 WL 314514, *2 (M.D.Pa., Feb. 9, 2006) (holding allegation that officer grabbed prisoner's penis and held it in her hand was *de minimis* under § 1997e(e)); Hancock v. Payne, 2006 WL 21751, *1, 3 (S.D.Miss., Jan. 4, 2006) (holding prisoners who alleged they were "sexually battered . . . by sodomy" did not satisfy § 1997e(e)). Non-physical sexual harassment is, of course, not physical injury. Gillespie v. Smith, 2007 WL 2002724, *1, 4 (N.D.Iowa, July 3, 2007); Maxton v. Quick, 2007 WL 1486142, *3 (D.S.C., May 18, 2007).

[593]Waggoner v. Comanche County Detention Center, 2007 WL 2068661, *4 (W.D.Okla., July 17, 2007) (holding plaintiff rendered unconscious by a shock shield after being pepper-sprayed, shaken, and punched sufficiently supported a showing of physical injury).

[594]Scarver v. Litscher, 371 F. Supp. 2d 986, 997–98 (W.D.Wis. 2005) (citing self-inflicted overdose of Thorazine as well as

- the consequences of failure to treat illness or injury, both immediate[595] and longer term or

---

self-inflicted razor cut in holding prisoner with mental illness had alleged physical injury), *aff'd*, 434 F.3d 972 (7th Cir. 2006); Ziemba v. Armstrong, 2004 WL 78063, *3 (D.Conn., Jan. 14, 2004) (holding that allegation of withdrawal, panic attacks, pain similar to a heart attack, difficulty breathing and profuse sweating, resulting from withdrawal of psychiatric medication, met the physical injury requirement); Wolfe v. Horn, 2001 WL 76332, *10 (E.D.Pa., Jan. 29, 2001) (holding physical consequences of withdrawal of hormone treatment to a pre-operative transsexual met physical injury requirement). *But see* Johnson v. Rawers, 2008 WL 752586, *5 (E.D.Cal., Mar. 19, 2008) (claim that medications were administered in a crushed form, causing plaintiff to feel depressed, anxious, nauseous, and paranoid, did not satisfy the statute), *report and recommendation adopted*, 2008 WL 2219307 (E.D.Cal., May 27, 2008); Robinson v. Johnson, 2008 WL 394977, *5 (E.D.Ark., Feb. 12, 2008) (allegation that plaintiff was forced to have an unnecessary PPD, which made his arm hurt, and take a second course of INH treatment, did not constitute injury); Chatham v. Adcock, 2007 WL 2904117, *16 (N.D.Ga., Sept. 28, 2007) (holding hallucinations, anxiety, and nightmares resulting from denial of Xanax did not meet physical injury requirement), *aff'd*, 334 Fed.Appx. 281 (11th Cir. 2009) (unpublished); Granger v. Naphcare Medical Contractor, 2007 WL 2825915, *4 (E.D.Tex., Sept. 26, 2007) (allegation of nosebleed and blurred vision from medication error did not meet the physical injury standard); Ladd v. Dietz, 2007 WL 160762, *1 (D.Neb., Jan. 17, 2007) (holding pain resulting from placing ear medication in plaintiff's eye was "not enough" to constitute physical injury); Morgan v. Dallas County Sheriff Dep't, 2005 WL 57282, *2 (N.D.Tex., Jan. 11, 2005) (holding that a complaint of "undue pain . . . on a regular basis" resulting from denial of medication is insufficient to establish physical injury), *report and recommendation adopted*, 2005 WL 2075796 (N.D.Tex., Aug. 26, 2005); Davis v. Bowles, 2004 WL 1205182, *2 (N.D.Tex., June 1, 2004) (holding an increase in blood pressure to 180/108 and headaches resulting from withholding of prescribed medication did not meet the physical injury threshold), *report and recommendation adopted*, 2004 WL 1381045 (N.D.Tex., June 18, 2004).

[595]*See* Perez v. U.S., 330 Fed.Appx. 388, 389-90 (3d Cir. 2009) (unpublished) (holding claim of untreated asthma attack resulting in "dizziness, headaches, weakness, back pain, and nausea," which required steroids, prescription medication, and other medical treatment to recover, presented a material issue of fact under the *de minimis* standard); Munn v. Toney, 433 F.3d 1087, 1089 (8th Cir. 2006) (holding claim of headaches, cramps, nosebleeds, and dizziness resulting from deprivation of blood pressure medication "does not fail . . . for lack of physical injury"); DeRoche v. Funkhouse, 2008 WL 881286, *7 (D.Ariz., Mar. 28, 2008) (further liver damage and daily pain, swelling, nausea and hypertension from lack of treatment for Hepatitis C satisfied the physical injury requirement); Maddle v. Correctional Medical Services, Inc., 2008 WL 839715, *6 (M.D.Tenn., Mar. 26, 2008) (presence of a thyroid mass requiring testing and then surgery satisfied the physical injury requirement, notwithstanding that the surgery was successful even though delayed; plaintiff complained of pain and complications including bleeding, nausea, and difficulties swallowing, eating, and breathing); Custard v. Young, 2008 WL 791954, *10 (D.Colo., Mar. 20, 2008) ("pain, bleeding, swelling, scarring" to gums and a significant loss of weight resulting from denial of denture adhesive, dental care or

a soft diet satisfied § 1997e(e) at the pleading stage); Perrey v. Donahue, 2007 WL 4277621, *6 (N.D.Ind., Dec. 3, 2007) (holding complaint of "prolonged and extreme pain, constant malaise, body soreness and aches, diarrhea, headaches, [and] loss of appetite" met the physical injury pleading standard); Boles v. Dansdill, 2007 WL 2770473, *21 (D.Colo., Sept. 20, 2007) (holding allegation that denial of medical care made plaintiff "physically ill" satisfied physical injury standard at pleading stage); Reeves v. Wallington, 2007 WL 1016979, *2 (E.D.Mich., Mar. 29, 2007) (holding standard met by shortness of breath, chest pain, hospitalization for observation and to rule out myocardial infarction following delay in receiving medication and exposure to chemical agents), *subsequent determination*, 2007 WL 2300798 (E.D.Mich., Aug. 7, 2007); Such v. Vincent, 2007 WL 906170, *3–5 (W.D.Pa., Mar. 22, 2007) (holding standard met by allegations that refusal to permit paralyzed prisoner to self-catheterize increased urinary tract infections, pain from being unable to urinate as needed, and incontinence); Clifton v. Eubank, 418 F. Supp. 2d 1243, 1248 (D. Colo. 2006) (addressing "prolonged" pain attendant upon labor and stillbirth), *on reconsideration on other grounds*, 2006 WL 893600 (D.Colo., Apr. 5, 2006); Fleming v. Clarke, 2005 WL 2170093, *2 (D.Neb., Sept. 6, 2005) (holding swelling, pain, and deterioration resulting from denial of prescribed knee brace met physical injury requirement); Martin v. Gold, 2005 WL 1862116, *9 (D.Vt., Aug. 4, 2005) (holding pain resulting from lack of dentures met physical injury requirement, though resulting headaches and hunger pains might not). *But see* Tuft v. Chaney, 2007 WL 3378347, *3 (S.D.Tex., Nov. 9, 2007) (holding complaints of "generalized 'fatigue' and 'stress'" resulting from MRSA and Hepatitis C were not physical injuries); Williams v. Caruso, 2007 WL 2710109, *7–8 (E.D.Mich., Sept. 13, 2007) (holding pain and suffering resulting from failure to provide a diet necessitated by kidney disease was not compensable); Mitchell v. Valdez, 2007 WL 1228061, *2 (N.D.Tex., Apr. 25, 2007) (holding chronic headaches causing extreme pain do not meet physical injury requirement); Giddings v. Valdez, 2007 WL 1201577, *3 (N.D.Tex., Apr. 24, 2007) (holding pain from two months' lack of treatment for a degenerative joint disease did not satisfy the physical injury requirement); Smith v. Dallas County Jail System, 2007 WL 1140215, *2 (N.D.Tex., Apr. 16, 2007) (staph infections did not satisfy physical injury requirement); Calderon v. Foster, 2007 WL 1010383, *8 (S.D.W.Va., Mar. 30, 2007) (pain, standing alone, is *de minimis*; plaintiff alleged two hours of chest pain which was resolved with nitroglycerine), *aff'd*, 264 Fed.Appx. 286 (4th Cir. 2008) (unpublished); Purtell v. Corrections Corp. of America, 2007 WL 1464376, *2 (N.D.Miss., Mar. 26, 2007) (severe headache for a day and a half was *de minimis*); Cooper v. Dretke, 2006 WL 3447679, *3 (S.D.Tex., Nov. 21, 2006) (holding that failure to repair a hearing aid that the prisoner used to alleviate symptoms associated with tinnitus did not show required "specific physical injury"); Cranford v. Payne, 2006 WL 2701273, *7 (S.D.Miss., Aug. 23, 2006) (holding a scalp infection is *de minimis*); Williams v. Smith, 2006 WL 938980, *2 (W.D.Ky., Apr. 10, 2006) (holding asthma attack requiring hospitalization was *de minimis*); Olivas v. Corrections Corp. of America, 408 F. Supp. 2d 251, 254, 259 (N.D.Tex. 2006) (resulting from delay in treatment of broken teeth with exposed nerve, resulting in pain reported as 10 on a scale of 1–10, did not meet physical injury requirement).

- prospective[596]
- denial of adequate food[597]
- food contamination or poisoning[598]
- denial of exercise[599]

- exposure to harmful substances[600]

---

[596]Young v. Beard, 2007 WL 1549453, *4 (W.D.Pa., May 22, 2007) (holding allegation that plaintiff sought damages for present and future injury from denial of cholesterol medication, and of testing of blood pressure, diabetes, and cholesterol more often than every six months, sufficed at the pleading stage), *vacated on other grounds*, 2007 WL 2012604 (W.D.Pa., July 3, 2007); Mejia v. Goord, 2005 WL 2179422, *5 (N.D.N.Y., Aug. 16, 2005) (denying summary judgment where prisoner was denied a low fat diet for potentially debilitating coronary condition); Perkins v. Kan. Dep't of Corr., 2004 WL 825299, *4 n.2 (D.Kan., Mar. 29, 2004) (holding allegation of progression of HIV infection met physical injury standard). *But see* Cotter v. Dallas County Sheriff, 2006 WL 1652714, *3–4 (N.D.Tex., June 15, 2006) (holding staphylococcus exposure and a "dormant" staph infection were *de minimis*).

[597]Williams v. Humphreys, 2005 WL 4905109, *7 (S.D.Ga., Sept. 13, 2005) (holding allegation of 12 pounds weight loss, abdominal pain, and nausea resulting from denial of pork substitute at meals sufficiently alleged physical injury). *But see* Davis v. District of Columbia, 158 F.3d 1342, 1394 (D.C. Cir.1998) (holding weight loss resulting from disclosure of HIV-positive status did not meet the physical injury standard); Linehan v. Crosby, 2008 WL 3889604, *13 (N.D.Fla., Aug. 20, 2008) (weight loss from denial of a kosher diet did not meet requirement); Bradford v. Caruso, 2008 WL 3843291, *3 (E.D.Mich., Aug. 14, 2008) (same as *Linehan*); Green v. Padula, 2007 WL 4124830, *2–3 (D.S.C., Sept. 25, 2007) (holding three-day denial of food and several hours' restraint during strip cell placement did not meet the physical injury requirement), *report and recommendation rejected in part on other grounds*, 2007 WL 4124663 (D.S.C., Nov. 19, 2007); Ghashiyah v. Wisconsin Dep't of Corrections, 2006 WL 2845701, *11 (E.D.Wis., Sept. 29, 2006) (holding 20–30 pound weight loss was not a physical injury).

[598]Bond v. Rhodes, 2006 WL 1617892, *3 (W.D.Pa., June 8, 2006) (holding allegation of serious diarrhea resulting from food tampering satisfied the requirement at the pleading stage); Young v. Medden, 2006 WL 456274, *20 (E.D.Pa., Feb. 23, 2006) (holding allegation that prison staff put substances in prisoner's food that made him urinate constantly "arguably demonstrate more than *de minimis* physical injury"); Gil v. U.S., 2006 WL 385088, *3 (M.D.Fla., Feb. 17, 2006) (awarding "intangible damages for pain and suffering, inconvenience, and loss of capacity for enjoyment of life" to prisoner who suffered food poisoning from tainted food). *But see* Mayes v. Travis State Jail, 2007 WL 1888828, *4–5 (W.D.Tex., June 29, 2007) (holding diarrhea allegedly caused by spoiled food was *de minimis*); Watkins v. Trinity Service Group Inc., 2006 WL 3408176, *4 (M.D.Fla., Nov. 27, 2006) (holding diarrhea, vomiting, cramps, nausea, and headaches from food poisoning were *de minimis*; noting a free person would not have to visit an emergency room or go to a doctor because of them); Cotter v. Dallas County Sheriff, 2006 WL 1652714, *3–4 (N.D.Tex., June 15, 2006) (holding two incidents of vomiting and diarrhea were *de minimis*).

[599]Williams v. Goord, 2000 WL 1051874, *8 n.4 (S.D.N.Y., July 28, 2000) (holding allegation of 28-day denial of exercise sufficiently alleged physical injury).

[600]Smith v. Leonard, 244 Fed.Appx. 583, 584 (5th Cir. 2007) (unpublished) (stating headaches, sinus problems, trouble breathing, blurred vision, irritated eyes, and fatigue, allegedly from exposure to toxic mold, might satisfy § 1997e(e) standard); Enigwe v. Zenk, 2006 WL 2654985, *5 (E.D.N.Y. Sept. 15, 2006) (declining to dismiss emotional injury claims in light of allegation of exposure to environmental tobacco smoke resulting in dizziness, uncontrollable coughing, lack of appetite, runny eyes, and high blood pressure); Bond v. Rhodes, 2006 WL 1617892, *3 (W.D. Pa. June 8, 2006) (holding allegation of serious diarrhea resulting from food tampering satisfied the requirement at the pleading stage); Young v. Medden, 2006 WL 456274, *20 (E.D. Pa. Feb. 23, 2006) (holding allegation that prison staff put substances in prisoner's food that made him urinate constantly "arguably demonstrate more than *de minimis* physical injury"); Gil v. U.S., 2006 WL 385088, *3 (M.D. Fla. Feb. 17, 2006) (awarding "intangible damages for pain and suffering, inconvenience, and loss of capacity for enjoyment of life" to prisoner who suffered food poisoning from tainted food); Caldwell v. District of Columbia, 201 F. Supp. 2d 27, 34 (D.D.C. 2001) (holding that evidence of heat exhaustion, skin rash, and bronchial irritation from smoke inhalation met the PLRA standard; injury need not be serious or lasting). *But see* cases cited in n.378, above, concerning asbestos exposure. *See also* Smith v. Leonard, 2008 WL 1912804, *6 n.7 (S.D.Tex., Apr. 28, 2008) (on remand from decision cited above, holding headaches, sinus problems, trouble breaathing, blurred vision, irritated eyes, and fatigue resulting from exposure to toxic mold were *de minimis*); Thompson v. Joyner, 2007 WL 4963007, *5 (E.D.N.C., May 29, 2007) (pepper spraying was *de minimis*), *aff'd*, 251 Fed.Appx. 826 (4th Cir. 2007) (unpublished); Ringgold v. Federal Bureau of Prisons, 2007 WL 2990690, *2, 4–5 (D.N.J., Oct. 5, 2007) (holding an injection that might have exposed the plaintiff to other people's blood did not meet the injury threshold); Patrick v. Bobby, 2007 WL 2446574, *3 (N.D.Ohio, Aug. 23, 2007) (rejecting claim based on failure to remove plaintiff from a unit where smoking is permitted, since his medical records show no resulting physical injury); Muhammad v. Sherrer, 2007 WL 2021789, *5 (D.N.J., July 9, 2007) (holding claim prisoner was "overcome" by silicon fumes and suffered high blood pressure as a result was *de minimis*); Mayes v. Travis State Jail, 2007 WL 1888828, *4–5 (W.D.Tex., June 29, 2007) (sinus infection allegedly caused by black mold and diarrhea allegedly caused by spoiled food were *de minimis*); Cotter v. Dallas County Sheriff, 2006 WL 1652714, *3–4 (N.D.Tex., June 15, 2006) (holding exposure to welding dust and metal shaving allegedly resulting in an undiagnosed nervous condition did not constitute physical injury); Moore v. Bucher, 2006 WL 1451544, *2 (N.D.Fla., May 23, 2006) (holding prisoner who said he was subjected to smoke and fumes from construction and renovation for 10–12 hours a day for about 10 days did not meet the physical injury standard because he complained only "that he has asthma, suffered pain, and had to be treated with medication such as antibiotics and ibuprofen"); Gill v. Shoemate, 2006 WL 1285412, *5 (W.D.La., May 8, 2006) (holding headaches and eye and throat irritation resulting from exposure to mold, mildew, dust, and fumes were *de minimis*); Reeves v. Jensen, 2005 WL 2090896, *1–2 (W.D.Mich., Aug. 30, 2005) (dismissing as *de minimis* a claim that plaintiff "became ill" after a chemical agent was used against another prisoner); Hogg v. Johnson, 2005 WL 139103, *1, *3 (N.D.Tex., Jan. 21, 2005) (dismissing allegation that plaintiff was "gassed three times for

- infliction of pain or illness through extreme conditions of confinement,[601] physical abuse[602] or denial of medical care[603] and
- stillbirth or miscarriage.[604]

However, there are plenty of cases that seem to involve similar or equally serious conditions but come out the other way, and often it is hard to see why.[605] Some courts have

_____

asking for a mattress and standing up for his rights" for lack of physical injury), *report and recommendation adopted*, 2005 WL 762137 (N.D.Tex., Apr. 1, 2005).

[601]Rinehart v. Alford, 2003 WL 23473098, *2 (N.D.Tex., Mar. 3, 2003) (holding that severe headaches and back pain, attributed by the jail nurse to bright 24-hour illumination and sleeping on a narrow bench, sufficiently alleged physical injury); Perez G. v. Lambert, 2001 WL 34736218, *3 (D.Or., Sept. 7, 2001) (holding that allegation of cramps, vomiting, constipation, compacted bowels, and anal bleeding, resulting from confinement in conditions so filthy the plaintiff could not eat and his subsequent denial of bathroom breaks while in restraints, met the physical injury standard).

In *Calhoun v. Hargrove*, 312 F.3d 730, 735 (5th Cir. 2002), the appeals court reversed the dismissal without a hearing of an allegation that being forced to perform medically contraindicated work caused high blood pressure at near-stroke levels and light-headedness, and directed the district court to determine factually whether physical injury had occurred. On remand, the court found it had not, and the appeals court affirmed. Calhoun v. Hargrove, 71 Fed.Appx. 371 (5th Cir. 2003) (unpublished).

[602]Payne v. Parnell, 246 Fed.Appx. 884, 889 (5th Cir. 2007) (unpublished) (holding that being jabbed with a cattle prod is not *de minimis*); Lawson v. Hall, 2008 WL 793635, *5-7 (S.D.W.Va., Mar. 24, 2008) (declining to apply § 1997e(e) to allegation of "severe pain" from being kneed); Zamboroski v. Karr, 2007 WL 541921, *5 (E.D.Mich., Feb. 16, 2007) (holding severe pain resulting from lack of mobility during nine months in restraints, along with rashes and scarring on his arms and inability to raise his arms over his head when released, were not *de minimis*); Mansoori v. Shaw, 2002 WL 1400300, *3 (N.D.Ill., June 28, 2002) (holding alleged "tenderness and soreness," for which plaintiff was taken to a hospital for treatment and received a diagnosis of "chest wall injury," met the standard); Romaine v. Rawson, 140 F. Supp. 2d 204, 214 (N.D.N.Y. 2001) (holding "minor" injuries—three slaps in the face—met the PLRA standard). *But see* Dixon v. Toole, 225 Fed. Appx. 797, 799 (11th Cir. 2007) (per curiam) (unpublished) (holding "mere bruising" from 17.5 hours in restraints was *de minimis*; prisoner actually complained of "welts").

[603]Clifton v. Eubank, 418 F. Supp. 2d 1243, 1248 (D.Colo. 2006) (addressing "prolonged" pain attendant upon labor and stillbirth), *on reconsideration on other grounds*, 2006 WL 893600 (D.Colo., Apr. 5, 2006).

[604]Clifton v. Eubank, 418 F. Supp. 2d 1243, 1245-51(D.Colo. 2006) (holding that losing one's child and the pain attendant upon labor and stillbirth both separately meet the physical injury standard).

[605]Many examples can be found in nn.594-602, above, in the cases listed after "*But see*" in each note. *See also* Darvie v. Countryman, 2008 WL 2725071, *7 (N.D.N.Y., July 10, 2008) (characterizing"anxiety,depression,stress,nausea,hyperventilation, headaches, insomnia, dizziness, appetite loss, weight loss, etc.," as

stated explicitly that the alleged infliction of severe physical pain does not satisfy the statute.[606] It is conceivable that outright torture may not be compensable as long as it is inflicted with sufficient care to leave no marks.[607]

_____

"essentially emotional in nature"), *report and recommendation adopted*, 2008 WL 3286250 (N.D.N.Y., Aug. 7, 2008); Geter v. Goode, 2006 WL 1129407, *2 (D.S.C. Apr. 25, 2006) (holding "superficial abrasions and scarred tissue" *de minimis*); Trevino v. Johnson, 2005 WL 3360252, *5 (E.D.Tex., Dec. 8, 2005) (holding a prisoner who was struck twice in the face and had his fingers pulled back had *de minimis* injury where he sustained only an abrasion to the forehead); Myers v. Valdez, 2005 WL 3147869, *2 (N.D.Tex., Nov. 17, 2005) (holding "pain, numbness in extremities, loss of mobility, lack of sleep, extreme tension in neck and back, extreme rash [and] discomfort" to be *de minimis*); Abney v. Valdez, 2005 WL 3147863, *2 (N.D.Tex., Oct. 27, 2005) (holding more frequent urination, near-daily migraine headaches, and itchiness and watery eyes did not meet the physical injury requirement); Vega v. Hill, 2005 WL 3147862, *3 (N.D.Tex., Oct. 14, 2005) (holding "bad headaches, sleeplessness, dizziness," and "feel[ing] like a 'zombie'" to be *de minimis*); Mitchell v. Horn, 2005 WL 1060658, *1 (E.D.Pa., May 5, 2005) (dismissing complaint of "severe stomach aches, severe headaches, severe dehydration, loss of weight, severe itching, due to the inability to take his prescribed medication, nausea, physical weakness and blurred vision," stating that such "transitory" injuries were not contemplated by the PLRA).

[606]Mahon v. Benoir, 2008 WL 4065834, *11 (D.S.C., Aug. 27, 2008) (holding allegation of "chronic pain and by the pain traveling throughout parts of his body and lost the use of his entire right hand and arm 'at one point during his incarceration'" did not satisfy the physical injury requirement); Calderon v. Foster, 2007 WL 1010383, *8 (S.D.W.Va., Mar. 30, 2007) (pain, standing alone, is *de minimis*), *aff'd*, 264 Fed.Appx. 286 (4th Cir. 2008) (unpublished); Ladd v. Dietz, 2007 WL 160762, *1 (D.Neb., Jan. 17, 2007) (holding pain resulting from placing ear medication in plaintiff's eye was "not enough" to constitute physical injury); Clifton v. Eubank, 418 F. Supp. 2d 1243, 1246 (D.Colo. 2006); Olivas v. Corrections Corp. of America, 408 F. Supp. 2d 251, 254, 259 (N.D.Tex. 2006) (dismissing as *de minimis* pain reported as 10 on a scale of 1-10, resulting from delay in treatment of broken teeth with exposed nerve).

[607]For example, see *Jarriett v. Wilson*, 162 Fed.Appx. 394 (6th Cir. 2005) (unpublished), in which a prisoner's complaint that he was forced to stand in a two-and-a-half-foot square cage for about 13 hours, naked for the first 8–10 hours, unable to sit for more than 30 or 40 minutes of the total time, in acute pain, with clear, visible swelling in a portion of his leg that had previously been injured in a motorcycle accident, during which time he repeatedly asked to see a doctor. *Id.*, *8 (dissenting opinion). The appeals court affirmed the dismissal of his claim as *de minimis* on the ground that the plaintiff did not complain about his leg upon release or shortly thereafter when he saw medical staff. *Id.*, *4. The decision was initially published, but Westlaw has removed the opinion from its original citation and replaced it with a note stating that it was "erroneously published." Jarriett v. Wilson, 414 F.3d 634 (6th Cir. 2005).

Jarriett contrasts with *Payne v. Parnell*, 246 Fed.Appx. 884 (5th Cir. 2007) (unpublished), in which the court, referring both to § 1997e(e) and the Eighth Amendment, held that being jabbed with a cattle prod was not *de minimis*, despite the lack of long-term

In addition, some courts have dismissed visible bodily injuries as *de minimis*.[608]

Unfortunately, most of these decisions make no attempt to define what "physical injury" means, other than "more than *de minimis*."[609] The meaning of physical injury might be

clarified by 18 U.S.C. § 242, a federal statute that makes it a crime for someone acting under color of state law to deprive another person of federal civil rights, and requires a showing of "bodily injury" before someone who violates the statute can be sentenced to more than one year in prison.[610] Bodily injury is not defined in the statute. However, several other federal criminal statutes define that term as meaning "(A) a cut, abrasion, bruise, burn, or disfigurement; (B) physical pain; (C) illness; (D) impairment of a function of a bodily member, organ, or mental faculty; or (E) any other injury to the body, no matter how temporary."[611] Several circuits have adopted that definition for purposes of § 242 as well,[612] and there is no apparent reason why it should not be applied under § 1997e(a).[613] We don't see much difference between "bodily" and "physical" injury. As far as we know, no court has yet considered this idea. If you are faced with an argument that your injury isn't severe enough to satisfy the PLRA, but it falls within the statutory definition of bodily injury, you should point these statutes out to the court and argue that if you meet the definition of bodily injury, you also satisfy the physical injury requirement.

F. ATTORNEYS' FEES

The PLRA limits the attorneys' fees that prisoners can recover compared to other civil rights litigants.[614] Most of the limitations do not affect prisoners directly, since prisoners proceeding *pro se* cannot recover attorneys' fees, but they may affect the ability of prisoners to get lawyers to represent them.

---

damage, in part because it was "calculated to produce real physical harm." 246 Fed.Appx. at 888–89.

[608]*See* cases cited in n.586, above; in addition, *see* Gibson v. Galaza, 2006 WL 829120, *10 (E.D.Cal., Mar. 29, 2006) (holding multiple abrasions, a small cut on lip, and a bruised right knee are *de minimis*); Wallace v. Brazil, 2005 WL 4813518, *1 (N.D.Tex., Oct. 10, 2005) (holding a knot on the head allegedly inflicted by an officer with an iron bar was *de minimis*); Cuciak v. Hutler, 2005 WL 1140690, *2–3 (D.N.J., May 13, 2005) (dismissing allegation that defendant pushed plaintiff, stepped on his bare foot and broke his toenail; court notes that the plaintiff did not allege his injury required medical attention); McDonald v. Smith, 2003 WL 22208554 (N.D.Tex., Sept. 25, 2003) (holding "large amount of muscle spasm across lumbar sacral area of back" after a use of force did not meet the physical injury requirement); Luong v. Hatt, 979 F. Supp. 481, 485–86 (N.D.Tex. 1997) ("A physical injury is an observable or diagnosable medical condition requiring treatment by a medical care professional"; holding abrasion of arm and chest, contusion and swelling of jaw did not meet that standard.). *Contra*, Cotney v. Bowers, 2006 WL 2772775, *7 (M.D.Ala., Sept. 26, 2006) (holding bruised ribs that took weeks to heal could be found not *de minimis*); Oliver v. Gaston, 2006 WL 2805343, *6 (S.D.Miss., Sept. 7, 2006) (holding "numerous swollen spots, bruises and abrasions to the face and scalp" were more than *de minimis*); Evans v. Alameida, 2006 WL 618298, *1 (E.D.Cal., Mar. 10, 2006) (noting prior decision that "abrasions and bleeding" met the standard), *report and recommendation adopted*, 2006 WL 1774875 (E.D.Cal., June 26, 2006); Hardin v. Fullenkamp, 2001 WL 35816398, *7 (S.D.Iowa, June 22, 2001) (holding evidence prisoner was cut and bruised and other prisoners' affidavits that they saw him beaten and later limping met the standard).

[609]One exception is a district court decision that cited dictionary definitions of "physical" as "of or relating to the body," and of "injury" as "an act that damages, harms, or hurts; an unjust or undeserved infliction of suffering or harm; wrong," and held that a reasonable jury could find that the statute was satisfied by exposure to noxious odors, including those of human wastes, and "dreadful" conditions of confinement (including inability to keep clean while menstruating, denial of clothing except for a paper gown, and exposure to prurient ogling by male prison staff and construction workers). Waters v. Andrews, 2000 WL 1611126, *7 (W.D.N.Y., Oct. 16, 2000). This case stretches the language of the statute pretty far; other courts have held similar facts not to satisfy the requirement. *See* Alexander v. Tippah County, Miss., 351 F.3d 626, 631 (5th Cir. 2003) (holding that prisoner who vomited as a result of exposure to noxious odors in a filthy holding cell full of raw sewage suffered only a *de minimis* injury, if any); Brooks v. Delta Correctional Facility, 2007 WL 2219303, *1 (N.D.Miss., July 30, 2007) (holding being forced to defecate in clothing and sleep in feces was *de minimis*); Jennings v. Weberg, 2007 WL 80875, *1 (W.D.Mich., Jan. 8, 2007) (holding a prisoner who was routinely spat upon and had urine thrown on him by an HIV-positive prisoner alleged only mental or emotional injury); Parter v. Valone, 2006 WL 3086900, *2–3 (E.D.Mich., Oct. 30, 2006) (holding a prisoner who was denied the use of a bathroom and urinated on

himself suffered only mental or emotional injury); Jarrell v. Seal, 2004 WL 241712 (E.D.La., Feb. 10, 2004) (holding that a prisoner who alleged he soiled himself after not being allowed to use a toilet was complaining of humiliation and had suffered no physical injury), *aff'd*, 110 Fed.Appx. 455 (5th Cir. 2004) (unpublished. *Cf.* Glaspy v. Malicoat, 134 F. Supp. 2d 890, 894–95 (W.D.Mich. 2001) (treating denial of toilet access to a non-prisoner, with predictable results, as a deprivation of liberty).

[610]18 U.S.C. § 242 (providing "if bodily injury results from the acts committed in violation of this section . . . [the defendant] shall be fined under this title or imprisoned not more than ten years, or both").

[611]18 U.S.C. § 831(f)(5); *accord*, 18 U.S.C. § 1365(h)(4); 18 U.S.C. § 1515(a)(5); 18 U.S.C. § 1864(d)(2).

[612]*See* U.S. v. Gonzales, 436 F.3d 560, 575 (5th Cir. 2006); U.S. v. Bailey, 405 F.3d 102, 111 (1st Cir. 2005); U.S. v. Myers, 972 F.2d 1566, 1572 (11th Cir. 1992). *Gonzales* excepts use of force cases from this holding because of other Fifth Circuit principles concerning such cases.

[613]"When Congress uses, but does not define a particular word, it is presumed to have adopted that word's established meaning." U.S. v. Myers, 972 F.2d 1566, 1572 (11th Cir. 1992) (citing Davis v. Mich. Dep't of Treasury, 489 U.S. 803, 813, 109 S. Ct. 1500 (1989)).

[614]*See* Ch. 10, § Y, concerning attorneys' fees.

Fees under 42 U.S.C. § 1988[615] are barred in "any action brought by a prisoner"[616] except when the fees are "directly and reasonably incurred in proving an actual violation of the plaintiff's rights" under a statute that allows fees to be awarded.[617] It is unclear whether this provision bars fee awards in cases that are settled, rather than cases that go to trial. Several courts have held that injunctive proceedings that are settled may support an award of fees if there are findings of legal violation or a record that supports such findings.[618] Fees may also be awarded if they are "directly and reasonably incurred in enforcing the relief ordered for the violation."[619] The statute says that fees must be "proportionately related to the court ordered relief for the violation."[620] It does not say in what proportion. However, defendants may be required to pay fee awards of up to 150% of any damages awarded—but no more.[621]

Hourly rates for lawyers are limited to 150% of the Criminal Justice Act (CJA) rates for criminal defense representation set in 18 U.S.C. § 3006A.[622] Courts have disagreed whether this means 150% of the rates authorized by the federal Judicial Conference or the actual, lower rates paid in the district based on how much money Congress actually provides.[623] Both rates are much lower than the market rates that lawyers usually charge and that are awarded in non-prisoner cases, and they will probably discourage many lawyers from taking prisoners' cases. (Although the hourly rate is 50% higher than the Criminal Justice Act rates, lawyers defending clients under the CJA get paid for their time whether they win or lose.)

Prisoners are more directly affected by the provision that says that "up to" 25% of a damage judgment is to be applied to the fee award. If the fee award is not greater than 150% of the judgment, defendants must pay the rest.[624] Most courts have held that the term "up to" allows the courts some discretion in determining how much of a winning prisoner-plaintiff's damage award must be applied to attorneys' fees.[625]

---

[615]42 U.S.C. § 1988 is the statute that authorizes attorneys' fees in actions under 42 U.S.C. § 1983. In cases where fees are based on some other law, the PLRA fees restrictions do not apply. *See, e.g.,* Armstrong v. Davis, 318 F.3d 965, 973–74 (9th Cir. 2003) (holding that fees in Americans with Disabilities Act and Rehabilitation Act suits are not governed by the PLRA fees limitations).

[616]For purposes of these provisions, ex-prisoners are not prisoners, and a case filed after the plaintiff's release is not governed by the PLRA fees provisions. Doe v. Washington County, 150 F.3d 920, 924 (8th Cir. 1998). The attorneys' fees provisions are not limited to cases about prison conditions. Robbins v. Chronister, 435 F.3d 1238, 1241–44 (10th Cir. 2006) (en banc) (applying PLRA restrictions to case about events before prisoner's incarceration); Jackson v. State Bd. of Pardons and Paroles, 331 F.3d 790, 794–95 (11th Cir. 2003) (applying PLRA restrictions to case about parole eligibility hearings).

[617]42 U.S.C. § 1997e(d)(1)(A).

[618]*See* Laube v. Allen, 506 F. Supp. 2d 969, 979–80 (M.D.Ala. 2007) (holding that fees may be awarded for injunctive settlements to the extent they satisfy the PLRA's "need-narrowness-intrusiveness" requirement and the fees were "directly and reasonably incurred" in obtaining it); Watts v. Director of Corrections, 2007 WL 1100611, *3 (E.D.Cal., Apr. 11, 2007) (awarding fees for "proving an actual violation" notwithstanding that case was settled), *amended on reconsideration on other grounds,* 2007 WL 1752519 (E.D.Cal., June 15, 2007); Lozeau v. Lake County, Mont., 98 F. Supp. 2d 1157, 1168 n.1 and 1170 (D.Mont. 2000) ("Defendants cannot settle a case, promise reform or continued compliance, admit the previous existence of illegal conditions, admit that Plaintiffs' legal action actually brought the illegal conditions to the attention of those in a position to change them and subsequently allege a failure of proof."); Ilick v. Miller, 68 F. Supp. 2d 1169, 1173 n.1 (D.Nev. 1999).

[619]42 U.S.C. § 1997e(d)(1)(B)(ii); *see* West v. Manson, 163 F. Supp. 2d 116, 120 (D.Conn. 2001) (holding fees are recoverable for post-judgment monitoring).

[620]42 U.S.C. § 1997e(d)(1)(B)(i).

[621]42 U.S.C. § 1997e(d)(2); *see* Pearson v. Welborn, 471 F.3d 732, 742–43 (7th Cir. 2006) (holding fees limited to $1.50 where plaintiff recovered only $1.00 in nominal damages); Boivin v. Black, 225 F.3d 36, 40–42 (1st Cir. 2000) (same); Clark v. Phillips, 965 F. Supp. 331, 336 (N.D.N.Y. 1997) (holding fees of $7921.96 to be proportionately related to $10,000 damage award). This 150%

limit does not apply to cases in which the plaintiff seeks and receives an injunction as well as damages. Walker v. Bain, 257 F.3d 660, 667 n.2 (6th Cir. 2001); Carbonell v. Acrish, 154 F. Supp. 2d 552, 566 (S.D.N.Y. 2001). *Cf.* Torres v. Walker, 356 F.3d 238, 243 (2d Cir. 2004) (holding that a case resolved by "so ordered" stipulation was not governed by the 150% limit, since there was no "money judgment").

[622]42 U.S.C. § 1997e(d)(3). As we write this, the rate authorized under the CJA is $118 an hour, 150% of which is $177.00 an hour. Graves v. Arpaio, 633 F. Supp. 2d 834, 854 (D.Ariz. 2009).

[623]*Compare* Hadix v. Johnson, 398 F.3d 863 (6th Cir. 2005) (holding Judicial Conference rates apply), *with* Hernandez v. Kalinowski, 146 F.3d 196, 201 (3d Cir. 1998) (holding the actual rates paid apply); *see also* Johnson v. Daley, 339 F.3d 582, 584 (7th Cir. 2003) (en banc).

[624]42 U.S.C. § 1997e(d)(2).

[625]One court has held that in deciding what proportion of an award to make the plaintiff pay, courts should consider factors including "(1) the degree of the opposing parties' culpability or bad faith, (2) the ability of the opposing parties to satisfy an award of attorneys' fees, (3) whether an award of attorneys' fees against the opposing parties could deter other persons acting under similar circumstances, and (4) the relative merits of the parties' positions." Kahle v. Leonard, 563 F.3d 736 (8th Cir. 2009). Previously, most decisions had said only that the court has discretion to apply less than 25% of the plaintiff's award. *See* Boesing v. Hunter, 540 F.3d 886, 891–92 (8th Cir. 2008) (affirming district court's application of 1% of $25,000 recovery); Siggers-El v. Barlow, 433 F. Supp. 2d 811, 822–23 (E.D.Mich. 2006) (applying $1.00 of the recovery to attorneys' fees, noting that the jury found that defendants had lied about their conduct and awarded significant damages as punishment and deterrent); Farella v. Hockaday, 304 F. Supp. 2d 1076, 1081 (C.D.Ill. 2004); Hutchinson v. McCabee, 2001 WL 930842, *8 n.11 (S.D.N.Y., Aug. 15, 2001) (holding that court has discretion to apply less than 25% of plaintiff's recovery to fees); Morrison v. Davis, 88 F. Supp. 2d 799, 811–13 (S.D. Ohio 2000) (applying only $1.00 of judgment against recovery); Hernandez v. Kalinowski, No. 96-6269 (E.D. Pa. Aug. 20, 1997) (applying 20% of

The courts have rejected arguments that the attorneys' fees restrictions deny equal protection.[626]

G. WAIVER OF REPLY

The PLRA provides:

> (g)   Waiver of Reply.
>
> (1)   Any defendant may waive the right to reply to any action brought by a prisoner confined in any jail, prison, or other correctional facility under [42 U.S.C. § 1983] . . . or any other Federal law. Notwithstanding any other law or rule of procedure, such waiver shall not constitute an admission of the allegations contained in the complaint. No relief shall be granted to the plaintiff unless a reply has been filed.
>
> (2)   The court may require any defendant to reply to a complaint brought under this section if it finds that the plaintiff has a reasonable opportunity to prevail on the merits.[627]

This means that in prisoners' suits, the defendants do not have to answer the complaint unless the court tells them to do so based on a finding that the prisoner has a "reasonable opportunity to prevail on the merits." In practice, courts generally direct defendants to answer if the case survives initial screening or a motion to dismiss, which means that the complaint states a claim for which relief can be granted.[628] The provision that "[n]o relief shall be granted to

the plaintiff unless a reply has been filed" raises a question about whether default judgments, the usual remedy when a defendant fails to answer the complaint, are still available in prisoner litigation. These questions are discussed elsewhere in this Manual.[629]

H. HEARINGS BY TELECOMMUNICATION AND AT PRISONS

The PLRA added a new section to the Civil Rights of Institutionalized Persons Act (CRIPA) providing:

> (f)   Hearings.
>
> (1)   To the extent practicable, in any action brought with respect to prison conditions in Federal court pursuant to section 1979 of the Revised Statutes of the United States (42 U.S.C. § 1983), or any other Federal law, by a prisoner confined in any jail, prison, or other correctional facility, pretrial proceedings in which the prisoner's participation is required or permitted shall be conducted by telephone, video conference, or other telecommunications technology without removing the prisoner from the facility in which the prisoner is confined.
>
> (2)   Subject to the agreement of the official of the Federal, State, or local unit of government with custody over the prisoner, hearings may be conducted at the facility in which the prisoner is confined. To the extent practicable, the court shall allow counsel to participate by telephone, video conference, or other communications technology in any hearing held at the facility.[630]

For years, many federal courts have used telephones and video in court proceedings, and some have held proceedings at prisons.[631] However, this PLRA provision concerning hearings at the prison raises important legal and

---

award to fee), *aff'd in part and rev'd on other grounds*, 146 F.3d 196, 199–201 (3d Cir. 1998); *see* Norwood v. Vance, 2008 WL 686901, *4 (E.D.Cal., Mar. 12, 2008) (where plaintiff received a punitive award of $39,000 and a nominal award of $11.00, requiring plaintiff to pay only 25% of the nominal award), *vacated on other grounds*, 572 F.3d 626 (9th Cir. 2009).

A few courts have either assumed (mistakenly, we think) that they must apply the 25% figure, or have done so without discussing why. *See* Johnson v. Daley, 339 F.3d 582, 584–85 (7th Cir. 2003) (en banc) (dictum); Jackson v. Austin, 267 F. Supp. 2d 1059, 1071 (D. Kan. 2003) (holding that 25% of the plaintiff's recovery must be applied to fees); Beckford v. Irvin, 60 F. Supp. 2d 85, 89–90 (W.D.N.Y. 1999) (applying 25% without discussion); Roberson v. Brassell, 29 F. Supp. 2d 346, 355 (S.D. Tex. 1998) (stating 25% "must be applied").

[626]Johnson v. Daley, 339 F.3d 582, 584 (7th Cir. 2003) (en banc); Jackson v. State Bd. of Pardons and Paroles, 331 F.3d 790, 796–98 (11th Cir. 2003); Foulk v. Charrier, 262 F.3d 267, 704 (8th Cir. 2001) (upholding cap of 150% of damages); Walker v. Bain, 257 F.3d 660, 665–70 (6th Cir. 2001) (same); Hadix v. Johnson, 230 F.3d 840 (6th Cir. 2000) (upholding limit on hourly rates); Boivin v. Black, 225 F.3d 36 (1st Cir. 2000) (same); Carbonell v. Acrish, 154 F. Supp. 2d 552, 561–66 (S.D.N.Y. 2001) (upholding 150% limit).

[627]42 U.S.C. § 1997e(g).

[628]*See, e.g.*, Rush v. Giurbino, 2007 WL 3473223, *2 (S.D.Cal., Nov. 14, 2007); Jones v. Bowersox, 2005 WL 1185598, *1–2 (W.D.Mo., May 18, 2005); Daniel v. Power, 2005 WL 1958350, *2 (S.D.Ill., July 20, 2005) (after initial screening, " [d]efendants are ORDERED to timely file an appropriate responsive pleading to the

Amended Complaint, and shall not waive filing a reply pursuant to 42 U.S.C. § 1997e(g)."); Sims v. Kernan, 29 F. Supp. 2d 952, 961 (N.D.Ind. 1998) (finding that the plaintiff has a reasonable opportunity to prevail on the merits, and ordering that defendants respond to the complaint as provided for in the Federal Rules of Civil Procedure); Proctor v. Vadlamudi, 992 F. Supp. 156, 159 (N.D.N.Y. 1998) (magistrate's recommendation that if case is not dismissed, defendants should be declared heretofore to have waived reply and should be directed to answer within 30 days).

[629]*See* Ch. 10, §§ D (concerning answers) and E (concerning default judgments).

[630]42 U.S.C. § 1997e(f); *see* Moss v. Gomez, 162 F.3d 1169 (9th Cir. 1998) (unpublished) (holding district court should have considered teleconferencing as an alternative to producing prisoner witness who was a security risk).

[631]*See, e.g.*, Hall v. Bellmon, 935 F.2d 1106, 1109 (10th Cir. 1991) (noting use of telephone evidentiary hearing to assess frivolousness of claim); Am. Inmate Paralegal Ass'n v. Cline, 859 F.2d 59, 62 (8th Cir. 1988) (upholding constitutionality of a pretrial conference by two-way audio–video connection between prison and courthouse).

practical problems. The statute refers to counsel's participation "[t]o the extent practicable" by telephone, video, etc. If a prisoner has an attorney, there seems to be no reason the attorney cannot attend the proceeding in person. If the prison is at such a remote location that neither counsel's presence nor her participation by telecommunication is practicable, it is questionable whether the proceeding should be held at the prison. It will generally be fairer to a prisoner with counsel to have pretrial proceedings conducted at a location where counsel can attend.

The statute refers to holding "hearings" but not "trials" at the prison, leaving it unclear whether evidentiary proceedings are included.[632] Conducting a trial or evidentiary proceeding by video conferencing raises questions of fairness, particularly in jury trials. In *United States v. Baker*,[633] a non-PLRA case, the court upheld the constitutionality of holding prisoners' psychiatric commitment hearings by video, but was careful to note that such decisions are generally based on expert testimony and do not depend either on the demeanor of the witnesses or the "impression" made by the person being committed, and that the proceeding does not involve fact-finding in the usual sense. That description does not fit most evidentiary proceedings in prisoner cases, and courts have traditionally expressed a strong preference for having prisoner plaintiffs physically present in court for trial.[634] On this basis, you may wish to oppose trial at the prison or by telecommunications. Or you may not. You may find it less oppressive to have your case heard in that manner rather than being transported back and forth to court in restraints.

If the court does hold a hearing by telephone or video in your case, it will be your responsibility to see that any witnesses you wish to present or cross-examine are subpoenaed to attend, just as in a live hearing in the courtroom.[635]

I. Revocation of Earned Release Credit

The PLRA adds a new section concerning earned release credit:

§ 1932. Revocation of earned release credit

In any civil action brought by an adult convicted of a crime and confined in a Federal correctional facility, the court may order the revocation of such earned good time credit under section 3624(b) of title 18, United States Code, that has not yet vested, if, on its own motion or the motion of any party, the court finds that:

(1) the claim was filed for a malicious purpose;

(2) the claim was filed solely to harass the party against whichit was filed; or

(3) the claimant testifies falsely or otherwise knowingly-presents false evidence or information to the court.[636]

This provision, which applies only to federal prisoners, takes away good time based on what a court thinks about a prisoner's litigation activities. Though it raises substantial questions about due process of law, the statute sets out no procedural protections. It is not clear what due process requirements would govern.[637] The only reported decisions applying this provision do not discuss the due process issue.[638]

The revocation of earned release credit provision of the PLRA governs proceedings in federal court, and presumably has no application in state court. There appear to be no decisions yet on this issue, however.

J. Diversion of Damage Awards

The PLRA includes a pair of provisions concerning the award of damages in a successful suit brought by a prisoner:

Any compensatory damages awarded to a prisoner in connection with a civil action brought against any Federal, State, or local jail, prison, or correctional facility or against any official or agent of such jail, prison, or correctional

---

[632]*But see* Bickham v. Blair, 1999 WL 627397 (E.D.La., Aug. 16, 1999) (noting that an evidentiary hearing was held by telephone); Edwards v. Logan, 38 F. Supp. 2d 463, 466–67 (W.D.Va. 1999) (authorizing video jury trial for Virginia prisoner held in New Mexico; analogizing to PLRA's provisions concerning pretrial proceedings).

[633]45 F.3d 837 (4th Cir. 1994).

[634]Hernandez v. Whiting, 881 F.2d 768, 770–72 (9th Cir. 1989); Muhammad v. Warden, Balt. City Jail, 849 F.2d 107, 113 (4th Cir. 1988); Poole v. Lambert, 819 F.2d 1025, 1029 (11th Cir. 1987). However, courts have authorized video trials in some instances without relying on the PLRA. *See* Ch. 10, § Q, concerning plaintiff's appearance at trial.

[635]*See* Bickham v. Blair, 1999 WL 627397, *1 (E.D.La., Aug. 16, 1999). Getting witnesses to court is discussed in Ch. 10, § Q.

[636]28 U.S.C. § 1932. Note that there is another statute with the same section number—entitled Judicial Panel on Multidistrict Litigation—but this citation is correct.

[637]Punishing persons with incarceration for things they do in litigation sounds to us a lot like criminal contempt, which requires the same protections that a defendant in a criminal prosecution receives. International Union, United Mine Workers of America v. Bagwell, 512 U.S. 821, 828–34, 114 S. Ct. 2552 (1994). If you are faced with proceedings under this section, you should make that argument, and in the alternative, you should argue that at least you should get the procedural protections that a prisoner is entitled to in a parole revocation proceeding. Since the proceeding would be about actions you took in the litigation, and not things you did contrary to internal prison rules, there would be no reason to compromise due process protections for the sake of prison order, as is the case with due process protections in disciplinary hearings. At a minimum, of course, you should receive the due process protections that are required in a disciplinary proceeding that leads to the loss of good time. *See* Ch. 4, §§ H.1, H.6.c., concerning disciplinary and parole revocation hearings.

[638]*See* Rice v. Nat'l Security Council, 244 F. Supp. 2d 594, 597, 605 (D.S.C. 2001) and cases cited, *aff'd*, 46 Fed.Appx. 212 (4th Cir. 2002) (unpublished).

facility, shall be paid directly to satisfy any outstanding restitution orders pending against the prisoner. The remainder of any such award after full payment of all pending restitution orders shall be forwarded to the prisoner.[639]

Prior to payment of any compensatory damages awarded to a prisoner in connection with a civil action brought against any Federal, State, or local jail, prison, or correctional facility or against any official or agent of such jail, prison, or correctional facility, reasonable efforts shall be made to notify the victims of the crime for which the prisoner was convicted and incarcerated concerning the pending payment of any such compensatory damages.[640]

There is very little case law about these statutes.[641] One important question is whether the phrase "compensatory damages *awarded*" includes settlement of damage claims. As a matter of plain English, it would seem not, and that is the holding of the only relevant decision we are aware of.[642]

K. Injunctions

The PLRA contains a number of provisions restricting courts' abilities to enter and to maintain "prospective relief" (mostly injunctions, or court orders[643]) in prison cases.[644]

1. Entry of Prospective Relief

Under the PLRA, courts may not enter prospective relief in prison cases "unless the court finds that such relief is narrowly drawn, extends no further than necessary to correct the violation of the Federal right, and is the least intrusive means necessary to correct the violation of the Federal right. The court shall give substantial weight to any adverse impact on public safety or the operation of a criminal justice system caused by the relief."[645] This standard is not significantly different from the law in effect before the PLRA,[646] although the requirement of specific court findings is new, as is the requirement (discussed below) that settlements meet these

---

[639]PLRA of 1995, Pub. L. No. 104–134, § 807, 110 Stat. 1321–66, 1321–76 (1996). This provision is not codified, and appears after 18 U.S.C. § 3626.

[640]PLRA of 1995, Pub. L. No. 104–134, § 808, 110 Stat. 1321–66, 1321–76 (1996). This provision is not codified, and appears after 18 U.S.C. § 3626.

[641]*See* Loucony v. Kupec, 2000 WL 1050905 (D.Conn., Feb. 17, 2000) (holding that a person who sued after he was released from prison was not a "prisoner" and the statute did not apply to him).

[642]Dodd v. Robinson, Civil Action No. 03-F-571-N, Order, *1 (M.D. Ala., Mar. 26, 2004). In that case, the court held that a damages settlement was not subject to the requirement of direct payment of restitution orders because the parties had reached a private settlement agreement.

[643]Orders issued in the course of pretrial case management are not prospective relief. *In re* Arizona, 528 F.3d 652, 658 (9th Cir. 2008) (direction that defendants submit a report on facts relevant to a *pro se* prisoner claim was not "relief"), *cert. denied*, 129 S. Ct. 2852 (2009).

[644]One federal appeals court has held that under the PLRA's language, punitive damages are "prospective relief" subject to the PLRA's limitations. Johnson v. Breeden, 280 F.3d 1308, 1325 (11th Cir. 2002); *see* Hudson v. Singleton, 2006 WL 839339, *2 (S.D.Ga., Mar. 27, 2006) (upholding a punitive award under *Breeden*). Other courts have mostly ignored this decision. We think it is wrong, because the prospective relief provisions are clearly written to deal with injunctions and make very little sense applied to punitive damages. *See* Tate v. Dragovich, 2003 WL 21978141, *6 n.7 (E.D.Pa., Aug. 14, 2003) ("At first blush, it seems that one can neither 'narrowly draw' punitive damages, not adjust them to better 'correct' a violation of rights, nor render them any more or less 'intrusive.'"). One court has gone further and has held that the PLRA has abolished punitive damages entirely. Margo v. Bedford

County, 2008 WL 857507, *10 (W.D.Pa., Mar. 31, 2008). We see no basis for this conclusion.

[645]18 U.S.C. § 3626(a); *see* Crawford v. Clarke, 578 F.3d 39, 43-44 (1st Cir. 2009) (granting injunction concerning religious practices for all "special management units" in non-class suit brought by residents of one unit); Morales Feliciano v. Rullan, 378 F.3d 42, 54–56 (1st Cir. 2004) (finding remedy of privatization of medical care appropriate in light of failure of less intrusive measures; "Drastic times call for drastic measures."); Clement v. California Dept. of Corrections, 364 F.3d 1148, 1152 (9th Cir. 2004) (affirming statewide injunction against prohibition on receipt of materials downloaded from the Internet); Gomez v. Vernon, 255 F.3d 1118, 1130 (9th Cir. 2001) (affirming injunction benefiting named individuals; though an unconstitutional policy had been found, it had been directed at those persons); Benjamin v. Fraser, 156 F. Supp. 2d 333, 344, 350 (S.D.N.Y. 2001) (applying PLRA standards in jail conditions litigation), *aff'd in part, vacated and remanded in part*, 343 F.3d 35, 53–57 (2d Cir. 2003); Morrison v. Garraghty, 239 F.3d 648, 661 (4th Cir. 2001) (affirming injunction prohibiting refusing the plaintiff a religious exemption from property restrictions solely based on his non-membership in the "Native American race"); Jordan v. Pugh, 2007 WL 2908931, *4 (D.Colo., Oct. 4, 2007) (holding a nationwide injunction appropriate where a rule was found facially overbroad under the First Amendment). *But see* Lindell v. Frank, 377 F.3d 655, 660 (7th Cir. 2004) (holding injunction against restrictions on receipt of clippings overbroad insofar as it applied to other prisoners besides the plaintiff); Leon v. Schaff, 2007 WL 3025694, *4 (D.N.J., Oct. 15, 2007) (citing adverse impact clause in denying injunction to remove plaintiff who was being investigated for assault from segregation).

[646]*See* Gilmore v. California, 220 F.3d 987, 1006 (9th Cir. 2000); Smith v. Arkansas Dep't of Correction, 103 F.3d 637, 647 (8th Cir. 1996) (holding PLRA "merely codifies existing law and does not change the standards for determining whether to grant an injunction"); Williams v. Edwards, 87 F.3d 126, 133 & n.21 (5th Cir. 1996) (PLRA "codifies the standards governing a district court's grant of prospective relief in prison reform litigation"); Hadix v. Caruso, 461 F. Supp. 2d 574, 586–87 (W.D.Mich. 2006) (holding PLRA's "actual standards are consistent with traditional norms of non-interference with state regulation of prisons"), *remanded on other grounds*, 248 Fed.Appx. 678 (6th Cir. 2007) (per curiam) (unpublished); *compare* Toussaint v. McCarthy, 801 F.2d 1080, 1086–87 (9th Cir. 1986) (pre-PLRA cases applying similar standard); Duran v. Elrod, 760 F.2d 756, 760–61 (7th Cir. 1985) (weighing public safety and criminal justice system concerns in enforcing jail crowding order).

requirements as well. The statute also prohibits injunctive relief that requires state or local law officials to exceed their authority or violate state or local law unless federal law requires such relief, such relief is necessary to correct a federal law violation, and no other relief will correct the violation.[647] This provision also appears reasonably consistent with prior law.[648] The PLRA does limit federal court prospective relief to correcting violations of "*Federal* rights," which means that a court cannot enter an injunction based on a violation of state or local law.[649] Under the PLRA, courts have continued to grant injunctions to protect federal constitutional rights.[650]

2. Preliminary Injunctions

Preliminary injunctions must meet the same standards described above for other prospective relief, and they automatically expire after 90 days unless the court has made the order final.[651] However, a court may grant a new preliminary injunction after the first one has expired if the plaintiff shows that the conditions justifying the injunction still exist.[652]

3. Prisoner Release Orders

The PLRA contains special rules for "prisoner release orders," which it defines as "any order . . . that has the purpose or effect of reducing or limiting the prison population, or that directs the release from or non-admission of prisoners to a prison."[653] Such orders are permitted only if

previous, less intrusive relief has failed to remedy the federal law violation in a reasonable time.[654] A release order must be supported by clear and convincing evidence that "crowding is the primary cause of the violation of a Federal right" and no other relief will remedy the violation.[655] One court has held that the limits on prisoner release orders do not apply to motions to modify pre-PLRA prisoner release orders, citing the statutory language that "no court *shall enter* a prisoner release order" without complying with the PLRA requirements.[656]

Procedurally, the PLRA requires that prisoner release orders be issued by a three-judge court, which may be requested either by the moving party or by the district court.[657] This requirement may give rise to procedural tangles in cases involving different kinds of relief.[658] One court has refused to convene a three-judge court to consider an individual prisoner's "[m]otion for [his own] Prisoner Release" that failed to allege, except in conclusory terms, how overcrowding violated any of his constitutional rights.[659] The prisoner release order procedure has been used only rarely.[660]

---

[647]18 U.S.C. § 3626(a)(1)(B); *see* Perez v. Hickman, 2007 WL 1697320, *2–4, 7 (N.D.Cal., June 12, 2007) (ordering increase in salaries paid to prison dentists, contrary to state law, and finding PLRA standards met).

[648]*See, e.g.*, Stone v. City & County of San Francisco, 968 F.2d 850, 861–65 (9th Cir. 1992) (holding, pre-PLRA, that provisions of consent decree that overrode state law were not the least intrusive option available and were thus prohibited). *See also* LaShawn A. v. Barry, 144 F.3d 847, 854 (D.C. Cir. 1998) (stating, pre-PLRA, that "[d]isregarding local law . . . is a grave step and should not be taken unless absolutely necessary").

[649]Handberry v. Thompson, 446 F.3d 335, 344–46 (2d Cir. 2006) (holding that in prison cases the PLRA overrides federal courts' "supplemental jurisdiction" to enforce state law).

[650]*See* cases cited in Ch. 8, §§ O.2, n.1081, and O.2.a, n.1096.

[651]18 U.S.C. § 3626(a)(2).

[652]Mayweathers v. Newland, 258 F.3d 930, 936 (9th Cir. 2001); Farnam v. Walker, 593 F. Supp. 2d 1000, 1004, 1018–19 (C.D.Ill. 2009) (holding successive preliminary injunctions are permissible, granting injunction and setting conference date near 90-day deadline to discuss possible entry of successive injunction); Riley v. Brown, 2006 WL 1722622, *7–16 (D.N.J., June 21, 2006) (granting second injunction after expiration of first), *see* Gammett v. Idaho State Bd. of Corrections, 2007 WL 2684750, *4 (D.Idaho, Sept. 7, 2007) (holding termination and automatic stay procedures do not apply to preliminary injunctions).

[653]18 U.S.C. § 3626(g)(4); *see* Berwanger v. Cottey, 178 F.3d 834, 836 (7th Cir. 1999) (noting that a maximum population provision is a prisoner release order). *But see* Inmates of Suffolk County Jail v. Sheriff of Suffolk County, 952 F. Supp. 869, 883

(D.Mass.) (holding that a population cap is not a prisoner release order in the absence of an order to release), *aff'd as modified and remanded on other grounds*, 129 F.3d 649 (1st Cir. 1997).

[654]18 U.S.C. § 3626(a)(3)(A). Some courts had adopted that view before the enactment of the PLRA. *See* Inmates of Occoquan v. Barry, 844 F.2d 828, 842–43 (D.C. Cir. 1988) (holding that population limit is a last resort remedy, not a first step).

[655]18 U.S.C. §§ 3626(a)(3)(E)(i)–(ii).

[656]Berwanger v. Cottey, 178 F.3d 834, 836 (7th Cir. 1999) (citing 18 U.S.C. § 3626(a)(3)(A)).

[657]18 U.S.C. §§ 3626(a)(3)(B)–(D).

[658]*See* Tyler v. Murphy, 135 F.3d 594, 598 (8th Cir. 1998) (unclear under PLRA whether "findings that will avoid termination of an existing injunction must in all cases be made by a three-judge court if the injunction includes a prisoner release order").

[659]Pangburn v. Goord, 1999 WL 222553, *7 (W.D.N.Y., Apr. 12, 1999).

[660]*See* Coleman v. Schwarzenegger, 2010 WL 99000 (E.D.Cal., Jan. 12, 2010) (entering order to reduce prison population); Coleman v. Schwarzenegger, 2009 WL 2430820 (E.D.Cal., Aug. 4, 2009) (ordering plan to reduce California prison population from nearly 200% of design capacity to 137.5% of capacity), *stay denied*, 2009 WL 2851846 (E.D. Cal., Sep. 3, 2009), *appeal dismissed for want of jurisdiction*, ___ S.Ct. ___, 2010 WL 154851 (Mem) (Jan. 19, 2010); Roberts v. County of Mahoning, Ohio, 495 F. Supp. 2d 784, 786 (N.D.Ohio 2007) (noting appointment of three-judge court and entry of prisoner release order by consent); *see also* Coleman v. Schwarzenegger, 2007 WL 2122636 (E.D.Cal., July 23, 2007), *appeal dismissed*, 2007 WL 2669591 (9th Cir., Sept. 11, 2007); Plata v. Schwarzenegger, 2007 WL 2122657 (N.D.Cal., July 23, 2007) (both requesting the Ninth Circuit to appoint a three-judge court to consider a population limit on the California prison system), *appeal dismissed*, 2007 WL 2669591 (9th Cir., Sept. 11, 2007).

The *Coleman v. Schwarzenegger* litigation cited above is almost certain to be reviewed by the Supreme Court, probably sometime in 2010.

The PLRA permits state and local officials to intervene to oppose prisoner release orders.[661]

4. Termination of Judgments

The PLRA provides that court orders in prison litigation, including consent judgments, may be terminated after two years unless the court finds that there is a "current and ongoing violation" of federal law. After this two-year period, orders may be challenged every year.[662] An order may be challenged at any time if it was entered without findings by the court that it "is narrowly drawn, extends no further than necessary to correct the violation of the Federal right, and is the least intrusive means necessary to correct the violation of the Federal right."[663] Such an order may be terminated immediately unless a current and ongoing federal law violation is shown. A "violation of the Federal right" means a violation of the federal Constitution, statutes, or regulations. Violation of the court order itself is not enough.[664]

Under this provision, numerous court orders that benefited prisoners—but that were entered before the PLRA and did not contain the findings required by the PLRA—have been terminated. In other cases, relief has been continued based on findings of a continuing and ongoing violation.[665] Constitutional challenges asserting that the provision violates the separation of powers, the Equal Protection Clause, and the Due Process Clause have been unsuccessful.[666]

5. Automatic Stay

The PLRA provides that courts must promptly rule on motions to terminate prospective relief, and that such prospective relief is automatically stayed on the 30th day after such a motion is made. The 30 days can be extended for an additional 60 days for good cause shown.[667] The Supreme Court has held that this provision does not violate the principle of separation of powers.[668]

6. Settlements

The PLRA provides that settlements that include prospective relief must meet the same requirements that the PLRA establishes for other court orders.[669] The court must find that these settlements are narrowly drawn, necessary to correct federal law violations, and the least intrusive way of doing so. (In practice, parties who are settling often agree to these findings and the court approves them.) It is no longer the case that parties can agree to a federal court settlement on whatever terms they choose. Parties can enter into "private settlement agreements" that do not meet the PLRA standards, but these agreements cannot be enforced in federal court.[670] In effect, they must be contracts enforceable in state court.

The PLRA does not restrict settlements that do not involve prospective relief (*i.e.*, damages settlements).

---

[661] 18 U.S.C. § 3626(a)(3)(F); *see* Ruiz v. Estelle, 161 F.3d 814, 818–21 (5th Cir. 1998) (holding that PLRA grants individual legislators the right to intervene in prison litigation).

[662] 18 U.S.C. § 3626(b)(1, 3).

[663] 18 U.S.C. § 3626(b)(2); *see* Tyler v. Murphy, 135 F.3d 594, 597 (8th Cir. 1998) (noting that absent the required findings, immediate termination provision rather than two-year provision applies).

[664] Plyler v. Moore, 100 F.3d 365, 370 (4th Cir. 1996); Harvey v. Schoen, 51 F. Supp. 2d 1001, 1005 (D.Minn. 1999); Thompson v. Gomez, 993 F. Supp. 749, 766 (N.D.Cal. 1997); Imprisoned Citizens Union v. Sharp, 11 F. Supp. 2d 586, 608–09 (E.D.Pa. 1998), *aff'd*, 169 F.3d 178 (3d Cir. 1999).

[665] *See, e.g.*, Pierce v. County of Orange, 526 F.3d 1190, 1208–13 (9th Cir. 2008) (finding ongoing violations with respect to exercise and religious access in segregation, terminating other judgment provisions), *cert. denied*, 129 S. Ct. 597 (2008); Benjamin v. Fraser, 264 F.3d 175 (2d Cir. 2001) (affirming findings of continuing and ongoing violations); Graves v. Arpaio, 2008 WL 4699770, *2–3 *et passim* (D.Ariz., Oct. 22, 2008) (partly terminating relief, partly preserving, or modifying relief based on current record; considering evidence covering a one-year period).

[666] Court of appeals decisions and significant district court decisions upholding the statute include: Berwanger v. Cottey, 178 F.3d 834 (7th Cir. 1999); Nichols v. Hopper, 173 F.3d 820 (11th Cir. 1999); Benjamin v. Jacobson, 172 F.3d 144 (2d Cir. 1999); Imprisoned Citizens Union v. Ridge, 169 F.3d 178 (3d Cir. 1999); Hadix v. Johnson, 133 F.3d 940 (6th Cir. 1998); Dougan v. Singletary, 129 F.3d 1424 (11th Cir. 1997); Inmates of Suffolk County Jail v. Rouse, 129 F.3d 649 (1st Cir. 1997); Gavin v. Branstad, 122 F.3d 1081 (8th Cir. 1997); Plyler v. Moore, 100 F.3d 365 (4th Cir. 1996); Vazquez v. Carver, 18 F. Supp. 2d 503 (E.D.Pa. 1998), *aff'd*, 181 F.3d 85 (3d Cir. 1999); Thompson v. Gomez, 993 F. Supp. 749 (N.D. Cal. 1997).

One circuit initially struck the provision down on separation of powers grounds; on rehearing, the court did not decide the constitutional question. Taylor v. U.S., 143 F.3d 1178 (9th Cir. 1998) (striking down provision as violating separation of powers), *superseded*, 181 F.3d 1017 (9th Cir. 1999) (en banc).

[667] 18 U.S.C. § 3626(e)(3).

[668] Miller v. French, 530 U.S. 327, 120 S. Ct. 2246 (2000).

[669] 18 U.S.C. § 3626(c)(1).

[670] 18 U.S.C. § 3626(c)(2).

7. Special Masters

The PLRA substantially restricts the use of special masters (court-appointed officials who help see that judgments are obeyed) in prison litigation.[671] The small amount of litigation over this section of the PLRA has been concerned with the definition of a special master, and whether the PLRA applies to masters appointed before the PLRA's enactment.[672]

---

[671] 18 U.S.C. § 3626(f). *But see* Roberts v. County of Mahoning, 495 F. Supp. 2d 670, (N.D.Ohio 2005) (finding case of overcrowded and understaffed jail sufficiently complex to warrant appointment of a special master).

[672] Benjamin v. Fraser, 343 F.3d 35, 44–48 (2d Cir. 2003) (holding a court monitor without quasi-judicial powers was not a special master, and the PLRA does not apply to special masters appointed before its enactment); Handberry v. Thompson, 446 F.3d 335, 351–52 (2d Cir. 2006) (applying *Benjamin* holding to find "special monitor" in jail education case not governed by PLRA special master provisions); Hadix v. Caruso, 465 F. Supp. 2d 776, 810-11 (W.D.Mich. 2006) (creating Office of Independent Monitor over medical care system without reference to special master provision), *amended on reconsideration*, 2007 WL 162279 (W.D.Mich., Jan. 16, 2007), *remanded on other grounds*, 248 Fed. Appx. 678 (6th Cir. 2007) (per curiam); Laube v. Campbell, 333 F. Supp. 2d 1234, 1239 (M.D.Ala. 2004) (holding a "healthcare monitor" was not governed by PLRA special master provisions); Jones v. City & County of San Francisco, 976 F. Supp. 896, 903 n.2 (N.D.Cal. 1997); Madrid v. Gomez, 940 F. Supp. 247, 251 n.7, 254 (N.D.Cal. 1996); Coleman v. Wilson, 933 F. Supp. 954 (E.D.Cal. 1996).

CHAPTER 10

How to Litigate

This chapter tells you how to start and to litigate a civil lawsuit. Because we cannot deal with 50 different state court systems, we focus on the procedures and practices in federal court. This does not mean you should always go to federal court. There are many kinds of cases that you are better off filing in state court and some that you must file in state court.[1]

Many states have used the federal courts as a model for their own court systems, and much of the contents of this chapter will also help you in state court. But you should always learn and follow the rules of the court you are in.

The Federal Rules of Civil Procedure (Fed.R.Civ.P.) govern civil cases in federal court.[2] These Rules are often amended in part, so you must be sure you have the current edition of the rules. At the end of 2007, a lot of the rules were re-worded and many of the sections and subsections were re-numbered, which makes reading older cases confusing; you sometimes have to compare the current rules to the case discussion to be sure what rule the case is talking about.

Federal district courts also have local rules with which you must comply, which you should be able to obtain from the local district court clerk. Some courts will provide these free, especially to indigent litigants; others may charge a small fee for them. Some federal judges have individual rules of practice as well, which you should be able to get from the judge's chambers by writing and requesting a copy. Local rules and individual judges' rules are also often available on the Internet, and your prison law library or someone you know outside the prison may be able to obtain them for you that way. If you are litigating in state court, you should find out if that court has local rules in addition to the state's general rules of civil procedure.

A. How a Lawsuit Works

A civil lawsuit in federal court proceeds through a series of well-defined procedural steps.

---

[1] *See* Ch. 8, § H, for discussion of the choice between state and federal court. In addition, in Chapters 2, 3, and 4, we explain the difference between many federal constitutional claims and state law claims. In some states, prisoners' rights organizations have published books, pamphlets, or information sheets on practice in state courts. Information about these can be found in Appendices B and D.

[2] The Federal Rules of Civil Procedure are included in Title 28 of the United States Code and are published separately in various books. These rules also apply in federal habeas corpus and other federal post-conviction proceedings, except when they conflict with the separate habeas corpus and post-conviction rules. *See* U.S. v. Frady, 456 U.S. 152, 166–67 n.15, 102 S. Ct 1584 (1982), for a

discussion of the application of the Fed.R.Civ.P. to proceedings 28 U.S.C. §§ 2254 and 2255.

To start a lawsuit about prison conditions, you must first *exhaust administrative remedies* by using all levels of the prison administrative process before filing in court.[3] Once you have done this, you may file a *complaint*[4] with the court, explaining how your legal rights have been violated and stating the relief you think you are entitled to.

Under the Prison Litigation Reform Act (PLRA), all prisoner civil actions are screened for merit before they are filed.[5] If you are without funds to pay litigation costs, you should ask to proceed *in forma pauperis* (IFP),[6] which excuses you from immediately paying the entire filing fee and also provides for *service of process*[7] by the U.S. Marshal. If the case survives screening and is filed, you must serve process on the defendants by arranging for formal delivery of the complaint and the summons to each of them; this gives the court *personal jurisdiction* to take action against the defendants.

The defendants must respond to your complaint by filing an *answer*[8] admitting or denying the complaint's factual allegations, or by filing a motion attacking the complaint—e.g., a *motion to dismiss*, which argues that even if your complaint is all true, you are not legally entitled to any relief.[9] If they make such a motion and it is denied, they must then file an answer. They may also file a motion to dismiss after the answer, though at that point it will be called a motion for *judgment on the pleadings*.

Once the complaint has been answered, both sides work to develop the facts of the case. They may engage in *discovery*,[10] a set of procedures by which one party obtains information, documents, or admissions from another party. If either party believes that the material facts are not in dispute, that party may move for *summary judgment*,[11]

arguing that there is no need for a trial, and asking the court to enter judgment on the undisputed facts as to part or all of the case. The defendants seem to move for summary judgment in most *pro se* prisoner cases that get past screening or a motion to dismiss.

If the case gets past the summary judgment motion, it will go to *trial* unless settled.[12] The trial may be before a jury if the plaintiff is seeking money damages and if either side has asked for a jury trial. The jurors will decide the facts after they hear the evidence and after the judge instructs them about the relevant law. If the plaintiff only seeks an *injunction*[13] (a court order telling the defendants to do something, or stop doing something, in order not to violate the plaintiff's rights), the court will decide both the facts and the legal issues. In some cases, the court will separate the determination of *liability* (whether the plaintiff's rights were violated) from the question of *remedy* or *relief* (how much in damages or what kind of injunction a plaintiff is entitled to after establishing liability).

Once there is a *final judgment* in the case, the losing party may *appeal*[14] (or both parties may appeal if each side won part of the case). The appeals court will review the record of the case to determine if the lower court made any significant errors of law, but will not hear new evidence that was not presented in the trial court, and will defer to the lower court's or jury's factual findings unless they are completely at odds with the evidence. The appeal decision may resolve all remaining issues, or the case may be sent back to the lower court fur further proceedings.

After a decision on appeal, the losing party may ask the United States Supreme Court to hear the case by filing a petition for *certiorari*.[15] The vast majority of these petitions are denied.

Sometimes some of these procedures can be skipped. For example, in an emergency or other urgent situation, a plaintiff may seek a *temporary restraining order* or a *preliminary injunction* rather than wait for trial to seek a *permanent injunction*.[16] In some cases the rules permit an *interlocutory appeal* before a final judgment is entered.

B. THE COMPLAINT: STATING A CLAIM

A civil lawsuit starts with a complaint.[17] The main object of a complaint is to *state a claim* against each defendant. This means the complaint should allege facts that, if you can prove them, will establish that the defendant violated your legal rights.

---

[3]Usually this means filing a grievance; in some cases it means using a different administrative appeal process, depending on the prison's rules. The exhaustion requirement of the federal Prison Litigation Reform Act (PLRA) is discussed in Ch. 9, § D. If your lawsuit is not about prison conditions, or if your suit is based on state rather than federal law, the PLRA exhaustion requirement does not apply, but another exhaustion requirement may apply instead. *See* Ch. 8, § K, concerning exhaustion of remedies generally. Many states have adopted exhaustion requirements similar to the PLRA that must be completed prior to filing a lawsuit in state court. *See, e.g.,* Mich. Compiled Law § 600.5503.

[4]Complaints are discussed in § B of this chapter.

[5]PLRA screening is discussed in Ch. 9, § C.

[6]IFP status is discussed in § C.3 of this chapter. The PLRA made many changes in the IFP rules for prisoners. These are discussed in Ch. 9, § A.

[7]Service of process is discussed in § C.4 of this chapter.

[8]Answers are discussed in § D of this chapter. Under the PLRA, defendants in prisoner cases need not file an answer unless the court directs them to do so. If the case passes the initial screening required by the PLRA, the court will generally direct defendants to reply. *See* Ch. 9, § G, concerning "waiver of reply."

[9]Motions to dismiss are discussed in § I of this chapter.

[10]Discovery is discussed in § K.2 of this chapter.

[11]Summary judgment is discussed in § L of this chapter.

[12]Trials are discussed in § R of this chapter.

[13]Injunctions are discussed in Ch. 8, § O.2.

[14]Appeals are discussed in § U of this chapter.

[15]Petition for certiorari are discussed in § U.2 of this chapter.

[16]These orders are discussed in Ch. 8, § O.2.

[17]This document is called a "petition" in federal habeas corpus and post-conviction proceedings and in some state court proceedings. In some state proceedings it is called a "claim."

1. Requirements of a Complaint[18]

A federal court complaint should be separated into numbered paragraphs. Each paragraph should be short and should be limited to "a single set of circumstances"[19]—usually meaning facts relating to the acts or omissions of a party, whether plaintiff or defendant. A civil complaint should contain the following specific information:

(1) A short and plain statement of the basis of the court's jurisdiction.[20] This section should have the heading "Jurisdiction" so the court can find it easily.

(2) The name and address of the plaintiff, usually you, and where you are incarcerated, along with the same information for any additional plaintiffs. This section and the next one should be headed "Parties."

(3) The name of each defendant and his job title and duties, with citation to any statutes, rules, or policy directives explaining those duties. If you don't know the identities of some defendants, you will have to list them as "John Doe" defendants and amend the complaint later to add their identities.[21]

(4) Optionally, you may wish to add a section headed "Exhaustion of Administrative Remedies" and a simple statement that you have exhausted all available remedies, if that is the case. In most prison conditions cases, exhaustion is not required to be pled, so if pleading it would be more complicated than a simple statement that you have exhausted, it is probably advisable to leave it out in most cases.[22] There are some claims for which the law does require a plaintiff to plead exhaustion of administrative remedies, and in those cases you must include an allegation of exhaustion.[23] State law may require pleading of administrative exhaustion;[24] if so, you should plead exhaustion of state law claims whether you bring them in state court or in federal court.

(5) A "short and plain statement of the claim showing that the pleader is entitled to relief"[25]—i.e., your factual allegations, usually in chronological order, showing that your legal rights have been violated and how each named defendant is connected to those legal violations. This section should be headed "Facts."

(6) A separate paragraph or paragraphs stating which of your legal rights were violated, and (briefly) how.[26] This section should be headed "Claims for Relief" or "Causes of Action."

(7) A request for the relief to which you are entitled, such as damages, an injunction, or both. This section should be headed "Relief Requested" or "Demand for Judgment." You may request more than one kind of relief.[27]

Many federal district courts require *pro se* litigants to use a standardized form complaint provided by the court.[28] The form will generally call for the same information as in the preceding list, plus additional items such as information on lawsuits you have previously filed and whether you have utilized administrative remedies. Concerning your litigation history, if you do not answer honestly, your case may

---

[18]Preparing a complaint is also discussed in Ch. 12, § B. A sample complaint is found at Appendix B.

[19]*See* Rule 10, Fed.R.Civ.P.

[20]Rule 8(a), Fed.R.Civ.P.

Prisoners alleging constitutional or other federal law violations should cite 28 U.S.C. § 1331(a), the general federal question jurisdiction statute. If your suit is based on diversity of citizenship, cite 28 U.S.C. § 1332(a)(1). *See* Ch. 8, §§ B.1, B.2, F.2, for further discussions of federal question and diversity jurisdiction. If you are including state law claims because they arise out of the same facts as federal claims, you should cite 28 U.S.C. § 1367, which provides for "supplemental" jurisdiction over such claims. *See* Ch. 8, § F.1, concerning supplemental jurisdiction.

[21]Concerning the use of John Doe defendants, *see* Davis v. Kelly, 160 F.3d 917, 921 (2d Cir. 1998) and cases cited; Soto v. Brooklyn Correctional Facility, 80 F.3d 34, 37 (2d Cir. 1996); Estate of Rosenberg by Rosenberg v. Crandell, 56 F.3d 35, 37 (8th Cir. 1995); Murphy v. Goord, 445 F. Supp. 2d 261, 266 (W.D.N.Y. 2006) (permitting plaintiff to use a pseudonym for unknown defendants, take discovery to identify them, then amend his complaint to add their correct names).

Amending the complaint is discussed in § J of this chapter. Issues involving John Doe defendants and the statute of limitations are discussed in Ch. 8, § N.

[22]This issue is discussed in Ch. 9, at the beginning of § D.8.

[23]For example, the Federal Tort Claims Act requires plaintiff to plead exhaustion, since exhaustion is necessary to the court's jurisdiction over the claim. *In re* Agent Orange Prod. Liab. Litig., 818 F.2d 210, 214 (2d Cir.1987).

[24]*See, e.g.*, Litzinger v. Bruce, 41 Kan.App.2d 9, 11, 201 P.3d 707 (Kan.App. 2008) (dismissing for failure to attach proof of exhaustion to petition); Boylen v. Ohio Dep't of Rehab. & Corr., 182 Ohio App.3d 265, 273, 912 N.E.2d 624 (2009) (citing statute requiring affidavit of exhaustion with the complaint); Pedraza v. Tibbs, 826 S.W.2d 695, 699 (Tex.App. 1992) (citing statute requiring documentary proof of exhaustion upon filing suit); Casteel v. McCaughtry, 168 Wis.2d 758, 484 N.W.2d 579, 585 (Wis.App. 1992) (exhaustion of administrative remedies and compliance with a notice of claim requirement must be pled in the complaint), *aff'd in part and rev'd in part on other grounds*, 176 Wis.2d 571, 500 N.W.2d 277 (Wis. 1993).

[25]Rule 8(a), Fed.R.Civ.P.

[26]*See* Chapters 2–6 for a discussion of these legal rights.

[27]Rule 8(a), Fed.R.Civ.P. *See* Ch. 8, § O for a discussion of different types of relief.

[28]*See* Appendix C, Form 1c, for a sample of a standardized complaint.

be dismissed.[29] Concerning exhaustion, if your answer is that you did not exhaust, or did not exhaust at the prison where you are presently held, be sure to clarify why, whether the form calls for an explanation or not.[30]

You may wish to verify your complaint. Verification means swearing or declaring under penalty of perjury that the facts alleged in your complaint are true. Swearing means signing a statement before a notary stating that the contents of the document are true and correct; declaring means that you write at the beginning or end of the document that you declare under penalty of perjury that its contents are true and correct, sign the statement, and date it.[31] The advantage of verifying your complaint is that if the defendants move for summary judgment, the verified complaint can be considered as if it were an affidavit in opposition to the motion; an unverified complaint cannot.[32]

The facts alleged in the complaint must support each element of the claim you are asserting.[33] For example, any complaint under 42 U.S.C. § 1983, the most frequently used civil rights statute, must contain facts showing that (a) you were denied a right protected by federal law, and (b) this was done by persons acting under color of state law.[34] Particular legal claims have their own additional elements; *e.g.*, to establish a violation of your Eighth Amendment medical care rights, you must show (a) that you had a serious medical need, and (b) the defendants acted with deliberate indifference towards it.[35] Your factual allegations must support both of those elements. In fact, if your factual allegations support a valid claim, the court should treat your complaint as raising that claim, even if you have not cited the right legal theory.[36]

There may be other pleading requirements depending on the kind of case you are bringing and the court you are in. Administrative exhaustion, as mentioned above, must be pled in some cases (but not in most federal civil rights actions). There are a few other items that must be specifically pled in federal court complaints,[37] but most of them have little application to prisoners' cases.

It is unclear how specific and detailed a complaint must be. The Federal Rules require "a short and plain statement of the claim showing that the pleader is entitled to relief,"[38] which means that federal court complaints generally need only give "fair notice of what the . . . claim is and the grounds upon which it rests."[39] However, recent Supreme Court decisions seem to have made the "fair notice" requirement much more demanding.

Formerly, the rule was that "a complaint should not be dismissed for failure to state a claim unless it appears beyond doubt that the plaintiff can prove no set of facts in support of his claim which would entitle him to relief."[40] The Supreme Court has now rejected that standard,[41] and has held that complaints must include enough factual matter to make the claims "plausible."[42] It then went on in *Ashcroft v. Iqbal*, a more recent case, to hold that the plausibility requirement "demands more than an unadorned, the-defendant-unlawfully-harmed-me accusation"; the "sheer possibility that a defendant has acted unlawfully" is insufficient, and pleading facts that are "merely consistent with" liability "stops short of the line between possibility and plausibility of 'entitlement to relief.'"[43] Further, the Supreme Court said, a court

---

[29]*See, e.g.*, Jackson v. Onondaga County, 549 F. Supp. 2d 204, 225–26 (N.D.N.Y. 2008); Dickerson v. Anderson, 2008 WL 4845226, *1 (S.D.Ga., Nov. 10, 2008).

[30]*See* Ch. 9, at the beginning of § IV.D.8, on this subject.

[31]28 U.S.C. § 1746.

[32]*See* § L.2.a for discussion of responding to a summary judgment motion.

[33]Phillips v. County of Allegheny, 515 F.3d 224, 234 (3d Cir. 2008).

[34]These element are discussed in Ch. 8, § B.1.

[35]*See* Ch. 2, § F for a discussion of medical care claims. Chapters 2–6 generally discuss the elements of most constitutional claims and state law tort claims that prisoners commonly bring.

[36]Phillips v. Girdich, 408 F.3d 124, 130 (2d Cir. 2005); O'Grady v. Village of Libertyville, 304 F.3d 719, 723 (7th Cir. 2002) ("A plaintiff is not required to set forth a legal theory to match the facts, so long as some legal theory can be sustained on the facts pleaded in the complaint."). Thus, in *Curry v. Kerik*, 163 F. Supp. 2d 232, 237 (S.D.N.Y. 2001), the plaintiff alleged he had been injured by hazardous jail conditions through the defendants' negligence, which does not state a federal constitutional claim; however, the facts he alleged supported a claim of deliberate indifference, and the case was allowed to go forward even though he had not pled a deliberate indifference claim.

[37]*See* Rule 9, Fed.R.Civ.P.

[38]Rule 8(a), Fed.R.Civ.P.

[39]*See* Bell Atlantic Corp. v. Twombly, 550 U.S. 544, 555, 127 S. Ct. 1955 (2007) (quoting Conley v. Gibson, 355 U.S. 41, 47, 78 S. Ct. 99 (1957)); *accord*, Swierkiewicz v. Sorema, 534 U.S. 506, 512, 122 S. Ct. 992 (2002).

[40]Conley v. Gibson, 355 U.S. 41, 45–46, 78 S. Ct. 99 (1957).

[41]Bell Atlantic Corp. v. Twombly, 550 U.S. 544, 561–62, 127 S. Ct. 1955 (2007).

[42]Bell Atlantic Corp. v. Twombly, 550 U.S. at 570 (". . . [W]e do not require heightened fact pleading of specifics, but only enough facts to state a claim to relief that is plausible on its face."); *see id.*, 550 U.S. at 555 ("While a complaint attacked by a Rule 12(b)(6) motion to dismiss does not need detailed factual allegations, . . . a plaintiff's obligation to provide the grounds' of his 'entitle[ment] to relief' requires more than labels and conclusions and a formulaic recitations of the elements of a cause of action will not do. . . ."); Phillips v. County of Allegheny, 515 F.3d 224, 234 (3d Cir. 2008) (under *Bell Atlantic*, each element of the claim must meet the plausibility standard; "'stating . . . a claim requires a complaint with enough factual matter (taken as true) to suggest' the required element. This 'does not impose a probability requirement at the pleading stage,' but instead 'simply calls for enough facts to raise a reasonable expectation that discovery will reveal evidence of the necessary element.'"); Ridge at Red Lawk, L.L.C. v. Schneider, 493 F.3d 1174, 1177 (10th Cir. 2007) (". . . [T]he complaint must give the court reason to believe that this plaintiff has a reasonable likelihood of mustering factual support for these claims.").

[43]Ashcroft v. Iqbal, ___ U.S. ___, 129 S. Ct. 1937, 1949 (2009).

must "draw on its judicial experience and common sense" in determining whether allegations are plausible.[44]

Exactly what all this means is not clear, especially because the *Ashcroft v. Iqbal* decision is so new that as we write this (late 2009, with a quick update in early 2010), there are only a few decisions that give any useful guidance. Clearly, mere recitations of legal conclusions or "conclusory statements" are not sufficient to state a claim.[45] Some courts have concluded that detailed pleading of facts is now required in order to state a claim.[46] In particular, some are demanding that plaintiffs plead supporting facts if they allege that defendants acted with illegal intent such as intent to discriminate, retaliate, etc.[47] As for plausibility, some courts seem to think that if there is an explanation of what happened to you that seems more plausible to the court than what you allege, then your allegations are not plausible and your complaint does not state a claim.[48] This is troublesome,

since some judges may not understand the extent to which law and rules are sometimes disregarded in prison. It also may infringe upon the jury trial provision of the Seventh Amendment, which "requires that the jury be allowed to make reasonable inferences from facts proven in evidence having a reasonable tendency to sustain them."[49] Other courts have taken a narrower view of the plausibility requirement, holding that an alternative explanation must be "so overwhelming that the [plaintiff's] claims no longer appear plausible."[50]

Under *Iqbal*, defendants will probably make motions routinely to dismiss prisoners' complaints on the ground that their allegations are not sufficiently plausible or factually supported. This is likely to be especially true of complaints against supervisory-level governmental defendants.[51]

---

[44]*Iqbal*, 129 S. Ct. at 1950.

[45]*Iqbal*, 129 S. Ct. at 1949; *Bell Atlantic*, 550 U.S. at 555 (citing Papasan v. Allain, 478 U.S. 265, 286, 106 S. Ct. 2932 (1986)). *See* Roberts v. Babkiewicz, 582 F.3d 418, 422 (2d Cir. 2009) (allegation in complaint that prosecution was dropped "because it was apparent from medical evidence that the plaintiff was innocent of the charge" was plausible and non-conclusory).

[46]*See, e.g.*, Vasquez-Hernandez v. Estrada-Adorno, 2009 WL 1586813, *1 (D.P.R., June 3, 2009) (holding an allegation of gender discrimination in access to rehabilitation and treatment programs is conclusory without allegations of particular programs that the plaintiff was denied); Carrea v. California, 2009 WL 1770130, *9 (C.D.Cal, June 18, 2009) (holding that allegation that no white inmate was ever treated as the plaintiff was did not state an equal protection claim because the complaint did not spell out how similarly situated white prisoners were treated).

[47]*See, e.g.*, Moss v. U.S. Secret Service, 572 F.3d 962, 970–71 (9th Cir. 2009) (allegations that Secret Service moved anti-Bush protesters because of their political views, and did so pursuant to an unwritten policy, were conclusory in the absence of supporting facts).

[48]*See, e.g.*, Monroe v. City of Charlottesville, Va., 579 F.3d 380, 388-89 (4th Cir. 2009) (holding that it was more plausible police stopped the plaintiff because he resembled the description of a suspect than because he was black); Lacy v. Tyson, 2009 WL 2777026, *4 (E.D.Cal., Aug. 27, 2009) (holding that plaintiff's claim of retaliatory placement in segregation for filing grievances against staff for assaulting him was not plausible because it was more likely he was placed there for his own protection); Blanchard v. Yates, 2009 WL 2460761, *3 (E.D.Cal., July 27, 2009) (holding that plaintiff's claim that the warden was deliberately indifferent to the risk that he would contract an infectious disease as a result of a transfer was implausible because it is "more likely" that the defendant transferred the plaintiff based on advice of medical professionals); *see* King v. United Way of Central Carolinas, Inc., 2009 WL 2432706, *8 (W.D.N.C., Aug. 6, 2009) (holding claim must be dismissed if a "lawful alternative explanation" appears more likely than the unlawful explanation put forward by the plaintiff). This view is based on *Iqbal*'s conclusion that it was more likely that the post-9/11 detainee plaintiffs were kept in restrictive conditions because of their suspected terrorist connections than because of their race, religion, or national origin.

[49]Galloway v. U.S., 319 U.S. 372, 396, 63 S. Ct. 1077 (1943); *accord*, Anderson v. Liberty Lobby, Inc., 477 U.S. 242, 255, 106 S. Ct. 2505 (1986) ("Credibility determinations, the weighing of the evidence, and the drawing of legitimate inferences from the facts are jury functions, not those of a judge."); Tennant v. Peoria & P.U.R. Co., 321 U.S. 29, 35, 64 S. Ct. 409 (1944) ("The very essence of [the jury's] function is to select from among conflicting inferences and conclusions that which it considers most reasonable." (quoted in Rogers v. Missouri Pac. R. Co., 352 U.S. 500, 504 n.8, 77 S. Ct. 443 (1957)). We haven't seen any case law on this point yet, but one law review article has argued that *Iqbal*'s interpretation of Rule 8, Fed.R.Civ.P., makes some applications of Rule 8 unconstitutional under the Seventh Amendment. Kenneth S. Klein, *Ashcroft v. Iqbal Crashes Rule 8 Pleading Standards on to Unconstitutional Shores*, 88 Neb. L. Rev. 261 (2009).

[50]Chao v. Ballista, 630 F. Supp. 2d 170, 177 (D.Mass. 2009) ("Allegations become 'conclusory' where they recite only the elements of the claim and, at the same time, the court's commonsense credits a far more likely inference from the available facts. . . . Yet in keeping with Rule 8(a), a complaint should only be dismissed at the pleading stage where the allegations are so broad, and the alternative explanations so overwhelming, that the claims no longer appear plausible."). In *Chao*, the court held that the plaintiff's specific factual allegations of "repetitive, long-lasting sexual abuse," along with the public attention given to sexual abuse in prisons generally, supported a claim that prison officials, including the Commissioner, were deliberately indifferent to it. *Chao*, 630 F. Supp. 2d at 178. *See also* Garfield v. Cook County, 2009 WL 4015553 (N.D. Ill. Nov. 19, 2009) ("While [plaintiff's use of force] claims largely lack detail, the escalation of a prison official-prisoner disagreement into violence is not so improbable that [plaintiff's] claims must be dismissed."); Schoppel v. Schrader, 2009 WL 1886090, *6-7 (N.D. Ind. June 30, 2009) (allegations that County Council knew that the jail was understaffed, provided inadequate medical care as a result, and did not have a classification system that would identify prisoners with medical problems, and that these factors caused a prisoner's death, and was deliberately indifferent in not providing funding to remedy these problems, sufficiently pled a deliberate indifference claim).

[51]*See* Kyle v. Holina, 2009 WL 1867671, *1-2 (W.D.Wis., June 29, 2009) (holding allegations that defendants were "aware and in control of the segregated environ[m]ents" and they "allow this practice to be carried out in the living qua[r]ters and chow halls of the prison or prison[s] under their control," and that they had

Iqbal held that such complaints must allege "that each Government-official defendant, through the official's own individual actions, has violated the Constitution."[52] In *Ashcroft*, the plaintiff had alleged intentional discrimination based on race, religion, or national origin, and the Supreme Court said that since such a claim required proof of intentional discrimination, the plaintiff must plead facts indicating that the supervisory officials acted with discriminatory intent,[53] not just that they were aware that their subordinates had done so.[54] So it may be, *e.g.*, that now prisoners alleging an Eighth Amendment violation and naming supervisory officials as defendants must allege, and have some factual basis supporting the allegation, that those defendants as well as line staff were deliberately indifferent, since deliberate indifference is generally required to show an Eighth Amendment violation.[55]

Here are a few things to keep in mind in preparing complaints and in responding to motions to dismiss after *Bell Atlantic* and *Iqbal*:[56]

(1) Avoid "conclusory allegations," *i.e.*, broad statements that defendants have violated your rights without factual support. Be clear about what you think each defendant did, or failed to do, to violate your legal rights.[57] If you allege that a defendant acted with improper intent, *e.g.*, to retaliate against you for complaining, or to discriminate against you based on race, religion, etc., state the factual basis for that belief.[58] If you think a defendant failed to perform a duty, make clear what you think the person's duty was, and why.

(2) Account for alternative explanations. State whatever facts you can that would contradict a defendant's claim, or a judge's belief, that there is some lawful explanation for what happened to you that is more likely than what you allege. For example, in a use of force case, state whatever facts would make it clear that staff were not using force lawfully to keep order: *e.g.*, that you did nothing to provoke force except to say something the officer did not like, or you did not physically resist the officer, or that you were in handcuffs when you were beaten, if any of those things are the case. If there were other officers present who did not stop an officer from beating you, be sure to make it clear that they had a realistic opportunity to intervene, if that is the case.

(3) Amend your complaint if needed. The Federal Rules of Civil Procedure allow amendment "as a

---

imposed an "unwritten policy of segregation," did not sufficiently plead a claim of intentional racial discrimination against prison warden, regional director, and national director of prisons). *But see* Young v. State of New York Office of Mental Retardation and Development Disabilities, 649 F. Supp. 2d 282, 294 (S.D.N.Y. 2009) (denying summary judgment on supervisory liability pending development of facts, despite court's doubts about claim); Vaden v. Campbell, 2009 WL 1919474, *3 (N.D. Fla., July 2, 2009) (Plaintiff alleged she was sexually assaulted by a deputy, that he had been sexually aggressive before, and that the Sheriff should have known it and put a stop to it. "The allegations plausibly assert a claim for negligent supervision or retention.").

Iqbal and supervisory liability are discussed further in Ch. 8, § B.4.a.

Iqbal may also be a problem in pleading municipal liability, since courts may be less willing than before to allow a claim of municipal policy to go forward based only on what a plaintiff has personally experienced. *See* 5 Borough Pawn, LLC v. City of New York, 640 F. Supp. 2d 268, 299-300 (S.D.N.Y. 2009) (allegation that police misconduct resulted from municipal policy was implausible because plaintiff did not identify other officers who acted similarly; it was more plausible that the defendant "was a rogue officer who disobeyed City policy"). *But see* Schoppel v. Schrader, 2009 WL 1886090, *6-7 (N.D. Ind., June 30, 2009) (plaintiff sufficiently pled a deliberate indifference claim against a county council by alleging that they knew the jail was understaffed, lacked a medical classification system, provided inadequate medical care, and still failed to provide adequate funding to cure the problems).

[52]Ashcroft v. Iqbal, 129 S. Ct. at 1948. Municipal liability is discussed further in Ch. 8, § B.4.b.

[53]*Iqbal*, 129 S. Ct. at 1952.

[54]*Iqbal*, 129 S. Ct. at 1949.

[55]*See* Ch. 2, § A.2, concerning deliberate indifference.

[56]This discussion has benefited considerably from presentations by Prof. Alexander Reinert of Cardozo Law School and Jane Perkins, Esq., of the National Health Law Program.

[57]One court recently said, when dismissing a complaint with leave to amend:

When drafting his amended complaint, [the plaintiff] should ask himself whether someone reading the complaint should be able to answer the following questions with respect to each claim:

- What are the facts that form the basis for plaintiff's claims?
- What did each defendant do that makes him or her liable for violating plaintiff's rights?
- How was plaintiff injured by a particular defendant's conduct?

Palmore v. Mass, 2009 WL 1749797, *2 (W.D.Wis., June 19, 2009). This standard is not necessarily very demanding. *See* Evans v. Tavares, 2009 WL 3187282 (N.D. Ill., Sept. 30, 2009) (allegations were "grounded in sufficient specific facts to render them plausible" where false arrest claim alleged that defendants " knew Plaintiff had committed no crime but arrested him anyway" and excessive force claim alleged that "although he was in no way resisting arrest, some or all of the Individual Defendants slammed him into a vehicle"). *But see* Arar v. Ashcroft, 585 F.3d 559, 569 (2d Cir. 2009) (holding plaintiff who "fail[ed] to specify any culpable action taken by any single defendant" failed to state a claim against any of them), *pet. for cert. filed*, No. 09-92378, U.S.L.W. 3461 (Feb. 1, 2010);.

[58]One court has suggested that since the deliberate indifference standard that governs many supervisory claims requires less of a showing of intent than the discrimination claim at issue in *Iqbal*, less may be required to plead a deliberate indifference claim than an intentional discrimination claim. Chao v. Ballista, 630 F. Supp. 2d 170, 178 (D.Mass 2009). The deliberate indifference standard and what facts can support a deliberate indifference claim are discussed in Ch. 2, §§ A.2, F.1, G.1.a, G.3.

matter of course" within 21 days after the service of a motion to dismiss, and provide that the court should grant leave "freely" at other times.[59] If a motion cites shortcomings in your complaint that you can correct by amending, you should do so. Most courts have also held that if your complaint is dismissed for inadequate pleading under *Iqbal*, you should have the option to amend your complaint at that point.[60]

(4) Emphasize that your case is different from *Iqbal*. That case involved "a national and international security emergency unprecedented in the history of the American Republic."[61] In addition, it sought damages against extremely high-level government officials. Remind the judge of these facts, which may have affected the way the Supreme Court decided the case. Your case will almost certainly be more ordinary than *Iqbal*, and courts may not demand such detailed pleading. The Supreme Court decided a prison case shortly after the *Twombly* decision, and held that a prisoner adequately stated a claim of Eighth Amendment violation by alleging that a doctor had stopped his prescribed hepatitis C medication, and was "endangering [his] life"; he said this medication was withheld "shortly after" petitioner had commenced a one-year treatment program, that he was "still in need of treatment for this disease," and that the prison officials were in the meantime refusing to provide treatment.[62] Since it is unlikely that *Iqbal* was intended to overrule this decision (and it certainly doesn't say so), you can argue that the level of detail and plausibility of the complaint in that case indicates the standard you have to meet.

(5) Remind the court that the Supreme Court has recently said that the Federal Rules do not require "heightened pleading" except where the Rules spell out such a requirement,[63] and that

courts are not free to impose such requirements on their own.[64] Those holdings, which the Court in *Iqbal* did not say it was overruling,[65] should limit the extent to which lower courts can demand extreme factual specificity in pleading.

(6) Remind the court that courts have generally held *pro se* complaints to less stringent standards than formal pleadings drafted by lawyers,[66] and have acknowledged the special problems in writing detailed complaints that are caused by incarceration.[67] Courts have also held that they should consider other documents a *pro se* prisoner has filed, in addition to the complaint, in determining whether the prisoner has stated a claim.[68] The *Iqbal* case was not *pro se* and the Supreme Court's decision gave no hint that it intended to overrule these decisions.

(7) Check the development of the law in your federal circuit and the Supreme Court—and in Congress. The *Iqbal* decision is very new and there will be many decisions interpreting it which will make it easier to know what is required and, we hope, easier to defend your complaint against a motion to dismiss. Also, there is already a bill in Congress to overrule

[59]Rule 15(a), Fed.R.Civ.P.

[60]*See* Moss v. U.S. Secret Service, 572 F.3d 962, 965 (9th Cir. 2009); Coleman v. Tulsa Cty. Bd. of Cty Comm'rs, 2009 WL 2513520, *3 (N.D. Okla., Aug. 11, 2009); Wilson v. Pallman, 2009 WL 2448577, *6 (E.D.Pa., Aug. 7, 2009); Brenston v. Wal-Mart, 2009 WL 1606935, *5 (N.D.Ind., June 8, 2009). *But see* Carrea v. California, 2009 WL 1770130, *10 (C.D.Cal., June 18, 2009) (denying leave to amend where plaintiff had tried three times without stating a claim against some defendants).

[61]Ashcroft v. Iqbal, ___ U.S. ___, 129 S. Ct. 1937, 1954 (2009).

[62]Erickson v. Pardus, 551 U.S. 89, 94, 127 S. Ct. 2197 (2007) (per curiam).

[63]Swierkiewicz v. Sorema, 534 U.S. 506, 512–13, 122 S. Ct. 992 (2002) (employment discrimination cases); Leatherman v. Tarrant County Narcotics Intelligence & Coordination Unit, 507 U.S. 163, 168, 113 S. Ct. 1160 (1993) (claims of municipal liability).

Both these cases emphasize that the only exceptions to the "notice pleading" standard of Rule 8(a) are those set out in Rule 9(b). *See* Morgan v. U.S., 323 F.3d 776, 780 (9th Cir. 2003) ("Heightened pleading standards no longer apply to constitutional claims involving improper motives.") The Court in Bell Atlantic Corp. v. Twombly, 550 U.S. 544, 569 n.14, 127 S. Ct. 1955 (2007), also said it was not establishing a heightened pleading standard, and *Iqbal* said it was applying *Twombly*. Ashcroft v. Iqbal, 129 S.Ct. at 1949–51.

[64]Swierkiewicz v. Sorema, 543 U.S. at 512–13.

[65]*See* Palmore v. Mass, 2009 WL 1749797, *1 (W.D.Wis., June 19, 2009) (assuming *Swierkewicz* and *Iqbal* are compatible). Some lower courts do seem to think that *Iqbal* overruled *Swierkiewicz* with respect to pleading requirements. *See* Fowler v. UPMC Shadyside, 578 F.3d 203, 211 (3d Cir. 2009).

[66]Erickson v. Pardus, 551 U.S. 89, 94, 127 S. Ct. 2197 (2007) (per curiam); Hughes v. Rowe, 449 U.S. 5, 9, 101 S. Ct. 173 (1980) (citing Haines v. Kerner, 404 U.S. 519, 520–21, 92 S. Ct. 594 (1972) (per curiam) (*pro se* complaints are entitled to liberal construction)).

[67]Billman v. Indiana Dep't of Corr., 56 F.3d 785, 789–90 (7th Cir. 1995) (Posner, C.J.) ("The peculiar perversity of imposing heightened pleading standards in prisoner cases . . . is that it is far more difficult for a prisoner to write a detailed complaint than for a free person to do so, and again this is not because the prisoner does not know the law but because he is not able to investigate before filing suit."); *accord*, Rodriguez v. Plymouth Ambulance Service, 577 F.3d 816, 821 (7th Cir. 2009); Alston v. Parker, 363 F.3d 229, 233 n.6 (3d Cir. 2004).

[68]Warren v. District of Columbia, 353 F.3d 36, 38 (D.C. Cir. 2004); Dellairo v. Garland, 222 F. Supp. 2d 86, 89 (D.Me. 2002); Preston v. New York, 223 F. Supp. 2d 452, 461 (S.D.N.Y. 2002), *aff'd*, 87 Fed.Appx. 221 (2d Cir. 2004) (unpublished).

Iqbal's pleading requirements, the Notice Pleading Restoration Act of 2009,[69] though we have no idea whether it will pass.

To try to make the distinction between pleading facts and pleading legal conclusions more concrete, here is an example of a legal conclusion or conclusory statement, of the sort that does not adequately state a claim:

Defendant Hoffman retaliated against me for exercising my constitutional rights.

Now here are allegations that give "fair notice of what the plaintiff's claim is *and the grounds upon which it rests*,"[70] by outlining the facts supporting each element of the claim:

(1) I have filed several prior lawsuits against prison staff.

(2) Defendant Hoffman told me that since I like filing lawsuits against officers he was going to place me in segregation for a long, long time.

(3) Defendant Hoffman then wrote a misconduct falsely claiming that I had threatened his life.

(4) I was found guilty of the threatening behavior at a disciplinary hearing.

(5) As a result of Defendant Hoffman writing the false misconduct, I spent two years in segregation until the misconduct was set aside.

(6) As a result of this false misconduct, I lost my prison job; I was denied parole; I could only have non-contact visitation instead of contact visiting; I was removed from prison programs recommended to complete prior to parole.

(7) My First Amendment right to petition the courts was violated by defendant Hoffman's filing of this false misconduct.

These factual allegations plausibly support the elements of a First Amendment retaliation claim, which are:

- that the speech or conduct at issue was protected (paragraph 1 refers to filing lawsuits, which is protected under the First Amendment);
- that the defendant took adverse action against the plaintiff (paragraphs 3 through 7 allege facts that constitute adverse action); and
- that there was a causal connection between the protected speech and the adverse action (paragraphs 2 and 3 state facts that support the argument that the plaintiff was disciplined in retaliation, rather than as a result of actually violating prison rules).[71]

2. Joinder: Multiple Claims, Defendants, or Plaintiffs

If someone is going to be a defendant in your case, you can bring as many claims as you have against that party in the same case.[72] In fact, if you have multiple claims against a party arising from the same factual situation, you may have to bring them in the same action, because under the rules of *res judicata* you may not be permitted to litigate additional claims later about those same facts.[73]

You can also sue more than one defendant in the same action *if* your claims against them "aris[e] out of the same transaction, occurrence, or series of transactions or occurrences" and if "any question of law or fact common to all defendants will arise in the action."[74] That is, you cannot bring different claims against different people in the same action if the claims are not related to each other. In the past, courts did not always pay much attention to this rule. However, nowadays they are concerned that prisoners will try to avoid the filing fee and "three strikes" provisions of the Prison Litigation Reform Act (PLRA) by joining claims in one complaint that really should be filed in separate actions which would require separate filing fees and would count as separate "strikes" if dismissed on certain grounds.[75]

You should therefore make clear in your complaint, and be prepared to argue if necessary, your basis for asserting that different claims do arise from the same "transaction, occurrence, or series of transaction or occurrences," and that questions of law or fact common to all defendants will arise. That does not mean you can never bring suit about incidents that happen at different times and places. It does mean you have to have some basis for arguing that the different claims are not unrelated.

Here are some examples of different ways that claims can be related.

- In one recent decision, a prisoner raised six different claims involving different defendants that arose at four different times, and the court held that the only ones that could be brought in

---

[69]S. 1504, 111th Cong. (2009). This statute would restore the *Conley v. Gibson* pleading standard referred to in n.40, above.

[70]Bell Atlantic Corp. v. Twombly, 550 U.S. 544, 555, 127 S. Ct. 1955 (2007) (emphasis supplied) (citation omitted).

[71]*See* Gill v. Pidlypchak, 389 F.3d 379, 380 (2d Cir. 2004); *see also* Ch. 3, § B.6, concerning First Amendment retaliation claims. That chapter shows that the elements of such a claim have been

stated in different ways, but they generally add up to the same thing.

[72]Rule 18(a), Fed.R.Civ.P.

[73]For example, if you bring suit alleging that an officer used excessive force against you in violation of the Eighth Amendment, and you also want to argue that this conduct constituted a state law assault and battery, you will probably need to bring these claims in the same lawsuit unless there is another legal rule that prevents you from doing so.

[74]Rule 20(a)(2), Fed.R.Civ.P.

[75]*See* George v. Smith, 507 F.3d 605, 607–08 (7th Cir. 2007); Valdez v. Dretke, 2007 WL 2177007, *8–9 (S.D.Tex., July 26, 2007); *see also* Pope v. Miller, 2007 WL 2427978, *4–5 (W.D.Okla., Aug. 21, 2007) (holding claims of two plaintiffs misjoined under Federal Rules where they involved distinct factual issues as to exhaustion and merits). The PLRA filing fees and "three strikes" provisions are discussed in Ch. 9, §§ A and B.

the same lawsuit were claims of excessive force, and of denial of medical or mental health care following that same use of force.[76]

- If you were prevented from receiving different books or magazines by different staff members at different prisons, but the denials were all pursuant to a statewide policy—or if the policy is fine, but if there is a pattern of failure to enforce it—then you have an argument that your claims against different defendants are related.

- If your claim is that you were subjected to deliberate indifference to your medical needs over a period of time by different medical practitioners, you would argue that the various failures to provide treatment were part of "the same . . . series of transactions or occurrences" as required by Rule 20(a).

- If your claim is that you were beaten on three different occasions by three different groups of prison staff, but you had some basis to argue that the incidents were linked (e.g., if there were a particular supervisor with authority over all the staff who tolerated or encouraged such behavior, or if there were a pattern of excessive force on a particular unit), then joinder might be proper. Otherwise you would have to file separate suits.

The Federal Rules also provide that *plaintiffs* may join together in one action, on the same basis as defendants may be joined: if the plaintiffs' claims "aris[e] out of the same transaction, occurrence, or series of transactions or occurrences" and if "any question of law or fact common to all plaintiffs will arise in the action."[77] This subject, too, has become complicated by the PLRA. Several courts have held that prisoners may not file joint complaints any more because the PLRA forbids it and overrides the joinder rules. Other courts have held that prisoners can file joint complaints just like anybody else, but unlike other litigants they must each pay an entire filing fee. We think both of these ideas are wrong, and explain why in another chapter.[78] However, if you are in a federal circuit that has ruled adversely on one of these questions, you will be stuck with that ruling, so be sure to find out the law in your jurisdiction.

C. STARTING YOUR LAWSUIT

To get a lawsuit started, you must file your complaint and serve process on the defendants. We explain how to do this in the next several sections. The bottom line is this: for an indigent prisoner, the easiest way to proceed is to file the

complaint by mail, ask the court to let you proceed *in forma pauperis* (without prepaying of the filing fees) if you are eligible to do so, and have process served by the U. S. Marshal.

However, a friend outside prison can file the complaint for you in person.[79] If you are in a hurry and have the money, you can pay the filing fee and move ahead more quickly, and you can also try to serve process by mail or through a friend or paid process server. You may also be able to expedite the case by moving for a preliminary injunction or a temporary restraining order, assuming you meet the legal requirements for obtaining such relief.[80]

Filing and service procedures for *pro se* litigants vary from court to court, and you (or a friend who is helping you) should try to find out the exact requirements of the court you will be filing in. The court clerk's office, or the *pro se* clerk's office if there is one, should be able to answer questions, and in many cases they can provide written instructions. Some courts have placed instructions for *pro se* litigants on the Internet.[81] A friend could download these and send them to you in prison, or the prison law library may have them or be able to obtain them for you.

1. Filing the Complaint

A federal court civil lawsuit "is commenced by filing a complaint with the court."[82] To file a complaint, you send it to the

---

[76]Vasquez v. Schueler, 2007 WL 5431016, *2 (W.D.Wis., Nov. 29, 2007), *clarified*, 2007 WL 5514113 (W.D. Wis., Dec. 10, 2007).

[77]Rule 20(a)(1), Fed.R.Civ.P.

[78]*See* Ch. 9, § A, nn.60–65.

[79]Someone trying to file a complaint in person may have to fill out civil cover sheets or the summons, in addition to paying the fee.

[80]Procedures and legal standards for obtaining these orders are discussed in Ch. 8, § O.2. They are reserved for litigants who face "irreparable harm" if they do not get quick relief from the court.

[81]*See, e.g., A Manual for Pro Se Litigants Appearing Before the United States District Court for the Southern District of New York* (2007), *available at* http://www1.nysd.uscourts.gov/cases/show.php?db=forms&id=71 (visited November 22, 2008).

[82]Rule 3, Fed.R.Civ.P.

Sometimes there is a question about the date an action is commenced, especially if you seek to proceed *in forma pauperis*, since your complaint will not be formally filed until your IFP application is decided, which may involve some delay. For purposes of satisfying the statute of limitations, your case is deemed to have been commenced either when the clerk receives the complaint, or when you put it into the prison legal mail system for mailing to the clerk. *See* Ch. 8, § N., nn.960–964, and § H of this chapter discussing the "prison mailbox" rule. Similarly, if a court is determining whether you waited until after you exhausted your administrative remedies before bringing suit, you are deemed to have brought suit when you submitted the complaint. *See* Ch. 9, § IV.D.1, n.241. However, the deadline for serving process runs from the time the complaint is formally filed. *See* § C.4.a of this chapter, n.184.

clerk of the court.[83] You must also submit either the filing fee or your motion to proceed *in forma pauperis*.[84]

Different courts have different requirements for how many copies of the summons and complaint to file. For example, for *pro se* litigants who wish to have process served by the Marshal, some federal courts require the plaintiff to supply

- a copy of the summons[85] and complaint for the court file;
- a copy of the summons and complaint for each defendant;
- an extra copy for the clerk to date-stamp and return to you;
- an extra copy for the judge's chambers.[86]

The clerk will then forward the summonses and complaints to the Marshal for service.[87]

A New York district court, by contrast, requires *pro se* litigants to submit only the original and two copies of the complaint. It prepares the summons itself and sends the complaint and the original summons back to the *pro se* plaintiff, with copies for each defendant, along with instructions and forms that must be filled out in order for the Marshal to serve the complaint. The plaintiff is then responsible for forwarding the proper numbers of summonses[88] and complaints for service on all defendants, along with properly filled out service forms, to the Marshal.[89] So be sure you read the rules of the court you are filing in to see what is required.

2. Venue

You must file your federal court complaint in the correct judicial district, or venue. Since Congress amends the venue statute every so often, be sure you have the current version, and that any court decisions you rely on are applying the current statutory provisions.

Under current law, in most civil actions, venue is proper in

(1) a judicial district where any defendant resides, if all defendants reside in the same State,

(2) a judicial district in which a substantial part of the events or omissions giving rise to the claim occurred, or a substantial part of property that is the subject of the action is situated, or

(3) a judicial district in which any defendant may be found, if there is no district in which the action may otherwise be brought.[90]

These provisions apply to suits against state and local prison officials or personnel both in their individual and in their official capacities. They also apply to suits against federal officials sued in their individual capacities (*i.e.*, for damages).[91] If the case is brought against federal officials in their official capacities—*i.e.*, for injunctive relief—venue is proper in any district where

(1) a defendant in the action resides,

(2) a substantial part of the events or omissions giving rise to the claim occurred, or a substantial part of

---

[83]Rule 5(e) states that the judge may permit papers to be filed with the judge. You can't file your complaint this way.

[84]*In forma pauperis* proceedings are discussed in § C.3 of this chapter.

[85]A summons informs the defendant that he or she has been sued and states the time period in which a response must be made. The required contents of a summons are set out in Rule 4(a), Fed.R.Civ.P. (formerly Rule 4[b]). *See* Appendix C, Form 4, for an example of a summons.

[86]*See, e.g.*, Rule 5.1[b], Local Rules for Civil Cases, United States District Court for the Eastern District of Michigan.

[87]If the Marshalls are responsible for service, they usually will use the mail to serve the complaint and summons on a named defendant. Service in this manner can take a fair amount of time.

[88]The original summons—the one with the embossed court seal on it—should be filed in court after service of process has been accomplished.

[89]*A Manual for Pro Se Litigants Appearing Before the United States District Court for the Southern District of New York* at 48–52 (2007).

[90]28 U.S.C. § 1391 (b); *see* Arnold v. Maynard, 942 F.2d 761, 162 n.2 (10th Cir. 1991) (claim against officials in prison in one district and central correctional offices in another district could be filed in either district); Gwynn v. Transcor America, Inc., 26 F. Supp. 2d 1256, 1260–63 (D.Colo. 1998) (where plaintiff alleged a course of sexual assault by transport personnel over seven states, venue was proper where some of the events occurred); Carillo v. Darden, 992 F. Supp. 1024, 1025 (N.D.Ill. 1998) (venue was proper in district where one of several defendants lived); Smiley v. Reno, 131 F. Supp. 2d 839, 841 (W.D.La. 2001) (where defendants lived in two districts, venue was proper in either, and court could not break up the case and transfer part to the other district); Perez v. Hawk, 302 F. Supp. 2d 9, 17–18 (E.D.N.Y. 2004) (similar to *Smiley*; court would not sever claims that were related in order to transfer some claims to another district); *see also* Myers v. Bennett Law Offices, 238 F.3d 1068, 1076 (9th Cir. 2001) (in determining venue in a tort action, the place where the injury occurred is a relevant factor), and cases cited.

[91]Stafford v. Briggs, 444 US. 527, 544, 100 S. Ct. 774 (1980); Flanagan v. Shively, 783 F. Supp. 922, 935 (M.D.Pa. 1992), *aff'd*, 980 F.2d 722 (3d Cir. 1992).

The District of Columbia federal courts are reluctant to hear cases brought by federal prisoners incarcerated in other parts of the country. If you claim that "events or omissions giving rise to the claim" took place in Washington, D.C., you must be prepared to substantiate your claim. Cameron v. Thornburgh, 983 F.2d 253, 256–57 (D.C. Cir. 1993) (expressing concern about "manufacturing venue" in D.C.; transferring case). A claim that federal defendants had enforced policies made in D.C. does not necessarily make D.C. a proper venue. Zakiya v. U.S., 267 F. Supp. 2d 47, 53–54 (D.D.C. 2003); Huskey v. Quinlan, 785 F. Supp. 4, 7 (D.D.C. 1992) (holding policies made in D.C. did not support venue in D.C. where plaintiff "principally takes issue with the conduct of individuals, not with the policies underlying that conduct," and because implementation of policy in another district was at issue, venue was more appropriate in the other district).

property that is the subject of the action is situated, or

(3) the plaintiff resides if no real property is involved in the action.[92]

Venue in a Federal Tort Claims Act (FTCA) suit against the federal government is proper in the district where the plaintiff resides or the act or omissions complained of occurred.[93]

In a diversity of citizenship[94] case, venue is proper in

(1) a judicial district where any defendant resides, if all defendants reside in the same State,

(2) a judicial district in which a substantial part of the events or omissions giving rise to the claim occurred, or a substantial part of property that is the subject of the action is situated, or

(3) a judicial district in which the defendants are subject to personal jurisdiction at the time the action is commenced.[95]

If you file in the wrong venue, the court may dismiss the case, or may transfer the case to a district where venue is proper.[96] Even if venue is proper in the district where the case was filed, a federal district court has discretion to transfer a case to a different district in which venue is also proper "[f]or the convenience of parties and witnesses, in the interest of justice."[97] However, defendants must meet a "heavy burden" to overcome the plaintiff's choice of venue, especially when the prisoner sues in the district he is in.[98] This change of venue statute is sometimes invoked in prison cases

to transfer the case to the district in which the plaintiff is incarcerated[99] or in which a substantial part of the alleged legal violation occurred.[100]

For venue purposes, the majority of courts hold that a prisoner "resides" in the district where he lived before his incarceration, or where he intends to live after release.[101] The "residence" of a public official or officer sued in his official capacity is the place where he performs his official duties.[102] Some courts have held that state officials who perform official duties in several districts may be deemed to "reside" in more than one judicial district.[103]

---

[92]28 U.S.C. § 1391 (e); Stafford v. Briggs, 444 U.S. at 543–45.

[93]28 U.S.C. § 1402(b); see Kimberlin v. Quinlan, 774 F. Supp. 1, 9–10 (D.D.C. 1991) (venue was proper in the District of Columbia for FTCA claims arising from the conduct of federal employees in that district but not for other claims unconnected with the district), rev'd on other grounds, 6 F.3d 789 (D.C. Cir. 1993), vacated and remanded on other grounds, 515 U.S. 321, 115 S. Ct. 2552 (1995).

[94]Diversity of citizenship means that the plaintiff and defendants are citizens of different states. You will need to rely on diversity jurisdiction only if you have no federal claims but are trying to bring a state law claim in federal court. See Ch. 8, § F.2, for a discussion of the federal courts' diversity jurisdiction.

[95]28 U.S.C. § 1391(a).

[96]28 U.S.C. § 1404; see Buchanan v. Manley, 145 F.3d 386, 389 & n.6 (D.C. Cir. 1998) (per curiam) (affirming dismissal rather than transfer under the circumstances); Zakiya v. U.S., 267 F. Supp. 2d at 58–60 (transferring case to district where venue is proper); see Janis v. Ashcroft, 348 F.3d 491, 493 (6th Cir. 2003) (questioning propriety of sua sponte dismissal for improper venue).

[97]28 U.S.C. § 1404(a).

[98]Clarkson v. Coughlin, 783 F. Supp. 789, 799–800 (S.D.N.Y. 1992) (declining to transfer case to the district where correction department headquarters is located); accord, In re Ricoh Corp., 870 F.2d 570, 572 (11th Cir. 1989). But see Nichols v. U.S. Bureau of Prisons, 895 F. Supp. 6, 8 (D.D.C. 1995) ("While ordinarily the plaintiff's choice of forum is entitled to deference, several decisions in this Circuit suggest that it is not entitled to any great weight where 'the activities [forming the basis of the suit] have little, if any,

connection with the chosen forum.'" (citations omitted)), mandamus denied, 1995 WL 551095 (D.C. Cir., Aug. 25, 1995).

[99]Banks v. Curtis Candy Co., 531 F. Supp. 826 (S.D.N.Y. 1982) (suit by inmate against candy company for damage caused by allegedly defective product transferred to district where inmate was located and incident occurred).

[100]Balawajder v. Scott, 160 F.3d 1066, 1067 (5th Cir. 1998) (transfer of a prisoner's case to the district in which claims allegedly arose proper); Boyd v. Snider, 44 F. Supp. 2d 966, 969–74 (N.D.Ill. 1999) (transferring case to where the prison is located); Carillo v. Darden, 992 F. Supp. 1024, 1026 (N.D.Ill. 1998) (transferring to district where the claim arose and all relevant records are located); Huskey v. Quinlan, 785 F. Supp. 4, 7 (D.D.C. 1992); Berry v. New York State Dep't of Correctional Services, 808 F. Supp. 1106, 10 (S.D.N.Y. 1992) (granting transfers to the district in which the operative facts occurred); Pierce v. Coughlin, 806 F. Supp. 426, 428 (S.D.N.Y. 1992) (transfers action to district where prison is located); Miller v. County of Passaic, New Jersey, 699 F. Supp. 409, 411 (E.D.N.Y. 1988) (court sua sponte transferred prisoners' claim to New Jersey where all the defendants resided and the events giving rise to the action transpired).

[101]See Ellingburg v. Connett, 457 F.2d 240, 241 (5th Cir.1972); Williams v. Bowman, 157 F. Supp. 2d 1103, 1106 (N.D.Cal. 2001); Bontkowski v. U.S., 2005 WL 2756029, *2 (M.D.Fla. 2005) (unpublished) and cases cited; Flanagan v. Shively, 783 F. Supp. 922, 935–36 (M.D.Pa. 1992) (inmate is not a resident of district in which he is incarcerated absent evidence of intent to remain there upon discharge), aff'd, 980 F.2d 722 (3d Cir. 1992); O'Brien v. Schweiker, 563 F. Supp. 301, 302 (E.D.Pa. 1983) (prisoner retains domicile he had at time of incarceration).

[102]GCG Austin, Ltd. v. City of Springboro, Ohio, 284 F. Supp. 2d 927, 930 (S.D.Ohio 2003) ("'[w]here a public official is a party to an action in his official capacity, he resides in the judicial district where he maintains his official residence, that is, where he performs his official duties.'" (quoting O'Neill v. Battisti, 472 F.2d 789, 791 (6th Cir. 1972)).

[103]See Cheeseman v. Carey, 485 F. Supp. 203, 207 (S.D.N.Y.), remanded on other grounds, 623 F.2d 1387 (2d Cir. 1980); Michigan State Chamber of Commerce v. Austin, 577 F. Supp. 651, 654–55 (E.D. Mich. 1983), rev'd on other grounds, 788 F.2d 1178 (6th Cir. 1986). Cf. Taylor v. White, 132 F.R.D. 636, 640 (E.D.Pa. 1990) (state officials can be sued where they maintain their offices, either in the state capitol or in district where regional offices are located in which substantial activities related to the claims took place). Courts have held that federal officials, unlike state officials, can have only one official residence for venue purposes. See Neville v. Dearie, 745 F. Supp. 99, 102 (N.D.N.Y. 1990) and cases cited.

If it does not matter to you what district you litigate in, the best way to avoid time-wasting venue controversies is generally to file damage cases in the district (or one of the districts) where your rights were violated, and file injunctive cases that deal with your current treatment in prison in the district where you are currently incarcerated.

Even if venue is otherwise proper in a district, you may not be able to obtain personal jurisdiction in that district over a particular defendant if he has not had sufficient contact with the state in which the case is pending.[104]

3. Proceeding *In Forma Pauperis*

If you can't afford to pay the federal court filing fee[105] and other litigation expenses, you can apply for permission to proceed *in forma pauperis* (IFP), which means "as a poor person."[106] For prisoners, IFP status does not mean being excused from paying the filing fee as it does for other indigent litigants. Rather, under the Prison Litigation Reform Act (PLRA), prisoners must pay the entire filing fee in full, in installments, as they have money in their prison accounts.[107] They must pay the entire fee even if they withdraw a case or it is dismissed immediately at the court's initial screening.[108] In addition, prisoners who have had three

strikes (three or more actions or appeals dismissed as frivolous, malicious, or failing to state a claim) are generally not allowed to proceed *in forma pauperis*.[109] The details of the PLRA filing fee scheme are discussed in another chapter.[110] Here, we present the information you need to know to decide what to do and to file your case.

Prisoners may ask why they should bother seeking IFP status if they will have to pay the filing fees anyway. If you do not proceed IFP, you will have to pay the entire fee *up front* (before you can file the case). Also, IFP litigants are eligible to have their summons and complaints served by the "officers of the court" (the U.S. Marshals Service)[111] and to be excused from payment of some costs (though not fees) on appeal.[112] Without IFP status, you will have to take care of service and pay appeal costs yourself.[113]

The PLRA filing fee requirements apply to "prisoners," which under the statute means "any person subject to incarceration, detention, or admission to any facility who is accused of, convicted of, sentenced for, or adjudicated delinquent for, violations of criminal law or the terms and conditions of parole, probation, pretrial release, or diversionary program."[114] Persons are not prisoners under the PLRA if they are civilly committed, held as immigration detainees, or released, including those on parole to non-institutional settings.[115] So if you expect to be released in the near future, you may wish to wait until your release to file suit so you can avoid the fees and other PLRA provisions.[116] The fee requirements apply to "civil actions," which do not include habeas corpus and other post-judgment proceedings relating to criminal matters, but may include some matters related to

---

[104]This problem is referred to as "long-arm jurisdiction." *See* Burger King Corp. v. Rudzewicz, 471 U.S. 462, 469, 105 S. Ct. 2174 (1985). It seldom arises in prison cases, and when it does, it is usually in cases involving interstate transfers. *See, e.g.*, Meyer v. Federal Bureau of Prisons, 929 F. Supp. 10, 13 (D.D.C. 1996) (long-arm jurisdiction statute did not establish personal jurisdiction in the District of Columbia over an employee working in Missouri absent any allegation that he conducted any business or made any contract for services in D.C., and the inmate did not allege that he was harmed in any way in D.C. by employee); Barry v. Whalen, 796 F. Supp. 885, 889–90 (E.D. Va. 1992); Pollack v. Meese, 737 F. Supp. 663, 665–66 (D.D.C. 1990); Delgado v. Federal Bureau of Prisons, 727 F. Supp. 24, 26–27 (D.D.C. 1989).

[105]At present, the fee for filing a federal court civil complaint is $350.00. 28 U.S.C. § 1914(a). For appeals, there is a $450.00 filing fee (effective Nov. 1, 2003). *See* Court of Appeals Miscellaneous Fee Schedule, *available at* http://www.uscourts.gov/fedcourtfees/courtappealsfee_january2009.pdf (last visited March 14, 2010).

[106]Many states have adopted similar procedures as discussed in this section. If you are considering filing in state court, you should review the state statutes and court rules pertaining to *in forma pauperis* in your jurisdiction.

[107]Courts have disagreed about how the filing fee requirement applies to cases involving more than one plaintiff; some courts have said that each plaintiff must pay a full filing fee, while others have said that prisoners cannot file multiple-plaintiff cases at all, but must file separately. This issue is discussed in Ch. 9, § A, nn.60–65.

[108]McGore v. Wrigglesworth, 114 F.3d 601, 607 (6th Cir. 1997); *In re* Tyler, 110 F.3d 528, 529–30 (8th Cir. 1997) (PLRA compels the payment of the respective fees at the moment the complaint or notice of appeal is filed.); Hains v. Washington, 131 F.3d 1248, 1250 (7th Cir. 1997); Robbins v. Switzer, 104 F.3d 895, 897–98 (7th Cir. 1997); Leonard v. Lacy, 88 F.3d 181, 184–85 (2d Cir. 1996) (". . . [W]e will apply the PLRA to impose any required obligation

for filing fees (subject to installment payments) upon all prisoners who seek to appeal civil judgments without prepayment of fees. That obligation will be imposed prior to any assessment of the frivolousness of the appeal.").

Initial screening is discussed below in § C.3.b of this chapter, and in Ch. 9, § C.

[109]28 U.S.C. § 1915(g). There is an exception for cases involving an "imminent threat of serious physical injury." *See* Ch. 9, § B for a discussion of this provision.

[110]*See* Ch. 9, § A.

[111]28 U.S.C. § 1915(d).

[112]28 U.S.C. § 1915(c).

[113]*See* §§ C.4, U.1.e of this chapter on those subjects; *see also* Mills v. Fischer, 2010 WL 364457, *1 (W.D.N.Y., Feb. 1, 2010) (discussing benefits of IFP status beyond payment of filing fee).

[114]28 U.S.C. § 1915(h).

[115]*See* Ch. 9, nn.8–17, for further discussion of this point.

[116]You should be careful in making this judgment. You should be sure that you will have enough time between your release and the expiration of the statute of limitations both to file your complaint and to conduct discovery and join any necessary new defendants within the statute of limitations. *See* § J of this chapter concerning amending your complaint, which you will have to do to add parties; § K.2 of this chapter, concerning discovery; Ch. 8, § N, concerning statutes of limitations.

criminal proceedings such as challenges to seizures of property.[117]

Once the IFP application is granted and an initial review of the complaint is completed, it is filed for the prisoner by the court. The U. S. Marshal will issue and serve process without your having to pay.[118] IFP status does not excuse you from paying all litigation expenses. You will probably have to pay witness fees to persons who are not parties to the lawsuit if subpoenaed to testify at depositions or at trial.[119] You are also responsible for other "incidental costs" of litigation, such as copies of documents[120] and postage for filing and serving papers after the complaint has been filed.

The statute also provides that a court may request an attorney to represent any person unable to afford counsel.[121] The statute contains additional provisions pertaining to appeals.[122]

a. Establishing Indigency To request *in forma pauperis* (IFP) status, you are required to submit an affidavit stating the nature of the action, listing all of your assets, stating that you are unable to pay the required fees or give security, and that you believe you are entitled to relief.[123] You are also required to attach "a certified copy of the trust fund statement (or institutional equivalent) for the prisoner for the 6-month period immediately preceding the filing of the complaint or notice of appeal. . . ."[124]

District courts have different procedures for acquiring the certified statements; in most courts prisoners must get them from prison officials, but in some, the court directs officials to submit the information directly to court. Some courts place in the order granting IFP, or in an attachment to it, a requirement that the prisoner agree to have funds removed monthly from his prison account by prison staff and that when the total amount removed exceeds $10 that the amount will be sent to the federal court.[125] Prisoners should obtain the necessary forms and instructions from the clerk of the court in which they intend to bring suit.[126]

Courts are divided on what steps to take when a prisoner has not provided the required affidavit or trust account statement to support a claim of indigency.[127] If the prisoner must obtain the trust fund statement from the record office of the prison, prison officials' cooperation is obviously required. Your case should not be dismissed because prison officials don't submit the information promptly.[128] If they fail

---

[117]*See* Ch. 9, nn.22–28, for further discussion of this point.

[118]28 U.S.C. § 1915(d). Service of process is discussed in § C.4 of this chapter.

Some courts have held that IFP status may excuse litigants from paying a variety of fees for items such as photocopies, retrieving records from a federal records center, and reproduction of magnetic tape recordings. Murphy v. Jones, 801 F. Supp. 283, 288 (E.D.Mo, 1992). The IFP statute does not say this, and we do not know how widespread these practices are. *Compare In re* Richards, 914 F.2d 1526, 1527 (6th Cir. 1990) (inmate appealing as an indigent does not have a right to have filed stamped copy of notice of appeal made and returned to him at government expense). Courts have also held that they may appoint court experts without charging IFP litigants. Court-appointed experts are discussed in §§ K.3 and S.1.e of this chapter.

[119]*See* § K.2.d(1) of this chapter on depositions and § Q of this chapter on trial witnesses.

[120]*See* Tabron v. Grace, 6 F.3d 147, 159 (3d Cir. 1993) (there is "no statutory authority for a court to commit federal funds to pay for deposition transcripts") and cases cited; Brandon v. Beard, 140 F.R.D. 328, 329 (M.D. Pa. 1991) (plaintiff required to pay costs of copying documents sought in discovery).

[121]28 U.S.C. § 1915(e)(1). Appointment of counsel is discussed in § C.5 of this chapter.

[122]These provisions are discussed in § U.1.e. of this chapter.

[123]28 U.S.C. § 1915(a).

[124]Section 1915(a)(2); *see* Spaight v. Makowski, 252 F.3d 78, 79 (2d Cir. 2001) (holding that the relevant time period on appeal is six months before filing the notice of appeal, not six months before moving for *in forma pauperis* status); McGore v. Wrigglesworth, 114 F.3d 601, 605 (6th Cir. 1997) (warning that failure to pay fee or to provide necessary affidavit of indigency or trust account

---

statement may eventually result in dismissal of case). You should do the best you can to comply with the statute, and if you can't, explain why to the court.

As a practical matter, courts have sometimes accepted information supplied by prison officials that was a little out of date. *See* Jackson v. Wright, 1999 WL 160782, *1 n.2 (N.D.Ill., Mar. 10, 1999) (accepting statement ending the month before the complaint was filed in light of the small amounts involved); Lam v. Clark, 1999 WL 90635, *1 (N.D.Ill., Feb. 10, 1999) (accepting account information ending three and a half weeks before the filing of the complaint, since there is a consistent pattern for the six months covered).

Some courts require a statement for the preceding 12 months, *see, e.g.*, Wilson v. Sargent, 313 F.3d 1315, 1317 (11th Cir. 2002), which appears contrary to the statute.

[125]Wilson v. Sargent, 313 F.3d at 1322; *see also* McGore v. Wrigglesworth, 114 F.3d at 606; Hatchet v. Nettles, 201 F.3d 651 (5th Cir. 2000).

[126]The addresses of the federal district courts, organized by Circuit, are provided in Appendix A.

[127]*Compare* Henderson v. Norris, 129 F.3d 481, 484–85 (8th Cir. 1997) (stating "failure to file prison account information will result in the assessment of an initial appellate partial fee of $35 or such other amount that is reasonable, based on whatever information the court has about the prisoner's finances") *with* McGore v. Wrigglesworth, 114 F.3d at 605 (directing district court to notify the prisoner of the deficiency and to give the prisoner 30 days from date of order to correct it; if the prisoner does not comply with the order, the district court must presume prisoner is not pauper and assess full amount of fees. If they are not paid the case should be dismissed for lack of prosecution.).

[128]*See* Lawton v. Ortiz, 2006 WL 2689508, *1 (D.N.J., Sept. 19, 2006) (granting IFP status where prisoner said officials didn't respond to plaintiff's requests for an account statement and other evidence showed he was indigent); Gant v. Dane County Sheriff Office, 2000 WL 34227527, *1 (W.D.Wis., Aug. 23, 2000) (requesting that sheriff provide a copy of the procedure for obtaining an account statement and ask jail officials to provide a statement, where prisoner said his repeated efforts had been unavailing).

Delay in submitting the financial information will not cause prisoners to miss the statute of limitations as long as the complaint

or refuse to provide a certified statement, the court can order them to do so.[129]

At every stage you must be completely honest with the court concerning your finances. If you misrepresent them, the court may dismiss your case.[130]

b. Dismissal as Frivolous, Malicious, or Failing to State a Claim Federal courts have long had the power to screen *in forma pauperis* (IFP) cases and to dismiss those that they found to be frivolous or malicious upon filing, without requiring service of process on the defendants.[131] The Prison Litigation Reform Act expanded that power to include, in addition, cases in which the complaint failed to state a claim on which relief could be granted and cases seeking damages from an immune defendant, and applied the expanded power to prisoner civil cases generally, even if the plaintiff is not proceeding IFP and has paid the filing fee.[132] If the court finds that the entire complaint is frivolous, malicious, fails to state a claim, or seeks damages from an immune defendant, it will dismiss it without service of process. If only some of the claims or defendants fall into those categories, the court will dismiss them and then refer the complaint to the U.S. Marshal for service upon the remaining defendants.[133]

A complaint that fails to state a claim upon which relief may be granted is one in which the facts alleged do not establish a violation of law.[134] A complaint is malicious if it is filed for an improper purpose or amounts to an abuse of the

legal system.[135] A complaint is frivolous if it "lacks an arguable basis either in law or fact."[136] A complaint is legally frivolous if it fails to raise an "arguable question of law" or is based on an "indisputably meritless legal theory."[137] A complaint may also be legally frivolous if the facts in the complaint make it absolutely clear that the case is barred by a defense—*e.g.*, that the statute of limitations has run,[138] or that the claim is barred by immunity[139] or *res judicata*.[140]

A complaint is factually frivolous only if the "claims describ[e] fantastic or delusional scenarios,"[141] which means that "the facts alleged rise to the level of the irrational or the wholly incredible, whether or not there are judicially noticeable facts available to contradict them."[142] If your complaint

---

itself is submitted in time. *See* Garrett v. Clarke, 147 F.3d 745, 746 (8th Cir. 1998) ("For purposes of the statute of limitations, the filing of a complaint commences a federal cause of action. . . . [T]he prisoner should be allowed to file the complaint, and then supply a prison account statement within a reasonable time." (citations omitted)).

[129]*See* Stinnett v. Cook County Med. Staff, 1999 WL 169327, *1 (N.D.Ill. Mar. 19, 1999) (requiring prison officials to send a certified copy of prisoner's financial statement to the court).

[130]28 U.S.C. § 1915(e)(2); Romesburg v.Trickey, 908 F.2d 258, 260 (8th Cir. 1990) and cases cited. An erroneous financial statement is not cause for dismissal if there is no evidence of bad faith on the plaintiff's part. Lee v. McDonald's Corp., 231 F.3d 456, 459 (8th Cir. 2000) ("Although Section 1915 mandates dismissal of the lawsuit if an affiant's assertion of poverty is not true, a court is not required to dismiss provided the true facts demonstrate that the affiant is sufficiently poor to qualify for *in forma pauperis* status."); Mathews v.Gaither, 902 F.2d 877, 881 (11th Cir. 1990).

[131]*See, e.g.,* Ford v. Johnson, 362 F.3d 395, 399–400 (7th Cir. 2004) (describing procedure).

[132]This power is conferred in 28 U.S.C. § 1915(e)(2)(B)(i); 28 U.S.C. § 1915(A)(b)(1); and 42 U.S.C. § 1997e(c); *see* Ruiz v. U.S., 160 F.3d 273, 274 (5th Cir. 1998) (28 U.S.C. § 1915A applies "regardless of whether the plaintiff has paid the filing fee or is proceeding [IFP])"; McGore v. Wrigglesworth, 114 F.3d 601, 604–05 (6th Cir. 1997). The screening and dismissal power is discussed further in Ch. 9, § C.

[133]28 U.S.C. § 1915(d); House v. Belford, 956 F.2d 711, 719–20 (7th Cir. 1992).

[134]*See* § B.1 of this chapter for discussion of this point.

[135]Pittman v. Moore, 980 F.2d 994, 995 (5th Cir. 1993) (citing repetitive litigation as malicious); Crisafi v. Holland, 655 F.2d 1305, 1309 (D.C. Cir. 1981) (per curiam) ("complaint that threatens violence or that contains disrespectful references to the court" properly characterized as malicious); Spencer v. Rhodes, 656 F. Supp. 458, 464 (E.D.N.C.), *aff'd*, 826 F.2d 1061 (4th Cir. 1987) (complaint filed for purposes of vengeance and not to redress a legal wrong was malicious); Ballentine v. Crawford, 563 F. Supp. 627, 629 (N.D.Ind. 1983) (complaint that repeated allegations of previous litigation was abusive and malicious); Hernandez v. Earney, 558 F. Supp. 1256, 1258 (W.D.Tex. 1983) (dismissal as malicious was proper where plaintiff wrote letter to defendants and offered to dismiss complaint if they would recommend to state court that he be granted habeas corpus relief on his state conviction). Sometimes courts make the same point without using the word "malicious." *See* Bailey v. Johnson, 846 F.2d 1019, 1021 (5th Cir. 1988) (". . . [A]n IFP complaint that merely repeats pending or previously litigated claims may be considered abusive and dismissed under the authority of section 1915(d) [now § 1915(e)(2)]."); Horsey v. Asher, 741 F.2d 209, 213 (8th Cir. 1984) (a complaint may be dismissed under § 1915(d) [now § 1915(e)(2)] if it is "plainly part of a longstanding pattern of abusive and repetitious lawsuits").

[136]Neitzke v. Williams, 490 U.S. 319, 327, 109 S. Ct. 1827 (1989); *see also* Denton v. Hernandez, 504 U.S. 25, 33, 112 S. Ct. 1728 (1992).

[137]*Neitzke*, 490 U.S. at 327–28. For example, claims that prisoners have a constitutional right to deodorant or steak dinners have been held legally frivolous. Lawler v. Marshall, 898 F.2d 1196, 1199 (6th Cir. 1990).

[138]Street v. Vose, 936 F.2d 38, 39 (1st Cir. 1991). *See* Ch. 8, § N concerning statutes of limitations.

[139]*Neitzke*, 490 U.S. at 327; Sun v. Forrester, 939 F.2d 924, 925–26 (11th Cir. 1991). *See* Ch. 8, § L concerning immunity.

[140]Ali v. Higgs, 892 F.2d 438, 440 (5th Cir. 1990). *See* Ch. 8, § M concerning *res judicata*.

[141]*Neitzke*, 490 U.S. at 328.

[142]Denton v. Hernandez, 504 U.S. 25, 31–32, 112 S. Ct. 1728 (1992). For example, one court observed, "Examples of claims lacking rational facts are prisoner petitions asserting that Robin Hood and his Merry Men deprived prisoners of their access to mail or that a genie granted a warden's wish to deny prisoners any access to legal texts." Lawler v. Marshall, 898 F.2d at 1199; *see* Dekoven v. Bell, 140 F. Supp. 2d 748, 756 (E.D. Mich. 2001) (plaintiff's claim that his conviction must be set aside since it was obtained by "secular authorities in contravention of the mandates of God as set

is not as far out as those examples, the court should not dismiss it as factually frivolous.[143]

Courts have also said that a case may be frivolous if it is "(1) of little or no weight, value, or importance; (2) not worthy of serious consideration; or (3) trivial,"[144] and that the small monetary value of a prisoner's claim may help make it frivolous.[145] We think this ruling is contrary to United States Supreme Court decisions which have recognized that some First Amendment and procedural due process violations may only result in nominal damages.[146]

Dismissal as frivolous, malicious, not stating a claim, or seeking damages from an immune defendant may be done without prior notice or an opportunity to respond,[147] though one federal circuit has cautioned that this ought to be done only where "it is unmistakably clear that the court lacks jurisdiction, or that the complaint lacks merit or is otherwise defective."[148] Most courts have held that under the PLRA, as under prior law, *pro se* litigants are allowed an opportunity to amend deficient complaints before the court finally dismisses them.[149] One court has held that the PLRA prohibits this opportunity to amend, but that holding is probably wrong under a recent Supreme Court decision.[150] The PLRA screening provisions do not affect the rule that a court reviewing a complaint must accept as true all allegations of material fact and construe them in the light most favorable to the plaintiff, or the rule that courts must construe *pro se* pleadings liberally.[151]

Some courts have special procedures for determining whether *pro se* prisoners' complaints are frivolous. The court may direct prison officials to prepare an investigation and report in order to develop an adequate factual record,[152] or may send the prisoner a questionnaire seeking further detail about the facts and claims.[153] The court may hold an evidentiary hearing by telephone[154] or even in person (usually at the prison) to permit the prisoner to "clarify, amend, and amplify" the pleadings.[155] Such procedures should be limited to helping decide whether a complaint is frivolous. It is improper to resolve factual disputes and to make credibility judgments at that point in the case.[156] It is also improper to rely on unauthenticated records and inadmissible testimony in such proceedings.[157] If the district court dismisses your case in such an inappropriate manner, you should consider appealing.[158]

c. Payment of Filing Fees If a prisoner is granted *in forma pauperis* (IFP) status, the court will assess an initial

---

forth in the Holy Bible" was dismissed as frivolous), *aff'd*, 22 Fed. Appx. 496 (6th Cir. 2001) (unpublished).

[143]*See* Clark v. Georgia Pardons and Paroles Board, 915 F.2d 636, 639–40 (11th Cir. 1990) (an allegation that the plaintiff's parole was denied because he was pursuing litigation against prison officials because of his brother's allegedly wrongful death was not fantastic); Lawler v. Marshall, 898 F.2d at 1199 (an allegation that the plaintiff observed officers' conduct through the reflection off his nail clipper may strain credulity, but is not so delusional as to be frivolous).

[144]*See, e.g.*, Deutsch v. U.S., 67 F.3d 1080, 1087 (3d Cir. 1995).

[145]Nagy v. FMC Butner, 376 F.3d 252, 257–58 (4th Cir. 2004) (dismissing claim for $25 for lost coat).

[146]*See, e.g.*, Memphis Community Sch. Dist. v. Stachura, 477 U.S. 299, 308 n.11, 106 S. Ct. 2537 (1986) (holding nominal damages should be granted for section 1983 claims when actual injury for procedural due process violation cannot be shown); Carey v. Piphus, 435 U.S. 247, 267, 98 S. Ct. 1042 (1978) (holding nominal damage award of $1.00 required for procedural due process violation). *See also* Hughes v. Lott, 350 F.3d 1157, 1162 (11th Cir. 2003) (holding section 1997e(e) does not preclude nominal damages); Risdal v. Halford, 209 F.3d 1071, 1073 (8th Cir. 2000) (holding court must award nominal damages in the amount of $1.00 for First Amendment violations). *See also* Ch. 8, § O.1 for a discussion on damages.

[147]*See* Ch. 9, § C, n.196.

[148]*See* Ch. 9, § C, n.197.

[149]*See* Ch. 9, n.198.

[150]*See* Ch. 9, n.199.

[151]*See* Ch. 9, n.200.

[152]Hall v. Bellmon, 935 F.2d 1106, 1109 (10th Cir. 1991) (report is often necessary in *pro se* cases such as this "to develop a record sufficient [for the trial judge] to ascertain whether there are any factual or legal bases for the prisoner's claims"). In the Tenth Circuit, these reports are called "*Martinez* reports." *See* Simkins v. Bruce, 406 F.3d 1239, 1240 n.2 (10th Cir. 2005) ("A *Martinez* report is a judicially authorized investigative report prepared by prison officials to help the court determine if 'a *pro se* prisoner's allegations have any factual or legal basis.'" (citation omitted)); Martinez v. Aaron, 570 F.2d 317, 318–19 (10th Cir. 1978) (holding that report is necessary to determine "preliminary issues including those of jurisdiction").

[153]Macias v. Raul A. (Unknown), Badge No. 153, 23 F.3d 94, 97 (5th Cir. 1994) (to "ensure that IFP claims are developed adequately, our circuit has encouraged district courts to hold hearings or provide questionnaires to IFP plaintiffs"); Parker v. Carpenter, 978 F.2d 190, 191 n.2 (5th Cir. 1992).

[154]Hall v. Bellmon, 935 F.2d at 1109.

[155]James v. Alfred, 835 F.2d 605, 606 (5th Cir. 1988). In the Fifth Circuit this procedure is called a "*Spears* hearing." *See* Carbe v. Lappin, 492 F.3d 325, 327–28 (5th Cir. 2007); Spears v. McCotter, 766 F.2d 179, 181–82 (5th Cir. 1985).

[156]*See* Hobbs v. Lockhart, 46 F.3d 864 (8th Cir. 1995) (court should not have dismissed after "pre-jury" hearing based on its view that no jury would find in the plaintiff's favor); Northington v. Jackson, 973 F.2d 1518, 1521, 1525 (10th Cir. 1992) (defendant's testimony in telephone hearing should not have been used as a basis to dismiss the complaint); Pedraza v. Meyer, 919 F.2d 317, 319 (5th Cir. 1990) (credibility judgment should not have been made at a *Spears* hearing); Wilson v. Barrientos, 926 F.2d 480, 483 (5th Cir. 1991) (court may make "limited" credibility assessments focusing on "the inherent plausibility of a prisoner's allegations based on objective factors, rather than the demeanor of witnesses or a witness's prior criminal record.")

[157]Gentile v. Missouri Dep't of Corrections and Human Resources, 986 F.2d 214, 217–19 (8th Cir. 1993); Gilbert v. Collins, 905 F.2d 61, 63 (5th Cir. 1990); *see* Wilson v. Barrientos, 926 F.2d at 483 (unsworn witnesses, unauthenticated documents, and lack of cross-examination are improper at a *Spears* hearing).

[158]Appeals are discussed in § U of this chapter.

partial filing fee of 20% of the average monthly deposits in the prisoner's account, or the average monthly balance, for the past six months, whichever is greater.[159] (Prisoners with no money at all are assessed an initial fee of $0.00.) The initial fee is to be collected "when funds exist," and the statute adds that prisoners shall not be prohibited from bringing suit or appealing a judgment because they cannot pay.[160] The remainder of the fee is to be collected monthly at the rate of 20% of the preceding month's deposits to the prisoner's account.[161] Courts have disagreed whether prisoners who file multiple suits must pay all the fees at the same time, which could mean that 100% of their money is taken in monthly payments, or whether there is a limit to how many fees can be collected at one time.[162]

In some jurisdictions, the fee is automatically sent to the court by the prison; in others, the prisoner must act to make the payment. A case should not be dismissed for non-payment without first determining if the prisoner has had the opportunity to pay and has taken the steps within his own control to make the payment.[163] However, if you intentionally do not pay, or if you fail to take the necessary steps to pay (e.g., by spending all your money on something else), your case is likely to be dismissed.[164]

Prisoners generally may not be prohibited from bringing an action because they owe fees from a prior action. However, one federal circuit has held that prisoners who seek dishonestly to evade payment of filing fees, or fail to pay fees that they incur because they are subject to the three strikes provision, can be denied *in forma pauperis* status or barred outright from filing.[165]

d. Appeals and Other Relief from IFP Decisions If the district court has dismissed your complaint as frivolous, malicious, failing to state a claim, or seeking damages from an immune defendant, you have several options.

If your complaint is dismissed on grounds that you could correct by amending it,[166] you should do so.[167] Most courts hold that such dismissals at the *in forma pauperis* (IFP)/initial screening stage should allow the plaintiff leave to amend the complaint.[168] Many federal courts have rules or procedures designed to give plaintiffs an opportunity to amend their complaints before they are dismissed as frivolous, or to re-file within a specified period of time after they are dismissed. Some courts will enter orders containing instructions, *e.g.*, to amend the complaint within a specified period of time. If the court enters such an order in your case, you should follow the court's instructions.

If the order of dismissal does not explicitly allow you leave to amend, you should just file a motion to amend the complaint.[169] One court has held (incorrectly, in our view) that prisoners cannot amend complaints which are dismissed at this stage.[170]

If you think your complaint is all right as it stands and the district court just missed or misunderstood something in it, you can file a motion under Rule 59(e), Fed.R.Civ.P., to alter or amend the judgment, within 28 days (formerly 10 days) of the entry of the order dismissing your complaint, or you may file a motion to reconsider within the time specified by local rules.[171] This motion should point out what you think the judge missed in the complaint.

---

[159]Section 1915(b)(1). For example, in *Wilson v. Sargent*, 313 F.3d 1315 (11th Cir. 2002), the prisoner received $215.00 in deposits over the preceding six months, for an average of $35.83 a month. Since this amount was larger than the average monthly balance, the court assessed an initial fee of 20% of $35.83, or $7.16. Wilson v. Sargent, 313 F.3d at 1319–20 (footnote omitted).

[160]28 U.S.C. § 1915(b)(4); *see* Taylor v. Delatoor, 281 F.3d 844, 850–51 (9th Cir. 2002) (a prisoner who cannot pay the initial fee must be allowed to proceed with his case and not merely be granted more time to pay).

[161]Skinner v. Govorchin, 463 F.3d 518, 523–24 (6th Cir. 2006).

[162]*See* Ch. 9, § A, nn.56–58.

[163]*See* Ch. 9, § A, n.40.

[164]*See* Cosmo v. Meadors, 351 F.3d 1324, 1332 (10th Cir. 2003) (affirming dismissal of case where plaintiff said he couldn't pay the fees but had spent his money on other items); Jackson v. N.P. Dodge Realty Co., 173 F. Supp. 2d 951, 952 (D.Neb. 2001) (rejecting prisoner's claim where he was clearly able to pay).

[165]*See* Ch. 9, § A, n.42–44.

[166]For example, if you filed suit because some officers had used excessive force against you, but you only sued the warden, without any explanation of why the warden should be held liable, you could file an amended complaint that either provided some basis for finding the warden liable for the officers' acts, or named the officers involved as defendants, or both.

[167]In particular, if the court directs you to file an amended complaint correcting a particular problem, you should do so. *See* Summers v. Salt Lake County, 713 F. Supp. 1415 (D. Utah 1989) (imposing sanctions against a prisoner who filed a Rule 59 motion rather than amending his complaint as directed).

[168]*See* cases cited in n.149 of the previous section.

[169]*See* § J of this chapter concerning amending complaints. If the order dismissing your complaint does not specifically grant you leave to amend the complaint, and if there is not law in your circuit clearly granting you the right to do so, your motion should probably also seek to alter, set aside, or vacate the judgment under Rule 59 or Rule 60 of the Fed.R.Civ.P., on the ground that you are submitting an amended complaint that addresses the reasons the court dismissed your first complaint. *See* Morse v. McWhorter, 290 F.3d 795, 799 (6th Cir. 2002); Curley v. Perry, 246 F.3d 1278, 1284 (10th Cir. 2001); Shea v. Wheeler, 2000 WL 34237497, *2 (W.D.Wis. 2000) (Rule 59 motion allowed to challenge dismissal based upon §1915A). Rules 59 and 60 are discussed in §§ R.15.c and T.1 of this chapter.

[170]*See* Ch. 9, § C, n.199.

[171]Rule 59(e) provides for motions to alter or amend a final judgment. A dismissal of a complaint at the IFP stage is generally without prejudice, and some courts hold that a dismissal without prejudice is not a final judgment.

Most federal courts allow motions to reconsider or for reargument of decisions that do not constitute a final judgment.

You can also appeal from the decision dismissing your complaint or from the denial of a motion seeking to amend the dismissed complaint.[172] Appellate courts regularly reverse decisions by district courts erroneously dismissing prisoners' complaints as frivolous or failing to state a claim.[173]

Dismissal of a complaint as frivolous, malicious, etc., is considered to be without prejudice because it is not a judgment on the merits, so you are technically entitled to refile the same complaint if you pay the filing fee.[174] This course of action is not wise; if the court thought the complaint was frivolous the first time around, it will probably grant a motion to dismiss made by the defendants the second time around, and all you will accomplish is wasting the filing fee. The better course of action is to correct the complaint's problems if possible in one of the ways described in this section.

The denial of IFP status is an appealable order.[175] If you appeal, you may move in the district court to proceed IFP on appeal.[176] However, if the district court has certified that the appeal is not taken in "good faith,"[177] you will need either to pay the filing fee or to file a motion to proceed as an indigent with the appellate court.[178]

4. Serving the Summons and Complaint

After you file the complaint, you have to arrange for service of process. That means delivering the summons and complaint to each defendant according to certain rules. Until proper service is made on a defendant, the court does not have "personal jurisdiction" over the defendant, the defendant is not required to respond to the complaint,[179] and the court cannot take any action against that defendant.[180] Defendants can, however, waive any defense based on insufficient service or lack of personal jurisdiction if they appear in the case but do not raise the defense timely.[181] In federal

---

These motions are discussed in § F of this chapter. If you are not sure which is appropriate, just call your motion one "to alter or amend the judgment, or to reconsider."

[172]*See* Curley v. Perry, 246 F.3d at 1284 ("A litigant whose complaint has been dismissed with prejudice could file a motion to alter or amend the judgment under Rule 59(e) or for relief from the judgment under Rule 60(b). The litigant can also bring an appeal, in which we conduct plenary review of the sufficiency of the complaint.").

If you make a timely Rule 59(e) motion, it suspends the finality of the judgment, and your time for filing a notice of appeal runs from the disposition of the Rule 59(e) motion. *See* § U.1.a of this chapter for further discussion of this point. If you miss the 28-day deadline of Rule 59(e), you can file a motion later under rule 60(b), Fed.R.Civ.P., if it fits one of the grounds for relief stated in that rule. Rule 60(b) motions are discussed in § T.1 of this chapter. Rule 60(b) motions do not affect the time for appeal unless they are filed within 28 days of the entry of judgment. Rule 4(a)(4)(A)(vi), Fed.R.App.P. An appeal from a Rule 60(b) motion also does not necessarily bring up for appellate review the validity of the judgment that you were trying to get modified. For those reasons, and because the grounds for relief under Rule 60(b) are limited, you should get your motion in under Rule 59(e) within 28 days.

Appeals from dismissals as frivolous or malicious are discussed further in § U.1.c of this chapter.

[173]*See, e.g.*, McEachin v. McGuinnis, 357 F.3d 197, 201 (2d Cir. 2004) (claim stated that "seven-day restrictive diet imposed upon him as discipline by the defendants impinged upon his observance of Ramadan by depriving him of properly blessed food with which to break his daily fast."); Hughes v. Lott, 350 F.3d 1157 (11th Cir. 2003) (*Heck v. Humphrey* is no bar to search and seizure claims); Moore v. Mabus, 976 F.2d 268, 271 (5th Cir. 1992) (inadequate treatment of prisoners with AIDS); La Fevers v. Saffle, 936 F.2d 1117, 1119–20 (10th Cir. 1991) (denial of religious diet).

[174]Denton v. Hernandez, 504 U.S. 25, 112 S. Ct. 1728, 1734 (1992). The term "on the merits" is discussed in Ch. 8, § N; dismissals without prejudice are discussed in § I of this chapter.

[175]Roberts v. U.S. Dist. Court, 339 U.S. 844, 845, 70 S. Ct. 954 (1950) (holding that "denial by a District Judge of a motion to proceed *in forma pauperis* is an appealable order"); Andrews v. Cervantes, 493 F.3d 1047, 1052 (9th Cir. 2007); Lister v. Department of Treasury, 408 F.3d 1309, 1310–11 (10th Cir. 2005); Woods v. Dahlberg, 894 F.2d 187, 187 & n.1 (6th Cir. 1990); Deutsch v. U.S., 67 F.3d 1080, 1083 (3d Cir. 1995). *But see* West v. Macht, 197 F.3d 1185, 1188 (7th Cir. 1999) (denial of IFP status for some claims was not final where other claims remained, unless the court entered partial final judgment under Rule 54(b)).

[176]Appeals are discussed in more detail in § U of this chapter.

[177]Section 1915(a)(3) and Rule 24(a), Fed.R.App.Proc.; *see also* Baugh v. Taylor 117 F.3d 197, 202 (5th Cir. 1997).

[178]*See* Henderson v. Norris, 129 F.3d 481, 484 (8th Cir. 1997). *See also* § U.3.e of this chapter for a discussion of proceeding as an indigent on appeal.

[179]See § D of this chapter for a discussion of when a defendant is required to answer a complaint.

[180]Friedman v. Estate of Presser, 929 F.2d 1151, 1156 (6th Cir. 1991).

There are some decisions that hold that minor deficiencies in service procedures can be overlooked where the defendant clearly had actual notice of the lawsuit. *See, e.g.*, Sidney v. Wilson, 228 F.R.D. 517 (S.D.N.Y. 2005) ("Rule 4 of the Federal Rules is to be construed liberally 'to further the purpose of finding personal jurisdiction in cases in which the party has received actual notice.'" (quoting Romandette v. Weetabix Co., Inc., 807 F.2d 309, 311 (2d Cir. 1986)). However, other decisions suggest that leniency about service comes into play only where the plaintiff has extended every effort to comply with the rules. Bogle-Assegai v. Connecticut, 470 F.3d 498, 508–09 (2d Cir. 2006), *cert. denied*, 128 S. Ct. 1121 (2008). Other courts may simply insist on strict compliance with the rules. So do your best to get it right.

[181]Rule 12(h), Fed.R.Civ.P., provides that these defenses, among others, are waived if the party does not include them in an initial motion to dismiss under Rule 12, or fails to raise them in a motion or a responsive pleading or amended responsive pleading. That means "a defendant must raise the defense of lack of personal jurisdiction or improper service 'at the time he makes his first

court, service of process is governed by Rule 4 of the Federal Rules of Civil Procedure.

If you have been granted *in forma pauperis* (IFP) status, the district court is responsible for service of the complaint, which it will usually direct the U. S. Marshal to carry out.[182] If you have been denied IFP status, or if you pay the filing fee without seeking it, you will be responsible for service of the complaint, though as discussed below you can still use the Marshals as long as you pay their fees.

a. Procedures for Service The summons and complaint are supposed to be served within 120 days after the complaint is filed.[183] *In forma pauperis* (IFP) complaints are not actually filed until after the IFP application is decided, so the 120 days doesn't start running until that point.[184] You should receive a date-stamped copy of the complaint back from the clerk indicating the date of filing; if not, the date on the summons will usually be the date the complaint is filed.[185]

If a plaintiff fails to meet the 120-day deadline but there is "good cause" for missing it, the court must extend the time for service for an appropriate period.[186] Good cause includes mistakes that are not the plaintiff's fault,[187] including errors

or delays by the clerk or the U.S. Marshal.[188] However, even if the Marshal is supposed to serve process for you, you must pay attention, and follow up on whether service is being completed in a timely fashion; if you don't, a court may find a lack of good cause even if the Marshal did not serve process properly.[189] You must also cooperate with the Marshal and provide any necessary information.[190] A *pro se* litigant's ignorance of the rules is not considered good cause for failure to serve timely.[191]

---

significant defensive move.'" Transaero, Inc. v. La Fuerza Aerea Boliviana, 162 F.3d 724, 730 (2d Cir.1998) (cited in Santiago v. C.O. Campisi Shield No. 4592, 91 F. Supp. 2d 665, 671 (S.D.N.Y. 2000)).

[182]*See* 28 U.S.C. §§ 1915(d) ("The officers of the court *shall* issue and serve all process, and perform all duties in [*in forma pauperis*] cases . . ." (emphasis added)); Fed.R.Civ.P. 4(c)(3) (the court must order "that service be made by a United States marshal or deputy marshal or by a person specially appointed by the court" in IFP cases); *see* Olsen v. Mapes, 333 F.3d 1199, 1204–05 & n.4 (10th Cir. 2003) (noting that under current Rule the court should direct service even without a request from the plaintiff); Moore v. Jackson, 123 F.3d 1082, 1085–86 (8th Cir. 1997) (Marshal, not IFP plaintiff, was required to complete forms for service on defendants).

[183]Rule 4(m), Fed. R.Civ. P.

This rule applies to cases in federal court. State courts may have different rules. *See, e.g.,* Gray v. Lacke, 885 F.2d 399, 409–10 (7th Cir. 1989) (state rule requiring service within 60 days of filing of complaint did not apply in federal court).

[184]Sidney v. Wilson, 228 F.R.D. 517, 523 (S.D.N.Y. 2005); Heenan v. Network Publications, Inc., 181 F.R.D. 540, 543–44 (N.D.Ga. 1998). At least one court has held (correctly, in our view) that in a case where the plaintiff does not proceed IFP and has paid the fee, the running of the 120-day period should be suspended until the court has also completed the initial screening to which prisoner cases are subject under the Prison Litigation Reform Act, 28 U.S.C. § 1915A. *See* Shabazz v. Franklin, 380 F. Supp. 2d 793, 799–800 (N.D.Tex. 2005).

[185]Remember that for statute of limitations purposes, your action commences on the date that the court received your *pro se* complaint, or the date that you placed it into the prison mail system, and not the date that it is filed after IFP and screening procedures. *See* Ch. 8, § N, n.960–964.

[186]Rule 4(m), Fed.R.Civ.P.

[187]*See, e.g.,* Prisco v. Frank, 929 F.2d 603, 604 (11th Cir. 1991) ("Good cause" exists "when some outside factor such as reliance on

faulty advice, rather than inadvertence or negligence, prevented service."); Baltrunas v. Sheahan, 161 F.R.D. 56 (N.D.Ill. 1995) (there was good cause for failure to serve process timely on employees of Sheriff's office where personnel in that office obstructed efforts to serve process and to identify unknown or mis-named defendants); Poulakis v. Amtrak, 139 F.R.D. 107, 108–09 (N.D.Ill. 1991) (being misinformed by court personnel about proper procedures was good cause in a *pro se* case); Patterson v. Brady, 131 F.R.D. 679, 684 and n.7 (S.D.Ind. 1990) (delay in appointing counsel, inaction by appointed counsel, and misinformation from the clerk's office constituted good cause for late service).

[188]Lindsey v. U.S. R.R. Retirement Bd., 101 F.3d 444, 447–48 (5th Cir. 1996) (". . . [G]ood cause is shown when *in forma pauperis* plaintiffs' failure to properly serve a defendant is attributable to government personnel who have improperly performed their duties."); Olsen v. Mapes, 333 F.3d at 1204–05 (holding that *in forma pauperis* plaintiffs were not culpable for failure to timely serve where there was no evidence that they failed to cooperate with the Marshals Service); Byrd v. Stone, 94 F.3d 217, 220 (6th Cir. 1996) ("Under the circumstances present here, the utter failure of the clerk and the Marshals Service to accomplish their respective duties to issue and serve process for plaintiff proceeding *in forma pauperis* constitutes a showing of good cause under Fed.R.Civ.P. 4."); Welch v. Folsom, 925 F.2d 666, 667, 670 (3d Cir. 1991); Puett v. Blandford, 912 F.2d 270, 275 (9th Cir. 1990); Fowler v. Jones, 899 F.2d 1088, 1094 n.5 (11th Cir. 1990); Rochon v. Dawson, 828 F.2d 1107, 1110 (5th Cir. 1987); Soto v. Keenan, 409 F. Supp. 2d 215, 217 (W.D.N.Y. 2006) (dismissal for failure by the Marshals to serve process timely is unwarranted where the plaintiff did what was required of him); Williams v. Allen, 616 F. Supp. 653, 656 (E.D.N.Y. 1985) (similar to *Soto*).

[189]*See* Lindsey v. U.S. R.R. Retirement Bd., 101 F.3d 444, 446–47 (5th Cir.1996) (good cause is not shown where the plaintiff does nothing about known lack of service on a defendant); Del Raine v. Williford, 32 F.3d 1024, 1030–31 (7th Cir. 1994) (claims dismissed where plaintiff did not get the amended complaint to the Marshal before the 120 days had expired); VanDiver v. Martin, 304 F. Supp. 2d 934, 938–43 (E.D.Mich. 2004) (where Marshals did not execute service but plaintiff did not inquire about status of service within the 120-day period, claims dismissed; reviewing case law).

[190]Graham v. Satkoski, 51 F.3d 710, 713 (7th Cir. 1995) (stating "if the failure to serve process was due to appellants' failure to cooperate with the Marshals Service, there may not be good cause and dismissal may be appropriate").

[191]Marozsan v. U.S., 849 F. Supp. 617, 648–49 (N.D. Ind. 1994) and cases cited, *aff'd,* 90 F.3d 1284 (7th Cir. 1996); *see* Novak v. National Broadcasting Co., Inc., 131 F.R.D. 44, 45–46 (S.D.N.Y. 1990) (loss of counsel did not excuse failure of *pro se* plaintiffs to serve process timely). *Cf.* McNeil v. U.S., 508 U.S. 106, 113, 113 S. Ct. 1980 (1993) (". . . [O]ur rules of procedure are based on the

If you miss the 120-day deadline and don't have good cause, the court may either dismiss your case without prejudice as to any defendant who was not timely served, or may direct that service be made within a specified time.[192] If the case is dismissed without prejudice against any defendant, you will have to file an amended complaint to get that defendant back into the case.[193] The court should grant you more time to complete service rather than dismiss if the statute of limitation has run.[194] If you are having trouble serving process within 120 days, you should move for an extension of time.[195]

Once you serve process and the defendants have appeared by counsel, you can serve further papers on their attorney.[196] There is one big exception to this: if you file an amended complaint that adds new defendants, you must serve process on the new defendants just as you did on the original defendants.[197]

There are several ways to serve the summons and complaint, described in Rule 4, Fed.R.Civ.P. Some district courts have also developed their own arrangements for service of process in *pro se* prison cases. For example, we are informed that in some federal courts, judges sometimes appoint a prison employee to serve process. You may wish to seek the advice of knowledgeable law library staff members, experienced *pro se* litigants, or local attorneys on these practical points.

Methods for serving process include the following.

1. *Have the U.S. Marshal serve process.* As mentioned above, the Marshal serves process free for IFP litigants.[198] Federal courts have different ways of arranging this; they may require you to fill out service instruction forms for the Marshal and send the forms in with the complaint, or they may send them to you to fill out after you file. Write to the *pro se* clerk (or to the court clerk if there is no *pro se* clerk) if you are not sure of the procedure used by your particular court.

If you are not proceeding IFP, you may still ask the court to issue an order requiring the Marshal to serve the summons and complaint.[199] However, you will have to pay the fees, which are set in regulations issued by the United States Attorney General.[200]

The advantages of relying on the Marshal are that it will cost you nothing if you are proceeding IFP, there will be an official record of service by a law enforcement agency, and the Marshal will probably have an easier time than you will in locating defendants who have changed jobs or moved.[201] On the other hand, Marshals can be very slow and sometimes do not follow instructions properly. If you use the Marshal for service, you may have to write to him or to the court at some point to make sure the job actually gets done. You should try to find out about other prisoners' experiences with the local Marshal before deciding how to serve process.

The courts have generally held that delay by the Marshal constitutes "good cause" for failure to complete service

---

assumption that litigation is normally conducted by lawyers . . ., [but] we have never suggested that procedural rules in ordinary civil litigation should be interpreted so as to excuse mistakes by those who proceed without counsel.").

[192]Rule 4(m), Fed.R.Civ.P.; *see* Umbenhauer v. Woog, 969 F.2d 25, 30 (3d Cir. 1992) ("dismissal of a complaint is inappropriate when there exists a reasonable prospect that service may yet be obtained").

The court should dismiss for lack of timely service only if the defendants make a motion to dismiss or if the court first gives you notice that it is considering this step. Thompson v. Maldonado, 309 F.3d 107, 110 (2d Cir. 2002) (per curiam).

[193]*See* § J of this chapter for a discussion of amending complaints and adding parties.

[194]Rule 4(m), Fed.R.Civ.P., Note of Advisory Committee on 1993 Amendment. That is because if the statute of limitations has run, you will not be able to bring a dismissed defendant back into the case. Petrucelli v. Bohringer and Ratzinger, 46 F.3d 1298, 1306 (3d Cir. 1995); Umbenhauer v. Woog, 969 F.2d 25, 30 n.6 (3d Cir. 1992). If you miss the 120-day deadline and the statute has run or is about to do so, be sure to point this out to the court when you ask for more time.

[195]Rule 4(m), Fed.R.Civ.P.

[196]Rule 5(b)(1), Fed.R.Civ.P.

[197]*See* Turner v. City of Taylor, 412 F.3d 629, 649–51 (6th Cir. 2005) (holding plaintiff was required to request issuance of summonses for service on new defendants).

[198]Rule 4(c)(3), Fed.R.Civ.P.

[199]*See* Gams v. Westchester County Dep't of Probation, 232 F.R.D. 202 (S.D.N.Y. 2005). Rule 4(c)(3) also provides that the court can appoint another person to serve process.

[200]28 U.S.C. § 1921(c)(2). The regulations are published in 28 C.F.R. § 0.114. At present, the fees are $8.00 per item for mail service. For personal service, the fee is $45.00 per hour (or portion thereof), per item served by one employee, plus travel costs including mileage. For each additional employee, the cost is $45.00 per hour, per item, plus travel costs including mileage. Travel costs are calculated according to 5 U.S.C. § 57.

[201]The Marshals in some districts do not agree that it is their job to track these defendants down. Case law suggests that it is the Marshal's responsibility as long as you provide enough information to identify the defendants. *See* Byrd v. Stone, 94 F.3d 217, 219 (6th Cir. 1996); Graham v. Satkoski, 51 F.3d 710, 713 (7th Cir. 1995) (stating "once the former prison employee is properly identified, the Marshals Service should be able to ascertain the individual's current address and, on the basis of that information, complete service"); Sellers v. U.S., 902 F.2d 598, 602 (7th Cir. 1990); Jones-Bey v. Wright, 876 F. Supp. 195, 197–98 (N.D.Ind. 1995) (if a defendant is no longer employed at an institution, the Marshal shall ask the prison or the prison department the defendant's current address and shall attempt service at that address); Sidney v. Wilson, 228 F.R.D. 517, 523 (S.D.N.Y. 2005) (Marshals have duty to determine change of address of defendant). However, it may be difficult to force the Marshal to do it, and you should probably try to get the necessary information through discovery. We explain how to do this in § K.2.c. of this chapter.

within 120 days; they do not blame *pro se* litigants for the Marshal's mistakes.[202]

The U.S. Marshal generally first tries to serve the summons and complaint by use of "waiver of service,"[203] described in more detail below. If that doesn't work, the Marshal is obligated to serve process personally.[204] If the Marshal has a problem serving a defendant, he may contact you for additional information. You should respond to any such inquiry. If you fail to provide accurate information, the court may find that your failure to serve within the 120 days was your fault and you have lost the right to serve that defendant.[205]

2. *Get someone else to serve the summons and complaint personally for you.* In a non-IFP case, anyone who is not a party and is 18 years of age or older can personally serve the summons and complaint.[206] You cannot perform personal service yourself since you are a party.

You can hire a professional process server, whom you will have to pay. You can also ask friends or family members to serve the summons and complaint. You should only do this if you can have it done by a trustworthy and competent person who you are confident can follow instructions and deal with prison bureaucracies. Bear in mind that a private person who attempts to serve process may have trouble getting access to prison personnel on the job. You should also consider whether a person trying to serve process on prison staff would be subjected to risk or intimidation.[207]

Personal service upon a competent adult must be made by delivering a copy of the summons and the complaint to him personally or by leaving copies at his "dwelling or usual place of abode with someone of suitable age and discretion who resides there" (*e.g.*, not a child or someone who is

mentally ill or senile), or by delivering them to "an agent authorized by appointment or by law to receive service of process."[208] (In practice, prisons sometimes designate a staff member to receive process for prison employees.)

There are additional special rules for serving the United States or federal government officers or agencies,[209] state or municipal governments,[210] and other defendants.[211] These rules must be carefully followed where they apply, or your action may be dismissed.

3. *Request a waiver of service.* The Federal Rules allow bypassing formal service of process if defendants will cooperate by filling out a waiver of service form and returning it. To request a service waiver, you send a notice and request to the defendant by first-class mail "or other reliable means" along with a copy of the complaint. The notice must state the date the request is sent and the court in which the action has been filed and must allow a "reasonable time' (at least 30 days) to return the waiver. You must also enclose an extra copy of the notice and request and "a prepaid means of compliance in writing" (*i.e.*, a copy of a waiver form and a stamped self-addressed envelope).[212] When a defendant returns an executed service waiver, you should file it with the clerk of the court; at that point you will have satisfied the obligation to serve process for that defendant.[213]

If a defendant fails to comply with a waiver request without good cause, the court is authorized to make that defendant pay the costs of personal service.[214] Despite this incentive, in some jurisdictions, prison personnel as a matter of policy do not respond to service waiver requests or mail service. You should try to find out if this is the case in your district before deciding which service method to use. If you try to use the service waiver procedure and one or more defendants fail to return the form, you will need to try another means of service. At that point, even if you are not proceeding IFP, you may wish to ask the court to direct the Marshal to serve the defendants personally. Point out that even if you are indigent, it will be the defendants who must pay the Marshal's fees.

The service waiver provisions apply to individual defendants and to corporations, partnerships, and unincorporated associations.[215]

4. *Use state law service procedures.* For individual defendants, corporations and associations, and state or local

---

[202]*See* cases cited in n.188, above.

[203]Rule 4(d), Fed.R.Civ.P. If you are responsible for ensuring that the complaint is filed, you can also use the waiver of service procedure, described below.

[204]Armstrong v. Sears, 33 F.3d 182, 188 (2d Cir. 1994).

[205]*See* Lee v. Armontrout, 991 F.2d 487, 489 (8th Cir. 1993) (claim dismissed where prisoner gave incorrect service address to Marshal and Department of Corrections did not employ the defendant or have a correct address for him); Johnson v. U.S. Postal Serv., 861 F.2d 1475, 1479–80 (10th Cir. 1988) (holding that the U.S. Marshal could not be held accountable for plaintiff's failure to serve where plaintiff's complaint named the wrong defendant).

[206]Rule 4(c)(2), Fed.R.Civ.P.

[207]Other inmates can serve process for you on prison staff with whom they come into contact. Benny v. Pipes, 799 F.2d 489, 493–94 (9th Cir, 1986), *amended*, 807 F.2d 1514 (9th Cir. 1987). If you can safely arrange this, it is probably the quickest and simplest way of getting process served. However, common sense suggests that it may expose the inmates involved to retaliation or discipline. You will have to assess this risk based on the atmosphere and attitudes in your prison. Also, if the prison has rules governing the manner in which papers are to be served, you should follow them or risk disciplinary action. *See* Schroeder v. Mabellos, 823 F. Supp. 806, 809–10 (D.Haw. 1993) (holding that service of process is a First Amendment right but may be restricted for security reasons), *rev'd on other ground*, 29 F.3d 634 (9th Cir. 1994).

[208]Rule 4(e)(2), Fed.R.Civ.P.

[209]Rule 4(i), Fed.R.Civ.P.

[210]Rule 4(j), Fed,R.Civ.P.

[211]Rules 4(f) – 4(h), Fed.R.Civ.P.

[212]Rule 4(d), Fed.R.Civ.P.

Forms for the notice and request and the waiver form appear as Forms 1A and 1B in the Appendix of Forms at the end of the Federal Rules of Civil Procedure.

[213]Rule 4(d)(4), Fed.R.Civ.P.

[214]Rule 4(d)(2), Fed.R.Civ.P.; *see* Ammons v. Gerlinger, 2007 WL 5595899, *3–4 (W.D.Wis. 2007) (assessing service costs against defendants who did not return service waiver).

[215]Rule 4(d)(1), Fed.R.Civ.P.

governments, you can serve a federal court summons and complaint in the manner prescribed by state law.[216]

States often have statutes authorizing particular officials, such as sheriffs, bailiffs, or court clerks, to serve process.[217] If they will serve federal court process at all, they may provide a quick and cheap alternative.[218] Check your state statutes to determine who has this responsibility, and inquire of experienced litigators or knowledgeable law library personnel how well these alternatives of serving process work out in practice.

5. *Federal defendants.* To serve the United States (*i.e.*, the federal government itself)—*e.g.*, under the Federal Tort Claims Act[219]–you must either deliver a copy of the summons and complaint to the United States Attorney for the district where the case is filed or someone he designates, or send them by registered or certified mail to the civil process clerk in the United States Attorney's office. You must also send copies by registered or certified mail to the Attorney General of the United States in Washington, D.C. If you are challenging an order by a federal officer or agency that is not made a party, you must also send the complaint by registered or certified mail to that officer or agency.[220]

To serve an officer of the United States in his official capacity, or an agency or corporation of the United States, you must serve the United States as just described *and* send the summons and complaint to the officer, agency, or corporation.[221] This rule applies *only* to "official capacity" claims (generally, claims for injunctive relief) against federal officials or employees. If you are suing federal employees or officials for damages in their individual capacities, this procedure is not valid service; you must serve the individuals,[222] and you need not serve the United States.[223]

Whatever service method you use, once the summons and complaint have been served, proof of service or a service waiver must be filed with the court.[224] If the Marshal serves process, he is responsible for filing proof of service. Professional process servers or state or local officers who serve process should provide you with an affidavit of service, which you can file. If you arrange for a private person to serve process, you should get that person to give you an affidavit verifying that service was properly made.

b. Practical Problems in Serving Process To serve process, you have to know where the defendant is. Usually, the Marshal can arrange to serve process on a prison employee or official at the prison, and sometimes prison administrations will make this accommodation for other process servers too. However, if defendants are not actually at the prison—if they are on sick leave, retired or resigned, or transferred to another prison—they can't be served at the prison. Prison staff are unlikely to accept service for them, and even if they do, such service may be legally questionable.[225] This problem arises even when the U.S. Marshal is trying to serve process.

Prison officials are extremely reluctant to provide the home addresses of staff or former staff because they think it would be an invasion of privacy and a possible threat to security.[226] It is not clear whether the Marshal is obligated to try to locate and serve defendants whose addresses you cannot provide.[227] In any case, the Marshal has no power to force prison officials to provide staff addresses.

If you face this problem, you should file a discovery request seeking the present or last known addresses of the defendants who are not yet served, and make a motion to compel discovery if the information is not provided.[228]

---

[216]Rules 4(e)(1), 4(h)(1)(A), 4(j)(2)(B), Fed.R.Civ.P.

[217]*See, e.g.,* Florida Statutes Annot. § 48.021; Vernon's Annotated Missouri Statutes § 506.140(1).

[218]For example, one practitioner informed us that in Florida, local sheriffs serve federal court process for $20.00, that their service is very quick except in the Miami area, and that they have an easier time getting access to prison personnel than other process servers.

[219]*See* Ch. 8, § C.2 concerning this statute.

[220]Rule 4(i)(1), Fed.R.Civ.P.

[221]Rule 4(i)(2), Fed.R.Civ.P.

[222]Robinson v. Turner, 15 F.3d 82, 84 (7th Cir. 1994); Lowe v. Hart, 157 F.R.D. 550, 551–52 (M.D. Fla.1994); *see* Ecclesiastical Order of the Ism of Am, Inc. v. Chasin, 845 F.2d 113, 116 (6th Cir. 1988) (when lawsuit is really against agents in official capacities, the government must be served).

[223]Vaccaro v. Dobre, 81 F.3d 854, 857 (9th Cir.1996); Armstrong v. Sears, 33 F.3d 182, 186–87 (2d Cir.1994); McCain v. Scott, 9 F. Supp. 2d 1365, 1368–69 (N.D.Ga. 1998); Dodson v. Reno, 958 F. Supp. 49, 54–55 (D.P.R. 1997), *aff'd*, 125 F.3d 841 (1st Cir. 1997) (unpublished).

[224]Rule 4(d)(4) (concerning service waivers), Rule 4(l) (concerning proof of service), Fed.R.Civ.P. A form for proof of service appears on the back of the original summons.

[225]Service may be made on "an agent authorized by appointment or by law to receive service of process." Rule 4(e)(2), Fed.R.Civ.P. Sometimes, the head clerk or another prison official is administratively designated to receive process for prison employees, and no one seems to challenge this practice. However, we doubt that this is really valid service for defendants who are not actually working at the institution at the time. Certainly it is not adequate for defendants who are no longer employed by the prison system. Howard v. Wilderson, 768 F. Supp. 1002, 1009 (S.D.N.Y. 1991).

[226]Sellers v. U.S., 902 F.2d 598, 602 (7th Cir. 1990) ("Prison guards do not want prisoners to have their home addresses, and the Bureau of Prisons is reluctant to tell prisoners even the current place of employment of their former guards.").

[227]*Compare* Sellers v. U.S., 902 F.2d at 602 (holding that Marshal must try to locate defendants whom the plaintiff identifies) *with* Lee v. Armontrout, 991 F.2d 487, 489 (8th Cir. 1993) (holding that the plaintiff is obliged to provide correct addresses for service).

[228]*See* § K.2 of this chapter, concerning discovery practice, and § K.2.1, concerning motions to compel, defendants may try to avoid producing this information by claiming that they do not personally have the records. There is case law holding that if they or their attorneys can get it, they must respond. *See* § K.2.f of this chapter.

The motion should state that you do not personally need this information but it is needed by the U.S. Marshal to complete service as ordered by the court, and that it is acceptable to have the addresses provided directly to the Marshal if prison officials prefer.[229]

Another possible solution is to persuade prison staff, or the attorney representing the defendants who have already been served, to arrange to accept service for the unserved defendants. They usually will have to contact defendants to get authorization to do this. You will probably have to agree that service in this manner will not bind the state, city, or county to represent these named defendants until the defendants request representation and a decision has been made on that request. If defense counsel or the unserved defendants will not agree to this, you can suggest this method in your motion to compel as an alternative to providing you or the U.S. Marshal with the actual addresses. Courts may find it an appropriate compromise between your need to effectuate service and the privacy of prison staff.

In some cases, you may have only the last name or the first name (or a description) of one or more defendants. You are entitled to conduct appropriate discovery to obtain sufficient information to name them accurately in the complaint and to serve process on them.[230]

5. Appointment of Counsel

There is no constitutional right to have counsel appointed in most civil lawsuits.[231] A federal court may request an attorney[232] to represent an indigent litigant under a provision of the *in forma pauperis* statute,[233] but has no power to force an attorney to do so[234]—or to pay the attorney.[235] Your chance of getting a lawyer appointed probably has as much to do with practical realities as with legal rules. Some areas simply have more lawyers willing to take *pro se* cases than others, and some federal courts have better-organized programs of recruiting lawyers than others.

We generally recommend that *pro se* litigants seek appointment of counsel. As one court put it, counsel can

> explain the applicable legal principles to the complainant and . . . limit litigation to potentially meritorious issues. In addition, appointment of a lawyer provides the unlettered inmate with an opportunity to obtain representation equally qualified with the professional counsel usually provided by the state for the defendants. Frequently, as in the present instance, a lawyer can negotiate the settlement of a meritorious claim. If the case goes to trial, counsel for

---

[229]Arrangements of this sort to obtain necessary service information without disclosure to the plaintiff are common in prisoner litigation. *See, e.g.*, Young v. Department of Mental Health, 2008 WL 4821002, *2 (D.Conn., Nov. 4, 2008) (directing court's *Pro Se* Prisoner Litigation Office to obtain defendants' full names and addresses from Department of Correction Legal Affairs Unit and send them service waivers, and to arrange for service by the Marshals on any defendant who fails to return the waiver); Munguia v. Frias, 2008 WL 4370272, *5 n.4 (S.D.Cal., Sept. 25, 2008) (noting entry of Order of Confidentiality Directing Attorney General to Provide Information as to Defendant Frias' Address to the U.S. Marshall, and Directing the U.S. Marshal to Effect Service of Process Pursuant to Fed.R.Civ.P. 4); Shockley v. University of Texas Medical Branch, 2008 WL 4138105, *1 (N.D.Tex., Sept. 4, 2008) (noting that the court directed the other defendants to provide an address for the unserved defendant, and provided that address to the U.S. Marshal for service); Vandiver v. Austin, 2008 WL 2622851, *3 (E.D.Mich., June 30, 2008) (noting that court directed state Attorney General's office to file defendants' addresses under seal for service purposes); Harris v. Ford, 32 F. Supp. 2d 1109, 1110 (D. Alaska 1999) (noting provision of defendants' addresses confidentially to Marshal).

[230]*See, e.g.*, Davis v. Kelly, 160 F.3d 917, 921 (2d Cir. 1998) (same) and cases cited; Murphy v. Keller, 950 F.2d 290, 293 (5th Cir. 1992 directing district court to allow discovery of documents such as duty rosters and personnel records that would assist the plaintiff in identifying the defendants).

[231]*See* Ch. 3, § C.1.

[232]Courts may not appoint lay persons, including other prisoners, to represent indigents. Hahn v. McLey, 737 F.2d 771, 772 (8th Cir. 1984) (". . . [W]e disapprove of the judicial appointment of inmates to serve as legal representatives when that appointment would allow them to leave the prison compound and actively participate in trial."). One court has also "strongly recommend[ed]" against a court's using its clerks to provide legal assistance to unrepresented persons. Johnson v. Schmidt, 83 F.3d 37, 40 (2d Cir. 1996).

[233]28 U.S.C. § 1915(e)(1). A question may arise whether the "three strikes" provision of the Prison Litigation Reform Act, which forbids prisoners with three prior dismissals on certain grounds from "bring[ing]" an action "under this section" (*i.e.*, 28 U.S.C. § 1915), also bars the appointment of counsel. Some courts have so held. Hairston v. Blackburn, 2010 WL 145793, *10 (S.D.Ill., Jan. 12, 2010); Ammons v. Gerlinger, 2007 WL 5595899, *1 (W.D.Wis., May 1, 2007). We think that is wrong. The counsel appointment provision says: "The court may request an attorney to represent *any person* unable to afford counsel." 28 U.S.C. § 1915(e)(1) (emphasis supplied). It does not refer to persons "bring[ing]" suit "under this section," as the three-strikes provision does. Further, it refers to persons "unable to afford counsel," unlike the other provisions of the statute that excuses persons from prepayment of the filing fee if they are "unable to pay such fees or give security therefor." 28 U.S.C. § 1915(a)(1). Given this statutory language, we think that the provision for appointment of counsel involves a separate analysis from "bringing an action" IFP, even though it appears in the IFP statute. *Cf.* Weir v. Potter, 214 F. Supp. 2d 53, 55 (D.Mass. 2002) (holding a person not indigent enough to proceed *in forma pauperis* may be eligible for appointment of counsel). So if you have three strikes, but you can pay the filing fee or are allowed to proceed under the "imminent danger of serious physical injury" exception to the three-strikes provision, we think you remain eligible for the appointment of counsel. The three-strikes provision is discussed in more detail in Ch. 9, § B.

[234]Mallard v. U.S. District Court of Iowa, 490 U.S. 296, 109 S. Ct. 1814 (1989).

[235]An attorney who is appointed and who wins the case may be able to recover attorneys' fees from the defendants. *See* § Y of this chapter.

the plaintiff can shorten the trial and limit evidence to relevant issues, benefitting his client, opposing parties and the court.[236]

Even if you are not "unlettered" and think you know the law pretty well, a lawyer can generally do a better job than a prisoner in conducting discovery (especially depositions), negotiating a settlement of meritorious claims, and performing the other difficult tasks of litigation, by virtue of experience and of not being locked up in the defendants' custody.

Different courts have made different statements of the standards governing appointment of counsel, but they generally involve similar factors.[237] You should address these factors in your motion.

1. *Whether the case appears to have merit.* Some courts have held that this factor is considered first, and if the case does not appear meritorious, counsel should not be appointed.[238]

2. *The plaintiff's ability to investigate the facts.* If your case requires extensive documentary discovery, depositions of prison officials, or access to witnesses you cannot get to (such as prisoners who have been released or transferred to other prisons) or documents you are not allowed to have, you should explain the circumstances in your motion for counsel.[239]

3. *Whether conflicting evidence implicating the need for cross-examination will be important to the case.* Be sure to inform the court in your motion if you expect the facts to be strongly disputed[240]—e.g., if you allege that you were assaulted by correctional officers, but they have charged you with assaulting them.

4. *The indigent's ability to present the case.* Explain to the court any factors that will present special difficulties for you. For example, tell the court if you lack education; if you are not an experienced "jailhouse lawyer"; or if you have a

---

[236]Knighton v. Watkins, 616 F.2d 795, 799 (5th Cir. 1980) (footnote omitted).

[237]*See* Pruitt v. Mote, 503 F.3d 647, 654 (7th Cir. 2007) (district court must ask "(1) has the indigent plaintiff made a reasonable attempt to obtain counsel or been effectively precluded from doing so; and if so, (2) given the difficulty of the case, does the plaintiff appear competent to litigate it himself?"); Baranowski v. Hart, 486 F.3d 112, 126 (5th Cir. 2007) (decision based on "type and complexity of the case, the litigant's ability to investigate and present the case, and the level of skill required to present the evidence" (citation omitted)), *cert. denied*, 128 S. Ct. 707 (2007); Gaviria v. Reynolds, 476 F.3d 940, 943 (D.C. Cir. 2007) (local court rule requires consideration of nature and complexity of the case, potential merit of claims, demonstrated ability of *pro se* party to retain counsel by other means, and the interests of justice, including benefit to the court from appointed counsel); Rucks v. Boergermann, 57 F.3d 978, 979 (10th Cir. 1995) (courts are to evaluate the merits of a prisoner's claims, the nature and complexity of the factual and legal issues, and the prisoner's ability to investigate the facts and present his claims; Abdullah v. Gunter, 949 F.2d 1032, 1035 (8th Cir. 1991).

Some courts have simply stated that "exceptional circumstances" must be shown to justify appointment of counsel. In practice, these courts' decisions generally focus on the same factors discussed in this section. *See, e.g.,* Lavado v. Keohane, 992 F.2d 601, 605–06 (6th Cir.1993) (". . . [C]ourts have examined 'the type of case and the abilities of the plaintiff to represent himself,' [which] generally involves a determination of the 'complexity of the factual and legal issues involved.'" (citations omitted)). *But see* Tabron v. Grace, 6 F.3d 147, 155 (3d Cir. 1993) (rejecting exceptional circumstances requirement).

[238]*See* Carmona v. U.S. Bureau of Prisons, 243 F.3d 629, 632 (2d Cir. 2001) (". . . [W]e look first to the 'likelihood of merit' of the underlying dispute."); Risley v. Hawk, 108 F.3d 1396, 1396 (D.C. Cir. 1997); Tabron v. Grace, 6 F.3d at 155; Hodge v. Police Officers, 802 F.2d 58, 60 (2d Cir. 1986) (holding as a threshold matter, "counsel is . . . unwarranted where the indigent's chances of success [on the merits] are extremely slim").

[239]*See, e.g.,* Agyeman v. Corrections Corp. of America, 390 F.3d 1101, 1104 (9th Cir. 2004) (noting that plaintiff never got access to relevant regulations through discovery); Montgomery v. Pintchak, 294 F.3d 492, 502 (3d Cir. 2002) (directing appointment of counsel because imprisoned plaintiff could not take necessary depositions and "encountered multiple obstacles [in discovery], both in the resistance of the defendants and in the intricacies of the discovery rules"); Tabron v. Grace, 6 F.3d at 156 (holding that need for discovery supports appointment of counsel); Parham v. Johnson, 126 F.3d 454, 459 (3d Cir. 1999) (". . . [T]he prisoner's lack of legal experience and the complex discovery rules clearly put him at a disadvantage in countering the defendant's discovery tactics [and that] . . . these [discovery] rules prevented [the Plaintiff] from presenting an effective case below."); Hendricks v. Coughlin, 114 F.3d 390, 394 (2d Cir. 1997) (noting importance of taking depositions rather than just written discovery in a case alleging First Amendment retaliation, since written discovery answers are typically prepared by the lawyers and not the witness); Abdullah v. Gunter, 949 F.2d at 1036 (noting need for counsel to investigate the application of and alternatives to a challenged prison regulation); Tucker v. Randall, 948 F.2d 388, 391–92 (7th Cir. 1991) (noting that prisoner could not effectively investigate case arising at a jail from which he had been transferred); Pendergrass v. Hodge, 53 F. Supp. 2d 838, 845 (E.D.Va. 1999) (claim that inmate assault was solicited by staff members required discovery by counsel); Johnson v. Howard, 20 F. Supp. 2d 1128, 1129 (W.D.Mich. 1998) (counsel should be appointed where prisoner was forbidden to obtain records that might help him discover and locate witnesses to his alleged beating, but lawyer could get them); Gatson v. Coughlin, 679 F. Supp. 270, 273 (W.D.N.Y. 1988) (similar to *Tucker*).

[240]*See, e.g.,* Solis v. County of Los Angeles, 514 F.3d 946, 958 (9th Cir. 2008) (prisoner with eighth grade education and no legal training is "ill-suited" to conduct a jury trial); Steele v. Shah, 87 F.3d 1266, 1271 (11th Cir. 1996) (noting case will turn on assessments of credibility; denial of counsel should be reconsidered); Rayes v. Johnson, 969 F.2d 700, 704 (8th Cir. 1992); Whisenant v. Yuam, 739 F.2d 160, 163 (4th Cir. 1984); Bright v. Hickman, 96 F. Supp. 2d 572, 577–78 (E.D.Tex. 2000) (need for cross-examination skills to deal with conflicting testimony supported appointment of counsel); Hetzel v. Swartz, 917 F. Supp. 344, 346 (M.D.Pa. 1996) (credibility issues supported appointment of counsel); Gatson v. Goughlin, 679 F. Supp. at 273 (same).

physical or mental disability that would make it difficult for you to present your case.[241]

5. *The complexity and difficulty of the case.* If there appear to be complex factors or legal issues that you don't think you can handle very well, you should identify these to the court.[242] Factual issues that may merit appointment of counsel include those requiring the use of expert witnesses,[243] such as many medical issues,[244]

or involving conflicting testimony of multiple witnesses,[245] or requiring the court to sort out the motivations or personal involvement of multiple defendants in an alleged civil rights violation,[246] or the potential liability of corporate and other kinds of defendants and the remedies available against each.[247]

The fact that a case will be tried before a jury also supports the appointment of counsel.[248] Legal issues that courts have considered complex enough to support the appointment of counsel include application of the Eighth Amendment "totality of the conditions" standard,[249] "state of mind" issues like deliberate indifference,[250] evaluating the justification for prolonged strip cell confinement,[251] the defense of qualified immunity,[252] the constitutionality of a federal statute,[253] questions of the extent of prisoners' rights

---

[241]Pruitt v. Mote, 503 F.3d 647, 655 (7th Cir. 2007) (en banc) ("... [T]he judge will normally take into consideration the plaintiff's literacy, communication skills, educational level, and litigation experience. To the extent there is any evidence in the record bearing on the plaintiff's intellectual capacity and psychological history, this, too, would be relevant."); Hamilton v. Leavy, 117 F.3d 742, 749 (3d Cir. 1997) (counsel should be appointed for prisoner with assault claim whose medical records showed he had a paranoid delusional disorder); Tabron v. Grace, 6 F.3d at 156 (plaintiff's education, literacy, prior work and litigation experience, and ability to understand English should be considered); Rayes v. Johnson, 969 F.2d at 703–04 (counsel should have been appointed for an inmate who lacked ready access to a law library, showed that he did not understand discovery procedures, and could not articulate all his claims); Bright v. Hickman, 96 F. Supp. 2d 572, 577 (E.D.Tex. 2000) (plaintiff's lack of education and experience with the judicial system supported counsel appointment); Hetzel v. Swartz, 917 F. Supp. 344, 345–46 (M.D.Pa. 1996) (appointing counsel for plaintiff who was very ill, not very literate, and had shown difficulties in presenting his case); *see also* Parham v. Johnson, 126 F.3d at 460 ("it may be difficult for indigent plaintiffs to understand the complex discovery rules" in investigating their claims). *Compare* Purnell v. Lopez, 903 F. Supp. 863, 864 (E.D.Pa. 1995) (denying counsel where plaintiff made no representations about his education, work experience, litigation experience, or literacy).

[242]*Cf.* Wood v. Idaho Dep't of Corrections, 391 F. Supp. 2d 852, 867 (D.Idaho 2005) (court appoints counsel because of "sensitive nature of the sexual abuse claims").

[243]Steele v. Shah, 87 F.3d 1266, 1271 (11th Cir. 1996); Tabron v. Grace, 6 F.3d at 156; Jackson v. County of McLean 953 F.2d 1070, 1073 (7th Cir. 1992).

The Supreme Court recently confirmed the important of expert testimony in upholding a grant of summary judgment against a prisoner on a First Amendment issue, stating that the prisoners "did not offer any fact-based *or expert-based* refutation [of prison officials' argument] in the manner the rules provide." Beard v. Banks, 548 U.S. 521, 534, 126 S. Ct. 2572 (2006) (emphasis supplied). Be sure to quote this to the court if you request appointment of counsel in a challenge to prison policies based on the need for expert testimony.

[244]*See, e.g.,* Greeno v. Daley, 414 F.3d 645, 658 (7th Cir. 2005) (in reversing refusal to appoint counsel, appellate court stated that district court was wrong in saying the case was "factually simple and legally straightforward," since it involved medical records and inmate's complaints and requests over a period of two years, and requires an assessment of the adequacy of treatment, which will likely require expert testimony); Montgomery v. Pintchak, 294 F.3d 492, 504 (3d Cir. 2002) (counsel should be appointed when medical issues are complex and expert is needed); Moore v. Mabus, 976 F.2d 268, 272 (5th Cir. 1992) (directing appointment of counsel in a case involving the treatment of HIV positive

inmates); Tucker v. Randall, 948 F.2d at 392 (citing conflicting medical evidence as a reason to appoint counsel); Tabron v. Grace, 6 F.3d at 156 (explaining that "where the law is not clear, it will often best serve the ends of justice to have both sides of a difficult legal issue presented by those trained in legal analysis"). *Compare* King v. Patterson, 999 F.2d 351, 353 (8th Cir. 1993) (counsel need not be appointed where "case was neither factually nor legally complex, the complaint alleged a single incident of excessive force, and the Court felt that King had clearly communicated his concerns and could adequately present the facts of his case to the Court").

[245]Bright v. Hickman, 96 F. Supp. 2d 572, 577–78 (E.D.Tex. 2000).

[246]Hendricks v. Coughlin, 114 F.3d 390, 394 (2d Cir. 1997) (finding First Amendment retaliation claim alleging supervisory liability to be complex).

[247]Agyeman v. Corrections Corp. of America, 390 F.3d 1101, 1103–04 (9th Cir. 2004) (noting "triple complexity" of case involving a private corporation contracting with the federal government requiring consideration of tort claims against the corporation, a Federal Tort Claims action against the government, or a *Bivens* action against individual federal defendants).

[248]Solis v. County of Los Angeles, 514 F.3d 946, 958 (9th Cir. 2008); Abdullah v. Gunter, 949 F.2d 1032, 1036 (8th Cir. 1991).

[249]Nilsson v. Coughlin, 670 F. Supp. 1186, 1189 (S.D.N.Y. 1987) ("The nature of the inquiry demanded in a 'totality of the conditions' action is complicated. The factual issues are difficult and intertwined." (citation omitted)).

[250]Swofford v. Mandrell, 969 F.2d 547, 552 (7th Cir. 1992) (pointing out that "difficult and subtle question" of state of mind required for deliberate indifference is too complex for *pro se* plaintiff to understand and present to jury).

[251]Johnson v. Williams, 788 F.2d 1319, 1324 (8th Cir. 1986).

[252]LaFrance v. Rampone, 678 F. Supp. 72, 73 (D. Vt. 1988) ("The Court appointed counsel to brief the sole question of whether the defendant parole officers were entitled to absolute or qualified immunity from suit."); Vines v. Howard, 676 F. Supp. 608, 616 (E.D. Pa. 1987) ("issue of qualified immunity, the related issue of damages, and possible trial on such issues would best be handled by an experienced attorney."); *cf.* Anderson v. Recore, 317 F.3d 194, 196 (2d Cir. 2003) (appellate court appointed counsel and requested supplemental brief on issue of qualified immunity).

[253]Lewis v. Sullivan, 135 F.Supp. 2d 954, 957 (W.D.Wis. 2001); *see* Charles v. Verhagen, 220 F. Supp. 2d 937, 955 (W.D.Wis. 2002)

under the federal disability statutes,[254] and determining whether a prison regulation violates the *Turner v. Safley* "reasonable relationship" standard.[255]

For what it is worth, we think that certain types of cases present particular difficulties for *pro se* litigants and are especially appropriate for the appointment of counsel. These include cases involving assault by other prisoners. In our experience, *pro se* prisoners have extreme difficulty in grasping the legal issues in these cases and figuring out which prison officials can properly be held liable.

Cases involving staff assaults are also especially difficult, since the facts are almost always disputed and there are seldom any neutral witnesses. These cases cannot be won without the exercise of a high degree of trial skills based on a firm foundation of depositions and other pretrial discovery and preparation that is usually beyond the abilities of a *pro se* prisoner.

Finally, medical and mental health care cases frequently involve technical issues that *pro se* prisoners are unable to deal with adequately and that in many cases require the use of expert witnesses.

6. *Whether the prisoner has sought to obtain counsel.* Some courts will first consider the effort of the prisoner in obtaining counsel on his own.[256] This means that you should

write at least two or three attorneys[257] and describe what your case concerns and ask that they represent you. You will need to keep a copy of the letter sent and any responses that you receive. Ways to try to get counsel on your own are discussed elsewhere in this Manual.[258]

You should file a motion for the appointment of counsel along with your application to proceed *in forma pauperis.*[259] In your motion for counsel, don't just tell the court that you have a great case and it is a winner. You need to provide the court with some factual or logical basis why you cannot adequately litigate the case yourself, along the lines suggested earlier in this section.

If your motion is denied, you should carefully study the reasons given by the court for denying it. Some judges believe that counsel motions should not be granted until after the case has developed and they can evaluate it better[260]—*e.g.,* after the case has survived a motion to dismiss or for summary judgment.[261] It may be appropriate to renew your motion for counsel after the court has denied dismissal or summary judgment.

It may also be appropriate to renew your motion for counsel if a problem comes up in the case that you can't

---

(deferring appointment of counsel to see if United States would intervene to defend the statute, which would obviate the need for counsel), *aff'd,* 348 F.3d 601 (7th Cir. 2003).

[254]Flakes v. Frank, 322 F. Supp. 2d 981, 983 (W.D.Wis. 2004), *reconsideration denied,* 2004 WL 1563190 (W.D.Wis., July 12, 2004).

[255]Abdullah v. Gunter, 949 F.2d 1032, 1036 (8th Cir. 1991). The Supreme Court has provided support on this point, emphasizing that though it is difficult to prevail under the *Turner* standard, "it is not inconceivable that a plaintiff's *counsel,* through rigorous questioning of officials by means of depositions, could demonstrate genuine issues of fact for trial." Beard v. Banks, 548 U.S. 521, 536, 126 S. Ct. 2572 (2006) (emphasis supplied).

[256]Gil v. Reed, 381 F.3d 649, 658 (7th Cir. 2004) (". . . [T]he threshold consideration in determining whether to appoint counsel is whether the inmate has attempted and failed to procure counsel on his own."); Purnell v. Lopez, 903 F. Supp. 863, 864 (E.D.Pa. 1995). One court has suggested that this requirement is not reasonable as applied to indigent prisoners. Rose v. Racine Correctional Institution, 141 F.R.D. 105, 106–07 (E.D. Wis. 1992); *see also* Cooper v. A. Sargenti Co., Inc., 877 F.2d 170, 173–74 (2d Cir. 1989) (". . . [T]he most important disability of the poor claimant may be not so much his lack of funds but his lack of practical access to attorneys. If the indigent plaintiff is a prison inmate or a homeless vagrant, he may have no effective means of bringing his claim to the attention of the lawyer marketplace to have its merit appraised."). *Cf.* McDonald v. Head Criminal Court Supervisor Officer, 850 F.2d 121, 124 (2d Cir. 1988) (taking notice "that most indigent incarcerated prisoners do not in fact have the resources, knowledge and experience needed to find counsel willing to represent them without charge (or at best with the hope of a contingent payment in some cases)").

[257]*See* Flakes v. Frank, 322 F. Supp. 2d 981, 983 (W.D.Wis. 2004) (noting usual practice of requiring plaintiff first to contact three lawyers who do civil rights work), *reconsideration denied,* 2004 WL 1563190 (W.D.Wis., July 12, 2004); Giles v. Tate, 907 F. Supp. 1135, 1139 (S.D.Ohio 1995) (same); *see also* Gil v. Reed, 381 F.3d at 658 (being turned down by lawyers is not a "reality check" about the merits of the case).

[258]*See* Ch. 1, § D.

[259]*See* Appendix C, Forms 3a–3c, for example of these papers. Many federal courts require prisoners to use form *pro se* complaints and IFP applications, and some of these contain form motions for appointment of counsel. Others do not. If there is no form for counsel, you will have to draft your own motion using our form as a guide.

[260]*See* King v. Frank, 328 F. Supp. 2d 940, 950 (W.D.Wis. 2004) (declining to appoint counsel for a plaintiff who said he was mentally ill, since it was too early to determine whether the complex questions raised were sufficiently meritorious to appoint counsel, given the shortage of willing lawyers).

[261]Some courts have criticized this practice. *See* Hendricks v. Coughlin, 114 F.3d 390, 392 (2d Cir. 1997) (stating such a policy "plainly poses Catch-22 problems" where assistance of counsel may be "vital to surviving" the motion); *see also* Hughes v. Joliet Correctional Center, 931 F.2d 425, 429–30 (7th Cir. 1991) (disapproving policy not to appoint counsel except for evidentiary proceedings; in this case, a summary judgment affidavit was required). In Michigan federal courts, in our observation, most judges will not seriously consider appointing counsel until after the prisoner has survived a dispositive motion. This can be a bad policy because without a lawyer, the plaintiff may not be able to develop the case at all. However, it means that if your request for counsel is denied, you should absolutely proceed with discovery as best you can. If you obtain documents relevant to your case, you are more likely to survive the summary judgment motion, and if the court sees documentary support for your claims, it is more likely to conclude that the case has sufficient merit to appoint counsel.

handle. For example, a court may be willing to reconsider appointing counsel if the defendants are completely unco-operative in responding to your discovery requests; if you have lost access to essential witnesses because they were transferred or released; or if a legal issue arises that is beyond your ability to comprehend. If you do make such a renewed motion, make it clear that you have something new to say and are not just repeating the same arguments that the court has already rejected.[262] Also, you cannot refuse to follow the rules of litigation or orders of the court while you wait for the court to rule on your counsel motion.[263]

District courts should explain their reasons for denying the appointment of counsel.[264] They should also rule on pending motions for counsel before dismissing the complaint.[265] If the court fails to do either of these things, the matter is worth raising on appeal.

A court may appoint counsel for a limited purpose and not for the whole case.[266] For example, your case might be factually straightforward, but it could also involve a difficult issue of the constitutionality of a statute; or you might need documentary discovery followed by depositions to identify the proper defendants. If these particular issues are beyond your capabilities, if the court has declined to appoint counsel for the whole case, it is possible it might change its mind in part if you point out a particular problem that you cannot handle by yourself.

The federal courts are split on the question whether the denial of appointment of counsel is immediately appealable or whether you have to wait until the end of the case to appeal.[267] On appeal, courts do not substitute their judgment for the district court, but merely determine whether the lower court abused its discretion in denying counsel.[268] In practice, when an appellate court thinks that a *pro se* plaintiff with a serious case was badly treated in the district court, it sometimes directs or strongly suggests that counsel be appointed when it sends the case back to the lower court.[269] For this reason, if the district court denies counsel and you lose and then appeal, if there is a basis for arguing that the denial of counsel was seriously wrong, don't forget to include that issue in your notice of appeal and brief so the issue will be properly before the appeals court. Also, if appointment of counsel is denied by a magistrate judge, be sure to object to that ruling to the district court, or you may be deemed to have waived the issue.[270]

If counsel is appointed for you, you are no longer proceeding *pro se*, and the court will only accept papers from your lawyer and not from you.[271] The defendants will generally only serve papers on your attorney and communicate

---

[262]A recent decision holds that courts are under no obligation to "revisit" the denial of appointed counsel based on later developments in the case. Pruitt v. Mote, 503 F.3d 647, 659 (7th Cir. 2007) (en banc). However, if you make a new motion and put new arguments before the court based on later developments, the court will be obliged to address those arguments. *See Pruitt*, 503 F.3d at 660.

[263]Johnson v. U.S. Dep't of the Treasury, 939 F.2d 820, 825 (9th Cir. 1991); McDonald v. Head Criminal Court Supervisor Officer, 850 F.2d 121, 124 (2d Cir. 1988) (". . . [W]hile pro se litigants may in general deserve more lenient treatment than those represented by counsel, all litigants, including pro ses, have an obligation to comply with court orders.").

[264]Allen v. Thomas, 388 F.3d 147, 150 (5th Cir. 2004); Howland v. Kilquist, 833 F.2d 639, 646 (7th Cir. 1987).

[265]Johnson v. U.S. Dep't of Treasury, 939 F.2d 820, 824–25 (9th Cir. 1991) (stating "a district court abuses its discretion if it fails to rule upon a motion for appointment of counsel before granting a motion of the defendant disposing of the case"); Tucker v. Randall, 948 F.2d 388, 390 (7th Cir. 1991); McElyea v. Babbitt, 833 F.2d 196, 199 (9th Cir. 1987).

[266]*See, e.g.*, Vera v. Utah Dep't of Human Services, 60 Fed. Appx. 228, 230 (10th Cir. 2003) (unpublished) (noting appointment of counsel for the limited purpose of seeking appointment of counsel); Donald v. Cook County Sheriff's Dep't, 95 F.3d 548, 556 (7th Cir. 1996) (". . .[T]he court may assist the plaintiff by providing counsel for the limited purpose of amending the complaint"); Smith v. Kansas Dep't of Corrections, 2008 WL 4534242, *1 (D. Kan., Oct. 7, 2008) (noting appointment of counsel to assist at a settlement conference); Bowser v. Montana, 2007 WL 1456012, *1 (D.Mont., May 14, 2007) (noting appointment of counsel to assist in drafting an amended complaint); Coto v. Bowen, 1989 WL 29995, *2 (E.D.N.Y., Mar. 14, 1989) (appointing counsel to explore equitable tolling question); Dooley v. Quick, 598 F. Supp. 607, 624 n.22 (D.R.I. 1984) (appointing counsel to help frame rules to implement a decision plaintiffs won *pro se*), *aff'd*, 787 F.2d 579 (1st Cir. 1986) (unpublished).

[267]Not immediately appealable: Barnes v. Black, 544 F.3d 807, 810 (7th Cir. 2008); Holt v. Ford, 862 F.2d 850, 852–54 (11th Cir. 1989) (en banc); Ficken v. Alvarez, 146 F.3d 978, 981 (D.C. Cir. 1998); Miller v. Simmons, 814 F.2d 962, 966–67 (4th Cir. 1987); Henry v. City of Detroit Manpower Dep't, 763 F.2d 757 (6th Cir. 1985) (en banc); Smith-Bey v. Petsock, 741 F.2d 22 (3d Cir. 1984). Immediately appealable: Robbins v. Maggio, 750 F.2d 405, 412–13 (5th Cir. 1985); Slaughter v. City of Maplewood, 731 F.2d 587, 588–89 (8th Cir. 1984).

[268]Pruitt v. Mote, 503 F.3d 647, 659 (7th Cir. 2007) (en banc); Bemis v. Kelley, 857 F.2d 14, 16 (1st Cir. 1988). In *Pruitt*, the court said that the district court's exercise of discretion must be assessed as of the time it was made, and not in light of later events in the case, even if they showed that the prisoner was unable to present his case adequately. However, later events are relevant to show whether the prisoner was prejudiced by an erroneous decision not to appoint counsel. *Pruitt*, 503 F.3d at 659–60.

[269]*See, e.g.*, Williams v. White, 897 F.2d 942, 945 (8th Cir. 1990); Black v. Lane, 824 F.2d 561, 563 (7th Cir. 1987); Wimmer v. Cook, 774 F.2d 68, 76 (4th Cir. 1985).

[270]Hill v. Smithkline Beecham Corp., 393 F.3d 1111, 1114–15 (10th Cir. 2004) (stating court's "firm waiver" rule would bar appeal of the denial of counsel if the plaintiff did not object in the lower court).

[271]U.S. v. Agofsky, 20 F.3d 866, 872 (8th Cir. 1994) (en banc) (citing Munz v. Fayram, 626 F. Supp. 197, 198–99 (N.D. Iowa 1985), *appeal dismissed*, 786 F.2d 1169 (8th Cir. 1986)); U.S. v. Hirschfeld, 911 F. Supp. 200, 201 (E.D. Va. 1995) (". . . [A] person can either proceed pro se or represented by an attorney, but not by both methods—a 'hybrid' representation—simultaneously.").

about the case with your attorney. It will be the attorney's job to keep you informed about the progress of the case.

D. Answer

After a complaint is served, the defendant is required to file an answer.[272] An answer is a response to a complaint that either admits or denies each statement in the complaint, or states that the defendant does not know whether a particular statement is true, which has the same legal effect as a denial of the allegation.[273] If the defendant's answer does not respond to one of the factual paragraphs in the complaint, that paragraph is taken as admitted.[274]

Usually a defendant is required to serve an answer to your complaint within 21 days (60 days for federal government defendants)[275] after a copy of the complaint and summons has been served upon him. If a defendant has waived service, he has 60 days after sending the waiver to serve an answer.[276] However, the Prison Litigation Reform Act (PLRA) permits a defendant to "waive the right to reply to any action brought by a prisoner" under federal law, and forbids the court to grant any relief "unless a reply has been filed."[277] But the next section says that "[t]he court may require any defendant to reply to a complaint brought under this section if it finds that the plaintiff has a reasonable opportunity to prevail on the merits."[278]

In practice, it appears that district courts generally direct defendants to reply to any complaint that passes initial screening or a motion to dismiss, and therefore states a claim.[279] We have not seen any pattern either in the case law or in our own or other lawyers' experience of defendants simply refusing to answer the complaint based on the PLRA. Ordinarily, if a defendant did fail or refuse to answer the complaint, you would seek a default judgment. However, the PLRA has limited default judgments in prisoner litigation.[280]

If you amend the complaint to add parties at a later point, after the initial screening, the court may neglect to direct the defendants to answer. When you are moving to amend a complaint, always request that the court direct the defendants to answer as well as grant your motion to amend. If you amend the complaint as a matter of course (i.e., when no motion is required), and if the defendants do not answer

the amended complaint, you may need to make a motion asking the court to direct them to answer.[281]

A defendant may elect not to file an answer initially, and may instead try to get your case dismissed by filing one of the motions permitted under Rule 12[282] or Rule 56, Fed.R.Civ.P.[283] If the defendant files a motion that is not granted, he will generally be required to answer within 14 days after the court decides the motion.[284]

A defendant may include a counterclaim against you in an answer.[285] A counterclaim is a claim for relief (usually damages) filed by the defendant against the plaintiff—e.g., you sue an officer for assaulting you and he counterclaims against you, alleging you injured him while he was properly performing his duties. If an answer contains a counterclaim, you must file a reply to the counterclaim within 21 days after it is served on you.[286] Failure to do so can result in a default judgment against you on the counterclaim.

Unless there is a counterclaim, you are not required or permitted to file a pleading in response to the answer unless the court directs you to.[287] Once the complaint has been answered, your task is to move the case forward by taking discovery and preparing for trial, or by moving for summary judgment or a preliminary injunction if the facts support such a motion.[288]

Defendants may ask for an extension of time to respond to your complaint.[289] In civil rights litigation against prison staff or other public employees, government lawyers almost always ask for more time, since they generally have to do some amount of investigation to determine if they will defend the employees or request them to get other counsel. Generally you should agree to this request unless there is a very good reason, such as an emergency, to refuse it. Lawyers routinely give each other extensions as a basic

---

[272]Rule 7(a), Fed.R.Civ.P. If several defendants are represented by the same attorney, the attorney may file either a single joint answer or a separate answer for each defendant.

[273]Rule 8(b), Fed.R.Civ.P.

[274]Rule 8(b)(6), Fed.R.Civ.P.

[275]See Rules 12(a)(1)(A), 12(a)(2)–(3), Fed.R.Civ.P.

[276]Rule 12(a)(1)(A)(ii), Fed.R.Civ.P. This time period is 90 days if the defendant is not within any judicial district of the United States.

[277]42 U.S.C. § 1997e(g)(1).

[278]42 U.S.C. § 1997e(g)(2).

[279]See Ch. 9, § G.

[280]Default judgments are discussed in the next section.

[281]Amendment by motion and as a matter of course are discussed in § J of this chapter.

[282]These include a motion to dismiss or for judgment on the pleadings (discussed in § I of this chapter), a motion for a more definite statement, or a motion to strike.

[283]Rule 56 governs motions for summary judgment, discussed in § L of this chapter.

[284]Rule 12(a)(4)(A), Fed.R.Civ.P.

[285]Rule 13, Fed.R.Civ.P.

[286]Rule 12(a)(1)(B), Fed.R.Civ.P.

[287]Rule 7(a), Fed.R.Civ.P.

Some prisoners erroneously file a "traverse" to the answer, probably because such a document is sometimes used in federal habeas corpus cases. See 28 U.S.C. § 2248; compare Rule 5, Rules Governing § 2254 Cases in the United States District Court, Advisory Committee Note (noting that a traverse is appropriate only under "special circumstances"). You should not file a traverse in an ordinary federal court civil lawsuit unless the court directs you to do so. The rules may be different in state courts.

[288]See § L of this chapter and Ch. 8, § O.2 for discussion of these motions.

[289]Extensions of time must be granted by the court, Rule 6(b), Fed.R.Civ.P., but parties commonly agree to extensions which are then approved by the court.

courtesy. The court will probably grant the extension even if you don't agree, and all you will accomplish is to make yourself look unreasonable, and motivate the defendants to deny you similar courtesy when you need it. If the defendants ask for repeated extensions adding up to long periods of time, it is reasonable to oppose the request by filing a declaration or affidavit in opposition, pointing out to the court how much time they have already had and any prejudice or harm the delay is causing you.

E. DEFAULT JUDGMENT

If a defendant simply does not answer or file a motion in response to a complaint, the usual remedy is to seek a default judgment, which means that the court grants judgment in your favor. However, as discussed in the previous section, the Prison Litigation Reform Act (PLRA) says that defendants in an action "brought by a prisoner" under federal law can waive the reply; though the court can direct a reply, it cannot grant any relief against the defendant "unless a reply has been filed."[290] Those provisions can be read as meaning that you cannot get a default judgment in a case you file while you are in prison, though the question is not settled.[291]

If you find yourself in the situation where a defendant simply refuses to answer after being ordered to do so, you should try to get a default judgment, and argue to the court that Congress could not really have meant to eliminate such an essential procedure from prisoner litigation.[292] If the court is not persuaded that it can enter a default judgment, we have speculated that the best way to proceed is to move for contempt of court, seeking as a remedy the same relief you would have been entitled to had the defendant filed an answer and had the case proceeded to trial.[293] You would

argue that the PLRA does not affect the court's contempt power.[294] Nobody to our knowledge has ever done this.

There are also situations where the PLRA will not affect your entitlement to a default judgment. If you filed your complaint when you were not in prison, the PLRA will not apply to your case. There are also some extreme situations where a court can enter a default judgment against a defendant who *has* answered the complaint but has refused to comply with court rules or procedures afterwards.[295]

Getting a default judgment is a two-step process. First, a default can be entered against a defendant who has been properly served[296] but who "has failed to plead or otherwise defend" as the rules require.[297] To get a default, you submit a request to the clerk, with an affidavit showing that the party is in default, and the clerk must enter the default.[298]

Then you must ask for a default judgment. If your claim in the complaint is for "a sum certain, or for a sum which can by computation be made certain,"[299] you should submit the request for default judgment to the clerk along with an affidavit establishing the amount due.[300]

If what you are seeking is not a sum certain or one which can be calculated, you must submit a motion for a default judgment to the court.[301] In either case, you should include an affidavit stating that the defendant is not in military service,[302] and a proposed judgment for the clerk or judge to sign. If the case does not involve a "sum certain," after the default judgment is entered, a hearing (sometimes called an "inquest") will be held to determine the amount of

---

[290]42 U.S.C. § 1997e(g)(1)–(2).

[291]Bell v. Lesure, 2009 WL 1290984, *3–4 (W.D.Okla., May 6, 2009) (holding the PLRA forbids entry of default judgments in prisoner cases); Vinning v. Walls, 2009 WL 839052, *1 (S.D.Ill., Mar. 31, 2009) (holding default judgment could be entered, but no relief ordered, under the PLRA). However, default judgments do continue to be granted in prison cases. *See* Cameron v. Myers, 569 F. Supp. 2d 762 (N.D.Ind., 2008).

[292]This argument would be based on the Supreme Court's decision in *Jones v. Bock*, 549 U.S. 199, 212–213, 221–24, 127 S. Ct. 910 (2007), in which the Court said that lower courts should not interpret the PLRA exhaustion requirement to depart from the usual practices under the Federal Rules of Civil Procedure or accepted litigation practice, except to the extent that the PLRA actually says to do so. *Accord*, Miller v. Donald, 541 F.3d 1091, 1099 (11th Cir. 2008) (applying same reasoning to PLRA "three strikes" provision). You would argue that since default judgments are part of the usual litigation practice under Rule 55, Fed.R.Civ.P., and the PLRA does not specifically mention default judgments, you can still obtain one.

[293]Concerning contempt damages, *see* § T.2.b(1) of this chapter.

[294]*See* Essex County Jail Inmates v. Treffinger, 18 F. Supp. 2d 445, 462 (D.N.J. 1998) (noting that another PLRA section, 18 U.S.C. § 3626(a), has no effect on the contempt power).

[295]*See* Rule 37(b)(2)(A)(vi), Fed.R.Civ.P. (authorizing default judgment for certain discovery violations); Rule 16(f)(1), Fed.R.Civ.P. (authorizing Rule 37(b)(2)(A)(vi) sanctions for violations of pretrial procedure requirements).

[296]*See* Feist v. Jefferson County Commissioners Court, 778 F.2d 250, 252 (5th Cir. 1985) (default judgment could not be granted without proper service of complaint).

[297]Rule 55(a), Fed.R.Civ.P.

[298]Rule 55(a), Fed.R.Civ.P.; Appendix C, Forms 8a–8b.

[299]This phrase means a definite amount of money that can be determined without any exercise of judgment by the court. For example, if prison officials withheld a check that someone sent you, the amount of the check would be a "sum certain." If they withheld six weeks' wages from you and you were paid a fixed amount each week, your wages would be "a sum which can by computation be made certain." Claims for non-monetary injuries, such as pain and suffering, emotional anguish and humiliation, or loss of privileges or amenities in prison, do not fall in either category.

[300]Rule 55(b)(1), Fed.R.Civ.P.

[301]Rule 55(b)(2), Fed.R.Civ.P. If the party in default has entered an appearance in the case by this time, you should serve the motion on that party's attorney. Rule 55(b)(2), Fed.R.Civ.P.

[302]If the defendant is in the military, he enjoys certain special protections from entry of default judgments. *See* 50 App. U.S.C. § 521(g) (Soldiers' and Sailors' Civil Relief Act of 1940).

damages to which you are entitled.[303] At the inquest the defendant will be allowed to dispute your evidence concerning damages, but will not be permitted to dispute that he is legally liable to you.[304]

A default judgment may not be entered against the federal government, its agencies, or its officers unless the plaintiff establishes that he is legally entitled to relief anyway[305]—a requirement that does not exist in cases against other defendants.

Courts are reluctant to enter default judgments because of "the usual preference that cases be heard on the merits rather than resorting to sanctions that deprive a litigant of his day in court."[306] Even when default judgments are granted, they often do not stick. The court can set aside a default if the defendant shows good cause for having defaulted, and may set aside a default judgment under Rule 60(b), Fed.R.Civ.P.[307] In deciding whether a default judgment should be set aside, the court should consider whether the party obtaining the default would be prejudiced, whether the defaulting party has a meritorious defense, and whether the default resulted from the defaulting parties' culpable or willful conduct.[308]

Given the difficulty in getting and keeping a default judgment, you may ask "Why bother seeking it?" The answer is that sometimes the default judgment will be granted and will stand, and sometimes seeking one is the only way to get your case moving. In addition, a court that sets aside a default judgment may impose sanctions or conditions on the defaulting party.[309]

F. Motion Practice

The way to ask a court to take action in your case, *i.e.*, to enter an order, is to make a motion. In other sections of this chapter, we discuss particular kinds of motions: motions to dismiss and for judgment on the pleadings, to file an amended complaint, for summary judgment, for a preliminary injunction, to compel discovery, to exclude evidence from the trial, for a new trial, and others.[310] In this section we discuss motions in general.

Before you bring any kind of motion you should be sure to read the local rules of the court you are in as well as any special rules employed by the judge in your case. Local rules and judges' rules often have special requirements about motions that are in addition to the requirements in the Federal Rules of Civil Procedure. They often require the moving party to seek the opposing party's consent to the relief sought before filing a motion[311] (if the parties agree, they can submit an agreed order to the court for approval rather than file motion papers), or require the moving party to notify the court or get the court's permission before filing any motions. They may require that a memorandum of law (*i.e.*, a brief) be filed in connection with some motions or all motions, and may specify page limits for motion papers. Many courts have detailed requirements for motions to compel discovery.

---

[303]Rule 55(b)(2), Fed.R.Civ.P.; *see* Graham v. Satkoski, 51 F.3d 710, 713–14 (7th Cir. 1995) (affirming inquest award of $550 for failure to treat scalp condition and confiscation and disposal of newspapers, mail, and portable radio); Kidd v. Andrews, 340 F. Supp. 2d 333, 338 (W.D.N.Y. 2004) (granting default judgment, withholding determination of damages until other defendants' liability is determined).

[304]Benny v. Pipes, 799 F.2d 489, 495 (9th Cir.1986) ("Well-pleaded allegations are taken as admitted on a default judgment."), *amended*, 807 F.2d 1514 (9th Cir.1987); *accord*, Jackson v. Sturkie, 255 F. Supp. 2d 1096, 1100 (N.D. Cal. 2003) ("Following default judgment, a defendant is deemed to have admitted the well-pleaded allegations in the complaint.").

[305]Rule 55(e), Fed.R.Civ.P.; *see* Commercial Bank of Kuwait v. Rafidain Bank, 15 F.3d 238, 242 (2d Cir. 1994) ("Rule 55(e) reflects Congress' recognition 'that the government is sometimes slow to respond and that the public fisc should be protected from claims that are unfounded but would be granted solely because the government failed to make a timely response.'" (citations omitted)).

[306]Mitchell v. Brown & Williamson Tobacco Corp., 294 F.3d 1309, 1316–17 (11th Cir. 2002) (default judgment is a "drastic remedy" for extreme situations); Caldwell v. Center for Correctional Health and Policy Studies, 228 F.R.D. 40, 46 (D.D.C. 2005) (declining to enter a default judgment for discovery violations that did not seriously prejudice the plaintiff).

[307]Rule 55(c), Fed.R.Civ.P.

Rule 60(b), Fed.R.Civ.P., provides for relief from a final judgment for various reasons; the one applicable to default judgments is likely to be "mistake, inadvertence, surprise, or neglect," Rule 60(b)(1), which requires that a motion be filed within one year; there is also a provision for "any other reason that justifies relief." Rule 60(b)(6). "To justify relief under subsection (6), a party must show "extraordinary circumstances" suggesting that the party is faultless in the delay. . . . If a party is partly to blame for the delay, relief must be sought within one year under subsection (1) and the party's neglect must be excusable." Pioneer Inv. Services Co. v. Brunswick Associates Ltd. Partnership, 507 U.S. 380, 393, 113 S. Ct. 1489 (1993).

[308]Benny v. Pipes, 799 F.2d 489, 494 (9th Cir. 1986) (guards who knowingly failed to answer the complaint were culpable; default not vacated), *amended*, 807 F.2d 1514 (9th Cir. 1987); Davis v. Musler, 713 F.2d 907, 915 (2d Cir. 1983); Widmer-Baum v. Chandler-Halford, 162 F.R.D. 545, 553–59 (S.D.Iowa 1995) (refusing to vacate default judgment where defendants' conduct appeared willful and defendants presented no meritorious defense); Harris v. District of Columbia, 159 F.R.D. 315, 316–17 (D.D.C. 1995) (vacating a default judgment, even where default seemed willful, because it appeared that defendants had a meritorious defense).

[309]*See, e.g.*, Harris v. District of Columbia, 159 F.R.D. at 317 (awarding attorneys' fees to plaintiff for time expended on default proceedings); Hall v. Mackey, 720 F. Supp. 261, 262 (S.D.N.Y. 1989) (prison officials fined $500 for the benefit of prison law library).

[310]You can look in the table of contents or the index of this Manual to find where these motions are discussed.

[311]They may also include incentives to agree. One local rule provides that "the court may tax costs for unreasonable withholding of consent." Local Rules for Civil Cases, Rule 7.1(a)(3), United States District Court for the Eastern District of Michigan.

If you have filed your case in state court, you must consult those court's rules. Do not assume that the rules and practices are the same in federal court.

Motions must be made in writing unless they are made during a trial or hearing. A written motion "shall state with particularity the grounds therefore, and shall set forth the relief or order sought"[312]—in other words, it must state exactly what you want and why you think you should get it.

Motions, like all other papers filed in federal court, must be signed, and your signature certifies that you have made a reasonable inquiry and believe that your motion has a proper basis in fact and in law and is not made for an improper purpose.[313] The form of motion papers is discussed elsewhere in this Manual.[314]

In some districts your motion should state a "return date,"[315] which is the date that the court will in theory hear the motion. In practice, the court will not hold oral argument on every motion, and will rarely do so in a *pro se* prisoner case.[316] The return date really serves as the deadline by which all papers must be filed so the court can consider the motion. It is not the deadline for the judge to decide the motion; judges are not held to any specific time within which motions must be decided.

Rule 6(c), Fed.R.Civ.P., requires you to serve motion papers at least 14 days before the return date, and Rule 6(d) adds three days for motions served by mail. In some cases, local rules require longer periods of time between service of the motion and the return date, and some courts only hear motions on particular days, sometimes one day a week or one day a month. The return date must be set far enough ahead to accommodate the time requirements of the Federal Rules of Civil Procedure, local rules, and individual judges' rules specifying the dates and times when they hear motions.

Parties often cannot respond to motions within the usual time periods, and the accepted practice is to ask the opposing party to agree to an extension before going to court about it. You should generally extend this normal courtesy to defendants upon request, though you may be justified in refusing if there are repeated requests involving long periods of time. If you need more time, you should ask your adversary first, then request it from the court if your adversary does not agree. If the parties agree to an extension and inform the court before the deadline for filing a response passes, the court can grant your request without your having to file a motion. If you have already missed the deadline, you must make a motion and show "excusable neglect."[317] There are a few motions for which the time deadlines cannot be extended.[318]

In urgent situations, you can bring a motion before the court by order to show cause. This procedure is not specifically mentioned in the Federal Rules of Civil Procedure but is generally accepted in federal practice. An order to show cause is a proposed order submitted directly to the court, along with supporting affidavits, commanding the defendants to respond to your motion by a particular date. The party making the motion drafts the order, leaving blanks for the court to fill in the dates. If the court signs it, the order is to be served on the defendants by a date stated in the order. The party who obtains the order to show cause is normally responsible for getting the order served. If you are proceeding *in forma pauperis*, you should put a provision in the order requiring the U. S. Marshal to serve the order.

Orders to show cause are not to be used routinely. The most common use of orders to show cause is to seek temporary restraining orders and preliminary injunctions in emergency situations. Procedures for seeking these orders are discussed elsewhere in this Manual.[319] If you do not have a genuine emergency, the judge is not likely to sign an order to show cause, and you may wind up losing more time than if you had used the ordinary motion procedures to begin with.

Decisions on motions mostly cannot be appealed unless they are "final decisions" on the merits of the whole case (*e.g.*, granting summary judgment or dismissing the entire

---

[312]Rule 7(b)(1)(B), Fed.R.Civ.P.

[313]Rule 11(b), Fed.R.Civ.P. Rule 11 provides for sanctions if a motion or other paper filed in court does *not* satisfy its requirements. *See* § W of this chapter.

[314]*See* Ch. 11, § D.

[315]In some courts, litigants are not expected to state return dates in their motion papers. Check the local court rules concerning motions.

[316]You may be able to persuade the court to hold a telephonic or video hearing on your motion. Federal courts do more and more of their business by telephone or video when the parties all have lawyers, and we see no reason why *pro se* cases should be any different, especially since the Prison Litigation Reform Act encourages the use of telecommunications in cases involving incarcerated parties. 42 U.S.C. § 1997e(f); *see* Ch. 9, § H, concerning this PLRA provision.

[317]Rule 6(b)(1)(B), Fed.R.Civ.P. The decision whether neglect is excusable is based on all the relevant circumstances, including "the danger of prejudice to the [opposing party], the length of the delay and its potential impact on judicial proceedings, the reason for the delay, including whether it was within the reasonable control of the movant, and whether the movant acted in good faith." Pioneer Investment Services Co. v. Brunswick Associates Limited Partnership, 507 U.S. 380, 394–95, 113 S. Ct. 1489 (1993) (footnotes omitted). *See also* Smith v. District of Columbia, 430 F.3d 450 (D.C. Cir. 2005) (extension to file later motion for summary denied; "[i]n the absence of any motion for an extension, the trial court had no basis on which to exercise its discretion."); Quigley v. Rosenthal, 427 F.3d 1232, 1238 (10th Cir. 2005) (it is "well established that inadvertence, ignorance of the rules, and mistakes construing the rules do not constitute excusable neglect for purposes of Rule 6(b)"); Cordero-Soto v. Island Finance, Inc., 418 F.3d 114, 118 (1st Cir. 2005) (excusable neglect not shown due to counsel's failure to timely inform court of basis for extension).

[318]Rule 6(b)(2), Fed.R.Civ.P. (referring to motions under Rules 50(b) and (d), 52(b), (d), and (e), and 60(b)).

[319]*See* Ch. 8, § O.2; Appendix C, Forms 11a–11c.

case) or they grant or deny an injunction.[320] If you wish the district court to reconsider a decision on a motion that is not appealable, you can file a motion for reargument or reconsideration. This motion is not referred to in the Federal Rules of Civil Procedure but is generally recognized in federal courts and is provided for in some courts' local rules.[321] Motions to reconsider are not designed to rehash matters the court has already considered and decided.[322] Such motions are only granted if a party shows that the court "overlooked controlling decisions or factual matters that were put before the court on the underlying motion"[323] or that the facts or law significantly changed after the matter was submitted to the court for decision.[324]

G. Serving Papers and Writing to the Court

Parties in litigation are not supposed to communicate privately (*ex parte*) with the court except in very rare circumstances. Anything you have to say to the court should be disclosed to the other side, and vice versa.

Once your complaint is served on a party, you should serve all subsequent litigation papers on that party's attorney if he has one. Service of papers after the complaint can be made by delivering the papers to the attorney or party or by mailing them to the attorney or party. After you have served the other side, you should file the papers in court along with proof of service.[325] After the complaint has been

served, you file subsequent papers by sending them to the clerk of the court.[326] All papers filed in court must be signed by the party, if *pro se*, or by the attorney if the party has one.[327] Many federal courts require you to file an original and a copy of each pleading; check the local rules and the judge's individual practice rules.[328]

If you have any occasion to write to the court about your case, you should send copies of your letter to the other parties. You should indicate that you have done this by noting it at the end of the letter (*e.g.*, "cc: John Doe, Esq., Assistant Attorney General"). Or you can enclose a certificate of service with the letter to the court so there will be no misunderstanding.

If you are addressing important issues in your case, it is preferable to do so by motion, or by declaration or affidavit if you are responding to the other side's motion. Letters do not always become part of the court record, and a court cannot base a substantive decision on factual assertions that are not in a sworn affidavit or a declaration under penalty of perjury.[329]

H. Calculating Time Deadlines

Rule 6, Fed.R.Civ.P., sets out the rules for calculating time deadlines in federal district court—when you or your adversary must file a motion, respond to a motion, etc. Generally, the day of the event that starts the time running does not get counted, but the day of the deadline is counted.[330] If the deadline would otherwise fall on a Saturday, Sunday, or legal holiday, the deadline is the next business day afterward. All days are counted, including intermediate Saturdays, Sundays, and legal holidays.[331] If you are responding to something served on you by mail, you get an additional three days.[332] For matters pertaining to appeals, there are similar rules in Rule 26 of the Federal Rules of Appellate Procedure.

There is a special rule for *pro se* prisoner litigants who file legal papers by mail. The Supreme Court held that a *pro se* prisoner's notice of appeal is deemed filed on the day it is delivered for mailing to prison authorities, rather than applying the usual rule that it is filed the day it arrives at court, since the litigant loses control over the notice as soon as he turns it over to prison personnel.[333] The lower federal courts have generally applied this "prison mailbox" rule to

---

[320]*See* § V.1.c. of this chapter for a discussion of what decisions can be appealed and when.

[321]These motions have generally been treated procedurally like motions to alter or amend a final judgment under Rule 59(e), Fed.R.Civ.P., which until recently meant you had to get them filed within 10 days of the decision. *See* Emory v. Secretary of Navy, 819 F.2d 291, 293 (D.C. Cir. 1987). Rule 59(e) has been amended, effective December 1, 2009, to change the deadline to 28 days. You should check the local court rules to see if there is a rule governing motions for reargument or reconsideration and if the deadline has been changed to 28 days. If not, it is probably safer to assume it is 10 days unless there is case law in your district to the contrary.

Pursuant to Rules 52(b) and 59(b), a motion for reconsideration of a *judgment* must be made within 28 days.

Reconsideration of a decision on a motion for summary judgment is authorized by Rule 54(b), Fed.R.Civ.P., which says that summary judgment decisions are subject to revision until final judgment is entered on all parties and claims. *See* Smook v. Minnehaha County, S.D., 353 F. Supp. 2d 1059, 1061 (D.S.D. 2005), *rev'd and remanded on other grounds*, 457 F.3d 806 (8th Cir. 2006), *cert. denied*, 549 U.S. 1317 (2007).

[322]*See, e.g.*, Graham ex rel. Estate of Graham v. County of Washtenaw, 358 F.3d 377, 385 (6th Cir. 2004).

[323]Ososki v. St. Paul Surplus Lines Ins. Co., 162 F. Supp. 2d 714, 718 (E.D. Mich. 2001).

[324]*See, e.g.*, Hittle v. Scripto-Tokai Corp., 166 F. Supp. 2d 159, 161 (M.D. Pa. 2001) (intervening change in the applicable law); Holstein v. City of Chicago, 149 F.R.D. 147, 148 (N.D. Ill. 1993).

[325]An example of proof of service appears in Appendix C, Form 15.

[326]Rule 5(d), Fed.R.Civ.P.

[327]Rule 11(a), Fed.R.Civ.P.; *see* § W of this chapter for further discussion of Rule 11.

[328]*See, e.g.*, See E.D. Mich. Local Rule 5.1(b), which requires that "[a]ll papers filed with the clerk must include an original and one copy." The copy is to be clearly marked "JUDGE'S COPY."

[329]These documents are discussed in Ch. 12, § C.

[330]Rule 6(a)(1)(A, C), Fed.R.Civ.P.

[331]Rule 6(a)(1)(B), Fed.R.Civ.P. This is a recent change in the rules, effective December 1, 2009. Older decisions will not reflect this change. Be sure you have the current rules.

[332]Rule 6(d), Fed.R.Civ.P.

[333]Houston v. Lack, 487 U.S. 266, 273–76, 108 S. Ct. 2379 (1988); *see* Stoot v. Cain, 570 F.3d 669, 671–72 (5th Cir. 2009) and

other civil litigation deadlines as well, including the filing of the complaint.[334] Courts have applied this rule to civil detainees as well as persons under criminal confinement.[335]

For notices of appeal, the Federal Rules of Appellate Procedure have been amended to spell out what is necessary to get the benefit of the prison mailbox rule.[336] While this rule is technically limited to notices of appeal, at least two federal circuits have held that its requirements should apply to other documents,[337] and we would expect courts generally to hold that if you comply with them, your document will be considered filed as of the date you put it in the prison mail system.

That rule provides that if there is a system designed specially for legal mail, the prisoner must use that system.[338] The prisoner must also submit a declaration or notarized statement indicating when the notice of appeal was put into the prison mail system and stating (truthfully) that first-class postage has been prepaid.[339] If the prison procedure is

to deduct postage automatically from your account rather than requiring you to prepay it, or if you are indigent and postage will be paid by the prison, your declaration or affidavit should say that. Courts have held that the affidavit or declaration need not be submitted with the notice of appeal, but can be submitted later[340] (though it is probably best to submit it with the notice or other document you are filing).

The "prison mailbox" rule does not apply when you don't use the prison mail system. If you send your papers to someone else for mailing, your document will not be deemed filed until it arrives at the court.[341] If you do use the prison mail system, but the deadline has already passed before you turn over the document to prison authorities for mailing, the prison mailbox rule will not help you.[342]

---

cases cited (rule applies to papers given timely to prison authorities for mailing, even if they never reach the court).

There are a lot of other rules pertaining to notices of appeal. These are discussed in § U.1.d of this chapter.

[334]As to complaints, *see* Douglas v. Noelle, 567 F.3d 1103, 1106–07 (9th Cir. 2009); Price v. Philpot, 420 F.3d 1158, 1164 (10th Cir. 2005); Richard v. Ray, 290 F.3d 810, 813 (6th Cir. 2002); Dory v. Ryan, 999 F.2d 679, 682 (2d Cir. 1993), *modified on other grounds*, 25 F.3d 81 (2d Cir. 1994). As to other documents, *see, e.g.,* Edwards v. U.S., 266 F.3d 756, 758 (7th Cir. 2001) (all *pro se* prisoner filings absent exceptional circumstances); Tapia-Ortiz v. Doe, 171 F.3d 150, 152 (2d Cir. 1999) (per curiam) (prison mailbox rule applied to administrative claim under FTCA); Faile v. Upjohn Co., 988 F.2d 985, 988 (9th Cir. 1993) (discovery responses); Dunn v. White, 880 F.2d 1188, 1190 (10th Cir. 1989) (filing of objections to magistrate's report and recommendation); Smith v. Evans, 853 F.2d 155, 161–162 (3d Cir. 1988) (*Houston* rationale applies to rule 59(e) motion for reconsideration). The prison mailbox rule may not be applicable to deadlines in criminal cases. *See* U.S. v. Emuegbunam, 268 F.3d 377, 397 (6th Cir. 2001) ("*Houston's* mailbox rule does not apply to Rules 29 and 33").

[335]*See, e.g.,* Jones v. Blanas, 393 F.3d 918, 926 (9th Cir. 2004) (mailbox rule applies to "civil detainee confined in state hospital as sexually violent predator").

[336]Rule 4(c)(1), Fed.R.App.P.

[337]Douglas v. Noelle, 567 F.3d 1103, 1108–09 (9th Cir. 2009); Price v. Philpot, 420 F.3d 1158, 1164–65 (10th Cir. 2005).

[338]Rule 4(c)(1), Fed.R.App.P.

[339]Rule 4(c)(1), Fed.R.App.P.; *see* Davis v. Woodford, 446 F.3d 957, 960 (9th Cir. 2006) (sworn proof of service form stating that another prisoner had placed plaintiff's notice of appeal in the prison system timely was sufficient despite the fact that the mail did not go out for a week); U.S. v. Ceballos-Martinez, 371 F.3d 713, 715–18 (10th Cir. 2004); Grady v. U.S., 269 F.3d 913, 918 (8th Cir. 2001). *But see* Ingram v. Jones, 507 F.3d 640, 644 (7th Cir. 2007) (prison mailbox rule requires filing a declaration or notarized statement with the date of deposit in the mail system and statement that first-class postage was pre-paid; statement "postage was prepaid by the institution" does not satisfy the rule where it isn't true); U.S. v. Craig, 368 F.3d 738, 740–41 (7th Cir. 2004) (refusing to apply rule where prisoner's declaration did not state that

first-class postage had been paid); U.S. v. Smith, 182 F.3d 733, 735 n.1 (10th Cir. 1999) (same).

Such a document would be similar to the proof of service included as Form 15 in Appendix C. In fact, in a document that is served as well as filed, you could simply add to your proof of service a statement that you are turning your papers over to prison officials on a particular date for mailing to the court. A sworn declaration stating this date will shift the burden to the defendants to prove you did not submit the document on time. Caldwell v. Amend, 30 F.3d 1199 (9th Cir. 1994).

One federal appeals court initially held that placement in a mailbox for non-legal mail did not satisfy the prison mailbox rule because it did not produce documentation of the date of mailing. Miller v. Sumner, 921 F.2d 202, 203 (9th Cir.1990). However, that court has acknowledged that *Miller* is abrogated by later decisions, and that placement of the document in a prison mailbox and provision of a declaration or affidavit of timely mailing satisfies the rule. Douglas v. Noelle, 567 F.3d 1103, 1108–09 (9th Cir. 2009).

[340]Sulik v. Taney County, Missouri, 316 F.3d 813, 814 (8th Cir. 2003) (prisoner could file the affidavit after timeliness was challenged, since the rule did not say when it has to be filed); Grady v. U.S., 269 F.3d at 918 ("the prisoner must *at some point* attest to [having deposited his legal papers in the mail system] in an affidavit or notarized statement"; noting that court may give less weight or decline to consider long-delayed affidavits or declarations (emphasis supplied)); *see* U.S. v. Ceballos-Martinez, 371 F.3d at 717 (dismissing appeal; noting prisoner did not include declaration or affidavit with notice of appeal, "and he has not subsequently" done so).

[341]Knickerbocker v. Artuz, 271 F.3d 35, 37 (2d Cir. 2001) (per curiam) (mailbox rule did not apply when *pro se* inmate gave legal pleadings to sister to mail); Wilder v. Chairman of Central Classification Board, 926 F.2d 367, 370–71 (4th Cir. 1991).

[342]Walker v. Jastremski, 430 F.3d 560, 561 (2d Cir. 2005) (holding "untimely filing was not attributable to mail in the prison system, and therefore the prison mailbox rule is inapplicable to his case"); Sulik v. Taney County, Mo., 316 F.3d 813, 815–16 (8th Cir. 2003).

Some states have adopted the mailbox rule for prisoners filing in state courts.[343] Others have not.[344]

If you need more time to meet a court deadline, the court may "for cause shown" give you more time. If you ask for an extension or "enlargement" before the deadline, you don't have to make a formal motion.[345] If you have already missed the deadline, the court can still give you an extension if you make a motion and show "excusable neglect."[346]

There are a few deadlines that the court has no authority or limited authority to extend.[347] These include the 28-day limit for post-trial motions for judgment as a matter of law, to alter or amend a judgment, for a new trial,[348] and the one-year limit for certain motions for relief from a judgment or order.[349]

At least one court has held that delays in the prison's delivery of court orders should not count against the prisoner in calculating when an appeal or motion to reconsider that order is due.[350] You should not count on getting the benefit of this holding, since you may have to show that the delay was caused by the prison and not just slow mail delivery, which could be difficult. Meet the deadline if you can, and if that is going to be a problem, write to the court immediately stating the date that you received the order from prison mail delivery. If the deadline is one that the court has the authority to extend, ask for more time.

I. Motion to Dismiss or for Judgment on the Pleadings

Defendants may make a motion to dismiss your case in whole or in part under Rule 12, Fed.R.Civ.P. Most often the defendants will move under Rule 12(b)(6) and argue that your complaint fails to state a claim upon which relief can be granted.[351] This means that even if all the facts you allege are true, they don't establish a violation of the Constitution or of any other law that the court can enforce. (Under the Prison Litigation Reform Act, the court is supposed to consider whether your complaint states a claim anyway, either at the beginning of your case or whenever it gets around to it.[352]) A motion to dismiss may be made on behalf of all defendants (e.g., arguing that what they did to you was not illegal) or some of the defendants (e.g., arguing that even if it was illegal, they weren't personally involved in it).

A motion to dismiss is to be made before an answer is filed.[353] However, after an answer is filed, the defendants can file a motion making the same arguments. At that point it is called a motion for judgment on the pleadings.[354] In practice, the two motions generally amount to the same thing and are governed by the same legal standards,[355] so we will use the term "motion to dismiss" to refer to both.

To survive a motion to dismiss, your complaint must include "enough facts to state a claim to relief that is plausible on its face,"[356] and do so for each element of your claim.[357] We discuss this pleading standard, and what you must do to state a claim, in more detail earlier in this chapter.[358]

---

[343]These courts have permitted pleadings of *pro se* prisoners to be deemed filed at the time they are deposited in the prison mail system or given to a person designated to receive prisoner mail. *See* Ex parte Williams, 651 So.2d 569, 571 (Ala. 1992); Mayer v. Arizona, 184 Ariz. 242, 908 P.2d 56,57 (App. 1995); *In re* Jordan, 4 Cal.4th 116, 13 Cal.Rptr.2d 878, 840 P.2d 983, 985 (1992); Haag v. Florida, 591 So.2d 614, 617 (Fla. 1992); Massaline v. Williams, 274 Ga. 552, 554 S.E.2d 720, 722 (2001); Setala v. J.C. Penney Company, 97 Hawai'i 484, 40 P.3d 886, 890–93 (Haw. 2002); Munson v. State, 128 Idaho 639, 917 P.2d 796, 799–800 (1996); Taylor v. McKune, 25 Kan.App.2d 283, 962 P.2d 566, 569–70 (1998); State ex rel. Egana v. Louisiana, 771 So.2d 638 (La. 2000); Commonwealth v. Hartsgrove, 407 Mass. 441, 553 N.E.2d 1299, 1301– 02 (1990); Sykes v. Mississippi, 757 So.2d 997, 1000–01 (Miss. 2000); Kellogg v. Journal Communications, 108 Nev. 474, 835 P.2d 12, 13–14 (1992); Woody v. Oklahoma ex rel. Dep't of Corrections, 1992 OK 45, 833 P.2d 257, 259–60 (Okla. 1992); Hickey v. Oregon State Penitentiary, 127 Or.App. 727, 874 P.2d 102, 105 (1994); Commonwealth v. Jones, 549 Pa. 58, 700 A.2d 423, 426 (1997); Ramos v. Richardson, 228 S.W.3d 671, 673 (Tex. 2007); Tenn.R. Civ. P. 5.06 (papers prepared by or filed on behalf of an incarcerated *pro se* prisoner are deemed to have been filed with the trial court when they are "delivered to the appropriate individual at the correctional facility."). In Utah, a state court said, "We understand why many of our sister states have decided to adopt *Houston*'s interpretation of the federal rules to their own state rules of procedure," but left the question for the state supreme court in its function of drafting rules of appellate procedure. State v. Parker, 936 P.2d 1118, 1120–21 (Utah App.1997). Afterward, the Utah rules were amended to adopt the prison mailbox rule. Utah R. App. P. 4(g).

[344]*See* Hamel v. State, 338 Ark. 769, 1 S.W.3d 434 (1999) (refusing to adopt the mailbox rule); Carr v. State, 554 A.2d 778 (Del. 1989) (same); Walker-Bey v. Dep't of Corrections, 222 Mich. App. 605, 608–11, 564 N.W.2d 171 (1997).

[345]In a federal court of appeals, you must make a formal motion to get an enlargement of time. Rule 26(b), Fed.R.App.P.

[346]Rule 6(b)(1)(B), Fed.R.Civ.P. The meaning of "excusable neglect" is discussed in § F of this chapter.

[347]Rule 6(b)(2), Fed.R.Civ.P.

[348]Rules 50(b), 50(d), 52(b), 59(b), 59(d), and 59(e), Fed.R.Civ.P.

[349]Rule 60(b), Fed.R.Civ.P.

---

[350]U.S. v. Fiorelli, 337 F.3d 282, 289–90 (3d Cir. 2003).

[351]Rule 12(b)(6), Fed.R.Civ.P.

[352]This judicial screening requirement is discussed in § X.C.3.b of this chapter and in Ch. 9, § C.

[353]Rule 12(b), Fed.R.Civ.P.

[354]Rule 12(c), Fed.R.Civ.P.

[355]Craigs, Inc. v. General Elec. Capital Corp., 12 F.3d 686, 688 (7th Cir. 1993); Delhomme v. Caremark Rx Inc., 232 F.R.D. 573, 576 n.2 (N.D.Tex. 2005).

[356]Bell Atlantic v. Twombly, 550 U.S 544, 570, 127 S. Ct. 1995 (2007).

[357]Phillips v. County of Allegheny, 515 F.3d 224, 234 (3d Cir. 2008) (stating a claim "requires a complaint with enough factual matter (taken as true) to suggest' the required element. [quoting *Bell Atlantic*, 550 U.S. at 576 n.3.] This 'does not impose a probability requirement at the pleadling stage,' but instead 'simply calls for enough facts to raise a reasonable expectation that discovery will reveal evidence of the necessary element.'").

[358]*See* § B.1 of this chapter.

There are two ways to respond to a motion to dismiss: fight it, or correct your complaint. If you think the defendants' arguments are simply wrong, you should file a response explaining why your case should not be dismissed. If the defendants make an incorrect legal argument, you will need to point out their error to the court and say what the correct law is. The defendants may also argue that the allegations in your complaint simply don't show a violation of law, or don't show that they are responsible for it. You will need to explain in your response how your allegations support your claim that the defendants violated the law, for each element of your legal claim—and for each defendant, if they argue that you haven't stated a claim against particular defendants.

Sometimes, however, a motion to dismiss will demonstrate that you have made a mistake or left something out of your complaint. If that is the case, you should be allowed to amend the complaint to eliminate the basis for the motion to dismiss.[359] A recent amendment to the rules gives you 21 days after the service of a motion to dismiss in which you can amend your complaint "as a matter of course" (i.e., without your opponent's agreement or court permission), and if you do need to seek permission, it should be given "freely."[360] You should then file a brief in opposition to the motion to dismiss explaining why the amended complaint corrects the defects raised by the defendants.

In deciding a motion to dismiss, the court is required to "accept the allegations of the complaint as true and construe those allegations, and any reasonable inferences that might be drawn from them, in the light most favorable to the plaintiff."[361] The court is not to resolve factual disputes at this stage of the lawsuit. If the defendants submit materials outside the complaint, such as affidavits or documentary exhibits, the court must either ignore them or convert the motion into a motion for summary judgment.[362] Most courts hold that if a motion to dismiss is converted to one for summary judgment, a *pro se* prisoner must be given notice of that fact and of the requirement that he submit his own affidavits or other evidence to counter any evidence submitted by the defendants.[363]

In some circumstances, you may wish to get your own case dismissed because you don't want to pursue it any more, or you can't or don't want to pursue it at that time.[364] This is called voluntary dismissal. You can file a notice of dismissal at any time before an answer or a motion for summary judgment is served, or you can obtain a stipulation from all parties allowing the dismissal. As long as you have not dismissed the same legal claims previously, the dismissal will be "without prejudice,"[365] meaning that you can file the claims again later as long as you don't miss the statute of limitations. You may also be able to persuade the court to dismiss your case at a later point without prejudice.[366]

If you don't meet any of these conditions, or if a stipulation or order of dismissal states that the dismissal is with prejudice, the dismissal "operates as an adjudication on the merits,"[367] which means you will be barred by the doctrine of *res judicata* from bringing the claims again.[368]

If for some reason, you cannot or do not want to continue litigating a case that you have filed, you should voluntarily dismiss the case. Don't just abandon it. If you do that, the court is likely to grant the defendants' motion to dismiss or summary judgment motion, considering only their side

---

[359]The Supreme Court has stated that a plaintiff with an "arguable" claim should be permitted to amend the complaint before a pending motion to dismiss is ruled on. Neitzke v. Williams, 490 U.S. 319, 329, 109 S. Ct. 1827 (1989). One federal circuit has said that prisoners are not entitled to amend their complaints to avoid dismissal under the screening provisions of the Prison Litigation Reform Act, but we understand that holding to be limited to the screening context, and not to apply where the case has survived screening and the defendants have filed a motion to dismiss. *See* Benson v. O'Brian, 179 F.3d 1014, 1016 (6th Cir. 1999) (holding amendment is not permitted where the PLRA screening provisions apply); *see generally* Ch. 9, § C, concerning the PLRA screening provisions. In any case, most federal courts have rejected the Sixth Circuit's rule, and hold that a plaintiff should have the opportunity to amend a deficient complaint both in connection with PLRA screening and when a motion to dismiss has been filed. *See, e.g.,* Grayson v. Mayview State Hosp., 293 F.3d 103, 108–09 (3d Cir. 2002).

[360]Rule 15(a), Fed.R.Civ.P. Procedures for amending a complaint are discussed in the next section.

[361]Kay v. Bemis, 500 F.3d 1214, 1217 (10th Cir. 2007) (quoting Gaines v. Stenseng, 292 F.3d 1222, 1224 (10th Cir. 2002)). *See also* Bell Atlantic v. Twombly, 550 U.S 544, 555, 127 S. Ct. 1995 (2007) (stating that the decisions on such motion to dismiss rest "on the assumption that all the allegations in the complaint are true"); Luney v. SGS Automotive Services, Inc., 432 F.3d 866, 867 (8th Cir. 2005); Roth Steel Products v. Sharon Steel Corp., 705 F.2d 134, 155

(6th Cir. 1982) (12(b)(6) motion to dismiss is directed solely to the complaint and any exhibits attached to it).

[362]Rule 12(b), Fed.R.Civ.P.; GFF Corp. v. Associated Wholesale Grocers, Inc., 130 F.3d 1381, 1384 (10th Cir. 1997) (quoting Fed.R.Civ.P. 12(b)); Lown v. Salvation Army, Inc., 393 F. Supp. 2d 223, 234 (S.D.N.Y. 2005).

[363]These requirements, and other aspects of summary judgment procedure, are discussed in § L of this chapter.

[364]For example, if your release date is coming up, you might want to dismiss voluntarily and then re-file after your release so your case would no longer be "brought by a prisoner" and you could avoid some of the disadvantages of the PLRA. You should only do this if you are sure there will be enough time between your release and the running of the statute of limitations that you will be able to get your case filed again and will have enough time to take discovery and amend the complaint or add parties within the limitations period if necessary. *See* Ch. 9 concerning the PLRA.

[365]Rule 41(a)(1), Fed.R.Civ.P.

[366]Rule 41(a)(2), Fed.R.Civ.P. The judge can dismiss in these circumstances "on terms that the court considers proper"; the dismissal is without prejudice unless the court says it is with prejudice.

[367]Rule 41(a)(1)(B).

[368]*Res judicata* is discussed in Ch. 8, § M.

of the story, resulting in another bad decision for prisoners.[369]

The court may also dismiss your case if you fail to prosecute it or if you do not comply with court rules or court orders.[370] However, courts must be patient with the problems of *pro se* litigants,[371] and it is improper to dismiss for failure to prosecute when a litigant who is known to be incarcerated fails to appear for trial or a conference.[372] Repeated failure to comply with court orders or deadlines or failure to move the case forward over a long period of time will justify dismissal even in a *pro se* case.[373] You are entitled

to receive notice before a court dismisses your case for failure to prosecute.[374]

J. Amending the Complaint

Under Rule 15(a), Fed.R.Civ.P., you can amend your complaint once "as a matter of course" (*i.e.*, without permission from the court or agreement from the defendant) if you do so within 21 days of serving the original complaint or within 21 days of being served with an answer or a motion to dismiss.[375] If these time periods have passed, or if you have already amended your complaint once, you must get your opponent's consent or the leave (permission) of the court.[376]

If you have to seek permission to amend your complaint, it will usually be granted. The rule says "[t]he court should freely give leave when justice requires,"[377] and the courts have said that means leave to amend should be granted unless there is some good reason like "undue delay, bad faith or dilatory motive on the part of the movant, repeated failure to cure deficiencies by amendments previously allowed, undue prejudice to the opposing party by virtue of allowance of the amendment, futility of amendment, etc."[378] Almost all federal courts have held that you should be granted leave to amend even if your complaint has been dismissed as frivolous or failing to state a claim at initial screening.[379]

---

[369]*See, e.g.,* Ballard v. Woodward, 641 F. Supp. 432, 433–34 (W.D.N.C. 1986); *cf.* Ghazali v. Moran 46 F.3d 52, 53 (9th Cir. 1995) (no abuse of discretion to dismiss *pro se* complaint where inmate filed no opposition to motion to dismiss).

[370]Rule 41(b), Fed.R.Civ.P.

[371]Nasious v. Two Unknown B.I.C.E Agents, 492 F.3d 1158 (10th Cir. 2007) (reversing dismissal for failure to comply with court orders to provide short statement of claim where orders may not have been understandable to *pro se* litigant and where court did not consider alternatives to dismissal with prejudice); Cintron-Lorenzo v. Departamento de Asuntos del Consumidor, 312 F.3d 522, 526–27 (1st Cir. 2002) (acknowledging that leniency for *pro se* litigants is sometimes appropriate, but holding that dismissal with prejudice for failure to prosecute was not an abuse of discretion because, *inter alia*, the district court gave the *pro se* litigant two explicit warnings before dismissing and the litigant was an attorney); Espinoza v. U.S., 52 F.3d 838, 842 (10th Cir. 1995) (district court should consider the difficulties inherent in the service rules for *pro se* litigants); Smith-Bey v. Cripe, 852 F.2d 592, 594 (D.C. Cir. 1988) (eight months of inactivity after the denial of counsel does not in itself warrant dismissal for lack of prosecution); Palmer v. City of Decatur, Ill., 814 F.2d 426, 428–29 (7th Cir. 1987) (*pro se* litigant's case should not have been dismissed for failure to prosecute while he was actively trying to obtain counsel); *see* Allen v. Calderon, 408 F.3d 1150, 1152 (9th Cir. 2005) (complaint should not have been dismissed for failure to prosecute when evidence showed *pro se* inmate was incompetent); Sterling v. U.S., 985 F.2d 411, 412 (8th Cir. 1993) (dismissal with prejudice is appropriate only where a plaintiff intentionally or willfully causes delay).

[372]Hernandez v. Whiting, 881 F.2d 768, 770–71 (9th Cir. 1989).

[373]Emerson v. Thiel College, 296 F.3d 184, 190–91 (3d Cir. 2002) (delays over two years justified dismissal); Jourdan v. Jabe, 951 F.2d 108, 110 (6th Cir. 1991) (upholding dismissal for repeated failure to meet court deadlines); West v. City of New York, 130 F.R.D. 522, 524–26 (S.D.N.Y. 1990) (dismissing case for failure to take action to move the case for 19 months). In determining whether dismissal with prejudice is appropriate, courts generally consider factors such as "(1) the extent of the party's personal responsibility; (2) the prejudice to the adversary caused by the failure to meet scheduling orders and respond to discovery; (3) a history of dilatoriness; (4) whether the conduct of the party or the attorney was willful or in bad faith; (5) the effectiveness of sanctions other than dismissal, which entails an analysis of alternative sanctions; and (6) the meritoriousness of the claim or defense." Emerson v. Thiel College, 296 F.3d at 190.

[374]Smith-Bey v. Cripe, 852 F.2d 592, 594 (D.C. Cir. 1988); Thompson v. Housing Auth., 782 F.2d 829, 831–32 (9th Cir. 1986) (per curiam) (affirming dismissal where district court had given plaintiff abundant opportunity to comply with its orders and local rules).

[375]Rule 15(a)(1), Fed.R.Civ.P. This is a change from prior law. The rule formerly provided that you could amend your complaint as a matter of course at any time before a responsive pleading was filed.

[376]Rule 15(a)(2), Fed.R.Civ.P.

[377]Rule 15(a)(2), Fed.R.Civ.P.

[378]Foman v. Davis, 371 U.S. 178, 82–83, 83 S. Ct. 227 (1962); *accord*, Interroyal Corp. v. Sponseller, 889 F.2d 108, 112 (6th Cir. 1990); Allen v. Ronan, 764 F. Supp. 738, 740 (D.Conn.1991) (complaint with conclusory allegations as to civil rights violations and conspiracy was dismissed without prejudice to amend with proper factual allegations). *But see In re* NAHC, Inc. Sec. Litig., 306 F.3d 1314, 1332 (3d Cir. 2002) ("We have made it clear that an amendment would be futile when 'the complaint, as amended, would fail to state a claim upon which relief could be granted.'"); Gay v. Petsock, 917 F.2d 768, 772 (3d Cir. 1990) (proposed amendments denied when they were not made until the first day of trial).

[379]*See, e.g.,* Lira v. Herrera, 427 F.3d 1164, 1169–70 (9th Cir. 2005) (it is improper to deny leave to amend a complaint unless it is clear that the complaint could not be saved by amendment (citation omitted)). One federal circuit, the Sixth, has held that the Prison Litigation Reform Act forbids prisoners from amending their complaints to avoid dismissal at screening. We think this is clearly wrong. *See* Ch. 9, § C, n.199, for further discussion of this issue.

Generally, amendments to a complaint that add new claims or parties must be made within the time set by the statute of limitations for filing the suit.[380] However, if a new claim or defense arises from the same facts alleged in the original pleadings, it may "relate back" to the time the original pleading was filed.[381] For example, suppose you were assaulted by officers, had your clothes ripped off, and were thrown naked in a strip cell without ever getting a hearing. If you initially filed a complaint alleging cruel and unusual punishment and denial of due process, and later amended to allege that ripping your clothes off was part of a search conducted unreasonably in violation of the Fourth Amendment, your Fourth Amendment claim would probably relate back. Relation back problems most frequently come up when plaintiffs amend to add new parties, including "John Doe" defendants, who are identified after the statute of limitations has passed.[382]

An amended complaint deals with events that occurred before the original complaint was filed. A supplemental complaint deals with events that have occurred since you filed your original complaint.[383] These events must have some relationship to the claims in the original complaint.[384] If they do not, you will have to raise them in a separate lawsuit. A supplemental complaint can add new parties.[385]

You may file a supplemental complaint only with the permission of the court, but this permission is supposed to be granted freely, just like permission to file an amended complaint.[386] Permission should be denied only in cases where the complaint is filed out of bad faith or an intent to delay.[387] However, some courts have interpreted the Prison Litigation Reform Act's administrative exhaustion requirement as barring prisoners from joining claims to an existing lawsuit unless they were exhausted before the original complaint was filed.[388]

To file a supplemental complaint, or to file an amended complaint after the time for amendment "as a matter of course" has passed, you must file a motion with the court and attach a copy of the proposed new complaint. Once the court grants permission to file the amended or supplemental complaint, you must serve it on counsel for the defendants already in the case. You can serve it as prescribed in Rule 5(b)(1), Fed.R.Civ.P., on defendants who have already been served with process. However, if there are new defendants in the amended or supplemental complaint, you will have to serve process on each one of them, just as you served the original defendants when you first filed the case.[389] Since defendants in a prisoner case are not required to answer the complaint unless the court directs them to do so, always ask the court to direct them to file an answer when you move to file an amended or supplemental complaint.[390]

There are two other ways, in addition to the usual amendment procedure, that the issues in a case may be changed.

Courts generally hold pretrial conferences pursuant to Rule 16(c), Fed.R.Civ.P., at which formulating the issues and amending the complaint may be discussed. Usually the main topics at conferences are scheduling of discovery, motions, and other activities. After such conference, the court may enter a pretrial order, which is usually agreed to between the parties. Once a pretrial order is signed by the court it supersedes all prior pleadings filed and becomes the controlling document unless modified by the Court.[391] The court may or may not use this procedure in a *pro se* prisoner case.[392]

---

[380]*See* Ch. 8, § N, for a discussion of statutes of limitations.

[381]Rule 15(c), Fed.R.Civ.P. (a new claim or defense relates back if it "arose out of the conduct, transaction, or occurrence set out—or attempted to be set out—in the original pleading"); *see* Tapia-Ortiz v. Doe, 171 F.3d 150, 152 (2d Cir. 1999) (per curiam) (holding an amended complaint adding new defendants cannot relate back if the newly-added defendants were not named originally because the plaintiff did not know their identities (citing Barrow v. Wethersfield Police Dep't, 66 F.3d 466, 470 (2d Cir. 1995)).

[382]*See, e.g.,* Tapia-Ortiz v. Doe, 171 F.3d 150, 152 (2d Cir. 1999) (per curiam) (holding an amended complaint adding new defendants cannot relate back if the newly-added defendants were not named originally because the plaintiff did not know their identities (citing Barrow v. Wethersfield Police Dep't, 66 F.3d 466, 470 (2d Cir. 1995))). These problems are discussed in Ch. 8, § N.

[383]Rule 15(d), Fed.R.Civ.P.; *see* U.S. ex rel. Kinney v. Stoltz, 327 F.3d 671, 673 (8th Cir. 2003) (". . . [S]upplemental pleadings, not amended pleadings, are intended to cover matters occurring after the original complaint is filed." (citation omitted)).

[384]Quaratino v. Tiffany & Co., 71 F.3d 58, 66 (2d Cir. 1995) (the proposed supplemental facts must connect the new pleading to the original pleading); Keith v. Volpe, 858 F.2d 467, 474 (9th Cir. 1989).

[385]Griffin v. County School Board of Prince Edward County, 377 U.S. 218, 227, 84 S. Ct. 1226 (1964).

[386]Walker v. United Parcel Service, Inc., 240 F.3d 1268, 1278 (10th Cir. 2001) (Such authorization "'should be liberally granted unless good reason exists for denying leave, such as prejudice to the defendants.' Even so, such motions 'are addressed to the sound discretion of the trial court.'. . ." (citing Gillihan v. Shillinger, 872

F.2d 935, 941 (10th Cir. 1989)); Novak v. National Broadcasting Co., Inc., 724 F. Supp. 141, 145 (S.D.N.Y. 1989).

[387]All West Pet Supply Co. v. Hill's Pet Products Div., Colgate-Palmolive Co., 152 F.R.D. 202, 204 (D.Kan. 1993) ("Unless good reason exists for denying leave, such as prejudice to the defendants, leave to supplement a complaint is to be liberally granted." (citations omitted)); Novak v. National Broadcasting Co., Inc., 724 F. Supp. at 145.

[388]We think this is wrong, as explained in Ch. 9, § D.1, nn. 242–245.

[389]Procedures for service of process are discussed in § C.4 of this chapter.

You must serve both a summons and a complaint on each new defendant. Since a summons is only good for 120 days, you will need to get a new summon issued by the clerk if the original summons is out of date.

[390]*See* § D of this chapter.

[391]Rule 16(d), Fed.R.Civ.P.; Anderson v. Genuine Parts Co., Inc., 128 F.3d 1267, 1270 (8th Cir. 1997).

[392]Pretrial conferences and orders are discussed further in § O of this chapter.

Rule 15(b), Fed.R.Civ.P., provides that if a party objects at trial that evidence is not within the issues raised by the pleadings, the court may permit the pleadings to be amended if doing so will aid in presenting the merits and the objecting party fails to show that it would be prejudiced.[393] The rule also provides that if "an issue not raised by the pleadings is tried by the parties' express or implied consent, it must be treated in all respects as if . . . raised in the pleadings."[394] This means that if evidence on a new issue is presented at trial and the opposing party does not object, the court will act as if the new issue had been raised in an amended pleading.[395]

K. Preparing Your Factual Case

1. Gathering Evidence

In most *pro se* cases, the most important evidence you have will be your own testimony, documents already in your possession, and witnesses you already know about. You may obtain helpful evidence from the defendants in discovery, but be sure to start by assessing what information you already have or are able to get independently.

You should start by trying to determine what facts are needed to prove each of your allegations and list what witnesses or documents can help you do so. For example, if you allege that officers beat you up, that you were given a disciplinary hearing that denied due process, and that you were denied medical card for your injuries, your initial list of witnesses would include all eyewitnesses to the beat-up, anyone who later observed your injuries, anyone who was present at your disciplinary hearing, and anyone who witnessed your requests for medical assistance.

Your document list would include all official reports, investigations and witness statements that the prison produces when there is a use of force, including any videotape; the documents you were given in connection with your disciplinary hearing; any documents produced from the disciplinary hearing that inmates are not normally given, including any tape recording that may have been made; your own medical records; and any records of requests for

medical assistance (*e.g.*, sick call sign-up sheets or grievances you may have filed).

Once you have developed such a list, you should try to narrow it down by determining which items or witnesses are likely to be most helpful and which are likely to be repetitive of others.[396] Then you should figure out which evidence you can get on your own and which you will have to pursue through discovery.

If there are prisoner witnesses (or cooperative prison employee witnesses) to whom you have access, interview them and get them to sign affidavits or write out statements if possible.[397] You should do this quickly, since you or your witnesses may be transferred to different prisons during the litigation.

If possible, you should send copies of these statements to someone outside prison to keep in case your legal documents are lost or destroyed. These should be notarized or otherwise sworn to.[398]

Obtaining these statements serves three purposes. First, they will help you keep track of what you can prove. Second, the statements can be submitted in response to defendants' summary judgment motion, or in support of your motion.[399] Third, they may help you convince a reluctant judge that the witnesses you are requesting be produced for trial have something important to say.[400]

Witness statements should state the specific facts that the particular witness observed; they should not be conclusory statements and should not state legal conclusions or opinions.[401]

---

[393]Rule 15(b)(1), Fed.R.Civ.P.; *see* Green Country Food Mkt., Inc. v. Bottling Group, LLC, 371 F.3d 1275, 1280–81 (10th Cir. 2004) (if the opposing party objects to such an amendment, the party proffering the evidence must file a motion to amend, and the opposing party must fail to demonstrate prejudice from the proposed amendment, before the amendment may be allowed).

[394]Rule 15(b)(2), Fed. R.Civ.P.

[395]If the opposing party *does* object, the court cannot allow the amendment. Green Country Food Mkt., Inc. v. Bottling Group, LLC, 371 F.3d 1275, 1280–81 (10th Cir. 2004) (holding that while Fed.R.Civ.P. 15(b) permits implied amendments to conform to the evidence, if an opposing party objects to an implied amendment, the party seeking it must file a motion to amend, and the opposing party must fail to demonstrate prejudice from the proposed amendment, before the district court may allow the amendment).

[396]For example, if there is a tape recording of the disciplinary hearing, testimony by people who were present at the hearing may not be necessary to establish what happened at it. Similarly, if you received an adequate medical examination that is reflected in your medical records, eyewitnesses to your physical condition may not add much to the case.

[397]Most prison employees will not give written statements to prisoners. Some of them may tell you that they cannot give you affidavits for fear of getting into trouble but will testify truthfully at trial if you subpoena them. Experience suggests that most prison staff will not in fact give favorable testimony for prisoners at trial. This is why it is important to get something in writing from staff at the time of the event, if you can.

Under some circumstances you or other prisoners can testify to statements made orally by prison employees. If the employees are defendants or the agents of defendants, such statements are not hearsay but are "admissions" that can be placed in evidence. Admissions are discussed in § S.2 of this chapter.

[398]*See* 28 U.S.C. § 1746, for the federal courts' procedure for swearing to the contents of documents without having them notarized.

[399]*See* § L of this chapter for a discussion of summary judgment.

[400]*See* § Q of this chapter for a discussion of getting your witnesses brought to court.

[401]For example, a witness statement that just says "I saw the plaintiff brutalized without justification by Officer X" will not carry any weight. Nor will identical or near-identical statements signed

If your state has a freedom of information act or public records act, you may be able to use that statute to obtain copies of documents relevant to your lawsuit before it is filed— *e.g.*, reports of completed investigations, regulations, or policy directives.[402] Some states have passed statutes barring or limiting prisoners from the use of their freedom of information laws.[403] These statutes may not prevent another person, such as a family member, from making the request. The federal government also has such provisions, most notably the Freedom of Information Act[404] and the Privacy Act.[405] These statutes differ in scope and purpose and contain significant exemptions affecting the information that can be disclosed, and to whom.[406] It may also be helpful to use the prison grievance procedure (which you have to do anyway to exhaust your administrative remedies), or just write a letter (or have a friend or family member write it) seeking information from the prison officials about the basis for their treatment of you or for policies that you wish to challenge.

2. Discovery

Discovery is a process for learning facts and obtaining evidence relevant to your case. The federal court discovery rules are based on the idea that justice is best served if each side knows what the other side will try to prove. In our opinion, cases are often lost or won in discovery.

Pro se prisoners are entitled to use the discovery rules on the same terms as other litigants.[407] However, prison officials sometimes are unresponsive to their discovery requests, and courts sometimes dismiss *pro se* cases without regard to the lack of response to outstanding discovery requests.[408] It is therefore important for prisoners to assert their discovery rights so the court will enforce them. Situations may arise where your status as a *pro se* prisoner does make it impossible to take discovery adequately; in such situations, the court should consider appointing counsel.[409]

Through discovery, you can obtain documents created by prison officials giving their versions of incidents and their justifications for their actions or policies.[410] You can obtain the statements of witnesses made while their memories are still fresh (which makes it more difficult for them to change their stories later). You can obtain information about the defendants and their prior records that may be relevant to their credibility and other issues,[411] as well as about policies,

---

by different witnesses, especially if they are all written in your handwriting.

[402]The use of public records and freedom of information laws is beyond the scope of this Manual; the laws, their scope and exclusions, and the means of using them vary from state to state. The Reporters Committee for Freedom of the Press has compiled information on those laws in their *State Open Government Guide*, which can be consulted free on the Internet at http://www.rcfp.org/ogg/index.php (last visited March 12, 2010). The compilation can be purchased for $100.00, or a booklet with the information on a single state can be purchased for $10.00, from Reporters Committee for Freedom of the Press, 1101 Wilson Blvd., Suite 1100, Arlington, VA 22209. The RCFP also publishes, and makes available on its website, other useful information such as state-by-state guides to access to electronic records, police records, and judicial records.

[403]*See, e.g.*, the Michigan statute, M.C.L. § 15.231(2).

[404]5 U.S.C. § 552b.

[405]5 U.S.C. § 552a. The Privacy Act allows persons to obtain records concerning themselves from federal agencies, 5 U.S.C. § 552a(d)(1), subject to certain limits and exemptions. It also requires agencies to keep accurate records concerning individuals and to respond to requests to correct errors, and provides civil remedies for aggrieved persons. *See* Ch. 3, § E.3, n.939, and Ch. 4, § H.7, nn.540–552.

[406]These details are beyond the scope of this Manual. The Reporters Committee for Freedom of the Press, mentioned in n.402 above, has prepared a *Federal Open Government Guide* which contains information about both statutes. It can be consulted free on the Internet, http://www.rcfp.org/fogg/index.php, or purchased for $10.00.

[407]Klingele v. Eikenberry, 849 F.2d 409, 412 n.1 (9th Cir. 1988); Finley v. Trent, 955 F. Supp. 642, 648 (N.D.W.Va. 1997); Castle v. Jallah, 142 F.R.D. 618, 620 (E.D.Va. 1992); *see* Holloway v. Lockhart, 813 F.2d 874, 880 (8th Cir. 1987) (district court rule requiring *pro se* prisoners to get leave of court before seeking discovery was invalid because it conflicted with Federal Rules of Civil Procedure).

[408]*See, e.g.*, Jones v. Blanas, 393 F.3d 918, 930–31 (9th Cir. 2004) (district court inappropriately granted summary judgment without allowing plaintiff the discovery he had been seeking); LaBounty v. Coughlin, 137 F.3d 68, 71–72 (2d Cir. 1998) (holding district court should not have granted summary judgment to defendants where his inability to provide certain evidence allegedly resulted from defendants' failure to respond to discovery); Salahuddin v. Coughlin, 993 F.2d 306, 309–10 (2d Cir. 1993); Dean v. Barber, 951 F.2d 1210, 1213–14 (11th Cir. 1992); Abdul-Wadood v. Duckworth, 860 F.2d 280, 282–83 (7th Cir. 1988); *see also* Sellers v. U.S., 902 F.2d 598, 602 (7th Cir. 1990) ("[o]ur impression is that prisoners appearing *pro se* get the runaround" from the federal Department of Justice when seeking information necessary to serve process).

[409]*See, e.g.*, Johnson v. Howard, 20 F. Supp. 2d 1128, 1129 (W.D.Mich. 1998) (where prison rules forbade prisoner to obtain records that might help plaintiff discover or locate witnesses, court should consider appointment of counsel).

[410]*See, e.g.*, Ingle v. Yelton, 439 F.3d 191, 195–96 (4th Cir. 2006) (allowing discovery of videotapes of police shooting); Jones v. Blanas, 393 F.3d 918, 930–31 (9th Cir. 2004) (holding discovery about strip searches to find out whether they were conducted pursuant to a county policy should have been allowed).

[411]*See, e.g.*, Ramirez v. County of Los Angeles, 231 F.R.D. 407, 411–12 (C.D.Cal. 2005) (requiring production of discipline and personnel complaints against defendant officer); Martinez v. Cornell Corrections of Texas, 229 F.R.D. 211, 212–13 (D.N.M. 2005) (requiring production of information about officer's prior misconduct); Scaife v. Boenne, 191 F.R.D. 590, 595–96 (N.D.Ind. 2000) (plaintiff was entitled to discover information about previous complaints against police officers, since past conduct is relevant to punitive damages; the fact that these were not "public records" under state law did not protect them from federal discovery); Cox v. McClellan, 174 F.R.D. 32, 34 (W.D.N.Y. 1997) ("Prior civilian

practices, and occurrences in the prison that may be relevant to your claim.[412] You can learn the identities and location of witnesses and potential defendants.[413] One very important point about identifying defendants is that courts have held that if you sue supervisory officials but they were not personally involved in violating your rights, they should still be required to respond to discovery, so you can identify those people who were responsible.[414] Sometimes, information

complaints made against the defendants and incidents of excessive force by individual defendants are clearly discoverable in § 1983 actions." Evidence that supervisors knew about prior assaults may be relevant to claims against the supervisors. Record of a prior assault arrest is discoverable.); Brandon v. Beard, 140 F.R.D. 328, 329 (M.D.Pa. 1991) (directing production of portions of personnel records). The relevance of this sort of information is discussed in § T.5 of this chapter. Information such as defendants' dates of birth, Social Security numbers, and addresses will probably not be ordered produced, since doing so might endanger their safety. Collens v. City of New York, 222 F.R.D. 249, 253–55 (S.D.N.Y. 2004); Kowalski v. Stewart, 220 F.R.D. 599, 600–01 (D.Ariz. 2004).

[412]Martinez v. Cornell Corrections of Texas, 229 F.R.D. 215, 220–21, 223 (D.N.M. 2005) (plaintiff in a sexual abuse case could obtain information about other such incidents in the jail and correspondence with the Department of Justice about jail policies); Kowalski v. Stewart, 220 F.R.D. 599, 602 (D.Ariz. 2004) (defendants ordered to produce policies, directives, and instructions to staff concerning medical services); Green v. Baca, 219 F.R.D. 485, 492–93 (C.D.Cal. 2003) (plaintiff alleging failure to release him timely was entitled to obtain records and a report on other instances of "overdetention").

[413]See, e.g., Murphy v. Keller, 950 F.2d 290, 293 (5th Cir. 1992) (directing district court to allow discovery of documents such as duty rosters and personnel records so the plaintiff could identify the officers who he alleged beat him); Hoyt v. Connare, 202 F.R.D. 71, 78–79 (D.N.H. 1996) (requiring defendants to provide the address and telephone number of a witness, the person who allegedly cleaned up the blood in the plaintiff's cell after he was assaulted); Scaife v. Boenne, 191 F.R.D. 590, 594 (N.D.Ind. 2000) (requiring production of witness's contact information).

If a court denies production of witness contact information for security reasons, it should make other arrangements for the plaintiff to have access to the witness. See Kowalski v. Stewart, 220 F.R.D. 599, 602 (D.Ariz. 2004) (requiring defendants to submit former employee's address to court clerk so he could be subpoenaed).

[414]Davis v. Kelly, 160 F.3d 917, 921 (2d Cir. 1998) and cases cited; accord, Carmona v. Toledo, 215 F.3d 124, 134–35 (1st Cir. 2000); Donald v. Cook County Sheriff's Dep't, 95 F.3d 548, 555–56 & n.3 (7th Cir. 1996) (discussing "allowing the case to proceed to discovery against high-level administrators with the expectation that they will identify the officials personally responsible"); Wellman v. Faulkner, 715 F.2d 269, 275 (7th Cir. 1983) (stating "the responsibility of senior prison officials can be assumed at the pleading stage, pending discovery of those who were directly responsible for whatever deprivation may have occurred"); Gillespie v. Civiletti, 629 F.2d 637, 642–43 (9th Cir. 1980) (finding the district court abused its discretion in dismissing the case with respect to the John Doe defendants without requiring the named defendants to answer interrogatories seeking the names and addresses of the supervisors in charge of the relevant facilities

obtained in discovery raises more questions, and you will have to pursue leads through additional discovery.

It is your responsibility to use the discovery rules to develop evidence to support your claims, and to do it promptly. If your case is not dismissed at the outset, the defendants will probably make a motion for summary judgment, and you may need evidence from discovery for your response to that motion.[415]

The general rules concerning discovery are contained in Rules 26 through 37, Fed.R.Civ.P. These rules are amended from time to time, so be sure you have the current edition of the rules.

The Federal Rules provide for "initial disclosures" that the parties are supposed to make automatically, without a request.[416] This provision does not apply to cases that are filed by prisoners proceeding *pro se*.[417] However, some courts

during the relevant time period); King v. Frank, 328 F. Supp. 2d 940, 949 (W.D.Wis. 2004); Cook v. City of New York, 578 F. Supp. 179, 184 (S.D.Y. 1984) (dismissed prison officials required to cooperate with discovery); see also Murray v. City of Chicago, 634 F.2d 365, 366 (7th Cir. 1980) (when defendants all blamed each other for the violation, the plaintiff was entitled to discovery to identify the "true culprit"); Murphy v. Goord, 445 F. Supp. 2d 261, 266 (W.D.N.Y. 2006) (permitting plaintiff to use a pseudonym for unknown defendants, take discovery to identify them, then amend his complaint to add their correct names). Defendants may, however, argue that these decisions are undermined by a recent Supreme Court decision emphasizing the protection of high-level officials against the burdens of discovery. Ashcroft v. Iqbal, ___ U.S. ___, 129 S. Ct. 1937, 1950 (2009).

Courts have also said that they have a duty to assist *pro se* plaintiffs in identifying the correct defendants. Valentin v. Dinkins, 121 F.3d 72, 75 (2d Cir. 1997) (when "a party is ignorant of defendants' true identity, it is unnecessary to name them until their identity can be learned through discovery or through the aid of the trial court" (citation omitted)); Donald v. Cook County Sheriff's Dep't, 95 F.3d at 555 ("To the extent the plaintiff faces barriers to determining the identities of the unnamed defendants, the court must assist the plaintiff in conducting the necessary investigation." (citing cases); see Spencer v. Doe, 139 F.3d 107, 113 (2d Cir. 1998) (district court inappropriately dismissed case for lack of prosecution though plaintiff had moved for assistance in identifying defendants).

[415]See § L of this chapter concerning summary judgment. As discussed in that section, courts can delay summary judgment motions to permit additional discovery, but the court may not do so if you have had time for discovery but have not done anything.

[416]Rule 26(a)(1)(A), Fed.R.Civ.P.

[417]Rule 26(a)(1), Fed.R.Civ.P., provides:

(B) *Proceedings Exempt from Initial Disclosure.* The following proceedings are exempt from initial disclosure:

* * *

(iv) an action brought without an attorney by a person in custody of the United States, a state, or a state subdivision; . . .

We don't think this rule applies to cases that are filed *pro se* but in which counsel is later appointed, since it is impossible to comply with an *initial* disclosure requirement at some later stage in the case; we haven't found any case law on this point.

have local rules providing for automatic discovery in *pro se* prisoner cases.[418] *Pro se* prisoners are also exempt from the Federal Rules' requirement that the parties have a conference to develop a discovery plan, to seek settlement and to arrange for the initial disclosures.[419] However, all cases, including *pro se* prisoner cases, are subject to the requirements of Rule 26(a)(2) concerning disclosure of expert testimony and of Rule 26(a)(3) for disclosure shortly before trial of all witnesses and exhibits.

The most important discovery devices available are depositions (Rules 27, 30, 31, Fed.R.Civ.P.), interrogatories to parties (Rule 33), requests for production of documents and things (Rule 34), and requests for admissions (Rule 36).[420] Each of these is discussed in more detail in the following several sections.

In the past, discovery requests and responses (including deposition transcripts, interrogatory answers, and admissions) were generally filed in court. However, the current rules prohibit filing them until they are actually used in the proceeding, unless the court orders that they be filed.[421]

a. Scope of Discovery: Relevance and Burden The scope of federal court discovery is set forth in Rule 26(b)(1), Fed.R.Civ.P.:

> Unless otherwise limited by court order, the scope of discovery is as follows: Parties may obtain discovery regarding any nonprivileged matter that is relevant to any party's claim or defense—including the existence, description, nature, custody, condition, and location of any documents, or other tangible things and the identity and location of persons having knowledge of any discoverable matter. For good cause, the court may order discovery of any matter relevant to the subject matter involved in the action. Relevant information need not be admissible at the trial if the discovery appears reasonably calculated to lead

to the discovery of admissible evidence. All discovery is subject to the limitations imposed by Rule 26(b)(2)(C).[422]

Rule 26(b)(2)(C) permits the court to limit discovery when it becomes "unreasonably cumulative or duplicative, or can be obtained from some other source that is more convenient, less burdensome, or less expensive," or when the party seeking discovery has already had ample opportunity to discover the information, or when the burden or expense of the proposed discovery outweighs its likely benefits.[423]

But even burdensome or expensive discovery may be required if it is relevant to the case.[424] If a party claims that certain discovery will be excessively burdensome, it must demonstrate why that is the case.[425] If the discovery will be burdensome only because of the way defendants keep their

---

Under this rule, if you wait until you are released from custody to file your suit, your case *will* be subject to the initial disclosure requirements.

[418]Rule 33.2, Local Rules of the United States District Courts for the Southern and Eastern Districts of New York, requires defendants in use of force cases, inmate–inmate assault cases, and disciplinary due process cases arising from New York State prisons or New York City jails, to respond to certain "standing discovery requests," automatically in the Southern District and if ordered by the court in the Eastern District.

[419]*See* Rule 26(f)(1), Fed.R.Civ.P., which provides that "[e]xcept in a proceeding exempt from initial disclosure under Rule 26(a)(1)(B) or when the court orders otherwise, the parties must confer as soon as practicable. . . ."

[420]The rules also provide for entry upon land for inspection and other purposes (Rule 34, Fed.R.Civ.P.) and the physical and mental examination of persons (Rule 35), which we do not discuss in detail. Rule 35 is most likely to come up in connection with defendants' attempts to obtain a physical or mental examination of prisoner plaintiffs, so we do address it in § K.2.i, below, concerning responding to discovery requests.

[421]Rule 5(d)(1), Fed.R.Civ.P.

[422]The scope of discovery was slightly narrowed by amendments to the Federal Rules in 2000. Formerly, Rule 26(b) provided that discovery automatically extended to "any matter not privileged, which is relevant to the subject matter involved in the pending action, whether it relates to the claim or defense of the party seeking discovery or to the claim or defense of any other party. . . ." Under the older rule, courts interpreted the scope of discovery "broadly to encompass any matter that bears on, or that reasonably could lead to other matter that could bear on, any issue that is or may be in the case." Oppenheimer Fund, Inc. v. Sanders, 437 U.S. 340, 351, 98 S. Ct. 2380 (1978) (footnote and citation omitted); *see* La Chemise Lacoste v. Alligator Co., Inc., 60 F.R.D. 164, 171 (D. Del. 1973) (discovery should be allowed "unless it is clear that the information sought can have no possible bearing upon the subject matter of the action"). Those statements are a bit outmoded and you should not rely on them under the current rule.

The current rule refers to material "that is relevant to any party's claim or defense"; if it is just relevant to the subject matter, and not to a claim or defense, you have to get a court order based on good cause to take discovery about it. Rule 26(b)(1), Fed.R.Civ.P. This is a very fine distinction and in general you should not waste a lot of time worrying about it. You are probably better off focusing on whether particular evidence that you wish to discover might actually help you or your adversary to prove or to disprove something that will be an issue in your case. That is what the argument will focus on if you get involved in a dispute about the scope of discovery.

[423]*See* Crawford-El v. Britton, 523 U.S. 574, 599–601, 118 S. Ct. 1584 (1998) (discussing district court's discretion to manage discovery).

[424]Fagan v. District of Columbia, 136 F.R.D. 5, 7 (D.D.C. 1991); Schaap v. Executive Industries, Inc., 130 F.R.D. 384, 387 (N.D.Ill. 1990); King v. Georgia Power Co., 50 F.R.D. 134, 136 (N.D.Ga. 1970).

[425]*See* Redland Soccer Club, Inc. v. Dep't of the Army, 55 F.3d 827, 856 (3d Cir. 1995) (mere statement that an interrogatory was overly broad, burdensome, oppressive, and irrelevant is not an adequate objection; the party resisting discovery must show specifically how each interrogatory is not relevant or how each question is overly broad, burdensome, or oppressive (citation omitted)); McLeod, Alexander, Powel & Apffel, P.C. v. Quarles, 894 F.2d 1482, 1485 (5th Cir. 1990) (same; standard equally applicable to interrogatories and document requests); St. Paul Reinsurance Co., Ltd. v. Commercial Financial Corp., 198 F.R.D. 508, 511–13 (N.D.Iowa 2000).

records, it will generally be allowed.[426] You can also respond to claims of burdensomeness by being flexible; *e.g.*, you could agree that if prison officials let you look through the relevant files, you will identify the particular documents that pertain to your case and they need not copy all the files for you.

Attorneys and *pro se* litigants are now required to certify with their signatures that their discovery requests or objections are lawful, not improperly motivated, and not unreasonably burdensome or expensive.[427] Those who abuse the discovery rules may be subjected to sanctions by the court.[428]

b. Privileges A privilege is a rule that excludes certain kinds of information from being used in court proceedings. Evidence that would be privileged at trial is also generally exempt from discovery.[429] There are a variety of privileges: the attorney–client privilege, the physician–patient privilege, the priest–penitent privilege, the husband–wife privilege, the privilege against self-incrimination, etc. These privileges vary from state to state, and not all of them are recognized by federal courts.[430]

Federal court privileges are governed by federal court case law and not by state law,[431] except when a state law claim (*e.g.*, a pendent or supplemental claim) is in question. A state law forbidding disclosure does not create a privilege in federal court and will not be enforced if it is inconsistent with the federal law or privileges,[432] although state law may be considered in interpreting the scope of the federal court privileges.[433] In general, privileges are to be narrowly construed, since they limit the courts' ability to get at the truth.[434]

A party claiming privilege in federal court must identify a particular privilege that federal courts recognize. The mere assertion that information is "confidential" establishes no privilege enforceable in federal court.[435] Nor may privileges be asserted in a generalized fashion. Documents or information claimed to be privileged must be specifically

[426]Fagan v. District of Columbia, 136 F.R.D. at 7 ("Plaintiffs should not suffer if the information is not easily accessible because defendants have an inefficient filing system. . ."); Kozlowski v. Sears, Roebuck & Co., 73 F.R.D. 73, 76 (D.Mass. 1976) ("The defendant may not excuse itself from compliance with Rule 34, Fed.R.Civ.P., by utilizing a system of record-keeping which conceals rather than discloses relevant records, or makes it unduly difficult to identify or locate them, thus rendering the production of the documents an excessively burdensome and costly expedition.").

[427]Rule 26(g)(1)(B), Fed.R.Civ.P.

[428]Rule 26(g)(3), Fed.R.Civ.P.; *see* Malautea v. Suzuki Motor Co., 987 F.2d 1536, 1545 (11th Cir. 1993), *aff'g*, 148 F.R.D. 362, 374 (S.D.Ga. 1991) (upholding Rule 26(g) sanctions for a "pattern of conduct" manifesting improper purpose that consisted of meritless objections to requests as irrelevant or overly burdensome, and partial answers to discovery questions that were evasive and misleading); *see also In re* Byrd, Inc., 927 F.2d 1135, 1137 (10th Cir. 1991) (bad faith of counsel is not a necessary element before sanctions can be awarded under Rule 26(g)).

[429]*See* Rule 501, Fed.R.Evid.; U.S. v. Reynolds, 345 U.S. 1, 6, 73 S. Ct. 528 (1953).

[430]For example, the physician–patient privilege did not exist at common law and is provided for by various state statutes. Whalen v. Roe, 429 U.S. 589, 602 n.28, 97 S. Ct. 869 (1977). Federal courts have generally refused to recognize it. Northwestern Memorial Hosp. v. Ashcroft, 362 F.3d 923, 926 (7th Cir. 2004); Hancock v. Dodson, 958 F.2d 1367, 1373 (6th Cir. 1992) (federal courts do not recognize a physician–patient privilege); Hancock v. Hobbs, 967 F.2d 462, 466 (11th Cir. 1992) and cases cited. Federal courts have also refused to recognize a privilege for medical "peer review" materials. Agster v. Maricopa County, 422 F.3d 836, 839 (9th Cir. 2005). However, the Supreme Court has recognized a psychotherapist–patient privilege that protects records of mental health treatment from disclosure. Jaffee v. Redmond, 518 U.S. 1, 116 S.Ct. 1923 (1996) (holding privilege applied to communications made confidentially to a licensed psychotherapist in the course of

diagnosis or treatment). *Compare* U.S. v. Romo, 413 F.3d 1044, 1047 (9th Cir. 2005) (statements to a prison counselor were not privileged because they were not made in the course of diagnosis or treatment). The privacy of medical records is now protected to a limited degree by the Constitution and by the federal Health Insurance Portability and Accountability Act (HIPAA), discussed in Ch. 2, § 4.f.j.

[431]This is what Rule 501, Fed.R.Evid., means when it directs courts to use "principles of the common law as they may be interpreted by the courts of the United States in the light of reason and experience." This provision is explained further in the legislative comments that are included in many editions of the Federal Rules of Evidence.

[432]Agster v. Maricopa County, 422 F.3d 836, 839 (9th Cir. 2005); Keith H. v. Long Beach Unified School District, 228 F.R.D. 652, 657 (C.D.Cal. 2005); Smith v. Goord, 222 F.R.D. 238, 240 (N.D.N.Y. 2004) (state law protecting public employees).

[433]Kerr v. U.S. District Court, 511 F.2d 192, 197 (9th Cir. 1975), *aff'd*, 426 U.S. 394, 96 S. Ct. 2119 (1976); Smith v. Goord, 222 F.R.D. 238, 241 (N.D.N.Y. 2004); Everitt v. Brezzel, 750 F. Supp. 1063, 1065–66 (D. Colo. 1990); Wei v. Bodner, 127 F.R.D. 91, 94–95 (D.N.J. 1989); King v. Conde, 121 F.R.D. 180, 187 (E.D.N.Y. 1988).

[434]U.S. v. Nixon, 418 U.S. 683, 708–10, 94 S. Ct. 3090 (1974); Mims v. Dallas County, 230 F.R.D. 479, 484 (N.D. Tex. 2005) ("Like all privileges, the work product doctrine must be strictly construed. . . ."); Allen v. Chicago Transit Authority, 198 F.R.D. 495, 500 (N.D.Ill. 2001). *But see* Swidler & Berlin v. U.S., 524 U.S. 399, 409–10, 118 S. Ct. 2081 (1998) (holding that strict construction principle does not apply to attorney–client privilege because it existed at common law).

[435]Pearson v. Miller, 211 F.3d 57, 68 (3d Cir. 2000) ("Merely asserting that a state statute declares that the records in question are 'confidential' does not make out a sufficient claim that the records are 'privileged' within the meaning of Fed.R.Civ.P. 26(b)(1) and Fed R. Evid. 501." (citations omitted)); *In re* Grand Jury Subpoena Dated December 17, 1996, 148 F.3d 487, 492 (5th Cir. 1998); Nguyen Da Yen v. Kissinger, 528 F.2d 1194, 1205 (9th Cir.1975) ("The records are confidential but not privileged."); Seales v. Macomb County, 226 F.R.D. 572, 576 (E.D.Mich. 2005) (same).

designated and described; the document doing this is called a privilege log.[436]

The most frequently raised privileges in federal court prison cases include the governmental or official information privilege (often referred to as "executive privilege"). One branch of this privilege is designed to protect "deliberative and decision-making processes of government officials" and "investigative reports of an administrative agency to the extent that they reflect advisory rather than factual material."[437]

Thus, even if prison officials can keep their decision-making processes secret, they must disclose purely factual matter relating to their decisions.[438] Moreover, a litigant can obtain "deliberative" or "advisory" materials when the litigant's need for the material is "compelling" or outweighs the policies favoring secrecy.[439] For example, if prison officials put a lot of prisoners who had recently filed grievances into segregation without notice or hearing, the prisoners' need to find out if prison officials really believed there was an emergency might outweigh any interest the defendants had in keeping their deliberations secret; if so, you could discover their internal memos on the subject.

Another branch of the governmental privilege is the law enforcement privilege, which covers matters such as the identity of informants and ongoing criminal or other investigations.[440] Defendants also sometimes claim a "self-critical analysis" privilege, which is not recognized by all courts and, where it is recognized, is given a very limited application.[441]

The deliberative and law enforcement privileges are subject to procedural requirements: they must be formally asserted and supported with specific factual allegations.[442] "An improperly asserted claim of privilege is no claim of privilege."[443]

The attorney–client privilege applies where there is "(1) a communication between client and counsel, which (2) was intended to be and was in fact kept confidential, and (3) made for the purpose of obtaining or providing legal advice."[444] The privilege does not extend to communications

---

[436]Rule 26(b)(5)(A), Fed.R.Civ.P.; SEC v. Beacon Hill Asset Mgmt LLC, 231 F.R.D. 134, 144 (S.D.N.Y. 2004) ("The standard for testing the adequacy of [a] privilege log is whether, as to each document, it sets forth specific facts that, if credited, would suffice to establish each element of the privilege or immunity that is claimed." Typically the log will identify each document and the persons who were parties to the communications, providing sufficient detail to permit judgment whether the document is at least potentially protected from disclosure.); St. Paul Reinsurance Co., Ltd. v. Commercial Financial Corp., 198 F.R.D. 508, 513–14 (N.D.Iowa 2000); see Burlington Northern & Santa Fe Ry. Co. v. U.S. Dist. Court for Dist. of Mont., 408 F.3d 1142, 1147–49 (9th Cir. 2005) (directing case-by-case approach to waiver questions where privilege log is inadequate).

[437]Kinoy v. Mitchell, 67 F.R.D. 1, 10–11 (S.D.N.Y. 1975) (footnote omitted); accord, DiPace v. Goord, 218 F.R.D. 399, 403 (S.D.N.Y. 2003); Kelly v. City of San Jose, 114 F.R.D. 653, 658–59 (N.D.Cal. 1987). But see Fonville v. District of Columbia, 230 F.R.D. 38, 43 (D.D.C. 2005) (deliberative privilege does not apply to documents concerning a particular investigation, but to materials concerning the adoption of a more general policy); Allen v. Chicago Transit Authority, 198 F.R.D. 495, 502 (N.D.Ill. 2001) (documents about individual discrimination complaints that do not relate to the formulation or exercise of agency policy-oriented judgment are not protected by the deliberative process privilege).

[438]Environmental Protection Agency v. Mink, 410 U.S. 73, 87–89, 93 S. Ct. 827 (1974); Castle v. Jallah, 142 F.R.D. 618, 622 (E.D. Va. 1992) (prisoner was entitled to discover factual portions of incident reports); Kinoy v. Mitchell, 67 F.R.D. at 12.

[439]Marriott Int'l Resorts, L.P. v. U.S., 437 F.3d 1302, 1307 (Fed. Cir. 2006); Sun Oil Co. v. U.S., 514 F.2d 1020, 1024 (Cl. Ct. 1975); Kinoy v. Mitchell, 67 F.R.D. at 11.

[440]Peate v. McCann, 294 F.3d 879, 885 (7th Cir. 2002) ("We recognize, however, that the government has an interest in maintaining the confidentiality of files containing sensitive information regarding on-going investigations."); Smith v. City of Detroit, 212 F.R.D. 507, 509 (E.D.Mich. 2003) and cases cited.

[441]Leon v. County of San Diego, 202 F.R.D. 631, 637 (S.D.Cal. 2001) (requiring production of nursing "peer review" records; the self-critical analysis privilege does not apply to "routine internal corporate reviews" of safety matters, though it does have limited applicability to post-accident reviews); Price v. County of San Diego, 165 F.R.D. 614, 618–19 (S.D.Cal. 1996) (stating that the self-critical analysis privilege may not exist in federal court, and if it does, it is limited to expressions of opinion or recommendations, and not to underlying facts, and not to routine internal reviews of matters related to safety concerns); Soto v. City of Concord, 162 F.R.D. 603, 612 (N.D.Cal. 1995) (internal affairs reports and witness statements are not protected by the self-critical analysis privilege; the idea "offends basic notions of openness and public confidence in our system of justice").

[442]Ramirez v. County of Los Angeles, 231 F.R.D. 407, 410–12 (C.D.Cal. 2005) (overruling claim of official information privilege where defendants did not submit a declaration from a responsible official with personal knowledge explaining the basis for the privilege); Fonville v. District of Columbia, 230 F.R.D. 38, 43 (D.D.C. 2005) (both the deliberative process and law enforcement privileges require "(1) a formal claim of privilege by the head of the department having control over the requested information; (2) assertion of the privilege based on actual personal consideration by that official; and (3) a detailed specification of the information for which the privilege is claimed, with an explanation why it properly falls within the scope of the privilege").

[443]Black v. Sheraton Corp. of America, 371 F. Supp. 97, 101 (D.D.C. 1974); accord, Neighborhood Development Collaborative v. Murphy, 233 F.R.D. 436, 442 (D.Md. 2005).

[444]U.S. v. Construction Prod. Research, Inc., 73 F.3d 464, 473 (2d Cir.1996) (citations omitted); see Allen v. Chicago Transit Authority, 198 F.R.D. 495, 499 (N.D.Ill. 2001) (Privilege exists "(1) Where legal advice of any kind is sought (2) from a professional legal advisor in his capacity as such, (3) the communications relating to that purpose, (4) made in confidence (5) by the client, (6) are at his instance permanently protected from disclosure by himself or by the legal adviser, (8) except the protection may be waived." (quoting 8 John Henry Wigmore, Evidence in Trials at Common Law § 2292) (John T. McNaughton rev.1961)).

not involving an attorney[445] or communications that are merely factual in nature and do not involve legal advice.[446] Parties asserting the attorney–client privilege, like the work product privilege discussed below, must sufficiently identify who was involved or present at the communication and the nature of the communication to permit assessment of the claimed privilege.[447]

There is also a privilege for "attorney work product" which is exempted from discovery pursuant to Rule 26(b)(3)(A).[448] The phrase has been defined broadly to include any materials "prepared in anticipation of litigation or for trial by or for another party or its representative (including the other party's attorney, consultant, surety, indemnitor, insurer, or agent). . . ."[449] But it does not include the documents and information compiled in the ordinary course of running the prison or other government agency, such as disciplinary reports, grievances, prison rules, etc.[450] The work

product privilege may be overcome by showing a substantial need and inability reasonably to obtain the information by other means.[451] A party or another person can obtain his own statement from counsel regardless of any claim of work product.[452]

The rules also set out a procedure for discovering the opinions of experts who will testify at trial.[453]

A privilege cannot be used to protect information about something that the litigant has himself put in issue.[454] If prison officials claim they did something on the advice of counsel, they cannot rely on the attorney–client privilege to keep the advice secret.[455] This principle cuts both ways; if you sue about an event, you cannot then refuse to answer questions about your own conduct during that event on the ground of the privilege against self-incrimination.[456] If you put your mental condition into issue, you cannot invoke the psychotherapist–patient privilege to refuse to provide information about your condition or treatment.[457] Your refusal to do so could result in your case being dismissed.

Prison officials may not assert that information is privileged if they have released it to other persons. A privilege "should not be regarded as a right which can be disclosed to some and withheld from others."[458] Thus, if you can show

---

[445]Allen v. Chicago Transit Authority, 198 F.R.D. 495, 499 (N.D.Ill. 2001) (communication from a corporate vice president to an EEO coordinator was not protected by the attorney–client privilege); Jackson v. County of Sacramento, 175 F.R.D. 653, 657–58 (E.D.Cal. 1997) (documentation of police investigation was not privileged because no attorney made or received the communications and they were not created by county claims representatives).

[446]Green v. Baca, 226 F.R.D. 624, 651–52 (C.D.Cal. 2005), *clarified*, 2005 WL 283361 (C.D.Cal., Jan. 31, 2005); National Congress for Puerto Rican Rights v. City of New York, 194 F.R.D. 105, 109 (S.D.N.Y. 2000).

[447]Bogle v. McClure, 332 F.3d 1347, 1358 (11th Cir. 2003) (memorandum from county counsel containing legal advice, but not designated "privileged" or "confidential," was properly admitted into evidence despite a claim of attorney–client privilege, absent evidence regarding who, if anyone, received it other than its addressees, or what the addressees did with it or whether they considered it confidential; further, it appeared to be disclosable under state Open Records Act); Green v. Baca, 226 F.R.D. 624, 651 (C.D.Cal. 2005) (refusing to preclude testimony by the Sheriff's Special Counsel where the Sheriff failed to identify specific information and communications that were privileged), *clarified*, 2005 WL 283361 (C.D.Cal., Jan. 31, 2005); St. Paul Reinsurance Co., Ltd. v. Commercial Financial Corp., 198 F.R.D. 508, 513–14 (N.D.Iowa 2000).

[448]*See* Hickman v. Taylor, 329 U.S. 495, 511, 67 S. Ct. 385 (1947).

[449]Rule 26(b)(3)(A), Fed.R.Civ.P.

[450]U.S. v. Adlman, 134 F.3d 1194, 1195 (2d Cir. 1998) (work product privilege does not apply to documents that would have been created regardless of litigation); *In re* Grand Jury Subpoena (Mark Torf/Torf Environmental Management), 357 F.3d 900, 907–08 (9th Cir. 2004); Hoptowit v. Ray, 682 F.2d 1237, 1262 (9th Cir. 1982) (report prepared by non-lawyers for director of prison and not in anticipation of litigation was not protected by work product privilege); Mims v. Dallas County, 230 F.R.D. 479, 483–84 (N.D. ex. 2005) (jail officials failed to establish that the lawsuit was "primary motivating purpose" for preparation of report evaluating health care services and programs); National Congress for Puerto Rican Rights v. City of New York, 194 F.R.D. 105, 109–10 (S.D.N.Y. 2000) (purely factual materials prepared for legislative body and

not litigation were not work product); Collins v. Mullins, 170 F.R.D. 132, 134–35 (W.D.Va. 1996) (use of force witness statements are not work product); Miller v. Pancucci, 141 F.R.D. 292, 303 (C.D.Cal. 1992) (internal affairs tort claim investigations were not work product because they were prepared regardless of whether litigation was anticipated); Santiago v. Miles, 121 F.R.D. 636, 641–42 (W.D.N.Y. 1988).

[451]Rule 26(b)(3), Fed.R.Civ.P.

[452]Rule 26(b)(3), Fed.R.Civ.P.

[453]Rule 26(a)(2), Fed.R.Civ.P.

[454]E.E.O.C. v. General Telephone Co. of Northwest, Inc., 885 F.2d 575, 578 (9th Cir. 1989).

[455]Glenmede Trust Co. v. Thompson, 56 F.3d 476, 486 (3d Cir. 1995) ("The attorney–client privilege may be waived by a client who asserts reliance on the advice of counsel as an affirmative defense." (citation omitted)); Mitzner v.Sobol, 136 F.R.D. 359, 361–62 (S.D.N.Y. 1991); Buford v. Holladay, 133 F.R.D. 487, 496 (S.D. Miss. 1990); Smith v. Montgomery County, Md., 573 F. Supp. 604, 609–10 (D.Md. 1983), *appeal dismissed*, 740 F.2d 963 (4th Cir. 1984).

[456]*See* § K.2.i of this chapter for further discussion of this issue.

[457]Price v. County of San Diego, 165 F.R.D. 614, 622 (S.D.Cal. 1996) (though there is a psychotherapist–patient privilege, "[w]here a patient-litigant has raised an issue as to his or her psychological state, the privilege will be waived."); Topol v. Trustees of Univ. of Pennsylvania, 160 F.R.D. 476, 477 (E.D.Pa. 1995) (holding that plaintiff waived any applicable psychotherapist–patient privilege by placing her mental state in issue).

[458]*In re* Grand Jury Proceedings, October 12, 1995, 78 F.3d 251, 254–55 (6th Cir. 1996) (voluntary disclosure of privileged communications by the client to a third party constitutes waiver of the attorney–client privilege); *In re* Columbia/HCA Healthcare Corp. 192 F.R.D. 575, 579 (M.D.Tenn. 2000) ("[V]oluntary disclosure of privileged materials to the government constitutes a

that information you need is or can be released to others (prison employees, their lawyers, insurance companies, etc.), defendants should not be able to deny it to you.[459] If there are laws or regulations governing release of information— e.g., a state freedom of information or public records law law—see if they have disclosure provisions that are inconsistent with defendants' claims that they must keep the information secret.[460]

c. Practical Issues in Discovery As a practical matter, discovery disputes can seriously bog down your case even if you ultimately win. Also, courts sometimes resolve discovery disputes according to their own ideas of what is reasonable rather than by following the letter of existing case law. Because federal discovery decisions are generally not appealable until a final judgment has been entered in the case,[461] you are stuck with whatever the district court decides. For these reasons, you should follow some simple rules to keep discovery disputes to a minimum and get what you need promptly.

- *Follow the rules.* Some courts are not sympathetic to *pro se* discovery attempts and some prison officials and their lawyers do their best to obstruct them. Don't give them any excuses to rule against you or to refuse to cooperate. Study the Federal Rules of Civil Procedure and the local rules and make sure your discovery requests comply with them. Do the same if you have to file a motion to compel discovery.
- *Keep the request short.* The less you ask for in a request, the more likely you are to get it quickly and without an argument.[462] You should never

use discovery just to make the defendants or their lawyer work. This tactic will almost certainly backfire, and it is prohibited by the rules.[463]

- *Spell it out.* Make the discovery request as clear as possible, describing exactly what you want. If you can describe the precise documents or information you want in the terminology used by prison officials (e.g., "critical incident reports," "major misconduct reports," or "Administrative Bulletin No. 66"), do so. Cite any regulation, directive, or policy statement that describes a document or requires that it be kept (e.g., "incident reports as mandated by Rule XYZ").

  Keep in mind that the defendants' attorney may know less than you do about prison policies and record-keeping, and the easier you make his job, the more likely it is that you will get the information you need and not a hard time. Also, the more specific you are, the harder it is for the defendants to pretend not to understand your request.

  A good tactic is to make a general request and then add specifics: e.g., "any and all documents and reports concerning a disturbance in H Block on January 4, 2007, including, but not limited to, the critical incident reports, use of force reports, disciplinary charges, statements of witnesses, findings and conclusions of disciplinary hearings, etc."
- *Know why you want the information.* If defendants refuse to give you something and you go to court by filing a motion to compel, you will have to explain to the court why the information is relevant. You should think through why you are making the request before you submit it to the defendants.
- *Establish priorities.* You should think about what information is most important to you and what will be easiest to get; you may want to seek discovery in stages rather than all at once. For example, if you are beaten by guards, you will

---

waiver of the attorney–client privilege to all other adversaries."), *aff'd*, 293 F.3d 289, 302 (6th Cir. 2002); Hearn v. Rhay, 68 F.R.D. 574, 580 (E.D.Wash. 1975).

[459]Melendez-Colon v. U.S., 56 F. Supp. 2d 142, 145 (D.P.R. 1999) (disclosure under Freedom of Information Act waived privilege in litigation); Clark v. Township of Falls, 124 F.R.D. 91, 94 (E.D. Pa. 1988).

[460]*See* Bogle v. McClure, 332 F.3d 1347, 1358 (11th Cir. 2003) (holding defendants could not reasonably expect document to remain confidential when it was "arguably" subject to state Open Records Act).

[461]Adapt of Philadelphia v. Philadelphia Housing Authority, 433 F.3d 353, 360 (3d Cir. 2006). *But see* Church of Scientology of California v. U.S., 506 U.S. 9, 18 n.11, 113 S. Ct. 447 (1992) (discovery order against a disinterested third party is immediately appealable).

[462]You should consider breaking down your discovery requests if your case involves different sets of defendants or different claims. For example, if you were improperly transferred to a mental hospital from prison, it might be appropriate to make separate discovery requests about what prison officials did before the transfer and about how you were treated at the mental hospital. Similarly, if you have one claim about a beating and one claim about interference with your mail, you may seek discovery about these claims in separate requests.

If you do submit more than one request, to avoid confusion make sure they are labeled in some fashion, *e.g.*, "Plaintiff's First Request for Documents," "Plaintiff's First Set of Interrogatories to the Defendant Office of Mental Health," "Plaintiff's First Request for Admissions," etc.

[463]Rules 26(g)(1)(B), 26(g)(3), Fed.R.Civ.P. (prohibiting discovery or objections made for improper purposes such as harassment and delay, providing sanctions for violating that prohibition). *See* Martin v. LaBelle, 7 Fed.Appx. 492, 496 (6th Cir. 2001) (unpublished) ("Requiring defendants to respond to requests to admit to which defendants previously responded and objected was unreasonable, unnecessary, and unduly burdensome. Fed R. Civ. P. 26(g)(2)(A) and 26(g)(3). In such a situation, bad faith of counsel is not a necessary element before sanctions can be awarded under Rule 26(g)." (citation omitted)).

want the defendants' reports of the incident. You may also want records of any prior complaints or disciplinary actions against the guards in order to show that their superiors should have been aware of their violent natures. However, prison officials rarely relinquish personnel records of any sort without a fight. You may wish to make separate requests: *e.g.*, in one request ask for the uncontroversial materials and in a later separate request ask for the materials that are likely to be disputed. If you ask for everything in the same request, the defendants may refuse to produce anything until the court has resolved the dispute about a few of the documents.

The highest priority discovery will generally be the names and addresses of all defendants for whom you do not already have this information, so you can arrange for service of process.[464] You should serve a discovery request seeking this information at the earliest possible point in the case. Prison officials will not willingly give you staff members' addresses, so you should state in your discovery request that prison officials can satisfy the request by providing that information directly to the U.S. Marshals who will serve the summons and complaint, or—if you are not eligible to have service handled by the Marshal—by arranging to accept service for these other defendants.[465]

- *Be reasonable.* If defendants offer you a compromise that will give you what is most important to you, consider it seriously. If they ask for more time to produce the information, agree to it as long as you are not dealing with an emergency and the time they ask for is not unreasonably long.[466] One 30-day extension is routinely granted by courteous litigators, and defendants will probably be able to get it from the court even if you do not consent. Any agreement should be in writing.

By being reasonable, you may be able to get what you need without a long court fight, and even if you do have to go to court, the judge may be more willing to exercise his discretion in your favor if you have previously been reasonable in dealing with the defendants.

You may have trouble with discovery even if you follow the rules and all of our suggestions. Even though *pro se* litigants have the same discovery rights as litigants with

counsel,[467] some prison officials and defense lawyers seem to think that they can get away with disregarding *pro se* discovery efforts. If this happens to you, you must seek the court's help[468] at a reasonably early point—preferably as soon as it is clear you can't resolve the problem.[469] If you wait until the time of trial, the court may not be willing to delay the proceedings, or the issue may simply get lost.[470] If the defendants file a motion for summary judgment[471] before they respond to your discovery request, or before you have had time to make any requests, and if the discovery would help you answer the motion, you should ask for an extension of time to respond to the motion until your request is answered or you have had time to take discovery.[472]

Unfortunately, some courts have a tendency to overlook discovery issues in *pro se* cases and dismiss the cases without addressing them.[473] Make sure the court is well aware of any discovery controversies if you are unable to resolve them by yourself. You should keep accurate records of your attempts to resolve discovery issues, such as copies of your letters to defendants' counsel, notes of conversations, etc., so you can present your side of any discovery controversy persuasively.

Prison officials sometimes argue that they should not have to give you certain discovery because it would present a security threat for you or other prisoners to have access to it.[474] If they make this argument and the court accepts it, you may wish to renew your request for the appointment of counsel on the ground that these discovery restrictions make it impossible for you to litigate adequately *pro se*.[475]

d. Depositions There are two types of depositions. First is the oral deposition, which consists of both parties asking questions of the witness before a stenographer

---

[464]This subject is discussed further in § C.4.b of this chapter.

[465]This issue is discussed in more detail in § C.4.b, nn.226–230.

[466]If defendants ask for an extension of time to provide discovery and the discovery time period is almost up, you should request that they stipulate to an extension of discovery, so if they produce material that suggests other information you need to discover, you will have time to do it.

[467]*See* cases cited in n.407, above.

[468]This can be done through a motion to compel discovery, discussed in § K.2.h of this chapter. Local court rules generally require you to attempt to resolve the problem informally before making a motion to compel.

[469]Prior to filing any motion to compel, you should write defendants' counsel asking when you can expect the discovery to be provided. When you file your motion to compel, you want to be seen as the reasonable person.

[470]*See, e.g.*, Buttler v. Benson, 193 F.R.D. 664, 666 (D.Colo. 2000) (citing DesRosiers v. Moran, 949 F.2d 15, 22–23 (1st Cir. 1991)).

[471]*See* § L of this chapter concerning summary judgment.

[472]Rule 56(f), Fed.R.Civ.P.

[473]*See, e.g.*, cases cited in n.408, above.

[474]*See* Stringfellow v. Perry, 869 F.2d 1140, 1143 (8th Cir. 1989); Castle v. Jallah, 142 F.R.D. 618, 622 (E.D.Va. 1992) (discovery of confidential operating procedures denied); Brandon v. Beard, 140 F.R.D. 328, 330 (M.D. Pa. 1991) (inmate evaluations not produced because of fears of retaliation).

[475]*See* Johnson v. Howard, 20 F. Supp. 2d 1128, 1129 (W.D.Mich. 1998) (holding court should consider appointment of counsel where prison rules forbade prisoner to obtain records that might help plaintiff discover or locate witnesses).

(court reporter).[476] Second is the written deposition, which consists of written questions submitted to be answered under oath before a stenographer.[477]

Leave of court is required in order to take any deposition of a prisoner.[478] This rule applies to you as well as to any other prisoner witnesses you or the other side may wish to depose. However, leave of court will obviously be granted to take the plaintiff's deposition.[479]

If the defendants notice your deposition without getting leave of court, you may wish to point that fact out to them and suggest that they follow the rules. Generally you should not refuse to proceed based on this technical defect.[480] All you will accomplish is delay of your case.

If you wish to review the deposition transcript, you must request this opportunity before the deposition is completed.[481] You will have 30 days from the time the transcript or record is made available to you in order to review it.

If changes in form or substance are necessary, you should write and sign a separate statement saying what the changes are and giving the reasons for them.[482] This statement will be appended to the deposition record. If the changes are substantial, the deposition may be reopened for further inquiry.[483]

1) Oral Depositions At an oral deposition, a party or a party's lawyer asks questions of an adverse party or a witness, who must answer the questions under oath. Depositions are one of the most useful discovery devices; one court has said that they are "incomparably preferable to written interrogatories as a vehicle for seeking out useful evidence, not only because of the greater ease in shaping later questions based on earlier answers but also because the interrogatory answers are typically prepared by lawyers rather than through the uncounselled responses of the witnesses."[484]

Oral depositions are governed by Rule 30, Fed.R.Civ.P. They are limited to seven hours of testimony unless the court directs or the parties agree otherwise.[485] They are very difficult for *pro se* prisoners to take.[486] In fact, some courts have said that the need for depositions in a case is a good reason for appointing counsel.[487] However, if you want to try to take one or more oral depositions, here is how to do it.

To take a deposition, you must give the other side's attorney and the person being deposed "reasonable written notice"

---

[476]Rule 30, Fed.R.Civ.P.

[477]Rule 31, Fed.R.Civ.P.

[478]Rule 30(a)(2), Fed.R.Civ.P.; *see* Whitehurst v. U.S., 231 F.R.D. 500, 501 (S.D.Tex. 2005); Charles v. Wade, 665 F.2d 661, 663–65 (5th Cir. 1982) (holding that refusal to permit taking a prisoner's deposition in lieu of having him produced at trial was an abuse of discretion).

[479]Williams ex rel. Williams v. Greenlee, 210 F.R.D. 577, 578–89 (N.D.Tex. 2002) ("The court should grant leave to depose an incarcerated witness unless the objecting party shows that: (1) the deposition would be unreasonably cumulative or duplicative; (2) the party seeking the deposition has had ample opportunity to obtain the information sought; or (3) the burden or expense of the deposition outweighs its likely benefit."); Miller v. Bluff, 131 F.R.D. 698, 699–700 (M.D. Pa. 1990); *see* Kendrick v. Schnorbus, 655 F.2d 727, 729 (6th Cir. 1981) (holding that the deposition of a prisoner–plaintiff will not be suppressed even if leave was not obtained).

[480]If no court order has been obtained and you refuse to be deposed, sanctions cannot be imposed against you. Ashby v. McKenna, 331 F.3d 1148, 1150 (10th Cir. 2003). If a court order *has* been issued and you refuse to have your deposition taken, sanctions, up to dismissal, can be imposed. Moon v. Newsome, 863 F.2d 835, 837 (11th Cir. 1989) (affirming dismissal of suit based on prisoner plaintiff's refusal to cooperate with deposition ordered by court on defendants' motion under Rule 30(a)(2), and failure to pay resulting sanctions).

[481]Rule 30(e), Fed.R.Civ.P. The former requirement that all deposition transcripts be submitted to the witness for signing has been eliminated.

[482]*See* Holland v. Cedar Creek Mining, Inc., 198 F.R.D. 651, 653 (S.D.W.Va. 2001) (disallowing changes where the witness failed to explain the reasons for them). We suggest you keep the explanations short: *e.g.*, "Error in transcription by the reporter," or "Original testimony in error." Do not write all over the transcript or otherwise mutilate it because a court can impose sanctions for such behavior. *See* Barlow v. Esselte Pendaflex Corp., Meto Div., 111 F.R.D. 404, 406–07 (M.D.N.C. 1986). *Cf.* S.E.C. v. Parkersburg Wireless, L.L.C., 156 F.R.D. 529, 535 (D.D.C. 1994) (noting modern

trend in which courts do not allow a party "to make any substantive change she so desires" in deposition testimony).

[483]Reilly v. TXU Corp., 230 F.R.D. 486, 491 (N.D.Tex. 2005). Both the original testimony and the changes remain part of the deposition. Holland v. Cedar Creek Mining, Inc., *id*; Coleman v. Southern Pac. Transp. Co., 997 F. Supp. 1197, 1205 (D.Ariz. 1998); Barlow v. Esselte Pendaflex Corp., Meto Div., 111 F.R.D. at 406–07.

[484]Hendricks v. Coughlin, 114 F.3d 390, 394 (2d Cir. 1997). *Hendricks* was referring to a case where the dispute was about defendants' reasons for taking certain action, but we think its comment is true to some degree about most kinds of cases.

[485]Rule 30(d)(2); *see* Malec v. Trustees of Boston College, 208 F.R.D. 23, 24 (D.Mass. 2002) (denying request for 14 hours to take a deposition, without prejudice to renewing the request after the first seven hours).

[486]Some courts do not approve of oral depositions in *pro se* prisoner cases. *See* Myers v. Andzel, 2007 WL 3256879, *1 (S.D.N.Y., Oct. 15, 2007) ("Depositions conducted by pro se, incarcerated litigants are generally disfavored in this District. . . . Instead, courts typically require such litigants to propound interrogatories to the adverse party.").

Prison rules may directly or indirectly prohibit you from taking depositions. We are not aware of any decisions directly addressing this issue. One federal appeals court has upheld in general a policy forbidding prisoners from attending depositions conducted by counsel in their civil actions. *In re* Wilkinson, 137 F.3d 911, 913 (6th Cir. 1998). However, that is a very different situation from a case where the prisoner has no lawyer and must conduct the deposition himself. *Wilkinson* went on to say that a federal court has the authority to order a prisoner produced at a deposition if it is shown that doing so "will contribute significantly to a fair adjudication of his claim." 137 F.3d at 915. We think that representing yourself is a circumstance that meets this standard.

[487]*See* § C.5 of this chapter, n.239.

of the time and place of the deposition.[488] Thirty days is usually considered reasonable unless there is some specific reason for haste. Local court rules may define reasonable notice more specifically.

A named defendant does not need to be subpoenaed to appear at the deposition, but a non-party must be subpoenaed,[489] and you must pay the statutory witness fee for non-party witnesses.[490]

Normally, depositions are taken stenographically by a court reporter, who is almost always a notary who can swear in the witness. Court reporters charge a fee for showing up and a fee per page of transcript; a half-day's deposition can easily cost several hundred dollars in some jurisdictions.

Since most prisoners do not have the money to pay for stenographic depositions,[491] we will focus on taped depositions. Rule 32(b)(3)(a) states "[u]nless the court orders otherwise, it may be recorded by audio, audiovisual, or stenographic means. The noticing party bears the recording costs."[492] The old rules required parties to obtain a written stipulation or court order to take a non-stenographic deposition. You should probably do this, even though it is no longer required, since things have a way of going wrong inside a prison and as a *pro se* litigant you will have a hard time getting quick relief from the court.[493] A document that spells out the arrangements may help avoid or resolve disputes. You should also obtain the stipulation or court order because without it the prison probably will not allow you to have access to a room where you can bring a tape recorder or allow a tape recorder to be brought into the prison.

You should present a proposal to the defendants' lawyer and ask him either to agree to it or else propose a better way of handling the depositions.[494] If you reach an agreement, it should be put in writing in the form of a stipulation and submitted to the court for its signature. If you can't agree, then you should file a motion requesting an order stating how the deposition will be taken.

The motion should describe your efforts to work things out, and state whom you wish to depose, what kind of information you expect them to provide, that you will need a room at the prison, and that you will need to either bring a tape recorder to the deposition or have one brought into the prison and taken out as soon as the deposition is completed.

Your arrangements for taping a deposition should include the following:

(1) *Person before whom the deposition shall be taken.* Unless the parties agree otherwise, depositions are to be "conducted before an officer appointed or designated under Rule 28,"[495] which means someone authorized to administer oaths, such as a notary public, or someone specially appointed by the court to do so.[496] The officer begins by stating his name and business address, the date, time and place of the deposition, and the deponent's name. Then he administers the oath or affirmation to the deponent and identifies those present.[497] He will then let you start asking questions, then defendant's counsel can ask questions, and you get to ask follow-up questions. At the end of the questioning, the officer will state that the deposition is complete and state any stipulations between the parties about the custody or transcript of the recording.[498]

The rules also provide that the parties can enter into written stipulations modifying deposition procedures,[499] so it may be more practical to stipulate to have the oath

---

[488]Rule 30(b)(1), Fed.R.Civ.P.

[489]Rule 45(a)(1)(B), Fed.R.Civ.P.

[490]Windsor v. Martindale, 175 F.R.D. 665, 670 (D.Colo. 1997) and cases cited; Wright v. U.S., 948 F. Supp. 61 (M.D.Fla. 1996); *see also* Smith v. Yarrow, 78 Fed. Appx. 529, 544 (6th Cir. 2003) (unpublished) ("A prisoner plaintiff proceeding *in forma pauperis* may seek waiver of certain pretrial filing fees, but there is no constitutional or statutory requirement that the government or the Defendant pay for an indigent prisoner's discovery efforts."); Pedraza v. Jones, 71 F.3d 194, 197 (5th Cir. 1995) (federal courts are not authorized to waive or pay these fees on behalf of an IFP litigant). At present, the witness fee is $40.00 a day, plus travel expenses. 28 U.S.C. § 1821(b)–(d). Incarcerated persons called as witnesses do not receive these fees. 28 U.S.C. § 1821(f).

[491]If you can afford stenographic depositions, you can probably afford a lawyer, and you should try to get one. If that is not the case and you wish to take stenographic depositions *pro se*, you should try to obtain a stipulation or court order spelling out how the deposition will be managed. It should address similar issues to those we discuss in connection with taped depositions: identifying the reporter before whom the deposition will be taken, the location of the deposition, who can be present at the deposition, and admission of the reporter along with any other necessary participant to the prison.

[492]In this discussion, we will assume that the deposition is to be audiotaped.

[493]In *Hudson v. Spellman High Voltage*, 178 F.R.D. 29, 31–33 (E.D.N.Y. 1998), the court entered an order spelling out the conduct of a taped deposition in a non-prisoner case.

[494]Before you do this, you should inquire at the prison whether there are any procedures already in place for handling taped depositions for a prisoner.

[495]Rule 30(b)(6), Fed.R.Civ.P.

[496]Rule 28(a)(1), Fed.R.Civ.P.; *see* Hudson v. Spellman High Voltage, 178 F.R.D. 29, 32 (E.D.N.Y. 1998) (court directed having a notary public present at the deposition would satisfy this requirement). *Compare* Ott v. Stipe Law Firm, 169 F.R.D. 380, 381 (E.D.Okla. 1996) (it was improper for the plaintiff to administer the oath, and doing so would make the deposition inadmissible at trial).

[497]Rule 30(b)(5)(A), Fed.R.Civ.P.

[498]Rule 30(b)(5)(C), Fed.R.Civ.P.

[499]Rule 29, Fed.R.Civ.P. (the parties may stipulate "that depositions may be taken before any person, at any time or place, on any notice, and in the manner specified—in which event it may be used in the same way as any other deposition").

administered by the defendants' attorney or by a prison employee who is also a notary public, and have the tape recorders operated by you and by the defendants' attorney.

(2) *The manner of recording the deposition.* The deposition notice should state the method by which the deposition will be recorded.[500] The stipulation should probably go into more detail. We suggest that there should be two tape recorders so there will be two copies of the tape (or to guarantee one copy, if one recorder malfunctions). Ideally, you would provide one tape recorder and the defendants or prison administration would provide another.

However, most prisons do not permit inmates to possess tape recorders, so you may need to arrange for your family or friends to provide one temporarily. If prison officials are unwilling to do this, suggest to them—or to the court—that the prison or defendants' attorney provide both recorders. There should also be an agreement as to who is to supply blank tapes, and how many of them will be needed. (To avoid confusion, different depositions should go on different tapes. The rules also provide that if a single deposition goes on more than one tape, the officer should repeat the information about the deposition that is required in Rule 30(b)(5)(i)–(iii) at "the beginning of each unit of the recording medium."[501])

(3) *The manner of preserving and filing the deposition.* If the deposition is taken before an "officer" such as a notary public, he should seal and label the deposition and send it to the attorney who arranged for the deposition; the attorney is then responsible for preserving it.[502] If there is no officer, the first problem is to make sure that the deposition tape gets out of the prison safely. One of the two taped depositions should also be filed with the court if possible.[503] You will need a copy of the tape

and the defense counsel will need a copy.[504] Unless you can have a friend or family member at the deposition, the most practical solution, if counsel will agree, is to make defense counsel responsible for taking the tapes, copying them, filing the original with the court, and returning a copy to you. If the prison does not allow you to have a tape player to listen to the tape deposition, you should seek a court order that you be allowed to listen to the deposition on a tape player provided by prison staff.

Alternatively, defense counsel could take the tapes and send them to your friends or family, who could be responsible for copying, filing, and sending copies to you and defense counsel. Either arrangement requires you to trust the defense lawyer. However, lawyers are trained to be careful, and few lawyers are willing to do something so unethical as to alter or destroy evidence outright (especially when a court order or stipulation makes them responsible for safeguarding it). If defense counsel is unwilling to take on this responsibility, and you can't have a friend or family member present at the deposition, you may wish to ask the court for help in finding a practical solution.

(4) *Place of the deposition.* The deposition will have to be taken somewhere in the prison. The stipulation or order should require prison officials to provide a quiet room where you will not be interrupted and no one can overhear the proceedings.

(5) *Who can be present.* You may be concerned that having prison staff present will intimidate inmate witnesses or make staff witnesses less likely to be candid. A stipulation or order should provide that the deposition will be attended only by you, the witness, the defendants' counsel, and the person before whom the deposition will be taken, if any.[505]

Staff members' friends, union representatives, or other extraneous persons should not be in the deposition room.[506] In depositions

---

Lawyers sometimes suggest that depositions be taken pursuant to "the usual stipulations," whatever they are. *Don't agree to this.* Ask your adversary to spell out any stipulations he wishes you to agree to, and consider them one by one. For example, sometimes one of the "usual stipulations" is waiver of the witness's opportunity to sign the transcript. That is a bad idea, since if the witness is going to say that there is an error in the transcript, or that he misspoke and some of his testimony is inaccurate, you will want to know that shortly after the transcript is done, rather than be surprised by it at trial.

[500]Rule 30(b)(3), Fed.R.Civ.P.

[501]Rule 30(b)(5)(B).

[502]Rule 30(f)(1), Fed.R.Civ.P.

[503]The rules formerly required filing of depositions, but that requirement has been eliminated, Rule 30(f)(1), Fed.R.Civ.P.; now they say only that if a deposition *is* filed, the party filing it must promptly notify all the other parties. Rule 30(f)(4), Fed.R.Civ.P.

Most courts now have local rules that prohibit the filing of discovery materials unless the court orders them filed. We think it is wise to request the court to order the filing of a taped deposition because it is easy for tapes to get lost, damaged, or tampered with.

[504]*See* Hudson v. Spellman High Voltage, 178 F.R.D. 29, 32 (E.D.N.Y. 1998) (directing the plaintiff to provide defense counsel with a duplicate of the tape immediately after the deposition in a non-prison case).

[505]Such orders are authorized by Rule 26(c)(1)(E), Fed.R.Civ.P.

[506]Synthes Spine Co., L.P. v. Walden, 232 F.R.D. 460, 466 (E.D Pa. 2005) (court issued order that non-parties may not

conducted in prison by lawyers, security staff are normally present outside the deposition room but not inside it; you may wish to ask for a similar arrangement, though this may not be granted in a *pro se* case. Parties to a case are generally permitted to be present at a deposition if they wish,[507] a rule which presents obvious problems if the plaintiff is a prisoner.[508]

(6) *Admission of all persons to the prison.* If you have anyone coming from outside the prison for the deposition, such as the witness, someone bringing you a tape recorder, or someone to administer the oath and record the deposition, the stipulation or order should specifically provide that that person shall be permitted to enter the prison and should require prison officials to arrange all necessary clearances in advance.

If you wish to use tape-recorded deposition testimony at trial, you must provide the court with a written transcript as well as the recording.[509] If you do not have a way to do this, you should bring the problem to the court's attention well before trial. The defendants may bring a court reporter to the deposition or may make their own transcript of the

tape-recording; you may wish to include in a request for production of documents any transcript that they have made of the deposition, or simply request that they provide a copy of the transcript to you and to the court. You can also make your own transcript of a tape-recorded deposition, have a friend or family member do it, or hire a stenographer to prepare a transcript from the tape. This is not an ideal arrangement, since transcripts made from tapes (especially if the transcriber was not present at the deposition) tend to have errors in them. There may also be legitimate disputes about what was actually said. In order for your transcript to be usable, you will probably either have to reach an agreement about its accuracy with defense counsel, or submit the transcript to the witness for review and to submit a signed statement of any errors to be corrected or other necessary changes in the transcript. Ordinarily this review opportunity is limited to 30 days and must be requested before the deposition is completed, and the officer before whom the deposition was taken must attach the deponent's changes to the transcript.[510] You and defense counsel might wish to agree on a different procedure depending on the circumstances.

Whether you use a stenographer or a tape recorder, the purpose of a deposition is to obtain a clear, complete statement of the facts known to the party being deposed.[511] You should be friendly and business-like and not antagonistic during the deposition. Make the witness as comfortable as possible and you will be more likely to obtain useful information.

Above all, you should listen to the witness. You should have basic questions written out before the deposition, but be prepared to depart from your list of questions to ask for more detail, or to follow up on new points that emerge during the deposition. You should let the witness speak freely even if he is not directly responding to your question. (You can always repeat the question if necessary.) When new questions occur to you, don't interrupt the witness; instead, make notes of the additional questions so you can ask them later.

Counsel for the other side may object to some of your questions. You should state that the objection is noted for the record and then request an answer from the deponent. The only basis for instructing a deponent not to answer is to preserve a privilege, to enforce a limit on evidence directed by the court, or to present a motion for a protective order.[512]

---

attend deposition); Dunlap v. Reading Co., 30 F.R.D. 129, 131 (E.D.Pa. 1962) ("We consider the camaraderie of employees who work together as 'good cause' for their separation on their pretrial examination.").

[507] *See, e.g.,* Galella v. Onassis, 487 F.2d 986, 997 (2d Cir. 1973) (although court has power to exclude a party from a deposition, such an exclusion should be ordered rarely); Alexander v. F.B.I., 186 F.R.D. 21, 53 (D.D.C. 1998) ("[T]here is no evidence Rule 26(c)(5) [now Rule 26(c)(1)(E)] was intended to bar parties from attending depositions." (citation omitted)).

[508] *See In re* Collins, 73 F.3d 614, 615–16 (6th Cir. 1995) (holding prisoner with violent history should be excluded from prison officials' depositions in light of security problems; state had agreed to provide counsel with access to the plaintiff during the deposition). The prisoner in *Collins* had counsel, which minimized the effect of this exclusion. Later, the court said that "[u]nder some circumstances an inmate may be able to make a specialized showing of the necessity of his attending a particular pretrial deposition" and should be allowed to attend in such cases. *In re* Wilkinson, 137 F.3d 911, 915 (6th Cir. 1998).

Collins and *Wilkinson* involved prisoners who had lawyers. If you are proceeding *pro se*, you may wish to request that you be present at any deposition that the defendants take of witnesses other than yourself. We would think that your *pro se* status would constitute the showing of necessity for you to attend that is required by *Wilkinson*. As a practical matter, that would probably require that the deposition be taken at the prison, rather than at the attorneys' offices. In your request, offer the alternative that you be allowed to attend by telephonic means so that you can object, if necessary, and be provided an opportunity to engage in cross-examination.

[509] Rule 32(c), Fed.R.Civ.P. The rule also says that a party *may* provide deposition testimony in "nontranscript form" in addition, and it must be presented in nontranscript form on any party's request, if it is available, in a jury trial.

[510] Rule 30(e), Fed.R.Civ.P. This rule is discussed further at nn.481–483, above.

[511] These comments concern depositions that you take of other persons. How to respond when your own deposition is being taken is discussed in § K.2.i of this chapter.

[512] Rule 30(c)(2), Fed.R.Civ.P.; Ralston Purina Co. v. McFarland 550 F.2d 967, 973 (4th Cir. 1977) ("The action of plaintiff's counsel in directing [the witness] not to answer the questions posed to him was indefensible and utterly at variance with the discovery provisions of the Federal Rules of Civil Procedure."); Gould Investors, L.P. v. General Ins. Co., 133 F.R.D. 103, 104–05 (S.D.N.Y. 1990); First Tennessee Bank v. Federal Deposit Ins. Corp., 108

However, if you try to use the deposition at trial, the court will rule on any objections made at the deposition, and may exclude testimony if a question is genuinely objectionable.[513]

If opposing counsel makes an objection to the form of a question, you should try to rephrase the question.[514] If the deponent refuses to answer, your remedy is a motion to compel discovery, discussed in § K.2.h of this chapter. Objections "must be stated concisely in a nonargumentative and non-suggestive manner."[515] It is improper for opposing counsel to "interpret" questions for the witness, coach them about their answers, make long "speaking" objections and engage in long off-the-record colloquies with the witness, or leave the room with a witness while a question is pending.[516]

Depositions, like other statements made out of court, are generally considered hearsay at trial. However, they may be introduced in a court proceeding, consistently with the rules of evidence, if the witness is not available to testify for any of several reasons, including imprisonment.[517] Depositions of defendants and their agents may also be

introduced as "admissions by [a] party-opponent."[518] They may also be used to impeach persons who testify at trial.[519]

Courts will not always allow a prisoner/plaintiff to attend his civil rights trial or to have prisoner witnesses brought to the courthouse to testify.[520] Since prison officials may transfer your witnesses to another prison or a prisoner may be paroled, you may wish to take the oral deposition of these witnesses as early as possible after you have filed your lawsuit.

On the other hand, if you are confident that you can keep track of the witnesses and are very concerned that they appear personally, you may prefer to avoid taking their depositions so you will not create a temptation for the court to dispense with their personal appearance and testimony.

2) Written Depositions For most prisoners, taking oral depositions is impractical. There is also a procedure for taking depositions upon written questions, in which you do not have to be present though you must arrange for an officer to record the deposition and to ask the questions.[521]

To take a deposition upon written questions, you must serve a notice and written questions upon the other party.[522] Within 14 days defendants' counsel must serve you with any questions that they want asked as cross-examination. You then have seven days to serve redirect questions, and the defendants have seven days to serve recross questions.[523] Defendants may object to some or all of your questions, but those objections do not prevent the questions from being asked; as with oral depositions, the testimony is taken subject to objection.[524] If the court sustains an objection, the relevant testimony may be excluded from evidence at trial.

You must then provide a copy of the notice and copies of all questions served to the officer who will take the deposition.[525] A copy of the deposition and of the notice and questions need not be filed with the court; if you do file them, you must notify all other parties of the filing.[526]

If the person to be deposed is not a party, you will be required to have a subpoena served upon them to have the

---

F.R.D. 640, 640 (E.D.Tenn.1985) ("It is well-settled that counsel should never instruct a witness not to answer a question during a deposition unless the question seeks privileged information or unless counsel wishes to adjourn the deposition for the purpose of seeking a protective order from what he or she believes is annoying, embarrassing, oppressive or bad faith conduct by adverse counsel."). This is especially the case if the witness is not even a client of the lawyer making the objection, *see* Shapiro v. Freeman, 38 F.R.D. 308, 312 (S.D.N.Y. 1965), as would be the case where the defense lawyer for prison staff sued as individuals objected to questions posed to persons who were not defendants.

[513]Rule 32(b), Fed.R.Civ.P. ("an objection may be made at a hearing or trial to the admission of any deposition testimony that would be inadmissible if the witness were present and testifying").

[514]Examples of objections to form include "compound questions," which mix up two different questions. For example, the question, "Did you see the altercation, or were you outside the housing unit?" is a compound question. You should break it into two questions. A question's form may be objectionable if it assumes a fact that has not been established. For example, you shouldn't ask, "When you saw Officer Smith hit me, where was he standing?" without first asking, "Did you see Officer Smith hit me?" An objection to form may also be made if a question is unclear for some reason.

[515]Rule 30(c)(2), Fed.R.Civ.P.

[516]Calzaturficio S.C.A.R.P.A. S.P.A. v. Fabiano Shoe Co., Inc., 201 F.R.D. 33, 39–41 (D.Mass. 2001); *see* McDonough v. Keniston, 188 F.R.D. 22, 23–24 (D.N.H. 1998) (noting that rules were amended to end speaking and coaching objections like "if you understand" and "if you remember"); Damaj v. Farmers Ins. Co., 164 F.R.D. 559, 560 (N.D.Okla. 1995) (condemning obstructionist tactics and suggestive objections at a deposition); Armstrong v. Hussman Corp., 163 F.R.D. 299, 303 (E.D.Mo. 1995).

[517]Rule 32(a)(4)(C), Fed.R.Civ.P. This point is discussed further in § S.4.c of this chapter.

[518]Rule 801(d)(2), Fed.R.Evid., permits the use of "a statement by the party's agent or servant concerning a matter within the scope of the agency or employment, made during the existence of the relationship," commonly called an admission. Admissions are discussed in § S.2 of this chapter.

[519]Impeachment is discussed in §§ T.3.c and T.5 of this chapter.

[520]Court appearances are discussed in § Q of this chapter.

[521]*See* Rule 31, Fed.R.Civ.P.

This may be the only means that you have to obtain discovery from a person not named as a defendant in a lawsuit, unless you or someone else can interview them.

[522]Rule 31(a)(3), Fed.R.Civ.P.

[523]Rule 31(a)(5), Fed.R.Civ.P.

[524]Whitehurst v. U.S., 231 F.R.D. 500, 501–02 (S.D.Tex. 2005).

[525]Rule 31(b), Fed.R.Civ.P.

[526]Rule 31(c)(2), Fed.R.Civ.P.

person appear for the written deposition.[527] You must include with the subpoena payment for the subpoena fee and mileage.[528]

As with oral depositions, you must either pay for a stenographer or arrange to tape record the deposition. If you intend to have the deposition taped, you will need to make arrangements for someone to swear the witness, operate the tape recorder, etc. It is unlikely that you will be present for the taking of the written deposition.

A deposition upon written questions is less effective than an oral deposition because you have no opportunity to observe the witness to assess his credibility and demeanor, to ask follow-up questions, or to change your approach depending on the answers you get. This procedure has the same disadvantage as interrogatories, discussed in the next section, in which written answers are provided to written questions. However, interrogatories may only be served on parties, while depositions on written questions may be taken of any witness. Also, with a deposition upon written questions, even though the witness will probably see the questions in advance and may be coached by the lawyer, he will have to answer in his own words rather than having the answers drafted by an attorney.

e. Interrogatories Interrogatories are governed by Rule 33, Fed.R.Civ.P. Interrogatories can be used to obtain information only from named parties or their agents. They consist of written questions submitted to the opposing party for a written answer.[529]

The party served with interrogatories must answer or object to the questions, under oath, within 30 days of service of interrogatories unless the court directs, or the parties agree to, a different schedule.[530] Answers to interrogatories must be in a form usable in court.[531]

If a party objects and refuses to answer an interrogatory, the reasons for objecting must be stated.[532] Failure to state objections in a timely manner waives the objections unless the party shows good cause for raising them late.[533]

The rules permit you to serve up to 25 interrogatories ("all discrete subparts" count against the 25) on each party; to serve more, you must obtain court permission.[534] A *pro se* prisoner's inability to take depositions might support an expansion of the interrogatory limit, though we don't know of any case law on that point. Some district courts have adopted rules requiring parties to use other discovery devices (usually depositions and requests for documents) before serving interrogatories.[535] This is a good practice anyway, since interrogatories give defendants and their lawyers the opportunity to formulate answers that best serve their interests.

Therefore, you should not rely solely on interrogatories for answers to questions about the facts of the case; you should try to obtain relevant documents first, if you can. A document that was written as part of ordinary prison operations is likely to be more reliable than an interrogatory answer prepared in the course of litigation.

Interrogatories are most useful for obtaining the names and locations of defendants, witnesses, and others with information about the case, for determining the existence and location of documents,[536] and for obtaining information about defenses and evidence or legal theories supporting them.[537]

---

[527]Rule 31(a)(1), Fed.R.Civ.P.

[528]*See* n.490, above.

[529]Unlike depositions by written questions, *see* § K.2.d(2) of this chapter, interrogatories don't require you to exchange questions with the other side or to have someone present to read the questions and to record the answers.

[530]Pursuant to Rule 6(d), Fed.R.Civ.P., a party served by mail with a discovery request has three additional days that are to be added on to the 30 days.

[531]Davidson v. Goord, 215 F.R.D. 73, 77 (W.D.N.Y. 2003) (answers that merely referenced allegations in the complaint were not acceptable).

[532]Rule 33(b)(4), Fed.R.Civ.P. Objections must be stated reasonably specifically. Caldwell v. Center for Correctional Health and Policy Studies, 228 F.R.D. 40, 44 (D.D.C. 2005) (objections must "show specifically how an interrogatory is overly broad, burdensome or oppressive, by submitting affidavits or offering evidence which reveals the nature of the burden"; answers like "overly broad" or "burdensome" are inadequate and waive the objection).

[533]Rule 33(b)(4), Fed.R.Civ.P. Waiver of discovery objections is discussed further in § K.2.h of this chapter, nn.578–581.

[534]Rule 33(a)(1), Fed.R.Civ.P.; *see* Skinner v. Uphoff, 410 F. Supp. 2d 1104, 1111 (D.Wyo. 2006) (relieving plaintiffs from 25-interrogatory limit); *see also* Nyfield v. Virgin Islands Telephone Corp., 200 F.R.D. 246, 247–48 (D.V.I. 2001) (subparts should count as separate interrogatories if they seek information about discrete subjects, but an interrogatory seeking communications of a particular type should be treated as a single interrogatory even if it asks that time, place, persons present, and contents be stated separately for each communication; plaintiff allowed to propound 25 interrogatories).

[535]*See, e.g.,* Rule 33(b), Local Rules of the United States District Courts for the Southern Districts of New York (allowing most interrogatories only "if they are a more practical method of obtaining the information sought than a request for production or a deposition").

[536]Roesberg v. Johns-Manville Corp., 85 F.R.D. 292, 300–01 (E.D.Pa. 1980).

[537]Rule 33(a)(2), Fed.R.Civ.P., says: "An interrogatory is not objectionable merely because it asks for an opinion or contention that relates to fact or the application of law to fact, but the court may order that the interrogatory need not be answered until designated discovery is complete, or until a pretrial conference or some other time."

This refers to "contention interrogatories," which essentially ask a party to explain his case and say what it is based on. These interrogatories are sometimes subject to abuse. See Lucero v. Valdez, 240 F.R.D. 591, 594 (D.N.M. 2007) (interrogatories asking for "each and every fact" and application of law to fact that supports every allegation in the complaint are unduly broad and burdensome; such interrogatories are permissible if they will

f. Request for Production of Documents, Electronically Stored Information, or Tangible Things Requests for production of documents, electronic information, or tangible items can only be served upon named parties to the lawsuit (requests to non-parties must be made via subpoena, as discussed below). Rule 34(a), Fed.R.Civ.P.,[538] authorizes a party to request any other party

> to produce and permit the requesting party or its representative to inspect, copy, test, or sample the following items in the responding party's possession, custody, or control:
> (A) any designated documents or electronically stored information—including writings, drawings, graphs, charts, photographs, sound recordings, images, and other data or data compilations—stored in any medium from which information can be obtained either directly, or, if necessary, after translation by the responding party into a reasonably usable form); or
> (B) any designated tangible things; . . .

A party is required to respond to a document request within 30 days unless the court directs, or the parties agree to, a different schedule.[539] If a party objects to any part of a request, it must specify the reason and allow inspection of the rest.[540] Objections not made in a timely fashion are waived.[541]

You must state with reasonable specificity the items you want prison officials to permit you to inspect and possibly copy.[542] Often the best way to do this is to state the request generally and then more specifically list the items that you know exist.[543] You should include a reasonable time, place, and manner of making the requested inspection.[544]

The rules do not prescribe who is to pay for copying documents. For convenience, in many cases the defendants simply will make copies and send them to you if small quantities are involved. In other cases they may insist that you pay. Our guess is that in most cases, if you demonstrate to the court that you cannot pay and that the documents are important to your case, the judge will direct or persuade the defendants to give them to you. Otherwise you may have to pay.[545]

Under Rule 34(a)(1), if the documents you need are not in the "possession, custody or control" of the defendants,[546] you cannot get them through a request to produce, but will have to serve a subpoena for production of documentary evidence (sometimes called a subpoena *duces tecum*) on the third party who has them.[547] You will have to serve the subpoena upon the person that is named in it. In *in forma pauperis* cases, the court through the U.S. Marshal is responsible for service of process.[548] If you are not proceeding *in forma pauperis*, "[a]ny person who is at least 18 years old and not a party may serve a subpoena."[549] Most courts have assumed that subpoenas must be personally served, like

---

"clarify the issues in the case, narrow the scope of the dispute, set up early settlement discussions, or expose a substantial basis for a motion" to dismiss or for summary judgment); *see also* Schaap v. Executive Industries, Inc., 130 F.R.D. 384, 387–88 (N.D.Ill. 1990) (interrogatories about purely legal issues were inappropriate, but interrogatory asking whether party took particular legal positions, and if so what their factual basis was, was permissible).

[538]*See also* Appendix C, Form 5a, for an example of a request for production of documents.

[539]Pursuant to Rule 6(d), Fed.R.Civ.P., a party served by mail with a discovery request has three additional days that are to be added on to the 30 days.

[540]Rule 34(b)(2)(B)–(C), Fed.R.Civ.P.

[541]*See* § K.2.h of this chapter, nn.577–580, concerning waiver of discovery objections.

[542]Rule 34(b)(1)(A), Fed.R.Civ.P. If the requested documents are voluminous, you should request to review them and let officials know what you want copied.

[543]An example of how to do this is given in § K.2.c of this chapter.

[544]Rule 34(b)(1)(B), Fed.R.Civ.P. If you wish to review prison records kept in a different location, prison officials may allege the records cannot leave that location without disrupting their operations. You can then suggest the examination of the records take place on a weekend at the prison where you are incarcerated

while a prison official is on duty to supervise the review. This should create a minimum of inconvenience to any of the parties.

[545]*See* Windsor v. Martindale, 175 F.R.D. 665, 672 (D.Colo. 1997) (prisoner proceeding *in forma pauperis* in civil rights litigation was "not entitled to copy of any document produced under subpoena without payment of appropriate copy cost, if required."); Brandon v. Beard, 140 F.R.D. 328, 329 (M.D.Pa. 1991) (declining to make defendants pay for copying documents without a showing that plaintiff could not afford to pay).

[546]The phrase "possession, custody or control" means that the party either has the document, has the legal right to obtain it, or has the practical ability to obtain the document. Klesch & Co. Ltd. v. Liberty Media Corp., 217 F.R.D. 517, 520 (D.Colo. 2003) and cases cited; Triple Five of Minnesota, Inc. v. Simon, 212 F.R.D. 523, 527 (D.Minn. 2002); *see* Comeau v. Rupp, 810 F. Supp. 1127, 1166 (D.Kan.) (requiring government agency to seek to obtain documents in possession of other agencies), *reconsideration granted in part on other grounds*, 810 F. Supp. 772 (D.Kan. 1992). In prison cases brought against officers or other lower level staff, official prison reports, policies, etc., are routinely produced, even though technically they may be in possession, custody, or control of the prison warden or clerk. In a few cases where defendants have made an issue of this, the courts have required the agencies or supervisors to provide the discovery. Cook v. City of New York, 578 F. Supp. 179, 184 (S.D.N.Y. 1984) (dismissed prison officials required to cooperate with discovery).

Documents in the possession of a party's attorney may be required to be produced. Schultz v. Butcher, 24 F.3d 626, 630 (4th Cir. 1994); *In re Ruppert*, 309 F.2d 97, 98 (6th Cir. 1962).

[547]Rule 45, Fed.R.Civ.P.

[548]28 U.S.C. § 1915(d) ("The officers of the court shall issue and serve all process, and perform all duties in such cases."). *See* U.S. v. Means, 741 F.2d 1053, 1055 (8th Cir. 1984) (en banc) (point conceded by government); Jackson v. Brinker, 147 F.R.D. 189, 193 & n.1 (S.D.Ind. 1993) ("The Marshals Service was directed to serve the plaintiff's subpoena pursuant to its duties under 28 U.S.C. § 1915(c).").

[549]Rule 45(b)(1), Fed.R.Civ.P.

the complaint.[550] However, the rule does not specifically say that, and some courts allow mail service, though not by regular mail.[551] You will have to research the question in your federal district to learn if you can dispense with personal service. You should not have to pay witness fees for a document subpoena, since the rule permits the subpoenaed party to produce the documents without appearing.[552]

Documents can be requested in a deposition notice, to be produced at or before the deposition.[553]

g. Request for Admission Requests for admission, which ask the opposing party to admit or deny the truth of particular facts,[554] are among the most useful tools of discovery. Facts that have been admitted are binding on the adverse party,[555] and you can use the admissions to establish those facts at trial or on a motion for summary judgment.

Requests for admission can be served at any time during litigation. The opposing party has thirty days after service to answer or object.[556] (You should file with the court the certificate of service showing when you served them.) If a party objects to a request, he must specifically state the reasons for the objection. Prison officials cannot claim they do not know the answer unless they state that they have made reasonable inquiry and still do not have sufficient information to admit or deny the request.[557]

If the defendants deny facts set forth in a request for an admission and you later prove them to be true, the defendants may be held liable for any expenses that are incurred

in proving the facts they earlier denied.[558] The same rules apply to you if requests for admissions are served on you.

The rules state that if a request for admission is not timely answered, the matter is deemed admitted.[559] However, the rule also provides that admissions may be withdrawn or amended "if it would promote the presentation of the merits of the action and if the court is not persuaded that it would prejudice the requesting party in maintaining or defending the action on the merits."[560] If the defendants don't answer your request on time, you have to choose between making efforts to get them to respond, so you will know what their position is, and relying on the admissions and risking that they will be withdrawn at the last minute.[561]

Opinions differ as to which is the better course. If you rely on the admissions and the defendants try to withdraw them, you must argue to the court that you have based your trial preparation on them and you will be prejudiced if they are withdrawn.[562] You will also need to argue that if the admissions are set aside, you should be allowed to undertake additional discovery, since you relied on the admissions in conducting your discovery.

If you decide to rely on the admissions, you will want to put them in evidence at the trial, so you should be sure to include them on your evidence list in any pretrial order or conference.[563] This will strengthen your argument that you

---

[550]*See, e.g.*, Chima v. U.S. Dep't of Defense, 23 Fed.Appx. 721, 724 (9th Cir. 2001) (unpublished).

[551]*See, e.g.*, Hall v. Sullivan, 229 F.R.D. 501, 505–06 (D.Md. 2005) (service by Federal Express was sufficient on non-party when subpoena requested documents only); Windsor v. Martindale, 175 F.R.D. 665, 670 (D.Colo. 1997) (regular mail was insufficient, but certified mail by the U.S. Marshals Service was sufficient); Doe v. Hersemann, 155 F.R.D. 630, 630–31 (N.D.Ind. 1994) (certified mail was sufficient).

[552]Rule 45(c)(2)(A); *see* Windsor v. Martindale, 175 F.R.D. 665, 670 (D.Colo. 1997) (no witness fee and mileage due where subpoenaed person did not have to appear at a depositon); Jackson v. Brinker, 1992 WL 404537, *2 (S.D.Ind., Dec. 21, 1992) (same).

There is one reported decision to the contrary. *See* Badman v. Stark, 139 F.R.D. 601, 604–06 (M.D.Pa. 1991). As *Jackson* explains, *Badman* is in error because it relies on cases involving subpoenas requiring witnesses to appear and not just to produce documents.

[553]*See* § K.2.i of this chapter, nn.597–598, for discussion of this option.

[554]The relevant rule actually says "facts, the application of law to fact, or opinions about either. . . ." Rule 36(a)(1)(A), Fed.R.Civ.P.

[555]Rule 36(b), Fed.R.Civ.P. ("Any matter admitted under this rule is conclusively established unless the court on motion permits withdrawal or amendment of the admission.").

[556]Rule 36(a)(3), Fed.R.Civ.P. Pursuant to Rule 6(d), Fed.R.Civ.P., a party served by mail with a discovery request has three additional days that are to be added on to the 30 days.

[557]Rule 36(a)(4), Fed.R.Civ.P.

[558]Rule 37(c)(2), Fed.R.Civ.P.

[559]Rule 36(a)(3), Fed.R.Civ.P.

[560]Rule 36(b), Fed.R.Civ.P.

[561]*See* Conlon v. U.S., 474 F.3d 616, 621–24 (9th Cir. 2007) (discussing standards for allowing withdrawal of admissions); Hadley v. U.S., 45 F.3d 1345, 1348 (9th Cir. 1995) (holding that the district court abused its discretion in refusing to allow the withdrawal of two inadvertent admissions that went to the heart of the case); Kerry Steel, Inc. v. Paragon Indus., Inc., 106 F.3d 147, 154 (6th Cir. 1997) ("The prejudice contemplated by [Rule 36(b)] is not simply that the party who initially obtained the admission will now have to convince the fact finder of its truth." (internal quotation marks omitted). Instead, prejudice under Rule 36(b) "relates to special difficulties a party may face caused by a sudden need to obtain evidence upon withdrawal or amendment of an admission." (internal quotation marks omitted)); Davis v. Noufal, 142 F.R.D. 258, 259 (D.D.C. 1992) (allowing party to withdraw admissions resulting from failure to respond, since they would block any consideration of the merits).

[562]In one case that co-author Manville litigated, the defendant never responded to a request to admit that he wrote a false misconduct, and Manville relied on his failure to deny it. During the pretrial conference, defendant's counsel objected to the statement's being taken as admitted, but never filed a motion to have it set aside. At trial, defendant's counsel requested for the first time that the admission be set aside. Manville argued that his client would be prejudiced since he had not taken certain depositions, one prison official had now retired and moved out of state and was not available for deposition, and Manville had not engaged in other discovery because he relied upon the admission. The trial court refused to set aside the admission and this decision was affirmed on appeal. Riley v. Kurtz, 1999 WL 801560, *2 (6th Cir. 1999).

[563]*See* § N of this chapter.

have relied on them and the defendants should not be allowed to withdraw them.

Requests for admission can be used to establish facts about the case, the application of law to facts, and the genuineness of documents. Requests for admission as to questions of law alone are not appropriate.[564]

The request for admission should be written in simple, straightforward, and neutral language. Each separate admission should contain only one idea. If there are a number of different points you want admitted, put each one into a separate, numbered item.

Requests for admission are most useful for simplifying matters that are not really in dispute, such as background facts about prison procedures and the authenticity of documents you wish to use at trial.[565] It is usually a waste of effort to request the defendants to admit that they mistreated you or violated the law during the event you are suing about.

However, you can use admissions to establish important elements of your *prima facie* case, such as "Admit that on December 4, 2006, at 12:00 noon, Officer Ward was on duty in cell block A."[566] You can prepare a series of admissions that will pinpoint exactly how far the defendants are willing to go in conceding your factual allegations, and how much of the incident is really in dispute. You can also combine interrogatories and document requests with admissions to get a very precise picture of the defendants' position.[567]

There are other kinds of admissions: admissions of a party-opponent, admissions against interest, and judicial admissions, which are addressed in another section.[568]

h. Compelling Discovery and Sanctions The discovery process is intended to work without the need for court intervention. However, if a party has refused to comply with a discovery request, or has failed to disclose information required by the rules,[569] the opposing party may file a motion pursuant to Rule 37(a)(2), Fed.R.Civ.P., for an order compelling discovery.[570] The party against whom the motion is filed will have a chance to answer the motion, and the court will decide whether an order compelling discovery should be issued.

Rule 37 requires that a motion to compel "include a certification that the movant has in good faith conferred or attempted to confer" with the other side in an effort to resolve the dispute without court action.[571] Some local court rules also require litigants to request an informal conference with the court before filing a motion.[572] If your discovery request is not answered within the time that the rules prescribe, you should write to defense counsel and request an answer promptly after the time has expired.[573]

If you do not receive the information you requested within a reasonable time such as 20 days after you have written the letter, you can advise defense counsel that you will have to file a motion to compel if defendants do not comply promptly. If defense counsel requests a reasonable amount of additional time, you should agree to it as long as the defense lawyer is willing to prepare a stipulation to that effect for approval by the court. (Courts generally approve such agreements unless they are inconsistent with a discovery schedule set by the court.)

You should also consider any reasonable compromise offered to you by defense counsel, and offer a reasonable compromise yourself if you can think of one.

If you have to file a motion to compel, read the local rules *and* the judge's own rules carefully. Many courts have specific requirements concerning what must be included in a motion to compel, such as either attaching copies of the discovery requests themselves to the motion, or quoting verbatim in the motion the discovery requests that are at issue.[574] Some courts or judges require a letter to the court about the issue before a motion is filed. Your motion should include a complete account of the discovery dispute and of your attempts to resolve it. It is therefore important that you keep copies of all letters and records of all conversations between you and opposing counsel.

If you have to file a motion to compel, don't delay. Once you have made the necessary attempts to resolve the problem informally, get your motion into court. Sometimes, when you file a motion to compel, prison

---

[564]McConkie v. Nichols, 392 F. Supp. 2d 1, 7 n.6 (D.Me. 2005), *aff'd on other grounds*, 446 F.3d 258 (1st Cir. 2006).

[565]Rule 36(a)(1)(A), Fed.R.Civ.P.

[566]If you get a defense lawyer who denies admissions based on the tiniest error or discrepancy, you may have to break the request for admissions down into smaller parts, *e.g.*, separate questions on whether the officer was on duty on the day, whether he was on duty on a particular unit, whether he was on that unit at a particular time of day, etc.

[567]*See* Appendix C, Form 5b, for an example of how to do this.

[568]*See* § T.2 of this chapter.

[569]*See* Rule 26(a), Fed.R.Civ.P. The disclosure requirement is discussed in § K.2 of this chapter.

[570]*See* Appendix C, Forms 6a–6c.

[571]Rule 37(a)(1), Fed.R.Civ.P. Most local court rules also impose "meet and confer" requirements. *See, e.g.*, Avent v. Solfaro, 210 F.R.D. 91, 95 (S.D.N.Y. 2002) (denying prisoner's motion to compel for failure to try to contact the defendants or ask for a conference with the court first); Van Westrienen v. Americontinental Collection Corp., 189 F.R.D. 441 (D.Or. 1999).

[572]*See, e.g.*, Rule 37.2, Local Civil Rules, United States District Court, Southern District of' New York.

[573]Some decisions, including those cited in n.571, above, say that more than a letter to opposing counsel is required to satisfy the "meet and confer" requirement. Presumably courts will understand that prisoners are not in a position to "meet" freely with opposing counsel (though you can and probably should suggest that the opposing attorney meet with you at the prison). If you have the ability to try to telephone defense counsel to discuss the discovery issues before filing a motion, you should probably do so.

[574]*See, e.g.*, Rule 37.1, Local Civil Rules, U.S. District Court, Southern District of New York; Rule 37.2, Local Rules for Civil Cases, U.S. District Court, Eastern District of Michigan.

officials will provide the answers immediately to avoid annoying the judge.

The sooner this happens the better. If they still don't answer, it may take the judge a while to decide the motion. You should try to get discovery disputes resolved well before the deadline for completing discovery so you will have the opportunity to follow up on any information that is produced. Discovery issues that are not raised until near the time of trial have a way of getting lost.

Defendants will sometimes claim that the information you want is privileged, or that it would be embarrassing, oppressive, or unduly burdensome or expensive to produce it.[575] (They may not wait for your motion to compel to make these claims; these arguments may also be raised by them in a motion for a protective order, provided for in Rule 26(c), Fed.R.Civ.P., or simply stated as objections in their discovery response.) You must counter these arguments.[576] Courts sometimes respond to privilege disputes by directing that documents be produced *in camera* (to the court) and ruling on the dispute after inspecting the documents.[577]

If the defendants failed to answer a discovery request within the time set by the rules or any extensions granted by the court, you should emphasize that fact in your motion to compel. There is ample case law that objections are waived if they are not made in a timely fashion,[578] even if the objections are based on a claim of privilege.[579] Objections must be

made with sufficient specificity to avoid waiver.[580] In practice, these waivers are not always enforced,[581] but sometimes they are, and even if they are not, defendants' failure to follow the rules will not make them look good to the court. (You should, of course, always comply with these time limits yourself when defendants seek discovery from you, and if you can't comply, ask for more time rather than just submitting responses late.)

If an order compelling discovery has been granted and the party refuses to comply with the order, you may file a motion under Rule 37(b), Fed.R.Civ.P., which provides for sanctions including assessment of expenses and attorneys' fees, establishing facts in the other party's favor, barring the disobedient party from pursuing certain claims or submitting certain evidence, striking out pleadings or parts of them, staying the case until the order is obeyed, dismissing the action or proceeding or any part thereof, or entering a default judgment against the disobedient party.[582] If a party

---

[575]*See* Rule 26(c)(1), Fed.R.Civ.P. (stating these factors as a basis for granting a protective order).

[576]Ways of doing this are discussed in §§ K.2.a, K.2.b of this chapter.

[577]Windsor v. Martindale, 175 F.R.D. 665, 671–72 (D.Colo. 1997) (directing production *in camera*); Freeman v. Fairman, 917 F. Supp. 586, 589 (N.D.Ill. 1996) (declining to order discovery after inspecting the document *in camera*). Courts often decline to inspect material *in camera* where the objecting party has not made a persuasive argument for non-production. Smith v. Goord, 222 F.R.D. 238, 242 (N.D.N.Y. 2004) (*in camera* inspection should not be done routinely as a substitute for full disclosure); Soto v. City of Concord, 162 F.R.D. 603, 613–14 (N.D.Cal. 1995) (*in camera* inspection should be ordered only if defendants first put forth a satisfactory basis for asserting the privilege).

[578]Morin v. Nationwide Federal Credit Union, 229 F.R.D. 364, 368 (D. Conn. 2005); Safeco Ins. Co. of America v. Rawstrom, 183 F.R.D. 668, 670–73 (C.D.Cal. 1998) (even if some objections are made timely, others made late are waived); Godsey v. U.S., 133 F.R.D. 111, 113 (S.D.Miss. 1990); Demary v. Yamaha Motor Crop., 125 F.R.D. 20, 22 (D.Mass. 1989) and cases cited.

With respect to interrogatories, this principle now appears in the rules themselves. *See* Rule 33(b)(4), Fed.R.Civ.P. (providing for waiver unless the party shows "good cause" for failure to object timely). It is equally applicable to requests for document production. Fonville v. District of Columbia, 230 F.R.D. 38, 42 (D.D.C. 2005); Drexel Heritage Furnishings, Inc. v. Furniture USA, Inc., 200 F.R.D. 255, 258 (M.D.N.C. 2001).

[579]Marx v. Kelly, Hart & Halman, P.C., 929 F.2d 8, 12 (1st Cir. 1991); Fonville v. District of Columbia, 230 F.R.D. 38, 42–43 (D.D.C. 2005); First Sav. Bank, F.S.B. v. First Bank System, Inc., 902 F. Supp. 1356, 1360 (D.Kan. 1995) ("The party asserting a privilege

or the work-product doctrine as a bar to discovery . . . must present the privilege objection 'in a timely and proper manner.'").

[580]Caldwell v. Center for Correctional Health and Policy Studies, 228 F.R.D. 40, 42 (D.D.C. 2005) (responses like "overly broad" or "burdensome," without more, waived the objections); Ritacca v. Abbot Laboratories, 203 F.R.D. 332, 336 (N.D.Ill. 2001) (failure to produce privilege log or object with the requisite specificity is grounds for waiver).

When defendants object to production of documents on grounds of privilege, they must produce a "privilege log," which is adequate if it "sets forth specific facts that, if credited, would suffice to establish each element of the privilege or immunity that is claimed." SEC v. Beacon Hill Asset Mgmt LLC, 231 F.R.D. 134, 144 (S.D.N.Y. 2004) (noting that privilege logs typically identify each document and the persons who were parties to the communications, providing sufficient detail to permit judgment whether the document is at least potentially protected from disclosure). A party cannot refuse to provide a privilege log on the ground that doing so will reveal counsel's thought processes. Aikens v. Deluxe Financial Services, Inc., 217 F.R.D. 533, 535 (D.Kan. 2003).

[581]*In re* DG Acquisition Corp., 151 F.3d 75, 84 (2d Cir. 1998) (honoring objection based on Fifth Amendment privilege where litigants did not act in bad faith and adequately supported their privilege claim); Scaturro v. Warren and Sweat Mfg. Co., Inc., 160 F.R.D. 44, 46 (M.D.Pa. 1995) (a "party who fails to make a timely objection 'may' be held to have waived his objections," but waiver is appropriate in cases of egregious conduct).

[582]Rule 37(B)(2)(A), Fed.R.Civ.P. *See* Caldwell v. Center for Correctional Health and Policy Studies, 228 F.R.D. 40, 46 (D.D.C. 2005) (declining to enter default judgment where discovery delays did not prejudice plaintiff's ability to go forward); Sanders v. City of New York, 218 F. Supp. 2d 538, 543 (S.D.N.Y. 2002) ($5000 sanction imposed for failure to produce discovery timely); Callwood v. Zurita, 158 F.R.D. 359, 361–62 (D.V.I. 1994) (after repeated failure to obey court orders to provide discovery, court finds bad faith; it declines to enter a default judgment, but deems the complaint's allegations established, precludes any defense or any evidence or argument refuting the admissions they had failed to respond to, and bars defendants from asserting counterclaims or filing dispositive motions); Green v. District of Columbia, 134 F.R.D. 1, 3–4 (D.D.C. 1991) (court establishes facts in plaintiffs'

fails to disclose information required by the automatic disclosure rules, it may be precluded from using the witnesses or information, and may also be subjected to other sanctions.[583] Harsh sanctions such as dismissal or a default judgment will only be used if the court finds that the party has willfully refused to comply with an order compelling discovery.[584]

i. Responding to Discovery Requests You are under the same obligation to respond to discovery requests as the defendants, and you must follow the rules discussed in the preceding sections.[585] Refusing to cooperate with discovery will not help you, and if you willfully disobey a court order concerning discovery, the court may dismiss your case[586] and may impose costs or sanctions against you.[587]

---

favor where prison officials had ignored discovery requests for months); *In re* Anthracite Coal Antitrust Litigation, 82 F.R.D. 364, 369–70 (M.D.Pa. 1979) (barring defendants from submitting certain evidence, but refusing to enter a default judgment in the absence of repeated bad faith obstruction of discovery).

[583]Rule 37(c)(1), Fed.R.Civ.P., *citing* Rule 26(e)(1); *see* Tarlton v. Cumberland County Correctional Facility, 192 F.R.D. 165, 169–71 (D.N.J. 2000) (imposing sanction of attorneys' fees and expenses against defendants who failed to make initial disclosures). These disclosure provisions do not apply in *pro se* cases. *See* § K.2 of this chapter.

[584]National Hockey League v. Metropolitan Hockey Club, Inc., 427 U.S. 639, 643, 96 S. Ct. 2778 (1975); Webb v. District of Columbia, 189 F.R.D. 180, 185–92 (D.D.C. 1999) (default judgment entered for long history of discovery abuses); *see* Lawrence v. Bowersox, 297 F.3d 727, 733–34 (8th Cir. 2002) (affirming monetary sanctions for failing to produce videotape of incident; striking pleadings and entering a default judgment would have been justified).

[585]McDonald v. Head Criminal Court Supervisor Officer, 850 F.2d 121, 124–25 (2d Cir. 1988) (affirming dismissal of *pro se* prisoner's complaint for failing to "play by the rules" of discovery); Moon v. Newsome, 863 F.2d 835, 837 (11th Cir., 1989); Davidson v. Goord, 215 F.R.D. 73, 77 (W.D.N.Y. 2003) (directing plaintiff to comply with various requests). Courts may consider your *pro se* status in determining whether you have met your obligations. *See* Porter v. Martinez, 941 F.2d 732, 733–34 (9th Cir. 1991) (noting that *pro se* homeless litigant had tried to comply with discovery obligations).

[586]Lindstedt v. City of Granby, 238 F.3d 933, 937 (8th Cir. 2002) (dismissing where plaintiff refused to answer defendants' interrogatories because he believed the defendants had abused discovery in other litigation); Farnsworth v. City of Kansas City, Mo., 863 F.2d 33, 34 (8th Cir. 1988); Ebeh v. Tropical Sportswear Intern. Corp., 199 F.R.D. 696, 698 (M.D.Fla. 2001) (dismissing where plaintiff had walked out of deposition and failed to pay resulting sanctions); Quiles v. Beth Israel Medical Center, 168 F.R.D. 15, 18–19 (S.D.N.Y. 1996) (*pro se* plaintiff's refusal to comply with discovery order resulted in dismissal of lawsuit).

[587]Mungin v. Stephens, 164 F.R.D. 275, 279–81 (N.D.Ga. 1995) (prisoner fined $500 for refusing to go forward with deposition because he had filed a motion requesting that it be deferred; court declines to dismiss for failure promptly to pay sanction).

In general, you must answer questions that are put to you, whether at a deposition, in interrogatories, document requests, or requests for admissions,[588] unless they seek information that is privileged. You can object to the questions asked you at a deposition, but you must answer them. Your objections will then be considered at trial when you are asked the same questions and you seek to keep the answers out of evidence.[589] The only questions a deponent may refuse to answer are those that involve privileged information or that violate a limitation on evidence directed by the court.[590]

Parties may decline to answer interrogatories, document requests, or admission requests on grounds of extreme burdensomeness or lack of relevance,[591] but keep in mind that the scope of relevance is very broad in discovery, and you may be ordered to respond, or sanctioned if the court thinks your objections are meritless.

Defendants are entitled to ask in discovery about your background, including your criminal record, your prison disciplinary record, and matters that may affect your credibility, such as the use of aliases.[592] You may have to answer questions about other prisoners if the questions are relevant to the events you are suing about or if the other prisoners are witnesses. Your ability to assert your Fifth Amendment privilege against self-incrimination about information relevant to matters that you have put into issue by bringing the lawsuit is likely to be significantly limited.[593] You will not be compelled to give testimony if you "take the Fifth" about

---

[588]*See, e.g.*, Davidson v. Goord, 215 F.R.D. 73, 77 (W.D.N.Y. 2003) (requiring prisoner to answer interrogatories asking the basis for his damage claim).

[589]Rule 32(b), Fed.R.Civ.P. If the defendants offer parts of the actual deposition into evidence, you can ask that they be excluded if you made objections to the relevant questions on the record during the deposition.

[590]Rule 30(d)(1), Fed.R.Civ.P. If a deposition is "being conducted in bad faith or in a manner that unreasonably annoys, embarrasses, or oppresses the deponent or party," the deposition may be suspended long enough to make a motion to the court for relief. Rule 30(d)(3), Fed.R.Civ.P. It is improper to refuse to answer questions under any other circumstances. Dravo Corp. v. Liberty Mut. Ins. Co., 164 F.R.D. 70, 75 (D.Neb. 1995).

[591]If you make a burdensomeness objection, you must explain why answering would be burdensome. Davidson v. Goord, 215 F.R.D. 73, 77 (W.D.N.Y. 2003).

[592]Storie v. U.S., 142 F.R.D. 317, 319 (E.D.Mo.1992) (holding criminal convictions discoverable through interrogatories); McDonald v. Head Criminal Court Supervisor Officer, 117 F.R.D. 55, 57–8 (S.D.N.Y. 1987), *aff'd*, 850 F.2d 121 (2d Cir. 1988); *see* Hickman v. Taylor, 329 U.S. 495, 511, 67 S. Ct. 385 (1947) (discovery for purposes of impeachment permitted).

The use of such information at trial is discussed in § S.5(a) of this chapter.

[593]Serafino v. Hasbro, Inc., 82 F.3d 515, 517–18 (1st Cir. 1996) (stating "in the civil context . . . one party's assertion of his constitutional right should not obliterate another party's right to a fair proceeding"); McMullen v. Bay Ship Management, 335 F.3d 215, 218–19 (3d Cir. 2003) ("Although the privilege is available,

issues relevant to your lawsuit, but if you do so, the court may dismiss your case.[594] Some courts have held that lesser measures should be used where practical, such as staying the case until the risk of criminal prosecution has passed, or allowing an adverse inference that the testimony would be disadvantageous to the party taking the Fifth.[595] The same rules apply to the defendants whom you sue.[596]

A deposition notice may be accompanied by a request under Rule 34 to produce documents.[597] You should obey the notice unless you believe you have good grounds for refusing to produce the documents.[598] If that is the case, you should be prepared to explain those reasons at the deposition. If you do this, the defendants may take part of the deposition and then adjourn it subject to reopening it if they get the court to order you to produce the documents.

You should not bring documents that were not requested unless you will need to refer to them in answering questions. Defense counsel has the right to look at anything you refer to while testifying. Even if you don't refer to the documents, there may be an argument about whether defense counsel can look at them, which you should avoid if you don't need to have the documents with you.

You should not treat defendants' discovery as a confrontation. This is especially true at depositions, where defendants' lawyer may try to get you angry or upset so you will say something that hurts your case. You should answer the questions as honestly and as briefly as possible. If you do not understand a question, ask for an explanation.

You should always listen to the question and take a moment to think about your answer before responding. The best answer is always the truth, usually in as few words as possible.

Do not be sarcastic or a smart aleck. This will not advance your case, especially when recorded in a written transcript. If you do not know part or all of the answer to a question— e.g., if you don't know the precise date that something happened—say so.

When a party takes a deposition, the other party has the right to ask questions at the end. At your deposition, if you feel that the defendants have managed to confuse you and get you to say damaging things, you are allowed to give additional testimony to set the record straight. Do not do this unless there was some genuine confusion earlier in the deposition. Instead of clarifying the transcript, you may only be offering the defendants additional information they had overlooked, and they will have the right to ask you more questions about your clarifying testimony.

Defendants may seek a physical or mental examination of you pursuant to Rule 35, Fed.R.Civ.P. A court may direct such an examination by "a suitably licensed or certified examiner" if your "mental or physical condition—including blood group—is in controversy."[599] The party seeking such an examination must make a motion, and if it is granted must provide on request a copy of the examiner's report;[600] after doing that, it may request from the party against whom the order was entered production of reports of any other examinations of the same condition.[601] Courts may enter further orders to safeguard the fairness of the proceeding when a Rule 35 examination is ordered.[602] The report resulting from a Rule 35 examination is not necessarily admissible in court.[603] A Rule 35 motion cannot be used by a plaintiff as

---

prejudice to the other party must be minimized and an equitable resolution adopted.").

[594]Serafino v. Hasbro, Inc., 82 F.3d at 517–19 (1st Cir. 1996); Penn Communications Specialties, Inc. v. Hess, 65 F.R.D. 510 (E.D. Pa. 1975); Brown v. Ames, 346 F. Supp. 1176 (D.Minn. 1972).

[595]See, e.g., McMullen v. Bay Ship Management, 335 F.3d at 219; Jones v. City of Indianapolis, 216 F.R.D. 440, 452 (S.D.Ind. 2003) (staying discovery about death in police custody for 90 days where criminal investigation was ongoing).

[596]Harris v. City of Chicago, 266 F.3d 750, 754 (7th Cir. 2001) (where police officer took the Fifth at his deposition, trial court should have precluded his testimony or allowed him to be impeached concerning taking the Fifth); Gutierrez-Rodriguez v. Cartagena, 882 F.2d 553, 576–77 (1st Cir. 1989) (affirming district court's refusal to allow defendant to testify at trial when he asserted Fifth Amendment privilege during discovery); Banks v. Yokemick, 177 F. Supp. 2d 239, 245 (S.D.N.Y. 2001) (noting police officer was precluded from preventing a defense on matters as to which he took the Fifth).

[597]Rule 30(b)(2), Fed.R.Civ.P. That would mean you have 30 days to comply with it, see Rule 34(b), Fed.R.Civ.P., unless the court directed or you agreed to a shorter time.

[598]The legitimate scope of discovery, which is broad, is discussed in §§ K.2.a and K.2.b of this chapter.

[599]Rule 35(a), Fed.R.Civ.P. The mere fact that a plaintiff alleges mental distress does not put his mental condition sufficiently in controversy to merit a Rule 35 examination. Bowen v. Parking Auth. of the City of Camden, 214 F.R.D. 188, 194 (D.N.J. 2003) ("No specific psychiatric malady has been alleged nor has Bowen asserted a claim of unusually severe emotional distress within the meaning of Rule 35."); Ricks v. Abbott Laboratories, 198 F.R.D. 647, 648–49 (D.Md. 2001) (Rule 35 requires more than a showing of relevance; the alleged emotional distress must be unusually severe, require an expert to explain, or be described in clinical terms for Rule 35 to apply).

[600]Rule 35(b)(1), Fed.R.Civ.P.

[601]Rule 35(b)(3).

[602]For example, in Hodges v. Keane, 145 F.R.D. 332 (S.D.N.Y. 1993), the court ordered a mental examination of the prisoner plaintiff based on defendants' argument that the plaintiff had a history of paranoid schizophrenia that affected his perceptions and could affect his trial testimony. However, it also required the defendants to pay for an expert to be hired by the plaintiff to address the results of the examination. Hodges, 145 F.R.D. at 334–35; see Sidari v. Orleans County, 174 F.R.D. 275, 291 (W.D.N.Y. 1996) (requiring mental health examination to be tape-recorded).

[603]In Hodges v. Keane, discussed in the previous footnote, the court later excluded from evidence the report of the mental examination, which diagnosed the plaintiff with "anti-social personality disorder," since his mental health records showed that he had been found free of psychiatric symptoms five years after the incident he sued about, and the trial was being held 13 years after that incident. Therefore, the court said, the mental examination

a way to get medical care.[604] Even if defendants do not seek a Rule 35 examination, or the court does not grant it, they may take other discovery concerning your mental or physical condition using other discovery methods,[605] subject to any applicable privileges.[606]

3. Expert Witnesses

Expert witnesses are persons with "scientific, technical, or other specialized knowledge" who are allowed to testify to their opinions on matters within their expertise.[607] In prison and other civil rights litigation, experts commonly testify concerning their opinions on subjects such as prison medical and mental health care,[608] the psychological effects of mistreatment by staff or harsh conditions of confinement,[609] prison security procedures,[610] police procedure, and the use of force.[611]

The Federal Rules require persons who are to testify as experts to be identified at least 90 days before trial (or 30 days later if the expert is solely to rebut defendants' expert testimony), and to submit at that time a written report including the expert's opinion, the data forming the basis for it, the witness's qualifications including publications, a list of other cases in which the expert testified, and what the expert is being paid.[612] Prison officials will sometimes wish to call their own employees, or themselves, as experts; courts have disagreed whether, in such cases, the same disclosure requirements apply as to any other expert.[613] Unless the court has already directed defendants to provide this information, you should serve an interrogatory asking them to identify all persons that they intend to qualify as expert witnesses or obtain opinion testimony from, and requesting the information that Rule 26(a)(2) requires them to produce.

Expert witnesses who will testify may be deposed after they submit their reports.[614] Neither the attorney–client nor the work-product privilege applies to communications or material provided to an expert witness, including one employed by the defendants, so you would be allowed to inquire into any communications from any of the defendants or their lawyers to the employee-expert.[615]

---

report was too remote to be relevant to credibility. Hodges v. Keane, 886 F. Supp. 352, 356 (S.D.N.Y. 1995).

[604]Green v. Branson, 108 F.3d 1296, 1304 (10th Cir. 1997).

[605]Merrill v. Waffle House, Inc., 227 F.R.D. 467, 471 (N.D.Tex. 2005); Bowen v. Parking Auth. of the City of Camden, 214 F.R.D. 188, 195 (D.N.J. 2003).

[606]*In re* Sims, 534 F.3d 117, 134–42 (2d Cir. 2008) (holding plaintiff did not forfeit his psychotherapist–patient privilege where he did not pursue damages for mental or emotional injuries).

[607]Rule 702, Fed.R.Evid., permits persons with "scientific, technical, or other specialized knowledge" to testify as experts and state their opinions on matters within their expertise. The scope and admissibility of expert testimony is discussed further in § S.1.e of this chapter.

[608]*See* McKinney v. Anderson, 924 F.2d 1500, 1511 (9th Cir.) (reversing decision that expert could not be appointed; suggesting court appoint expert to analyze health effects of secondary cigarette smoke), *vacated on other grounds sub nom.* Helling v. McKinney, 502 U.S. 903, 112 S. Ct. 291 (1991); Greason v. Kemp, 891 F.2d 829, 835 (11th Cir. 1990); Cabrales v. County of Los Angeles, 864 F.2d 1454, 1460 (9th Cir. 1988), *vacated*, 490 U.S. 1087 (1989), *reinstated*, 886 F.2d 235 (1989).

[609]*See* Jordan v. Gardner, 986 F.2d 1521, 1525–26 (9th Cir. 1993) (en banc); Davis v. Locke, 936 F.2d 1208, 1213 (11th Cir. 1991); Davenport v. DeRobertis, 844 F.2d 1310, 1315 (7th Cir. 1988); Fisher v. Koehler, 692 F. Supp. 1519, 1543–46 (S.D.N.Y. 1988), *aff'd*, 902 F.2d 2 (2d Cir. 1990).

[610]Taylor v. Michigan Dep't of Corrections, 69 F.3d 76, 82–83 (6th Cir. 1995); Marria v. Broaddus, 200 F. Supp. 2d 280, 287–88 (S.D.N.Y. 2002); Ruiz v. Estelle, 154 F. Supp. 2d 975, 987, 992–94 (S.D.Tex. 2001).

[611]*See* Champion v. Outlook Nashville, Inc., 380 F.3d 893, 907–09 (6th Cir. 2004); Samples v. City of Atlanta, 916 F.2d 1548, 1551–52 (11th Cir. 1990); Russo v. City of Cincinnati, 953 F.2d 1036, 1047 (6th Cir. 1992); Slakan v. Porter, 737 F.2d 368, 375 (4th Cir. 1984).

[612]Rule 26(a)(2), Fed.R.Civ.P.; Hilt v. SFC Inc., 170 F.R.D. 182, 185 (D.Kan. 1997) (expert's report "must provide the substantive rationale in detail with respect to the basis and reasons for the proffered opinions. It must explain factually why and how the witness has reached them."); *see also* Fidelity National Title Ins. Co. of New York v. Intercounty National Title Ins. Co., 412 F.3d 745, 750–51 (7th Cir. 2005) (litigant "must disclose any information 'considered' by the litigant's testifying expert" including "whatever materials are given him to review in preparing his testimony, even if in the end he does not rely on them in formulating his expert opinion, because such materials often contain effective ammunition for cross-examination"). The rule does not explicitly state that parties may obtain in discovery copies of previous publications or expert reports, transcripts of previous expert testimony or depositions, etc., but in practice such discovery is often done, so you may wish to seek such materials if they are about similar issues to those involved in your case.

[613]*Compare* McCulloch v. Hartford Life and Acc. Ins. Co. 223 F.R.D. 26, 27–28 (D.Conn.2004) (holding employees must comply with same discovery requirements as other experts), *clarified*, 2004 WL 1688529 (D.Conn., Apr. 26, 2004) and cases cited *with* Bank of China, New York Branch v. NBM LLC, 359 F.3d 171, 182 n.10 (2d Cir. 2004) (holding employee expert need not file report); Bowling v. Hasbro, Inc., 2006 WL 2345941, *1–2 (D.R.I. 2006); *see* Rice v. Kempker, 374 F.3d 675, 681 (8th Cir. 2004) (treating opinions of prison officials as lay opinion based on their personal knowledge, holding they need not have been identified as experts).

[614]Rule 26(b)(4)(A), Fed.R.Civ.P. Parties sometimes retain experts to assist them in preparing for trial, but do not present their testimony at trial. Discovery of their opinions is allowed only under very limited circumstances. Rule 26(b)(4)(B), Fed.R.Civ.P.

[615]Dyson Technology Ltd. v. Maytag. Corp., 241 F.R.D. 247, 251–52 (D.Del. 2007); Estate of Manship v. U.S., 236 F.R.D. 291, 295 n.3 (M.D. La. 2006), *vacated on other grounds*, 237 F.R.D. 141 (M.D.La. 2006); JB and Jeb by and through Palmer v. Asarco, Inc., 225 F.R.D. 258, 261 (N.D.Okla. 2004). *Contra, In re* Teleglobe Communications Corp., 392 B.R. 561, 576–77 (Bkrtcy.D.Del. 2008). *See also* Granger v. Wisner, 656 P.2d 1238, 1242 (Ariz. 1982) (holding attorney–client privilege does not cover communications between a lawyer and expert witness).

Many prison cases cannot be won without the use of an expert[616] and will be lost at summary judgment or trial for lack of expert evidence.[617] Others will be made much stronger or weaker by the presence or absence of such testimony. However, few *pro se* prisoners can afford to hire an expert. In general, experts are expensive; typically the costs include an hourly rate to the expert for performing the tasks that are necessary to form a reliable opinion about the case, such as reviewing documents, viewing the area where the incident happened, reviewing discovery responses and depositions of defendants (if any), preparing a report, and testifying, plus the travel costs of coming to court and to the place where the relevant events happened. In addition, preparing and presenting an expert is a difficult task for someone without legal training.

If your case will require an expert, or the defendants have said that they will call one, you may wish to ask the court to appoint counsel, citing the need for an expert (the basis of which you should explain) and your inability to afford one among the reasons. The importance of expert testimony is one of the factors that supports appointment of counsel,[618] though getting counsel will still be a long shot.

If you can't get counsel appointed, you may wish to ask the court to appoint an independent expert, which it may do on its own motion or that of a party.[619] Such an expert works for the court and not for the plaintiff.[620] Expert appointments have been made, or suggested by appellate courts, in several prison cases,[621] though most requests for an expert

are denied.[622] The court is not required to appoint an expert, even if prison officials have listed an expert as a witness.[623] You must explain to the court how the expert will assist the court or jury in understanding the issues.[624] You must also make this request timely.[625] If the court does appoint an expert, it can order that prison officials pay the entire costs of the expert if you are indigent.[626]

---

[616]For example, in medical malpractice cases, expert evidence is necessary to establish the required standard of care and to show that defendants deviated from it, unless the issues are within the common knowledge of lay people. *See* Ch. 2, § F.5, nn.796–799. Cases alleging deliberate indifference to serious medical needs in violation of the Eighth Amendment may also require expert evidence, depending on what is at issue. *See* Ch. 2, § F.1, n.326, and § F.2, n.395. (As pointed out in the sections just cited, sometimes something less than a retained expert witness can meet this requirement.)

[617]The Supreme Court recently confirmed the importance of expert testimony in upholding a grant of summary judgment against a prisoner on a First Amendment issue, stating that the prisoners "did not offer any fact-based *or expert-based* refutation [of prison officials' argument] in the manner the rules provide." Beard v. Banks, 548 U.S. 521, 534, 126 S. Ct. 2572 (2006) (emphasis supplied). Be sure to quote this to the court if you request appointment of an expert or of counsel in a challenge to prison policies.

[618]*See* n.243 of this chapter.

[619]Rule 706(a), Fed.R.Evid.

[620]General Electric Co. v. Joiner, 522 U.S. 136, 150, 118 S. Ct. 512 (1997); Pedraza v. Jones, 71 F.3d 194, 197 (5th Cir. 1995).

[621]Steele v. Shah, 87 F.3d 1266, 1271 (11th Cir. 1996) (stating that appointment of an expert for the indigent plaintiff may "avoid a wholly one-sided presentation of opinions on the issue"); Taylor v. Michigan Dep't of Corrections, 69 F.3d 76, 82–83 (6th Cir. 1995) (effect of overcrowding on risk of rape); Williams v. McKeithen, 963 F.2d 70, 71–72 (5th Cir. 1992) (jail conditions); McKinney v. Anderson, 924 F.2d 1500, 1510–11 (9th Cir.) (suggesting the

appointment of expert witnesses on the health risks of environmental tobacco smoke), *vacated and remanded*, 112 S. Ct. 291 (1991), *reinstated*, 959 F.2d 853 (9th Cir. 1992), *aff'd sub nom.* Helling v. McKinney, 509 U.S. 25, 113 S. Ct. 2475 (1993); Crabtree v.# Collins, 900 F.2d 79, 81 (6th Cir. 1990) (noting appointment of an expert neurologist by the district court); Smith v. Jenkins, 919 F.2d 90, 94 (8th Cir. 1990) (suggesting that the district court "may" appoint an independent expert or obtain an opinion from the doctor who treated the plaintiff before his imprisonment); Fugitt v. Jones, 549 F.2d 1001, 1006 (5th Cir. 1977) (noting court's authority to appoint expert); Reynolds v. Goord, 103 F. Supp. 2d 316, 318–19 (S.D.N.Y. 2000) (noting appointment of medical expert); Delker v. Maass, 843 F. Supp. 1390, 1395 (D.Or. 1994) (noting appointment of medical expert); Balla v. Board of Corrections, 656 F. Supp. 1108, 1110 (D.Idaho 1987) (appointing expert on prison crowding); *see* Webster v. Sowders. 846 F.2d 1032, 1038–39 (6th Cir. 1988) (requiring findings of fact and conclusions of law to support appointment of an asbestos-removal expert); *see also* Christy v. Robinson, 216 F. Supp. 2d 398, 404–05, 411 (D.N.J. 2002) (noting that court directed prison medical provider to arrange for plaintiff's examination by independent doctors); Hodges v. Keane, 145 F.R.D. 332, 335–36 (N.D.N.Y. 1993) (requiring defendants who sought to have their psychiatrist examine the plaintiff to pay for the indigent plaintiff to hire his own expert).

[622]*See, e.g.*, Gaviria v. Reynolds, 476 F.3d 940, 945–46 (D.C. Cir. 2007) (affirming denial of appointment where prisoner had not demonstrated independently that there was a serious issue as to his medical care); Ledford v. Sullivan, 105 F.3d 354, 359 (7th Cir. 1997) (affirming denial of appointment where medical issues did not appear to be complex).

[623]*See, e.g.*, Ledford v. Sullivan, 105 F.3d at 356, 358–59 (no abuse of discretion denying request to appoint medical expert in case where defendants presented one). *But see* Spann v. Roper, 453 F.3d 1007, 1008 (8th Cir. 2006) (per curiam) (disapproving district court's denial of motion for an expert followed by grant of summary judgment to defendants because plaintiff lacked expert evidence in medical case).

[624]*See, e.g.*, Walker v. American Home Shield Long Term Disability Plan, 180 F.3d 1065, 1071 (9th Cir. 1999) (affirming appointment of independent expert where district court apparently "found the evidence concerning fibromyalgia to be confusing and conflicting"); Steele v. Shah, 87 F.3d 1266, 1271 (11th Cir. 1996) (stating that appointment of an expert for the indigent plaintiff may "avoid a wholly one-sided presentation of opinions on the issue").

[625]*See* Hannah v. U.S., 523 F.3d 597 (5th Cir. 2008) (affirming refusal to appoint expert, and dismissal of case for lack of expert testimony, where prisoner did not make the request before the deadline for naming expert witness and did not ask to have that deadline extended).

[626]Rule 706(b), Fed.R.Evid. ("In other civil actions and proceedings, the compensation [of an expert] shall be paid by the parties in such proportion and at such times as the court directs,

L. SUMMARY JUDGMENT

Summary judgment is a procedure designed to dispose of cases without trial[627] where there are no factual disputes that require a trial. One court has called it "the 'put up or shut up' moment in a lawsuit, when a party must show what evidence it has that would convince a trier of fact to accept its version of the events."[628] If you get past initial screening and a motion to dismiss, you will probably face a summary judgment motion, and you should plan to deal with it from the time you start your case.

Summary judgment is to be granted if the record before the court shows "that there is no genuine issue as to any material fact and that the movant is entitled to a judgment as a matter of law."[629] If the court finds that there is a genuine issue of material fact, then there will be a trial to determine the facts.

A "material" fact is one that "might affect the outcome of the suit under the governing law. . . . Factual disputes that are irrelevant or unnecessary will not be counted."[630] A "genuine" issue exists "if evidence is such that a reasonable jury could return a verdict for the nonmoving party."[631]

In determining whether there is a genuine issue of material fact, the court must view all facts and make all reasonable inferences in favor of the nonmoving party[632] (*i.e.*, if defendants move for summary judgment, the court should accept your version of the facts, and vice versa.) Circumstantial evidence can create an issue of material fact barring summary judgment,[633] as can important unanswered questions in the moving party's factual claims.[634]

---

and thereafter charged in like manner as other costs."). A number of circuits have recognized that Rule 706(b) grants a district court the discretion to apportion all the costs of an expert to one side. *See, e.g.,* Ledford v. Sullivan, 105 F.3d 354, 360–61 (7th Cir. 1997); Steele v. Shah, 87 F.3d 1266, 1271 (11th Cir. 1996) (remanding the case because the lower court failed to exercise its discretion to appoint and compensate an expert if the plaintiff was in fact indigent); McKinney v. Anderson, 924 F.2d 1500, 1511 (9th Cir.), *vacated and remanded on other grounds,* 502 U.S. 903, 112 S. Ct. 291 (1991) (finding that the phrase "such proportion as the court directs," *in an appropriate case,* permits the district court to apportion all costs to one side); Webster v. Sowders, 846 F.2d 1032, 1038–39 (6th Cir. 1988) (stating that "[a] District Court has authority to apportion costs under this rule [706(b)], including excusing impecunious parties from their share"); U.S. Marshals Serv. v. Means, 741 F.2d 1053, 1059 (8th Cir. 1984) (stating that discretionary power to advance fees of expert witnesses should be exercised *only under compelling circumstances*). *Contra,* Boring v. Kozakiewicz, 833 F.2d 468, 473–74 (3d Cir. 1987) (holding there is no way to pay experts appointed for indigents under Rule 706). *Cf.* Hodges v. Keane 145 F.R.D. 332, 335–36 (S.D.N.Y. 1993) (court ordered defendants to pay, pursuant to Fed.R.Civ.P. 26(c), the cost for the indigent plaintiff to hire an expert to address or rebut any opinion that defendants' expert may proffer at trial).

[627]This section discusses summary judgment in federal court. State courts will generally have a similar procedure, but the rules and the terminology may be different from those in federal court.

[628]Schacht v. Wisconsin Dep't Of Corr., 175 F.3d 497, 504 (7th Cir.1999); *see* Celotex Corp. v. Catrett, 477 U.S. 317, 323, 106 S. Ct. 2548 (1986) (party must submit evidence supporting each element of its case to avoid summary judgment).

[629]Rule 56(c)(2), Fed.R.Civ.P. If there is no genuine factual issue, summary judgment does not violate the right to a jury trial, since the purpose of trials is only to decide factual issues. *See* Plaisance v. Phelps, 845 F.2d 107, 108 (5th Cir. 1988).

Summary judgment cannot be granted just because a party doesn't respond to a summary judgment motion; the moving party still has to show that it is entitled to win based on the record. Reed v. Bennett, 312 F.3d 1190, 1194–95 (10th Cir. 2002); Martinez v. Stanford, 323 F.3d 1178, 1182 (9th Cir. 2003); Amaker v. Foley, 274 F.3d 677, 681 (2d Cir. 2001).

[630]Anderson v. Liberty Lobby, Inc., 477 U.S. 242, 248, 106 S. Ct. 2505 (1986); Gray v. York Newspapers, Inc., 957 F.2d 1070, 1078 (3d Cir. 1992).

[631]Anderson v. Liberty Lobby, Inc., 477 U.S. at 248.

[632]Matsushita Electric Industrial Co., Ltd. v. Zenith Radio Corp., 475 U.S. 574, 587, 106 S. Ct. 1348 (1986); *see* Curry v. Scott, 249 F.3d 493, 507–08 (6th Cir. 2001) (where record showed history of misconduct by officer, court should not have inferred on summary judgment that higher officials did not know about it on their motion for summary judgment); Fischl v. Armitage, 128 F.3d 50, 56–59 (2d Cir. 1997) (showing proper and improper inferences from record in prisoner assault case); Miller v. Leathers, 913 F.2d 1085, 1088 (4th Cir. 1990) (per curiam) ("Miller's version of the incident supports a reasonable inference that Leathers intended to provoke an incident so as to allow Leathers to beat him under the guise of maintaining order or defending himself."); Baker v. Zlochowon, 741 F. Supp. 436, 439–40 (S.D.N.Y. 1990) (decision not to pay plaintiff for his absences from work and to transfer him to a lower paying job after he filed a lawsuit challenging prison officials' actions could sustain reasonable inference of retaliation sufficient to defeat summary judgment); Wilson v. City of Chicago, 707 F. Supp. 379, 381–82 (N.D.Ill. 1989) (summary judgment could not be granted to a police supervisor whose conduct permitted the inference that he condoned or encouraged excessive force).

[633]*See* Fischl v. Armitage, 128 F.3d at 56 (the fact that one defendant was assigned to a particular control area and was present there raised a factual question whether he unlocked the plaintiff's cell, even though other officers also had keys to the area); Smith v. Maschner, 899 F.2d 940, 949 (10th Cir. 1990) (plaintiff's retaliation claim supported by "suspicious timing of his discipline, coincidental transfers of his witnesses and assistants, and an alleged pattern by defendants of blocking his access to legal materials and assistance"); Simms v. Hardesty, 303 F. Supp. 2d 656, 667 (D.Md. 2003) (plaintiff's severe injuries raised a factual issue as to whether he was beaten, though the defendants denied it and he could not remember because of his injuries), *aff'd,* 104 Fed.Appx. 853 (4th Cir. 2004) (unpublished).

[634]In *Bradich v. City of Chicago,* 413 F.3d 688 (7th Cir. 2005), an arrestee killed himself shortly after being locked up in the police station. Although the three officers involved swore that they were "frantically trying to save" him, the court could not grant summary judgment based on that assertion because to do so would have been to draw inferences in the moving party's favor. There were three officers and they waited 10 minutes to summon help. The court asked why could one of them not have called for help

The court is not supposed to decide disputed facts or assess credibility on a summary judgment motion.[635] Thus, a court may not grant summary judgment because it thinks the prisoner's assertions about an incident or an injury are inconsistent with prison medical records.[636] Courts have held that a litigant cannot create a factual dispute by contradicting his own earlier sworn statement, but they have cautioned that this rule must be limited to cases of clear contradiction and those where it appears that a summary judgment affidavit is intended to create a sham factual issue. [637]

Summary judgment may be granted on the whole case or on part of the case. It may be granted on some legal claims and not others;[638] for or against some parties but not others;[639] or on liability but not on damages.[640] If one party moves for summary judgment, the court may grant summary judgment for the other party if the record before it so justifies.[641]

The court is supposed to decide a summary judgment motion based on facts that are properly put before it. This usually means facts stated on personal knowledge in sworn affidavits or declarations under penalty of perjury.[642] Declarations or affidavits by prisoners have the same status as those by anyone else, and it is improper to discount or disregard them on summary judgment.[643] Other documents containing sworn statements—depositions, interrogatory answers, etc.—may be used on a summary

---

immediately? Why did the one officer who had CPR training not use it? *Bradich*, 413 F.3d at 691.

[635]Masson v. New Yorker Magazine, Inc., 501 U.S. 496, 520, 111 S. Ct. 2419 (1991); Anderson v. Liberty Lobby, Inc., 477 U.S. 242, 255, 106 S. Ct. 2505 (1986); Wilson v. Williams; 997 F.2d 348, 350–51 (7th Cir. 1993); Gray v. Spillman, 925 F.2d 90, 95 (4th Cir. 1991); Titran v. Ackman, 893 F.2d 145, 147 (7th Cir. 1990).

[636]Scott v. Coughlin, 344 F.3d 282, 289–90 (2d Cir. 2003) (court should not have granted summary judgment based on perceived disparity between plaintiff's sworn statement and medical records; doing so was an impermissible credibility determination and weighing of contradictory evidence); Calhoun v. Thomas, 360 F. Supp. 2d 1264, 1280 (M.D.Ala. 2005) (failure of an emergency room physician to notice visible injuries did not show force used was *de minimis*, since the doctor's main concern was an earlier gunshot wound, and other evidence showed severe swelling and discoloration); Sanders-El v. Spielman, 38 F. Supp. 2d 438, 439 n.1 (D.Md. 1999) (stating "it would seem that the law must entertain the possibility that health care providers in a prison setting might bring certain biases to their occupation"); *see* Brooks v. Kyler, 204 F.3d 102, 107–08 & n.4 (3d Cir. 2000) (noting that *pro se* prisoners generally cannot get independent medical evidence and their own sworn statements are the best evidence available to them); Green v. Branson, 108 F.3d 1296, 1304 (10th Cir. 1997) (noting claim of falsification of medical records after a use of force).

[637]In *Jeffreys v. City of New York*, 426 F.3d 549 (2d Cir. 2005), the court held that summary judgment was proper despite factual disputes where the plaintiff's factual presentation was so hopelessly contradictory that no reasonable person could believe it, but it went on to caution that if there is "a plausible explanation for discrepancies," the court should not "disregard the later testimony because of an earlier account that was *ambiguous, confusing, or simply incomplete*." *Jeffreys*, 426 F.3d at 555 n.2 (emphasis by court, citations omitted); *see* DeSpain v. Uphoff, 264 F.3d 965, 972 n.1 (10th Cir. 2001) ("Conflicts between the sworn testimony in an affidavit and that of a deposition are not automatic grounds for disregarding the affidavit, unless the record suggests the affidavit likely was introduced merely to create a 'sham fact issue' for purposes of summary judgment."); Thomas v. Roach, 165 F.3d 137, 144 (2d Cir. 1999) (plaintiff's affidavit did not contradict his "vague and inconclusive" prior statements); Hayes v. New York City Dep't of Correction, 84 F.3d 614, 619–20 (2d Cir. 1996) (prior deposition testimony was not clear and circumstances did not suggest plaintiff was creating a sham issue).

[638]*See* Spann v. Roper, 453 F.3d 1007, 1008–09 (8th Cir. 2006) (per curiam) (affirming summary judgment for prison nurse for giving plaintiff the wrong medication, but denying summary judgment for failure to respond to his symptoms afterwards); Richardson v. Coughlin, 763 F. Supp. 1228 (S.D.N.Y. 1991) (granting summary judgment to the plaintiff on one issue and to the defendants on one issue, and denying it on a third issue).

[639]*See, e.g.*, Ziemba v. Armstrong, 430 F.3d 623 (2d Cir. 2005) (supervisor dismissed based on lack of evidence of liability whereas genuine issue of material fact as to whether prison nurse and medic were deliberately indifferent to inmate's serious medical needs precluded summary judgment); Curry v. Scott, 249 F.3d 493, 499 (6th Cir. 2001) (supervisors dismissed and individual officer summary judgment motion denied).

[640]Rule 56(d)(2), Fed.R.Civ.P.; *see* Patterson v. Coughlin, 905 F.2d 564, 570–71 (2d Cir. 1990) (affirming summary judgment on liability but reversing summary judgment for damages because of factual dispute over the amount of damages); Alexander v. Perrill, 836 F. Supp. 701, 706 (D.Ariz. 1993) (summary judgment is granted as to liability).

[641]Ramsey v. Coughlin, 94 F.3d 71, 73–74 (2d Cir. 1996) (cautioning that the moving party must have a chance to contest summary judgment for the other party, and must have had sufficient chance for discovery); Wilson v. Continental Development Co., 112 F. Supp. 2d 648, 663 (W.D.Mich. 1999) (citing Eckford-El v. Toombs, 760 F. Supp. 1267, 1272 (W.D.Mich. 1991)).

[642]"A supporting or opposing affidavit must be made on personal knowledge, set out facts that would be admissible in evidences, and show that the affiant is competent to testify on the matters stated." Rule 56(e)(1), Fed.R.Civ.P.

A federal statute provides that in federal court proceedings written declarations made under penalty of perjury are acceptable in lieu of notarized affidavits. 28 U.S.C. § 1746. Affidavits and declarations are discussed in Ch. 11, § C.

[643]Scott v. Coughlin, 344 F.3d 282, 289 (2d Cir. 2003); Carroll v. Yates, 362 F.3d 984, 985 (7th Cir. 2004); Taylor v. Rodriguez, 238 F.3d 188, 195 (2d Cir. 2001) (prisoner's affidavit was sufficient without corroboration by other affidavits or documentation); Wilson v. Williams, 997 F.2d 348, 350–51 (7th Cir. 1993) (rejecting district court's view that the plaintiff's affidavits could not establish a material factual issue); Harris v. Ostrout, 65 F.3d 912, 916–17 (11th Cir. 1995) (noting that lower court had "overlooked" prisoners' affidavits); Gawloski v. Dallman, 803 F. Supp. 103, 111 (S.D.Ohio 1992); Rembert v. Holland, 735 F. Supp. 733, 737–38 (W.D.Mich. 1990).

judgment motion.[644] Unsworn statements generally cannot be considered.[645] If the facts you need to establish are not within your personal knowledge (*e.g.*, if another inmate saw an officer remove your legal papers from your cell), you will usually need the affidavit or declaration of the person who does have personal knowledge; hearsay cannot be considered on summary judgment[646] unless it falls into an exception to the hearsay rule.[647] The court also cannot consider

statements, even if they are in affidavit or declaration form, that are merely conclusions that do not state any factual basis.[648]

Documentary evidence may also be used to support or oppose a motion for summary judgment as long as it would be admissible at trial under the rules of evidence. Documents must be authenticated to be considered, which technically means that "a sworn or certified copy must be attached to or served with the affidavit."[649] In practice, courts often accept less formal means of authentication.[650] When you submit documents, you must "lay a foundation" for each one by explaining in your affidavit or declaration what it is and how you got it and providing enough other information for the court to determine if it is admissible.[651] Documents that would be inadmissible at trial cannot be considered on summary judgment.[652]

The summary judgment rule refers to "the pleadings, the discovery and disclosure materials on file, and any affidavits. . . ."[653] Discovery and disclosure materials are

---

[644]Thus, if the defendants take your deposition, you can use the transcript on a summary judgment motion since it was taken under oath. *See* Scicluna v. Wells, 345 F.3d 441, 445 (6th Cir. 2003) (plaintiff's deposition testimony that he told a prison employee about a risk of assault was enough to defeat summary judgment; documentary support was unnecessary); Bozeman v. Estate of Haggard, 302 F. Supp. 2d 1310, 1311 & n.1 (M.D.Ala. 2004) (deposition could be used on summary judgment even unsigned, since it was taken under oath), *aff'd*, 422 F.3d 1265 (11th Cir. 2005).

[645]Woloszyn v. County of Lawrence, 396 F.3d 314, 323 (3d Cir. 2005) (in a jail suicide case, an unsworn statement by another prisoner that the deceased prisoner had been yelling, screaming, and kicking for 45 minutes before he killed himself was prperly excluded from consideration (citing Adickes v. S.H. Kress & Co., 398 U.S. 144, 158 n.17, 90 S. Ct. 1598 (1970)); Okoye v. Univ. of Tex. Houston Health Sci. Ctr., 245 F.3d 507, 515 (5th Cir. 2001) (holding that an unsworn statement was not competent summary judgment evidence because it did not meet the requirements of Rule 56(e)); Mays v. Rhodes, 255 F.3d 644, 648 (8th Cir. 2001) (unsworn statements about death of a prisoner could not be considered); Mason v. Clark, 920 F.2d 493, 495 (8th Cir. 1990) (summary judgment cannot be granted based on an unsigned affidavit); Beyah v. Coughlin, 789 F.2d 986, 989 (2d Cir. 1986) (unverified letters could not support summary judgment); Harris v. Dugger, 757 F. Supp. 1359, 1363–64 (S.D.Fla. 1991) (prisoner's unsworn statement was insufficient to resist summary judgment).

There are some exceptions to the rule against considering unsworn statements. Some courts have procedures under which they request a "report" from prison officials, and that report may be treated like an affidavit on a summary judgment motion. Northington v. Jackson, 973 F.2d 1518, 1521 (10th Cir. 1992). Also, some unsworn statements may be admissible as admissions of a party defendant. *See* § T.2 of this chapter for a discussion of admissions.

[646]Boyce v. Moore, 314 F.3d 884, 889 (7th Cir. 2002) (plaintiff's testimony about a prison supervisor's callous racist remark about his complaints was inadmissible because the plaintiff heard about it from another prisoner); Ellis v. Washington County and Johnson City, Tenn., 198 F.3d 225, 229 (6th Cir. 1999); Beyah v. Coughlin, 789 F.2d at 989 (attorney's hearsay affidavit was insufficient).

This is where you should plan from the beginning for the summary judgment motion. If your case depends on testimony from another person, you should try to get an affidavit or declaration from that person right away, because he may not be available to you later when you want to make a summary judgment motion or have to respond to the defendants' motion.

[647]Stelwagon Mfg. Co. v. Tarmac Roofing Sys., Inc., 63 F.3d 1267, 1275 n.17 (3d Cir. 1995) (hearsay statements can be considered on a motion for summary judgment if they are capable

of admission at trial). The hearsay rule and its exceptions are discussed in § T.2 of this chapter.

[648]Fitzgerald v. Corrections Corp. of America, 403 F.3d 1134, 1142–43 (10th Cir. 2005) (an expert affidavit stating that the failure to treat plaintiff's medical condition was appropriate, without explaining the basis for the conclusion, could not support summary judgment even with no contrary evidence); Palmer v. Marion County, 327 F.3d 588, 596–97 (7th Cir. 2003) (affidavit alleging racial discrimination but citing no facts in support could not defeat summary judgment); Samuels v. Mockry, 77 F.3d 34, 36 (2d Cir. 1996) (court should not have granted summary judgment based on conclusory allegations, not based on personal knowledge, of the reason for plaintiff's placement in restrictive conditions); Weber v. Dell, 804 F.2d 796, 802 (2d Cir. 1986) (sheriff's assertion that 70% of arrestees carry contraband in jail, "a conclusory estimate based neither on personal observation nor on an analysis of the jail's records," was an improper basis for summary judgment); *see also* n.670, below.

[649]Rule 56(e)(1), Fed.R.Civ.P.; Carmona v. Toledo, 215 F.3d 124, 131 (1st Cir. 2000); Moore v. Holbrook, 2 F.3d 697, 699 (6th Cir. 1993); Wells v. Franzen, 777 F.2d 1258, 1262 (7th Cir. 1985) (medical records unaccompanied by certifying affidavits or other means of authentication should not have been considered on summary judgment motion). *See* § S.4 of this chapter for further discussion of authenticity.

[650]*See, e.g.*, Bozeman v. Orum, 199 F. Supp. 2d 1216, 1222–23 (M.D.Ala. 2002) (unauthenticated documents could be considered if it was apparent they could be authenticated at trial), *aff'd*, 422 F.3d 1265 (11th Cir. 2005); Payne v. Collins, 986 F. Supp. 1036, 1056 (E.D.Tex. 1997) (the fact that the adverse party produced the document in discovery held adequate to establish its authenticity).

[651]The rules of evidence and the means of laying a foundation for the admission of documents into evidence are discussed in § S.4 of this chapter.

[652]Wells v. Boston Ave. Realty, 125 F.3d 1335, 1340 (10th Cir. 1997) (unsigned investigator report is not admissible in summary judgment since it is hearsay).

[653]Rule 56(c), Fed.R.Civ.P.

generally not filed with the court. They will only be "on file" if you or your adversary files them with the motion papers or responses to them, as is now required by many local rules.[654]

Local courts rules often have special provisions concerning summary judgment. In particular, they commonly require a party moving for summary judgment to file a statement of the undisputed facts that the party believes entitle him to a summary judgment; the party opposing summary judgment must file a statement of the disputed facts he believes prevent the court from granting summary judgment.[655] If you fail to file a statement of disputed facts, you may be deemed to have admitted the defendants' statement of undisputed facts.[656]

Sometimes a party submits a motion to dismiss or a motion for judgment on the pleadings,[657] but includes with it additional material such as affidavits or documents, which are not supposed to be considered on such motions. The court must either exclude those materials or convert the motion to one for summary judgment.[658] If it converts the motion, it must give all parties "a reasonable opportunity to present all the material that is pertinent to the motion."[659]

Most courts agree that a *pro se* prisoner faced with a summary judgment motion must receive an understandable notice of the requirements of the summary judgment rules, including the necessity of submitting affidavits if the facts are in dispute.[660]

A summary judgment motion can be made by either party at any time up to 30 days after the close of discovery.[661] The opposing party must file a response within 21 days after the motion is served, or 21 days after a responsive pleading is due, whichever is later.[662] If you need more time for your response, you should ask the other side to agree, and if they do not agree, you should ask the court for the time you need. A reasonable adjournment will seldom be refused to a *pro se* litigant. The rules also provide for delaying summary judgment proceedings if the non-moving party needs additional discovery.[663] When the parties' papers on a summary judgment motion are filed, the court will decide the motion, with or without oral argument at its discretion.[664]

1. Moving for Summary Judgment

In order to bring and win a summary judgment motion, you must show that there is no genuine issue of material fact as to each element of your legal claim. You must show these facts in a way that meets the requirements of the rules described in the preceding section.

For example, if you allege that you were placed in punitive segregation without adequate notice of the charges, without being allowed to speak at your hearing, and without a meaningful statement of reasons, you would write an affidavit describing the hearing and your placement in segregation; you would attach the inadequate notice and statement of reasons to the affidavit as exhibits. (It would also be wise

---

[654]*See, e.g.*, Rule 29.2, Local Rules for Civil Cases, U.S. District Court for the Eastern District of Michigan.

[655]One typical rule provides:

> (a) Upon any motion for summary judgment pursuant to Rule 56 of the Federal Rules of Civil Procedure, there shall be annexed to the notice of motion a separate, short and concise statement, in numbered paragraphs, of the material facts as to which the moving party contends there is no genuine issue to be tried. Failure to submit such a statement constitutes grounds for denial of the motion.
>
> (b) The papers opposing a motion for summary judgment shall include a correspondingly numbered paragraph responding to each numbered paragraph in the statement of the moving party, and if necessary, additional paragraphs containing a separate, short and concise statement of additional material facts as to which it is contended that there exists a genuine issue to be tried.
>
> (c) Each numbered paragraph in the statement of material facts set forth in the statement required to be served by the moving party will be deemed to be admitted for purposes of the motion unless specifically controverted by a correspondingly numbered paragraph in the statement required to be served by the opposing party.
>
> (d) Each statement by the movant or opponent pursuant to Rule 56.1(a) and (b), including each statement controverting any statement of material fact, must be followed by citation to evidence which would be admissible, set forth as required by Federal Rule of Civil Procedure 56(e).

Rule 56.1, Local Civil Rules, United States District Courts for the Southern and Eastern Districts of New York.

[656]*See, e.g.*, Hewes v. Magnusson, 350 F. Supp. 2d 222, 225 (D.Me. 2004); Kramer v. Gwinnett County, Ga., 306 F. Supp. 2d 1219, 1221 (N.D.Ga. 2004), *aff'd*, 116 Fed.Appx. 253 (11th Cir. 2004) (unpublished).

[657]These motions are discussed in § I of this chapter.

[658]Rule 12(d), Fed.R.Civ.P.

[659]Rule 12(d), Fed.R.Civ.P.; *see* Whitesel v. Sengenberger, 222 F.3d 861, 866 (10th Cir. 2000); Amaker v. Weiner, 179 F.3d 48, 57 (2d Cir. 1999); McElyea v. Babbitt, 833 F.2d 196, 200 (9th Cir. 1987).

[660]Irby v. New York City Transit Auth., 262 F.3d 412, 414 (2d Cir. 2001); Houston v. Sidley & Austin, 185 F.3d 837, 838 n.1 (7th Cir. 1999); Rand v. Rowland, 154 F.3d 952, 960–61 (9th Cir. 1998) (en banc); Neal v. Kelly, 963 F.2d 453, 456 (D.C. Cir. 1992); Brown v. Shinbaum, 828 F.2d 707, 708 (11th Cir.1987); Hummer v. Dalton, 657 F.2d 621, 624–25 (4th Cir. 1981). *Contra*, Beck v. Skon, 253 F.3d 330, 333 (8th Cir. 2001; Martin v. Harrison County Jail, 975 F.2d 192, 193 (5th Cir. 1992); *see* Brock v. Hendershott, 840 F.2d 339, 343 (6th Cir. 1988) (holding *pro se* non-prisoners are not entitled to individual notice).

[661]Rule 56(c)(1)(A), Fed.R.Civ.P.

[662]Rule 56(c)(1)(B), Fed.R.Civ.P.

[663]*See* § L.2.d, below.

[664]The rules previously provided for a hearing on summary judgment motions, but the present rule has eliminated that provision. Rule 56(c)(2), Fed.R.Civ.P. Even before that revision, courts had held that the hearing requirement could be satisfied by the court's consideration of written submissions. *See* Geear v. Boulder Community Hospital, 844 F.2d 764, 766 (10th Cir. 1988).

to attach the prison's disciplinary procedures to give the court a clear understanding of what the documents mean.) The affidavit should lay a foundation for the exhibits by stating what they are—for example:

> Exhibit 1, attached to this affidavit, is the notice of infraction that I was handed on August 1, 1992 by Lieutenant Smith to start my disciplinary proceeding, pursuant to Rule 5 of the prison Disciplinary Rules. The Disciplinary Rules are attached to this affidavit as Exhibit 2. These rules were handed to me when I was admitted to the prison, and handed to other inmates who were admitted with me, by a reception officer who stated that they were the official rules of the prison.

The affidavit should make clear the personal role of each defendant in the violation of law that you allege— *e.g.,* "The notice of infraction, which fails to specify the acts I was accused of committing, was signed by Lieutenant Smith and was handed to me by Lieutenant Smith." You should also submit a memorandum of law (a brief) explaining how your factual submissions prove that your rights were violated.

If the defendants do not dispute your factual allegations, and do not make material factual assertions that you dispute, the court should then decide the case based on those undisputed facts. If the parties do dispute the material facts, the judge should deny summary judgment, holding a trial to determine the facts.

If you move for summary judgment, the defendants may cross-move for summary judgment themselves. You must then respond to their cross-motion for summary judgment as described in the next section.

2. Responding to a Summary Judgment Motion

The defendants can move for summary judgment on a variety of grounds. For example, they may argue

- that the factual allegations in your complaint are false, or that they don't tell the whole story;
- that even accepting your version of the facts, what they did to you was not against the law;
- that they are immune from liability;[665]
- that they were not personally involved in any legal violation;[666]
- that your claim is not timely under the statute of limitations;[667] or
- that your suit is barred by a prior court decision under the rules of *res judicata* or collateral estoppel.[668]

You can respond to a motion for summary judgment in several ways: (1) dispute the facts, (2) concede the facts and

argue that they do not justify judgment for the defendants (or cross-move for summary judgment yourself), (3) attack the adequacy of the defendants' factual presentation, or (4) request that the motion be denied or stayed because you have not had sufficient opportunity to obtain the necessary facts.

a. Disputing the Facts If you argue that the defendants' factual allegations are not correct or are incomplete, your response must "set out specific facts showing a genuine issue for trial."[669] The requirement of setting forth specific facts is enforced strictly by the courts.[670]

You *must* file an affidavit or declaration[671] in opposition to the motion stating which facts alleged by the defendants you dispute, or which material facts the defendants left out, and how you know these facts. If you or other prisoners submit affidavits disputing the material facts alleged in the defendants' motion, the district court should not grant summary judgment.[672] (In fact, in *pro se* cases, courts are supposed to consider any factual material sworn to or declared under penalty of perjury, whatever form it is in,[673] but it is best to do it right and submit affidavits or declarations.) Sometimes judges grant summary judgment against prisoners in disregard of affidavits or declarations creating a material factual dispute; this is wrong, and should be reversed on appeal.[674] As noted above, in most federal courts, the local rules will require you to file a separate statement identifying the disputed facts that merit a trial.

---

[669]Rule 56(e), Fed.R.Civ.P.

[670]*See, e.g.,* Reese v. Anderson, 926 F.2d 494, 499 (5th Cir. 1991) (an affidavit stating only that the decedent was surrounded by police officers when he was shot and offering an opinion that he posed no danger to the officers was conclusory and insufficient to withstand summary judgment in the officers' favor); Caputo v. Fauver, 800 F. Supp. 168, 171 (D.N.J. 1992), *aff'd,* 995 F.2d 216 (3d Cir. 1993); Meadows v. Hattonsville Correctional Center, 793 F. Supp. 684, 687 (N.D.W.Va. 1992) ("[Plaintiff] simply cannot rest on conclusory legal claims when Defendants have submitted affidavits and documents countering these naked allegations."), *aff'd,* 991 F.2d 790 (4th Cir. 1993); Castillo v. Bowles, 687 F. Supp. 277 (N.D.Tex. 1988) ("General conclusory allegations … do not become sufficient simply because they are put in an affidavit form and stated by someone other than the plaintiff."); *see also* n.648, above.

[671]A declaration is a document reciting facts which bears a statement signed and dated by the person who wrote the document stating, *e.g.,* "I declare under penalty of perjury that the following is true and correct." 28 U.S.C. § 1746. Affidavits and declarations are discussed in Ch. 11, § C.

[672]Wilson v. Williams, 997 F.2d 348, 350–51 (7th Cir. 1993).

[673]Jones v. Blanas, 393 F.3d 918, 923 (9th Cir. 2004) (holding that where the plaintiff is *pro se,* the court "must consider as evidence in his opposition to summary judgment all of [plaintiff's] contentions offered in motions and pleadings, where such contentions are based on personal knowledge and set forth facts that would be admissible in evidence, and where [plaintiff] attested under penalty of perjury that the contents of the motions or pleadings are true and correct").

[674]*See* cases cited in n.643, above.

---

[665]Immunities are discussed in Ch. 8, § L.

[666]The "personal involvement" requirement is discussed in Ch. 8, § B.4.a.

[667]Statutes of limitations are discussed in Ch. 8, § N.

[668]These doctrines are discussed in Ch. 8, § N.

A good approach to preparing your opposition papers is to go through the defendants' motion line by line and make notes of which factual statements you disagree with, and what proof you have that supports your version of the case. If the facts you seek to establish are demonstrated by documents, attach copies of the documents as exhibits to your affidavit or declaration, and lay a foundation for them as discussed in the previous section.

In cases involving the question whether a prison rule or practice bears a reasonable relationship to legitimate penological interests,[675] if prison officials state their justifications for the rule or practice, those statements are considered evidence.[676] The burden will be on you to respond with "fact-based or expert-based refutation" of their claims.[677] It is not enough just to criticize their reasoning or question their motives, or cite other decisions from other prisons that have gone your way.[678] If their justifications make any sense at all, you must come up with something factual,[679] or present an admissible expert opinion[680] or equivalent,[681] refuting them. In cases involving medical or other technical issues, you may also need an expert opinion or equivalent.[682]

Your factual presentation must be complete enough to show that there is a genuine issue of material fact as to each point on which you bear the burden of proof.[683]

When served with a summary judgment motion, you cannot simply claim that you will prove your case at trial; if you do, the court will grant summary judgment against you.[684] You also cannot rely on your complaint as a response to the motion.[685] There is one exception: if your complaint was verified, the court should consider it as an affidavit in opposition to summary judgment.[686] However, your verified complaint will withstand a summary judgment motion only if it presents specific facts based on personal knowledge admissible in evidence,[687] and does so with respect to every factual issue raised by the defendants in their summary judgment motion.[688] For this reason, you should generally file an affidavit responding specifically to the allegations in the defendants' motion.

b. Conceding the Facts and Arguing the Law You may agree that the defendants' factual allegations are true and that they tell the whole story, but still believe that those facts show that your rights were violated. If that is the case, you should file a brief explaining why the facts as alleged by the defendants do not entitle them to summary judgment.

---

[675]This reasonable relationship standard, set out in *Turner v. Safley*, 482 U.S. 78, 89, 107 S. Ct. 2254 (1987), governs most claims of prison restrictions on constitutional rights. This standard is discussed at length in Ch. 3, § A.

[676]Beard v. Banks, 548 U.S. 521, 530–33, 126 S. Ct. 2572 (2006). The reason prison officials' views are treated as evidence, whereas your opinion will not be, is that under the *Turner* standard, courts are required to defer to the professional judgment of prison officials. *Beard*, 548 U.S. at 528–30.

[677]Beard v. Banks, 548 U.S. at 534.

[678]Beard v. Banks, *id.* The Court does say: "A prisoner may be able to marshal substantial evidence that, given the importance of the interest [infringed upon], the Policy is not a reasonable one. *Cf.* [*Turner*,] 482 U.S., at 97–99, 107 S. Ct. 2254 (striking down prison policy prohibiting prisoner marriages)." *Beard*, 548 U.S. at 535–36.

[679]See, e.g., Jacklovich v. Simmons, 392 F.3d 420, 431–32 (10th Cir. 2004) (describing factual record supporting decision for plaintiffs).

In *Beard v. Banks*, the Supreme Court said "it is not inconceivable that a plaintiff's counsel, through rigorous questioning of officials by means of depositions, could demonstrate genuine issues of fact for trial." 548 U.S. at 536. In a case governed by the *Turner* standard, you may wish to call this statement to the court's attention if you request the appointment of counsel. *See* § C.5 of this chapter concerning appointment of counsel.

[680]If you can't afford a lawyer, you probably can't afford to retain an expert either. You can request that the court appoint an expert, who will work for the court and not for you. Such requests are granted in prison cases only on rare occasions. Expert witnesses are discussed in § K.3 of this chapter.

[681]For example, if prison officials have ever admitted that a particular policy is not necessary or fails to serve its purpose, and you can prove it, that evidence can come is as an admission by a party-opponent. *See* § T.2 of this chapter concerning admissions.

[682]In *Spann v. Roper*, 453 F.3d 1007 (8th Cir. 2006) (per curiam), a medical care case, the court found it "incongruous" that the district court denied the plaintiff's motion for appointment of

an expert witness and then granted summary judgment in part because of his failure to supply medical evidence.

[683]Celotex Corp. v. Catrett, 477 U.S. 317, 322–23, 106 S. Ct. 2548 (1986); *see* Holloway v. Pigman, 884 F.2d 365, 367 (8th Cir. 1989) (upholding summary judgment for prison officials on a religious freedom claim because the prisoner failed to detail what his religion actually required or assert facts showing the extent of the deprivation of his religious rights).

[684]Oltarzewski v. Ruggiero, 830 F.2d 136, 138 (9th Cir. 1987); MacLeod v. Kern, 379 F. Supp. 2d 103, 108 (D.Mass. 2005); Wilson v. Maben, 676 F. Supp. 581d, 583 (M.D.Pa. 1987).

[685]Rule 56(e)(2), Fed.R.Civ.P.

[686]Ward v. Moore, 414 F.3d 968, 970 (8th Cir. 2005); Hart v. Hairston, 343 F.3d 762, 765 (5th Cir. 2003) (verified complaint may serve as competent summary judgment evidence); Schroeder v. McDonald, 55 F.3d 454, 460 (9th Cir. 1995); Neal v. Kelly, 963 F.2d 453, 457 (D.C. Cir. 1992) and cases cited.

"To 'verify' a complaint, the plaintiff must swear or affirm that the facts in the complaint are true 'under the pains and penalties of perjury.'" Hayes v. Garcia, 461 F. Supp. 2d 1198, 1204 (S.D.Cal. 2006) (citations omitted), *aff'd*, 293 Fed.Appx. 447 (9th Cir. 2008) (unpublished), *cert. denied*, 130 S. Ct. 226 (2009).

[687]Causey v. Balog, 162 F.3d 795, 803 n.4 (4th Cir. 1998) (a verified complaint containing factual statements that are made on information and belief, rather than personal knowledge, is insufficient to oppose summary judgment); Schroeder v. McDonald, 55 F.3d at 460.

[688]For example, suppose you file a suit alleging that your constitutional rights were violated, and the defendants move for summary judgment on the ground that your claim is barred by a prior lawsuit under the doctrine of *res judicata*. Unless your complaint specifically refutes this argument—which it probably will not—the complaint will not be an adequate response to the summary judgment motion, even if it is verified.

You can also cross-move for summary judgment yourself, arguing that on the undisputed facts, you should win.

c. Attacking the Defendants' Factual Presentation

Sometimes prison officials move for summary judgment without submitting an adequate evidentiary basis for it. If they fail to establish the necessary facts in the manner required by the rules, you should ask the court to deny their motion on that ground. In particular, most courts have held that prison officials who argue that a prison rule or practice should be upheld as reasonably related to legitimate penological objectives must submit evidence to that effect, and not just argument.[689]

This means that prison officials generally should not be able to get summary judgment based on a lawyer's affidavit; they will have to submit their own affidavits or declarations attesting to the reasons for their practices.

You should never rely solely on attacking the adequacy of the defendants' motion. Even if the other side submits no affidavits, under some circumstances the party opposing summary judgment must still show that there is a genuine issue of material fact as to each essential element of its case.[690]

In addition to arguing that the defendants have not submitted an adequate factual case, you should also put sufficient facts before the court to show that there is a genuine factual issue as to each point on which you bear the burden of proof.

d. Requesting More Time and Discovery

If there is some reason why you cannot submit the necessary affidavits or other evidence to oppose a summary judgment motion, you should submit an affidavit asking the court to deny the motion, or at least stay it, until you have obtained the necessary information.[691] This is the proper course if you have not had an opportunity to complete discovery or if the defendants have not yet complied with your discovery requests.[692]

". . . [W]here the facts are in the possession of the moving party, a continuance of a motion for summary judgment should be granted as a matter of course."[693]

Such a request is also appropriate if there are other reasons you cannot get the necessary evidence[694]—e.g., if you need the affidavit of a prisoner who is now at another prison, and prison officials will not let you correspond with him.[695] Whatever the problem is, you must spell out for the court what information you expect to get, how you expect to get it, and why you haven't been able to obtain it previously; if you don't have good reasons, your request will likely be denied.[696] For this reason, you should pursue discovery promptly after

---

[689]*See, e.g.*, Beerheide v. Suthers, 286 F.3d 1179, 1189 (10th Cir. 2002); Davis v. Norris, 249 F.3d 800, 801 (8th Cir. 2001); Flagner v.# Wilkinson, 241 F.3d 475, 486 (6th Cir. 2001); Walker v. Sumner, 917 F.2d 382, 386–87 (9th Cir. 1990); Hunafa v. Murphy, 907 F.2d 46, 48 (7th Cir. 1990); Swift v Lewis, 901 F.2d 730, 731–32 (9th Cir. 1990); Pressley v. Brown, 754 F. Supp. 112, 117 (W.D.Mich. 1990). *But see* Beard v. Banks, 548 U.S. 521, 530–33, 126 S. Ct. 2572 (2006) (holding that prison officials' explanations of the justifications for their policies *are* evidence). This issue is discussed above at nn.676–682, above.

[690]Celotex Corp. v. Catrett, 477 U.S. 317, 322–23, 106 S. Ct. 2548 (1986).

[691]Rule 56(f), Fed.R.Civ.P.

[692]A court should not grant summary judgment against a party who has not had an opportunity to pursue discovery or whose discovery requests have not been answered. Ingle v. Yelton, 439 F.3d 191, 196 (4th Cir. 2006) (denial of Rule 56(f) motion "is particularly inappropriate when . . . 'the materials sought are the object of outstanding discovery'" (citations omitted)); Leigh v. Warner Bros., Inc., 212 F.3d 1210, 1219 (11th Cir. 2000) (summary

judgment is generally inappropriate when the party opposing the motion has been unable to obtain responses to his discovery requests); LaBounty v. Coughlin, 137 F.3d 68, 71–72 (2d Cir. 1998); Salahuddin v. Coughlin, 993 F.2d 306, 309–10 (2d Cir. 1993); Klingele v. Eikenberry, 849 F.2d 409, 412–13 (9th Cir. 1988); Nauman v. Bugado, 374 F. Supp. 2d 893, 900–01 (D.Haw. 2005) (where plaintiff had no evidence to support his municipal liability claim, but had made a discovery request for the defendant officers' disciplinary and complaint records, court denied summary judgment pending compliance with the discovery requests).

[693]Costlow v. U.S., 552 F.2d 560, 564 (3d Cir. 1977); *accord*, Ingle v. Yelton, 439 F.3d 191, 196 (4th Cir. 2006); Baker v. McNeil Island Corrections Center, 859 F.2d 124, 127 (9th Cir. 1988); Jackson v. Procunier, 789 F.2d 307, 312 (5th Cir. 1986); Major League Baseball Promotion Corp. v. Colour-Tex, Inc., 729 F. Supp. 1035, 1043 (D.N.J. 1990).

In *Jones v. Blanas*, 393 F.3d 918 (9th Cir. 2004), the court held that summary judgment was improperly granted on plaintiff's strip search claim without allowing discovery concerning defendants' search policies. However, it upheld summary judgment on the plaintiff's access to courts claim, since the discovery sought on that claim concerned the nature of the injury to him, which involved facts within his control. *Jones*, 393 F.3d at 930–31.

[694]Foster v. Delo, 130 F.3d 307, 308 (8th Cir. 1997) (summary judgment should not have been granted where prisoner said he could not get affidavits from prisoners because they were afraid of retaliation, and reported in his papers what they had told him); La Batt v. Twomey, 513 F.2d 641, 650 (7th Cir.1975) (summary judgment was improper where prisoner made several material offers of proof and said that "the strenuous security system within the prison prevented him from securing affidavits").

[695]In a case like that, you should also ask the court for an order that prison officials permit you to correspond for the limited purpose of requesting the affidavit.

[696]Dulany v. Carnahan, 132 F.3d 1234, 1238 (8th Cir. 1997) ("The plaintiffs said that they sought 'to discover critical facts,' . . . but they did not articulate what particular critical facts they needed to develop or hoped to unveil."); Terrell v. Brewer, 935 F.2d 1015, 1018 (9th Cir. 1991) (upholding the refusal to adjourn a summary judgment motion pending further discovery because the plaintiff "failed to show the existence of additional essential and discoverable evidence"); Barfield v. Brierton, 883 F.2d 923, 931–33 (11th Cir. 1989) (upholding the district court's refusal to adjourn a summary judgment motion because the *pro se* plaintiff had had amply time and opportunity but failed to diligently pursue discovery); Baird v. Alameida, 407 F. Supp. 2d 1134, 1139 (C.D.Cal. 2005) (refusing to defer decision where plaintiff did not move under Rule 56(f) or file

filing your complaint rather than waiting for defendants to make a summary judgment motion and then making your requests. (Sometimes courts grant a stay of discovery at defendants' request because the defendants say they are going to file a "dispositive motion." If that has happened, but there is information you need to respond to the summary judgment motion, you should ask the court to lift the stay of discovery, at least to allow you to obtain that necessary information.)

If the summary judgment motion involves more than one issue, you may need to adopt a different strategy for each issue. For example, if you brought suit over a beating and a disciplinary proceeding, defendants might move for summary judgment arguing that (1) you were not beaten, (2) the notice and statement of reasons did not deny due process, and (3) the Superintendent had no personal involvement in the case.

You might respond (1) by describing the beating in your affidavit, demonstrating that there is a disputed factual issue; (2) by arguing that on the undisputed facts (*i.e.*, what is on the disciplinary documents), your notice and statement of reasons did not meet due process standards; and (3) by asking that the motion be denied or be postponed as to the personal involvement issue because the defendants have not yet answered your discovery request for their internal procedures spelling out who is responsible for reviewing disciplinary appeals.

3. Appeals from Summary Judgment Decisions

Whether a summary judgment decision can be appealed depends on whether summary judgment is granted or denied and whether the decision is on the whole case or part of the case.

If summary judgment is granted dismissing the entire case, that judgment is final and appealable. However, if summary judgment is granted only as to part of the case, the order is not considered final unless the court "expressly determines that there is no just reason for delay" and directs entry of final judgment.[697] If the court does make such a determination, the order is appealable immediately, and you must appeal at that time. In most cases, the court will not make such a determination, and the summary judgment decision will not become final and appealable until final judgment is entered on the whole case.

The denial of summary judgment generally cannot be appealed. There is one very important exception to this rule. If the defendants move for summary judgment on the ground that they are entitled to qualified or absolute

immunity, they may appeal a decision against them immediately.[698]

If a court grants summary judgment to the defendants and dismisses your case, you should seriously consider appealing if you think the court was wrong,[699] especially if the district court did not follow your federal circuit's rules concerning notice of summary judgment motions.[700] Federal district courts are sometimes careless in prison cases in determining whether there is a genuine issue of material fact, and in other cases they seem to hold prisoners to unusually difficult standards in establishing factual disputes. Appellate courts reverse these decisions with some frequency.[701]

However, you must be very sure that you have done your homework and made the necessary record to show that there is a genuine factual dispute. If you have not put the proper facts before the lower court in the proper manner, the appeals court will not save you from your mistakes.

M. PRELIMINARY INJUNCTIONS AND TEMPORARY RESTRAINING ORDERS

If you ask for an injunction in your complaint, the judge will consider that request at the time of trial. If your situation is urgent and you can't wait that long, you can move for a preliminary injunction or for a temporary restraining order. Both the legal standards and the procedures for seeking these types of relief are discussed elsewhere in this Manual.[702]

N. MAGISTRATE JUDGES

United States Magistrate Judges are judicial officers who are appointed by the federal district courts for eight-year terms,[703] unlike federal district judges, who are appointed by the President for life. Cases are routinely referred to magistrate judges for specific purposes by the district judges to whom the cases are assigned.

Although magistrate judges' powers are limited relative to those of district judges, they play a very important role in federal court litigation.

---

an affidavit stating what facts were expected to be uncovered and how they might help defeat summary judgment).

[697]Rule 54(b), Fed.R.Civ.P.

The district court may also make a partial summary judgment order appealable by certifying that it involves a "controlling question of law" that the appeals court should decide quickly. 28 U.S.C. § 1292(b). Requests for such certification are very rarely granted.

[698]Qualified immunity appeals are extremely common. They are discussed in Ch. 8, § L.4.

[699]Appeal procedures are discussed in § U of this chapter.

[700]These rules are discussed in § L of this chapter. The most common error of this sort is granting a motion to dismiss based on matters outside the complaint without formally converting the motion to one for summary judgment and giving you notice and a chance to respond.

[701]*See, e.g.*, Dale v. Lappin, 376 F.3d 652, 655–56 (7th Cir. 2004) (per curiam) (rejecting district court's view that plaintiff's statement consisted of "bald assertions" without "concrete facts" where he identified the employees from whom he requested forms, identified the forms requested, and recited other circumstances in detail); *see also* cases cited in n.643, above.

[702]*See* Ch. 8, § O.2.

[703]28 U.S.C. § 631(e).

Magistrate judges exercise their power in three important ways in civil cases.

1. Decision of Nondispositive Matters

A district judge may refer matters to a magistrate judge, if they do not finally dispose of a claim or defense in the case, without the consent of the parties. Magistrate judges frequently supervise discovery and decide discovery disputes, deal with scheduling issues and requests for extension of time, and supervise preparation for trial and the development of pretrial orders. "Dispositive" matters that may not be referred to a magistrate judge for decision include motions for injunctive relief, to dismiss or for judgment on the pleadings, for summary judgment, or for certification of a class.[704]

The magistrate judge's decision of a nondispositive matter may be reviewed by the district court if a party serves and files specific objections within 14 days of service of the magistrate judge's order. However, the decision will be modified or set aside only if it is "clearly erroneous or contrary to law."[705]

2. Proposed Findings and Recommendations on Dispositive Motions and Prisoner Cases

On a district judge's referral, a magistrate judge may conduct hearings and propose finding of fact and recommendations on dispositive matters, applications for post-conviction relief, and "prisoner petitions challenging conditions of confinement."[706] The prisoner petitions category includes virtually all prison cases, including those based on isolated incidents as well as those challenging continuing conditions of confinement.[707]

In some district courts, all prisoner petitions are automatically referred to a magistrate judge.

When magistrate judges are assigned these kinds of matters, the district judges retain greater powers of review. The magistrate judge issues findings and a recommendation, not a decision, and if a party objects to any part of the findings or recommendation, the district judge is required to make a completely new (*de novo*) determination of the matter. After being served with the finding and recommendations, the parties have 14 days to serve and file written objections.[708]

If you don't file objections within 14 days, unless you get an extension of time from the court, they will be waived, meaning the district judge need not consider them and you will probably not be able successfully to appeal the district court's judgment if it adopts the magistrate judge's findings.[709] The objections must specifically identify the findings that you object to.[710] The district judge may accept, reject, or modify the findings or recommendations in whole or in part, or may take further evidence or send the matter back

---

[704]28 U.S.C. § 636(b)(1)(A). *Cf.* U.S. v. Rivera-Guerrero, 377 F.3d 1064, 1069 (9th Cir. 2004) (holding magistrate judge may not issue final decision on authorization of involuntary medication to render a defendant competent for trial, since such an order has direct consequences for the defense of lack of competency to stand trial, and disposes of his right to avoid involuntary medication; district court must exercise *de novo* review).

[705]28 U.S.C. § 636(b)(1); *accord*, Rule 72(a), Fed.R.Civ.P. The time limit of Rule 72(a) was formerly 10 days excluding weekends and holidays; it was changed to 14 days counting *all* days (which usually amounts to the same thing), effective December 1, 2009. The statute still says 10 days. We assume you can rely on the amended rule.

[706]28 U.S.C. § 636(b)(1)(B); *accord*, Rule 72(b), Fed.R.Civ.P.

[707]McCarthy v. Bronson, 500 U.S. 136, 139–41, 111 S. Ct. 1737 (1991).

[708]28 U.S.C. 636(b)(1)(C); *accord*, Rule 72(b), Fed.R.Civ.P. The time limit of Rule 72(b) was formerly 10 days excluding weekends and holidays; it was changed to 14 days counting *all* days (which usually amounts to the same thing), effective December 1, 2009. The statute still says 10 days. We assume you can rely on the amended rule unless the court advises you otherwise, since courts have held that even under the former rule, the magistrate judge must inform parties of the time limit and they do not waive their right to object by missing the deadline if they were not informed of it. U.S. v. Carrillo-Morales, 27 F.3d 1054, 1062 (5th Cir. 1994) (time limit "does not apply, however, unless the magistrate judge informs the parties of the time limits for filing objections."); Moore v. U.S., 950 F.2d 656, 659 (10th Cir. 1991) (magistrate judge must inform the *pro se* party "'not only of the time period for filing objections, but also of the consequences of a failure to object, i.e. waiver of the right to appeal from a judgment of the district court based upon the findings and recommendations of the magistrate [judge]."); *see also* Talley v. Hesse, 91 F.3d 1411, 1413 (10th Cir. 1996) (holding that *pro se* litigant must be informed that failure to object will, rather than may, bar appellate review of both legal and factual conclusions of magistrate judge). Some courts have applied this rule to *pro se* litigants only. *See* Small v. Secretary of Health and Human Services, 892 F.2d 15, 16 (2d Cir. 1989); Wright v.Collins, 766 F.2d 841, 846 (4th Cir. 1985).

[709]*See, e.g.*, Negron v. Celebrity Cruises, Inc., 316 F.3d 60, 62 (1st Cir. 2003) (affirming district court's refusal to entertain late objections); Knox v. Palestine Liberation Organization, 229 F.R.D. 65, 68–69 (S.D.N.Y. 2005) (finding late objections waived). In some cases, courts have considered late objections or allowed appeal after late objections, usually where the party had some good reason for being late. *See, e.g.*, Snyder v. Nolen, 380 F.3d 279, 284–85 (7th Cir. 2004) (holding waiver of late objections would "defeat the ends of justice" where the reason for lateness was prison's failure to forward mail after a temporary transfer); Wirsching v. Colorado, 360 F.3d 1191, 1197 (10th Cir. 2004) (finding "interests of justice" exception to court's "firm waiver rule" where party is not at fault in failing to object timely); Williams v. Meyer, 346 F.3d 607, 613–14 (6th Cir. 2003) (late objections were not waived; plaintiff requested extensions of time, one of which was granted, and had good reasons for seeking them); Vogel v. U.S. Office Products Co., 258 F.3d 509, 515 (6th Cir. 2001) (where a party files objections late, a district court can still consider them).

[710]Rule 72(b)(2), Fed.R.Civ.P., refers to "specific written objections." *See* Johnson v. Zema Sys. Corp., 170 F.3d 734, 741 (7th Cir. 1999) (rule requires the party "to specify each issue for which review is sought.").

to the magistrate judge with instructions.[711] If you present new evidence in your objections, the district court has discretion to consider it or not,[712] so it is a good idea to make sure you present everything you have to the magistrate judge.

If one of the parties has demanded, and is entitled to, a jury trial, the case may not be referred to a magistrate judge for trial without the parties' consent.[713] However, it may be referred for pretrial proceedings.

3. Decision by Consent

The parties can consent to a magistrate judge's hearing, and entering final judgment in, "any and all" civil matters, including jury and non-jury proceedings.[714] The parties are supposed to be notified of the availability of a magistrate judge for this purpose at the beginning of the case.[715] If the parties consent, the magistrate judge will handle the case from that point on as if he were a district judge, including conducting the trial. The magistrate judge's decisions in consent cases are appealable to the court of appeals like decisions of the federal district court.[716] The relevant statute and rule stress that consent to having a case handled by a magistrate judge must be voluntary,[717] though many districts encourage litigants to give consent. If there is a mistake and the court thinks you *have* consented when you have not, you will need to speak up if you want to have your trial before the district judge. If you voluntarily participate in a trial before a magistrate judge, you have impliedly consented to it.[718]

Although magistrate judges have more restricted powers than district judges, you should not feel that you are getting second-rate justice if you must appear before one. In many districts the magistrate judges are about as distinguished and competent as the district judges. Because of the limits on their jurisdiction, they are often less overworked

than the district judges and therefore may have more time to pay attention to your case. For this reason, too, you may be able to get a trial and decision more quickly by consenting to trial before a magistrate judge.

You should consider these factors, as well as anything you can learn about how particular magistrate judges have ruled in other cases, in deciding whether to consent to have your case heard and decided by a magistrate judge. If you do consent, it is probably best to do so early in the case so you will have the same person handling both the pretrial proceedings and the trial.

O. PRETRIAL CONFERENCES AND PROCEEDINGS

In the usual civil case where both sides have attorneys, the parties are required to meet early in the case to discuss the nature and basis of their claims, the possibility of early settlement, etc., and to develop a discovery plan, and to report these matters to the court.[719] The court is required to issue a scheduling order, which it may do based on the parties' report of their conference, or based on a scheduling conference with the court or on telephone, mail, or other communications.[720] This order is to be issued within 90 days of a defendant's "appearance" (serving an answer or a motion) or within 120 days of the service of the complaint upon a defendant, whichever is earlier.[721] The scheduling order must set time limits for joining parties, amending the pleadings, completing discovery, and filing motions, and may include other material as well.[722] Once issued, a scheduling order can only be modified with the court's permission based on good cause.[723]

There is generally at least one more pretrial conference shortly before a civil case is tried, which serves purposes such as clarifying the legal and factual issues; determining whether the complaint or answer needs to be amended; getting stipulations (agreements) concerning facts which are not disputed,[724] the admissibility of evidence, and the authenticity of documents; identifying witnesses and documents, and eliminating unnecessary or repetitive evidence; discussing the possibility of settlement; and other aspects of managing the case and the trial.[725]

These procedures may not be followed in full, or at all, in a *pro se* prisoner case. The scheduling order rule applies "[e]xcept in categories of actions exempted by district court rule as inappropriate,"[726] and *pro se* prisoner cases are

---

[711]28 U.S.C. 636(b)(1)(C); *accord*, Rule 72(b)(3), Fed.R.Civ.P.

[712]*See* Jones v. Blanas, 393 F.3d 918, 935 (9th Cir. 2004) (finding an abuse of discretion in refusal to consider new evidence where a *pro se* plaintiff offered facts as soon as he understood what was necessary).

[713]McCarthy v. Bronson, 500 U.S. at 143–44.

[714]28 U.S.C. § 636(c)(1); *accord*, Rule 73(a), Fed.R.Civ.P.

Habeas corpus proceedings are generally considered civil matters for purposes of this statutory provision. Farmer v. Litscher, 303 F.3d 840, 842 (7th Cir. 2002). However, one federal appeals court has held that magistrate judges may not issue final rulings in proceedings under 28 U.S.C. § 2255, which involves review of federal convictions and sentences. *See* U.S. v. Johnston, 258 F.3d 361, 369 (5th Cir. 2001). Others have disagreed. *See* Farmer v. Litscher, 303 F.3d 840 (7th Cir. 2002).

[715]28 U.S.C. § 636(c)(2); *accord*, Rule 73(b), Fed.R.Civ.P.

[716]28 U.S.C. § 636(c)(3); *accord*, Rule 73(c), Fed.R.Civ.P. Formerly, parties could agree to appeal from the magistrate judge to the district court, but that provision was repealed.

[717]28 U.S.C. § 636(c)(2); *accord*, Rule 73(b).

[718]Roell v. Withrow, 538 U.S. 580, 586–91, 123 S. Ct. 1696 (2003).

[719]Rule 26(f)(1)–(2), Fed.R.Civ.P.

[720]Rule 16(b)(2), Fed.R.Civ.P.

[721]Rule 16(b), Fed.R.Civ.P.

[722]Rule 16(b)(3), Fed.R.Civ.P.

[723]*Id.*

[724]For an example of such a factual stipulation, *see* Frett v. Government of Virgin Islands, 839 F.2d 968, 971–72 (3d Cir. 1988).

[725]*See* Rule 16(b)(1), Fed.R.Civ.P.

[726]*Id.*

exempted in some districts.[727] The rule requiring the parties to confer exempts litigants who are exempted from the initial disclosure requirements, which includes *pro se* prisoners.[728] Practices will vary among districts and in some cases between judges, so you will have to consult the local rules of your district and the judge's individual rules (which you should be able to get by requesting them from the judge's chambers), if any.

If the court enters a scheduling order in your case, it may do so without a conference, or after a conference attended only by the defendants' lawyers. The federal courts generally do not have prisoners produced for conferences. However, you can ask to attend the conference or any later conference by telephone,[729] or if that is not possible, if a family member or a friend may attend the conference on your behalf. You can also request that a transcript be prepared and made available to you of any conference you are unable to attend. In some districts, federal courts hold some proceedings in the prisons.[730]

Courts generally do not produce prisoners in court for pretrial conferences either.[731] However, if the court in your district holds proceedings at the prison,[732] it may hold a pretrial conference in your case, and you should make the most of the opportunity. If the conference is held (as it probably will be) shortly before your trial, you should be prepared to ask the defendants to stipulate to the authenticity and the admissibility of any documents you wish to introduce into evidence (especially if those documents were produced by the defendants during the course of discovery).[733]

If the defendants don't agree, you may be able to get the court to make a ruling on the documents' admissibility, and if not, you may get an idea from the discussion of what you have to do before the trial in order to get the documents admitted. You should be prepared to say whom you wish to call as witnesses, and why, and you should have subpoenas and writs of habeas corpus ad testificandum[734] ready at the conference, since the judge may wish to deal with them on the spot.

You should also ask the court for assistance in resolving any remaining issues concerning discovery. In addition to dealing with these practical problems, part of your purpose will be to demonstrate to the judge and to the defendants' lawyers that you are well prepared and that they should take you seriously.

If the court does not plan to hold a pretrial conference, it is possible that you can persuade it to do so if you think one is needed. If there are serious issues concerning discovery, the admissibility of documents, or obtaining witnesses (*e.g.*, prisoners who are incarcerated at other prisons), you may wish to write to the court and request a pretrial conference four to eight weeks before the case is scheduled for trial.[735]

You should explain the reason why such a conference is needed. If you have good reasons, the court may make an exception to its usual practice and have you produced for a pretrial conference, or may make some other arrangement such as a telephone conference to deal with the problems you raise. Or it may simply deal with your issues based on your written request.

Courts typically require the parties to prepare a joint pretrial order, which the court signs and which address matters such as agreed or stipulated facts, disputed legal issues and questions of admissibility of evidence, exhibit lists, lists of deposition testimony that will be used as evidence, etc. This can either be done in connection with a pretrial conference that is intended to narrow and resolve the issues,[736] or the court can simply direct the parties to confer and work out a joint pretrial order, or to prepare pretrial statements that contain the same necessary information but do not get combined into a single document. In that case, you should raise all your issues in the document you send to court, and specifically call the court's attention to any matter that requires its attention or action such as signing writs for your witnesses.

The court may or may not utilize such a procedure in a *pro se* case. It is probably to your advantage for the court to do so if you are capable of understanding the procedure,

---

[727]*See, e.g.*, Rule 16.1(c), Local Practice Rules, United States District Court, Northern District of New York (exempting from Rule 16 procedures all cases excluded by court's General Order 25, including "prisoner petitions").

[728]Rule 26(f)(1), Fed.R.Civ.P.

[729]Courts may arrange conferences by telephone or by audio-video connection. *See* 42 U.S.C. § 1997e(f) (authorizing conduct of pretrial proceedings by telephone, video conference, or other telecommunications technology); American Inmate Paralegal Association v. Cline, 859 F.2d 59, 62 (8th Cir. 1988).

[730]This practice too is authorized by 42 U.S.C. § 1997e(f).

[731]The rule provides that district courts' local rules may exempt categories of cases from the the the conference requirement. Be sure to find out whether *pro se* prisoner cases are exempted in your district.

[732]*See* § C.3.b of this chapter, n.155.

[733]These issues are discussed in § S.4 of this chapter.

[734]The subjects are discussed in § Q of this chapter.

[735]If you have problems with discovery, you should not wait too long; you should raise them with the court at the earliest practical opportunity. *See* § K.2.c of this chapter.

[736]For example, one district court requires the parties to exchange, 10 or more days before a final pretrial conference, statements including contested and uncontested facts, issues of law and any unusual questions about admissibility of evidence, proposed jury instructions, witness lists and brief statements of their anticipated testimony, summaries of the qualifications and testimony of any expert witnesses, a list of exhibits, a list of deposition testimony to be offered in evidence, and details of damages or other relief sought. Rule 16.1(d), Local Rules of Civil Procedure, United States District Court for the Western District of New York. Before the conference, counsel are required to mark and list all exhibits. At the pretrial conference, all the exhibits are to be produced and objections to their admission discussed. Rule 16.1(e), *id.* After these proceedings, the court may enter a final pretrial order and certify the case as ready for trial. Rule 16.1(f)(2), *id.*

since it will provide you with a lot of information about the defendants' case before the trial. However, the court may not penalize a *pro se* litigant for failure to comply with procedures that he does not understand.[737]

P. Preparation for Trial

After the pretrial conference, if any, and before the trial, there are certain things you must do.

First, you should draft the questions you wish to ask each witness.[738] You don't want your witnesses to ramble while testifying, and the best way to avoid this is to organize your questions logically and in advance. The same is true about preparing your own testimony.

Second, you need to talk to your witnesses, or write to them if they have been transferred or released, to ensure that they are still willing to testify.[739] You should go over your questions with those witnesses to whom you have access so they will know what to expect and you will be sure of what their answers are. It is also worthwhile to do a practice cross-examination of these witnesses (or have someone else do it), for the same reason.

Third, you should draft proposed jury instructions concerning each of your claims so you can submit them at the beginning of the trial.[740]

Fourth, you should number and mark all the documents that you want admitted at trial (Plaintiff's Exhibit 1, Plaintiff's Exhibit 2, etc.).[741] It will be less confusing if you try to number them in the order in which you expect to offer them. Use clean copies of the documents. A court likely will not admit exhibits that you have underlined or written on.

Fifth, if the trial is to occur at the courthouse, you must make sure the court has issued writs of habeas corpus ad testificandum to have your prisoner witnesses and yourself brought to court.[742] (The same is true if the trial will be at the prison but some of your witnesses are at another prison.) You should also make sure that you get subpoenas issued for any witnesses who are not in prison, including prison officials you may wish to call.[743]

Sixth, if the judge will conduct the voir dire (as is the practice in most federal courts), you should submit your proposed voir dire questions before trial.[744]

Seventh, you should make a motion *in limine*[745] if you expect the defendants to offer evidence that you would prefer to keep out, such as your criminal record or disciplinary history.

Q. Getting Yourself and Your Witnesses to Court

An incarcerated person has no constitutional right to appear personally at a hearing or trial in a civil suit.[746] However, there is a constitutional right to a fair trial in a civil case, which requires that plaintiffs have the opportunity to present their cases so that the trier of fact can make a meaningful search for the truth.[747] It is arguable that exclusion from trial may deny that opportunity. In any case, a federal court has the discretion to order a prisoner produced in a civil case.[748] In exercising their discretion to produce prisoners, federal district courts have been directed to consider factors including:

> the costs and inconvenience of transporting a prisoner from his place of incarceration to the courtroom, any potential danger or security risk which the presence of a particular inmate would pose to the court, the substantiality of the matter at issue, the need for an early determination of the matter, the possibility of delaying trial until the prisoner is released, the probability of success on the merits, the integrity of the correctional system, and the interest of the inmate in presenting his testimony in person rather than by deposition.[749]

Using this standard, federal courts have generally required prisoners to be produced for trial unless there is substantial justification for not doing so.[750] Some courts

---

[737]Kilgo v. Ricks, 983 F.2d 189, 193–94 (11th Cir. 1993) (requiring district court either to appoint counsel, assist the *pro se* litigant in completing the procedures, or skip some of the procedures).

[738]The proper form for asking questions of witnesses is discussed in § S.3.b–S.3.d of this chapter.

[739]Most letters from one prisoner to another are opened and scanned if not read by prison staff so be careful what you put in that letter.

[740]Jury instructions are discussed in § F.12 of this chapter.

[741]Handling of documentary exhibits at trial is discussed in § S.4 of this chapter.

[742]Getting yourself and your witnesses to court is discussed in § Q of this chapter.

[743]Subpoenas are discussed in § Q of this chapter.

[744]*Voir dire* is discussed in § R.3 of this chapter.

[745]Motions *in limine* are discussed in § S.6 of this chapter.

[746]Thornton v. Snyder, 428 F.3d 690, 697 (7th Cir. 2005); Jacobson v. McIlwain, 145 F.R.D. 595, 601 (S.D. Fla. 1992); *see* Price v. Johnston, 334 U.S. 266, 285, 68 S. Ct. 1049 (1948) (same, as to argument of appeal).

[747]Latiolais v. Whitley, 93 F.3d 205 (5th Cir. 1996); *see also* Lemmons v. Law Firm of Morris and Morris, 39 F.3d 264, 268 (10th Cir. 1994) (although a prisoner generally has no constitutional right to attend trial, once a court has ordered his production, obstructing his court appearance may deny the right of court access).

[748]Michaud v. Michaud, 932 F.2d 77, 81 (1st Cir. 1991); *see* Price v. Johnston, 334 U.S. at 284–85 (same, as to appellate argument). Some courts have held that under the circumstances before them, the prisoner is responsible for the costs of transportation. *See* Manning v. Tefft, 839 F. Supp. 126, 129–30 (D.R.I. 1994).

[749]Stone v. Morris, 546 F.2d 730, 735–36 (7th Cir. 1976).

[750]*See, e.g.,* Latiolais v. Whitley, 93 F.3d 205, 208 (5th Cir. 1996) (reversing decision to hold trial on deposition testimony rather

have held that the decision should not be affected by the trial court's view of the plaintiff's likelihood of success[751] or the amount at stake in the case.[752]

In determining how to try a *pro se* prisoner case, the court should first consider producing the prisoner for trial. If doing so is unfeasible, "all other reasonably available alternatives to trial with his presence should be considered, with indefinite stays and dismissals for failure to prosecute only being considered, if at all, as last resorts."[753] Those alternatives include trying the case without the prisoner's presence, permitting the prisoner to testify by affidavit, deposition, or video, or holding the trial in whole or in part at the prison.[754] Courts have acknowledged that trial by videoconference "is not the same as a trial where the witnesses testify in the same room as the jury" and that video proceedings "have their shortcomings," so a decision to deny a prisoner's physical appearance in the courtroom "is not one that should be taken lightly."[755] That view is consistent with Rule 43,

Fed.R.Civ.P., which allows trial testimony by video only "for good cause shown in compelling circumstances and upon appropriate safeguards,"[756] and with the Prison Litigation Reform Act, which authorizes and encourages use of telecommunications for hearings but not for trials.[757]

The appointment of counsel may be considered as an alternative to producing the prisoner, or at least as a way of minimizing the damage from non-production.[758] If the case is to be tried without producing the plaintiff and without appointing counsel, "the district court should fully inform the plaintiff as to the exact manner in which the trial will be conducted and carefully instruct him as to how he may present his evidence and testimony to the court."[759]

Federal courts have generally not been willing to order production in court for pretrial proceedings and motions.[760]

In deciding whether incarcerated witnesses should be produced, courts have relied on the same considerations as they do in connection with producing the plaintiff.[761] However, the plaintiff "must demonstrate to the court the nature and materiality of the testimony" of the prisoner witnesses requested.[762]

---

than producing plaintiffs; lower court appropriately considered the expense and security risks of bringing the prisoners to the trial, but failed to weigh the extent to which plaintiffs' presence would aid resolution of the case, which turned on credibility assessment); Pollard v. White, 738 F.2d 1124, 1125 (11th Cir. 1984) (upholding refusal to produce prisoner from Illinois prison to Alabama court where he was represented by counsel, he was able to testify by deposition, and evidence suggested that he was a substantial security risk); Taylor v. Slatkin, 2003 WL 21104918, *1 (N.D.Tex., May 13, 2003); Hawks v. Timms, 35 F. Supp. 2d 464, 467–68 (D. Md. 1999) (ordering plaintiff produced from Pennsylvania for trial in Maryland because his claim depends on his own testimony and credibility, so appearing by affidavit or deposition would put him at a serious disadvantage; the distance is relatively short and the trial will take only three days the court regularly has prisoners produced for criminal and civil proceedings; since the plaintiff has completed 5 years of a 26 year sentence, a stay is not reasonable); Martin v. Potter, 635 F. Supp. 645, 647–48 (D.V.I. 1986) (refusing to produce prisoner whose long sentence made him a security risk from Pennsylvania federal prison to Virgin Islands court; appointing counsel instead), *aff'd*, 877 F.2d 56 (3d Cir. 1989).

[751]Poole v. Lambert, 819 F.2d 1025, 1029 (11th Cir. 1987).

[752]Sisk v. U.S., 756 F.2d 497, 500 (7th Cir. 1985).

[753]Muhammad v. Warden, Baltimore City Jail, 849 F.2d 107, 113 (4th Cir. 1988); *accord*, Hernandez v.Whiting, 881 F.2d 768, 770–72 (9th Cir. 1989).

[754]Hawks v. Timms, 35 F. Supp. 2d 464, 465 (D.Md. 1999) (citing Muhammad v. Warden, Baltimore City Jail, 849 F.2d at 113); Hernandez v. Whiting, 881 F.2d 768, 771–72 (9th Cir. 1989); *see* Jones v. Hamelman, 869 F2d 1023, 1030 (7th Cir 1989) (upholding the refusal to produce the plaintiff for that part of the trial held outside the prison).

[755]Thornton v. Snyder, 428 F.3d 690, 697–98 (7th Cir. 2005). In *Thornton*, a video trial was found justified based on evidence that the plaintiff was classified an "extremely high escape risk" with a "moderate aggression level" who would ordinarily be escorted by at least two staff members when he came to court, and who was housed in a prison about 120 miles from the prison. The court said there were sufficient safeguards in place where the jury, in the courtroom, watched a four-way screen showing the judge, the plaintiff, the witness, and defendants' counsel, and both the plaintiff

and the jury could see everyone at the same time. *Thornton*, 428 F.3d at 698–99. *See* Edwards v. Logan, 38 F. Supp. 2d 463, 464 n.1, 466-68 (W.D.Va. 1999) (directing Virginia trial of a prisoner transferred to New Mexico because of his "extensive enemy situation" should be held by video; delay until release is not acceptable where that would be 10 years later; noting plaintiff's case is simple).

A decision authorizing psychiatric commitment hearings by video emphasized that (unlike trials) such decisions are generally based on expert testimony and do not depend much on either the witnesses' demeanor or the "impression" made by the person being committed, and that the proceeding does not involve factfinding in the usual sense. U.S. v. Baker, 45 F.3d 837, 845 (4th Cir. 1994).

[756]Rule 43(a), Fed.R.Civ.P. (referring to "contemporaneous transmission from a different location").

[757]42 U.S.C. § 1997e(f); *see* Ch. 9, § H, concerning this provision.

[758]Heidelberg v. Hammer, 577 F.2d 429, 431 (7th Cir. 1978); Martin v. Potter, 635 F. Supp. 645, 647–48 (D.V.I. 1986). While appointment of counsel has many advantages, it is still not a perfect solution, since you would not be in the courtroom to testify and to assist counsel.

[759]Poole v. Lambert, 819 F.2d 1025, 1029 (11th Cir. 1987).

[760]*In re* Wilkinson, 137 F.3d 911, 914 (6th Cir. 1998) (prisoner has no right to attend depositions taken in his case); Demoran v. Witt, 781 F.2d 155, 158 (9th Cir. 1985) (prisoner need not be produced for summary judgment motion on which he was able to submit papers); Holt v. Pitts, 619 F.2d 558, 561 (6th Cir. 1980) (stating "the court is required to make a lesser degree of accommodation during the proceedings prior to trial").

[761]Carter v. Hutto, 781 F.2d 1028, 1031–32 (4th Cir. 1986); Jerry v. Francisco, 632 F.2d 252, 255–56 (3d Cir. 1980).

[762]Cook v. Bounds, 518 F.2d 779, 780 (4th Cir. 1975); *accord*, Walker v. Sumner, 14 F.3d 1415. 1422 (9th Cir. 1994) (upholding refusal to produce witness when plaintiff would not say what the witness would testify to); Carter v. Hutto, 781 F.2d at 1032

In arguing for your production in court, you should make the following points. If the case involves factual disputes (and it must, if it is going to trial), the court or jury should be able to see and hear you in order to evaluate your credibility based on your demeanor.[763] The more the case relies on your testimony, rather than on documents or on testimony by other witnesses who will be present, the stronger this argument will be.[764]

If you do not have counsel, there will be no one to manage the presentation of your proof, cross-examine adverse witnesses, present a rebuttal case to the defendants' evidence, object to improper evidence or arguments, and give opening and closing arguments.[765] Even if you do have counsel, it is important for counsel and the client to be able to consult during the trial. No matter how well counsel prepares, it is common for matters to come up at trial that counsel has not anticipated, does not know about, and needs to discuss with his client.

Courts sometimes decide that the testimony of a prisoner plaintiff or his witnesses should be presented by deposition.[766] If the prisoner has counsel and there are other, non-incarcerated witnesses who will testify in support of his claims, this may be a barely acceptable solution, though it will disadvantage the prisoner. If the prisoner is proceeding *pro se*, depositions are not adequate because someone needs to be in court to manage the presentation of the case. If the court requires you to testify by deposition and you have counsel, your counsel will presumably arrange and conduct the deposition as if you were testifying at trial. If you do not have counsel, we think fairness requires the court to arrange such a deposition. It would be very unfair to require you to rely on depositions taken by the defendants' lawyer since these depositions will reflect the defendants' interest in attacking your case rather than your interest in presenting it successfully.

State courts have taken different approaches to court appearances by prisoners in civil cases.[767] Some take a similar approach to the federal courts by balancing the prisoner's interest in appearing against the state's interest in not having to produce the prisoner.[768] Some state courts are more protective of prisoners' ability to appear in court when the prisoner is the defendant, rather that the plaintiff, in a civil suit.[769]

Other state courts refuse to produce prisoners in civil cases.[770] In these courts, the prisoner generally has the right to present his testimony by oral or written deposition. If a state court's refusal to produce a prisoner prevents his case from going forward at all, it may violate the Constitution.[771]

The procedure by which a prisoner, including a plaintiff, is produced to testify in a federal court is a writ of habeas corpus *ad testificandum* directed to the person with custody

---

(where plaintiff supplied information about substance of witnesses' testimony, court could not refuse to produce them where plaintiff did not supply a statement that they were willing to testify); Cupit v. Jones, 835 F.2d 82, 85–86 (5th Cir. 1987) (upholding refusal to issue subpoenas in the absence of a showing of need); Poole v. Lambert, 819 F.2d at 1029 (upholding district court's refusal to produce imprisoned witnesses whose testimony would be duplicative); Cookish v. Cunningham, 787 F.2d 1, 5 (1st Cir. 1986) (upholding refusal to produce all of the plaintiff's witnesses because there was no showing of need for all of them and the court permitted them to testify by affidavit).

[763]Heidelberg v. Hammer, 577 F.2d at 431.

[764]Latiolais v. Whitley, 93 F.3d 205, 208 (5th Cir. 1996); Hawks v. Timms, 35 F. Supp. 2d 464, 467–68 (D.Md. 1999).

[765]See Latiolais v. Whitley, 93 F.3d at 209–10 (noting that plaintiffs' absence left them unable to object to trial errors).

[766]Depositions are discussed in § K.2 of this chapter.

[767]This issue comes up frequently in state court family law-related proceedings, and additional citations and discussion can be found in Ch. 3, § G.2, n.1002–1003, § G.3, n.1073.

[768]See, e.g., Seth D. v. State, Dep't of Health and Social Services, Office of Children Services, 175 P.3d 1222, 1226–31 (Alaska 2008) (prisoner has no due process right to be transported to a parental termination trial, but courts must examine whether the parent's absence means that the trial itself denies due process; in future cases, state must make a specific showing of cost and risk of producing prisoner); In re Jesusa V., 32 Cal.4th 588, 601, 85 P.3d 2 (Cal. 2004) (right of court access entitles litigants to a meaningful opportunity to be heard, but that does not mean physical presence in every case); In re Z.L.T., 124 S.W.3d 163, 166 (Tex.S.Ct. 2003) "[T]he trial court did not abuse its discretion by implicitly denying Thompson's request for a bench warrant," "[b]ecause Thompson failed to make the required showing, and the trial court is not required, on its own, to seek out the necessary information."); Arpaio v. Steinle, 201 Ariz. 353, 355, 35 P.3d 114 (Ariz.App.Div. 1, 2001) ("a rebuttable presumption exists that an inmate is entitled to attend 'critical proceedings,' such as the trial itself, on timely request"); State ex rel. Kittrell v. Carr, 878 S.W.2d 859, 862 (Mo. App.E.D. 1994).

[769]See, e.g., Payne v. Superior Court of Los Angeles County, 17 Cal.3d 908, 132 Cal.Rptr. 405, 553 P.2d 565, 575–77 (1976) (indigent civil defendant has a due process right to appear in court or to have counsel appointed); Piper v. Popp, 167 Wis.2d 633, 482 N.W.2d 353, 355 (Wis. 1992) (indigent civil defendant must be permitted to appear personally, have counsel appointed, or obtain a continuance until he is released or can obtain private counsel).

This is an issue that rarely comes up in federal court because most suits against prisoners are not within the federal courts' jurisdiction.

[770]Clements v. Moncrief, 549 So.2d 479, 481 (Ala. 1989) (holding that there is no right to be produced); Myers v. Emke, 476 N.W.2d 84, 85 (Iowa 1991) (holding that the court lacked power to order production of a prisoner held in a different county).

If your case is one that can be filed either in state or in federal court, you should find out your state's law on this point before you decide which court to file in. You may also be able to argue that if your legal claim is based on federal law (*e.g.*, a state court § 1983 action), the state court is obligated to follow federal law governing court appearances. See Howlett v. Rose, 496 U.S. 356, 375–78, S. Ct. 2430 (1990); Felder v. Casey, 487 U.S. 131, 151, 108 S. Ct. 2302 (1988) (both cases requiring application of certain federal law in state court § 1983 actions). We are not aware of any case law on this precise point.

[771]See Lynk v. LaPorte Superior Court No. 2, 789 F.2d 554, 560–61 (7th Cir. 1986).

over the prisoner.[772] Such a writ is effective anywhere in the country.[773] If the purpose of the court appearance is something other than testimony, the issuance of a writ of habeas corpus is authorized by the All Writs Act.[774]

You should submit your proposed writ to the court several weeks in advance of the trial date. Often, courts wait until the last minute to "writ down" prisoners because of inadequate or overcrowded detention facilities near the courthouse. Prisoners who are subpoenaed to testify are not entitled to statutory witness fees, unlike other witnesses.[775]

If you wish to call witnesses who are not prisoners, you should make sure each of your non-prisoner witnesses receives a subpoena at least two weeks prior to trial date requiring their presence. To obtain witness subpoenas, write the clerk of the court, ask for some blank witness subpoenas, and fill them out.[776]

Subpoenas must be personally served. You can arrange for a friend or family member 18 years of age or older, or a professional process server, to do this. A copy of the subpoena is to be served; the original subpoena (the one with the embossed court seal) is retained and filed with the court after the person who served the subpoena fills out the form on the back.

In theory, if you are proceeding *in forma pauperis*, you can send your completed subpoenas to the U.S. Marshals Service, along with a copy of the order granting *in forma pauperis* (IFP) status, requesting the Marshal to serve the subpoenas. The Marshal's fee for serving the subpoenas should be waived if you have been granted *in forma pauperis* status. In practice, we understand, some Marshals have taken the position that IFP status only covers service of the summons and the complaint. You should therefore ask

the district judge to direct the Marshal to serve your subpoenas.

Most courts have held that an indigent litigant must generally tender the witness fees and mileage to be served with the subpoena.[777] Some courts have held that the IFP statute permits the court to direct the U. S. Marshal to advance the witness fees if the witnesses are shown to be material and necessary.[778]

The most important point about getting witnesses (including yourself) to court is that it is your responsibility to take the proper steps to get them produced. Just putting them on your witness list will not do the job; if you want them there, you must make sure that the court issues the necessary writ or subpoena.[779]

Do not rely on the defendants' witness list either; they are not required to call all the witnesses on their list, and if they think they can beat you by dropping a witness, they will surely do so. Sometimes defense counsel or prison officials will agree to produce you or other necessary witnesses without requiring you to prepare a writ. Make sure that this agreement is in writing or that it is made in court in the presence of the judge. If you can't ensure this, you are better off preparing the writs.

Prisoners who are produced for court may be subjected to necessary security measures during transportation, including shackles and other restraints.[780] However, the court should avoid the use of shackles, or minimize their use and visibility, in the courtroom during a jury trial.[781] The use

---

[772] 28 U.S.C. §§ 2241(c), 2243; *see* Pennsylvania Bureau of Correction v. U.S. Marshals Service, 474 U.S. 34, 38–39, 106 S. Ct. 355 (1985). A model writ and supporting affidavit appear in Appendix C, Forms 7a and 7b. However, you should probably write to the court clerk, the *pro se* clerk, or the judge's chambers and ask if they can provide you with a form writ used in that district.

[773] U.S. v. Moussaoui, 382 F.3d 453, 466 (4th Cir. 2004) ("It is thus clear that a district court can reach beyond the boundaries of its own district in order to issue a testimonial writ."); Hawks v. Timms, 35 F. Supp. 2d 464, 468 n.4 (D.Md. 1999); Greene v. Prunty, 938 F. Supp. 637, 639 (S.D.Cal. 1996).

[774] Price v. Johnston, 334 U.S. 266, 278–79, 68 S. Ct. 1049 (1948) (addressing production of prisoner for appellate argument). The All Writs Act, now found at 28 U.S.C. § 1651(a), authorizes federal courts to "issue all writs necessary or appropriate in aid of their respective jurisdictions and agreeable to the usages and principles of law."

[775] 28 U.S.C. § 1821(f).
The Supreme Court held that under an earlier version of the statute prisoners were entitled to witness fees. Demarest v. Manspeaker, 498 U.S. 184, 111 S. Ct. 599 (1991). Congress then changed the statute and eliminated the witness fee for prisoners. *See* U.S. v. Tippett, 975 F.2d 713, 715–16 (10th Cir. 1992).

[776] Rule 45(a)(3), Fed.R.Civ.P.

[777] Malik v. LaVallee, 994 F.2d 90 (2d Cir. 1993); Tedder v. Odel, 890 F.2d 210, 211–12 (9th Cir. 1989) and cases cited; McNeil v. Lowney, 831 F.2d 1368, 1373 (7th Cir. 1987); Lloyd v. McKendree, 749 F.2d 705, 706–07 (11th Cir. 1985); Gonzalez v. Fenner, 128 F.R.D. 606, 607–08 (S.D.N.Y. 1989); Hodge v. Prince, 730 F. Supp. 747, 749–52 (N.D.Tex. 1990), *aff'd*, 923 F.2d 853 (5th Cir. 1991).
At present, the statutory witness fee is $40.00 a day plus travel expenses. 18 U.S.C. § 1821(b).

[778] Guy v. Maio, 227 F.R.D. 498, 501 (E.D.Wis. 2005) (citing Coleman v. St. Vincent de Paul Society, 144 F.R.D. 92, 95–96 (E.D.Wis. 1992)); *see* U.S. v. Means, 741 F.2d 1053, 1057–58 (8th Cir. 1984) (en banc) (in "compelling circumstances," trial court may rely on Federal Rule of Evidence 614(a) to authorize witnesses expenses to be paid for by solvent party to lawsuit).

[779] *See* McGill v. Duckworth, 944 F.2d 344, 353 (7th Cir. 1991) (prisoner should have subpoenaed witnesses rather than relying on his witness list and the court's "inherent power" to compel their attendance).

[780] Castillo v. Stainer, 983 F.2d 145, 148 (9th Cir. 1992) (upholding chaining of prisoner during transport), *amended*, 997 F.2d 669 (9th Cir. 1993); Goff v. Nix, 803 F.2d 358, 368 (8th Cir. 1986) (upholding visual body cavity searches in connection with court appearances); Datz v. Hutson, 806 F. Supp. 982, 989–90 (N.D Ga. 1992) (upholding shackling of prisoners in court holding cells), *aff'd*, 14 F.3d 58 (11th Cir. 1994).

[781] The Supreme Court has said there is a consensus of courts that "during the guilt phase of a trial, a criminal defendant has a right to remain free of physical restraints that are visible to the jury; that the right has a constitutional dimension; but that the right may be overcome in a particular instance by essential state interests such as physical security, escape prevention, or courtroom

of stun belts in court is governed by the similar concerns.[782] The misuse of security procedures against prisoners who

decorum." Deck v. Missouri, 544 U.S. 622, 628, 125 S. Ct. 2007 (2005). The same is true of the penalty phase of capital prosecutions, which is a jury proceeding. *Deck*, 544 U.S. at 632–33. Courts must make "case-specific" decisions about the risk posed by a particular individual. *Id.* at 633–34.

The same considerations apply to civil trials. Davidson v. Riley, 44 F.3d 1118, 1122 (2d Cir. 1995) ("The principles consistently applied are that the trial court has discretion to order physical restraints on a party or witness when the court has found those restraints to be necessary to maintain safety or security; but the court must impose no greater restraints than are necessary, and it must take steps to minimize the prejudice resulting from the presence of the restraints.") The court must make an independent decision as to the need for shackles and cannot abdicate decision to correctional personnel. *See* Woods v. Thieret, 5 F.3d 244, 247–50 (7th Cir. 1993); Lemons v. Skidmore, 985 F.2d 354, 356 (7th Cir. 1992) (restraints must be justified at a hearing and must be the minimum required by security); Holloway v. Alexander, 957 F.2d 529, 530 (8th Cir. 1992).

[782]U.S. v. Durham, 287 F.3d 1297, 1306 (11th Cir. 2002); *accord*, U.S. v. Miller, 531 F.3d 340, 345 (6th Cir. 2008), *cert. denied*, 129 S. Ct. 307 (2008). The *Dunham* court said:

> [S]tun belts plainly pose many of the same constitutional concerns as do other physical restraints, though in somewhat different ways. Stun belts are less visible than many other restraining devices, and may be less likely to interfere with a defendant's entitlement to the presumption of innocence. However, a stun belt imposes a substantial burden on the ability of a defendant to participate in his own defense and confer with his attorney during a trial. If activated, the device poses a serious threat to the dignity and decorum of the courtroom.

287 F.3d at 1306. Therefore, close judicial scrutiny is required of the justification for its use.

> Due to the novelty of this technology, a court contemplating its use will likely need to make factual findings about the operation of the stun belt, addressing issues such as the criteria for triggering the belt and the possibility of accidental discharge. A court will also need to assess whether an essential state interest is served by compelling a particular defendant to wear such a device, and must consider less restrictive methods of restraint. Furthermore, the court's rationale must be placed on the record to enable us to determine if the use of the stun belt was an abuse of the court's discretion.

Dunham, 287 F.3d at 1306–07; *see* U.S. v. Honken, 541 F.3d 1146, 1164 (8th Cir. 2008) (upholding use of stun belt in light of defendant's martial arts training and dangerousness); U.S. v. Miller, 531 F.3d at 345–46 (holding court abused its discretion using a stun belt without holding a hearing and making findings). One court has held that the use of a stun belt is more justifiable in *pro se* cases where the prisoner is moving around the courtroom. Weaver v. State, 894 So.2d 178, 194–95 (Fla. 2004).

If a prisoner fails to object to use of the stun belt during the trial, courts will hold the issue waived, or will only find it reversible if it was "plain error." *See, e.g.,* U.S. v. Miller, 531 F.3d at 345–46 (finding error harmless); Belisle v. State, 11 So.3d 256, 281–82 (Ala. Crim.App. 2007), *aff'd*, 11 So.3d 323 (Ala. 2008), *cert. denied*, 129

are to appear in court may violate the right of court access.[783]

R. TRIALS

This section will introduce the basics of trial practice. We cannot cover all aspects of this subject, but we hope to provide enough information to help you present your case correctly and clearly to a court or jury.

1. What Happens at a Trial?

The purpose of a trial is to decide facts that are in dispute. If there is no factual dispute, there is no need for a trial, and the judge can decide the case without one.[784]

There may be a few differences in the way different courts conduct trials, but most federal civil trials follow the same basic outline. We will list the steps in this section and then explain them in more detail in the sections that follow.

A trial begins with the selection of a jury, if the parties have asked for a jury trial. If they have not asked (or if the case is one where there is no right to a jury), the judge will decide the case. A non-jury trial is called a bench trial.

Next, the plaintiff makes an opening statement, telling the judge or jury what he expects to prove. The defendants may make an opening statement after the plaintiff's statement, or may wait until after the plaintiff's evidence has been presented.

After opening statements, the plaintiff will present his evidence. When the plaintiff's case is finished, the defendants may move for judgment as a matter of law[785] on the ground that the plaintiff's evidence, even if believed, does not establish a violation of law by the defendants.

If the judge denies the defendants' motion, the defendants present their evidence. If new issues are raised in the defendants' case, the plaintiff may then present rebuttal evidence; if more new issues are introduced, the defendants may be allowed to present "surrebuttal" evidence.

After all the evidence is in, either party may move for judgment as a matter of law, arguing that they are entitled to win the case regardless of how any factual disputes are resolved. If those motions are denied, the parties make their closing arguments. In a bench trial, the case is ready for decision after closing argument; in a jury trial, the judge will charge, or instruct, the jury as to what its duties are and how it is to evaluate the parties' proof. The jury will then deliberate and return with a verdict.

S. Ct. 2865 (2009); Scieszka v. State, 259 Ga.App. 486, 487, 578 S.E.2d 149 (Ga.App. 2003).

[783]May v. Sheahan, 226 F.3d 876, 883 (7th Cir. 2000) (claim stated against policy of shackling inmates with AIDS and not allowing them to attend court proceedings); Penny v. Shansky, 884 F.2d 329, 330 (7th Cir. 1989).

[784]*See* § L of this chapter concerning summary judgment.

[785]This motion used to be called a motion for a directed verdict in a jury trial or a motion to dismiss in a non-jury trial.

In a bench trial, the judge will either issue an oral decision at the time ("rule from the bench") or will "reserve decision" and issue a written decision later. In a bench trial, the judge can also ask the parties to submit post-trial briefs containing proposed findings of fact and conclusions of law, and legal authorities supporting them, for consideration in reaching a decision.

After the verdict or decision, the losing party may make a motion for judgment as a matter of law[786] or for a new trial.

2. The Right to Trial by Jury

The Seventh Amendment to the United States Constitution provides, "In Suits at common law, where the value in controversy shall exceed twenty dollars, the right of trial by jury shall be preserved, and no fact tried by a jury, shall be otherwise re-examined in any Court of the United States, than according to the rules of the common law."[787] The Seventh Amendment guarantees the right to a jury trial in federal court civil rights suits for money damages against prison officials or other government employees.[788]

In a jury trial, the jury decides the facts; the court decides all legal questions. You have the right to a jury trial only if your case presents a factual issue that, if decided your way, would entitle you to win. If a judge decides that there is no factual dispute, or that you would lose the case even if the facts were decided your way, the judge may decide the case on that basis by granting summary judgment without violating your right to a jury trial.[789]

The Seventh Amendment does not apply when you are seeking an injunction[790] or when you are suing the federal government under the FTCA; there are no jury trials in these cases.[791] The Seventh Amendment does not apply to the states,[792] so if you are pursuing state law claims in state court, your right to a civil jury trial is governed by state law.

To get a jury trial you have to ask for it. The best time and place to make a jury demand is in the complaint. If you do not do this, you must serve a jury demand on the other side within 14 days of the service of the last pleading directed to the issue you want a jury trial on, and then file it with the court.[793] This generally means within 14 days after the defendants serve their answer. If you do not ask for a jury trial in time, you will waive the right to a jury trial;[794] however, the court has discretion to give you a jury trial anyway.[795] Either party can ask for a jury trial, and a party may not withdraw a jury demand without the other side's consent.[796]

Whether to ask for a jury trial is a major decision. A jury trial is harder to conduct than a bench trial, and you should consider whether your skills are adequate.[797] You should consider:

- how sympathetic the judge might be if you do not have a jury;

---

[786]This motion, when made at the end of the case, used to be called a motion for judgment notwithstanding the verdict, or JNOV.

[787]U.S. Const., Amend. VII.

[788]City of Monterey v. Del Monte Dunes at Monterey, Ltd., 526 U.S. 687, 729, 119 S. Ct. 1624 (1999) (Scalia, J., concurring); *see* Curtis v. Loether, 415 U.S. 189, 94 S. Ct. 1005 (1974) (discussing scope of Seventh Amendment).

[789]*See* § L of this chapter, n.629.

[790]City of Monterey v. Del Monte Dunes at Monterey, Ltd., 526 U.S. at 719.

If you seek damages *and* an injunction, you have the right to a jury trial on the damages portion of the trial. *See also* Ch. 8, § O.2, concerning this point.

[791]28 U.S.C. § 2402; *see* Ch. 8, § C.2, concerning the FTCA.

[792]City of Monterey v. Del Monte Dunes at Monterey, Ltd., 526 U.S. at 720 (Seventh Amendment right to jury trial does not apply to suits decided by state courts); Elliott v. City of Wheat Ridge, 49 F.3d 1458, 1460 (10th Cir. 1995).

[793]Rule 38(b), Fed.R.Civ.P. The deadline in this rule was changed from 10 days, excluding weekends and holidays, to 14 days including all days, effective December 1, 2009. *See* Marshall v. Knight, 445 F.3d 965, 970 (7th Cir. 2006) (allowing plaintiff to amend complaint to add jury demand); Lutz v. Glendale Union High Sch., 403 F.3d 1061, 1066 (9th Cir. 2005) ("If these additional claims were new 'issue[s]' under Rule 38(b), then [the plaintiff's] jury trial demand . . . was timely as to them.").

[794]Rule 38(d), Fed.R.Civ.P.; *see* Mile High Industries v. Cohen, 222 F.3d 845, 855 n.8 (10th Cir. 2000).

If you have asked for a jury trial but the court erroneously proceeds with a bench trial instead, you must object at the beginning of the trial or your right to a jury is waived. Fillmore v. Page, 358 F.3d 496, 503 (7th Cir. 2004) ("A failure to object to a proceeding in which the court sits as the finder of fact 'waives a valid jury demand as to any claims decided in that proceeding, at least where it was clear that the court intended to make fact determinations.'" (citation omitted)).

[795]Rule 39(b), Fed.R.Civ.P.; *see* Members v. Paige, 140 F.3d 699 (7th Cir. 1998) (district court may require a reason for not asking for a jury timely, but "[o]nce such a reason has been advanced, the district court 'ought to approach each application under Rule 39(b) with an open mind and an eye to the factual situation of that particular case, rather than with a fixed policy'"; lack of counsel may be a sufficient justification for having failed to request a jury timely (citation omitted)); Lewis v. Thigpen, 767 F.2d 252, 257–59 (5th Cir. 1985) (*pro se* plaintiff should be relieved from jury waiver unless there are "strong and compelling reasons" to the contrary); Johnson v. Dalton, 57 F. Supp. 2d 958, 960 (C.D.Cal. 1999) (court has discretion to grant untimely jury demand when not due to "oversight" or "inadvertence"). *But see* Salahuddin v. Harris, 684 F. Supp. 1224, 1228–29 (S.D.N.Y. 1988) (plaintiff denied relief from jury waiver because he waited a year after appointment of counsel to ask for it). *See also* Lutz v. Glendale Union High Sch., 403 F.3d 1061, 1066 (9th Cir. 2005) (even when you add a new issue in an amended complaint, the district court can deny the jury request because "'the issues in the original complaint and the amended complaint turn[ed] on the same matrix of facts, . . . '" (citation omitted)).

[796]Rule 38(d), Fed.R.Civ.P.; *see* Dell'Orfano v. Romano, 962 F.2d 199, 202 (2d Cir. 1992) (plaintiff was entitled to a jury trial because the defendants asked for one).

[797]On the other hand, the fact that a case will be tried to a jury is a factor supporting the appointment of counsel. Solis v. County

- what is the attitude of the people in the community from which the jury will come toward prisoners;[798]
- whether you have a legal claim that ordinary people will easily understand (*e.g.*, they beat you up and broke your arm), or one that is more technical (*e.g.*, they did not give you adequate notice and statement of reasons in connection with a disciplinary hearing);
- how long it takes to get a jury trial (usually longer than a bench trial in most jurisdictions); and
- whether the factual issues are more complicated than a jury is likely to understand.

Expert trial lawyers often believe that juries are more likely to be moved by sympathetic appeals than judges,[799] and that judges are more likely to stick strictly to the facts and the law. Which way this cuts obviously depends on the facts of the case, including facts about you, such as the nature of your criminal record[800] and whether you come across as a dangerous or dishonest person to the kinds of people who serve on juries.[801]

3. Selecting a Jury

A federal civil jury consists of six to twelve jurors. Unless the parties stipulate otherwise, the jurors' verdict must be unanimous, and a jury that has been reduced to fewer than six members cannot render a verdict.[802] After the jury returns a verdict, but before it is discharged, a party may request that the jurors be polled, or the court may do so on its own initiative; if the decision is not unanimous or consistent with a stipulation for a non-unanimous verdict, the court may direct the jury to deliberate further or may order a new trial.[803] State courts may have different rules on these subjects and on other aspects of jury procedure; always check the rules of the court you are in.

You have the right to an impartial jury. Impaneling an impartial jury has two main parts. First, a number of prospective jurors (an "array") will be called to the courtroom. Second, the judge will supervise the selection of specific jurors through a voir dire examination.

By statute, people must be called for jury duty on a random basis,[804] and anyone is deemed to be qualified for jury service if he is a United States citizen at least eighteen years old who has lived for a year in the judicial district, can speak English, is capable of filling out the required forms, is physically and mentally able to serve, and does not have a conviction or pending charge of a serious crime.[805]

The voir dire examination consists of asking each prospective juror a number of questions designed to find out if he can decide the case fairly. In federal court, the voir dire may be conducted either by the judge or by counsel.[806] Usually the judge does it because it is faster that way; check the local court rules to see if there is a prescribed practice in your jurisdiction. Sometimes the judge will permit counsel to ask additional questions after the judge has finished. The judge has broad discretion in the way voir dire is conducted.[807]

Voir dire questions should be designed to learn if there are any reasons why a particular juror cannot decide the case fairly based on the evidence.[808] A juror should not sit on your case if the juror has preconceived ideas about the case;

---

of Los Angeles, 514 F.3d 946, 958 (9th Cir. 2008); Abdullah v. Gunter, 949 F.2d 1032, 1036 (8th Cir. 1991). Appointment of counsel is discussed in § C.5 of this chapter.

[798]This is hard to be sure about. Generally, prisoner advocates assume that people in urban areas and/or areas with significant minority representation will mostly be more liberal, and more prone to be open-minded about claims that convicted criminals have been mistreated by law enforcement personnel, than will be people in more rural areas with few minority residents, or people in areas where prisons are a major employer and a basis of the economy. But people don't always conform to such gross stereotypes. Also, the community from which the jury is selected may be large enough to include different kinds of areas and populations. For example, the federal court sitting in Detroit picks from an area about 80 miles by 40 miles. Within that large an area, you will not know until you actually are picking the jury where the members of the jury pool live—and even then, their attitudes may surprise you.

[799]*See, e.g.*, Robert E. Keeton, *Trial Tactics and Methods* at § 7.2 (2d ed., Little, Brown & Co., 1973).

[800]This evidence may be, but is not required to be, excluded from the trial. *See* § S.5.a of this chapter for a discussion of this subject.

[801]*See* § F.3 of this chapter for a discussion of jury selection.

[802]Rule 48, Fed.R.Civ.P.

The recommended practice is to seat more than six jurors so if one or more jurors cannot continue for some reason, there will still be six jurors to decide the case. *See* Rule 48, Fed.R.Civ.P., Notes of Advisory Committee to 1991 Amendment. Many district courts are now seating eight jurors and all will deliberate unless one is excused prior to deliberation.

[803]Rule 48(c), Fed.R.Civ.P. This is a new provision, effective December 1, 2009.

[804]28 U.S.C. § 1863(a).

[805]28 U.S.C. § 1865(b).

[806]Rule 47(a), Fed.R.Civ.P.

[807]Mu'Min v. Virginia, 500 U.S. 415, 423, 111 S. Ct. 1899 (1991); Richie v. Rogers, 313 F.3d 948, 961 (6th Cir. 2002) (affirming trial court's denial of individual voir dire and of questioning about specific contents of news reports); Wolfe v. Brigano, 232 F.3d 499, 504 (6th Cir. 2000) (Wellford, J., concurring) (trial court's broad discretion in the conduct of voir dire is nevertheless "subject to essential demands of fairness" (quoting U.S. v. Nell, 526 F.2d 1223, 1229 (5th Cir. 1976)).

[808]*See* Scott v. Lawrence, 36 F.3d 871, 874 (9th Cir. 1994) (citing Darbin v. Nourse, 664 F.2d 1109, 1112–13 (9th Cir. 1981)).

prejudices based on race, religion, your status as a prisoner or some other factor; prior knowledge of the case which might influence his decision; or personal or business relationships with parties to the case or their relatives.

Your voir dire questions should focus on these issues. You should submit proposed voir dire questions to the court in advance of the trial. The court is obligated "to probe the jury adequately for bias or prejudice about material matters on request of counsel."[809]

If a juror's answers reveal some bias about the case, you may challenge that juror for cause.[810] The judge will then either excuse the juror or overrule your challenge.[811]

If your challenge for cause is overruled, or if you think a juror may be biased but you cannot cite a specific reason, you may exercise a "peremptory challenge" and have that juror removed.[812] Typically, litigants are provided with the jurors' qualification forms to rely on in exercising their peremptory challenges.[813]

Peremptory challenges can be used for any reason and do not need to be explained, with one exception. They may not be used to exclude jurors based on race or gender,[814] and you or the defendants' lawyer can be required to explain your reasons for excluding jurors if it appears that race or gender was a factor.[815]

Ordinarily, each party is limited to three peremptory challenges. If there are multiple plaintiffs or defendants, the judge will decide whether each of them gets three peremptory challenges, or whether they are restricted to a total of three among them.[816] If there are multiple defendants in your case, be sure to ask the court to restrict the other side to a total of three (or else give you more challenges) so each side will have an equal influence on the selection of the jury.[817]

After the voir dire, the judge will swear in the jury. If you have any objections to the way the jury was selected, you must make them before the jury is sworn or you will waive them.[818]

Before the jury selection starts, you should ask the judge to explain to you exactly how he intends to proceed. Practices may vary from place to place and from judge to judge, and it is easy to get confused about things such as when and how to make peremptory challenges.[819]

You should understand that you do not have a right to a "jury of your peers" in the sense of people who come from similar social or racial backgrounds. The purpose of jury selection is to provide a cross-section of the community, and if your trial is taking place in a white, middle-class or rural area, you will probably get a white, middle-class, or rural jury.

Moreover, juries in general tend to underrepresent minorities and low-income people (in part because jury rolls are made up in whole or in part from voters lists,[820] and these groups have low voter registration rates), and to overrepresent people who will receive their full salaries while serving (like many government employees) and people who do not have to work or take care of children (like retired people). Many people simply cannot afford to sit on juries and lose time from work, and others are subject to family obligations that prevent them from serving; the judge is likely to excuse these people.[821] Also, prospective jurors who seem sympathetic to prisoners, minority group members, or poor people are likely to be removed from the jury by the defendants' peremptory challenges. These facts should be kept in mind in deciding whether to ask for a jury trial.

---

[809]Darbin v. Nourse, 664 F.2d at 1114; see Rainey v. Conerley, 973 F.2d 321, 325 (4th Cir. 1992) (trial judge in a use of force case should have asked jury panel members "whether they would tend to credit the testimony of a law enforcement official over that of a prisoner, simply because of their respective positions").

[810]Fields v. Brown, 431 F.3d 1186, 1196–97 (9th Cir. 2005), on rehearing, 503 F.3d 755 (9th Cir. 2007), cert. denied, 128 S. Ct. 1875 (2008); U.S. v. Torres, 128 F.3d 38, 43, 49 (2d Cir. 1997) (discussing actual bias and implied bias standards, and upholding the trial judge's decision to strike a potential juror based on bias inferred from the similarity between the juror's own conduct and the accusation against the defendant).

[811]28 U.S.C. § 1870.

[812]U.S. v. Broussard, 987 F.2d 215, 221 (5th Cir. 1993) ("The denial or impairment of the right to exercise peremptory challenges is reversible error without a showing of prejudice."), abrogated on other grounds by J.E.B. v. Alabama, 511 U.S. 127, 114 S. Ct. 1419 (1994).

[813]Edmonson v. Leesville Concrete Co., Inc., 500 U.S. 614, 622–23, 111 S. Ct. 2077 (1991) (citing G. Berman, Jury Selection Procedures in United States District Courts at 7–8 (Federal Judicial Center 1982)).

[814]J.E.B. v. Alabama, 511 U.S. 127, 114 S. Ct 1419 (1994) (gender); Edmonson v. Leesville Concrete Co., Inc., 501 U.S. at 624–29 (race). Edmonson makes clear that such discrimination is forbidden in civil cases as well as criminal ones.

[815]See Snyder v. Louisiana, 552 U.S. 472, 477–85, 128 S. Ct. 1203 (2008) (holding claimed reasons for peremptory challenges were a pretext for racial discrimination); Kahle v. Leonard, 563 F.3d 736, 739–40 (8th Cir. 2009) (affirming district court finding of gender discrimination in striking women in a jail rape case); Barnes v. Parker, 972 F.2d 978, 980 (8th Cir. 1992) (defense attorney gave a legitimate nonracial reason for striking the only black member of the jury panel).

[816]28 U.S.C. § 1870; see Rodriguez v. Riddell Sports, Inc., 242 F.3d 567, 581 (5th Cir. 2001) (additional challenges are usually given where multiple defendants may not share the same strategy, but there is no "definite rationale" governing the question).

[817]See Goldstein v. Kelleher, 728 F.2d 32, 37 (1st Cir. 1984) (granting an unequal number of challenges was an abuse of discretion); Fedorchick v. Massey Ferguson, Inc., 577 F.2d 856, 858 (3d Cir. 1978).

[818]Robert S. Hunter, Federal Trial Handbook at § 24.27 (West, 4th ed. 2007).

[819]See Carr v. Watts, 597 F.2d 830, 832–33 (2d Cir. 1989).

[820]28 U.S.C. § 1863(b)(2).

[821]See 28 U.S.C. § 1866(c) (providing for excuses from jury service on grounds of "undue hardship or extreme inconvenience").

4. Starting the Trial

To begin the trial, the court normally introduces counsel and then asks plaintiff's counsel whether he is ready to proceed. Presumably the court will treat a *pro se* plaintiff in the same fashion.

If the parties have stipulated to certain facts that need not be proved at trial, these stipulated facts may be read to the jury after opening statements before the first witness testifies.[822] This is probably appropriate if they are background facts such as the location or size of the prison. However, if they are closely related to a particular witness's story, they should probably be read in connection with that witness's testimony. They also may (and probably should) be offered into evidence in writing.[823]

How and when stipulated facts are presented is within the trial judge's discretion[824] and should be arranged with the judge and the opposing party before the trial. The use of factual stipulations can cause the trial to go very fast, reducing the jury's opportunity to hear the witnesses (including yourself) testify and assess their credibility. Depending on how credible each side's witnesses are, this may or may not be to your advantage.

5. Opening Statements

Both parties are entitled to present opening statements. The plaintiff will present his opening statement first, and the defendants can either present their opening statement right after the plaintiff or reserve opening statements until after the plaintiff's case is finished.[825]

Opening statements are intended to tell the court or jury the issues that will be presented and the facts that will be proved. They should not be argumentative. They are also not evidence. If you assert a fact in your opening statement, you must later submit testimony or other evidence proving that fact, or the judge or jury will not be able to consider it. Also, if you make a claim and then fail to support it with evidence, your credibility will be damaged.

The opening statement should set out facts that will be sufficient to establish your legal claim if you can prove them. If it does not do so, the defendants may be able to move for dismissal (now called judgment as a matter of law) at the end of your opening statement.[826] If the defendants make such a motion in your case, and you realize that you left something out of the opening statement, you should ask the judge for permission to add to your opening statement.

Your opening statement should also give the judge or jury a preview of the evidence you will be presenting so they will know what to expect and be able to understand it better. This is particularly important if you will have several witnesses whose testimony will cover various times and places. You may also wish to explain some things about the prison setting with which a judge or jury may be unfamiliar—though, as with other facts you refer to in your opening statement, you must submit sworn testimony or other evidence in order for those facts to be in evidence.

The other purpose of an opening statement is to introduce yourself as well as your case. The judge or jury will be assessing you as a person and judging your credibility, and the opening statement will be your first chance to try to make a favorable impression. Be respectful and calm and avoid rhetoric and name-calling.

You should also try to tell the jurors something about yourself so they can begin to see you as a human being and not just as a convict. (This should be kept brief. The judge will probably allow you some latitude as a *pro se* litigant, but do not try to tell your life story.) If your criminal record is going to be brought out in the trial,[827] you should be the one to do it.

We have drafted a sample opening statement to illustrate these points.

> Good morning. My name is Dan Manville. I am 32 years old and I am an inmate at the State Prison of Southern Michigan, where I am serving a sentence for manslaughter. Until the events you are going to hear about, I had a job in the prison tailor shop and I was studying for my high school equivalency certificate.
>
> On the morning of January 19, 2006, I was placed in handcuffs in my cell, maced, and then beaten with an axe handle while I was being taken to the hole. (The hole is a term used for a special unit the prison uses for solitary confinement and segregation of prisoners they say broke the rules.) I was handcuffed during this entire period and was not fighting back. The reason I was treated this way was because I had had a verbal argument with an officer the day before.
>
> You will hear my testimony about how I asked to be let out of my prison cell to take a shower on January 18, and Officer Jones got mad at me because he was busy and I insisted on my shower. You will hear that I was locked in my cell for the noon count of prisoners on January 19 when Lieutenant Smith and Officer Jones approached my cell and Lieutenant Smith told me to place my hands

---

[822]*See, e.g.*, Hiltgen v. Sumrall, 47 F.3d 695, 703 (5th Cir. 1995) (stipulated facts read to the jury at the beginning of the trial).

[823]Frett v. Government of Virgin Islands, 839 F.2d 968, 971–72 (3d Cir. 1988) (quoting stipulated facts read and submitted to the jury).

[824]*See* Johnson v. Sawyer, 120 F.3d 1307, 1331 (5th Cir. 1997) ("The district court refused to read to the jury the facts stipulated in the pretrial order. This is [a] question best left to the court on remand."); Garnes v. Gulf & W. Mfg. Co., 789 F.2d 637, 643 (8th Cir. 1986) (finding "no merit" to claim that stipulated facts instruction unduly highlighted the admitted facts).

[825]Kent Sinclair, *Federal Civil Practice* § 15.20 at 822 (Practicing Law Institute, 4th ed. 2004).

[826]Kent Sinclair, *Federal Civil Practice* at § 15.20.

[827]Whether your criminal record can be referred to should be established before trial through a motion *in limine*. These motions are discussed in § S.6 of this chapter.

between the bars so I could be handcuffed. I will tell you how Officer Jones, following an order by Lieutenant Smith, maced me even though I was locked in my cell in handcuffs, and how Officer Brown later beat me with an axe handle as we walked to the hole.

You will hear testimony of prisoner Ronald Lev that his cell is directly across from mine and that he saw Officer Jones mace me without provocation while I was handcuffed. Prisoner Stuart Steinberg will testify that as I was being led out of the cell block, he saw Officer Brown strike me on the head and shoulders with an axe handle.

You will see the prison medical records that verify that I had severe bruises on my shoulders and neck and lumps on my head after all this happened, and I will testify about the pain and suffering that I experienced from the beating, including dizziness and blurred vision for a period of a week and being unable to engage in any exercise for three or four weeks.

6. Plaintiff's Evidence

As the plaintiff, you will present your case first, including all the witnesses and all the documents that you think will help show that your rights were violated. This is called your "direct case" or "case-in-chief." Do not try to surprise the defendants by holding back a crucial piece of evidence until after they have presented their case. It is your burden to present a *prima facie*[828] case at the beginning, and if you fail to do this, the judge may grant judgment as a matter of law to the defendants, which means your case will be dismissed.

Also, rebuttal is restricted to answering new issues raised by the defendants when they put in their evidence, and if they do not handle their case as you expect, you may not be permitted to put in the rebuttal evidence that you planned. If your case depends in part on the testimony of prison personnel—or even the defendants themselves—you must call them as part of your case.[829]

When you put on witnesses to support your case, you will get their testimony on the record by asking them questions. This is direct examination. After you are finished, the other side gets to ask them questions; this is called cross-examination. The rules governing direct and cross-examination are discussed later.[830]

Your main witness may be yourself. Since it would be silly to ask yourself questions, you should prepare your testimony in the form of a narrative story, which you will tell from the witness stand. You may wish to write out an outline to help you remember everything. However, the other side will be permitted to examine and use any notes you have with

you while on the witness stand.[831] You should be familiar enough with what you want to say that you can do it without notes if you have to. If you keep referring to notes, it will not help your credibility. If you do take notes to the stand, they should be no more than a broad outline of topics you wish to cover.

While the case is being presented, you or the defendants' lawyer may believe that an improper question has been asked. (What questions are proper is discussed later in this chapter.[832]) In that case, you or the opposing lawyer will make an objection. An objection should indicate "the specific ground of objection, if the specific ground was not apparent from the context."[833]

Judges generally prefer that objections be kept short and not argumentative, especially in a jury trial. You can make your objection clear by saying, *e.g.*, "Your Honor, I object on the ground of hearsay," or just, "Objection, hearsay." (It is not a ground for objection that you think the witness is not telling the truth; that is for you to establish through cross-examination or your own evidence.) The judge may rule on an objection immediately or may ask for further comment from either side.

If the other side objects to one of your questions, do not respond or continue asking questions; wait until the judge rules. An objection is like a stoplight in the trial; do not proceed until the judge gives you the green light by ruling on the objection. You should be sure you understand the basis for the objection and the court's ruling. You do not have to abandon a topic just because an objection is sustained. You may be able to rephrase your question so it is not objectionable.

If the judge sustains objections to testimony that you are convinced is proper and admissible, and you don't understand why, ask if you can approach the bench, and very politely request an explanation so you can get your case in consistently with the court's rulings. If you are clearly trying to follow the court's direction, the judge is likely to explain his rulings further.

If you have more than one witness or a large number of documents, you will have to decide in what order to present your evidence. You want your case to be as forceful as possible and as clear as possible. To be forceful, you will generally want to present your strongest witness (usually yourself) first; to be clear, you will usually want to present witnesses in chronological order of the events they will testify about. Sometimes these two considerations are in conflict and you will have to make a judgment about what will be more effective.

You can put documents into evidence at any point in your case, with the exception that some documents may need to have a foundation laid during the testimony of a

---

[828]This term is discussed in § S.1.f of this chapter.

[829]When examining an adverse party or a witness identified with an adverse party, you are permitted to use leading questions as if you were cross-examining. *See* § S.3.b of this chapter for further discussion of this point.

[830]*See* § S.3.b of this chapter.

[831]Rule 612, Fed.R.Evid.

If opposing counsel asks why you need notes, you can reply, "To make sure all the truth comes out in court."

[832]*See* § S.3 of this chapter.

[833]Rule 103(a)(1), Fed.R.Evid.

particular witness.[834] It is often very effective to put documents in as their subject matter comes up in testimony. For example, if you claim that an officer beat you because you had earlier filed a complaint against him, you could put that complaint in evidence when you mention it at the beginning of your testimony; you could put medical records showing your injuries into evidence later, after you describe the beating or your treatment at the prison clinic.

You should also consider how you want the documents communicated to the jury. The judge has discretion to read them to the jury or let you or the witness read them, or to give them to the jury to read, or both. It is probably most effective to have the witness read the document, or at least the important parts of the document, to the jury. If the jurors are to read the documents themselves, it will speed things up if you can have enough extra copies for each juror.

In either case, when you give your closing argument, you should explain the documents' significance to your case and urge the jury to review them when they deliberate. If a document is long or hard to read, call the jury's attention to the key points and tell them what you think the document means for your case.

7. Offer of Proof

If the court has refused to allow you to use evidence, such as prior acts of a defendant to show the defendant's intent or opportunity or to impeach, you must ask the district court to let you make an "offer of proof" in order to preserve your right to raise the issue on appeal (and in some cases to try to persuade the court to reconsider).[835] This would occur outside of the presence of the jury. During the "offer of proof" you would state what the evidence would have shown if admitted and why the evidence should be admitted.[836]

The court may not let you make an offer of proof while the relevant witness is on the stand; it may tell you to do it at the next break or at the end of the day. Be sure to remember to make the offer; if you forget, you will waive the issue.[837]

An offer of proof is no more than a statement for the record what the testimony would have been if the person had testified, what the evidence would have established if admitted, and the potential impact it could have had on the case. For example:

> If inmate Jones was allowed to testify, he would have testified that he was standing by the officer's desk filling out a kite. He heard Defendant Jones state that this was the last time he was going to listen to inmate Manville tell him what he was legally required to do in his job. Jones went on to state that it has been a while since a weapon had been found in the block. This testimony would show that Defendant Jones had a motive to plant a weapon in Manville's cell and would have also contradicted, for impeachment purposes, Defendant Jones's statement that inmate Manville was just another inmate in the block and he had no dealings with him.

8. Motions After the Plaintiff's Evidence

After you have presented your case, the defendants have the right to make a motion to throw part or all of your case out on the ground that your evidence, even if it is believed, does not show that your rights were violated—*i.e.*, you have failed to prove a *prima facie* case.[838] If you fail to produce some evidence as to every element of your legal claim, you will have failed to make a *prima facie* case. These motions are almost always made orally and not on paper.

There are two things you can do in responding to such a motion. First, you can show the judge that you have

---

[834]Laying a foundation is discussed in § S.4.d of this chapter.

[835]Rule 103(a)(2), Fed.R.Evid. ("Error may not be predicated upon a ruling which admits or excludes evidence unless a substantial right of the party is affected, and . . . (2) Offer of Proof.—In case the ruling is one excluding evidence, the substance of the evidence was made known to the court by offer or was apparent from the context within which questions were asked."); *see, e.g.*, Surprevant v. Rivas, 424 F.3d 5, 22 (1st Cir. 2006) (prison staff failed to make offer of proof why incident from seven years earlier was relevant); Medcom Holding Co. v. Baxter Travenol Lab., Inc., 106 F.3d 1388, 1395 (7th Cir. 1997) (plaintiff made offer of proof in attempt to introduce Rule 404(b) evidence); People v. Mills, 2008 WL 625093, *6 (Cal.App. 4 Dist. 2008) ("The court's decision to exclude evidence of Eric's knife assault on the Centinela prison guard was not final, and the court was willing to revisit the issue upon an offer of proof that Eric admitted to being found in possession of the knife."); Com. v. Spearin, 446 Mass. 599, 607, 846 N.E.2d 390 (2006) (inmate failed to make offer of proof as to facts of controversy between him and another inmate, so testimony of animosity between two was excluded).

[836]*See* U.S. v. Martinez, 988 F.2d 685, 700 (7th Cir. 1993) (holding that trial court's exclusion of Rule 404(b) evidence on grounds of failure to make a proper offer of proof was justified). *Cf.* U.S. v. Harvey, 959 F.2d 1371, 1374–75 (7th Cir. 1992) (excluding

evidence where party seeking its admission made only vague response regarding its admissibility).

[837]*See* Walden v. Georgia-Pacific Corp., 126 F.3d 506 517 (3d Cir. 1997) ("Although decisions to exclude evidence are generally reviewed for abuse of discretion, when a party fails to preserve the right to appeal an exclusion, we review for plain error. Under Fed.R.Evid. 103(a), a party may not appeal a ruling excluding evidence unless the party asserting error made an offer of proof at trial.").

[838]This motion was formerly called a motion to dismiss in a bench trial and a motion for a directed verdict in a jury trial. Now it is called a motion for judgment as a matter of law in a jury trial and a motion for judgment on partial findings in a non-jury trial. Rules 50(a), 52(c), Fed.R.Civ.P.

The rules actually provide that such a motion can be made any time as long as you have "been fully heard" on the issues involved in the motion. In most cases they are made at the end of the plaintiff's case. However, if such a motion is made at an earlier point, and if you have additional evidence to present that is relevant to the defendants' motion, you should tell the court that you have not yet "been fully heard."

The meaning of *prima facie* case is discussed in § S.1.f of this chapter.

produced some evidence in support of each element of your claim. (It is useful to keep a checklist of what you have to prove and check off each fact as it is put into evidence.) The defendants may also claim that you have failed to prove something that you are not legally required to prove. For example, they may say that you did not prove that a particular officer struck you during a beating; however, if you proved that the officer did stand by while others beat you, you should remind the judge of that and of the fact that that evidence is legally sufficient to hold that officer liable.[839]

Second, if it turns out that the defendants are right and you have accidentally left something out of your proof, you can ask to reopen your case and put in the missing evidence. Whether to permit this is in the judge's discretion.[840]

9. Defendants' Evidence

If the court finds you have proved a *prima facie* case, the defendants will be required to present their evidence. During the defendants' case, their lawyer will conduct the direct examination of witnesses, and you will cross-examine them. The defendants will introduce whatever documents support their case.

On occasion, you may introduce a document in evidence during defendants' case when you use it to cross-examine one of the defendants' witnesses.

10. Rebuttal and Surrebuttal

After the defendants' case has been presented, the plaintiff may present rebuttal evidence to counter evidence presented by the defendants.[841] Rebuttal evidence is usually limited to responding to new issues raised by the defendants. Evidence that should logically have been presented as part of the plaintiff's direct evidence (or "case-in-chief") may not be permitted on rebuttal, although the court has discretion to relax this rule.

The defendant may be permitted "surrebuttal" to respond to the plaintiff's rebuttal evidence.[842]

As mentioned earlier, you should not hold back evidence that supports your legal claim in order to present it on rebuttal. If you think the evidence is important and helpful, present it during your direct case.

11. Motions After the Evidence Is Closed

Once both sides' evidence is closed in a jury trial, either side may make a motion for judgment as a matter of law

(formerly called a motion for a directed verdict), either on the whole case or on selected issues. Such a motion will be granted if "the court finds that a reasonable jury would not have a legally sufficient evidentiary basis to find for the party on that issue."[843]

The defendants will argue that you have not proved a *prima facie* case.[844] You will argue that the defendants' evidence does not establish a defense even if it is true. For example, suppose you show that prison guards waited four days before sending you to a doctor for your broken arm, and the defendants prove only that they provided adequate medical care after you got to the doctor. That fact does not provide a defense for the original four-day delay, so you would be justified in asking for judgment as a matter of law against the guards on the issue of delayed care.[845]

You can make a motion for judgment as a matter of law after you have received an adverse decision, but only if you made such a motion at the close of the evidence, and only on the same grounds that were argued in the pre-verdict motion.[846] A post-verdict motion for judgment as a matter of law was formerly called a motion for judgment notwithstanding the verdict, or JNOV.

12. Closing Arguments

After all the evidence is in, you and the defendants' lawyer will be permitted to make closing arguments to the jury or to the judge concerning what the evidence shows and why you should win the case. Most commonly, the plaintiff argues first, followed by the defendants, and the plaintiff is then permitted rebuttal.

Some judges or some local rules may vary this procedure. You should ask the judge before the start of trial how closing arguments will be handled so you can prepare properly.

Closing arguments should be limited to the issues in the case and the evidence that has been presented. Facts that are not supported by evidence in the record may not be argued,[847] although you may argue reasonable inferences

---

[839]*See* Ch. 2, § G.2.b(5).

[840]Zenith Radio Corp. v. Hazeltine Research, Inc., 401 U.S. 321, 331–32 91 S. Ct. 795 (1971); Blinzler v. Marriott Intern., Inc., 81 F.3d 1148, 1160 (1st Cir. 1996) ("A trial court's decision to reopen is premised upon criteria that are flexible and fact-specific, but fairness is the key criterion.").

[841]Robert S. Hunter, *Federal Trial Handbook* at § 27 (West, 4th ed., 2007).

[842]*Id.* at § 27.4.

[843]Rule 50(a)(1), Fed.R.Civ.P.

This motion must be made before the case is submitted to the jury so accidental failures to submit evidence may be corrected. Rule 50(c), Fed.R.Civ.P., Note of Advisory Committee on 1991 Amendment.

[844]This term is defined in § S.1.f of this chapter.

[845]*See* Ch. 2, § F.1 concerning delays in medical care.

[846]Rule 50(b), Fed.R.Civ.P., Notes of Advisory Committee on 1991 Amendment; Hurst v. Dezer/Reyes Corp., 82 F.3d 232, 237 (8th Cir. 1996); Meriwether v. Coughlin, 879 F.2d 1037, 1043 (2d Cir. 1989). These post-decision motions are discussed in § R.14 of this chapter.

[847]U.S. v. Small, 74 F.3d 1276, 1280 (D.C. Cir. 1996) (in closing argument counsel may not refer to, or rely upon, evidence unless the trial court has admitted it); Reed v. Philadelphia, Bethlehem & New England R.R. Co., 939 F.2d 128, 133–34 (3d Cir. 1991) ("'The remarks of counsel [are] required to be confined to the evidence admitted in the case. . . . Reversible error is committed when

from facts that are in the record.[848] For example, in a civil case, if a party has failed to call a witness or to produce other evidence in his control that would be expected to help his case, you can argue that the jury or court should infer that the evidence would not have been favorable to that party.[849]

It is improper to argue your personal beliefs about the honesty of witnesses, though you may argue that the evidence shows that particular witnesses are credible or incredible.[850] You may know that a particular guard is a notorious liar, but you aren't entitled to say so unless you have produced evidence to back it up (and even if you have, you'd better use more polite language in court). You may not appeal to the jury's sympathy, prejudice, or passion,[851]

e.g., by relying on racial, religious, economic, or political biases.[852]

You should not ask the jury how they would feel if they or members of their families had to undergo what happened to you.[853] It is improper to mention any settlement offers that were made. Personal attacks on opposing parties or witnesses are inappropriate; comment about them should be restricted to what the evidence will support.[854] Criticisms of opposing counsel must not be abusive.

These rules concerning proper argument apply both to you and to the other side's lawyer. If you think argument is improper, you can object to it just as you would object to an improper question during the trial. If the judge agrees that it is improper, he may give the jury a "curative" instruction. If you don't object at trial, an appellate court will not reverse based on the improper argument unless it is so extreme as to constitute "plain error."[855] Even if a proper objection was made, appellate courts are very reluctant to overturn jury verdicts on this ground and tend to conclude that improper

---

counsel's closing argument to the jury introduces extraneous matter that has a reasonable probability of influencing the verdict." (quoting Ayoub v. Spencer, 550 F.2d 164, 170 (3d Cir. 1977)); Simpson v. City of Maple Heights, 720 F. Supp. 1306, 1309–10 (N.D.Ohio 1989) (the plaintiff was entitled to a new trial on damages because of defendants' counsel's references to unsupported allegations about past incidents involving the plaintiff).

[848]Harris v. Steelweld Equipment Co., Inc., 869 F.2d 396, 406–07 (8th Cir. 1989); U.S. v. White, 241 F.3d 1015, 1023 (8th Cir. 2001) (prosecutor must limit the closing argument to "the evidence and the reasonable inferences that may be drawn from it," although the prosecutor may use colorful language and argue "a personal interpretation of the evidence." (citations omitted)).

[849]*See* Sagendorf-Teal v. County of Rensselaer, 100 F.3d 270, 275 (2d Cir. 1996) (trial court may, in its discretion, give a missing witness charge "when a party has it peculiarly within his power" to call a relevant witness but does not do so (citation omitted)); Goldberger Foods, Inc. v. U.S., 23 Cl.Ct. 295, 308 (1991) (when a party has the ability to introduce available evidence to support its claim and yet fails to do so, a negative inference arises that the evidence is unfavorable to the party's claim, unless the party proffers a sufficient explanation for the omission of the evidence), *aff'd*, 960 F.2d 155 (Fed. Cir. 1992); Niehus v. Liberio, 973 F.2d 526, 530–31 (7th Cir. 1985) (upholding "missing evidence" instructions by judge to jury).

For example, if the warden who reviews all disciplinary convictions claims that he actually passed this work on to a subordinate in your case, and if the subordinate does not testify, you can argue that the jury should infer that the subordinate would not have supported the warden's story.

[850]Spicer v. Rossetti, 150 F.3d 642, 644 (7th Cir. 1998) ("Just as counsel may not express his beliefs regarding the honesty of the opposing party's witnesses, . . . he may not express his belief regarding opposing counsel's opinions of honesty." (citation omitted)); U.S. v. Necoechea, 986 F.2d 1273, 1276 (9th Cir. 1993) (improper vouching consists of "placing the prestige of the government behind a witness through personal assurances of the witness's veracity. . . ." (citations omitted)); U.S. v. Rivera, 971 F.2d 876, 884 (2d Cir. 1992) (arguments in summation did not improperly vouch for witnesses where arguments were permissible inferences from evidence at trial).

[851]Moses v. Union Pacific R.R., 64 F.3d 413, 417 (8th Cir. 1995) (appeals to prejudice against insurance companies were improper).

[852]Bird v. Glacier Elec. Coop., Inc., 255 F.3d 1136, 1151–52 (9th Cir. 2001) (appeal to racial prejudice in closing argument offended fundamental fairness and violated due process); Moore v. Morton, 255 F.3d 95, 120 (3d Cir. 2001) (race); Ramsey v. American Air Filter Co., Inc., 772 F.2d 1303, 1311 (7th Cir. 1985) (race); Hong v. City of St. Louis, 698 F. Supp. 180, 183 (E.D. Mo. 1988) (repeated references to Marxism and Communism were improper in a case brought by a Chinese plaintiff).

[853]Lovett ex rel. Lovett v. Union Pacific R. Co., 201 F.3d 1074, 1083 (8th Cir. 2000); Joan W. v. City of Chicago, 771 F.2d 1020, 1022 (7th Cir. 1985) (upholding trial court's decision to sustain objections to plaintiff's asking the jury "how would you feel?" if they were in the plaintiff's position).

[854]Spicer v. Rossetti, 150 F.3d at 644; Fineman v. Armstrong World Indus., Inc., 980 F.2d 171, 206–07 (3d Cir. 1992) (affirming district court's order granting defendants a new trial where plaintiffs' counsel characterized defendants' witnesses as "liars" and "perjurers," repeatedly relied on facts not in evidence, and engaged in repeated personal attacks on opposing counsel during summation); Pickett v. DeTella, 163 F. Supp. 2d 999, 1005–06 (N.D.Ill. 2001) (defense counsel's reference to the plaintiff as a "rule violator" with a "long disciplinary history" who was "out of control" did not require a new trial; "rule violator" was supported by the record; "long disciplinary history" was contrary to the court's prior rulings but was harmless error; "out of control" is argument that jurors would recognize as such).

[855]This is a very difficult standard to meet. *See, e.g.,* Gee v. Pride, 992 F.2d 159, 162 (8th Cir. 1993) (holding that defense counsel's reference to the plaintiff as a "gun-toting, dope-eating stick-up man" was not plain error); Vineyard v. County of Murray, Ga., 990 F.2d 1207, 1213–14 (11th Cir. 1993) (finding no plain error where plaintiff's counsel's "egregiously improper arguments to the jury" asked jury to "send a message" to the sheriff regarding excessive force); People v. Childress, 633 N.E.2d 635, 652–653, 158 Ill.2d 275 (1994) (holding that prosecutor's suggestion that defendant posed an escape risk was improper, since there was no evidence he had ever tried to escape or been treated as an escape risk, and so was his reference to prison as like a "college campus," but they were not plain error).

argument was harmless error as long as the evidence clearly supports the verdict.[856]

It is the judge's job, not yours, to instruct the jury about the law. That doesn't mean you shouldn't mention the law; it means you should try to use the law as a way of commenting on the evidence. For example, in a brutality case you might say, "Under our Constitution, prison staff are permitted to use reasonable force to keep order, prevent escapes, etc., but they are not permitted to use force maliciously or sadistically for the purpose of harming prisoners. The evidence shows that the force used against me was far in excess of anything required to keep order and that the guards beat me because they were mad at me and wanted to hurt me." Then you would move on to the actual evidence that proved this statement.

In discussing the law, be sure your statements are consistent with the judge's instructions. If you are given a written copy of the instructions, which is the practice in some courts, you may wish to read from it to make your points.[857] (If you do this, keep it short and to the point.)

In your closing argument, you will have three goals. First, you want to make sure that the judge or jury understands your case. To do this, you should go over each element of your legal claim and summarize the evidence that was produced in support of each one. If there are elements of your case that the defendants admit, emphasize them.

Second, you want to persuade the judge or jury that you are right on those issues where there is a factual dispute. You should be sure to emphasize any reason supported by the record for finding your evidence more credible than the other side's. For example, if a guard's testimony about an altercation with you is inconsistent with the guard's written report, with the kind of injuries you received, or with some other evidence in the case, cite that fact as a reason why the guard's testimony should not be believed in any respect.

Third, you want to convince the judge or jury that you are a worthwhile human being and that they should not be prejudiced against you simply because you are a prisoner.

The best way to do this is to conduct yourself in a dignified and businesslike manner during your argument.

In a damage case, you will have to deal with the amount of damages you are entitled to.[858] This can be very difficult in cases which involve intangible constitutional rights. How do you translate the denial of a meaningful statement of reasons or a year's confinement in a substandard disciplinary cell into dollars and cents? This problem has become even more difficult because of the Prison Litigation Reform Act, which prohibits damages for "mental or emotional injury" without physical injury.[859]

We don't have any magic answers to this question, but we suggest the following approach. Break down what happened to you into as many separate elements as you can think of, and ask the jury to consider each one. For example, in a case of improper disciplinary segregation, you might say

> In deciding how much I am entitled to in damages, I want you to think about my spending a year locked up in a steel box five feet wide by eight feet long. I want you to think about my being deprived of all my personal property—my books, my clean clothing, my personal letters and pictures, my drawing and painting materials. I want you to think about my sitting there for 24 hours a day with nothing to do. I want you to think about my not having a mop or any disinfectant to clean my cell. I want you to think about the lack of hot water for washing, and the fact that I only got one shower a week, and that I had to wear the same clothes for a week at a time.

In arguing damages, keep in mind that some courts have held that is improper to request a specific dollar amount in damages for pain and suffering.[860]

In a bench trial, particularly a complicated one, the judge may want the parties to write post-trial briefs in place of giving closing arguments. You should find out before the trial (at the pretrial conference, if there is one) what the judge's preference is; if you have a preference, you should

---

[856]*See, e.g.*, Scott v. James, 902 F.2d 672, 674 (8th Cir. 1990) (defense counsel's statement that prisoners can file civil suits free and obtain free lawyers was reprehensible but not reversible where the record clearly supported the verdict); Matthews v. CTI Container Transport Int'l, Inc., 871 F.2d 270, 278 (2d Cir. 1989) ("Not every improper or poorly supported remark made in summation irreparably taints the proceedings; only if counsel's conduct created undue prejudice or passion which played upon the sympathy of the jury, should a new trial be granted."). In most cases cited in this section, the appellate court concluded that the improper argument was harmless error. Harmless error is defined in § U.1.a of this chapter.

[857]For example, suppose your claim is for deliberate indifference to your serious medical needs. You could read the judge's definition of a serious medical need, and then explain why your medical problems fit that definition. You could read the judge's instruction on deliberate indifference, and explain why each defendant's conduct fit that instruction. You could use the same procedure for other disputed issues in the case.

[858]Damages are discussed in Ch. 8, § O.

[859]42 U.S.C. § 1997e(e); *see* Ch. 9, § E, concerning that provision.

[860]Waldorf v. Shuta, 896 F.2d 723, 743–44 (3d Cir. 1990) (plaintiff's counsel may not, in closing argument, request a dollar figure for pain and suffering); Caldwell v. District of Columbia, 201 F. Supp. 2d 27, 32 (D.D.C. 2001) (citing Queen v. Washington Metropolitan Area Transit Authority, 901 F.2d 135, 140 (D.C. Cir. 1990)). Most circuits have left the matter to the discretion of the trial judge, who may either prohibit counsel from mentioning specific figures or impose reasonable limitations, including cautionary jury instructions. *See, e.g.*, Consorti v. Armstrong World Indus., Inc., 72 F.3d 1003, 1016 (2d Cir.1995) (encouraging trial judges to prohibit counsel from suggesting specific monetary awards for pain and suffering), *vacated on other grounds*, 518 U.S. 1031, 116 S. Ct. 2576 (1996); Evoy v. CRST Van Expedited, Inc., 430 F. Supp. 2d 775, 783 (N.D.Ill. 2006) (counsel allowed to suggest awards for non-economic damages if cautionary instruction is given that counsel's argument is not evidence).

state it at that time. If the parties make closing arguments in court, the judge is more likely to decide on the spot or very soon.

If you are afraid that the evidence was confusing or that the judge may miss something that is very important, writing a brief may be more advantageous. If you are not a particularly good writer, you may be better off taking your chances with the spoken word.

13. Jury Instructions and Special Verdicts

In a jury trial, the judge will instruct the jury about the law before the jury decides the case.[861] These jury instructions (or "charge" to the jury) will generally come after the closing arguments.[862]

Parts of the jury instructions will be standardized, such as the instruction that the plaintiff in a civil case has the burden of proof, that all people are considered equal before the law, etc. These instructions are often taken from published sets of "pattern" instructions.[863] Sometimes pattern instructions address more specific issues of liability, such as the constitutional standards in use of force or medical care cases.[864]

Other parts of the jury instructions will be tailored to the issues in your case, and the judge will explain to the jury what is involved in proving whatever legal claim you have made.[865] For example, if you claim that your correspondence was illegally interfered with, the judge will explain to the jury what your legal rights are with respect to correspondence. If you have more than one legal theory, the court must charge separately concerning each one.[866] Jury instructions should not be given about issues that are not actually in the case.[867]

The parties should submit proposed jury instructions to the court before the trial.[868] A *pro se* litigant should probably not worry about standard matters like the burden of proof, how to weigh evidence, etc. You will have too many other things to take care of. However, you should submit proposed instructions on those issues which are likely to be the most controversial and the most important.

These will generally include the explanation of the legal rights you claim were violated, the personal responsibility of supervisory officials,[869] the definition of recklessness or deliberate indifference,[870] and the way damages are to be determined.[871]

If there is a pattern instruction that is used in your federal circuit, you should probably use it as a starting point (and tell the court you have done so). Otherwise, the best way to write proposed jury instructions is to find one or more cases in the Supreme Court or your federal circuit dealing with the issue you are concerned with, and take language out of these cases.[872] For example, if your claim is one

---

[861]*See* Appendix C, Form 12c, for an examples of jury instructions.

[862]The court has discretion to instruct the jury before or after closing arguments, or both. Rule 51(b)(3), Fed.R.Civ.P. (stating that the court "may instruct the jury at any time before the jury is discharged").

[863]*See, e.g.,* Hon. Leonard B. Sand *et al., Modern Federal Jury Instructions* (Lexis-Nexis ed. 1991) (four volumes); O'Malley, Grenig & Lee, *Federal Jury Practice and Instructions* (West Pub. Co., 6th ed. 1998) (nine volumes).

[864]Martin A. Schwartz & George C. Pratt, 4 *Section 1983 Litigation: Jury Instructions* (Wolters Kluver, Supp. 2008), compiles jury instructions specifically for civil rights litigation, including prisoners' claims.

[865]*See* Burton v. Armontrout, 975 F.2d 543, 546 n.4 (8th Cir. 1992), for an example of instructions tailored to the issues in the case.

[866]Davis v. Lane, 814 F.2d 397, 400–01 (7th Cir. 1987) (Eighth Amendment use of force claim and state law battery claim should have received separate instructions).

[867]Baskerville v. Mulvaney, 411 F.3d 45, 48–49 (2d Cir. 2005) (court need not instruct that malicious use of force violates the Eighth Amendment even if not serious or harmful, where plaintiff did not allege force that was not serious or harmful); Poullard v. Turner, 298 F.3d 421, 423 (5th Cir. 2002) (court should not have

instructed jury concerning mental anguish damages where plaintiff did not seek such damages); Spicer v. Rossetti, 150 F.3d 642, 644 (7th Cir. 1998) (court should not have given instruction that force is lawful if it is reasonably believed to be necessary, where defendants denied using force at all except for handcuffs); Davenport v. DeRobertis, 653 F. Supp. 649, 659–60 (N.D.Ill. 1987) (court need not instruct that professional standards do not establish constitutional rights in a case where no one had claimed that they did), *aff'd,* 844 F.2d 1310 (7th Cir. 1988).

[868]Rule 51(a), Fed.R.Civ.P. The rule actually says requests for jury instructions may be submitted "[a]t the close of the evidence or at any earlier reasonable time that the court orders," but many judges require that you get them in earlier. Certainly the earlier you get them in the more time the judge will have to think about them. If issues come up during the trial that could not reasonably have been anticipated, you can file requests for jury instructions on those issues after the close of the evidence. Rule 51(a)(2), Fed.R.Civ.P.

[869]Personal responsibility is discussed in Ch. 8, § B.4.a.

[870]These issues are discussed in Ch. 2, §§ A.2, F.1, G.1.a; Ch. 8, § 4.b.

[871]Damages are discussed in Ch. 8, § O.1.

[872]Sometimes courts quote jury instructions in their opinions. *See, e.g.,* Baskerville v. Mulvaney, 411 F.3d 45, 47–48 (2d Cir. 2005) (Eighth Amendment use of force standard); Fillmore v. Page, 358 F.3d 496, 508–09 (7th Cir. 2004) (Eighth Amendment use of force standard); Johnston v. Breeden, 280 F.3d 1308, 1313–14 (11th Cir. 2002) (Eighth Amendment use of force standard); Gorman v. Easley, 257 F.3d 738, 750–51 (8th Cir. 2001) (disability statutes), *rev'd on other grounds sub nom.* Barnes v. Gorman, 536 U.S. 181, 122 S. Ct. 2097 (2002); Blissett v. Coughlin, 66 F.3d 531, 537 (2d Cir. 1995) (unconstitutional conditions of confinement); Williams v. Patel, 104 F. Supp. 2d 984, 988–89 (C.D.Ill. 2000) (medical care claim against individual prison doctor); Beckford v. Irvin, 49 F. Supp. 2d 170, 181–82 (W.D.N.Y. 1999) (damages for pain and suffering in disability case).

for deprivation of medical care, you might adapt the Supreme Court's language in *Estelle v. Gamble* and write:

> Deliberate indifference to serious medical needs of prisoners constitutes cruel and unusual punishment. This is true whether the indifference is manifested by prison doctors in their response to the prisoner's needs or by prison guards in intentionally denying or delaying access to medical care or intentionally interfering with the treatment once prescribed.[873]

You should identify where the language in your proposed instructions came from.

Whether you start with a pattern instruction or with language from a case, you may also wish to add a more specific statement relating to the facts of your case. For example, a plaintiff might add to the above deliberate indifference instructions, "If you find that Dr. Smith prescribed a back brace for the plaintiff but that Officer Jones took it away from him, you may find that Officer Jones was deliberately indifferent to the plaintiff's serious medical needs."

When you take proposed jury instructions from a previously decided case, be sure that that case actually reflects the current state of the law.

The court is supposed to tell the parties of its decisions concerning their requested jury instructions before they make closing arguments.[874] This discussion is generally called a "charge conference." If either party objects to any of the proposed instructions, it must make the objection before jury instructions and closing argument, so the court will have a chance to reconsider in time to change the instructions.[875]

An erroneous jury instruction requires reversal on appeal unless the error is harmless.[876] However, if your objection is not made in time, it is waived and cannot be raised on appeal.[877] You should study the instructions submitted by the defendants closely and object to anything that you do not believe is supported by the law[878] or that

does not state the law in a way that is fair to both sides. Look closely at anything the defendants try to add to a pattern instruction.

Traditionally, juries have returned a "general verdict," consisting of a finding for the plaintiff or the defendants and an amount of damages if the plaintiff won. However, the court may in its discretion give the jury additional guidance by requiring it to return a "special verdict" by answering a series of written questions about each of the basic factual issues in the case.[879] Courts often use special verdicts in connection with the qualified immunity defense.[880] A sample special verdict form appears elsewhere in this Manual.[881]

Special verdicts are used frequently in civil rights cases. A common opinion about special verdicts is that they are most useful in cases where it is important to focus the jury's attention on the factual and legal issues and away from their attitudes towards the parties—a description which fits most prison cases. They are also useful to help avoid jury confusion in cases with multiple plaintiffs, defendants, or legal claims.

14. Verdict or Decision

In a jury trial, the jury will retire to consider the case after hearing closing arguments and the court's instructions.

---

[873]*See* Estelle v. Gamble, 429 U.S. 97, 104–05, 97 S. Ct. 285 (1976). This is not a precise quotation.

[874]Rule 51(b)(1), Fed.R.Civ. P.

[875]Rule 51(c)(2), Fed.R.Civ.P. The rule also provides that if the party is not informed of an instruction or the refusal to give an instruction in time to object at the proper time, it may object promptly upon learning of it.

[876]Cobb v. Pozzi, 363 F.3d 89, 116 (2d Cir. 2004).

[877]Rule 51(d)(1), Fed.R.Civ.P. The only exception to this rule is errors so extreme as to constitute "plain error." *See* Rule 51(d)(2), Fed.R.Civ.P. ("A court may consider a plain error in the [jury] instructions that has not been preserved as required by Rule 51(d)(1) if the error affects substantial rights."); Johnson v. U.S., 520 U.S. 461, 466–67, 117 S. Ct. 1544 (1997) (explaining that unpreserved errors may be corrected when there is (1) an error, (2) that is plain, (3) that affects substantial rights, and (4) seriously affects the fairness, integrity, or public reputation of judicial proceedings); Rodriguez-Marin v. Rivera-Gonzalez, 438 F.3d 72, 83 (1st Cir. 2006); Ivey v. Wilson, 832 F.2d 950, 955 (6th Cir. 1987).

[878]For example, defendants sometime try to have the defense of qualified immunity presented to the jury, even though it is an

issue for the court. *See* Ch. 8, § L.4. They sometimes try to have the jury instructed that the plaintiff must prove that the defendants acted maliciously and sadistically in cases where the deliberate indifference standard should be applied. *See* Ch. 2, § A.2.

[879]Rule 49(a), Fed.R.Civ.P.; *see* Douglas v. Owens, 50 F.3d 1226 (3d Cir. 1995); Mateyko v. Felix, 924 F.2d 824, 827 (9th Cir. 1990) (special verdict forms may be used "provided the questions asked are adequate to obtain a jury determination of the factual issues essential to judgment"). If a jury returns seemingly inconsistent answers to special verdicts, the court should look for a way of viewing them as consistent, Corpus v. Bennett, 430 F.3d 912, 915 (8th Cir. 2005), and may in its discretion resubmit them to the jury with a request for clarification. Mateyko v. Felix, *supra*, and cases cited; Duk v. MGM Grand Hotel, Inc., 320 F.3d 1052, 1058 (9th Cir. 2003). *Contra*, McCollum v. Stahl, 579 F.2d 869, 871–72 (4th Cir. 1978) (". . . [T]he remand of the questions to the jury was tantamount, in its effect, to a direction to the jury to find liability in order to warrant the award of damages."). If the answers are inconsistent no matter how the court looks at them, there must be a new trial. Stephenson v. Doe, 332 F.3d 68, 79 (2d Cir. 2003).

Rule 49(b) provides for a general verdict accompanied by answers to written questions (formerly called "special interrogatories"), questions addressing some or all of the factual issues in the case. This device appears to be less frequently used than special verdicts.

[880]*See* Ch. 8, § L.5, concerning qualified immunity.

[881]Appendix C, Form 12b. For other examples of how special verdict forms are written, *see* Corpus v. Bennett, 430 F.3d 912, 914 n.3 (8th Cir. 2005) (police brutality case); Johnson v. Breeden, 280 F.3d 1308, 1319 (11th Cir. 2002) (Eighth Amendment excessive force case); Walker v. Bain, 257 F.3d 660, 672 n.4 (6th Cir. 2001) (First Amendment retaliation claim); Giron v. Corrections Corp. of America, 191 F.3d 1281, 1285 (10th Cir. 1999) (failure to protect from sexual assault); Fletcher v. O'Donnell, 867 F.2d 791, 793 (3d Cir. 1989) (arrest without probable cause, excessive force).

The jury may ask to have particular portions of the record read back to it, to have exhibits brought into the jury room, or to receive further instruction from the judge. The parties should be permitted to be present in the courtroom if the judge gives further instructions or reads parts of the record to the jury.[882]

When the jury returns with a verdict, it will be read by the foreperson or the court clerk. The jury may be polled (asked individually if they agree with the verdict). In a bench trial, the judge may rule orally from the bench or may issue a written decision later.

15. Motions After the Verdict or Decision

There are several kinds of motions that can be made immediately after a trial to overturn or modify the decision. These motions have important effects on the parties' appeal rights, which we discuss elsewhere.[883] The rules also authorize motions at a later stage to obtain relief from a judgment or modification of the judgment.[884]

a. Motion for Judgment as a Matter of Law If a party unsuccessfully made a motion for judgment as a matter of law at the end of the trial,[885] that party can renew the motion on paper by serving and filing it not later than 28 days after entry of judgment.[886] The renewed motion is restricted to the same issues that were raised in the initial motion during the trial.[887] This motion is designed for situations where there were no real factual issues to go to the jury.

b. Motion for a New Trial Within 28 days after the entry of judgment, a party may make a motion for a new trial.[888] Such a motion may be based on a claim that the verdict was against the weight of the evidence, that the damages were excessive or inadequate, that evidence was improperly rejected, that the jury instructions were erroneous, or that other errors were made in the conduct of the trial.[889] This motion, unlike a motion for judgment as a matter of law, does not require that the moving party have made a motion during the trial.[890]

New trials are rarely granted unless there are gross errors in the way the trial was conducted or there is significant newly discovered evidence. If you claim newly discovered evidence, you should submit an affidavit explaining why the evidence was not available to you before or during the trial.[891]

c. Motion to Alter or Amend the Judgment A motion to alter or amend the judgment must also be filed within 28 days.[892] This motion may not be used to re-examine factual issues decided by a jury,[893] but it is appropriate for addressing errors of law by the court[894] or inadvertent errors such as omission of matters that the court obviously intended to include.[895]

---

[882]Robert S. Hunter, *Federal Trial Handbook* at §§ 88.16, 88.17 (West Pub. Co., 4th ed., 2007); *see* Chicago, R. I. & P. R. Co. v. Speth, 404 F.2d 291, 294 (8th Cir. 1968).

[883]*See* § U.1.d(1) of this chapter.

[884]*See* § T of this chapter.

[885]*See* § R.11 of this chapter.

[886]Rule 50(b), Fed.R.Civ.P. This deadline was extended from 10 to 28 days effective December 1, 2009. *See* Freeman v. Berge, 2005 WL 1168311 (W.D.Wis., May 16, 2005) (granting prison officials' renewed motion for judgment as a matter of law as to $1.2 million verdict to inmate), *aff'd*, 441 F.3d 543 (7th Cir. 2006); Littlewind v. Rayl, 839 F. Supp. 1369, 1376 (D.N.D. 1993) (granting judgment as a matter of law to prisoner plaintiff), *appeal dismissed*, 33 F.3d 985 (8th Cir. 1994).

[887]*See* Rule 50(b), Fed.R.Civ.P., Note of Advisory Committee on Rules, 1991 Revision; Surprenant v. Rivas, 424 F.3d 5 (1st Cir. 2005) (officer waived issue for appeal when he moved for judgment as a matter of law at close of inmate's case but did not renew motion at the close of all the evidence, and verdict did not work a clear and gross injustice).

[888]Rule 59(b), Fed.R.Civ.P. This rule formerly allowed only 10 days but was amended effective December 1, 2009.

[889]*See* Bell v. Johnson, 404 F.3d 997, 1003–05 (6th Cir. 2005) (affirming district court grant of new trial as to damages only); Poullard v. Turner, 298 F.3d 421, 423–24 (5th Cir. 2002) (grant of new trial as to both compensatory and punitive damages but not liability); Ruffin v. Fuller, 125 F. Supp. 2d 105, 109–10 (S.D.N.Y. 2000) (granting new trial where jury's verdict against prisoner was against the weight of the evidence in light of medical evidence, "frankly incredible" testimony of officers that they did not see how he was injured, and fact that crucial portion of surveillance tape was destroyed); Littlewind v. Rayl, 839 F. Supp. 1369, 1376 (D.N.D. 1993) (granting new trial to prisoner plaintiff), *appeal dismissed*, 33 F.3d 985 (8th Cir. 1994). *But see* Giles v. Rhodes, 171 F. Supp. 2d 220, 225 (S.D.N.Y. 2001) (refusing a new trial despite plaintiff's argument that medical evidence was contrary to defendants' claims in a use of force case).

[890]Giles v. Rhodes, 171 F. Supp. 2d at 224 and cases cited.

[891]*See* Waul v. Coughlin, 177 F.R.D. 173, 176–78 (S.D.N.Y. 1997) (new trial denied in part because plaintiff failed to exercise due diligence in moving to compel discovery or otherwise pursuing evidence defendants did not produce), *reconsideration denied*, 1998 WL 295481 (S.D.N.Y., June 4, 1998).

[892]Rule 59(e), Fed.R.Civ.P. This deadline was extended from 10 to 28 days effective December 1, 2009.

[893]Garshman Co., Ltd. v. General Elec. Co., Inc., 993 F. Supp. 25, 28 (D.Mass. 1998) (citing Robinson v. Watts Detective Agency, 685 F.2d 729, 742 (1st Cir. 1982)), *aff'd*, 176 F.3d 1 (1st Cir. 1999)).

[894]Arrieta-Colon v. Wal-Mart Puerto Rico, Inc., 434 F.3d 75, 89 (1st Cir. 2006) (improper jury instruction that is harmful to the case can be reviewed); U.S. ex rel. A+ Homecare, Inc. v. Medshares Management Group, Inc., 400 F.3d 428 (6th Cir. 2005) (verdict inconsistencies reviewable pursuant to Rule 59(e)); Finch v. City of Vernon, 845 F.2d 256, 258–59 (7th Cir. 1988).

[895]Ingle ex rel. Estate of Ingle v. Yelton, 439 F.3d 191, 197 (4th Cir. 2006) ("Rule 59(e) motions will be granted in three circumstances: '(1) to accommodate an intervening change in controlling law; (2) to account for new evidence not available at trial; or (3) to correct a clear error of law or prevent manifest injustice.'"); Messina v. Krakower, 439 F.3d 755, 759 (D.C. Cir. 2006) (same). Rule 59(e) motions are not to be used to raise arguments that a party could have and should have raised at an

These motions are not limited to judgments entered after a trial; they may also be used if the court has entered judgment without trial, *e.g.*, by granting a motion to dismiss or for summary judgment.[896]

Other motions aimed at modifying or overturning a judgment are discussed later in this chapter.[897] Appeals are also discussed in a separate section.[898]

S. Evidence

This section identifies some basic concepts of the law of evidence and some evidentiary problems that frequently come up in prisoners' cases. It focuses on the Federal Rules of Evidence (Fed.R.Evid.), which govern proceedings in federal courts. State rules of evidence will often be similar to the federal rules, but if you are litigating in state court, you must find out what the state rules are. The rules of evidence determine both what evidence is admissible at trial and what the court can consider on a motion for summary judgment.

The rules of evidence have been the subject of many long books, and we can only scratch the surface of the subject here. If you want to pursue the subject further, you should obtain one of the short guides to evidence prepared for lawyers and law students.[899]

Also, many editions of the Federal Rules of Evidence contain the Notes of Advisory Committee on Proposed Rules and on later amendments, which provide useful background information about the rules.

One important evidentiary subject, privileges, is discussed in another section.[900]

1. Basic Concepts

a. Direct and Circumstantial Evidence Direct evidence is evidence of the precise fact in issue (*e.g.*, whether Officer X hit you with an axe handle). It generally consists either of testimony from witnesses who saw or heard the act or statements in question (*e.g.*, prisoners A and B testify that

they saw the officer hit you with the axe handle), or of documents prepared by such witnesses.

Circumstantial evidence is evidence of facts from which one can reasonably infer or deduce a fact in issue. For example, suppose two prisoners testify they saw Officer X, carrying an axe handle, lead you shackled into a closed room five minutes before you were found unconscious and bloody, with your hands still shackled. It is reasonable to infer that (1) Officer X struck you with the axe handle, and (2) his statement that you attacked him with a knife is not true, since your hands were still shackled. Circumstantial evidence is as valid legally as direct evidence, though it may not be as persuasive.[901]

b. Relevance and Materiality Evidence must be relevant to be admissible. Relevant evidence is defined as "evidence having any tendency to make the existence of any fact that is of consequence to the determination of the action more probable or less probable than it would be without the evidence."[902] In other words, evidence is relevant if it helps prove or disprove a fact that is important to the outcome of the lawsuit. Whether evidence is relevant is determined not just by the subject matter of the lawsuit, but also by the legal and factual positions that the parties take.[903]

The court may exclude evidence which is relevant "if its probative [proof] value is substantially outweighed by the danger of unfair prejudice, confusion of the issues, or misleading the jury, or by considerations of undue delay, waste of time, or needless presentation of cumulative evidence."[904]

In the past it was generally said that evidence had to be "material" as well as relevant. The difference between

---

earlier point. Sault Ste. Marie Tribe of Chippewa Indians v. Engler, 146 F.3d 367, 374 (6th Cir. 1998).

[896]*See, e.g.*, Lance v. United Mine Workers of America 1974 Pension Trust, 400 F. Supp. 2d 29, 31 (D.D.C. 2005).

Rule 59 refers to judgments, and is generally applied when the court enters final judgment on part or all of the case. If you want the court to reconsider its decision of a motion that does not result in a final judgment—*e.g.*, a denial of summary judgment, or a discovery decision—the proper vehicle is a motion for reconsideration or reargument. These motions are discussed in § F of this chapter.

[897]*See* § T of this chapter.

[898]*See* § U of this chapter.

[899]*See, e.g.*, Michael H. Graham, *Federal Rules of Evidence in a Nutshell* (West Pub. Co., 7th ed., 2006). A more comprehensive treatise is Edward W. Cleary, *McCormick on Evidence* (West Pub. Co., 6th ed., 2006).

[900]*See* § K.2.b of this chapter.

[901]*See* Farmer v. Brennan, 511 U.S. 825, 842, 114 S. Ct. 1970 (1994) ("Whether a prison official had the requisite knowledge of a substantial risk is a question of fact subject to demonstration in the usual ways, including inference from circumstantial evidence. . . ."); Bennett v. Goord, 343 F.3d 133, 139 (2d Cir. 2003) (stating "where . . . circumstantial evidence of a retaliatory motive is sufficiently compelling, direct evidence is not invariably required"); Gayle v. Gonyea, 313 F.3d 677, 684 (2d Cir. 2002) (similar to *Bennett*); Henderson v. U.S. Parole Comm'n, 13 F.3d 1073, 1077 (7th Cir. 1994) (circumstantial evidence is sufficient at prison misconduct hearing to support guilty finding); Colon v. Coughlin, 58 F.3d 865, 872–73 (2d Cir. 1995) (circumstantial evidence of clean prison record and direct proof of retaliation, together with temporal proximity, held to be sufficient proof of retaliation to withstand summary judgment); *see also* Crawford El v. Britton, 93 F.3d 813, 817–19 (D.C. Cir. 1996) (per curiam) (rejecting distinction between circumstantial and direct evidence concerning intent of officials), *aff'd*, 523 U.S. 574, 118 S. Ct. 1584 (1998).

[902]Rule 401, Fed.R.Evid.

[903]For example, in a criminal prosecution for excessive force, the officer defendants tried to put in evidence of prior inmate violence in the jail, saying it was evidence of their state of mind. However, since they all claimed either that they were not present or that they did not beat the prisoner, their state of mind was not an issue in the case, and evidence of it was not relevant. U.S. v. Tines, 70 F.3d 891, 898–99 (6th Cir. 1995).

[904]Rule 403, Fed.R.Evid.

relevance and materiality was never very clear, and the Federal Rules of Evidence have dropped the concept of materiality and adopted a broad definition of relevance instead.[905]

c. Inferences and Presumptions

An inference consists of deducing a fact you are trying to prove from other facts already proved or admitted.[906] Inferences are often made from circumstantial evidence. For example, claims that prisoners have been disciplined or transferred in retaliation for lawsuits or other constitutionally protected activity must often be proven by inferences from the time sequence of the prisoner's and the prison officials' actions.[907]

Deliberate indifference or malicious intent on the part of prison personnel are often inferred from their actions.[908] The existence of a municipal policy or custom may be inferred from the widespread character or general knowledge of the practices in issue.[909]

If a party fails to produce evidence that is within his control, it may be inferred that that evidence would be unfavorable to him.[910]

A presumption is a rule that one fact may be inferred from another fact unless there is evidence to the contrary.[911] A presumption may be rebutted if the opposing party presents some evidence to the contrary. For example, a prisoner's domicile is presumed to be where he lived before his incarceration, but the presumption can be rebutted by evidence that he intends to live somewhere else after release.[912]

d. Judicial Notice

Courts may take "judicial notice" of facts which are "not subject to reasonable dispute" because they are either "(1) generally known within the territorial jurisdiction of the trial court or (2) capable of accurate and ready determination by resort to sources whose accuracy cannot reasonably be questioned."[913] The adverse party has the right to be heard as to whether judicial notice of particular evidence is proper.[914]

Although it is sometimes said that judicial notice can be taken of "matters of public record," that is true only for facts that are "not subject to reasonable dispute"; if there is a reasonable dispute about them, judicial notice is not appropriate.[915] Courts can take notice of their own records and those of other courts, at least for matters such as the fact that a case was filed, or what its disposition was.[916] However, courts have cautioned that "[f]actual findings in one case

---

[905]Rule 401, Fed.R.Evid., Notes of Advisory Committee on Proposed Rules. The term "material fact" is still used in connection with summary judgment. *See* Rule 56(e), Fed.R.Civ.P. Summary judgment is discussed in § L of this chapter.

[906]*See* Farmer v. Brennan, 511 U.S. 825, 842, 114 S. Ct. 1970 (1994) (prison officials' knowledge of a risk of assault may be inferred from the fact that the risk was obvious); Fischl v. Armitage, 128 F.3d 50, 56 (2d Cir. 1997) (it was reasonable to infer that the officer who had responsibility for a housing unit, and the keys, was the person who opened plaintiff's cell resulting in an assault); Wood v. Sunn, 865 F.2d 982, 988 (9th Cir. 1988) (failure to provide medication could be inferred from the absence of a record of it and from testimony that it should have been reported if dispensed), *vacated*, 880 F.2d 1011 (9th Cir. 1989); Howard v. Adkison, 887 F.2d 134, 139 (8th Cir. 1989) (harm compensable in damages can be inferred from unconstitutional conditions).

[907]*See* cases cited in Ch. 3, § C.6.

[908]*See* Ch. 2, §§ A.2, and G.2.b.3.

[909]Vann v. City of New York, 72 F.3d 1040, 1049 (2d Cir. 1995) ("deliberate indifference may be inferred if the complaints are followed by no meaningful attempt on the part of the municipality to investigate or to forestall further incidents"); Spell v. McDaniel, 824 F.2d 1380, 1391 (4th Cir. 1987); *see* Ch. 8, § B.4.b.

[910]Sagendorf-Teal v. County of Rensselaer, 100 F.3d 270, 275–76 (2d Cir. 1996) (jury could infer from defendants' failure to call certain witnesses that their testimony would not have been favorable to defendants); McCrary-El v. Shaw, 992 F.2d 809, 812–13 (8th Cir. 1993) (jury should have been told that prison officials' failure to produce videotape of incident could support an inference that it would have helped the prisoner's case); Romaine v. Rawson, 140 F. Supp. 2d 204, 210 (N.D.N.Y. 2001) (court in bench trial gave weight to fact that prison officials "mislaid" all the inmate statements supporting plaintiff's allegations but not the ones that didn't support them); *see also* U.S. v. West, 393 F.3d 1302, 1309 (D.C. Cir. 2005) ("A missing-evidence instruction is appropriate if it is peculiarly within the power of one party to produce the evidence and the evidence would elucidate a disputed transaction."); Niehus v. Liberio, 973 F.2d 526, 530 (7th Cir. 1992) (addressing

propriety of missing-evidence instruction). Some courts require a showing of bad faith to justify a missing evidence instruction. Beaudry v. Corrections Corp. of America, 331 F.3d 1164, 1168–69 (10th Cir. 2003). *Cf.* Pelletier v. Magnusson, 195 F. Supp. 2d 214, 233–37 (D.Me. 2002) (evidence of spoliation of evidence, in the form of missing records, barred summary judgment against the plaintiff; question of missing evidence inference left to trial); Wackenhut Corrections Corporation v. de la Rosa, 305 S.W.3d 594, 625–27 (Tex.App. 2009) (spoliation instruction properly given where videotape of incident disappeared).

[911]*See* Rule 301, Fed.R.Evid. (stating that "a presumption imposes on the party against whom it is directed the burden of going forward with evidence to rebut or meet the presumption, but does not shift to such party the burden of proof in the sense of the risk of nonpersuasion. . . ."). For example, if it is shown that a person made use of a reliable means of communication, a fact-finder can infer that the communication was received. Kennell v. Gates, 215 F.3d 825, 829–30 (8th Cir. 2000).

[912]Smith v. Cummings, 445 F.3d 1254, 1260 (10th Cir. 2006); Sullivan v. Freeman, 944 F.2d 334, 337 (7th Cir. 1991).

[913]Rule 201(b), Fed.R.Evid.

[914]Rule 201(e), Fed.R.Evid.; *see* Fenner v. Suthers, 194 F. Supp. 2d 1146, 1148–49 (D.Colo. 2002) (information on website was not suitable for judicial notice, in part because the prisoner couldn't look at it and therefore had no opportunity to be heard meaningfully).

[915]Lee v. City of Los Angeles, 250 F.3d 668, 689–90 (9th Cir. 2001) (waiver of extradition forms and hearing transcript in which the plaintiff said he understood what rights he was giving up were not appropriate for judicial notice where it was disputed what the mentally disabled plaintiff could understand).

[916]Akers v. Watts, 589 F. Supp. 2d 12, 15 (D.D.C. 2008).

ordinarily are not admissible for their truth in another case through judicial notice."[917]

Judicial notice will rarely be useful in a prison case. Many things that you may consider to be facts not subject to reasonable dispute (*e.g.*, that racism is rampant among prison staff) will be viewed as very debatable in court, and matters pertaining to prison practices and conditions are seldom "generally known" outside the prison. "Sources whose accuracy cannot reasonably be questioned" will probably be limited to dictionaries, encyclopedias, technical books, maps, charts, etc.

Examples of the kinds of facts of which court are likely to take judicial notice are the prevalence of heavy traffic in New York City at rush hour and the time the sun rises and sets on a particular day.

e. Opinion and Expert Testimony In general, witnesses are supposed to testify to facts and not to opinions or conclusions. However, drawing the line between them can be hard, and "lay" (non-expert) witnesses are therefore permitted to testify to opinions or inferences as long as they are based on the perception of the witness and are helpful to a clear understanding of the testimony or the issues.[918]

Examples of lay opinions that courts have admitted include statements that the witness's physical condition was improved by medical treatment,[919] that an individual was drunk,[920] and that a substance found in a prisoner's cell was fermented.[921]

You should try to keep lay opinion testimony to a minimum, since the other side's lawyers will almost certainly object to it, and judges will be cautious about

permitting it.[922] For example, you or other inmates might be permitted to testify that an officer appeared angry or upset; a court is less likely to allow testimony that the officer appeared to be trying to harm you rather than get you under control.[923] You should plan to bring out the facts about the officer's behavior that cause you to have such an opinion— *e.g.*, whether he was cursing at you, whether he struck you, whether you were resisting at the time, etc.

Persons with "scientific, technical, or other specialized knowledge" may testify as expert witnesses and give their opinions on issues within their specialties.[924] Experts should not be allowed to give opinions concerning the credibility of witnesses[925] or the "ultimate issue" of whether the defendants acted illegally.[926] The defendants may try to present themselves or other prison personnel as expert witnesses who can give their opinions about prison practices, and the court may qualify them as experts.[927]

The presentation and cross-examination of expert witnesses is one of the more complicated aspects of trial practice and is beyond the scope of this Manual.[928] If it appears that expert testimony is likely to be important in your case, it makes sense to request the appointment of counsel.[929]

The evidence rules also provide for court-appointed experts,[930] and several courts have appointed experts in prison cases.[931] However, this is not a routine procedure, and courts are unlikely to appoint experts unless they are presented with extremely good reasons for doing so.

---

[917]Wyatt v. Terhune, 315 F.3d 1108, 1114 n.5 (9th Cir. 2003); *accord*, Holloway v. Lockhart, 813 F.2d 874, 879 (8th Cir. 1987) (finding in previous case that gassing of prisoners was reasonable and necessary was not suitable for judicial notice; it could be determined only by evaluating the testimony and credibility of witnesses).

A court also "cannot take judicial notice of a factual finding in the less procedurally rigid prison disciplinary hearing." Rivera v. Hamlet, 2003 WL 22846114, *5 (N.D.Cal. 2003). However, documentation from disciplinary hearings may be admissible for purposes other than the truth of what it asserts, and may be admissible for the truth of what it asserts under the business records and public records exceptions to the hearsay rule, discussed below in § S.4.b of this chapter.

[918]Rule 701, Fed.R.Evid.

[919]U.S. v. Guzzino, 810 F.2d 687, 699 (7th Cir. 1987) ("... [L]ay opinion testimony as to the mental state of another is indeed competent under [Rule 701]."); Dallis v. Aetna Life Ins. Co., 768 F.2d 1303, 1305–06 (11th Cir. 1985).

[920]U.S. ex rel. Williams v. Washington, 913 F. Supp. 1156, 1162 (N.D.Ill. 1995); Gaynor v. Atlantic Greyhound Corp., 183 F.2d 482, 485 (3d Cir. 1950).

[921]Griffin v. Sprat, 969 F.2d 16, 22 (3d Cir 1992) (dictum) (lay witness testimony that substance found in cell was fermented can be bases of disciplinary proceeding guilty finding).

[922]*See* U.S. v. Whalen, 940 F.2d 1027, 1033–34 (7th Cir. 1991) (prisoner could not testify about what witnesses were able to see on his cellblock because he had not observed the condition of the particular location on the night of the incident).

[923]*See* U.S. v. Brown, 938 F.2d 1482, 1488 (1st Cir. 1991) (testimony regarding defendant's "inchoate state of mind" was inadmissible).

[924]Rule 702, Fed.R.Evid.; *see* Jones v. Hamelman, 869 F.2d 1023, 1028–29 (7th Cir. 1989) (upholding the refusal to qualify an inmate as an expert witness on prison procedures and disciplinary units).

Additional provisions concerning expert testimony appear in Rules 703–05, Fed.R.Evid.

[925]Nimely v. City of New York, 414 F.3d 381, 398–99 (2d Cir. 2005); Westcott v. Crinklaw, 68 F.3d 1073, 1076–77 (8th Cir. 1995).

[926]Berry v. City of Detroit, 25 F.3d 1342, 1353–54 (6th Cir.1994) (expert opinion on whether defendants were deliberately indifferent was not admissible).

[927]There are procedural requirements for naming expert witnesses, and special discovery provisions concerning them, discussed in § K.3 of this chapter.

[928]A useful discussion of this subject appears in James W. Jeans, *Trial Advocacy* at §§ 14.1–14.23, 15.38–15.55 (West Pub. Co. ed. 1993).

[929]The need for expert testimony is one of the reasons that courts have cited for appointing counsel in civil rights cases. *See* § C.5 of this chapter.

[930]Rule 706(a), Fed.R.Evid.

[931]*See* § K.3 of this chapter, nn.619–626, concerning court-appointed experts.

f. Burden of Proof and *Prima Facie* Case The burden of proof is the requirement that a party produce a certain amount of evidence in order to establish that something is true. The burden of proof on most issues is on the plaintiff in a civil case. However, there may be certain issues, often called affirmative defenses, on which the defendants have the burden of proof. For example, if the defendants claim that your lawsuit is barred by *res judicata* or collateral estoppel, they have the burden of proof on that question.[932] Exhaustion of administrative remedies is generally an affirmative defense, so defendants have the burden of proving it.[933]

However, if defendants claim that they were not personally involved in the unlawful acts you complain about, or that these acts never happened, the burden of proof will be on you to prove that a particular defendant violated your rights.

In civil cases, the party with the burden of proof must prove the facts by a "preponderance of the evidence." That means alleged facts must be shown to be more likely true than not true.[934] The preponderance of the evidence is not determined just by the number of witnesses on either side but also by the credibility of the evidence. One credible witness may carry more weight than 10 incredible ones.

The party with the burden of proof on an issue also has the burden of going forward with the evidence. That is, he must establish a *prima facie* case. This is done by producing enough evidence to justify a finding in the party's favor unless the evidence is explained or discredited by the other side.[935] Once a party has made a *prima facie* case, the burden of going forward with the evidence shifts to the other side. The burden of proof does not shift.

An example may make these points clearer. Suppose you sue a guard for beating you up. You have the burden of proof and the burden of going forward. If you testify that you were minding your own business and the guard suddenly slugged you, you have met your burden of going forward and have made a *prima facie* case.

The burden of going forward then shifts to the guard. If he then testifies that you were slashing someone with a knife and he slugged you to protect the other prisoner's life, the guard has met his burden of going forward. At that point, the judge or jury will decide if you have proved your case by a preponderance of the evidence.

If the judge or jury thinks your story is credible in the light of all the evidence, you win. If the guard's story appears more credible, the guard wins. If the stories are equally credible, the guard wins, because the burden of proof is on you.

Procedurally, you must meet your burden of going forward when you present the plaintiff's evidence, or the defendants will be entitled to judgment as a matter of law at the close of your case.[936] The defendants must meet their burden of going forward when they present their evidence or you will be entitled to judgment as a matter of law.

2. Hearsay and Admissions

Hearsay is defined as "a statement, other than one made by the declarant while testifying at the trial or hearing, offered in evidence to prove the truth of the matter asserted."[937] The Federal Rules of Evidence provide that "[h]earsay is not admissible except as provided by these rules" or by other properly enacted rules.[938]

In other words, you cannot introduce a statement made by a person at some other time and place if you are putting it in to prove what the statement says. For example, if you sue Officer Smith for beating you up, and prisoner Jones tells you, "I saw Officer Smith hitting you while you were handcuffed," you cannot testify to what Jones said because it is hearsay. To get this evidence before the court, you have to get Jones into court to testify.

Written evidence is often hearsay. Thus, if prisoner Jones writes a statement for you about what he saw, it ordinarily cannot come into evidence at trial even if it is notarized or declared to be true under penalty of perjury.

A statement is not hearsay if it is not offered to prove the truth of what the statement says. For example, if you wrote a statement and sent it to the warden complaining that Officer Smith beat you up, it would not be admissible to show that Smith beat you up. But if you are trying to prove something else—for example, that you made a complaint against Smith, or that the warden knew about such complaints—your complaint could be admitted for that purpose.[939]

---

[932]Hayles v. Randall Motor Co., 455 F.2d 169, 173 (10th Cir. 1972). *Res judicata* and collateral estoppel are discussed in Ch. 8, § M.

[933]*See* Ch. 9, § D.8.

[934]*In re* Winship, 397 U.S. 358, 371, 90 S. Ct. 1068 (1970) (Harlan, J., concurring) (citation omitted) (preponderance standard "simply requires the trier of fact 'to believe that the existence of a fact is more probable than its nonexistence'").

[935]A *prima facie* case is "[a] party's production of enough evidence to allow the fact-trier to infer the fact at issue and rule in the party's favor." Black's Law Dictionary (8th ed. 2004).

[936]*See* §§ R.11, R.15(a) of this chapter concerning judgment as a matter of law.

[937]Rule 801(c), Fed.R.Evid.

[938]Rule 802, Fed.R.Evid.

[939]*See* Moore v. Plaster, 313 F.3d 442, 444 (8th Cir. 2002) (documents allegedly showing plaintiff committed a disciplinary offense were not hearsay because they were not submitted for the truth of what they asserted, but to show that officials had some evidence on which to find him guilty); Gutierrez-Rodriguez v. Cartagena, 882 F.2d 553, 575 (1st Cir. 1989) (past civilian complaints against a defendant were properly admitted to prove that his supervisors were on notice of the complaints and not to prove what the complaints said); Lane v. Griffin, 834 F.2d 403, 407–08 (4th Cir. 1987) (testimony concerning what the chaplain told the superintendent about the plaintiff was not hearsay because it was offered to explain the superintendent's state of mind and not for the truth of what it asserted); Johnson v. Herman, 132 F. Supp. 2d 1130, 1133 (N.D.Ind. 2001) (jail employee's statement about what an unidentified court employee told him was admissible because it

A statement is also not hearsay if it is a prior statement by a witness who testifies at the trial and it is used to impeach that witness's credibility, or to restore the witness's credibility after it has been attacked, or it concerns the identification of a person that the witness has seen.[940]

A statement is not hearsay if it is an "admission by a party-opponent." This is one of the most important aspects of the hearsay rule because it permits you to use past statements made by the defendants and their agents, employees, etc. The full definition of an admission by a party-opponent is:

> The statement is offered against a party and is (A) the party's own statement, in either an individual or a representative capacity or (B) a statement of which the party has manifested an adoption or belief in its truth, or (C) a statement by a person authorized by the party to make a statement concerning the subject, or (D) a statement by the party's agent or servant concerning a matter within the scope of the agency or employment, made during the existence of the relationship, or (E) a statement by a co-conspirator of a party during the course and in furtherance of the conspiracy. . . . [941]

Thus, if the warden says to you, "I'm having you transferred because I am sick of your complaining," you can testify that he said this if you have sued the warden claiming a retaliatory transfer. It is an admission by the defendant that is relevant to your claim.[942] Also, if the transfer order is written by a prison employee stating, "Prisoner to be transferred at the Warden's authorization because of constant complaints," that statement can be admitted into evidence against the warden as an admission "by a person authorized by him

to make a statement concerning the subject" (*i.e.*, to write transfer orders) or "by his agent or servant concerning a matter within the scope of his agency or employment."[943]

In general, any written or oral statement by a defendant, or by a subordinate of a defendant made while he was employed in that position, that is related to his job responsibilities and that helps you in your lawsuit is likely to be an admission by a party-opponent, and therefore to be admissible in evidence, despite the hearsay rule.[944]

There are several other kinds of admissions. Responses to requests for admission pursuant to the discovery rules are discussed in another section.[945] Admissions against interest, now known as statements against interest, are exceptions to the hearsay rule provided for by another of the Federal Rules of Evidence.[946] Judicial admissions are concessions made in pleadings, stipulations or other formal means that concede a fact at issue in the case so there is no need to submit proof of it.[947]

---

was not offered for the truth of what the court employee said, but to show what the jail staff did to investigate the plaintiff's complaint that he was held after his release date).

[940]Rule 801(d)(1), Fed.R.Evid.

The use of prior statements by witnesses is discussed in more detail in § S.2 of this chapter.

[941]Rule 801(d)(2), Fed.R.Evid.; Larez v. City of Los Angeles, 946 F.2d 630, 642 (9th Cir. 1991) (statements by police chief indicating approval of officers' misconduct could come in as admissions to support claim of chief's liability).

Rule 801(d)(2) continues by stating: "The contents of the statement shall be considered but are not alone sufficient to establish the declarant's authority under subdivision (C), the agency or employment relationship and scope thereof under subdivision (D), or the existence of the conspiracy and the participation therein of the declarant and the party against whom the statement is offered under subdivision (E)." That means you have to provide additional evidence of those matters. For example, if you were offering a report by the mail delivery officer stating his understanding of the prison's policy on opening mail, you could obtain an admission from the defendants in discovery, *see* § K.2.g of this chapter, that the person was indeed the mail delivery officer at the relevant time, or you could testify from your own observation that he was the person who delivered your mail to your cell almost all the time.

[942]*See* Hoptowit v. Ray, 682 F.2d 1237, 1262 (9th Cir. 1982) (holding prisoners could testify to statements made by guards because they were admissions).

[943]Rule 801(d)(2), Fed.R.Evid.

The term "agent or servant" is construed broadly, and there is no requirement that an employee has managerial responsibility for his statements to constitute admissions against the employer. Union Mutual Life Ins. Co. v. Chrysler Corp. 793 F.2d 1, 8 (1st Cir. 1986); *see* Pappas v. Middle Earth Condominium Ass'n, 963 F.2d 534, 537–38 (2d Cir. 1992) (employee who responded with bucket and shovel to complaint about icy conditions); Davis v. Mobil Oil Exploration & Production S.E., 864 F.2d 1171, 1174 (5th Cir. 1989) (speaker identified only as a "Mobil Company man" wearing a Mobil hard hat); Wright v. Farmers Co-Op of Arkansas and Oklahoma, 681 F.2d 549, 552–53 (8th Cir. 1982) (employee who filled propane tank).

[944]*See* Hoptowit v. Ray, 682 F.2d 1237, 1262–63 (9th Cir. 1982) (statements by prison guards and an unspecified "prison employee" were admissions in a suit against prison administrators); Green v. Baca, 226 F.R.D. 624, 636 (C.D.Cal. 2005) (holding report of a Special Counsel retained to review Sheriff's Department operations was an admission of a party-opponent since the counsel acted as the Sheriff's agent), *clarified*, 2005 WL 283361 (C.D.Cal., Jan. 31, 2005); Lipton v. County of Orange, N.Y., 315 F. Supp. 2d 434, 449–50 (S.D.N.Y. 2004) (statements by officers about their supervisor's intentions were admissible as admissions where the officers executed the orders at issue); Coleman v. Wilson, 912 F. Supp. 1282, 1294–96 (E.D.Cal. 1995) (excerpts from depositions of persons who were prison employees when deposed were admissible against higher prison officials as admissions).

[945]*See* § K.2.g of this chapter.

[946]*See* Rule 804(b)(3), Fed.R.Evid. Under that rule, if a declarant is unavailable as a witness, the court may admit into evidence "[a] statement that was at the time of its making so far contrary to the declarant's pecuniary or proprietary interest, or so far tended to subject the declarant to civil or criminal liability, or to render invalid a claim by the declarant against another, that a reasonable person in the declarant's position would not have made the statement unless believing it to be true."

[947]Help At Home Inc. v. Medical Capital, L.L.C., 260 F.3d 748, 753 (7th Cir. 2001); Stelco Holding Co. v. U.S., 44 Fed.Cl. 703, 709 n.12 (Fed.Cl. 1999), *dismissed*, 31 Fed.Appx. 663 (Fed. Cir. 2002) (unpublished).

There are also many other exceptions to the hearsay rule—*i.e.*, types of statements that are admissible even though they are hearsay. These are listed in Rules 803 and 804, Fed.R.Evid. Since there are a couple of dozen of them, we will only discuss the ones that are most likely to come up in prisoner litigation.

Among the most important of the hearsay exceptions are the "present sense impression" and "excited utterance" exceptions, which admit as evidence statements "describing or explaining an event or condition made while the declarant was perceiving the event or condition, or immediately thereafter," or "relating to a startling event or condition made wile the declarant was under stress of excitement caused by the event or condition."[948]

Thus, if you are beaten by guards and then brought into the view of a group of inmates, and the inmates look at you and say things like, "Oh my God, he's half dead!," those statements made on the scene should be admissible to show what your physical condition was at the time. Another important exception admits statements reflecting "then existing mental, emotional, or physical condition."[949] This exception would permit a witness to testify that he heard you screaming, "Stop! You're killing me!" while officers were in your cell beating you, because it reflects the pain you were suffering at the time.

Statements made for purposes of medical diagnosis or treatment, describing medical history, symptoms, pain, or sensations, or "the inception or general character of the cause or external source" of medical complaints to the extent that they are pertinent to diagnosis or treatment, are also admissible.[950]

There are various hearsay exceptions pertaining to documentary evidence,[951] which will be discussed in more detail later in this chapter.

3. Testimonial Evidence

a. Competency Every person, including children and the insane, is presumed competent to testify until challenged.[952] A person may testify if he is willing to take an oath or affirmation,[953] has personal knowledge of what he will testify about,[954] and can communicate that knowledge.

b. Direct Examination Direct examination of a witness is done by the party calling the witness. You will conduct direct examination of your witnesses, and the defendants will conduct direct examination of theirs. Direct examination is usually limited to "non-leading" questions. What constitutes a leading question is hard to explain, and judges may differ in their rulings.[955]

The basic idea is that a leading question is one which suggests to the witness what the answer is. For example, if you are trying to establish that Officer Smith was carrying an axe handle at a particular time, it is leading to ask, "Did Officer Smith have an axe handle in his hands?" It is probably leading to ask, "What did Officer Smith have in his hands?" It is not leading to ask, "Did Officer Smith have anything in his hands?" and then ask, "What did he have in his hands?" As a *pro se* litigant, you may not be held to as strict a standard in this respect as an attorney would be. However, you should do your best to avoid leading questions on direct examination.

The rules about leading questions apply to defendants' lawyers too. If your adversary asks a leading question of a defense witness, you may object.

You are allowed to use leading questions on direct examination under certain circumstances. The most important of these circumstances is when you call a hostile witness, an adverse party, or a witness identified with an adverse party as part of your case.[956] This means that if you call any of the defendants or their agents to give testimony during your case, you should be able to use leading questions with them in order to keep the testimony focused on what you want to bring out. However, if you intend to use leading questions with a witness on your direct case, you should ask the judge's permission and be prepared to proceed with non-leading questions if he so directs. This issue is best dealt with before trial—at a pre-trial conference, if there is one—if at all possible.

You may also use leading questions "as may be necessary to develop [the witness's] testimony."[957] This provision refers to establishing preliminary matters which are not

---

[948]Rules 803(1), 803(2), Fed.R.Evid.

[949]Rule 803(3), Fed.R.Evid.

[950]Rule 803(4), Fed.R.Evid.; *see* Rascon v. Hardiman, 803 F.2d 269, 278–79 (7th Cir. 1986) (plaintiff's statement to medical personnel that his injuries were caused by a beating was properly admitted).

[951]Rules 803(5), 803(6), 803(7), 803(8), Fed.R.Evid.

[952]Rule 601, Fed.R.Evid.; *see* Andrews v. Neer, 253 F.3d 1052, 1062–63 (8th Cir. 2001) (state statute making persons with mental illness incompetent to testify did not apply in federal court, where Rule 601 governs).

[953]Rule 603, Fed.R.Evid.

[954]Rule 602, Fed.R.Evid.

[955]One writer states:

> A leading question is one that suggests to the witness the answer that is desired. That is, it puts words into the witness's mouth. It may assume to be proved a fact which has not been proved. If it meets that test, it may be leading even though it is put into the alternative. A question that may be answered by a simple yes or no may or may not be leading, but is not leading where it is no more suggestive of one answer than the other. On the other hand, a leading question may be one that calls for something more than a yes or no answer. Questions that are intended to call attention to a subject or subjects about which testimony is desired, but not in themselves suggesting the answers expected, are not leading.

Robert S. Hunter, *Federal Trial Handbook* at § 40.3 (West Pub. Co., 4th ed., 2007).

[956]Rule 611, Fed.R.Evid.

[957]*Id.*

disputed, such as the witness's presence at a particular time and place, to dealing with witnesses who have difficulty testifying because of age or mental or physical condition, and to dealing with confused witnesses. If your witness does get seriously confused on the stand, you should ask the court's permission to ask a leading question to get the witness back on track.

The purpose of direct examination for you is to establish your claim, and your questions should be designed to prove your case and not to disprove something you think the other side may try to show later. For example, if you think the defendants will try to show that you have threatened your witness to make him testify in a particular way, do not ask the witness on direct examination if he has been threatened. Save it for redirect examination (if the defendants raise it on cross-examination) or for your rebuttal case (if they make this accusation during the defendants' case).

Whenever possible, you should go over each of your witnesses' testimony with the witness a day or two before trial. You should have your questions written out and should go through them just as if the witness was on the stand.

When you get a witness on the stand, things never go exactly as you expect. You must listen to the witness as he testifies to make sure that he answers the question you ask. Often you will ask a witness a question and the witness will give an answer that covers the next several questions on your list, forcing you to skip ahead. Or the witness may leave out a key fact, requiring you to go back and ask a follow-up question to bring it out.

It is helpful to check off the questions on your list as they are answered to make sure you don't skip something important. If you get confused, do not hesitate to ask the judge to let you take a minute to get straightened out.

c. Cross-Examination

Cross-examination is conducted by the party who did not call the witness. It takes place after direct examination and is generally limited to the subjects that were covered in direct examination and matters relating to the witness's credibility.[958] Each side gets the chance to cross-examine the other side's witnesses.

Cross-examination is probably the trickiest part of a trial and the one where you must think the most quickly and clearly. When you are on the stand being cross-examined, remember that your adversary is trying to do two things: to discredit your testimony, and to discredit you as a person. In order to do the latter, the opposing lawyer will probably try to make you angry, hostile, or confused on the witness stand so he can make you look undeserving or take advantage of the jury's or judge's stereotypes about prisoners.

Remember this, and do not lash out at the opposing attorney when you are cross-examined. Keep your dignity, answer the questions, do not try to argue, and if you do not understand the question, ask to have it repeated. If the

attorney badgers you or shouts at you, you can ask the judge calmly and politely to tell him to stop. (Don't do this unless it gets badly out of hand for a long time.) If the judge does not curb the attorney, accept it and do not argue with the judge. By keeping your dignity on the stand, you will keep the court or jury focused on the issues in the case and not on the personalities.

On cross-examination, leading questions are permitted;[959] in fact, they are preferred by most lawyers, because they permit the questioner to keep greater control over the situation. Thus, when cross-examining, you would be permitted to ask, "Did Officer Smith have an axe handle in his hand?" For that matter, you could ask, "Officer Smith had an axe handle in his hand, didn't he?"

Your questions—like these examples—should be narrowly focused on particular factual issues. Avoid questions that give the witness free rein to say whatever he wants. For example, don't ask a question like, "Why did you hit me?" Ask questions that focus on relevant facts that may help you, such as, "When you hit me, I was surrounded by you and three other officers, wasn't I?"

When you are cross-examining, you are not permitted to argue with the witness or badger the witness. The other side is subject to the same limitations when cross-examining you or your witness. If the witness does not answer the question you ask, you should repeat it (e.g., "But officer, my question is . . .") If the witness persists in giving a response that does not answer the question, ask the judge for help (e.g., "Your Honor, the answer is not responsive. Would you direct the witness to answer the question that was asked?").

The most important aspect of cross-examination is planning in advance and having a clear idea of what it is that you want to accomplish. It is a big mistake simply to get up and ask a lot of questions that result only in the witness's repeating his story. This only bolsters the witness's testimony.

Instead, you should focus on particular points where you can help your case or hurt the other side's case through cross-examination. Stick to these points and keep it short. Try to finish your cross-examination with questions on a point that is particularly helpful to your case.

If a witness testifies against you but does not actually provide any harmful testimony, you are not required to cross-examine him at all, and you should not unless you are certain you will get helpful testimony from him.[960]

---

[958]Rule 611(b), Fed.R.Evid.

The court may in its discretion permit a witness to be asked about additional matters as if direct examination were continuing.

[959]Rule 611(c), Fed.R.Evid.

[960]For example, suppose there is an issue in your case concerning whether you engaged in some kind of misconduct. If an officer who was on the scene testifies about the incident and does not mention your alleged misconduct, leave it alone. Otherwise the officer may say, "Oh, yes, I forgot, I saw you doing so-and-so."

On the other hand, if you have a report by the officer that describes the incident but does not mention the alleged misconduct, you might ask the officer, "So you didn't see me doing so-and-so, did you?" If the officer then says, "I forgot," etc., you can

If a defense witness says nothing to hurt your case, be sure to point this out in closing argument.

Some basic cross-examination techniques are as follows.

Establishing the witness's bias, prejudice, or interest. A witness's testimony can be attacked by showing that the witness has some reason to lie. For example, if several guards are buttressing each other's false testimony to cover up the misconduct of one of them, you might try to bring out the fact that they work together, see each other every day, rely on each other in tight spots, hang out together after work, etc.

If you previously complained about a prison employee who is testifying, that fact might indicate a motivation to testify falsely against you.

If an employee violated prison rules and would be subject to discipline if he were found out, there is another motive to testify falsely against you.

Generally, you can ask the witness about these subjects on cross-examination; if you have evidence to prove something the witness denies, you can put it into evidence on rebuttal.

These same tactics can and will be used by the defense against you.

Cross-examination on the basis of bias, prejudice, or interest is one of several forms of "impeachment" of a witness's credibility.

Testing the witness's opportunity to observe. Sometimes witnesses will testify to things it is doubtful they really were able to see or hear. If a guard testifies that he saw you strike for first blow in an altercation, but you know he was at the other end of a long gallery and you were surrounded by other inmates at the time, you can bring these facts out with appropriate questions.

Limiting the witness's testimony. Sometimes a witness will help the other side in some small respect but will not be able to testify at all about some other major aspect of the case. It can be helpful to emphasize this on cross-examination. For example, if a guard testifies that you walked out of a housing unit with two other guards peacefully and in good physical condition, and you claim that you were beaten in a stairwell, you might ask, "You didn't see me after we left the housing unit, did you? You couldn't see into the stairwell, could you? So if they did something to me in the stairwell, you couldn't have seen it, could you?"

Also, a prison official may testify as to certain prison practices without knowing whether the practice was followed in your case. For example, if a deputy warden testifies about disciplinary procedures at the prison, you might ask, "You don't have any idea whether I actually received notice of these particular charges in advance of the hearing, do you?"

Highlighting helpful parts of the testimony. Sometimes an adverse witness will give some testimony that is helpful to you. Often this testimony will consist of something that contradicts another defense witness. You can make this clear to the judge or jury by asking questions about the testimony that helped your case. For example, if two guards claim that you assaulted one of them and had to be removed from the housing unit by force, and a third guard testifies that you did commit the assault but that you left the housing unit peacefully, on cross-examination you could ask the third guard, "You testified, didn't you, that you saw me leaving the housing unit peacefully?" Getting him to repeat this testimony on cross-examination may help undermine the testimony of the other guards.

Stating your case again. Sometimes it is effective to state your case again through accusatory leading questions. You have to be careful to avoid getting into an argument with the witness, and you have to keep it short and punchy. After all, since the witness will presumably deny everything, you are looking for dramatic effect rather than information. For example, you might ask at the end of a cross-examination, "Isn't it true that you hit me in the face while I was handcuffed? Isn't it true that you stood by while Officer Smith hit me in the head with an axe handle? Isn't it true that you walked out of my cell leaving me handcuffed and bleeding? Isn't it true that you ignored me when I called for medical help?"

Since the answer to each of these questions will probably be a loud "No," you should probably avoid this tactic with a self-confident witness whose credibility has not been successfully attacked, or you will run the risk of bolstering the defendants' case. If the witness is not self-confident, or if you have successfully impeached his credibility, an accusatory cross-examination may be more effective.

Impeachment by use of prior inconsistent statements. If a witness testifies in a way that is inconsistent with a prior statement he made, you can cross-examine the witness about the statement. There is an accepted way to do this properly and effectively. First, get the witness to repeat the inconsistent testimony. Then ask the witness if he made the other statement, giving the time and place it was made. For example:

Q: You testified on direct examination, didn't you, that the only officer present when you took me to segregation was Officer Smith?
Q: Do you recall giving a deposition at the prison on January 11 of this year?
Q: And were you under oath?
Q: And were you asked these questions, and did you give these answers, at page 45?
[Read the inconsistent testimony]
Q: Were you asked those questions, and did you give those answers?

Use a similar sequence of questions if the prior inconsistent statement was made in an official report, in conversation, or in some other form.

---

cross-examine him using his report. The contradiction between his "remembering" that you committed misconduct and not having mentioned it in his report at the time is likely to weaken the defense case's credibility.

If the witness denies making the statement, you may place the statement into evidence. If it is in a report or other document, you can put the document in evidence; if it is a statement that you or another witness heard, the person who heard it can take the stand during your rebuttal case and testify that it was made. But before you can do this, you must impeach the witness with the statement. Prior inconsistent statements can only come into evidence if "the witness is afforded an opportunity to explain or deny the [statement] and the opposite party is afforded an opportunity to interrogate him thereon. . . ."[961]

Do not try to impeach with every possible inconsistency you find in the record. No witness is perfectly consistent, and the judge or jury will not be impressed with minor discrepancies. Be selective and choose the ones that make the most dramatic points.

A prior *consistent* statement may be put into evidence if the witness has been subjected to an "express or implied charge against the declarant of recent fabrication or improper influence or motive."[962] If your credibility is attacked in those ways, and if you have prior statements— *e.g.*, a complaint to the warden or a letter to your family—that show you have been telling the same story all along, you should be able to place these prior statements on the record.

Impeachment by reference to criminal convictions, prior bad acts, character, etc. These subjects are dealt with later in this chapter.[963]

d. Redirect Examination Redirect examination is available to the party calling the witness once the cross-examination has been completed. Leading questions are generally prohibited on redirect examination. If your witness has given harmful or confusing testimony on cross-examination, you may seek to cure the harm or confusion on redirect examination.

On redirect, you are limited to the subjects covered during cross-examination. You cannot introduce new evidence on redirect that you should have introduced on direct examination but forgot. (If you have made a serious mistake on direct, the judge may permit you to rectify it on redirect, but you should ask permission before you try this.)

After redirect examination, re-cross may be permitted, limited to the subjects covered in the redirect.

4. Documentary Evidence

In most cases, documents you will want to use at trial will fall into one of several categories: documents created by prison personnel in the course of their duties, documents created by you or by other prisoners (such as lists of lost property, grievances, or eyewitness accounts or events), or prior testimony at depositions or court proceedings. We have focused on these types of documents. The rules of

evidence cited in this section will also be your starting point if you have a problem concerning a different kind of document.

a. The Authenticity of Documents The party offering a document into evidence must demonstrate its authenticity—*i.e.*, that the document is what it claims to be and is not a fake. If you created the document (*e.g.*, a complaint or grievance that you filed), your testimony is sufficient to authenticate it. In some cases, your testimony may be sufficient to authenticate an official document— *e.g.*, a notice or statement of reasons given to you in connection with a disciplinary proceeding. Where you do not have personal knowledge of the nature of the document, you cannot authenticate it. If the document is a record or report from the prison files, in theory you must either get a certified copy,[964] subpoena the person responsible for keeping the files to testify that your copy is authentic, or as part of the discovery process get prison officials to admit that it is an authenticated copy. In practice, federal judges generally expect the parties to deal with authenticity questions before trial so they do not have to hear about them unless there is actually a dispute about a particular document. Some courts have held that when a party produces a document in discovery, that fact is sufficient to establish its authenticity when the adverse party offers it in evidence.[965]

You can establish the authenticity of documents before trial by serving requests for admission on the defendants.[966] You can also ask the defendants to stipulate that documents are authentic, either by letter or at a pretrial conference, if the court holds one. Additional details on the requirements of authenticity are set out in the evidence rules.[967]

Authenticating a document simply shows that it is genuine. It does not necessarily make it admissible, and it does not mean that the judge or jury must believe what the document says.

Generally, to prove what a document says, you must introduce the document or a copy of it. Duplicate copies of documents are admissible to the same extent as the originals unless there is a genuine question as to the copies' authenticity or there is some other reason their admission would be unfair.[968]

---

[961] Rule 613(b), Fed.R.Evid.

[962] Rule 801(d)(1)(B). Fed.R.Evid.

[963] *See* § S.5 of this chapter.

---

[964] "Certified" means that the custodian of the document, or other person authorized to make the certification, makes a certificate under seal stating that the document is a correct copy. Rule 902(4), Fed.R.Evid.

[965] *See* Payne v. Collins, 986 F. Supp. 1036, 1056 (E.D.Tex. 1997) and cases cited.

[966] *See* § K.2.g of this chapter concerning requests for admission. An example of such a request is "Admit that Attachment 1 to this Request is an authentic copy of the plaintiff's prison medical record for the period from January 5, 2009 to January 20, 2009."

[967] Rules 901, 902, Fed.R.Evid.

[968] Rules 1001(4), 1003, Fed.R.Evid. *See also* U.S. v. Westmoreland, 312 F.3d 302, 311 (7th Cir. 2002).

Testimony about the document or references to it in another document are not good enough to get the content of the document before the jury. However, this limitation does not apply if the document itself is lost, destroyed, or otherwise unavailable, or if the other side has it and fails to produce it despite knowing it will be an issue.[969]

b. Hearsay Problems with Documents Any document may appear to be hearsay.[970] You should be prepared to explain why any document you wish to introduce either is not hearsay or falls into an exception to the hearsay rule. This is not difficult when the document is part of the regular prison record keeping system.

Often, a prison document will be a statement by one of the defendants or by an agent of one of the defendants, and can therefore come in as an admission by a party-opponent.[971]

In many cases, prison documents will be admissible as "records of regularly conducted activity" (often termed "business records")[972] or "public records and reports."[973]

These rules are construed broadly; the fact that a document was prepared by a prison staff member, lodged in the prison files and retained in them is generally sufficient to support its admission as a business or public record[974] unless there are circumstances indicating it is unreliable.

Public records that set forth "factual findings resulting from an investigation made pursuant to authority granted by law" may be admitted in their entirety; "opinions" and "conclusions" need not be removed.[975] This rule generally permits the admission of investigative reports on or by prison and law enforcement agencies, which sometimes contain material helpful in individual prisoners' suits.[976]

Even if a document is generally admissible as a business or a public record, there may be things in it that are not admissible. If the document quotes or reports statements by

---

[969]Rule 1004, Fed.R.Evid. Some courts have held that summaries are admissible as best evidence of destroyed records, pursuant to Fed.R.Evid. 1004. *See, e.g.,* U.S. v. Dudley, 941 F.2d 260, 264 (8th Cir.1991) (allowing admission of business records summary of federal reserve bank concerning currency source as "best evidence" of destroyed records).

[970]Hearsay is discussed in § S.2 of this chapter.

[971]*See* Rule 801(d)(2), Fed.R.Evid. Admissions by party-opponents are discussed in § S.2 of this chapter.

[972]Rule 803(6), Fed.R.Evid. The rule defines such a record as:

A memorandum, report, record, or data compilation, in any form, of acts, events, conditions, opinions, or diagnoses, made at or near the time by, or from information transmitted by, a person with knowledge, if kept in the course of a regularly conducted business activity, and if it was the regular practice of that business activity to make memorandum, report, record or data compilation, all as shown by the testimony of the custodian or other qualified witness, or by certification . . . unless the source of information or the method or circumstances of preparation indicate lack of trustworthiness. The tem "business" as used in this paragraph includes business, institution, association, profession, occupation, and calling of every kind, whether or not conducted for profit.

See Wheeler v. Sims, 951 F.2d 796, 802–05 (7th Cir. 1992) (prison disciplinary records and records of staff observations of prisoner's physical condition were admissible as business records).

[973]Rule 803(8), Fed.R.Evid. This rule permits the admission of:

Records, reports, statements, or data compilations, in any form, of public offices or agencies, setting forth (A) the activities of the office or agency, or (B) matters observed pursuant to duty imposed by law as to which matters there was a duty to report, excluding, however, in criminal cases matters observed by police officers and other law enforcement personnel, or (C) in civil actions and proceedings and against the Government in criminal cases, factual findings resulting from an investigation made pursuant to authority granted by law, unless the sources

of information or other circumstances indicate lack of trustworthiness.

[974]Stone v. Morris, 546 F.2d 730, 738 (7th Cir. 1976); *see* Combs v. Wilkinson, 315 F.3d 548, 554–56 (6th Cir. 2002) (report prepared by use of force committee admissible pursuant to Rule 808(8)); U.S. v. Reyes, 157 F.3d 949, 951–53 (2d Cir. 1998) (prison visitor log book generated and kept by the prison was admissible).

[975]Beech Aircraft Corp. v. Rainey, 488 U.S. 153, 161–70, 109 S. Ct. 439 (1988) (interpreting Rule 803(8)(C), Fed.R.Evid.). Portions of such reports may be excluded under the "trustworthiness" exception to the rule or under other rules such as those dealing with relevance and prejudice. *See* Bank of Lexington & Trust Co. v. Vining-Sparks Securities, Inc., 959 F.2d 606, 616 (6th Cir.1992) ("To determine whether a report is trustworthy, the Advisory Committee suggests four factors to consider: (1) the timeliness of the investigation, (2) the special skill or experience of the investigators, (3) whether the agency held a hearing, and (4) possible motivational problems." (citation omitted)).

[976]*See* Combs v. Wilkinson, 315 F.3d 548, 555–56 (6th Cir. 2002) (rejecting argument that investigative report was not admissible under Rule 602 or 803(8) for lack of authors' personal knowledge because such reports "embody the results of investigation and accordingly are often not the product of the declarant's firsthand knowledge" (quotation omitted)); Bridgeway Corp. v. Citibank, 201 F.3d 134, 143 (2d Cir. 2000) (holding United States State Department Country Reports for Liberia admissible under Fed.R.Evid. 803(8)(C) and noting the rule "renders presumptively admissible not merely . . . factual determinations in the narrow sense, but also . . . conclusions or opinions that are based upon a factual investigation" (internal quotations omitted)); Hill v. Marshall, 962 F.2d 1209, 1215 n.2 (6th Cir. 1992) (admitting legislative report on problems in prison medical care system under Rule 803(8)(C) based on interviews with witnesses where author did not have personal knowledge of events); Green v. Baca, 226 F.R.D. 624, 636 (C.D.Cal. 2005) (holding report of a Special Counsel retained to review Sheriff's Department operations admissible as a public record setting forth factual findings), *clarified*, 2005 WL 283361 (C.D.Cal., Jan. 31, 2005); Pelletier v. Magnusson, 195 F. Supp. 2d 214, 217–19 (D.Me. 2002) (holding admissible the report of a physician's assistant assigned by prison department to investigate prison suicides). *But see* Evans v. Dugger, 908 F.2d 801, 809 (11th Cir. 1990) (upholding the admission of material concerning history of prison medical neglect only in redacted form to eliminate prejudicial and misleading material).

people other than the author of the document, those statements are likely to be "double hearsay" or "hearsay within hearsay." Such evidence can only be admitted "if each part of the combined statements conforms with an exception to the hearsay rule. . . ."[977]

For example, suppose a prison employee writes on a transfer form, "Warden directed this transfer because of prisoner's constant complaining." The form itself can be admitted under the business records exception to the hearsay rule. The warden's statement, reported by the employee, is "hearsay within hearsay," and is not necessarily admissible for the truth of what it asserts. However, a plaintiff who sued the warden over the transfer could offer the statement as an admission by a party opponent.[978] The two hearsay exceptions—business or public records and admission by a party opponent—would work together to make the whole document admissible.

By contrast, in one case, a nurse wrote in a prisoner's medical records that an officer told her that the plaintiff told him that he had inflicted an injury himself. (This amounts to triple hearsay.) The defendants were not permitted to use this evidence. The medical records were admissible as business records, and the inmate's statement would have been an admission of a party opponent if it had been made to the nurse who wrote the medical record. But instead it was reported by the officer. The officer's hearsay statement was not admissible under the business records exception because it was not clear that the officer had a "business duty" to report the matter to the medical staff. Therefore, a "link in the hearsay chain" was missing.[979]

Hearsay within hearsay is often an issue in reports of public agencies. The factual findings of investigations may be admissible under Rule 803(8)(C), Fed.R.Evid., but the reports and statements on which the findings are based may not be.[980] However, they may be admissible under other

rules. For example, in a use of force investigation, statements by officers involved may be admissible under Rule 803(8)(A), as reports of "the activities of the office or agency," or Rule 803(8)(B), as "matters observed pursuant to duty imposed by law as to which matters there was a duty to report."[981] Statements by prison personnel whom you have sued, or their subordinates, may be admissible under Rule 801(d)(2) as admissions of a party-opponent. However, witness statements by prisoners do not fit into any of these categories and may not be admissible. So if a prison investigation includes a statement by a prisoner witness that is helpful to you, you will need to get that witness's testimony at trial or by deposition.

Documents qualifying as records of regularly conducted activity or as public records and reports may not be admitted "if sources of information or other circumstances indicate lack of trustworthiness."[982] One court has held that reports by prison guards concerning events for which they are being sued are "dripping with motivations to misrepresent" and for that reason are not trustworthy enough to be admitted.[983]

In practice, courts will seldom exclude prison records just because they are written by prison personnel. You should review each document carefully to see if there is an

---

of interviews with witnesses, victim, and prosecutor that contained "neither factual findings made by the report's preparers nor conclusions and opinions based upon such factual findings" inadmissible under Rule 803(8)(C)).

[981]*See* Hynes v. Coughlin, 79 F.3d 285, 294–95 (2d Cir. 1996) (document was not admissible under this section where the author of the document did not actually observe what she reported).

[982]Rules 803(6), 803(8), Fed.R.Evid.

[983]Bracey v. Herringa, 466 F.2d 702, 704–05 (7th Cir. 1972) (citation omitted). Similarly, in *Lewis v. Velez*, 149 F.R.D. 474 (S.D.N.Y. 1993), the court held that incident reports generated by correction officers were not admissible under Rule 803(6) because they lacked reliability:

> Where reports of inmate beatings show a lack of reliability and trustworthiness due to the self-interest of the correction officers responsible for the records, such records are inadmissible. . . . Self-interest functions strongly in the case at hand, where correction officers involved could be subject to disciplinary action, including dismissal, for using excessive force and could, furthermore, be brought up on criminal charges or incur civil liability. The fact that, as the defendants point out, correction officers receive strict instructions to make their reports truthfully does not diminish the motives that undermine the trustworthiness of such reports.

F.R.D. at 486 (citing *Bracey*). *Accord*, Romano v. Howarth, 998 F.2d 101, 108 (2d Cir. 1993) (". . . [E]ven if the defendants could establish that the officers had a business duty to report accurately to the nurses, there is still a dark cloud hovering over this particular business record: the officer's motive to fudge the truth of what really happened in Romano's cell."); Morales Feliciano v. Hernandez Colon, 697 F. Supp. 37, 40 (D.P.R. 1988) (noting unreliability of prison documentation). *But see* Harris v. Dugger, 757 F. Supp. 1359, 1363–64 (S.D.Fla. 1989) (rejecting *Bracey*).

---

[977]Rule 805, Fed.R.Evid.

[978]Rule 801(d)(2), Fed. R. Evid. Admissions are discussed in § S.2 of this chapter.

[979]Romano v. Howarth, 998 F.2d 101, 107–08 (2d Cir. 1993) ("If, however, the supplier of the information does not act in the regular course, an essential link is broken; the assurance of accuracy does not extend to the information itself, and the fact that it may be recorded with scrupulous accuracy is of no avail." (quoting Fed.R.Evid. 803(6) advisory committee's note)); *compare* Payne v. Collins, 986 F. Supp. 1036, 1055 (E.D.Tex. 1997) (prison "operational review report" was admissible as a business record because all the hearsay in it was from persons acting in the regular course of business); *see also* U.S. v. Ortiz, 125 F.3d 630, 632 (8th Cir. 1997) (report consisting of double hearsay not admissible); U.S. v. Pendas-Martinez, 845 F.2d 938, 942–43 (11th Cir. 1988) (concluding that, even if one level of double-hearsay statement was not hearsay, second level of hearsay was not excepted from the hearsay rule and, therefore, was inadmissible); Eng v. Scully, 146 F.R.D. 74, 79–80 (S.D.N.Y. 1993) (report consisting mostly of double hearsay was not admissible).

[980]*See* Miller v. Field, 35 F.3d 1088, 1091 (6th Cir. 1994) (holding investigative police reports which comprised summaries

individual basis for keeping that document out. A document may not really be relevant to the issues at the trial. It may contain material, such as extraneous derogatory remarks about you, that supports your argument that it is untrustworthy. A "report" may be nothing more than a summary of what the defendants claim to have happened, rather than an independent investigation with findings.[984]

Even if the court refuses to exclude the entire document, it may exclude parts of it as being particularly irrelevant, prejudicial, or untrustworthy. If the defendants try to put in a very long document or a whole file of documents (*e.g.*, your complete institutional file), you may wish to ask that only the relevant portions be admitted.[985]

Conversely, if they offer a document selectively, and there are other parts of the document that help you or give a more balanced picture, you may wish to ask the court to admit the entire document or none of it,[986] though portions of the document that are inadmissible hearsay cannot be admitted.[987]

You should also keep in mind that the defendants' lawyer may wish to put documents in evidence to avoid calling certain witnesses, so excluding the documents may mean that more witnesses will be called to testify against you. This can be good or bad, depending on who the witnesses are and how impressive they are likely to be.

Documents which are not written by defendants or their agents and which are not part of regular prison practice are harder to get into evidence. Generally, written statements that you obtain from witnesses will not be admissible at trial, even if they are sworn to. You should plan on calling the witnesses to testify if you need their evidence. The adverse party has a right to cross-examine your witnesses and if only the statement is admitted they cannot do so.

Even if a witness is unavailable, a prior statement by the witness is usually admissible only if it is prior testimony in court or at a deposition, or is a statement made under certain other very limited circumstances.[988] The court has discretion to admit a hearsay statement of an unavailable witness if the statement appears to be trustworthy and a number of other requirements are met,[989] but you should not expect this to happen in a factually contested prison case.

When a witness's credibility has been attacked in certain specified ways, such as by claims that the witness's testimony was a recent fabrication or the witness was subject to improper influence or motive, documents containing prior consistent statements by that witness may be admissible to support his credibility.[990]

Sometimes you or one of your witnesses will have written something down when it happened but will not be able to testify from memory by the time of trial. For example, you might have made a list of your lost property right after it was lost, or have made a list of volumes missing from the law library while you were working or doing research there. You cannot place this document into evidence; however, you can testify that the document was written when the matter was fresh in your mind and that it was accurate when you wrote it, and then read it into the record.[991]

---

[984]*See, e.g.*, Klein v. Vanek, 86 F. Supp. 2d 812, 820 (N.D.Ill. 2000) (police investigator's conclusion that plaintiff was not credible held not admissible as a public record because of lack of trustworthiness: there was no hearing, the investigator never actually interviewed those involved, and was not shown to have any specialized expertise in judging credibility or in assessing plaintiff's mental illness); *see also* Reynolds v. Green, 184 F.3d 589, 596 (6th Cir. 1999) (upholding exclusion of report by Corrections Ombudsman's Office because it consisted in part of a self-serving statement by the plaintiff, which lacks "the reliability attributable to the independent conclusions of a public official," plus additional "hearsay within hearsay").

[985]Your objections to your entire medical or prison file being introduced is that 90% or more is irrelevant; it will be confusing to the jury; and/or it will delay the trial.

[986]Rule 106, Fed.R.Evid. You will need to explain why admission of other portions of the document "ought in fairness to be considered" along with the part defendants offer. *Id.*; *see* U.S. v. Sweiss, 814 F.2d 1208, 1212 (7th Cir. 1987) (party urging admission of an excluded conversation must "specify the portion of the testimony that is relevant to the issue at trial and that qualifies or explains portions already admitted.").

[987]*See* Trepel v. Roadway Express Inc., 194 F.3d 708, 718 (6th Cir. 1999) ("[T]he completeness doctrine embodied in Rule 106 should not be used to make something admissible that would otherwise be excluded.").

[988]Rule 804(b), Fed.R.Evid.

Even prior testimony may not be admitted if there are reasons it would be misleading or unfair to admit it. *See* Reilly v. Natwest Markets Group Inc., 181 F.3d 253, 269 (2d Cir. 1999) (court did not abuse its discretion in barring employer from using employee's deposition to impeach his trial testimony, where he could not answer many deposition questions because the employer had not produced certain necessary files).

[989]Rule 807, Fed.R.Evid. (formerly Rules 803(24) and Rule 804(b)(5). Fed.R.Evid. *See* U.S. v. Thunder Horse, 370 F.3d 745, 747 (8th Cir. 2004), for a discussion of the standard that must be met for statements to be admitted under this "residual" hearsay exception.

[990]Rule 801(d)(1)(B), Fed.R.Evid. This rule is strictly limited to the specific situations it refers to, and cannot be used to counter all forms of impeachment or to bolster the witness generally. It also is limited to statements made *before* the alleged fabrication, influence, or motive came into being. Tome v. U.S., 513 U.S. 150, 156–60, 115 S. Ct. 696 (1995).

[991]Rule 803(5), Fed.R.Evid.; *see* Parker v. Reda, 327 F.3d 211, 213–15 (2d Cir. 2003) (per curiam) (lower court could properly allow prison sergeant who said he remembered nothing about an incident to read his contemporaneous memorandum into the record, even if memo did not have sufficient indicia of reliability to be admitted as a business record).

A document may also be used to refresh a witness's recollection. If the witness then remembers the matters at issue, the document need not be offered or admitted into evidence. *See* U.S. v. Humphrey, 279 F.3d 372, 377 (6th Cir. 2002) (document need not be admitted or admissible in evidence in order to be used to refresh the recollection of a witness) (citing U.S. v. Faulkner, 538 F.2d 724,

c. Depositions and Prior Testimony Depositions and testimony from prior court proceedings are always admissible to impeach the testimony of a witness.[992] Depositions and prior testimony of adverse parties or their agents may also be introduced directly as admissions.[993] The court has discretion to require that voluminous deposition testimony be reduced to a summary.[994]

Depositions may be used as a substitute for live testimony if the witness is dead, more than 100 miles from the court, unavailable because of age, illness, infirmity, imprisonment, or his attendance cannot be obtained by subpoena; other exceptional circumstances may also justify admitting a deposition.[995] (A prisoner is not "unavailable" by reason of imprisonment if he can be produced by the adverse party or through a writ of habeas corpus *ad testificandum*, but if he is more than 100 miles away, his deposition may be introduced regardless of availability.[996]) A deposition may be used even if it is from another action if it involves the same parties and subject matter, or is otherwise admissible under the Federal Rules of Evidence.[997]

---

727 (6th Cir. 1976)). However, the document must be provided to the adverse party, who may cross-examine the witness about it and may introduce relevant portions of it into evidence. Rule 612, Fed.R.Evid.

[992]Rule 32(a)(2), Fed.R.Civ.P.; Rule 801(d)(1), Fed.R.Evid.

[993]Admissions of a party opponent are discussed in § S.2 of this chapter.

[994]Planned Parenthood of Columbia/Willamette, Inc. v. American Coalition of Life Activists, 290 F.3d 1058, 1083 (9th Cir. 2002); Oostendorp v. Khanna, 937 F.2d 1177, 1179–80 (7th Cir. 1991).

[995]Rule 32(a)(4), Fed.R.Civ.P.; Rule 804(b)(1), Fed.R.Evid.; *see* Ueland v. U.S., 291 F.3d 993, 995–97 (7th Cir. 2002) (deposition of prisoner who was incarcerated more than 100 miles from the site of the trial should have been admitted); Vaughn v. Willis, 853 F.2d 1372, 1378 (7th Cir. 1988) (inmate witness who refused to testify out of fear was unavailable and his deposition could be used at trial under Rule 804(b), Fed.R.Evid.); Rascon v. Hardiman, 803 F.2d 269, 277 (7th Cir. 1986) (deposition of former inmate was admitted under Rule 32(a)(3)(D) where a private investigator testified he could not find the witness, showing he was not available by subpoena). *But see* Gregory v. Shelby County, Tenn., 220 F.3d 433, 449 (6th Cir. 2000) (where prisoner refused to testify because he had been harassed by officers and other prisoners, he should not have been ruled unavailable for purposes of using his deposition, because Rule 804(a), Fed.R.Evid., requires that a witness "persist[] in refusing to testify . . . despite an order of the court," and no order had been entered; but error found harmless).

"For a party to be 'unable' to procure a witness's attendance at trial by subpoena implies that the party used reasonable diligence to get him to attend." Griman v. Makousky, 76 F.3d 151, 153 (7th Cir. 1996) (where party thought witness was in jail, but he had been released, deposition could not be admitted in the absence of prior efforts to secure attendance at trial).

[996]Ueland v. U.S., 291 F.3d at 996–97.

[997]Rule 32(a)(8), Fed.R.Civ.P. The most important provision of the Federal Rules of Evidence affecting prior depositions is Rule 801(d), which allows the use of depositions as impeachment and allows the use of statements by a party or the party's agent as

Under this rule, a court may be tempted to refuse to produce you or your incarcerated witnesses for trial if the defendants have taken depositions.[998] You should argue vigorously that it is unfair for you to have to present your case through depositions which were taken by the other side to prepare their case and that these depositions do not adequately reflect the nature of your case, assuming that is correct.

Deposition testimony can be excluded if it would not be admissible from a witness on the stand.[999] For example, if a witness gives hearsay testimony in a deposition, that part of the deposition should not be admissible at trial, if you timely objected at the deposition on hearsay grounds,[1000] unless it falls within one of the exceptions to the rule against hearsay. If a party offers part of a deposition, the adverse party may require it to offer other parts "that in fairness should be considered with the part introduced," and other parties may introduce other parts.[1001]

d. Handling Documentary Evidence Federal courts generally try to streamline the use of documents; they have little patience with technical disputes at trial, particularly about subjects like authenticity, or whether a document is a business or public record. You should therefore try to work these problems out before trial. One way to do this with your documents is to file a request for admissions[1002] that the documents you wish to introduce are authentic, that they are admissible as business or public records, etc.[1003] If you want to keep certain documents out of evidence, file a motion *in limine* explaining your reasons well before trial.[1004]

If you do not do either of these things but the court holds a pretrial conference,[1005] bring the documents that you wish to introduce and ask the other side to stipulate that they are authentic and admissible, and inform the court at that time of any evidence you know of that you think should be excluded. The court may resolve the issues at the

---

admissions by a party-opponent. The latter are discussed in § S.2 of this chapter.

[998]*See* § Q of this chapter for a discussion of issues concerning court appearances by you and your witnesses.

[999]Rule 32(b), Fed.R.Civ.P.

[1000]Rule 32(d)(3)(B), Fed.R.Civ.P.

[1001]Rule 32(a)(6), Fed.R.Civ.P.; *see* Trepel v. Roadway Exp., Inc., 194 F.3d 708, 719 (6th Cir. 1999) (party offering part of deposition could be required to introduce enough of it to put the initially offered statement into context).

[1002]Requests for admissions are discussed in § K.2.g of this chapter.

[1003]For example, you could ask the defendants to admit that:

1. The attached document, dated February 19, 2009, and headed "Adjustment Committee Notice," is a true copy of a disciplinary charge lodged against the plaintiff.
1. The attached document headed "Adjustment Committee Notice," dated February 19, 2009, is a public record setting forth the actions of a public agency.

[1004]Motions *in limine* are discussed in § S.6 of this chapter.

[1005]Pretrial conferences are discussed in § O of this chapter.

conference or may instruct the parties on what to do to get them resolved.

Do not make notes, underlines, or other marks on documents you wish to put into evidence.[1006] Since your notes and marks are not admissible, you may wind up in a long argument about whether the whole document has to be excluded, or there may be a delay while the parties search for a clean copy of the document. If there is no clean copy of the document, the exhibit may be excluded and your case may be significantly harmed by its being excluded.

The standard procedure for putting a document into evidence is as follows. State on the record what the document is and hand it to the court reporter to be marked and listed as an exhibit. At that point, it will be given a number or letter and be deemed "marked for identification." (This step can be shortened if the parties pre-mark their exhibits and provide the court and each other with lists of their exhibits.[1007])

Next, give it to the lawyer for the other side to inspect. Tell the judge if there is an admission or stipulation as to its authenticity or admissibility. If not, you may have to "lay a foundation" by testifying, having a witness testify, or producing other evidence that the document is authentic, that it is a business record, and whatever else is necessary to show it is admissible. The other side will have a chance to object, and the judge will rule on any objection after hearing the parties' arguments.

You should keep a list of all the exhibits, noting which ones are only marked for identification and which ones are actually admitted into evidence. Before you close your case, you should be sure that all the documents you want in the record have been admitted into evidence. If the judge has delayed a ruling on any of the documents, be sure to remind the judge and request a ruling before the taking of evidence is closed.

5. Prior Records of Plaintiff and Prison Personnel

The rules of evidence place limits on when and how evidence of prior crimes and other misconduct can be used in litigation.

a. Criminal Convictions Under Rule 609, Fed.R.Evid., a witness's prior convictions can be admitted into evidence for impeachment purposes in a civil case if the crime "was punishable by death or imprisonment in excess of one year

under the law under which the witness was convicted,"[1008] or without regard to the punishment if the crime "required proof or admission of an act of dishonesty or false statement by the witness."[1009] Traditionally, prior convictions are brought out through cross-examination, and if the witness denies the conviction, the record of conviction may be admitted.

It is only convictions that are used to impeach, and not arrests, or criminal charges or accusations that don't result in a conviction.[1010] Juvenile adjudications are not admissible in civil cases.[1011] Proper impeachment is generally limited to the crime, the date, and the disposition; the details of the crimes usually are not admitted.[1012] You should object to the

---

[1006]Since you don't always know when you receive a document that you will want to use in court, it is wise simply not to mark on any official documents you receive. If you need to make some notation (*e.g.*, to record the date received), do it in pencil on the back of the document. If you mark up the printed side of a document it may be very difficult to remove the markings so it can be used.

[1007]Many federal judges' pretrial procedures require the parties to pre-mark their exhibits before trial and to exchange them no later than a day or two before trial.

[1008]Rule 609(a)(1), Fed.R.Evid.

[1009]Rule 609(a)(2), Fed.R.Evid.; *see* McHenry v. Chadwick, 896 F.2d 184, 188–89 (6th Cir. 1990) (misdemeanor shoplifting conviction should have been excluded, but misdemeanor conviction of concealing stolen property should have been admitted because it involved dishonesty); Brundidge v. City of Buffalo, 79 F. Supp. 2d 219, 225 (W.D.N.Y. 1999) (criminal impersonation is a crime involving dishonesty or false statement); Eng v. Scully, 146 F.R.D. 74, 78–79 (S.D.N.Y. 1993) (attempted escape is not a crime of dishonesty or false statement). Some courts have taken the view that theft offenses involve dishonesty under Rule 609(a)(2). *See, e.g.*, U.S. v. Kinslow, 860 F.2d 963, 968 (9th Cir. 1988) (holding armed robbery is a crime of dishonesty). However, the people in charge of writing the rules have said that this is "an unduly broad view of 'dishonesty.' . . ." Note of the Advisory Committee to the 1990 Amendment to Rule 609.

This rule was amended in 2006 to clarify that it includes only those crimes which require proof of dishonesty or false statement (perjury, fraud, etc.), and not other kinds of crimes (*e.g.*, murder) in which the defendant may have acted dishonestly or deceitfully. Note of Advisory Committee on 2006 Amendments.

[1010]Jordan v. Medley, 711 F.2d 211, 218 (D.C. Cir. 1983) ("Arrest without more does not, in law any more than in reason, impeach the integrity or impair the credibility of a witness." (citation omitted)); *see* U.S. v. Adedoyin, 369 F.3d 337, 343–44 (3d Cir. 2004) (felony convictions based on *nolo contendere* pleas can be admitted under Rule 609). Evidence of crimes or "bad acts" other than actual criminal convictions is discussed in § S.5b, below. See Rule 404(b), Fed.R.Evid. (barring evidence of uncharged crimes when offered "to prove the character of a person in order to show action in conformity therewith").

[1011]Rule 609(d), Fed.R.Evid.

[1012]U.S. v. Capozzi, 486 F.3d 711, 721 n.4 (1st Cir. 2007); Wilson v. Williams, 182 F.3d 562, 568 (7th Cir. 1999) (district court should have allowed defendants to use the fact that plaintiff had been convicted of murder and sentenced to life imprisonment, and not that he had been convicted of killing two police officers); Cummings v. Malone, 995 F.2d 817, 826 (8th Cir. 1993); Gora v. Costa, 971 F.2d 1325, 1330 (7th Cir. 1992); James v. Tilghman, 194 F.R.D. 402, 405 (D.Conn.1999). *But see* Young v. James Green Management, Inc., 327 F.3d 616, 626 (7th Cir. 2003) (noting general rule, but finding basis in facts of the case for cross-examining about further details of convictions).

admission of records from your prison file that provide further information about your criminal history.[1013]

Convictions are not admissible if a period of more than ten years has passed since the date of conviction, or since the date of release from prison for that conviction, whichever is later, unless the court finds "that the probative value of the conviction supported by specific facts and circumstances substantially outweighs its prejudicial effect."[1014] Therefore, if your (or your witness's) prior conviction is old enough, or if the maximum sentence for it was a year or less in prison and it did not involve dishonesty or false statement, it should generally not come into evidence.

You may be able to get other crimes excluded from evidence as well. Rule 609(a) says its provisions are "subject to Rule 403," which provides that relevant evidence "may be excluded if its probative value is substantially outweighed by the danger of unfair prejudice. . . ."[1015] A court may exclude more recent, serious convictions from evidence if they do not have much to do with credibility and if there is a likelihood that they would prejudice a jury against you,[1016]

though decisions on this subject vary greatly from case to case and judge to judge.[1017] In some instances, courts have allowed impeachment with the fact that the witness was convicted of a crime, but have excluded the nature of the crime under Rule 403 because it was excessively prejudicial.[1018] However, the Rule 403 balancing does not apply to convictions of crimes requiring proof or admission of acts of dishonesty or false statement.[1019]

Prior convictions are generally used only to impeach the credibility of a party or witness.[1020] They are not supposed to be used to show that you are a bad character and therefore ought to lose your lawsuit, or that you did something bad in the past so you probably also did something bad in the case before the court.[1021]

However, your prior convictions may be admitted if there is some other reason they may be relevant, e.g., to prove "motive, opportunity, intent, preparation, plan, knowledge, identity, or absence of mistake or accident."[1022] In addition, the rules provide, "Evidence of the habit of a person or of the routine practice of an organization, whether corroborated or not and regardless of the presence of eyewitnesses, is relevant to prove that the conduct of the

---

[1013]Sometimes defendants' lawyers will list a prisoner's entire prison file as an exhibit. Since your file will probably contain additional detail about your criminal history (not to mention allegations about matters you were not convicted of, and claims of prison misconduct), you should object at the first opportunity (i.e., when your file first shows up on a defendants' exhibit list or their part of a pretrial order). You should argue that each document in your file must be considered individually, and only those specific documents that are relevant to the claims and defenses in the lawsuit, or otherwise admissible under the Rules of Evidence, should be admitted.

[1014]Rule 609(b), Fed.R.Evid.

[1015]Rule 403, Fed.R.Evid.

The Supreme Court ruled that an earlier version of Rule 609 was not subject to Rule 403 and that courts had no discretion to exclude evidence of criminal convictions based on concerns about unfair prejudice. Green v. Bock Laundry Machine Co., 490 U.S. 504, 109 S. Ct. 1981 (1989). Rule 609 was amended in 1990 to change this result, so Green is no longer valid law. See Kunz v. DeFelice, 538 F.3d 667, 675 (7th Cir. 2008).

[1016]See, e.g., Walker v. Horn, 385 F.3d 321, 332–35 (3d Cir. 2004) (noting exclusion of convictions for assault, firearms violations, and terroristic threats on the ground that their prejudicial effect was greater than their probative value; holding robbery convictions should have been excluded because they do not involve "communicative or expressive dishonesty"); Abshire v. Walls, 830 F.2d 1277, 1281 (4th Cir. 1987) (receiving stolen property is "not highly probative of credibility"); Wierstak v. Heffernan, 789 F.2d 968, 971–72 (1st Cir. 1986) (15-year-old breaking, entering, larceny, and drug convictions were properly excluded as having little bearing on truthfulness; drug offenses excluded because of their prejudicial nature); Christmas v. Sanders, 759 F.2d 1284, 1292 (7th Cir. 1985) (upholding exclusion of rape conviction); U.S. v. Alberti, 470 F.2d 878, 882 (2d Cir. 1972) (assault conviction "does not relate to truthfulness or untruthfulness"); U.S. v. Puco, 453 F.2d 539, 542 (2d Cir. 1971) (stating ". . .we do not believe that a narcotics conviction is particularly relevant to in-court veracity"), appeal after remand, 476 F.2d 1099 (1973); Brandon v. Village of Maywood, 179 F. Supp. 2d 847, 853–54

(N.D.Ill. 2001) (minor drug convictions excluded); see also Morello v. James, 797 F. Supp. 223, 228 (W.D.N.Y. 1992) (admitting the fact that the plaintiff had a felony conviction, but excluding the fact that it was for sexual offenses); Eng v. Scully, 146 F.R.D. 74, 78 (S.D.N.Y. 1993) (murder conviction excluded); U.S. v. Alberti, 470 F.2d 878, 882 (2d Cir. 1972) (assault conviction "does not relate to truthfulness or untruthfulness").

[1017]Donald v. Wilson, 847 F.2d 1191, 1197–98 (6th Cir. 1988) (upholding the admission of a rape conviction); Lewis v. Sheriff's Department for the City of St. Louis, 817 F.2d 465, 467 (8th Cir. 1987) (upholding the admission of various convictions because they were not similar to the incident at issue in the case); Brundidge v. City of Buffalo, 79 F. Supp. 2d 219, 226 (W.D.N.Y. 1999) (admitting drug convictions as "high on the scale of veracity-related crimes").

[1018]These rulings often involve sex offenses. See, e.g., U.S. v. Ford, 17 F.3d 1100, 1103 (8th Cir. 1994) (only the fact of felony allowed); Foulk v. Charrier, 262 F.3d 687, 699–700 (8th Cir. 2001) (cross-examination limited to the number of plaintiff's felony convictions, the length of his sentence, and how long he had served; court notes that plaintiff's sex offenses had little bearing upon credibility); Morello v. James, 797 F. Supp. 223, 228 (W.D.N.Y. 1992) (only the fact that plaintiff had a felony conviction allowed); Marvel v. Snyder, 2003 WL 22134838, *4 (D.Del. 2003) (same).

[1019]Rule 609(a)(2), Fed.R.Civ.P.; see U.S. v. Field, 625 F.2d 862, 871 (9th Cir. 1980) ("Such crimes are always admissible; rule 609(a) (2) grants no judicial discretion for their exclusion.").

[1020]Rule 609(a), Fed.R.Evid.

[1021]Rule 404(b), Fed.R.Evid. ("Evidence of other crimes. . .is not admissible to prove the character of a person in order to show that he acted in conformity therewith.").

[1022]Rule 404(b), Fed.R.Evid. See Heath v. Cast, 813 F.2d 254, 259 (9th Cir. 1987) (evidence of arrestee's prior arrest and his brother's prior misdemeanor convictions were probative of their bias against police and of arrestee's motive in bringing civil rights action against police officers).

person or organization on a particular occasion was in conformity with the habit or routine practice."[1023]

Prison officials may argue that your criminal record is relevant to establish a "habit" of a particular kind of conduct. The courts have required an extremely strong showing before accepting such an argument.[1024] Habit evidence may "be weighed and considered by the trier of fact in the same manner as any other type of direct or circumstantial evidence."[1025]

Prison officials may also argue that your criminal record is relevant because they took it into account in deciding how to deal with you.[1026]

If your criminal record, or that of one of your witnesses, is going to come in, you should probably bring it out yourself at the beginning of the testimony ("pull its teeth," as trial lawyers say).[1027] If you do this, the defendants should not be allowed to put in further evidence duplicating your testimony. However, if you or your witnesses try to explain away prior convictions during direct examination by giving your own version of events, you have "opened the door" to impeachment by the prosecution on the details of the conviction.[1028] But "opening the door" does not give license for defendant's counsel to dwell on the details of a prior conviction and shift the focus of the trial to the plaintiff's prior history.[1029]

Be sure you are accurate in stating your criminal record; nothing is worse than having the defendants show on cross-examination that you misstated such basic facts. In order to know whether to bring out your criminal record, you obviously need a prior ruling as to whether your convictions will be admitted. This ruling can be obtained through a motion *in limine.*[1030]

b. Prior Bad Acts Rule 404(b), Fed.R.Evid., provides, "Evidence of other crimes, wrongs, or acts is not admissible to prove the character of a person in order to show that he acted in conformity therewith. It may, however, be admissible for other purposes, such as proof of motive, opportunity, intent, preparation, plan, knowledge, identity, or absence of mistake or accident. . . ." This means, *e.g.*, that prison officials should not be able to show that you have a record of prior misbehavior in prison in order to prove that you misbehaved in an incident about which you are suing.[1031]

[1023]Rule 406, Fed.R.Evid. "Habit" has been defined as "a regular practice of meeting a particular situation with a specific type of conduct, such as the habit of going down a particular stairway two stairs at a time, or of giving a hand-signal for a left turn, or of alighting from railway cars while they are moving. The doing of the habitual acts may become semi-automatic." Camfield v. City of Oklahoma City, 248 F.3d 1214, 1232 (10th Cir. 2001) (internal quotation marks omitted)); *accord*, Loughan v. Firestone Tire & Rubber Co., 749 F.2d 1519, 1524 (11th Cir. 1985) (quoting *McCormick on Evidence* §§ 195 at 462–63).

[1024]*See* Reyes v. Missouri Pacific Railway Co., 589 F.2d 791, 794–95 (5th Cir. 1979) (holding that four convictions for public intoxication do not establish a habit of excessive drinking).

[1025]*See* Loughan v. Firestone Tire & Rubber Co., 749 F.2d 1519, 1523 (11th Cir. 1985). See nn.1040–1041, below, concerning habit evidence.

[1026]*See* Purnell v. Lord, 952 F.2d 679, 685 (2d Cir. 1992) (in inmate's civil rights suit, brought because his privilege of corresponding with a female inmate in another facility had been terminated, evidence of the female inmate's propensity for violence, while prejudicial, was outweighed by its probative effect); Geitz v. Lindsey, 893 F.2d 148, 151 (7th Cir. 1990); Palmerin v. City of Riverside, 794 F.2d 1409, 1413–14 (9th Cir. 1986) (plaintiffs' guilty pleas to "resisting, delaying or obstructing" police and to resisting arrest during incident at issue in the suit were properly admitted as relevant to the appropriateness of the officers' behavior). See nn. 1042–1043, below, on this point.

[1027]However, if you place your conviction in during your testimony, you can't later claim error for it being admitted. *See* Ohler v. U.S., 529 U.S. 753, 760, 120 S. Ct. 1851 (2000) (stating party "who preemptively introduces evidence of a prior conviction on direct examination may not on appeal claim that the admission of such evidence was error").

[1028]U.S. v. White, 222 F.3d 363 (7th Cir. 2000); U.S. v. Baylor, 97 F.3d 542 (D.C. Cir. 1996) (government witness opened door to more extensive cross-examination by attempting to minimize conduct for which he was convicted; usual need for protection from unfair prejudice diminished since witness is not on trial). *But see* U.S. v. Robinson, 8 F.3d 398, 409–10 (7th Cir. 1993) (witness did not open door by acknowledging conviction, denying guilt, and saying he was not guilty).

[1029]U.S. v. Robinson, 8 F.3d at 410; Geitz v. Lindsey, 893 F.2d 148, 151 (7th Cir. 1990); Charles v. Cotter, 867 F. Supp. 648, 656 n.3, 660 (N.D.Ill. 1994) (cautioning that in civil rights cases, which often pit unsympathetic plaintiffs against the guardians of community safety, it is easy (albeit unfairly prejudicial) to use prior convictions to transform the claim into an attack on plaintiff's character).

[1030]Motions *in limine* are discussed in § S.6 of this chapter.

[1031]U.S. v. Serrata, 425 F.3d 886, 904–05 (10th Cir. 2005) (upholding refusal to allow evidence of a prior instance of resisting handcuffing, which "could have impermissibly suggested that Mr. Duran had a propensity to act in a certain manner"); Surprenant v. Rivas, 424 F.3d 5, 22 (1st Cir. 2005) (evidence that prisoner had "converged" on an officer seven years previously could not be admitted to show he was a "perpetrator" or to show his "plan" in the current incident); Hynes v. Coughlin, 79 F.3d 285, 291–92 (2d Cir. 1996) (holding disciplinary history should have been excluded, since record made clear that defense used it to show character); Lataille v. Ponte, 754 F.2d 33, 37 (1st Cir. 1985) ("At best, this is an argument that since Lataille had assaulted guards with food in the past, it is likely that he did it again in this situation. This is clearly forbidden by Rule 404."); Lewis v. Velez, 149 F.R.D. 474, 481 (S.D.N.Y. 1993) (asserting issue of self-defense does not allow inmate's past assaultive record to be placed before jury); Avila v. Knight, 475 F. Supp. 1054, 1055 (S.D.N.Y. 1978); *see* Harris v. Davis, 874 F.2d 461, 464–65 (7th Cir. 1989) (disapproving admission of disciplinary record); McGill v. Duckworth, 726 F. Supp. 1144, 1147 (N.D. Ind. 1989) (excluding evidence of prior homosexual conduct from a prison rape case), *rev'd on other grounds*, 944 F.2d 344 (7th Cir. 1991); Davenport v. DeRobertis, 653 F. Supp. 649, 658–50 (N.D.Ill. 1987) (excluding reasons prisoner witnesses were in segregation), *aff'd as modified on other grounds*, 844 F.2d 1310 (7th Cir. 1988). *But see* Perrin v. Anderson, 784 F.2d 1040, 1045–46 (10th Cir. 1986) (evidence of prior violent encounters with police

It also means that you cannot show that an officer mistreated other prisoners in order to show that he mistreated you too. However, if you or your adversary has some other reason for the evidence to come in, it may be admitted. For example, you might argue that an officer's prior (or subsequent) assaults show a motive (hostility to prisoners) or an intent (to harm prisoners who are outspoken), which would be relevant to whether the officer used excessive force against you.[1032] Thus, one court held that testimony should have been admitted that a police officer used a shock device on another person only a few days before the plaintiff alleged the officer did it to him, since that evidence could help show intent, opportunity, preparation, and plan, as well as for impeachment of the official's denial. Another witness's testimony that after his arrest, the same officer, with others, beat him for several hours shortly before the arrest of the plaintiff, also could show the officer's intent, opportunity, and plan.[1033]

The difference between proving character (not permitted) and proving motive, opportunity, intent, preparation, plan, knowledge, identity, or absence of mistake or accident (permitted) is not always clear,[1034] so courts are sometimes skeptical of such evidence, and decisions on admitting it are not always consistent.[1035] Courts may find reasons in the legal standard or the factual questions at issue in a particular case to admit or exclude such evidence.[1036] If a party "opens the door" by presenting evidence about the same subject matter, evidence of prior bad acts may be admitted.[1037]

If the court has refused to allow you to use evidence to impeach or to use prior acts to show defendant's intent or opportunity, you must ask the district court for an opportunity to make an offer of proof in order to preserve the issue for a possible appeal.[1038]

Remember that a defendant can seek to use your "prior bad acts" against you in the same way: your disciplinary record or other past actions may be used to show your motive, intent, etc.[1039]

Another way that prior acts can be used is through "habit" evidence. Rule 406, Fed.R.Evid., provides, "Evidence of the habit of a person or of the routine practice of an organization, whether corroborated or not and regardless of the presence of eyewitnesses, is relevant to prove that the conduct of the person or organization on a particular

---

was not admissible under Rule 404(b), Fed.R.Evid., but was admissible as "habit" evidence under Rule 406).

[1032]*See* U.S. v. Brown, 250 F.3d 580, 584–85 (7th Cir. 2001) (in police brutality case, prior incident where officer had abused a civilian and called attention to his police authority was admissible to show officer's intent to punish people who defied his authority); Ismail v. Cohen, 899 F.2d 183, 188–89 (2d Cir. 1990); U.S. v. Dise, 763 F.2d 586, 592 (3d Cir. 1985); Martinez v. Cornell Corrections of Texas, 229 F.R.D. 211, 212 (D. N.M. 2005) (plaintiff held entitled to discover information about an officer's misconduct during the course of his employment, since it could be relevant to the claim against the private management corporation; evidence might also show that the officer acted with the requisite intent to support an award of punitive damages, or be admissible under Rule 404(b) to show motive, opportunity, preparation, plan, etc.); Edwards v. Thomas, 31 F. Supp. 2d 1069, 1074 (N.D.Ill. 1999) (plaintiff allowed to use evidence of a sustained excessive force complaint against police officer in order to establish officer's intent to use excessive force during his interrogation of the plaintiff); Sharpe v. City of Lewisburg, Tenn., 677 F. Supp. 1362, 1365 (M.D. Tenn.1988); Hayden v. Maldonado, 110 F.R.D. 157, 159 (N.D.N.Y. 1986) (evidence of other incidents could refute a claim that the defendants were "calm men" who would not assault anyone); *see also* Lamar v. Steele, 693 F.2d 559, 561 (5th Cir. 1982) (testimony that a guard had asked a prisoner to kill another "writ writer" was admissible as relevant to the guard's plan or motive). *But see* Robinson v. City of St. Charles, Mo.,972 F.2d 974, 976 (8th Cir. 1992) (personnel records that might show police officers' malicious intent were not admissible because state of mind is not relevant in a police use of force case).

[1033]Wilson v. City of Chicago, 6 F.3d 1233, 1238 (7th Cir. 1993).

[1034]*See* Robert S. v. Stetson School, Inc., 256 F.3d 159, 170 (3d Cir. 2001) (evidence of prior incidents of staff abuse, offered to show a "permissive attitude" towards such misbehavior, excluded because it would likely have been considered as showing staff acted similarly towards the plaintiff).

[1035]*Compare* Berkovich v. Hicks, 922 F.2d 1018, 1021–23 (2d Cir. 1991) (upholding exclusion of evidence) *with* Ismail v. Cohen, 899 F.2d 183, 188–89 (2d Cir. 1990) (upholding admission of evidence); O'Neill v. Krzeminski, 839 F.2d 9, 11 (2d Cir. 1988) (dividing three ways on admissibility of evidence).

[1036]*See, e.g.*, DiRico v. City of Quincy, 404 F.3d 464, 467–68 (1st Cir. 2005) (evidence of police officer's past misconduct couldn't be used as evidence of mistake or accident by the officer because the officer didn't say that the plaintiff's injuries were caused by mistake or accident); Tanberg v. Sholtis, 401 F.3d 1151, 1167–68 (10th Cir. 2005) (excluding evidence of previous incidents of excessive force or arrest without probable cause by police officers, offered to show intent and absence of mistake, because the plaintiffs' Fourth Amendment claim was governed by an objective standard and state of mind was not relevant); Hynes v. Coughlin, 79 F.3d 285, 291–92 (2d Cir. 1996) (plaintiff's prior disciplinary record should have been excluded, since plaintiff did not put his intent at issue, and defendants did not claim they were aware of his record and based their actions on it); Laws v. Cleaver, 140 F. Supp. 2d 145, 156 (D.Conn.2001) (prior discipline of officer for failing to report other officers' hanging a noose from the ceiling was not admissible in excessive force case because it had minimal probative value as to truthfulness and the incidents were not similar).

[1037]*See* Westcott v. Crinklaw, 68 F.3d 1073, 1077–78 (8th Cir. 1995) (police officer who testified he had not previously discharged his firearm and had worked continuously for the police department opened the door for evidence that he had been suspended twice for prior shootings); Waul v. Coughlin, 177 F.R.D. 173, 176–78 (S.D.N.Y. 1997) (questions about whether plaintiff's positive evaluations had been considered in transfer decision opened the door to admitting his disciplinary record), *reconsideration denied*, 1998 WL 295481 (S.D.N.Y., June 4, 1998).

[1038]For a discussion of offers of proof, *see* § S.7 of this chapter.

[1039]Norton v. Colyer, 828 F.2d 384, 386 (6th Cir. 1987) (medical records of drug use were properly admitted to show that the plaintiff's motive for seeking infirmary admission was to get drugs and not medical care).

occasion was in conformity with the habit or routine practice."[1040] This rule could in theory be used to admit evidence of past misconduct. Courts appear to require a showing of many similar incidents before they will admit evidence on that basis.[1041]

The defendants may also argue that your criminal or prison record should be admitted because it influenced the way they treated you.[1042] This argument, of course, has no merit if the defendants were not aware of your record at the time they acted.[1043] Even if the relevance of the evidence is established, the court may exclude it if the danger of unfair prejudice outweighs its value as proof.[1044]

Evidence of prior or subsequent misconduct by prison or law enforcement personnel, and of inadequate investigative or disciplinary responses to it, may also be admissible against supervisory personnel or municipal government to show deliberate indifference on their part to prisoner's or citizen's rights.[1045]

Under a different rule, a witness may be cross-examined about prior instances of misconduct if the court believes that the misconduct is probative of truthfulness or untruthfulness.[1046] However, if the witness denies those instances or disputes some aspect of them, the cross-examiner may not submit independent ("extrinsic") evidence showing that they occurred as stated.[1047]

c. Character Evidence Evidence of a person's character is admissible only under strictly limited circumstances which are set forth in Rules 404, 405, and 608, Fed.R.Evid. Character evidence is restricted because it is likely to be a distraction from the facts of the case.[1048]

[1040]*See, e.g.*, Bowman v. Corrections Corp. of America, 350 F.3d 537, 548 (6th Cir. 2003) (finding no plain error in admitting evidence of warden's "'informal procedure' for dealing with phone calls received from 'outside sources'" even without evidence of "degree of specificity and frequency of uniform response").

[1041]*See* U.S. v. Serrata, 425 F.3d 886, 906 (10th Cir. 2005) (evidence relating to two previous incidents in which inmate had resisted handcuffing and arrest was not admissible as evidence of habit or routine); Mobil Exploration and Producing U.S., Inc. v. Cajun Constr. Servs., Inc., 45 F.3d 96, 99–100 (5th Cir. 1995) ("Evidence of the defendant's actions on only a few occasions or only in relation to the plaintiff are not enough; the plaintiff must show regularity over substantially all occasions or with substantially all other parties. . . ." (footnote omitted)); Perrin v. Anderson, 784 F.2d 1040, 1046 (10th Cir. 1986) (noting that five violent incidents would normally fail to establish a habit, but upholding their admission because there were offers of proof of many more incidents); *see* nn.1023–1025, above, concerning this rule as applied to criminal convictions.

[1042]McCrary-El v. Shaw, 992 F.2d 809, 812 (8th Cir. 1993) (video tapes of past violent behavior of plaintiff admitted to show state of mind of officers with respect to violent nature of plaintiff); Donald v. Wilson, 847 F.2d 1191, 1194 (6th Cir. 1988) (evidence admitted of inmate's prior use of prosthesis to carry contraband); West v. Love, 776 F.2d 170, 174 (7th Cir. 1985) (evidence that plaintiff was housed in a unit for violent inmates was relevant to the reasonableness of the defendants' actions).

[1043]Lataille v. Ponte, 754 F.2d 33, 37 (1st Cir. 1985); Avila v. Knight, 475 F. Supp. 1054, 1055 (S.D.N.Y. 1978). For this reason, in taking depositions of prison staff concerning their treatment of a prisoner, it is always important to ask what they knew about the prisoner or how they regarded the prisoner before the incident. If the staff say that they knew nothing, or that he was just another prisoner like the rest of them, they will not be able to claim later that they acted as they did because of the prisoner's record.

[1044]Rule 403, Fed.R.Evid.; *see* Harris v. Davis, 874 F.2d 461, 464 (7th Cir. 1989) (evidence of inmate drinking alcohol one week after incident that is basis of lawsuit not admissible); Ismail v. Cohen, 899 F.2d 183, 188 (2d Cir. 1990) (evidence of police officer's subsequent use of force admitted to show absent of mistake and intent).

[1045]Parrish v. Luckie, 963 F.2d 201, 205–06 (8th Cir. 1992) (stating "reports of violent behavior are relevant to show that Chief Bruce had knowledge of Luckie's propensity toward violence"); Foley v. City of Lowell, Mass., 948 F.2d 10, 14–16 (1st Cir. 1991); Sherrod v. Berry, 827 F.2d 195, 204–05 (7th Cir. 1987) (admission of evidence regarding separate suit brought against police officer upheld even though incident giving rise to separate suit occurred one month after the event upon which current litigation was based), *vacated on other grounds*, 835 F.2d 1222 (7th Cir.), *remanded for new trial*, 856 F.2d 802 (1988) (en banc); Grandstaff v. City of Borger, 767 F.2d 161, 170 (5th Cir. 1985) ("Where police officers know at the time they act that their use of deadly force in conscious disregard of the rights and safety of innocent third parties will meet with approval of city policymakers, the affirmative link/moving force requirement is satisfied.").

[1046]Rule 608(b), Fed.R.Evid.; *see* U.S. v. Davis, 183 F.3d 231, 255 (3d Cir. 1999) (defendant allowed to be impeached by departmental charges when he testified that his firing was for reasons unrelated to these charges), *amended*, 197 F.3d 662 (1999); Hynes v. Coughlin, 79 F.3d 285, 293–94 (2d Cir. 1996) (court should have allowed cross-examination of an officer who had made a false workers' compensation claim and was once suspended for providing false information to a supervisor); Brundidge v. City of Buffalo, 79 F. Supp. 2d 219, 226–27 (W.D.N.Y. 1999) (plaintiff could be cross-examined about use of false names and Social Security numbers). *But see* U.S. v. McCourt, 925 F.2d 1229, 1232–33 (9th Cir. 1991) (stating that Rule 608 does not permit inquiry into prior bad acts when the sole purpose is to show propensity toward criminal conduct); Crimm v. Missouri Pacific Railway, 750 F.2d 703, 707–08 (8th Cir. 1984) (evidence of marijuana use excluded).

[1047]Rule 608(b), Fed.R.Evid.; *see* Searles v. van Bebber, 251 F.3d 869, 877–78 (10th Cir. 2001) (testimony that plaintiff who alleged denial of kosher food had been observed eating non-kosher food, if offered for impeachment, was "inadmissible as extrinsic evidence of specific instances of the plaintiff's conduct under Fed.R.Evid. 608(b)").

[1048]Rule 404(a), Fed.R.Evid., Notes of Advisory Committee on Proposed Rules; *see* Davidson v. Smith, 9 F.3d 4, 7–8 (2d Cir. 1993) (testimony concerning plaintiff's past psychiatric history was improper); Cohn v. Papke, 655 F.2d 191, 193 (9th Cir. 1981) (evidence that plaintiff was bisexual was not admissible to show that he probably solicited a same-sex police officer for sexual activity). Evidence of prior lawsuits is not admissible where it amounts to an attempt to prove the character trait of litigiousness.

You will generally not be able to put in favorable evidence from your institutional record or the testimony of counselors, ministers, etc., in order to show that you are a good person.[1049] This kind of evidence will only be admitted if there is some other reason why it is relevant. For example, if you claim that you were put in administrative segregation in retaliation for legal action, evidence of a good institutional record could be relevant to discredit the defendants' claim that they did it because you were a danger to security.

6. Pretrial Rulings on Evidence: Motions *In Limine*

Most decisions on admission of evidence come during the trial when an objection is made. The problem with this procedure is that the evidence may come out before the objection can be made, or the jury may get an idea of what it is while the objection is being argued. Also, sometimes you need to know before the trial what is coming in so you can plan your case.

If you know there will be an important evidentiary issue, you can request a pretrial ruling by filing a motion *in limine* (which means "at the beginning").[1050] The best way to make this motion is in writing at least several weeks (preferably longer) before the trial. You can also make the motion orally at a pretrial conference, if there is one, or just before the trial begins. In your motion, you should tell the court what the evidence is and why you think it should be kept out or let in.[1051]

In some cases the judge may be reluctant to rule before trial because he may feel that hearing other evidence will make it easier to make the right ruling.[1052] In that case, you should stress to the court any reason why you need a ruling to prepare your case—*e.g.*, to know if you should mention your criminal record at the beginning of your testimony.[1053]

Gastineau v. Fleet Mortgage Corp., 137 F.3d 490, 495–96 (7th Cir. 1998) (to be admissible, evidence of prior litigation "must tend to show something other than a plaintiff's tendency to sue"); Outley v. City of New York, 837 F.2d 587, 591–95 (2d Cir. 1988); Eng v. Scully, 146 F.R.D. 74, 79 (S.D.N.Y. 1993).

[1049]*See* United State v. Davis, 546 F.2d 583, 592–93 and n.22 (5th Cir. 1977) (upholding exclusion of favorable prison record despite plaintiff's claim that it showed he had no intent to escape).

[1050]*In re* Japanese Electronic Products Antitrust Litigation, 723 F.2d 238, 260 (3d Cir. 1983), *rev'd on other grounds*, 475 U.S. 574, 106 S. Ct. 1348 (1986); U.S. v. 215.7 Acres of Land, More or Less, 719 F. Supp. 273, 275 (D.Del. 1989). Many of the rulings discussed in the preceding several sections were made in response to motions *in limine*.

[1051]*See* Martino v. Korch, 131 F. Supp. 2d 313, 316 (D.Conn. 2000) (deciding prisoner plaintiff's motion *in limine*).

[1052]Hunter v. Blair, 120 F.R.D. 667 (S.D.Ohio 1987); *see* Gaines v. Farese, 915 F.2d 1571, 1990 WL 153937, *4 (6th Cir. 1990) (unpublished) (upholding such ruling by lower court).

[1053]*See* Pena v. Leombruni, 200 F.3d 1031, 1034–35 (7th Cir. 1999) ("It is highly desirable that the trial judge rule on motions *in limine* well before trial so that the parties can shape their trial

T. Procedures After a Decision

In earlier sections we have discussed motions that must be made immediately after an adverse decision to correct it or set it aside,[1054] or for reconsideration or reargument of decisions on interlocutory matters.[1055] In this section we discuss motions that may be appropriate at a later post-judgment stage.

1. Relief from Judgment or Order

Rule 60, Fed.R.Civ.P., permits a final judgment or order to be corrected or vacated under certain circumstances. This rule does not provide a substitute for an appeal or a way of avoiding the time limits for appeal.[1056]

One part of the rule provides that clerical errors in judgments, orders, or other parts of the record, and errors arising from oversight or omissions, may be corrected at any time.[1057] This part of the rule is construed very strictly and may not be used to correct errors involving the substance of the case.[1058]

A party may obtain relief from a judgment within one year on a showing of "mistake, inadvertence, surprise, or excusable neglect,"[1059] newly discovered evidence,[1060] or fraud, misrepresentation or other misconduct by an

---

preparation in light of his rulings without having to make elaborate contingency plans.").

[1054]*See* § R.15 of this chapter, concerning motions for judgment as a matter of law, for a new trial, or to alter or amend the judgment.

[1055]*See* § F of this chapter, nn.321–324.

[1056]*See* §U.1.d.1 of this chapter, n.1204.

[1057]Rule 60(a), Fed.R.Civ.P.

[1058]Dudley ex rel. Estate of Patton v. Penn-America Ins. Co., 313 F.3d 662, 671 (2d Cir. 2002) ("A motion to correct a clerical error under Rule 60(a) must seek to conform the written judgment to the judgment actually rendered by the court; it cannot seek to alter the substantive rights of the parties."); *In re* W. Tex. Mktg. Corp., 12 F.3d 497, 503 (5th Cir. 1994) ("'Rule 60(a) finds application where the record makes apparent that the court intended one thing but by merely clerical mistake or oversight did another. Such a mistake must not be one of judgment or even of misidentification, but merely of recitation, of the sort that a clerk or amanuensis might commit, mechanical in nature.'" (quoting Dura-Wood Treating Co., Div. of Roy O. Martin Lumber Co. v. Century Forest Ind., Inc., 694 F.2d 112, 114 (5th Cir.1982) (internal citations and quotations omitted in original)).

[1059]Rule 60(b)(1), Fed.R.Civ.P.

[1060]Rule 60(b)(2), Fed.R.Civ.P. *See* Jones v. Lincoln Elec. Co., 188 F.3d 709, 732 (7th Cir. 1999) (litigant seeking a new trial under Rule 60(b)(2) must show that: (1) the evidence was discovered after the trial; (2) the movant exercised due diligence; (3) the evidence is not merely cumulative or impeaching; (4) the evidence is material; *and* (5) the evidence is such that a new trial would probably result in a different outcome); *see* Salter v. Hooker Chemical, Darez Plastic & Chemical Division, 119 F.R.D. 7, 8–9 (W.D.N.Y. 1988) (failure of plaintiff to discover newly presented evidence earlier was not excused by his *pro se* status).

adverse party.[1061] (You cannot accuse the other side of fraud or misrepresentation just because they have opposed your claims and won; you must have strong evidence of fraud and not just of a conflict of evidence.[1062])

A party may also obtain relief from a judgment which is void, which has been satisfied or which, for some reason, should not continue to be effective,[1063] or for "any other reason justifying relief from the operation of the judgment."[1064]

Rule 60(b)(1) through 60(b)(3) motions must be made during the one-year period noted above, and Rule 60(b)(4) through 60(b)(6) motions must be made "within a reasonable time."[1065]

2. Enforcement and Modification of Judgments

If you win your case, sometimes you have to take further action to enforce or execute[1066] the judgment or to obtain additional relief to vindicate your rights.

a. Collecting a Money Judgment A money judgment is not automatically enforceable the moment it is signed. The judgment is automatically stayed, and the prevailing party cannot seek to collect, for 14 days after its entry.[1067] If the losing party timely files a motion for judgment as a matter of law, to amend the findings or for additional findings, for a new trial or to alter or amend the judgment, or for relief from judgment, the court may continue to stay enforcement of the judgment until it decides the motion.[1068] Enforcement may also be stayed if the defendants appeal, but the defendants will generally be required to post a security bond.[1069]

Once any post-trial motions or appeals are disposed of in your favor, the defendants are obligated to pay the judgment. You should ask defendants' attorney in writing how long it will take the state or other governmental agency to issue a check if a defendant was found officially liable, or how long it will take the defendant to pay if he was held personally liable.[1070] It normally takes a state or local government several weeks or several months to issue a check, and you will probably have to fill out some forms.

As long as there is no claim that they do not intend to pay the judgment and no evidence that they are acting in bad faith, the court is unlikely to interfere in these normal but slow processes. The good news is that you are entitled to interest on a judgment, starting from the date the judgment is entered.[1071]

If a defendant hasn't paid after several months and you have communicated with his attorney to no avail, you should complain to the court, which may be able to get the

---

[1061]Rule 60(b)(3), Fed.R.Civ.P. *See* General Universal Systems, Inc. v. Lee, 379 F.3d 131, 156 (5th Cir. 2004) ("This subsection of the Rule is aimed at judgments which were unfairly obtained, not at those which are factually incorrect." (quotation and citation omitted)). *See also* Anderson v. Cryovac, Inc., 862 F.2d 910, 923 (1st Cir.1988) (holding that, for the term "misconduct" to "have meaning in the Rule 60(b)(3) context, it must differ from both 'fraud' and 'misrepresentation'").

[1062]Cleveland Demolition Co., Inc. v. Azcon Scrap Corp., 827 F.2d 984, 986–87 (4th Cir. 1987); *see* Ervin v. Wilkinson, 701 F.2d 59, 61 (7th Cir. 1983) (holding that fraud must be established by clear and convincing evidence).

To justify Rule 60(b)(3) relief, misconduct of an adverse party must be of such a nature as to prevent the other party from fully and fairly presenting his case. West v. Love, 776 F.2d 170, 176 (7th Cir. 1985); *see* Anderson v. Cryovac, Inc., 862 F.2d at 923 (withholding evidence in discovery may be sufficient misconduct to justify relief); Jordan v. Paccar, Inc., 97 F.3d 1452, 1996 WL 528950, *6 (6th Cir. 1996) (unpublished) ("other misconduct" may include "accidents that should have been avoided, for instance a reckless approach to searching one's files for discoverable material.").

[1063]Rules 60(b)(4), 60(b)(5), Fed.R.Civ.P.

[1064]Rule 60(b)(6), Fed.R.Civ.P.; *see* Klapprott v. U.S., 335 U.S. 601, 613–14, 69 S. Ct. 384 (1949) (civil defendant who was ill, penniless, and incarcerated, and therefore unable to appear and defend his case, granted relief), *modified*, 336 U.S. 942, 69 S. Ct. 877 (1950). Use of this rule is generally restricted to cases of "exceptional circumstances or undue hardship." Gil v. Vogilano, 131 F. Supp. 2d 486, 494 (S.D.N.Y. 2001). Relief has been granted under this section to prisoners whose cases were dismissed when they did not receive notice of proceedings because they were transferred or for other reasons, *see* Smith v. Muccino, 223 F. Supp. 2d 396, 403–04 (D.Conn. 2002), or did not understand proper procedures because of language difficulties. Gil v. Vogilano, 131 F. Supp. 2d at 494.

This part of the rule is not to be used for matters that are covered by any other part of the rule. Liljeberg v. Health Services Acquisition Corp., 486 U.S. 847, 863, 108 S. Ct. 2194 (1988).

[1065]Rule 60(c)(1), Fed. R.Civ.P.; *see* Briley v. Hidalgo, 981 F.2d 246, 249 (5th Cir. 1993) (no time limit on Rule 60(b)(4) attack on a judgment as void for lack of jurisdiction).

[1066]Obtaining compliance with a court order is called "enforcement"; this term is most frequently used in connection with injunctive orders. Enforcement of a money judgment is often referred to as "execution" of the judgment.

[1067]Rule 62(a), Fed.R.Civ.P. Under this rule, an injunction is not automatically stayed, so you can enforce an injunction immediately unless the court orders it stayed.

[1068]Rule 62(b), Fed.R.Civ.P. These motions are provided for by Rules 50, 52(b), 59, and 60 respectively.

[1069]*See* Rule 8(a)(2)(E), Fed.R.App.P., and Rule 62(d), Fed.R.Civ.P. (providing that when an appeal is taken, the appellant may seek a stay of execution of the judgment by filing a bond).

[1070]In some jurisdictions, the state or municipal government will pay the judgment against an individual employee or officer under an indemnity statute. *See, e.g.*, N.Y. Public Officers' Law § 17. Be sure to find out if your state or locality has this type of statute. Some of these indemnification statutes are discretionary, which means that even though the State has provided representation to the individual officer being sued, the government agency involved may decide not to pay, leaving you to collect your judgment from the individual defendant. *See* Mich. Compiled Laws § 691.1408.

[1071]28 U.S.C. § 1961.

defendants to pay without formal proceedings. If this doesn't work, consider seeking a writ of execution. This is the preferred means for collection of a federal court money judgment.[1072] Federal courts utilize state court execution procedures unless federal statutes dictate otherwise,[1073] so you must consult state law to determine the exact form of papers required.

However, papers seeking a writ of execution should be supported, at a minimum, by an affidavit or declaration stating the name of the court in which the judgment was entered, the type of claim, the date and amount of the judgment, against whom it was entered, and that the amount hasn't been paid.[1074] If possible, you should also attach a copy of the judgment to your motion. A writ of execution is a type of process and can be served by the U.S. Marshals or a person appointed by the court, or consistently with state law practice and procedure.[1075]

Be sure to ask the court to order the Marshal to serve the writ, and in your papers, identify property of the defendant to be seized to satisfy the judgment. Discovery is permitted in aid of execution of a money judgment,[1076] and you can use discovery to identify and locate individual defendants' houses, bank accounts, and other property. If the judgment is against a municipality rather than an individual, or if the government agency is required to indemnify an individual defendant, you can seek a writ seizing property such as the sheriff's official automobiles, the Department of Corrections' computers, etc.

Even though federal courts are directed to use state law in executing judgments, they may override state law if necessary in order to ensure that the judgment is paid.[1077] If there is a statute or an agreement making a third party responsible for paying the judgment, you may be able to enforce that obligation in federal court.[1078]

If the third party is a state or a state agency, the Eleventh Amendment may prevent a federal court from enforcing an indemnification law.[1079] However, if a state agency has agreed to pay a specific judgment, it cannot later claim that the Eleventh Amendment prevents a federal court from enforcing it against the agency.[1080]

If you are having trouble collecting a money judgment, you should consider asking the court to appoint counsel to assist you, even if the court declined to appoint counsel earlier. Once you have won a judgment, your case is obviously meritorious, which is the most important factor in deciding whether to appoint counsel.[1081]

Also, enforcing a money judgment is a familiar procedure for many lawyers, so it may be easier to find a lawyer willing to help you at this stage of the case. If the judgment is for a substantial sum, you may be able to get a private lawyer to assist you in collecting it on a contingency basis.

[1072]Rule 69(a)(1), Fed.R.Civ.P., provides: "A money judgment is enforced by a writ of execution, unless the court directs otherwise. The procedure on execution—and in proceedings supplementary to and in aid of judgment or execution—must accord with the procedure of the state where the court is located, but a federal statute governs to the extent it applies." The court in its discretion may "direct otherwise" by utilizing other state law procedures. Laborers' Pension Fund v. Dirty Work Unlimited, Inc., 919 F.2d 491, 494 (7th Cir. 1990) (upholding use of contempt proceeding to enforce an order for turnover of assets), *appeal dismissed*, 223 F.3d 459 (7th Cir. 2000). Other remedies that may exist under state law include garnishment, arrest, mandamus, and appointment of a receiver. *In re* Merrill Lynch Relocation Management, Inc., 812 F.2d 1116, 1120 (9th Cir. 1987) ("State law has been applied under Rule 69(a) to garnishment, mandamus, arrest, contempt of a party, and appointment of receivers."). If state remedies are insufficient to ensure that the judgment is paid, the court may utilize its powers to order the performance of specific acts under Rule 70, Fed.R.Civ.P. Hankins v. Finnel, 964 F.2d 853, 856–57 (8th Cir. 1992).

[1073]Rule 69(a)(1), Fed.R.Civ.P.; *see* Strong v. Laubach, 371 F.3d 1242, 1247 (10th Cir. 2004).

[1074]*See* Bower v. Cassanave, 44 F. Supp. 501, 504 (S.D.N.Y. 1941).

[1075]Rules 4.1, 69(a)(1), Fed.R.Civ.P., *see* Apostolic Pentecostal Church v. Colbert, 169 F.3d 409, 414 (6th Cir. 1999).

[1076]Rule 69(a)(2), Fed.R.Civ.P., *see* First City, Texas Houston, N.A. v. Rafidain Bank, 281 F.3d 48, 54 (2d Cir. 2002).

[1077]Hankins v. Finnell, 964 F.2d at 859–61 (federal court properly enjoined state from attaching the proceeds of a judgment under state Incarceration Reimbursement Act); Spain v. Mountanos, 690 F.2d 742, 745–47 (9th Cir. 1982); Collins v. Thomas, 649 F.2d 1203, 1205–06 (5th Cir. 1981).

[1078]Courts had held that a judgment in federal court could be enforced against an entity that had agreed or was required by law to pay such judgments against public employees. Argento v. Village of Melrose Park, 838 F.2d 1483 (7th Cir. 1988); Skevofilax v. Quigley, 810 F.2d 378 (3d Cir. 1987) (en banc). The Supreme Court then held that federal courts lack jurisdiction to enforce judgments against third parties under certain circumstances. Peacock v. Thomas, 516 U.S. 349, 116 S. Ct. 862 (1996) (Employment Retirement Income Security Act case). The Seventh Circuit has held that the *Argento* case is still good law, insofar as it allows plaintiffs who have obtained a federal court judgment against defendants to seek payment from persons or entities who are legally obliged to pay the judgment, as long as they do so within the original suit rather than filing a new one. Yang v. City of Chicago, 137 F.3d 522, 525–26 (7th Cir. 1998); Wilson v. City of Chicago, 120 F.3d 681, 684–85 (7th Cir. 1997). Similarly, the Third Circuit held that *Skevofilax* is still good law in a garnishment proceeding based on an indemnification requirement. IFC Interconsult, AG v. Safeguard Intern. Partners, LLC., 438 F.3d 298 (3d Cir. 2006). However, at least one federal circuit has held that an indemnification requirement cannot be enforced in federal court after *Peacock*. *See* Hudson v. Coleman, 347 F.3d 138 (6th Cir. 2003).

[1079]Ortiz-Feliciano v. Toledo-Davila, 175 F.3d 37, 39–40 (1st Cir. 1999); *In re* Secretary of Dep't of Crime Control, 7 F.3d 1140, 1146–48 (4th Cir. 1993).

[1080]Hankins v. Finnell, 964 F.2d at 857; Williams v. Lane, 818 F. Supp. 1212, 1213 (N.D.Ill. 1993), *amendment denied*, 1993 WL 326680 (N.D.Ill., Aug. 25, 1993).

The Eleventh Amendment is discussed in more detail in Ch. 8, § L.1.

[1081]Standards governing the appointment of counsel are discussed in § C.5 of this chapter.

Many states and the federal government have laws that allow the seizure of prisoners' money to pay restitution, compensate crime victims, pay for the cost of incarceration, etc. These laws may affect your ability to keep any damages you recover. They are addressed elsewhere in this Manual.[1082]

b. Enforcing or Modifying an Injunctive Order An injunction order may be enforced through a motion for finding of contempt or through a motion that may be called a "motion to enforce" or a "motion for further relief." It is not totally clear which approach is best. On the one hand, courts are reluctant to hold public officials in contempt; on the other, one court has held that a judgment of contempt is the only proper way to deal with noncompliance problems.[1083] The safest approach is probably to ask for the relief you need and rely on both the contempt power and the court's equitable and statutory power to enforce its order.

The Prison Litigation Reform Act has limited courts' ability to grant additional relief to ensure compliance, since any new order must satisfy the "prospective relief" restrictions of that statute.[1084] An enforcement motion in a case where there there is an order or judgment does not require exhaustion of administrative remedies.[1085]

1) Contempt A party who disobeys a court order may be held in contempt.[1086] There are two types of contempt: criminal and civil. Criminal contempt punishes a litigant who has disobeyed an order, while civil contempt, which we focus on here, is intended to coerce future compliance with orders and, if appropriate, compensate the other party for losses caused by past noncompliance.[1087]

To seek a judgment of contempt, you must file a motion supported by affidavits or other documents that show that the defendants have unjustifiably failed to comply with the order. The party seeking a contempt finding has the burden of proving noncompliance by "clear and convincing" evidence.[1088] If the adverse party claims that compliance was impossible, it bears the burden of proof on that point.[1089] Self-induced inability to comply does not support an impossibility defense.[1090]

In deciding civil contempt motions, courts consider whether the defendants "have been reasonably diligent and energetic in attempting to accomplish what was ordered"[1091] and whether they have taken "all reasonable steps within their power to ensure compliance with the court's orders."[1092] Intentional or willful disobedience need not be shown to establish contempt, and good faith is not a defense to a contempt claim.[1093] If a party has failed to comply with some substantial portion of the court order, the fact that he has

---

[1082]*See* Ch. 4, § IV.H.8.d.; *see also* Ch. 9, § J, concerning provisions of the Prison Litigation Reform Act.

[1083]Newman v. State of Alabama, 683 F.2d 1312, 1319–21 (11th Cir. 1982); *see also* Reynolds v. Alabama Dep't of Transp., 996 F. Supp. 1130, 1154 (M.D.Ala. 1998) (citing *Newman*).

[1084]*See* Ch. 9, § K.1, concerning these provisions.

An order that does nothing more than enforce already existing injunctive provisions does not present an issue under the prospective relief provisions. Jones-El v. Berge, 374 F.3d 541, 545 (7th Cir. 2004); Marion County Jail Inmates v. Anderson, 270 F. Supp. 2d 1034, 1036–37 (N.D.Ind. 2003); Essex County Jail Inmates v. Treffinger, 18 F. Supp. 2d 445, 462 (D.N.J. 1998).

[1085]Arce v. O'Connell, 427 F. Supp. 2d 435, 440–41 (S.D.N.Y. 2006); Figueroa v. Dean, 425 F. Supp. 2d 448, 454 (S.D.N.Y. 2006).

[1086]Rule 70(e), Fed.R.Civ.P. This is the case even if the party believes in good faith that the order is unlawful, U.S. v. Underwood, 880 F.2d 612, 618 (1st Cir.1989), or if it is later ruled erroneous. Mones v. Commercial Bank of Kuwait, S.A.K. 399 F. Supp. 2d 412, 416 (S.D.N.Y. 2005).

[1087]Int'l Union, United Mine Workers of Am. v. Bagwell, 512 U.S. 821, 827–30, 114 S. Ct. 2552 (1994); U.S. v. United Mine Workers, 330 U.S. 258, 302–03, 67 S. Ct. 677 (1947) (sanction imposed to compel obedience to a lawful court order or to provide compensation to a complaining party is civil); Paramedics Electromedicina Comercial, Ltda v. GE Medical Systems

Information Technologies, Inc., 369 F.3d 645, 657 (2d Cir. 2004); New York State NOW v. Terry, 886 F.2d 1339, 1351 (2d Cir. 1989).

[1088]*In re* Grand Jury Investigation, 545 F.3d 21, 25 (1st Cir. 2008); Duquin v. Dean, 423 F. Supp. 2d 411, 418 (S.D.N.Y. 2006). "Clear and convincing evidence is 'that weight of proof which produces in the mind of the trier of fact a firm belief or conviction as to the truth of the allegations sought to be established, evidence so clear, direct and weighty and convincing as to enable the fact finder to come to a clear conviction, without hesitancy, of the truth of the precise facts' of the case." Shafer v. Army & Air Force Exchange Service, 376 F.3d 386, 396 (5th Cir. 2004) ((citations omitted)).

[1089]U.S. v. Santee Sioux Tribe of Nebraska, 254 F.3d 728, 736 (8th Cir. 2001); Morales Feliciano v. Parole Board of Com. of Puerto Rico, 887 F.2d 1, 5 (1st Cir. 1989); Inmates of Allegheny County v. Wecht, 874 F.2d 147, 152 (3d Cir. 1989), *vacated and remanded on other grounds*, 110 S. Ct. 355 (1989); Twelve John Does v. District of Columbia, 855 F.2d 874, 877–78 (D.C. Cir. 1988); Palmigiano v. DiPrete, 710 F. Supp. 875, 882 (D. R.I. 1989).

[1090]U.S. v. Santee Sioux Tribe of Nebraska, 254 F.3d at 736; *In re* Power Recovery Sys., Inc., 950 F.2d 798, 803 (1st Cir. 1991); Carty v. Turnbull, 144 F. Supp. 2d 395, 416–17 (D.V.I. 2001) (failure to provide funds to comply with order about prison conditions did not excuse noncompliance, nor did failure of a contractor to perform where defendants failed to pay him).

[1091]Goluba v. School Dist. of Ripon, 45 F.3d 1035, 1037 (7th Cir. 1995) (citation omitted); Marion County Jail Inmates v. Anderson, 270 F. Supp. 2d 1034, 1035 (S.D.Ind. 2003); Morales Feliciano v. Rosello Gonzales, 124 F. Supp. 2d 774, 78623w (D.P.R. 2000) (contempt found based on "sluggish and disorganized" efforts to comply); Aspira of New York v. Board of Education, 423 F. Supp. 647, 654 (S.D.N.Y. 1976) and cases cited.

[1092]Stone v. City and County of San Francisco, 968 F.2d 850, 856 (9th Cir. 1992) (citation omitted); *accord*, U.S. v. Santee Sioux Tribe of Nebraska, 254 F.3d at 736; Chairs v. Burgess, 143 F.3d 1432, 1437 (11th Cir. 1998); Peppers v. Barry, 873 F.2d 967, 969 (6th Cir. 1989).

[1093]Chao v. Transocean Offshore, Inc., 276 F.3d 725, 728 (5th Cir. 2002); Rolex Watch U.S.A., Inc. v. Crowley, 74 F.3d 716, 720 (6th Cir. 1996) (the intent of a party to disobey a court order is "irrelevant to the validity of [a] contempt finding;" willfulness is

partially complied or made efforts to comply is not a defense to contempt.[1094]

No one can be held in contempt of an order unless it is clear and specific enough that they can understand it and unless the acts they committed are clearly in violation of the order.[1095] A person must have had actual notice of a court order to be held in contempt of it.[1096] The "officers, agents, servants, employees, and attorneys" of a party can also be held in contempt if they have actual notice of the order, as can "other persons who are in active concert with them" or with a party.[1097] Thus, prison guards and other employees may be subject to contempt sanctions if they violate an injunction against the prison administration.[1098] A party may also be found in contempt for failing to make sure that subordinates obey the order.[1099]

Civil contempt remedies can serve two purposes: to coerce the judgment violator into compliance with the court order, or to compensate a party for losses or damages caused by the other party's violation of the order.[1100] Courts have broad discretion to enter orders to make sure a prior order is carried out or its purposes are accomplished.[1101] Courts may award nominal[1102] or compensatory damages, sometimes called remedial fines, to persons injured by violation of a court order.[1103] If injury is demonstrated, a compensatory award is mandatory and not discretionary.[1104]

---

not an element of civil contempt); Benjamin v. Sielaff, 752 F. Supp. 140, 147 (S.D.N.Y. 1990).

[1094]Sizzler Family Steak House v. Western Sizzlin Steak, 793 F.2d 1529, 1534 n.5 (11th Cir. 1986); Fortin v. Commissioner of Mass. Dep't of Public Welfare, 692 F.2d 790, 796–97 (1st Cir. 1982); Aspira of New York v. Board of Education, 423 F. Supp. at 654.

[1095]Rule 65(d), Fed.R.Civ.P.; Paramedics Electromedicina Comercial, Ltda. v. GE Medical Systems Information Technologies, Inc., 369 F.3d 645, 655 (2d Cir. 2004) (order must be "clear and unambiguous" to support contempt finding); Gates v. Shinn, 98 F.3d 463, 471 (9th Cir. 1996) (defendants could not be held in contempt of order requiring "appropriate level" of psychiatric care where the order did not make clear what "appropriate" meant); N.L.R.B. v. Brooke Industries, 867 F.2d 434, 435 (7th Cir. 1989); Balla v. Idaho State Board of Corrections, 869 F.2d 461, 465 (9th Cir. 1989); Stotler & Co. v. Able, 870 F2d 1158, 1163 (7th Cir. 1989).

[1096]Rule 65(d)(2), Fed.R.Civ.P. Some courts have held that a party need only have "constructive" notice, which means "no actual knowledge, but the ability to acquire knowledge by reasonably diligent inquiry." Eckstein v. Balcor Film Investors, 58 F.3d 1162, 1168 (7th Cir. 1995). However, the rule was amended in 2007 to make clear that actual notice is required for a contempt finding. Rule 65(d)(2), Advisory Committee Notes on 2007 Amendments.

Some courts have held that injunction must be placed in writing and given to the other party before contempt can be found. McClendon v. City of Albuquerque, 79 F.3d 1014, 1021 (10th Cir. 1996) ("It has been held that '[o]ral statements are not injunctions,' and that a defendant is under no judicial compulsion when an injunction is not recorded on a separate document in accordance with Rules 58 and 65(d)." (citations omitted)), stay vacated, 100 F.3d 863 (10th Cir. 1996).

[1097]Rule 65(d)(2), Fed.R.Civ.P.; see Morales Feliciano v. Hernandez Colon, 704 F. Supp. 16, 19 (D.P.R. 1988) (prison staff with notice could be held liable).

Actual notice, like any other fact, can be inferred from circumstantial evidence. Morales Feliciano v. Hernandez Colon, 704 F. Supp. at 19 ("actual notice can be reasonably inferred" from a requirement that an order be made known to all employees).

[1098]Morales Feliciano v. Hernandez Colon, 704 F. Supp. at 19.

[1099]National Basketball Ass'n v. Design Management Consultants, Inc., 289 F. Supp. 2d 373, 377 (S.D.N.Y. 2003); E.E.O.C. v. Wal-Mart Stores, 147 F. Supp. 2d 980, 982–83 (D.Ariz. 2001) (contempt found for failure to train staff); Jordan v. Arnold, 472 F.

Supp. 265, 289 (M.D.Pa. 1979) ("[F]inding of civil contempt may be made if it is shown that a party has violated his obligations imposed by a court decree by failure of diligence, ineffective control, and lack of purpose in effectuating the requirements of the decree."), appeal dismissed, 831 F.2d 725 (3d Cir. 1980); Landman v. Royster, 354 F. Supp. 1292, 1294, 1301–02 (E.D.Va. 1973). Compare Stotts v. Quinlan, 139 F.R.D. 321, 325 (E.D.N.C. 1991) (declining to hold in contempt the Bureau of Prisons director because he "took reasonable steps" to ensure compliance by his subordinates).

[1100]Int'l Union, United Mine Workers of Am. v. Bagwell, 512 U.S. 821, 829, 114 S. Ct. 2552 (1994); U.S. v. United Mine Workers, 330 U.S. 258, 303-04, 67 S. Ct. 677 (1947)

[1101]McComb v. Jacksonville Paper Co., 336 U.S. 187, 193–94, 69 S. Ct. 497 (1949); E.E.O.C. v. Local 580, International Assn. Of Bridge, Structural and Ornamental Ironworkers, 925 F.2d 588, 595 (2d Cir. 1991); Carty v. Turnbull, 144 F. Supp. 2d 395, 418 (D.V.I. 2001) (court may require actions not provided for in original order to cure contempt); see Newman v. State of Alabama, 683 F.2d 1312, 1318 (11th Cir. 1982) (noting that noncomplying parties may be imprisoned). But see Glover v. Johnson, 721 F. Supp. 808, 849 (E.D.Mich. 1989) (incarcerating prison officials was not one of the "best remedies"), aff'd in part and rev'd in part on other grounds, 934 F.2d 703 (6th Cir. 1991).

[1102]See Powell v. Ward, 643 F.2d 924 (2d Cir. 1981) (affirming an award of nominal damages to inmates in response to the violation of an earlier court order, although the inmates had not suffered any actual damages).

Nominal damages does not always mean $1.00 in contempt proceedings. See Aldape v. Lambert, 34 F.3d 619, 620 (8th Cir. 1994) (noting award of "nominal damages in the amount of $10 from each defendant"); Welch v. Spangler, 939 F.2d 570, 571 (8th Cir. 1991) (affirming $10 nominal damages to each prisoner). See Ch. 8, § O.1.b, concerning nominal damages.

[1103]American Rivers v. U.S. Army Corps of Engineers, 274 F. Supp. 2d 62, 70 (D.D.C. 2003); Merriweather v. Sherwood, 250 F. Supp. 2d 391, 394–95 (S.D.N.Y. 2003) (damages for civil contempt limited to compensation for losses suffered; punitive fines disallowed); Benjamin v. Sielaff, 752 F. Supp. 140, 148-49 (S.D.N.Y. 1990); Morales Feliciano v. Hernandez Colon, 704 F. Supp. at 20 and cases cited; Powell v. Ward, 487 F. Supp. 917, 936 (S.D.N.Y. 1980), aff'd as modified, 643 F.2d 924 (2d Cir. 1981); see Hutto v. Finney, 437 U.S. 678, 691, 98 S. Ct. 2565 (1978) ("If a state agency refuses to adhere to a court order, a financial penalty may be the most effective means of insuring compliance.").

[1104]Vuitton et Fils S.A. v. Carousel Handbags, 592 F.2d 126, 130 (2d Cir. 1979) ("The district court is not free to exercise its discretion and withhold an order in civil contempt awarding damages," to the extent damages are established.); Morales Feliciano v. Hernandez Colon, 704 F. Supp. at 20, and cases cited.

Contempt damages, like other compensatory damages, must reflect the party's actual loss.[1105] Once contempt is established by clear and convincing evidence, damages need be proved by only a preponderance of the evidence.[1106]

Courts may also order coercive fines to make a party comply with an order, but these will generally be payable to the court.[1107] To be considered coercive, fines must be imposed in such a way the party can avoid them by complying with the order.[1108] If fines are neither coercive nor remedial, they are criminal in nature and cannot be imposed in a civil contempt proceeding.[1109]

2) Further Relief and Modification of Judgments A court has inherent power to make additional orders when a judgment has been disobeyed or has failed to achieve its purpose.[1110] This power of enforcement by the court is supported by several rules and statutes, though it has also been limited to some extent by the Prison Litigation Reform Act (PLRA).[1111]

Rule 70(a), Fed.R.Civ.P., provides that if a party fails to perform a specific act required by a judgment, the court "may order the act to be done—at the disobedient party's expense—by another person appointed by the court."[1112]

The All Writ Act permits federal courts to "issue all writs necessary or appropriate in aid of their respective jurisdictions,"[1113] including orders "necessary or appropriate to effectuate and prevent the frustration of orders [the court] has previously issued."[1114]

Rule 60(b)(5), Fed.R.Civ.P., provides for the modification of a judgment "when it is no longer equitable that the judgment should have prospective applications." Under this rule, a party may obtain modification of a judgment by establishing "that a significant change in facts or law warrants revision of the decree and that the proposed modification is suitably tailored to the changed circumstances."[1115]

In the past, prison officials often sought to use Rule 60(b)(5) to escape their obligations under court orders and consent decrees.[1116] Nowadays, they are more likely to rely on the PLRA's "prospective relief" provisions, which allow them to be relieved of orders and consent decrees unless it is shown that there remains a "continuing and ongoing violation" of federal law.[1117] However, prison officials may still seek adjustment of injunctions under Rule 60(b)(5) if they are not ready to seek termination. Even under the PLRA, they may not simply violate an order or decree; they must obtain modification or termination from the court.[1118]

[1105]Paramedics Electromedicina Comercial, Ltda v. GE Medical Systems Information Technologies, Inc., 369 F.3d 645, 658 (2d Cir. 2004) (sanction paid to other party "should correspond at least to some degree with the amount of damages"); Elkin v. Fauver, 969 F.2d 48, 52 (3d Cir. 1992); *see also* E.E.O.C. v. Local 638, 81 F.3d 1162, 1177 (2d Cir. 1996) (the amount of the compensatory award must be based on a showing of actual injury).

[1106]F.T.C. v. Kuykendall, 371 F.3d 745, 754 (10th Cir. 2004); McGregor v. Chierico, 206 F.3d 1378, 1386–87 (11th Cir. 2000).

[1107]*In re* Chase and Sanborn Corp., 872 F.2d 397, 400–01 (11th Cir. 1989); Morales Feliciano v. Parole Board of Com. Of Puerto Rico, 887 F.2d 1, 6 (1st Cir. 1989). In *Glover v. Johnson*, 199 F.3d 301, 313 (6th Cir. 1999), prison officials were fined $5000 a day (totalling $385,000) for failure to obey orders requiring equal programming for female prisoners; the court held it a proper coercive measure, and upheld placing the money in a fund for the prisoners' benefit.

[1108]Int'l Union, United Mine Workers of Am. v. Bagwell, 512 U.S. 821, 829–30, 114 S. Ct. 2552 (1994); Bradley v. American Household Inc., 378 F.3d 373, 378 (4th Cir. 2004); *see* American Rivers v. U.S. Army Corps of Engineers, 274 F. Supp. 2d 62, 70 (D.D.C. 2003) (giving defendants a deadline after which they are to be fined for every day of noncompliance).

[1109]Int'l Union, United Mine Workers of Am. v. Bagwell, 512 U.S. at 829.

[1110]Root v. Woolworth, 150 U.S. 401, 410–411, 14 S. Ct. 136 (1893) (1983) ("It is well settled that a court of equity has jurisdiction to carry into effect its own orders, decrees and judgments. . . ."); U.S. v. United Shoe Machinery Corp., 391 U.S. 244, 248–49, 88 S. Ct. 1496 (1968); System Federation v. Wright, 364 U.S. 642, 647–48, 81 S. Ct. 368 (1966); King-Seeley Thermos Co. v. Aladdin Industries, Inc., 418 F.2d 31, 35 (2d Cir. 1971); National Law Center v. U.S. Veterans Admin., 98 F. Supp. 2d 25, 26–27 (D.D.C. 2000) ("A court's powers to enforce its own injunction by issuing additional orders is broad, . . . particularly where the enjoined party has not 'fully complied with the court's earlier orders.'" (citations omitted)); *see* Hook v. State of Arizona Dep't of Corrections, 972 F.2d 1012, 1014 (9th Cir. 1992) (district court had jurisdiction to grant an injunction enforcing a prior consent decree against prison officials).

[1111]18 U.S.C. § 3626; *see* Ch. 9 for a discussion of the PLRA; *see also* n.1085, above.

[1112]*See* Gilbert v. Johnson, 490 F.2d 827, 829–30 (5th Cir. 1974); *see also* Gary W. v. State of La., 622 F.2d 804, 806 (5th Cir. 1980) (citing Gates v. Collier, 616 F.2d 1268 (5th Cir. 1980)).

[1113]28 U.S.C. § 1651(a); *see* Anderson v. Romero, 42 F.3d 1121, 1124 (7th Cir. 1994) (court could if necessary order defendants to disclose next of kin of deceased plaintiff under All Writs Act).

[1114]U.S. v. New York Telephone Co., 434 U.S. 159, 172, 98 S. Ct. 364 (1977).

[1115]Rufo v. Inmates of Suffolk County Jail, 502 U.S. 367, 388, 112 S. Ct. 748 (1992) (appropriate to grant a Rule 60(b)(5) motion when the party seeking relief from an injunction or consent decree can show "a significant change either in factual conditions or in law"; such subsequent changes can be in either statutory or decisional law); *see* Agostini v. Felton, 521 U.S. 203, 215, 117 S. Ct. 1997 (1997) (change in decisional law supported Rule 60 relief).

[1116]*See, e.g.*, Gates v. Rowland, 39 F.3d 1439, 1444 (9th Cir. 1994); Thompson v. Enomoto, 915 F.2d 1383 (9th Cir. 1990); Kozlowski v. Coughlin, 871 F.2d 241, 246–48 (2d Cir. 1989).

[1117]18 U.S.C. § 3626; *see* Ch. IX, § K.4, concerning termination of judgments under the PLRA.

[1118]Hook v. Arizona Dep't of Corrections, 107 F.3d 1397, 1402–05 (9th Cir. 1997) and Hook v. State of Arizona Dep't of Corrections, 972 F.2d 1012, 1016–17 (9th Cir. 1992). If prison officials do attempt to disregard a previously entered judgment, your first step should be to notify the attorneys (if any) who obtained that judgment and who should be in a position to enforce it.

c. **Declaratory Relief** If you obtain a declaratory judgment,[1119] you may need to seek enforcement of it. The court has the power to grant an injunction if prison officials fail to follow the requirements of a declaratory judgment.[1120]

U. APPEALS

1. Court of Appeals

If you lose your case in the district court and you believe the district court was wrong, you can appeal to the court of appeals for the federal circuit in which the district court is located.[1121] If you win in the district court, the defendants can appeal. If the court ruled for you on some issues, and for the defendants on others, both sides can appeal the parts of the case they lost.

Appeals in federal court are governed by the Federal Rules of Appellate Procedure (Fed.R.App.P.).[1122] Since these rules are amended fairly often, be sure you have the current edition of them. Courts of appeals also have local rules, which you should be able to obtain from the court clerk, or which a friend or the prison law library may be able to get for you from the court's website, and which sometimes add significant points to the Rules of Appellate Procedure.

a. **What Appeals Courts Do** Appeals courts do not reconsider all aspects of a case from scratch. Their main job is to correct errors of law. They use several different "standards of review" depending on what issue they have to decide. They exercise "plenary" (full), or *de novo*, review over questions of law.[1123] They have less power with respect to factual questions. An appeals court must uphold a district court's factual findings unless they are "clearly erroneous," which means that "the reviewing court on the entire evidence is left with the definite and firm conviction that a mistake has been committed."[1124] Jury verdicts are even harder to overturn; they will be set aside only if no reasonable jury could have reached the same verdict based on the

evidence submitted.[1125] This happens only rarely; when jury verdicts are overturned, it is usually because the jury has been incorrectly instructed on the law, or the district court has made some other *legal* error in the trial.

On many other issues, the district court is given a very general legal standard and must use its discretion (judgment) in applying it to a particular case. In these cases, the appeals court will uphold the district court's decision unless the district court used the wrong legal standard or its decision was so extreme as to constitute an "abuse of discretion."[1126]

For example, the Federal Rules of Evidence provide that relevant evidence "may be excluded if its probative [proof] value is substantially outweighed by the danger of unfair prejudice. . . ."[1127] The district court exercises discretion in deciding whether unfair prejudice outweighs probative value, and the appeals court will only reverse if it finds that the lower court abused its discretion.[1128] Other decisions governed by the abuse of discretion standard include determining when an *in forma pauperis* case is factually frivolous,[1129] whether to appoint counsel in a civil case,[1130] whether to exercise pendent or supplemental jurisdiction over state law claims,[1131] whether and how to grant an

---

[1119]*See* Ch. 8, § O.3, concerning declaratory judgments.

[1120]Wolff v. McDonnell, 418 U.S. 539, 555, 94 S. Ct. 2963 (1974) (once prisoner obtained declaratory relief, he could obtain an injunction against future application of invalid prison regulation).

[1121]*See* Appendix A for the addresses of the federal court of appeals.

[1122]These rules are published as part of Title 28 of the United States Code. They are also published separately in various books.

[1123]*See, e.g.*, Arbon Steel & Serv. Co. v. U.S., 315 F.3d 1332, 1334 (Fed. Cir. 2003) (matters of constitutional interpretation receive plenary review); Boyle v. U.S., 200 F.3d 1369, 1371 (Fed. Cir. 2000) (whether court has jurisdiction and whether complaint states a claim are questions of law reviewed *de novo*).

[1124]U.S. v. U.S. Gypsum Co., 333 U.S. 364, 395, 68 S. Ct. 525 (1948) (quoted in Anderson v. City of Bessemer City, North Carolina, 470 U.S. 564, 573, 105 S. Ct. 1504 (1985)).

[1125]Sailor Inc. F/V v. City of Rockland, 428 F.3d 348, 351 (1st Cir. 2005); Ivey v. Wilson, 832 F.2d 950, 953 (6th Cir. 1987) and cases cited.

[1126]U.S. v. Pelullo, 964 F.2d 193, 199 (3d Cir. 1992) ("To the extent the district court's admission of evidence was based on an interpretation of the Federal Rules of Evidence, our standard of review is plenary. But we review the Court's decision to admit the evidence if premised on a permissible view of the law for an abuse of discretion."); *see* U.S. v. Taylor, 487 U.S. 326, 335–37, 108 S. Ct. 2413 (1988) (explaining abuse of discretion standard); Coleman v. Gen. Motors Acceptance Corp., 296 F.3d 443, 446 (6th Cir. 2002) ("Abuse of discretion is defined as 'a definite and firm conviction that the trial court committed a clear error of judgment.'" (citation omitted)).

[1127]Rule 403, Fed.R.Evid.

[1128]Costantino v. Herzog, 203 F.3d 164, 173 (2d Cir. 2000) (Rule 403 rulings "are entitled to considerable deference and will not be overturned absent a clear abuse of discretion.").

[1129]Denton v. Hernandez, 504 U.S. 25, 33, 112 S. Ct. 1728 (1992) ("a §§ 1915(d) [now, § 1915(e)(2)] dismissal is properly reviewed for an abuse of that discretion,"); *see also* § C.3.b of this chapter.

[1130]Terrell v. Brewer, 935 F.2d 1015, 1017 (9th Cir. 1991) (no abuse of discretion in denying motion for appointment of counsel since exceptional circumstances not demonstrated); *see* § C.5 of this chapter.

[1131]Smith v. Dearborn Fin. Servs., Inc., 982 F.2d 976, 983 (6th Cir. 1993) (stating "because the district court properly dismissed plaintiff's federal claims for lack of subject matter jurisdiction, the district court also was within its discretion to dismiss plaintiff's pendent state law claims without prejudice." (citations omitted)); *see* Ch. 8, § F.1.

injection,[1132] and whether to produce a prisoner in court.[1133]

In many cases, appeals courts conclude that the district court made mistakes but that they did not affect the outcome of the case. These mistakes are called "harmless error"—defined as "errors or defects which do not affect the substantial rights of the parties"[1134]—and the appeals court will affirm the lower court's decision in spite of them.

The harmless error rule is used very frequently in connection with decisions during trials, such as the admission or exclusion of evidence or the way jury instructions are phrased.[1135]

The foregoing discussion gives some hints as to when it is worthwhile appealing and when it is not. If you think the district court is simply wrong on the law, and you have case law or the rules on your side, you may be successful on appeal. If you think the district court or the jury got the facts wrong, you are unlikely to win unless there is no evidence in the record that supports their conclusion. If you think the district court mismanaged your trial in some fashion, you will have the difficult task of convincing the appeals court that it abused its discretion.

The category of cases in which prisoners most frequently win appeals is that in which the district court treated a *pro se* case in a careless or perfunctory way. These include:

- cases in which the district court dismissed an *in forma pauperis* complaint as legally or factually frivolous without understanding or paying attention to the actual facts and legal theories in the complaint;[1136]
- cases in which the district court dismissed a *pro se* case without ever ruling on pending

motions for discovery, appointment of counsel, or other important items;[1137]

- cases in which summary judgment was granted against a prisoner who did not receive proper notice of the nature of the motion and the necessity to file affidavits in response;[1138]
- cases in which the district court granted summary judgment without looking closely enough at the record to see that there were genuine material factual disputes;[1139]
- other cases in which the district court's actions have denied the *pro se* plaintiff a fair opportunity to be heard.[1140]

b. What Appeals Courts Will Consider An appeals court will only consider issues that are properly before it. To get an issue before an appeals court, you must lay the right groundwork.

First, the issue must be "preserved" in the trial court. That means you must raise it at an appropriate time. Legal arguments that were never presented to the trial court will generally not be considered for the first time on appeal.[1141] Errors in the way a trial was conducted will not be considered on appeal unless an objection was made at the time in the trial court. Trial issues that were not properly preserved will only be considered on appeal if they were so extreme as to constitute "plain error."[1142]

[1132]Ashcroft v. American Civil Liberties Union, 542 U.S. 656, 664, 124 S. Ct. 2783 (2004) ("'This Court, like other appellate courts, has always applied the abuse of discretion standard on the review of a preliminary injunction.'" (citation omitted)); *see* Ch. 8, § O.2.

[1133]*See* § Q of this chapter.

[1134]28 U.S.C. § 2111. *See, e.g.,* Scott v. James, 902 F.2d 672, 674 (8th Cir. 1990) (allowing the jury to see the plaintiff in handcuffs, if it happened, was harmless error because the jury knew he was in prison from his own testimony).

[1135]*See, e.g.,* Walker v. Horn, 385 F.3d 321, 334–36 (3d Cir. 2004) (erroneous admission of plaintiff's criminal record was harmless error because there was so much other evidence undermining his credibility); Wolff v. Moore, 199 F.3d 324, 327 (6th Cir. 1999) (court should not have admitted evidence that a witness had offered to take a polygraph test, but the error was harmless because other evidence corroborated his testimony); U.S. v. Gometz, 879 F.2d 256 (7th Cir. 1989) (admission of inmate's prior bad acts was harmless error). *But see* Lewis v. City of Irvine, Kentucky, 899 F.2d 451, 456–57 (6th Cir. 1990) (error not harmless when trial court erroneously instructed the jury on the legal standard applicable to the plaintiff's claim).

[1136]*See* cases cited in § C.3.d of this chapter, n.173.

[1137]*See* §§ C.5, n.265, and K.2., n.408, of this chapter.

[1138]*See* § L of this chapter.

[1139]*See, e.g.,* Phelps v. Dunn, 965 F.2d 93, 99–100 (6th Cir. 1992); Longmire v. Guste, 921 F.2d 620, 624–25 (5th Cir. 1991); Madewell v. Roberts, 909 F.2d 1203, 1206–07 (8th Cir. 1990); Jamison-Bey v. Thieret, 867 F.2d 1046, 1047–48 (7th Cir. 1989); *see* § L of this chapter concerning summary judgment.

[1140]*See, e.g.,* McGuckin v. Smith, 974 F.2d 1050, 1057–58 (9th Cir. 1992) (case should not have been dismissed against a defendant because the *pro se* plaintiff misspelled his name); DeBardeleben v. Quinlan, 937 F.2d 502, 504–06 (10th Cir. 1991) (case should not have been dismissed for failure to notify the court of the plaintiff's address when plaintiff had been trying to move the case along and there was no evidence of bad faith); Porter v. Martinez, 941 F.2d 732, 733–34 (9th Cir. 1991); Hernandez v. Whiting, 881 F.2d 768, 770–71 (9th Cir. 1989) (case should not have been dismissed for failure to prosecute when the plaintiff, known to be incarcerated, did not appear for a court conference); Hay v. Waldron, 834 F.2d 481, 487 (5th Cir. 1987).

[1141]Lekas v. Briley, 405 F.3d 602, 614–15 (7th Cir. 2005) (retaliation claim waived because plaintiff never presented legal arguments or cited authority to support his claim in the district court); Conn.Gen. Life Ins. Co. v. New Images of Beverly Hills, 321 F.3d 878, 882 (9th Cir. 2003) (declining to consider contentions raised for the first time on appeal); Warren v. District of Columbia, 353 F.3d 36, 38–39 (D.C. Cir. 2004) (jail officials could not pursue argument that complaint did not state a claim where they had failed to raise it below).

[1142]Keeper v. King, 130 F.3d 1309, 1315 (8th Cir. 1997) (appeals court would not review exclusion of evidence where plaintiff did not make an offer of proof); Reynolds v. Green, 184 F.3d 589,

Second, the order or judgment that you are challenging must be properly identified in the notice of appeal.[1143]

Third, the issue must be identified in your appeal briefs.[1144] You must include all issues in your first brief, and not add issues in the reply brief—the reply brief is for responding to your opponent's brief.

There are a few exceptions to these rules. The most important is that a court may consider at any point whether it has jurisdiction over the case.[1145]

c. What Can Be Appealed District court decisions cannot always be appealed at the time they are made. Generally, appeals courts only review "final decisions" of a district court.[1146] Most "interlocutory" (interim) orders, such as discovery and evidentiary rulings, are not appealable until final judgment is entered on the whole case.[1147]

A final decision is one "which ends the litigation on the merits and leaves nothing for the court to do but execute the judgment."[1148] There is some confusion about decisions that dismiss a whole complaint but provide for leave to file an amended complaint, or are "without prejudice," meaning that in theory the complaint can be amended or refiled. (Dismissal of a complaint as frivolous under the *in forma pauperis* statutes is often without prejudice.[1149]) Such dismissals are sometimes said to be non-final and therefore not appealable, since the plaintiff has the option of re-filing the complaint after correcting anything that was wrong with it.[1150] However, courts have held that a plaintiff can choose to "stand on his complaint" and appeal it, rather than amend or

re-file, and the judgment will be treated as final.[1151] As a practical matter, if there seems to be a way you can amend your complaint to cure whatever the district court said is wrong with it, you should generally do so;[1152] if the court then dismisses your amended complaint, you can appeal at that point. If your complaint has been dismissed based on a reason you cannot correct, then the dismissal is final and appealable regardless of whether it is without prejudice.[1153]

There is some confusion about when the time for appeal begins to run in this situation—when the court acts on a proposed amended complaint, when the order of dismissal is entered,[1154] or when the deadline, if any, for filing an

---

593–94 (6th Cir. 1999) (applying "plain error" standard to a review of jury instructions where plaintiff had not objected at trial). *See* § R.12 of this chapter, n.855, concerning plain error. Offers of proof are discussed in § R.7 of this chapter. Objections at trial are discussed in §§ R.6, R.12, and R.13 of this chapter.

[1143]This point is discussed in § U.1.d(2) of this chapter.

[1144]Rule 28(a)(9)(B), Fed.R.App.P.; *see* Ramani v. Ashcroft, 378 F.3d 554, 558–559 (6th Cir. 2004) ("It is proper for an appellate court to consider waived all issues not raised in an appellant's briefs, even if the issue has been raised in the notice of appeal."). The contents of appellate briefs are discussed in § U.1.g of this chapter.

[1145]Bender v. Williamsport Area School Dist., 475 U.S. 534, 541, 106 S. Ct. 1326 (1986).

[1146]28 U.S.C. § 1291.

[1147]McCook Metals LLC v. Alcoa, Inc., 249 F.3d 330, 335 (4th Cir. 2001) (discovery orders are "inherently interlocutory" and typically not appealable); Matter of Fischel, 557 F.2d 209, 213 (9th Cir. 1977) (denial of a motion to strike evidence is not appealable).

[1148]Catlin v. U.S., 324 U.S. 229, 233, 65 S. Ct. 631 (1945); *accord,* Lauro Lines s.r.l. v. Chasser, 490 U.S. 495, 498, 109 S. Ct 1976 (1989); *see* Franklin v. District of Columbia, 163 F.3d 625, 628–29 (D.C. Cir. 1998) (a judgment on liability that does not also address relief is not final and not appealable).

[1149]*See* Denton v. Hernandez, 504 U.S. 25, 33–34, 112 S. Ct. 1728 (1992). Such dismissals are discussed in § C.3.c of this chapter, and appeals from them are discussed further in § C.3.d.

[1150]Glaus v. Anderson, 408 F.3d 382, 385–86 (7th Cir. 2005); Martinez v. Gomez, 137 F.3d 1124, 1125 (9th Cir. 1998).

[1151]Unfortunately, there is no uniform rule about how to do this, and you will have to see what your federal circuit has held. Some courts have held or suggested that the plaintiff must explicitly state his intention to "stand on his complaint." *See* Frederico v. Home Depot, 507 F.3d 188, 192 (3d Cir. 2007) (stating "the dismissal of the complaint is final and appealable because Frederico clearly indicated an intent to stand on the original complaint"); Connecticut Nat. Bank v. Fluor Corp., 808 F.2d 957, 960–961 (2d Cir. 1987). Others assume that the fact that the plaintiff is appealing is sufficient to show that he is standing on his complaint, *see* McKusick v. City of Melbourne, 96 F.3d 478, 482 n.2 (11th Cir. 1996); Indian Oasis-Baboquivari Unified School Dist. v. Kirk, 91 F.3d 1240, 1244 (9th Cir. 1996), or that letting the time designated for amending a complaint lapse serves that purpose. *See* Davis v. Ruby Foods, Inc., 269 F.3d 818, 819 (7th Cir. 2001). One federal circuit has held that "a plaintiff, who has been given leave to amend, may not file a notice of appeal simply because he does not choose to file an amended complaint. A further district court determination must be obtained" by filing a notice in the *district* court indicating an intent not to file an amended complaint, but to appeal. WMX Technologies, Inc. v. Miller, 104 F.3d 1133, 1135–36 (9th Cir. 1997) (en banc). This court makes a distinction between an order dismissing the *complaint* and an order dismissing the *action*, and says you must have the latter to appeal.

[1152]For example, if a court holds that your complaint does not sufficiently allege why the defendants you sued were personally involved and responsible for what happened to you, you could file an amended complaint providing the missing information. Or, if you realized from the court's decision that you had sued the wrong people, you could file an amended complaint suing the right people.

[1153]Glaus v. Anderson, 408 F.3d 382, 385–86 (7th Cir. 2005) (no amendment to a habeas corpus petition could cure it where the district court had held that plaintiff's claim could not be raised in habeas at all); Young v. Nickols, 413 F.3d 416, 418 (4th Cir. 2005) (no amendment could cure a complaint barred by *Heck v. Humphrey*); Redmond v. Gill, 352 F.3d 801, 803 (3d Cir. 2003) (dismissal denying indigent person the right to proceed *in forma pauperis*); Martinez v. Gomez, 137 F.3d 1124, 1125–26 (9th Cir. 1998) (dismissal holding statute of limitations had expired and was not tolled could not be cured by amended complaint); Welch v. Folsom, 925 F.2d 666, 668 (3d Cir. 1991) (dismissal without prejudice for failure of U.S. Marshals to serve process was final because the *in forma pauperis* plaintiff was presumably unable to pay for private service of process).

[1154]Sooner Prods. Co. v. McBride, 708 F.2d 510, 511 (10th Cir. 1983). In *Sooner*, the court held that since the plaintiff's motion to

amended complaint passes.[1155] When in doubt, file your notice of appeal within 30 days of the *earliest* date that the judgment could have become final. Rule 4(a)(2), Fed.R.App.P., states that if you file your notice of appeal too early, the court will treat it as having been filed at the beginning of the proper time period. If you file too late, the court will not hear your appeal.[1156]

There are several exceptions to the "final decision" requirement. Orders granting, modifying, or continuing an injunction, or refusing to do so, are appealable.[1157] If the district court certifies that a non-appealable order involves a "controlling question of law" that needs to be resolved quickly, the court of appeals may in its discretion permit a party to appeal.[1158] Such permission is rarely granted.

Immediate appeal is also allowed from a "collateral order," which is an interlocutory order that decides an important and disputed issue that is separate from the merits of the action, and does so in a way that cannot effectively be reviewed on appeal at the end of the case,[1159] because the "legal and practical value" of the right involved would be destroyed by waiting (*i.e.*, the damage will already be done by then).[1160] Examples of collateral orders include the denial of permission to proceed *in forma pauperis*,[1161] decisions to subject a mentally incompetent criminal defendant to involuntary medication,[1162] and orders to disclose privileged documents.[1163] The courts disagree whether the denial of appointment of counsel is an appealable collateral order.[1164] Most importantly, the denial of a motion claiming that a government official is immune from suit is immediately appealable.[1165] This very important subject is discussed at length elsewhere.[1166]

If you have sued multiple parties or raised multiple legal claims, and the court makes a decision concerning only part of the case, that order is not final unless the court expressly finds there is no reason to delay and therefore directs the entry of final judgment as to that part of the case.[1167]

Thus, if the court dismisses the warden from your lawsuit but leaves the guards as defendants, or if it grants summary judgment dismissing one of your claims but not another claim, the order is not final and appealable unless the court specifically says so.[1168] If you file a premature notice of appeal from a partial judgment and the district court later issues a final order disposing of the rest of the case, some courts hold that the premature appeal can go forward, but others say no, meaning that you must file a new notice of

---

amend the complaint was not one that would toll the time for filing a notice of appeal under Rule 4(a)(4), Fed.R.App.P., the time ran from the original dismissal. Therefore an appeal taken from the denial of the motion to amend was not timely as to the dismissal, but only as to the denial of the amendment.

[1155]Van Poyck v. Singletary, 11 F.3d 146, 149 (11th Cir. 1994); Festa v. Local 3, Intl. Brotherhood of Electrical Workers, 905 F.2d 35, 36–37 (2d Cir. 1990); Otis v. City of Chicago, 29 F.3d 1159, 1166–68 (7th Cir. 1994) (en banc); Schuurman v. Motor Vessel Betty K V, 798 F.2d 442, 445 (11th Cir. 1986) (per curiam).

[1156]The time for filing a notice of appeal is discussed further in § U.1.d(1) of this chapter.

[1157]28 U.S.C. § 1291(a)(1). This statute contains several other provisions about appealability.

The grant of a declaratory judgment is not appealable unless it is a final judgment that disposes of the whole case. Henrietta D. v. Giuliani, 246 F.3d 176, 180 (2d Cir. 2001).

[1158]28 U.S.C. § 1292(b); *see* White v. Nix, 43 F.3d 374, 376–77 (8th Cir. 1994) (certification should be "granted sparingly" only in "exceptional" cases); Marriott v. County of Montgomery, 426 F. Supp. 2d 1, 13–14 (N.D.N.Y. 2006) (refusing to certify for appeal where statutory standard was not met).

[1159]Digital Equip. Corp. v. Desktop Direct, Inc., 511 U.S. 863, 867, 114 S. Ct. 1992 (1994) (Collateral orders are orders "that are conclusive, that resolve important questions completely separate from the merits, and that would render such important questions effectively unreviewable on appeal from final judgment in the underlying action"; violation of private agreement not to stand trial is not subject to collateral order review). The collateral order doctrine is given a "practical . . . construction." *Compare* Transtech Indus., Inc. v. A & Z Septic Clean., 5 F.3d 51, 56 (3d Cir. 1993) (erroneous ruling which may result in additional litigation expenses is not alone sufficient to justify immediate review); Morales Feliciano v. Parole Board of Com. of Puerto Rico, 887 F.2d 1, 3 (1st Cir. 1989) (contempt order involving very large penalties was immediately appealable).

[1160]Lauro Lines s.r.l. v. Chasser, 490 U.S. 495, 498–99, 109 S. Ct. 1976 (1989).

[1161]*See* § C.3.d of this chapter, n.175.

[1162]Sell v. U.S., 539 U.S. 166, 176–77, 123 S. Ct. 2174 (2003).

[1163]*In re* Sealed Case (Medical Records), 381 F.3d 1205, 1209–10 (D.C. Cir. 2004); U.S. v. Philip Morris Inc., 314 F.3d 612, 617–21 (D.C. Cir. 2003); Pearson v. Miller, 211 F.3d 57, 64–65 (3d Cir. 2000). *But see* Carpenter v. Mohawk Industries, Inc., 541 F.3d 1048, 1054 (11th Cir. 2008) (disagreeing that order for disclosure over privilege objection is a collateral order), *aff'd*, __ U.S. __,130 S. Ct. 599 (2009).

[1164]*See* § C.5 of this chapter, n.267.

[1165]Mitchell v. Forsyth, 472 U.S. 511, 526–30, 105 S. Ct. 2806 (1985).

The *grant* of summary judgment on qualified immunity is generally not appealable unless it disposes of the entire case and is therefore a final judgment. Coleman v. Parkman, 349 F.3d 534, 547 (8th Cir. 2003).

[1166]*See* Ch. 8, § L.4 for additional discussion of qualified immunity appeals.

[1167]Rule 54(b), Fed.R.Civ.P. *See* Doe v. City of Chicago, 360 F.3d 667, 673 (7th Cir. 2004) (holding judge should not have entered partial final judgment); *see also* DeMelo v. Woolsey Marine Industries, Inc., 677 F.2d 1030, 1033–35 & n.9 (5th Cir. 1982) (discussing differences between partial final judgment under Fed. R. Civ. P. 54(b) and certification for appeal under 28 U.S.C. §§ 1292(b)); PYCA Industries, Inc. v. Harrison County Waste Water Management Dist., 81 F.3d 1412, 1421 (5th Cir. 1996) (noting that an appeal will be dismissed if the Rule 54(b) certifications is found to be an abuse of discretion).

[1168]Appeals from summary judgment decisions are discussed further in § L.3 of this chapter.

appeal in order to bring the entire case before the court of appeals.[1169]

If a party appeals an interlocutory order over which the appeals court has jurisdiction, such as an injunction or a collateral order, the court has the discretion to hear other issues that are not appealable under the doctrine of "pendent appellate jurisdiction."[1170] Appeals courts are reluctant to exercise this jurisdiction without a strong reason.[1171]

In "exceptional circumstances amounting to a judicial 'usurpation of power,'"[1172] a non-appealable order may be challenged via petition for a writ of mandamus.[1173] Mandamus is not a substitute for an appeal[1174] and should not be used in connection with an appealable order.

d. Notice of Appeal The first step in an appeal is filing a notice of appeal.[1175] This notice must be filed with the clerk of the district court—not the court of appeals.[1176] If the court rules partly for you and partly for your adversary, and the adversary appeals, you cannot rely on the adversary's notice of appeal, but must file your own notice of appeal or cross-appeal.

1) *Timing of the Notice of Appeal* The Federal Rules of Appellate Procedure prescribe time limits for filing the notice of appeal, and also provide for ways to get the limits extended. These time limits are jurisdictional, so if you miss the deadline, your appeal will be dismissed.[1177]

A notice of appeal must generally be filed within 30 days[1178] of entry of the judgment or order you are appealing; if one of the parties is the United States, a federal officer, or a federal agency, the time limit is 60 days to file the notice for any of the parties.[1179] (It is not settled whether the 60-day time limit applies to cases involving federal officers sued in their individual capacities,[1180] or exactly who qualifies as a federal "officer."[1181]) Once a party has filed a notice of appeal, any other party has at least 14 more days to file his own notice of appeal.[1182] However, if you filed a timely motion for

---

[1169]*Compare* Good v. Ohio Edison Co., 104 F.3d 93, 95 (6th Cir. 1997); Clausen v. Sea-3, 21 F.3d 1181, 1184 (1st Cir. 1994); Lewis v. B.F. Goodrich Co., 850 F.2d 641, 645 (10th Cir. 1988) (en banc) (premature appeal can go forward when district court disposes of the whole case before the appeals court dismisses the appeal, whether or not a party has obtained Rule 54(b) certification in the meantime); Sacks v. Rothberg, 845 F.2d 1098, 1099 (D.C. Cir. 1988) (per curiam) (similar to *Lewis*) *with* Miller v. Special Weapons, L.L.C., 369 F.3d 1033, 1034–35 (8th Cir. 2004) (premature appeal does not become effective when rest of case is decided; citing contrary authority); Useden v. Acker, 947 F.2d 1563, 1570 (11th Cir. 1991) (premature notice of appeal is not effective).

[1170]Gates v. Cook, 234 F.3d 221, 228 n.5 (5th Cir. 2000) (where court had jurisdiction over an injunctive order, it exercised discretion to address issues of substitution of counsel and intervention).

[1171]*See, e.g.*, Davidson v. Chestnut, 193 F.3d 144, 151 (2d Cir. 1999) (per curiam) (on defendants' qualified immunity appeal, refusing to exercise pendent appellate jurisdiction over plaintiff's appeal of adverse rulings because the issues did not overlap those in the qualified immunity appeal; that jurisdiction is available only when "the otherwise unappealable issue is inextricably intertwined with the appealable one, or . . . review of the otherwise unappealable issue is necessary to ensure meaningful review of the appealable one." (citations omitted)).

[1172]Will v. U.S., 389 U.S. 90, 95, 88, S. Ct. 269 (1967) (citations omitted) (quoted in Ramirez v. Rivera-Dueno, 861 F.2d 328, 334 (1st Cir. 1988)).

[1173]*See* Hulsey v. West, 966 F.2d 579, 582–83 (10th Cir. 1992) (mandamus granted ordering the district court to ensure petitioner's right to jury trial); McNeil v. Guthrie, 945 F.2d 1163, 1165 (10th Cir. 1991) (granting mandamus to compel district court clerk to file the plaintiff's papers); Rowland v. U.S. District Court for the Northern District of California, 849 F.2d 380 (9th Cir. 1988) (granting mandamus to forbid district court from sending a court-appointed monitor into a prison where no constitutional violation had been shown).

[1174]*In re* Weston, 18 F.3d 860, 864 (10th Cir. 1994); *In re* Epps, 888 F.2d 964, 966 (2d Cir. 1989).

[1175]Rule 3(a), Fed.R.App.P.

[1176]Rule 3(a), Fed.R.App.P.; *see* Appendix C for a sample notice of appeal. If a notice of appeal is mistakenly filed with the court of appeals, its clerk will write on the notice the day of receipt, which will be considered the day the notice was filed, and send it to the district court clerk. Rule 4(d), Fed.R.App.P.

[1177]Bowles v. Russell, 551 U.S. 205, 208–13, 127 S. Ct. 2760 (2007). In *Bowles*, the prisoner was late in filing because he relied on the deadline as erroneously stated by the district court, and the Supreme Court said his appeal still had to be dismissed.

[1178]Time periods and deadlines are computed on appeal the same way they are in the district court, *see* § H, nn.330–332, of this chapter: by excluding the day of the event that starts the period, counting all days including weekends and legal holidays, and including the last day of the period. If that last day falls on a weekend or legal holiday, the period continues until the next business day. Rule 26(a)(1), Fed.R.App.P.

[1179]Rule 4(a)(1), Fed.R.App.P.

[1180]Several courts have adopted the view that "[w]henever the alleged grievance arises out of a government activity, the 60-day filing period of Rule 4(a) applies if: (a) the defendant officers were acting under color of office, or (b) the defendant officers were acting under color of law or lawful authority, or (c) any party in the case is represented by a government attorney." Wallace v. Chappell, 637 F.2d 1345, 1348 (9th Cir. 1981) (en banc) (per curiam) and cases cited; *accord*, Buonocore v. Harris, 65 F.3d 347, 352 (4th Cir. 1995); Williams v. Collins, 728 F.2d 721, 724 (5th Cir. 1984). Unless your circuit has clearly held that the 60-day time limit applies, you should assume you only have 30 days.

[1181]NeSmith v. Fulton, 615 F.2d 196, 198–99 (5th Cir. 1980) (civilian technician was not a federal "officer" because he did not have a managerial role or "other significant authority," nor did his suit "involve the U.S. as a real party in interest requiring various government officials to review the decision to appeal," nor was he actively serving in the military). On this issue, too, it is best to assume you only have 30 days to appeal unless there is clear case law in your circuit indicating you have 60.

[1182]A party who wishes to cross-appeal gets the regular 30- or 60-day period, or 14 days after the initial notice of appeal is filed, whichever period ends later. Rule 4(a)(3), Fed.R.App.P.

judgment as a matter of law, to amend or make additional fact findings, to alter or amend the judgment, or for a new trial, under Rules 50(b), 52(b), or 59, Fed.R.Civ.P., the time period to file a notice of appeal for either party does not start running until the motion is denied.[1183] The same is true of a motion for relief from judgment under Rule 60, Fed.R.Civ.P., *if* the motion is filed within 28 days after entry of judgment.[1184]

The time period for filing the notice of appeal begins to run on the day judgment or an appealable order is entered. Judgment is generally considered entered when the clerk enters it in the civil docket,[1185] which *may* be a day or more after the day an order or opinion is signed.[1186] The date entered on the docket sheet stating that the judgment was filed is the official date of entry of judgment. There is an exception to this rule. Judgments are required to be set out in a separate document and not just entered in the civil docket. Judgment is considered entered when it is entered in the civil docket and the separate document is created. But if somebody forgets to create the separate document, then judgment is considered entered 150 days after the entry is made in the civil docket.[1187]

Generally, a notice of appeal is considered "filed" on the day the clerk receives it.[1188] However, there is a special rule for prisoners. The notice of appeal is considered filed on the day that the prisoner places it in the prison's internal mail system; if there is a system designed for legal mail, the prisoner must use that system to have the benefit of this rule.[1189] The prisoner must submit a declaration or notarized statement indicating when the notice of appeal was put into the prison mail system and that first-class postage has been prepaid.[1190] If you do not use the prison's mailing system, or its separate legal mail system if there is one, this rule does not apply,[1191] and in that case your notice must be *received* by the clerk within 30 days of the entry of judgment.[1192]

If the notice of appeal is filed before the judgment or order is entered, it will be treated as if filed on the day the judgment is entered.[1193]

You need not serve a notice of appeal on the other parties to the case; it is the clerk's responsibility to do that.[1194] However, it is good practice to serve the notice on your adversary; it may be helpful if there is a dispute over the timelines of the notice.

A notice of appeal that is filed before the disposition of any of the post-judgment motions listed in Rule 4(a), Fed.R.App.P., has no effect until the motion is disposed of, and then it will only apply to the original judgment.[1195] If you want to appeal the disposition of the post-judgment motion as well, you must file a new notice of appeal, or amend the original one, within 30 days of the disposition.[1196]

[1183]Rule 4(a)(4)(A), Fed.R.App.P.; *see* McCarthy v. Mayo, 827 F.2d 1310, 1313 n.1 (9th Cir. 1987) (stating that a timely Rule 59(e) motion tolls the time period for filing a notice of appeal and that the 30-day time period for filing the notice of appeal begins when the district court denies the Rule 59(e) motion).

[1184]Rule 4(a)(4)(A), Fed.R.App.P.

[1185]Rule 58(c), Fed.R.Civ.P.

[1186]Burrell v. Newsome, 883 F.2d 416, 418 (5th Cir. 1989) (noting docket entry was one day later than filing of decision). Don't count on a delay in entry of judgment unless you have proof that it occurred; sometimes judgment is entered on the same day that a decision is made or an order filed.

[1187]Rule 58(c), Fed.R.Civ.P.; *see* Rule 79(a), Fed.R.Civ.P., concerning the civil docket.

[1188]Houston v. Lack, 487 U.S. 266, 274, 108 S. Ct. 2379 (1988).

[1189]Rule 4(c)(1), Fed.R.App.P.; *see* Davis v. Woodford, 446 F.3d 957, 960 (9th Cir. 2006) (sworn proof of service form stating that another prisoner had placed plaintiff's notice of appeal in the prison system timely was sufficient despite the fact that the mail did not go out for a week).

Rule 4(c) incorporates the holding of *Houston v. Lack*, which stated that "the *pro se* prisoner has no choice but to entrust the forwarding of [mail] to prison authorities whom he cannot control or supervise and who may have every incentive to delay," and therefore held that *pro se* prisoner's notice of appeal must be regarded as "filed" when delivered to prison authorities for mailing. *Houston*, 487 U.S. at 273–76; *see* Vaughan v. Ricketts, 950 F.2d 1464, 1466 (9th Cir. 1991) (prisoner whose lawyer informally withdrew after the trial was entitled to the benefit of the *Houston* rule).

This "prison mailbox" rule is discussed further in § H of this chapter.

[1190]Rule 4(c)(1), Fed.R.App.P.; *see* U.S. v. Ceballos-Martinez, 371 F.3d 713, 715–18 (10th Cir. 2004); Grady v. U.S., 269 F.3d 913, 918 (8th Cir. 2001). *But see* U.S. v. Craig, 368 F.3d 738, 740–41 (7th Cir. 2004) (appeal dismissed where prisoner's declaration did not state that first-class postage had been paid). If the standard prison procedure is to deduct postage automatically from your account, or if you were indigent and prison procedure was to pay the postage in those circumstances, explain those facts in your affidavit.

Courts have held that the affidavit or declaration need not be submitted with the notice of appeal, but can be submitted later. Sulik v. Taney County, Missouri, 316 F.3d 813, 814 (8th Cir. 2003) (prisoner could file the affidavit after timeliness was challenged, since the rule did not say when it has to be filed); Grady v. U.S., 269 F.3d at 918 ("the prisoner must *at some point* attest to [having deposited his legal papers in the mail system] in an affidavit or notarized statement"; noting that court may give less weight or decline to consider long-delayed affidavits or declarations (emphasis supplied)); *see* U.S. v. Ceballos-Martinez, 371 F.3d at 717 (dismissing appeal; noting prisoner did not include declaration or affidavit with notice of appeal, "and he has not subsequently" done so).

[1191]Knickerbocker v. Artuz, 198 F. Supp. 2d 415, 417–19 (S.D.N.Y. 2002) (prisoner who asked his sister to mail the notice of appeal was not entitled to the benefit of the mailbox rule when the notice arrived late).

[1192]Wilder v. Chairman of Central Classification Bd., 926 F.2d 367, 370–71 (4th Cir. 1991); Miller v. Sumner, 921 F.2d 202, 203–04 (9th Cir. 1990).

[1193]Rule 4(a)(2), Fed.R.App.P.

[1194]Rule 3(d), Fed.R.App.P.; *see* Smith v. White, 857 F.2d 1042, 1043 (5th Cir. 1988).

[1195]Rule 4(a)(4)(B)(i), Fed. R. App.P.

[1196]Rule 4(a)(4)(B)(ii), Fed.R.App.P.; Smith v. Barry, 502 U.S. 244, 247–48, 112 S. Ct. 678 (1992).

The courts have disagreed whether a post-judgment motion that is timely filed but not timely served affects the timing or validity of the notice of appeal.[1197]

You can obtain from the district court an extension of the time for filing a notice of appeal if you can show "excusable neglect" or good cause for your delay.[1198] You must make a motion for such an extension no later than 30 days after the notice of appeal was supposed to be filed—*i.e.*, within 60 days after the judgment was entered.[1199] (If you have not already filed the notice at the time you make your motion, be sure to include the notice of appeal along with the motion.) Depending on when you file, the district court can give you another 30 days or 14 days.[1200] If the district court does not grant your motion to extend time to file a notice to appeal, this denial is an immediately appealable final judgment.[1201]

Your motion should include an affidavit explaining the reason for the delay. The court can only grant you 30 days after the original deadline, or 14 days from the date of the order granting the extension.[1202] If you have sent the court a notice of appeal with your motion, and the court grants the motion, it will treat your notice as timely filed.

If you miss the deadline for filing your notice of appeal because you did not receive notice of a judgment or order within 21 days of its entry, the court may give you an additional 14 days to file your notice of appeal. You must file a motion to reopen the time to file an appeal. This motion to reopen must be filed within 180 days of the entry of judgment or within 14 days of your receiving the judgment, whichever is earlier.[1203] In the past, Rule 60(b), Fed.R.Civ.P., was sometimes used to reopen the time for appeal, but it appears that this is no longer an option.[1204] Under current law, if you miss the appeal deadline, then file a Rule 60(b) motion, and then appeal from the denial of that motion, that appeal "brings up for review only the denial of the motion and not the merits of the underlying judgment for errors that could have been asserted on direct appeal."[1205]

This 180-day deadline means, in practice, that if you are awaiting a decision on a motion or bench trial, it is your job to find out what happened if a few months pass and you don't get notice of a decision. It is also your job to keep the court informed of any changes in your address so the clerk can mail the judgment to the correct place.

2) Contents of the Notice of Appeal

The notice of appeal must specify the party or parties who are appealing, the judgment, order, or part thereof appealed from, and the court to which the appeal is taken.[1206]

A *pro se* notice of appeal is considered filed only on behalf of the party signing the notice (and the signer's spouse and minor children, if they are parties), "unless the notice of appeal clearly indicates a contrary intent."[1207] Therefore, if your case involves multiple plaintiffs, and the others do not file their own notices of appeal, you must list the names of all who wish to appeal.[1208] You must also get them to sign the notice. However, the signature is not a jurisdictional requirement, and lack of it can be corrected later.[1209] So if you can't get the signatures of all those who wish to appeal before the deadline for filing the notice of appeal, file the notice without the signatures so that it will be timely, and then file a corrected notice with the signatures later.[1210] At least one court has held that it is the court's responsibility to give *pro se* parties who failed to sign the notice of appeal an

---

[1197]*Compare* Simmons v. Ghent, 970 F.2d 392, 393 (7th Cir. 1992) (holding that service is required to toll the appeal deadline) *with* Welch v. Folsom, 925 F.2d 666, 669 (3d Cir. 1991) (if complaint is dismissed prior to service, then Rule 59 motion does not have to be served upon parties named in the complaint and not yet served); Craig v. Lynaugh, 846 F.2d 11 (5th Cir. 1988) (holding service is not required).

[1198]Rule 4(a)(5)(A)(ii), Fed.R.App.P. *See* Pearson v. Gatto, 933 F.2d 521, 524–25 (7th Cir. 1991) (counsel's overcommitment to *pro bono* cases constituted excusable neglect); Weekley v. Jones, 927 F.2d 382, 385–86 (8th Cir. 1991) (prisoner's *pro se* status, his impaired mental health, and his use of psychotropic medications constituted good cause); Merritt v. Broglin, 690 F. Supp. 739, 743–44 (N.D.Ind. 1988) (court considered late request for an extension because the court clerk made an error and returned prisoner's papers). *But see* Bishop v. Corsentino, 371 F.3d 1203, 1207 (10th Cir. 2004) (failure to decide whether to appeal and seeking advice on that subject were not good cause or excusable neglect). The definition of excusable neglect is discussed in § F of this chapter.

[1199]Rule 4(a)(5)(A)(i), Fed.R.App.P.

[1200]Rule 4(a)(5)(C), Fed.R.App.P.

[1201]*See* Bishop v. Corsentino, 371 F.3d 1203, 1206 (10th Cir. 2004) (noting such appeals are reviewed for abuse of discretion).

[1202]Rule 4(a)(5), Fed.R.App.P.

[1203]Rule 4(a)(6), Fed.R.App.P.

[1204]*See* Snyder v. Nolen, 380 F.3d 279, 293 (7th Cir. 2004) (concurring opinion) (after 180 days, judgment is "beyond review"); Cent. Vt. Pub. Serv. Corp. v. Herbert, 341 F.3d 186, 190 (2d Cir. 2003) ("Because final judgments should not be lightly reopened, Rule 60(b) may not be used as a substitute for timely appeal." (citation and internal quotations omitted)); Dunn v. Cockrell, 302 F.3d 491, 493 (5th Cir. 2002); Clark v. Lavallie, 204 F.3d 1038, 1041 (10th Cir. 2000) (Rule 60(b) cannot be used to get around time limits set by Rule 4(a)(5) and (6)); Zimmer St. Louis, Inc. v. Zimmer Co., 32 F.3d 357, 360 (8th Cir. 1994). A decision that says Rule 60(b) can still be used for this purpose did not consider the effect of the amendment to Rule 4(a)(6), Fed.R.App.P. Clark v. Lavallie, 204 F.3d at 1041 n.4 (citing Lewis v. Alexander, 987 F.2d 392, 395–96 (6th Cir. 1993)).

[1205]Branum v. Clark, 927 F.2d 698, 704 (2d Cir. 1991).

[1206]Rule 3(c), Fed.R.App.P.

[1207]Rule 3(c)(2), Fed.R.App.P.

[1208]*See* Rule 3(b), Fed.R.App.P., concerning joint or consolidated appeals.

[1209]Becker v. Montgomery, 532 U.S. 757, 764–66, 121 S. Ct. 1801 (2001)

[1210]Becker v. Montgomery, 532 U.S. at 765–68; *accord*, Wash v. Johnson 343 F.3d 685, 688–689 (5th Cir. 2003) (overruling Mikeska v. Collins, 928 F.2d 126 (5th Cir. 1991) *and* Carter v. Stalder, 60 F.3d 238, 239 (5th Cir. 1995)).

opportunity to do so, as part of the court's obligation to read *pro se* complaints generously.[1211]

In specifying the "judgment, order, or part thereof appealed from," it is generally sufficient simply to identify the final judgment, since a notice of appeal from a final judgment is supposed to bring up for review the entire judgment and all the nonfinal rulings in the case.[1212] Also, if the notice of appeal specifically identifies a particular prior order or part of the final judgment, the court may refuse to address other issues or parts of the judgment not mentioned in the notice.[1213]

For these reasons, it is probably safest simply to list the final judgment, identifying it by date.[1214] If there is no final judgment and you are appealing from an interlocutory order, you must identify that order in the notice of appeal. If you have appealed from a final judgment, and you also wish to appeal from a postjudgment order of some sort that came after your notice of appeal, you must file a second notice of appeal or an amended notice of appeal to be sure the postjudgment order will be before the appellate court.

The rules recommend that parties use the form notice of appeal in the Federal Rules of Appellate Procedure, but they also provide that appeals "shall not be dismissed for informality of form or title of the notice of appeal."[1215] Thus, courts have construed letters to the court and other documents as notices of appeal as long as they were timely filed and contained the required information.[1216] Courts have generally construed motions to extend the time for filing a notice of appeal as amounting to the notice of appeal.[1217]

e. *In Forma Pauperis* Under the Prison Litigation Reform Act (PLRA), the appellate filing fee is not waived for prisoners, even for those who are completely indigent.[1218] The rule is the same as in the district court: if you are granted *in forma pauperis* (IFP) status, you will be required to pay an initial filing fee, and then pay the rest of the fee as you have money in your prison account,[1219] though you must be allowed to proceed even if you don't have money to pay the initial fee.[1220]

Prisoners, unlike most litigants, must request permission to proceed IFP on appeal, even if they were previously permitted to proceed IFP in the district court.[1221] To request IFP status on appeal, you must file a new motion in the *district* court, along with a supporting affidavit showing that you can't afford to pay or give security for fees and costs, stating that you are entitled to redress and stating the issues that you intend to present on appeal,[1222] and a certified copy

---

[1211]Casanova v. Dubois, 289 F.3d 142, 146 (1st Cir. 2002) (at the court's direction, the clerk contacted the non-signing plaintiffs to give them an opportunity to sign).

[1212]*See* Alejo v. Heller, 328 F.3d 930, 935 (7th Cir. 2003); Weiss v. Cooley, 230 F.3d 1027, 1031 (7th Cir. 2000) (where two defendants were dismissed early in the case, their dismissal was reviewable on appeal from the final judgment); Akin v. PAFEC Ltd., 991 F.2d 1550, 1563 (11th Cir. 1993) ("When a district court enters a final judgment, 'all prior non-final orders and rulings which produced the judgment' are merged into the judgment and subject to review on appeal."); Caldwell v. Moore, 968 F.2d 595, 598 (6th Cir. 1992).

There are occasional exceptions. *See* Berdella v. Delo, 972 F.2d 204, 208–09 (8th Cir. 1992) (notice of appeal from order that included a final judgment did not bring up for review earlier order granting partial summary judgment against one party).

[1213]Cook v. Powell Buick, Inc., 155 F.3d 758, 761 (5th Cir. 1998) ("... [W]here a party designates in the notice of appeal particular orders *only*, and *not* the final judgment, we are without jurisdiction to hear challenges to other orders not specified." (emphasis in original)); Chaka v. Lane, 894 F.2d 923, 924–25 (7th Cir. 1990) (although a notice of appeal from a final judgment brings up the whole case for review, a notice that specifies a particular interlocutory order limits the appeal to review of that order); McLaurin v. Fischer, 768 F.2d 98, 102 (6th Cir. 1985) ("If an appellant ... chooses to designate specific determinations in his notice of appeal—rather than simply appealing from the entire judgment—only the specified issues may be raised on appeal.").

You may be excused from a mistake of this sort if your intent to appeal the whole judgment is clear from the notice of appeal and the appellee has not been misled by the mistake. Foman v. Davis, 371 U.S. 178, 181–82 S. Ct. 227 (1962); Benn v. First Judicial Dist. of Pa., 426 F.3d 233, 237 (3d Cir. 2005) ("... [A] notice may be construed as bringing up an unspecified order for review if it appears from the notice of appeal itself and the subsequent proceedings on appeal that the appeal was intended to have been taken from the unspecified judgment, order, or part thereof.").

[1214]Form 1, at the end of the Fed R.App.P., makes it clear that listing only the final judgment is acceptable.

[1215]Rule 3(c) and Form 1, Fed.R.App.P.; *see* Hilliard v. Scully, 667 F. Supp. 97, 98 (S.D.N.Y. 1987) (notice of appeal submitted on the wrong size paper should be considered timely filed).

[1216]Smith v. Barry, 502 U.S. 244, 247–48, 112 S. Ct. 678 (1992) (appellate brief filed within the time for filing a notice of appeal); Tijerina v. Plenti, 984 F.2d 148, 150 n.5 (5th Cir. 1993) (*in forma pauperis* application); Cooper v. Sheriff, Lubbock County Texas, 929 F2d. 1078, 1082 (5th Cir. 1991) (letter to the court).

[1217]*See, e.g.*, Andrade v. Attorney General of State of California, 270 F.3d 743, 752 (9th Cir. 2001) and cases cited; Rinaldo v. Corbett, 256 F.3d 1276, 1279 (11th Cir. 2001); U.S. v. Smith, 182 F.3d 733, 735–36 (10th Cir. 1999); Haugen v. Nassau County Dep't of Social Services, 171 F.3d 136, 137–38 (2d Cir. 1999) (per curiam). *But see* Harris v. Ballard, 158 F.3d 1164, 1166 (11th Cir. 1998) (declining to construe motion as a notice of appeal where it indicated uncertainty whether to appeal or not).

[1218]28 U.S.C. § 1915(b)(1). *See* § C.3 of this chapter, and Ch. 9, § A, for a more detailed discussion of filing fees under the PLRA. *See* Ch. 9, nn.3–21, for discussion of who is a "prisoner" subject to these PLRA provisions.

[1219]28 U.S.C. § 1915(b)(1).

[1220]28 U.S.C. §§ 1915(b)(4).

[1221]Morgan v. Haro, 112 F.3d 788, 789 (5th Cir. 1997); *see* 28 U.S.C. § 1915(a)(2); Rule 24(a)(3), Fed.R.App.P.

Rule 24(a)(3)(B) provides that a party who was granted IFP status in the district court requires no further authorization to proceed IFP on appeal *unless* "a statute provides otherwise." The Advisory Committee note on the 2002 amendment to the Rule makes it clear that this provision refers to the PLRA requirement that prisoners submit an IFP application on appeal.

[1222]Rule 24(a)(1), Fed.R.App.P.; Form 4, Fed.R.App.P. Samples of these papers appear in Appendix C. *See* Boling-Bey v. U.S.

of your prison trust fund account statement for the six months before the filing of the notice of appeal.[1223]

The district court may deny you IFP status if it certifies that your appeal is not taken in good faith, or that you are not otherwise entitled to proceed IFP; if it does this, it must state the reasons for doing so.[1224] An appeal is not taken in good faith when the issues the appellant raises are all frivolous.[1225] If the district court has dismissed the lawsuit as frivolous, it is unlikely to think that an appeal is being taken in good faith.[1226] In its findings, the district court is also to determine whether you now have three "strikes," *i.e.*, lawsuits which have been dismissed for being frivolous, malicious, or failing to state a claim. If you already have three strikes, you will not be allowed to appeal without paying the whole appellate filing fee up front,[1227] even if the appeal is taken in good faith, unless you convince the court that you are under imminent danger of serious physical injury at the time the appeal is filed.[1228]

If you were not already proceeding *in forma pauperis* in the district court, you must file a motion to proceed IFP on appeal; this motion is filed in the district court.[1229] The motion should include an affidavit showing that you can't afford to pay or give security for fees and costs, stating that you are entitled to redress and stating the issues that you intend to present on appeal, and should be accompanied by a certified statement of your prison account for the six months preceding your notice of appeal.[1230] While this motion is pending in the district court, you can file a motion with the appellate court for appointment of counsel.[1231] You should state in that motion that you are seeking IFP from the district court or, if already granted IFP, that IPF was granted by the district court and on what date.

If you are appealing an adverse judgment after a jury trial or an actual hearing where witnesses testified, it is likely you will need to provide portions of the transcripts to the appellate court for it to rule on your issues.[1232] This subject is addressed in the next section.

If the district court certified that your appeal is not taken in good faith or denies you *in forma pauperis* status, but you wish to appeal IFP anyway, you have 30 days after service of the notice of the district court's action to file a motion to proceed on appeal IFP with the appellate court.[1233] You must attach to the motion a copy of the affidavit filed in the district court in support of IFP and the statement of the district court supporting its finding of refusing to certify a good faith appeal. If no affidavit was filed with the district court, you must include an affidavit as set forth in Rule 24(a)(1).

If you choose to challenge the certification of lack of good faith by filing a motion to proceed IFP on appeal, your motion must be directed to why the reasons provided by the district court in denying the certification of good faith were wrong, which usually means why your case is not frivolous.[1234] If the appellate court will not grant your IFP motion, the only way your appeal will be heard is for you to pay the entire filing fee up front. If the appellate court grants the IFP motion, it will then remand to the district court for a determination of the initial partial appellate filing fee and the collection of the balance.[1235] If the appellate court finds that the denial of a "good faith" certification was in error, an order will be issued setting a briefing schedule for the appeal.[1236] You will still be required to pay the complete filing fee, but you will be able to do it in installments according to the usual procedure.[1237]

Parole Commission, 559 F.3d 1149, 1153–54 (10th Cir. 2009) (describing process).

[1223]28 U.S.C. § 1915(a)(2).

[1224]Rule 24(a)(3), Fed.R.App.P.; *see also* Baugh v. Taylor, 117 F.3d 197, 202 (5th Cir. 1997) (district court required to provide reasons for certifying that appeal was not taken in good faith).

[1225]Coppedge v. U.S., 369 U.S. 438, 445, 82 S. Ct. 917 (1962). *Coppedge* was a criminal case, but the same standard applies in civil cases. *See* Wooten v. District of Columbia Metropolitan Police Dep't, 129 F.3d 206, 208 (D.C. Cir. 1997); DeBardeleben v. Quinlan, 937 F.2d 502, 505 (10th Cir.1991).

[1226]*See, e.g.,* Prophete v. Gilless, 869 F. Supp. 537, 539 (W.D.Tenn.1994) (citing Williams v. Kuhlman, 722 F.2d 1048, 1050 n.1 (2d Cir. 1983)).

[1227]28 U.S.C. § 1915(g); *see* Ch. 9, § B.1, for a discussion of the three strikes provision. Appellate courts have disagreed, in cases where a district court decision is the third strike, whether the plaintiff should be able to appeal that decision without having to pay the filing fee in advance. *See* Ch. 9, § B.1, nn.146–48.

[1228]*See* Ch. 9, § B.2, concerning the imminent danger exception.

[1229]Rule 24(a)(1), Fed.R.App.P.

[1230]The motion is described in Rule 24(a)(1); Fed.R.App.P.; Form 4, Fed.R.App.P. Samples of these papers appear in Appendix C. The account statement is required by 28 U.S.C. § 1915(b)(2).

[1231]*See* 28 U.S.C. § 1915(e)(1).

[1232]Rule 10(b)(1)(A), Fed.R.App.P (requiring an appellant to "order from the reporter a transcript of such parts of the proceedings not already on file as the appellant considers necessary").

[1233]Rule 24(a)(5), Fed.R.App.P.

[1234]*See* McIntosh v. U.S. Parole Comm'n, 115 F.3d 809, 812 (10th Cir. 1997) (Prisoner "is required to demonstrate not only a financial inability to pay the required fees, but also 'a reasoned, nonfrivolous argument on the law and facts in support of the issues raised on appeal.'" (internal quotation marks omitted)); Newlin v. Helman, 123 F.3d 429, 433 (7th Cir. 1997) ("A plaintiff who has been told that the claim is foreclosed and then files a notice of appeal without offering any argument to undermine the district court's conclusion is acting in bad faith.").

[1235]*See* Henderson v. Norris, 129 F.3d 481, 484–85 (8th Cir. 1997) (per curiam).

[1236]*See, e.g.,* Hains v. Washington, 131 F.3d 1248, 1250 (7th Cir. 1997) ("Under the PLRA, it is at least theoretically possible that an appeal from a §§ 1915A dismissal (and accompanying denial of leave to proceed *in forma pauperis* in district court) could be taken in 'good faith.' . . . Exceptional cases may arise in which a district courts grants leave to appeal *in forma pauperis* to a plaintiff who appeals a close question under § 1915A in good faith.").

[1237]*See* 28 U.S.C. § 1915(b)(1)–(4); *see also* Leonard v. Lacy, 88 F.3d 181 (2d Cir. 1996) (interpreting the fee-payment requirements of the PLRA).

Most appellate courts will deem the motion to proceed on appeal *in forma pauperis* as a notice of appeal if you have failed to file a separate notice.[1238]

If the appellate court affirms the district court's denial of a "good faith" certification, or if you do not follow these procedures, you will have to pay the full filing fee, probably within 30 days, or the appeal will be dismissed for want of prosecution.[1239]

f. Transmission of the District Court's Record The appellant (person appealing) is responsible for getting the record of the case prepared and transmitted to the court of appeals and for preparing an appendix containing the relevant parts of the record.[1240] An appellant proceeding IFP can request that the appeal be heard on the full record from the court below[1241] so as not to have to prepare an appendix.[1242] If you do prepare an appendix, you must consult with your opponent about its contents.[1243]

As the appellant (the person taking the appeal), if you "intend to urge on appeal that a finding or conclusion is unsupported by the evidence or is contrary to the evidence," you are required to provide to the appellate court "a transcript of all evidence relevant to that finding or conclusion" that you are challenging.[1244] To get a transcript made and paid for in an *in forma pauperis* case, you must get the district court or a circuit judge to certify "that the appeal is not frivolous (but presents a substantial question)."[1245] In order to do this, you must file a motion explaining why those portions of the transcript are necessary for your appeal.[1246]

If you do not receive permission to proceed IFP on appeal, you will need to obtain and pay for portions or all of the transcript,[1247] obtain copies of documents in the file needed for the appendix, and provide the court with 10 copies and each opposing counsel with one copy of the appendix.[1248]

If the defendants are the appellants, they will be responsible for preparing the appendix, and must consult with you about its contents.[1249]

g. Appellate Briefs When the court of appeals receives the district court record, the clerk of that court will notify all parties of the date on which it was filed.[1250] The clerk will also issue a briefing schedule which will set the dates that the parties are required to file their respective briefs. The Fed.R.App.P. gives the appellant 40 days to file and serve his brief; the appellee then has 30 days to serve and file his brief, and the appellant may file a reply brief within 14 days after service of the appellee's brief.[1251] The local rules of each federal appeals court may alter these periods or contain additional or different requirements.[1252]

[1238]Mosley v. Cozby, 813 F.2d 659, 660 (5th Cir. 1987), and cases cited.

[1239]Callihan v. Schneider, 178 F.3d 800, 804 (6th Cir. 1999); Baugh v. Taylor, 117 F.3d 197, 202 (5th Cir. 1997).

[1240]Rules 10(b), 11(a), 30(a), Fed.R.App.P.

[1241]Rule 24(c), Fed.R.App.P.

[1242]It is probably desirable to prepare an appendix, because then the court can more conveniently locate the documents you want it to see, but it may not be practical or affordable to do so from within prison unless it is very short. A litigant without counsel proceeding IFP is required to file four legible copies of the appendix with the court and serve one copy on counsel for each defendant who has a separate lawyer. The appendix is generally filed with the brief. Rule 30(a)(3), Fed.R.App.P.

[1243]Rule 30(b)(1), Fed.R.App.P.

The required contents of the appendix are set out in Rule 30(a)(1), Fed.R.App.P. The appendix is not supposed to contain the whole record, since that is available to the court anyway. Rule 30(b)(1), Fed.R.App.P.

[1244]Rule 10(b)(2), Fed.R.App.P. Failure to obtain a relevant transcript in such a case is grounds for dismissing the appeal. Wrighten v. Glowski, 232 F.3d 119, 120 (2d Cir. 2000) (". . . [W]e dismiss this appeal with prejudice because the plaintiff failed to provide this Court with the trial transcripts needed to conduct meaningful appellate review, despite two extensions of time and advice from this Court to move in the district court for trial transcripts."); Richardson v. Henry, 902 F.2d 414, 416 (5th Cir.1990); *see* Learning Curve Toys, Inc. v. PlayWood Toys, Inc., 342 F.3d 714, 731 n.10 (7th Cir. 2003) (refusing to consider issue where party failed to provide necessary transcript).

[1245]28 U.S.C. § 753(f) ("Fees for transcripts furnished in . . . proceedings to persons permitted to appeal *in forma pauperis* shall . . . be paid by the U.S. if the trial judge or a circuit judge certifies that the appeal is not frivolous (but presents a substantial question)."); *see* McCarthy v. Bronson, 906 F.2d 835, 841 (2d Cir.1990) (free transcripts may only be provided to an appellant whose appeal is non-frivolous), *aff'd*, 500 U.S. 136, 111 S. Ct. 1737 (1991). You should first move in the district court, and if the motion is denied, you can file a motion in the court of appeals.

At least one court has construed the statute as providing for transcripts for the use of IFP litigants who have won their cases and are defending against appeals. Stanley v. Henderson, 590 F.2d 752, 753–54 (8th Cir. 1979).

[1246]*See* Harvey v. Andrist, 754 F.2d 569, 571 (5th Cir. 1985); Nolt v. Strausser, 761 F. Supp. 18, 19–20 (E.D.Pa. 1990) (both denying transcript where it did not appear necessary for the appeal). In *Oliver v. Collins*, 904 F.2d 278, 281–82 (5th Cir. 1991), the prisoner didn't explain why the transcript was necessary, and the district court denied it; the appeals court directed the magistrate judge to reconsider in light of the arguments made in the prisoner's appellate brief. Don't count on getting this kind of break.

[1247]Rule 10(b), Fed.R.App.P.

[1248]Rule 30(a)(3), Fed.R.App.P. Check the court's local rules on this point. Some courts require fewer copies.

[1249]Rule 30(b)(1), Fed.R.App.P.

[1250]Rule 12(c), Fed.R.App.P.

[1251]Rule 31(a), Fed.R.App.P. Reply briefs must be filed at least seven days before oral argument unless the court allows a later filing.

[1252]For example, in the Sixth Circuit, the parties are given specific times to file what is known as the "draft" brief. This draft brief will contain citations to the record and will provide a space for adding a "Joint Appendix" citation later. Once the draft briefs are filed by the parties, then the joint appendix is prepared by the

Briefs and other papers filed by an inmate of a prison or other institution are considered timely filed if they are placed in the institution's internal mail system on or before the deadline and an affidavit is filed with the court stating the date it was deposited there and that first-class postage was prepaid. If there is a separate system for legal mail, you must use it to get the benefit of the rule.[1253]

If you cannot prepare your brief and file it within the time period allowed, you may be able to get an enlargement of time by filing a motion with the court showing good cause for your need for more time.[1254] You should ask for your opponent's consent first. Failure to file your brief on time, or to get an enlargement of time, can result in your appeal being dismissed if you are the appellant, or oral argument being denied to you if you are the appellee.[1255]

Unless the court or local rules direct otherwise, the principal briefs of each side, if typewritten, are limited to 30 pages, and the reply brief to 15 pages, not including the table of contents, tables of citations, and any addendum containing statutes, rules, regulations, etc.[1256] Alternatively, if you are able to have your brief word-processed, it is acceptable if it contains no more than 14,000 words or 1300 lines of monospaced type (you will have to certify your compliance with this requirement[1257]). A separate rule contains length limits for briefs in cases involving a cross-appeal.[1258]

Briefs must be double-spaced on 8 ½ by 11 inch paper, and there are other requirements about typeface, typestyles, etc., that assume everyone has access to word processing or at least to a typewriter.[1259] You should study the requirements of Rule 32, Fed.R.App.P., and comply with them as best you can; if you are not able to comply in all respects, you should explain the reasons in a cover letter when you submit your brief. You should also obtain a copy of the local rules of the appellate court you are appealing to, which may contain additional requirements about the form of briefs, and may also contain special provisions for *pro se* litigants.

The appellant's brief should contain the following:[1260]

(1)   A table of contents, with page references, and a table of authorities including the cases, statutes, and other materials you have cited, listing the pages of the brief where they are cited.[1261]

(2)   A statement of subject matter and appellate jurisdiction. This must contain a statement of the basis for the lower court's jurisdiction and a statement of the basis of the appeals court's jurisdiction citing the relevant statutes, facts that show they are applicable, and dates that show that the appeal is timely (*i.e.*, when the judgment or order was entered and when you filed your notice of appeal).[1262]

(3)   A statement of the issues presented for review. For example, "Whether the defendants' macing of the plaintiff while he was handcuffed and confined in his cell violated the cruel and unusual punishments clause of the Eighth Amendment."[1263]

(4)   A statement of the case, consisting of a brief statement of the nature of the case, the course of proceedings in the lower court, and the lower court's decision.[1264] (This can be called a Statement of Proceedings.)

(5)   A statement of facts, which contains the facts relevant to the issues on appeal, with reference to the parts of the record that contain those facts.[1265]

(6)   An argument. You will present an argument for each issue that is raised on appeal. For each issue, the argument should include "a concise statement of the applicable standard of review."[1266] The argument will also contain your contentions with respect to the issues you listed in the statement of issues, the reasons you think the court should rule in your favor, and citations to cases, statutes, rules, or parts of the record that support your argument. Each issue on appeal should have its own "point" which briefly states your claim as to that issue. The argument should be preceded by a summary of the argument, "which must contain a succinct,

---

appellant and it is filed with the court and served upon opposing party. The parties are usually given 14 days after the filing of the joint appendix to place the joint appendix citation with the pleading citations and then filed a "Final Brief" with the Sixth Circuit. See Sixth Circuit Rule 28(a). Other Federal Courts of Appeals may require different procedures for filing of the appellate brief so make sure that you read the appellate rules from the court of appeals where you are filing your appellate brief.

[1253]Rule 25(a)(2)(C), Fed.R.App.P. This "prison mailbox" rule is discussed in more detail in § H, nn.333–342, and in § U.1.d(1), nn.1188–1192, of this chapter.

[1254]Rule 26(b), Fed.R.App.P. For example, if prison officials have limited your access to the law library, or if you did not timely receive the notice that the record had been filed, you should include this fact in an affidavit attached to your motion.

[1255]Rule 31(c), Fed.R.App.P.

[1256]Rule 32(a)(7) (A), Fed.R.App.P.

[1257]Rule 32(a)(7)(B, C), Fed.R.App.P.

[1258]Rule 28.1, Fed.R.App.P.

[1259]Rule 32(a)(4, 5), Fed.R.App.P.

[1260]Rule 28(a), Fed.R.App.P. A sample appellate brief appears in Appendix C, Form 13b. Writing briefs is discussed in Ch. 12, § E.

[1261]Rule 28(a)(2, 3), Fed.R.App.P.

[1262]Rule 28(a)(4), Fed.R.App.P.; *see* Appendix C, Form 13b, for an example of how to meet these requirements.

[1263]Rule 28(a)(5), Fed.R.App.P.

[1264]Rule 28(a)(6), Fed.R.App.P.

[1265]Rule 28(a)(7), Fed.R.App.P.

[1266]Rule 28(a)(9), Fed.R.App.P. Standards of review are discussed in § U.1.a of this chapter.

clear, and accurate statement of the arguments made in the body of the brief. . . ."[1267]

(7) Conclusion. This should include a statement of exactly what you think the appellate court should do.[1268]

You should also include a certification of compliance with the length limit, if you are relying on the word count or the line count.[1269]

The appellee's brief must contain the same items, except that it need not include a jurisdictional statement, statement of the issues, statement of the case, statement of facts, and statement of the standard of review unless the appellee is dissatisfied with the appellant's version of them.[1270]

In your brief, when you are referring to the parties, you need not use the terms "appellant" or "appellee"; in fact the rules discourage doing so. You can use the terms used in the lower court (*e.g.*, "plaintiff" and "defendant"), or the parties' names or titles (*e.g.*, "Jones," or "the warden"), or combine them (*e.g.*, "defendant Jones" or "the defendant warden").[1271] The point is to be clear, and using the parties' names is probably the best way to do this.

When you make statements about the case record, you should always provide a citation to the part of the record in question. If the particular item is included in the appendix, you should cite the relevant page of the appendix. If the item is not included in the appendix, you should identify it by title and docket number, and page within the document or by transcript page number.[1272]

If you are proceeding *in forma pauperis* without a lawyer, you must file an original and three copies of your brief with the court and send one copy to counsel for defendants.[1273] If you are not proceeding *in forma pauperis*, you must have your brief printed or duplicated so the court receives 25 copies and each opposing counsel gets two copies,[1274] unless a local rule of the court prescribes a different number.

h. Oral Argument The appellate rules provide that oral argument normally should be allowed unless a panel of three judges decides that oral argument is not needed.[1275] However, few courts of appeals will allow an incarcerated person to present oral argument, even though federal courts

have the power to issue a writ of habeas corpus for this purpose.[1276]

You may request by motion that you be allowed to present oral argument; alternatively, you may wish to request that if you are not permitted to argue orally, the other side should not be permitted to do so either. In at least a few cases, *pro se* litigants have been provided with a transcript of the argument and permitted to submit written comments afterward. We do not know whether this procedure is currently used in any appeals court. Video hookups are widely used for oral argument in federal appellate courts now; we don't know if they have been used in prisoner cases, but the Prison Litigation Reform Act encourages the use of telecommunications in pretrial proceedings,[1277] and we don't see any reason why the practice could not be extended to appellate argument.

If oral argument is permitted, the appellant will present his argument first and can reserve some of the time allocated to respond to appellee's argument.[1278] The court normally grants each party a specific amount of time for oral argument,[1279] which may be short; one appeals court routinely grants five minutes in *pro se* cases.[1280]

If time permits, the appellant should start with a short, fair statement of the facts and case history. Do not read at length from your brief, the record, or other authorities.[1281] The court is interested in hearing in what way you think the district court was wrong, though you may wish to call the court's attention to particular parts of the record or particular case authority that support your argument.

You should expect the court to ask you questions, and you should be prepared to answer them. When the court asks a question, always answer it immediately, even if you think it is not important. (After you answer it, of course, you are free to explain why you don't think it is important.) Since nobody ever has enough time at oral argument, you should pick out the two or three most essential points you need to get across, and be prepared to drop everything else in order to make them.

Before argument, you should study the other side's brief and be prepared to respond to any statement or argument in it. You should be able to answer questions about the facts and to tell the court where in the record it can find any fact that you wish to emphasize.

i. Decisions on Appeal After a case is argued orally or submitted on the briefs, the appeals court may render a decision

---

[1267]Rule 28(a)(8), Fed.R.App.P.

[1268]Rule 28(a)(10), Fed.R.App.P.

[1269]Rule 28(a)(11), Fed.R.App.P.

[1270]Rule 28(b), Fed.R.App.P.

[1271]Rule 28(d), Fed.R.App.P.

[1272]*See* Rule 28(e), Fed.R.App.P.

[1273]Rule 31(b), Fed.R.App.P.

[1274]Rule 31(b), Fed.R.App.P. The court gets 10 copies of the appendix, and each opposing counsel gets one copy. Rule 30(d), Fed.R.App.P. Check the local rules of the court on this point; some appeals courts require fewer copies of the Appendix.

[1275]Rule 34(a), Fed.R.App.P.

[1276]Price v. Johnson, 334 U.S. 266, 284–85, 68 S. Ct. 1049 (1948).

[1277]42 U.S.C. § 1997e(f).

[1278]Rule 34(c), Fed.R.App.P.

[1279]Rule 34(b), Fed.R.App.P. (directing clerk to notify parties how much time is allowed); Rule 34(b), Sixth Circuit Rules (15 minutes per side).

[1280]Rule 34(b), Rules Supplementing Federal Rules of Appellate Procedure, United States Court of Appeals for the Second Circuit.

[1281]Rule 34(c), Fed.R.App.P.

in a few days, several months, or longer in some cases. It can affirm the district court's decision, which means that what the district court decided will stand. At that point, if the district court had entered a final judgment, the case is over unless someone petitions for rehearing in the appeals court or tries to take the case to the United States Supreme Court. If there is no final judgment yet, the case will generally go back to the district court for further proceedings.

If the appeals court finds a significant error in the district court's actions, it may modify the judgment, which means correcting an error without sending the case back to the district court. It may vacate the judgment and remand to the district court for further proceedings to correct the error. It may reverse the judgment and either direct the entry of a different judgment or order that a new trial or other further proceedings be conducted. It may remand the case to the district court for various purposes such as additional findings of fact or additional evidence, reconsideration in light of changed circumstances or law, etc.

An appeals court can also dismiss an appeal if it determines that it lacks jurisdiction or if the appellant fails to follow proper procedures in the appellate court.

After the decision, the court clerk enters judgment and serves a copy of the opinion (or the judgment, if there is no opinion) and notice of the date of entry of the judgment on the parties[1282] (*i.e.*, mails it to them). The court of appeals issues its "mandate" (usually consisting of its judgment, opinion, and any direction about costs) 21 days after judgment is entered, unless the mandate is stayed because of a petition for rehearing or for certiorari.[1283]

j. Rehearing or Rehearing En Banc You may file a petition for rehearing by the panel that decided the case, or for rehearing en banc (sometimes spelled "in banc") within 14 days after entry of the judgment of the court of appeals.[1284] You must state in your petition "with particularity" the points of law or facts which you feel the court overlooked or misapprehended.[1285] There may be additional requirements in the local rules of the appellate court you are in.

Rehearing is very rarely granted and rehearing en banc is almost never granted.[1286] Sometimes the court will amend its opinion in response to a petition for rehearing without actually granting the petition.

If the other side files a motion for rehearing or rehearing en banc, you need not respond to the petition until and unless the court requests you to do so.[1287]

k. Appointment of Counsel There is no right to appointed counsel on appeal of a civil action. However, the courts of appeals are authorized to request counsel to represent you,[1288] and we recommend that you file a motion asking the court to do so.[1289] Even if the district court refused to appoint counsel for you, the court of appeals may take a different view and may also be in a better position to find a lawyer for you.

2. Supreme Court

If you lose your case in the court of appeals and you believe the court of appeals was wrong, you may consider petitioning for review in the United States Supreme Court.[1290]

a. Jurisdiction and Role of the Supreme Court The Supreme Court has the power to review virtually any decision of a federal court of appeals;[1291] it has more limited powers to review decisions of the highest court of a state.[1292] There are very few cases that the Supreme Court is required to hear, and prison cases almost never fall into these categories.[1293]

[1282]Rule 36(b), Fed.R.App.P.

[1283]Rule 41, Fed.R.App.P. Rule 41(b) says that the mandate is issued seven days after expiration of the 14-day period for filing a petition for rehearing, *see* Rule 40, Fed.R.App.P., or seven days after denial of a rehearing petition or motion for stay or the mandate. Rule 41(d) provides that a party may move to stay the mandate pending filing and disposition of a petition for certiorari.

[1284]Rules 35(c), 40(a), Fed.R.App.P. Since the decision in the case will have been mailed to you, your time will be reduced by the days it takes to get to you. To compensate for this loss of time, you get an additional three days because of the mail service. Rule 26(c), Fed.R.App.P.

A rehearing en banc is a rehearing by all the active judges of the court rather than by the usual three-judge panel. You need only file one motion to seek one, designating it as a "Motion for Rehearing With Suggestion of Rehearing En Banc."

[1285]Rule 40(a), Fed.R.App.P.

[1286]Rule 35(a), Fed.R.App.P. En banc consideration is reserved for cases where it is needed "to secure or maintain uniformity of the court's decisions" (*i.e.*, a decision conflicts with other decisions of the same appeals court) and cases that involve a question of "exceptional importance," *e.g.*, the decision is in conflict with authoritative decisions of other federal appeals courts. Rule 35(b), Fed.R.App.P.

[1287]Rule 40(a)(3), Fed.R.App.P. (no response permitted unless the court requests).

[1288]28 U.S.C. § 1915(e)(1).

[1289]Sample papers requesting the appointment of counsel are presented in Appendix C. If you had appointed counsel in the district court, that appointment does not automatically carry over into the court of appeals. DiAngelo v. Illinois Dep't of Public Aid, 891 F.2d 1260, 1262 (7th Cir. 1989). You should ask your appointed lawyer if he is willing to continue representing you on appeal. If not, you should file a motion for appointed counsel in the appellate court.

A lawyer appointed by the court of appeals is not obligated to continue to represent you in the district court if there are further proceedings after the appeal. However, you should not hesitate to ask the attorney politely if he would continue to represent you. Some will and some will not.

[1290]*See* Appendix A for the address of the Supreme Court.

[1291]28 U.S.C. § 1254(1).

[1292]28 U.S.C. § 1257.

[1293]For a more detailed description of the jurisdiction of the Supreme Court, read 28 U.S.C. §§ 1251–58 and cases interpreting these statutes.

Proceedings in the Supreme Court are governed by the Rules of the Supreme Court of the United States.[1294]

The Supreme Court takes very few cases and selects them carefully. It generally restricts itself to cases that present issues of importance to the federal judicial system or to the nation, not just to the people involved in the case. Usually these cases involve important and unsettled issues of federal constitutional or statutory law, conflicts with an earlier Supreme Court decision, or conflicts in decisions between federal courts of appeals or between state and federal courts about significant issues of federal law.[1295] The Supreme Court is not in the business of correcting every mistake that the lower courts make.

b. Petition for Writ of Certiorari To apply for Supreme Court review, you must file a petition for a writ of certiorari within 90 days after entry of the judgment or decree in the court of appeals.[1296] The clerk is supposed to enter judgment by noting it on the court's docket after receiving the court's opinion, unless you filed a petition for rehearing; in that case, entry of judgment takes place on the date the petition is denied.[1297]

A petition for a writ of certiorari is a miniature brief which should include the following:[1298]

(1) Questions presented. These questions should be short and to the point, not argumentative or repetitious. The Court will only consider those questions specifically identified in the petition.

(2) Lists of parties. You should list, either in the caption or in one of the footnotes, the names of all the plaintiffs and defendants.

(3) Table of contents and table of authorities, if the petition is longer than five pages or 1500 words. The table of authorities is an alphabetical listing of the cases, constitutional provisions, statutes, books, etc., that you cite, listing the pages where they are cited in the petition.

(4) Reference to the official and unofficial reports[1299] of opinions in the case by the lower courts or administrative agencies.

(5) Jurisdictional grounds. This section must contain the date of the entry of the judgment or decree you are appealing; the date of entry of any order concerning a request for rehearing;

the date and terms of any order granting an extension of time for filing the petition for certiorari; and the statutory provision that gives the Supreme Court jurisdiction to hear the case.[1300]

(6) Constitutional provisions, statutes, ordinances, and regulations relied on. If these are not too lengthy, you should list them as part of your brief; if they are lengthy, include them in the appendix.

(7) A concise statement of the case. This should contain the facts that are important to the questions presented.

(8) The basis for federal jurisdiction. If you are asking the Supreme Court to review a case from a state court, you must provide information about when and how questions of federal law were raised.[1301] If your case was decided by a federal appeals court, you should explain why the federal district court had jurisdiction in the first place.[1302]

(9) Argument. This section should be called "Reasons for Granting the Writ" and should contain a direct and concise argument why the Supreme Court should grant your petition for certiorari.

(10) Appendix. This should contain a copy of any orders, decisions, etc., you received from the lower and appellate courts, including any order denying a petition for rehearing, any other documents from the case record that the Supreme Court should consider in order to understand the petition, and the judgment that you want the Court to review.

Petitions for certiorari are usually printed in booklet form.[1303] Most *pro se* prisoners will have to use the option to submit it typed, double-spaced except for quotations, on 8 ½ by 11 inch white paper, bound at the upper left-hand corner, and signed by the *pro se* litigant.[1304] In that form, the petition for certiorari may not exceed 40 pages, not counting the questions presented, the list of parties, the table of contents and table of authorities, and the appendix.[1305]

A copy of the petition for certiorari must be served on counsel for the other side and a proof of service filed with

---

[1294]28 U.S.C., Rules of the Supreme Court. These rules may also be obtained from the Clerk of the Supreme Court.

[1295]*See* Rule 10, Supreme Court Rules.

[1296]28 U.S.C. § 2101(c); Rule 13.1, Supreme Court Rules.

[1297]Rule 36(a), Fed.R.App.P. The date that the time runs from is not the date that the mandate of the court of appeals is issued. It is the date that the court enters its order resolving the case. Rule 13.3, Supreme Court Rules.

[1298]*See* Rule 14.1, Supreme Court Rules; *see also* Appendix C for a sample petition for a writ of certiorari.

[1299]These are discussed in Ch. 11, § B.1.

[1300]If you are cross-petitioning in response to the other side's petition, additional information is required, as stated in Rule 14.1(e)(iii), Supreme Court Rules.

[1301]Rule 14.1(g)(i), Supreme Court Rules.

[1302]Rule 14.1(g)(ii), Supreme Court Rules.

[1303]Rule 33.1, Supreme Court Rules (describing requirements for booklet-form petitions).

[1304]Rule 33.2, Supreme Court Rules. Persons proceeding *in forma pauperis* are expected to file papers in this form except when it is impossible. Rule 39.3, Supreme Court Rules.

[1305]Rule 33.2, Supreme Court Rules.

the Clerk of the Supreme Court.[1306] These documents can be served by mail.[1307] If you are suing the United States or any department, office, agency, officer, or employee, you must serve a copy on counsel for the person being sued and send a copy to the Solicitor General of the United States, Room 5614, Department of Justice, 950 Pennsylvania Ave., N.W., Washington, D.C. 20530-0001.[1308]

The purpose of a petition for certiorari is not to convince the Supreme Court that you have been mistreated, or just that the court below was wrong, but to convince it that your case is important enough to justify devoting the Court's limited time to it. In your statement of questions presented and in your argument, you should emphasize the importance of the issues, the lack of guidance from the Supreme Court to the lower courts on these issues, or any conflicts on the issue in the lower district and appellate courts.[1309] If you cannot make a convincing argument on those grounds, your petition for certiorari will not receive serious consideration.

c. *In Forma Pauperis* If you wish to proceed in the Supreme Court without payment of fees and costs and without having to print a large number of copies of your papers, you will need to submit a motion to proceed *in forma pauperis* (IFP) and a supporting affidavit.[1310] The motion shall state the reasons you should be allowed to proceed IFP, whether or not leave to proceed IFP was sought in the lower courts, and if so, whether it was granted.[1311]

The affidavit need not contain a list of the issues you are presenting in your petition for certiorari but should be similar to your IFP affidavit in the court of appeals. The IFP motion must be filed along with the petition for certiorari.[1312] If you are an "inmate confined in an institution and . . . not represented by counsel," you need only file the original petition (though of course you must have served the other side). If you are no longer confined but are seeking to proceed *in forma pauperis*, you are required to file the original and 10 copies.[1313]

Once the Clerk of the Court has received these documents, along with proof of service, the petition for certiorari will be filed and placed on the docket.[1314]

d. Counsel If the Supreme Court grants a petition for a writ of certiorari, it will appoint counsel for an indigent party upon a timely motion or request. The Clerk of the Court will write to you promptly after the petition is granted to ask if you want counsel appointed; you should request counsel immediately. The proper procedure is to file a single copy of a motion if you are still an inmate and if not, to file an original and 10 copies.[1315]

Since the Supreme Court grants all timely requests for appointment of counsel, our discussion of Supreme Court practice ends here.

V. Costs

Generally, costs are awarded to the prevailing party in a lawsuit unless there is another rule, a statute, or a court order that provides otherwise.[1316] The costs referred to do not include every expenditure that a litigant makes in the course of a lawsuit; they are limited to the specific items listed in 28 U.S.C. § 1920, including clerks' and marshals' fees, witness fees, copies of necessary document, transcripts that were necessarily obtained, and a few other items.[1317] District courts have substantial discretion whether and to what extent to tax costs for those items.[1318]

A *pro se* litigant may be awarded costs on the same basis as any other litigant,[1319] and may have costs imposed against him even if he is proceeding *in forma pauperis* (IFP).[1320]

[1306]Rules 29.3, 29.5, Supreme Court Rules. These rules give more detail on service requirements. Your motion to proceed *in forma pauperis*, and the supporting affidavit, should be served along with the petition.

[1307]Rule 29.3, Supreme Court Rules.

[1308]Rule 29.4(a), Supreme Court Rules.

[1309]*See* Rule 10, Supreme Court Rules.

[1310]Rule 39.1, Supreme Court Rules. *See also* Appendix C for a sample motion and affidavit to proceed IFP.

[1311]Rule 39.1, Supreme Court Rules.

[1312]Rule 39.2, Supreme Court Rules.

[1313]Rule 39.2, Supreme Court Rules.

[1314]Rule 39.4, Supreme Court Rules.

[1315]Rule 39.2, Supreme Court Rules; *see* Robert L. Stern *et al.*, *Supreme Court Practice* § 8.13(b) (Bureau of National Affairs, Washington, D.C., 2002).

[1316]Rule 54(d)(1), Fed.R.Civ.P.

Under that rule, costs can be imposed against the federal government or its officers or agencies "only to the extent allowed by law." Under 28 U.S.C. § 2412(b) (commonly called the Equal Access to Justice Act), the federal government and its agencies and officials sued in official capacities are liable for costs on the same basis as everyone else. However, the *in forma pauperis* (IFP) statute says that costs may not be taxed against the federal government in IFP cases. 28 U.S.C. § 1915(f)(1); *see* Maida v. Callahan, 148 F.3d 190, 193 (2d Cir. 1998) (holding costs may not be taxed for or against the United States in an IFP case).

[1317]*See* Crawford Fitting Co. v. J. T. Gibbons, Inc., 482 U.S. 437, 441–42, 107 S. Ct. 2494 (1987); Brisco-Wade v. Carnahan, 297 F.3d 781, 782–83 (8th Cir. 2002).

[1318]Crawford Fitting Co. v. J. T. Gibbons, Inc., 482 U.S. at 441–42; *see, e.g.*, Association of Mexican-American Educators v. State of California, 231 F.3d 572, 591–93 (9th Cir. 2000) (en banc) (affirming denial of costs against civil rights plaintiff); Torres v. City of New York, 262 F. Supp. 2d 317, 318 (S.D.N.Y. 2003) (declining to award costs against civil rights plaintiff).

[1319]Coleman v. Turner, 838 F.2d 1004, 1005 (8th Cir. 1988); *cf.* Hadix v. Johnson, 322 F.3d 895, 900 (6th Cir. 2003) (recognizing right of *pro se* person to recover costs but denying costs on facts in that case).

[1320]*See, e.g.*, McGill v. Faulkner, 18 F.3d 456, 460 (7th Cir. 1994) (trial court has discretion to award costs despite present indigency of prisoner proceeding IFP); Weaver v. Toombs, 948 F.2d 1004, 1014 (6th Cir. 1991) (holding court has "authority to assess

The IFP statute provides that "[j]udgment may be rendered for costs at the conclusion of the suit or action as in other proceedings."[1321] The Prison Litigation Reform Act (PLRA) has added the provision that if a judgment for costs is entered against a prisoner, he must pay the entire costs ordered,[1322] *i.e.*, the award is not subject to further review or appeal, on grounds of the plaintiff's lack of funds or otherwise.[1323] However, the court still has discretion despite the PLRA to refrain from assessing costs, or to reduce the costs assessed, against an IFP litigant, based on factors including "the losing party's good faith, the difficulty of the case, the winning party's behavior, and the necessity of the costs."[1324] Under the PLRA, awards of costs are to be collected in the same manner as filing fees.[1325]

Costs do not include attorneys' fees. However, courts have held that the attorneys' fees statutes also permit the recovery of some litigation expenses, and that *pro se* plaintiffs may recover these expenses, even though they are not entitled to attorneys' fees.[1326]

To recover costs, the prevailing party files a "bill of costs" with the court, supported by an affidavit verifying its correctness and that the costs were necessary for the litigation.[1327] The Fed.R.Civ.P. do not set a deadline for seeking costs, but some local court rules do. Costs are taxed by the clerk on 14 days' notice; you have 7 days thereafter to serve a motion asking the court to review the clerk's action.[1328] Therefore, if you lose a case and you are served with a bill of costs by the defendants, you should review it to determine if you wish either to challenge the legitimacy of the costs claimed, or to request that the court deny costs or reduce them because of your financial situation or other reasons cited above.

Costs on appeal are addressed by a separate rule providing for procedures similar to those in the district court.[1329]

W. SANCTIONS[1330]

Rule 11 of the Federal Rules of Civil Procedure provides for sanctions (penalties) against attorneys or parties who file papers that have no basis in fact or law or are filed for improper purposes such as harassment, delay, or increased costs. This rule provides that attorneys or parties proceeding *pro se* must certify, whenever they file a document in court, that

> to the best of the person's knowledge, information or belief, formed after an inquiry reasonable under the circumstances:
>
> (1) it is not being presented for any improper purpose, such as to harass, cause unnecessary delay, or needlessly increase the cost of litigation;
> (2) the claims, defenses, and other legal contentions are warranted by existing law or by a nonfrivolous argument for extending, modying, or reversing existing law or for establishing of new law;
> (3) the factual contentions have evidentiary support or, if specifically so identified, will likely have evidentiary support after a reasonable opportunity for further investigation or discovery; and
> (4) the denials of factual contentions are warranted on the evidence or, if specifically so identified, are reasonably based on belief or a lack of information.[1331]

---

reasonable costs . . . against unsuccessful *in forma pauperis* plaintiffs even if their claims are not deemed frivolous, malicious or vexatious"); Lay v. Anderson, 837 F.2d 231, 232–33 (5th Cir. 1988) (per curiam). For example, one prisoner was assessed $7,989.90 in costs and $15,750 in attorneys' fees. *See* Sanders v. Seabold, 188 F.3d 509, 509 (6th Cir. 1999) (unpublished).

[1321]28 U.S.C. § 1915(f)(1).
Such awards cover costs that the other party has actually paid, not costs that the IFP litigant was excused from prepaying to the court. Evans v. Tennessee Dep't of Corrections, 514 F.2d 283, 284–85 (6th Cir. 1975). (Under PLRA, prisoners proceeding IFP now pay filing fees anyway. *See* Ch. 9, § A for further discussion of the PLRA's effect on filing fees and costs.)

[1322]28 U.S.C. § 1915(f)(2)(A).

[1323]*See* Talley-Bey v. Knebl, 168 F.3d 884, 886 (6th Cir. 1999) ("Because a prisoner can no longer challenge the assessment of fees . . . on the grounds that the prisoner is unable to pay the assessment, if a court chooses to tax a prisoner, the prisoner is required to pay the assessment in full."); Whitfield v. Scully, 241 F.3d 264, 273 (2d Cir. 2001) (noting PLRA prevents appellate courts from reviewing cost awards in prisoner cases).

[1324]Singleton v. Smith, 241 F.3d 534, 539 (6th Cir. 2001) (citing White & White, Inc. v. American Hosp. Supply Corp., 786 F.2d 728, 732–33 (6th Cir. 1986)); Feliciano v. Selsky, 205 F.3d 568, 572 (2d Cir. 2000) (noting "the ability of a court to require, as a matter of discretion, that the indigent prisoner pay the costs, or some part of them"); *see* Johnson v. Freeburn, 2002 WL 1009572, *3 (E.D.Mich. 2002) (discussing factors affecting discretion in award of costs).

[1325]28 U.S.C. § 1915(f)(2); *see* Skinner v. Govorchin, 463 F.3d 518, 523–24 (6th Cir. 2006); Johnson v. McNeil, 217 F.3d 298, 301–02 (5th Cir. 2000).

[1326]Burt v. Hennessey, 929 F.2d 457, 459 (9th Cir. 1991) (*pro se* plaintiff may recover litigation expenses to extent attorney could receive them under award of attorney fees pursuant to 42 U.S.C. § 1988); Jermosen v. Smith, 733 F. Supp. 13, 14 (W.D.N.Y. 1990). *Contra*, Mayberry v. Walters, 862 F.2d 1040, 1042 (3d Cir. 1988) (a *pro se* plaintiff may not be awarded the costs of paralegal services under the fees statute).

[1327]28 U.S.C. § 1924; *see* Candelaria v. Coughlin, 181 F.R.D. 278, 282–83 (S.D.N.Y. 1998) (denying some costs to prisoner because of inadequate documentation and explanation).

[1328]Rule 54(d)(1), Fed.R.Civ.P. Calculating time deadlines and asking for an extension of time are discussed in § H of this chapter.

[1329]Rule 39(d), Fed.R.App.P.

[1330]This section does not address contempt sanctions, which are discussed in §T.2.b.1 of this chapter, or awards of attorneys' fees, which are discussed in § Y of this chapter. Nor does it address orders restricting prisoners' ability to file lawsuits in the future, which are discussed in the next section.

[1331]Rule 11(b), Fed.R.Civ.P.

Rule 11 penalties can include "nonmonetary directives," monetary penalties, or some or all of the attorney's fees or other expenses caused by the violation.[1332] Similar or more severe sanctions can be imposed for misconduct related to discovery[1333] or noncooperation with pretrial procedures,[1334] and a statute provides for sanctions against counsel who "multiplies the proceedings . . . unreasonably and vexatiously."[1335] Appeals courts can sanction litigants for frivolous appeals.[1336] Courts also have inherent power to sanction abuses of the judicial process.[1337] For example, the knowing presentation of a falsified document to a court is grounds for dismissal,[1338] as is abusive or threatening conduct.[1339] Repeated violation of rules and court orders may result in dismissal for failure to prosecute.[1340] Sanctions should be proportionate to the seriousness of the violations and the degree of fault of the sanctioned party.[1341]

Despite the general rule that *pro se* filings are to be construed liberally, courts have imposed Rule 11 and other sanctions against a number of *pro se* litigants whom they believe to have abused the court system.[1342] Monetary sanctions are sometimes enforced by directing prison officials to withdraw the money from prisoners' accounts.[1343]

The use of sanctions against *pro se* litigants is one more reason to do what you should do anyway: be sure you have a basis for everything you file in court, and follow the rules of court and all relevant court orders.[1344]

[1332]Rule 11(c)(2), Fed.R.Civ.P.; *see* Bout v. Bolden, 22 F. Supp. 2d 653, 658–59 (E.D.Mich. 1998) (where plaintiff submitted a forged document, striking the relevant claim and requiring plaintiff to pay expenses of the handwriting expert who exposed falsification).

[1333]Rule 37(b), Fed.R.Civ.P.; *see* § K.2.h of this chapter concerning discovery sanctions. Rule 11 does not apply to discovery issues. Rule 11(d), Fed.R.Civ.P.

[1334]Rule 16(f), Fed.R.Civ.P.

[1335]28 U.S.C. § 1927; *see* Gomez v. Vernon, 255 F.3d 1118, 1134–35 (9th Cir. 2001) (granting § 1927 sanctions); Avent v. Solfaro, 223 F.R.D. 184, 188 (S.D.N.Y. 2004) (denying § 1927 sanctions).

[1336]Rule 38, Fed.R.App.P.

[1337]Montgomery v. Davis, 362 F.3d 956, 957 (7th Cir. 2003) (per curiam); Gomez v. Vernon, 255 F.3d 1118, 1133–34 (9th Cir. 2001).

[1338]Pope v. Federal Exp. Corp., 974 F.2d 982, 984 (8th Cir.1992); Combs v. Rockwell Int'l Corp., 927 F.2d 486, 488 (9th Cir. 1991); Campos v. Correction Officer Smith, 418 F. Supp. 2d 277, 279 (W.D.N.Y. 2006).

[1339]Nelson v. Eaves, 140 F. Supp. 2d 319, 322–23 (S.D.N.Y. 2001) (dismissing claim of plaintiff who sent sexually graphic and threatening letters to the Assistant Attorney General); Gantt v. Maryland Division of Correction, 894 F. Supp. 226, 229–30 (D.Md. 1995) (dismissing all pending cases of plaintiff who disobeyed order to stop filing documents containing threats, obscenities, or excrement), *aff'd*, 73 F.3d 357 (4th Cir. 1996) (unpublished).

[1340]Gist v. Lugo, 165 F.R.D. 474, 477–78 (E.D.Tex. 1996) (case dismissed where plaintiff ignored at least six court orders, did not comply with local rules regarding participating in drafting of a joint final order and disclosing information, and failed to serve papers on the defendants).

[1341]Long v. Steepro, 213 F.3d 983, 986–88 (7th Cir. 2000) (dismissal of *pro se* prisoner's case for missing the deadline for filing his list of witnesses, exhibits, and contentions was excessive where he had missed no prior deadlines and had believed that proceedings were stayed); Lucas v. Miles, 84 F.3d 532, 535 (2d Cir. 1996) (Dismissal for violating an order should be reserved for "extreme" circumstances. Court should consider "(1) the duration of the plaintiff's failure to comply with the court order, (2) whether plaintiff was on notice that failure to comply would result in dismissal, (3) whether the defendants are likely to be prejudiced by

further delay in the proceedings, (4) a balancing of the court's interest in managing its docket with the plaintiff's interest in receiving a fair chance to be heard, and (5) whether the judge has adequately considered a sanction less drastic than dismissal."); Mendez v. Walker, 110 F. Supp. 2d 209, 216–17 (W.D.N.Y. 2000) (refusing to dismiss for failure to follow an order to submit documents to the court in English; plaintiff was given no warning that his case might be dismissed).

[1342]Montgomery v. Davis, 362 F.3d 956, 957–58 (7th Cir. 2003) (prisoners fined $500 each under inherent powers for filing civil rights actions in the guise of habeas petitions to avoid prior restrictions on civil filings); Vestal v. Clinton, 106 F.3d 553, 555 (4th Cir. 1997) (prisoner fined $500 under Rule 38, Fed.R.App.P., for completely frivolous claim); Carman v. Treat, 7 F.3d 1379, 1381 (8th Cir. 1993) (affirming Rule 11 dismissal of inmate's civil rights action with prejudice for filing of motion with no factual support); Joiner v. Delo, 905 F.2d 206, 208 (8th Cir. 1990) (all claims dismissed because the plaintiff misrepresented facts to the court); American Inmate Paralegal Association v. Cline, 859 F.2d 59 (8th Cir. 1988) (dismissal imposed as a sanction for disobeying a court order); Knoll v. Webster, 838 F.2d 450, 451 (10th Cir. 1988) ($10 sanction imposed for repetitive suit against an immune defendant); Lay v. Anderson, 837 F.2d 231, 233 (5th Cir. 1988) (litigant sanctioned for failing to exhaust prison grievance procedure after being directed to do so); Gabel v. Lynaugh, 835 F.2d 124, 125 (5th Cir. 1988) (sanctions imposed for frivolous appeal); Lyons v. Sheets, 834 F.2d 493, 496 (5th Cir. 1987) (monetary sanctions imposed, district court directed to accept no more suits on the same subject until they are paid); Robinson v. Moses, 644 F. Supp. 975, 982–83 (N.D.Ind. 1986) (sanctions of $3600 imposed). *But see* Thomas v. Evans, 880 F.2d 1235, 1240 (11th Cir. 1989) (*pro se* status should be taken into account in determining whether a filing was reasonable).

[1343]*See* Olson v. Coleman, 997 F.2d 726, 729 n.3 (10th Cir. 1993); Freeze v. Griffith, 849 F.2d 172, 176 (5th Cir. 1988); Lay v. Anderson, 837 F.2d at 233 n.1 (prison officials ordered to withdraw funds from prisoner's account until costs are paid); Whittington v. Lynaugh, 842 F.2d 818, 820–21 (5th Cir. 1988); Simmons v. Poppell, 837 F.2d 1243, 1244 (5th Cir. 1988) (costs awarded against *pro se* litigant, to be withdrawn in amounts not to deplete his account below $10.00); Summers v. Salt Lake County, 713 F. Supp. 1415 (D.Utah 1989) (*all* prisoner's money to be taken until costs are paid).

[1344]White v. General Motors Corp., 908 F.2d 675, 680 (10th Cir. 1990) (in order to avoid Rule 11 sanctions, a *pro se* party's actions must be objectively reasonable).

Rule 11 sanctions cannot be imposed without providing some measure of due process protections. These include, at a minimum, notice (either from the court or the adverse party) and an opportunity to respond.[1345] In the case of a *pro se* prisoner, due process may require an opportunity for discovery, specific notice of the sanction that is proposed, and more time to respond than a litigant with a lawyer might receive.[1346]

Rule 11 provides that if a party moves for sanctions, he is required to serve the motion on the other side and wait 21 days before filing with the court it to give the adverse party a chance to withdraw or correct the paper that violates the rule.[1347] A court that wishes to impose Rule 11 sanctions on its own initiative must enter an order describing the conduct that allegedly violated Rule 11 and directing the party to show cause why it has not violated the rule.[1348]

Sanctions can be imposed against prison officials and their lawyers, and have been in several cases.[1349] Don't get carried away with the idea of getting your adversaries sanctioned.

In our experience, many things that *pro se* litigants consider outrageous are actually within the normal limits of litigation. Also, the time and energy you put into pursuing sanctions is taken away from the main object of winning your lawsuit.

X. Restrictions on *Pro Se* Litigants

In the Prison Litigation Reform Act (PLRA), Congress provided that prisoners who have had three actions or appeals dismissed as frivolous, malicious, or failing to state a claim may not proceed *in forma pauperis* unless they are "under imminent danger of serious physical injury."[1350] This "three strikes" provision is discussed in another chapter.[1351]

Courts have also taken measures on an individual basis against litigants (prisoners and others) who they believe (often correctly) are abusing the judicial system with meritless litigation. Courts clearly have the power to enter injunctions to curb abusive litigants,[1352] appellate courts have set limits to protect the right of access to courts. One court has described such injunctions as "an extreme remedy [that] should be used only in exigent circumstances,"[1353] and only after the litigant has received notice and an opportunity to be heard and the court has made "substantive findings about the frivolous or harassing nature of the plaintiff's litigation."[1354] Courts cannot rely solely on the number of cases someone has filed to justify an injunction, but must consider the nature, motivation, and consequences

---

[1345]Mendoza v. Lynaugh, 989 F.2d 191 (5th Cir. 1993) (district court abused its discretion when it failed to give notice to prisoner that conduct was subject to sanctions pursuant to Rule 11). *See also* Donaldson v. Clark, 819 F.2d 1551, 1559–61 (11th Cir. 1987). When a party files a motion for sanctions, the motion papers should provide adequate notice to the other side, thus giving them a chance to be heard in the form of papers responding to the motion. If the court wishes to impose sanctions *sua sponte* (on its own), the court must itself provide notice and an opportunity to be heard. Securities Industry Ass'n v. Clarke, 898 F.2d 318, 322 (2d Cir. 1990); Tome Growney Equipment, Inc. v. Shelley Irrigation Development, Inc., 834 F.2d 833, 835–36 (9th Cir. 1987). If a court imposes sanctions on you without providing those protections, you should consider an appeal.

[1346]*See* Thomas v. Evans, 880 F.2d 1235, 1243 (11th Cir. 1989).

[1347]Rule 11(c)(1)(A), Fed.R.Civ.P.; *see* Marrie v. Nickels, 70 F. Supp. 2d 1252, 1267 (D.Kan. 1999). This provision is called the "safe harbor" provision.

[1348]Rule 11(c)(1)(B), Fed.R.Civ.P.

[1349]*See* Gomez v. Vernon, 255 F.3d 1118, 1134–35 (9th Cir. 2001) (sanctions imposed for invading prisoners' attorney–client privilege); Hall v. Mackey, 720 F. Supp. 261, 262 (S.D.N.Y. 1989) (prison officials sanctioned for delaying proceedings; fine donated to prison law library); Boone v. Elrod, 706 F. Supp. 636, 638–39 (N.D.Ill. 1989) (sanctions imposed against jail captain's lawyer for baseless motion); Knop v. Johnson, 667 F. Supp. 512, 515–22 (W.D. Mich. 1987) (sanctions imposed for abusive motion practice), *aff'd in pertinent part*, 977 F.2d 996, 1014 (6th Cir. 1992). In other decisions, prison officials' lawyers have been ordered to show cause why they should not be sanctioned for making frivolous arguments and other Rule 11 violations. *See* Carroll v. Yates, 362 F.3d 984, 986 (7th Cir. 2004); Lawson v. Trowbridge, 153 F.3d 368, 372 (7th Cir. 1998); Pope v. Shafer, 86 F.3d 90, 92 (7th Cir. 1996); Salahuddin v. Coughlin, 999 F. Supp. 526, 539–40 (S.D.N.Y. 1998); Riley v. Coutu, 172 F.R.D. 224, 228 (E.D.Mich. 1997); *see also* Fink v. Gomez, 239 F.3d 989, 994 (9th Cir. 2001) (sanctions could be imposed for "an attorney's reckless misstatements of law and fact, when coupled with an improper purpose"); Goka v. Bobbitt, 862 F.2d 646, 650–52 (7th Cir. 1988) (appellate court directs district court to consider sanctions against prison officials' lawyers).

[1350]28 U.S.C. § 1915(g).

[1351]*See* Ch. 9, § B.

[1352]*In re* McDonald, 489 U.S. 180, 184–85, 109 S. Ct. 993 (1989) (*pro se* litigant forbidden to proceed *in forma pauperis* in seeking extraordinary writs from the Supreme Court); *see* Molski v. Evergreen Dynasty Corp., 500 F.3d 1047, 1057 (9th Cir. 2007) (citing 28 U.S.C. § 1651(a), the All Writs Act, as giving courts power to enjoin abusive litigation), *cert. denied*, 129 S. Ct. 594 (2007).

[1353]*In re* Powell, 851 F.2d 427, 431 (D.C. Cir. 1988); *accord*, Molski v. Evergreen Dynasty Corp., 500 F.3d at 1057 ("such pre-filing orders are an extreme remedy that should rarely be used"); Cromer v. Kraft Foods North America, Inc., 390 F.3d 812 (4th Cir. 2004) ("Such a drastic remedy must be used sparingly, however, consistent with constitutional guarantees of due process of law and access to the courts."); DeLong v. Hennessey, 912 F.2d 1144, 1148 (9th Cir. 1990).

[1354]Molski v. Evergreen Dynasty Corp., 500 F.3d at 1057; *accord*, DeLong v. Hennessey, 912 F.2d at 1148; *In re* Powell, 851 F.2d at 434; *see* Lau v. Meddaugh, 229 F.3d 121, 123 (2d Cir. 2000) ("unequivocal rule" is that litigants are entitled to notice and an opportunity to be heard before they are enjoined from litigating, and must receive a written order stating precisely what they are forbidden to do).

of the litigation.[1355] Forbidding a litigant to file lawsuits without an attorney's assistance has been held overbroad.[1356]

Further, injunctions must be "narrowly tailored to fit the specific circumstances at issue."[1357] They are often restricted to particular subject matter as to which the litigant has behaved abusively.[1358] Rather than broadly barring prisoners from filing suit, courts impose less drastic measures such as requiring the litigant to seek leave of court and show the action is not frivolous before filing.[1359] The same is true of restrictions on proceeding *in forma pauperis*.[1360]

[1355]Molski v. Evergreen Dynasty Corp., 500 F.3d at 1057–58, 1061 (citing Safir v. U.S. Lines, Inc., 792 F.2d 19, 24 (2d Cir.1986)); Cromer v. Kraft Foods North America, Inc., 390 F.3d at 818 (Courts must weigh "(1) the party's history of litigation, in particular whether he has filed vexatious, harassing, or duplicative lawsuits; (2) whether the party had a good faith basis for pursuing the litigation, or simply intended to harass; (3) the extent of the burden on the courts and other parties resulting from the party's filings; and (4) the adequacy of alternative sanctions."); In re Powell, 851 F.2d at 434; Abdul-Akbar v. Watson, 901 F.2d 329, 332 (3d Cir. 1990).

[1356]Procup v. Strickland, 792 F.2d 1069, 1071 (11th Cir. 1986); see Kolocotronis v. Morgan, 247 F.3d 726, 728 (8th Cir. 2001) (mental patient could not be forbidden to file suit except through his guardian; he could be required to obtain leave of court before filing further suits); Cauthon v. Rogers, 116 F.3d 1334, 1337 (10th Cir. 1997) (enjoining plaintiff from suing without counsel unless he first obtains court permission to proceed *pro se* by filing a petition with the clerk providing specified information).

[1357]Cromer v. Kraft Foods North America, Inc., 390 F.3d at 818; accord, Brow v. Farrelly, 994 F.2d 1027, 1038 (3d Cir. 1993); DeLong v. Hennessey, 912 F.2d 1144, 1148 (9th Cir. 1990) (order should be narrowly tailored to "the specific vice encountered"); Castro v. U.S., 775 F.2d 399, 410 (1st Cir. 1985) (holding that injunctions "should be narrowly drawn to fit the specific vice encountered" in order to avoid impermissible infringement on the right of access to the courts).

[1358]Cromer v. Kraft Foods North America, Inc., 390 F.3d at 818; O'Loughlin v. Doe, 920 F.2d 614, 618 (9th Cir. 1990); Polur v. Raffe, 912 F.2d 52, 56 (2d Cir. 1990); Safir v. U.S. Lines, Inc., 792 F.2d 19, 24 (2d Cir. 1986); Castro v. U.S., 775 F.2d at 410.

[1359]Iwachiw v. New York State Dep't of Motor Vehicles, 396 F.3d 525, 529 (2d Cir. 2005) (per curiam); In re Chapman, 328 F.3d 903, 905–06 (7th Cir. 20003) (per curiam); Kolocotronis v. Morgan, 247 F.3d 726, 728 (8th Cir. 2001); Ortman v. Thomas, 99 F.3d 807, 811 (6th Cir. 1996) (absolute bar on suit about particular subject is overbroad; litigant can be required to show that a proposed lawsuit is not frivolous or vexatious before filing).

[1360]Abdul-Akbar v. Watson, 901 F.2d 329, 332–33 (3d Cir. 1990) (barring the plaintiff from proceeding IFP in future § 1983 actions was impermissibly broad; plaintiff should be required to seek leave of court for future claims and to certify under penalty of contempt that they are new claims with factual merit and not legally foreclosed); Matter of Davis, 878 F.2d 211, 212–13 (7th Cir. 1989) (filings could be controlled by reviewing them as they are submitted; complete ban on *in forma pauperis* filings could deny right of access to courts); Abdullah v. Gatto, 773 F.2d 487, 488 (2d Cir. 1985) (litigant could not be barred from all IFP filings concerning a particular subject; he could be required to seek leave of court before filing them); Franklin v. Murphy, 745 F.2d 1221,

In light of these decisions, it would seem that the PLRA three strikes provision is unconstitutional, since it imposes filing restrictions based solely on the number of cases dismissed, does not consider the specific circumstances of each prisoner's case, and bars filing *in forma pauperis* entirely (except for the narrow "imminent danger" category of cases) rather than requiring the litigant to seek leave of court or certify that the claims have factual and legal basis before filing. However, that statute has been upheld against constitutional challenge.[1361]

Courts have entered injunctions against the practice of some prisoners of filing liens against the property of prison, court, or law enforcement officials who they believe have not performed their duties properly; this practice is not protected by the First Amendment.[1362]

Y. Attorneys' Fees

Plaintiffs who are "prevailing parties" in civil rights cases against state or local officials are ordinarily entitled by statute to recover attorneys' fees determined by the court and paid by the defendants.[1363] Attorneys' fees are awarded only to plaintiffs who have attorneys; a *pro se* litigant cannot recover attorneys' fees.[1364] The importance of attorneys' fees to a *pro se* litigant is that their availability may help persuade an attorney to take your case. The Prison Litigation Reform Act (PLRA) limits attorneys' fees in cases where fees are authorized by 42 U.S.C. § 1988(b), which include most prisoner civil rights suits against state and local officials.[1365]

1231–32 (9th Cir. 1984) (holding that an order limiting plaintiff to six IFP filings a year must provide opportunity for plaintiff to show a need for additional filings); Carter v. U.S., 733 F.2d 735 (10th Cir. 1984) (holding that total preclusion from IFP status "unduly impairs appellant's constitutional right of access to the courts"); In re Green, 669 F.2d 779, 786 (D.C. Cir. 1981) (same as Carter).

[1361]See Ch. 9, § B.3, for further discussion of this issue and other reasons we believe the statute is unconstitutional.

[1362]U.S. v. Barker, 19 F. Supp. 2d 1380, 1384–85 (S.D.Ga. 1998); accord, U.S. v. Martin, 356 F. Supp. 2d 621, 627–28 (W.D.Va. 2005); see Monroe v. Beard, 536 F.3d 198, 207–09 & n.11 (3d Cir. 2008) (upholding prison rule barring legal materials related to filing of fraudulent liens, noting that prisoners have been criminally prosecuted and convicted for this conduct).

[1363]42 U.S.C. § 1988(b).

[1364]Kay v. Ehrler, 499 U.S. 432, 435–36 and n.6, 111 S. Ct. 1435 (1991) and cases cited. *Pro se* litigants have, however, been awarded some litigation expenses under this statute. *See* cases cited in § V of this chapter.

[1365]42 U.S.C. § 1997e(d)(1). Fees are authorized by § 1988(b) in cases brought under 42 U.S.C. 1983 (the basic civil rights statute applicable to state and local officials under which most prisoner suits are brought); 42 U.S.C.A. § 2000bb *et seq.* (the Religious Freedom Restoration Act of 1993); and 42 U.S.C.A. § 2000cc *et seq.* (the Religious Land Use and Institutionalized Persons Act of 2000). These are the statutes that prisoners most often use. In addition, § 1988(b) is the basis of fee awards in cases under 42 U.S.C. §§ 1981, 1981a, 1982, 1983, 1985, and 1986; 20 U.S.C.A. § 1681 *et seq.* (sex discrimination); and 42 U.S.C.A. § 2000d *et seq.* (title VI of the

The major exception are the Americans with Disabilities Act (ADA) and the Rehabilitation Act, which have their own fee provision; fees are awarded at market rates in prisoner disability cases.[1366] Attorneys' fees can also be awarded *against* civil rights plaintiffs, but only for actions found to be frivolous, unreasonable, or without foundation—not just because the defendants prevailed.[1367]

Plaintiffs who prevail in civil actions other than tort actions against the United States, or against federal officials sued in their official capacities, may recover fees under the Equal Access to Justice Act (EAJA) unless the government's position was "substantially justified" or "special circumstances make an award unjust."[1368] The PLRA limits do not apply to EAJA fees, which are subject to their own set of statutory limits. Fees may not generally be awarded against federal officials sued in their individual capacities.[1369]

Plaintiffs may be "prevailing parties" entitled to fees if they partially prevail in the case.[1370] They are entitled to fees if they get the relief they seek through a settlement but are not entitled to fees for relief obtained through voluntary action by the defendants rather than an actual court decision.[1371]

Civil Rights Act of 1964). These statutes are rarely used by prisoners. The PLRA restrictions on fees are discussed in Ch. 9, § F.

[1366]Armstrong v. Davis, 318 F.3d 965, 973–74 (9th Cir. 2003); Beckford v. Irvin, 60 F. Supp. 2d 85 (W.D.N.Y. 1999). These disability statutes are discussed in Ch. 2, § F.4.h.2.

[1367]Hughes v. Rowe, 449 U.S. 5, 14–15, 101 S. Ct. 173 (1980) ("These limitations apply with special force in actions initiated by uncounseled prisoners."); *accord*, Houston v. Norton, 215 F.3d 1172, 1174–75 (10th Cir. 2000) (lower court must explain justification for awarding fees against prisoner plaintiff); Legal Servs. v. Arnett, 114 F.3d 135, 141 (9th Cir. 1997) ("A prevailing defendant may receive an award of attorney's fees under §§ 1988 'only where the action is found to be unreasonable, frivolous, meritless or vexatious.'" (internal quotation marks omitted)).

[1368]28 U.S.C. § 1412(d)(1)(A) (Equal Access to Justice Act).

[1369]Kreines v. U.S., 33 F.3d 1105, 1107–09 (9th Cir. 1994).

[1370]Texas State Teachers Assn. v. Garland Independent School District, 489 U.S. 782, 790–91, 109 S. Ct. 1486 (1989).

[1371]Buckhannon Board and Care Home, Inc. v. West Virginia Department of Health and Human Resources, 532 U.S. 598, 600, 121 S. Ct. 1835 (2001) (prevailing party does not include a party that has failed to secure a judgment on the merits or a court-ordered consent decree, but has nonetheless achieved the desired result because the lawsuit brought about a voluntary change in the defendant's conduct). *See also* Torres v. Walker, 356 F.3d 238, 243 (2d Cir. 2004) (under PLRA, money judgment must be entered if fees are to be awarded; however, if settlement is reached that references non-application of PLRA's fees provision it is binding on the parties).

CHAPTER 11

Legal Research

If you are reading this Manual, it will probably be the starting point for your legal research on most questions, since we have tried to assemble as much useful information as practical on most of the questions that are likely to come up in civil litigation about your treatment in prison. However, this Manual will start to get out of date immediately as new cases are decided and new statutes are enacted and old ones amended, and anyway we probably missed something. Also it is impossible for us to cite every case in every federal or state jurisdiction. So you may find useful authority on a subject here, but still need to know if your federal circuit or district court, or your state courts, take the same approach as that authority. You will need to supplement what we have done with your own legal research in order to assess whether a case can be successful, and then to have a chance of succeeding.

This chapter explains the basics of doing legal research. We can't discuss every aspect of these legal research methods in this Manual.[1] But the information in this chapter sets

forth the basic skills you need to do legal research in a prison law library.[2] This is not a complete review of legal research in prisons and jails, because some institutions have done away with law libraries and have made other arrangements for legal access. Others provide some degree of computerized legal research assistance. These points are discussed at the end of the chapter.

and writing. *See* Christopher G. Wren, *The Legal Research Manual: A Game Plan for Legal Research and Analysis* (Legal Education Pub. ed., 1996) (out of print; often available through Amazon, Abebooks, or other second-hand booksellers); Robert Berring & Elizabeth Edinger, *Legal Research Survival Manual* (West Group Publishing ed., 2002) (paperback, $31); Amy E. Sloan, *Basic Legal Research: Tools and Strategies* (Aspen Pub., 4th ed. 2009) (paperback, $72); Morris L. Cohen & Kent Olson, *Legal Research in a Nutshell* (Thomsen West, 9th ed. 2007) (paperback, $33). The prices are current as of mid-2009, but may change. You may also be able to find these books cheaper at Amazon or other discount sellers if prison rules allow.

[2]The law concerning prison law libraries and access to these libraries are discussed in Ch. 3, § C.

---

[1]There are a number of other good books at various price levels that deal more in depth with legal research, problem-solving,

A. MARSHALLING THE FACTS

Legal research is ultimately based on *facts*, because the facts determine what legal questions you must research. To do meaningful legal research, you must have a clear understanding of the facts to which the law will be applied. We suggest that you meticulously write down all the facts that relate to your problem in a narrative (story) form, telling *what* happened,[3] *to whom* it happened, *when* and *where* it happened, *how* it happened, and *why* it happened. This statement of facts will assist you in organizing your thoughts and your research. You can also use it later when you write your complaint, motion, or brief. The following is an example of "marshalling the facts":

1. On November 16, 2007, I arrived at Jackson Prison and was then assigned to 4-block, a general population block.
2. After I was placed in cell 52-3-4, I went to the yard and saw Lt. Peters and walked up to him since I knew him from the last time I was at Jackson Prison. I informed Lt. Peters that when I was at Jackson Prison about 6 months ago I was stabbed while confined in 4-block.
3. I told Lt. Peters that I was stabbed in 4-block about 6 months ago and after spending time in the hospital for the stab wounds I was placed in protective custody and then transferred from Jackson Prison. I asked Lt. Peters to read a copy of my Notice of Intent where I was classified to protective custody as a result of that stabbing, which I tried to hand him.
4. Lt. Peters stated that "you like suing our officers and winning don't you." I told Lt. Peters that since being transferred back to Jackson Prison and placed in 4-block I have received numerous threats stating "they won't miss this time."
5. I offered Lt. Peters to read a couple of the kites that had been placed in my cell since my return to Jackson which threatened my life. Instead of looking at any of these documents Lt. Peters said I should have thought about needing prison staff help some day to protect me before filing lawsuits. Lt. Peters went on to state that "you made your own bed, now lie in it." Lt. Peters walked away from me at that time.
6. After Lt. Peters left me I walked back to 4-block, prepared a grievance against him, placed the grievance in the cell block mailbox, and went to evening chow. After chow, as I entered the door of 4-block a blanket was thrown over my head and I was assaulted with prison-made knives and hard objects. After what seems a long-time I heard an inmate yell "screw coming." The beating and stabbing stopped and I heard people running away from where I was. When the guard found me I was on the floor and bleeding. I had trouble breathing.
7. I was given some treatment by prison medical staff and was then transferred to an outside hospital. I was taken to the emergency room there and operated on. I was told by the doctor after the operation that I was lucky to be alive since a knife had nicked my heart. The doctor also told me that my skull had been caved in and I had started to develop swelling on the brain. The doctor told me he had placed a stent in my head to allow the draining of any fluids.
8. I was returned to the prison from the outside hospital on November 30, 2007 and this is when I found the first-step grievance against Lt. Peters had been denied on November 21st. On December 1, 2007, a Saturday, I filed a second-step grievance against Lt. Peters. In this second-step I explained why the grievance was being filed untimely, *i.e.*, I had just been returned from the hospital and no one had taken this first-step grievance denial to me at the hospital. I filed the second and third steps of the grievance process as to Lt. Peters but these were denied.
9. When I left the outside hospital I was given a copy of the medical order from the doctor that I was to return on December 27, 2007, so they could determine whether to take the stent out of my head. The medical order also stated that I was to receive physical therapy.
10. On or about December 16, 2007, I sent a medical kite to the nurse asking whether I would be returned to the outside hospital on December 27 and asked her why I had not been scheduled for physical therapy. I attached a copy of the medical order to the medical kite.
11. On December 28, 2007, I received a response from Nurse Foresman stating that she had reviewed my records and had determined that I did not need to return to see the outside doctor and that she had determined that if I just walked around the exercise track each day, I would not need physical therapy.
12. Nurse Foresman did not conduct an examination of me or refer me to a doctor before I was informed that I would not see the outside doctor or receive physical therapy. I exhausted the grievance process against Nurse Foresman without obtaining any relief. The head of Prison Medical Providers denied any relief from the medical decisions made by Nurse Foresman.
13. After I filed my grievance against Nurse Foresman, I stopped receiving my pain medication.

---

[3] Just stating that someone violated your rights, or violated a specific right such as the right to medical care, is not "meticulously writing down the facts." It is what courts call a "conclusory statement," and it will not help you much in marshalling your facts.

I suffered headaches throughout the day. The pain becomes so unbearable that I usually cannot stand. The area where my skull was shattered is where I feel the most severe pain. When I have severe pain I lose my vision and when the pain lessens it can take up to an hour before I can see again. The area around my heart constantly is painful. At times it feels as if I am having a heart attack. When I write Nurse Foresman and explain to her the pain I am feeling I receive a response telling me to buy aspirin at the prison store.

14. Finally, in July of 2008, I was sent to see the outside doctor for the pain in my head. This doctor could not believe that the stent had remained in my head for an extra seven months and I was still alive. I was taken to the emergency room by this doctor and the stent was removed from my head the same day I saw him.

15. It is now six months later and I am still having severe headaches, not all day, but at least a few hours a day. When I have severe headaches I will lose my vision. The outside doctor has ordered that I receive physical therapy but Defendants Nurse Foresman and Prison Medical Providers have refused to provide physical therapy.

Next, list any prison rule or regulation that you think pertains to your possible lawsuit. For example:

1. Prison Rule # 719.03, paragraph 5, states an inmate will be placed in protective segregation when a threat to his safety or well-being exists.

2. Prison Rule # 719.03, paragraph 5, states that an inmate should not be confined in the same institution with his known enemies, and an inmate who has been seriously injured by unknown persons should not be placed in the same institution where he was injured.

3. Administrative Rule 05.03(C) states an inmate is entitled to humane treatment.

4. Prison Rule # 503.01, paragraph 3, states that when good reason is shown by an inmate for not timely filing a grievance or an appeal of a response, the grievance should be processed as if timely filed. See also Mich. Compiled Laws XXXX.00.

5. Prison Rule 600.13, paragraph 17, states medical decisions are to be made by appropriate medical staff.

6. Administrative Rule 05.03(C) states that prison staff is not to retaliate against an inmate for filing grievances or lawsuits.

Once you have marshaled the facts and possible violations of rules, you will then form legal questions based on these facts and alleged rule violations to guide you in your research. These "legal questions" are just short statements asking what your rights might be. The following are some examples of questions you might want to answer before deciding whether or not to file a lawsuit:

1. Am I excused from complying with the time limits for filing a grievance appeal when I was not available due to my being confined in an outside hospital?[4]

2. When prison officials know that I am at a local hospital are they required to send the grievance response to the hospital so that I can appeal it on time?

3. Can a nurse decide not to return me to an outside hospital when the outside treating physician ordered a follow-up visit?

4. Can a nurse decide not to provide physical therapy when the outside treating physician ordered it?

5. Can I sue a private medical provider in federal court?

6. What is the standard of liability for a private medical provider in federal court?

7. What is the standard of liability for a nurse working for a private medical provider who is sued in federal court?

8. Am I required to name both the nurse and the private medical provider in the lawsuit?

9. Can I receive both compensatory and punitive damages from the private medical provider and/or the nurse that works for them?

10. Can the Lieutenant ignore my request for protective segregation after I have informed her about a previous stabbing of me at Jackson Prison?

11. Is the Lieutenant required to read the documents showing a threat on my life?

12. Is the Lieutenant required to check my prison file to determine whether I had previously been stabbed at Jackson Prison?

13. Can the Lieutenant ignore my request for protective segregation after I informed him and provided evidence that since being confined in 52-3-4 I received threats on my life?

14. What legal standard must I meet under the federal constitution to establish liability against the Lieutenant?

15. What legal standard must I meet under state law for failure to protect me from an assault to establish liability against the Lieutenant?

16. Can I recover more than nominal damages as a result of the nurse denying me to see the outside doctor again and for denying me physical therapy?

---

[4]Exhaustion of administrative remedies is discussed in Ch. 9, § D.

Once you have formulated your legal questions, you will need to do the legal research to determine what the answers are. Once you have done some research, you may be able to restate the questions in a more precise fashion, using the terms and ideas you have learned through your research. The following are some restated questions:

1. Can prison officials refuse to process a second step grievance filed late when I was not responsible for the late filing since at that time I was under a doctor's care at the outside prison?[5]

2. Can a nurse working for the prison private medical provider overrule an order of the outside treating doctor for physical therapy?[6]

3. Can a cause of action for failure to protect from a known risk of harm be established by showing that the Defendant was negligent?[7]

4. Is a known risk of harm established as to the Lieutenant when the prison file shows that I had been stabbed twice previously in 4-block and I have received threats since being recently confined there and I informed the Lieutenant of this information?[8]

5. Does the Lieutenant have a duty to investigate my claim that I had previously been stabbed in 4-block and am now receiving threats on my life?[9]

6. Will the Prison Litigation Reform Act limit my recovery from the nurse to nominal damages since I have not suffered a physical injury as a result of being denied to see the outside doctor and being provided prescribed physical therapy?[10]

7. Will the Prison Litigation Reform Act limit my recovery from the private medical provider to nominal damages since I have not suffered a physical injury as a result of being denied to see the outside doctor and being provided physical therapy?[11]

When framing the legal questions, you must keep in mind what you will need to prove at trial in establishing (1) that the facts you allege are true, (2) that your rights were violated, and (3) that you suffered injuries for which damages may be awarded. You should only include in your legal questions those facts you have support for, or are sure you can obtain support for during discovery.[12]

B. READING CASES

There is no magic to legal research; it is mostly just hard work and thinking. You must first learn how to find a case and, once you find it, learn how to use the research aids included in reporters to analyze it. These aids will also assist you in finding additional cases "on point," and in analyzing and evaluating them quickly.

1. "Reports" and "Reporters"

Most important court decisions are published in a court "report" or "reporter."[13] A report is the official publication of the court, while a reporter is the unofficial publication of the same cases by a private publishing company. West Publishing Company (now part of Thomson Reuters) publishes the unofficial reporters, which contain all of the decisions of the federal and state courts that will be published in the official reports. Some states, like Colorado and Delaware, no longer have an official reporter, so the West reporter is the only set of books where you can find their cases. Your prison law library should have West's reporters containing federal cases and should have either the state's official reports or the national reporter for the region in which your state is located (*e.g.*, the North Western Reporter for Michigan). Many states have their own West reporters, such as the New York Supplement, the Minnesota Reporter, and the California Reporter.

United States Supreme Court cases are published in three different sets of books. The official publication is the United States Reports, which is abbreviated as "U.S." West publishes Supreme Court decisions in the Supreme Court Reporter, abbreviated "S.Ct." The Lawyers' Cooperative Publishing Company publishes the United States Supreme Court Reports, Lawyers' Edition, abbreviated "L.Ed." and "L.Ed.2d." This reporter contains a summary of briefs of counsel and annotations on significant legal issues in reported cases, as well as the Supreme Court opinions themselves. The pages of both the Supreme Court Reporter and the Lawyers' Edition are marked to indicate the corresponding pages in the United States Reports. This permits you to

---

[5]*See* Ch. 9, §§ D.3, D.6, for a discussion of the grievance process.

[6]*See* Ch. 2, §§ F.1 (suing the right defendants), 3.d (access to outside medical care).

[7]*See* Ch. 2, § G.1.f, for a discussion of a state tort claims for inmate assault.

[8]*See* Ch. 2, § G.1, for a discussion of the standard for protection from an inmate assault.

[9]*See* Ch. 2, §§ G.1.b (risk to a particular prisoner), 1.e (causation and suing the right defendants).

[10]*See* Ch. 9, § E, for a discussion of limitations on recovery of damages pursuant to the PLRA.

[11]*Id.*

---

[12]For a discussion of medical care, *see* Ch. 2, § F.

[13]Courts generally do not publish decisions that they regard as routine or of minor importance. If you know that there is an unpublished decision that is important to your case, you may be able to obtain it from the court clerk, but you will probably have to pay copying costs.

Many procedural issues are decided orally or by orders that are not accompanied by written opinions. Orders and oral decisions are almost never published. Jury verdicts are not published either, although sometimes judges' decisions on motions challenging the validity of jury verdicts are published.

give the U.S. Reports page citation even if your prison law library does not have the U.S. Reports, as is often the case.

The following is a list of reports and reporters containing decisions of the federal and state courts. Even though most states have their own reports, the reporters listed below are probably what will be available to you.

Federal Reports and Reporters of the National Reporter System

Full Name of Publication	Official Abbreviation	Type of Cases Reported
United States Reports	U.S.	U.S. Supreme Court
Supreme Court Reporter	S.Ct.	U.S. Supreme Court
U.S. Supreme Court Reports, Lawyers' Edition	L.Ed./L.Ed.2d	U.S. Supreme Court
Federal Reporter, Second and Third Series	F.2d, F.3d	Federal Courts of Appeals
Federal Appendix	Fed.Appx	Federal Courts of Appeals, "unpublished" (non-precedential) decisions[14]
Federal Supplement and Federal Supplement, Second Series	F.Supp./F.Supp.2d	Federal District Courts
Federal Rules Decisions	F.R.D	Federal District Courts

Regional Reporters Of The National Reporter System

Full Name of Publication	Official Abbreviation	Type of Cases Reported
Atlantic Reporter	A.2d	Reports cases from Pa., Md., N.J., Ct., Vt., R.I., N.H., Me., Del., and D.C.
North Eastern Reporter	N.E.2d	Reports cases from Ill., Ind., Mass., N.Y., and Ohio
North Western Reporter	N.W.2d	Reports cases from Iowa, Mich., Minn., Neb., N.D., S.D., and Wis.
Pacific Reporter	P.2d	Reports cases from Alaska, Ariz., Cal., Colo., Hawaii, Idaho, Kan., Mont., Nev., N.M., Okla., Ore., Utah, Wash., and Wyo.

Full Name of Publication	Official Abbreviation	Type of Cases Reported
South Eastern Reporter	S.E.2d	Reports cases from Ga., N.C., S.C., Va., and W.Va.
Southern Reporter	So.2d	Reports cases from Ala., Fla., La., and Miss.
South Western Reporter	S.W.2d	Reports cases from Ark., Ky., Mo., Tenn., and Tex.

The "2d" behind the citation of a reporter means it is the second series of that reporter. Some reporters have a third series ("3d"). These later series contain more recently decided cases.

2. Citations

Each reported decision has its own individual "citation," which tells you in abbreviated form where to find the case, what court decided it and what happened to it. For example, the citation *Austin v. Wilkinson*, 189 F. Supp. 2d 719 (N.D.Ohio 2002), *order modified*, 204 F. Supp. 2d 1024 (N.D.Ohio 2002), *aff'd in part, rev'd in part, and remanded*, 372 F.3d 346 (6th Cir. 2004), *aff'd in part, rev'd in part*, 543 U.S. 1032, 125 S. Ct. 686 (2005), tells you that the plaintiff (the person suing) is named Austin[15] and the defendant (the person being sued) is named Wilkinson. The number "189" in the citation is the volume in which the case will be found. The "F. Supp. 2d" tells you that the case is reported in the Federal Supplement, Second Series. The "719" indicates that the case begins on page 719 of volume 485. The "(N.D.Ohio 2002)" informs you that the case was decided in 2002 by the United States District Court for the Northern District of the State of Ohio.[16] You next see "*order modified*, 240 F. Supp. 2d 1024," which tells you that the district court took action, now reported in volume 240 of the Federal Supplement, Second Series, to modify its original order issued in 189 F. Supp.2d 719, and you should read that second decision to see how the original order was modified. Next is "*aff'd in part, rev'd in part and remanded*, 372 F.3d 346 (6th Cir. 2004)," which tells you that in 2004 the lower court decision was affirmed in part and reversed in part by the United States Court of Appeals for the Sixth Circuit and that the case was remanded (sent back) to the trial court for further consideration; the appeals court decision is reported in volume 372 of the Federal Reporter, Third Series (F.3d)

---

[14]Formerly, federal appellate decisions that were not designated for publication by the court generally could not be cited under the local rules of the federal circuits. An amendment to the Federal Rules of Appellate Procedure provides that courts may not prohibit or restrict the citation of such opinions. Rule 32.1, Fed.R.App.P. However, a decision that the court designated as non-precedential remains non-precedential, so citing it is of limited value to your argument, though its reasoning may be persuasive to the court.

[15]Even though this case is a class action and has hundreds of actual class members, the first name on the complaint is the name that will be given to the case in the short caption and the name the case will be listed in the court reporters.

[16]Many states are divided into two or more federal judicial district (*e.g.*, Ohio is divided into Northern and Southern Districts). When citing a case from a state which has two or more district courts, indicate which district the court is located in (*e.g.* "(N.D.Ohio 2002)").

starting on page 346. Next is "*aff'd in part, rev'd in part*, 543 U.S. 1032, 125 S. Ct. 686 (2005)," which tells you that the United States Supreme Court heard and decided the case in 2005 by affirming in part and reversing in part the decision of the Sixth Circuit. This decision is reported in volume 543 of the United States Reports (U.S.) on page 1032.[17]

The proper citation format can be obtained from *The Bluebook: A Uniform System of Citation* (18th ed. 2005). This book should be in your prison's law library.[18] You can also look at the citations in the footnotes in this Manual (and especially in the sample papers in Appendix C) to see how cases are to be cited in briefs. Do not worry too much about getting the citation form exactly right. Just be sure you have the case name, where the case is published, the year it was decided, the court that decided it, and information on any later decisions or actions in the case by the higher courts.

Prison law libraries are likely to have the unofficial reporters published by West. You may also wish to cite to the official report, since that may be what the court has, and you want to make it easy for an overworked judge to find a case that is helpful to you. Or you may have the official citation and need the West citation so you can find the case in the prison library. These different citations to the same case are called "parallel citations,"[19] and there are four ways to find them. Most of the time, the official cite is printed in the West reporter right above the case name. You can also use *Shepard's Citations*.[20] A third way is to look in the "Table of Cases" volume of the Federal Practice Digest or the digest from the region from which your case is reported.[21] Finally, if your law library has it, you can use the National Reporter Bluebook to find the unofficial citation when you have the official citation. Parallel citations can also be found in electronic databases such as Westlaw and Lexis if you have access to them.

Statutes and regulations have citations too. They usually consist of a number designating the chapter or "title" that the statute or regulation appears in, the name or abbreviation of the code or statutory compilation, and the specific section number of the law. For example, the most frequently used civil rights statute is cited as 42 U.S.C. § 1983. This refers to section 1983 of Title 42 of the United States Code; this title is called "Public Health and Welfare."

A few citations in this Manual have blanks in them, for example, ___ F.3d ___. That means the case was so new when we finished this Manual that it had not yet appeared in the reporters. We generally report a Westlaw citation

(one that looks like 2009 WL 12345) for those cases because that is all that was available at the time. You should use the Table of Cases volumes of the digests to get the citations for these cases.

3. Research Aids from a Case

In the West reporters, after the names of the parties and the date of the decision, there is an unofficial summary of the case, called a "synopsis," written by an employee of the publishing company. The synopsis is not part of the decision and you should not quote it to the court. It will give you a quick idea of what the case is about, but synopses are often seriously incomplete, and sometimes get things wrong.

After the synopsis are short paragraphs called "headnotes," with numbers, a word or short phrase, and a key followed by a number. Each headnote paragraph corresponds to a section in the body of the actual court decision. For example, in *Austin v. Wilkinson*, in volume 189 of the Federal Supplement, Second Series, headnote 5 corresponds to the section in the opinion that begins with [5], which is found on page 742 of the decision. These headnotes also are not part of the decision, and should not be quoted in your briefs.

Headnotes can be very useful in helping you find the part of the opinion that you are most interested in.[22] But they are not always perfectly accurate and they do not always cover all the important points in a case. You cannot rely on a case until you have actually read it through.

Headnote 5 in *Austin v. Wilkinson* has the phrase and key number "Prisons Key Cite Notes 319k13.3." Key numbers are a very important part of the West legal research system because they are designed to help you find other cases, which deal with similar issues. The digest topic and key number "Prisons Key Cite Notes 319k13.3" is used in all the West digests[23] and all the West reporters. You can look in the Federal Practice Digest or the General Digest and find other cases that have been reported which deal with the same legal issue or subject matter. This is not quite as good as it sounds, since the West indexing is not always consistent or complete.[24] You may have to use several key numbers to research a particular subject, and you still may not find everything that is relevant.

At the end of a headnote there may be a citation to a section of federal or state constitution (such as U.S.C.A. Const. Amend. 14), or to a statute (such as 42 U.S.C.A.

---

[17]This citation also shows that the decision is reported in volume 125 of the Supreme Court Reporter (S. Ct.) on page 686.

[18]It is published by the Harvard Law Review Association, Gannett House, 1511 Massachusetts Ave., Cambridge, Mass. 02138. The current price is $25.00.

[19]Remember that the federal courts and some states do not have official reports and rely exclusively on West reporters. Cases from these jurisdictions do not have parallel citations.

[20]Shepardizing is discussed in § C.4 of this chapter.

[21]Digests are discussed in § C.2 of this chapter.

---

[22]The headnote numbers can also be used in Shepardizing, discussed in § C.4 of this chapter.

[23]West publishes the Federal Practice Digest (federal cases only), the General Digest (cases from all states and the federal courts), digests for some of the regional reporters, and digests for most of the individual states.

[24]For example, *see* Wood v. Sunn, 852 F.3d 1205 (9th Cir.), *superseded*, 865 F.2d 982 (9th Cir. 1988), *vacated*, 880 F.2d 1011 (9th Cir. 1989). The opinion in 865 F.2d is only slightly changed from the earlier one in 852 F.2d, but it has twice as many headnotes.

§ 1983) or a regulation. This means that this part of the opinion has interpreted or construed the statute, regulation, or constitutional provision.

Reports and reporters generally will list the names of the attorneys representing the parties involved. You may wish to contact them to request some of the legal documents filed in a case that is similar to yours. Some attorneys will provide you a free copy; others will charge you for photocopying and postage; others will not respond to your letters at all.[25] (You may also wish to request a lawyer who has handled a case similar to yours to represent you.) You may be able to obtain copies of documents filed in court from the court clerk; however, federal courts will probably charge you at least 50 cents per page, and state courts will probably have similar charges.

4. Reading and Briefing the Case

When you find a case that appears relevant, you should do two things: read the whole case, and *brief* it. Briefing means writing a short analysis and evaluation of the case. Briefing helps you understand what the case means and helps you separate the *holding* (the court's actual ruling on the facts before it) from dictum (statements by the judge about what the law might be on some other set of facts). Briefing also is the most useful way to take notes on your research so you won't have to go back and reread the same cases repeatedly. In briefing the case, you will be looking for those *questions of law* the court had to resolve to render a decision, and the holdings the court had to make to render a decision.

In some cases, you may only brief part of the case. For example, if the case involves claims of excessive force, denial of medical care, and denial of due process in a disciplinary proceeding, you may be interested only in the due process discussion. But you should first read through the whole case to be sure of what is in it.

The following method of briefing a case is suggested.

a. Facts State in a short paragraph the precise facts in the case you are briefing. For example, from *Wolff v. McDonnell*:[26]

> Nebraska statute provided that a prisoner could lose statutory good time if found guilty of a major disciplinary violation. The procedures required by the state law entitled the prisoner to appear before an Adjustment Committee where the report is read to her and she could ask questions of the writer of the ticket. The Committee could conduct additional investigations if it desired. A finding of guilty would usually result in loss of good time.

b. Judicial History This short paragraph will state the history of the case, which is generally summarized by the court. For example:

> The district court, based on prior decisions of the Circuit, had rejected the prisoners' procedural due process claim after an evidentiary hearing.[27] The Court of Appeals reversed, holding that the procedural requirements outlined recently by the Supreme Court should be followed in prison disciplinary hearings.[28]

c. Issue Usually, there is more than one issue in a decision, and each issue should be stated in a separate short paragraph. For example:

> Whether state prisoners are entitled to procedural protection by the Due Process Clause of the Fourteenth Amendment when charged with disciplinary actions that could result in the loss of statutory good time?
> What procedural protection is an inmate entitled to at a disciplinary hearing?

d. Result/Holding The holding of the court tells you what the court said about the issue. For example:

> Prisoners facing disciplinary charges of major misconduct that could result in loss of statutory good time are entitled to the minimum requirements of procedural due process.

There may be more than one result/holding, and each of these should be listed separately.

e. Reasoning/Rationale You want to state exactly what reasons the court used in the decision to reach each of its holdings. The rationale consists of the rule of law and the facts found by the court in the present case to support its rule of law. For example:

> A state need not create the right to receive statutory good time, which results in shortened prison sentence. But, once it has created a right to good time and its deprivation is a sanction authorized for major misconduct, the prisoner has a state-created "liberty" interest that is entitled to minimum procedural protection to ensure that the state-created right is not arbitrarily abrogated.

f. Subsequent Judicial History You will usually need to "Shepardize"[29] the citation to determine whether the case was appealed to a higher appellate court and whether, after a remand to the lower, court, another judgment has been rendered. The subsequent judicial history is important because an appellate court may reverse or vacate the lower court's judgment or may decide that the lower court's rationale was wrong, or the lower court may reconsider some aspect of its

---

[25]You should not write to a lawyer and ask for all the documents in a case. You are more likely to get a response if you ask for specific items that you actually expect you can use, such as the complaint or any memorandum of law concerning the merits of the legal claim.

[26]418 U.S. 539, 94 S. Ct. 2963 (1974). The facts stated relate only to one issue in the case.

[27]McDonnell v. Wolff, 342 F. Supp. 616 (D.Neb. 1972).

[28]McDonnell v. Wolff, 483 F.2d 1059 (8th Cir. 1973).

[29]Shepardizing is discussed in § C.4 of this chapter.

earlier decision. Either way, it may mean that the original decision is no longer good law. However, a lower court decision that is appealed may be reversed on some issues and affirmed on others. You should be sure you understand how the higher court has dealt with the particular issue you are concerned with.

Briefing cases is time-consuming and requires meticulous attention to detail. We think it is worth it, especially for prisoners just learning the law, because it is a way of focusing your attention on all the essential points. If you master the discipline of briefing, the quality of your legal work will probably improve considerably.

C. Methods of Research

In doing legal research, often the hardest part is getting started. Once you find a case or two on the subject you are researching, you can use the key numbers in the case's headnotes to find similar cases, or you can Shepardize the case to find later cases that have cited it. In this section, we list several methods of legal research, beginning with the ones that are easiest for a prisoner who is starting from scratch.

1. Using This Manual and Other Treatises

If someone has written a Manual or treatise on the subject you are interested in, that may be the fastest route to the information you need. In this Manual we have done our best to include discussions of most issues faced by prisoners in civil litigation, with case citations. By using the table of contents and the index of this Manual, you may find what you need easily.

As you have probably seen, the case citations in this Manual are found in the footnotes. Each footnote is intended to provide support for the statement in the text to which the footnote is appended. (In a few cases, there is a statement in the footnote itself that some of the cases are related to.) Some of the footnotes contain a large number of citations and may be confusing. Many of the citations have "introductory signals" before them that indicate why they are there. A citation that has no signal in front of it directly supports the statement it is cited for. "*Accord*" means that the case or cases says the same thing as the case just previously cited. "*See*" means that the case clearly supports the statement it is cited for, but does not directly state it. "*See also*" means that the case supports the statement, but generally less directly (we have used it often in citing cases that support a related proposition or address related subject matter). On the other hand, "*Contra*" means that the case is directly to the contrary of cases previously cited in the footnote. "*But see*" means that the case is clearly contrary to previously cited cases but may not be as explicit about it as a "*contra*" case. "*Compare* [case] *with* [case]" means that looking at both cases will illustrate the point that is being discussed. "*Cf.*" and "*But cf.*" refer to cases that have something to do with the subject under discussion; there is usually a phrase in parentheses after them that explains what the point is. "*E.g.*" after a signal (like "*see, e.g.*") means "for example,"

indicating that there are a lot of cases that could be cited and we have just picked one or a few.[30]

There are many other books on legal subjects written by law professors, practicing attorneys, and others. For example, there are many treatises on civil procedure and practice in the federal courts. The best of them are Moore's *Federal Practice* and Wright and Miller's *Federal Practice and Procedure*, each of which have multiple volumes; there are other, shorter books as well. There are two major legal encyclopedias that cover most areas of the law: *American Jurisprudence* and *Corpus Juris Secundum*. A prison law library is unlikely to have the whole set, but they may have selected volumes. The *American Law Reports* (A.L.R.) is a series that contains selected cases decided by state and federal courts with an extensive commentary and annotations for each. A.L.R. is now in its sixth series; there is also a separate A.L.R. Federal focusing on federal law issues. The A.L.R. sets contain articles on a number of prison-related issues. Many states have treatises, or even encyclopedias, on the law of their states—for example, *New York Jurisprudence*. A leading treatise on tort law is often known as "Prosser and Keeton on Torts."[31]

If books like these are available to you in the prison law library or through some other means it is always worthwhile starting with them when you research a legal issue. They will generally lead you to the most important cases on a subject, and they may also explain the issue and make it easier for you to understand the cases when you read them.

2. Using the Digests

The most useful research tools in the West reporter system are the digests. These are multi-volume sets of books that collect all the headnotes from the cases in the West reporters and organize them according to subject matter, so all the Federal Civil Procedure headnotes are together, all the Civil Rights headnotes are together, etc. There are several sets of digests. For the federal courts, there is the *Federal Practice Digest*; the third series of these digest covers 1975–1985 and the fourth series covers everything after that. For all courts, there is the *General Digest*; volumes of this digest are issued monthly, and periodically they are collected into the *Decennial Digest*. The most recent *Decennial Digest* (the Eleventh Series) covers 2001–2004; the previous one covers 1996–2001. Some states also have their own separate West digests.[32] The digests consist of hardcover books, which are supplemented with "pocket parts" (paperbound

---

[30]These signals are explained in Harvard Law Review Ass'n, *The Bluebook: A Uniform System of Citation*, Rule 1.2 at 46–47 (18th ed. 2005).

[31]W. Page Keeton, et al., *Prosser and Keeton on the Law of Torts* (West Publishing Co., 5th ed., 1984).

[32]There are some digests that are not put out by West. For example, the United States Supreme Court Reporters, Lawyers' Edition, has its own digest that does not use the West key number system. Annotated statute books also have digest sections, often called "Notes of Decisions," as discussed in § C.5 of this chapter.

supplements that go into the back of the main volume) or separate bound paperback update volumes. These supplements will list more recent cases published after the hardcover volumes were printed.

All the West digests are organized in the same way. There is a list of subject headings that starts with Abandoned and Lost Property and ends with Zoning and Planning. (A prison law library may only have selected volumes and not the whole set.) Each subject heading is broken down into subheads for particular specialized topics. These subheads correspond to the West key numbers. Under each subheading, there will be headnotes from cases about the particular topic. In the *Federal Practice Digest* and the *General Digest*, United States Supreme Court cases are listed first, then federal appeals court cases, then federal district court cases listed alphabetically by state. The *General Digest* also has state court cases listed alphabetically by state.

Unfortunately, cases about prisons and prisoners' rights are found in a wide variety of the West key number sections. As the key number system is organized now (*i.e.*, in mid-2009, when we are writing this), the largest number of relevant key numbers appear in the sections on Prisons and on Sentencing and Punishment—Cruel and Unusual Punishment—Conditions of Confinement. There is also a small section on Convicts with only a few key numbers, and a section on Sheriffs and Constables with one key number (k105) titled "Ill treatment of and injuries to prisoners." In the Civil Rights section, key numbers 1089-1098 deal with prisons, as do many others; many of the subjects dealt with under Civil Rights have subheadings titled "Criminal law enforcement; prisons." Similarly, in Constitutional Law, there are subsections concerning prisons under First Amendment (key numbers 1193-97), Right to Privacy (1274-75), and Freedom of Religion and Conscience (1421-27), and other constitutional rights. Some cases involving prisoners may not be listed in any of these. For that reason, you should be sure to Shepardize the most important cases you find so you can locate relevant cases that do not appear in the prison-related digest headings.

Since they have the largest number of prison-related key numbers, at the end of this chapter we list the key numbers in the Prisons section and in Sentencing and Punishment—Cruel and Unusual Punishment—Conditions of Confinement.

To find the most recent decisions, once you have looked in the digests and in their pocket parts or supplements, you should look in any reporter volumes or "advance sheets" that include later cases than the digests. (The advance sheets are paperback volumes of the case reporters that appear quickly and then are discarded when the hardcover reporter volumes appear.) For example, if the most recent reported case in the digest supplement is volume 526 F. Supp. 2d, to find the most recently reported cases, you will need to look at each reporter or advance sheet after volume 526 of the Federal Supplement, Second Series. These will include the paperback "advance sheets," which are issued weekly, for the different reporters in your law library. You should look

at the "Key Number Digest" found in the back of each hardcover volume and in the front of each paperbound advance sheet volume to see if there are additional cases in the digest topic of interest to you.

3. Researching a Case

If you have found one or more cases that deal with your particular point of interest, you can use these as a basis for additional research. You can use the headnotes to locate the section of the decision that deals with the issue you are interested in. Usually, there will be citations to earlier cases on the same subject in that part of the decision. You can also get the digest topic name and key numbers of the headnotes concerning the subject and look in the digests under that name and number to find other cases on the same subject.

Another method of researching is to Shepardize the case you start with to find other cases that cite it. Often, these cases will involve the same issue. Shepardizing a case will lead you to cases decided after the case you start with; using the digests will give you prior cases as well.

4. Shepardizing

Shepard's Citations is a collection of books that list places where a particular court decision is cited or mentioned, including later court decisions, law reviews, and annotations in the American Law Reports. "Shepardizing" serves several purposes. First, it tells you whether the cases you are citing are valid law or have been reversed or overruled by a higher court. Second, it assists your research efforts, since cases that cite the case you are Shepardizing will often deal with the same subject as that case.

There are also *Shepard's* volumes for statutes. Shepardizing a statute will allow you to find the original legislation number, any legislative changes (appeal, amendment, revision, etc.), cases interpreting the statute, and any other publication citing it. Shepardizing court rules and law reviews will provide additional research materials.

There are numerous sets of *Shepard's Citations*, each dealing with a particular court system or set of statutes. Each set consists of at least one permanent bound volume plus temporary paperbound supplements. To determine whether you have all the correct *Shepard's* volumes, you need to look at the box on the front cover of the most recent supplemental pamphlet. It will tell you "What Your Library Should Contain."

Once you have found the right set of *Shepard's* and have made sure that all the volumes are there, you should examine the first few pages of one of these volumes. Find the "Table of Abbreviations," located in the front, and familiarize yourself with it. These abbreviations are used throughout *Shepard's Citations* and tell you what the other cases citing your decision have done. If you see an "e" before a citation, you know the case is explained; an "o" tells you the case has been overruled; and an "f" tells you the court that cited the case you are Shepardizing "followed" that holding.

If you are Sheparding a case, you should start with the most recent *Shepard's* and work your way backward. Once you have the right section of the most recent *Shepard's*, look for the volume and page number of the case you want to Shepardize. You can simplify your search by identifying the issue you are researching. Some of the *Shepard's* cites will have a small raised number at the end. This number tells you which headnote in the original case the case cited in *Shepard's* relates to. You can use these numbers to identify cases dealing with the issue you are researching.

Shepardizing more than one case on a particular point—especially cases from different courts decided in different years—will probably help you find a larger number of additional useful cases.

Shepardizing a statute, such as 28 U.S.C. § 1334(4), is a little different from using case *Shepard's*, in that you must look under the title of the statute first ("Title 28"), then the section ("1334"), then any subsection ("4").

This is a very limited discussion of Shepardizing, and we recommend that you study the Preface of a bound *Shepard's* volume until you have mastered this method of legal researching. Your law library should also contain the pamphlet entitled *How to Use Shepard's Citations*. If it doesn't, you should ask the librarian to get it, since it is free to subscribers.

You should always Shepardize cases you cite to make sure they have not been reversed or overruled. That advice includes the cases in this Manual. We Shepardized them as we finished the Manual, but our work mostly does not reflect decisions after mid- to late 2009.

5. Researching a Statute

Statutes are published in multiple-volume sets of books. They are usually organized by general subject matter in "codes" or statutory compilations. For example, the United States Code has one large section, Title 28, that takes up a number of volumes and contains all the statutes concerning the federal courts as well as the Federal Rules of Civil Procedure and other court rules. In New York, all the state statutes concerning prisons appear in the Correction Law, which takes up two volumes in the New York statutes.

New statutes passed by legislatures, and amendments to old statutes, are first printed in volumes generally called "session laws" which will not usually be available in prison law libraries. Then they are added to codes and statutory compilations by means of pocket parts in the back of the statute volumes or paperback supplements to the volumes. If a statute has been amended in part, you may have to look both at the pocket part *and* the main volume in order to find the whole statute in its current version. If a statute book does not have a current pocket part or paperback supplement, you should complain to whoever is in charge of the law library or file a grievance to get it updated.

To find a statute on a particular subject, you should look in the index to the statutes. Generally, there is a separate set of index volumes covering the whole set of statutes, as well as indexes to each individual volume. To make use of

a statutory index, you should use the "word approach" described in § C.6 of this chapter. For example, to find out what must be alleged in a federal civil rights complaint to establish the court's jurisdiction, you would look in the index to the United States code under the general topics of "federal court," "district court," "jurisdiction," "civil rights," "complaint," etc. Under each of these general topics would be listed numerous headings and subheadings you should scan to obtain a citation to a statute. Once you have obtained citations of statutes that might contain the information you seek, go to each statute and read it. Since statutes are often amended, you should look in the pocket part or paperback supplement to be sure you have the most recent version.

One of the statutes you should have found and listed is 28 U.S.C. § 1331. If you look in the volume of the United States Code Annotated, which includes §§ 1292 to 1331 of Title 28, you will find § 1331. Read it to see if it is what you are looking for.

Codes and statutory compilations often exist in more than one edition. If it is available to you, you should always try to use the annotated version of the statutes (*e.g.*, the U.S. Code Annotated or McKinney's Consolidated Laws of New York Annotated), since they have additional research aids. These include "Historical and Revision Notes," which tell you where to find the legislative history and when, if ever, the statute was amended or revised.[33] There are often "Cross References," which refer you to other statutes that cover topics similar to this one. The "Library References" listing will give topical subject headings with their Key Numbers used in the West Digests, and also may give a reference to one of the legal encyclopedias (such as C.J.S., or *Corpus Juris Secundum*). There are other references to books and law reviews that may be helpful.

The "Notes of Decisions" after each statute contain a series of paragraph summaries explaining court decisions that have interpreted and applied that statute. These notes are similar in certain respects to the West Digests and are used in the same way. At the beginning of each Notes of Decisions section is an index to assist you in finding cases. Once you have found the phrases in the index that you feel are related to your area of interest, turn to these numbered sections of the annotation and skim them for cases of interest. Remember to check the pocket part and any bound paperback supplements dated later than the pocket part. The Notes of Decisions in the U.S. Code Annotated for 42 U.S.C. § 1983 are particularly extensive. However, they are generally less complete than the West Digests, so you should use them in addition to the digests and not instead of them.

---

[33]Most prison law libraries will not have the U.S. Code Congressional and Administrative News (U.S.C.C.A.N.), which lists the origins of federal statutes, what committee of the legislative branch worked on it, comments of congressional members during debate on legislation, etc. If it is available, it can be useful to show the intent of the statute.

You can also Shepardize the statute and its subsections to determine if there have been any legislative changes and to find court decisions interpreting these changes.

6. Researching by Word

The "word approach" is most useful in researching a legal problem when you know of no statutes or cases to start your research and do not know what key numbers to look at in the digests, in short, when you have no idea where to begin. The prison law library should contain the "Descriptive Word Index" volumes of the digests. These volumes list words alphabetically and state where they can be found under Digest Topics and Key Numbers in the regular volumes of the digest. For example, you can look up the general heading "Criminal Law" in the Descriptive Word Index of the Federal Practice Digest 4th. You will find cross-references to other index topics. One of these is "Prisons." If you look under that heading; you will find a couple of references to conditions of confinement. These will refer you to key numbers in the digest that will contain cases about prison conditions. The same approach may help you in using the index of this Manual or other legal treatises.

7. What If There Is No Law Library?

Not every jail or prison has an adequate law library, and some have no law libraries at all, or do not allow some or all prisoners to have direct access to the library. They may provide computerized legal research, or a "paging" system, which requires prisoners to identify the materials they need, or a system of assistance by persons with legal training.

a. **Computerized Legal Research** Lawyers and courts increasingly do their research in on-line databases via computers, or computer-accessed CD-ROMs, rather than in books. Prisons and jails are moving in this direction as well, though more slowly, in part because of the reluctance of officials to allow prisoners to have direct on-line access or to use expensive and delicate computer equipment. However, some prisons and jails do allow prisoners to do their research on-line or in CD-ROM systems, and others have the research done by prison staff members, either instead of or in addition to a paper library. There are two main systems of computerized legal research, Westlaw (part of the same corporate conglomerate as the West Publishing Company) and Lexis.

It is not practical for us to try to explain in detail how to do computerized legal research. You need hands-on training and practice to be able to do it right. The main thing you should keep in mind is that anything you can do in a paper library, you can do on-line, and more. So you can use the West digest headings in Westlaw to collect cases that may be relevant, and you can use KeyCite, which is similar to Shepard's, to see if a case has been reversed or overruled, or whether other courts have cited it. Lexis has its own system of digest headings, and Shepard's is available through Lexis. You can move from case to case, or case to statute or back,

more easily on the computer screen than in a paper library. For example, if the case you are reading on the computer cites another case or a statute, you can move directly to the cited case or statute by clicking on an on-screen link.

You can also conduct word searches of cases or statutes. For example, if you wanted to know what the courts have said about tuberculosis testing of prisoners, you could use Westlaw or Lexis to search for all cases that include the words tuberculosis, prison or prisoner, and test or testing in the same paragraph. You could direct this search to state court cases, federal law cases, federal appeals court or district court cases only, or cases within a single federal circuit or federal district court, or even decided by a particular judge. These kinds of searches can be extremely helpful and efficient, but it takes a lot of time and practice to learn to do it right so you find the cases you want without also bringing up dozens or even hundreds of cases that are not useful to you. If a staff member or legal assistant at the prison law library is going to do the research for you, you will need to be able to describe very specifically what it is you are looking for.

Westlaw and Lexis both provide free instruction materials for their services. Westlaw has such publications at *Westlaw User Guide*, *Welcome to Westlaw*, and *Westlaw Quick Reference Guide: Getting Started on Westlaw*, among others. These can be obtained via the Internet at http://west. thomson.com/support/user-guide/westlaw/gen-info.aspx, or by telephone at 1-800-WESTLAW (1-800-937-8529), if your prison allows these methods of access, or if there is someone outside who can get them for you. If not, you can write to West Headquarters, 610 Opperman Drive, Eagan, MN 55123.

Lexis similarly offers items titled *The Value of Doing Legal Research*, *Lexis.com At-A-Glance*, *LexisNexis Quick Reference Guide*, *Learning Lexis*, and *10 Tips for Cost Effective Research*, available on the Internet at http://law.lexisnexis. com/lexis/brochures. Lexis can be reached by telephone at (800) 253-5624 or by mail at LexisNexis Matthew Bender, 1275 Broadway, Albany, NY 12204.

b. **Paging Systems** Some prisons and jails do not allow prisoners, or some categories of prisoners such as those in segregation, to use their law libraries directly. Others may not have libraries, and instead obtain requested materials from a law library elsewhere. To use such a system, you must know what to ask for.[34] How you do this will depend on how much assistance from legally trained persons comes with the system. For example, you might be able to identify the most important cases on a particular subject from this book, and then ask for all later cases that have cited those cases, or cited them in connection with the point you are

---

[34]In the past, some courts have held such systems unconstitutional unless they provide sufficient trained legal assistance or other aids to make it possible for prisoners without legal training to use them effectively. *See* Ch. 3, § C.2.a, nn.515–517.

interested in. This would require someone to use Shepard's Citations or KeyCite to identify the cases and then obtain them for you.

If you don't have that level of assistance, you may need to ask for the reference volumes yourself. For example, you could ask for the volumes of *Shepard's* that have entries for the cases you are interested in, or the KeyCite list of citations for them, and then request the cases, which are listed as citing the case you started with. Or you could ask for the recent digest volumes that have the digest sections for the topics you wish to research, and request the cases that seem to be most relevant. (Some prison paging systems have mini-libraries that have reference volumes like digests, just for this purpose.) One thing you should do, if you do not have direct access to a law library, is ask for a list of the contents of the library. It may have treatises or textbooks, such as books on federal jurisdiction or on civil procedure; they may make your research easier than starting from scratch researching case law.

c. Legal Assistance Systems Some prisons and jails do not have law libraries, and some have even gotten rid of libraries they used to have, and instead provide limited assistance from legally trained persons. These programs undoubtedly differ widely in the services offered and how well they work. If you are lucky, someone will do your legal research for you, and possibly draft papers for you (or at least the initial complaint). If you are not so lucky, you may encounter a program that is seriously understaffed and that has narrow limits on what work they will do and how much time they will devote to it.[35] Under those circumstances, you will need to be as specific as possible as you can be about what you want done, and how it should be done, using this Manual as a guide where possible.

8. List of Digest Headings

As mentioned earlier, here are the key numbers from the West sections on Prisons and on Sentencing and Punishment—Cruel and Unusual Punishment—Conditions of Confinement. The purpose of presenting them here it to assist you in using the West research system, since it is the system you are most likely to have access to.

310 PRISONS
    I. In General
    100   In general
    101   Establishment and maintenance
    102   Management and operation
      103—In general
      104—Proceedings

---

105   Judicial supervision, intervention, or review

II. Prisoners and Inmates
(A)   IN GENERAL
110   In general
111   Status, rights, and disabilities in general
112   Regulation and supervision in general; role of courts
113   Particular rights and disabilities
114   Contracts
115   Property and conveyances
   116—In general
   117—Money and finances; inmate accounts
(B)   CARE, CUSTODY, CONFINEMENT, AND CONTROL
120   In general
121   Discipline, security, and safety in general
122   Retaliation in general
123   Particular violations, punishments, deprivations, and conditions
124   Use of force
125   Sexual conduct
126   Protection from violence, assault, or abuse
127   Shackles or other restraints
128   Association in general; prisoner organizations
129   Expression, communications, and censorship in general
130   Privacy in general
131   Threats, intimidation, and harassment; abusive language
132   Personal property and effects; contraband
133   Purchases; commissaries
134   Search, seizure, and confiscation
   135—In general
   136—Particular issues and applications
   137—Strip searches
   138—Samples and tests
   139—Disposition of seized material
140   Reading and writing material; libraries
141   Visitors
   142—In general
   143—Contact and conjugal visits
144   Mail and correspondence
   145—In general
   146—Incoming
   147—Outgoing
   148—Internal; inmate-to-inmate
149   Telephones
150   Computers; e-mail
151   Religious practices and materials
   152—In general
   153—Hair, grooming, and clothing
   154—Diet and meals
   155—Services, ceremonies, texts, study, and prayer
156   Hazardous and unhealthful conditions; housing
157   Food and drink
158   Clothing and grooming; bedding and sleeping conditions

---

[35]The operation of one such program is described in *Bear v. Kautzky*, 305 F.3d 802, 804–05 (8th Cir. 2002); *see also* White v. Kautzky, 269 F. Supp. 2d 1054, 1056 (N.D.Iowa 2003), *rev'd and vacated on other grounds*, 494 F.3d 677 (8th Cir. 2007). The constitutional adequacy, or lack of it, of such programs is discussed in Ch. 3. § 2.a, nn.507–512.

CHAPTER 12

Writing Legal Documents

The best advice we can give you on legal writing is what we said in Chapter 1: **Keep it simple, keep it short, use plain English and don't try to sound like a lawyer.**[1] (We have provided a number of examples of this kind of writing in Appendix C.) You should stick to the factual and legal issues in the case and avoid engaging in personal attacks on anyone—the defendants, their lawyers, or a lower court that has ruled against you.[2] If you think someone involved in the case has done something wrong, make that point in neutral language, with facts and not by name-calling or accusations you can't prove.[3] Avoid a hostile or threatening tone or you will divert the court's attention from the issues in the case to your own character. By the language that you use, you should present a picture of yourself as a reasonable and thoughtful person.

You should type your legal papers, double-spaced, if you can, and if you must handwrite them, you should print clearly, double-spaced, and leave ample margins at the top, bottom and sides of the page. In federal court, your signature constitutes a certificate that you have read the document, that to the best of your knowledge it is well grounded in fact and law, and that it is not submitted for an improper purpose.[4] In multi-plaintiff litigation, each plaintiff must sign every document you submit to the court if it is to be effective with respect to that plaintiff.[5]

---

[1]There are plenty of books that discuss legal writing in much more detail. *See* Bryan A. Garner *et al.*, *The Redbook: A Manual on Legal Style* (West Publishing Co., 2d ed. 2006) (spiral bound, $40); Elizabeth Fajans *et al.*, *Writing for Law Practice: Advanced Legal Writing* (Foundation Press, 2004) (paperback, $58); Bryan A. Garner, *Legal Writing in Plain English: A Text with Exercises* (University of Chicago Press, 2001) (paperback, $16); Stephen D. Stark, *Writing to Win: The Legal Writer* (Main Street Books, 1999) (paperback, $16.95). The prices are current as of mid-2009, but may change. You may also be able to find these books cheaper at Amazon or other discount sellers if prison rules allow.

[2]*See* Vinson v. Colom, 228 F.3d 409 (5th Cir. 2000) (unpublished) (warning *pro se* plaintiffs their papers can be stricken for use of derogatory personal comments about the district judge) (citing Theriault v. Silber, 574 F.2d 197 (5th Cir. 1978)). In *Theriault*, a prisoner's notice of appeal was stricken because it contained disrespectful and impertinent remarks concerning the trial judge.

[3]For example, if a judge draws a factual conclusion that has no relationship to the evidence in the case, don't say she made it up; point out that it is unsupported by the record. Similarly, if your adversary makes a legal argument that ignores an important case that supports your position, don't accuse her of lying; point out that her argument is flawed because she ignores important precedent.

[4]Rule 11(a), Fed.R.Civ.P. ("Every pleading, written motion, and other paper must be signed . . . by a party personally if the party is unrepresented."); *see* Warren v. Guilker, 29 F.3d 1386, 1389–90 (9th Cir. 1994) (Rule 11 applies to *pro se* inmate). Rule 26(g)(1), Fed.R.Civ.P., contains a similar requirement for signing of discovery requests. *See* Gyore v. Krausz Precision Mfg. Corp., Inc., 954 F.2d 727 (9th Cir. 1992) (unpublished) (holding Rule 26(g)(1) applicable to *pro se* litigants). *See* Ch 10, § W, for a more extensive discussion of Rule 11.

[5]If *pro se* parties fail to arrange for all plaintiffs to sign a document before filing, courts will often allow an opportunity for all to sign later. *See* Wash v. Johnson, 343 F.3d 685, 688–89 (5th Cir. 2003); Casanova v. DuBois, 289 F.3d 142, 146 (1st Cir. 2002); Zolnowski v. County of Erie, 944 F. Supp. 1096, 1098 (W.D.N.Y. 1996). Courts will dispense with the requirement that all *pro se* plaintiffs sign papers only in the rarest of circumstances; since federal statutes allow parties to plead their cases only "*personally* or by counsel," 28 U.S.C. § 1654, and not by non-attorneys, one *pro se* litigant will generally not be allowed to sign on behalf of others. For one of the rare exceptions, *see* Santiago v. C.O. Campisi Shield No. 4592, 91 F. Supp.2d 665, 671–72 (S.D.N.Y. 2000) (accepting papers prepared for plaintiff by another prisoner without plaintiff's signature where the plaintiff was transferred and could not sign them but informed the court that he wished to adopt them). If you are filing court papers in a multi-plaintiff case and cannot get them signed by all parties before filing, *e.g.*, because other plaintiffs have been transferred, you should send copies to the other plaintiffs with instructions to sign them and file them individually, and notify the court you have done that. If you are unable to do this,

Beyond that basic advice, which applies to everything you write, different kinds of legal documents must be written in different ways.

A. CAPTION

Any document you file in court should start with a caption stating the name of the court and the names of the parties. The caption of the complaint should state the names of all the plaintiffs and all the defendants.[6] If there are a large number of plaintiffs or defendants named in the caption of the complaint, you can generally use a "short caption" on documents filed after the complaint, listing the first plaintiff and the first defendant and adding "*et al.*" (which means "and others") after each.[7] (*You should not use this "short caption" on a notice of appeal or on an order or judgment.*) The caption should also contain the docket number of the case and the name of the judge and magistrate judge, when these are known. When they are not known, a space should be left to fill in the information later. The caption should contain a title explaining what the document is—*e.g.*, Complaint, Affidavit in Opposition to Defendants' Motion for Summary Judgment, Memorandum of Law in Support of Plaintiffs' Motion to Compel Discovery.

The following is an example of a caption, minus the document title:

UNITED STATES DISTRICT COURT
FOR THE EASTERN DISTRICT OF MICHIGAN
Southern Division

DANIEL E. MANVILLE,
Plaintiff

v.   Case No. 08-cv-071297
                                      Hon. Mark J. Smithville
                                      Mag. Judge Pete Leeway

PRISON MEDICAL PROVIDERS;
MARK FORESMAN, Nurse;
JERRY PETERS, Lieutenant, sued
in their individual capacities;
Defendants.
                JURY TRIAL DEMANDED[8]

---

call the situation to the court's attention and ask for its assistance in getting the papers to the other plaintiffs for signature.

Some courts have held that *pro se* prisoners cannot bring multi-plaintiff litigation at all, but must instead file separate complaints. Other courts have disagreed, and we think those courts are right. This issue is discussed in Ch. 9, § A, nn.60–65.

[6]If you are bringing a civil action, you are called a plaintiff, and the other party is called the defendant. If you are bringing a habeas corpus or a mandamus action, you are the petitioner and the opposing party is the respondent.

[7]*See* Rules 7(b)(2), 10(a), Fed.R.Civ.P. An example of a full caption appears in Appendix C, Form 1a; a short caption appears in Form 1b.

[8]Author Manville always places the request for a jury trial in the caption of his complaints, even though the rules do not require putting it there.

There are more examples of captions in Appendix C.

B. COMPLAINT

The complaint is the document that starts a lawsuit.[9] (In some kinds of cases, it may be called a petition or a claim.) The purpose of a complaint is to put your factual allegations before the court and identify the legal basis for your claims. It generally should not contain legal argument or case citations.

a) *Title and Introduction.* A complaint should start with a title after the caption. The body of the complaint (which you should double space if possible) should begin with a very short paragraph summing up what the case is about, for example:

VERIFIED[10] COMPLAINT FOR DAMAGES
AND INJUNCTIVE RELIEF
I. Introduction
1. This is a § 1983 action filed by Plaintiff Daniel Manville, a state prisoner, alleging violation of his constitutional rights to receive medical care and seeking injunctive relief and money damages. Plaintiff also seeks an injunction and damages pursuant to the Americans with Disabilities Act and the Rehabilitation Act.

After this introductory paragraph, you should add a series of short paragraphs covering the following subjects:

b) *Jurisdiction.* You should inform the court that it has jurisdiction over your lawsuit by citation to statutes, court rules, or the facts.[11] There may be more than one basis for jurisdiction and you should cite to each one in the jurisdictional section of the complaint. For example:

II. Jurisdiction
2. Jurisdiction of this Court is invoked pursuant to 28 U.S.C. § 1331 in that this is a civil action arising under the Constitution of the United States.
3. Jurisdiction of the Court is invoked pursuant to 28 U.S.C. § 1343(a)(3) in that this action seeks to redress the deprivation, under color of state law, of rights secured by Acts of Congress providing for equal rights of persons within the jurisdiction of the United States.

In some cases, you must file an administrative claim or notice of claim before filing suit in order for the court to

---

[9]Additional discussion of preparing complaints appears in Ch. 10, § B.1. A sample complaint appears in Appendix C, Form 1a.

[10]A verified complaint (one which you swear to or declare under penalty of perjury is true) may be used as an affidavit opposing summary judgment under Rule 56, or in other motion practice, to the extent it is based on personal knowledge and sets forth specific facts admissible in evidence. *See* Ch. 10, § L.2.a concerning verified complaints in summary judgment proceedings.

[11]*See* Ch. 8, §§ B.1, B.2, concerning jurisdiction in federal civil rights actions.

have jurisdiction. In that case, you should allege compliance in your complaint, *e.g.*:

> The plaintiff filed an administrative tort claim concerning the occurrences complained of on [date], within two years after those occurrences, and brought suit within six months of the mailing of the notice of final agency denial of that claim, as required by 28 U.S.C. § 2401. [For a claim under the Federal Tort Claims Act.]

Or:

> The plaintiff filed a notice of claim concerning the occurrences complained of with the Comptroller of [state or city] within 90 days of those occurrences, as required by [state or local law], and the Comptroller has failed to settle the plaintiff's claim. [For a state law claim with a notice of claim requirement.]

c) *The parties.* You must identify each plaintiff and defendant, both by name and by office, if any. You should spell out relationships between the parties. If a party is an agent, subordinate, or employee of another person or agency, you should allege that fact. If a party is an agency or department of state, federal, or local government, you should allege that fact too. If you are a prisoner, you should allege where you are imprisoned (or were imprisoned at the time relevant to the complaint), and in whose custody, and you should do the same for any other prisoners who are co-plaintiffs with you. In cases under 42 U.S.C. § 1983, you must allege and state facts showing that the defendants acted under color of state law,[12] and in all cases you should state whether you are suing them in their personal capacity, official capacity, or both.[13] For example:

III. Parties

4. Plaintiff Dan Manville at all times relevant was confined by the Michigan Department of Corrections (MDOC) at Southern Michigan Correctional Facility (SMCF).

5. Defendant PRISON MEDICAL PROVIDERS (PMR) is a private Michigan Corporation which has been, at all relevant times, under a contract with Michigan Department of Corrections to provide medical care and services to inmates confined with MDOC, including Dan Manville.

6. Defendant MARK FORESMAN at all relevant times was a nurse employed by PMR.

7. Defendant JERRY PETERS at all relevant time was a Lieutenant at SMCF employed by MDOC.

8. Defendants Foresman and Peters at all relevant times were acting under color of state law and are being sued in their individual capacities.

d) *Exhaustion of remedies.* You are required to exhaust administrative remedies prior to filing any federal court lawsuit while confined in prison that relates to the conditions of confinement.[14] Even though the United States Supreme Court has held a complaint filed by an inmate need not allege exhaustion,[15] we suggest that you include the allegation in your complaint that you have fully exhausted all available administrative remedies, *if* that is the case and you can state it truthfully and simply.[16] For example:

IV. Exhaustion of Available Remedies

9. Plaintiff exhausted his administrative remedies before filing this complaint.

If you are raising a state law claim that requires exhaustion, you must allege exhaustion in your complaint if exhaustion is necessary to the court's jurisdiction or if there is a state court rule that requires pleading of exhaustion. (In federal civil actions, exhaustion under the Prison Litigation Reform Act is an affirmative defense that the defendants, not the plaintiff, must plead. However, you may need to put facts about your grievances in the complaint for some other purpose, such as showing that the defendants had knowledge of your problem.)

e) *The facts.* You should allege only those facts that you think you can prove and which are relevant to your legal claims. We suggest that you allege only one fact per numbered paragraph.

You don't need to cite case law in your complaint. Rather, you need to be familiar with the law governing your different legal claims so you will know what the elements of each claim are. Then you need to allege facts that if proved would establish each of these elements. In this sample complaint we are discussing, we have stated factual allegations that support each of the legal claims: (1) failure to protect from a known risk of substantial harm;[17] (2) deliberate indifference to medical needs;[18] and (3) retaliation for filing lawsuits.[19]

V. Factual Statement

10. On November 18, 2007, Plaintiff stopped Lt. Peters and informed him that he needed protection from the dan-bites, a prison gang.

11. Plaintiff told Lt. Peters that he had been stabbed in 4-block 6 months ago and after spending time in the hospital for the stab wounds he was placed in protective custody and then transferred from Jackson Prison.

---

[12]Color of state law is discussed in Ch. 8, § B.1.c. In *Bivens* actions seeking damages against federal employees or officials, you must generally establish that they acted under color of *federal* law. This subject is discussed in Ch. 8, § B.2.c. Usually the fact that someone is employed at a prison should be sufficient for this purpose.

[13]Capacity is discussed in Ch. 8, § B.4.c.

[14]*See* Ch. 9, § D, for a discussion of the exhaustion requirement of the Prison Litigation Reform Act.

[15]Jones v. Bock, 549 U.S. 199, 127 S. Ct. 910 (2007) (exhaustion is an affirmative defense that defendants must plea).

[16]*See* Ch. 9, § D.8 concerning this point.

[17]For a discussion of the elements of a failure to protect claim, *see* Ch. 2, § G.1.

[18]For a discussion of the elements of a medical claim, *see* Ch. 2, § F.1.

[19]For a discussion of the elements of a retaliation claim, *see* Ch. 3, §§ B.6, C.1.b and C.1.c.

12. Plaintiff also offered Lt. Peters to read a copy of his Notice of Intent indicating he was classified to protective custody as a result of that stabbing.

13. Lt. Peters stated that Plaintiff "likes to sue our officers and win, don't you?"

14. Plaintiff told Lt. Peters that since being transferred back to Jackson Prison and placed in 4-block he had received numerous threats that they won't miss this time.

15. Plaintiff offered to Lt. Peters to read a couple of the kites that had been placed in his cell threatening his life.

16. Instead of looking at any of these documents, Lt. Peters told Plaintiff he should have thought about needing prison staff some day to protect him before he filed a lawsuit.

17. Lt. Peters went on to state that Plaintiff made his own bed, now he should lie in it.

18. Lt. Peters walked away from Plaintiff.

19. After Lt. Peters left, Plaintiff walked back to 4-block and filed a grievance against Lt. Peters.

20. Plaintiff went to chow that evening and as he returned to 4-block and entered the door, a blanket was thrown over his head and he was assaulted with prison-made knives and hard objects.

21. After what seemed a long time Plaintiff heard an inmate yell "screw coming." The beating and stabbing stopped and Plaintiff heard people running away from him.

22. When the guard found him, Plaintiff was lying on the floor and bleeding.

23. Plaintiff told the officer he had trouble breathing.

24. Plaintiff was given some treatment by prison medical staff and was then transferred to an outside hospital.

25. Plaintiff was taken to an outside emergency room and then operated on as a result of the injuries he suffered from the assault.

26. Plaintiff was told by the doctor after the operation that he was lucky to be alive since a knife had nicked his heart.

27. The doctor also told Plaintiff that his skull had been caved in and he had started to develop swelling on the brain.

28. The doctor told Plaintiff he had placed a stent in his head to allow draining of any fluids.

29. Plaintiff was returned to the prison from the outside hospital on November 30, 2007 and learned that the first-step grievance against Lt. Peters had been denied on November 23d.

30. On December 1, 2007, a Saturday, Plaintiff filed a second-step grievance against Lt. Peters. In this second-step he explained why the grievance was being filed untimely, *i.e.*, Plaintiff had just been returned from the hospital and no one had sent the first-step grievance denial to him at the hospital.

31. The second-step grievance was denied, and when Plaintiff filed a third-step grievance concerning Lt. Peters' conduct, that was denied too.

32. When Plaintiff left the outside hospital he was given a copy of a medical order from the doctor that he was to return to the hospital on December 27, 2007, so hospital staff could determine whether to take the stent out of his head. The medical order also stated that he was to receive physical therapy.

33. On or about December 16, 2007, Plaintiff sent a medical kite to the nurse asking whether he would be returned to the outside hospital and December 27 and asked her why he had not been scheduled for physical therapy. Plaintiff attached a copy of the medical order to the medical kite.

34. On December 28, 2007, Plaintiff received a response from Nurse Foresman stating that she had reviewed my records and had determined that he did not need to return to see the outside doctor and that she had determined that if he just walked around the exercise track each day, he would not need physical therapy.

35. Nurse Foresman did not conduct an examination of Plaintiff or refer him to a doctor before informing him that he would not see the outside doctor or receive physical therapy.

36. Plaintiff exhausted the grievance process against Nurse Foresman without obtaining any relief.

37. The head of Prison Medical Providers denied any relief from the medical decisions made by Nurse Foresman.

38. After he filed the grievance against Nurse Foresman, Plaintiff stopped receiving his pain medication.

39. Plaintiff suffers headaches throughout the day. The pain becomes so unbearable that he usually cannot stand.

40. The area where Plaintiff's skull was fractured is where he feels the most severe pain.

41. When he has severe pain he loses his vision and when the pain lessens it can take up to an hour before he can see again.

42. The area around his heart is constantly painful. At times it feels as if Plaintiff is having a heart attack.

43. When he wrote Nurse Foresman and explained to her the pain he suffered, Plaintiff received a response telling him to buy aspirin at the prison store.

44. Finally, in July of 2008, Plaintiff was sent to see the outside doctor for the pain in his head.

45. The outside doctor could not believe that the stent had remained in Plaintiff's head for an extra seven months and he was still alive.

46. Plaintiff was taken to the emergency room by this doctor and the stent was removed from my head the same day I saw him.

47. It is now six months later and Plaintiff is still having severe headaches for at least a few hours a day. When he has severe headaches he still loses his vision.

48. The outside doctor ordered that Plaintiff receive physical therapy but Defendants Nurse Foresman and Prison Medical Providers have refused to provide physical therapy.

f) Claims for relief (sometimes called "causes of action" or "counts"). These paragraphs should explain which of your legal rights have been violated and identify the facts that establish that violation of law. For example:

Claims for Relief

A. Failure to Protect

49. The failure of Defendant Peters to act on his knowledge of a substantial risk of serious harm to Plaintiff violated his Eighth Amendment right to be free from deliberate indifference to his safety.

50. As a result of Defendant Peters' failure, Plaintiff was viciously assaulted and received serious physical and emotional injuries.

B. Deliberate Indifference to Medical Needs

51. The refusal of Defendant Nurse Foresman to authorize the removal of Plaintiff's stent after 30 days and to provide physical therapy to him constituted deliberate indifference to Plaintiff's serious medical needs in violation of the Eighth Amendment.

52. Defendant Prison Medical Providers have a policy of restricting, if not outright denying, follow-up care ordered by a doctor when such care is expensive.

53. Defendant Nurse Foresman was following the policy of Prison Medical Providers when she denied any follow-up care to Plaintiff that had been ordered.

54. The failure of Defendant Prison Medical Providers to take steps to ensure that Plaintiff received the needed treatment, despite its knowledge of Plaintiff's serious medical needs, constituted deliberate indifference to Plaintiff's serious medical needs.

55. As a result of Defendant Prison Medical Providers' and Defendant Nurse Foresman's failure to provide needed medical treatment, Plaintiff suffered further injury and physical and emotional pain and injury.

C. Retaliation

56. The refusal of Defendant Peters to provide protection to Plaintiff as a result of Plaintiff's having filed a lawsuit against prison staff constituted retaliation for petitioning government for redress of grievances and therefore violated the First Amendment.

57. As a result of Defendant Peters' failure, Plaintiff was viciously assaulted and received serious physical and emotional injuries.

Sometimes a little more explanation is needed. For example, if you are making a state law claim of negligence,[20] your legal research should have told you the elements of that cause of action: the defendant owed you a duty of care, the defendant breached that duty, you were injured in some fashion, and your injury was proximately caused by the breach of duty. Each element should have a separate paragraph. For example, if you are alleging a claim of negligent failure to protect you from assault:

Negligent Failure to Protect

58. Defendant Peters owed Plaintiff a duty of reasonable care to protect him from assaults by other prisoners.

59. Defendant Peters breached that duty by failing to provide protection when Plaintiff informed him of his fear of being assaulted and showed Defendant Petters the documents supporting his fear.

60. The breach of duty resulted in serious physical and emotional injury and damages.

61. The breach of duty proximately caused those damages.

You should include a separate claim for relief for each of your legal rights that you think was violated. For example, if you think that the defendants' actions violated a constitutional provision and a state statute and also constituted a common law tort, you should have three separate claims for relief reflecting these three different legal theories.

g) *Relief requested.* You should set out in separate paragraphs the relief you think you are entitled to—damages, injunctive relief, a declaratory judgment, reversal of a disciplinary proceeding—from each defendant. It is customary to add a final paragraph requesting the court to grant "such other relief as it may appear Plaintiff is entitled to." For example:

Relief Requested

WHEREFORE, Plaintiff requests that this Court grant the following relief:

A. Declare that Defendant Peters violated Plaintiff's Eighth Amendment rights when he failed to protect him from a known risk of assault and he was severely assaulted;

B. Declare that Defendant Foresman violated Plaintiff's Eighth Amendment right to medical care;

C. Declare that Defendant Prison Medical Provider violated Plaintiff's Eighth Amendment rights to medical care;

D. Declare that Defendant Peters violated Plaintiff's First Amendment right not to be retaliated against for filing lawsuits;

E. Issue an injunction requiring that Defendants Prison Medical Providers provide physical therapy to Plaintiff as ordered by the outside doctor;

F. Award compensatory damages for plaintiff's physical and emotional injuries, and punitive damages against each defendant; and

G. Grant Plaintiff such other relief as it may appear Plaintiff is entitled to.

h) *Signature and address.* You should then sign the document, date it, and include your mailing address.

i) *Verification.* Some complaints need to be verified (*i.e.,* sworn to), and others do not, depending on the rules of the court you are in. **It is wise to verify all complaints**, both to avoid making a mistake and because a verified complaint can sometimes be used like an affidavit in responding to motions by the defendants.[21] To verify a complaint or petition, you sign an affidavit or declaration stating that the facts stated in the complaint are true to your knowledge, and that

---

[20]Negligence claims are discussed in various places in this Manual. These can be located by consulting the Index.

[21]In federal court, a complaint that is verified and based upon personal knowledge satisfies the requirement of Rule 56(e), Fed.R.Civ.P., that an affidavit be filed in response to a motion for summary judgment. *See* Ch. 10, § L.2.a.

any facts stated on information and belief are true to the best of your knowledge and belief. It should be notarized or signed under penalty of perjury, as described in the next section.

C. AFFIDAVIT OR DECLARATION

An affidavit is a written statement that is sworn to before a notary public. It is used when you need to put facts before the court in writing. Falsehoods in an affidavit, like falsehoods on the witness stand, could subject the person who submits them to prosecution for perjury, false swearing, contempt or court, or fraud.

The federal courts and some state courts permit litigants to submit a declaration under penalty of perjury instead of an affidavit. (Be sure you know whether the court system you are litigating in accepts declarations or whether it insists on notarized affidavits.) A declaration is not notarized, but the person making it declares under penalty of perjury that it is true, and can be prosecuted if he signs a false declaration.[22] For example:

> Pursuant to 28 U.S.C. 1746, I declare (or certify, verify, or state) under penalty of perjury that the following is true and correct.
>
> * * *
>
> [Signature]
> [Date]

An affidavit or declaration should begin with the case caption. Beneath that, for affidavits, is a short affidavit heading which shows where the affidavit was sworn to, such as:

> STATE OF MICHIGAN)
>   ) AFFIDAVIT OF DAN MANVILLE
> COUNTY OF WAYNE)

The affidavit continues with an unnumbered paragraph, such as "Dan Manville, being first duly sworn, deposes as follows:" You will then state the facts to which you wish to swear in numbered paragraphs.

The person swearing to the facts is called the affiant or deponent. At the bottom of the affidavit, allow a place for the signature of the affiant. Below the affiant's signature, provide a statement that the affidavit was sworn to before the notary on such and such a date, and leave a space for the notary's signature.

You should swear only to those facts which are within your personal knowledge. If you have reason to believe something is true, but did not personally observe it, you may state that it is true "on information and belief."

Declarations are similar in form to affidavits except that they do not need the heading indicating where the affidavit

was sworn or the references to the notary. The person making the declaration is called the declarant.

The most common types of affidavits or declarations you will use are:

(1) *Proof of Service.*[23] The affiant swears or declares that a document was mailed or served on a particular date.
(2) *Affidavit or Declaration of Indigency.*[24] The affiant swears that she is too poor to afford court costs and fees, or is so poor that she cannot afford an attorney, etc. It should include the facts about your financial situation.
(3) *Affidavit or Declaration of Verification.* The affiant swears or declares that the facts stated in a document (*e.g.*, the complaint) are true to her knowledge, and that the facts stated on information and belief are true to the best of her knowledge and belief.
(4) *Affidavit or Declaration Supporting or Opposing Summary Judgment.*[25] A party moving for summary judgment, and a party opposing summary judgment, must generally file affidavits stating the facts that support their positions.

If other people support your version of the facts, and they have personal knowledge of the facts, you may submit their affidavits or declarations as well as your own.

D. MOTIONS

A motion is a request to a court to take some action in a case that is pending before it. Motions that are commonly filed by parties to federal court civil rights cases include motions to file an amended complaint, motions to dismiss or for judgment on the pleadings, motions for summary judgment, motions to compel discovery, motions for a temporary restraining order or a preliminary injunction, and motions *in limine* to exclude certain evidence from the trial.

The Federal Rules of Civil Procedure require that motions be in writing unless they are made during a hearing or trial, that they "state with particularity the grounds" for the motion, and that they "state the relief sought."[26] You may submit a document called a "motion" that sets out the required information, along with a notice giving the return date for the motion.[27] You may also include the grounds and the relief sought in the notice of motion. Often the motion or notice of motion states the grounds and relief sought

---

[22]Hatchet v. Nettles, 201 F.3d 651, 654 (5th Cir. 2000) ("false statements in an affidavit or unsworn declaration made under penalty of perjury may result in prosecution for perjury. 18 U.S.C. § 1621.").

[23]*See* Appendix C, Form 15.

[24]*See* Appendix C, Form 21. Indigency and *in forma pauperis* proceedings are discussed in Ch. 10, § C.3.

[25]*See* Appendix C, Forms 9b, 10a; *see also* Ch. 10, § L, for a discussion of summary judgment.

[26]Rule 7(b)(1), Fed.R.Civ.P.

[27]Return dates are explained in Ch. 10, § F.

in an abbreviated form, with a more detailed affidavit or declaration submitted with the motion. In urgent situations, a motion may be brought by order to show cause; the moving party submits an order to the court, generally supported by affidavits, which if signed by the judge will require the opposing party to respond within a short time.[28]

It is helpful to look at a motion submitted by a competent attorney in the court where you are litigating and use it as a model, since there are some variations in practice in different courts.[29] However, don't worry too much about details of form; as long as you meet the basic requirements of the rules, the court should give your motion the proper consideration.

Local court rules may contain additional requirements for certain motions. They often require the party filing the motion to contact counsel for the other side to determine whether they will agree to the relief asked in the motion, and to report on that effort in an affidavit or declaration. These rules also require that motions to compel discovery include an explanation of the efforts you have made to settle the dispute out of court.[30] For summary judgment motions, they usually require that the party making the motion submit a list of the undisputed facts that she believes justify summary judgment, and require the opposing party to submit a list of the disputed facts that she believes prevent the court from entering summary judgment.[31]

If your motion is one that is governed by a specific court rule, you should cite the rule in your motion papers and make sure that you have met any requirements that are stated in the rule. For example, motions for summary judgment are governed by Rule 56(c), Fed.R.Civ.P., which states that summary judgment is authorized if "there is no genuine issue as to any material fact and . . . the moving party is entitled to judgment as a matter of law." Your motion papers should allege that these requirements are met and should demonstrate that that is the case.

Motions must often be supported by documentation. For example, you should attach to a motion to compel discovery a copy of the discovery request that is in dispute, and any response that has been made to it. Similarly, if you move for summary judgment alleging that your disciplinary proceeding denied due process, you should attach the documentation you received concerning the disciplinary charges

and disposition. When you submit documents to court with a motion, you should number them and explain what the documents are in your declaration or affidavit. For example:

> Exhibit 1 attached to this declaration is the notice of disciplinary charges that was handed to me by Lieutenant Smith on October 18, 2008.

Motions must often be supported by a brief or a memorandum of law. In some cases, court rules require you to submit a brief. In any case in which there is any question of your legal right to the relief you request, you should submit a brief containing your legal argument.

If the other side files a motion, you will need to file a response. The form of the response will depend on local practice and on what the motion involves. If the motion alleges facts that you dispute, you will need to file an affidavit or declaration stating your version of the facts, supported by documentary exhibits if those are necessary to support the facts you allege. You will generally need to file a brief stating your legal position about any legal issues the defendants raise and about the legal significance of disputed facts. (For example, suppose you claim excessive force, and the defendants move for summary judgment alleging that they only used holds to restrain you and that doesn't violate the Eighth Amendment. If in fact they banged your head against the wall and kicked you, you would respond with an affidavit or declaration stating those facts, and in your brief you would argue that those facts *do* make out a violation of the Eighth Amendment.)

E. BRIEF OR MEMORANDUM OF LAW

A brief or memorandum of law is a document that argues your legal position on one or more points and briefly restates those facts that are necessary to support your legal argument. The term "brief" has usually been used for appeal briefs and post-trial briefs while "memorandum of law" has been used for briefs in the trial court in support of motions or in opposition to them. This difference in terminology makes no difference in substance. Several sample briefs are provided in Appendix C.[32]

1. Contents of a Brief

A brief typically includes a table of contents, a statement of the case or procedural history, a statement of facts, an argument stating your legal position, a statement of the relief requested, and your signature. Appellate briefs will also contain a table of cases and authorities, a statement of questions presented, and a statement of the standard of review the court is required to apply.[33] You should always include a

---

[28]*See* Ch. 10, § F. This procedure is not to be used routinely. It is most likely to be useful to a prisoner who is seeking a temporary restraining order and preliminary injunction. *See* Ch. 8, § O.2; Appendix C, Forms 11a–11c.

[29]For example, in the Southern and Eastern Districts of New York, there is rarely a document called a "motion"; usually there is a very brief notice of motion, a declaration or affidavit stating the facts the motion is based on, and a memorandum of law explaining the legal basis for the motion.

[30]Discovery motions are discussed further in Ch. 10, § K.2.h. *See also* Appendix C, Forms 6a–6c.

[31]Summary judgment motions are discussed further in Ch. 10, § L. *See also* Appendix C, Forms 9a–9d, 10a–10c.

[32]*See* Appendix C, Forms 3c, 6c, 9d, 10c, and 11c for examples of briefs in lower court proceedings.

[33]These items are discussed in a little more detail in Ch. 10, § U.1.g. An example of an appellate brief appears in Appendix C,

table of contents, even if the court rules do not require it, because it makes it easier for the judge to find particular points in your brief.

The statement of facts in a brief concentrates on the facts of the case that are relevant to your legal argument. Thus, in a motion to compel discovery, you would state the facts of the discovery dispute. However, you would only state the facts of the incident alleged in the complaint insofar as they were relevant to the discovery dispute (*e.g.*, to show that the discovery sought was relevant to the complaint).[34] Note that a court cannot rely on facts that are stated only in a brief. You get facts before the court through a sworn affidavit or declaration, by sworn testimony in court, or through documents that you either submit with a proper foundation in connection with a motion or place into evidence in a trial or hearing. The statement of facts in a brief summarizes these materials.

2. Writing a Brief

The most important point about writing a legal brief is to make clear what the issue is. Often, lawyers for prison officials will argue in generalities—*e.g.*, that mere disagreements with prison medical staff do not establish constitutional violations, or that prison disciplinary convictions only need to be supported by "some evidence." If these generalities do not really apply to your case, you must make that fact clear to the court. For example, if the defendants refused without justifications to call witnesses or to give you notice of a disciplinary hearing, they have denied due process regardless of whether there is "some evidence" to support the charges.

Briefs frequently involve more than one legal issue. Each issue should have its own separate portion, or "point," of the brief. Each point should have a numbered "point heading" that states your basic argument in a complete sentence. For example, one point might be headed:

I. The District Court Erred By Failing To Give Notice That It Was Converting Defendants' Motion To Dismiss To A Summary Judgment Motions.

Another one might be headed:

II. Summary Judgment Was Improper Because The Plaintiff's Evidence That He Was Beaten Without Provocation Created A Disputed Question Of Material Fact.[35]

If your point takes several logical steps to establish, you should try to break it down into sub-points, each with its own heading,[36] and each listed in the table of contents.

This makes your brief easier to read and to understand, and it makes it easier for the judge to come back to your brief and find a particular item. It also may help you think through your case—and the weaknesses in the other side's case—more clearly. Within points and sub-points, you should be careful to break up your argument into short paragraphs. Each paragraph should deal with one basic idea, and if possible it should start with a "topic sentence" that states that basic idea clearly.

Each point and sub-point should include relevant authority to support your position. This authority can be cases, statutes, constitutional provisions, court rules, administrative rules, city ordinances, etc. You may also use "secondary" authority, such as quotations from legal treatises or encyclopedias, law review articles, or other books and materials.

Cases may provide different degrees of support for your arguments. The strongest authority is a case that directly states a legal rule that closely fits your case. Cases with facts similar to yours ("on point") are stronger authority than cases with facts that are different (or "distinguishable"). Often you will not find cases that are on point or that directly state a legal rule that helps you. In those instances, you may need to argue by analogy. For example, the Supreme Court has held that an illiterate inmate is entitled to assistance with a defense in a disciplinary proceeding. You can argue by analogy that an inmate with a mental disorder or with impaired vision or hearing should also be entitled to assistance because she is likely to have problems similar to an illiterate person in understanding what is going on.[37]

Cases from the United States Supreme Court are stronger authority than cases from federal appellate courts, and appellate court cases are stronger authority than district court authority. Cases from the federal circuit or district you are litigating in are stronger authority than cases from other jurisdictions. Similarly, in state courts, decisions of the state Supreme Court are stronger than authority from the intermediate appellate courts or trial courts, and cases from the judicial district or circuit you are in are stronger than cases from other districts or circuits.

You can't always find a case directly on point in the jurisdiction you are litigating in. In these situations, it is effective to combine different kinds of authority. For example, suppose you file suit in a federal district court in New York, which is part of the Second Circuit, challenging a jail or prison practice of having untrained correctional officers screen requests for medical care. There is no authority that we have found in the Second Circuit or the New York federal courts on this specific point. You might write:

The Second Circuit has recognized that "systemic deficiencies in staffing, facilities, or procedures [which] make unnecessary suffering inevitable" constitute deliberate indifference to prisoners' medical needs. *Todaro v. Ward*, 565 F.2d 48, 52 (2d Cir. 1977). [This case is from the right

---

Form 13b. Local rules or judges' individual rules may also require a table of authorities in district court briefs.

[34]*See* Appendix C, Forms 61–6c, for sample of papers on a motion to compel discovery.

[35]Summary judgment is discussed in Ch. 10, § L.

[36]The model brief section later in this chapter shows how to do this, as does Appendix C, Form 9d.

[37]*See* Ch. 4, § H.1.f.

federal circuit and directly states a legal rule that fits your case in a general way.] The use of untrained personnel to make medical decisions is a systemic deficiency in staffing. Several courts have squarely held that permitting persons without medical training to decide whether prisoners receive medical attention states a deliberate indifference claim. *Kelley v. McGinnis*, 899 F.2d. 612, 616 (7th Cir. 1990); *Mitchell v. Aluisi*, 872 F.2d 577, 581 (4th Cir. 1989); *Boswell v. Sherburne County*, 849 R.2d 1117, 1123 (10th Cir. 1988). [These are cases that are directly on point, but they are from other jurisdictions.] In *Todaro v. Ward*, the court held unconstitutional a system in which medical screening was carried out by trained medical personnel, but under conditions that did not permit them sufficient time, facilities and information to make use of their training. *Todaro*, 565 F.2d at 50–51. If that practice is unconstitutional, surely the use of personnel who do not even have such training is also unconstitutional. [On this point, *Todaro* provides an analogy to the use of untrained personnel, and the brief explains the basis of the analogy.]

If a legal point is well founded or obvious, you can use a single case to support it. If a proposition is likely to be challenged, you should use all the authorities you can muster, within reason.

If your adversary cites cases and claims that they are contrary to your legal position, you should explain wherever possible that these cases are not similar to yours ("distinguish" the cases) or that they are not really contrary to your position, if that is the case. You can also argue that they were wrongly decided. You are in the strongest position to argue that a decision is wrong if there is a case from a higher court that is inconsistent with it at least in part.[38] You can also try to point out logical flaws in the decision's reasoning. If you are relying on a statute, regulation, or court rule, you can argue that the decision is contrary to the language or the purposes of the rule.[39] You can argue that a prior decision should not be applied in your case because it would result in extreme unfairness or injustice under the circumstances of your case.[40] You can also argue that the law should be a

certain way as a matter of "public policy"—*i.e.*, that ruling your way would have a good result for society and ruling against you would have a bad result.[41] You can show that if the position of the other side is carried to its logical extreme, the results will be absurd, ridiculous, or unfair. For example, if the Supreme Court had accepted prison officials' position that misuse of force does not violate the Constitution unless it inflicts "significant injury," it would in effect have authorized them to torture prisoners with electric shock, rubber hoses, and other methods that cause only temporary pain. The Supreme Court realized this and rejected the prison officials' argument.[42]

Your argument should be logical, as short as possible, and in the best English you can manage. Do not use a word if you do not know what it means, and do not use a rare or unusual word if a more common word will do. Do not try to "write like a lawyer" to impress the judge. Using plain English will make your documents easier to read and reduces the chance of making an embarrassing mistake.

It may help to have others read over your brief once you have finished it. If your friends cannot understand what you are saying, chances are the judge will not understand either.

You should avoid overusing words such as "clearly," "plainly," "obviously," etc. If something really is clear, plain, or obvious, the court does not need you to tell it so.

You should bring your argument "down to earth" by connecting it with the facts as often as possible. Your purpose is not to write a scholarly essay on the law; it is to convince the court that you should win a specific case involving specific facts.

If your brief is to be filed before your opponent's brief, you will have to decide whether to answer an argument that you predict your opponent may use against you. As a general rule, you should not do this, because you might call your opponent's attention to an issue she might otherwise miss. However, if the issue is certain to be raised by your opponent, you should address it head-on in your brief at the earliest possible opportunity.

In the following example, we have drafted a portion of a brief so as to demonstrate some of the points made in the preceding discussion. In particular, it demonstrates breaking a point up into sub-points and using short paragraphs, each one expressing a single idea. It also demonstrates

---

[38]For an example of an argument that a decision is wrong, *see* Ch. 4, § H.1.c, in which we argue that a decision of one federal appeals court concerning the calling of witnesses at disciplinary hearing is inconsistent with relevant authority from the United States Supreme Court.

[39]For an example of a case discussing legislative intent in the context of prisoner litigation, *see* Greig v. Goord, 169 F.3d 165, 167 (2d Cir. 1999) (holding Congress did not intend for Prison Litigation Reform Act exhaustion requirement to apply to persons who have been released).

[40]An example of a successful argument of this kind appears in *Patterson v. Coughlin*, 905 F.2d 564 (2d Cir. 1990). Plaintiffs usually have the burden of proving that an unconstitutional disciplinary proceeding would have come out differently if proper procedures had been followed. In *Patterson*, the court held that prison officials' actions had made it impossible for the prisoner to locate witnesses to meet this burden of proof. Therefore, the court

held that in that particular case, the burden of proof would be on prison officials. 905 F.2d at 570.

[41]An example of this kind of argument appears in *Bell v. City of Milwaukee*, 746 F.2d 1205 (7th Cir. 1984), *overruled on other grounds*, Russ v. Watts, 414 F.3d 783, 788 (7th Cir. 2005), where the court held that a claim of civil rights violation should "survive" the death of the victim if that death was caused by the civil rights violation. To rule that the claim did not survive would be undesirable because "it would be more advantageous to the unlawful actor to kill rather than injure." *Id.* at 1239.

[42]*See* Hudson v. McMillan, 503 U.S. 1, 12–14, 112 S. Ct. 995 (1992) (concurring opinion).

connecting the legal argument with the facts and citing and distinguishing authority.

Here is the background for the example: Suppose you have severe migraine headaches and a doctor prescribes medication to help control them, but prison officials fail to provide the medication. Suppose you sue them, but prison officials file a motion to dismiss on the grounds that your complaint does not state a constitutional claim because your medical problem is not serious, that you are only disagreeing with prison medical staff, that you received some medical treatment, and they are not intentionally trying to hurt you. You might respond as follows:

Argument
Point 1
The Complaint States a Claim Under the Eighth Amendment

The Supreme Court has ruled that "deliberate indifference to serious medical needs of prisoners" is cruel and unusual punishment. *Estelle v. Gamble*, 429 U.S. 97, 104 (1976). The complaint alleges facts that state a constitutional claim under this standard.

A. The Plaintiff Has a Serious Medical Need

The defendants argue that the plaintiff's medical problem is not "serious" because it consists of "mere headaches." Defendants' Memorandum of Law at page X. They are wrong for the following reasons.

First, courts generally agree that a medical need is "serious" if it "has been diagnosed by a physician as mandating treatment." *Brown v. Johnson*, 387 F.3d 1344, 1351 (11th Cir. 2004); *Johnson v. Busbee*, 953 F.2d 349, 351 (8th Cir. 1991); *Gaudreault v. Municipality of Salem, Mass.*, 923 F.2d 203, 208 (1st Cir. 1990); *Monmouth County Correctional Institution Inmates v. Lanzaro*, 834 F.2d 326, 347 (3d Cir. 1987). In this case, the prison doctor thought the plaintiff's problem was serious enough to require treatment, and she prescribed medication for it. Complaint at ¶ XX. The plaintiff's problem is therefore "serious" under the holdings of the above-cited cases.

Second, a medical condition may be serious if it "significantly affects an individual's daily activities." *Hayes v. Snyder*, 546 F.3d 516, 523 (7th Cir. 2008) (citations omitted); *McGuckin v. Smith*, 974 F.2d 1050, 1060 (9th Cir. 1992). Plaintiff's "mere headaches" have had serious consequences for him. The complaint alleges that his migraine headaches are so serious that at times he is unable to work, read, write, or leave his cell for meals or activities. Complaint at ¶ XX. Thus, they "significantly affect" the plaintiff's daily activities.

Finally, courts have acknowledged that conditions that cause significant pain are serious medical needs. *Brock v. Wright*, 315 F.3d 158, 162 (2d Cir. 2003) ("chronic and substantial pain" indicates that a medical need is serious); *McGuckin v. Smith*, 974 F.2d 1050, 1060 (9th Cir. 1992) (same as *Brock*); *Gutierrez v. Peters*, 111 F.3d 1364, 1371 (7th Cir. 1997) ("delays in treating painful medical conditions that are not life-threatening can support Eighth Amendment claims"; infected pilonidal cyst); *Boretti v. Wiscomb*, 930 F.2d 1150, 1154-55 (6th Cir. 1991) (needless pain is actionable even if there is not permanent injury). This is true because a chief purpose of the Cruel and Unusual Punishments Clause is to prevent the "unnecessary and wanton infliction of pain." *Estelle v. Gamble*, 429 U.S. at 104 (citation omitted). The Complaint alleges that the plaintiff has suffered significant and recurrent pain from his headaches. Complaint at ¶ XX. This pain is sufficient to make the plaintiff's medical need "serious."

Defendants argue that migraine headaches are not really serious, citing *Boring v. Kozakiewicz*, 833 F.2d 468, 473 (3d Cir, 1987). Defendants' Memo. at X. In fact, *Boring* does not say that. *Boring* dismissed a particular prisoner's complaint of migraine headaches on the ground that the seriousness of his problem was not "apparent to a lay person" and that he provided no expert testimony about seriousness. In this case, by contrast, the plaintiff has stated facts that would permit a lay person to conclude that his problem was serious. These facts are the pain he suffered, the degree of interference with his daily activities, and the fact that the prison doctor prescribed medication for him. Complaint at ¶ ¶ XX-XX. The *Boring* opinion does not indicate that the plaintiff in that case pled specific facts of this nature, and *Boring* is therefore distinguishable.

Boring was also at a completely different procedural stage from this case. There, the defendants had moved for summary judgment, and the issue was whether the plaintiffs' *evidence* created a "genuine issue of material fact." Rule 56(c), Fed.R.Civ.P. Here, the defendants have moved to dismiss the complaint, and the only issue is whether the complaint's *allegations* state a constitutional claim. *Roth Steel Products v. Sharon Steel Corp.*, 705 F.2d 134, 155 (6th Cir. 1982). What either party might or might not show on a motion for summary judgment is simply not before the court at this point.

For these reasons, the Complaint sufficiently alleges a serious medical need on the part of the plaintiff.

B. Defendants' Conduct Amounts to Deliberate Indifference

The complaint alleges that the prison doctor prescribed medication to control the plaintiff's headaches, but that prison officials have on some occasions failed to keep that medication in stock in the pharmacy and on other occasions have failed to allow the plaintiff to go to the medication window to get his medication. Complaint at ¶¶ XX-XX.

"[I]ntentionally interfering with the treatment once prescribed" is one of the forms of deliberate indifference cited by the Supreme Court. *Estelle v. Gamble*, 429 U.S. at 105. Many decisions have held that failing or refusing to provide medication prescribed by physicians constitutes deliberate indifference. *Gil v. Reed*, 381 F.3d 649, 661 (7th Cir. 2004); *Aswegan v. Bruhl*, 965 F.2d 676, 677-78 (8th Cir. 1992); *Hill v. Marshall*, 962 F.2d 1209, 1213-14 (6th Cir. 1992); *Johnson v. Hay*, 931 F.2d 456, 461-62 (8th Cir. 1991); *Boretti v. Wiscomb*, 930 F.2d 1150, 1156 (6th Cir. 1991); *Johnson v. Hardin County, Ky.*, 908 F.2d 1280, 1284 (6th Cir. 1990); *Ellis v. Butler*, 890 F.2d 1001, 1003-04 (8th Cir. 1989).

The defendants argue that failure to provide prescribed medication does not violate the Constitution, citing *Mayweather v. Foti*, 958 F.2d 91 (5th Cir. 1992). What *Mayweather* actually says is that "*occasionally*, a dose of medication may have been forgotten. . . ." (Emphasis supplied.) Here, by contrast, it was more than "occasionally" that the plaintiff was denied his medication. The complaint at ¶ XX alleges that the plaintiff was denied his prescribed medication more than half the time. *Mayweather* is therefore distinguishable.

The defendants also argue, and cite cases holding, that a prisoner's disagreement with her medical treatment does not violate the Constitution. That is true, but it is not applicable to this case. Here, the prison doctor *agreed* that the plaintiff should receive medication, and she prescribed it. It is the other defendants—the warden, the pharmacy manager, and the unit supervisor of plaintiff's housing unit—who have obstructed the plaintiff's prescribed medical care by failing to give him access to his medication and to ensure that it was available in the pharmacy.

The foregoing is an example of the Argument section of the brief. Complete sample briefs that include statement of facts and other sections appear in Appendix C.

Finally, a word about citing and quoting cases. Citations are discussed elsewhere,[43] and you will see indications of how to cite cases properly throughout the footnotes of this Manual. When you cite a case, you should give its full citation the first time you cite it, *e.g.*, *Smith v. Jones*, 123 F.3d 456, 458 (10th Cir. 2002). The second page number, 458, would be the "pin cite," which is the page where the court makes the particular point you are citing it for. When you cite the case again, you can use a "short form" cite, *e.g.*, *Smith v. Jones*, 123 F.3d at 458—though it may be a good idea to use the full cite if the previous cite was much earlier in your papers. When you cite a case repeatedly, you can abbreviate the citation even more, *e.g.*, *Smith*, 123 F.3d at 458. Just be sure it is absolutely clear what case you are citing so the court won't get confused about what you are saying.

When you use the full cite to a case, you should include any subsequent judicial history.[44] For example, if you are citing a district court case that was affirmed on appeal, you would indicate that fact, *e.g.*, *Smith v. Jones*, 123 F.Supp.2d 456 (D.Colo. 2001), *aff'd*, 123 F.3d 456 (10th Cir. 2002). Sometimes it isn't that simple, and an appellate court will reverse the district court, or affirm, reverse, and/or remand some parts and not others. In cases like that, you should first be sure that the point you are citing the case for was not reversed on appeal. If it was reversed on the ground you are citing it for, it is no longer authoritative and will generally not help you.[45] If the appellate decision does not simply affirm everything the lower court did, you will want to cite the case in a way that tells the court the status of the holding you are relying on. For example, if the appellate court did not rule on your point but reversed for some other unrelated reason, your citation would say *rev'd on other grounds*. Look at the conclusion of the appellate decision for a clear statement of what it did to the lower court decision. You can also look at the footnotes in this Manual to get an idea of the different ways of describing what appellate courts have done.

When the Supreme Court denies certiorari (refuses to hear a case), your citation should conclude *cert. denied*, 123 U.S. 456, or *cert. denied*, 123 S.Ct. 456. (The S.Ct. cite is always available before the U.S. cite.) However, *cert. denied* cites need not be included if they are more than two years old.[46] If the Supreme Court actually did hear and decide the case, you should include the Supreme Court disposition no matter how old it is.

When you use a quotation from a case, be sure you use the court's exact words, and do not quote selectively so as to alter the meaning of what the court said. There will be cases where you need to cut down a quotation from a case, *e.g.*,

---

[43]*See* Ch. 11, § B.2.

[44]*See* Ch. 11, § B.1.4(f).

[45]There are rare exceptions. If a lower court ruled your way in another jurisdiction, and an appellate court outside your jurisdiction reversed it, you might want to argue that the court in your case should follow the lower court decision because it is more logical and convincing than the appellate reversal. An example of this kind of argument appears in Ch. 4, § H.1.c, n.325.

[46]Harvard Law Review Ass'n, *The Bluebook: A Uniform System of Citation*, Rule 10.7 at 92 (18th ed. 2005).

where you need to quote the first and fourth sentences in a paragraph to make your point, but the other sentences are not relevant, or there is a long string of citations that takes up space. If you omit anything from a quotation, you must insert ellipsis marks consisting of three periods (four periods if the ellipsis is at the end of a sentence) to show that you have left something out. Sometimes it is necessary to insert or substitute something into a quotation to make it understandable. For example, a court might say: "Under the above discussed rule, a statement of reasons for a disciplinary decision that merely says 'based on reports submitted, the prisoner is guilty as charged,' denies due process." That statement does not make clear that the "above discussed rule" is the holding of *Wolff v. McDonnell*, the Supreme Court's leading

disciplinary due process. To make the quotation usable, you can insert the case name, in brackets, so the court will know you have altered the quotation for clarity, *e.g.*, "Under the [*Wolff v. McDonnell*] rule, a statement of reasons," etc. You should do this very sparingly and very carefully, since if the court thinks you are misrepresenting case holdings, it will not trust anything you say, and you might be sanctioned.

APPENDIX A

United States Federal Courts Directory

United States Supreme Court

United States Supreme Court
1 First Street, N.E.
Washington, DC 20543

United States Court of Appeals

DISTRICT OF COLUMBIA CIRCUIT
United States Courthouse
Third and Constitution Avenues, N.W.
Washington, DC 20001

FIRST CIRCUIT
United States Courthouse
1 Courthouse Way
Boston, MA 02109

SECOND CIRCUIT
United States Courthouse
500 Pearl Street
New York, NY 10007

THIRD CIRCUIT
United States Courthouse
601 Market Street
Philadelphia, PA 19106

FOURTH CIRCUIT
United States Courthouse
1100 East Main Street
Richmond, CA 23219-3525

FIFTH CIRCUIT
Federal Building
600 S. Maestri Place
New Orleans, LA 70130

SIXTH CIRCUIT
United States Courthouse
100 E. Fifth Street, Ste. 500
Cincinnati, OH 45202

SEVENTH CIRCUIT
United States Courthouse
219 S. Dearborn Street
Chicago, IL 60604

EIGHTH CIRCUIT
United States Courthouse
111 S. Tenth Street
St. Louis, MO 63102-1116

NINTH CIRCUIT
United States Courthouse
95 Seventh Street
San Francisco, CA 94103-1518

TENTH CIRCUIT
United States Courthouse
1823 Stout Street, 1st Floor
Denver, CO 80202-2505

ELEVENTH CIRCUIT
Court of Appeals Building
56 Forsyth Street, N.W.
Atlanta, GA 30303

United States District Court

ALABAMA MIDDLE
P.O. Box 711
Montgomery, AL 36101

ALABAMA NORTHERN
United States Courthouse
1729 Fifth Avenue North
Birmingham, AL 35203-2000

ALABAMA SOUTHERN
123 John A. Campbell
United States Courthouse
113 St. Joseph Street
Mobile, AL 36602

ALASKA
Internal Box 4
Anchorage, AK 99513-9513

ARIZONA
United States Courthouse
401 W. Washington Street
Phoenix, AZ 85003-2146

ARKANSAS EASTERN
United States Courthouse
600 W. Capitol Avenue
Little Rock, AR 72201

ARKANSAS WESTERN
P.O. Box 1547
Fort Smith, AR 72902

CALIFORNIA CENTRAL
G-8 United States Courthouse
312 North Spring Street
Los Angeles, CA 90012-4701

CALIFORNIA EASTERN
4-200 United States Courthouse
501 I Street
Sacramento, CA 95814-7300

CALIFORNIA NORTHERN
450 Golden Gate Avenue
Box 36060
San Francisco, CA 94102-3434

CALIFORNIA SOUTHERN
Federal Building, Ste. 4290
880 Front Street
San Diego, CA 92101

COLORADO
United States Courthouse, 2nd Fl.
901 19th Street
Denver, CO 80294

CONNECTICUT
United States Courthouse
141 Church Street
New Haven, CT 06510

DELAWARE
Federal Building
844 North King Street
Wilmington, DE 19801-3519

DISTRICT OF COLUMBIA
United States Courthouse
333 Constitution Avenue, N.W.
Washington, DC

FLORIDA MIDDLE
United States Courthouse, Ste. 1200
401 W. Central Boulevard
Orlando, FL 32801

FLORIDA NORTHERN
United States Courthouse Annex, 3rd Fl.
111 North Adams Street
Tallahassee, FL 32301

FLORIDA SOUTHERN
United State Courthouse
400 North Miami Avenue
Miami, FL 33128

GEORGIA MIDDLE
P.O. Box 128
Macon, GA 31202

GEORGIA NORTHERN
United States Courthouse
75 Spring Street, S.W.
Atlanta, GA 30303-3309

GEORGIA SOUTHERN
P.O. Box 8286
Savannah, GA 31412

GUAM
United States Courthouse, 4th Fl.
520 West Soledad Avenue
Hagatna, GU 96910-4950

HAWAII
Federal Building
300 Ala Moana Boulevard
Honolulu, HI 96850-0001

IDAHO
United States Courthouse
550 West Fort Street
Boise, ID 83724-0101

ILLINOIS CENTRAL
United States Courthouse
600 East Monroe Street
Springfield, IL 62701

ILLINOIS NORTHERN
United States Courthouse, 20th Fl.
219 South Dearborn Street
Chicago, IL 60604

ILLINOIS SOUTHERN
United States Courthouse
750 Missouri Avenue
East St. Louis, IL 62201

INDIANA NORTHERN
United States Courthouse
204 South Main Street
South Bend, IN 46601

INDIANA SOUTHERN
United States Courthouse
46 East Ohio Street
Indianapolis, IN 46204

IOWA NORTHERN
4200 C. Street WS
Cedar Rapids, IA 52404

IOWA SOUTHERN
P.O. Box 9344
Des Moines, IA 50306-9344

KANSAS
United States Courthouse
500 State Avenue
Kansas City, KS 66101-2400

KENTUCKY EASTERN
United States Courthouse, 2nd Fl.
101 Barr Street
Lexington, KY 40507-1313

KENTUCKY WESTERN
United States Courthouse, Ste. 106
601 West Broadway
Louisville, KY 40202-2227

LOUISIANA EASTERN
United States Courthouse
500 Poydras Street
New Orleans, LA 70130

LOUISIANA MIDDLE
Federal Building, Ste. 139
777 Florida Street
Baton Rouge, LA 70801

LOUISIANA WESTERN
United States Courthouse, Ste. 1167
300 Fannin Street
Shrevport, LA 71101

MAINE
Federal Courthouse
156 Federal Street
Portland, ME 04101-4152

MARYLAND
United States Courthouse
101 West Lombard Street
Baltimore, MD 21201-2605

MASSACHUSETTS
United States Courthouse, Ste. 2300
One Courthouse Way
Boston, MA 02210-3002

MICHIGAN EASTERN
United States Courthouse
231 West Lafayette Boulevard
Detroit, MI 48226

MICHIGAN WESTERN
Federal Building
110 Michigan Street, N.W.
Grand Rapids, MI 49503

MINNESOTA
United States Courthouse, Ste. 202
300 South Fourth Street
Minneapolis, MN 55415

MISSISSIPPI NORTHERN
United States Courthouse
911 Jackson Avenue East
Oxford, MS 38655

MISSISSIPPI SOUTHERN
P.O. Box 23552
Jackson, MS 39225-3552

MISSOURI EASTERN
United States Courthouse
111 South Tenth Street
St. Louis, MO 63102-1116

MISSOURI WESTERN
United States Courthouse
400 East Ninth Street
Kansas City, MO 64106

MONTANA
P.O. Box 8537
Missoula, MT 59807-8527

NEBRASKA
United State Courthouse, Ste. 1152
111 South 18th Plaza
Omaha, NE 68102

NEVADA
United State Courthouse, 1st Fl.
333 Las Vegas Boulevard South
Las Negas, NV 89101-7065

NEW HAMPSHIRE
United States Courthouse
55 Pleasant Street
Concord, NH 03301

NEW JERSEY
United States Courthouse
50 Walnut Street
Newark, NJ 07102

NEW MEXICO
United States Courthouse, Ste. 270
333 Lomas Boulevard, N.W.
Albuquerque, NM 87102

NEW YORK EASTERN
1185 United States Courthouse
225 Cadman Plaza East
Brooklyn, NY 11201-1818

NEW YORK NORTHERN
P.O. Box 7367
Syracuse, NY 13261-7367

NEW YORK SOUTHERN
United States Courthouse
500 Pearl Street
New York, NY 10007-1312

NEW YORK WESTERN
United States Courthouse
68 Court Street
Buffalo, NY 14202-3328

NORTH CAROLINA EASTERN
P.O. Box 25670
Raleigh, NC 27611

NORTH CAROLINA MIDDLE
Federal Building, Ste. 1
324 West Market Street
Greensboro, NC 27401-7455

NORTH CAROLINA WESTERN
Federal Building
401 West Trade Street
Charlotte, NC 28202

NORTH DAKOTA
P.O. Box 1193
Bismarck, NC 58502-1193

NORTHERN MARIANA ISLANDS
P.O. Box 500687
Saipan, MP 96950

OHIO NORTHERN
United States Courthouse
801 West Superior Avenue
Cleveland, OH 44113

OHIO SOUTHERN
United States Courthouse
85 Marconi Boulevard
Columbus, OH 43215-2835

OKLAHOMA EASTERN
P.O. Box 607
Muskogee, OK 74402

OKLAHOMA NORTHERN
United States Courthouse
333 West Fourth Street
Tulsa, OK 74103-3819

OKLAHOMA WESTERN
United States Courthouse
200 Northwest Fourth
Oklahoma City, OK 73102

OREGON
United States Courthouse
1000 Southwest Third Avenue
Portland, OR 97204-2802

PENNSYLVANIA EASTERN
United States Courthouse
601 Market Street
Philadelphia, PA 19105-1797

PENNSYLVANIA MIDDLE
P.O. Box 1148
Scranton, PA 18501

PENNSYLVANIA WESTERN
United States Courthouse
700 Grant Street
Pittsburgh, PA 15219-1906

PUERTO RICO
Federal Building
150 Carlos Chardon Avenue
San Juan, PR 00918-1767

RHODE ISLAND
United States Courthouse
One Exchange Terrace
Providence, RI 02903-1270

SOUTH CAROLINA
United States Courthouse
901 Richland Street
Columbia, SC 29201

SOUTH DAKOTA
United States Courthouse
400 South Phillips Avenue
Sioux Falls, SD 57104-6581

TENNESSEE EASTERN
United States Courthouse, Ste. 130
800 Market Street
Knoxville, TN 37902-7902

TENNESSEE MIDDLE
United States Courthouse
801 Broadway
Nashville, TN 37203-3816

TENNESSEE WESTERN
Federal Building
167 North Main Street
Memphis, TN 38103

TEXAS EASTERN
United States Courthouse
211 West Ferguson Street
Tyler, TX 75702

TEXAS NORTHERN
United States Courthouse
1100 Commerce Street
Dallas, TX 75242-1310

TEXAS SOUTHERN
P.O. Box 61010
Houston, TX 77208

TEXAS WESTERN
United States Courthouse
655 East Durango Boulevard
San Antonio, TX 78206

UTAH
United States Courthouse
350 South Main Street
Salt Lake City, UT 84101

VERMONT
P.O. Box 945
Burlington, VT 05402

VIRGIN ISLANDS
Federal Building
3013 Estate Golden Rock
St. Croix, VI 00820-0820

VIRGINIA EASTERN
United States Courthouse
600 Granby Street
Norfolk, VA 23510-1915

VIRGINIA WESTERN
P.O. Box 1234
Roanoke, VA 24006

WASHINGTON EASTERN
United States Courthouse, Ste. 840
920 West Riverside Avenue
Spokane, WA 99201-1010

WASHINGTON WESTERN
United States Courthouse
700 Stewart Street
Seattle, WA 98101-1271

WEST VIRGINIA NORTHERN
P.O. Box 1518
Elkins, WV 26241

WEST VIRGINIA SOUTHERN
United States Courthouse
300 Virginia Street East
Charleston WV 25301

WISCONSIN EASTERN
Federal Building
517 East Wisconsin Avenue
Milwaukee, WI 53202

WISCONSIN WESTERN
United States Courthouse
120 North Henry Street
Madison, WI 53703-4304

WYOMING
Federal Building
2130 Capitol Avenue
Cheyenne, WY 82001

APPENDIX B

Prisoners' Assistance Organizations

The information in this appendix is taken from the *Prisoners' Assistance Directory* published by the National Prison Project of the American Civil Liberties Union, as updated in 2008, and is reprinted with that office's kind permission.

The directory lists organizations that provide legal and other assistance to prisoners. Keep in mind that as time passes, organizations change personnel and addresses, and sometimes go out of existence entirely, so we cannot guarantee the accuracy of this information at the time you are consulting this Manual.

The directory is updated on a regular basis by the National Prison Project of the ACLU, 915 15th Street, NW, 7th Floor, Washington, DC 20005, and any future editions can be obtained from that office.

NATIONAL AND REGIONAL ORGANIZATIONS

Corrections/Criminal Justice/Legal

American Civil Liberties Union (ACLU)
Address: 125 Broad Street
           New York, NY 10004
Phone: (212) 549-2500
Website: www.aclu.org
Services: See the listing of state affiliates for services available in your area.

ACLU National Prison Project
Address: 915 15th Street, N.W., 7th Floor
           Washington, DC 20005
Phone: (202) 393-4930; (202) 393-4931 fax
E-mail: npp@npp-aclu.org
Website: www.aclu.org/prisons
Services: Handle class action suits involving prison conditions and related issues in state and federal institutions. Litigation is usually limited to cases involving major class actions challenging prison conditions or otherwise of national significance. Also provide advice and materials to individuals or organizations involved in prison issues. Do not handle cases on behalf of individual prisoners (except sexual assault cases) or post-conviction cases. Several publications are available from the NPP, including the biannual Journal - $2 a year for prisoners and $35 a year for non-prisoners. See Publications section (now in Appendix D) for a complete list.

American Friends Service Committee

Contact: Joyce D. Miller
Address: 1501 Cherry Street, Philadelphia, PA 19102
Phone: (215) 241-7000
E-mail: afscinfo@afsc.org
Website: www.afsc.org
Services: National and local healing justice programs focus on advocacy, education, policy development and organizing. Publish analysis and action reports (free to prisoners), including: Survivors Manual, a manual written by and for people living in control units; The Prison Inside the Prison: Control Units, Supermax Prisons, and Devices of Torture. Also online StopMax Campaign (www.afsc.org/stopmax) to promote and support a national movement to end solitary confinement and related forms of torture in US prisons; and Rights 101: How and when to assert your rights with the Police (www.afsc.org/rights101), an online manual for youth workers and facilitators of youth workshops.

Center on Juvenile and Criminal Justice (CJCJ)

Contact: Dan Macallair
Address: 54 Dore Street
San Francisco, CA 94103
Phone: (415) 621-5661; (415) 621-5466 fax
E-mail: cjcj@cjcj.org
Website: www.cjcj.org
Services: Offer Alternative Sentencing Program (ASP) reports, which are written proposals that CJCJ presents to courts, parole boards, or other agencies that control juvenile and adult sentencing. A proposal is developed in conjunction with the defendant and his/her attorney. It usually includes a social history, analysis of the instant offense, and a sentence recommendation. The sentence recommendation generally includes a rationale based on sentencing rules and several sentencing options, such as treatment, community service, restitution, and a volunteer community advocate. CJCJ is available to make adjustments in the elements of a plan should the client be unable to meet any of the conditions. Prisoners and persons facing imprisonment who are interested in ASP services should have their attorneys contact Dan Macallair. Also publish a wide variety of articles and booklets on prison conditions, the criminal-justice system, and other issues. See Publications section (now in Appendix D) for a complete list.

Centurion Ministries

Address: 221 Witherspoon Street
Princeton, NJ 08542
Services: Only handles cases in which a prisoner has been sentenced to either death or life in prison without parole, cases in which a prisoner has exhausted most or all appeals, and cases in which a prisoner is claiming absolute innocence. No self-defense or accidental-death cases.

Citizens United for Rehabilitation of Errants (CURE)

Contact: Charlie Sullivan
Address: P.O. Box 2310
Washington, DC 20013
Phone: (202) 789-2126
Website: www.curenational.org
Services: Organize prisoners, their families and other concerned citizens to achieve reforms in the criminal-justice system. CURE has a presence in 40 states. See listings for individual states in this directory or write for complete listing of addresses of state chapters. Does not handle individual cases.

Families Against Mandatory Minimums (FAMM)

Contact: Julie Stewart
Address: 1612 K Street, N.W. - #700
Washington, DC 20006
Phone: (202) 822-6700; (202) 822-6704 fax
E-mail: FAMM@FAMM.org
Website: www.FAMM.org
Services: Work to change mandatory sentencing laws. Provide information about the laws and how to change them. FAMM's local chapters hold rallies, meet with the media, give speeches, and distribute information so a wider audience will understand the need for alternatives to incarceration and fair punishment. Offers a newsletter, *FAMM-gram*. Contributions accepted.

Fortune Society

Contact: Sherri Goldstein
Address: 53 W. 23rd Street
New York, NY 10010
Phone: (212) 691-7554 x501; (212) 633-6845 fax
E-Mail: sgoldstein@fortunesociety.org
Website: www.fortunesociety.org
Services: Ex-offender self-help program. Provide educational programs, general counseling, HIV-AIDS assistance and court advocacy. Publishes *Fortune News*, free to prisoners upon request.

The Innocence Project

Address: 100 Fifth Avenue, 3rd Floor
New York, NY 10011

Phone: (212) 364-5340

Services: Case submissions are only handled by mail. This chapter only handles cases in which physical or biological evidence could prove innocence. Innocence Projects provide representation and/or investigative assistance to prison inmates who claim to be innocent of the crimes for which they were convicted. There is now at least one Innocence Project serving each state except Hawaii, North Dakota and South Dakota. Most of these innocence projects are new and over-whelmed with applications, so waiting time between application and acceptance is long. Wrongfully convicted persons should not be dissuaded from applying to Innocence Projects because of this, but should have realistic expectations regarding acceptance and time lags. Please go to the following website for informa-tion about other affiliates: http://www.innocenceproject.org/Content/313.php.

Law Offices of Alan Ellis, California Office

Contact: Alan Ellis

Address: 495 Miller Avenue - #201
Mill Valley, CA 94941

Phone: (415) 380-2550; (415) 380-2555 fax

E-mail: aelaw1@alanellis.com

Website: www.alanellis.com

Services: Provide post-conviction representation of federal criminal defendants including plea negotiations, sentencing, Rule 35 motions, appeals, § 2241 and § 2255 habeas corpus petitions and prison and parole matters. Publish *The Federal Prison Guidebook*, available to prisoners for $29.95.

Law Offices of Alan Ellis, Pennsylvania Office

Contact: Peter Goldberger or James H. Feldman

Address: 50 Rittenhouse Place
Ardmore, PA 19003

Phone: (610) 658-2255, (610) 649-8200

E-mail: aelaw2@aol.com

Website: www.alanellis.com

Services: Provide post-conviction representation of federal criminal defendants including plea negotiations, sentencing, Rule 35 motions, petitions under 28 U.S.C. § 2255, appeals, and Supreme Court petitions. Occasionally publish *Federal Sentencing and Postconviction News*, free for federal prisoners.

Law Office of Marcia G. Shein

Contact: Marcia G. Shein

Address: 2392 N. Decatur Road
Decatur, GA 30033

Phone: (404) 633-3797; (404) 633-7980 fax

Website: www.msheinlaw.com

Services: Handle federal criminal law pre- and post-conviction cases. Fees may be charged for services. Provide objective background reports for attorneys; interpretation of psychological informa-tion and related reports. Handle initial parole hearings; regional and national appeals; pre- and post-custody consulta-tion and early termination of probation and parole. All services are offered for pro se litigants. Research and development issues; sentencing mitigation; federal and supreme court appeals; habeas corpus § 2255; INS petitions to stay; deportation and prison transfers; clemency petitions. Distribute the *Federal Criminal Law News*.

Mennonite Central Committee, U.S. Office on Justice and Peacebuilding

Contact: Lorraine Stutzman Amstutz

Address: 21 S. 12th Street, P.O. Box 500
Akron, PA 17501

Phone: (717) 859-1151 or (888) 563-4676

Website: http://mcc.org/us/peacebuilding

Services: Educational and resource program, pro-viding a variety of materials on subjects such as prisons, alternatives to prison, and the death penalty. Several publica-tions are available free to prisoners and their families; contact the program for a resource list. Also provides consultation and information to individuals and groups involved in victim-offender reconciliation programs (VORPs).

National Association for the Advancement of Colored People

National Headquarters

Address: 4805 Mt. Hope Drive
Baltimore, MD 21215

Phone: (800) NAACP-98; (410) 580-5777 (local)

Website: www.naacp.org

Services: Eliminate disparate treatment in all aspects of law enforcement and criminal-justice systems. Eliminate capricious racial profiling practices. Ensure fair and equitable trials and sentences. Ensure felony re-entry. Promote a moratorium on the death penalty. We have offices in all 50 states, including Washington, DC.

We also have offices in Germany, Italy, Japan and Korea. Please see our website to get information for your local office.

National Center on Institutions and Alternatives

Address: 7222 Ambassador Road
              Baltimore, MD 21244
Phone: (410) 265-1490; (410) 597-9656 fax
E-mail: aboring@ncianet.org
Website: www.ncianet.org
Services: Offer private pre-sentence investigative services; technical assistance to jurisdictions regarding prison overcrowding, as well as jail suicide prevention. Conduct research on criminal-justice issues.

National Commission on Correctional Health Care

Contact: Cherie Minor
Address: 1145 W. Diversey Parkway
              Chicago, IL 60614
Phone: (773) 880-1460; (773) 880-2424 fax
Website: www.ncchc.org
Services: Publish standards for health services for jails, prisons and juvenile-detention confinement facilities. Serve as an accreditation body; develop programs for training correctional and health-care personnel; provide technical assistance to facilities; develop and distribute publications and uniform documentation; conduct annual national conference on correctional health care and other programs; and conduct research on selected aspects of correctional health care. Publish a quarterly newspaper, *CorrectCare*, which is available free to prison libraries but cannot be sent free to individual prisoners. Write for a complete list of publications.

Partnership for Safety and Justice

Contact: Kathleen Pequeno or Brigette Sarabi
Address: P.O. Box 40085
              Portland, OR 97240
Phone: (503) 335-8449; (503) 232-1922 fax
Website: www.safetyandjustice.org
Services: Partnership for Safety and Justice unites people convicted of crime, survivors of crime, and the families of both to advance approaches that redirect policies away from an over-reliance on incarceration to effective strategies that reduce violence and increase safety.

Prisoners' Rights Research Project

Address: University of Illinois College of Law
              332 Law Building, m/c 594
              504 East Pennsylvania Avenue
              Champaign, IL 61820
Phone: (217) 333-4205; (217) 244-1478 fax
Services: Students provide back-up legal research assistance for prisoners nationwide. Cannot give advice or represent prisoners and can answer only specific questions. Will copy no more than 10 pages.

Safer Society Foundation

Contact: Tammy Kennedy
Address: P.O. Box 340
              Brandon, VT 05733
Phone: (802) 247-3132; (802) 247-4233 fax
E-mail: tammyk@sover.net
Website: www.safersociety.org
Services: Provide sexual-abuse prevention and treatment publications and operate a national referral line for those seeking treatment providers for sexually offending behaviors. This program is free and confidential, and open to all: offenders, family and friends of offenders, social workers, court and corrections personnel and therapists. Also answer general resource requests from prisoners, such as, providing contact information on self-help groups, and providing worksheets on general information regarding sexual abuse, etc.

The Sentencing Project

Contact: Marc Mauer
Address: 514 Tenth Street, N.W. - #1000
              Washington, DC 20004
Phone: (202) 628-0871; (202) 628-1091 fax
E-mail: staff@sentencingproject.org
Website: www.sentencingproject.org
Services: Provide technical assistance to develop alternative sentencing programs and conduct research on criminal-justice issues. No direct services to prisoners.

Southern Poverty Law Center

Contact: Rhonda Brownstein
Address: 400 Washington Avenue
              Montgomery, AL 36104
Phone: (334) 956-8200
Website: www.splcenter.org
Services: Handle class action civil-rights suits involving prison conditions, access to health care, education, voting rights, and hate crimes.

Stop Prisoner Rape

Address: 3325 Wilshire Boulevard - #340
              Los Angeles, CA 90010
Phone: (213) 384-1400; (213) 384-1411 fax

E-mail: info@spr.org
Website: www.spr.org
Services: Seek to end sexual violence against men, women, and minors in all forms of detention. SPR's website provides information for survivors, a legal section with legislation and case law, appeals for action, a comprehensive bibliography, and links to articles, reports, and other resources. Prisoners wishing to communicate with SPR should address their correspondence to Ms. Melissa Rothstein, Esq.

U.S. Department of Justice, Civil Rights Division, Special Litigation Section

Address: Special Litigation Section
             U.S. Department of Justice
             Civil Rights Division
             950 Pennsylvania Avenue, N.W.
             Washington, DC 20530
Phone: (202) 514-6255 or (877) 218-5228; (202) 514-0212 fax
Website: www.usdoj.gov/crt/split
Services: Enforce the Civil Rights of Institutionalized Persons Act (CRIPA), which authorizes the Attorney General to conduct investigations and initiate litigation relating to conditions of confinement in state or locally operated institutions. Investigate facilities to determine whether there is a pattern or practice of violations of residents' federal rights. Maintain enforcement responsibility for Title III of the Civil Rights Act of 1964, which prohibits racial discrimination in public facilities. Enforce the portion of the Religious Land Use and Institutionalized Persons Act (RLUIPA) that protects institutionalized individuals' right to the free exercise of their religion. Also, enforce provisions of two different federal statutes relating to law-enforcement misconduct: the police misconduct provision of the Violent Crime Control and Law Enforcement Act of 1994, and the Safe Streets Act of 1968, which authorize the Attorney General to initiate civil litigation to remedy a pattern or practice of discrimination by federally funded law-enforcement agencies based on race and other characteristics.

AIDS/Hepatitis

AIDS Education Project of the National Prison Project

Contact: Jackie Walker
Address: 915 15th Street, N.W., 7th Floor
             Washington, DC 20005

Phone: (202) 393-4930; (202) 393-4931 fax
E-mail: jwalker@npp-aclu.org
Services: Serve as a clearinghouse for information on HIV/AIDS, Hepatitis, and STDs in prisons and jails. Provide assistance to HIV/AIDS/Hepatitis peer-education groups, advocacy on individual cases, legal information, and referrals. Publish *Play It Safer*—free single copies and paid bulk orders available. See Publications section (now in Appendix D) for more information.

CDC National Prevention Information Network (National AIDS Clearinghouse)

Address: P.O. Box 6003
             Rockville, MD 20849-6003
Phone: (800) 458-5231 (toll-free);
             (404) 679-3860 international; (888) 282-7681 fax
E-mail: info@cdcnpin.org
Website: www.cdcnpin.org
Services: The Center for Disease Control's NPIN develops, identifies, and collects information on the prevention and control of HIV/AIDS, sexually transmitted diseases, and tuberculosis and disseminates this information to the CDC, national prevention hotlines, state and local health departments, grassroots community groups, and health professionals. These groups, in turn, use NPIN materials to educate individuals at risk for these diseases about the critical role that environment and behavior play in disease prevention. A core feature of the NPIN is comprehensive databases housing up-to-date information on community resources and services, educational materials, funding opportunities, and news summaries from the popular press and scientific and medical journals. Other services provided include a toll-free 800 number; CDC-approved publications such as resource guides and prevention brochures; a website featuring searchable databases and full-text publications; resource centers that offer onsite technical assistance and training; and an HIV/AIDS resource service designed specifically for businesses.

CDC National STD/HIV Hotline

Phone: (800) 232-4636; (888) 232-6348 TTY
E-mail: dstd@cdc.gov
Website: www.cdc.gov/std
Services: Call for information about STDs and referrals to STD clinics.

Hepatitis C (HCV) Prison Support Project

Contact:	Phyllis Beck
Address:	P.O. Box 41803
	Eugene, OR 97404
Phone:	(541) 607-5725; (541) 607-5684 fax
E-mail:	pkbeckinor@aol.com
Website:	www.hcvinprison.org
Services:	Educate prisoners and advocate for better testing, diagnosis, and prevention of Hepatitis and HIV/HCV co-infection. Distribute bimonthly newsletter and Hepatitis C, HIV/HCV co-infection packets free to prisoners.

National Minority AIDS Council

Address:	Prison Initiative
	1931 13th Street, N.W.
	Washington, DC 20009
Phone:	(202) 483-6622, x333; (202) 483-1135 fax
E-mail:	info@nmac.org
Website:	www.nmac.org
Services:	Develop and disseminate HIV/AIDS education and training interventions for target groups, including prisoners living with and at risk for HIV/AIDS, prison health-care providers and community-based HIV/AIDS service personnel. Provide technical assistance to community groups participating in the CDC/ HRSA Corrections Demonstration Project. The demonstration project aims to reduce recidivism and ensure continuity of care for HIV+ ex-offenders by connecting HIV+ prisoners with community HIV/AIDS services three to six months before they are released.

Book Programs/Pen Pals

Books to Prisoners

Address:	c/o Left Bank Books
	92 Pike Street, Box A
	Seattle, WA 98101
Phone:	(206) 442-2013 (voicemail)
E-mail:	bookstoprisoners@cs.com
Website:	www.bookstoprisoners.net
Services:	Provide free books to prisoners in all states except California. Books cannot be sent to prisons that only allow new books. BTP believes that books are tools for learning and opening minds to new ideas and possibilities. Prisoners should send specific requests (by title, author, topic or genre) and allow several months' reply time.

Prison Book Program

Address:	c/o Lucy Parsons Bookstore

	1306 Hancock Street - #100
	Quincy, MA 02169
Phone:	(617) 423-3298
E-mail:	info@prisonbookprogram.org
Website:	www.prisonbookprogram.org
Note:	Requests for books are accepted by mail only. Please use phone number only for book donations, financial contributions, or other information.
Services:	Dedicated to promoting literacy and education in the prison population nationwide. Provide free books to all prisoners. Prisoners can request specific titles or books on general topics, including politics, law, AIDS, feminism, economics, and history. Also supply academic texts and instructional materials, as well as publications in Spanish. Orders take three months to process.

Prison Library Project

Address:	915 West Foothill Boulevard - #128
	Claremont, CA 91711
Services:	Provide books and cassette tapes to individual prisoners, study groups, prison libraries and prison chaplains free of charge. Also publish *Ways and Means: A Resource List for Inmates.*

Prison Pen Pals

Address:	P.O. Box 120074
	Ft. Lauderdale, FL 33312
Services:	We list all names of prisoners who write to us without descriptions. We do not match pen pals, but rather the lists of prisoner names are distributed to various individuals, ministries, etc., and around the country. We also send names to half a dozen websites

Prisoners' Literature Project

Address:	c/o Bound Together Book Store
	1369 Haight Street
	San Francisco, CA 94117
Services:	Provide prisoners with free books, magazines and pamphlets. No books sent to Texas.

Prisoners' Reading Encouragement Project

Contact:	Annette Johnson
Address:	145 Nassau Street - #3D
	New York, NY 10038
Phone:	(212) 349-6741
E-mail:	info@prisonreader.org
Website:	www.prisonreader.org
Services:	A support organization to prison libraries and educational programs. Our mission

is threefold: to enhance literacy and educational opportunities for inmates by soliciting and making gifts to prison libraries; to educate the public about the need for libraries and educational programming within correctional facilities; and to establish scholarship funds for tuition and textbooks for inmates engaged in courses or independent study while in prison. All donations are tax deductible.

WriteAPrisoner.com

Address:	P.O. Box 10
	Edgewater, FL 32132
Phone:	(386) 427-5857
E-mail:	general-information@writeaprisoner.com
Website:	www.writeaprisoner.com
Services:	Prison pen pal organization providing Personal and Legal ads to inmates. We also offer a free resume service to inmates being released within the year; a program called "Back to Work"; and the Children Impacted by Crime Scholarship Fund. Our goal is to reduce recidivism through correspondence, education, employment, resources, and prevention.

WriteAPrisoner.com's Books Behind Bars

Address:	P.O. Box 10
	Edgewater, FL 32132
Phone:	(386) 427-5857
E-mail:	general-information@writeaprisoner.com
Website:	www.writeaprisoner.com/books-behind-bars
Services:	Established to help prison teachers, prison librarians, and prison chaplains obtain books and other educational materials they need through public donations. Our mission is to improve the overall effectiveness of the correctional system by bridging the gap between the public and these sometimes underfunded yet vitally important educational departments.

Death Penalty

ACLU Capital Punishment Project

Address:	201 West Main Street - #402
	Durham, NC 27701
Phone:	919-682-5659; 919-682-5961 fax
Website:	www.aclu.org/capital
Services:	The ACLU's Capital Punishment Project works toward the abolition of the death penalty.

Amnesty International, USA

Address:	5 Penn Plaza - 16th Floor
	New York, NY 10001
Phone:	(212) 807-8400; (212) 627-1451 fax
Website:	www.amnestyusa.org
Services:	Work to abolish the death penalty and publish death-penalty reports, available online.

National Coalition to Abolish the Death Penalty

Address:	1705 DeSales Street, N.W., 5th Floor
	Washington, DC 20036
Phone:	(202) 331-4090; (202) 331-4099 fax
E-mail:	info@ncadp.org
Website:	www.ncadp.org
Services:	Provide information and advocacy against the death penalty. Do not provide legal assistance. Publish a newsletter, *LIFELINES*, six times a year for members. Membership, $25/year. Also publish the *Abolitionist Directory*, which lists organizations working to end the death penalty. Updated annually, $2/copy.

Southern Center for Human Rights

Address:	83 Poplar Street, N.W.
	Atlanta, GA 30303-2122
Phone:	(404) 688-1202; (404) 688-9440 fax
E-mail:	rights@schr.org
Website:	www.schr.org
Services:	Provide representation of persons facing the death penalty and assistance to attorneys in death-penalty cases.

Drug Law Reform

ACLU Foundation Drug Law Reform Project

Contact:	Graham Boyd
Address:	1101 Pacific Avenue - #333
	Santa Cruz, CA 95060
Phone:	(831) 471-9000; (831) 471-9676 fax
Website:	www.aclu.org/drugpolicy
Services:	Our goal is to end punitive drug policies that cause the widespread violation of constitutional and human rights, as well as unprecedented levels of incarceration.

Families/Visitation

The Center for Children of Incarcerated Parents

Contact:	Denise Johnston
Address:	P.O. Box 41-286
	Eagle Rock, CA 90041
Phone:	(626) 449-2470; (626) 449-9001 fax
E-mail:	ccip@earthlink.net
Website:	www.e-ccip.org

Services: Provide clearinghouse of materials for prisoners and their families; a catalog is available by mail. Host correspondence parent education course for prisoners and conduct child-custody advocacy.

Family & Corrections Network

Address: 93 Old York Road, Suite 1 - #510
            Jenkintown, PA 19046
Phone: (215) 576-1110; (215) 576-1815 fax
E-mail: fcn@fcnetwork.org
Website: www.fcnetwork.org
Services: Offer information on children of prisoners, parenting programs for prisoners, prison visiting, incarcerated fathers and mothers, hospitality programs, keeping in touch, returning to the community, the impact of the justice system on families, and prison marriage. Provide extensive website on families of offenders and the FCN Report. FCN cannot mail out free publications, but agencies, counselors, friends and family may download free materials from our website and distribute them to prisoners. FCN does not provide legal assistance.

Foreverfamily

Address: 691 Garibaldi Street SW
            Atlanta, GA 30310
Phone: (404) 223-1200; (404) 223-1010 fax
E-mail: sbarnhill@mindspring.com
Website: www.foreverfam.org
Services: Volunteers aid children of imprisoned mothers by providing after-school programs, summer camp, recreational activities, service projects, and trips to visit their mothers. Imprisoned mothers are also provided with educational materials, re-entry assistance and psychological support.

National Coalition Against Domestic Violence

Address: 1120 Lincoln Street - #1603
            Denver, CO 80203
Phone: (303) 839-1852; (303) 839-1681 TTY;
            (303) 831-9251 fax
E-mail: mainoffice@ncadv.org
Website: www.ncadv.org
Services: NCADV is comprised of people dealing with the concerns of battered women and their families. We represent both rural and urban areas. Our programs support and involve battered women of all racial, social, religious and economic groups, ages and lifestyles. We oppose the use of violence as a means of control over others

and support equality in relationships and the concept of helping women assume power over their own lives. We strive toward becoming independent, community-based groups in which women make major policy and program decisions. We have over 50 offices nationwide. Please see our website for a complete list and contact information.

National Reproductive Freedom Project of the ACLU

Address: 125 Broad Street, 18th Floor
            New York, NY 10004-2400
Phone: (212) 549-2633; (212) 549-2652 fax
Website: www.aclu.org/reproductiverights
Services: Protects everyone's right to make informed decisions free from government interference about whether and when to become a parent.

Prisoner Visitation and Support (PVS)

Contact: Eric Corson
Address: 1501 Cherry Street
            Philadelphia, PA 19102
Phone: (215) 241-7117; (215) 241-7227 fax
E-mail: pvs@afsc.org
Website: www.prisonervisitation.org
Services: Provide visitation to prisoners at most federal and military prisons in the U.S. The visitors provide supportive services such as acting as nonjudgmental listeners, visiting once a month, and reaching out to prisoners in a spirit of mutual respect, trust and acceptance. With a national network of visitors, PVS maintains contact with prisoners who are transferred from prison to prison and who are in solitary confinement. Do not visit state prisons.

Tele-Net, Inc.

Phone: 1-888-925-7800
Website: www.telenetinc.net
Services: Dedicated to reducing the cost of collect calls placed by inmates from correctional facilities.

Volunteers of America

Address: 1660 Duke Street
            Alexandria, VA 22314
Phone: (800) 899-0089 or (703) 341-5000 (local);
            (703) 341-7000 fax
Website: www.volunteersofamerica.org
Services: Dedicated to helping those in need rebuild their lives and reach their full potential through providing emergency services and resources to ex-offenders

and their families. Services include employment training, technical assistance, bus tokens, clothing, tools, food, etc. Please visit the website to find one of their 40 offices throughout the country.

Gays/Lesbians

ACLU Lesbian Gay Bisexual Transgender and AIDS Project
Address: 125 Broad Street, 18th Floor
New York, NY 10004-2400
Phone: (212) 549-2627
Website: www.aclu.org/getequal
Services: The combined Project staff members are experts in constitutional law and civil rights, specializing in sexual orientation, gender identity, and HIV. Fights discrimination and moves public opinion on LGBT rights through the courts, legislatures and public education. Brings impact lawsuits in state and federal courts throughout the country; cases designed to have a significant effect on the lives of LGBT people and those with HIV/AIDS. In coalition with other civil-rights groups, we also lobby in Congress and support grassroots advocacy from local school boards to state legislatures.

Gay and Lesbian Advocates and Defenders (GLAD)
Contact: Intake Staff
Address: 30 Winter Street - #800
Boston, MA 02108
Phone: (617) 426-1350 or (800) 455-GLAD; (617) 426-3594 fax
E-mail: gladlaw@glad.org
Website: www.glad.org
Services: Impact litigation on gay, lesbian, bisexual, transgender and HIV-related civil-rights and discrimination issues within New England. No direct representation. Legal information line in English and Spanish, Monday through Friday, 1:30 to 4:30 p.m.

Gay and Lesbian Prisoner Project
Address: P.O. Box 1481
Boston, MA 02117
Services: Provide limited pen pal service for G/L/B/T prisoners and send resource information and articles related to G/L/B/T prisoner issues. Publish *Gay Community News* 3 or 4 times a year, free to lesbian and gay prisoners. Volunteer-run, services are limited.

Out of Control Lesbian Committee to Support Women Political Prisoners
Address: 3543 18th Street, Box 30
San Francisco, CA 94110
Services: Send resource information to women prisoners. Publish *Out of Time* newsletter 5 times a year, free to all prisoners. We are volunteer-run. Services are limited, but include activism and advocacy for women political prisoners.

PFLAG (Parents Family and Friends of Lesbians and Gays)
Address: 1726 M Street, N.W. - #400
Washington, DC 20036
Phone: (202) 467-8180; (202) 467-8194 fax
E-mail: info@pflag.org
Website: www.pflag.org
Services: In addition to providing support to families and friends of GLBT people, PFLAG members are advocates for legislation that promotes equality for GLBT people, as well as for educational efforts to do the same. We also advocate for GLBT quality through civil-rights legislation and legal protections. We have chapters located all over the U.S. Please see our website to find your local office.

Immigrants' Rights

National Immigrants Rights Project of the ACLU
Address: 125 Broad Street, 18th Floor
New York, NY 10004-2400
Phone: (212) 5490-2660; (212) 549-2654 fax
Address: 405 14th Street - #300
Oakland, CA 94612
Phone: (510) 625-2010; (510) 622-0050 fax
Services: Works to defend the civil and constitutional rights of immigrants through a comprehensive program of impact litigation and public education. The IRP files constitutional and class action lawsuits protecting the historic guarantee to judicial review, enforcing fair-employment practices, and maintaining constitutional safeguards against detention practices and biased asylum adjudication.

Juveniles

Center on Juvenile and Criminal Justice (CJCJ)
Address: 54 Dore Street
San Francisco, CA 94103
Phone: (415) 621-5661; (415) 621-5466 fax
Website: www.cjcj.org

Services: Promote balanced and humane criminal-justice policies that reduce incarceration and promote long-term public safety for juveniles, through the development of model programs, technical assistance, research/policy analysis, and public education.

Youth Law Center

Address: 200 Pine Street - #300
San Francisco, CA 94104
Phone: (415) 543-3379; (415) 956-9022 fax
E-mail: info@ylc.org
Website: www.ylc.org
Services: Handle major institutional and class action cases on behalf of juveniles only. *Cannot assist individuals.* Issues include conditions of confinement, special education up to age 22 and treatment of juveniles in adult correctional facilities

Mental Health

National GAINS Center/TAPA Center for Jail Diversion

Address: 345 Delaware Avenue
Delmar, NY 12054
Phone: (800) 311-4246; (518) 439-7612 fax
Website: www.gainscenter.samhsa.gov
Services: Collect and disseminate information about mental health and substance abuse services for incarcerated people with mental disorders. Supports and engages in creative initiatives and collaboration with public and private organizations in an advisory capacity.

Religious

Aleph Institute

Contact: Rabbi Menachem Katz
Address: P.O. Box 547127
Surfside, FL 33154
Phone: (305) 864-5553; (305) 864-5675 fax
E-mail: admin@aleph-institute.org
Website: www.aleph-institute.org
Services: Offers Jewish religious instruction to prisoners; religious articles; correspondence courses; counseling; religious-freedom advocacy. Provide personal visits to prisoners by Rabbis and rabbinical students, family support groups. Maintain network of local contacts in all states. Weekly Torah literature is available free and quarterly newsletter, *The National Liberator*, is also available. Send requests in writing to Rabbi Katz.

Forgiven Ministry, Inc.

Contact: Scottie Barnes
Address: P.O. Box 117
Taylorsville, NC 28681
Phone: (828) 632-6424 or (866) 900-4463
E-mail: scottie@forgivenministry.org
Website: www.forgivenministry.org
Services: Advocacy organization that reaches out to the unsaved and unlovable with the forgiveness and love of Jesus Christ through the power of the Holy Spirit.

International Prison Ministry

Contact: Bob Hoekstra
Address: P.O. Box 2868
Costa Mesa, CA 92628-2868
Phone: (714) 972-0288; (800) 527-1212 (toll-free); (714) 972-0557 fax
Services: Help other jail and prison ministries obtain Bibles, Bible Study books, *Lifechanging* books and greeting cards at affordable, reduced prices. Provide free Bibles, Bible Study and *Lifechanging* books to prisoners.

Mennonite Central Committee, US

Contact: Lorraine Stutzman Amstutz
Address: 21 S. 12th Street, P.O. Box 500
Akron, PA 17501-0500
Phone: (717) 859-1151; (717) 859-3875 fax
Website: www.mcc.org
Services: Provide information on issues such as ministry to victims and offenders, alternatives to prison, victim-offender reconciliation and restorative justice. Coordinate presentations, workshops and written materials on principles and application of restorative justice. Provide consultation and information through VORP, and develop educational and training materials on a variety of issues.

Program on Freedom of Religion and Belief of the ACLU

Contact: Jeremy Gunn
Address: 915 15th Street, N.W., 2nd Floor
Washington, DC 20005
Phone: (202) 675-2330; (202) 546-0738 fax
Website: www.aclu.org/religion
Services: To preserve our freedom of speech and ensure that religious liberty is protected by keeping the government out of religion.

Technology

National Technology and Liberty Program of the ACLU

Address: 915 15th Street, N.W., 6th Floor
Washington, DC 20005

Phone: (202) 715-0817; (202) 546-0738 fax
Website: www.aclu.org/privacy
Services: The tremendous explosion in surveil-lance-enabling technologies, combined with the ongoing weakening in legal restraints that protect our privacy, have us drifting toward a surveillance society. The ACLU's Technology and Liberty Project fights this trend and works to pre-serve the American tradition that the government not track individuals or vio-late privacy unless it has evidence of wrongdoing.

Veterans/Military

National Veterans Legal Services Program

Contact: Intake Section
Address: P.O. Box 65762
            Washington, D.C. 20035
Phone: (202) 265-8305; (202) 328-0063 (fax)
E-mail: info@nvlsp.org
Website: www.nvlsp.org
Services: Provide information on Agent Orange benefit issues for Vietnam veterans and referrals for veteran-law issues only. Self-help guides on Agent Orange, Gulf War, and VA Claims: $7.50 for one and $5.50 for each additional. Publish the *Veterans Benefits Manual,* a comprehensive guide to veterans' law. *The Veterans Advocate,* a newsletter of veter-ans law and advocacy ($50/year for incarcerated veterans: $80/year for law-yers, government); and *Manual on Military Discharge Upgrading,* $95. Correspondence training course for veterans' advocates, $75 for prisoners. Please call to verify all prices. Prices are subject to change.

Voting Rights

ACLU Voting Rights Project

Contact: Nancy Abudu
Address: 2600 Marquis One Tower
            245 Peachtree Center Avenue, NE
            Atlanta, GA 30303-1227
Phone: (404) 523-2721; (404) 653-0331 fax
E-mail: vrpaclu@aol.com
Website: www.votingrights.org
Services: Works to protect the gains in political participation won by minorities since passage of the 1965 Voting Rights Act, including felony disenfranchisement. The Project encourages the reporting of discriminatory voting practices by calling

the Voting Section of the U.S. Department of Justice Civil Rights Division at (800) 253-3931.

Women

ACLU Reproductive Freedom Project

Address: 125 Broad Street, 17th Floor
            New York, NY 10004
Phone: (212) 549-2633; 549-2652 fax
E-mail: rfp@aclu.org
Website: www.aclu.org/reproductiverights
Services: The Project handles issues related to reproductive rights and abortion. Contacts should first be made through state ACLU affiliates.

ACLU National Women's Rights Project

Contact: Claudia Flores
Address: 125 Broad Street, 18th Floor
            New York, NY 10004
Phone: (212) 549-2665; (212) 549-2580 fax
Website: www.aclu.org/womensrights
Services: Through litigation, community outreach, advocacy and public education, WRP empowers poor women, women of color, and immigrant women who have been victimized by gender bias and face perva-sive barriers to equality.

National Clearinghouse for the Defense of Battered Women

Contact: Sue Osthoff
Address: 125 South 9th Street - #302
            Philadelphia, PA 19107
Phone: (215) 351-0010 or (800) 903-0111 x3;
            (215) 351-0779 fax
Website: www.ncdbw.org
Services: Provide technical assistance to women charged with crimes and their defense teams. The organization assists advocates for women who have injured or killed their batterers in self-defense; battered women who have been coerced into criminal activity; and women charged with "failing to protect" their children from the batterers' violence. Accepts collect calls from women in prison.

Out of Control Lesbian Committee to Support Women Political Prisoners

Address: 3543 18th Street, Box 30
            San Francisco, CA 94110
Services: Send resource information to women prisoners. Publish *Out of Time* newsletter 5 times a year, free to all prisoners. We are volunteer-run. Services are limited, but

include activism and advocacy for women political prisoners.

State and Local Organizations

Alabama

Aid to Inmate Mothers

Contact: Carol Potok
Address: P.O. Box 986
Montgomery, AL 36101-0986
Phone: (334) 262-2245; (800) 679-0246; (334) 262-2296 fax
E-mail: carol@inmatemoms.org
Website: www.inmatemoms.org
Services: Transitional program for mothers who are between 18 and 24 months of their release dates. Offer educational programs for women prisoners, release plans, and follow-up casework for one year after release. Arrange monthly visitation for mothers who do not already have transportation for their children. Provide outreach to children while their mothers are incarcerated.

Alabama CURE

Contact: Rosemary Collins
Address: P.O. Box 190504
Birmingham, AL 35219-0504
Phone: (205) 481-3781; (800) 665-3602; (205) 481-3991 fax
E-mail: rosemarytc@bellsouth.net
Services: Prison-reform legislative organization interested in improving the Alabama and federal criminal-justice systems.

Alabama Prison Project

Contact: Lucia Penland
Address: 619 N. Bridge Street
Wetumpka, AL 36092
Phone: (334) 264-7416; (334) 567-7845 fax
E-mail: halbert@mindspring.com
Services: Provides no legal services. Organizes advocacy community on anti-death-penalty issues and prison conditions. Visits death-row prisoners and offer family support. Investigates for defense in sentencing phase of capital trials and tracks death-row convictions. Offers a program for families of death-row prisoners. Publishes the *Alabama Prison Project* newsletter. Sponsors the Alabama CURE chapter.

ACLU of Alabama

Contact: Lori Raphan, Staff Attorney
Address: 207 Montgomery Street - #910
Montgomery, AL 36104
Phone: (334) 262-0304; (334) 269-5666 fax
E-mail: info@aclualabama.org
Website: www.aclualabama.org
Services: Prison conditions; limited direct referrals.

Equal Justice Initiative of Alabama

Address: 122 Commerce Street
Montgomery, AL 36104
Phone: (334) 269-1803; 334-269-1806 fax
E-mail: contact_us@eji.org
Website: www.eji.org
Services: Represent death-row prisoners in direct appeals to the appellate courts in Alabama and in post-conviction challenges in state and federal courts.

Montgomery AIDS Outreach

Contact: Lucero Sitz
Address: 820 W. South Boulevard
Montgomery, AL 36105
Phone: (334) 280-3388; (800) 510-4704; (334) 280-3315 fax
E-mail: lsitz@maoi.org
Website: www.maoi.org
Services: Support group and discharge planning services to HIV+ female prisoners at Julia Tutwiler Prison in Wetumpka. HIV-prevention education classes to pre-release inmates.

Alaska

ACLU of Alaska

Contact: Jason Barndeis, Staff Attorney
Address: P.O. Box 201844
Anchorage, AK 99520-1844
Phone: (907) 276-2258; (907) 258-0288 fax
E-mail: akclu@akclu.org
Website: www.akclu.org
Services: Handle litigation on constitutional issues on a *limited* basis.

Alaska Human Rights Commission

Address: 800 A Street - #204
Anchorage, AK 99501-3669
Phone: (907) 274-4692; Toll-Free: (800) 478-4692 (in-state only)
Website: http://gov.state.ak.us/aschr
Services: Investigate discrimination and other human-rights abuses statewide.

Alaskan AIDS Assistance Association

Address: 1057 West Fireweed Lane - #102
Anchorage, AK 99503

Phone: (907) 263-2050, Hotline: (800) 478-AIDS, Syringes: (907) 276-1400; (907) 263-2051 fax
E-mail: aaaa@alaskanaids.org
Website: www.alaskanaids.org
Services: Offer case management, referrals and education. Provide emotional support services to people with AIDS/HIV infection and their families; support groups; 24-hour helpline; buddy volunteer program; and advocacy and practical support. Publish free triannual newsletter.

Alaskan AIDS Assistance Association –Juneau
Address: P.O. Box 21481
            Juneau, AK 99802
Phone: (907) 586-6089; (888) 660-AIDS; (907) 586-1089 fax
E-mail: aaaase@alaskanaids.org
Website: www.alaskanaids.org
Services: Offer case management, referrals and education. Provide emotional support services to people with AIDS/HIV infection and their families; support groups; 24-hour helpline; buddy volunteer program; and advocacy and practical support. Publish free tri-annual newsletter.

Alaska Legal Services Corporation –Anchorage
Address: 1016 W. 4th Avenue - #200
            Anchorage, AK 99501
Phone: (907) 272-9431; (888) 478-2572; (907) 279-7417 fax
E-mail: anchorage3@alsc-law.org
Services: Provide free civil (non-criminal) legal assistance to low-income Alaskans. Advocates reducing the legal consequences of poverty. We are sorry, but we cannot respond to requests for legal assistance made by e-mail. Any information that you send to us by e-mail is not confidential and is not protected by the attorney/client privilege. Referrals will be given if possible.

Alaska Legal Services Corporation – Bethel
Address: P.O. Box 248
            Bethel, AK 99559-0248
Phone: (907) 543-2237; (800) 478-2230; (907) 543-5537 fax
E-mail: bethel@alsc-law.org
Website: www.alaskalawhelp.org

Alaska Legal Services Corporation –Dillingham
Address: P.O. Box 176
            Dillingham, AK 99576

Phone: (907) 842-1452; (888) 391-1475; (907) 842-1430 fax
E-mail: dillingham@alsc-law.org
Website: www.alaskalawhelp.org

Alaska Legal Services Corporation – Fairbanks
Address: 1648 Cushman - #300
            Fairbanks, AK 99701-6202
Phone: (907) 452-5181; (800) 478-5401; (907) 456-6359 fax
E-mail: fairbanks@alsc-law.org
Website: www.alaskalawhelp.org

Alaska Legal Services Corporation – Juneau
Address: 419 6th Street - #322
            Juneau, AK 99801-1096
Phone: (907) 586-6425; (800) 789-6426; (907) 456-6359 fax
E-mail: fairbanks@alsc-law.org
Website: www.alaskalawhelp.org

Alaska Legal Services Corporation—Ketchikan
Address: 306 Main Street - #218
            Ketchikan, AK 99901-6483
Phone: (907) 225-6420; (907) 225-6896 fax
E-mail: Ketchikan@alsc-law.org
Website: www.alaskalawhelp.org

Alaska Legal Services Corporation—Kotzebue
Address: P.O. Box 526
            Kotzebue, AK 99901-6483
Phone: (907) 225-6420; (907) 225-6896 fax
E-mail: Kotzebue@alsc-law.org
Website: www.alaskalawhelp.org

Arizona

ACLU of Arizona
Contact: Alessandra Soler Meetze
Address: P.O. Box 17148
            Phoenix, AZ 85011-0148
Phone: (602) 650-1967; (602) 650-1376 fax
E-mail: intake@acluaz.org
Website: www.acluaz.org
Services: Prison conditions (limited to state prisons); limited direct referrals; general community education.

American Friends Service Committee
Address: 103 N. Park Avenue
            Tucson, AZ 85719
Phone: (520) 623-9141; (520) 623-5901 fax
E-mail: afscaz@afsc.org
Website: www.afsc.org/az
Services: Serve as a resource for prisoners, ex-prisoners, and their family members to find information and resources to address

their questions and needs, and a place to get involved in bringing their voices to the seats of power in Arizona.

Middle Ground Prison Reform, Inc.

Contact:	Donna Leone Hamm
Address:	139 East Encanto Drive
	Tempe, AZ 85281
Phone:	(480) 966-8116; (801) 409-8536 fax
E-mail:	middleground@msn.com
Website:	www.middlegroundprisonreform.org
Services:	Provide education/training programs; counseling; legislative advocacy for prison reform; litigation on policies and procedures affecting visitors; public speaking on criminal- and social-justice issues; referrals to social-service agencies. Advocacy and public education is performed on state and national levels; direct services are provided statewide in Arizona. Publish periodic newsletter; membership is $3/year for prisoners, $20/year non-prisoners.

Southern Arizona AIDS Foundation

Contact:	Danny Blake
Address:	375 S. Euclid Avenue
	Tucson, AZ 85719
Phone:	(520) 628-7223; (800) 771-9054; (520) 628-7222 fax
E-mail:	info@saaf.org
Website:	www.saaf.org
Services:	Provides limited legal assistance for guardianship arrangements. Referrals are provided to assist with wills, power of attorney, and other legal matters.

Arkansas

ACLU of Arkansas

Contact:	Rita Sklar
Address:	904 West Second Street - #1
	Little Rock, AR 72201
Phone:	(501) 374-2660; (501) 374-2842 fax
Website:	www.acluarkansas.org
Services:	Prison conditions; county jail conditions/treatment referrals; litigation; referrals to Compliance Coordinator.

Women's Project

Contact:	Felicia Davidson
Address:	2224 Main Street
	Little Rock, AR 72206
Phone:	(501) 372-5113; (501) 372-0009 fax
Website:	www.womens-project.org

Services:	All services are provided only in Arkansas at the state women's prison and community punishment center. They include a weekly battered women's support group; biweekly peer AIDS-education program; a child transportation project; yearly caretakers' retreat. Provide prison library through donations of books and periodicals and support with job search for women parolees in Arkansas.

California

ACLU of Northern California

Contact:	Alan Schlosser
Address:	39 Drumm Street
	San Francisco, CA 94111
Phone:	(415) 621-2493; (415) 255-1478
Website:	www.aclunc.org
Services:	Handle rare post-conviction matters; habeas corpus; prison conditions; direct referrals.

ACLU of San Diego and Imperial Counties

Contact:	David Blair-Loy
Address:	P.O. Box 87131
	San Diego, CA 92138
Phone:	(619) 232-2131; (619) 232-0036 fax
E-mail:	info@aclusandiego.org
Website:	www.aclusandiego.org
Services:	Handle rare post-conviction matters; habeas corpus; prison conditions; direct referrals.

ACLU of Southern California

Contact:	Mary Tiedeman
Address:	1616 Beverly Boulevard
	Los Angeles, CA 90026
Phone:	(213) 977-9543; (213) 250-3919 fax
E-mail:	acluinfo@aclu-sc.org
Website:	www.aclu-sc.org
Services:	L.A. County jail conditions; rare habeas corpus, post-conviction and prison conditions; referrals.

California Coalition for Women Prisoners

Contact:	Karen Shain
Address:	1540 Market Street - #490
	San Francisco, CA 94102
Phone:	(415) 255-7036 x4; (415) 552-3150 fax
Services:	Raise public consciousness about the cruel and inhumane conditions under which women in prison live and advocate for positive change. Promote the leadership of and give voice to women prisoners and former prisoners. Publish newsletter,

The Fire Inside, available free to prisoners and by donation from others.

California Prison Focus

Contact: Corey Weinstein
             Georgia Schreiber (HIV education)
Address: 1904 North Franklin Street - #507
             Oakland, CA 94612
Phone: (510) 836-7222; (510) 836-7333 fax
E-mail: contact@prisons.org
Website: www.prisons.org
Services: Investigate conditions of confinement in California's job-unit prisons at Pelican Bay, Corcoran and Valley State Prison for Women. Seek to monitor and end the human-rights violations in California's Security Housing Unit facilities through regular investigative visits, advocacy and education. Publish a newsletter and various educational materials. Offer HIV/Hepatitis C education.

Catholic Charities of the East Bay Detention Ministry (CCEB)

Contact: Michael Radding
Address: 433 Jefferson Street
             Oakland, CA 94607
Phone: (510) 768-3139; (510) 451-6998 fax
E-mail: mradding@cceb.org
Services: Provide religious, pastoral services in the jails and juvenile halls of Alameda and Contra Costa Counties and victim/offender mediation services. Also offer counseling and emergency-assistance referrals.

The Center for Children of Incarcerated Parents

Contact: Dolores Thomas
Address: P.O. Box 41-286
             Eagle Rock, CA 90041
Phone: (626) 449-2470; (626) 449-9001 fax
E-mail: ccip@earthlink.net
Website: www.e-ccip.org
Services: Therapeutic services for children of criminal offenders and family-reunification projects for prisoners and their children.

Centerforce

Address: 2955 Kerner Boulevard, 2nd Floor
             San Rafael, CA 94901
Phone: (415) 456-9980; (415) 456-2146 fax
Website: www.centerforce.org
Services: Centerforce is a private, non-profit California organization that demonstrates concern for prison visitors through a network of Prison Visitor Hospitality Centers. A Centerforce visitor center has been established at 20 state prisons, one federal prison and one California Youth Authority facility, providing a variety of direct services such as transportation, drop-in childcare, information and referrals, shelter and general hospitality. Also provide health-education services to the incarcerated community through our Health Services Division. Write for a complete list of centers and free Centerforce brochure.

Center for Juvenile and Criminal Justice

Address: 440 9th St.
             San Francisco, CA 94103
Phone: (202) 737-7270; (202) 737-7271 fax
Website: www.cjcj.org
Services: Promote balanced and humane criminal-justice policies that reduce incarceration and promote long-term public safety, for juveniles, through the development of model programs, technical assistance, research/policy analysis, and public education.

Community Connection Resource Center

Contact: Dwight James
             Lillian Kellison (Incarcerated Youth Offender Program)
Address: 4080 Centre Street
             San Diego, CA 92103
Phone: (619) 543-8500; (888) 800-2272
Services: Provide services exclusively for prisoners and ex-offenders. Comprehensive re-entry services include: pre-release planning in local, state and federal correctional institutions; vocational assessment; assistance with emergency needs such as shelter, food and clothing; life-skills workshops and job development and placement. Also provide residential recovery/re-entry for women on parole, a comprehensive outpatient substance-abuse program, and an ex-offender support group called Freedom First. Contact us for addresses of other California offices.

Families With a Future

Contact: Ida Robinson
Address: c/o LSPC
             1540 Market St. - #490
             San Francisco, CA 94102
Phone: (415) 255-7036 x307
E-mail: idais1@comcast.net
Services: Provide limited funding for visitation transportation for children of women prisoners serving sentences of 10 or more years. Offer support services for children

of incarcerated parents as well as limited crisis intervention in the San Francisco Bay area. Provide training for those interested in working with children of incarcerated parents.

Friends Outside

Address: P.O. Box 4085
              Stockton, CA 95204
Phone: (209) 955-0701; (209) 955-0735 fax
E-mail: gnewby@friendsoutside.org
Website: www.friendsoutside.org
Services: Headquarters for 12 Friends Outside Chapters in California and Nevada that provide various social services to state and county prisoners and their families. Pre-release and family services and a Parenting Program are provided to prisoners through case managers at all 33 California State Prisons. Visitor centers are also operated at all California State Prisons. The Friends Outside Creative Conflict Resolution Program are in jails, prisons, juvenile programs, and in the community.

Justice Now

Address: 1322 Webster Street - #210
              Oakland, CA 94612
Phone: (510) 839-7654; (510) 839-7615 fax
Website: www.jnow.org
Services: Works with women prisoners and local communities to build a safe compassionate world without prisons. The first teaching law clinic in the country solely focused on the needs of women prisoners. Interns and staff provide legal services in the areas of need identified by women prisoners, including: compassionate release; health-care access; defense of parental rights; sentencing mitigation; placement in community-based programs.

Law Center for Families

Address: 510 16th Street - #300
              Oakland, CA 94612
Phone: (510) 451-9261
E-mail: info@lcff.org
Website: www.lcff.org
Services: Provide individual representation, advice, referrals and community education concerning: housing rights, family law/domestic violence, consumer law, economic support/public benefits, and language access.

Legal Services for Prisoners with Children

Contact: Karen Shain
Address: 1540 Market Street - #490
              San Francisco, CA 94102
Phone: (415) 255-7036; (415) 552-3150 fax
E-mail: karen@prisonerswithchildren.org
Website: www.prisonerswithchildren.org
Services: Legal advocacy and litigation on behalf of incarcerated parents, their children, families, attorneys and other prisoners' rights advocates. Currently focusing on test-case litigation, legislative reform, and administrative advocacy on behalf of incarcerated parents and their children, particularly in the areas of medical care, prenatal medical care for pregnant women prisoners, foster care and termination of parental-rights issues, and alternatives to incarceration. Does not currently have funding to provide individual legal assistance to prisoners, but does respond to hundreds of inquiries each month, and provides information and referrals to incarcerated parents.

Northern California Service League

Contact: Shirley Melnicoe
Address: 28 Boardman Place
              San Francisco, CA 94103
Phone: (415) 863-2323; (415) 863-1882 fax
E-mail: ncsl@norcalserviceleague.org
Website: www.norcalserviceleague.org
Services: Offer counseling and referral services for prisoners and their families. Re-entry assistance includes job-development assistance, in-jail substance-abuse treatment, and life-skills training. County and state prisoners/ex-offenders only.

Penal Law Project

Contact: Director
Address: 25 Main Street - #102
              Chico, CA 95929
Phone: (530) 898-4354; (530) 898-4911 fax
E-mail: clic@exchange.csuchico.edu
Website: www.aschico.com/?Page=252
Services: Habeas corpus; direct referrals; legal research. Provide legal information only, including information on record-sealing and expungement; no legal counseling. Provide services to prisoners at the Susanville Correctional Facility and Northern California Women's Facility in Stockton.

Prison Activist Resource Center

Address: P.O. Box 339
              Berkeley, CA 94701
Phone: (510) 893-4648; (510) 893-4607 fax

Website: www.prisonactivist.org
Services: Support for prisoners and prison activists; public-education project.

Prison Law Clinic

Contact: Millard Murphy
Address: UC Davis School of Law
One Shields Avenue
Building TB30
Davis, CA 95616
Phone: (530) 752-6942; (530) 752-0822 fax
E-mail: mmmurphy@ucdavis.edu
Services: Prison conditions; parole revocation; legal research. Services are provided to prisoners of California State Prisons.

Prison Law Office

Contact: Donald Specter
Address: General Delivery
San Quentin, CA 94964
Phone: (415) 457-9144; (415) 457-9151 fax
Website: www.prisonlaw.com
Services: Provide direct legal assistance for the range of problems encountered by California prisoners, excluding attacks on criminal convictions. The focus is on conditions of confinement. Provide pamphlets pertaining to various problems free of charge to prisoners.

Prisoner Services

Contact: Peggy Harrell
Address: Marin County Jail
13 Peter Behr Drive
San Rafael, CA 94903
Phone: (415) 499-3203
Services: Provide direct services for prisoners in the Marin County Jail and their families, including referrals to community agencies regarding counseling on drugs and alcohol dependency; food and clothing; literacy programs; family counseling; and orientation for prisoners and families moving on to state prisons. Excellent resource for San Quentin prisoners temporarily detained here.

Public Interest Law Firm

Contact: Kyra Kazantzis
Address: 111 West Street Jon - #315
San Jose, CA 95113
Phone: (408) 280-2417
Services: A program of the Law Foundation of Silicon Valley, the mission is to protect human rights of individuals and groups in the Silicon Valley area who are under-represented in the civil-justice system.

PILF accomplishes its mission by leveraging the skills and resources of pro bono attorneys to provide high quality representation in class action and impact litigation, advocacy in state and local government, and litigation support to local legal services programs.

State Public Defender—San Francisco

Contact: Lynne S. Coffin
Address: 221 Main Street, 10th Floor
San Francisco, CA 94105
Phone: (415) 904-5600; (415) 904-5635 fax
Services: Capital appeals (only) for convicted felony indigents.

Colorado

ACLU of Colorado

Contact: Catherine Hazouri
Address: 400 Corona Street
Denver, CO 80218-3915
Phone: (303) 777-5482; (303) 777-1773 fax
E-mail: info@aclu-co.org
Website: www.aclu-co.org
Services: Handle habeas corpus and prison-conditions matters, damage suits. Provide direct referrals.

Colorado CURE

Contact: Dianne Tramutola-Lawson
Address: 3470 S. Poplar - #406
Denver, CO 80224
Phone: (303) 758-3390 (also fax #)
E-mail: dianne@coloradocure.org
Website: www.coloradocure.org
Services: Work primarily through legislative channels to reduce crime through reform of the criminal-justice system. Provide prisoners and their families with information about rehabilitative programs. Provide no legal services. Publish quarterly newsletter.

Empowerment Program

Contact: Kathy Howard
Address: 1600 York Street
Denver, CO 80206
Phone: (303) 320-1989; (303) 320-3987 fax
E-mail: kat-howard@empowermentprogram.org
Website: www.empowermentprogram.org
Services: Provide education, employment assistance, health, housing referrals and support services to women who are in disadvantaged positions due to incarceration, poverty, homelessness, HIV/AIDS infection or involvement in the criminal-justice system.

Our goal is to decrease rates of recidivism by providing case management, support services, basic skills education, housing and resource coordination that can offer viable alternatives to habits and choices that may lead to criminal behaviors.

New Foundations Non-Violence Center

Address: 901 W. 14th Avenue - #7
Denver, CO 80204
Phone: (303) 825-2562; (303) 623-3492 fax
Website: www.home.earthlink.net/~nfnc
Services: Offer a one-to-one visitation program at the Denver County Jail that includes advocacy and informal counseling. Organize intensive three-day Alternatives to Violence Project (AVP) workshops in some Colorado penal facilities, and some community settings.

Volunteers of America Colorado Branch

Contact: Calvin McGee, Program Supervisor
Address: 22877 Lawrence Street
Denver, CO 80205
Phone: (303) 295-2165; (303) 298-8169 fax
Services: Provide emergency services and resources to ex-offenders and their families, including technical assistance, bus tokens, clothing, tools, food, etc.

Connecticut

ACLU Connecticut

Contact: Renee Redman
Address: 32 Grand Street
Hartford, CT 06106
Phone: (860) 247-9823; (860) 728-0287 fax
E-mail: info@acluct.org
Website: www.acluct.org
Services: Provide assistance to a limited number of class actions. No individual prisoner assistance is available.

Community Partners in Action

Contact: Maureen Price-Boreland
Address: Parkville Business Center
110 Bartholomew Avenue - #3010
Hartford, CT 06106
Phone: (860) 566-2030; (860) 566-8089 fax
E-mail: mprice@cpa-ct.org
Website: www.cpa-ct.org
Services: Provides a wide range of services to offenders and ex-offenders, including alternatives to incarceration, pretrial-release programs, resettlement program, employment services, substance-abuse programming, community-service

opportunities, work-release residential program, family reunification for men (post-release), and HIV/AIDS programs.

Connecticut Correctional Ombudsman

Contact: James R. Bookwalter
Address: 110 Bartholomew Avenue - #4010
Hartford, CT 06106
Phone: (860) 951-8867; (860) 951-8872 fax
Services: Receives and investigates complaints from prisoners in Connecticut institutions about the actions and decisions of the Department of Corrections. We accept collect calls.

Families in Crisis, Inc.

Contact: Susan Quinlan
Address: 30 Arbor Street, North Wing
Hartford, CT 06106
Phone: (860) 236-3593; (860) 231-8430 fax
E-mail: administration@familiesincrisis.org
Website: www.familiesincrisis.org
Services: Provides a comprehensive range of counseling and support services to offenders and their families: individual and family counseling, crisis intervention, court outreach, transportation, childcare programs, parent education groups, support groups and training programs. Areas served include: Greater Hartford, New Haven, Waterbury, and Bridgeport. Publish *Going Home: A Pre-Release Training Manual for Successful Family Reintegration*, $23.95 per copy.

Families in Crisis New Haven Office

Address: 48 Howe Street
New Haven, CT 06511
Phone: (203) 498-7790; (203) 562-3660 fax
Website: www.familiesincrisis.org

Families in Crisis Waterbury Office

Address: 232 N. Elm Street
Waterbury, CT 06702
Phone: (203) 573-8656; (203) 573-1132 fax
Website: www.familiesincrisis.org

Inmates' Legal Assistance Program, Law Offices of Sydney T. Schulman

Contact: Jane Starkowski
Address: 78 Oak Street, P.O. Box 260237
Hartford, CT 06126-0237
Phone: (860) 246-1118; (800) 301-4527; (860) 246-1119 fax
Services: Provide legal assistance in civil matters only. Assistance does not include representation and/or entering an appearance

in a case. Assist prisoners in identifying, articulating and researching legal claims. Enable prisoners' access to the judicial system via advice, counsel and preparation of meaningful legal papers such as writs, complaints, motions and legal memorandum or law for claims having legal merit. Our legal services are limited to sentenced prisoners and prisoners incarcerated in Connecticut institutions.

Isaiah 61:1, Inc.

Contact:	Ed Davies
Address:	P.O. Box 1399
	Bridgeport, CT 06601
Phone:	(203) 368-6116; (203) 576-0616 fax
E-mail:	Eddav72@aol.com
Services:	Offer pre-release programs for offenders to help them achieve a smooth transition back to their families and communities. Services include: work release, career guidance, spiritual and individual counseling groups, life-skills training, anger management, HIV/AIDS education and counseling, AA/NA/Alanon, and mandatory family therapy. Programs last approximately 6-9 months for women and 3-4 months for men.

Jerome N. Frank Legal Services Organization

Address:	Yale Legal Services
	P.O. Box 209090
	New Haven, CT 06520
Phone:	(203) 432-4800; (203) 432-1426 fax
Services:	Limited resources. Offer legal services to Connecticut federal and state prisoners. Specialize in parole-related litigation, post-conviction, habeas corpus, prison conditions and direct referrals. Damages suits can be handled on a contingency-fee basis only if client is a pauper and s/he cannot get a local law firm to take the case. Publish *Connecticut Prisoners' Rights*, which includes a detailed reference guide to resources for prisoners and ex-offenders, $4 if able to pay.

Perception Programs, Inc.

Address:	54 North Street, P.O. Box 407
	Willimantic, CT 06226
Phone:	(860) 450-7122; (860) 450-7127 fax
E-mail:	linda.mastrianni@
	perceptionprograms.org
Website:	www.perceptionprograms.org
Services:	Limited to Connecticut residents only. Programs include residential work-release and treatment programs for male

and female offenders, residential substance-abuse treatment for male offenders, Alternative to Incarceration Center, Intentional Skills Development groups available in Department of Correction Institutions, outpatient substance-abuse counseling and supportive housing for HIV+ inmates ending their sentences.

Delaware

AIDS Delaware

Contact:	John Baker
Address:	100 W. 10th Street - #315
	Wilmington, DE 19801
Phone:	(302) 652-6776; (302) 652-5150 fax
E-mail:	baker@aidsdelaware.org
Website:	www.aidsdelaware.org
Services:	Offer free and anonymous HIV counseling and testing; case management, prevention, and educational programs; support groups, STD/HIV hotline, and more. Provide safer-sex literature and a *Dispatch* newsletter, free upon written request for information.

AIDS Delaware Kent and Sussex County Office

Address:	706 Rehoboth Avenue
	Rehoboth, DE 19971
Phone:	(302) 226-5350; (302) 226-3519 fax

ACLU of Delaware

Contact:	Legal Department
Address:	100 W. 10th Street - #309
	Wilmington, DE 19801
Phone:	(302) 654-3966; (302) 654-3689 fax
E-mail:	aclu@aclu-de.org
Website:	www.aclu-de.org
Services:	Handle litigation on constitutional issues on a limited basis.

Delaware Center for Justice, Inc.

Contact:	Janet Leban
Address:	100 West 10th Street - #905
	Wilmington, DE 19801
Phone:	(302) 658-7174; (302) 658-7170 fax
E-mail:	center@dcjustice.org
Website:	www.dcjustice.org
Services:	Advocate on behalf of prisoners and their families to resolve problems in the criminal-justice system. Services include prisoner grievances; alternatives to incarceration; legislative advocacy; AIDS education. Special emphasis on incarcerated women's issues. Provide volunteer tutoring services to juvenile institutions. Quarterly newsletter is

available free to Delaware prisoners upon request.

District Of Columbia

ACLU of the National Capital Area

Contact: Legal Department *or*
Fritz Mulhauser
Address: 1400 20th Street, N.W. - #119
Washington, DC 20036-5920
Phone: (202) 457-0800
Website: www.aclu-nca.org
Services: Limited constitutional issues litigation.

Mid-Atlantic Innocence Project

Address: 4801 Massachusetts Ave NW
Washington, DC 20016
Phone: (202) 274-4404
Fax: (202) 274-4226
Email: VanBuskirkC.MAIP@gmail.com
Website: www.exonerate.org
Services: The Mid-Atlantic Innocence Project (MAIP) is a non-profit organization dedicated to correcting and preventing the conviction of innocent people in the District of Columbia, Maryland, and Virginia. Through our Board of Directors, a staff of one full-time and one part-time lawyer, a project assistant and attorney and student volunteers, we identify innocent prisoners in our region. We then provide them with pro bono investigative and legal assistance so they can obtain their freedom.

D.C. Prisoners' Project

Address: 11 Dupont Circle, N.W. - #400
Washington, DC 20036
Phone: (202) 319-1010
E-mail: philip_fornaci@washlaw.org
Services: Provide legal services to D.C. Code offenders, wherever they are incarcerated, in confinement and non-confinement-related civil matters. Serve as an individual representation clearinghouse on prisoners' rights issues related to D.C.; provide social services and health education (AIDS/HIV-related); information and referrals. Distribute a free basic AIDS/HIV information brochure.

National CURE

Address: P.O. Box 2310
Washington, DC 20013
Phone: (202) 789-2126
E-mail: cure@curenational.org
Website: www.curenational.org

Services: Organize prisoners, their families and other concerned citizens to achieve reforms in the criminal-justice system. No individual cases.

Prisons Foundation

Address: 1718 M Street, N.W. - #151
Washington, DC 20036
Phone: (202) 393-1511; (727) 538-2095 fax
Website: www.prisonsfoundation.org
Services: Sponsors prisons arts and crafts shows around the country with the support of the National Endowment for the Arts. Currently have about 100 inmates in 40 states in the U.S. and England involved in this show.

Prison Art Gallery

Address: 1600 K Street, N.W. - #501
Washington, D.C. 20006
Services: Open 9:30am to 5:30pm M-F, and 12:30pm to 5:30pm Saturday and Sunday.

Prisoners' Rights Program

Contact: Ryan Roberts
Address: Public Defender Service
633 Indiana Avenue, N.W.
Washington, DC 20004
Phone: (202) 628-1200; (202) 626-8423 fax
Services: Services limited to prisoners confined in D.C. correctional facilities. Provide legal advice and assistance with conditions-of-confinement issues generally, including living conditions, access to adequate medical, dental, and psychiatric care, access to the courts, confinement to special housing units, visitation issues, and the right to practice one's religion. No criminal matters, motions to reduce sentence or detainers. Distribute free informational memos on various prison law topics upon written request only.

Visitors' Services Center

Contact: Ann Cunningham-Keep
Address: 1422 Massachusetts Avenue, S.E.
Washington, DC 20003
Phone: (202) 544-2131; (202) 543-1572 fax
E-mail: vscdcjails@aol.com
Website: www.vscdcjails.net
Services: Provide volunteers who visit prisoners at the D.C. Jail and help them with problems on the outside, including: referrals to drug treatment, jobs and housing. Also offer a third-party custodianship program.

Florida

ACLU of Florida

Contact: Randall Marshall
Address: 4500 Biscayne Boulevard - #340
Miami, FL 33137-3227
Phone: (786) 363-2700; (305) 576-1106 fax
E-mail: aclufl@aclufl.org
Website: www.aclufl.org
Services: Handle litigation on constitutional issues.

Capital Defense Project

Address: P.O. Box 14273
Tallahassee, FL 32317
Phone: (850) 915-0695
Services: Criminal defense investigations, both trial and post-conviction; fact development; mitigation; witness location.

Federal Cure, Inc.

Address: P.O. Box 15667
Plantation, FL 33317
Phone: (408) 549-8935
E-mail: fedcure@fedcure.org
Website: www.fedcure.org

Florida Families with Loved Ones in Prison (FLIP)

Address: 710 Flanders Avenue
Daytona, FL 32114
Phone: (904) 254-8453
Website: www.afn.org/flip
Services: Provide counseling to family members through Action and Support Groups. Publish biannual newsletter. See our website for a full listing of chapters throughout Florida.

Florida Institutional Legal Services, Inc. (FILS)

Address: 1010-B NW 8th Avenue
Gainesville, FL 32601
Phone: (352) 375-2494; (352) 271-4366 fax
Services: Legal assistance to prisoners incarcerated in state institutions in Florida. Handle primarily class actions. Cases involving conditions of confinement, medical care, civil rights, and brutality will receive priority.

Florida Justice Institute, Inc.

Contact: Randall C. Berg, Jr.
Address: 3750 Miami Tower
100 S.E. Second Street
Miami, FL 33131-2309
Phone: (305) 358-2081; (305) 358-0910 fax
E-mail: rcberg@floridajusticeinstitute.org

Services: Handle civil-rights actions affecting conditions in Florida's prisons and jails; referral arrangements with members of the private bar for damages suits and civil-rights cases; prison advocacy; and lobbying for criminal-justice reform. (No collect calls.)

Transition

Address: 1550 N.W. 3rd Avenue
Miami, FL 33136
Phone: (305) 571-2001; (305) 571-2002 fax
Services: Job-training and job-placement services for ex-offenders.

Georgia

ACLU of Georgia

Contact: Legal Department
Address: P.O. Box 54406
Atlanta, GA 30308
Phone: (404) 523-5398; (404) 577-0181 fax
E-mail: info@acluga.org
Website: www.acluga.org
Services: Litigate prison-condition problems. No post- conviction cases.

Prison and Jail Project

Contact: John Cole Vodicka
Address: P.O. Box 6749
Americus, GA 31709
Phone: (229) 928-2080; (229) 924-7080 fax
Services: Watchdog agency that monitors conditions in jails and prisons and treatment of defendants in courtrooms. Advocate on behalf of prisoners, criminal defendants, and their families. Focus is on Southwest Georgia, not statewide. Publish *Freedomways,* a newsletter free to prisoners six times a year.

Southern Center for Human Rights

Address: 83 Poplar Street, N.W.
Atlanta, GA 30303-2122
Phone: (404) 688-1202; (404) 688-9440 fax
E-mail: rights@schr.org
Website: www.schr.org
Services: Civil-rights actions affecting conditions and practices in Alabama and Georgia prisons. Represent people facing the death penalty and assist attorneys handling jail, prison and death-penalty cases.

Southern Prison Ministry

Contact: Murphy Davis
Address: 910 Ponce de Leon Avenue, N.E.
Atlanta, GA 30306-4212

Phone: (404) 874-9652; (404) 874-7964 fax
Website: www.opendoorcommunity.org
Services: Visitation; correspondence; advocacy for individual prisoners. Provide hospitality and transportation for family members to visit prisons. Services for Georgia prisons only and primarily death-row prisoners.

Thomas M. West, Attorney at Law
Address: 400 Colony Square - #200
            1201 Peachtree Street, NE
            Atlanta, GA 30361
Phone: (404) 589-0136; (404) 881-2875 fax
E-mail: tom_mcwest@hotmail.com
Services: Post-conviction; habeas corpus; prison conditions; direct referrals; damage suits and criminal defense.

Hawaii

ACLU of Hawaii
Contact: Lois Perrin
Address: P.O. Box 3410
            Honolulu, HI 96801
Phone: (808) 522-5900; (808) 522-5909 fax
E-mail: office@acluhawaii.org
Website: www.acluhawaii.org
Services: Handle prison-conditions and individual abuse cases; limited to state prisons.

Office of the Ombudsman
Contact: Robin K. Matsunaga
Address: 465 S. King Street, 4th Floor
            Honolulu, HI 96813
Phone: (808) 587-0770; (808) 587-0774 TTY; (808) 587-0773 fax
E-mail: complaints@ombudsman.hawaii.gov
Website: www.ombudsman.hawaii.gov
Services: Receive complaints from prisoners regarding conditions of confinement at facilities operated by the State of Hawaii.

Idaho

ACLU of Idaho
Contact: Jack Van Valkenburgh
Address: P.O. Box 1897
            Boise, ID 83701
Phone: (208) 344-9750; (208) 344-7201 fax
E-mail: admin@acluidaho.org
Website: www.acluidaho.org
Services: Advocate for civil liberties in Idaho, including the rights of prisoners.

Illinois

ACLU of Illinois
Contact: Harvey Grossman
Address: 180 N. Michigan Avenue - #2300
            Chicago, IL 60601-7401
Phone: (312) 201-9740; (312) 201-9760 fax
E-mail: acluofillinois@aclu-il.org
Website: www.aclu-il.org
Services: Civil-rights actions; priority to class action issues.

Illinois CURE
Contact: Dr. Maria Rudisch
Address: 3134 E. 92nd Street
            Chicago, IL 60617
Phone: (773) 933-7919

Institute of Women Today
Contact: Sister Donna Quinn, RSM
Address: 7315 S. Yale Avenue
            Chicago, IL 60621
Phone: (773) 651-8372; (773) 783-2673 fax
E-mail: IWT7315@aol.com
Services: Civil-rights actions; habeas corpus; direct referrals; legal research; prison health care; employment and vocational guidance; skills training; counseling; advocates for children of incarcerated mothers. We also have two shelters for former female prison residents and their children in Chicago: Maria Shelter (transitional shelter with 4-month stay) and Casa Notre Dame (second-stage shelter with maximum 2-year stay for women who need more time to accomplish their goals).

Jewish Prisoners Assistance Foundation
Contact: Rabbi Binyomin Scheiman
Address: 9401 N. Margail
            Des Plaines, IL 60016
Phone: (847) 296-1770; (847) 296-1823 fax
Website: www.chabadandfree.com
Services: Help protect the rights of Jewish prisoners in Illinois. Pre- and post-release counseling with prisoners and their families, and support programs to obtain housing and employment for ex-offenders.

John Howard Association
Address: 300 West Adams Street - #423
            Chicago, IL 60606
Phone: (312) 782-1901; (312) 782-1902 fax
E-mail: Info@john-howard.org
Website: www.john-howard.org

Services: Limited direct services within Illinois; monitoring of Illinois prisons and jails and advocacy on prison conditions and prisoners' rights.

MacArthur Justice Center

Contact: Locke Bowman
Address: Northwestern University School of Law
            375 E. Chicago Avenue
            Chicago, IL 60611
Phone: (312) 503-1271; (312) 503-1272 fax
Services: Does impact litigation on criminal-justice issues, especially prison conditions. While we do conduct litigation on behalf of prisoners, we do not accept all cases. Services for Federal and state prisoners.

Prisoner Release Ministry, Inc.

Address: P.O. Box 69
            Joliet, IL 60434-0069
Phone: (815) 723-8998; (815) 723-5544 fax
E-mail: prministry@sbcglobal.net
Website: www.prisonerreleaseministry.com
Services: Job preparation, counseling and placement for persons on probation, parole, and work release in Will, Kankakee, Kane, DuPage, Kendall, Grundy and Cook Counties. Emergency assistance with food, work clothes, and transportation. Computerized job bank for entire State of Illinois.

Safer Foundation

Contact: Ewing A. Foulks
Address: 571 West Jackson Boulevard
            Chicago, IL 60661-5701
Phone: (312) 922-2200; (312) 922-7640 fax
Website: www.saferfoundation.org
Services: Provide job-readiness training, job placement, basic education, drug-abuse counseling, emergency services (by referral for food, clothing, shelter) to men and women released from prison to Chicago area and to the Quad Cities area (Rock Island, Illinois and Davenport, Iowa). Operate the Crossroads Community Correctional Center for men. Publish informational materials on the Safer programs and a quarterly newsletter.

Indiana

ACLU Indiana

Contact: Ken Falk
Address: 1031 E. Washington Street
            Indianapolis, IN 46202
Phone: (317) 635-4056; (317) 635-4105 fax

Website: www.aclu-in.org
Services: Handle prison-conditions matters; provide referrals.

Damien Center

Address: 26 N. Arsenal Avenue
            Indianapolis, IN 46201
Phone: (317) 632-0123; (800) 213-1167; (317) 632-4363 fax
E-mail: info@damien.org
Website: www.damien.org
Services: Offer services to prisoners who have AIDS or are HIV-positive. Assist former prisoners with employment services and housing assistance. Also assist families of people with AIDS. Publish the *Damien Center Newsletter*, available upon request. (No collect calls.)

Indiana CURE

Address: P.O. Box 199256
            Indianapolis, IN 46219
Phone: (317) 357-2606
E-mail: director@incure.org
Services: Advocacy organization that works to reduce crime through criminal-justice reform and the rehabilitation of errants. Also work with the families of prisoners.

Public Defender of Indiana

Contact: Susan Engelland
Address: 1 N. Capitol - #800
            Indianapolis, IN 46204
Phone: (317) 232-2475; (317) 232-2307 fax
Services: Provide legal representation to indigent prisoners in post-conviction actions challenging Indiana convictions/sentences in state court *only*. Represent juveniles in parole revocation proceedings. Also accept appointments, at county expense, for trial or appeal.

Iowa

ACLU Iowa

Contact: Randall Wilson
Address: 901 Insurance Exchange Building
            Des Moines, IA 50309
Phone: (515) 243-3576; (515) 243-8506 fax
Website: www.iowaclu.org
Services: Provide direct referrals. Handle prison-conditions litigation and legislative issues on prison conditions. Handle no post-conviction matters.

Iowa CURE

Contact: Jean Basinger

Address: P.O. Box 41005
              Des Moines, IA 50311-4718
Phone: (515) 277-6296
Services: Work toward reform of sentencing laws, including clemency procedure and sentence length. Assist in job training and enhancement of prisoner-family relationships.

Iowa Citizens' Aide Ombudsman
Contact: William Angrick
Address: Ola Babcock Miller Building
              1112 E. Grand Avenue, 1st Floor, W. Wing
              Des Moines, IA 50319
Phone: (515) 281-3592; (515) 242-6007 fax
Services: Handle issues related to prisons, jails, and the Iowa Department of Corrections.

Iowa Medical Society
Contact: Office of Legal Affairs
Address: 1001 Grand Avenue
              West Des Moines, IA 50265
Phone: (515) 223-1401; (515) 223-0590 fax
E-mail: thellman@iowamedical.org
Website: www.iowamedical.org/ola.htm
Services: The core purpose of the IMS is to assure the highest quality of health care in Iowa through our role as physician and patient advocate. Handle inmate grievances against prison doctors or hospitals.

University of Iowa College of Law—Legal Clinic
Contact: John Whiston
Address: University of Iowa College of Law
              Iowa City, IA 52242
Phone: (319) 335-9023; (319) 353-5445 fax
E-mail: law-legal-clinic@uiowa.edu
Services: Handle post-conviction, habeas corpus and prison-conditions cases and provide direct referrals. Maintain a waiting list in order to limit the number of cases assigned to students. Legal research is subject to delays. Services limited to prisoners in Iowa or serving Iowa sentences in other jurisdictions.

Kansas

ACLU of Kansas and Western Missouri
Address: 3601 Main Street
              Kansas City, MO 64111
Phone: (816) 756-3113
Website: www.aclukswmo.org
Services: Handle prison-conditions cases and provide direct referrals. Do not handle post-conviction matters.

Paul E. Wilson Defender Project
Contact: Jean K. Gilles Phillips
Address: University of Kansas, School of Law
              409 Green Hall
              Lawrence, KS 66045
Phone: (785) 864-5571; (785) 864-5054 fax
Services: Handle post-conviction and habeas corpus cases; only provide advice on civil matters. Assist prisoners in Kansas and Leavenworth Federal Penitentiary. No money damages.

Kentucky

ACLU of Kentucky
Contact: Lili Lutgens
Address: 315 Guthrie Street - #300
              Louisville, KY 40202
Phone: (502) 581-1181; (502) 589-9687 fax
E-mail: info@aclu-ky.org
Website: www.aclu-ky.org
Services: Handle prison- and jail-conditions matters.

Kentucky Department of Public Advocacy, Capital Post-Conviction Branch
Address: 100 Fair Oaks Lane - #301
              Frankfort, KY 40601
Phone: (502) 564-3948; (502) 564-3949 fax
Services: Handle post-conviction cases at state and federal level. Also provide training for legal services and referrals.

Louisiana

ACLU of Louisiana
Contact: Katie Schwartzmann
Address: P.O. Box 56157
              New Orleans, LA 70156
Phone: (504) 522-0617; (504) 522-0618 fax
E-mail: admin@laaclu.org
Website: www.laaclu.org
Services: Provide post-conviction referrals. Consider prison-condition and civil-rights violations for impact litigation.

Community Service Center, Inc.
Contact: Octavia Edinburg
Address: 4000 Magazine Street
              New Orleans, LA 70115
Phone: (504) 897-6277; (504) 897-6281 fax
E-mail: cscnouw@aol.com
Services: Free counseling, case management, emergency, GED preparatory classes, substance-abuse referrals, socialization classes and support groups (including family reunification, women-to-women

and parenting) for former prisoners convicted of a felony.

Juvenile Justice Project of Louisiana

Address: 1600 Oretha C. Haley Boulevard
New Orleans, LA 70113
Phone: (504) 522-5437; (504) 522-5430 fax
Website: www.jjpl.org
Services: Provide legal services for juveniles.

Louisiana CURE

Address: P.O. Box 181
Baton Rouge, LA 70821
Website: www.curelouisiana.org
Services: Advocacy organization that works to reduce crime through criminal-justice reform and the rehabilitation of errants.

Project Return

Contact: Dr. Robert E. Roberts
Address: 51 Yosemite Drive
New Orleans, LA 70131
Phone: (504) 452-5585; (504) 988-1019 fax
E-mail: bob@projectreturn.com
Website: www.projectreturn.com
Services: Offer a proven, cost-effective method of transitioning convicted felons successfully from incarceration to free society and finally to employment. Services include GED preparation, addiction treatment and counseling and job-training and placement assistance. A brochure outlining the program (which is a part of Tulane University Medical Center-SPH&TM) is available free upon request.

Maine

ACLU Maine

Contact: Shenna Bellows
Address: 401 Cumberland Avenue - #105
Portland, ME 04101
Phone: (207) 774-5444; (207) 774-1103 fax
E-mail: info@mclu.org
Website: www.mclu.org
Services: Handle prison-conditions cases. Direct representation by MCLU is available in cases involving violations of constitutional rights.

Cumberland Legal Aid Clinic

Contact: Diane Arbour
Address: University of Maine School of Law
246 Deering Avenue
Portland, ME 04102
Phone: (207) 780-4370; toll-free: (877) 780-2522

Website: www.mainelaw.maine.edu/cumberlandlegal.aspx
Services: Provide legal representation for low-income individuals in Cumberland, York, and Southern Androscoggin. Assist in civil cases including divorce, parental rights and responsibilities, general civil litigation, civil-rights litigation, and non-fee-generating tort litigation. Provide criminal defense for any class of crime at the state level and in the U.S. District Court for the District of Maine. Also, protection from abuse and harassment litigation in all service areas. Clients are represented by seniors in law school who are specially licensed to practice law in the State of Maine. Does not provide legal advice or information over the phone. Does not maintain a waiting list of potential clients. Does not provide services on a walk-in basis.

Maine CURE

Address: 6 Boulder Lane
Lyman, ME 04002
Phone: (207) 449-7334
Services: Advocacy organization that works to reduce crime through criminal-justice reform and the rehabilitation of errants.

NDRAN CURE (National Death Row Assistance Network)

Address: *June 1 - October 1:*
6 Tolman Rd
Peaks Island, ME 04108
October 1 - June 1:
12200 Rd. 41.9
Mancos, CO 81328
Phone: *June 1 - October 1:*
(207) 766-2418
October 1 - June 1:
(970) 533-7383
E-mail: claudia@ndran.org
Website: www.ndran.org

Maryland

ACLU of Maryland

Contact: Debbie Jeon
Address: 3600 Clipper Mill Road - #350
Baltimore, MD 21211
Phone: (410) 889-8555; (410) 889-8558 TTY;
(410) 366-7838 fax
E-mail: aclu@aclu-md.org
Website: www.aclu-md.org
Services: Handle prison-conditions cases. Direct representation by the ACLU is available only in cases involving violation of

constitutional rights. The Baltimore office also handles all cases concerning prisoners in Eastern Shore jails.

Alternative Directions, Inc.
Address: 2505 N. Charles Street
Baltimore, MD 21218
Phone: (410) 889-5072; (410) 889-5092 fax
Services: Alternative Directions provides free legal assistance to persons in prison or recently released from incarceration. Most cases handled involve family and domestic legal issues. The program also provides monthly workshops to prisoners on legal rights and responsibilities.

Health Education Resource Organization (HERO)
Address: 1734 Maryland Avenue
Baltimore, MD 21201
Phone: (410) 685-1180; (410) 685-3101 fax
Website: http://hero-mcrc.org
Services: Sponsor volunteers who go to the Maryland State Penitentiary to provide counseling, facilitating meetings, contacting families and lawyers. Distribute some literature and videos related to health issues. Contact them for specifics.

Maryland CURE
Address: P.O. Box 1583
Annapolis, MD 21404
Phone: (301) 869-8180
E-mail: mdcure@curenational.org
Website: www.curenational.org/mdcure
Services: Promote and provide information about rehabilitative programs. Advocate for sensible use of prison space, alternatives to incarceration, and resources and programs that will assist prisoners. Local and National CURE newsletters available with a MD CURE membership.

Office of the Public Defender, Collateral Review Division
Address: 300 W. Preston Street - #213
Baltimore, MD 21201
Phone: (410) 767-8460; (410) 333-7609 fax
Website: www.opd.state.md.us
Services: Handle post-convictions, parole revocation and extradition matters for prisoners throughout Maryland. Services limited to Maryland state prisoners only.

Prisoner Rights Information System of Maryland
Contact: Stephen Meehan
Address: P.O. Box 929
Chestertown, MD 21620
Phone: (410) 778-1700

Services: Handle civil-rights cases pertaining to conditions-of-confinement issues (no criminal work). Limited to state prisons. Provide direct referrals, free legal service to retain counsel and representation at Inmate Grievance Office hearings in select cases. Also handle medical complaints, sentencing reviews and miscellaneous legal problems.

Prisoners Aid Association of Maryland, Inc.
Contact: Michael Brown
Address: 204 E. 25th Street
Baltimore, MD 21218
Phone: (410) 662-0353; (410) 662-0358 fax
Website: www.prisonersaid.org
Services: Provide services to prisoners and ex-offenders through community involvement and professional programs, including: counseling, employment and housing placement. Run residential facility for homeless and jobless ex-offenders. Fact sheet available.

Massachusetts

ACLU of Massachusetts
Contact: John Reinstein
Address: 211 Congress Street
Boston, MA 02110
Phone: No incoming calls; (617) 451-0009 fax
E-mail: info@aclum.org
Website: www.aclu-mass.org
Services: Handle cases involving civil-liberties violations; provide limited direct referrals.

Goldfarb Behavioral Health Clinic Integration Program
Address: Shattuck Hospital
170 Morton Street
Jamaica Plain, MA 02130
Phone: (617) 971-3375
Website: www.shattuckhospital.org
Services: This project is for ex-offenders returning to the community who need mental-health and/or substance-abuse services. The project also serves people who are on parole and probation.

Harvard Prison Legal Assistance Project (PLAP)
Contact: Pamela Cameron
Address: Gannett House 100
Harvard Law School
Cambridge, MA 02138
Phone: (617) 495-3969 (non-collect)
Hotline: (617) 495-3127 (in-state prisoners *only*)
Services: Representation of prisoners at disciplinary and/or parole hearings. Also assist

State prisoners with other prison-related problems via hotline. Services for Massachusetts prisoners only. No self-help manuals. Does not send legal materials in the mail.

Massachusetts Correctional Legal Services, Inc.

Contact: Leslie Walker
Address: 8 Winter Street, 11th Floor
Boston, MA 02108
Phone: (617) 482-2773; (617) 451-6383 fax
E-mail: lwalker@mcls.net
Website: www.mcls.net
Services: Provide direct services to Massachusetts prisoners on the following matters: civil-rights violations, denial of medical care, brutality, detainers and warrants, recovery of "lost" property, sentence calculation, parole application and revocation, advice and referrals for disciplinary hearings and post-conviction proceedings (no direct representation), and visitation. Publish a free quarterly newsletter, *MCLS Notes*, in English and Spanish. MCLS accepts collect calls from Massachusetts prisoners on Monday afternoons from 1 to 4 p.m.
(800) 882-1413/(617) 482-4124 (County Facilities) (877) 249-1342 (DOC Facilities).

Massachusetts CURE

Contact: Dave Elvin
Address: 409 Main Street
Amherst, MA 01002
Phone: (413) 687-7363
E-mail: delvin@javanet.com
Services: Education and outreach. Do not provide direct assistance.

Suffolk County House of Correction, Inmate Legal Services

Address: 20 Bradston Street
Boston, MA 02118
Phone: (617) 635-1000
Services: General legal services, exclusively serving indigent prisoners confined to the Suffolk County House of Correction in Boston. By appointment and referral, assist with routine jail credit, sentencing, and habeas corpus; claims for bail money and personal property; post-conviction motions, parole and disciplinary hearings; and assistance with pro se civil matters, including referral and coordination with outside counsel.

Michigan

ACLU of Michigan

Contact: Michael Steinberg
Address: 2966 Woodward Avenue
Detroit, MI 48201
Phone: (313) 578-6800; (313) 578-6811 fax
E-mail: bbove@aclumich.org
Website: www.aclumich.org
Services: Handle prison-conditions cases and provide direct referrals. Services are limited to state prisons and jails.

CURE—Enough

Address: P.O. Box 15655
Detroit, MI 48230
Phone: (269) 383-0028; (269) 373-2545 fax
E-mail: ar1220@wayne.edu
Services: Organizes to remove felony restrictions on jobs, etc.

Michigan CURE

Contact: Kay D. Perry
Address: P.O. Box 2736
Kalamazoo, MI 49003-2736
Phone: (269) 383-0028; (269) 373-2545 fax
E-mail: kayperry@aol.com
Services: Grassroots criminal-justice-reform organization that includes prisoners, their families and other concerned citizens. Through advocacy, work to establish a humane and effective criminal-justice system. Publish quarterly newsletter for members and self-help brochures and booklets.

SORT (Sex Offenders Restored through Treatment)

Address: P.O. Box 1191
Okemos, MI 48805
Phone: (517) 482-2085
E-mail: sata@satasort.org
Website: www.satasort.org
Services: Offers education about types of abuses, ways to control abuse, and positive approaches to therapy and restorative justice. Also lends support through referrals, networking, and sharing positive information for those at risk as victims and offenders, those victimized, those who have offended, therapists, the justice system, policy makers, and the public.

Minnesota

ACLU Minnesota

Contact: Teresa Nelson

Address: 450 N. Syndicate Avenue - #230
              St. Paul, MN 55104
Phone: no incoming calls; (651) 647-5948 fax
E-mail: support@aclu-mn.org
Website: www.aclu-mn.org
Services: Handle various matters, including post-conviction, habeas corpus, and prison conditions only if they present a Bill of Rights violation. Provide direct referrals.

AMICUS

Address: 15 S. 5th Street - #1100
              Minneapolis, MN 55402
Phone: (612) 348-8570; (612) 348-6782 fax
Website: www.amicususa.org
Services: Provide one-on-one volunteer services for prisoners in Minnesota State prisons. Reconnect and assist ex-offenders with housing, clothing and job-seeking resources. Offer scholarships and pre- and post-release programs.

Legal Assistance to Minnesota Prisoners

Contact: Brad Colbert
Address: LAMP Clinic
              875 Summit Avenue
              St. Paul, MN 55105
Phone: (651) 290-8651; (651) 290-6406 fax
Services: Provide civil legal services to persons incarcerated in Minnesota state prisons who cannot afford or in any manner obtain a private attorney.

Legal Rights Center

Contact: Community Worker
Address: 1611 Park Avenue South
              Minneapolis, MN 55404
Phone: (612) 337-0030; (612) 337-0797 fax
E-mail: office@legalrightscenter.org
Website: www.legalrightscenter.org
Services: Handle post-conviction, direct referrals and criminal defense cases only. No appeals except for cases previously handled by the Center.

Mississippi

ACLU of Mississippi

Contact: Nsombi Lambright
Address: P.O. Box 2242
              Jackson, MS 39225-2242
Phone: (601) 355-6464; (601) 355-6465 fax
E-mail: msacluoffice@msaclu.org
Website: www.msaclu.org
Services: Conduct civil-rights actions. Cases are limited to constitutional issues; no criminal work.

Mississippi CURE

Contact: Jonathan Edwards
Address: P.O. Box 1620
              Philadelphia, MS 39350-9998
E-mail: jonathan@mississippicure.org
Website: www.mississippicure.org

Missouri

4-H Living Interactive Family Education
Missouri Department of Corrections

Contact: Institutional Activities Coordinator
Address: 11593 State Highway O
              Mineral Point, MO 63660
Phone: (573) 438-6000 x1534
Services: Provide enhanced visiting, parenting education and group activities to incarcerated individuals and their families at Potosi Correctional Center. Program uses National 4-H organization framework.

ACLU of Eastern Missouri (Eastern)

Contact: Anthony Rothert
Address: 454 Whittier Street
              St. Louis, MO 63108
Phone: (314) 652-3111
Website: www.aclu-em.org
Services: Pursue prison-conditions issues and provide research, information and referrals to prisoners.

Agape House

Contact: Linda Lamb, Manager
Address: 810 East High
              Jefferson City, MO 65101
Phone: (573) 636-5737
Services: Provide overnight lodging for family and friends visiting inmates in prison areas. Also provide family-reunification support.

Center for Women in Transition

Contact: Sister Rose McLarney
Address: 7529 S. Broadway
              St. Louis, MO 63111
Phone: (314) 771-5207
Fax: (314) 771-0066
Email: cwit@cwitstl.org
Website: http://cwitstl.org/
Services: Provides information, referrals and volunteer mentors for women exiting incarceration. Provides advocacy for needs of children of offenders and alternative sentencing for women.

C.H.I.P.S. (Challenging Incarcerated Parents and Spouses)

Contact: Institutional Activities Coordinator

Address: 8501 No More Victims Rd.
Jefferson City, MO 65101

Phone: (573) 751-3911

Services: Provide enhanced visiting, parent education, marriage seminars, family reunification, support and referrals for fathers at Algoa Correctional Center.

Criminal Justice Ministry

Contact: Carleen Reck

Address: 4127 Forest Park Avenue
St. Louis, MO 63108

Phone: (314) 652-8062; (314) 531-6712 fax

Website: www.svdpstl.org/cjm

Services: Provide information, referrals, mentoring, public information and advocacy.

Girl Scout Council of Greater St. Louis

Address: 2130 Kratky Road
St. Louis, MO 63114

Phone: (314) 890-9569

Website: www.gscgsl.org

Services: Provide transportation and expenses for Girl Scouts Beyond Bars, Girl Scout troop meetings in St. Louis and activities with moms and their daughters at the correctional center.

Good Samaritan Project

Address: 3030 Walnut Street
Kansas City, MO 64108-3811

Phone: (816) 561-8784; (816) 753-4582 fax

Website: www.gspkc.org

Services: Provide supportive and responsive care for individuals affected by HIV/AIDS, through education and advocacy.

Let's Start

Contact: Cynthia Stevenson

Address: 1408 South 10th Street
St. Louis, MO 63104

Phone: (314) 241-2324

Services: Provide support for women coming out of prison, their children and the caregivers of the children. Also provide public education and advocacy.

Long Distance Dads
Missouri Department of Corrections

Contact: Joe Miller

Address: 2729 Plaza Drive
Jefferson City, MO 65102

Phone: (573) 751-2389

Services: Provide parent education; self-help and family-reunification support for incarcerated fathers at several Missouri facilities.

Lutheran Ministries/Humanitri

Contact: Sarah Barnes

Address: P.O. Box 6385
St. Louis, MO 63107

Phone: (314) 652-4300 x14

Services: Provide transportation, self-help support group, mentoring, religious ministry and referrals.

Missouri CURE

Address: P.O. Box 6034
Chesterfield, MO 63006

Phone: (816) 413-0186

E-mail: missouricure@hotmail.com

Website: www.mocure.org

Services: Advocacy organization that works to reduce crime through criminal-justice reform and the rehabilitation of errants.

Parents as Teachers

Contact: Melanie Richter

Address: 920 South Jefferson
Mexico, MO 65265

Phone: (573) 581-3773 x154

Services: Provide parent education, counseling, information, referrals, gifts for children and family reunification support. Serve Audrain County.

PATCH of Chillicothe

Contact: Colleen Scotch, Director

Address: P.O. Box 871
Chillicothe, MO 64601

Phone: (660) 646-6462

Services: Provide enhanced mother-child visits in a home-like setting, pre- and post-visit counseling, parent education, re-entry preparation and support group, information, referrals, gifts for children, mentoring, public education and advocacy, family therapy, family reunification support and transportation to visits at Chillicothe Correctional Center.

PATCH of W.E.R.D.C.C.
(Women's Eastern Reception and Diagnostic Correctional Center)

Address: Highway E 54
Vandalia, MO 63382

Phone: (573) 594-6686

Services: Provide transportation, overnight lodging, children's center in the visiting area, gifts for children and enhanced visiting for incarcerated mothers at W.E.R.D.C.C.

Prisoner Family Services

Contact: Susan Smith
Address: 3540 Marcus Avenue
St. Louis, MO 63115
Phone: (314) 807-4352
Services: Provide transportation once or twice per month to 19 Missouri correctional centers. Also provide overnight lodging, information, referrals, gifts for children, public education and advocacy.

Project COPE: Congregation Offender Partnership Enterprise

Address: 3529 Marcus Avenue
St. Louis, MO 63115
Phone: (314) 389-4804; (314) 389-4804 fax
E-mail: office@projcope.org
Website: www.projcope.org
Services: Ecumenical agency engaging congregations in supportive partnerships with individually selected ex-offenders as they re-enter the St. Louis community.

Regeneration Courage 2 Change, Inc.

Contact: Wilma Warren
Address: P.O. Box 300573
St. Louis, MO 63132
Phone: (314) 368-2426
Email: regencourage2chg@aol.com
Services: Provides a mentoring/life-skills program for children with incarcerated parents, parent education, self-help support group, information, referrals, religious ministry, family reunification support, community residential services, public education and advocacy.

Montana

ACLU of Montana

Contact: Scott Crichton
Address: P.O. Box 1317
Helena, MT 59624
Phone: (406) 248-1086; (406) 248-7763 fax
E-mail: aclu@aclumontana.org
Website: www.aclumontana.org
Services: Provide representation in prison-conditions cases.

Nebraska

ACLU of Nebraska

Contact: Amy Miller
Address: 941 O Street - #706
Lincoln, NE 68508
Phone: (402) 476-8091; (402) 476-8135 fax
E-mail: info@aclunebraska.org

Website: www.aclunebraska.org
Services: Handle civil-rights actions and habeas corpus. Cases are limited to constitutional issues. Provide direct referrals.

Nebraska AIDS Project

Address: 139 S. 40th Street
Omaha, NE 68131
Phone: (800) 782-2437 (in-state only)
(402) 552-9260; (402) 552-9251 fax
Website: www.nap.org
Services: Statewide AIDS service organization providing prevention strategies, support services and case management to persons living with HIV/AIDS. Provides practical support, volunteers, support groups, emergency assistance and statewide hotline. Clients must be diagnosed as HIV-positive. Support services available for family members and significant others.

Nevada

ACLU of Nevada

Contact: Gary Peck
Address: 732 South 6th Street - #200A
Las Vegas, NV 89101
Phone: (702) 366-1226; (702) 366-1331 fax
E-mail: aclunv@aclunv.org
Website: www.aclunv.org
Services: Handle habeas corpus and prison- and jail-conditions cases. All services depend on the availability of volunteer counsel.

Friends and Family of Incarcerated Persons, Inc.

Address: P.O. Box 27708
Las Vegas, NV 89126
Phone: (702) 223-6600
E-mail: ffipffip1@cox.net
Services: Provide support and help for the "out-mates," those on the outside who have a loved one in prison or jail. Hold meetings every Friday evening, 7:00 p.m., at Christ Episcopal Church, 2000 South Maryland Parkway, Meeting Room #1.

Nevada AIDS Foundation

Address: 900 West First Street - #200
Reno, NV 89503
Phone: (775) 348-9888; (775) 324-9339 fax
E-mail: info@nvaf.net
Website: www.nvaf.net
Services: Services limited to HIV-positive prisoners. Write and/or visit prisoners, depending upon volunteers. Residence assistance for qualified persons with HIV infection (in latest stages). Try to find homes for

prisoners upon release. Housing is subsidized up to $300 a month, depending on existing funds. Maintain a food bank that is available for HIV-positive former prisoners. Several free brochures.

New Hampshire

New Hampshire CLU
Contact:	Claire Ebel
Address:	18 Low Avenue
	Concord, NH 03301
Phone:	(603) 225-3080; (603) 226-3149 fax
Services:	Handle prison conditions, First Amendment and prisoners' rights cases.

New Jersey

ACLU of New Jersey
Contact:	Legal Department
Address:	P.O. Box 32159
	Newark, NJ 07102
Phone:	(973) 642-2084; (973) 642-6523 fax
E-mail:	info@aclu-nj.org
Website:	www.aclu-nj.org
Services:	Legal defense of serious violations of constitutional rights; violations must originate within the State of New Jersey.

Garden State CURE
Address:	c/o Office of Jail & Prison Ministry
	P.O. Box 5147
	Trenton, NJ 08638
Phone:	(609) 406-7400, x5655
E-mail:	rschul@dioceseoftrenton.org
Services:	Advocacy organization that works to reduce crime through criminal-justice reform and the rehabilitation of errants.

H.O.P.E. For Ex-Offenders, Inc.
Contact:	Rev. Jonathan Whitfield
Address:	259 Passaic Street
	Hackensack, NJ 07601
Phone:	(201) 646-1995 (phone and fax)
Services:	Provide employment referrals, temporary housing, clothing, food, transportation, medication, etc., for prisoners in Bergen and Passaic counties.

Horton Dance! Inc.
Contact:	Rev. Adrienne Unae
Address:	P.O. Box 311
	Clementon, NJ 08021
Phone:	(856) 783-7314
E-mail:	info@hortondance.org
Website:	www.hortondance.org
Services:	Ministers to the incarcerated via dance movement therapy and teaches the art form as a mode of prayer and embodied prayer for mental and physical healing.

Hyacinth AIDS Foundation
Address:	317 George Street - #203
	New Brunswick, NJ 08901
Phone:	(732) 246-0204; (732) 246-4137 fax
	(800) 443-0254 (in-state only)
E-mail:	info@hyacinth.org
Website:	www.hyacinth.org
Services:	Offer the following services to prisoners with AIDS or who are HIV-positive: buddies/volunteers who offer one-on-one support; support groups; liaison with paroled/released prisoners; and AIDS information for corrections staff. Services are available to state and county prisoners, but not at every facility since access to each facility must be granted separately. Also offer support groups for families and a rental-assistance program in Essex County only.

New Jersey Association on Correction (NJAC)
Address:	986 S. Broad Street
	Trenton, NJ 08611
Phone:	(609) 396-8900; (609) 396-8999
Services:	Provide direct services to offenders and ex-offenders and advocates to improve the criminal-justice system. Direct services are offered through two pre-release facilities, Clinton House and Bates House. The two resource centers serve probationers and parolees. Residential facilities are restricted to state prisoners on community release. Also publish *News and Views*, a quarterly newsletter discussing criminal-justice and corrections issues, available as a membership benefit. Membership is free to prisoners and $20/year for non-prisoners.

NJAC's Clinton House
Address:	21 N. Clinton Avenue
	Trenton, NJ 08609
Phone:	(609) 396-9186; (609) 396-0099 fax
Services:	Clinton House is a 40-bed residential community-release program for adult male offenders. Most of the residents are A304s (classified violent offenders). Eligibility criteria include full minimum status and being within 18 months of parole eligibility. The program includes work release with a strong focus on reintegration and deinstitutionalization.

Distribute newsletters and kindness from the Human Kindness Foundation.

NJAC's Sanford Bates House

Address:	33 Remsen Avenue New Brunswick, NJ 08901
Phone:	(732) 846-7220
Services:	Residential program for female state pre-release prisoners. Services include individual, group and family counseling, employment assistance, substance-abuse counseling and financial counseling. Assist in the transition from incarceration to living in the community. Residents pay house fees on a sliding scale.

Office of the Ombudsman, New Jersey Department of Corrections

Address:	Department of Corrections, Ombudsman's Office P.O. Box 855 Trenton, NJ 08625
Phone:	(609) 292-8020 (Inmate Line, collect calls accepted)
Services:	Provide assistance to prisoners with problems and complaints. The office functions independently of the state prison facilities to ensure the development of trust, confidentiality and objectivity between Ombudsmen and prisoners. Ombudsmen are expected to be alert and to follow through on any violation of due process; to observe that basic living standards are met; to be especially responsive to all allegations of staff brutality; and to observe searches and crisis situations as required.

New Mexico

ACLU of New Mexico

Contact:	Peter Simonson
Address:	P.O. Box 80915 Albuquerque, NM 87198
Phone:	(505) 266-5915; (505) 266-5916 fax
E-mail:	psimonson@aclu-nm.org
Website:	www.aclu-nm.org
Services:	No direct services to prisoners; referrals only. Investigate complaints alleging that an indigent defendant has not been appointed a Public Defender. Refer complaints from penitentiary prisoners to the appropriate Public Defender office or to the prison compliance monitor in Santa Fe. Refer prisoners looking for statutes or cases to the Prison Research Staff at the UNM Law Library. Check complaints regarding food, sanitation, medical

treatment, mail, lawyer access and visiting privileges for city and county jail inmates.

Coalition for Prisoners' Rights

Contact:	Mara Taub
Address:	702 Franklin Ave. Santa Fe, NM 87505
Phone:	(505) 982-9520; (505) 982-9520 fax
Services:	Publish a national monthly newsletter. Provide information and referrals about prison support groups. Work to educate people about prison-related issues. Newsletter is free to prisoners; modest sliding-scale fee for others.

Dismas House, Inc.

Contact:	Peter Rinn
Address:	P.O. Box 6101 Albuquerque, NM 87197
Phone:	(505) 343-0746
Fax:	(505) 345-4513
Services:	Transitional housing program for men and women who are parolees from New Mexico prisons. Room, board, utilities, laundry facilities and unlimited local phone calls are provided at an affordable cost for a maximum of 10 people at any given time. There is a multi-step admission process and a minimum 90-day supervised stay.

FACES New Mexico/CURE

Address:	1083 Mesa Loop NW Los Lunas, NM 87031
Phone:	(505) 865-7571
E-mail:	royalmesa@comcast.net
Services:	Advocacy organization that works to reduce crime through criminal-justice reform and the rehabilitation of errants.

New Mexico Public Defender Department, Post-Conviction Unit

Contact:	Chris Bulman
Address:	301 N. Guadalupe - #001 Santa Fe, NM 87501
Phone:	(505) 827-3900 x146; (505) 476-0273 fax
Services:	Provide court appointed representation services for conditions-of-confinement issues and substantive underlying case challenges.

New Mexico Women's Justice Project

Address:	c/o Peanut Butter and Jelly, Inc. 1101 Lopez Road, S.W. Albuquerque, NM 87105
Phone:	(505) 877-7060; (505) 877-7063 fax

E-mail: info@pbjfamilyservices.org
Website: www.pbjfamilyservices.org
Services: Provide a broad range of technical assistance, advocacy, training, planning, and oversight on issues involving women in prison and jails and the children of incarcerated parents.

Protection and Advocacy System
Address: 1720 Louisiana Blvd. NE - #204
            Albuquerque, NM 87110
Phone: (800) 432-4682; (505) 256-3184 fax
Services: Provide information and referrals; advocacy; negotiation or court action on behalf of individuals and groups; training regarding legal rights; benefits and assistance with other disability issues. (In-state calls only.)

New York

ACCESS/Argus Community Inc.
Contact: Dianna Diaz
Address: 760 East 160th Street
            Bronx, NY 10456
Phone: (718) 401-5741; (718) 993-9662 fax
E-mail: ddiaz@arguscommunity.org
Services: Intensive case management for HIV+ persons, including ex-offenders and their families with or without Medicaid. Provide referrals, escort to appointments, and home visits. Can work with prisoners with a 30-day discharge date. Will work with parole, if clients agree/consent.

AIDS Related Community Services
Contact: Hugo Mendez
Address: 473 Broadway
            Newburgh, NY 12550
Phone: (845) 562-5005; (845) 562-5212 fax
AIDS-line: (800) 992-1442
Website: www.arcs.org
Services: Provide support groups, short-term counseling, AIDS crisis intervention, comprehensive case-management services. Prison service initiative for state correctional facilities. Jail services program for county correctional facilities. Referrals available for medical, legal, dental, funeral, and other services. Will provide materials on current HIV/AIDS and updated medical information.

Cephas Attica, Inc.
Contact: Robert Miller
Address: 102 N. Union Street
            Rochester, NY 14607
Phone: (585) 546-7472; (585) 546-8579 fax
E-mail: cephas3@rochester.rr.com
Website: www.cephas.org
Services: Provide group counseling in Attica, Wyoming, Collins, Orleans, Albion, Rochester, Gowanda, and State School for Youth at Industry prisons (13 groups weekly) and aid prisoner families. Post-release services include housing for parolees with a commitment to Cephas, Attica's 90-day program. Also offer assistance with educational opportunities, transportation, housing and job opportunities and substance-abuse aftercare. Available 24 hours a day for counseling.

The Children's Center
Contact: Sister Elaine Roulet
Address: Bedford Hills Correctional Facility
            247 Harris Road
            Bedford Hills, NY 10507
Phone: (914) 241-3100 x4050; x3199 fax
Services: Offer a wide range of services to prisoner mothers and their children. Programs include: foster-care workshops, parenting classes, nursery, Infant Development Center, children's advocacy, family literacy, seasonal and holiday activities, story corner and transportation assistance. The Children's Playroom is open every day of the year. Provide the *Foster Care Handbook for Incarcerated Parents* and *Parenting from Inside/Out: The Voices of Mothers in Prison*.

CURE New York
Contact: Amy and George Oliveras
Address: P.O. Box 1314
            Wappingers Falls, NY 12590
E-mail: cureny@bestweb.net
Website: www.bestweb.net/~cureny
Services: Educational and advocacy organization that works for criminal-justice reform and the rehabilitation of errants. Produce a quarterly newsletter focusing attention on New York criminal-justice issues.

Civil Rights Clinic
Contact: Claudia Angelos
Address: N.Y.U. Clinical Law Center
            245 Sullivan Street, 5th Floor
            New York, NY 10012
Phone: (212) 998-6430; (212) 995-4031 fax
Services: In conjunction with a law school program, students handle an extremely limited number of civil-rights cases. At present, the clinic focuses on police

misconduct, but has represented some New York State prisoners incarcerated close to New York City and may resume doing so in the future.

Fortune Society
Contact: Kristen Kidder
Address: 53 W. 23rd Street, 8th Floor
New York, NY 10010
Phone: (212) 619-7554; (212) 255-4948 fax
Website: www.fortunesociety.org
Services: Ex-offender self-help organization with a national membership of 30,000. Work with ex-offenders in the New York area. Offer one-on-one counseling (ex-offender to ex-offender); one-on-one tutoring; job-training placement; tutoring in preparation for the high school GED diploma; and outpatient substance-abuse services. No legal services. Act as a referral agency for halfway houses, drug- or alcohol-addiction programs, and numerous other social services. Conduct an alternatives-to-incarceration program and AIDS counseling. Publish *Fortune News*, free to prisoners upon request.

Legal Action Center
Contact: Paralegal on Call
Address: 225 Varick Street - 4th Floor
New York, NY 10014
Phone: (800) 223-4044; (212) 243-1313; (212) 675-0286 fax
E-mail: lacinfo@lac.org
Website: www.lac.org
Services: Concerned primarily with employment, housing, and other types of discrimination against ex-offenders, ex-addicts, ex-alcoholics, and people with HIV. Provide law libraries and pre-release centers in New York State facilities with a publication, *How to Get and Clean Up Your New York State Rap Sheet*. Non-prisoners interested in receiving this publication should contact the LAC.

New York City Board of Correction
Contact: Cathy Potler
Address: 51 Chambers Street, Rm. 923
New York, NY 10007
Phone: (212) 788-7840; (212) 788-7860 fax
Services: Evaluate the performance of the Department of Correction, establish and ensure compliance with minimum standards of confinement, health care, and mental-health care in all city correctional facilities. Review prisoner and employee grievances, investigate serious incidents and make recommendations in critical areas of correctional planning.

New York CLU
Contact: Arthur Eisenberg
Address: 125 Broad Street, 19th Floor
New York, NY 10004
Phone: (212) 607-3300; (212) 607-3318 fax
Website: www.nyclu.org
Services: Handle rare post-conviction and habeas corpus cases, only if they raise new civil-liberties issues. Refer most prison issues to either the Prisoners' Rights Project of Legal Aid or Prisoners' Legal Services of New York.

The Osborne Association
Address: 809 Westchester Avenue
Bronx, NY 10455
Phone: (718) 707-2600; (718) 707-3105 fax
E-mail: egaynes@osborneny.org
Website: www.osborneny.org
Services: Operate model programs and provide direct services to defendants, prisoners, ex-offenders and their families in the South Bronx, Brooklyn, and Manhattan and at five upstate prisons to those who qualify. Do not provide direct legal services. Most programs require court referrals. Publications are available, including literature on the effects of incarceration on children and services available to HIV-positive prisoners and parolees.

Ossining Prison Ministry, Inc.
Contact: Marion Farrell
Address: 34 S. Highland Avenue
Ossining, NY 10562
Phone: (914) 941-0540; (914) 941-3929 fax
Services: Provide breakfast and supervised child-care on Saturdays and Sundays to visiting families and friends of prisoners at Sing Sing Prison. Some counseling is also provided and other hospitality as needed.

Prisoners' Legal Services of New York
Website: www.plsny.org
Services: Provide civil legal services to indigent prisoners in New York State correctional facilities in cases where no other counsel is available. Handle cases involving disciplinary procedures, medical care, excessive force, mental-health care, conditions of confinement, sentence computation, parole and jail-time credit. No collect calls.

PLS Ithaca (including Central Intake)

Contact:	Betsy Hutchings
Address:	114 Prospect Street
	Ithaca, NY 14850
Phone:	(607) 273-2283; (607) 272-9122 fax
E-mail:	bhutchings@plsny.org
Services:	Serve prisoners in Auburn, Butler, Camp Georgetown, Camp Monterey, Camp Pharsalia, Cape Vincent, Cayuga, Elmira, Five Points, Southport, Watertown, and Willard.

PLS Albany

Contact:	James Bogin
Address:	41 State Street, Suite M112
	Albany, NY 12207
Phone:	(518) 438-8046; (518) 438-6643 fax
E-mail:	jbogin@plsny.org
Services:	Serve prisoners in Arthur Kill, Bayview, Beacon, Bedford Hills, Camp Fallsburg, Camp Mt. McGregor, Camp Summit, CNYPC, Coxsackie, Downstate, Eastern, Edgecombe, Fishkill, Fulton, Great Meadow, Green Haven, Greene, Hale Creek, Hudson, Johnstown, Lincoln, Marcy, Mid-Orange, Midstate, Mohawk, Oneida, Otisville, Queensboro, Shawangunk, Sing Sing, Sullivan, Taconic, Ulster, Wallkill, Walsh, Washington, and Woodbourne

PLS Buffalo

Contact:	Maria Pagano
Address:	237 Main Street, Suite 1125
	Buffalo, NY 14202
Phone:	(716) 854-1007; (716) 854-1008 fax
E-mail:	mpagano@plsny.org
Services:	Serve prisoners in Albion, Attica, Buffalo, Collins, Gowanda, Groveland, Lakeview, Livingston, Orleans, Rochester, Wende, and Wyoming.

PLS Plattsburgh

Contact:	Michael Cassidy
Address:	121 Bridge Street. - #202
	Plattsburgh, NY 12901
Phone:	(518) 561-3088; (518) 561-3262 fax
E-mail:	mcassidy@plsny.org
Services:	Serve prisoners in Adirondack, Altona, Bare Hill, Camp Gabriels, Chateaugay, Clinton, Franklin, Gouverneur, Lyon Mountain, Moriah, Ogdensburg, Riverview, and Upstate.

Prisoners' Rights Project of the Legal Aid Society

Address:	199 Water Street
	New York, NY 10038
Phone:	(212) 577-3530; (212) 509-8433 fax
Website:	www.legal-aid.org
Services:	Primary work involves conditions-of-confinement litigation in federal court. Also provide referrals and offer information, advice, and various forms and information packets to individual prisoners seeking information on their legal rights and remedies. Services limited to prisoners in New York State prisons and New York City jails.

Providence House, Inc.

Contact:	Monzura Rhue
Address:	703 Lexington Avenue
	Brooklyn, NY 11221
Phone:	(718) 455-0197; (718) 455-0692 fax
Services:	Provide transitional housing and support to homeless, abused and formerly incarcerated women and their children. Residents are linked to support services in the community, learn basic skills and receive help obtaining permanent housing.

Society of St. Vincent de Paul

Contact:	Dismas Committee
Address:	249 Broadway
	Bethpage, NY 11714
Phone:	(516) 822-3132; (516) 822-2728 fax
E-mail:	rwood@svdprvc.org
Services:	Provide bail assistance, transportation in emergencies and reasonable assurance of housing and emergency clothing. Services are limited to Long Island residents who are returning to Long Island from prison and those incarcerated in Long Island.

Southern Tier AIDS Program

Address:	122 Baldwin Street
	Johnson City, NY 13790
Phone:	(607) 798-1706; (607) 798-1977 fax
E-mail:	info@stapinc.org
Website:	www.stapinc.org
Services:	Provide group and individual support group services, case management upon release, educational programs and materials for corrections officials and parole officers.

Women's Prison Association and Home, Inc.

Contact:	Ann L. Jacobs
Address:	110 Second Avenue
	New York, NY 10003
Phone:	(212) 674-1163; (212) 677-1981 fax
Services:	Assist women in making the transition from incarceration to independent living

in the community through halfway houses, foster-care prevention and visitation advocacy, housing and job-placement assistance, vocational-training programs, family and child welfare programs, and substance-abuse programs. Emphasize self-reliance through independent living-skills development, self-empowerment, peer support, and client involvement in the community. Strive to increase public awareness of and support for effective, community-based responses to crime.

North Carolina

ACLU of North Carolina
Contact: Katherine Lewis Parker
Address: P.O. Box 28004
Raleigh, NC 27611
Phone: (919) 834-3390; (919) 828-3265 fax
E-mail: aclunc@nc.rr.com
Website: www.acluofnorthcarolina.org
Services: Handle habeas corpus and prison-conditions cases. Provide direct referrals, including referrals for damage suits.

North Carolina Prisoner Legal Services, Inc.
Contact: Brenda Richardson
Address: P.O. Box 25397
Raleigh, NC 27611-5397
Phone: (919) 856-2200
Website: www.ncpls.org
Services: Legal services to North Carolina prisoners only. Provide a range of services from advice about prisoners' legal rights to representation in all state and federal courts. Handle a variety of legal matters involving prison conditions and criminal convictions. Write NCPLS for a brochure detailing which types of cases receive top priority, providing information on how to request assistance from NCPLS, and listing information packets and legal forms available to prisoners.

Prison-Ashram Project
Address: c/o Human Kindness Foundation
P.O. Box 61619
Durham, NC 27715
Phone: (919) 383-5160; (919) 383-5140 fax
Website: www.humankindness.org
Services: Publish an interfaith spiritual newsletter and distribute some free books. Publications discuss the foundation of self-honesty, courage, kindness, humor, and wonder.

Summit House, Inc.
Contact: Raymond Matz
Address: 122 N. Elm Street - #910
Greensboro, NC 27403
Phone: (336) 691-9888; (336) 275-5042 fax
E-mail: ray@summithouse.org
Website: www.summithouse.org
Services: Summit House is an alternative correctional facility that helps non-violent female offenders and their children under 7. The intensive residential program focuses on rehabilitation, teaching responsible citizenship, respect for the law, behavior modification, and life-skills training. Strict guidelines and a point system regulate the residents' daily lives, but also allow them to make choices. A team of case managers is present 24 hours a day. During their stay, residents are expected to earn a GED, if not a high school graduate; attend college or other vocational training; participate in substance-abuse counseling and skills-training programs; obtain employment; achieve independent living arrangements with their children; and be cooperative and involved members of the house. Information brochures are available upon request.

North Dakota

ACLU of the Dakotas
Contact: Jennifer Ring
Address: 112 North University Drive - #301
Fargo, ND 58102
Phone: (701) 461-7290; (701) 461-7291 fax
E-mail: info@acludakotas.org
Website: www.acludakotas.org

Ohio

AIDS Volunteers of Cincinnati
Contact: Victoria Brooks
Address: 220 Findlay
Cincinnati, OH 45202
Phone: (513) 421-2437; (513) 421-0301 fax
Website: www.avoc.org
Services: Services include an AIDS information and referral line; a buddy program; and support groups for HIV-positive persons and their families. Provide case management, support groups, forums, financial counseling, transportation, advocacy, and home-health-care coordination. Assistance with chemical- and alcohol-dependency referrals, crisis intervention, and prevention.

ACLU of Ohio

Contact: Jeff Gamso
Address: 4506 Chester Avenue
Cleveland, OH 44103
Phone: (216) 472-2200; (216) 472-2210 fax
E-mail: contact@acluohio.org
Website: www.acluohio.org
Services: Review complaints about prison and jail conditions. For state prison complaints, prisoner is asked to file a grievance and appeal and send the response if s/he is dissatisfied with it.

Books 4 Prisoners

Contact: The Books 4 Prisoners Crew
Address: P.O. Box 19065
Cincinnati, OH 45219
Website: www.freewebs.com/books4prisoners
Services: An all-volunteer group providing free progressive political and educational material to prisoners. *Only have services available* in Ohio, Indiana and 4 state facilities in Texas (Lane Murray Unit, Ramsey I Unit, Gatesville Unit, and Polunsky Unit). Prisoners are limited to two books, postage included, every six months.

CURE Ohio

Contact: Kunta Kenyatta
Address: P.O. Box 14080
Columbus, OH 43214
Phone: (937) 299-8298; (614) 784-9696 fax
Website: http://cureohio.us/
Services: Provide a legislative voice for Ohio prisoners and their families. Talk to legislators, public officials, and the general public about the need for criminal-justice reform. Publish a bimonthly newsletter, *Against All Odds*.

Columbus AIDS Task Force

Contact: Peggy Anderson
Address: 1751 East Long Street
Columbus, OH 43212
Phone: (614) 299-2437; (614) 291-7162 fax
Hotline: (800) 332-2437
Website: www.catf.net
Services: Offer education about AIDS transmission and prevention for pre-release prisoners, prisoners in drug-treatment programs, and prisoners in programs for sex offenders (upon request from state institutions). Upon release, ex-offenders with AIDS may become CATF clients. Client services include support groups for clients and their families, legal and medical

referrals, and a buddy program. Distribute a wide variety of literature about HIV/ AIDS for all ages. Operate statewide toll-free hotline. Hotline for hearing impaired is (800) DEAF-TTY.

Community Connection for Ohio Offenders, Inc.

Contact: Ginger Cermelj
Address: P.O. Box 341347
Columbus, OH 43234
Phone: (614) 760-1902; (614) 760-1908 fax
Website: www.communityconnectionohio.com
Services: Provide an overall support network for offenders and ex-offenders to help them be responsible, contributing members of society. Educate the community to support and nurture this target population and educate clients to successfully return to the community. Provide a Community Connection Program brochure and a packet listing services available in the state of Ohio.

Ohio Justice and Policy Center

Address: 215 E. 9th Street - 6th Floor
Cincinnati, OH 45202
Phone: (513) 421-1108; (513) 562-3200 fax
E-mail: contact@ohiojpc.org
Website: www.ohiojpc.org
Services: Educate and assist Ohio prisoners with use of grievance and administrative remedies to solve complaints dealing with conditions of confinement and protect prisoner rights under the PLRA and Ohio H.B. 455. Help prisoners' families understand prison procedures and their rights as family members. Also litigate on significant prisoner rights issues and run an empowerment program for Ohio incarcerated women.

Women's Re-Entry Resource Network

Contact: Mary Kozina
Address: 1468 West 25th Street
Cleveland, OH 44113
Phone: (216) 696-7535; (216) 658-4727 fax
Services: Provide mental-health services, parenting classes, support services for children, job-readiness and placement assistance, educational assistance, legal assistance, onsite baby sitting during groups and classes, specialized services for Welfare-to-Work participants, clothing assistance, referrals for substance-abuse treatment, housing information, creative-writing groups, temporary transportation, and case-management and counseling services at Cuyahoga County Jail.

Oklahoma

ACLU of Oklahoma

Contact: Tina Izadi
Address: 3000 Paseo Drive
               Oklahoma City, OK 73103
Phone: (405) 524-8511; (405) 524-2296 fax
E-mail: acluok@acluok.org
Website: www.acluok.org
Services: Handle prison-conditions cases and civil-liberties violations. Provide limited referrals. Do not provide post-conviction assistance or research services to prisoners.

Oklahoma CURE

Address: P.O. Box 9741
               Tulsa, OK 74157-0741
Phone: (918) 744-9857 (and fax)
E-mail: okcure@earthlink.net
Website: www.home.earthlink.net/~okcure
Services: Advocacy organization that works to reduce crime through criminal-justice reform and the rehabilitation of errants.

Oregon

ACLU of Oregon

Contact: David Fidanque
Address: P.O. Box 40585
               Portland, OR 97204-0585
Phone: (503) 227-3186; (503) 227-6948 fax
E-mail: info@aclu-or.org
Website: www.aclu-or.org
Services: Handle limited post-conviction, habeas corpus, and prison-conditions cases. Direct referrals are provided to agencies but not to private attorneys. This office has no staff attorneys.

Community Court Project

Multnomah County Adult Community Justice District Offices

Address: 421 Southwest Fifth Avenue - #600
               Portland, OR 97204
Phone: (503) 988-3007; (503) 988-4574 fax
Services: By collaborating with citizens, law enforcement, court and social-service agencies, the Community Court Project encourages defendants to contribute positively to their community through community-service projects and offers them social-service assistance to address underlying problems that can lead to criminal behavior.

Better People

Contact: Clariner Boston
Address: 4310 NE MLK, Jr. Boulevard
               Portland, OR 97211
Phone: (503) 281-2663; (503) 281-2667 fax
Website: www.betterpeople.org
Services: A living-wage employment and counseling program for adult offenders.

Center on Juvenile and Criminal Justice (CJC)

Northwest Regional Office

Address: Western Oregon University
               HHS 223A
               345 N. Monmouth
               Monmouth, OR 97361
Phone: (503) 838-8401
Services: Promote balanced and humane criminal-justice policies that reduce incarceration and promote long-term public safety for juveniles, through the development of model programs, technical assistance, research/policy analysis, and public education.

Federal Public Defender, District of Oregon

Portland (Main) Office

Address: 101 SW Main Street - #1700
               Portland, OR 97204
Phone: (503) 326-2123; (503) 326-5524 fax

Eugene Office

Address: 151 W. 7th Street - #510
               Eugene, OR 97401
Phone: (541) 465-6937; (541) 465-6975 fax

Medford Office

Address: 15 Newton Street
               Medford, OR 97501
Phone: (541) 776-3630; (541) 776-3624 fax

Hepatitis C (HCV) Prison Support Project

Contact: Phyllis Beck
Address: P.O. Box 41803
               Eugene, OR 97404
Phone: (541) 607-5725; (541) 607-5684 fax
E-mail: pkbeckinor@aol.com
Website: www.hcvinprison.org
Services: Educate prisoners and advocate for better testing, diagnosis, and prevention of Hepatitis and HIV/HCV co-infection. Distribute bimonthly newsletter and Hepatitis C, HIV/HCV co-infection packets free to prisoners.

Legislative Commission on Indian Services

Address: 900 Court Street, NE - #167
               Salem, OR 97301
Phone: (503) 986-1067; (503) 986-1071 fax
Email: cassandra.webber@state.or.us
Website: www.leg.state.or.us/cis

Services: The state regulated office to aid in legislative issues dealing with Tribe and Nation peoples.

Multnomah County Legal Aid
Address: 700 SW Washington - #500
           Portland, OR 97205
Phone: (503) 224-4086; (503) 295-9496 fax
Website: www.oregonlawhelp.org
Services: Assist residents in family law, public benefits, landlord tenants, and other civil matters.

Oregon CURE
Address: 1631 NE Broadway - #460
           Portland, OR 97232
Phone: (866) 357-2873
Website: www.oregoncure.org
Services: Advocacy organization that works to reduce crime through criminal-justice reform and the rehabilitation of errants.

Oregon Office of the Governor
Address: Citizens' Representative Office
           Office of the Governor
           900 Court Street NE
           Salem, OR 97301
Phone: (503) 378-4582; (503) 378-6827 fax
Services: Handle issues that come to the Governor's Office dealing with corrections, board of parole, post-prison supervision, and other law-enforcement areas.

Oregon State Public Defender
Contact: Peter Gartlan
Address: 1320 Capitol Street, NE - #200
           Salem, OR 97301-7869
Phone: (503) 378-3349 or (503) 378-2371
E-mail: peter.gartlan@opds.state.or.us
Website: www.opds.state.or.us
Services: Handle direct criminal appeals for indigent defendants convicted of felonies in state circuit courts; misdemeanors in state district courts and parole appeals, together with parole set appeals.

Oregonians for Alternatives to the Death Penalty
Address: P.O. Box 361
           Portland, OR 97207-0361
Phone: (503) 236-1686
E-mail: info@oadp.org
Website: www.oadp.org
Services: Criminal-justice activists joined in a concerted effort to increase the effectiveness of Oregon's response to violent interpersonal crime. Our members include victims, survivors, attorneys, religious leaders, teachers and other concerned citizens. OADP works toward repeal of the death penalty; support life sentence alternatives in response to aggravated murder as effective and sufficient; promote research, education and discussion of issues relating to the death penalty; work to promote principles of restorative justice for all those affected by murder, including victims' family members, prisoners and prisoners' families.

Pennsylvania

AIDS Law Project of Pennsylvania
Contact: Rhonda Goldfein
Address: 1211 Chestnut Street - #600
           Philadelphia, PA 19107
Phone: (215) 587-9377; (215) 587-9902 fax
Services: Provide a range of legal services, including information on compassionate release and referrals to community-based organizations for prisoners living with HIV/AIDS. Publish *AIDS and the Law: Your Rights in Pennsylvania*, available free to prisoners and low-income residents.

ACLU of Pennsylvania
Contact: Vic Walczak
Address: P.O. Box 40008
           Philadelphia, PA 19106
Phone: (215) 592-1513; (215) 592-1343 fax
E-mail: info@aclupa.org
Website: www.aclupa.org
Services: Primarily provide direct referrals. Occasionally handle habeas corpus and prison-conditions cases.

ACLU of Pennsylvania, Greater Pittsburgh Chapter
Address: 313 Atwood Street
           Pittsburgh, PA 15213
Phone: (412) 681-7736; (412) 681-8707 fax
E-mail: info@aclupgh.org
Website: www.pgh.aclu.org
Services: Handle prison-conditions cases and provide referrals.

American Friends Service Committee
Contact: Joyce D. Miller
Address: 1501 Cherry Street
           Philadelphia, PA 19102
Phone: (215) 241-7000
E-mail: afscinfo@afsc.org
Website: www.afsc.org
Services: National and local healing justice programs focus on advocacy, education, policy development and organizing.

Publish analysis and action reports (free to prisoners), including: Survivors Manual, a manual written by and for people living in control units; The Prison Inside the Prison: Control Units, Supermax Prisons, and Devices of Torture. Also online StopMax Campaign (www.afsc.org/stopmax) to promote and support a national movement to end solitary confinement and related forms of torture in US prisons; and Rights 101: How and when to assert your rights with the Police (www.afsc.org/rights101), an online manual for youth workers and facilitators of youth workshops.

BEBASHI

Contact:	Ebony Davis
Address:	1217 Spring Garden Street, 1st Floor
	Philadelphia, PA 19123
Phone:	(215) 769-3561, x132; (215) 769-3860 fax
Website:	www.bebashi.org
Services:	Provide discharge-planning and case-management services to HIV+ prisoners in Pennsylvania State Correction Institutions. Assist with housing, medical and behavioral health care, public benefits, and support in re-entry. Limited to HIV+ prisoners who are returning to Philadelphia County upon release. Furnish agency brochures and discharge planning forms upon request.

Centre Peace, Inc.

Contact:	Tom Brewster
Address:	3013 Benner Pike
	Bellefonte, PA 16823-8303
Phone:	(814) 353-9081; (814) 353-9083 fax
E-mail:	thom@centrepeace.org
Website:	www.centrepeace.org
Services:	Run Prayer-Mate Program. Prisoners and community members communicate by mail through this office on a first-name-only basis. Provide SCI-Rockview family-visitation assistance for PA prisoners, corrections personnel, and community. We pay half the cost of transportation to Rockview Prison in Bellefonte, PA. Run conflict-resolution training that teaches non-violent resolution of conflicts and introduction to mediation. Organize PA Prison Runathon—prisoners run a marathon to raise funds for alternatives to incarceration of youth. Publish *Criminal Justice Advocacy and Support Directory*, free for PA prisoners, victims, and their families.

Community Justice Project

Contact:	Donald Driscoll
Address:	1705 Allegheny Building
	Pittsburgh, PA 15219
Phone:	(412) 434-6002

Concerned Seniors/Gray Panthers of Graterford

Contact:	Dr. Julia Hall
Address:	Drexel University
	Philadelphia, PA 19104
Phone:	(215) 895-2472; (215) 895-1333 fax
E-mail:	hall@drexel.edu
Services:	Advocate for older prisoners incarcerated in Pennsylvania prisons and jails. Provide information, advocacy, external contacts and opportunities to prepare for return to the community. Medical, legal, financial and family experts frequently serve as guest speakers to the group. Services are limited to the State Correctional Institute at Graterford in Pennsylvania.

Defender Association of Philadelphia

Address:	1441 Samson Street
	Philadelphia, PA 19102
Phone:	(215) 568-3190; (215) 988-0208 fax
Services:	Represent indigent adults and juveniles in criminal cases for which Association is appointed as counsel by the courts.

Pennsylvania Innocence Project at Temple University Beasley School of Law

Contact:	Marissa B. Bluestine, Esq.
Address:	1719 N. Broad Street
	Philadelphia, PA 19122
Phone:	(215) 204-3818 (direct)
	(215) 204-4255 (main)
Services:	The mission of the Pennsylvania Innocence Project is to secure the exoneration, release from imprisonment, and restoration to society of persons who are innocent and have been wrongly convicted. We accept cases with or without potential DNA evidence, but are limited to working only with those inmates who were convicted in Pennsylvania and are currently or have yet to serve the sentence arising out of that conviction.

Lewisburg Prison Project, Inc.

Address:	P.O. Box 128
	Lewisburg, PA 17837
Phone:	(570) 523-1104; (570) 523-3944 fax
E-mail:	prisonproject@dejazzd.com
Website:	www.eg.bucknell.edu/~mligare/LPP.html

Services: Provide direct civil legal services without charge to indigent prisoners who are victims of crime or abuse, or who have been denied their constitutional rights due to their conditions of confinement. Serve prisoners in the Middle District of Pennsylvania, including 2 Federal Corrections Complexes, 11 State Prisons, and 34 County Jails. Offer a number of publications distributed nationwide of specific interest to prisoners. Contact the LPP for their most recent list of manuals and bulletins on prisoner rights and pro se litigation. Cannot provide legal services by mail; assist with criminal law, sentencing law, or divorce; forward anything to other prisoners; or find citations, review briefs, or make copies.

Pennsylvania Institutional Law Project

Contact: Angus Love
Address: 718 Arch Street
            Suite 304 South
            Philadelphia, PA 19106
Phone: (215) 925-2966; (215) 925-5337 fax
Website: www.pailp.org
Services: Represent prisoners on prison-conditions issues and a full range of civil services. Assistance provided to prisoners in the federal, state, or county jails throughout the Commonwealth. Distribute various self-help publications regarding disciplinary actions, political asylum, name change, and a report of leading cases in 3rd Circuit Court of Appeals, as well as a local referral guide.

Pennsylvania Prison Society

Contact: William DiMascio
Address: 245 N. Broad Street - #300
            Philadelphia, PA 19107-1518
Phone: (215) 564-6005; (215) 564-7926 fax
E-mail: geninfo@prisonsociety.org
Website: www.prisonsociety.org
Services: Provide support for prisoners while incarcerated and upon return to the community, in addition to providing services for their families. The Re-Entry Services Program (RESP) assists former offenders with life and employment skills to become productive members of their communities. The Services to Elderly Inmates (STEP) provides case-management and direct services for aging prisoners in state prisons. The Inmate Family Services (IFS) program teaches parenting skills to individuals incarcerated throughout the state.

The IFS facilitates Support of Kids with Incarcerated Parents (SKIP), a support group for children between the ages of 8-12 years. The Virtual Visitation program offers prisoners and their families the opportunity to visit via teleconference when distance prevents families from traveling to visit loved ones. Staff and volunteers operate the family resource center at the State Correctional Institution at Graterford.

The Program for Female Offenders, Inc.

Contact: Carol Hertz
Address: 100 N. Braddock Ave.
            Pittsburgh, PA 15208
Phone: (412) 281-7380; (412) 642-9118 fax
E-mail: chertz@tpfo.org
Services: Work with women who are on probation or parole or who have ever been in trouble with the law. Provide ongoing support in the areas of counseling, parole planning, career, workshops, referrals and job placement. Operate the Program Center, a work-release center that functions as an alternative program to serving time in the Allegheny County Jail.

The Program for Female Offenders, Inc., Greater Harrisburg Office

Contact: Valerie G. Simmons
Address: 1515 Derry Street
            Harrisburg, PA 17104
Phone: (717) 238-9950; (717) 236-3585 fax
Services: Work with women who are on probation or parole or who have ever been in trouble with the law. Provide ongoing support in the areas of counseling, HIV/AIDS prevention, parole planning, career education, mentoring, workshops, referrals, and job placement. Operate the Woodside Family Center, which functions as an alternative program to serving time in the Dauphin County Prison.

Program for Women and Families

Contact: Dr. Joyce Dougherty
Address: 1030 Walnut Street
            Allentown, PA 18102
Phone: (610) 433-6556; (610) 433-1983 fax
E-mail: contactus@thepwf.org
Website: www.thepwf.org
Services: Work exclusively with women offenders at the local level. Provide employment counseling, housing counseling, individual and group counseling, case management, parenting classes, and HIV/AIDS

prevention programs. Also operate a small transitional residence.

Project IMPACT
Contact: Rhonda Hummel or David Deibler-Gorman
Address: S.C.I. Muncy
P.O. Box 180
Muncy, PA 17756
Phone: (570) 546-3171 x419 or x420
Services: Run a children's center at SCI-Muncy where prisoners can spend individual time with their children. Project IMPACT also offers activity workshops, prenatal classes and parenting support groups. Provide a workbook for incarcerated parents written by staff, professionals and prisoners at SCI-Muncy, called *I Love You This Much*. The workbook provides parents with ideas and suggestions for actively staying part of their children's lives despite the physical separation. Cost is $5 plus $2 s/h. Write for an order form. Services are limited to prisoners at SCI-Muncy.

Urban League Employment Program
Contact: David Tugume
Address: 502 S. Duke Street
Lancaster, PA 17602
Phone: (717) 394-1966: (717) 295-5044 fax
Services: Provide job-search workshops, individualized job-search assistance, counseling, and follow-up employment services. Also, offer a free job-listing service for employers.

www.prisoners.com
Contact: Sandra Feigley
Address: P.O. Box 5251
Harrisburg, PA 17110
Phone: (717) 236-6045
Website: www.prisoners.com
Services: Present prison-related issues to the world through our website and present prisoner issues to Pennsylvania legislators.

Puerto Rico

ACLU of Puerto Rico
Contact: William Ramirez, Esq.
Address: Union Plaza Building - #205
416 Avenida Ponce de Leon
San Juan, PR 00918
Phone: (787) 753-8493; (787) 753-4268 fax
E-mail: aclupr@prtc.net
Services: Provide limited assistance to prisoners. Services are restricted to general counseling

and direct referrals. Provide advocacy against the death penalty and work in coalition with local prison-advocacy organizations.

Rhode Island

ACLU of Rhode Island
Contact: Steven Brown
Address: 128 Dorrance Street - #220
Providence, RI 02903
Phone: (401) 831-7171; (401) 831-7175 fax
E-mail: riaclu@riaclu.org
Website: www.riaclu.org
Services: Provide limited assistance to prisoners. Services are restricted to post-conviction, habeas corpus, prison conditions, and direct referrals. Especially concerned with prison problems that raise significant First Amendment or due process issues.

South Carolina

ACLU of South Carolina
Contact: Valerie Shannon
Address: 2712 Middleburg Drive - #104
Columbia, SC 29204
Phone: (803) 799-5151; (803) 254-7374 fax
E-mail: intake@aclusc.org
Website: www.aclusc.org
Services: Provide limited assistance to prisoners. Services are restricted to post-conviction, habeas corpus, prison conditions, and direct referrals.

Alston Wilkes Society
Contact: S. Anne Walker
Address: 3519 Medical Drive
Columbia, SC 29203
Phone: (803) 799-2490; (803) 540-7223 fax
E-mail: glockhart@alstonwilkessociety.org
Website: www.alstonwilkessociety.org
Services: Statewide social-service organization that provides a broad range of direct services and referral assistance to offenders, ex-offenders and their immediate families. Provide assistance to prisoners regarding parole and release planning, as well as advocacy and legislative services. Operate halfway houses for adult offenders, group homes for emotionally disturbed juveniles, and a facility for homeless male veterans. Provide public information and educational programs to citizens of South Carolina, and provide a range of volunteer services to adults and juveniles.

Accept out-of-state referrals of residents of South Carolina and of probationers under jurisdiction of the Federal Bureau of Prisons.

South Dakota

ACLU of the Dakotas

Contact: Jennifer Ring
Address: Manchester Building
            112 N. University Drive - #301
            Fargo, ND 58102-4661
Phone: (701) 461-7290: (701) 461-7291 fax
E-mail: dakaclu@cs.com
Website: www.acludakotas.org

Tennessee

ACLU of Tennessee

Contact: Melody Fowler-Green
Address: P.O. Box 120160
            Nashville, TN 37212
Phone: (615) 320-7142
Website: www.aclu-tn.org
Services: Handle habeas corpus, if a civil-rights question is involved, and prison- and jail-conditions cases. Provide direct referrals and legal assistance regarding discrimination based on AIDS/HIV.

Reconciliation Ministries, Inc.

Contact: Alice Arceneaux
Address: 702 51st Avenue North
            Nashville, TN 37209
Phone: (615) 292-6371; (615) 292-6383 fax
E-mail: reconciliation_@hotmail.com
Services: We only respond to requests relating to Tennessee prisoners. Provide a guest-house for families coming to Nashville to visit a prisoner in a Middle Tennessee correctional facility. Accommodations are free to visiting families and some transportation assistance is available. Reservations are required. For ex-offenders looking to relocate, contact the Tennessee Board of Probation and Parole. Offer a weekly support group for adults with loved ones in prison. Provide advocacy for families, information, and referrals. Offer publications of interest to prisoners and their families: *Separate Prisons Newsletter*, available free; *Handbook for Families and Friends of Tennessee Prisoners*, contact office for cost; *Two in Every 100*, a workbook for young children with a parent in prison, contact office for cost. Parole packets with information about preparing for parole in Tennessee are $8.

Tennessee Coalition to Abolish State Killing

Address: Box 120552
            Nashville, TN 37212
Phone: (615) 256-3906
E-mail: tcask@tcask.org
Website: www.tcask.org
Services: Coordinate legislative and community opposition to the death penalty. Publish quarterly newsletter, *Tennessee Lifelines*, free to Tennessee death-row prisoners.

Texas

ACLU of Texas

Contact: Lisa Graybill
Address: P.O. Box 12905
            Austin, TX 78711-2905
Phone: (512) 478-7309; (512) 478-7303 fax
E-mail: info@aclutx.org
Website: www.aclutx.org
Services: Handle city, county, state and federal prison-conditions cases.

Dallas County Jail Programs Division

Contact: Jim Strickland
Address: 133 N. Industrial Boulevard, LB31
            Dallas, TX 75207
Phone: (214) 653-2837; (214) 653-2832 fax
Services: Coordinate education courses (literacy and GED through community college), recreation, library, and substance-abuse programs for prisoners *within* the Dallas County Jail system. Assist in referrals to outside community agencies for released prisoners.

FIND-CURE (Furnishing Imprisoned Non-Citizens with Direction)

Contact: Dr. Luis Payan
Address: 705 Mississippi Avenue
            El Paso, TX 79902
Phone: (915) 747-7985
E-mail: lapayan@utep.edu

Texas CURE

Address: 4121 Burning Tree Lane
            Garland, TX 75042
Phone: (972) 276-9865
E-mail: dill.c@tx.rr.com
Website: www.txcure.org
Services: Provide referrals and information, no legal assistance. Organize prisoners, their families and other concerned citizens to achieve reforms in the Texas

criminal-justice system. Publish a quarterly newsletter, *News & Notes*, free to Texas prisoners and Texas CURE members contributing $10 or more.

Texas Inmates Families Association (TIFA)

Address: P.O. Box 300220
Austin, TX 78703-0004
Phone: (512) 371-0900
E-mail: tifa@tifa.org
Website: www.tifa.org
Services: Advocacy organization for families with incarcerated loved ones. Help families help their incarcerated family members with conditions issues, such as medical care, abuse, and violence. Provide educational and other information. Advocate for legislative and criminal justice reform and public awareness.

Welcome House, Inc.

Contact: Jackie Thompson
Address: 921 N. Peak Street
Dallas, TX 75204
Phone: (214) 887-0696; (214) 827-9582 fax
E-mail: jmthompson9@sbcglobal.net
Services: Offer housing, food, clothing, and the introduction to recovery as described by AA guidelines. Provide a safe place to live for prisoners, HIV-infected individuals, and women. Affiliated with Dallas's court system, we frequently accompany offenders to court and testify to their program adherence. Also offer a mentoring program, GED assistance, life-skills, family and marital counseling, and a recovery support group. Assist parolees in establishing a home in a structured drug-free environment. Distribute a free client brochure on agency specifics.

Texas Advocacy Project, Inc.

Contact: Andrea Sloane
Address: P.O. Box 833
Austin, TX 78767-0833
Phone: (512) 476-5377; (800) 777-3247 (toll-free)
E-mail: info@women-law.org
Website: www.women-law.org
Services: Provide free legal assistance for any victim of violence or sexual assault in Texas.

Utah

ACLU of Utah

Contact: Margaret Plane

Address: 355 North 300 W - #1
Salt Lake City, UT 84103
Phone: (801) 521-9289; (801) 532-2850 fax
E-mail: aclu@acluutah.org
Website: www.acluutah.org
Services: Review complaints resulting in systemic violations of prisoner rights. Monthly meetings with prison officials to resolve ongoing problems; medical care, mental health, and general conditions.

Prisoner Information Network (PIN)

Contact: Marianne Johnstone
Address: P.O. Box 165171
Salt Lake City, UT 84116
Phone: (801) 355-0234; (801) 521-6282 fax
E-mail: pin@prisonernetwork.com
Services: A resource for prisoners and their families in Utah. Provide hygiene kits to prisoners being released in Utah. Hold monthly outreach meetings and publish newsletter, *Behind the Wire*. Also publish the *Utah Prisoner Resource Guide*, $4 for prisoners and $10 for people in the free world.

Vermont

ACLU of Vermont

Contact: Laura Philipps
Address: 137 Elm Street
Montpelier, VT 05602
Phone: (802) 223-6304; (802) 233-6304 fax
E-mail: info@acluvt.org
Website: www.acluvt.org
Services: Handle post-conviction cases involving civil-liberties issues; limited prison-conditions cases; damage suits (no fees). Provide direct referrals. Services limited to Vermont prisoners, residents, and prisoners transferred to other states.

Prisoners' Rights Office

Contact: Dawn Seibert
Address: 6 Baldwin Street - 4th Floor
Montpelier, VT 05633
Phone: (802) 828-3194; (802) 828-3163 fax
Website: www.defgen.state.vt.us
Services: Handle limited civil-rights actions, post-conviction relief, habeas corpus and prison-conditions cases; direct referrals; parole revocation; and prison disciplinary matters. *Only assist Vermont prisoners charged with Vermont crimes.*

Vermont Catholic Charities, Inc.

Address: 351 North Avenue
Burlington, VT 05401

Phone: (802) 658-6110 x312; (802) 860-0451 fax
E-mail: charities@vermontcatholic.org
Services: Provide one-on-one pastoral counseling, family visitation, prisoner-supervised passes, and referral services. Services are limited to Vermont offenders, ex-offenders and their families. Also provide Catholic Mass and other Church services. Ensure that each prisoner receives a Christmas gift—*i.e.*, socks, shampoo, writing paper, etc. Furnish clothing whenever possible to needy prisoners. Assist ex-offenders with employment and housing assistance.

Virginia

AIDS/HIV Services Group
Contact: Bruce Taylor
Address: P.O. Box 2322
            Charlottesville, VA 22902
Phone: (434) 979-7714; (434) 979-8734 fax
E-mail: info@aidsservices.org
Website: www.aidsservices.org
Services: Offer services to individuals with HIV/AIDS who are in the local jail, including emotional support, information packets, and assistance with post-release planning— housing, employment, etc. Also offer supportive services to family members and friends of individuals with HIV/AIDS who are incarcerated.

ACLU of Virginia
Contact: Rebecca Glenberg
Address: 530 East Main Street - #310
            Richmond, VA 23219
Phone: (804) 644-8022; (804) 649-2733 fax
E-mail: intake@acluva.org
Website: www.acluva.org
Services: Handle select litigation limited to state prison facilities and county jails.

Assisting Families of Inmates
Contact: Fran Bolin
Address: 1 N. 5th Street - #400
            Richmond, VA 23219
Phone: (804) 643-2401; (804) 643-2464 fax
E-mail: family@afoi.org
Website: www.afoi.org
Services: Provide visiting-day transportation for families and friends of state prisoners between Richmond and most major state prisons (goes to 30 facilities). Provide information and referrals for community resources that assist families and provide chaperones to accompany children on visits with incarcerated mothers. Collaborate with CIS to run a school-based counseling program for children of incarcerated parents, called *Milk and Cookies*. Cooperate with United Methodist Church to recruit and enroll eligible children for the *All God's Children* summer camp.

The Beautiful Struggle
Contact: Billie Jones
Address: P.O. Box 223152
            Chantilly, VA 20153
Phone: (703) 361-4645
E-mail: thebeautifulstruggle@ yahoogroups.com
Website: http://groups.yahoo.com/group/ thebeautifulstruggle
Services: Advocacy to change society's perception of how prisoners are viewed.

Offender Aid and Restoration of Arlington County
Contact: Transition Advisor
Address: 1400 N. Uhle Street - #704
            Arlington, VA 22201
Phone: (703) 228-7030; (703) 228-3981 fax
E-mail: info@oaronline.org
Website: www.oaronline.org
Services: Provide support, emergency assistance, identification, direct referrals, and planning for transition into the community. Prepare clients to obtain and maintain suitable employment. *Limited* to residents of Arlington County, City of Alexandria, and City of Falls Church.

Offender Aid and Restoration of Charlottesville/Albemarle
Contact: Patricia Smith
Address: 750 Harris Street - #207
            Charlottesville, VA 22903
Phone: (434) 296-2441; (434) 979-4038 fax
E-mail: cdodds@oar-jacc.org
Services: Offer pretrial services, supervision of community service and restitution, job assistance, and emergency assistance for offenders and families.

Offender Aid and Restoration of Richmond, Inc.
Contact: Barbara Slayden
Address: 1 N. 3rd Street - #200
            Richmond, VA 23219
Phone: (804) 643-2746; (804) 643-1187 fax
E-mail: info@oarric.org
Website: www.oarric.org
Services: Post-release services are provided to inmates released from a jail in the greater

Richmond area and inmates from a state or federal prison returning to the Richmond area. A Post-Release Services Client Guide is available free through the mail to inmates requesting information.

Opportunities, Alternatives & Resources of Fairfax County, Inc.

Address: 10640 Page Avenue - #250
          Fairfax, VA 22030-4000
Phone: (703) 246-3033; (703) 273-7554 fax
E-mail: info@oarfairfax.org
Website: www.oarfairfax.org
Services: Provide referrals to community resources, employment and vocational guidance, one-on-one volunteers (prisoner visitation) at Fairfax County Adult Detention Center and emergency assistance for ex-offenders to obtain food, clothing and temporary housing. Family assistance services include: family support group, one-on-one counseling (by appointment), emergency assistance to obtain food, clothing and temporary housing and Saturday Friends, a support group for children of offenders and the children's main care givers. Assistance available only for Fairfax County residents and ex-offenders from Fairfax County returning from state correctional institutions. Limited resources also available to residents and ex-offenders in Loudon and Prince William Counties.

Virginia Capital Representation Resource Center

Contact: Rob Lee
Address: 2421 Ivy Road - #301
          Charlottesville, VA 22903
Phone: (434) 817-2970; (434) 817-2972 fax
E-mail: roblee@vcrrc.org
Services: Provide expert legal consultative services to attorneys and law firms that represent death-sentenced prisoners in Virginia.

Virginia CURE

Address: P.O. Box 19307
          Alexandria, VA 22320-0307
Phone: (703) 765-6549; (703) 765-6549 fax
E-mail: virginiacure@cox.net,
          VirginiaPrisoners@yahoogroups.com
Website: www.vacure.org
Services: All-volunteer membership organization. Provide referrals, public information and education on the criminal-justice system, and prison and criminal-justice-reform advocacy. Network with state legislature, prisoner family-support groups, religious leaders, and administrative agencies that deal with prison and criminal justice issues. Publish infrequent newsletter on Virginia prison issues, *Inside Out.* Dues: $2 (or 6 stamps) prisoners; $15 individuals; $25 family; $50 supporter; $150 life member/organization; $250 benefactor.

Virginia Institutionalized Persons (VIP) Project of the Legal Aid Justice Center

Contact: Helen Trainor, Project Director
Address: 1000 Preston Ave., Suite A,
          Charlottesville, VA 22903
Phone: 434-977-0553, ext. 130
E-mail: helen@justice4all.org
Services: Investigates conditions in Virginia's prisons and jails to bring systemic change where civil and human rights are being violated. Does not represent individual prisoners but instead builds class action lawsuits and initiates policy reform, both through community engagement and legislative activism.

Washington

ACLU of Washington

Contact: Julya Hampton
Address: 705 Second Avenue - #300
          Seattle, WA 98104-1799
Phone: (206) 624-2180; (206) 624-2190 fax
E-mail: administration@aclu-wa.org
Website: www.aclu-wa.org
Services: Handle complaints, on a limited basis, regarding jail and prison conditions and treatment of prisoners (depending on available staff resources). No post-conviction appeals.

Columbia Legal Service

Contact: Beth Colgan
Address: 101 Yesler Way - #301
          Seattle, WA 98104
Phone: (206) 382-3399 (collect) or (206) 464-0838; (206) 464-0856 fax
Services: Handle conditions-of-confinement and civil-rights claims.

Law Office of Leta J. Schattauer

Contact: Leta J. Schattauer
Address: 705 Second Avenue - #1300
          Seattle, WA 98104
Phone: (206) 623-0366; (206) 623-2186 fax
Services: Represent Washington State prisoners in post-conviction matters in State and Federal court. Provide representation

before the ISRB (parole board), the Clemency Board, and other institutional administrative bodies. Also represent sexual predators facing civil commitment and/or release to the community.

Spokane County Public Defender
Contact: John Rodgers
Address: 1033 W. Gardner
Spokane, WA 99260-0280
Phone: (509) 477-4246; (509) 477-2567 fax
Services: By court appointment only, handle adult felony, juvenile felony and misdemeanor and county misdemeanor crimes. Also handle civil commitments and juvenile dependency cases.

West Virginia

ACLU of West Virginia
Address: P.O. Box 3952
Charleston, WV 25339-3952
Phone: (304) 345-9246; (304) 345-9262 fax
E-mail: mail@acluwv.org
Website: www.acluwv.org
Services: Handle complaints on a very limited basis, regarding jail and prison conditions.

Alderson Hospitality House
Contact: Tina Marquart
Address: P.O. Box 579
Alderson, WV 24910
Phone: (304) 445-2980
Website: www.aldersonhospitalityhouse.org
Services: Provide free lodging, meals, transportation and support to families and loved ones visiting women incarcerated in Alderson Federal Prison Camp. Publish free quarterly newsletter, *The Trumpet.* Donations are accepted.

Wisconsin

ACLU of Wisconsin
Contact: Lawrence Dupuis
Address: 207 East Buffalo Street - #325
Milwaukee, WI 53202
Phone: (414) 272-4032 x16; (414) 272-0182 fax
E-mail: inquiries@aclu-wi.org
Website: www.aclu-wi.org
Services: Do limited prison-conditions work. Prefer cases that involve constitutional issues and that may have a broad enough impact to succeed in changing legislation or administrative remedies.

AIDS Network
Contact: Jenny Shaffer
Address: 600 Williamson Street
Madison, WI 53703
Phone: (608) 252-6540; (800) 486-6276; (608) 252-6559 fax
E-mail: info@aidsnetwork.org
Services: Provide information, referrals and advocacy by mail, and when permitted, by phone and visits. Assist in obtaining medical care, AODA treatment and housing. Educate prisoners' attorneys on possible effect of HIV infection on a client's case. Services are limited to prisoners in county, state or federal correctional facilities within South Central Wisconsin. A newsletter is available.

Horizon, Inc.
Contact: Constance Shaver
Address: 2511 W. Vine Street
Milwaukee, WI 53205
Phone: (414) 342-3237; (414) 342-3258 fax
E-mail: horizoni@horizonshouse.org
Website: www.horizonshouse.org
Services: Provide alternatives to incarceration (halfway house) for women.

Madison-area Urban Ministry
Contact: Jackie Austin, Program Coordinator
Address: 2300 South Park Street - #5
Madison, WI 53713
Phone: (608) 256-0906; (608) 256-4387 (fax)
E-mail: mum@emum.org
Website: www.emum.org
Services: Work on issues of affordable housing, re-entry of formerly incarcerated people, healthy neighborhoods, and mentoring children who have an incarcerated parent.

Project RETURN
Contact: Wendel Hruska
Address: 2821 N. 4th Street - #202
Milwaukee, WI 53212
Phone: (414) 374-8029; (414) 374-8033 fax
E-mail: projectreturn@asapnet.net
Website: www.projectreturnmilwaukee.org
Services: Assist people leaving prison with finding permanent family-supporting jobs and affordable housing, while remaining drug-free. Affirm and challenge ex-offenders to become productive Milwaukeeans.

Wisconsin Community Services Inc.
Contact: Stephen Swigart
Address: 3732 W. Wisconsin Avenue - #200
Milwaukee, WI 53208

Phone:	(414) 290-0400; (414) 271-4605 fax
E-mail:	sswigart@wiscs.org
Website:	www.wiscs.org
Services:	Operate community and alternative programs for offenders, including adult and juvenile halfway houses, a pretrial-release program, court intervention, alcohol/drug and mental-health services, a home-detention program, mediation services and a Parents Support and Advocate Program.

Wisconsin CURE

Contact:	Kathleen Hart
Address:	P.O. Box 183
	Greendale, WI 53129
Phone:	(414) 384-1000 x32
E-mail:	harthouse9@yahoo.com
Services:	Advocacy organization that works to reduce crime through criminal-justice reform and the rehabilitation of errants.

Wyoming

ACLU-Wyoming Chapter

Contact:	Linda Burt
Address:	P.O. Box 20706
	Cheyenne, WY 82003
Phone:	(307) 637-4565; (307) 637-4565 fax
E-mail:	wyoaclu@aol.com
Website:	www.aclu-wy.org
Services:	Provide general prisoner assistance primarily by screening and referral.

Wyoming Defender Aid Program

Contact:	Dianne Courselle
Address:	1000 E. University Avenue, Dept. 3035
	Laramie, WY 82071
Phone:	(307) 766-3223; (307) 766-2105 fax
E-mail:	dcoursel@uwyo.edu
Services:	Handle post-conviction and habeas corpus cases. Provide direct referrals and legal research.

University of Wyoming Legal Services

Contact:	John Burman
Address:	1000 E. University Avenue, Dept. 3010
	Laramie, WY 82071
Phone:	(307) 766-2104; (307) 766-4823 fax
E-mail:	uwlsp@uwyo.edu
Services:	Provide legal assistance for civil matters that are not fee-generating.

INTERNATIONAL ORGANIZATIONS

Amnesty International

| Address: | 322 Eighth Avenue |
| | New York, NY 10001 |

Phone:	(212) 807-8400
Website:	www.amnesty.org
Services:	An independent worldwide movement working for the international protection of human rights. Seek the release of men and women detained because of their beliefs, ethnic origin, language, or religious creed, provided they have not used violence (prisoners of conscience). Work for a fair and prompt trial for all political prisoners and work on behalf of such people detained without charge or trial. Oppose the death penalty, torture or other inhumane treatment of prisoners. For prisoners who have been ill-treated by prison personnel, will provide a "Questionnaire on Torture and Ill-treatment." (Do not send transcripts.) Publish numerous reports on human-rights violations around the world, including death-penalty reports. Write for complete list. All AI reports are available on the website.

Books to Prisoners Montreal

Address:	2130 Rue Mackay
	Montreal, QC H3G 2J1
	Canada
Phone:	(514) 848-7585
E-mail:	bookstoprisoners@excite.com
Services:	Send books to prisoners free of charge.

Canadian Association of Elizabeth Fry Societies (CAEFS)

Contact:	Kim Pate
Address:	151 Slater Street - #701
	Ottawa, ON K1P 5H3
	Canada
Phone:	(613) 238-2422; (613) 232-7130 fax
E-mail:	caefs@web.ca
Website:	www.elizabethfry.ca
Services:	Provide a wide range of social-service programs, including direct services, policy, and law reform for institutionalized and marginalized women and girls. There are 25 member societies located in Canada. Please write for more information.

Human Rights Watch

Address:	350 5th Avenue, 34th Floor
	New York, NY 10118-3299
Phone:	(212) 290-4700; (212) 736-1300 fax
Website:	www.hrw.org
Services:	Conduct fact-finding investigations into human-rights abuses in all regions of the world. Working with local partners,

monitor conditions of detention around the world. Publish findings in books and reports.

Penal Reform International

Address: Unit 450, The Bon Marche Centre
             241-251 Ferndale Road
             London SW9 8BJ
             United Kingdom
Phone: +44 20 7924 9575;
             +44 20 7924 9697 fax
E-mail: info@penalreform.org
Website: www.penalreform.org
Services: Provide assistance to local human rights organizations, NGO's, and local governments in the reform of criminal-justice and prison systems and in fighting to abolish the death penalty. Work through regional offices in Moscow, Bucharest, and Washington.

Prisoners Abroad

Address: 89-93 Fonthill Road
             Finsbury Park
             London N4 3JH
             United Kingdom
Phone: +44 20 7561 6820;
             +44 20 7561 6821 fax
E-mail: info@prisonersabroad.org.uk
Website: www.prisonersabroad.org.uk
Services: Provide information, advice and support to Britons detained overseas, to their families and friends, and to released prisoners trying to re-establish themselves in society. We negotiate with prison authorities; advise on prison transfers and finding lawyers; provide essentials such as medicine, food and clothing; link prisoners with pen pals; send magazines and

books to clients; give advice and support to families of prisoners abroad; and provide resettlement services for returning clients, including support in finding accommodations, counseling, and applying for benefits.

Prison Fellowship International

Contact: Suzanne Fisher
Address: P.O. Box 17434
             Washington, DC 20041
Phone: (703) 481-0000; (703) 481-0003 fax
E-mail: info@pfi.org
Website: www.pfi.org
Services: Through our national ministries in 112 countries, offer the following service: Angel Tree for prisoners' children and families.

Prison Reform Trust

Address: The Old Trading House
             15 Northburgh Street
             London EC1V 0JR
             United Kingdom
Phone: +44 20 7251 5070;
             +44 20 7251 5076 fax
E-mail: prt@prisonreformtrust.org.uk
Website: www.prisonreformtrust.org.uk
Services: Lobby government for changes in conditions for prisoners and inform the public of issues regarding imprisonment. Provide advice and information service to prisoners and their families and publish research books and papers on aspects of imprisonment. Current projects include a three-year study of the problems faced by young parents in prison, the mentally ill in prison, facilities for visiting at various prisons around the UK, and prisoner voting rights.

APPENDIX C

Forms and Sample Papers for Civil Rights Cases

This Appendix contains examples of documents that prisoners often file in civil rights lawsuits in federal court. Most of the forms are based on a hypothetical case that we have invented. Some of these forms can also be used in state courts, but you are always better off if you can look at properly drafted state court papers to use as models.

We have added notes and references to other parts of this Manual where we think they would be helpful. If these forms raise other issues that you want to know more about, consult the alphabetical Index at the end of the Manual to see where they are discussed.

These sample papers are single-spaced. Everything you submit to a court should be double-spaced. Briefs and memoranda of law should also have cover pages with the caption in the upper part of the page, the title of the document (*e.g.*, "Plaintiff's Memorandum of Law in Opposition to Defendants' Motion for Summary Judgment") in the middle of the page and the plaintiff's name and address in the lower part of the page. (Sometimes local court rules have additional requirements for brief covers and for briefs.) We have not included cover pages for space reasons.

1. Complaint

Note: Complaints are discussed in Ch. 10, § B, and in Ch.12, § B. The following is a state prisoner's complaint and therefore alleges that the defendants acted under color of state law. A complaint against federal prison officials would allege that the defendants acted under color of federal law. *See* Ch. 8, § B.2.

This complaint is fairly complicated because we wanted to include several different legal issues. There are samples of simpler complaints in non-prisoner cases in Forms 1-8 at the end of the Federal Rules of Civil Procedure.

There is disagreement whether a complaint should request a specific amount of damages and this is discussed in Ch. 8, § O.1.d. At the end of the complaint we have presented an alternative version of the damage demand that does not specify amounts of damages. We have also presented a version of the damage demand that reflects the limitations on compensatory damages imposed by the Prison Litigation Reform Act, discussed in Ch. 9, § E.2.

1a. Civil Rights Complaint

UNITED STATES DISTRICT COURT
WESTERN DISTRICT OF _____

JOSEPH WILLIAMS
     Plaintiff,

-v-

JAMES GREEN, RICHARD BROWN,
JANE WHITE, ROBERT GRAY,
GEORGE COLE, HOWARD LEVETT,
JOHN DOE, sued in their individual
capacities, and JORGE GARCIA, MARY
WARREN, and ARTHUR CHRISTOPHER,
sued in their official capacities,
Defendants.

Case No.
Hon.

/

COMPLAINT WITH JURY DEMAND

Introduction

This is a civil rights action filed by Joseph Williams, a state prisoner, for damages and injunctive relief under 42 U.S.C. § 1983, alleging excessive use of force and denial of medical care in violation of the Eighth Amendment to the United States Constitution and confinement in segregation in violation of the Due Process Clause of the Fourteenth Amendment to the Constitution. The plaintiff also alleges the torts of assault and battery and negligence.

Jurisdiction

1. The Court has jurisdiction over the plaintiff's claims of violation of federal constitutional rights under 42 U.S.C. §§ 1331(1) and 1343.

2. The Court has supplemental jurisdiction over the plaintiff's state law tort claims under 28 U.S.C. § 1367.

Parties

3. The plaintiff, Joseph Williams, was incarcerated at Stonehaven Correctional Facility ("Stonehaven") during the events described in this complaint.

4. Defendants James Green, Richard Brown, and Jane White are correctional officers employed at Stonehaven. They are sued in their individual capacities.

5. Defendant John Doe is a correctional officer employed at Stonehaven whose name is presently unknown to plaintiff. He is sued in his individual capacity.

6. Defendant Robert Gray is a correctional lieutenant in charge of the Administrative Segregation Unit at Stonehaven. He is sued in his individual capacity.

7. Defendant George Cole is the Deputy Warden for Security at Stonehaven and is in charge of the supervision and discipline of all correctional staff at Stonehaven. He is sued in his individual capacity.

8. Defendant Jorge Garcia is the Medical Administrator at Stonehaven and is generally responsible for ensuring provision of medical care to prisoners and specifically for scheduling medical appointments outside the prison when a prisoner needs specialized treatment or evaluation. He is sued in his individual and official capacities.

9. Defendant Mary Warren is the Deputy Warden for the Administrator at Stonehaven and is in charge of transportation of prisoners to medical appointments. She is sued in her official and individual capacities.

10. Defendant Howard Levett is a correctional lieutenant at Stonehaven and is responsible for conducting disciplinary hearings for prisoners accused of breaking prison rules. He is sued in his individual capacity.

11. Defendant Arthur Christopher is the warden of Stonehaven and is responsible for reviewing all administrative appeals of disciplinary charges filed by Stonehaven inmates. He is sued in his individual and official capacities.

12. All the defendants have acted, and continue to act, under color of state law at all times relevant to this complaint.

Facts

13. On March 14, 2008, the plaintiff was top-locked (confined to his general population cell at Stonehaven) without explanation.

14. On March 15, 2008, at about 5:00 a.m., defendant Gray came to plaintiff's cell door and directed him to pack his property because he was "moving out."

15. Plaintiff repeatedly asked defendant Gray where he was being taken and defendant Gray refused to answer.

16. Defendant Gray said: "I know how to deal with a wise guy," and left.

17. The plaintiff then began to pack his property as ordered.

Misuse of Force

18. Shortly after these events, defendant Gray returned to plaintiff's cell, accompanied by Defendants Green, Brown, White, and Doe, who were wearing riot helmets, gas masks and jackets, and carrying batons and a tear gas dispenser.

19. The plaintiff stated that he was cooperating and packing his property as ordered.

20. Without warning, defendant Gray said, "Spray him," and defendant Brown sprayed tear gas into plaintiff's cell.

21. Defendant Green then opened plaintiff's cell door and defendants Green, Brown, White, and Doe entered his cell.

22. Defendant Brown knocked the plaintiff to the floor, where he was kicked and struck with batons by defendants Brown and Green.

23. Defendants White and Doe did not intervene to prevent these kicks and blows, and the plaintiff believes that these defendants also kicked and struck him.

24. During this assault one of the defendants stamped on the plaintiff's left ankle, breaking it. The plaintiff also received lacerations to his face and scalp and numerous bruises and abrasions to his arms, legs, torso, face, and head.

25. During these events defendant Gray remained outside plaintiff's cell and did not intervene.

26. During these events the plaintiff did not resist or threaten the officers in any fashion or break any prison rules.

27. Defendants Green, Brown, White, and Doe are members of the Stonehaven Emergency Response Team.

28. Defendants Green and Brown have repeatedly engaged in excessive force against inmates in the past.

29. Defendant Cole has been placed on notice of the abusive conduct of defendants Green and Brown by a number of complaints and grievances over many months, but has failed to take disciplinary action against them or otherwise to control their behavior.

30. After the above-described assault, plaintiff was taken to the prison infirmary, where he received sutures for two of his lacerations and treatment for his exposure to tear gas.

31. The plaintiff was then taken by ambulance to the emergency room of Mercy Hospital, where his ankle was examined, found to be broken, and placed in a cast.

Denial of Due Process

32. The next day, March 16, 2008, the plaintiff was placed in punitive segregation.

33. On March 17, 2008, the plaintiff was served with disciplinary charges for assaulting staff, inciting to riot, threatening staff, and refusing a direct order, based on the above-described events.

34. The plaintiff requested that the hearing officer call as witnesses Roy Phillips, who was housed in the cell across from him in general population, and the inmates housed on either side of Mr. Phillips and on either side of Plaintiff, who had been in a position to see and hear parts of the incident on which the charges were based.

35. The plaintiff did not know the names of these other witnesses, but he provided their cell locations.

36. The plaintiff also asked that defendants Green, Brown, White, and Doe be called as witnesses.

37. On March 19, 2008, the plaintiff received a disciplinary hearing before defendant Levett.

38. Defendant Levett failed to call any of the witnesses requested by the plaintiff, stating that he was not going to call witnesses from general population to a hearing involving a segregation inmate and that the staff reports gave a full picture of the incident.

39. After the hearing, the plaintiff received a written deposition signed by defendant Levett stating, "Guilty as charged based on staff statements," and sentencing the plaintiff to three years in punitive segregation.

40. The staff statements provided to the plaintiff alleged that the plaintiff had refused to leave his cell when ordered, had assaulted defendants Green, Brown, White, and Doe, and had threatened them.

41. The staff statements did not state any facts showing that the plaintiff had incited other inmates to riot.

42. Pursuant to prison procedure, the plaintiff filed an administrative appeal with defendant Christopher, pointing out that none of his witnesses had been called, that there was no evidence supporting the charge of inciting to riot, and that the written disposition did not explain the reasons for the finding of guilt.

43. Defendant Christopher denied the plaintiff's appeal.

Denial of Medical Care

44. While the plaintiff was at Mercy Hospital on March 15, 2008, Dr. Chadhuri, the emergency room physician on duty, told him, and wrote in an order that was to be sent back to the prison, that his ankle would remain in a cast for four weeks and that he would then require a course of physical therapy to regain full use of it.

45. On or about March 22, 2008, the plaintiff submitted a sick call request seeking an appointment for the removal of his sutures and the scheduling of the removal of his cast and his physical therapy.

46. About a week later, the plaintiff was taken to the medical clinic and his sutures were removed by a physician's assistant, Mr. Jones.

47. When he asked about this cast and this physical therapy, Mr. Jones said he didn't know and the plaintiff would have to submit another request.

48. Since then, the plaintiff has submitted repeated sick call requests and has filed a grievance requesting the removal of his cast and the provision of physical therapy for his ankle.

49. On information and belief, when a prisoner files a grievance, the grievance staff calls the matter to the attention of those individuals responsible for the matter that the grievance concerns.

50. Defendant Garcia is responsible for medical care generally and for arranging for specialized medical care outside the prison.

51. Defendant Warren is responsible for arranging for specialized care outside the prison.

52. After seven weeks, the plaintiff has received no response from the medical department.

53. The plaintiff is in great pain and his ankle is stiff and does not turn properly.

54. On information and belief, if the plaintiff is not promptly provided with physical therapy as directed by Dr. Chadhuri, he risks permanent disability.

Exhaustion of Administrative Remedies[1]

55. The plaintiff has exhausted his administrative remedies with respect to all claims and all defendants.

Claims for Relief

56. The actions of defendants Green, Brown, White, Doe, and Gray in using physical force against the plaintiff without need or provocation, or in failing to intervene to prevent the misuse of force, were done maliciously and sadistically and constituted cruel and unusual punishment in violation of the Eighth Amendment of the United States Constitution.

57. The actions of defendants Green, Brown, White, and Doe in using physical force against the plaintiff without need or provocation constituted the tort of assault and battery under the law of [your state].

58. The failure of defendant Cole to take disciplinary or other action to curb the known pattern of physical abuse of inmates by defendants Green and Brown constituted deliberate indifference to the plaintiff's and other prisoners' safety, and contributed to and proximately caused the above-described violation of Eighth Amendment rights and assault and battery.

59. The actions of defendant Levett in refusing to call the witnesses requested by the plaintiff, finding him guilty of inciting to riot with no evidence to support the charge, and providing an inadequate written disposition of the charges, and of Christopher in upholding the disciplinary decision, denied the plaintiff due process of law in violation of the Fourteenth Amendment to the United States Constitution.

60. The failure of defendants Garcia and Warren to provide for the removal of the plaintiff's ankle cast, follow-up examination and treatment of his broken ankle, and physical therapy for his ankle, constitutes deliberate indifference to the plaintiff's serious medical needs in violation of the Eighth Amendment to the United States Constitution.

61. The failure of defendants Garcia and Warren to provide for the removal of the plaintiff's ankle cast, follow-up examination and treatment of his broken ankle, and physical therapy for his ankle, constitutes the tort of negligence under the law of [your state].

---

[1] Even though a prisoner is not required to affirmatively allege exhaustion of prison administrative remedies, there is an advantage to doing so: it makes responding to a motion to dismiss for non-exhaustion easier. *See* Ch. 9, § D.8, for further discussion of this point. If you plead exhaustion, we suggest that you keep it simple. If for some reason you prefer to plead exhaustion in more detail, here is an example of how to do it:

55. The plaintiff filed a grievance complaining about use of excessive force by defendants Gray, Green, Brown, White, and Doe, and completed all three steps of the grievance process. He also filed a grievance against defendant Cole for his failure to supervise and control the use of force by these defendants when he had prior knowledge of excessive use of force, and completed all three steps of the grievance process.

56. The plaintiff filed an administrative appeal concerning denial of due process at the disciplinary hearing by defendants Levett, Cole, and Christopher. The plaintiff completed the two steps of the administrative appeal process.

Relief Requested

WHEREFORE, plaintiff requests that the court grant the following relief:

A. Issue a declaratory judgment stating that:
1. The physical abuse of the plaintiff by defendants Green, Brown, White, and Doe violated the plaintiff's rights under the Eighth Amendment to the United States Constitution and constituted an assault and battery under state law.
2. Defendant Cole's failure to take action to curb the physical abuse of prisoners violated the plaintiff's rights under the Eighth Amendment to the United States Constitution and constituted an assault and battery under state law.
3. Defendant Levett's actions in conducting the plaintiff's disciplinary hearing, and defendant Christopher's actions in sustaining it, violated the plaintiff's rights under the Due Process Clause of the Fourteenth Amendment to the United States Constitution.
4. Defendant Garcia's and defendant Warren's actions in failing to provide adequate medical care for the plaintiff violated, and continue to violate, the plaintiff's rights under the Eighth Amendment to the United States Constitution.

B. Issue an injunction ordering defendants Garcia, Warren, or their agents to:
1. Immediately arrange for the plaintiff's cast to be removed and his ankle to be examined by a qualified physician;
2. Immediately arrange for the plaintiff's need for physical therapy or other follow-up medical treatment to be evaluated by a medical practitioner with expertise in the treatment and restoration and function of broken ankles; and
3. Carry out without delay the treatment directed by such medical practitioner.

C. Issue an injunction ordering defendant Christopher to:
1. Release the plaintiff from punitive segregation and place him in general population, with restoration of all rights and privileges.
2. Expunge the disciplinary convictions described in this complaint from the plaintiff's institutional record.

D. Award compensatory damages in the following amounts:
1. $100,000 jointly and severally against defendants Green, White, Gray, Doe, and Cole for the physical and emotional injuries sustained as a result of the plaintiff's beating.
2. $10,000 jointly and severally against defendants Levett and Christopher for the punishment, including deprivation of liberty and amenity, and emotional injury resulting from their denial of due process in connection with the plaintiff's disciplinary proceeding.
3. $50,000 jointly and severally against defendants Garcia and Warren for the physical and emotional injury resulting from their failure to provide adequate medical care to the plaintiff.

E. Award punitive damages in the following amounts:
1. $20,000 each against defendants Green, White, Gray, Doe, and Cole;
2. $10,000 each against defendants Levett and Christopher;
3. $20,000 each against defendants Garcia and Warren.

F. Grant such other relief as it may appear that plaintiff is entitled.

[Date]
Respectfully submitted,
[Plaintiff's Name and Address]

Alternate version of damage demand:
D. Award compensatory damages jointly and severally against:
1. Defendants Green, White, Gray, Doe, and Cole for the physical and emotional injuries sustained as a result of the plaintiff's beating.
2. Defendants Levett and Christopher for the punishment and emotional injury resulting from their denial of due process in connection with the plaintiff's disciplinary proceedings.
3. Defendants Garcia and Warren for the physical and emotional injury resulting from their failure to provided adequate medical care of the plaintiff.

Alternate version of damage demand for segregated confinement reflecting Prison Litigation Reform Act (PLRA) physical injury requirement:
D. Award compensatory damages jointly and severally against:
1. Defendants Green, White, Gray, Doe, and Cole for the physical and emotional injuries sustained as a result of the plaintiff's beating.

2. Defendants Levett and Christopher for the punishment and emotional injury resulting from their denial of due process in connection with the plaintiff's disciplinary proceedings. By this demand, plaintiff seeks compensatory damages for the loss of privileges and quality of life in his prison living conditions, and loss of the limited liberty enjoyed by prisoners, resulting from his segregated confinement, in that he was confined for 23 hours a day in a cell roughly 60 feet square, and deprived of most of his personal property as well as the ability to work, attend educational and vocational programs, watch television, associate with other prisoners, attend outdoor recreation in a congregate setting with the ability to engage in sports and other congregate recreational activities, attend meals with other prisoners, attend religious services [and whatever other privileges you may have lost]. Plaintiff separately and in addition seeks compensatory damages for the mental or emotional distress resulting from his prolonged confinement in segregation without due process of law, to which he is entitled because of the physical injuries sustained in his beating and as a result of the deprivation of medical care pled herein.

3. Defendants Garcia and Warren for the physical and emotional injury resulting from their failure to provided adequate medical care of the plaintiff.

Note: The PLRA provides: "No Federal civil action may be brought by a prisoner confined in a jail, prison, or other correctional facility, for mental or emotional injury suffered while in custody without a prior showing of physical injury." 42 U.S.C. § 1997e(e). Many courts have held or assumed that segregated confinement inflicts only mental or emotional injury. Our view is that the concrete deprivations of segregated confinement are separate from any mental or emotional injury that may be inflicted, and prisoners should be able to recover damages for them. The above damages demand reflects that view. Further, our hypothetical case is one in which the plaintiff *did* suffer physical injury—not from the segregated confinement, but from the beating and deprivation of medical care. Since those injuries are closely related to the plaintiff's being placed in segregation, we think that under the statute, those injuries should allow recovery of damages for emotional injury resulting from segregation too. So we have written this damages demand to say (a) plaintiff suffered injuries from segregation that are not just mental or emotional, and he can recover compensatory damages for them, and (b) he can also recover for mental or emotional injury because of the physical injuries he sustained. These issues are discussed more fully in Ch. 9, § E.2. (We're sorry this is so complicated. If we wrote the law, it would be simpler.)

1b. Amended Complaint

1) Motion for Leave to File an Amended Complaint

Note: Amending a complaint is discussed in Ch. 10, § J. See Ch. 10, § F on motion practice and Ch. 12, § B on motion papers. The rules and form of motion papers do vary from district to district. Some courts require a notice of motion (see below for a sample), and others require that every motion be supported by a memorandum of law. Read the local court rules and follow them. We have not prepared a sample memorandum of law for this motion, but there are several examples of memoranda of law in other parts of this Appendix.

UNITED STATES DISTRICT COURT
WESTERN DISTRICT OF _____

JOSEPH WILLIAMS
    Plaintiff,

-v-
                                    Case No.
                                      Hon.

JAMES GREEN, *et al.*,[2]
Defendants.

/

MOTION FOR LEAVE TO FILE AN AMENDED COMPLAINT

Plaintiff, Joseph Williams, pursuant to Rule 15(a), Fed.R.Civ.P., requests leave to file an amended complaint adding a party.

1. The plaintiff in his original complaint named a John Doe defendant.

2. Since the filing of the complaint the plaintiff has determined that the name of the John Doe defendant is Wayne Blue. In the proposed amended complaint, paragraphs 5, 18, 21, 23, 27, 36, 40, 56, and 57 of the allegations, and paragraphs A.1, D.1, and E.1 of the relief requested, are amended to reflect the identity and the actions of Officer Blue.

3. This Court should grant leave freely to amend a complaint. *Foman v. Davis*, 371, 178, 182, 83 S.Ct. 227 (1962); *Williams v. Cargill, Inc.*, 159 F.Supp.2d 984, 997-98 (S.D. Ohio 2001).

---

[2]Once the original of the complaint has been filed listing all the parties, any further pleadings only need to list the first defendant, followed by *et al.*, which means "and others."

[Date]
Respectfully submitted,
[Plaintiff's Name and Address]

2) Proposed Amended Complaint

Note: To save space, this form includes only the paragraphs of the complaint that the motion proposes to amend. You will need to file a complete new complaint. It is probably better to include the complete amended complaint with your motion, but it should be acceptable to include with the motion only those paragraphs that you actually wish to change. You can then file the complete amended complaint after the motion is granted. If you take the latter course, the amended complaint should contain only those changes that the court has approved in granting your motion.

[CAPTION]

5. Defendant Wayne Blue is a correctional officer employed at Stonehaven. He is sued in his individual capacity.

* * *

21. Defendant Green then opened plaintiff's cell door and defendants Green, Brown, White, and Blue entered his cell.

* * *

23. Defendants White and Blue did not intervene to prevent these kicks and blows, and the plaintiff believes that these defendants also kicked and struck him.

* * *

27. Defendants Green, Brown, White, and Blue are members of the Stonehaven Emergency Response Team.

* * *

36. The plaintiff also asked that defendants Green, Brown, White, and Blue be called as witnesses.

* * *

40. The staff statements provided to the plaintiff alleged that the plaintiff had refused to leave his cell when ordered, had assaulted defendants Green, Brown, White, and Blue, and had threatened them.

* * *

58. The actions of defendants Green, Brown, White, Blue, and Gray in using physical force against the plaintiff without need or provocation, or in failure to intervene to prevent the misuse of force, were done maliciously and sadistically and constituted cruel and unusual punishment in violation of the Eighth Amendment of the United States Constitution.

59. The actions of defendants Green, Brown, White, and Blue in using physical force against the plaintiff without need or provocation constituted the tort of assault and battery under the law of [your state].

* * *

1. The physical abuse of the plaintiff by defendants Green, Brown, White, and Blue violated the plaintiff's rights under the Eighth Amendment to the United States Constitution and constituted an assault and battery under state law.

* * *

1. $100,000 jointly and severally against defendants Green, White, Gray, Blue, and Cole for the physical and emotional injuries sustained as a result of the plaintiff's beating.

* * *

1. $20,000 each against defendants Green, White, Gray, Blue, and Cole;

[Date]
Respectfully submitted,
[Plaintiff's Name and Address]
Note: Author Manville usually does not state a specific amount of damages in the complaint. We have shown how to write a damage demand without specific amounts in Form 1a of this Appendix.

3) Notice of Motion

Note: A notice of motion states the date that the motion theoretically will be heard (the "return date"). In fact, the court may not "hear" a motion in a pro se case but may decide based on the papers, and if it does hear the motion, it will probably set a date based on its own calendar and convenience. The main function of the notice of motion is to set a deadline for all papers to be filed. *See* Ch. 10, § F, concerning motion practice, for a discussion of how to determine the proper date. Also check the local court rules; not all courts require notices of motion.

This form can be used for any motion; just remove the phrase "granting the Plaintiff leave to file an amended complaint" and substitute whatever you are moving for, *e.g.*, "compelling discovery" or "granting partial summary judgment."

[CAPTION]

NOTICE OF MOTION

PLEASE TAKE NOTICE that on the enclosed declaration of the Plaintiff Joseph Williams, attached exhibits, and memorandum of law, plaintiff will move the Court on [date], at the United States District Court, [address], at such time as the Court may direct, for an order granting the Plaintiff leave to file an amended complaint.

TO:　　[Name of defense lawyer]
　　　　[Address]
　　　　Attorney for Defendants

[Date]
Respectfully submitted,
[Name]

1c. Standardized § 1983 Federal Court Complaint Form

Note: This form is taken from the Federal Judicial Center, Recommended Procedures for Handling Prisoner Civil Rights Cases in the Federal Courts (1980). Some district courts have modified it, and some have made up their own forms, so you should try to get the form used by the court in which you wish to file your case. Note that this form does not provide for a demand for a jury trial. If you want a jury trial and the court's form does not have a space for it, you should probably write JURY TRIAL DEMANDED prominently on the first page of the form complaint.

This form is accompanied by a separate form for requesting permission to proceed *in forma pauperis*. That form appears in § 2b of this Appendix.

INSTRUCTIONS FOR FILING A COMPLAINT BY A PRISONER
UNDER THE CIVIL RIGHTS ACT, 42 U.S.C. § 1983

This packet includes four copies of a complaint form and two copies of a forma pauperis petition. To start an action you must file an original, one copy of your complaint for each defendant you name, and one for the court. For example, if you name two defendants you must file the original and three copies of the complaint. You should also send an extra copy of the complaint to the court so it can be stamped with the filing information and then returned to you for your own records. *All copies of the complaint must be identical to the original.*

The clerk will not file your complaint unless it conforms to these instructions and to these forms.

Your complaint must be legibly handwritten or typewritten. You, the plaintiff, must sign and declare under penalty of perjury that the facts are correct. If you need additional space to answer a question, you may use the reverse side of the form or an additional blank page.

Your complaint can be brought in this court only if one or more of the named defendants is located within this district. Further, you must file a separate complaint for each claim that you have unless they are all related to the same incident or issue.

You are required to furnish, so that the United States Marshal can complete service, the *correct name and address of each person you have named as a defendant*. A PLAINTIFF IS REQUIRED TO GIVE INFORMATION TO THE UNITED STATES MARSHAL TO COMPLETE SERVICE OF THE COMPLAINT UPON ALL PERSONS NAMED AS DEFENDANTS.

In order for this complaint to be filed, it must be accompanied by the filing fee of $350. In addition, the United States Marshal will require you to pay the cost of serving the complaint on each of the defendants.

If you are unable to pay the filing fee and service costs for this action, you may petition the court to proceed *in forma pauperis*. Two blank petitions for this purpose are included in this packet. One copy should be filed with your complaint; the other copy is for your records.

You will note that you are required to give facts. THIS COMPLAINT SHOULD NOT CONTAIN LEGAL ARGUMENT OR CITATIONS.

When these forms are completed, mail the original and the copies to:
　　Clerk of the United States District Court for the
　　_____ District of _____
　　[Local court address is inserted here.]

PRISONER CIVIL RIGHTS COMPLAINT

Instructions

1. **This form is for use by state prisoners filing under 42 U.S.C. § 1983 and federal prisoners filing pursuant to *Bivens v. Six Unknown Named Agents of Federal Bureau of Narcotics*, 403 U.S. 388 (1971).**

2. You may file a complaint in the United States District Court for the Eastern District of Michigan if one or more of the named defendants is located within the Eastern District of Michigan or if the cause of action arose in this District.

3. You **must** file a separate complaint for each claim, unless all the claims are related to the same incident, issue, or defendant.

4. You **must** complete the entire complaint form. No exhibits are necessary at this stage. Submit the following items to the Clerk's Office:

   a. A complete and accurate list of the name of **each** defendant, the address for **each** defendant, and the capacity in which **each** defendant is being sued.

   b. The original complaint with attachments and one copy of the complaint (including attachments). You **may** be directed to provide the court with additional copies of the complaint (including attachments) at a later date.

5. The complaint **must** be typed or neatly written and each page **must** be numbered. If additional pages are needed, they **must** be typed or neatly written on 8½" x 11" white paper and securely attached to the complaint.

6. You **must** tell the truth and **each** plaintiff **must** sign and date the form. If you make a false statement of a material fact, you may be prosecuted for perjury.

7. You **must** pay a filing fee of $350.00. If you cannot pay the fee, you may ask to proceed without prepayment of fees and costs. To do that, **each** plaintiff **must** fill out an Application to Proceed Without Prepayment of Fees and Costs and provide a certified copy of the prison trust fund account statement for the preceding 6 month period. **You are obligated to pay the entire amount of the filing fee even if: (1) the court dismisses your complaint or (2) you voluntarily dismiss your complaint.**

8. Checks or money orders **must** be made payable to: "Clerk, U.S. District Court" and sent **with** the complaint to the address indicated in number 10 below.

9. If you pay the $350.00 filing fee when you file your complaint, you will be responsible for serving the defendants. (See Instructions for Preparation and Service of Summons Forms.)

10. Send all of your completed paperwork to this address:

> **Clerk, United States District Court for the Eastern District of Michigan**
> **Theodore Levin U.S. Courthouse**
> **231 W. Lafayette Boulevard, Fifth Floor**
> **Detroit, MI 48226**

Official Use Only

Case Number	Judge	Magistrate Judge

PRISONER CIVIL RIGHTS COMPLAINT

This form is for use by state prisoners filing under 42 U.S.C. § 1983 and federal prisoners filing pursuant to Bivens v. Six Unknown Named Agents of Federal Bureau of Narcotics, 403 U.S. 388 (1971).

Plaintiff's Information

Name	Prisoner No.

Place of Confinement

Street	City	State	Zip Code

Are there additional plaintiffs? ☐ Yes   ☐ No

If yes, any additional plaintiffs to this action should be listed on a separate 8½" x 11" sheet of paper and securely attached to the back of this complaint. You must provide names, prisoner numbers and addresses for all plaintiffs.

Defendant's Information

Name	Position

Street/P.O. Box	City	State	Zip Code

Are you suing this defendant in his/her: ☐ Personal Capacity   ☐ Official Capacity   ☐ Both Capacities

Are you suing more than one defendant?   ☐ Yes   ☐ No

If yes, any additional defendants to this action should be listed on a separate 8½" x 11" sheet of paper and securely attached to the back of this complaint. You must provide their names, positions, current addresses and the capacity (personal, official or both) in which you are suing them.

I. PREVIOUS LAWSUITS

Have you filed any other lawsuits in state or federal court relating to your imprisonment?

☐ Yes   ☐ No

If "Yes," complete the following section. If "No," proceed to Part II.

Please list all prior civil actions or appeals that you have filed in federal court while you have been incarcerated.

Docket or Case Number:
Name of Court:
Parties (Caption or Name of Case):
Disposition:

Docket or Case Number:
Name of Court:
Parties (Caption or Name of Case):
Disposition:

Docket or Case Number:
Name of Court:
Parties (Caption or Name of Case):
Disposition:

Any additional civil actions should be listed on a separate sheet of 8½" x11" paper and securely attached to the back of this complaint.

II. STATEMENT OF FACTS

State here, as briefly as possible, the facts of your case. Describe how each defendant is involved. Include the names of other people, dates and places involved in the incident. Do not give any legal arguments or cite any cases or statutes. If you intend to allege several related claims, number and set forth each claim on a separate 8½" x 11" sheet of paper and securely attach the papers to the back of this complaint.

_____

_____

_____

_____

_____

_____

_____

_____

_____

_____

III. RELIEF

State briefly and exactly what you want the Court to do for you.

_____

_____

_____

_____

_____

_____

_____

_____

_____

I declare (or certify, verify, or state) under penalty of perjury that the foregoing is true and correct.

Executed (signed) on _____ (date).

_____
Signature of Plaintiff

2. *In Forma Pauperis*

Note: Proceeding *in forma pauperis* in federal district court is discussed in Ch. 9, § A, and Ch. 10, § C. In addition to the documents discussed here, the Prison Litigation Reform Act requires prisoners seeking to proceed *in forma pauperis* to "submit a certified copy of the trust fund account statement (or institutional equivalent) for the prisoner for the 6-month period immediately preceding the filing of the complaint or notice of appeal, obtained from the appropriate official of each prison at which the prisoner is or was confined." 28 U.S.C. § 1915(a)(2).

2a. Declaration in Support of Request to Proceed *In Forma Pauperis*

Note: You can use the court-provided form, or you can use this model form.

[CAPTION]

**DECLARATION IN SUPPORT OF REQUEST FOR
LEAVE TO PROCEED *IN FORMA PAUPERIS***

JOSEPH WILLIAMS states:

1. I am the plaintiff in the above-entitled action. I make this declaration in support of my application for leave to proceed *in forma pauperis* pursuant to 28 U.S.C. § 1915.

2. I am incarcerated in the Stonehaven Correctional Facility.

3. Because I am held in punitive segregation, I am not permitted to work and have no steady income.

4. Before I was placed in punitive segregation on March 19, 2008, I was employed in the prison tailor shop and received a wage of $3.00 a day for five days' work each week.

5. I have received approximate $100.00 in gifts from family members over the past 12 months.

6. I have no other source of income and do not own any cash, bank accounts, real estate, stocks, bonds, notes, automobiles, or other valuable property.

Pursuant to 28 U.S.C. § 1746, I declare under penalty of perjury that the foregoing is true and correct.

[Date]
[Name and Address]

2b. Form Declaration in Support of Request to Proceed in Forma Pauperis

Note: This form is taken from the Federal Judicial Center, Recommended Procedures for Handling Prisoner Civil Rights Cases in Federal Courts. As with the complaint form, different district courts may have their own variations on this form, and you should try to obtain the form used by the district court you will file your case in. The form should be submitted to the court along with your complaint.

**DECLARATION IN SUPPORT OF REQUEST TO
PROCEED *IN FORMA PAUPERIS***

Instructions to court:

This form is to be sent to the prisoner-plaintiff.

If there is reason to believe that the information received is not accurate or complete, the court may want to use form 3 in addition. Form 3 is an order asking the record officer at the institution to submit a certificate stating the current balance in the plaintiff's institutional account.

[CAPTION]

**DECLARATION IN SUPPORT OF REQUEST TO PROCEED
*IN FORMA PAUPERIS***

I, [your name], am the petitioner in the above-entitled case. In support of my motion to proceed without being required to prepay fees or costs or give security therefore, I state that because of my poverty I am unable to pay the costs of said proceeding or to give security therefor; that I believe I am entitled to redress.

I declare that the responses which I have made below are true.

1. Are you presently employed? Yes___ No ___

   a. If the answer is yes, state the amount of your salary per month and give the name and address of your employer.

b. If the answer is no, state the date of last employment and the amount of the salary per month which you received.

_____

2. Have you received within the past 12 months any money from any of the following sources?

a. Business, profession, or form of self-employment? Yes___ No___ .

b. Rent payment, interest, or dividends? Yes___ No___ .

c. Pensions, annuities, or life insurance payments? Yes___ No___ .

d. Gifts or inheritances? Yes___ No___ .

e. Any other sources? Yes___ No___ .

If the answer to any of the above is yes, describe each source of money and state the amount received from each during the past 12 months. _____

3. Do you own any cash or do you have money in a checking or savings account?

Yes___ No___ . (Include any funds in prison accounts.)

4. Do you own any real estate, stocks, bonds, notes, automobiles, or other valuable property (excluding ordinary household furnishings and clothing)? Yes___ No___ .

If the answer is yes, describe the property and state its approximate value.

_____.

5. List the persons who are dependent upon you for support; state your relationship to those persons; and indicate how much you contribute toward their support.

_____

I understand that a false statement or answer to any questions in this declaration will subject me to penalties of perjury.

[Signature and printed name.]

I declare under the penalty of perjury that the foregoing is true and correct.
Signed this ___ day of _____, 20___.
[Signature]

3. Counsel

Note: There is no right to appointed counsel in a civil rights suit, but federal courts may request attorneys to represent indigent plaintiffs. *See* Ch. 10, § C.5.

3a. Motion for Appointment of Counsel

Note: In some courts, motions are to be accompanied by a notice of motion setting a return date. *See* Ch. 10, § F on motion practice and Ch. 12, § B on motion papers. A sample notice of motion appears in Form 1a.3, above. Practice as to the form of motions may differ from state to state, but the court will not care if you don't get the form exactly right.

[CAPTION]

MOTION FOR THE APPOINTMENT OF COUNSEL

Plaintiff, Joseph Williams, pursuant to § 1915, requests this Court to appoint counsel to represent him in this case for the following reasons.

1. The plaintiff is unable to afford counsel.

2. The issues involved in this case are complex.

3. The plaintiff, as a segregation inmate, has extremely limited access to the law library.

4. Over 30 days ago, the plaintiff wrote letters to three attorneys, Daniel Manville, John Boston, and Jerome Wallace, asking them to handle his case but he has not heard from any of them.

5. The plaintiff has a limited knowledge of the law.

WHEREFORE, this Honorable Court should appoint counsel to represent the plaintiff.

[Dated]
[Name and Address]

3b. Declaration in Support of the Plaintiff's Motion for the Appointment of Counsel

Note: When you make a motion, any facts that you wish to put before the court must be sworn to. This may be done either in an affidavit sworn to before a notary public or in a declaration under penalty of perjury. *See* Ch. 12, § C. This sample is in the form of a declaration. Documents that you submit with your motion should be identified and explained in the declaration.

[CAPTION]

**DECLARATION IN SUPPORT OF PLAINTIFF'S MOTION
FOR THE APPOINTMENT OF COUNSEL**

JOSEPH WILLIAMS states:

1. I am the plaintiff in the above-entitled case. I make this declaration in support of my motion for this appointment of counsel.

2. The complaint in this case alleges that the plaintiff was subjected to the misuse of force by several correctional officers, some of whom actively beat and kicked him and others of whom watched and failed to intervene. It alleges that supervisory officials were aware of the violent propensities of some of the officers and are liable for failing to take action to control them. The plaintiff was subsequently denied due process in a disciplinary hearing by a hearing officer, and the appeal was denied by the warden. Plaintiff was denied ordered medical care by the prison medical administrator and the deputy warden for the administration.

3. This is a complex case because it contains several different legal claims, with each claim involving a different set of defendants.

4. The case involves medical issues that may require expert testimony.

5. The plaintiff has demanded a jury trial.

6. The case will require discovery of documents and depositions of a number of witnesses.

7. The testimony will be in sharp conflict, since the plaintiff alleges that the defendants assaulted him, while the defendants in their disciplinary reports asserted that he assaulted them.

8. The plaintiff has only a high school education and has no legal education.

9. The plaintiff is serving a sentence in punitive segregation. For this reason, he has very limited access to legal materials and has no ability to investigate the facts of the case, for example, by locating and interviewing other inmates who were eyewitnesses to his beating.

10. As set forth in the Memorandum of Law submitted with this motion, these facts, along with the legal merit of plaintiff's claims, support the appointment of counsel to represent the plaintiff.

WHEREFORE, the plaintiff's motion for appointment of counsel should be granted.

Pursuant to 28 U.S.C. § 1746, I declare under penalty of perjury that the foregoing is true and correct.

Signed this ___ day of _____, 20__ .
[Signed.]

3c. Memorandum of Law in Support of Plaintiff's Motion for Appointment of Counsel

Note: A memorandum of law or a brief that refers to facts in a declaration or to allegations in a complaint should cite the relevant paragraphs of the declaration or complaint.

A legal argument in a memorandum of law or brief is ordinarily divided into numbered Points. This memorandum only has one point. Other examples in this Appendix have multiple points and are numbered.

[CAPTION]

**MEMORANDUM OF LAW IN SUPPORT OF PLAINTIFF'S
MOTION FOR THE APPOINTMENT OF COUNSEL**

Statement of the Case

This is a civil rights case filed under 42 U.S.C. § 1983 by a state prisoner and asserting claims for the unconstitutional misuse of force, the denial of due process in subsequent disciplinary proceedings, and the denial of medical care for injuries inflicted during the misuse of force. The plaintiff seeks damages as to all claims and an injunction to ensure proper medical care and expungement of his disciplinary convictions.

Statement of Facts

The Complaint alleges that the plaintiff was assaulted by several correctional officers, receiving a number of injuries including a broken ankle. He was taken to a hospital where his ankle was placed in a cast; the doctor gave instructions to remove the cast after four weeks and to provide the plaintiff with a course of physical therapy. The cast was not removed for seven weeks and no physical therapy or evaluation for physical therapy has been performed. The plaintiff was convicted at a disciplinary hearing of assaulting staff, inciting to riot, threatening staff, and refusing a direct order. The hearing officer denied the plaintiff's request to call as witnesses inmates and staff members who were present during the incident. He convicted the plaintiff of all charges despite the complete lack of any evidence, even in the officers' reports, of inciting to riot. The hearing officer's written report of the charges said only "Guilty as charged based on staff statements," with no further explanation. The defendant Warden denied the disciplinary appeal.

ARGUMENT

THE COURT SHOULD APPOINT COUNSEL FOR THE PLAINTIFF.

In deciding whether to appoint counsel for an indigent litigant, the court should consider "the factual complexity of the case, the ability of the indigent to investigate the facts, the existence of conflicting testimony, the ability of the indigent to present his claim and the complexity of the legal issues." *Abdullah v. Gunter*, 949 F.2d 1032, 1035 (8th Cir. 1991) (citation omitted). In addition, courts have suggested that the most important factor is whether the case appears to have merit. *Carmona v. U.S. Bureau of Prisons*, 243 F.3d 629, 632 (2d Cir. 2001). Each of these factors weighs in favor of appointment of counsel in this case.

1. *Factual Complexity.* The plaintiff alleges that several correctional officers physically abused him, while others stood by and watched. He also asserts that certain prison supervisors were on notice of the violent propensities of some of those officers and did nothing about them. He challenges the denial of medical care after the incident by two other defendants. Finally, he claims denial of due process by a disciplinary hearing officer and a warden. The sheer number of claims and defendants makes this a factually complex case.

In addition, one of the plaintiff's claims involves the denial of medical care; it will probably be necessary to present a medical expert witness or to cross-examine medical witnesses called by the defendants, or both. The presence of medical or other issues requiring expert testimony supports the appointment of counsel. *Montgomery v. Pinchak*, 294 F.3d 492, 503-04 (3d Cir. 2002); *Moore v. Mabus*, 976 F.2d 268, 272 (5th Cir. 1992); *Jackson v. County of McLean*, 953 F.2d 1070, 1073 (7th Cir. 1992).

2. *The plaintiff's ability to investigate.* The plaintiff is locked up in punitive segregation and has no ability to investigate the facts. For example, he is unable to identify, locate, and interview the inmates who were housed in nearby cells and who saw some or all of the misuse of force. He is in the same situation with regard to developing the facts as an inmate who has been transferred to a different institution, a factor that several courts have cited in appointing counsel. *Tucker v. Randall*, 948 F.2d 288, 391-92 (7th Cir. 1991); *Gatson v. Coughlin*, 679 F.Supp. 270, 273 (W.D.N.Y. 1988). In addition, this case will require considerable discovery concerning the identity of witnesses, the officers' reports and statements about the incident, any prior history of misuse of force by the officers, and the plaintiff's medical history. *See Parham v. Johnson*, 126 F.3d 454, 459 (3d Cir. 1997) (holding counsel should have been appointed because "prisoner's lack of legal experience and the complex discovery rules clearly put him at a disadvantage in countering the defendant's discovery tactics . . . these [discovery] rules prevented [the Plaintiff] from presenting an effective case below.").

3. *Conflicting testimony.* The plaintiff's account of his beatings by officers is squarely in conflict with the statements of the officers. This aspect of the case will be a credibility contest between the defendants and the plaintiff (and such inmate witnesses as can be located). The existence of these credibility issues supports the appointment of counsel. *Steele v. Shah*, 87 F.3d 1266, 1271 (11th Cir. 1996); *Gatson v. Coughlin*, 679 F.Supp. at 273.

4. *The ability of the indigent to present his claim.* The plaintiff is an indigent prisoner with no legal training, a factor that supports the appointment of counsel. *Forbes v. Edgar*, 112 F.3d 262, 264 (7th Cir. 1997). In addition, he is confined to segregation with very limited access to legal materials. *Rayes v. Johnson*, 969 F.2d 700, 703-04 (8th Cir. 1992) (citing lack for ready access to a law library as a factor supporting appointment of counsel).

5. *Legal complexity.* The large number of defendants, some of whom are supervisory officials, presents complex legal issues of determining which defendants were sufficiently personally involved in the constitutional violations to be held liable. *Hendricks v. Coughlin*, 114 F.3d 390, 394 (2d Cir. 1997) (holding complexity of supervisory liability supported appointment of counsel). In addition, the plaintiff has asked for a jury trial, which requires much greater legal skill than the plaintiff has or can develop. *Solis v. County of Los Angeles*, 514 F.3d 946, 958 (9th Cir. 2008) (prisoner with eighth grade education and no legal training is "ill-suited" to conduct a jury trial).

6. *Merit of the case.* The plaintiff's allegations, if proved, clearly would establish a constitutional violation. The unprovoked and injurious beating alleged in the complaint clearly states an Eighth Amendment violation. *See Hudson v. McMillian,* 503 U.S. 1, 112 S.Ct. 995 (1992). The allegations of denial of medical care amount to "intentionally interfering with the treatment once prescribed," which the Supreme Court has specifically cited as an example of unconstitutional deliberate indifference to prisoners' medical needs. *Estelle v. Gamble,* 429 U.S. 97, 105, 97 S.Ct. 285 (1976). The unjustified denial of witnesses, conviction of a disciplinary offense with no supporting evidence, and the failure to give a meaningful statement of reasons for the decisions are all violations of clearly established due process principles. *See Ponte v. Real,* 471 U.S. 491, 497, 105 S.Ct. 2192 (1985); *Superintendent v. Hill,* 472 U.S. 445, 457, 105 S.Ct. 2768 (1985); *Wolff v. McDonnell,* 418 U.S. 539, 559, 94 S.Ct. 2963 (1974). On its face, then, this is a meritorious case.

CONCLUSION

For the foregoing reasons, the court should grant the plaintiff's motion and appoint counsel in this case.

[Date]
[Name and Address]

4. Summons

Note: The summons is discussed in Ch. 10, § C.1. You can obtain the standard form summons from the clerk of the court, or you can write your own. You must prepare a separate summons for each defendant. The caption of a summons, like that of a complaint, should name all parties and not just the first plaintiff and the first defendant. Under the rules, defendants get 20 days to answer the complaint, although that time is frequently extended. Federal government defendants get 60 days to answer. *See* Ch. 10, § D.

[CAPTION]

SUMMONS

TO: [Defendant's name]:

You are hereby summoned and required to serve upon plaintiff Joseph Williams, whose address is [mailing address], an answer to the complaint that is herewith served upon you, within 20 days after service of this summons upon you, exclusive of the day of service. If you fail to do so, judgment by default may be taken against you for the relief demanded in the complaint.

Clerk of the Court

[Leave space for the seal of the
U.S. District Court.]

Dated:
[Leave this date blank for the clerk to fill in.]

5. Discovery

Note: Discovery is discussed in Ch. 10, § K.2.

5a. Request for Production of Documents

Note: Document requests are discussed in Ch. 10, § K.2.f.

[CAPTION]

PLAINTIFF'S FIRST REQUEST FOR PRODUCTION OF DOCUMENTS

Pursuant to Rule 34, Fed.R.Civ.P., the plaintiff requests that the defendants produce the documents listed within 30 days, either by providing the plaintiff with copies or by making them available to the plaintiff for inspection and copying.

1. Any and all grievances, complaints, or other documents received by prison staff Defendant Christopher or his agents at Stonehaven concerning the mistreatment of inmates by Defendants Green, Brown, White, or Gray, and any memoranda, investigative files, or other documents created in response to such complaints, since January 1, 2004.

2. Any and all policies, directives, or instructions to staff concerning the use of tear gas or other chemical agents by Stonehaven staff.

3. Any and all policies, directives, or instructions to staff concerning the use of force by Stonehaven staff.

4. Any and all policies, directives, or instructions to staff governing sick call procedures, both in general population and in segregation.

5. All sick call request sheets from May 22, 2008 to the date of your response.

6. The plaintiff's complete medical records from March 15, 2008 to the date of your response.

7. Any logs, lists, or other documentation reflecting grievances filed by Stonehaven inmates from April 1, 2008 to the date of your response.

8. Any and all documents created by any Stonehaven staff member or any other Department of Correction employee or official in response to a grievance filed by the plaintiff in April 2008 concerning his medical care, or any appeals of that grievance.

9. Any and all documents created by any Stonehaven staff member from March 15, 2008 to date concerning the plaintiff's medical care and not included in items 6, 7, or 8 of this request.

10. Any and all documents, including but not limited to use of force reports, created by any Stonehaven staff member or any other Department of Correction employee or official concerning any use of force incident involving the plaintiff on or about March 15, 2008, or any investigation or action concerning that incident.

[Date]
[Name and Address]

5b. Interrogatories Combined with Request for Production of Documents.

Note: Interrogatories are discussed in Ch. 10, § K.2.e.

[CAPTION]

PLAINTIFF'S INTERROGATORIES AND REQUEST FOR PRODUCTION OF DOCUMENTS

Pursuant to Rules 33 and 34, Fed.R.Civ.P., the plaintiff submits the following interrogatories and requests for documents to the defendants. You are directed to answer each of the interrogatories in writing under oath, and provide the plaintiff with copies of each of the requested documents or make them available to the plaintiff for inspection and copying.

1. State the duties of defendant Jorge Garcia, Medical Administrator at Stonehaven Correctional Facility ("Stonehaven"). If those duties are set forth in any job description or other document, produce the document(s).

2. State the duties of defendant Mary Warren, Deputy Warden for Administration at Stonehaven, insofar as they pertain to providing medical care to prisoners or transportation of prisoners to medical appointment or facilities. If those duties are set forth in any job description or other document, produce the document(s).

3. State the names, titles, and duties of all staff members at Stonehaven, other than the defendants Garcia and Warren, who have responsibility for scheduling prisoners' medical appointments outside the prison, for arranging transportation to medical appointments outside the prison, or for evaluation requests for specialized treatment or evaluation. If those duties are set forth in any job description or other document, produce the document(s).

4. State the names, titles, and duties of all staff members at Stonehaven, other than defendants Garcia and Warren, who have responsibility for ensuring that inmates' request for medical attention are responded to. If those duties are set forth in any job description or other document, produce the document(s).

5. State the procedure in effect during March of 2008 at Stonehaven for conducting sick call, including the procedure by which inmates sign up for or request sick call. If the procedure is different for segregation inmates than for general population inmates, state both procedures. If these procedures are set forth in any policy, directive, or other document, produce the document(s).

6. State the names, titles, and duties of all staff members at Stonehaven who have responsibility for responding to, investigating or deciding inmate grievances. If those duties are set forth in any job description, policy directive, or other document, produce the document(s).

7. State the procedure in effect during March 2008 at Stonehaven for responding to, investigating, and deciding inmate grievances. If the procedure for handling grievances based on medical complaints is different from the procedure for handling other kinds of grievances, state both procedures. If those procedures are set forth in any directive, manual, or other document, produce the documents(s).

[Date]
[Name and Address]

5c. Request for Admissions

Note: Requests for admissions are discussed in Ch. 10, § K.2.g.

[CAPTION]

PLAINTIFF'S REQUEST FOR ADMISSIONS

Pursuant to Rule 36, Fed.R.Civ.P., plaintiff requests the defendants to make the following admissions within 30 days after the service of this request.

1. The plaintiff was transported to the emergency room of Mercy Hospital on March 15, 2008.

2. The plaintiff was examined at Mercy Hospital by a physician, Dr. Chadhuri.

3. Dr. Chadhuri concluded that the plaintiff was suffering from a broken ankle.

4. The plaintiff's ankle was placed in a cast on March 15, 2008 at Mercy Hospital.

5. Dr. Chadhuri directed that the cast be removed four weeks after it was placed on the plaintiff's ankle.

6. Dr. Chadhuri directed that the plaintiff receive a course of physical therapy after the cast was removed.

7. It is the routine and established practice at Stonehaven to send a Stonehaven Prison Hospital Referral Form ("Referral Form") along with every inmate who is taken to a hospital.

8. It is the routine and established practice at Mercy Hospital to write on the Stonehaven Prison Hospital Referral Form the patients' diagnosis, the treatment provided at the hospital and the directions for follow-up treatment after the patient's return to the prison.

9. It is the routine and established practice at Stonehaven for the Medical Administrator to review all Referral Forms to ensure that the patient received appropriate follow-up treatment.

10. Dr. Chadhuri's direction regarding removal of the plaintiff's cast and provision of physical therapy was placed in writing on the Stonehaven Prison Hospital Referral Form.

11. Dr. Chadhuri's direction regarding provision of physical therapy was placed in writing on a Stonehaven Prison Hospital Referral Form.

12. The Referral Form containing Dr. Chadhuri's directions was returned to the prison.

13. The return of the Referral Form containing Dr. Chadhuri's directions was consistent with the prison's routine and established practice.

14. The Stonehaven Medical Administrator, Jorge Garcia, reviewed the Referral Form bearing Dr. Chadhuri's directions consistently with the prison's routine and established practice.

15. The cast was not removed from the plaintiff's ankle until seven weeks after it had been placed there.

16. As of the date of this admission request, the plaintiff had not been provided with physical therapy for his ankle.

17. There is an informal policy at Stonehaven giving low priority to the medical needs of inmates in punitive segregation.

18. The failure to remove the plaintiff's cast in a timely manner resulted from the application of the informal policy stated in Request No. 17 above.

19. Defendant Garcia knew of the policy stated in Request No. 17, above, and took no action to prevent or correct its application to the plaintiff.

20. Defendant Garcia took no action to ensure that the plaintiff's cast was removed in a timely manner.

21. There is an informal policy at Stonehaven that inmates in punitive segregation are not sent out of the prison for medical care unless their lives are at risk.

22. Physical therapy is not provided on-site at Stonehaven.

23. The failure to provide physical therapy to the plaintiff resulted from the application of the informal policy stated in Request No. 21 above.

24. Defendant Garcia knew of the policy stated in Request 21, above, and took no action to prevent or correct its application to the plaintiff.

25. Defendant Garcia took no action to ensure that the plaintiff received physical therapy.

26. Defendant Warren knew of the policy described in Request No. 21, above, and took no action to prevent or correct its application to the plaintiff.

27. The failure to provide physical therapy to the plaintiff presents a substantial risk of permanent disability to plaintiff's ankle.

[Date]
[Name and Address]

6. Compelling Discovery

Note: Motions to compel discovery are discussed in Ch. 10, § K.2h. As that section points out, federal courts generally require that parties attempt to resolve discovery disputes themselves before filing motions to compel, and their efforts to resolve the dispute must be described in the motion papers.

6a. Motion to Compel Discovery

Note: In some courts, motions are to be accompanied by a notice of motion setting a return date. *See* Ch. 10, § F on motion practice and Ch. 12, § B on motion papers. A sample notice of motion appears in Form 1a.3, above. Practice as to the form of motions may differ from state to state, but the court will not care if you don't get the form exactly right.

[CAPTION]

PLAINTIFF'S MOTION TO COMPEL DISCOVERY

The plaintiff moves pursuant to Rule 34(b) and 37(a), Fed.R.Civ.P., for an order compelling the defendants to produce for inspection and copying the documents requested on June 1, 2008.

[Date]
[Name and Address]

6b. Declaration in Support of Motion to Compel

Note: When you make a motion, any facts that you wish to put before the court must be sworn to. This can be done either by declaration under penalty of perjury or by affidavit sworn to before a notary public. Documents that you submit with your motion should be identified and explained in the affidavit.

[CAPTION]

DECLARATON IN SUPPORT OF MOTION TO COMPEL

JOSEPH WILLIAMS declares under penalty of perjury:

1. I am the plaintiff in this case. I make this affidavit in support of my motion to compel discovery.

2. On June 1, 2008, I served on the defendants' counsel a request for production of documents, which is attached to this affidavit as Exhibit 1.

3. Defendants did not respond to this request within the 30 days allowed, nor did they request an extension of time from this Court or agreement from the plaintiff to an extension of time.

4. On July 30, 2008, I wrote to the defendants' counsel pointing out that their responses were a month late and requesting that they respond immediately. A copy of my letter is attached as Exhibit 2.

5. Defendants' counsel did not respond to my letter. On August 24, 2008, defendant responded to my document request by filing objections to the production of any of the materials sought. A copy of their objections is attached as Exhibit 3.

6. I wrote to defendants' counsel on August 31, 2008, in an attempt to resolve the dispute informally as required by Local Rule. A copy of my letter is attached as Exhibit 4. Two months have passed since I mailed Exhibit 4 and defendants' counsel has not responded to it.

7. Defendants' objections are waived as a result of their failure to make them in a timely manner, as set forth in the brief accompanying this motion.

8. Defendants' objections on the ground that the discovery sought is irrelevant, burdensome, and privileged have no merit, as set forth in the brief accompanying this motion.

[Date]
[Name and Address]

6c. Brief in Support of Motion to Compel

Note: A brief in support of a motion is often called a memorandum of law.

Generally, a brief with more than two or three sections should have a table of contents, even though the rules do not require it in the federal district court.

[CAPTION]

BRIEF IN SUPPORT OF MOTION TO COMPEL DISCOVERY

Statement of the Case

This is a § 1983 action filed by a prisoner at Stonehaven Correctional Facility seeking damages, a declaratory judgment, and injunctive relief based on the use of excessive force, the denial of procedural due process, and the denial of medical care.

Statement of Facts

On June 1, 2008, the plaintiff served a request for production of documents pursuant to Rule 34, Fed.R.Civ.P. As set forth in the plaintiff's declaration, the defendants failed to respond within 30 days, and did not make any effort to obtain an extension from the court or by contacting the plaintiff. After two months, the plaintiff requested a response. After several more weeks, the defendants served a response in which they objected to the plaintiff's entire request. Defendants' counsel has not responded to the plaintiff's efforts to resolve this dispute. *See* plaintiff's declaration at ¶¶ 2-6.

ARGUMENT

POINT I
**DEFENDANTS HAVE WAIVED THEIR OBJECTIONS BY THEIR FAILURE
TO RESPOND TIMELY TO THE REQUEST**

The rules provide that responses and objections to requests for production of documents are to be served within 30 days of the requests unless the court grants a shorter or longer time. Rule 34, Fed.R.Civ.P. The defendants, however, waited almost three months before responding, without obtaining or even seeking permission from the court, or agreement from the plaintiff, for this delay.

It is well established in federal practice that "discovery objections are waived if a party fails to object timely to interrogatories, production request, or other discovery efforts." *Godsey v. United States*, 133 F.R.D. 111, 113 (S.D. Miss. 1990); *accord, Morin v. Nationwide Federal Credit Union*, 229 F.R.D. 364, 368 (D. Conn. 2005); *Safeco Ins. Co. of America v. Rawstrom*, 183 F.R.D. 668, 670-73 (C.D. Cal. 1998); *Demary v. Yamaha Motor Crop.*, 125 F.R.D. 20, 22 (D. Mass. 1989) and cases cited. This waiver is enforced even if the objections are based on a claim of privilege. *Marx v. Kelly, Hart & Halman, P.C.*, 929 F.2d 8, 12 (1st Cir. 1991); *Fonville v. District of Columbia*, 230 F.R.D. 38, 42-43 (D.D.C. 2005); *Fretz v. Keltner*, 109 F.R.D. 303, 309 (D. Kan. 1986) and cases cited. The noncomplying party is excused from the waiver only if the discovery is "patently improper," *Godsey v. United States*, 133 F.R.D. at 113, or if it "far exceeds the bounds of fair discovery," *Krewson v. City of Quincy*, 120 F.R.D. 6, 7 (D.Mass. 1988); *accord, U.S. ex rel. Burroughs v. DeNardi Corp.*, 167 F.R.D. 680, 687 (S.D.Cal.1996).

As shown in the next point, the discovery sought is not only proper but is highly appropriate and relevant.

POINT II
THE DISCOVERY SOUGHT IS RELEVANT TO THE CLAIMS AND DEFENSES IN THIS CASE

Defendants' belated objections state that the documents requested by the plaintiff are irrelevant to the action. Their argument is frivolous.

Rule 26(b)(1), Fed.R.Civ.P., permits discovery of "any nonprivileged matter that is relevant to any party's claim or defense. . . . Relevant information need not be admissible at the trial if the discovery appears reasonably calculated to lead to the discovery of admissible evidence."

Each item sought by the plaintiff is relevant to the claims and defenses in the case, as explained below.

A. Documents relevant to past mistreatment of inmates by Defendants Green, Brown, White, or Doe.

Item 1 of the plaintiff's request seeks "Any and all grievances, complaints, or other documents received by the defendants or their agents at Stonehaven concerning mistreatment of inmates by defendants Green, Brown, White, or Gray and any memoranda, investigative files or other documents created in response to such documents, since January 1, 2004."

The defendants state generally in their objections that "personnel records of officers are not relevant to this action." Their description of the documents sought is incorrect.

First, the plaintiff does not seek "personnel records" in any general way. He seeks documents pertaining to particular kinds of complaints and allegations about these defendants, whether or not they are part of "personnel records." He does not seek other matters that may be in the personnel records, such as medical data or information about their records of lateness, leaves, vacations, etc.

Second, the kind of information sought is highly relevant. The plaintiff has alleged that repeated complaints about mistreatment of inmates have been made about two of the four defendants, and that nothing has been done about them. Evidence to that effect would be highly relevant to the claim of supervisory liability against defendant Cole, the Deputy Warden for Security, set out in ¶¶ 29 and 58 of the complaint. *See Beck v. City of Pittsburgh*, 89 F.3d 966, 973-74 (3d Cir. 1996) (citing *Parrish v. Luckie*, 963 F.2d 201, 205-06 (8th Cir. 1992)); *Foley v. City of Lowell, Mass.*, 948 F.2d 10, 14-16 (1st Cir. 1991).

This evidence may also support the claim against the officers themselves. Rule 404(b), Fed.R.Evid., provides, "Evidence of other crimes, wrongs, or acts is not admissible to prove the character of a person in order to show that he acted in conformity therewith. It may, however, be admissible for other purposes, such as proof of motive, opportunity, intent, preparation, plan, knowledge identity, or absence of mistake or accident." Evidence of prior incidents of abuse by prison or law enforcement personnel has been admitted by several courts as relevant to "motive, opportunity, intent, preparation, plan, knowledge, identity or absence of mistake or accident." *See Barnes v. City of Cincinnati*, 401 F.3d 729, 741-42 (6th Cir. 2005) ("intent" to discriminate); *Heno v. Sprint/United Mgmt. Co.*, 208 F.3d 847, 856 (10th Cir. 2000) (anecdotal evidence of discrimination admissible if incident can be tied to plaintiff's circumstances through, for example, common supervisors and same time frame); *Hynes v. Coughlin*, 79 F.3d 285, 290-01 (2d Cir. 1996); *Gutierrez-Rodriguez v. Cartagena*, 882 F.3d 553, 572 (1st Cir. 1989) (evidence of 13 prior incidents of misbehavior by officer admissible against supervisor to show knowledge).

For these reasons the material sought is relevant and should be produced.

[*Note*: Similar arguments should be drafted for the other items in the discovery request to which the defendants objected, and for any other reasons besides relevance that they gave for not responding.]

CONCLUSION

For the foregoing reasons, the court should grant plaintiff's motion to compel discovery.

[Date]
[Name and Address]

7. Writ of Habeas Corpus Ad Testificandum for Production of Incarcerated Witness.

Note: The procedures for getting witnesses to court are discussed in Ch. 10, § Q. This form is to be used to obtain the production in court of an incarcerated person. It is drafted for the plaintiff in our hypothetical case, but a similar form would be used to obtain the production of an incarcerated witness.

The presence of a non-incarcerated witness must be obtained by subpoena. Subpoena forms may be obtained from the clerk of the court.

7a. Petition for a Writ of Habeas Corpus Ad Testificandum

[CAPTION]

PETITION FOR A WRIT OF HABEAS CORPUS AD TESTIFICANDUM

Pursuant to 28 U.S.C. § 2241(c)(5), the plaintiff Joseph Williams requests that this Court issue a writ of habeas corpus *ad testificandum* requiring Warden Christopher to bring the plaintiff before the court for a trial scheduled to commence on January 10, 2009, and states in support:

1. The plaintiff's case depends in large part on his own testimony. Since the credibility of witnesses will be an issue in this matter, the jury should be allowed to hear the plaintiff testify personally and observe his demeanor.

2. The plaintiff is proceeding *pro se* in this matter and should therefore be produced to manage the presentation of his case, to cross-examine the defendants who testify and their witnesses, and to hear the defendants' case and present appropriate rebuttal.

Plaintiff requests that the defendants bear the costs of the implementation of the terms of this writ.

[Date]
[Name and Address]

7b. Proposed Order Granting Writ of Habeas Corpus Ad Testificandum

Note: With your petition, you should submit a proposed order granting the writ and directing production of you or your witness. (Depending on how neatly you can prepare the order, the court may prefer to prepare its own order, but you should provide one and let the court decide.)

[CAPTION]

ORDER GRANTING WRIT OF HABEAS CORPUS AD TESTIFICANDUM

At a session of said Court held in the City of Stonehaven, New York, this ___ day of ____, ___:

PRESENT: HON. JOHN D. JONES
United States District Judge
 IT IS ORDERED that a writ of habeas corpus be issued for JOSEPH WILLIAMS, Prison No. 135706, to be brought before this Court on the following day and at the following time.

_____
UNITED STATES DISTRICT JUDGE

WRIT OF HABEAS CORPUS AD TESTIFICANDUM

WHEREAS, it has been made to appear to this Court that JOSEPH WILLIAMS, 135706, is now confined at the Stonehaven Correctional Facility, Stonehaven, N.Y., and that his presence will be necessary in this Court, in CIVILIAN CLOTHES, no later than 8:00 a.m., on January 10, 2009, and to be returned to this Court each day thereafter until discharged from said writ.

NOW THEREFORE, in the Name of the United States of America, WE COMMAND ARTHUR CHRISTOPHER, Warden of said institution, to have the body of said PRISONER JOSEPH WILLIAMS, 135706, in the U.S. District Court for the Western District of _____, [address of court], on the RETURN DATE indicated above.

WITNESS, the Honorable John D. Jones, U.S. District Judge, and the seal of the U.S. District Court, on December ___, 2008.

CLERK
BY: .
DEPUTY CLERK

8. Default Judgment

Note: Default judgments are discussed in Ch. 10, § E.

8a. Request for Entry of Default

[CAPTION]

REQUEST FOR ENTRY OF DEFAULT

TO: Clerk of the Court for the Western District of [State]:
 You will please enter the default of Defendant Mary Warren for failure to plead or otherwise defend as provided by the Federal Rules of Civil Procedure, as appears from the attached declaration of Joseph Williams.

[Date]
[Name and Address]

8b. Declaration for Entry of Default

[CAPTION]

DECLARATION IN SUPPORT OF ENTRY OF DEFAULT

Plaintiff, Joseph Williams states:

1. I am the *pro se* Plaintiff in the above-entitled matter.

2. The Defendant Mary Warren was served with a copy of the summons and complaint as appears from the proof of service on file.

3. The Defendant Mary Warren has not filed or served an answer or taken other actions as may be permitted by law although more than 55 days have passed since the date of service.

Pursuant to 28 U.S.C. § 1746, I declare under penalty of perjury that the foregoing is true and correct.

[Date]
[Name and address]

8c. Request for Entry of Default Judgment by the Clerk

[CAPTION]

REQUEST FOR ENTRY OF DEFAULT JUDGMENT

TO: Clerk of the Court:

Plaintiff Joseph Williams requests that you enter judgment in default based upon the attached declaration against defendant Mary Warren in the above-entitled matter for $ ___, plus interest at the rate of ___% and costs.

[Date]
[Name and address]

8d. Declaration in Support of Request for Default Judgment

[CAPTION]

DECLARATION IN SUPPORT OF REQUEST FOR DEFAULT JUDGMENT

Plaintiff Joseph Williams states:

1. I am the *pro se* plaintiff in the above-entitled matter.

2. The amount due plaintiff from defendant Mary Warren is	$91.00:
a. Value of law book destroyed	$45.00
b. Value of legal papers	$15.00
Total	$60.00
c. Interest for one year at 6%	$3.60
d. Costs:	
Service of process	$20.00
Postage, paper, and copying	$27.40
TOTAL	$91.00

3. The default of the defendant has been entered for failure to appear in this action.

4. The amount listed above is due and owing and no part has been paid.

5. The costs sought to be recovered have occurred in this action.

6. The defendant is not in the military service as shown by the attached declaration.

Pursuant to 28 U.S.C. § 1746, I declare under penalty of perjury that the foregoing is true and correct.

[Date]
[Name and Address]

8e. Declaration that Defendant is Not in Military Service

[CAPTION]

DECLARATION AS TO MILITARY SERVICE

Joseph Williams states:

1. I am the *pro se* plaintiff in the above-entitled matter. I make this declaration pursuant to the requirements of the Soldiers' and Sailors' Civil Relief Act, 50 U.S.C., Appendix § 520.

2. The Defendant Mary Warren has worked at the Stonehaven Correctional Facility since plaintiff was incarcerated in July 2001.

3. Based on that fact, the plaintiff is convinced that defendant Warren is not in the military service of the United States.

Pursuant to 28 U.S.C. § 1746, I declare under penalty of perjury that the foregoing is true and correct.

[Date]
[Name and Address]

8f. Default Judgment by the Clerk

[CAPTION]

JUDGMENT

Defendant Mary Warren having failed to plead or otherwise defends in this action and her default having been entered,

Now upon application of the plaintiff and upon declaration that that defendant is indebted to plaintiff in the sum of $60.00, that defendant has been defaulted for failure to appear and that the defendant is not an infant or incompetent person, and is not in the military service of the United States, it is hereby

ORDERED, ADJUDGED, AND DECREED that plaintiff recover the sum of $60.00, with interest of $3.60, at the rate of 6% per year from the date of February 13, 2008, and costs in the sum of $27.40.

Clerk

[Date]

8g. Motion for Default Judgment by the Court

Note: If your claim is not for a "sum certain," you must make a motion to the court for a default judgment. The court will hold a hearing—or a jury trial, if you asked for one—on the damages for which you are entitled. See Ch. 10, § E.

This motion should be accompanied by proof of service. It should also be accompanied by a declaration that the defendant is not in military service, if that is the case. *See* form 8e.

[CAPTION]

MOTION FOR DEFAULT JUDGMENT

Plaintiff Joseph Williams moves the court to enter a default judgment against defendant Mary Warren for $20,000, and states:

1. A default has been entered against defendant Mary Warren for failure to answer or otherwise defend in the above-entitled matter.

2. Defendant Mary Warren is not in the military service as shown by the attached declaration.

[Date]
[Name and Address]

8h. Notice of Motion for Default Judgment

Note: Motion practice, including notices of motion, is discussed in Ch. 10, § F; another sample notice of motion appears at § 1a.3 of this Appendix.

[CAPTION]

NOTICE OF MOTION FOR DEFAULT JUDGMENT

TO: Mary Warren

Please take notice that plaintiff will make application to the court, at room, United States Courthouse, [ADDRESS], on the [DATE], at [TIME] or as soon thereafter as he may be heard, for entry of a default judgment in favor of the plaintiff and against you for $20,000.

[Date]
[Name and Address]

8i. Default Judgment by the Court

[CAPTION]

JUDGMENT

The court has ordered that the plaintiff herein recover of the defendant the damages sustained by him and that an inquest be taken before a jury to assist plaintiff's damages and that, upon rendering of a verdict by the jury, judgment be entered in accordance therewith. This case was regularly brought on for hearing on the [DATE], before the court and a jury, after due notice thereof to said defendant, and the jury has rendered a verdict for the plaintiff and against defendant Mary Warren in the sum of $ _____ compensatory and $ _____ punitive damages. It is hereby

ORDERED, ADJUDGED, AND DECREED, that the plaintiff recover of the defendant Mary Warren the sum of $ _____, together with costs.

_____
United States District Judge

[Date]

9. Plaintiff's Motion for Summary Judgment

Note: Moving for summary judgment is discussed in Ch. 10, § L.1.

9a. Motion for Summary Judgment

Note: The next few forms assume that the plaintiff in our hypothetical case moves for summary judgment on one of his claims (partial summary judgment).

In some courts, motions are to be accompanied by a notice of motion setting a return date. *See* Ch. 10, § F on motion practice and Ch. 12, § B on motion papers. A sample notice of motion appears in Form 1a.3, above. Practice as to the form of motions may differ from state to state, but the court will not care if you don't get the form exactly right.

[CAPTION]

PLAINTIFF'S MOTION FOR PARTIAL SUMMARY JUDGMENT

Pursuant to Rule 56, Fed.R.Civ.P., plaintiff Joseph Williams requests this court to grant him summary judgment as to the liability of defendants Levett and Christopher for damages for denial to the plaintiff of due process of law. The reasons therefor are set forth in the plaintiff's declaration and brief in support of this motion.

[Date]
[Name and Address]

9b. Declaration in Support of Motion for Summary Judgment

Note: Facts supporting a motion for summary judgment must be sworn to in the motion. This can be done either by affidavit sworn to before a notary public or through a declaration under penalty of perjury. See Ch. 12, § C. If some of the facts are established or supported by documents, those documents should be identified and explained in the declaration. You will need to attach those documents to the declaration.

[CAPTION]
**DECLARATION IN SUPPORT OF
PLAINTIFF'S MOTION FOR PARTIAL SUMMARY JUDGMENT**

JOSEPH WILLIAMS states:

1. I am the plaintiff in this case. The Complaint alleges that I was assaulted by prison staff, convicted of serious disciplinary charges and punished without due process of law, and denied necessary medical care. I submit this declaration in support of my motion for partial summary judgment on my claim of denial of due process. (I have not moved for summary judgment on the assault and medical care claims because there are material factual disputes concerning them.)

2. I am an inmate at Stonehaven Correctional Facility. On March 15, 2008, I was assaulted by prison staff, as set forth in my complaint at paragraphs 18-31.

3. As a result of the March 15, 2008, incident, I was served with disciplinary charges for assaulting staff, inciting to riot, threatening staff, and refusing a direct order. I was immediately placed in segregation.

4. I received a disciplinary hearing on March 19, 2008. Before the hearing, pursuant to the usual institutional procedures, I requested that the hearing officer call five inmates as witnesses for me. I provided the name of one of them and the cell locations of the other four.

5. At the same time I requested that the hearing officer call the officers who had been involved in the altercation. I identified three of them by name and the fourth as "the other officer who came to my cell."

6. The hearing officer, defendant Levett, refused to call any of these witnesses, stating that he would not call witnesses from general population to a hearing involving a segregation inmate and that the staff reports gave a "full picture" of the incident.

7. The usual practice in the prison is to remove any general population inmate to segregation when he is charged with a serious disciplinary offense. I base this statement about prison practice on my observation that inmates in my housing area have almost always been removed after being charged with serious disciplinary offenses and on numerous statements by correctional officers who are agents of the defendant Warden Christopher that inmates with disciplinary charges had been taken to segregation.

8. The evidence at the hearing consisted solely of the written reports of the four defendant officers and my testimony.

9. After the hearing I received a written disposition stating only, "Guilty as charged based on staff statements," and sentencing me to three years in punitive segregation. A copy of the deposition is attached to this declaration.

10. The staff statements alleged that I refused to leave my cell when ordered, assaulted the four officers, and threatened them. The statement did not state any facts showing that I had incited other inmates to riot, and I specifically denied doing so at the hearing. Copies of the officers' statements are attached to this affidavit as Exhibit 3.

11. Consistently with institutional procedure, I filed an administrative appeal with the Warden, defendant Christopher, pointing out the failure to call any of the witnesses, the lack of evidence to support my inciting to riot, and the failure of the written disposition to explain the reason for the finding of guilt. Defendant Christopher denied my appeal. Copies of my appeal and defendant Christopher's appeal decision are attached as Exhibits 4 and 5, respectively.

12. For the reasons stated in the brief submitted with this motion, these undisputed facts establish that defendants Levett and Christopher denied my right to the due process of law. Accordingly, I am entitled to summary judgment on my due process claim.

Pursuant to 28 U.S.C. § 1746, I declare under penalty of perjury that the foregoing is true and correct.

[Date]
[Name]

9c. Statement of Undisputed Facts

Note: Many federal courts have local rules that require a party moving for summary judgment to submit a statement of the undisputed facts that entitle him to summary judgment.

[CAPTION]

STATEMENT OF UNDISPUTED FACTS

Pursuant to Local Rule of this court's Civil Rules, the plaintiff submits the following list of undisputed facts that entitle him to partial summary judgment on his claim of denial of due process of law.

1. The plaintiff was charged by prison officials with the serious disciplinary offenses of assaulting staff, inciting to riot, threatening staff, and refusing a direct order.

2. The plaintiff requested defendant Levett, the hearing officer, to call five inmate eyewitnesses to the incident.

3. Defendant Levett refused on the ground that the plaintiff was in segregation and the witnesses were in general population.

4. It is the routine practice in the prison to remove prisoners charged with serious disciplinary offenses from general population to segregation pending their disciplinary charges.

5. The plaintiff requested defendant Levett to call four officers who were directly involved in the incident.

6. Defendant Levett refused to call these witnesses on the ground that their written reports provided a "full picture" of the incident.

7. Defendant Levett did not make individualized decisions as to the appropriateness of calling each witness.

8. Defendant Levett found the plaintiff guilty of all offenses charged, including inciting to riot.

9. No evidence was submitted during the hearing that supported the charge of inciting to riot.

10. The written disposition prepared by defendant Levett stated only, "Guilty as charged based on staff statements" with no further explanation.

11. The plaintiff appealed to the Warden, defendant Christopher, pointing out the deficiencies described in items 1 through 10 of this statement.

12. Defendant Christopher affirmed the disciplinary conviction.

13. The plaintiff is presently serving a sentence of three years in punitive segregation.

[Date]
[Name and Address]

9d. Brief in Support of Summary Judgment Motion

Note: When a brief refers to facts set out in a declaration or affidavit, it should cite the relevant paragraphs of the declaration or affidavit.

[CAPTION]

BRIEF IN SUPPORT OF
PLAINTIFF'S MOTION FOR PARTIAL SUMMARY JUDGMENT

Statement of the Case

This is a § 1983 action filed by a prisoner at Stonehaven Correctional Facility seeking damages, a declaratory judgment, and injunctive relief based on the use of excessive force, the denial of procedural due process, and the denial of medical care. In this motion the plaintiff seeks summary judgment on his claims arising from the denial of due process.

Statement of Facts

As set forth in the accompanying declaration of the plaintiff, Joseph Williams, he was convicted of serious prison disciplinary charges at a hearing in which none of the witnesses he requested were called. The hearing officer, defendant Levett, stated that the inmate witnesses were not called because they were in general population and the plaintiff was in segregation. Prison practice is to remove all inmates charged with serious offenses to segregation from general population pending their hearings. The hearing officer stated that the staff witnesses were not called because their written reports provided a "full picture."

No evidence was submitted at the hearing in support of the charge of inciting to riot and the plaintiff specifically denied the charge. The written disposition by defendant Levett stated only, "Guilty as charged based on staff statements," with no further explanation. The plaintiff was sentenced to three years in segregation. The plaintiff appealed to the Warden, defendant Christopher, pointing out the due process violations in the hearing, but defendant Christopher affirmed the convictions.

Note: Statements in a Statement of Facts should identify the evidence that supports them, *e.g.*, "Williams Decl. at ¶ __," or "Exhibit 1, disciplinary hearing disposition."

ARGUMENT

POINT I
THE CONDUCT OF THE PLAINTIFF'S DISCIPLINARY HEARING BY
DEFENDANT LEVETT DENIED HIM THE DUE PROCESS OF LAW

When prison officials subject inmates to "atypical and significant hardship . . . in relation to the ordinary incidents of prison life" they must observe the safeguards of due process. *Sandin v. Conner*, 512 U.S. 472, 115 S.Ct. 2293 (1995). The Second Circuit has recognized the existence of a liberty interest entitled to due process when an inmate is confined in segregation for more than 305 days. *Colon v. Howard*, 215 F.3d 227, 231-32 (2d Cir. 2000); *accord, Palmer v. Richards*, 364 F.3d 60, 64-5 (2d Cir. 2004). Plaintiff has been sentenced to punitive confinement for at least 1095 days (three years). He has a liberty interest in not being so confined unless he has received due process. *Colon v. Howard, supra; Palmer v. Richards, supra; cf. Wolff v. McDonnell*, 418 U.S. 539, 556-59, 94 S.Ct. 2963 (1974).

A. The Refusal to Call the Plaintiff's Witnesses Denied Due Process

Prisoners have the right to call witnesses when it is not "unduly hazardous to institutional safety or correctional goals." *Wolff v. McDonnell*, 418 U.S. at 566. Witnesses may be denied for reasons such as "irrelevance, lack of necessity, or the hazards presented in individual cases." *Id.* None of these reasons apply to this case, and none of them were stated by the hearing officer.

Defendant Levett stated that he would not call the inmate witnesses because they were in general population and the plaintiff was in segregation. If this justification were accepted, it would effectively abolish the right to call inmate witnesses, since it is standard prison procedure to place inmates charged with disciplinary offenses in segregation pending their hearings.

This justification, therefore, amounts to the kind of blanket policy of denying witnesses or types of witnesses that courts have repeatedly struck down as violating due process. *Whitlock v. Johnson*, 153 F.3d 380, 388 (7th Cir. 1998); *Mitchell v. Dupnik*, 75 F.3d 517, 525 (9th Cir. 1996); *King v. Wells*, 760 F.2d 89, 93 (6th Cir. 1985); *McCann v. Coughlin*, 698 F.2d 112, 122-23 (2d Cir. 1983).

The witnesses were not irrelevant or unnecessary. They were in a position to see and hear all or part of the incident at the plaintiff's cell. Had they been called, they could have testified that when the officers came to the plaintiff's cell, he was packing his property for transfer; that he offered no resistance to the officers or their orders; that they fired tear gas into his cell without provocation; and that they entered his cell and beat and kicked him without provocation or resistance.

Courts have repeatedly held that the refusal to call witnesses with personal knowledge of the incident in question denied due process. This is especially so when a prisoner "faces a credibility problems trying to disprove the charges of a prison guard," *Ramer v. Kerby*, 936 F.2d 1102, 1104 (10th Cir. 1991), and when the hearing officer refuses to hear *any* witnesses corroborating the accused inmate, *Graham v. Baughman*, 772 F.2d 441, 445 (8th Cir. 1985); *Green v. Nelson*, 442 F.Supp. 1047, 1057 (D. Conn. 1977), both of which apply to this case.

B. The Failure to Provide a Meaningful Explanation of the Finding of Guilt Denied Due Process

Prisoners who are found guilty of disciplinary charges are entitled to a "written statement by the factfinders as to the evidence relied on and the reasons' for the disciplinary action." *Wolff v. McDonnell*, 418 U.S. at 565 (quoting *Morrissey v. Brewer*, 408 U.S. 471, 489, 92 S.Ct. 2593 (1972)). Several courts have held that the practice of simply adopting the report of staff members with no further explanation denies due process. *Scrugg v. Jordan*, 485 F.3d 934, 941 (7th Cir. 2007) (quoting *Chavis v. Rowe*, 643 F.2d 1281, 1287 (7th Cir. 1981)) ("Without a detailed statement of the [disciplinary] Committee's findings and conclusions, a reviewing court (or agency) cannot determine whether the finding of guilt was based on substantial evidence or whether it was sufficiently arbitrary so as to be a denial of the inmate's due process rights."). *See also King v. Wells*, 760 F.2d 89, 93 (6th Cir. 1985); *Dyson v. Kocik*, 689 F.2d 466, 467 (3d Cir. 1982). Prison officials must provide some degree of explanation for the conclusions they reach. *Whitford v. Bogling*, 63 F.3d 527, 536-37 (7th Cir. 1995); *Stone-Bey v. Swihart*, 898 F.Supp. 1287, 1299-1300 (N.D. Ind. 1995); *Washington v. Chrans*, 769 F.Supp. 1045, 1052 (C.D. Ill. 1991).

Here, defendant Levett provided no explanation whatever for believing the written reports of the officers over the personal testimony of the plaintiff.

C. The Plaintiff's Conviction of Inciting to Riot, Unsupported by Any Evidence, Denied Due Process

Due process forbids officials to convict prisoners of disciplinary offenses unless there is "some evidence" to support the charges. *Superintendent v. Hill*, 472 U.S. 445, 457, 105 S.Ct. 2768 (1985). In this case, there was *no* evidence to support the charge of inciting to riot.

The only evidence at the hearing was the written reports of the four officers and the testimony of the plaintiff. There is nothing in any of their reports to support the conclusion that the plaintiff spoke to or communicated with any other inmates in any fashion, much less "incited" them. Nor is there any such evidence in the plaintiff's testimony; he specifically denied inciting the other inmates in any fashion.

In the absence of any evidence, the conviction for inciting to riot denied due process.

POINT II

**DEFENDANT CHRISTOPHER IS LIABLE FOR THE DUE PROCESS
VIOLATIONS BY REASON OF HIS FAILURE TO CORRECT THEM
ON ADMINISTRATIVE APPEAL**

Although Warden Christopher did not commit the due process violations, he became responsible for them when he failed to correct them in the course of his supervisory responsibilities, and affirmed the plaintiff's disciplinary conviction. A supervisor who learns of a constitutional violation through a report or appeal may be held liable for failing to correct it. *Williams v. Smith*, 781 F.2d 319, 323-24 (2d Cir. 1986) (warden could be liable if he accepted a policy or custom of due process denials in disciplinary hearings); *see also Hicks v. Frey*, 992 F.2d 1450, 1455 (6th Cir. 1993) (noting that an official may be held liable for failure to supervise and control subordinates even though the official was not directly involved in the specific incident of misconduct). In particular, wardens and other high-level prison officials who are designated to decide disciplinary appeals have the duty to conduct at least a "minimal investigation" when confronted with evidence of due process violations, and they may be held liable for failing to perform this duty. *Sira v. Morton*, 380 F.3d 57, 80 (2d Cir. 2004); *Wright v. Smith*, 21 F.3d 496, 502 (2d Cir. 1994) (holding that a supervisor may be held personally responsible for the deprivation of constitutional rights if, inter alia, the supervisor (a) is aware of the deprivation and fails to remedy it; or (b) created, or allowed to continue, a policy in which unconstitutional practices occurred); *Lewis v. Smith*, 855 F.2d 736, 738 (11th Cir. 1988); *King v. Higgins*, 702 F.2d 18, 21 (1st Cir.

1983) (Superintendent who was designated to hear disciplinary appeals had a duty to conduct at least a "minimal investigation" and could be held liable for failure to do so upon receiving reports giving notice of due process violations).

It cannot be argued that the Warden did not learn of the due process violations in this case. The inadequate statement of reasons, the failure to call *any* of the plaintiff's witnesses, and the lack of evidence in the reports for the charge of inciting to riot were all apparent from the documents created in the course of the disciplinary proceeding. Moreover, the plaintiff identified the due process violations in his appeal letter, so the Warden knew just what to look for.

Nor can it be argued that this is merely a case of "knowledge and acquiescence" in a subordinate's violation, which may not itself violate the Constitution. See Ashcroft v. Iqbal, ___ U.S. ___, 129 S.Ct. 1937, 1949 (2009). This is a case where the Warden "*personally* had a job to do, and he did not do it," and his failure to do his job was "so likely to result in the violation of the inmates' constitutional rights" as to establish deliberate indifference on his part. *Hill v. Marshall*, 962 F.2d 1209, 1213-14 (6th Cir. 1992); *accord, Foltz v. Michigan Dep't of Corrections*, 69 F.3d 76, 81 (6th Cir. 1995). Deliberate indifference by supervisory officials to inmates' constitutional rights is sufficient to establish liability under 42 U.S.C. § 1983. *Jett v. Penner*, 439 F.3d 1091, 1098 (9th Cir. 2006) (Prison administrators "are liable for deliberate indifference when they knowingly fail to respond to an inmate's requests for help."); *Thompson v. Upshur County, Texas*, 245 F.3d 447, 459 (5th Cir. 2001); *Aswegan v. Bruhl*, 965 F.2d 676, 677 (8th Cir. 1992).

CONCLUSION

For the foregoing reasons, the court should grant partial summary judgment on liability to the plaintiff on his due process claims. The amount of damages due to the plaintiff must be determined at trial. *Patterson v. Coughlin*, 905 F.2d 564, 570 (2d Cir. 1990).

[Date]
Respectfully submitted,
[Name and Address]

10. Response to Defendants' Summary Judgment Motion

Note: Responding to a summary judgment motion is discussed in Ch. 10, § L.2.

10a. Declaration in Opposition to Summary Judgment Motion

Note: When you respond to a motion, any facts that you wish to put before the court must be sworn to. This may be done either in a declaration under penalty of perjury or an affidavit sworn to before a notary public. See Ch. 12, § C. This sample is in the form of a declaration. Documents that you submit with your motion should be identified and explained in the declaration.

[CAPTION]

DECLARATION IN OPPOSITION TO
DEFENDANTS' MOTION FOR SUMMARY JUDGMENT

Joseph Williams states:

1. I am the plaintiff in the above-entitled case. I make this declaration in opposition to defendants' motion for summary judgment on my claims concerning the use of force against me by defendants Green, Brown, White, and Blue.

2. The defendants' affidavit claims, in summary, that they ordered me to leave my cell to be transferred, that I refused, and that when they opened my cell, I assaulted them and had to be subdued. They claim that they used only enough force to restrain me and that my injuries resulted from my attempts to escape their grasp. They state that they employed tear gas against me only after I had made it impossible for them to subdue me without it.

3. The defendants are not entitled to summary judgment because there are genuine issues of materials fact to be resolved. These issued are identified in the accompanying Statement of Disputed Factual Issues filed by the plaintiff pursuant to Local Rule ___ of this district court. The facts are set out in this declaration.

4. On March 14, 2008, I was removed from general population at Stonehaven and placed in administrative segregation without explanation.

5. On March 15, 2008, at about 5:00 a.m., defendant Gray came to the cell door and told me to pack my property for transfer.

6. I asked defendant Gray where I was being sent and defendant Gray refused to answer. Instead, he said, "I know how to deal with a wise guy," and left.

7. I then began to pack my property as ordered.

8. Shortly after defendant Gray left, Defendants Green, Brown, White, and Blue came to my cell door wearing riot helmets, gas masks and jackets and carrying batons and a tear gas dispense.

9. I stated that I was cooperating and packing my property. Contrary to the defendants' affidavits, I did not refuse to pack or leave my cell.

10. Without warning, defendant Green said, "Spray him," and defendant Brown sprayed tear gas into my cell. Contrary to the defendants' affidavits, they gassed me before they gave me any orders, before they opened my cell door, and before there was any physical contact between any of the defendants and myself.

11. Defendant Green then opened my cell door and defendants Green, Brown, White, and Blue entered my cell. Defendant Brown knocked me to the floor, where I was kicked and struck with batons by defendants Brown and Green.

12. Defendants White and Blue did not intervene to prevent these kicks and blows, and I believe that these defendants also kicked and struck me.

13. During this assault one of the defendants stamped on my left ankle, breaking it. I also received lacerations to my face and scalp and numerous bruises and abrasions to my arms, legs, torso, face, and head.

14. Contrary to defendants' affidavits, during these events I did not resist or threaten the officers in any fashion or break any prison rules. Rather, I lay on the floor and tried to protect my face from the defendants' blows and kicks.

15. The foregoing factual allegations create a genuine issue of material fact and will, if proved at trial, support a judgment in my favor, as explained in the brief submitted with this declaration.

Pursuant to 28 U.S.C. § 1746, I declare under penalty of perjury that the foregoing is true and correct.

[Date]
[Name and Address]

10b. Statement of Disputed Facts

Note: Many federal courts have local rules requiring the party opposing a summary judgment motion to file a separate statement of any genuine issues of material facts that the party claims prevent the court from granting summary judgment. The court may find you have waived the right to dispute any facts that you do not include in this statement—or, if you don't file the statement at all, that you have waived all factual disputes. The name of this document will vary from court to court, so be sure you read the rule of the court in which your case is pending.

[CAPTION]

PLAINTIFF'S STATEMENT OF DISPUTED FACTUAL ISSUES

Defendants have moved for summary judgment on the plaintiff's claim concerning the use of force. Pursuant to Local Rule of this court, the plaintiff submits the following list of genuine issues of material fact that require the denial of defendants' motion.

1. Whether the plaintiff refused to pack his property and leave his cell for transfer when so ordered.

2. Whether the plaintiff offered any resistance or disobedience to defendants Green, Brown, White, and Blue before they tear-gassed him.

3. Whether the plaintiff offered a resistance or disobedience to those defendants before they opened his cell door.

4. Whether the plaintiff offered any resistance or disobedience to those defendants when they entered his cell.

5. Whether the force utilized by the defendants against the plaintiff was applied in good-faith effort to maintain or restore discipline or maliciously and sadistically to cause harm.

6. Whether the plaintiff's injuries resulted from his own acts of resistance to the defendants or from their purposeful use of unnecessary force.

[Date]
[Name and Address]

10c. Brief in Opposition to Defendants' Summary Judgment Motion

Note: When a brief refers to facts set out in a declaration or affidavit, it should cite the relevant paragraphs of the declaration or affidavit.

[CAPTION]

PLAINTIFF'S BRIEF IN OPPOSITION TO
DEFENDANTS' SUMMARY JUDGMENT MOTION

Statement of the Case

This is a § 1983 action filed by a prisoner at Stonehaven Correctional Facility seeking damages, a declaratory judgment, and injunctive relief based on the use of excessive force, the denial of procedural due process, and the denial of medical care. Defendants have filed a motion for summary judgment as to the plaintiff's use of force claim against defendants Green, Brown, White, and Blue, arguing that their conduct did not violate the Constitution.

Statement of Facts

The plaintiff's declaration submitted in response to the defendants' motion states that on the morning of March 15, 1993, the four defendants appeared at the plaintiff's cell door after he had been told to pack for a transfer. Although he had previously questioned the order, he was packing when the defendants arrived. He offered no resistance, but nevertheless he was summarily tear-gassed while locked in his cell; the four defendants then entered his cell, knocked him down, and kicked and beat him, inflicting substantial injuries including a broken ankle.

The defendants' affidavits tell a different story. They claim that when they came to the plaintiff's cell, he refused to pack his property or leave his cell; that he assaulted them when they opened his cell; and that they had to tear-gas him because of his continued physical resistance. His injuries, they say, resulted from his own actions.

ARGUMENT

POINT I
THERE ARE GENUINE ISSUE OF MATERIAL FACT THAT PRECLUDE
SUMMARY JUDGMENT FOR THE DEFENDANTS ON THE PLAINTIFF'S
USE OF FORCE CLAIM

Summary judgment is to be granted only if the record before the court shows "that there is no genuine issue as to any material fact and that the moving party is entitled to a judgment as a matter of law." Rule 56(c), Fed.R.Civ.P. A "material" fact is one that "might affect the outcome of the suit under the governing law." *Anderson v. Liberty Lobby, Inc.*, 477 U.S. 242, 248, 106 S.Ct. 2505 (1986).

The declarations of the plaintiff and the defendants are squarely contradictory as to what force was used, when it was used, and why it was used. The allegations in the plaintiff's declaration portray a completely needless use of force against an inmate who was locked in his cell and was attempting to cooperate with the order he had been given. The defendants, by contrast, claim that they used only necessary force to control a prisoner who resisted them violently. There is clearly a genuine issue of fact.

The factual dispute is also material. Under the governing law, whether the use of force by prison staff violates the Eighth Amendment depends on whether it was "applied in a good-faith effort to maintain or restore discipline or maliciously and sadistically to cause harm." *Hudson v McMillian*, 503 U.S. 1, 5-6, 112 S.Ct. 995 (1992); *Whitley v. Albers*, 475 U.S. 312, 320-21, 106 S.Ct. 1078 (1986). The fact that force was used when unnecessary, or in a manner excessive to any need, is in itself evidence that the defendants were acting "maliciously and sadistically to cause harm." *Miller v. Leathers*, 913 F.2d 1085, 1088 (4th Cir. 1990); *Oliver v. Collins*, 914 F.2d 56, 59 (5th Cir. 1990); *Orwat v. Maloney*, 360 F.Supp. 2d 146, 153-54 (D. Mass. 2005). A reasonable jury could find for the plaintiff based on the facts in the plaintiff's declaration, and summary judgment must therefore be denied. *Anderson v. Liberty Lobby, Inc.*, 477 U.S. 242, 248, 106 S.Ct. 2505 (1986).

CONCLUSION

For the foregoing reasons, the defendants' motion for summary judgment should be denied.

[Date]
[Name and Address]

11. Motion for a Temporary Restraining Order and a Preliminary Injunction

Note: Temporary restraining orders (TROs) and preliminary injunctions are discussed in Ch. 8, § O.2.

11a. Order to Show Cause and Temporary Restraining Order

Note: A party seeking a TRO and preliminary injunction should draft an order granting the TRO and setting a date for a hearing on the preliminary injunction, leaving the exact place and date blank for the judge to fill in. Ordinarily a party who obtains an order to show cause is responsible for serving it on the other side. A prisoner proceeding *in forma pauperis* should request the court to direct the United States Marshal to serve the order.

[CAPTION]

ORDER TO SHOW CAUSE AND TEMPORARY RESTRAINING ORDER

Upon the supporting declaration of the plaintiff and the accompanying memorandum of law it is

ORDERED that defendants Mary Warren and Jorge Garcia show cause in room of the United States Courthouse, [address], on the day of, 200, at o'clock, why a preliminary injunction should not issue pursuant to Rule 65(a), Fed.R.Civ.P., enjoining the said defendants, their successors in office, agents, and employees and all other persons acting in concern and participation with them, to provide a medically appropriate course of physical therapy to the plaintiff designed to restore and maintain the full function of his left ankle.

IT IS FURTHER ORDERED that effective immediately, and pending the hearing and determination of this matter, defendants Warren and Garcia shall arrange for the plaintiff to be examined by a qualified orthopedic specialist and to obtain from that specialist an evaluation of the condition of plaintiff's left ankle and a prescription for a course of physical therapy that will restore and maintain the full function of his left ankle.

IT IS FURTHER ORDERED that this order to show cause, and all other papers attached to this application, shall be served on defendants Warden and Garcia by, 2008, and the United States Marshals Service is hereby directed to effectuate such service.

_____

United States District Judge

[Date]

11b. Declaration in Support of TRO and Preliminary Injunction

Note: When you make a motion, any facts that you wish to put before the court must be sworn. This may be done either in a declaration under penalty of perjury or in an affidavit sworn to before a notary public. *See* Ch. 12, § C. This sample is in the form of a declaration. Documents that you submit with your motion should be identified and explained in the declaration or affidavit.

[CAPTION]

DECLARATION IN SUPPORT OF PLAINTIFF'S MOTION FOR A TEMPORARY RESTRAINING ORDER AND PRELIMINARY INJUNCTION

Joseph Williams states:

1. I am the plaintiff in this case. I make this declaration in support of my motion for a temporary restraining order and a preliminary injunction to ensure that I receive necessary medical care.

2. As set forth in the Complaint in this case, I was assaulted by prison staff on March 15, 1993. During the assault, one of the defendants stepped or stomped on my ankle.

3. I was taken to the emergency room of Mercy Hospital, where the physician on duty, Dr. Chadhuri, examined me and told me that my ankle was broken. He placed my ankle in a cast and told me that the cast should remain on for four weeks and then I should receive a course of physical therapy to regain full use of it.

4. Dr. Chadhuri wrote my diagnosis and the directions concerning the cast and physical therapy on a standard Prison Hospital Referral Form. I was not given a copy of the form, but I watched Dr. Chadhuri fill it out. He gave the form to one of the escort officers who brought me to the emergency room and returned me to the prison.

5. Contrary to Dr. Chadhuri's direction, the cast was not removed from my ankle until seven weeks after it was placed there.

6. Contrary to Dr. Chadhuri's direction, I have not been provided with a course of physical therapy despite my repeated requests, or provided with a consultation with a physician qualified to assess and treat my condition.

7. On information and belief, I have not been provided with physical therapy because there is an informal policy at Stonehaven to giving low priority to the medical needs of segregation inmates and of refusing to provide them with medical care outside the prison unless their medical condition is life-threatening.

8. Physical therapy services are not provided in prison at Stonehaven; prisoners needing such services must be taken to an outside facility.

9. My left ankle is stiff and painful. I cannot walk normally and my ankle does not have the full range of motion it had before it was broken.

10. I am suffering irreparable harm in the form of continued physical and mental pain and suffering and an increasing risk that my ankle will never be restored to its full usefulness.

10. Defendant Jorge Garcia is the Medical Administrator at Stonehaven and is responsible for scheduling medical appointments outside the prison when a prisoner needs specialized treatment or evaluation.

12. Defendant Mary Warren is the Deputy Warden for Administration at Stonehaven and is in charge of transportation of prisoners to medical appointments.

13. Together, these defendants have the responsibility for providing the plaintiff the necessary physical therapy as well as the ability to arrange it.

14. For the reasons set forth in the memorandum of law filed with this motion, the plaintiff is entitled to a temporary restraining order requiring the defendant to arrange for an examination and a plan of treatment by a qualified specialist, and to a preliminary injunction requiring the defendants to carry out that plan of treatment.

15. For the foregoing reasons, the court should grant the plaintiff's motion in all respects.

Pursuant to 28 U.S.C. § 1746, I declare under penalty of perjury that the foregoing is true and correct.

[Date]
[Name and Address]

11c. Memorandum of Law in Support of Motion for a TRO and Preliminary Injunction

Note: When a brief refers to facts set out in a declaration or affidavit, it should cite the relevant paragraphs of the declaration or affidavit.

[CAPTION]

MEMORANDUM OF LAW IN SUPPORT OF
PLAINTIFF'S MOTION FOR A TEMPORARY RESTRAINING ORDER AND PRELIMINARY INJUNCTION

Statement of the Case

This is a civil rights action brought under 42 U.S.C. § 1983 by a state prisoner whose ankle was broken by prison staff and who is presently being denied appropriate medical care. The plaintiff seeks a temporary restraining order and a preliminary injunction to ensure that he received proper medical care.

Statement of Facts

As stated in the declaration submitted with this motion, the plaintiff was assaulted by prison staff and his ankle was broken. (Dec. at ¶¶ 2-3) The emergency room physician who treated him directed that his cast be removed within four weeks and that he be provided a course of physical therapy. (Dec. at ¶¶ 3-4) The defendant did not provide him with physical therapy or with a consultation with a physician qualified to assess and treat his condition. (Dec. at ¶ 6) The plaintiff is experiencing continued pain, stiffness, and limited motion in his ankle and cannot walk properly. (Dec. at ¶¶ 9-10)

ARGUMENT

POINT I
THE PLAINTIFF IS ENTITLED TO A TEMPORARY RESTRAINING
ORDER AND A PRELIMINARY INJUNCTION

In determining whether a party is entitled to a temporary restraining order or a preliminary injunction, courts generally consider several factors: whether the party will suffer irreparable injury, the "balance of hardships" between the parties, the likelihood of success on the merits, and the public interest. Each of these factors favors the grant of this motion.

A. The Plaintiff is Threatened with Irreparable Harm

The plaintiff alleges that he has been denied care for a serious medical need contrary to a physician's instruction. Such conduct by prison officials is a clear violation of the Eighth Amendment. *Estelle v. Gamble*, 429 U.S. 97, 105, 97 S.Ct. 285 (1976) (noting that "intentionally interfering with the treatment once prescribed" is a form of unlawful deliberate indifference); *see also* cases cited in § C of this point.

As a matter of law, the continuing deprivation of constitutional rights constitutes irreparable harm. *Elrod v. Burns*, 427 U.S. 347, 373, 96 S.Ct. 2673 (1976); *American Trucking Associations, Inc. v. City of Los Angeles*, 559 F.3d 1046, 1058-59 (9th Cir. 2009). This principle has been applied in prison litigation generally, *see Jolly v. Coughlin*, 76 F.3d 468, 482 (2d Cir. 1996); *Newsom v. Norris*, 888 F.2d 371, 378 (6th Cir. 1989); *Mitchell v. Cuomo*, 748 F.2d 804, 806 (2d Cir. 1984); *McClendon v. City of Albuquerque*, 272 F.Supp.2d 1250, 1259 (D.N.M. 2003), and specifically in prison medical care cases. *Phillips v. Michigan Dep't of Corrections*, 731 F.Supp. 792, 801 (W.D. Mich. 1990), *aff'd*, 932 F.3d 969 (6th Cir. 1991).

In addition, the plaintiff is threatened with irreparable harm because of the nature of his injury, a broken ankle with loss of movement and function. If he does not receive proper treatment at the proper time, he may never walk normally again.

B. The Balance of Hardships Favors the Plaintiff

In deciding whether to grant TRO's and preliminary injunctions, courts ask whether the suffering of the moving party if the motion is denied will outweigh the suffering of the non-moving party if the motion is granted. *See, e.g., Mitchell v. Cuomo*, 748 F.2d 804, 808 (2d Cir. 1984) (holding that dangers posed by prison crowding outweighed state's financial and administrative concerns); *Duran v. Anaya*, 642 F.Supp. 510, 527 (D.N.M. 1986) (holding that prisoners' interest in safety and medical care outweighed state's interest in saving money by cutting staff).

In this case, the present suffering of the plaintiff and his potential suffering if he permanently loses the normal use of his ankle and foot are enormous. The "sufferings" the defendants will experience if the court grants the order will consist of taking the plaintiff to a suitable doctor and then carrying out the doctor's orders—something that the defendants do, and are obligated to do, for members of the prison population on a daily basis. The defendants' hardship amounts to no more than business as usual.

C. The Plaintiff is Likely to Succeed on the Merits

The plaintiff has a great likelihood of success on the merits. What defendants have done—"intentionally interfering with [medical] treatment once prescribed"—was specifically singled out by the Supreme Court as an example of unconstitutional "deliberate indifference" to prisoners' medical needs. *Estelle v. Gamble*, 429 U.S. 97, 105, 97 S.Ct. 285 (1976). Many other courts have held that the failure to carry out physicians' orders is unconstitutional. *See, e.g., Johnson v. Wright*, 412 F.3d 398, 406 (2d Cir. 2005) (denial of Rebetron therapy for Hepatitis C contrary to the recommendations of all the plaintiff's treating physicians); *Lawson v. Dallas County*, 286 F.3d 257, 263 (5th Cir. 2002) (disregard for follow-up care instructions for paraplegic); *Lopez v. Smith*, 203 F.3d 1122, 1132 (9th Cir. 2000) (en banc) (failure to provide prescribed liquid diet for prisoner with a broken jaw, and substitution of a pureed diet that could not be drunk through a straw, stated a claim of interference with prescribed treatment); *Koehl v. Dalsheim*, 85 F.3d 86, 88 (2d Cir. 1996) (denial of prescription eyeglasses sufficiently alleged deliberate indifference); *Erickson v. Holloway*, 77 F.3d 1078, 1080-81 (8th Cir. 1996) (officer's refusal of emergency room doctor's request to admit the prisoner and take x-rays); *Aswegan v. Bruhl*, 965 F.2d 676, 677-68 (8th Cir. 1992) (failure to honor doctors' orders and refrain from cuffing the plaintiff's hands behind his back); *Boretti v. Wiscomb*, 930 F.2d 1150, 1156 (6th Cir. 1991) (nurse's failure to perform prescribed dressing change).

D. The Relief Sought Will Serve the Public Interest

In this case, the grant of relief will serve the public interest because it is always in the public interest for prison officials to obey the law, especially the Constitution. *Phelps-Roper v. Nixon*, 545 F.3d 685, 690 (8th Cir. 2008); *Duran v. Anaya*, 642 F.Supp. 510, 527 (D.N.M. 1986) ("Respect for law, particularly by officials responsible for the administration of the State's correctional system, is in itself a matter of the highest public interest."); *Llewelyn v. Oakland County Prosecutor's Office*, 402 F.Supp. 1379, 2393 (E.D. Mich. 1975) (stating "the Constitution is the ultimate expression of the public interest.").

POINT II
THE PLAINTIFF SHOULD NOT BE REQUIRED TO POST SECURITY

Usually a litigant who obtains interim injunctive relief is asked to post security. Rule 65(c), Fed.R.Civ.P. However, the plaintiff is an indigent prisoner and is unable to post security. The court has discretion to excuse an impoverished litigant from posting security. *Elliott v. Kiesewetter*, 98 F.3d 47, 60 (3d Cir. 1996) (stating that district courts have discretion to waive the bond requirement contained in Rule 65(c) of the Federal Rules of Civil Procedure if "the balance of the[] equities weighs overwhelmingly in favor of the party seeking the injunction"); *Moltan Co. v. Eagle-Pitcher Industries, Inc.*, 55 F.3d 1171, 1176 (6th Cir. 1995). In view of the serious medical danger confronting the plaintiff, the court should grant the relief requested without requiring the posting of security.

CONCLUSION

For the foregoing reasons, the court should grant the motion in its entirety.

[Date]
[Name and Address]

12. Trial

12a. *Voir Dire* Questions

Note: Jury selection and *voir dire* are discussed in Ch. 10, § R.3.

[CAPTION]

PLAINTIFF'S PROPOSED *VOIR DIRE* QUESTIONS

Plaintiff submits the following list of proposed *voir dire* questions.

Background

1. How long have you lived in the area?

2. Do you own your own home?

3. What are the ages of your children and what do they do?

4. Where are you employed?

  What is your title?

5. To what clubs and social organizations do you belong?

6. What are your hobbies?

7. What magazines do you regularly read?

8. How many years of formal education do you have?

9. Were you ever in the military?

  What rank did you hold?

  What duties did you have?

  Were you ever in the military police?

10. The following persons may be called as witnesses in this case. Do you know or have you ever heard of any of these persons? [List witnesses you or the defendants may call.]

11. Do you know any of the defendants in this case?

12. Do you have any opinions concerning the [name of the prison where the allegations of the complaint arose]?

  What are they?

13. Have you or any member of your family or a close friend ever been the victim of a crime?

  What was the nature of the crime?

  Was the perpetrator punished?

  What was the result?

  Were you satisfied with the results?

14. Have you or has any member of your family ever held any job in (a) a law enforcement agency, such as the police or prosecutor office, (b) any government agency, or (c) a private detective or security guard agency?

15. Do you know anyone who was or is employed by or in any way connected with the [prison where the allegations of the complaint arose]?

16. Do you know anyone who was or is employed by or in any way connected with the [corrections department that operates the prison]?

17. Do you know anyone, including your neighbors, friends, co-workers, or relatives, who works or has worked in a jail or prison or as a parole or probation officer?

18. Does your job cause you to work with any law enforcement officer or agency?

19. In this case, the defendants are represented by attorneys for the Attorney General's Office. Do you understand that this title has no particular significance, and that these attorneys are merely lawyers employed by the government?

20. In this case you may hear testimony from medical doctors and psychiatrists. Have you ever had any experience with either doctors or psychiatrists which affected you in some way so that you could not be in impartial jurors in a case involving such testimony?

21. What TV programs do you regularly watch?

22. What are the names of the radio stations that you listen to with any frequency?

Attitudes Toward Prisons, Use of Force

23. Have you ever been inside a jail or prison?

   In what circumstances?

24. Do you think prisoners are treated too lightly?

25. Do you think prisoners are afforded too many privileges?

26. Do you think a person loses any rights when he or she is sent to prison?

27. What is the purpose of prison?

28. If a prisoners disobeys an order, should he or she be punished, and if so, how?

29. Under what circumstances, if any, do you think corporal punishment of a prisoner is appropriate?

30. Under what circumstances do you think it would be appropriate for a prison official to hit a prisoner or use physical force against a prisoner when the prisoner is in restraints and unable to resist?

31. Do you believe that prisoners are entitled to humane and fair treatment?

32. Do you believe there are circumstances under which a prisoner forfeits his or her right to humane and fair treatment?

33. If a prisoner is harmed by the actions of another person, under what circumstances should he bring a lawsuit and be compensated for the harm inflicted by the prison officials?

34. What do you think should be done if a prison official is shown to have beaten a prisoner without provocation or to have seen others doing so without intervening?

Race

35. Do you know anyone who is black or African-American, such as a co-worker, friend, or neighbor?

36. How would you feel if a black or African-American family moved onto your street?

37. Do you belong to social clubs or organizations that bar membership to some individuals based on their race or ethnic origins?

Note: The foregoing questions assume that racial prejudice against African-Americans may affect the outcome of the case. If you or someone else involved in that case as a party or witness is a member of another ethnic group that is often the object of prejudice, you may wish to substitute that ethnic group in these questions.

Credibility

38. Do you know anyone who has been in prison?

   What is your relationship with that person?

   What was the person imprisoned for?

   How long was the sentence?

39. If a prisoner and a prison official give conflicting testimony about the same incident, which one would you be inclined to believe and why?

40. If you know someone has been convicted of a crime, would that make you less likely to believe he or she was telling the truth?

41. Under what circumstances, if any, would a prison official be likely to give false testimony?

42. Under what circumstances do you think people who work together on the same job are likely to protect a co-worker they suspect of wrong?

43. If you were in a position to hire someone, under what circumstances would you hire a person with a criminal record?

[Date]
[Name and Address]

12b. Special Verdict Form

Note: Special verdicts are discussed in Ch. 10, § R. 12.

Special verdicts must be adapted to the facts of the case and the judge's charge. This special verdict form is based on the hypothetical case used throughout this Appendix.

Question 1 is based on the holding of the Supreme Court that the "wanton and unnecessary inflict of pain" constitute cruel and unusual punishment. The Court has also held that in use of force cases, the defendants must act "maliciously and sadistically" in order for their acts to be found "wanton." *See Hudson v. McMillian*, 503 U.S. 1, 112 S.Ct. 995 (1992); *see also* Ch. 2, §§ A.1, A.2, G.2a(3). A court that uses the phrase "wanton and unnecessary" in special verdicts will probably charge the jury that they must find that the defendants acted maliciously and sadistically. Alternatively, the court may prefer to use the phrase "maliciously and sadistically" in the special verdicts themselves.

Questions 5 through 11 concerning the due process claim incorporate the rules concerning proof of damages in due process cases that are discussed in Ch. 4, § D.1.r(4). We have never seen special verdicts from this kind of case, but we think this is what they would have to look like.

[CAPTION]

PLAINTIFF'S PROPOSED SPECIAL VERDICT FORM

Misuse of Force Claim

1. Do you find that any of the following defendants inflicted pain wantonly and unnecessarily in using force against the plaintiff?

Green	Yes	No
Brown	Yes	No
White	Yes	No
Blue	Yes	No

2. If your answer to question 1 was "Yes" for defendant Green or Brown, do you find that defendant Cole knew that these defendants were disposed to misuse force against prisoners, and that defendant Cole acted with deliberate indifference in failing to take action to prevent them from continuing to abuse prisoners?

Yes   No

3. If your answer to question 1 was "yes" for any defendant, what amount of compensatory damages will fairly compensate the plaintiff for any injury, loss, pain, or suffering resulting from the misuse of force against the plaintiff?

$____.

4. If your answer to question 1 or 2 was "yes" for any defendant, what amount of punitive damages, if any, do you find appropriate against that defendant?

Green	$____.
Brown	$____.
White	$____.
Blue	$____.
Cole	$____.

Due Process Claim

5. Do you find that defendant Levett denied due process in conducting the plaintiff's disciplinary hearing?

Yes   No

6. If your answer to questions 5 was "Yes," do you find that defendant Christopher was deliberately indifferent to the denial of due process in denying the plaintiff's appeal?

     Yes   No

7. If your answer to question 5 was "Yes," do you find that the denial of due process caused the plaintiff to be convicted rather than exonerated, or to receive a more severe punishment, than he would have received at a hearing complying with due process requirements?

     Yes   No

8. If your answer to question 7 was "Yes," what amount of damages will fairly compensate the plaintiff for any punishment that he would not have suffered if due process had been followed?

                  $____.

9. If your answer to question 5 or question 6 was "Yes," what amount of punitive damages, if any, do you find appropriate against each defendant whom you found liable?

     Levett $____.

     Christopher $____.

Medical Care Claim

10. Do you find that either of the following defendants displayed deliberate indifference to the plaintiff's serious medical needs?

     Garcia Yes   No

     Warren Yes   No

11. If your answer to Question 10 was "Yes" as to either defendant, what amount of compensatory damages will fairly compensate the plaintiff for any injury, loss, pain, or suffering caused by the defendants' deliberate indifference to his serious medical needs?

     $____.

12. If your answer to question 10 was "Yes" as to either defendant, what amount of punitive damages, if any, do you find appropriate against that defendant?

     Garcia $____.

     Warren $____.

[Date]
Jury Foreperson

12c. Jury Instructions

Note: Jury instructions are discussed in Ch. 10, § R. 12. The right to a jury trial and selecting a jury are discussed in Ch. 10, §§ R.2 and R.3.

    The following jury instructions do not relate to our hypothetical case. They are slightly modified from instructions that were proposed by the plaintiff and adopted by the court in a prison assault case tried in federal court. We have added instructions on the use at trial of depositions, interrogatories, and expert opinions, since these were not at issue in the trial.

    Remember that jury instructions should reflect the law of the court where the case is tried as well as the nature of the evidence the parties will present.

[CAPTION]

PLAINTIFF'S PROPOSED INSTRUCTIONS TO THE JURY

Introduction

Members of the Jury:

    Now that you have heard all of the evidence and the argument of counsel, it is my duty to give you the instructions of the Court considering the law applicable to this case.

It is your duty as jurors to follow the law as I shall state it to you, and to apply the law to the facts as you find them from the evidence in the case. You are not to single out one instruction alone as stating the law, but must consider the instructions as a whole.

(Counsel have quite properly referred to some of the governing rules of law in their arguments. If, however, any difference appears to you between the law as stated by counsel and that stated by the court in these instructions, you are of course to be governed by the Court's instructions.)

Nothing I say in these instructions is to be taken as an indication that I have any opinion about the facts of this case, or what that opinion is. It is not my function to determine the facts, but rather yours.

You must perform your duties as jurors without bias or prejudice as to any party. The law does not permit you to be governed by sympathy, prejudice, or public opinion. All parties expect that you will carefully and impartially consider all of the evidence, follow the law as it is now being given to you, and reach a just verdict, regardless of the consequences.

All Persons Equal Before the Law

This case should be considered and decided by you as an action between persons of equal standing in the community, of equal worth, and holding the same or similar stations in life. A person convicted by the State is entitled to the same fair trial at your hands as is any individual. The law is no more respectful of one person than another, and all persons, including prisoners, stand equal before the law and are to be dealt with as equals in a court of justice.

Evidence in the Case— Attorneys' Statements Not Evidence; Admission by Attorney

Arguments, statements, and remarks of attorneys are not evidence, and you should disregard anything said by an attorney that is not supported by evidence or by your own general knowledge and experience. However, an admission of a fact by an attorney is binding on his client.

Unless you are otherwise instructed, the evidence in the case consists of the sworn testimony of the witnesses, regardless of who may have called them; and all exhibits received in evidence, regardless of who may have produced them; and all facts which may have been admitted or stipulated; and all facts and events which may have been judicially noticed.

Any evidence as to which an objection was sustained by the Court, and any evidence ordered stricken by the Court, must be entirely disregarded.

Evaluation of Evidence

As the sole judges of the facts, you must determine which of the witnesses you believe, what portion of their testimony you accept and what weight you attach to it. At times during the trial I may have sustained objections to questions asked without permitting the witness to answer or, where an answer has been made, may instruct that it be stricken from the record and that you disregard it and dismiss it from your minds. You may not draw any inference from an unanswered question nor may you consider testimony which has been stricken in reaching your decision. The law requires that your decision be made solely upon the competent evidence before you. Such items as I exclude from your consideration will be excluded because they are not legally admissible.

The law does not, however, require you to accept all of the evidence I shall admit, even though it be competent. In determining what evidence you will accept you must make your own evaluation of the testimony given by each of the witnesses, and determine the degree of weight you choose to give to his testimony. There is no magical formula by which one may evaluate testimony. You bring with you to this courtroom all of the experience and background of your lives. In your everyday affairs you determine for yourselves the reliability or unreliability of statements made by you and by others. The same tests that you use in your everyday dealings are the tests which you apply in your deliberations. The interest or lack of interests of any witness in the outcome of this case, the bias or prejudice of a witness, if there be any, the age, the appearance, the manner in which the witness gives his testimony on the stand, the opportunity that the witness had to observe the facts concerning which he testifies, the probability or improbability of the witness' testimony when viewed in light of all of the other evidence in the case, are all items to be taken into your consideration in determining the weight, if any, you will assign to that witness' testimony. If such considerations make it appear that there is a discrepancy in the evidence, you will have to consider whether the apparent discrepancy may not be reconciled by fitting the two stories together. If, however, that is not possible, you will then have to determine which of the conflicting versions you will accept.

In weighing the testimony of a witness you should consider his relationship to the plaintiff or to the defendant; his interest, if any, in the outcome of the case; his manner of testifying; his opportunity to observe or acquire knowledge concerning the facts about which he testified; his candor, fairness, and intelligence; and the extent to which he has been supported or contradicted by other credible evidence. Consider the witness's ability to observe the matters as to which he has testified, and whether he impresses you as having accurate recollection of these matters. You may, in short, accept or reject the testimony of any witness in whole or in part.

After making your own judgment, you will give the testimony of each witness such weight, if any, as you may think it deserves.

Evidence: Direct, Indirect, Circumstantial

There are, generally speaking, two types of evidence from which a jury may properly find the truth as to the facts of a case. One is direct evidence—such as the testimony of an eyewitness. The other is indirect or circumstantial evidence—the proof of a chain of circumstances pointing to the existence of or non-existence of certain facts.

As a general rule, the law makes no distinction between direct and circumstantial evidence, but simply requires that the jury find the facts in accordance with the preponderance of all the evidence in the case, both direct and circumstantial.

When the attorneys on both sides have stipulated or agreed to the existence of a fact, the jury must, unless otherwise instructed, accept the stipulation and regard that fact as proved.

Unless you are otherwise instructed, the evidence in the case consists of the sworn testimony of the witnesses, regardless of who may have called them; and all exhibits received in evidence, regardless of who may have produced them; and all facts which may have been admitted or stipulated.

Any evidence as to which an objection was sustained by the Court, and any evidence ordered stricken by the Court, must be entirely disregarded.

Unless you are otherwise instructed, anything you may have seen or heard outside the courtroom is not evidence, and must be entirely disregarded.

It is the duty of the attorney for each side of a case to object when the other side offers testimony or other evidence which the attorney believes is not properly admissible. You should not show prejudice against an attorney or his client because the attorneys made objections.

Impeachment—Inconsistent Statements or Conduct

A witness may be discredited or impeached by contradictory evidence; or by evidence that at some other time the witness has said or done something, or has failed to say or do something which is inconsistent with the witness' present testimony.

If you believe any witness has been impeached and thus discredited, it is your exclusive province to give the testimony of that witness such credibility, if any, as you may think it deserves.

Jurors May Take into Account Ordinary Experience and Observations

You have a right to consider all the evidence in the light of your own general knowledge and experience in the affairs of life, and to take into account whether any particular evidence seems reasonable and probable. However, if you have personal knowledge of any particular fact in this case, such knowledge may not be used as evidence.

Notice, Knowledge—Duty of Inquiry

The means of knowledge are ordinarily the equivalent in law to knowledge. So, if it appears from the evidence in the case that a person had information which would lead a reasonably prudent person to make inquiry through which he would surely learn certain facts, then this person may be found to have had actual knowledge of those facts, the same as if he had made such inquiry and had actually learned such facts.

That is to say, the law will charge a person with notice and knowledge of whatever he would have learned, upon making such inquiry as it would have been reasonable to expect him to make under the circumstances.

Knowledge or notice may also be established by circumstantial evidence. If it appears that a certain condition has existed for a substantial period of time, and that the defendant had regular opportunities to observe the condition, then you may draw the inference that he had knowledge of the condition.

Depositions—Use as Evidence

During the trial of this case, certain testimony has been presented to you by way of deposition, consisting of sworn recorded answers to questions asked of the witness in advance of trial by one or more of the attorneys for the parties to the case. The testimony of a witness who, for some reason, cannot be present to testify from the witness stand may be read to you. Such testimony is entitled to the same consideration, and is to be judged as to credibility, and weighed, and otherwise considered by the jury, insofar as possible, in the same way as if the witness had been present, and had testified from the witness stand.

Expert Testimony

The rule of evidence provides that if scientific, technical, or other specialized knowledge might assist the jury in understanding the evidence or in determining a fact in issue, a witness qualified as an expert by knowledge, skill, experience, training, or education may testify and state an opinion concerning such matters.

You should consider each expert opinion received in evidence in this case and give it such weight as you may think it deserves. If you should decide that the opinion of any expert witness is not based upon sufficient education and experience, or if you should conclude that the reason given in support of the opinion are not sound, or that the opinion is outweighed by other evidence, then you may disregard the opinion entirely.

DEFINITIONS INTRODUCED

I shall now give you the definitions for some important legal terms. Please listen carefully to these definitions so that you will understand the terms when they are used later.

Meaning of Burden of Proof

I shall now explain to you the burden of proof which the law places on the parties to establish their respective claims. When I say that a party has the burden of proof, I mean the evidence must satisfy you that the proposition on which that party has the burden of proof has been established by evidence which outweighs the evidence against it.

You must consider all the evidence regardless of which party produced it.

Burden of Proof—Preponderance of the Evidence

The burden is on the plaintiff in a civil action such as this to prove his claim by a preponderance of the evidence. This does not mean that plaintiff must prove his case to an absolute certainty, since proof to an absolute certainty is seldom possible in any case. If the proof should fail to establish any essential element of plaintiff's claim by a preponderance of the evidence in the case, and the jury should find for the defendant as to that claim.

To "establish by a preponderance of the evidence" means to prove that something is more likely so than not so. In other words, a preponderance of the evidence in the case means such evidence as, when considered and compared with that opposed to it, has more convincing force, and produces in your minds belief that what is sought to be provided is more likely true than not true.

In determining whether any fact in issue has been proved by a preponderance of the evidence in the case, the jury may, unless otherwise instructed, consider the testimony of all witnesses, regardless of who may have called them, and all exhibits received in evidence, regardless of who may have produced them.

Stipulation of Facts

A stipulation of facts is an agreement among the parties that a certain fact is true. You must regard such agreed facts as true. *Note*: The stipulated facts, if any, should be listed here and read to the jury.

Knowledge of the Law Presumed; Specific Intent Not Required

Everyone is required to know what the law is and to act according to the law. If someone engages in an activity which violates the law, that person is responsible for his actions whether he intended to violate the law or not.

Specific Intent not Required

In order to find in favor of the Plaintiff in this case, it is not necessary to find that the defendant had the specific intent to violate the Plaintiff's constitutional rights. If the Defendant specifically intended to engage in activities which violated the Plaintiff's constitutional rights, Plaintiff can recover money damages from the Defendant whether the Defendant intended to violate Plaintiff's rights or not. In other words, the Plaintiff can recover money damages if the Defendant intended the actions which resulted in a violation of the Plaintiff's constitutional rights.

Prison Conditions, Generally

Convicted prisoners do not forfeit all constitutional protections by reason of their conviction and confinement in a prison. But simply because prison inmates retain certain constitutional rights does not mean that these rights are not subject to restrictions and limitations. The fact of confinement as well as the legitimate goals and policies of the penal institution limits these retained constitutional rights. There must be mutual accommodation between institutional needs and objectives and the provisions of the Constitution that are of general application.

Maintaining institutional security and preserving internal order and discipline are essential goals that may require limitations on or retraction of the retained constitutional rights of convicted prisoners. Prison officials must be free to take appropriate action to ensure the safety of inmates and corrections personnel. However, prisoners have a right to be free from cruel and unusual punishment.

Statute—42 U.S.C. Sec. 1983

Section 1983 of Title 42 of the United States Code under which this action is brought provides that any inhabitant of this judicial district may seek redress in this Court, by way of damages, against any person or persons who, under color of law, statute, ordinance, regulation, or custom, knowingly subjects such inhabitant to the deprivation of any rights, privileges, or immunities, secured or protected by the Constitution or laws of the United States.

The foregoing statute comprises one of the Civil Rights Acts enacted by the Congress under the Fourteenth Amendment to the Constitution of the United States, which provides:

No State shall make or enforce any law which shall abridge the privileges or immunities of citizens of the United States; nor shall any State deprive any person of life, liberty, or property, without due process of law; nor deny to any person within its jurisdiction the equal protection of the law.

Constitutional Claim

Plaintiff claims that Defendants' actions or failure to act amounted to a deprivation of Mr. Manville's right to reasonable protection from assault as provided by the Eighth Amendment to the United States Constitution.

Constitutional Rights; Eighth Amendment

I will now instruct you on Mr. Manville's Eighth Amendment claim.

The Eighth Amendment to the United States Constitution guarantees that no prisoner shall be subjected to cruel and unusual punishment. The constitutional prohibition against cruel and unusual punishment not only prohibits certain kinds of physical punishment, such as torture, but embodies broad and idealistic concepts of dignity, civilized standards, humanity, and decency. The Eighth Amendment requires conduct compatible with the evolving standards that mark the progress of a maturing society. Thus, the Eighth Amendment requires that a jail official, under the circumstances as I shall define them for you, must not be deliberately indifferent to a prisoner's need for protection against physical assault. A prisoner who is deprived of such protection because of a jail official's deliberate indifference to a physical assault has suffered a violation of his constitutional rights as guaranteed by the Eighth Amendment.

To be cruel and unusual punishment, conduct which does not purport to be punishment at all must involve more than ordinary lack of due care for the prisoner's interest or safety. It is obduracy or wantonness, not inadvertence or error in good faith that characterizes the conduct prohibited by the cruel and unusual punishment clause.

Essential Elements of Plaintiff's Claim—Eighth Amendment

In order to prove his claim concerning violation of the Eighth Amendment, the burden is upon the Plaintiff to establish by a preponderance of the evidence each of the following elements:

1. that the Defendant acted under the color of law;
2. that the Defendant's act or omission constituted deliberate indifference to Plaintiff's physical well-being;
3. that the conduct of the Defendant was the proximate cause of injury and consequent damage to the Plaintiff.

I will now define each element for you.

"Under Color of State Law"—Defined

Acting under color of law means acting in one's capacity as a state official.

Note: If Defendants have stipulated to acting under color of state law, or if they do not dispute it, this instruction can be eliminated, or replaced with a statement that it is stipulated or undisputed.

Violation of Eighth Amendment: Definition/Burden of Proof

In this case, in order to find that the Defendant is liable for the violation of Mr. Manville's constitutional right to be protected from physical assault from other inmates, you must find that the Defendant acted or failed to act with deliberate indifference to Mr. Manville's physical safety.

In order to be deliberately indifferent, a defendant's conduct must amount to more than inadvertence, lack of due care, negligence or error. Instead it must reflect reckless behavior, callous neglect or thoughtless disregard equivalent to a flagrant or remarkably bad failure to protect. It is obduracy and wantonness, not inadvertence or error in good faith that characterize the prohibited conduct.

In establishing "deliberate indifference," Plaintiff has the burden of proving the following:

1) that there existed a great degree of risk of physical harm to Plaintiff at the prison on November 12, 2008;
2) that the Defendant knew of this risk;
3) that the Defendant took no or wholly inadequate action in the face of actual knowledge of a risk to Mr. Manville; and
4) that the Defendant's action or omission was more than inadvertence, lack of due care, negligence or error.

If you are satisfied that the Plaintiff has met this burden of proof, then you may infer that the Defendant was deliberately indifferent to Mr. Manville's constitutional rights.

"Proximate Cause"—Defined

I shall now define for you proximate cause.

An injury or damage is proximately caused by an act whenever it appears from the evidence in the case that the act or omission played a substantial part in bringing about or actually causing the injury or damage, and that the injury or damage was either a direct result or a reasonably probable consequence of the act or omission.

More Than One Proximate Cause

There may be more than one proximate cause of the Plaintiff's injuries. To be a proximate cause, the acts of the Defendant need not be the only cause nor the last cause. A cause may be proximate although it and another cause acted at the same time or in combination to produce the occurrence.

Intervening Negligence or Conduct of Person not a Party

If you decide that the Defendant has violated Mr. Manville's constitutional rights and that such violation was a proximate cause of the injury of Plaintiff, it is not a defense that the conduct of other jail officials or persons who are not parties to this suit also may have been a cause of this occurrence.

However, if you decide that the primary proximate cause of the occurrence was the conduct of others, then your verdict should be for the Defendant.

Damages: Defendant Take the Plaintiff as he finds him

You are instructed that the Defendant takes the Plaintiff as he finds him. If you find that the Plaintiff was unusually susceptible to injury, that fact will not relieve the Defendant from liability for any and all damages resulting to Plaintiff as a proximate result of Defendants' wrongful conduct.

Measure of Damages—Personal

Any bodily injury sustained by the Plaintiff and any resulting pain and suffering, disability or mental anguish experienced in the past or to be experienced in the future constitutes personal injury. No evidence of the value of such intangible things as physical pain and suffering has been or need be introduced. In that respect, it is not value you are trying to determine, but an amount of money that will fairly compensate the Plaintiff for the damages suffered. There is no exact standard for fixing the compensation to be awarded on account of such elements of damage. Any such award should be fair and just in light of the evidence.

You should include each of the following elements of damage which you decide has been sustained by the Plaintiff to the present time:

1. physical pain;
2. mental anguish;
3. fright and shock;
4. embarrassment, humiliation, or mortification.

If any element of damage is of a continuing nature, you shall decide how long it may continue. If an element of damage is permanent in nature, then you shall decide how long the Plaintiff is likely to live.

Which, if any, of these elements of damage has been proved is for you to decide based upon evidence and not upon speculation, guess, or conjecture. The amount of money to be awarded for certain of these elements of damage cannot be proved in a precise dollar amount. The law leaves such amount to your sound judgment. Your verdict must be solely to compensate Plaintiff for his damages.

Punitive Damages

You may also decide whether the Plaintiff is entitled to the award of any punitive damages. The purpose of an award of punitive damages is to punish a wrongdoer for his misconduct and to deter similar conduct by others. In order to award punitive damages, you must find one of the following:

1. that the Defendant acted intentionally or purposefully to deprive the Plaintiff of his rights: or
2. that the Defendant acted in reckless disregard of or with callous indifference to the Plaintiff's rights: or
3. that the Defendant carried out lawful activities with unnecessary harshness, or abused his official power, or took unfair advantage of the Plaintiff.

If you find that the Defendant did any one or more of these things, then you may award punitive damages.

If you award punitive damages, you should fix the amount using calm discretion and sound reason. You must not be influenced by sympathy for or dislike of any party in the case.

Jury Deliberations

When you go to the jury room, your deliberations should be conducted in a businesslike manner. You should first select a foreperson. She or he should see to it that the discussion goes forward in a sensible and orderly fashion and that each juror has the opportunity to discuss the issues fully and fairly.

When the eight of you agree upon a verdict, it will be received as your verdict. In your deliberations, you should weigh the evidence with due regard and consideration for each other's opinions. You should listen to each other's arguments with open minds, and make every reasonable effort to reach a verdict.

Before deciding the case, give impartial consideration to the views of your fellow jurors. This means you should give respectful consideration to one another's views and talk over differences of opinion in a spirit of fairness and frankness.

It is natural that differences of opinion will arise. When they do, each of you should not only express your opinion but also the facts and reasons upon which you base it.

In the course of your deliberations, do not hesitate to reexamine your own views and change your opinion if you are convinced that it is wrong.

However, none of you should surrender your honest conviction as to the weight and effect of the evidence solely because of the opinion of your fellow jurors or for the mere purpose of returning a verdict.

If you wish to communicate with the Court while you are deliberating, please have your foreperson write a note and deliver it to the bailiff. It is not proper to talk directly with the judge, attorneys, court officers, or other persons involved in the case, even if the discussion has nothing to do with the case.

During your deliberations, you must not disclose the state of your deliberations to others outside the jury room. Therefore, unless you reach a verdict, do not disclose this information even in the courtroom.

The exhibits that have been admitted into evidence will be given to you and you may examine them in the jury room.

Election of Foreperson

Upon retiring to the jury room, you will select one of your number to act as your foreperson. The foreperson will preside over your deliberations, and will be your spokesman here in Court.

Special Verdict Form

A form of special verdict has been prepared for your convenience. Nothing in this form of verdict is to suggest or convey in any way or manner as to what verdict I think you should find. What the verdict shall be is the sole and exclusive duty and responsibility of the jury.

[Forms of special verdict read]

You will take this form to the jury room and, when eight of eight of you have reached agreement as to your verdict, you will have your foreperson fill in, date and sign the special verdict form as so completed. The foreperson will then prepare a note indicating that you have reached a verdict, but not revealing the verdict, and will date and sign the note, and ring the bell for the bailiff.

Communications Between Court and Jury During Jury's Deliberations

If it becomes necessary during your deliberations to communicate with the Court, you may send a note by a bailiff, signed by your foreperson or by one or more members of the jury. No member of the jury should ever attempt to communicate with the Court by any means other than a signed writing, and the Court will never communicate with any member of the jury on any subject touching the merits of the case otherwise than in writing, or orally here in open Court.

You will note from the oath about to be taken by the bailiffs that they too, as well as all other persons, are forbidden to communicate in any way or manner with any member of the jury on any subject touching the merits of the case.

Bear in mind also that you are never to reveal to any person—not even to the Court—how the jury stands, numerically or otherwise, on the questions before you, until after you have reached a verdict.

13. Appeal

Note: Appeals are discussed in Ch. 10, § U.

13a. Notice of Appeal

Note: This sample notice is based on the notice at the end of the Federal Rules of Appellate Procedure, Form 1.

[CAPTION]

NOTICE OF APPEAL

Notice is hereby given that Joseph Williams, plaintiff in the above-entitled matter, appeals to the United States Court of Appeals for the Circuit from the final judgment entered in this action on [date of entry of judgment].

[Date]
[Name and Address]

13b. Appellate Brief

Note: Appellate briefs are discussed in Ch. 10, § U.g. Brief writing in general is discussed in Ch. 12, § E.

This brief assumes that the use of force claim in our hypothetical case was the only claim and that the district court granted summary judgment to the defendants, disposing of the whole case. If there were several claims and the court only granted summary judgment on some of them, the order would not be appealable until the end of the case. *See* Ch. 10, § L.3.

Rule 28(a)(9), Fed.R.App.P., requires the argument section to include "for each issue, a concise statement of the applicable standard of review (which may appear in the discussion of the issue or under a separate heading placed before the discussion of the issues)." In this sample brief, which raises only one issue, the standard of review is stated in the first paragraph under Argument, rather than making it a separate section. Standards of review are explained in Ch. 10, § U.1.a.

The first page of an appellate brief should be a cover page. The rules set out specific requirements for a cover page but say they do not apply to "unrepresented parties." Rule 32(a)(2), Fed.R.App.P. You should try to comply with those requirements to the extent you can.

The Table of Contents should come right after the cover page and need not have a caption. In the Table of Contents, the number of the page on which each item begins should be listed on the right.

Table of Contents

Table of Authorities

Note: The page or pages on which each authority is cited should be listed on the right.

Cases

Anderson v. Liberty Lobby, Inc., 477 U.S. 242, 106 S.Ct. 2505 (1986) . . . .

Hudson v. McMillian, 503 U.S. 1, 112 S.Ct. 995 (1992) . . . .

Jenkins v. Winter, 540 F.3d 742 (8th Cir. 2008) . . . .

Kaucher v. County of Bucks, 455 F.3d 418 (3d Cir. 2006) . . . .

Miller v. Leather, 913 F.2d 1085 (4th Cir. 1990) (en banc) . . . .

Noonan v. Staples, Inc., 539 F.3d 1, 5 (1st Cir. 2008) . . . .

Oliver v. Collins, 914 F.2d 56 (5th Cir. 1990) . . . .

Titran v. Ackman, 893 F.2d 145 (7th Cir. 1990) . . . .

Washington v. Haupert, 481 F.3d 543 (7th Cir. 2007) . . . .

Whitley v. Albers, 475 U.S. 312, 106 S.Ct. 1078 (1986) . . . .

Ziemba v. Armstrong, 433 F.Supp. 248 (D. Conn. 2006) . . . .

Constitutional Provisions, Statutes, and Rules

U.S. Const., Amend. VIII . . . .

42 U.S.C. § 1983 . . . .

Rule 56(c), Fed.R.Civ.P . . . .

BRIEF OF APPELLANT

Statement of Subject Matter and Appellate Jurisdiction

The district court has subject matter jurisdiction under 42 U.S.C. § 1331(a) because the complaint raises a question whether the defendants violated the plaintiff's rights under the United States Constitution. This court has appellate jurisdiction under 28 U.S.C. § 1291 because the grant of summary judgment to the defendants is a final judgment. Judgment was entered on December 1, 2008, and the plaintiff's notice of appeal was filed on December 20, 2008.

Statement of Issues Presented for Review

1. Whether the district court in granting summary judgment improperly decided disputed factual issues.

2. Whether the plaintiff's factual allegations of an unprovoked beating by prison staff raised a material issue under the Eighth Amendment.

Statement of the Case

A. Statement of the Proceedings

This is a civil rights action under 42 U.S.C. § 1983 brought by a state prisoner who alleges that he was unlawfully beaten. The district court granted summary judgment to the defendants on the ground that the warden's internal investigation established that the defendants used force against the plaintiff in order to make him obey a legitimate order and not to harm him.

B. Statement of Facts

The plaintiff alleged in a declaration under the penalty of perjury that the defendants tear-gassed him while he was locked in his cell and after he had told them that he would cooperate with their order to pack his property. They then entered his cell, knocked him down, and beat and kicked him. During these events he offered no resistance.

The defendants submitted the affidavits of three of the defendant officers, which stated that the plaintiff had refused to leave his cell for transfer and had resisted their efforts to remove him from his cell, injuring himself in the process. They also submitted the affidavit of the prison warden, who stated that he had the incident thoroughly investigated and the investigation supported the account of the officers. The warden's affidavit was accompanied by various unsworn witness statements and an "investigative summary" by a deputy warden of the prison.

The district court held that the defendants were entitled to summary judgment because the plaintiff's "unsupported allegations" were insufficient to establish a genuine issue of material facts in light to the warden's "thorough investigation."

Summary of Argument

The plaintiff's affidavit squarely contradicted the factual allegations of the defendants, and the facts it alleged would have supported a judgment for the plaintiff under the Eighth Amendment. Summary judgment was therefore improper on the record before the district court.

Standard of Review

Whether a party is entitled to summary judgment is a question of law over which this Court exercises plenary review. *Noonan v. Staples, Inc.*, 539 F.3d 1, 5 (1st Cir. 2008); *Kaucher v. County of Bucks*, 455 F.3d 418, 422 (3d Cir. 2006).

ARGUMENT

POINT I

THE DISTRICT COURT SHOULD NOT HAVE GRANTED SUMMARY JUDGMENT BASED ON ITS RESOLUTION OF DISPUTED FACTS

Summary judgment is to be granted only if the record before the court shows "that there is no genuine issue as to any material facts and that the moving party is entitled to a judgment as a matter of law." Rule 56(c), Fed.R.Civ.P.

The plaintiff's affidavit squarely contradicts the defendants' story concerning what force was used, when it was used, and why it was used. The district court's statement that the plaintiff's sworn declaration consists of "unsupported allegations" and that the warden's investigation was "thorough" amounts to a judgment about the credibility of the plaintiff's factual allegations. The district court may not make credibility determinations or otherwise resolve disputed factual issues on a motion for summary judgment. *Jenkins v. Winter*, 540 F.3d 742, 750 (8th Cir. 2008); *Washington v. Haupert*, 481 F.3d 543, 550 (7th Cir. 2007).

POINT II

THE PLAINTIFF'S FACTUAL ALLEGATIONS RAISE A MATERIAL ISSUE UNDER THE EIGHTH AMENDMENT

A "material" fact is one that "might affect the outcome of the suit under the governing law." *Anderson v. Liberty Lobby, Inc.*, 477 U.S. 242, 248, 106 S.Ct. 2505 (1986). The disputed facts alleged by the plaintiff are material. His affidavit portrays a completely needless use of force against an inmate who was locked in his cell and was attempting to cooperate with the order he had been given.

Whether the use of force by prison staff violates the Eighth Amendment depends on whether it was "applied in a good-faith effort to maintain or restore discipline or maliciously and sadistically to cause harm." *Hudson v. McMillian*, 503 U.S. 1, 5, 112 S.Ct. 995 (1992). The facts alleged by the plaintiff are evidence that the defendants were acting "maliciously and sadistically to cause harm"; they would support a jury verdict in the plaintiff's favor. *See Miller v. Leathers*, 913 F.2d 1085, 1088 (4th Cir. 1990); *Oliver v. Collins*, 914 F.2d 56, 59 (5th Cir. 1990); *Ziemba v. Armstrong*, 433 F.Supp. 248, 251 (D. Conn. 2006).

CONCLUSION

For the foregoing reasons, the grant of summary judgment should be reversed and the case should be remanded to the district court for trial.

[Date]
[Name and Address]

14. Petition for Certiorari to the United States Supreme Court

Note: Petitions for certiorari to the United States Supreme Court are discussed in Ch. 10, § U.2.b. We have changed our hypothetical case slightly from the one used in earlier forms because that case did not present issues that meet the Supreme Court's criteria for granting certiorari.

The legal issue presented in this sample petition is discussed in Ch. 4., § D.1.c.

It is customary to number the pages that precede the "Decisions Below" section with lower-case Roman numerals—(i), (ii), (iii), etc. Starting with Decisions Below, the pages are given ordinary numbers. The Appendix is at the end of the petition and is numbered in the form "1a, 2a" or "A-1, A-2."

A petition for writ of certiorari should have a cover page in the following form.

IN THE
SUPREME COURT OF THE UNITED STATES
OCTOBER TERM 2008
No. _____

JOSEPH WILLIAMS,
Petitioner,
-against-
HOWARD LEVETT, et al.,
Respondents

PETITION FOR A WRIT OF CERTIORARI
TO THE UNITED STATES COURT OF APPEALS
FOR THE ___ CIRCUIT

[Petitioner's name]
[Address]

QUESTION PRESENTED

Whether witnesses called by a prisoner subject to institutional disciplinary charges should testify at the hearing in the accused prisoner's presence, in the absence of threats to institutional safety or correctional goals.

PARTIES

The petitioner is Joseph Williams, a prisoner at Stonehaven Correctional Facility in [where prison is located]. The respondents are Howard Levett, a correctional lieutenant at Stonehaven Corrections Facility, and Arthur Christopher, the warden at Stonehaven Correctional Facility.

Table of Contents

Note: The Table of Contents should list the number of the page on which each item starts at the right

Table of Authorities

Cases:

Bartholomew v. Watson, 665 F.2d 915 (9th Cir. 1982) . . . .
Baxter v. Nebraska Dep't of Correctional Services, 11 Neb. App. 842, 663 N.W. 136 (2003) . . . .
Baxter v. Palmigiano, 425 U.S. 308, 322, 96 S.Ct. 1551 (1976) . . . .
Bolden v. Alston, 810 F.2d 353 (2d Cir. 1987). . . . .
Hrbek v. State, 478 N.W. 617 (Iowa 1991) . . . .
King v. Wells, 760 F.2d 89 (6th Cir. 1985). . . . .
Ponte v. Real, 471 U.S. 491, 105 S.Ct. 2192 (1985) . . . .
Powell v. Ward, 487 F.Supp. 917 (S.D.N.Y. 1980), *aff'd as modified*, 643 F.2d 924 (2d Cir. 1981). . . . .
Ramer v. Kerby, 936 F.2d 1102 (10th Cir. 1991) . . . .
Wolff v. McDonnell, 418 U.S. 539 94 S.Ct. 2963 (1974). . . . .

Note: The Table of Authorities should list the number of the page or pages where each authority is cited.

DECISIONS BELOW:

The decision of the United States Court of Appeals for the _____ Circuit is unreported. It is cited in the table at 643 F.3d 999 (___ Cir. 2008) and a copy is attached as Appendix A to this petition (A.1). The order of the United States District Court for the Western District of _____ is not reported. A copy is attached as Appendix B to this petition (A.11).

JURISDICTION

The judgment of the United States Court of Appeals for the _____ Circuit was entered on December 1, 2007. An order denying a petition for rehearing was entered on January 29, 2008, and a copy of that order is attached as Appendix B to this petition (A.10). Jurisdiction is conferred by 28 U.S.C. § 1254(1).

CONSTITUTIONAL AND STATUTORY PROVISIONS INVOLVED

This case involves Amendment XIV to the United States Constitution, which provides:

Section 1. All persons born or naturalized in the United States, and subject to the jurisdiction thereof, are citizens of the United States and of the State wherein they reside. No State shall make or enforce any law which shall abridge the privileges or immunities of citizens of the United States; nor shall any State deprive any person of life, liberty, or property, without due process of law; nor deny to any person within its jurisdiction the equal protection of the laws.

*   *   *

Section 5. The Congress shall have power to enforce, by appropriate legislation, the provisions of this article.

The Amendment is enforced by Title 42, Section 1983, United States Code:

Every person who, under color of any statute, ordinance, regulation, custom, or usage, of any State or Territory or the District of Columbia, subjects, or causes to be subjected, any citizen of the United States or other person within the jurisdiction thereof to the deprivation of any rights, privileges, or immunities secured by the Constitution and laws, shall be liable to the party injured in an action at law, suit in equity, or other proper proceeding for redress, except that in any action brought against a judicial officer for an act or omission taken in such officer's judicial capacity, injunctive relief shall not be granted unless a declaratory decree was violated or declaratory relief was unavailable. For the purposes of this section, any Act of Congress applicable exclusively to the District of Columbia shall be considered to be a statute of the District of Columbia.

STATEMENT OF THE CASE

The petitioner's complaint alleged that he was charged with several serious disciplinary offenses by prison officials. It further alleged that the charges were false and that in reality the petitioner had been beaten by prison staff without justification. Pursuant to the usual procedure, the petitioner requested that the disciplinary hearing officer, respondent Levett, call five inmate witnesses who were in the adjacent and opposite cells at the time of the incident that gave rise to the disciplinary charges. The hearing officer did not call them at the disciplinary hearing. Instead, he stated to the petitioner that he had spoken to the witnesses and none of them claimed to have seen the plaintiff being beaten by officers as he alleged. He declined the request to bring the witnesses to the hearing so they could be asked additional questions. The petitioner was convicted of all charges and sentenced to three years in punitive segregation. His administrative appeal, which described the refusal to call the witnesses and stated the reasons for calling the witnesses, was denied by the Warden, respondent Christopher.

The district court granted summary judgment to the defendants on the ground that the Due Process Clause does not require that witnesses "called" in a prison disciplinary hearing actually testify at the hearing. The court of appeals affirmed the grant of summary judgment for the reasons stated by the district court.

BASIS FOR FEDERAL JURISDICTION

This case raises a question of interpretation of the Due Process Clause of the Fourteenth Amendment to the United States Constitution. The district court had jurisdiction under the general federal question jurisdiction conferred by 28 U.S.C. 1331.

REASONS FOR GRANTING THE WRIT

A. Conflicts with Decisions of Other Courts

The holding of the courts below that witnesses need not personally appear in prison disciplinary hearing is directly contrary to the holding of three federal circuits. *See Ramer v. Kerby*, 936 F.2d 1102, 1104 (10th Cir. 1991); *King v. Wells*, 760 F.2d 89, 92 (6th Cir. 1985); *Bartholomew v. Watson*, 665 F.2d 915, 917-18 (9th Cir. 1982). In addition, the Supreme Court of Iowa has held that "[a]n unjustified refusal to permit live testimony of a defense witness . . . will warrant reversal." *Hrbek v. State*, 478 N.W. 617, 619 (Iowa 1991); *accord, Baxter v. Nebraska Dep't of Correctional Services*, 11 Neb. App. 842, 849-50, 663 N.W. 136 (2003).

B. Importance of the Question Presented

This case presents a fundamental question of the interpretation of this Court's decision in *Wolff v. McDonnell*, 418 U.S. 539, 566, 94 S.Ct. 2963 (1974). The question presented is of great public importance because it affects the operations of the prison systems in all 50 states, the District of Columbia, and hundreds of city and county jails. In view of the large amount of litigation over prison disciplinary proceedings, guidance on the question is also of great importance to prisoners, because it affects their ability to receive fair decisions in proceedings that may result in months or years of added incarceration or harsh punitive confinement.

The issue's importance is enhanced by the fact that the lower courts in this case have seriously misinterpreted *Wolff*. This Court held in *Wolff* that prisoners have a limited right to call witnesses. The Court reiterated this point in *Ponte v. Real*, 471 U.S. 491, 497, 105 S.Ct. 2192 (1985), and added that prison officials have the burden of explaining the reasons for refusing to call witnesses in a particular case.

The common sense understanding of "calling" a witness is bringing the witness into the proceeding to give testimony, and nothing in *Wolff* or *Ponte* suggests otherwise. Both cases acknowledge that there are security and other concerns that may require limiting prisoners' due process rights in particular cases. However, those concerns are accommodated by permitting prison officials to bar witnesses when calling them would be "unduly hazardous to institutional safety or correctional goals." 418 U.S. at 566. As one court observed, the reasoning of *Wolff* simply does not support

> a blanket policy against allowing witnesses to be present at the hearing. The Court appears to have contemplated individualized determinations of the potential threat to security created by the presence of the inmate at the interview. True, prison administrators are to be given broad discretion in determining whether such a threat exists. . . . But administrative necessity does not require a blanket rule which precludes the presence of witnesses when there are no countervailing concerns warranting that prohibition. Requiring prison officials to determine on an individual basis whether witnesses can be present encourages them to exercise their discretion to strike the appropriate balance between the prisoner's right to call witnesses and the prison's need to maintain order.

Powell v. Ward, 487 F.Supp. 917, 928 -929 (S.D.N.Y. 1980), *aff'd as modified*, 643 F.2d 924 (2d Cir. 1981).

The lower court's reasoning that witnesses never need actually appear at the hearing is unconvincing. It relied on a case from the Second Circuit that does contain that holding. *See Bolden v. Alston*, 810 F.2d 353, 358 (2d Cir. 1987). However, *Bolden* based its conclusion on *Baxter v. Palmigiano*, 425 U.S. 308, 322, 96 S.Ct. 1551 (1976)—a case that upheld the denial of confrontation and cross-examination of witnesses *against* the inmate. The *Baxter* Court made this distinction crystal clear, describing its holding as that "there is no general right to confront and cross-examine *adverse* witnesses." *Baxter*, 425 U.S. at 322 n.5 (emphasis supplied). The Court in *Wolff* had also held that a prisoner has no right in a disciplinary hearing to confront and cross-examine the witnesses *against* him. *Wolff*, 418 U.S. at 567-69. However, this holding did not address the treatment of witnesses called by the prisoner. The Court stated a completely different standard for them, providing for the exclusion of witnesses called *by* the prisoner only when "unduly hazardous to institutional safety or correctional goals." *Wolff*, 418 U.S. at 566. This standard permits prison officials to exercise their discretion to exclude witnesses when a particular case warrants it, while preserving the prisoner's right to call witnesses when there is no reason to exclude them. Nothing in *Baxter* is contrary to the distinction made in *Wolff* between adverse witnesses and the accused prisoner's own witnesses, and nothing in *Baxter* alters the *Wolff* holding concerning calling of the prisoner's witnesses.

Thus the court below seriously misinterpreted *Wolff* by failing to distinguish between witnesses against the prisoner and witnesses called by and for the prisoner. The Court should correct that misinterpretation and make it clear that witnesses called by the prisoner should appear at the hearing unless such a personal appearance in a particular case would be unduly hazardous to institutional safety or correctional goals.

CONCLUSION

For the foregoing reasons, certiorari should be granted in this case.

[Date]
Respectfully submitted,
[Name and Address]

Note: The Appendix to the petition is not included.

15. Proof of Service

Note: Once the summons and complaint have been properly served as described in Ch. 10, § C.4, all subsequent papers can be served on counsel for the defendants. When you file papers with the court clerk, you should include a sworn affidavit or declaration under penalty of perjury stating that you have served them. *See* Ch. 10, § G.

[CAPTION]

Joseph Williams declares under penalty of perjury pursuant to 28 U.S.C. § 1746 that he mailed a copy of the enclosed [describe papers you are filing] to defendant's counsel, John Jones, Assistant Attorney General, [Address], by placing them in an envelope and placing the envelope in the Mail Hall Legal Mailbox at Stonehaven Correctional Facility, [Address], on [date].

[Name]
[Date]

16. Standard Form 95 for Federal Prisoners' Claims for Damage, Injury or Death (Federal Tort Claims Act)

Note: This form must be submitted to the proper agency before filing a claim under the Federal Tort Claims Act (FTCA). The FTCA is discussed in Ch. 8, § C.2.

The form, which is a one-page document with printing on both sides, has been reformatted to fit the page size of this book. The material on the back of the form would not fit on one book page, so our version of the form takes up three pages.

It is preferable to use the Government's version of the form because it has more space to write in. If you can't get the official form, "other written notification" is acceptable. Therefore, you should be able to use a photocopy of our version of the form, or write your own form or letter. Whatever you submit must include all the information that the form calls for. In our opinion it should look as much like the official form as is practical.

CLAIM FOR DAMAGE, INJURY, OR DEATH	INSTRUCTIONS: Please read carefully the instructions on the reverse side and supply information requested on both sides of this form. Use additional sheet(s) if necessary. See reverse side for additional instructions.	FORM APPROVED OMB NO. 1105-0008

1. Submit To Appropriate Federal Agency:	2. Name, Address of claimant and claimant's personal representative, if any. (See instructions on reverse.) (Number, Street, City, State and Zip Code)

3. TYPE OF EMPLOYMENT ☐ MILITARY ☐ CIVILIAN	4. DATE OF BIRTH	5. MARITAL STATUS	6. DATE AND DAY OF ACCIDENT	7. TIME (A.M. OR P.M.)

8. Basis of Claim (State in detail the known facts and circumstances attending the damage, injury, or death, identifying persons and property involved, the place of occurrence and the cause thereof. Use additional pages if necessary.)

9.   **PROPERTY DAMAGE**

NAME AND ADDRESS OF OWNER, IF OTHER THAN CLAIMANT (Number, Street, City, State, and Zip Code).

BRIEFLY DESCRIBE THE PROPERTY, NATURE AND EXTENT OF DAMAGE AND THE LOCATION WHERE PROPERTY MAY BE INSPECTED. (See Instructions on reverse side.)

10.   **PERSONAL INJURY/WRONGFUL DEATH**

STATE NATURE AND EXTENT OF EACH INJURY OR CAUSE OF DEATH, WHICH FORMS THE BASIS OF THE CLAIM. IF OTHER THAN CLAIMANT, STATE NAME OF INJURED PERSON OR DECEDENT.

11.   **WITNESSES**

NAME	ADDRESS (Number, Street, City, State, and Zip Code)

12. (See instructions on reverse.)	**AMOUNT OF CLAIM** (in dollars)		
12a. PROPERTY DAMAGE	12b. PERSONAL INJURY	12c. WRONGFUL DEATH	12d. TOTAL (Failure to specify may cause forfeiture of your rights.)

I CERTIFY THAT THE AMOUNT OF CLAIM COVERS ONLY DAMAGES AND INJURIES CAUSED BY THE INCIDENT ABOVE AND AGREE TO ACCEPT SAID AMOUNT IN FULL SATISFACTION AND FINAL SETTLEMENT OF THIS CLAIM

13a. SIGNATURE OF CLAIMANT (See instructions on reverse side.)	13b. Phone number of person signing form	14. DATE OF SIGNATURE

CIVIL PENALTY FOR PRESENTING FRAUDULENT CLAIM	CRIMINAL PENALTY FOR PRESENTING FRAUDULENT CLAIM OR MAKING FALSE STATEMENTS
The claimant is liable to the United States Government for the civil penalty of not less than $5,000 and not more than $10,000, plus 3 times the amount of damages sustained by the Government. (See 31 U.S.C. 3729.)	Fine, imprisonment, or both. (See 18 U.S.C. 287, 1001.)

95-109   NSN 7540-00-634-4046   STANDARD FORM 95
PRESCRIBED BY DEPT. OF JUSTICE
28 CFR 14.2

INSURANCE COVERAGE

In order that subrogation claims may be adjudicated, it is essential that the claimant provide the following information regarding the insurance coverage of his vehicle or property.

15. Do you carry accident insurance? ☐ Yes   If yes, give name and address of insurance company (Number, Street, City, State, and Zip Code) and policy number.   ☐ No

16. Have you filed a claim on your insurance carrier in this instance, and if so, is it full coverage or deductible? ☐ Yes   ☐ No | 17. If deductible, state amount.

18. If a claim has been filed with your carrier, what action has your insurer taken or proposed to take with reference to your claim? (It is necessary that you ascertain these facts.)

19. Do you carry public liability and property damage insurance? ☐ Yes   If yes, give name and address of insurance carrier (Number, Street, City, State, and Zip Code).   ☐ No

INSTRUCTIONS

Claims presented under the Federal Tort Claims Act should be submitted directly to the "appropriate Federal agency" whose employee(s) was involved in the incident. If the incident involves more than one claimant, each claimant should submit a separate claim form.

Complete all items - Insert the word NONE where applicable.

A CLAIM SHALL BE DEEMED TO HAVE BEEN PRESENTED WHEN A FEDERAL AGENCY RECEIVES FROM A CLAIMANT, HIS DULY AUTHORIZED AGENT, OR LEGAL REPRESENTATIVE, AN EXECUTED STANDARD FORM 95 OR OTHER WRITTEN NOTIFICATION OF AN INCIDENT, ACCOMPANIED BY A CLAIM FOR MONEY

Failure to completely execute this form or to supply the requested material within two years from the date the claim accrued may render your claim invalid. A claim is deemed presented when it is received by the appropriate agency, not when it is mailed.

If instruction is needed in completing this form, the agency listed in item #1 on the reverse side may be contacted. Complete regulations pertaining to claims asserted under the Federal Tort Claims Act can be found in Title 28, Code of Federal Regulations, Part 14. Many agencies have published supplementing regulations. If more than one agency is involved, please state each agency.

The claim may be filed by a duly authorized agent or other legal representative, provided evidence satisfactory to the Government is submitted with the claim establishing express authority to act for the claimant. A claim presented by an agent or legal representative must be presented in the name of the claimant. If the claim is signed by the agent or legal representative, it must show the title or legal capacity of the person signing and be accompanied by evidence of his/her authority to present a claim on behalf of the claimant as agent, executor, administrator, parent, guardian or other representative.

If claimant intends to file for both personal injury and property damage, the amount for each must be shown in item #12 of this form.

DAMAGES IN A **SUM CERTAIN** FOR INJURY TO OR LOSS OF PROPERTY, PERSONAL INJURY, OR DEATH ALLEGED TO HAVE OCCURRED BY REASON OF THE INCIDENT. THE CLAIM MUST BE PRESENTED TO THE APPROPRIATE FEDERAL AGENCY WITHIN **TWO YEARS** AFTER THE CLAIM ACCRUES.

The amount claimed should be substantiated by competent evidence as follows:

(a) In support of the claim for personal injury or death, the claimant should submit a written report by the attending physician, showing the nature and extent of injury, the nature and extent of treatment, the degree of permanent disability, if any, the prognosis, and the period of hospitalization, or incapacitation, attaching itemized bills for medical, hospital, or burial expenses actually incurred.

(b) In support of claims for damage to property, which has been or can be economically repaired, the claimant should submit at least two itemized signed statements or estimates by reliable, disinterested concerns, or, if payment has been made, the itemized signed receipts evidencing payment.

(c) In support of claims for damage to property which is not economically repairable, or if the property is lost or destroyed, the claimant should submit statements as to the original cost of the property, the date of purchase, and the value of the property, both before and after the accident. Such statements should be by disinterested competent persons, preferably reputable dealers or officials familiar with the type of property damaged, or by two or more competitive bidders, and should be certified as being just and correct.

(d) **Failure to specify a sum certain will render your claim invalid and may result in forfeiture of your rights.**

PRIVACY ACT NOTICE

This Notice is provided in accordance with the Privacy Act, 5 U.S.C. 552a(e)(3), and concerns the information requested in the letter to which this Notice is attached.
  A. *Authority:* The requested information is solicited pursuant to one or more of the following: 5 U.S.C. 301, 28 U.S.C. 501 et seq., 28 U.S.C. 2671 et seq., 28 C.F.R. Part 14.

B. *Principal Purpose:* The information requested is to be used in evaluating claims.
C. *Routine Use:* See the Notices of Systems of Records for the agency to whom you are submitting this form for this information.
D. *Effect of Failure to Respond:* Disclosure is voluntary. However, failure to supply the requested information or to execute the form may render your claim "invalid".

PAPERWORK REDUCTION ACT NOTICE

This notice is <u>solely</u> for the purpose of the Paperwork Reduction Act, 44 U.S.C. 3501. Public reporting burden for this collection of information is estimated to average 6 hours per response, including the time for reviewing instructions, searching existing data sources, gathering and maintaining the data needed, and completing and reviewing the collection of information. Send comments regarding this burden estimate or any other aspect of this collection of information, including suggestions for reducing this burden, to the Director, Torts Branch, Attention: Paperwork Reduction Staff, Civil Division, U.S. Department of Justice, Washington, D.C. 20530 or to the Office of Management and Budget. Do not mail completed form(s) to these addresses.

APPENDIX D

Other Publications of Interest

We have cited books on various subjects in the text of the Manual. *See* Ch. 1, n.1 (a book on police misconduct litigation), n.19 (prisoner legal manuals for New York and California); Ch. 2, n. 787 (a leading treatise on torts); Ch. 8, n.6 (comprehensive books on 42 U.S.C. § 1983); Ch. 10, n.402 (books on open records and freedom of information laws), nn. 799, 818 (books on trial practice), n.899 (books on evidence), n. 863 (books on jury instructions); Ch. 11, n.1 (books on legal research); Ch. 12, n.1 (books on legal writing). General books on constitutional law that are reasonably readable and affordable include *Constitutional Law: Principles and Policies* by Erwin Chemerinsky (Aspen Publishers, 3d ed., 2006, $64.00) and *Constitutional Law in a Nutshell* by Jerome A. Barron and C. Thomas Dienes (West Publications, 6th ed., 2005, $33.00). These books can be obtained from their publishers, or in some cases from discount booksellers if you are allowed to use them.

Other books and periodicals that may be helpful or interesting are listed in the *Prisoners' Assistance Directory* published by the National Prison Project of the American Civil Liberties Union, which has kindly given us permission to reproduce their bibliography in this Appendix, below.

A. Publications

ACLU National Prison Project Publications

The following publications can be ordered prepaid from the National Prison Project of the ACLU, 915 15th Street, N.W., 7th Floor, Washington, D.C. 20005; (202) 393-4930 or fax (202) 393-4931.

The National Prison Project Journal—The NPP's biannual newsletter featuring articles, reports, legal analysis, legislative news, and other developments in prisoners' rights. An annual subscription is $30 or $2 for prisoners.

Play it Safer—This booklet describes sexually transmitted diseases, the signs of disease, the importance of safer sex, and the need for treatment. Eleven of the most common STDs are explained, from Chancroid to Trichomoniasis. The 27-page booklet also includes a national resource list for prisoners. Booklet bulk rates are 100 copies for $35, 500

copies for $150 or 1000 copies for $280. Send order requests to Jackie Walker at the NPP. This publication is free to prisoners.

Prisoners' Assistance Directory—The *Directory* lists and describes local, state, national, and international organizations that provide services to prisoners, ex-offenders and prisoners' families. The *Directory* is available for $35 prepaid.

American Civil Liberties Union Publications

ACLU Fact Sheet: Mail in Prison—Available for $1.

ACLU Fact Sheet: Prisoner Transfers—Available for $1.

ACLU Fact Sheet: Smoking in Prison—Available for $1.

ACLU Fact Sheet: Visitation in Prison—Available for $1.

ACLU Fact Sheet Set (all four listed above)—Available for $3.50.

American Correctional Association

The following publication is available from the American Correctional Association, Attention: Roberta Gibson, 206 N. Washington St., Suite 200, Alexandria, VA. 22314; (800) 222-5646 x 0129.

Corrections Compendium—A peer-reviewed research-based journal of the American Correctional Association for corrections professionals. Reports on trends in corrections, legal developments and provides monthly surveys on various corrections issues. Published six times a year. The cost is $72 for one year.

Biddle Publishing

To order the following, contact the publisher at 13 Gurnet Road, PMB 103, Burnswick, ME. 04011; (207) 833-5016. Website: www.biddleaudenreed.com.

Going to Prison? 5th Edition—A guide to help prepare those en route to prison. The new edition is expanded to include updated information on Federal facilities and Community Corrections Management offices and States' DOC. The cost is $9.95 (plus $2.50 shipping).

Center on Juvenile and Criminal Justice Publications

To order any of the following publications, write the Center at: 54 Dore St., San Francisco, CA. 94103; (415) 621-5661. Contact the Center for prices. All listed publications are also available free on the Center's website at: www.cjcj.org.

An Analysis of San Francisco Juvenile Justice Reforms During the Brown Administration (2001).

A California Juvenile Court Advocate's Guide to Noninstitutional Placement (2002).

The Color of Justice: An Analysis of Juvenile Adult Court Transfers in California (2000).

Community-Based Treatment: The Impact of the Homeless Pretrial Release Project (2000).

Dispelling the Myth: An Analysis of Youth and Adult Crime Patterns in California over the Past 20 Years (2000).

Drug Use and Justice 2002: An Examination of California Drug Policy Enforcement (2002).

From House of Refuge to 'Youth Corrections': Same Story, Different Day (2005).

It's More Profitable to Treat the Disease than to Prevent it: Why the Prison Industrial Complex Needs Crime (2004).

Poor Prescription: The Costs of Imprisoning Drug Offenders in the United States (2000).

Racial Disparities and the Drug War (2005).

Reducing Disproportionate Minority Confinement: The Multnomah County Oregon Success Story and its Implications (2002).

School House Hype: Two Years Later (2000).

Shattering 'Broken Windows': An Analysis of San Francisco's Alternative Crime Policies (1999).

Slavery in the Third Millennium (2005).

Texas Tough? An Analysis of Incarceration and Crime Trends in the Lone Star State (2000).

Too Little, Too Late: President Clinton's Prison Legacy (2001).

Why are we so Punitive? Some Observations on Recent Incarceration Trends (2004).

Widening the Net in Juvenile Justice and the Dangers of Prevention and Early Intervention (2001).

Columbia Human Rights Law Review

The Jailhouse Lawyer's Manual, 7th Edition—A handbook of legal rights and procedures designed for use by people in prison. The JLM informs prisoners of their legal rights, shows them how to secure these rights through the complex array of procedures and legal vocabulary which make up this system. The JLM also instructs prisoners in techniques of legal research and explains the need to take note of important legal developments. Available online at http:www.columbia.edu/cu/hrlr/jlm.html $90 for non-inmates and $45 for inmates. To place your order or get more information, please call or write to Columbia Human Rights Law Review, Attn: JLM Order, 435 West 116th Street, New York, N.Y. 10027; (212) 854-1601; (212) 854-7946 (fax).

Foreverfamily Publications

The following publications are available from Foreverfamily, 691 Garibaldi Street, SW, Atlanta, GA. 30310; (404) 223-1200. Publications are free to prisoners and their families or $10 prepaid for non-prisoners:

Parenting from Prison: A Handbook for Incarcerated Mothers—A guidebook for mothers who are incarcerated.

Jail and Justice—A handbook for incarcerated women.

Gay & Lesbian Advocates & Defenders Publications

To order the following publications, write GLAD, 30 Winter Street, #800, Boston, MA. 02108; (617) 426-1350:

National Resource List for Prisoners—A resource listing for prisoners nationally (2 pages). Free to prisoners.

New England Prisoner Packet—A collection of legal research for people in prison facing discrimination or abuse. Free to prisoners.

Law Office of Alan Ellis Publications

Publications available from the offices of Alan Ellis, P.C. at P.O. Box 150, Lemont, PA. 16851-0150 include:

The Federal Prison Guidebook 2005–2006 Edition—This book contains comprehensive descriptions of every federal prison in the United States and costs $29.95 for prisoners and their families.

Federal Sentencing and Postconviction News—This newsletter contains practice tips, news updates, and recent favorable case law descriptions. Available free to federal prisoners.

Legal Action Center Publications

Prisoners can receive the following publications from the Legal Action Center at 225 Varick Street, New York, N.Y. 10014; (212) 243-1313 or (800) 223-4044. Publications are also available online at www.lac.org/pubs/gratis.html:

Are you. . . .—This booklet helps prisoners prevent job discrimination before it happens.

Certificate of Relief from Disabilities and Certificate of Good Conduct: What you Can Do About Criminal Convictions When Looking for Work—This updated pamphlet helps people with criminal histories understand the process of obtaining New York State certificates that can be helpful in seeking employment.

How to Obtain Important Documents—This guide tells people in New York how to apply for and obtain important documents, including driver's licenses, non-driver I.D.

cards, social security cards, birth certificates, and other documents.

Lewisburg Prison Project Publications

The following publications are available from the Project, P.O. Box 128, Lewisburg, PA. 17837; (570) 523-1104:

Barron's Law Dictionary—Available for $12.50.

Legal Bulletins—Each bulletin provides information on constitutional law as applied to federal and state institutions. Each one covers a specific topic (First Amendment, due process, medical care, post-conviction, etc.), and includes case citations and practical instructions for legal actions. Write the Project for a current listing of bulletins. Price ranges from $1.50–$3.00. Most cost $1.50 and are distributed nationwide.

Self-Defense Manual for Pennsylvania State Prisoners Accused of Misconduct—This booklet only applies to Pennsylvania prisoners and is available for $1.75.

Michigan—CURE Publications

The following publications are available from MICURE, P.O. Box 2736, Kalamazoo, MI. 49003-2736; (269) 383-0028:

Booklets: *Directory of Michigan Adult Sex-Offender Treatment Programs*, $2.00; *Keeping Love Alive While in Prison*, $1.50.

Brochures: *Getting Out Contacts*—A listing, by county, of agencies and organizations that may be helpful to persons leaving prison; *Self-Help Recovery Bibliography*—A list of helpful readings for sex offenders and their loved ones; *Thoughts on Getting Out*; *What You Can Do to Ensure that Best Possible Health Care While You Are in Prison.*

National Coalition to Abolish the Death Penalty Publications

The following publications are available from the Coalition, 1717 K Street, #510, Washington, D.C. 20036; (202) 331-4090:

Abolitionist Directory—The directory lists organizations and contacts, by state, working to end the death penalty. It is updated annually and costs $3 per copy plus $1.70 for postage.

National Execution Alert—This newsletter highlights the monthly stories of prisoners who are scheduled to be executed. Annual subscription costs $15.

National Legal Aid and Defender Association Publications

The following publication is available from the NLADA, 1140 Connecticut Avenue N.W. #900, Washington, D.C. 20006; (202) 452-0620:

Directory of Legal Aid and Defender Services—A directory of civil and criminal public law offices throughout

the United States. The price is $35.00 for program members, $55.00 for individual members, and $95.00 for non-members.

National Veterans' Legal Services Project Publications

To purchase the following documents, contact the Veterans' Project, 2001 S. Street, N.W. #610, Washington, D.C. 20009-1125; (202) 265-8305:

The Veterans Advocate—This newsletter addresses veteran law and advocacy issues. For incarcerated veteran organizations and accredited service organizations, the cost is $80 for a one-year subscription or $120 for a two-year subscription.

Veterans Benefits Manual—This Manual is a comprehensive guide to veteran's law. To purchase call (800) 533-1637.

Prisons Foundation

The following publications are available from the Foundation, 1718 M Street, N.W. #151, Washington, D.C. 20036; (202) 393-1511; (727) 538-2095 (fax); or online at www.prisonsfoundation.org:

Death Row Resource Guide—An extensive compilation of significant information about the death penalty worldwide, with special emphasis on executions in the United States. The cost is $79.

Prison Artists and Their Work—Profiles over 80 prison artists, reproducing hundreds of their works, many in full color; bonus CD, 71 minutes of music recorded in prison. The cost is $127.

Prisoners Rights Resource Guide—The rights of prisoners in America have evolved from the dismal past into a hopeful present and a promising future. Landmark Supreme Court cases have been decided along the way. We provide clear explanations of what they mean for inmates and staff. The cost is $84.00.

Prisons Almanac 2006—A compilation of a full year of the most significant news stories about prisons. Also includes a current, comprehensive statistical profile of who is in prison, why they are there and where they are located. Finally, there are original essays written by experts and inmates. Available for $58.

Prisons Help Sourcebook—A thorough reference that provides profiles and gives contact information for hundreds of sources. Ideal for volunteers, students, friends, and families of prisoners. The book also presents a modern prison memoir, a management guide for wardens and a resource guide for anyone interested in the way prisons operate. Finally, over 100 films, videos, novels, and nonfiction books about prisons are reviewed and summarized. The cost is $75.

PSI Publishing, Inc.

To purchase the following, contact PSI Publishing, 413-B 19th Street, #168, Lynden, WA. 98264; (800) 557-8868:

The Prisoner's Guide to Survival—Legal research guide covering all aspects of federal litigation common to prisoners. Designed for novice pro se litigants and experienced attorneys involved in federal criminal appeals and prison civil rights actions. Available to prisoners for $49.95 and non-prisoners for $64.95, plus $5 shipping and handling.

Reconciliation Ministries Publications

The following publications are available from Reconciliation Ministries, 702 51st Avenue North, Nashville, TN. 37209; (615) 292-6371:

Handbook for Families and Friends of Tennessee Prisoners—A handbook for family members of Tennessee prisoners. Contact the office for cost.

Parole Packets—The packets provide information on preparing for parole in Tennessee. Available for $8.

Two in Every 100. This workbook is for young children with a parent in prison. It is designed to be completed with a parent, teacher, or counselor. Contact the office for cost.

The Sentencing Project Publications

To order the following publications, contact the Project, 514 10th Street, N.W. #1000, Washington, D.C. 20004; (202) 628-0871. Most publications can be found at the website and downloaded for free, except the books:

Aging Behind Bars: "Three Strikes" Seven Years Later (2001), $5.00.

Americans Behind Bars: One Year Later (1992), $6.00.

Americans Behind Bars: U.S. and International Use of Incarceration (1995), $8.00

An Analysis of the Economics of Prison Siting in Rural Communities, $5.00.

Big Prisons, Small Towns: Prison Economics in Rural American (2003), $3.00.

Diminishing Returns: Crime and Incarceration in the 1990s (2000), $5.00.

Incarceration & Crime: A Complex Relationship (2005), $2.00.

Intended and Unintended Consequences: State Racial Disparities in Imprisonment (1997), $8.00.

The "Meaning of Life": Long Prison Sentences in Context (2004), $8.00

State Sentencing and Corrections Policy in an Era of Fiscal Restraint (2002), $3.50.

Books:

Invisible Punishment—The Collateral Consequences of Mass Imprisonment (2002), edited by Marc Mauer and Meda Chesney-Lind. Available for $17.95.

Race to Incarcerate (1999), by Marc Mauer. Available for $22.95.

Race to Incarcerate (2000), by Marc Mauer. Available for $14.95.

Starlite, Inc. Publications

The following publication is available from the publisher, P.O. Box 20004, St. Petersburg, Fl., 33742; (727) 392-2929 or (800) 577-2929:

The Citebook—A legal reference book listing case citations on many issues, from access to the courts to witnesses. It also includes an overview of the federal and state court systems, a basic guide to filing legal pleadings, addresses for all federal courts and state and federal adult prisons, the U.S. Constitution, and a glossary of legal terms. Latest edition is available for $41.95, including shipping/handling/priority mail.

Thomson/West Group Publishing

The following publications are available from Thomson/West Group Publishing, 610 Opperman Drive, Eagan, MN. 55164; (800) 328-9352:

Criminal Law in a Nutshell, by Arnold H. Loewy. This book provides an overview of criminal law. Available for $27.00, including shipping.

Criminal Procedure in a Nutshell, by Jerold H. Israel and Wayne LaFave. This book concentrates on constitutional criminal procedures and their limitations. The Fourth, Sixth, and Fourteenth Amendments are heavily covered. A table of cases is also included. Available for $26.50, including shipping.

The Law and Policy of Sentencing and Corrections, by Lynn S. Branham. This book provides an overview of the sentencing process, the status of pretrial detainees and convicted offenders, prisoners' rights and responsibilities, and a chapter on prisoner remedies. The book ends with a chapter on the restoration of rights for released offenders. Available for $29.00, including shipping.

Prisoners and the Law, by Ira P. Robbins. This six-volume, 6,500 page comprehensive set covers a full range of issues and legal questions concerning prisoners' rights, including AIDS, drugs, overcrowding, security, appeal, weapons, correspondence, visitation issues, prisoner safety, probation, parole, etc. Available for $986, plus tax and shipping.

The Women's Project Publications

The following publications are available from the Women's Project, 2224 S. Main Street, Little Rock, AR. 72206; (501) 372-5113:

HIV, AIDS and Reproductive Health: A Peer Trainer's Manual—Available free to prisoners.

Transformation—A bimonthly newsletter available free to prisoners.

B. Newsletters

Note: Many organizations listed in the National Prison Project Directory, see Appendix B, publish newsletters that are usually available at minimal cost. See organizations' listing for additional details in Appendix B. The following newsletters cover a broad range of corrections and criminal justice issues. Subscription rates are subject to change.

Against all Odds—Published by CURE-Ohio, P.O. Box 14080, Columbus, OH. 43214; (937) 299-8298. Available on CURE-Ohio's website: http://cureohio.us.

AIDS Network Survival—This bimonthly publication includes profiles of prison artists, previews of prison art to be exhibited at upcoming Prison Foundation shows, news of prisoners, staff, activists, and programs that are improving the prison environment. Available to prisoners for a donation of $2 (postage stamps accepted) and donations of $25 for non-prisoners. Contact Prisons Foundation, 1718 M Street, # 151, Washington, D.C. 20036; (202) 383-1511; www.prisonsfoundation.org.

Coalition for Prisoners' Rights Newsletter—National monthly newsletter published by the Coalition, P.O. Box 1911, Santa Fe, N.M. 87504-1911; (505) 982-9520. Available free to prisoners, their family members, and ex-prisoners. The rate for others is $12 per year for individuals, and $25 per year for government agencies and for-profit institutions.

Compassion—Bimonthly newsletter written by death-row prisoners. Compassion, c/o St. Rose Peace and Justice, 140 W. South Bondary Street, Perrysburg, OH. 43551. There are various donation/participation rates; however, a one-year subscription is $50. Your subscription will also underwrite $25 in scholarships benefiting family members of murdered victims.

Correct Care—Quarterly newspaper on correctional health care. Prison libraries may request copies. Go to www.ncchc.org/pubs/correctcare.html. Printed in its entirety online and copies are mailed only to members. Contact National Commission on Correctional Health Care (NCCHC), 1145 W. Diversey Parkway, Chicago, IL. 60614; (773) 880-1460.

Correctional Law Reporter—Covers recent decisions and developments in corrections and criminal justice law. Cost is $169.95 for six issues. Contact Civic Research Institute, P.O. Box 585, Kingston, N.J. 08528; (609) 683-4450.

Corrections Professional—Semi-monthly publication, provide corrections news for corrections staff. Subscriptions are $215 per year (plus shipping). Contact LRP Publications, 74 Dresher Road, #500, Horsham, PA. 19044; (215) 784-0920; (800) 341-7874.

Damien Center Newsletter—A bimonthly newsletter on AIDS-related issues. Subscription available free upon written request. Contact Damien Center, 26 N. Arsenal, Indianapolis, IN. 46205; (317) 632-0123 or (800) 213-1163 (in-state only).

Delaware Center for Justice Commentary—Quarterly newsletter available free to Delaware prisoners upon request. Also available online at: www.dcjustice.org/news.html.

Contact the Delaware Center, 100 West 10th Street, #905, Wilmington, DE. 19801; (302) 658-7174.

Dispatch—A newsletter on AIDS-related issues. Available from AIDS Delaware, 100 W. 10th Street, #315, Wilminigton DE. 19801; (302) 653-6776.

FAMMGram—Available from Families Against Mandatory Minimums (FAMM), 1612 K. Street, N.W. #700, Washington, D.C. 20006; (202) 822-6700. Donations are requested.

Fortune News—Available free to prisoners. Contact the Fortune Society, 53 W. 23rd Street, 8th Floor, New York, N.Y. 10010; (212) 691-7554. Also available on the Fortune Society's website: www.fortunesociety.org.

Freedom Inside—Newsletter designed for and written by inmates. It is based on the Conversations with God materials and its message. The publication is free to inmates. Please send a written request to P.O. Box 74007, Phoenix, AZ. 85068.

GRATERFRIENDS the Newsletter—Published monthly. Subscriptions are $3 for prisoners and $15 for non-prisoners. Contact the Pennsylvania Prison Society, 245 Broad Street, #300, Philadelphia, PA. 19107-1518; (215) 412-7917. Also available on the Pennsylvania Prison Society's website: www.prisonsociety.org.

Hepatitis C Awareness News—Published periodically. Current and back issues are only available online at www.hcvinprison.org. Contact the Hepatitis C Awareness Project, P.O. Box 41803, Eugene, OR. 97404; (541) 607-5725.

Illinois Coalition to Abolish the Death Penalty Newsletter—Quarterly newsletter free to prisoners. Contact Illinois Coalition Against the Death Penalty, 180 N. Michigan Avenue, #2300, Chicago, IL. 60601; (312) 849-2279.

Inside Out—Infrequent newsletter on Virginia prison issues. Available free with membership. Dues are $2 (or 6 stamps) for prisoners, $15 for individuals, $25 for families, $50 for supporting members, $150 for life members/organizations, and $250 for benefactors. Contact Virginia CURE, P.O. Box 19307, Alexandria, VA. 22320-0307; (703) 765-6549.

Justitia Newsletter—Published by the Justice Studies Association. Contact Department of Criminal Justice, Hudson Valley Community College, 80 Vanderburgh Avenue, Troy. N.Y. 12180; (518) 629-7331). Also available online at www.justicestudies.org/Justice-Pub.html.

Justice Quarterly—Published four times a year. Subscription rates are $419. Justice Quarterly is published by Routledge Journals with editorial control by the Academy of Criminal Justice Services. Contact Routledge Journals, 325 Chestnut Street, 8th Floor, Philadelphia, PA. 19110; (800) 354-1420.

Lifelines—Published every three months for members. To obtain a subscription contact the National Coalition to Abolish the Death Penalty, 1717 K Street N.W. #510, Washington, D.C. 20009; (202) 331-4090.

Maryland CURE Newsletter—Local and national CURE newsletters are available with a Maryland CURE membership. Dues are $2 a year for prisoners and $10 a year for non-prisoners. To purchase the newsletter only is $5.

Contact MD CURE, P.O. Box 23, Simpsonville, MD. 21150; marylandcure@hotmail.com.

Michigan CURE Newsletter—Quarterly newsletter available to members. Contact MI-CURE, P.O. Box 2736, Kalamazoo, MI. 49003-2736; (616) 383-0028.

The National Prison Project Journal—A biannual newsletter featuring articles, reports, legal analysis, legislative news, and other developments in the corrections and criminal justice fields. Includes the Case Law Report, a review of recent federal court decisions relevant to corrections. An annual subscription is $2 for prisoners and $35 for non-prisoners. Contact the NPP, 915 15th Street, N.W. 7th Floor, Washington, D.C. 20005; (202) 393-4930.

News and Views—This quarterly newsletter discusses criminal-justice and corrections issues and is available free to NJAC members. Membership is free to prisoners and $20 for non-prisoners. Contact the New Jersey Association on Correction, 986 S. Broad Street, Trenton, N.J. 08611; (609) 396-8900.

Out of Time—A newsletter focusing on women prisoners, published monthly. Articles include cases of political prisoners and human-rights violations in prisons. Available free to prisoners and the community. See our website for archived issues. Contact Out of Control Lesbian Committee, 3543 18th Street, P.O. Box 30, San Francisco, CA. 94110; abodyke@earthlink.net.

Prison Legal News—This monthly journal covers prison-related news and analysis from across the country. A one-year subscription is $18 for prisoners, $25 for individuals, and $60 for lawyers and institutions. Contact Prison Legal News, P.O. Box 2420, West Brattleboro, VT. 05303; (802 257-1342; www.prisonlegalnews.org.

The Prison Mirror—Monthly newsletter published by and for men of the Minnesota Stillwater Correctional Facility. Subscriptions are $12. Contact Pat Meineke, 970 Pickett Street North, Bayport, MN. 55003-1490; (651) 779-2700.

The Prisoner's Guide to Survival—This legal-assistance Manual, published in 2001, covers post-conviction remedies and prisoner civil rights complaints. Current legislation, including the PLRA, the AEDPA, and the RFRA, is discussed. Also included: a guide to the FOIA and Privacy Act, a prisoner resource directory, legal glossary, actual size forms and sample documents. There is an extensive case law section with over 3000 Shepardized prisoner-related case law decisions. Soft cover, 750 pages. Non-prisoners $64.95, plus $5 shipping and handling; prisoners $49.95, plus $5 shipping and handling. Pease contact us at 413-B 19th Street #168, Lynden, WA. 982644; (800) 557-8868. Further information is available at www.prisonerlaw.com.

Razor Wire Newsletter—Published three to four times a year. The newsletter covers criminal justice public education and advocacy work. The cost is $6 for prisoners, $15 for students, and $30 for all others. Contact the November Coalition, 282 W. Astor, Colville, WA. 99114; (509) 684-1550.

Resist Newsletter—This newsletter is published six times a year. The suggested donation is $20. Contact Resist, 259 Elm Street, Somerville, MA. 02144; (617) 623-5110. Also available on Resist website: www.resistinc.org/newsletters/newsletters.html.

Separate Prisons Newsletter—This monthly newsletter is free to families of Tennessee prisoners and is sent to many Tennessee prison libraries and prisoner newspapers. Contact Reconciliation Ministries, 702 51st Avenue, N, Nashville, TN. 37209; (615) 292-6371.

The Trumpet—Free quarterly newsletter accepts donations. Contact Alderson Hospitality House, P.O. Box 579, Alderson, W.V. 24910; (304) 445-2980.

The Veterans Advocate—Monthly newsletter covers veterans' law and advocacy issues. Subscriptions are $80 a year. Contact the National Veterans Legal Services Project, 2001 S. Street N.W., #610, Washington, D.C. 20009-1125; (202) 265-8305.

C. Duplicating Services

Photo Duplicating Service
Provide copies of collections from the Library of Library of Congress, manuscripts, prints, photographs, maps, etc. Copyrighted materials cannot be copied without special permission. Fees vary according to the nature of the request. Order forms and price schedules are available. Written request and prepayment are required. Contract the Library of Congress, Photo Duplication Service, 101 Independence Avenue, S.E., Washington, D.C. 20540-4570; (202) 707-5640.

INDEX